THE PENGUIN ENCYCLOPEDIA
OF PLACES

W. G. Moore was educated at Burton-on-Trent Grammar School, where a film review brought him his first pen-money, and later took his B.Sc. at London University. He has spent most of his working life teaching, tutoring, lecturing, and writing, and has contributed to a variety of journals, from daily newspapers to quarterly reviews. In 1938 he published The Geography of Capitalism, and then wrote the geographical section of Odhams, Complete Self-Educator. At the start of the Second World War he was commissioned in the meteorological branch of the R.A.F., spent some years in Iraq, Persia, and the Middle East, organized the meteorological service for Persia, and completed his R.A.F. career by lectures on meteorology and climatology. He has since written, in addition to this volume, A Dictionary of Geography for Penguin Books, The World's Wealth, which the Economist described as 'a brilliantly carried out survey of the resources – animal, vegetable, and mineral – from which man gets his living, The Soil is a Live One, and a number of series of books including Essential Geography, Adventure in Geography, and New Visual Geography, and contributed to the Larousse Encyclopédie Universelle (English edition). He has also edited a large number of geographical filmstrips.

# The Penguin Encyclopedia of Places

W. G. MOORE

PENGUIN BOOKS

Penguin Books Ltd, Harmondsworth, Middlesex, England
Penguin Books Inc., 7110 Ambassador Road, Baltimore, Maryland 21207, U.S.A.
Penguin Books Australia Ltd, Ringwood, Victoria, Australia

—

First published 1971

—

Copyright © W. G. Moore, 1971

—

Made and printed in Great Britain
by Hazell Watson & Viney Ltd
Aylesbury, Bucks
Set in Monotype Times

# AUTHOR'S NOTE

In the *Encyclopedia of Places* we have attempted to include those places throughout the world on which the reader is most likely to seek information, and, keeping in mind its limitations as to length, we have aimed at preserving a balance between comprehensiveness and lucidity – between the number of entries and the space devoted to each entry. The reader will require more information about 'places' of outstanding significance, such as continents and oceans, than about minor 'places', such as small towns and villages, and the lengths of articles vary accordingly. Even the minor 'places', however, are regarded as important enough to require more than a simple statement of their location: their inclusion in the encyclopedia implies some significance. To assist the reader in locating places on a map, the less well known features are referred by distance and direction to others of major significance: e.g. small towns are referred to near-by large cities. In these cases distances are given in miles 'as the crow flies', not by road or rail, and directions by the points of the compass.

Population figures are taken from the most recent census of the country concerned or from the latest official estimates. When recent estimates have been highly speculative, e.g. on the provinces and cities of China, earlier and more reliable figures have been preferred; on the other hand, the recent UN estimate of the national population of China (for 1968) appears to be soundly based and is quoted in the article on China. The preliminary results of certain censuses were being announced while the book was passing through the final stages of production. In the case of the 1970 census in the USSR, the figures for constituent republics, national areas, largest cities, etc. were received and were incorporated in the encyclopedia.

With regard to place-names, which often arouse controversy: we have adopted the versions which we consider to be those most familiar to English-speaking readers: e.g. Florence (not Firenze), Munich (not München), though the native equivalents are also given. In some instances it is felt that the native equivalents are already well known to and are being used by English-speaking peoples, and the fact has been acknowledged in certain place-names: e.g. Göteborg (not Gothenburg), Tbilisi (not Tiflis) – again with the equivalents. In the case of the languages which do not use the Latin alphabet, e.g. Chinese and Arabic, we have adhered to the anglicized names to which English-speaking readers have become accustomed *in the written form*. This seemed preferable to a possibly ingenious but undoubtedly misleading attempt at transliteration.

The reader will appreciate that a number of changes involving places mentioned in the encyclopedia were taking place after the book had been sent to press. We have brought facts up-to-date as far as possible with the brief items in the Addenda, and some additional entries have been included. It is suggested, therefore, that the reader, after seeking an entry in the main part of the book, should then consult the Addenda. An asterisk (*) accompanying an entry indicates that further relevant information will be found under the same heading in the Addenda.

In the compilation of an encyclopedia, even of relatively modest dimensions, an author has constantly to call on the services of others, to whom he owes a considerable debt, and I should particularly like to express my gratitude to Mr George S. Dugdale (Librarian, Royal Geographical Society) and Mr D. C. Money (geographer and author) for their contributions. I must also acknowledge the innumerable officials in embassies, legations, high commissions and specialist libraries who have so readily assisted with information.

W. G. M.

# SYMBOLS AND ABBREVIATIONS

| | | | |
|---|---|---|---|
| AR | Autonomous Region | m. | mile(s) |
| Ar. | Arabic | Mt | Mount |
| ASSR | Autonomous Soviet | N | North |
| | Socialist Republic | NA | National Area |
| b. | born | NE | North-East |
| BC | British Columbia | NNE | North-North-East |
| C | degrees Centigrade | NNW | North-North-West |
| c. | circa | NW | North-West |
| cap. | capital | pop. | population |
| cent. | century, centuries | R. | River |
| Co. | County | rel. | religion(s) |
| d. | died | RSFSR | Russian Soviet Federal |
| DC | District of Columbia | | Socialist Republic |
| E | East | S | South |
| e.g. | for example | SE | South-East |
| ENE | East-North-East | Sp. | Spanish |
| Eng. | English | sq. m. | square miles |
| ESE | East-South-East | SSE | South-South-East |
| esp. | especially | SSR | Soviet Socialist Republic |
| F | degrees Fahrenheit | SSW | South-South-West |
| FGR | Federal German Republic | St | Saint, Street |
| Fr. | French | SW | South-West |
| ft | feet | UN | United Nations |
| GDR | German Democratic | US | United States |
| | Republic | USA | United States of America |
| Ger. | German | USSR | Union of Soviet Socialist |
| Gr. | Greek | | Republics |
| inc. | include(s), including | W | West |
| ins. | inches | WNW | West-North-West |
| Is. | Islands | WSW | West-South-West |
| L. | Lake | ⇨ | see |
| lang. | language(s) | ⇨⇨ | see also |
| lat. | latitude | * | see Addenda |
| long. | longitude | | |

# CONVERSION TABLES

In general, measures and weights are given in the British Imperial system; the following tables will help readers to convert to the metric system.

| Distances | | | Altitudes | |
| --- | --- | --- | --- | --- |
| *miles* | *kilometres* | | *feet* | *metres* |
| 1 | 1·609 | | 1 | 0·305 |
| 2 | 3·218 | | 2 | 0·610 |
| 3 | 4·827 | | 5 | 1·525 |
| 4 | 6·436 | | 10 | 3·050 |
| 5 | 8·045 | | 20 | 6·100 |
| 6 | 9·654 | | 50 | 15·250 |
| 7 | 11·263 | | 100 | 30·500 |
| 8 | 12·872 | | 200 | 61·000 |
| 9 | 14·481 | | 500 | 152·500 |
| 10 | 16·090 | | 1,000 | 305 |
| 20 | 32·180 | | 2,000 | 610 |
| 50 | 80·450 | | 5,000 | 1,525 |
| 100 | 160·900 | | 10,000 | 3,050 |
| 150 | 241·350 | | 20,000 | 6,100 |
| 200 | 321·800 | | 25,000 | 7,625 |
| 500 | 804·500 | | 30,000 | 9,150 |
| 1,000 | 1,609 | | | |

| Areas | | | | |
| --- | --- | --- | --- | --- |
| *sq. m.* | *sq. km.* | | *sq. m.* | *sq. km.* |
| 1 | 2·590 | | 2,000 | 5,180 |
| 2 | 5·180 | | 5,000 | 12,950 |
| 5 | 12·950 | | 10,000 | 25,900 |
| 10 | 25·900 | | 20,000 | 51,800 |
| 20 | 51·800 | | 50,000 | 129,500 |
| 50 | 129·500 | | 100,000 | 259,000 |
| 100 | 259 | | 200,000 | 518,000 |
| 200 | 518 | | 500,000 | 1,295,000 |
| 500 | 1,295 | | 1,000,000 | 2,590,000 |
| 1,000 | 2,590 | | | |

*Small areas*
1 acre = 0·405 hectare

*Sea depths*
1 fathom (6 feet) = 1·828 metres

*Depth of rainfall*
1 inch = 25·4 millimetres

*Temperatures*
To convert temperatures on the Fahrenheit scale to temperatures on the Centigrade scale, or vice versa, use the following equations:

$$C = (F - 32) \div 1{\cdot}8; \qquad F = (1{\cdot}8 \times C) + 32.$$

*Weights*
1 ton = 1·016 metric tons (tonnes)

# A

**Aabenraa** Denmark. Port on the Aabenraa Fiord (Jutland) 50 m. SE of Esbjerg. Pop. (1965) 14,591. Fishing, brewing. In Germany 1864–1920.

**Aachen** (Fr. **Aix-la-Chapelle**) Federal German Republic. Ancient Aquis Granum. Town in N Rhine-Westphalia 40 m. WSW of Cologne, near the Belgian and Dutch borders. Pop. (1968) 176,608. Industrial town in a coalmining district. Manufactures textiles, glass, chemicals, needles, etc. Important railway centre. Famous for its thermal springs for many centuries. Has a 14th-cent. Rathaus; the cathedral (begun 796, rebuilt 983) contains the tomb of Charlemagne, who made it his N capital. The Holy Roman Emperors were crowned here 813–1531. Annexed by France 1801; ceded to Prussia 1815. After the 1st World War it was occupied by the Allies. During the 2nd World War it was severely damaged by air raids, and was the first important German city to fall to the Allies (1944).

**Aalborg** Denmark. Port on the S side of Lim Fiord (N Jutland) 64 m. NNW of Aarhus. Pop. (1965) 85,632. Shipbuilding; cement, textile, and other industries. Linked with Nörresundby by a bridge across the fiord.

**Aalen** Federal German Republic. Town in Baden-Württemberg 30 m. NNE of Ulm. Pop. (1963) 33,700. Manufactures textiles etc.

**Aalst** ◊ *Alost.*

**Aarau** Switzerland. Capital of the Aargau canton on the Aar R. at the foot of the Jura mountains, 24 m. SE of Basel. Pop. (1969) 17,800. Manufactures scientific instruments, textiles, bells. Capital of the Helvetic Republic 1798–1803.

**Aare River** ◊ *Aar River.*

**Aargau** Switzerland. Canton in the N. Area 542 sq. m. Pop. (1969) 422,000 (German-speaking, mainly Protestant). Cap. Aarau. Bounded by the Rhine (N), crossed by the Aar and its tributary the Reuss. Fertile valleys, with cultivation of cereals and fruits. Sulphur springs at Baden and Schinznach and saline springs at Rheinfelden. Manufactures textiles, metal goods. Chief towns Aarau, Brugg. The region was the headquarters of the Habsburgs, who lost it to the Swiss Confederates 1415. A

dependency of Berne till 1798; became a separate canton 1803.

**Aarhus** Denmark. Second largest city, on the E coast of Jutland. Pop. (1965) 117,748. Seaport. Railway junction. Commercial centre. Oil refining, iron founding, brewing. University (founded 1928, opened 1933).

**Aar (Aare) River** Switzerland. The largest river entirely within Switzerland, 180 m. long, rising in the Aar glaciers, flowing N past Meiringen (the Aar Gorge), W through L. Brienz, past Interlaken and through L. Thun, then NW past Thun and Berne, entering L. Biel as the Hagneck Canal and leaving it as the Aar Canal, then flowing generally NE past Solothurn, Olten, and Aarau and joining the Rhine opposite Waldshut (Germany). Navigable from the Rhine confluence as far as Thun.

**Aba** Nigeria. Town in Eastern Nigeria 33 m. NE of Port Harcourt, on the railway to Kaduna. Pop. (1960) 58,000. Commercial centre. Trade in palm oil and kernels.

**Abadan** Iran. Port in Khuzistan (SW), on an island in the Shatt-al-Arab 33 m. from the head of the Persian Gulf. Pop. (1966) 272,962. Major oil-refining and exporting centre; supplied by pipelines from the Khuzistan oilfields.

**Abadla** ◊ *Algeria; Sahara.*

**Abakan** USSR. Capital of the Khakass Autonomous Region, Krasnoyarsk Territory, RSFSR, just N of the confluence of the Abakan and the Yenisei rivers. Pop. (1970) 90,000. Industrial centre. Sawmilling, metal working. Founded 1707.

**Abbai River** ◊ *Tana, Lake.*

**Abbazia** ◊ *Opatija.*

**Abbeville** France. Town in the Somme department, on the banks of the Somme 25 m. NW of Amiens. Pop. (1968) 25,072. Manufactures sugar, carpets, etc. Severely damaged in the 2nd World War.

**Abbots Bromley** England. Village in Staffordshire 12 m. E of Stafford. Pop. (1961) 1,190. Famous for the Sept. fair, at which the Horn Dance is performed.

**Abbotsford** Scotland. Home (1812–32) of Sir Walter Scott, on the S bank of the Tweed 3 m. W of Melrose (Roxburghshire).

**Abbots Langley** England. Small town in

SW Hertfordshire 3 m. N of Watford. Pop. (1961) 18,157. Birthplace of Nicholas Breakspear (Pope Adrian IV; 1080–1159).

**Abeokuta** Nigeria. Town in Western Nigeria on the Ogun R. 48 m. N of Lagos, on the railway to Kano. Pop. (1960) 84,000. Surrounded by a mud wall. In a fertile valley; agricultural products yams, palm oil and kernels, cacao, timber. Main industries cotton weaving and dyeing. Founded c. 1830. Before 1914 capital of the independent Egba state.

**Aberavon** ◊ *Port Talbot.*

**Aberbrothock** ◊ *Arbroath.*

**Abercarn** Wales. Urban district in W Monmouthshire 7 m. NW of Newport. Pop. (1961) 19,221. Coalmining. Manufactures iron and steel, tinplate.

**Aberconway** ◊ *Conway.*

**Aberdare** Wales. Urban district in NE Glamorgan, on the R. Cynon 4 m. SW of Merthyr Tydfil. Pop. (1961) 39,044. Coalmining, brewing. Manufactures cables, radio and television sets, etc.

**Aberdare Mountains** ◊ *Kenya; Tana River.*

**Aberdeen** Scotland. County town of Aberdeenshire, a royal burgh, and third city of Scotland, on the bay between the mouths of the Don and the Dee, on the E coast. Pop. (1961) 185,379. The harbour has been continually improved since the completion of the Victoria Dock (1848). Chief seaport of the NE; Scotland's major fishing port, with the third largest fish market in Britain. Manufactures knitwear, hosiery, paper. Shipbuilding. Known as 'the Granite City' as many of its buildings are constructed of this local stone; granite dressing is a large industry. An important town as early as the 12th cent.; chartered a royal burgh by William the Lion (1179). In the N part of the city, Old Aberdeen, is King's College (founded 1494), which joined with Marischal College (founded 1593) to form the University of Aberdeen (1860). The granite St Machar's Cathedral (dating in parts from the 14th cent.) and the 13th/14th-cent. 'Auld Brig o'Balgownie' are also in Old Aberdeen.

**Aberdeenshire** Scotland. County in the NE, bounded on the N and E by the North Sea. Area 1,971 sq. m. Pop. (1961) 298,503. County town Aberdeen. Mountainous in the SW, containing part of the Cairngorm Mountains, with Ben Macdhui (4,296 ft) the highest peak. Coastal plains in the E. Drained by the Dee, Don, Deveron, and Ythan rivers. Agriculture, fishing. The NE

is famous for cattle. Braemar (Highland Games) and Ballater are tourist centres. Balmoral Castle is the principal royal residence in Scotland. Chief towns Aberdeen, Peterhead, Fraserburgh, Huntly.

**Aberdovey** (Welsh **Aberdyfi**) Wales. Small seaside resort on Cardigan Bay in Merionethshire, at the mouth of the Dovey. Pop. (1961) 1,260.

**Aberfan** Wales. Coalmining village in Glamorgan 4 m. SSE of Merthyr Tydfil. Scene of a disaster in Oct. 1966: a mass of mine waste, sludge, etc. from a coal tip slid down and buried a school and several houses, killing 144 people, including 116 children.

**Aberfeldy** Scotland. Small burgh in Perthshire on the S bank of the R. Tay 22 m. NW of Perth. Pop. (1961) 1,469. Whisky distilling. Near by are the picturesque Falls of Moness.

**Abergavenny** Wales. Municipal borough in Monmouthshire, at the confluence of the Usk and the Gavenny rivers 16 m. N of Newport. Pop. (1961) 9,625. Market town. Collieries in the neighbourhood.

**Abergele** Wales. Market town in N Denbighshire, 5 m. WSW of Rhyl. Pop. (1961) 7,982. Forms an urban district with the seaside resort of Pensarn.

**Abertillery** Wales. Urban district in Monmouthshire 12 m. NNW of Newport. Pop. (1961) 25,160. Coalmining. Manufactures tinplate.

**Aberystwyth** Wales. Municipal borough in Cardiganshire at the mouth of the Ystwyth and Rheidol rivers on Cardigan Bay. Pop. (1961) 10,418. Seaside resort. Seat of a college of the University of Wales (1872) and of the National Library of Wales (1911).

**Abidjan** Ivory Coast. Capital, on the Ebrié Lagoon. Pop. (1963) 247,000. Rail terminal for exports, esp. cacao, cotton, palm oil and kernels, timber. Connected by rail with its outport Port-Bouet; jointly with it the main seaport. Formerly capital of the French colony (1934–58). ◊◊ *Ouagadougou.*

**Abilene** USA. Town in Texas 145 m. WSW of Fort Worth. Pop. (1960) 90,368. Commercial centre. Trade in cotton, wheat, livestock, oil. Clothing, foodprocessing, and other industries. Seat of the Hardin-Simmons University (1891).

**Abingdon** England. Municipal borough in Berkshire, on the R. Thames 6 m. S of Oxford. Pop. (1961) 14,283. Manufactures cars, leather goods. Brewing. Agricultural trade. Remains of an ancient Benedictine abbey.

**Abitibi, Lake** Canada. A lake of very irregular shape, covering 350 sq. m. on the border between Quebec and Ontario provinces. Touching its wooded N banks is the Quebec–Winnipeg railway, a line of penetration for French-Canadian farmers and lumbermen who are increasingly settling in the scantily peopled area.

**Abitibi River** Canada. River in Ontario 340 m. long, draining L. Abitibi, flowing N, and joining the Moose R. Its power is harnessed at Abitibi Canyon near Fraserdale, used in local gypsum and lignite mines, and carried to several other mining centres in Ontario.

**Abkhaz ASSR (Abkhazia)** USSR. Autonomous Republic in the NW of the Georgian SSR between the Black Sea and the S slopes of the Greater Caucasus. Area 3,320 sq. m. Pop. (1970) 487,000 (mainly Georgian and Abkhazian). Cap. Sukhumi. Mountainous and well wooded. The majority of the population is concentrated in the narrow coastal plain, which has a sub-tropical climate. On the plain maize, tobacco, tea, citrus fruits, and vines are cultivated; there are several health resorts, inc. Sukhumi, Gudauty, and Gagry. Hydroelectric power and coal produced. Annexed by Russia 1864; became an ASSR 1921.

**Abnikum** ♢ *Ani*.

**Åbo** ♢ *Turku*.

**Aboukir (Abu Qir)** United Arab Republic. Small village on the bay of the same name, 14 m. NE of Alexandria, with which it is connected by rail. Nelson defeated the French in Aboukir Bay (the 'Battle of the Nile'; 1798).

**Abruzzi e Molise** Italy. S central region. Area 5,880 sq. m. Pop. (1961) 1,584,777. Abruzzi (N) comprises the provinces of Aquila, Chieti, Pescara, and Teramo; Molise (S) the province of Campobasso. In the highest and most rugged part of the Apennines. No large towns. In the fertile valleys main occupations are stock rearing and cultivation of cereals, grapes, sugarbeet, etc.

**Abu, Mount** India. Isolated mountain (5,650 ft) in Rajasthan 60 m. W of Udaipur, near the Aravalli Range. A well-known place of pilgrimage; two of the Jain temples at Dilwara are of white marble (11th/13th cent.). The near-by small town of Abu is a hot-weather resort.

**Abu Qir** ♢ *Aboukir*.

**Abu Simbel** United Arab Republic. Site of two temples built by Rameses II (1304–1237 B.C.) in the sandstone cliffs on the left bank of the Nile 145 m. SW of Aswan. The temples were threatened by the rise in water level of the reservoir behind the ♢ *Aswan* High Dam, and UNESCO in cooperation with the UAR government had them removed in sections and rebuilt 200 ft above the original site and 12 ft above the highest expected water level (1964–8).

**Abydos** Turkey. Ancient town in Asia Minor on the Hellespont (♢ *Dardanelles*) whence Xerxes crossed with his army on a bridge of boats (480 B.C.). Also scene of the legend of Hero and Leander.

**Abyssinia** ♢ *Ethiopia*.

**Acadia (Fr. Acadie)** N America. Early name – introduced into Europe (1524) by the Florentine traveller Verrazano – for a large area in eastern N America settled by the French, from the lower St Lawrence valley as far S as Philadelphia. De Monts was given a patent by Henry IV of France in 1603; 18 years later Sir William Alexander was granted the land, and changed the name of the coastal portion to ♢ *Nova Scotia*. The French inhabitants were in almost continuous rebellion; when the Treaty of Utrecht (1713) ceded Acadia to Britain, about 6,000 of them were deported. The US Acadia National Park is a forested area mainly on Mt Desert Island, off the coast of Maine.

**Acapulco (officially Acapulco de Juárez)** Mexico. Popular seaside resort in Guerrero state, 195 m. SSW of Mexico City. Pop. (1960) 49,000. Fine sandy beaches and many hotels. Commercial centre. Trade in fruit, cotton, etc.

**Acarnania** Greece. District in ancient Greece, W of the Aspropotamos R. Now forms a *nome* with ♢ *Aetolia*.

**Accad** ♢ *Akkad*.

**Accra** Ghana. Capital, largest city, and former 'surf' port, on the Gulf of Guinea. Pop. (1964) 491,000. Grew up round the three fortresses of Fort James, Fort Crèvecoeur (later Fort Ussher), and Christiansborg, built by the English, Dutch, and Danes respectively. Replaced Cape Coast as capital of the Gold Coast 1876. Rail and road terminal from the interior. Government administrative buildings, schools, hospitals, the National Museum, two cathedrals, headquarters of the broadcasting system, factories, etc. Near by at Legon is the University of Ghana.

**Accrington** England. Municipal borough in Lancashire 5 m. E of Blackburn. Pop. (1961) 40,987. Cotton weaving, calico printing and dyeing. Manufactures textile machinery, bricks, etc.

**Achaea** Greece. 1. Region of ancient Greece, on the N coast of the Peloponnese between the mountains of Erymanthos and the Gulf of Corinth. Its cities combined to form the Achaean League, the main power in Greece (280–146 B.C.) until the Roman conquest.
2. *Nome* of modern Greece. Area 1,210 sq. m. Pop. (1961) 236,770. Cap. and chief seaport Patras. Produces currants, olives. Sheep and goats raised. Formerly part of Achaea and Elis *nome*.

**Achelous River** ⟡ *Aspropotamos River*.

**Achill Island** Irish Republic. Island off the W coast of Co. Mayo. Area 57 sq. m. Pop. (1966) 3,598. Connected with the mainland by a bridge across the narrow Achill Sound. Mountainous, rising to 2,204 ft in Slievemore (N). Main occupations fishing, cultivation of oats and potatoes, raising of livestock. Chief villages and tourist centres Dugort, Keel.

**Aconcagua** Argentina. Highest peak of the Andes (22,835 ft), in W Argentina near the Chile frontier and the Uspallata Pass.

**Aconcagua River** Chile. River 120 m. long, rising on Aconcagua and entering the Pacific 12 m. N of Valparaiso. Irrigates a fertile valley producing fruit, tobacco, etc. Followed by the Trans-Andine railway.

**Acre** Brazil. State in the W, bounded by Peru, Bolivia, and Amazonas state. Area 58,899 sq. m. Pop. (1960) 160,208. Cap. Rio Branco. Named after the Acre R. (tributary of the Purús), which crosses it. Formerly part of Bolivia; passed to Brazil 1903.

**Acre** (Ar. **'Akka**) Israel. Town on the Bay of Acre 9 m. NNE of Haifa. Pop. 20,000. Formerly an important port; superseded by Haifa. Its strategic position was responsible for a stormy history; some of its ruins date from the time of the Crusades. Taken by the Muslims 638; captured by the Crusaders 1104; fell to Saladin 1187; recaptured (1191) by the Crusaders, who made it their chief port. Finally lost to the Muslims 1291. Taken by the Turks 1517. Successfully defended against Napoleon

1799. Taken by Ibrahim Pasha of Egypt (1832) but recaptured (1840) by combined British, Austrian, and Turkish fleets and restored to Turkey. Occupied by the British in the 1st World War.

**Actium** Greece. Promontory in ancient Greece, in NW Acarnania opposite the modern Preveza. Famous for the naval victory of Octavian over Antony and Cleopatra (31 B.C.).

**Acton** England. Former municipal borough in Middlesex; from 1965 part of the London borough of Ealing. Pop. (1961) 65,274. Engineering and other industries. Former residents include Richard Baxter and Henry Fielding.

**Adam, Mount** ⟡ *Falkland Islands*.

**Adam's Bridge (Rama's Bridge)** Ceylon/ India. Chain of sandbanks 17 m. long between Rameswaram Island (SE India) and Mannar Island (NW Ceylon). According to Hindu legend, the remains of a great causeway built by Rama (hero of the *Ramayana*) to take his army from India to Ceylon. Geological evidence suggests that it was once an isthmus.

**Adam's Peak** Ceylon. Mountain 7,360 ft high, in SW 45 m. ESE of Colombo. Much visited by pilgrims. On the conical summit is a platform with a hollow about 5 ft long resembling a human footprint; to Buddhists it is that of Buddha, to Hindus that of Siva, and to Muslims that of Adam.

**Adana** Turkey. Capital of Adana province, in SE Asia Minor on the Seyhan R. Pop. (1965) 289,900. Industrial and commercial centre. Manufactures cotton goods, tobacco products, etc. Trade in cereals, cotton. Has a stone bridge dating in part from the time of Justinian, and the ruins of a castle founded (782) by Harun al-Rashid.

**Adapazari** Turkey. Town in the Kocaeli province 130 m. WNW of Ankara. Pop. (1965) 90,000. Manufactures textiles, etc. Trade in rugs, tobacco, etc. Partly destroyed by earthquake, with the loss of 83 lives, in July 1967.

**Adare, Cape** ⟡ *Ross Sea*.

**Addis Ababa** Ethiopia. In Amharic, 'New Flower'. Capital, on a plateau 8,000 ft above sea level; site chosen (1887) by Emperor Menelek II. Pop. (1964) 449,021. Connected with ⟡ *Djibouti* (French Territory Afars and Issas) by a 486-m. railway (1917). International airport. Became the capital of Abyssinia 1896. After the occupation of the country by the Italians (1936), became the capital of Italian E Africa (including Eritrea and Italian Somaliland). Captured (1941) from the Italians during the 2nd World War; Ethiopian rule was restored. Seat of the University College of Addis Ababa (founded 1950) and the Haile Selassie University (inaugurated 1961).

**Adelaide** Australia. Capital of S Australia, on the Torrens R. just W of the Mt Lofty Range, near the E shore of Gulf St Vincent. Pop. (1966) 726,930. Founded (1836) as the centre of a planned colony for free immigrants. Contains over three fifths of the state's population and is the chief outlet for exports of wheat, wool, fruit, wine, meat, hides, and wattle bark. Cultural and commercial centre. Expanding industries, inc. the manufacture of agricultural implements, cars, electrical equipment, paint, textiles. The Torrens has been dammed and converted into a lake, while water for the city is partly supplied by a 46-m. pipeline from a reservoir at Mannum on the Murray R. Summer droughts are typical of its Mediterranean type of climate; most of its rain, 21 ins. annually, falls in winter; temperatures range from 74° F in Jan. to 52° F in July. Large airport 5 m. W of the city. Ships dock at the outer harbour to Port Adelaide, 16 m. from the city centre.

**Adelboden** Switzerland. Resort in the Bern canton 22 m. SW of Interlaken in the Bernese Oberland at a height of 4,450 ft. Pop. (1960) 2,900.

**Adélie Land** Antarctica. Antarctic territory between Wilkes Land and King George V Land (between long. 136° E and 142° E) bordering the Indian Ocean. Area 155,000 sq. m. Discovered by Dumont d'Urville 1840; explored by Sir Douglas Mawson 1912–13. Placed under French sovereignty 1938. From 1955 part of ◊ *French Southern and Antarctic Territories.*

**Aden** S Yemen. Former British Crown Colony, on the SW coast of the Arabian peninsula 100 m. E of the S entrance to the Red Sea; formerly included Perim, Kamaran, and the Kuria Muria Is. Area 75 sq. m. Pop. (1964) 225,000 (mostly Arab and Yemeni). Consists of two volcanic peninsulas of barren rock, Aden (E) and Little Aden (W), enclosing Aden Back Bay. Important fuelling station on the route to the E. Entrepôt trade. Produces salt from seawater. Oil refining and minor industries. The old Arab town of Crater (pop. 55,000)

is on the E side of the main peninsula; Sheikh Othman (pop. 29,000) at the head of the isthmus; the modern port of Steamer Point on the W. Aden has considerable strategic significance and is strongly fortified. Important commercially in very early times, but declined after the discovery of the Cape route to India (1497). Captured by the British 1839. Revived after the opening of the Suez Canal (1869). Scene of many political disturbances in the 1960s. Became part of the Federation of S Arabia (1963), which became the People's Republic of S Yemen (1967).

**Aden Protectorate.** Former British protectorate, divided into W and E and held by Arab chiefs, E, W, and N of Aden; includes the island of Socotra. Area 112,000 sq. m. Pop. 660,000. Much of the area, with Aden, formed the Federation of S Arabia (1963), which became the People's Republic of S Yemen (1967). Produces dates, gums. Sheep and goats raised. Principal port Mukalla.

**Adige (Ger. Etsch) River** Italy. Ancient Athesis. Second longest (220 m.) and most important river after the Po, rising in small lakes on the Resia Pass, flowing S and E to Merano, and then SE to Bolzano (where it is joined by the Isarco), turning SW (receiving the Noce and the Avisio) past Trento and Rovereto, then SE past Verona and Legnago, and then E to enter the Adriatic Sea a few miles N of the Po. Used for hydroelectric power and irrigation.

**Adirondack Mountains** USA. Group of mountains in the N part of New York state, rising from a plateau of 2,000 ft to a height of 5,345 ft in Mt Marcy, structurally a southerly continuation of the Laurentian Shield of Canada. Heavily glaciated during the Great Ice Age; many beautiful lakes and waterfalls. Poor soil has not encouraged settlement; some lumbering, but the greater part of the forest cover remains. Many resorts.

**Admiralty Islands** Australasia. Group of about 40 islands in the ◊ *Bismarck Archipelago* NE of New Guinea; part of the Australian Trust Territory of New Guinea. Area 800 sq. m. Pop. (1966) 20,647. Main island Manus. Chief town Lorengau. Main occupations coconut planting, shell fishing. Discovered (1616) by the Dutch. Annexed by Germany 1885. Recaptured (1944) from the Japanese in the 2nd World War.

**Adour River** France. River 208 m. long, rising in the Hautes-Pyrénées department S of the Pic du Midi de Bigorre, flowing in a wide curve through Gers and Landes, and entering the Bay of Biscay below Bayonne.

**Adowa** ◊ *Aduwa*.

**Adria** Italy. Ancient Atria. Town in Rovigo province, Veneto, between the Po and the Adige rivers 27 m. NE of Ferrara. Pop. (1961) 26,027. A prosperous seaport on the Adriatic (to which it gave its name) in Etruscan and later in Roman times, but now 14 m. inland owing to silting. Manufactures bricks, cement, etc.

**Adrianople** ◊ *Edirne*.

**Adriatic Sea** Europe. Arm of the Mediterranean, extending 500 m. NW between Italy and the Balkan Peninsula, from the strait of Otranto (45 m. wide) to the Gulf of Trieste. The W coast is low-lying and straight, the E coast steep, rocky, and much indented, with many offshore islands. The chief rivers are the Po and the Adige, which continually deposit silt on the coast; Adria (from which the name derives) and other former ports are now inland. Chief modern ports Brindisi, Bari, Venice, Trieste (Italy); Rijeka, Split, Dubrovnik (Yugoslavia); Durrës (Albania). Famous for its blue water and fine scenery. Many popular tourist centres on the Italian and Dalmatian coasts.

**Aduwa (Adowa; Adwa)** Ethiopia. Capital of Tigre province, village 75 m. S of Asmara at a height of 6,500 ft in an agricultural region. Pop. 6,000. Invading force of Italians repulsed by Ethiopian forces 1896. Bombed and captured by the Italians 1935. Reoccupied by Ethiopian and British troops 1941.

**Adygei AR USSR.** Autonomous Region in the Krasnodar Territory of the S European RSFSR, N of the Caucasus and S of the Kuban and Laba rivers. Area 2,934 sq. m. Pop. (1970) 386,000. Cap. Maikop. Maize, wheat, sun-flowers, tobacco cultivated. Food processing. The people are largely Adygei, Circassians from the mountain valleys who were forced by the Russians to settle in the lowlands (1861). The Region was established in 1922.

**Adzhar ASSR (Adzharistan) USSR.** Autonomous Republic in the SW of the Georgian SSR at the W end of the Lesser Caucasus, bordered on the S by Turkey. Area 1,160 sq. m. Pop. (1970) 310,000 (mainly Adzhar and Georgian). Cap. Batumi. The mountainous E is thinly populated. Most of the inhabitants live in the narrow coastal plain, which has a subtropical climate with heavy rainfall and where most of the USSR's tea and citrus fruits are produced. Many seaside resorts, inc. Batumi (also the chief industrial centre). Under the Muslim Turks in the 17th and 18th cent.; annexed by Russia in the 19th cent. Became an ASSR 1921.

**Aegean Sea** Europe. Arm of the Mediterranean 400 m. long (N–S) and up to 200 m. wide (W–E); between Greece and Asia Minor (Turkey), linked by the Dardanelles with the Sea of Marmara and the Black Sea. Studded with islands (the great majority belonging to Greece), inc. the Dodecanese, the Cyclades, the N Sporades, and Euboea. Leading ports Piraeus, Thessaloniki (Greece); Izmir (Turkey). The name may derive from Aegeus, father of Theseus in ancient Greek legend.

**Aegina** ◊ *Aigina*.

**Aelana** ◊ *Aqaba*.

**Aetolia** Greece. Region on the N side of the Gulf of Patras, forming with Acarnania (from which it is separated by the Aspropotamos R.) the *nome* of Aetolia and Acarnania. Combined area 2,081 sq. m. Pop. (1961) 237,407. Cap. Missolonghi. Largely mountainous. Cereals, olives, and other crops cultivated on the coastal plain. Aetolia became important with the formation of the Aetolian League (314 B.C.). Joined Rome to defeat the Macedonians 197 B.C. Later opposed the Romans, lost power, and was incorporated into Achaea.

**Afghanistan.** An independent, mountainous, somewhat isolated kingdom in Central Asia. Area 250,000 sq. m. Pop. (1962) 13,800,000 (60 per cent Afghan, 15 per cent Tajik, 10 per cent Hazara). Cap. Kabul. Lang. Persian, Pushtu. Rel. Muslim.

Bounded by the USSR (N), Pakistan (E and S), Iran (W); in the NE (Wakhan) it touches on China. Most of the country is arid and barren; cultivation is successful only in the fertile plains and valleys, generally by means of irrigation. Administratively divided into 29 provinces. TOPOGRAPHY, CLIMATE. The country is dominated by the Hindu Kush (NE), rising to over 25,000 ft and extending W by the Koh-i-Baba, the Safed Koh, and the Paropamisus Range. The central highlands are called the Hazarajat (after the native Hazara). Along part of the N frontier flows the Amu Darya; the longest river, the Helmand, drains SW to the Seistan depression, and the Kabul R. E to the Indus. In general the climate is dry continental, exceptionally rigorous in winter in the NE, hot and dusty in summer in the sandy desert of the SW, the Dasht-i-Margo. Annual precipitation is less than 10 ins. in many areas.

RESOURCES, PEOPLE, etc. Both agriculture and stock rearing are practised. Crops include wheat and other cereals, cotton, and grapes and other fruits. Large numbers of fat-tailed sheep; the valuable karakul ('Persian lamb') breed is also raised. Mineral resources scarcely exploited. No railways; as most of the roads are unsuitable for vehicular traffic, goods are usually carried by camel or mule caravan. Main exports karakul skins, dried fruits, nuts, carpets, cotton, wool. Foreign trade is chiefly with the USSR. Chief towns Kabul, Kandahar, Herat. Most of the people belong to the Sunni sect of Islam; a minority (esp. the Hazara) is Shiah Muslim. They are divided into tribes and clans; some are nomadic. The country adopted parliamentary democracy under a new constitution which took effect in 1965, with a National Assembly of 216 elected members.

HISTORY. In early times Afghanistan was occupied by Persians, Greeks, and various Asiatic and Semitic peoples. The great Persian monarch Nadir Shah absorbed the entire country in his empire; on his death (1747) one of his Afghan officers, Ahmed Khan, took the royal title and founded modern Afghanistan. For a time it extended far beyond its present frontiers, but under Ahmed Shah's successors many possessions were lost. In the 19th cent. the rivalry between Britain and Russia led to the Afghan Wars; peace was restored when British troops occupied Kabul (1879). Relations with Britain improved, until King Amanullah's invasion of India (1919) precipitated the 3rd Afghan War but this ended in a few months, and Britain recognized the complete independence of Afghanistan in 1921. Amanullah abdicated in 1929.

Africa. Second largest of the world's land masses; three times the size of Europe. Area 11,641,000 sq. m. Pop. (1961) about 261 million. Extent N–S 5,000 m. from

Cape Blanc to Cape Agulhas (S Africa) and E–W 4,500 m. from Cape Verde to Cape Guardafui. The last continent to be fully explored by Europeans; hence 'the dark continent'. Falls into two very distinct parts, effectively separated by the Sahara: N Africa, essentially a Mediterranean area, together with the Nile valley, a part of the Old World since antiquity; and a larger part S of the Sahara, discovered only slowly by European exploration, where permanent settlement by Europeans is limited to certain parts (e.g. S Africa, Kenya), sparsely inhabited by a great variety of Negro peoples with varying cultures and languages. Much of the area is unpropitious, but there are great potentialities and considerable mineral wealth. Recently the 'wind of change' has swept many of the African peoples (at varying levels of preparedness and, as regards the mass of the population, still at a tribal stage of culture) to the status of independent countries.

The equator runs almost exactly through the centre, but more than two thirds of Africa lies to the N. The Greenwich meridian passes through NW and W Africa; most of the continent is in E longitudes. Bounded by the Mediterranean Sea (N), the Atlantic Ocean (W), and the Red Sea, the Gulf of Aden, and the Indian Ocean (E). Joined to SW Asia by the isthmus of Suez. At the Straits of Gibraltar only 9 m. from Europe. Peninsulas and bays are few; the coastline is relatively short (16,000 m.). Off the SE coast is the Malagasy Republic (Madagascar), fourth largest island in the world. Few other islands: Socotra, Zanzibar, Pemba to the E; the Comoro Is., Fernando Póo, São Thomé, Principe, Annobon Island in the Gulf of Guinea; and the Cape Verde Is., Canary Is., and Madeira off the NW coast. Those of the NW and Guinea coasts are of volcanic origin.

TOPOGRAPHY. Largely a vast plateau. Generally higher in the S and E than in the N and W. Broken in the extreme NW by the folded ranges of the Atlas Mountains. In the extreme SE the Drakensberg forms a high rim. Mean elevation greater than that of Europe but less than that of Asia. A prominent feature is the Great Rift Valley with its many lakes; E of L. Victoria (the largest in the continent) are the highest mountains, the volcanic Mt Kilimanjaro and Mt Kenya. Other heights are the Ruwenzori Highlands beside the W branch of the Great Rift Valley (NW of L. Victoria) and Ras Dashan in Ethiopia. RIVERS. The Nile, Africa's longest river, leaves the N side of L. Victoria and enters the N end of L. Albert, as the White Nile; joined at Khartoum by the Blue Nile (fed mainly from L. Tana in the Ethiopian highlands), it flows N to the Mediterranean, receiving no tributaries as it crosses the immense desert region of NE Africa. In spite of its greater length its basin area is much smaller than that of the Congo R., Africa's second great waterway, whose E headstreams rise on the lofty plateau between L. Malawi and L. Tanganyika; fed by many tributaries, it flows N and W to the Atlantic Ocean. The headstreams of the Niger flow from the Futa Jallon plateau NE towards the Sahara; in a roughly semi-circular course it turns E and then S, entering the Gulf of Guinea. The Zambezi (shortest of Africa's four great waterways, but the largest of those flowing into the Indian Ocean) has many tributaries, including the Shiré from L. Malawi, but the basin area is less than half that of the Nile. Other rivers in southern Africa include the Orange – which receives the Vaal (both rising on the W slopes of the Drakensberg) and flows into the Atlantic Ocean – and the Limpopo, which follows a roughly semicircular course to the Indian Ocean. ⟡ under DEVELOPMENT below.

CLIMATE. Almost three quarters of Africa lies within the tropics, and experiences the vertical sun. No area extends far into temperate latitudes, but in some regions altitude tempers the heat. Temperature, humidity, and annual rainfall (over 60 ins.) are high throughout the year in equatorial central Africa and on the Guinea coast. In equatorial E Africa temperatures are lower on the plateau, rainfall is lighter, and the cooler climate is more congenial to Europeans. On both sides of the equatorial region temperatures are high but there are marked rainy and dry seasons; despite drought in the cool season, annual rainfall in the coastal areas of Sierra Leone and Liberia is more than 120 ins. N of the equator rainfall decreases northwards, and a vast area influenced by the dry NE Trade Winds has a hot desert type of climate and an annual rainfall of less than 10 ins. The Sahara extends virtually from the Atlantic Ocean to the Red Sea, with some of the

highest shade temperatures on record, though as the skies are cloudless rapid radiation causes the hot days to be followed by relatively cool nights. In corresponding latitudes S of the equator is the Kalahari Desert: the SE Trade Winds carry rain only to the E part of the plateau, esp. to E Malagasy. Along the N African coast, and again around Cape Town, the climate is of dry sub-tropical Mediterranean type: summers are long, dry, and hot, and rain falls chiefly in the mild winters.

VEGETATION AND CROPS. Tropical rain-forest covers most of the Congo basin and the Guinea coast, the belt along the E side of Malagasy, and part of the narrow coastal fringe of E Africa; it yields tropical hardwoods, e.g. mahogany. Other products, e.g. palm oil and rubber, now come largely from plantations; the cacao tree has been successfully introduced into forest clearings, and bananas grow widely. Savannah extends in a broad belt round these forests and occupies most of the W of Malagasy; the characteristic vegetation is tall coarse grass with scattered trees, including the baobab and varieties of acacia. Cattle are raised, millet and maize cultivated; groundnuts, cotton, sisal, tobacco, and coffee are important export crops. Around the drier edge of the savannah the grassland passes gradually to scrub, merging into desert. Scrub and desert together cover a high proportion of the continent. The Sahara contains sandy, rocky, and stony areas, but over its greater part there is a sparse vegetation of stunted shrubs. In oases the date palm is important; cotton, cultivated on irrigated land, is an important crop. In the Mediterranean regions of the NW and the S, forests and woodlands contain evergreen trees and shrubs; olives are widely cultivated in the NW and grapes and citrus fruits in both areas.

ANIMALS. Wild life abounds in many parts. On the savannah live some of the world's largest herbivores – elephant, rhinoceros, hippopotamus, giraffe – with various species of antelope, and carnivores, e.g. lions, leopards, hyenas. Monkeys and apes are widespread; gorillas and chimpanzees inhabit the tropical rain-forests, which also have abundant bird and insect life. The world's largest bird, the ostrich, occurs on grasslands and in the semi-desert regions in the S. The camel is the principal animal of the semi-desert and desert regions. Many wild animals are in danger of extinction, and nature reserves, e.g. the Kruger National Park, have been created.

Certain insects profoundly affect the human and economic life of Africa. The tsetse fly infests enormous areas of E, W, and central Africa, bringing sleeping sickness to man and *nagana* to cattle. The anopheles mosquito carries malaria over much of Africa. Locusts are a plague in many areas (outside the tropical rainforests). Various control methods against these and other harmful insects, e.g. insecticides, the destruction of insect breeding-places, the dipping and inoculation of cattle, are achieving some success.

RESOURCES. There is considerable mineral wealth, e.g. uranium, gold, platinum, diamonds (both gemstones and industrial). Rich copper deposits are worked in the Katanga province of Congo (Kinshasa) and the Copperbelt of Zambia. Congo (Kinshasa) produces the bulk of the world's cobalt. Chrome ore and phosphates are extensively mined, but Africa is poor in power resources; coal is found only rarely (e.g. in S Africa). Rich oilfields have recently been discovered in Algeria, Libya, and Nigeria. Hydroelectric power is developed on a relatively small scale, chiefly in Morocco and the Katanga province of Congo (Kinshasa); among recent schemes the Owen Falls Dam (Uganda) and the Kariba Dam (Rhodesia/Zambia) are noteworthy.

DEVELOPMENT. Hampered by poor transport. Many rivers have waterfalls and rapids which impede navigation; others are useless in the dry season, a factor which also hinders the use of water power. There are steamer services over long stretches of the Nile and Congo rivers, however, as well as on the larger lakes. Rail and road construction has usually been piecemeal, depending upon the advance of European colonization, and only S Africa has what can be termed a network of railways. There is a Portuguese-built coast-to-coast railway between Benguela (Angola) and Beira (Moçambique); the three former French colonies in NW Africa – Algeria, Morocco, Tunisia – are linked by rail. The Cape to Cairo and the Trans-Sahara railway routes are unlikely to be completed, in view of airtransport development.

POPULATION. A density of about 22 per sq. m. – slightly greater than that of S America, but only one tenth that of Europe.

The lower valley and delta of the Nile (where the river provides water for irrigation) are the most densely populated; Cairo is by far the largest city in Africa. Otherwise population density is high only in small areas around large towns, e.g. Ibadan, Johannesburg. Aridity causes limited settlement; vast areas of the Sahara, Libyan, Kalahari, and Namib deserts and lesser areas of the eastern Horn of Africa (SE Ethiopia, NE Kenya) are uninhabited. The coastal fringe of NW Africa, the Nile valley, the Guinea land (Gambia to E Nigeria), the plateau area round L. Victoria, and the E parts of S Africa and of the Malagasy Republic (regions where in general rainfall favours agriculture) are well peopled compared with the rest of the continent.

PEOPLES. Two main indigenous groups, roughly divided by the S edge of the Sahara (always a barrier to large-scale migrations). N of the Sahara, a mixture of Hamitic and Semitic peoples, more akin to S Europeans than to trans-Saharan Africans. The Hamites include the Berbers and the Tuareg, centred on the Ahaggar plateau; the Ethiopians are largely of mixed Hamitic and Semitic origin. With the Arab conquest (7th cent. A.D.) the Semites spread across N Africa; they now occupy most of Egypt, N Sudan, and Libya, and much of NW Africa; but there has been so much mingling of Arabs and Berbers that they are often indistinguishable, and all are Muslim. S of the Sahara the population is Negro. Some, e.g. the Hausa and the Fulani of N Nigeria and the Dinka and the Shilluk of the Upper Nile Valley, show strong Hamitic admixture. The rest are sometimes divided into two major groups: the Sudanese (inhabiting W Africa, e.g. the Yoruba, the Kru, and the Mandinga); the Bantu (inhabiting most of Africa S of the equator). Some Bantu, e.g. the Kikuyu, are agriculturists, some, e.g. the Masai, are pastoralists; others, e.g. the Zulu, combine agriculture and stock raising. The Bushmen (S Africa), shorter and with paler skins, are remnants of an earlier people driven by the Bantu and later by the Europeans into the least hospitable areas; they now live by their primitive hunting economy in the Kalahari Desert, and – like the Hottentots (believed to derive from the Bushmen and Hamitic stock) – they face extinction. The pygmies (negrillos) in the tropical forests of central Africa are another dwindling group. The inhabitants of Malagasy are mainly of Polynesian stock.

HISTORY AND DISCOVERY. Ancient Egypt was one of the earliest civilizations. The Mediterranean littoral was settled and developed first by the Carthaginians, from the 9th cent. B.C. After expelling them, the Romans (who gave the name Africa to their new provinces) continued the process. In the 5th cent. B.C. Herodotus knew something of the Upper Nile and Libya. Later the Arab geographers showed a growing though imprecise knowledge of wider areas. The Arab conquest (7th cent. A.D.) gave N Africa some unity and a common religion. Later the Portuguese explored the W coast; Diaz rounded the Cape of Good Hope in 1488 and Vasco da Gama reached the E coast by the same route. To the Portuguese (and to the British, the Dutch, and the French, who followed them) Africa was a valuable source of slaves, ivory, and gold, obtained at various points along the W coast; the interior remained unknown. During the late 18th and the 19th cent. a number of famous explorers gradually penetrated 'the dark continent', esp. Mungo Park in the Niger basin, Bruce in Abyssinia (now Ethiopia), Livingstone in the Zambezi and Upper Congo basins, Burton in Somaliland and round L. Tanganyika, Speke at the source of the Nile and L. Victoria, and Stanley in the Congo basin and at L. Tanganyika and L. Albert and in the Ruwenzori Highlands. In the second half of the 19th cent. and the early 20th cent. various European powers colonized Africa; Abyssinia (Ethiopia) and Liberia alone remained independent. After the 1st World War the German colonies became Mandated Territories of the League of Nations. They became Trust Territories of the United Nations after the 2nd World War, when the Italians also lost their colonies. The 2nd World War led to increased political consciousness among African peoples, and most of the former colonies and protectorates have now achieved independence.

Agade ◊ Akkad.

Agadès ◊ Aïr Highlands; Niger.

Agadir Morocco. Port on the Atlantic coast 75 m. S of Essaouira. Pop. 45,000. Serves the fertile Sous region. Linked by road with Essaouira and Marrakesh. Fish-canning industry. Devastated by earthquake 1960, when over 12,000 people were killed.

Agaña ◊ Guam.

Agartala ◊ Tripura.

Agen France. Market town on the N side of the Garonne R. (here crossed by a bridge) 58 m. NW of Toulouse. Pop. (1968) 37,470. Prefecture of the Lot-et-Garonne department. In a fruit-growing and market-gardening region, well known for preserved fruits and other food products. Cathedral dates in part from the 12th cent.

Agincourt (modern Azincourt) France. Village in the Pas-de-Calais department, 30 m. SE of Boulogne-sur-mer. Pop. (1968) 220. Famous for the victory (1415) of Henry V and English forces over a much larger French army during the Hundred Years War.

Aginskoye ◊ Buryat-Aginsky NA.

Agordat Ethiopia. Town in Eritrea 70 m. W of Asmara (with which it is connected by rail) where the Italians defeated the Khalifa and his followers (1893). Pop. 2,000.

Agra India. City in Uttar Pradesh, on the Jumna R. 115 m. SSE of Delhi. Pop. (1961) 462,029. Industrial and commercial centre. Manufactures cotton goods, carpets, footwear, etc. Trade in hides, wool. Famous for its buildings, esp. the Taj Mahal (probably the world's most celebrated mausoleum), built 1632–50 in pure white marble by Shah Jahan as a memorial to his wife. In the fortress built by Akbar (1566) are the Moti Masjid (Pearl Mosque) of Shah Jahan, and the Jahangiri Mahal of Akbar (whose tomb is 6 m. N at Sikandra). Founded (1566) by Akbar; capital of India for many years, but began to decline when Aurangzeb moved to Delhi (1658). Captured by the British 1803. Capital of the NW Provinces 1835–62.

Agrigento Italy. Ancient Agrigentum. Formerly (until 1927) Girgenti. Capital of Agrigento province near the S coast of Sicily, 55 m. SSE of Palermo. Pop. (1961) 47,919. Trade in sulphur. Harbour at Porto Empedocle (SW). Founded (582 B.C.) by Greek colonists from Gela. Plundered by the Carthaginians 406 B.C. Occupied by the Romans 210 B.C. Greek remains, inc. several temples. Severely damaged during the 2nd World War. Birthplace of Empedocles (490–430 B.C.).

Aguascalientes Mexico. 1. State on the central plateau at a height of 6,000 ft. Area 2,499 sq. m. Pop. (1969) 316,000. Mainly agricultural, producing maize, fruit, vegetables. Cattle ranches provide bulls for Mexican bull rings.

**2.** Capital of Aguascalientes state 115 m. NE of Guadalajara. Pop. (1969) 166,900. Important railway workshops; flour mills, tanneries, potteries. Named after the medicinal hot springs near by.

**Agulhas, Cape** S Africa. In Portuguese, 'Needles'. The most southerly point of Africa, in the Cape Province between the Atlantic and Indian oceans. A rocky headland, with reefs dangerous to shipping. Lighthouse.

**Ahaggar (Hoggar) Mountains** Algeria. Highland region in the central Sahara, rising to 9,850 ft in Mt Tahat. Annual rainfall up to 10 ins.; many wadis have been formed. Population mainly Tuareg. Chief oasis town Tamanrasset.

**Ahlen** Federal German Republic. Town in N Rhine-Westphalia 18 m. SSE of Münster. Pop. (1963) 42,200. Coalmining centre. Manufactures hardware, footwear, etc. In the Prussian province of Westphalia until 1945.

**Ahmadabad** India. Capital of the Ahmadabad district in Gujarat, on the Sabarmati R. 280 m. N of Bombay. Pop. (1961) 1,149,918. Important railway junction. Cotton milling. Manufactures pottery, brocades, jewellery, etc. A cultural centre; seat of the University of Gujarat (1950). Many fine buildings, including the Jama Masjid and other mosques and the modern Jain temple (1848). Founded (1411) by Ahmad Shah; declined in the 18th cent. but revived with the establishment of the cotton industry in the mid 19th cent.

**Ahmadnagar** India. Capital of the Ahmadnagar district in Maharashtra, 125 m. E of Bombay. Pop. (1961) 119,020. Commercial and industrial centre. Trade in cotton, grain, etc. Cotton milling, tanning. Manufactures copper and brass articles. Founded (1494) by Ahmad Nizam Shah.

**Ahuachapán** Salvador. Capital of the Ahuachapán department, on the W coast. Pop. (1961) 40,359. Centre of an important coffee-producing area. A recently built bridge across the Paz R. carries the Pan-American highway from Guatemala.

**Ahuriri, Port** ▷ *Napier.*

**Ahvenanmaa** (Swedish **Åland** Islands) Finland. Archipelago of over 6,000 granite islands and rocky islets, about 80 of them inhabited, at the entrance to the Gulf of Bothnia. Area 581 sq. m. Pop. (1968) 21,500. Cap. Maarianhamina (Mariehamn), a free

port, on Ahvenanmaa (Åland), the largest island (area 285 sq. m., pop. 15,000). The inhabitants, of Swedish descent and Swedish-speaking, are mainly fishermen. Some cattle rearing. Rye, barley, flax cultivated. Swedish almost continuously from the Middle Ages; ceded to Russia 1809. After the 1st World War, despite a plebiscite in favour of secession to Sweden, Finnish sovereignty was confirmed by the League of Nations (1921).

**Ahwaz** Iran. Capital of Khuzistan, on the Karun R. 80 m. NNE of Abadan. Pop. (1966) 206,265. Railway junction, commercial centre, and river port. Once important, and revived recently with the construction of the railway and development of oilfields.

**Aigina (Aiyina)** Greece. Ancient Aegina. Island 18 m. SW of Athens. Area 33 sq. m. Pop. 11,000. Produces olives, vines, figs, etc. Commercially important in ancient times, but conquered by Athens 457 B.C. Its people were exiled (431 B.C.), and it declined. The modern town of the same name stands on the site of the old, on the NW coast.

**Aigues-Mortes** France. Town in the Gard department, 15 m. ESE of Montpellier on the W edge of the Rhône delta. Pop. (1968) 4,197. In the Middle Ages an important seaport, built by Louis IX (St Louis), who embarked here for his two crusades (1248, 1270); now 3 m. from the sea owing to silting. The 13th-cent. walls and the Tour de Constance, built by St Louis, are preserved.

**Ailsa Craig** Scotland. Rocky granite island in the Firth of Clyde 10 m. W of Girvan, rising sharply to 1,114 ft. Area 1 sq. m. Lighthouse. Sanctuary of gannets and other sea-birds.

**Ain** France. Department in the E between the Rhône and Saône rivers, bounded on the NE by Switzerland. Area 2,249 sq. m. Pop. (1968) 339,262. Prefecture Bourg. E of the Ain R., which flows SSW through it, are the Jura mountains, where cattle and sheep are grazed and cheese is manufactured; W of the river are the fertile Bresse, where cereals, vines, etc. are cultivated and pigs and poultry raised, and, to the S, the Dombes region, with its many ponds and its cattle and pig rearing. Important hydro-electric installations on the Rhône (Génissiat) and the Ain. Chief towns Bourg, Belley.

**Ain River** France. River 124 m. long rising in the central Jura and flowing SSW through the Jura and Ain departments to join the Rhône 18 m. above Lyons. Provides hydroelectric power.

**Aintree** England. Village in S W Lancashire just N of Liverpool. Racecourse where the annual Grand National steeplechase has been run since its inception (1839).

**Air (Azben, Azbine) Highlands** Niger. Highlands in the S Sahara region, rising to over 6,000 ft. Several oases. Chief centre Agadès, a caravan town.

**Airdrie** Scotland. Large burgh and industrial town in N Lanarkshire 11 m. E of Glasgow. Pop. (1961) 33,620. Coalmines, iron foundries, engineering works, etc.

**Aire River** England. River in Yorkshire 70 m. long, rising in Pennines and flowing S E and E past Skipton, Bingley, and Leeds to receive the Calder at Castleford and join the Ouse above Goole. The upper valley (Airedale) is the original home of the Airedale breed of dogs. The Aire Gap is an important route by rail, road, and canal through the Pennines.

**Aireborough** England. Urban district in the W Riding of Yorkshire 5 m. NNE of Bradford. Pop. (1961) 27,643. Includes Rawdon, Guiseley, and Yeadon. Woollen mills. Ancestors of the poet Longfellow are buried in Guiseley churchyard.

**Aisne** France. Department in the N E comprising parts of the Île-de-France, Picardy, and Champagne, taking its name from the Aisne R. Area 2,867 sq. m. Pop. (1968) 526,346. Prefecture Laon. Sugar-beet and cereals cultivated. Cattle raised. Manufactures textiles, leather, mirrors, chemicals. Chief towns Laon, St Quentin, Soissons. Scene of much fighting in both world wars.

**Aisne River** France. River 150 m. long, rising in the Meuse department, flowing NNW and then W to join the Oise R. near Compiègne. Connected by canals with the Oise and Marne rivers. Scene of important battles during the 1st World War.

**Aix-en-Provence** France. Ancient Aquae Sextiae. Town in the Bouches-du-Rhône department 18 m. NNE of Marseille. Pop. (1968) 93,671. Spa. Industrial and commercial centre. Trade in olives, almonds, fruits. Manufactures agricultural implements, fertilizers, matches. Famous as a cultural centre. Seat of the faculties of law and letters of the Aix-Marseille University (founded 1409). Outstanding buildings are the 12th/15th-cent. cathedral and the 17th-cent. baroque town hall. Founded

(123 B.C.) by the Roman consul Sextius Calvinus and named Aquae Sextiae because of the thermal springs. Scene of the defeat of the Teutones by Marius (102 B.C.). Capital of Provence during the Middle Ages; lost importance after the union of Provence to the Crown. Birthplace of Cézanne (1839–1906).

**Aix-la-Chapelle** ♢ *Aachen.*

**Aix-les-Bains** France. Ancient Aquae Gratianae. Town in the Savoie department 8 m. N of Chambéry, near the E side of the Lac du Bourget. Pop. (1968) 20,718. Resort and spa. The mineral springs were known to the Romans; Roman remains in the neighbourhood. Winter sports centre at near-by Mont Révard.

**Aiyina** ♢ *Aigina.*

**Ajaccio** France. Capital (prefecture) and seaport of Corsica, on the W coast near the head of the Gulf of Ajaccio. Pop. (1968) 42,300. Resort and commercial town. Trade in timber etc. Fishing. The house where Napoleon was born is now a museum. Occupied by the Germans in the 2nd World War; liberated Sept. 1943.

**Ajanta** India. Village in Maharashtra, in the Ajanta Hills 120 m. NNE of Ahmadnagar. Famous for the near-by Buddhist cave temples cut into the side of a ravine, consisting of monasteries and meeting halls, many of them decorated with frescoes, constructed between 100 B.C. and the 7th cent. A.D.

**Ajmer** India. City in Rajasthan 220 m. S W of Delhi. Pop. (1961) 231,240. Railway junction. Industrial and commercial centre. Railway engineering. Manufactures textiles, soap, footwear, etc. Trade in grain, oilseeds, etc. Has the white marble tomb of a Muslim saint, and an ancient Jain temple converted into a mosque. Probably founded in the 2nd cent. A.D. Formerly capital of the Ajmer state.

**Akhtyrka** USSR. Town in the Ukrainian SSR 64 m. WNW of Kharkov. Pop. 31,500. Agricultural centre. Railway terminus. Founded by Poles in the 17th cent. Fine 18th-cent. cathedral.

**Akimiski Island** ♢ *James Bay.*

**Akita** Japan. Capital of Akita prefecture, on the N W coast of Honshu at the mouth of the Omono R. Pop. (1965) 216,606. Minor seaport. Exports petroleum products. Railway workshops, oil refinery (supplied from local oilfield). Manufactures fertilizers, wood pulp, etc.

**'Akka** ♢ *Acre.*

**Akkad (Accad)** Asia Minor. Ancient region in N Babylonia. Named after the capital, Akkad (Agade). Flourished in the 3rd millennium B.C. after Sargon had conquered the surrounding lands, including Sumer.

**Aklavik** Canada. Village in Eskimo country on the W channel of the Mackenzie delta, in the NW Territories. Built (1912) as a Hudson's Bay Company trading post. Arctic administration and the seat of the Anglican Bishop of the Arctic have been moved 33 m. NE to a site with more stable foundations, ◊ *Inuvik*.

**Akmolinsk** ◊ *Tselinograd.*

**Akola** India. Industrial and commercial town in Maharashtra 50 m. WSW of Amravati. Pop. (1961) 115,760. Manufactures cotton goods, soap, etc. Important trade in cotton.

**Akron** USA. Industrial town in Ohio 30 m. SSE of Cleveland at the highest point on the Erie Canal between the Great Lakes and the Ohio R. Pop. (1960) 290,351. Founded 1825. Its great growth occurred when its rubber factories expanded to meet the demand for tyres for the automobile industry; it remains the leading tyre-manufacturing centre of the USA. Also manufactures synthetic rubber and plastic products, machinery, chemicals, etc. University (1870).

**Aksu (Aqsu)** China. Town in Sinkiang-Uighur 250 m. ENE of Kashgar in the Aksu oasis. Pop. 40,000. Caravan centre. Manufactures textiles, carpets, leather.

**Aksum (Axum)** Ethiopia. Ancient town in the Tigre province 13 m. WSW of Aduwa at a height of 7,000 ft. Trade in coffee, cereals, etc. According to tradition, the Jewish Ark of the Covenant was deposited here.

**Aktyubinsk** USSR. Capital of the Aktyubinsk Region, Kazakh SSR, 90 m. SW of Orsk. Pop. (1970) 150,000. Important industrial centre. Manufactures chemicals, ferro-alloys, electrical equipment. Engineering. Flour milling. Founded 1869 as a fort.

**Akyab** Burma. Capital of the Arakan division, a seaport on the Bay of Bengal. Pop. 43,000. Exports rice. Rice-milling industry. Developed in the 19th cent. from a small fishing village. Occupied by the Japanese 1942–5.

**Alabama** USA. One of the southern states, about the size of England. Area 51,609 sq. m. Pop. (1970) 3,373,006. Cap. Montgomery. Admitted to the Union in 1819 as the 22nd state; popularly known as the 'Cotton' state. The largest heavy-industry state in the S, with important coal and iron deposits in the region of Birmingham, a busy manufacturing area. The rest of the state is largely agricultural. The N boundary reaches the Tennessee R. in a fertile valley now controlled by the ◊ *Tennessee* Valley Authority. Farther S the southern end of the Appalachians (Allegheny and Cumberland ranges) protrudes into the state. Rain falls at all seasons, decreasing from 60 ins. annually on the S coast to 40 ins. inland. The rich fertile soil of central Alabama was once covered with cotton plantations, using Negro labour, but now has more diversified agriculture. With increased mechanization, labour requirements were reduced; cotton is increasingly grown in rotation with hay, legumes, or grain. The cultivation of fruit, groundnuts, soya beans, vegetables, and sugar-cane, and cattle rearing and dairy farming are also being developed. Large-scale emigration of the Negro cultivators (to the textile and agricultural machine factories in the towns, and to the northern states) has followed, reducing the percentage of Negroes to less than 30. The S coastlands of Alabama, low-lying, hot, humid, unhealthy, and sparsely populated, are thickly wooded and yield turpentine and resin. Chief towns Birmingham, Mobile, Montgomery. Explored in the 16th cent. by Spaniards, who named it after an Indian tribe; settled by the French in the 17th cent. and the English in the 18th.

**Alabama River** USA. River 312 m. long formed by the union of the Coosa and Tallapoosa rivers, flowing generally SW to join the Tombigbee R. and form the Mobile R. 44 m. above Mobile.

**Alagôas** Brazil. State in the NE shoulder. Area 10,704 sq. m. Pop. (1960) 1,271,062. Cap. Maceió. Sugar-cane is grown along the seaboard and cotton inland.

**Alai Mountains** USSR. Mountain range extending W from the Tien Shan through the Kirghiz SSR into the Tadzhik SSR, rising to over 16,000 ft. To the S is the Trans-Alai range rising to 23,382 ft in Lenin Peak. Between the two ranges is the fertile pastoral Alai Valley, watered by the Kyzyl-Su R.

**Alameda** USA. Residential town in California, on an island in San Francisco Bay. Pop. (1960) 61,316. Favoured by San Francisco businessmen for their homes, because it has fewer fogs and less chilly winds than the city. Minor port. Has an important naval air station. Shipbuilding centre for pleasure craft. Seaside resort.

**Alamein, El** United Arab Republic. Village on the coastal railway in N Egypt, 65 m. WSW of Alexandria. Scene of the decisive victory (1942) of the British over the Germans during the N African campaign in the 2nd World War, which ended the imminent threat of German occupation of Egypt.

**Alamo** USA. Fort at San Antonio, Texas, heroically defended during the Texan revolt against Mexico (1836) by its 183 guards, who were all killed.

**Åland** ◊ *Ahvenanmaa.*

**Alaska** USA. State in the extreme NW of N America. Area 586,400 sq. m. Pop. (1970) 294,607. Cap. Juneau. Admitted to the Union in 1959 as the 49th state. Largely mountainous, with much volcanic activity; Mt McKinley (20,269 ft) in the Alaska range is the highest peak in N America. Much of Alaska is permanently snow-covered, but the lower mountain slopes are forested. The coast is deeply indented; sinking has reduced the W end of the Pacific mountain system – which includes the volcano Katmai – to the line of the Aleutian Is. Barren tundra occupies much of the basin of the Yukon R., which flows W to the Bering Sea. N of the Arctic Circle is the Brooks Range, a remote and almost inaccessible Arctic wilderness, the domain of Eskimo caribou hunters. Many airstrips have been constructed; the state has 228 general airports (1961). The Eskimos have been encouraged to settle, with the substitution of reindeer for wild caribou. The climate of the W island belt is equable but wet and foggy; the interior has continental extremes with a warm but very short summer. The Arctic region is polar in climate, with long cold winters and short cool summers. Main export formerly fish (esp. salmon), now superseded by oil; others are furs (esp. sealskins), minerals, timber. Petroleum and natural gas first produced 1959. Chief towns Anchorage, on the S coast, Fairbanks, and Juneau, which is in the 'panhandle', a coastal strip extending 600 m. SE. Bought from Russia in 1867 for $7,200,000.

**Alaska Highway** Canada/USA. A strategic road from Dawson Creek in N British Columbia to Fairbanks, Alaska. Built by USA (1942) as a defensive precaution against possible Japanese invasion in the 2nd World War. Continued by a good road to Edmonton, Alberta, it is used as a military and tourist road, opening up the Canadian Yukon territory, and forms the N part of a projected Inter-American Highway from Alaska to Argentina.

**Álava** Spain. One of the ◊ *Basque Provinces* in the N, with the Ebro R. on its S boundary. Area 1,176 sq. m. Pop. (1961) 138,934. Cap. Vitoria. Cereals, fruits, potatoes cultivated in the fertile valleys. Industries concentrated in Vitoria.

**Albacete** Spain. **1.** Province in the SE. Area 5,737 sq. m. Pop. (1961) 370,976. Mainly hilly. Main occupations agriculture (cereals, vines, olives) and stock raising (sheep).
**2.** Capital of the Albacete province, 86 m. WSW of Valencia. Pop. (1967) 83,495. Market town in an irrigated region. Famous for its cutlery, daggers, and knives. Also manufactures chemicals, soap, etc.

**Alba Longa** Italy. Ancient city in Latium, probably on the W shore of L. ◊ *Albano*, about 12 m. SE of Rome, near the modern Castel Gandolfo. Traditionally the oldest Latin city, founded by Ascanius, son of Aeneas. Destroyed by its daughter city Rome in the 7th cent. B.C.

**Albania.** Small republic in SE Europe. Area 11,097 sq. m. Pop. (1966) 1,914,000. Cap. Tiranë. Lang. Gheg (N) and Tosk (S) dialects. Rel. Muslim 65 per cent, Orthodox 23 per cent, Roman Catholic 11 per cent.

The most backward as well as the smallest of the Balkan republics. Bounded by Yugoslavia (NE, sharing lakes Shkodër, Ohrid, and Prespa), Greece (S), and the Adriatic (W).

TOPOGRAPHY, CLIMATE. Rugged, mountainous, and difficult of access, rising to 9,063 ft in Korab on the E Yugoslav border, with marshy but generally fertile coastal lowlands which widen considerably in the centre. Crossed by the Drin, Shkumbi, Seman, Vijosë, and other rivers, which are useless for navigation because they almost dry up in the summer and become torrents in the winter. The climate is Mediterranean along the coast and continental in the mountains, where the rainfall is heavier and winters are much cooler.
RESOURCES, PEOPLE, *etc.* Agricultural methods are primitive. Principal crop maize; wheat, tobacco, and sugar-beet also cultivated. Olives and citrus fruits are grown near the coast. In the mountains the rearing of sheep and goats is the main

occupation, and extensive areas are covered with forests. There has been little development of mineral resources. Oil is produced at Kuçovë and sent by pipeline to the port of Vlonë. Chrome, copper, and iron ore are exported. The fourth 5-year plan (1966–70) aimed at substantially increasing mineral, agricultural and industrial production. There are hydroelectric power installations at Selitë, at Mt Daita near Tiranë, at the Karl Marx plant on the Mati R. and at the Friedrich Engels plant at Shkopeti. The few industries include flour-milling and the manufacture of cement. Roads are poor. Many mountain districts are inaccessible to wheeled vehicles; the total length of railways is only 68 m. (1964). Chief towns Tiranë, Shkodër, Korçë, Vlonë, Durrës, Elbasan. The people, long organized in clans, belong to two main groups, the Ghegs N and the Tosks S of the Shkumbi R. Primary education is nominally compulsory, but the majority of the population is illiterate.

HISTORY. The region was nominally under Roman rule in the 1st cent. A.D., was overrun by the Goths in the 4th and 5th cent., and was reconquered (535) for the Byzantine Empire by Justinian, but in these and subsequent invasions the mountain tribes were never completely overcome. Turkish rule was imposed in 1478, despite a determined resistance led by Scanderbeg, the national hero, and persisted for more than 4 centuries. Independence was proclaimed in 1912. The German Prince William of Wied accepted the crown, but left after the outbreak of the 1st World War (1914). Became a republic 1925. Ahmed Bey Zogu, a former prime minister and president, proclaimed himself King Zog I in 1928. Some economic and educational progress was made but Albania was invaded by the Italians in 1939 and the King fled. After the 2nd World War a Communist single-party government was established under Enver Hoxha. Britain and the USA broke off relations with Albania (1946) and vetoed her admission to the UN, but she was finally admitted in 1955. In recent years Soviet influence has been replaced by that of Communist China, and diplomatic relations between Albania and the USSR were broken off in 1961.

**Albano, Lake** Italy. Ancient Albanus Lacus. A crater lake in an extinct volcano, drained into a tributary of the Tiber by a tunnel constructed (398–397 B.C.) because of a pronouncement by the Delphic oracle that Veii could not be conquered until its waters reached the sea. On the E bank is Monte Cavo (ancient Albanus Mons), 3,115 ft high. On the W shore is the probable site of ◊ *Alba Longa*.

**Albany** Australia. Seaport and resort in Western Australia on King George Sound 245 m. SE of Perth. Pop. (1966) 11,417. Fish and meat canning. Exports fruit. Founded as a penal colony; first settled 1826.

**Albany** (Georgia) USA. Market town on the Flint R. in the SW 75 m. SE of Columbus. Pop. (1960) 55,890. In the centre of a rich agricultural area. Locally grown cotton led to the manufacture of cotton goods. Food processing (esp. pecans, peanuts) now more important.

**Albany** (New York) USA. State capital, on the W bank of the Hudson R. 135 m. N of New York City. Pop. (1960) 129,726. Chief industries printing, publishing, and the manufacture of foodstuffs and electrical goods. Renowned for its fine public buildings. One of the oldest cities in N America: founded 1614 by the Dutch as a trading post (Fort Nassau); renamed in honour of the Duke of York and Albany (afterwards James II) 1664. The importance of the site, near the confluence of the Mohawk and the Hudson, was realized during the American War of Independence. Became state capital 1797. Later grew as a railway and commercial centre.

**Albemarle Island** ◊ *Galápagos Islands*.

**Albert, Lake** Congo (Kinshasa)/Uganda. Lake in the W branch of the Great Rift Valley, 100 m. long and up to 22 m. wide. Area 2,000 sq. m. Part of the frontier between Congo (Kinshasa) and Uganda. Fed by the Victoria Nile (NE) and the Semliki R. (S). Drains N through the Albert Nile into the Bahr el Jebel. Discovered (1864) by Sir Samuel Baker. Named after the Prince Consort. ◊ *Edward, Lake*.

**Alberta** Canada. The most westerly of the three prairie provinces, between British Columbia (W) and Saskatchewan (E), bounded on the S by Montana (USA). Area 255,285 sq. m. Pop. (1966) 1,463,203. Cap. Edmonton. Consists of a plateau descending E and NE from the Rocky Mountains, which form the S part of its boundary with British Columbia. The N part is drained N by the Peace and Athabaska rivers, and the S is drained E to L. Winnipeg. Climate typically continental.

Mainly agricultural. Chief crops wheat, oats, barley. Cattle-rearing in the S. Largely forest in the N. Important coalfields: produces about one quarter of Canada's output. The discovery (1947) of a major oilfield at Leduc, near Edmonton, led to rapid development: now produces two thirds of Canada's oil output. Vast reserves of natural gas. Chief towns Edmonton, Calgary.

**Albert Canal** Belgium. Canal in the NE, 80 m. long, joining the Scheldt (at Antwerp) to the Meuse (at Liège). Completed 1939. Navigable by barges up to 2,000 tons. Part of Belgium's E defence line, but was easily crossed by the Germans in the 2nd World War, owing to failure to destroy two of its bridges.

**Albertville** ⟡ *Kalemie.*

**Albi** France. Prefecture of the Tarn department, on the Tarn R. 42 m. ENE of Toulouse. Pop. (1968) 46,613. Textile, glass, dyeing, and other industries. Brickbuilt cathedral (13th/16th-cent.). Musée Toulouse-Lautrec. Gave its name to the Albigensian heresy (11th–12th cent.) which resulted in the Albigensian Crusade and the creation of the Inquisition.

**Albion.** Ancient name for Great Britain, but now usually restricted to England. Possibly a reference to the chalk cliffs of Dover, from Latin *albus* ('white').

**Albula Pass** Switzerland. Pass in the Graubünden (Grisons) canton, in the Rhaetian Alps, reaching a height of 7,595 ft, leading from the upper Engadine to the valley of the Albula R., a tributary of the upper Rhine (Hinter Rhein). The Albula railway tunnel is nearly 4 m. long and 6,000 ft above sea level.

**Albuquerque** USA. Railway centre and health resort in New Mexico, at a height of 5,000 ft on the Rio Grande 60 m. SW of Santa Fé. Pop. (1960) 201,189. Pastoral farming in the surrounding countryside. Railway engineering, food-processing, canning, and other industries. Founded (1706) by the Spaniards. Many distinctively Spanish buildings. Seat of the University of New Mexico (1892).

**Albury** Australia. Town in New South Wales 135 m. WSW of Canberra on the N bank of the meandering, braided Murray R. Pop. (1966) 32,019. Commercial centre. Trade in wool, wheat, wine, fruit, etc.

**Alcalá de Guadaira** Spain. Market town and resort in Seville province in Andalusia, on the Guadaira R. 12 m. ESE of Seville. Pop.

(1961) 31,004. Well known for its bread and its olive oil.

**Alcalá de Henares** Spain. Town in Madrid province in New Castile, on the Henares R. 18 m. ENE of Madrid. Pop. (1961) 25,123. Several minor industries. Famous for its historical associations; birthplace of Cervantes (1547–1616). Noteworthy buildings include the old university (founded 1510; removed to Madrid 1836). The Complutensian Polyglot Bible, named after the Roman town Complutum (which stood across the river), was published here (1517).

**Alcalá la Real** Spain. Town in Jaén province in Andalusia, 24 m. SSW of Jaén. Pop. (1961) 23,314. Market town with minor industries. Trade in wine, cereals. Named la Real ('the royal') to commemorate recapture from the Moors by Alfonso XI (1340).

**Alcatraz** USA. Rocky island in San Francisco Bay, California, opposite the Golden Gate. From 1933 to 1963, when it was closed, a civil prison used for dangerous long-term criminals.

**Alcázar de San Juan** Spain. Town in Ciudad Real province in New Castile, 50 m. NE of Ciudad Real. Pop. (1961) 24,963. Railway junction. Market town. Trade in wine. Associated with Cervantes and the story of *Don Quixote.*

**Alcoy** Spain. Town in the Alicante province in Valencia, 25 m. N of Alicante. Pop. (1961) 51,096. Manufactures textiles, paper, etc.

**Aldabra Island** Indian Ocean. Group of small islands in the form of an atoll, administratively part of the Seychelles until 1965, when they became part of the new colony of the British Indian Ocean Territory. The atoll is regularly visited for the collection of coconuts and turtles.

**Aldan** USSR. Town in the SE of the Yakut ASSR, RSFSR, 260 m. SSW of Yakutsk. Pop. 12,000. Goldmining centre. On the road from Yakutsk to the Trans-Siberian Railway.

**Aldan River** USSR. River 1,700 m. long, rising in the W of the Stanovoi range, flowing generally NE, then N and W, and joining the Lena R. near Ust Aldan.

**Aldeburgh** England. Municipal borough in E Suffolk, 20 m. ENE of Ipswich near the estuary of the Alde. Pop. (1961) 2,972. Seaside resort. Timbered moot hall (16th-cent.). Birthplace of the poet George Crabbe (1754–1832). Home of the composer

Benjamin Britten, who inspired the annual music festival.

**Aldermaston** England. Village in Berkshire, 9 m. SW of Reading. Site of the Atomic Weapons Research Establishment. From 1958 to 1963 starting point of the Aldermaston marches organized by the Campaign for Nuclear Disarmament.

**Alderney** England. Most northerly of the larger Channel Is., a dependency of Guernsey. Area 3 sq. m. Pop. (1961) 1,449. Cap. St Anne (near the centre of the island). Separated from the coast of Normandy by a dangerous channel, the Race of Alderney, 9 m. wide. To the W are the Casquets, a group of dangerous rocks (with a lighthouse), where many ships have been wrecked. Alderney cattle reared. Exports early potatoes.

**Aldershot** England. Municipal borough in Hampshire 8 m. W of Guildford. Pop. (1961) 31,260. An unimportant village until the permanent military camp was established (1854). Minor industries.

**Aldridge-Brownhills** England. Urban district in S Staffordshire between Walsall and Lichfield, formed in 1966 from the urban districts of Aldridge and Brownhills. Pop. (1968) 86,780. Engineering. Manufactures bricks and tiles, etc. Coalmining in the neighbourhood.

**Alençon** France. Prefecture of the Orne department, on the Sarthe R. 30 m. N of Le Mans. Pop. (1968) 33,388. Market town. Once famous for lace (*point d'Alençon*). Manufactures textiles etc.

**Aleppo** (Ar. **Haleb**) Syria. Capital of the Aleppo province in the NW, Syria's second largest city, and the chief industrial and commercial centre of the N. Pop. (1962) 496,231. Manufactures cotton and silk goods, carpets, soap, cement, etc. Trade in cereals, fruit, wool, livestock, etc. With the ancient citadel on a mound in the centre, it is one of the most picturesque of Eastern cities. Fell to the Hittites c. 2,000 B.C. Taken by the Arabs in A.D. 638, it flourished as a centre of the caravan trade between Europe and Asia. Under the Turks from 1517; declined with the opening of sea routes to the East. Revived when the railways were constructed early in the 20th cent. and again when Syria achieved independence (1946).

**Alès** France. Town in the Gard department 25 m. NW of Nîmes at the foot of the Cévennes. Pop. (1968) 44,607. Centre of a mining area (coal, iron, zinc). Market for raw silk. Metallurgical, glass, chemical, and other industries.

**Alessandria** Italy. Capital of Alessandria province, in Piedmont, on the Tanaro R. 48 m. ESE of Turin. Pop. (1961) 92,760. Railway centre. Engineering, hat manufacture, and other industries.

**Aletsch Glacier** Switzerland. Glacier in the Bernese Alps, the largest in Europe. Length 16 m. Consists of the Great Aletsch (10 m. long), Upper Aletsch, and Middle Aletsch. To the NW is the Aletschhorn (13,721 ft), one of the highest peaks in the Bernese Alps.

**Aleutian Islands** USA. Chain of over 150 islands, the W continuation of the summits of the Aleutian range of Alaska, extending towards the E Siberian peninsula of Kamchatka. The islands are mountainous, with summits rising to 8,000 ft. Many volcanoes. Owing to the cold Alaska Current and the northerly situation the climate is inhospitable – cold, damp, and very foggy. Soil uncultivable. The scanty population (of mixed Russian and Eskimo descent) are mainly fur trappers and fishermen. Though the salmon fisheries are valuable, the main importance of the islands today is strategic. Following the Japanese occupation of Kiska and Attu islands (1942) in the 2nd World War, the USA has built several air bases here.

**Alexander Archipelago** USA. Group of over 1,000 mountainous islands off the Pacific coast of the Alaskan 'panhandle', the summits of a submerged mountain chain. Main occupation fishing. Chief towns Ketchikan, Sitka.

**Alexander Bay** ◊ *Orange River*.

**Alexandria** (Ar. **Al Iskandariya**) United Arab Republic. Chief seaport and second city of Egypt, on a strip of land separating L. Mareotis (Mariut) from the Mediterranean. Pop. (1960) 1,513,000. Main export raw cotton. Industries include cotton ginning and cottonseed-oil pressing. Manufactures paper, soap, etc. Connected by rail with Cairo, Suez, and the Nile delta. Airports. Many foreign residents, largely Greeks and Syrians, engaged in trade. Founded (332 B.C.) by Alexander the Great, partly on the mainland and partly on the island of Pharos ('the lighthouse'), the two being linked by a mole (the Heptastadium), which in time was widened by the accumulation of silt and became an isthmus, forming two harbours, the old (Great) harbour (E) and the present harbour (W). In antiquity Alexandria was a centre of Greek and Jewish culture, with a great university and two famous libraries, a museum, royal palaces, and temples; also the most important commercial port of the Mediterranean. The Romans' greatest provincial capital, second city in importance to Rome, with a population of 300,000 citizens and a vast number of slaves. Under the later Romans and the Byzantines, a centre of Christian theology. The famous libraries were destroyed or dispersed, largely by the zeal of Theodosius, who destroyed most of the pagan buildings (A.D. 391). Alexandria fell to the Arabs in the 7th cent. Its commercial importance waned, esp. after the discovery of America and of the Cape route to India; its decline was accelerated when ◊ *Cairo* was chosen as capital. Regained its former splendour in the 19th cent. when Mehemet Ali ordered the construction of the Mahmudiya Canal to the Nile, bringing trade to the city and facilitating irrigation in the neighbourhood. The construction of the Suez Canal (1869) diminished Alexandria's importance, but it has continued to handle the bulk of Egypt's foreign trade. Little of ancient Alexandria remains beyond the granite shaft called Pompey's Pillar, the catacombs, and the ruins at Pharos. The two obelisks called Cleopatra's Needles were removed to London and New York in the 19th cent. The modern city is a mixture of ancient and modern, oriental and occidental. Pleasant residential suburbs.

**Alexandria** (Louisiana) USA. Market town on the Red R. 96 m. NW of Baton Rouge. Pop. (1960) 40,279. Centre of a rich cotton-growing area. Engineering, sawmilling, cottonseed-oil pressing, brickmaking, etc.

**Alexandria** (Virginia) USA. Town on the W bank of the Potomac R. near Washington (DC), of which it is virtually a suburb. Pop. (1960) 91,023. Once a river port of some importance; now mainly residential. Several historic buildings associated with George Washington.

**Alexandroupolis** Greece. Formerly Dedeagach. Capital of the Évros *nome*, in Thrace, on the Gulf of Ainos, an inlet of the Aegean Sea. Pop. (1961) 18,712. Formerly Turkish (as Dedeagach); became Greek after the 1st World War.

**Alexandrovsk-Grushevsky** ◊ *Shakhty*.

**Alfreton** England. Urban district in Derby-

shire 13 m. NNE of Derby. Pop. (1961) 22,998. Industrial and coalmining centre. Ironworks. Manufactures clothing, etc.

**Algarve** Portugal. The southernmost and smallest province, separated from the rest of the country by mountain ranges ending in Cape St Vincent. Area 1,958 sq. m. Pop. (1960) 314,841. Cap. Faro. Produces Mediterranean fruits in the S. Fishing. Last stronghold of the Moors in Portugal; reconquered 1249.

**Algeciras** Spain. Seaport and resort in the Cádiz province, Andalusia, 55 m. SE of Cádiz, on Algeciras Bay opposite Gibraltar. Pop. (1967) 73,292. Exports cork, oranges. Founded (713) by the Moors. Taken by Alfonso XI of Castile (1344) and destroyed. The modern town was built in 1760. Scene of the Algeciras Conference (1906) of European powers meeting to settle their dispute over Morocco.

**Algeria.** Independent state in N Africa, between Morocco and Tunisia. Area 922,000 sq. m. Pop. (1963) 10,453,600 (mainly Berber and Arab Muslims, with some Europeans, principally French). Cap. Algiers. Comprises 13 N departments and 2 large sparsely peopled Saharan departments (area about 7 times that of the N).

TOPOGRAPHY, RESOURCES, *etc.* The N is crossed by the Atlas Mountains (the coastal ranges are called the Tell Atlas); in the fertile coastal region are concentrated most of the population and the agriculture, producing cereals (wheat, barley), wine, and citrus fruits. To the S of this range are the semi-arid high plateaux, containing salt lakes (*shotts*); esparto grass for manufacturing high-grade paper is gathered for export, mainly to the UK. Farther S are the Saharan Atlas, also parallel to the coast; the ranges form a climatic line between the Mediterranean littoral and the Sahara. Dates are exported from the oases. Algerian waters are fished for sardines, anchovies, tunny-fish, etc. Mineral resources include petroleum, iron ore, phosphates. Important fields of oil and natural gas are in production in S Algeria, under French ownership; royalties are paid to the Algerian government. The important towns of N Algeria are linked by a road and rail network from Tunisia through Algeria to Morocco; a section of the long-planned Trans-Saharan railway now reaches Abadla (S of Colomb-Béchar). Principal exports oil (over half), wine, iron ore, phosphates, citrus fruits, vegetables, flowers.

HISTORY. Part of the N African littoral, where the Berbers were the indigenous people. Came under Turkish rule in the 16th cent. but the Turks never established control beyond the Tell. They were followed by the Deys, independent rulers who maintained a precarious authority throughout the ◊ *Barbary Coast.* Annexed by France 1865; became a department of France. French colonists entered in considerable numbers, and with stable government and better communications the population grew rapidly. French policy was to integrate Algeria completely into France itself, but the opposition of the *colons* (established French settlers) to granting equal rights to the Algerians caused an Algerian nationalist movement, and the National Liberation Front (FLN, founded 1951) organized open revolt. The *colons* created the Secret Army Organization (OAS), led by army officers, and both factions opposed the French government's attempts at conciliation during years of violence and terrorism. After a referendum Algeria opted for complete independence (1962), but the nationalization of large estates and the return to France of hundreds of thousands of *colons* gravely weakened the economy, which France supports by continuing financial help and special trade facilities. A major problem is a very high birthrate, with a population increase of some 200,000 a year. ◊ *Numidia.*

**Alghero** Italy. Seaport in NW Sardinia 18 m. SW of Sassari. Pop. (1961) 26,688. Fishing. Cathedral (12th-cent.), damaged in the 2nd World War.

**Algiers (Ar. Al-Jezair)** Algeria. Capital, chief seaport, and largest town, on the W side of the Bay of Algiers. Pop. (1967) 943,000. Behind the city rises the mountain Bouzaréa (1,240 ft). The modern French quarter is below the old town and the Kasbah (citadel), which was the residence of the last two native rulers (Deys). Noteworthy buildings are the great mosque, the cathedral, the national library, the museum of antiquities, and the university (1879). Varied industries, many associated with wine making. Exports (mainly to France) half the total Algerian output of wine, fruits, cereals, cork, tobacco, etc. Muslim city founded in the 10th cent. A.D. Flourished under Turkish rule. A base for

Barbary pirates from *c.* 1500 until captured by the French (1830). Adhered to Vichy France in the 2nd World War until the Allied invasion (1942); then headquarters of General de Gaulle's Free French government. Scene of much violence and bloodshed during the Algerian nationalists' post-war struggle for independence.

**Alhambra** USA. Suburb of Los Angeles, California, with commuter residences. Pop. (1960) 54,807. Market centre for local fruit and vegetable farmers. Manufactures oil-refining equipment, plastics, etc.

**Alhucemas** ◊ *Morocco.*

**Alicante** Spain. **1.** Mediterranean province in the SE formed (1833) from parts of the old provinces of Valencia and Murcia. Area 2,259 sq. m. Pop. (1961) 711,942. Largely barren. Irrigated areas produce wine and fruits.
**2.** Capital of Alicante province, seaport 80 m. S of Valencia. Pop. (1967) 153,742. Exports wine, fruits, olive oil. Oil refinery. Manufactures textiles, chemicals, tobacco products, soap, etc.

**Alice Springs** Australia. Formerly Stuart. Town in the Northern Territory in the Macdonnell ranges at 1,900 ft. Pop. (1966) 6,001. Terminus of the transcontinental railway from the S and of the Stuart Highway from Darwin, 800 m. to the NNW. Airport and Flying Doctor base near by. Serves Central Australia, catering for cattlemen, prospectors, and tourists. Capital of the old territory of Central Australia 1926–31.

**Aligarh** India. Commercial town in the W of Uttar Pradesh, 78 m. SE of Delhi. Pop. (1961) 185,020. Trade in grain, cotton, etc. Cotton milling, metal working, etc. Butter production. Seat of the famous Aligarh Muslim University (1920). Taken from the Mahrattas by the British 1803.

**Alima River** ◊ *Congo (Brazzaville),* Republic of.

**Al Iskandariya** ◊ *Alexandria.*

**Al Ittihad** ◊ *South Yemen.*

**Aliwal North** S Africa. Town on the Cape Province bank of the Orange R. 115 m. SSE of Bloemfontein at a height of 4,350 ft. Pop. (1960) 10,706. Health resort, noted for its hot mineral springs.

**Aliwal South** ◊ *Mossel Bay.*

**Al-Jezair** ◊ *Algiers.*

**Alkmaar** Netherlands. Town in the N Holland province, on the N Holland Canal 20 m. NNW of Amsterdam. Pop. (1968) 51,542. Commercial centre with a famous cheese market. Manufactures furniture, clothing, cigars, etc.

**Allahabad** India. Ancient Prayag. City in the SE of Uttar Pradesh, on the Jumna R. near the confluence with the Ganges, 350 m. SE of Delhi. Pop. (1961) 411,955. Commercial centre. Trade in grain, cotton, sugar, etc. Textile, flour-milling, and other industries. Of great importance to Hindus as a place of pilgrimage because of its position: a religious festival is held annually at the confluence of the sacred Ganges with the Jumna; every 12th year the festival has special significance and is attended by as many as a million pilgrims. Seat of a university (1887). Within the fort is the famous pillar (252 B.C.) with inscriptions of the edicts of Asoka. Near by are the garden and tomb of Khusru. Ceded to the British 1801. Capital of the United Provinces 1901–49.

**Allegheny Mountains** USA. W portion of the Appalachian mountain system, forming the watershed between river drainage to the Atlantic and (by Mississippi tributaries) to the Gulf of Mexico. Built up of mainly horizontally bedded rocks of Carboniferous age, including coalbearing strata, they form a high plateau which has been finely dissected by numerous deep river valleys to become an area of well-rounded uplands 3,000–4,000 ft high. Early English colonists coming from the E coast found the plateau difficult to cross, and the region was long a frontier zone between the French (in the Mississippi basin) and the English (along the coast). Still heavily wooded, the Alleghenies are of only limited agricultural use. Principal products hay, eggs.

**Allen, Bog of** Irish Republic. Region of peat bogs in central Ireland. Area 370 sq. m. Drained by the Brosna, Barrow, and Boyne rivers. Cultivated in parts. Some of the turf is now cut for use as fuel in power stations.

**Allenstein** ◊ *Olsztyn.*

**Allentown** USA. Town in Pennsylvania on the Lehigh R. 50 m. NNW of Philadelphia. Pop. (1960) 108,347. On the edge of the Pennsylvanian anthracite field. Cement, textile, and other industries.

**Alleppey** India. Seaport and industrial town in Kerala on the Malabar coast 80 m. NNW of Trivandrum. Pop. (1961) 138,834. Exports coir, copra, coconuts. Manufactures coir ropes and matting, coconut oil, etc.

**Alliance** USA. Town in Ohio 15 m. ENE of Canton. Pop. (1960) 28,362. Iron and steel, engineering, and other industries.

**Allier** France. Department in the centre in the old Bourbonnais province, extending over the upper basins of the Loire, Allier, and Cher rivers where they leave the Massif Central. Area 2,850 sq. m. Pop. (1968) 386,553. Prefecture Moulins. Cereals and vegetables produced in the Allier basin (Limagne). Pigs and poultry raised. Coalmines (Commentry). Chief towns Moulins, Montluçon (where the industries are centred).

**Allier River** France. River 269 m. long, rising in the Cévennes in the Lozère department, flowing NNW through the fertile Limagne (cereals, vegetables, stock rearing), and joining the Loire near Nevers.

**Alloa** Scotland. Small burgh and industrial town in Clackmannanshire 6 m. E of Stirling on the Forth R. Pop. (1961) 13,895. Whisky distilling, brewing. Manufactures hosiery, etc.

**Alloway** Scotland. Village in Ayrshire 2 m. S of Ayr. Birthplace of Robert Burns (1759–96).

**Alma-Ata** USSR. Formerly (until 1927) Verny. Capital of the Kazakh SSR and of the Alma-Ata Region, on the Turksib Railway 425 m. ENE of Tashkent. Pop. (1970) 730,000. Beautifully situated at 2,600 ft beneath snow-capped mountains. Commercial and industrial centre in an agricultural and fruit-growing area. Trade in wheat, sugar-beet, apples, grapes. Manufactures machinery, textiles, food and tobacco products, etc. Seat of a university (1928) and of the Kazakh Academy of Sciences (1946). Founded by Russians (1854) as a fort on the site of the old Kazakh city of Alma-Ata. Virtually destroyed by earthquakes 1887 and 1911. Developed rapidly after the construction of the Turksib Railway.

**Almada** Portugal. Town in the Setúbal district on the S bank of the Tagus estuary, opposite and S of Lisbon. Pop. (1960) 30,688. Flour milling, fish canning, etc. Linked with Lisbon by the Salazar bridge (opened 1966). Has a huge statue of Christ (total height 357 ft) overlooking the Tagus, sculpted (1954–9) by Francisco Franco.

**Almadén** Spain. Town in the Ciudad Real province in New Castile, 52 m. WSW of Ciudad Real. Pop. (1961) 13,587. Rich mercury mines, worked for many centuries.

**Almadies, Cape** ◊ *Verde, Cape.*

**Almelo** Netherlands. Industrial town in Overijssel province 13 m. N W of Enschede. Pop. (1968) 58,155. Manufactures textiles, furniture, etc. Has a 17th-cent. town hall.

**Almería** Spain. 1. Mediterranean province in Andalusia, formed from parts of the ancient kingdom of Granada. Area 3,388 sq. m. Pop. (1961) 360,777. Mainly mountainous. Important for minerals (iron, lead). Produces esparto grass and fruits (chiefly grapes). 2. Capital of Almería province, seaport on the Gulf of Almería 68 m. ESE of Granada. Pop. (1967) 99,653. Exports products of the province, inc. large quantities of grapes. Flourished under the Moors (8th–15th cent.), when the population approached 200,000, but its commercial importance declined. The ruins of the San Cristóbal castle overlook the town. Gothic cathedral (16th-cent.).

**Alnwick** England. Urban district in Northumberland on the Aln R. 30 m. N of Newcastle upon Tyne. Pop. (1961) 7,482. Market town. Brewing. Manufactures fishing tackle. Dominated by Alnwick Castle (14th-cent. in parts). Remains of Alnwick Abbey (12th-cent.).

**Alofi** ◊ *Wallis and Futuna Islands.*

**Alost** (Flemish **Aalst**) Belgium. Town in the E Flanders province on the Dender R. 15 m. WNW of Brussels. Pop. (1968) 45,881. Industrial and commercial centre. Manufactures textiles (cotton, linen), clothing. Brewing. Trade in hops. The Church of St Martin (15th-cent.) has a famous Rubens. Birthplace of Dirk Maartens, who set up one of the first printing presses in Europe here (1473).

**Alpes-Maritimes** France. Department in the S E in Provence, bounded on the E by Italy, on the S by the Mediterranean Sea, and surrounding the principality of Monaco; formed (1860) from the county of Nice and the district of Grasse. Area 1,659 sq. m. (inc. the 202-sq.-m. frontier strip acquired by the Franco-Italian peace treaty of 1947). Pop. (1968) 722,070. Prefecture Nice. Mountainous, with the Maritime Alps along the N boundary. Principal river the Var. Flowers, fruits, and early vegetables cultivated in the narrow coastal strip. Manufactures perfumes, essences, olive oil. Along the coast (Côte d'Azur, the W part of the Riviera) are the famous resorts, Nice, Cannes, Antibes, Menton.

**Alps.** Mountain system of S central Europe curving in a general S W–N E direction from the Mediterranean coast of S France and N W Italy, where they link with the Apennines, through S and central Switzerland and most of Austria, into S Germany, then SE along the Adriatic coast of Yugoslavia, covering in all about 80,000 sq. m. Drained to the North Sea by the Rhine, to the Mediterranean by the Rhône, and to the Adriatic by the Po. Usually divided, rather arbitrarily, into Western, Central, and Eastern Alps. 1. *Western Alps*: Maritime, Cottian, Dauphiné, and Graian Alps; highest peaks Pic des Écrins (13,461 ft), Gran Paradiso (13,323 ft), Monte Viso (12,602 ft). 2. *Central Alps*: in the S the Pennine, Lepontine, Rhaetian, and Ötztal Alps, in the N the Bernese Alps, Alps of the Four Forest Cantons, Glarus, Allgäu, and Bavarian Alps; highest peaks Mont Blanc (15,781 ft; loftiest mountain in the Alps), Monte Rosa (15,217 ft), Matterhorn (14,701 ft), Finsteraarhorn (14,032 ft), Jungfrau (13,653 ft), Piz Bernina (13,304 ft). 3. *Eastern Alps*: Zillertal Alps, Hohe Tauern, and Niedere Tauern, flanked to the S by the Dolomites, Carnic Alps, which are continued E by the Karawanken and are linked by the Julian Alps to the Dinaric Alps; highest peaks Gross Glockner (12,460 ft), Marmolada (10,965 ft). There are numerous passes through the Alps, including the Mont Cenis, Little and Great St Bernard, Simplon, St Gotthard, Maloja, Stelvio, Splügen, and Brenner, with railway tunnels at the Mont Cenis, Lötschberg, Simplon, and St Gotthard. There are road tunnels at ◊ *Mont Blanc* (1965) and San Bernardino (Graubünden, 1967). The snowline varies from about 8,000 ft on the N to about 10,000 ft on the S side, and below this is the zone of characteristic Alpine flora, including the well-known edelweiss, while the timber line is at 6,000 to 7,000 ft above sea level.

The Alps were created by movements which forced the earth's crust into a complex series of folds and creases, including great recumbent folds ('nappes'); atmospheric and other agencies subsequently carved them into their present form. Of these agencies, the glaciers have contributed much to the magnificent Alpine scenery, as also have the many lakes on the N and S sides of the mountains. Largely because of their scenery, but also because of the opportunities they afford for mountaineering and winter sports, the Alps have become one of the principal playgrounds of Europe, and tourism is the outstanding industry. Dairy farming is important on the mountain pastures, while vines and other crops are grown in the valleys. The increasing development of hydroelectric power has stimulated the manufacturing industries, and textiles, condensed milk, clocks and watches are typical products.

**Alps** (Australia) ◊ *Australian Alps*.

**Alps** (New Zealand) ◊ *Southern Alps*.

**Als** Denmark. Island in the Little Belt, separated from coast of S Jutland by Als Sound but linked with the mainland by a bridge since 1930. Area 121 sq. m. Pop. 49,000 (almost entirely Danish-speaking). Chief town Sönderborg. Ceded to Prussia 1864, but returned to Denmark after a plebiscite 1920.

**Alsace** (Ger. **Elsass**) France. Ancient Alsatia. Region in the NE between the Vosges and the Rhine, now occupied by the Haut-Rhin and Bas-Rhin departments. On the fertile lowlands cereals, hops, tobacco, vegetables, fruit cultivated. Wine produced on the E slopes of the Vosges. Potash mined near Mulhouse. Cotton goods and chemicals manufactured in the Mulhouse-Colmar area. Chief towns Strasbourg, Mulhouse, Colmar, Belfort. Alsace was for long part of Germany, but in 1648 much of it was ceded to France. More was taken by Louis XIV, and the remainder added after the French Revolution (1789). In 1871, after the Franco-Prussian War, all Alsace except the Territory of Belfort was incorporated into Germany to form, with part of Lorraine, the imperial territory of Alsace-Lorraine. By the Treaty of Versailles after the 1st World War, the latter was returned to France, and Alsace was divided into its old departments of Haut-Rhin and Bas-Rhin. In addition to preserving their own dialect, the people of Alsace display a strong local patriotism, insisting that they are primarily Alsatian rather than French or German.

**Alsace-Lorraine** (Ger. **Elsass-Lothringen**). Frontier region between France and Germany, bounded on the E by the Rhine. Incorporated into Germany as an imperial territory (*Reichsland*) after the Franco-Prussian War (1871). Although the inhabitants at that time were mainly Teutonic, since the French Revolution their political sympathies had been with France. They were moving more closely to Germany at the outbreak of the 1st World War, but the region was returned to France by the Treaty of Versailles (1919); Alsace became the departments of Haut-Rhin and Bas-Rhin, and Lorraine the Moselle department. Again under German rule during the 2nd World War (1940–44).

**Altai Mountains** USSR. Extensive mountain system in the S of Siberia, continuing SE into Mongolia as the Great Altai. The highest USSR peak is Belukha (14,783 ft). Lead, zinc, silver mined. The principal USSR centre of the atomic industry is at Ust Kamenogorsk. In the NW the lower slopes are thickly forested; in the drier SE there is only semi-desert vegetation.

**Altai Territory** USSR. Territory in the S of Siberia (RSFSR), bordering on the Kazakh SSR (W); drained by the upper Ob R. Area 101,000 sq. m. Pop. 2,500,000. Cap. Barnaul. Includes part of the Altai Mountains and much fertile agricultural land (wheat, sugar-beet, dairy produce, etc.). Crossed by the Turksib Railway. Linked by road with Mongolia.

**Altamira Cave** Spain. Cave 17 m. SW of Santander, in the Santander province in the N. Palaeolithic wall drawings, discovered 1879.

**Altamura** Italy. Town in the Bari province in Apulia, 27 m. SW of Bari. Pop. (1961) 43,735. Built on the site of a pre-Roman town. Centre of an agricultural district producing cereals, grapes, olives. Manufactures macaroni. Cathedral (13th-cent.).

**Alta River** Norway. River 120 m. long, in the Finnmark county in the N, rising near the Finnish border and flowing generally N to enter the Arctic Ocean by the Alta Fiord.

**Altbreisach** ◊ *Breisach*.

**Altdorf** Switzerland. Capital of the Uri canton, near the S end of L. Lucerne. Pop. (1960) 7,477. Scene of the adventures of William Tell, with a statue of him where the shooting of the apple from his son's head is supposed to have taken place. Has a Tell Theatre.

**Altenburg** German Democratic Republic. Town in the Gera district in Thuringia, 26 m. S of Leipzig. Pop. (1963) 46,866. Commercial and industrial centre in a lignite-mining area. Manufactures sewing machines, playing cards, hats, etc. Former capital of the duchy of Saxe-Altenburg.

**Altiplano** ◊ *Andes*; *Bolivia*.

**Alto Adige** ◊ *Trentino Alto Adige*.

**Alton** England. Urban district in Hampshire on the R. Wey 9 m. SSE of Basingstoke. Pop. (1961) 9,158. Market town. Brewing. Has a 15th-cent. church which exhibits bullet marks from the fighting between parliamentary and royalist troops (1643). The village of ◊ *Selborne* is 4 m. SSE.

**Alton** USA. Industrial town in Illinois 17 m. NNE of St Louis on the E side of the Mississippi. Pop. (1960) 43,047. Oil refining, flour milling. Manufactures glass, paper, etc.

**Altona** Federal German Republic. Industrial town and port on the right bank of the Elbe just below Hamburg (into which it was incorporated 1938). Pop. 250,000. The trade resembles that of ◊ *Hamburg*. Fish-processing, textile, tobacco, machine-tool, chemical, and other industries. Became Danish 1640. Burned by the Swedes 1713. Passed to Prussia 1866. Severely damaged in the 2nd World War.

**Altoona** USA. Industrial town in Pennsylvania 82 m. E of Pittsburgh. Pop. (1960) 69,347. Railway workshops and extensive marshalling yards. Manufactures clothing, electrical equipment, etc. Developed by the Pennsylvania Railroad (1849), when the line was being constructed across the Alleghenies.

**Altötting** Federal German Republic. Town in Upper Bavaria 52 m. E of Munich. Pop. 9,000. Traditional pilgrimage centre with chapel containing famous image of the Virgin Mary. Count Tilly, a celebrated general of the imperial armies in the Thirty Years War, is buried in the 13th-cent. parish church.

**Altrincham** England. Municipal borough in Cheshire, 8 m. SW of Manchester. Pop. (1961) 41,104. Market gardens supply the Manchester area. Engineering industries.

**Alwar** India. Town in the E of Rajasthan, 85 m. SSW of Delhi. Former capital of the state of Alwar (which joined the Rajasthan Union 1949). Pop. (1961) 72,707. Oilseed and flour milling, etc. Trade in millet, cotton goods, etc. Notable palace.

**Amagasaki** Japan. Industrial town in Hyogo prefecture, Honshu, on Osaka Bay just NNW of Osaka. Pop. (1965) 500,977. Manufactures textiles, chemicals, metal products, glass, etc.

**Amager** Denmark. Island in The Sound, opposite Copenhagen (part of which is in the N). Area 25 sq. m. Connected to the mainland by a bridge.

**Amajuba Hill** ◊ *Majuba Hill*.

**Amalfi** Italy. Town in Salerno province in Campania, on the Gulf of Salerno 22 m. SE of Naples. Pop. (1961) 12,365. Popular tourist centre. In the 9th cent. an independent republic. Became a duchy in 953, rivalling Pisa, Genoa, and Venice. Taken by the Pisans in the 12th cent. It quickly declined, but its maritime code, the *Tavole Amalfitane*, was recognized in the Mediterranean till 1570.

**Amapá** Brazil. Federal territory in the NE, N of the Amazon mouth. Area 54,147 sq. m. Pop. (1960) 68,889. Cap. Macapá. Mostly rain-forest; coastal mangrove swamps. Large manganese deposits have been discovered and are being exploited.

**'Amara** Iraq. Capital of the 'Amara province, on the Tigris R. 180 m. SE of Baghdad. Pop. 53,000. Trade in dates, grain, wool, etc. Well known for its silverware.

**Amarapura** Burma. Town in the Mandalay district, on the Irrawaddy R. just S of Mandalay. Pop. 8,000. Silk weaving. Manufactures *lungyis*. Founded (1783) as the capital; the population rose to 170,000, but the capital was temporarily moved to Ava 1823. Largely destroyed by earthquake 1839; after Mandalay had become the capital, it was abandoned (1860). Pagodas, the ruins of the old palace, and a great statue of Buddha remain.

**Amarillo** USA. Town in Texas 320 m. NW of Fort Worth. Pop. (1960) 137,969. Commercial and industrial centre, in a region producing oil, natural gas, and wheat, and raising cattle. Oil refining, meat packing, flour milling, synthetic rubber manufacture, etc.

**Amaro, Monte** ◊ *Apennines*.

**Amazonas** Brazil. Largest state. In the Amazon basin. Area 603,876 sq. m. Pop. (1960) 721,215. Cap. Manáus. Population density little more than 1 per sq. m.; one quarter live near Manáus, the remainder along the waterways of the vast rain-forest.

**Amazon River** S America. The world's largest river system, mainly in Brazil, receiving water from the Andes between 2° N and 20° S, where tributaries in S Bolivia supply the middle Amazon via the Madeira. From sources 100 m. from the Pacific, water flows thousands of miles to the Atlantic: 3,300 m. via the Marañón, and 3,900 m. via the Ucayali–Apurímac. The main river is formed in Peru by the Marañón–Ucayali confluence (called the Solimões as far as Manáus). The main north-bank tributary, the Rio Negro, brings water from 5° N in the Guiana Highlands. Other great tributaries, e.g. the Tocantins, Xingu, and Tapajos, rise far S in the interior plateaux of Brazil, and on their banks live the few surviving tribes of primitive Indians, under the guardianship of the Indian Protection Service of the Brazilian government. The great discharge at the Amazon mouth makes the river water identifiable 200 m. out to sea. Tidal effects are felt 500 m. inland, and in the lower reaches there is a bore (the *pororoca*) up to 16 ft high. Steamers of 11,000 tons regularly serve Manáus (1,000 m. upstream) and vessels of 14-ft draught can reach Iquitos (Peru), 2,300 m. from the Atlantic.

The whole system covers 2½ million sq. m. The lowlands extend for 800 m. N–S; here the rivers have little gradient (the Amazon falls only 35 ft in its last 2,000 m.), and floods can widen the channels by scores of miles. The surface (partly-consolidated sands, clays, and gravels) is swampy and covered by silt from the shifting rivers, with low levees; low bluffs separate flat flood plains.

The equatorial lowlands have little seasonal or daily temperature variation (monthly averages 27° C (80° F)). Annual rainfall 70–120 ins. No dry months, but Sept.–Nov. generally less rainy. Tropical rain-forest covers nearly the whole of the Amazon basin, which occupies 40 per cent of the area of Brazil but has less than 7 per cent of its population (which is concentrated around Manáus, Santarém, and Belém). The climate is not unbearable, but economic possibilities are very limited; once the tropical forest is cleared, the soil is thin and infertile. The Amazon enjoyed a boom period *c.* 1880–1910, when its scattered wild rubber trees were the world's main source of raw rubber supplies; the capital of Amazonas, ◊ *Manáus*, had a brief burst of magnificence. With the development of rubber plantations in SE Asia, profits from the forests dwindled, and the vast area now yields little wealth: rubber, babassu nuts, Brazil nuts, hardwoods, jute, animals, skins.

**Ambala** India. Town in the E of the Punjab 70 m. SE of Ludhiana. Pop. (1961) 105,543. Railway junction. Industrial and commercial centre. Cotton ginning, flour milling, food processing, etc. Trade in grain, cotton, etc.

**Ambato** Ecuador. Capital of Tungurahua province, in a hollow near the N base of Mt Chimborazo, at a height of 8,345 ft, 70 m. S of Quito. Pop. (1966) 89,541. Commercial centre. Resort, the 'garden city of Ecuador', noted for fruit trees and gardens. Manufactures textiles. Fruit canning, tanning, etc. Suffered severe earthquake damage 1949.

**Amberg** Federal German Republic. Town in Bavaria, on the Vils R. 38 m. E of Nuremberg. Pop. (1964) 42,300. Manufactures enamels, textiles, cement, etc. Iron mines in the neighbourhood. Capital of the Upper Palatinate till 1810.

**Ambleside** England. Small town and tourist centre in Westmorland, in the Lake District 1 m. N of L. Windermere and 12 m. NW of Kendal. Pop. 2,000. An urban district 1895–1935. Many associations with the poet Wordsworth.

**Amboina (Ambon)** Indonesia. **1.** Island in the Moluccas, just SW of Ceram, in the Maluku province. Area 386 sq. m. Pop. 73,000. Mountainous, with fertile coastal plains. Main products nutmegs, rice, coconuts, cloves. Chief town Amboina. In 1605 the island was taken from the Portuguese by the Dutch, who in 1623 massacred the inhabitants of a British settlement there – for which Cromwell obtained compensation (1654).
**2.** Chief town and seaport of Amboina Island. Pop. 40,000. Exports copra, spices.

**America** ◊ *Central America*; *North America*; *South America.*

**Amersfoort** Netherlands. Industrial town in the Utrecht province 13 m. ENE of Utrecht. Pop. (1968) 76,285. Manufactures chemicals, bicycles, carpets, etc. The Koppelpoort is a 14th-cent. watergate. Birthplace of the Dutch statesman J. van Oldenbarneveldt (1547–1619).

**Amersham** England. Market town in S Buckinghamshire 7 m. ENE of High Wycombe near the Chiltern Hills. Pop. (rural district, 1961) 56,565. Brewing. Manufactures radio isotopes, furniture, etc. Has a 17th-cent. market hall. Just SW is Coleshill, birthplace of Edmund Waller (1606–87).

**Ames** USA. Town in Iowa 32 m. N of Des

Moines. Pop. (1960) 27,003. Centre of a rich maize-growing area. Seat of the Iowa State University (1858).

**Amesbury** England. Small town in Wiltshire, on the R. Avon 7 m. N of Salisbury. Pop. (rural district, 1961) 22,594. In a district possessing remains of prehistoric man, inc. ♢ *Stonehenge*.

**Amiens** France. Prefecture of the Somme department, in the N, on the Somme R. 74 m. N of Paris. Pop. (1968) 122,864. Capital of Picardy till 1790. Route and industrial centre. Manufactures cotton, woollen, linen, velvet goods, carpets, clothing, machinery, etc. Market gardens (*hortillonnages*) abound to the NE. Trade in grain, beet-sugar, wool, etc. The famous Cathedral of Notre Dame (built mainly 1220–88), one of the outstanding French Gothic cathedrals, is the largest church in France. In the Hôtel de Ville (begun 1550) was signed the Treaty of Amiens (1802) between Britain, France, Spain, and Holland. Suffered considerable damage in both world wars. Famous citizens were Peter the Hermit and Charles Du Cange, of whom there are statues.

**Amirante Islands** Indian Ocean. Archipelago 120 m. SW of the Seychelles (of which they are a dependency). Pop. about 100. Chief product copra.

**Amman** Jordan. Ancient Rabbath Ammon; Philadelphia. Capital, 54 m. ENE of Jerusalem at a height of 2,400 ft. Pop. (1967) 330,220. Chief industrial centre. Manufactures textiles, cement, tobacco products, etc. Airport. As Rabbath Ammon, capital of the Ammonites. Rebuilt by Ptolemy Philadelphus and named Philadelphia in the 3rd cent. B.C. Declined after the Arab conquest. The great influx of refugees following the war with Israel (1948) more than quadrupled the population in the 1950s; the refugee problem arose again after the war with Israel in 1967.

**Amoy** China. Seaport in Fukien province, on Amoy island in the Formosa Strait. Pop. 224,000. Exports sugar, tobacco, paper, etc. Hinterland restricted to SE Fukien until the building of the Yingtan–Amoy railway (1956). Industrial and commercial centre. Manufactures chemicals, paper, etc. Seat of a university founded (1921) by a Fukienese who became wealthy in Malaya. One of the first Chinese ports to trade with Europeans (1842); its once flourishing tea exports diminished in the late 19th cent.

**Amphissa** ♢ *Phocis*.
**Amraoti** ♢ *Amravati*.
**Amravati** India. Formerly Amraoti. Town in the N of Maharashtra, 90 m. WSW of Nagpur. Pop. (1961) 137,875. Commercial centre. Important cotton trade. Cotton ginning, etc.

**Amritsar** India. Town in the Punjab 32 m. E of Lahore (Pakistan). Pop. (1961) 376,295. Railway junction. Industrial and commercial centre. Manufactures carpets, textiles, chemicals, etc. Trade in cotton, wool, hides, etc. The religious centre of the Sikhs, founded in the 16th cent. around a sacred tank (pool), the Amrita Saras, on a small island of which is the famous Golden Temple. Scene of the Amritsar Massacre (1919), when British troops fired on Indian demonstrators, killing nearly 400.

**Amsterdam** Netherlands. Capital and largest city, seaport and industrial centre, mainly on the S bank of the Ij R. (an arm of the Ijsselmeer) where it is joined by the canalized Amstel R. (from which the name derives). Pop. (1968) 857,635. Built on piles; intersected by a network of concentric and radial canals crossed by about 400 bridges. Linked with the sea by the North Holland Canal to the Helder (1825) and the North Sea Canal to Ijmuiden (1876). The Merwede Canal (1892) was widened and deepened 1935–52 and extended from Utrecht to the Waal, accommodating Rhine barges up to 2,000 tons. Important centre of diamond cutting and polishing. Shipbuilding, sugar refining, brewing. Manufactures chemicals, textiles, etc. Enjoyed its greatest prosperity as a seaport in the 17th cent., when the Treaty of Westphalia (1648) closed the Scheldt to navigation and destroyed the trade of Antwerp. Today overshadowed by Rotterdam. Outstanding buildings include the Rijksmuseum, with a priceless collection of Dutch and Flemish paintings, inc. several by Rembrandt; the 13th-cent. Oude Kerk and 15th-cent. Nieuwe Kerk; and the 17th-cent. royal palace (formerly a town hall). Seat of the University of Amsterdam (1632) and the Free University (1882). Airport at Schiphol, 5 m. to the SW.

**Amsterdam** USA. Town in New York State on the Mohawk R. 30 m. NW of Albany. Pop. (1960) 28,772. Manufactures carpets, textiles, plastics, etc.

**Amsterdam Island** ♢ *Nouvelle Amsterdam*.
**Amu Darya** USSR/Afghanistan. Ancient

Oxus. Important river of Central Asia rising in the Pamirs in a headstream called the Pyandzh R. Total length 1,500 m. Flows generally W, forming much of the Afghanistan–USSR boundary, then turns NW through Turkmenistan and Uzbekistan, separating the Kara Kum and Kyzyl Kum deserts, and entering the Aral Sea by an extensive delta. Much used for irrigation (e.g. Khiva oasis). Navigable for more than 800 m.

**Amur River** (Chinese **Heilung-kiang**) China/USSR. River in E Asia, formed on the USSR–China frontier by the union of the Shilka and Argun rivers, flowing nearly 1,800 m. first SE and then NE, entering the Sea of Okhotsk opposite the N end of Sakhalin. Total length with the Shilka headstream 2,690 m. Chief tributaries the Sungari and the Ussuri, both from the S. Above its confluence with the Ussuri, the Amur with the Argun forms part of the frontier between the USSR and China; below the confluence the Ussuri forms another long section of the frontier. The river is ice-free May–Oct., and much of it is navigable. Important towns on its banks are Blagoveshchensk, Khabarovsk, Komsomolsk, and Nikolayevsk. Blagóveshchensk, capital of the Amur Region of the RSFSR, is the centre of the Amur Railway, linked with the Trans-Siberian Railway and giving the USSR a route to the Pacific independent of the more direct route through NE China. The area was long under dispute between China and Russia; by 1860 Russia had been ceded all land on the left bank of the Amur, on the right bank of the Ussuri, and on the right bank of the Amur below the Ussuri confluence.

**Anadyr** USSR. Formerly Novo Mariinsk. Town in RSFSR on the estuary of the Anadyr R. Pop. 5,600. Lignite mining. Fish-canning. Airport.

**Anadyr Range** USSR. Mountain range in the extreme NE of Siberia (RSFSR) extending SE from the coast of the E Siberian Sea. Rises to over 5,000 ft.

**Anadyr River** USSR. River 500 m. long, rising at the N end of the Gydan range in NE Siberia, flowing SW and then E, and entering the Gulf of Anadyr on the Bering Sea.

**Anáhuac** Mexico. 'The land near the waters': pre-Conquest name for the Mexico basin, the densely populated part of the central plateau where Mexico City stands.

The name derives from the many former lakes, now mainly dry.

**Anápolis** Brazil. Commercial town in the S of the Goiás state, 80 m. SW of Brasilia. Pop. 60,000. In an agricultural region. Trade in livestock, coffee, maize, etc.

**Anatolia** ◊ *Asia Minor.*

**Anchorage** USA. Largest and most important industrial town in Alaska, in the S, at the head of the Cook Inlet. Pop. (1960) 44,237. On the railway to Fairbanks. Railway workshops. Salmon canneries. Fur market, airport, seaport. Coal and gold mined near by. Severely damaged by earthquake in 1964, with some loss of life.

**Ancohuma, Mount** ◊ *Illampu, Mount.*

**Ancona** Italy. Capital of Ancona province, in the Marches; also capital of the Marches. Pop. (1968) 107,542. Seaport and industrial centre. Shipbuilding, sugar refining, etc. Founded in the 4th cent. B.C. by Greeks from Syracuse. Flourished under the Romans, and has a white triumphal arch erected in honour of Trajan (A.D. 115). Harbour improved in the late 19th cent. Suffered from bombardments in both world wars.

**Ancud** ◊ *Chiloé Island.*

**Åndalsnes** Norway. Small town in the Möre og Romsdal county, at the head of Romsdal Fiord 105 m. WSW of Trondheim. Pop. 1,400. Scene of the first British landings in the 2nd World War (1940). Severely damaged in the ensuing battle.

**Andalusia** Spain. Region and former province in the S, bordering S on the Mediterranean and Atlantic. Comprises the modern provinces of Almería, Granada, Málaga, Cadiz, Huelva, Seville, Córdoba, and Jaén. Much of it consists of the basin of the Guadalquivir, and in the SE is the Sierra Nevada, which has Mulhacén (11,421 ft), the highest peak in Spain. Irrigation has made it one of the most fertile parts of Spain, producing olives, vines, cereals, citrus fruits, and even sugarcane. Also rich in minerals. Fishing important along the coast. Attained its greatest glory under Moorish rule, which lasted from the 8th to the end of the 15th cent. and left outstanding monuments in such cities as Seville, Córdoba, and Granada.

**Andaman Islands** Indian Ocean. Islands 120 m. SSW of Cape Negrais (Burma); with the Nicobar Is., a territory of India. Area 2,500 sq. m. Pop. 19,000 (excluding aborigines). Chief town Port Blair (S

Andaman). A N–S band; the five large N islands (the Great Andamans, inc. N, Middle, and S Andaman) are separated from Little Andaman (S) by the Duncan Passage. Also about 200 islets. Generally hilly; well covered with tropical forests, which yield padouk (Andaman redwood) and other valuable timbers. Coconuts, rice, coffee, and rubber cultivated. Copra and timber exported from Port Blair. The extremely primitive aboriginal Negritos live in the forests and are now few in number (probably less than 100). A penal settlement established on the islands by the Indian Government (1858) was abandoned in 1945. Occupied by the Japanese 1942–5.

**Andermatt** Switzerland. Village in the Uri canton, 16 m. S of Altdorf in the Urseren valley at a height of 4,700 ft. Pop. (1960) 1,500. Summer resort and winter-sports centre. On the Furka–Oberalp railway and the road to the St Gotthard Pass.

**Anderson** (Indiana) USA. Industrial town on the White R. 35 m. NE of Indianapolis. Pop. (1960) 49,061. Manufactures motor-car parts, machinery, etc.

**Anderson** (S Carolina) USA. Industrial town 30 m. SW of Greenville. Pop. (1960) 41,316. Manufactures cotton goods, chemicals, etc.

**Andes** S America. A vast mountain system, raised, folded, and faulted in late Tertiary times, extending 4,500 m., continuous with the mountains of N America, in a general N–S alignment (though in Venezuela the minor Cordillera sweeps E, and in S Peru and Bolivia the trend is NW–SE). It narrows in Chile, and is much lower in the S, where it is cut through by glaciated valleys. In Bolivia and S Peru the E and W Cordilleras enclose the Altiplano (12,000–13,000 ft), a high, bleak tableland containing various basins, deep river-cut valleys, and the large L. Titicaca. Rivers from the high W Cordillera cut far into the plateaux and through the E foothills, and here, only 100 m. from the Pacific, the first tributaries of the Amazon start their 3,000-m. course to the Atlantic. The N and central Andes enclose many high basins, which are important pockets of population. North from S Colombia are three parallel Cordilleras, separated by deep valleys containing the Cauca and Magdalena rivers; the E Cordillera has many high basins.

The Andes divide S America into two very distinct parts: the average height of the chain is 13,000 ft, and the E–W passes are seldom lower than 10,000 ft. Several peaks are of great height: Aconcagua rises to 22,835 ft. There are several peaks of over 20,000 ft in the main Cordilleras, many of volcanic origin and many still active, which have spread volcanic ash over wide areas. The Andes and foothills are subject to severe earthquakes. The snowline is at 15,000 ft in Ecuador, 21,000 ft in N Chile, and only 2,300 ft in extreme S Chile, where large permanent icefields and glaciers occur. As a whole the Andes provide magnificent scenery.

Amerindians, e.g. the Chibchas of Colombia, were established in the Andes before the rise of the Inca Empire. From the 13th cent. millions lived under the Inca administration, centred mainly on the Cuzco region of Peru. Gold, silver, and copper were worked from early times. Potatoes and maize were first cultivated here. In the 16th cent. the Spanish conquerors destroyed Inca agriculture but intensified the mining of silver.

Today many metals come from the high Andes: copper, tin, silver, lead, zinc. From the W flanks (where the Andean slopes are separated from the coastal range by debris-filled troughs) come iron ore, nitrates, and iodine, and petroleum from the adjoining lowlands E and W. Settlement is concentrated in the high basins; there is much poverty among the tenant-farming highland Indians. Wool from the sheep, llama, and vicuña is the main commodity of exchange.

**Andhra Pradesh** India. State in the SE, formed (1953) from the Telugu-speaking area of N Madras; further boundary adjustments made in 1956 and 1960. Area 106,286 sq. m. Pop. (1961) 35,983,447. Cap. Hyderabad. Chief seaport Vishakhapatnam. Principal crops rice, sugar-cane, groundnuts.

**Andizhan** USSR. Capital of the Andizhan Region, Uzbek SSR, in the fertile Fergana valley, 160 m. ESE of Tashkent. Pop. (1970) 188,000. Trade in cotton. Produces cotton goods, cottonseed oil, foodstuffs, etc. Destroyed by earthquake in 1902 and rebuilt.

**Andorra.** *Small independent state in the E Pyrenees, on the Franco-Spanish frontier. Area 190 sq. m. Pop. (1967) 15,000 (distributed among 6 villages; Catalan in origin and speech). Cap. Andorra la Vieja (Fr. Andorre la Vieille). Mountainous, rising to nearly 10,000 ft, with deep valleys and gorges. Drained by the Valira R. Climate harsh. Main occupation sheep rearing. Some barley and tobacco cultivated. Its autonomy is supposed to have been instituted by Charlemagne. Now under the joint suzerainty of the President of France and the Spanish bishop of Urgel, to both of whom nominal tributes are paid. The two 'co-princes' are represented in Andorra by the 'Viguier de France' and the 'Viguier Episcopal'. Administered by a council of 24 members.

**Andover** England. Municipal borough in Hampshire, 12 m. NW of Winchester. Pop. (1961) 17,808. Market town. Flour milling, malting, etc.

**Andria** Italy. Town in Bari province in Apulia, 32 m. WNW of Bari. Pop. (1961) 70,831. Produces wine, olive oil, macaroni, etc. Founded in the 11th cent. Favourite residence of Emperor Frederick II (1194–1250).

**Andros** Greece. 1. Most northerly island of the Cyclades, in the Aegean Sea. Area 117 sq. m. Pop. (1961) 12,925. Mountainous, with many fertile valleys. Famous for wine since ancient times.
2. Chief town of Andros Island, on the E coast. Pop. 1,900.

**Andújar** Spain. Town in the Jaén province in Andalusia, on the Guadalquivir R. 24 m. NW of Jaén. Pop. (1961) 32,185. Commercial centre. Famous for *alcarrazas* (jars for keeping water cool). Soap, textile, and other industries. Uranium plant supplying material for nuclear energy (opened 1960). **Anécho** ◊ *Togo*.

**Angara River** USSR. River 1,150 m. long in SE Siberia, flowing from L. Baikal (SW) NNW past Irkutsk and then W, joining the Yenisei R. at Strelka. In the lower course sometimes called the Upper Tunguska. Navigable for most of the course. Much utilized for hydroelectric power, e.g. at Bratsk (completed 1967).

**Angarsk** USSR. Industrial town in the Irkutsk Region (RSFSR), on the Angara R. 30 m. NW of Irkutsk. Pop. (1970) 204,000. Has developed rapidly since the 2nd World War. Manufactures petrochemicals, machinery, etc.

**Angel Falls** Venezuela. Waterfall in the SE, on a tributary of the Caroni R. At 3,212 ft probably the highest in the world.

**Ångerman River** Sweden. River 280 m. long, rising near the Norwegian frontier and flowing generally SSE to the Gulf of Bothnia near Harnosand. Hydroelectric plants. Used for floating timber down to sawmills on the estuary.

**Angers** France. Ancient Juliomagus. Prefecture of the Maine-et-Loire department in the W, on the Maine R. 52 m. ENE of Nantes. Pop. (1968) 134,959. Commercial and industrial centre. Produces wine, textiles, footwear, agricultural machinery, etc. Seat of the Counts of Anjou from the 9th to the 13th cent. Architecturally one of the finest French towns, with the 13th-cent. castle (built by Louis IX), the 12th/13th-cent. cathedral, the Logis Barrault (a 15th-cent. Renaissance house), and various churches and museums. Educational and art centre. Damaged by bombardment in the 2nd World War (1944).

**Angkor** Cambodia. Ruins just N of Siemreap, N of L. Tonlé Sap. A remnant of the Khmer civilization; dates from the 9th–12th cent. Angkor Thom, the ancient Khmer capital, is enclosed by a wall and contains the royal palace and remarkable Bayon temple. Just S is the great temple of Angkor Wat (or Angkor Vat), the best preserved example of Khmer architecture and one of the world's outstanding buildings. Abandoned in the 15th cent. Discovered in dense jungle in the 1860s; later cleared.

**Anglesey (Anglesea)** Wales. Ancient Mona. Island and county off the NW coast, separated from the mainland (Caernarvonshire) by the Menai Strait. Area 276 sq. m. Pop. (1961) 51,700. County town Beaumaris. Low-lying, generally flat. Linked with the mainland by road and railway bridges. Chief occupations agriculture and sheep rearing. Tourism important. Chief towns Holyhead (on Holy Island off the W coast), a packet station for the Irish Republic (Dun Laoghaire), Beaumaris, Amlwch, Menai Bridge.

**Angmagssalik** Greenland. Small trading post and settlement (mainly of Eskimo) on Angmagssalik Island in the E, about 60 m. S of the Arctic Circle. Pop. 700. The US base (established 1941) has an important meteorological and radio station.

**Angola (Portuguese West Africa).** Portuguese overseas territory on the Atlantic seaboard of Africa, mainly S of the Congo estuary; includes ◊ *Cabinda*, an enclave N of the estuary. Area 481,226 sq. m. (divided into 13 districts). Pop. (1960) 4,832,677 (principally Bantu, with about 250,000 Europeans). Cap. Luanda (São Paulo de Luanda). Bounded on the N by Congo (Brazzaville) and Congo (Kinshasa), on the E by Congo (Kinshasa) and Zambia, and on the S by SW Africa. Consists of a narrow coastal plain (1,000-m. coastline) and a broad dissected tableland (at a height of 4,000–6,000 ft) which descends eastwards to the basins of the Congo and the Zambezi. Sugar-cane, cacao, and cotton plantations on the hot unhealthy lowlands of the N. Coffee and sisal produced on the plateau. Subsistence crops include maize, cassava, rice. Cattle raised on parts of the plateau free from the tsetse fly. Diamonds mined in the NE. Important towns are the seaports of Lobito, Benguela, Moçâmedes; and Nova Lisboa, the future capital. The Benguela railway runs from Lobito across Angola through Katanga – Congo (Kinshasa) – and Zambia to Beira in Moçambique. Exports include coffee, maize, diamonds, sugar. The N coast was discovered by the Portuguese (late 15th cent.); Luanda was founded in 1575. Portuguese sovereignty over the coastline has remained almost continuous. From the 17th to the 19th cent. the colony's prosperity depended on the slave trade; economic development has been slow. There was open rebellion in the N in 1961–2, suppressed in ways much criticized elsewhere; a UN committee reported 150,000 refugees.

**Angora** ◊ *Ankara.*

**Angostura** ◊ *Ciudad Bolívar.*

**Angoulême** France. Prefecture of the Charente department, 68 m. NNE of Bordeaux on a 300-ft-high promontory overlooking the Charente R. Pop. (1968) 50,883. Route centre. Important paper mills, breweries, distilleries, etc. Became the seat of the Counts of Angoumois in the 9th cent. Cathedral (12th-cent., restored in the 19th cent.).

**Anguilla** British W Indies. One of the Leeward Is., 60 m. NNW of St Kitts. Area 35 sq. m. Pop. (1966) 5,395. Forms, with St Kitts, Nevis, and Sombrero, the territory of St Kitts-Nevis-Anguilla. Produces and exports sea-island cotton, salt. Demands for independence from St Kitts led to the landing of British troops and police (1969).

**Angus** Scotland. Formerly Forfarshire. County in the E, bounded by Aberdeenshire and Kincardine (N), the Firth of Tay (S), and Perthshire (W). Area 874 sq. m. Pop. (1961) 278,370. County town Forfar. Between the wild and picturesque Gram-

pian Mountains and the Sidlaw Hills is the fertile Strathmore, where oats, barley, and potatoes are cultivated and livestock raised. Chief towns Dundee, Arbroath, Montrose, Brechin, Forfar. ◊ *Coupar-Angus; Glamis.*

**Anhalt** German Democratic Republic. Former state; part of Saxony-Anhalt 1945–52. Area 888 sq. m. Pop. (1939) 437,000. Cap. Dessau. The former rulers were a German family descended from Albert the Bear (1100–1170), among whom it was divided. United again 1863. Joined the German Empire 1871 and the Weimar Republic 1919.

**Anhwei** China. Province in the E, on both sides of the Yangtse R. Area 54,000 sq. m. Pop. 33,560,000. Cap. Hofei. Chief crops wheat, millets, beans (in the N); rice, tea, cotton (in the hillier S).

**Ani** Turkey. Ancient Abnikum. Ruined city of medieval ◊ *Armenia*, in the Kars province in NE Turkey, E of Kars near the USSR frontier. Remains of cathedral, churches, etc. Capital of Armenia in the 10th cent. Destroyed by earthquake in the 14th cent.

**Aniene (Teverone) River** Italy. Ancient Anio. River 73 m. long, rising in the Apennines and joining the Tiber just above Rome. Has supplied Rome with water for centuries. Now a source of hydroelectric power. A famous waterfall at Tivoli.

**Anio River** ◊ *Aniene River.*

**Anjou** France. Former province, in the Paris Basin, now approximately forming the Maine-et-Loire department. Cap. Angers. Geoffrey Plantagenet, Count of Anjou, was the father of the English king Henry II. Annexed by Louis XI of France 1480.

**Ankara** Turkey. Formerly Angora. Capital of Turkey and of Ankara province, on a hill above the Anatolian plateau, 200 m. ESE of Istanbul, at a height of 2,900 ft. Pop. (1965) 905,700. Commercial and industrial centre. Trade in grain, wool, and in mohair from Angora goats. Manufactures textiles, cement, leather goods, etc. In spite of its long history, almost entirely a modern city. Seat of a university (1946) and a technical university (1956). Its outstanding relic is the temple on the walls of which is the *Monumentum Ancyranum*, a valuable record of Augustan times. Taken by the Tatars 1402. Recaptured by the Turks 1415, and has since belonged to Turkey. Declined until chosen as capital by Kemal Atatürk (1920), after which it developed rapidly. The Atatürk mausoleum is one of its foremost buildings.

**Ankaratra Mountains** ◊ *Malagasy Republic.*

**Anking** China. Formerly (1912–49) Hwaining. Commercial town and river port in Anhwei province on the N bank of the Yangtse R. 150 m. SW of Nanking. Pop. 105,000. Trade in rice, cotton, etc. Once an important regional centre and capital of Anhwei province; declined with the building of the railway to Wuhu and Kiukiang.

**Annaba** Algeria. Formerly Bône. A Mediterranean seaport in the Annaba department, 260 m. E of Algiers. Pop. (1967) 165,000. The third most important seaport (after Algiers and Oran). Exports phosphates, iron ore, cork, wine, etc. Manufactures chemicals. A centre of early Christianity; for 35 years the episcopal see of St Augustine. Taken by the French 1832. Developed rapidly after the discovery of iron ore and phosphates in NE Algeria. ◊ *Numidia*; *Tebessa.*

**Annam.** Former kingdom and French protectorate in SE Asia. Part of ◊ *Vietnam* since 1946.

**Annan** Scotland. Royal burgh and market town in Dumfriesshire, on the Annan R. 15 m. ESE of Dumfries. Pop. (1961) 5,572. Flour milling, whisky distilling. Manufactures fertilizers. Birthplace of the African explorer Hugh Clapperton (1788–1827). The first nuclear power station to operate in Scotland was opened near by in 1959.

**Annan River** Scotland. River 49 m. long, rising in the Moffat Hills and flowing S into the Solway Firth 2 m. S of Annan.

**Annapolis** USA. State capital of Maryland, near the mouth of the Severn R. 23 m. S of Baltimore. Pop. (1960) 23,385. Residential town, with historic buildings. Seat of the US Naval Academy (1845). Founded 1649, as Providence; renamed (1694) after Princess Anne (later Queen Anne).

**Annapolis Royal** Canada. Small town in Nova Scotia, on the Annapolis Basin, an arm of the Bay of Fundy, and at the mouth of the Annapolis R. whose valley is famous for its apple orchards. Founded (1605) by de Monts as Port Royal. Ceded to Britain 1713 and renamed in honour of Queen Anne.

**Ann Arbor** USA. Town in Michigan, 32 m. W of Detroit. Pop. (1960) 67,340. Manufactures scientific instruments, cameras, motor-car accessories, etc. Seat of the University of Michigan (1841).

**Annecy** France. Prefecture of the Haute-Savoie department on the N shore of L. Annecy 22 m. S of Geneva, at a height of 1,470 ft. Pop. (1968) 56,689. Industrial centre. Manufactures textiles, paper, watches, etc. The arcaded streets, lakeside aspect, and pleasant climate have made it a popular resort. Annecy-le-Vieux (2 m. NNE) has a famous bell foundry. At the reconstructed convent of the Visitation is the tomb of St Francis of Sales (1567–1622), bishop of Geneva, who was born near by.

**Annecy, Lake** France. Lake in the SE in the Haute-Savoie department. Area 10 sq. m. Many resorts around the shores.

**Annobón** Equatorial Guinea. Former Spanish island in the Gulf of Guinea. Area 6½ sq. m. Pop. (1960) 1,415. Chief town San Antonio. Discovered by the Portuguese (1473) on New Year's Day: the name means 'Happy New Year'. Ceded (with Fernando Póo) to Spain 1778. The inhabitants are probably descendants of Africans shipwrecked in the 16th cent. ◊ *Equatorial Guinea.*

**Annonay** ◊ *Ardèche.*

**Ansbach** Federal German Republic. Formerly also Anspach. Town in Bavaria 26 m. WSW of Nuremberg. Pop. (1964) 32,600. Manufactures machinery, textiles, etc. Residence of the Hohenzollerns 1331–1791. Transferred from Prussia to Bavaria 1806.

**Anshan** China. Industrial town in Liaoning province in the NE, 60 m. SW of Shenyang. Pop. (1957) 805,000. A leading metallurgical centre. Important iron and steel plant. Manufactures chemicals, cement. Development of the steel industry led to an enormous increase in population from the early 1930s.

**Anstruther** Scotland. Fishing port and seaside resort in E Fifeshire, on the Firth of Forth 8 m. SSE of St Andrews. Pop. (1961) 2,888. Consists of Anstruther Easter, Anstruther Wester, and Kilrenny.

**Antakya** ◊ *Antioch.*

**Antalya** Turkey. Capital of the Antalya province in the SW, on the Gulf of Antalya 235 m. W of Adana. Pop. (1965) 71,800. Seaport. Trade in grain, timber. Flour milling, canning, etc.

**Antananarivo** ◊ *Tananarive.*

**Antarctica.** Continental land mass between 5 and 6 million sq. m. in area, mainly snow-covered plateau 6,000–10,000 ft above sea level surrounding the S Pole, with mountain ranges and extensive ice sheets and glaciers. Graham Land and other parts of the continent facing Tierra del Fuego have a structure resembling the S parts of S America; Graham Land itself consists of a range of fold mountains bordered by horizontal sediments. The remainder of the continent beyond the Ross and Weddell seas resembles Australia and S Africa structurally, with vast uplifted blocks and a pre-Cambrian basement covered by early sedimentary rocks. Much remains to be discovered of its geology, but there are later sedimentaries; coal, bedded horizontally, exists in the W. Mt Erebus (13,202 ft), on Ross Island, is an active volcano.

The Antarctic Ocean is subdivided into a number of seas – the Ross, Weddell, King Haakon VII, and Amundsen seas; the huge inlets of the Ross and Weddell seas give a smaller land area to the W than the E, and shorter journeys to the Pole from coastal bases. Pack ice covers the ocean except in midsummer and drifts with the E and SE winds; it reaches a minimum at the end of Feb. and beginning of March, when ships can best reach the coast and touch land far into the Weddell Sea inlet. The Ross Sea underwater ridge prevents warmer water from reaching the deep inner sea, where a broad ice shelf exists.

Surface temperatures depend on both latitude and altitude: the mean annual temperature at the S Pole is $-51°$ C at 9,200 ft, but stations at greater altitude to the N have lower mean temperatures. Temperature inversions over the cold surfaces can cause strong down-slope winds, and gustiness and intense local blizzards result. Occasional surges of polar air move N into the westerlies which encircle the Antarctic, and a cyclonic storm may move into the perimeter of the Antarctic, but the average precipitation is only of the order of 5–8 ins. annually. Few forms of plant life exist, except mosses, lichens and algae. Animal life is found on the sea and the coast, and includes many seabirds, with penguins among them, and seals.

Capt. Cook reached $71°10'$ S on his voyages of 1772–5, and previous to this the search for a 'great south land' had provided a motive for southern exploration, though none survived to describe land S of the Antarctic Circle. In the late 18th and early 19th cent. sealers and whalers began to discover islands off Antarctica. In 1821 a Russian expedition under F. von Bellingshausen reached land within the Antarctic Circle. Whaling and sealing interests brought Weddell, Biscoe, and Balleny to make discoveries, and scientific investigations and explorations were successfully made in 1839–43 by Wilkes from the USA, Dumont d'Urville from France, and Sir James Ross from Great Britain. Investigations of Antarctic waters by Sir John Murray in H MS *Challenger* (1874) and by the Norwegian captains Larsen and Christensen (1892–5) added to knowledge of the continent. Exploration by well-equipped expeditions followed: under Scott (1901–4), Shackleton (1908–9), and Amundsen, who in 1911 first reached the S Pole, a month before Scott, who perished with his companions on the return journey. In 1929 Byrd, who had previously explored in Antarctica, flew to the S Pole. Shortly before his death he directed the 1955–8 expedition, formed to gain scientific information, as a contribution to the International Geophysical Year. Also contributing knowledge was a Commonwealth Trans-Antarctic expedition under Sir Vivian Fuchs, whose tracked vehicles crossed from Shackleton Base on Weddell Sea to Scott Base at McMurdo Sound, Ross Sea, via the pole. The area S of 60° S is reserved for international peaceful scientific investigation under the International Antarctic Treaty (1959); otherwise various territories are claimed, except in the sector S of the Pacific between 80° and 150° W, where the USA has made much exploration. The first nuclear reactor in Antarctica, on the Ross Ice Shelf, went into operation in 1962.

**Antibes** France. Port and resort in the Alpes-Maritimes department, on the French Riviera 12 m. SW of Nice. Pop. (1968) 48,013. Exports flowers. Manufactures perfumes, chocolate. The famous resorts of Juan-les-Pins and Cap d'Antibes (on the peninsula of the same name) are near by. Important in Roman times; Roman remains. The Château Grimaldi, a museum, has works by Picasso.

**Anticosti** Canada. Large island in Quebec province, in the Gulf of St Lawrence, 135 m. long and up to 30 m. wide. Well wooded (mainly conifers); the chief occupation of the scanty population is lumbering. Discovered (1534) by Cartier.

**Antigua** West Indies. One of the Leeward Is., 45 m. N of Guadeloupe. Area 108 sq. m. Pop. (1963) 61,664. Cap. and chief seaport St John's (pop. 13,000). Forms, with Barbuda and Redonda, the

Antigua territory. It has a relatively dry climate and occasional hurricanes, but is fertile. Sugar-cane and sea-island cotton cultivated. Principal exports sugar, molasses, rum, cotton. Tourism is of increasing importance. Discovered (1493) by Columbus. First colonized by the English 1632; declared a British possession 1667. Became an associated state within the Commonwealth 1967.

**Antigua (Antigua Guatemala)** Guatemala. Ancient capital (hence the name), 16 m. W of Guatemala city, whence the capital was removed when it was virtually destroyed by earthquakes in 1773. Pop. (1964) 21,984. Now a commercial centre in a coffee-growing region. Its picturesque situation and historic buildings, some of which are intact, attract many tourists.

**Antilles.** A great arc of islands extending more than 2,000 m. round the Caribbean Sea and including all the W Indies except the Bahamas. The Greater Antilles consist of Cuba, Jamaica, Hispaniola (Haiti and Dominican Republic), and Puerto Rico. The Lesser Antilles consist of the Leeward Is., the Windward Is., and the islands off the coast of Venezuela (including the Netherlands Antilles).

**Antilles, Netherlands** ◊ *Netherlands Antilles.*

**Antioch (Antakya)** Turkey. **1.** Capital of the Hatay province in the S, 55 m. W of Aleppo in Syria, on the Orontes R. Pop. (1965) 57,900. Commercial centre. Trade in grain, cotton, etc. Founded by Seleucus I *c.* 300 B.C. Became a great commercial city. An early centre of Christianity. Fell to the Persians (A.D. 538), the Arabs (636), the Seljuk Turks (1084), the Mamelukes (1268), and the Ottoman Turks (1516). Thereafter declined.

**2.** Ancient city of Pisidia, near modern Akşehir on the Anatolian plateau. Founded by Seleucus I *c.* 280 B.C. Visited by St Paul.

**Antipodes Islands** New Zealand. Small group of uninhabited rocky islands at 49°45′ S, 178°40′ E, in the S Pacific about 450 m. SE of South Island. The nearest land to the antipodes of London, England.

**Antisana** Ecuador. Volcano in the Andes, 18,885 ft high, 30 m. ESE of Quito. Part of a large snow-capped massif, with a village settlement at over 12,000 ft on the W slopes.

**Antofagasta** Chile. Capital of the Antofagasta province, largest town on the arid N coast, 650 m. N of Valparaiso. Pop. (1966) 75,000. Seaport with an artificial harbour. Exports nitrates, copper, etc. Ore refining, brewing, canning, etc. The railway from La Paz carries much of Bolivia's exports and imports. There is a secondary line over the Andes (opened 1948) to Salta in Argentina.

**Antony** France. Residential suburb of S W Paris, in the Hauts-de-Seine department. Pop. (1968) 56,878.

**Antrim** Northern Ireland. **1.** Maritime county in the NE, bounded on the W by the R. Bann and Lough Neagh, and on the S by the R. Lagan. Area 1,098 sq. m. Pop. (1961) 273,923. County town Belfast. Largely a low basalt plateau, rising to 1,817 ft in Mt Trostan, reaching the N coast in the columnar basalt of the Giant's Causeway. Famous for picturesque river valleys, the Glens of Antrim. Chief crops oats, potatoes, flax. Cattle, pigs, sheep reared. Principal industry linen manufacture. Shipbuilding at Belfast. Cotton and woollen manufactures. Chief towns Belfast, Larne, Lisburn, Ballymena, Portrush.

**2.** Town in Co. Antrim on the NE shore of Lough Neagh 13 m. NW of Belfast. Pop. (1961) 1,448. Linen mills. A famous round tower (10th-cent.).

**Antung** China. Seaport in the Liaoning province, near the mouth of the Yalu R. on the N Korea frontier. Pop. 360,000. Exports soya bean oil, timber, etc. Outport Tatungkow. Industrial centre. Sawmilling, silk milling, food processing. Manufactures paper, textiles, etc. Developed with the advent of the railway (1907). Became capital of the Antung province of Manchukuo (1932–45) and later of the Liaotung province.

**Antwerp (Flemish Antwerpen; Fr. Anvers)** Belgium. **1.** Province in the N, bounded on the N by the Netherlands. Area 1,104 sq. m. Pop. (1968) 1,518,464 (mainly Flemish-speaking). Chief towns Antwerp, Mechelen, Turnhout, Merksem, Lierre.

**2.** Capital of Antwerp province, on the Scheldt R. 55 m. from the open sea and 24 m. N of Brussels. Pop. (1968) 239,848. Chief seaport and commercial centre of Belgium. Considerable transit trade with W Germany, esp. the Ruhr area. Competes with Rotterdam as a leading port of continental Europe. Important industrial centre. Oil and sugar refineries, flour mills, motor-car assembly plants, textile factories, etc. Diamond cutting. Of great artistic and historic interest. The Gothic cathedral (begun 1352) has a spire 400 ft high and contains three Rubens masterpieces. The tombs of Rubens and his family are in the Church of St James. The house of the 16th-cent. printer C. Plantin is now a museum. The Stock Exchange (Bourse) was built (1868–72) to replace the 16th-cent. building destroyed by fire. Birthplace of Van Dyck (1599–1641); many fine examples of his work. In the late 15th cent. it became the principal commercial centre of Europe, but declined after being sacked by the Spaniards (1576) and again when the Treaty of Westphalia closed the Scheldt to navigation (1648). After the Scheldt was reopened (1795), the Dutch exercised their right to levy tolls on shipping until 1863, when Belgium redeemed this right by purchase; Antwerp rapidly regained its commercial prosperity. Severely damaged by German rockets after being taken by Allied forces in the 2nd World War (1944).

**Anuradhapura** Ceylon. Capital of the North-Central province, 110 m. NNE of Colombo. Pop. 18,000. In a rice-growing area (irrigated). Also an ancient ruined city, former capital of Ceylon, founded in the 5th cent. B.C. Remains of shrines, palaces, bathing pools, etc. The famous Bo-tree of Gautama. An important Buddhist place of pilgrimage.

**Anzhero Sudzhensk** USSR. Coalmining and industrial town in the Kuznetsk basin in the Kemerovo Region (RSFSR), 50 m. NNW of Kemerovo on the Trans-Siberian Railway. Pop. (1970) 106,000. Manufactures plastics, dyes, and drugs (mainly from coal by-products), machinery, etc. Formed (1928) from Anzherka and Sudzhenka.

**Anzio** Italy. Ancient Antium. Port in the Roma province in Latium, on the Tyrrhenian Sea 33 m. S of Rome. Pop. (1961) 15,889. Resort. Fishing centre. Birthplace of Nero (A.D. 37–68), among the ruins of whose villa was found the famous statue of Apollo Belvedere. Severely damaged in the 2nd World War; scene of Allied landings (Jan. 1944).

**Aomori** Japan. Capital of the Aomori prefecture, on Mutsu Bay on the N coast of Honshu. Pop. (1965) 224,431. Seaport; large local trade, esp. with Hokkaido. Exports rice, timber, fish, etc.

**Aorangi** ◊ *Cook, Mount.*

**Aosta** Italy. Capital of the Valle d'Aosta province on the Dora Baltea R. 52 m. NNW of Turin. Pop. (1961) 30,633. Tourist centre for the lovely Valle d'Aosta. Metal-working and other industries. Many

Roman remains. Cathedral (12th-cent.). Birthplace of Archbishop Anselm (1033?–1109).

**Apeldoorn** Netherlands. Town in the Gelderland province, 17 m. N of Arnhem. Pop. (1968) 118,694. Railway junction. Manufactures paper, etc. Het Loo, the summer residence of the Dutch royal family, is near by.

**Apennines** Italy. Mountain chain 800 m. long, extending throughout the peninsula from the Maritime Alps in the N to the Strait of Messina. Divided into three sections (northern, central, and southern). The N part is subdivided into the Ligurian Apennines, the Tuscan Apennines (inc., in the Apuan Alps, the famous Carrara marble quarries), and the Umbrian Apennines. In the central part are the highest groups; the Gran Sasso d'Italia rises to 9,560 ft in Monte Corno, and the Maiella to 9,170 ft in Monte Amaro. The S part extends to the Gulf of Taranto and curves SSW into the 'toe' of Italy, with Aspromonte (6,417 ft) near the S tip. Many mineral springs. Near Naples is the still active volcano Vesuvius. The S has long been subject to earthquakes. Forests are now much reduced (though some reforestation has taken place), but well-watered areas have pastures. Cereals, vines, olives, fruits, and nuts cultivated on the more fertile lower slopes.

**Apia** Western Samoa. Capital, seaport on the N coast of Upolu. Pop. (1961) 21,699. Exports bananas, copra, cacao.

**Appalachian Mountains** USA. A great system of mountain ranges and plateaux extending NE–SW more than 1,500 m. along the E side of N America from the Gulf of St Lawrence to central Alabama. Three distinct regions are recognized. The Older Appalachians of mainly crystalline rocks form the most easterly belt and include such individual ranges as the White Mountains and Green Mountains (N) and the Blue Ridge (S). To the W of this belt is the Great Appalachian Valley and then the Newer Appalachians, consisting of younger strata, with long ridges of folded mountains separated by longitudinal valleys. Still farther W is the third belt, the Appalachian plateau, including the extensive Allegheny Mountains. The highest peak in the Appalachians is Mt Mitchell (6,684 ft). in the Black Mountains of N Carolina. Within the Appalachians are the richest anthracite and bituminous coalfields in the US, chiefly in the N. Rich deposits of iron ore in the extreme S.

**Appenzell** Switzerland. 1. Canton in the NE, an enclave of the St Gallen canton. A full canton till 1597, when as a result of the Reformation it broke up into two independent half-cantons: Appenzell Ausser Rhoden (area 94 sq. m.; pop. (1969) 50,500; cap. Herisau; Protestant) and Appenzell Inner Rhoden (area 66 sq. m.; pop. (1969) 13,500; cap. Appenzell; Roman Catholic). Appenzell Ausser Rhoden is mainly industrial, and manufactures textiles. The principal occupation in Appenzell Inner Rhoden is pastoral farming (dairy produce). 2. Capital of Appenzell Inner Rhoden, on the Sitter R. 7 m. S of St Gallen, at a height of 2,590 ft. Pop. (1960) 2,575. Tourist centre. Manufactures embroidery.

**Appleby** England. Municipal borough, county town of Westmorland on the R. Eden 30 m. SE of Carlisle. Pop. (1961) 1,751. Has a castle (Norman keep). Traditionally a meeting-place for gypsies at the annual horse fair (June).

**Appleton** USA. Industrial town in Wisconsin, on the Fox R. 90 m. NNW of Milwaukee. Pop. (1960) 48,411. Paper and textile mills, etc., deriving hydroelectric power from the river. Just S is the picturesque L. Winnebago.

**Apra** ◊ *Guam.*

**Apulia (Puglia)** Italy. Region in the S, along the Adriatic Sea, comprising the provinces of Foggia, Bari, Brindisi, Ionio, and Lecce. Area 7,468 sq. m. Pop. (1961) 3,409,687. Largely hilly, with lowlands in the N and the S (the 'heel' of Italy). Cereals, vines, olives, almonds, tobacco cultivated. Much olive oil produced.

**Apuré River** Venezuela. River 420 m. long (over 300 m. navigable), rising in the E Cordillera, flowing NE and E across the W llanos, and joining the Orinoco. Cattle raised and some maize and other crops cultivated in the basin.

**Apurímac River** Peru. River 550 m. long, rising in the small L. Villafra in the Andes of S Peru, flowing (deeply entrenched) generally NNW, and joining the Urubamba R. to form the Ucayali, one of the main headstreams of the Amazon. In the lower reaches known as the Ene and the Tambo.

**Aqaba** Jordan. Ancient Elath; Aelana. Seaport at the N end of the Gulf of Aqaba, Jordan's only outlet to the sea. Pop. (1961) 9,000. Site of biblical Elath, one of the ports from which Solomon's fleets sailed to Ophir. Was the Roman military post of Aelana. Near by is the modern port of Eilat in Israel.

**Aqsu** ◊ *Aksu.*

**Aquila** Italy. Capital of the Aquila province, and of Abruzzi e Molise, on the Pescara (Aterno) R. 55 m. NE of Rome, at a height of 2,360 ft, near the Gran Sasso d'Italia. Pop. (1961) 56,019. Trade in agricultural produce, livestock. Manufactures textiles, macaroni, etc. Has several notable churches and a famous 13th-cent. fountain with 99 jets. Severely damaged by earthquake in 1703, and in the 2nd World War.

**Aquitaine** France. Ancient Aquitania. Region and ancient province in the SW. Conquered by the Romans in 56 B.C. Occupied by the Visigoths in the 5th cent. and by the Franks in the 6th cent. Became an independent duchy in the 7th cent. About the 10th cent. the name was corrupted to Guienne, and Gascony was joined to it. The two duchies went to the French crown in 1137 and to the English crown in 1152, reverting to France when conquered by Charles VII (1451). The Aquitaine Basin, a fertile plain bounded by the Massif Central (E), the Pyrenees (S), and the Bay of Biscay (W), and drained by the Garonne R. and its tributaries, produces wheat, maize, wine, fruits, and vegetables. Principal towns Bordeaux, Toulouse.

**Arabia.** Great peninsula in SW Asia, 1,200 m. long and on average 700 m. wide. Area about 1,000,000 sq. m. Bounded by the Persian Gulf and the Gulf of Oman (E), the Arabian Sea and the Gulf of Aden (S), and the Red Sea (W); separated from the rest of the continent by the desert of the Nafud (N), to the N of which is the Syrian Desert, which ancient geographers included in Arabia. Sometimes called Jazirat al 'Arab ('Isle of the Arabs') because of its geographical isolation. An enormous plateau; the high W edge overlooks the Red Sea, and peaks in the Yemen rise to over 10,000 ft; it slopes more gently E and NE to the Persian Gulf. Also mountainous in the SW and SE.

The distinguishing feature of the climate is extreme dryness; rainfall is negligible except in the highlands, where 15–20 ins. or more fall during the summer monsoon. Summer temperatures high. No perennial rivers; numerous wadis which carry water only after rain. Much of Arabia is true desert, without vegetation, in three main types: 'dahanah' (hard gravel); 'nafud' (deep sand, often in dunes); and 'harrah' (rough lava). In the centre is Nejd, with widely scattered groups of oases; in the S is the vast Rub 'al Khali ('Empty Quarter'), part dahanah and part nafud. Apart from the oases (where dates are the main crop) the most fertile region is highland Yemen (SW; the 'Arabia Felix' of the ancients), home of the famous Mocha coffee; nomadic Bedouin tribes of the interior eke out a meagre livelihood by rearing camels, goats, and sheep. The largest city in the interior is Riyadh in Nejd; Mecca and Medina in Hejaz are important pilgrimage centres. The other principal centres of population, Jidda, Aden, Kuwait City, etc., are on the coast.

Early Arabian history is obscure. The chaos prevailing in the 6th cent. was evidently the result of protracted tribal wars. Mohammed united the tribes, attracting followers with a mixture of religion and patriotism; the new era is dated from his flight from Mecca to Medina (622). His successors extended their dominion over Persia, Mesopotamia, Syria, Palestine, Egypt, N Africa, and even into Spain. Despite this spread of Arab influence, the peninsula itself lost its cohesion and broke up into several minor principalities. A new chapter of Arabian history opened in the mid 18th cent. with the Wahhabi movement, later eclipsed but revived in the 20th cent. by Ibn Saud, who with his rival, Hussein Ibn Ali of Mecca, ejected the Turks and annexed Hejaz (then Asir). The new state, named (1932) Saudi Arabia, has since been the dominant country in the peninsula. Oil was struck on the island of Bahrain in 1932; other rich oil deposits have been discovered and developed, and the economies of Saudi Arabia and of the sheikhdoms of Kuwait, Bahrain, and Qatar have been transformed. The Arab League was formed (1945), in an attempt to reunite the Arab world, from Egypt, Iraq, Saudi Arabia, Syria, Lebanon, Jordan, and Yemen, and was later joined by Libya (1953), Sudan (1956), Tunisia and Morocco (1958), Kuwait (1961), and Algeria (1962).

**Arabian Desert** United Arab Republic. A rocky desert in Egypt, between the Nile (W) and the Gulf of Suez and the Red Sea (E). To the S is the Nubian Desert. Largely mountainous, some peaks rising to over 6,000 ft.

**Arabian Sea.** The NW section of the Indian Ocean, between Arabia (W) and India (E). Two arms: the Gulf of Aden leads to the Red Sea, the Gulf of Oman to the Persian Gulf.

**Aracajú** Brazil. Capital of the Sergipe state, in the NE, port 6 m. above the mouth of the Cotinguiba R. Pop. (1960) 115,713. Exports sugar, cotton, rice, hides, etc. Sugar refining, tanning. Manufactures textiles.

**Arad** Rumania. Industrial town on the Mures R. 30 m. NNE of Timişoara, near the Hungarian frontier. Pop. (1968) 130,801 (inc. many Hungarians). Railway junction. Railway engineering. Manufactures textiles, spirits, leather, etc. Trade in grain, cattle, etc. Formerly a Turkish fortress (16th cent.). Passed to Austria, then Hungary, and to Rumania after the 1st World War.

**Arafura Sea.** A section of the SW Pacific Ocean, between Australia (S) and New Guinea (N). Adjoins the Timor Sea (W) and the Torres Strait (E).

**Aragón** Spain. Region and former kingdom in the NE, comprising the modern provinces of Huesca, Teruel, and Zaragoza; drained by the Ebro R. and its tributaries. Area 18,382 sq. m. Chief towns Zaragoza, Huesca, Teruel. Thinly populated, apart from some valleys and irrigated areas. Conquered by the Moors in the 8th cent. United with Catalonia in the 12th cent. and with Castile in the 15th cent. through the marriage of Ferdinand of Aragón and Isabella of Castile.

**Aragón River** Spain. River 80 m. long, rising in the Central Pyrenees and flowing generally SW to join the R. Ebro.

**Araguaia River** Brazil. River 1,400 m. long, rising on the Mato Grosso plateau, flowing generally NNE to join the Tocantins R. at São João do Araguaia. Forks in the middle course to enclose the large Bananal Island.

**Arak** Iran. Formerly Sultanabad. Town on the Trans-Iranian Railway 160 m. SW of Tehran at a height of 5,900 ft. Pop. (1966) 72,087. Manufactures rugs and carpets, matches, etc. It was capital of the former province of Iraq (i.e. Persian Iraq), corresponding to ancient Media and later spelled Arak, since 1938 part of the province of Gilan.

**Arakan** Burma. Region of Lower Burma,

on the Bay of Bengal. Chief town Akyab. The coastal strip extends from the E Pakistan frontier (N) to the Irrawaddy delta (S), and is flanked by the Arakan Yoma, which rise to over 10,000 ft. Heavy monsoon rains. Main crop rice; tobacco and fruits also cultivated. Passed to Burma 1782. Ceded to Britain 1826.

**Arakan Yoma** Burma. Range of mountains 400 m. long, between and parallel to the Irrawaddy R. and the Arakan Coast (Bay of Bengal), extending from the Chin Hills (N) to the Irrawaddy delta (S) and rising to over 10,000 ft in the N. A climatic barrier, shielding the 'dry zone' of central Burma from the monsoon rains. Tropical rain-forest on the W slopes, teak forest on the E slopes.

**Araks River** ◊ *Arax River*.

**Aral Sea** USSR. Fourth largest lake (inland sea) in the world. Separated from the Caspian Sea (W) by the Ust Urt Plateau. Area 24,000 sq. m. Slightly saline. Fed by the Syr Darya (NE) and the Amu Darya (S) rivers. No outlet. Generally shallow. Fished for sturgeon and carp, but frozen about 3 months annually. Navigation difficult. There are many islands: the Kirghiz name, Aral Denghiz, means 'Island Sea'.

**Aran Islands** Irish Republic. Group of three rocky islands – Aranmore (or Inishmore; the largest, with many antiquities), Inishmaan, and Inisheer – 25–30 m. WSW of Galway. Area 18 sq. m. Pop. (1966) 1,612. Fishing. A little agriculture. Associated with the works of J. M. Synge.

**Arapuni** ◊ *Waikato River*.

**Ararat, Mount** (Turkish Ağri Daği) Turkey. Volcanic mountain mass in the extreme NE, near the border with Soviet Armenia and Iran. Consists of two main peaks: Great Ararat (16,916 ft), the traditional resting place of Noah's Ark after the flood (◊ *Armenia*); and Little Ararat (12,843 ft).

**Aras River** ◊ *Arax River*.

**Aravalli Range** India. Hills extending 350 m. SW–NE through Rajasthan. Generally 1,500–3,000 ft high. Mt Abu near by is 5,650 ft.

**Arax (Araks; Aras) River.** Ancient Araxes. River 600 m. long, rising in Turkish Armenia S of Erzurum, flowing generally E, forming parts of the frontier between Turkey and USSR and between Iran and USSR. The old course joins the Kura R., but the new course (since 1896) flows direct into the Caspian Sea.

**Arbroath** Scotland. Formerly Aberbrothock. Royal burgh in SE Angus, 16 m. ENE of Dundee. Pop. (1961) 19,533. Resort. Fishing port. Manufactures sailcloth, canvas, footwear, etc. Ruins of a 12th-cent. abbey. Scene of Robert I's Declaration of Independence (1320).

**Arcachon** France. Fishing port and resort in the Gironde department in the SW, on the shore of the Arcachon Basin (a 60-sq.-m. lagoon almost enclosed by sand dunes and pine forests), 32 m. WSW of Bordeaux. Pop. (1968) 15,755. Famous for oyster beds.

**Arcadia** Greece. *Nome* in the central Peloponnese. Area 1,664 sq. m. Pop. (1961) 134,950. Cap. Tripolis (pop. 18,500). Mainly mountainous. Largely infertile. Wheat, tobacco, grapes cultivated. Sheep and goats reared. The inhabitants of ancient Arcadia were shepherds and hunters, worshipping nature deities.

**Archangel (Arkhangelsk)** USSR. Capital of Archangel region (RSFSR), on the right bank of the N Dvina R. 20 m. from its point of entry into Dvina Bay (White Sea). Pop. (1970) 343,000. Seaport, chief timber-exporting and sawmilling centre of USSR. Centre of White Sea fisheries. Railway terminus. Shipyards, fish canneries, rope mills. Most of the trade is carried on June–Oct., though the port is also kept open in May and November with the help of ice-breakers. Founded (1553) as a result of the establishment of Anglo-Muscovite trade. Russia's only seaport until 1702, when St Petersburg (now Leningrad) was founded; after that date it declined. Its importance increased again with the construction of the railway (1897), and it was a leading supply port in both world wars.

**Arctic Ocean.** Ocean surrounding the N Pole and lying N of about 70° N, connected by the Bering Strait with the Pacific, and by Baffin Bay and Davis Strait (W) and Greenland Sea and Norwegian Sea (E) with the Atlantic. Area about 5½ million sq. m. Its greatest depth (17,850 ft) was recorded in 1927 NW of Point Barrow (Alaska). Many great rivers, inc. the Mackenzie, Ob, Yenisei and Lena, flow into it. Evaporation slight. Salinity is the lowest of all the oceans. During the winter most of it is covered with ice, which in summer breaks up into masses of pack ice that drift S with the outflowing currents. The first surface crossing from Point Barrow (Alaska) via the N Pole to a

small island off Spitsbergen, was made
by the British Trans-Arctic Expedition
1968–9.

**Ardebil (Ardabil)** Iran. Town in Azerbaijan
115 m. E of Tabriz. Pop. (1966) 83,548.
Commercial and road centre. Trade with
USSR. Manufactures carpets, rugs, etc.
Mausoleum of Sheik Safiuddin (1252–
1334), the religious leader.

**Ardèche** France. Department in the former
Languedoc province, crossed in the W by
the Monts du Vivarais and in the SE by
the Ardèche R., and bounded on the E by
the Rhône. Area 2,145 sq. m. Pop. (1968)
256,927. Prefecture Privas. Mulberry and
chestnut trees, vineyards, and orchards in
the S. Produces cereals, wines. Coal and
iron ore mined. Manufactures silk. Chief
towns Annonay (pop. 21,567), with silk
spinning and weaving and paper industries,
and Privas (pop. 10,660), famous for
*marrons glacés*.

**Ardèche River** France. River 75 m. long,
rising in the Cévennes and flowing generally
SE to the Rhône. Near Vallon is the Pont
d'Arc, a natural bridge which it has
carved in the limestone.

**Arden, Forest of** England. District in
Warwickshire, originally part of a large
Midlands forest between the R. Avon and
modern Birmingham. Setting of Shakespeare's *As You Like It*.

**Ardennes.** A forested plateau, mainly in
SE Belgium but extending into Luxembourg and the Ardennes department of
France, at a height generally of 1,200–
1,600 ft but rising to over 2,200 ft in the
NE. Some pastoral farming, but agriculture is poor. The woods still contain
much wild game. Much less extensive than
were the Arduenna Silva of the Romans.
Scene of severe fighting in both world wars.

**Ardennes** France. Department in the N,
containing part of the Ardennes and the
Argonne, drained by the Meuse and the
Aisne rivers and their tributaries. Area
2,038 sq. m. Pop. (1968) 309,380. Prefecture Mézières. Lumbering and stock
rearing in the hills. Agriculture in the
fertile Aisne valley. Slate quarries. Iron
mines. Chief towns Mézières and Charle-
ville (twin towns) and Sedan.

**Ardnacrusha** Irish Republic. Village in SE
Co. Clare, on the opposite side of the
Shannon R. to Limerick. Site of the great
Shannon hydroelectric scheme.

**Ardnamurchan Point** Scotland. Rocky
headland at the W extremity of the

peninsula of the same name, in NW
Argyll. The most westerly point on the
mainland of Great Britain. Lighthouse
(1849).

**Ardrossan** Scotland. Small burgh, seaport,
and resort in NW Ayrshire, on the Firth
of Clyde 14 m. NNW of Ayr. Pop. (1961)
9,574. Small oil refinery. Exports coal.

**Arequipa** Peru. Capital of the Arequipa
department in the S, at a height of 7,500 ft
in an irrigated area beneath the volcanic
El Misti (19,200 ft). Pop. (1961) 156,657.
Important commercial city, serving the S
Peruvian highlands. Mainly a wool market.
Tanning, brewing, flour milling, etc. Manufactures textiles, soap. Linked by rail with
its port, Mollendo, 55 m. SW. Pleasant
sunny climate; even temperatures throughout the year and little rain. An Inca city,
refounded by the Spanish (1540). Narrow
cobbled streets lead from the Plaza de
Armas, with a 17th-cent. cathedral mostly
rebuilt in the 19th cent., and typify the
mixture of native Indian, colonial, and
modern cultures. Has suffered much from
earthquakes, esp. in 1868; severely damaged
in 1960.

**Arezzo** Italy. Capital of Arezzo province,
in Tuscany, in the upper Arno valley, 38
m. SE of Florence. Pop. (1961) 74,992.
Commercial centre. Trade in cereals, wine,
olive oil. Manufactures textiles, clothing,
furniture, etc. Gothic cathedral (1277–
1510), Romanesque Church of Santa Maria
della Pieve, and the Palazzo della Frater-
nità (the two last in the famous Piazza
Grande). Birthplace of Petrarch (1304–74)
and Vasari (1511–74). Severely damaged in
the 2nd World War.

**Argenteuil** France. Town in the Val d'Oise
department, a NW suburb of Paris on
the right bank of the Seine. Pop. (1968)
90,929. Manufactures motor-car parts,
aircraft engines, electrical equipment,
rayon, etc. Market gardens supply Paris
with asparagus, beans, peas, etc. Grew up
around a convent (founded 7th cent.)
where Héloïse was abbess. '*La Sainte
Tunique*', said to be Christ's robe (presented to the convent by Charlemagne),
is in the church.

**Argentina.** Federal republic in the extreme
S of S America. Area 1,084,120 sq. m.
Pop. (1962) 21,247,420. Cap. Buenos
Aires. Lang. Spanish. Rel. mainly Roman
Catholic.

Second largest country in S America,
extending from 21° S to 55° S. Bounded by

Bolivia and Paraguay (N), Brazil, Uruguay, and the Atlantic (E), and Chile (W). Its prosperity depends very largely on the vast grassy plains or pampas around the R. Plate. Apart from Uruguay, it has the highest standard of living and literacy in S America. The people are predominantly of European stock. Its resources are mainly agricultural, and it has long been a major exporter of meat. Administratively divided into 22 provinces, the federal district of Buenos Aires, and a National Territory.

TOPOGRAPHY, CLIMATE, *etc.* Very varied in relief, vegetation, and climate, from tropical in the N (the Chaco) through the pleasant climate of the great pampas to the bitter cold of Patagonia in the far S. Four main areas. 1. *The Andes*, which define the long W frontier with Chile, along which are found 'oases' of cultivable land. 2. *The north*, with the great forests of the Chaco and the rolling plains between the Paraná and the Paraguay rivers. 3. *The pampas*, the geographical and economic heart of the country, an area of 250,000 sq. m. covering vast plains, uninterrupted by hills or even trees, suitable for pasture and agriculture. 4. *Patagonia*, in the far S, an infertile, windswept land where little but sheep can be raised, ending in the cold barren Tierra del Fuego.

RESOURCES, PEOPLE, *etc.* Export trade is almost wholly in agricultural produce, mainly obtained within 300–400 m. of Buenos Aires (though a third of the sheep are in the far S). Cattle, sheep, wheat, maize, and flax are produced on the pampas, of which 40 per cent is under pasture and the rest is agricultural. Estates are often of immense size, divided by wire fences into fields of several thousand acres. Wheat predominates in a great belt from Bahía Blanca towards Rosario; maize and flax to the N of Rosario; dairying and fruit farming in the milder NW pampas. In the W foothills of the Andes, 'oases' of irrigated land produce fruit and wine; sugar-cane comes from the NW, and cotton growing is increasing in the E Chaco. Oil, recently discovered, is produced by a national undertaking. In spite of the few mineral resources, Buenos Aires has become a large industrial area, with a variety of light manufactures in addition to food-packing enterprises. There are now as many industrial workers as agricultural.

The political system closely resembles that of the USA. The emergence of a great urban population led to a decline in the influence of the land-owning classes, and culminated after the 2nd World War in the dictatorship of Perón, who favoured the industrial working class at the expense of other interests. The Perón régime was overturned in 1955, but successor governments continue to face economic difficulties, largely caused by falling exports, increased internal consumption (which hampers meat exports), and by past and continued overemphasis on industrialization.

HISTORY. The first Spanish attempts at settlement on the R. Plate were frustrated by the fierce opposition of the Indians. Having settled in friendlier territory in Asunción, the Spanish later (1580) colonized Buenos Aires. Under the viceroyalty of Peru, the country was neglected. It declared itself independent (1816) with the help of the liberator San Martín; but internal strife and later the tyrannical rule of de Rosas retarded development. Argentina became a federal republic after the expulsion of de Rosas (1852).

Capital (largely British) flowed into the country for the construction of the railways, which transformed the pampas from a primitive pastoral economy to a rich region of intensive cattle rearing and agriculture. With the advent of refrigeration Argentina became a major meat supplier to the UK. The population grew rapidly through immigration (7 million immigrants, mainly Italian and Spanish, 1857–1930). The Indians were virtually exterminated, and thus the present population is overwhelmingly white.

**Argolis** Greece. *Nome* in the NE Peloponnese (formerly combined with Corinthia), including islands in the Gulf of Argolis. Area 873 sq. m. Pop. (1961) 88,716. Cap. Nauplia. An agricultural region; produces wine, currants, sultanas. The ancient region of Argolis included the important cities Mycenae and Argos.

**Argolis, Gulf of** Greece. Inlet of the Aegean Sea, in the E Peloponnese, with the island of Spetsai at the entrance and Nauplia on the NW coast.

**Argonne** France. A wooded hilly region 1,100 ft high, about 40 m. long and 10 m. wide, on the border of the Meuse and the Marne departments and partly in the Ardennes department. Formerly of strategic importance. Much fighting in the 1st World War.

**Argos** Greece. Ancient town, one of the oldest in Greece, in the NE Peloponnese 28 m. SSW of Corinth. Pop. 16,700. In the 7th cent. B.C. it dominated the Peloponnese. A ruined temple, the Heraeum, is 5 m. NNE.

**Argostólion (Argostoli)** Greece. Capital of Cephalonia, in the Ionian Is., on the SW coast. Pop. (1961) 7,322. Trade in wine etc. Destroyed by earthquake 1953.

**Argun River** China/USSR. River 900 m. long, rising in the Great Khingan Mountains (NE China) as the Hailar, flowing generally W to the USSR frontier. Here linked with L. Hulun Nor. Turns NNE, forms part of the China–USSR frontier, and joins the Shilka to form the Amur R.

**Argyllshire** Scotland. County in the W, bounded on the W by the Atlantic Ocean. Area 3,110 sq. m. Pop. (1961) 59,345. County town Inveraray. The coast is deeply indented with sea lochs (Sunart, Linnhe, Fyne, etc.). Includes many S islands of the Inner Hebrides (Mull, Coll, Tiree, Iona, Colonsay, Islay, Jura, etc.) and the peninsula of Kintyre. Wild, picturesque, and mountainous; rises to 3,766 ft in Bidean Nam Bian and 3,689 ft in Ben Cruachan (near the N end of Loch Awe, a freshwater lake). Principal occupations fishing, sheep and cattle rearing. Oats and barley grown in limited coastal areas. Slate and granite quarried. Industries include aluminium working (Kinlochleven) and whisky distilling (Campbeltown). Dunoon and Oban are resorts.

**Arica** Chile. Oasis town in the rainless N; the most northerly seaport. Pop. 46,542. Oil terminal, with a pipeline to Sicasica in Bolivia (completed 1958). A railway climbs 285 m. to La Paz and takes about half Bolivia's trade. Much Peruvian trade also passes through Arica. Above the town is the site of Chile's great victory over Peru (1879).

**Ariège** France. Department in the S, formed from parts of the provinces of Gascony and Languedoc and the county of Foix, bounded on the S by Spain and Andorra. Area 1,893 sq. m. Pop. (1968) 138,478. Prefecture Foix. The S is occupied by the N slopes of the Pyrenees, with the Pic de Montcalm rising to 10,105 ft, and the N is fertile lowland producing cereals, wine, fruits, and potatoes. Iron and lead mined.

Chief towns Foix, Tarascon, Pamiers.

**Ariège River** France. River 100 m. long, rising in the E Pyrenees near the Andorra border, flowing generally NNW, and joining the Garonne near Toulouse. Several hydroelectric installations.

**Arizona** USA. Mountainous state on the Mexican border. Area 113,909 sq. m. Pop. (1970) 1,752,122. Cap. Phoenix. Admitted to the Union in 1912 as the 48th state; popularly known as the 'Apache' state, being the home of most of the Apache Indians. Much of it is desert, with a rainfall varying from 1 in. in the extreme W to 35 ins. in the E. The N is part of the Colorado Plateau, in which the Colorado R. has cut the famous Grand Canyon. The high mountain ranges are forested; highest point Humphrey's Peak (12,670 ft). Several enormous irrigation works have been built to store water, notably the Roosevelt, Coolidge, Yuma, and Horse Mesa dams, on which depends practically all the agriculture of the state (its main resource). With irrigation good-quality cotton is grown, using highly mechanized methods. Wheat, barley, sugar-beet, citrus fruits, and vegetables also cultivated. The mineral resources are valuable, esp. copper and lead. Chief industry smelting and refining metals. Principal towns Phoenix, Tucson. Largest Indian population of any US state, with Hopi, Apache, and Navajo reservations.

**Arkansas** USA. State in S central region. Area 53,104 sq. m. Pop. (1970) 1,886,210. Cap. Little Rock. Admitted to the Union in 1836 as the 25th state; popularly known as the 'Bear' state. There is a sharp contrast between the NW and SE areas; the former is highland, the latter low-lying and covered by fertile Mississippi alluvium. In the W are the Ozark and Ouachita Mountains, separated by the valley of the Arkansas R. Warm, humid air from the Gulf of Mexico brings considerable rain (up to 60 ins.) and causes high summer temperatures, but precludes winter frost. Cotton still the main crop; soya beans are important and maize and rice are grown. Over 95 per cent of the US production of bauxite is mined; coal and petroleum also obtained. The natural hot mineral water occurring at Hot Springs attracts sufferers from rheumatism. Chief towns Little Rock, Fort Smith, North Little Rock, Pine Bluff. Secured from France as part of the Louisiana Purchase (1803).

**Arkansas River** USA. River 1,500 m. long rising in the Rocky Mountains of central Colorado and flowing generally ESE to the Mississippi. Chief tributary the Canadian R. Wide variations in its volume; though banked by levees, the lower valley is subject to extensive flooding.

**Arkhangelsk** ◊ *Archangel*.

**Arklow** Irish Republic. Small fishing port and resort in SE Co. Wicklow, at the mouth of the Avoca R. 13 m. SSW of Wicklow. Pop. (1966) 6,083. Manufactures pottery. Remains of the castle of the Ormondes, destroyed by Cromwell (1649).

**Arkona** ◊ *Rügen*.

**Arlberg** Austria. Mountain and pass (5,912 ft) in the W. The road over the latter and the railway through the Arlberg Tunnel (1884, over 6 m. long), which was electrified in 1923, link Vorarlberg and Tirol.

**Arles** France. Market town in the Bouches-du-Rhône department, mainly on the left bank of the Rhône 47 m. NW of Marseille. Pop. (1968) 46,136. Trade in sheep, wine, olives. Manufactures chemicals, paper, sausages, etc. Important in Roman times; capital of Gaul in the 4th cent. By the 10th cent. the capital of the kingdom of Arles, formed from the kingdoms of Burgundy and Provence, which passed to the Dauphin (later Charles VI) in 1378. Although it was damaged in the 2nd World War, few of the historical monuments suffered. Among the Roman remains are a famous amphitheatre (seating over 20,000) and a theatre. Ancient cathedral of St Trophime and a museum of Provençal arts and crafts, founded by the poet Mistral (1830–1914), who was born near by.

**Arlington** (Massachusetts) USA. Town 6 m. NW of Boston. Pop. (1960) 49,953. Commercial centre in a market-gardening and dairy-farming area. Manufactures leather goods etc.

**Arlington** (Texas) USA. Town 12 m. E of Fort Worth. Pop. (1960) 44,775 (7,692 in 1950). Industrial and commercial centre. Manufactures aircraft, missiles, etc. Expanded rapidly in the 1950s.

**Arlington** (Virginia) USA. Urban county on the Potomac R., near Washington (DC), with which it is connected by the Arlington Memorial Bridge. Area 24 sq. m. Pop. (1960) 163,401. The military Arlington National Cemetery of 408 acres, on what was once the estate of General Robert E. Lee, contains the graves of about 60,000 soldiers killed in the American Civil War, with the tombs of the US Unknown Soldier and of President J. F. Kennedy (as a war hero). Also in Arlington County are Fort Myer, the National Airport (for Washington), and the Pentagon building.

**Armagh** Northern Ireland. **1**. Inland county in the SE, low-lying in the N and hilly in the S, rising to 1,893 ft in Slieve Gullion. Area 489 sq. m. Pop. (1961) 117,580. Main crops potatoes, flax. Cattle reared. Main industry linen manufacture. Chief towns Armagh, Portadown, Lurgan.

**2**. County town of Co. Armagh, 33 m. SW of Belfast. Pop. (1961) 9,982. Main industry linen manufacture. Seat of both Protestant and Roman Catholic archbishops. Outstanding buildings are the Protestant cathedral, built on the site of a church said to have been founded by St Patrick (445), where Brian Boru was buried, and the 19th-cent. Roman Catholic cathedral. The ecclesiastic metropolis of Ireland from the 5th to the 9th cent. Suffered much from Danish raids and the English wars; declined, but revived in the 18th and 19th cent.

**Armagnac** France. Hilly district, formerly a province in Gascony with capital Auch; now mainly in the Gers department. Famous for its brandy, made from local grapes at Condom and other small towns.

**Armavir** USSR. Town in Krasnodar Territory (RSFSR), on the Kuban R. 105 m. E of Krasnodar. Pop. (1970) 146,000. Flour milling, meat packing, distilling, etc. Manufactures agricultural machinery, vegetable oils. On the oil pipeline from Grozny.

**Armenia** (Armenian **Hayastan**) Asia Minor. Region and former kingdom. Ancient capital ◊ *Artaxata*. The frontiers have varied throughout history, but in general corresponded roughly with the modern ◊ *Armenian SSR* and near-by areas in Turkey and Iran. Mainly a plateau region, of average height 6,000–8,000 ft, with ridges and isolated volcanic peaks, inc. the lofty *Mt* ◊ *Ararat* (16,916 ft); Armenian legend claims that their first king, Haik, was a descendant of Noah. Includes the lofty L. Van and the sources of the Euphrates and Tigris. By the 6th cent. B.C. the Armenians had become a distinct nation, settled in Asia Minor, governed by

51                                                                ARRAS

a Persian satrap till 330 B.C. After brief independence in the 2nd cent. B.C. they were conquered by the Romans. In A.D. 66 Nero recognized Tiridates I as king of Armenia. Under Tiridates III it became the first country to adopt Christianity as state religion (303); this led to conflict with Persia, and in 387 it was divided into Persian and Roman spheres of influence. For 5 centuries it was repeatedly under Persian, Byzantine, or Arab domination. Autonomous under native Bagratid rulers from the 9th to the 11th cent., it was again conquered by the Byzantines and then by the Seljuks. It was divided between Persia and Turkey from the 16th cent. till Russia obtained what is now the Armenian SSR in part from Persia (1828) and in part from Turkey (1878). Under the Ottoman Empire, Armenians in Turkey were discriminated against as non-Muslim and frequently persecuted, but they played an important role as bankers and merchants. The ties of religion and language kept alive a sentiment of nationality, which provoked Abdul Hamid to instigate a series of massacres (1894–1915) in which thousands were killed and many fled to other countries. After the Russian Revolution the people of Russian Armenia enjoyed a short-lived independence. The country was proclaimed a Soviet Socialist Republic 1920.

Armenia Colombia. Town in a productive coffee-growing district, at 5,000 ft, in the Central Cordillera. Pop. 110,000. Railhead for the journey E over the Quindío Pass. A modern city, founded 1889.

Armenian SSR USSR. Constituent SSR in Transcaucasia, bounded on the S and W by Iran and Turkey. Area 11,490 sq. m. Pop. (1970) 2,493,000 (about 85 per cent Armenians; the remainder Georgians, Russians, Kurds, Azerbaijani, Persians, and Jews). Cap. Yerevan. Mainly high plateaux and mountain ranges, rising to 13,432 ft in Mt Aragaz. Soils fertile, but require irrigation in areas of low rainfall. The Yerevan district and the Arax valley are the chief agricultural regions, where wheat, cotton, and vines are cultivated on collective and state farms. Stock rearing important on the plateaux. Copper, zinc, and molybdenum mined. Hydroelectric power derived from a series of stations on the Razdan R. between L. Sevan and the Arax R. (scheme completed 1962). Chief industrial towns Yerevan, Leninakan.

Formed 1920. Part of the Transcaucasian SFSR 1922–36. Became a constituent republic of the USSR 1936. For early history ◊ Armenia.

Armentières France. Town in the Nord department on the Lys R. 9 m. WNW of Lille. Pop. (1968) 28,469. Manufactures linen, hosiery, etc. Entirely destroyed in the 1st World War and again damaged in the 2nd World War. Made famous in the song Mademoiselle from Armentières.

Armidale Australia. Market town and mining centre (gold, antimony) in New South Wales 165 m. N. of Newcastle, on the New England plateau at 3,313 ft. Pop. (1966) 14,990. Trade in wool, dairy produce, fruit.

Arnhem Netherlands. Capital of the Gelderland province, on the Rhine R. 35 m. ESE of Utrecht. Pop. (1968) 135,090. Railway junction. Engineering and boatbuilding. Manufactures rayon, clothing, pharmaceutical products, etc. Scene of an unsuccessful British airborne landing during the 2nd World War (Sept. 1944) in an attempt to turn the Siegfried Line.

Arnhem Land Australia. Region about 60,000 sq. m. in area in the N of the Northern Territory, named after the Dutch vessel Arnhem which explored the coast in the 17th cent. Mainly a reserve for aborigines, the majority of whom are semi-nomadic. Plentiful rain Dec.–March, followed by long drought, supports grassland with trees, while mangroves grow along the coasts and estuaries.

Arno River Italy. River 150 m. long, rising on Monte Falterona and flowing mainly W past Florence and Pisa to the Ligurian Sea. Barely 20 m. are navigable. The valley (Val d'Arno) is fertile and picturesque. The river burst its banks and caused disastrous floods in ◊ Florence Nov. 1966.

Arnstadt German Democratic Republic. Town in Erfurt district, on the Gera R. 11 m. SSW of Erfurt. Pop. (1965) 27,368. Railway junction. Manufactures gloves, machinery, footwear, etc. J. S. Bach was organist at the Church of St Boniface 1703–7.

Arran Scotland. Island in Buteshire, in the Firth of Clyde, separated from Kintyre by Kilbrannan Sound. Area 166 sq. m. Pop. (1961) 3,705. Mountainous, rising to 2,866 ft in Goat Fell. Picturesque; a popular tourist centre.

Arras France. Prefecture of the Pas-de-

Calais department on the canalized Scarpe R. 27 m. SSW of Lille. Pop. (1968) 53,573. Trade in cereals. Engineering, brewing. Manufactures beet sugar, vegetable oils, agricultural implements. Once famous for tapestry. In pre-Christian times, chief town of the Atrebates. Became capital of Artois; finally passed to France 1640. In the 1st World War the famous town hall and cathedral were virtually destroyed. Again suffered damage in the 2nd World War. Birthplace of Robespierre (1758–94).

**Arromanches-les-Bains** France. Village in the Calvados department, 15 m. NW of Caen. Site of the prefabricated Mulberry harbour built by Allied troops to permit landings in German-occupied territory during the 2nd World War (D-Day, 6 June 1944).

**Artaxata (Artashat)** USSR. Ancient capital of ◊ *Armenia*, S of Yerevan. Founded by Artaxias 189 B.C. Destroyed by the Romans, but restored and renamed Neronia. Modern town known as Kamarlu till 1945, then renamed after the ancient town.

**Artemovsk** USSR. Formerly Bakhmut. Town in the E of the Ukrainian SSR, in the Donbas, 43 m. NNE of Donetsk. Pop. 61,000. Has the largest salt mines in USSR. Iron and glass manufacture and other industries. Founded 1571.

**Artois** France. Ancient Artesium. Former province, with capital Arras; now in the Pas-de-Calais department. Mainly agricultural. Includes the W part of the Franco-Belgian coalfield. Belonged in turn to Flanders, France, Burgundy, Austria, and Spain; returned to France 1640. Gave its name to 'artesian' wells: the first European examples were sunk here (1126).

**Aru Islands** Indonesia. Island group in the S Moluccas, between New Guinea and the Tanimbar Is. Area 3,300 sq. m. Pop. 27,000. Five main islands, separated by narrow channels; about 90 islets. Low-lying and forested. Chief products pearls, mother-of-pearl, trepang.

**Aruba** Netherlands Antilles. Island in the W Indies WNW of Curaçao. Area 73 sq. m. Pop. (1968) 59,020. Chief town Oranjestad. Refines oil (from Venezuela). Manufactures petrochemicals.

**Arundel** England. Municipal borough in W Sussex, on the Arun R. 8 m. WNW of Worthing. Pop. (1961) 2,614. Market town. Stands below Arundel Castle (seat of the

Dukes of Norfolk), built in the 11th cent. and restored in the 18th cent.

**Arusha** Tanzania. Capital of the Arusha region, in the N, just SW of Mt Meru (14,490 ft). Pop. 10,000. Terminus of the railway from Tanga via Moshi. Market town in a coffee-growing area. Headquarters of the East African Community (Kenya, Uganda, Tanzania).

**Arve River** France/Switzerland. River 62 m. long, rising in the Savoy Alps, flowing SW past Chamonix and then generally NW, crossing the Swiss frontier to join the Rhône just below L. Geneva.

**Arvida** Canada. Industrial town in Quebec, 5 m. W of Chicoutimi. Pop. (1966) 15,342. Electric power harnessed from falls on the Saguenay R. (a tributary of the St Lawrence) is used in one of the world's greatest aluminium smelters.

**Asahikawa** Japan. Town in Hokkaido, on the Ishikari R. 75 m. NE of Sapporo. Pop. (1965) 245,243. Industrial and commercial centre of N Hokkaido. Brewing (*sake*). Manufactures wood products, textiles, etc.

**Asansol** India. Industrial town in W Bengal, on the Raniganj coalfield 120 m. NW of Calcutta. Pop. (1961) 103,405. Railway engineering. Manufactures iron and steel, chemicals, etc.

**Ascalon** ◊ *Ashkelon.*

**Ascension Island** S Atlantic Ocean. British island of volcanic origin 750 m. NW of St Helena. Area 34 sq. m. Pop. (1967) 1,486 (concentrated in Georgetown, an international cable station). Noted breeding place for sea turtles. Discovered by the Portuguese on Ascension Day 1501. Remained uninhabited until the British established a garrison when Napoleon was sent to St Helena (1815). Controlled by the Admiralty until 1922, when it was transferred to the Colonial Office as a dependency of St Helena. The first British civil satellite communications centre, intended for an important part in the American programme to land men on the moon, began to operate here 1966.

**Aschaffenburg** Federal German Republic. Town in NW Bavaria, on the Main R. 23 m. ESE of Frankfurt. Pop. (1963) 55,000. River port. Trade in timber, coal, etc. Manufactures textiles, clothing, scientific and optical instruments, etc. Originally a Roman fortress. Ceded to Bavaria 1814. Among important buildings is Johannisburg Castle, former summer residence of the Archbishop of Mainz. Severely damaged in the 2nd World War.

**Aschersleben** German Democratic Republic. Town in Halle district 30 m. NW of Halle. Pop. (1965) 35,641. In a potash- and lignite-mining region. Manufactures textiles, beet sugar, paper, etc.

**Ascoli Piceno** Italy. Capital of Ascoli Piceno province, in the Marches, on the Tronto R. 43 m. NW of Pescara. Pop. (1961) 50,114. Produces macaroni, textiles, pottery, etc. Roman remains. Outstanding buildings include the cathedral, Church of San Francesco, and Palazzo del Popolo.

**Ascot** England. Village in E Berkshire, 5 m. SW of Windsor. The famous racecourse of Ascot Heath was laid out (1711) by order of Queen Anne, who inaugurated the Royal Ascot Meeting (June).

**Ashanti** Ghana. Administrative region in the S. Area 9,700 sq. m. Pop. (1960) 1,108,548. Cap. Kumasi. Hilly, with large areas of tropical rain-forest, much of which has been cleared for cacao cultivation. Also produces kola nuts, tropical hardwoods (e.g. mahogany). Food crops cassava (manioc), yams, maize. Formerly a British protectorate: at various times in the 19th cent. the Ashanti people were at war with Britain; King Prempeh was deposed and exiled in 1896, but allowed to return in 1924. The Ashanti Confederacy was restored in 1935. Ashanti was virtually part of the Gold Coast colony until its independence as Ghana (1957).

**Ashbourne** England. Urban district in W Derbyshire on the R. Dove 12 m. NW of Derby, near picturesque Dovedale. Pop. (1961) 5,656. Market town. Varied light industries. Has a 13th-cent. church. Scene of a traditional Shrovetide football game played in the main street.

**Ashburton** New Zealand. Market and industrial town on the Canterbury Plains, S Island, 50 m. SW of Christchurch. Pop. (1966) 12,672. Flour and woollen mills, creameries.

**Ashburton River** Australia. River in Western Australia rising 150 m. S of Nullagine and flowing 300 m. WNW to the Indian Ocean near Onslow; flow, however, is intermittent.

**Ashby de la Zouch** England. Urban district in W Leicestershire 16 m. WNW of Leicester in a coalmining area. Pop. (1961) 7,425. Market town. Minor industries. Name derived from the Norman family of la Zouch. The ruined 15th-cent. castle,

where Mary Queen of Scots was imprisoned (1569), appears in Scott's *Ivanhoe*.

**Ashdown Forest** England. Former forest in E Sussex, now heath and woodland. Most of the trees were felled for the furnaces of the one-time iron industry.

**Asheville** USA. Town in the S Appalachian Mountains of N Carolina, 100 m. WNW of Charlotte, at a height of 2,300 ft. Pop. (1960) 60,192. Tourist centre. Manufactures textiles, paper, furniture, etc. Birthplace of Thomas Wolfe (1900–1938).

**Ashford** England. Urban district in Kent, 17 m. ESE of Maidstone. Pop. (1961) 27,962. Market town. Important railway workshops. Brewing. A noteworthy Perpendicular church (St Mary's), with a lofty four-pinnacled tower.

**Ashington** England. Urban district in Northumberland, 14 m. N of Newcastle upon Tyne. Pop. (1961) 27,294. Coalmining. Iron foundries.

**Ashkelon (Ascalon)** Israel. Ancient city in Palestine 14 m. NNE of Gaza. Captured by Rameses II in the 13th cent. B.C. Later held by the Philistines, the Assyrians, and the Persians. Taken by the Crusaders and twice recaptured by Saladin (1187, 1192). Destroyed by the Sultan Baybars 1270. Roman and Crusader remains. Birthplace of Herod the Great (*c.* 73–4 B.C.).

**Ashkhabad** USSR. Formerly (1919–27) Poltoratsk. Capital of the Turkmen SSR, at the foot of the Kopet Dagh, near the Iran frontier, in a fertile oasis. Pop. (1970) 253,000. Manufactures textiles, footwear, glass, etc. Meat packing, food processing, etc. On the Trans-Caspian Railway. Founded 1881. Seat of a university (1951) and the Turkmen Academy of Sciences (1951). Seriously damaged by earthquake 1948.

**Ashland** USA. Industrial town and river port in Kentucky, on the Ohio R. 100 m. ENE of Lexington. Pop. (1960) 31,283. Oil refineries. Nickel and iron and steel works.

**Ashton-in-Makerfield** England. Urban district in SW Lancashire, 5 m. S of Wigan. Pop. (1961) 19,262. Coalmining and cotton-milling centre.

**Ashton-under-Lyne** England. Municipal borough in SE Lancashire, 6 m. E of Manchester. Pop. (1961) 50,165. Coalmining and cotton-milling centre. Manufactures machinery, plastics, leather goods, etc.

**Ashuanipi, Lake** ◊ *Churchill River* (2).

**Ashur (Assur)** Iraq. Capital of ancient

Assyria. A site beside the Tigris R. 55 m. S of Mosul near modern Sharqat. Superseded by Nineveh in the 9th cent. B.C. Excavations have revealed palaces, temples, etc.

**Asia.** Largest of the continents, occupying almost one third of the world's land surface. Area (with offshore islands) 17 million sq. m. Bounded by the Arctic Ocean (N), the Pacific Ocean (E), and the Indian Ocean (S). The W boundary with Europe (which is geographically a peninsula of Asia) is generally considered to run along the Ural Mountains, the Caspian Sea, the Caucasus Mountains, the Black Sea, the Bosporus, and the Dardanelles. Joined to Africa across the Sinai Peninsula. Features of the E and S coastline are a number of peninsulas, of varied size: Kamchatka, Korea, Indo-China (with its appendage the Malay peninsula), and the peninsulas of India, Arabia, and Asia Minor. Off the same coasts are festoons of islands, e.g. Sakhalin and the Kuril Is., the islands of Japan, Formosa, the Philippines, Indonesia, and Ceylon.

TOPOGRAPHY, CLIMATE, *etc.* A continent of contrasts, it includes both the highest point on the earth's surface (Mt Everest) and the lowest (the Dead Sea). It may be divided into a number of major physical units. From the lofty Pamirs to the NW of India radiate several great mountain ranges: the Tien Shan (NE), the Kunlun and Altyn Tagh (E), the Karakoram and the Himalayas (SE), the Sulaiman Range and the Hindu Kush (SW). Between these ranges and others are high plateaux such as those of Tibet (the highest and most extensive on the earth) and Mongolia. N of the central mountain ranges are the W Siberian plain and the low central Siberian plateau, drained to the Arctic by the Ob, Yenisei, and Lena rivers. E Asia includes the great river basins of the Amur, the Hwang-ho, the Yangtse-kiang, and the Sikiang, separated and partially enclosed by mountain spurs. SE and S Asia have the great river plains of the Mekong and the Irrawaddy; the Brahmaputra, the Ganges, and the Indus (the extensive Indo-Gangetic Plain); and the Tigris and the Euphrates (Mesopotamia). On the SW margins of the continent are the plateaux of peninsular India, Arabia, and Asia Minor. The central mass of mountains and plateaux forms an effective N–S and E–W barrier, encloses regions of inland drainage such as the Tarim and the Turfan basins, and is an important climatic divide.

Asia has the coldest known spot on earth (Verkhoyansk in Siberia) as well as some of the hottest, and the wettest (Cherrapunji in Assam) as well as some of the driest. The climates range from Arctic in the N (where large areas have a permanently frozen subsoil) to equatorial in the S. To the S and E of the central mountains and plateaux is the world's great monsoon region, where changes of temperature and pressure in the interior bring cool dry out-blowing winds in winter and hot moisture-laden in-blowing winds in summer. SW Asia, a continuation of the hot desert lands of N Africa, extends E to NW India; a broad belt of mid-latitude desert stretches across the plateaux of central Asia to the Gobi Desert. The coastal fringes of Israel, Syria, and Asia Minor have a Mediterranean climate; that of N Asia is cold continental, merging in the far N into Arctic. There are correspondingly wide variations in the natural vegetation: S of the Arctic tundra is the vast area of coniferous forest called the Siberian taiga, and in SW Siberia and Manchuria there are much smaller regions of steppe or mid-latitude grassland, but in E Asia the natural vegetation consists largely of mixed forest, now much depleted. The SE still has considerable areas of evergreen tropical rain-forest (esp. in the islands of Indonesia and the Malay peninsula) and of deciduous monsoon forest in Burma, Thailand, and NE India.

RESOURCES, PEOPLE, HISTORY. In the monsoon lands of S and E Asia rice is the principal food crop; wheat and millets are grown in the drier regions. Vegetable oils are obtained from soya beans (China), groundnuts (India, China), and copra (Philippines, Indonesia). Dates are produced in the desert lands (Iraq, etc.). Tea is an important export of India and Ceylon. Non-food products include rubber (Malaya, Indonesia), cotton (USSR), and jute (Pakistan, India). Many regions produce metallic ores, as well as coal (USSR, China); but the most spectacular recent mineral development has been the increase in petroleum output from SW Asia (Kuwait, Saudi Arabia, Iran, Iraq). Industrialization has progressed slowly, except in Japan, parts of USSR, and latterly China. The majority of Asian peoples are still agriculturists.

Asia has the greatest population of all the continents, well over half mankind: 2,052 million out of 3,581 million (1968), excluding USSR. About two thirds belong to the Mongoloid groups (the so-called 'yellow' peoples), inc. the Japanese, the Chinese, the Koreans, the Thai, the Malay, and the Burmese; the remainder are mainly the brown-skinned Indo-Europeans, natives of India and Pakistan, Arabs, and kindred folk of SW Asia. Sundry primitive tribes survive in the heart of Ceylon, the Malay peninsula, and elsewhere. Asia gave the world its principal religions; Christianity, Judaism, and Islam originated in the SW, Hinduism and Buddhism in India, Confucianism in China. Today Islam is the religion of SW and W central Asia and of Pakistan, Indonesia, and Malaysia; Hinduism is that of India, Buddhism that of Ceylon, Burma, Thailand, and Mongolia. A mixture of Confucianism and Taoism prevails in China and of Confucianism and Shinto in Japan. In Asia flourished some of the great civilizations of antiquity, inc. the Sumerian, the Babylonian, the Assyrian, the Median, the Persian, and the Arab, and notably that of China in the E. When European nations sought trade in S and SE Asia, from the 17th cent. onwards, many areas gradually came under their direct rule and formed parts of their overseas empires. An outstanding 20th-cent. political development in Asia has been the achievement of independence by one country after another since the end of the 2nd World War.

**Asia Minor (Anatolia)** Turkey. Peninsula in W Asia between the Black Sea (N), the Mediterranean (S), and the Aegean (W); forms the greater part of Turkey. Essentially a plateau, average height 2,500 ft. The Pontic Mountains (N) and the Taurus Mountains (S) merge in the Armenian Knot (E), which culminates in the peak of Mt Ararat. The dry steppe-like interior has many salt lakes; the W and S coastal regions have a Mediterranean climate. Lying between the Eastern and Western worlds it was the scene of numerous conflicts. Passed to the Ottoman Turks in the 13th–14th cent.

**Asir** Saudi Arabia. Region in the SW, bordering on the Red Sea between Hejaz and Yemen. Area 40,000 sq. m. An arid coastal plain, rising to mountains which exceed 9,000 ft and descend E to the desert interior. Resembles East Africa rather than inland Arabia. The highlands have a moderate rainfall and produce coffee, grain, and fruits. Incorporated into Saudi Arabia by Ibn Saud in 1933.

**Askja** Iceland. Volcano, 56 m. SE of Akureyri in the Odadahraun lava field. Height 4,574 ft. Large crater (34 sq. m.). Became active again 1961.

**Asmara** Ethiopia. Town on the Hamasen plateau at 7,600 ft, 38 m. SW of Massawa, to which it is linked by railway. Pop. 138,000. Surrounded by rich agricultural land. Manufactures textiles, matches, soap. Occupied by the Italians 1889; became capital of the Italian colony of ◊ *Eritrea*. Captured by the Allies during the 2nd World War (1941). Remained under British military rule till Eritrea was federated with Ethiopia by a UN resolution (1952).

**Asnières** France. Suburb of NW Paris, in the Hauts-de-Seine department on the left bank of the Seine. Pop. (1968) 80,530. Aircraft, machine-tool, motor-car, perfume, and other industries. Boating centre for Parisians.

**Aspromonte** Italy. Mountain mass in the Reggio di Calabria province, in the 'toe' of Italy, rising to 6,417 ft. Scene of Garibaldi's defeat and capture (1862).

**Aspropotamos River** Greece. Ancient Achelous ('White') R. Second longest river in Greece (130 m.), rising in the Pindus Mountains and flowing generally S to the Ionian Sea opposite Ithaca.

**Assab** Ethiopia. Port on the Red Sea. Pop. 10,000. Second to Massawa in handling Ethiopia's foreign trade. Salt works. Purchased by an Italian steamship company as a coaling station after being first settled in 1869. Acquired by the Italian government (1882) as a base for the colonization of ◊ *Eritrea*. Captured by British and Indian forces during the 2nd World War (1941).

**Assam** India. State in the extreme NE. Area (excluding the NE Frontier Agency) 47,091 sq. m. Pop. (1961) 11,872,772 (66 per cent Hindus, 23 per cent Muslims). Cap. Shillong. Bounded by Tibet (N), Burma (E), E Pakistan (W), and Bhutan (NW). Almost enclosed by mountains; crossed by the broad fertile valley of the Brahmaputra R. Monsoon climate, characterized by heavy rainfall, reaching over 400 ins. a year on the S slopes of the Khasi Hills. Dense tropical forests; elephant, rhinoceros, tiger, and leopard abound. About 90 per cent of the people are engaged in agriculture; rice is extensively grown, but tea is the main cash crop. Coal and petroleum are produced; an oil refinery was opened at Gauhati in 1962. Ceded to Britain after the First Burmese War (1826). Became an autonomous province of British India 1937. On the partition of India (1947), the mainly Muslim district of Sylhet was included in E Pakistan. The integration of the NE Frontier Agency (area 31,438 sq. m.; pop. 337,000) with Assam was agreed in 1963.

**Assen** Netherlands. Capital of the Drenthe province, 15 m. S of Groningen. Pop. (1968) 36,940. Railway and canal junction. Clothing, food-processing, and other light industries.

**Assiniboia** Canada. 1. Area near Winnipeg (then Fort Garry) formed by the Hudson's Bay Company 1835. Transferred to the Dominion of Canada 1870.
2. A much larger area, S of the Assiniboine R. within the NW Territories, so named in 1882, but divided in 1905, one fifth to Alberta, four fifths to Saskatchewan.

**Assiniboine River** Canada. River 590 m. long, rising in E Saskatchewan and flowing SE and then E through S Manitoba to join the Red R. at Winnipeg. Its basin is one of Canada's main wheat-growing regions. The name derives from the Assiniboin Indian tribe.

**Assisi** Italy. Town in the Perugia province in Umbria, 13 m. ESE of Perugia. Pop. (1961) 24,372. Birthplace of St Francis (1182–1226), founder of the Franciscan religious order, above whose tomb two churches were built (1228–53); they contain frescoes by Cimabue, Giotto, and others. Birthplace of St Clare (1194–1253), whose tomb is in the 13th-cent. Church of Santa Chiara.

**Assiut** ◊ *Asyût*.

**Assuan** ◊ *Aswan*.

**Assur** ◊ *Ashur*.

**Assynt, Loch** Scotland. Lake 7 m. long in SW Sutherland, with an outlet to the sea by the R. Inver. Near the E end are the ruins of the 15th-cent. Ardvreck Castle, where Montrose was captured (1650).

**Assyria.** Ancient empire in SW Asia, around the city of Ashur on the upper Tigris R., in the N of the plain of Mesopotamia. In the 13th cent. B.C. Calah became the capital. The power of Assyria grew, and Babylonia was conquered. A period of still greater expansion followed in the 9th and 8th cent. B.C. The conquests of Sargon and his suc-

cessors raised Assyria to the peak of its glory. Esarhaddon (681–668 B.C.) conquered Egypt; in the reign of his son Assurbanipal the signs of approaching decay were evident, though his library of cuneiform tablets at Nineveh, his capital, were to become a valuable source of historical information. Nabopolassar of Babylonia and Cyaxares of Media combined to destroy Nineveh in 612 B.C. Babylonia grew in power as Assyria fell.

**Asti** Italy. Capital of Asti province, in Piedmont, 28 m. ESE of Turin. Pop. (1961) 61,044. Route, industrial, and commercial centre. Noted for sparkling wine (Asti spumante). Distilleries, rayon mills, etc. Gothic cathedral (14th-cent.). Birthplace of Vittorio Alfieri (1749–1803).

**Astrakhan** USSR. Capital of the Astrakhan Region (RSFSR), on the delta of the Volga R. 60 m. from the Caspian Sea. Pop. (1970) 411,000. Chief Caspian port, though icebound for 4 months a year. Dispatches timber, grain, metals, etc. downstream, and oil, cotton, fruit, rice, etc. upstream. Shipbuilding, fish processing (esp. the preparation of caviare), sawmilling. Manufactures textiles, footwear, etc. Standing 70 ft below sea level, it is protected from Volga floods by dykes. Consists of the 16th/17th-cent. Kreml (citadel) which includes a cathedral, the White Town (containing offices, shops, etc.), and the suburbs (wooden houses). Its name is given to the fur made from the skins of newborn Persian lambs. Formerly capital of a Tatar khanate. Captured by Ivan the Terrible 1556. Its importance increased with the exploitation of the Baku oilfields in the late 19th cent., but has diminished since the opening of the Volga–Don Canal (1952).

**Asturias** Spain. Region and former kingdom in the NW, corresponding to the present Oviedo province; almost isolated from the rest of the country by the Cantabrian mountains. Chief industry mining. The coalmines (the richest in Spain) have been worked for many centuries. Chief towns Oviedo, Gijón, Avilés, Mieres. Conquered by the Romans in the 3rd and 2nd cent. B.C. During the Moorish invasion, became a Christian stronghold; the reconquest of Spain was started from Asturias, and a Christian kingdom founded here.

**Asunción** Paraguay. Capital, on the E bank of the Paraguay R. near the confluence with the Pilcomayo. Pop. (1962) 305,160 (a quarter of the country's population live in the district). Transacts most of Paraguay's business. River transport and a central winding railway to Buenos Aires (938 m.); a ferry link to the Pan-American highway at Pilcomayo. Flour milling, food processing. Manufactures textiles, footwear, etc. Settled by the Spaniards (1538), who found the Guarani Indians friendly; became the centre from which Spanish colonization of the S part of the continent proceeded.

**Aswan (Assuan)** United Arab Republic.* Ancient Syene. Town in Upper Egypt, on the E bank of the Nile just below the First Cataract. Pop. (1960) 48,000. On the railway to Cairo. Commercial and tourist centre and winter resort. Syenite (granite) quarries in the neighbourhood. 3 m. upstream is the great Aswan irrigation dam (completed 1902), which created a vast artificial lake on the Nile. Its height was twice raised (1912, 1933). The new Aswan High Dam was begun in 1960.The project, which was worked out by British engineers but received Soviet financial and technical aid, creates a vast reservoir, stretching 300 m. to the Third Cataract, the world's second largest man-made lake (Kariba is slightly larger). The High Dam is 365 ft high and nearly 3 m. long. The first stage was completed on time in May 1964; the dam was scheduled to be ready in 1970. It will greatly increase the irrigation potential of the Nile waters; the flow will serve a large hydroelectric power station, generating about 2,000 megawatts. ⟡ *Abu Simbel.*

**Asyût (Assiut)** United Arab Republic. Ancient Lycopolis. Chief city in Upper Egypt, on the W bank of the Nile. Pop. (1960) 122,000. On the railway to Cairo. Caravan-trading centre. Cotton spinning, wood and ivory carving, pottery making. One of the chief centres of the Copts. The Asyût barrage (1902) across the Nile provides water for irrigation.

**Atacama Desert** S America. Part of the arid area W of the Andes, stretching from N central Chile to S Ecuador and comprising the barren lands of N Chile and S Peru. One of the driest areas on earth. Between the Andean slopes and the coast (falling steeply to the Pacific) discontinuous basins of dried-up lakes, 40–50 m. wide, bear caliche deposits yielding nitrates and iodine. Great copper mines in the W Andes. Iron-ore reserves in desert Chile.

**Atbara** Sudan. Town on the right bank of the Atbara R. at its confluence with the Nile. Pop. (1964) 45,000. Important railway junction for Port Sudan. Railway engineering. Manufactures cement. Trade in cotton etc.

**Atbara River** Sudan. River over 700 m. long, rising in the Ethiopian highlands, flowing NNW, and joining the Nile at Atbara. The only tributary of the Nile between the Blue and the White Nile confluence and the Mediterranean. After the flood season (July–Aug.) becomes a chain of pools.

**Atchafalaya River** USA. An outlet of the Red R. in Louisiana, leading to the bay of the same name in the Gulf of Mexico. Also carries Mississippi water in flood time. For most of its 220 m. it has been strengthened by levees.

**Athabaska (Athabasca), Lake** Canada. Lake 200 m. long and 3,000 sq. m. in area, in NW Saskatchewan and NE Alberta. It receives the Athabaska and Peace rivers in the SW and discharges NW by the Slave R. into the Great Slave L. and thence into the Mackenzie R. The discovery of uranium ores on the N shore led to the growth of Uranium City in the 1950s.

**Athabaska (Athabasca) River** Canada. River 765 m. long, rising in the Rocky Mountains near Mt Columbia and flowing generally NE to L. Athabaska. Oil-bearing sands extend 120 m. along the lower course.

**Athelney, Isle of** England. Small area near the confluence of the Tone and Parrett rivers in Somerset. Formerly isolated by marshes. Hiding place of Alfred the Great after his defeat by the Danes (878); he founded (888) the Athelney monastery.

**Athens** (Gr. **Athínai**) Greece. Capital of Greece, and of the Attica *nome*, on the chief plain of Attica 5 m. from the Saronic Gulf and its port Piraeus (with which it now forms one large city). Total pop. (1961) 1,852,709. Economic and cultural centre of Greece. Manufactures textiles, rugs, chemicals, wine, etc. (concentrated mainly in Piraeus). Above the plain rise a number of limestone ridges, two of which, the Lycabettus (909 ft) just outside the ancient walls, and the Acropolis (512 ft), dominate the city. The former is waterless and was unused in ancient times.

Modern Athens, principally to the N and E of the Acropolis, is centred on Constitution Square and Concordia Square, and includes the university, the parliament house, the national library, and museums. New residential and industrial suburbs have extended the city boundaries during the 20th cent. and seaside resorts have sprung up on the Saronic Gulf. The population increased considerably after each world war, owing to the great influx of refugees. The present development dates from Greek independence (1834). Under King Otto I (from Munich) German architects gave it broad streets and squares and erected solid uninspiring buildings; but for the wonderful clear light of Greece, and the vivacious bustle of the streets, present-day Athens would be undistinguished. Beyond the modern city and still secure from the spreading rash of suburbs, stands the Acropolis, with its cluster of superb temples, the beauty of which draws increasing thousands of tourists each year. Of ancient Athens there are still considerable remains testifying to its former glory: the Parthenon, in white marble, set in a framework of 46 Doric columns; the Ionic Erechtheum; the temple of Athena Nike; and the Propylaea, a gateway. S of the Acropolis are the theatre of Dionysus (dating from the 6th cent. B.C.) and the Odeum of Herodes Atticus (2nd cent. A.D.). To the W and N are the Hephaesteum or Theseum (5th cent. B.C., the best-preserved temple of ancient Greece), the Dipylon gate, the Agora (market), and the Roman Tower of the Winds. Among the hills W of the Acropolis are the Areopagus (scene of ancient murder trials), the Pnyx, and the hills of the Nymphs (site of the modern observatory), and the Muses.

Athens (named after its patron goddess Athena) was ruled by Ionian kings until about 1000 B.C. The first signs of its approaching greatness came in the 6th cent. B.C. with the democratic reforms of Solon and Cleisthenes. In the following cent. it became the leading Greek city-state, and decisively defeated the Persians, thanks to its powerful navy. This was the golden age, when art and literature flourished (under Themistocles, Cimon, and Pericles), when the city was linked to Piraeus by the famous Long Walls, and the Parthenon, Erechtheum, and Propylaea were built – the age of Aeschylus, Sophocles, and Euripides the dramatists, of Socrates the philosopher, and of Herodotus the historian. Athens was defeated by Sparta in the Peloponnesian War of 431–404 B.C. but recovered and renewed its cultural supremacy with such figures as Aristophanes, Plato, and Aristotle, but then lost political power after defeat by Philip of Macedon at Chaeronea (338 B.C.). Next under Roman rule, Athens was plundered by Sulla in 86 B.C. but prospered again in the 2nd cent. A.D. (esp. under Hadrian). Although taken by the Visigoths in 267 and 395, it maintained its academic standing until Justinian closed the schools of philosophy in 529, after which it soon sank to the level of a provincial Byzantine town. It fell to the Turks in 1458. By the time of the Greek War of Independence (1834) it had sunk to a miserable township of less than 5,000. When independence from Turkey was gained it grew rapidly.

**Athens** USA. Town in Georgia, on the Oconee R. 58 m. ENE of Atlanta. Pop. (1960) 31,355. In an important cotton-growing area. Commercial and industrial centre. Manufactures textiles, cottonseed oil, fertilizers, etc. Seat of the University of Georgia (1785).

**Atherstone** England. Market town in Warwickshire 4 m. NW of Nuneaton. Pop. (rural district, 1961) 24,394. On the Roman road Watling Street. In the neighbouring village of Merevale are the remains of the 12th-cent. Merevale Abbey.

**Atherton** England. Urban district in Lancashire 10 m. WNW of Manchester. Pop. (1961) 19,755. Industrial centre. Coal-mining, cotton milling, etc.

**Athlone** Irish Republic. Town in Co. Westmeath, on the Shannon R. 70 m. W of Dublin. Pop. (1966) 9,623. Almost in the geographical centre of Ireland. Main Irish broadcasting station 2 m. E. Textile mills. Birthplace of the tenor John McCormack (1884–1945).

**Atholl** Scotland. Mountainous district in Perthshire, on the S slopes of the Grampian Mountains. Area 450 sq. m. About one third deer forest. Chief towns Pitlochry, Dunkeld, and Blair Atholl (seat of the Dukes of Atholl).

**Athos, Mount** (Gr. **Hagion Oros**, 'Holy Mountain') Greece. Highest point (6,570 ft) of the Chalcidice peninsula, in Macedonia, at the SE end of Acte (Akti), the most easterly of the three prongs extending into the Aegean Sea. Connected to the mainland by an isthmus, where there are still traces of a canal cut by Xerxes before 480 B.C. Area 131 sq. m. Pop. (1961) 2,687 (mainly Basilian monks). Administrative centre Karyai (pop. 429). A self-governing community of 20 monasteries, formed in the 10th cent. Autonomy was granted by the Greek government in 1927.

**Atitlán** Guatemala. Volcano (11,633 ft) just S of L. Atitlán in the S. Active 16th–19th cent.

**Atitlán, Lake** Guatemala. Lake 24 m. long and 10 m. wide, 40 m. W of Guatemala City at a height of 5,000 ft. Depth 1,000 ft. Famed for its beauty. Believed to occupy the crater of an extinct volcano. Near its S shores are inactive volcanoes (inc. Atitlán). No visible outlet.

**Atlanta** USA. State capital of Georgia, principal state commercial and railway centre. Pop. (1960) 487,455. Railway engineering. Manufactures textiles, clothing, furniture, chemicals, cottonseed oil, machinery, etc. Seat of the Emory University for white students (1915) and the Atlanta University for Negroes (1865). Founded 1837. Partly destroyed by Union troops under Sherman during the American Civil War (1864), but developed rapidly when hostilities were over.

**Atlantic City** USA. Holiday resort in New Jersey, on Absecon Beach, a low sandy island 10 m. long, 55 m. SE of Philadelphia. Luxury and other hotels, amusement piers, recreational facilities. Varied industries.

**Atlantic Ocean.** World's second largest ocean, lying between Europe and Africa (E) and N and S America (W), named after the Atlas Mountains in N Africa. Area about 32 million sq. m. Divided by the equator into the N Atlantic and S Atlantic. Its greatest depth (30,246 ft) is in the Milwaukee Deep N of Puerto Rico (W Indies), but the average depth is about 13,000 ft. A ridge rising some 6,000 ft above the ocean floor runs N–S down the middle of the N and S Atlantic, inc. the islands of the Azores in the former and Ascension and Tristan da Cunha in the latter. Other island groups are the Canary Is., Cape Verde Is., and Madeira off Africa; the British Isles and Iceland in Europe; Newfoundland, W Indies, and Bermuda off N America; the Falkland Is., S Georgia, etc. off S America. The salinity of the Atlantic is by far the highest of the great oceans. In the N Atlantic the main currents follow a clockwise direction and include the Gulf Stream and the N Atlantic Drift, while in the S Atlantic they have an anti-clockwise flow, as exemplified by the Benguela and Brazil Currents. With the economically developed and densely populated regions of E North America and NW Europe on opposite sides of the N Atlantic, the latter has become the world's busiest ocean highway.

**Atlas Mountains** Africa. System of folded mountain chains extending WSW–ENE across NW Africa. Related to similar folded chains in S Europe. A physical and climatic barrier between the Mediterranean region and the Sahara. Among the ranges are the Tell (Maritime) Atlas and the Saharan Atlas; between these are the high plateaux (◊ *Algeria*). The highest range is the Great (High) Atlas in Morocco, with snow-capped peaks, rising to 13,664 ft in Djebel Toubkal. Some well-watered Atlas slopes are covered with forests of oak, cedar, etc., where cork is the main product. They enclose fertile cultivated valleys. The people are mainly of Berber stock, with a considerable Arab admixture.

**Atrato River** Colombia. River 400 m. long, rising in the W Cordillera (the headwaters receive about 400 ins. of rain annually), flowing N through the forests between the Sierra de Baudo and the W Cordillera, and entering the Gulf of Darien. Navigable in the upper course, where there is gold and platinum dredging.

**Atria** ◊ *Adria*.

**Attica** (Gr. **Attiki**) Greece. *Nome* in central Greece, including the SE peninsula (part of ancient Attica) and several islands in the Saronic Gulf and farther S. Area 1,458 sq. m. Pop. (1961) 2,057,994. Cap. Athens. Cereals, olive oil, and wine produced.

**Attleboro** USA. Town in SE Massachusetts 12 m. NE of Providence (RI). Pop. (1960) 27,118. Manufactures jewellery, silverware, etc. Founded (1669) by immigrants from Attleborough (Norfolk, England).

**Aube** France. Department in Champagne, SE of Paris, on the edge of the Paris Basin. Area 2,326 sq. m. Pop. (1968) 270,325. Prefecture Troyes. The chalk area of the centre and NW ('*Champagne pouilleuse*') is arid and infertile, except along the Aube R. In the wooded and more fertile SE, cereals and vines are cultivated. Manufactures hosiery. Chief towns Troyes, Arcis-sur-Aube, Bar-sur-Aube.

**Aube River** France. Navigable river 150 m. long, rising on the Plateau de Langres, and flowing NW through the Haute-Marne and Aube departments to the Seine.

**Aubervilliers** France. Formerly Notre-Dame-des-Vertus. Industrial suburb NNE of Paris in the Seine-St Denis department. Pop. (1968) 73,808. Manufactures fertilizers, paints, varnishes, perfumes, leather goods, etc.

**Auburn** (Maine) USA. Industrial town on the Androscoggin R. 30 m. N of Portland. Pop. (1960) 24,449. Manufactures shoes.

**Auburn** (New York) USA. Town at the N end of L. Owasco, 22 m. WSW of Syracuse. Pop. (1960) 35,249. Manufactures diesel engines, plastics, etc. Site of a famous state prison (founded 1816).

**Aubusson** France. Town in the Creuse department on the Creuse R. 46 m. ENE of Limoges. Pop. (1968) 6,761. Famous since the 16th cent. for carpets and tapestries. Birthplace of Cardinal Pierre d'Aubusson (1423–1503).

**Auch** France. Ancient Augusta Auscorum. Prefecture of the Gers department in the SW, on the Gers R. 45 m. W of Toulouse. Pop. (1968) 23,718. Market town. Trade in Armagnac brandy, wine, cereals. Flour-milling, furniture, hosiery, and other industries. Famous for *pâté de foie gras*. Gothic cathedral (15th/17th-cent.). An important city in Roman Gaul. Capital of Armagnac and later of Gascony.

**Auchinleck** Scotland. Small town in Ayrshire 13 m. E of Ayr. Pop. (1961) 4,800. Coalmining centre. Near by is Auchinleck House, seat of the Boswell family. James Boswell (1740–95) is buried in the churchyard.

**Auckland** New Zealand. Largest city, chief seaport, and former capital (1840–65) of New Zealand, founded 1840, on a narrow isthmus in the N of the N Island, between Manukau Harbour (S) and Waitemata Harbour (N). Pop. (1966) 149,660 (urban area 547,900). Most of its trade is handled by Waitemata Harbour, the wharves being reached by a dredged channel. New harbour bridge opened 1959. Deals with one third of the country's overseas trade. Exports dairy produce, wool, hides, timber. Imports machinery, petroleum, coal, fertilizers. Manufactures textiles, chemicals, foodstuffs, etc. Shipyards, engineering works, vehicle-assembly plants. The main passenger seaport and trans-Pacific airport. Many extinct volcanic cones in the neighbourhood.

**Auckland Islands** New Zealand. Group of 6 uninhabited islands of volcanic origin about 300 m. S of Invercargill (S Island). Area 234 sq. m. Discovered 1806.

**Aude** France. Department on the Gulf of Lions in Languedoc. Area 2,448 sq. m. Pop. (1968) 278,323. Prefecture Carcassonne. Largely mountainous, rising to 4,039 ft in the Corbières. Crossed W–E by the valley of the Aude R. Wine, cereals, olives, fruit produced in the fertile N. Salt produced along the lagoon-fringed coast. Chief towns Carcassonne, Narbonne, Castelnaudary, Limoux.

**Aude River** France. River 140 m. long, rising in the Pyrenees near the Pic de Carlitte, and flowing N past Carcassonne and then E to the Gulf of Lions.

**Aue** German Democratic Republic. Industrial town in the Karl-Marx-Stadt district 12 m. SE of Zwickau. Pop. (1965) 31,720. Centre of a uranium-mining region in the Erz Gebirge. Manufactures textiles, metal goods, etc.

**Aughrabies Falls** ◊ *Orange River*.

**Aughrim** Irish Republic. Small village in Co. Galway, 4 m. WSW of Ballinasloe. Pop. 100. Scene of the battle (1691) in which the forces of William III (under General Ginkel) utterly defeated those of James II (under the French General St Ruth).

**Augsburg** Federal German Republic. Ancient Augusta Vindelicorum. Industrial city in Bavaria on the Lech R. near its confluence with the Wertach, 35 m. WNW of Munich. Pop. (1968) 210,573. Important railway junction. Principal textile centre of S Germany (cotton, woollen, linen). Also manufactures diesel engines, agricultural machinery, machine tools, precision instruments, chemicals, etc. Noteworthy buildings are the 10th/15th-cent. cathedral, the 17th-cent. Renaissance town hall, the 15th/16th-cent. Church of St Ulrich. Augustus founded a Roman colony here in 14 B.C. Became a free imperial city 1276. Birthplace of Holbein (1497–1543). Home of the Fugger merchant-banker family. Important commercial and banking centre in the 15th and 16th cent. During the 2nd World War the factories making submarine and aircraft engines were heavily bombed, and some historic buildings suffered severe damage.

**Augusta.** Name given (usually in honour of the Emperor Augustus) to many ancient towns in the Roman Empire, e.g. Augusta Auscorum (◊ *Auch*), Augusta Taurinorum (◊ *Turin*), Augusta Vindelicorum (◊ *Augsburg*).

**Augusta** Italy. Seaport in E Sicily 12 m. NNW of Syracuse on a small island connected to the mainland by a bridge. Pop. (1961) 27,950. Fisheries. Salt works. Founded by Emperor Frederick II 1232.

**Augusta** USA. Town and river port in

Georgia, on the Savannah R. at the head of navigation, 110 m. NNW of Savannah. Pop. (1960) 70,626. Connected by bridges with Hamburg (S Carolina). Cotton market with important cotton manufactures. Founded as a trading post 1735. State capital 1786–95.

**Aulnay-sous-Bois** France. Residential suburb of NE Paris, in the Seine-St Denis department. Pop. (1968) 61,758.

**Aunis** France. Former province, on the Bay of Biscay, forming (with part of Saintonge) the department of Charente-Maritime. Includes the islands of Ré and Oléron. The capital was La Rochelle.

**Aurangabad** India. Town in Maharashtra, 175 m. ENE of Bombay. Pop. (1961) 87,579. Textile manufactures. Trade in grain. Founded in the early 17th cent. Became the capital of the Mogul emperor Aurangzeb; has the mausoleum he erected to his wife. Seat of the Marathwada University (1958).

**Aurès Mountains** ◊ *Timgad*.

**Aurillac** France. Prefecture of the Cantal department in S central France, on the Jordanne R. 68 m. SSW of Clermont-Ferrand. Pop. (1968) 31,143. Market town. Trade in cheese and livestock. Manufactures umbrellas, leather goods, etc. Grew up round the 9th-cent. Abbey of St Géraud, a centre of medieval learning. Birthplace of Pope Sylvester II (d. 1003) and Paul Doumer (1857–1932).

**Aurora** USA. Industrial town in Illinois, 34 m. W of Chicago. Pop. (1960) 63,715. Manufactures steel equipment for offices and schools, also pumps, machinery, etc.

**Auschwitz** ◊ *Oświęcim*.

**Austerlitz** (Czech **Slavkov**) Czechoslovakia. Town in Moravia, 13 m. ESE of Brno. Pop. 4,000. Scene of what was probably Napoleon's most brilliant victory (2 Dec. 1805), when he defeated the combined Russian and Austrian armies.

**Austin** (Minnesota) USA. Town 92 m. SSE of Minneapolis. Pop. (1960) 27,908. Railway engineering, meat packing, etc.

**Austin** (Texas) USA. State capital, on the Colorado R. 150 m. WNW of Houston. Pop. (1960) 186,545. Food-processing and other industries. Educational and artistic centre. Seat of the University of Texas (1883). Named after the Texan colonizer S. F. Austin (1793–1836).

**Austral (Tubuai) Islands** (◊ *French Polynesia*) S Pacific Ocean. Group of islands S of the Society Is. Total area 67 sq. m. Pop.

(1962) 4,371 (Polynesian). Rurutu and Tubuai are the largest of the four main islands; far to the S is Rapa. Discovered (1777) by Capt. Cook. Annexed by France 1880.

**Australasia** S Pacific Ocean. Term applied somewhat loosely to the islands of the S Pacific including Australia, New Zealand, New Guinea, and their adjacent islands, but assumed by some authors to be equivalent to Oceania. It is not favoured by many geographers on account of its ambiguity.

**Australia.** Independent member of the Commonwealth of Nations. Area 2,967,909 sq. m. Pop. (1968) 12,030,820. Cap. Canberra. Lang. English. Rel. mainly Anglican and Roman Catholic.

The largest island in the world and the smallest continent, about ¾ the size of Europe. It lies between the Indian Ocean (W) and the Pacific Ocean (E) and is almost bisected by the Tropic of Capricorn. Sheep rearing is the main occupation, but in spite of the importance of pastoral farming and agriculture there is a large urban population. Much of it is desert and the average population density is low (3·75 per sq. m.). The standard of living is high, social stratification is slight. Comprises six states (New South Wales, Victoria, Queensland, South Australia, Western Australia, Tasmania), the Northern Territory, and the Australian Capital Territory (Canberra).

TOPOGRAPHY, CLIMATE. The W part of the mainland consists of arid plateau 600–1,000 ft high, with dissected tablelands rising above this level. E of this a central plain extends from the Gulf of Carpentaria to the S edge of the Murray R. basin, underlain in the N by the Great Artesian Basin. The Great Dividing Range runs parallel to the E (Pacific) coast, its uplifted blocks generally having steep E faces and sloping more gently inland. The highest point is Mt Kosciusko (7,328 ft) in the Australian Alps. The E coastlands, nowhere over 250 m. and generally less than 70 m. wide, are the most fertile and adequately watered region where the majority of the large towns and population are concentrated. Offshore the Great Barrier Reef runs through the Coral Sea to about lat. 24° S. Tasmania, an island of 26,383 sq. m., is separated from the mainland (SE) by the Bass Strait.

The N half is tropical, the SE and SW have warm temperate climates, with hot dry summers and mild rainy winters, while

Tasmania is mild throughout the year. Rainfall diminishes sharply inland from the N and E coasts. Most of the interior has less than 20 ins. annually, much of it below 10 ins., and the rainfall is often unreliable. Many river systems are a maze of wandering channels, filled only after storms. The Murray R. system is the only large perennial one. The L. Eyre basin is the largest area of inland drainage and is usually dry. Artesian water, present in many parts, is often brackish but generally suitable for livestock.

FLORA AND FAUNA. The dry interior has considerable areas of desert, but there is much semi-arid land with tussock grass and scrub. Between this and the better-watered coastlands a great arc of grass country stretches from the SE to the NW, with eucalyptus forest in the wetter regions and some tropical forest in the NE. In the SW there are forests of jarrah and karri, valuable hardwoods. The fauna of Australia, like the flora, has certain exclusive features. There are no native cats, pigs, or dogs; the destructive dingo or wild dog was introduced long ago and is already doomed. Typical mammals are the marsupials (of which the kangaroo is the largest), the koala bear, and the platypus. The rabbit was introduced by settlers and so increased in numbers as to become a threat to sheep and cattle pastures. Its numbers were greatly reduced by myxomatosis after 1952.

RESOURCES. Since the days of the early settlements, when squatters took up much of the new agricultural lands, farm mechanization, the selective breeding of stock and plants, the use of fertilizers, and the development of soil science have established Australia as a major exporter of wool and wheat. Wheat comes mainly from the SE and SW areas receiving 10–25 ins. of rain a year. Most of the 158 million (1966) sheep are in the SE and SW where the annual rainfall is 20–30 ins., though millions are grazed at low densities in less favourable southern and interior areas, aided by artesian water. Dairy cattle prosper on the moist coastlands of S Queensland, the SE and SW, and on irrigated land. Beef cattle are raised on hill country in these regions and on huge ranches in the N, NW, and the Great Artesian Basin. Sugar-cane, bananas, and pineapples come from coastal Queensland and N New South Wales, deciduous fruits from Victoria, Tasmania, and the SW. Irrigated lands in the Murray basin and near Adelaide and Perth support citrus and deciduous fruits and vines.

Australia has extensive mineral resources. Zinc, lead, and silver come from New South Wales, Queensland, and NW Tasmania, copper from Queensland, tin from the Great Dividing Range and Tasmania, gold from Western Australia and Victoria, and large iron-ore deposits are worked in the NW and in S Australia. Coal comes from coastal New South Wales and Queensland, smaller amounts from S and Western Australia, lignite from S Victoria. Uranium exists in the Northern Territory and N Queensland and there is some oil in S Queensland. Hydroelectric power resources are limited except in Tasmania and the SE mountains, where the Snowy Mountains project is a large modern development scheme.

In recent years industry has developed and there are now over 1 million industrial workers. There is a growing steel industry. Other manufactures include industrial metals, machinery, foodstuffs, chemicals, textiles, paper, and petroleum products, mainly for home consumption. The greatest industrial areas are those of Newcastle–Sydney–Port Kembla in E New South Wales, and Melbourne and S Victoria; others are near Adelaide, S of Perth, and inland of Brisbane. Imports are mainly of metals, machinery, crude oil, textiles, and chemicals. Wool is far ahead of other exports, followed by wheat, meat, metals and metal manufactures, fruits, dairy produce (esp. butter), and sugar. The UK is Australia's best customer; other European countries and the US buy mainly wool. Trade with Asian countries has increased significantly in recent years, Japan having become a major wool buyer.

PEOPLE, GOVERNMENT. Most of the people live in or near the coastal lands of the E, SE, and SW, in the temperate areas. In the occupied interior, agricultural stations and townships are widely dispersed. Over half the population live in the metropolitan areas of the state capitals: Sydney, Melbourne, Brisbane, Adelaide, Perth, Hobart. The people are mainly of British descent, but since 1946 many immigrants ('New Australians') have come from other European countries. At the time of the discovery of Australia various tribes of aborigines with a Stone

Age culture were scattered throughout the land. Their numbers declined in the 19th cent. Today there are some 30,000, of whom 18,000 are in the Northern Territory.

There is a parliament of two houses, and administration is in the hands of a prime minister and cabinet. Each of the states has its own government, which retains those powers not specifically delegated to the central government.

HISTORY. Australia was the last continent to be 'discovered'. The N was visited early in the 17th cent. by Dutch navigators, and in 1642 Tasman sailed via Tasmania to New Zealand. In 1770 Capt. Cook landed to the S of the present Sydney, and this led to the region being claimed and settled by the British as New South Wales. It was at first used largely as a penal settlement (transportation virtually ceased by 1839), and though the colonies (later states) were founded one by one, it was not till the discovery of gold at Bathurst (1851) that settlers arrived in considerable numbers. The population began to increase rapidly: it rose from 405,000 in 1850 to 3,770,000 in 1900. The continent was first crossed N–S by J. M. Stuart in 1862. Long before then, however, men had moved in from the early coastal settlements to the lands which have since provided the major part of the country's wealth in wool and wheat. In 1901 the colonies were fused into the Commonwealth and became states; the federal capital was at Melbourne until 1927, when it was transferred to Canberra. The Northern Territory, annexed to S Australia in 1863, was taken over by the Commonwealth in 1911. Australia played a notable part at the side of Britain in both world wars.

**Australian Alps** Australia. Mountain ranges in the SE, at the S end of the Great Dividing Range. Contain Mt Kosciusko (7,328 ft), the highest peak in Australia. Popular winter-sports area.

**Australian Antarctic Territory.** All islands and territories other than ◊ *Adélie Land* S of 60° S and between 45° and 160° E, under Australian authority since 1933. Scientific bases were established at Mawson in MacRobertson Land (1954) and at Davis in Princess Elizabeth Land (1957); in 1959 Australia also took custody of Wilkes station, in Wilkes Land, sharing research with the USA. By the International Antarctic Treaty (1959), the area S of 60° S is reserved for international peaceful scientific investigation.

**Australian Capital Territory** ◊ *Canberra.*

**Austria** (Ger. Österreich). Federal republic in central Europe. Area 32,366 sq. m. Pop. (1961) 7,073,807. Cap. Vienna. Lang. German. Rel. predominantly Roman Catholic.

Almost entirely within the Alps. Bounded by the Federal German Republic (Bavarian Alps, etc.) and Czechoslovakia (N), Hungary (E), Yugoslavia (Karawanken) and Italy (Carnic, Zillertal, and Ötztal Alps) (S), Switzerland and Liechtenstein (Rhaetian Alps, the Rhine, and L. Constance) (W). Administratively divided into 9 provinces: Vienna, Lower Austria, Burgenland, Upper Austria, Salzburg, Styria, Carinthia, Tirol, Vorarlberg.

TOPOGRAPHY, RESOURCES, *etc.* In the SW the Ötztal Alps rise to 12,382 ft in the Wild Spitze, and the Hohe Tauern to 12,461 ft in the Gross Glockner; the latter is continued E towards the centre of Austria by the Niedere Tauern. Drained principally by the Danube (flowing W–E across the N region) and by its tributaries the Lech, the Inn, the Traun, the Raab, and the Drave. Continental climate, with cold winters, warm summers, and a moderate rainfall; temperatures decrease and rainfall increases with altitude.

The beautiful mountain scenery, esp. in the Tirol, the lakes of Carinthia, and the many winter-sports centres and spas, attract large numbers of visitors; tourism has become a major industry. The mountainous character of the country restricts agriculture and necessitates imports of grain, fats, and other foodstuffs. Nearly half of the arable land is in Lower Austria, which occupies less than a quarter of the total area. Forest covers about one third of the area; timber is a valuable product. Chief crops wheat, rye, barley, potatoes. Cattle and pigs extensively reared. Considerable mineral wealth. Lignite mined in many districts. The rich iron-ore deposits of Styria form the basis of a considerable steel industry. Production of petroleum, begun in the 1930s, has decreased. Copper, lead, zinc, graphite also mined. The industries (increasingly using hydroelectric power) are located chiefly in Vienna, Graz, and Linz. The other large towns, Salzburg and Innsbruck, are primarily cultural and tourist centres.

HISTORY. In early times inhabited by Celtic tribes. The land S of the Danube was conquered by the Romans (14 B.C.) and divided into three provinces of the Empire. From the 5th cent. A.D. the area was overrun by Vandals, Goths, Huns, Lombards, and Avars. Conquered by Charlemagne, who established the Eastern Mark in the present Upper and Lower Austria at the end of the 8th cent. Otto II presented Austria to the Babenberg family (976), who ruled until 1246 and initiated the long rise to prestige and power. Rudolf of Habsburg, the German king, appointed his son Albert governor of Austria and Styria in 1282 and the house of Habsburg ruled Austria almost continuously from then until 1918. Bohemia and Hungary were united with Austria in the 16th cent. After the second siege of Vienna by the Turks (1683) and the liberation of most of Hungary from the Turks, Bohemia, Moravia, and Hungary all underwent thorough Germanization. For a time Prussia was a formidable rival, but Austria gained considerably from the Partitions of Poland (1772, 1793, 1795). With the rise of Napoleon came the end of the Holy Roman Empire, and Francis II proclaimed himself Emperor of Austria (1804). Austria played a substantial part in the final defeat of Napoleon and was rewarded with Lombardy, Venetia, Istria, and Illyria (abandoning the Netherlands). Internal unrest showed itself in the revolution of 1848, which began in Hungary. Lombardy and Venetia were lost after wars with Sardinia (1859) and Prussia (1866) respectively; nationalist feeling in Hungary was for a time placated by the establishment of the Dual Monarchy (1867), but the disaffection of the Slav minorities remained. The instability of Austria–Hungary helped to bring about the 1st World War, at the end of which the monarchy collapsed and Austria was reduced to an insignificant republic. It was forcibly incorporated into Nazi Germany (1938). After the 2nd World War it recovered its independence and 1938 frontiers, following military occupation by the Allies, on the conclusion of the Austrian State Treaty (1955).

**Auvergne** France. Region and former province in the Massif Central, forming the present Cantal and Puy-de-Dôme departments and part of the Haute-Loire department. The Auvergne Mountains include many volcanic peaks (Plomb du Cantal, Puy de Dôme, Mont Dore), and rise to 6,188 ft in the Puy de Sancy. Mineral springs. Chief town Clermont-Ferrand. Early inhabitants were the Arverni, a Celtic tribe whose chieftain Vercingetorix was Caesar's chief opponent in the Gallic war. Finally united with France 1527.

**Auxerre** France. Ancient Autissiodurum. Prefecture of the Yonne department, on the Yonne R. 43 m. SW of Troyes. Pop. (1968) 38,066. Market town. Trade in wine (from local vineyards). Manufactures metal goods and paints (from locally quarried ochre). Became the seat of a bishop in the 3rd cent. Gothic cathedral (13th/16th-cent.). The Church of St Germain has a 6th-cent. and later crypts. The 13th-cent. bishop's palace is now the seat of the prefecture.

**Avalon** Canada. The SE peninsula of Newfoundland, with half the island's population. At its E tip is the capital, St John's.

**Avebury** England. Village in Wiltshire on the R. Kennet 9 m. SSW of Swindon. Site of a large neolithic structure (discovered by John Aubrey in the 1660s) including an outer stone circle 400 yards in diameter and two small circles; the stones are 5–20 ft high and 3–12 ft broad. Near by is the artificial mound of Silbury Hill, the largest prehistoric structure in Britain. The village and site were acquired by the National Trust in 1943.

**Avellaneda** Argentina. Major industrial suburb of Buenos Aires, where the Riachuelo R. enters the La Plata estuary. Pop. 330,000. Huge *frigoríficos* (meatpacking plants). Oil refining, tanning. Manufactures textiles, matches, etc. Docks for shipping animal products from the pampas.

**Avellino** Italy. Capital of Avellino province, in Campania, in the Apennines 28 m. ENE of Naples. Pop. (1961) 41,825. Sulphur mining and refining. Flour milling. Manufactures hats. The ruins of ancient Abellinum are $2\frac{1}{2}$ m. NE. 4 m. NW is the Benedictine convent and shrine of Monte Vergine (founded in the 12th cent.).

**Averno** Italy. Ancient Avernus. A small crater lake, nearly 2 m. in circumference, in Campania 10 m. W of Naples. In ancient times the sulphurous fumes were believed to kill passing birds; it was represented as the entrance to hell.

**Aveyron** France. Department in the SW of the Massif Central, almost corresponding to the ancient county of Rouergue. Area 3,386 sq. m. Pop. (1968) 281,568. Prefecture Rodez. Mountainous and largely barren, with the Monts d'Aubrac in the NE and the Cévennes in the SE. Includes much of the limestone Causses region. Cattle and sheep raised. Cereals and potatoes cultivated, and vines, fruits, and vegetables in the sheltered valleys. Coal mined at Decazeville and Aubin. The town of Roquefort is famous for cheese. Chief towns Rodez, Millau (glove manufacture).

**Aveyron River** France. River 150 m. long, in the Aveyron and Tarn-et-Garonne departments in the S, rising on the Aveyron–Lozère border and flowing generally WSW to join the Tarn R. near Montauban.

**Avignon** France. Historic town, prefecture of the Vaucluse department, on the left bank of the Rhône R. 57 m. NNW of Marseille. Pop. (1968) 88,958. Trade in wines. Manufactures chemicals, soap, cement, paper, rayon, etc. Tourist centre for visitors to Provence. Dominated by the massive papal palace, a 14th-cent. combined castle, fortress, and convent, which took 30 years to build. Only 4 arches of the 12th-cent. bridge of St Bénézet (subject of the folk song *Sur le pont d'Avignon*) now extend across the Rhône, and among its ruins is the original Romanesque chapel. Almost encircled by enormous crenellated walls built (14th cent.) by the popes when it was the residence of Pope Clement V and his successors during the 'Babylonian exile' (1309–77) and of two antipopes (1378–1408). Remained in the possession of the popes till it was incorporated into France (1791).

**Ávila** Spain. 1. Province in Old Castile, forming part of the Meseta in the N; mountainous in the S. Area 3,107 sq. m. Pop. (1961) 238,372. Chiefly agricultural. Cereal cultivation. Livestock (mainly merino sheep) raised.
2. Capital of Ávila province, on the Adaja R. 54 m. WNW of Madrid, at a height of nearly 4,000 ft. Pop. 25,000. Medieval architecture, inc. 12th-cent. granite walls and 11th/14th-cent. cathedral, makes it a popular tourist centre. Has declined in importance since the 17th cent. Birthplace of St Teresa (1515–82).

**Avoca (Ovoca) River** Irish Republic. River in Co. Wicklow, formed by the union of the Avonbeg and the Avonmore,

flowing SE and entering the Irish Sea at Arklow. The beauty of its valley is celebrated in Thomas Moore's *The Meeting of the Waters* ('Sweet Vale of Avoca . . .').

**Avon (Afon)** British Isles. In Celtic, 'stream' or 'river'. Applied to several rivers, e.g. East (Hampshire) Avon, Lower Avon, Upper Avon; three in Scotland (tributaries of the Clyde, the Forth, and the Spey); and one (the Afon) in S Wales, with the mouth at Aberavon.

**Avonmouth** England. Seaport at the mouth of the Lower Avon in Gloucestershire, 6 m. NW of and included in the port of Bristol. Docks, flour mills, chemical works; zinc smelting.

**Avon River, Lower** England. The Bristol Avon, 75 m. long, rising on the E slope of the Cotswold Hills near Tetbury in Gloucestershire, flowing in a wide curve past Chippenham, Melksham, Bradford-on-Avon, Bath, and Bristol, and entering the Severn estuary at Avonmouth. Below Bristol, an important commercial waterway.

**Avon River, Upper** England. The Warwickshire Avon, 96 m. long, rising near Naseby in Northamptonshire, flowing generally SW past Rugby, Warwick, Stratford-upon-Avon, and Evesham, and joining the Severn at Tewkesbury.

**Avranches** France. Town in the Manche department, on a hill above the Sée R. 30 m. E of St Malo. Pop. (1968) 11,102. Market town. Trade in grain, fruit, cider, dairy produce. Tanning. On the site of the former cathedral (destroyed 1790) is a stone to mark the spot where Henry II received absolution for the murder of Thomas à Becket. Badly damaged during fighting in the Normandy campaign in the 2nd World War (1944).

**Awe, Loch** Scotland. Freshwater lake in Argyllshire, 22 m. long SW–NE and up to 3 m. wide at the N end (near which is Ben Cruachan, 3,689 ft). Drains into Loch Etive by the R. Awe, 4 m. long.

**Axminster** England. Town in Devonshire, on the R. Axe 24 m. E of Exeter. Pop. (rural district, 1961) 14,350. Once famous for carpets, first manufactured 1755.

**Axum** ◊ *Aksum.*

**Ayacucho** Peru. Capital of the Ayacucho department, on the Lima-Cuzco highway 150 m. WNW of Cuzco. Pop. 24,000. A historical colonial city, in a basin at 9,500 ft. Manufactures woollen and leather goods, etc. Cobbled streets, colonial mansions, many churches. Seat of a university, closed 1886, reopened 1958. Founded (1539) by Pizarro. A battle on the near-by plain of Ayacucho (1824) ended Spanish rule and led to the independence of Peru.

**Ayacucho, La Paz de** ◊ *La Paz*.

**Aylesbury** England. County town of Buckinghamshire, municipal borough 35 m. NW of London. Pop. (1961) 27,891. Food processing (esp. dairy products), flour milling, engineering, printing. Formerly well known for ducks, and for lace. Taken by the Saxons in the 6th cent. The mainly 13th-cent. Church of St Mary was restored (1849–69) by Gilbert Scott.

**Aylesford** England. Town in Kent, on the R. Medway 3 m. NW of Maidstone. Pop. (1961) 4,500. Paper mills. Cement works. About a mile to the NE is a dolmen known as Kit's Coty House.

**Ayr** Scotland. Royal burgh and county town of Ayrshire, on the Firth of Clyde at the mouth of the Ayr 31 m. SSW of Glasgow. Pop. (1961) 45,297. Small port and resort. Exports coal. Engineering, metal working. Manufactures woollen and leather goods, machinery, etc. In the burgh, 2 m. S, is the village of Alloway, birthplace of Robert Burns. His parents' cottage is now a museum. Two bridges over the Ayr were the subject of his poem *Twa Brigs*. Prestwick airport is 2 m. NNE of Ayr.

**Ayrshire** Scotland. County in the SW, bounded on the W by the Firth of Clyde. Area 1,132 sq. m. Pop. (1961) 342,855. County town Ayr. Hilly in the S and E, rising to 2,299 ft in Black Craig (SE). Drained by the Ayr, Irvine, Doon, Girvan, and Stinchar rivers. Dairy farming important; this is the home of the Ayrshire breed of cattle. Oats and potatoes cultivated. Coalmines. Manufactures textiles, carpets, leather goods, explosives. Chief towns Ayr, Kilmarnock, Prestwick. Several resorts along the coast, e.g. Saltcoats, Largs.

**Aysgarth** England. Village in the N Riding of Yorkshire, 28 m. NW of Harrogate, with a picturesque waterfall, the Aysgarth Force (on the R. Ure).

**Ayutthaya (Ayuthia)** Thailand. Ancient capital (1350–1767), on the Chao Phraya R. 45 m. N of Bangkok. Pop. 31,000. In a rice-growing region. Commercial and tourist centre. Many ruins, including temples and pagodas. Destroyed by the Burmese 1767.

**Azben (Azbine) Highlands** ◊ *Aïr Highlands*.

**Azerbaijan** Iran. Region in the NW, bounded by Soviet Azerbaijan and Armenia (N), the Caspian Sea (E), and E Iraq and Turkey (W). Administratively divided into the two provinces of E Azerbaijan (cap. Tabriz) and W Azerbaijan (cap. Rezaiyeh). Mountainous. The extinct volcano Savalan (W of Ardebil) rises to 15,784 ft. Main river the Arax (Aras) on the N frontier. Near the W border is the large salt-water L. Urmia. An attempt to achieve autonomy after the 2nd World War was suppressed (1946).

**Azerbaijan SSR** USSR. Constituent SSR in E Transcaucasia, bounded by the Caspian Sea (E) and Iran (S). Area 33,430 sq. m. Pop. (1970) 5,111,000 (63 per cent Azerbaijani Turks (Muslims), 14 per cent Russians, 12 per cent Armenians, 3 per cent Georgians). Cap. Baku. Includes the Nakhichevan Autonomous Republic (separated from it by Armenia) and the Nagorno–Karabakh Autonomous Region. Across the N part runs the main Caucasus range, rising to over 14,000 ft. In the SW is the E part of the Lesser Caucasus. Between these mountainous areas are the hot dry steppes of the Kura and Arax rivers, which provide water for irrigation and hydroelectric power. Principal crop cotton; wheat, maize, potatoes also cultivated. Tea, citrus fruits, and other sub-tropical plants cultivated on the humid Caspian lowlands. Main industry oil production on the Apsheron peninsula, centred on Baku, formerly the richest oilfield in the USSR, with associated refining and chemical industries. Crude and refined petroleum carried by tanker up the Volga and by pipeline to Batumi. Other minerals include copper, iron, aluminium, sulphur. Chief towns Baku, Kirovabad, Sumgait. Nakhichevan (pop. 27,000) is capital of the Nakhichevan ASSR, and Stepanakert (pop. 23,000) of the Nagorno–Karabakh AR. Long a source of dispute between Turkey and Persia, the present Azerbaijan was ceded to Russia 1828. After the 1917 Revolution, Soviet rule was not established till 1920. Azerbaijan became a member of the Transcaucasian SFSR 1922 and a constituent republic of the USSR 1936.

**Azores** (Portuguese **Açores**) Portugal. Archipelago belonging to Portugal, the nearest island about 900 m. W of Lisbon in the N Atlantic. Area 888 sq. m. Pop.

(1960) 327,480. They consist of three widely separated groups: São Miguel and Santa Maria (SE); Terceira, Graciosa, São Jorge, Faial (Fayal), Pico (centre); Flores, Corvo (NW). Administratively they are divided into three districts, named after the capitals and chief seaports – Ponta Delgada, Angra do Heroísmo, Horta. Mountainous, rising to 7,600 ft on Pico Island, with rugged coasts, their volcanic origin has led to frequent eruptions and earthquakes. Their climate is unusually mild and equable, with a moderate rainfall, their vegetation luxuriant, and some of them have become winter resorts. Crops include pineapples, oranges, early vegetables. Described by Arab geographers in the 12th cent.; first settled by the Portuguese in the mid 15th cent. The famous naval battle between Sir Richard Grenville in the *Revenge* and the Spanish fleet took place off Flores (1591).

**Azov** USSR. Town in RSFSR on the left bank of the Don R. near the mouth, 20 m. WSW of Rostov-on-Don. Pop. 39,000. Its former importance as a seaport was lost owing to silting of the harbour and the growth of Rostov-on-Don and Taganrog. Fishing port. Fish-canning industry.

**Azov, Sea of** USSR. Ancient Palus Maeotis. A shallow arm of the Black Sea, with which it is connected by the Strait of Kerch (ancient Bosporus Cimmerius). Area 14,500 sq. m. Low salinity, owing to the discharge into it of several rivers, esp. the Don, which empties into the Gulf of Taganrog, an inlet in the NE. Usually frozen around the shores Nov–March. Sea currents have created a number of sandspits along the N and E coasts and the Tongue of Arabat, 70 m. long, which separates it from the Sivash Lagoon. Important fisheries (the Turkish name means 'Fish Sea'). Principal seaports Rostov-on-Don, Taganrog, Kerch.

**Azul** Argentina. Cattle town in the Buenos Aires province, 180 m. SSW of Buenos Aires in rolling grazing land. Pop. 45,000. Flour milling, meat packing, tanning.

# B

**Baalbek** Lebanon. Ancient Heliopolis. Town 40 m. ENE of Beirut at the foot of the Anti-Lebanon at 3,850 ft. Pop. 12,000. A tourist centre, world famous for its extensive ruins. The early Phoenician city was associated with the worship of the sun-god Baal (hence the name) and also the Greek name Heliopolis ('City of the Sun'). It reached its greatest splendour in Roman times: within the area of the Acropolis (excavated in the early 20th cent.) are the ruins of the great temple of Jupiter, with 6 enormous columns still standing, and of a smaller but better-preserved temple near by. Baalbek was sacked by the Saracens and others, and has suffered severely from earthquakes.

**Bab-el-Mandeb** Red Sea. In Arabic, 'Gate of Tears'. Strait 15–20 m. wide connecting the Red Sea with the Gulf of Aden. Separates SW Arabia from Africa. Contains the island of ◊ *Perim*.

**Babol (Babul)** Iran. Formerly Barfrush. Town in E Mazandaran 95 m. NE of Tehran. Pop. (1966) 49,973. Linked by road with its former port, Babol Sar (now a seaside resort) on the Caspian Sea. Commercial centre. Trade in rice and cotton.

**Babylon** Iraq. Ancient city of ◊ *Babylonia* on the R. Euphrates near the town of Hilla, 55 m. S of Baghdad. Became important when made capital of Babylonia under Hammurabi. Virtually destroyed by the Assyrians under Sennacherib in the 7th cent. B.C. Reached its greatest splendour in the time of Nebuchadnezzar. Captured by Cyrus and by Alexander; declined from the 3rd cent. B.C. when superseded by Seleucia. The famous Hanging Gardens were one of the Seven Wonders of the World. The ruins revealed by excavations date from the reign of Nabopolassar (Nebuchadnezzar's father) and later. In the N is the mound of Babil, probably the site of a palace of Nebuchadnezzar and possibly of the Hanging Gardens; a central mound, Al Qasr, contained Nebuchadnezzar's chief palace; to the S was the great temple of Marduk, the city's god.

**Babylonia.** Ancient empire in Mesopotamia, watered by the Euphrates and Tigris rivers; a principal part of Iraq. Strictly, the state created by Hammurabi, in the 2nd millennium B.C., with Babylon as its capital. Later a subject province of Assyria. Asserted its independence in the 7th century B.C., under Nabopolassar, and helped to overthrow the Assyrian empire. Nebuchadnezzar raised it to the peak of its power and prosperity, extended his rule over the whole of Mesopotamia, and defeated the Egyptians, taking Jerusalem, and carrying many of the people of Judah into captivity. Following Cyrus's capture of Babylon (539 B.C.), however, Babylonia was a minor province of the Persian empire.

**Bacău** Rumania. Capital of a district of the same name in Moldavia, on the Bistriţa R. 95 m. NNW of Galaţi. Pop. (1968) 79,079. Industrial town. Manufactures oilfield equipment, textiles, leather goods, etc.

**Bacolod** Philippines. Commercial town and minor port on the NW coast of Negros island. Pop. (1960) 119,315. In an important sugar-producing region. Trade in rice, sugar-cane. Sugar refining, fishing.

**Bactria.** Ancient country in central Asia, between the upper R. Oxus (◊ *Amu Darya*) and the Hindu Kush, with capital Bactra (◊ *Balkh*, Afghanistan). One of the petty kings was Vishtaspa, protector of Zoroaster. It became a satrapy of the Persian empire in the 6th cent. B.C. Conquered by Alexander the Great (328 B.C.) and then part of the Seleucid empire. A powerful independent state (*c.* 255–139 B.C.), but conquered by the Scythians. Gave its name to the Bactrian (two-humped) camel.

**Bacup** England. Municipal borough in E Lancashire, 15 m. N of Manchester. Pop. (1961) 17,295. Manufactures cotton goods, felt, footwear. Coalmining near by.

**Badajoz** Spain. 1. The largest province, in the W, bordering on Portugal. Area 8,360 sq. m. Pop. (1961) 834,370. Stock rearing (chiefly sheep); cereals, olives, vines grown in the more fertile areas. Agriculture much improved from the early 1950s by irrigation schemes.

2. Capital of Badajoz province, on the left bank of the Guadiana R. near the

frontier with Portugal, with which it has a considerable trade. Pop. (1967) 101,422. Flour milling, distilling, brewing, food processing. Because of its strategic position it was frequently attacked by invaders. Birthplace of the artist Luis Morales (1509–86).

**Badalona** Spain. Town in the Barcelona province in Catalonia, an industrial suburb of NE Barcelona. Pop. (1967) 130,722. Chemical, textile, glass, and other industries.

**Bad Ems** ◊ *Ems.*

**Baden** Austria. Spa in Lower Austria, beautifully situated at the foot of the Wiener Wald, 15 m. SSW of Vienna. Pop. (1961) 22,484. Warm sulphur springs, known since Roman times.

**Baden** Federal German Republic. Former state in the SW. Area 5,820 sq. m. Bounded S and W by the Rhine. Mountainous (contains the Black Forest and part of the Swabian Jura) except for the Rhine valley, which is rich agriculturally, producing cereals, fruits, wine, etc. Forestry and woodworking in the Black Forest, a popular tourist area. Manufactures clocks, textiles, chemicals. Formed (1771) from the Margraviates of Baden-Baden and Baden-Durlach. Became a Grand Duchy 1806. In 1952 in the new arrangement of the *Länder* ('States') it became part of Baden-Württemberg. ◊ *Baden-Baden.*

**Baden** Switzerland. Spa and resort in Aargau, on the Limmat R. 13 m. NW of Zürich. Pop. (1969) 15,700. Famous for hot saline and sulphur springs, suitable for the treatment of gout and rheumatism. Electrical engineering, textile manufacture. The Confederation Diet sat in the Rathaus from 1424. Thus virtually capital of Switzerland until 1712.

**Baden-Baden** Federal German Republic. Spa in Baden-Württemberg, in the Oos valley 21 m. SSW of Karlsruhe. Pop. (1963) 40,200. The hot springs, known to the Romans, are used for the treatment of rheumatism, gout, etc. Promenades and public gardens are attractively laid out. The old town is dominated by the ruined Old Castle and the restored New Castle.

**Baden-Württemberg** Federal German Republic. A *Land* formed (1952), following a plebiscite, from the *Länder* of Baden, Württemberg-Baden, and Württemberg-Hohenzollern. Area 13,800 sq. m. Pop. (1968) 8,565,500. Cap. Stuttgart. Other important towns Mannheim, Karlsruhe, Heidelberg.

**Bad Godesberg** ◊ *Godesberg.*

**Bad Homburg** ◊ *Homburg vor der Höhe.*

**Bad Kreuznach** Federal German Republic. Spa and health resort in the Rhineland-Palatinate, on the Nahe R. 24 m. SW of Wiesbaden. Pop. (1963) 35,800. Saline springs. Manufactures optical instruments, chemicals, etc. Tanning.

**Badlands** USA. Dry area in S Dakota c. 100 m. long and 40 m. wide, SE of the Black Hills. Eroded by stream action into peaks, pillars, and steep-sided gullies. The name is also applied to similar regions elsewhere.

**Badminton (Great Badminton)** England. Village in the Cotswold hills, Gloucestershire, 14 m. ENE of Bristol. Seat of the dukes of Beaufort. The game of badminton is named after it.

**Badrinath** India. Village in the Garhwal district in the N of Uttar Pradesh in the central Himalayas. Famous for the temple of Vishnu, an important place of pilgrimage, at 10,300 ft. The peak of Badrinath,' 23,200 ft, is near by.

**Baeza** Spain. Market town in the Jaén province in Andalusia, 23 m. NE of Jaén. Pop. (1961) 15,431. Flour milling, tanning, distilling, etc. Once capital of a small Moorish kingdom with a population of c. 50,000. Sacked by Ferdinand III of Castile (1237); never completely recovered.

**Baffin Bay** Canada/Greenland. Gulf 700 m. long and up to 400 m. wide; part of the NW Passage which joins the Atlantic and Arctic Oceans. Linked with the Atlantic by the Davis Strait and with the Arctic by the Smith, Jones, and Lancaster Sounds. Navigation dangerous because of icebergs carried by the Labrador Current. Discovered by William Baffin 1616.

**Baffin Island** Canada. The largest and most easterly island in the Canadian Arctic, in the SE Franklin District, NW Territories. Area 184,000 sq. m. Pop. 2,000 (mostly Eskimo). Resembles N Labrador, from which it is separated by the Hudson Strait; in the E there are mountains rising to c. 8,000 ft, with ice-caps, snowfields, and glaciers. Principal occupations whaling, hunting, and fur trapping.

**Bafing River** ◊ *Senegal River.*

**Bagé** Brazil. Regional trading centre in the Rio Grande do Sul state, 200 m. WSW of Pôrto Alegre near the Uruguay frontier. Pop. (1960) 47,930. Meat packing. Trade in livestock. An experimental agricultural station.

**Baghdad** Iraq. Capital of Iraq and of Baghdad province on the R. Tigris. Pop. (1965) 1,745,328. Commercial and route centre. Manufactures textiles, cigarettes, cement, leather. Connected by rail with Basra and Kirkuk, and with Istanbul by the Baghdad Railway through Mosul (opened in 1940). Focal point of many roads. Airport. University (1926). Remains of the ancient walls and a few old mosques, but it reflects little of its former glories. A centre of desert routes from Sumerian times, modern Baghdad was founded in A.D. 762 by the Abbasid caliph Al-Mansur, on the site of a Babylonian town. Enlarged by caliph Harun al-Rashid, and under him and his successor Mamun acquired fame for learning and commerce, as the 'Abode of Peace' and the fabled city of the *Thousand and One Nights*. Sacked (1258) by the Mongols, who destroyed the irrigation system, the foundation of Mesopotamian prosperity. The caliphate fell, and with it the splendour of Baghdad. By 1638, when it was taken by the Turks, it had shrunk to a town of minor significance. When Iraq became an independent state after the 1st World War (1927) Baghdad became the capital and its fortunes began to revive.

**Bagnères-de-Bigorre** France. Ancient Vicus Aquensis. Spa in the Hautes-Pyrénées department on the Adour R. 12 m. SSE of Tarbes. Pop. (1968) 11,122. Mineral springs, known since Roman times. Textile and engineering industries.

**Bagnolet** France. Industrial suburb to the E of Paris, in the Seine-St Denis department. Pop. (1968) 34,039. Manufactures plaster of Paris, furniture, etc.

**Baguio** Philippines. Mountain resort, summer capital, and goldmining centre in Luzon, 130 m. N of Manila at a height of 4,500 ft. Pop. (1960) 50,331. Severely damaged during the 2nd World War. A conference of SE Asian countries and Australia was held here 1950.

**Bahamas** W Indies. British archipelago in the Atlantic Ocean, extending SE over 700 m., from 50 m. E of the SE Florida coast. Total area 4,404 sq. m. (but only about 20 of the hundreds of islands, rocks, and cays are inhabited). Pop. (1963) 131,428 (about 80 per cent Negroes, descendants of liberated slaves from the USA). Cap. and chief seaport Nassau, on the island of New Providence. The islands are built of coral and are low-lying, nowhere exceeding 500 ft in height. The soil is thin, dry, and not favourable to agriculture, though vegetation may obtain moisture from the porous subsoil. They lie between lat. 21° N and 27° N, and are subject to hurricanes, which may cause considerable damage; rainfall is heavy in summer, when temperatures are high. Frosts are unknown, and the mild winter climate attracts many visitors (esp. from the USA and Canada), who are the principal source of revenue. A large area is unproductive, but there are forests of yellow pine, and timber is exported. Little more than 1 per cent of the land is arable, producing vegetables and fruit (inc. pineapples, bananas, citrus fruit) for local consumption. The sponge fisheries, once important, are now of little value, but crawfish are caught and exported to the USA. Salt panning is one of the principal industries; salt is a valuable export.

**San Salvador** (Watling's Island) was probably Columbus's first landfall in America (12 Oct. 1492). British settlers arrived in the 17th cent. British possession of the islands was confirmed by the Treaty of Versailles (1783). The islands served as a base for blockade runners during the American Civil War, and for bootleggers during Prohibition times. The colony was granted internal self-government 1964.

**Bahariya Oasis** ◊ *Western Desert.*

**Bahawalpur** Pakistan. Capital of the Bahawalpur division of W Pakistan, near the Sutlej R. 60 m. SSE of Multan. Pop. (1961) 84,377. Former capital of the Bahawalpur state. Industrial and commercial centre. Manufactures cotton goods, soap, etc. Trade in rice, cotton, etc.

**Bahia (Baía)** Brazil. Maritime state in the E. Area 216,556 sq. m. Pop. (1960) 5,990,605. Cap. Salvador. A fertile coastal plain up to 50 m. wide, backed by a stepped escarpment, with valleys parallel to the coast and a broad N–S mountain range. Inland is the central Brazilian plateau, crossed by the middle São Francisco R. About 90 per cent of Brazil's cacao crop produced in the SE. Sugar-cane, tobacco, and cotton grown in the Recôncavo district near Salvador. Principal mineral industrial diamonds.

**Bahía Blanca** Argentina. Rail centre and seaport in Buenos Aires province, serving the S pampas, at the head of the Bahía Blanca (Blanca Bay). Pop. (1960) 136,137. Exports grain, wool, meat, hides. Meat packing, oil refining, flour milling, tanning, etc. A fort and trading post since 1828.

**Bahrain (Bahrein) Islands** Persian Gulf. Group of islands between the Qatar peninsula and the mainland of Saudi Arabia; an independent Arab sheikhdom under British protection. Area 231 sq. m. Pop. (1965) 182,203 (mainly Shia and Sunni Muslims). Cap. Manama. The main island, Bahrain ('Two Seas'), 30 m. long and 10 m. wide, is connected by causeway with Muharraq Island, 4 m. long and 1 m. wide. Other islands are Sitra and Umm An-Nasaan. Oil was discovered on Bahrain 1932. The wells are linked by pipeline with a refinery which also processes oil carried by pipeline from Dhahran in Saudi Arabia. Also dhow building and other minor industries. The once famous pearl fishing has greatly declined.

**Bahr el Ghazal** Sudan. In Arabic, 'Gazelle River'. River formed from several streams. It joins the Bahr el Jebel near L. No, and forms the Bahr el Abiad (White ◊ *Nile*). Impeded by sudd, but navigable for steamers July–Oct. as far as Wau on the Jur R. ◊◊ *Chad, Lake*.

**Bahr el Jebel** Sudan. In Arabic, 'Mountain River'. A section of the White ◊ *Nile*, between Nimule and the point where it joins the Bahr el Ghazal (near L. No), below which it is called the Bahr el Abiad (White Nile). Flows through sudd swamps, but is navigable between Juba and Nimule, except along rapids.

**Baía** ◊ *Bahia*.

**Baiae** (modern **Baia**) Italy. A favourite resort of the ancient Romans, on the Gulf of Pozzuoli 9 m. WSW of Naples, notorious for luxury and immorality. Julius Caesar and Nero had villas there. A theatre and three sets of baths were discovered 1953. Modern Baia is a small village (pop. *c.* 1,000).

**Baia-Mare** Rumania. Capital of Maramures district in the NW, 34 m. ESE of Satu-Mare. Pop. (1968) 68,077 (inc. many Hungarians). Industrial centre. Important chemical industry; lead and zinc smelting, etc.

**Baikal, Lake** USSR. The largest freshwater lake in Asia and the deepest lake in the world, in SE Siberia (RSFSR). Area 12,700 sq. m. Greatest depth 5,300 ft. Altitude 1,500 ft. Receives over 300 streams, mostly mountain torrents, as well as the Selenga, Barguzin, and Upper Angara rivers. The only outlet is the Angara R. Frozen for over 4 months of the year; otherwise navigated by steamers. The Trans-Siberian Railway skirts the S shore. Unusual fauna, inc. a deep-sea fish and the Baikal seal. Well stocked with edible fish, e.g. sturgeon, herring, salmon. The largest island is Olkhon.

**Baja (Lower) California** Mexico. A rugged mountainous peninsula in the NW, 730 m. long, extending SE from, and geographically a continuation of, California (USA). Divided into the state of Baja California – area 27,064 sq. m.; pop. (1969) 1,044,000; cap. Mexicali – and the territory of Baja California Sur – area 28,439 sq. m.; pop. (1969) 106,000; cap. La Paz. From its mountain ranges, rising to 10,100 ft in the Sierra San Pedro Mártir, short unnavigable streams drain W to the Pacific and E to the Gulf of California. The climate is generally hot and arid and the region largely barren, with settlements concentrated mainly near the US border, where irrigation has enabled cotton, fruits, vegetables, and vines to be grown. Some minerals are worked, and there is pearl and deep-sea fishing off the S coast.

**Bajada de Santa Fé** ◊ *Paraná*.

**Bakersfield** USA. Town in California on the Kern R. 110 m. NNW of Los Angeles. Pop. (1960) 56,848. In an important oilfield, with refineries. Manufactures refinery equipment, chemicals, etc.

**Bakewell** England. Urban district in Derbyshire, 10 m. W of Chesterfield. Pop. (1961) 3,603. Market town. Home of Bakewell tarts. Chatsworth House (Duke of Devonshire) and Haddon Hall (Duke of Rutland) are near by.

**Bakhchisarai** USSR. In Tatar, 'Garden Palace'. Town in S Crimea (RSFSR), 16 m. SW of Simferopol. Pop. 16,000. Manufactures copper and leather goods. Former capital of the Crimean khans (princes), whose palace, the Khan Sarai, was destroyed (1736) but restored by Potemkin (1787).

**Bakhmut** ◊ *Artemovsk*.

**Bakony Forest** Hungary. Densely forested hill country N of L. Balaton. Chief town Veszprem. Vineyards on the S slopes. Deposits of bauxite and manganese.

**Baku** USSR. Capital of Azerbaijan SSR, on the S coast of the Apsheron peninsula on the Caspian Sea. Pop. (1970) 1,261,000. Important seaport and oil-producing centre. Oil refining, shipbuilding. Manufactures oil-drilling equipment, chemicals, cement, textiles, etc. Connected by double pipeline with the Black Sea port of Batumi.

Oil is also shipped to Astrakhan. Principal cultural centre of Azerbaijan. Seat of a state university (1919) and the Azerbaijan Academy of Science (1945). In the old city in the SW are the 12th-cent. Maiden's Tower (now a lighthouse) and the remains of the 15th-cent. Palace of the Khans. The main residential area and public buildings are in the new city. Baku was known to Arab geographers in the 10th cent. Its oil and gas wells (which sometimes burned spontaneously) were revered by Zoroastrian fire-worshippers. From the 16th to the 18th cent. it was under Persian rule and was incorporated in Russia 1806. Rapid growth came with the development of the oil industry in the 1870s. Output has declined since 1940 and has been overtaken by the 'Second Baku' in the Volga–Ural region.

**Bala** Wales. Urban district in Merioneth, on the R. Dee at the N end of L. Bala (4 m. long, the largest natural lake in Wales). Pop. (1961) 1,603. Market town.

**Balaklava** USSR. Small port in S Crimea (RSFSR), 8 m. S of Sevastopol, famous for the battle (1854) during the Crimean War when the charge of the Light Brigade took place. Pop. 2,000.

**Balaton, Lake** Hungary. The largest lake in Central Europe, SW of Budapest. Area 230 sq. m. Shallow; frozen in winter. Vineyards and orchards around the shores. Many summer tourist resorts.

**Balbi, Mount** ⟡ *Bougainville*.

**Balboa** Panama Canal Zone. Port at the Pacific end of the Panama Canal, just W of Panama City. Pop. (1960) 3,100. Extensive docks and wharves; ship repairing, etc. Named after Vasco Nuñez de Balboa, who first crossed the Panama isthmus (1513).

**Balbriggan** Irish Republic. Small town in Co. Dublin on the Irish Sea 20 m. N of Dublin. Pop. (1966) 3,248. Famous for hosiery.

**Baldock** England. Urban district in Hertfordshire, on the R. Ivel 4 m. NE of Hitchin. Pop. (1961) 6,764. Manufactures hosiery etc.

**Bâle** ⟡ *Basel*.

**Balearic Islands** Spain. Archipelago off the E coast, in the Mediterranean Sea; a province. Area 1,935 sq. m. Pop. (1961) 443,327. Cap. Palma (Majorca). Consists of four large islands – Majorca (Mallorca); Minorca (Menorca); Iviza (Ibiza); Formentera – and several islets. Generally undulating, rising to 4,741 ft in Puig Mayor near the N coast of Majorca. Vines, almonds, olives, and cereals are grown. Fishing is important. The climate has made the islands (esp. Majorca) popular with tourists. The people, who are akin to the Catalans, provided both Carthaginian and Roman armies with regiments of stoneslingers. Later the islands came under Vandal, Byzantine, and Moorish rule. Became a dependency of Aragon 1349.

**Bali** Indonesia. Island just E of Java, across the Bali Strait. Area 2,100 sq. m. Pop. 1,633,000. Chief town Singaraja. Largely mountainous and volcanic, rising to over 10,000 ft in Mt Agung. Equable climate, fertile soil, and luxuriant vegetation; often called 'the Jewel of the East'. The women are famed for their beauty and graceful dancing. Hinduism, the principal religion, was brought from India in the 7th cent. Rice, copra, and coffee are leading products. Trade with the Netherlands began in the 17th cent. but the island did not come wholly under Dutch rule until 1908.

**Balikesir** Turkey. Capital of the Balikesir province in the NW, 100 m. SSW of Istanbul. Pop. (1965) 69,300. Commercial centre. Trade in cereals, opium, etc. Flour milling. Manufactures textiles, rugs, etc.

**Balikpapan** Indonesia. Seaport in SE Borneo on the Strait of Makassar. Pop. 30,000. Oil refinery. Scene of a naval battle between US and Japanese forces in the 2nd World War (1942).

**Balkan Mountains** (Bulgarian **Stara Planina**) Bulgaria. In Bulgarian, 'Old Mountains'. Mountain range extending across the country from the Yugoslav border to the Black Sea, rising to 7,795 ft in Yamrukchal and forming the watershed between the Danube and the Maritsa rivers. The most famous pass is the Shipka.

**Balkan Peninsula.** Extensive peninsula in SE Europe, between the Adriatic and the Ionian seas (W) and the Aegean and the Black seas (E). The N boundary is generally considered to lie along the Sava and the lower Danube rivers. Comprises Greece, Turkey-in-Europe, Bulgaria, Albania, and most of Yugoslavia. Mainly mountainous. Climate continental in the N, Mediterranean in the S. After the fall of the Byzantine Empire, it became one of the most backward areas of Europe, esp. under the Ottoman Empire. The wars of independence against Turkey, and subsequent conflicts between the independent Balkan countries, made the Balkans a most unstable and disruptive element in Europe in international politics in the late 19th and early 20th cent.

**Balkh** (now usually known as **Wazirabad**) Afghanistan. Town in the N, 12 m. WNW of Mazar-i-Sharif. Pop. 10,000. Built on the site of ancient Bactra (◊ *Bactria*) and called by natives 'the Mother of Cities'. Sacked (1220) by Genghis Khan; did not recover its earlier importance.

**Balkhash** USSR. Town on the N shore of L. Balkhash in the Kazakh SSR. Pop. 70,000. Connected by rail with the copper mines at Kounradski, 15 m. N. Copper smelting.

**Balkhash, Lake** USSR. Large shallow salt lake in the SE Kazakh SSR at a height of 900 ft. Area 7,000 sq. m. Fed chiefly by the Ili R. No outlet. Frozen for about 5 months annually. Probably once formed part of a much larger lake.

**Ballachulish** Scotland. Village in Argyllshire, on the S shore of Loch Leven. Large slate quarries, worked since 1760. Glencoe village is just E.

**Ballarat** Australia. Town in Victoria 67 m. WNW of Melbourne on a plateau at 1,420 ft. Pop. (1966) 56,304. Industrial and commercial centre and railway junction, having risen as a boom settlement in the 1851 gold rush. It survived the declining mineral production to become a market town for the surrounding agricultural area, with textile mills, railway workshops, paper mills, metal works, etc. The 'Eureka Stockade' incident, involving bloodshed among the miners, took place here 1854. The Welcome gold nugget, weighing over 2,200 oz., was found 1858.

**Ballater** Scotland. Small burgh in Aberdeenshire on the R. Dee 36 m. WSW of Aberdeen and 7 m. E of ◊ *Balmoral Castle*. Pop. (1961) 1,132. Resort, near picturesque moors and woods.

**Ballina** Irish Republic. Market town in Co. Mayo, on the R. Moy near the mouth on Killala Bay. Pop. (1966) 6,084. Salmon fisheries.

**Ballinasloe** Irish Republic. Town in Co. Galway on the R. Suck, 35 m. E of Galway. Pop. (1966) 5,828. Terminus of the Grand Canal. Agricultural centre. Famous annual livestock fair (Oct.). Brewing, flour milling, limestone quarrying.

**Ballinrobe** Irish Republic. Market town in Co. Mayo on the R. Robe, near the mouth on Lough Mask. Pop. (1966) 1,240. Noted for trout fishing. Near by is Lough Mask

House, home of Captain Boycott (1832–97), the ostracism of whom (as an absentee landlord's agent) during the Land League's 'Plan of Campaign' (1880) is the origin of the word 'boycott'.

**Ballybunion** Irish Republic. Fishing village and popular resort in Co. Kerry, at the mouth of the R. Shannon 9 m. WNW of Listowel. Pop. (1966) 1,160.

**Ballycastle** Northern Ireland. Town and resort in Co. Antrim, on Ballycastle Bay 44 m. NNW of Belfast. Pop. (1961) 2,643.

**Ballyclare** Northern Ireland. Town in Co. Antrim, 10 m. SW of Larne. Pop. (1961) 4,441. Linen and bleaching works.

**Ballymahon** Irish Republic. Small market town in Co. Longford, on the R. Inny 11 m. S of Longford. Pop. 700. Pallas (2 m. E) is the probable birthplace of Oliver Goldsmith (1730–74); near-by Lissoy is the 'Sweet Auburn' of his *Deserted Village*.

**Ballymena** Northern Ireland. Town in Co. Antrim, on the R. Braid 18 m. W of Larne. Pop. (1961) 14,740. Manufactures linen. Bleaching and dyeing works.

**Ballymoney** Northern Ireland. Market town in Co. Antrim, 7 m. SE of Coleraine. Pop. (1961) 3,409. Linen manufacture, milk processing, etc.

**Ballyshannon** Irish Republic. Town in Co. Donegal, at the mouth of the R. Erne on Donegal Bay 11 m. SSW of Donegal town. Pop. (1966) 2,233. Salmon-fishing centre. Seaside resort. Hydroelectric plant on the river.

**Balmoral Castle** Scotland. In Gaelic, 'Majestic Dwelling'. A private home of British monarchs, in Aberdeenshire on the right bank of the R. Dee 7 m. W of Ballater. Bought by Prince Albert for Queen Victoria, who built the castle (1854) in white granite in 'Scottish-baronial' style.

**Balsas, Río de las** ◊ *Mexico*.

**Baltic Sea** (Ger. **Ostsee**) Europe. Ancient Mare Suevicum. Sea in N Europe, bounded by Denmark, Sweden, Finland, USSR, Poland, and Germany. Connected with the North Sea by the Sound, the Great Belt, the Little Belt, the Kattegat, and the Skagerrak. Area 163,000 sq. m. (inc. the Kattegat). Unusually shallow, reaching its greatest depth (253 fathoms) off Gotland; very small tides. A large number of rivers empty into it, giving low salinity; this and the shallowness cause large areas to become icebound for 3–5 months in winter. Major inlets are the Gulf of Bothnia (N), the Gulf of Finland (E), the Gulf of Riga, and the

Gulf of Gdańsk. Principal islands are those of Denmark; Fehmarn (FGR); Gotland and Öland (Sweden): Ahvenanmaa (Finland); Saaremaa and Hiiumaa (USSR); Rügen (GDR). Linked with the North Sea by the Kiel Canal and the Göta Canal (through Swedish lakes).

**Baltimore** USA. Important seaport, also the largest city and chief industrial and commercial centre in Maryland, at the head of a 12-m.-long branch of Chesapeake Bay, with a deep natural harbour formed by the estuary of the Patapsco R. Pop. (1970) 895,222. Chief exports grain, coal, iron and steel. Main imports metallic ores (esp. iron) and petroleum. Manufactures machinery, tractors, railway equipment, aircraft, chemicals, textiles, clothing. Steel mills, copper refineries, printing works, canneries, meat-packing plants, sugar and oil refineries. A great steelworks was built (1916) on a tidewater site at Sparrows Point 10 m. away, and large shipyards are there. In the 19th cent. 'Baltimore clippers' gained a world reputation.

Despite the disastrous fire of 1904, which destroyed much of the business quarter, it is noted for its public buildings, monuments, squares and parks, and has been nicknamed 'Monumental City'. Seat of the Johns Hopkins University (1876), some schools of the University of Maryland, and several colleges. Its Roman Catholic archbishop ranks as Primate of the USA. Founded 1729. Grew rapidly in the 19th cent., shipping goods from the interior to Europe. The defence of Fort McHenry against the British (1814) inspired Francis Scott Key to write *The Star-spangled Banner*. It was the Atlantic port closest to the National Pike Road, the first trans-Appalachian highway, and the Baltimore and Ohio RR (begun 1828) was the first railway in the USA. The world's first nuclear-powered lighthouse, to guide shipping in and out of the harbour, was put into operation 1964.

**Baltistan** India. Region in the W Ladakh district, in Kashmir, inhabited by Balti, a Muslim people of Tibetan origin. Chief town Skardu. Mountainous, containing K2 (28,250 ft) and other peaks of the Karakoram mountains.

**Baluchistan** Pakistan. Region of W Pakistan, bounded by Afghanistan (N), the Arabian Sea (S), and Iran (W). Area 134,000 sq. m. Chief town Quetta. The N was formerly under British control; the S comprised the princely states of Kalat, Kharan, Las Bela, and Makran. Largely mountainous, with lofty ridges, e.g. the Sulaiman, Kirthar, and Central Makran ranges, separating arid deserts from fertile valleys. Rainfall scanty; rivers intermittent. Cereals and fruits produced where there is water. Camels, sheep, goats raised. Quetta is reached by the famous Bolan Pass. Natural gas, produced at Sui, is sent by pipeline to Karachi and Multan. A railway runs through the Bolan Pass and via Quetta to the Afghan frontier; a branch line turns W into Iran. The three main sections of the population (predominantly Muslim) are the Baluchi, the Pathans, and the Brahui, who speak different languages (Baluchi, Pushtu, Brahui). Crossed several times by the invaders of India; Alexander the Great passed through the S on his return to Persia from India (325 B.C.). Much of it was held by the Arabs in the 7th–10th cent. Later ruled by tribal chiefs. British control of the N was secured during the Afghan Wars of the 19th cent. and a military base was established at Quetta. Passed to Pakistan 1947.

**Bamako** Mali. Capital, on the R. Niger. Pop. (1967) 170,000. Formerly capital of the French Soudan. Connected by rail with Dakar. Important trading centre for the W Sudan.

**Bamberg** Federal German Republic. Town in N Bavaria on the canalized Regnitz R. near the confluence with the Main, 32 m. NNW of Nuremberg. Pop. (1963) 73,700. Engineering, brewing. Manufactures textiles, footwear, etc. Trade in vegetables, fruit, etc. From 1007 to 1802 the seat of independent prince-bishops. The Romanesque cathedral, founded (1004) by the Emperor Henry II, contains the marble tomb of the founder and his wife.

**Bamburgh** England. Village and resort in Northumberland, on the E coast 16 m. SE of Berwick. Pop. (1961) 410. Capital of the kings of Northumbria in the 6th cent. Birthplace, home, and burial-place of Grace Darling (1815–42).

**Bamu** ◊ *Stanley Pool*.

**Bananal Island** ◊ *Araguaia River*.

**Banat** Rumania. Former administrative region (till 1968), in the W. Area 8,415 sq. m. Cap. Timişoara. The name *banat* was originally given to any Hungarian frontier province or territory governed by a *ban* (viceroy), but came to be applied specifically to the Banat of Temesvár (Timişoara), mainly a fertile plain between the Tisza R. and the Transylvanian Alps. This belonged mainly to Hungary from the 11th cent. onwards. After the 1st World War it was divided, except for a small district near Szeged, between Rumania and Yugoslavia, and the name was then used only of the Rumanian region.

**Banbridge** Northern Ireland. Market town in Co. Down, on the R. Bann 22 m. SW of Belfast. Pop. (1961) 6,115. Manufactures linen, rope, fishing nets.

**Banbury** England. Municipal borough in Oxfordshire on the R. Cherwell 22 m. N of Oxford. Pop. (1961) 20,996. Market town. Manufactures aluminium products, electrical goods, etc. Food processing. Iron ore mined in the neighbourhood. Famous for over 300 years for its cakes. The Banbury Cross celebrated in nursery rhyme was destroyed by Puritans in the 17th cent. but replaced by another in the 19th cent.

**Banda Islands** Indonesia. Group of volcanic islands in the S Moluccas, S of Ceram. Total area 20 sq. m. Pop. 14,000. Largest island Bandalontar (Great Banda). Products nutmegs, mace, copra.

**Bandama River** ◊ *Ivory Coast*.

**Bandar** ◊ *Masulipatnam*.

**Bandar Pahlavi (Pahlavi)** Iran. Port in Gilán province on a lagoon of the Caspian Sea 14 m. NW of Rasht. Pop. (1964) 33,990. Exports rice, hides, etc. Fishing.

**Bandjarmasin (Banjermasin)** Indonesia. Capital of the S Kalimantan province (S Borneo) and port on the Barito R. 24 m. from the mouth. Pop. (1961) 214,096. Exports timber, rattan, rubber, etc. Seat of the Lambung Mangkurat University (1960).

**Bandon** Irish Republic. Town in Co. Cork on the R. Bandon 15 m. SW of Cork City. Pop. (1966) 2,294. Tanning, brewing, whisky distilling. Founded in the early 17th cent. by Richard Boyle, 1st Earl of Cork, father of the chemist Robert Boyle.

**Bandung** Indonesia. Capital of the W Java province 80 m. SE of Jakarta, at a height of 2,400 ft. Pop. (1961) 972,566. Manufactures textiles, quinine, rubber products, etc. Also a health resort and cultural centre. Seat of a university (1958) and an Institute of Technology. Beautiful mountain and forest scenery in the neighbourhood.

**Banff** Canada. Resort in SW Alberta, on the Bow R. 63 m. WNW of Calgary in the Rocky Mountains at 4,538 ft. Pop. 2,500. The Canadian Pacific Railway station for the Banff National Park, famous for spectacular scenery (with several peaks over 10,000 ft), mountain lakes, and glaciers. Hot sulphur springs.

**Banff** Scotland. County town of Banffshire, a royal burgh, on the Moray Firth at the mouth of the R. Deveron. Pop. (1961) 3,329. Seaside resort. Fishing. Whisky distilling.

**Banffshire** Scotland. County in the NE, on the Moray Firth. Area 630 sq. m. Pop. (1961) 46,400. County town Banff. A low-lying coastal strip in the N; mountainous in the S, the Cairngorm mountains rising to over 4,000 ft along the S border. Drained by the Spey and the Deveron rivers. Cattle rearing. Fishing. Largest town Buckie.

**Bangalore** India. Capital of Mysore, 180 m. W of Madras, at a height of 3,000 ft. Pop. (1961) 905,134. Road and railway junction. Important textile industry. Also manufactures electrical apparatus and radio sets, machinery, footwear, etc. Seat of a university (1964) and the Indian Institute of Science (1911). Founded in the 16th cent. Under British rule, had the largest cantonment in S India (returned to Mysore 1947). Has expanded rapidly in recent years with the development of industries.

**Bangka (Banka)** Indonesia. Island separated from the SE coast of Sumatra by the Bangka Strait. Area (with near-by islets) 4,611 sq. m. Pop. 280,000. Chief town Pangkalpinang. One of the world's chief tin-mining centres; also deposits of iron, lead, etc.

**Bangkok (Thai Krung Thep)** Thailand. Capital and chief seaport, on the Chao Phraya R. 15 m. from the mouth. Pop. (1964) 1,656,747. Exports rice, rubber, tin, etc. Industrial centre. Rice milling, saw-milling, railway engineering, oil refining, cement manufacture, etc. At the centre of the city is the 18th-cent. royal town, founded by Rama I as his capital, after the fall of Ayutthaya. The royal temple of Wat Phra Keo (1785) has a remarkable image of Buddha. Numerous government offices and public buildings. Transport through the city was formerly by boat along the many canals (*klongs*) but since the 1890s modern roads have been constructed. Seat of 5 universities: Chulalongkon (1917), Thammasart (1934), and the Universities of Medical Science, Agriculture, and Fine Arts.

**Bangor** Northern Ireland. Municipal borough and seaside resort in Co. Down, on the S side of Belfast Lough 11 m. ENE of Belfast. Pop. (1961) 23,865. Ruins of an abbey founded by St Comgall in the 6th cent.

**Bangor** USA. Town in Maine on the Penobscot R. 110 m. NE of Portland. Pop. (1960) 38,912. Manufactures wood pulp, paper, clothing, etc. A prosperous lumbering and shipbuilding centre in the 19th cent.

**Bangor** Wales. Municipal borough in Caernarvonshire, at the N end of the Menai Strait. Pop. (1961) 13,977. Educational centre, seat of the University College of N Wales (founded 1884), a constituent college of the University of Wales since 1893. The 15th/16th-cent. cathedral was restored in the late 19th cent. Slate exported from Port Penrhyn within the borough.

**Bangui** Central African Republic. Capital of the republic, formerly capital of Ubangi-Shari, on the Ubangi R. and on the S border with Congo (Kinshasa). Pop. (1964) 82,500. Commercial centre. Produces palm oil, soap, etc.

**Bangweulu, Lake** Zambia. Shallow lake on a plateau at a height of 3,700 ft, bordered by swamps. Area 3,800 sq. m. Fed by the Chambezi (♢ *Congo*) R. and drained by the Luapula R. Discovered (1868) by David Livingstone, who died on its shore in 1873.

**Banias (Baniyas)** Syria. Small fishing port on the Mediterranean 90 m. SW of Aleppo. Terminal of the oil pipeline from Kirkuk (Iraq). ♢ *Caesarea Philippi*.

**Banja Luka** Yugoslavia. Town in Bosnia and Hercegovina, on the Vrbas R. 90 m. NW of Sarajevo. Pop. (1961) 51,158. Commercial centre. Manufactures textiles. Brewing, flour milling, etc. An Orthodox cathedral, a 16th-cent. mosque (and many others), and remains of Roman baths.

**Banjermasin** ♢ *Bandjarmasin*.

**Banka** ♢ *Bangka*.

**Banks Island** (British Columbia) Canada. Island 43 m. long, in the Hecate Strait off the Pacific coast.

**Banks Island** (NW Territories) Canada. The most westerly island of Canada's Arctic Archipelago, in the SW Franklin District. Area 26,000 sq. m. Mainly plateau, rising to over 2,000 ft in the S. First explored (1851) by McClure.

**Bannockburn** Scotland. Small town in Stirlingshire, 2 m. SSE of Stirling, on the Bannock Burn, a tributary of the R. Forth. Pop. (1961) 4,760. Near by is the site of the battle (1314) in which Robert Bruce defeated Edward II of England and ensured Scottish independence.

**Bann River** Northern Ireland. River rising in the Mourne mountains as the Upper Bann, and flowing 40 m. NW, past Banbridge and Portadown, into the S end of Lough Neagh. The Lower Bann leaves the N end of Lough Neagh, flows 40 m. NNW, through Lough Beg and past Coleraine, to the sea. Famous for salmon fishing.

**Banstead** England. Urban district in E central Surrey, near Epsom; 14 m. from London, one of its dormitory towns. Pop. (1961) 41,573.

**Bantry** Irish Republic. Town at the head of Bantry Bay, 45 m. WSW of Cork. Pop. (1966) 2,341. Manufactures tweed.

**Bantry Bay** Irish Republic. Picturesque inlet on the SW coast of Co. Cork, 23 m. long and 4–6 m. wide. Fine natural anchorage. Contains Whiddy Island and Bear Island. Scene of the famous attempted landing of a French force under General Hoche, whose 14 warships were scattered by storms (Christmas 1796). Whiddy Island was chosen as the site of a large oil storage depot.

**Bapaume** France. Town in the Pas-de-Calais department 72 m. SE of Calais. Pop. (1968) 4,114. Flour milling, brickmaking, and other industries. Scene of a French victory over the Prussians (1871). In the 1st World War, changed hands several times and was almost entirely destroyed. Again suffered severe damage in the 2nd World War.

**Baranagar** India. Industrial town in W Bengal, on the Hooghly R. just N of Calcutta. Pop. (1961) 107,837. Jute and cotton milling. Manufactures chemicals, machinery, etc.

**Barbados** W Indies. Former British colony; a low-lying island, the most easterly of the W Indies. Area 166 sq. m. Pop. (1969) 250,686. Cap. and chief seaport Bridgetown. The highest point is Mt Hillaby (1,203 ft), in the centre. Volcanic dust from the neighbouring island of St Vincent has covered the coral limestone and produced a fertile soil which is intensively cultivated. The tropical heat is moderated by the NE Trade Wind Dec.–May; rainfall is heavy and comes mainly during the hot season. Chief crop sugar-cane. Sugar is by far the most important export, followed by molasses and rum. Bridgetown, in Carlisle Bay on the SW coast, has the only harbour; the island, almost encircled by coral reefs, was provided with new deep-water berths 1961. Probably first visited by the Portuguese, who named it Los Barbados ('Bearded') on account of the many bearded fig trees. The English landed in 1605; colonization began in 1628, and from then Barbados was continuously held by Britain. Became independent 1966. Disastrous hurricanes occurred in 1780, 1831, and 1898. The present greatest problem is the high density of population – 1,510 per sq. m.

**Barbary Coast** Africa. The N African coast from Morocco to Tripolitania. Named after the Berber (the principal inhabitants). Notorious from the 16th to the 19th cent. as the haunt of pirates: Moors joined with Algerian and Tunisian corsairs and preyed on shipping in the Mediterranean or levied 'appeasement' tribute from European countries. Several European and US expeditions were sent against the pirates in the 19th cent.: piracy was not wiped out till the French stormed ◊ *Algiers* (1830).

**Barberton** S Africa. Town in the SE of the Transvaal, near the Swaziland frontier, at a height of 2,825 ft. Pop. (1960) 11,016. Developed 1882–6 as the result of a gold rush, which was over by 1887; declined as a mining town, but became the centre of a prosperous agricultural area producing cotton and citrus fruits.

**Barberton** USA. Industrial town in Ohio just SW of Akron. Pop. (1960) 33,805. Manufactures tyres, chemicals, boilers, etc.

**Barbizon** France. Village in the Seine-et-Marne department, on the edge of the forest of Fontainebleau. Gave its name to the 'Barbizon School' of painters – Corot, Millet, Rousseau, Daubigny, and other 19th-cent. artists who made it their home.

**Barbuda** W Indies. A low-lying coral island in the Leeward Is., a dependency of ◊ *Antigua*, which is 28 m. to the S. Area 62 sq. m. Pop. (1960) 1,145. Produces sea-island cotton, sugar-cane.

**Barca (Barce, El Merg)** Libya. Town in Cyrenaica, 50 m. ENE of Benghazi, with which it is connected by rail. Pop. 10,000. Founded by the Greeks and Libyans in the 6th cent. B.C. Captured by the Persians 512 B.C. Later ruled by the Ptolemies. Fell to the Arabs in the 7th cent. A.D. Severely damaged by earthquakes, with loss of life, 1963.

**Barcellona Pozzo di Gotto** Italy. Market town in the Messina province in Sicily, 18 m. W of Messina. Pop. (1961) 32,138. Trade in wine and olive oil.

**Barcelona** Spain. **1.** Province in the NE, in Catalonia, on the Mediterranean Sea. Area 2,985 sq. m. Pop. (1961) 2,877,966. Mountainous in the N. Narrow coastal plain. Drained by the Llobregat R. and its tributaries. The most densely populated and highly industrialized province in Spain.
**2.** Ancient Barcino. Capital of Barcelona province, on the Mediterranean. Pop. (1967) 1,697,102. The second largest city in Spain, its main seaport and industrial and commercial centre. Exports textiles and machinery, which it manufactures along with chemicals, leather goods, plastics, etc. Also exports wine, olive oil, and cork from the interior. Overlooked from the S by the castle on the Montjuich hill (574 ft). Bisected by the Ramblas, a famous avenue constructed over a dry river-bed. In the old city are the 13th/15th-cent. cathedral (damaged in the Civil War, 1937), the 14th-century Church of Santa María del Mar, the 16th-cent. Episcopal Palace, and the Palacio de la Diputación (seat of the old parliament of Catalonia). Centre of Catalan culture. University (1430). Founded by the Carthaginians, named after Hamilcar Barca. Prospered under the Romans and Visigoths. Captured by the Moors and Franks. Ruled by independent Counts of Barcelona from the 9th to the 12th cent. After the union of Catalonia with Aragon (1137), became one of the leading Mediterranean seaports. Its maritime code, the *Consulado del Mar*, was widely recognized. When Catalonia was incorporated into Spain relations with the central government were frequently strained. Barcelona became the centre of Catalan separatism, and also of anarcho-syndicalism and socialism. In the Spanish Civil War (1936–9) it was the seat of the government, but after many air attacks finally surrendered to the Franco forces Jan. 1939.

**Barcelona** Venezuela. Capital of the Anzoátegui state in the NE, on the Neveri R. 3 m. from the mouth. Pop. (1961) 40,733. Commercial centre. Exports cattle, hides, skins, etc. through its port, Guanta.

**Bardia** Libya. Village and port on the Mediterranean coast of Cyrenaica, near the United Arab Republic frontier. Came into prominence during the 2nd World War as the starting-point of the Italian campaign against Egypt (1940). Subsequently captured and recaptured by the British and the Germans alternately, changing hands five times in 1941–2 until finally held by the British.

**Bardsey** Wales. Island in Caernarvonshire, 2 m. long and 1 m. wide, separated from the Lleyn peninsula by Bardsey Sound. Ruins of an abbey founded in the 6th cent. A medieval place of pilgrimage. Lighthouse.

**Bareilly** India. Industrial and commercial town and railway junction in Uttar Pradesh, 135 m. ESE of Delhi. Pop. (1961) 254,409. Trade in grain and sugarcane. Produces carpets, furniture, sugar, etc. Founded 1537. Passed to the British 1801.

**Barents Sea** Arctic Ocean. Shallow part of the Arctic, bounded by Norway, European USSR, Novaya Zemlya, Spitsbergen, and Franz Josef Land. Named after Willem Barents, a 16th-cent. Dutch navigator who made three voyages in search of the NE passage. Navigation in the N part is hampered by pack-ice. The S part is warmed by the N Atlantic Drift and has become an important fishing ground.

**Barfleur** France. Small fishing port in the Manche department, 16 m. E of Cherbourg. Pop. (1968) 874. An important point of embarkation for England in the Middle Ages. William, only son of Henry I of England, was drowned when the *White Ship* sank off Barfleur (1120); traditionally Henry 'never smiled again'.

**Barfrush** ◊ *Babol.*

**Bari** Italy. Ancient Barium. Capital of Bari province, in Apulia, a seaport on the Adriatic Sea 140 m. ENE of Naples. Pop. (1968) 345,108; has grown rapidly from 77,000 (1901) and 162,000 (1936). Iron foundries, oil refinery, canneries, flour mills. Manufactures textiles, soap, etc. Exports wine, olive oil, fruit, etc. A Roman colony, later governed by Goths, Lombards, Byzantines, and Normans. An embarkation port for the Crusades. Cathedral (12th-cent.). University (1924).

**Barinas** Venezuela. Capital of Barinas state, 140 m. SW of Barquisimeto, in the cattle-rearing and oil-producing llanos. Pop. (1961) 25,707.

**Barisal** Pakistan. Town in E Pakistan, on the Ganges–Brahmaputra delta 70 m. S of Dacca. Pop. (1961) 70,025. Rice and flour milling. Manufactures soap etc. Trade in rice, jute, oilseeds. Suffered severely, with considerable loss of life, from cyclone and tidal waves in May 1965.

**Barking** England. Greater London borough (1965) comprising the former municipal borough of Barking (Essex) on the R. Roding (except the part W of Barking Creek) and the former municipal borough of Dagenham (Essex) (except the N part of Chadwell Heath Ward). Pop. (1963) 178,645. It has a large power station, rubber, chemical and paint factories, and the huge Ford Motor Works (Dagenham).

**Barkly East** S Africa. Town in Cape Province near the S end of the Drakensberg at 5,950 ft. Pop. (1962) 3,648. Sheep-farming centre. Noted for fine mountain scenery. Connected by rail with Aliwal North. Named after Sir Henry Barkly, Governor of the Cape 1870–77.

**Bar-le-Duc** France. Prefecture of the Meuse department, on the Ornain R. and the Marne–Rhine Canal 45 m. W of Nancy. Pop. (1968) 20,384. Metal working, brewing. Manufactures textiles, jam, etc. Capital of the medieval counts (later dukes) of Bar. Several 15th/17th-cent. houses and remains of the ducal palace. Birthplace of the 2nd Duke of Guise (1519–63), Charles Oudinot (1767–1847), Count Exelmans (1775–1852), and Raymond Poincaré (1860–1934).

**Barletta** Italy Seaport in the Bari province in Apulia, on the Adriatic Sea 35 m. WNW of Bari. Pop. (1961) 68,035. Chemical, soap, cement, and other industries. Important trade in wine and fruits. A 12th/15th-cent. cathedral. During the French siege of Barletta (1503), a famous combat took place between 13 picked knights of Italy and France – the *Disfida di Barletta* of d'Azeglio.

**Barmouth** Wales. Urban district in Merioneth, on Cardigan Bay at the mouth of the R. Mawddach 6 m. W of Dolgellau. Pop. (1961) 2,348. Seaside resort.

**Barnard Castle** England. Urban district in Durham, on the R. Tees 15 m. W of Darlington. Pop. (1961) 4,969. Market town. Remains of the 12th-cent. castle, built by Bernard de Baliol, which figures in Scott's *Rokeby*.

**Barnaul** USSR. Capital of the Altai Territory (RSFSR), on the Ob R. and the Turksib Railway. Pop. (1970) 439,000. Engineering, sawmilling, food processing. Manufactures textiles, footwear, etc. Founded as a mining centre 1739. Expanded rapidly as a manufacturing town in the 1930s.

**Barnes** England. Former municipal borough in Surrey, on the R. Thames, 6 m. WSW of London; from 1965 part of the Greater London Borough of Richmond upon Thames. Pop. (1961) 39,757. A dormitory suburb which includes Mortlake and E Sheen. The famous 17th-cent. Kitcat Club held its meetings in a cottage here. Barnes Bridge is the finishing point of the annual boat race between Oxford and Cambridge universities. St Paul's School (Boys') moved here from Hammersmith in 1968.

**Barnet** England. Greater London borough (1965) comprising the former urban districts of Barnet and E Barnet (Hertfordshire), Friern Barnet (Middlesex), and the municipal boroughs of Finchley and Hendon (Middlesex). Pop. (1963) 318,051. Scene of a battle (1471) in the Wars of the Roses in which the Earl of Warwick (the Kingmaker) was killed.

**Barnoldswick** England. Urban district in the W Riding of Yorkshire, 12 m. WNW of Keighley. Pop. (1961) 10,267. Manufactures cotton goods.

**Barnsley** England. County borough in the W Riding of Yorkshire, on the R. Dearne 11 m. N of Sheffield. Pop. (1961) 74,650. Coalmining. Engineering, clothing, and carpet industries.

**Barnstaple** England. Municipal borough in Devonshire, on the estuary of the R. Taw 34 m. NW of Exeter. Pop. (1961) 15,907. Market town. Holiday resort. Manufactures lace, gloves, pottery ('Barum ware'), etc. A 15th-cent. stone bridge of 16 arches across the Taw and a 14th-cent. parish church. Birthplace of John Gay (1685–1732), composer and librettist of *The Beggar's Opera*.

**Baroda** India. Former capital of the princely state of Baroda, now in Gujarat, 240 m. N of Bombay. Pop. (1961) 295,144. Industrial and cultural centre. Railway junction. Manufactures textiles, chemicals, matches, metal goods, etc. Trade in cotton. Distinguished by its handsome public buildings. Seat of the Maharaja Sayajirao University (1949).

**Baro River** ◊ *Sobat River.*

**Barotseland** Zambia. The most westerly province, in the Upper Zambezi basin. Area 48,798 sq. m. Pop. (1965) 390,600. Administrative centres Mongu, Lealui. Consists mainly of tropical grasslands or savannah, where African tribes (inc. the paramount Barotse) raise cattle and cultivate maize.

**Barquisimeto** Venezuela. Formerly Nueva Segovia. Capital of the Lara state, in the NW, on the Barquisimeto R., in a hilly coffee-growing district on the Pan-American Highway. Pop. (1961) 199,691. Trade in coffee, sugar, cacao, rum. Flour milling, tanning. Manufactures textiles, cement, leather goods, etc. Founded (as Nueva Segovia) 1552. Destroyed by earthquake 1812.

**Barra** Scotland. Island in the Outer Hebrides, in Inverness-shire, separated from S Uist by the Sound of Barra. Area 35 sq. m. Pop. (1961) 1,467 (2,250 in 1931). Chief town Castlebay. Mountainous, rising to 1,260 ft. Herring fishing; but the fishing industry has declined, causing depopulation.

**Barrackpore (Barrackpur)** India. Town in W Bengal on the Hooghly R. 15 m. N of Calcutta. Pop. (1961) 63,778. Jute and rice milling and other industries. Formerly an important military station.

**Barrancabermeja** Colombia. River port on the E bank of the middle Magdalena R. Pop. 65,000. A leading oil-drilling and refining centre, with a 335-m. pipeline to Cartagena; the refined products are piped to Medellín, Manizales, and Bogotá.

**Barranqueras** ◊ *Resistencia.*

**Barranquilla** Colombia. Capital of the Atlántico department, important seaport and international airport, on the Magdalena R. 10 m. from the mouth. Pop. (1968) 498,301. Now accessible to ocean-going vessels by a dredged channel. Industrial centre. A wide range of manufactures, e.g. textiles, vegetable oils, chemicals, foodstuffs. ◊ *Cartagena* (Colombia).

**Barreiro** Portugal. Town in the Setúbal district, on the S bank of the Tagus estuary opposite and SE of Lisbon. Pop. (1960) 30,399. Manufactures cork products, fertilizers, etc. Flour milling. Linked with Lisbon by ferry.

**Barren Island, Cape** ◊ *Furneaux Islands.*

**Barrhead** Scotland. Small burgh and industrial town in Renfrewshire, 7 m. SW of Glasgow. Pop. (1961) 14,422. Textile, bleaching and dyeing, sanitary-ware, and light-engineering industries.

**Barrier Reef** ◊ *Great Barrier Reef.*

**Barrow-in-Furness** England. County borough of NW Lancashire, on the coast of Furness. Pop. (1961) 64,824. Sheltered seawards by Walney Island, to which it is connected by a road bridge. Its growth from a small fishing village of 325 people

(1847) to a major industrial centre was due chiefly to the discovery in the area of rich hematite iron ore (1840). Large iron and steel works were established. Shipbuilding followed (both merchant and naval vessels, inc. many submarines; the first British nuclear submarine was launched here 1960). Engineering. Manufactures paper, chemicals, etc.

**Barrow Island** ◊ *Monte Bello Islands.*

**Barrow River** Irish Republic. River 120 m. long, rising in the Slieve Bloom Mountains and flowing first E and then S to Waterford Harbour. Navigable to Athy, 65 m. up-river, and then linked to Dublin by a canal.

**Barrow Strait** Canada. Channel 40 m. wide separating the Bathurst, Cornwallis, and Devon islands (N) from the Prince of Wales and Somerset islands (S). On the route from Baffin Bay through the Canadian Arctic archipelago to the Beaufort Sea. Named after Sir John Barrow.

**Barry** Wales. Municipal borough in Glamorganshire, on the Bristol Channel 8 m. SW of Cardiff. Pop. (1961) 42,039. Seaport. Exports coal, cement, steel goods, etc. Flour milling etc. Barry Island (just S, and joined to the mainland) is a popular holiday resort.

**Bartlesville** USA. Town in Oklahoma, on the Caney R. 41 m. N of Tulsa. Pop. (1960) 27,893. Commercial centre in an oil-producing region. Oil refining, zinc smelting, etc.

**Barwon River** ◊ *Darling River.*

**Basel** (Fr. **Bâle**, English **Basle**) Switzerland. Ancient Basilia. Town in the NW, on the Rhine, on the French and German frontiers, forming (with three villages) the half-canton of Basel-Stadt. Pop. (1969) 216,600 (the second largest in Switzerland). Important commercial, industrial, and railway centre. Chemical, metal, silk, and printing industries. Divided by the Rhine (navigable downstream) into Greater Basel (left bank) and Lesser Basel. Founded by the Romans. Became a free imperial city in the 11th cent. Joined the Swiss Confederation 1501. The minster (cathedral) of red sandstone is the burial-place of Erasmus. A 16th-cent. Rathaus and a museum with a fine Holbein collection. Seat of a university (founded (1460) by Pope Pius II), the oldest in Switzerland.

**Basel Canton** Switzerland. Divided into two half-cantons in 1833. 1. *Basel-Land*: The countryside surrounding Basel-Stadt, on

the N slopes of the Jura mountains. Area 165 sq. m. Pop. (1969) 200,500. Produces cereals. Watch-making. Textile industry. Salt mines. 2. *Basel-Stadt*: Practically coterminous with the town of ◊ *Basel*. Area 14 sq. m. Pop. (1969) 238,600.

**Bashkir ASSR** USSR. Autonomous republic of RSFSR, at S end of and mainly W of the Urals. Area 55,430 sq. m. Pop. (1970) 3,819,000 (40 per cent Russians, 24 per cent Bashkirs – formerly nomadic people of Muslim religion). Cap. Ufa. It has important oilfields, part of the Volga–Ural ('Second Baku') region, with the longest pipeline in the USSR connecting the Tuimazy oilfield with refineries at Omsk (1955). Iron, copper, manganese, and other metallic ores also mined. Cereals, potatoes, sugar-beet cultivated. Butter and cheese produced. Chief industrial centres Ufa, Sterlitamak, Beloretsk.

**Basildon** England. Urban district, 'new town' in S Essex, 10 m. S of Chelmsford. Pop. (1961) 88,459. Formed (1955) from the townships of Billericay, Laindon, Pitsea, and Wickford. Engineering, printing, etc. Manufactures tobacco products, aircraft equipment, etc.

**Basilicata (Lucania)** Italy. Region in the S, between the Gulf of Taranto and the Tyrrhenian Sea, comprising the provinces of Potenza and Matera. Area 3,855 sq. m. Pop. (1961) 648,085. Mountainous in the W, rising to over 6,000 ft. Cereals, olives, vines cultivated. Chief towns Potenza, Matera.

**Basingstoke** England. Municipal borough in Hampshire, 27 m. NNE of Southampton. Pop. (1961) 25,940. Market town and road and rail centre. Manufactures agricultural implements, clothing, leather, bricks, etc. Near by are the ruins of Basing House, burned down (1645) by Cromwell's Parliamentary forces after a two years' siege.

**Basle** ◊ *Basel.*

**Basque Provinces** Spain. The provinces of Álava, Guipúzcoa, and Vizcaya in the NE, on the Bay of Biscay. Total area 2,803 sq. m. Total pop. (1961) 1,371,654. Álava is mainly agricultural, producing maize, sugar-beet, vines, and fruits. The two maritime provinces, Guipúzcoa and Vizcaya, are highly industrialized, with mining, engineering, shipbuilding, and fishing industries. The Basques are an ancient people; their language is distinct from any other European or world tongue.

Converted late to Christianity (from the 3rd to the 5th cent.), they have remained fervent Catholics but preserve a strong tradition of being independent of either Spain or France. The Guernica Oak, an ancient tree under which the Council met, remained for centuries a symbol of liberty. Two of their most famous figures were St Ignatius Loyola and St Francis Xavier. They settled in their present region in the 9th cent. and founded the kingdom of Navarre. Later, under the Castilian kings, they enjoyed special democratic rights, but their prosperity diminished after the conquest of Navarre by Ferdinand of Aragon in the 16th cent. The special rights were abolished in 1876. In the Spanish Civil War (1936–9) they supported the government, setting up an autonomous Basque government in Guernica, but were subjugated by Franco's forces (1937) after the bombing of Guernica by air squadrons from Nazi Germany.

**Basra** Iraq. Chief port, and capital of Basra province, on the Shatt-al-Arab 70 m. from the Persian Gulf, linked by rail with Baghdad. Pop. (1965) 313,327. Exports chiefly dates, also wool, barley, oil. Originally founded at Az Zubeir, about 8 m. distant. Became famous in the time of Harun al-Rashid but later declined, and silting sealed it off from the Persian Gulf. Its modern port was opened up by the British in the 1st World War. Became an important supply base for the USSR in the 2nd World War. Conversion of the Basra–Baghdad railway from metre to standard gauge was completed in 1964.

**Bas-Rhin** France. Department in the E, comprising the N part of Alsace, bounded on the E and N by the Federal German Republic and on the W by the Vosges mountains. Area 1,850 sq. m. Pop. (1968) 827,367. Prefecture Strasbourg. The lowlands are fertile, growing cereals, hops, fruits, vegetables. Wine produced on the E slopes of the Vosges. The region is highly industrialized. Manufactures machinery, locomotives, leather, textiles. Chief towns Strasbourg, Haguenau.

**Bassano del Grappa** Italy. Town in Vicenza province in the NE, 19 m. NNE of Vicenza. Pop. (1961) 30,497. Manufactures metal goods, pottery, etc. Tanning, printing, etc. The cathedral, several churches, and the museum contain works by the 16th–17th-cent. da Ponte family of artists, surnamed Bassano after their birthplace. Napoleon defeated the Austrians near by in 1796.

**Bassein** Burma. Port in Lower Burma, on the Bassein R. (the westernmost distributary of the Irrawaddy R.), 70 m. from the mouth. Pop. 78,000. Centre of the rice trade. Rice milling. Pottery manufacture.

**Bassenthwaite, Lake** England. Lake 4 m. long and ¾ m. wide, in the Lake District in Cumberland 3 m. NW of Keswick. Skiddaw (3,054 ft) is 2 m. E.

**Basses-Alpes** France.* Department in the SE, in Provence, bordering on Italy in the NE. Area 2,697 sq. m. Pop. (1968) 104,813 Prefecture and chief town Digne. Mountainous and infertile in the N and E. Drained by the Durance and its tributaries, inc. the Verdon. Olives, fruits, vines produced in the valleys.

**Basses-Pyrénées** France. Department in the SW, formed from Béarn and part of Gascony, bordering on Spain, and bounded by the Bay of Biscay (W), and the crest of the Pyrenees (S). Area 2,977 sq. m. Pop. (1968) 508,734 (largely Basque). Prefecture Pau. Drained by the Adour R. and its tributaries. Hydroelectric power developed from the mountain streams. Maize, wheat, fruits, wine produced in the lowlands. Livestock raised in the highlands. Many popular spas and resorts: Biarritz, St-Jean-de-Luz, Hendaye on the coast; Pau and several smaller towns such as Salies and Cambo inland. Chief towns Pau, Bayonne.

**Bass Rock** Scotland. Islet in E Lothian, 350 ft high and 1 m. in circumference, at the entrance to the Firth of Forth. Used as a prison in the 17th cent. Now has a lighthouse. Sea-bird sanctuary.

**Bass Strait** S Pacific Ocean. Channel 75–150 m. wide separating mainland Australia and Tasmania, linking the Indian Ocean (W) with the Tasman Sea (E), and containing King Island and the ◊ *Furneaux Islands*. Identified as a strait (1798) by Surgeon George Bass, R.N.

**Bastia** France. Chief town and seaport of Corsica, on the NE coast. Pop. (1968) 50,100. Exports wine, fish, fruits, etc. Fishing. Manufactures tobacco products etc. Founded by the Genoese in the 14th cent. The *bastiglia* (fortress), built 1383, was later replaced by a citadel, which dominates the port and old town. Severely damaged in the 2nd World War.

**Basutoland** ◊ *Lesotho*.

**Bataan** Philippines. Peninsula in S Luzon

30 m. long and 15-20 m. wide on the W side of Manila Bay. Heroically defended during the 2nd World War for 3 months (1942) against the Japanese by American and Filipino forces. Recaptured 1945.

**Batangas** Philippines. Seaport and capital of Batangas province, on S Luzon. Pop. (1960) 82,819. Trade in rice, sugarcane, etc.

**Batavia** ◊ *Jakarta*.

**Bath** England. Ancient Aquae Sulis. County borough in NE Somerset, on the R. Avon 10 m. ESE of Bristol. Pop. (1961) 80,856. Minor industries, e.g. biscuit manufacture. Chiefly known as a spa. The Romans probably discovered the hot springs *c.* A.D. 50, and excavations have revealed remains of their watering-place. In the Middle Ages wool-weaving was important. In the 18th cent., through the inspiration of Beau Nash (1674–1761) and the architectural genius of John Wood and his son (also John Wood), such features as Royal Crescent, Lansdown Crescent, and the Assembly Rooms were built. The Assembly Rooms were destroyed by bombing in the 2nd World War, and were restored and reopened in 1963. Bath, one of England's most beautiful cities, also has a 16th-cent. abbey church, and old houses built with Bath stone, quarried locally. University (1966). It has given its name to an invalid chair and a bun. Birthplace of the journalist C. P. Scott (1846–1932).

**Bathgate** Scotland. Industrial town in W Lothian, 16 m. WSW of Edinburgh. Pop. (1961) 12,686. Coal and shale-oil mining. Automobile engineering. Manufactures metal goods, paper, etc. Birthplace of the physician Sir James Simpson (1811–70).

**Bathurst** Australia. Town in New South Wales, on the Macquarie R. 100 m. WNW of Sydney. Pop. (1966) 17,220. One of the first settlements W of the Blue Mountains (1815) and scene of an early gold rush (1851). Still a mining and stock-rearing centre, with tanning and flour-milling industries, in a sheep-farming and wheat-growing region.

**Bathurst** Canada. Port on the NE coast of New Brunswick, in the Gulf of St Lawrence. Pop. (1966) 15,526. Pulp and paper mill, raw material for which comes from near-by forests of black spruce. Salmon fisheries. Large deposits of lead, zinc, and copper were discovered (1953) in the district.

**Bathurst** Gambia. Capital and chief sea-port, on St Mary's Isle at the mouth of the Gambia R. Pop. (1963) 27,809. Exports chiefly groundnuts and groundnut oil, also palm kernels. Has two deep-water wharves.

**Bathurst, Cape** Canada. Promontory on the N coast of the mainland, in the NW Territories, projecting into the Beaufort Sea. Like several other localities of the same name, it commemorates Earl Bathurst, British Colonial Secretary 1812–28.

**Bathurst Inlet** Canada. Arm of the Arctic Ocean, extending S nearly 140 m. from Coronation Gulf into the NW Territories. Also a trading post.

**Bathurst Island** Canada. One of the Parry Is. in the Arctic Ocean N of the Barrow Strait. Area 7,300 sq. m.

**Batley** England. Municipal borough in the W Riding of Yorkshire, 6 m. SSW of Leeds. Pop. (1961) 39,390. Centre of heavy woollen manufacture. Shoddy was first manufactured here. Coalmines in the neighbourhood.

**Baton Rouge** USA. State capital, industrial town, and river port of Louisiana, at the head of navigation for ocean-going ships on the Mississippi, 70 m. WNW of New Orleans. Pop. (1960) 152,419. Oil refineries and petrochemical industries. Seat of the Louisiana State University (1860).

**Battersea** England. Former metropolitan borough of SW London, on the S bank of the R. Thames, here crossed by the Battersea (1890), Albert (1873), and Chelsea (1937) bridges; from 1965 part of the Greater London borough of Wandsworth. Pop. (1961) 105,758. Battersea Park (200 acres) beside the river is one of London's playgrounds, has sculptures by Henry Moore, and in 1951 accommodated the amusement section of the Festival of Britain. The power station is one of the largest in Europe. The Battersea Dogs' Home is almost equally famous. Formerly (18th cent.) noted for enamel ware. Much damaged by bombing during the 2nd World War.

**Battle** England. Town in E Sussex, 6 m. NW of Hastings. Pop. (1961) 4,300. Named after the Battle of Hastings, actually fought at Battle in 1066. Ruins of Battle Abbey, founded by William the Conqueror to commemorate his victory.

**Battle Creek** USA. Town in S Michigan at the confluence of the Kalamazoo R. and Battle Creek, 110 m. W. of Detroit. Pop. (1960) 44,169. In a maize- and wheat-growing region. Manufactures cereal foods (Post and Kellogg factories), agricultural implements, etc.

**Batumi** (Russian **Batum**) USSR. Capital of the Adzhar ASSR, SW Georgia, on the E coast of the Black Sea. Pop. (1970) 101,000. One of the chief seaports. Naval base. Exports petroleum and manganese. Connected by an oil pipeline with Baku and Alyaty. Main industries oil refining, marine and railway engineering, fruit and vegetable canning. Manufactures metal cans, clothing, etc. Tea, tobacco, and citrus-fruit plantations in the neighbourhood. Resort, with a mild sub-tropical climate. Ceded to Russia by Turkey 1878.

**Bauchi (Jos) Plateau** Nigeria. Highlands in Central Nigeria, rising to over 5,000 ft. The name, 'Land of Slaves', refers to the long practice of slave raiding in the area. Important tin mines had been worked by the Africans; large-scale European exploitation began in 1902, and ◊ *Jos* became the principal mining centre.

**Bautzen** German Democratic Republic. Industrial town in the Dresden district, on the Spree R. 32 m. ENE of Dresden. Pop. (1965) 43,853. Manufactures textiles, railway rolling stock, machinery, etc. The 15th-cent. cathedral has been used since 1635 by both Protestants and Roman Catholics (kept apart by an iron screen). Scene of the defeat of a combined Russian and Prussian army by Napoleon (1813).

**Bavaria** (Ger. **Bayern**) Federal German Republic. A *Land* in the S, bordering in the NE on the German Democratic Republic, in the E on Czechoslovakia, in the SE and S on Austria. Area 27,232 sq. m. Pop. (1964) 9,846,600. Cap. Munich. Bounded on the S by the Alps, on the E by the Bohemian Forest (Böhmerwald), and on the NE by the Fichtelgebirge and the Franconian Forest (Frankenwald); crossed by lower ranges, e.g. the Franconian Jura, between which there are wide plains and fertile valleys. Drained chiefly by the Danube and the Main (linked by the Ludwig Canal) and their tributaries. Predominantly agricultural and pastoral: cereals and potatoes are the main crops; large numbers of cattle and pigs are raised. Valuable forests. Industries are centred on Munich, Nuremberg, Augsburg, Regensburg, Würzburg. Brewing is important. Abounds in beautiful mountain and lake scenery, and has many picturesque towns and villages, some of which preserve much of their medieval appearance, e.g. Rothen-

burg. This, together with the Wagner opera festival at Bayreuth and the Passion Play at Oberammergau, make it a popular tourist area.

The earliest inhabitants were Celts. Conquered by the Romans near the end of the 1st cent. B.C. Became a duchy, ruled from 1180 by the House of Wittelsbach, which became the oldest dynasty in Europe. Fought in alliance with Prussia against France 1870. Joined the German Empire 1871. The last Wittelsbach king abdicated in 1918, there was an abortive Communist revolution, and Bavaria became a republic. Hitler's first attempt to seize power took place in Bavaria (1923), and the headquarters of the Nazi party were in Munich. After the 2nd World War the Rhenish Palatinate (the detached territory on the W bank of the Rhine) and the Lindau district were lost to Bavaria, and it was made a *Land* of the Federal German Republic in 1949.

Since the 18th cent. the largest of the S German states, Bavaria has always preserved a strong sense of individuality. About 71 per cent of the population are Roman Catholic, 27 per cent Protestant. The universities at Munich and Würzburg are Catholic, that at Erlangen is Protestant.

**Bay City** USA. Port in Michigan, at the head of Saginaw Bay on L. Huron, 100 m. NNW of Detroit. Pop. (1960) 53,604. Manufactures automobile parts, cranes, prefabricated buildings, lake boats, etc. Sugar refineries.

**Bayeux** France. Ancient market town in the Calvados department in the NW, 17 m. WNW of Caen. Pop. (1968) 12,871. Manufactures lace and pottery. Noteworthy 12th/13th-cent. cathedral. In the museum is the famous 'Bayeux Tapestry', illustrating William the Conqueror's invasion and conquest of England, possibly made by his wife Queen Matilda. One of the first French towns to be liberated from the German occupation (1944).

**Bay Islands** (Sp. **Islas de la Bahía**) Honduras. Group of islands in the Gulf of Honduras, forming a department. Area 144 sq. m. Pop. (1964) 8,961. Largest island Roatán, 30 m. long and 9 m. wide. Chief products coconuts, bananas, pineapples. Discovered by Columbus 1502. Occupied by British settlers in the 17th cent, and made a British colony 1852. Ceded to Honduras 1859.

**Bay of Biscay** N Atlantic Ocean. Ancient

Sinus Aquitanicus. Wide inlet of the Atlantic Ocean, between the W coast of France and the N coast of Spain. The name is a corruption of Basque 'Vizcaya'. Notorious for sudden storms and choppy seas.

**Bay of Islands** Canada. Bay on the W coast of Newfoundland, studded with many small islands. Several fishing settlements along the shores.

**Bay of Plenty** New Zealand. Wide inlet into the NE coast of the N Island. Contains several small islands (Makatana, Mayor, White).

**Bayonne** France. Town in the Basses-Pyrénées department in the SW, at the confluence of the Nive and the Adour rivers near the Bay of Biscay. Pop. (1968) 45,175. Chief port of the Basque country. Exports steel products, timber, brandy, etc. Distilling, flour milling. Manufactures fertilizers. Steel works at Boucau near by. Gothic cathedral (13th/15th-cent.). Birthplace of the artist Bonnat (1833–1922), whose house is now an art museum. Formerly renowned for the manufacture of cutlery and swords (possibly the origin of the word 'bayonet').

**Bayonne** USA. Industrial town in New Jersey, on a long narrow peninsula just S of Jersey City between Newark Bay and Upper New York Bay. Pop. (1960) 74,125. Terminal of the oil pipeline from Texas. Chief industries oil refining and manufactures of chemicals, cables, boilers.

**Bayreuth** Federal German Republic. Town in Upper Franconia, Bavaria, 40 m. NE of Nuremberg. Pop. (1963) 61,700. Manufactures textiles, pottery, etc. Noted for its connexion with Richard Wagner; an annual festival of his works is held in the Festspielhaus. Burial-place of Franz Liszt, Richter, and Wagner. Has an 18th-cent. opera house. Severely damaged in the 2nd World War.

**Bayswater** England. Residential district in the former metropolitan borough of Paddington, W London (from 1965 in the City of Westminster). Named after Baynard's Water, the former name of the Westbourne, which flowed into the Serpentine. Tyburn Tree, the famous gallows, stood near Marble Arch.

**Baytown** USA. Industrial town in Texas, founded 1947, on Galveston Bay 23 m. E of Houston. Pop. (1960) 28,159. Centre of an oil-producing region. Oil refining. Manufactures chemicals, synthetic rubber, etc.

**Beachy Head** England. Headland 570 ft high, on the Sussex coast between Eastbourne and Seaford, consisting of chalk cliffs at the E end of the S Downs. Lighthouse. Scene of a naval battle (1690) when combined English and Dutch fleets were defeated by the French.

**Beaconsfield** England. Urban district in S Buckinghamshire, 22 m. WNW of London. Pop. (1961) 10,019. Home of Edmund Burke, who is buried here. Many associations with Disraeli, who took (1876) the title of Earl of Beaconsfield.

**Beardmore Glacier** Antarctica. Huge glacier, one of the world's largest, moving from the Queen Alexandra Range to the Ross Ice Shelf. Discovered (1908) by Sir Ernest Shackleton.

**Béarn** France. Former province in the SW, now part of the Basses-Pyrénées department, into which it was incorporated in 1790. The people are partly Basque. Agriculture and stock rearing. United with France in 1589 when Henry of Navarre ('le Béarnais') became king of France. Incorporated into the French kingdom 1620.

**Bearsden** Scotland. Small burgh in Dunbartonshire 6 m. NW of Glasgow, formed in 1958. Pop. (1968) 22,625. Mainly residential.

**Beas River** India. One of the 5 rivers of the Punjab, rising at 13,000 ft in the Himalayas and flowing 290 m. generally W and SW, joining the Sutlej 25 m. ENE of Ferozepore.

**Beauce** France. Natural region (pays) in the Paris Basin, a dry, fertile limestone plain, comprising parts of the Eure-et-Loir, Loir et-Cher, Loiret, Essonne and Yvelines departments. Chief town Chartres. Known as 'the granary of Paris' because of its wheat production.

**Beaufort Sea** Arctic Ocean. That part of the Arctic between N Alaska and ◊ Banks Island. Shallow in the S and E, deepening to 12,000 ft or more in the NW. Usually covered with drifting ice.

**Beaufort West** ◊ Karroo.

**Beaujolais** France. Region formerly in the Lyonnais province, now forming the N part of the Rhône department and part of the Loire department, on the NE edge of the Massif Central. Famous for Burgundy wines, produced on the valley slopes. Chief trading centre Villefranche.

**Beaulieu** England. Pronounced Bewly. Village in S Hampshire, on the Beaulieu

R. at the edge of the New Forest 6 m. SSW of Southampton. Ruins of a Cistercian abbey, founded by King John (1204). The refectory is restored and serves as the parish church. At the Palace House, seat of Lord Montagu, is the Montagu motor museum, a collection of veteran cars, etc.

**Beauly** Scotland. Pronounced 'Bewly'; a corruption of Beaulieu. Village in N Inverness-shire, at the head of Beauly Firth, on the Beauly R. (formed by the confluence of the Farrar and the Glass; the Glass is formed by the confluence of the Cannich and the Affric, the latter flowing through the beautiful Glen Affric). Ruins of the Cistercian Priory of St John, founded in the 13th cent.

**Beaumaris** Wales. Municipal borough in Anglesey, at the N end of the Menai Strait. Pop. (1961) 1,960. Seaside resort. Ruins of a 13th/14th-cent. castle built by Edward I. Elizabethan grammar school (1603).

**Beaumont** USA. Town in Texas, 80 m. ENE of Houston, at the end of the deepwater canal from Port Arthur. Pop. (1960) 119,175. Commercial and industrial centre. Trade in petroleum, timber, rice, cotton. Oil-refining, synthetic rubber, paper, meat-packing, and other industries.

**Beaune** France. Town in the Côte d'Or department 23 m. SSW of Dijon. Pop. (1968) 17,377. Famous for Burgundy wines. Manufactures agricultural implements, casks, etc. The historic buildings include the famous 15th-cent. Hôtel-Dieu, with a polyptych of the Last Judgement by van der Weyden, and the 12th/13th-cent. Church of Notre Dame.

**Beauvais** France. Ancient Caesaromagus and Bellovacum. Prefecture of the Oise department, on the Thérain R. 40 m. NNW of Paris. Pop. (1968) 49,347. Market town. Trade in dairy produce, apples, cereals, etc. Manufactures tiles, brushes, rayon, etc. Formerly noted for Gobelin tapestries; the industry was moved to Paris after the factory was destroyed in the 2nd World War. An annual festival, dating from 1472, when Jeanne Hachette defended the town against Charles the Bold. The famous cathedral (begun 1227 and never completed) has the highest of all Gothic choirs (157 ft). Scene of the R 101 airship disaster (1930).

**Bebington** England. Municipal borough just S of Birkenhead on the Wirral peninsula in Cheshire. Pop. (1961) 52,202. Includes Bromborough (docks and chem-ical works), Eastham (at the W end of the Manchester Ship Canal), and Port Sunlight (a model town built in 1888 for the workers of Lever Bros, now Unilever, where soap, margarine, etc. are manufactured).

**Bec Abbey** France. Ruined Benedictine abbey in the village of Le Bec-Hallouin in the Eure department 20 m. SW of Rouen. Founded 1034. Became a medieval centre of learning, from which Lanfranc and Anselm went to Canterbury.

**Beccles** England. Municipal borough in NE Suffolk, on the R. Waveney. Pop. (1961) 7,330. Market town. Flour milling, malting, printing. Noted for crayfish. Has a 14th-cent. church with a detached belfry.

**Bechuanaland** ◊ *Botswana*.

**Beckenham** England. Former municipal borough of NW Kent, a dormitory suburb of SE London, including W Wickham; from 1965 part of the Greater London borough of Bromley. Pop. (1961) 77,265. In Beckenham is the Bethlem Royal Hospital, the first mental hospital in England, founded 1247 and moved here from London 1930.

**Beddgelert** Wales. Village and holiday resort in Caernarvonshire, S of Snowdonia, 10 m. SE of Caernarvon. Pop. (1961) 760. Associated with the story of Gelert, the faithful hound of Llewelyn ap Iorweth, which protected Llewelyn's son from a wolf; but Llewelyn, thinking it had slain his child, killed it. The name, however, probably means 'St Kelert's grave'.

**Beddington and Wallington** England. Former municipal borough in NE Surrey, a dormitory suburb of S London; from 1965 part of the Greater London borough of Sutton. Pop. (1961) 32,588.

**Bedford** England. County town of Bedfordshire, municipal borough, on the R. Ouse 45 m. NNW of London. Pop. (1961) 63,317. Manufactures agricultural implements, electrical goods, pumps, beer, confectionery, bricks. Associated with John Bunyan (born at the near-by village of Elstow), who wrote parts of *The Pilgrim's Progress* during his 12-year imprisonment in Bedford jail. The philanthropist and prison reformer John Howard was High Sheriff of Bedfordshire; there are statues to him and to Bunyan. The well-known public school (founded 1552) was endowed by Sir William Harper (d. 1573), Lord Mayor of London, a native of Bedford.

**Bedfordshire** England. County in the S Midlands. Area 473 sq. m. Pop. (1961) 380,704. County town Bedford. Generally low-lying, drained by the Great Ouse and its tributary the Ivel. Hilly in the S (Chiltern Hills). Primarily agricultural, with wheat cultivation and market gardening. Other towns Luton (where industries are largely centred), Dunstable, Leighton Buzzard, Biggleswade. Many associations with John Bunyan (◊ *Bedford*).

**Bedlington** (**Bedlingtonshire**) England. Urban district in SE Northumberland, 11 m. N of Newcastle upon Tyne, inc. the coalmining town of Bedlington. Pop. (1961) 29,373. Famous for a breed of terriers.

**Bedwas and Machen** Wales. Urban district in Monmouthshire, on the R. Rhymney 7 m. N of Cardiff. Pop. (1961) 10,231. In a coalmining area.

**Bedwellty** Wales. Urban district in Monmouthshire 5 m. SSE of Tredegar. Pop. (1961) 27,336. In a coalmining area.

**Bedworth** England. Urban district in Warwickshire, 3 m. S of Nuneaton. Pop. (1961) 32,501. Coalmining and other industries.

**Beersheba** Israel. Town 46 m. SW of Jerusalem. Pop. (1968) 69,500. In biblical times it was at the S extremity of Palestine, Dan being at the N extremity – hence the phrase 'from Dan to Beersheba'. In the 1st World War it was captured by the British (1917). Has become an important commercial centre for the N Negev. Manufactures pottery, glass, etc.

**Beeston and Stapleford** England. Urban district in Nottinghamshire, 3 m. SW of Nottingham. Pop. (1961) 56,720. Engineering. Manufactures pharmaceutical products, hosiery, lace, etc.

**Behistun** (**Bisutun**) Iran. Village in the W, 18 m. E of Kermanshah, with a precipitous rock 1,700 ft high carrying a cuneiform inscription by Darius I in Old Persian, Susian, and Babylonian recording his defeat of the usurper Gaumata. Sir Henry Rawlinson climbed the rock (1835), copied the inscription, deciphered the Persian by 1846, and so made possible the decipherment of the Susian and Babylonian texts.

**Beira** Moçambique. Seaport on the Moçambique Channel, at the mouth of the Pungwe and Busi rivers 470 m. NNE of Lourenço Marques; capital of the Manica and Sofala district. Pop. 50,000. Built on a sandy spit, it has a relatively healthy climate. Linked by rail with Congo (Kinshasa), Malawi, Rhodesia, and Zambia; considerable trade with these, since improvements in harbour accommodation. Administered by the Moçambique Company 1891–1941; the charter was not renewed. Now administered by the Portuguese government.

**Beirut** Lebanon. Capital and chief seaport, on St George's Bay. Pop. (1961) 298,000. Educational centre with four universities – Lebanese (1951), American (1866), French (1881), and Arab (1937), the last a branch of Alexandria University. Food processing, engineering, textile manufacture. It existed in the 15th cent. B.C., and prospered under Seleucids, Romans, and Byzantines, but was severely damaged by earthquakes in the 6th cent. and again suffered from the Arab occupation in the 7th cent. From the 16th cent. it was held by the Turks almost continuously, though in fact dominated by the Druses, till after the 1st World War, when it became capital of Syria and Lebanon under French mandate; in 1941 it was made capital of the newly independent Lebanon.

**Beisan** (Hebrew **Beit Shean**) Israel. Ancient Bethshan; Scythopolis. Small town in the NE, 36 m. SE of Haifa, on the site of an ancient fortress, the biblical Bethshan. Excavations from 1921 onwards revealed remains dating back to 1500 B.C. and beyond, including temples mentioned in the Old Testament, Egyptian stelae, and the sarcophagus of Antiochus, cousin of Herod the Great. In Roman times the city of Scythopolis, capital of the Decapolis, stood here.

**Béja** Tunisia. Ancient Vaga (Vacca). Capital of the Béja governorate 55 m. W of Tunis. Pop. (1966) 72,034. Market town in the fertile Medjerda valley, in a district well known for centuries for its wheat. An important centre in Roman times.

**Békés** Hungary. Market town in the county of the same name, in the SE, on the White Körös R. 7 m. NNE of Bekescsaba. Pop. 29,000. In an agricultural region producing cereals, tobacco, etc.

**Bekescsaba** (**Csaba**) Hungary. Chief town of Békés county, 110 m. SE of Budapest. Pop. (1968) 53,000. Commercial centre and railway junction, in a fertile agricultural region. Flour mills, brickworks. Manufactures textiles, machinery, etc.

**Belaya River** USSR. River 700 m. long in the Bashkir ASSR, rising in the S Urals and flowing SW past Beloretsk, then N and NW past Sterlitamak and Ufa to join the Kama R. Important for transport and irrigation.

**Belaya Tserkov** USSR. Town in the Ukrainian SSR 50 m. SSW of Kiev. Pop. (1970) 109,000. Commercial centre. Flour mills. Manufactures leather goods, clothing, etc.

**Belcher Islands** ◊ *Hudson Bay*.

**Belém** Brazil. Capital of the Pará state, seaport, and major airport, on the Pará R. 85 m. from the open sea and just S of the equator. Pop. (1960) 359,988. Handles the products of the Amazon basin: rubber, Brazil nuts, hardwoods, babassu nuts, jute. Linked by an unpaved road with the new capital Brasilia. Originally a colonial fortified settlement. Developed rapidly with the rubber boom, but its trade is now more varied.

**Belfast** Northern Ireland. Capital, chief seaport, and industrial centre of Ulster; a county borough, at the mouth of the R. Lagan, on Belfast Lough, a deep navigable inlet from the Irish Sea. Pop. (1961) 416,094. Important shipyards and linen factories. Manufactures tobacco products, rope, clothing, whisky, etc. Pleasantly situated with the hills of Antrim to the N and those of Down to the S. Among its principal buildings are the City Hall and St Anne's Cathedral (Protestant), begun 1899, in Romanesque style. Seat of the Queen's University (founded 1845). Many fine public parks. Near by, at Stormont, is the classical-style Parliament building of Northern Ireland, built 1928–32. The history of Belfast goes back to the building of a castle at a ford over the Lagan in 1177. English and Scottish settlers were brought in during the 16th–17th-cent. 'Plantations', and the 'Old Irish' were expelled. The linen industry was stimulated by the influx of French Huguenots, after the revocation of the Edict of Nantes (1685). Shipbuilding developed with the aid of Scottish coal and iron towards the end of the 18th cent. The major growth came with the Industrial Revolution. Became a city 1888. Capital of Northern Ireland since 1920. Damaged by air raids in the 2nd World War. Birthplace of Lord Kelvin (1824–1907) and Sir John Lavery (1856–1941).

**Belfort** France. Prefecture of the Territoire de Belfort, 25 m. WSW of Mulhouse. Pop. (1968) 55,833. Commands the Belfort Gap between the Vosges and the Jura mountains; of strategic importance. Manufactures textiles, electrical machinery, locomotives, turbines, etc. The long siege in the Franco-Prussian War (1870–71) is commemorated by a huge carving of a lion (by Bartholdi, sculptor of the Statue of Liberty in New York harbour).

**Belfort, Territoire de** France. Department in the E, the only part of the former province of ◊ *Alsace* left to France after 1871. Area 235 sq. m. Pop. (1968) 118,450. Prefecture Belfort.

**Belgaum** India. Town in Mysore 240 m. SSE of Bombay at over 2,000 ft. Pop. (1961) 127,885. Manufactures textiles, leather, furniture, etc. Trade in rice etc. Taken by the British 1818.

**Belgian Congo** ◊ *Congo (Kinshasa)*.

**Belgium** (Fr. **Royaume de Belgique;** Flemish **Koninkrijk België**). Kingdom in NW Europe. Area 11,778 sq. m. Pop. (1968) 9,605,601. Cap. Brussels. Lang. Flemish and French. Rel. mainly Roman Catholic.

One of the smallest countries in Europe, bounded by the North Sea and the Netherlands (N), the Federal German Republic and Luxembourg (E), and France (S and SW). Also one of the most highly industrialized and most densely populated countries (816 per sq. m. in 1968). Intensive farming is also important. For administrative purposes it is divided into 9 provinces (with provincial capitals): Antwerp (Antwerp); Brabant (Brussels); W Flanders (Bruges); E Flanders (Ghent); Hainaut (Mons); Liège (Liège); Limbourg (Hasselt); Luxembourg (Arlon); Namur (Namur).

TOPOGRAPHY, CLIMATE. Mainly lowlying. Three regions. 1. In the N is the low sandy area of Flanders and the Campine (in Flemish, Kempen) with an almost straight coast fringed by dunes on which stands the port of Ostend, the largest of several popular seaside resorts. 2. The fertile central plain, between the Scheldt and Meuse rivers, both of which are navigable and, with a network of canals, provide an excellent system of inland waterways more than 1,000 m. in length. 3. In the SE is the largely forested plateau of the Ardennes, rising to over 2,000 ft. Near the coast the climate is maritime temperate, somewhat similar to that of SE England, but in the Ardennes conditions are more continental, with more severe winters and heavier rainfall.

RESOURCES, PEOPLE, *etc.* On the small farms heavy crops of cereals, potatoes, flax, sugar-beet, and hops are produced, and cattle are raised, but grain and other foodstuffs have to be imported. Industry is based on the coalfields of Hainaut (centred on Mons and Charleroi) and the Campine; output has fallen considerably in recent years, but iron and steel production – for which iron ore is imported from Lorraine (France) – has increased at Liège and other towns. Textiles rank second to metallurgy, the principal centre being Ghent. The great bulk of the country's trade is handled by Antwerp, on the Scheldt estuary, one of Europe's leading seaports, serving much of W Germany as well as Belgium. The Belgians are divided into two language groups by a line running approximately E–W just S of Brussels. To the N are the Flemings, who speak Flemish, and to the S the Walloons, whose language is French. Brussels is bilingual. Both Flemish and French are now official languages, but this has not prevented continuing controversy between the two groups as to their respective status and rights.

HISTORY. The country is named after the Belgae, the Celtic peoples who inhabited the area when it was conquered by Julius Caesar. In medieval times it was divided into several counties (Flanders etc.), duchies (Brabant etc.), and the bishopric of Liège; the great textile and commercial cities, e.g. Ghent, Bruges, then achieved virtual independence. In the 15th cent. what is now Belgium passed to the duchy of Burgundy and later to the Habsburgs. From Spain it was transferred to Austria (1713), France (1797), and then the Netherlands (1815). The Roman Catholic Belgians soon quarrelled with the Protestant Dutch, revolted, and had their independence recognized (1830). Prince Leopold of Saxe-Coburg became king, and his successor, Leopold II, gained wealth and some notoriety through his personal interest in the development of the Congo (annexed 1908). Belgium was invaded and occupied by the Germans in the 1st World War and again in the 2nd World War; it was largely the attitude of Leopold III during the second occupation which led to criticism and to his abdication in favour of his son Baudouin (1950). After the 2nd World War Belgium made a quick economic recovery and with the

Netherlands and Luxembourg formed a customs union known as Benelux (1947). The country's relations with its enormously wealthy Colony, the Belgian Congo, were less happy; independence was at last granted to Congo (Kinshasa) in 1960, but the people were ill prepared for self-government, and with the withdrawal of Belgian authority they were plunged into civil war.

**Belgorod** USSR. Town in RSFSR on the N Donets R. 50 m. NNE of Kharkov. Pop. (1970) 151,000. Flour milling, meat packing, tanning, etc. Chalk quarried in the neighbourhood.

**Belgorod-Dnestrovsky** USSR. Ancient Tyras. Formerly Cetatea Alba (Rumanian). Seaport on the Black Sea coast in Bessarabia, Ukrainian SSR, on a lagoon at the mouth of the Dniester R. Pop. 26,000. Trade in salt, canned fish, wine, etc. Held at various times by the Russians and the Turks. Became Rumanian 1918. Returned to the USSR in 1944 and renamed.

**Belgrade** (Serbo-Croat Beograd – 'White Town') Yugoslavia. Capital of Yugoslavia and of Serbia, at the confluence of the Danube and the Sava rivers. Pop. (1961) 598,346. River port, railway and road junction. Commercial centre. Manufactures electrical goods, textiles, chemicals; food processing. University (1863). In a strategic position between Central Europe and the Balkans, it has been frequently attacked and destroyed. There are few monuments to its past apart from Kalemegdan, the old Turkish fortress. First fortified by the Celts in the 3rd cent. B.C. Changed hands several times; became capital of Serbia 1403, but fell to the Turks 1521. The Turkish garrison finally withdrew in 1867. Again capital of Serbia from 1878, and became capital of Yugoslavia 1918. Severely damaged in the 2nd World War.

**Belgravia** England. Residential district in W London, S of Knightsbridge, mainly in the City of Westminster. Includes Belgrave, Eaton, and Cadogan Squares. Developed (*c.* 1826) on a reclaimed marsh.

**Belitung** ◊ *Billiton*.

**Belize** British Honduras. Capital and chief seaport, in a swampy area on both banks and at the mouth of the Belize R.; the harbour is shallow and obstructed with coral reefs and sandbanks. Pop. (1966) 38,482. Chief exports hardwoods (mahogany), bananas, coconuts, grapefruit. In

1961 Belize suffered severe damage and loss of life from a hurricane and a 15-ft tidal wave; plans were made to move the capital to an inland site.

**Bellagio** Italy. Village and holiday resort on L. Como, on a promontory dividing the two southern arms of the lake. Picturesque gardens and villas. Wood carving.

**Bellary** India. Town and railway junction in Mysore, 200 m. N of Mysore. Pop. (1961) 85,673. Manufactures textiles. Sugar milling. Trade in cotton. The ancient fort stands on a 450-ft granite rock.

**Bellegarde-sur-Valserine** France. Town in the Ain department at the confluence of the small Valserine R. with the Rhône, 16 m. SW of Geneva. Pop. (1968) 9,690. Manufacturing centre. Metallurgical, textile, and other industries. On the Rhône 4 m. S is the great Génissiat Dam and hydroelectric plant. The former gorge (La Perte du Rhône) has been submerged owing to the drowning of the valley above the dam.

**Belle-Île-en-Mer** France. Island in the Morbihan department, in the Bay of Biscay S of the Quiberon peninsula (Brittany). Area 32 sq. m. Pop. 5,000. Chief town Le Palais. The impressive cliffs are a tourist attraction. Main occupations fishing, sardine canning. Held by the British 1761–3, then ceded to France in exchange for Nova Scotia.

**Belle Isle** Canada. Small island at the E end of the strait of the same name separating Newfoundland from the coast of Labrador; the first land sighted by ships crossing the Atlantic. The strait, closed by ice Nov.–May, provides the shortest route from Europe to the St Lawrence estuary and seaway.

**Belleville** Canada. Town in SE Ontario, on L. Ontario 40 m. W of Kingston. Pop. (1966) 32,785. Meat packing, cheese making. Manufactures cement, plastics, machinery, etc.

**Belleville** (Illinois) USA. Town 15 m. SE of St Louis. Pop. (1960) 37,264. Industrial centre. Manufactures stoves, clothing, etc. Coal mined in the neighbourhood. US Air Force training school at near-by Scott Field.

**Belleville** (New Jersey) USA. Industrial town just N of Newark. Pop. (1960) 35,005. Manufactures machinery, chemicals, etc.

**Bellingham** USA. Seaport in NW Washington, on the bay of the same name, 80 m. N of Seattle. Pop. (1960) 34,688. Fruit and salmon canning. Processes dairy produce, timber, etc. from the surrounding area.

**Bellingshausen Sea** Southern Ocean. Section of the Southern Ocean W of Graham Land (Palmer Peninsula) (Antarctica). Visited by a Russian expedition under F. von Bellingshausen (1819–21) and named after him.

**Bellinzona** Switzerland. Capital of the Ticino canton, on the Ticino R. near the N end of L. Maggiore. Pop. (1969) 16,500. Road, railway, and tourist centre. Railway engineering, woodworking, printing, and other industries. Three picturesque 15th-cent. castles.

**Bell Island** Canada. Small island in Conception Bay off SE Newfoundland. Area 11 sq. m. Pop. 8,000. High-quality hematite iron mines (first worked 1895) extending under the sea.

**Bell (Inchcape) Rock** Scotland. Reef in the N Sea, off the coast of Angus 12 m. SE of Arbroath. Lighthouse erected (1807–11) by Robert Stevenson. The legend of the warning bell is told in Southey's *Ballad of the Inchcape Rock*.

**Belluno** Italy. Capital of the Belluno province in Veneto, N. Italy, on the Piave R. 50 m. N of Venice. Pop. (1961) 31,403. Tourist centre (serves the Dolomites). Manufactures electrical equipment, furniture, etc. Cathedral (16th-cent.), and a Renaissance palace.

**Belo Horizonte** Brazil. Capital of the Minas Gerais state, on the plateau at 2,500 ft, 210 m. N of Rio de Janeiro, to which it is linked by motorway and railway; also motorways to Brasilia and São Paulo. Pop. (1960) 642,912. Pleasant climate. Centre of a mining (iron, manganese) and agricultural (cotton, cattle) region. Food processing, diamond cutting. Manufactures iron and steel, textiles, footwear. University (1927). Brazil's first planned city, founded at the turn of the century to replace the decaying gold centre of Ouro Prêto as state capital.

**Belomorsk** USSR. Formerly Soroka. Seaport in the Karelian ASSR (RSFSR), on the White Sea at the N end of the Baltic–White Sea Canal and on the Murmansk railway. Pop. 14,000. Sawmilling, fish canning. Exports timber.

**Beloretsk** USSR. Industrial town in the Bashkir ASSR (RSFSR), in the S Urals 55 m. NW of Magnitogorsk. Pop. 59,000. Metallurgical centre. Manufactures steel, wire, nails, etc. from local iron and manganese ores.

**Belorussia** ◊ *Byelorussia*.

**Belovo** USSR. Industrial town in the RSFSR, in the Kuznetsk Basin 55 m. NW of Novokuznetsk on a branch of the Trans-Siberian Railway. Pop. (1970) 108,000. Metallurgical and other industries. Coal mined near by.

**Belper** England. Urban district in Derbyshire, on the R. Derwent 7 m. N of Derby. Pop. (1961) 15,563. Industrial centre and market town. Cotton and hosiery mills. Chemical works. The cotton industry was founded (1776) by Jedediah Strutt, inventor of a ribbing machine.

**Belsen** Federal German Republic. Village in Lower Saxony near Celle. Site of a notorious concentration camp during the Nazi régime.

**Belt, Great** ◊ *Great Belt*.

**Belt, Little** ◊ *Little Belt*.

**Belterra** ◊ *Tapajós River*.

**Beltsy** USSR. Town in the Moldavian SSR 70 m. NW of Kishinev. Pop. (1970) 102,000. Agricultural centre. Sugar refining, flour milling, meat packing, etc. In Rumania (as Bălţi) between the 1st and 2nd World Wars.

**Benares** ◊ *Varanasi*.

**Benbecula** Scotland. Island in the Outer Hebrides in Inverness-shire, between N Uist and S Uist. Area 36 sq. m. Pop. 900. Main occupation fishing.

**Bendigo** Australia. Formerly Sandhurst. Mining centre in Victoria 85 m. NNW of Melbourne. Pop. (1966) 42,191. Developed in the gold rush of 1851; goldfield characterized by deep saddle reefs. Now also a market town. Flour-milling, tanning, textile manufacture, and other industries.

**Benevento** Italy. Ancient Beneventum. Capital of the Benevento province in Campania, on the Calore R. 32 NE of Naples. Pop. (1961) 55,381. Produces confectionery, matches, a liqueur (Strega), etc. Chief town of the Samnites, but taken by the Romans in the 3rd cent. B.C. Became an important town on the Appian Way. Mainly under papal rule from medieval times until 1860, when it was incorporated in the kingdom of Italy. A triumphal arch erected in A.D. 114 in honour of Trajan. The cathedral was severely damaged in the 2nd World War and later rebuilt.

**Benfleet** England. Residential urban district in S Essex, 5 m. W of Southend. Pop. (1961) 32,372. Includes S Benfleet (on Benfleet Creek which separates Canvey Island from the mainland), Hadleigh, and Thundersley.

**Bengal** India/Pakistan. 1. Former presidency of British India, in the NE at the head of the Bay of Bengal, approximating to the great Ganges–Brahmaputra delta and bounded on the N by mountainous Sikkim and Bhutan. It has a humid tropical climate, with rainfall varying from 50 ins. to well over 100 ins. annually, and is important for the production of rice and jute. Its chief city, Calcutta, was capital of India from 1833 to 1912, when it was superseded by Delhi. In the 19th cent. Bengal at times included neighbouring regions, e.g. Assam, but the Bengali-speaking core was made a province in 1912 and became autonomous in 1937. With the partition of India (1947), Bengal was divided: the larger, mainly Muslim, area (E) was assigned to Pakistan, and the chiefly Hindu area (W) to India.
2. *East Bengal*: the detached E province of Pakistan. Area 55,126 sq. m. Pop. (1961) 50,840,235. Capital Dacca. Chief seaport Chittagong.
3. *West Bengal*: state of the republic of India. Area 33,829 sq. m. Pop. (1961) 34,926,279. Capital and chief seaport Calcutta.

**Bengal, Bay of.** Arm of the Indian Ocean between peninsular India and Burma. Receives the combined Ganges and Brahmaputra, Irrawaddy, Mahanadi, Godavari, Krishna, and Cauvery rivers. Islands include the Andaman, Nicobar, and Mergui groups.

**Benghazi (Bengasi)** Libya. Ancient Hesperides; Berenice. Seaport at the E end of the Gulf of Sidra; capital of Cyrenaica and (with Tripoli) joint capital of Libya. Pop. 80,000. Connected by rail with Barca and Soluk. Founded by the Greeks as Hesperides. Renamed Berenice (in honour of his wife) by Ptolemy III. Important centre of colonization under the Italians 1911–42. Changed hands several times during the 2nd World War; finally captured by the British 1942.

**Benguela (Benguella)** Angola. Seaport 25 m. SW of Lobito. Pop. 15,000. Flourished during the slave-trade period. Has now lost most of its foreign trade to ◊ *Lobito*, ocean terminus of the railway linking it to Angola central plateau, Katanga (Congo

(Kinshasa)), Malawi, Moçambique, Rhodesia, and Zambia.

**Benin** Nigeria. Ancient kingdom of W Africa, with a coastline extending from the Volta R. to the Rio del Rey and including the shores of the Bight of Benin, the Niger delta, and some of the country E of the delta. Small but powerful. The Bini (Beni) were governed by a theocracy; their ritual involved considerable human sacrifice. The coast came under British protection in 1885; human sacrifice and the slave trade were stopped. Became the Benin Province of S Nigeria 1914.

**Benin, Bight of** Atlantic Ocean. Bay in the Gulf of Guinea (W Africa), bordered by the coasts of E Ghana, Togo, Dahomey, and W Nigeria as far as the Niger delta. Formerly known as the Slave Coast.

**Benin City** Nigeria. Town in a forest clearing 155 m. E of Lagos. Pop. (1962) 54,000. Trade in palm oil and kernels, timber, etc. Wood carving, brassware. Former capital of the kingdom of ◊ *Benin*. Formerly a centre of the slave trade.

**Beni River** ◊ *Madeira River*.

**Beni Suef** United Arab Republic. Capital of Beni Suef governorate, on the W bank of the Nile 70 m. SSW of Cairo. Pop. (1960) 79,000. Linked by rail with Cairo and with El Faiyum oasis, for which it is an important trade centre. Cotton ginning and other industries.

**Ben Lomond** Scotland. Mountain 3,192 ft high, on the E side of *Loch* ◊ *Lomond* in Stirlingshire.

**Ben Nevis** Scotland. Highest mountain in the British Isles (4,406 ft), in Invernessshire 4 m. ESE of Fort William, overlooking the picturesque Glen Nevis. On the NE side is a 1,500-ft precipice.

**Benoni** S Africa. Town in the S of the Transvaal, on the Witwatersrand 17 m. E of Johannesburg, at a height of 5,600 ft. Pop. (1967) 126,701 (44,000 whites, 82,435 Bantu). Goldmining. Engineering etc.

**Bensberg** Federal German Republic. Town in N Rhine-Westphalia 9 m. ENE of Cologne. Pop. (1963) 33,400. Mainly residential. Manufactures leather goods etc. Has an early 18th-cent. castle and ruins of a 13th-cent. castle.

**Benue River** Cameroun/Nigeria. River 900 m. long, chief tributary of the Niger, rising in the Adamawa mountains N of Ngaoundéré (Cameroun), flowing N and then generally WSW past Yola and

Makurdi (Nigeria), and joining the Niger at Lokoja 230 m. above the mouth. Navigable to Garoua (Cameroun) in the flood season (July–Oct.).

**Beograd** ◊ *Belgrade*.

**Berar** India. Territory of Madhya Pradesh consisting largely of the broad, fertile valley of the Purna R. (a tributary of the Tapti), between the Satpura and Ajanta ranges, one of the richest cotton-growing regions in India. It was administered as Hyderabad Assigned Districts 1853–1903, and then became an administrative division of the Central Provinces and Berar; in 1950 the two latter became the state of Madhya Pradesh.

**Berbera** Somali Republic. Seaport on the Gulf of Aden. Pop. (1960) 40,000. Exports sheep, goats, skins, and gums, mainly to Aden.

**Berbice River** Guyana. River 300 m. long, flowing N from the Guiana Highlands, over falls, to the coastal plain, and entering the Atlantic near New Amsterdam. Navigable for 125 m. Diamonds are worked in the middle course.

**Berchtesgaden** Federal German Republic. Village in the Bavarian Alps, 11 m. SSW of Salzburg (Austria), at a height of 1,700 ft amid fine mountain scenery. Pop. 5,000. Popular resort. Salt mining, wood carving. Became famous as the site of Hitler's mountain retreat.

**Berdichev** USSR. Town in Ukrainian SSR 95 m. WSW of Kiev. Pop. 53,000. Industrial centre and railway junction. Sugar-refining, tanning, engineering, etc. Founded 1482. Belonged to Lithuania, Poland, and finally (1793) Russia.

**Berezina River** USSR. River 350 m. long in the Byelorussian SSR, rising in the N and flowing S through low-lying wooded country to join the Dnieper R. Linked with the W Dvina R. and the Baltic Sea by the Berezina Canal, thus forming the Baltic–Black Sea waterway. Near Borisov, on the upper course, Napoleon crossed the river with great losses (Nov. 1812) during the retreat from Moscow.

**Berezniki** USSR. Industrial town in RSFSR 95 m. N of Perm. Pop. (1970) 145,000. An important centre of the chemical industry. Manufactures fertilizers, dyes, sulphuric acid, soda, etc., using local common salt, potash, and coal.

**Bergamo** Italy. Capital of the Bergamo province in Lombardy, 28 m. NE of Milan, at the foot of the Bergamasque

Alps. Pop. (1968) 123,518. Industrial centre. Engineering, textile manufacture, etc. In the old town, on a 1,200-ft hill, are a 12th/14th-cent. Romanesque church and the 15th-cent. Colleoni chapel. Birthplace of Gaetano Donizetti (1797–1848).

**Bergen** (Belgium) ◊ *Mons*.

**Bergen** (German Democratic Republic) ◊ *Rügen*.

**Bergen** Norway. Seaport and second city of Norway, in the SW at the head of the Byfjord. Pop. (1968) 116,794. Built round a sheltered and spacious harbour; a *fylke* (county) in itself. Trade chiefly in fish and fish products. Shipbuilding and engineering. Manufactures paper, furniture, pottery, rope, etc. Important tourist and cultural centre. University (1948). Founded (1070) by Olaf III as Bjorgvin. The chief city in medieval times, later surpassed as a trading centre by Oslo. In 1665 an English fleet pursuing a Dutch merchant fleet into Bergen harbour was heavily bombarded: the 'Bergen incident' contributed to the fall of Clarendon and the rise of the Cabal. Suffered severely from fires at various times; the central area was rebuilt 1916. In the 2nd World War it was again heavily damaged. Birthplace of Edvard Grieg (1843–1907).

**Bergen-op-Zoom** Netherlands. Town in the N Brabant province in the SW, on the small Zoom R. near its confluence with the Scheldt. Pop. (1968) 38,489. Sugar-refining, iron-founding, distilling, and other industries. Strongly fortified (16th cent.) and often besieged.

**Bergerac** France. Town in the Dordogne department in the SW, on the Dordogne R. 47 m. E of Bordeaux. Pop. (1968) 28,015. Famous for wines and chestnuts. Distilling, tanning. Manufactures footwear etc.

**Berhampur** India. Town in Orissa 110 m. SW of Cuttack. Pop. (1961) 76,931. Commercial centre. Trade in rice, sugarcane, oilseeds, etc.

**Bering Sea.** A N section of the Pacific Ocean between NE Siberia and Alaska, bounded on the S by the Aleutian Is., connected N through the Bering Strait with the Arctic Ocean. Named after the Danish navigator Vitus Bering, who explored the region for Peter the Great of Russia from 1728. Contains several islands, including St Lawrence, St Matthew, and the Pribilof Is., in US waters, and the Komandorskiye Is., in Russian waters. Bering died (1741) of scurvy on one of the last-named group.

**Berkeley** England. Small town in SW Gloucestershire, 15 m. SW of Gloucester. Pop. (1961) 1,116. The fertile dairy-farming Berkeley Vale is famous for Double Gloucester cheese. Nuclear power station (opened 1963). Edward II was murdered in Berkeley Castle (1327). Birthplace of Dr Edward Jenner (1749–1823).

**Berkeley** USA. Residential and university city in California, across the Bay from San Francisco, relatively free from the prevailing sea mists. Pop. (1960) 111,268. Manufactures soap, paint, chemicals. Berkelium, discovered in the university laboratories in 1950, is named after it.

**Berkhamsted (Great Berkhamsted, Berkhampstead)** England. Urban district in SW Hertfordshire, 10 m. W of St Albans. Pop. (1961) 13,048. Largely residential. Chemical industry. It has a well-known public school. The Foundling Hospital was transferred here in 1935. Birthplace of William Cowper (1731–1800).

**Berkshire** England. Inland county in the S, bordered in the N by the R. Thames. Area 725 sq. m. Pop. (1961) 503,357. County town Reading. The Berkshire Downs run W–E across the middle of the county, with White Horse Hill reaching 856 ft; but the highest point is Inkpen Beacon (975 ft) in the extreme SW. Sheep, pigs, and dairy cattle raised. Wheat and oats cultivated in the fertile valleys, esp. the Vale of the White Horse and the valley of the R. Kennet.

**Berlin** Federal German Republic/German Democratic Republic. Largest city in Germany (in 1939 the second largest city in continental Europe), on the Spree R. Capital of Germany till 1945. Of relatively recent origin, having developed from two 13th-cent. villages on the Spree, lying in a sandy, rather infertile plain (of glacial origin) studded by lakes. Became capital of the Electorate of ◊ *Brandenburg*, and then (being closely bound up with the rise of the Hohenzollerns) of the kingdom of ◊ *Prussia*. The most spectacular growth came in the 19th cent., when it became the centre of the German railways and of an important system of inland waterways, being linked by canals with the Elbe and the Oder rivers. On the creation of the German Empire (1871) it became the capital. There were many fine streets, the most famous being the Unter den Linden (extending almost a mile to the Brandenburg Gate), the Kurfürstendamm (well known for its fashionable shops), the

Wilhelmstrasse (government offices), and the Tiergartenstrasse (embassies). During the 2nd World War the city was virtually destroyed by air raids and the heavy artillery bombardments of the Russians in the final battle for the capital. In 1945 Berlin was divided into four zones of occupation, British, French, American, and Soviet. In 1948 the USSR withdrew from the Berlin administration (*Kommandatura*); Berlin became two administratively separate entities. The Soviet authorities also stopped all road and rail traffic from the west, in the hope of causing the western allies to abandon their sector, but the Anglo-American airlift maintained supplies to W Berlin until the blockade was lifted in 1949. W Berlin became the chief point at which Germans fleeing from the E crossed to the W. In 1961 the E German authorities erected a concrete wall along the boundary between the two sectors to stem the outflow. The wall greatly restricts contact, commercial or social, between E and W Berlin.

WEST BERLIN. Area 188 sq. m. Pop. (1968) 2,163,306. Still the largest city in the Federal German Republic (of which it forms a *Land*). Maintains a somewhat difficult existence as an enclave within the German Democratic Republic (which controls and levies dues on all civilian traffic entering the city). Its economy is hampered by the difficulty of communications and by being cut off from its immediate economic hinterland, E Germany. It has been aided by considerable US investment and by regular subventions from the German Federal Republic, and has the appearance of a reconstructed, lively, and prosperous metropolis. Numerous industries: printing, publishing, manufacture of electrical equipment, clothing, chemicals, etc.

EAST BERLIN. Area 156 sq. m. Pop. (1968) 1,082,019. Capital of the German Democratic Republic. Its reconstruction has lagged, and its general appearance is neglected. In 1953 the people of E Berlin revolted against the régime: the attempt was put down by force with Soviet assistance. Before the building of the wall many E Berliners worked in W Berlin.

**Bermejo River** Argentina/Paraguay. River 650 m. long, rising in the extreme NW, and flowing SE to join the Paraguay R. near Pilar (Paraguay). In the middle course it divides into two streams (the N one is called the Teuco), which later rejoin.

**Bermondsey** England. Former metropolitan borough of SE London, on the S bank of the Thames, linked with Stepney by Tower Bridge and Rotherhithe Tunnel; from 1965 part of the Greater London borough of Southwark. Pop. (1961) 51,815. Long famous for tanneries. Other industries, docks (Surrey Commercial), wharves, and warehouses. Name probably derived from 'Beormund's Island', referring to a Saxon overlord and the insular, marshy nature of the district.

**Bermudas.** Group of over 300 islands, about 20 inhabited, 700 m. SE of New York City, forming the British colony of Bermuda. Total area 21 sq. m. Pop. (1968) 50,097. Cap. Hamilton, on Bermuda (Main) Island. The islands are low-lying and rocky; the highest point is 240 ft above sea level. They have been formed by the growth of coral on the base of a submarine volcanic cone. Coral fragments from the surrounding coral reefs, broken off by wave action, have drifted or been blown to form extensive coral sand dunes. Connected by bridges and causeways, they form an almost continuous arc 20 m. long. The subtropical climate ensures a mild winter, and the equable temperatures are beneficial to delicate invalids. Summer heat is tempered by the NE Trade Winds. The rainfall, which is evenly distributed throughout the year, amounts to 60–70 ins., and the air is always moist. Owing to the permeability of the soil and rocks there are no surface streams or wells, yet the vegetation is prolific. The cover of juniper trees is being restored after considerable destruction by blight (1940–45). On the small area of cultivated land (little more than 1 sq. m.) the smallholders grow mainly tropical fruit and vegetables; early potatoes, tomatoes, onions, arrowroot, and bananas were once grown for the N American market, now protected by tariffs. The chief exports are lily-bulbs and pharmaceutical oils; the main revenue comes from American tourists. The group derives its name from Juan Bermúdez, a Spaniard, who discovered them in 1515. They were first inhabited when a number of colonists under Sir George Somers was shipwrecked here (1609). Taken over by the Crown 1684. During the 2nd World War (1941) sites were leased for 99 years to the USA for naval and air bases.

**Bern (Berne)** Switzerland. Capital, also capital of the Bern canton, on the Aar R. at a height of 1,800 ft. Pop. (1969) 168,600.

Manufactures knitwear, furniture, chocolate, musical instruments. Printing and publishing. University (1834). Headquarters of the Universal Postal Union. Medieval streets with arcades and ornate fountains; the 15th/16th-cent. Gothic cathedral, the 15th-cent. Rathaus, and the Federal Palace are outstanding buildings. The name is supposed to refer to bears, and a bear-pit is still a tourist attraction. Founded (1191) by Berchtold V of Zähringen. Became a free imperial city 1218. Continually extended its power; became capital of the Swiss Confederation 1848.

**Bernburg** German Democratic Republic. Town in the Halle district, 26 m. NNW of Halle on the Saale R. Pop. (1965) 45,845. Centre of a potash and rock-salt mining district. Chemical, engineering, and other industries. Formerly capital of the duchy of Anhalt-Bernburg.

**Bern (Berne) canton** Switzerland. The second largest canton, between the Bernese Alps and the French frontier. Area 2,658 sq. m. Pop. (1969) 1,005,000. Cap. Bern (Berne). Hydroelectric power. Manufactures watches, textiles, food products. Divided geographically into three regions. The Bernese Oberland, in the S, includes the Alpine peaks of Finsteraarhorn and Jungfrau, the lakes of Thun and Brienz, and many resorts, e.g. Interlaken, Mürren, Grindelwald, Kandersteg, Meiringen. The Mittelland (central area) includes the lower valley of the Aar R., the Emmental (Emme valley) – famous for scenery and for cheese – and the city of Bern. The Seeland (lake area), in the N, includes the lakes of Biel and Neuchâtel and the Bernese Jura.

**Bernicia** England/Scotland. Kingdom in the NE believed to have been founded by Ida in A.D. 547 and to have extended later from the Tees to the Forth. United with Deira, to form the kingdom of Northumbria, 605.

**Bernkastel-Kues** Federal German Republic. Town in Rhineland-Palatinate, on the Mosel R. 22 m. NE of Trier. Pop. 5,000. Famous for wines.

**Berre, Étang de** France. Lagoon in the Bouches-du-Rhône department in the SE. Area 60 sq. m. Connected to the Gulf of Fos by the 4-m. Étang de Caronte. Eel fisheries. Important oil refineries round its shores, also saltworks.

**Berry** France. Former province, in the S of the Paris Basin, now forming the Indre and Cher departments and parts of other departments. Bought by the French crown

1101. Became a duchy 1360. Divided into the present departments 1790. The capital was Bourges.

**Berwick-upon-Tweed** England. Municipal borough at the mouth of the R. Tweed on the N bank, forming with Spittal and Tweedmouth on the S bank the County of the Borough of Berwick-upon-Tweed, though usually regarded as being in the county of Northumberland. Pop. (1961) 12,166. Three bridges across the Tweed: an old road bridge (1634), a much larger road bridge (1928), and a railway viaduct (1850). Engineering. Manufactures fertilizers, hosiery. Salmon fishing. For centuries involved in English-Scottish border troubles, Berwick changed hands 13 times between 1147 and 1482. Declared neutral territory 1551. Became part of Northumberland 1885.

**Berwickshire** Scotland. County in the SE, bordering in the SE on England (the lower Tweed forming most of the boundary) and in the E on the North Sea. Area 457 sq. m. Pop. (1961) 22,441. County town Duns (pop. 1,838). Sheep raised on the Lammermuir Hills in the N, whence the county slopes down to the fertile lowland (the Merse) N of the Tweed, where cereals are cultivated.

**Berwyn** USA. Town in Illinois 9 m. WNW of Chicago. Pop. (1960) 52,244. Residential and industrial centre. Manufactures electrical equipment, machine tools, etc.

**Besançon** France. Ancient Vesontio. Prefecture of the Doubs department in the E, on the peninsula formed by a loop of the Doubs R. at the foot of the Jura mountains, 48 m. E of Dijon. Pop. (1968) 119,471. Chief centre in France of watch and clock making. Manufactures rayon, hosiery, chocolate, etc. Brewing, engineering. Several Roman remains. Cathedral (founded in the 4th cent.; mainly built in the 11th/13th cent.). Renaissance Palais Granvelle (16th-cent.). Seat of a university (moved from Dôle 1691). Chief town of the Sequani. Taken by Julius Caesar 58 B.C. Became an important Roman military post and later a colony. Belonged to Burgundy and then to Franche-Comté. After a period of Austro-Spanish rule, ceded to France in 1678 and replaced Dôle as capital of the Franche-Comté province. Birthplace of François Fourier (1772–1837), Pierre Proudhon (1809–65), Victor Hugo (1802–85).

**Beskids** Czechoslovakia/Poland. Two ranges, West and East, of the Carpathian mountains, along the Czechoslovak–Polish frontier, rising to 5,659 ft in Babia Góra (W Beskids). Well forested. Popular tourist area.

**Bessarabia** USSR. Region bounded by the Dniester R. (N and E), the Danube R. (S), and the Prut R. (W); the N and S parts are in the Ukrainian SSR and the larger central part is in the Moldavian SSR. Area 17,100 sq. m. Pop. mainly Moldavians, Ukrainians, and Russians. Chief town ◊ *Kishinev*. Principally agricultural. Maize, wheat, sugar-beet, vines cultivated. Sheep, cattle, pigs raised. Became part of the Roman province of Dacia in the 2nd cent. A.D. Afterwards overrun by Goths, Huns, Avars, Bulgars, and others, inc. the Thracian Bessi (from whom the name derives) in the 7th cent. Conquered by the ruling prince of Moldavia in the 14th cent., and long disputed between the Turks and the Russians. Ceded to Russia 1812. Annexed by Rumania (1918) after the 1st World War. Retaken by the USSR 1940.

**Bessemer** USA. Industrial town in Alabama just SW of Birmingham. Pop. (1960) 33,054. Manufactures iron and steel goods, chemicals. Coal and iron mined in the neighbourhood. Named after Sir Henry Bessemer, inventor of the Bessemer process for steel manufacture.

**Bethesda** Wales. Urban district in N Caernarvonshire, 4 m. SE of Bangor. Pop. (1961) 4,151. The Penrhyn slate quarries are near by.

**Bethlehem** (Ar. **Beit Lahm**) Jordan. Town in the W, 5 m. SSW of Jerusalem. Pop. 24,000. The reputed birthplace of Christ. Manufactures souvenirs in olivewood etc. The Emperor Constantine built a basilica here (A.D. 330), subsequently added to and restored, beneath which is the Grotto of the Nativity, where Christ is said to have been born. Latin, Greek, and Armenian convents stand near the Church of the Nativity, and the cell where St Jerome translated the Bible, as well as his tomb, may be seen.

**Bethlehem** USA. Industrial town in Pennsylvania, on the Lehigh R. 47 m. NNW of Philadelphia. Pop. (1960) 75,408. Important steel centre (Bethlehem Steel Corporation). Also manufactures textiles, electrical equipment, etc. Seat of the Lehigh University (1866). Famous for an annual music festival and a Bach choir. Founded (1741) by Moravians and has the Central Moravian Church and a Moravian college.

**Bethnal Green** England. Former metropolitan borough of E London; from 1965 part of the Greater London borough of Tower Hamlets. Pop. (1961) 47,018. Once noted for silk weaving (introduced by Huguenots and spread here from Spitalfields), replaced by cabinet making, tailoring, etc. Contains part of Victoria Park (217 acres).

**Béthune** France. Town in the Pas-de-Calais department in the N, 21 m. WSW of Lille. Pop. (1968) 28,379. Route centre and market town in a coalmining and agricultural area. Manufactures beet sugar, footwear, etc. Severely damaged during German advances in both world wars.

**Betsiboka River** ◊ *Majunga*.

**Betwys-y-Coed** Wales. Urban district in Caernarvonshire, 16 m. S of Llandudno, in a picturesque wooded area on the R. Llugwy near its confluence with the R. Conway. Pop. (1961) 778. Resort. The Swallow Falls are 2 m. WNW.

**Beuthen** ◊ *Bytom*.

**Beveland, North** ◊ *North Beveland*.

**Beveland, South** ◊ *South Beveland*.

**Beverley** England. Municipal borough and county town in the E Riding of Yorkshire, 8 m. NNW of Hull. Pop. (1961) 16,024. Market town. Tanning, brewing, etc. A 13th-cent. minster on the site of a monastery founded by John of Beverley (640–721); a 14th-cent. parish church and a 15th-cent. gateway. Birthplace of the martyr Bishop John Fisher (1459–1535).

**Beverly** USA. Industrial town and fishing port on the NE coast of Massachusetts 7 m. NNE of Lynn. Pop. (1960) 36,108. Manufactures footwear, shoe machinery, clothing.

**Beverly Hills** USA. Suburb of W Los Angeles, California. Famous as the home of film stars.

**Beverwijk** Netherlands. Town in the N Holland province, 7 m. N of Haarlem. Pop. (1968) 42,008. Market gardening. Engineering; jam manufacture, fruit and vegetable canning, etc.

**Bewdley** England. Municipal borough in N Worcestershire, on the R. Severn 3 m. WSW of Kidderminster. Pop. (1961) 5,033. Market town. Manufactures combs etc. Ancient Forest of Wyre to the W. Birthplace of Earl Baldwin (1867–1947).

**Bexhill-on-Sea** England. Municipal borough in E Sussex 4 m. WSW of Hastings. Pop. (1961) 28,926. Seaside resort. Inland, in the old town, the Norman church of St

Peter. Suffered much damage from air raids in the 2nd World War.

**Bex-les-Bains** Switzerland. Spa in the Vaud canton in the SW, on the Avançon R. near its confluence with the Rhône. Pop. (1960) 4,800. Brine and sulphur baths. Salt mined in the neighbourhood.

**Bexley** England. Greater London borough (1965) comprising the former municipal boroughs of Bexley and Erith, the urban district of Crayford, and the part of the urban districts of Chislehurst and Sidcup N of the A20 road, all in N W Kent. Pop. (1963) 209,937. The former municipal borough of Bexley (pop. 89,629), now partly industrial, was the home of William Morris for some years.

**Bezhitsa** USSR. Formerly (1935–43) Ordzhonikidzegrad. Industrial town on the Desna R. (RSFSR), just N W of Bryansk (with which it was incorporated 1956). Manufactures locomotives, railway rolling stock, agricultural implements, etc.

**Béziers** France. Town in the Hérault department, on the Orb R. and the Canal du Midi, 92 m. ESE of Toulouse. Pop. (1968) 82,271. An important wine-trade centre. Manufactures barrels, corks, insecticides, fertilizers, confectionery. Scene of a massacre after its capture (1209) by Simon de Montfort (the elder) during the Albigensian crusade (◊ *Albi*). Expanded rapidly after 1850 with the development of viticulture in Languedoc.

**Bhagalpur** India. Town in Bihar, on the Ganges R. 120 m. ESE of Patna. Pop. (1961) 143,850. Trade in rice, oilseeds, etc. Manufactures textiles, esp. silk. University (1960).

**Bhatgaon (Bhadgaon)** Nepal. Town 7 m. ESE of Katmandu. Pop. 84,240. Chiefly important as a Hindu religious centre, with many finely carved temples. Founded in the 9th cent.

**Bhatpara** India. Industrial town in W Bengal, on the Hooghly R. 23 m. N of Calcutta. Pop. (1961) 147,630. Important jute-milling centre; also cotton milling, engineering.

**Bhavnagar (Bhaunagar)** India. Port of Gujarat, on the Gulf of Cambay 92 m. SSW of Ahmadabad. Pop. (1961) 171,039. Trade in cotton etc. Manufactures textiles, bricks and tiles, brassware. Capital of the former princely state of Bhavnagar, which was merged into Saurashtra in 1948 and into Gujarat in 1960.

**Bhopal** India. Capital of Madhya Pradesh,

105 m. ENE of Indore. Pop. (1961) 185,374. Manufactures electrical equipment, textiles, matches, ghee, etc. Capital of the former state of Bhopal.

**Bhubaneswar** India. Capital of Orissa, 18 m. S of Cuttack. Pop. (1961) 38,211. Ancient town and place of pilgrimage, famous for its temples, of which the principal example dates from the 11th cent.

**Bhutan.** State in the E Himalayas bounded by Tibet (N), India (E and S), and Sikkim (W). Area 19,000 sq. m. Pop. 750,000. Cap. Thimphu. Entirely mountainous, with some peaks exceeding 20,000 ft. Drained by several tributaries of the Brahmaputra R. Climate varies with altitude and so too does the natural vegetation, with dense forests in the lower valleys and permanent snow on the mountain summits. Rice, maize, and millet are cultivated and ponies are bred; metal working and weaving are among the few minor industries. Tashi Chho Dzong, the former summer capital, contains the country's principal lamasery with over 1,000 priests. The dominant people, the Bhotias, are of Tibetan origin, their language is a dialect of Tibetan, and their religion, a form of Buddhism, is similar to that of Tibet. Bhutan was converted to Buddhism in the 8th cent. The original inhabitants were conquered by Tibetan soldiers in the 9th cent. When the Bhotias invaded Cooch Behar (1772), they were driven out by a British force, and after further raids part of S Bhutan was annexed (1865). By a treaty of 1910 the British government doubled the annual subsidy paid to Bhutan (since 1865), while the latter agreed to be guided by Britain in external affairs; a similar treaty was concluded with India in 1949. From the 16th cent. to 1907 Bhutan was under the dual control of a spiritual and a temporal ruler, but since then it has been governed by a hereditary maharajah, who has adopted the title of king.

**Biafra** ◊ *Nigeria.*

**Biafra, Bight of** Atlantic Ocean. Bay at the E end of the Gulf of Guinea between the Niger delta and Cape Lopez, bordered by the coasts of Cameroun, N Gabon, E Nigeria, Río Muni. Contains the island of Fernando Póo.

**Bialystok** Poland. Capital of the Bialystok voivodship, in the NE, 110 m. NE of Warsaw. Pop. (1968) 158,500. Important industrial centre and railway junction. Manufactures textiles (esp. woollen), agricultural machinery, etc. Founded 1320. Passed to Prussia (1795) and then to Russia (1807). Returned to Poland 1919.

**Biarritz** France. Resort in the Basses-Pyrénées department, on the Bay of Biscay, close to the Spanish frontier. Pop. (1968) 26,985. Famous for its mild climate and sandy beaches. Developed from a small fishing village into a fashionable resort of international repute under the patronage first of Napoleon III and the Empress Eugénie (France), later of Queen Victoria and Edward VII (Britain).

**Bicester** England. Urban district in Oxfordshire, 11 m. NNE of Oxford. Pop. (1961) 5,513. Market town and hunting centre. Roman remains at near-by Alchester.

**Bida** ◊ *Doha.*

**Bideford** England. Municipal borough on the N coast of Devonshire, on the R. Torridge estuary (crossed by an ancient 24-arch bridge). Pop. (1961) 10,265. Small seaport. Holiday resort. Manufactures pottery. An active port in the 16th cent., used by Drake, Grenville, and Raleigh as starting point for their voyages. Kingsley wrote part of *Westward Ho!* here, and the district figures prominently in the novel.

**Biel (Bienne)** Switzerland. Town in the Bern canton, at the NE end of L. Biel on the Schüss R. Pop. (1969) 67,800. Important industrial centre. Noted for watch making. Also manufactures special steels, machine tools, cars, paper, etc. Has the Schwab Museum of Archaeology, and the W Cantonal Technical Institute. Connected by funicular railway with the resorts of Macolin and Évilard on the Jura slopes.

**Biel (Bienne), Lake** Switzerland. Lake in the W, at a height of 1,400 ft at the foot of the Jura mountains. Area 16 sq. m. Drains the Lake of Neuchâtel through the Thièle (Zihl) R. Receives the waters of the Aar R, via the Hagneck Canal and loses them via the Aar Canal to the old bed. Lake dwellings were discovered in the 19th cent.

**Bielefeld** Federal German Republic. Industrial town in N Rhine-Westphalia, at the foot of the Teutoburger Wald 58 m. WSW of Hanover. Pop. (1968) 169,224. Noted for linen. Also manufactures clothing, sewing machines, bicycles, furniture, etc.

**Biella** Italy. Industrial town in the Vercelli province in Piedmont, 40 m. NE of Turin. Pop. (1961) 47,423. A leading centre of the woollen industry. Also manufactures cotton goods, hats, etc.

**Bielsko-Biala** Poland. Town in the Kato-wice voivodship in the S, 30 m. S of Katowice. Pop. (1968) 87,100. Formed (1951) from the towns of Bielsko and Biala Krakowska. An important textile industry since the 16th cent. Also manufactures machinery, paper, etc. Founded in the 13th cent. Returned to Poland from Austria 1919.

**Bienne** ◊ *Biel.*

**Bié Plateau** ◊ *Nova Lisboa; Okavango River.*

**Biggin Hill** ◊ *Orpington.*

**Biggleswade** England. Urban district in Bedfordshire, on the R. Ivel 9 m. ESE of Bedford. Pop. (1961) 8,047. Market-gardening centre. Engineering.

**Bihar** India 1. State in the NE, bounded on the N by Nepal. Area 67,196 sq. m. Pop. (1961) 46,455,610. Cap. Patna. The N part is a flat, fertile plain, watered by the Ganges and its tributaries, where rice is by far the most important crop; the S is hilly and rises in places to over 3,000 ft. Bihar is noted as the main mineral-producing state, yielding principally coal and also iron ore and mica, with a great iron and steel works at Jamshedpur. Other important towns are Patna, Gaya, Bhagalpur, Darbhanga, Ranchi, and Muzaffarpur. Chief language Bihari. Formed part of the province of Bihar and Orissa from 1912 to 1937, when it became an autonomous province, and in 1948 was made a state of the Indian Union. 2. Town in Bihar state (to which it gave its name), 40 m. SE of Patna. Pop. (1961) 78,581. Trade in rice, oilseeds, etc.

**Biisk** USSR. Town in Altai territory (RSFSR) near the confluence of the Biya and Katun rivers (which form the Ob R.), 80 m. SE of Barnaul. Pop. (1970) 186,000. Meat packing, sugar refining. Manufactures textiles. Centre of trade between the USSR and Mongolia, being the terminus of the railway from Novosibirsk.

**Bijagós (Bissagos) Islands** Portuguese Guinea. Small archipelago off the Guinea coast. Four large islands (Orango, Formosa, Caravela, Roxa), about 10 smaller islands, and many islets; all low-lying and unhealthy. Area 600 sq. m. Main products coconuts and rice. The port of Bolama is on the island of the same name.

**Bijapur** India. Ancient city in Mysore, 60 m. SSW of Sholapur. Pop. (1961) 78,854. Cotton ginning, oilseed milling, and other industries. Trade in cotton and grain. Formerly capital of the independent kingdom of Bijapur, which fell to Aurangzeb in 1686; never recovered its splendour. Many remains of temples, palaces, and mosques, the outstanding building being the Gol Gumbaz, the 17th-cent. tomb of Mohammed Adil Shah, with a large dome 198 ft high.

**Bikaner** India. Industrial and commercial town of Rajasthan, on the edge of the Thar Desert 170 m. WNW of Jaipur. Pop. (1961) 150,634. Manufactures carpets, blankets. Trade in wool, hides, etc. Surrounded by a stone wall 6 ft thick. Founded (1488) by Bika, a Rajput chief. Became capital of the former state of Bikaner.

**Bikini Atoll** (Marshall Islands) S Pacific Ocean. Now uninhabited atoll in the Ralik Chain. Scene of US atom-bomb tests (1946) after removal of the population.

**Bilá Hora (White Mountain)** Czechoslovakia. Hill (1,246 ft) in Bohemia, 4 m. ESE of the centre of Prague. Scene of the defeat of Bohemian forces under Frederick V by a combined Austrian and Bavarian army (1620). Bohemia passed to Austria; independence was not regained till 1918.

**Bilbao** Spain. Capital of the Vizcaya province, near the mouth of the Nervión R. (Bay of Biscay). Pop. (1967) 371,851. One of Spain's major seaports. Accessible to large freight steamers via the canalized river; the outer harbour is protected by breakwaters. Noted since the Middle Ages for the manufacture of iron goods, esp. swords; the iron and steel works are still the most important in Spain. Exports iron ore, lead, wine. Shipbuilding, fishing. Manufactures railway rolling stock, tyres, machinery, chemicals, paper, cement, etc. The old town, on the right bank of the river, is connected with the new town by several bridges. Suffered severely in the wars with France. Besieged in the Carlist Wars (1835–6, 1874). Seat of the Basque autonomous government (1936) during the Spanish Civil War. Taken by the Franco forces 1937.

**Billingham** England. Industrial town in Durham, 3 m. NNE of Stockton-on-Tees. Pop. (1961) 32,130. Important centre of the chemical industry, with one of the world's largest plants. Has grown rapidly from a small village. In the town, on the Tees estuary, is Port Clarence. ◊ *Teesside.*

**Billings** USA. Town in Montana, on the Yellowstone R. 180 m. ESE of Helena. Pop. (1960) 52,851. In an irrigated region. Trade in wool, livestock, beet sugar, etc. Large sugar refinery. Meat packing, flour milling.

**Billingsgate** England. Chief fish market of London, just below London Bridge on the N bank of the R. Thames, on the site of one of the gates of Roman London's river-wall. Originally a general port, in 1699 it became a free port for fish. The bad language of the fish porters is proverbial.

**Billiton (Belitung)** Indonesia. Island between Bangka and SW Borneo. Area 1,860 sq. m. Pop. 92,000. Chief town and port Tanjungpandan. Important mainly for its tin mines, worked largely by Chinese.

**Bilma (Kawar)** Niger. Town in a small Saharan oasis 800 m. S of Tripoli (Libya). Pop. 1,000. On caravan routes from Tripoli to L. Chad and to Agadès. Considerable trade in salt, obtained from the salt lakes. Dates also produced in the oasis. Mean annual rainfall 0·8 in.

**Biloxi** USA. Fishing port and seaside resort in SE Mississippi, on a peninsula on Mississippi Sound (Gulf of Mexico). Pop. (1960) 44,053. Fish canning, boat-building, etc.

**Bilston** England. Industrial town in S Staffordshire, from 1966 part of the county borough of Wolverhampton. Pop. (1961) 33,077. Manufactures iron and steel products, machinery, enamelled goods, pottery.

**Bingen** Federal German Republic. Town in the Rhineland-Palatinate, on the Rhine at the mouth of the Nahe R. just above the Bingerloch whirlpool. Pop. (1963) 20,500. Tourist and commercial centre. Important wine trade. Near by, on a rock in the Rhine, is the Mäuseturm (Mouse-tower), where legend says that Archbishop Hatto II was devoured by mice for ill-treating his subjects.

**Binghamton** USA. Industrial town in S New York State at the confluence of the Chenango and Susquehanna rivers, 77 m. SSW of Utica. Pop. (1960) 75,941. Manufactures aircraft parts, cameras, footwear, machinery, etc.

**Bingley** England. Urban district in the W Riding of Yorkshire, on the R. Aire 5 m. NW of Bradford. Pop. (1961) 22,308. Manufactures woollens, worsteds, textile machinery, paper, etc.

**Bintan** ◊ *Riouw Archipelago.*

**Bío-Bío River** Chile. River 220 m. long, rising in the Andes near the Chile–Argentina frontier, flowing NW, and entering the Pacific near Concepción. The upper

tributaries provide hydroelectric power.
**Birdum** Australia. Small town in the Northern Territory 280 m. SE of Darwin, terminus of the railway therefrom, on the Stuart Highway. Centre of an extensive cattle-ranching area.

**Birkenhead** England. County borough on the Wirral peninsula in NW Cheshire, on the S bank of the R. Mersey opposite Liverpool, with which it is connected by rail (1886) and road (1934) tunnels and ferry. Pop. (1961) 141,683. Seaport. Exports flour, machinery. Imports grain, cattle. The flour mills are among the world's largest. Shipbuilding also important. Other industries include boiler making, engineering, food processing. Its great expansion dates from the opening of the docks (1847).

**Birmingham** England. County borough in NW Warwickshire in the Midlands; the second largest city in England and in Great Britain, with suburbs extending into Staffordshire and Worcestershire. Pop. (1961) 1,105,651. Of outstanding importance in the metal-working industry; claims to manufacture 'everything from a pin to a motor car'. Among its innumerable products are cars, motor cycles, and bicycles; fire-arms and ammunition; chemicals; electrical equipment; machine tools; nails and screws; jewellery; tyres (Fort Dunlop); and chocolate (Bournville). Known colloquially as 'Brum' or 'Brummagem'; the latter was adopted into the English language ('Brummagem ware'), as denoting goods of cheap and meretricious type, chiefly because of the manufacture of counterfeit coins in the 17th cent. and quite unjustly in terms of today's products. Situated near the geographical centre of the country, 110 m. NW of London, it is the meeting point of important railways, roads, and canals.

Well endowed with public parks, gardens, and recreation grounds, but (owing to the fact that its main expansion was due to the Industrial Revolution) the majority of the leading buildings date only from the 19th cent. The oldest church, for example, is St Martin's, originally erected in the 13th cent. but completely rebuilt in 1873. There is an 18th-cent. Anglican cathedral with stained-glass windows by Burne-Jones, damaged (like St Martin's) in the 2nd World War, and a Roman Catholic cathedral. The university (main buildings at Edgbaston) dates from 1900; the oldest educational institution is the King Edward

VI grammar school (1552). Other noteworthy buildings include the Town Hall (1834), where Mendelssohn conducted the first performance of *Elijah* (1847), the City Museum and Art Gallery (1855), and the Museum of Science and Industry (1950).

At the end of the 11th cent. Birmingham was a town of no great significance, but two centuries later it had become an important market town, developed around the junction of several roads at the Bull Ring. In the 16th cent. Leland wrote that 'a great parte of the towne is mayntayned by smithes', who (he adds) obtained their iron and coal from Staffordshire and Warwickshire. Standing on the edge of the Black Country, Birmingham grew and prospered with the Industrial Revolution; the famous Soho ironworks of Watt and Boulton may still be seen. Yet it was not incorporated till the 19th cent. (1838). It became a centre of nonconformism, as exemplified by Joseph Priestley and others, and continued in the late 19th cent. by one of its most distinguished MPs, John Bright. During this period the Chamberlain and the Cadbury families, in their different spheres, contributed much to its development. In 1889 it was made a city; in 1897 its chief magistrate was given the title of Lord Mayor. Its limits were considerably extended in 1911 and again in 1928 and 1931, until the area amounted to 80 sq. m.

**Birmingham** USA. Industrial town in Alabama, near the S end of the Appalachian mountains. Pop. (1960) 340,887. Local deposits of coal, iron ore, and limestone provide raw materials for the important iron and steel industry. Also manufactures cement, cotton goods, chemicals, etc. Important rail and air route centre. Seat of several colleges.

**Birobidzhan** USSR. Capital of the Jewish Autonomous Region, in Khabarovsk Territory, RSFSR, on the Trans-Siberian Railway 100 m. WNW of Khabarovsk. Pop. (1970) 56,000. Sawmilling, woodworking. Manufactures clothing, footwear. The name is also applied to the Jewish AR.

**Birr** Irish Republic. Formerly Parsonstown. Town in W Co. Offaly, on the R. Brosna. Pop. (1966) 3,265. Market town. Brewing. In Birr Castle William Parsons, 3rd Earl of Rosse, installed his famous telescope (1845).

**Biscay, Bay of** ⟡ *Bay of Biscay*.

**Bisceglie** Italy. Seaport in the Bari province

in Apulia, on the Adriatic Sea 22 m. WNW of Bari. Pop. (1961) 41,451. Trade in wine and olives. Engineering, sawmilling. Manufactures furniture etc. Cathedral (11th-cent.).

**Bischoff, Mount** (Tasmania) Australia. Tin-mining centre in Tasmania, near Waratah, 90 m. W of Launceston. Production began in 1870.

**Bishop Auckland** England. Urban district in Durham, near the confluence of the R. Gaunless with the R. Wear, 9 m. SSW of Durham. Pop. (1961) 35,276. Coalmines and ironworks in the neighbourhood. Seat of the bishops of Durham since the 12th cent.

**Bishop's Stortford** England. Municipal borough in E Hertfordshire, on the R. Stort 12 m. ENE of Hertford. Pop. (1961) 18,308. Brewing. Manufactures matches, electrical equipment. Remains of a Norman castle, formerly belonging to the bishops of London, with a dungeon (the 'Bishop's Hole') long used as an ecclesiastical prison. Birthplace of Cecil Rhodes (1853–1902).

**Biskra** Algeria. Town and oasis 120 m. SSW of Constantine, in the Constantine department. Pop. 53,000. Vast numbers of date palms: an important date market. Also olive and pomegranate trees. Connected by rail with Constantine and Touggourt. Hot in summer, but a popular resort owing to the cool sunny winters and the very light annual rainfall (about 7 ins.). In a small oasis 12 m. SE is the mosque with the tomb of Sidi Okbar, the Arab leader who conquered N Africa for Islam and was killed by the Berber in A.D. 682.

**Bisley** England. Village in Surrey, 3 m. WNW of Woking. Venue of the annual meeting of the National Rifle Association since 1890.

**Bismarck** USA. State capital of N Dakota, on the Missouri R. where it is crossed by the Northern Pacific railway route to the W. Pop. (1960) 27,670. Market centre for the agricultural produce of the surrounding spring-wheat area.

**Bismarck Archipelago** SW Pacific Ocean. Volcanic group of islands E of New Guinea, in the Territory of New Guinea. Area 20,000 sq. m. Pop. (1966) 218,265 (mostly Melanesians). Largest island New Britain; others include New Ireland, Lavongai, Admiralty Islands. Mountainous, with active volcanoes, and densely forested. Produce copra, cacao, and some copper and gold. Became a German protectorate (1884) and part of the Australian mandated territory of New Guinea (1921).

**Bissagos Islands** ◊ *Bijagós Islands.*

**Bissão (Bissau)** Portuguese Guinea. Capital (since 1942) and chief seaport, on the estuary of the Geba R. Pop. 3,000. Exports copra, palm oil, rice, etc. Slave-trade centre from the late 17th to the late 19th cent.

**Bisutun** ◊ *Behistun.*

**Bitolj** (Turkish **Monastir**) Yugoslavia. Town in Macedonia 70 m. S of Skoplje. Pop. (1961) 49,001. Agricultural centre. Carpet making, tanning, etc. Near by was the ancient Heraclea Lyncestis. Captured from the Turks by the Serbs and incorporated in Serbia in 1913.

**Bitonto** Italy. Ancient Butuntum. Town in the Bari province in Apulia, 10 m. W of Bari. Pop. (1961) 37,395. Market town. Produces wine, olive oil. Romanesque cathedral (12th/13th-cent.).

**Bitter Lakes** ◊ *Suez Canal.*

**Bizerta** (Fr. **Bizerte**) Tunisia. Seaport and naval base on the Mediterranean. Pop. (1966) 95,023. On the canalized channel which forms the outlet of the Lake of Bizerta to the sea, with good outer and inner harbours. At the SW corner·of the lake is the naval base of Sidi Abdallah. After centuries of neglect, the port was reopened (1895) by the French. Taken by the Germans in the 2nd World War, heavily bombed, almost completely destroyed, and recaptured by the Allies in 1943. Post-war reconstruction was rapid. After Tunisian independence France retained the naval base; this caused friction between the French and the Tunisians, and fighting in 1961. After UN discussions, Tunisia agreed to temporary French retention of the base. The first steel works in Tunisia were inaugurated at Menzel Bourguiba (formerly Ferryville), near Bizerta, in 1966.

**Björneborg** ◊ *Pori.*

**Blackburn** England. County borough in Lancashire 8 m. E of Preston, on the Leeds–Liverpool Canal. Pop. (1961) 106,114. Became a leading centre of cotton weaving with the invention (1764) of the spinning-jenny by James Hargreaves (a native of the town). Also manufactures textile machinery, chemicals, paint, paper, electrical and leather goods. Brewing, engineering. The ancient Church of St Mary's was rebuilt in the 19th cent. and became the cathedral in 1926. Birthplace of Viscount Morley (1838–1923). **Black Country** England. Industrialized region in the Midlands, mainly in S Staffordshire but also comprising adjoining parts of Worcestershire and Warwickshire. The name derives from the smoke and soot formerly emitted by the many foundries and furnaces. Towns include Wolverhampton, Walsall, West Bromwich, Wednesbury.

**Black Forest** (Ger. **Schwarzwald**) Federal German Republic. Thickly wooded mountainous district in Baden-Württemberg, separated from Switzerland by the R. Rhine, rising to 4,898 ft. in the Feldberg. Area 1,800 sq. m. Source of the Danube, the Neckar, and various tributaries of the Rhine. Manufactures cuckoo-clocks, musical boxes, and wooden toys, as an adjunct to the tourist trade.

**Blackfriars** England. District of the City of London, near where the Fleet Ditch enters the Thames. Linked with Southwark by Blackfriars Bridge. The name derives from the Dominican priory (1238) destroyed in the Great Fire (1666).

**Blackheath** England. Residential district of S E London in the Greater London boroughs of Lewisham and Greenwich, formerly a heath crossed by the Roman road from Dover to London. Wat Tyler, leader of the Peasants' Revolt (1381), and Jack Cade, leader of another peasant rebellion (1450), mustered their forces here. England's first game of golf (brought in by James I and his Scots courtiers) was played on Blackheath (1608). The present open space (267 acres), a remnant of the former heath, is shared by Lewisham and Greenwich.

**Black Hills** USA. Isolated group of mountains on the borders of SW South Dakota and NE Wyoming, rising in Harney Peak to 7,242 ft, and generally about 2,000 ft above the surrounding plains. Much of the area is now a national park. In 1874 gold was discovered and it became the scene of a gold rush. A remarkable feature is a group of gigantic sculptures carved from the granite side of Mt Rushmore (◊ *Mount Rushmore National Memorial*).

**Black Mountain** Wales. Ridge on the border between Breconshire and Carmarthenshire, rising to 2,632 ft in Carmarthen Van.

**Black Mountains** Wales. Range in E Breconshire, on the borders with Monmouthshire and Herefordshire, rising to 2,660 ft in Waun Fach.

**Blackpool** England. County borough in Lancashire, on the Irish Sea. Pop. (1961) 152,133. One of Britain's leading holiday resorts, attracting annually about 8

million visitors, esp. from the industrial north and the Midlands. Climate bracing. Sandy beaches, promenades, swimming baths, cinemas, theatres, aquarium, famous illuminations, and a 520-ft-high tower modelled on the Eiffel Tower in Paris. Conferences of various kinds are held here.

**Black Sea (Euxine Sea)** Europe/Asia. Ancient Pontus Euxinus. Large inland sea between Europe and Asia, bounded by the USSR (N and E), Turkey (S), and Bulgaria and Rumania (W). Area 164,000 sq. m. (excluding the Sea of Azov). Connected to the Aegean Sea and the Mediterranean in the S W by the Bosporus, the Sea of Marmara, and the Dardanelles, and with the Sea of Azov in the NE by the Kerch Strait. In general the E and S coasts are backed by mountains; the W and N coasts are mostly low-lying, with several extensive *limans* or lagoons at river mouths. The many rivers emptying into it (inc. the Danube, the Dniester, the S Bug, and the Dnieper, and the Don and the Kuban into the Sea of Azov) give the surface waters a low salinity. A unique feature is that below about 80 fathoms it is stagnant, charged with sulphuretted hydrogen, and without any marine life. Almost tideless, with an outward surface flow through the Bosporus. Principal fisheries in the N and W: the varied catch includes anchovy, sardine, mackerel, tunny. Virtually a Turkish lake from the 15th to the 19th cent. With the collapse of the Ottoman Empire and the growth of Russian power in the area, it increased in importance as an international trade highway. Turkey's right to fortify the Bosporus and the Dardanelles was removed by the Treaty of Lausanne (1923) but restored by the Montreux Convention (1936). ◊ *Crimea*.

**Blackwater River** Irish Republic. River 104 m. long, rising near Castleisland in Co. Kerry, flowing E through Co. Cork to Co. Waterford, turning S, and entering the Atlantic at Youghal. Noted for trout and salmon.

**Blackwater River** Irish Republic/Northern Ireland. River 50 m. long, rising near Fivemiletown in Tyrone (NI), flowing generally E and N as the S E border with Monaghan (IR) and Armagh (NI), and entering the SW end of Lough Neagh.

**Blaenavon** Wales. Urban district in Monmouthshire, 6 m. NNW of Pontypool. Pop. (1961) 8,424. Coalmines. Iron and steel works.

**Blagoveshchensk** USSR. Town and river port in the Amur region (RSFSR), on the Amur R. at the confluence with the Zeya R., on a branch of the Trans-Siberian Railway. Pop. (1970) 128,000. Flour milling, sawmilling. Manufactures machinery, furniture, footwear, etc.

**Blair Atholl** Scotland. Village and resort in Perthshire, at the confluence of the Tilt and the Garry rivers 6 m. NW of Pitlochry. Pop. 1,900. Whisky distilling. Blair Castle, seat of the dukes of Atholl, was built in the 13th cent. and restored in the 19th.

**Blairgowrie and Rattray** Scotland. Small burgh in E Perthshire, comprising two towns on opposite banks of the R. Ericht, linked by a bridge and amalgamated in 1929. Pop. (1961) 5,168. Market town in a fruit-growing region (esp. raspberries).

**Blanc (Blanco), Cape** Mauritania. Headland at the S end of the Cape Blanc peninsula, just S of the frontier between Spanish Sahara and Mauritania. Port Étienne stands on the E coast of the peninsula.

**Blanc, Cape** Tunisia. Headland on the Mediterranean coast of N Tunisia 5 m. NNW of Bizerta. Often considered the northernmost point of Africa (though the neighbouring coast extends slightly farther N).

**Blanc, Mont** ◊ *Mont Blanc*.

**Blanco, Cape** ◊ *Blanc, Cape* (Mauritania).

**Blandford (Blandford Forum)** England. Municipal borough in Dorset, on the R. Stour 22 m. SW of Salisbury. Pop. (1961) 3,558. Market town in a dairy- and sheep-farming region. Almost completely destroyed by fire in 1731, it was rebuilt in uniform Georgian style.

**Blantyre** Malawi. Town in the Shiré highlands at 3,600 ft. Pop. (1966) 109,461 (inc. about 4,000 Europeans). On the railway from Beira to L. Malawi. Chief commercial centre. Headquarters of the missionary societies. Founded 1876, when the Church of Scotland Mission building was erected. Named Blantyre after Livingstone's birthplace. Became a municipality 1895. Joined with Limbe 1956, and named Blantyre-Limbe; renamed Blantyre 1966.

**Blantyre** Scotland. Town in N Lanarkshire 8 m. SE of Glasgow. Pop. 16,800. In a coalmining region. Engineering etc. Includes the village of Low Blantyre, birthplace of David Livingstone (1813–73), with a Livingstone museum.

**Blarney** Irish Republic. Village in Co. Cork 3 m. WNW of Cork. Pop. (1966) 932. Woollen mills. Ruins of the 15th-cent. Blarney Castle contain the famous Blarney Stone, kissing which is reputed to endow one with 'blarney', the gift of persuasive speech.

**Blasket Islands** Irish Republic. Group of rocky islands off Slea Head in Co. Kerry, uninhabited since 1953. The people used to subsist mainly on fishing.

**Blaydon** England. Municipal borough in Durham, on the R. Tyne 4 m. W of Newcastle upon Tyne. Pop. (1961) 30,615. Coalmining and industrial centre. Manufactures coal by-products, firebricks, bottle glass. Immortalized in the song *Blaydon Races*.

**Blenheim** (Ger. **Blindheim**) Federal German Republic. Village in W Bavaria, 30 m. NE of Ulm. Pop. 1,000. Near Blenheim took place an important battle (1704) in the War of the Spanish Succession, when the English and the Austrians, under Marlborough and Prince Eugene, defeated the French and the Bavarians, under Marshals Tallard and Marsin.

**Blenheim** New Zealand. Capital of Marlborough district in the NE of the S Island 160 m. NNE of Christchurch. Pop. (1966) 13,242. In a farming area. Flour milling, brewing.

**Blenheim Palace** England. Seat of the dukes of Marlborough, near Woodstock in Oxfordshire. Presented to the 1st Duke of Marlborough, for his many victories in the French wars, and named in honour of his greatest victory, the Battle of Blenheim. Designed by Vanbrugh, it was begun in 1705, but Marlborough did not see the work completed. Birthplace of Sir Winston Churchill (1874–1965), who is buried in the near-by village churchyard at Bladon.

**Bletchley** England. Urban district in NE Buckinghamshire, 10 m. E of Buckingham, including the small town of Fenny Stratford. Pop. (1961) 17,093. Railway junction. Market town. Engineering, brickmaking, etc.

**Blida** Algeria. Town in the S of the fertile Mitidja plain, 30 m. SW of Algiers. Pop. (1967) 87,000. On the railway between Algiers and Oran. Vineyards, citrus orchards, and olive groves in the region. Considerable trade in oranges, wine, etc. Flour milling. Manufactures olive oil, soap, etc. Almost destroyed by an earthquake in 1825, rebuilt, and again damaged by earthquake 1867.

**Block Island** USA. Island 7 m. long off the

S coast of Rhode Island, from which it is separated by Block Island Sound. Summer resort, catering esp. for yachtsmen and deep-sea fishermen.

**Blocksberg** ◊ *Brocken.*

**Bloemfontein** S Africa. Capital of the Orange Free State and judicial capital of the Republic (since 1910), 300 m. WNW of Durban at a height of 4,600 ft. Pop. (1967) 146,000 (inc. 63,200 whites). Trading centre for much of the OFS and ◊ *Lesotho.* Railway engineering, meat canning. Manufactures furniture etc. Because of its central position it is the venue of agricultural, religious, political, and other conferences. Also an educational centre, seat of the Orange Free State University (1855). Because of the altitude and clear air, the US universities of Harvard and Michigan have built observatories near by. Founded 1846.

**Blois** France. Prefecture of the Loir-et-Cher department, on the Loire R. 33 m. SW of Orléans. Pop. (1968) 44,762. Market town. Trade in wine, brandy, grain. Manufactures furniture, vinegar, etc. The château, part of which dates from the 13th cent., is one of the most famous in the middle Loire valley.

**Bloomfield** USA. Formerly Wardsesson. Residential and industrial town in New Jersey, just NNW of Newark. Pop. (1960) 51,867. Manufactures metal and electrical goods, pharmaceutical products, etc. Renamed (1796) after General Joseph Bloomfield.

**Bloomington** (Illinois) USA. Industrial town 120 m. SW of Chicago, in the Corn Belt. Pop. (1960) 36,271. Railway engineering and other industries. Seat of the Illinois Wesleyan University (1850).

**Bloomington** (Indiana) USA. Industrial town 47 m. SSW of Indianapolis. Pop. (1961) 31,357. Manufactures furniture, gloves, etc. Seat of Indiana University (1838).

**Bloomsbury** England. District in central London, from 1965 in the Greater London borough of Camden. Famous for its many squares (Bedford, Brunswick, Gordon, Mecklenburgh, Russell, Tavistock, etc.) and for the 'Bloomsbury School' of writers and artists in the 1930s. Its standing as a residential district deteriorated in the early 20th cent. but it remains a major educational and cultural centre. Seat of the British Museum, much of the University of London, the Royal Academy of Dramatic Art, the headquarters of the YMCA, etc. Home of many famous 19th- and early-20th-cent. artists and authors. Dickens lived at 48 Doughty Street (now a museum) 1837–9 and Disraeli was born at 22 Theobald's Road (1804). The grounds of the famous 18th-cent. Foundling Hospital are now public gardens named after the founder, Thomas Coram (1668–1751).

**Bluefields** Nicaragua. Chief Caribbean port, near the mouth of the Bluefields (Escondido) R. Pop. (1967) 17,706. Exports hardwoods, bananas. Outport El Bluff. ◊◊ *Mosquito Coast.*

**Blue Mountains** (Australia) ◊ *Great Dividing Range.*

**Blue Mountains** Jamaica. Range in the E, of average height about 3,500 ft, but rising to 7,402 ft in Blue Mountain Peak. Thickly wooded and picturesque; a popular tourist area. Coffee grown on the slopes.

**Blue Ridge** USA. Range of the Appalachian mountains extending SW–NE 650 m. from N Georgia to the Maryland border. Average height 2,000–4,000 ft, rising to 6,684 ft in Mt Mitchell. Attractive scenery; a popular tourist area with many resorts.

**Blumenau** Brazil. Market town in Santa Catarina state, on the Itajaí R. 110 m. S of Curitiba. Pop. 48,000 (largely of German origin).

**Blyth** England. Municipal borough in Northumberland, at the mouth of the R. Blyth 11 m. NNE of Newcastle. Pop. (1961) 35,933. Seaport. Exports coal. Imports timber. Coalmining centre. Shipbuilding. Fishing.

**Boa Vista** ◊ *Roraima.*

**Bobo-Dioulasso** Upper Volta. Commercial town in the SW, 210 m. WSW of Ouagadougou, on the railway to the latter from Abidjan (Ivory Coast). Pop. (1967) 68,000. Trade in groundnuts, shea nuts, etc.

**Bobriki** ◊ *Novomoskovsk.*

**Bobruisk** USSR. Town in the Byelorussian SSR on the Berezina R. 85 m. SE of Minsk. Pop. (1970) 138,000. Commercial centre. Trade esp. in timber and grain. Large paper and cellulose works. Engineering. Manufactures clothing, footwear.

**Bocholt** Federal German Republic. Industrial town in N Rhine-Westphalia, 30 m. N of Duisburg, near the Dutch frontier. Pop. (1963) 46,100. Manufactures textiles, machinery, etc.

**Bochum** Federal German Republic. Industrial town in N Rhine-Westphalia, in the Ruhr district. Pop. (1968) 348,620. Coalmining. Manufactures steel, mining equipment, chemicals, television sets, textiles, etc. A small market town before the development of the coal and iron industries in the 19th cent. Severely damaged in the 2nd World War.

**Bodélé Depression** ◊ *Chad, Lake.*

**Bodensee** ◊ *Constance, Lake.*

**Bodmin** England. Municipal borough and county town of Cornwall, 27 m. WNW of Plymouth. Pop. (1961) 6,209. Market town. To the NE is Bodmin Moor, which rises to 1,375 ft in Brown Willy.

**Boeotia** Greece. *Nome* in the Attica peninsula, bounded on the S by the Gulf of Corinth. Area 1,225 sq. m. Pop. (1961) 114,474. Cap. Levadia (pop. 12,609). Agriculture is important in the fertile valleys. Wheat, wine, and olives produced; livestock reared. The ancient Boeotian League was a confederacy of cities led by Thebes in the 6th cent. B.C. and including Orchomenus and Plataea.

**Bofors** ◊ *Karlskoga.*

**Bognor Regis** England. Urban district in W Sussex, 13 m. W of Worthing, on the English Channel. Pop. (1961) 28,144. Seaside resort. Several convalescent homes. Pleasure gardens, promenade, etc. The suffix *Regis* was added after King George V's convalescence in Bognor (1929).

**Bogor** Indonesia. Formerly Buitenzorg. Resort 30 m. S of Jakarta at a height of 850 ft. Pop. (1961) 154,092. It was the residence of the governor-general of the Dutch East Indies, and has famous botanical gardens (1817). Seat of part of the University of Indonesia.

**Bogotá** Colombia. Capital of Colombia and of the Cundinamarca department, on the slopes of the fertile Cundinamarca basin, in the E Cordillera, at a height of 8,661 ft. Pop. (1964) 1,487,920. Remote from the rest of the country, but served by regular airlines, by highways from Carácas (via Cúcuta) and from the W coast (via Girardot in the Magdalena valley), and by light railways. Mild climate with even temperatures. A suburban sprawl surrounds the old colonial heart of the city, and broad avenues cut across narrow colonial streets. Manufactures textiles, tobacco products, chemicals, food products, etc. University (1572). Originally a centre of Chibcha culture. Founded (1538) by the Spaniards as Santa Fé de Bogotá; the name derives from Bacatá, the Chibcha

name for the district. Became the capital of the Spanish viceroyalty of New Granada, and an important cultural centre.

**Bogue Islets** ◊ *Montego Bay.*

**Bohemia** (Ger. **Böhmen,** Czech **Čechy).** Former kingdom in central Europe, bounded by the Sudeten Mountains, the Moravian Heights, the Böhmerwald, and the Erzgebirge. Area 20,102 sq. m. A province of Czechoslovakia 1918–49; then administratively divided into regions. Mainly a plateau cut by the Elbe (Labe) and the Vltava rivers and their tributaries. Many fertile areas, esp. in the river valleys. Produces cereals, sugar-beet, potatoes, fruit, hops. The chief wealth is mineral: one of Europe's main sources of uranium; also coal, lignite, iron ore, graphite, silver, etc. Metallurgical, textile, and other industries in Prague, Plzeň (Pilsen; world-famous for beer), and a number of towns along the S foot of the Erzgebirge, e.g. Ústi nad Labem, Most, etc. The famous watering-places of Karlovy Vary (Karlsbad) and Mariánské Lazne (Marienbad) are in the NW.

**Bohemian Forest** ◊ *Böhmerwald.*

**Böhmerwald (Bohemian Forest;** Czech **Český Les)** Czechoslovakia/Federal German Republic. Forested mountain range, 150 m. long, forming the frontier between Czechoslovakia and Bavaria (FGR), rising to 4,777 ft in Mt Arber. Divided by the Furth pass into a NW portion and a higher SE portion. Little agriculture. Coal, lignite, and graphite deposits. Main product timber.

**Bohol** Philippines. Island N of Mindanao. Area 1,588 sq. m. Pop. (1960) 620,000. Chief town Tagbilaran, in the SW. Rice, coconuts, and Manila hemp cultivated.

**Bois de Boulogne** France. A park and fashionable district in W Paris, extending from the former fortifications to the Seine R. Area 2,100 acres. The name derives from Boulogne-sur-Seine (now Boulogne-Billancourt). Contains the racecourses of Auteuil and Longchamp, and the Jardins d'Acclimatation for plants and animals. Given to the city by Napoleon III when he became emperor (1852).

**Boise** USA. State capital of Idaho, on the Boise R. in the SW. Pop. (1960) 34,481. Commercial centre, marketing agricultural produce. Food-processing and other industries.

**Bokhara** ◊ *Bukhara.*

**Boksburg** S Africa. Industrial town in the

Transvaal, 13 m. E of Johannesburg, at a height of 5,348 ft. Pop. (1967) 83,300 (29,950 whites, 44,300 Bantu). Chief centre of the E Rand goldmining industry. Manufactures railway and electrical equipment, soap, pottery, etc.

**Bolama** ◊ *Bijagós Islands*.

**Bolan Pass** Pakistan. Pass about 60 m. long through the Brahui Range in W Pakistan, used by the railway and the road between Sibi and Quetta. Rises to nearly 5,900 ft. In the past it was an important route into India from the NW.

**Bolivia** Republic of central S America. Area 424,160 sq. m. Pop. (1967) 4,294,000. Cap. Sucre; administrative cap. La Paz. Official lang. Spanish; the Indians speak Aymará, Quechua, and Guaraní. Rel. Roman Catholic.

Completely land-locked, bounded by Brazil (N and E), Paraguay and Argentina (S), and Chile and Peru (W). Mountainous, with difficult communications. Deficient in food production; minerals (esp. tin) are the main resources. The people are divided into widely differing strata, the bulk being illiterate and poor. Political life is turbulent. The country is divided administratively into 9 departments: La Paz, Cochabamba, Potosí, Santa Cruz, Chuquisaca, Tarija, Oruro, Beni, Pando.

TOPOGRAPHY, CLIMATE. The mountain system of the Andes reaches a width of 400 m. (W). Between the W Cordillera, studded with large volcanoes along the Chile frontier, and the E Cordillera is the open, wind-swept, and treeless Altiplano, a high tableland with large lakes (Titicaca, Poopó), salt flats, and loose, dry, porous soil. The high Cordillera Real has forested slopes in the N and drops steeply to the E lowlands. The S slopes are drier and are cut by the tributaries of the Río Grande, Mamoré, and Pilcomayo rivers. In the NE are tropical rain-forests; in the SE a more open woodland alternates with savannah, swamp, and scrub.

RESOURCES, PEOPLE, *etc.* Handicapped by difficulties of communication, and by the fact that most of the population live on the Altiplano, where agriculture is unrewarding. The main industry is mining, for which the Indians supply cheap labour and have been long exploited. Tin (the most important mineral), lead, zinc, wolfram, and some decreasing silver are the chief exports. The region E of the Andes produces sugar-cane, rice, coffee, and other food crops, but the cost of transporting them to the Altiplano is great and the potentialities of these more fertile areas remain underdeveloped. The Indians of the Altiplano (physically adapted to life at high altitudes by a remarkable lung development) are backward, superstitious, and firmly attached to their traditional way of life; efforts to educate them and persuade them to move to more productive areas make slow progress. Their chief crops are potatoes and barley.

HISTORY. Near L. Titicaca (on the Altiplano) there are remains of an ancient pre-Inca civilization. Under the Incas the area was prosperous, but with the destruction of their roads and economic organization by the Spanish, the surviving Indians fell to subsistence level. The Spanish, attracted to the Altiplano by the silver mines of ◊ *Potosí* (then the most obvious source of wealth), grossly exploited the Indians; there were frequent risings. Sucre, one of Bolívar's generals, freed the colony from Spain (1825) and named it after the great liberator. But it remained in the grip of rapacious and incompetent rulers, and lost land to Chile, Paraguay, and Brazil. In the war with Chile (1879–83) it lost its strip of Pacific coast, but in return Chile built the railway from La Paz to Arica, where Bolivia has the use of a free port which has become her main export outlet. Part of the N territory of Acre was lost to Brazil (1903), and most of the Chaco passed to Paraguay (1938) after a war which left both countries exhausted. The 2nd World War brought wealth to the mine-owners, but no general prosperity; social unrest and rebellion grew. The National Revolutionary Movement came to power in 1952 and nationalized the tin mines (both those of the Bolivian millionaire Patiño and those belonging to foreigners). Efforts are being made to improve the standard of living of the Indians and of workers in general.

**Bollington** England. Urban district in E Cheshire, 3 m. NNE of Macclesfield. Pop. (1961) 5,642. Textile printing and dyeworks.

**Bologna** Italy. Ancient Bononia. Capital of Bologna province in Emilia-Romagna, on a fertile plain at the foot of the Apennines, on the Aemilian Way 52 m. N of Florence. Pop. (1968) 485,435. Chief industry engineering. Well known for macaroni and sausages. Arcaded streets and historic buildings give it a medieval appearance. The Cathedral of San Pietro (first built in 910 and twice rebuilt) and the 13th-cent. Church of San Francesco were severely damaged in the 2nd World War. Many other fine churches (e.g. the great Gothic church of San Petronio), palaces, and the early-12th-cent. leaning towers of Asinelli and Garisenda. In the 2nd cent. B.C. Bononia was made a Roman colony. Became a free city in the 12th cent. In the Middle Ages a leading centre of learning in Europe. The university (founded 1200) was distinguished for the early study of human anatomy. Dante and Petrarch were among the students. Galvani (1737–98), a native of Bologna, lectured here. The civic museum has an excellent collection of local antiquities, and the art gallery many fine works of the Bolognese school of painting. Under papal rule almost continuously 1506–1860, then absorbed into the kingdom of Italy. Birthplace of Marconi (1874–1937).

**Bolsover** England. Urban district in NE Derbyshire, 6 m. E of Chesterfield. Pop. (1961) 11,770. Coalmining. Limestone quarrying. Grew up round a Norman castle, rebuilt in the 17th cent. The famous Elizabethan mansion, Hardwick Hall, is 4 m. S.

**Bolton** England. County borough in Lancashire 11 m. NW of Manchester. Pop. (1961) 160,887. Important centre of the cotton industry, esp. spinning. Engineering. Manufactures textile machinery, chemicals, etc. Known from the 14th cent. for its woollen manufactures; with the invention and development of spinning machinery by Arkwright and Crompton in the late 18th cent. it became a leading cotton-manufacturing town. Birthplace of Samuel Crompton (1753–1827), whose half-timbered house 'Hall-i'-th'-Wood' is now a museum, and of the 1st Lord Leverhulme (1851–1925).

**Bolzano** Italy. Capital of Bolzano province, in Trentino-Alto Adige, on the Isarco R. near its confluence with the Adige, 37 m. S of the Brenner Pass. Pop. (1968) 101,825. Tourist centre. Industrial and commercial town. Fruit canning, flour milling. Manufactures textiles etc. Trade in fruits, wines, etc. Passed from Austria to Italy 1919.

**Boma** Congo (Kinshasa). Port on the N bank of the Congo R. 180 m. WSW of Kinshasa. Pop. 32,000. Exports palm oil, coffee, etc. Flourishing slave-trade centre from the 16th to the 18th cent. Became the capital of the Congo Free State 1886. Later capital of the Belgian Congo; succeeded by Léopoldville (Kinshasa) 1926.

**Bombay** India. Capital of Maharashtra and the largest city in India, on the Arabian Sea. Pop. (1961) 4,152,056. The country's leading seaport; exports cotton goods, oilseeds, cotton, etc. Important industrial and commercial centre, with the cotton industry pre-eminent; also manufactures chemicals, machinery, paper, carpets, etc. Stands at the S end of Bombay Island, which is about 11 m. long and 3 m. wide, and has a magnificent natural harbour on the sheltered E side, overlooked by the impressive arch known as the 'Gateway of India', built to commemorate the visit of King George V (1911). Beside the harbour there are oil refineries, while power for the factories and mills (mainly in the N part of the city) is derived from hydroelectric plants in the Western Ghats on the mainland. Bombay has many fine public buildings, and almost as imposing are the residences of the wealthier citizens on Malabar Hill and Back Bay, which, despite its name, faces the open sea. The university (founded 1857) has 42 constituent colleges. Bombay Island was acquired from a Gujarat sultan by the Portuguese in 1534, and was ceded to Charles II of England (1661) as part of the dowry of Catherine of Braganza; from him it passed to the E India Company. Trade gradually increased, and the city expanded considerably in the 19th cent. through the building of the railways, the opening of the Suez Canal, and the establishment of the textile industry. Under British rule it was capital of Bombay Presidency; with the partition (1947) it became capital of Bombay state in the Indian Union, and with the reorganization of 1960 capital of Maharashtra. The population is mainly Hindu, but is very cosmopolitan in character, and includes about 70,000 Parsees, whose influence is out of all proportion to their number.

**Bonaire** ◊ *Netherlands Antilles.*

**Bonanza Creek** ◊ *Klondike River.*

**Bondy** France. Suburb of NE Paris, in the Seine-St Denis department, on the Ourcq Canal. Pop. (1968) 51,692. Manufactures chemicals, glass, biscuits, etc.

**Bône** ◊ *Annaba.*

**Bo'ness (Borrowstounness)** Scotland. Small

burgh, industrial town, and port in W Lothian, on the Firth of Forth 16 m. WNW of Edinburgh. Pop. (1961) 10,194. Coal-mining. Manufactures pottery, fertilizers. To the S are traces of Antoninus's Wall (Graham's Dyke).

**Bonin Islands** (Japanese **Ogasawara-gunto**) Pacific Ocean. Volcanic island group about 600 m. S of Tokyo. Area 40 sq. m. Pop. (1965) 203. Three main groups: Bailey Is., Beechey Is., Parry Is. The largest island is Chichi-jima, with the main harbour and a US naval base. Breadfruit and bananas are grown. The Japanese name derives from the reputed 16th-cent. discoverer Ogasawara. Annexed by Japan 1876. Occupied by the US after the 2nd World War (1945). Returned to Japan 1968.

**Bonn** Federal German Republic. Ancient Castra Bonnensia. Capital (since 1949), in N Rhine-Westphalia, on the Rhine 15 m. SSE of Cologne. Pop. (1968) 137,960. Engineering workshops, tobacco factories, publishing houses, printing works. Manufactures office equipment, pharmaceutical products, etc. An ancient city; in Roman times a military settlement. Passed from France to Prussia 1815. Occupied by British and French troops 1918–26. Seat of the West German Constituent Assembly in 1948. Many buildings of interest; outstanding among them is the University (founded 1786), housed since 1818 in the electoral palace of the archbishops of Cologne. Minster (mainly 11th/13th-cent.). The birthplace of Beethoven (1770–1827) is now a museum. Among modern buildings, the Bundeshaus (Parliament).

**Bonneville, Lake** USA. A large body of water which in the Quaternary era occupied much of present-day Utah; the Great Salt Lake of today is a remnant. The former lake bed is now a dry flat plain, where shallow *playas* form after heavy rain and soon disappear. In 1935–9 the Bonneville Salt Flats were used for attempts on the motor-car speed record.

**Bonnyrigg and Lasswade** Scotland. Small burgh in Midlothian 6 m. SE of Edinburgh, formed when the two towns were united (1929). Pop. (1961) 6,331. Manufactures carpets, cement.

**Boothia** Canada. Formerly Boothia Felix. Low-lying peninsula, reaching Murchison Point, 71°55′ N, the most northerly limit of the N American mainland. Joined to the mainland by the Boothia Isthmus. Discovered and explored by Sir James Ross (1829–33), who placed the N magnetic pole here. Named after Ross's patron, Sir Felix Booth.

**Boothia, Gulf of** Canada. Gulf nearly 200 m. long, an inlet of the Arctic Ocean between the Boothia Peninsula and Baffin Island.

**Bootle** England. County borough in SW Lancashire, on the R. Mersey adjoining Liverpool, including much of the Mersey dock system. Pop. (1961) 82,829. Seaport. Extensive timber trade. Tanning, engineering, tin-smelting, and other industries.

**Boppard** Federal German Republic. Town in the Rhineland-Palatinate, on the left bank of the Rhine R. 8 m. S of Coblenz. Pop. 8,000. Tourist centre. Trade in wine.

**Borås** Sweden. Industrial town in the SW, on the Viske R. 35 m. E of Göteborg. Pop. (1968) 70,144. Centre of the textile industry. Manufactures hosiery, clothing, etc. Founded (1622) by King Gustavus Adolphus.

**Bordeaux** France. Ancient Burdigala. Prefecture of the Gironde department on the Garonne R. 60 m. from the sea. Pop. (1968) 270,996. Chief port of SW France. Large export trade in wines (known generally as 'Bordeaux'), the produce of four districts of the Gironde department, Graves, Sauternes, Médoc, St Émilion. Also exports petroleum products. Manufactures many of the requisites of the wine trade, e.g. bottles, casks, corks, crates. Shipbuilding, sugar refining. Oil refineries at Bec d'Ambès, Pauillac, on the Gironde. Chemical and food-processing industries. A well planned city, with many 18th-cent. buildings. At the centre is the Place des Quinconces, which has imposing statues of Montaigne (1533–92) and Montesquieu (1689–1755), both born in the neighbourhood. Cathedral (12th/15th-cent.), several old churches, and an 18th-cent. theatre. University (1441). Important commercial centre in Roman times. In the 4th cent. A.D. became capital of Aquitania Secunda, but declined after the collapse of the Roman Empire. Prospered again under the English (1154–1453). Became capital of the Guienne province under Louis XI. Much improved during the 18th cent. Headquarters of the Girondists during the French Revolution. Temporarily the seat of the French government during the Franco-Prussian War (1870–71) and in both world wars.

**Border, the** Scotland/England. The area

on both sides of the border between England and Scotland. The border counties are Northumberland and Cumberland on the English side, and Berwick, Roxburgh, and Dumfries, on the Scottish side. The Scottish shires of Selkirk and Peebles are also often reckoned as border counties.

**Bordighera** Italy. Town and seaport in Imperia province, in Liguria, on the Gulf of Genoa. Pop. (1961) 10,561. Popular winter resort; fine coastal scenery and gardens. Exports flowers, and large quantities of palm branches for use in churches on Palm Sunday.

**Borgholm** ⇔ *Öland Island*.

**Borislav** USSR. Industrial town in the Ukraine 50 m. SW of Lvov. Pop. 32,000. A petroleum and natural gas centre. Oil refining. Manufactures oilfield equipment. Passed from Austria to Poland (1919), and under the Potsdam Agreement (1945) to the USSR.

**Borisoglebsk** USSR. Town in RSFSR on the Khoper R. 130 m. ESE of Voronezh. Pop. 54,000. Meat packing, flour milling, tanning. Trade in grain. Founded (1646) as a Muscovite defence against the Crimean Tatars.

**Borku** Chad. Region in the L. Chad depression S of the Tibesti highlands. Chief town Faya (Largeau). Mostly sandy desert, with many *khors* (intermittent streams) and oases, where dates and barley are grown and goats raised. Formerly important in the slave trade between N and Central Africa.

**Borkum** Federal German Republic. Town at the W end of Borkum Island. Popular holiday resort.

**Borkum Island** Federal German Republic. Island off the estuary of the Ems R.; the westernmost of the E ⇔ *Frisian Islands*. Area 14 sq. m. Pop. 6,000.

**Borlänge** Sweden. Industrial town in Kopparberg county, 120 m. NW of Stockholm. Pop. (1968) 29,060. Important steelworks.

**Borneo.** Largest island of the Malay Archipelago, lying E of the Malay peninsula and Sumatra. Area 287,000 sq. m. Pop. about 6 millions. It is divided politically into four sections, the largest of which forms part of Indonesia, occupies more than two thirds of the island, and is known to the Indonesians as Kalimantan; this section is subdivided into four provinces, W, S, E and Central Kalimantan. The other three sections, all in the N, are the two former British colonies of Sarawak and North Borneo (renamed Sabah), since 1963 part of the Federation of Malaysia, and the British protectorate of Brunei. Much of the interior is mountainous, with Mt Kinabalu in Sabah rising to 13,697 ft. A central core of ranges extends NE-SW across the island, and the many rivers rising therein include the Kapuas and Rajang, which flow W, and the Barito, which flows S. The climate is hot and humid throughout the year, the rainfall exceeding 100 ins. annually, and a large proportion of the island is densely forested.

Rice and sago are grown as subsistence crops both on the broad coastal lowlands and inland on cleared sections of forest. Rubber and copra are exported. There are important oilfields: in Kalimantan near the port of Balikpapan and on Tarakan Island, in Brunei around Seria, and in Sarawak around Miri. In general the island is thinly populated, the various pagan Dyak tribes of the interior living mainly along the banks of the rivers, which form the principal highways; around the coasts there are many Malays (who, like the Dyaks, largely subsist on rice and fish, but are Muslims by religion) and Chinese, who are frequently traders. Apart from those mentioned the chief towns are Bandjarmasin (Kalimantan), Kota Kinabalu (Sabah), Kuching (Sarawak), Brunei.

Borneo has never had political unity, and its name is derived from Brunei, once a much more powerful and extensive sultanate than it is at present. The Portuguese and Spaniards established trading relations with the island in the 16th cent. and the Dutch and British in the 17th cent. With European influence removed in the early 19th cent., the coastal natives indulged in large-scale piracy, but British authority was later restored in the N and Dutch in the S, boundaries being defined by treaty in 1891. During the 2nd World War Borneo was occupied by the Japanese 1942-5. In 1950 the former Dutch Borneo became part of the republic of Indonesia.

**Bornholm** Denmark. Island in the Baltic Sea, off the SE coast of Sweden. Area 227 sq. m. Pop. (1965) 48,620. Chief town and seaport Rönne. With 8 small near-by islands it forms the *amt* of Bornholm. Principal industries agriculture and fishing. Popular seaside resort. Taken by the Hanseatic League 1510. Passed to Denmark 1522 and to Sweden 1645. Returned to Denmark 1660.

**Bornu** Nigeria. A formerly independent Muslim state, dating from the 11th cent. Divided into British, French, and German spheres of influence by the end of the 19th cent. The greater part was incorporated into Nigeria as a province in 1902. The German sphere of influence became part of the mandated territory of the British Cameroons in 1922.

**Borobudur** Indonesia. Ruin of an enormous Buddhist shrine in central Java, near Jogjakarta, consisting of a truncated and terraced pyramid, elaborately carved, and a seated Buddha. Probably built in the 9th cent.

**Borodino** USSR. Village in the RSFSR 75 m. W of Moscow. Scene of a bitter battle between Napoleon's army and the Russians during the march on Moscow (1812).

**Boroughbridge** England. Market town in the W Riding of Yorkshire, 6 m. ESE of Ripon on the R. Ure. Pop. (1961) 1,850. Three prehistoric monoliths, called the Devil's Arrows.

**Borromean Islands** Italy. Four islands in L. Maggiore. Pop. 300. Named after Count Vitaliano Borromeo, who constructed the famous palace and terraced gardens on Isola Bella in the 17th cent.

**Borrowdale** England. Picturesque valley in S Cumberland, in the Lake District, leading down to the S end of Derwentwater. Graphite mines (now exhausted) formerly supplying the pencil industry at Keswick.

**Borrowstounness** ◊ *Bo'ness.*

**Borsippa** Iraq. City of ancient Babylonia 15 m. SSW of Babylon near the Euphrates R. The site is marked by two large mounds, one of which may have represented the Tower of Babel.

**Borstal** England. Village in Kent, 2 m. S of Rochester. Seat of the original institution for the rehabilitation of juvenile delinquents (set up in 1902) from which the Borstal system developed and after which other such institutions are named.

**Boscastle** England. Small fishing port and tourist resort in N Cornwall 15 m. N of Bodmin. Pop. 700. Picturesque coastal scenery.

**Bosnia-Hercegovina** Yugoslavia. One of the constituent republics consisting of Bosnia in the N and the smaller Hercegovina in the S. Area 19,736 sq. m. Pop.

(1961) 3,277,948 (Serbs and Croats). Cap. Sarajevo. Mountainous, lying mainly in the Dinaric Alps. Agriculture in the valleys, where cereals, vegetables, fruit (chiefly plums), and tobacco are cultivated. Chief towns Sarajevo, Banja Luka, Tuzla, Mostar. From the 10th to the 12th cent. Bosnia was independent. While under Turkish rule 1463–1878 it incorporated Hercegovina. The area then came under Austro-Hungarian rule; annexed 1908. Serbian opposition led to the assassination of the Archduke Francis Ferdinand at Sarajevo (1914), which precipitated the 1st World War. Bosnia and Hercegovina became part of the newly created Yugoslavia 1918.

**Bosporus** (Turkish **Karadeniz Boğazi**) Asia/Europe. Ancient Bosporus Thracius (to distinguish it from Bosporus Cimmerius, the Strait of Kerch). Formerly also known as Bosphorus. Strait 18 m. long and $\frac{1}{2}$–$2\frac{1}{2}$ m. wide, joining the Black Sea to the Sea of Marmara and separating Asiatic from European Turkey, thus forming part of the boundary between Asia and Europe. The name means 'Oxford' and refers to the legend of Io, who crossed it in the form of a heifer. Several inlets along both shores; one of these, the Golden Horn, forms the harbour of Istanbul. Of great strategic importance, the strait was under the control of an international commission from 1918, but in 1936 Turkey was allowed to refortify it.

**Boston** England. Municipal borough in Parts of Holland, SE Lincolnshire, on the R. Witham 4 m. from the mouth. Pop. (1961) 24,903. Market town and seaport. Canning and other industries. The name (Botolph's Town) derives from St Botolph, founder of a monastery here (654). A leading English port, second only to London, in the 13th cent. The fine parish church of St Botolph is famous for its 273-ft tower (the 'Boston Stump'). Some of the Pilgrim Fathers were imprisoned in the 15th cent. Guildhall in 1607; they later helped to found Boston (Massachusetts), and in memory of this the American city has contributed funds for the restoration of St Botolph's Church. Regained some of its former importance as a port by the deepening of the Witham (1882–4) and the opening of a new quay (1938). Birthplace of John Foxe (1516–87).

**Boston** USA. State capital of Massachusetts, a major seaport and the leading fishing port of the USA, at the head of Massachusetts Bay; an ice-free and almost land-locked harbour 6½ m. from the open sea. Pop. (1970) 628,215. The commercial, industrial, and financial centre of New England; nicknamed 'the Hub of the Universe' on account of its position of leadership in the 19th cent. Imports are largely raw materials, e.g. wool, cotton, hides, coal, and oil, for local industries making textiles, leather goods, footwear, machinery, food products, soap, and chemicals, many of which are exported. A leading educational centre; seat of Boston University (1869), Northeastern University (1898), and part of Harvard University (the remainder being at neighbouring Cambridge); Boston Latin School, one of the country's first free public schools, was established in 1635. In the second half of the 19th cent. Boston was the literary centre of the USA; Emerson, Hawthorne, Thoreau, Whittier, Longfellow, Oliver Wendell Holmes, and Lowell all lived in and around the city. Among its historic buildings are Christ Church (1723), the old State House (1748, restored 1880), near which the Boston Massacre (1770) took place, Faneuil Hall (1762), and the State Capitol (1798). More modern buildings include the Boston Museum of Fine Arts and the Symphony Hall, home of the famous Boston Symphony Orchestra.

Founded (1630) by Puritans; named after the town in Lincolnshire from which many of its first citizens had come. Flourished as the principal colony of the Massachusetts Bay Company, and played an outstanding part in the struggle for independence. At the Boston Massacre (1770) several people were killed by British soldiers; at the Boston Tea Party (1773) British-taxed tea was thrown in the harbour; the Battle of Bunker Hill was fought in 1775, and in the following year the British withdrew. Incorporated as a city 1822. Again came into prominence with the formation (1831) of the Boston anti-slavery movement. In 1872 it suffered a disastrous fire in which much of the commercial quarter of the city was destroyed.

**Bosworth Field** ◊ *Market Bosworth.*

**Botany Bay** Australia. Inlet on the coast of New South Wales 5 m. S of Sydney. Captain Cook and Joseph Banks landed here (1770), and reported favourably on its suitability for colonization and pro-

claimed British sovereignty over the E Australian coast. Chosen as the site of a penal settlement (1788) and a party of 1,030 (inc. 736 convicts) landed, but were later transferred to Port Jackson (Sydney Cove). Modern Sydney has spread S, and now there are industries producing chemicals, plastics, etc. and oil refineries, while the outer suburbs of the city lie about the bay.

**Bothnia, Gulf of.** Arm of the Baltic Sea N of Ahvenanmaa (Åland Is.), between Sweden and Finland, named after the former maritime region of Bothnia (now divided between Sweden and Finland). Shallow and of low salinity, it is closed by ice in winter, but has several important timber ports on its coasts.

**Botoşani** Rumania. Town in Moldavia, 60 m. NW of Iaşi. Pop. (1968) 35,707. Named after Batu Khan, grandson of Genghis Khan. Important flour-milling industry. Manufactures textiles, clothing, etc.

**Botswana** Africa. Republic in southern Africa, formerly the British High Commission Territory of Bechuanaland, bounded by Rhodesia (NE), S Africa (SE and S) and SW Africa (W and N). Area 222,000 sq. m. Pop. (1964) 543,105 (3,921 Europeans). Cap. Gaberones. A dry plateau area, average height over 3,000 ft. Annual rainfall about 20 ins. (mainly in summer). In the N the large depressions of the Okavango Swamp, the Makarikari Salt Pan, and L. Ngami become lakes during the rainy season. In the dry grassland of the Kalahari in the S the mean annual rainfall is less than 20 ins. Maize and millets are grown, but unreliability of rainfall makes agriculture precarious except with irrigation. Main occupation cattle rearing. Principal exports beef carcasses, cattle, hides and skins. The population is chiefly in the E and SE, through which runs the railway from Mafeking (in Cape Province, S Africa) to Bulawayo (Rhodesia). Mafeking was formerly the extra-territorial headquarters of the administration. The most important tribe is the Bamangwato, whose capital is Serowe.

First taken under British protection in 1885; the area N of the Molopo R. became the Bechuanaland Protectorate, that S of the river a Crown Colony known as British Bechuanaland, which was annexed to Cape Colony (S Africa) 1895. The British government proposed to transfer the Protectorate to the British S Africa Company, but after protests from the Bechuana chiefs agreed to continue the Protectorate, which later became one of the three British High Commission Territories in southern Africa (the others were Basutoland and Swaziland). A new constitution providing for a legislative council with an elected majority and an executive council was introduced in 1961. Bechuanaland became the republic of Botswana, an independent member of the Commonwealth, in 1966. The former British Bechuanaland is a district in Cape Province (S Africa).

**Bouaké** Ivory Coast. Town 175 m. N N W of Abidjan, on the railway to the interior. Pop. (1964) 80,000. Important trade centre for coffee, cacao, etc. Cotton ginning. Manufactures textiles, sisal products.

**Bouches-du-Rhône** France. Department in the S E, formed (1790) from W Provence. Area 2,026 sq. m. Pop. (1968) 1,470,271. Prefecture Marseille. The W part (the Camargue) is a marshy plain where livestock are raised. East of this is the arid plain of the Crau and to the E and N are E–W ranges of hills (Maritime Alps). Along the Mediterranean coast are several lagoons (Étang de Berre, Étang de Vaccarès); inland there are many pools. Produces olive oil, wine, fruit; also lignite, salt. Marseille is the chief commercial and industrial centre. Other towns are Arles and Aix-en-Provence.

**Bougainville** (Solomon Islands) S W Pacific Ocean. Mountainous island, largest of the Solomon Is. Area 4,100 sq. m. Pop. (1966) 72,490. Rises to 8,500 ft in the volcanic Mt Balbi (N). The lowlands are densely forested. Produces copra, tagua nuts, etc. Discovered (1768) by Bougainville. Held by Germany from 1884. Occupied by Australia 1914. Retained since 1920 as part of the Territory of New Guinea.

**Bougie** Algeria. Seaport in the Constantine department, 95 m. W N W of Constantine. Pop. (1967) 63,000. Favourably situated in abundant sub-tropical vegetation on the slopes of the Jebel Guraya. Annual rainfall 40 ins. Chief port of Kabylia. Exports olive oil, fruits, cereals, petroleum, iron ore, phosphates. Connected by a branch line with the main railway from Constantine to Oran. Terminal of the oil pipeline from Hassi Messaoud. Gave its name to the wax candle (Fr. *bougie*), first exported to Europe from here. An ancient Roman city; became the capital of the Vandals in the 5th cent. A.D. Passed in turn to the Arabs, the Berber,

the Barbary pirates, the Spaniards, and the Turks. Occupied by the French 1833. Developed rapidly with the exploitation of the near-by mines and improvements to the harbour. ♦ *Touggourt*.

**Boulder** U S A. Town in Colorado, 25 m. N W of Denver, at a height of 5,350 ft. Pop. (1960) 37,718. Mining and ranching centre. Health resort. Seat of the University of Colorado (1877). Atomic-energy plant near by.

**Boulder Dam** ♦ *Hoover Dam*.

**Boulogne (Boulogne-sur-mer)** France. Ancient Gesoriacum, Bononia. Seaport in the Pas-de-Calais department, at the mouth of the Liane R. on the English Channel. Pop. (1968) 50,138. Cross-channel steamer services to Folkestone and Dover. France's chief fishing port. Fish curing, salting, etc. Manufactures cement, iron and steel, bricks, tiles. The old upper town contains the 19th-cent. Church of Notre Dame, severely damaged in the 2nd World War, the Hôtel-de-ville, and the castle. The lower town is built round the harbour. Near by is a column commemorating Napoleon's projected invasion of England (1804). Taken by Philip, Duke of Burgundy, 1419. United to the crown by Louis XI 1477. Seized by the English 1544; restored to France 1550. Birthplace of Godfrey of Bouillon (c. 1060–1100) and Sainte-Beuve (1804–69).

**Boulogne-Billancourt** France. Industrial and residential suburb to the S W of Paris, in the Hauts-de-Seine department, on the Seine. Pop. (1968) 109,380. Motor-car, aircraft, rubber, soap, cosmetics, and other industries. Formed (1925) from Boulogne-sur-Seine and Billancourt.

**Bounty Islands** New Zealand. Group of uninhabited islets in the S Pacific, 400 m. E S E of Dunedin (S Island). Discovered (1788) by Capt. Bligh in the *Bounty*.

**Bourbon** ♦ *Réunion*.

**Bourbonnais** France. Former province, in central France. Cap. Moulins. Divided in 1790 to form the present Allier department and parts of the Cher, Creuse, and Puy-de-Dôme departments. Formed the duchy of Bourbon 1327–1527, then united to the French crown. Belonged to the Bourbon-Condé family from 1661 until the Revolution (1789).

**Bourg (Bourg-en-Bresse)** France. Prefecture of the Ain department, on the Reyssouze, a tributary of the Saône, 35 m. N N E of Lyon. Pop. (1968) 40,407. Market town and railway junction. Trade in grain, wine, poultry.

Manufactures pottery. Flour milling, cheese making. In the suburb of Brou is the remarkable 16th-cent. late Gothic church, built by Marguerite of Austria.

**Bourges** France. Ancient Avaricum. Prefecture of the Cher department, on the Canal du Berry at the confluence of the Auron and the Yèvre rivers. Pop. (1968) 73,998. Military, route, and industrial centre. State ordnance factories. Manufactures woollens, linoleum, hardware, agricultural implements, etc. Among important buildings are the beautiful 12th/16th-cent. Gothic cathedral (remarkable for its stained glass and the absence of transepts), the 15th-cent. Hôtel de Jacques Coeur (c. 1395–1456; born here), and the Berry museum. In Roman times capital of Aquitania Prima. Residence of Charles VII, who proclaimed the Pragmatic Sanction (known as 'the King of Bourges'), in the 15th cent. The university (1463) was suppressed during the French Revolution. Birthplace of Louis XI (1423–83).

**Bourget, Lac du** France. Lake 11 m. long and up to 2 m. wide in the Savoie department. Near by are the resort of Aix-les-Bains and the Abbey of Hautecombe. Celebrated in Lamartine's poem *Le Lac*.

**Bourget, Le** France. Town in the Seine-St Denis department, 7 m. NNE of Paris. Pop. (1968) 9,797. One of the two chief metropolitan airports. Charles Lindbergh landed here after his historic trans-Atlantic flight (May 1927).

**Bourne** England. Urban district in Parts of Kesteven in S Lincolnshire, 15 m. SE of Grantham. Pop. (1961) 5,339. Market town. Associated with Hereward the Wake. Birthplace of Lord Burghley (1520–98).

**Bournemouth** England. County borough in SW Hampshire, on Poole Bay. Pop. (1961) 153,965. Popular holiday resort. Long sandy beach, two piers, long drives (Undercliff and Overcliff), winter gardens. Equable climate and sheltered position. Many nursing and convalescent homes. The sea front is reached by several picturesque dells (the 'chines'). Many parks and open spaces. Museum, art gallery. Boatbuilding. Settled in ancient times, but by the mid 19th cent. merely a village of a few hundred houses. Began to develop as a resort in the late 19th cent. Birthplace of Sir Hubert Parry (1848–1918). Burial-place of William Godwin and Mary Wollstonecraft and their daughter Mary Shelley.

**Bournville** England. Residential and industrial district in S Birmingham. Founded (1879) by George Cadbury for the workers at his cocoa and chocolate factories. One of the earliest examples of town-planning.

**Bouvet Island** S Atlantic Ocean. Island 1,800 m. SSW of Capetown, S Africa. Area 22 sq. m. Discovered (1739) by a French naval officer, Pierre Bouvet. Claimed for Britain 1825. Norwegian dependency since 1930.

**Bovey Tracey** England. Market town in Devonshire, 11 m. SW of Exeter. Pop. (1961) 3,650. Manufactures pottery from local china-clay.

**Bow (Stratford-le-Bow)** England. District in the former metropolitan borough of Poplar, in E London; from 1965 in the Greater London borough of Tower Hamlets. The name derives from the 12th-cent. bow-arched bridge over the R. Lea. Not to be confused with the Bow of 'Bow bells', the Church of St Mary-le-Bow in Cheapside, within the sound of whose bells every true cockney is supposed to be born.

**Bowness** England. Village in NW Cumberland, on the Solway Firth, 12 m. WNW of Carlisle. At the W end of Hadrian's Wall, only traces of which may still be seen.

**Bowness-on-Windermere** England. Tourist centre in Westmorland, on the E shore of L. Windermere. Part of the urban district of Windermere since 1905.

**Bow River** Canada. River 315 m. long, in Alberta, flowing generally SE from the Rocky Mountains, through the fine scenery of the Banff National Park, past Banff and Calgary to the S Saskatchewan R. From Calgary to the W its course is followed by the Canadian Pacific Railway.

**Box Hill** England. Picturesque spur of the North Downs in Surrey, just NNE of Dorking, 596 ft high. Property of the National Trust. Named after the many box trees here.

**Boyacá** Colombia. Small town in the Boyacá department in the E Cordillera, at a height of 7,750 ft. Scene of Bolívar's defeat of the Spanish (1819), which led to independence for Colombia and Venezuela.

**Boyle** Irish Republic. Market town in Co. Roscommon, on the R. Boyle 22 m. SSE of Sligo. Pop. (1966) 1,789. Remains of a Cistercian abbey (founded 1161).

**Boyne River** Irish Republic. River 80 m. long, rising in the Bog of Allen, flowing generally NE through Co. Meath, and entering the Irish Sea 4 m. below Drogheda. The Battle of the Boyne (1690), in which

James II was defeated by William III, was fought at Oldbridge, 3 m. W of Drogheda.

**Boys' Town** USA. Village in E Nebraska, 10 m. W of Omaha, founded (1917) by Father Edward J. Flanagan as a settlement for homeless boys, occupying 320 acres of farm land. Remarkable for its successful application of the principles of self-rule and self-discipline.

**Brabant** Belgium/Netherlands. Former province of the Low Countries, between the Meuse and the Scheldt rivers. Became a duchy in the Middle Ages, and later changed hands several times. When Belgium became independent (1830), it was divided: the S part became two provinces of Belgium and the N part a province of the Netherlands. 1a. *Antwerp (Antwerpen)*: A province of Belgium; drained by the Scheldt, Dyle, Nèthe, and Rupel rivers. Area 1,104 sq. m. Pop. (1968) 1,518,464. Cap. Antwerp. Largely agricultural. Food-processing and sugar-refining industries. 1b. *Brabant*: A province of Belgium; drained by the Dyle, Demer, and Senne rivers. Area 1,267 sq. m. Pop. (1968) 2,148,513. Cap. Brussels. Largely agricultural. Manufactures machinery, textiles, etc. The 1830 revolution began here, and the revolutionary song *La Brabançonne* became the Belgian national anthem. 2. *North Brabant (Noord-Brabant)*: A province of the Netherlands; drained by the Mark and Dommel rivers. Area 1,903 sq. m. Pop. (1968) 1,725,292. Cap. 's Hertogenbosch. Textile and electrical industries.

**Brač** Yugoslavia. The largest of the Dalmatian islands, in the Adriatic Sea, 10 m. SE of Split. Area 152 sq. m. Tourist and fishing centre. Chief town Supetar, on the N coast.

**Brackley** England. Municipal borough in Northamptonshire 8 m. ESE of Banbury on the R. Ouse. Pop. (1961) 3,202. Flour milling, brewing. Formerly a prosperous trade in wool. Magdalen College School (founded 1447).

**Bracknell** England. 'New town' in E Berkshire 10 m. ESE of Reading. Pop. (1961) 20,380. Planned pop. 60,000. Headquarters of the Meteorological Office from 1961. Manufactures clothing, furniture, etc.

**Bradford** England. County borough in the W Riding of Yorkshire, 9 m. W of Leeds. Pop. (1961) 295,768. Important centre of worsted and woollen manufacture. Also produces velvet, mohair, silk, and rayon goods. Dyeing, electrical and other engineering. Manufactures textile machinery. Probably already associated with the woollen industry in the early 14th cent. The former parish church of St Peter, dating to the 15th cent., became the cathedral in 1920. Other noteworthy buildings include the Cartwright Memorial Hall, with art gallery and Museum (1904), dedicated to the inventor of the power-loom; the Town Hall (1873); and the Wool Exchange (1867). Birthplace of Frederick Delius (1863–1934).

**Bradford-on-Avon** England. Urban district in Wiltshire, on the R. Avon 5 m. ESE of Bath. Pop. (1961) 5,757. Market town. Formerly important in the woollen industry. Largely built of local stone. Ancient 9-arched stone bridge with a bridge chapel. Small Saxon church with a nave only 26 ft long.

**Braemar** Scotland. 1. District in SW Aberdeenshire, extending E–W from Ballater to Glen Dee. Deer forests. Several villages up to 1,000 ft above sea level. Tourist centre. Small knitting industry. Includes ◊ *Balmoral Castle*.
2. Principal village of the Braemar district, a holiday resort on Clunie Water, 13 m. WSW of Ballater. Scene of the gathering of the clans to the standard of the Earl of Mar in the Jacobite rebellion (1715). Now scene of the annual Highland Games (the Braemar Gathering).

**Braga** Portugal. Ancient Bracara Augusta. Capital of the Braga district in the N, 28 m. NNE of Oporto. Pop. (1960) 40,977. Manufactures hats, cutlery, etc. Important religious centre since the Middle Ages. Seat of the Roman Catholic Primate of Portugal. The sanctuary of Bom Jesus do Monte, a famous place of pilgrimage, is 3 m. SE. Taken by the Suevi and then the Visigoths in the 5th cent., and by the Moors in the 8th; retaken by Ferdinand I of Aragon in 1040.

**Brahmaputra River** S Asia. Major river 1,800 m. long rising in SW Tibet on a Himalayan glacier. As the Tsangpo it flows generally E across S Tibet at a height of about 12,000 ft to the E end of the Himalayas. Here, near the mountain mass of Namcha Barwa (25,445 ft), it turns N, then curves round to flow S through a series of deep gorges and, now known as the Dihang, leaves Tibet and enters NE Assam (India). It flows WSW as the Brahmaputra through the fertile valley of Assam, flanked by tea gardens and rice fields, then turns S into E Pakistan and merges its delta with that of the Ganges before entering the Bay of Bengal. Navigable by steamer for 800 m. to Dibrugarh, but most river traffic ascends only to ◊ *Gauhati*.

**Brăila** Rumania. River port in the Brăila district, on the Danube R. Pop. (1968) 144,623. Leading centre of the train trade. Flour mills, railway workshops, timber yards. Manufactures paper, cardboard, textiles, footwear, etc. In Turkish hands 1544–1828.

**Braintree and Bocking** England. Urban district in Essex, 15 m. W of Colchester; formed from the two towns in 1934. Pop. (1961) 20,553. Manufactures metal windows, textiles, brushes. The woollen industry introduced by 15th/16th-cent. Flemish refugees was superseded by lace manufacture introduced by 16th/17th-cent. Huguenot refugees.

**Brakpan** S Africa. Town in the Transvaal, on the Witwatersrand 20 m. E of Johannesburg, at a height of 5,400 ft. Pop. (1967) 84,421 (34,000 whites, 50,000 Bantu). Important goldmining centre.

**Brampton** England. Market town in NE Cumberland, 8 m. ENE of Carlisle. Pop. (1961) 3,130. Roman remains. Near by are Lanercost Priory (founded 1169) and Naworth Castle (built in the reign of Edward III).

**Brandenburg** German Democratic Republic/Poland. 1. Former Electorate. Originally inhabited by Slavs (and early a part of the kingdom of ◊ *Poland*); partially conquered by Charlemagne in the 9th cent. and more successfully by the Margrave Albert the Bear in the 12th cent. Passed to Frederick I of Hohenzollern in 1415 and became an Electorate. Expanded considerably in the 17th cent. The Elector Frederick III took the title 'King of ◊ *Prussia*' in 1701. At the end of the 2nd World War the Potsdam Agreement restored the area E of the Oder (Odra) and Neisse (Nysa) rivers to Poland. The remainder became a *Land* of the German Democratic Republic (E Germany) which was divided into the districts of Frankfurt-an-der-Oder, Cottbus, and Potsdam in 1952.
2. Industrial town in the GDR, in the Potsdam district of the former Brandenburg *Land*, on the Havel R. 38 m. WSW of Berlin. Pop. (1965) 89,754. Formerly capital of the Prussian province of Brandenburg. Manufactures tractors, machinery, textiles, etc. A 14th-cent. cathedral and a 13th/14th-cent. town hall.

**Brandon** Canada. Town in SW Manitoba, on the Assiniboine R. 130 m. W of Winnipeg. Pop. (1966) 29,981. Commercial centre in a wheat-growing region. Oil refining, engineering, etc. Manufactures agricultural implements etc.

**Brandywine Creek** USA. Stream 20 m. long, rising in SE Pennsylvania and flowing SE through N Delaware to join the Christina R. near its confluence with the Delaware R. Famous as the scene of a battle near Chadds Ford, when Washington was defeated by English forces under Howe (1777).

**Brantford** Canada. Town in S Ontario, on the Grand R. 20 m. WSW of Hamilton. Pop. (1966) 59,854. Industrial centre. Manufactures refrigerators, agricultural implements, pottery, etc. Named after Joseph Brant (1742–1807), a Mohawk Indian chief.

**Bras d'Or, Lake** Canada. Tidal lake in NE Nova Scotia, almost dividing Cape Breton Island into two parts. Area 360 sq. m. At the lake-shore village of Baddeck Dr Alexander Graham Bell founded (1907) the Aerial Experiment Association.

**Brasilia** Brazil. Capital (since 1960), in a Federal District within the state of Goiás, 600 m. NW of Rio de Janeiro, at the junction of two small rivers in a bare rolling upland 3,000 ft above sea level. Pop. (1960) 141,172. Built to the plan of the Brazilian architect Lucio Costa, in the shape of an aeroplane, with the government offices and cathedral in the nose, other important buildings along the fuselage, and a succession of autonomous community blocks forming the residential area along the wings (7 m. long). Pleasant climate; noon is hot, but the nights are cool, and humidity is low (heavy rains in summer). The transfer of the capital to this region was provided for in the 1891 Constitution, but it was not until after 1955 (under President Kubitschek) that the scheme, intended to stimulate the development of Brazil's sparsely populated and underdeveloped interior, came into being. A large part of the administration has not yet been transferred and continues to operate in Rio de Janeiro. The city, which lies roughly at the geographic centre of Brazil, is joined by road to São Paulo and Rio, and by frequent air services to most parts of the country.

**Braşov** Rumania. Formerly (1950–61) Stalin (Orasul Stalin). Capital of the Braşov district in Transylvania, on the slopes of the Transylvanian Alps 90 m. NNW of Bucharest. Pop. (1968) 172,342. Important commercial and industrial town. Manufactures aircraft, tractors, machinery, oil-drilling equipment, textiles, etc. Iron and copper smelting. Tourist and winter-sports centre. A 14th/15th-cent. church, called the Black Church because the walls are smoke-blackened from the fire of 1689. Founded (1211) by the Teutonic Knights. Became an important centre of German population. Passed from Hungary to Rumania 1920.

**Bratislava** Czechoslovakia. Formerly Pressburg. Capital of Slovakia, and of the administrative region of Zápodoslovenský, on the Danube R. near the S end of the Little Carpathian Mountains. Pop. (1967) 277,000. River port. Railway and industrial centre. Of strategic importance owing to its position on an international waterway and near the frontiers of Austria and Hungary. Large agricultural trade. Important oil refinery. Oil pipeline from Brody (Ukraine), put into operation in 1962. Engineering, brewing, printing. Manufactures chemicals, textiles, paper, etc. Flour milling, sugar refining. Seat of the Comenius University (1919). Capital of Hungary 1541–1784. Many Hungarian kings were crowned in the 13th-cent. Gothic cathedral. Other noteworthy buildings are the 13th-cent. town hall (now a museum) and Franciscan church. Called Pressburg while within the Austro-Hungarian empire. Became the capital of Slovakia 1918. Capital of the Slovakian republic 1938–45.

**Bratsk** USSR. Industrial town in the Irkutsk Region, RSFSR, on the Angara R. 285 m. NNW of Irkutsk. Pop. (1970) 155,000. Site of a large hydroelectric power station, completed 1967. Expanded rapidly in the 1960s: pop. (1959) 43,000. Sawmilling. Manufactures wood pulp, cellulose, furniture, etc.

**Braunschweig** ◊ *Brunswick*.

**Bray** England. Village in Berkshire, on the R. Thames 1 m. SE of Maidenhead. Made famous by the song *The Vicar of Bray*, which is said to refer to Simon Aleyn (vicar 1540–88), who retained his incumbency through all the religious vicissitudes of the reigns of Henry VIII, Edward VI, Mary I, and Elizabeth I.

**Bray** Irish Republic. Seaside resort in Co. Wicklow, on the Irish Sea near Bray Head, 11 m. SSE of Dublin. Pop. (1966) 12,699. Became popular in the mid 19th cent.

**Brazil.**\* Republic of S America. Area 3,287,195 sq. m. Pop. (1967) 87,209,000. Cap. Brasilia. Lang. Portuguese. Rel. more than 90 per cent Roman Catholic.

Fourth largest country in the world, covering nearly half the area and containing half the population of S America. Frontiers with all the S American republics except Chile and Ecuador. Sparsely populated. Almost nine tenths of the people and the great majority of the agriculture, industry, roads, and railways are found along the Atlantic coastal belt; the vast basin of the Amazon and the immense interior plateau are scarcely developed at all. There are great resources, but the enormous scale of the country creates formidable problems of transportation etc. In a population of many races and nationalities, colour consciousness and discrimination are minimal. Brazil is a union of 22 states, 4 territories, and the Federal District. The states are Acre, Amazonas, Pará, Maranhão, Piauí, Ceará, Rio Grande do Norte, Paraíba, Pernambuco, Alagôas, Sergipe, Bahia, Minas Gerais, Espirito Santo, Rio de Janeiro, Guanabara, São Paulo, Paraná, Santa Catarina, Rio Grande do Sul, Mato Grosso, Goiás; the territories are Rondônia, Roraima, Amapá, Fernando de Noronha.

TOPOGRAPHY, CLIMATE. In the N the tropical rain-forests of the Amazon basin (once the centre of a rubber boom), with a hot humid climate, cover one third of the country. The 'shoulder' of Brazil (NE) is mainly dry and covered with thorn scrub. Central Brazil is a vast tableland; much of it stands at a height of 2,000–3,000 ft, with higher scarp edges, and an even higher series of ridges, with peaks over 8,000 ft high, to the E and SE. Except for the large São Francisco R. and smaller rivers such as the Doce and Paraíba, which flow to the Atlantic, the plateau is drained mostly N to the Amazon or W and S to the Paraná-Paraguay system, and has adequate rainfall for savannah and some woodland. The climate is more invigorating than that of the humid coastal lands, which are wide in the N, narrow to the S and then broaden again in the far S in the more temperate Rio Grande do Sul. This configuration hampers communications between the coastlands and the interior, and has helped to confine economic development to the former, leaving the latter, the immense, thinly peopled *sertão*, largely undeveloped. RESOURCES, PEOPLE, *etc.* Typically a one-crop economy: sugar in early colonial times, replaced by coffee since the 19th cent. Brazilian coffee has long dominated the world market; though its share has fallen (to about 40 per cent), coffee remains the mainstay of Brazilian exports (half, by value). Cotton is next in importance among the exports; others are cacao, sugar, oranges, bananas, tobacco. Brazil has become a major livestock producer, with more cattle, pigs, and goats than Argentina. Mineral deposits have been scarcely scratched. There are vast reserves of iron ore, and about 20 million tons are produced annually, a great deal of which is exported. Manganese and industrial diamonds are also exported, but Brazil is poor in coal and petroleum; the one large oil-field, in Bahia, produces about one third of the petroleum requirements. There is immense hydroelectric potential; several large generating stations have been built, but demand exceeds supply.

Industries are concentrated mainly in the states of Guanabara (Rio), São Paulo, and Minas Gerais. The most important is the manufacture of cotton goods, which employs about one quarter of all industrial workers. Steel production is located chiefly at Volta Redonda. The country is largely self-sufficient in consumer goods and in a growing variety of engineering, chemical, electrical, and other goods. Few manufactured goods except cotton textiles are exported. The problems of communications are on a continental scale: there are 23,700 m. of railways, most of which are in need of re-equipment, and roads are mainly rudimentary (except in the Rio–São Paulo area), though a road-building programme to link Brasilia with other cities is in progress. Air services are far-flung, frequent, and much used. The Constitution closely resembles that of the USA, but politics depend more upon personalities than upon party programmes. Not immune to revolutions, but those that have occurred have been brief and usually bloodless.

HISTORY. The Treaty of Tordesillas (1494) gave the Portuguese control of territories in S America E of about long. 50° W; Cabral visited Brazil in 1500. By 1537 three settlements existed: São Vicente (near Santos), Olinda (near Recife), and Salvador de Bahia; 15 hereditary 'captaincies' were created along the coastlands, but few flourished. The NE coastland, centred on Salvador, was developed for sugar, and Negro slaves were introduced. From Santos the Jesuits founded ◊ *São Paulo*. The French controlled the coastland near Rio de Janeiro 1555–60, and the Dutch held the NE sugar lands from 1630 for nearly 30 years. Mineral finds in Minas Gerais led to the first real settlement of the interior, by Paulistas, towards the end of the 17th cent. Rio de Janeiro became colonial capital in place of Salvador 1763. As a result of the Napoleonic Wars, the Portuguese royal family lived in Brazil 1808–21; Dom Pedro, son of King João of Portugal, declared Brazil an independent kingdom 1822. Under Dom Pedro II Brazil enjoyed wise and liberal rule: immigration and development went forward rapidly. Slavery was abolished 1888. Became a republic 1889. A succession of stable and relatively uneventful presidencies followed until 1930, when Getúlio Vargas, Governor of Rio Grande do Sul, deposed the President, assumed power, and ruled as dictator 1930–45. He was again elected President 1951, but committed suicide 1954. Kubitschek (President 1956–60) built the new capital Brasilia and greatly encouraged industrial development. The rapid pace of industrialization has created acute financial, social, and political unrest.

**Brazzaville** Congo (Brazzaville). Capital. River port beside Stanley Pool on the Congo R. opposite Kinshasa (Congo (Kinshasa)). Pop. (1965) 156,000. Formerly capital of French Equatorial Africa and Middle Congo. Connected by railway with the chief seaport, Pointe Noire. Railway workshops. Manufactures shoes, textiles, etc. Founded by de Brazza 1883. Became an important base for French colonization.

**Brechin** Scotland. Royal burgh and market town in Angus, on the S Esk R. 10 m. NE of Forfar. Pop. (1961) 7,114. Manufactures linen, paper, whisky. A 13th-cent. parish church (former cathedral) and 11th-cent. round tower.

**Brecon (Brecknock)** Wales. Municipal borough and county town of Breconshire, at the confluence of the R. Honddu with the Usk, in the centre of the county. Pop. (1961) 5,797. Produces textiles, leather. The Priory Church of St John became a cathedral (1923) when the new diocese of Swansea and Brecon was formed. Birthplace of Sarah Kemble (Mrs Siddons, 1755–1831).

**Breconshire (Brecknockshire)** Wales. County in the SE. Area 733 sq. m. Pop. (1961) 55,544. County town Brecon. Generally mountainous, esp. in the S, where the Brecon Beacons rise to 2,906 ft. Drained chiefly by the Usk and the Wye rivers. Main occupation farming. Coal mined in the S. Chief towns Brecon, Brynmawr.

**Breda** Netherlands. Industrial town in the N Brabant province, at the confluence of the Merk and the Aa rivers. Pop. (1968) 119,880. Food canning. Manufactures textiles, textile machinery, matches, footwear, etc. Having strategic importance, it changed hands many times. The Spanish capture (1625) is the subject of Velasquez's painting, *The Surrender of Breda*. Charles II regained the throne of Britain by signing the Declaration of Breda (1660), guaranteeing indemnity and religious liberty. The colonies of New York and New Jersey were awarded to England by the Peace of Breda (1667).

**Bregenz** Austria. Ancient Brigantium. Capital of Vorarlberg, at the E end of L. Constance. Pop. (1961) 21,331. Tourist resort. Textile, electrical, and other industries. Cable railway to the summit of Mt Pfänder (3,490 ft).

**Breisach (Altbreisach)** Federal German Republic. Town in Baden-Württemberg, on the right bank of the Rhine, opposite Neuf-Brisach (France), 12 m. WNW of Freiburg. Pop. 5,000. Produces sparkling wines. The surrounding district is named Breisgau. For centuries a German stronghold, frequently besieged by the French. Incorporated into Baden 1805. Severely damaged in the 2nd World War.

**Breisgau** Federal German Republic. District in Baden-Württemberg extending along the right bank of the Rhine, including the main peaks of the S Black Forest. Chief town Freiburg. Frequently changed hands from the 17th cent. onwards. Divided between Baden and Württemberg 1805.

**Breitenfeld** German Democratic Republic. Village 5 m. NW of Leipzig. Scene of two famous battles in the Thirty Years War: the victory of the Swedes (under Gustavus Adolphus) over the imperialists (under Tilly) in 1631; and that of the Swedes (under Torstensson) over the imperialists (under Piccolomini) in 1642.

**Bremen** Federal German Republic. 1. *Freie Hansestadt Bremen*: A *Land* of the FGR consisting of two enclaves in Lower Saxony centred on the cities of Bremen and Bremerhaven, both on the lower Weser R. Area 156 sq. m. Pop. (1968) 751,800.
2. Second most important seaport of the FGR, in the Bremen *Land*, on the lower Weser R. 50 m. from the sea. Pop. (1968) 603,600. Exports iron and steel and other manufactured goods. Oil refining, shipbuilding, flour milling, brewing, sugar refining. Manufactures chocolate, tobacco products. The Old Town (Altstadt), on the right bank of the Weser, has the 12th-cent. cathedral and the 15th-cent. Rathaus. Many medieval buildings were destroyed or damaged during the 2nd World War. On the left bank of the river, which is spanned by five bridges, is the New Town (Neustadt), founded in the 17th cent. Bremen became a leading member of the Hanseatic League in the 14th cent., and a free imperial city in the 17th. Overseas trade expanded considerably with the establishment of the North German Lloyd shipping line (1857). It became a Republic and Free Hansa City in the German Empire and then in the Weimar Republic, and, with Bremerhaven, a *Land* in the FGR in 1949.

**Bremerhaven** Federal German Republic. Seaport on the Weser estuary 34 m. NNW of Bremen, of which it is the outport. Pop. (1968) 148,185. Fishing, fish processing, ship repairing. Developed rapidly after the founding of the North German Lloyd shipping line (1857).

**Bremerton** USA. Town in Washington, on a peninsula in Puget Sound 14 m. WSW of Seattle. Pop. (1960) 28,922. Naval dockyards, shipbuilding, etc. Expanded rapidly during the 2nd World War.

**Brenner Pass (Italian Passo Brennero)** Austria/Italy. The lowest of the main Alpine passes (4,500 ft), connecting Innsbruck (Austria) with Bolzano (Italy). A road was built over it in 1772 and a railway (with many tunnels and bridges) in 1864–7. Frequent meeting place of Hitler and Mussolini (1940–41).

**Brent** England. Greater London borough (1965) comprising the former municipal boroughs of Wembley and Willesden (Middlesex). Pop. (1963) 295,678.

**Brentford and Chiswick** England. Former municipal borough of Middlesex and suburb of W London, the two towns being united in 1927; from 1965 part of the Greater London borough of Hounslow. Pop. (1961) 54,832. Brentford stands at the confluence of the R. Brent with the Thames. Manufactures soap, pharmaceutical products, tyres, etc. At Brentford Edmund Ironside defeated the Danes (1016) and Prince Rupert defeated the Parliamentarians (1642). ⟡ *Chiswick*.

**Brentwood** England. Urban district in S W Essex, 18 m. N E of London, of which it is a dormitory town. Pop. (1961) 51,959.

**Brescia** Italy. Ancient Brixia. Capital of the Brescia province (area 1,834 sq. m.) in Lombardy, at the foot of the Alps 51 m. E of Milan. Pop. (1968) 201,414. Industrial centre. Manufactures iron goods, firearms, textiles, hosiery, etc. A temple erected by Vespasian in A.D. 73 (now a museum of antiquities); two cathedrals (11th/12th- and 17th-cent.); medieval museum, with many valuable relics. Many buildings damaged in the 2nd World War. Birthplace of the religious reformer Arnoldo di Brescia (d. 1155).

**Breslau** ⟡ *Wrocław*.

**Bresse** France. District in the Ain, Jura, and Saône-et-Loire departments, between the Saône R. and the Jura mountains. Chief town Bourg. A fertile plain 600-800 ft above sea level. Noted for pigs and poultry. Ceded to France by the Duke of Savoy in 1601.

**Brest** France. Fortified seaport and naval station in the Finistère department, on the Atlantic coast of Brittany, on the N side of Brest Roads, which are entered by Le Goulet, a channel 1–2 m. wide. Pop. (1968) 159,857. Exports fruit, vegetables. Imports wheat, wine, coal, oil, timber. Fishing, flour milling, engineering, brewing. Manufactures chemicals. Extensive dockyards. Arsenal and naval academy. Richelieu built a harbour here 1631; Vauban fortified the port 1688. The French fleet was defeated off Brest by the English under Howe 1794. Used as a submarine base by the Germans during the 2nd World War, and severely damaged by Allied bombing. The siege of 1944 completely destroyed the old town.

**Brest (Brest-Litovsk)** USSR. Capital of Brest region, in S W Byelorussia on the Bug R. (Polish frontier). Pop. (1970) 122,000. Important agricultural centre, railway junction, and river port. Trade in timber, cereals, cattle. Sawmilling, cotton spinning, food processing, engineering. Founded in the 11th cent. as Brest-Litovsk. Passed to Russia 1795. Reverted to Poland 1921. Restored to the USSR under the Potsdam Agreement 1945. The separate Russo-German peace treaty of the 1st World War was signed here 1918.

**Bretton Woods** USA. Small resort in New Hampshire, in the White Mountains. Scene of an international conference (1944) which led to the establishment of the International Monetary Fund and the World Bank.

**Briançon** France. Ancient Brigantium. Tourist and winter-sports centre in the Hautes-Alpes department, 48 m. ESE of Grenoble, in the valley of the upper Durance R. Pop. (1968) 10,497. Consists of the old town, at a height of over 4,000 ft, fortified by Vauban, and the lower new town (Sainte-Catherine). Trade in silk, cheese, etc.

**Bridgend** Wales. Urban district in S Glamorganshire, on the R. Ogwr 16 m. W of Cardiff. Pop. (1961) 15,156. Market town. Manufactures footwear, etc.

**Bridge of Allan** Scotland. Small burgh and resort in Stirlingshire, on the Allan Water 2 m. N of Stirling. Pop. (1961) 3,312. Mineral springs. Minor industries.

**Bridgeport** USA. Industrial town and seaport in S W Connecticut on Long Island Sound. Pop. (1960) 156,748. Large engineering plants. Manufactures machinery, sewing machines, electrical equipment, hardware, etc. From 1846, the home of P. T. Barnum, circus showman, who contributed much to the improvement of the town.

**Bridgetown** Barbados. Capital and chief seaport, on Carlisle Bay, on the S W side of the island, sheltered from the N E Trade Winds. Pop. (1969) 12,283. Principal exports sugar, molasses, rum. In 1961 a new deep-water harbour was opened, with berths for 8 ships, and the runway at Seawell airport was extended to take the largest jet aircraft. The equable climate and fine beaches have made it a popular tourist resort. Trafalgar Square, in the centre of the town, has public buildings and a monument of Nelson.

**Bridgnorth** England. Market town in Shropshire, on the R. Severn 13 m. WSW of Wolverhampton. Pop. (1961) 7,552. Manufactures carpets, electrical equipment. Picturesque; divided by the river into the High Town and the Low Town, connected by flights of steps and a funicular railway. Half-timbered 17th-cent. town hall; 16th-cent. house where Bishop Percy of the 'Reliques' (1729–1811) was born.

**Bridgwater** England. Municipal borough

and port in Somerset, on the R. Parrett 9 m. NNE of Taunton. Pop. (1961) 25,582. Manufactures bath bricks (from sand and clay deposited by the tides), cement, bricks, electrical equipment. Near by is the site of the Battle of Sedgemoor (1685), in which the Monmouth rebellion was crushed and after which Judge Jeffreys conducted the Bloody Assize. Birthplace of Admiral Robert Blake (1599–1657).

**Bridlington** England. Municipal borough in the E Riding of Yorkshire, on Bridlington Bay 5 m. WSW of Flamborough Head. Pop. (1961) 26,007. Port. Seaside resort. Remains of a 12th-cent. Augustinian priory in the nave of the parish church. Queen Henrietta Maria landed here in 1643, and when the town was bombarded she took refuge in Boynton Hall 3½ m. W.

**Bridport** England. Municipal borough in Dorset, on the R. Brit 14 m. W of Dorchester. Pop. (1961) 6,517. Market town. Manufactures ropes, fishing nets, sailcloth, and cordage. The fishing village and seaside resort of West Bay is 1½ m. S.

**Brie** France. Agricultural region (*pays*) mainly in the Seine-et-Marne department between the Seine and Marne rivers E of Paris. Chief commercial centre Meaux. Produces wheat and sugar-beet, but chiefly famous for dairy produce, esp. the soft Brie cheese. Partly wooded; includes the Forêt de Sénart.

**Brieg** ◊ *Brzeg*.

**Brienz** Switzerland. Town in the Bern canton, on the NE side of L. Brienz. Pop. (1960) 2,950. Tourist resort. Wood carving, violin making.

**Brienz, Lake** Switzerland. Lake in the Bern canton, in the Bernese Alps, at 1,860 ft. Area 11 sq. m. Chief town Brienz. The Aar R. enters at the NE end and leaves at the SW, discharging into L. Thun. On the S shore are the famous Giessbach Falls.

**Brierley Hill** England. Industrial town in S Staffordshire, 9 m. W of Birmingham, on the edge of the Black Country. Pop. (1961) 56,377. Manufactures iron and steel, glassware, pottery, bricks.

**Brig** Switzerland. Town in the Valais canton, on the R. Rhône, important as a route centre because of its position at the N end of the Simplon Pass and tunnel and at the junction of the Simplon, Lötschberg, and Furka railways. Pop. (1960) 2,234.

**Brighouse** England. Municipal borough in the W Riding of Yorkshire, on the R. Calder 4 m. N of Huddersfield. Pop. (1961) 30,783. Industrial town. Woollen, cotton, and silk mills. Manufactures carpets, textile machinery, etc.

**Brightlingsea** England. Urban district in E Essex, on the estuary of the R Colne. Pop. (1961) 4,788. Yachting and holiday resort. Oyster fishing.

**Brighton** England. County borough in E Sussex, on the Channel coast 48 m. S of London. Pop. (1961) 162,757. Popular seaside resort, at the foot of the S Downs, with a sea front over 5 m. long. Joins Hove in the W. Some fishing. Manufactures footwear, food products. Seat of the University of Sussex (1959), just NE, and of Roedean Girls' School. Described as 'a poor fishing town' (then known as Brighthelmstone) in the early 18th cent.; popularized by Dr Russell (who advocated sea bathing) and the Prince Regent (George IV) who had the Royal Pavilion rebuilt (1817) in oriental style. The opening of the railway (1841) further stimulated its growth as a resort. Birthplace of Aubrey Beardsley (1872–98).

**Brindisi** Italy. Ancient Brundisium. Capital of the Brindisi province in Apulia, in the 'heel' of Italy on the Adriatic Sea. Pop. (1961) 70,657. Seaport. Exports wine, olive oil. Important as the gateway to Greece. An outer and an inner harbour. Castle of Frederick II; cathedral (12th-cent., restored in the 18th cent.); a column believed to mark the S end of the Appian Way. Was a Roman naval station. Declined after the Crusades. Severely damaged by earthquake 1456. Revived with the opening of the Suez Canal (1869).

**Brisbane** Australia. Capital of Queensland, 14 m. up the Brisbane R., which reaches Moreton Bay through much silt and sand; with a dredged channel the city is a major seaport, accommodating vessels of 32-ft draught, and has a large graving dock. Pop. (1966) 719,140. Its climate is subtropical, rainfall amounting to about 45 ins. annually and mean monthly temperatures varying from 58° F to 77° F. Railways run N to Cairns, S to Sydney and industrial New South Wales, and inland to the growing industrial area round Ipswich and to rural collecting centres. Exports frozen meat, butter, cheese, sugar, wool, hides, and canned fruit, etc. Shipbuilding, food processing, etc. Manufactures cement, furniture, clothing, footwear, etc. Seat of the University of Queensland (1911). Fine streets and parks; among outstanding buildings is the City Hall (1930). Its site was selected (1824) by Sir Thomas Brisbane, Governor of New South Wales, as a penal settlement. Opened to free settlement 1842. Became capital of the colony of Queensland 1859.

**Bristol** England\*. County borough in the SW, on the R. Avon 7 m. above the mouth on Bristol Channel, partly in Gloucestershire and partly in Somerset. Pop. (1961) 436,440. Important seaport and industrial centre. Port includes the docks at Avonmouth and Portishead, at the river mouth. Imports grain, fruit (esp. bananas), wine, tobacco, petroleum, etc. Manufactures aircraft, tobacco products, chocolate, soap, etc. The cathedral, dating from the 12th cent. but much restored in later times, is surpassed by the magnificent 14th-cent. Church of St Mary Redcliffe, described by Queen Elizabeth I as 'the fairest, the goodliest, and the most famous parish church in England'. Much of the city (inc. Merchant Venturers' Hall) was destroyed by bombing during the 2nd World War, though the Almshouses (1699) have been restored. In front of the 18th-cent. Exchange (designed by John Wood of Bath) are four bronze pillars, the 'Nails', where merchants used to carry out cash transactions. giving rise to the expression 'pay on the nail'. Seat of a university (1909) and a 16th-cent. grammar school. On Brandon Hill is the Cabot tower (1897), commemorating John Cabot's expedition to N America (1497). City Art Gallery and Museum; Theatre Royal (1766), reopened 1943. Just NW at Clifton the Avon gorge is spanned by Brunel's famous suspension bridge (1845).

Settled in late Saxon times, Bristol developed primarily through its trade, and by the 12th cent. was an important port. Early trade largely with Ireland (wool). Much of its later trade was with the Americas, and in the 17th–18th cent. it prospered from the slave trade. Declined somewhat after abolition and the rise of Liverpool. One of the first trans-Atlantic steamships, the *Great Western*, was built and sailed from here in 1838. As ships increased in size the city docks became inadequate, and the docks at Avonmouth and Portishead were taken over (1884). Birthplace of Thomas Chatterton (1752–70), Robert Southey (1774–1843), Sir Thomas Lawrence (1769–1830), Samuel Plimsoll (1824–98), J. A. Symonds (1840–93).

**Bristol** USA. Industrial town in Connecti-

cut 14 m. SW of Hartford. Pop. (1960) 45,499. Noted for clock making since the end of the 18th cent. Also manufactures ball bearings, springs, sports equipment, etc.

**Bristol Channel** England/Wales. Inlet of the Atlantic Ocean between Wales and SW England, extending 80 m. E to the Severn estuary and narrowing from 50 m. to 5 m. in width. It has the greatest tidal range in England. On the Welsh side the chief inlets are Milford Haven, Carmarthen Bay, and Swansea Bay; chief ports Cardiff and Swansea; chief rivers the Taf and the Towy. On the English side the chief inlets are Bideford Bay and Bridgwater Bay; chief towns Ilfracombe and Weston-super-Mare; chief rivers the Severn, Parrett, Taw, and Torridge.

**British Antarctic Territory.** British colony of the S Atlantic created on 3 March 1962, comprising all the Antarctic mainland and islands between 20° W and 80° W long. and S of 60° S lat., including S Shetland and S Orkney Islands and Graham Land – formerly part of ◊ *Falkland Islands* dependencies. Area 150,000 sq. m. No permanent inhabitants.

**British Columbia** Canada. The most westerly province, on the Pacific coast. Area 366,255 sq. m. Pop. (1966) 1,873,674. Cap. Victoria, on Vancouver Island. Largest city and chief seaport Vancouver, on the mainland, the W terminus of the Canadian Pacific and Canadian National Railways. Almost entirely mountainous, 4 distinct ranges running roughly parallel N–S. The most westerly range, invaded by the sea, forms a chain of mountainous islands along the coast; the most easterly, the high, rugged, snow-capped ridge of the Rocky Mountains, towers above the prairies, and until the building of the railroad discouraged travel farther W. The ranges are cut by the valleys of the main rivers (the Fraser, Kootenay, Thompson, and Columbia) and their tributaries. These rivers are fast-flowing, and the water-power potential is enormous. The climate varies considerably: maritime temperate along the coast, continental in the interior. At Prince Rupert the mean annual temperature range is 23° F and rainfall 98 ins. and at Kamloops they are 57° F and 10 ins.

The forests are valuable, with rich stands of Douglas fir, Western hemlock, Sitka spruce, and red cedar; lumbering is a major industry. Only about 3 per cent of the land is suitable for agriculture. Dairying and mixed farming are practised in the S; much fruit is grown. The Okanagan valley is famous for apples, grown in irrigated orchards. On the coast there are important salmon and herring fisheries. Mineral deposits are extensive; coal, gold, silver, lead, zinc, and copper are mined. Industries – associated with the forestry, farming, fishing, and mining which form the basis of the economy – include sawmilling, pulp and paper milling, fish and fruit canning, ore smelting and refining. They are aided by abundant hydroelectric power, e.g. the aluminium smelters at Kitimat. Chief towns Vancouver, Victoria, New Westminster.

From 1821 British Columbia was the preserve of the Hudson's Bay Company; after the Fraser R. gold rush (1858) the mainland colony was established, to be joined by Vancouver Island in 1886. It joined the Dominion of Canada in 1871, on the understanding that a trans-continental railway would be constructed; in 1885 the CPR reached Vancouver.

**British Honduras.** British colony in Central America, on the Caribbean coast, forming the SE part of the Yucatán peninsula; bounded on the N by Mexico and on the W by Guatemala. Area 8,866 sq. m. Pop. (1966) 114,255 (more than one third Negro, about one quarter native Indian and Carib, 4 per cent European, the remainder mainly of mixed mulatto and *mestizo* stock). Cap. and chief seaport Belize. Inland in the S are the Maya Mountains rising to over 3,500 ft, but the land is mainly low-lying and flat; along the swampy coast are lagoons and many keys (cays) and reefs. Climate tropical, but the NE Trade Winds temper the heat; rainfall is heavy, and damage has often been caused by hurricanes. Dense forests cover much of the colony, and forest products (mahogany, cedar, pine, chicle) are valuable exports. Sugar-cane and citrus fruits are grown along the coast; sugar, grapefruit, and oranges are important exports. Communications in the interior are extremely difficult, being practically confined to the rivers, down which timber is floated.

The first regular settlements were established (1662) by the English (from Jamaica), who exploited the logwood and mahogany. Despite opposition and frequent attacks from the Spaniards, the English remained; their occupation was recognized in 1798. In 1862 British Honduras became a dependency of Jamaica, and in 1884 an independent colony. It has long been claimed by Guatemala; in 1946 the British government offered to refer the matter to the International Court of Justice, but the dispute remains unresolved. A greater measure of internal self-government was granted on 1 Jan. 1964.

**British Indian Ocean Territory.** British colony formed in 1965 consisting of the Chagos Archipelago (formerly a dependency of Mauritius), and the Aldabra Is., the Farquhar Is., and Des Roches (formerly dependencies of the Seychelles).

**British Isles** ◊ *England*; *Great Britain*; *Ireland*; *Scotland*; *Wales*.

**British Virgin Islands** W Indies. Group of 36 islands in the E of the Virgin Is. archipelago. Area 59 sq. m. Pop. (1965) 9,119. Cap. Road Town (pop. 2,000) on Tortola (area 21 sq. m., pop. 6,762), the main island. Other leading islands are Virgin Gorda, Anegada, and Jost Van Dyke; altogether only 11 are inhabited. Most of them are hilly and they have a pleasant sub-tropical climate; their chief products are livestock (cattle), fish, fruit, vegetables. Became part of the Federation of the Leeward Is. in 1871, but when this came to an end (1956) the Colony of the Virgin Is. was established.

**Brittany** (Fr. **Bretagne**) France. Ancient Armorica. Former duchy and province, occupying the peninsula between the English Channel and the Bay of Biscay. Divided administratively into the departments of Finistère, Côtes-du-Nord, Morbihan, Ille-et-Vilaine, and Loire-Atlantique. The coast is rocky and indented like that of Cornwall (England). The picturesque fishing ports and beaches, the many megalithic monuments (e.g. ◊ *Carnac*), and the observance of local customs have made it popular with holiday-makers. Inland much of the area consists of unproductive moorland. Around Rennes (on the main river, the Vilaine) cider apples, potatoes, etc. are cultivated. Market gardening has developed on the coastal plains, and early vegetables are exported to Britain, where the Breton onion-seller is a familiar figure. Main occupations agriculture, fishing. Ruled by the Romans from Caesar's invasion (56 B.C.) till the 5th cent. A.D. Then settled by Celtic refugees from Britain, who gave it its name and account for the affinity of the Breton language (still spoken in rural areas) with Cornish and Welsh. Became a duchy in the 10th cent. and a province of France 1532. During the Revolution (1789–94) showed divided sympathies.

**Brive (Brive-la-Gaillarde)** France. Market town in the Corrèze department, on the Corrèze R. 52 m. SSE of Limoges. Pop. (1968) 49,325. Trade in fruit and vegetables, cattle, wool, chestnuts, etc. Manufactures food products, paper, etc. The 12th-cent. Church of St Martin stands in the centre of the old town.

**Brixham** England. Small town in Devonshire, 5 m. S of Torquay. Pop. (1961) 10,679. Fishing port and tourist resort with a picturesque harbour. The landing of William of Orange (1688) is commemorated by a statue on the quay. ♢ *Torbay.*

**Brixton** England. District in the London borough of Lambeth, S of the Thames. One of London's largest prisons (founded 1820).

**Brno** Czechoslovakia. Capital of the Jihomoravský region, just above the confluence of the Svitava and the Svratka rivers, 110 m. SE of Prague. Pop. (1967) 333,000. The country's second largest city; an industrial, commercial, and cultural centre. Important textile industry. Manufactures cars, machinery, clothing, furniture, soap, etc. Produced the Bren gun. The city is dominated by the fortress of Spilberk, on a hill 945 ft high, an Austrian political prison 1621–1857 (where the Italian poet Silvio Pellico was confined 1822–30). In the old town of narrow crooked streets, there are many old buildings, e.g. the cathedral (15th-cent.), the old town hall (16th-cent.) and 14th/16th-cent. churches. University (1919). Withstood a long siege by the Swedes under Torstensson 1645. J. G. Mendel (1822–84) was abbot of the Augustinian monastery.

**Broach** India. River port in Gujarat on the Narmada R. 40 m. NNE of Surat. Pop. (1961) 73,639. Manufactures textiles. Taken by the British in 1772 and again in 1803.

**Broads (Norfolk Broads)** England. A region of shallow lakes amid marshland (mainly in Norfolk, with a small part in Suffolk) centred on the R. Bure and its tributaries the Ant and Thurne, partly caused by the widening ('broadening') of rivers. A popular area for holiday-making, yachting, fishing, bird-watching. Wroxham and Barton are among the more picturesque broads.

**Broadstairs** England. Seaside resort in the Isle of Thanet in NE Kent, forming an urban district with near-by St Peter's. Pop. (1961) 16,929. The house where Dickens frequently stayed is called Bleak House after his novel.

**Brocken (Blocksberg)** German Democratic Republic. Highest peak (3,747 ft) of the Harz Mountains, in the Magdeburg district. In fog or mist the 'Spectre of the Brocken' (the magnified shadow of the observer) may be seen. Traditionally the witches' meeting place on Walpurgis Night (1 May). Location of the witch scene in Goethe's *Faust.*

**Brockman, Mount** ♢ *Hamersley Range.*

**Brockton** USA. Industrial town in Massachusetts 19 m. S of Boston. Pop. (1960) 72,813. Leading centre of shoe manufacture. Also produces footwear machinery and tools, leather.

**Broken Hill** Australia. Mining and industrial town in the W interior of New South Wales 220 m. NE of Port Pirie. Pop. (1966) 30,001. Lode 3 m. long of metallic sulphides, lead and silver above, zinc below, worked since 1883. Metal concentrates are smelted and refined at Port Pirie and Risdon (Tasmania). The water supply is piped from the Menindee storage on the Darling R.

**Broken Hill** (Zambia) ♢ *Kabwe.*

**Bromberg** ♢ *Bydgoszcz.*

**Bromley** England. Greater London borough (1965) comprising the former municipal boroughs of Beckenham and Bromley and the urban districts of Chislehurst and Sidcup (S of the A20 road), Orpington, and Penge, all in NW Kent. Pop. (1963) 294,344. Birthplace of H. G. Wells (1866–1946).

**Brompton** England. Residential district in S Kensington in SW London. Contains the Roman Catholic Brompton Oratory (built in the Italian Renaissance style); Brompton Chest Hospital; the Victoria and Albert Museum, the Science Museum, the Natural History department of the British Museum, and the Geological Museum.

**Bromsgrove** England. Urban district in N Worcestershire, 12 m. NNE of Worcester. Pop. (1961) 35,296. Iron foundries. Manufactures nails, buttons. The grammar school (founded 1553; refounded 1693) was attended by A. E. and Laurence Housman.

**Bronx, the** ◊ *New York.*

**Brooklyn** ◊ *New York.*

**Brownsville** USA. Town in S Texas, on the Rio Grande 22 m. from the mouth, opposite Matamoros (Mexico). Pop. (1960) 48,040. Commercial centre. Trade in petroleum, citrus fruits, cotton, etc. Canning, chemical, and other industries.

**Bruce, Mount** ◊ *Hamersley Range.*

**Bruges** (Flemish **Brugge**) Belgium. Capital of West Flanders province, 25 m. WNW of Ghent. Pop. (1968) 51,885. Market town. Railway and canal junction. Tourist centre. Engineering, flour milling, brewing. Manufactures lace, yeast. Linked by ship-canal with Zeebrugge. Has preserved much of its medieval character. Gothic church of Notre Dame containing Michelangelo's marble *Virgin and Child.* Market hall (13th/15th-cent.) with the famous belfry and 46-bell carillon. Leading market of the Hanseatic League (13th cent.). Reached the peak of its importance in the 15th cent., the population at one time exceeding 200,000. Repressive measures against the inhabitants after a revolt, religious persecution, and the silting up of the Zwin estuary led to a decline. In the late 19th and early 20th cent. some revival of trade was achieved by the construction of new docks and the ship-canal to Zeebrugge.

**Brugg** Switzerland. Small town in Aargau canton, on the Aar R. 17 m. NW of Zürich. Pop. (1960) 6,700. Near by is the site of Vindonissa, the chief Roman camp in Helvetia, where remains of an amphitheatre etc. were found; also ruins of the 11th-cent. Habsburg castle. Birthplace of Johann Zimmermann (1728–95).

**Brühl** Federal German Republic. Town in N Rhine-Westphalia, 7 m. S of Cologne. Pop. (1963) 37,200. In a lignite-mining area. Manufactures briquettes, machinery, etc.

**Brunei. 1.** British-protected sultanate of NW Borneo forming an enclave of Sarawak (Malaysia). Area 2,226 sq. m. Pop. (1966) 127,195 (mainly Malays and native Borneans). Its prosperity depends largely on the Seria oilfield (discovered 1929), which appears to have passed its peak output; the interior is heavily forested. The sultanate reached the height of its power in the 16th cent., when it controlled much of Borneo and neighbouring islands. Be-

came a British protectorate 1888. Administered by a British resident 1906. The only former British dependency inhabited by Malays that did not join the Federation of Malaysia in 1963.

**2.** Capital of Brunei, on the Brunei R. 9 m. from the mouth, partly built on piles. Pop. (1966) 30,000.

**Brunnen** Switzerland. Port and tourist resort on L. Lucerne, in the Schwyz canton. Pop. (1960) 4,445. Linked with Morschach by rack-and-pinion railway. Scene of the reaffirmation by the Forest Cantons (1315) of the Everlasting League (1291), the foundation of Swiss independence.

**Brunswick (Braunschweig)** Federal German Republic. **1.** Former duchy in N Germany, comprising 3 larger and 6 smaller enclaves in the Prussian provinces of Hanover and Saxony. Area 1,417 sq. m. The property of the Guelphs in the 12th cent., becoming later the duchies of Brunswick-Lüneburg (whose Duke became Elector of Hanover 1692) and Brunswick-Wolfenbüttel. Hanover was annexed by Prussia 1866. The last king's grandson was made Duke of Brunswick 1913. Incorporated in the new *Land* of Lower Saxony 1945.

**2.** City in Lower Saxony on the Oker R., formerly capital of the duchy of Brunswick. Pop. (1968) 228,696. Varied industries: fruit and vegetable canning, flour milling, sugar refining, publishing; manufactures bicycles, calculating machines, etc. Many historic buildings, inc. the town hall (14th/15th-cent., now restored), were damaged or destroyed in the 2nd World War.

**Brussels** Belgium. Capital of Belgium and of Brabant province, on the Senne, a tributary of the Scheldt. Pop. (1968) 1,079,181. Important railway junction. Manufactures textiles, clothing, lace, carpets, chemicals, paper, furniture, etc. Divided into the commercial 'lower town' and the residential 'upper town'. In the famous Grand' Place is one of the finest buildings in Europe, the magnificent 15th-cent. Hôtel de Ville; also the smaller but equally ornate Maison du Roi. The Royal Palace and the Palais de la Nation (housing the Parliament) date from the 18th cent., and the Palais de Justice and the University (founded 1834) from the 19th. The 13th-cent. St Gudule and the 14th-cent. Notre-Dame-du-Sablon are outstanding among the churches. Described in the 17th cent. as 'one of the finest cities in Europe', Brussels has been vastly improved in modern times by the construction of handsome boulevards and avenues. It absorbed several neighbouring communes in 1921. Improvements have also been made in its harbour: the Willebroek Canal, constructed in the 16th cent. and giving the city direct access to the sea, was enlarged, and the outer port was completed in 1922.

Probably originating on one of the islands in the Senne marshes, Brussels flourished as a commercial centre from the 10th cent. largely owing to its position on the route from Cologne to Ghent and Bruges. It began to expand, and a new wall was built in the 14th cent. to enclose a much greater area; the course of this wall is followed by modern boulevards. It became capital of the duchy of Brabant, and passed to Burgundy and then to the Habsburgs. The centre of the city was destroyed by French bombardment 1695. Became capital when Belgium won independence (1830). Occupied by German forces in both world wars. Site of the first great international exhibition after the 2nd World War (1958); the dominating feature of this was appropriately the Atomium, displaying man's achievements in the field of atomic energy.

**Bryansk** USSR. Capital of the Bryansk region (RSFSR), on the Desna R. 215 m. SW of Moscow. Pop. (1970) 318,000. Railway and industrial centre. Important railway workshops; also sawmills, ironworks, brickworks, etc. Manufactures electrical equipment, woollen goods. Founded (1146) as Debryansk. An independent principality till 1356. Became Russian in the 17th cent.

**Brynmawr** Wales. Urban district in SE Breconshire, 2 m. NE of Ebbw Vale. Pop. (1961) 6,471. The coalmining and steel industries of the neighbourhood, which suffered severely in the economic depression of the 1930s, have been replaced largely by light industries.

**Brzeg** (Ger. **Brieg**) Poland. Ancient town in the Opole voivodship, on the Odra (Oder) R. 25 m. SE of Wroclaw. Pop. (1968) 29,900. Manufactures textiles, leather goods, chemicals, etc. Originally part of the medieval Polish state, then in German Silesia (Polish Śląsk). Restored to Poland after the 2nd World War, under the Potsdam Agreement (1945). Called Brieg during the German administration.

**Bucaramanga** Colombia. Capital of the Santander department, in the E Cordillera, at 3,000 ft. Pop. (1968) 229,748. Commercial and industrial city, in mountainous country growing coffee, tobacco, and cotton. Manufactures cement, cigars and cigarettes, textiles, straw hats, etc. Founded 1622; expanded rapidly from the late 19th cent.

**Bucharest** (Rumanian **București**) Rumania. Capital of Rumania and of the Ilfov district, in Walachia, on the Dambovița R., a tributary of the Danube. Pop. (1968) 1,414,643. Important industrial, commercial, and cultural centre. Oil refining, tanning, flour milling. Manufactures aircraft, machinery, textiles, chemicals, etc. Considerable trade in petroleum, timber, agricultural produce. The main thoroughfare is the Calea Victoriei, continued as the Kiselev Avenue, along which are the former royal palace (now the Palace of the Republic), the triumphal arch, the Kisilev Park, and the Baneasa racecourse. Generally modern in appearance; developed from a rather primitive medieval town only in the late 19th cent. Seat of the Patriarch of the Eastern Orthodox church. A 17th-cent. Metropolitan cathedral and several 18th cent. churches. University (1864). Bucharest was founded (according to one story) by a shepherd named Bucur. Became capital of Walachia 1698, and for more than a century suffered considerably from plagues and fires. Became capital of Rumania 1861. The Treaty of Bucharest (1812) ended the Russo-Turkish War; that of 1913 ended the Balkan Wars.

**Buckfastleigh** England. Urban district in Devonshire, on the R. Dart 11 m. W of Torquay. Pop. (1961) 2,550. Manufactures woollen goods. Near by is Buckfast Abbey, built by Benedictine monks (1907–37) on the site of a medieval Cistercian abbey.

**Buckhaven and Methil** Scotland. Small burgh in Fifeshire, on the Firth of Forth; formed by the union of the two towns (1891). Pop. (1961) 21,104. Coalmining. Exports coal. Fishing.

**Buckingham** England. Municipal borough in Buckinghamshire, on the R. Ouse 15 m. NW of Aylesbury. Pop. (1961) 4,377. Market town. Engineering. Manufactures dairy products. Stowe House, former seat of the dukes of Buckingham, since 1923 occupied by the public school, is 3 m. NNW.

**Buckinghamshire** England. County in the

S Midlands. Area 749 sq. m. Pop. (1961) 486,183. County town Aylesbury. The Thames forms the S boundary; drained also by the Thame and the Wye (Thames tributaries) and in the N by the Ouse. The land rises gently N from the Thames to the chalk ridge of the Chiltern Hills, and descends more abruptly on their N slopes to the fertile Vale of Aylesbury, where cereals, fruit, and vegetables are cultivated and dairy cattle and poultry are raised. The famous woods of the Chilterns were chiefly responsible for the local furniture industry; ◊ *Slough* and ◊ *High Wycombe* are the largest manufacturing centres. Many small towns and villages are notable for their associations with poets or statesmen, e.g. Chalfont St Giles (Milton), Stoke Poges (Gray) Hughenden (Disraeli), Beaconsfield (Burke).

**Budapest** Hungary. Capital of Hungary and of Pest county, on the R. Danube. Pop. (1968) 1,990,000. Important commercial centre, largely because of its position at a crossing of the Danube and on the edge of the Hungarian plain. Trade in grain, wine, cattle, hides, wool. With its suburbs has a great part of the country's industrial activity: flour milling, brewing, manufacture of iron and steel, machinery, textiles, chemicals. Comprises two separate towns, the older Buda, on the hilly right bank of the Danube, and the low-lying Pest on the left bank, united into a single municipality 1872. Chief centre of Magyar culture. Seat of a university (1635) and a technical university (1857). Relatively few buildings of historic interest. In Buda was built the coronation church of St Matthias in the 13th–15th cent. (rebuilt in the 19th), and in Pest the 19th-cent. Basilica of St Stephen with its 315-ft-high dome. The Roman colony of Aquincum, of which remains were found, fell to the barbarians in the 4th cent. Both Buda and Pest were ruled by the Turks 1541–1686, recovered under the Habsburgs, and grew rapidly in the late 19th cent. After the 1st World War Budapest developed many new industries. The city suffered severely when besieged by the Russian army in the 2nd World War (1945) and again in the national uprising (1956).

**Budaun** India. Town in Uttar Pradesh 25 m. SW of Bareilly. Pop. (1961) 58,770. Minor industries. Trade in grain, cotton,

etc. Has the 13th-cent. Jama Masjid (Great Mosque), later restored several times.

**Buddh Gaya** India. Village in Bihar 6 m. S of Gaya. Site of a temple (built over the remains of an Asokan temple) and the sacred Bo-tree under which Buddha is said to have received enlightenment.

**Bude** England. Small port and holiday resort on the N coast of Cornwall, forming with Stratton the urban district of Bude-Stratton. Pop. (urban district, 1961) 5,095. Picturesque coastal scenery, especially to the S.

**Budleigh Salterton** England. Urban district in Devonshire, on Lyme Bay (English Channel) 4 m. ENE of Exmouth. Pop. (1961) 3,871. Fishing port. Holiday resort. E Budleigh, 2 m. inland, was the birthplace of Sir Walter Raleigh.

**Budweis** ◊ *České Budejovice*.

**Buea** ◊ *Cameroun*.

**Buenaventura** Colombia. Chief Pacific seaport, in the Valle del Cauca department 40 m. NW of Cali. Pop. (1968) 96,708. Outlet for the fertile Cauca valley and the Chocó mining region. Exports coffee, sugar, hides, gold, platinum. Fish canning etc. Founded 1540. Expanded with the building of the picturesque railway to Cali (1914).

**Buenos Aires** Argentina. Capital, on the W bank of the Río de la Plata estuary. Pop. (1960) 2,966,816. The country's chief seaport and industrial and commercial centre. Principal exports meat (beef), grain (wheat, maize), wool. Manufactures textiles, paper, paint, chemicals, metal goods, etc. Around the docks there are great meat-packing plants and grain elevators. Power stations use imported coal, and natural gas and petroleum products are piped into the city. Terminal for a network of railways serving the pampas and linking it with Bolivia and Chile. The city has been largely rebuilt in the 20th cent. on the typical N American block pattern, with residential suburbs, broad avenues, numerous parks, fine shopping centres, and an underground railway. Has one of the largest opera houses in the world. University (1821). The main thoroughfare, the Avenida de Mayo, is an imposing tree-lined boulevard extending between the two chief squares, the Plaza de Mayo and the Plaza del Congreso. The cathedral (1804) contains the tomb of the Liberator, San Martín. Founded (1536) by Spaniards, who were driven out by the Indians. Permanently settled 1580. Remained small and relatively unimportant for the next 200 years, though it was made capital of a viceroyalty (1776) and was freed from the trade restrictions imposed by Spain (1778). Expanded and prospered greatly in the second half of the 19th cent. with the development of the immense hinterland of the pampas. Became capital of the republic 1880.

**Buffalo** USA. Industrial city, lake port, and commercial centre in New York, at the E end of L. Erie. Pop. (1960) 532,759. At the W end of the easiest route across the Appalachian highlands, the Hudson-Mohawk gap, which is followed by roads, railways, and canal to New York City; near the S end of the Welland Canal from L. Ontario. An important gateway to the Middle West. Also linked with Ontario (Canada) by a railway bridge across the Niagara R., and by a road bridge, opened (1927) to commemorate a century of peace between Canada and the USA. The lakeside harbour, protected by a breakwater 4½ m. long, handles enormous quantities of iron ore, coal, and grain. Manufactures iron and steel, aircraft, plastics, electrical equipment, machinery, etc. Electric power is drawn from Niagara Falls, 20 m. distant. Seat of the University of Buffalo (1846) and several colleges. First settled in 1803, under the name of New Amsterdam; renamed *c.* 1810. Almost destroyed in the Anglo-American War (1813). Its rapid development followed the opening of the Erie Canal to New York (1825).

**Buganda** Uganda. One of the four regions into which Uganda is administratively divided. Area 25,600 sq. m. Pop. (1959) 1,881,149. Cap. Kampala (also cap. of Uganda). Chief commercial centre Entebbe. Divided into the administrative districts of Mengo, Masaka, and Mubende. Mainly savannah; dense forests along the rivers. Chief products cotton, coffee, bananas. Taken under British protection 1894. Granted native self-government 1900. During the preparations for the independence of Uganda, the people of Buganda (the Baganda) sought autonomy, but have remained within the state. After Uganda had been granted independence (1962), the Kabaka of Buganda became the first President (1963). When Dr Milton Obote, the Prime Minister of Uganda, suspended the constitution and assumed full powers, the Kabaka of Buganda fled the country (1966).

**Bug River (Western Bug)** Poland/USSR. River 480 m. long, rising in W Ukraine near Zolochev, flowing generally NW, and joining the Vistula below Warsaw. Navigable below Brest(-Litovsk), where the Mukhanets R. links it to the Dnieper-Bug Canal. Forms the Polish-Soviet frontier for over 100 m.

**Bug River (Southern Bug)** USSR. River 530 m. long, rising in W Ukraine 75 m. ESE of Zolochev, flowing generally SE, and entering the Dnieper estuary and the Black Sea below Nikolayev. Navigable for about 60 m. of its lower course. The upper reaches are impeded by rapids.

**Builth Wells** Wales. Urban district in N Breconshire, on the R. Wye 14 m. N of Brecon. Pop. (1961) 1,602. Market town. Resort. Mineral springs.

**Buitenzorg** ♢ *Bogor*.

**Bujumbura (Usumbura)** Burundi. Capital and chief port, at the NE end of L. Tanganyika. Pop. 70,000. Exports cotton, coffee, hides, etc. Manufactures pharmaceutical products, canoes, nets. Formerly capital of Ruanda-Urundi.

**Buka Atoll** ♢ *Solomon Islands*.

**Bukavu** Congo (Kinshasa). Formerly Costermansville. Capital of ♢ *Kivu* province, at the S end of L. Kivu near the Rwanda frontier, at a height of 4,750 ft. Pop. 10,000. Commercial and route centre. Cinchona processing. Manufactures pharmaceutical products, insecticides, cement. Grew rapidly owing to European settlement.

**Bukhara (Bokhara)** USSR. Capital of the Bukhara region in Uzbekistan, 280 m. WSW of Tashkent. Pop. (1970) 112,000. Commercial centre. Manufactures silk and woollen goods; once famous for its rugs and carpets. An ancient city, in a fertile oasis near the Zeravshan R., surrounded by walls, and with many mosques and bazaars. Under Arab rule from the 7th to the 9th cent. and Persian rule from the 9th to the 10th cent. it was a centre of Muslim learning, and is still noted for its theological colleges. The early state of Bukhara was conquered and the city destroyed by Genghis Khan (1220). Taken by the Uzbeks in the early 16th cent., became capital of the emirate of Bukhara. At the Russian revolution the Emir was driven out (1920) and his territory was made an SSR, but in 1924 it was divided between the Uzbek, Tadzhik, and Turkmen SSRs. A pipeline 1,250 m. long from Bukhara, taking natural gas to Chelyabinsk in the Urals, was opened 1963.

**Bukovina.** Region of SE Europe E of the Carpathians, drained by the Siret and Prut rivers, now divided between the USSR (W Ukraine) and Rumania. Passed from Turkey to Austria (1775), and to Rumania (1918). N Bukovina was ceded to the USSR 1940, occupied by Rumania 1941–4, and returned to the USSR 1947; chief town Chernovtsy (Cernǎuti). S Bukovina remained in Rumania as a province, abolished 1952. Peopled by a mixture of Rumanians, Ruthenians, and Ukrainians.

**Bulawayo** Rhodesia. Chief commercial and railway centre and second largest town, in Matabeleland, 240 m. SW of Salisbury at a height of 4,469 ft. Pop. (1968) 271,000 (inc. 210,000 Africans). Railway workshops, iron foundries, sugar refinery. Manufactures agricultural implements, textiles. Airport. Founded (1893) on the site of the kraal of Lobengula (chief of the Matabele). About 30 m. S, in the Matopo Hills, is the tomb of Cecil Rhodes.

**Bulgaria.** Republic in the Balkan Peninsula in SE Europe. Area 42,818 sq. m. Pop. (1965) 8,226,564. Cap. Sofia. Lang. Bulgarian (88 per cent) and Turkish (10 per cent). Rel. mainly Eastern Orthodox, some Muslim.

Bounded by Rumania (N), the Black Sea (E), Turkey and Greece (S), and Yugoslavia (W). Primarily agricultural: before 1945 it was a country of small-holdings; since 1946 the Communist régime has limited individual land ownership to 20 hectares (49·4 acres). Administratively divided into 30 provinces, three of which are the largest towns: Sofia, Plovdiv, and Varna.

TOPOGRAPHY, CLIMATE. To the S of the Danube (which forms most of the N frontier) a plain stretches E–W across the country, succeeded farther S by the Balkan Mountains, with several peaks exceeding 7,000 ft. These mountains separate the N lowlands from the plains of the SE, largely the Maritsa basin. In the SW are the still higher Rhodope Mountains, rising to 9,596 ft in Peak Musala. The Balkan Mountains form an E–W watershed; the N plains are drained by tributaries of the Danube flowing N, and the S part of the country is drained by the Maritsa, Mesta, and Struma rivers, flow-ing generally S to the Aegean Sea. On the whole the climate is continental, with warm summers and cold winters; conditions are more moderate in the sheltered valleys.

RESOURCES, PEOPLE, *etc.* Nearly half the land is under cultivation. Principal crops cereals, sugar-beet, tobacco (an important export), sunflowers (for seed), vines. Attar of roses (from the famous Valley of Roses) is still an important source of revenue. Large numbers of sheep reared. After the establishment of the People's Republic, 932 co-operative and 67 state farms were set up 1946–60. Agricultural as well as industrial production is controlled by successive Five-year Plans. Tractors and other machines have been introduced where even ploughs and draught animals had been unknown. Mineral resources have been little exploited, but coal output is increasing. Oil is produced near Balchik on the Black Sea; a new and promising oilfield was discovered near Pleven 1962. Great emphasis is placed on increasing industrialization; capital investment in industry has far exceeded that in other sectors of the economy. The main centres of industry are Sofia, Plovdiv, and Pleven. The chief ports are Varna and Burgas on the Black Sea and Ruse on the Danube. About two thirds of the population live in villages. The illiteracy rate (23 per cent in 1946) has decreased. The great majority of the population belongs to the Eastern Orthodox Church, but there are over 900,000 Muslims: 190,000 Pomaks (Bulgarian Muslims), and the remainder descendants of Turks.

HISTORY. Invaded in the 7th cent. A.D. by the Bulgars, who gradually adopted the language and culture of the conquered Slavs and acquired considerable power in SE Europe. Annexed by the Ottoman Empire 1395; remained under oppressive Turkish rule until 1878. Liberated by Russia during the Russo-Turkish wars, but did not achieve full sovereignty until Ferdinand of Saxe-Coburg-Gotha, the ruling prince, proclaimed himself king (1908). Took part in the Balkan Wars (1912–13) and joined the German side in the 1st World War. Lost S Dobruja to Rumania, the Aegean coastline to Greece, and some territory to Yugoslavia (1919). Again supported the German cause in the 2nd World War. S Dobruja was restored 1945. After a referendum, the monarchy was abolished (1946) and a People's Republic was proclaimed. The greater part of the foreign trade has since been with the USSR.

**Bull Run** USA. Small stream in N Virginia. Scene of two Confederate victories (1861, 1862) in the American Civil War. Jackson's stand in the first battle earned him the nickname of 'Stonewall'.

**Bunbury** Australia. Seaport in S W Western Australia 100 m. S of Perth on Geographe Bay. Pop. (1966) 15,453. Exports timber, wheat, wool. Manufactures superphosphates, textiles.

**Buncrana** Irish Republic. Town on the E side of Lough Swilly in N E Co. Donegal. Pop. (1966) 2,916. Seaside resort, market town, and fishing centre.

**Bundaberg** Australia. Port in SE Queensland, 180m. NNW of Brisbane. Pop. (1966) 25,404. Exports sugar. Sugar refining, brewing, distilling (rum).

**Bundoran** Irish Republic. Fishing port and seaside resort in S Co. Donegal, on Donegal Bay. Pop. (1966) 1,421.

**Bungay** England. Urban district in N E Suffolk, on the R. Waveney 13 m. W of Lowestoft. Pop. (1961) 3,581. Market town. Printing. Manufactures agricultural implements. Ruins of a Norman castle.

**Bunker Hill** USA. Small hill in Charlestown, now part of Boston, in Massachusetts; connected by a ridge with Breed's Hill. Scene of the first important battle of the American Revolution (1775); the Bunker Hill Monument marks the battlefield.

**Buraida** Saudi Arabia. Town and oasis in Nejd 200 m. NW of Riyadh. Pop. 70,000. Trade in dates, grain, etc.

**Burbank** USA. Industrial town in California, on the outskirts of Los Angeles. Pop. (1960) 90,155. Film and television studios. Manufactures aircraft.

**Burdekin River** Australia. River 425 m. long rising 85 m. N W of Townsville in E Queensland, flowing generally S E and then N to enter the Pacific through an unnavigable delta at Upstart Bay. The flow varies greatly, but increases to produce widespread flooding in summer.

**Burdwan** India. Capital of the Burdwan division of W Bengal, 60 m. NW of Calcutta. Pop. (1961) 108,224. Rice milling. Manufactures cutlery, hosiery. Trade in rice, sugar-cane, jute, etc. University (1960).

**Burgas** Bulgaria. Capital of the province of Burgas, on the Gulf of Burgas on the Black

Sea. Pop. (1965) 106,127. Seaport and industrial centre. Exports tobacco, wool, leather, etc. Manufactures agricultural machinery, textiles, soap. Flour milling. Fishing. A new oil refinery began to operate in 1963.

**Burgdorf** Switzerland. Town in the Bern canton, on the Emme R. 11 m. N E of Bern. Pop. (1969) 16,700. Manufactures textiles etc. Trade in Emmenthal cheese. In the old castle (now a museum) above the modern town Pestalozzi established his first school (1799).

**Burgenland** Austria. Province in the E, bordered in the E by Hungary. Area 1,530 sq. m. Pop. (1961) 271,001. Cap. Eisenstadt (pop. 7,600). Mainly low-lying in the N (partly occupied by L. Neusiedler); hilly in the centre and S. Chief occupations agriculture and stock rearing. Ruled by Austria from 1491 and by Hungary from 1647. Restored to Austria after the 1st World War. After a plebiscite, the Sopron salient was returned to Hungary (1921), almost separating the N part of the province from the S.

**Burghead** Scotland. Small burgh in N Morayshire, on a headland at the E end of Burghead Bay, in the Moray Firth, 7 m. NW of Elgin. Pop. (1961) 1,346. Fishing port. Resort.

**Burgos** Spain. 1. Province in Old Castile, in the N. Area 5,531 sq. m. Pop. (1961) 380,791. Forms part of the Meseta. Largely forested. Drained by the Ebro and the Douro (Duero) rivers. Cereals and other crops cultivated. Sheep reared.
2. Capital of Burgos province, on the Arlanzón R., a tributary of the Douro, 75 m. SW of Bilbao. Pop. (1967) 100,413. Flour milling, engineering. Manufactures tyres, paper, woollen and leather goods, chemicals, etc. Tourist centre. Famous for its architecture; the magnificent Gothic cathedral (begun 1221, completed 1567) with its 15 chapels, is the burial-place of El Cid. Several other Gothic churches. The life of the city centres on the arcaded Plaza Mayor. Founded 884. Became capital of the kingdom of Castile, but declined with the rise of Madrid. Franco's provisional capital during the Civil War (1936–9). Near by is the birthplace of El Cid (c. 1043–99).

**Burgundy** (Fr. **Bourgogne**) France. Former province, comprising the present departments of Ain, Saône-et-Loire, Côte-d'Or, and parts of Haute-Marne, Aube, and Yonne. Long famous for wines. Conquered by Julius Caesar. Settled in the 5th cent. A.D. by the Burgundii (a Germanic tribe), who established a kingdom of Burgundy. Divided for a time, then reunited in the 10th cent. as a second kingdom (Kingdom of Arles). Fell to the Holy Roman Empire 1032. The imperial dominion included the county of Burgundy (later Franche-Comté), between the Jura mountains and the Saône R. The duchy of Burgundy, created from land W of the Saône, became very powerful, and ruled most of modern Holland, Belgium, and N and E France. With the death of Charles the Bold (1477) the duchy itself passed to France and the remaining territories to the Empire. Franche-Comté was annexed to France (1678) by Louis XIV.

**Burhanpur** India. Town in Madhya Pradesh on the Tapti R. 280 m. NE of Bombay. Pop. (1961) 82,090. Manufactures textiles and shellac. Founded in the early 15th cent. Long famous for fine fabrics decorated with gold and silver thread.

**Burlington** (Iowa) USA. Industrial town on the Mississippi R. 140 m. ESE of Des Moines. Pop. (1960) 32,430. Manufactures furniture, boilers, electrical equipment, etc.

**Burlington** (Vermont) USA. Port and largest city of Vermont, on L. Champlain. Pop. (1960) 35,531. Trade by rail and lake. Manufactures food products (inc. maple sugar), furniture, tools, etc. Seat of the University of Vermont (1791).

**Burma.** Independent republic of SE Asia. Area 261,789 sq. m. Pop. (1968) 26,390,000 (about 80 per cent Burmese). Cap. Rangoon. Rel. chiefly Buddhist.

Officially known as the Union of Burma. Bounded on the E by China, Laos, and Thailand, and on the W by the Bay of Bengal, E Pakistan, and India. It is primarily an agricultural country, its heart the basin of the great Irrawaddy R. and the main tributary, the Chindwin, and it is one of the world's leading exporters of rice. Divided into Burma proper, which occupies the central part of the country, the Kachin (NE), Shan (E), Kayah and Karen (SE) states, and the Chin special division (NW). TOPOGRAPHY, CLIMATE, *etc.* Separated from India and E Pakistan by a succession of ranges known N–S as the Patkai, Naga, and Chin Hills and continued as the Arakan Yoma, which rises to 10,018 ft in Mt Victoria and also divides the coastal strip of Arakan from the rest of the country. The Irrawaddy and Chindwin flow S from the mountainous N (the valley of the former being separated in its lower course from the Sittang basin by the Pegu Yoma range) to enter the sea by a broad delta. E of the central plain of Burma is a plateau averaging 3,000 ft in altitude and cut by the deep N–S gorges of the Salween R. To the S of the plateau is the long narrow coastal strip of Tenasserim, extending as far as the Isthmus of Kra and fringed by the chain of islands known as the Mergui Archipelago.

Typical monsoon climate similar to that of India, with a rainy season June–Oct., a cool dry season Nov.–Feb., and a hot, dry season March–May. Along the Arakan and Tenasserim coasts the rainfall approaches 200 ins. annually, but on the lee side of the Arakan Yoma, in the central dry belt, there is as little as 20 ins. a year. The natural vegetation varies with the rainfall: where the latter exceeds about 80 ins. annually the lower lands are clothed with tropical rainforests, while the somewhat drier regions (40–80 ins.) support deciduous monsoon forests, home of the teak; the dry belt has only scrub and semi-desert vegetation.

RESOURCES, PEOPLE, *etc.* About two thirds of the cultivated area is sown with rice, which is concentrated in the wet alluvial lands of the Irrawaddy delta and the valleys of the lower Chindwin and Sittang rivers, and Burma is normally able to produce a considerable surplus for export. In the dry belt, where about $1\frac{1}{4}$ million acres are irrigated, the principal crops are cotton, groundnuts, millet, and sesamum. There is room for agricultural expansion, as government policy has recognized, but in general the Burmese farmer traditionally preserves an easy-going attitude to his life's work. Teak is floated down the rivers from the monsoon forests to sawmills at Rangoon and elsewhere and is exported. Oil production at Yenangyaung and Chauk in the dry belt has not yet reached the pre-war amount. Jade and rubies are mined in the N, silver and lead in the E, and tin and tungsten in the S. For centuries the main trade routes have been provided by the Irrawaddy and its tributaries; the waterways are now supplemented by railways from Rangoon into the interior, but Burma has no rail connexion with any neighbouring country. After Rangoon the chief cities are Mandalay and Moulmein.

Inhabited by a number of different races speaking different languages. The Burmese, who are of Mongolian stock and Buddhist by religion, represent the most advanced section of the population and live mainly on the fertile lowlands. Each of the hill tribes occupies the region named after it (see above) and has its own language and customs; they are generally described as Animists, though many of the Karens of the Kayah and Karen states have adopted Christianity. The main immigrant groups are the Indians, about 600,000 in number, who originally supplied most of the coolie labour, and the 350,000 Chinese, who are usually traders and artisans. As long as Burma was a parliamentary democracy (1948–58), the Shans, Kachins, Karens, and Chins enjoyed a measure of local autonomy and were represented in the government.

HISTORY. The Burmese people of today are the descendants of various Mongolian tribes which moved into the country from W China and Tibet, probably in the 7th cent. Unity was achieved in 1054 with the founding of the Pagan dynasty by Anawrahta, who introduced Buddhism, and lasted till 1287, when Burma fell to the Mongols under Kublai Khan. For much of the following five centuries the land was split into petty states, but in 1752 Alangpaya (Alompra) brought the whole country under his sway. His successors came into conflict with the British, however, and as a result of the Burmese Wars (1823–6, 1852, 1885–6) the country was gradually annexed by Britain; in 1886 it was made a province of India. Burma was separated from India in 1937. During the 2nd World War it was occupied by the Japanese (1942–5), and the destruction and demoralization of these years left the country disorganized and difficult to govern. In 1948 Burma became an independent republic, its parliament consisting of a Chamber of Deputies and a Chamber of Nationalities. In 1958 and again in 1962, however, government was taken over by a Revolutionary Council.

Burma Road. Highway about 800 m. long from Lashio, the railway terminus in E Burma, to Kunming and Chungking in China. Begun by the Chinese 1937; completed 1939. Utilized for the transport of war materials to the Chinese forces in the Sino-Japanese War until closed by the Japanese (1942).

Burnham England. Small town in Buckinghamshire, just NW of and within the municipal borough of Slough. Near by is the woodland area (375 acres) of Burnham Beeches, the remains of an ancient forest,

purchased (1879) by the City of London.
Burnham-on-Crouch England. Urban district in SE Essex, on the estuary of the R. Crouch. Pop. (1961) 4,167. Noted for yachting. Oyster culture.
Burnham-on-Sea England. Urban district in Somerset, on Bridgwater Bay (Bristol Channel). Pop. (1961) 9,850. Seaside resort.
Burnley England. County borough in E Lancashire, at the confluence of the Brun and Calder rivers. Pop. (1961) 80,588. In a coalmining district. Important textile centre. Cotton weaving; also spinning and dyeing. Engineering. Manufactures textile machinery, chemicals, etc. Towneley Hall (acquired by the corporation in 1902) is a museum and art gallery. Suffered from the 'cotton famine' during the American Civil War (1861–5), and from the 20th-cent. decline in the Lancashire cotton trade.
Burntisland Scotland. Royal burgh, port, industrial town, and resort in S Fifeshire, on the Firth of Forth opposite Edinburgh. Pop. (1961) 6,036. Aluminium works. Shipbuilding. Exports coal. The name may derive from the site having once been an island.
Burrinjuck Dam ◊ Murrumbidgee River.
Burry Port Wales. Urban district in S Carmarthenshire, 4 m. W of Llanelli. Pop. (1961) 5,671. Market town. Port. Exports coal. Anthracite mining. Manufactures tinplate.
Bursa Turkey. Capital of Bursa province, 55 m. S of Istanbul. Pop. (1965) 211,600. Trade in tobacco, fruit, grain, etc. Manufactures textiles, carpets. Several imposing mosques and tombs of Ottoman sultans. Probably founded by King Prusias I of Bithynia in the 2nd cent. B.C. Taken by the Ottoman Turks (1326), it was their capital for nearly a century.
Burslem England. One of the 'Five Towns' of the Potteries, in N Staffordshire, since 1910 incorporated in ◊ Stoke-on-Trent. Called the 'mother of the Potteries'; the oldest of the pottery towns, the industry having been established here in the 17th cent. Site of the Wedgwood Institute (1863). Birthplace of Josiah Wedgwood (1730–95), who set up his first works here 1759.
Burton-upon-Trent England. County borough in E Staffordshire, on the R. Trent 10 m. SW of Derby. Pop. (1961) 50,766. Its famous brewing industry (partly due to the presence of sulphate of lime in the local well-water) may date back to the Benedictine abbey founded in 1002; it became

131

BUTESHIRE

important in the 18th cent. Cooperages, engineering works, timber yards. Manufactures tyres, food products, etc.

**Burujird** Iran. Town in Khuzistan province at a height of 5,500 ft, 60 m. S of Hamadan. Pop. (1966) 71,486. Commercial centre. Trade in grain and fruit. Manufactures carpets and rugs, textiles.

**Burundi.** Republic in Central Africa bounded by Rwanda (N), Tanzania (E and S), and L. Tanganyika and Congo (Kinshasa) (W). Area 10,747 sq. m. Pop. (1963) 2,600,000. Cap. Bujumbura. Consists mainly of a high broken plateau at 4,000–6,000 ft, rising to over 8,000 ft in the S. The Luvironza, the most southerly headstream of the Nile, rises in the S. Cattle, sheep, goats raised. Maize, cassava, plantains cultivated. Exports livestock, hides, coffee, cotton. Three ethnic groups: the tall, aristocratic Watutsi; the peasant Bahutu of Bantu stock (the great majority); and a small number of pigmy Batwa. After the 1st World War (1923), as the S part of Ruanda-Urundi, it was administered by Belgium under League of Nations mandate, and after the 2nd World War (1946) as a UN Trust Territory. When Ruanda-Urundi was granted independence (1962), Burundi (Urundi) remained a monarchy, while Rwanda became a republic. It was declared a republic in 1966.

**Bury** England. County borough in SE Lancashire, on the R. Irwell. Pop. (1961) 59,984. Important in the 14th cent. for the woollen industry, superseded by the cotton industry in the 18th cent. Cotton spinning and weaving, wool spinning, dyeing. Manufactures textile and paper-making machinery, felts, chemicals, paint, etc. Birthplace of John Kay (1704–64), co-inventor of the flying shuttle, and Sir Robert Peel (1788–1850).

**Buryat ASSR** USSR. Autonomous republic of the RSFSR, till 1958 known as the Buryat-Mongol ASSR, bordering on Mongolia (S) and on L. Baikal (W). Area 135,650 sq. m. Pop. (1970) 812,000. Cap. and chief industrial centre Ulan-Ude. Much of it lies on the Vitim Plateau, and forests of larch, fir, and cedar cover the slopes of the Barguzin Mountains. Cattle and sheep rearing are important occupations. Cereals cultivated in the river valleys. The Buryats, a Mongol people, are Buddhists by religion; they were conquered by the Russians in the 17th cent., and now form about half the population.

**Buryat-Aginsky NA** USSR. National Area in S Siberia, in the Chita Region (RSFSR). Area 9,000 sq. m. Pop. (1970) 66,000 (largely Buryat Mongols). Cap. Aginskoye (75 m. SSE of Chita). Stock rearing, lumbering, etc.

**Bury St Edmunds** England. Municipal borough and county town of W Suffolk. Pop. (1961) 21,144. Market town. Brewing, sugar refining. Manufactures agricultural machinery. St Edmund, last king of the East Angles (martyred 870), was buried (903) in the now ruined abbey, which later became a place of pilgrimage; hence the name (originally St Edmund's Bury). Two 15th-cent. churches: St James's (which became a cathedral 1914) and St Mary's, burial-place of Mary Tudor, Duchess of Suffolk (sister of Henry VIII and grandmother of Lady Jane Grey).

**Bushey** England. Urban district in SW Hertfordshire, 2 m. SE of Watford. Pop. (1961) 20,653. Mainly residential. Several well-known schools.

**Bushire** (Persian **Bushehr**) Iran. Port on the Persian Gulf, 110 m. WSW of Shiraz, with which it is connected by road. Pop. 27,000. Exports wool, rugs, cotton, etc. Founded in 1736, it superseded the near-by port of Rishire, but has declined in recent years with the development of trade in the Abadan region.

**Bussum** Netherlands. Town in N Holland province 13 m. ESE of Amsterdam. Pop. (1968) 41,833. Largely residential: a 'dormitory' town of Amsterdam. Manufactures chocolate etc. Has noteworthy 20th-cent. churches and other buildings.

**Busto Arsizio** Italy. Industrial town in Varese province in Lombardy, 20 m. NW of Milan. Pop. (1961) 64,367. Important centre of cotton and rayon manufacture. Also produces iron and steel, textile machinery, footwear, dyes, etc. Noteworthy 16th-cent. church, Santa Maria di Piazza, designed by Bramante.

**Bute** Scotland. Island in Buteshire, in the Firth of Clyde, separated from the Cowal peninsula by the narrow Kyles of Bute. Area (inc. Inchmarnock Island) 47 sq. m. Chief town Rothesay (on the E coast), a well-known holiday resort. Hilly in the N, rising to 875 ft. Farming in the centre.

**Buteshire** Scotland. County comprising several islands in the Firth of Clyde and Kilbrannan Sound: the most important are Arran, Bute, Great Cumbrae, and Little

Cumbrae. Area 218 sq. m. Pop. (1961) 15,129. County town Rothesay.

**Butte** USA. Mining town in Montana 47 m. SSW of Helena. Pop. (1960) 27,877. Produces nearly one third of the copper mined in the USA; also silver, zinc, and manganese. Manufactures mining machinery, chemicals. Seat of the Montana School of Mines (1900) and the offices of the Anaconda Copper Mining Co.

**Buttermere, Lake** England. Lake in SW Cumberland (in the Lake District), 1¼ m. long and ⅓ m. wide. Connected with Crummock Water by a short stream. Popular with tourists for its picturesque scenery. Buttermere village is near the N end.

**Buxton** England. Municipal borough in NW Derbyshire, on the R. Wye 20 m. W of Chesterfield, in the Peak District 1,000 ft above sea level; the highest town of its size in England. Pop. (1961) 19,236. Health resort. Long famous for thermal and chalybeate springs, used in the treatment of gout, rheumatism, etc. The Crescent and the Devonshire Royal Hospital are noteworthy. Near by is Poole's Hole, a limestone cave with stalactites and stalagmites. Limestone quarried in the neighbourhood.

**Buzău** Rumania. Town in the SE, on the Buzău R. 60 m. NE of Bucharest. Pop. (1968) 59,114. Trade in grain, timber, petroleum. Oil-refining, flour milling, textile, and other industries.

**Bydgoszcz** (Ger. **Bromberg**) Poland. Capital of the Bydgoszcz voivodship, on the Brda R. 140 m. WNW of Warsaw. Pop. (1968) 275,200. Industrial town. Manufactures machinery, textiles, clothing, footwear, paper, etc. Trade in timber. Passed to Prussia 1772. Called Bromberg during the German administration. Returned to Poland (1919) after the 1st World War.

**Byelorussia (Belorussia, White Russia)** USSR. Constituent republic (SSR) of the USSR, bordering in the W on Poland. Area 80,134 sq. m. Pop. (1970) 9,003,000. Cap. Minsk. Mainly low-lying, with the extensive Pripet Marshes in the S. Drained by the Dnieper and its tributaries to the Black Sea, and by the W Dvina and the Neman rivers to the Baltic Sea. All these rivers are used for floating timber from the forests, which occupy over one quarter of the total area. Cultivated land has been considerably increased by draining the marshlands. Main crops flax, potatoes, sugar-beet, fodder crops. Large numbers of beef and dairy cattle and pigs reared. Much attention has been paid to the development of the peat industry; peat is used in power stations and chemical plants and provides most of the country's fuel needs. Industries are concentrated chiefly in Minsk, Gomel, Mogilev, Vitebsk, Bobruisk, Grodno, and Brest. Divided administratively into 6 regions: Brest, Gomel, Grodno, Minsk, Mogilev, Vitebsk. About four fifths of the population are Byelorussian (usually considered the purest of the three great Slav divisions); the remainder are Russian, Polish, Ukrainian, and Jewish.

From the 14th cent. Byelorussia was ruled alternately by Russia and Poland. In the three Partitions of Poland (1772–95) it passed finally to Russia. Suffered severely in the various wars (17th and 18th cent.), during Napoleon's march on Moscow (1812), and in both world wars. The Byelorussian SSR (formed 1919) joined the USSR in 1922. Subsequently enlarged with territory from RSFSR, and later increased in area by almost two thirds through the acquisition of a large area of E Poland under the Potsdam agreement (1945).

**Bytom** (Ger. **Beuthen**) Poland. Industrial town in the Katowice voivodship (Upper Silesia) 8 m. NNW of Katowice. Pop. (1968) 186,700. Coal, zinc, and lead mining centre. Manufactures machinery etc. Taken by Prussia 1742. Called Beuthen during the German administration. Severely damaged in the 2nd World War. Returned to Poland under the Potsdam Agreement (1945).

**Byzantium.** Ancient Greek city on the shore of the Bosporus, on the site of modern ◊ *Istanbul*. Founded *c*. 658 B.C. by Greeks from Megara and Argos. Prospered on account of the favourable position for trade and the excellent harbour. Taken by the Romans A.D. 196. Constantine I built the new city of Constantinople (later the capital of the Byzantine Empire) here in A.D. 330.

# C

**Cabanatuan** Philippines. Market town in Luzon 60 m. N of Manila. Pop. 55,000. Trade in rice and other agricultural produce.

**Cabinda (Kabinda)** Angola. District on the Atlantic seaboard. Area 3,000 sq. m. Pop. 51,000. Chief town and seaport Cabinda (pop. 12,000). An enclave separated from the rest of Angola by a strip of land belonging to Congo (Kinshasa) along the Congo R. Produces cocoa, coffee, palm oil, timber. Scene of fighting between Africans and Portuguese in the Angola rebellion (1961).

**Cáceres** Spain. 1. Province, bounded on the W by Portugal, forming part of Estremadura. Area 7,699 sq. m. Pop. (1961) 544,407. Produces cereals, olive oil, etc. Sheep and pigs raised.
2. Capital of Cáceres province, on the Cáceres R. Pop. 52,000. Market town. Trade in grain, olive oil, wool, ham, and the red sausages (*embutidos*) for which the province is famous. Manufactures cork and leather goods, textiles, fertilizers, etc. The upper, old town has medieval walls.

**Cadenabbia** Italy. Village and resort in Como province in Lombardy, on the W side of L. Como. Near by is the Villa Carlotta (1747) with gardens and art treasures, now the property of the Italian government.

**Cader Idris** Wales. Mountain ridge in W Merionethshire, rising to 2,927 ft in the peak of Pen-y-Gader, with a remarkable *cwm* (cirque) in the steep slope down to the tarn of Llyn-y-Cau. Frequently mentioned in Welsh legends.

**Cádiz** Spain. 1. Province in Andalusia, the most southerly of the Iberian peninsula, bounded by the Mediterranean (SE), the Strait of Gibraltar (S), and the Atlantic (SW). Area 2,851 sq. m. Pop. (1961) 818,847. Fertile. Famous for sherry (named after Jerez de la Frontera). Produces olives, vines, oranges, cork. Salt obtained by evaporation of sea water.
2. Capital of Cádiz province, Atlantic seaport, at the end of the spit projecting NW from the Isla de León, commanding the entrance to the Bay of Cádiz. Pop. (1967) 133,114. Exports wine, salt, olive oil, cork. The harbour has been much improved this century. Within the bay there are shipyards

and a naval base. Modern and clean in appearance, with whitewashed houses and fine marine promenades. Medical faculty of the University of Seville. Two cathedrals (13th-cent. and 18th/19th-cent.); the Torre Vigía (watch-tower); art gallery (with paintings by Spanish masters); chapel of the Capuchins, containing Murillo's unfinished picture *The Marriage of St Catherine*, while painting which Murillo fell from the scaffold and was killed (1682). Founded (*c.* 1100 B.C.) by the Phoenicians. Passed in turn to the Carthaginians, the Romans and the Moors. Recaptured by Alfonso X of Castile 1262. Columbus's port of departure on his second voyage. Rose to wealth and importance during the colonial era, but declined in the 19th cent. Scene of the meeting of the Cortes to promulgate the new liberal constitution (1812). Birthplace of the composer Manuel de Falla (1876–1946).

**Caen** France. Prefecture of the Calvados department, in Normandy, on the Orne R. Pop. (1968) 114,398. Port; industrial, commercial, and educational centre. Manufactures steel, pottery, textiles, cement. Exports iron ore, dairy produce, cement, building stone (several cathedrals and churches of S England were built with Caen limestone). Imports coal, timber, grain. Seat of a university (founded 1432), whose buildings were destroyed in the Normandy campaign of the 2nd World War (1944), with most of the city centre; the churches of St Étienne (l'Abbaye aux Hommes), founded by William the Conqueror, and la Trinité (l'Abbaye aux Dames), founded by his wife Queen Matilda, escaped damage. Became important under William. Taken by the English 1346 and 1417. A centre of Girondist resistance to the Revolutionary Convention 1793. Birthplace of François de Malherbe (1555–1628) and D. F. E. Auber (1782–1871).

**Caerleon** Wales. Urban district in S Monmouthshire, on the R. Usk 2 m. NE of Newport. Pop. (1961) 4,184. Site of the Roman fortress of Isca (*c.* A.D. 75); considerable remains. Long associated with Arthurian legend.

**Caernarvon** Wales. Municipal borough, county town, port, and resort in Caernarvonshire, on the Menai Strait. Pop. (1961) 8,998. Exports slate. Near by is the site of the Roman Segontium. The well-preserved castle, built by Edward I (1284), is reputedly the birthplace of Edward II, first Prince of Wales. Here Prince Charles was invested as 21st Prince of Wales (1969).

**Caernarvonshire** Wales. Maritime county in the NW, extending SW into the Lleyn peninsula. Area 569 sq. m. Pop. (1961) 121,194. County town Caernarvon. Mountainous; Snowdon (3,560 ft) is the highest peak in England and Wales. Snowdonia's mountain and lake scenery make it a popular tourist region. Principal other industries slate quarrying (declining), sheep farming. Main river the Conway (forming most of the E border). Principal towns Caernarvon, Bangor, Conway, Llandudno, Pwllheli.

**Caerphilly** Wales. Urban district in E Glamorganshire, 7 m. N of Cardiff. Pop. (1961) 36,008. Coalmining. Market town. Originated Caerphilly cheese. The castle (13th/14th-cent.) is the largest in Wales.

**Caesarea Palestinae** Israel. Ancient city and seaport 22 m. SSW of modern Haifa, founded (13 B.C.) by Herod the Great as the port to his capital Sebaste (Samaria). Roman remains. Declined as a port after being occupied by the Muslims (638). Temporarily revived under the Crusaders, but destroyed by the Muslims (1265).

**Caesarea Philippi** Syria. City of ancient Palestine, now the village of ◊ *Banias* in the extreme SW of Syria, near the Israeli frontier. Site of the Greek Paneas, renamed Caesarea Philippi by the Romans. Near by are the traditional springs of the Jordan.

**Cagliari** Italy. Seaport in S Sardinia; chief town of the island and capital of Cagliari province, on the Gulf of Cagliari. Pop. (1968) 215,807. Salt lagoons on both sides. Exports salt, lead, zinc, etc. Flour milling, tanning, fishing, etc. Built at the foot and on the slopes of a long steep hill. Cathedral (13th/14th-cent., later rebuilt); Byzantine churches; Punic necropolis; Roman amphitheatre; two early-14th-cent. Pisan towers, Torre dell'Elefante and Torre di San Pancrazio. University (1626).

**Caguas** Puerto Rico. Town 18 m. S of San Juan. Pop. (1960) 65,098. Industrial and commercial centre in an agricultural region (tobacco, sugar-cane, etc.). Manufactures cigars, leather goods, etc.

**Caher (Cahir)** Irish Republic. Market town in Co. Tipperary, on the R. Suir. Pop.

(1966) 1,740. Salmon-fishing centre. Castle (12th-cent.), built by Conor O'Brien, later rebuilt and restored.

**Cahirciveen (Cahersiveen)** Irish Republic. Small port in Co. Kerry, on the estuary of the R. Valentia. Pop. (1966) 1,649. Fishing. The church contains a memorial to Daniel O'Connell (1775–1847), who was born near by.

**Cahors** France. Ancient Divona. Prefecture of the Lot department and formerly capital of Quercy; in a loop of the Lot R. 57 m. N of Toulouse. Pop. (1968) 20,903. Market town. Food processing. Trade in wine, truffles, etc. The 13th/14th-cent. Pont Valentré is the outstanding medieval fortified bridge in France, with three towers. Cathedral (12th/15th-cent.); museum (formerly an episcopal palace). In Roman times famous for linen. A leading banking centre in the 13th cent. Birthplace of Pope John XXII (1249–1334), founder of the university (1331), which united with that of Toulouse in 1751. Also birthplace of Léon Gambetta (1838–82).

**Cairngorm Mountains** Scotland. A range of the Grampians in Aberdeenshire, Banffshire, and Inverness-shire. Includes Ben Macdhui (4,296 ft, the second highest peak in Scotland), Braeriach (4,248 ft), Cairn Toul (4,241 ft), and Cairn Gorm (4,084 ft, after which the local brown or yellow quartz is named). The area was declared a nature reserve 1954.

**Cairns** Australia. Seaport in Queensland 180 m. NNW of Townsville. Pop. (1966) 29,185. Exports sugar, timber, etc. A picturesque, attractively built town in an agricultural (sugar-cane, tropical fruits, etc.), lumbering, and mining region. Also a tourist centre.

**Cairo** (Ar. **El Qahira**) United Arab Republic. Capital, the largest city in Africa and the Middle East, on the right bank of the Nile, at the head of the delta. Pop. (1960) 3,346,000 (with considerable non-Egyptian communities, inc. Syrians, Sudanese, Greeks, Italians). Connected by rail with Upper Egypt, Alexandria, etc. An important international airport. The chief commercial centre, with a variety of manufactures: cement, textiles, vegetable oils, beer, etc. The Mosque and University of El Ashar (founded 972), the principal theological seminary of Islam (with over 10,000 students); also Cairo University (1908) and the Ein Shamse University (1950). Over 200 mosques, including those of Tulun (9th-cent.) and Hasan (14th-cent., near the great citadel); the mosques, representative of different phases of Islamic architecture, make Cairo outstanding among Arab cities. Several museums of Islamic art. Important ancient Egyptian treasures are housed in the Museum of Antiquities.

The Arab city with its mosques and narrow tortuous streets, the Coptic (Egyptian Christian) area, and the Jewish quarter are in the E; modern Cairo, with government offices, hotels, opera house, etc., built in more European style, is in the W. To the NE is the modern suburb of ◊ *Heliopolis*. Al Gezireh, an island in the Nile, is the centre for country clubs and horse racing. The river port of Bulag is a NW suburb, with a paper and printing industry. The famous pyramids of Giza are 8 m. SW of Cairo.

When the Arabs conquered Egypt they founded El Fustat (A.D. 641) near the Roman fortress town of Babylon, where 'Old Cairo' now stands. Opposite is the island of Roda, where traditionally Pharaoh's daughter found Moses in the bulrushes. The most important of the later towns, El Qahira (founded *c.* 968), gave the city its name. After the Crusaders' unsuccessful attack (1176), Saladin built the citadel on the Moqattam Hills but within the city precincts. Under Turkish rule (1517–1798) Cairo declined, but it grew rapidly in size and importance in the 19th and 20th cent.

**Caistor** England. Small market town in N Lincolnshire, 11 m. SW of Grimsby. Pop. (rural district, 1961) 13,397. Built on the site of a Roman camp and early British fort.

**Caistor St Edmunds** England. Roman Venta Icenorum. Now a suburb of Norwich (3 m. S). Excavations and aerial photography have revealed evidence of a large Roman encampment.

**Caithness** Scotland. County in the extreme NE of the Scottish mainland, separated from the Orkneys by the Pentland Firth in the N; bounded by the North Sea (E and SE) and Sutherland (W). Area 686 sq. m. Pop. (1961) 27,345. County town Wick. The only two towns, Wick and Thurso, are on rivers of the same names. Generally infertile region of moorland and mountains (in the S). Main occupations sheep farming, crofting, fishing. On the rugged N coast are Dunnet Head (the northernmost point of mainland Scotland) and Duncansby Head (the most north-easterly point, to the

W of which is the site of John o'Groat's house).

**Cajamarca** Peru. Capital of the Cajamarca department, in the W Cordillera (NW), in a basin at a height of over 9,000 ft. Pop. 48,000. Market town in an agricultural (maize, alfalfa, wheat) and mining (gold, copper, silver, zinc) region. Manufactures textiles, leather goods, straw hats. Here Pizarro ambushed and executed Atahualpa, the Inca ruler (1533).

**Calabria** Italy. Region in the S comprising the 'toe' of Italy – provinces of Cosenza, Catanzaro, and Reggio di Calabria, between the Ionian and the Tyrrhenian seas. Area 5,828 sq. m. Pop. (1961) 2,045,215. Chief town Reggio. Mainly mountainous; still partly forested. Vines, citrus fruits, and olives cultivated. Sheep and goats raised. Has suffered much from earthquakes, droughts, deforestation, erosion, and malaria. Economic progress has also been retarded by poor communications. Hydroelectric plants in the La Sila mountains. In Roman times the 'heel' of Italy was called Calabria; the Byzantines transferred the name to the 'toe' (previously known as Bruttium).

**Calais** France. Industrial town and seaport in the Pas-de-Calais department, on the Strait of Dover 145 m. N of Paris and 22 m. ESE of Dover. Pop. (1968) 74,908. Owes its importance to its position on the shortest sea crossing between France and England. Heavy traffic in continental passengers and mail. Imports raw materials for the NE industrial region (ores, timber, etc.). Fishing, boatbuilding. Manufactures lace, tulle, rayon, clothing. Important since the end of the 10th cent. In English hands 1347–1558. Rodin's group *The Burghers of Calais* commemorates the long heroic siege of 1346–7. The old town around the harbour was virtually destroyed in the 2nd World War.

**Calapan** ◊ *Mindoro*.

**Calcutta** India. Capital of W Bengal and the second largest city in India, on the left bank of the Hooghly R. about 80 m. by river from the Bay of Bengal. Pop. (1961) 2,927,289. Major seaport. Exports manganese ore, pig iron, raw jute and jute products, tea, oil seeds, etc. Road and railway junction and industrial city. Centre of jute milling, railway engineering, tanning. Manufactures cotton goods, chemicals, paper, soap, etc. Seat of a university, founded (1857) on the pattern of the University of London. Has been described as a city of palaces, but might equally well be called a city of slums; much has been done in recent years, however, to eradicate former squalor. Its life is centred on the Maidan or park (area 2 sq. m.), which contains the later Fort William (1757–73). The outstanding building is the marble Victoria Memorial (opened 1921), erected on the site of the old jail, which houses an enormous collection of pictures, documents, etc. illustrating Indian history. To the N of the Maidan are Government House, until 1912 the residence of the viceroy, and the site of the earlier Fort William (1696) and of the notorious 'Black Hole of Calcutta'. On the E side of the Maidan is Chowringhee Road, which has the Indian Museum, the Bengal School of Art and the Asiatic Society, as well as many imposing hotels, shops, and clubs. In the S of the city, beside a canal, is the Kali Ghat, with the famous Kali temple.

Calcutta was virtually founded in 1690 by Job Charnock of the English East India Company with the occupation of the former village of Sutanati, now within the city boundary; the original Fort William was built for its defence. In 1698 the villages of Sutanati, Govindpur, and Kalikata were purchased by the English, and the settlement was named after the third of these. Because of its defensive position and its excellent anchorage – and in spite of the unhealthy site – Calcutta developed and prospered. In 1756, however, it was captured by Suraj-ud-Dowlah, Nawab of Bengal, who confined 146 prisoners in a small guard-room of Fort William during a torrid June night: there were only 23 survivors from this, the 'Black Hole of Calcutta', on the following morning. Calcutta was recaptured in 1757, a new Fort William was built, the Maidan was formed, and the modern city began to arise. It was the capital of British India from 1773 to 1912, when it was superseded by Delhi, but its commercial importance increased again with the extension of the harbour (1920). The large industrial centre of Howrah, on the opposite side of the Hooghly, is geographically part of Calcutta but now constitutes a separate municipality.

**Caldera** ⟡ *Copiapó*.

**Caledonia** Scotland. Roman name, occurring first in the works of Lucan (1st cent. A.D.) for the part of Britain N of the line traced by the Wall of Antoninus, between the Firth of Forth and the Firth of Clyde. Now used (esp. poetically) for the whole of Scotland.

**Caledonian Canal** Scotland. Waterway 60 m. long, from Loch Linnhe to the Moray Firth along the Great Glen. It comprises Loch Ness, Loch Oich, and Loch Lochy, which are linked by canals 22 m. long in all. Construction began in 1803; opened in 1823; completed in 1847. Now little used.

**Calgary** Canada. Town in S Alberta, at the confluence of the Bow and the Elbow rivers. Pop. (1966) 330,575 (88,904 in 1941). The largest city of Canada's high plains. Important railway junction in a ranching area, near the Turner Valley oilfields (linked by pipelines). Main industries meat packing, flour milling, oil refining; manufactures explosives. Founded 1883. The annual Calgary Stampede is a great tourist attraction.

**Cali** Colombia. Capital of the Valle del Cauca department, in the Cauca valley, at a height of 3,200 ft. Pop. (1968) 637,929. Industrial and commercial city, in a rich agricultural area growing sugar-cane, rice, coffee, and tobacco and with pastures for livestock. Manufactures textiles, clothing, footwear, soap, etc. Founded 1536, but developed little until the 20th cent., esp. after the construction of the railway to Buenaventura (1914) and the opening of the Panama Canal.

**Calicut** ⟡ *Kozhikode*.

**California** USA.* Third largest state (now first in population), bordering the Pacific. Area 158,693 sq. m. Pop. (1970) 19,696,840. Cap. Sacramento. Admitted to the Union in 1850 as the 31st state; popularly known as the 'Golden' state (because of its gold production). Inland from the Coast Range (N–S, parallel to the coast) is the long Central Valley, in which flow the Sacramento R. from the N and the San Joaquin R. from the S; after joining, they emerge from the valley into San Francisco Bay. Further E is the high range of the Sierra Nevada, along the E border, with many peaks exceeding 10,000 ft, rising to 14,495 ft in Mt Whitney. In the extreme SE is Death Valley, a deep depression 280 ft below sea level. The climate is as diverse as the topography: the N is cool, wet, and often foggy; the S has a typically Mediterranean climate with abundant sunshine, summer drought, and rainfall mainly in winter. In the sheltered interior of the SE are the Mojave and Colorado Deserts, containing the Imperial Valley and the Salton Sea. The slopes of the Coast Range and the Sierra Nevada are forested; Californian redwoods are among the world's most magnificent trees. The state is second in lumber production, mainly softwoods.

The leading fruit-producing state; chief crops citrus fruits, grapes. Cotton, cereals, sugar-beet, vegetables also important. About 40 per cent of the country's fish are landed at its ports. One of the three main oil-producing states; important output of gold, mercury, and other minerals. Long the undisputed giant in the production of motion pictures. Since the 2nd World War, industry has expanded considerably. The processing of farm produce and the manufacture of aircraft, machinery, electrical equipment, and chemicals are of major importance. The population is rising more rapidly than that of any other state; it is the only one to rise by over 5 million 1950–60, and became the most populous state in 1964. Leading cities Los Angeles, San Francisco, San Diego; 10 others have populations of over 100,000.

The Californian coast was first explored by Juan Rodriguez Cabrillo (1542); Drake repaired his ships in one of its bays (1579). But not till 1769 did Spanish settlers arrive in San Francisco Bay; from then till 1823 California was under the control of Franciscans and Dominicans, who established a number of missions. The territory was associated politically with Mexico; it was ceded to the USA (1848) after the Mexican War.

**Callan** Irish Republic. Small town in Co. Kilkenny, on the Owenree R. 9 m. SW of Kilkenny. Pop. (1966) 1,263. Market town. Augustinian abbey (15th-cent.).

**Callander** Scotland. Small burgh and resort in Perthshire, on the R. Teith. Pop. (1961) 1,654. Tourist centre for the Trossachs and Loch Katrine. The region is described in Scott's *The Lady of the Lake*.

**Callao** Peru. Chief seaport, 8 m. W of the centre of Lima, to which it is linked by railways and roads. Pop. (1961) 161,286. Large deep harbour on Callao Bay. Handles most of Peru's imports (esp. machinery and metal goods) and one quarter of the exports. Fishing, fish processing and canning. Meat packing, flour milling, brewing, etc. Connected by railway and road to highland centres via the Rimac valley, and to coastal towns by the Pan-American Highway. Founded 1537. Frequently raided by

Drake and other adventurers. Destroyed by earthquake and tidal wave (1746) but rebuilt and fortified.

**Calne** England. Municipal borough in Wiltshire 6 m. N of Devizes. Pop. (1961) 6,559. Market town. The manufacture of woollen cloth, once important, has been superseded by bacon curing. Site of a palace of the West Saxon kings in the 10th cent.

**Calshot** England. Promontory on the W side of the entrance to Southampton Water in S Hampshire. Site of a castle built by Henry VIII for coastal defence. Important RAF seaplane base in the 1930s.

**Caltagirone** Italy. Town in the Catania province in Sicily, 38 m. SW of Catania, at a height of 2,000 ft. Pop. (1961) 44,212. Noted for terra-cotta and majolica work. To the SE is a Greek necropolis of the 6th and 5th cent. B.C.

**Caltanissetta** Italy. Capital of Caltanissetta province, in Sicily, 58 m. W of Catania. Pop. (1961) 63,027. Headquarters of the Sicilian sulphur industry. Manufactures cement, soap, etc. Cathedral (17th-cent.); 17th-cent. baroque palace. School of Mines.

**Calvados** France. Department in Normandy, bounded on the N by the English Channel. Area 2,197 sq. m. Pop. (1968) 519,695. Prefecture Caen. Mainly lowlying, with the Normandy hills in the SW rising to 1,197 ft. A reef extending about 15 m. along the coast, between the Orne and Vire rivers, was named Les Calvados after a Spanish vessel was wrecked there (1588). Extensive stock rearing and dairy farming. Produces cider and Calvados apple brandy. Textile industry also important. Deauville and Trouville are fashionable seaside resorts. Chief towns Caen, Bayeux, Falaise, Lisieux.

**Camagüey** Cuba 1. Capital of the Camagüey province in E Cuba, 40 m. WSW of its port, Nuevitas, to which it is linked by rail. Pop. (1960) 191,379. Route centre; outlet for a region producing sugar-cane, fruit, and timber and raising cattle. Founded in the 16th cent. Cathedral (17th-cent.); many distinguished churches.
2. Archipelago off the N coast of the Camagüey province. Chief islands Romano, Sabinal, Coco.

**Camargue, La** France. The delta of the Rhône R., in the Bouches-du-Rhône department. Lying between the Grand Rhône (E) and the Petit Rhône (W), much of it is marshy, and there are several shallow *étangs* (lagoons) in the S, the largest being the Étang de Vaccarès. The marshes are the haunt of flamingoes and other birds. Fishing and the production of marine salt in salt-pans in the S; the rearing of sheep, cattle, and bulls (for the bull-ring) in the N. In recent years communications have been improved, more land has been reclaimed, and rice and other crops (inc. vines) are cultivated.

**Cambay** India. Town in Gujarat, on the Gulf of Cambay 53 m. S of Ahmadabad. Pop. (1961) 51,291. Manufactures textiles, matches, etc. Trade in cotton, grain, etc. It was an important port in the days of Marco Polo and earlier but declined owing to the silting up of the harbour.

**Cambay, Gulf of** India. Inlet of the Arabian Sea between the S coast of Gujarat and the Kathiawar peninsula. Its ports have lost importance through the silting of their harbours.

**Camberley** England. Residential town in the urban district of Frimley and Camberley in W Surrey, 6 m. N of Aldershot. Pop. (urban district, 1961) 30,342. Seat of the Royal Staff College. Burial-place of the American author Bret Harte (1839–1902).

**Camberwell** England. Former metropolitan borough in S London: from 1965 in the Greater London borough of Southwark. Pop. (1961) 174,697. Mainly residential; includes Dulwich, Peckham, and Nunhead. Once the home of George, Prince of Denmark (Queen Anne's consort), after whom Denmark Hill is named. Site of the South London Fine Art Gallery. Birthplace of Robert Browning (1812–89).

**Cambodia\***. Independent republic in S Indochina bounded by Thailand (W and N), Laos (NE), Vietnam (E and SE), and the Gulf of Siam (SW). Area 71,000 sq. m. Pop. (1962) 5,748,842 (about 81 per cent Cambodians (Khmers), with 500,000 Vietnamese and 300,000 Chinese). Cap. Pnom Penh. Most of the Cambodians are Buddhists. The country consists in the main of an alluvial plain drained by the Mekong and centred on the extensive L. Tonlé Sap. Monsoon climate; more than half the cultivated land is devoted to rice production. Considerable area of forests, yielding valuable timber. A large catch of freshwater fish is taken, chiefly from L. Tonlé Sap. Principal exports rubber, rice, maize, timber. Pnom Penh is the chief port and the only town with more than 50,000 inhabitants. The new port of Sihanoukville was opened in 1960.

Early in the Christian era Cambodia formed the kingdom of Fu-nan, which extended beyond the present boundaries into Thailand, Cochin China (S Vietnam), and Laos. Absorbed late in the 6th century by the Khmers, under whose rulers Angkor was built. Attacked by Siam (Thailand) and Annam (Vietnam), Cambodia was saved by the establishment of a French protectorate (1863). After the 2nd World War it joined the French Union (1949), but declared complete independence 1953.

**Camborne** England. Town in Cornwall 11 m. WSW of Truro, forming (since 1934) with ◊ *Redruth* the urban district of Camborne-Redruth. Pop. (urban district, 1961) 36,090. Engineering etc. School of Metalliferous Mining. The birthplace of the engineer Richard Trevithick (1771–1833), who worked in the neighbourhood, is near by.

**Cambrai** France. Ancient Camaracum (of the Nervii). Industrial town in the Nord department, at the junction of the Escaut (Scheldt) R. and the St Quentin Canal. Pop. (1968) 39,922. Long famous for fine cambric (named after it). Cloth dyeing and bleaching. Sugar refining (from locally grown beet), flour milling. Scene of the formation of the League of Cambrai against Venice (1508) and of the signing (1529) of the Treaty of Cambrai (Paix des Dames). Burial-place (in the original cathedral destroyed in the French Revolution) of Fénelon, Archbishop of Cambrai 1695–1715. Suffered considerable damage in both world wars.

**Cambridge** England. City, municipal borough, and county town of Cambridgeshire, on the R. Cam (also known as the Granta). Pop. (1961) 95,358. Radio and electronic, printing, and other industries. Chiefly famous for the university. Most of the outstanding features are connected with the colleges: the celebrated stretch of river known as the 'Backs' (along the backs of some of the colleges), and such buildings as King's College Chapel (begun 1446, a superb example of the Perpendicular style) and the modern University Library. The oldest college is Peterhouse (founded 1284), and the others are Clare (1326), Pembroke (1347), Gonville Hall (1349, which became Gonville and Caius in 1558), Trinity Hall (1350), Corpus Christi (1352), King's (1441), Queen's (1446, refounded 1475), St Catharine's (1475), Jesus (1497), Christ's (1505), St

John's (1511), Magdalene (1542), Trinity (1546), Emmanuel (1584), Sidney Sussex (1588), Downing (1800), Selwyn (1882), and Churchill (1962). The women's colleges are Girton (1873), Newnham (1875), and New Hall (1954). Noteworthy ecclesiastical buildings include the 10th-cent. Saxon Church of St Benedict, the 12th-cent. Church of the Holy Sepulchre (oldest of the four round Norman churches in England), and the 13th-cent. Church of St Edward King and Martyr (where Latimer preached). Evidence of pre-Roman settlement has recently been found, and Roman remains indicate the existence of a settlement near a ford over the river. William the Conqueror built a castle to assist his campaign against Hereward the Wake. In the Middle Ages the town grew in importance commercially both as a river port (at the head of navigation) and because of its position on the route between E England and the Midlands. By the 12th cent. there were several schools; early in the 13th cent. the nucleus of the university had been established.

**Cambridge** USA. City in Massachusetts, on the Charles R. opposite Boston. Pop. (1960) 107,716. One of the chief educational centres of the USA; seat of Harvard University (founded 1636, America's first college) and of the Massachusetts Institute of Technology. The earliest printing press in America was set up here (1639); printing and publishing have continued to be leading industries. Manufactures soap, confectionery, etc. Washington established his headquarters (1775–6) at a house which later became the home of Henry Wadsworth Longfellow.

**Cambridgeshire** England. Inland county in E Anglia; includes the separate administrative county of the Isle of ◊ *Ely*. Area (excluding Ely) 492 sq. m. Pop. (1961) 189,913. County town Cambridge. Flat, except for low uplands in the S (e.g. the Gog Magog Hills to the SE of Cambridge city); lies largely in the ◊ *Fens*. Soil extremely fertile. Produces cereals, sugar-beet, fruit, vegetables. Chief rivers the Great Ouse (with its main tributaries the Cam, the Lark, and the Little Ouse) and the Nene (N); their courses are partly artificial, and there are numerous drainage channels. In the S are great earthworks, of which the best-known is Devil's Dyke, 7½ m. long, lying over the ancient Icknield Way. Chief towns Cambridge, Ely, March, and Wisbech (the three last in the Isle of Ely).

**Camden** England. Greater London borough (1965) comprising the former metropolitan boroughs of Hampstead, Holborn, and St Pancras. Pop. (1963) 245,776.

**Camden** USA. Industrial town and port in New Jersey, on the Delaware R. opposite Philadelphia, with which it is connected by bridge. Pop. (1960) 117,159. Manufactures textiles, canned soups, radio and television apparatus, pens, etc. Shipbuilding, oil refining. Originally settled by Quakers. Named after Lord Chancellor Camden (1773). Home of Walt Whitman from 1873.

**Camden Town** England. Part of the Greater London borough of Camden (NW) from 1965. Built (1791) when Lord Camden allowed his land to be leased for building houses.

**Camelford** England. Market town and rural district in Cornwall, on the R. Camel 10 m. NNE of Bodmin. Pop. (rural district, 1961) 6,610. One of the places identified with King Arthur's Camelot.

**Camelot** Britain. Seat of the court of the quasi-legendary British King Arthur. Variously identified with Caerleon, Camelford, Winchester, and other places in the S.

**Camembert** France. Village in the Orne department in Normandy, 32 m. SE of Caen. The famous Camembert cheese, first made by Marie Harel, is now chiefly produced at Vimoutiers, 3 m. to the NNE.

**Cameroun**. Federal republic in Africa, on the Bight of Biafra, extending N to L. Chad. Area 183,000 sq. m. Pop. (1965) 5,229,000. Cap. Yaoundé. Cap. of W Cameroun (formerly British) Buea. Mainly plateau, at a height of 2,000 ft. Tropical climate. Annual rainfall varies from 412 ins. at Debundscha and 155 ins. at Douala (both on the coast) to 62 ins. at Yaoundé (on the plateau) and under 20 ins. around L. Chad. The S is covered with tropical rain-forest, with valuable trees, e.g. mahogany and ebony. The N is largely savannah. Food crops include cassava and plantains (S), millets and durra (N). Aluminium smelted and refined at Edéa. Douala is an important commercial centre. Chief exports cocoa, coffee, aluminium.

Formerly the German colony of Kamerun. Occupied by French and British troops during the 1st World War (1916). The larger E part became a French mandate and the smaller W portion was assigned to Britain 1919. After the 2nd World War the whole became a U N Trust Territory. French Cameroun became independent as the Cameroun Republic (1960). The N part of the British Cameroons joined Nigeria and the S became part of the Cameroun Republic (1961).

**Cameroun Mountains** Cameroun. Isolated volcanic group S W of the Adamawa Massif. The major peak, Great Cameroun (the highest mountain in W Africa), rises to 13,350 ft. Annual rainfall on the W slopes is over 400 ins. Last eruptions 1909 and 1922.

**Camiri** ◊ *Cochabamba*.

**Campagna di Roma** Italy. Undulating plain in the Roma province in Latium, bounded on the S W by the Tyrrhenian Sea. Drained by the lower Tiber R. and several small intermittent streams. Largely covered with volcanic earth. Once fertile; deteriorated through over-grazing (sheep) and malaria. Long neglected, it has been to a considerable extent restored by drainage and anti-malarial measures.

**Campania** Italy. Region in the S, bordering in the W on the Tyrrhenian Sea; comprises the provinces of Avellino, Benevento, Caserta, Napoli, and Salerno, and includes the islands of Capri, Ischia, Procida, and the Pontine Islands. Area 5,248 sq. m. Pop. (1961) 4,756,094. Chief town Naples. Long famed for its fertility. Produces fruits, vegetables, hemp, and tobacco as well as vines, olives, and cereals. Industries are centred mainly on Naples. Other important towns Salerno, Benevento, Caserta. Site of the Roman centres of Herculaneum and Pompeii. Many popular modern resorts along the coast. Ancient Campania was much smaller than the modern region. As part of the kingdom of Naples, it was united with Italy 1861.

**Campbeltown** Scotland. Royal burgh in Argyllshire, on the S E coast of the Kintyre peninsula. Pop. (1961) 6,525. Fishing port. Whisky distilling, rope making. Seaside resort. A 12th-cent. granite cross. Important about the 6th cent. A.D. as the seat of the Dalriad monarchy.

**Campeche** Mexico. 1. State in the S E, on the Gulf of Campeche, bounded on the S by Guatemala, occupying the S W part of the Yucatán peninsula. Area 21,660 sq. m. Pop. (1969) 239,000. Chief port Ciudad del Carmen, on a sand bar separating the Laguna de Términos from the gulf. Mainly lowlands, with dense forests in the S, from which logwood is obtained.
2. Capital of Campeche state, on the Gulf of Campeche 100 m. S W of Mérida, with which it is connected by rail. Pop. 44,000. Port with shallow roadstead and much diminished trade since Spanish colonial times. Manufactures cigars, leather, footwear, Panama hats, etc. Picturesque. Founded 1540.

**Campeche, Gulf of** ◊ *Mexico*.

**Campinas** Brazil. Town in the São Paulo state, 50 m. N W of São Paulo. Pop. 123,000. Considerable trade in coffee. Now a growing industrial area. Sugar refining. Manufactures sewing machines, textiles, tyres, wine, cottonseed oil, etc. Experimental agricultural station.

**Campobasso** Italy. Capital of Campobasso province, in Abruzzi e Molise, 55 m. N N E of Naples. Pop. (1961) 34,011. Market town. Manufactures cutlery, soap, etc. Restored 15th-cent. castle.

**Campo Grande** Brazil. Rapidly growing market town in the S of the Mato Grosso state. Pop. 66,000. On the São Paulo–Corumbá railway, serving the high and almost treeless country of the divide between the Paraguay and the Paraná rivers. Exports livestock, packed and dried meat, hides and skins, and agricultural produce to São Paulo.

**Campos** Brazil. Industrial town in the Rio de Janeiro state, on the Paraíba R. 30 m. from the mouth, 150 m. N E of Rio de Janeiro. Pop. 132,000. In a rich agricultural region. Sugar refining. Manufactures textiles, leather goods, soap, etc.

**Camptown** ◊ *Irvington*.

**Canaan.** Name applied to ancient Palestine before being occupied by the Israelites; generally considered to signify the land between the Mediterranean Sea (W) and the R. Jordan and Dead Sea (E): the 'promised land' of the Israelites.

**Canada.** An independent member of the Commonwealth of Nations, in N America. Area 3,851,809 sq. m. Pop. (1966) 20,014,880. Cap. Ottawa. Lang. English and French. Rel. mainly Roman Catholic and Protestant.

Occupies all the N American continent N of the U S apart from the U S state of Alaska on the N W and the two small French islands of St Pierre and Miquelon. Although it has a larger area than the U S, its population is only slightly more than one tenth as great, and the majority are concentrated in the SE within 150 m. of the US border. Vast areas in the N consist of uninhabited wasteland; about 48 per cent of the land area is forested. The products of these forests represent by far the most important part of the country's exports, and its wheatfields and mines are also of great commercial importance. Nevertheless, industrialization has progressed rapidly in recent years, and twice as many workers are employed in manufacturing as in farming and lumbering together (1963). Perhaps the outstanding feature of Canada's position in the world is her economic dependence on the US, which is responsible for nearly two thirds of her total foreign trade. The country consists of 10 provinces and 2 territories. *Provinces*: Newfoundland, Nova Scotia, New Brunswick, Prince Edward Island, Quebec, Ontario, Manitoba, Saskatchewan, Alberta, British Columbia. *Territories*: Northwest Territories, Yukon.

TOPOGRAPHY. Canada stretches from about 42° N latitude in the S, approximately the latitude of Rome, to within 500 m. of the N Pole; it extends W–E through about 88° longitude and includes five different time zones. Its most mountainous region is the Western Cordillera, which occupies the Yukon, most of British Columbia, and a narrow strip of SW Alberta. This region is dominated by the Rocky Mountains in the E and the Coast Range in the W, between them a lofty plateau broken by the Selkirk Mountains (S) and the Stikine Mountains (N); in the St Elias Mountains of SW Yukon are the country's highest peaks, Mt Logan (19,850 ft) and Mt St Elias (18,008 ft). E of the Cordillera are the Interior Plains, which descend E from the foothills of the Rockies towards the Great Lakes in three great steps. They are an extension of the Great Plains and the central lowlands of the US, their natural vegetation gradually changing from grassland or prairie in the S through coniferous forest to tundra in the far N. To the E of the plains is the Canadian, Laurentian, or Pre-Cambrian Shield, a vast region occupying one third to one half of the entire country, stretching around Hudson Bay from the Labrador coast to the Arctic. It consists essentially of an enormous mass of ancient rocks, dotted with innumerable lakes and streams, forest-covered in the S and merging into tundra in the N. N of the Canadian Shield

are the numerous islands of the Arctic Archipelago, a region of tundra with patches of ice-cap, e.g. on Ellesmere and Baffin islands, and a permanently frozen subsoil. S of the Canadian Shield are the St Lawrence Lowlands, which include those lying along the shores of L. Erie and L. Ontario, the most intensively farmed, the most industrialized, and the most populous part of Canada. Finally, there is the Appalachian region, an extension of the Appalachians of the US, occupying the Maritime Provinces, the adjacent part of Quebec including the Gaspé peninsula, and Newfoundland: a region largely of parallel ridges and valleys, much forested but with considerable areas of good farmland.

CLIMATE. In so vast a country, there are great variations of climate. Along the coast of British Columbia the climate may be described as maritime temperate. The prevailing westerly winds deposit an abundant and well-distributed rainfall, particularly on the windward slopes of the mountains, and winters are mild and summers cool; a drier climate, with more extreme temperatures, is experienced on the plateau of the Western Cordillera, which is shielded from the rain-bearing winds by the coastal mountain ranges. In the Arctic Archipelago and along the Arctic coast the winters are long and very severe, while summers are short and cool. To the S the climate gradually becomes less rigorous, but even on the S prairies it has continental characteristics: the winter is still cold, though the summer is warm, and annual precipitation (rainfall and snowfall together) is light. In SE Canada the precipitation increases generally from W to E, and along the Atlantic coast is moderately heavy and evenly distributed; here the winters, though fairly cold, are less severe than in the interior.

RESOURCES. Although less than 8 per cent of the total land area is classified as cultivated land, agriculture occupies an extremely important place in the Canadian economy. Spring wheat is by far the leading single crop. In 1963 Canada harvested the largest wheat crop in its history – over 720 million bushels. More than 95 per cent of this enormous output comes from the Prairie Provinces, with Saskatchewan easily first, followed by Alberta and then Manitoba. Between them these provinces also produce most of the oats and barley.

Dairy farming, involving the production of a considerable hay crop, is important in the Great Lakes–St Lawrence lowlands of Quebec and Ontario; fruit (esp. apples) is grown chiefly in Ontario and British Columbia.

Of the enormous area of forested land, about 720,000 sq. m. are regarded as both accessible and capable of producing merchantable timber. In the forests of British Columbia grow the Douglas fir, red cedar, and other 'big' trees; E of the Rockies spruce and other species provide the smaller softwood timber used in the manufacture of wood pulp and paper, and are cut mainly in Ontario, Quebec, and Newfoundland. Canada is the world's leading exporter of newsprint, the majority of its great output being taken by the US. Furs, with mink the most important type, are now produced chiefly on fur farms. Fishing, the country's oldest industry, is practised on the Pacific and Atlantic coasts. The most valuable catch is salmon from British Columbia; the principal species fished from the Maritime Provinces and Newfoundland are cod, haddock, herring, and lobsters.

Mineral resources are considerable. The output of coal, mined chiefly in Alberta and Nova Scotia, has fallen slightly to an annual average of about 10 million tons, but large quantities of petroleum and natural gas are now produced in Alberta, the former sent by pipeline to Sarnia (Ont.) for refining and the latter to Toronto and Montreal. Hydroelectric power has also been developed on a tremendous scale and is used, e.g., in the production of aluminium. The principal metallic ores are nickel, copper, gold, and uranium; a high proportion of the world's asbestos comes from Quebec. Industries are concentrated in the Great Lakes–St Lawrence area (particularly in Montreal and Toronto, the largest cities) and in Hamilton and Windsor, the leading centre in the W being Vancouver; in the lead are wood pulp and paper manufacture, the smelting and refining of metallic ores, and oil refining.

TRANSPORTATION, TRADE. The railways played an outstanding part in opening up the interior of this vast country and in developing and maintaining trade across the three great physical barriers, the Appalachians, the Canadian Shield, and the Rockies. Since the opening of the St Lawrence Seaway (1959) the Great Lakes, now accessible to ocean shipping, have acquired an added importance. The Trans-Canada Highway, from St John's (Newfoundland) to Victoria (BC), was opened in 1962. In the E, Montreal is the leading seaport, though it suffers the disadvantage, like the Great Lakes, of being closed by ice in winter, when Halifax takes its place. Vancouver handles the major part of the Pacific trade.

Canada's chief exports are the products of the forest (timber, wood pulp, newsprint) and the prairie (wheat), followed by a group of mineral products – petroleum, nickel, aluminium, iron ore, copper, uranium, asbestos. Imports consist principally of machinery, automobile parts, agricultural implements, and other manufactured goods. Of the exports 64 per cent go to the US and about 10 per cent to Britain, while 72 per cent of the imports come from the US and 6 per cent from Britain (1967).

PEOPLE, GOVERNMENT. About 44 per cent of the population are of British origin and 30 per cent are French Canadians, the latter being found mainly in Quebec province; the next largest group, those of German origin, numbers about 1 million. There are about 192,000 American Indians (1961), most of them living in Indian Reserves, and a few thousand Eskimos in the far N. Roman Catholics constitute 46 per cent of the population, well over half of them being in Quebec; the leading Protestant denominations are the United Church, the Anglican Church, and the Presbyterian.

By the British North America Act (1867) the constitution was required to be 'similar in principle to that of the United Kingdom'. Executive authority is vested in the Queen and is carried on in her name by the Governor-General, while legislative power is exercised by a Parliament of two Houses, the Senate (102 members) and the House of Commons (264 members). Each province has its own government, which deals with matters of local concern, the Queen being represented by a Lieutenant-Governor.

HISTORY. The Canadian coast was reached by John Cabot, who sailed from Bristol, in 1497, but the first permanent settlement came only in 1608, when Champlain founded Quebec. In 1663 this settlement, known as New France, was made into a royal province of France. French explorers and missionaries journeyed into the interior beyond the Great Lakes and as far as the Mississippi, while fur traders of the Hudson's Bay Company, chartered in England in 1670, concentrated their activities on the immense territories around Hudson Bay. The French and the British inevitably came into conflict: in 1756 the Seven Years War began, Wolfe defeated Montcalm and took Quebec (1759), and by the Peace of Paris (1763) Canada was ceded to Britain. During the American War of Independence the Canadians defeated a revolutionary invasion, and thousands of loyalists fled N and played a great part in the development of the country. In 1791 it was divided at the Ottawa R. into Lower Canada and Upper Canada, the former predominantly French and the latter British. After armed revolts had been quelled in both provinces, the two were united (1841), and then by the British North America Act a confederation of Lower Canada (Quebec), Upper Canada (Ontario), Nova Scotia, and New Brunswick was brought about (1867). Two years later the vast territory of Rupert's Land, extending W to the Rockies, was bought from the Hudson's Bay Company. In 1870 the province of Manitoba was created from it, in 1871 British Columbia joined Canada and in 1873 Prince Edward Island. Despite tremendous difficulties, E and W were at last linked in 1885, when the Canadian Pacific Railway was completed; the provinces of Alberta and Saskatchewan were formed from the NW Territories in 1905. Economic prosperity increased with the exploitation of forests, fisheries, and mineral deposits, with the conversion of the prairies into 'the bread-basket of the world', later with the development of hydroelectric power and manufacturing industries, and, despite setbacks, e.g. in the years of the great trade depression (1929–35), Canada became and remained one of the world's great trading nations. Inevitably the nation began to demand an increasing degree of autonomy. After the 1st World War Canada's international status was expressed in independent membership of the League of Nations, while her equality of status with Britain in the Commonwealth was defined in the Statute of Westminster (1931). In 1949 Newfoundland joined Canada as the tenth province.

**Canary Islands** N Atlantic Ocean. Group of Spanish islands 60 m. off the NW coast of Africa. Divided into two provinces named after the two capitals. Las Palmas contains the islands of Lanzarote, Fuerteventura, and Grand Canary (Gran Canaria); Santa Cruz de Tenerife contains those of Tenerife, Palma, Gomera, and Hierro. Total area 2,807 sq. m. Total pop. (1961) 944,448. Of volcanic origin; mountainous. The mild healthy climate makes them popular winter resorts. Water is scarce; some areas are almost desert. Where irrigation is possible, abundant crops are produced. Principal exports bananas, tomatoes, potatoes. Leading industries fishing, canning. The two chief ports, Las Palmas and Santa Cruz de Tenerife, are important fuelling stations. The Canary Is. were known to the Phoenicians, Greeks, Carthaginians, and Romans. The elder Pliny attributed the name Canaria to the large number of dogs; they may have been Plutarch's 'Fortunate Islands'. Came into the possession of Ferdinand and Isabella of Aragon–Castile in 1476; Spanish sovereignty was established (1479) by treaty between Aragon–Castile and Portugal. Became wholly Spanish; the original Guanches (probably of Berber stock) have been assimilated.

**Canaveral, Cape** ♢ *Kennedy, Cape.*

**Canberra** Australia. Capital of the Commonwealth, in the Australian Capital Territory, on an upland plain dotted with small hills and crossed by the Molonglo R., 150 m. SW of Sydney. Pop. (1966) 92,199 (7,300 in 1933; 13,300 in 1943). The site, consisting of 911 sq. m. of grazing land, was adopted in 1909; the new city was planned by W. B. Griffin, a Chicago architect, and the foundation stone was laid in 1913. Much building followed the 1st World War and in 1927 the Commonwealth Parliament was transferred here from Melbourne. Since then, the growth of government departments, the establishment of the Australian National University and of offices controlling research, commerce, and manufactures have led to a considerable increase in population. The original 'cobweb' plan remained unchanged until 1958, when a National Capital Development Commission proposed new residential, commercial, and industrial areas to take ultimately 500,000 people, and a landscaped lake area about the Molonglo R. New roads, suburbs, and water supplies are being developed.

**Candia** ◊ *Iráklion*.

**Canea** (Gr. **Khaniá**) Greece. **1.** *Nome* in W Crete. Area 926 sq. m. Pop. (1961) 130,898. Mainly agricultural.
**2.** Capital of Crete (since 1840) and of Canea *nome*, in the NW of the island. Pop. (1961) 38,268. Seaport, probably on the site of ancient Cydonia. Coastal trade in citrus fruits, carob beans, wine, olive oil. Flourished in the 13th–17th cent. under Venetian rule; remains of Venetian fortifications. Captured by the Turks 1645. Severely damaged during the German invasion in the 2nd World War (1941). The birthplace of the Greek statesman Eleutherios Venizelos (1864–1936) is near by.

**Cannae** (modern **Canna**) Italy. Town in ancient Apulia, near the mouth of the Aufidus (Ofanto) R., 6 m. NE of Canusium (Canosa). Scene of Hannibal's great victory over the Romans (216 B.C.).

**Cannes** France. Resort in the Alpes-Maritimes department on the French Riviera, 16 m. SW of Nice. Pop. (1968) 68,021. Fruits and flowers extensively grown in the neighbourhood. Essential oils and candied fruits produced. Its development as a fashionable resort dates from 1834, when Lord Brougham, attracted by its position and its mild healthy climate, built himself a villa. Sheltered by low hills. Wide boulevards, many hotels, villas, casinos, and sports facilities. On the Mont Chevalier (in the old town), a 17th-cent. church and a medieval watch-tower. Offshore are the Îles de Lérins: on the Île Ste Marguerite the 'Man in the Iron Mask' was imprisoned (1687–98), and the Île St Honorat has the oldest monastery in W Europe.

**Canning Dam** ◊ *Darling Range*; *Perth* (Australia).

**Cannock** England. Urban district in Staffordshire, 8 m. NNE of Wolverhampton. Pop. (1961) 42,186. Coalmining. Cannock Chase (once a royal preserve) is just to the E.

**Canso, Strait (Gut) of** Canada. Strait between Cape Breton Island and the mainland of Canada, at its narrowest part 1 m. wide. Crossed by a causeway (1955) carrying a road and a railway, with a lock and drawbridge to allow the passage of shipping.

**Cantabrian Mountains** Spain. Mountain range in the N, extending 300 m. E–W from the Pyrenees, parallel to the coast of the Bay of Biscay. Forms a barrier between the central Meseta and the narrow coastal plain. The highest peaks (in the central area) include Peña Cerredo (8,794 ft) and Peña Vieja (8,628 ft). Rich in minerals, esp. coal and iron.

**Cantal** France. Department in the Auvergne region. Area 2,231 sq. m. Pop. (1968) 169,330 (steadily decreasing owing to migration). Prefecture Aurillac. Mountainous (volcanic Monts du Chantal occupying the central area), rising to 6,096 ft in the Plomb du Cantal. Drained by the Dordogne R. and its tributaries. Harsh climate. Cattle rearing, dairy farming. Produces cheese and butter.

**Canterbury** England. Roman Durovernum; Saxon Cantwaraburh ('Borough of the Men of Kent'). Cathedral city and county borough in E Kent on the R. Stour 55 m. ESE of London. Pop. (1961) 30,376. Market town. Trade in hops, grain, etc. Dominated by the great cathedral; famous chiefly because the archbishop is the Anglican Primate of All England. Situated at a ford over the Stour and a focus of routes across SE England, it flourished and became the capital of the Saxon kingdom of Kent, the fourth Saxon king of which, Ethelbert, was converted to Christianity and presented St Augustine (who arrived from Rome in A.D. 597) with land on which to found an abbey; St Augustine became the first Archbishop of Canterbury (597–604) and Canterbury has remained the headquarters of the English Church. The early cathedral occupied by St Augustine was destroyed by fire in 1067; Archbishop Lanfranc (1070–89) began the building of a completely new cathedral, not finished until the 15th cent. Thus the architectural styles range from Norman to Perpendicular; the most striking exterior feature, the 235-ft central (Bell Harry) tower, is late 15th-cent. Perpendicular. The two principal periods of building may be distinguished in the two parts into which the interior is divided, the choir being raised in unusual fashion above the nave, with the altar above the choir. When Archbishop Thomas à Becket was murdered in the cathedral (1170) and at once canonized, a magnificent shrine was erected in the Trinity Chapel, which for more than three centuries drew throngs of pilgrims (who provided material for Chaucer's *Canter-*

*bury Tales).* Noteworthy features within the cathedral are the fine Norman crypt, the tombs of Edward the Black Prince and Henry IV, the site of Becket's murder, and beautiful stained-glass windows illustrating miracles said to have been performed after Becket's martyrdom. The treasure accumulated at Becket's shrine was confiscated by Henry VIII (1535), in the course of the Reformation.

Probably the oldest part of Canterbury is the artificial mound known as the Dane John (now in a public park), with a memorial to Christopher Marlowe (1564–93), who was born in Canterbury, as was Richard Barham (1788–1845). Near by is the large Norman keep, sole remnant of the 11th-cent. castle. There are remains of the old city walls, but of the six former gates only the 14th-cent. West Gate has survived. The remains of St Augustine's abbey were converted into a missionary college in 1844. St Martin's Church (restored) was used for Christian worship even before the coming of St Augustine. St Dunstan's Church has in its vault the head of Sir Thomas More (1478–1535). At the King's School (refounded by Henry VIII in 1541, built on the site of the monastery hall) is preserved a superb Norman entry-stair. Some of the old buildings, including parts of the cathedral, were seriously damaged in German air raids during the 2nd World War (1942).

**Canterbury** New Zealand. Provincial district covering the E central part of the S Island. Area 16,769 sq. m. Pop. (1966) 376,441. Chief town Christchurch. It includes the high mountain country of the Southern Alps, the eastern foothills, and the Canterbury Plains, and extends from the Waitaki R. in the S roughly to the Kaikoura Ranges in the N. The central Canterbury Plains, with Christchurch the largest city, form the most closely settled part of the S Island. Formerly used for extensive wheat farming, they now support mixed farms for sheep, fat lambs, dairy cattle, and the cultivation of grain and fodder crops, with special areas for horticulture and vegetables. The surface is apt to be dry, and tree belts act as windbreaks. S of Christchurch the Rangitata and Rakaia rivers provide irrigation water. Hydroelectric power is developed on several rivers. Inland, hill country supports extensive sheep farming, as does the Banks Peninsula. Chief seaport Lyttelton.

**Canton** (China) ◊ *Kwangchow.*

**Canton** USA. Industrial town in Ohio, 21 m. SSE of Akron. Pop. (1960) 113,631. Outlying centre of the Pittsburgh iron and steel manufacturing district. Steel works and rolling mills. Manufactures roller bearings, vacuum cleaners, enamelware, etc. Home of President McKinley (1843–1901).

**Canton Island** ◊ *Phoenix Islands.*

**Canvey Island** England. Residential urban district in S Essex, in the Thames estuary. Pop. (1961) 15,599. Connected by bridge with S Benfleet on the mainland. Suffered considerable flood damage 1953.

**Cape Barren Island** ◊ *Furneaux Islands.*

**Cape Breton Island** Canada. Island in NE Nova Scotia (named after a headland on the E coast), separated from the mainland by the Canso Strait which is crossed by a causeway (1955). Area 3,975 sq. m. Pop. 164,000 (many of Scottish and French origin). Coastline deeply indented. Almost bisected by the Bras d'Or Lake. Climate cool and damp, the cold Labrador Current reducing the temperature of the coastal water; fogs are common. Farming is largely dairying, much of it a part-time occupation with fishing and lumbering. Mineral wealth is important, esp. coal, mined in the Sydney-Glace Bay area and used at the Sydney steel works. Gypsum mined in the N. Much of the NW peninsula, with outstanding coastal scenery, has become the Cape Breton Highlands National Park. From 1713 the island was a French colony named Île Royale. Not taken by the British until 1758. Joined to Nova Scotia, but became a separate province 1784. Rejoined Nova Scotia 1820.

**Cape Coast** Ghana. Formerly Cape Coast Castle (from the castle built here by the Swedes in 1652). Capital of the Central Region, seaport 85 m. WSW of Accra. Pop. (1960) 41,143. Main export cacao. Taken from the Swedes by the Dutch. Passed to Britain 1664. Chief city of the Gold Coast till 1876, when Accra became capital.

**Cape Girardeau** USA. Town in Missouri, on the Mississippi R. 100 m. SSE of St Louis. Pop. (1960) 24,947. Industrial centre. Manufactures footwear, clothing, etc.

**Cape Province** S Africa. In full, Cape of Good Hope province (after the headland). The southernmost part of Africa; largest of the four provinces of the Republic of S

Africa. Area 278,465 sq. m. Pop. (1960) 5,362,853 (3,011,080 Bantu; 1,330,089 Coloured; 18,477 Asian; 1,003,207 white). Cap. Cape Town. An extensive plateau, at a height of about 3,000 ft, reaching N to the arid Kalahari Desert. In the S are the lower Karroo plateaux, the Zwarteberg and Langeberg folded ranges, and a narrow coastal plain. The main waterway, the Orange R., flows W to the Atlantic Ocean. Rivers flowing to the Indian Ocean (e.g. the Great Kei) are shorter but carry more water, owing to the heavier rainfall in the E. The area around Cape Town has a Mediterranean climate: many vineyards. Maize, wheat, citrus fruits. Sheep grazed in the drier areas. Agriculture has been extended by irrigation schemes. Chief minerals are diamonds (◊ Kimberley) and copper (Okiep). Principal towns Cape Town, Port Elizabeth, East London. The first permanent European settlement was that of the Dutch, who founded a colony in 1652. Many Huguenot immigrants arrived later in the 17th cent. The British annexed the colony 1806. The colony became a province of the Union of S Africa on its formation (1910).

**Capernaum** Israel. Ancient town on the N shore of L. Tiberias (Sea of Galilee), closely associated with Christ's teaching. The remains of a synagogue of the 2nd cent. A.D. were excavated early in the present cent.

**Cape Town (Capetown)** S Africa. Legislative capital and also capital of Cape Province, on Table Bay in the SW. Pop. (1967) 625,000 (199,000 white; 328,000 Coloured; 90,000 Bantu; 7,500 Asian). Chief passenger seaport and third largest city. Its harbour has two graving docks, oil storage tanks, cold storage plants, and a large grain elevator. A city of great scenic beauty, to which much is contributed by Table Mountain (3,549 ft), standing just to the S. University (1918). The 17th-cent. castle (now housing the Department of Defence) and Groote Schuur (at Rondebosch on the SE outskirts) are examples of Dutch colonial architecture. Groote Schuur, once the home of Cecil Rhodes, is now the official residence of the Prime Minister, and the university buildings are in its grounds. Other important buildings and places of interest are the Houses of Parliament, the National Art Gallery, and the Municipal Botanical Gardens; Adderley Street is the principal thoroughfare. The National Botanical Gardens are at Kirstenbosch (S),

originally part of the Groote Schuur estate, on the slopes of Table Mountain. Founded (1652) by Jan van Riebeeck, who established a victualling station for ships of the Dutch East India Company; the oldest white settlement in S Africa.

**Cape Verde Islands.** Archipelago and Portuguese overseas territory in the Atlantic Ocean 350 m. WNW of Cape Verde (Senegal); consists of 10 islands and 5 islets. Pop. (1960) 201,549 (mostly mulattoes and Negroes). Cap. Praia (pop. 9,980), on São Tiago. Divided into two groups, Barlavento (Windward) and Sotavento (Leeward): the NE Trade is the prevailing wind. The former includes São Vicente, Santo Antão, São Nicolau, Santa Luzia, Sal, and Boa Vista; the latter includes São Tiago, Maio, Fogo, and Brava. São Vicente is a fuelling station on the route to S America. The islands are mountainous and of volcanic origin; the highest peak, Pico do Cano (9,281 ft), last erupted severely in 1847. Climate hot, humid, and unfavourable to Europeans. Exports coffee. Cattle and goats raised. Some fishing.

**Cape York Peninsula** Australia. Peninsula projecting N into Torres Strait between the Gulf of Carpentaria (W) and the Coral Sea (E), with Cape York at the N end. Mainly tropical forest and grassland.

**Cap Haïtien (Le Cap)** Haiti. Seaport on the N coast. Pop. (1961) 30,000. Exports coffee, sugar-cane, bananas, etc. from the fertile coastal plain. Under French rule it was capital of the colony ('the Paris of Haiti'). Largely destroyed by earthquake (1842) but trade later recovered.

**Caporetto** ◊ Kobarid.

**Cappadocia.** Ancient region of Asia Minor, of varying extent but occupying a mountainous area of present-day central Turkey. For a time it was an independent kingdom, its capital at Mazaca (modern Kayseri). Became a Roman province A.D. 17.

**Capri** Italy. Ancient Capreae. Rocky island in Napoli province, in Campania, at the S entrance to the Bay of Naples. Area 4 sq. m. Pop. (1961) 7,332. Popular tourist resort, with picturesque scenery and pleasant climate. Produces white wine. The two towns (at different levels), Capri (450 ft) and Anacapri (980 ft), were connected only by a flight of steps until 1874, when a carriage road was constructed. Highest point Monte Solaro (1,920 ft). Along the precipitous coast there are two landing places, Marina Grande (from which a funicular railway leads to the town) and Marina Piccola. Famous for the Grotta Azzurra (Blue Grotto, rediscovered 1826), accessible only by small boat; Axel Munthe's villa San Michele at Anacapri (with an exquisite garden and magnificent views); and the remains of villas built by the Emperor Tiberius.

**Caprivi Zipfel (Caprivi Strip)** SW Africa. Strip of land in the NE, 300 m. long and about 30 m. wide, giving the Territory access to the Zambezi R. Named after Count Caprivi, the German Chancellor, who negotiated its cession from Britain (1893).

**Capua** Italy. Ancient Casilinum. Market town in Caserta province in Campania, on the Volturno R. 18 m. N of Naples. Pop. (1961) 17,578. The 9th-cent. cathedral, severely damaged in the 2nd World War, was rebuilt. Ancient Capua (on a site 3 m. to the SE), of great strategic importance, was linked with Rome by the Appian Way. Remains of a large amphitheatre. After its destruction by Saracens (840) the inhabitants moved, and founded modern Capua.

**Carácas** Venezuela. Capital of Venezuela and of the Federal District, in a basin at a height of 3,000 ft. Pop. (1961) 1,336,119 (200,000 in 1939). The centre of economic and cultural life, it derives its wealth mainly from oil, and is the headquarters of the oil companies and large business houses. Manufactures textiles, clothing, and many other consumer goods. There are great contrasts between the ultra modern administrative, office, hotel, and entertainment buildings and the older colonial buildings and the miserable dwellings of the outer suburbs. Climate warm but pleasant; mean annual temperature 68° F. Stretches 9 m. along the valley, beneath deeply gullied hills. Connected with its seaport ⟡ La Guaira and the coastal airport by an 11-m. tunnelled motorway. Inland a main road leads to the Valencia basin and the W, as part of the Pan-American Highway. Founded 1567. Became the capital of the captaincy-general of Carácas. Birthplace of Simón Bolívar (1783–1830). Became capital of independent Venezuela 1829. Devastated by earthquakes in 1755 and 1812; again severely damaged, with considerable loss of life, by an earthquake in 1967.

**Carbonia** Italy. Lignite-mining town in Cagliari province in Sardinia, 34 m. W of Cagliari. Pop. (1961) 35,327. The lignite is used to produce electricity.

**Carcassonne** France. Prefecture of the Aude department, on the Canal du Midi and the Aude R., divided by the Aude into the old town (Cité) and the new Ville Basse. Pop. (1968) 46,329. Tourist centre. Trade in wine. Tanning, hosiery manufacture, and other industries. The old town, built on a hill, is a medieval fortified city of great architectural interest: a 12th-cent. castle, the 11th/14th-cent. Romanesque and Gothic cathedral of St Nazaire and the massive ramparts and towers. Within the new town (the business and residential area) is the 13th-cent. cathedral (restored). Suffered severely during the Albigensian Crusade (⟡ Albi); taken by Simon de Montfort (the elder) (1209).

**Carchemish.** Ancient city on the Euphrates R., in modern S Turkey on the Syrian border. Centre of a neo-Hittite culture. Scene of a battle (605 B.C.) in which Nebuchadnezzar defeated the Egyptians.

**Cárdenas** Cuba. Seaport in Matanzas province, 23 m. E of Matanzas. Pop. 48,000. Exports sugar. Sugar refining, rum distilling, rice milling. Manufactures rope, matches, etc.

**Cardiff** Wales. Capital of Wales (since 1955), city, county borough, and county town of Glamorganshire, on the R. Taff 2 m. from the mouth (on the Severn estuary). Pop. (1961) 256,270. Seaport. Exports coal, iron and steel products. Imports timber, iron ore, grain. Ship repairing, steel milling, engineering, flour and paper milling. Manufactures chemicals, cement, etc. The castle, built in the 11th cent. and partly destroyed by Owen Glendower (1404), was presented to the city by the 3rd Marquis of Bute in 1947. Among outstanding buildings in and around Cathays Park are the Law Courts, the City Hall, the Welsh National Museum, the Glamorganshire County Hall, the Cardiff Technical College, the University College of South Wales and Monmouthshire, and the Temple of Peace and Health. Of modern growth, though it dates from a 1st-cent. A.D. Roman station. Expanded rapidly with the development of the S Wales coal and iron fields, largely through the efforts of the 2nd Marquis of Bute, who initiated the construction of a dock in 1839. The population rose from 1,870 to 32,954 1801–61. The present extensive dock system includes those of Penarth and Barry. The world's leading coal exporter before the 2nd World War; the trade has since declined.

**Cardigan** Wales. Municipal borough and county town of Cardiganshire, on the R. Teifi 3 m. above the mouth. Pop. (1961) 3,780. Market town, having declined as a port through the silting of the river mouth and the advent of steamships. Traces of a 12th-cent. castle.

**Cardiganshire** Wales. County in the W, on Cardigan Bay (Irish Sea). Area 693 sq. m. Pop. (1961) 53,564. County town Cardigan. Mainly a plateau, rising in the extreme NE to 2,468 ft in Plynlimmon. Extends from the mouth of the R. Dovey (N) to the R. Teifi; drained also by the Rheidol and Ystwyth rivers. Farming is an important occupation. Oats and barley cultivated. Cattle and sheep reared. Chief towns Cardigan, Aberystwyth, Lampeter. Many British and Roman remains.

**Caria.** Ancient region in SW Asia Minor, on the Aegean Sea S of Lydia (the modern SW Turkey). The chief towns were Halicarnassus and Cnidus.

**Caribbean Sea** W Atlantic Ocean. Part of the W Atlantic, bounded by the Greater and Lesser Antilles (N and E) and the coasts of Venezuela, Colombia, and the neighbouring states of Central America (S and W). Linked with the Gulf of Mexico by the Yucatán Channel. Area 1,000,000 sq. m. Named after the warlike Caribs who formerly inhabited parts of the region.

**Cariboo** Canada. Mining district in the W foothills of the Cariboo Mountains, British Columbia. Scene of the Cariboo gold rush (1860). Named after the near-by Cariboo Lake.

**Cariboo Mountains** Canada. Mountain range 200 m. long, in E British Columbia, running W of and roughly parallel to the main range of the Rocky Mountains, separated from them by the Fraser R.

**Carinthia** (Ger. **Kärnten**) Austria. Province bordering in the S on Italy and Yugoslavia. Area 3,680 sq. m. Pop. (1961) 495,226. Cap. Klagenfurt. Mainly mountainous, containing the highest peak in Austria, the Gross Glockner (12,461 ft). Chief river the Drau. Many small lakes, including the Weissensee and the Millstättersee, with resorts. Lumbering, stock rearing, and mining (iron, lignite, etc.). Principal towns Klagenfurt, Villach. Became Austrian in the 14th cent. Small areas were lost to Italy (SW) and Yugoslavia (SE) in 1919.

**Carisbrooke** England. Village in the Isle of Wight (Hampshire) just SW of Newport. In the now partly ruined 11th-cent. castle Charles I was imprisoned for 10 months (1647–8) before his execution.

**Carlisle** England. Ancient Luguvallum (Roman); Caer Luel (British). City, county borough, and county town of Cumberland, at the confluence of the Caldew and the Petteril with the R. Eden. Pop. (1961) 71,112. Railway, industrial, and commercial centre. Flour milling. Manufactures textiles, biscuits, agricultural machinery, etc. Liquor trade under state management since 1921. Castle (11th-cent.), in which Mary Queen of Scots was imprisoned for a time; 12th-cent. cathedral. Destroyed by the Danes 875. Restored by William Rufus 1092. An important fortress in the border wars with the Scots. Withstood a 9-month siege (1644–5) in the Civil Wars.

**Carlow** Irish Republic. **1.** County in Leinster. Area 346 sq. m. Pop. (1966) 33,593. Gently undulating, with a range of barren mountains in the SE. Highest point Mt Leinster (2,610 ft). Drained by the Barrow and the Slaney rivers. Stock rearing, dairy farming. Oats and potatoes cultivated.
**2.** County town of Co. Carlow, at the confluence of the R. Burren with the R. Barrow. Pop. (1966) 7,791. Market town. Flour milling, sugar refining, brewing. Has an ancient castle (in ruins), a 19th-cent. Roman Catholic cathedral, and an 18th-cent. theological college.

**Carlsbad** USA. Town in SE New Mexico, on the Pecos R. 225 m. SE of Albuquerque. Pop. (1960) 25,541. Tourist resort for visitors to the Carlsbad Caverns National Park (17 m. to the SW), containing limestone caves of which the largest (the Big Room) is more than half a mile long. Potash (discovered near by in 1931) mined and refined. Commercial centre. Trade in cotton, wool, alfalfa, etc.

**Carlton** England. Urban district in Nottinghamshire, just E of Nottingham. Pop. (1961) 38,790. Manufactures bricks, hosiery, furniture, etc.

**Carluke** Scotland. Industrial town in Lanarkshire, 5 m. NNW of Lanark. Pop. 7,000. In a coalmining and fruit-growing area. Manufactures jam.

**Carmarthen** Wales. Municipal borough and County town of Carmarthenshire, on the R. Towy 8 m. above the mouth on Carmarthen Bay. Pop. (1961) 13,249. Railway junction. Market town. Flour milling.

Manufactures dairy products. Remains of a Norman castle; mainly 14th-cent. church.
**Carmarthenshire** Wales. The largest county in Wales, bounded on the S by Carmarthen Bay (Bristol Channel). Area 920 sq. m. Pop. (1961) 167,736. Mountainous in the N and E, rising to 2,632 ft in Carmarthen Van. Chief river the Towy. Stock rearing in the uplands. Agriculture in the lowlands (S). Coalmining and metallurgical industries (especially tin and copper smelting and tinplate manufacture) in the SE, centred on Llanelli. Chief towns Carmarthen, Ammanford, Burry Port, Kidwelly, Llandovery, Llanelli.
**Carmel, Mount** Israel. Limestone ridge extending 14 m. NW from the Samarian Hills to the Mediterranean Sea at Haifa, rising to 1,732 ft. In the Bible, the scene of Elijah's struggle with the priests of Baal. The Order of Carmelites was founded here in the 12th cent.
**Carmona** Spain. Market town in Andalusia, 20 m. ENE of Seville. Pop. (1961) 28,216. In a region producing wine and olive oil. Flour milling, tanning, and other industries. A large necropolis and other Roman remains have been excavated. Taken from the Moors (whose influence on the architecture is still apparent) by Ferdinand III of Castile 1247.
**Carnac** France. Village in the Morbihan department 17 m. SE of Lorient. Famous for the standing stones or menhirs, extending about 3 m. in parallel rows. A common-burial ground of the Iberians (c. 2000 B.C.).
**Carnforth** England. Urban district in N Lancashire, 6 m. N of Lancaster. Pop. (1961) 4,113. Market town. Railway junction. Gravel pits.
**Carniola** Yugoslavia. Former crownland and duchy of Austria; the capital was Ljubljana (Laibach). Occupied by the Slovenes (6th cent.). Passed to the Habsburg monarchy in the 14th cent. Divided between Yugoslavia and Italy (1919), the former receiving about five sixths of the 3,850 sq. m.; the whole became part of Slovenia (Yugoslavia) in 1947.
**Carnot, Cape** ◊ *Great Australian Bight.*
**Carnoustie** Scotland. Small burgh and holiday resort in Angus, on the North Sea 10 m. ENE of Dundee. Pop. (1961) 5,511. Famous golfing centre.
**Caroline Islands** W Pacific Ocean. Archipelago of Micronesia in the W Pacific, W of the Marshall Is., including the important

Palau, Truk, and Yap island groups, the large volcanic islands of Kusaie and Ponape, and many atolls. Pop. about 60,000. Little variation in mean monthly temperatures from 80° F, rainfall being plentiful and well distributed. The islands produce copra, sugar, taro, arrowroot, tapioca; deposits of bauxite, phosphates, iron ore. Discovered (1526) by Spaniards. Purchased from Spain by Germany 1899. Occupied by the Japanese in the 1st World War and held under mandate until 1935, when they were claimed by Japan. In 1947 they became part of the US Trust Territory of the Pacific Is.
**Caroní River** Venezuela. River 500 m. long, rising in the Guiana Highlands (extreme SW) flowing generally W and then N to join the lower Orinoco R. Above the confluence is a large hydroelectric plant, associated with the steelworks at San Torre de Guayana, which first operated in 1962. ◊ *Angel Falls.*
**Carpathian Mountains.** Mountain system of central and E Europe, a connecting link in the great Alpine uplift between the Alps and the Balkan Mountains, extending in a vast arc 900 m. long. From near Bratislava (Czechoslovakia) they form part of the Czechoslovak-Polish frontier, crossing the SW of the Ukrainian SSR into Rumania, and re-approach the Danube at the Iron Gate on the Rumanian–Yugoslav frontier. Enclose the Plain of Hungary. The main W–E divisions are the Little Carpathians, the White Carpathians, the W and E Beskids, the High and the Low Tatra, and the Transylvanian Alps. In general considerably lower than the Alps. Crossed by several low passes. The highest peak is Gerlachovka (8,737 ft) in the High Tatra, a popular tourist region noted for its beautiful Alpine scenery with jagged peaks, mountain lakes, and glacial features. Well wooded to a height of more than 4,000 ft. Rich in minerals, but of little economic importance and sparsely peopled.
**Carpentaria, Gulf of** Australia. Large inlet in the N, between Arnhem Land and Cape York Peninsula, about 300 m. W–E and 370 m. N–S. Receives many rivers. Contains the islands of Groote Eylandt, the Sir Edward Pellew Group and the Wellesley Is.
**Carpentras** France. Ancient Carpentoracte. Market town in the Vaucluse department 15 m. NE of Avignon. Pop. (1968) 22,130. In a hilly region on the edge of the wide valley of the R. Rhone. Famous for sweet-

meats and candied fruits. Capital of the Meminians, and later of the Comtat Venaissin. A 15th/16th-cent. Gothic church (formerly a cathedral); 17th-cent. former bishop's palace; 14th-cent. gateway, the Porte d'Orange.

**Carpi** Italy. Town in the Modena province in Emilia–Romagna, 10 m. N of Modena. Pop. (1961) 45,208. Produces wine, food products. Cathedral (16th-cent.).

**Carrara** Italy. Town in the Massa-Carrara province in Tuscany, near the Ligurian Sea, 30 m. N N W of Pisa. Pop. (1961) 64,091. Famous for marble, quarried and worked in the neighbourhood and exported throughout the world from its port Marina di Carrara. Cathedral (13th/14th-cent.).

**Carrickfergus** Northern Ireland. Municipal borough and fishing port in Co. Antrim, on the N side of Belfast Lough. Pop. (1961) 10,211. Manufactures linen, rayon, etc. Castle (12th-cent.). Scene of William III's landing (1690) before the Battle of the Boyne.

**Carrickmacross** Irish Republic. Market town in Co. Monaghan, 13 m. W S W of Dundalk. Pop. (1966) 1,946. Famous for lace. Manufactures alcohol (from potatoes), shoes.

**Carrick-on-Shannon** Irish Republic. County town of Leitrim, on the R. Shannon. Pop. (1966) 1,394. Fishing centre. Market for dairy produce, livestock, potatoes.

**Carrick-on-Suir** Irish Republic. Market town in Co. Tipperary on the R. Suir. Pop. (1966) 4,874. Slate quarrying. Tanning. Salmon fishing. Castle (14th-cent., re-stored).

**Carron** Scotland. Village in Stirlingshire, on the R. Carron 2 m. N N W of Falkirk. Famous for the ironworks (established 1760). The carronade gun (first cast here) and carron oil are named after it.

**Carshalton** England. Former urban district in N E Surrey, S of London, for which it acts as a dormitory suburb; from 1965 part of the Greater London borough of Sutton. Pop. (1961) 57,462.

**Carson City** U S A. State capital of Nevada, near the Californian border, 26 m. S of Reno. Pop. (1960) 5,163. In a silver-mining district. Commercial centre. Resort. Named after Kit Carson (1809–68), a famous hunter and scout.

**Cartagena** Colombia. Capital of the Bolívar department and principal seaport of the N W, on the Caribbean coast. Pop. (1968) 242,085. Linked by canalized waterway to the Magdalena R. and by a highway to southern cities. Terminal of the pipeline from the Barrancabermeja oilfields. Exports agricultural produce (sugar, rice, maize, tobacco, etc.) from an extensive hinterland, and gold and platinum from the Atrato valley. Manufactures textiles, footwear, tobacco products, chemicals, soap. University (1827). Founded and fortified by the Spanish 1533; an export centre for precious metals and stones. Frequently attacked by pirates and hostile squadrons, and sacked on several occasions. Later over-shadowed by Barranquilla. Remained one of the most Spanish and picturesque cities of Latin America.

**Cartagena** Spain. Ancient Carthago Nova. Fortified naval base and seaport in Murcia, on the Mediterranean Sea 27 m. SSE of Murcia. Pop. (1967) 140,944. Exports lead and iron mined in the neighbourhood. Lead and iron smelting, metal working, boat building. Manufactures chemicals, glass, bicycles, etc. Founded in the 3rd century B.C. by Hasdrubal, it became the Carthaginian headquarters in Spain. Captured (209 B.C.) by Scipio Africanus (the elder), and thrived under the Romans as a mineral-exporting port (silver, lead). Almost destroyed by the Goths A.D. 425. Flourished again in the 16th cent. when it was rebuilt and fortified by Philip II of Spain.

**Cartago** Colombia. Commercial town in the Valle del Cauca department, 40 m. S W of Manizales. Pop. 65,000. Trade in coffee, tobacco, cattle, etc. Founded 1540.

**Carthage** Tunisia. Ancient city state on the N coast of Africa, near modern Tunis, of which it is now a residential suburb. Founded in the 9th cent. B.C. by the Phoenicians. From the 6th cent. B.C. the Carthaginians developed both trade and sea power, controlled the coasts of N W Africa, Sardinia, Malta, the Balearic Is., and much of Sicily, and established colonies in what are now Senegal and Guinea. They became wealthy by selling Negro slaves, ivory, gold, etc. from tropical Africa, but their rivalry with Rome led to the Punic Wars; in the first (268–241 B.C.) they were defeated in Sicily but conquered much of Spain; in the second (218–201 B.C.), despite victories in Italy itself, Hannibal was finally defeated at Zama (202 B.C.). Largely owing to the insistence of Cato that Carthage must be destroyed ('*Delenda est Carthago*') Rome attacked again; in the 3rd Punic War (149–146 B.C.) Roman armies utterly defeated the Carthaginians and razed the city. More than a century later (under Augustus) Carthage was rebuilt; it became one of the greatest cities in the Roman Empire. Later it was of importance in the early history of Christianity. Subsequently taken by the Vandals (A.D. 439), it became their capital. Recaptured by the Byzantine army 534. Totally destroyed by the Hillali Arabs 698. Almost nothing of Punic Carthage has survived, but extensive Roman ruins testify to its past grandeur. The Bardo museum in Tunis contains a rich collection of Roman art, esp. mosaics.

Carúpano Venezuela. Seaport in the Sucre state (NE). Pop. 44,000. Exports coffee, cacao. Manufactures straw hats, pottery, soap.

Casablanca Morocco. Chief seaport and largest city, on the Atlantic coast 50 m. SW of Rabat. Pop. (1964) 1,177,000 (rapidly expanding). Handles more than three quarters of Morocco's foreign trade. Constant harbour improvements since 1913 have made it one of the world's largest artificial ports. Exports phosphates, manganese ore. Manufactures textiles, glass, cement, soap, superphosphates. Fishing. Founded in the early 16th cent. (on the site of ancient Anfa) by the Portuguese, as Casa Branca ('White House'). Occupied by the French 1907. The modern suburb of Anfa was the scene of the Casablanca Conference between Roosevelt and Churchill during the 2nd World War (1943).

Casale Monferrato Italy. Town in the Alessandria province in Piedmont, on the Po R. Pop. (1961) 40,827. Industrial and commercial centre. Important cement works. Manufactures agricultural machinery, silk, rayon, footwear. Trade in fruit, rice, etc. Romanesque cathedral (11th/ 12th-cent.). Became the capital of the marquisate of Montferrat in the 15th cent.

Cascade Range USA. Range of mountains extending from the Fraser R. in British Columbia through W Washington and Oregon practically parallel to the Pacific coast, in general 4,000–5,000 ft in height but rising to over 10,000 ft in several snow-capped extinct volcanoes, including Mt Rainier (14,408 ft) and Mt Adams (12,307 ft). Continued S by the Sierra Nevada of California. Named after the cascades of the Columbia R. where this river cuts through the range. The mountain slopes are well forested, with large stands of Douglas fir and other conifers.

Caserta Italy. Capital of the Caserta province (dissolved in 1927, reconstituted in 1945) in Campania, 15 m. NNE of Naples. Pop. (1961) 50,381. Market town. Trade in cereals, citrus fruits, wine, olive oil. Manufactures chemicals, soap. A 12th-cent. cathedral at Caserta Vecchia, 3 m. to the NE. A village until 1752, when the magnificent royal palace was begun (completed in 1774). An Allied HQ during the 2nd World War; scene of the surrender of the German forces in Italy (29 April 1945).

Cashel Irish Republic. Town in Co. Tipperary, 12 m. ENE of Tipperary. Pop. (1966) 2,682. Seat of a Protestant bishop. The Rock of Cashel (300 ft), 'the holiest spot in Ireland', is crowned by the remains of the 13th-cent. St Patrick's Cathedral, the 12th-cent. Cormac's Chapel, and an ancient cross where the kings of Munster were crowned.

Casper USA. Ranching town and route centre on the N Platte R. in central Wyoming. Pop. (1960) 38,930. Airport. An oil well was established near by in 1890; oil production rose considerably during the 1st World War. The town now has oil refineries and manufactures tents, bricks, etc.

Caspian Sea Iran/USSR. The largest inland sea (salt lake) in the world; 750 m. long N–S and on average 220 m. wide. Area 152,000 sq. m. Lies between Asia and the extreme SE of Europe, within the USSR except for the S coast, which is in Iran. With the Black Sea and the Aral Sea it once formed part of a much greater inland sea. Receiving large volumes of fresh water from the Volga, Ural, and other rivers, it has a lower salinity than the Black Sea. No outlet. Tideless. In the N, where it is shallow, it is frozen for 2–3 months annually. Crossed by a submarine ridge extending E from the Apsheron peninsula; the depth increases to the S. The level has fluctuated (partly owing to differential evaporation and partly to varying amounts of water received from the rivers) and since 1929 has dropped by 8 ft to 92 ft below sea level. Quantities of salt (chiefly Glauber's salt) are deposited through evaporation in Kara Bogaz Gol, an almost land-locked gulf on the E. Principal ports Astrakhan, Makhachkala, Baku, Krasnovodsk. Its fisheries are famous for the finest caviare.

Cassel ⟡ Kassel.

Castellammare di Stabia Italy. Seaport in Napoli province, Campania, on the Bay of

Naples 16 m. SE of Naples. Pop. (1961) 64,618. Resort, with mineral springs. Industrial and commercial centre. Naval dockyard. Macaroni factories. Manufactures aircraft equipment, marine engines, textiles, etc. The near-by Roman resort of Stabiae was buried by the eruption of Vesuvius (A.D. 79). The ruined castle (which gives the name) was built in the 13th cent. by the Emperor Frederick II.

**Castellón de la Plana** Spain. **1.** Province in Valencia. Area 2,578 sq. m. Pop. (1961) 339,229. Mountainous in the N and W, with a fertile coastal plain. Mainly agricultural. Produces cereals, vines, fruits, olives in the lowlands.
**2.** Capital of the Castellón de la Plana province, 3 m. from the Mediterranean, 42 m. NNE of Valencia. Pop. (1967) 81,187. Manufactures cement, paper, textiles, tiles. Exports oranges, almonds, etc. through the harbour of El Gráo de Castellón. Chiefly modern. Has a 14th-cent. church and a 17th-cent. octagonal bell tower.

**Castelvetrano** Italy. Market town in the Trapani province in W Sicily. Pop. (1961) 31,282. Railway junction. Produces Marsala wine. Ruins of the ancient Greek colony of Selinus near by.

**Castile** (Sp. **Castilla**) Spain. Former kingdom of central and N Spain, extending from the Bay of Biscay (N) to the Sierra Morena (S), on the central plateau or Meseta at a height of 2,500–3,000 ft. Generally bare and monotonous. Subject to a harsh continental climate; suffers from frequent droughts. Divided by the Sierra de Guadarrama and the Sierra de Gredos into Old Castile (N) and New Castile (S), the former drained by the Ebro and Duero (Douro) rivers and the latter by the Tagus and the Guadiana. Old Castile (area 19,390 sq. m.) consists of the 6 provinces of Ávila, Burgos, Logroño, Santander, Segovia, and Soria (Palencia and Valladolid are also sometimes included). New Castile (area 27,933 sq. m.) comprises the 5 provinces of Ciudad Real, Cuenca, Guadalajara, Madrid, and Toledo. The name Castile probably derives from the number of castles erected against the Moors. Originally a county of the kingdom of León; became virtually independent in the 10th cent. The kingdoms of Castile and León were united in 1230. The marriage of Ferdinand II of Aragon and Isabella of Castile (1469) united the kingdoms of Aragon and Castile; thereafter the history of Castile is that of Spain.

**Castlebar** Irish Republic. County town of Mayo, at the E end of Castlebar Lough. Pop. (1966) 5,629. Market town. When a mixed French-Irish force landed at Killala (1798) the British garrison fled so precipitately that the incident was named the 'Races of Castlebar'.

**Castle Douglas** Scotland. Small burgh in Kirkcudbrightshire, on Carlingwark Loch 9 m. NE of Kirkcudbright. Pop. (1961) 3,253. Market town. Fishing centre. Livestock market. On an island in the R. Dee, 2 m. W, is the ruined 14th-cent. Threave Castle, stronghold of the Douglas family, presented to the National Trust in 1948.

**Castleford** England. Municipal borough in the W Riding of Yorkshire, on the R. Aire near its confluence with the Calder. Pop. (1961) 40,345. Coalmining. Manufactures glass, earthenware, chemicals. Birthplace of Henry Moore, the sculptor (1898–      ).

**Castleton** England. Village in the Peak district in N Derbyshire, 8 m. NE of Buxton. Near by are several caves and mines (fluorspar), and the ruined Castle of the Peak (Peveril Castle) made famous by Scott's *Peveril of the Peak.*

**Castletown** (Manx **Bully Cashtel**) England. Former capital of the Isle of Man; port and market town on the S coast 9 m. SW of Douglas. Pop. (1961) 1,549. Has the 14th-cent. Castle Rushen; near by is the Old House of Keys (where the Manx parliament once sat).

**Castres** France. Town in the Tarn department on the Agout R. 38 m. E of Toulouse. Pop. (1968) 42,920. Important textile centre since the 14th cent. Manufactures woollen and cotton cloth. Tanning, engineering, metal working. Grew up round a 7th-cent. Benedictine abbey. Became a Huguenot stronghold in the 16th cent.

**Castries** ◊ *St Lucia.*

**Castrop-Rauxel** Federal German Republic. Town in N Rhine-Westphalia, just NW of Dortmund. Pop. (1963) 88,500. Coalmining. Manufactures chemicals (coal byproducts), textiles, cement, bricks, etc. Formed (1926) by the union of Castrop, Rauxel, and other towns.

**Catalonia** Spain. Region (formerly a principality) in the NE, extending from the Pyrenees along the Mediterranean Sea, comprising the provinces of Barcelona, Gerona, Lérida, and Tarragona. Area 12,329 sq. m. Pop. (1961) 3,925,779. Cap.

Barcelona. Mainly hilly. Drained by the lower Ebro R., its tributaries, and the Llobregat and the Ter rivers. Wines, olive oil, almonds, citrus and other fruits extensively produced. Lacks raw materials, but is well provided with hydroelectric power and has thus become Spain's most highly industrialized region. Manufactures textiles, metal goods, chemicals. Many bathing resorts.

Under Roman rule, the NE of Hispania Tarraconensis. Later fell to the Alani, the Goths, and the Moors; the Moors were conquered by Charlemagne 788. United with Aragon in the 12th cent. Both were united with Castile in the 15th cent. The region changed hands several times, between France and Spain, in the succeeding centuries. There is a very strong regional patriotism. The Catalan language (akin to Provençal) is widely spoken, but its use in broadcasting or in printed publications is virtually forbidden under the Franco régime. An autonomous Catalan government was set up in 1932 and lasted through the Spanish Civil War (1936–9), in which Catalonia played a leading part on the Government side. Fully incorporated into the Spanish state after the victory of the Franco rebellion (1939).

**Catamarca** Argentina. Old colonial city, capital of the Catamarca province (NW), 120 m. S of Tucumán, in a sub-Andean valley, at a height of 1,600 ft. Pop. 29,000. Agricultural centre. Famous for hand-woven ponchos. Thermal springs near by.

**Catania** Italy. Capital of the Catania province in Sicily, on the Gulf of Catania, just S of Mt Etna. Pop. (1968) 406,794. Seaport and industrial city. Food processing, sulphur and sugar refining, shipbuilding. Manufactures textiles, footwear, paper. Almost completely destroyed several times by eruptions of Etna (esp. 1669) and by earthquakes (esp. 1693). An 18th-cent. appearance. A former Benedictine monastery, S. Nicolò, with a vast 17th-cent. church. Cathedral (11th-cent., restored in the 18th cent.). University (1434). Founded (729 B.C.) by the Greeks. Conquered by the Romans 263 B.C. Remains of a Roman theatre and Roman baths and aqueducts. Birthplace of Vincenzo Bellini (1801–35).

**Catanzaro** Italy. Capital of the Catanzaro province in Calabria, on a hill near the Gulf of Squillace, in a district noted for its orange and lemon groves. Pop. (1961) 74,037. Former centre of the silk industry. Now

largely residential. Suffered in several earthquakes, notably in 1783. Damaged in the 2nd World War (1943).

**Catbalogan** ◊ *Samar*.

**Caterham and Warlingham** England. Urban district in E Surrey, 7 m. S of Croydon. Pop. (1961) 34,808. Pleasantly situated on the N Downs; mainly residential. A military depôt. Engineering and cosmetics industries.

**Catskill Mountains** USA. Group belonging to the Allegheny Plateau, at the N end of the Appalachians; deeply dissected by river gorges ('cloves') into flat-topped, steep-sided mountains. Average height 3,000 ft; the two highest peaks exceed 4,000 ft. Despite extensive felling and destructive fires, still thickly wooded. The Catskills provide water for New York City. Owing to easy access they are a favourite resort region of New Yorkers in summer and winter. They include the area of Washington Irving's Rip Van Winkle story.

**Catterick** England. Village in the N Riding of Yorkshire, on the R. Swale 10 m. SSW of Darlington. Important military camp. Racecourse near by.

**Cauca River** Colombia. River 840 m. long, chief tributary of the Magdalena R.; flows generally N between the W and central Cordilleras. Partly navigable for small vessels. The valley is extremely fertile, with a great variety of crops, including sugar-cane and tobacco. Has given its name to two departments: Cauca (cap. ◊ *Popayán*) and Valle del Cauca (cap. ◊ *Cali*).

**Caucasus** USSR. Geographical region in S European USSR, between the Black Sea and the Caspian Sea, consisting of the N Caucasus, the Great Caucasus, and Transcaucasia. 1. *N Caucasus*: Mainly plains, with the Stavropol Plateau and the Kuban Steppe. Drained by the Kuban and Terek rivers in the S and the Don (the only navigable river) in the N. Cereals, cotton, and other crops cultivated in the W. Principal industrial and commercial centres Armavir, Astrakhan, Krasnodar, Rostov-on-Don, Stavropol.

2. *Great Caucasus*: The chief mountain ranges, extending 750 m. WNW–ESE, from the Taman Peninsula (Black Sea) to the Apsheron Peninsula (Caspian Sea), and rising to 16,558 ft in Mt Kazbek, 17,054 ft in Dykh Tau, and 18,481 ft in Mt Elbruz (the highest peak in Europe). Mt Elbruz and Mt Kazbek are extinct volcanoes. There is evidence of volcanic activity in the ther-

mal springs at Pyatigorsk, Kislovodsk, etc. Many snowfields and glaciers; the snowline varies from 9,000 to 11,000 ft. The railways follow the narrow coastal plains at the ends of the mountain barrier. There are a few high passes, notably the Mamison Pass (9,550 ft, on the Ossetian Military Road) and the Krestovaya Gora (7,815 ft, on the equally famous and spectacular Georgian Military Road). Annual rainfall 90–100 ins. on the S slopes (in the Abkhaz ASSR), where the richest vegetation (with extensive forests) is to be found; decreases W–E, and is scarcely 10 ins. on the Apsheron Peninsula. Most important mineral petroleum, produced chiefly on the Apsheron Peninsula (around Baku) and in the N foothills (at Grozny and Maikop). Important manganese mines at Chiatura (Georgia), in the S foothills.

3. *Transcaucasia*: Largely mountainous; the Surami Range links the Great Caucasus with the much lower Little Caucasus and the Armenian Highlands, and separates the Colchis lowlands (W) from the Kura lowlands (E). Known to the ancient Greeks; connected with the Prometheus legend and with the story of Jason and the Argonauts seeking the Golden Fleece in Colchis (the Rioni basin in Georgia).

Armenia and Georgia, long the dominant states, were at first independent but later subject to Rome, Byzantium, and Persia and were invaded by successive waves of Huns and Mongols, partitioned between Turkey and Persia in the 16th–18th cent., and gradually conquered by Russia. Georgia became a Russian protectorate in 1783, but the last resistance of the mountain peoples was not crushed till 1864; tens of thousands of Circassians and Abkhazians then emigrated to Turkey. During the Bolshevik revolution (1917–22) there were attempts to make Transcaucasia independent; nationalist sentiment, though pacified by concessions from the Soviet government (e.g. recognition of national languages), was by no means extinguished.

Politically the Caucasus comprises Armenia and the S areas of Azerbaijan and Georgia (the three republics which formed the Transcaucasian SFSR 1922–36).

**Causses** France. Limestone plateau region, in the S of the Massif Central. Divided by deeply-cut river channels into a number of smaller plateaux (causses; the term derives from *cau*, the local form of *chaux*, 'lime'). Typical limestone (karst) scenery: under-

ground streams, caves, and swallow-holes (*avens*). Spectacular features like the Tarn gorge are tourist attractions. The E Causses, at a height of 3,000–4,000 ft, include the famous Causse Méjean, S of the Tarn R. The Causses du Quercy, to the W, chiefly in the Lot department, are lower and less arid. Sparsely populated. Main occupation sheep rearing. Produces Roquefort (ewes' milk) cheese.

**Cauterets** France. Fashionable spa and tourist resort, in the Hautes-Pyrénées department at a height of 3,000 ft near the Spanish frontier. Pop. (1968) 1,130. Well known for thermal springs and winter sports. Centre for visits to Pyrenean peaks, e.g. the Pic de Chabarrou (9,550 ft) and Mont Vignemale (10,820 ft).

**Cauvery (Kaveri) River** India. River 470 m. long rising in the W Ghats and flowing generally ESE through Mysore and Madras to the Bay of Bengal. Here it forms a broad delta, its principal channel being the most northerly, the Coleroon, and the area is irrigated by canals. The river is dammed at Mettur and Krishnarajasagara and hydroelectric power is developed. It is sacred to the Hindus.

**Caux** France. Natural region (*pays*) in the Seine Maritime department in Normandy, bordering on the English Channel and extending from Le Havre to Dieppe. A chalk plateau. The fertile loess produces oats, sugar-beet, flax, etc.

**Cava de'Tirreni** Italy. Holiday resort in Salerno province in Campania, 3 m. NW of Salerno. Pop. (1961) 42,231. In a beautiful, well-cultivated valley among wooded hills. Manufactures textiles etc. Near by is the Benedictine abbey of La Trinità della Cava (founded 1025).

**Cavan** Irish Republic. **1.** County in the province of Ulster. Area 730 sq. m. Pop. (1966) 54,022 (76,670 in 1936). Generally hilly, rising to 2,188 ft in Mt Cuilcagh (NW). Drained by the Annalee and the Erne rivers. Boggy, damp, and largely infertile. Many lakes. Cattle and pigs raised. Potatoes cultivated. Becoming depopulated.

**2.** County town of Co. Cavan near the E shore of Lough Oughter. Pop. (1966) 3,244. Market town. Modern Roman Catholic cathedral; ruined Dominican abbey. The abbey graveyard is the burial-place of the 17th-cent. hero Eoain Ruagh (Owen Roe) O'Neill, subject of Thomas Davis's famous elegy.

**Cawdor** Scotland. Village in Nairnshire,

5 m. SW of Nairn. The castle is traditionally the scene of Macbeth's murder of Duncan (1040).

**Cawnpore** ◊ *Kanpur.*

**Cayenne** French Guiana. Capital and chief seaport, on an island at the mouth of the Cayenne R. Pop. (1967) 24,581. A shallow harbour; large vessels discharge into lighters. Imports foodstuffs for the largely undeveloped hinterland. Exports chiefly gold. A French penal settlement 1854–1938. Gave its name to Cayenne pepper, made from a plant of the Capsicum genus common in the vicinity.

**Cayman Islands** W Indies. Three low-lying coral islands 150 m. NW of Jamaica. Total area 100 sq. m. Pop. (1960) 8,511. The largest is Grand Cayman, on which stands Georgetown, the chief town and port; the others are Little Cayman and Cayman Brac. They are famed for their turtles, which (with turtle products and shark skin) are the chief exports. Discovered (1503) by Columbus, who named them Las Tortugas because of the many turtles; they were not colonized until the 17th cent. when they were settled by Britons from Jamaica. A dependency of Jamaica until 1962, when they became a British colony.

**Ceanannus Mór (Kells)** Irish Republic. Town in NW Meath, near the Blackwater R. Pop. (1966) 2,274. Grew up round the monastery founded by St Columba in the 6th cent. Many antiquities, esp. the Book of Kells, a uniquely and very remarkably illustrated 8th-cent. MS of the Gospels in Latin (now in the library of Trinity College, Dublin), which in 1962 left Ireland for the first time, to be exhibited in London side by side with the 9th-cent. Lindisfarne Gospel MS.

**Ceará** Brazil. State in the NE 'shoulder'. Area 57,134 sq. m. Pop. (1960) 3,337,856. Cap. ◊ *Fortaleza.* Exports produce of the dry but irrigated interior: cotton, sugar, hides and skins, carnauba wax, etc.

**Cebu** Philippines. 1. Long, narrow, hilly island between Negros (W) and Bohol and Leyte (E), forming, with several smaller islands, Cebu province. Area 1,703 sq. m. Pop. 1,350,000. Mainly agricultural, producing maize, sugar-cane, abacá, coconuts, tobacco. Maize (not rice) is the chief food crop. Coal and copper mined, limestone quarried.
2. Capital of Cebu province, on the E coast of Cebu island. Pop. (1960) 251,146. An inter-island port. Exports abacá, copra,

cement, etc. Manufactures cement, pottery. Opposite the city is Mactan Island, where Magellan lost his life (1521).

**Cedar Rapids** USA. Industrial town in Iowa, on the Cedar R. 105 m. ENE of Des Moines. Pop. (1960) 92,035. In a maize-growing and stock-rearing area. Meat packing. Manufactures food products (esp. cereals), starch, agricultural and road-building machinery.

**Celaya** Mexico. Town on the central plateau at a height of 5,900 ft. Pop. 59,000. Market town. Railway junction. Noted for its sweetmeats. Manufactures textiles. Trade in grain, cotton, livestock, etc. Birthplace of the Mexican architect F. E. de Tresguerras (1765–1833), whose buildings add distinction to the town.

**Celebes** (Indonesian **Sulawesi**) Indonesia. Island E of Borneo, of irregular shape and once described as 'a handful of peninsulas tied in the middle'. Area 72,000 sq. m. Pop. (1961) 7 millions. Largely mountainous, rising to 11,286 ft in Rantemario; much of it is forested. Exports copra, coffee, spices, rattan. Divided into two provinces, N and S Sulawesi, the capitals being Manado and Macassar respectively, the latter being also the chief seaport. The Portuguese, who settled in the Macassar area in the 17th cent., were driven out by the Dutch, and the island later formed two presidencies of the Netherlands E Indies.

**Celle** Federal German Republic. Town in Lower Saxony, on the Aller R. 24 m. NE of Hanover. Pop. (1963) 59,000. Railway junction. Manufactures machinery, chemicals, textiles, foodstuffs. Many 16th/18th-cent. half-timbered houses in the old quarter of the town. Former residence (1378–1705) of the dukes of Brunswick-Lüneburg.

**Central African Republic.** Formerly one of the four territories (Ubangi-Shari) of French Equatorial Africa. Area 234,000 sq. m. Pop. (1967) 1,466, 000. Cap. Bangui. Bounded by Chad (N), Sudan (E), Congo (Kinshasa) (S), and Cameroun (W). Largely savannah; forest belts along the rivers. Drained by tributaries of the Ubangi R. and by the headstreams of the Shari R. flowing to L. Chad. Chief products and exports diamonds, cotton. Became a member of the French Community 1958 and an independent member of the UN 1960.

**Central America.** The part of the American continent between the Isthmus of Tehuantepec and the Isthmus of Panama: comprises the Mexican states of Chiapas, Tabasco, Campeche, and Yucatán, and the territory of Quintana Roo, together with the republics of Guatemala, Honduras, Salvador, Nicaragua, Costa Rica, and Panama, and the colony of British Honduras. Total area 230,000 sq. m. Total pop. about 12 million. A tropical, mountainous region, structurally related (except for the Sierra Madre of Guatemala) more to the ranges of the Antilles than to the Pacific ranges of N America. Many volcanoes; the highest, Tajumulco, rises to 13,812 ft. Earthquakes have been frequent. Climate and natural vegetation are determined largely by altitude; three distinct zones are recognized: hot (*tierra caliente*), on the lowlands and coastal plains; temperate (*tierra templada*), on the lower mountain slopes; cool (*tierra fria*), on the upper mountain slopes. The Caribbean coastlands, more exposed to the N E Trade Winds, are wetter than those on the Pacific side; rainfall is everywhere plentiful. On the lowlands bananas are the chief crop; coffee widely cultivated on the temperate mountain slopes. Most of the people are mestizos, of mixed Indian and Spanish descent. Communities of pure Maya Indians are found in the N, notably in Guatemala. Many Negroes along the Caribbean coast. Spaniards predominate in Costa Rica. Chief language Spanish.

The Maya civilization flourished in N W Central America as early as the 2nd cent. A.D., but the people later migrated to the Yucatán peninsula, where at the time of the Spanish conquest they were engaged in civil war. Columbus visited the Caribbean coast in 1502; in 1513 Balboa crossed the Isthmus of Panama to the Pacific. Independence from Spain was won in 1821; two years later the Central American Federation of Costa Rica, Honduras, Nicaragua, Guatemala, and Salvador was formed, but in 1838 it broke up into the present small republics.

**Central Asia, Soviet** USSR. Term applied since the Russian Revolution to the Soviet republics of Russian Turkestan, including the Kirghiz, Tadzhik, Turkmen and Uzbek SSRs and sometimes the Kazakh SSR.

**Cephalonia** (Gr. **Kefallinía**) Greece. The largest of the ◊ *Ionian Islands*, W of the Gulf of Patras, forming, with near-by islands, a *nome*. Area 357 sq. m. Pop. (1961)

46,302. Cap. Argostolion. Mountainous, rising to 5,341 ft in Mt Ainos. Mainly agricultural, producing currants, wine, olive oil. Sided with Athens in the Peloponnesian War (431–404 B.C.). A member of the Aetolian League in the 4th–3rd cent. B.C. Taken by the Romans 189 B.C. Held at times by the Byzantines, the Turks, and the Venetians. Devastated by earthquake 1953.

**Ceram** Indonesia. Island in the S Moluccas W of New Guinea, from which it is separated by the Ceram Sea. Area 6,622 sq. m. Pop. 97,000. Chief port Wahai, on the N coast. Crossed W–E by a densely forested mountain range which rises to 11,007 ft in Binaja. Exports copra, sago, timber, dried fish.

**Cerdaña** (Fr. **Cerdagne**) France/Spain. Valley in the E Pyrenees, in the Pyrénées-Orientales department (France) and the Gerona and Lérida provinces (Spain). Divided between the two countries by the Peace of the Pyrenees (1659). Llivia is a Spanish enclave in France.

**Cerignola** Italy. Market town in Foggia province, in Apulia, 23 m. SE of Foggia. Pop. (1961) 49,287. Trade in wine, olive oil, wool. Manufactures cement, footwear, etc. The Spanish defeated the French near by (1503) to make the kingdom of Naples a Spanish province.

**Cerne Abbas** England. Village in Dorset 7 m. N of Dorchester. On the face of Trundle Hill is the Cerne Giant (or Long Man), a 180-ft representation of a man formed by cutting away the grass from the chalk, of unknown but very ancient date. The hill and Giant are now owned and maintained by the National Trust.

**Cerro del Mercado** ◊ *Durango*.

**Cerro de Pasco** Peru. Capital of the Pasco department, a mining and smelting town in the Central Andes at a height of 14,000 ft; one of the highest towns in the world. Pop. 19,000. Silver was formerly the principal mineral; now chiefly copper, also zinc, lead, bismuth. Near by is the vanadium-mining centre of Minaragra.

**Cerro Gordo** Mexico. Mountain pass in the foothills of the Sierra Madre Oriental 60 m. WNW of Veracruz, on the highway to Mexico City. Scene of a battle in the Mexican War (1847) in which American forces under General Scott decisively defeated the Mexicans under Santa Anna.

**Cesena** Italy. Town in Forli province in Emilia-Romagna, on the Savio R. 13 m.

SE of Forlì. Pop. (1961) 79,704. Produces macaroni, beet sugar, wine, etc. The Malatesta library (1452) contains many valuable MSS. Birthplace of Pius VI (pope 1775–99) and Pius VII (pope 1800–1823).

České Budejovice (Ger. Budweis) Czechoslovakia. Capital of the Jihočeský region, on the Vltava R. 80 m. S of Prague. Pop. (1967) 72,000 Principal industrial and commercial centre of S Bohemia. Manufactures beer (Budweiser), pencils, enamel goods, furniture. Trade in cereals, timber. Founded in the 13th cent. by Budivoj Vitkovec. Renaissance town hall (18th-cent.).

Cessnock Australia. Town in New South Wales 24 m. WNW of Newcastle. Pop. (1966) 15,329. In a region noted for fruit and dairy farming. Coalmining and agricultural centre, developing rapidly. Produces wine, clothing, etc.

Cetinje Yugoslavia. Town in SW Montenegro, 18 m WSW of Titograd, at a height of 2,068 ft in a valley among limestone mountains. Pop. 9,000. Founded by Ivan the Black in the 15th cent. Formerly capital of Montenegro. Former royal palace. Monastery of St Gospodija, burial-place of the Montenegrin prince-bishops. Occupied by the Austrians in the 1st World War and by the Italians in the 2nd. Liberated by Marshal Tito 1944. Subsequently rebuilt.

Cette ⟡ Sète.

Ceuta (Sebta) Spanish Morocco. Spanish military station and seaport on a peninsula on the NW coast; an enclave in Morocco, opposite Gibraltar, administratively part of the Cadiz province of Spain. Pop. (1967) 71,108. Captured by Portugal 1415. Fell to Spain (which has held it ever since) 1580.

Cévennes France. Mountain range on the SE edge of the Massif Central, extending 150 m. generally SW–NE. Average height 3,000–4,000 ft. Highest peaks Mont Mézenc (5,755 ft) and Mont Lozère (5,584 ft). Watershed between the Loire and the Garonne rivers (W) and the Rhône and the Saône rivers (E); also source of the Allier, Loire, Lot, Tarn, and other rivers. Largely barren limestone. A small coalfield N of Alès. Sheep rearing. Olives, vines, and mulberries grown on the S slopes.

Ceylon. Independent member of the British Commonwealth. Area 24,959 sq. m. Pop. (1963) 10,582,064 (about 70 per cent Sinhalese). Cap. Colombo. Lang. mainly Sinhalese. Rel. mainly Buddhist.

A pear-shaped island off the SE coast of India, from which it is separated by Palk Strait and the Gulf of Mannar. Although tropical, it exhibits considerable variety in climate and vegetation and has some delightful scenery. Primarily agricultural, tea being by far the most important cash crop, followed by rubber and coconut products. The country is divided into the following 9 provinces: Western, Central, Southern, Northern, Eastern, North-Western, North-Central, Uva, Sabaragamuwa.

TOPOGRAPHY, CLIMATE, etc. Consists of a south central mountainous area surrounded by broad coastal plains; the highest peak is Pidurutalagala (8,281 ft), but more famous is Adam's Peak (7,360 ft). Rivers radiating from the mountain mass are generally short and of limited value, the most important being the Mahaweli Ganga (206 m.), which flows NNE to Koddiyar Bay. Much of the coast is fringed with coconut palms and lined with sandbanks and lagoons: in the NW Mannar Island is almost joined to Rameswaram Island (India) by the line of sandbanks known as Adam's Bridge.

Ceylon's insular situation gives it more equable temperatures and a generally pleasanter climate than the neighbouring mainland of India. At Colombo, on the SW coast, the mean monthly temperature varies little from 80° F, but at the hill station and health resort of Nuwara Eliya (6,200 ft), overlooked by Pidurutalagala, it fluctuates between 57° F and 62° F. Most of the island has abundant rainfall, distributed by the two monsoons: the W and S coasts and mountains receive rain mainly from the SW monsoon (May–Oct.) and the NE and E mainly from the NE monsoon (Nov.–Dec.), the annual total varying from 40 ins. to well over 100 ins.; the N plain is a relatively dry region. A great deal of the original tropical forest has been cleared for rubber plantations and tea gardens.

RESOURCES, PEOPLE, etc. Rice, the main food crop, occupies about one third of the cultivated land, but more has to be imported. Coconuts are grown chiefly along the W and SW coasts, tea in the hills, especially between Kandy and Nuwara Eliya, and rubber in the SW. Coffee was the earliest cash crop, but it all but disappeared from the island after being attacked by a fungus disease c. 1870; the economy was saved by the introduction of tea and rubber. Graphite is the principal mineral, and certain precious and semi-precious stones, inc. sapphires and rubies, are found. The great majority of the foreign trade passes through Colombo, which is also the only city with more than 100,000 inhabitants; Jaffna, Kandy, and Galle are other important towns. Tea represents about two thirds of the total exports, rubber and coconut products (copra, coconut oil, desiccated coconut) most of the remainder.

The two groups of Sinhalese people, lowland and Kandyan, are descendants of the colonists from NE India who came to Ceylon in the 6th cent. B.C.; they are Buddhists, the centre of their religion being the old capital, Kandy. Tamils from S India, divided now into Ceylon Tamils and Indian Tamils, and Hindus by religion, form the next largest group; others are the Moors, who came from Arabia and are Muslims, the Burghers, who are descendants of Portuguese and Dutch settlers, with much mixed Sinhalese blood, and a small and diminishing number of primitive aboriginal Veddas.

HISTORY. The aborigines of Ceylon were first conquered by Vijaya, an Aryan prince from NE India, in the 6th cent. B.C. Buddhism was introduced about three centuries later, and a branch of the sacred Bo-tree was planted at Anuradhapura. Ceylon was often invaded by Tamils, but in the 12th cent. A.D. a despotic monarch, Prakrama Bahu I, inaugurated a native dynasty and the so-called 'golden age of Lanka'. The Portuguese established trading settlements in the 16th cent., to be driven out by the Dutch, who in turn were expelled by the British. The whole island was annexed by Britain 1815. Having achieved the status of a self-governing member of the Commonwealth (1948) Ceylon decided on becoming a republic in 1956; from 1957 to 1963 the country suffered from continual discord between the Sinhalese and the Tamils.

**Chad.** Formerly the northernmost of the four territories of French Equatorial Africa. Area 488,000 sq. m. Pop. (1964) 2,675,000. Cap. Fort Lamy. Mainly N, E, and SE of L. ◊ *Chad*; bounded by Libya (N), Sudan (E), the Central African Republic (S), and Cameroun, Niger, Nigeria (W). The N contains the Tibesti highlands and is a Saharan region with a great daily range of temperature. The S is mainly dry savannah, but the Shari and the Logone rivers overflow in the summer rainy season and create swamps in the SW. Chief occupations cotton cultivation, stock rearing. The main caravan routes cross the Sahara to Benghazi and Tripoli. Became a member of the French Community 1958, and an independent member of the UN 1960.

**Chad, Lake** Chad/Nigeria. A shallow lake mainly in the W of Chad, bordering on the NE shoulder of Nigeria. Area variable according to seasons and water supply. A remnant of a former inland sea; now considerably smaller than when discovered (1823), by Denham, Clapperton, and Oudney. Many islands and mudbanks; indeterminate marshy shores. Fed chiefly by the Shari R. (S). No apparent outlet, but its waters percolate into the Soro and Bodélé depressions.

**Chadderton** England. Urban district in Lancashire, just W of Oldham. Pop. (1961) 32,494. Manufactures cotton goods, electrical equipment, etc.

**Chadileufú River** ◊ *Salado River*.

**Chagos Archipelago (Oil Islands).** Group of islands in the Indian Ocean, formerly a dependency of Mauritius, about 1,200 m. NE of the latter, belonging to Britain; from 1965 part of the British Indian Ocean Territory. Five main coral atolls, the chief being Diego Garcia. Pop. about 1,000. Copra exported.

**Chagra River** ◊ *Gogra River*.

**Chalcedon** Turkey. Ancient city in Asia Minor almost opposite Byzantium, on a site now occupied by modern Kadiköy. Founded 685 B.C. Passed to Rome 74 B.C. Scene of the Council of Chalcedon (the fourth ecumenical council of the Catholic Church) A.D. 451.

**Chalchuapa** El Salvador. Town in the Santa Ana department at a height of 2,100 ft 10 m. W of Santa Ana, in a coffee-growing district. Pop. 35,000.

**Chalcidice (Gr. Khalkidikí)** Greece. *Nome* in Macedonia, formed by a peninsula terminating SE in three prongs, Kassandra, Sithonia, and Akti. Area 1,237 sq. m. Pop. (1961) 79,838. Cap. Polygyros (pop. 3,381). At the tip of the Akti peninsula stands the autonomous Mt ◊ *Athos*. Produces wheat, olive oil, wine. Magnesite mined. The name is derived from Chalcis (Khalkis), from which it was colonized in the 7th–6th cent. B.C.

**Chalcis (Gr. Khalkis)** Greece. Capital of the Euboea *nome*, 35 m. NNW of Athens, at the narrowest point of the Euripus strait. Pop. (1961) 23,786. Seaport. Trade in wine, citrus fruits, olives, olive oil, cereals, livestock. Founded many colonies, e.g. Chalcidice (Khalkidiki), from the 8th cent. B.C. Called Negropont in the Middle Ages, from the black wooden bridge (built 411 B.C.) joining it to the mainland, now replaced by a swing bridge.

**Chaldaea (Chaldea).** Name sometimes applied to Babylonia as a whole, being derived from the people (Chaldaeans) who invaded the region in the 11th cent. B.C.; more strictly, the lower Tigris-Euphrates basin, in S Babylonia.

**Chalfont St Giles** England. Village in Buckinghamshire, 7 m. E of High Wycombe. Milton's Cottage, where he lived during the Great Plague (1665–6) and completed *Paradise Lost*, has been national property since 1887. Near by at Jordans is the grave of William Penn (1644–1718), the Quaker founder of Pennsylvania.

**Chalfont St Peter** England. Village in Buckinghamshire, 8 m. ESE of High Wycombe. Mainly residential.

**Chalna** Pakistan. Port in E Pakistan, on the Pussur R. 60 m. from the sea and 15 m. S of Khulna, developed from 1950 to relieve pressure on Chittagong. Pop. (1961) 3,900. Exports jute.

**Châlons-sur-Marne** France. Ancient Catalaunum. Prefecture of the Marne department, on the Marne R. and its lateral canal 27 m. SE of Reims. Pop. (1968) 54,075. Important centre of the wine trade of Champagne. Brewing. Manufactures barrels, leather goods, wallpaper. Has a 13th/17th-cent. cathedral and the 12th/13th-cent. Church of Notre Dame en Vaux. Aetius and Theodoric decisively defeated Attila and the Huns near by at the Battle of the Catalaunian Plains (451). Famous in the Middle Ages for worsted cloth ('shalloon').

**Chalon-sur-Saône** France. Ancient Cabillonum. River port in the Saône-et-Loire department, at the junction of the Saône R. and the Canal du Centre. Pop. (1968) 52,746. Leading commercial centre of the Saône valley. Engineering, boatbuilding, sugar refining, brewing, etc. Capital of the Kings of Burgundy in the 6th cent. The 12th/15th-cent. Church of St Vincent was formerly a cathedral.

**Chambal River** India. River 550 m. long rising in the Vindhya Range and flowing N and NE across Madhya Pradesh and Rajasthan to join the Jumna R. below Etawah.

**Chambéry** France. Prefecture of the Savoie department, 29 m. NNE of Grenoble. Pop. (1968) 53,813. Market town in a gorge joining the upper Rhône and the Isère valleys, also containing the Lac du Bourget. On the chief route to the Mont Cenis and the Little St Bernard passes. A favourite Alpine tourist centre. Aluminium works. Well known for vermouth and silk. Cathedral (14th/15th–cent.). A tower of the castle belongs to the original castle of the dukes of Savoy, of whom Chambéry was the capital.

**Chambord** France. Village in the Loir-et-Cher department on the Cosson R. 28 m. SW of Orléans. Famous for the Renaissance château of Chambord, originally a hunting lodge of the counts of Blois, rebuilt under Francis I from 1526, and extensively altered under Louis XIV in the 17th–18th cent. Its outstanding feature is the double staircase. It was the scene of the first performance of Molière's *Le Bourgeois Gentilhomme* (1671) and was the residence of the kings of France, King Stanislas Poniatowski (the last king of Poland), Marshal de Saxe, and Marshal Berthier.

**Chamdo** China. Chief town of the Chamdo area, in E Tibet, on the Mekong R. 370 m. ENE of Lhasa at a height of 11,000 ft. Trading centre on the route between Lhasa and S China.

**Chamonix (Chamonix-Mont-Blanc)** France. All-year Alpine resort in the Haute-Savoie department 37 m. E of Annecy, in the Chamonix valley at a height of 3,400 ft. Pop. (1968) 8,403. Through the valley flows the Arve R. The usual base for the ascent of peaks in the Mont Blanc massif to the S. The Brévent and Aiguilles Rouges ranges are to the N.

**Champagne** France. Former province in the NE, now forming the Ardennes, Marne, Aube, and Haute-Marne departments, with parts of the Aisne, Seine-et-Marne, Yonne, and Meuse departments. The name ('Country of Fields') derives from the plains around Reims, Châlons-sur-Marne, and Troyes (formerly the capital). Divided by parallel ridges into sub-regions. In the centre, a dry chalk area (the original *Champagne pouilleuse*); sheep rearing provides wool for the hosiery industry. To the E, the clay dairy-farming *Champagne humide*. To the W (along the slopes between Reims and Épernay) the vine-growing area where the world-famous Champagne wines are produced. The region is traversed by the fertile valleys of the Aisne, Marne, Aube, and Seine rivers. Ruled in the Middle Ages by its own counts, who ensured commercial prosperity by promoting famous fairs. Attached to the French crown 1314. Declined, but flourished again because of its sparkling wines and its textiles. From the defeat of the Huns (451) a frequent battle-ground for many centuries.

**Champaign** USA. Town in Illinois 48 m. SE of Bloomington, forming a single community with Urbana. Pop. (1960) 49,583. Manufactures dairy and soyabean products, clothing, etc. Seat of the University of Illinois (1867).

**Champigny-sur-Marne** France. Town in the Val-de-Marne department on the Marne R., a suburb of Paris. Pop. (1968) 70,564. Largely residential. Flour milling. Manufactures furniture, pharmaceutical products, etc. Favourite venue of Parisians for boating and camping.

**Champlain, Lake** USA. Picturesque narrow lake, 107 m. long and 1–14 m. wide, between the Green Mountains (Vermont) and the Adirondacks (New York State). Occupies part of the valley which leads N from New York to Montreal. The shores are lined with summer fishing resorts. Named after the French explorer who discovered it (1609).

**Chandernagore** India. Former French settlement, now in W Bengal, on the Hooghly R. 22 m. N of Calcutta. Pop. (1961) 67,105. Jute milling. Manufactures cotton goods, etc. Became a French settlement 1674; flourished commercially for a time but later declined. Ceded to India 1950.

**Chandigarh** India. Joint capital of Punjab and Haryana, 140 m. N of Delhi. Pop. (1961) 89,321. Replaced Lahore, which passed to Pakistan with the partition of India (1947). A completely new city, planned in part by the French architect Le Corbusier; divided into residential neighbourhood units each with its bazaar, clinic, police station, cinema, etc.; designed for a

pop. of 150,000. University (1947). Inaugurated 1953. Neighbourhood became a Union Territory 1966.

**Changchun** China. Formerly Kwangchengtse, Hsinking. Capital of Kirin province in the NE, 150 m. SW of Harbin. Pop. (1957) 975,000. Railway junction on the S Manchuria Railway. Industrial centre. Railway engineering, sawmilling, food processing (soya beans, flour), etc. Seat of the People's University of NE China (1958). Originally called Kwangchengtse, it developed as the junction of the wide-gauge Chinese Eastern Railway with the standard-gauge S Manchuria Railway (1905). Became capital of Manchukuo (1934), being greatly enlarged and renamed Hsinking. Made the first major lorry-producing centre in China (1956). Its present name was restored after 1945.

**Changsha** China. Capital of Hunan province, on the Siang R. 185 m. SSW of Wuhan. Pop. 651,000. Important river port and industrial centre. Large trade in rice; also tea, timber, etc. Lead, zinc, and antimony smelting. Manufactures textiles, glass, fertilizers, etc. Famous for handicraft industries (porcelain, embroidery, paper umbrellas, etc.). University (1959). A former treaty port and a leading educational and cultural centre.

**Chankiang** ◊ *Tsamkong*.

**Channel Islands** (Fr. Îles Normandes) France/England. Group of islands on the S side of the English Channel, W of the Cotentin Peninsula in NW France; British except the Chausey Is. Total area 75 sq. m. Pop. (1961) 104,378. Chief islands Jersey, Guernsey, Alderney, Sark. Others include the Casquets (with a famous lighthouse), Brechou, Herm, Jethou. The attractive scenery, mild sunny climate, and annual rainfall of only 30–40 ins. make them a popular holiday and honeymoon resort. The fertile soil facilitates cultivation of early tomatoes, potatoes, flowers, etc. Jersey, Guernsey, and Alderney have produced famous breeds of dairy cattle. Administered according to laws and customs of their own. French is the official language in Jersey, English in Guernsey; a Norman patois is spoken in rural districts. The islands became part of the duchy of Normandy in the 10th cent. and are the only part of it still belonging to Britain. Sark still has a feudal sovereign, always a woman, la Dame de

Sark. Early in the 2nd World War they were demilitarized and many of their inhabitants were evacuated to Britain. Heavily bombed; then occupied by the Germans (1940–45). One of the Casquet Is. is the scene of Victor Hugo's *Les Travailleurs de la Mer*.

**Chantilly** France. Town in the Oise department, 24 m. N of Paris, near the Forest of Chantilly. Pop. (1968) 10,501. Famous horse-racing centre and popular Parisian resort. Formerly noted for lace and porcelain manufacture. The château was destroyed in the French Revolution but rebuilt in the 19th cent. by the Duc d'Aumale, who presented it and its art collections to the Institut de France.

**Chao Phraya River** ◊ *Menam Chao Phraya*.

**Chapala, Lake** Mexico. Largest lake in Mexico (70 m. long and 15–20 m. wide), 30 m. SE of Guadalajara at a height of 6,000 ft on the central plateau. Many islands. The fine scenery has made it a favourite resort area.

**Chapel-en-le-Frith** England. Town in Derbyshire 5 m. N of Buxton. Pop. (rural district, 1961) 18,366. Market town. Manufactures brake and clutch linings. Limestone quarrying in the neighbourhood. The name derives from the royal forest (frith) of the Peak District.

**Chapra** India. Town in Bihar 27 m. WNW of Patna. Pop. (1961) 75,580. Railway and road junction. Trade in cereals etc.

**Chapultepec** Mexico. Rocky hill about 3 m. SW of Mexico City, with a beautiful park and a castle (18th-cent.), now the National Museum of History. Scene of the last great battle in the Mexican War (1847). In 1945 the Inter-American Conference of American Republics met here and signed the Act of Chapultepec, which declared 'reciprocal assistance and American solidarity'.

**Chard** England. Municipal borough in Somerset, 11 m. SSE of Taunton. Pop. (1961) 5,778. Market town. Manufactures agricultural machinery, gloves, lace. Named after Cerdic, founder of the ancient kingdom of Wessex. Birthplace of Margaret Bondfield (1873–1953), the first British woman cabinet minister.

**Chardzhou** USSR. Second largest town in the Turkmen SSR, 300 m. ENE of Ashkhabad on the Amu Darya R. and the Trans-Caspian Railway. Pop. (1967) 85,000.

Railway junction. River port. Manufactures textiles (mainly cotton) etc.

**Charente** France. Department in the W, comprising the former province of Angoumois and parts of Limousin, Marche, Périgord, Poitou, and Saintonge. Area 2,305 sq. m. Pop. (1968) 331,016. Prefecture Angoulême. In the hilly NE (*Terres Froides*) cattle are raised. The remainder (*Terres Chaudes*), drained by the Charente and Vienne rivers, is rich in agriculture: wheat, oats, barley, and potatoes cultivated; the wine of the Cognac district is distilled into brandy. Chief towns Angoulême, Cognac.

**Charente-Maritime** France. Formerly (till 1941) Charente-Inférieure. Department in the W, bounded on the W by the Bay of Biscay, comprising the former provinces of Saintonge and Aunis, part of Poitou, and the Ré, Oléron, Aix, and Madame islands. Area 2,792 sq. m. Pop. (1968) 483,622. Prefecture La Rochelle. Mainly low-lying and flat. Drained by the Charente, Seudre, and Sèvre Niortaise rivers. Chiefly agricultural. Cereals, fodder crops cultivated. Dairy farming. N of the Charente R. the grapes are used for making wine and brandy. Oyster and mussel beds at Marennes. Chief towns La Rochelle, Rochefort (chief port), Saintes.

**Charente River** France. River 220 m. long, rising in the Haute-Vienne department, flowing generally W through the Charente and the Charente-Maritime departments, and entering the Bay of Biscay opposite the Île d'Oléron. Navigable for small vessels below Angoulême.

**Charenton-le-Pont** France. Suburb SE of Paris, in the Val-de-Marne department at the confluence of the Marne and the Seine rivers. Pop. (1968) 22,658. Wine bottling, fruit canning. Manufactures porcelain. The name derives from the 10-arched stone bridge across the Marne, once part of the defences of Paris.

**Chari River** ◊ *Shari River*.

**Charleroi** Belgium. Town in the Hainaut province, on the Sambre R. 30 m. S of Brussels. Pop. (1968) 24,540. Industrial centre in a coalmining and steel-manufacturing area. Manufactures heavy electrical machinery, glass, cement, beer, etc. Church of St Christophe (17th-cent., rebuilt 1957); modern town hall (1936). Founded (1666) on the site of a village called Charnoy; named after Charles II of Spain by the Spanish governor.

**Charleston** (S Carolina) USA. Second city, chief commercial centre of S Carolina; seaport on a narrow peninsula at the confluence of the Ashley and the Cooper rivers, 7 m. from the Atlantic, with a naval station just N, on the Cooper R. Pop. (1960) 75,940. Exports timber, fruit, cotton, etc. Manufactures fertilizers, wood products, pulp and paper, steel, etc. Founded 1670. Scene of the first action in the American Civil War, when the Confederates bombarded Fort Sumter (1861). Severely damaged when under siege by Union forces (1863–5) and later by earthquake (1886), but many fine colonial buildings survive. World-famous for its gardens, esp. the magnolias and azaleas.

**Charleston** (W Virginia) USA. State capital, on the Kanawha R. Pop. (1960) 85,796. Industrial centre. Oil refining. Manufactures chemicals, glass, paints, etc. (utilizing coal, oil, brine, and other natural resources of the region). First settled 1788. Home of Daniel Boone (1734–1820), famous American pioneer and backwoodsman.

**Charlotte** USA. Largest town in N Carolina, in the piedmont zone, near the S Carolina border. Pop. (1960) 201,564. Industrial centre. Manufactures textiles (cotton and woollen), machinery, chemicals, etc. Seat of the Johnson C. Smith Negro University (1867).

**Charlottenburg** Federal German Republic. Residential suburb of W Berlin, incorporated into the city in 1920. Pop. 225,000. Manufactures glass, paper, etc. Originally Lietzenburg; renamed (1696) after Sophie Charlotte, wife of the Elector Frederick. Scene of the 1936 Olympic Games.

**Charlottesville** USA. Town in Virginia 70 m. WNW of Richmond. Pop. (1960) 29,427. Manufactures textiles etc. Seat of the University of Virginia, founded by Thomas Jefferson (1819). Near by is Monticello, Jefferson's home, preserved as a national memorial.

**Charlottetown** Canada. Capital and chief seaport of Prince Edward Island, on the S coast. Pop. (1966) 18,257. Exports dairy produce, potatoes. Canning, meat packing. Manufactures textiles. Founded 1768; named after Queen Charlotte, wife of George III. Seat of St Dunstan's University (1855, Roman Catholic).

**Charnwood Forest** England. Upland area in N Leicestershire, SW of Loughborough and just E of the Leicestershire coalfield, rising to 912 ft in Bardon Hill. Largely barren, with patches of woodland.

**Charters Towers** Australia. Town in E Queensland 68 m. SW of Townsville. Pop. (1966) 7,533. Centre of a cattle-rearing region. Gold was discovered here in 1871 and mined from 1875, but little is now yielded.

**Chartres** France. Prefecture of the Eure-et-Loir department, on the Eure R. 47 m. SW of Paris. Pop. (1968) 36,881. Chief market town of the Beauce region. Considerable trade in cereals, livestock. Sawmilling, brewing, tanning. Manufactures agricultural machinery etc. The hill is crowned by the famous 12th/13th-cent. cathedral, Notre Dame, with two lofty spires, the 12th-cent. Clocher Vieux (351 ft) and the 16th-cent. Clocher Neuf (377 ft), and magnificent portals and 13th-cent. stained glass. Many other noteworthy churches. One of the chief towns of the Carnutes. Became capital of the county (later duchy) of Chartres.

**Châteauroux** France. Prefecture of the Indre department, on the Indre R. 42 m. SW of Bourges. Pop. (1968) 51,201. Manufactures woollen goods, furniture, tobacco products, etc. Brewing. Trade in grain, livestock. Owes its name (and origin) to the castle, founded in the 10th cent. by Raoul, prince of Déols. The present Château-Raoul (14th/15th-cent.) is occupied by the Préfecture. In the suburb of Déols (capital of lower Berry in the Middle Ages) are the remains of a famous 10th-cent. Benedictine abbey. Birthplace of Count Henri Bertrand (1773–1844), close friend of Napoleon I.

**Château-Thierry** France. Market town in Brie, in the Aisne department on the Marne R. 26 m. W of Épernay. Pop. (1968) 11,629. Manufactures mathematical and musical instruments, food products, etc. Scene of many battles throughout history and of much fighting in both world wars. Birthplace of La Fontaine (1621–95).

**Chatham** Canada. Town in Ontario, on the Thames R. 46 m. ENE of Windsor. Pop. (1966) 32,424. Industrial and commercial centre in an agricultural region. Sugar refining, canning, meat packing, etc.

**Chatham** England. Municipal borough in N Kent, on the Medway estuary 30 m. ESE of London. Pop. (1961) 48,989. Naval base, established by Henry VIII and Elizabeth I. Dockyard with dry docks, ship-repairing yard. Forms a conurbation with the other two 'Medway towns', Rochester (W) and

Gillingham (E). The naval barracks was opened in 1897 and the naval hospital in 1907. The Naval War Memorial (1924) was extended in 1952.

**Chatham (San Cristóbal) Island ◊** *Galápagos Islands*.

**Chatham Islands** New Zealand. Group consisting of two main islands, Chatham (Whairikauri) (348 sq. m.) and Pitt (Rangihaute) (24 sq. m.), and several rocky islets, volcanic in origin, about 400 m. ESE of Wellington in the Pacific. Pop. about 500 (mostly Maoris). Chief occupations sheep rearing, fishing. Discovered (1791) by Lieutenant Broughton; named after the Earl of Chatham. The last of the native Morioris, almost exterminated in 1831 by Maoris, died here in 1933.

**Chatsworth** England. Parish in Derbyshire, 3 m. ENE of Bakewell. Contains Chatsworth House (seat of the dukes of Devonshire), a large Ionic building with gardens and art collections begun by the 1st Duke (1688).

**Chattanooga** USA. Industrial and commercial town in SE Tennessee, in hilly country on the Tennessee R. Pop. (1960) 130,009. Developed rapidly following the provision of cheap electric power by the Tennessee Valley Authority: the Chickamauga Dam is on the N outskirts. Manufactures machinery, textiles, stoves and boilers, furniture, etc. University (1886). During the American Civil War the city and its neighbourhood were the scene of several important engagements, including the battles of Chickamauga, Lookout Mountain ('Battle above the Clouds'), and Missionary Ridge (all 1863).

**Chaumont (Chaumont-en-Bassigny)** France. Prefecture of the Haute-Marne department, on high ground above the confluence of the Marne and the Suize rivers. Pop. (1968) 27,569. Tanning. Manufactures gloves, footwear. Scene of the signing of the treaty by which Britain, Austria, Russia, and Prussia bound themselves to pursue the war against Napoleon to a successful end (1814).

**Chaumont-sur-Loire** France. Village in the Loir-et-Cher department on the Loire R. 25 m. E of Tours. Famous for the 15th-cent. château, in Gothic and Renaissance styles; residence of both Catherine de Medici and the celebrated mistress of her husband (Henri II), Diane de Poitiers, in the 16th cent.

**Chautauqua** USA. Village on the W shore of L. Chautauqua, New York. Seat of the Chautauqua Institution (1874), founded to help Sunday-school teachers in their work, which now provides summer lectures, concerts, etc.

**Chautauqua, Lake** USA. Picturesque lake, 17 m. long and 1–3 m. wide, in the extreme W of New York state at a height of 1,300 ft.

**Chaux-de-Fonds, La** Switzerland. Industrial town in the Neuchâtel canton, in the valley of the same name, 9 m. NW of Neuchâtel at a height of 3,250 ft. Pop. (1969) 43,200. Important centre of the Jura watch- and clock-making industry. Has a technical school and a museum (mainly horological).

**Cheadle and Gatley** England. Urban district in Cheshire, 2 m. WSW of Stockport. Pop. (1961) 45,599. Engineering. Manufactures chemical and pharmaceutical products, bricks, etc.

**Cheb** (Ger. **Eger**) Czechoslovakia. Town in W Bohemia, on the Ohre (Eger) R. 95 m. W of Prague, near the German frontier. Pop. (1967) 25,633. Industrial centre. Manufactures agricultural machinery, textiles, beer, etc. Important railway junction. Its strategic position has meant a stormy history. Wallenstein was murdered (1634) in the 12th-cent. castle. A leading centre of the Sudeten-German movement after the 1st World War. The expulsion of the former large German population took place after the 2nd World War.

**Cheboksary** USSR. Capital of the Chuvash ASSR (RSFSR), on the right bank of the Volga R. 130 m. E of Gorki. Pop. (1970) 216,000. Linked by branch line with the Trans-Siberian Railway. Manufactures electrical equipment, textiles, matches, etc.

**Checheno-Ingush ASSR** USSR. Autonomous republic of the RSFSR, on the N slopes of the Great Caucasus, extending N to the plain of the Terek R., bordering in the E on the Dagestan ASSR and in the S on the Georgian SSR. Area 7,350 sq. m. Pop. (1970) 1,065,000 (chiefly Chechen and Ingush, Muslim herdsmen and farmers). Cap. Grozny. Important oilfield centred on Grozny (opened 1893). Petrochemical and engineering industries. A Chechen autonomous region was formed in 1922 and an Ingush autonomous region in 1924; united in 1934, they became an autonomous republic 1936. Dissolved for collaboration with the Germans (1944); reconstituted 1957. Over 200,000 Chechen and Ingush returned to their homes 1957–9.

**Cheddar** England. Village in N Somerset just S of the Mendip Hills, 7 m. NW of Wells. Agricultural market in a dairy-farming area. Famous for cheese, manufactured since the 17th cent. Near by is the Cheddar Gorge: tall limestone cliffs, and caves containing magnificent stalactites and stalagmites.

**Chefoo** China. Officially Yentai. Former Treaty port in Shantung, on the N coast of the Shantung peninsula. Pop. 227,000. Exports soya beans, vegetable oil, fruits, etc.; formerly had important trade in raw silk. The original harbour at Chefoo silted up in the 19th cent. and the name is still applied to the new harbour at Yentai. Opened to foreign trade 1858. Trade increased when linked by rail with the main Tsingtao–Tsinan line 1955.

**Cheju Island** S Korea. Island 45 m. long and up to 17 m. wide, 60 m. S of the coast of S Korea. Area 718 sq. m. Pop. (1960) 281,720 (Korean). Cap. Cheju (pop. 68,000). Mountainous, rising to over 6,000 ft. Well wooded. Fishing, cattle rearing. Chief crops cereals, soya beans.

**Chekiang** China. Maritime province on the E China Sea. Area 39,300 sq. m. Pop. (1957) 25,280,000. Cap. Hangchow. Smallest province, but one of the most densely populated. Largely mountainous. Climate varies from sub-tropical (S) to temperate (N). Chief crops tea, rice, cotton. Principal towns Hangchow, Ningpo, Wenchow, all seaports.

**Chelm** Poland. Market town in the Lublin voivodship, 43 m. ESE of Lublin. Pop. (1968) 37,100. Flour milling, brickmaking, etc. Founded in the 13th cent.

**Chelmsford** England. County town of Essex, municipal borough on the R. Chelmer at its confluence with the R. Cann 30 m. ENE of London. Pop. (1961) 49,810. Market town. Manufactures electrical equipment. Flour milling, brewing, malting. Important in the Middle Ages owing to its position on the London–Colchester road. St Mary's parish church, originally completed in 1424 but rebuilt after collapsing in 1800, became a cathedral in 1914. The Shire Hall was built 1789–92.

**Chelsea** England. Residential area in London, on the N bank of the Thames where it is crossed by the Chelsea, Albert, and Battersea bridges; from 1965 part of the Royal Borough of Kensington and Chelsea. Pop. (1961) 47,085. Long literary and artistic associations, esp. in the 18th and 19th cent.

Among those who have lived in Chelsea are Sir Thomas More, Steele, Swift, Carlyle (whose house in Cheyne Row is a public memorial), George Eliot, Turner, Rossetti, Whistler, Oscar Wilde. The 14th-cent. Old Church was destroyed by bombing in the 2nd World War (except for the More chapel) and was rebuilt. Chelsea Royal Hospital for old and invalid soldiers (Chelsea Pensioners), founded by Charles II and designed by Wren (completed 1692), was also damaged. Ranelagh Gardens and later Cremorne Gardens were well-known places of entertainment in the late 18th cent. The Chelsea bun is famous; the original bun-house stood till 1839. The Chelsea porcelain works was removed to Derby in 1769.

**Chelsea** USA. Suburb of NE Boston, Massachusetts, separated from it by the estuary of the Mystic R. Pop. (1960) 33,749. Manufactures shoes, chemicals, paints, etc.

**Cheltenham** England. Municipal borough in Gloucestershire, on the R. Chelt (a small tributary of the Severn) 7 m. ENE of Gloucester. Pop. (1961) 71,968. Residential town, favoured by retired civil servants and army officers. Educational centre: Cheltenham College (1841) and Cheltenham Ladies' College (1853). Its fame as a spa dates from the discovery of mineral springs in 1716. Several light industries. Centre of hunting and steeplechasing, with a famous racecourse. Birthplace of Gustav Holst (1874–1934).

**Chelyabinsk** USSR. Capital of the Chelyabinsk Region (RSFSR), in the E foothills of the S Urals 450 m. ENE of Kuibyshev, on the Trans-Siberian Railway. Pop. (1970) 874,000. Major industrial centre. Iron and steel, zinc-refining plants. Manufactures tractors, agricultural machinery, chemicals, etc. Founded (1658) as a military post. Developed as a commercial centre, trading in grain and coal, with a flour-milling industry. Expanded rapidly with the advent of the Trans-Siberian Railway (1892) and the development of heavy industry in the 1930s.

**Chelyuskin, Cape** USSR. The most northerly point of Asia and of continental USSR, in the Krasnoyarsk Territory (RSFSR), at the N end of the Taimyr peninsula.

**Chemnitz** ◊ *Karl-Marx-Stadt.*

**Chemulpo** ◊ *Inchon.*

**Chenab River** India. One of the 5 rivers of

the Punjab, 700 m. long, rising in the Himalayas and flowing first NW and then generally SW. It joins the Jhelum R., later receives the Ravi, and then joins the Sutlej E of Alipur. Extensively used for irrigation.

**Chengchow** China. Formerly (1913–49) Chenghsien. Capital of Honan province, in the N near the Hwang-ho. Pop. 595,000. Important railway junction on the Peking–Kwangchow (N–S) and Lienyun–Lanchow (E–W) lines. Also a commercial centre. Trade in grain, hides and skins, etc. Manufactures machinery, textiles, etc. Flour milling, vegetable oil processing, etc.

**Chengtu** China. Capital of Szechwan province, on the fertile Chengtu plain 170 m. NW of Chungking. Pop. (1957) 1,107,000. Commercial centre for trade between the mountainous region of NW Szechwan and the Red Basin, in an area irrigated by a system created in the 3rd cent. B.C. Railway engineering. Manufactures textiles, bricks and tiles, etc. Important educational centre; seat of Szechwan University (1931) and a Technical University (1954).

**Chepstow** Wales. Urban district in Monmouthshire, on the R. Wye 2 m. above its mouth in the Severn estuary. Pop. (1961) 5,980. Market town. River port. Has a ruined castle (mainly 14th-cent.) and a tubular bridge by Brunel (1852). Tintern Abbey is near by.

**Chequers** England. Tudor mansion and estate on a historic site in Buckinghamshire, 2 m. SW of Wendover, presented to the nation (1921) by Lord Lee of Fareham to be used as the official country residence of the Prime Minister.

**Cher** France. Department comprising parts of the former provinces of Berry, Bourbonnais, and Nivernais. Area 2,819 sq. m. Pop. (1968) 304,601. Prefecture Bourges. Drained by the Cher and the middle Loire rivers. Fertile in the lowlands. Cereals, vines, vegetables, fodder crops cultivated. Extensive pastures for raising sheep and cattle. Many hilly parts are well wooded. Chief towns Bourges, Vierzon.

**Cherbourg** France. Seaport in the Manche department on the English Channel on the N coast of the Cotentin peninsula. Pop. (1968) 40,333. The harbour, protected by a breakwater over 2 m. long, can accommodate the largest transatlantic liners. Shipbuilding, ship repairing. Probably on the site of Roman Coriallum. Fortified under Louis XIV in the 17th–18th cent. Harbour works were begun under Louis

XVI and continued by Napoleon I and Napoleon III. An important naval base before the 2nd World War. When the arsenal was destroyed (1944) parts of the commercial harbour were also damaged.

**Cheremkhovo** USSR. Coalmining town of the Irkutsk region (RSFSR), on the Trans-Siberian Railway 80 m. NW of Irkutsk. Pop. (1968) 107,000. Manufactures machinery, chemicals, etc.

**Cherepovets** USSR. Port on the N side of the Rybinsk Reservoir (RSFSR), 130 m. NW of Yaroslavl. Pop. (1970) 189,000. Route and industrial centre. Manufactures iron and steel, agricultural machinery, footwear, matches, etc. Shipbuilding, sawmilling. Developed rapidly with the construction of the Rybinsk Reservoir (1941). The integrated iron and steel works (1955) was established to supply steel to the Leningrad area.

**Cheribon** ◊ *Tjirebon*.

**Cherkassy** USSR. River port and industrial town in the Ukrainian SSR, on the right bank of the Dnieper R. 100 m. SE of Kiev. Pop. 159,000. Sawmilling, metal working, engineering, food processing.

**Cherkessk** USSR. Formerly Batalpashinsk, Sulimov, Yezhovo-Cherkessk. Capital of the Karachayevo-Cherkess AR (RSFSR), on the Kuban R. 55 m. S of Stavropol. Pop. (1970) 67,000. N Caucasus railway terminus. Industrial centre. Metal working, flour milling. Manufactures chemicals. Founded (as Batalpashinsk) 1825.

**Chernigov** USSR. Town in the Ukrainian SSR on the Desna R. 80 m. NNE of Kiev. Pop. (1970) 159,000. River port and industrial town, in a region producing grain, flax, potatoes. Manufactures textiles, knitwear, footwear, chemicals, etc. An ancient city; Byzantine cathedral (11th-cent.). Capital of the independent principality of Syeversk in the 11th cent. Destroyed by Tatars 1239. Changed hands several times; fell to Russia in the 17th cent.

**Chernovtsy** USSR. Formerly (1918–40) Cernăuţi. Capital of the Chernovtsy Region, in the W of the Ukrainian SSR on the Prut R. Pop. (1970) 187,000. Sawmilling, engineering, food processing. Manufactures textiles, rubber products, etc. Cathedral (19th-cent.). University (1875). Grew in economic importance under Austro-Hungarian rule (1775–1918) as capital of Bukovina. In Rumania (1918–40) as Cernăuţi. Ceded to Russia 1940.

**Chernyakhovsk** USSR. Formerly Insterburg. Town in the Kaliningrad region (RSFSR) 50 m. E of Kaliningrad on the Angerapp R. Pop. (1963) 29,000. Railway junction. Industrial centre. Food processing. Manufactures chemicals etc. Founded in the 14th cent. In E Prussia (Germany), as Insterburg, until 1945. Ceded to Russia under the Potsdam Agreement (1945); renamed after Marshal Chernyakhovsky, who captured it during the 2nd World War.

**Cherrapunji** India. Village in Assam, on the S slope of the Khasi Hills at 4,309 ft, 25 m. SSW of Shillong. Pop. 2,000. Famous for world record in mean annual rainfall, 428 ins. In one year (1861) more than 900 ins. of rain fell.

**Cher River** France. River 199 m. long, rising in the Massif Central, flowing N and then W, and joining the Loire 10 m. WSW of Tours. Navigable in lower course.

**Cherski Range** USSR. Curved mountain system extending NW-SE in NE Siberia (RSFSR), over 600 m. long, rising to 10,325 ft in Pobeda. The Indigirka R. flows S-N through the range.

**Chertsey** England. Residential urban district in Surrey, on the Thames 18 m. WSW of London. Pop. (1961) 40,376. Market gardening: the produce is sent to London markets. Has a 7-arch bridge built in 1785. Grew up round a 7th-cent. Benedictine monastery, burial-place of Henry VI.

**Cherwell River** England. River 30 m. long, rising in Northamptonshire, flowing S through Oxfordshire, and joining the Thames at Oxford.

**Chesapeake Bay** USA. Largest inlet in the country's Atlantic coast, nearly 200 m. long and up to 30 m. wide, with the mainland parts of Maryland and Virginia on the W and the Delmarva peninsula on the E; into it flow the Susquehanna, Potomac, Rappahannock, York, and James rivers. Famous for crab and oyster fishing. A 17½-m. series of causeways, tunnels, and bridges spanning its entrance was opened in 1964.

**Chesham** England. Urban district in Buckinghamshire 8 m. NE of High Wycombe, on the S slopes of the Chiltern Hills. Pop. (1961) 16,236. Market town. Manufactures wood products (local beech), pencils, shoes, etc.

**Cheshire** England. County in the NW bounded on the W by Denbighshire and Flintshire (Wales) and on the NW (where the Wirral peninsula separates the Dee and

the Mersey estuaries) by the Irish Sea. Area 1,015 sq. m. Pop. (1961) 1,367,860. County town Chester. Generally low-lying and flat, or gently undulating. Numerous small lakes or meres, with the R. Mersey on the N boundary and the R. Dee in the W; crossed SE-NW by the R. Weaver. Also several canals, including most of the Manchester Ship Canal. Dairy farming important. Long famous for cheese. Salt, extracted (mainly as brine) around the R. Weaver (chiefly at Northwich, Winsford, Middlewich, and Sandbach), furnishes raw material for the chemical industry. Coal mined in the E. Principal towns Chester, Birkenhead, Stockport, Wallasey, Crewe, Bebington, Sale.

**Cheshunt** England. Residential urban district in SE Hertfordshire, 14 m. N of London, for which it is a dormitory suburb. Pop. (1961) 35,297. Market-gardening centre. Horticultural research station. Seat (1792-1905) of the Countess of Huntingdon's College, now Cheshunt College, Cambridge.

**Chesil Bank** England. Shingle beach 170-200 yards wide on the coast of Dorset, extending NW from Portland for 9 m. to Abbotsbury, where there is a famous swannery; separated from the mainland by the Fleet inlet. It continues along the coast for 7 m. more to a point near Bridport. The pebbles increase in size towards the seaward end, as though graded.

**Chester** England. Ancient Deva (Devana Castra). County town of Cheshire; county borough mainly on the right bank of the R. Dee 6 m. above its shallow estuary. Pop. (1961) 59,283. Important railway centre. Cheese market. Brewing. Manufactures clothing, metal windows, etc. An ancient and picturesque city: unique in England for its intact surrounding walls (red sandstone) divided into four main sections by the two principal streets, which intersect at right angles; 'the Rows' (covered ways, arcades) are an outstanding feature. The cathedral (the church of St Werburgh's Abbey till 1541) dates from Norman times. The castle (except 'Caesar's Tower') was removed about 1790. Many 16th/17th-cent. timbered houses. Racecourse outside the city walls. The Roman fort, destroyed by Aethelfrith of Northumbria *c.* A.D. 614, was rebuilt 907. Last English city to fall to William the Conqueror (1066). Taken by the Parliamentarians in the English Civil Wars only after a long siege (1643-6).

**Chester** USA. Industrial town and port in SE Pennsylvania, on the Delaware R. 12 m. SW of Philadelphia. Pop. (1960) 63,568. Settled (as Uppland) by Swedes *c.* 1645; renamed by William Penn, who landed here in 1682. Shipbuilding, oil refining. Manufactures locomotives, textiles, etc.

**Chesterfield** England. Municipal borough in Derbyshire, on the R. Rother 10 m. S of Sheffield. Pop. (1961) 67,833. Industrial town in a coalmining region. Iron founding, engineering. Famous 14th-cent. parish church with a twisted spire. Stephenson Memorial Hall (1879), commemorating George Stephenson the engineer (who died in Chesterfield). Modern town hall (1938).

**Chester-le-Street** England. Urban district in Durham, 6 m. N of Durham City. Pop. (1961) 18,948. Coalmining and iron-smelting district. Manufactures confectionery. Near by is the 14th-cent. Lumley Castle.

**Cheviot Hills** England/Scotland. Range of hills extending 35 m. SW–NE along the border between England and Scotland. The highest peak is The Cheviot (2,676 ft) in Northumberland. Sources of the N Tyne and the Coquet rivers. Ample grazing land. The Cheviot breed of sheep is famous.

**Cheyenne** USA. State capital of Wyoming, in the extreme SE, at a height of 6,000 ft, 95 m. N of Denver (Colorado). Pop. (1960) 43,505. Commercial centre in ranching country. Railway workshops, light industries.

**Chiana River** Italy. Ancient Clanis. River 60 m. long, rising in the Apennines near Arezzo, flowing through the flat Val di Chiana, and emptying partly into the Arno R. and partly into the Tiber. In the Middle Ages the Val di Chiana was an uninhabitable swamp, but it was reclaimed in the 19th cent. The region is now almost entirely cultivated.

**Chiang Mai** Thailand. Chief town in the N and capital of Chiang Mai province, on the Ping R. 380 m. NNW of Bangkok. Pop. (1964) 65,736. N terminus of the railway from Bangkok. Centre of the teak trade. Founded in the late 13th cent. Long capital of a Lao or N Thai kingdom. Ruins of several ancient temples.

**Chianti, Monti** Italy. Small range in the Apennines in Tuscany, 15 m. long, rising to over 2,900 ft. Grapes for the famous Chianti wine are grown on the slopes.

**Chiapas** Mexico. Pacific state, on the Guatemala frontier. Area 28,520 sq. m. Pop. (1969) 1,556,000 (largely Indians). Cap. Tuxtla Gutiérrez. Mountainous, with a narrow coastal plain. Backward agriculture, but exports tropical products (hardwoods, fruit, coffee, cocoa, cotton, etc.). Maya ruins in the NE.

**Chiatura** USSR. Town in the Georgian SSR on the Kvirila R. Pop. (1963) 25,000. One of the world's leading centres of manganese mining (since 1879). The refined ore is exported through Poti.

**Chiba** Japan. Capital of the Chiba prefecture, Honshu, on Tokyo Bay 25 m. ESE of Tokyo. Pop. (1965) 332,174. Manufactures steel, textiles, paper, etc.

**Chicago** USA. Second city of the USA, hub of the vast Middle West, in Illinois on the lower W. shore of L. Michigan. Pop. (1970) 3,325,263. Contains the largest stockyards and meat-packing plants in the world, and is the greatest railway centre and one of the busiest airports. Leading market for grain and one of the greatest industrial regions in the USA, manufacturing iron and steel, agricultural machinery, electrical equipment, railway rolling stock, chemicals, textiles, food products. Its Merchandise Mart is the largest commercial office building in the world. Railway development has somewhat reduced the importance of its harbour, but large quantities of coal, iron ore, and limestone are still imported and grain exported via the Great Lakes.

The city (which covers an area of 200 sq. m.), stretches more than 20 m. along L. Michigan; on the lake front are the famous Michigan Boulevard and Grant Park, with the Natural History Museum and the Art Institute, while near by are the Adler Planetarium and Soldier Field, a large sports stadium. Among the educational institutions are the University of Chicago (1892), the Northwestern University (1851), the Loyola University (1870), the De Paul University (1898), and the Oriental Institute, perhaps the world's greatest centre of Oriental studies.

Chicago stands near the site of Fort Dearborn (built 1803). It did not begin to grow until the settling of the Middle West accelerated on the completion of the Erie Canal. It became a city in 1837, but its great expansion came with the construction of the railways. In 1871, the city (then mainly of wood) was devastated by fire. When it was rebuilt, great new industries developed, and immigrants poured in, esp. from Germany, Ireland, Poland, Scandinavia. In 1893 the World's Columbian Exposition was held, where Sullivan the architect made Chicago the leading centre of architectural design and devised the first skyscrapers. In Prohibition times Chicago was notorious for its lawlessness, associated particularly with Al Capone. The Century of Progress Exposition (1933–4) celebrated the immense strides that Chicago had made from village to metropolis in the course of a century.

Chichén Itzá Mexico. A ruined Maya city in Yucatán 75 m. ESE of Mérida. One of the outstanding archaeological sites of the American continent, with pyramids, temples, and statues. Founded in the 6th cent. A.D. by the Itzá, it was abandoned, then reoccupied in the 10th cent., but finally abandoned in the 15th cent.

Chichester England. Municipal borough, ancient cathedral city, and county town of W Sussex, between the S Downs and the English Channel 13 m. ENE of Portsmouth. Pop. (1961) 20,118. Agricultural and livestock markets; little industry. The wool trade for which it was famous in the Middle Ages has declined. The streets show evidence of Roman planning. Features of interest include the cathedral (begun in the late 11th cent. and unique in having a detached bell tower, in Perpendicular style), part of the ancient walls (on Roman foundations), a 16th-cent. octagonal market cross, and a Roman amphitheatre (discovered 1935). The new 'theatre-in-the-round' under Sir Laurence Olivier was opened in 1962. The famous Goodwood racecourse ('Glorious Goodwood') is near by.

Chichi-jima ◊ Bonin Islands.

Chickamauga USA. Town in Georgia 11 m. S of Chattanooga, on the small river of the same name, a tributary of the Tennessee R. Pop. (1960) 1,824. The Battle of Chickamauga (1863) in the American Civil War took place near by.

Chickamauga Dam USA. Dam on the Tennessee R. just NE of Chattanooga, near the confluence with the Chickamauga R. An important Tennessee Valley Authority dam, designed to provide hydroelectric power, control flooding, etc.

Chiclayo Peru. Capital of the Lambayeque department, on the dry coastal plain of the NW, in the Lambayeque valley, irrigated from the Andes. Pop. (1961) 86,904. Commercial centre of a region growing sugar-cane, rice, cotton. Rice milling, cotton ginning, brewing, tanning, etc.

Chicopee USA. Town in S Massachusetts at the confluence of the Chicopee and the Connecticut rivers, just N of Springfield. Pop. (1960) 61,553. Manufactures tyres, fire-arms, textiles, etc.

Chicoutimi Canada. Lumber town and river port in Quebec, 112 m. N of Quebec at the confluence of the Chicoutimi and the Saguenay rivers. Pop. (1966) 32,526. Hydroelectric power. Pulp milling. Manufactures paper, furniture.

Chicoutimi River Canada. River 100 m. long in Quebec, a tributary of the Saguenay R. Hydroelectric power station near Chicoutimi.

Chiemsee Federal German Republic. The largest lake in Bavaria, in the SE, at a height of 1,700 ft. Area 33 sq. m. Fed by the Ache R. Discharges via the Alz R. into the Inn. On Herreninsel (largest of its 3 islands) is a castle built in imitation of Versailles by Ludwig II of Bavaria.

Chieti Italy. Ancient Teate (Theate). Capital of the Chieti province in Abruzzi e Molise, 8 m. SSW of Pescara. Pop. (1961) 47,792. Manufactures textiles, macaroni, bricks, etc. Cathedral (11th-cent., restored) with a fine Gothic campanile. Remains of Roman temples. The Theatine monastic order was founded in 1524.

Chignecto Bay Canada. Inlet of the Bay of Fundy, about 35 m. long and 10 m. wide, between SE New Brunswick and Nova Scotia. Exceptionally high tides.

Chignecto Isthmus Canada. Neck of land between Chignecto Bay and the Northumberland Strait, 15 m. wide at the narrowest point, across which runs the border between Nova Scotia and New Brunswick. The name (of Micmac origin) means 'the great marsh district'.

Chigwell England. Urban district in Essex, 12 m. NE of London, of which it is a dormitory suburb. Pop. (1961) 61,001. The King's Head Inn is the 'Maypole Inn' of Dickens's *Barnaby Rudge*. William Penn, founder of Pennsylvania, was a pupil at the 17th-cent. grammar school.

Chihuahua Mexico. 1. State in the N, on the Rio Grande R. Area 95,376 sq. m. Pop. (1969) 1,826,000. Climate cool in the mountainous W (Sierra Madre Occidental), mild in the centre, and hot in the desert (E). Main industry mining (gold, silver, copper, zinc, lead). Cotton cultivated; cattle reared, esp. in the W and N. The miniature Chihuahua dogs are bred here.

2. Capital of Chihuahua state and chief town in the N, in a valley surrounded by spurs of the Sierra Madre Occidental, at a height of 4,667 ft. Pop. (1969) 247,100. In a mining and cattle-rearing district. Smelting. Manufactures textiles. University (1954). Hidalgo y Costilla, a hero of Mexican independence, was executed here in 1811. Later it was the headquarters of Pancho Villa, who once captured the city (1910) by disguising his men as peasants on their way to market.

**Chile.** Republic on the W coast of S America. Area 286,397 sq. m. Pop. (1964) 8,515,023. Cap. Santiago. Lang. Spanish.

A long narrow strip of territory, over 2,600 m. from 17°30′ S to 56° S (Cape Horn). Bounded by the Pacific (W), and by the Andes (E), which cut it off from the rest of S America. Maximum width about 250 m. One of the smallest countries in S America, but the largest producer of minerals (other than oil); copper is the most important, accounting for nearly 70 per cent of the exports. The largely homogeneous population, a compound of the original Spanish settlers and the native Indians, are intelligent, energetic, and in general literate. Agriculture is deficient, partly because of the unfavourable climate in the N and the S but largely owing to outmoded patterns of land ownership and production. A large proportion of the population is undernourished. There are efficient and growing industries, based on indigenous coal, hydroelectric power, and iron. The rate of population increase, however, is high and outruns increases in productivity. Divided administratively into 25 provinces. TOPOGRAPHY, CLIMATE. In a country of such latitudinal extent there is great diversity of climate and vegetation. Starting from the N (the frontier with Peru), the first 1,000 m. comprise the completely rainless hot Atacama desert, without vegetation but containing copper and nitrate deposits, and a semi-desert stretch where some cultivation is possible with irrigation. Then comes the most fertile part of Chile, from Illapel to Concepción, where the farmlands are concentrated in the central valley, an area of abundant winter rains and dry summers, containing the bulk of the population and the three largest cities, Santiago, its port Valparaiso, and Concepción. Next comes a country of lakes and forests and some cultivated land, with frequent rain, extending to Puerto Montt. The final 1,000 m. consist of wild and almost uninhabited country, mountainous, with fiords and glaciers, heavy rains, and a cold stormy climate. In the extreme S there is a small region with an Atlantic coastline, less rainy, where sheep raising, coalmining, and oil production are the main occupations.

RESOURCES, PEOPLE, *etc.* Minerals provide the greatest wealth; besides nitrates and iodine, huge copper deposits are worked on the W Andean slopes, at Chuquicamata and Potrerillos (N), and at El Teniente farther S. Iron ore is mined in N Chile, for export and for the steelworks at Huachipato, near Concepción. Petroleum from Tierra del Fuego is sent to the refinery at Concón, just N of Valparaiso, and provides almost all the petrol requirements. Coal is mined S of Concepción. Large hydroelectric stations are mostly in central Chile; others are planned. Copper contributes two thirds or more of the exports, other minerals over a fifth. Wool (chiefly from the far S) supplies the home textile industries; some is exported. Timber exploitation is increasing. Fishing is important; the production and export of fishmeal have grown rapidly. Santiago and Valparaiso are by far the largest cities, and with Concepción (S) are the chief industrial centres. Most of the other towns of central Chile are agricultural centres; the majority have suffered earthquake damage. The N ports serve the mineral areas; Arica and Antofagasta are also ports for Bolivia.

The estate ('*hacienda*') system still obtaining in the agricultural regions is a feudal system, with workers raising subsistence crops on allotted areas and often living in primitive conditions. Though the country grows insufficient foods for the rapidly increasing population, large pastoral estates still occupy valuable agricultural land, although some have been divided for cultivation.

Governed by a bicameral parliamentary system, broadly similar to that of the USA but with longer terms of office. Chile has recently been ruled by left-wing governments; many of the industries and public utilities are State controlled. The large copper companies, however, are owned by US corporations, and the land problem has not been fully resolved.

HISTORY. The Spanish conquistadors

found central Chile under Inca domination. Valdivia founded Santiago (1541) but the Spanish were turned back by the fierce Araucanian Indians (S), who remained independent until the 19th cent. (when they made a treaty with the Chileans). The mingling of Spaniards and Indians produced a largely *mestizo* population; few of the people are of pure European descent. Colonial Chile became part of the viceroyalty of Peru. Independence was proclaimed in 1810 by General O'Higgins, son of an Irish-born Viceroy of Peru and a Chilean mother; final liberation came in 1818. Chile fought Peru and Bolivia 1879–84, and on victory extended her N frontier, acquiring nitrates in the N desert.

**Chilkoot Pass** Canada/USA. Pass at a height of 3,500 ft on the border between the Alaska panhandle and NW British Columbia (Canada), N of Skagway (Alaska). A route used by many gold prospectors during the Klondike gold rush (1896).

**Chillán** Chile. Capital of the Ñuble province, in the central valley, 56 m. ENE of Concepción. Pop. 79,000. Trade in fruit, wine, etc. Manufactures leather goods, footwear. Flour milling. Founded 1594. Moved to its present site 1836. Has suffered severely from earthquakes; destroyed by the 1939 earthquake and rebuilt. The original site, Chillán Viejo, was the birthplace of the Chilean liberator, Bernardo O'Higgins (1778–1842).

**Chillicothe** USA. Commercial and industrial town in Ohio, on the Scioto R. 44 m. S of Columbus. Pop. (1960) 24,957. Manufactures footwear, paper, furniture, etc. State capital 1803–10 and 1812–16.

**Chillon** Switzerland. Castle just S of Montreux, at the E end of L. Geneva, dating mainly from the 13th cent.; now a museum. Formerly a stronghold of ◊ *Savoie*. The state prison where François Bonivard (made famous by Byron's *The Prisoner of Chillon*) was imprisoned 1530–36.

**Chiloé Island** Chile. Island off the SW coast, N of the Chonos Archipelago. Area 3,241 sq. m. Chief town Ancud (pop. 22,000), an agricultural and timber centre (N). Closely forested, with clearings for potatoes, barley, etc. Many fishing hamlets. With a section of the mainland, and numerous other sparsely inhabited islands, it forms the province of Chiloé (area 9,050 sq. m.; pop. (1960) 98,662; cap. Ancud). ◊ *Puerto Montt*.

**Chiltern Hills** England. Low range of chalk hills extending 55 m. NE from the Goring Gap in the Thames valley, through parts of Oxfordshire, Buckinghamshire, Hertfordshire, and Bedfordshire, and continuing as the East Anglian Heights. Highest point Coombe Hill (852 ft), 1½ m. SW of Wendover. A well defined escarpment, facing NW. Several main railways and roads from London to the Midlands use the gaps in the range. Formerly clothed in dense beech forests, the haunts of robbers, to restrain whom the office of Steward of the Chiltern Hundreds was created; this now nominal post is presented to any member of the House of Commons desiring to retire from Parliament (since an MP may not hold a Crown 'office of profit'). The supplies of beechwood stimulated the furniture industry, esp. at High Wycombe.

**Chimborazo** Ecuador. Inactive volcano, in the N of the Chimborazo province; the highest peak (20,577 ft) in the Ecuadorian Andes, an impressive snow-capped cone, standing out from the massif. The large glaciers are sometimes visible from the Pacific coast. The summit was first reached by Whymper (1880).

**Chimbote** Peru. Seaport with a sheltered natural harbour, in the Ancash department 230 m. NNW of Lima. Pop. (1961) 63,970. Site of Peru's first iron and steel plant (opened 1958), using ore from S Peru and power from the Santa R. Fishing port. Exports fish products, sugar, etc.

**Chimkent** USSR. Industrial town in the Kazakh SSR 90 m. N of Tashkent on the Turksib Railway. Pop. (1970) 247,000. Important lead-zinc refinery. Manufactures chemicals, cement, cotton goods, etc. Flour milling, canning. Taken by the Russians 1864.

**China.** A people's republic of E Asia. Area 3,768,000 sq. m. Pop. (1968) *c*. 730 million. Cap. Peking. Lang. mainly Mandarin Chinese. Rel. Confucian, Buddhist, Taoist.

The second largest (after the USSR) and the most populous country in the world. It has the world's oldest contemporary civilization, and throughout its long history agriculture has been the mainstay of its economy, still employing about four fifths of its enormous population, with a social system which has preserved its unity over more than four millennia; the three basic food crops are rice, in the S, and wheat and millet farther N. Farming has been of a small-scale subsistence type, practised by millions of peasants on minute plots of land, more accurately described as horticulture rather than agriculture, but adequate to support a rural population density of up to 3,000 per sq. m. Only since the establishment of the Communist régime (1949) has any serious co-ordinated attempt at mechanization of agriculture or greater industrialization been made. The country is divided into 22 provinces, 5 autonomous regions, and 2 municipalities. The provinces are: in the N E Region Heilungkiang, Kirin, Liaoning; in the N Region, Hopei, Shansi; in the E Region, Shantung, Kiangsu, Anhwei, Chekiang, Fukien, Formosa (Taiwan) – which the Peking régime regards as part of China; in the Central–S Region, Honan, Hupei, Hunan, Kiangsi, Kwangtung; in the SW Region, Szechwan, Kweichow, Yunnan; in the NW Region, Shensi, Kansu, Tsinghai. The 5 autonomous regions are Inner Mongolia, Sinkiang-Uighur, Kwangsi-Chuang, Ningsia-Hui, Tibet, and the municipalities under direct government administration are Peking and Shanghai. China proper, as usually understood, comprises the old 18 provinces and excludes Manchuria (NE), Mongolia, Tibet, and Sinkiang.

TOPOGRAPHY, CLIMATE, etc. China proper falls into three main natural regions which coincide with the basins of the three great rivers. N China is the basin of the Hwang-ho, including the loess plateau of the NW, which merges N into the extensive Mongolian plateau, and the Great Plain which is crossed by the lower section of the river; to the NE are the central plain and the E highlands of Manchuria. Central China, separated from the N by the Tsinling Mountains, is drained by the Yangtse-kiang; it consists of the mountainous region of the far west, which passes into the vast, lofty Tibetan plateau, the Red Basin, occupying much of Szechwan province, and E of the Great Gorge the central lowlands and the delta area. S China, separated from the Yangtse basin by the S China Highlands, includes the plateau of Yunnan in the W, the Si-kiang basin, and the narrow coastal plains of the SE. Off the Luichow peninsula in the extreme S is the large island of Hainan.

The climate of China proper is dominated by the monsoons, with cold, dry winds from the N in winter and warm rain-bearing winds from the S and SE in summer. In N China the winters are very cold, the strong winds sometimes bringing duststorms, while summers are hot, and the rainfall averages 25–30 ins. annually. In Central China the winters are rather less cold and include some rain, the annual total amounting to 40–60 ins. S China has a sub-tropical type of monsoon climate, winters being mild and the mean annual rainfall reaching 80 ins. or more. The great plateaux of Tibet and Mongolia have a dry climate with extremes of temperature. Most of the original forest cover of China has long been removed for fuel, and the results may be seen in the bare, eroded hills of many areas: a situation which the present government is attempting to rectify by schemes of afforestation.

RESOURCES, PEOPLE, etc. With so much of the country consisting of infertile mountains and plateaux, its peasant farmers are necessarily confined to the river valleys, deltas, and limited plains. Farming is intensive to the utmost degree, every scrap of organic matter, including human excrement, being used to enrich the soil. Although in general every available square yard is cultivated, the Chinese villager's traditional veneration for his ancestors often causes him to devote some of the best land to burial grounds. By the end of 1958, when socialization of agriculture was declared complete, the peasant population had been organized in over 26,000 'People's Communes', each Commune representing about 10,000 active workers.

In the S rice occupies about three quarters of the cultivated land, and tea is grown in the hills but has decreased in importance as an export crop; the warm climate of the S also allows oranges, lichees, and other fruits to be grown. N of the Yangtse wheat and millets are the principal food crops, and the acreage of soya beans has increased considerably in recent years. Every farm has its vegetable garden, and pigs and poultry are numerous, living mostly by scavenging and providing a welcome reserve of food; fish is a significant item in the Chinese diet. Coal is the most important mineral and output is estimated at 320 million tons or well over 8 times that of the 1930s; China is the world's leading producer of tungsten (Kiangsi) and antimony (Hunan); iron ore (Liaoning, Hupei) and tin (Yunnan) are also produced. Iron and steel are manufactured at Anshan (Liaoning), Wuhan (Hupei), and Paotow (Inner Mongolia), and textiles at a number of centres, inc. Shanghai and Wuhan. The largest cities are Shanghai, Peking, and Tientsin, and there are 11 others with more than 1 million inhabitants. Industrial development has been long hampered by poor communications; not till 1936, when the Yangtse was bridged at Wuhan, was there a direct railway link between N and S (Peking-Kwangchow). Under the various 5-year plans much progress has been made with railway and road construction; on the other hand, the entire internal economy was dislocated by the disastrous harvests of 1959-61, necessitating heavy emergency imports of grain from Canada and elsewhere, and not till 1963 did it appear that the normal 'simultaneous development of industry and agriculture' could proceed.

Widespread illiteracy is another obstacle to progress which the Communist government has attempted to overcome; in 1949 higher education was taken over by the state and was reorganized with the emphasis on technical education. In 1956 a 30-letter version of the Latin alphabet was adopted to replace gradually the 30,000 characters of the Chinese script. The highest organ of state authority is the National People's Congress, elected for 4 years by provinces, autonomous regions, municipalities, armed forces, and Chinese residents abroad; the highest administrative organ is the State Council, headed by the Prime Minister.

HISTORY. Chinese history may be said to begin in the 3rd millennium B.C., the Hsia dynasty (2205-1766 B.C.) being followed by the better-known Shang (1766-1122 B.C.) and Chou (1122-249 B.C.) dynasties; under the Shang the Chinese were already making bronze vases of unsurpassed beauty, and under the Chou dynasty lived the great Chinese philosophers, Confucius and Lao Tse. The short-lived Ch'in dynasty, from which the name China may be derived, had one remarkable ruler, Shih Huang Ti (246-210 B.C.), the 'First Emperor', who united the country, completed the Great Wall against the northern barbarians – and ordered all historic records to be destroyed. Then came the Han dynasty (206 B.C.-A.D. 221), which was distinguished for its prosperity and its artistic and other achievements, not the least of which was the invention of paper; the country expanded, contact was made

with the Roman Empire, and Buddhism was introduced.

The Tang (618-906) and Sung (960-1280) dynasties were separated by a period of decline and disorder, and in 1280 the Mongol conquest, begun in 1211 by Genghis Khan, was completed by Kublai Khan, whose court was described by Marco Polo. By 1368 the Mongol Yuan dynasty had been overthrown and replaced by the Ming dynasty, which lasted till 1644, and Chinese rule was again established as far as the Great Wall. In the 16th cent. relations were opened between China and the European nations. The Portuguese reached Kwangchow (Canton) in 1516 and were later allowed to settle in Macao, to be followed by Spaniards, Dutch, and English. Meanwhile the Manchu tribes of E Manchuria had invaded the Liaotung peninsula, captured Peking, which had been capital since 1421, and gradually conquered China, establishing the last imperial dynasty, the Ch'ing (1644-1912).

Trade with Europe slowly increased, but the Chinese were obstructive and unfriendly; a British embassy was sent to Peking in 1792, but a second embassy was dismissed in 1816 because the ambassador refused to 'kowtow'. War broke out with Britain on the question of opium imports (1839-42), and as a result five ports, Canton, Amoy, Foochow, Ningpo, and Shanghai, were opened to foreign trade and Hong Kong was ceded to Britain. The Taiping rebellion (1850-64) destroyed much of S China, and a war against Britain and France (1856-60) ended with further concessions, including the opening of Tientsin to foreign trade. Chinese power was crumbling. Korea obtained independence, Formosa was ceded to Japan; Russia secured railway rights in Manchuria and the lease of Port Arthur, Britain the lease of Wei-hai-wei and Germany of Kiaochow. The Boxer Rebellion (1900) was a final effort to expel the hated foreigner, and exhibited the crying need for reforms. Revolution, led by Sun Yat-sen, broke out in 1911, the last Manchu emperor abdicated (1912), and a republic was established with Yüan Shih-kai as president. The latter died in 1916, however, and China was once more plunged into chaos and civil war. Sun Yat-sen died in 1925, and his successor, Chiang Kai-shek, all but unified the country under Kuomintang rule and removed the capital from Peking to Nanking (1928).

Japan seized Manchuria, setting up the nominally independent state of Manchukuo (1931), and then invaded China proper (1937). China was not liberated from the Japanese till the end of the 2nd World War (1945). Kuomintang corruption and incompetence contrasted markedly with the efficiency of the Communists, Chiang Kai-shek and his dwindling Nationalist forces fled to Formosa before the Red Armies, and the People's Republic of China was proclaimed in Peking (1949). China recognized the independence of the Mongolian People's Republic (1946), but annexed Tibet (1950). A noteworthy result of China's subsequent foreign policy has been the strain put upon the 30-year treaty of 'friendship, alliance and mutual aid' with the USSR (1950) owing to the apparently divergent interpretations of Marxist philosophy by the two Communist governments. The so-called Cultural Revolution led to considerable internal unrest (1967–8). Relations with the USSR were further strained by border incidents along the ◊ *Ussuri R.*

Chinandega Nicaragua. Capital of the Chinandega department, 70 m. WNW of Managua. Pop. (1967) 36,885. Market town. Sugar refining, flour milling. Manufactures cotton goods, furniture.

China Sea. Section of the Pacific Ocean bordering on China and divided by Formosa (Taiwan) into the E China Sea (N) and the S China Sea (S).

Chincha Alta Peru. Town in the Ica department, 120 m. SE of Lima in a cotton- and vine-growing region. Pop. 29,000. Cotton ginning, brandy distilling.

Chinchow China. Formerly (1913–47) Chinhsien. Industrial town in Liaoning province 135 m. WSW of Shenyang on the railway to Peking. Pop. 352,000. Manufactures chemicals, synthetic fuels, textiles, paper, food products, etc. Developed by the Japanese in the 1930s. It was capital of the former Liaosi province.

Chindwin River Burma. Chief tributary of the Irrawaddy R., 650 m. long, formed in the extreme N from several headstreams and flowing generally S to join the latter 13 m. NE of Pakokku. Navigable for shallow-draught vessels for about 300 m.

Chingford England. Former municipal borough in Essex, on the edge of Epping Forest and 10 m. NE of London, for which it is a dormitory suburb; from 1965 part of the Greater London borough of Waltham

Forest. Pop. (1961) 45,777. A half-timbered 16th-cent. house, one of the hunting lodges of Queen Elizabeth I, is now a museum.

Chinghai ◊ *Tsinghai.*

Chinhsien ◊ *Chinchow.*

Chinkiang China. Town in the Kiangsu province, on the Yangtse-kiang at its junction with the Grand Canal. Pop. 201,000. Flour milling. Manufactures textiles, matches, etc. Trade in rice, wheat, soya beans. Opened to foreign trade 1859. Lost importance later owing to competition from Shanghai and the decline of the Grand Canal as a significant waterway.

Chinon France. Ancient town in the Indre-et-Loire department on the Vienne R. 26 m. WSW of Tours. Pop. (1968) 8,035. Produces wine, baskets, ropes, leather. The ruined castle (3 separate strongholds) on a rock above the town was the death-place of Henry II of England (1189) and the scene of Joan of Arc's first meeting with the Dauphin, later Charles VII of France (1429). Ancient churches: St Mexme (Romanesque), St Étienne, St Maurice. Near by is the birthplace of Rabelais (1494–1553).

Chioggia Italy. Town in Venezia province, in Veneto, on an island at the S end of the Venetian lagoon 16 m. S of the city; connected to the mainland by a bridge. Pop. (1961) 47,151. Important fishing port. Shipbuilding. Manufactures soap, textiles, cement. Has the 14th-cent. Church of San Martino, and an 11th-cent. cathedral rebuilt in the 17th cent. Scene of naval warfare between Genoa and Venice until Venice triumphed in 1378–81.

Chios (Gr. Khíos) Greece. 1. Island in the Aegean Sea off the coast of Asiatic Turkey, forming a *nome* with the neighbouring islands of Psará and Oinousa. Area 336 sq. m. Pop. (1961) 62,090. Famous for centuries for wine, figs, and mastic; also produces olives, almonds, citrus fruits. Sheep and goats raised. Its inhabitants suffered severely in the Turkish massacre of 1822.

2. Capital of the Chios *nome*, seaport on the E coast. Pop. (1961) 24,361. Exports wine, mastic, fruits. Boatbuilding, wine making, tanning. One of the twelve Ionian city states of antiquity, with a famous school of epic poets. A free city under the Romans. Prospered under Byzantine rule. Passed in turn to the Venetians, the Genoese, the Turks, and finally (1913) the Greeks.

**Chippenham** England. Municipal borough in Wiltshire, on the R. Avon 12 m. ENE of Bath. Pop. (1961) 17,525. Market town in a dairy-farming region. Bacon curing. Manufactures cheese, condensed milk. Engineering. Formerly important for trade in the wool obtained from sheep reared on the Cotswolds.

**Chipping Campden** England. Picturesque small town in the Cotswold Hills in NE Gloucestershire, 7 m. ESE of Evesham. Pop. 2,600. Many fine old houses, mainly 15th/16th-cent. and all built of local stone. Very important in the wool trade in the later Middle Ages.

**Chipping Norton** England. Municipal borough in Oxfordshire 11 m. SW of Banbury. Pop. (1961) 4,241. Market town. Manufactures tweeds. Has the 15th-cent. Church of St Mary the Virgin in Decorated and Perpendicular styles; 17th-cent. alms-houses. Churchill, 4 m. SW, was the birthplace of Warren Hastings (1732–1818).

**Chiquimula** Guatemala. Capital of the Chiquimula department, on the Chiquimula R. 65 m. ENE of Guatemala. Pop. 35,000. Market town in a region producing fruit, tobacco, sugar-cane, maize.

**Chiquinquirá** Colombia. Town in the Boyacá department at a height of 8,365 ft in the E Cordillera, 70 m. NNE of Bogotá. Pop. 24,000. Market for coffee, sugar-cane, cotton, wheat, maize, cattle. The famous Muzo emerald mines to the SW. Has the shrine of Our Lady of Chiquinquirá, a famous place of pilgrimage.

**Chirchik** USSR. Industrial town in the Uzbek SSR, on the Chirchik R. 20 m. NE of Tashkent. Pop. (1970) 108,000. Manufactures fertilizers, agricultural machinery, footwear, etc.

**Chiriqui, Gulf of** Panama. Gulf 90 m. wide and 15–20 m. long, on the Pacific coast.

**Chiriqui, Mount** Panama. Highest peak in Panama (11,397 ft), in the Chiriqui province near the Costa Rica frontier. An inactive volcano.

**Chiriqui Lagoon** Panama. Lagoon 35 m. long and 10–15 m. wide, on the Caribbean coast, enclosed by the Bocas del Toro archipelago.

**Chislehurst** England. Residential town in Kent, 11 m. SE of London, of which it is a dormitory suburb, from 1965 in the London borough of Bromley. Pop. (1961) 86,907. Camden Place, home of William Camden the antiquary, was the exile residence and death-place of Napoleon III. Ancient man-made cave-dwellings ('dene holes') in the chalk beneath Chislehurst Common.

**Chiswick** England. Residential district in Middlesex on the N bank of the Thames, formerly a municipal borough with Brentford; from 1965 part of the Greater London borough of Hounslow. Many attractive houses, including those of William Morris and Hogarth. Chiswick House, now national property, was a residence of the dukes of Devonshire. Burial-place of Hogarth and Whistler.

**Chita** USSR. Capital of the Chita Region (RSFSR), on the Trans-Siberian Railway and on the Chita R. near its confluence with the Ingoda R. Pop. (1970) 242,000. Industrial centre. Railway engineering, tanning, flour milling, etc. Developed with the advent of the railway (1897).

**Chitral** Pakistan. Former state in the Peshawar Division of W Pakistan. Area 5,700 sq. m. Pop. 113,000. Cap. Chitral. Extremely mountainous, rising to 25,260 ft in Tirich Mir. Cereals and fruits grown in the valleys. A small British and Sikh force was besieged and relieved at the town of Chitral in 1895.

**Chittagong** Pakistan. Chief seaport of E Pakistan, on the Karnaphuli R. 10 m. from the mouth and 135 m. SE of Dacca. Pop. (1961) 364,205. Exports jute, jute products, tea. Naval base. Industrial centre. Manufactures chemicals, textiles, soap, etc. Has developed greatly as a port since the partition of India (1947), having been overshadowed before by Calcutta. Suffered severely from cyclones in 1963 and 1965. Pakistan's first steel mill opened here in 1967.

**Chkalov** ♦ *Orenburg.*

**Chocó** ♦ *Buenaventura.*

**Choisy-le-Roi** France. Industrial suburb SSE of Paris, in the Val-de-Marne department on the Seine R. Pop. (1968) 41,711. Manufactures pottery, linoleum, hosiery, etc. Suffered much damage in the 2nd World War before the liberation of Paris.

**Cholet** France. Industrial town in the Maine-et-Loire department, 32 m. SW of Angers. Pop. (1968) 43,281. Manufactures textiles, footwear, etc. Suffered severely in the Vendée rebellion (1793–5).

**Cholon** S Vietnam. Industrial and commercial town 3 m. SW of Saigon, since 1932 administered as part of that city. Rice milling is a leading industry and is largely in the hands of the Chinese, who form about half the population. Sawmilling, tanning, etc. Manufactures pottery. Large river trade in rice and dried fish.

**Cholula (Cholula de Rivadavia)** Mexico. Town on the central plateau 6 m. W of Puebla at a height of 6,900 ft, on the Inter-American Highway. Pop. 13,000. Market town. Produces wine. An old Toltec city, it has the tallest pyramid in Mexico (177 ft), built of sun-dried bricks and earth, of great antiquity.

**Choluteca** Honduras. Capital of Choluteca department, on the Choluteca R. 60 m. S of Tegucigalpa, and on the Inter-American Highway. Pop. 11,000. Market town in an area producing maize, beans, coffee, sugar-cane.

**Chomutov** Czechoslovakia. Industrial town in NW Bohemia 52 m. NW of Prague. Pop. (1967) 38,000. In a coalmining district. Manufactures steel products, glass, paper, etc.

**Chonju** S Korea. Town 130 m. S of Seoul. Pop. (1960) 188,726. Rice milling. Manufactures textiles, paper, etc. Formerly noted for its handicraft industries.

**Chorley** England. Municipal borough in Lancashire, 9 m. NW of Bolton. Pop. (1961) 31,262. Industrial town. Cotton spinning and weaving, engineering, and other industries. Birthplace of Sir Henry Tate (1819–99).

**Chorzów** Poland. Formerly Królewska Huta (Ger. Königshutte). Industrial town in the Katowice voivodship, 4 m. NW of Katowice town. Pop. (1968) 150,400. In the Śląsk (Upper Silesia) coal and iron district. Manufactures steel, railway rolling stock, chemicals, glass, etc. Under German administration during the Partition (1794–1921); restored to Poland after the 1st World War. With the industrial development of the area the population rose rapidly, and after the 2nd World War again rose (129,000 in 1950).

**Chowkowtien** China. Village in Hopei province 35 m. SW of Peking where bones of the Peking Man (*Sinanthropus pekinensis*) were discovered in 1929.

**Christchurch** England. Municipal borough in SW Hampshire, just ENE of Bournemouth, on Christchurch Harbour and at the confluence of the Avon and the Stour rivers. Pop. (1961) 26,498. Holiday resort. Named after the famous Augustinian priory church, Holy Trinity. Has remains of the 12th-cent. castle and the Norman House.

**Christchurch** New Zealand. City on an almost flat site in the E of the Canterbury Plains, S Island, just NW of its port, Lyttelton. Pop. (1966) 161,566. Founded 1850. The success of its early planning and development owed much to the Anglican Canterbury Association. Parts of the city have an 'English atmosphere' by virtue of the old buildings, such as the cathedral and the provincial council chambers, schools and colleges, and through the use of stone and English trees; spacious suburbs, however, have made it now a large sprawling city. Numerous meat works, woollen mills, flour mills, tanneries, and canning plants process the produce of the eastern plains. Other factories manufacture chemicals, fertilizers, footwear, etc. and there are railway workshops and various light industries. An electrified railway and a highway pass S through tunnels to Lyttelton.

**Christianshaab** Greenland. Settlement in the W, on Disko Bay. Pop. (district) 600. Base for hunting and fishing. Seal-oil refinery. Founded 1734.

**Christiansted** ⬦ *St Croix*.

**Christmas Island** Indian Ocean. Originally Moni. Island in the Indian Ocean 200 m. S of the W end of Java. Area 52 sq. m. Pop. (1966) 3,381 (inc. 2,228 Chinese). Irregular in shape, with a central plateau, rising in places to over 1,000 ft, on which there is large-scale phosphate mining. Annexed by Britain 1888. Administered by Singapore 1900–1958, then transferred to Australia.

**Christmas Island** Pacific Ocean. One of the Line Is. in the central Pacific (1°58′ N, 157°27′ W). The largest atoll in the Pacific; area 223 sq. m. Pop. (1966) 356. Coconut plantations, producing copra. Discovered (1777) by Capt. Cook. Annexed by Britain; included in Gilbert and Ellice Is. colony 1919.

**Chukot NA USSR.** National Area in the RSFSR, in the extreme NE of Siberia. Area 275,000 sq. m. Pop. (1970) 101,000 (about one quarter Chukchi). Cap. Anadyr. Mainly tundra. Chief occupations reindeer herding, fishing, hunting (fur-bearing animals).

**Chungking** China. Important river port in Szechwan province, on the Yangtse R. at its confluence with the Kialing R. Pop. (1957) 2,121,000. As the chief outlet for Szechwan, trades in tung oil, hog bristles, tea, etc. Iron and steel plants. Manufactures textiles, paper, chemicals, matches, etc. (industries mainly developed since the 2nd World War). Linked with Burma via Kunming and the famous Burma Road, with Chengtu by rail (1952). Airport. Its history dates back to the Hsia dynasty, in the 3rd millennium B.C. Chungking was the wartime capital of China (1937–46); severely damaged by Japanese bombing.

**Chuquicamata** Chile. Mining town in the Antofagasta province, on an arid plateau in the Andes at a height of over 10,000 ft. Pop. 30,000. One of the world's largest opencast mines (copper). Smelting is carried out by utilizing electric power from Tocopilla, and water is piped from Andean streams.

**Chuquisaca** ♢ *Sucre*.

**Chur** (Fr. **Coire**) Switzerland. Ancient Curia Rhaetorum. Capital of the Graubünden (Grisons) canton, on the Plessur R. at a height of 1,950 ft, surrounded by mountains. Pop. (1969) 30,900. Commercial and tourist centre. Trade in wine. The meeting-point of routes from the Splügen and the San Bernardino passes. Long an episcopal see (5th cent.). Has a 12th/13th-cent. Romanesque and Gothic cathedral and a 15th-cent. Rathaus. Birthplace of the artist Angelica Kauffmann (1741–1807).

**Churchill** Canada. Seaport and railway terminus in Manitoba, at the mouth of the Churchill R. on Hudson Bay. Pop. (1966) 1,689. The trading post established (1688) by the Hudson's Bay Company was named after Lord Churchill (later the Duke of Marlborough). Replaced in 1718 by Fort Churchill, which in 1733 was replaced by Fort Prince of Wales; this was destroyed by the French (1782) and Fort Churchill was re-established. It was reached by the railway in 1929, and grain was shipped (mid Aug.–mid Oct.) from 1931.

**Churchill River** Canada. **1**. River 925 m. long, rising in L. Methy in NW Saskatchewan and flowing generally E through several lakes to Hudson Bay at Churchill. Long known as the English R. (the route to the interior used by English or Hudson's Bay Company fur traders). Hydroelectric power plant at Island Falls.
**2**. Formerly Hamilton R. River in Labrador 560 m. long, rising near the Quebec border in L. Ashuanipi. Flowing N and then SE, through several lakes, at Churchill Falls (formerly Hamilton Falls) just below Lobstick L. it descends over 800 ft in 10 m., with one spectacular drop of 245 ft; hydroelectric power is being developed here.

Then continues generally E to L. Melville and the Atlantic.

**Church Stretton** England. Small market town in Shropshire, 13 m. S of Shrewsbury. Pop. (1961) 2,712. The name Stretton (Street Town) derives from its situation on a Roman road. 2 m. NE is the site of an ancient British camp.

**Chusan** (**Chushan**) **Archipelago** China. Group of islands in the E China Sea off Hangchow Bay, on important fishing grounds but dangerous to navigation owing to fogs and strong currents. Largest island Chusan (230 sq. m.).

**Chuvash ASSR** USSR. Autonomous republic in RSFSR, in the middle Volga valley, bordered on the N by the Volga and on the W by the Sura R. Area 7,064 sq. m. Pop. (1970) 1,224,000 (about three quarters Chuvash, of Finno-Tatar origin; the remainder mainly Russian). Cap. Cheboksary. Agriculture (esp. the cultivation of cereals and fodder crops) and lumbering have long been important occupations, on which the industries developed since the 1917 revolution (e.g. flour milling, tanning, woodworking) are largely based.

**Cicero** USA. Industrial town in Illinois, just W of Chicago. Pop. (1960) 69,130. Manufactures radio, telephone and electrical equipment, metal products, building materials, hardware, etc. Founded 1857.

**Ciénaga** Colombia. Seaport in the Magdalena department on the Caribbean coast 40 m. E of Barranquilla. Pop. 70,000. Exports bananas, cotton, etc.

**Cienfuegos** Cuba. Seaport on the S coast, on Cienfuegos (Jagua) Bay 135 m. ESE of Havana. Pop. (1960) 99,530. Exports sugar. Manufactures cigars, soap, etc. Sugar refining, coffee processing. Trade in tobacco, coffee, molasses. One of the most picturesque cities in Cuba. Founded (1819) by the French General Luis d'Clouet, from Louisiana.

**Cieszyn** (**Těšín**, Ger. **Teschen**) Poland. Town in the Katowice voivodship in Silesia. Pop. (1968) 24,700. Former capital of a principality, long disputed. Passed to the Habsburgs in the 16th cent. After the 1st World War the newly re-created Poland received Cieszyn town and the new state of Czechoslovakia the W suburb of Těšín. Poland occupied the whole area on the dismemberment of Czechoslovakia by Nazi Germany (1938). The division was restored under the Potsdam Agreement (1945).

**Cilicia.** Ancient region in Asia Minor, now

in S Turkey, between the Taurus Mountains and the Mediterranean Sea. The road from Tarsus, one of its chief towns, through the Taurus Mountains by the pass called the Cilician Gates was an important route to the interior. In the 11th cent. a small Armenian (Christian) principality was established here, developed into a kingdom, and lasted for almost 3 centuries.

**Cimarron River** USA. River 650 m. long, rising in NE New Mexico and flowing generally E through the Oklahoma Panhandle and SE Colorado, then across SW Kansas, and re-entering Oklahoma to join the Arkansas R.

**Cincinnati** USA. Second largest city in Ohio, on the Ohio R. Pop. (1960) 502,550. Route and commercial centre for an extensive region of Ohio, Kentucky, and Indiana. Industries include meat packing and the manufacture of chemicals, machine tools, clothing, paper, motor vehicles, plastics, and machinery. Seat of the Xavier University (1831) and the University of Cincinnati (1874). Standing largely on two terraces above a bend in the Ohio R., it has spread into the surrounding hills. Founded in 1788, it was named Losantiville (a hybrid word meaning 'the city opposite the mouth of the Licking River'); in 1790 it was renamed Cincinnati in honour of General St Clair, Governor of the Northwest Territory and president of the Pennsylvania Society of the Order of Cincinnati. Many German, Irish, and British immigrants arrived during the 19th cent., many Italians and Russians in the early 20th cent.

**Cinderford** England. Town in Gloucestershire, 11 m. WSW of Gloucester. Pop. (1961) 7,100. In a coalmining and agricultural district in the Forest of Dean.

**Cinque Ports** England. Originally, the 5 ports (Hastings, Romney, Hythe, Dover, Sandwich) which in the 11th cent. were given privileges amounting almost to autonomy, in return for furnishing the English Crown with ships in time of war. Later Winchelsea and Rye were added, and then subsidiary 'limbs' or 'members', e.g. Deal, Folkestone. Their importance declined in the 17th and 18th cent. The office of Lord Warden formerly carried important civil, military, and naval powers; it survives as a title of honour awarded for outstanding service to the Crown: Sir Winston Churchill received it in 1946.

**Cintra** ◊ *Sintra*.

**Cirencester** England. Ancient Corinium.

Urban district in Gloucestershire, on the R. Churn (a headstream of the Thames) 15 m. SE of Gloucester. Pop. (1961) 11,836. Market town. Hunting centre. Engineering. Many Roman remains, including an amphitheatre. The parish church is in Perpendicular style. Remains of a 12th-cent. Augustinian abbey. An important wool centre in the Middle Ages, but the trade declined.

**Citlaltépetl** ◊ *Orizaba, Pico de.*

**Città di Castello** Italy. Walled town in Perugia province, in Umbria, on the Tiber R. 20 m. E of Arezzo. Pop. (1961) 37,413. Manufactures agricultural machinery, cement, etc. Cathedral. Renaissance palaces.

**Città Vecchia (Mdina)** Malta. Former capital, 6 m. W of Valletta. Roman remains. Cathedral (12th-cent., rebuilt after the destruction of the town by earthquake in 1693). Severely damaged in the 2nd World War.

**Ciudad Bolívar** Venezuela. Formerly Angostura. Capital of the Bolívar state, river port on the Orinoco R. 250 m. from the delta, on narrows: hence the former name (in Spanish, 'Narrows'). Pop. 56,000. Accessible to ocean-going vessels. Exports cattle, hides, balata gum, chicle, gold, etc. Angostura bitters were invented here (1824) but the distillery moved (1875) to Port of Spain (Trinidad).

**Ciudad Juarez** Mexico. Formerly El Paso del Norte. City in the Chihuahua province, on the Rio Grande and the US border, opposite El Paso (Texas). Pop. (1969) 522,000. Commercial centre. Flour milling, cotton ginning, etc. Thriving souvenir trade with American tourists. Enclosed by desert, except for the river valley, where maize, cotton, and alfalfa are grown and cattle raised. Originally a base for Spanish colonial expansion northwards. City founded 1681–2. Renamed (1888) in honour of President Benito Juárez, who had made it his capital for a time.

**Ciudad Real** Spain. 1. Province formed (1833) from parts of New Castile, mostly occupying the La Mancha plain. Area 7,622 sq. m. Pop. (1961) 583,948. Agriculture. Mercury, lead, etc. mined.
2. Capital of the Ciudad Real province, on the plain between the Guadiana and Jabalón rivers. Pop. (1961) 36,000. Trade in cereals, olive oil, wine. Flour milling, brandy distilling. Textile industry. Founded in the mid 13th cent. by Alfonso X of Castile.

**Ciudad Trujillo** ◊ *Santo Domingo*.

**Ciudad Victoria** Mexico. Capital of the Tamaulipas province, at the E foot of the Sierra Madre Oriental at a height of 1,100 ft 130 m. NNW of Tampico. Pop. 51,000. Agricultural and mining centre. Textile and tanning industries.

**Civitavecchia** Italy. Seaport in Roma province in Latium, 37 m. WNW of Rome, which it serves. Pop. (1961) 38,138. Fishing. Manufactures cement, calcium carbide, etc. Has a citadel designed by Michelangelo. Founded by Trajan in the 1st cent. A.D.

**Clackmannan** Scotland. Former county town of Clackmannanshire, 2 m. ESE of Alloa. Pop. 2,350. Coalmining.

**Clackmannanshire** Scotland. The smallest county in Scotland, between the Ochil hills (where it rises to 2,363 ft) and the R. Forth. Area 55 sq. m. Pop. (1961) 41,391. County town Alloa. Coalmining. Woollen milling, brewing, whisky distilling. Chief towns Alloa, Alva, Clackmannan, Dollar, Tillicoultry.

**Clacton-on-Sea** England. Urban district in E Essex 12 m. ESE of Colchester. Pop. (1961) 27,543. Popular seaside resort.

**Clamart** France. Residential suburb in SW Paris. Pop. (1968) 55,299.

**Clapham** England. Residential district in SW London; from 1965 in the Greater London borough of Wandsworth. Contains Clapham Common (205 acres). Clapham Junction, handling over 2,000 trains daily, is Britain's busiest railway station. Home of William Wilberforce (1759–1833), slave-trade abolitionist and member of the 'Clapham Sect'.

**Clare** England. Picturesque market town in SW Suffolk, on the R. Stour 13 m. SSW of Bury St Edmunds. Pop. (1961) 1,320. A former stronghold of the E Anglian kingdom. Remains of an ancient castle and of a 13th-cent. priory.

**Clare** Irish Republic. County in Munster, on the W coast between Galway Bay and the Shannon estuary. Area 1,231 sq. m. Pop. (1966) 73,702. County town Ennis. Hilly in the E and N, low-lying and more fertile along the Shannon estuary (S), with a rugged Atlantic coastline (Cliffs of Moher). Chief rivers the Shannon (with Lough Derg and the Ardnacrusha power station) and its tributary the Fergus. Salmon fishing. Dairy farming. Oats and potatoes cultivated. Many round towers and other historic remains. Chief towns Ennis, Kilrush.

**Clarke Island** ◊ *Furneaux Islands*.

**Clarksburg** USA. Industrial town in W Virginia, on the West Fork (headstream of the Monongahela R.). Pop. (1960) 28,112. In a region producing coal and natural gas. Manufactures glass, pottery, clothing, etc. Birthplace of Thomas J. ('Stonewall') Jackson (1824–63).

**Clay Cross** England. Urban district in Derbyshire, 5 m. S of Chesterfield. Pop. (1961) 9,173. In a coalmining district. Iron founding, engineering, brickmaking.

**Clear, Cape** Irish Republic. Headland on Clear Island off the SW coast of Co. Cork; the most southerly point in Ireland. Lighthouse.

**Clearwater** USA. Town in W Florida 20 m. W of Tampa. Pop. (1960) 34,653. Resort. Citrus-fruit packing and market-gardening centre.

**Cleator Moor** England. Former urban district in Cumberland, 3 m. SE of Whitehaven; dissolved and incorporated in Ennerdale rural district (1934). Pop. (1961) 6,411. Coalmining declined during the depression of the 1930s.

**Cleckheaton** ◊ *Spenborough*.

**Cleethorpes** England. Municipal borough in Lincolnshire, on the Humber estuary 2 m. ESE of Grimsby. Pop. (1961) 32,705. Seaside resort.

**Clent Hills** England. Short range in Worcestershire, SW of Birmingham. At the N end is St Kenelm's Chapel, built over a spring, formerly a famous place of pilgrimage.

**Clerkenwell** England. District in the former metropolitan borough of Finsbury, London; from 1965 in the Greater London borough of Islington. Named after the well, long lost but rediscovered in 1924, where parish clerks used to perform miracle plays. Once noted for watchmaking, later replaced by watch-repairing. Grew up as two parishes round the nunnery of St Mary and the priory of St John, the latter the headquarters in England of the Knights Hospitallers of the Order of St John of Jerusalem.

**Clermont-Ferrand** France. Ancient Augustonemetum. Prefecture of the Puy-de-Dôme department, at the foot of a volcanic range including the Puy de Dôme (4,806 ft). Pop. (1968) 154,110. Chief industrial centre of the Massif Central. Important rubber factories. Manufactures tyres and rubberized clothing, also machinery, chemicals, clothing, footwear. Gothic cathedral (13th/15th-cent.). University (1808). Founded by the Romans. Capital of the duchy of Auvergne in the 16th cent. Birthplace of Blaise Pascal (1623–62).

**Clevedon** England. Urban district in Somerset, on the Bristol Channel 12 m. W of Bristol. Pop. (1961) 10,642. Seaside resort. Clevedon Court (14th-cent.) is 'Castlewood' in Thackeray's *Henry Esmond*.

**Cleveland** England. Hilly district in the N Riding of Yorkshire, S and SE of Middlesbrough, rising in the S to nearly 1,500 ft. Formerly an important iron-mining district. The iron and steel industry is centred on Middlesbrough.

**Cleveland** USA. Largest city in Ohio, eleventh largest in the USA, on L. Erie, at the mouth of the Cuyahoga R. Pop. (1970) 738,956. A leading Great Lakes port, ideally placed to manufacture steel from L. Superior iron ore and Ohio coal. The steel mills are among the world's largest; also oil refineries, machine shops, foundries, meat-packing plants, and factories manufacturing chemicals, cement, cars, electrical appliances, etc. Seat of the Western Reserve University (1826) and the Case Institute of Technology (1880). First settled in 1796. Laid out by Moses Cleaveland (1754–1806), agent of the Connecticut Land Company, after whom it was named (the 'a' in Cleaveland was dropped in 1832). Developed rapidly with the coming of the Ohio and Erie Canal (1832) and the railway (1851). The rise of the Rockefeller family began here.

**Cleves** (Ger. **Kleve**) Federal German Republic. Town in N Rhine-Westphalia near the Dutch border. Pop. 23,000. Manufactures margarine, biscuits, footwear. Among buildings damaged in the 2nd World War were the Schwanenburg, the 11th-cent. castle of Wagner's *Lohengrin*, and the 14th/15th-cent. collegiate church. Birthplace of Anne of Cleves (1515–57), 4th wife of Henry VIII.

**Clichy** (**Clichy-la-Garenne**) France. Industrial suburb of NW Paris, in the Hauts-de-Seine department. Pop. (1968) 52,704. Oil refining. Manufactures motor-vehicle and aircraft parts, chemicals, plastics, electrical equipment, etc. The famous Beaujon hospital was moved here in 1935.

**Clifton** USA. Industrial town in NE New Jersey, just SSE of Paterson. Pop. (1960) 82,084. Manufactures aircraft propellers, clothing, machine tools, textiles, chemicals, etc.

**Clinton** USA. Town on the Mississippi R., in Iowa 75 m. ESE of Cedar Rapids. Pop. (1960) 33,589. Industrial centre. Manufactures machine tools, pumps, hardware, cellophane, etc. Named after De Witt Clinton, former Governor of New York. Grew as a sawmilling centre, but when timber supplies diminished turned to other industries.

**Clitheroe** England. Municipal borough in E Lancashire, on the R. Ribble at the foot of Pendle Hill (1,831 ft). Pop. (1961) 12,147. Manufactures cotton goods, paper. Limestone quarried in the neighbourhood. A ruined Norman castle and its grounds serve as a war memorial.

**Cloncurry** Australia. Town in Queensland 415 m. WSW of Townsville, to which it is linked by railway. Pop. (1966) 2,149. Once a small goldmining centre; now serves a huge beef cattle area, sending livestock to the coast. Mineral production now overshadowed by Mt Isa, 70 m. W. Important airport.

**Clonmacnoise** Irish Republic. Village in Co. Offaly, on the R. Shannon 10 m. E of Ballinasloe. Ireland's most remarkable ecclesiastical ruins, inc. the Seven Churches (the oldest built in 904), two round towers, and three Celtic crosses. Site of monastery (founded by St Kieran 541) which became a seat of learning where the famous medieval works *The Book of the Dun Cow* and *Abbot Tigenach's Annals* were written.

**Clonmel** Irish Republic. County town of Co. Tipperary, on the R. Suir. Pop. (1966) 11,031. Market town. Sporting centre (hunting, fishing, horseracing). Flour milling, ham and bacon curing. Original starting-point of the 'bians', rapid and regular coaches carrying both goods and passengers, which were Ireland's sole public transport until the railway age, named after Bianconi, who established the service (1815). Birthplace of Laurence Sterne (1713–68).

**Clovelly** England. Small seaside resort and fishing village in Devonshire, on Bideford Bay in the Bristol Channel. Pop. 500. The steep main street rises 400 ft in wide steps, making the use of any wheeled transport impossible.

**Cluj** Rumania. Capital of the Cluj district and former capital of Transylvania, on the Little Somes R. 210 m. NW of Bucharest. Pop. (1968) 191,411. Has developed from a mainly residential town into an important commercial and industrial centre. Manufactures metal products, hardware, chemicals, textiles, etc. Several educational institutions, including a university (1945). Has the 14th/15th-cent. Gothic Church of St Michael. Seat of 4 bishoprics (Eastern Orthodox, Uniate, Reformed, Unitarian). Birthplace of Matthias Corvinus of Hungary (1440–90).

**Cluny** France. Town in the Saône-et-Loire department, 12 m. NW of Mâcon, on the Grosne R. Pop. (1968) 4,268. Grew up round the famous Benedictine abbey (founded 910), a leading religious and cultural centre in the Middle Ages. Until the erection of St Peter's in Rome the abbey church (a Romanesque building completed in the 12th cent., of which only parts remain) was the largest in Christendom. Birthplace of Prud'hon (1758–1823).

**Clutha River** New Zealand. Longest river in the S Island (150 m.), rising in Lakes Wanaka and Hawea and flowing SE through Otago to the delta near Kaitangata. Navigable by small vessels to Roxburgh, where it is dammed for a large hydroelectric station.

**Clydebank** Scotland. Large burgh in Dunbartonshire, on the R. Clyde 6 m. WNW of Glasgow. Pop. (1961) 49,654. Many of the world's largest ships (*Queen Mary*, *Queen Elizabeth*, etc.) have been built in the great shipyards. Manufactures sewing machines etc. Severely damaged by air raids during the 2nd World War.

**Clyde River** Scotland. The most important (though not the longest) river in Scotland, rising (as the Daer Water) in S Lanarkshire, and flowing 106 m. N and NW past Lanark, Hamilton, Glasgow, Clydebank, and Dumbarton (where it widens into the Firth of Clyde). Near Lanark it descends 230 ft in less than 4 m. in the four famous Falls of Clyde. Below Lanark it passes through a fertile fruit-growing area, then through the main industrial region of Scotland. Below Glasgow (which is accessible to ocean-going vessels) the banks are lined with shipyards for some 20 m. Linked with the R. Forth by a canal.

**Cnidus.** Ancient Greek city of SW Asia Minor, from *c.* 330 B.C. on Cape Krio. A prosperous port, famous for its educational institutions. Here in one of the temples was the celebrated statue of Aphrodite by Praxiteles. The Athenians defeated the Spartans in a naval battle off Cnidus (394 B.C.).

**Cnossus** ◊ *Knossos*.

**Coahuila** Mexico. State in the N, bounded on the N and NE by Texas (USA), consisting mainly of broken plateau, crossed by the Sierra Madre Oriental and sloping gently down to the Rio Grande. Area 58,067 sq. m. Pop. (1969) 1,225,000. Cap. Saltillo. In the W is Mexico's main cotton-growing area. Coal, silver, lead, and copper mined. First settled by the Spanish (around Saltillo) *c.* 1575.

**Coalbanks** ◊ *Lethbridge*.

**Coalville** England. Urban district in NW Leicestershire, 12 m. NW of Leicester. Pop. (1961) 26,159. Coalmining centre. Engineering, brickmaking, and other industries.

**Coatbridge** Scotland. Large burgh in N Lanarkshire, 9 m. E of Glasgow. Pop. (1961) 53,946. Coalmining centre. Manufactures iron and steel, wire ropes, etc.

**Coats Island** ◊ *Hudson Bay*.

**Coatzacoalcos (Puerto Mexico)** Mexico. Port near the mouth of the Coatzacoalcos R. on the Gulf of Campeche. Pop. 37,000. Linked by rail across the Isthmus of Tehuantepec with Salina Cruz, on the Pacific. Exports petroleum products etc.

**Cobán** Guatemala. Capital of Alta Verapaz department, 70 m. N of Guatemala at a height of 4,300 ft. Pop. (1964) 38,426. Market town in a coffee-growing region.

**Cóbh** Irish Republic. Formerly Queenstown. Seaport on the S shore of Great Island in Cork harbour. Pop. (1966) 5,613. Port of call for Atlantic liners. Holiday resort. The cathedral (St Colman) is the burial-place of Charles Wolfe (1791–1823), author of *The Burial of Sir John Moore*. Renamed Queenstown after a visit by Queen Victoria (1849); the old name was restored in 1922.

**Coblenz (Ger. Koblenz)** Federal German Republic. Ancient Confluentes. City in the Rhineland-Palatinate on the Rhine R. at its confluence with the Mosel R.; the name is a corruption of the Roman name. Pop. (1968) 102,859. Centre of the wine trade. Manufactures pianos, furniture, footwear, paper, etc. In the old city are the 13th-cent. castle and a fine 13th/15th-cent. church; in the new city is the 18th-cent. palace of Clement Wenceslaus. Across the Rhine is the fortress of Ehrenbreitstein. Founded *c.* 9 B.C. as a Roman military post. Held by the archbishop-electors of Trier 1018–1794, was taken by France, passed to Prussia (1815), and was capital of the

Rhine province 1824–1945. In 1946 it became capital of the new Rhineland-Palatinate *Land*, but was superseded by Mainz (1950). Severely damaged in the 2nd World War. Birthplace of Prince Metternich (1773–1859).

Coburg Federal German Republic. Town in N Bavaria, on the Itz R. 57 m. N of Nuremberg. Pop. (1963) 43,100. Manufactures machinery, toys, porcelain, etc. Has a 16th-cent. ducal palace, and a castle (mentioned in the 11th cent.) where Luther lived during the Diet of Augsburg (1530). Former capital of Saxe-Coburg but united to Bavaria in 1920. Near by is the birthplace of Prince Albert (1819–61), consort of Queen Victoria.

Cochabamba Bolivia. Formerly Oropeza. Capital of the Cochabamba department, the second largest city in Bolivia, in a fertile, closely settled basin, at a height of 8,570 ft in the E Andes, 80 m. ENE of Oruro. Pop. (1962) 92,008. Centre for Bolivia's main agricultural area, producing grain and fruit. Oil piped from the Camiri oilfield and refined. Manufactures furniture, footwear, tyres. Also a resort, with a mild climate. University (1832).

Cochin India. 1. Former state in the SW between the Anaimalai Hills and the Malabar coast; later in Travancore-Cochin state and now part of Kerala. Area 1,493 sq. m. 2. Seaport in Kerala, on the Malabar coast 110 m. NNW of Trivandrum. Pop. (1961) 35,076. Exports copra, coir ropes and mats, tea, etc. Imports rice, petroleum products, etc. Manufactures coir products, plywood, etc. Harbour considerably improved since 1920. Site of a naval base. The earliest European settlement in India (1503).

Cochin-China. Former French colony of Indo-China, since 1949 S Vietnam.

Cockatoo Island ◊ *Yampi Sound.*

Cockburn Sound ◊ *Kwinana.*

Cockenzie and Port Seton Scotland. Small burgh in E Lothian, on the Firth of Forth, comprising two neighbouring fishing ports. Pop. (1961) 3,462.

Cockermouth England. Urban district in W Cumberland, at the confluence of the Cocker and the Derwent rivers on the NW edge of the Lake District. Pop. (1961) 5,823. Manufactures footwear. Birthplace of William Wordsworth (1770–1850).

Coco River Nicaragua. Formerly Wanks R. River 400 m. long, rising in Honduras, flowing generally ENE through Nicaragua, forming the boundary with Honduras for

much of its length, and entering the Caribbean Sea by a delta at Cabo Gracias a Díos. Partly navigable; used mainly for floating timber.

Cocos Island (Sp. Isla del Coco) Pacific Ocean. Uninhabited island in the E Pacific 200 m. SW of the Osa Peninsula in Costa Rica (to which it belongs). Area 9 sq. m. Famous for stories of buried treasure; searched unsuccessfully by many expeditions.

Cocos (Keeling) Islands Indian Ocean. Group of 27 coral islands in the Indian Ocean, 1,700 m. NW of Perth (Australia); since 1955 forming a Territory of the Commonwealth of Australia. Area 5 sq. m. Pop. (1967) 631 (largely Malays). The main islands, which are low-lying and covered with coconut palms (hence the name), are West, Home, and Direction islands. Exports coconuts, copra, coconut oil. The airport on West Island is a refuelling point on the air route between Australia and S Africa. Discovered (1609) by Captain Keeling of the East India Company. Settled (1825) by a Scotsman, John Clunies Ross. Annexed to the Crown 1857; then attached in turn to Ceylon (1878), Straits Settlements (1882), and Singapore (1903).

Cod, Cape USA. Low sandy peninsula 65 m. long in SE Massachusetts, curving round to enclose Cape Cod Bay, on the shore of which the Pilgrim Fathers landed in 1620 (◊ *Plymouth*, USA). Produces cranberries. Many summer resorts and fishing villages, including Barnstable, Falmouth, Truro, Chatham.

Cognac France. Ancient town in the Charente department, on the Charente R. 60 m. NNE of Bordeaux. Pop. (1968) 22,515. The famous brandy is distilled from wine made with local grapes. Subsidiary industries, e.g. making bottles, corks, crates, barrels, hoops. Birthplace of François I; scene of his alliance against the Emperor Charles V (1526).

Coimbatore India. Industrial town in Madras on the Noyil R. 265 m. SW of Madras, in a pleasant situation at a height of 1,437 ft in the Nilgiri Hills. Pop. (1961) 286,305. Rice and flour milling. Manufactures textiles, fertilizers, leather; industries powered by the Pykara hydroelectric scheme. Near by at Perur is an 18th-cent. temple.

Coimbra Portugal. Capital of the Coimbra district, on a hill above the Mondego R. 115 m. NNE of Lisbon. Pop. (1960) 46,313.

Market for wine, grain, olives. Manufactures pottery. An important cultural centre. Seat of Portugal's oldest university (founded in Lisbon 1290; permanently transferred here 1537). Two cathedrals. The famous Quinta das Lagrimas (House of Tears), where Inés de Castro was murdered (1355). Capital of Portugal 1139–1260.

**Colbeck, Cape** ◊ *Ross Sea.*

**Colchester** England. Ancient Camulodunum. Municipal borough in NE Essex, on the R. Colne. Pop. (1961) 65,072. Market town. Engineering. Market gardening, rose growing. Manufactures agricultural implements, chemicals, footwear. Seat of the University of Essex (1961). Capital of the British chief Cunobelinus (Cymbeline); sacked in Boadicea's rebellion (A.D. 62). Many remains, inc. part of the Roman wall. The Norman castle has a museum of Roman and other antiquities. Augustinian priory, St Botolph (12th-cent., built chiefly of Roman brick). An important port in the 13th cent. The oyster fisheries at the mouth of the Colne have been famous for many centuries.

**Colchis.** In ancient times a region on the E coast of the Black Sea along the lower Rion R., now in the Georgian SSR. Famous in Greek mythology as the home of Medea and the destination of the Argonauts. Now known as Kolkhida: a low-lying swampy area, much of which has been drained and cultivated in recent years (citrus fruits etc.).

**Coldstream** Scotland. Small burgh in Berwickshire, on the R. Tweed 12 m. SW of Berwick-on-Tweed, linked by bridge with Cornhill (England). Pop. (1961) 1,227. Once the resort of runaway couples intent on marriage, which was solemnized at the old Toll House. From here General Monck marched into England with the troops he had raised (1660); in commemoration of the event, the pick of his regiments was named the Coldstream Guards.

**Colenso** S Africa. Village in Natal on the Tugela R. Pop. (1960) 2,034. Scene of a defeat of the British forces attempting to relieve Ladysmith during the Boer War (1899). Named after the first Anglican bishop of Natal, J. W. Colenso (1814–83), a scholar of the Zulu language.

**Coleraine** Northern Ireland. Municipal borough in Londonderry, on the R. Bann estuary. Pop. (1961) 11,912. Seaport. Salmon fishing. Whisky distilling. Bacon and ham curing. Manufactures shirts and linen. Seat of the New University of Ulster (1968).

**Coleshill** ◊ *Amersham.*

**Colima** Mexico. 1. Small state in the W, on the Pacific, including the Revilla Gigedo Is. 500 m. offshore. Area 2,016 sq. m. Pop. (1969) 238,000. Mainly agricultural, producing sugar-cane, rice, maize, etc.
2. Capital of Colima state, on the Colima R. 45 m. ENE of Manzanillo, its port. Pop. 44,000. Market town processing maize, rice, sugar-cane, etc. Manufactures cigars, shoes.

**Colima, Mount** Mexico. Volcano (12,278 ft) in the Jalisco state, near the Colima border. Erupted, with loss of life, in 1941. Just N is Nevado de Colima (14,235 ft), an inactive volcano.

**Colmar** France. Prefecture of the Haut-Rhin department, on the plain just E of the Vosges, 23 m. N of Mulhouse. Pop. (1968) 62,341. Centre of the Alsatian cotton industry. Manufactures woollen, silk, and rayon goods, starch. Brewing, flour milling. Trade in Alsatian wines. Typically Alsatian in character. Many notable buildings, e.g. the 16th-cent. Maison Pfister, the 17th-cent. Maison des Têtes, and a 13th/14th-cent. Dominican monastery (now a museum). Became a free imperial city 1226. Annexed to France 1681. Held by Germany 1871–1919 and 1940–5. Birthplace of F. Bartholdi, the sculptor (1834–1904).

**Colne** England. Municipal borough in NE Lancashire, 6 m. NNE of Burnley. Pop. (1961) 19,410. Industrial town. Cotton, rayon, and woollen industries. Tanning.

**Colne River** England. 1. River 35 m. long, rising in NW Essex, flowing SE past Halstead and Colchester, and entering the North Sea at Mersea Island.
2. River 35 m. long, rising near Hatfield (Hertfordshire), flowing SW and S past Watford and Uxbridge, forming part of the boundary between Buckinghamshire and Middlesex, and joining the Thames at Staines.

**Colne Valley** England. Urban district in the W Riding of Yorkshire, 5 m. WSW of Huddersfield. Pop. (1961) 21,309. Manufactures woollen goods, chemicals, textile machinery.

**Cologne (Ger. Köln)** Federal German Republic. Ancient Colonia Agrippinensis. Largest city in N Rhine–Westphalia and third largest city in W Germany, on the Rhine R. Pop. (1968) 854,482. River port. Industrial city. Banking and insurance centre. Manufactures motor vehicles, railway rolling stock, machine tools, cables, chemical and pharmaceutical goods, perfume (inc. eau de Cologne, first produced here early in the 18th cent.), chocolate, etc. The famous Gothic cathedral (begun 1248; not completed till 1880) was not seriously damaged in the 2nd World War, but many other historic buildings were destroyed. University (founded 1388; suspended from 1798; refounded 1919). Originally the chief town of the Ubii. Made a Roman colony (A.D. 50) by the Emperor Claudius for his wife Agrippina, who was born here. A bishopric from the 4th cent., it was raised to an archdiocese by Charlemagne in 785, and its archbishops long wielded great political power. In medieval times it prospered commercially, became a leading member of the Hanseatic League (1201), and in 1474 was created a free imperial city. Captured by the French in 1794, the see was secularized (1801) and its territories assigned to Prussia (1815). Once more the city prospered, and from 1881 to 1921 its area was considerably increased.

**Colomb-Béchar** Algeria. Capital of the Saoura department (the more westerly of the two Saharan departments), near the frontier with Morocco 500 m. SW of Algiers. Pop. (1967) 27,000. Oasis town, with many date palms. On the projected Trans-Saharan railway from Ghazaouet (on the Mediterranean coast), which ends at Abadla (50 m. SSW). Linked by rail with Algeria's only coalmining area, Kenadsa (13 m. WSW).

**Colombes** France. Industrial and residential suburb in NW Paris, in the Hauts-de-Seine department. Pop. (1968) 80,616. Well-known sports stadium. Engineering, chemical, hosiery, and other industries.

**Colombey-les-deux-Églises** France. Village in the Haute-Marne department, 8 m. E of Bar-sur-Aube. Private residence of the late President de Gaulle.

**Colombia.** Republic in the NW of S America, the fourth largest country in the continent, and the only one with both Atlantic and Pacific coastlines. Area 462,000 sq. m. Pop. (1964) 17,484,508 (20 per cent white, 10 per cent Indian, and the rest mixed, apart from some Negroes along the coast). Cap. Bogotá. One of the country's greatest difficulties is transport; Bogotá and other centres of population are in mountainous districts far from the ocean. The population, which is increasing rapidly, is not homogeneous and differs in composition in the various isolated clusters. Main crop coffee (over 70 per cent of all exports); broadly self-supporting in food production. Substantial petroleum exports. Many diseases are endemic; housing is poor and both the birth-rate and the death-rate are very high. Industry has been growing; nearly half the employed are in industrial or commercial occupations. The amended constitution of 1957 provides that the Congress should consist of equal numbers of the main parties (Liberals and Conservatives) and that the President should be from each party alternately for four-year terms. There is freedom of the press and religion. Administratively divided into 20 departments, 3 intendencies, and 5 commissaries.

TOPOGRAPHY AND CLIMATE. Three fifths of the country is almost uninhabited tropical lowland. In the SW the Andes divide into parallel Cordilleras, separated by long deep valleys open to the N. Along the Pacific coast is a relatively low range, inland of which is lowland drained to the Caribbean by the Atrato R. and to the Pacific by the San Juan. The W and central Cordilleras are separated in the S by a high rift valley, with the upper course of the Cauca R. Farther N the Cauca valley is wide and fertile, then narrow and steep-sided, until the river emerges on to flat marshy lowland and joins the Magdalena R., which rises about 2° N (where the central and E Cordilleras separate) and flows N through a wide level-floored valley to the N lowlands. The W Cordillera is the lowest, and the central the highest, with Mt Huila rising to 18,865 ft. The E Cordillera is a broad mountain mass with snow-capped peaks and intermontane basins at 8,000–9,000 ft. SW of L. Maracaibo the system divides, continuing as the Sierra de Perija (N) and the Cordillera de Mérida (E). In the extreme N lies the high isolated Sierra Nevada de Santa Marta, with Cristóbal Colón (18,950 ft) within sight of the coast. The Cauca–Magdalena plains are marshy, with shallow lakes and permanent swamp.

The W hills and lowlands have a high rainfall and a hot humid climate throughout the year, and are largely clothed with dense rain-forests. The NE has long dry seasons and consists mainly of *llanos* (grasslands). There are forests again in the SE. In the mountains climate, vegetation, and agricultural products vary with altitude, two wet seasons alternating with two dry. Below 3,000 ft is the *tierra caliente*, with cacao, rice, bananas, and tropical lowland products; from 3,000 to 6,500 ft is the *tierra templada*, producing coffee, sugar, and maize; from 6,500 to 10,000 ft is the *tierra fria*, with wheat, barley, maize, potatoes, and temperate fruits. Above lie the *páramos*, as far as the snowline, with alpine meadows and pastures.

ECONOMY. Just over half the population are agriculturalists, the majority growing subsistence crops, e.g. maize, wheat, rice, sugar-cane. Coffee production is second only to that of Brazil. Next to coffee, petroleum (from the NW and the Magdalena valley) is the most valuable export, followed by bananas; others include tobacco, timber, and platinum (from the W river valleys). Industrial production has expanded: Medellín and Cali, though remote from ports, have many industries, with textiles to the fore; Bogotá, even more remote, is the administrative and cultural centre of the country, and has light industries. Air transport is important in a land of such difficult relief, while the Magdalena R. is a leading artery for passengers and goods. Chief seaports Barranquilla, Cartagena, Buenaventura.

HISTORY. Before the Spanish conquest, Chibcha Indians practised sedentary farming in the high basins of the E Cordillera; others mined gold and silver in the valleys of the central Cordillera. The Spanish settled first on the Caribbean coast, founding Santa Marta (1525) and Cartagena (1533); by 1538 Bogotá had been founded, in the Cundinamarca basin. The country formed part of the presidency of New Granada until 1718, then became a viceroyalty independent of that of Peru. Struggles for independence took place 1810–19; Bolívar's forced march through the Andes brought him to Bogotá, and 'Gran Colombia' was proclaimed, but by 1830 Venezuela and Ecuador had become separate states. The name was changed from New Granada to Colombia in 1863. Government was stable 1922–49; there was a civil war 1949–53 and further troubles subsequently.

Colombo Ceylon. Capital and chief seaport, on the W coast just S of the mouth of the Kelani R. Pop. (1963) 510,947. Exports tea, rubber, coconut oil, copra, desiccated coconut. With its large artificial harbour, it replaced Galle as the island's leading port when improvements were carried out and the first breakwater was completed (1874–86). Also the principal commercial centre, the business section of the city being still known as the Fort. Since 1942 seat of the University of Ceylon, formed from Ceylon Medical College (1870) and Ceylon University College (1921). Taken by the Dutch 1656; handed over to Britain 1796.

Colón Panama. Formerly Aspinwall. Capital of the Colón province, the second largest city in Panama, on Manzanillo Island at the Caribbean end of the Panama Canal. Pop. (1960) 59,360. Divided by the Canal Zone boundary from its twin city and port Cristóbal, but the Trans-Isthmian Highway (to Panama City) belongs to Panama. Founded in 1850 as Aspinwall, after one of the builders of the railway, but later renamed (Cristóbal Colón is the Spanish form of Christopher Columbus). Long notorious for yellow fever and malaria, which were overcome by public-health measures at the commencement of work on the Panama Canal (1903).

Colón Archipelago ◊ *Galápagos Islands*.

Colophon. Ancient city in Ionia 15 m. N of Ephesus, its port being Notium or New Colophon. One of the places claimed as the birthplace of Homer. The final charge of the Colophon cavalry in action was said to be decisive – hence the use of the word for the finishing touch to a book or manuscript.

Colorado (Argentina) ◊ *Río Colorado*.

Colorado USA. State in the W, rectangular in shape. Area 104,247 sq. m. Pop. (1970) 2,195,887. Cap. Denver. Admitted to the Union in 1876 as the 38th state; popularly known as the 'Centennial' or 'Silver' state. A Rocky Mountain state with an average height of 6,800 ft, the highest state in the USA; more or less bisected by the Continental Divide. Highest peak Mt Elbert (14,431 ft); about 50 others exceed 14,000 ft. Climate in general dry, with wide variations in rainfall and temperature. Mainly a stock-raising, farming, and mining state. Dairy farming has developed round the urban centres, and irrigation agriculture is important, esp. for alfalfa; wheat and sugar-beet are also leading crops. Principal minerals bituminous coal, petroleum; main US producer of uranium, radium, molybdenum (of which it has the world's largest mine at Climax), vanadium. Gold, silver, zinc, and lead also produced. Industries, concentrated mainly in the towns just E of the Rockies, include meat packing, sugar refining, vegetable canning, ore processing. Chief towns Denver, Pueblo (iron and steel industry), Colorado Springs (resort).

The first explorers were Spaniards from Mexico in the 16th cent. Coronado entered the region in 1540; Spanish expeditions continued throughout the 17th and 18th cent. In 1799 Jean de la Maisonneuve arrived at the present site of Denver; in the 19th cent. fur traders helped to explore and develop the territory. Became a state (1876) 100 years after the Declaration of Independence; hence the sobriquet 'Centennial' state. The farmers of Colorado suffered from the droughts of 1932-7, which created dust-bowls on the plains, but both farming and mining prospered in the two world wars.

**Colorado Desert** USA. Arid region in SE California W of the Colorado R.; separated from the Mojave Desert by the San Bernardino and other mountains. It contains the Salton Sea, 249 ft below sea level, and the Imperial Valley, which is fertile where irrigated.

**Colorado River** USA. River 1,440 m. long, rising in the Rocky Mountain National Park in N Colorado, flowing generally S W through Utah and Arizona and then S, and entering the Gulf of California. Forms the state boundaries between Nevada and Arizona, between California and Arizona, and in Mexico between Baja California and Sonora; also a short stretch of the international frontier between Arizona and Baja California. Flowing through a mountainous region, it cuts many deep gorges, while its lower course ends in a large delta which includes part of the Imperial Valley. Its tributaries include the Dolores and the Gunnison rivers in Colorado, the Green and the San Juan rivers in Utah, and the Little Colorado and the Gila rivers in Arizona. Below its confluence with the Little Colorado it has carved a path through a great plateau, forming the world-famous Grand Canyon. This enormous gorge, 218 m. long and 4-15 m. wide, reaches a depth of nearly 6,000 ft. The river has been utilized to a remarkable degree for irrigation and power. Large dams along its course include the Hoover Dam (formerly known as Boulder Dam), the Davis Dam, the Parker Dam (with aqueducts to Los Angeles and San Diego), and the Imperial Dam, which diverts water into the All-American Canal for the irrigation of the Imperial and Coachella Valleys in S California.

**Colorado River** USA. River 970 m. long, rising on the Llano Estacado and flowing generally SE to Matagorda Bay on the Gulf of Mexico. Used for irrigation and power. Several important dams.

**Colorado Springs** USA. Health resort and tourist centre just E of Pikes Peak in Colorado, at a height of 6,000 ft. Pop. (1960) 70,194. Near by are the US Air Force Academy and the famous ◊ *Garden of the Gods*.

**Colossae.** Ancient city of S W Phrygia, Asia Minor, near the modern Denizli (Turkey). St Paul addressed his Epistle to the Colossians to the members of the early Christian Church here.

**Columbia** (Missouri) USA. Town near the Missouri R. 28 m. N N W of Jefferson City. Pop. (1960) 36,650. Manufactures clothing, furniture, etc. Flour milling. Seat of the University of Missouri (1839).

**Columbia** (S Carolina) USA. Capital and largest city of S Carolina, at the head of navigation on the Congaree R. Pop. (1960) 97,433. Important textile (cotton) mills. Manufactures fertilizers, cottonseed oil, etc. Cultural and educational centre. Seat of the University of S Carolina (1801) and the Allen University (1880, Negro). Founded 1786.

**Columbia, District of** USA. Federal district, on the Potomac R. Area 69 sq. m. Pop. (1970) 764,000. Co-extensive with the city of Washington. Chosen as the site of the capital in order to overcome inter-state rivalry, and ceded by Maryland. The oldest building, the President's residence, was completed in 1799, and the seat of government was transferred there in 1800. When the British sacked Washington (1814) they set fire to the residence; subsequently painted white to cover the marks, it has remained the 'White House'. Planned by a French engineer, Pierre l'Enfant, the city is laid out in rectangular blocks crossed by diagonal arteries. The skyline is dominated by the Capitol with its great rotunda and dome, where Congress meets, and by the Washington Monument (555 ft). Other notable buildings are the Lincoln and Jefferson Memorials and the Supreme Court. The residents of the District of Columbia have no representation in Congress, and the city is administered by

Commissioners appointed by the President. Population grew considerably in the present century until 1950, but then fell by nearly 5 per cent 1950–60; about half a million people also live in near-by suburbs, outside the District of Columbia proper.

**Columbia River** Canada/USA. River 1,150 m. long (460 m. in Canada); among US rivers, second in volume only to the Mississippi. Rises in the small L. Columbia in the Rocky Mountains (British Columbia), flows N and doubles round to the N of the Selkirk Range, then S through the Arrow Lakes to the US border, then W, SE, and again W, forming the boundary between Washington (N) and Oregon (S), and enters the Pacific by a long estuary. Has cut many gorges and canyons, e.g. through the Cascade Range. Enormous power potential; important dams along its course include the Grand Coulee Dam, the Bonneville Dam, and the McNary Dam. Chief tributary the Snake, others being the Kootenay, Spokane, and Willamette rivers. Named after the *Columbia*, the ship of Capt. Gray, a Boston trader who explored its mouth (1792).

**Columbus** (Georgia) USA. Town at the head of navigation of the Chattahoochee R., 96 m. SSW of Atlanta. Pop. (1960) 116,779. Commercial and industrial centre. Textile mills. Manufactures bricks and tiles, fertilizers, agricultural implements, food products. Hydroelectric power from the Chattahoochee. Founded (1828) as a trading post where the water power and the transport facilities of the river could be used.

**Columbus** (Ohio) USA. State capital on the Scioto R. Pop. (1970) 533,418. Industrial centre. Meat packing, printing and publishing. Manufactures aircraft and motor-car parts, electrical equipment, machinery, footwear, etc. Seat of the Ohio State University (1872). Founded 1812.

**Colwyn Bay** Wales. Municipal borough in NW Denbighshire, on the Irish Sea; comprises Colwyn Bay, Old Colwyn, and Rhos-on-Sea. Pop. (1961) 23,090. Seaside resort.

**Combaconum** ◊ *Kumbakonam*.

**Commander Islands** ◊ *Komandorski Islands*.

**Como** Italy. Ancient Comum. Capital of Como province, in Lombardy, at the SW end of L. Como, 24 m. N of Milan. Pop. (1961) 81,983. Tourist centre. Lake port. Railway junction. Important silk industry. Manufactures textile machinery, motor

cycles, furniture, glass, etc. Marble cathedral (mainly 15th-cent.); several ancient churches; 13th-cent. Gothic town hall. Fell to the Visconti 1335. Later came under Austrian rule; liberated by Garibaldi 1859. Birthplace of the elder (A.D. 23–79) and the younger Pliny (61–113), Pope Innocent XI (1611–89), Alessandro Volta (1745–1827).

**Como, Lake** Italy. Third largest lake in Italy, in Lombardy at a height of 650 ft. Area 55 sq. m. (length 30m., maximum width $2\frac{1}{2}$ m.). Formed by the expansion of the Adda R., which enters in the N and leaves in the SE. In the S it is divided by the promontory of Bellagio into two arms, L. Como (W) and the Lake of Lecco (E). Beautifully situated among mountains. Many noted resorts around the shores, including Bellagio, Cadenabbia, Como, Lecco, Tremezzo.

**Comodoro Rivadavia** Argentina. Port on the Gulf of San Jorge, 560 m. SSW of Bahía Blanca. Pop. 40,000. Oil wells near by (discovered 1907), the main source of Argentina's output. Oil refining. A pipeline 1,100 m. long takes natural gas to Buenos Aires.

**Comorin, Cape** ◊ *Nagercoil*.

**Comoro Islands** Indian Ocean. Group of volcanic islands belonging to France, in the Indian Ocean between the African mainland and the N end of Malagasy, consisting of 4 large islands and many islets. Area 838 sq. m. Pop. (1966) 248,517 (largely Muslims of mixed Negro, Arab, and Malagasy stock). Grande Comore is the largest and most westerly island and has over half the total population. Islands mountainous, well forested, and fertile. Climate tropical; rainy season Nov.–April. Chief exports vanilla, copra, and essential oils (citronella, ylang-ylang, etc.). The archipelago was long under Arab influence. Mayotte was taken by France in 1843, the other 3 islands being placed under French protection in 1886; all were attached to Madagascar (now Malagasy) 1914–46, and then became a French overseas territory, represented in the French parliament.

**Compiègne** France. Ancient Compendium. Town in the Oise department, on the Oise R. 43 m. NNE of Paris; the forest of Compiègne (55 sq. m.) is near by. Pop. (1968) 32,563. Popular resort. Engineering, sawmilling, and other industries. At the siege of Compiègne Joan of Arc was captured by the English (1430). The 1918

Armistice ending the 1st World War was signed in a railway carriage in the forest, and in the same carriage the French capitulation to Germany in the 2nd World War was signed in Hitler's presence (1940).

**Compton** USA. Industrial town in California 11 m. S of Los Angeles. Pop. (1960) 71,812. Oil refining. Manufactures oil-well equipment, steel and glass products, etc. Founded 1868. Became a city 1888. Grew rapidly in the 1950s.

**Conakry (Konakry)** Guinea. Capital and chief seaport, on the offshore island of Tombo, connected with the mainland by a causeway. Pop. (1964) 120,000. Terminus of the railway from Kankan. Exports alumina, iron ore, bananas, palm kernels, etc. Grew rapidly after iron ore, mined on the near-by Kaloum peninsula, was first exported (1952).

**Concarneau** France. Sardine-fishing port and seaside resort in the Finistère department on the Bay of Biscay 12 m. SE of Quimper. Pop. (1968) 18,150. Fish canning.

**Concepción** Chile. Capital of the Concepción province, the most important city in the S, on the Bio-Bio R. 9 m. SE of its port, Talcahuano. Pop. (1966) 158,941. Manufactures textiles, leather goods, paper, cement, glass, etc. Chile's principal coal mines are near by. University (1919). Founded 1550. Destroyed by earthquakes in 1570, 1730, and 1751, then removed to its present site. Again severely damaged in the earthquakes of 1939 and 1960.

**Concepción** Paraguay. Capital of the Concepción department; port on the Paraguay R. 135 m. NNE of Asunción. Pop. (1962) 33,886. Commercial centre. Trade in yerba maté, timber, quebracho, hides, livestock. Sawmilling, cotton ginning, flour milling.

**Concepción del Uruguay** Argentina. River port on the Uruguay R., in the Entre Ríos province. Pop. 40,000. Terminus of the Entre Ríos railway. Exports grain, beef.

**Conchos River** ◊ Mexico.

**Concord** (California) USA. Town 10 m. NE of Oakland. Pop. (1960) 36,208. Mainly residential. Expanded rapidly in the 1950s: pop. (1950) 6,953.

**Concord** (Massachusetts) USA. Town on the Concord R. 17 m. WNW of Boston. Pop. (1960) 3,188. Largely residential. Famous as scene of the first battle of the Revolution (1775) and home of several American writers: Hawthorne, Emerson, Thoreau, and the Alcotts.

**Concord** (New Hampshire) USA. Capital of New Hampshire, on the Merrimack R. Pop. (1960) 28,991. Printing and publishing. Manufactures leather goods. Settled (as Pennycook) 1725. Incorporated (as Rumford) 1733. Renamed Concord 1765. Home of Benjamin Thompson (Count Rumford).

**Concordia** Argentina. River port on the Uruguay R. in the Entre Ríos province, opposite Salto (Uruguay). Pop. 56,000. Exports cereals and citrus fruits, trading with Uruguay, Brazil, and Paraguay. Manufactures vegetable oils, leather, etc. Tourist centre.

**Coney Island** USA. Seaside resort in New York, part of Brooklyn (New York City), in the SW of Long Island. A playground for the people of New York City, noted for its amusement parks, side-shows, cafés, and dance halls, and for its 5-m. beach and promenade.

**Congleton** England. Municipal borough in Cheshire, on the R. Dane 11 m. ENE of Crewe. Pop. (1961) 16,802. Industrial town. Manufactures cotton goods, hosiery, cardboard boxes, etc.

**Congo (Brazzaville), Republic of.** Formerly (as ' Moyen Congo', Middle Congo) one of the four territories of French Equatorial Africa. Area 132,000 sq. m. Pop. (1964) 864,000 (mainly Bantu). Cap. Brazzaville; chief seaport Pointe Noire. Bounded by Cameroun and the Central African Republic (N), Congo (Kinshasa) (E and S), the Atlantic Ocean (SW), and Gabon (W). Hot, humid climate. Annual rainfall 80–100 ins. Largely equatorial forest, interspersed with wooded savannah. Chief exports tropical hardwoods (e.g. mahogany, okoumé) and palm oil and kernels. Some lead mining. The coast was discovered in the 17th cent. by the Portuguese and was a French trading base from the 17th to the 19th cent. De Brazza explored the Alima R., reached Stanley Pool, and claimed the area for France (1880). Originally named French Congo, later Middle Congo (1903–58). Became a member of the French Community 1958 and an independent member of the UN 1960.

**Congo (Kinshasa), Republic of.** Republic in Central Africa, formerly the Belgian Congo. Area 895,000 sq. m. Pop. (1962) 14,797,000 (mainly Bantu, with some Nilotic and Sudanese Negroes and aboriginal Pygmies). Cap. Kinshasa (formerly Léopoldville).

TOPOGRAPHY, CLIMATE. Occupies about two thirds of the basin of the Congo R., consisting of a vast depression in the African plateau mainly over 1,000 ft above sea level, fringed on the E and S by highlands. The E highlands, on the edge of the W branch of the Great Rift Valley, rise to 16,795 ft in Ruwenzori. The N half, lying on both sides of the equator, has a typical equatorial climate, with constant high temperatures and all-year rainfall (60–80 ins. annually), and is chiefly covered with tropical rain-forest. The S half has a tropical climate, always hot but with a well-marked dry season, and is principally savannah country, with belts of forest along the rivers. Wild life is abundant and preserved in national parks.

ECONOMY. The principal agricultural exports are palm oil and kernels, cotton, and coffee; food crops include cassava, maize, and plantains. Congo (Kinshasa) is the world's leading producer of industrial diamonds, chiefly from the former Kasai province, and cobalt, from the mineral-rich Katanga. Katanga is also an important producer of copper (the main export) and uranium ore; tin, zinc, manganese, gold, and silver are mined. Lubumbashi (Katanga) – formerly Elisabethville – is linked by rail with Lobito (Angola) and with the Zambian system. The Congo R. is navigable for over 1,000 m. above Kinshasa to Kisangani (Stanleyville), and hundreds of miles of tributaries are also navigable. Matadi, the chief seaport, at the head of the Congo estuary, is linked by rail with Kinshasa. Other important towns are Luluabourg, Jadotville, Bukavu. From 1967 the country has been divided administratively into Kinshasa city and 8 provinces.

HISTORY. Although the Portuguese Diogo Cão discovered the mouth of the Congo R. in 1482, travel difficulties prevented European exploration until H. M. Stanley's historic journey down the river (1876–7). He was charged by King Leopold II of Belgium (on behalf of the International Association of the Congo) with continued exploration and the conclusion of agreements with native chiefs. After the Berlin Conference (1884–5), Leopold II was recognized as the head of the state founded by the International Association, the Congo Free State. The Arab slave trade and cannibalism were suppressed, but serious charges of ill-treatment of natives and the abolition of freedom of trade were made against the administration; Belgium assumed responsibility for government in 1908, and the country became a colony, the Belgian Congo. It became independent in 1960, but disorder followed the withdrawal of the Belgian administrators, doctors, and others: tribal violence, attacks on Europeans, army mutiny, famine. Katanga province proclaimed its independence. The UN recognized the Adoula government as the central government of the republic in 1961, UN forces invaded Katanga, and fighting with Katangan troops continued into 1963. The secession of Katanga suddenly collapsed, however, and peace and a semblance of law and order was imposed.

Congonhas do Campo Brazil. Hill town in Minas Gerais. Pop. 12,000. The famous pilgrimage church of Bom Jesus, built 1773; in the chapels in a garden leading to the church are a series of episodes, portrayed in wooden statues by the remarkable 18th-cent. Brazilian sculptor Francisco Lisboa, generally known as Aleijadinho ('Little Cripple'). Other statues by him, in soapstone, are on the terrace.

Congo River Africa. River 3,000 m. long, the second longest in Africa; one of the world's great rivers, second only to the Amazon, with its tributaries draining a basin of over 1,400,000 sq. m. The E headstream, the Chambezi, rises on the plateau S of L. Tanganyika, passes through L. Bangweulu and continues as the Luapula R., which enters L. Mweru, leaving it as the Luvua R. The W headstream, the Lualaba R., rises on the Katanga plateau near the Zambia frontier and joins the Luvua; below the confluence the stream is still called the Lualaba R. It receives the Lukuga R., which connects it with L. Tanganyika. Below Stanley Falls it is called the R. Congo; along this middle course, it is very wide, studded with islands, and receives several great tributaries, including the Ubangi R. from the N and the Kasai R. from the S. The flow in the lower course is regular, because these tributaries are fed during the rainy seasons of both the N and the S hemispheres. Some 350 m. above its mouth the river widens into Stanley Pool, then cuts through the Crystal Mountains by a gorge and descends 886 ft in 220 m., by the Livingstone Falls, widening again into an estuary nearly 100 m. long. Matadi, just below the falls, is accessible to ocean-going vessels. Steamers navigate over 1,000 m. of the river between Kinshasa and Kisangani; with its tributaries the Congo provides over 7,500 m. of navigable waterways. Some unnavigable stretches are linked by railways, e.g. Matadi–Kinshasa, Kisangani–Ponthierville, Kindu–Kabalo. The mouth of the Congo was discovered by the Portuguese in 1482; the middle and upper courses remained virtually unknown until Livingstone reached Nyangwe (on the Lualaba R.) in 1871 and Stanley journeyed down-river from Nyangwe to Boma in 1876–7.

**Conisbrough (Conisborough)** England. Urban district in the W Riding of Yorkshire, on the R. Don 5 m. S W of Doncaster. Pop. (1961) 17,956. Coalmining centre. Ruins of a 12th-cent. Norman castle with an outstanding circular keep.

**Coniston Water** England. Lake 5 m. long and $\frac{1}{2}$ m. wide, in N Lancashire in the Lake District, 5 m. W of L. Windermere, at the foot of the Old Man of Coniston (2,633 ft). On the E shore is Brantwood, the home of Ruskin, who is buried in Coniston village churchyard (W of the lake). Scene of the establishment of the world water-speed record of 141·7 m.p.h. by Sir Malcolm Campbell (1939), and of a new record of 260 m.p.h. by his son Donald Campbell (1959).

**Conjeeveram** ◊ *Kanchipuram.*

**Connaught (Connacht)** Irish Republic. Province in the W, between the R. Shannon and the Atlantic, comprising the counties of Galway, Leitrim, Mayo, Roscommon, and Sligo. Area 6,611 sq. m. Pop. (1966) 401,950.

**Connecticut** USA. State in New England. Area 5,009 sq. m. (third smallest in the Union). Pop. (1970) 2,987,950. Cap. Hartford. One of the original 13 states; popularly known as the 'Nutmeg' state. Main rivers the Connecticut, draining the central lowlands, the Thames (E) and the Housatonic and the Naugatuck (W). Highest point Bear Mountain (2,322 ft), in the extreme NW. Many glacial lakes. The coast, indented by river mouths and bays, has several good harbours. Climate humid continental. Annual rainfall 40–50 ins. Agriculture important, esp. tobacco growing, market gardening, poultry and dairy farming. Forests of beech, chestnut, birch, maple, and poplar cover some 2 million acres. Minerals are of minor importance, but granite, limestone, clay, and sandstone are quarried. The state is mainly industrial, specializing in precision instruments; its manufactures include fire-arms and ammu-

nition, brassware, textiles, clocks and watches, jewellery, machinery, pins and needles, wire products, and precision tools. Chief towns Hartford, Bridgeport, New Haven, Waterbury. Adriaen Block, a Dutch explorer, discovered the Connecticut R.; a Dutch trading post established in 1633 on the site of Hartford was later abandoned. English colonists from Massachusetts formed the first permanent settlements at Windsor, Wethersfield, and Hartford in 1634–5. In the American War of Independence Connecticut strongly supported the colonists; in the American Civil War it was on the side of the Union.

**Connemara** Irish Republic. Barren, boggy area in the W of Co. Galway, including the mountain group called the Twelve Bens, which rise to 2,393 ft, and a great number of small lakes. Wild, picturesque scenery, both coastal and inland, popular with tourists. Fishing.

**Consett** England. Urban district in N Durham, 12 m. SW of Newcastle upon Tyne. Pop. (1961) 38,927. Iron and steel works. Collieries.

**Constance (Ger. Konstanz)** Federal German Republic. Town in Baden-Württemberg on the Rhine R. at its exit from L. Constance. Pop. (1963) 55,100. Port. Tourist centre. Railway junction. Manufactures textiles, machinery, chemicals, etc. Its minster (formerly cathedral) dates from the 11th cent.; an old Dominican monastery is now a hotel. Famous in medieval times for its linen industry. Scene (1414–18) of the Church Council of Constance, which condemned and burned John Huss (1415) and Jerome of Prague (1416). Surrendered to Austria 1548. Ceded to Baden 1805. Birthplace of Count Zeppelin (1838–1917).

**Constance, Lake (Ger. Bodensee)**. Ancient Lacus Brigantinus. Lake at a height of 1,300 ft bordering on Austria, Federal German Republic, and Switzerland. Area 205 sq. m. (length 40 m., width 8 m.). The Rhine enters in the SE near Bregenz and leaves in the NW (from the Untersee) at Stein am Rhein. The greater part of the lake (the Obersee) is in the E and SE. Near Constance in the W it divides into the Untersee (S) and the Überlingersee (N). Fishing villages and holiday resorts around the shores are linked by steamers. Chief towns Constance, Lindau, Friedrichshafen (Germany), Bregenz (Austria).

**Constanța (Constanza)** Rumania. Ancient Constantiana. Capital of the Constanța district; chief Rumanian seaport, on the Black Sea. Pop. (1968) 161,627. Exports petroleum, grain, timber. Oil pipeline from Ploeşti. Seaside resort. Manufactures furniture, bricks, textiles, soap, etc. Founded by Greeks in the 6th cent. B.C., rebuilt by Constantine the Great in the 4th cent. A.D. Its modern development dates from 1878, when it was ceded to Rumania by Turkey.

**Constantine** Algeria. Ancient Cirta. Capital of the Constantine department, 210 m. ESE of Algiers. Pop. (1967) 255,000. Third largest city. On a rocky plateau, cut off on all sides except the W by a deep ravine formed by the Rummel R. Modern suburbs to the SW. Chief centre for the trade of the High Plateaux and the interior (grain, wool, leather, esparto grass, etc.). Flour milling etc. Manufactures woollen and leather goods. An important town in ancient ◊ *Numidia*. Destroyed A.D. 311; restored by Constantine the Great 313. Taken by the French 1837.

**Constantinople** ◊ *Istanbul*.

**Constanza** ◊ *Constanţa*.

**Conway (Aberconway)** Wales. Municipal borough in Caernarvonshire, on the estuary of the R. Conway. Pop. (1961) 11,392. Seaside resort. Market town. Impressive remains of a 13th-cent. castle and town walls. The river is crossed by a road suspension bridge designed by Telford (1826) and a tubular railway bridge designed by Stephenson (1848).

**Conway River** Wales. River 30 m. long, rising in SE Caernarvonshire, flowing N, forming most of the border between Caernarvonshire and Denbighshire, and entering the Irish Sea at Conway.

**Cooch Behar (Kuch Bihar)** India. Former princely state in the NE; since 1950 part of W Bengal. Area 1,321 sq. m. Rice, jute, and tobacco grown. Chief town Cooch Behar (pop. 42,000).

**Cook (Aorangi), Mount** New Zealand. Highest peak (12,349 ft) in New Zealand, in the Southern Alps, S Island. Permanently snow-capped, the surrounding snowfields feeding large glaciers.

**Cook Islands** S Pacific Ocean. Islands of Polynesia in the S Pacific between 8° S and 23° S lat. and 156° W and 167° W long., roughly in two groups: Northern Group of atolls, including Manihiki (Humphrey), Pukapuka (Danger), Penrhyn (Tongareva), and Rakahanga (Reirson), each of which has several hundred people and produces copra and pearl shell; Southern or Lower Group (Cook Is. proper), including Rarotonga and Mangaia, of volcanic origin, and Aitutaki, Atiu, and 4 others, all coral islands. Total area 93 sq. m. Pop. (1966) 19,247. Seat of administration Rarotonga (pop. 9,971), which, with Mangaia, exports copra and fruits. Niue (Savage) Island, W of the other islands, belongs to the group but is under separate administration; it is a raised coral atoll exporting copra and bananas. Some of the islands were discovered by Capt. Cook (1773), others by the English missionary John Williams (1823). Became a British protectorate 1888; annexed to New Zealand 1901.

**Cookstown** Northern Ireland. Urban district in NE Co. Tyrone, on the R. Ballinderry 32 m. W of Belfast. Pop. (1961) 4,964. Dairy-farming centre. Manufactures linen, hosiery. Founded (1609) by Allan Cook.

**Cook Strait** New Zealand. Strait separating the N Island and the S Island, 16 m. wide at the narrowest point. Well known for its strong, gusty winds.

**Coolgardie** ◊ *Kalgoorlie*.

**Coorg** India. Former small state in the W Ghats, now in the extreme S of Mysore. Area 1,591 sq. m. Chief town Mercara. Mountainous and wooded, with several peaks exceeding 5,000 ft. Heavy rainfall. Rice, coffee, oranges grown.

**Copenhagen (Danish Köbenhavn)** Denmark. In Danish, 'Merchants' Haven'. Capital and largest city, on the E coast of Zealand island near the S end of The Sound (Öresund); linked by bridges with the suburb of Christianshavn on the N coast of Amager island. Pop. (1965) 874,417. Denmark's chief port and commercial centre. The excellent harbour occupies the channel between Zealand and Amager islands. Exports butter, cheese, eggs, bacon. Shipbuilding, engineering, brewing. Manufactures porcelain, textiles, chocolate, paper, etc. At the centre is the Kongens Nytorv square, from which the main thoroughfares radiate. Near by are the 17th-cent. Charlottenborg Palace (now housing the Academy of Arts), the Royal Theatre, and the 17th-cent. Thotts palace. Also has a cathedral (rebuilt in the early 19th cent.), Trinity Church, with a remarkable round tower ascended by a spiral incline, and the 18th-cent. Christiansborg Palace on the Slottsholm (an island formed by a narrow arm of the harbour), last restored in 1903 and now used as the parliament house. A leading centre of Scandinavian culture. Seat of a university (1479), several learned societies, and the Thorvaldsen and other museums.

Only a fishing village until 1167, when the Bishop of Roskilde built a castle on the site of the present Christiansborg Palace. The settlement gradually acquired importance as a trading centre. Became capital of Denmark 1443. Attacked by the Hanseatic League in the 15th cent. and by the Swedes in the 17th. Bombarded by the English, Dutch, and Swedish fleets 1700. Suffered severely from fires in 1728 and 1795. The Danish fleet was destroyed by Nelson at the Battle of Copenhagen (1801). Again bombarded by the English fleet 1807.

**Copiapó** Chile. Capital of the Atacama province, on the Copiapó R. at a height of 1,200 ft, 40 m. ESE of its port, Caldera, and 250 m. S of Antofagasta. Pop. (1960) 37,224. Centre of a copper- and iron-mining region and of an irrigated belt along the river.

**Coppermine** Canada. Village at the mouth of the Coppermine R. in the NW Territories. Pop. mainly Eskimo. Caribou and polar-bear hunting, whaling. Trading post. Royal Canadian Mounted Police post. Meteorological and radio station.

**Coppermine River** Canada. River 525 m. long, in the Mackenzie District, NW Territories, rising in a small lake, flowing S to L. De Gras N of the Great Slave Lake, then flowing generally N, and entering the Coronation Gulf.

**Coptos (Koptus)** United Arab Republic. Ancient Egyptian city near the Nile 20 m. NE of Thebes. Trade with India and Arabia via the Red Sea made it a great commercial centre from *c.* 300 B.C. After rebelling against Diocletian it was almost destroyed, but recovered and was again important in later Roman times. The village of Kuft (Qift) occupies the site.

**Coquimbo** Chile. Town in the Coquimbo province on Coquimbo Bay; port for La Serena, 9 m. NE. Pop. (1960) 41,304. Market town. Trade in grain, fruit, minerals (chiefly copper). The bay provides winter quarters for the Chilean navy.

**Coral Gables** USA. Residential town and resort in Florida just SW of Miami. Pop. (1960) 34,793. Seat of the University of Miami (1925).

**Coral Sea** SW Pacific Ocean. Section of the SW Pacific between Australia (W) and the New Hebrides and New Caledonia (E), containing the Great Barrier Reef. In the 2nd World War, US naval aircraft won a vital battle here with the Japanese fleet (1942).

**Corby** England. Urban district in Northamptonshire, 6 m. N of Kettering. Pop. (1961) 36,322 (1,596 in 1931; 16,704 in 1951). Industrial town. Owes its rapid growth to the large iron and steel industry. Designated a 'new town' (1950), with a planned pop. of 80,000; designated area increased in 1963.

**Córdoba** Argentina. Capital of the Córdoba province, on the Río Primero at a height of 1,400 ft 420 m. NW of Buenos Aires. Pop. (1960) 589,153. Commercial centre. Resort. Manufactures cars, tractors, textiles, cement, glass, etc. Derives hydroelectric power from the great San Roque dam across the Río Primero above the city. Founded 1573. Has many fine old buildings including a cathedral (17th/18th-cent.). Cultural centre; seat of a university (1613), the first in Argentina.

**Córdoba** Mexico. Market town in the Veracruz state, in the Sierra Madre Oriental at a height of 3,000 ft 60 m. WSW of Veracruz. Pop. (1960) 32,883. In a coffee-growing region. Coffee roasting, sugar refining.

**Córdoba (Cordova)** Spain. **1.** Province in Andalusia, divided by the Guadalquivir R. into the mountainous N (crossed by the Sierra Morena) and the fertile plain of the S. Area 5,295 sq. m. Pop. (1961) 798,437. Mainly agricultural. Produces olives, fruit, cereals. Silver, lead, copper, coal mined.
**2.** Capital of Córdoba province, an ancient typically Moorish city, on the Guadalquivir R. and on the S slopes of the Sierra de Córdoba. Pop. (1967) 220,226. Industrial, commercial, and tourist centre. Engineering, brewing, distilling. Manufactures textiles, pottery, leather, leather goods. Trade in cereals, olives, wine. Colonized by the Romans 152 B.C. In Moorish hands 711–1236 (and still has many narrow twisting streets with fine Moorish houses). Became capital of Moorish Spain 756; reached the peak of its fame in the 10th cent. The outstanding building is the *mezquita* (mosque), built in the 8th–10th cent., now a cathedral. Declined after conquest by Ferdinand III of Castile (1236). The production of goatskin leather (*cordovan*, cordwain) for which it was long famous has almost disappeared. Birthplace of the two Senecas, Lucan, and Maimonides.

**Corfe Castle** England. Picturesque stone-built village in SE Dorset, on the Isle of Purbeck, 6 m. SSW of Poole. Ruins of an ancient castle (destroyed by Cromwell) where Edward the Martyr was said to have been murdered (978). Edward II after his deposition was imprisoned here.

**Corfu (Gr. Kerkira)** Greece. 1. Ancient Corcyra; probably Homer's Scheria. Second largest and most beautiful of the Ionian Is., forming, with small neighbouring islands, a *nome*. Area 246 sq. m. Pop. (1961) 101,555. The island lies mainly off the coast of Epirus, but at its N end, where the Corfu Channel narrows, comes within 2 m. of the Albanian coast. Mountainous in the N. Chief products olive oil, wine, citrus fruits. Settled *c*. 734 B.C. by Corinth; the two cities became rivals, and fought the first recorded naval battle in Greek history (*c*. 664 B.C.). Under Venetian rule 1386–1797 and British 1815–64, being then ceded to Greece.
2. Capital of Corfu *nome*, on the E coast of Corfu. Pop. (1961) 26,991. Seaport. Exports olive oil, fruit, etc. Industries textile and soap manufacture, fishing, tourism. Seat of Greek and Roman Catholic archbishops. The town, having been built within walls, is a maze of narrow, winding streets.

**Corinth (Gr. Korinthos)** Greece. Capital of the Korinthia *nome*; port on the Gulf of Corinth near the W end of the 4-m.-long Corinth Canal. Pop. (1961) 15,892. Trade in wine, currants (which are supposed to have been named after it). Founded 1858, when Old Corinth, 3 m. SW, was destroyed by earthquake; itself destroyed by earthquake in 1928 and rebuilt. One of the wealthiest and most powerful of ancient Greek cities, guarded by its citadel or Acrocorinthus (1,886 ft). Excavations from 1896 onwards have revealed the *agora* (market-place), temple of Apollo, amphitheatre, and other Greek and Roman remains. Probably founded *c*. 1350 B.C. By the 7th cent. B.C. it had become a great commercial and industrial centre, famed for its pottery and metal-work and numbering Syracuse and Corfu among its colonies. Athenian help for Corcyra (Corfu) led Corinth to join forces with Sparta against Athens, long a formidable rival, in the Peloponnesian War (431–404 B.C.), but in the Corinthian War (395–387 B.C.) it combined with Athens, Thebes, and Argos against Sparta. Became a member of the Achaean League 243 B.C. In 146 B.C. it was plundered of its art treasures and destroyed by the Romans. Refounded by Julius Caesar 44 B.C.; it regained its commercial prosperity, and the famous Isthmian Games at near-by Isthmia were restarted. Under the Turks (1458–1687 and 1715–1822) it declined to an insignificant village, and then finally passed to Greece.

**Corinth Canal** Greece. Ship canal 4 m. long constructed 1881–93, crossing the Isthmus of Corinth and joining the Gulf of Corinth (NW) to the Saronic Gulf (SE), thus separating the Peloponnese from the Greek mainland. Shortens the journey from the Adriatic to the Piraeus by 200 m.

**Corio Bay** ♢ *Port Phillip Bay*.

**Cork (Corcaigh)** Irish Republic. 1. County in the province of Munster, in the SW, bordering on the Atlantic in the S; the largest county in Ireland. Area 2,880 sq. m. Pop. (1966) 339,703. County town Cork. The deeply indented coastline extends from the Kenmare R. (W) to Youghal Harbour (E). Other inlets include Bantry Bay (around which is some of Ireland's loveliest scenery), Dunmanus Bay, and Cork Harbour. Crossed more or less W–E by mountain ranges rising to over 2,000 ft in the Boggeragh Mountains (W), between which are the fertile valleys of the Blackwater, Lee, and Bandon rivers. Dairy farming. Potatoes and root crops grown. Chief towns Cork, Cóbh, Mallow, Youghal.
2. County town of Co. Cork, second largest city in the Irish Republic, built on and around an island at the mouth of the R. Lee and at the head of Cork Harbour. Pop. (1966) 122,146. Seaport (though the largest vessels use Cóbh). Exports dairy produce, cattle, etc. Distilling, brewing, bacon curing, motor-vehicle assembly. Manufactures tyres, woollen goods and fertilizers. Protestant and Roman Catholic cathedrals. Seat of the University College of Cork, part of the National University. An 18th-cent. church, St Ann Shandon, with a parti-coloured steeple. A monastery was founded by St Finbar (Finnbarr) in the 6th or 7th cent. An Anglo-Norman settlement had been established by the 12th cent. Scene of landings by the pretenders Lambert Simnel (1487) and Perkin Warbeck (1497) and their brief acceptance as Yorkist kings of England: hence the cognomen 'the Rebel City'. Part of Spenser's *Faery Queen* was written near by. Taken by Cromwell's forces (1649) and by Marl-

borough's (1690). Birthplace and burial-place of Francis Mahony (1804–66), author of *The Bells of Shandon*.

**Corner Brook** Canada. Town in W New-foundland, on the Humber R. near the mouth. Pop. (1966) 27,116. One of the world's largest paper mills, producing newsprint for export. Iron foundries, cement works, and gypsum mill. Grew rapidly after the building of the paper mills (1925).

**Corniche** France. Three highways on the Riviera, running S of the Maritime Alps between Nice and Menton. The Grande Corniche (built as a military road by Napoleon I 1806) ascends to over 1,700 ft; the Moyenne Corniche links the inter-mediate towns; the Petite Corniche runs along the coast through Beaulieu and Monte Carlo.

**Cornwall** Canada. Industrial town and port in SE Ontario, on the St Lawrence R. 53 m. ESE of Ottawa. Pop. (1966) 45,766. Manufactures rayon, cotton goods, paper, chemicals, etc. Linked by bridge (1934) with Rooseveltown (NY), USA.

**Cornwall** England. County in the extreme SW, bounded by the Atlantic (N and NW), the English Channel (S and SW), and Devonshire (E). Area (inc. the Scilly Isles) 1,356 sq. m. Pop. (1961) 341,746. County town Bodmin. The southernmost point is Lizard Point; the most westerly is Land's End, 25 m. WSW of which are the Scilly Isles. Much of the coast is rocky and picturesque; gaunt headlands are inter-spersed with bays and sheltered coves. Much of the interior consists of hills and moors; Bodmin Moor rises to 1,375 ft in Brown Willy. Chief rivers the Tamar, the Fowey, the Fal, and the Camel. The scenic attractions and mild climate (which in places, e.g. the Scilly Isles, produces almost sub-tropical vegetation) have made it extremely popular with tourists. Seaside resorts include Falmouth, Newquay, Pen-zance, St Ives. Fishing is still practised though on a diminished scale. Dairy farm-ing and the production of early vegetables and flowers are important. Tin and copper mining (for which the county was long famous) have declined practically to ex-tinction. By far the most valuable mineral is china clay (kaolin). Granite and slate are quarried. Chief towns Truro (adminis-trative centre), Camborne-Redruth, St Austell. Cornish (a Celtic language) has not been spoken since the late 18th cent.

**Coro** Venezuela. Capital of Falcón state 200 m. WNW of Carácas. Pop. (1961) 44,757. Linked by road and rail with its port La Vela (7 m. ENE). Industrial and commercial centre. Manufactures cigars, soap, etc. Trade in coffee, maize, etc. Founded 1527.

**Coromandel Coast** India. The SE coast, on the Bay of Bengal, between the Krishna (Kistna) R. delta and Point Calimere (S); it has no natural harbours and is severely buffeted during the NE monsoon (Oct.–April). The name is probably de-rived from Cholamandalam, the land of the ancient Chola dynasty.

**Coronation Gulf** Canada. An arm of the Arctic Ocean, separating Victoria Island from the mainland. Named (1821) by Franklin in honour of the coronation of George IV.

**Coronel** Chile. Port in the Concepción province, 15 m. SSW of Concepción. Pop. (1960) 60,234. In a coalmining area; the chief coaling station on the Chilean coast. Flour milling. Manufactures soap. Scene of a British naval defeat by the German Admiral von Spee during the 1st World War (1914).

**Coronel Oviedo** Paraguay. Capital of the Caaguazú department, 80 m. E of Asun-ción. Pop. (1962) 44,254. Commercial centre. Sawmilling. Sugar refining.

**Corpus Christi** USA. Port in S Texas on Corpus Christi Bay, connected by a deep-water channel to the Gulf of Mexico. Pop. (1960) 167,690. Exports cotton, petroleum, sulphur, fish, etc. Oil refining, cotton ginning. Manufactures chemicals, cottonseed oil, cement, etc. Popular resort, with excellent beaches. Industries developed rapidly after the discovery of natural gas and then oil from 1913 onwards.

**Corregidor** Philippines. Fortified island at the entrance to Manila Bay. During the 2nd World War it was heroically defended by the American garrison against the Japanese (April–May 1942).

**Corrèze** France. Department formed from the old province of Limousin, in the NW Massif Central, crossed in the N by the Monts du Limousin and drained by the Corrèze, the Vézère, and the Dordogne rivers. Area 2,273 sq. m. Pop. (1968) 237,858. Prefecture Tulle. Largely infertile. Agriculture in the river valleys. Produces cereals, fruit, vegetables, wine. Sheep and pig rearing. Several hydroelectric plants. Chief towns Brive, Tulle.

**Corrèze River** France. River 60 m. long, in the Corrèze department, flowing SW past Tulle and Brive to the Vézère R.

**Corrib, Lough** Irish Republic. Irregular-shaped lake, mainly in Co. Galway, with a small part in Co. Mayo. Area 68 sq. m. Drained to Galway Bay by the short R. Corrib.

**Corrientes** Argentina. Capital of the Corrientes province, port on the Paraná R. 25 m. below the confluence of the Alto Paraná with the Paraguay R. Pop. 104,000. Linked by ferry with Barranqueras on the opposite bank of the Paraná. Above Corrientes shallow-draught vessels are used. Trade in agricultural products (cotton, rice, etc.). Manufactures vegetable oils, textiles, etc. Sawmilling, tanning. Seat of a college of the National University of the Litoral (1922). Founded 1588.

**Corsica** (Fr. *Corse*) France. Island in the Mediterranean Sea immediately N of Sardinia, from which it is separated by the Strait of Bonifacio; a department of France. Area 3,367 sq. m. Pop. (1968) 269,831. Prefecture Ajaccio. The interior is mountainous (with plains only along the E coast), rising to 8,891 ft in Monte Cinto. The rocky W coast has many headlands and gulfs. Over the lower mountain slopes is spread a tangled undergrowth of shrubs (Fr. *maquis*, Italian *macchia*) which used to provide cover for bandits. Farming primitive. Sheep and goats raised in large numbers. Produces olives, vines, citrus fruits, chestnuts. Growing tourist industry. The seaports Ajaccio and Bastia are the largest towns. Exports olive oil, wine, fruits, etc. Belongs, geographically and historically, more to Italy than to France; outside the towns a dialect akin to Italian is spoken. Held in turn by the Etruscans, the Carthaginians, the Romans, the Vandals, and the Saracens. Fell to Pisa in the 11th cent. and to Genoa in the 14th. Ceded to France 1768. Under French rule the long-practised brigandage and the vendetta (blood feud) were gradually suppressed.

**Cortona** Italy. Town in Arezzo province in Tuscany, 14 m. SSE of Arezzo, overlooking the Val di Chiana and L. Trasimeno. Pop. (1961) 26,718. Etruscan and Roman remains. Paintings by Luca Signorelli in the cathedral. The 13th-cent. palace houses the museum of the Etruscan Academy (founded 1726). Birthplace of Luca Signorelli (1450–1523).

**Corumbá** Brazil. Market town and river port in the Mato Grosso state, on the Paraguay R. Pop. 39,000. Linked by rail with São Paulo and Santa Cruz (Bolivia). Exports the products of a large area, chiefly dried beef and hides and skins.

**Corunna (La Coruña)** Spain. **1.** Province in Galicia, bounded on the N and W by the Atlantic. Area 3,051 sq. m. Pop. (1961) 991,729. The rocky coastline has many deep inlets (rias). The heaviest rainfall in Spain. Main occupations fishing, stock rearing, and the cultivation of cereals, vegetables, and fruit.
**2.** Capital of Corunna province, Atlantic seaport on Corunna Bay. Pop. (1967) 187,859. Important sardine-fishing and canning centre. Manufactures cigars, cotton goods, glassware, etc. To the NW is the 157-ft Roman Tower of Hercules, now a lighthouse. Scene of the sailing of the Spanish Armada (1588), of Drake's burning of the city (1598), and of the Peninsular War battle in which Sir John Moore was killed (1809). Burial-place of Moore (the old-town San Carlos gardens).

**Corwen** Wales. Small market town and angling resort in NE Merionethshire, on the R. Dee at the foot of the Berwyn Mountains. Pop. (1961) 2,160. Headquarters of Owen Glendower before the battle of Shrewsbury (1403).

**Cos** (Gr. *Kos*) Greece. **1.** Island in the Aegean Sea, the second largest of the Dodecanese, separated from the Bodrum peninsula (Turkey) by the narrow Cos Channel. Area 109 sq. m. Pop. 21,000. Mainly low-lying and fertile, producing cereals, olive oil, fruits, wine. Cos lettuce originally grown here. It has frequently suffered from earthquakes, being severely damaged in 1933. In ancient times it won fame as a literary and medical centre: birthplace of Hippocrates (*c.* 460 B.C.).
**2.** Capital of Cos, on the NE coast. Pop. 8,000. Trade in agricultural products. Castle built by the Knights of St John. In the market square is a famous old plane tree under which Hippocrates is said to have taught.

**Coseley** England. Industrial town in S Staffordshire, 3 m SSE of Wolverhampton in the Black Country. Pop. (1961) 39,557. Metal working. Manufactures machinery etc.

**Cosenza** Italy. Ancient Consentia. Capital of Cosenza province in Calabria, on the Crati R. Pop. (1961) 78,611. Market town and road junction in a region producing figs and other fruits. Manufactures furniture, textiles, etc. Cathedral (12th-cent.).

**Costa Mesa** USA. Town in California 32 m. SE of Los Angeles. Pop. (1960) 37,550. Manufactures fibreglass products, electronic equipment, etc. Expanded rapidly in the 1950s: pop. (1950) 11,844.

**Costa Rica.** Republic of Central America. Area 19,653 sq. m. Pop. (1964) 1,369,659 (97 per cent white and mestizo, 2 per cent Negro, 1 per cent Indian). Cap. (and only large city) San José. Lang. Spanish. Rel. Roman Catholic.

On an isthmus between the Caribbean Sea and the Pacific Ocean, with Nicaragua to the N and Panama to the SE. A mountainous country with high volcanoes, now dormant, rising to over 10,000 ft. Has suffered several severe earthquakes. Two thirds of the population live in the Meseta Central, an upland region with a pleasant climate and a fertile volcanic soil. The country is divided administratively into 7 provinces.

Forests cover three quarters of the total area, and yield balsa, sandalwood, mahogany, rosewood, and cedar. Mainly agricultural: largely dependent on coffee, the chief crop of the uplands, which provides nearly half the exports. Bananas are an important export, and cacao and sugarcane are also grown in the coastal plains, which are hot and humid on the Caribbean but drier and cooler on the Pacific coast.

Columbus discovered the Caribbean coast on his last voyage (1502) and named it the Rich Coast (Costa Rica), possibly because of the gold ornaments of the natives. As part of Guatemala, the country was under Spanish rule until 1821 and a member of the Central American Federation 1823–38. The population is well integrated, and enjoys stable government. Literacy is high, and expenditure on education is four times that on the armed forces.

**Costermansville** ◊ *Bukavu*.

**Côte d'Argent** France. Popular holiday-resort area, at the S end of the Bay of Biscay, between Biarritz and the mouth of the Adour R.

**Côte d'Azur** France. The Mediterranean coast of the French Riviera, so named because of the deep blue of the sea. Includes the resorts of Antibes, Cannes, Juan-les-Pins, Menton, Monte Carlo (in Monaco), Nice, Villefranche.

**Côte d'Or** France. Department in Burgundy. Area 3,392 sq. m. Pop. (1968) 421,192. Prefecture Dijon. Crossed by the S part of the Plateau de Langres, which separates the basins of the Saône and Seine (linked by the Burgundy Canal), and by the Côte d'Or (range of hills), after which the department is named. On the E slopes are the famous vineyards of Beaune, Chambertin, Montrachet, Nuits St Georges, etc. Cereals and vegetables are also cultivated; cattle and sheep raised. A network of railways converges on Dijon. Beaune is an important centre of the wine trade.

**Cotentin** France. Peninsula forming the N part of the Manche department. Cherbourg, the chief town and only good seaport, is on the N coast. Noted for stock rearing, dairy farming, and apple growing. The most northerly points are Cap La Hague (NW) and Barfleur Point (NE).

**Côtes-du-Nord** France. Department in Brittany, on the English Channel, with a broken coastline, and many small offshore islands. Area 2,786 sq. m. Pop. (1968) 506,102. Prefecture St Brieuc. Mainly low-lying. Produces cider apples, hemp, cereals. Chief towns St Brieuc, Dinan, Guingamp, Lannion.

**Cotonou** Dahomey. Chief seaport and commercial centre, 20 m. WSW of Porto Novo, on a narrow sandy spit between L. Nokoué (a lagoon) and the sea. Pop. (1965) 111,000. Connected by rail with Parakou and Pobé (in the interior). Exports agricultural products, esp. palm oil and kernels, groundnuts. Manufactures vegetable oils, soap, etc.

**Cotopaxi** Ecuador. World's highest active volcano (19,344 ft), in the Andes 30 m. SSE of Quito. An almost symmetrical snow-capped cone. Frequently active, causing devastation in the surrounding settlements. First climbed by Reiss (1872).

**Cotswold Hills** England. Range of hills, mainly in Gloucestershire, extending SSW–NNE from Bath to Chipping Campden, at an average height of 500–600 ft, rising to 1,083 ft in Cleeve Cloud near Cheltenham. The Severn–Thames watershed. Many sheep are reared. Much visited for the beautiful villages (e.g. Bourton-on-the-Water, Burford, Painswick) built of the local limestone. The fortunes made from wool in the 14th–17th cent. helped to pay for some of the magnificent churches.

**Cottbus (Kottbus)** German Democratic Republic. Industrial town in the Cottbus district, on the Spree R. 68 m. SE of Berlin. Pop. (1965) 73,257. Manufactures woollen goods, carpets, machinery, soap, etc. Passed to ⟡ *Brandenburg* in 1462, and for a short time (1807–13) belonged to Saxony.

**Coulsdon and Purley** England. Former residential urban district in NE Surrey 13 m. S of London, which it serves as dormitory suburb; from 1965 part of the Greater London borough of Croydon. Pop. (1961) 74,738.

**Council Bluffs** USA. Town in SW Iowa at the foot of the bluffs along the Missouri R., opposite Omaha (Nebraska). Pop. (1960) 54,361. Railway and commercial centre. Railway workshops. Grain elevators. Manufactures agricultural implements, railway equipment, batteries, etc.

**Coupar-Angus** Scotland. Small burgh and market town in Perthshire, on the R. Isla 11 m. NNE of Perth; to be distinguished from Cupar in Fife. Pop. (1961) 2,049. Manufactures linen. Part of it was formerly in Angus.

**Courbevoie** France. Industrial and residential suburb in NW Paris, in the Hauts-de-Seine department, on the Seine R. Pop. (1968) 58,283. Manufactures cars, perfumes, cosmetics, soap, etc.

**Courland (Ger. Kurland, Lettish Kurzeme)** USSR. Region and former duchy in the Latvian SSR, between the Gulf of Riga and the Lithuanian border. Partly wooded but mainly agricultural, producing cereals, flax and potatoes. Inhabited originally by the Curi, a powerful, warlike people in the 10th–11th cent. Later a duchy under Polish sovereignty 1561–1795. It was then ceded to Russia; became part of independent Latvia in 1920 (except for a small area given to Lithuania), being divided into two provinces, Kurzeme (W) and Zemgale (E). In 1940 it returned to Russia as part of the Latvian SSR.

**Courland Lagoon** ⟡ *Kurisches Haff*.

**Courtrai (Flemish Kortrijk)** Belgium. Town in the W Flanders province, on the Lys R. 47 m. W of Brussels. Pop. (1968) 45,170. Important textile centre (linen, cotton, rayon, nylon, lace). In the 12th/13th-cent. Church of Notre Dame is Van Dyck's *Erection of the Cross*. Has a 16th-cent. Gothic town hall and the Broelbrug, an old bridge with 15th-cent. towers. Reached its peak of prosperity in the Middle Ages, when the population was probably 200,000. Scene of the defeat of a French army by the burghers of Ghent and Bruges in the 'Battle of the Spurs' (so called because the French fled) in 1302.

**Coutances** France. Town in the Manche department 42 m. S of Cherbourg, on the Cotentin peninsula. Pop. (1968) 10,993. Market town. Trade in agricultural produce. Textile and leather industries. Fine 13th-cent. Gothic cathedral, damaged in the 2nd World War.

**Coventry** England. City and county borough in Warwickshire, 16 m. ESE of Birmingham. Pop. (1961) 305,060 (70,000 in 1901; 167,000 in 1931). A leading centre of the motor-car industry, which developed from bicycle manufacture. Also produces machinery, hosiery, rayon, electrical equipment, etc. Grew up round a Benedictine monastery, founded in the 11th cent. by Leofric, husband of Lady Godiva. In the 13th–17th cent. the principal industry was weaving, with important trade in wool and cloth. Suffered severely from air raids during the 2nd World War; the cathedral church, St Michael, was destroyed (1940) except for the 303-ft spire and some outside walls, and the early 15th-cent. St Mary's Hall (built for the local trade guilds) and the 16th-cent. half-timbered Ford's Hospital were damaged. After the war the devastated city centre was replanned and rebuilt, with a shopping precinct, the Belgrade Theatre, the Hotel Leofric, and other noteworthy buildings; the magnificent but highly controversial new cathedral, containing works by Epstein, Graham Sutherland, etc., and retaining the ruins of the old cathedral church as a memorial shrine, was consecrated in 1962.

**Covington** USA. Industrial town in Kentucky on the Ohio R., connected with Cincinnati by a suspension bridge (1866). Pop. (1960) 60,376. Manufactures X-ray equipment, tobacco products, machine tools, tiles, bricks, paper, etc. Named after General Leonard Covington (1768–1813).

**Cowdenbeath** Scotland. Small burgh and coalmining town in S Fifeshire, 5 m. NE of Dunfermline. Pop. (1961) 16,974.

**Cowes** England. Urban district on the N coast of the Isle of Wight, on both banks of the estuary of the R. Medina (West Cowes, East Cowes). Pop. (1961) 16,974. Port. Famous yachting and yacht-building centre. Manufactures hovercraft. Headquarters of the Royal Yacht Squadron (founded 1812) and scene of the annual 'Cowes Week' (Aug.). In E Cowes is Osborne House, built in Palladian style for Queen Victoria (1845). Scene of the sailing of the founders of Maryland, USA (1633).

Cowley England. Suburb of Oxford where William Morris (later Lord Nuffield) began the manufacture of motor-cars on the production-line system. Now an important unit in the UK automobile industry. Headquarters of the Cowley Fathers, an Anglican religious community (1865).

Cracow (Polish Kraków) Poland. Capital of Kraków voivodship, Poland's third largest city, on the Vistula R. 160 m. SSW of Warsaw. Pop. (1968) 560,300 (221,000 in 1931). Railway junction. Commercial and industrial centre. Trade in salt, timber, cattle, agricultural produce. Manufactures iron and steel (at Nowa Huta), railway rolling stock, agricultural machinery, chemicals, clothing, food, and tobacco products, etc. It has long been a leading centre of Polish culture; the famous Jagiellonian University, at which Copernicus was a student, was founded in 1364 – one of the oldest in Europe. Renowned for its many fine buildings and historic monuments. On the Wawel, a hill just SW of the old town, are the 14th-cent. cathedral, which contains the tombs of Polish kings and half of Kosciuszko, Mickiewicz, and Pilsudski, and the royal castle, begun in the 12th cent. and enlarged in the 16th. The 13th/14th-cent. Church of Our Lady has a magnificent triptych by Veit Stoss; near by is the 14th-cent. frequently restored Cloth Hall. Probably founded early in the 8th cent. Polish capital 1305–1609. At the Third Partition (1795) it passed to Austria; became part of the duchy of Warsaw (1809) and the republic of Cracow (1815); was incorporated in Austria (1846), and returned to Poland (1918).

Cradock S Africa. Town in the Cape Province, on the Great Fish R. 130 m. N of Port Elizabeth. Pop. (1960) 19,000. Market town in a rich sheep-farming district. 3 m. N are hot sulphur springs. The Mountain Zebra National Park is near by. Founded 1814. Named after Sir John Cradock, Governor of the Cape 1811–13. Home and burial-place of Olive Schreiner, S African authoress.

Craigavon Northern Ireland. Urban district in N E Co. Armagh, formed in 1967 from the rural district of Lurgan. Pop. (1968) 10,830.

Crail Scotland. Small burgh in E Fifeshire, near the mouth of the Firth of Forth, 2 m. W of Fife Ness. Pop. (1961) 1,066. Seaside resort. Fishing.

Craiova Rumania. Ancient Castra Nova. Capital of the Dolj district, on the Jiu R. in Walachia, 120 m. W of Bucharest. Pop. (1968) 158,651. Industrial town. Manufactures textiles, machinery, leather goods, etc. Food processing.

Cranbrook England. Market town in Kent, 12 m. S of Maidstone. Pop. (1961) 4,150. Agricultural centre of the Kent Weald. Trade in hops, fruit, etc. From the 14th to the 17th cent. had a flourishing broadcloth industry, introduced from Flanders. Has the largest working windmill in England.

Cranston USA. Industrial town in Rhode Island on the Pawtuxet R. just S of Providence. Pop. (1960) 66,766. Manufactures textiles, machinery, rubber products, etc. Named after Samuel Cranston, Governor of Rhode Island 1698–1727.

Cranwell England. Village in Parts of Kesteven in Lincolnshire, 11 m. NE of Grantham. Site of the Royal Air Force College (1920).

Crawley England. Urban district in W Sussex 7 m. NE of Horsham, created a 'new town' in 1956. Pop. (1961) 53,786. Light engineering. Manufactures furniture, electronic equipment, plastics, etc.

Crayford England. Urban district in NW Kent, on the R. Cray 2 m. WNW of Dartford; a dormitory suburb of London. Pop. (1961) 31,265. Engineering, flour milling. Manufactures furniture.

Crécy (Crécy-en-Ponthieu) France. Village in the Somme department, 10 m. NNE of Abbeville. Pop. (1968) 1,398. Scene of the famous victory of Edward III of England over the French (1346).

Crediton England. Urban district in Devonshire, 7 m. NW of Exeter, on the R. Creedy. Pop. (1961) 4,422. Market town. Engineering. Manufactures cider, confectionery. Traditionally the birthplace of St Boniface (680–754).

Crema Italy. Market town in the Cremona province in Lombardy, 24 m. NW of Cremona. Pop. (1961) 30,035. Manufactures textiles etc. Cathedral (13th/14th-cent.).

Cremona Italy. Capital of Cremona province in Lombardy, on the Po R. 50 m. SE of Milan. Pop. (1961) 73,902. Industrial and commercial centre for the fertile Po valley. Manufactures confectionery, dairy products (cheese, butter), macaroni, silk, musical instruments, etc. Impressive main square, with magnificent cathedral and octagonal baptistry (12th-cent.) and the 13th-cent. Torrazzo (the highest campanile in Italy). Founded by the Romans *c.* 220 B.C. Famous in the 16th–18th cent. for violins, made by the Amati, Guarnieri, and Stradivari. Birthplace of the composer Claudio Monteverdi (1567–1643).

**Cres** Yugoslavia. Island in the Gulf of Kvarner on the Adriatic Sea, SSW of Rijeka. Area 130 sq. m. Pop. 12,000. Chief village and principal port Cres. Main occupations agriculture, sheep farming, fishing. Belonged to Austro-Hungary till 1919 and to Italy 1919–47.

**Crete (Gr. Kríti)** Greece. Fourth largest island in the Mediterranean Sea, to the S of the Aegean Sea. Area 3,217 sq. m. Pop. (1961) 483,258. Cap. Canea (Khanía). Mostly mountainous, rising to over 8,000 ft in Mt Ida (Psiloríti) in the centre. The N coast is deeply indented. The mountain slopes have been almost denuded of forests. In the limited plains and valleys large numbers of olive trees are grown. Main products olive oil, citrus fruits, wine. Sheep and goats raised. Divided administratively (with neighbouring small islands) into the four *nomes* of Canea, Iráklion, Lasíthi, Rethymnon. Chief towns Canea (Khanía), Candia (Iráklion). Archaeological discoveries have revealed that Crete was the home of the Minoan civilization, one of the world's oldest; development has been traced *c.* 3400–1100 B.C. The palace at Knossos in particular yields information of immense value. The island played an insignificant part in Greek history. Fell to Rome (67 B.C.), Byzantium (A.D. 395), the Muslims (826), the Venetians (1204), and the Turks (1669). After a number of rebellions in the 19th cent. it was finally united with Greece in 1912. Taken by the Germans in the first airborne invasion of the 2nd World War (1941).

**Creuse** France. Department comprising most of the Marche and parts of the Berry and other provinces, in the NW corner of the Massif Central. Area 2,164 sq. m. Pop. (1968) 156,876. Prefecture Guéret. In the S is the Plateau de Millevaches. Main river the Creuse. The soil is thin and the climate inhospitable. Agriculture (cereals, potatoes) limited to the valleys. Livestock reared on the uplands. Chief towns, Guéret, Aubusson.

**Creuse River** France. River 150 m. long, rising in the Plateau de Millevaches, flowing NNW, and joining the Vienne R. A famous gorge in the upper course.

**Crewe** England. Municipal borough in Cheshire, 20 m. ESE of Chester. Pop. (1961) 53,394. Where only a farmhouse stood in 1841 grew up one of Britain's most important railway junctions with some of the world's largest railway workshops. Railway engineering. Manufactures cars, chemicals, clothing, etc.

**Crewkerne** England. Urban district in S Somerset, 17 m. SE of Taunton. Pop. (1961) 4,215. Market town. Manufactures leather goods, textiles. A 15th-cent. church; 17th-cent. almshouses.

**Criccieth** Wales. Urban district in Caernarvonshire, on the S coast of the Lleyn peninsula (Cardigan Bay). Pop. (1961) 1,671. Seaside resort. Home and burial-place of Lloyd George (1863–1945).

**Crieff** Scotland. Small burgh on the R. Earn in Strath Earn, 15 m. W of Perth. Pop. (1961) 5,773. Health resort. Whisky distilling, tanning. An ancient market cross with Runic carving. Famous before 1770 for cattle fairs. Had a notorious tree used as a gallows for cattle thieves and other criminals.

**Crimea (Krim)** USSR. Peninsula 210 m. long W–E and 120 m. N–S, on the N side of the Black Sea, joined to the mainland by the narrow Perekop isthmus; a region in the Ukrainian SSR. Area 9,880 sq. m. Pop. 1,500,000 (chiefly Russian and Ukrainian). Cap. Simferopol. To the NE is the shallow Sivash lagoon, separated from the Sea of Azov by the long sandy Arabat spit or tongue. To the E is the Kerch strait and beyond it the Taman peninsula. Most of the Crimea is arid but generally fertile steppe, drained by the Salgir R. and other intermittent streams, with many small salt lakes. Wheat and cotton cultivated. Mountains extend SW–NE parallel to the S coast and a few miles inland. In contrast to the dusty summers and frosty winters of the steppe, the coastal climate is Mediterranean; the region is called the Russian Riviera and is an important tourist area, centred on Yalta. Here vines, fruits, and tobacco are grown. Fisheries around all the coasts. Metallurgical industry is based on the rich iron-ore deposits of Kerch. Sevastopol is the chief seaport, and a naval base. Colonized in turn by the Scythians and the Greeks, it became subject to Rome, and later was overrun by the Goths, the Huns, and the Khazars. Conquered by the Turks (1475) and under Turkish rule until annexed by Russia (1783). The W Crimea was the scene of the Crimean War (1854–6) in which Britain, France, and Turkey were allied against Russia. After the Bolshevik revolution (1917) the Crimean ASSR was formed (within the RSFSR) in 1921. Collaboration of some of the population with the Germans during the 2nd World War caused subsequent downgrading to the status of a region (1946), transferred to the Ukrainian SSR in 1954. The Yalta Conference between Roosevelt, Churchill, and Stalin took place at Livadia (near Yalta) in 1945.

**Crimmitschau** German Democratic Republic. Industrial town in the Karl-Marx-Stadt district 25 m. W of Karl-Marx-Stadt. Pop. (1965) 31,074. Manufactures textiles, textile machinery, etc.

**Crna Gora** ◊ *Montenegro*.

**Croagh Patrick** Irish Republic. Cone-shaped mountain (2,510 ft) in Co. Mayo, on the S shore of Clew Bay. Traditionally the spot where St Patrick first preached. Now a notable place of annual pilgrimage on the last Sunday in July.

**Croatia** (Serbo-Croatian **Hrvatska**) Yugoslavia. Constituent republic in the NW. Area 21,824 sq. m. Pop. (1961) 4,159,696. Cap. Zagreb. Bordered on the SW by the Adriatic, it stretches to the Drava R. in the N bordering on Hungary, and includes most of Istria and a narrowing strip of the Dalmatian coast as far S as the Gulf of Kotor (except for the corridor giving Hercegovina access to the Adriatic). Many islands (Krk, Cres, Brač, Korčula, etc.) along the coast. Mountainous and barren in the SW (Dinaric Alps). Much lower and more fertile in the NE. Mainly agricultural. Produces cereals, fruits, vegetables. Principal towns Zagreb, Rijeka (chief seaport), Split, Osijek. Settled in the 7th cent. A.D. by the Croats, who still form the majority of the population and are Roman Catholic (the large Serb minority are Eastern Orthodox). Conquered by Hungary 1091. Enjoyed some degree of autonomy till the creation of Yugoslavia (1918), when it became the province of Croatia-Slavonia.

Became the People's Republic of Croatia 1946.

**Crocodile River** ◊ *Limpopo River*.

**Cromarty** ◊ *Ross and Cromarty*.

**Cromer** England. Urban district in Norfolk on the North Sea 21 m. N of Norwich. Pop. (1961) 4,895. Seaside resort. Protected by a sea wall from marine erosion, which encroached on the cliffs for many centuries. The 15th-cent. Perpendicular Church of St Peter and St Paul has a 159-ft tower.

**Crompton** England. Urban district in SE Lancashire, a suburb of Oldham. Pop. (1961) 12,707. Cotton mills.

**Crook and Willington** England. Urban district in Durham 8 m. SW of Durham. Pop. (1961) 25,218. Coalmining. Manufactures machinery, firebricks, etc.

**Crosby** England. Municipal borough in SW Lancashire, just NW of Bootle; a residential suburb of Liverpool. Pop. (1961) 59,707.

**Cross Fell** England. Highest mountain (2,930 ft) in the Pennines, in E Cumberland 11 m. ENE of Penrith.

**Crotone** Italy. Ancient Crotona. Town in the Catanzaro province in Calabria, on the Gulf of Taranto. Pop. (1961) 43,256. Important chemical works and zinc-smelter, drawing power from hydroelectric plants in the La Sila mountains. Founded (710 B.C.) by the Achaeans. Became a wealthy and powerful city. The inhabitants (esp. Milo) won fame at the Olympic Games. Seat of the school established by Pythagoras 540–530 B.C.

**Croton River** USA. River 60 m. long in New York, flowing generally SW to join the Hudson R. at Croton Point. An important source of water supply for New York city since 1842; the water of the Croton R. reservoirs is carried by the two Croton Aqueducts.

**Crouch River** England. River 24 m. long, rising near Brentwood in Essex, flowing E past Burnham-on-Crouch to enter the North Sea at Foulness Point. The estuary is a celebrated yachting centre.

**Crowborough** England. Small market town in NE Sussex 7 m. SW of Tunbridge Wells near Crowborough Beacon (792 ft, the highest point in Ashdown Forest). Pop. (1961) 8,109.

**Crowland (Croyland)** England. Small market town in Parts of Holland, S Lincolnshire, on the R. Welland 7 m. NNE of Peterborough. Pop. (1961) 2,835. Ruins of a Benedictine abbey, founded in the 8th cent.

by King Aethelbald and restored in the 12th; the restored N aisle is used as the parish church. A 14th-cent. triangular bridge.

**Crow's Nest Pass** Canada. Pass 4,450 ft high in the Rocky Mountains on the border of Alberta and British Columbia, through which runs a branch line of the Canadian Pacific Railway. The name is a translation of the Cree Indian name.

**Croydon** England. Greater London borough (1965) comprising the former county borough of Croydon and the former urban district of Coulsdon and Purley (Surrey). Pop. (1963) 327,125. Chiefly residential. Manufactures clocks, pharmaceutical products, foodstuffs, etc. As London's first airport, Croydon was superseded by Northolt. Site of a palace of the Archbishops of Canterbury from the Conquest till 1780; the hall and chapel are used as a girls' school. The Whitgift Grammar School and 'hospital' (almshouses) were founded in the late 16th cent. by Archbishop Whitgift (1530–1604).

**Croyland** ◊ *Crowland.*

**Crozet Islands** Indian Ocean. Archipelago in the S W Indian Ocean 1,500 m. ESE of Port Elizabeth, consisting of 5 larger and 15 smaller islands in two groups. Area 116 sq. m. Mountainous and virtually uninhabited. Discovered 1772; annexed for France. A meteorological station was set up on Possession Island in 1964. From 1955 part of the ◊ *French Southern and Antarctic Territories.*

**Csaba** ◊ *Bekescsaba.*

**Csongrád** Hungary. Market town in the Csongrád county, at the confluence of the Tisza and the Körös rivers. Pop. 26,000. Flour milling, sawmilling.

**Ctesiphon** Iraq. Ancient city on the Tigris R. 20 m. SE of Baghdad. Famous for the remains of the great vaulted hall of the Sassanian palace. Became capital of the Sassanian empire in the 2nd cent. but was captured and plundered by the Arabs in 637. Scene of a battle between the British and the Turks in the 1st World War (1915).

**Cuba.** Island republic, the largest and most westerly of the W Indies, at the entrance to the Gulf of Mexico. Area 44,206 sq. m. Pop. (1963) 7,134,044 (73 per cent white and mulatto, 27 per cent Negro and mixed). Cap. Havana. Lang. Spanish. Rel. Roman Catholic.

Mainly flat or gently undulating; in the Sierra Maestra range (SE) the Pico Turquino rises to 6,496 ft, and near the centre is the Sierra de Trinidad. The N coast, largely steep and rocky with numerous coral reefs and small islands, is washed by the Atlantic, and the S coast, chiefly low and swampy, by the Caribbean. Off the S W coast is the Isle of Pines (area 1,180 sq. m.). There are many coastal inlets which provide sheltered harbours. The climate is subtropical, with a small seasonal variation. Hurricanes occur: in 1963 hurricane 'Flora' caused the deaths of at least 1,150 people and enormous losses in crops etc.

The main crop is sugar, which with by-products earns nearly nine tenths of Cuba's foreign exchange. Other exports are tobacco (esp. cigars) in second place, pineapples, bananas, citrus fruits. Industries are sugar refining, rum distilling, sisal and tobacco processing. Recent political events have completely changed the direction of Cuban foreign trade: in 1958 about 70 per cent of exports and imports were destined for and came from the USA, but this trade rapidly declined, and by 1964 85 per cent of foreign trade was with the Communist countries, chiefly the USSR and China. Cuba is divided administratively into 6 provinces.

Discovered (1492) by Columbus. By 1511 it had been settled by Spain. In the 18th cent. it became the haunt of buccaneers. Remained Spanish till the Spanish-American War (1898); after a short occupation by US forces it became independent in 1902, but remained closely linked with the USA. Under the Castro régime Cuba broke away and developed close ties with the USSR (1959). The establishment of rocket bases (1962) led to a critical confrontation between the USA and the USSR, and for a time Cuba was blockaded by the US Navy. The USA, however, has continued to maintain her naval base at Guantánamo.

**Cubatão** ◊ *Santos.*

**Cúcuta** (officially **San José de Cúcuta**) Colombia. Capital of the Norte de Santander department, on the Pan-American Highway (Bogotá–Carácas) 10 m. from the Venezuela frontier. Pop. (1964) 147,250. Commercial centre. Large trade in coffee. Coffee roasting. Manufactures textiles, soap, etc. Founded 1734. Used by Bolívar as his base for the march on Carácas. Rebuilt after destruction by earthquake (1875).

**Cuddalore** India. Seaport on the Coromandel Coast, in Madras, 100 m. SSW of

Madras. Pop. (1961) 79,168. Exports groundnuts, cotton goods. Weaving and dyeing. Passed from the French to the British 1785.

**Cuenca** Ecuador. Capital of the Azuay province, 80 m. SE of Guayaquil, in a fertile basin at a height of 8,500 ft. Pop. (1962) 60,021. Trade in cinchona bark, sugar-cane, cereals, etc. Flour milling. Manufactures tyres, Panama hats, textiles, leather, etc. University (1868). Founded 1557. A town of cobbled streets and old colonial buildings.

**Cuenca** Spain. 1. Province in New Castile. Area 6,586 sq. m. Pop. (1961) 315,433. Largely mountainous; part of the Meseta and (S) of La Mancha. Mainly used for rearing sheep and goats. Agriculture in the lower areas. Lumbering on the Serranía de Cuenca.
2. Capital of Cuenca province, on a hill above the Júcar R. at a height of 3,000 ft. Pop. 27,007. Market town. Minor flour milling, sawmilling, tanning, and other industries. Cathedral (13th-cent.). Taken from the Moors by Alfonso VIII of Castile 1177. Became a textile centre in the later Middle Ages; declined from the 17th cent.

**Cuiabá** Brazil. Capital of the Mato Grosso state, at the head of navigation on the Cuiabá R. Pop. 46,000. Accessible by river from Corumbá and by road from Campo Grande. Collecting centre for cattle, hides, dried meat, ipecacuanha, etc. Founded (1719) by gold prospectors.

**Cuiabá River** Brazil. River 300 m. long, rising on the divide of the Mato Grosso tableland, flowing generally SSW, joining the São Lourenço R. and then the Paraguay R.

**Cuillin Hills** Scotland. Mountain group in S Skye in Inverness-shire, rising to 3,309 ft in Sgurr Alasdair, the highest peak on the island.

**Culiacán** Mexico. Capital of Sinaloa state, at the foot of the Sierra Madre Occidental 190 m. WNW of Durango. Pop. (1960) 82,045. In an irrigated agricultural region, producing maize, beans, sugar-cane, etc. Manufactures textiles etc. Founded 1531.

**Cullinan** S Africa. Town in the Transvaal 20 m. ENE of Pretoria. Pop. (1961) 4,211. Founded 1903; built up round the Premier diamond mine, where the world's largest diamond (the 'Cullinan') was found (1905).

**Culloden Moor (Culloden Muir)** Scotland. Moorland area in Inverness-shire 5 m. E of Inverness; part of Drummossie Muir.

Scene of the defeat (1746) of the Jacobite forces under the Young Pretender ('Bonnie Prince Charlie', grandson of James II) by the Hanoverian forces under the Duke of Cumberland (son of George II), and of the massacres after the battle which earned the victor the title of 'Butcher Cumberland'. Greatly celebrated in songs, poems, and novels.

**Culross** Scotland. Royal burgh in Fifeshire, on the Firth of Forth 6 m. WSW of Dunfermline. Pop. (1961) 514. Holiday resort. Noted for 16th- and 17th-cent. houses exemplifying Scottish domestic architecture. Remains of a 13th-cent. Cistercian abbey.

**Cumae** Italy. Ancient city on the W coast of Campania, 11 m. W of Naples. Said by Strabo to be the earliest Greek settlement in Italy; founded in the 8th cent. B.C. Established colonies at Naples, Pozzuoli, etc. Defeated the Etruscan fleet with the help of Hiero of Syracuse in 474 B.C. Conquered by the Samnites before the end of the 5th cent B.C. Pre-Hellenic, Greek, Samnite, and Roman graves have been discovered.

**Cumaná** Venezuela. Formerly Nueva Toledo. Capital of the Sucre state, on the Manzanares R. 1 m. above the mouth and its port Puerto Sucre. Pop. (1964) 110,201. Exports coffee, cacao, tobacco. Fishing, fish canning, cotton milling. Founded (as Nueva Toledo) c. 1521; the oldest European settlement in South America. Severely damaged by earthquakes (esp. 1766, 1797, and 1929).

**Cumberland** England. County in the NW, bordering on Scotland (N) and on the Irish Sea and the Solway Firth (W). Area 1,520 sq. m. Pop. (1961) 294,162. County town Carlisle. Picturesque, mountainous in the S (which is drained by the Ellen, the Derwent, and the Esk rivers and comprises a considerable part of the ◊ *Lake District*): Scafell (3,210 ft), Helvellyn (3,118 ft), Skiddaw (3,053 ft). In the NW is the broad plain of Carlisle, drained by the R. Eden and its tributaries, rising in the E to the Pennines (Cross Fell, 2,930 ft) and in the NE to the Cheviot Hills. Dairy farming and the cultivation of oats and root crops in the lowlands. Sheep farming in the hills. Granite and slate quarried. Industries in the three small ports of Workington, Whitehaven, and Maryport are based on local coal deposits. Constant border strife for many centuries until the union of the crowns of England and Scotland (1603). Britain's first atomic-energy power station was opened at Calder Hall in 1956.

**Cumberland** USA. Industrial town in NW Maryland, on the Potomac R. 115 m. WNW of Baltimore, in the Appalachian Mountains. Pop. (1960) 33,415. Trade in coal, mined in the neighbourhood. Railway engineering. Manufactures tyres, glassware, etc.

**Cumberland Peninsula** Canada. Peninsula in SE Baffin Island in the NW Territories, extending 200 m. E into the Davis Strait. Mountainous, rising to over 8,000 ft. Named in honour of the 3rd Earl of Cumberland (1558–1605).

**Cumberland Plateau (Cumberland Mountains)** USA. The S part of the westernmost division of the Appalachians, mainly in Tennessee. Source of the Cumberland and the Kentucky rivers. The Cumberland Gap, an old settlers' route important in the American Civil War, is a pass in the extreme SW of Virginia. Named in honour of William, Duke of Cumberland, the victor of ◊ *Culloden*.

**Cumberland River** USA. River 690 m. long, rising on the Cumberland Plateau and flowing generally W to join the Ohio R. at Smithland (Kentucky).

**Cumbernauld** Scotland. Former village in the detached part of Dunbartonshire, 13 m. ENE of Glasgow, constituted a 'new town' in 1955 to accommodate people from Glasgow. Pop. (1968) 24,383 (4,924 in 1961). Varied industries.

**Cumbraes, The** Scotland. Two islands in Buteshire, in the Firth of Clyde; separated by the ½-m.-wide Tan strait. Area: Great Cumbrae 5 sq. m.; Little Cumbrae 1 sq. m. Pop. (1961) 1,645. On Great Cumbrae is the holiday resort of Millport.

**Cumbre, La** ◊ *Uspallata Pass*.

**Cumbria** Britain. Region (approximating to modern Cumberland and Westmorland) which remained an autonomous British kingdom after the Anglo-Saxon conquest in the 5th cent. A.D. Had become part of England by the 12th cent. The Cumbrian Mountains of the Lake District (highest point Scafell, 3,210 ft) are within the region.

**Cumnock and Holmhead** Scotland. Small burgh in Ayrshire, 14 m. E of Ayr. Pop. (1961) 5,403. New Cumnock, a coalmining village, is 5 m. SE. Burial-place of the Covenanter Alexander Peden, 'the Prophet' (1626–86). Home of the British labour leader Keir Hardie (1856–1915).

**Cunaxa.** Ancient town in Babylonia near the Euphrates R. Scene of the defeat (401 B.C.) of Cyrus the Younger (with about 13,000 Greek mercenaries) by his brother Artaxerxes II, which was followed by the famous 'Retreat of the Ten Thousand' under Xenophon.

**Cunene River** ◊ *Kunene River*.

**Cuneo** Italy. Capital of Cuneo province in Piedmont, 47 m. S of Turin. Pop. (1961) 46,065. Important trade in raw silk. Manufactures textiles (silk) etc. Metal working, food processing, etc. Important road and rail junction.

**Cupar** Scotland. Royal burgh and county town of Fifeshire, 8 m. WSW of St Andrews. Pop. (1961) 5,495. Tanning. Manufactures fertilizers. Beet sugar refined near by. A school stands on the site of the 12th-cent. castle of the Macduffs.

**Curaçao** Netherlands Antilles. Largest island of the two ◊ *Netherlands Antilles* groups in the Caribbean Sea between Aruba and Bonaire 40 m. N of the coast of Venezuela. Area 183 sq. m. Pop. (1968) 139,211. Cap. Willemstad. Agricultural products include sisal and citrus fruits. Orange peel is used in the manufacture of the famous Curaçao liqueur. The chief industry is the refining of petroleum from the L. Maracaibo region in Venezuela. Discovered by the Spaniards 1499. Taken by the Dutch 1634. Apart from a short British occupation, has remained Dutch ever since.

**Curicó** Chile. Capital of the Curicó province, in the fertile central valley 110 m. SSW of Santiago. Pop. (1960) 52,000. Market town. Trade in cattle. Flour milling, wine making, distilling. Founded 1742. Severely damaged by earthquake 1928.

**Curitiba** Brazil. Capital of the Paraná state, on a plateau at 3,000 ft, 43 m. W of its port, Paranaguá. Pop. (1960) 344,560. Important commercial and industrial centre. Trade in coffee, timber, maté. Manufactures paper, textiles, etc. Seat of the University of Paraná (1946). A rapidly growing city, esp. since the large-scale immigration of Poles, Germans, and Italians from the mid-19th cent. onwards.

**Curragh, The** Irish Republic. Plain in Co. Kildare, just E of Kildare, famous for its turf. Area about 5,000 acres. Site of a racecourse probably since the 1st cent. A.D. and of a military camp since 1646. The 'revolt' of some British Army officers against the coming into force of the 1913 Home Rule Act, influential in Irish history, is known as 'the Curragh Incident'. The Irish Derby is run on the racecourse (June).

**Curzola** ◊ *Korčula*.

**Cutch, Rann of** ◊ *Kutch, Rann of*.

**Cuttack** India. River port and commercial town in Orissa, at the head of the Mahanadi R. delta. Pop. (1961) 146,303. Trade in rice, oilseeds, etc. Engineering, tanning, gold and silver filigree work, etc. Formerly capital of Orissa. Seat of the Utkal University from 1943 to 1962, when it was moved to Bhubaneswar.

**Cuxhaven** Federal German Republic. Seaport in Lower Saxony at the entrance to the Elbe estuary. Pop. (1963) 44,900. Serves as the outport to Hamburg. Fishing, fish canning. Shipbuilding. Summer resort.

**Cuyabá River** ◊ *Cuiabá River*.

**Cuyahoga Falls** USA. Town in NE Ohio on the Cuyahoga R. Pop. (1960) 47,922. Manufactures machinery, tools, rubber and paper products, etc., but largely residential.

**Cuzco** Peru. Ancient city; now capital of the Cuzco department, in the fertile valley of the Vilcanota, at a height of 11,440 ft. Pop. (1961) 78,289. Commercial centre. Several small industries, e.g. brewing, tanning, textile manufacture. Severely damaged by earthquake 1950. Rich in examples of Spanish colonial architecture and in remains of Inca buildings (inc. the famous Temple of the Sun), of which enough survives to show the massive perfection of the stonework. Capital (from the 11th cent. until the Spanish conquest early in the 16th cent.) of the Inca empire, a fully planned and regulated state, ruled by a benevolent Inca élite, which gradually extended its rule over the whole area that is now Peru and Bolivia, and over parts of modern Ecuador, Chile, and Argentina. The Incas maintained centralized control by an extensive system of roads, over which messengers travelled quickly. They had no writing, but used a mnemonic and reckoning system in the form of *quipus*, cords knotted to record statistical information. Economic security was ensured for all, but at the price of initiative or freedom for the mass of the Indians; the empire crumbled when Pizarro destroyed the ruling class in his conquest (1533). Near by stands the Inca fortress of Sacsahuamán, remarkable for the enormous and perfectly fitting blocks of rock of which it is built.

**Cwmbran** Wales. Urban district in Monmouthshire 4 m. N of Newport, designated a 'new town' in 1949, with an ultimate population of 55,000. Pop. (1968) 30,290 (21,690 in 1961). The coalmines closed in 1927; various industries have since been set up, with government help, to absorb redundant labour.

**Cyclades** (Gr. **Kikládhes**) Greece. Group of over 200 islands in the Aegean Sea, forming a *nome*. Area 995 sq. m. Pop. (1961) 99,931. Cap. Hermoupolis (pop. 14,403) on Syros. Produce wine, tobacco, olives, some minerals (emery, iron ore, etc.). Generally rugged but picturesque. Ruled by Turkey from the 16th cent.; passed to Greece 1832.

**Cyprus** (Gr. **Kypros**). Island republic in the E Mediterranean, 50 m. S of Turkey, 60 m. W of Syria. Area 3,572 sq. m. Pop. (1967) 614,000 (about 77 per cent Greek-speaking and Eastern-Orthodox Christian, 18 per cent Turkish-speaking and Muslim). Cap. Nicosia. The greatest length is 140 m., 46 m. of this being the narrow tapering Karpas peninsula (NE). The greatest breadth is 60 m. Largely mountainous; the rugged Kyrenia mountains extend along the N coast, the higher Troödos Mountains in the SW rise to 6,403 ft in Mt Olympus. Between the two ranges is the broad fertile Mesaoria plain. The rivers are torrents in winter but run dry in summer. The anciently-famous forests are reduced to less than one fifth of the total area. Large numbers of sheep and goats raised. Wheat, barley, olives, carobs, citrus fruits, and wine produced. Celebrated in antiquity for its copper mines ('copper' derives from Kypros). Principal minerals iron, cupreous pyrites. Famagusta is the only seaport capable of accommodating large vessels; Limassol and Larnaca have open roadsteads, Paphos and Kyrenia small harbours. Administratively divided into 6 districts (named after the above towns). Cyprus is rich in archaeological remains testifying to, e.g., a Bronze Age culture probably before 3000 B.C. Settled by the Phoenicians *c.* 800 B.C. Fell to Assyria, Egypt, and Persia. Taken by Rome 58 B.C. For some centuries part of the Byzantine Empire, then changed hands several times until conquered by the Turks 1571. Occupied (1878) and annexed (1914) by Britain; a Crown Colony 1925–60, then became an independent republic within the British Commonwealth. Open violence later demonstrated continuing tension between the Greek and the Turkish communities.

**Cyrenaica** Libya. Largest and most easterly

province 1951–63 (◊ *Libya*). Area 330,000 sq. m. Pop. 320,000. Cap. Benghazi. Bounded by the United Arab Republic and Sudan (E), Chad (S), Tripolitania and Fezzan (W). Second largest town (after Benghazi) Derna. The fertile districts in the narrow coastal plain produce barley, wheat, grapes, olives. Dates are grown farther S. Dry farming practised on the Barca plateau, but the raising of livestock (chiefly goats and sheep) is the main occupation. Tunny fishing important. To the S an extensive arid depression gradually rises to the Libyan desert and the Kufra oases. In, the extreme S W are the Tibesti highlands. The chief towns are linked by a coastal road running S and W to Tripoli. A short railway joins Benghazi to Barca and Soluk. Caravan routes lead S to Saharan oases. The coastal region was first settled by the Greeks, who founded ◊ *Cyrene* (hence 'Cyrenaica'). Passed to the Ptolemies and then to Rome; became a Roman province 67 B.C. Conquered by the Arabs in the 7th cent. Occupied by the Turks in the 16th cent. and part of the Turkish empire until they were driven out by the Italians in 1911, when it became part of the Italian colony of Libya. Scene of many battles in the N African campaigns of the 2nd World War. Under British military administration 1942–51. Became one of the three provinces of the new independent federal kingdom 1951; the Amir became King Idris I el-Mahdi el-Senussi.

**Cyrene** (Ar. **Shahat**) Libya. Original capital of Cyrenaica, on the coast road 50 m. W of Derna. Pop. 500. Founded by Greek colonists from Thera *c.* 630 B.C. Passed to the Ptolemies 322 B.C. and to Rome 96 B.C. Anciently famed for its medical school and intellectual life; Callimachus and Eratosthenes were among its outstanding citizens. Many Greek and Roman remains, including temples, baths, gymnasium, acropolis.

**Cythera** (Gr. **Kíthira**) Greece. Island off the S E Peloponnese at the entrance to the Gulf of Laconia. Area 106 sq. m. Pop. 6,000. Rocky, with some fertile areas. Produces olive oil, wine, etc. Chief town Kíthira. In ancient times it was sacred to Aphrodite, who was supposed to have risen from the sea there.

**Czechoslovakia.\*** Republic in central Europe. Area 49,359 sq. m. Pop. (1967) 14,271,547 (66 per cent Czech, 28 per cent Slovak (both Slavonic), 3 per cent Hungarian, 1·2 per cent German). Cap. Prague. Rel. 80 per cent Roman Catholic, 10 per cent Protestant.

Bounded by Poland and the German Democratic Republic (N), the USSR (E), Hungary and Austria (S), and the Federal German Republic (W). Many of the frontiers are marked by natural features: the Erzgebirge, the Sudeten and the Carpathian Mountains in the N, the Danube R. in the S, the Bohemian Forest (Böhmerwald) in the W. The former provinces of Bohemia, Moravia-Silesia, and Slovakia were replaced after the 1948 revolution by 19 administrative regions (1949), which were reduced to 10 (plus Prague) in 1960: Jihočeský, Jihomoravský, Severočeský, Severomoravský, Středočeský, Východočeský, Západočeský (in Bohemia and Moravia-Silesia); and Středoslovenský, Východoslovenský, Západoslovenský (in Slovakia).

TOPOGRAPHY, CLIMATE. The three political regions (Bohemia, Moravia, Slovakia) correspond to physical divisions. Bohemia (W) is a plateau, rising round the edges to the Sudeten Mountains (NE), the Moravian Heights (SE), the Böhmerwald (SW), and the Erzgebirge (NW), and drained by the Elbe (Labe) and the Vltava rivers and their tributaries. Moravia (E of Bohemia) is largely lowland, drained to the Danube by the Morava and its tributaries, and rising gently to the Moravian Heights in the W and the Carpathian Mountains in the E; the Moravian Gate (between the Sudeten and the Carpathian Mountains, including part of the Morava valley) is the historic route between the Oder and the Danube. Slovakia (E of Moravia) is mainly highland; the greater part of the area (all but the extreme S) is occupied by the W Carpathian Mountains (including the Little and the White Carpathians), and S of the main range is the High Tatra, with the highest peak in Czechoslovakia, Gerlachovka (8,737 ft). Climate varies considerably with altitude; in general, it becomes more continental from W to E.

RESOURCES, PEOPLE, *etc.* Highly industrialized economy, but agriculture is still important. About 40 per cent of the land is arable. Principal crops cereals, sugar-beet, potatoes, hops; many of the manufactures, e.g. beer (from Pilsen), sugar (from Prague), and other foodstuffs, are derived from these products. Cattle and pigs raised in large numbers. After the republic was created (1918) the former large estates were broken up; under the Communist régime since the 2nd World War (from 1948) farming has been organized on Soviet lines. Collective farms (8,784) and State farms (364) accounted for 89 per cent of all the farmed land in 1962; but agricultural production has fallen far short of the requirements of the 5-year plans, and had still not reached the 1939 level by 1958. Rich in forests; lumbering is an important occupation. The output of the basic minerals for the principal industries (bituminous coal, lignite, and iron ore) greatly increased under the two first plans (1949–53 and 1956–60). Other minerals are copper, lead, silver, uranium. Among the leading industries (all of which are nationalized) are iron and steel, textiles, chemicals, glass, and porcelain. Chief industrial centres Bratislava, Brno, Ostrava, Pilsen, Prague. Well-known spas Jachymov (Joachimsthal), Karlovy Vary (Karlsbad), and Mariánské Lázně (Marienbad). There was a considerable infiltration of Germans (esp. into the industrialized areas of Bohemia) and Hungarians (into S Slovakia) in the inter-war years, but the great majority of the Germans were expelled after the 2nd World War.

HISTORY. Before the republic was created (1918) the territories had separate histories.

Bohemia and Moravia, early peopled by Slavs, were converted to Christianity by the Greek monks Cyril and Methodius. Both formed part of Sviatopluk's kingdom of 'Great Moravia' in the 9th cent. and in 1029 Moravia was incorporated into Bohemia, ruled first by dukes of the Přemyslide dynasty and then (from 1310) by the house of Luxemburg; the rulers took the title of king in 1197. Charles IV, one of the greatest rulers of Bohemia, founded a university in Prague in the 14th cent. and made it the leading cultural centre in Central Europe. The church-reform movement of John Huss (15th cent.) was inspired by anti-German national sentiment as well as religious feeling; the subsequent Hussite wars seriously weakened the country, which came under the domination of the Habsburgs in 1526 (and remained so until 1918). In the revolt of 1618–20 the Czechs were defeated at the Battle of the White Mountain (1620); nationalism and Protestantism were ruthlessly suppressed, and demands for independence were not revived until the 19th cent.

The Slovaks are a Slav people, closely related to the Czechs; Slovakia too formed part of 'Great Moravia' in the 9th cent. but was occupied by the Magyars in the 10th and remained subject to Hungary (and later was part of the Austro-Hungarian empire) until 1918.

The rise of Nazism and the Hitler régime in Germany resulted in the Munich Pact (1938) by which the Sudeten lands were ceded to Germany and other land to Hungary and to Poland, and in 1939 the Germans dismembered the republic, making Bohemia-Moravia a German protectorate and Slovakia an independent state. After the 2nd World War independence was regained, but Ruthenia (E Slovakia) was ceded to the USSR. Since the communists seized control (1948) the country has been politically and economically part of the Soviet bloc. When the Czechs demanded greater political and economic freedom, Soviet forces invaded the country and occupied Prague and other leading cities (1968).

Częstochowa Poland. Important industrial town and railway junction in the Katowice voivodship, on the Warta R. 70 m. SSW of Łódź. Pop. (1968) 184,500. Manufactures iron and steel, textiles, chemicals, paper, etc. In a famous monastery, on the hill Jasna Góra (938 ft), is an image of the Virgin believed to have been painted by St Luke; reputed to shed tears, it attracts many thousands of pilgrims annually.

# D

**Dabrowa Górnicza** Poland. Industrial town in the Katowice voivodship, 8 m. ENE of Katowice. Pop. (1968) 60,100. Coalmining centre since the late 18th cent. Has one of the thickest coal seams in the world, the 'Reden' seam. Iron founding etc.

**Dacca** Pakistan. Capital of E Pakistan, on the Burhi-ganga R. Pop. (1961) 556,712. Manufactures textiles (jute etc.), hosiery, carpets, chemicals, etc. Trade in rice, jute, oilseeds, etc. Its port is Narayanganj, 10 m. SE. University (1921). Former capital of Bengal (1608–1704) and of E Bengal and Assam (1905–12). The manufacture of fine muslins, for which Dacca was once famous, declined in the 19th cent. owing to competition from Lancashire.

**Dachau** Federal German Republic. Town in Bavaria, 11 m. NNW of Munich. Pop. (1963) 30,000. Manufactures electrical equipment, paper, textiles, etc. Site of a notorious concentration camp of the Nazi régime.

**Dacia.** Ancient region in SE Europe comprising the greater part of modern Rumania, inhabited in pre-Christian times by people known to the Romans as Daci. Became a Roman province early in the 2nd cent. A.D., abandoned late in the 3rd cent.

**Dadra and Nagar Aveli** India. Union Territory forming an enclave in Maharashtra; formerly Portuguese territory attached for administrative purposes to Daman (just NW) and transferred to India in 1961. Area 189 sq. m. Pop. (1962) 57,963.

**Dagenham** England. Former municipal borough of SW Essex, on the N bank of the R. Thames, incorporated in 1938; from 1965 part of the Greater London borough of Barking (excluding the N part of Chadwell Heath Ward). Pop. (1961) 108,363. In 1921 it was a parish of 9,127 people, and owes its rapid expansion to the establishment of the Becontree LCC housing scheme and the Ford motor works (completed 1932) and other industries. Besides the automobile industry, manufactures knitted goods, chemicals, paints and veneers, etc.

**Dagestan ASSR USSR.** Autonomous republic in the RSFSR, between the E part of the Great Caucasus and the Caspian Sea. Area 19,416 sq. m. Pop. (1970) 1,429,000 (a complex mixture of peoples, inc. Rus-

sians and Azerbaijanis). Cap. Makhachkala. Chiefly mountainous, with a narrow coastal plain. Cattle and sheep reared. Wheat, vines, cotton, etc. cultivated. Some oil and natural gas produced. Chief towns Makhachkala, Derbent. There was much destruction during the Revolution (1918–20), and, after being made an autonomous republic (1921), it suffered severely from famine. Agriculture and industry have developed considerably under the Soviet régime.

**Dahlak Islands** Ethiopia. Archipelago in the Red Sea, off the Bay of Massawa (Eritrea). Mainly coral. Two large islands (Nora; Dahlak Kebir) and many smaller; only three are inhabited. Noted for pearl fisheries; the catch is marketed at Massawa.

**Dahomey.** Republic on the Gulf of Guinea (Slave Coast), formerly one of the territories of French W Africa. Area 44,649 sq. m. Pop. (1965) 2,370,000. Cap. Porto Novo. Chief seaport Cotonou. Bounded by Niger and Upper Volta (N), Nigeria (E), and Togo (W). Equatorial climate in the low-lying lagoon-fringed coastal area, largely covered with tropical rain-forest. The coastal railroad has inland branches to Parakou and Pobé. Principal exports palm kernels, palm oil, groundnuts. Food crops cassava, maize, millet, yams. Cotton and coffee have been introduced successfully. In the early 19th cent. a powerful Negro kingdom, famed for bronzes and for its Amazon troops, highly-trained women warriors; also notorious for mass human sacrifice ('Dahomey customs'). Became a French sphere of influence in the mid 19th cent. and a French colony after the defeat of the king of Dahomey (1894); a territory of French W Africa 1904–58. Became a member of the French Community 1958 and an independent member of the UN 1960.

**Dairen** ◊ *Lü-ta.*

**Dakar** Senegal. Capital and chief seaport, on the Atlantic coast at the S end of the Cape Verde peninsula. Pop. (1965) 474,000. Formerly a French naval base. An international airport, half-way between Europe and Brazil; an important cable station. Connected by rail with Kaolack and St Louis, and with Kayes, Bamako, and

Koulikoro in Mali. Seat of a university (1957), a Pasteur Institute, a medical school, hospitals. Hot climate with distinct rainy and dry seasons. Chief exports groundnuts, groundnut oil, oil-cake. Oil extraction, food processing, cement manufacture, titanium refining. The Dutch occupied Gorée Island (opposite Dakar) 1588; it was seized by the French 1677. The slave trade was long the main activity. Became the capital of French W Africa 1902. Supported the Vichy government during the 2nd World War and resisted attacks by the British and the Free French (1940). Joined the Allies 1942.

**Dalkeith** Scotland. Small burgh and market town in Midlothian 8 m. SE of Edinburgh between the N and S Esk rivers. Pop. (1961) 8,864. Important trade in grain. Brewing. Manufactures carpets, brushes, etc. Near by is Dalkeith Palace, seat of the dukes of Buccleuch, rebuilt c. 1700 by Vanbrugh.

**Dallas** USA. City in N Texas, second largest in the state, 32 m. E of Fort Worth. Pop. (1970) 836,121. Route, commercial, and industrial centre. Important cotton market. Headquarters of several oil companies. Cotton ginning. Manufactures cotton goods, aircraft, leather goods, oilfield equipment, petroleum products, chemicals, etc. A leading centre of women's fashions. Seat of the Southern Methodist University (1911). Named (1845) after Vice-president Dallas. Scene of the assassination of President J. F. Kennedy (1963).

**Dalmatia** Yugoslavia. A strip of the Adriatic coast in Croatia, with a narrow corridor giving Hercegovina an outlet to the sea, extending from the Velebit Channel (N) to the Gulf of Kotor (S). The neighbouring Adriatic waters are festooned with islands, inc. Pag, Dugi Otok, Brač, Hvar, and Korčula. Mountainous and largely barren (Dinaric Alps), it is extremely picturesque and has several resorts and ports (inc. Split, Dubrovnik, Šibenik, Zadar). Settled by Slavs in the 7th and 8th cent. From 1420 ruled by Venice. Passed to Austria (1797), to Italy (1805), and again to Austria (1815). Became part of Yugoslavia (1919) except for Zara (Zadar) and some islands, which remained Italian, but were transferred to Yugoslavia 1947.

**Dalton-in-Furness** England. Urban district in N Lancashire, 4 m. NE of Barrow-in-Furness. Pop. (1961) 10,317. Important ironworks. Birthplace of George Romney, the artist (1734–1802). Near by are the ruins of the 12th-cent. Furness Abbey.

**Daly Waters** Australia. Small settlement in the Northern Territory about 300 m. SSE of Darwin in poor stock country. Has a memento of J. M. Stuart's journey (1862): an 'S' carved into a tree.

**Daman (Damão)** India. Former Portuguese settlement consisting of the district and town of Daman, on the Gulf of Cambay, with the districts of Dadra and Nagar Aveli inland. Area 211 sq. m. Pop. 69,000. The town of Daman was taken by the Portuguese in 1558, and the district in 1559. Daman as a whole was forcibly incorporated into the Indian Union, along with the other settlements of Portuguese India, in 1961. The town and district of Daman were made part of the Union Territory of Goa, Daman, and Diu.

**Damanhûr** United Arab Republic. Town in the Nile delta 38 m. ESE of Alexandria, on the railway to Cairo. Pop. (1960) 126,000. Capital of the rich agricultural governorate of Beheira. Important in the cotton trade. Cotton ginning etc.

**Damão** ◊ *Daman.*

**Damascus** (Ar. **Esh Sham**) Syria. Capital of the republic, at the E foot of the Anti-Lebanon at a height of 2,200 ft. Pop. (1962) 507,503. Reputedly the oldest city in the world to be continuously inhabited. Long famous for its silks, leather, gold and silver filigree work, brass and copper ware. The waters of the Barada R. irrigate fine gardens and orchards of apricots, figs, almonds, etc. University (1924). It has few buildings to bear witness to its long history apart from the 13th-cent. citadel and the Great Mosque (severely damaged in the fire of 1893 and restored); nevertheless, its white minarets amid the green trees, with the adjacent desert stretching into the distance, are an unforgettable sight. The covered 'Street called Straight' with its bazaars crosses the city from W to E, with a gate at each end. Still a great centre of commerce, with motor trucks now largely taking the place of camel caravans. First mentioned in the Bible in Genesis. Conquered by the Assyrians in the 8th cent. B.C., by Alexander the Great 332 B.C., and by the Romans 64 B.C. Christianized at an early date, but taken by the Arabs (635) and became Muslim. Fell to the Mongols (1260), Tamerlane (1399), the Ottoman Turks (1516). In 1924 it became capital of the French mandate of Syria and in 1941 capital of the republic.

**Damietta** (Ar. **Dumyat**) United Arab Republic. Town on the Damietta branch of the Nile 8 m. from the mouth, 95 m. NNE of Cairo, to which it is linked by rail. Pop. (1960) 72,000. Manufactures cotton goods. Just S of old Damietta (ancient Tamiathis). Declined in importance with the development of Alexandria and Port Said. Probably gave its name to dimity, a striped cotton cloth for which it was famous.

**Dammam** Saudi Arabia. Town and port on the Persian Gulf 8 m. N of Dhahran. Pop. 30,000. Developed in the 1940s after the discovery of oil (1936).

**Damodar River** India. River in Bihar and W Bengal rising on the Chota Nagpur plateau and flowing 370 m. generally ESE to join the Hooghly R. India's most important coalfield is in the Damodar Valley. The Damodar Valley scheme, providing for hydroelectric power, irrigation, flood control, etc., was begun in 1948.

**Dampier, Mount** New Zealand. Peak rising to 11,287 ft, in Tasman National Park, Southern Alps, in the S Island.

**Dampier Archipelago** Indian Ocean. Group of rocky islands off NW Western Australia, the largest being Enderby Island (21 sq. m.). Sheep farming on some islands.

**Dan.** Biblical town in the extreme N of the Holy Land (now Israel), with which the mound Tell-el-Kadi near the Syrian border is often identified. Beersheba was in the extreme S – hence the phrase 'from Dan to Beersheba'.

**Danakil Land (Dankalia)** Ethiopia/French Somaliland. Desert region, mainly in NE Ethiopia but partly in the French Territory of the Afars and the Issas, bounded by the Red Sea and an escarpment of the Great Rift Valley. Between the Ethiopian highlands and the mountain ranges parallel to the Red Sea coast is the extensive Danakil Depression, falling to nearly 400 ft below sea level. The nomadic Danakils raise camels, goats, sheep, cattle.

**Danger Island** ♢ *Cook Islands*.

**Dankalia** ♢ *Danakil Land*.

**Danube River** (Ger. **Donau**, Czech **Dunaj**, Hungarian **Duna**, Serbo-Croatian **Dunav**, Rumanian **Dunărea**).* The second longest river in Europe (1,750 m.), and the most important in Central and SE Europe. Flows through or forms the boundary of 8 countries. It is formed from two headstreams, the Brigach and Brege, which rise in the Black Forest (Federal German Republic) and unite near Donaueschingen,

and it flows generally ESE to the Black Sea. Through Württemberg its course is NE, at Ulm it becomes navigable, and above Regensburg (Bavaria) it receives the Altmühl, whence it is linked by canal with the Main and Rhine. It turns SE, receives the Inn at Passau, enters Austria, and passes through Linz and Vienna. Below Bratislava (Czechoslovakia) it forms part of the Czechoslovak–Hungarian border, and turns S through Budapest to cross the Hungarian plain. In Yugoslavia it is joined by several of its chief navigable tributaries – the Drava, Tisza, Sava (at Belgrade), and Morava; it narrows to pass through the famous Iron Gate, then broadens as it traverses the flat, marshy Walachian plain, forming most of the Rumanian–Bulgarian boundary. Turning N to pass through Brăila and Galaţi and then E, receiving the Prut, it enters the Black Sea by a great delta, which is a labyrinth of reed-covered marshes and swamps, with three main channels. Shipping on the Danube was formerly controlled by the international Danube Commission; in 1948 the interested Communist countries of central and E Europe repudiated the Paris convention of 1921 at the Belgrade conference, but reaffirmed free navigation from Regensburg to Izmail (USSR). Austria joined the new commission in 1959 and the Federal German Republic in 1963.

**Danville** (Illinois) USA. Town on the Vermilion R. 120 m. S of Chicago. Pop. (1960) 41,856. Commercial centre of an agricultural and coalmining region. Manufactures mining machinery, chemicals, hardware, food products, etc.

**Danville** (Virginia) USA. Town on the Dan R. 57 m. SE of Roanoke. Pop. (1960) 46,577. Important tobacco market. Manufactures textiles, furniture, etc. The last capital of the Confederacy in the American Civil War, for 7 days (April 1865).

**Danzig** ♢ *Gdańsk*.

**Darbhanga** India. Commercial town and railway and road junction in N Bihar, on the Little Baghmati R. 67 m. NE of Patna. Pop. (1961) 103,016. Trade in rice, wheat, oilseeds, etc. Seat of Darbhanga Sanskrit University (1961).

**Dardanelles** Turkey. Ancient Hellespont. Narrow strait, 45 m. long and 1–5 m. wide, connecting the Aegean Sea and the Sea of Marmara and separating European and Asiatic Turkey. Of great strategic and commercial importance throughout history.

About 480 B.C. Xerxes I crossed it into Europe, and in 334 B.C. Alexander the Great crossed it into Asia. In Greek mythology it was the scene of the legend of Hero and Leander. The name was derived from the ancient Greek town of Dardanus on the Asiatic shore. ⬦ *Gallipoli*.

**Dar-es-Salaam** Tanzania. In Arabic, 'Haven of Peace'. Capital and chief seaport, on the Indian Ocean 40 m. S of Zanzibar. Pop. (1967) 372,515. Terminus of the railway crossing Tanzania from Kigoma (on L. Tanganyika). Handles over half the country's exports, including sisal, cotton, coffee, hides and skins, diamonds, gold. A lighterage port until 1956, when deep-water berths were opened. Oil refining, rice milling, tanning. Manufactures soap, paint, etc. College of the University of East Africa (1963). Founded by the Sultan of Zanzibar 1862. Occupied by the Germans in 1889; became capital of German E Africa in 1891. Occupied by British troops during the 1st World War (1916).

**Darién** Panama. The E part of the republic, between the Gulf of Darién on the Caribbean coast of the isthmus and the Gulf of San Miguel on the Pacific coast, and including the province of Darién; bordering on Colombia. Area (province) 6,000 sq. m. Pop. (1968) 24,100. Cap. La Palma. Mainly agricultural, producing maize, rice, beans. Discovered by the Spaniards; it was in 1513 that Vasco Núñez de Balboa stood 'silent upon a peak in Darién'. In 1698–1700 two Scottish expeditions unsuccessfully attempted to colonize the region, which they named 'New Caledonia'.

**Darjeeling** India. Hill station in W Bengal 315 m. N of Calcutta, at a height of 6,000–8,000 ft. on the S slopes of the Himalayas. Pop. 40,000. Tea plantations in the neighbourhood. Remarkable views of some of the highest snow-clad peaks of the Himalayas, inc. Kanchenjunga (28,168 ft).

**Darlaston** England. Industrial town in Staffordshire 4 m. ESE of Wolverhampton in the Black Country. Pop. (1961) 21,732. Manufactures nuts and bolts, hardware, castings, etc.

**Darling Downs** Australia. Undulating plateau at 2,000–3,000 ft in SE Queensland, W of the Great Dividing Range. Toowoomba is the chief town. Much sheep and dairy farming. Wheat, barley, fodder crops cultivated.

**Darling Range** Australia. Ridge 250 m.

long in the SW of Western Australia, parallel to the coast, generally 800–1,500 ft high and rising to 1,910 ft in Mt Cooke. Wooded slopes dissected by many streams. Water storages include Mundaring and Canning Dam reservoirs.

**Darling River** Australia. The longest tributary of the Murray R., from the confluence of headstreams near the Queensland–New South Wales border flowing generally SW across New South Wales for about 1,900 m. to the Murray R. at Wentworth. Known in the upper course as Macintyre (headstream) and Barwon. Its flow fluctuates considerably, rising at times from a mere trickle to flood large areas. Storages have been constructed on its lower course for water supply and irrigation.

**Darlington** England. County borough in Durham on the R. Skerne near its confluence with the R. Tees, 13 m. WSW of Middlesbrough. Pop. (1961) 84,162. Engineering, bridge building, etc. Manufactures woollen goods etc. A market town before the Industrial Revolution, it owes its modern development to the opening of the Stockton–Darlington railway (1825); 'Locomotive No. 1' is exhibited at Bank Top station. The 12th-cent. Church of St Cuthbert was restored in the 19th cent.

**Darmstadt** Federal German Republic. Industrial town in Hessen 17 m. S of Frankfurt. Pop. (1968) 139,424. Former capital of Hesse. Railway engineering. Manufactures diesel engines, machinery, chemicals, pharmaceutical products, etc. Seat of a technical university (1895). Severely damaged in the 2nd World War. Birthplace of the chemist Justus von Liebig (1803–73).

**Dartford** England. Municipal borough in NW Kent on the R. Darent 7 m. W of Gravesend, 3 m. from the R. Thames. Pop. (1961) 45,643. Market town and industrial centre. Important paper manufacture, site of the first paper mill in England. Flour milling, engineering. Manufactures pharmaceutical products, cement. Probable birthplace of Wat Tyler, who led the Peasants' Revolt from here in 1381. The Dartford Tunnel under the R. Thames, linking it with Purfleet (Essex), was opened in 1963.

**Dartmoor** England. Upland region in S Devonshire well known for its wild moorland scenery, conspicuous features being the isolated masses of granite ('tors'). Area over 300 sq. m. Rises to 2,039 ft in High Willhays and 2,028 ft in Yes Tor. Most of the rivers of Devonshire rise here.

Cattle, sheep, and half-wild ponies live on the moor. Princetown is the chief centre of population, and near by is the famous prison founded (1806) for French prisoners of war and used for convicts since 1850. In 1951 365 sq. m. of Dartmoor Forest were made a national park.

**Dartmouth** Canada. Industrial town in Nova Scotia opposite Halifax, with which it is connected by a suspension bridge across Halifax Harbour, completed 1955. Pop. (1966) 58,745. Shipbuilding, sugar refining, oil refining, etc. First settled 1750. Has grown rapidly since the 2nd World War.

**Dartmouth** England. Municipal borough in S Devonshire on the W side of the R. Dart estuary 8 m. SSW of Torquay. Pop. (1961) 5,757. Seaport. Yachting centre, holiday resort. Seat of the Royal Naval College (since 1905). An important seaport in the 11th cent.; in 1190 Richard Coeur de Lion set sail from here on his crusades. Sir Humphrey Gilbert, John Davis, and Thomas Newcomen were born in the neighbourhood.

**Darwen** England. Municipal borough in Lancashire 4 m. S of Blackburn. Pop. (1961) 29,452. Manufactures cotton goods, paper, plastics, chemicals, paints, etc.

**Darwin** Australia. Capital and chief seaport of the Northern Territory in the extreme N, overlooking the harbour of Port Darwin (formerly known as Palmerston). Pop. (1966) 20,261. Connected by 317-m. railway to Birdum and by further 630 m. of Stuart Highway to Alice Springs. International airport (Sydney–Singapore route). Regular shipping services to Australian states. The terminal of the overland telegraph from Adelaide and cable from Java; serves the mineral workings at Rum Jungle and South Alligator R. Founded 1869; named after Charles Darwin.

**Dasht-i-Kavir** Iran. Extensive salt desert on the central plateau of Iran, in W Khurasan. Almost rainless. Beneath the salt crust the ground is marshy and treacherous.

**Daugavpils** USSR. Formerly Dünaburg (Ger., till 1893), Dvinsk (Russian 1893–1920). Town in the Latvian SSR on the W Dvina R. Pop. (1970) 101,000. Railway and road junction. Railway engineering. Manufactures food products, textiles, etc. Trade in grain, flax, timber. Founded by the Livonian Order in the 13th cent. Passed to Russia 1772.

**Dauphiné** France. Former province in the SE, now comprising the departments of Drôme, Hautes-Alpes, and Isère. Cap. Grenoble. Its rulers took the title *dauphin*, the last to hold a semi-independent position being Louis XI. Annexed to the crown 1456.

**Davao** Philippines. Seaport in SE Mindanao on Davao Gulf. Pop. (1960) 231,833. Exports abacá, copra, timber. During the 2nd World War the Japanese landed here (Dec. 1941).

**Davenport** USA. Industrial town in Iowa, on the Mississippi R., opposite Rock Island. Pop. (1960) 88,981. Manufactures locomotives, railway rolling stock, agricultural implements, washing machines, etc. Named after Colonel George Davenport, the Englishman who founded it (1836).

**Daventry** England. Municipal borough in Northamptonshire, 11 m. W of Northampton. Pop. (1961) 5,846. Just to the E on Borough Hill (653 ft) is a large prehistoric and Roman camp; a powerful radio transmitting station was erected here 1925.

**Davis** ◊ *Australian Antarctic Territory*.

**Davis Strait** N Atlantic. An arm of the Atlantic, between SE Baffin Island and SW Greenland, 400 m. long and 200–400 m. wide. Usually navigable from midsummer to late autumn. Named after John Davis, who discovered it (1587).

**Davos** Switzerland. Mountain valley of the Landwasser R. 13 m. ESE of Chur in Graubünden (Grisons) canton. Pop. (1960) 9,588. Contains two famous health resorts and winter-sports centres: Davos Platz and Davos Dörfli, 2 m. apart and both at a height of about 5,100 ft. At the N end of the valley is the picturesque Davosersee or L. Davos.

**Dawlish** England. Urban district in S Devonshire near the mouth of the R. Exe 3 m. SW of Exmouth. Pop. (1961) 7,807. Seaside resort. Trade in flowers.

**Dawson** Canada. Town in Yukon Territory, on the Yukon R. Pop. (1966) 881. Former capital of the territory. Trade and communications centre for the Klondike mining region. Founded (1896) during the Klondike gold rush, when the population rose to about 25,000. Named after George M. Dawson, director of the Geological Survey of Canada.

**Dayton** USA. Industrial town in Ohio on the Great Miami R. 67 m. WSW of Columbus. Pop. (1960) 262,332. Manufactures refrigerators, cash registers, air-conditioning equipment, machine tools, aircraft instruments, etc. Home of the

Wright brothers, who set up an aircraft research factory in 1911. Now a centre for military aviation development, with the Wright-Patterson Air Force Base. University (1850).

**Daytona Beach** USA. Seaside resort in NE Florida on the Atlantic and on the Halifax R. (a lagoon). Pop. (1960) 37,395. Since 1903 the venue of motor speed trials, on the famous hard white beach, 30 m. long and 500 ft wide at low tide. Named after Mathias Day, who founded it (1870).

**DC** ◊ *Columbia, District of.*

**De Aar** S Africa. Important railway junction in the Cape Province, 400 m. NE of Cape Town at a height of 4,079 ft. Pop. (1960) 14,357. Large railway workshops.

**Dead Sea** (Ar. **Bahret Lut**). Salt lake on the border of Israel and Jordan, 46 m. long and 3-9 m. wide, its surface 1,286 ft below sea level; only 3-30 ft deep at the S end, up to 1,300 ft deep in the N; flanked on the E and W shores by steep hills. Occupies part of a rift valley which includes the Sea of Galilee and the Gulf of Aqaba. At its N end receives the Jordan R. and several intermittent streams, but has no outlet, losing water solely by evaporation. Therefore has a very high salinity, about 25 per cent or 7 times that of the ocean, and contains large quantities of sodium chloride (common salt) as well as potassium, magnesium, and calcium salts, which are exploited. From 1947 onwards a number of important MSS. dating from the 2nd cent. B.C.-1st cent. A.D. were discovered in caves near the Dead Sea and are known as the Dead Sea scrolls. The Dead Sea is associated with the biblical story of Lot and the cities of Sodom and Gomorrah – hence the Arabic name, which means 'Sea of Lot'.

**Deal** England. Municipal borough in E Kent, 8 m. NNE of Dover opposite the Downs roadstead and Goodwin Sands. Pop. (1961) 24,791. A 'limb' or member of the Cinque Ports. Seaside resort. The parish church of St Leonard's in Upper Deal dates from Norman times. Probable landing place of Julius Caesar in Britain (55 B.C.). Lifeboat station at Walmer, in the borough 1 m. S. Walmer Castle is the official residence of the Lord Warden of the Cinque Ports, and here the 1st Duke of Wellington died (1852).

**Dean, Forest of** England. Hilly district and ancient royal forest in W Gloucestershire, between the Severn and the Wye rivers. Almost completely deforested by the latter half of the 17th cent. but later reforested. Coalmining on a small scale.

**Dearborn** USA. Town in SE Michigan, 9 m. W of Detroit on the Rouge R. Pop. (1960) 112,007. Birthplace of Henry Ford (1863–1947), who established the first great mass-production motor-car factory there after the 1st World War. In the city is the Edison Institute of Technology (established by Henry Ford 1933), a feature of which is Greenfield Village, a reproduction of an early American village.

**Death Valley** USA. Arid rift valley in E California and S Nevada, part of the Great Basin region, lying N of the Mojave Desert. Badwater, 282 ft below sea level, is the lowest point in the W hemisphere. Telescope Peak, on the W edge of the valley, rises to 11,045 ft. The valley contains extensive sand dunes, salt flats, and many desert plants. Summers are very hot. Named (1849) by a party of 'forty-niners' seeking gold, some of whom died of thirst and exposure when trying to cross it. Created the Death Valley National Monument 1933.

**Deauville** France. Fashionable resort in the Calvados department, at the mouth of the Touques R. opposite Trouville. Pop. (1968) 5,370. Well-known racecourse and casino.

**Debrecen** Hungary. Capital of Hajdú-Bihar county 120 m. E of Budapest. Pop. (1968) 151,000. Railway junction and market town. Trade in livestock, tobacco. Flour milling. Manufactures agricultural machinery, pharmaceutical products, salami, etc. University (1912). Seat of the revolutionary government of 1849. In 1944 after the German retreat in the 2nd World War the provisional Hungarian government was formed here.

**Debryansk** ◊ *Bryansk.*

**Decatur** (Alabama) USA. Industrial town on the Tennessee R. 76 m. N of Birmingham. Pop. (1960) 29,217. Manufactures synthetic fibres, metal goods, food products, etc. Developed industrially after the establishment of the Tennessee Valley Authority (TVA).

**Decatur** (Illinois) USA. Town on the Sangamon R. 37 m. E of Springfield. Pop. (1960) 78,004. Railway engineering, maize and soya-bean processing. Manufactures motor-car accessories, tractors, plastic and metal products, etc. Lincoln's log-cabin courthouse is in Fairview Park. Named after Stephen Decatur. Seat of the Millikin University (1901).

**Deccan** India. Triangular plateau of peninsular India S of the Satpura Range and enclosed between the Western Ghats and the Eastern Ghats. Slopes generally E from about 3,000 ft to 1,500 ft; the main rivers Godavari, Krishna, and Cauvery flow W–E to the Bay of Bengal. The term is sometimes restricted to the area between the Narmada and the Krishna rivers, sometimes to the S and SE parts of the plateau.

**Děčín** Czechoslovakia. River port and railway junction in the Severočeský region at the confluence of the Polzen (Ploučnice) and Elbe rivers. Pop. (1967) 42,000. Manufactures chemicals, textiles, paper. A 17th-cent. castle; 16th-cent. bridge.

**Dedeagach** ◊ *Alexandroupolis*.

**Dee River** Scotland. **1.** River 87 m. long rising on Ben Braeriach in the Cairngorms, and flowing E past Braemar, Balmoral Castle, Ballater, and Aboyne, forming part of the Aberdeenshire–Kincardine border, to the North Sea by an artificial channel at Aberdeen. Good salmon fishing. Has supplied Aberdeen with water since 1864. **2.** River 38 m. long issuing from Loch Dee, Kirkcudbrightshire, and flowing generally S to the Irish Sea at Kirkcudbright. Salmon and trout fishing.

**Dee River** Wales/England. River 70 m. long rising in Bala Lake, Merioneth, and flowing generally N past Corwen, Llangollen, Chester (which it almost encircles), and Flint to the Irish Sea. The estuary, 13 m. long and about 5 m. wide, is a monotonous expanse of sand at low tide.

**Dehra Dun** India. Town in NW Uttar Pradesh 130 m. NNE of Delhi. Pop. (1961) 126,918. Trade in rice, wheat, oilseeds, etc. Noted chiefly as the seat of the Indian Military Academy (1932) and the Indian Forest Research Institute and College (1867). Founded in the late 17th cent. by the Sikh guru, Ram Rai, whose temple is an outstanding building.

**Deir ez Zor** Syria. Town in the E, on the Euphrates R. 170 m. ESE of Aleppo. Pop. (1962) 59,757. Road centre for W Syria, S Turkey, and Iraq. Population has rapidly increased in recent years. Petroleum has been sought in the neighbourhood.

**Delagoa Bay (Lourenço Marques Bay)** Moçambique. Inlet of the Indian Ocean, in the S. Discovered (1502) by António do Campo, commander of a ship on Vasco da Gama's expedition. Lourenço Marques stands on the inner bay.

**Delaware** USA. State on the E seaboard, forming the NE part of the Delmarva peninsula between Chesapeake Bay and Delaware Bay, with Pennsylvania to the N and Maryland to the S; second smallest state of the union. Area 2,057 sq. m. Pop. (1970) 542,979. Cap. Dover. One of the original 13 states, and the first to ratify the Constitution; popularly called the 'Diamond' or 'Blue Hen' state. Generally low-lying, hilly in the extreme N. Climate humid and hot in summer, cool in winter; because of its peninsular location the growing season is long. Varied agriculture. Wheat, maize, fruit, vegetables cultivated. Substantial poultry raising and fishing. Manufacturing centred on Wilmington, the one large city (headquarters of the great chemical Du Pont company). Shipbuilding, cotton dyeing, etc. Delaware Bay was discovered (1609) by Henry Hudson. In 1610 Lord de la Warr touched there, giving it his name. Although a slave state, Delaware declined to secede from the Union in the American Civil War.

**Delft** Netherlands. Town in S Holland province, 5 m. SSE of The Hague on the Schie canal. Pop. (1968) 80,545. Famous for the pottery and porcelain industry begun in the 16th cent. Also manufactures chemicals, cigars, cables, etc. Among its buildings are the Prinsenhof (formerly a monastery, then a palace, now a museum) where William the Silent was assassinated (1584). An Old Church with the tombs of Leeuwenhoek and van Tromp, and a New Church, with the tombs of William the Silent and Grotius. Seat of a technical university (1906). Birthplace of Grotius (1583–1645) and Vermeer (1632–75).

**Delhi** India. **1.** Union territory in the N, formerly a chief commissioner's state, and a province 1912–50. Area 573 sq. m. Pop. (1961) 2,658,612. **2.** Capital of the republic and of Delhi territory, on the right bank of the Jumna R. Pop. (1961) 2,061,758. Important largely because of its strategic position on the Indo-Gangetic plain. Great railway centre. Manufactures textiles, hosiery, chemicals, gold and silver filigree articles, etc. Old Delhi, seventh in the series of cities which have stood in this district, is sometimes locally called Shahjahanabad after the Mogul Emperor Shah Jahan who reconstructed it in the 17th cent. Within its walls are the Fort, which contains the beautiful Imperial Palace (1638–48) of Shah Jahan, the magnificent Jama Masjid or Great

Mosque of the same monarch (1648–50), and the once far-famed Chandni Chauk or 'Street of the Silversmiths'. New Delhi, about 3 m. S of the Fort, was chosen as capital of India in 1912 and became capital of the republic in 1947. It was designed chiefly by Sir Edwin Lutyens, and among its buildings, which skilfully blend the Eastern and Western styles of architecture, are Government House, the Secretariat buildings, and the former Viceregal Lodge. University (1922).

**Delmarva Peninsula** USA. Peninsula lying between Chesapeake Bay (W) and the Delaware R., Delaware Bay, and the Atlantic (E). Comprises most of Delaware and parts of Maryland and Virginia, the name deriving from abbreviations of the names of the three states. Main occupations market gardening, poultry farming, forestry, fishing.

**Delmenhorst** Federal German Republic. Industrial town in Lower Saxony 9 m. WSW of Bremen. Pop. (1963) 59,300. Manufactures textiles, linoleum, machinery, clothing, soap, etc.

**Delos** (Gr. **Dhilos**) Greece. One of the smallest islands in the Cyclades, in the Aegean Sea, sometimes called Mikra Dhilos (Little Delos) to distinguish it from Rinia or Megali Dhilos (Great Delos), just to the W. Traditionally the centre of the Cyclades, adrift in the Aegean Sea until moored by Zeus as a birthplace for Apollo and Artemis. Served as treasury of the Delian League 478–454 B.C. until the removal to Athens.

**Delphi** (Gr. **Delphoi**) Greece. Ancient city of Phocis and seat of the famous Delphic oracle, at the S foot of Parnassus. Here were held the Pythian Games every four years from 582 B.C. By the end of the 4th cent. A.D. the Oracle was no longer consulted. Excavations in the 19th cent. revealed many of the remains of Delphi; a village, Kastri, had been built on the site but was moved S and renamed Delphoi.

**Demavend** ◊ *Elburz*.

**Demerara River** Guyana. River 215 m. long, rising in the central forest area, flowing N, and entering the Atlantic at Georgetown. Large quantities of bauxite are shipped from Mackenzie, 60 m. up river.

**Denain** France. Town in the Nord department, on the Escaut R. 7 m. WSW of Valenciennes. Pop. (1968) 27,988. Important coalmining and steel-manufacturing centre. Sugar refining, brewing, railway engineering. Scene of Marshal Villars's victory over Prince Eugène (1712).

**Denbigh** Wales. Municipal borough and county town of Denbighshire in the Vale of Clwyd 10 m. S of Rhyl. Pop. (1961) 8,044. Market town. Produces butter etc. Remains of a 14th-cent. castle where Charles I took refuge 1645. Birthplace of H. M. Stanley (1841–1904), the African explorer.

**Denbighshire** Wales. County in the NE, on the Irish Sea. Area 669 sq. m. Pop. (1961) 173,843. County town Denbigh. Mainly mountainous, with fertile valleys of scenic beauty (e.g. those of the Clwyd, Conway, and Dee). Main occupations agriculture, stock rearing. Chief towns Denbigh, Wrexham (on which coalmining is centred), Colwyn Bay (seaside resort), and Llangollen.

**Denby Dale** England. Urban district in the W Riding of Yorkshire, 7 m. SE of Huddersfield. Pop. (1961) 9,304. Woollen industry. Formed 1938 from a group of small neighbouring towns.

**Denizli** Turkey. Capital of Denizli province, 110 m. ESE of Izmir. Pop. (1965) 64,300. Market town. Once famous for its gardens. Important in the 14th cent. for its textiles; later declined.

**Denmark** (Danish **Kongeriget Danmark**). A kingdom of N Europe forming part of Scandinavia. Area 16,611 sq. m. Pop. (1965) 4,767,597. Cap. Copenhagen.

Consists of the N and greater part of the Jutland peninsula, which is bounded on the S by the Federal German Republic; several islands in the Baltic Sea between this peninsula and Sweden, including Zealand, Falster, Laaland, and Fünen, and, much farther E, Bornholm; some of the N Frisian Is. in the North Sea. One of the smaller countries of Europe, its wealth is largely dependent on agriculture; the emphasis is on dairy farming, and much of the land is divided into smallholdings. For administrative purposes it is divided into the following 25 counties, in addition to the city of Copenhagen and the borough of Frederiksberg: Copenhagen, Roskilde, Frederiksborg, Holbaek, Sorö, Praestö, Bornholm, Maribo, Svendborg, Odense, Assens, Vejle, Skanderborg, Aarhus, Randers, Aalborg, Hjörring, Thisted, Viborg, Ringköbing, Ribe, Haderslev, Aabenraa, Sönderborg, Tönder. The overseas possessions of Greenland and the Faeroe Is. are represented in the *Folketing* or Diet, though the latter also has its own parliament.

TOPOGRAPHY, CLIMATE. Entirely low-lying, the highest point being Ejer Bavnehöj (564 ft) in E Jutland, but very gently undulating rather than flat; well drained. Along the W coast of Jutland is an almost continuous line of sand dunes, planted with trees and grasses and enclosing lagoons. Other coasts are much indented with fiords; the largest is the Limfjord, which separates the N extremity from the remainder of Jutland. The chief straits leading through the islands from the Kattegat to the Baltic are The Sound (Öresund), the Great Belt, and the Little Belt. Owing to maritime influences the climate is relatively mild and damp, similar to but rather cooler than that of E England; only rarely are the straits impassable because of ice.

AGRICULTURE, RESOURCES, PEOPLE. With a favourable climate and fertile soil, especially on the islands, the Danes have become outstanding as dairy farmers, their methods being intensive and highly scientific. They keep a moderate area in permanent pasture, but their crops (esp. barley and root crops) are cultivated mainly to feed to the large numbers of cattle and pigs. Vast quantities of butter, cheese, eggs, and bacon are exported to Britain and the Federal German Republic, their principal markets. Almost half of the farms are less than 25 acres in area, but the proprietors are assisted by an efficient system of co-operative processing and marketing. Few mineral resources, apart from the kaolin on Bornholm, used in porcelain manufacture; industries, though varied, are generally on a small scale. Fishing has become increasingly important since the 2nd World War. About one fifth of the total population lives in Copenhagen, the leading seaport as well as capital; the only other towns with more than 100,000 people (1965) are Aarhus and Odense. Esbjerg, the chief seaport on the W coast of Jutland, is linked by railway with Copenhagen, with a train ferry crossing the Great Belt. Ethnically and linguistically the Danes are Scandinavian. They are governed by a constitutional monarchy, with a single-chamber *Folketing* elected by proportional representation, the *Landsting* (Senate) having been abolished in 1953.

HISTORY. The Danes probably migrated to their present home from S Sweden in the 5th and 6th cent. Ruled at first by local chieftains, they were united and converted to Christianity in the 10th cent. by Harald Bluetooth. Canute ruled Denmark, Norway, and England, but at his death (1035) the kingdoms separated. In 1389, however, Denmark, Norway, and Sweden were united, and, although Sweden became independent in 1523, Norway remained under Danish rule until 1814. In 1536 Lutheranism was introduced as the national religion. Throughout the 16th and 17th cent. attempts to regain supremacy in the Baltic led to disastrous wars with Sweden; then, having supported Napoleon, Denmark was compelled to cede Norway to Sweden (1814), and lost Schleswig-Holstein to Prussia (1864). Nevertheless, the 19th cent. saw a great cultural renaissance, led by Andersen, Thorvaldsen, and others; education was immensely stimulated by the work of Grundtvig; the economy prospered with the development of the co-operative movement among the farmers. Denmark was neutral in the 1st World War, but recovered N Schleswig after a plebiscite (1920). In the 2nd World War the country was occupied by the Germans. Iceland, previously united with Denmark, became independent in 1944.

**Dent du Midi** Switzerland. Massif in the Alps near the French border comprising several peaks, inc. Haute Cime, the highest, 10,696 ft; Cime de l'Est or Dent Noire, 10,433 ft; Dent Jaune, 10,456 ft; Cathédrale, 10,387 ft.

**Denton** USA. Market town in Texas 34 m. NNE of Fort Worth. Pop. (1960) 26,844. Flour milling, cheese making, etc. Manufactures clothing, etc. Seat of the North Texas State University (1901) and the Texas Women's University (1903).

**D'Entrecasteaux Islands** Pacific Ocean. Group of volcanic islands off the SE coast of New Guinea, administered as part of the Australian Territory of Papua and New Guinea. Area 1,200 sq. m. Pop. 30,000. Three large islands, Goodenough, Fergusson, and Normanby, and many islets. Chief product copra.

**Denver** USA. State capital of Colorado, on the S Platte R. at a height of 5,280 ft. Pop. (1970) 512,691. Has an unequalled system of mountain parks within easy access and an excellent climate, making it a popular health and recreational centre. Important cattle and sheep markets. Meat packing. Manufactures agricultural and mining machinery, rubber products, etc. A

US coinage mint. Seat of the University of Denver (1864) and of the University of Colorado medical school. Founded 1859. Grew as a mining centre (gold, silver). Named after General James W. Denver, Governor of the territory.

**Deptford** England. Former metropolitan borough of SE London on the S bank of the Thames; from 1965 part of the Greater London borough of Lewisham. Pop. (1961) 68,267. Industrial and workers' residential district. Engineering. Manufactures soap, chemicals, furniture, etc. The name is probably due to the existence of a ford over the Ravensbourne, a stream which enters the Thames through Deptford Creek. Here John Evelyn the diarist lived, Peter the Great of Russia studied shipbuilding, and Christopher Marlowe was killed. The royal naval dockyard established (1513) by Henry VIII was closed in 1869.

**Dera Ghazi Khan** Pakistan. Town in W Pakistan 50 m. WSW of Multan. Pop. (1961) 47,105. Commercial centre. Much of the earlier town was destroyed by the Indus R. floods in 1908–9, and another town was built on the present site W of the river.

**Dera Ismail Khan** Pakistan. Capital of the Dera Ismail Khan division of W Pakistan, on the Indus R. 160 m. SSW of Peshawar. Pop. (1961) 46,140. Commercial centre. Trade in grain, oilseeds, etc. Minor industries.

**Derbent** USSR. Port in the Dagestan ASSR (RSFSR), on the Caspian Sea 75 m. SSE of Makhachkala. Pop. 46,000. Fishing. Fish canning. Manufactures textiles, wine, etc. Important glassworks at Dagestanskiye Ogni near by. Ruins of the 6th-cent. Caucasian Wall, erected by the Persians to defend their frontier. Taken by the Arabs (728) and the Mongols (1220). Finally passed to Russia 1813.

**Derby** England. County town of Derbyshire, on the R. Derwent. Pop. (1961) 132,324. Important railway junction. Varied industries. Railway engineering. Manufactures aircraft engines, lawn mowers, hosiery, textiles, electrical equipment, porcelain, paints. Previously a flourishing commercial centre; industrialization began with the introduction of the country's first silk mill (1719). All Saints' Church, with its 16th-cent. tower, became the cathedral with the creation of the bishopric (1927). Birthplace of Herbert Spencer (1820–1903).

**Derbyshire** England. County in the N Midlands. Area 1,006 sq. m. Pop. (1961) 877,548. County town Derby. Mountainous and picturesque in the N and NW, rising to 2,088 ft in The Peak. Flat or gently undulating in the S and E. Drained by the Derwent, Dove, Wye, and Trent rivers. Buxton, the Matlocks, and Bakewell are resorts noted for mineral springs. Sheep raised on the uplands and dairy cattle on the lowlands. Coalmining important in the E and S. Limestone quarried near Buxton. Principal industries (centred on Derby, Chesterfield, Ilkeston, Long Eaton, Heanor, Alfreton) iron smelting, engineering, textile manufacture.

**Dereham** ◊ *East Dereham.*

**Derg, Lough** Irish Republic. 1. Lake 25 m. long and 1–3 m. wide at the boundary of Counties Galway, Clare, and Tipperary, in the lower course of the R. Shannon. On Holy Island or Inishcaltra are a 10th-cent. round tower and the ruins of four ancient churches.
2. Small lake in S Donegal, 3 m. NNW of Pettigo. Station Island, traditional scene of St Patrick's purgatory, is a place of pilgrimage.

**Derna** Libya. Town in Cyrenaica, on the coastal road 150 m. ENE of Benghazi, in an oasis producing dates, etc. Pop. 16,000. Occupied by American troops after they had captured it from pirates in 1805. Under Turkish rule 1835–1911, then taken by Italy. Changed hands several times during the 2nd World War; finally taken by the British 1942.

**Derry** ◊ *Londonderry.*

**Derwent River** Australia. River in Tasmania rising in L. St Clair and flowing 130 m. SE to a wide estuary on Storm Bay, Tasman Sea, at Hobart. Supplies power to several hydroelectric installations.

**Derwent River** England. Name derives from Celtic Dwrgent ('Clear Water').
1. River 35 m. long in Cumberland, rising in the Lake District (Borrowdale Fells) and flowing N through Derwentwater and Bassenthwaite, then W to the Irish Sea at Workington.
2. River 60 m. long in Derbyshire, rising near The Peak and flowing S to the R. Trent. Supplies water to Derby, Leicester, Nottingham, and Sheffield from the Derwent, Howden, and Ladybower reservoirs.
3. River 30 m. long rising in the Pennines near the Durham–Northumberland border, flowing generally ENE and forming part

of their boundary, to the R. Tyne near Newcastle.

**4.** River 70 m. long, rising in the N York Moors and flowing generally SSW to join the R Ouse 5 m. NW of Goole, forming part of the boundary between the N and E Ridings.

**Derwentwater** England. Lake 3 m. long and about 1 m. wide in the Lake District, Cumberland, just S of Keswick. Surrounded by mountains and picturesque, with several small islands and the Falls of Lodore at the upper (S) end. The R. Derwent enters at the S end and leaves at the N end to connect it with Bassenthwaite L.

**Desaguadero River** ◊ *Salado River*.

**Des Moines** USA. State capital of Iowa, on the Des Moines R. at the confluence with the Raccoon R. Pop. (1960) 208,982. In the heart of the Corn Belt and in a coal-mining area. Route and industrial centre. Manufactures agricultural machinery, tyres, cement, leather goods, etc. Printing and publishing. Seat of the Drake University (1881). First settled (1843) as Fort Des Moines.

**Des Moines River** USA. River 540 m. long rising in SW Minnesota and flowing generally SSE to join the Mississippi R. near Keokuk, in SE Iowa. Used for hydroelectric power. The name probably derives from the French '*la Rivière des Moines*', perhaps owing to an association with Trappist monks.

**Desna River** USSR. River 700 m. long rising about 50 m. ESE of Smolensk, in the RSFSR, and flowing generally SSW past Bryansk to the Dnieper R. above Kiev. Important waterway for timber, agricultural produce, etc. Navigable below Bryansk.

**Dessau** German Democratic Republic. Industrial town in the Halle district, on the Mulde R. near its confluence with the Elbe. Pop. (1965) 95,546. Formerly capital of Anhalt state. Manufactures railway rolling stock, machinery, chemicals, etc. Site of the Junkers aircraft works before 1945. In the former ducal palace are works by Rubens, Titian, and Van Dyck.

**Dessie** Ethiopia. Market town 160 m. NNE of Addis Ababa at a height of 8,000 ft. Pop. 39,000. Linked by road with Addis Ababa, Asmara, Assab. Trade in coffee, cereals, hides, etc.

**Detmold** Federal German Republic. Town in N Rhine-Westphalia 17 m. ESE of Bielefeld. Pop. (1963) 30,600. Formerly capital of Lippe. Manufactures furniture, biscuits, etc. Brewing. On the Grotenburg in the Teutoburger Wald SW of the town is von Bandel's massive statue of Arminius.

**Detroit** USA. Largest city in Michigan, and fifth largest in the USA, on the Detroit R. opposite Windsor (Ontario), with which it is linked by tunnel and bridge. Pop. (1970) 1,492,914. The greatest concentration of automobile manufacture in the world; Ford, General Motors, and Chrysler operate vast plants which account for three quarters of its industrial activity. Also manufactures aircraft engines and accessories, electrical and television equipment, adding machines. Oil refineries, shipyards, salt works. It has a large port, fourth in exporting rank in the USA, serving the vast commerce of the Great Lakes. Seat of the University of Detroit (1911) and the Wayne University (1933). Noteworthy parks, esp. on Belle Isle in the river. Founded (1701) by French settlers under Antoine de la Mothe Cadillac; became the most important city W of the E seaboard.

**Deurne** Belgium. Suburb of E Antwerp. Pop. (1968) 77,159. Mainly residential. Some industries. Antwerp airport.

**Deux-Sèvres** France. Department in the W formed mainly from Poitou. Area 2,337 sq. m. Pop. (1968) 326,462. Prefecture Niort. Mainly agricultural; wheat, oats, potatoes, vegetables widely cultivated. Dairy farming important. Name derived from Sèvre-Nantaise and Sèvre-Niortaise, the rivers by which the department is drained. Chief towns Niort, Parthenay.

**Deventer** Netherlands. Industrial town and railway junction in Overijssel province, on the Ijssel R. 9 m. ENE of Apeldoorn. Pop. (1968) 62,777. Manufactures chemicals, textiles, cigars, etc. Flour milling, engineering. Famous for its honey gingerbread (*Deventer koek*). In the Middle Ages it was a commercial, educational, and religious centre where Erasmus, Thomas à Kempis, and Pope Adrian VI were educated. An 11th/16th-cent. church (Groote Kerk); 17th-cent. town hall.

**Devizes** England. Municipal borough in Wiltshire on the disused Kennet-Avon canal 16 m. ESE of Bath. Pop. (1961) 8,497. Market town. Till the 19th cent. an important cloth market. Main industries now bacon and ham curing and the manufacture of dairy products. Grew round the 12th-cent. castle, destroyed by Cromwell 1645.

**Devonport** Australia. Port in Tasmania at the mouth of the Mersey R. 45 m. WNW of Launceston; formed (1890) from Torquay and Formby on opposite sides of the river. Pop. (1966) 14,848. Exports dairy produce, vegetables, timber, etc. Market town. Resort.

**Devonport** England. Naval and military station in Devonshire on the R. Tamar estuary; a county borough till incorporated into Plymouth (1914). Birthplace of Capt. R. F. Scott (1868–1912), Antarctic explorer.

**Devonport** New Zealand. Suburb of Auckland, N Island, on the NE shore of Waitemata Harbour. Linked to the central commercial area by harbour bridge.

**Devonshire (Devon)** England. Maritime county in the SW between the Bristol Channel (N) and the English Channel (S). Area 2,612 sq. m. Pop. (1961) 822,906. County town Exeter. In the NE is Exmoor and in the E the Blackdown Hills, but the highest part of the county is the granitic mass of Dartmoor, which reaches 2,039 ft in High Willhays and 2,028 ft in Yes Tor. Chief rivers the Tamar, Exe, Dart, Teign, Taw, and Torridge, most of their valleys being wooded and all picturesque. The attractive coastal and inland scenery, coupled with the mild climate, has stimulated tourism, now the main industry, leading resorts being Torquay, Paignton, and Ilfracombe. Fishing from Brixham and Plymouth. In the fertile areas beef and dairy cattle are raised, and the county is as well known for its clotted ('Devonshire') cream as for the cider from its apple orchards. On the upland pastures sheep are grazed. Many great seafaring men have come from Devonshire; its history is woven into the maritime fortunes of England; Plymouth, with Devonport, is still an important seaport and naval station. Other towns are Exeter, Exmouth, Newton Abbot, Barnstaple.

**Dewsbury** England. County borough in the W Riding of Yorkshire, on the R. Calder 7 m. SSW of Leeds. Pop. (1961) 52,942. Industrial town. Important centre of the shoddy trade. Also manufactures blankets, carpets, heavy woollen goods, leather goods, etc. Coalmining in the neighbourhood.

**Dhahran** Saudi Arabia. Town in Hasa (E), near the Persian Gulf. Pop. 12,000. Headquarters of the Saudi Arabian oilfields, to which it is linked by pipelines. Airport. Connected by rail with Riyadh. Developed after 1936, when oil was discovered at near-by Dammam.

**Dharwar** India. Town in Mysore 245 m. NW of Bangalore. Pop. (1961) 77,235. Manufactures textiles. Rice and oilseed milling, etc. Trade in cotton, grain. Seat of Karnatak University (1950).

**Dhulia** India. Town in Maharashtra, on the Panjhra R. 190 m. NE of Bombay. Pop. (1961) 98,893. Manufactures textiles, soap. Oilseed milling etc. Trade in groundnuts, linseed, millet, cotton.

**Diamantina** Brazil. Town in the Minas Gerais state, in the Serra do Espinhaço 125 m. NNE of Belo Horizonte, at a height of 3,700 ft. Pop. 25,000. Centre of the once active diamond industry. Tanning. Manufactures textiles.

**Dibrugarh** India. River port in Assam, on the Dibru R. near its confluence with the Brahmaputra, 240 m. NE of Shillong. Pop. (1961) 58,480. In a tea-growing district. Trade in tea, rice, etc.

**Didcot** England. Small town and railway junction in Berkshire 10 m. S of Oxford. Ordnance depots. The atomic research station of Harwell is 2 m. WSW.

**Diégo-Suarez** Malagasy Republic. Seaport on the bay of the same name, at the N end of the island, with an excellent natural harbour. Pop. (1965) 38,484. Formerly a French naval base (first occupied by the French 1885). Occupied by British troops during the 2nd World War (1942). Importance diminished by its remoteness from the main producing areas. Exports coffee, sisal, frozen and canned meats, etc.

**Dieppe** France. Fishing port and resort in the Seine-Maritime department, at the mouth of the Arques R. Pop. (1968) 30,404. Cross-channel ferry service to Newhaven. Shipbuilding, fishing. Manufactures rope, pharmaceutical goods, ivory and bone articles, etc. Trade in wine, fish, textiles. With the Revocation of the Edict of Nantes (1685), Dieppe, being Protestant, lost its former position as France's leading port. Suffered considerable damage in the 2nd World War; scene of an Allied commando raid (1942), the first landing on the continent after the Dunkirk withdrawal (1940).

**Dihang River** ◊ *Brahmaputra River*.

**Dijon** France. Capital of the Côte-d'Or department, on the Ouche R. and the Burgundy canal. Pop. (1968) 150,791. Important railway and road junction. Considerable trade in Burgundy wines.

Manufactures motor-cycles, bicycles, chemicals, biscuits, gingerbread, liqueurs, mustard. The 14th/15th-cent. palace of the dukes of Burgundy (almost entirely rebuilt in the 17th and 18th cent.), now the hôtel de ville, houses one of the finest museums in France. Cathedral (13th/14th-cent.); 13th-cent. Gothic Church of Notre Dame; 15th/16th-cent. Church of St Michel. University (1722). Acquired by the dukes of Burgundy early in the 11th cent.; became their capital in the 13th cent. By the 15th cent. one of the country's leading cultural centres; but on passing to the crown (1477) it was reduced to the status of a provincial capital. Flourished again in the 18th cent., when it became the seat of a bishopric. In 1870 it was twice occupied by the Germans, but gained through the influx of Alsatian immigrants. Birthplace of Bossuet (1627–1704) and Rameau (1683–1764).

**Dili (Dilly)** Portuguese Timor. Capital and chief port, on the N coast. Pop. 7,000. Exports cotton, coffee, copra. In the 2nd World War occupied by the Japanese 1942–5.

**Dimitrovgrad** Bulgaria. Industrial town on the Maritsa R. 45 m. ESE of Plovdiv. Pop. (1965) 41,787. Important chemical industry (esp. fertilizers). Manufactures cement, earthenware. Developed rapidly from 1947, when it was named after Georgi Dimitrov, the famous Bulgarian Communist leader.

**Dimitrovo** ◊ *Pernik*.

**Dinajpur** Pakistan. Town in E Pakistan 170 m. NW of Dacca. Pop. (1961) 37,711. Commercial centre. Trade in rice, jute, etc. Seat of a college of Rajshahi University.

**Dinan** France. Town and holiday resort in the Côtes-du-Nord department, on a height above the Rance R., at the head of its estuary 15 m. S of St Malo. Pop. (1968) 16,605. Manufactures hosiery, cider, beer. Has 11th-cent. walls and a 14th-cent. castle. In the Church of St Sauveur is the heart of Bertrand du Guesclin.

**Dinant** Belgium. Town in Namur province on the Meuse R. 16 m. S of Namur. Pop. (1968) 9,901. The name derives from the French *dinanderie* ('copperware'): copper, brass, and bronze ware were manufactured here in the Middle Ages. Main tourist centre for the Belgian Ardennes. Sacked by Charles the Bold 1466. During the 1st World War (1914) it was almost destroyed and about 600 inhabitants were shot by the Germans.

**Dinard** France. Fashionable resort in the Ille-et-Vilaine department in Brittany, on the Rance estuary opposite St Malo. Pop. (1968) 9,162. Excellent bathing beach. Many hotels. Noted for its lobster and crayfish dishes.

**Dinaric Alps (Serbo-Croat Dinara Planina)** Yugoslavia. Range of mountains separating the coastal strip of Dalmatia from Bosnia and Hercegovina, joined to the main Alpine system by the Julian Alps. Highest peak Troglav (6,277 ft). Sometimes the name is applied to the entire belt of limestone ranges and plateaux between the Julian Alps and the Balkan system, occupying about one third of Yugoslavia.

**Dindigul** India. Town in Madras 33 m. NNW of Madurai. Pop. (1961) 92,947. Manufactures cheroots (from locally grown tobacco).

**Dingwall** Scotland. Royal burgh (since 1226) and county town of Ross and Cromarty, at the head of Cromarty Firth 11 m. NW of Inverness. Pop. (1961) 3,752. Market town. Railway junction. The name derives from the Scandinavian *Thingvöllr* ('Field of the Assembly').

**Dinslaken** Federal German Republic. Industrial town in N Rhine-Westphalia, 9 m. N of Duisburg. Pop. (1963) 46,400. Coal mining. Manufactures iron and steel products.

**Dire Dawa** Ethiopia. Town on the Addis Ababa–Djibouti railway 210 m. ENE of Addis Ababa. Pop. 48,800. Main commercial outlet for the Harar province. Trade in hides and skins, coffee. Manufactures textiles, cement.

**Dismal Swamp (Great Dismal Swamp)** USA. Coastal marshland in SE Virginia and NE North Carolina. Now partly reclaimed; once much larger and thickly wooded with cypress, black gum, etc. In the centre is L. Drummond, connected with the Dismal Swamp Canal, which links Chesapeake Bay with Albemarle Sound.

**Diss** England. Urban district in Norfolk, on the R. Waveney 20 m. SSW of Norwich. Pop. (1961) 3,682. Market town. Manufactures pottery, brushes, mats. The poet John Skelton (1460–1529), who satirized Cardinal Wolsey, was rector from 1498 and nicknamed himself 'the vicar of Hell' (*Dis*, another name for Hades).

**Diu** India. Former Portuguese settlement on the Gulf of Cambay consisting of the island and town of Diu and small mainland areas. Area 14 sq. m. Pop. 20,000. Taken by the Portuguese 1534. Forcibly incorporated into the Indian Union, along with other settlements of Portuguese India, 1961. Became part of the Union Territory of Goa, Daman, and Diu 1962.

**Diwaniya** Iraq. Capital of Diwaniya province, on the Hilla branch of the Euphrates R. and on the Baghdad–Basra railway, 100 m. SSE of Baghdad. Pop. 33,000.

**Diyarbakir** Turkey. Capital of Diyarbakir province, in Kurdistan, on the Tigris R. 105 m. ESE of Malatya. Pop. (1965) 102,700. Commercial centre for an agricultural region. Trade in grain, wool, mohair. Textile and leather manufactures. Became a Roman colony A.D. 230. Fell to the Persians (363), and to the Arabs (638). Ruled by the Ottoman Turks from 1515.

**Dizful** Iran. Town in Khuzistan 75 m. N of Ahwaz, on the Diz R., a tributary of the Karun. Pop. (1966) 105,381. Flour milling, dyeing.

**Djailolo** ⟡ *Halmahera*.

**Djakarta** ⟡ *Jakarta*.

**Djebel Toubkal** ⟡ *Atlas Mountains*.

**Djerba (Jerba)** Tunisia. Island at the S entrance to the Gulf of Gabès, connected to the mainland by causeway. Area 197 sq. m. Pop. 62,000 (mostly Muslims, with a community of nearly 3,000 Jews). Produces olives, dates, etc. Manufactures textiles, pottery. Sponge diving, fishing. Some development of tourism in the 1960s. Traditionally Homer's island of the lotus-eaters.

**Djibouti (Jibuti)** French Territory of the Afars and the Issas. Capital and chief seaport, on the Gulf of Aden 150 m. SW of Aden. Pop. (1966) 70,000. A free port from 1949. Terminus of the railway from Addis Ababa. Became capital 1892. Ethiopia's only outlet to the sea (handling most of her trade) until the Ethiopia–Eritrea federation (1952).

**Djokjakarta** ⟡ *Jogjakarta*.

**Dneprodzerzhinsk** USSR. Industrial town in the Ukrainian SSR, on the Dnieper R. 20 m. WNW of Dnepropetrovsk. Pop. (1970) 227,000. Important metallurgical centre. Manufactures iron and steel, cement, fertilizers.

**Dneproges** USSR. Suburb of Zaporozhye, in the Ukrainian SSR on the Dnieper R. Site of the largest dam and power station in Europe. The dam (called Dneprostroi until its completion in 1932) raised the level of the Dnieper more than 100 ft, and submerged the rapids below Dnepropetrovsk; navigation is facilitated by locks. Partially

destroyed by the retreating Russians during the 2nd World War (1941), the dam was rebuilt by 1947.

**Dnepropetrovsk** USSR. Formerly (till 1926) Ekaterinoslav. Capital of the Dnepropetrovsk Region in the Ukrainian SSR, on the right bank of the Dnieper R. at its confluence with the Samara R. Pop. (1970) 863,000. Important railway junction and industrial centre. Manufactures iron and steel, agricultural machinery, machine tools, chemicals, clothing, flour, etc. Obtains coal from the Donets basin, iron from Krivoi Rog, manganese from Nikopol, and power from Dneproges. Founded by Potemkin (1786) as Ekaterinoslav (after Catherine II). The nearness of coal, iron, and manganese deposits assisted rapid industrial expansion late in the 19th cent. The completion (1932) of the Dneproges dam further stimulated development.

**Dnepr River** ⟡ *Dnieper River*.

**Dnestr River** ⟡ *Dniester River*.

**Dnieper (Dnepr) River** USSR. River 1,400 m. long (third longest in Europe), rising S of the Valdai Hills in the Smolensk Region of RSFSR, flowing S and W past Dorogobuzh (the head of navigation), Smolensk, Mogilev (all in Byelorussia), then generally SE (through the Ukraine) past Kiev, Kremenchug, Dneprodzerzhinsk, and Dnepropetrovsk – where it turns from E to S on the great 'Dnieper bend' and then passes Zaporozhye and turns SW past Kherson – and entering the Black Sea by a large estuary. The completion of the Dneproges dam (1932) caused the submergence of the rapids below Dnepropetrovsk and rendered the river navigable throughout its course to Dorogobuzh. In the upper course it is closed by ice for about 4 months annually, in the lower course for 3. Connected by canals with the W Dvina and the Bug rivers, both flowing to the Baltic Sea. Chief tributaries the Berezina, the Pripet, the Sozh, and the Desna rivers. Important hydroelectric plants: Kakhovka, Dneproges, Kremenchug.

**Dniester (Dnestr) River** USSR. River 870 m. long, rising in the Carpathian Mountains in the Drogobych Region of the Ukrainian SSR and following a very meandering course, flowing generally SE through the W of the Ukraine and the E of the Moldavian SSR and entering the Black Sea by an extensive estuary. Closed by ice for about 2 months annually. Formed the boundary between the USSR and Rumania 1918–40.

**Döbeln** German Democratic Republic. Industrial town in the Leipzig district, on the Freiberger Mulde R. 36 m. ESE of Leipzig. Pop. (1965) 28,639. Manufactures steel, agricultural machinery, soap, etc.

**Dobruja (Dobrogea)** Bulgaria/Rumania. Region in SE Rumania and NE Bulgaria, between the lower R. Danube and the Black Sea; the central part is crossed by the Danube–Black Sea Canal. The N part was (till 1968) the Rumanian Dobrogea Region (area 5,968 sq. m.; pop. (1963) 517,000; cap. Constanța). Mainly agricultural: cereals, beans, etc. In Roman times part of Moesia. Belonged in turn to the Byzantine, the Bulgarian, and the Ottoman empires. Suffered severely in the Russo-Turkish wars of the 18th–19th cent. N Dobruja passed to Rumania and S Dobruja to Bulgaria after the Berlin Congress (1878). S Dobruja became Rumanian 1913, but was restored to Bulgaria 1940.

**Dodecanese (Gr. Dhodhekanisos)** Greece. In Greek, 'The 12 Islands'. Group of islands and islets in the SE Aegean Sea, forming a *nome*. Area 1,050 sq. m. Pop. (1961) 122,346 (mainly Greek). Cap. Rhodes (Ródhos). The largest and most important islands are Rhodes and Cos (Kos); the others are Astypalaia, Kalymnos, Karpathos, Kasos, Kastellorizon, Khalke, Laros, Lipsos, Nisyros, Patmos, Syme, Telos. Produce olives, fruits, sponges. Gained from the Knights Hospitallers by the Turks 1522. Seized by the Italians 1912. Passed to Greece after the 2nd World War (1947).

**Dogger Bank** North Sea. Extensive sandbank 100 m. E of the Northumberland coast. Depth of water mostly 10–20 fathoms. A rich fishing ground, esp. for cod. Scene of a naval battle between British and German forces in the 1st World War (1915).

**Dogs, Isle of** England. District in Poplar (E London), on the N bank of the Thames, bounded on three sides by a horseshoe bend in the river. Opposite Greenwich and connected to it by an under-river tunnel for pedestrians. Contains the West India and the Millwall docks. The origin of the name is unknown.

**Doha (Bida)** Qatar. Capital and chief seaport, on the E coast of the peninsula. Pop. 65,000.

**Dôle** France. Town in the Jura department

on the Doubs R. 27 m. WSW of Besançon. Pop. (1968) 28,774. Industrial centre. Manufactures agricultural implements, chemicals, etc. Trade in cheese, wine, etc. Capital of Franche-Comté from the 14th cent. Birthplace of Louis Pasteur (1822–95).

**Dolgano-Nenets NA** ◊ *Taimyr*.

**Dolgellau (Dolgelly, Dolgelley)** Wales. Urban district and county town of Merionethshire, on the Wnion R. just N of Cader Idris. Pop. (1961) 2,267. Market town. Tourist centre, amid fine mountain scenery. Once famous for cloth manufactured from the wool of Welsh mountain sheep.

**Dolhain** ◊ *Limbourg*.

**Dollar** Scotland. Small burgh in Clackmannanshire, 6 m. NE of Alloa, at the foot of the Ochil Hills. Pop. (1961) 1,955. Market town. Well-known academy (founded 1818).

**Dolomites** Italy. Alpine region in the SE Tirol, rising to 10,965 ft in Marmolada. Impressive scenery, with jagged dolomitic limestone peaks, ridges, scree slopes, etc. A popular tourist area. Principal resort Cortina d'Ampezzo.

**Dominica** W Indies. Island of the Windward Is., in the Lesser Antilles, between the French islands Martinique and Guadeloupe. Area 290 sq. m. Pop. (1966) 68,552 (mainly Negro, with a few Carib Indians in a reserve). Cap. Roseau (pop. 11,600). The island is crossed N–S by a range of mountains, rising in Morne Diablotin to 4,747 ft. Solfataras, hot springs, and subterranean vapours indicate volcanic activity; Boiling L. in the S gives off gases which are sometimes poisonous. Noteworthy scenery, with spectacular waterfalls, ravines, and forests. Cacao, limes, bananas, mangoes, oranges, vanilla, coconuts, and avocado pears cultivated. Exports rum, lime juice, copra, citrates. Named by Columbus, to commemorate the date of his discovery of the island, Sunday (*Dies Dominica*) 3 Nov. 1493. After changing hands between the French and the British several times, it finally became British during the Napoleonic Wars. It was a presidency of the Leeward Is. 1833–1940; then counted as part of the Windward Is. Became an associated state within the British Commonwealth 1967.

**Dominican Republic** W Indies. Republic occupying the larger E part of the island of Hispaniola (of which Haiti occupies the remainder). Area 18,699 sq. m. Pop. (1964) 3,451,700 (mainly of mixed European, African, and Asian origin, unlike the predominantly Negro Haitians). Cap. Santo Domingo. Divided administratively into the National District (containing Santo Domingo) and 25 provinces. Distinguished by its unsettled history, with 56 revolutions in less than a century (1844–1930). Largely dependent on its sugar plantations, developed with the help of US capital.

Mountainous: the Cordillera Central exceeds 10,000 ft (the greatest altitude in the W Indies). Fertile, well-watered. Mainly agricultural. Chief crop and export sugar; coffee, cacao, bananas, tobacco also exported. Few industries apart from sugar refining; cigars, cigarettes, foodstuffs produced. Bauxite and rock salt mined.

Hispaniola was discovered (1492) by Columbus. The E part remained Spanish when the W was ceded to France (1697). The Dominican Republic has been independent since 1844, except for a short period of Spanish rule (1861–3) and a US military occupation (1916–24). General Trujillo became President in 1930 and remained in power for 18 of the next 22 years; he was assassinated in 1961. After the end of the Trujillo dictatorship the first free elections for 38 years were held (1962), but the government was overthrown by a military coup (1963). Civil war broke out and lasted for 4 months (1965).

**Donaghadee** Northern Ireland. Urban district and seaside resort in Co. Down, 16 m. ENE of Belfast. Pop. (1961) 3,226. Till 1849 terminus of the mail steamer service with Portpatrick, Scotland, which was superseded by the Larne–Stranraer service.

**Donbas** ⟡ *Donets River.*

**Doncaster** England. County borough in the W Riding of Yorkshire, on the R. Don 17 m. NE of Sheffield. Pop. (1961) 86,402. On the main London–Edinburgh railway and the Great North Road. Main industries coalmining, railway engineering. Manufactures nylon, machinery, rope, bricks, etc. Near by is the racecourse, Town Moor, where the St Leger (originated 1778) is run (Sept.). Among its buildings are the 19th-cent. Church of St George, with a 170-ft tower, and the 18th-cent. Mansion House. Site of the Roman station of Danum.

**Donegal** Irish Republic. **1.** County of Ulster, in the NW, bounded on the NW

and SW by the Atlantic, on the E and SE by Counties Londonderry, Tyrone, and Fermanagh (all in Northern Ireland), and on the SW by Co. Leitrim. Area 1,865 sq. m. Pop. (1966) 108,549. County town Lifford. The coast is rocky and deeply indented, the main inlets being Loughs Foyle and Swilly, Sheep Haven, and Donegal Bay, and there are many offshore islands, including Aran and Tory; Malin Head is the northernmost point of Ireland. Inland it is wild, picturesque, and mountainous, with the Derryveagh Mountains in the NW rising to 2,466 ft in Mt Errigal, and the Blue Stack Mountains farther S. Chief rivers the Foyle, the Finn, and the Erne. Some fishing. Sheep and cattle raised. Potatoes cultivated. Homespun cloth made. The soil is generally poor and resources few, and the population is decreasing. Near Ballyshannon are hydroelectric power stations on the R. Erne (1952).

**2.** Small market town in Co. Donegal, at the head of Donegal Bay. Pop. (1966) 1,507. Ruins of a 15th-cent. Franciscan monastery; here the famous *Annals of the Four Masters*, a history of Ireland up to 1616, was probably written (1632–6).

**Donetsk** USSR. Formerly Yuzovka, Stalin, Stalino. Capital of the Donetsk region, in the Ukrainian SSR, 160 m. SSE of Kharkov. Pop. (1970) 879,000. Chief industrial centre of the Donbas. Coalmining. Manufactures iron and steel, machinery, chemicals, cement, clothing, etc. The great metallurgical industry here was founded by a British industrialist named Hughes *c.* 1870, and the town was called Yuzovka (Hughesovka) after him; it was renamed Stalin after the Revolution, then Stalino, and in 1961 the name was changed to Donetsk.

**Donets River** USSR. River 680 m. long rising in the RSFSR 80 m. NNE of Kharkov and flowing generally S and SE through the Ukraine to join the Don R. 60 m. ENE of Rostov. The Donets Basin, or Donbas, including the towns of Donetsk, Makeyevka, Gorlovka, and Lugansk, is the country's most productive coalfield and a great industrial region.

**Don River** England. River 70 m. long in the W Riding of Yorkshire, rising in the Pennines 7 m. W of Penistone, flowing SE and then NE through Sheffield, Rotherham, and Doncaster to join the R. Ouse at Goole.

**Don River** Scotland. River 82 m. long in Aberdeenshire, rising near the Banffshire border and flowing generally E to enter the North Sea just N of Aberdeen. Well known for salmon fishing.

**Don River** USSR. Ancient Tanaïs. River in European RSFSR, 1,200 m. long, rising near Tula and flowing generally S and then E within 48 m. of the Volga R., to which it is joined by canal (1952) near Volgograd; from here it turns SW past Rostov to enter the Sea of Azov by a delta. It rises at an altitude of only 580 ft, and has an average fall of about 5 ins. per mile. Navigable to small craft as far upstream as Voronezh. Closed by ice for 3–4 months annually. Important fisheries. Used for transportation of grain, coal, timber. Chief tributaries the Voronezh, the Donets and the Medveditsa.

**Doorn** Netherlands. Town and health resort in Utrecht province 11 m. SE of Utrecht where Kaiser William II of Germany lived in exile from 1919 till his death (1941). Pop. 5,000.

**Doornik** ◊ *Tournai.*

**Dorchester** (Dorset) England. Ancient Durnovaria. Municipal borough and county town of Dorset, on the R. Frome 24 m. W of Bournemouth. Pop. (1961) 12,266. Market town. Known chiefly for its associations with Thomas Hardy (1840–1928), being the 'Casterbridge' of his Wessex novels. His birthplace and the house where he spent his last years are both near by. Many Roman and pre-Roman remains: 2 m. SW is the great earthwork of ◊ *Maiden Castle*; near by at Poundbury is another encampment, and at Maumbury Rings are the remains of a Roman amphitheatre. ◊ *Tolpuddle* is 7 m. ENE. Dorchester is also associated with William Barnes, the Dorset poet (1800–1886).

**Dorchester** (Oxfordshire) England. Village on the R. Thame near its confluence with the R. Thames 8 m. SSE of Oxford. Abbey Church (mainly 13th-cent.) with a remarkable 'Jesse window'. Important in Saxon times, when it was the seat of a bishopric.

**Dordogne** France. Department formed (1790) mainly from the old district of Périgord. Area 3,561 sq. m. Pop. (1968) 374,073. Prefecture Périgueux. The E part, on the W slopes of the Massif Central, is rather dry and stony. The W, esp. in the river valleys, is fertile: vines, wheat, tobacco, etc. cultivated; chestnuts, walnuts, truffles also important. Chief towns Périgueux, Bergerac.

**Dordogne River** France. River 290 m. long rising on Mont Dore in the Auvergne Mountains, flowing SW and W to join the Garonne R. and form the Gironde estuary. Famous vineyards (e.g. St Émilion) beside its lower course. Several hydroelectric installations.

**Dordrecht** Netherlands. Sometimes abbreviated to Dordt or Dort. Industrial town and port in S Holland province, 12 m. SE of Rotterdam, mainly on the S bank of the Oude Maas R. Pop. (1968) 88,461. Shipbuilding, marine engineering. Manufactures electrical equipment, chemicals, glass, etc. A 14th-cent. church (Groote Kerk). Chief port of the Netherlands until the 17th cent., then superseded by Rotterdam. First meeting place of the United Provinces (1572) and scene of the Synod of Dort (1618–19). Birthplace of Johann de Witt (1625–72), mathematician and statesman.

**Dorking** England. Urban district in Surrey, on the R. Mole near the N Downs, with Box Hill (596 ft) 1 m. NE. Pop. (1961) 22,594. Market town. A 5-clawed breed of poultry was named after it. Birthplace of T. R. Malthus (1766–1834). Also associated with Fanny Burney, Keats, Dickens, and Meredith.

**Dornbirn** Austria. Town in Vorarlberg province 6 m. S of Bregenz near the Swiss frontier. Pop. (1961) 28,075. Manufactures textiles.

**Dornoch** Scotland. Royal burgh and county town of Sutherland on Dornoch Firth. Pop. (1961) 933. Seaside resort with well-known golf course. Former 13th-cent. cathedral, burned in 1570, restored 1835–7 as the parish church. Scotland's last burning of a witch took place here (1722).

**Dorset (Dorsetshire)** England. County in the SW, bounded on the S by the English Channel. Area 973 sq. m. Pop. (1961) 309,176. County town Dorchester. The chalk range of the N Dorset Downs runs across the centre, rising in the E to 902 ft; in the S are the lower S Dorset Downs and in the N Cranborne Chase, the rest of the county being low-lying. Chief rivers the Frome and the Stour. Dorset is noted for its quiet but varied charms, immortalized in the novels of Thomas Hardy; the coast also is picturesque and has such resorts as Weymouth, Swanage, and Lyme Regis.

Sheep raised on the downs and dairy cattle in the valleys. Portland building stone quarried. Largest town Poole.

**Dort** ◊ *Dordrecht*.

**Dortmund** Federal German Republic. Industrial town and port in N Rhine-Westphalia on the Emscher R. at the head of the Dortmund–Ems Canal 20 m. ENE of Essen. Pop. (1968) 648,244. A major centre of coalmining and steel manufacture. Brewing, engineering. Expanded with the development of the Ruhr coalfield. A town of importance by the 9th cent., it benefited commercially by joining the Hanseatic League in the 13th. Ceded to Prussia 1815. Among its old buildings are the 13th-cent. Reinoldikirche and the 12th-cent. Marienkirche; many were severely damaged by Allied bombing in the 2nd World War.

**Douai** France. Ancient Duacum. Industrial town in the Nord department, on the Scarpe R. 18 m. S of Lille. On the northern coalfield at the centre of routes by road, rail, and canal. Pop. (1968) 51,657. Manufactures iron and steel, coke, machinery, glass, etc. Many associations with British Catholics: in 1568 a college for English Catholics was set up here and in 1592 another for Scottish Catholics, and the 'Douai Bible', used by Roman Catholics, was published at the former 1610. Taken from Spain by Louis XIV 1667, later ceded to France. Its university, founded (1562) by Philip II of Spain, was suppressed in the French Revolution, and was transferred to Lille 1887.

**Douala** Cameroun. Chief seaport and largest town, 125 m. W of Yaoundé. Pop. 150,000. Terminus of the railway from Yaoundé. Exports tropical hardwoods, cacao, bananas, etc. Brewing, flour milling. Manufactures textiles, footwear. Formerly capital of the German colony of Kamerun (1901–16).

**Douarnenez** France. Fishing port in the Finistère department, on the S shore of Douarnenez Bay 25 m. SE of Brest. Pop. (1968) 20,184. Sardine and tunny fishing. Boatbuilding, fishing-net making, fish canning.

**Doubs** France. Department in the E formed from Montbéliard and part of Franche-Comté, bounded on the E by Switzerland and crossed by the Doubs R. Area 2,030 sq. m. Pop. (1968) 426,363. Prefecture Besançon. Largely mountainous, with four parallel chains of the Jura running NE-

SW across it. The NW area is lower and more fertile, producing cereals, vegetables, etc. Manufactures motor vehicles, bicycles, clocks and watches, etc. Chief towns Besançon, Montbéliard, Pontarlier.

**Doubs River** France. River 267 m. long, rising in the E Jura, flowing first NE through picturesque limestone gorges, forming part of the Franco-Swiss frontier, turning W, N, then SW to join the Saône R. at Verdun-sur-le-Doubs. Distance in direct line from source to mouth only 56 m. Towns along its course include Pontarlier, Besançon, Dôle.

**Douglas** (Isle of Man) England. Capital of the Isle of Man, municipal borough in the picturesque Douglas Bay on the E coast. Pop. (1961) 18,837. Seaport. Resort. Douglas Head, with a lighthouse, is just SE. The Tower of Refuge, built (1832) by Sir William Hillary, founder of the Royal National Lifeboat Institution, marks the dangerous Conister Rocks N of the harbour entrance. Among noteworthy buildings are the Manx Museum and the legislative buildings. Douglas was the first seaport in the UK to be equipped with radar (1948). Scene of annual motorcycle races.

**Dounreay** ◊ *Thurso*.

**Douro** (Sp. **Duero**) **River** Portugal/Spain. River 480 m. long, one of the longest in the Iberian peninsula, rising at the W end of the Sierra de Cebollera, flowing S, and then swinging W to drain much of the N Meseta; forms part of the Portuguese-Spanish border and enters the Atlantic near Oporto. Navigation impeded by rapids; used chiefly for irrigation and hydroelectric power. Vineyards in its lower valley produce the finest Port wines.

**Dover** England. Ancient Dubris (Portus Dubris). Municipal borough in E Kent, on the Strait of Dover, 65 m. ESE of London. Pop. (1961) 35,248. A Cinque Port, the only one still an important seaport, terminus of the shortest sea route to the continent (to Calais, 22 m. distant), with a service also to Ostend, car ferries, and a train ferry (to Dunkirk). Its harbour is enclosed by breakwaters (1898–1909); the large car ferry terminal was completed 1953. Within the precincts of the Norman castle, which overlooks the town, are a Roman pharos (lighthouse), which guided the legions across the Channel, and the ancient church of St Mary in Castro (rebuilt in the 12th cent.). The town hall incorporates the hall of a Maison Dieu founded by Hubert de Burgh in the 13th cent. Named after the small R. Dour, which pierces the famous chalk cliffs here. At the SE end of Watling Street, it was for the Romans an important gateway to England from the continent as it is today. The castle, successfully defended (1216) against the French by Hubert de Burgh, was long considered to be the key to England. In the 1st World War it was the headquarters of the famous Dover Patrol; in the 2nd World War it suffered severely from air raids and long-range bombardments.

**Dover, Strait of** (Fr. **Pas de Calais**). Strait between England and France, connecting the English Channel with the North Sea; at its narrowest (between Dover and Cap Gris Nez) 21 m. wide. This is the route taken by most Channel swimmers, the first successful one being Capt. Webb (1875, Dover–Calais).

**Dove River** England. Picturesque river 40 m. long, rising 3 m. SW of Buxton, flowing S and SE, and forming much of the Derbyshire–Staffordshire border, joining the R. Trent near Burton-on-Trent. Dovedale, between Dove Holes and Thorpe Cloud, is especially well known for its scenery, while the stream is familiar to anglers because of its associations with Izaak Walton.

**Dovey River** ⟡ *Cardiganshire*.

**Dovrefjell** Norway. Mountainous plateau in the S, separated from the Jotunheim Mountains (SSW) by the Gudbrandsdal, rising to 7,498 ft in Snöhetta. Crossed by the Oslo–Trondheim railway (opened 1921).

**Down** Northern Ireland. Maritime county in the E, facing the Irish Sea, bounded by Belfast Lough (N) and Carlingford Lough (S). Area 952 sq. m. Pop. (1961) 267,013. County town Downpatrick. Coastline indented, the principal inlet being Strangford Lough, almost enclosed by the low-lying Ards peninsula. Hilly, with Slieve Donard in the Mourne Mountains (SE) rising to 2,796 ft. The fertile valleys of the Lagan, Upper Bann, and other rivers produce oats, potatoes, and turnips, and cattle are reared. Main industry linen manufacture. Chief towns Downpatrick, Bangor, Newry, Newtownards.

**Downey** USA. Suburb 10 m. SE of Los Angeles in California. Pop. (1960) 82,505.

Manufactures aircraft, cement, soap, etc. Named after J. G. Downey, California's seventh Yankee governor (1860–62).

**Downpatrick** Northern Ireland. County town of Co. Down, urban district 22 m. SSE of Belfast. Pop. (1961) 4,219. Market town. Manufactures linen. Tanning, brewing. The name is derived from the large *dun*, the Mound of Down, and the associations with St Patrick, who is supposed to have founded a monastery here *c.* 440; he and St Columba are said to have been buried here. Near by are the remains of Saul Abbey, where St Patrick died, and of the 12th-cent. Inch Abbey.

**Downs** England. Chalk hills in the S, the name being generally applied to two roughly parallel ranges running W–E known as the N Downs and the S Downs. The N Downs extend through Surrey and Kent, ending at the white cliffs of Dover, the S Downs through Sussex to Beachy Head, and the scarp slopes of the two ridges face each other across the Weald. Their highest points are Leith Hill (965 ft) in the N Downs and Butser Hill (865 ft) in the S Downs. They provide good sheep pasture and have produced the well-known Southdown breed. Farther W are the Hampshire, Berkshire, and Marlborough Downs, with Inkpen Beacon in S Berkshire reaching 975 ft.

**Downs, The** England. Roadstead off the E coast of Kent opposite Deal, about 8 m. by 6 m., protected by the Goodwin Sands, except during strong southerly gales.

**Drachenfels** Federal German Republic. Mountain (1,053 ft) in the Siebengebirge on the right bank of the Rhine R. near Honnef, 8 m. SE of Bonn. Ruins of a 12th-cent. castle at the summit. So named ('Dragon's Rock') because according to legend Siegfried here slew the dragon.

**Drakensberg** S Africa. Principal mountain range in southern Africa: the E escarpment of the plateau, extending through the Transvaal, Natal, and the Cape Province (S Africa) and forming the W frontier of Swaziland and the E frontier of Lesotho. The highest peaks are in Lesotho: Thaban Ntlenyana (11,425 ft) and Mont-aux-Sources (10,822 ft, near which is the Natal National Park). An important watershed: the Tugela R. flows to the Indian Ocean, the Orange R. (with its tributaries the Vaal and the Caledon) to the Atlantic.

**Drama** Greece. 1. *Nome* in Macedonia, with Bulgaria on its N border. Area 1,353 sq. m. Pop. (1961) 120,936. Drained by the Mesta R. Chief crop tobacco.

**2.** Ancient Drabescus. Capital of Drama *nome*, 73 m. ENE of Salonika. Pop. (1961) 32,195. Market town. Trade mainly in tobacco.

**Drammen** Norway. Port at the mouth of the Drammen R. and the head of Drammen Fiord (Dramsfiord), 23 m. SW of Oslo. Pop. (1968) 47,827. Manufactures and exports paper, wood pulp, cellulose, etc. Engineering.

**Drammen (Drams) River** Norway. River 190 m. long, rising as the Hallingdal R. on the Hallingskarv Mountains, flowing generally E and then SSE to Drammen Fiord (Dramsfiord). Provides hydroelectric power for sawmills etc.

**Drancy** France. Suburb of NE Paris, in the Seine-St Denis department. Pop. (1968) 69,528. Mainly residential, with many large blocks of flats.

**Drava (Drave) River.** River 450 m. long rising in the Carnic Alps near Dobbiaco (Italy), flowing E into Austria and then Yugoslavia, turning ESE to join the Danube R. 12 m. E of Osijek, forming part of the Yugoslav-Hungarian border. Navigable by steamers below Barcs (95 m.).

**Drenthe** (Drente) Netherlands. Province in the NE, bordered on the E by the Federal German Republic. Area 1,021 sq. m. Pop. (1968) 354,124. Cap. Assen. Much infertile heathland, steadily being reclaimed. Potatoes, rye, etc. cultivated. Cattle reared. Peat digging. Oil and natural gas produced in the SE.

**Dresden** German Democratic Republic. Capital of Dresden district, on the Elbe R. 63 m. ESE of Leipzig. Pop. (1968) 500,158. Important commercial and industrial centre. Railway and road junction. Manufactures machine tools, optical and musical instruments, electrical equipment, chemical and pharmaceutical goods, cigarettes, etc. (but the famous Dresden china is made at Meissen). Formerly regarded as one of the most beautiful of German cities and noted for its Baroque architecture, Dresden was severely damaged in the 2nd World War (1945). Many of its finest buildings were destroyed, including the Baroque Hofkirche and Frauenkirche, the Opera House, and the world-famous Zwinger, with its valuable art collections; most of the treasures, however, had been kept in safety outside the city. Among its principal outdoor features are the great public park known as the Grosser Garten and the Brühl Terrace, an attractive promenade built (1738) along the S bank of the Elbe. Once a Slav settlement, Dresden became the capital of Henry, Margrave of Meissen, in 1270. Later capital of the electors and kings of Saxony. Became an art centre in the 17th and the 18th cent., esp. under the electors Augustus I and II, and was often known as 'the German Florence'. Suffered severely in the Seven Years War (1760) and at the Battle of Dresden (1813), the last of Napoleon's great victories.

**Driffield (Great Driffield)** England. Urban district in the E Riding of Yorkshire, 19 m. NNW of Hull. Pop. (1961) 6,890. Market town. Flour milling. Manufactures oil-cake, agricultural machinery.

**Drina River** Yugoslavia. River 290 m. long, formed by the union of the Tara and the Piva rivers on the N border of Montenegro, flowing generally NNE to join the Sava R.

**Drin River** Albania. River 100 m. long, formed by the union of the White Drin R. and the Black Drin R. at Kukës, flowing generally W; divides on the plain of Shkodër, the old course continuing S to the Adriatic, with an arm flowing W to join the Bojana R.

**Drogheda** Irish Republic. Seaport in Co. Louth on the R. Boyne 4 m. above its mouth on Drogheda Bay. Pop. (1966) 17,908. Exports cattle. Linen and cotton milling, brewing, engineering. Manufactures cement, fertilizers, etc. Taken by the Danes in the 10th cent., later an Anglo-Norman stronghold. In 1494 a parliament held here enacted 'Poynings' Law', by which Irish legislation had to be ratified by the English Privy Council. During the Civil War it was captured by Cromwell (1649) and its inhabitants massacred or transported to the W Indies. The name means 'Bridge over the Ford'.

**Drogobych (Drohobycz)** USSR. Town in the Ukrainian SSR 42 m. SW of Lvov. Pop. 42,000. Centre of petroleum and natural gas production. Oil refining, metal working. Manufactures chemicals, soap. Trade in agricultural produce. Passed from Poland to Austria 1772. Returned to Poland 1919. Taken by the USSR 1939.

**Droitwich** England. Municipal borough in Worcestershire 6 m. NNE of Worcester on the R. Salwarpe. Pop. (1961) 7,975.

Spa: salt springs (wyches), among the strongest in Europe and known since Roman times, no longer used for salt manufacture but for treatment of rheumatic ailments. Saltworks at Stoke Prior, 4 m. to the N E. Manufactures heating equipment etc. Birthplace of Edward Winslow (1595–1655), Pilgrim Father and first governor of New Plymouth.

**Drôme** France. Department in the SE, formed (1790) from parts of Dauphiné and Provence. Area 2,533 sq. m. Pop. (1968) 342,891. Prefecture Valence. Mountainous in the E, where spurs of the Cottian Alps reach 7,890 ft (Dévoluy); slopes W to its W boundary, the Rhône. On the lowlands vines, mulberries, maize, truffles, and olives are grown, Rhône wines are produced, and textiles are manufactured. Chief towns Valence, Montélimar (famous for nougat).

**Drôme River** France. River 65 m. long flowing generally W N W across the Drôme department to join the Rhône R. 15 m. N of Montélimar.

**Dromore** Northern Ireland. Urban district in Co. Down, on the R. Lagan 16 m. S W of Belfast. Pop. (1961) 2,125. Market town. Linen industry. Cathedral destroyed 1641; present church built in 1661 by Bishop Jeremy Taylor (1613–67), who is buried here along with Bishop Thomas Percy (1729–1811).

**Droylsden** England. Urban district in SE Lancashire just E of Manchester. Pop. (1961) 25,457. Manufactures textiles, chemicals. Engineering.

**Drummondville** Canada. Industrial town in Quebec, on the St Francis R. 60 m. E N E of Montreal. Pop. (1966) 29,216. Manufactures synthetic fibres, hosiery, paper, etc. Has an important hydroelectric plant.

**Drygalski Island** Antarctica. Island off the coast of Queen Mary Land, discovered (1914) by Sir Douglas Mawson and named after the German explorer Erich von Drygalski.

**Dubai** Trucial States. Chief seaport and largest town, on the Persian Gulf, in the Sheikhdom of Dubai. Pop. 60,000.

**Dubbo** Australia. Town in New South Wales, on the Macquarie R. 185 m. N W of Sydney. Pop. (1966) 15,568. Centre of a wool- and wheat-producing district. Flour milling. Manufactures clothing.

**Dublin** Irish Republic. **1.** Maritime county in Leinster, bordering on the Irish Sea (E). Area 356 sq. m. Pop. (1966) 795,047

(three quarters of whom live in Dublin city). The N and central parts are low-lying but the S is mountainous, rising to 2,473 ft in Kippure (Wicklow Mountains). Chief river the Liffey. Oats and potatoes cultivated. Cattle raised. Apart from Dublin, the principal town is Dún Laoghaire (seaport).
**2.** Irish **Baile Átha Cliath** ('Town of the Hurdle Ford'). Capital of the republic, county borough at the mouth of the R. Liffey on Dublin Bay, facing the Irish Sea. Pop. (1966) 568,772. Seaport. Leading commercial and cultural centre. Has the famous Guinness brewery, reputedly the largest in the world. Engineering, flour milling, whisky distilling. Manufactures poplin, biscuits. The principal roads and railways converge on the city, and it exports much of the livestock, bacon, eggs, and dairy produce from the interior, chiefly to Britain via Liverpool and Holyhead. The harbour, begun with the building of the North Wall (1714), has been considerably improved during the present century, and docks serve both the Royal and Grand Canals.

The city is more or less bisected by the R. Liffey, and its best-known thoroughfare, O'Connell Street, runs N from O'Connell Bridge to Parnell Square. Attractive open spaces S of the river include St Stephen's Green, Merrion Square, and College Park. Near the last-named is Trinity College, or the University of Dublin, founded 1591, but mainly 18th-cent., like many other distinguished Dublin buildings; in its famous library, which has the right to receive a copy of every book published in the British Isles, is the 9th-cent. *Book of Kells*, often described as 'the most beautiful book in the world'. Near St Stephen's Green is University College, one of the constituent colleges of the National University of Ireland. On College Green is one of Dublin's most striking buildings, that of the Bank of Ireland (begun 1729), which formerly housed the Irish parliament. Leinster House (1745), originally the town mansion of the dukes of Leinster, has been the seat of the Irish parliament since 1922; adjoining it are the National Gallery, National Museum, and National Library. Besides the two leading colleges there are many other educational institutions and learned societies in Dublin, and the Irish national drama has long been worthily represented at the Abbey Theatre (founded 1904) which occupied the old Queen's Theatre from 1951, when its original home in Abbey Street was burned down; the new Abbey Theatre was opened in 1966. Two Protestant cathedrals, Christ Church, founded (1038) by Sigtryg the Dane, restored 1870–78, and St Patrick's, the national cathedral of the Church of Ireland, founded 1190, where Swift was dean (1713–45) and where he is buried. Also a Roman Catholic metropolitan pro-cathedral (1816). On the N W outskirts of the city is Phoenix Park, one of the largest and finest parks in Europe, 1,750 acres in area, containing the People's Garden, the Zoological Gardens, recreation grounds, and the former Viceregal Lodge, now the residence of the President.

As the Irish name for the city suggests, there was probably a ford across the Liffey at Dublin in very early times, long before it was settled by the Danes in the 9th cent. Although defeated by Brian Boru at Clontarf (1014) the Danes ruled the city for more than three centuries, but were finally driven out by the Anglo-Normans 1171. In the following year Henry II visited Dublin and presented it by Charter to 'his subjects of Bristol', thus inaugurating 7½ centuries of English rule. In 1689 James II, attempting to recover his throne, held his last parliament in Dublin, and was followed, after his defeat at the Battle of the Boyne, by William III, who gave thanks for victory in St Patrick's Cathedral. The 19th cent. was largely a period of violence and disorder. After the United Irishmen had planned to seize the city in 1798, a revolt broke out in 1803 and Robert Emmet and other leaders were executed. In 1873 the first Home Rule conference was held in the Rotunda, where later (1905) the Sinn Fein movement was founded; in 1882 Lord Frederick Cavendish and Thomas Burke were murdered in Phoenix Park. The Easter Monday rising of 1916 was suppressed, but the first Sinn Fein parliament met in the Mansion House under the presidency of De Valera in 1919, and disturbances and bloodshed continued until the establishment of the Irish Free State in 1922 – and for 5 years afterwards. Although the republic was neutral in the 2nd World War, Dublin was bombed in error by German aircraft (1941), causing damage and casualties.

Of the many famous citizens that Dublin has produced, the city has shone most brilliantly in the sphere of literature, with Swift (1667–1745), Steele (1672–1729), Thomas Moore (1779–1852), R. B. Sheridan (1751–1816), Oscar Wilde (1854–1900), G. B. Shaw (1856–1950), W. B. Yeats (1865–1939), J. M. Synge (1871–1909) and James Joyce (1882–1941); others are Edmund Burke (1729–97), the Duke of Wellington (1769–1852), Lord Carson (1854–1935), and Sir William Orpen (1878–1931).

**Dubrovnik** (Italian **Ragusa**) Yugoslavia. Seaport on the Dalmatian coast 100 m. SE of Split. Pop. (1961) 22,961. Tourist centre; picturesque, medieval in appearance. Modern harbour at the suburb of Gruž. Among the many historic buildings are the 17th-cent. cathedral with altarpiece by Titian, the 15th-cent. rector's palace, and cloisters of 14th-cent. Dominican and Franciscan monasteries, while the city is justifiably proud of its ancient walls. Just off Dubrovnik is the small island of Lokrum, where Richard I was said to have been shipwrecked (1190). Founded in the 7th cent. by refugees from Epidaurus (the modern Cavtat). Became a great commercial centre, an independent republic and rival of Venice, but declined from the 16th cent. Passed to Austria (1814), then to Yugoslavia (1918), when it was given its present name. The word 'argosy' is derived from its Italian name.

**Dubuque** U S A. Industrial town, river port, and railway centre in Iowa 62 m. NE of Cedar Rapids on the Mississippi R. Pop. (1960) 56,606. Meat packing. Manufactures tractors, machinery, furniture, clothing, etc. Named after Julien Dubuque, a French trader who settled here (1788) and worked the lead deposits.

**Ducie Island** ◊ *Pitcairn Island.*

**Dudley** England. County borough in Worcestershire, an enclave in Staffordshire 8 m. WNW of Birmingham in the Black Country. Pop. (1961) 61,748. Centre of the wrought-iron industry. Manufactures boilers, chains, welding equipment, and other metal goods, as well as bricks and tiles. Coalmining in the neighbourhood. Remains of Dudley Castle (mainly 16th cent.); among later buildings are the Guest Hospital (1868) and the new town hall (1928).

**Dudweiler** Federal German Republic. Industrial town in Saarland 4 m. NE of Saarbrücken. Pop. (1963) 29,700. Coalmining. Metal working. Manufactures electrical equipment etc.

**Duero River** ◊ *Douro River*.

**Duff Islands** S W Pacific Ocean. Small group of volcanic islands in the British ◊ *Solomon Islands* Protectorate in Melanesia.

**Dugi Otok** Yugoslavia. Island 28 m. long and 3 m. wide off the Dalmatian coast. Fishing villages and seaside resorts, the largest being Sali, on the S coast, 14 m. S of Zadar. Name means 'Long Island'.

**Duisburg** Federal German Republic. Industrial town and river port in N Rhine-Westphalia, at the confluence of the Rhine and the Ruhr rivers, 13 m. N of Düsseldorf. Pop. (1968) 468,526. One of the world's largest and busiest inland ports. Important iron and steel industry; also coalmining, shipbuilding, engineering. Manufactures chemicals, textiles, etc. An ancient town, it developed rapidly after the establishment of the steel industry in the 19th cent. Severely damaged by bombing during the 2nd World War.

**Dukeries, The** England. District in N W Nottinghamshire in Sherwood Forest, between Mansfield and Worksop, consisting of the great parks of a group of former ducal seats (hence the name): Welbeck, Worksop, Clumber, and Thoresby.

**Dukhan** ◊ *Qatar*.

**Dukinfield** England. Municipal borough in N E Cheshire 6 m. E of Manchester. Pop. (1961) 17,318. Engineering. Manufactures wood and metal products, cotton goods, bricks and tiles, etc.

**Duluth** U S A. Industrial town and port in Minnesota at the mouth of the St Louis R. at the W end of L. Superior. Pop. (1960) 106,884. Built on a picturesque site above the lake, it has an excellent harbour, ice-bound for 4 months annually. Handles grain, iron ore and coal shipments. Manufactures telephone equipment, cement, etc. Flour milling, sawmilling, brewing, etc. An aerial lift bridge spans the ship canal (through Minnesota Point) which forms the harbour entrance. Named after Daniel Greysolon, Sieur du Lhut (Duluth), a French trader and explorer who built a trading post in the neighbourhood *c.* 1678.

**Dulwich** England. Residential suburb in the Greater London borough of Southwark, in S London. Well-known public school, Dulwich College, founded (1619) by Edward Alleyn; large park (72 acres), and famous art gallery (founded 1811).

**Dumbarton** (Gaelic **Dun Breatann**) Scotland. Royal burgh and county town of Dunbartonshire near the confluence of the R. Leven with the R. Clyde 14 m. W N W of Glasgow. Pop. (1961) 26,335. Main industry shipbuilding; also engineering, whisky distilling, etc. The Gaelic name means 'Fort of the Britons'. Dumbarton Rock (240 ft) was once capital of the British kingdom of Strathclyde.

**Dum-Dum** India. Town in W Bengal, just N E of Calcutta. Pop. (1961) 20,159. Engineering etc. The first soft-nosed 'dum-dum' bullets were made at the arsenal in the late 19th cent. and were used against the tribesmen on the N W frontier. Now the site of Calcutta international airport. North Dum-Dum (pop. 38,451) and South Dum-Dum (pop. 111,284) are adjoining municipalities.

**Dumfries** Scotland. Royal burgh and county town of Dumfriesshire, on the R. Nith 29 m. W N W of Carlisle. Pop. (1961) 27,275. Market town. Manufactures tweed, hosiery. Since 1929 includes Maxwelltown, on the opposite bank of the river. In St Michael's churchyard is the Burns Mausoleum (1815); the house where the poet spent his last 5 years is now a museum. In the market place is the old town hall (1708), known as the Mid Steeple. The Old Bridge, built (1280) of stone, is now reserved for pedestrians.

**Dumfriesshire** Scotland. County in the S, bordering Cumberland, England (S E), and Solway Firth (S). Area 1,073 sq. m. Pop. (1961) 88,423. County town Dumfries. Slopes gradually from the Southern Uplands in the N (where White Coomb reaches 2,695 ft and Hart Fell 2,651 ft) towards the coast. Drained to the Solway Firth by the Nith, Annan, and Esk rivers; the valleys of the first two, Nithsdale and Annandale, provide routes by railway and road through the Southern Uplands. Sheep and cattle raised. Oats, root crops cultivated. Chief towns Dumfries, Annan.

**Dunajec River** Poland. River 130 m. long formed by the union of the Czarny (Black) Dunajec and the Bialy (White) Dunajec, rising in the High Tatra and flowing generally E and N to join the Vistula R. Used for hydroelectric power.

**Dunbar** Scotland. Royal burgh in E Lothian, on the North Sea 26 m. E of Edinburgh. Pop. (1961) 4,003. Fishing port. Resort. The ruined castle was the scene of a successful defence by 'Black Agnes' (Countess of March) against the English (1336). Cromwell defeated the Scots at the Battle of Dunbar (1650).

**Dunbartonshire (Dumbartonshire)** Scotland. County in the W, lying between Loch Lomond (E), the Clyde estuary (S), and Loch Long (W), and including a detached area between Stirlingshire and Lanarkshire. Area 244 sq. m. Pop. (1961) 184,546. County town Dumbarton. Mountainous in the N and W, with Ben Vorlich (N) rising to 3,092 ft; here the picturesque scenery attracts many tourists in summer. The R. Leven drains Loch Lomond to the Clyde; dyeing, bleaching, and textile printing have long been important in the Vale of Leven. Shipbuilding is the principal industry at Clydebank and Dumbarton, the chief towns, both on the Clyde. Coal mined in the detached area around Kirkintilloch.

**Dunblane** Scotland. Small burgh in Perthshire, on Allan Water 5 m. N of Stirling. Pop. (1961) 2,922. Market town. Spa. Woollen mills. The first church here is said to have been built by St Blane in the 7th cent. Cathedral (founded in the 12th cent., restored 1893).

**Dundalk** Irish Republic. County town and seaport of Co. Louth, near the mouth of the R. Castletown, Dundalk Bay, 20 m. N of Drogheda. Pop. (1966) 20,002. Exports cattle, beef, grain, etc. Railway engineering, brewing. Manufactures linen, hosiery, etc. Here Edward Bruce proclaimed himself king of Ireland (1315) and was killed in battle near by (1318).

**Dundee** Scotland. Royal burgh in Angus, on the N shore of the Firth of Tay 36 m. NNE of Edinburgh. Pop. (1961) 182,959. Seaport, fourth largest city in Scotland, and chief centre of the British jute industry. Since the partial decline in jute manufacturing owing to competition from Indian mills, other industries have been developed. Engineering. Manufactures linen, canvas, linoleum, jam, marmalade, confectionery, cash registers, electrical equipment, clocks and watches, etc. Linked with Edinburgh and the S by railway via the Tay Bridge, completed in 1888 to replace the earlier bridge, which was destroyed in a gale (1879); a new road bridge was opened in 1966. Its buildings include the modern Caird Hall, the Albert Institute, and the three City Churches under one roof, surmounted by the 156-ft Old Steeple, dating from the 15th cent. The former University College (founded 1883), which was reorganized and renamed Queen's College in 1953, is part of St Andrews University. Within the burgh is the resi-

dential and resort town of Broughty Ferry, on the Firth of Tay 4 m. E.

**Dunedin** New Zealand. Seaport and industrial town on the SE coast of the S Island, at the head of Otago Harbour. Pop. (1966) 77,149. Manufactures woollen goods, clothing, footwear, agricultural machinery, etc. Most of its trade is handled at Port Chalmers, 8 m. NE along the harbour. Main exports wool, meat, fruit, cheese, condensed milk. The city is beautifully situated, with forested hills preserved in the Town Belt overlooking the harbour. Founded (1848) by Scottish settlers; grew with the discovery of gold in Otago in 1861; merchants prospered, labour became available for development. Seat of the University of Otago (1869). The principal streets, Princes Street and George Street, were named after those of Edinburgh; Scottish affiliations have remained strong. The first shipment of frozen New Zealand meat was dispatched from here 1881.

**Dunfermline** Scotland. Ancient royal burgh in SW Fifeshire. Pop. (1961) 47,159. Famous from the early 18th cent. for damask and linen; now manufactures silk, rayon, rubber products. Also engineering, bleaching and dyeing. Coalmining in the neighbourhood. The palace, little of which remains, was a favourite residence of Scottish kings, and many of them with their queens were buried in the 11th-cent. abbey. Birthplace of Andrew Carnegie (1835–1919), who presented Pittencrieff Park and Glen, the public library and baths and other gifts to the town; several of his endowment trusts are administered from here.

**Dungannon** Northern Ireland. Urban district in Co. Tyrone 35 m. WSW of Belfast. Pop. (1961) 6,503. Market town. Manufactures linen, bricks, etc. The chief seat of the O'Neills, the earls of Tyrone, until the early 17th cent.

**Dungarvan** Irish Republic. Urban district in Co. Waterford, on Dungarvan Harbour 25 m. SW of Waterford. Pop. (1966) 5,380. Seaport. Market town. Manufactures glue and gelatine, leather, dairy products. 6m. SE is Helvick Head (230 ft).

**Dungeness** England. Low shingle headland, the southernmost point of Kent, slowly extending seawards by accumulation of shingle. Old lighthouse; a new automatic lighthouse was opened in 1960. Work on a nuclear power station here was begun in 1960.

**Dunkeld** Scotland. Village in Perthshire on the R. Tay 13 m. NNW of Perth. Ruined cathedral partly dating from the 12th cent., presented to the nation by the Duke of Atholl 1918. About 1 m. S is the probable remnant of Birnam Wood, immortalized in Shakespeare's *Macbeth*.

**Dunkirk** (Fr. **Dunkerque**) France. Northernmost seaport of France, in the Nord department on the North Sea 24 m. ENE of Calais. Pop. (1968) 28,082. Shipbuilding, oil and sugar refining, cotton and jute spinning. Manufactures fishing nets, soap, etc. Probably grew round a church built in the Dunes of St Éloi in the 7th cent. – hence the name ('Church in the Dunes'). Changed hands many times: in 1388 it was burned by the English, in 1658 was ceded to Cromwell, in 1662 was sold by Charles II to Louis XIV. In the 2nd World War the harbour was completely destroyed, to be partially reopened in 1946, the Dover–Dunkirk train ferry first operating again in 1948. Scene of the heroic evacuation of over 300,000 Allied troops, hemmed in by German forces, in 1940. Birthplace of the famous French admiral, Jean Bart (1651–1702).

**Dún Laoghaire** Irish Republic. Pronounced Dunleary. Formerly Dunleary, Kingstown. Passenger seaport for Dublin, in Co. Dublin on the S shore of Dublin Bay, with steamer service to Holyhead. Pop. (1966) 51,772. Also a seaside resort and yachting centre. Its original name was changed to Kingstown after George IV had embarked here (1821), and to its present name in 1921.

**Dunmow** (**Great Dunmow**) England. Market town in Essex on the R. Chelmer 8 m. E of Bishop's Stortford. Pop. (1961) 3,904. Here the ancient Dunmow Flitch trial is held annually, a married couple who can testify that they have not quarrelled for one year being awarded a flitch of bacon – the custom having been revived in 1855. The village of Little Dunmow is 2 m. ESE. Birthplace of Lionel Lukin (1742–1834), inventor of the lifeboat.

**Dunoon** Scotland. Small burgh in Argyllshire, on the Firth of Clyde 6 m. W of Greenock. Pop. (1961) 9,211. Seaside resort; yachting centre. Traces of an ancient castle. Just N is Holy Loch, which became a base for US Polaris submarines 1960.

**Duns** ◊ *Berwickshire*.

**Dunstable** England. Municipal borough in Bedfordshire, at the N end of the Chiltern Hills 4 m. W of Luton. Pop. (1961) 25,618. Printing, engineering. Manufactures lorries and vans, paper, cement. In the centre of the town is the intersection of the Roman Watling Street and the ancient Icknield Way. Near by are Dunstable Downs, used for gliding; 3 m. S is Whipsnade Zoo.

**Dunwich** England. Village in E Suffolk 4 m. SSW of Southwold. In Anglo-Saxon times it was the chief commercial centre of East Anglia; in the 7th cent. it was made capital by Sigebert and was also the seat of a bishopric. By the mid 11th cent. erosion by the sea had begun, and through the centuries the old port was gradually engulfed.

**Durance River** France. River 218 m. long rising near the Mont Genèvre Pass in the High Alps of Dauphiné, flowing generally SSW, at first through several deep gorges, then turning W to join the Rhône R. near Avignon. Used for hydroelectric power in the upper course, for irrigation and the Marseille water supply farther downstream.

**Durango** Mexico. 1. State in the N; a high tableland, with the Sierra Madre Occidental in the W. Area 46,184 sq. m. Pop. (1969) 959,000. Rich mining areas in the mountains produce silver, gold, iron, copper, etc. Cotton, wheat, and other crops are grown, esp. in the Nazas R. valley.

2. Capital of the Durango state, in the Sierra Madre Occidental, 130 m. SW of Torreón, at a height of 6,314 ft. Pop. (1969) 152,200. Railway junction and mining town. Iron ore is mined on the famous hill Cerro del Mercado, 2 m. N. Iron founding, sugar refining. Manufactures textiles, glass, etc. Founded 1563.

**Durazno** Uruguay. Capital of the Durazno department, on the Yí R. 110 m. NNW of Montevideo. Pop. 28,000. Road and rail junction. Market town in a cattle- and sheep-rearing area. Trade in livestock, hides, grain, etc. Meat packing, flour milling.

**Durazzo** ◊ *Durrës*.

**Durban** S Africa. Largest city and chief seaport in Natal, on the Indian Ocean 800 m. ENE of Cape Town. Pop. (1967) 662,894 (180,000 Europeans, 254,000 Asians (chiefly Indians), 200,000 Africans (many Zulu)). Fine harbour and excellent dock and bunkering facilities. Serves the Transvaal and the Orange Free State. Greater overseas trade than Cape Town, being nearer the main agricultural and mining regions. Exports coal, manganese and chrome ore, maize, wool (from the interior), sugar, oranges, pineapples (from the coastal region), etc. Motor-car assembly, oil and sugar refining, railway engineering. Manufactures machinery, metal goods, furniture, etc. Warm humid climate. A leading seaside resort with magnificent beaches. With Pietermaritzburg, seat of the University of Natal (1909). The first European settlers (1824) were British elephant-hunters. Founded 1835; named after the then Governor of Cape Colony, Sir Benjamin D'Urban. Scene of serious rioting between Africans and Indians 1949.

**Düren** Federal German Republic. Industrial town in N Rhine-Westphalia on the Rur R. 22 m. WSW of Cologne. Pop. (1963) 52,600. Manufactures metal goods, textiles, paper, glass, etc. Severely damaged in the 2nd World War.

**Durham** England. 1. County in the NE, bounded on the E by the North Sea. Area 1,015 sq. m. Pop. (1961) 1,517,039. County town Durham. Hilly in the W, where it rises to the crest of the Pennines. Descends in the E to a coastal plain. Drained by the Tyne, the Wear, and the Tees rivers. Sheep are grazed on the hill slopes. Oats, wheat, and other crops cultivated in the fertile river valleys. Its wealth, however, is based on the important coalfield, located in the E half of the county, which has given rise to the heavy industries of Sunderland, Gateshead, Jarrow, the Hartlepools, Stockton-on-Tees, and Darlington – chiefly iron and steel manufacture, shipbuilding and engineering, with chemical manufacture at Billingham. Sunderland, South Shields, and the Hartlepools are ports.
2. Municipal borough and county town of Co. Durham, built round a hill in a loop of the R. Wear 14 m. S of Newcastle upon Tyne. Pop. (1961) 20,484. Dominated by its cathedral and castle, which stand on the hill, the city contrasts vividly with the great manufacturing centres elsewhere in the county – though it has some small industries (e.g. carpet weaving), and there is coalmining in the neighbourhood. The magnificent Norman cathedral (begun 1093) was built on the site of a shrine erected for the body of St Cuthbert, brought here in 995. Bede is also buried here. Bishop Flambard and Bishop Pudsey, who were largely responsible for the construction of the cathedral, were also concerned in the building of the castle, which was founded by William the Conqueror in

1072 and is now occupied by the University of Durham. The latter (founded 1832) comprises several Durham colleges, and from 1937 to 1963 included King's College, Newcastle.

**Durham** USA. Town in N Carolina 20 m. NW of Raleigh. Pop. (1960) 78,302. Commercial and industrial centre in a tobacco-growing region, producing about a fifth of the US cigarettes. Also manufactures hosiery, textiles, etc. Large business interests here are held by Negroes. Seat of the Duke University (1924), named after Washington Duke (1820–1905), one of the founders of the tobacco industry.

**Durrës** (Italian **Durazzo**) Albania. Ancient Epidamnus, Dyrrachium. Country's chief seaport, on the Adriatic 19 m. W of Tiranë. Pop. (1967) 53,000. Exports olive oil, tobacco. Minor flour-milling, tobacco, and soap industries. Seat of a Roman Catholic bishop and a Greek Metropolitan, but the majority of the population are Muslims. Founded in the 7th cent. B.C. as Epidamnus by Corcyra (Kerkira, Corfu) and Corinth. As Dyrrachium, an important port under the Romans. It later changed hands many times, and declined under Turkish rule (1501–1913), reviving with the modernization of the port in the 1930s.

**Dushanbe** USSR. Formerly Stalinabad. Capital of the Tadzhik SSR, 195 m. S of Tashkent, with which it is linked by road. Pop. (1970) 374,000. Meat packing. Manufactures textiles, machinery, cement, leather etc. Connected with the Trans-Caspian Railway via Termez (1929) and by narrow gauge with the cotton-growing Vakhsh valley. Seat of the Tadzhik state university (1948). Developed rapidly after 1929; in 1961, when the name Stalinabad was dropped, it was renamed after the old village that formerly stood here.

**Düsseldorf** Federal German Republic. City in N Rhine-Westphalia, on the Rhine R. 20 m. NNW of Cologne. Pop. (1968) 688,503. Important river port and industrial centre. Manufactures iron and steel, machinery, cars, chemicals, glass, textiles, clothing, etc. Also the leading commercial centre for the Ruhr and Wupper industrial areas. Despite its many industries it is an attractive city, justly renowned for its parks, gardens, and squares. Of small significance until 1288, when it was made a town; later became capital of the duchy of Berg. Passed to Prussia 1815. Frequently bombed in the 2nd World War and suffered considerable damage. Birthplace of Johann (1740–1814) and Friedrich (1743–1819) Jacobi, the philosophers, Heinrich Heine (1797–1856), the poet, and Peter von Cornelius (1783–1867), the painter.

**Dutch Guiana** ◊ *Surinam*.

**Dúvida, Rio da** ◊ *Roosevelt River*.

**Dvina River** USSR. 1. *Northern* (Russian *Severnaya*) *Dvina*: river 470 m. long, formed by the union of the Sukhona and Yug rivers in European RSFSR, flowing NW to Dvina Bay, White Sea, below Archangel. Navigable for most of its course May–Nov. Linked with the Mariinsk canal system via the Sukhona R. and the N Dvina Canal. Chief tributaries the Vychegda, Pinega, Vaga.
2. *Western* (Russian *Zapadnaya*) *Dvina*: river 640 m. long, rising in the Valdai Hills, RSFSR, flowing SW and then NW past Riga to the Gulf of Riga. Navigable in part May–Nov. Used for timber floating and hydroelectric power.

**Dzerzhinsk** USSR. Modern industrial town in RSFSR, on the Oka R. 20 m. W of Gorki. Pop. (1970) 221,000. Important centre of fertilizer and other chemical manufactures. Sawmilling, engineering, flour milling. Expanded rapidly in the 1930s.

**Dzhambul** USSR. Capital of the Dzhambul region, in the Kazakh SSR, 285 m. W of Alma-Ata, on the Turksib Railway. Pop. (1970) 188,000. Industrial centre. Manufactures superphosphates, prefabricated houses, etc. Sugar refining (sugar-beet), fruit canning. Occupies the site of a 5th-cent. city, and was given its present name in 1937.

**Dzierzoniow** (Ger. **Reichenbach**) Poland. Industrial town in the Wroclaw voivodship, 32 m. SSW of Wroclaw. Pop. (1968) 32,600. Manufactures textiles, electrical equipment, etc. Passed to Prussia 1742. Returned to Poland 1945.

**Dzungaria** China. Arid plateau region in N Sinkiang-Uighur between the Altai Mountains (N) and the Tien Shan (S), bounded by the USSR (W) and the Mongolian People's Republic (E). Most of its rivers drain into inland lakes. As a Mongolian kingdom it extended over a much wider area in the late 17th cent., but was conquered by the Chinese in the mid 18th cent. Chief town Urumchi. The Dzungarian Gate on the border provides an important route between China and the USSR.

# E

**Ealing** England. From 1965 a Greater London borough, in W London, comprising the former municipal boroughs of Acton, Ealing, and Southall (all in Middlesex). Pop. (1963) 299,762. Mainly residential. Birthplace of Thomas Huxley (1825–95).

**Earls Court** England. Residential district in the Greater London borough of Kensington and Chelsea. Probably named after the Earls of Warwick, who resided here. Since 1884 the venue of many exhibitions in Earls Court Exhibition Building.

**Earlston** Scotland. Ancient Ercildoune (of which the present name is a corruption). Town in SW Berwickshire on Leader Water 5 m. ENE of Galashiels. Pop. 1,800. Market town. Manufactures tweeds. Has the ruins of 'Rhymer's Tower', the traditional home of Thomas the Rhymer or Thomas of Ercildoune, the 13th-cent. poet and prophet.

**Earn River** Scotland. River 46 m. long, flowing E from Loch Earn through Strathearn to the Tay estuary 6 m. SE of Perth. Well-known fishing stream.

**Easington** England. Coalmining town in E Durham 9 m. E of Durham, near the North Sea coast. Pop. (1961) 10,456.

**East Anglia** England. Region and ancient kingdom in the E, comprising the modern counties of Norfolk and Suffolk. Founded by the Angles in the 6th cent. and later conquered by Mercia and the Danes. The East Anglia of today is known for its agriculture, producing crops of wheat, barley, sugar-beet, etc., and also for its quiet beauty, illustrated in the paintings of Constable and other artists.

**East Barnet** England. Former urban district in Hertfordshire, ESE of and adjacent to Barnet; from 1965 part of the Greater London borough of Barnet. Pop. (1961) 40,599.

**Eastbourne** England. County borough in E Sussex, on the English Channel at the foot of the S Downs, with Beachy Head 3 m. to the SW. Pop. (1961) 60,897. Formerly a group of villages, it developed into a popular seaside resort under the patronage of the 7th Duke of Devonshire (1808–91). Many open spaces and gardens, inc. Hampden Park and Devonshire Park; a terraced marine parade nearly 3 m. long. In the Old Town, 1 m. inland, a fine parish church in Transitional Norman style.

**East Chicago** USA. Industrial town in NW Indiana on L. Michigan, just SE of Chicago. Pop. (1960) 57,669. Oil refining, railway engineering. Manufactures steel, chemicals, cement, etc.

**East Dereham (Dereham)** England. Urban district in Norfolk 15 m. WNW of Norwich. Pop. (1961) 7,197. Market town. Flour milling. Manufactures agricultural implements. A 12-cent. church with the grave of William Cowper. Birthplace (near by at Dumpling Green) of George Borrow (1803–81).

**Easter Island** (Spanish **Isla de Pascua**) Pacific Ocean. An isolated island in the S Pacific 2,300 m. W of Chile, to which it belongs. Area 64 sq. m. Pop. 800 (chiefly Polynesians). Sheep and cattle are raised on extensive grasslands, and tobacco, sugarcane, etc. are cultivated. Best known for its huge stone statues, carved out of tufa from the volcano Rano Roraku, and the wooden tablets carrying an ideographic script, all of unknown origin; these were probably the work of the ancestors of the present Polynesian inhabitants. Discovered by the Dutchman Roggeveen on Easter Day 1722 (hence the name). The population was once many times larger than at present, but was much reduced by disease, warfare, and emigration. Annexed by Chile 1888.

**East Flanders** ◊ *Flanders.*

**East Grinstead** England. Urban district of E Sussex, 11 m. SE of Reigate near Ashdown Forest. Pop. (1961) 15,421. Market town. An almshouse, Sackville College, founded 1608, and many timbered houses. During the 2nd World War the hospital became renowned for plastic surgery. Iron mining and smelting in the neighbourhood from Roman times.

**East Ham** England. Former county borough in SW Essex and suburb of E London; from 1965 part of the Greater London borough of Newham. Pop. (1961) 105,359. Industrial and residential centre. Manufactures chemicals etc. Contains the Royal Albert and King George V docks and the large Beckton gasworks.

**East Hartford** USA. Industrial town in

Connecticut, on the Connecticut R. opposite Hartford. Pop. (1960) 43,977. Manufactures aircraft engines, machinery, paper, furniture, etc.

**East Indies.** Name formerly applied rather loosely to SE Asia in general, inc. India and the Malay Archipelago, then to the whole Malay Archipelago, inc. the Philippines and New Guinea; then to the Netherlands E Indies – the islands of the Malay Archipelago which became the republic of Indonesia after the 2nd World War.

**East Kilbride** Scotland. Formerly a small town in NW Lanarkshire 7 m. SSE of Glasgow, designated a 'new town' in 1947 with a planned population of 70,000. Pop. (1961) 31,972 (5,136 in 1951). Manufactures aircraft engines, machinery, electrical appliances. Printing etc. Birthplace of the brothers John (1728–93) and William (1718–83) Hunter, noted surgeons.

**East Lansing** USA. Town in Michigan just E of Lansing. Pop. (1960) 30,198. Mainly residential. Seat of the Michigan State University of Agriculture and Applied Science (1855).

**Eastleigh** England. Municipal borough in Hampshire 5 m. NNE of Southampton. Pop. (1961) 36,577. Railway engineering.

**East London** S Africa. Formerly Port Rex. Seaport in the Cape Province 150 m. ENE of Port Elizabeth, at the mouth of the Buffalo R. Pop. (1967) 134,071. Port for the NE of the Cape Province, the Orange Free State, Lesotho, and the Transkeian Territories. Exports maize, wool, hides, fruits. Fishing. Railway engineering. Manufactures soap, furniture, leather goods, clothing, etc. Popular holiday resort. First called Port Rex when visited by the brig *Kingsna* in 1836; renamed 1847. Railway construction began 1874, harbour improvements 1886.

**East Lothian** Scotland. Formerly Haddingtonshire. County bounded on the NE by the North Sea and on the NW by the Firth of Forth. Area 267 sq. m. Pop. (1961) 52,653. County town Haddington. Low-lying in the N, it rises in the S to the Lammermuir Hills, which reach 1,750 ft. Main river the Tyne. Chief occupations agriculture, sheep rearing, coalmining. Several holiday resorts. Chief towns Haddington, Dunbar, N Berwick.

**Easton** USA. Industrial town in Pennsylvania 51 m. N. of Philadelphia at the confluence of the Lehigh and the Delaware rivers. Pop. (1960) 31,955. Manufactures agricultural machinery, textiles, cement, paper, etc.

**East Orange** USA. Residential and industrial town in New Jersey, just NW of Newark, largest of 5 neighbouring municipalities known as 'the Oranges'. Pop. (1960) 77,259. Manufactures electrical equipment, clothing, paint, etc.

**East Pakistan** Pakistan. One of the two provinces of Pakistan, in the NE of the Indian sub-continent, separated by 850 m. from the other, W Pakistan, in the NW. Area 55,126 sq. m. Pop. (1961) 50,840,235. Cap. Dacca. Comprises the E part of the former Indian province of Bengal and most of the Assam district of Sylhet. Though less than one fifth of the area of W Pakistan, it is the more populous. Primarily agricultural. Main food crop rice. Produces about 80 per cent of the world supply of jute. Large quantities of sea and freshwater fish are caught. A network of inland waterways, the chief being the Ganges, Brahmaputra, and Meghna. Principal towns Dacca, Chittagong (main seaport). For administrative purposes it is divided into the Dacca, Chittagong, Rajshahi, and Khulna Divisions.

**East Point** USA. Industrial town in Georgia just SSW of Atlanta. Pop. (1960) 35,633. Manufactures textiles, fertilizers, furniture, etc.

**East Providence** USA. Industrial town in Rhode Island on the Seekonk and the Providence rivers, opposite Providence. Pop. (1960) 41,945. Textile dyeing and printing. Manufactures machinery, chemicals, wire products, paper, etc.

**East Prussia.** Former province of Prussia, on the Baltic Sea SW of Lithuania. From 1919 it was separated from the rest of Germany by the Polish Corridor and the Free City of Danzig. In 1945 it was divided between Poland and the USSR, the former receiving 8,106 sq. m. (the S) and the latter about 6,100 sq. m. (the N). The capital, Königsberg, was renamed Kaliningrad. Situated between the Vistula and the Neman, the area is low-lying and marshy with many small lakes, inc. the extensive Masurian Lakes region in the E. It was an area of large agricultural estates owned by the Prussian 'Junkers'. The pre-war German population has been completely replaced by Russians and Poles.

**East River** USA. Tidal strait and navigable waterway of New York City, 16 m. long, connecting New York Bay with Long

Island Sound, and separating the boroughs of Manhattan and the Bronx from Brooklyn and Queens.

**East St Louis** USA. Formerly Illinoistown. Town in SW Illinois on the Mississippi R. opposite St Louis. Pop. (1960) 81,712. Important industrial and railway centre. Large aluminium works. Meat packing, oil refining. Manufactures paints, fertilizers, chemicals, glass, etc. Laid out (1816) as Illinoistown; incorporated as E St Louis 1865.

**Eau Claire** USA. Town in Wisconsin at the confluence of the Chippewa and the Eau Claire rivers, 75 m. E of St Paul (Minnesota). Pop. (1960) 37,987. Market town in a dairy-farming and stock-rearing area, having developed first as a lumbering centre. Manufactures rubber and leather goods, paper. Meat packing, food processing, etc.

**Ebbw Vale** Wales. Urban district in W Monmouthshire on the R. Ebbw 20 m. N of Cardiff. Pop. (1961) 28,361. Coalmining. Manufactures iron and steel, tinplate. A victim of the trade depression of the 1930s; revived somewhat with the establishment of new steel works (1935).

**Eberswalde** German Democratic Republic. Town in the Frankfurt-on-Oder district 30 m. NE of Berlin. Pop. (1965) 33,092. Manufactures iron and steel products (esp. cranes), chemicals, building materials, etc. The former cutlery industry has died out.

**Ebro River** Spain. Ancient Iberus (Hiberus). River 570 m. long rising in the Cantabrian Mountains in Santander province and flowing generally SE to the Mediterranean. Navigable by seagoing vessels only to Tortosa (20 m. inland). The delta is canalized. Chief tributaries the Aragón, Gállego, Guadalope, Huerva, Jalón, and Segre rivers. Zaragoza and Logroño are the principal towns on its banks. Much used for hydroelectric power. Has been used for irrigation since Moorish times. Gave its name to the Iberii, originally the people living along its banks, and the Iberian peninsula.

**Ecclefechan** Scotland. Village in Dumfriesshire, in Annandale 13 m. E of Dumfries. Birthplace and burial-place of Thomas Carlyle (1758-1832), whose home is now National Trust property.

**Eccles** England. Municipal borough in SE Lancashire, on the R. Irwell and the Manchester Ship Canal 5 m. W of Manchester. Pop. (1961) 43,184. Manufactures textiles, machinery, chemicals. Noted for Eccles cakes, now made in Manchester.

**Écija** Spain. Ancient Astigis. Town in Seville province, Andalusia, on the Genil R. 52 m. ENE of Seville. Pop. (1961) 49,762. Produces olive oil, wine, soap, textiles, etc. Long noted for its cobblers; according to one story it was the see of St Crispin, patron saint of shoemakers. Picturesque; many remnants of Moorish architecture. One of the hottest places in Spain in summer; known as the 'frying-pan of Andalusia'.

**Ecuador.** Second smallest republic of S America, on the NW coast. Area 104,505 sq. m. Pop. (1967) 5,585,400. Cap. Quito. Lang. mainly Spanish. Rel. mainly Roman Catholic.

Bounded by Colombia (N), Peru (E and S), and the Pacific Ocean (W). Resources, mainly agricultural, are largely undeveloped and communications are difficult. It is self-sufficient in most foodstuffs, however, and the standard of living, though low, is rising slowly. Illiteracy is widespread. About 40 per cent of the population are pure Indian, another 40 per cent mixed; 10 per cent are white and 10 per cent Negro or mulatto. For administrative purposes the country is divided into 20 provinces.

TOPOGRAPHY, CLIMATE. Crossed in the N by the equator. Consists of three distinct regions: the mountainous backbone of the Andes; the coastal plain between the Andes and the Pacific (W); and part of the basin of the upper Amazon (E). The Andes extend N–S as two main cordilleras, separated by a long trough in which lies a series of basins 7,000–9,000 ft high, drained by rivers flowing to the Amazon or the Pacific. Above the Cordilleran crests tower lofty volcanic cones, e.g. Chimborazo (20,577 ft) and Cotopaxi (19,344 ft); several (incl. Cotopaxi) are active. In the W are the broad lowlands of the Guayas R., N and E of Guayaquil, and low sandstone and limestone hills farther W and N. E of the Andes are the densely forested foothills and the Amazon plains, with scattered Indian tribes.

Climate is extremely varied and dependent largely on altitude. In the NW there are long rainy periods and the land is closely forested, but the hot Guayas lowlands, with a single rainy period (Dec.–June), consist of grassy savannah. In the SW, near the Peruvian frontier, conditions are arid, with xerophytic vegetation; the cold

Peruvian current swings W away from the coast about lat. 4°S. On the highlands forests occur up to about 10,000 ft, vegetation depending on shelter and soil: many of the porous volcanic soils are very dry, supporting tussock grass well below the usual altitude of the *páramos*.

RESOURCES, PEOPLE, *etc.* Economy based on agriculture. The Guayas lowlands produce most of the commercial crops, e.g. bananas, coffee, and cacao, which represent over 80 per cent of the exports. The hilly districts N W of Guayaquil are renowned for their toquilla straw ('Panama') hats. Ecuador's chief oilfield is on the Santa Elena peninsula; the petroleum is refined at La Libertad and Salinas. Quito, at a height of 9,350 ft, lies on the Pan-American Highway, which passes from Colombia to Peru via the highland basins. Railways run to Guayaquil, the main seaport, and to the small N outlet of San Lorenzo. Esmeraldas (N) is the chief banana port. Three fifths of the population occupy the intermont basins, cultivating maize, wheat, potatoes, fruit, vegetables, pyrethrum. Some dairy farming. Sheep, alpacas, and llamas are grazed on the *páramos*. Market centres, e.g. Ambato and Riobamba, have textile mills; these towns have frequently suffered from earthquakes. Agricultural methods have remained backward in many areas; overpopulation has caused considerable migration to the lowlands. The highlands contained 90 per cent of the population in 1780 and 60 per cent in 1960 (some of the increase in the lowlands is due to immigration, however).

HISTORY. The highland basins were well populated in Inca times. Quito, the centre of authority, was occupied by the Spanish 1534. Cattle, sheep, and wheat were introduced. For nearly three centuries the region formed part of the viceroyalty of Peru. In the 18th cent. Negro slave labour was brought to the coastal plantations. The struggle for independence from Spain was won in 1822; in 1830 Ecuador broke away from 'Gran Colombia' and became an independent republic.

**Edam** Netherlands. Town in N Holland province 12 m. NNE of Amsterdam. Pop. 8,300. A market for the famous cheese made in the neighbourhood, named after it, and exported in large quantities. Also manufactures earthenware etc.

**Eddystone Rocks** England. Dangerous group of rocks in the English Channel 14 m. SSW of Plymouth. Its first lighthouse, built by Winstanley (1698), was swept away in a storm; the second (1709) was destroyed by fire (1755); the third, built by Smeaton (1759), was the first lighthouse in which dovetail-jointed stones were used, and was replaced by another in 1882.

**Ede** Netherlands. Industrial town in Gelderland province 10 m. WNW of Arnhem. Pop. (1968) 68,772. Important rayon industry. Also metal working etc.

**Eden River** England. 1. River 65 m. long, rising in the Pennines, flowing N W through Westmorland and Cumberland past Appleby and Carlisle, and entering the Solway Firth.

2. River 12 m. long, rising in SE Surrey, flowing E, and joining the Medway R. at Penshurst (Kent).

**Eden River** Scotland. River 30 m. long, rising near the Fife–Kinross border, flowing ENE across Fifeshire, and entering the North Sea near St Andrews.

**Eder River** Federal German Republic. River 85 m. long rising in N Rhine-Westphalia and flowing ENE through Hessen to join the Fulda R. S of Kassel. The Eder Dam, controlling one of Germany's largest reservoirs and providing hydroelectric power, was heavily bombed by RAF planes during the 2nd World War (1943).

**Edessa (Gr. Edhessa)** Greece. Ancient Aegae. Capital of Pella *nome*, in Macedonia, 50 m. WNW of Salonika. Pop. (1961) 15,534. Market town in a picturesque, fertile district. Trade in wine, fruit, tobacco. Manufactures textiles, rugs and carpets, etc. Ancient capital of Macedonia. Scene of the assassination of Philip II (336 B.C.).

**Edfu (Idfu)** United Arab Republic. Ancient Apollinopolis Magna. Town on the W bank of the Nile 58 m. N of Aswan. Pop. 18,000. Earthenware manufactured in the district. Trade in cotton, cereals, dates. Has an almost complete sandstone temple, dedicated to the god Horus, begun by Ptolemy III in 237 B.C. and completed in the reign of Ptolemy XIII in 57 B.C.

**Edgehill** England. Ridge in S Warwickshire on the border with Oxfordshire, rising to 743 ft and forming part of the watershed between the Severn and Thames basins. Here was fought the first large (but indecisive) battle of the Civil War (1642).

**Edgware** England. District in the former municipal borough of Hendon, Middlesex; from 1965 in the Greater London borough of Barnet; on the Edgware Road (the

Roman Watling Street), a residential suburb of London. The smithy here was said to have inspired Handel's *The Harmonious Blacksmith*, but the story is unsubstantiated.

**Edinburgh** Scotland. Capital of Scotland, royal burgh, and county town of Midlothian, near the S shore of the Firth of Forth 41 m. E of Glasgow. Pop. (1961) 468,378. Administrative and business centre and leading cultural centre of Scotland. Printing and publishing, brewing, whisky distilling. Manufactures biscuits, confectionery, chemicals, etc. Leith, its port, was incorporated in the city in 1920. Nicknamed 'Auld Reekie' because of the curtain of smoke that used to hang over the lower parts of the city, Edinburgh has a more dignified and certainly more accurate sobriquet in 'Athens of the North'. It stands on and around a group of hills, with Castle Rock (445 ft) at the centre, Calton Hill (349 ft) to the E, Arthur's Seat (823 ft) to the S E, the Braid Hills to the S, and Corstorphine Hill (520 ft) to the W; on the N side it slopes gently down to the Firth of Forth. Its principal thoroughfare is Princes Street, one of the finest in Europe, on account of its setting rather than its buildings, dominated by the castle on Castle Rock and flanked by Princes Street Gardens. To the N of Princes Street is the New Town, largely dating from the 18th cent., and to the S the Old Town. In the heart of the Old Town is the 'Royal Mile', the city's second famous thoroughfare, so called because kings and queens so often passed along it on their official duties. It follows the ridge running from the castle to Holyroodhouse; on both sides are tall tenements and narrow wynds (alleys) – for, when the city was enclosed by walls, its people were forced to build upwards.

The oldest building in the castle and in Edinburgh is the restored Norman Chapel of St Margaret, dating from 1093, where Queen Margaret, wife of Malcolm Canmore, worshipped. Here, too, is the Old Palace, containing the crown room, the royal apartments, and the old parliament hall, while near by is the impressive National War Memorial (1927) for the 1st World War. The Palace of Holyroodhouse, begun *c.* 1500 by James IV, is still the official residence of the monarch when in Scotland; this was the residence of Mary Queen of Scots, scene of her marriage to Bothwell and of the murder of Rizzio

(1566). Little remains, however, of the Chapel Royal, once part of the adjoining Abbey. Among the existing ecclesiastical buildings probably the best known are the Church of St Giles, restored 1872–83, with a fine 'crown' steeple, and the 19th-cent. St Mary's Cathedral. Other noteworthy buildings are the 17th-cent. Parliament House, John Knox's House, the Canongate Tolbooth, Royal Scottish Academy, National Gallery, the unfinished National Monument, the Scott Monument. Register House, containing Scottish national records etc., was designed by Robert Adam, as was much else in the New Town. The University (founded 1583) has long been famous for its medical school, with which the Royal Infirmary is closely associated.

Edinburgh takes its name from Edwin, king of Northumbria, who defeated the Picts and set up a military post here in the 7th cent., and a settlement grew up round the castle on Castle Rock. In 1329 it was made a burgh by Robert the Bruce, and in 1437 it replaced Perth, where James I was assassinated, as the national capital; James II was crowned at Holyrood Abbey instead of at Scone. On the departure of James VI, who was born in the castle, to become James I of Great Britain and Ireland (1603), Edinburgh lost political though not cultural prestige, a change which was emphasized by the Act of Union in 1707. Later in the 18th cent. came a revival, particularly in the literary and academic fields; during the same period the Nor' Loch, N of the castle, was drained, the North Bridge was built, and the New Town with its handsome streets and squares was laid out. Since the 2nd World War the city has added to its cultural reputation and attracted great numbers of new visitors with the annual Edinburgh Festival, inaugurated 1947. Birthplace of David Hume (1711–76), Allan Ramsay (1713–84), the painter, and Robert Fergusson (1750–74).

**Edirne** Turkey. Formerly Adrianople. Capital of Edirne province in European Turkey, at the confluence of the Maritsa and Tundzha rivers near the Greek frontier. Pop. (1965) 46,000 (having decreased from about 80,000 in 1905 owing to emigration). Manufactures textiles, carpets, soap, leather etc. Oriental in appearance, it has among its buildings the famous 16th-cent. mosque of Sultan Selim II, the ruined palace of the sultans, and the bazaar of Ali Pasha. It was enlarged in the 2nd cent. A.D. on the site of the ancient Uskadama by the Roman Emperor Hadrian, after whom it was named. Here in 378 the Romans were decisively defeated by the Goths. It was the residence of the Turkish sultans from 1365 (after it had been captured from the Bulgarians) to 1453, when Constantinople fell. In the Russo-Turkish Wars it twice fell to the Russians (1829 and 1878). Taken by the Bulgarians and recovered by the Turks in 1913. After the 1st World War it became Greek, but was returned to Turkey 1923.

**Edjélé** Algeria. Oil-producing centre in the Sahara, near the Libyan frontier 135 m. S of Ghadames. Oilfield first operated in 1957. Pipeline to La Skhirra (Tunisia).

**Edmonton** Canada. Provincial capital of Alberta, on the N Saskatchewan R. Pop. (1966) 376,925. (2,626 in 1901; 79,197 in 1931). Industrial city in an agricultural, coal, oil, and fur-trading region. Principal gateway to the Peace R. area and the Mackenzie District. Linked by road with the Alaska Highway, the Mackenzie Highway, and the Trans-Canada Highway. Major airport. Oil refining, meat packing, tanning. Manufactures chemicals, clothing, etc. Seat of the University of Alberta (1906).

**Edmonton** England. Former municipal borough in Middlesex and residential suburb of N London; from 1965 part of the Greater London borough of Enfield. Pop. (1961) 92,062. Keats and Cowper lived here, the Bell Inn having been immortalized in the latter's *John Gilpin*. Charles and Mary Lamb are buried in the graveyard of All Saints' Church.

**Edom (Idumaea)**. District in S Palestine (Israel) between the Dead Sea and the Gulf of Aqaba, presented to Esau.

**Edward (Albert Edward Nyanza), Lake** Congo (Kinshasa)/Uganda. Lake in the W branch of the Great Rift Valley (N of L. Kivu) at a height of 3,000 ft, on the frontier between Congo (Kinshasa) and Uganda. Area 820 sq. m. One of the W reservoirs of the R. Nile. Connected with L. George (Dweru) (NE), which it drains, by a 25-m. channel. Fed also by the Rutshuru R. (S). Empties through the Semliki R. (NW) into L. Albert. Discovered (1888) by H. M. Stanley; named after the then Prince of Wales (later Edward VII). Salt from the surrounding saltpans is sold over a large area. Abundant fish, waterfowl, crocodiles, and (S) hippopotami.

**Efate Island** ⟡ *New Hebrides*.

**Eger** Hungary. Capital of Heves county on the Eger R. 24 m. SW of Miskolc. Pop. (1968) 44,000. Market town. Produces and trades in wine. Also an ecclesiastical centre with many churches, causing it to be known formerly as 'the Rome of Hungary'.

**Egham** England. Urban district in Surrey 18 m. WSW of London on the S bank of the R. Thames, containing Runnymede and Virginia Water. Pop. (1961) 30,553. Mainly residential. Light engineering. Site of the Royal Holloway College (1886). On Cooper's Hill is the Commonwealth Air Forces memorial (1953). ⟡ *Runnymede*.

**Egmont, Mount** New Zealand. Extinct volcanic peak (8,260 ft) in Taranaki, N Island, 15 m. S of New Plymouth, in the shape of an almost perfect cone; stands in Egmont National Park. Named by Capt. Cook 1770; the Maori name was Taranaki.

**Egypt** ⟡ *United Arab Republic*.

**Eider River** Federal German Republic. River 117 m. long in Schleswig-Holstein, rising SW of Kiel and flowing generally WNW to the North Sea at Tönning. Before the opening of the Kiel Canal it connected the Baltic and the North Sea via the Eider Canal.

**Eifel** Federal German Republic. Bleak, desolate plateau of volcanic origin between the Rhine, the Mosel, the Ahr, and the Our rivers, in general 1,500–2,500 ft above sea level. Many volcanic cones and small crater lakes.

**Eigg** Scotland. Small island in the Inner Hebrides, Inverness-shire, 7 m. from the mainland. Area 11 sq. m. Rises to 1,289 ft in the Scuir of Eigg (S).

**Eilat** Israel.* Small port in the S, at the head of the Gulf of Aqaba, near the Jordanian frontier and 5 m. WNW of the Jordanian port of ⟡ *Aqaba*.

**Eildon Hills** Scotland. Range in Roxburghshire 1m. S of Melrose, consisting of three conical peaks, the highest rising to 1,385 ft. Associated with many legends, including those of Thomas the Rhymer.

**Eindhoven** Netherlands. Chief industrial centre of N Brabant province. Pop. (1968) 184,519. Owes its rapid growth from a small town of 5,700 people (1910) to the great expansion of the radio and electrical industry. Also manufactures motor vehicles, textiles, plastics, cigars, matches, etc. Railway junction. Seat of a technical university (1957).

**Einsiedeln** Switzerland. Town in Schwyz canton, 20 m. SE of Zürich. Pop. (1960)

8,792. Famous for its 10th-cent. Benedictine abbey; in the church is the statue of the 'Black Madonna', much visited by pilgrims. Ulrich Zwingli was parish priest here 1516–18.

Éire ◊ *Ireland.*

**Eisenach** German Democratic Republic. Industrial town in the Erfurt district, 32 m. W of Erfurt on the edge of the Thuringian Forest. Pop. (1965) 50,059. Rock-salt mining. Manufactures motor vehicles, machine tools, chemicals, etc. Summer resort. On a hill overlooking the town is the Wartburg, ancient castle of the landgraves of Thuringia. Birthplace of J. S. Bach (1685–1750).

**Eisenhower, Mount** Canada. Formerly Castle Mountain. Peak (9,390 ft) in SW Alberta, in the Banff National Park in the Rocky Mountains. Renamed (1946) in honour of General (later President) Eisenhower.

**Eisenhüttenstadt** German Democratic Republic. Industrial town and river port in the Frankfurt-an-der-Oder district, on the Oder R. 15 m. SSE of Frankfurt-an-der-Oder. Pop. (1965) 36,619. Terminus of the Oder–Spree Canal. Formed (1961) from the towns of Stalinstadt and Fürstenberg around blast furnaces and steelworks which use imported fuel and raw materials. Also manufactures glass, dyes, etc.

**Eisenstadt** ◊ *Burgenland.*

**Eisleben** German Democratic Republic. Town in the Halle district, 20 m. WNW of Halle. Pop. (1965) 33,000. Copper smelting, cigar making. Manufactures textiles, clothing, machinery, etc. Birthplace of Martin Luther (1483–1546), who was also baptized and died here.

**El Aaiún** ◊ *Spanish Sahara.*

**Elam (Susiana)** Ancient country in SW Asia, E of the Tigris R. and approximating to modern Khuzistan, in SW Iran. It warred frequently with Babylonia and was conquered by Assurbanipal in the 7th cent. B.C. After the fall of Assyria, towards the close of that century, it became a Persian province and was known as Susiana, its capital being Susa.

**Elan River** Wales. River rising in the Cambrian Mountains of central Wales just inside the Cardiganshire border and flowing generally ESE across W Radnorshire to join the R. Wye below Rhayader. On the Elan and its tributary the Claerwen four dams were built between 1904 and 1952, the reservoirs formed supplying water by

a 73½-m. aqueduct to Birmingham and surrounding areas. The valley is well known for its scenery. Trout fishing in the reservoirs.

**El Araish** ◊ *Larache.*

**Elath** ◊ *Aqaba.*

**Elâziğ** Turkey. Capital of Elâziğ province, 50 m. ENE of Malatya. Pop. (1965) 78,600. Market town. Trade in cereals, fruit, etc.

**Elba** Italy. Ancient Aethalia (Gr.), Ilva (Latin). Island off the W coast, the largest in the Tuscan Archipelago, in Livorno (Leghorn) province. Area 86 sq. m. Pop. 32,000. Separated from the mainland by the Strait of Piombino. Steep, rocky coastline; rises to 3,340 ft in Monte Capanne. Iron ore has been mined for more than 2,000 years, and some is smelted at Portoferraio, the chief town and port on the N coast. Produces wine. Anchovy, sardine, and tunny fisheries. Expanding tourist industry. Napoleon was exiled here (1814–15), being given full sovereign rights over the island.

**Elbasan** Albania. Market town on the Shkumbi R. 20 m. SE of Tiranë. Pop. (1967) 39,000 (chiefly Muslims). Terminus of the railway from Durrës. Manufactures textiles, leather, soap, olive oil. Trade in olives, tobacco, maize. Near by is the oil refinery of Çerrik (1957).

**Elbe (Czech Labe) River.** River in central Europe, 725 m. long, rising on the S side of the Riesengebirge in NE Bohemia (Czechoslovakia). Flowing first S, it turns W below Hradec Králové, then flows generally NW across the Czechoslovak-GDR frontier, past Dresden and Magdeburg to Hamburg (FGR), entering the North Sea by a 56-m. estuary. At the mouth, which is 9 m. wide, is Cuxhaven. Navigable by barges for over 500 m. Connected with the Rhine and the Weser via the Mittelland Canal system. By the Treaty of Versailles (1919) it was internationalized below the confluence with the Vltava, but this was repudiated by Germany in 1938. The volume of international trade was much reduced after the end of the 2nd World War.

**Elblag (Ger. Elbing)** Poland. Town in the Gdańsk voivodship, on the Elblag R. 5 m. above the mouth on the Vistula Lagoon (Frisches Haff), 35 m. ESE of Gdańsk. Pop. (1968) 86,000. Industrial centre and seaport. Shipbuilding, engineering. Manufactures textiles, etc. Seaborne trade is now limited, the port having been eclipsed by

Gdańsk. Founded in the 13th cent. Admitted to the Hanseatic League. Belonged to Poland for most of the period 1466–1772, and then passed to Prussia. Returned to Poland 1945.

**Elbruz (Elbrus), Mount** USSR. Massif in the Caucasus Mountains in the Kabardino-Balkar ASSR on the border with the Georgian SSR, N of the main range. Consists of two extinct volcanic peaks, the E summit rising to 18,356 ft and the W summit to 18,481 ft – the highest in the range and in Europe. Many snowfields and glaciers, from which flow the Kuban and other rivers.

**Elburz** Iran. Range of mountains in the N, curving round near, and more or less parallel to, the S shores of the Caspian Sea, rising to 18,934 ft in the extinct volcano Demavend. Forms a climatic divide, the N slopes being rainy and forested, while the S slopes are arid and cultivable only by irrigation. Tehran, the capital, stands on the lower S slopes of the central Elburz.

**Elche** Spain. Town in Alicante province, Valencia, 13 m. WSW of Alicante. Pop. (1967) 97,849. Manufactures footwear, textiles, fertilizers, soap, etc. but chiefly noted for its groves of date-palms. The fruit, though inferior to the N African, are exported, and the leaves are sold throughout Spain for Palm Sunday. Its white, flat-roofed houses and the many date-palms give Elche an oriental appearance: it was held from the 8th to the 13th cent. by the Moors, who provided it with its irrigation system.

**El Dorado** USA. Town in S Arkansas, 110 m. SSW of Little Rock. Pop. (1960) 25,292. Important centre of the oil industry. Oil refining. Manufactures oil-well equipment, petroleum products. Also trade in timber, cotton. Founded 1843.

**Elektrostal** USSR. Industrial town in the Moscow region, RSFSR, 32 m. E of Moscow. Pop. (1970) 123,000. Important steel industry. Manufactures machinery, stainless-steel goods, etc. Heavy engineering. Grew rapidly in the 1920s.

**Elephanta** India. Small island in Bombay harbour, 4 m. in circumference, famous for the cave temples dedicated to Siva. The Great Temple, in the main cave, probably dating from the 8th or 9th cent., is supported by pillars cut out of the rock, and around it are many statues of Hindu deities, the most striking a three-headed bust of Siva.

**El Ferrol del Caudillo** Spain. Formerly El Ferrol. Chief Atlantic naval base, in Coruña province, 13 m. NE of Corunna. Pop. (1967) 84,866. Strongly fortified, with a deep natural harbour. Besides the arsenal and dockyard, has fishing, fish-processing, boatbuilding, and other industries. Birthplace of General Franco (El Caudillo) (1892–    ), the name being changed officially in 1939.

**Elgin** Scotland. Royal burgh and county town of Morayshire, on the R. Lossie 36 m. ENE of Inverness. Pop. (1961) 11,971. Market town. Whisky distilling, brewing, flour milling, etc. Ruins of a 13th-cent. cathedral and a bishop's palace. Gordonstoun School is near by.

**Elgin** USA. Town in Illinois, on the Fox R. 35 m. WNW of Chicago. Pop. (1960) 49,447. Noted for watches; also manufactures electrical equipment, radio sets, motor-car accessories, pianos, etc. First settled 1832.

**Elginshire** ◊ *Morayshire*.

**Elgon, Mount**. Extinct volcano on the Kenya–Uganda border NE of L. Victoria, rising to 14,178 ft. The crater is about 5 m. in diameter. On the fertile lower slopes coffee, bananas, etc. are cultivated. Caves on the S slopes were long used by Africans as dwelling places.

**El Gráo de Castellón** ◊ *Castellón de la Plana*.

**Elis** (Gr. **Eleia**) Greece. *Nome* of the W Peloponnese. Area 1,178 sq. m. Pop. (1961) 188,718. Cap. Pyrgos (pop. 20,558). Produces currants, citrus fruits, etc. Ancient Elis was a district bounded by Achaea (N), Arcadia (E), Messenia (S), and the Ionian Sea (W). Its fertile coastal lowlands were drained by the Alpheus and Peneus rivers. Famed for its horses. The Olympic Games were held at Olympia, but it declined after their abolition (394 B.C.). The capital was Elis, now in ruins.

**Elisabethville** ◊ *Lubumbashi*.

**Elizabeth** USA. Formerly Elizabethtown. Town in NE New Jersey just SSW of Newark. Pop. (1960) 107,698. Long an industrial centre; the Singer sewing-machine factory was established in 1873. Also manufactures motor-car and aircraft accessories, furniture, printing presses, etc. Oil refining. First settled 1664. Known as Elizabethtown till 1740; named after Sir George Carteret's wife.

**Elkhart** USA. Industrial town in N Indiana 135 m. N of Indianapolis at the confluence of the Elkhart and the St Joseph rivers. Pop. (1960) 40,274. Manufactures electrical equipment, musical instruments (producing nearly three quarters of all the wind and percussion instruments made in the USA), metal goods, machinery, etc.

**Elk Island National Park** Canada. The largest fenced animal reserve in Canada; in Alberta 21 m. E of Edmonton. Area 75 sq. m. Since 1906 a sanctuary for elk, moose, buffalo, deer; established as a National Park 1913. Mainly forested, with bathing and camping facilities.

**Ellesmere** England. Urban district in NW Shropshire, 15 m. NNW of Shrewsbury on the Ellesmere Canal, linking the R. Severn and the R. Mersey. Pop. (1961) 2,254. Market town. In a dairy-farming district on the W shore of The Mere (small lake) from which its name is derived.

**Ellesmere Island** Canada. Arctic island in NE Franklin District, NW Territories, off NW Greenland; the northernmost island of Canada, largest of the Queen Elizabeth Is. Area 82,000 sq. m. The coast is indented with fiords, dividing the island into 4 parts (N–S): Grant Land, Grinnell Land, Sverdrup Land, Lincoln Land. Mountainous, rising to over 9,000 ft. There is sparse vegetation in many areas; the musk-ox is common. Small settlements at Craig Harbour (SE) and Alexandra Fiord (E); a meteorological station on Eureka Sound (NW). Named (after the 1st Earl of Ellesmere) by Sir E. A. Inglefield, who first explored the island in 1852.

**Ellesmere Port** England. Municipal borough and port in NW Cheshire on the S bank of the Manchester Ship Canal 9 m. SSE of Liverpool. Pop. (1961) 44,714 (18,911 in 1931). Within the borough is the important oil refinery of Stanlow. Besides the manufacture of petroleum products there are motor-car, flour-milling, and engineering industries.

**Ellice Islands** S Pacific Ocean. Formerly the Lagoon Is. Archipelago consisting of 9 groups of atolls in the S Pacific between the Fiji and Gilbert Is., extending 5°30′–11° S lat. and 176°–180° E long. Total area 9½ sq. m. Pop. (1965) 7,000. Cap. Funafuti. Plentiful rainfall; temperatures are uniformly high. Coconuts are grown and copra is exported. Most of the Polynesian inhabitants speak Samoan, their ancestors having probably come from Samoa. Protestant missions have long worked in the islands. A British protectorate was established in 1892, and in 1915 the islands became part of the British colony of the ◊ *Gilbert and Ellice Islands*. US naval and air bases were established here in the 2nd World War.

**Ellis Island** USA. Small island in Upper New York Bay, New York. Area 27 acres. Used as an immigrant station 1892–1954. Named after Samuel Ellis, a Manhattan merchant who bought it in the 18th cent. It was artificially enlarged from 3 acres to its present size, mainly in 1898 and 1905.

**Ellora** India. Village in Maharashtra 18 m. NW of Aurangabad. Famous for the rock temples excavated in the hillside and extending for more than 1 m. They are in three groups, Buddhist, Hindu, and Jain, the outstanding one being the Kailasa temple of the Hindu group, which was carved externally as well as internally out of the rock.

**Ellore** ◊ *Eluru*.

**El Merg** ◊ *Barca*.

**Elmhurst** USA. Town in Illinois 16 m. W of Chicago. Pop. (1960) 36,991. Mainly residential. Limestone quarried in the neighbourhood.

**Elmira** USA. Industrial town in New York, 85 m. SSE of Rochester on the Chemung R. Pop. (1960) 46,517. Manufactures firefighting and office equipment, glass bottles, etc. Site of the New York State Reformatory, which has had a great influence on correctional methods in the USA and elsewhere.

**Elmshorn** Federal German Republic. Industrial town in Schleswig-Holstein 20 m. NW of Hamburg. Pop. (1963) 35,400. Shipbuilding, food processing. Manufactures textiles, leather goods, etc.

**El Paso** USA. Town in W Texas on the Rio Grande opposite Ciudad Juarez (Mexico). Pop. (1960) 276,687. Tourist resort. Industrial centre. Copper smelting, oil refining, meat packing. Manufactures textiles, glass, cement, clothing, etc. Considerable trade with Mexico. Mexican handicrafts are practised; there is a large population of Mexican descent. The S (Mexican) bank of the river was originally settled by Spaniards in the 17th cent.; the first settlement on the N (US) bank was made in 1827.

**El Teniente** ◊ *Rancagua*.

**Elsinore** ◊ *Helsingör*.

**Eltham** England. Residential district in the Greater London borough of Greenwich (SE). Remains of 14th-cent. former royal

ELURU

palace. Burial-place of Thomas Doggett (d. 1721), founder of the prize of 'Doggett's Coat and Badge' for Thames watermen.

**Eluru (Ellore)** India. Town in Andhra Pradesh 180 m. ESE of Hyderabad, at the junction of the Godavari and Krishna R. canal systems. Pop. (1961) 108,321. Manufactures textiles, carpets, leather, etc. Rice and jute milling. Trade in rice, oilseeds, tobacco.

**Elvas** Portugal. Town in the Portalegre district, Alto Alentejo province, near the Spanish border. Pop. 13,600. Once a strong fortress; a 17th-cent. aqueduct and 15th-cent. cathedral. Now well known for the preserving of fruit (esp. plums).

**Ely** England. Cathedral city and urban district on the R. Ouse in the administrative county of the Isle of Ely, Cambridgeshire, 14 m. NNE of Cambridge. Pop. (1961) 9,815. Market town. Manufactures beet sugar, baskets, agricultural implements. Its cathedral, a famous landmark, dates back to the 11th cent., with 7th-cent. Saxon relics; it has a remarkable Norman nave, a Decorated octagon, and examples of the Early English and Perpendicular styles. The King's Grammar School, founded in the 11th cent. and refounded 1541, includes the Ely Porta, the old monastery gatehouse, and Prior John de Cranden's chapel, both of the 14th cent. Ely grew originally round a 7th-cent. nunnery, and here the Saxons under Hereward the Wake offered their final resistance to William the Conqueror. The name is supposed to be derived from the eels in the R. Ouse.

The Isle of Ely, originally so named because it consisted of slightly elevated land surrounded by fens, is mainly agricultural, producing sugar-beet, potatoes, cereals, fruit, etc. Area 375 sq. m. Pop. (1961) 89,112.

**Elyria** USA. Town in Ohio, on the Black R. 23 m. WSW of Cleveland. Pop. (1960) 43,782. Manufactures foundry products, plastics, pumps, chemicals, etc. Named after himself by the first settler, Heman Ely, a New Englander, in 1817.

**Emba River** USSR. River 380 m. long in the W Kazakh SSR, flowing generally SW to the NE part of the Caspian Sea, passing in its lower course through the rich Emba oilfield with centres at Makat, Koschagyl, and elsewhere.

**Emden** Federal German Republic. Seaport in Lower Saxony, on the R. Ems estuary near the Netherlands border 72 m. WNW

of Bremen. Pop. (1963) 46,100. Terminus of the Dortmund–Ems canal. Exports coal. Imports ores, grain, timber. Shipbuilding, oil refining, fishing, fish canning, etc. Became a free imperial city 1595. Passed to Prussia 1744, to Hanover 1815, and returned to Prussia 1866. Suffered severely in the 2nd World War; most of the historic buildings were destroyed.

**Emilia-Romagna** Italy. Region in the N comprising the provinces of Bologna, Ferrara, Modena, Parma, Piacenza, Reggio nell'Emilia, Forlì, and Ravenna. Area 8,542 sq. m. Pop. (1961) 3,646,507. Cap. Bologna. The Apennines run WNW–ESE along its S border; N of them are the fertile plains of the R. Po, producing wheat, sugar-beet, tomatoes, and other crops. Food processing is the principal industry. Several popular resorts on the Adriatic coast, e.g. Rimini, Riccione, Cattolica.

**Emmen** Netherlands. Town in Drenthe province 32 m. SSE of Groningen near the German border. Pop. (1968) 76,599. A 'new town', formed since the 2nd World War from several separate hamlets. Formerly a centre of peat digging, a much reduced industry. Manufactures agricultural machinery, chemicals, nylon, cement, etc.

**Emmental (Emmenthal)** Switzerland. Valley of the upper Emme R., Bern canton. Noted for its dairy produce, esp. Emmental cheese. Chief market Langnau.

**Empoli** Italy. Town in Firenze province, Tuscany, on the Arno R. 17 m. WSW of Florence. Pop. (1961) 34,989. Manufactures macaroni, hosiery, etc. Paintings and sculptures by Bartolommeo, the della Robbias, etc. in its churches.

**Ems (Bad Ems)** Federal German Republic. Town in the Rhineland-Palatinate on the Lahn R. 7 m. ESE of Coblenz. Pop. 10,000. Well-known spa, famous since Roman times for its hot alkaline springs. At a conference here (1786) four German archbishops made the famous pronouncement against papal interference known as the Punctuation of Ems. The meeting here (1870) between William I of Prussia and the French ambassador, and Bismarck's version of the encounter – the so-called Ems Telegram – led to the Franco-Prussian War.

**Ems River** Federal German Republic. River 230 m. long, rising in the Teutoburger Wald and flowing generally NNW to the Dollart and the North Sea. Linked at Meppen to the Ruhr by the Dortmund–Ems Canal.

**Enakievo** ⬦ *Yenakievo*.

**Encarnación** Paraguay. Capital of the Itapúa department, river port on the Alto Paraná R. opposite Posadas in Argentina and linked with it by train ferry. Pop. (1962) 35,186. Exports maté, timber, tobacco, cotton, hides. Sawmilling, tanning, etc.

**Endeavour Strait** Australia. The S part of Torres Strait between the N coast of Cape York Peninsula, Queensland, and Prince of Wales Island. Named after Capt. Cook's vessel *Endeavour*, which passed through on his return voyage (1770).

**Enderbury Island** ⬦ *Phoenix Islands*.

**Enderby Island** ⬦ *Dampier Archipelago*.

**Enderby Land** Antarctica. The most westerly part of the Australian Antarctic Territory, extending between 45° E and 55° E long. Discovered (1831) by John Biscoe; visited by Sir Douglas Mawson 1929–31

**Ene River** ⬦ *Apurímac River*.

**Enfield** England. Former municipal borough of Middlesex (created 1955); from 1965 a Greater London borough. Pop. (1963) 273,637. Once a market town, now a residential and industrial suburb 10 m. N of London. Manufactures metal goods, electrical equipment, cables, etc. A 13th/16th-cent. church. Near by is Enfield Chase, over 3,000 acres of which were purchased by the LCC (1938) for the Green Belt scheme.

**Enfield** USA. Town in Connecticut, on the Connecticut R. 15 m. NNE of Hartford. Pop. (1960) 31,464. Manufactures hardware, wood products, etc.

**Engadine** Switzerland. Upper (Swiss) part of the valley of the Inn R., in Graubünden (Grisons) canton, extending from the Maloja Pass about 60 m. to the Austrian frontier; divided into Upper Engadine (SW) and Lower Engadine (NE). Villages have whitewashed stone houses. Several resorts and winter sports centres, e.g. St Moritz. The Swiss National Park (61 sq. m.), founded 1909, famous for its Alpine flora and fauna, is reached from Zernez in the Lower Engadine.

**Engelberg** Switzerland. Village and resort in the Obwalden half-canton, 18 m. SSE of Lucerne at a height of 3,343 ft, hemmed in by lofty mountains including Titlis (10,627 ft). Pop. (1960) 2,650. Grew round a Benedictine abbey founded in the 12th cent.

**Engels** USSR. Formerly Pokrovsk. Town in RSFSR on the Volga R. opposite Saratov. Pop. (1970) 130,000. Industrial centre. Railway engineering, meat packing, flour milling, etc. Manufactures textiles, leather goods, etc. Capital of the Volga German ASSR from 1923 until the latter was dissolved in 1941.

**England.** The S and largest part of Great Britain. Area (excluding Monmouthshire) 50,331 sq. m. Pop. (1961) 43,430,972. Cap. London.

Constitutes the largest political division both of Great Britain and of the United Kingdom of Great Britain and Northern Ireland; also the most populous of the four units (England, Scotland, Wales, Northern Ireland), with more than four fifths of the total population. With Scotland to the N and Wales to the W it is separated from the continent of Europe by the North Sea and the English Channel (inc. the narrow Strait of Dover) and from Ireland by the Irish Sea. Although rather more than three quarters of its land surface is classified as agricultural (arable, permanent pasture, rough grazing land), the country depends for its economic wealth on its manufacturing industries, and only one other major country in Europe, the Netherlands, has a higher density of population. For administrative purposes it is divided into the following counties: Bedfordshire, Berkshire, Buckinghamshire, Cambridgeshire and Isle of Ely, Cheshire, Cornwall, Cumberland, Derbyshire, Devonshire, Dorsetshire, Durham, Essex, Gloucestershire, Hampshire and Isle of Wight, Herefordshire, Hertfordshire, Huntingdonshire, Kent, Lancashire, Leicestershire, Lincolnshire (Parts of Holland, Kesteven, and Lindsey), London, Norfolk, Northamptonshire and Soke of Peterborough, Northumberland, Nottinghamshire, Oxfordshire, Rutlandshire, Shropshire, Somerset, Staffordshire, E Suffolk, W Suffolk, Surrey, E Sussex, W Sussex, Warwickshire, Westmorland, Wiltshire, Worcestershire, Yorkshire (E Riding, N Riding, and W Riding). For a geographical description of the country (topography, climate, etc.) ⬦ *Great Britain*.

AGRICULTURE, INDUSTRY. Slightly more than half of the agricultural land is arable. The principal crops are wheat, barley – both particularly in the drier, sunnier eastern counties – turnips and similar root crops, sugar-beet – again chiefly in the eastern counties – potatoes – largely in the Fens – hay. Kent is the leading county in the production of hops and fruit, which are also grown in Herefordshire and Worcestershire; some fruits are cultivated in most S counties. Market gardening is important in the vicinity of the large industrial areas. Permanent pasture occupies about two thirds as large an area as arable land, emphasizing the importance of livestock in English agriculture. Dairy farming is located mainly in the western counties which, because of their mild, moist climate, can support rich pastures, and Cheshire and Somerset are outstanding. Of the beef cattle, the Hereford, named after its county of origin, has won fame on the ranches of N and S America as well as at home. Sheep are grazed on the poorer upland pastures, e.g. in the Lake District and the Pennines and on the chalk hills of S England, esp. the N and S Downs. The fishing industry, though somewhat less important than formerly, is still substantial, and is centred mainly on the E coast ports of Hull and Grimsby. Coal has long formed the basis of the country's leading industries, and is the principal mineral, the Yorkshire, Notts., and Derby coalfield having the highest output. Iron ore is found in the E Midlands and elsewhere, and china clay in Cornwall; salt beds in Cheshire and S Durham supply the near-by chemical industries. Iron and steel are manufactured at various centres in the Midlands and NE, inc. Sheffield and Middlesbrough. Associated industries are shipbuilding, chiefly in the NE (on the Tyne, Wear, and Tees estuaries); the construction of locomotives and railway rolling stock, at Crewe, Derby, and other railway centres; the manufacture of motor vehicles (now of great significance in foreign trade) at Coventry, Birmingham, Dagenham, Oxford, and Luton. Of the textiles, the cotton industry is concentrated in Lancashire and the woollen industry in the W Riding of Yorkshire. Boots and shoes are manufactured in the E Midlands (Northants), pottery in N Staffs. (Stoke-on-Trent), and glass in S Lancashire (St Helens), while a large number of varied industries are located in Greater London.

POPULATION. In 1801 the population of England and Wales together was 8,892,536, and within 50 years this number had doubled; by 1901 the population of England alone was 30,813,043, and in 1951 it had risen to 41,159,213. In 1961, as in 1931, 80 per cent of the people of England and Wales were living in urban areas. More than one third of the urban population of England were massed in 6 great conurbations; Greater London was by far the largest, with over 8 million people, followed in order of size by SE Lancashire, W Midlands, W Yorkshire, Merseyside, Tyneside. After London the largest cities in order of population are Birmingham, Liverpool, Manchester, Leeds, Sheffield, Bristol. The English people are mainly of Anglo-Saxon and Danish origin (although along the Welsh border and in SW England the earlier Celtic strain is more apparent) while over the centuries there has been a continuous intermingling of newcomers: Scots, Welsh, and Irish, as well as Normans, Flemings, Dutch, Poles, and many others. The influx of coloured immigrants from distant parts of the Commonwealth, chiefly from the W Indies and Pakistan, is a feature of post-1946 conditions. The established Church of England is Protestant Episcopal and is divided into the two archiepiscopal provinces of Canterbury and York; in 1961 it had 27·3 million baptized members. The various Nonconformist bodies, chiefly the Methodist, Baptist, and Congregational, number several millions, while Roman Catholics are estimated at 3·7 millions.

HISTORY. When Julius Caesar invaded England (55 B.C.) he found the land inhabited by Celts, who had crossed from the mainland more than six centuries earlier. The Roman occupation began in A.D. 43, and in the 2nd cent. Hadrian's Wall was built at the instance of the Emperor Hadrian to defend the line from the Tyne to the Solway Firth in N England. The upper classes were Romanized and spoke Latin, each town had its forum, amphitheatre, temples, and baths, but with the departure of the Romans in the 5th cent. all effective traces of Roman influence were submerged, and the Celts withdrew into Wales and Cornwall before the invading Angles, Saxons, and Jutes. The invaders, within the next two centuries converted to Christianity, established several kingdoms, of which Wessex gained the supremacy in the 9th cent. Persistent Danish raids were resisted by King Alfred of Wessex, but recommenced, and for a time (1016–42) the country was ruled by Danish kings. The Norman Conquest (1066) brought the Anglo-Saxon period to an end, and the new line of kings attempted to establish national unity through a strong monarchy. While the small village community still formed the basis of English life, towns now began to grow up and trade developed. Meanwhile, the struggle for power between king and barons came to a head under King John; he was compelled to sign Magna Carta (1215), which was gradually to lead to a parliamentary system of government. An Anglo-Norman colony was established in Ireland, the conquest of Wales was completed, English possessions in France were extended but later lost in the Hundred Years War (1337–1453). The 14th cent. saw much internal unrest, with the Black Death (1348) and the Peasants' Revolt (1381), and in the following century the Wars of the Roses between the Houses of Lancaster and York ended with the accession (1485) of Henry Tudor (Henry VII).

The Reformation came to England under Henry VIII, who made himself head of the Church, dissolving the monasteries and confiscating their property. Commercial expansion (esp. the rise in the woollen trade) and political rivalry brought conflict with Spain, and in the reign of Elizabeth I led to the defeat of the Spanish Armada (1588) and the emergence of England as a great naval power. Elizabethan England was distinguished by the work of Shakespeare and his contemporaries. Elizabeth's successor was James VI of Scotland, who became James I of England (1603). The Stuarts, however, failed to maintain the harmony that had been created under the Tudors between king and Parliament, and the outcome was the Civil War, to be followed by the execution of Charles I (1649) and the dictatorship of Cromwell. If the restoration of the monarchy, in the person of Charles II, was welcomed, it was more as a reaction against Puritanism than in anticipation of further Stuart follies, and in 1688 James II, an avowed Catholic, was dethroned and succeeded by William III and Mary. Overseas, England had been laying the foundations of the Empire in N America and India, and in the reign of Queen Anne the parliaments of England and Scotland were united (1707).

The end of the Stuarts had demonstrated the supremacy of Parliament over the monarchy, and this was emphasized under the new Hanoverian line by the development of Cabinet government. It was under the Hanoverians that the American colonies revolted and were lost, but before the close of this period there came changes of great significance to the country's economic life in the Industrial Revolution, which converted the English from an agricultural nation into the foremost industrial nation in the world.

Many political and social reforms were inaugurated with the Reform Bill of 1832, by which political power passed from the aristocracy to the middle classes. A policy of free trade increased the prosperity of the country, control over India and over the route to India was strengthened, Canada, Australia, and New Zealand were developed, new colonies were established in Africa. At home the working classes, at first denied both the franchise and a share in the country's wealth, created the trade unions; by the beginning of the 20th cent. the latter had helped to form a third political party, the Labour Party, to challenge both the Conservatives and the Liberals. In Europe Britain was threatened commercially and politically by Germany, but victory in the 1st World War, far from resolving the country's difficulties, only brought new problems: independence had to be granted to southern Ireland as the Irish Free State (1922), later to become a republic (1949); a general strike occurred in 1926; the world economic depression of 1929–31 led to widespread unemployment. On the other hand, universal suffrage was now established (1918 and 1928), and considerable advances were made in the standards of education and housing and in insurance against sickness and unemployment. With the end of the 2nd World War came the election of a Labour government which for the first time had an overall majority (1945). At the same time the nature of the Empire, now termed the Commonwealth, began to change, with ever-widening grants of independence. Some countries, e.g. India, Pakistan, Ghana, Nigeria, became republics but remained within the Commonwealth; others, e.g. Burma, S Africa, left the Commonwealth. It was the economic crisis at home, however, which finally defeated the Labour Party and brought about the return of the Churchill government of 1951, inaugurating a long period of Conservative rule (till 1964). For further information on economic development, ◊ *Great Britain.*

**Englewood** (Colorado) USA. Residential suburb of Denver, on the S Platte R. at a height of 5,200 ft. Pop. (1960) 33,398. Many greenhouses. Manufactures brooms etc.

**Englewood** (New Jersey) USA. Residential town 13 m. NNE of Jersey City. Pop. (1960) 26,057. Manufactures elevators, leather goods, etc.

**English Channel** (Fr. La Manche, 'The Sleeve'). Arm of the Atlantic Ocean, between England and France, 350 m. long and 100 m. wide at the W end (between Ushant and the Scilly Isles) and 21 m. at the Strait of Dover (E end) where it joins the North Sea. Abounds in fish. Many seaside resorts on both coasts. The principal islands are the Channel Is. and the Isle of Wight. Several cross-channel steamer services. First crossed by balloon 1785; first swum 1875; first crossed by aircraft 1909 (Blériot), by hovercraft 1959. Since the early 19th cent. the construction of a Channel tunnel has been advocated, and plans are being drawn up.

**English River** ◊ *Churchill River* (1).

**Enid** USA. Town in N Oklahoma 66 m. NNW of Oklahoma City. Pop. (1960) 38,859. Commercial centre and wheat market. Oil refining, flour milling. Manufactures oilfield equipment etc. Seat of the Phillips University (1906).

**Enna** Italy. Formerly (till 1927) Castrogiovanni. Capital of Enna province, in central Sicily, 13 m. ENE of Caltanissetta, on a plateau at 2,600 ft. Pop. (1961) 28,323. In a sulphur-mining district. Ancient Enna was a centre of the worship of Demeter (Ceres). The town was held by the Saracens 859–1087.

**Ennerdale Water** England. Lake 2½ m. long and up to ½ m. wide in SW Cumberland in the Lake District 7 m. ESE of Whitehaven, which it supplies with water. Part of Ennerdale, the valley above the lake, was presented to the nation in 1936.

**Ennis** Irish Republic. County town of Co. Clare on the R. Fergus 19 m. NW of Limerick. Pop. (1966) 5,834. Brewing, distilling, flour milling. Restored 13th-cent. Franciscan abbey.

**Enniscorthy** Irish Republic. Market town in Co. Wexford, on the R. Slaney 12 m. NNW of Wexford, with which it is connected by canal. Pop. (1966) 5,762. Brewing, flour milling, bacon and ham curing, pottery manufacture. Roman Catholic cathedral; the keep of a 13th-cent. Norman castle. Taken by Cromwell 1649. Sacked by Irish insurgents 1798.

**Enniskillen** Northern Ireland. Municipal borough and county town of Fermanagh on an island in the R. Erne, between Upper and Lower Lough Erne. Pop. (1961) 7,438. Trade in agricultural produce. Cattle market. Famous as a Protestant stronghold. James II's forces were defeated here 1689.

**Enschede** Netherlands. Town in Overijssel province near the German frontier, linked by the Twente Canal with the Ijssel and Rhine rivers. Pop. (1968) 135,677. Leading centre of the Dutch cotton industry. Also manufactures clothing, paper, chemicals, tyres, etc. Much of the town was burned in 1862 and was rebuilt.

**Ensenada** Mexico. Port in Baja (Lower) California, 60 m. SE of Tijuana. Pop. 43,000. Exports cotton. Fishing, fish canning, wine making.

**Entebbe** Uganda. Town in the Buganda region, on the NW shore of L. Victoria, at a height of 3,760 ft. Pop. 11,000. Important international airport. Mainly an administrative centre. Botanical gardens, a virus research institute, and a hospital. Founded as a garrison post 1893.

**Entre Minho e Douro** Portugal. Popularly known as Minho. Former province between the Minho (N) and the Douro (S) rivers, containing the administrative districts of Braga, Viana do Castelo, and Pôrto, divided in 1936 between the new province of Minho and the N part of Douro Litoral province. Intensively cultivated, producing maize, vines, fruit, olives, etc. Chief towns Oporto, Braga.

**Enugu** Nigeria. Former capital of the Eastern Region, 120 m. NNE of Port Harcourt, with which it is linked by rail. Pop. (1963) 68,000. Main coalmining centre in W Africa; supplies the railways, tin mines, and shipping. Railway engineering, sawmilling. Became capital of the breakaway state of Biafra (◊ *Nigeria*) in 1967.

**Épernay** France. Town in the Marne department, on the Marne R. 16 m. SSW of Reims. Pop. (1968) 27,767. One of the two main headquarters of the Champagne wine industry (the other being Reims). Manufactures corking equipment, corks, bottles, and casks; the wine is bottled and stored in vast underground cellars dug in the chalk. Other industries sugar refining, textile manufacture.

**Ephesus.** Ancient Ionian city on the W coast of Asia Minor, 30 m. SSE of the modern Izmir (Turkey). Famous for its wealth and for its temple of Artemis (Diana). Taken by Alexander the Great 333 B.C. Passed to the Romans 133 B.C., later becoming capital of Roman Asia. Visited by St Paul, who addressed an epistle to the Christians here; in A.D. 262 both city and temple were destroyed by the Goths. Never fully recovered and was later abandoned. Excavations in the late 19th and the early 20th cent. revealed ruins of the temple and other buildings.

**Epidaurus** Greece. Ancient town in Argolis, in the NE Peloponnese on the Saronic Gulf. Famous for the sacred precinct of Asclepius; remains of the temple and the theatre, among the finest in Greece, have been excavated. Just NW is the small modern town of Nea Epidhavros ('New Epidaurus'), where Greek independence was proclaimed 1822.

**Épinal** France. Prefecture of the Vosges department, on the Moselle R. 42 m. SSE of Nancy. Pop. (1968) 39,991. Flourishing cotton industry, introduced by Alsatian immigrants. Also manufactures Kirsch liqueur, cheap engravings, lithographs, etc. (*images d'Épinal*). Grew round a 10th-cent. monastery founded by the Bishop of Metz. Ceded to the duchy of Lorraine 1465. Incorporated into France 1766.

**Epirus** (Gr. Ípiros). **1.** Ancient Epeiros. Region in ancient Greece in the NW between the Pindus Mountains and the Ionian Sea; the name means 'the Mainland'. Mountainous and not very fertile. Famous for cattle and horses. One of the tribes, the Molossians, attained their greatest power under Pyrrhus (318–272 B.C.), whose costly defeats of the Romans were the original 'Pyrrhic victories'. Passed to the Turks in the 15th cent.; after Greek independence it was ceded to Greece (S part) and Albania (N part).
**2.** Region in modern Greece comprising the *nome*s of Árta, Ioánnina, Préveza, and Thesprotia. Area 3,495 sq. m.

**Epping** England. Urban district in W Essex 15 m. NNE of London. Pop. (1961) 9,998. Market town. In a dairy-farming region. Stands on the N edge of Epping Forest, part of the ancient Waltham Forest which once covered most of Essex; after reduction by enclosures, 5,600 acres were purchased by the Corporation of the City of London and opened to the public in 1882.

**Epsom and Ewell** England. Municipal borough and residential district of Surrey 13 m. SSW of London. Pop. (1961) 71,177. On Epsom Downs just S is the racecourse where several famous races, including the Derby (founded 1780) and the Oaks – named after Lord Derby and his estate – are held. Because of mineral springs containing magnesium sulphate, Epsom became a celebrated 17th-cent. spa, and gave its name to Epsom salts. Epsom College, a well-known public school, was founded 1855. The neighbouring village of Ewell, which was absorbed in 1937, contains part of Nonsuch Park (259 acres), included in the Green Belt.

**Equatorial Guinea.** Former Spanish territory on the Gulf of Guinea; two provinces: Río Muni (a section of the mainland, with the offshore islands of Corisco, Elobey Grande, Elobey Chico) and Fernando Póo (the islands of Fernando Póo and Annobón). Area 10,830 sq. m. (Río Muni 10,045). Pop. (1960) 245,989 (7,084 Europeans). Cap. Santa Isabel (pop. 19,869) on Fernando Póo. Río Muni is bounded by Cameroun (N) and Gabon (E and S). A narrow coastal plain rises to a dissected plateau (average height 2,000 ft). Typically equatorial climate; annual rainfall 80 ins. Chief exports cacao, coffee, tropical hardwoods. Chief seaport Bata (capital of Río Muni). Gained independence and became a member-state of the United Nations 1968.

**Erbil (Arbil, Irbil)** Iraq. Ancient Arbela. Capital of Erbil province, 50 m. E of Mosul. Pop. 35,000. Commercial centre. Trade in grain, livestock. Terminus of the railway from Baghdad and Kirkuk. Important in Assyrian times.

**Erciyas Daği** Turkey. Extinct volcano in central Turkey 13 m. S of Kayseri, 12,850 ft in height.

**Ercolano** ◊ *Herculaneum.*

**Erebus, Mount** Antarctica. Active volcano (13,202 ft) on Ross Island in the Ross Sea. Discovered (1841) by Sir James Ross and named after one of his ships.

**Erevan** ◊ *Yerevan.*

**Erfurt** German Democratic Republic. **1.** Administrative district formed in 1952 from part of the *Land* of Thuringia. Area 2,827 sq. m. Pop. (1968) 1,256,034.
**2.** Capital of Erfurt district, on the Gera R. 65 m. WSW of Leipzig. Pop. (1968) 193,285. Railway junction. Industrial and commercial centre. Manufactures machinery, electrical equipment, typewriters, clothing, etc. Trade in flowers, vegetables, seeds. One of the oldest of German cities, it has a 13th/15th-cent. cathedral, the 13th-

cent. Church of St Severus, and the buildings of the former university, opened in 1392 and suppressed in 1816, where Luther studied.

**Ericht, Loch** Scotland. Lake 15 m. long and ½–1 m. wide on the Perthshire–Inverness-shire border at a height of 1,150 ft. From the S end water is led by tunnel to a hydro-electric plant on Loch Rannoch.

**Erie** USA. Port and manufacturing town in NW Pennsylvania, on L. Erie. Pop. (1960) 138,440. Handles coal, petroleum, timber, grain, fish. The harbour is sheltered by the Presque Isle peninsula. Manufactures refrigerators, electrical equipment, metal goods, paper, etc. Fort Presque Isle was built by the French in 1753 but later abandoned; occupied by the British in 1760, and passed to the USA 1785.

**Erie, Lake** Canada/USA. Fourth largest (9,889 sq. m.) of the Great Lakes between the USA and Canada, at a height of 572 ft above sea level; the shallowest of the Great Lakes, with a maximum depth of 210 ft. It freezes easily, and is closed to navigation from mid Dec. to March or April. Through the Detroit R. it receives the waters of the upper lakes; it empties via the Niagara R. into L. Ontario. Chief ports Toledo, Cleveland, Erie, Buffalo, and Sandusky in the USA and Port Colborne (at the entrance to the Welland Canal leading to L. Ontario) in Canada. Named after the Erie Indians. Discovered by the French in the early 17th cent. In the 18th cent. it became an important fur-trade route, and forts and trading posts were built along its shores.

**Erie Canal** USA. Waterway 360 m. long, from Albany (Hudson R.) to Buffalo (L. Erie); the main canal in the New York State Barge Canal System. Opened 1825. The object (amply fulfilled) was to make eastern markets accessible to farmers of the Great Lakes region, and to facilitate the westward movement of settlers; it also enhanced the commercial importance of New York. Tolls were paid until 1882.

**Erith** England. Former municipal borough in Kent 14 m. E of London; from 1965 part of the Greater London borough of Bexley. Pop. (1961) 45,403. Formerly a naval station on the S bank of the R. Thames. Manufactures chemicals, paints, paper, electrical equipment, cables, etc. The Church of St John the Baptist, largely rebuilt, dates from Norman times.

**Eritrea** Ethiopia. Territory bordering on the Red Sea, from Ras Kasar to the strait of Bab el Mandeb. Area 45,754 sq. m. Pop. (1963) 1,100,000. Cap. Asmara. Chief seaport Massawa (linked by rail with Asmara and Agordat). The narrow coastal strip, hot and arid, includes part of the desert of Danakil Land. The upland zone (an extension of the Ethiopian highlands), rising to 9,800 ft in Mt Soira, is cooler and wetter. Principal occupation stock rearing (cattle, sheep, goats). Coffee is grown in the uplands, gum arabic collected in the lowlands. Salt produced, and pearls fished off the Dahlak Is. – but the volume of trade is small. Italy secured various possessions along the Red Sea coast in the late 19th cent. and in 1890 formed the colony of Eritrea, the base for the invasions (1896 and 1935) of Abyssinia (Ethiopia). Occupied by British forces during the 2nd World War (1941) and then under British military administration. Became an autonomous unit, in federation with Ethiopia, by UN decision 1952. Completely integrated with Ethiopia 1962.

**Erivan** ◊ *Yerevan*.

**Erlangen** Federal German Republic. Town in Bavaria at the confluence of the Regnitz and Schwabach rivers 10 m. N of Nuremberg. Pop. (1963) 73,200. Manufactures electrical equipment, gloves, cotton goods (first introduced by the Huguenots). Noted for its beer. Seat of a Protestant university (1743). Birthplace of Georg Simon Ohm (1787–1854).

**Ermelo** Netherlands. Market town in Gelderland province 16 m. WNW of Apeldoorn. Pop. (1968) 35,434. In a poultry- and dairy-farming region.

**Ernakulam** India. Industrial town in Kerala 35 m. N of Alleppey. Pop. (1961) 117,253. Linked by bridges with the seaport of Cochin. Manufactures soap, coir rope and mats, etc. Educational centre, with 5 colleges affiliated to Kerala University.

**Erne, Lough** Northern Ireland. Lake in Co. Fermanagh consisting of Upper Lough Erne (11 m. long and up to 3 m. wide) and Lower Lough Erne (18 m. long and up to 5½ m. wide), the latter being often known simply as Lough Erne. They are joined by part of R. Erne. Both contain many islands; Devenish island, near the S end of Lower Lough Erne, is famous for its 6th-cent. ruins.

**Erne River** Irish Republic. River 64 m. long, rising in Lough Gowna on the border of Counties Longford and Cavan and flowing NW through Lough Oughter and Lough Erne past Ballyshannon, near which are hydroelectric plants (1952), to Donegal Bay on the Atlantic.

**Erzerum** ◊ *Erzurum*.

**Erzgebirge** (Czech **Krušné Hory**, 'Ore Mountains'). Mountain range on the border of Bohemia (Czechoslovakia) and Saxony (GDR), extending about 90 m. WSW–ENE, and about 25 m. wide. Rises to 4,081 ft in Klinovec (Czechoslovakia). Many minerals, inc. silver, copper, lead, were formerly worked, but are now practically exhausted; since the 2nd World War uranium ore has been obtained, chiefly at Jachymov (Czechoslovakia) and Aue (GDR). Several spas and winter-sports centres.

**Erzincan** Turkey. Capital of Erzincan province, near the Euphrates R. 95 m. WSW of Erzurum. Pop. (1965) 45,000. Manufactures textiles, clothing, copper goods. Has suffered severely from earthquakes, the most recent in 1939.

**Erzurum (Erzerum)** Turkey. Capital of Erzurum province, in the E, on a fertile plateau at a height of 6,300 ft. Pop. (1965) 105,300. Tanning, sugar-refining, and other industries. Trade in grain, vegetables. Seat of Atatürk University (1957). An ancient town, in an important strategic position, it fell to the Turks in 1515 and was taken three times by the Russians (1828, 1878, 1916).

**Esbjerg** Denmark. North Sea port in Jutland opposite Fanö island 80 m. SW of Aarhus. Pop. (1965) 57,255. Grew from a village (13 people in 1868) owing to the construction of the railway and harbour in 1874. Denmark's chief fishing port. Exports dairy produce, bacon, etc., chiefly to Britain. Steamer services to Harwich, Newcastle. Manufactures margarine, rope, etc.

**Esch (Esch-sur-l'Alzette)** Luxembourg. Industrial town and second largest city, on the Alzette R. 10 m. SW of Luxembourg. Pop. (1968) 27,466. Iron mining; centre of the steel industry. Manufactures steel goods, fertilizers, etc.

**Eschwege** Federal German Republic. Town in Hessen, on the Werra R. 27 m. ESE of Kassel. Pop. (1963) 24,000. Manufactures soap, textiles, footwear, etc.

**Eschweiler** Federal German Republic. Industrial town in N Rhine-Westphalia 8 m. ENE of Aachen. Pop. (1963) 40,000.

Coalmining. Brewing, tanning. Manufactures metal goods, cables, etc.

**Escondido River** ◊ *Bluefields*.

**Escorial (Escurial)** Spain. Small town at the foot of the Sierra de Guadarrama, 26 m. NW of Madrid, near which is one of the most magnificent buildings in Europe, comprising monastery, palace, and mausoleum. The monastery, *El real monasterio de San Lorenzo del Escorial*, was erected by Philip II (1563–84). The famous library and art treasures of El Escorial were added later.

**Esdraelon (Jezreel), Plain of** Israel. Fertile plain watered by the Kishon R., extending SE–NW from the Jordan valley to the foot of Mt Carmel. Site of the battlefield of Megiddo.

**Esfahan** ◊ *Isfahan*.

**Esher** England. Urban district in NE Surrey 15 m. SW of London, for which it is a dormitory suburb. Pop. (1961) 60,586. Gatehouse of the 15th-cent. Esher Place, where Cardinal Wolsey lived (1529). Claremont, built by Lord Clive (1768) and now a school. Also Sandown Park racecourse.

**Eskilstuna** Sweden. Industrial town in Södermanland, on the Hjälmar R., which joins L. Hjälmar and L. Mälar, 55 m. W of Stockholm. Pop. (1968) 65,605. Important centre of the iron and steel industry, long noted for the manufacture of cutlery, swords, and hardware. Also produces machinery, precision instruments, electrical equipment. Named after St Eskil, an English missionary martyred here 1181.

**Eskişehir** Turkey. Capital of Eskişehir province 135 m. W of Ankara. Pop. (1965) 173,900. Industrial centre. Sugar refining. Manufactures textiles, cement, agricultural implements, etc. Trade in grain and other agricultural produce. Centre of the meerschaum industry, now of diminished importance. Known since the 3rd cent. for its hot sulphur springs. Near by was the ancient Phrygian city Dorylaeum.

**Esk River** England. 1. River rising on Scafell, Cumberland, and flowing 20 m. SW to the Irish Sea near Ravenglass.
2. River in the N Riding of Yorkshire, rising in the Cleveland Hills and flowing 24 m. generally E to enter the North Sea at Whitby.

**Esk River** England/Scotland. River 36 m. long formed by the union of the Black Esk and the White Esk, flowing SSE through

Dumfriesshire (Scotland), crossing the border into Cumberland (England), and turning SSW to enter Solway Firth 8 m. NNW of Carlisle.

**Esk River** Scotland. 1. *North Esk*: River 29 m. long rising in the Grampians and flowing SE to enter the North Sea 4 m. NNE of Montrose, forming part of the Angus–Kincardine border.

2. *South Esk*: River in Angus, 49 m. long, rising in the Grampians and flowing SE and then E to enter the North Sea at Montrose.

3. River in Midlothian, 4 m. long, formed by the union of the North Esk (17 m.) and the South Esk (19 m.) and flowing N to enter the Firth of Forth at Musselburgh.

**Esmeraldas** Ecuador. Capital of Esmeraldas province, at the mouth of the Esmeraldas R. 125 m. NW of Quito. Pop. 33,000. Chief seaport in the NW. Exports bananas, timber.

**Esna (Isna)** United Arab Republic. Ancient Latapolis. Town on the W bank of the Nile R. 62 m. SSW of Qena. Pop. 26,000 (many Copts). Site of an important barrage (rebuilt 1948). Manufactures pottery. Ruins of a temple dedicated to Khnum, the ram-headed god.

**Espirito Santo** Brazil. Maritime state in the E; a low coastal strip 230 m. long, rising in the W to mountain ranges. Area 15,196 sq. m. Pop. (1960) 1,188,665. Cap. Vitória. Chief river the Rio Doce. The marshy coast has only one good harbour, Vitória. Produces coffee, sugar-cane, fruits.

**Espiritu Santo Island** ⟡ *New Hebrides*.

**Esquimalt (Esquimault)** Canada. Port and naval base at the S end of Vancouver Island, British Columbia; a suburb of Victoria. Large dry-dock and other facilities. Taken over by the Canadian government from the British 1906. Headquarters of the Canadian Maritime Command (Pacific).

**Essaouira** Morocco. Formerly Mogador. Seaport on the Atlantic coast 105 m. W of Marrakesh, with which it is connected by road. Pop. 30,000. Exports wool, olive oil. Fish canning, sugar refining, tanning.

**Essen** Federal German Republic. Town in N Rhine-Westphalia between the Ruhr R. and the Rhine–Herne Canal 20 m. NNE of Düsseldorf. Pop. (1968) 705,203. Leading industrial centre of the Ruhr coalfield, owing its impressive growth to the establishment of the Krupp steel works early in the 19th cent. Besides coalmining and steel manufacture, there are chemical, textile, glass, and furniture industries. Railway engineering. Founded originally round a 9th-cent. convent. Very severely damaged in the 2nd World War.

**Essequibo River** Guyana. River 630 m. long, rising in the Guiana highlands on the Brazil frontier, flowing generally N over many falls and rapids, and entering a wide estuary. Navigable for small ocean-going vessels for about 50 m. Receives several large tributaries; on one of them, the Potaro, are the famous Kaieteur Falls (741 ft).

**Essex** England. County in the SE, bounded by the North Sea (E) and the Thames estuary (S). Area 1,528 sq. m. Pop. (1961) 2,286,970. County town Chelmsford. From the flat coastal plain the county becomes gently undulating inland, particularly in the NW, with several hills 300–400 ft in height; the rivers are either affluents of the Thames (e.g. the Lea and the Roding) or flow to the North Sea (the Stour, which forms much of the N boundary with Suffolk, the Colne, Blackwater, Chelmer, and Crouch – the estuary of the Colne is noted for its oysters). Along the low but indented coast there are several popular resorts, including Southend-on-Sea and Clacton; Tilbury is a seaport, Harwich has ferry services to the continent, and there is a large oil refinery at Shell Haven. The N is mainly agricultural, producing cereals, sugar-beet, fruits, and vegetables, while in the S, where Epping Forest is a mere remnant of the former woodlands, dairy farming is important. In the SW the county has become part of Greater London, and is both industrial and residential, inc. parts of the boroughs of Redbridge, Barking, Newham; some districts, e.g. the 'new towns' of Basildon and Harlow, have experienced a remarkable expansion in recent years.

**Esslingen** Federal German Republic. Industrial town in Baden-Württemberg on the Neckar R. 6 m. ESE of Stuttgart. Pop. (1963) 83,900. Manufactures machinery, electrical equipment, textiles, gloves, etc. Old town hall (15th-cent.). Founded in the 8th cent. A free imperial city from 1273. Incorporated into Württemberg 1802.

**Essonne** France. Department S of Paris formed in 1964, when the former Seine and Seine-et-Oise departments were reorganized. Area 699 sq. m. Pop. (1968) 674,157. Prefecture Ivry.

Estelí Nicaragua. Capital of Estelí department, 60 m. NNW of Managua on the Inter-American Highway. Pop. (1963) 26,764. Market town. Sawmilling, tanning.

Esthwaite Water England. Lake in N Lancashire in the Lake District, 1½ m. long and ¼ m. wide, between Coniston Water and L. Windermere. Near the N end is the village of Hawkshead, at whose grammar school Wordsworth was a pupil 1778–83.

Eston England. Industrial town in the N Riding of Yorkshire, on the R. Tees estuary 4 m. ESE of Middlesbrough. Pop. (1961) 37,160. Steel mills, shipyards, chemical works. ♢ Teesside.

Estonia (Estonian Eesti) USSR. Constituent republic of the USSR, bounded by the Gulf of Finland (N), the RSFSR (E), the Latvian SSR (S), and the Gulf of Riga and the Baltic (W), and including Saaremaa, Hiiumaa, and neighbouring islands. Area 17,410 sq. m. Pop. (1970) 1,357,000 (75 per cent Estonians, 20 per cent Russians). Rel. mainly Lutheran. Cap. Tallinn. Generally low-lying, being an extension of the great Russian plain, it has moraine ridges in the S which rise at one point to over 1,000 ft. One fifth of the area is covered with forests, which provide raw material for various manufactures (wood-pulp, paper, furniture, matches), but agriculture and dairy farming are the chief occupations, yielding cereals, potatoes, dairy produce, and eggs. There are valuable oil-shale deposits in the NE, and shale gas is supplied to Tallinn and Leningrad. The large L. Chudskoye (Peipus) on the E boundary is drained to the Gulf of Finland by the Narva R., on which an important hydroelectric power station was built in 1955. After Tallinn the principal towns are Tartu, which has a university founded 1632, and Kohtla-Järve, a new town at the centre of the oil-shale industry.

For many centuries the Estonians, a Finno-Ugrian people, were subject to various foreign powers. In the 13th cent. the N part of their territory was conquered by the Danes, who founded Reval (now Tallinn), and the S by the Teutonic Knights. By the 17th cent. (1629) all Estonia had passed to Sweden, but in less than a century (1721) it had become a province of Russia. Not till 1920 did Estonia achieve complete independence, after a struggle against both Germans and Russians, but in 1940 it was occupied by Soviet forces and annexed to the USSR; German occupation followed in the 2nd World War (1941–4), and since that time the country has been dominated, politically and economically, by the Soviet Union.

Estoril Portugal. Internationally famous seaside resort on the 'Portuguese Riviera', 13 m. W of Lisbon, with which it is connected by electric railway. Pop. 40,000. Made popular by its mild climate, beach, casino, and many excellent hotels. A magnificent avenue of palm trees leads from the casino to the sea front. Monte Estoril is a neighbouring resort (W).

Estremadura Portugal. Maritime province comprising most of the Lisboa district and parts of the Leiria and Setúbal districts. Area 2,065 sq. m. Pop. 1,600,000. Cap. Lisbon. Much reduced in 1936 from the old province (6,941 sq. m.). Chief products wine, fruit, cork, salt. Several popular resorts, e.g. Estoril, Cascais.

Estremadura (Extremadura) Spain. Historic region in the W bordering on the old Portuguese Estremadura, lying between the latter and New Castile and comprising Cáceres and Badajoz provinces. Area 16,059 sq. m. Pop. 1,379,000. Largely tableland (Meseta), crossed by the Tagus and Guadiana rivers. Agriculture, formerly backward, has been improved by extensive irrigation schemes. Chief products olives, wheat. Sheep and pigs raised.

Esztergom (Ger. Gran) Hungary. Town in Komárom county on the Danube R. almost opposite its confluence with the Hron R. and near the Czechoslovak frontier. Pop. (1962) 23,716. Resort (thermal springs). Manufactures textiles, machinery, etc. Famous as the birthplace of St Stephen (979), who in 1001 became the first Christian king of Hungary. The cathedral (1821–70), which is modelled on St Peter's, Rome, stands on a hill overlooking the Danube.

Etawah India. Town in Uttar Pradesh, 70 m. ESE of Agra. Pop. (1961) 69,681. Oilseed milling. Manufactures textiles. Trade in cotton, agricultural produce. Principal building the 16th-cent. Jama Masjid or Great Mosque, originally a Hindu temple.

Ethiopia (Abyssinia). Independent empire in NE Africa (including Eritrea). Area 345,000 sq. m. Pop. (1966) 22,977,000. Cap. Addis Ababa. Bounded by the Red Sea (N and NE), the French Territory of the Afars and the Issas and Somalia (E), Kenya (S), and Sudan (W). A lofty plateau, descending sharply on the E to the narrow coastal fringe of Eritrea and the Red Sea. Divided into a NW region (rising to 15,158 ft in Ras Dashan) and a smaller SE section (rising to 14,131 ft in Mt Bale) by the Great Rift Valley, which cuts across from the Red Sea to L. Rudolf. The largest lake, L. Tana, is the source of the Blue Nile. The Sobat R. (tributary of the White Nile) and the Atbara R. (the Nile's only substantial affluent below Khartoum) also rise in the NW part of the plateau. Three zones, according to altitude. 1. *Kolla*: Up to 5,000 ft. The long-berry Mocha coffee is cultivated, chiefly in the Harar district. 2. *Woina Dega*: 5,000–8,000 ft. The principal agricultural zone. Cereals, vines, tobacco. 3. *Dega*: Over 8,000 ft. Coniferous forests and open grasslands. Cattle, sheep, and horses reared.

Almost self-supporting in agricultural produce. The volume of foreign trade is small. Coffee by far the most important export. Addis Ababa is linked by rail (via Dire Dawa) with Djibouti in the French Territory of the Afars and the Issas; this is the principal trade route. Another line connects Asmara with the Red Sea at Massawa. Other important towns are Dessie and Harar.

The Hamitic Gallas (Muslim, Christian, and pagan) constitute about half the total population. The ruling group, the Amharas (of mixed Hamitic and Semitic origin), number some 2 million and live chiefly in the central highlands; like the Tigréans (to the N) they are Coptic Christians. In the SE are the Somalis (Muslim), in the SW the Nilotic Negro tribes, and N of L. Tana the Falashas (Judaic).

Ancient Ethiopia was an ill-defined territory S of Egypt (which included the N of modern Ethiopia). Traditionally, the founder of the Ethiopian royal line (*c.*1000 B.C.) was Menelik, son of Solomon and the Queen of Sheba. Christianity was introduced in the 4th cent. The period of greatest prosperity was after the conquest of Yemen, in the 6th cent. By vanquishing Egypt in the 7th cent. the Arabs isolated the Ethiopians from the civilized world for many centuries. A local chief, Lij Kassa, proclaimed himself Emperor Theodore II of Ethiopia 1855. A successor Menelik II (Shoa) defeated the invading Italians at Aduwa in 1896, and preserved Ethiopian independence. The Italians again attacked and occupied Ethiopia 1935. After their defeat by British forces during the 2nd World War (1941) the Emperor Haile Selassie was restored. The former Italian colony of Eritrea was federated to Ethiopia in 1952 and was integrated into Ethiopia in 1962.

**Etna** Italy. Highest volcano in Europe and highest mountain in S Italy (10,741 ft), in Catania province, E Sicily, 18 m. NNW of Catania. An isolated peak, it has the shape of a truncated cone, the uniformity of the slope broken on the E by an immense gully, 2,000–4,000 ft deep and over 3 m. wide; on its sides are more than 200 secondary cones. Three distinct zones on its slopes. The lowest, the cultivated zone, extending to about 4,000 ft, is one of the most densely populated agricultural regions in the world; up to 1,500 ft it produces citrus fruits, olives, and figs and above that height vines, almonds, etc. In the middle, up to 7,000 ft, is the wooded zone, with pines, chestnuts, etc., and above this the desert zone, a desolate area of lava and volcanic ash, almost devoid of vegetation and covered with snow for much of the year. The mountain may be viewed either from a road or a railway around its base, and a motor-road (completed 1935) ascends to over 6,000 ft. Of its many eruptions some of the most noteworthy were those of 475 B.C., described by Pindar and Aeschylus; A.D. 1169, when Catania was destroyed; 1669, the most destructive of all recorded eruptions, when Catania was again destroyed; and 1928, when Mascali was obliterated by lava. On average there have been eruptions about every 6 years during historic times.

**Eton** England. Urban district in Buckinghamshire on the R. Thames opposite Windsor. Pop. (1961) 3,901. Site of Eton College, England's largest and probably most famous public school (but not the oldest), founded by Henry VI in 1440–41 simultaneously with King's College, Cambridge.

**Etruria** Italy. Ancient district in NW Italy, of varying extent but latterly forming what is now Tuscany and part of Umbria. It may once have included all N Italy from the Tiber R. to the Alps, but by the 1st cent. B.C. it had been reduced to the territory between the Tiber, the Apennines, and the Arno. Its people, the Etruscans, were probably immigrants from Asia Minor; they occupied much of Italy, founded many important cities, and reached the peak of their power in the 6th cent. B.C. They had succumbed to Rome by the end of the 4th cent. B.C. As excavaations have shown, they had great artistic skill, particularly in sculpture.

**Etsch River** ♢ *Adige River*.

**Ettrick** Scotland. Village and parish in S W Selkirkshire on Ettrick Water, a river rising on Capel Fell and flowing 32 m. N E to join the R. Tweed. Birthplace of James Hogg (1770–1835), the 'Ettrick Shepherd'. Ettrick Forest formerly covered Selkirkshire and parts of Peeblesshire and Midlothian, was deforested, and in the 16th cent. converted into sheep pasturage.

**Euboea** (Gr. Évvoia) Greece. Largest of the Greek islands, forming a *nome* with neighbouring islands and Skyros (N Sporades) with its offshore islands, off the E coast of the mainland in the Aegean sea. Area (*nome*) 1,492 sq. m. Pop. (1961) 165,758. Cap. Chalcis. The island extends over 100 m. N W–S E, and is largely mountainous, rising to 5,718 ft in Mt Delphi. Cereals, vines, and olives cultivated in the fertile lowlands, sheep and goats raised in the mountains. Chalcis is linked with the mainland by a road bridge at the narrowest part of the Euripus channel. Taken by the Athenians (506 B.C.). Fell to the Romans (191 B.C.), the Venetians (1204), and the Turks (1470), and passed to Greece 1830.

**Euclid** USA. N E suburb of Cleveland, Ohio, on L. Erie. Pop. (1960) 62,998. Manufactures electrical equipment, metal goods, tractors, etc. Settled 1798. Named after the Greek mathematician by the surveyors.

**Euganean Hills** (Italian **Colli Euganei**) Italy. Range of hills of volcanic origin about 11 m. long in Veneto, S W of Padua, rising to nearly 2,000 ft. Thermal springs. Several villas, including Petrarch's home at Arqua.

**Eugene** USA. Town in W Oregon, on the Willamette R. 110 m. S S W of Portland. Pop. (1960) 50,977. Sawmilling, fruit canning, etc. Seat of the University of Oregon (1872).

**Eupen and Malmédy** Belgium. Two districts bordering on the Federal Republic of Germany (E), ceded to Belgium by the Treaty of Versailles in 1919; in 1925 they were incorporated in Liège province. Chief towns Eupen, Malmédy. Eupen

manufactures woollen goods, cables, etc.; pop. (with neighbouring villages) 26,000. Malmédy manufactures paper, leather, etc.; pop. (with neighbouring villages) 22,000.

**Euphrates River (Ar. Al Furat)**. Important river in S W Asia, 2,100 m. long, rising in two headstreams in the highlands N and N W of L. Van, in Turkey: the Murat Su, which flows 400 m. W S W, and the Kara Su or W Euphrates, which flows 280 m. S W to their confluence. The combined river now flows generally S W, turns S into Syria, then S E past Deir ez Zor, to enter Iraq. It continues S E through Iraq, past Haditha, Hit, Falluja, and Nasiriya, and joins the Tigris R. just below Al Qurna, to form the Shatt-al-Arab, which flows 113 m. to the head of the Persian Gulf. Reaches its highest level in May, lowest in Sept. Navigable for light craft as far as Hit. Many great cities of the past, inc. Babylon, Borsippa, and Carchemish, stood on or near its banks. The area between the Euphrates and the Tigris – Mesopotamia ('Between the Rivers') – was in ancient times elaborately irrigated and fertile. Modern irrigation schemes have not yet equalled the ancient systems.

**Eure** France. Department in the N W, formed (1790) from part of Normandy. Area 2,330 sq. m. Pop. (1968) 383,385. Prefecture Évreux. Mainly flat and fertile, but well wooded. Drained by the lower Seine and Eure rivers. Cereals, apples, flax cultivated. Dairy cattle raised; cheese and cider made. Textile and metal-working industries are important. Chief towns Évreux, Les Andelys.

**Eure-et-Loir** France. Department formed (1790) from parts of Orléanais and Normandy. Area 2,293 sq. m. Pop. (1968) 302,207. Prefecture Chartres. Drained by the Eure and the Loir rivers. Flat in the rich wheat-growing Beauce; in the W are the Perche Hills, a stock-rearing area famous for its Percheron horses. Chief towns Chartres, Châteaudun.

**Eureka** USA. Fishing port, seaport, and commercial centre in N W California, on Humboldt Bay 235 m. N N W of San Francisco. Pop. (1960) 28,137. An important sawmilling centre. Named by the first settler, James Ryan, who in 1850 drove his ship on to mud flats in Humboldt Bay, joyfully shouting 'Eureka!'.

**Eure River** France. River 140 m. long, rising in the Perche Hills (Orne) and flowing ESE and then N through the Eure-et-Loir and Eure departments to the Seine R.

**Europe.** Apart from Australia, the smallest of the continents, only slightly larger in area than the USA; it occupies about 7 per cent of the earth's land surface. On the other hand, it is second to Asia among the continents for size of population, containing over 20 per cent of the world total.

EXTENT, PHYSICAL FEATURES. Europe is a W peninsula of the great land mass of Eurasia. There is no well-marked geographical boundary with Asia, but the line between the two continents is generally considered to run along the low Ural Mountains (USSR) to the Caspian Sea, to include the lower Volga, and along the Caucasus, to include the Soviet republics of Georgia, Armenia, and Azerbaijan. The continent is bounded on the N by the Arctic Ocean; on the S by the Mediterranean Sea, linked through the Dardanelles with the Sea of Marmara and thence, through the Bosporus, with the Black Sea; on the W by the Atlantic Ocean, with its inlets the Bay of Biscay, English Channel, Irish Sea, North Sea, and Baltic Sea. From the extreme NE to Cape St Vincent in the SW it has a length of 3,400 m., and from Nordkyn, the northernmost point of Norway, to Cape Matapan, the southernmost point of continental Greece, a breadth of 2,400 m. A vast number of islands around its coasts include Spitsbergen and Novaya Zemlya (N), the British Isles, Faeroes, and Iceland (NW), and the Balearic Is., Corsica, Sardinia, Sicily, Crete and the other Greek islands in the Mediterranean, and with the mainland give it a total area of about 3,900,000 sq. m. Its coastline is further lengthened by several extensive peninsulas: Kola, Scandinavia, and Jutland in the N and the Iberian peninsula, Italy, and the Balkan peninsula, with the Peloponnese, in the S.

A great mountain system stretches W–E across S Europe, with the Pyrenees in the W, the Alps and Apennines in the centre, and the Carpathians, Balkan Mountains, and Caucasus Mountains in the E. The highest peaks are in the Caucasus, Elbruz (18,481 ft), Dykh Tau (17,054 ft), and Kazbek (16,558 ft) all exceeding the loftiest peak of the Alps, Mont Blanc (15,781 ft). The highest mountain in the Scandinavian peninsula is Galdhöpiggen (8,097 ft) in Norway. Between the two mountainous areas of the N and S is the vast N European Plain, which extends from N France through the Low Countries to Poland, broadening out until it occupies the entire N–S width of the USSR in Europe; this great plain covers about two thirds of the continent. Europe has many lakes (esp. in Finland) but they are small compared with the largest of Africa and N America, with the exception of the Caspian Sea, which is a salt lake and in any case belongs to Asia rather than Europe; the greatest European lakes are Ladoga and Onega in the USSR, Saimaa in Finland, and Väner and Vätter in Sweden. By far the longest river in Europe is the Volga, which rises in the Valdai Hills and flows E and S to the Caspian Sea. The Don, Dnieper, and Dniester, also Russian rivers, flow into the Black Sea, as does the Danube, the second longest river, but of greater economic importance is the Rhine, which rises in the Alps, flows generally NNW, and enters the North Sea; it is linked by a system of canals with many other rivers of N and W Europe, e.g. the Weser, Elbe, Oder, Danube, and Rhône. A ship canal, the Kiel Canal, connects the Baltic with the North Sea across Schleswig-Holstein (Federal German Republic).

CLIMATE, VEGETATION, *etc.* Owing to the influence of the N Atlantic Drift, the NW and W regions of Europe enjoy an exceptionally mild, equable type of climate for their latitudes, and such ports as Narvik (Norway) and Murmansk (USSR), well N of the Arctic Circle, are ice-free throughout the year. The influence of the sea diminishes progressively towards the E, with the result that the climate becomes more and more continental: winters are colder, summers are warmer, and in general the rainfall is less in the E – but nowhere are conditions so extreme as they are still farther E, in central Siberia. Lands of S Europe around the margins of the Mediterranean Sea experience a climate which is usually classified as Mediterranean or dry sub-tropical, characterized by hot dry summers and mild rainy winters. Away from the coastal areas (as, e.g., on the central plateau or Meseta of Spain and in the central Balkans) the climate is continental.

The regions of natural vegetation correspond closely to the climatic zones.

In the extreme N (N Scandinavia, Finland, and the USSR), with the sub-Arctic climate of long cold winters, short cool summers, and scanty rainfall, the tundra produces mosses, lichens, and dwarf shrubs – a region of reindeer herding. To the S is a broad belt of coniferous forests, occupying much of Scandinavia, Finland, and the N USSR, which furnishes immense quantities of timber for manufacture into wood pulp, paper, etc. Much farther S, on the Alps, Carpathians, and other mountain ranges, where climate is modified by altitude, there are other forests of pine, spruce, fir, and the like. S of the coniferous forests of N Europe is a belt of mixed coniferous and deciduous forest – but it must be added that the natural vegetation of most of this part of the continent, from Britain and France to the USSR, has been changed almost beyond recognition by agricultural and industrial development. Grasslands cover the Hungarian plain (pusztas) and a much more extensive area in the S USSR (steppes), the latter a great wheat-growing region merging into an arid semi-desert zone round the N shores of the Caspian Sea. The Mediterranean region has its own characteristic vegetation, such trees and shrubs as the evergreen oak and myrtle being typical, and among cultivated plants the olive.

INDUSTRIAL DEVELOPMENT, POPULATION, etc. The rich coalfields of Britain, Germany, France, and Belgium enabled W Europe to take the lead in industrial development from the Industrial Revolution of the 19th cent., and more recently the USSR, with abundant coal and iron deposits in the Ukraine, has come to the fore. France, Sweden, and E England, too, have substantial resources in iron ore, and there are important deposits of many other minerals. Industrialization and the growth of great manufacturing centres and conurbations based on mineral wealth were chiefly responsible for the high density of population in NW Europe, particularly marked in England and Wales, W Germany, Belgium, and Holland. Oil resources are richest in the USSR, notably in the Baku area at first and more recently in the Ural–Volga region (the 'second Baku').

The peoples of Europe may be divided into three main racial types, though mixing is apparent everywhere. In the NW is the Nordic type, with fair hair and skin and blue eyes; around the Mediterranean is the so-called Mediterranean type, with dark hair, eyes, and skin and generally of shorter stature. Between them are the Alpine people, who have brown hair, brown to grey eyes, and a rather stocky frame, the Slavs of E Europe being similar to them. Although there is some relationship between language and race, these do not always coincide. Most languages of Europe belong to the Indo-European group. Celtic tongues (Irish, Gaelic, Welsh, Breton) are still spoken in the W parts of the British Isles and Brittany; the Teutonic languages include English, German, Dutch, and Flemish and, among the Scandinavians, Norwegian, Swedish, Danish, and Icelandic. French, Spanish, Portuguese, Italian, and Rumanian are among the Romance languages, and Russian, Polish, Serbo-Croatian, Czech, Slovak, and Bulgarian among the Slavonic. The languages of the Basques, Maltese, Finns, Lapps, Estonians, Magyars, Turks, Georgians, and Azerbaijanis fall outside the Indo-European group. In religion the vast majority of the peoples of Europe belong, nominally at least, to the various branches of the Christian Church, but there is a considerable number of Muslims in Turkey, Albania, and Yugoslavia, and Jews are scattered throughout most parts of Europe.

POLITICAL DIVISIONS. The Romans imposed some sort of political unity on much of Europe, conferring the benefits of the Pax Romana – law and order – over a large area; they promoted the development of trade and the languages of Latin derivation, together with something of Graeco-Roman culture and the Christian religion. But by the end of the 4th cent. the Roman Empire had disintegrated; the W part, with its capital at Rome, was overrun by barbarians, while the much weakened E part, the Byzantine Empire, with its capital at Constantinople (Istanbul), survived till the 15th cent., when it finally succumbed to the Turks. In the W unity was again briefly achieved by Charlemagne, who ruled from the Elbe to the Ebro and in 800 was crowned Emperor by the Pope.

Thereafter the Holy Roman Empire was a pious idea rather than a reality, and Europe was divided into a large number of kingdoms and principalities, many of which bore little relationship to either ethnographic or linguistic groupings. However, a sense of nationhood began to emerge in several countries, and by the latter Middle Ages England, France, and Spain were recognizably nations. The urge for a national identity, in fact, gradually brought about national states in most of Europe except in Austria, Hungary, and the Ottoman Empire. After the 1st World War the political map of Europe took shape much as it stands today, although some major modifications were brought about by the 2nd World War (e.g. changes in the Polish frontiers, the division of Germany, and the integration of the Baltic States in the USSR).

ECONOMIC ORGANIZATION. The nations of Europe have long maintained strict independence in economic matters, and each developed its own tariff structure to protect and promote its favoured industries. The German Zollverein (begun in 1833) was a customs union which not only promoted economic progress, but paved the way for the unification of Germany under the leadership of Prussia. It was not till after the 2nd World War that any similar effort was made to unite Europe economically: in the European Economic Community (Belgium, France, the Federal German Republic, Italy, Luxembourg, and the Netherlands), set up in 1958, there was agreement to progress rapidly to internal free trade and a common external tariff. Britain did not initially join this Community and her efforts to do so in 1964 and 1967 were unsuccessful. In 1959 seven of the European countries not members of the EEC (Austria, Denmark, Norway, Portugal, Sweden, Switzerland, and the United Kingdom) joined together in a European Free Trade Association which aimed at promoting trade between its members by progressive reduction of tariffs and their eventual elimination. In eastern Europe after 1945 trade was largely channelled between members of the Communist bloc and other Communist countries, but recently there has developed a desire for trade on a wider international basis.

**Europoort** ◊ *Rotterdam*.

**Euxine Sea** ◊ *Black Sea*.

**Evanston** USA. Residential town in NE Illinois, just N of Chicago on L. Michigan. Pop. (1960) 79,283. Manufactures steel goods, paints, chemicals, etc. Seat of the Northwestern University (1851), and named after John Evans, one of the university's founders.

**Evansville** USA. Town in SW Indiana, on the Ohio R. Pop. (1960) 141,543. Manufactures refrigerators, agricultural machinery, furniture, etc. Meat packing, flour milling. Named after Robert M. Evans (1783–1844), one of its founders.

**Evenki NA** USSR. National Area in the Krasnoyarsk Territory, RSFSR, in central Siberia, drained by the Lower Tunguska and Stony Tunguska rivers. Area 286,000 sq. m. Pop. (1970) 13,000 (mainly Evenki). Cap. Tura (pop. 2,000). Mainly coniferous forest and tundra. Main occupations reindeer breeding, hunting, and fishing. Founded 1930.

**Everest, Mount** (Chinese **Chomolungma**). Peak of the Himalayas, highest on the earth's surface (29,028 ft), on the ill-defined Nepal–Tibet border. Named after Sir George Everest (1790–1866), former surveyor-general of India. Mallory and Irvine, members of the 1924 expedition, reached a height of about 28,000 ft but died there; a Swiss expedition of 1952 attained 28,215 ft. Finally, on the British expedition (1953) led by Sir John Hunt, Sir Edmund Hillary of New Zealand and the Sherpa Tensing reached the summit. The summit was later reached by a Swiss expedition (1956) and a US expedition (1963).

**Everett** (Massachusetts) USA. Residential and industrial town just N of Boston. Pop. (1960) 43,544. Manufactures pig-iron, machinery, chemicals, etc. Named after Edward Everett (1794–1865), an American statesman.

**Everett** (Washington) USA. Port on Puget Sound, at the mouth of the Snohomish R. 26 m. N of Seattle. Pop. (1960) 40,304. Exports timber, paper. Sawmilling. Manufactures wood pulp and paper etc.

**Everglades** USA. Sub-tropical marshy region in S Florida, a morass of saw-grass prairies extending in the S to mangrove swamps, with scattered clumps of trees (inc. cypress). Occupies most of Florida S of L. Okeechobee, covering over 4,000 sq. m. Partly drained and reclaimed; a large area was allotted to sugar-cane cultivation and cattle breeding. In the Everglades National Park (1947; area 1,719 sq. m.) the regional fauna and flora are preserved; the birds (inc. the pelican, egret, ibis, and spoonbill) are esp. noteworthy.

**Evesham** England. Municipal borough in Worcestershire, on the R. Avon 13 m. SE of Worcester. Pop. (1961) 12,608. In the fertile and beautiful Vale of Evesham, famous for fruit growing and market gardening. Market town. Fruit and vegetable canning, jam making. Remains of an 8th-cent. Benedictine abbey. At the Battle of Evesham (1265) Prince Edward defeated Simon de Montfort and the barons.

**Évora** Portugal. Ancient Ebora. Capital of the Évora district, in Alto Alentejo, 68 m. ESE of Lisbon. Pop. (1960) 24,144. Manufactures textiles. Trade in agricultural produce. Ancient and picturesque. Ruins of a Roman temple (the so-called temple of Diana). Archiepiscopal cathedral (12th/13th-cent., restored). Taken by the Moors 712; was not recaptured till 1166.

**Évreux** France. Prefecture of the Eure department, in the Iton R. valley 30 m. S of Rouen. Pop. (1968) 45,441. Market town. Manufactures metal goods, chemicals, etc. Much of the town (inc. the 12th/16th-cent. cathedral) damaged in the 2nd World War.

**Evritania (Euritania)** Greece. Mountainous *nome* in central Greece. Area 775 sq. m. Pop. (1961) 39,710. Cap. Karpenísion (pop. 3,445). Sheep and goats reared.

**Évros (Hevros)** Greece. *Nome* in E Thrace bordering on Bulgaria (N) and Turkey (E), and including the island of Samothrace. Area 1,618 sq. m. Pop. (1961) 157,901. Cap. Alexandroupolis. Produces wheat, tobacco, cotton. Fishing.

**Evros River** ◊ *Maritsa River*.

**Ewell** ◊ *Epsom and Ewell*.

**Exe, River** England. River 60 m. long rising on Exmoor and flowing generally SSE past Tiverton and Exeter to enter the English Channel by an estuary at Exmouth.

**Exeter** England. County borough, cathedral city, and county town of Devonshire, on the R. Exe 36 m. NE of Plymouth. Pop. (1961) 80,215. Railway junction. Commercial centre. Manufactures agricultural machinery, leather goods, etc. The famous cathedral (1270–1369), mainly in Decorated Gothic style but with Norman transeptal towers, was severely damaged, along with other buildings in the city, in air raids of the 2nd World War (1942), St James's Chapel being destroyed. Guildhall (14th/16th-cent.), one of the oldest municipal buildings in the country. Grammar school,

now housed in modern buildings, founded 1332. Seat of Exeter University (1955), founded (1922) as the University College of the Southwest. Birthplace of Sir Thomas Bodley, founder of the Bodleian Library (1545–1613), and Archbishop William Temple (1881–1944).

**Exmoor** England. High moorland in W Somerset and NE Devon, largely forest until the early 19th cent., now covered with heather, bracken, and grass, rising to 1,706 ft in Dunkery Beacon. Wild red deer and Exmoor ponies abound, and sheep are grazed. The Exe, Barle, and other rivers have picturesque valleys and are well known for trout fishing. Immortalized in R. D. Blackmore's *Lorna Doone*. Established as a National Park (area 265 sq. m.) in 1954.

**Exmouth** England. Urban district in Devon on the estuary of the R. Exe. Pop. (1961) 19,740. In a sheltered position, with a sandy beach and a mild climate. Resort. Fishing port. Sir Walter Raleigh (1552–1618) was born at Hayes Barton (4 m. NE).

**Exploits River** Canada. River 200 m. long in Newfoundland, rising in the SW and flowing generally NE through Red Indian L. and past Grand Falls (hydroelectric power station) to Notre Dame Bay on the NE coast.

**Extremadura** ◊ *Estremadura* (Spain).

**Eyre, Lake** Australia. Shallow salt lake in S Australia 400 m. N of Adelaide, 35 ft below sea level. Water only occasionally flows through many tributary channels to fill both the large N part (3,000 sq. m.) and the S part (450 sq. m.), and it is dry except during the rainy season. It was completely filled to depths of 7–13 ft, after exceptional rains, in 1890–91 and 1949–50. Named after E. J. Eyre (1815–1901), who discovered it (1840).

**Eyre (Eyre's) Peninsula** Australia. Triangular peninsula in S Australia projecting some 200 m. S between Spencer Gulf and the Great Australian Bight. The Middleback Range in the NE is rich in iron ore, mined at Iron Knob, Iron Monarch, and Iron Baron. Whyalla, in the E, has become a steel-producing, shipbuilding port, with irrigated dairy farming land near by. Main crops wheat, barley.

# F

**Faenza** Italy. Ancient Faventia. Town in Ravenna province, Emilia-Romagna, 29 m. SE of Bologna. Pop. (1961) 51,085. Important road and railway junction, on the ancient Aemilian Way. Noted since the Middle Ages for majolica pottery (or 'faience', from the French name of the town). Also manufactures furniture, textiles, etc. Cathedral (15th-cent.); famous museum of ceramics, rebuilt after the 2nd World War.

**Faeroe (Faroe) Islands** (Danish Faeröerne, 'Sheep Islands') Denmark. Group of 21 basalt islands (17 inhabited) in the N Atlantic, between Iceland and the Shetland Is. Total area 540 sq. m. Pop. (1966) 37,122. Cap. Thorshavn (on Strömö). Largest islands Strömö and Österö. All are rugged and have no native trees; on Österö the land rises to 2,900 ft. Main occupations sheep farming, fishing. Principal exports fresh, frozen, salted, and dried fish, chiefly cod. Passed from Norway to Denmark 1380. Have remained Danish, but were granted a separate legislature (*lagting*) in 1948.

**Faial** ♢ *Azores.*

**Fairbanks** USA. Town in Alaska 275 m. NNE of Anchorage. Pop. (1960) 13,311. N terminus of the Alaska Highway and the Alaska Railroad. Sawmilling, gold mining. Founded 1902, when gold was discovered in the neighbourhood. The University of Alaska (1922) is at College, 3 m. NW.

**Fairfield** USA. Industrial town in SW Connecticut, on Long Island Sound near Bridgeport. Pop. (1960) 46,183. Manufactures chemicals, motor-car accessories, etc. University (1942). Founded 1639.

**Fair Isle** Scotland. Isolated rocky island in the Shetlands, half way between the main group and the Orkneys. Area 6 sq. m. Pop. about 100. Noted for multi-coloured handmade knitwear. Bird-migration observatory. Fishing, sheep rearing. Since 1954 property of the National Trust for Scotland.

**Fairmont** USA. Coalmining and industrial town in W Virginia, on the Monongahela R. 110 m. NE of Charleston. Pop. (1960) 27,477. Manufactures glass, mining machinery, coal by-products, etc.

**Faiyum, El (Medinet el Faiyum, Medina)** United Arab Republic. Capital of El Faiyum governorate, 55 m. SW of Cairo. Pop. (1960) 102,000. Chief town in the fertile El Faiyum oasis, linked by rail and road with the Nile valley. Cotton ginning, spinning and weaving (cotton, wool), dyeing, tanning. Near-by (N) excavations have revealed the site of ancient Crocodilopolis (renamed Arsinoë by Ptolemy Philadelphus) where a sacred crocodile in the Lake of Moeris (Birket Qarun) was worshipped.

**Faizabad** India. Town in Uttar Pradesh, on the Gogra R. 80 m. E of Lucknow. Pop. (1961) 88,296. Railway junction. Sugar refining. Trade in sugar-cane, grain, oilseeds. Just E is the historic site of Ajodhya.

**Falaise** France. Town in the Calvados department on the Ante R. 23 m. SSE of Caen. Pop. (1968) 7,599. Livestock trade. Cheese making etc. The ruined castle of the dukes of Normandy, where William the Conqueror was born, stands on a cliff (*falaise*) above the town. Almost destroyed in the 2nd World War, during the Allied advance from Normandy (1944).

**Falémé River** ♢ *Senegal River.*

**Falkirk** Scotland. Large burgh, industrial town, and ancient market town in E Stirlingshire, on the Forth–Clyde Canal 10 m. SE of Stirling. Pop. (1961) 38,043. Centre of an iron-founding industry; the famous Carron ironworks is 2 m. to the NNW, producing light castings (stoves, grates, etc.) and other metalware. Other manufactures chemicals, beer, etc. At Westerglen (2 m. SW) is a BBC radio transmitter. The Wall of Antoninus ran through Falkirk. Scene of Edward I's defeat of Wallace (1298) and Prince Charles Edward's defeat of General Hawley (1746).

**Falkland Islands (Sp. Islas Malvinas)** S Atlantic Ocean. British crown colony in the S Atlantic, 300 m. E of the Strait of Magellan, consisting of two main islands, E Falkland and W Falkland, and many small islands. Area 4,700 sq. m. Pop. (1964) 2,132, of whom 1,074 live in Stanley, the chief town, on E Falkland. The main islands, separated by Falkland Sound, have many fiords and bays. They consist mainly of rocky moorland with peaty soils and few trees, the highest point being Mt Adam (2,315 ft) on W Falkland. Climate cool, windy, and bracing. Sheep farming is the only industry, the wool being exported to England; Stanley, the only important town, has a good harbour. Almost all the islanders are of British origin, half of them working and living on the sheep farms.

Visited by Capt. Davis (1592) and by Sir John Hawkins (1594); named (1690) by Capt. Strong. First colonized by the French (1764); passed to Spain; occupied by the British in 1832–3, after the expulsion of an Argentine garrison. Argentina still does not recognize British occupation, referring to the islands by their old Spanish name, Islas Malvinas. Far to the S are the Falkland Island Dependencies of ▷ *South Georgia* and ▷ *South Sandwich Islands*; in 1962 the former dependencies of the ▷ *South Shetland Islands*, ▷ *South Orkney Islands*, and ▷ *Graham Land* became the separate colony of British Antarctic Territory.

**Fall River** USA. Port, industrial and commercial town in SE Massachusetts at the mouth of the Taunton R. Pop. (1960) 99,942. Important centre of the cotton industry. Also manufactures rubber products, hats, clothing, etc. The name derives from the Quequechan or Fall R., which flows through the town.

**Falmouth** England. Municipal borough on the W shore of Carrick Roads (the estuary of the Fal and other rivers) in SW Cornwall. Pop. (1961) 15,427. Resort. Seaport. Important ship-repairing industry. Fishing (pilchards, oysters). At the entrance to the harbour are the 16th-cent. castles of Pendennis and St Mawes.

**Falster** Denmark. Island in the Baltic Sea, linked with Zealand (N) by a bridge across Storström Strait and with Lolland (W) by two bridges; with Lolland, forms the county of Maribo. Area 198 sq. m. Pop. 46,000. Chief town Nyköbing. Dairy and pig farming. Sugar-beet, fruit cultivated.

**Famagusta** (Gr. **Ammochostos**) Cyprus. Port in the E, on Famagusta Bay 3 m. S of ancient Salamis, on the site of ancient Arsinoë. Pop. (1967) 40,000 (almost one third Turkish). Became an important port of call during the Crusades and under Venetian rule. Declined under the Turks; ruined by earthquake 1735. Since the completion of the harbour (1906) and the construction of a major road to Nicosia, trade

has revived. Exports citrus fruits, carobs, potatoes. Manufactures footwear, clothing, etc. With its long sandy beaches, has become a popular seaside resort.

**Fanning Island** ▷ *Line Islands*.

**Fanö** Denmark. Island in the N Frisian Is., opposite Esbjerg. Area 22 sq. m. Pop. 2,750. Fishing industry. Holiday resorts.

**Fano** Italy. Ancient Fanum Fortunae. Adriatic seaport in Pesaro e Urbino province, The Marches, 7 m. SE of Pesaro. Pop. (1961) 41,033. Resort. Manufactures silk goods, shoes. Fishing. Has a triumphal arch of Augustus, the 15th-cent. Malatesta palace, and some noteworthy churches.

**Far East.** Term used rather loosely of E and SE Asia, but more strictly applied to regions along the Pacific seaboard of E Asia–E Siberia (USSR), China, Korea, and Japan, and possibly to include the Philippines, Indonesia, and Malaysia.

**Far Eastern Area** USSR. Former administrative division of E ▷ *Siberia*, dissolved in 1938 and divided into Khabarovsk and Primorye (Maritime) Territories; the capital was Khabarovsk.

**Fareham** England. Urban district in S Hampshire, on a creek in the NW corner of Portsmouth harbour, 6 m. NW of Portsmouth. Pop. (1961) 58,277. Market town. Manufactures earthenware, bricks. Engineering, boatbuilding, tanning. At Portchester, 3 m. ESE, is a ruined castle partly of Roman origin.

**Farewell, Cape** Greenland. Headland at the S tip of Egger Island; the southernmost point of Greenland, reaching a height of over 2,000 ft. Fringed by islets and rocks. Notorious for bad weather and heavy seas.

**Farewell, Cape** New Zealand. Most northerly point of the S Island. Lighthouse. Point of departure of Capt. Cook (April 1770) on his voyage of discovery along the E coastlands of Australia.

**Fargo** USA. Town in N Dakota, on the Red R. opposite Moorhead (Minnesota). Pop. (1960) 47,106. Largest town in the state. Manufactures agricultural machinery, food products, etc. Named after W. G. Fargo (1818–81) of Wells, Fargo, and Co., the organizer of the first extensive stagecoach system in N America.

**Faridpur** Pakistan. Town in E Pakistan 30 m. WSW of Dacca. Pop. (1961) 28,333. Trade in rice, jute, etc. Has the shrine of the Muslim saint, Farid Shah.

**Farnborough** England. Urban district in NE Hampshire 8 m. WNW of Guildford.

Pop. (1961) 31,437. Royal Aircraft Establishment, the largest aeronautical research centre in the UK. Military camps. In St Michael's (Roman Catholic) church Napoleon III, the Empress Eugénie (who had it built), and the Prince Imperial are buried.

**Farne Islands (The Staples)** England. Group of about 30 rocky islets off the coast of Northumberland, separated from it by the Fairway, a channel 1½ m. wide. Farne Island or Inner Farne, the largest, was the home of St Cuthbert, who died here (687). Longstone Island lighthouse was the scene of Grace Darling's heroic rescue of survivors from the *Forfarshire* (1838).

**Farnham** England. Urban district in Surrey, on the R. Wey 10 m. WSW of Guildford. Pop. (1961) 26,927. Market town. Just N is the castle, formerly the palace of the bishops of Winchester. Also near by is Moor Park, where Swift met 'Stella'. Birthplace and burial-place of William Cobbett (1763–1835).

**Farnworth** England. Municipal borough in S Lancashire 3 m. SE of Bolton. Pop. (1961) 27,474. Cotton and rayon mills, bleaching and dyeing works; engineering.

**Faro** Portugal. Capital of the Algarve province, on the S coast near Cape Santa Maria. Pop. (1960) 18,909. Port, sheltered by islands. Exports wine, dried figs, almonds, cork. Fishing (sardine, tunny). Cork processing, basket making. Airport, with fast developing tourist traffic. Recovered from the Moors 1249. Burned by the English 1596. Severely damaged by earthquake 1755.

**Faroe Islands** ◊ *Faeroe Islands*.

**Farrukhabad** India. Town in Uttar Pradesh, near the Ganges R. 80 m. NW of Kanpur. Pop. (1961) 94,591. Railway junction. Trade in grain, sugar-cane, oilseeds, etc. Manufactures cotton and metal goods. Sugar refining. Forms a joint municipality with neighbouring Fatehgarh.

**Fars** Iran. Ancient Persis. Province in the S, on the Persian Gulf. Area 75,000 sq. m. Pop. 1,600,000. Cap. Shiraz. Chief port Bushire. The coastal lowlands are hot and humid; inland the uplands are drier, with cold winters. Cereals, cotton, opium, dates, etc. cultivated. Ancient Persis, from which the Persians created their empire, contained the cities of Persepolis and Pasargadae.

**Fasher, El** Sudan. Capital of the Darfur province, 500 m. WSW of Khartoum. Pop.

(1964) 30,000. Caravan centre. Trades chiefly in gum arabic.

**Fashoda** ◊ *Kodok*.

**Fatehgarh** ◊ *Farrukhabad*.

**Fatehpur** India. Town in Uttar Pradesh, 47 m. SE of Kanpur. Pop. (1961) 28,323. Trade in cereals, oilseeds.

**Fatshan (Namhoi)** China. Town in Kwangtung province 11 m. SW of Kwangchow (Canton). Pop. 123,000. Industrial and commercial centre. Manufactures iron and steel, textiles (esp. silk), matches, porcelain, etc.

**Faversham** England. Municipal borough in N Kent, on a creek off the Swale 8 m. WNW of Canterbury. Pop. (1961) 12,983. Market town. Oyster fisheries. Fruit and vegetable canning, brewing, brickmaking. Early a 'Member' of the Cinque Port of Dover. King Stephen, his wife Matilda, and their son are buried in the now ruined Cluniac abbey founded by the king.

**Fayal** ◊ *Azores*.

**Fayetteville** USA. Formerly Campbelltown. Industrial town in N Carolina on the Cape Fear R. 50 m. SSW of Raleigh. Pop. (1960) 47,106. Manufactures textiles, furniture, etc. Food processing, sawmilling. Trade in cotton, tobacco, etc. Originally called Campbelltown by its Scottish founders (1739). Incorporated 1784 and named after Lafayette.

**Fear, Cape** USA. The southernmost point of Smith Island, and of N Carolina, in the Atlantic near the mouth of the Cape Fear R. The dangerous Frying-pan Shoals extend to the S and SE.

**Fécamp** France. Seaside resort and fishing port in the Seine Maritime department on the English Channel. Pop. (1968) 21,745. Noted for the Bénédictine liqueur, first prepared from local herbs by monks in the 16th cent. Fish curing, boatbuilding. Manufactures fishing nets, cod-liver oil, etc.

**Federal German Republic** ◊ *Germany*.

**Felixstowe** England. Urban district in E Suffolk, 10 m. SE of Ipswich. Pop. (1961) 17,220. Seaside resort. Port. Main industry tourism. Flour milling etc. Named after St Felix, first bishop of Dunwich.

**Felling** England. Urban district in NE Durham, just E of Gateshead. Pop. (1961) 36,130. Coalmining, engineering. Manufactures chemicals, paint, etc.

**Feltham** England. Former urban district in Middlesex 12 m. WSW of London; from 1965 part of the Greater London borough of Hounslow. Pop. (1961) 51,041. Residential and industrial. Manufactures aircraft and automobile parts, electrical equipment, etc. Kempton Park racecourse is in the district.

**Fenit** ◊ *Tralee.*

**Fens** England. Flat low-lying area in E England, W and S of the Wash, in the counties of Lincolnshire, Huntingdonshire, Cambridgeshire, and Norfolk; 70–75 m. N–S and about 35 m. E–W at its greatest width. Once formed an extensive bay of the North Sea, which was gradually silted up by the Witham, Welland, Nene, and Great Ouse rivers, leaving the Wash as the final remnant. From Roman times attempts at reclamation were made, but the Fens remained largely a region of marsh and swamp (apart from 'islands' of higher and firmer ground) until the 17th cent. when Cornelius Vermuyden introduced Dutch methods (1621), with the help of the Earl of Bedford (after whom the tract known as the Bedford Level was named). The work continued in sections until the 19th cent. Today little of the original Fens remains, apart from Wicken Fen, NE of Cambridge. The soil of the area (once known for its wildfowl and freshwater fish), now crisscrossed with watercourses and drainage canals, has proved extraordinarily fertile, and produces cereals, sugar-beet, fruit, vegetables, bulbs, etc. Remains of the monasteries built on the once isolated 'islands' may still be seen, e.g. at Crowland and Kirkstead.

**Feodosiya** USSR. Ancient Theodosia. Black Sea port and resort in SE Crimea (RSFSR). Pop. (1963) 54,000. Main export wheat. Fishing. Flour milling, brewing, fish canning, etc. Many sanatoria, rest homes, etc. Founded in the 6th cent. B.C. by Greeks from Miletus. Genoese (as Kaffa) from 1265. Passed to the Turks (1475) and to Russia (1774).

**Fergana (Ferghana)** USSR. 1. Valley in the Uzbek and Kirghiz SSRs N of the Pamirs; also region of the Uzbek SSR. Almost completely hemmed in by lofty mountains, with the Fergana and Chatkal ranges to the N and the Alai Mountains to the S; easily accessible only from the W. Drained by the Syr Darya and other mountain streams, extensively used for irrigation. In 1939 irrigation was improved by the construction of the Fergana Canal (170 m.), and subsequently by other canals; important crops of cotton, alfalfa, and grapes are grown. Chief towns Andizhan, Namangan, Ko-

kand. At various periods it has been under Persian, Arab, Mongol, and Uzbek domination.
2. Town in the Fergana region, 145 m. ESE of Tashkent, in the Uzbek SSR. Pop. 111,000. Manufactures cotton goods and clothing. Founded by the Russians as Novy Margelan in 1876; later called Skobelev and renamed Fergana after the Revolution.

**Fermanagh** Northern Ireland. County in SW Ulster; hilly in the NE and SW, rising to 2,188 ft in Cuilcagh on the SW border, the central area being occupied by Upper and Lower Lough Erne and the R. Erne. Area 715 sq. m. Pop. (1961) 51,613. County town Enniskillen. Mainly pastoral and agricultural. Potatoes cultivated. Cattle raised.

**Fermoy** Irish Republic. Market town in Co. Cork, on the R. Blackwater 19 m. NE of Cork. Pop. (1966) 3,207. Roman Catholic cathedral. Founded 1789 by a Scotsman. Became an important British garrison town.

**Fernando de Noronha** Brazil. Island in the S Atlantic, 230 m. NE of Cape São Roque on the 'shoulder' of Brazil; with neighbouring islands, forms the federal territory of Fernando de Noronha. Area 10 sq. m. Pop. (1960) 1,389. Has served as a penal colony since the 18th cent.

**Fernando Póo (Fernando Po)** Equatorial Guinea. Volcanic island in the Bight of Biafra, 20 m. from the Cameroun coast. Area 779 sq. m. Pop. (1960) 61,197. Cap. Santa Isabel (pop. 19,689). Rises to 9,351 ft in Santa Isabel Peak. Hot, humid climate; dense vegetation. Chief product and export cacao. Named after Fernão do Po, the Portuguese discoverer (1472). Ceded by Portugal (with Annobón island) to Spain 1778. Used by the British as a base for the suppression of the slave trade 1827–44, and then reverted to Spain.

**Ferozepore** India. Town in Punjab 50 m. SSW of Amritsar near the Pakistan frontier. Pop. (1961) 97,932. Cotton ginning. Trade in grain, cotton. Strategically important in the mid 19th cent. under British rule.

**Ferrara** Italy. Capital of Ferrara province, in Emilia-Romagna, 27 m. NNE of Bologna. Pop. (1968) 157,217. Manufactures fertilizers, plastics, beet sugar, macaroni, etc. Trade in grain, fruit, wine. The outstanding building is the brick moated castle of the house of Este (14th/15th-cent.); others include the cathedral, dating from the 12th cent., the university (1391), and several palaces, among them the Palazzo dei Diamanti, the Palazzo Schifanoia, and the Palazzo di Ludovico il Moro. Became the seat of the Este family in the 13th cent. and flourished as a centre of literature and the arts, with a population of 100,000. Declined after 1598 on being incorporated into the Papal States. Birthplace of Savonarola (1452–98) and Guarini (1537–1612).

**Ferrol, El** ◊ *El Ferrol del Caudillo*.

**Festiniog** ◊ *Ffestiniog*.

**Fez (Fès)** Morocco. Traditional northern capital, 110 m. E of Rabat; chief religious centre. Pop. (1964) 249,450. Two important mosques: the Karueein (largest in Africa), which is also a university, and that of Muley Idris, who founded Fez (A.D. 808). Pilgrimages were made to Fez instead of Mecca in the 10th cent. Reached the peak of its fame in the 14th cent. Gave its name to the man's cap of red felt which became the prevalent head-dress throughout the Ottoman Empire and is still much worn by Muslims. Centre of Moroccan handicrafts, e.g. carpets, Morocco leather goods, musical instruments. Textile industry, soap manufacture.

**Fezzan** Libya. Ancient Phazania. Formerly (until 1963) a province in the Sahara, S of Tripolitania. Area 213,000 sq. m. Pop. (1960) 65,000. Cap. Sebha (pop. 7,000). Mainly rocky desert (hammada) and sandy desert (erg); scattered oases. Sebha, Murzuk, Ghadames, and other centres of population are all oasis towns. In Roman times the area was crossed by several trans-Saharan caravan routes. Lost importance with the decline of the slave trade. Seized by Italy 1911. Captured by French forces during the 2nd World War (1943); under French military control until it became part of Libya, by UN resolution, in 1951.

**Ffestiniog (Festiniog, Llan Ffestiniog)** Wales. Urban district in Merionethshire 10 m. NE of Harlech, in a picturesque valley. Pop. (1961) 6,677. Tourist centre. Includes the slate-quarrying centre of Blaenau Ffestiniog, which has the world's largest pumped storage hydroelectric station (opened 1963). Near by are the well-known Cynfal Falls.

**FGR (Federal German Republic)** ◊ *Germany*.

**Fianarantsoa** Malagasy. Capital of Fianarantsoa province, 180 m. SSW of Tananarive at a height of 4,000 ft. Pop. (1962) 36,189. Market for cattle and agricultural produce. Meat canning, rice processing, etc. Linked by rail (1936) with the port of Manakara.

**Fichtelgebirge** Czechoslovakia/Federal German Republic. Mountain group on the W German-Czechoslovak frontier, from which radiate the Erzgebirge (NE), the Bohemian Forest (SE), the Franconian Jura (SW), and the Franconian and Thuringian Forests (NW). Partly covered with spruce forests. Rises to 3,448 ft in the Schneeberg.

**Fiesole** Italy. Ancient Faesulae. Town in Firenze province, Tuscany, on a hill (968 ft) overlooking the Arno R. Pop. (1961) 12,520. Now mainly a residential suburb 4 m. NE of Florence. Manufactures straw hats. An Etruscan and then a Roman town; has remains of the Etruscan town wall, a Roman theatre and baths, and an 11th-cent. (restored) Romanesque cathedral. Fra Angelico (1387–1455) lived and worked here.

**Fife** Scotland. Peninsular county between the Firths of Tay and Forth, bounded on the E by the North Sea. Area 505 sq. m. Pop. (1961) 320,541. County town Cupar. Hilly in the W, rising to 1,713 ft in W Lomond. Cultivated valleys and coastal plains. Cereals grown. Coal mined, limestone quarried. Various industries in the main towns, Cupar, Kirkcaldy, Dunfermline. Seaside resorts include St Andrews and Crail.

**Fiji Islands** SW Pacific Ocean.* British colony: Melanesian group of about 320 islands, about 100 of which are inhabited. Area 7,055 sq. m. Pop. (1967) 483,247. Cap. and chief seaport Suva (Viti Levu). The largest islands are Viti Levu (4,010 sq. m.) and Vanua Levu (2,137 sq. m.), others being Taveuni and Kandavu. These are mountainous, rising to about 4,500 ft, with dense forests on windward slopes and grass and pandanus in sheltered areas. Soils are fertile and support sugar-cane, taro, rice, coconuts, pineapples, bananas, cotton. Leading exports are sugar, coconut oil, gold, copra, bananas. Discovered by Tasman (1643) and visited by Capt. Cook (1774). Since 1874 the islands, with Rotuma (300 m. to the NW), have been a British Crown Colony, administered from Suva by a governor with an executive council and a legislative council which includes Fijians and Indians. The Indians, most of whom are Hindus, number about 242,000, Melanesian Fijians some 201,000, the remainder being Polynesians, Europeans, and Chinese.

The Indians are mostly descendants of men brought to work on the sugar plantations in the 19th cent. The Fijians were chiefly farmers and fishermen, as they are today, though some have worked in the gold-mines. The islands are linked by sea and air; Nadi (Viti Levu) is a major airport on the North America–Australasia routes.

**Filey** England. Urban district in the E Riding of Yorkshire, 7 m. SE of Scarborough on Filey Bay. Pop. (1961) 4,705. Seaside resort, with a sandy beach extending to the rocky headland of Filey Brigg.

**Finchley** England. Former municipal borough in Middlesex; from 1965 part of the Greater London borough of Barnet. Pop. (1961) 69,311. Finchley Common, once a haunt of highwaymen, has virtually disappeared.

**Findhorn River** Scotland. River 62 m. long, rising in the Monadhliath Mountains, flowing NE, and entering the Moray Firth near the village of Findhorn.

**Findlay** USA. Industrial town in Ohio on the Blanchard R. 42 m. S of Toledo. Pop. (1960) 30,344. Manufactures agricultural machinery, tyres, beet sugar, etc. Developed after the discovery of natural gas (1836).

**Fingal's Cave** ◊ *Staffa*.

**Finger Lakes** USA. Group of lakes in New York state, in the area immediately W and SW of Syracuse; so called because of their length and narrowness. The principal lakes in the group are the following (W–E): Honeoye, Canandaigua, Keuka, Seneca (the largest, 67 sq. m.), Cayuga (the longest, 38 m.), Owasco, Skaneateles, Otisco. Several holiday resorts in the region, because of its scenic beauty.

**Finistère** France. Department formed from the W part of Brittany; bounded by the English Channel (N), the Bay of Biscay (S), and the Atlantic Ocean (W). Area 2,729 sq. m. Pop. (1968) 768,929. Prefecture Quimper. The coast is rugged and indented. The interior is crossed by the granitic Montagnes d'Arrée (rising to 1,283 ft) and the Montagnes Noires (1,070 ft). Much of the land consists of heath, but cereals, cider apples, and early vegetables are grown. Fishing (sardines) important along the coast. Many tourists are attracted by such picturesque fishing ports as Douarnenez and Concarneau. Chief towns Quimper, the port and naval base of Brest, and Morlaix.

**Finisterre, Cape** Spain. Headland in the Coruña province, in the NW. Usually considered the westernmost point of the Spanish mainland.

**Finland (Suomi, Suomen Tasavalta).** Republic in NE Europe. Area 130,120 sq. m. Pop. (1968) 4,676,000 (92 per cent Finnish-speaking, 7 per cent Swedish-speaking). Cap. Helsinki. Rel. mainly Lutheran.

Bounded by Norway (N), the USSR (E), the Gulf of Finland (S), and the Gulf of Bothnia (W). A land of forests and lakes, about two thirds covered with forests; timber and wood products form the mainstay of the economy. Administratively divided into 12 provinces (Swedish names in brackets): Uusimaa (Nyland); Turku-Pori (Åbo-Björneborg); Ahvenanmaa (Åland); Häme (Tavastehus); Kymi (Kymmene); Mikkeli (St Michel); Kuopio; Pohjois-Karjala (Norra Karelen); Keski-Suomi (Mellersta Finland); Vaasa (Vasa); Oulu (Uleåborg); Lappi (Lappland).

TOPOGRAPHY, CLIMATE. Included in Finland is Ahvenanmaa (Åland Is., Swedish-speaking population) at the entrance to the Gulf of Bothnia. Much of Lapland (N) lies within the Arctic Circle: here Mt Haltia rises to 4,344 ft. The centre and S are mainly low-lying. There are thousands of lakes in the S half; the largest are L. Saimaa and L. Päijänne. The reconstructed Saimaa Canal, linking the L. Saimaa region with the Gulf of Finland, but mainly in Soviet territory, was inaugurated 1968. L. Oulu and L. Inari are farther N. The chief rivers are the Torne, the Kemi, and the Oulu, all flowing into the Gulf of Bothnia. Lakes, rivers, and canals (joining the lakes) are widely used for transport, esp. by the lumbering industry. Winters, esp. inland, are long and severe; summers are short and warm.

RESOURCES, PEOPLE, *etc.* In the N the forest gradually merges into tundra, a region where the Lapps gain a livelihood by reindeer raising and fishing. Logs from the mainly coniferous forests are floated down the rivers and canals in summer; the rivers also provide hydroelectric power. Lumbering is a leading occupation; many workers are employed in the manufacture of wood products, e.g. wood pulp, cellulose, plywood, paper, furniture. Timber, wood pulp, paper, and cardboard make up about three quarters of the exports. Agriculture is limited to the more fertile parts of the S; oats, rye, barley, and potatoes are grown; dairy farming is important. Helsinki, chief seaport and capital, is icebound in winter (like the other ports) but the harbour is usually kept open by icebreakers. Tampere and Turku are the only other towns with more than 100,000 inhabitants. Finnish literature includes the *Kalevala*, one of the world's outstanding epics, passed on orally for centuries and finally written down in the 19th cent. The republic is governed by a single-chamber House of Representatives, chosen for 4 years by direct and proportional election; the President is elected for 6 years.

HISTORY. Occupied by Finno-Ugrian tribes, who drove the Lapps to the N; conquered and converted to Christianity by Eric IX of Sweden in the 12th cent. Disputed for hundreds of years between Sweden and Russia. Became a grand duchy in the 16th cent. The Swedish language and culture spread, and a Diet was established. Ceded to Russia 1809; still enjoyed a considerable measure of autonomy, but by the early 20th cent. severe repression had followed. After the Russian Revolution (1917) independence was proclaimed. In 1939 Soviet troops invaded Finland, and for a time the Finns were allied with the Germans. By the peace treaty of 1940 Finland ceded the Karelian Isthmus, Viipuri (Vyborg), and the Finnish shores of L. Ladoga to the USSR; in 1944 the Petsamo (Pechenga) area was added. The Porkkala headland was also leased to the USSR, as a military base; this was returned to Finland in 1956.

**Finland, Gulf of.** E arm of the Baltic Sea, between Finland (N) and the USSR (E and S), 250 m. long and 40–80 m. wide. Shallow, and of low salinity. Frozen for 4–6 months annually. On the shores are the seaports of Helsinki and Kota in Finland and Vyborg, Leningrad, and Tallinn in the USSR.

**Finnart** Scotland. Oil terminal in Dunbartonshire, on the E shore of Loch Long 2 m. N of Garelochhead. Linked by 57 m. pipeline with Grangemouth (refinery). Enlarged to become the first oil terminal in Europe able to handle tankers of 100,000 tons (opened 1959).

**Finsbury** England. Former metropolitan borough of London, N of the Thames, bordering on the City (S); from 1965 part of the Greater London borough of Islington. Pop. (1961) 32,989 (increasing to about 150,000 by day). Residential, commercial, and industrial district. In the Bunhill

Fields cemetery Bunyan, Defoe, and William Blake are buried; Milton died in Bunhill Row. Also contains Sadler's Wells Theatre, John Wesley's Chapel, and the Mount Pleasant parcel-sorting office.

**Finsteraarhorn** Switzerland. Highest peak in the Bernese Oberland (14,026 ft), 7 m. SSE of Grindelwald on the border of the Bern and Valais cantons.

**Fiordland** ◊ *Otago*.

**Firenze** ◊ *Florence*.

**Firozabad** India. Town in Uttar Pradesh 25 m. E of Agra. Pop. (1961) 98,611. Leading centre for the manufacture of glass bangles. Trade in grain, oilseeds, etc.

**Fishguard and Goodwick** Wales. Urban district in N Pembrokeshire, on Fishguard Bay (Irish Sea). Pop. (1961) 4,898. Railway terminus; steamer services to Cork and Rosslare (Irish Republic). Also fishing port.

**Fitchburg** USA. Industrial town in Massachusetts on the Nashua R. 23 m. N of Worcester. Pop. (1960) 43,021. Manufactures machinery, paper, saws, footwear, etc.

**Fitzroy River** Australia. 1. River in Queensland, 170 m. long, formed from the Dawson and Mackenzie rivers and other headstreams and flowing generally E past Rockhampton to Keppel Bay.
2. River in Western Australia, 350 m. long, rising near the E end of the King Leopold Range and flowing generally SW and NW to King Sound. Swollen after the summer rains; partly dried up in the dry season.

**Fiume** ◊ *Rijeka*.

**Flamborough Head** England. High chalk headland on the coast of the E Riding of Yorkshire, at the N end of Bridlington Bay. Lighthouse. Many sea birds breed on the cliffs.

**Flanders (Fr. Flandre, Flemish Vlaanderen)** Belgium/France. Former county in the SW of the Low Countries, varying considerably in size throughout its history; now divided between Belgium and France. French Flanders approximates to the ◊ *Nord* department. Belgian Flanders comprises the two westernmost provinces: W Flanders (area 1,248 sq. m.; pop. (1968) 1,042,586; cap. Bruges) and E Flanders (area 1,147 sq. m.; pop. (1968) 1,305,717, cap. Ghent). The two provinces form Belgium's chief industrial region, esp. for coalmining and the manufacture of iron and steel and other metals and textiles. ◊ *Netherlands*.

**Fleet River** England. River formed by the

union of two streams rising in Hampstead and Highgate, flowing S, and joining the Thames near Blackfriars Bridge, London. Barges used it in the Middle Ages, but it was later choked by mud. It was built over and is now a sewer under Farringdon Street. The Fleet Prison stood on the E bank.

**Fleetwood** England. Municipal borough in Lancashire, at the SW end of Morecambe Bay and at the mouth of the R. Wyre. Pop. (1961) 27,760. Fishing port. Resort. Steamer service to the Isle of Man. Rossall school is 2½ m. SW. Named after the founder, Sir Peter Fleetwood (1801–66).

**Flensburg** Federal German Republic. Seaport in Schleswig-Holstein, near the Danish frontier 44 m. NW of Kiel at the head of the Flensburg Fiord. Pop. (1963) 97,000. Fish curing, shipbuilding, metal working, etc. Probably founded in the 12th cent. Passed from Denmark to Prussia 1864.

**Flinders Chase** ◊ *Kangaroo Island.*

**Flinders Island** Australia. Largest island in the Furneaux Group, in the Bass Strait off the NE coast of Tasmania. Area 802 sq. m. Pop. 900. Chief settlement Whitemark.

**Flinders Range** Australia. Mountains in S Australia extending N between L. Torrens and L. Frome, rising to 3,822 ft in St Mary Peak. Some copper, lead, and other minerals yielded in small quantity; uranium found at Mt Painter and elsewhere, but overshadowed by production in N Australia.

**Flinders River** Australia. River 520 m. long, in Queensland, rising in the E highlands 140 m. WSW of Townsville, flowing W and N, and entering the Gulf of Carpentaria. Named after Matthew Flinders (1774–1814), the English navigator who explored the coasts of Australia.

**Flin Flon** Canada. Town in Manitoba near the Saskatchewan border 390 m. NNW of Winnipeg. Pop. (1966) 10,201. Mining and smelting centre, producing copper, zinc, gold. Serious mining began in 1927. Incorporated 1946.

**Flint** USA. Industrial town in Michigan on the Flint R. 58 m. NW of Detroit. Pop. (1960) 196,940. Chiefly important for the motor-car industry; manufactures finished vehicles as well as bodies and parts. Manufacture of carts and carriages (important in the late 19th cent.) was followed by the motor-car industry *c.* 1904, when it was already popularly known as the 'vehicle city'.

**Flint** Wales. Municipal borough in Flintshire, on the Dee estuary 11 m. WNW of Chester. Pop. (1961) 13,690. Coalmining. Manufactures rayon, paper. Ruins of a 13th-cent. castle.

**Flintshire** Wales. County bordering on the Irish Sea and the Dee estuary, with a separate portion (SE) surrounded by Cheshire, Denbighshire, and Shropshire. Area 256 sq. m. Pop. (1961) 149,888. County town Mold. Drained by the Dee and the Clwyd rivers; the Clwydian Hills lie between them, along the Denbighshire border. Coalmining. Steel milling etc. Chief towns Mold, Flint, St Asaph, and the seaside resorts of Rhyl and Prestatyn.

**Flodden** England. Hill in Northumberland 3 m. ESE of Coldstream. Famous as the scene of the Battle of Flodden Field (which surrounds it), when James IV of Scotland was defeated and killed by the English under the Earl of Surrey (1513).

**Florence** (Italian **Firenze**) Italy. Ancient Florentia. Capital of the Firenze province in Tuscany, on both banks of the Arno R. near where it emerges from the Apennines. Pop. (1968) 455,081. Railway junction, linked with Bologna by a tunnel through the Apennines. Engineering, food processing. Manufactures chemicals, textiles, pottery, furniture, leather goods, etc. Trade in wine, olive oil, etc. Also considerable tourist industry, but best known as one of the world's great art centres, rich in works of the Italian Renaissance by such masters as Michelangelo, Leonardo da Vinci, Raphael, Cellini. Near the great Gothic cathedral of Santa Maria del Fiore (13th/15th-cent.) are the campanile by Giotto, possibly the most beautiful in the world, and the baptistery of San Giovanni, with its three famous bronze doors. The Church of Santa Croce has frescoes by Giotto; that of San Lorenzo has Michelangelo's tombs of the Medici.

Among the many palaces are the Palazzo della Signoria (the city hall), near which is the Loggia, with Cellini's bronze masterpiece, *Perseus*; the Palazzo degli Uffizi, with the Uffizi gallery, housing Italy's most important collection of paintings; the Palazzo Pitti, now an art gallery, and the Palazzo Strozzi, both of the 15th cent. Also has the Italian National Library, and several learned institutions, including the Accademia delle Belle Arti and the Accademia della Crusca. University (1924). The beautiful Boboli Gardens were designed in the 16th cent.

An early Roman colony, as Florentia ('City of Flowers'). In the 13th cent. witnessed the bitter rivalry between the Guelphs and Ghibellines (the papal and imperial factions). Suffered severely from famine and plague in the 14th cent. but became the centre of a powerful republic, largely by waging war on its neighbours, and grew commercially prosperous. Its artistic reputation was enhanced by the house of Medici, which ruled, with interruptions, for 3 centuries (1434–1737). Then followed a period under Austria, which lasted (again with breaks) till 1859, when the city was united with Italy. Capital of Italy 1865–70. Many of the historic buildings were damaged during the 2nd World War; much of the medieval section was destroyed by the Germans as they retreated. When the Arno burst its banks and flooded the city in 1966, many buildings and art treasures suffered severely, the damage being estimated at 100,000 million lire; 112 lives were lost in the flood disaster, which was considered the worst in Italy's recorded history. Birthplace of Dante (1265–1321), the greatest of Italian poets.

**Florence** USA. Industrial town in Alabama on the Tennessee R. 100 m. NNW of Birmingham. Pop. (1960) 31,649. Meat packing. Manufactures textiles etc. Power derived from the Wilson Dam 4 m. upstream. Developed industrially with the establishment of the Tennessee Valley Authority (TVA).

**Flores** Indonesia. One of the Lesser Sunda Is., with the Flores Sea to the N and the Sawu Sea to the S. Area 6,622 sq. m. Pop. 803,000. Chief town and port Ende. Mountainous, with several active volcanoes; interior heavily forested and little explored. Exports copra.

**Flores** Portugal. Westernmost island of the Azores, in the Atlantic Ocean. Area 55 sq. m. Pop. (1960) 6,617. Chief town Santa Cruz. Rises to over 3,000 ft. Noted for flowers (hence the name). Hot springs. Off Flores took place the famous battle between a Spanish fleet and Sir Richard Grenville in the *Revenge* (1591).

**Florianópolis** Brazil. Formerly Desterro. Capital of the Santa Catarina state 310 m. SSW of São Paulo, on Santa Catarina island, connected to the mainland by a long suspension bridge. Pop. (1960) 74,323. Seaport, with an excellent harbour. Ex-

ports sugar, tobacco, fruit, etc. Founded 1700. Renamed after President Floriano Peixoto 1893.

**Florida** USA. State in the extreme SE, mainly peninsular, between the Atlantic and the Gulf of Mexico; separated from Cuba by the Florida Strait. Area 58,560 sq. m. Pop. (1970) 6,671,162. Cap. Tallahassee. Admitted to the Union in 1845 as the 27th state; popularly known as the 'Peninsular' or 'Everglade' state. Largely swampy and low-lying, with many lakes, the largest being L. Okeechobee in the S. Climate humid and sub-tropical, with hot rainy summers and occasional hurricanes in the autumn. Pines and cypresses grow in profusion in the Everglades and the Big Cypress Swamp. Contains famous Atlantic resorts, e.g. Palm Beach, Miami, Daytona Beach. Citrus fruits produced in large quantities. Other crops maize, sugar-cane, tobacco. Market gardening and fishing (sponges) important. Chief mineral phosphates. Industries include food processing and the manufacture of cigars and wood products. Largest cities Miami, Tampa, Jacksonville. First explored by the Spaniards 1513. Remained a Spanish possession – apart from 20 years under British control (1763–83) – until 1821, when it was purchased by the USA.

**Florida Keys** USA. A chain of small islands over 100 m. long extending WSW in a curve from Biscayne Bay, in S Florida, towards the Gulf of Mexico. The largest islands are Key Largo and Key West (the westernmost); the city of Key West is the southernmost in the USA. Others in the group (which is separated from Cuba by the Florida Strait) are Long Key, Big Pine Key, Sugarloaf Key. Mainly covered with small trees and shrubs. Limes cultivated. Mainly noted as resorts for big-game fishing. The islands are linked with one another and with the mainland by the Overseas Highway, replacing the railway destroyed in the hurricane of 1935.

**Flórina** Greece. 1. Sparsely populated mountainous *nome* in Macedonia, bordering on Yugoslavia (N) and Albania (W). Area 718 sq. m. Pop. (1961) 67,238. Main occupations stock rearing, cultivation of cereals.

2. Capital of Flórina *nome*, near the frontier of Yugoslavia (to which it is connected by the Monastir Gap), 83 m. WNW of Thessaloniki. Pop. (1961) 12,270. Trade in cereals, fruit, livestock.

**Florissant** USA. Formerly (1920–40) St Ferdinand. Residential town in Missouri, near the Missouri R. 13 m. NNW of St Louis. Pop. (1960) 38,166, having grown rapidly (3,737 in 1950).

**Flushing** (Dutch **Vlissingen**) Netherlands. Seaport and resort in Zeeland province, on the S coast of Walcheren Island at the mouth of the W Scheldt. Pop. (1968) 39,061. Oil and coal bunkering. Shipbuilding, engineering, fishing. Closely associated with the Dutch struggle for independence; the first Dutch city to throw off Spanish rule (1572). Birthplace of Admiral de Ruyter (1607–76).

**Fly River** New Guinea. River 800 m. long, rising in the Victor Emmanuel Mountains in the centre and flowing generally SE to the Gulf of Papua. Navigable for over 500 m. but commercially unimportant.

**Focşani** Rumania. Capital of the Vrancea district, Moldavia, 105 m. NE of Bucharest. Pop. (1968) 36,644. Trade in cereals, wine. Manufactures soap, leather. Scene of the defeat of the Turks by Austrian and Russian armies (1789).

**Foggia** Italy. Capital of Foggia province, in the middle of the Apulian plain, 75 m. WNW of Bari. Pop. (1968) 136,293. Important trade in wheat. Flour milling, cheese making; produces macaroni, olive oil. Cathedral (12th-cent.); gateway to the palace of the Emperor Frederick II.

**Fokis** ▷ *Phocis*.

**Foligno** Italy. Town in Perugia province in Umbria, 20 m. SE of Perugia. Pop. (1961) 48,069. Railway junction. Sugar refining. Manufactures textiles, paper, etc. Cathedral (12th/13th-cent.). The first edition of Dante's *Divina Commedia* was printed at the Palazzo Orfini (1472).

**Folkestone** England. Municipal borough in SE Kent, 7 m. WSW of Dover. Pop. (1961) 44,129. At the foot of chalk hills rising to over 500 ft, with the broad promenade of the Leas along its cliffs. Seaside resort. Important packet station, with services to Boulogne. Also a fishing port. A 'limb' or member of the Cinque Ports. Birthplace of William Harvey (1578–1657), discoverer of the circulation of the blood.

**Fond du Lac** USA. Industrial town in Wisconsin, at the S end of L. Winnebago (hence the name), 58 m. NNW of Milwaukee. Pop. (1960) 32,719. Manufactures machine tools, refrigerators, textiles, etc. Also a holiday resort with lake boating

attractions. A French trading post in 1785; first permanently settled 1836.

**Fontainebleau** France. Town in the Seine-et-Marne department near the Seine R. 36 m. SSE of Paris, in the Forest of Fontainebleau. Pop. (1968) 19,803. Popular resort. Furniture industry. A residence of the French kings; the most famous building is the magnificent palace, built largely by Francis I, where Napoleon signed his abdication (1814). The forest (66 sq. m.), one of the most beautiful in France, has been the inspiration of many artists (▷ *Barbizon*).

**Fontenoy** Belgium. Village in the Hainaut province, 4 m. SE of Tournai. Scene of the defeat (1745) of the British and their Dutch and Austrian allies (under the Duke of Cumberland) by French forces (under Marshal Saxe).

**Foochow** China. Formerly Minhow. Capital of Fukien province, on the Min-kiang 35 m. from its mouth. Pop. 616,000. Port. Exports timber, bamboo shoots, sugarcane, etc. Manufactures machinery, chemicals, textiles, paper, etc. It was made one of the original five treaty ports 1842, and was linked by two bridges with the foreign settlement on Nantai island. Became important in the tea trade; declined with decreasing tea and lacquerware exports and river silting.

**Fordlandia** ▷ *Tapajós River*.

**Foreland Point** England. Headland on the N coast of Devon, 2 m. ENE of Lynmouth. ▷ *North Foreland*.

**Forest Hills** USA. Residential district of Queens borough, New York city, on Long Island. Chiefly noted for the West Side Tennis Club, where the US national lawn tennis championships and international matches are held.

**Forfar** Scotland. County town of Angus, an ancient royal burgh 13 m. NNE of Dundee. Pop. (1961) 10,252. Market town. Jute, linen, and rayon industries. The castle, residence of early Scottish kings, was destroyed (1307) by Robert Bruce; the site is marked by the town cross.

**Forlì** Italy. Ancient Forum Livii. Capital of Forlì province in Emilia-Romagna, on the Montone R. and the Aemilian Way, 38 m. SE of Bologna. Pop. (1968) 102,107. Manufactures textiles, furniture, footwear, felt, etc. Cathedral with 17th-cent chapel. The church of San Mercuriale has a fine 12th-cent. campanile.

**Formby** England. Urban district in SW

Lancashire, 11 m. NNW of Liverpool. Pop. (1961) 11,730. Market town. Mainly residential. Altcar, the venue of the Waterloo Cup (coursing), is 2 m. ESE.

**Formosa** Argentina. Capital of the Formosa province, on the Paraguay R. 70 m. SSW of Asunción (Paraguay). Pop. 40,000. River port. Market town. In an agricultural and stock-rearing region. Tanning. Meat packing.

**Formosa** (China) ◊ *Taiwan*.

**Formosa** (Portuguese Guinea) ◊ *Bijagós Islands*.

**Forres** Scotland. Royal burgh in Morayshire, on the R. Findhorn 12 m. WSW of Elgin. Pop. (1961) 4,810. Market town. Woollen and flour mills. Whisky distilling, engineering. An early castle was traditionally the scene of Macbeth's murder of Duncan; the later castle was a residence of Scottish kings in the 12th–14th cent. Sweno's stone near by is an elaborately carved monolith which probably commemorates the victory of Sweno (son of Harold, king of Denmark) over Malcolm II (1008).

**Forst** German Democratic Republic. Industrial town in the Cottbus district, on the Neisse R. and the Polish frontier 13 m. E of Cottbus. Pop. (1965) 29,861. Manufactures textiles, machinery, etc. Zasieki, formerly a suburb on the opposite side of the river, was transferred to Poland after the 2nd World War (1945).

**Fortaleza (Ceará)** Brazil. Capital of the Ceará state (NE), an Atlantic port, with an improved harbour. Pop. (1960) 514,818. Exports cotton, hides, carnauba wax, etc. Sugar refining, flour milling. Manufactures textiles, soap.

**Fort Augustus** Scotland. Village in Inverness-shire, at the S end of Loch Ness on the Caledonian Canal. A fort erected in 1716 and enlarged in 1730 was later named after William Augustus, Duke of Cumberland (the victor of ◊ *Culloden*); the buildings have been occupied by a Benedictine abbey since 1876, when the site was presented to the Order by Lord Lovat.

**Fort Collins** USA. Commercial town in Colorado 58 m. N of Denver, at a height of 5,000 ft. Pop. (1960) 25,027. In a stock-rearing and agricultural region. Sugar refining, flour milling, etc.

**Fort-de-France** Martinique (French W Indies). Formerly Fort-Royal. Capital and chief seaport, on the W coast, on Fort-de-France Bay, with a sheltered deep-water harbour. Pop. (1967) 99,051. Exports sugar, rum, cacao. French naval base. Main commercial centre since the destruction of St Pierre by volcanic eruption (1902). Near by is the birthplace of the Empress Josephine (1763–1814).

**Fort Dodge** USA. Town in Iowa, on the Des Moines R. 72 m. NNW of Des Moines. Pop. (1960) 28,399. Manufactures gypsum products, bricks and tiles, etc. Abundant gypsum deposits in the neighbourhood.

**Fortescue River** Australia. Intermittent river in Western Australia, 350 m. long, flowing generally WNW through broken country N of the Hamersley Range to the Indian Ocean.

**Forth River** Scotland. River 66 m. long, formed by the union of two headstreams (the Avondhu and Duchray Water) near Aberfoyle (Perthshire), flowing E by a meandering course past Stirling to Alloa, at the head of the Firth of Forth, which extends 51 m. to the North Sea and is crossed by a road bridge (1936) at Kincardine, the Forth Rail Bridge (1882–90) at Queensferry, and the Forth Road Bridge (1964). Islands include Bass Rock, Inchcolm, and Inchkeith. Principal ports Leith and Grangemouth; just above the Forth Rail Bridge is the naval base of Rosyth. At Grangemouth the river is connected by the Forth and Clyde Canal with Bowling on the Clyde estuary.

**Fort Knox** USA. Military reservation and air base in Kentucky, 27 m. SSW of Louisville. Purchased in 1917 by the US government, for use as a 1st World War training camp. The Gold Bullion Depository (built 1936) stores most of the US gold reserves.

**Fort Lamy** Chad. Capital of the republic, at the confluence of the Shari and Logone rivers S of L. Chad, near the Cameroun frontier. Pop. (1965) 86,000. Caravan centre. Airport. Trade in salt, dates, millet, livestock. Founded (1900) by the French.

**Fort Lauderdale** USA. Seaside resort in SE Florida, 25 m. N of Miami, near the Everglades. Pop. (1960) 83,648. Trade in citrus fruits, market-garden produce.

**Fort Smith** USA. Formerly Belle Pointe. Town in Arkansas, on the Arkansas R. and the Oklahoma border. Pop. (1960) 52,991. Chief manufacturing centre in the state. Produces glass, textiles, furniture, metal goods, etc. Founded (as Belle Pointe) 1817. Renamed after General Thomas A. Smith, the commander who ordered its construction.

**Fort Victoria** ◊ *Zimbabwe National Park*.

**Fort Wayne** USA. Industrial town and railway junction in NE Indiana at the confluence of the St Mary's and the St Joseph rivers. Pop. (1960) 161,776. Manufactures mining, agricultural, and electrical machinery, radio and television equipment, pumps and tanks, etc. Named after General Anthony Wayne, who built a fort here 1794. Grew as a fur-trading centre.

**Fort William** Canada. Lake port in Ontario, on the NW shore of L. Superior; with its twin city Port Arthur, the W terminus of the St Lawrence–Great Lakes Waterway. Pop. (1966) 48,208. Important outlet for prairie grain; huge elevators along the waterfront. Flour milling, sawmilling, engineering, brewing. Manufactures wood pulp and paper. Founded by the French as a fur-trading post 1678. A fort was built in 1801.

**Fort William** Scotland. Small burgh in Inverness-shire, near the foot of Ben Nevis at the NE end of Loch Linnhe. Pop. (1961) 2,715. Tourist centre. Important aluminium works and whisky distilleries. The fort, built by General Monk (1655), enlarged (1690) and renamed after William III, was dismantled 1866.

**Fort Worth** USA. Industrial town in Texas 32 m. W of Dallas. Pop. (1960) 356,268. Important grain and livestock market and oil-refining centre. Manufactures aircraft, clothing, agricultural machinery, etc. Meat packing, flour milling, etc. Seat of the Texas Christian University (1873). Many parks and famous botanical gardens.

**Fougères** France. Town in the Ille-et-Vilaine department, 27 m. NE of Rennes. Pop. (1968) 26,854. Manufactures footwear, clothing, etc. Granite quarried in neighbourhood. Famous castle (12th/15th-cent.).

**Fountains Abbey** ◊ *Ripon*.

**Fouta Djallon (Futa Jallon)**. Highland region in W Africa, mainly in Guinea but extending into Sierra Leone and Liberia. Much dissected; generally at a height of 3,000 ft, but rising to over 4,000 ft. Source of the Niger, Senegal, and Gambia rivers. Chiefly savannah. Principal occupation cattle rearing. Main crops rice, bananas.

**Foveaux Strait** ◊ *Stewart Island*.

**Fowey** England. Small seaport in Cornwall, on the estuary of the R. Fowey 22 m. W of Plymouth. Pop. (1961) 2,237. Seaside resort. Exports china clay. Fishing. Its maritime trade was important in the 14th–15th cent. The 'Troy Town' of Sir Arthur Quiller-Couch (1863–1944), who lived here. From 1968 part of the municipal borough of St Austell with Fowey.

**Foxe Channel** ◊ *Hudson Bay*.

**Foyers** Scotland. Village in Inverness-shire, on the E shore of Loch Ness at the mouth of the R. Foyers 18 m. SW of Inverness. Aluminium works. The first hydroelectric plant in Britain (1896).

**Foyle, Lough** Ireland. Inlet of the Atlantic, 15 m. long and 8 m. maximum width, between Co. Donegal (Irish Republic) and Co. Londonderry (Northern Ireland). Fed by the R. Foyle, on which the town of Londonderry stands.

**Framlingham** England. Market town in E Suffolk, 15 m. NNE of Ipswich. Pop. (1961) 1,945. Ruined 13th-cent. castle. Well-known public school, founded (1864) as a memorial to the Prince Consort.

**Francavilla Fontana** Italy. Market town in Brindisi province, Apulia, 19 m. ENE of Taranto. Pop. (1961) 30,300. Railway junction. Trade in wine, olive oil, wheat, etc. Has the former castle of the Imperiali family.

**France** Republic in W Europe. Area 212,919 sq. m. (roughly twice that of the UK). Pop. (1968) 49,778,540. Cap. Paris. Lang. French. Rel. mainly Roman Catholic. The richest in natural resources (both agricultural and mineral) and the most favoured by climate and geographical position of all the countries in western Europe, it lies between the Atlantic and the Mediterranean, separated from Spain by the Pyrenees, from Italy by the Alps, from Switzerland by the Jura, and from Germany (in part) by the Rhine R. Metropolitan France is administratively divided into 95 departments (see separate articles): Ain, Aisne, Allier, Alpes-Maritimes, Ardèche, Ardennes, Ariège, Aube, Aude, Aveyron, Bas-Rhin, Basses-Alpes, Basses-Pyrénées, Belfort (Territoire), Bouches-du-Rhône, Calvados, Cantal, Charente, Charente-Maritime, Cher, Corrèze, Corse (Corsica), Côte-d'Or, Côtes-du-Nord, Creuse, Deux-Sèvres, Dordogne, Doubs, Drôme, Essonne, Eure, Eure-et-Loir, Finistère, Gard, Gers, Gironde, Haute-Garonne, Haute-Loire, Haute-Marne, Hautes-Alpes, Haute-Saône, Haute-Savoie, Hautes-Pyrénées, Haute-Vienne, Haut-Rhin, Hauts-de-Seine, Hérault, Ille-et-

Vilaine, Indre, Indre-et-Loire, Isère, Jura, Landes, Loire, Loire-Atlantique, Loiret, Loir-et-Cher, Lot, Lot-et-Garonne, Lozère, Maine-et-Loire, Manche, Marne, Mayenne, Meurthe-et-Moselle, Meuse, Morbihan, Moselle, Nièvre, Nord, Oise, Orne, Paris (Ville), Pas-de-Calais, Puy-de-Dôme, Pyrénées-Orientales, Rhône, Saône-et-Loire, Sarthe, Savoie, Seine-et-Marne, Seine-Maritime, Seine-St Denis, Somme, Tarn, Tarn-et-Garonne, Val-de-Marne, Val d'Oise, Var, Vaucluse, Vendée, Vienne, Vosges, Yonne, Yvelines.

TOPOGRAPHY. The SE half is mainly mountainous, containing (besides the Pyrenees, Alps, and Jura along the frontiers) the Cévennes, the Auvergne, and the Vosges. Plains occupy most of the N W half. The great Central Plateau (the Massif Central) takes up nearly one sixth of the total area; it is a crystalline formation overlaid in parts with lava sheets and volcanic cones (*puys*) and fringed in the SW and S by limestone deposits (*causses*). It rises to 6,188 ft in the Puy de Sancy, and is largely infertile and sparsely inhabited, the rural population gradually moving away to the towns. The Pyrenees, with several peaks exceeding 10,000 ft, have always proved a considerable barrier between France and Spain. Higher still are the Alps, with the subsidiary ranges of the Maritime, Cottian, and Graian Alps lying across the SE frontier; the loftiest point, the Mont Blanc massif (15,781 ft), is on the Italian frontier. To the N are the Jura (5,652 ft), and still farther N the Vosges (4,649 ft), facing the Black Forest of Germany across the rift valley of the Rhine. Most of the lowland area of France consists of two extensive basins, Aquitaine and the Paris Basin, which, with the Île-de-France as its central area, is the true heartland of France; at its centre is Paris, whence the most important roads and railways radiate in all directions. It is crossed by the Seine (commercially France's principal river), which, with its tributaries the Oise, Marne, and Yonne and interconnecting canals, forms a network of busy inland waterways. In the S it includes the middle course of the Loire, famous for its beautiful châteaux. Through the Gate of Poitou the Paris Basin is linked with Aquitaine, which is drained by the Garonne, the third of France's great rivers, joined at the head of its estuary (the Gironde) by the Dordogne. W of the Paris Basin are the low hills, granite moorlands, and rocky indented coastline of Brittany and W Normandy. E of the Paris Basin, around the Vosges, are Alsace and Lorraine, linked via the Burgundian Gate with the narrow Rhône–Saône corridor, long the main route between the N and the Mediterranean region. In its lower course the valley of the Rhône, the fourth of France's great rivers, broadens out into the Mediterranean coastlands, with the celebrated resorts of the French Riviera (Côte d'Azur) in the E.

CLIMATE. Situated on the W coast of Europe, and thus influenced by the N Atlantic Drift, France in its NW half has a maritime temperate climate of cool summers, mild winters, and moderate rainfall. The climate of Brittany, for example, closely resembles that of Devon and Cornwall, but that of the SW is a little warmer. To the E the climate gradually becomes more continental, with warm summers and cold winters; this is particularly noticeable on the Central Plateau, where altitude increases the severity of the winters. Paris affords an illustration of the transition W–E from a maritime temperate to continental climate: in spite of the difference in latitude, it has virtually the same mean annual temperature as London (50° F) and almost equal rainfall, but the summers are slightly warmer and the winters slightly cooler. The third climatic zone, the S coast and the lower Rhône valley (with the island of Corsica), enjoys a Mediterranean climate, with hot dry summers and mild showery winters, marred at times by the cold *mistral*.

AGRICULTURAL RESOURCES. With its generally favourable climates and large fertile areas, France is much more of an agricultural country than Great Britain; the population density is less than one third of that of England and Wales: 37 per cent of the area is cultivated, including 3 per cent under vines; 24 per cent is pasture and 20 per cent forest. Wheat takes up the greatest acreage of arable land, followed by barley and oats; potatoes and sugar-beet are also important crops. The Paris Basin and Aquitaine are the main wheat-growing regions. France is the world's leading wine producer; only the N lies outside the vine-growing areas, and here hops are grown for beer (NE) and apples for cider (NW). The great wine-producing areas are Champagne, Burgundy, the lower Charente and Garonne valleys (noted for clarets, light

Bordeaux wines and brandy), Languedoc (producing large quantities of *vin ordinaire*), and the lower Rhône and Loire valleys. There is a considerable production of apples, pears, plums, and peaches. Market gardening is important, esp. in the Paris Basin and the NW. Large numbers of cattle, sheep, and pigs are raised. Fishing is a substantial industry, esp. along the Breton coast.

MINERAL RESOURCES. Considerable coal comes from the NE coalfield, which extends across the frontier into Belgium; there are scattered deposits around the edge of the Central Plateau, but some has also to be imported (mainly from the Ruhr). The rich iron-ore deposits of Lorraine, however, are more than sufficient to supply the domestic iron and steel industry, centred there and at St Étienne and Le Creusot; iron ore is exported to the Ruhr. Hydroelectric power has been extensively developed, notably in the Alps, and represents well over half the rapidly increasing quantity of electricity consumed, stimulating the production of aluminium, for example, from bauxite mined in the S. Potash is mined in Alsace. The Limoges porcelain industry uses local china clay.

INDUSTRY. The textile industry is of great importance, esp. in the Lille district (cotton), Lyons (rayon, silk), Alsace (cotton), and Rouen. Automobile manufacture has developed mainly around Paris, which also produces chemicals and a host of luxury articles. The post-war expansion of French industry, initiated by the first Monnet plan (1946–50) and continued under succeeding 5-year plans, led to an increased output of steel, cement, and fertilizers 1946–60: the first two were almost quadrupled and the third more than quadrupled. Imports are chiefly raw materials for the principal industries – coal, petroleum (feeding a vastly increased refining capacity), raw cotton and wool, and vegetable oils. Exports include iron and steel goods, machinery, cars, textiles, and chemicals. Noteworthy among the invisible exports is the tourist trade, which brings foreign visitors not only to the Riviera, to Biarritz on the Bay of Biscay, to Dinard and Deauville on the Breton and Normandy coasts, and to many other seaside resorts, but to Chamonix and other Alpine centres and to a great number of historic and picturesque towns such as Carcassonne, Nîmes, Arles, and Avignon.

SOCIAL AND CULTURAL. Despite industrialization, France is still in the main a country of villages and small towns. Only three centres have more than half a million inhabitants: Paris, Marseille (chief seaport), and Lyons; the main concentrations of population are around these three largest towns and in the industrial NE. The 1962 census, however, revealed two interesting trends: first, a rise in the number of towns with over 100,000 inhabitants (from 22 to 32 since 1946); second, the continuing slow but steady drift of population from the inhospitable and mainly rural Central Plateau. Other sparsely inhabited areas are the Alps and the Pyrenees, mountainous Corsica, and the Landes (S of the Gironde estuary), once an important sheep-grazing region but now largely planted with pines. The total population remained almost static, at just over 40 million, 1911–46, but has risen at a gradually increasing rate since the end of the 2nd World War. Although the French are predominantly Roman Catholic, Church and State have been separated since 1905. For centuries France has been a leader of Western culture; her capital has been the home of countless scholars and artists, and her educational institutions, museums, and art galleries have gained world renown. There are 23 universities, two of them (Toulouse and Montpellier) dating from the 13th cent. French culture is Latin in character, but local influences have been preserved: a German dialect is spoken in Alsace, Breton in Brittany, Flemish in the extreme NE, Basque in the extreme SW, and an Italian dialect in Corsica.

HISTORY. Previously disunited, ancient ◊ *Gaul* had a common language and form of government imposed on it by the Roman conquest of Julius Caesar (57–52 B.C.), and for some centuries it prospered. The '*Pax Romana*' was broken by the invasions of Germanic tribes (the Visigoths, Burgundians, and Franks) in the 5th cent. A.D., but Clovis, King of the Franks, embraced Christianity after his conquests and gained the support of the Church, brought unity again, and laid the foundations of the French state. Charlemagne extended the Frankish kingdom over a great part of W Europe, and was crowned Emperor of the West (800). After his death the land was again partitioned; feudalism fostered the disintegration, and after the Norman conquest of England (1066) much of France fell into the hands of the English. However, by the end of the Hundred Years War (1337–1454) only Calais remained to England, and this too was recovered in 1558 (though England held Dunkirk 1656–62). The commanding position that France now held was due mainly to the House of Capet, founded (987) by Hugh Capet, which had gradually established the authority of the monarch. When the Capetian line became extinct, their successors, the Valois, proved less able, if sometimes equally determined. Louis XI (1461–83) inaugurated the autocratic rule which ultimately became the despotism of Louis XIV (1643–1715). In the 18th cent. France suffered defeat in Louis XIV's War of the Spanish Succession, lost her colonial empire, and finally, under Louis XVI, faced bankruptcy. With the French Revolution (1789) and the execution of the king the 'ancien régime' came to an end, to be followed by the dictatorship of Napoleon, who led France through a short period of military glory, abdicated, and was defeated at Waterloo (1815). After a period of restored monarchy came the Revolution of 1848, and the Second Republic under Louis Napoleon, which became the Second Empire; this collapsed in the defeat in the Franco-Prussian War (1870–71). Recovery came quickly during the Third Republic, and a new colonial empire was built up. The 1st World War took a heavy toll of French life; in the 2nd World War France was rapidly overrun by the German army (1940). After liberation (1944) the Fourth Republic was established (1946). In spite of political dissensions, France renewed her economic strength, consolidated her position in W Europe, joined the N Atlantic Treaty Organization (1948), formulated the plan for the highly successful European Coal and Steel community (1950), and worked for a European Economic Community. Her colonial empire began to break up; the use of force, both in Indo-China and in Algeria, could not stifle the demands for independence. The substitution of the French Union (by the constitution of 1946) for the former colonial organization did not satisfy these demands. In 1958 the Fifth Republic was established, under General de Gaulle, and with the new constitution the French Community came into existence; but by 1962 the membership had shrunk to France, 6 African republics with a total population of less than 15 million, and overseas territories and possessions with a total population of scarcely 1 million. France's economic ties with most of her former possessions, however, remained close and effective.

**Franche-Comté** France. Former province lying between the Swiss frontier and the Saône R. First an independent state, then part of Burgundy. Annexed to France 1678. In 1790 it was divided into the present departments of Doubs, Haute-Saône, and Jura. Dôle was capital until 1678, when it was replaced by Besançon.

**Franconia** (Ger. **Franken**) Germany. Medieval duchy, first inhabited by the Germanic tribe of the Franks, extending along the valley of the Main R. from the Rhine to Bohemia. Later divided into W (Rhenish) Franconia, which disintegrated into free cities and ecclesiastical states, and E Franconia, which passed to the bishops of Würzburg and then to Bavaria. The name fell into disuse but was revived (1837) when Lower, Middle, and Upper Franconia were made administrative provinces of Bavaria.

**Frankfurt-am-Main** (**Frankfurt**) Federal German Republic. Largest city in Hessen, on the right bank of the Main R. Pop. (1968) 662,351. Important commercial, industrial, and route centre. Printing and publishing. Banking. Manufactures chemicals, machinery, electrical equipment, textiles, etc. Also an active river port. The *Altstadt* (old town) with its narrow streets and medieval buildings is in contrast with the more spacious *Neustadt* (new town). The former was severely damaged by bombing in the 2nd World War; among buildings destroyed were the 15th-cent. *Römer* (town hall) and the birthplace of Goethe (1749–1832). University (1914). Became the headquarters of the great I.G. Farbenindustrie (chemicals), and has long been famous for trade fairs. Site of an annual international book fair. Probably founded in the 1st cent. A.D. Capital of the E Frankish kingdom in the 9th cent. Already known for its fairs by the 13th cent. Free imperial city 1372–1806. Seat of the Diet of the German Confederation 1815–66, but supported Austria and was seized by Prussia 1866. The treaty ending the Franco-Prussian War was signed here (1871).

**Frankfurt-an-der-Oder** German Democratic Republic. **1.** Administrative district formed in 1952 from part of Brandenburg. Area 2,774 sq. m. Pop. (1968) 670,293.

**2.** Capital of the Frankfurt-an-der-Oder district, on the left bank of the Oder R. 50 m. ESE of Berlin. Pop. (1965) 58,006. Railway and road junction. Sugar refining, vegetable canning, sausage making. Manufactures machinery, furniture, etc. Founded in the mid-13th cent. by Franconian merchants. Belonged to the Hanseatic League in the 14th–15th cent. Its university (founded 1506) was moved to Breslau (Wroclaw) 1811. When the Oder (Odra) R. was made the German-Polish frontier (1945) its suburb on the E bank became the Polish town of Slubice. Severely damaged in the 2nd World War.

**Frankfurt-on-Main** ◊ *Frankfurt-am-Main*.

**Frankfurt-on-Oder** ◊ *Frankfurt-an-der-Oder*.

**Franklin** Canada. Administrative district of the NW Territories, comprising all the Canadian Arctic Archipelago and the Melville and Boothia peninsulas on the mainland. Area 549,253 sq. m. Pop. (1961) 5,758 (mainly Eskimo). Main occupation fur trapping.

**Franz-Josef Land** (Russian **Zemlya Frantsa Josifa**) USSR. Arctic archipelago of about 80 islands, N of Novaya Zemlya in the RSFSR. Area 8,000 sq. m. Uninhabited save for meteorological observers and migrant fur trappers. Mostly ice-covered, with mosses and lichens here and there. Animal life consists of bears, foxes, seals, and sea birds. Chief islands Aleksandra, George, and Wilczek Lands, and Graham Bell Island. Discovered (1873) by von Payer and Weyprecht. Annexed by the USSR 1926.

**Frascati** Italy. Town and summer resort in Roma province in Latium, on the N slopes of the Alban Hills 13 m. SE of Rome. Pop. (1961) 15,524. Famed for its villas and gardens (Aldobrandini, Torlonia, Falconieri, etc.) many of them severely damaged in the 2nd World War.

**Fraserburgh** Scotland. Small burgh and herring-fishing port in N Aberdeenshire, on the North Sea near Kinnaird Head. Pop. (1961) 10,462. Fish curing and canning. Manufactures pneumatic tools. Founded in the 16th cent. by Sir Alexander Fraser, after whom it is named.

**Fraser River** Canada. Chief river of British Columbia, 850 m. long, rising near the Yellowhead Pass and flowing NW, S, and then W to enter the Strait of Georgia below New Westminster. Main tributary the Thompson. In its lower course the Fraser passes through spectacular canyons; about 100 m. from the mouth it becomes navigable. Has the principal salmon spawning grounds along the Pacific coast. The lower valley is an important farming area. The upper valley was the scene of a gold rush (1858).

**Fray Bentos** Uruguay. Capital of the Río Negro department, on the Uruguay R. 170 m. NW of Montevideo. Pop. 18,000. Port, accessible to ocean-going ships. Commercial and industrial centre, long important for meat packing and canning. The meat extracts of Justus von Liebig were first produced here in 1861.

**Fredericia** Denmark. Seaport in E Jutland at the N end of the Little Belt. Pop. (1965) 32,964. Manufactures cotton and metal goods, fertilizers, etc. Founded 1652.

**Fredericton** Canada. Capital of New Brunswick, at the head of navigation on the St John R. Pop. (1966) 22,460. Sawmilling, woodworking. Manufactures shoes, plastics. Seat of the University of New Brunswick (1823). Founded (1783) by United Empire Loyalists.

**Fredrikstad** Norway. Port on the E shore of Oslo Fiord, at the mouth of the Glomma R. 48 m. S of Oslo. Pop. (1968) 30,089. Exports timber etc. Sawmilling, fishing, fish canning, etc.

**Freeport** (Illinois) USA. Town 107 m. WNW of Chicago. Pop. (1960) 26,628. Manufactures food products (cheese etc.), patent medicines, hardware, etc. Scene of one of the famous Lincoln–Douglas debates (1858).

**Freeport** (New York) USA. Town and resort on the SW coast of Long Island. Pop. (1960) 34,419. Big-game fishing centre. Manufactures clothing, furniture, etc.

**Freetown** Sierra Leone. Capital, chief seaport, and naval base, on the estuary of the Sierra Leone R. Pop. (1963) 128,000. Excellent natural harbour. Chief exports diamonds, palm kernels; iron ore exported from Pepel, 12 m. ENE. Tuna fishing. Railway engineering, rice and groundnut milling. Seat of Fourah Bay College, founded (1827) by the Church Missionary Society and part of the University of Sierra Leone. Hot wet climate, unfavourable to Europeans: formerly called 'the white man's grave'. Health conditions have been much improved by a modern drainage system and anti-malaria measures. Founded (1792) as a home for freed slaves.

**Freiberg** German Democratic Republic. Industrial town in the Karl-Marx-Stadt district, at the N foot of the Erzgebirge 18 m. WSW of Dresden. Pop. (1965) 48,438. Manufactures machinery, textiles, porcelain, etc. The 15th-cent. cathedral has a famous Romanesque portal known as the Golden Gate.

**Freiburg** (Switzerland) ◊ *Fribourg*.

**Freiburg-im-Breisgau** Federal German Republic. Town in Baden-Württemberg on the W edge of the Black Forest 33 m. NNE of Basel. Pop. (1968) 160,007. Manufactures textiles, chemicals, paper, furniture, etc. Also a cultural and tourist centre, with a famous 13th/16th-cent. Gothic cathedral and a university (1457). Founded in the 12th cent. Under Austrian rule from 1368. Passed to Baden 1805. Severely damaged in the 2nd World War.

**Freising** Federal German Republic. Town in Bavaria on the Isar R. 20 m. NNE of Munich. Pop. (1963) 28,800. Manufactures tractors, hosiery, gloves, etc. Brewing. Cathedral (12th-cent.); bishopric established here by St Korbinian in 724.

**Freital** German Democratic Republic. Industrial town in the Dresden district, 5 m. SSW of Dresden. Pop. (1965) 42,070. Manufactures glass, cameras, musical instruments, etc.

**Fréjus** France. Ancient Forum Julii. Town in the Var department near the Mediterranean 33 m. SW of Nice. Pop. (1968) 25,736. The harbour, built by the Romans, is now completely silted up, and Fréjus is nearly 2 m. from the sea. Roman remains include an amphitheatre, an aqueduct, and the old town walls. In 1959 more than 300 inhabitants of Fréjus and neighbouring St Raphael lost their lives when the Malpasset dam collapsed. Birthplace of Agricola (A.D. 40–93).

**Fremantle** Australia. Chief seaport of Western Australia, at the mouth of the Swan R. 10 m. SW of Perth. Pop. (1964) 24,400. Dredged harbour protected by moles. Terminus of the Trans-Australian Railway. Exports wheat, wool, timber, fruit. Manufactures fertilizers and soap. Engineering. Founded in 1829, it is one of the oldest settlements in Australia.

**French Equatorial Africa** ◊ *Central African Republic*; *Chad*; *Congo (Brazzaville)*, *Republic of*; *Gabon*.

**French Guiana.** French overseas department in S America, bounded by Surinam (Dutch Guiana) (W), Brazil (E and S), and the Atlantic (N). Area 35,000 sq. m. Pop. (1967) 44,330. Cap. and chief seaport Cayenne. Rises from the coast to the Tumuc-Humac Mountains. in the extreme S. Largely forested. Well watered. Little developed. Tropical climate, with heavy rainfall. Main exports gold, timber, rum. First colonized by the French in the 17th cent. A notorious penal settlement was maintained on the Île du Diable (Devil's Island), 27 m. NW of Cayenne, 1854–1938. French Guiana became an overseas department of France, with the territory of Inini as a dependency, in 1946.

**French India.** Former group of French settlements consisting of Pondicherry, Karikal, and Yanam on the E coast and Mahé on the W coast, with Chandernagore, an enclave in Bengal. Area 193 sq. m. Administrative centre Pondicherry. Chandernagore was transferred to India in 1950 and the remainder in 1954.

**French Polynesia** (Oceania) S Pacific Ocean. Formerly called French Settlements in Oceania. Island groups in the Pacific, a colony 1903–46, since 1958 an overseas territory of the French Community. Area 1,545 sq. m. Pop. (1967) 98,378. Cap. Papeete, on Tahiti in the Society Is., the most important group; the Marquesas, the Austral (Tubuai), Tuamotu, and Gambier Is. are the other main groups. Administered by a governor and a government council. Most of the islands are mountainous; some are of volcanic origin and coral-fringed, some are atolls. Chief exports copra, phosphates, vanilla, mother-of-pearl, pearls.

**French Shore** Canada. Part of the S and E coasts of Newfoundland, in which France had fishing rights from Britain under the terms of various treaties from 1713 to 1904. By the Treaty of Versailles (1783) the limits were Cape St John (N) and Cape Ray (S). The arrangement caused constant friction; in 1904 France sold all her rights.

**French Somaliland** ◊ *French Territory of the Afars and the Issas*.

**French Soudan** ◊ *Mali*.

**French Southern and Antarctic Territories** Indian Ocean. French Overseas Territory formed in 1955, comprising the ◊ *Crozet Islands* and ◊ *Kerguelen Islands*, the islands of ◊ *Nouvelle Amsterdam* and ◊ *St Paul*, and the Antarctic territory of ◊ *Adélie Land*. Area 158,000 sq. m. Total pop. 132 (meteorologists, scientists, etc.).

French Territory of the Afars and the Issas. Formerly French Somaliland. French overseas territory in E Africa, on the strait of Bab el Mandeb and the Gulf of Aden, bounded by Ethiopia (N, W, and S) and Somalia (SE). Area 8,500 sq. m. Pop. (1966) 108,000 (55,000 Somali, 30,500 Danakil). Cap. and chief seaport Djibouti. Largely desert. Occupied by the French 1881. Became an overseas territory of the French Union in 1946 and of the French Community in 1958. At a referendum in 1967 a majority of the electorate voted for continued association with France rather than independence; the Territory was renamed.

French West Africa ♦ Dahomey; Ivory Coast; Niger; Senegal; Upper Volta.

Fresh Water Canal ♦ Ismailia.

Fresnillo Mexico. Officially Fresnillo de González Echeverría. Town in the Zacatecas state, on the central plateau, at a height of 7,300 ft. Pop. (1960) 35,582. Market town, in a cereal-growing area. Also a mining centre, producing mainly silver.

Fresno USA. Town in California 165 m. SE of San Francisco. Pop. (1960) 133,929. Produces raisins, olive oil, agricultural equipment, pottery, etc. The drying and packing of fruit is an important industry; the Sun Maid Raisin Plant is the largest of its kind in the world. The name (Spanish for 'ash tree') was given by the railroad builders, because of the ash trees in the neighbouring foothills.

Fribourg (Ger. Freiburg) Switzerland. 1. Canton in the W lying NW of the Bernese Oberland. Area 645 sq. m. Pop. (1969) 174,000 (mainly French-speaking). Mountainous in the S. Cattle reared; cereals and sugar-beet cultivated. Noted for cheese (esp. Gruyère).
2. Capital of the Fribourg canton, on the Sarine R. 18 m. SW of Berne. Pop. (1969) 40,500. Manufactures chocolate, beer, electrical equipment, etc. Principal buildings the cathedral of St Nicholas (13th/15th-cent) and the university (1889). Founded (1157) by a duke of Zähringen. Belonged to the Habsburgs 1277–1452. Joined the Swiss Confederation 1481.

Friedrichshafen Federal German Republic. Town in Baden-Württemberg on the N shore of L. Constance. Pop. (1963) 39,330. Port, resort, and industrial centre. Manufactures cars etc. Tanning. Formerly the site of the Zeppelin works and a centre of aircraft construction, it was heavily bombed during the 2nd World War.

Friendly Islands ♦ Tonga.

Friern Barnet ♦ Barnet.

Friesland Netherlands. Ancient Frisia. Province in the N bounded by the Wadden Zee (N) and the Ijsselmeer (W). Area 1,325 sq. m. Pop. (1968) 511,330. Cap. Leeuwarden. Port Harlingen. Pastoral and agricultural, home of the famous Friesian breed of cattle.

Frimley ♦ Camberley.

Frinton and Walton England. Urban district in Essex comprising the seaside resorts of Frinton-on-Sea and Walton-on-the-Naze, 15 m. ESE of Colchester. Pop. (1961) 9,571.

Frisia ♦ Friesland.

Frisian Islands. Chain of islands off the coasts of the Netherlands, Federal German Republic, and Denmark, separated from the mainland by shallows 3–20 m. wide, extending from the Wadden Zee to Jutland. They are low-lying, and, despite sand dunes and artificial embankments, are constantly subject to marine erosion. Three groups: the W Frisian Is. belong to the Netherlands and consist of Texel, Vlieland, Terschelling, Ameland, Schiermonnikoog, and 4 smaller islands; the E Frisian Is., belonging to the Federal German Republic, include Borkum, Juist, Norderney, Baltrum, Langeoog, Spiekeroog, and Wangeroog, all used as seaside resorts, and 4 uninhabited islands; of the separate N Frisian Is., Nordstrand, Pellworm, Amrum, Föhr, and Sylt belong to the Federal German Republic, and Römö, Koresand, Manö, and Fanö to Denmark.

Friuli Italy/Yugoslavia. Ancient Forum Julii. Region between the Carnic Alps and the Gulf of Venice. A Lombard duchy in the 6th cent. and a possession of the Habsburgs after 1500. In 1866 the W part, in 1919 the whole area was included in Venezia Giulia (Italy); in 1947 E Friuli, excluding Gorizia, was ceded to Yugoslavia. ♦ Friuli-Venezia Giulia.

Friuli-Venezia Giulia Italy. Region in the NE formed (1947) from W Friuli and part of E Friuli, retained by Italy after the cession of Istria etc. to Yugoslavia; includes the provinces of Udine, Gorizia, and Trieste. Area 3,030 sq. m. Pop. (1961) 1,205,222. Cap. Trieste.

Frome England. Urban district in Somerset on the R. Frome 10 m. S of Bath. Pop. (1961) 11,440. Market town. Brewing, printing, light engineering. Manufactures woollen cloth. Bishop Thomas Ken (1637–1711) is buried in the 14th-cent. parish church.

**Frosinone** Italy. Capital (since 1926) of Frosinone province, in Latium, 50 m. ESE of Rome, on a hill (955 ft) in the Apennines. Pop. (1961) 31,155. Market town.

**Frunze** USSR. Formerly Pishpek. Capital of the Kirghiz SSR, in the Chu R. valley 120 m. WSW of Alma Ata, on a branch line of the Turksib Railway. Pop. (1970) 431,000. Industrial and commercial centre in a fertile irrigated region. Manufactures agricultural machinery, textiles, etc. Meat packing, flour milling, tanning. Founded as a fort (Pishpek) in the 19th cent.; renamed (1925) after M. V. Frunze, the revolutionary leader (1885–1925), who was born here.

**Fthiotis** ◊ *Phthiotis*.

**Fuenterrabía** Spain. Fishing port in Guipúzcoa province, on the Bay of Biscay, at the mouth of the Bidassoa R. Pop. 7,000. Fish canning, boatbuilding. The picturesque old town has a ruined castle dating from the 12th cent. The new town has become a popular resort. As a frontier fortress it was often attacked; here Condé was defeated when he invaded Spain (1638).

**Fuerteventura** ◊ *Canary Islands*.

**Fujiyama (Fuji, Fuji-san)** Japan. Country's highest mountain (12,395 ft), in Shizuoka prefecture in central Honshu, 68 m. WSW of Tokyo. An isolated extinct volcano, famous for its almost perfect symmetry and its snow-capped summit, it is sacred to the Japanese. Last active 1707.

**Fukien** China. Maritime province in the SE, on Formosa Strait. Area 47,500 sq. m. Pop. (1957) 14,650,000. Cap. Foochow. Generally mountainous and well wooded. Chief river the Min. Climate humid subtropical with rainfall 60–80 ins. annually. Principal crops rice, tea; timber (pine, fir, camphor) important. Chief towns Foochow and Amoy, both seaports. There has been much emigration of Chinese from Fukien, esp. to other countries in SE Asia, e.g. the Philippines.

**Fukui** Japan. Capital of Fukui prefecture, in central Honshu, 78 m. NNE of Kyoto. Pop. (1965) 169,634. Important textile centre (rayon, silk); also manufactures paper, leather goods, food products, etc. Severely damaged by earthquake 1948.

**Fukuoka** Japan. Capital of Fukuoka prefecture, in NW Kyushu. Pop. (inc. port Hakata, 1965) 749,808. Seaport and industrial centre. Exports machinery, porcelain, etc. Shipbuilding. Manufactures chemicals, textiles, metal goods, paper, pottery, etc. Seat of the Imperial University of Kyushu (1910).

**Fukushima** Japan. Capital of Fukushima prefecture, in N Honshu, 150 m. NNE of Tokyo. Pop. (1965) 173,680. Important silk-manufacturing centre.

**Fulda** Federal German Republic. Town in Hessen, on the Fulda R. 55 m. S of Kassel. Pop. (1963) 44,900. Manufactures textiles, tyres, ball bearings, etc. Trade in agricultural produce. Grew round a Benedictine abbey founded (744) by St Boniface, who is buried in the cathedral.

**Fulda River** Federal German Republic. River 95 m. long, rising in the Rhön and flowing N to join the Werra R., forming the Weser R.

**Fulham** England. Former metropolitan borough of London; from 1965 part of the Greater London borough of Hammersmith. Pop. (1961) 111,912. On the N bank of the R. Thames, here crossed by Putney Bridge. Fulham Palace, built from 1506 onwards, is the residence of the Bishop of London.

**Fullerton** USA. Town in S California 22 m. SE of Los Angeles. Pop. (1960) 56,180. Fruit packing, canning, and processing (esp. citrus fruits). Also a centre of petroleum production.

**Funafuti** ◊ *Ellice Islands*.

**Funchal** Madeira. 1. District of Portugal comprising the Madeira archipelago. Area 308 sq. m. Pop. (1960) 268,937.
2. Capital of Funchal district, on the SE coast of Madeira island. Pop. (1960) 100,476. Chief seaport and commercial centre. Exports Madeira wines. The mild winter and scenic beauty have made it a popular resort. Because of the steepness of some of the streets there were formerly no wheeled vehicles.

**Fundy, Bay of** Canada. An elongated inlet of the N Atlantic, between New Brunswick and Nova Scotia, 145 m. long and 60 m. wide at the mouth, narrowing at the head and dividing into Chignecto Bay and the Minas Basin. Chief harbour St John. Remarkable for the great rise and fall of the tides (up to 70 ft).

**Fünen** ◊ *Fyn*.

**Furka Pass** Switzerland. Alpine pass on the boundary between Valais and Uri cantons through which runs the Furka Road between Andermatt and Gletsch; one of the highest in Europe (7,976 ft). Under it is a railway tunnel 1 m. long.

**Furneaux Islands** Australia. Group in the Bass Strait off the NE coast of Tasmania, the main islands being Flinders (largest), Cape Barren, and Clarke islands. Main occupations sheep rearing, dairy farming. Named after their discoverer, Tobias Furneaux (1735–81), commander of one of Capt. Cook's vessels on his second voyage.

**Furness** England. District in NW Lancashire consisting of a peninsula bounded by the R. Duddon estuary (W), the Irish Sea (S), and Morecambe Bay (E). The N part is in the Lake District. Chief town Barrow-in-Furness.

**Fur Seal Islands** ◊ *Pribilof Islands*.

**Fürstenwalde** German Democratic Republic. Town in the Frankfurt-an-der-Oder district, 20 m. W of Frankfurt-an-der-Oder on the Spree R. Pop. (1965) 30,489. Manufactures tyres, electrical equipment, footwear, etc. Seat of the bishops of Lebus from the late 14th to the late 16th cent.

**Fürth** Federal German Republic. Industrial town in Bavaria just NW of Nuremberg, to which it is connected by Germany's first railway (opened 1835). Pop. (1963) 98,300. Manufactures mirrors, toys, radio and television apparatus, textiles, chemicals, etc. Founded in the 8th cent. Became prosperous largely because of its tolerance (until the Hitler régime) to the Jews, who found refuge here from persecution in Nuremberg.

**Fuse** Japan. Industrial town in Osaka prefecture, Honshu, just E of Osaka. Pop. (1965) 271,699. Manufactures machinery, textiles, chemicals, leather and rubber products, etc.

**Fushun** China. Industrial town and major coalmining centre in Liaoning province (Manchuria), 25 m. ENE of Shenyang. Pop. (1957) 985,000. Manufactures cement, mining equipment, etc. Coalmining began on a large scale in 1902, and the old town stands near a vast opencast mine. Oil-shale mining was developed by the Japanese *c.* 1930.

**Futa Jallon** ◊ *Fouta Djallon*.

**Futuna** ◊ *Wallis and Futuna Islands*.

**Fylde** England. Flat region in Lancashire between the estuaries of the Wyre and the Ribble rivers. Dairy and poultry farming. Chief towns Blackpool, Fleetwood, Lytham St Anne's.

**Fyn** (Ger. **Fünen**) Denmark. The second largest island, bounded on the E by the Great Belt and separated from the mainland (W) by the Little Belt. Area 1,150 sq. m. Pop. (1965) 389,404. Mainly flat and fertile. Dairy farming; cereals and sugar-beet cultivated. Chief towns Odense, Svendborg, Nyborg. Linked by bridge at Middelfart to the mainland, and by train ferry to Zealand (Nyborg–Korsör).

**Fyne, Loch** Scotland. Sea loch in Argyllshire 40 m. long and 1–4 m. wide, extending N and NE from the Sound of Bute. Inveraray is near the N end. Herring and other fishing.

# G

Gaberones Botswana.* Capital, in the SE 90 m. NNE of Mafeking (S Africa). Pop. (1967) 20,000. A small village until chosen as the capital of the new republic, building having commenced in Feb. 1964.

Gabès Tunisia. Seaport on the Gulf of Gabès 200 m. S. of Tunis. Pop (1966) 76,356. Exports large quantities of dates. Fishing. Terminus of the railway from Tunis via Sousse and Sfax. The oasis of Gabès is famous for its orchards (pomegranates, apricots, etc.) as well as its 300,000 date palms.

Gabès, Gulf of Tunisia. Ancient Syrtis Minor. An inlet of the Mediterranean Sea. Fisheries. On the coast are the towns of Sfax and Gabès (linked by coastal railway). ⇧> Sidra, Gulf of.

Gablonz ⟡ Jablonec.

Gabon. Republic of equatorial Africa, formerly one of the 4 territories of French Equatorial Africa. Area 103,000 sq. m. Pop. (1962) 455,000 (mainly Bantu). Cap. Libreville. Bounded on the NW by Equatorial Guinea (Río Muni), on the N by Cameroun, on the E and S by Congo (Brazzaville). Largely tropical rain-forest. Main exports manganese ore, hardwoods (e.g. okoumé), and petroleum. Food crops bananas, cassava, maize. The estuary of the Gabon R. was discovered (1485) by the Portuguese. The French established a settlement 1839. Known (with Middle Congo) as the French Congo 1888–1908. Became a French colony (1908), an overseas territory of the French Union (1946), a member of the French Community (1958), and an independent member of the UN (1960). An attempted change of government by *coup d'état* (1964) was prevented by the intervention of French forces.

Gadag India. Town in Mysore 35 m. E of Hubli. Pop. (1961) 76,614. Railway junction. Trade in textiles, grain. Manufactures cotton goods, leather, etc.

Gadames ⟡ Ghadames.

Gadsden USA. Industrial town in Alabama, on the Coosa R. 58 m. NE of Birmingham, in a district important for coal and iron. Pop. (1960) 58,088. Manufactures tyres, textiles, iron and steel goods, etc. Founded 1840.

Gaeta Italy. Port on a promontory on the Bay of Gaeta, in Latina province, Latium, 43 m. NW of Naples. Pop. (1961) 20,569. Also a resort. Fishing. Manufactures glass. The adjoining coast was much admired by the ancient Romans. Scene of the final defeat of Francis II of Naples by Italian troops (1860–61).

Gafsa Tunisia. Ancient Capsa. The largest town in the phosphate-mining area; on the Sfax–Tozeur railway 115 m. WSW of Sfax. Pop. 30,000. Oasis, producing dates, olives, and other fruits. Famous for hot springs (important in Roman times) and for near-by prehistoric discoveries.

Gainesville USA. Town in Florida 62 m. SW of Jacksonville. Pop (1960) 29,701. Meat packing. Manufactures electronic equipment, wood products, etc. Trade in market-garden produce, etc. Seat of the University of Florida (1905).

Gainsborough England. Urban district in Lincolnshire, on the R. Trent 15 m. NW of Lincoln. Pop. (1961) 17,276. Market town. Flour milling. Manufactures wood products, machinery, clothing. Founded in the 11th cent. by the Danish king Sweyn I, who died here. Buildings include the timbered Old Hall, which was rebuilt in the 15th cent., and an 18th-cent. parish church. Identified with St Ogg's in George Eliot's *The Mill on the Floss*.

Gairdner, Lake Australia. Shallow salt lake N of the Eyre Peninsula, S Australia, 100 m. long and 30 m. wide. Sometimes dry in summer.

Gairloch Scotland. Sea loch of W Ross and Cromarty about 5 m. long and 3 m. wide at its entrance. On its shore stands the fishing village and resort of Gairloch.

Galápagos Islands (Colón Archipelago) Ecuador. Group of Pacific islands, on the equator 600 m. W of Ecuador; 12 large islands and many small ones, with extinct volcanic cones. Area 2,868 sq. m. Pop. (1967) 3,100. The largest, Isabela (Albemarle) (75 m. long) and San Cristóbal (Chatham), have most of the population. The coastal fringes usually have little vegetation, but there is forest at higher levels. Most of the reptiles and half the plants are peculiar to the islands, which have now been made a nature sanctuary.

The name derives from the Spanish *galápago* ('tortoise'), after the monster tortoises which were once numerous but are now dying out. Darwin visited the Galápagos (1835) and there gathered valuable evidence to support his theory of the evolution of species.

**Galashiels** Scotland. Small burgh in Selkirkshire on the Gala Water near its confluence with the R. Tweed. Pop. (1961) 12,374. Important manufacture of tweeds and knitwear. Technical college associated with the woollen industry.

**Galaţi** Rumania. Capital of Galaţi district and river port in Moldavia, on the R. Danube 90 m. WNW of the mouth at Sulina. Pop. (1968) 157,920. Exports grain, timber. Shipbuilding. Manufactures textiles, chemicals, hardware, etc. Naval base. Scene of the Danube conference (1953).

**Galatia.** Ancient region in Asia Minor around the modern Ankara, so named because Gauls invaded and dominated it (278 B.C.). They were defeated, however, and their territory was much reduced by Attalus I of Pergamum (*c.* 230 B.C.). Became a Roman province 25 B.C.

**Galesburg** USA. Industrial town in Illinois, 43 m WNW of Peoria. Pop. (1960) 37,243. Manufactures agricultural implements, washing machines, hardware, etc. Railway engineering. Coalmines in the neighbourhood. Named after the Rev. George Washington Gale, a Presbyterian minister who founded both the town and Knox College in 1836. Birthplace of Carl Sandburg (1878–1967).

**Galicia** Poland/USSR. Region in SE Poland and the NW Ukrainian SSR, extending N from the Carpathians and drained by the Vistula and Dniester and other rivers. The Polish (W) part includes the towns of Cracow, Tarnow, Rzeszow, Przemyśl, and Nowy Sacz, and the Ukrainian part (E) Lvov, Stanislav, Drogobych, and Kolomyya. Considerable mineral wealth, particularly oil and natural gas. A Russian principality in the 12th cent. Passed to Poland in the 14th cent., and, with the 1st Partition (1772), to Austria. In 1815 Cracow became an independent republic, but, after the unsuccessful Polish rising, it was incorporated in Galicia (1846). Some measure of autonomy was now granted to Galicia, but Polish and Ukrainian (Ruthenian) nationalism continued to grow. In 1919 W Galicia was assigned to Poland, and in

1923 E Galicia was also recognized as Polish. After the 2nd World War the E part was ceded to the USSR and incorporated in the Ukrainian SSR.

**Galicia** Spain. Region and former kingdom in the NW, bounded by the Bay of Biscay (N), the Atlantic Ocean (W), and Portugal (S), now comprising the provinces of Corunna, Lugo, Orense, and Pontevedra. An area of mountains, plateaux, and deep valleys, highest in the E where the land rises to over 6,000 ft. Rocky coastline with many deep inlets (rias). Chief river is the Miño, forming part of the boundary with Portugal. Cattle and pigs raised. Maize, potatoes grown. Important sardine fishing. Chief towns Vigo, Corunna, Santiago de Compostela.

**Galilee** Israel. Region in the N, bounded by Lebanon (N), Syria and Jordan (E), and the Plain of Esdraelon (S). Divided into Upper Galilee (N), which is hilly and rises to nearly 4,000 ft, and Lower Galilee (S), lower and more fertile. Chief towns Tiberias (on the W shore of the Sea of Galilee), Nazareth.

**Galilee, Sea of (Lake Tiberias)** Israel. Lake 13 m. long and up to 7 m. wide, in the NE on the border with Syria; its surface 696 ft below sea level, it occupies part of the Great Rift Valley. The Jordan R. flows through it. In the Old Testament it is also called the Sea of Chinnereth and in the New Testament the Lake of Gennesaret.

**Gallarate** Italy. Town in Varese province, Lombardy, 25 m. WNW of Milan. Pop. (1961) 35,477. Manufactures textiles etc. Has a 12th/13th-cent. church.

**Galle** Ceylon. Formerly Point de Galle. Seaport and commercial town on the SW coast 65 m. SSE of Colombo. Pop. (1963) 64,942. Exports coconut oil, coir rope, etc. Became the island's chief port in the 16th and 17th cent.; declined with the improvement of Colombo harbour in the late 19th cent.

**Gallipoli** (Turkish **Gelibolu**) Turkey. **1.** Peninsula extending 55 m SW between the Dardanelles (S) and the Gulf of Saros (N). Scene of unsuccessful landings by British, Australian, and New Zealand troops in an attempt to force the Dardanelles in the 1st World War (1915).
**2.** Port in Canakkale province, on the Dardanelles at the entrance to the Sea of Marmara. Pop. (1965) 13,000. Trade in grain, livestock. Fishing. The first place in

Europe to be conquered by the Turks (c. 1356).

**Gällivare** Sweden. Town in Norrbotten county 50 m. SSE of Kiruna. Pop. (1968) 26,625. Iron-mining centre linked to Luleå on the Gulf of Bothnia and Narvik (Norway) by railway, the ore being transported thereby for export. Modern working of these rich deposits began in 1893.

**Galloway** Scotland. District in the SW comprising the counties of Wigtown and Kirkcudbright, formerly also the Carrick region of S Ayrshire. In the W is a double peninsula, the Rhinns of Galloway, with Corsewall Point at the N end and the Mull of Galloway, the most southerly point of Scotland, at the S end. Main occupation dairy farming; Galloway is the home of the breed of black cattle named after it. The Galloway hydroelectric scheme was established in 1935.

**Galt** Canada. Formerly Shade's Mills. Industrial town in Ontario, on the Grand R. 23 m. WNW of Hamilton. Pop. (1966) 33,491. Manufactures textiles, shoes, machinery, etc. Founded 1816; renamed (1827) after John Galt, the Scottish novelist.

**Galveston** USA. Seaport and industrial town in Texas on Galveston Island, at the entrance to Galveston Bay, an arm of the Gulf of Mexico, connected to the mainland by two causeways. Pop. (1960) 67,175. Shipyards and dry docks. Handles large exports of sulphur, cotton, wheat, etc. Flour and rice milling, meat packing, brewing. Manufactures chemicals, metal goods, hardware, etc. Seat of the medical school of the University of Texas. Popular resort ('the Oleander City'). A hurricane destroyed it in 1900, with the loss of about 5,000 lives; special precautionary measures were taken when it was rebuilt, including the building of a high sea wall. When it was struck by another violent hurricane (1961), fewer than 50 lives were lost and the damage to property was much reduced.

**Galway** Irish Republic. **1.** County in Connacht, in the W, bounded on the W by the Atlantic Ocean, with Galway Bay to the S. Area 2,293 sq. m. Pop. (1966) 149,887. Coast deeply indented, with many islands, including the Aran Is. The W part is mountainous, with the Twelve Pins (2,395 ft) and the Maamturk Mountains (2,307 ft); here is the wild but beautiful Connemara, a region of moors, bogs, and lakes. To the E of the large Lough Corrib

the land is low-lying and in part fertile, the Suck and the Shannon flowing along the E border. Potatoes grown; sheep raised. Chief towns Galway, Ballinasloe, Tuam.
**2.** County town of Co. Galway, at the mouth of the short R. Corrib, which drains Lough Corrib, on the N shore of Galway Bay. Pop. (1966) 24,597. Seaport and fishing centre, well-known for its salmon. Manufactures fishing nets, rope, furniture, etc. Flour milling. Several old houses ('mansions'); 14th-cent. church; University College (1849), part of the National University of Ireland and a centre of Gaelic studies. The Lynch Stone commemorates the execution of a mayor's son (by his father) for murder (1493).

**Gambela** ◊ *Sobat River*.

**Gambia.*** Former British colony and protectorate in W Africa, an enclave within Senegal, extending about 200 m. inland from the estuary of the Gambia R., along both banks. Area 4,008 sq. m. Pop. (1963) 315,486. Cap. Bathurst. Mainly savannah. Main product and export groundnuts; also palm kernels. The Gambia R. is the chief trade highway. Discovered by the Portuguese in the late 15th cent. Britain became interested in the region in the 17th cent. Became a British colony 1843, and part of the British W African settlements 1866. Regained its status as a separate colony 1888. Became independent within the British Commonwealth 1965.

**Gambia River.** River 700 m. long, rising in the Fouta Djallon plateau (in Guinea), flowing generally NW and W through Senegal and Gambia, and entering the Atlantic Ocean. Navigable to ocean-going vessels for nearly 200 m.

**Gambier Islands** (French Polynesia) S Pacific Ocean. Group of 4 coral islands and several uninhabited islets inside a barrier reef about 40 m. long, SE of the Tuamotu Is. Total area 12 sq. m. Largest island Mangareva; chief settlement Rikitea. Produce copra, coffee, mother-of-pearl.

**Ganale River** ◊ *Juba River*.

**Gander** Canada. Town and airport in E Newfoundland just N of Gander L. Pop. (1966) 7,183. Chosen as a trans-atlantic air base by the British Air Ministry 1935. Flights began in 1939; during the 2nd World War it became a leading Allied base, and later it became a major N American terminal for flights to Europe. The town has grown near the airport.

**Ganges Canals** India. Irrigation system in

Uttar Pradesh comprising the Upper and Lower Ganges Canals. The Upper Ganges Canal (1855–6) leaves the Ganges at Hardwar and divides, one branch continuing to Kanpur and the other to the Jumna; the Lower Ganges Canal (1879–80) leaves the Ganges near Dibai and splits into a number of branches.

**Ganges (Ganga) River.** Great river of India and Pakistan, 1,557 m. long, formed in the Himalayas from the union of the Bhagirathi R., which issues from an ice cave, and Alaknanda R. As the Ganges it flows generally SW past Hardwar, then turns SE past Farrukhabad and Kanpur to Allahabad, where it receives the Jumna. Continues E across the plain, past Varanasi (Benares) and Patna, being joined by the Gogra and Gandak, turns S and SE and begins to divide, about 220 m. from the Bay of Bengal, into the many distributaries which cross its great delta. Its main stream, the Padma, enters E Pakistan, is joined by the Jamuna, the main stream of the Brahmaputra, and as the Meghna enters the Bay of Bengal on the E side of the delta; on the W side is the Hooghly R., the main channel of navigation. The Ganges, the most sacred of Hindu rivers, is much used for irrigation.

**Gangtok** Sikkim. Capital and largest town, 30 m. NE of Darjeeling (India). Pop. (1964) 12,000. Trade in rice, maize, fruit, etc. Linked by road with Siliguri (India).

**Ganzo Azul** ◊ *Pucallpa*.

**Gard** France. Department in Languedoc bordering on the lower Rhône R. and delta (E) and on the Gulf of Lions (S). Area 2,270 sq. m. Pop. (1968) 478,544. Prefecture Nîmes. Flat in the S with many lagoons and marshes, rising to over 5,000 ft in the NW. Produces olives, mulberries (for silkworms), fruit, wine. Some coal mined. Industries (mainly metallurgy, textiles, paper) concentrated chiefly in Alès and Nîmes. Near Remoulins the Gard R. is crossed by the Pont du Gard aqueduct, constructed in 19 B.C. to carry water from springs near Uzès to Nîmes, which has some of the most famous Roman remains in France.

**Garda, Lake** (Italian **Lago di Garda**) Italy. Ancient Lacus Benacus. The largest lake in Italy (143 sq. m.), its S end 65 m. E of Milan. Fed by the Sarca R. in the N and drained by the Mincio R. in the SE. Well stocked with fish. Vines, olives, citrus fruits grown around its W and S shores.

Sirmione on the S shore was a favourite residence of Catullus, and many lakeside villages, linked by steamer services, have long been holiday resorts.

**Garden of the Gods** USA. A region of strangely eroded red sandstone just NW of Colorado Springs, Colorado. The rocks resemble animals, gargoyles, etc. Popular tourist attraction. Named by R. E. Cable, a Kansas City lawyer who visited the site in 1859.

**Gardez** Afghanistan. Commercial town 55 m. S of Kabul on the road to Kandahar, at a height of 7,500 ft on the central plateau. Pop. (1965) 46,000. Developed in recent years owing to the increase in road traffic.

**Garfield** USA. Industrial town in New Jersey, on the Passaic R. 10 m. NNE of Newark. Pop. (1960) 29,253. Manufactures textiles, chemicals, rubber products, etc.

**Garibaldi Park** Canada. Provincial park in the Coast Mountains of SW British Columbia, NE of Vancouver. Area 973 sq. m. Well-known scenic area, with mountain lakes, peaks, and glaciers. Facilities for camping, boating, etc.

**Garmisch-Partenkirchen** Federal German Republic. Resort and winter-sports centre in Upper Bavaria 52 m. SW of Munich at a height of 2,300 ft. Pop. (1963) 26,600. Rack-and-pinion railway to the Zugspitze. Woodworking etc. Site of the winter Olympic Games 1936.

**Garonne River** France. Ancient Garumna. River 360 m. long in the SW, rising in the Val d'Aran in the central Pyrenees (about 30 m. of the upper course being in Spain) and flowing NE and NW through the Haute-Garonne, Tarn-et-Garonne, Lot-et-Garonne, and Gironde departments. About 20 m. below Bordeaux it is joined by the Dordogne R. and forms the Gironde estuary, entering the Atlantic at the Pointe de Grave. With its tributaries, the Ariège, Tarn, Lot, etc., it drains the Aquitaine basin, and at Toulouse it is linked by the Canal du Midi with the Mediterranean. Wheat and maize extensively cultivated in its basin. The lower basin is famous for its wines.

**Gartok** China. Main commercial centre in W Tibet, at the W end of the Kailas Range at a height of 15,000 ft. Trade in wool, barley, salt, etc.

**Garut** Indonesia. Town in W Java 25 m. SE of Bandung at a height of 2,300 ft.

Pop. 56,000. Commercial centre and resort in an agricultural region (tea, rubber, cinchona), amid fine scenery (mountains, lakes, hot springs).

**Gary** USA. Major industrial city in NW Indiana at the S end of L. Michigan. Pop. (1960) 178,320. One of the world's leading steel-producing centres. Also manufactures tinplate, cement, chemicals, etc. Its 'platoon' school system, in which physical training is an important feature, is well-known. Named after Elbert H. Gary (1846–1927), first chairman of the US Steel Corporation.

**Gascony** France. Former province in the SW bounded by the Pyrenees (S) and the Bay of Biscay (W), in the Aquitaine basin, now comprising the departments of Gers, Hautes-Pyrénées, and Landes and parts of Haute-Garonne, Lot-et-Garonne, and Tarn-et-Garonne. The name is derived from the Vascones (Basques), a Spanish tribe which crossed the Pyrenees and conquered it in the 6th cent., later setting up the duchy of Vasconia (Gascony). In English hands 1154–1453, with Auch as capital. Divided into the present departments 1790.

**Gash River** ◊ *Kassala.*

**Gaspé** Canada. Peninsula in E Quebec between the St Lawrence R. (N) and Chaleur Bay (S). Area 11,000 sq. m. The interior is mountainous and wooded, with many streams and lakes. The Shickshock Mountains rise to 4,160 ft in Mt Jacques Cartier. Chief occupations cod fishing, lumbering, pulp milling. The people (largely French Canadians) live mainly in coastal villages. A provincial park (328,960 acres) was established 1937.

**Gastein (Bad Gastein)** Austria. Picturesque valley in Salzburg province near the E end of the Höhe Tauern at a height of 3,000–3,500 ft. Famous for its thermal springs. Principal resorts Bad-Gastein (pop. 5,700) and Hof-Gastein (pop. 4,700).

**Gastonia** USA. Town in N Carolina 19 m. W of Charlotte. Pop. (1960) 37,276. Important textile centre, esp. for the manufacture of cotton goods. Scene of a serious strike in the textile industry in 1929.

**Gateshead** England. County borough in Durham on the S bank of the R. Tyne opposite Newcastle-upon-Tyne, with which linked by tunnel and 5 bridges. Pop. (1961) 103,232. Engineering, shipbuilding, flour milling. Manufactures chemicals, pharmaceutical products, glass, etc. Many light industries were established in the 1930s in the Team Valley trading estate to relieve unemployment, esp. in the neighbourhood's coalmining industry. Probably founded in Saxon times. Largely destroyed by fire 1854; the 13th-cent. parish church was rebuilt.

**Gatineau River** Canada. River 230 m. long, rising near Parent (Quebec) and flowing generally SSW to join the Ottawa R. just below Ottawa. Important timber highway and source of hydroelectric power. Named after Nicholas Gatineau, a 17th-cent. fur trader.

**Gatooma** ◊ *Mashonaland.*

**Gatwick** England. Village in Surrey 6 m. SSE of Reigate on the London–Brighton road and railway. Site of London's subsidiary airport.

**Gauhati** India. Town in Assam, on the Brahmaputra R. 43 m. N of Shillong. Pop. (1961) 100,707. Trade in rice, jute, cotton, etc. Cotton, flour, and oilseed milling and other industries. The oil refinery began production in 1962. University (1948). Capital of the Ahom kingdom in the 18th cent. Later the centre of British administration in Assam. Near by are the ruins of two ancient Hindu temples.

**Gaul.** Ancient Gallia. Ancient country of W Europe inhabited by the Gauls and roughly corresponding to modern France. It consisted of Cisalpine Gaul (Gallia Cisalpina), the region of N Italy between the Alps and the Apennines, divided by the Po R. into Cispadane Gaul (Gallia Cispadana) and Transpadane Gaul (Gallia Transpadana); and the larger and more important Transalpine Gaul (Gallia Transalpina), extending from the Pyrenees as far N and E as the Rhine and the Alps. Its SE part had become a Roman province before 100 BC.; Julius Caesar conquered the whole of Transalpine Gaul (58–51 B.C.). It was divided into 5 administrative areas: Narbonensis, Aquitania, Lugdunensis, Belgica (roughly modern Belgium), and a fifth region comprising two military districts along the Rhine.

**Gävle** Sweden. Formerly Gefle. Capital of Gävleborg county, seaport on the Gulf of Bothnia at the mouth of the Gävle R. 100 m. NNW of Stockholm. Pop. (1968) 60,990. Exports iron, timber, wood pulp, paper. Shipbuilding, fish canning. Manufactures wood pulp, paper, chemicals, textiles, etc. Sometimes ice-bound for 3 months in the winter. Castle (16th-cent., rebuilt later); courthouse (18th-cent.).

**Gaya** India. Town in Bihar 58 m. S of Patna. Pop. (1961) 151,105. Trade in rice, oilseeds, sugar-cane, etc. Important place of Hindu pilgrimage. Buddh Gaya, 6 m. S, is sacred to Buddhists. Seat of Magadha University (1962).

**Gaza.** Ancient city of the Philistines, in SW Palestine; biblical history tells how Samson pulled down its temple. Taken by Alexander the Great (332 B.C.) and later by Maccabees and Romans. Scene of three battles in the 1st World War. The modern town of Gaza, 43 m. SSW of Tel Aviv (Israel), was occupied by the United Arab Republic, along with the Gaza coastal strip, from 1949 till the Israeli-Arab war of June 1967.

**Gaziantep** Turkey. Capital of Gaziantep province, 110 m. E of Adana. Pop. (1965) 160,200. Important market town. Manufactures textiles. Trade in grain and other agricultural produce. Strategically important throughout history. Besieged by the French and taken during their conquest of Syria (1921); returned to Turkey 1922.

**Gdańsk** Poland. Formerly Danzig. Baltic seaport and capital of the Gdańsk voivodship, near the mouth of the Vistula R. on Gdańsk Bay. Pop. (1968) 364,000. Exports coal, timber, grain, etc. Shipbuilding, food processing, distilling. Manufactures machinery, wood pulp and paper. Its outport for ocean-going vessels is Nowy Port, 4 m. NNW. The city had preserved much of its picturesque medieval appearance, with narrow streets and gabled houses, but it suffered severely in the 2nd World War; the famous 14th/16th-cent. Church of St Mary, e.g., was severely damaged. At first a Slavonic settlement, it joined the Hanseatic League in the 13th cent. and became an important Baltic port. Remained a free city under Polish sovereignty from 1455 to 1793, when at the 2nd Partition of Poland it passed to Prussia. A free city again 1807–14, it was returned to Prussia and made capital of the province of W Prussia. After the 1st World War it was made capital of the territory of the Free City of Danzig under the League of Nations, but in 1939 it was annexed by Germany – an action which was soon followed by the invasion of Poland and the outbreak of the 2nd World War. In 1945 it was returned to Poland, and with Gdynia and Szczecin handles the majority of the country's sea-borne trade. Birthplace of Fahrenheit (1686–1736) and Schopenhauer (1788–1860).

**GDR (German Democratic Republic)** ◊ *Germany*.

**Gdynia** Poland. Seaport in the Gdańsk voivodship, on Gdańsk Bay 12 m. NNW of Gdańsk. Pop. (1968) 179,200 (1,300 in 1921; 34,400 in 1931). Exports coal, timber, etc. Deliberately developed from a small fishing village in 1924 as a purely Polish port to replace Danzig (Gdańsk); within ten years became a major Baltic seaport, handling more of Poland's trade than Danzig. Now shares the majority of Poland's overseas trade with Gdańsk and Szczecin.

**Geba River** ◊ *Bissão*.

**Geelong** Australia. Port in Victoria on the flat W shore of Corio Bay, an arm of Port Phillip Bay, 42 m. SW of Melbourne. Pop. (1966) 104,974. Exports wool, wheat, meat, etc. Also railway junction and industrial centre. Manufactures tweeds and other woollen goods, cars, agricultural machinery. Oil refinery and cement and chemical works near by. The first woollen mill in Victoria was established here. Founded 1837. Grew rapidly after the gold rush of 1851.

**Gefle** ◊ *Gävle*.

**Geislingen (Geislingen an der Steige)** Federal German Republic. Town in Baden-Württemberg, in the Swabian Jura 32 m. ESE of Stuttgart. Pop. (1963) 25,800. Manufactures metal goods (inc. silverware), glassware, etc.

**Gela** Italy. Formerly Terranova di Sicilia. Town and port in Caltanissetta province, Sicily, on the S coast. Pop. (1961) 54,774. Founded as a Greek colony *c.* 690 B.C.; enjoyed its greatest prosperity under Hippocrates at the beginning of the 5th cent. B.C. Deserted *c.* 281 B.C. Refounded by Frederick II (1233) as Terranova di Sicilia. Scene of one of the first Allied landings in the invasion of Sicily in the 2nd World War (1943).

**Gelderland** Netherlands. Province between Ijsselmeer (NW) and W Germany (E and SE). Area 1,937 sq m. Pop. (1968) 1,456,554. Cap. Arnhem. Drained by the Ijssel, Waal, and Lower Rhine rivers; the fertile region of Betuwe in the SW and the infertile heathland of Veluwe in the N. Main crops wheat, rye, buckwheat, tobacco. Chief towns Arnhem, Nijmegen, Apeldoorn. Formerly a duchy. The E part (inc. the town of Geldern, from which the

name derives) was ceded to Prussia 1715.
**Geleen** Netherlands. Industrial town in
Limburg province 10 m. NE of Maastricht.
Pop. (1968) 36,254. Manufactures chemicals, fertilizers, textiles, etc. Coalmining in
the neighbourhood.

**Gelibolu** ◊ *Gallipoli*.

**Gelligaer** Wales. Urban district in Glamorgan 6 m. NE of Pontypridd, in a coalmining area. Pop. (1961) 34,572.

**Gelsenkirchen** Federal German Republic.
Industrial town in N Rhine-Westphalia,
just NE of Essen. Pop. (1968) 356,391
Leading coalmining centre of the Ruhr
coalfield. Blast furnaces, foundries, steel
mills. Manufactures machinery, stoves,
chemicals, glass, etc. Suffered severe
damage from bombing in the 2nd World
War.

**General José F. Uriburu** ◊ *Zárate*.

**Geneva** (Fr. Genève, Ger. Genf) Switzerland. 1. Small canton in the SW, almost
surrounded by French territory. Area 109
sq. m. Pop. (1969) 326,600, of whom the
majority live in the capital, Geneva, and its
suburbs, being mainly French-speaking and
Protestant. Fruit, vegetables, wine produced in the rural districts.
2. Capital of the Geneva canton, the third
largest city in Switzerland, at the point
where the Rhône R. leaves L. Geneva
(SW corner). Pop. (1969) 173,400. Cultural and commercial centre. Manufactures watches, optical and scientific instruments, machinery, confectionery, etc.
Cathedral (12th/13th-cent., restored); town
hall (16th/17th-cent.); Museum of Art and
History; university (1873), founded (1559)
as Calvin's Academy. Also the seat of the
International Red Cross (1864) and the
International Labour Office, and (1920–46)
of the League of Nations. A town of the
Allobroges, taken by the Romans with the
rest of S Gaul. Passed with Burgundy to
the Holy Roman Empire (1032), its bishops
later becoming imperial princes. In the
16th cent. with the advent of Calvin, it
became the centre of the Reformation and
a refuge for persecuted Protestants. Its
fame as a cosmopolitan and cultural centre
grew, esp. in the 18th cent. Annexed to
France 1798–1814. Became capital of the
22nd and last canton of the Swiss Confederation 1815. Birthplace of Rousseau
(1712–78), de Saussure (1740–99), and
Necker (1732–1804).

**Geneva, Lake** (Fr. Lac Léman, Ger. Genfersee) France/Switzerland. Crescent-
shaped lake between SW Switzerland and
the Haute-Savoie department of France, at
a height of 1,230 ft, about 45 m. long and
up to 8 m. wide. Area 223 sq. m. (140 sq. m.
Swiss, remainder (S) French). The Rhône
R. enters it at the E end, making its water
muddy, but to the W it becomes deep blue
and extraordinarily transparent; the river
leaves it at Geneva. Its beauty, with snow-
covered mountains to the S and vineyards
and pastures to the N, has been celebrated
by Byron, Voltaire, and others, and there
are several resorts along its shores, e.g.
Montreux, Vevey (Switzerland), Évian-les-
Bains (France). Its surface is subject to
temporary changes of level (*seiches*), similar
to tides, both longitudinally and transversely; these are probably caused by
variations in atmospheric pressure and
wind.

**Genf** ◊ *Geneva*.

**Génissiat** ◊ *Bellegarde-sur-Valserine*.

**Genk** Belgium. Coalmining town in Limbourg province 23 m. N of Liège. Pop.
(1968) 56,031 (inc. many Italians and other
foreigners). Manufactures mining machinery etc. Has expanded rapidly with the
development of the three local collieries.

**Gennevilliers** France. Industrial suburb of
NW Paris in the Hauts-de-Seine department, in a loop of the Seine R. Pop. (1968)
46,099. River port. Manufactures aircraft,
electrical equipment, etc.

**Genoa** (Italian Genova) Italy. Capital of
Liguria and of Genoa province, on the Gulf
of Genoa. Pop. (1968) 844,499. Italy's chief
seaport; exports olive oil, wine, textiles,
etc., also serving much of central Europe,
with considerable passenger traffic. Shipbuilding, engineering, oil refining, sugar
refining, food canning, brewing, distilling.
Manufactures iron and steel, aircraft, textiles, soap, paper, etc. Behind the excellent
harbour, which is protected by moles, the
city rises up the lower slopes of the Ligurian
Apennines, setting off to advantage its fine
architectural features. Outstanding among
them are its many churches, including the
cathedral of San Lorenzo, consecrated
1118, with campanile and cupola of the
16th cent.; and the churches of Sant'-
Ambrogio, reconstructed in the 16th cent.
from a 4th-cent. church, and Santa Maria
di Castello (11th-cent.). The palaces, too,
are magnificent, esp. those on the Via
Garibaldi, the Palazzo Rosso and Palazzo
Bianco, opposite one another and both
now museums; in the Palazzo Municipale

are letters of Columbus and Paganini's violin. University (1243). In the Middle Ages Genoa became a great maritime republic, at times vanquishing its two chief rivals, Pisa and Venice, but eventually becoming subject to France; its last overseas possession, Corsica, was ceded to France 1768. The city (inc. some of its most famous buildings) was severely damaged by bombing in the 2nd World War. Birthplace of Columbus (c. 1451–1506), John Cabot (1450–98), Paganini (1784–1840), and Mazzini (1805–72).

**George, Lake** (Uganda) ◊ *Edward, Lake.*

**George, Lake** USA. Long narrow lake (32 m. long and up to 3 m. wide) in NE New York, in the foothills of the Adirondack Mountains, with an outlet to the N into L. Champlain. Favourite summer resort, noteworthy for mountain scenery and islands. The original Indian name was 'Andiatarocte' ('Place Where the Lake Contracts'); the present name was given by General William Johnson (1755) in honour of George II.

**Georgetown** Guyana. Capital and chief seaport, on the right bank of the Demerara R., at the mouth; protected by a sea wall. Pop. (1967) 186,824. Exports sugar, rice, bauxite, etc. Airport inland. Coastal railway. Ferry across the river. the botanical gardens are famous, esp. the collections of palms and orchids. After disastrous fires (1945 and 1951) many of the old wooden buildings were replaced by concrete structures.

**George Town** (Malaya) ◊ *Penang.*

**Georgia** USA. State in the SE, bordered by Tennessee and N Carolina (N), S Carolina and the Atlantic (E), Florida (S), and Alabama (W). Area 58,876 sq. m. Pop. (1970) 4,492,038. Cap. Atlanta. One of the original 13 states; popularly known as the 'Empire State of the South'. The land rises gradually from the coast NW to the Appalachians; the highest point is Brasstown Bald (4,768 ft) in the NE. On the coastal plain there are swamps and forests of pine, cypress, oak, and magnolia, with Okefenokee Swamp in the SE. Climate humid and sub-tropical, rainfall averaging about 50 ins. annually. Agriculture is of major importance; chief crops maize, cotton, tobacco, groundnuts. The state produces most of the US kaolin output. Principal industries cotton milling, wood processing. Chief towns Atlanta, Savannah (chief seaport), Columbus, Augusta, Macon.

Explored by the Spaniards in the 16th cent. Became a British colony 1754, taking its name from George II. In the American Civil War it suffered considerably in Sherman's 'March to the Sea' (1864), commemorated in the song *Marching Through Georgia.*

**Georgian Bay** Canada. The NE part of L. Huron, in Ontario. Area 5,800 sq. m. Many summer resorts on the shores and islands. The Georgian Bay Islands National Park, comprising 30 small islands, was established in 1929.

**Georgian SSR** USSR. Constituent republic, in W Transcaucasia, bounded by Turkey (SW) and the Black Sea (W). Area 26,900 sq. m. Pop. (1970) 4,688,000 (about 64 per cent Georgians, 11 per cent Armenians, 10 per cent Russians, and 4 per cent Azerbaijanis). Cap. Tbilisi (Tiflis). Includes the Abkhaz ASSR, Adzhar ASSR, and S Ossetian AR. The N part lies on the S slopes of the Great Caucasus, the S part is on the Lesser Caucasus, and between the mountainous areas are the valleys of the Kura and Rion; these rivers and others have been harnessed for hydroelectric power, and there are large irrigation schemes. On the Black Sea lowlands (Colchis), with their humid sub-tropical climate, tea, citrus fruits, tung oil, and tobacco are produced, and (inland) wines. In the Chiatura district are the richest manganese deposits in the USSR, and coal, baryta, oil, and other minerals are exploited. Since the 2nd World War metallurgical and other industries have been developed. Chief towns Tbilisi, Kutaisi, the three main seaports (Batumi, Sukhumi, and Poti), Rustavi, and Gori, birthplace of Stalin. Many coastal and mountain resorts. An independent kingdom for more than 2,000 years; reached the peak of its power in the 12th and 13th cent. – the Golden Age of its culture and political influence, which came to an end with the Mongol invasion beginning in 1234. At times subject to Turkey and Persia, its principalities were gradually annexed by Russia (1810–67). After civil war (1917–21), the Georgian SSR joined the USSR as a member of the Transcaucasian SFSR (1922), and in 1936 became a separate constituent republic.

**Gera** German Democratic Republic. **1.** Administrative district created (1952) from part of the former *Land* of Thuringia. Area 1,546 sq. m. Pop. (1968) 735,952.

**2.** Capital of the Gera district, on the White Elster R. 37 m. W of Karl-Marx-Stadt. Pop. (1968) 109,402. Railway junction and industrial town. Manufactures textiles, machinery, furniture, carpets, etc. Has a 16th-cent. town hall.

**Geraldton** Australia. Seaport in Western Australia 230 m. NNW of Perth. Pop. (1966) 12,118. Outlet for the Murchison goldfield and also for a wide agricultural area. Exports wheat, wool. Manufactures superphosphates. Brewing, crayfish canning. Also a tourist centre.

**German Democratic Republic** ◊ *Germany*.

**German East Africa** ◊ *Rwanda*; *Tanzania*.

**Germantown** USA. Residential suburb of NW Philadelphia, Pennsylvania. Noted for 18th-cent. 'colonial' houses. An early centre of printing and publishing. Founded by 13 German families *c.* 1683. Site of the battle of Germantown (1777) in the American War of Independence.

**Germany** (Ger. **Deutschland**). Country of central Europe divided since 1945 into W Germany (Federal German Republic) and E Germany (German Democratic Republic). *West Germany (Federal German Republic)*: Area (inc. W Berlin) 95,930 sq. m. Pop. (1968) 59,948,500. Cap. Bonn. Rel. 50 per cent Protestants, 46 per cent Roman Catholics. *East Germany (German Democratic Republic)*: Area (inc. E Berlin) 41,802 sq. m. Pop. (1968) 17,089,884 Cap. E Berlin. Rel. 81 per cent Protestants, 11 per cent Roman Catholics.

Even after the territorial losses following the two world wars, Germany as a whole is still one of the larger countries of Europe, and the Federal German Republic alone is slightly larger than the United Kingdom. Germany is predominantly an industrial country, its manufacturing industries being concentrated mainly in Westphalia (W Germany) and Saxony (E Germany). Scientific methods of farming have raised productivity to a high level, but large quantities of foodstuffs as well as raw materials have to be imported. W Germany (FGR) is divided for administrative purposes into W Berlin and the following *Länder*: Schleswig-Holstein, Hamburg, Lower Saxony, Bremen, N Rhine-Westphalia, Hessen, Rhineland-Palatinate, Baden-Württemberg, Bavaria, and Saarland. E Germany (GDR) is divided for administrative purposes into the following Districts: Rostock, Schwerin, Neubrandenburg, Potsdam, Frankfurt-an-

der-Oder, Cottbus, Magdeburg, Halle, Erfurt, Gera, Suhl, Dresden, Leipzig, Karl-Marx-Stadt, and E Berlin.

TOPOGRAPHY, CLIMATE. The country may be divided into four main physical regions. In the N a low-lying sandy plain extends W–E from the Netherlands to Poland, forming part of the N European Plain and containing much heath (e.g. Lüneburg Heath) and moorland. S of this plain is the region of plateau and block mountains which comprises Central Germany, including the Harz, Thüringerwald, and other uplands and the two great industrial regions of Westphalia and Saxony. In the SW is the Rift Valley of the Rhine with its associated highlands (Black Forest, etc.) and the ridge of the Swabian and Franconian Jura. In the extreme S the land rises to the Bavarian Alps, which contain Germany's highest peak, the Zugspitze (9,721 ft). The principal rivers drain N and NW to the North Sea, outstanding in importance being the Rhine, with its tributaries the Main, Moselle, and Ruhr, also the Elbe and Weser; the Oder, on the Polish frontier with E Germany, flows to the Baltic, and the Danube through Bavaria to the SE. The commercial value of these rivers has been considerably enhanced by an interconnecting system of canals (Mittelland, Dortmund–Ems), while the Kiel Canal links the Baltic with the North Sea across Schleswig-Holstein. In the NW the climate is maritime temperate, and conditions become more continental (i.e. extreme) to the E, while in the S temperatures are somewhat reduced by altitude; rainfall is moderate (20–30 ins. annually) and well distributed throughout the year.

AGRICULTURE, INDUSTRY. On the poorer soils of the N rye is the main cereal, and here and elsewhere potatoes are an important crop. Sugar-beet is widely cultivated in Central Germany, and wheat to the S; grapes for the Rhine and Moselle wines are grown along the banks of those rivers and hops for the beers of Munich in Bavaria. The rich coal deposits of the Ruhr basin form the basis of the great iron and steel industry of that area, centred on Dortmund, Duisburg, and Essen, and much lignite is mined near Cologne; also in N Rhine-Westphalia Düsseldorf is an important commercial centre, Wuppertal is famous for its textiles, and Solingen for its cutlery. E Germany has the world's greatest output of lignite, mined in Saxony and largely utilized for the generation of electricity; in this area Leipzig is well-known for its printing and publishing, Dresden for its optical and precision instruments, Karl-Marx-Stadt (Chemnitz) for its textiles, Meissen for its porcelain. Chemicals are manufactured here and, in W Germany, along the Rhine at Ludwigshafen and other centres. Germany has an efficient system of railways and roads, the latter having been amplified during the Nazi régime by the construction of fast motorways. Hamburg and Bremen are the chief seaports of W Germany, while in E Germany Rostock is being developed to handle the country's entire sea-going traffic. There is a relatively small volume of trade between W and E Germany. The US has the largest share of W Germany's foreign trade, followed by France, the Netherlands, Italy, and Belgium. By a trade agreement (1959) nearly half of the trade of E Germany, which is a state monopoly, is with the USSR and more than three quarters with the Communist bloc as a whole.

PEOPLE, GOVERNMENT, *etc.* In the divided Germany subsequent to the 2nd World War a feature of the distribution of population has been the heavy stream of migrants leaving E Germany for W Germany. The number reached 396,000 in 1956, and was 225,000 in 1960, but in 1961 the E German government stemmed the flow by erecting the 'Berlin wall'. A much smaller number had meanwhile left W Germany for E Germany: 47,000 in 1956 and 29,000 in 1960. Most of the people of N Germany are Protestants, the Roman Catholics being strongest in Bavaria and the Rhineland. Education is compulsory for all children between the ages of 6 and 14. W and E Germany have different forms of government. W Germany is a federal republic, with a Federal Diet (*Bundestag*) elected for 4 years and a Federal Council (*Bundesrat*); E Germany, on the other hand, is a people's republic after the Soviet pattern, and as such is not recognized by any non-Communist government. W and E Germany each has its own unit of currency, the Deutsche Mark, but the rate of exchange fixed by the E German government for its D M (East) is not recognized by the International Monetary Fund.

HISTORY. The ancient Germanic tribes, who originated in Scandinavia, were long held by the Romans between the Rhine, Elbe, and Danube, but in the 3rd cent. a group of tribes in the NW, known as Franks, appeared. They gradually extended their power in Belgium and France, and by the time of Charlemagne Germany had become part of their kingdom. After the death of Charlemagne (814) Germany was separated from France and was ruled by its own kings, with the local dukes virtually independent until the establishment of the Saxon dynasty (919). The third of this elected line of kings, Otto I, was crowned Emperor by Pope John XII in 962, and so founded the Holy Roman Empire, which was to last till 1806. He also began the colonization of the Slav territories E of the Elbe, and, despite the later conflict between Emperors and Popes, the German people continued to expand, pushing their frontier as far E as the Vistula by the 14th cent., largely through the exploits of the Teutonic Knights. In the 16th cent. Charles V brought to the Empire extensive new possessions in Spain, Italy, the Netherlands, and elsewhere. At the same time the Reformation brought disunity to the German people; by the Peace of Augsburg (1555) most of N Germany was Protestant, and the ensuing Thirty Years War (1618–48) left the land depopulated, agriculture and commerce in ruin, and the imperial power merely nominal. Prussia now appeared as a military power, and under Frederick II conquered Silesia and became strong enough to challenge Austria; it was Napoleon, however, who united W Germany in the Confederation of the Rhine (1806) and simultaneously brought the Empire to an end. From 1815 Germany was a Confederation of 39 states, in many of which the democratic and nationalistic ideas inspired by the French Revolution of 1848 expressed themselves in open violence. Under Bismarck, Prussia supplanted Austria as the dominant German power, defeated Austria (1866) and then France (1870–71), and united Germany, with the King of Prussia as the hereditary German Emperor. At home industry developed, abroad a colonial empire was founded, but ambitious and aggressive policies led to defeat in the 1st World War (1914–18); the monarchy was overthrown and the democratic Weimar Republic established, while the colonies, chiefly in Africa, were placed under League of Nations mandate. A democratic system of government was short-lived, however, and the extreme right-wing Nazi party, taking advantage of the economic crisis of 1929–33, secured control and established the totalitarian Third Reich. Once more an aggressive foreign policy led to defeat in the 2nd World War (1939–45). E Prussia was partitioned between Poland and the USSR; the area of Germany, which in 1871 had been 208,780 sq. m. was reduced to 137,000 sq. m. and, moreover, the country was divided into four occupation zones by the US, Britain, France, and the USSR; in 1949 the three western zones became the Federal German Republic (W Germany) and the eastern zone became the German Democratic Republic (E Germany), while the former capital was similarly divided into W Berlin and E Berlin. In 1952, in W Germany, Baden, Württemberg-Baden, and Württemberg-Hohenzollern were amalgamated into the new *Land* of Baden-Württemberg, and in E Germany the five *Länder* were replaced by 15 Districts. A feature of the post-war years in W Germany was the remarkable recovery of the country's leading industries from the devastation of the 2nd World War; in E Germany, on the other hand, there was no such revival of economic prosperity, and in 1953, for example, widespread strikes were largely an expression of opposition to the Sovietization of industry and agriculture. With the passage of time the reunification of Germany, which most Germans on both sides of the Iron Curtain desired, seemed to be no nearer realization.

**Germiston** S Africa. Town in the Transvaal, at a height of 5,478 ft, 9 m. ESE of Johannesburg. Pop. (1967) 189,600 (119,200 Bantu, 65,000 whites). Important railway junction. Site of the world's largest gold refinery, serving the Witwatersrand mines. Railway engineering. Manufactures textiles, furniture, chemicals, steel goods, hardware, etc. Founded (1887) two years after the discovery of gold in the Witwatersrand.

**Gerona** Spain. 1. Province in the extreme NE, in Catalonia, bounded on the N by the Pyrenees, separating it from France, and on the E by the Mediterranean, with the small enclave of Llivia in France. Area 2,272 sq. m. Pop. (1961) 351,369. Mainly agricultural. Produces wheat, maize, wine, etc. Includes both the fertile Ampurdán plain and the Costa Brava with its many seaside resorts.
2. Ancient Gerunda. Capital of the Gerona province, on the Ter R. at its confluence with the Oñar R. 55 m. NE of Barcelona. Pop. (1961) 32,784. Flour milling. Manufactures textiles, chemicals, etc. Still has remains of the old city walls. Gothic cathedral (13th/16th-cent., 18th-cent. façade) with a remarkable single nave 73 ft wide.

**Gers** France. Department in the SW in Gascony at the foot of the Pyrenees, sloping down N towards the Garonne R. and drained by its tributaries (the Save, Gimone, Gers, and Baïse rivers) and the Adour R. Area 2,428 sq. m. Pop. (1968) 181,577. Prefecture Auch. Chiefly agricultural, famous for Armagnac brandy; also produces cereals, wine, fruit, poultry. Chief towns Auch, Condom.

**Gersoppa Falls** India. Cataract on the Sharavati R. in Mysore, renowned for its scenic beauty, 95 m. N of Mangalore. There are 4 cascades, the highest 829 ft. There is a hydroelectric power station near the falls.

**Gettysburg** USA. Small town (borough) in S Pennsylvania 35 m. SW of Harrisburg. Famous as the site of the Battle of Gettysburg (July 1863), the turning-point of the American Civil War, in which the Federal army under Meade defeated the Confederates under Lee. The National Cemetery (dedicated by Lincoln in his famous 'Gettysburg Address') is in the National Military Park, which includes the battlefield.

**Gevelsberg** Federal German Republic. Industrial town in N Rhine-Westphalia 7 m. ENE of Wuppertal. Pop. (1963) 32,100. Manufactures stoves, locks, bicycles, etc.

**Gezira, El** Sudan. In Arabic, 'The Island'. Plain between the White Nile and the Blue Nile, above their confluence at Khartoum, irrigated from the Sennar Dam on the Blue Nile (completed 1925). Chief town Wad Medani. Main crop cotton.

**Ghadames (Gadames, Rhadames)** Libya. Town in the Sahara, in the oasis of the same name 290 m. SW of Tripoli. Pop. 2,500. Near the intersection of the frontiers of Libya, Tunisia, and Algeria. Centre of caravan routes, but less important than formerly.

**Ghana.** Formerly Gold Coast. Republic in W Africa, a member of the British Commonwealth. Area 92,100 sq. m. Pop. (1968) 8,400,000. Cap. Accra. Bounded by Upper Volta (N), Togo (E), and the Ivory Coast (W). Principal waterway the Volta R.

(formed by the union of the White Volta and the Black Volta), which crosses NW–SE. Tropical monsoon climate. The SW coastal area is particularly hot and rainy; farther N the humidity is somewhat alleviated by the harmattan. Vegetation consists mainly of tropical rain-forest (S), changing gradually to savannah (N). Tropical hardwoods (e.g. mahogany) are shipped from the forest zone. Most important product and leading export cacao (grown by the Africans on small farms). Still produces about one third of the world's supply of cacao, despite destruction of cacao trees by 'swollen shoot' in recent years. Leading mineral export gold (mined in several areas); also diamonds, manganese. Railways run inland from Accra and Takoradi (chief seaport), joining at Kumasi. A new harbour was opened at Tema (E of Accra) in 1962.

The Portuguese, the Dutch, and the British established claims along the coast from the late 15th cent. The British Colony of the Gold Coast was created in 1874. The Northern Territories and Ashanti became a British protectorate in 1901. The development of cacao cultivation brought prosperity to many Africans; much progress was made in education. Became independent 1957; the Trust Territory of British Togoland was united with the Gold Coast to form the new state, named after the ancient kingdom of Ghana on the Niger R. Became a republic (within the British Commonwealth) and an independent member of the UN in 1960. Formed a union with Guinea and Mali to coordinate policies on economic and other matters 1960. After much political unrest and treason trials (1963), President Nkrumah introduced the single-party state (1964). He was deposed as the result of a military *coup* while visiting China in 1966.

**Ghats** India. Two mountain ranges of peninsular India, the Western and Eastern Ghats, forming the W and E margins respectively to the Deccan. The Western Ghats extend NNW–SSE from the Tapti R. valley to near Cape Comorin in the extreme S, reaching their highest point in Anai Mudi (8,841 ft) in Kerala (S); they have a profound climatic influence, for they cause the SW monsoon to deposit abundant moisture on their windward slopes, where the rainfall amounts to 100 ins. or more annually in places, while on the Deccan it averages only 20–40 ins. The

Eastern Ghats, a much more broken range than the other, has its highest point in Doda Betta (8,640 ft), in the Nilgiri Hills, where it meets the Western Ghats; their average height is 1,500 ft, compared with the 3,000 ft of the Western Ghats.

**Ghazaouet** ⟡ *Colomb-Béchar*; *Sahara*.

**Ghazipur** India. Town in Uttar Pradesh, on the Ganges R. 45 m. ENE of Varanasi (Benares). Pop. (1961) 37,147. Flour and oilseed milling. Manufactures perfumes.

**Ghazni** Afghanistan. Town 75 m. SSW of Kabul on the road to Kandahar, at a height of 7,280 ft on the central plateau. Pop. (1960) 26,000. Trade in livestock, wool, fruit, etc. It is walled, and above it stands the ancient citadel. From the late 10th cent. it flourished under the great Mahmud of Ghazni, and was capital of the Ghaznevid dynasty until destroyed in the mid 12th cent. by the Ghorids.

**Ghent** (Flemish **Gent**, Fr. **Gand**) Belgium. Capital of E Flanders province, on the Scheldt R. at its confluence with the Lys R. Pop. (1968) 155,717. Port, linked by canal with Terneuzen, making it accessible to large vessels. Also an industrial centre. Manufactures textiles (cotton, linen, jute), chemicals, fertilizers, glassware, paper. Flour milling, sugar refining, brewing, tanning, etc. Cathedral of St Bavon (12th/16th-cent.), which contains the masterpiece of the brothers van Eyck, *Adoration of the Lamb*; Belfry (12th/14th-cent.), with a 300-ft tower; Cloth Hall (14th-cent.); castle of the counts of Flanders (12th-cent. restored). The university was founded in 1816 and since 1930 has been Flemish. Ghent, historic capital of Flanders, grew up round the 9th-cent. castle of the first count, and spread to neighbouring islands which are still connected by numerous bridges. By the 13th cent. it had become an important centre of the textile industry, wealthy and powerful enough to enjoy a considerable measure of independence. Played a leading part in the struggle of the Netherlands against Spain, the Pacification of Ghent (1576) establishing a league in opposition to Spanish rule, but it was taken by the Spaniards in 1584. Freed from Habsburg domination 1794. Its commercial prosperity revived in the 19th cent. Birthplace of John of Gaunt (Ghent) (1340–99) and Maurice Maeterlinck (1862–1949).

**Ghivemba** ⟡ *Moçâmedes*.

**Ghor, El.** Depression 2–15 m. wide in Jordan and Israel between the Sea of Galilee and the Dead Sea, respectively 696 and 1,286 ft below sea level, forming part of the Great Rift Valley and continued S to the Gulf of Aqaba as the Araba depression.

**Giant's Causeway** Northern Ireland. Promontory of columnar basalt on the N coast of Co. Antrim 7 m. ENE of Portrush. Consists of several thousand pillars, mainly hexagonal, each 15–20 ins. across and of varying height.

**Gibraltar.** Ancient Calpe. British Crown Colony off the extreme S of Spain and at the W entrance to the Mediterranean Sea. Area 2½ sq. m. Pop. (1967) 25,281 (mainly of Italian, Portuguese, and Spanish descent and Roman Catholic in religion, speaking Spanish and English). The Rock of Gibraltar rises abruptly to 1,396 ft from the low, sandy isthmus which joins it to the Spanish mainland; it consists of limestone, and has many caves as well as tunnels excavated for defensive purposes. At its S end is the famous lighthouse of Europa Point. To the W of the Rock are the town and the harbour, the latter bounded by two long moles and a third detached mole. Gibraltar is a strongly fortified naval base, and much of the town, which is partly built on land reclaimed from the sea, is occupied by barracks, hospitals, etc. A free port; its trade is chiefly of transit type and the fuelling of ships. Tourist industry of increasing importance. Roman Catholic and Anglican cathedrals. The Calpe of the Greeks and Romans, with the ancient Abyla on the African coast it formed the Pillars of Hercules, which for centuries represented the W edge of the Mediterranean world. Its modern name is derived from Jebel-al-Tarik, after its Moorish conqueror, Tarik (711), the remains of whose castle may still be seen. Regained by the Spaniards 1462. Taken by Admiral Rooke 1704; has remained in British hands in spite of many Spanish and French attacks, notably the long siege of 1779–83. It was granted a considerable measure of internal self-government in 1964. Spain urged the decolonization of Gibraltar, and in accordance with a UN resolution a referendum was held (1967): the people of Gibraltar voted by 12,138 to 44 in favour of retaining the links with Britain.

**Gibraltar, Strait of.** Ancient Fretum Herculeum. Channel 36 m. long connecting the Atlantic and the Mediterranean, between S Spain and NW Africa; 27 m. wide at the W end, 8 m. at its narrowest, 15 m. at the

E end between the Rock of Gibraltar and Almina Point, near Ceuta (the ancient Pillars of Hercules). A surface current flows through it E from the Atlantic, while at greater depth another current flows W.

**Giessen** Federal German Republic. Industrial town in Hessen on the Lahn R. 32 m. N of Frankfurt-am-Main. Pop. (1963) 69,800. Manufactures machine tools, rubber and leather goods, tobacco products, etc. The university (1607) was temporarily an agricultural and veterinary college after the 2nd World War.

**Gifu** Japan. Capital of Gifu prefecture, in central Honshu 20 m. NNW of Nagoya. Pop. (1965) 358,130. Industrial centre. Manufactures textiles, paper goods (lanterns, parasols, fans, etc.), cutlery. Centre of fishing with trained cormorants on the Nagara R. – a popular tourist attraction.

**Gijón** Spain. Industrial town and seaport in Oviedo province, Asturias, 14 m. NE of Oviedo. Pop. (1967) 144,987. Important iron and steel industry, producing machinery, hardware, etc. Also manufactures chemicals, glass, cement, etc. Oil refining. Exports coal and iron ore. Modern importance dates from the construction of the railways in the late 19th cent. In the Spanish Civil War it was the last port in N Spain to fall to the Nationalists (1937).

**Gila River** USA. River 650 m. long rising in SW New Mexico and flowing generally SW across Arizona to join the Colorado R. near Yuma. The Coolidge Dam (built 1928) irrigates large areas for alfalfa, maize, and cotton. The river passes several Indian reservations and the Gila Cliff Dwellings National Monument.

**Gilbert and Ellice Islands** SW Pacific Ocean. British colony administered by the Western Pacific High Commission. Pop. (1967) 53,457. Cap. Tarawa (Gilbert Is.). The Gilbert and Ellice Is. became a protectorate in 1892 and Ocean Island was added in 1900; the islands were made a crown colony in 1915, and later included some of the Line Is. (1916–19) and the Phoenix Is. (1937). Copra and phosphate exported; fish forms a staple food. Apart from coconuts, pandanus palms, and breadfruit trees, vegetation is sparse. ⇨ *Ellice Islands, Gilbert Islands.*

**Gilbert Islands** SW Pacific Ocean. Group of atolls including 10 islands N of the equator (Little Makin, Makin, Marakei, Nikunau, Abaiang, Maiana, Tarawa, Abemama, Kuria, Aranuka) and 6 islands

S of the equator (Nonouti, Tabiteuea, Beru, Onotoa, Tamana, Arorae). Pop. (1967) 46,453. Cap. and main port Tarawa. The islands N of the equator have a plentiful rainfall, but many of those in the S suffer droughts. Temperatures uniformly high. Copra exported. The group was included in the British colony of the ◊ *Gilbert and Ellice Islands* in 1915. Several of them were occupied by the Japanese during the 2nd World War (1941), but were retaken by US forces in 1943.

**Gilboa** Israel. Hilly district in the N on the Jordan border, between the Plain of Esdraelon and the Jordan R. In biblical times the scene of Saul's defeat and death.

**Gilead** Jordan. Mountainous district in ancient Palestine, now in NW Jordan, E of the Jordan R., rising to 3,652 ft in Mt Gilead or Jebel Yusha, about 3 m. N of the modern As Salt.

**Gilgit** India. Mountainous district in NW Jammu and Kashmir, bounded on the W by Peshawar (W Pakistan) and on the NE by Sinkiang-Uigur (China). Area 14,680 sq. m. Pop. 77,000 (mainly Muslims). Dominated by several Himalayan peaks, including Nanga Parbat (26,660 ft) and Rakaposhi (25,550 ft). Drained by the Gilgit and Indus rivers. A British political agency was established here in 1878, and transferred to Kashmir in 1947. Since then under the control of Pakistan, as part of Azad Kashmir (Free Kashmir).

**Gillingham** (Dorset) England. Market town on the R. Stour 23 m. NNE of Dorchester. Pop. (1961) 3,445.

**Gillingham** (Kent) England. Municipal borough on the R. Medway estuary just NE of Chatham, containing much of the dockyard. Pop. (1961) 72,611. Centre of a fruit-growing district. Birthplace of William Adams (1564–1620), the first Englishman to enter Japan.

**Gippsland** Australia. District in SE Victoria. Chief town Sale. Wooded mountains in the N. Fertile plains in the S with numerous dairy farms and butter and cheese factories; maize, oats, hops, and vegetables cultivated. Huge lignite deposits in the Latrobe valley, supplying briquettes for Melbourne and fuel for power stations.

**Girardot** Colombia. River port on the upper Magdalena R. 55 m. WSW of Bogotá. Pop. 50,000. In a coffee-growing region. Exports coffee and cattle and hides. Manufactures textiles, leather, tobacco products.

**Girgenti** ◊ *Agrigento*.

**Gironde** France. Department in the SW, bounded on the W by the Bay of Biscay and drained by the Garonne and Dordogne rivers, which unite to form the Gironde estuary. Area 4,140 sq. m. (largest department in France). Pop. (1968) 1,009,390. Prefecture Bordeaux. Has some of the country's finest vineyards, the districts of Médoc, Graves, and Sauternes having given their names to famous wines. Maize, tobacco, fruit also cultivated. The infertile Landes is covered with pine forests. Industry concentrated in Bordeaux. Other towns Arcachon (resort), Libourne (wine trade).

**Girvan** Scotland. Small burgh in Ayrshire 18 m. SW of Ayr. Pop. (1961) 6,159. Holiday resort. Fishing port. The island of Ailsa Craig is 10 m. W.

**Gisborne** New Zealand. Town and port on Poverty Bay, on the E coast of the N Island. Pop. (1966) 24,939. Exports wool, meat, dairy produce.

**Giurgiu** Rumania. River port and market town in Walachia, in the Ilfov district on the left bank of the Danube R. 38 m. SSW of Bucharest. Pop. (1960) 34,248. Linked by oil pipelines with Ploeşti. Exports petroleum, grain, timber. Boat building, sugar refining, brewing, flour milling. Trade with Ruse (Bulgaria), on the opposite bank of the Danube. Founded (as San Giorgio) by the Genoese.

**Giza, El (El Gizeh; Giza)** United Arab Republic. Capital of Giza governorate, on the W bank of the Nile opposite Cairo. Pop. (1960) 250,000. Manufactures textiles, footwear, etc. 5 m. SW is the Great Pyramid of Cheops (Khufu), covering 13 acres, one of the Seven Wonders of the ancient world, the pyramids of Khafra and Menkaura, and the Sphinx.

**Glace Bay** Canada. Town in Nova Scotia, on the E coast of Cape Breton Island. Pop. (1966) 23,516. Coalmining centre. Small harbour used in the fishing industry.

**Glacier National Park** Canada. Reserve in SE British Columbia, in the Selkirk Mountains. Area 521 sq. m. Fine mountain scenery, with resorts for climbers, campers, etc. Established 1886.

**Glacier National Park** USA. Reserve in NW Montana in the Rocky Mountains, bounded on the N by the Canadian frontier, containing many glaciers and lakes, forests, and waterfalls. Area 1,560 sq. m. Highest peak Mt Cleveland (10,448 ft). Established 1910. Combined with the

Waterton Lakes National Park (Alberta, Canada) as the Waterton-Glacier International Peace Park in 1932.

**Glåma River** ⟡ *Glomma River*.

**Glamis** Scotland. Village in Angus 5 m. WSW of Forfar. Near by is the 17th-cent. Glamis Castle, birthplace of Queen Elizabeth the Queen Mother; the earlier structure belonged to Macbeth, thane of Glamis, hero of Shakespeare's play.

**Glamorgan (Glamorganshire)** Wales. County in the SE, bordering (S) on the Bristol Channel. Area 813 sq. m. Pop. (1961) 1,227,828. County town Cardiff. Mountainous in the N, rising to nearly 2,000 ft; farther S is the fertile Vale of Glamorgan, and in the extreme SW is the Gower peninsula. The main rivers, the Neath, the Tawe, and the Taff, flow generally S to the Bristol Channel. The most densely populated and industrially the most important Welsh county. In the N it contains the major part of the S Wales coalfield, mining being concentrated along the Rhondda and other valleys. Cardiff and Swansea are the chief ports, the latter has tinplate manufacture and copper smelting, and great steel works are in operation at Port Talbot. During the economic depression of the 1930s the industrial areas suffered severely, and to alleviate unemployment many new light industries were introduced. The Royal Mint was moved from London to Llantrisant, 10 m. WNW of Cardiff, in 1968.

**Glarus** Switzerland. 1. Canton comprising the basin of the Linth R., almost enclosed by lofty mountains, esp. in the S, e.g. Tödi (11,887 ft). Area 264 sq. m. Pop. (1969) 42,500 (chiefly Protestant and almost all German-speaking). Many cattle are raised on the alpine pastures, and cheese is made. Some cotton spinning.
2. Capital of the Glarus canton, on the Linth R. Pop. (1960) 5,852. Textile and wood-working industries. Almost completely destroyed (1861) by a fire spread by a violent föhn wind. Zwingli the Reformer was parish priest here 1506–16.

**Glasgow** Scotland. Royal burgh, largest city in Scotland and third largest in the UK, in Lanarkshire on both banks of the R. Clyde 20 m. from its mouth and 42 m. W of Edinburgh. Pop. (1961) 1,054,913 (77,385 in 1801; 761,709 in 1901). Important seaport. Centre of a great industrial region. Shipbuilding is the outstanding industry here and in neighbouring towns along the Clyde, and engineering is important. Other industries include flour milling, brewing, distilling; manufactures textiles, chemicals, soap, clothing, tobacco and food products. Also a centre of whisky blending and bottling. In export trade it ranks next in Britain to London and Liverpool, its docks being accessible to ocean-going vessels. Although an ancient city, present-day Glasgow is chiefly a product of the past two centuries – since the deepening of the river channel enabled ships to reach its centre; hence the statement that 'Glasgow made the Clyde and the Clyde made Glasgow'. Trade and industry created the wealth that built many fine streets and squares, as well as the notorious slums of the Gorbals. The most noteworthy historic building is the Cathedral of St Mungo, dating from the 12th cent. Glasgow University (founded 1451, the oldest in Scotland) since 1889 has occupied buildings at Kelvingrove designed by Sir Gilbert Scott. Other buildings are the Royal Exchange, Art Gallery and Museum, Mitchell Library, with a Burns collection, Merchants' Hall, the 17th-cent. Tron steeple (remnant of a church burned down in 1793), and the Crown steeple (the remains of the ancient tolbooth or prison). Sauchiehall St and Buchanan St are two of the principal thoroughfares, and the Green and Kelvingrove Parks two of the best-known open spaces. Glasgow receives its water supply from Lochs Katrine and Arklet. The name of the city is probably derived from the Celtic Glasghu, meaning 'beloved green spot', a settlement discovered here by St Kentigern (Mungo) in the 6th cent. Little is known of its subsequent history till the 12th cent., when it was made a burgh of barony (1178). Became a royal burgh 1636. In the mid 17th cent. it suffered from plague, famine, and fire, but the Treaty of Union (1707) gave it equal status with English ports and it acquired a major share of the American tobacco trade. Its commerce increased with the deepening of the Clyde channel (1768), then the textile, shipbuilding, and engineering industries developed, stimulated by the nearness of the Lanarkshire coal and iron mines, and Glasgow became one of the leading industrial centres in the UK. Severely damaged by bombing in the 2nd World War.

**Glastonbury** England. Municipal borough in Somerset, on the R. Brue 22 m. SW of Bath. Pop. (1961) 5,796. Market town.

293                                                  GLOUCESTER

Tanning. Manufactures footwear. According to legend this was where Joseph of Arimathea founded the first Christian church in England, and where his staff, planted on Wearyall Hill, took root and blossomed annually at Christmas. Another legend gives it as the burial-place of King Arthur. In the town are the ruins of the famous Benedictine Abbey, founded by the Saxon king Ine in the 8th cent., restored by St Dunstan in the 10th cent., burned down in 1184, rebuilt (by 1303), and suppressed by Henry VIII (1539), finally to be bought by the Church of England (1908). On the near-by Glastonbury Tor (525 ft) is a tower, the remains of St Michael's Chapel; NW of the town are the sites of ancient lake villages.

**Glauchau** German Democratic Republic. Town in the Karl-Marx-Stadt district 7 m. NNE of Zwickau. Pop. (1965) 33,318. Manufactures textiles, machinery, etc. Birthplace of Georg Agricola (1490–1555), the 'father of mineralogy'.

**Glencoe** Scotland. Valley ('glen') of the small R. Coe in Argyllshire, about 7 m. long, streching from Rannoch Moor to Loch Leven, flanked by steep mountains including Bidean nam Bian (3,766 ft.) and Buachaille Etive (3,129 ft). Legendary birthplace of Ossian. Scene of the massacre of the Macdonalds by the Campbells and English soldiers (1692).

**Glendale** USA. Residential and industrial suburb of N Los Angeles, California. Pop. (1960) 119,442. Manufactures aircraft, optical instruments, furniture, pottery, plastic goods, etc. Contains the Forest Lawn Memorial Park, a cemetery well known for its reproductions of works of art.

**Glendalough, Vale of** Irish Republic. Picturesque valley in Co. Wicklow 15 m. SSW of Bray, with two small lakes. Famous for its ecclesiastical ruins, including the cathedral, St Kevin's Cross (a granite monolith 11 ft high), the Round Tower, St Kevin's Kitchen (Church). St Kevin founded a monastery here in the 6th cent.

**Glenelg** Australia. Town and resort in SE South Australia, in the metropolitan area SW of Adelaide. Pop. (1961) 14,492. Near by is the 'Old Gum Tree', beneath which the colony of S Australia was proclaimed (1836).

**Glenelg River** Australia. River 280 m. long, rising in the Grampians, SW Victoria, flowing W and then S to Discovery Bay. Main course often dry, but Rocklands

Reservoir in the upper reaches diverts water to supply the Wimmera–Mallee districts.

**Glenrothes** Scotland 'New town' in the centre of Fifeshire, 6 m. N. of Kirkcaldy. Pop. (1961) 12,746. Developed since 1948. Target pop. 55,000.

**Gliwice** (Ger. **Gleiwitz**) Poland. Industrial town in the Katowice voivodship, Upper Silesia, on the Klodnica R. 17 m. W of Katowice. Pop. (1968) 166,600. Centre of coalmining and steel industries. Manufactures machinery, chemicals, etc. Food processing. A city in the 13th cent. Passed to Prussia 1742. Returned to Poland 1945.

**Glomma** (Norwegian **Glåma**) **River** Norway. The longest river in Scandinavia, 350 m. long, rising in a small lake 58 m. SE of Trondheim, flowing generally S past Röros, Elverum, and Kongsvinger, through L. Öyeren and past Sarpsborg to the Skagerrak at Fredrikstad. Important waterway for carrying timber to sawmills, paper mills, etc. Also supplies power for many hydroelectric installations.

**Glossop** England. Municipal borough in Derbyshire 12 m. ESE of Manchester at the NW edge of The Peak. Pop. (1961) 17,490. Cotton-manufacturing centre. Textile printing. Manufactures paper.

**Gloucester** England. Ancient Glevum. County town of Gloucestershire, on the R. Severn 8 m. WSW of Cheltenham. Pop. (1961) 69,687. River port, connected by the Gloucester–Berkeley Ship Canal (16½ m. long) with Sharpness, at the Severn mouth. Manufactures aircraft components, matches, toys, etc. Trade in timber, grain, etc. Its beautiful cathedral, with a 225-ft tower dating from the 15th cent., was the church of an 11th-cent. Benedictine abbey; with Worcester and Hereford cathedrals it is the scene of the annual Three Choirs Festival. Among the old timbered buildings is the 15th-cent. New Inn, and there is also the 12th-cent. church of St Mary-de-Crypt. Founded by the Romans towards the end of the 1st cent. A.D. Birthplace of Robert Raikes (1735–1811), who founded one of the first Sunday schools here (1780), Cardinal Vaughan (1832–1903), and W. E. Henley (1849–1903).

**Gloucester** USA. Fishing port and summer resort in Massachusetts 27 m. NE of Boston. Pop. (1960) 25,789. For over 200 years fishing for cod, mackerel, haddock, and halibut was the main occupation. Now boatbuilding, fish processing, and the making of oilskins, sails, and nets are more important. First settled 1623.

**Gloucestershire** England. County in the W Midlands. Area 1,257 sq. m. Pop. (1961) 1,000,493. County town Gloucester. Situated around the lower Severn and its estuary, and drained also by the Wye, which forms part of the W boundary, the Warwickshire Avon (N), Bristol Avon (S), and the upper Thames, the county falls into three distinct regions: the Cotswold Hills (E); the lower Severn valley, comprising the Vales of Gloucester and Berkeley (centre); and the Forest of Dean (W). Coal is mined in the last-named and near Bristol, and sheep are raised on the Cotswolds, but it is chiefly known for its dairy (butter, cheese) and fruit (cider apples) farming. Bristol, which geographically is partly in Somerset, is the principal industrial centre; other towns are Gloucester, Cheltenham, and Stroud, where there is still a vestige of the ancient woollen industry.

**Gloversville** USA. Industrial town in New York 40 m. NW of Albany. Pop. (1960) 21,741. Important centre of tanning and glove manufacture since the early 19th cent. (hence the name). Also manufactures handbags and other leather goods, etc.

**Glynde** England. Village in E Sussex 2 m. ESE of Lewes. Near by is Glyndebourne mansion, where opera festivals have been held since 1934.

**Gmünd (Schwäbisch Gmünd)** Federal German Republic. Town in Baden-Württemberg on the Rems R. 28 m. E of Stuttgart. Pop. (1963) 40,500. Noted since the Middle Ages for gold and silver working. Also manufactures clocks and watches, optical instruments, etc.

**Gmunden** Austria. Summer resort in Upper Austria in the beautiful scenery of the Salzkammergut at a height of 1,400 ft, where the Traun R. issues from L. Traun (Traunsee). Pop. 14,000. Brewing, wood carving. Salt mining in the neighbourhood.

**Gniezno (Ger. Gnesen)** Poland. Town in the Poznań voivodship 30 m. ENE of Poznań in region of hills and lakes. Pop. (1968) 50,000. Railway junction. Flour milling, sugar refining, brewing, etc. One of the oldest cities in Poland; in its 10th-cent. cathedral the Polish kings were crowned until 1320 and there St Adalbert was buried.

**Goa, Daman, and Diu** India. Union territory on the W coast, formerly a Portuguese overseas territory. Area 1,426 sq. m. Pop. (1961) 626,978. Cap. Panjim (Nova Goa). Goa, the largest area (1,350 sq. m.), is bounded on the N by Maharashtra and on the E and S by Mysore. Main crop rice; coconuts, timber, and manganese also produced. Under Portuguese rule since 1510, the district of Goa was invaded by Indian troops in 1961 and forcibly incorporated into the Indian Union, along with ◊ *Daman* and ◊ *Diu*.

**Gobi** (Chinese **Shamo**, 'Sandy Desert'). In its widest sense the vast area of desert in central Asia extending from the Pamirs through Sinkiang-Uighur and Mongolia to Manchuria. The Gobi proper, however, the E part of this region (the W being known as the Takla Makan), stretches 1,000 m. W–E and 300–600 m. N–S. It is a plateau of average altitude 3,000–5,000 ft, and consists partly of sandy desert, partly of stony desert, with areas of short-grass steppe where sheep, cattle, horses, and camels are raised by the Mongolian nomads; its S extension within the great N bend of the Hwang-ho is the Ordos plateau and to the W of this the Ala Shan range. The Gobi is crossed by the Ulan Bator–Tsining railway and several caravan routes.

**Godalming** England. Municipal borough in Surrey on the R. Wey 4 m. SSW of Guildford. Pop. (1961) 15,771. Mainly residential. Light engineering etc. The well-known public school Charterhouse (1611) moved here from London in 1872.

**Godavari River** India. River 900 m. long rising in the Western Ghats and flowing ESE across the Deccan, penetrating the Eastern Ghats by a gorge and entering the Bay of Bengal by a delta; the extensive irrigation canal system of the delta is linked with that of the Krishna delta. The river is sacred to the Hindus.

**Godesberg (Bad Godesberg)** Federal German Republic. Town and spa in N Rhine-Westphalia on the left bank of the Rhine R. just S of Bonn. Pop. (1963) 66,700. Mineral springs; pharmaceutical industry. Here on 22 Sept. 1938 Neville Chamberlain and Hitler held a meeting in preparation for the later Munich Pact.

**Godthaab** Greenland. Town in the SW, on the Godthaab Fiord at the entrance from Davis Strait. Pop. 6,100. Small seaport, with a radio station and a hospital. Hans Egede, a missionary, landed in 1721, and later established the first Danish colony in Greenland (1728).

**Godwin Austen (K2)** India. World's second highest peak (28,250 ft), in the Karakoram range in N Kashmir, named after Lt-Col. Godwin-Austen of the Survey of India. First climbed by two members of an Italian expedition in 1954.

**Gogra (Chagra) River.** River 600 m. long rising in the Himalayas SW of Rakas L. in Tibet, flowing SE into Nepal, turning generally S and then ESE through Uttar Pradesh (India) to join the Ganges R. near Chapra.

**Goiânia** Brazil. Capital of Goiás state; on the central Brazilian plateau at a height of 2,500 ft, 130 m. WSW of Brasilia. Pop. 133,000. Market in livestock, coffee. Built on modern lines. Replaced Goiás City as state capital 1937.

**Goiás** Brazil. State on the central plateau, at an average height of 2,500 ft. Area 247,848 sq. m. Pop. (1960) 1,954,862. Cap. Goiânia. Forested in the N; savannah in the S, which is more developed. Main crops coffee, tobacco, rice. In this state provision was made for a Federal District to receive the new capital ◊ *Brasilia*, inaugurated 1960.

**Gold Coast** ◊ *Ghana.*

**Golden Gate** USA. Strait 5 m. long and nearly 2 m. wide, at the entrance to San Francisco Bay, California. The Golden Gate Bridge, crossing it from San Francisco to Marin county, is the world's longest single-span suspension bridge, measuring 4,200 ft between the towers.

**Golden Horn** ◊ *Istanbul.*

**Goldsboro** USA. Town in N Carolina, on the Neuse R. 45 m. SE of Raleigh. Pop. (1960) 28,873. Railway junction. Important market for bright-leaf tobacco. Manufactures textiles etc.

**Gomal Pass** ◊ *Gumal Pass.*

**Gomel** USSR. Capital of the Gomel region, Byelorussian SSR, on the Sozh R. 180 m. SE of Minsk. Pop. (1970) 272,000. Important railway junction and industrial centre. Railway engineering. Manufactures agricultural implements, electrical goods, footwear, textiles, furniture, matches, etc. Belonged to Poland and Russia alternately until 1772, when it passed to Russia.

**Gomera** ◊ *Santa Cruz de Tenerife.*

**Gonda** India. Town in Uttar Pradesh, 70 m. ENE of Lucknow. Pop. (1961) 43,496. Railway junction. Trade in grain, oilseeds.

**Gondar** Ethiopia. Town 25 m. N. of L. Tana, at a height of 7,500 ft. Pop. 25,000. Linked by road with Asmara and Massawa. Formerly the capital, but suffered considerably in the civil wars. The last Italian

stronghold in Ethiopia during the 2nd World War; captured by the Allies 6 months after the campaign had officially ended (1941).

**Good Hope, Cape of** S Africa. Headland in the SW of the Cape Province, at the W entrance to False Bay. Named Cape of Storms by Bartholomew Diaz, who first rounded it (1486); renamed Cape of Good Hope by Prince Henry the Navigator, because it offered hope of finding a sea route to India. Also the official name of the ◊ *Cape Province.*

**Goodwick** ◊ *Fishguard and Goodwick.*

**Goodwin Sands** England. Stretch of sandbanks 10 m. long separated from the E coast of Kent by The Downs, a roadstead 6 m. wide, and partly exposed at low water. The sands, whose ends are marked by lightships, shelter The Downs but are a menace to shipping; many vessels have been wrecked here.

**Goodwood** England. Village in W Sussex 3 m. NE of Chichester. Goodwood House, seat of the dukes of Richmond. Racecourse with an annual summer meeting ('glorious' Goodwood). Motor-racing circuit.

**Goole** England. Municipal borough in the W Riding of Yorkshire, on the R. Ouse at the confluence with the R. Don. 47 m. from the North Sea through the Humber estuary. Pop. (1961) 18,875. Port. Exports coal, woollen goods. Imports raw wool, timber, etc. Shipbuilding, flour milling. Manufactures machinery, chemicals. Linked by canal, rail, and road with industrial Yorkshire and the Midlands; developed as a port with the construction of the canal system based on the Aire and Calder Navigation.

**Goose Bay** Canada. Village in SE Labrador, on Goose Bay, L. Melville. The airport was first used in the 2nd World War as a ferrying base.

**Göppingen** Federal German Republic. Industrial town in Baden-Württemberg, on the Fils R. 22 m. ESE of Stuttgart. Pop. (1963) 48,600. Manufactures textiles, machinery, precision instruments, toys, plastics, etc. 3 m. N is the ruined Hohenstaufen castle.

**Gorakhpur** India. Town and railway junction in Uttar Pradesh 105 m. NNE of Varanasi. Pop. (1961) 180,255. Railway engineering. Manufactures textiles, paper, etc. Trade in grain, oilseeds, etc. University (1957).

**Gorgonzola** Italy. Town in Milano province in Lombardy, 11 m. ENE of Milan, noted for the famous cheese named after it. Pop. (1961) 8,564.

**Gori** USSR. Town in the Georgian SSR, on the Kura R. 40 m. WNW of Tbilisi (Tiflis). Pop. (1968) 33,100. Industrial centre in a fruit-growing and market-gardening region. Canning, sawmilling, and other industries. Birthplace of Stalin (1879–1953).

**Gorizia** Italy. Capital of Gorizia province, in Friuli-Venezia Giulia, on the Isonzo R. and on the Yugoslav border, formerly capital of Austrian Görz-Gradisca. Pop. (1961) 42,187. Almost surrounded by mountains. Winter resort. Industrial town. Manufactures textiles, machinery, etc. Has a cathedral (14th-cent.) and the old castle of the counts of Görz. In the 1st World War it was the scene of much fighting between Austrians and Italians and suffered considerable damage.

**Gorky (Gorki)** USSR. Formerly Nizhni Novgorod. 1. Region in the European RSFSR drained by the Volga and lower Oka rivers. Area 28,900 sq. m. Pop. 3,683,000. Largely coniferous forest in the N, wooded steppe in the S. Many industries, power being supplied by local peat and wood, with oil and coal. Became a territory in 1929 and an *oblast* (region) in 1936.
2. Capital of Gorky region, at the confluence of the Volga and Oka rivers 260 m. ENE of Moscow. Pop. (1970) 1,170,000. Major river port. Railway junction. Important industrial centre. Manufactures locomotives, cars, aircraft, machine tools, generators, radio sets, chemicals, textiles, etc. Oil refining, shipbuilding (including hydrofoils), sawmilling, woodworking. Has a 13th-cent. kremlin (citadel) and two 13th-cent. cathedrals. University (1918). Founded (1221) as the frontier fortress of Nizhni Novgorod by Yuri, prince of Suzdal-Vladimir. Sacked by Tatars 1377–8. Annexed to Moscow 1417. Its great fairs gained a European reputation in the 19th cent. Birthplace of Balakirev (1836–1910), the composer, and Maxim Gorki (1868–1936), the novelist, in whose honour it was renamed (1932).

**Görlitz** German Democratic Republic. Industrial town in the Dresden district, on the Neisse R. and on the Polish border 55 m. E of Dresden. Pop. (1965) 88,824. Manufactures textiles, machinery, chemicals, glass, etc. Railway engineering.

Gothic church (15th-cent.). Near by is the Chapel of the Holy Cross with a 15th-cent. reproduction of the Holy Sepulchre at Jerusalem. A former district on the opposite bank of the river is now the Polish town of Zgorzelec.

**Gorlovka** USSR. Town in the Ukrainian SSR, in the Donbas 20 m. N of Makeyevka. Pop. (1970) 335,000 (23,000 in 1926; 109,000 in 1939). Coalmining and industrial centre. Manufactures mining machinery, chemicals, fertilizers.

**Gorno-Altai AR** USSR. Autonomous region in the Altai Territory, RSFSR, in the Altai Mountains on the Mongolian frontier. Area 35,740 sq. m. Pop. (1970) 168,000. Cap Gorno-Altaisk. Largely forested. Main occupations cattle rearing, lumbering, mining (gold, mercury). Formed (1922) as the Oirot AR. Renamed 1948.

**Gorno-Altaisk** USSR. Formerly Oirot-Tura. Capital of the Gorno-Altai AR, RSFSR, 140 m. SE of Barnaul. Pop. (1970) 34,000. Meat packing. Manufactures textiles, furniture. Linked with Mongolia by road across the Altai Mountains.

**Gorno-Badakhshan AR** USSR. Autonomous region in the Tadzhik SSR, in the Pamir massif on the borders of Afghanistan and China. Area 24,590 sq. m. Pop. (1970) 98,000. Cap. Khorog (pop. 12,000). Mountainous. Main occupation cattle and sheep rearing.

**Gorzów Wielkopolski (Ger. Landsberg-an-der-Warthe)** Poland. Industrial town in the Zielona Góra voivodship, on the Warta (Warthe) R. 48 m. SE of Szczecin (Stettin). Pop. (1968) 70,300. Manufactures textiles, chemicals, wood products, etc. Formerly in the Prussian province of Brandenburg. Returned to Poland 1945.

**Gosforth** England. Urban district in Northumberland 2 m. N of Newcastle upon Tyne. Pop. (1961) 27,072. Coalmining. Site of a racecourse, near which George Stephenson built his first locomotive (1814).

**Goslar** Federal German Republic. Town in Lower Saxony, 25 m. S of Brunswick on the NW slope of the Harz Mountains. Pop. (1963) 41,000. Railway junction. Mining and tourist centre. Manufactures furniture, chemicals, clothing, etc. Founded c. 920. A free imperial city from the late 13th cent. till 1802. Still medieval in appearance. Among its noteworthy buildings are the imperial palace (Kaiserhaus), the oldest secular building in Germany, built by the Emperor Henry III in the 11th cent. and restored in the 19th, and the Zwinger, a 16th-cent. round tower with walls 23 ft thick.

**Gosport** England. Municipal borough in Hampshire, on Portsmouth Harbour opposite Portsmouth. Pop. (1961) 62,436. Port, naval base. Has naval barracks and hospital as well as stores. Yacht building, engineering, etc. 3 m. W is the seaside resort of Lee-on-Solent.

**Göta Canal** Sweden. Waterway with 54 m. of canals, between Göteborg on the Kattegat and the Baltic Sea near Söderköping. Opened in 1832. The W part includes the Göta R., which avoids the Trollhättan Falls by a series of locks and continues to L. Väner; then a canal extends through several small lakes to L. Vätter, whence another canal leads through L. Rox to the Baltic.

**Göteborg (Gothenburg)** Sweden. Second largest city in Sweden and capital of Göteborg och Bohus county, at the mouth of the Göta R. on the Kattegat and W terminus of the Göta Canal. Pop. (1968) 445,448. Leading seaport, ice-free all year, and fishing port. Shipbuilding, marine engineering. Manufactures ball bearings, cars, textiles, etc. Here in 1865 was instituted the famous Gothenburg licensing system for spirituous liquors. University (1891). Cathedral (17th/19th-cent., restored); 17th cent. old town hall. Founded (1619) by Gustavus Adolphus. Became a major European port largely as a result of Napoleon's continental blockade.

**Gotha** German Democratic Republic. Town in the Erfurt district, 15 m. W of Erfurt. Pop. (1965) 57,256. Manufactures railway rolling stock, machinery, musical instruments, textiles, food products, etc. A village in the time of Charlemagne, it was a town by the close of the 12th cent. Became a famous publishing centre, and here the first *Almanach de Gotha* was published in 1764. Capital of Saxe-Coburg-Gotha 1826–1918.

**Gotham** England. Village 6 m. SSW of Nottingham. Pop. 1,400. Its inhabitants, the Wise Men of Gotham, won a reputation for stupidity: according to story their foolish behaviour was assumed in order to prevent King John, by no means a popular monarch, from residing in their midst – a ruse which succeeded.

**Gothenburg** ⟡ *Göteborg.*

**Gotland** Sweden. Island in the Baltic Sea comprising, with certain smaller islands, the county of Gotland. Total area 1,225 sq. m. Pop. (1968) 53,939. Cap. Visby. Main occupations the cultivation of cereals and sugar-beet and sheep rearing. Tourism also important. Engaged in trade as early as the Stone Age. Settled by German merchants in the 12th cent. Became Swedish in 1280, Danish in 1570, and Swedish again in 1645.

**Göttingen** Federal German Republic. Town in Lower Saxony, on the Leine R. 25 m. NE of Kassel. Pop. (1963) 82,600. Has a famous university founded (1724) by the Elector of Hanover, later King George II of England; the expulsion of seven professors, including the brothers Grimm (1837), because they had protested against the revocation of the liberal constitution of 1833 by King Ernest Augustus of Hanover, led to its decline, but it revived later. In medieval times a centre of cloth manufacture. Now manufactures optical and scientific instruments, machinery, etc.

**Gottwaldov** Czechoslovakia. Formerly Zlín. Town in Moravia 48 m. E of Brno. Pop. (1967) 64,000. Owes its economic importance to the establishment of the great footwear industry by Thomas Bata in 1913. Also manufactures wood products, machinery, etc. Renamed (1948) in honour of Klement Gottwald, then President of Czechoslovakia.

**Gouda** Netherlands. Town in S Holland province 12 m. NE of Rotterdam. Pop. (1968) 46,262. Famous cheese market (Gouda cheese). Also manufactures pottery, candles, etc. Among its buildings are the Groote Kerk, with a celebrated organ and stained-glass windows, and the Gothic town hall.

**Gough Island** ⟡ *Tristan da Cunha.*

**Goulburn** Australia. Town in New South Wales, on the Hawkesbury R. 53 m. NE of Canberra. Pop. (1966) 20,849. Railway junction. Wool and livestock markets. Woollen mills. Local granite quarries. Founded 1820.

**Goulburn River** Australia. River 345 m. long, rising in the Great Dividing Range in Central Victoria and flowing generally NW to the Murray R. near Echuca. Irrigates an extensive area of orchards, vineyards, vegetable fields, and pastures.

**Goulette, La** Tunisia. Town and port 7 m. ENE of Tunis, on a sand bar between the Lake of Tunis (El Bahira) and the Gulf of

Tunis. Pop. 20,000. Exports iron ore. Fishing. Also a summer resort.

**Gourock** Scotland. Small burgh in Renfrewshire, on the S shore of the Firth of Clyde 2 m. WNW of Greenock. Pop. (1961) 9,609. Seaside resort. Yachting centre. Marine engineering, yacht building.

**Gower** Wales. Peninsula in SW Glamorganshire between Burry Inlet and Swansea Bay, of considerable geological and archaeological interest. Along the picturesque S and W coasts there are several small holiday resorts.

**Gozo (Gozzo)** Malta. Island in the Mediterranean off the NW coast of Malta, to which it belongs. Area 26 sq. m. Pop. (1961) 27,506. Chief town Victoria (pop. 6,491). More fertile than Malta; fruit and vegetables cultivated.

**Graaff-Reinet** S Africa. Town in Cape Province, on the Sundays R. 140 m. NNW of Port Elizabeth. Pop. (1960) 16,703. Irrigated gardens, orchards, and vineyards make it an oasis on the dry Karroo Veld. Wool and mohair produced in the neighbourhood. Founded 1786.

**Gračanica** ◊ *Priština*.

**Grafton** Australia. Town in New South Wales, on the Clarence R. 150 m. S of Brisbane. Pop. (1966) 15,944. In a sugarcane and banana-growing and dairy-farming area. Trade in sugar, bananas, timber. Brewing etc.

**Graham Land** Antarctica. Barren, mountainous peninsula on the W side of the Weddell Sea, 650 m. S of Cape Horn. Formerly part of the Falkland Is. dependencies; since 1962 part of the ◊ *British Antarctic Territory*. Claimed by Argentina and Chile. Also known as Palmer Peninsula.

**Grahamstown** S Africa. Town in Cape Province 72 m. NE of Port Elizabeth. Pop. (1968) 40,867. Called the 'most English' town in the province. Important educational and religious centre. Seat of the Rhodes University (1904). Anglican cathedral and Roman Catholic pro-cathedral. Founded as a military post against Kaffir tribesmen by Colonel Graham (1812); settled 1820.

**Grain, Isle of** England. Island between the R. Thames and the R. Medway in N Kent. Area 5 sq. m. Connected to the mainland by road and railway across the narrow Yantlet Creek. Site of a large oil refinery.

**Grain Coast** ◊ *Guinea, Gulf of*.

**Grampians** Scotland. Name generally applied to the mountain system of the Scottish

Highlands lying between Glenmore and the Central Lowlands. Its N boundary is roughly the line Helensburgh–Stonehaven; it includes Ben Nevis (4,406 ft) and the peaks of the Cairngorm Mountains: Ben Macdhui (4,296 ft), Braeriach (4,248 ft), and Cairn Gorm (4,084 ft). Rivers flowing N from the Grampians include the Spey, Don, Dee, Findhorn and tributaries; those flowing S are the Esk, Tay, Forth and tributaries. The name is derived from Mons Graupius, the scene of Agricola's defeat of Galgacus and the northern Picts (A.D. 84), this having been misread as Grampius.

**Granada** Nicaragua. Capital of the Granada department in the SW, on L. Nicaragua. Pop. (1967) 40,200. Manufactures clothing, furniture, soap. Distilling. Trade in coffee, sugar-cane. Founded 1524. Raided several times by pirates in the 17th cent. and partly burned in 1856, but some of the old buildings from Spanish colonial times remain.

**Granada** Spain. 1. Province in the S, in Andalusia, bounded on the S by the Mediterranean. Area 4,838 sq. m. Pop. (1961) 769,408. Crossed by the Sierra Nevada, which rises to 11,421 ft in Mulhacén (the highest peak in Spain), and several less formidable ranges. The coastal plain and many of the valleys are fertile, and with irrigation cereals, sugar-cane, tobacco, etc. are produced.

2. Capital of Granada province, on the Genil R. Pop. (1967) 163,912. Trade in agricultural produce. Manufactures sugar, brandy, leather, soap, textiles, etc. Also a famous tourist resort, largely because of the magnificent Alhambra palace, built chiefly in the 13th and 14th cent., the finest example of Moorish art in Spain. On a neighbouring hill is the Generalife, the royal summer residence, with its beautiful gardens. The 16th/18th-cent. cathedral contains in its Chapel Royal the tomb of Ferdinand and Isabella; near by is the university (founded 1531). With its narrow, tortuous streets and oriental buildings, old Granada preserves many remnants of its long Moorish occupation. The city became capital of the Moorish kingdom of Granada, which included the modern provinces of Granada, Almería, and Málaga, in 1238, flourished as a centre of commerce and learning, and fell to the Spaniards in 1492.

**Granby** Canada. Industrial town in Quebec 42 m. E of Montreal. Pop. (1966) 34,349 (mainly French-speaking). Manufactures textiles, rubber and plastic products, furniture, etc.

**Gran Chaco** S America. An immense plain, about 250,000 sq. m. of lowland between the Andean foothills and the Paraguay and Paraná rivers. Drained to the Paraná by the Pilcomayo and Bermejo rivers. Shared by Bolivia, Paraguay, and Argentina. Hot rainy summers; mild generally dry winters with sudden cold spells. Huge areas are inundated in the rainy season. Largely scrub forest (where the quebracho is cut down for timber and tannin) and grassland (where there is some ranching). Very sparsely settled, 2 people per sq. m. Over this unpromising area Paraguay and Bolivia fought a costly and exhausting war (1932–5).

**Grand Banks** N Atlantic. A section of the continental shelf extending about 500 m. SE from Newfoundland, mainly at a depth of 50–100 fathoms. A famous fishing ground, esp. for cod, visited by the trawlers of many nations. Notorious for fogs, and icebergs are carried down by the Labrador Current, esp. in spring.

**Grand Bassam** ◊ *Ivory Coast*.

**Grand Canal** (Chinese Yun-ho) China. The longest canal in China (about 1,000 m.), linking Tientsin (N) with Hangchow (S). The central section, joining the Yangtse to the Hwang-ho, is the oldest, probably dating from the 6th cent., the S section having been added in the 7th cent. and the N section in the 13th cent. (by Kublai Khan). Still used in the S, it has lost much of its importance because of silting.

**Grand Canary (Gran Canaria)** Canary Islands. The most important island in the archipelago, between Tenerife and Fuerteventura. Area 592 sq. m. Pop. (1960) 400,837. Cap. Las Palmas. Extinct volcanoes rise to over 6,000 ft. The fine scenery and pleasant climate have made it a popular resort. Fertile: produces bananas, sugar-cane, tomatoes, potatoes. Exports through Las Palmas and its outport Puerto de la Luz.

**Grand Canyon** USA. Gorge of the Colorado R. extending E–W from its confluence with the Little Colorado R. to L. Mead; 218 m. long, 4–15 m. wide, and in places over 1 m. deep. Cut into a high plateau, it reveals in its rock strata of varied shape and colour, eroded into 'towers', 'temples', and other bizarre formations, the long geological past; it exhibits vertical river erosion on the grandest scale. A popular tourist region, with excellent facilities. Part of the Canyon, including 105 m. of gorge, was made into the Grand Canyon National Park in 1919.

**Grande Chartreuse** France. Limestone massif in the Isère department between Grenoble and Chambéry, rising to 6,847 ft in Chamechaude, with many cliffs and deep gorges. In a valley 13 m. NNE of Grenoble is the Monastery of La Grande Chartreuse. The original Carthusian monastery was founded (1085) by St Bruno near a village then known as Cartusia (hence the name), now St-Pierre-de-Chartreuse. It was destroyed frequently, and in 1792 the monks were expelled, returning in 1816, to be expelled again in 1903, and returning again in 1938. They continued to prepare their famous liqueur, Chartreuse, which they are said to distil from fine brandy and aromatic herbs gathered on the Dauphiné slopes.

**Grande Comore** ◊ *Comoro Islands*.

**Grand Falls** (Newfoundland) Canada. Town on the Exploits R. Pop. (1966) 7,451. Manufactures newsprint (since 1909). The near-by falls supply power to an important hydroelectric plant.

**Grand Forks** USA. Town in N Dakota at the confluence of the Red River of the North and the Red Lake R. Pop. (1960) 34,451. Railway junction. Trade in wheat, livestock, etc. Flour milling, meat packing. Seat of the University of N Dakota (1883).

**Grand Island** USA. Town in Nebraska 125 m. WSW of Omaha. Pop. (1960) 25,742. Railway junction. Railway engineering, beet-sugar refining, flour milling, etc. Founded by German settlers 1857.

**Grand Prairie** USA. Town in Texas 12 m. WSW of Dallas. Pop. (1960) 30,386. Expanded rapidly in the 1940s and 1950s after the establishment of an aircraft industry. Also manufactures rubber products etc.

**Grand Rapids** USA. Industrial and commercial town in SW Michigan at the rapids on the Grand R. 100 m. W of Flint. Pop. (1960) 177,313. Leading US centre of furniture manufacture and distribution. Now utilizes imported timber. Also an agricultural market (dairy produce, fruit). Manufactures refrigerators, automobile parts, hardware, paper, chemicals, etc. The town began as a trading post and lumbering centre in the 1820s; the furniture industry developed from the lumber trade.

**Grangemouth** Scotland. Small burgh and port in Stirlingshire on the S bank of the Firth of Forth and at the E end of the

Forth–Clyde Canal 2 m. ENE of Falkirk. Pop. (1961) 18,860. Important oil refinery. Chemical, engineering, and shipbuilding industries.

**Grange-over-Sands (Grange)** England. Urban district in N Lancashire on Morecambe Bay. Pop. (1961) 3,117. Seaside resort.

**Granite City** USA. Industrial town in Illinois 7 m. NNE of St Louis. Pop. (1960) 40,073. Railway junction. Manufactures iron and steel, tinplate, railway equipment, chemicals, etc.

**Grantham** England. Municipal borough in Parts of Kesteven, Lincolnshire, 22 m. SSW of Lincoln. Pop. (1961) 25,030. Railway junction. Engineering. Manufactures agricultural machinery, road rollers. Church of St Wulfram (13th-cent.); medieval Angel Hotel, where Richard III signed the death warrant of the Duke of Buckingham (1483); the grammar school which was attended by Sir Isaac Newton (1642–1727) – born near by at Woolsthorpe.

**Grasmere** England. Village and former urban district in Westmorland, in the Lake District 3 m. NW of Ambleside. Now forms part of the Lakes urban district: pop. (1961) 6,061. Tourist centre beside lake Grasmere amid beautiful scenery. The graves of William and Dorothy Wordsworth are in the churchyard; the house where they lived (1799–1808) is a museum.

**Grasse** France. Town and resort in the Alpes-Maritimes department overlooking the Mediterranean Sea 7 m. NNW of Cannes. Pop. (1968) 32,096. Stands among orange groves and extensive flower gardens (esp. roses) – from the produce of which perfumes and essences are distilled. Demand much reduced by competition from cheap synthetic perfumes; cut flowers, fruit (esp. peaches), and early vegetables now produced. Birthplace of Fragonard (1732–1806).

**Graubünden (Grisons)** Switzerland. The largest but most sparsely populated canton, in the E. Area 2,744 sq. m. Pop. (1969) 153,000. Cap. Chur. Mountainous, with many glaciers. Has the upper valleys of the Rhine and Inn; in the latter (the Engadine) and elsewhere are several well-known resorts, inc. Davos, St Moritz, Arosa, Chur. Joined the Swiss Confederation 1803. German, Romansch, and Italian are spoken.

**Graves** France. Region in the Gironde department in the SW, extending along the left bank of the Garonne R. between Langon and Bordeaux. Produces from its gravel soil (hence the name) the well-known Graves wines.

**Gravesend** England. Municipal borough in N Kent on the S bank of the R. Thames opposite Tilbury. Pop. (1961) 51,388. Port. Customs and pilot station within the Port of London. Yachting centre. Manufactures paper, cement. Printing, engineering, market gardening. Connected by ferry (passengers and vehicles) with Tilbury. In St George's Church is the tomb of the American Indian princess Pocahontas (1617).

**Grays (Grays Thurrock)** ◊ *Thurrock.*

**Graz** Austria. Second largest city and capital of Styria province, on the Mur R. where its valley broadens into the fertile plain known as Grazer Feld, 90 m. SSW of Vienna. Pop. (1961) 237,080. Cultural, commercial, and industrial centre. Also a resort and spa. Industries have expanded with the exploitation of coal and iron deposits and the development of hydroelectric power. Manufactures iron and steel, bicycles, precision instruments, paper, glass, textiles, leather, etc. The old town is dominated by the Schlossberg, on which there are parks, a famous clock tower, and the ruins of a fortress (destroyed 1809). University (1586). Gothic cathedral (15th-cent.); 16th-cent. Landhaus; an opera house (1899).

**Great Australian Bight** Indian Ocean. Wide bay of the Indian Ocean in the S coast of Australia, extending some 700 m. between Cape Pasley (W) and Cape Carnot (E). Shores generally inhospitable owing to the cliffs of the low semi-arid plateau along much of the perimeter. Surveyed by Flinders 1802.

**Great Barrier Reef** Australia. Greatest coral reef in the world, in the Coral Sea, extending about 1,200 m. SSE from Torres Strait to about lat. 24° S off the coast of Queensland. The corals rise from submerged ridges parallel to the Eastern Highlands; in the W the tops of partly submerged folds form islands, separated from the shore by narrow, navigable channels. Its natural beauty attracts tourists. Mother-of-pearl and trepang ('*bêche de mer*') obtained.

**Great Basin** USA. Interior region, roughly triangular in shape, nearly 200,000 sq. m. in area, between the Sierra Nevada and the

Cascade Range on the W and the Colorado Plateau and the Wasatch Range on the E. Mostly in Nevada and Utah, with a large area in California and small areas in Oregon, Idaho, and Wyoming. Not a single basin-shaped depression, but about 100 independent drainage basins, with lofty mountain ranges, deserts (Mohave, Great Salt Lake, Black Rock, Colorado, Death Valley), and salt lakes (Great Salt, Utah, Pyramid, Walker). The entire region is semi-arid, and agriculture is possible only with irrigation.

**Great Bear Lake** Canada. Lake in the Mackenzie District, NW Territories. Area 12,275 sq. m. Irregular in shape, with 5 'arms' and many small islands. Drained by the Great Bear R. into the Mackenzie R. Owing to surface ice (even in summer), only navigable for 4 months in the year. Discovered in the late 18th cent. Named after the bears found on its shores.

**Great Belt** (Danish *Store Bælt*) Denmark. Strait about 40 m. long and between 10 m. and 20 m. wide between Fyn and Zealand islands and linking the Kattegat with the Baltic Sea.

**Great Britain.** Largest island of the British Isles, comprising England, Scotland, and Wales, and including islands governed with the mainland (Isle of Wight, Scillies, Hebrides, Orkneys and Shetlands), but excluding the Channel Is. and the Isle of Man, which are separately governed. With Northern Ireland it is known as the United Kingdom of Great Britain and Northern Ireland, and this is often what is meant when the term Britain is used; in this sense the Channel Islands and Isle of Man should also be included. The areas and populations of the various parts (excluding Northern Ireland) are:

|  | Area (sq. m.) | Population (1961) |
|---|---|---|
| England | 50,331 | 43,430,972 |
| Wales (inc. Monmouth-shire) | 8,016 | 2,640,632 |
| Scotland | 30,405 | 5,178,490 |
| Isle of Man | 211 | 48,151 |
| Channel Is. | 75 | 104,378 |
| TOTALS | 89,038 | 51,402,623 |

TOPOGRAPHY, CLIMATE. Great Britain is bounded on the N, NW, and SW by the Atlantic Ocean, on the E by the North Sea, on the S by the English Channel, which

separates it from France, and on the W by St George's Channel, Irish Sea, and North Channel, which separate it from Ireland. Its greatest length N–S (Cape Wrath–Lizard Point) is 600 m.; greatest width (Land's End–N Foreland) 320 m. Like the remainder of the British Isles, it stands on the continental shelf, having once been joined to the mainland of Europe. Its highest land is in the N and W, with the result that most of the principal rivers flow to the E coast, the exceptions being the Severn and the Clyde.

Scotland consists of three distinct regions, the Highlands, the Central Lowlands, and the Southern Uplands. The Highlands, which lie N of the line Helensburgh–Stonehaven, are divided into two sections by the deep gash of Glen More (Great Glen), through which runs the Caledonian Canal; N of it are the NW Highlands and S of it the Grampians, in which stand the highest mountains of Great Britain (and of the British Isles), including Ben Nevis (4,406 ft) and Ben Macdhui (4,296 ft). This is a wild region, with few resources and a sparse and steadily decreasing population, though hydroelectric power is obtained from its lochs and rivers. The Central Lowlands comprise a broad rift valley, its S edge along the line Girvan–Dunbar, broken by lines of volcanic hills, including the Ochil and Sidlaw Hills (N) and the Pentland Hills (S), much of the area lying within the basins of the Clyde and Forth. About four fifths of the population of Scotland is concentrated in this region, its industrial importance being due mainly to the presence of the country's principal coalfields. On the rounded hills of the Southern Uplands, which extend S to the English border, sheep are grazed, but there is fertile farming land in the lower Tweed valley, as there is farther N throughout the drier, sunnier coastal lowlands of E Scotland.

To the S of the border the Pennines form the spinal column of England, extending as far S as the Midlands and rising to 2,930 ft in Cross Fell. On its E flanks are Britain's two chief coalfields, the Yorkshire, Notts., and Derby and the Northumberland and Durham, and on the W the S Lancashire coalfield; thus two of the most highly industrialized areas of Britain, the W Riding of Yorkshire (woollens etc.) and SE Lancashire (cottons etc.), have arisen here. W of the Pennines are the Cumbrian Mountains and the Lake District. The entire S E half of England is a low-lying area, its relatively level surface alleviated by ridges of limestone (Cotswolds etc.) and chalk (Chilterns, N and S Downs, etc.). Within it are two further industrialized and densely populated areas, the Midlands and the vast agglomeration of Greater London, which contains almost one fifth of the entire population of Great Britain. In this region, too, are the country's richest farmlands, esp. in E Anglia, yielding heavy crops of wheat, barley, sugar-beet, etc. There are uplands again in the S W Peninsula, with the granite mass of Dartmoor rising to 2,000 ft. Wales is a plateau dissected by many rivers (Severn, Wye, etc.) and surrounded by narrow coastal plains, Snowdonia in the N W containing the highest peak in England and Wales, Snowdon (3,560 ft). The most important industrial region of Wales is the S, where the coalfield has given rise not only to mining but to smelting, steel and tinplate manufacture, etc. Around the coasts of Great Britain many river estuaries have provided sites for great seaports – those of the Clyde, Forth, and Tay in Scotland, and those of the Thames, Mersey, Severn, and Humber in England. The coastline, indeed, offers an immense variety of scenery, from the sea lochs or fiords of N W Scotland and the rugged cliffs of Cornwall to the soft, low-lying sands and clays of E Anglia which are constantly being eaten away by marine erosion.

The climate of Great Britain may be described as maritime temperate, signifying that, because of its insular position off the N W coast of Europe, conditions are chiefly influenced by the sea. Temperatures, for example, are modified by the N Atlantic Drift, which gives the W unusually mild winters; the 40° F isotherm for January runs almost N–S as far as S England, so that Cape Wrath has the same midwinter temperatures on average as London. All parts of Great Britain enjoy both milder winters and cooler summers than places of the same latitude in continental Europe. At the same time the prevailing S W winds bring abundant rainfall, esp. to the upland W areas such as the N W Highlands of Scotland and the Lake District, where at some spots, e.g. Ben Nevis, well over 100 ins. have been measured in a year. It should be added

that a normal feature of the British climate is its changeability, due to the succession of depressions reaching its shores from the Atlantic for most of the year.

GOVERNMENT, ECONOMIC CONDITIONS. England, Wales, and Scotland have been ruled by the same monarch since 1603, and since the Treaty of Union (1707) they have formed the single political unit of Great Britain. The Irish rebellion (1798) led to the parliamentary Union of Ireland with Great Britain (1801), broken (1921) with the partition. Now the 6 counties of Northern Ireland are represented at Westminster, whilst retaining their own parliament which has limited powers. The supreme legislative power in Great Britain is vested in Parliament, which consists of the House of Commons and the House of Lords. The House of Commons comprises 630 members, representing county and borough constituencies, and elected by universal suffrage by persons over 18 years of age; the House of Lords is made up of hereditary and life peers and peeresses, archbishops, and bishops. Executive authority, vested nominally in the Crown, in practice rests with a committee of Ministers known as the Cabinet, chosen from the majority party in the House of Commons – a system which has been in force since the accession of the Hanoverian royal line in 1714 (◊ England).

Having initiated the Industrial Revolution, Great Britain became the world's leading manufacturing, banking, and investing nation, paying for imported foodstuffs and raw materials with the profits obtained therefrom. In the 20th cent., however, the cost of two world wars and the activities of foreign competitors have imposed a severe strain on the economy, and financial leadership has passed to the USA, while Britain maintains an influential position in the sterling bloc. Manufactured goods and services still pay for imported foodstuffs and raw materials, but their nature has somewhat changed: machinery, motor vehicles, and chemicals are leading exports; Great Britain now has the third largest active mercantile marine; in 1969, for example, the country took only fourth place in ship-building to Japan, Sweden, and the Federal German Republic; the textile industry has not regained its former overseas markets. Relatively small quantities of coal, once a principal export, are now shipped abroad.

On the other hand, agriculture, neglected in the years of industrial supremacy, has been revitalized. Meanwhile, the state has played an ever-increasing role in the economic and social life of the country, particularly since the 2nd World War: the coalmines, railways, gas and electricity supplies, the main airlines and broadcasting services are under government control. A National Insurance scheme and National Health Service have been introduced.

**Great Dividing Range** Australia. Name for the E highlands, running roughly parallel to the coast, consisting mainly of a series of tablelands in varying stages of erosion, 2,000–7,000 ft in height, named according to location, e.g. Blue Mountains, New England Ranges, Atherton Plateau. Highest point Mt Kosciusko (7,328 ft) in the Australian Alps. The highlands expose rocks of all ages; in Tertiary times there was great volcanic activity, so that some highlands have fertile soils weathered from basalt, e.g. parts of the Atherton Plateau. They form the watershed between rivers flowing to the Coral and Tasman Seas and those flowing to the Gulf of Carpentaria and Indian Ocean.

**Great Falls** USA. Town in Montana, on the Missouri R. Pop (1960) 55,357. Industrial centre, in a mining and agricultural region. Copper and zinc refineries, oil refinery. Manufactures electrical equipment, copper and aluminium wire and cables, bricks, etc. Named after the falls near by on the Missouri R. which supply hydroelectric power.

**Great Indian Desert** ♢ *Thar Desert*.

**Great Lake** Australia. Shallow lake at a height of 3,800 ft on the central plateau of Tasmania. Area 44 sq. m. Depth increased by Miena Dam on the S shore.

**Great Lakes** N America. Group of lakes on the Canadian-US frontier: (W-E) lakes Superior, Michigan, Huron, Erie, Ontario. Area of water surface 95,000 sq. m. The international frontier passes through all the lakes except L. Michigan, which is entirely within the USA. Their importance as a waterway has been increased by the St Lawrence Seaway. When they are open to navigation (about May–Dec.) vast quantities of iron ore, coal, grain, etc. pass through them and through the various ship canals to the St Lawrence R. Also important fisheries. Many lakeside resorts.

**Great Marlow** ♢ *Marlow*.

**Great Oasis** ♢ *Kharga Oasis*.

**Great Plains** N America. Region E of the Rocky Mountains, about 380 m. wide, including parts of Alberta and Saskatchewan (Canada) and extending S to New Mexico and Texas. Height varies from 6,000 ft (W) to 1,500 ft (E). Crossed by broad, shallow river valleys and covered largely with short grass. Main occupations stock rearing, grain cultivation.

**Great Rift Valley** Middle East/E Africa. Vast elongated depression extending from the Jordan R. valley (Syria) through the Sea of Galilee, the Dead Sea, and the Gulf of Aqaba, along the Red Sea into Ethiopia, then across Kenya, Tanzania, and Malawi into Moçambique. In E Africa it is marked by a chain of lakes, mainly long and narrow, including (N–S) Rudolf, Natron, and Malawi (Nyasa); in its vicinity there are examples of volcanic activity, e.g. Mt Kilimanjaro and Mt Kenya. A W branch extends from the N end of L. Malawi and takes in Lakes Tanganyika, Kivu, Edward, and Albert. Between the two branches, on a plateau, is L. Victoria. The altitude of the Great Rift Valley varies from over 6,000 ft above sea level in S Kenya to 1,286 ft below sea level on the floor of the Dead Sea.

**Great Salt Lake** USA. Inland salt lake in the Great Basin, in NW Utah, at a height of 4,200 ft, between the Wasatch Range and the Great Salt Lake Desert, with no outlet. The area has varied considerably, from about 2,200 sq. m. in 1877 to half that area in 1940 (the lowest recorded figure), but increasing again to nearly 1,500 sq. m. in 1950. The salinity increases with a decrease in area, and at about 25 per cent is too high for fish. It is the remnant of the vastly larger L. Bonneville.

**Great Slave Lake** Canada. Lake in the S Mackenzie District of the NW Territories. Area 11,000 sq. m. Of irregular shape, it receives the Yellowknife, Slave, and Hay rivers and is drained by the Mackenzie R. Navigable July–Oct. Main settlements Yellowknife, Reliance, Fort Resolution, Hay River. Named after the Slave Indians, who once inhabited its shores.

**Great Torrington (Torrington)** England. Municipal borough in Devonshire, on the R. Torridge 10 m. SSW of Barnstaple. Pop. (1961) 2,930. Market town. Manufactures dairy products, gloves.

**Great Wall** China. Defensive wall in N China extending about 1,500 m. from the Gulf of Liaotung W to Kansu, about 20 ft wide at the base and 12 ft at the top, height 15–30 ft, with taller towers at intervals. The E part, built of stone, earth, and brick, is well preserved, but the W part, constructed of earth, is much eroded. Originally built by Shih Huang Ti of the Ch'in dynasty in the 3rd cent. B.C. as a defence against the Mongols. Restored by the Ming emperor Hsien-tung in the 15th cent.

**Great Yarmouth (Yarmouth)** England. County borough in E Norfolk, on a long narrow peninsula between the North Sea (E) and the R. Bure, Breydon Water (formed by the R. Yare and the R. Waveney), and the R. Yare (W). Pop. (1961) 52,860. Herring port and seaside resort, once famous for its Yarmouth 'bloaters' (cured herring). Flour milling, engineering, brewing, etc. The main streets of the old town, parallel to the R. Yare, are connected by scores of narrow lanes ('rows'). The modern town has absorbed Southtown and Gorleston on the opposite (W) side of the estuary. Its Church of St Nicholas, founded in 1101 and one of the largest in England, was destroyed in the 2nd World War (1942) and rebuilt; other buildings include the 14th-cent. Tollhouse, now a museum, and the 17th-cent. Fishermen's Hospital. Birthplace of Anna Sewell (1820–78).

**Greece (Gr. Ellas, Hellas)**. Kingdom of S E Europe. Area 50,534 sq. m. Pop. (1966) 8,610,000. Cap. Athens. Lang. 96 per cent Greek. Rel. 89 per cent Eastern Orthodox.

Occupies the S part of the Balkan Peninsula and many islands in the Aegean and Ionian Seas – the islands have an area of 9,862 sq. m. Bounded on the N by Albania, Yugoslavia, and Bulgaria, on the N E by European Turkey. Primarily an agricultural country; in spite of the fact that only about one quarter of the land is cultivable, peasant farming supports one half of the population. Few industries, but foreign tourists are bringing increasing wealth. The country is divided for administrative purposes into 9 regions: Central Greece and Euboea, Peloponnese, Ionian Is., Thessaly, Macedonia, Epirus, Crete, Aegean Is., and Thrace, each subdivided into prefectures or *nome*s (nomoi), 51 in all.

TOPOGRAPHY, CLIMATE. A country of mountains, peninsulas, and islands. In the N the central backbone of the Pindus Mountains, virtually a continuation of the Dinaric Alps of Yugoslavia and Albania, separates Epirus (W) from Thessaly and Macedonia (E). Branches of this range to the E include the Othrys Mountains and Olympus (9,550 ft), the country's highest peak and legendary seat of the gods, continuing in the islands of Euboea, Andros, etc., and to the S E Parnassus (8,061 ft) and Gióna (8,235 ft), reappearing in the more W islands of the Cyclades. The Peloponnese, or Morea, the extensive S peninsula, is joined to central Greece by the narrow Isthmus of Corinth, now cut by the Corinth Canal, and rises in the Taygetus Mountains (S) to 7,887 ft. Crete, the Ionian Is., and many of the numerous Aegean islands are also mountainous. Macedonia and Thrace in the N E have limited plains, crossed by the country's principal rivers – the Vardar (Axios), Struma (Strimón), Mesta (Nestos), and Maritsa (Evros); the last-named separates Thrace from Turkey, while the Rhodope Mountains separate it from Bulgaria. In general the climate is Mediterranean in character, the hot dry summers making irrigation essential, but the highlands are cooler and less hospitable.

RESOURCES, PEOPLE, *etc.* The uplands were once well wooded, but deforestation led to further destruction by soil erosion, and they are now used for the grazing of large numbers of sheep and goats. Although agricultural machinery has been introduced since the 2nd World War, the peasant farmers' methods are primitive, the soil suffers from lack of fertilizers, and yields of cereals and other crops are low, so that wheat and flour, e.g., have to be imported. On the fertile plains and valleys the emphasis is on commercial crops, and tobacco and grapes (chiefly in the form of currants and sultanas) represent nearly half the total exports; others are olives, olive oil, citrus fruits. Some progress has been made in the production of hydro-electric power, but Greece has no coal and little lignite; a variety of other minerals (inc. iron ore, bauxite) is obtained in relatively small quantities. The main industries, also on a small scale, are oil refining, shipbuilding, and the manufacture of tobacco products, textiles, steel, cement. They are concentrated chiefly in the districts of Athens, neighbouring Piraeus, its port, which handles most of the foreign trade, and Salonika (Thessaloniki), the only other city with more than 100,000 inhabitants. Greece has the sixth largest merchant navy in the world; the highest proportion of its foreign trade is with the Federal German Republic. Of the minority religious groups, the most numerous are the Muslims (108,000). The illiteracy rate, 42 per cent of the population in 1928, had been reduced to 13 per cent in urban centres and 23 per cent in rural areas by 1961.

HISTORY. Some of the earliest civilizations in Europe flourished in Greece, notably the Minoan, on Crete, and the Mycenaean, which fell before invasions by Aeolians, Ionians, and Dorians, and had disappeared by c. 1100 B.C. The mountainous nature of the country and the virtual isolation of the various regions led to the development of the city-states, prevented national unity, and drove the people into an association with the sea which has lasted to the present day. From the 8th cent. B.C. the Greeks founded colonies around the coasts of the Black Sea and the Mediterranean, inc. Magna Graecia in S Italy. When the Persians under Darius invaded Greece (490 B.C.) they were defeated by the Athenians at Marathon; again under Xerxes they were defeated by the Athenians and Spartans together at Salamis (480) and Plataea (479). There now followed the great age of Greek drama, poetry, sculpture, architecture and philosophy, but the attempt at unity through an Athenian empire only led to the Peloponnesian War (431–404), in which Athens was defeated by Sparta, the latter to fall in turn to Thebes (379–371). Strife between the city-states allowed Philip II of Macedon to establish his supremacy (338), paving the way for his son, Alexander the Great, who through his conquests carried Greek culture to Egypt and as far E as India. By 146 B.C. Greece had been conquered by the Romans, and it then remained in the Byzantine Empire (A.D. 395) until the Turkish conquest (1453). Under Turkish rule parts of Greece were occupied at times by the Venetians, and the country was backward and oppressed. Not till 1821, when the War of Independence began, was there a national revival. Recognized as free in 1829, Greece had Prince Otto of Bavaria placed on the throne in 1832, only to be deposed in 1862 and replaced by Prince George of Denmark. In the Greco-Turkish War (1896–7) Greece was defeated, but turned the tables on the old enemy in the Balkan Wars (1912–13), and gained

considerable territory. Led by the Prime Minister, Venizelos, and against the wishes of King Constantine, Greece supported the Allied cause in the 1st World War (1917) and was rewarded with a large section of Thrace. Hundreds of thousands of Greek refugees from Turkey were resettled, and many Turks and Bulgarians left the country. A republic was set up in 1923, but the monarchy was restored in 1935. In the 2nd World War the Greeks repelled the Italians but were overwhelmed by the Germans, and at the end the country, already in a state of political and economic chaos, was torn by civil war. George II returned to the throne in 1946, to be succeeded in the following year by Paul I, who was succeeded in 1964 by Constantine II. Following a military *coup* (1967), the King fled the country, and government was taken over by a junta.

**Greeley** USA. Town in Colorado 50 m. NNE of Denver. Pop. (1960) 26,314. Commercial centre in an irrigated agricultural region. Sugar refining (beet), vegetable canning, etc. Founded 1870 as a co-operative agricultural settlement.

**Green Bay** USA. Port and industrial town in Wisconsin at the head of Green Bay on L. Michigan. Pop. (1960) 62,888. Excellent harbour, open April–Dec. Ships large quantities of cheese and other dairy products. Paper mills, engineering works, furniture and clothing factories, etc.

**Greenland.** Island off the NE of N America, lying mainly within the Arctic Circle, formerly a colony of Denmark; since 1953 an integral part of the Danish kingdom. Area 840,000 sq. m. Pop. (1966) 39,600 (inc. 3,000 Europeans, mostly Danes; the remainder are pure Eskimo or of mixed Eskimo and Danish descent). Cap. Godthaab. Separated in the extreme NW from Ellesmere Island (Canada) by the Kane Basin and the Kennedy Channel, and in the W and SW from Baffin Island (Canada) by the Davis Strait and Baffin Bay; bounded by the Arctic Ocean (N), the Greenland Sea (E), the Denmark Strait (SE), and the Atlantic (S). The world's largest island (apart from Australia): from Cape Morris Jesup (the northernmost point of land in the world) to Cape Farewell it measures 1,660 m.; the greatest width is nearly 800 m. The greater part of the surface is covered with an ice-cap estimated to be 7,000–8,000 ft thick, in the form of a basin or depression surrounded by coastal mountains rising to 12,139 ft in Mt Gunnbjorn in the SE. Recent soundings have shown that some of the land beneath the ice-cap is below sea level; thus Greenland may be not one large island but a number of smaller ones. Peary Land in the extreme N has no ice-cap. Many glaciers flow from the ice-cap to coastal fiords, the largest being Humboldt Glacier in the NW. The polar climate is uncertain and changeable, with frequent fogs and a wide range of temperatures and of amounts of precipitation.

Divided into W Greenland (cap. Godthaab), E Greenland, and N Greenland (Thule). The inhabitants live mainly on the W coast. Important settlements include Godthaab, Godhavn, Sukkertoppen, and Angmagssalik (E coast). Main occupation fishing for cod and halibut; whaling and seal hunting have declined. Some sheep raised in the SW. Most important mineral cryolite (mined at Ivigtut).

Discovered (c. 982) by Eric the Red, who named it Greenland to attract settlers. The first settlers came from Iceland; by the 14th cent. there were several thousand inhabitants. Godthaab dates from 1721, when Hans Egede, a Danish missionary, began the 'modern' colonization of the country. The first crossing of the interior was made by Nansen, who travelled E–W in 1888. Since the 2nd World War the USA has maintained air bases at Thule and Söndre Strömfjord on the W coast.

Greenland Sea Arctic Ocean. The S part of the Arctic, between Greenland and Spitsbergen. Largely covered by ice, driven S through it by the E Greenland Current.

Greenock Scotland. Large burgh and seaport in Renfrewshire on the S bank of the R. Clyde estuary 21 m. WNW of Glasgow. Pop. (1961) 74,578. Important shipbuilding, engineering, and sugar-refining industries. Also manufactures woollen goods, aluminium ware, chemicals, etc. Has the reputation of being the wettest town in Scotland, with a rainfall of 64 ins. annually. Birthplace of James Watt (1736–1819), commemorated by the Watt Institution (1837), and probably of Capt. Kidd.

Greensboro USA. Industrial town in N Carolina 83 m. NE of Charlotte. Pop. (1960) 119,574. Manufactures textiles, hosiery, stoves, chemicals, etc. Important insurance and educational centre. Named after General Nathanael Green, hero of the battle of Guilford Court House (1781). Birthplace of O. Henry (1862–1910).

Greenville (Mississippi) USA. River port on the Mississippi R. 100 m. NW of Jackson. Pop. (1960) 41,502. In a fertile cotton-growing region in the Mississippi–Yazoo delta. Manufactures chemicals, metal goods, cottonseed oil, etc.

Greenville (S Carolina) USA. Town on the Reedy R. 100 m. NW of Columbia. Pop. (1960) 66,188. Important industrial and commercial centre. Manufactures textiles, chemicals, metal goods, etc. Seat of the Furman University (1826).

Greenwich England. Former metropolitan borough of SE London, on the S bank of the R. Thames; from 1965 a Greater London borough including also Woolwich (except the part N of the Thames). Pop. (1963) 230,082. Connected to Poplar on the N bank by Greenwich Tunnel (pedestrians) and the Blackwall Tunnel (vehicles). In Greenwich Park (185 acres) is the original Royal Observatory, designed by Wren (1675), accepted internationally as being on the prime meridian of longitude (from 1884) and source of Greenwich Mean Time, moved to Herstmonceux in 1950. Greenwich Hospital, also by Wren, which became a Royal Naval College in 1873, stands on the site of a former royal palace, the birthplace of Henry VIII, Elizabeth I, and Mary. In the 19th cent. Greenwich was the venue of the famous annual 'whitebait dinners' for cabinet ministers, the last one being held in 1894.

Greenwich USA. Town in SW Connecticut 5 m. WSW of Stamford. Pop. (1960) 53,793. Picturesque. Largely residential. Boatbuilding. Manufactures marine engines, pumps, etc.

Greenwich Village USA. Part of the borough of Manhattan, New York City, bordered on the W by the Hudson R. A popular bohemian quarter, with old houses, winding streets, and exotic shops, restaurants, and night clubs. Grew up in colonial times as a separate village, and soon became a high-class residential quarter much frequented by authors, artists, and actors. Thomas Paine, Walt Whitman, Henry James, and Mark Twain were all associated with it.

Greifswald German Democratic Republic. Town in the Rostock district, on the Ryck R. near its mouth, 51 m. E of Rostock. Pop. (1965) 47,424. Railway junction.

Brewing. Manufactures textiles etc. Also a cultural centre. University (1456).

**Greiz** German Democratic Republic. Town in the Gera district, on the White Elster R. 18 m. SSE of Gera. Pop. (1965) 39,424. Engineering. Manufactures textiles, paper, etc.

**Grenada** West Indies. The southernmost of the Windward Is. group. Area 120 sq. m. Pop. (1963) 91,967 (2 per cent white, the remainder Negro). Cap. St George's (pop. 7,305). Formerly administered with the S Grenadines as a British Crown Colony; later in the W Indies Federation (1958–62). One of the most picturesque of the W Indian islands. Roughly oblong in shape. Mountainous, rising in Mt St Catherine to 2,756 ft. Grand Étang, at a height of 1,740 ft, is a large crater lake. Exports cacao, mace, nutmegs, bananas, etc. Manufactures rum, lime juice. Cotton ginning important. Discovered (1498) by Columbus. Held by Britain from 1783. Became an associated state within the British Commonwealth 1967.

**Grenadines** British W Indies. Chain of small islands in the Windward Is., extending 60 m. between St Vincent and Grenada and divided between them. The largest of the group, Carriacou (area 11 sq. m., pop. 6,433), belongs to Grenada.

**Grenoble** France. Prefecture of the Isère department and former capital of the Dauphiné, on the Isère R. 58 m. SE of Lyons. Pop. (1968) 165,902. Long famous for the manufacture of kid gloves, now important also for ferro-alloys, turbines, electrical equipment, machine tools, cement, paper, etc., the metallurgical industries being largely dependent on hydroelectric power. Ancient and strongly fortified city. Cathedral (11th/13th-cent.); 16th-cent. Palais de Justice; celebrated university (founded 1339). Beautifully situated; a major tourist centre for the French Alps. Its name is a corruption of Gratianopolis, the town founded here by the Emperor Gratian in the 4th cent. Birthplace of Stendhal (1783–1842).

**Gretna Green** Scotland. Village in S Dumfriesshire, on the English border 9 m. NW of Carlisle. Long famous as the venue of runaway English marriages, usually performed by the local blacksmith. The practice was severely restricted in 1856, when a law was passed requiring 3 weeks' residence in Scotland by one of the

parties. The marriages were declared illegal from 1940.

**Greymouth** New Zealand. Town and port on the W coast of the S Island at the mouth of the Grey R. Pop. (1966) 8,654. Exports coal, timber. Linked with Christchurch by rail through the Southern Alps.

**Grijalva River** ◊ *Mexico.*

**Grimsby** England. County borough and seaport in Parts of Lindsey, Lincolnshire, on the S side and near the mouth of the Humber estuary. Pop. (1961) 96,665. Claims to be the world's leading fishing port, with associated industries, e.g. manufacture of fertilizers, nets, ice. Also brewing; manufactures food products, chemicals. Trade in coal, grain, timber. Its development as a fishing port was chiefly due to extensive harbour improvements from 1846 onwards and provision of fast rail services to distribute the catch.

**Grindelwald** Switzerland. Famous resort in the Bern canton in a picturesque valley at a height of 3,400 ft, 9 m. ESE of Interlaken; mountain climbing centre at the foot of the Wetterhorn, Eiger and other peaks. Pop. (1960) 3,250.

**Gris-Nez, Cap** France. In French, 'Grey Nose'. Limestone headland 180 ft high, in the Pas-de-Calais department at the narrowest part of the Strait of Dover. The nearest point to the English coast. Lighthouse.

**Grisons** ◊ *Graubünden.*

**Grodno** USSR. Capital of the Grodno region in the Byelorussian SSR, on the Neman R. near the Polish border. Pop. (1970) 132,000. Railway junction. Manufactures electrical equipment, fertilizers, textiles, leather goods, etc. Sugar refining. Trade in grain and timber. Important as early as the 12th cent. Capital of Lithuania in the 14th cent. Changed hands later between Poland and Russia; ceded to the USSR 1945.

**Groningen** Netherlands. 1. Province in the NE. Area 899 sq. m. Pop. (1968) 511,753. Fertile, particularly in the N. Dairy farming. Potatoes, sugar-beet, vegetables cultivated.

2. Capital of Groningen province, 32 m. E of Leeuwarden. Pop. (1968) 157,093. Sugar refining. Manufactures chemicals, clothing, furniture, etc. Trade in grain and cattle. Railway junction and canal centre. University (1614). Principal church the 15th-cent. Martinikerk, which has an organ constructed by Rodolphus Agricola

(1443–85), who was born near Groningen.

**Grosseto** Italy. Capital of Grosseto province, in Tuscany, 44 m. SSW of Siena. Pop. (1961) 51,730. Market town on a reclaimed swamp. Trade in cereals, wine, olive oil. Manufactures agricultural implements etc. Cathedral (12th/13th-cent., restored). In the mid 18th cent. its population had been reduced to less than 700 by malaria.

**Grozny** USSR. Capital of the Checheno-Ingush ASSR and former capital (1944–57) of the Grozny region, RSFSR, on the Sunzha R. 125 m. NNE of Tbilisi (Tiflis). Pop. (1970) 341,000. Major centre of the petroleum industry, linked by pipelines with the near-by oilfields and with the oil ports of Makhachkala (Caspian Sea) and Tuapse (Black Sea) and with Rostov. Oil first discovered 1893. Also manufactures oil-drilling machinery, chemicals, etc. Sawmilling, food processing.

**Grudziaz** (Ger. **Graudenz**) Poland. Ancient town and river port on the Vistula R. in Bydgoszcz province. Pop. (1968) 74,700. Railway junction. Manufactures agricultural machinery, chemicals, glass, footwear, etc. Passed from Poland to Prussia in 1772 but was returned in 1919.

**Grünberg** ◊ *Zielona Góra.*

**Gruyère** Switzerland. District in Fribourg canton in the middle Saane valley, famous for the cheese named after it and for its cattle. The small town of Gruyères (pop. 1,349) stands on a hill at 2,713 ft. above the valley.

**Guadalajara** Mexico. Capital of Jalisco state, on the central plateau, at a height of 5,100 ft. Pop. (1969) 1,352,100. The second largest city in Mexico. Important commercial and route centre. Manufactures textiles, clothing, soap, vegetable oils, shoes, etc. Flour milling, tanning. Noted for pottery and glassware made by Indians. Cathedral (16th/17th-cent.); 17th-cent. Governor's Palace. Airport. Seat of two universities (1792, 1935).

**Guadalajara** Spain. **1.** Sparsely populated province in New Castile, on the Meseta, with a harsh continental climate. Area 4,705 sq. m. Pop. (1961) 183,545. Cereals, olives, vines, etc. grown in the valleys. Salt produced.

**2.** Capital of Guadalajara province, on the Henares R. 30 m. NE of Madrid. Pop. 19,000. In an agricultural region producing cereals, vines, olives, etc. Flour milling, tanning, etc. The note-worthy Infantado Palace (late 15th-cent.) was severely damaged in the civil war (1936–9), and later restored.

**Guadalcanal** (Solomon Islands) S Pacific Ocean. Volcanic island in the British Solomon Is. Protectorate, largest of the group. Area 2,500 sq. m. Pop. about 15,000. Honiara is capital of the Protectorate. Mountainous and closely forested, rising to about 8,000 ft. Main export copra. In the 2nd World War it was occupied by the Japanese (1942); recaptured by the Americans after heavy fighting (1943).

**Guadalquivir River** (Ar. **Wadi-el-Kebir,** 'Great River') Spain. River 360 m. long, rising in the Sierra de Segura in Jaén province and flowing generally WSW through Córdoba to Seville. Navigable below the city of Seville; divides into several branches as it crosses the swampy region known as Las Marismas; then, reunited, enters the Gulf of Cadiz and the Atlantic. Between Córdoba and Seville it is extensively used for irrigation. Several hydroelectric plants on its tributaries.

**Guadalupe** (Spain) ◊ *Sierra de Guadalupe.*

**Guadalupe Hidalgo** Mexico. Former town; now part of Gustavo A. Madero, Federal District, just NE of Mexico City, the most famous place of pilgrimage in the Americas, containing a great brick basilica with a shrine of Our Lady of Guadalupe. Built after an Indian had described having seen visions on the hill of Tepeyacac in 1531. Scene of the signing of the treaty ending the US–Mexican War (2 Feb. 1848).

**Guadeloupe** W Indies. A pair of neighbouring islands in the Leeward Is.; with dependencies, an overseas department of France. Total area 657 sq. m. Pop. (1967) 312,724 (mainly mulattoes and Negroes). Cap. Basse-Terre. The two main islands, Guadeloupe proper or Basse-Terre (W) and Grande-Terre (E), are separated by a narrow strait, the Rivière Salée; the former is the higher, rising to 4,869 ft in the dormant volcano, La Soufrière. The island dependencies are Marie-Galante (pop. 20,000), Désirade (pop. 1,592), Les Saintes (pop. 3,269), St Barthélemy (pop. 2,300), and the N half of St Martin (pop. 4,502). Main occupation agriculture. Chief products bananas, sugar, rum, coffee, cacao. Chief commercial centre and seaport Point-à-Pitre (Grande-Terre). Discovered (1493) by Columbus and named after a monastery in Spain. Continuously under French rule since 1816, it became an overseas department in 1946.

**Guadiana River.** Ancient Anas River. River 510 m. long in Spain and Portugal rising in several headstreams and becoming the Guadiana proper near Ciudad Real, flowing generally W to Badajoz. Here it turns S, forming the Spanish-Portuguese boundary, except for about 100 m., where it is flowing through S E Portugal, and enters the Gulf of Cadiz near Ayamonte (Spain). Owing to its lack of volume it has little economic value.

**Guainía River** ♢ *Rio Negro* (Brazil).

**Guaira, La** ♢ *La Guaira*.

**Guaíra Falls** ♢ *Paraná River*.

**Gualeguay** Argentina. Town in the S of the Entre Ríos province, 80 m. ESE of Rosario. Pop. 26,000. Has a port, Puerto Ruiz, 5 m. S, on the Gualeguay R. leading to the Paraná R. Trade in livestock, cereals.

**Gualeguaychú** Argentina. River port in the SE of the Entre Ríos province, on the Gualeguaychú R. 7 m. from the confluence with the Uruguay R. Pop. 43,000. Opposite Fray Bentos (Uruguay). Meat packing, tanning.

**Guam** (Marianas Islands) W Pacific Ocean. Southernmost and largest of the group. Area 209 sq. m. Pop. (1960) 67,044. Cap. Agaña (pop. 1,642). Mountainous and volcanic in the S, rising to 1,334 ft; lowlying coral in the N. Rice, coconuts, bananas, etc. cultivated. Cattle and pigs raised. Main export copra, through the only good port, Apra Harbour, in the W. Probably discovered in 1521 by Magellan. Ceded to the USA in 1898 after the Spanish-American War. Occupied by the Japanese in the 2nd World War (1941); recaptured by the Americans (1944) and became a major naval and air base.

**Guanabara** Brazil. State created (1960) when Rio de Janeiro ceased to be federal capital. Area 523 sq. m. Pop. (1960) 3,307,163. Includes the great metropolitan area of Rio de Janeiro on Guanabara Bay.

**Guanajuato** Mexico. 1. State on the central plateau. Average height 6,000 ft. Area 11,807 sq. m. Pop. (1969) 2,326,000. One of the main mining states of Mexico, rich in silver; also produces gold, zinc, copper, mercury, lead.
2. Capital of Guanajuato state, in the Sierra Madre Occidental at a height of 6,588 ft. Pop. 28,000. Mining centre (principally silver and gold). Manufactures

pottery, textiles. Built in a ravine, it has narrow tortuous streets rising steeply to the hillside mining villages. University (1732).

**Guanta** ♢ *Barcelona* (Venezuela).

**Guantánamo** Cuba. Town in the Oriente province, 40 m. ENE of Santiago de Cuba. Pop. (1960) 124,685. Commercial and processing centre for an agricultural region. Sugar milling, coffee roasting, tanning. Manufactures chocolate, liqueurs, etc. Founded (1822) by French refugees from Haiti.

**Guantánamo Bay** Cuba. Inlet in the Oriente province, 10 m. S of Guantánamo. Site of a US naval and air base, with strong fortifications, ceded to the USA (1901) after the Spanish-American War. Named Cumberland Bay in 1741, when an English force landed under Admiral Vernon and General Wentworth, but the name was soon changed.

**Guaporé** (Brazil) ♢ *Rondônia*.

**Guatemala.** The northernmost republic of Central America. Area 42,042 sq. m. Pop. (1964) 4,278,341. Cap. Guatemala City. Lang. Spanish and several Indian dialects. Rel. Roman Catholic.

Between the Gulf of Honduras on the Caribbean Sea (NE) and the Pacific Ocean (S); by land bordered by Mexico (N and W), British Honduras (NE), Honduras (E), and Salvador (SE). The most populous republic in Central America and the only one predominantly Indian. Over half the population are Indians, who retain their colourful traditional costume and follow a mode of life not essentially changed from Mayan times; few of them speak Spanish, and their economy is largely self-contained, with maize and beans as the staple foods. The remainder are of mixed Indian and Spanish descent (*ladinos*). The country is divided administratively into 22 departments.

TOPOGRAPHY, CLIMATE. Interior mountainous, with several volcanoes. Tajamulco (13,812 ft) is the highest peak in Central America. Fuego (12,582 ft) and Santa María (12,362 ft) are active volcanoes. W of Guatemala City is the picturesque L. Atitlán, surrounded by volcanic peaks. Chief rivers the Motagua, the Polochik (flowing through L. Izabal, the largest lake), and the Usumacinta. Earthquakes are not uncommon. Climate hot and humid on the coastal lowlands (*tierra caliente*), but healthy and pleasant in the upland valleys (*tierra templada*); above about 10,000 ft is the cool zone (*tierra fria*). Annual rainfall (mainly May-Oct.) 50 ins. on the average but much greater in some areas.

ECONOMY. Chiefly agricultural. Coffee, which provides 60 per cent of the exports, is grown on the upland slopes; cotton is the second most important export, and bananas and essential oils are also exported. In the extensive tropical forests mahogany, cedar, balsa, and cinchona are produced. Prominent in the country's rich bird life is the beautiful quetzal, which has become the national emblem. Guatemala City has textile mills, a cement factory, and a few light consumer industries. Other towns are Quezaltenango, Cobán, Mazatenango, Zacapa, and Puerto Barrios (the Caribbean port).

HISTORY. In pre-Columbian times a great centre of the Mayan civilization; the remarkable ruins at Quiriguá and elsewhere demonstrate its level of culture. In 1523-4 the Spanish conquered the country and formed the captaincy-general of Guatemala, with the capital at Antigua. It formed the nucleus of the Central American Federation (1828–38) but in 1839 Rafael Carrera founded the present republic. Its subsequent history was marred by revolutions and dictatorships. It claims the territory of British Honduras; the question was amicably discussed, though not settled, at San Juan (Puerto Rico) in 1962.

**Guatemala City** Guatemala. Capital of the republic and of the Guatemala department, in the SE, on the Inter-American Highway, at a height of 4,900 ft. Pop. (1964) 572,937. The largest city in Central America. Controls most of the country's coffee trade. Manufactures textiles, cement, soap, etc. Among notable features are the National Palace (completed 1943) in the Parque Central and the cathedral (18th/19th-cent.). Seat of the famous University of San Carlos (1676). Founded (1776) to take the place of the earlier capital, Antigua, which was destroyed by earthquake. Almost entirely destroyed by earthquakes 1917–18; rebuilt to the original plan.

**Guayama** Puerto Rico. Town 33 m. S of San Juan. Pop. (1960) 33,678. In an agricultural region producing sugar-cane etc. Sugar milling, textile manufacture, etc.

**Guayaquil** Ecuador. Largest city and chief seaport, also capital of Guayas province, on the Guayas R. 35 m. from its mouth on the Gulf of Guayaquil. Pop. (1966) 680,209. Exports bananas, cacao, coffee. Sugar refining, iron founding, tanning, sawmilling, brewing. Manufactures soap, textiles, etc. Linked by rail and road with Quito. University (1897). Founded 1537. Suffered frequently from fires and was severely damaged by earthquake in 1942; has been largely rebuilt in recent years.

**Gubbio** Italy. Ancient Iguvium. Town in Perugia province, Umbria, 19 m. NE of Perugia. Pop. (1961) 32,857. Long famous for majolica; also manufactures textiles and metal goods. With its 13th-cent. cathedral and its many palaces, it has a distinctly medieval appearance. In the Palazzo dei Consoli are the famous bronze Tabulae Iguvinae, from which much information about the ancient Umbrians was obtained.

**Gudbrandsdal** Norway. Fertile valley of the Lågen R. running NW–SE between the Rondane Mountains (E) and the Jotunheim Mountains (W). Agriculture, stock rearing (esp. horses), dairy farming. It has a distinctive dialect and folklore and is associated with the Peer Gynt legend. Trade route for many centuries; the Oslo–Trondheim railway (opened 1921) passes through it.

**Guelph** Canada. Industrial town in S Ontario, on the Speed R. 28 m. NW of Hamilton. Pop. (1966) 51,377. Manufactures electrical equipment, leather goods, hardware, etc. University (1964). Founded 1827.

**Guernica** Spain. Town in Vizcaya province 12 m. ENE of Bilbao. Pop. (1961) 8,089. Has the old oak tree beneath which the Basque parliament used to meet. Metalworking and furniture industries. On 27 April 1937, German aircraft supporting the nationalists in the Spanish Civil War bombed and destroyed the town, killing hundreds of civilians, and Guernica became the symbol of Fascist ruthlessness, inspiring one of Picasso's most famous paintings.

**Guernsey** England. Second largest of the Channel Is., 30 m. W of the Normandy coast. Area 24 sq. m. Pop. (1961) 45,150. Cap. St Peter Port. Tomatoes, grapes, and flowers are cultivated, mostly under glass, and the island has given its name to a famous breed of dairy cattle. Popular with holiday-makers from mainland Britain in summer. Dependencies are Alderney,

Brechou, Great Sark, Little Sark, Herm, Jethou, and Lihou.

**Guerrero** Mexico. A Pacific coast state in the SW. Area 24,624 sq. m. Pop. (1969) 1,620,000. Cap. Chilpancingo. Chief seaport Acapulco. Largely mountainous; crossed by the Sierra Madre del Sur. Mainly agricultural. Crops include cereals, cotton, sugar-cane, coffee.

**Guianas.** Region in the NE of S America, bounded by the Orinoco R. (N and W), the Rio Negro and the Amazon (S), and the Atlantic (E). Encloses the Guiana highlands, largely in Venezuela but partly in N Brazil and in the S of the three territories to which the name Guiana is specifically applied: ◊ *Guyana* (formerly British Guiana), Dutch Guiana (◊ *Surinam*), and ◊ *French Guiana*. The S highlands are lofty sandstone plateaux, mainly forested, with deep ravines, high cascades (e.g. the 741-ft Kaieteur Falls on the Potaro R.), and some areas of savannah. N of these is a heavily eroded belt of hilly crystalline rocks, also densely forested, containing diamonds, gold, and bauxite. Beyond lie flat marshy coastlands, agricultural areas containing most of the population, where the temperatures are uniformly high (the mean monthly figures vary little from 80° F) and humidity is also high.

**Guienne (Guyenne)** France. Former province in the SW, divided (1790) into the present departments of Aveyron, Dordogne, Gironde, and Lot and parts of the Tarn-et-Garonne and Lot-et-Garonne departments. In the 12th cent. it formed the duchy of Aquitaine with Gascony. Held by England 1154–1451. Its capital was Bordeaux.

**Guildford** England. Municipal borough in Surrey, on the R. Wey 26 m. SW of London. Pop. (1961) 53,977. Market and dormitory town. Manufactures plastics etc. Engineering, brewing. Among its buildings are Archbishop Abbot's Hospital, founded 1619; the 17th-cent. guildhall; the grammar school (16th-cent.); the new cathedral (1936); remains of a Norman castle. It was a royal borough in the Middle Ages, when it had an important cloth trade. Seat of the University of Surrey (1966).

**Guinea.** Republic in W Africa; formerly a French colony. Area 94,927 sq. m. Pop. (1964) 3,000,000. Cap. Conakry. Bounded on the NW by Portuguese Guinea, on the

S by Liberia and Sierra Leone. Chief feature the Fouta Djallon plateau, cut by the valleys of the Niger R. headstreams, a savannah region; main occupation cattle rearing. Tropical monsoon climate, with rain-forest in the coastal areas, producing the main agricultural exports, bananas and palm kernels. Chief exports iron ore (Kaloum peninsula), bauxite (Boké, Kindia, and the Los islands). Conakry is linked by rail with Kankan on the Milo R. (a tributary of the Niger). The French established the colony of Rivières du Sud in 1882, renaming it French Guinea 1895. After a referendum (1958) it declined to join the French Community, and became an independent member of the UN. Has an agreement with Ghana and Mali to co-ordinate policies in defence, economic, and foreign affairs. ◊ *Equatorial Guinea*; *Portuguese Guinea*.

**Guinea, Gulf of** W Africa. Broad Atlantic inlet, from Cape Palmas (Liberia) to Cape Lopez (Gabon). The Niger delta separates two large bays, the Bights of Biafra and Benin. Parts of the Gulf coast are named after the commodities in which Europeans formerly traded, e.g. the Grain Coast ('grains of paradise', i.e. Guinea pepper), the Ivory Coast, the Gold Coast (Ghana), the Slave Coast. Islands in the Gulf are Fernando Póo, Principe, São Tomé, Annobón. Receives the waters of the Volta, the Niger, and the Ogowé rivers.

**Guipúzcoa** Spain. One of the ◊ *Basque Provinces*; the smallest in Spain but one of the most densely populated, bounded on the N by the Bay of Biscay and on the NE by France. Area 771 sq. m. Pop. (1961) 478,337. Cap. San Sebastian. Largely industrial. Stock rearing. Fishing.

**Guisborough** England. Urban district in the N Riding of Yorkshire, 8 m. ESE of Middlesbrough at the foot of the Cleveland Hills. Pop. (1961) 12,079. Market town in a former iron-mining district. Tanning, brewing. Ruins of a 12th/14th-cent. Augustinian priory.

**Gujarat** India. State in the Indian Union, formed (1960) from the N and W part of the former Bombay state and including the former states of Saurashtra and Kutch, bordered by W Pakistan (NW) and the Arabian Sea (W). Area 72,245 sq. m. Pop. (1961) 20,633,350. Cap. Ahmadabad. Official languages Gujarati and Hindi. The State consists largely of a fertile plain on which cereals and cotton are grown, but includes the marshy Rann of Kutch and the partly arid Kathiawar peninsula.

**Gujranwala** Pakistan. Town in W Pakistan 43 NNW of Lahore. Pop. (1961) 197,000. Manufactures textiles, leather, metal goods, etc. Trade in cereals, cotton. Birthplace of the famous Sikh ruler, Ranjit Singh (1780–1839).

**Gujrat** Pakistan. Town in the Rawalpindi division of W Pakistan, 30 m. N of Gujranwala. Pop. (1961) 59,608. Trade in grain, cotton, etc. Handicraft industries (textiles, pottery, etc.).

**Gulbarga** India. Town in Mysore, 65 m. ESE of Sholapur. Pop. (1961) 97,069. Cotton manufactures. Flour and oilseed milling. Trade in cereals, cotton. Capital of the Bahmani kings in the 14th and 15th cent.; the ruins of their palaces, mosques, etc. remain. The most noteworthy building is a mosque modelled on that at Córdoba, Spain.

**Gulfport** USA. Seaport in Mississippi, on Mississippi Sound 65 m. WSW of Mobile. Pop. (1960) 30,204. Exports wood, cotton-seed products. Manufactures textiles, fertilizers, etc. Also a resort.

**Gulf Stream.** Warm ocean current in the N Atlantic, originating in the Gulf of Mexico and flowing through the Florida Strait and NE along the US Coast. At the Grand Banks off Newfoundland it fans out, slows down, and becomes less clearly defined, so much modified that it is now more correctly termed the N Atlantic Drift. It reaches the coasts of W and NW Europe and considerably influences their climate. First observed in the early 16th cent. Not scientifically studied until the 19th cent.

**Gumal (Gomal) Pass** Afghanistan/Pakistan. Pass 4 m. long at a height of about 5,000 ft on the Afghanistan–W Pakistan border 90 m. W of Dera Ismail Khan. Traversed by the Gumal R., a tributary of the Indus. Serves as a trade route for Afghan merchants.

**Gumti River** India. River 500 m. long in Uttar Pradesh, rising in the N and flowing generally SE past Lucknow and Jaunpur to join the Ganges R. Navigable for small vessels in its lower course.

**Guna (Goona)** India. Town in Madhya Pradesh, 120 m. SSW of Gwalior. Pop. (1961) 31,031. Commercial centre. Trade in grain, oilseeds.

**Guntur** India. Town in Andhra Pradesh 150 m. ESE of Hyderabad. Pop. (1961)

187,122. Trade in cotton, tobacco. Oil-seed, jute, and rice milling; engineering. Passed from French to British possession 1788.

**Guryev** USSR. Port and capital of the Guryev region, Kazakh SSR, on the Ural R. near its mouth on the Caspian Sea (NE). Pop. (1970) 113,000. Terminus of the Orsk–Kandagach railway and of the pipelines from the Emba oilfield. Oil refining. Fishing. Fish canning.

**Güstrow** German Democratic Republic. Town in the Schwerin district 20 m. S of Rostock. Pop. (1965) 37,982. Railway junction. Engineering, woodworking, etc. Capital of the duchy of Mecklenburg-Güstrow in the 16th–17th cent.

**Gütersloh** Federal German Republic. Industrial town in N Rhine-Westphalia 10 m. SW of Bielefeld. Pop. (1963) 53,300. Manufactures machinery, furniture, textiles, food products, etc.

**Guyana.** Formerly British Guiana. Former British colony in S America. Area 83,000 sq. m. Pop. (1967) 692,780 (about 51 per cent E Indian, 30 per cent Negro, 3 per cent European; about 20,000 Amerindians live in the interior). Cap. Georgetown. Mostly covered by jungle; only a narrow coastal belt is cultivable. Overpopulated in relation to the exploitable land. Chief products sugar-cane (mainly grown on large estates), bauxite; a considerable development of rice as a subsistence crop has recently been promoted. The birth-rate is high; both economic and social problems are enormous. First settled by the Dutch W India Company early in the 17th cent. Occupied by the British 1796. Finally ceded to Britain 1814. Internal self-government was achieved in 1961, but serious economic difficulties caused rioting and bloodshed; a state of emergency was declared in 1962. Became independent within the Commonwealth (as Guyana) 1966.

**Guyenne** ◊ *Guienne*.

**Gwadar (Gwadur)** Pakistan. Port in Baluchistan 300 m. W of Karachi, formerly, with adjoining territory (area 300 sq. m.), a dependency of Oman, but handed over to Pakistan in 1958. Pop. (1961) 8,146. Coastal trade and fishing industry.

**Gwalior** India. 1. Former princely state in central India consisting of one large area and several detached districts. Area 26,000 sq. m. Its rulers belonged to the Sindhia family of the Mahrattas, by whom

it was founded in the 18th cent. Its first capital was Ujjain. In 1948 it was merged with Madhya Bharat, which became part of Madhya Pradesh in 1956.
2. Former capital of Gwalior and of Madhya Bharat, now in Madhya Pradesh, 65 m. SSE of Agra. Pop. (1961) 300,587. Industrial centre. Flour and oilseed milling. Manufactures cotton goods, pottery, footwear, etc. University (1963). An ancient town centred round an imposing fort containing palaces and temples. Now includes the 19th-cent. town of Lashkar.

**Gwelo** Rhodesia. Town 90 m. ENE of Bulawayo, at a height of 4,650 ft. Pop. (1967) 39,500. Chief town of the midland region. Farming and industrial centre. Engineering. Manufactures footwear, ferrochrome, asbestos products, cement, etc. Founded 1894.

**Gyangtse (Gyantse)** China. Town in S Tibet 100 m. SW of Lhasa at a height of 13,000 ft. Pop. 10,000. Trade in wool, barley, salt, borax, tea, etc. Manufactures carpets, woollen cloth.

**Gympie** Australia. Town in SE Queensland on the Mary R. 90 m. NNW of Brisbane. Pop. (1966) 11,277. In a region of dairy farming and the cultivation of sugar-cane and bananas. Former gold-mining centre.

**Györ** Hungary. Capital of Györ-Sopron county, on the Rába R. near its confluence with an arm of the Danube 68 m. WNW of Budapest. Pop. (1968) 80,000. Important industrial centre and river port. Flour milling, distilling. Manufactures textiles etc. About 11 m. SE is the famous Benedictine abbey of Pannonhalma, founded (1101) by King Stephen.

# H

**Haag, Den** ⟡ *Hague, The.*

**Ha'apai** ⟡ *Tonga.*

**Haarlem** Netherlands. Capital of N Holland province, 11 m. W of Amsterdam. Pop. (1968) 173,133. Centre of Dutch bulb growing, with world wide exports. Also old-established printing industry. Manufactures textiles, chemicals, cocoa and chocolate, etc. Typically Dutch in appearance, with many canals and gabled houses. *Groote Kerk* (15th/16th-cent.); town hall, originally a palace of the counts of Holland, rebuilt in the 17th cent.; Frans Hals museum, with a fine collection of his paintings.

**Haarlemermeer** Netherlands. Formerly a shallow lake in N Holland province between Haarlem, Amsterdam, and Leiden, completely drained 1840–52; the polder so formed, mostly fertile, has been used for dairy farming and the cultivation of wheat, flax, etc. Now constitutes a commune of the same name. Pop. (1968) 54,995.

**Habbaniya, Lake** Iraq. Lake 19 m. long just S of the Euphrates R. 50 m. W of Baghdad. Near by is an airfield, formerly used by the British RAF.

**Hachinohe** Japan. Industrial town and port in Aomori prefecture, NE Honshu, 50 m. SE of Aomori. Pop. (1965) 189,385. Important fishing centre; fish canning. Manufactures chemicals, iron and steel, cement, etc.

**Hachioji** Japan. Industrial town in Honshu 25 m. W of Tokyo. Pop. (1965) 207,754. Manufactures textiles etc.

**Hackensack** USA. Residential and industrial town in New Jersey, on the Hackensack R. 12 m. N of Jersey City. Pop. (1960) 30,521. Manufactures furniture, glass, wallpaper, jewellery, etc. First settled in 1639 by Dutch colonists from Manhattan.

**Hackney** England. Former metropolitan borough in NE London; from 1965 a Greater London borough including Shoreditch and Stoke Newington. Pop. (1963) 257,301. Once residential, now largely industrial. Manufactures furniture, clothing, confectionery, etc. Hackney Marsh (340 acres), formerly a haunt of highwaymen and robbers, is now the largest playing-field in London. Many buildings destroyed in the air raids of the 2nd World War have been replaced by model housing estates.

**Haddington** Scotland. Small burgh and county town of E Lothian, on the R. Tyne 15 m. E of Edinburgh. Pop. (1961) 5,506. Market town. Woollen and hosiery manufactures. A 13th-cent. parish church. Birthplace of Alexander II (1198–1249), John Knox (1505–72), Jane Welsh Carlyle (1801–66), and Samuel Smiles (1812–1904).

**Haddingtonshire** ⟡ *East Lothian.*

**Hadhramaut** S Yemen. Region in S Yemen bordered on the N by Saudi Arabia and on the S by the Gulf of Aden and the Indian Ocean. Roughly co-extensive with the former E Aden Protectorate; consists of the former Qu'aiti State of Shihr and Mukalla and the former Kathiri State of Sai'un. Mainly desert; dates, millet, etc. cultivated. Chief ports Mukalla, Shihr.

**Hadleigh** England. Urban district in W Suffolk 9 m. W of Ipswich. Pop. (1961) 3,460. Market town. Malting, flour milling. The woollen industry introduced by the Flemings declined after the plagues of 1636 and 1687. A 14th-cent. church; 15th-cent. Deanery Tower (gateway).

**Hadrian's Wall** England. Remains of Roman fortifications against the N tribes of Britain, extending for 73 m. between Bowness (Solway Firth) and Wallsend (R. Tyne). Built on the instructions of the Emperor Hadrian *c.* A.D. 122–6.

**Hagen** Federal German Republic. Industrial town in N Rhine-Westphalia, in the Ruhr district 12 m. S of Dortmund. Pop. (1968) 199,734. Important railway junction. Engineering, brewing. Manufactures paper, food products, etc. Much damaged in the 2nd World War.

**Hagerstown** USA. Industrial and commercial town in the Cumberland Valley, W Maryland, 65 m. WNW of Baltimore. Pop. (1960) 36,660. Manufactures aircraft, dust-control equipment, leather goods, furniture, etc. Named after Jonathan Hager, a German who settled here (1737) on land which he called 'Hager's Delight'.

**Hagion Oros** ⟡ *Athos, Mount.*

**Hague, The** (Dutch **Den Haag, 's Gravenhage**) Netherlands. Seat of government of the Netherlands and capital of S Holland province, 32 m. SW of Amsterdam and 2 m. from the North Sea. Pop. (1968) 576,160. Chiefly residential, with some industries, e.g. distilling, printing, manufacture of clothing, etc. One of the finest cities in Europe, with handsome streets and buildings, e.g. the Binnenhof, founded in the 13th cent., where both chambers of the legislature are housed; the 17th-cent. Mauritshuis, now a famous picture gallery; the Huis ten Bosch ('House in the Wood'), a 17th-cent. royal residence; and the Peace Palace (1913), headquarters of the International Court of Justice. In the 13th cent. it was merely the site of a hunting lodge of the counts of Holland, but before the end of the 16th cent. it had become the meeting place of the States-General and residence of the stadholders. Later it was the scene of many treaties and conferences, inc. the Peace Conferences of 1899 and 1907.

**Haguenau** France. Industrial town in the Bas-Rhin department in Alsace, on the Moder R. 16 m. N of Strasbourg. Pop. (1968) 24,379. Trade in hops. Manufactures textiles, footwear, etc.

**Haifa** Israel. Chief seaport and important industrial centre, 55 m. NNE of Tel Aviv at the foot and on the slopes of Mt Carmel. Pop. (1968) 209,900. Manufactures textiles, chemicals, soap, cement, electrical equipment, etc. Its oil refinery is linked by pipeline with the oilfields of Kirkuk, but the flow of oil was stopped by Iraq after the Israeli-Arab war of 1948. Seat of an Institute of Technology (1912).

**Hail** Saudi Arabia. Town in Jebel Shammar, N Nejd, 350 m. NW of Riyadh. Pop. 30,000. On an important pilgrim and caravan route from Iraq to Medina and Mecca. Capital of the Ibn Rashid dynasty in the 19th cent. Fell to Ibn Saud 1921.

**Hailar River** ▷ *Argun River.*

**Hainan** China. Island off the S coast, in Kwangtung province, separated from the Luichow peninsula by Kiungchow Strait. Area 13,500 sq. m. Pop. 2,800,000. Chief town and port Hoihow (N). Mountainous in the centre and S, rising to 5,800 ft in the Wuchih Shan. Produces timber (mahogany, rosewood, etc.), rice, sugarcane, tobacco, pineapples, etc., also iron ore and other minerals. Has been under Chinese control since the 2nd cent. B.C. Occupied by the Japanese 1939–45.

**Hainaut (Hainault)** Belgium. Province in the SW, drained by the Scheldt, Dender, and Sambre rivers. Area 1,437 sq. m. Pop. (1968) 1,336,677. Cap. Mons. Low-lying and fertile in the N; the centre and S contain the important coalmining and iron and steel manufacturing region centred on Mons and Charleroi. A countship from the 9th cent.; united with that of Holland during the 14th and the 15th cent. and later shared the history of the Netherlands.

**Haiphong** N Vietnam. Chief seaport and second largest city, on the Red R. delta 55 m. ESE of Hanoi, to which it is linked by railway. Pop. (1963) 369,000. Exports rice, minerals, etc. Manufactures cement, textiles, plastics, etc. Developed in the late 19th cent. Recent industrial expansion assisted by USSR, China, and Czechoslovakia.

**Haiti** W Indies. Republic occupying the western third of the island of Hispaniola, in the Greater Antilles. Area 10,700 sq. m. Pop. (1962) 4,346,000. Cap. and chief seaport Port-au-Prince. Has an E frontier (193 m.) with the Dominican Republic, which occupies the remainder of Hispaniola; on the W it is separated from Cuba by the Windward Passage. Consists mainly of two peninsulas extending into the Windward Passage; also two islands, Île de la Tortue and Île de la Gonâve. Four fifths of the area is covered by wooded mountains, rising in the Massif de la Selle (SE) to 8,793 ft. Other ranges are the Massif du Nord (N) and the Massif de la Hotte (SW). The remainder consists of fertile plains, where the bulk of the population lives. Climate tropical, with little seasonal variation, though somewhat cooler in the mountains. The economy depends on agriculture; main commercial crops coffee, sugar-cane, sisal. Forest products include mahogany, rosewood, and cedar. Mineral resources are largely unexploited, but bauxite is mined and exported. Industry is still on a small scale; there are textile mills producing a cheap denim, a soap factory (opened 1954), a cement factory, and a number of food-processing and other plants. Apart from Port-au-Prince, the chief towns are Cap Haïtien and Les Cayes. Divided administratively into 9 departments.

Hispaniola was a Spanish possession from its discovery by Columbus (1493) until 1697, when the French took possession of the W part of the island (now Haiti, an Indian name meaning 'Mountainous Country'); it became France's most prosperous colony. Large numbers of African slaves were sent to work the cotton and sugar plantations, and the present population is mainly descended from them. In 1798 Toussaint l'Ouverture, a former slave, led a successful rebellion against the French and became a national hero and symbol of the fight against tyranny, but the real founder of Haitian independence was General Jean-Jacques Dessalines, who proclaimed himself Emperor of Haiti in 1804. From 1822 to 1844 the country was politically united with the Dominican Republic, France recognizing its independence in 1839. There was US occupation 1915–34. Overpopulation has led Haitians to penetrate into the Dominican Republic, resulting in border incidents and political tension. The Negroes (who are greatly influenced by the cult of voodoo) form about 95 per cent of the population and speak a French-derived patois (Créole). The remainder are mulattoes, who maintain the French cultural tradition. French is the official language. A UN investigation (1949) found that about 85 per cent of the population were illiterate.

**Hakodate** Japan. Seaport in Hokkaido, on the Tsugaru Strait (S). Pop. (1965) 243,418. Also an important fishing centre. Exports salted and canned fish, timber, etc. Shipbuilding, woodworking. Manufactures cement, food products, matches. Linked by ferry with Aomori (Honshu).

**Halberstadt** German Democratic Republic. Town in the Magdeburg district, N of the Harz Mountains and 32 m. SW of Magdeburg. Pop. (1965) 45,903. Sugar refining. Manufactures paper, machinery, textiles, sausages, etc. Cathedral (13th/14th-cent., severely damaged in the 2nd World War); 12th-cent. Liebfrauenkirche (Church of Our Lady); 14th-cent. town hall.

**Halesowen** England. Municipal borough in Worcestershire just WSW of Birmingham. Pop. (1961) 44,150. Industrial centre. Manufactures machine tools, anchors, nails, rivets, etc. Ruins of a 13th-cent. abbey near by. Birthplace of William Shenstone (1714–63), the poet.

**Halifax** Canada. Capital, largest city, and chief seaport of Nova Scotia, on the W shore of Halifax Harbour, an Atlantic inlet. Pop. (1966) 86,792. Has a fine natural harbour, ice-free at all seasons. Leading Canadian seaport for transatlantic shipping lines in winter, also E terminus of the Canadian National and Canadian Pacific railways. Shipbuilding, oil refining, fish processing, sugar refining. Manufactures food products, furniture, clothing, etc. Exports fish, fish products, timber, etc. Seat of the Dalhousie University (1818). Early buildings include the 18th-cent. Citadel and St Paul's Church. Canada's first newspaper, the *Halifax Gazette*, was started here (1752). Founded (1749) as a naval base, it was important in this capacity in both world wars. Part of the town was destroyed by the explosion of a munitions ship in the harbour in 1917.

**Halifax** England. County borough in the W Riding of Yorkshire, near the R. Calder 7 m. SW of Bradford. Pop. (1961) 96,073. Worsted, woollen, and carpet industries of major importance. Also manufactures clothing, confectionery, textile machinery, etc. Grammar school (founded in 1585); Piece Hall (1779), the town hall (1863, designed by Sir Charles Barry), and the 15th/17th-cent. Shibden Hall, just to the E (containing the West Yorkshire folk museum), are other noteworthy buildings. Its cloth trade dates from the 15th cent., and was later stimulated by the arrival of refugee Flemish merchants.

**Halle** German Democratic Republic. **1.** Administrative district, formerly part of the *Land* of Saxony-Anhalt. Area 3,386 sq. m. Pop. (1968) 1,932,938.
**2.** Capital of Halle district, formerly capital of Saxony-Anhalt, on the Saale R. 20 m. NW of Leipzig. Pop. (1968) 265,987. Industrial town, river port, and railway junction in a lignite-mining region. Manufactures sugar, paper, beer, chemicals, machinery, etc. University (founded 1694, incorporated in the University of Wittenberg 1817). A member of the Hanseatic League from the 13th to the 15th cent., Halle owed its commercial importance largely to its saline springs, which still produce. Birthplace of Handel (1685–1759).

**Hallstatt** Austria. Village in the Salzkammergut, Upper Austria, on the SW shore of the Hallstättersee. Salt mines near by. Owing to the discovery of prehistoric remains here in the mid 19th cent., it gave its name to the early Iron Age (Hallstatt period) of Europe.

**Halmahera (Djailolo)** Indonesia. Island in the Moluccas E of Celebes across the Molucca Sea, consisting of 4 peninsulas enclosing 3 bays, all of which open to the E. Area 7,000 sq. m. Pop. 55,000. Mountainous and well wooded, with several active volcanoes. Chief products nutmeg, sago, rice, coconuts.

**Halmstad** Sweden. Capital of Halland county, on the Kattegat 75 m. SSE of Göteborg. Pop. (1968) 46,548. Seaport. Industrial town. Resort. Exports timber, granite (quarried locally), dairy produce. Engineering. Manufactures textiles, wood pulp and paper.

**Hälsingborg** Sweden. Seaport in Malmöhus county, on The Sound 32 m. NNW of Malmö, with train ferry to Helsingör (Elsinore), in Denmark. Pop. (1968) 80,648. Industrial centre. Copper refining. Manufactures machinery, fertilizers, textiles, etc. Exports timber, paper, chemicals, etc. Changed hands several times between Denmark and Sweden, finally passing to the latter in 1710.

**Halstead** England. Urban district in N Essex, on the R. Colne 12 m. WNW of Colchester. Pop. (1961) 6,465. Market town. Manufactures wood products etc.

**Haltemprice** England. Urban district in the E Riding of Yorkshire; a residential and industrial suburb of NW Hull. Pop. (1961) 42,338. Boatbuilding, light engineering, cement manufacture, etc.

**Haltwhistle** England. Market town in Northumberland on the S Tyne R. 14 m. W of Hexham. Pop. (1961) 6,884. Coal-mining. Bishop Ridley (1500–1555) was born near by.

**Hama** Syria. Capital of the Hama administrative district, on the Orontes R. 120 m. NNE of Damascus. Pop. (1962) 116,098. Commercial centre. Trade in cereals, fruit. Tanning and weaving industries. Famous for its huge wooden water-wheels (*norias*), up to 90 ft in diameter, used for irrigation. An early Hittite settlement; passed to the Muslims in the 7th cent. A.D.

**Hamadan** Iran. Ancient Ecbatana. Town in Kermanshah province 180 m. WSW of Tehran at a height of 6,000 ft. Pop. (1966) 161,944. Trade in hides and skins, wool, etc. Long famous for its rugs and carpets. Also produces leather goods. Has the tomb of Avicenna, who died here in 1037. Capital of Media in the 7th–6th cent B.C. and summer capital of the Achaemenian Persian Empire in the 6th–4th cent. B.C. Fell to the Arabs in the 7th cent. A.D.

**Hamamatsu** Japan. Industrial town in Shizuoka prefecture, Honshu, 55 m. SE of Nagoya. Pop. (1965) 392,632. Manufactures motor-cycles, textiles, musical instruments (esp. pianos, organs), chemicals, etc.

**Hamburg** Federal German Republic. Second largest city (after W Berlin) and a *Land* of the Republic, on the Elbe R. 55 m. from its mouth on the North Sea. Pop. (1968) 1,832,560. Chief seaport, with an outport at Cuxhaven, and meeting place of ocean-going and river traffic. It has a great transit trade, importing raw materials and foodstuffs for the industrial regions of W Germany and exporting their manufactured goods. Shipbuilding, electrical engineering, food processing. Manufactures soap, margarine, chemicals, textiles, etc. Few old buildings, for most of those which survived the disastrous fire of 1842 were destroyed or heavily damaged by bombing in the 2nd World War. The site of a fortress of Charlemagne, Hamburg became an archbishopric in 834, and by the end of the 12th cent. a town had been founded near the old cathedral. In 1241 it formed a defensive alliance with Lübeck which gave rise to the Hanseatic League. Developed considerably as an international seaport in the 19th cent., with a particular interest in the transatlantic trade. Joined the German Empire in 1871, became a constituent state of the German Reich, and in 1949 a *Land* of the German Federal Republic. Birthplace of Mendelssohn (1809–47) and Brahms (1833–97).

**Hamden** USA. Residential and industrial town in Connecticut, 5 m. N of New Haven. Pop. (1960) 41,056. Manufactures hardware, fire-arms, metal goods, etc.

**Hämeenlinna (Tavastehus)** Finland. Capital of the Häme province, 58 m. NNW of Helsinki. Pop. (1968) 36,858. Manufactures textiles, plywood, etc. Castle dating from the 13th cent. Birthplace of Sibelius (1865–1957).

**Hameln** Federal German Republic. Town in Lower Saxony, on the Weser R. 25 m. SW of Hanover. Pop. (1963) 49,500. Famous for the legend of the Pied Piper of Hamelin, said to have been enacted here in 1284 and illustrated by frescoes at the 17th-cent. Rattenfängerhaus or Ratcatcher's House. Also an industrial centre. Iron founding, flour milling. Manufactures carpets, paper, textiles, chemicals, etc.

**Hamersley Range** Australia. Mountain range in the W of Western Australia, extending W–E about 170 m., between the Fortescue and the Ashburton rivers. Highest peaks Mt Bruce (4,024 ft) and Mt Brockman (3,654 ft). Rich deposits of iron ore.

**Hamhung (Hamheung)** N Korea. Industrial

and commercial town 115 m. NE of Pyongyang. Pop. 150,000. Manufactures textiles. Developed by the Japanese (1910–45) but severely damaged in the Korean War (1950–51). Just SE is the seaport and industrial centre of Hungnam (Heungnam), with important chemical and fertilizer plants.

**Hamilton** Australia. Market town and railway junction in SW Victoria, 165 m. W of Melbourne, in a dairy-farming area. Pop. (1966) 10,052.

**Hamilton** Bermuda. Capital and chief port, on an inlet of Bermuda Island. Pop. 3,000. Centre of commercial and social life, and a tourist resort. Founded 1790. Succeeded St George as capital in 1815.

**Hamilton** Canada. Town in Ontario at the W end of L. Ontario. Pop. (1966) 298,121. Lake port. Railway and industrial centre. Important steel works. Manufactures heavy machinery, electrical apparatus, typewriters, agricultural machinery, wire, textiles, clothing, etc. Seat of the McMaster University (1930). Named after George Hamilton, who founded the town (1813).

**Hamilton** New Zealand. Town in the N Island, on the Waikato R. 70 m. SSE of Auckland. Pop. (1966) 63,024. Manufactures dairy and wood products, clothing, etc. Engineering, brewing.

**Hamilton** Scotland. Large burgh in Lanarkshire near the R. Clyde 10 m. SE of Glasgow. Pop. (1961) 41,928. Manufactures metal goods, electrical equipment, etc. Because of subsidence due to coalmining many old buildings have been pulled down, including Hamilton Palace, seat of the dukes of Hamilton. Rudolf Hess landed on the latter's estate after flying from Germany (May 1941).

**Hamilton** USA. Formerly Fairfield. Industrial town in SW Ohio on the Great Miami R. 20 m. N of Cincinnati. Pop. (1960) 72,354. Manufactures paper, machinery, diesel engines, safes, etc. Laid out near the site of Fort Hamilton as Fairfield (1794); later renamed.

**Hamm** Federal German Republic. Industrial town in N Rhine-Westphalia, on the Lippe R. 19 m. ENE of Dortmund. Pop. (1963) 71,300. In a coalmining region. Manufactures wire and cables, machinery, stoves, etc. Because of its extensive railway marshalling yards and its factories, it was frequently bombed in the 2nd World War and was severely damaged.

**Hammerfest** Norway. Town in Finnmark, the most northerly in the world, on the W coast of Kvalöy Island. Pop. (1961) 5,862. Fishing, sealing, and whaling station with an ice-free port all the year. Exports cod-liver oil, salted fish, etc. The sun does not set here between 13 May and 29 July and does not rise between 18 Nov. and 23 Jan. During the 2nd World War it was used as a submarine base by the Germans, who destroyed it on retreating. It was rebuilt and reinhabited 1945–50.

**Hammersmith** England. Former metropolitan borough in W London on the N bank of the Thames, here crossed by Hammersmith Bridge, replacing an earlier suspension bridge; from 1965 a Greater London borough including ♢ *Fulham*. Pop. (1963) 222,059. Largely residential, with varied industries. St Paul's School, a leading public school (founded 1509), here 1884–1968. The large exhibition building of Olympia is in the borough, also the White City Stadium and the BBC Television centre and studios. William Morris, Turner, and Kneller lived in the Mall.

**Hammond** USA. Industrial town in NW Indiana near L. Michigan, on the Grand Calumet R. between Chicago and Gary. Pop. (1960) 111,698. Manufactures railway equipment, agricultural machinery, petroleum products, soap, etc. Named after George H. Hammond, who established a packing plant in 1868.

**Hampshire** England. County on the S coast, including the Isle of ♢ *Wight* which is separated from the mainland by the Solent. Area (excluding Isle of Wight) 1,503 sq. m. Pop. (1961) 1,336,084. County town Winchester. Crossed by the Hampshire Downs in the N and the South Downs in the SE. Drained by the Itchen, Test, and E Avon rivers. The New Forest, noted for its scenic beauty, is in the SW and borders on Southampton Water. Sheep reared on the downs. Cereals and root crops cultivated. Chief towns Winchester, Southampton, Portsmouth, Bournemouth, Gosport. Several seaside resorts on the Isle of Wight and on the mainland.

**Hampstead** England. Former metropolitan borough and residential suburb of NW London, in a hilly district rising in the N to 443 ft on Hampstead Hill; from 1965 part of the Greater London borough of Camden. Pop. (1961) 98,902. Hampstead Heath is one of London's most popular open spaces, famous for its Bank Holiday fairs and for the inns Jack Straw's Castle, the

Spaniards, and the Bull and Bush. Ken Wood has a fine Adam mansion. Parliament Hill is on the E boundary; in the extreme SE is Primrose Hill. Once a spa, Hampstead has long been favoured by artists and authors, inc. Constable, Romney, Keats, Leigh Hunt, John Galsworthy, and H. G. Wells.

**Hampton** England. Former urban district of Middlesex on the R. Thames 12 m. SW of London; from 1965 part of the Greater London borough of Richmond-upon-Thames. Contains Hampton Court Palace, an outstanding example of Tudor architecture, built by Cardinal Wolsey in 1515 and presented by him to Henry VIII in 1526. It remained a royal residence until the reign of George II. In Queen Victoria's reign the state apartments and picture galleries were opened to the public; the palace is also well-known for the Maze and the great vine planted in 1768. The Hampton Court Conference of the clergy was held here in 1604.

**Hampton** USA. Port in SE Virginia, on Hampton Roads just NE of Newport News. Pop. (1960) 89,258. Packs and exports fish, oysters, etc. Seat of the Hampton Institute, a college for Negroes (1868). Formed (1952) by amalgamating Hampton, Phoebus, and Elizabeth City county.

**Hamtramck** USA. Town in SE Michigan, completely surrounded by Detroit. Pop. (1960) 34,137 (largely of Polish extraction). Manufactures cars, paints, varnishes, etc. Named after Colonel J. F. Hamtramck, the first American commander of Detroit fort after its surrender by British troops in 1796.

**Hanau** Federal German Republic. Industrial town in Hessen at the confluence of the Kinzig and the Main rivers 10 m. E of Frankfurt. Pop. (1963) 48,500. Centre of the jewellery industry. Also manufactures rubber products, chemicals, etc. Diamond cutting and polishing. Most of its historic buildings were destroyed in the 2nd World War. Birthplace of the brothers Grimm (Jacob, 1785–1863; Wilhelm, 1786–1859) and Paul Hindemith (1895–1963), the composer.

**Hangchow** China. Capital of Chekiang province, on the Fuchun (Tsientang) R. at the head of Hangchow Bay, 100 m. SW of Shanghai. Pop. 784,000. S terminus of the Grand Canal. Commercial centre. Trade in silk, tea, rice. Manufactures textiles, matches, etc. Inaccessible to ocean-going ships owing to silting; waterborne trade limited to river and canal. Seat of two universities (1927, 1959). Flourished chiefly in the 12th cent. during the later Sung dynasty, when it became capital of S China. Chiefly because of its picturesque setting, it was considered by Marco Polo, who called it Kinsai (Chinese Kingshih), to be the world's finest city. Still a popular resort. Destroyed in the Taiping rebellion (1861) and rebuilt.

**Hangchow Bay** China. Funnel-shaped bay in Chekiang province, on the E China Sea, about 100 m. long and 60 m. wide (at the mouth); forms the estuary of the Fuchun (Tsientang) R. Notorious for its tidal bore.

**Hankow** ◊ *Wuhan*.

**Hanley** England. Town in the Potteries, N Staffordshire, one of the 'Five Towns'; since 1910 part of ◊ *Stoke-on-Trent*. Birthplace of Arnold Bennett (1867–1931).

**Hannibal** USA. Town on the Mississippi R. in NE Missouri. Pop. (1960) 20,028. Manufactures shoes, cement, metal goods, etc. Railway engineering. Once an important river port. Mark Twain (whose home is preserved) spent his boyhood in the town, which provided the setting for *Huckleberry Finn* and *Tom Sawyer*.

**Hanoi** N Vietnam. Capital of the republic, on the Red R. Pop. (1964) 850,000. Industrial centre. Railway junction and river port. Engineering, rice milling, tanning, brewing. Manufactures textiles, leather goods, matches, etc. University (refounded 1956). Capital of French Indo-China 1902–45, and of N Vietnam from 1954.

**Hanover** (Ger. **Hannover**) Federal German Republic. **1.** Former province in Prussia, in the W part of the N German lowlands, including Lüneburg Heath. Area 14,953 sq. m. There is a considerable area of heath and moor, but cereals, potatoes and sugar-beet are cultivated and cattle are raised on the more fertile lowlands; the region is drained by the navigable Ems, Weser, Aller, and Elbe rivers. In 1692 Duke Ernest Augustus of Brunswick-Lüneburg was granted the rank of elector, took the city of Hanover as his capital, and was popularly known as the Elector of Hanover. His wife was Sophia, grand-daughter of James I of England, and their son, the Elector George Louis, succeeded to the English throne in 1714; Britain and Hanover were thus ruled by the same monarch until the accession of Queen Victoria (1837). Hanover, a kingdom from 1815, was annexed by Prussia as a province in 1866. After the 2nd World War it was incorporated into the *Land* of Lower Saxony.

2. Capital of Lower Saxony and former capital of Hanover province, on the Leine R. and on the Weser–Elbe (Mittelland) Canal. Pop. (1968) 527,192. Industrial and commercial centre. Manufactures machinery, electrical equipment, textiles, fertilizers, tyres, food products, etc. Seat of a technical university (1879). Many of its old buildings, inc. the house of Leibniz and the Herrenhausen castle, once a residence of the kings of Hanover, were destroyed or badly damaged in the 2nd World War. Birthplace of Sir William Herschel (1738–1822), the astronomer.

**Hanyang** ⟶ *Wuhan*.

**Harar** Ethiopia. Capital of Harar province, 230 m. E of Addis Ababa at a height of over 5,000 ft. Pop. 38,000. Trade in coffee, cotton, hides, etc. An old walled town; the country's chief Muslim centre, with several mosques. Seat of the Haile Selassie Military Academy (1957). Captured from the Italians by British forces during the 2nd World War (1941).

**Harbin** China. Capital of Heilungkiang province, in Manchuria, 325 m. NNE of Shenyang on the Sungari R. Pop. (1957) 1,552,000. Important industrial, commercial, and route centre. Flour milling, soyabean processing, sugar refining, railway engineering. Manufactures machinery, chemicals, textiles, glass, etc. Its importance is largely due to its position at the junction of the Chinese Eastern and the S Manchurian Railways. It was founded by the Russians in 1897, in fact, during the construction of the Chinese Eastern line, and developed rapidly as an industrial town; it is still more Russian than Chinese in character.

**Hardanger Fiord** Norway. Inlet of the North Sea in Hordaland county, penetrating 75 m. inland; its mouth, 30 m. SSE of Bergen, is fringed by islands. Popular with tourists on account of its magnificent scenery, with lofty mountains and waterfalls on its flanks.

**Hardoi** India. Town in Uttar Pradesh 65 m. NW of Lucknow. Pop. (1961) 36,725. Trade in grain, oilseeds.

**Hardt Mountains** ⟶ *Neustadt-an-der-Weinstrasse*.

**Hardwar** India. Town in NW Uttar Pradesh, on the Ganges R. 108 m. NE of Delhi. Pop. (1961) 58,513. A well-known Hindu place of pilgrimage, with the temple of Gangadwara and an adjoining bathing ghat which has the footprint of Vishnu. Here the Upper Ganges Canal leaves the river.

**Harfleur** France. Town in the Seine-Maritime department, on the Seine estuary 4 m. E of Le Havre. Pop. (1968) 15,598. Manufactures metal goods, flour, vinegar. During the Middle Ages it was the chief port of NW France, but it declined with the silting up of the Seine estuary and the rise of Le Havre; it was somewhat improved by the cutting of the Tancarville Canal to Le Havre. Besieged and captured by Henry V of England 1415.

**Hargeisa** Somalia. Town 150 m. SSE of Djibouti. Pop. (1963) 40,255. Trading centre for the nomadic herdsmen of the region. Capital of British Somaliland 1941–60.

**Haringey** England. From 1965 a Greater London borough, comprising the former municipal boroughs of Hornsey, Tottenham, and Wood Green, all in Middlesex. Pop. (1963) 258,908.

**Hari Rud (Tedzhen River).** River 700 m. long in SW Asia, rising in the Koh-i-Baba in central Afghanistan, flowing W past Herat, turning N to form the Afghanistan–Iran border and the USSR–Iran border, then turning NW as the Tedzhen into the Turkmen SSR, finally losing itself in the sands of the Kara Kum desert. Irrigates parts of Herat province, Afghanistan, and the Turkmen SSR.

**Harlech** Wales. Seaside resort and former county town of Merionethshire, on Cardigan Bay 9 m. NNW of Barmouth. The now ruined castle (built by Edward I) surrendered to the Yorkists in 1468 after a bitter struggle, inspiring the song *The March of the Men of Harlech*.

**Harlingen** USA. Port in S Texas on an offshoot of the Gulf Intracoastal Waterway. Pop. (1960) 41,207. In an intensively cultivated agricultural area. Exports citrus fruits, vegetables, etc. Canning; manufactures chemicals etc.

**Harlington** ⟶ *Hayes and Harlington*.

**Harlow** England. Urban district in W Essex 6 m. SSW of Bishop's Stortford, with a small part in Hertfordshire. Pop. (1961) 53,496 (5,825 in 1951). Designated a 'new town' in 1947 with an ultimate pop. of 80,000. Residential town. Manufactures glass, surgical instruments, scientific equipment, furniture.

**Harpenden** England. Urban district in W

Hertfordshire 5 m. NNW of St Albans. Pop. (1961) 18,218. Mainly residential. Rothamsted Experimental Station for agricultural research is near by.

**Harpers Ferry** USA. Small resort and residential town in West Virginia at the confluence of the Potomac and Shenandoah rivers. Pop. 600. Famous for the raid on the US arsenal carried out by John Brown in 1859, which led to his surrender, trial, and execution (commemorated in the song *John Brown's Body*). In the American Civil War it was captured by Confederate forces under Jackson 1862.

**Harris** Scotland. The S part of the island of ◊ *Lewis-with-Harris* in the Outer Hebrides, Inverness-shire, joined to the N part by a narrow isthmus at Tarbert. Pop. (1961) 3,285. Famous for handwoven Harris tweeds.

**Harrisburg** USA. State capital of Pennsylvania, on the Susquehanna R. Pop. (1960) 79,697. Important railway junction. In a coalmining region. Manufactures steel, machinery, bricks, clothing, shoes, food products. Named after John Harris, the first settler, who arrived *c.* 1715.

**Harrogate** England. Municipal borough in the W Riding of Yorkshire, 14 m. N of Leeds. Pop. (1961) 56,332. Spa, famous for the chalybeate, sulphur, and saline springs discovered in 1596. The Royal Pump Room is now a museum. Standing at 400–500 ft in the foothills of the Pennines, it is an admirable centre for the Yorkshire moors and dales; also a popular conference town.

**Harrow-on-the-Hill (Harrow)** England. Former municipal borough in Middlesex 11 m. NW of London, for which it is a residential suburb; from 1965 a Greater London borough. Pop. (1963) 208,963. The name derives from the isolated hill 408 ft high, on the summit of which is the church of St Mary, founded in the 11th cent. Site of one of the country's oldest and most famous public schools, founded by John Lyon in 1571, former pupils having included Byron, Palmerston, Peel, Sheridan, Galsworthy, Cardinal Manning, and Winston Churchill; the names of many are carved on the panels of the fourth form room, which dates from 1611. In 1934 Harrow urban district absorbed Wealdstone, Pinner, Harrow Weald, and Stanmore, and in 1954 it became a municipal borough.

**Hartford** USA. State capital and largest city of Connecticut, on the Connecticut R.

Pop. (1960) 162,178. The most important business is insurance. Manufactures typewriters, fire-arms, electrical equipment, tools, machinery. Seat of the schools of law and insurance of the University of Connecticut. Settled (1635–6) as Newtown; renamed (1637) after Hertford, England. Birthplace of Noah Webster, the lexicographer (1758–1843).

**Hartlepool** England. Former municipal borough in E Durham, on Hartlepool Bay just NE of ◊ *West Hartlepool*, with which it combined (1967) to form the new county borough of Hartlepool. Pop. (county borough, 1968) 98,760. Port. Shipbuilding. Fishing. Grew up round a 7th-cent. convent; has the 12th-cent. Church of St Hilda.

**Harvey** USA. Industrial town in Illinois 19 m. S of Chicago. Pop. (1960) 29,071. Engineering, metal working, etc.

**Harwell** England. Village in Berkshire 2 m. WSW of Didcot. Pop. 2,200. Atomic research station (established 1947).

**Harwich** England. Municipal borough in NE Essex, on the estuary of the R. Stour and the R. Orwell, including the seaside resort of Dovercourt (SW). Pop. (1961) 13,569. Seaport. Fishing, engineering, etc. Steamer services to the Hook of Holland (Netherlands) and Esbjerg (Denmark). In the 2nd World War, when the town was frequently bombed, Harwich was an important naval base.

**Haryana** India. State formed in 1966 from the Hindi-speaking parts of Punjab. Area 17,600 sq. m. Pop. 7,600,000. Cap. (shared with Punjab) Chandigarh.

**Harz Mountains** Federal German Republic. Wooded range between the Elbe and the Weser rivers, rising to 3,747 ft in the Brocken. Formerly well known for mineral deposits, esp. silver and lead. Now attracts tourists on account of mineral springs, scenery, and climate.

**Hasa, Al** Saudi Arabia. The eastern region of Nejd, on the Persian Gulf, bounded on the N by Kuwait and its neutral zone. Chief town Hofuf. Dates and cereals grown in the oases of Hofuf and Qatir; sheep, camels, and donkeys bred by the Bedouin. The country's oil-producing region: petroleum was first discovered here in 1935; rapid development began after the 2nd World War. Taken from the Turks by Ibn Saud 1914. ◊⟩ *Saudi Arabia*.

**Haskovo** ◊ *Khaskovo*.

**Haslemere** England. Urban district in

SW Surrey, 12 m. SSW of Guildford. Pop. (1961) 12,528. Residential. Has the annual Dolmetsch festival of early music. Near by, on Blackdown (918 ft), is Aldworth, the home of Tennyson, who died there.

**Haslingden** England. Municipal borough in Lancashire 7 m. ESE of Blackburn. Pop. (1961) 14,370. Market town. Manufactures textiles, footwear, etc.

**Hassan** India. Town in Mysore 60 m. NW of Mysore at a height of 3,000 ft. Pop. (1961) 32,172. Rice milling, engineering, etc. Founded in the 12th cent.

**Hasselt** Belgium. Capital of Limbourg province, on the Demer R. and near the Albert Canal, 42 m. ENE of Brussels. Pop. (1968) 38,886. Industrial and market town. Flour milling, brewing, distilling, etc. Just N is the Campine coalfield. Noted for its septennial Feast of the Assumption pilgrimage. The Belgians were defeated here by the Dutch in their War of Independence (1831).

**Hassi Messaoud** Algeria. Oil-producing centre in the Sahara, 200 m. S of Biskra. Oilfield first operated in 1957. Oil pipeline to Bougie. Gas pipeline to Algiers via Mostaganem and Oran.

**Hastings** England. County borough in SE Sussex on the English Channel, including St Leonards-on-Sea (W). Pop. (1961) 66,346. Residential town. Seaside resort. Small fishing industry; main occupation catering for holiday-makers. Promenade (3 m. long), beaches, public gardens; overlooking the town is the ruined Norman castle, and there are 14th- and 15th-cent. churches. Formerly chief of the Cinque Ports. Became popular as a resort in the 18th cent. The Battle of Hastings (1066) was fought at Battle, 6 m. NW.

**Hastings** New Zealand. Town in the N Island 11 m. SSW of Napier. Pop. (1966) 26,867. In a region noted for fruit orchards and dairy farms. Fruit canneries.

**Hatfield** England. Market and residential town in Hertfordshire 5 m. ENE of St Albans. Pop. (rural district, 1961) 39,630. Aircraft and engineering industries. It has Hatfield House (built 1607–11), seat of the Marquess of Salisbury, and the remains of Hatfield Palace (1497), where Elizabeth I heard the news of her accession. On the outskirts a modern planned 'new town', known as Hatfield New Town, ultimately to house 25,000, has been developed.

**Hathras** India. Town in Uttar Pradesh 32 m. NNE of Agra. Pop. (1961) 64,045. Trade in grain, cotton, sugar. Cotton ginning and spinning.

**Hatteras, Cape** USA. Promontory in N Carolina, on Hatteras Island between Pamlico Sound and the Atlantic. Has had a lighthouse since 1798, owing to the frequent storms causing danger to shipping; long known as the 'Graveyard of the Atlantic'.

**Hattiesburg** USA. Town in SE Mississippi 86 m. SE of Jackson. Pop. (1960) 34,989. Sawmilling. Manufactures clothing, fertilizers, etc. Named after the wife of an early railway official. Seat of the University of Southern Mississippi (1910).

**Hattingen** Federal German Republic. Town in N Rhine-Westphalia, on the Ruhr R. 9 m. N of Wuppertal. Pop. (1963) 30,700. Coalmining. Manufactures steel.

**Haugesund** Norway. North Sea fishing port in Rogaland county 36 m. NNW of Stavanger. Pop. (1968) 27,294. Exports fresh, canned, and frozen herring. Fish canneries and saltworks. Near by is a monument to Harald Haarfager.

**Hauraki Gulf** New Zealand. Inlet of the Pacific in the E of the Auckland Peninsula, N Island, 38 m. E–W and 25 m. N–S, with the Great Barrier Island near the entrance and several islands within. In the S is the Firth of Thames, and to the SW are Waitemata Harbour and Auckland City.

**Haute-Garonne** France. Department in the S formed in 1790 from parts of Gascony and Languedoc, bordering S on Spain, from which it is separated by the Pyrenees. Area 2,458 sq. m. Pop. (1968) 690,712. Prefecture Toulouse. Drained by the Garonne and Ariège rivers; the Canal du Midi crosses the NE. Mainly agricultural; leading crops wheat, maize, and vines. Livestock raised. Industries concentrated at Toulouse.

**Haute-Loire** France. Mountainous department in the Massif Central formed in 1790 from Auvergne, with parts of Languedoc and Lyonnais. Area 1,930 sq. m. Pop. (1968) 208,337 (slowly decreasing). Prefecture Le Puy. In the SW are the Monts de la Margeride, in the centre the Monts du Velay, separating the Loire and Allier rivers, and in the E the Monts du Vivarais. Cereals grown around Le Puy. Livestock raised in the mountains.

**Haute-Marne** France. Department in the NE formed chiefly from part of Champagne. Area 2,415 sq. m. Pop. (1968)

214,336. Prefecture Chaumont. Rises in the S to the Plateau de Langres. Drained by the Meuse, Marne, and Aube rivers; crossed by the Marne–Saône Canal. Chief towns Chaumont, Langres, St Dizier.

**Hautes-Alpes** France. Mountainous department in the SE formed in 1790 from parts of Dauphiné and Provence, bordering NE on Italy. Area 2,178 sq. m. Pop. (1968) 91,790. Prefecture Gap. In the N is the Massif du Pelvoux, rising to 13,461 ft, and in the E are the Cottian Alps. Occupies the upper basin of the Durance R. Sheep rearing important. Chief towns Gap, Briançon, Embrun.

**Haute-Saône** France. Department in the E formed in 1790 from the N part of Franche Comté, bounded on the NE by the Vosges and drained NE–SW by the Saône R. and its tributary the Ognon R. Area 2,075 sq. m. Pop. (1968) 214,776. Prefecture Vesoul. Dairy farming and agriculture, including the cultivation of wheat, potatoes, and cherries – from which kirsch is distilled.

**Haute-Savoie** France. Department in the SE formed in 1860 from the N part of Savoie, bounded by L. Geneva (N), Switzerland (E), Italy (SE), and the Rhône (W). Area 1,775 sq. m. Pop. (1968) 378,550. Prefecture Annecy. Mountainous, occupied by the N part of the French Alps, with the Mont Blanc massif (15,781 ft) in the SE. Several rivers harnessed for hydroelectric power. Vines and cereals grown in the lower areas; cattle raised and cheese produced in the uplands. Popular tourist resorts include Annecy, on the Lake of Annecy, and Chamonix; Évian-les-Bains and Thonon-les-Bains are spas.

**Hautes-Pyrénées** France. Department in the SW formed in 1790 from part of Gascony, bordering S on Spain, from which it is separated by the Pyrenees. Area 1,750 sq. m. Pop. (1968) 225,730. Prefecture Tarbes. In the extreme S are Mont Perdu (10,995 ft) and Vignemale (10,820 ft). Several mountain streams provide hydroelectric power, the chief being the Adour. Many resorts and spas. Chief towns Tarbes, Lourdes, Bagnères-de-Bigorre.

**Haute-Vienne** France. Department in W central France formed in 1790 mainly from Marche and Limousin. Area 2,144 sq. m. Pop. (1968) 341,589. Prefecture Limoges. Generally hilly: the Monts de la Marche are separated from the Monts du Limousin by the valley of the Vienne R. The rather harsh climate limits crops in many areas to potatoes, buckwheat, and rye; livestock are raised. Kaolin is quarried and used in the porcelain industry of Limoges; other towns St Junien, St Yrieix.

**Haut-Rhin** France. Department in the NE, in Alsace, bordering E on W Germany (Rhine R.) and S on Switzerland. Area 1,354 sq. m. Pop. (1968) 585,018. Prefecture Colmar. From the Rhine valley it rises W to the Vosges, containing their highest peak, Ballon de Guebwiller (4,665 ft), and it is drained by the Ill R. and its tributaries. Crossed by the Rhône–Rhine Canal. Cereals, vines, hops, and fruits grown – the cherries for kirsch distilling. Potash mined. Important textile and other industries. Chief towns Colmar, Mulhouse, Guebwiller.

**Hauts-de-Seine** France. Department just W of Paris, formed in 1964 when the former Seine and Seine-et-Oise departments were reorganized. Area 68 sq. m. Pop. (1968) 1,461,619. Prefecture Nanterre.

**Havana (La Habana)** Cuba. Capital, leading seaport, and largest city; capital of the Havana province; the largest and one of the finest cities in the W Indies, on Havana Bay, in the Gulf of Mexico. Pop. (1960) 787,765. Excellent harbour. Exports tobacco, sugar-cane, tropical fruit; handles most of the country's imports. The main industry is the manufacture of cigars (the world-famous 'Havanas'). Sugar refining; manufactures textiles, chemicals, perfumes, etc. The tourist trade, chiefly from the USA, declined severely with the advent of the Castro régime (1959). Buildings are a colourful mixture of the old Spanish 'colonial' and the modern styles, the most noteworthy being the cathedral (built 1656–1724). Founded (1514) as San Cristóbal de la Habana by Diego Velásquez and soon moved to its present location. Capital since 1552. In 1898 the Spanish-American war was precipitated by the blowing up of the US battleship *Maine* in the harbour; this led to the US occupation (1898–1902).

**Havant and Waterloo** England. Urban district in SE Hampshire, on Langstone Harbour 6 m. NE of Portsmouth. Pop. (1961) 74,564. Connected to Hayling Island by road and railway bridges. Market town. Manufactures pharmaceutical products, toys, plastic goods, etc.

**Havel River** German Democratic Republic. River 213 m. long rising in a small lake and flowing generally S to Spandau (Berlin), here receiving the Spree R., turning W past Potsdam and then NNW to join the Elbe R.

**Haverford** USA. Town in Pennsylvania, just NW of Philadelphia, of which it is a residential suburb. Pop. (1960) 54,019. Minor industries.

**Haverfordwest** Wales. Municipal borough and county town of Pembrokeshire, 8 m. NNE of Milford Haven at the head of navigation of the W Cleddau R. Pop. (1961) 8,872. Market town. Ruins of a 12th-cent. castle and an Augustinian priory. Many Flemish weavers were settled here by Henry I in the 12th cent.

**Haverhill** USA. Important shoe-manufacturing town in NE Massachusetts, at the head of navigation on the Merrimack R. Pop. (1960) 46,346. The industry was established in 1795. Named after Haverhill, Suffolk (England). Birthplace of J. G. Whittier (1807–92).

**Havering** England. Greater London borough (1965) comprising the former municipal borough of Romford and the urban district of Hornchurch (both in Essex). Pop. (1963) 242,706.

**Havre, Le** France. Important passenger and cargo transatlantic seaport in the Seine-Maritime department, on the English Channel at the mouth of the Seine R. Pop. (1968) 200,940. A major import centre for coffee, cotton, and wool. Oil refining (pipeline to Paris), flour milling, sawmilling. Manufactures wire, machinery, chemicals, etc. The harbour, protected by two breakwaters, accommodates the largest liners. Severely damaged in the 2nd World War, but had practically recovered its former trade by 1949. Founded by Francis I (1516) as Le Havre de Grâce, the name being derived from the chapel dedicated to Notre Dame de Grâce in the former fishing village.

**Hawaii** USA. Group of islands in the N Pacific; since 1959 a state of the USA. Area 6,424 sq. m. Pop. (1970) 748,575. Cap. Honolulu. Seven inhabited islands: Hawaii, the largest (area 4,021 sq. m., pop. 61,332); Maui (area 728 sq. m., pop. 35,717); Oahu (area 589 sq. m., pop. 500,409), containing the bulk of the population and the capital; Kauai (area 551 sq. m., pop. 27,922); Molokai (area 259 sq. m., pop. 5,023); Lanai (area 141 sq. m., pop. 2,115); Niihau (area 72 sq. m., pop. 254). The islands contain some of the world's largest volcanoes: on Hawaii are the Kilauea volcano on Mauna Loa (13,675 ft), noteworthy for the size of its crater (2 m. across) and still active, and Mauna Kea (13,825 ft), dormant. The mild climate and fertile soil, formed in the lowlands from disintegrated lava, are excellent for agriculture. Chief crops pineapples, sugar-cane. A junction of international shipping and airline routes, the islands are easily accessible from the USA, the Far East and Australia. Tourist industry of great importance. Mixed population: Japanese and Caucasians each constitute about a third of the total and Hawaiians a sixth; intermarriage is common.

The Hawaiian Is. were discovered (1778) by Capt. Cook; he named them the Sandwich Is., after Lord Sandwich, but the name went out of use. An obelisk at Kaawaloa on Hawaii marks the spot where Cook was killed (1779). Ruled by native monarchs until 1893, when a republic was proclaimed; in 1898 the USA annexed the islands, which officially became US territory in 1900. The Japanese attack on the American naval base at Pearl Harbor (1941) was largely instrumental in bringing the USA into the 2nd World War.

**Hawarden** Wales. Market town in Flintshire 6 m. W of Chester. Pop. (rural district, 1961) 36,290. The 18th-cent. castle was the residence of W. E. Gladstone for 60 years until his death.

**Hawes Water** England. Lake in Westmorland, in the Lake District 9 m. S of Penrith, formerly 2½ m. long but extended by damming to 4 m. and deepened in order to supply Manchester with water.

**Hawick** Scotland. Small burgh in Roxburghshire, on the R. Teviot 40 m. SE of Edinburgh. Pop. (1961) 16,204. Noted for the manufacture of hosiery, knitwear, and tweeds of high quality. Also a large sheep market. In 1514 an English force was defeated at near-by Hornshole, an event commemorated annually by the ceremony 'Riding the Common'. 3 m. SW is Branxholm or Branksome Castle, scene of Scott's *The Lay of the Last Minstrel*.

**Hawke's Bay** New Zealand. Provincial district in the E of the N Island, consisting of hill country and plain E of the Ruahine Range. Area 4,260 sq. m. Pop. (1966) 124,960. The dry eastern hill country supports many sheep and cattle; lowlands noted for orchards, vineyards, fodder crops. Encloses the inlet Hawke Bay, on the S W shore of which is Napier.

**Hawkshead** ◊ *Esthwaite Water*.

**Haworth** England. Moorland village and former urban district in the W Riding of Yorkshire, 3 m. S W of Keighley, with which it was incorporated in 1938.The parsonage, home of the Brontë family, is now a museum and library; Charlotte and Emily Brontë are buried in the church.

**Hawthorne** U S A. Industrial and residential town in California 12 m. S W of Los Angeles. Pop. (1960) 33,035. Expanded rapidly in the 1950s after the establishment of the aircraft industry. Also manufactures electrical equipment etc. Named after Nathaniel Hawthorne, the author.

**Hayastan** ◊ *Armenia*.

**Haydock** England. Urban district in S W Lancashire 3 m. E N E of St Helens. Pop. (1961) 12,070. In a coalmining area. Haydock Park racecourse.

**Hayes and Harlington** England. Former urban district in Middlesex 12 m. W of London; from 1965 part of the Greater London borough of Hillingdon. Pop. (1961) 67,912. Residential and industrial. Manufactures radio and television sets, gramophones and records, food products, etc.

**Hayling Island**. England. Island off the S E coast of Hampshire, connected by road bridge with Havant on the mainland. Area 8 sq. m. Important mainly as a holiday resort.

**Hay River** Canada. River 350 m. long rising in N W Alberta, flowing W into British Columbia, turning N and E into Alberta, then N E into Mackenzie District, N W Territories, entering the Great Slave Lake at the settlement of Hay River (pop. 2,002). The Mackenzie Highway runs parallel to it in its lower course.

**Hayward** U S A. Town in W California 15 m. S E of Oakland. Pop. (1960) 72,700. Fruit canning. Manufactures electrical equipment, metal goods, etc. One of the largest poultry centres in the U S A. Founded 1854. Named after William Hayward, an early settler.

**Haywards Heath** England. Residential town in E Sussex on the London–Brighton railway, incorporated in the urban district of Cuckfield in 1934.

**Hazaribagh** India. Town in Bihar 43 m. N of Ranchi. Pop. (1961) 40,958. Trade in rice, oilseeds, etc.

**Hazleton** U S A. Town in Pennsylvania 21 m. S S W of Wilkes-Barre. Pop. (1960) 32,056. In an anthracite-mining region. Manufactures textiles, clothing, metal goods, etc.

**Heard Island** S Indian Ocean. Volcanic island 300 m. S S E of the Kerguelen Is., 27 m. long and 13 m. wide, rising to about 11,000 ft. Largely under snow and ice. Occasionally used as a meteorological station. Discovered (1853) by the American Capt. J. J. Heard. Under Australian administration since 1947.

**Heathrow** England. Site of the main London airport, 15 m. W of the centre of London, just S of the A4 (Bath) road.

**Hebburn** England. Urban district in N E Durham, on the S bank of the R. Tyne 4 m. E of Newcastle upon Tyne. Pop. (1961) 25,042. Industrial centre. Coalmining. Shipbuilding, engineering. Manufactures electrical machinery.

**Hebrides (Western Isles)** Scotland. Group of about 500 islands off the W coast, about 100 being inhabited, comprising the Inner Hebrides and Outer Hebrides, separated by the North Minch, Little Minch, and the Sea of the Hebrides. The principal islands of the Inner Hebrides are Skye, Rhum, Eigg, Coll, Tiree, Mull, Iona, Staffa, Jura, and Islay, those of the Outer Hebrides being Lewis with Harris, N and S Uist, Benbecula, Barra, and St Kilda. Little of the land is arable, and the main occupations are stock rearing, fishing, crofting, and the weaving of tweeds. Administratively they are divided between the counties of Ross and Cromarty, Inverness, and Argyll. From the 6th to the 13th cent. they were under Norwegian rule. In recent years their population has declined.

**Hebron (Ar. El Khalil)** Jordan. Town 18 m. S S W of Jerusalem, at a height of 2,000 ft in the biblical valley of Eshcol. Pop. (1967) 43,000. Reputed one of the world's oldest towns, at times the home of Abraham and of David. Its principal feature is the Haram, built over the Cave of Machpelah, where Abraham, Isaac, and Jacob are said to have been buried.

**Heckmondwike** England. Urban district in the W Riding of Yorkshire, 6 m. N E of Huddersfield. Pop. (1961) 8,420. Manufactures woollen goods, carpets, textile machinery. Birthplace of John Curwen (1816–80), founder of the tonic sol-fa system of musical teaching.

**Hedjaz** ◊ *Hejaz*.

**Heemstede** Netherlands. Town in N Holland province 3 m. S of Haarlem. Pop. (1968) 26,242. Mainly residential. Bulb growing.

**Heerenveen** Netherlands. Town in Friesland province 18 m. SSE of Leeuwarden. Pop. (1968) 30,282. Manufactures bicycles, mopeds, plastics, etc.

**Heerlen** Netherlands. Town in Limburg province 13 m. ENE of Maastricht. Pop. (1968) 76,515. Railway junction. Coalmining and industrial centre. Manufactures briquettes, textiles, cement, etc. Headquarters of the state mining administration.

**Heidelberg** Federal German Republic. Town in Baden-Württemberg on the Neckar R. 11 m. SE of Mannheim. Pop. (1968) 121,882. In a picturesque valley clad with orchards and vineyards. Brewing, printing. Manufactures metal goods, electrical equipment, cigars, etc. Considerable tourist trade. Chiefly famous for its university (founded 1386) and the ruined castle overlooking the town, begun in the 13th cent. and containing a celebrated wine cask made in 1751 with a capacity of about 49,000 gallons. Other buildings include the 15th-cent. churches of St Peter and the Holy Ghost. Heidelberg was the residence of the Electors Palatine from the 13th to the 18th cent., suffered a great deal during the Thirty Years War, and was again damaged in the 2nd World War. In 1907 the jawbone of the prehistoric Heidelberg man was found near Mauer, 6 m. SE.

**Heidenheim** Federal German Republic. Industrial town in Baden-Württemberg 21 m. NNE of Ulm. Pop. (1963) 50,000. Manufactures turbines, electrical machinery, textiles, furniture, etc. Dominated by the ruined castle of Hellenstein, on a hill nearly 2,000 ft high.

**Heilbronn** Federal German Republic. Town in Baden-Württemberg on the Neckar R. 24 m. N of Stuttgart. Pop. (1963) 92,400. Railway junction, river port, and industrial centre. Manufactures metal goods, chemicals, textiles, paper, etc. An ancient town, of commercial importance since the Middle Ages, it was originally called Heiligbronn ('Holy Spring'), owing to the spring at the 11th/12th-cent Church of St Kilian. Severely damaged in the 2nd World War.

**Heilungkiang** China. Province in the NE, in Manchuria, bounded on the N across the Amur R. by USSR and called after the Chinese name for this river, the Heilung-kiang. Area 179,000 sq. m. Pop. (1957) 14,860,000. Cap. Harbin. Largely mountainous, with the Little Khingan Mountains in the N, extending NW–SE S of the Amur R., and the Changkwansai Mountains in the S, separated from the former by the basin of the Sungari R. Spurs of the Great Khingan Mountains are well forested, and on the fertile lowlands crops of soya beans, wheat, and flax are grown. Coal and gold are mined. Chief towns Harbin, Tsitsihar, Kiamusze.

**Hejaz (Hedjaz)** Saudi Arabia. The W part of Saudi Arabia, extending along the Red Sea from the Gulf of Aqaba and Jordan (N) to Asir (S). Area 150,000 sq. m. Pop. 2,000,000 (mainly Bedouin). Cap. Mecca. Consists of a narrow coastal plain and inland a highland region, both largely barren, cultivation being possible only where water is available for irrigation, near wadis and springs. Principal towns Mecca and Jidda, the chief port. The population of both Mecca and Medina is temporarily swollen annually by the influx of some 100,000 pilgrims. Hejaz was under the control of the Turks from 1517, and in 1908 they completed the Hejaz railway from Damascus to Medina; the section S of Ma'an (Jordan), however, was destroyed in the 1st World War and has not been repaired. In 1925 Ibn Saud occupied the country, and in 1932 it was united with Nejd as ◊ *Saudi Arabia*, though each has retained its separate identity and capital. ◊ *Arabia*.

**Hekla** Iceland. Active volcano (5,110 ft) 68 m. ESE of Reykjavik, with several craters. Since the 12th cent. it has erupted 24 times, in 1766 with considerable loss of life, and last in 1970.

**Helder, Den** Netherlands. Seaport and important naval base in N Holland province, on the Marsdiep channel separating it from Texel island. Pop. (1968) 58,356. Naval barracks, arsenal, meteorological station. N terminus of the N Holland Canal. Fishing. Shipbuilding etc. Fortified by Napoleon 1811.

**Helena** USA. State capital of Montana, 48 m. NNE of Butte, in the Prickly Pear valley, at a height of 4,000 ft. Pop. (1960) 20,227. Commercial centre. Resort. In a mining and agricultural region. Manufactures concrete products, bricks and tiles, pottery, etc. Goldmines near by. Owes its origin to the gold discoveries in Last Chance Gulch (1864). Much earthquake damage 1935-7.

**Helensburgh** Scotland. Small burgh in Dunbartonshire on the N bank of the R. Clyde estuary at the entrance to Gare Loch. Pop. (1961) 9,605. Holiday resort. Named after the wife of Sir James Colquhoun, founder of the town (1777). Birthplace of J. L. Baird (1888-1946), the inventor, and home of Henry Bell (1767-1830), whose steamboat the *Comet* travelled from Port Glasgow to Helensburgh in 1812.

**Helicon** (Gr. **Elikón**) Greece. Mountain range in Boeotia rising to 5,735 ft, known in Greek mythology as the home of the Muses. On its slopes are the springs of Aganippe and Hippocrene, whose waters were believed to give poetic inspiration.

**Heligoland** (Ger. **Helgoland**) Federal German Republic. Small rocky island of Schleswig-Holstein in the North Sea, off the mouths of the Elbe and the Weser rivers. Pop. (1961) 1,824. Formed of red sandstone, it consists of Unterland ('Lower Town') on a sandy spit and Oberland ('Upper Town') on the cliffs above. Acquired by Britain from Denmark 1807. Ceded to Germany (1890) in exchange for Zanzibar. Its fortifications were destroyed after the 1st World War, but it became an important German submarine base in the 2nd World War; the fortifications were again destroyed (1947) and the island was returned to Germany in 1952.

**Heligoland Bight** Federal German Republic. Bay between Heligoland and the mouths of the Elbe and the Weser rivers. Scene of an important naval battle between British and German forces (28 Aug. 1914) in the 1st World War.

**Heliopolis** United Arab Republic. 1. In Greek, 'City of the Sun'. Chief centre of sun-worship in ancient Egypt, 6 m. NE of Cairo. Its famous schools of philosophy and astronomy were eclipsed by those of Alexandria. Cleopatra's Needle in London (and a similar one in New York) once stood as obelisks before the great temple, where another still marks the site.
**2.** Residential suburb of modern Cairo near the site of ancient Heliopolis.
**3.** ◊ *Baalbek*.

**Hellas** ◊ *Greece*.

**Hellendoorn** Netherlands. Town in Over-

ijssel province 9 m. WNW of Almelo. Pop. (1968) 28,766. Manufactures textiles.
**Hellville** ◊ *Nossi-bé*.
**Helmand River** Afghanistan. Country's longest river (870 m.), rising W of Kabul and flowing generally SW across the Hazarajat, turning W and then N to empty into a marshy lake known as Hamun-i-Helmand, on the border of Iran. Most of its valley is cultivated.

**Helmond** Netherlands. Industrial town in N Brabant province 10 m. ENE of Eindhoven. Pop. (1968) 56,976. Manufactures textiles, cocoa and chocolate, soap, margarine, etc.

**Helmstedt** Federal German Republic. Town in Lower Saxony 23 m. E of Brunswick (Braunschweig) on the frontier between the Federal German Republic and the German Democratic Republic. Pop. (1963) 29,100. In a lignite-mining region. Manufactures machinery, textiles, etc. The Juleum, where the former university was housed, is a noteworthy building.

**Helsingfors** ◊ *Helsinki*.

**Helsingör** (**Elsinore**) Denmark. Seaport in NE Zealand, separated by The Sound from Hälsingborg, Sweden, with which it is connected by car and train ferry. Pop. (1965) 29,327. Shipbuilding, food processing, etc. E of the town is Kronborg, the Elsinore castle of Shakespeare's *Hamlet*.

**Helsinki** (**Helsingfors**) Finland. Capital of Finland and of the Uusimaa province, on the Gulf of Finland. Pop. (1968) 527,478. The largest city, chief seaport, and a cultural centre. Exports timber, wood pulp, plywood, paper, etc. Shipbuilding, sugar refining. Manufactures paper, plywood, textiles, machinery, etc. The harbour, protected by the island fortress of Suomenlinna, is kept open by ice-breakers Jan.–April. The city is well laid out and modern in appearance, many of its chief buildings having been erected in the 20th cent., and has a university moved here from Turku in 1828. Founded (1550) by Gustavus I of Sweden. Replaced Turku as capital in 1812 while under Russian rule.

**Helston** England. Municipal borough in Cornwall, on the R. Cober 9 m. WSW of Falmouth. Pop. (1961) 7,085. Market town. Well known for its floral Furry Dance (8 May). The fishing village of Porthleven, 3 m SW on Mount's Bay, was incorporated with it in 1934.

**Helvellyn** England. Mountain (3,118 ft) in

the Lake District, on the Cumberland–Westmorland border between Ullswater and Thirlmere, with a sharp ridge known as Striding Edge projecting E.

**Helwan** United Arab Republic. Town in Giza province 16 m. S of Cairo, with which it is linked by rail. Pop. (with suburbs) 51,000. Has a dry equable climate, warm sulphur springs; a favourite health resort. Observatory (built 1903). Manufactures cement, iron and steel, etc.

**Hemel Hempstead** England. Municipal borough in Hertfordshire, on the R. Gade 6 m. W of St Albans, in 1946 designated a 'new town'. Pop. (1961) 55,164. Market town. Manufactures fireworks, office equipment, paper, etc. St Mary's Church is partly Norman.

**Hempstead** USA. Residential town in New York state, in W Long Island. Pop. (1960) 34,641. Manufactures textiles, radio equipment, etc.

**Hemsworth** England. Urban district in the W Riding of Yorkshire, 7 m. SE of Wakefield. Pop. (1961) 14,401. Coalmining centre. Has a 16th-cent. grammar school and hospital.

**Henderson Island** ◊ *Pitcairn Island.*

**Hendon** England. Former municipal borough in Middlesex and residential suburb of NW London; from 1965 part of the Greater London borough of Barnet. Pop. (1961) 151,500. Includes Mill Hill, with its well-known public school, and the University of London observatory. At Colindale is the newspaper department of the British Museum. The famous Hendon airfield (founded 1909) saw the start of the first non-stop flight to Paris (1911) and was the scene of the annual RAF display 1920–37; it was closed in 1957.

**Hengelo** Netherlands. Industrial town and railway junction in Overijssel province, on the Twente Canal 5 m. NW of Enschede. Pop. (1968) 68,348. Manufactures textiles, machinery, electrical equipment, etc.

**Hengyang** China. Town in Hunan province, on the Siang R. 95 m. SSW of Changsha. Pop. 235,000. Important route centre, on the Peking–Kwangchow (Canton) railway and at the junction of the line to Kweilin. Has considerable river traffic: at the head of navigation for large junks.

**Henley-on-Thames** England. Municipal borough in Oxfordshire, on the left bank of the R. Thames and 7 m. NNE of Reading at the foot of the Chiltern Hills. Pop. (1961) 9,131. Famous for its annual rowing festival, Henley Royal Regatta, first held in 1839. The Thames is crossed here by a stone bridge of 5 arches, built in 1786.

**Herakleion** ◊ *Iráklion.*

**Herat** Afghanistan. Capital of Herat province in the NW, on the Hari Rud 400 m. W of Kabul at a height of 3,000 ft. Pop. (1965) 62,000. Commercial and road centre. Flour milling. Manufactures textiles, rugs. Enclosed by a wall standing on a great earthwork and dominated by the citadel, the city has 5 gates and the partly ruined Jama Masjid or Great Mosque as well as remains of many other buildings testifying to its former glory. Fell to the Arabs in the 7th cent. and under them acquired great importance. Sacked by Genghis Khan (1220) and other invaders, to flourish again in the 15th cent. Suffered further attacks, generally declined, and was incorporated into Afghanistan by Dost Mohammed Khan 1863.

**Hérault** France. Department in the S, in Languedoc, named after the chief river, which flows S across it. Area 2,042 sq. m. Pop. (1968) 591,397. Prefecture Montpellier. Bordering on the Gulf of Lions, where there are three long coastal lagoons, it rises inland to the dry, limestone hills of the Garrigues and then to the S extension of the Cévennes. One of the country's chief wine-producing regions. Also grows olives, mulberries, fruits. Chief towns Montpellier, Béziers, Sète.

**Hercegovina** ◊ *Bosnia-Hercegovina.*

**Herculaneum** (Italian **Ercolano**) Italy. Ancient city in Campania 5 m. SE of Naples and just W of Vesuvius. Roman residential city and resort, severely damaged by earthquake in A.D. 63 and completely buried by semi-liquid lava, which afterwards solidified, in the eruption of Vesuvius along with Pompeii in A.D. 79. Its site was discovered in 1709, and excavations were begun in 1738 and continued at various times into the 20th cent., yielding relics of greater value than those of Pompeii.

**Hereford** England. Municipal borough and county town of Herefordshire, on the R. Wye 24 m. NW of Gloucester. Pop. (1961) 40,431. Important trade in agricultural produce. Manufactures leather, cider, beer, etc. The cathedral (begun 1079) exhibits every style from Norman to Perpendicular, and with Gloucester and Worcester is the venue of the Three Choirs Festival; among its treasures is the 14th-cent. *Mappa Mundi,* one of the oldest maps in the world. The Old House, a picturesque half-timbered building now a museum, dates from the 17th cent. The grammar school was founded in 1384. A new bridge over the R. Wye, with a single span 290 ft long, was opened in 1966. Birthplace of David Garrick (1717–79) and possibly of Nell Gwynn (1651–87).

**Herefordshire** England. County in the W, on the Welsh border. Area 842 sq. m. Pop. (1961) 130,919. County town Hereford. Consists of broad plains and hills, with the Malvern Hills rising to 1,395 ft in the E and the Black Mountains in the SW. Chief rivers the Wye, which has salmon, and the Teme, Lugg, and Monnow, well known for their trout. Hops, apples, and pears are grown, cider and perry being produced. Famous for its breed of beef cattle. Principal towns Hereford, Leominster, Ross-on-Wye.

**Herford** Federal German Republic. Industrial town in N Rhine-Westphalia 10 m. NE of Bielefeld. Pop. (1963) 55,700. Manufactures textiles, carpets, machinery, furniture, etc. Grew up round a Benedictine nunnery of the 9th cent.

**Herm** ♢ *Channel Islands*; *Guernsey*.

**Hermannstadt** ♢ *Sibiu*.

**Hermon, Mount (Ar. Jebel esh Sheikh).** A picturesque snow-capped mountain of the Anti-Lebanon, 9,232 ft high, on the Syria–Lebanon border 25 m. WSW of Damascus.

**Hermosillo** Mexico. Capital of Sonora state, on the Sonora R. Pop. (1969) 196,500. Commercial centre for an agricultural region (maize, cotton, fruit) and for a mining area (gold, copper, silver). Also a winter resort. Cathedral. University (1938).

**Hermoupolis** ♢ *Cyclades*.

**Herne** Federal German Republic. Industrial town in N Rhine-Westphalia in the Ruhr district, on the Rhine–Herne Canal. Pop. (1968) 103,783. Coalmining centre. Coke ovens, foundries, textile mills, chemical plant.

**Herne Bay** England. Urban district in NE Kent on the Thames estuary. Pop. (1961) 21,273. Seaside resort with a sea front 7 m. long. The village of Herne, with an Early English church, is 1½ m. inland.

**Herreninsel** ♢ *Chiemsee*.

**Hersham** ♢ *Walton and Weybridge*.

**Herstal** Belgium. Industrial town in Liège province, on the Meuse R. 3 m. NE of Liège. Pop. (1968) 29,894. Manufactures fire-arms, electrical equipment, motor cycles, etc. Claims to be the birthplace of Charlemagne.

**Herstmonceux (Hurstmonceux)** England. Village in E Sussex 8 m. NNE of Eastbourne. Pop. 1,800. The castle (1440, restored 1907) has since 1950 housed the Royal Observatory after its transfer from Greenwich. The 98-in. Sir Isaac Newton telescope, the largest in Europe, came into service 1967. Wooden garden baskets (trugs) made in the village. Name derived from Waleran de Monceux, lord of the manor at the close of the 12th cent.

**Hertford** England. Municipal borough and county town of Hertfordshire, on the R. Lea 20 m. N of London. Pop. (1961) 15,734. Market town. Manufactures brushes etc. Brewing, flour milling, printing. Important in Saxon times. The castle, of which little remains, was built in the 10th cent. and later rebuilt. About 2 m. SE is Haileybury College, a public school.

**Hertfordshire** England. Inland county in the S, bounded on the S by Greater London. Area 632 sq. m. Pop. (1961) 832,088. County town Hertford. Mainly low-lying, highest in the NW (Chiltern Hills). Drained to the R. Thames by the Lea, Stort, and Colne rivers. While most of it is agricultural (cereals, fruit, market-garden and dairy produce), the S lies on the fringe of the Greater London area, and in recent years the 'new towns' of Stevenage and Hemel Hempstead have developed within the county. Other towns Watford, St Albans, East Barnet, Welwyn Garden City, Hertford.

**Hertogenbosch, 's** ♢ *'s Hertogenbosch*.

**Hessen** Federal German Republic. **1.** Former grand duchy, known before 1866 as Hesse-Darmstadt, with capital Darmstadt; one of several petty states into which Hesse was divided, others including Hesse-Kassel, Hesse-Homburg, and Hesse-Marburg. After the Austro-Prussian War (1866), they were all absorbed by Prussia or Hesse-Darmstadt, and the latter became known simply as Hesse or Hessen. It was divided into two main areas, the N part (Oberhessen) being separated from the S part (Starkenburg and Rheinhessen) by a strip of Prussian territory; Mainz was the largest town. After the 2nd World War (1946), it was divided between the new *Länder* of Hessen and Rhineland-Palatinate.
**2.** *Land* of W Germany, comprising the territory of the Hessen grand duchy on the right bank of the Rhine with most of the

former Prussian province of Hesse-Nassau. Area 8,148 sq. m. Pop. (1968) 5,262,700. Cap. Wiesbaden. Largely uplands, it includes parts of the Odenwald, Westerwald, Hohe Rhön, and the Taunus, and is well forested; the Rheingau is famous for its wine. Several spas, inc. Wiesbaden, Bad Homburg, Bad Nauheim. Other important towns Frankfurt, Kassel, Darmstadt, Offenbach.

**Heston and Isleworth** England. Former municipal borough in Middlesex and suburb (mainly residential) of W London; from 1965 part of the Greater London borough of Hounslow. Pop. (1961) 102,897.

**Hetton-le-Hole (Hetton)** England. Urban district in NE Durham 6 m. NE of Durham. Pop. (1961) 17,463. Coalmining centre.

**Heungnam** ◊ *Hamhung.*

**Hexham** England. Urban district in Northumberland, on the R. Tyne 20 m. W of Newcastle upon Tyne. Pop. (1961) 9,897. Market town. Famous for the 13th-cent. priory church, containing remains of the monastery founded c. 674 by St Wilfrid. Also in the town are two towers known as the Moot Hall (15th-cent.) and Manor Office (14th-cent.). In 1464 the Lancastrians were defeated by Edward IV at the Battle of Hexham.

**Heysham** ◊ *Morecambe and Heysham.*

**Heywood** England. Municipal borough in SE Lancashire, 3 m. E of Bury. Pop. (1961) 24,053. Cotton and paper milling, engineering, tanning, etc.

**Hialeah** USA. Residential suburb of Miami, Florida; merges W with the Everglades. Pop. (1960) 66,972. Famous for the Hialeah Park racecourse (built 1931), with a vine-covered grandstand seating 10,500; the oval track surrounds a 92-acre area of lawns and flower-beds, with a 32-acre artificial lake in the centre where live about 200 pink flamingoes. Manufactures food products, furniture, etc. Founded in the early 1920s by James Bright, a Missouri rancher, and Glenn Curtiss, an aeronaut and sportsman.

**Hidalgo** Mexico. Mountainous state in central Mexico, traversed by the Sierra Madre Oriental. Area 8,101 sq. m. Pop. (1969) 1,282,000. Cap. Pachuca. Produces maize, tobacco, cotton, maguey (from which 'pulque' is made), and other crops. Silver, gold, copper, lead, etc. mined. Site of the ancient Toltec culture, with its capital at Tula.

**Hidalgo del Parral** Mexico. Important mining town (chiefly silver) in S Chihuahua, 120 m. SSE of Chihuahua city at a height of 6,400 ft. Pop. 26,000. Flour milling. Scene of the assassination of Francisco Villa (1923).

**Higham Ferrers** England. Municipal borough in Northamptonshire on the R. Nene 4 m. E of Wellingborough. Pop. (1961) 3,756. Market town. Tanning. Manufactures shoes. Birthplace of Archbishop Chichele (1364–1443).

**Highbury** England. Residential district in the London borough of Islington, containing the Arsenal football ground and Highbury Fields, a 30-acre park.

**Highgate** England. Residential suburb in N London mainly in the borough of Haringey; so named because of the toll-gate erected by the Bishop of London in the 14th cent. Whittington Stone, at the foot of Highgate Hill, is supposed to be where Dick Whittington sat and heard Bow Bells chime 'Turn again . . . '. Highgate School was founded (1565) by Sir Roger Cholmley, the Lord Chancellor. In Highgate cemetery are the graves of Michael Faraday, Mrs Henry Wood, George Eliot, Karl Marx, and Herbert Spencer.

**High Peak** ◊ *Peak District.*

**High Point** USA. Town in N Carolina 14 m. SW of Greensboro. Pop. (1960) 62,063. Important centre of the furniture industry, established in the 1880s. Manufactures hosiery, textiles, plywood, crates, chemicals, etc.

**High Wycombe** England. Municipal borough in S Bucks, at the entrance to a gap through the Chiltern Hills and on the R. Wye, a short tributary of the R. Thames. Pop. (1961) 50,301. Largely residential, but long noted for the manufacture of furniture. The industry originated in chairmaking, using wood from the beech forests of the Chilterns. Also manufactures paper, metal goods, clothing, precision instruments, etc. A 13th/16th-cent. parish church. Within the borough is the village of West Wycombe, 2 m. WNW, and just N is Hughenden Manor, the home of Disraeli 1847–81.

**Hiiumaa** ◊ *Baltic Sea.*

**Hildesheim** Federal German Republic. Industrial town in Lower Saxony, on the Innerste R. 18 m. SE of Hanover. Pop. (1963) 98,800. Manufactures machinery, textiles, carpets, cosmetics, etc. Grew and prospered through the establishment of a bishopric in the 9th cent. Joined the Hanseatic League in the 13th cent. The 11th-cent. cathedral and most of the old churches and timbered houses were either destroyed or severely damaged during the 2nd World War.

**Hillah (Al Hillah)** Iraq. Capital of Hillah province, 60 m. S of Baghdad on the Hillah branch of the Euphrates R. Pop. (1965) 84,717. Market town. Trade in cereals, dates. Manufactures rugs, leather goods. Largely built of bricks taken from the near-by ruins of ancient Babylon.

**Hillingdon** England. Greater London borough (1965) comprising the former municipal borough of Uxbridge and the urban districts of Hayes and Harlington, Yiewsley and West Drayton, and Ruislip–Northwood (all in Middlesex). Pop. (1963) 227,913.

**Hillmorton** ◊ *Rugby*.

**Hilo** USA. Seaport and chief town of Hawaii Island, Hawaii, on Hilo Bay on the E coast. Pop. (1960) 25,966. Exports sugar, coffee, fruit, etc. Fruit canning, rice milling. Tourist centre for visiting the island volcanoes. At various times (e.g. 1946) it has suffered severely from tidal waves.

**Hilversum** Netherlands. Industrial and residential town, railway junction, and summer resort in N Holland province 16 m. SE of Amsterdam. Pop. (1968) 101,685. Manufactures carpets, textiles, dyes, electrical machinery, furniture, etc. Main Dutch radio and television centre.

**Himachal Pradesh** India. Territory of the Indian Union in the W Himalayas bounded on the E by Tibet (China). Area 10,885 sq. m. Pop. (1961) 1,351,144 (mainly Hindus). Cap. Simla, in Punjab. Formed (1948) from 30 former Hill States, Bilaspur being added in 1954. Mountainous and forested; its main resource is softwood timber. Certain new areas were transferred to it from Punjab in 1966.

**Himalaya.** In Sanskrit, 'Abode of Snow'. Vast mountain system in central Asia lying along the S edge of the Plateau of Tibet, enclosed by the Indus and Brahmaputra rivers. It extends generally ESE in an immense curve about 1,500 m. long from the Pamirs (W) to the deep gorges of the Brahmaputra (E), and is 100–150 m. in width. Its ranges may be divided into 3 longitudinal zones, ascending from S to N: the Outer Himalayas, consisting mainly of the Siwalik Range, with an average height of 3,000–4,000 ft; the Lesser Himalayas,

closely related to and sometimes merging with the Great Himalayas, having an average height of 12,000–15,000 ft; and the Great Himalayas, the main range, which have an average height of about 20,000 ft and contain the highest peaks, inc. Everest (29,028 ft, highest in the world), Kanchenjunga (28,165 ft), and Nanga Parbat (26,660 ft). All the high peaks are permanently snow-capped, the snowline varying between about 15,000 ft and 19,000 ft; glaciers descend to levels about 4,000 ft below the snowline. The Himalayas form an effective climatic barrier, shielding the plains of N India from the cold, dry winds from the N in winter and the Tibetan plateau from the moisture-laden winds from the S in summer. At the same time there are great climatic variations within the mountain system, partly due to differences of altitude and partly to the more pronounced influence of the summer monsoon in the E than in the W. In the E, where the rainfall may exceed 100 ins. annually, the land rises from the formerly swampy jungle known as the *terai* through different forest belts to the alpine zone and the snowline; the sal forest of the hills provides valuable timber. In the W, where the rainfall averages 30–40 ins. annually, scrub and bamboo give way to temperate forest and then the alpine zone and the snowline. The 'hill stations' of the Himalayas (e.g. Simla, Darjeeling) at altitudes of 7,000–8,000 ft offer welcome relief from the torrid summer heat of the Indo-Gangetic Plain. The Himalayan ranges are a formidable barrier to N–S communications: railways merely reach the foothills, e.g. Simla and Darjeeling; of the few tracks through the mountains two of the more important are those from Srinagar via the Zoji La pass to Leh and from Kalimpong via the Chumbi Valley to Gyangtse.

**Himeji** Japan. Industrial town in Hyogo prefecture, Honshu, 30 m. WNW of Kobe. Pop. (1965) 367,798. Manufactures cotton and leather goods, chemicals, etc.

**Hims** ◊ *Homs*.

**Hinckley** England. Urban district in Leicestershire 12 m. SW of Leicester. Pop. (1961) 41,573. Manufactures hosiery, footwear, etc. Engineering.

**Hindenburg** ◊ *Zabrze*.

**Hindu Kush.** A westward extension of the Himalayan mountain system, from which it is separated by the Indus valley, extending WSW from the Pamirs for nearly 400

m. Highest peak Tirich Mir (25,260 ft). The mountain system is crossed by several passes at 12,000–13,000 ft, one of which, the Khawak, was negotiated by Alexander the Great. The Salang road-tunnel, 1½ m. long, between Kabul and Doshi (Afghanistan) was opened in 1964. The slopes of the Hindu Kush are generally barren and treeless.

**Hirosaki** Japan. Industrial town in Aomori prefecture, N Honshu, 21 m. SW of Aomori. Pop. (1965) 151,624. Noted for its green lacquer ware. Other industries textile manufacture, soya-bean processing, woodworking. To the W is the isolated conical peak of Iwakisan, a place of pilgrimage.

**Hiroshima** Japan. Capital of Hiroshima prefecture, in SW Honshu, 174 m. W of Osaka. Pop. (1965) 504,227. Industrial centre and seaport. Manufactures cars and lorries, machinery, textiles, rubber products, etc. Shipbuilding, brewing. Exports canned goods, rayon, etc. In Hiroshima Bay is the sacred island of Itsukushima. During the 2nd World War the city was the target of the first atomic bomb to be dropped in action (6 Aug. 1945): over 78,000 people were killed, about the same number were wounded, and most of the buildings were destroyed or severely damaged.

**Hirschberg** ◊ *Jelenia Góra*.

**Hispaniola** W Indies. Island in the Greater Antilles, E of Cuba. The W third is occupied by Haiti, the E two-thirds by the Dominican Republic. Discovered (1492) by Columbus, who named it 'La Isla Española', later abbreviated to Española and corrupted to Hispaniola. The pre-Columbian Arawak Indians had called it Haiti ('Mountainous Country') or Quisqueya; during the 19th cent. it was called both Haiti and Santo Domingo.

**Hissar** India. Town in Punjab, on a branch of the W Jumna Canal 92 m. WNW of Delhi. Pop. (1961) 60,222. Trade in cattle, cotton, grain, etc. Large government livestock farm. Founded (1356) by Feroze Shah.

**Histon** England. Village in Cambridgeshire 3 m. N of Cambridge. Pop. (1961) 3,260. In a fruit-growing district. Large jam and canning factory.

**Hitchin** England. Urban district in N Hertfordshire 14 m. NW of Hertford. Pop. (1961) 24,243. Market town. Engineering, tanning, cultivation and distilling of lavender. A 12th/15th-cent. parish church. Part of a 14th-cent. Gilbertine priory remains in an old almshouse. Birthplace of George Chapman (1559–1634).

**Hivaoa** ◊ *Marquesas Islands*.

**Hjälmar, Lake** Sweden. Lake 40 m. long and up to 10 m. wide (area 190 sq. m.) S W of L. Mälar, into which it drains by the Eskilstuna R. The town of Örebro is at its W end.

**Hobart** Australia. Capital and chief seaport of Tasmania, on the W shore of the Derwent R. estuary. Pop. (1966) 119,415. Excellent natural harbour of 40–48 ft depth and tidal range of only 3–4 ft. Linked with the E shore by a floating concrete bridge (1941), 3,168 ft long, a lift-span permitting vessels to pass through. The city has a beautiful setting dominated by Mt Wellington (4,166 ft) to the W. Founded 1804. The nucleus of the city has old sandstone buildings about the original harbour; new housing has spread outwards with industrial districts to the N and S. Seat of the University of Tasmania (1890). Hydroelectric power from the hinterland supplies industries, inc. zinc refining, flour milling, fruit canning, and chemical, cement, and woollen manufactures. Paper mills lie upstream; and ◊ *Risdon*, opposite, is a metal-refining centre. Primary exports include apples, wool, timber, dairy produce, meat, hops.

**Hobbs** USA. Market town in SE New Mexico on the Llano Estacado. Pop. (1960) 26,275. In a ranching and agricultural area. Oil refining. Founded 1907. Grew rapidly after the discovery of oil in the neighbourhood (1927).

**Hoboken** Belgium. Residential suburb of SW Antwerp, in Antwerp province, on the Scheldt R. Pop. (1968) 32,184. Main industry shipbuilding. Also metal working, wool combing, etc.

**Hoboken** USA. Port in New Jersey on the Hudson R. opposite Manhattan (New York City), with which it has tunnel, subway, and ferry connexions. Pop. (1960) 48,441. Manufactures electrical equipment, furniture, textiles, chemicals, etc. Shipbuilding. First settled by Dutch farmers in 1640, in 1658 it was deeded by the Indians to Peter Stuyvesant. The present town was laid out in 1804. The name derives from 'hobocan', an Indian word meaning a tobacco pipe.

**Hochheim** Federal German Republic. Town in Hessen, on the Main R. 3 m. above its confluence with the Rhine. Pop. 8,000.

Noted for its wine; the term 'hock' for white Rhine wines is probably a corruption of the name.

**Hoddesdon** England. Urban district in Hertfordshire 3 m. SE of Hertford. Pop. (1961) 17,902. Market town. Glasshouse cultivation of cucumbers, tomatoes, flowers. Manufactures electrical equipment, pharmaceutical goods, etc. Just NE is Rye House, scene of the plot (1683) against Charles II.

**Hodeida** Yemen. Chief seaport, on the Red Sea. Pop. 30,000. Exports Mocha coffee, hides and skins. Minor industries. Occupied by the Turks in the mid 19th cent. and developed by them. A road has been constructed with Chinese help to San'a, the capital.

**Hódmezővásárhely** Hungary. Capital of Csongrád county in the S, 15 m. NE of Szeged near the Tisza R. Protected from its floods by a large dike. Pop. (1968) 53,000. Centre of a rich agricultural region. Manufactures agricultural implements, pottery, bricks. Flour milling, distilling, etc.

**Hoek van Holland** ◊ *Hook of Holland.*

**Hof** Federal German Republic. Industrial town in NE Bavaria on the Saale R., near the frontiers with Czechoslovakia and the GDR. Pop. (1963) 56,200. Manufactures textiles, machinery, chemicals. Brewing, distilling, etc. Founded in the 13th cent. Several old churches. Suffered severely in various wars and was largely destroyed by fire in 1823.

**Hofei** China. Capital of Anhwei province 95 m. WSW of Nanking. Pop. 184,000. Commercial centre in an agricultural region producing rice, tobacco, beans, etc. Manufactures textiles, chemicals, etc. Just S is the large lake Chao Hu. Birthplace of Li Hung-chang (1823–1901).

**Hofuf** Saudi Arabia. Chief town of Hasa, Nejd, 70 m. SSW of Dhahran, near the Riyadh–Dammam railway. Trading centre in the Hasa oasis (dates, cereals, fruits).

**Hoggar Mountains** ◊ *Ahaggar Mountains.*

**Hohenlimburg** Federal German Republic. Industrial town in N Rhine-Westphalia 5 m. ESE of Hagen. Pop. (1963) 26,800. Steel mills. Manufactures wire, glass, etc. Grew up round the 13th-cent. castle.

**Hohensalza** ◊ *Inowroclaw.*

**Hokkaido** Japan. The most northerly and the second largest of the 4 main islands, separated from Honshu (S) by the Tsugaru Strait. Area (inc. offshore islands) 30,077 sq.

m. Pop. (1960) 5,039,206. Cap. Sapporo. Largely mountainous, with some peaks exceeding 6,000 ft and several volcanic cones. Has the country's longest river, the Ishikarigawa. Its climate is more rigorous than that of the other main Japanese islands, and the winters are especially long and severe in the N, while the E coast suffers from summer fogs. Well forested. Soya beans, potatoes, rice cultivated. The Ishikari district has one of the country's main coalfields. Main resource fisheries; great quantities of salmon, cod, herring, and sardines are caught. Forms a prefecture. Principal seaports Otaru, Muroran, Hakodate. First settled by the Japanese in the 16th cent. (when it was known as Yezo). Systematically developed from 1871. The Japanese do not take easily to the harsh climate of Hokkaido, but the population has increased fairly rapidly in recent years – at the same time as the number of aboriginal Ainu has diminished, from about 50,000 in 1600 to 15,000 today.

**Holbeach** England. Market town in Parts of Holland, Lincolnshire, 7 m. E of Spalding. Pop. (1961) 6,736. In a bulb- and fruit-growing district. Brewing, malting. A Decorated church with a 189-ft spire.

**Holborn** England. Former metropolitan borough of London, N of the Thames; from 1965 part of the Greater London borough of Camden. Pop. (1961) 21,596. In this district are the British Museum, Hatton Garden (centre of the diamond trade), two of the four Inns of Court (Lincoln's Inn and Gray's Inn, severely damaged in the 2nd World War), and Lincoln's Inn Fields; Wren's Church of St Andrew (1686) was destroyed in the 2nd World War. New office blocks have been erected on the sites of many buildings gutted in air raids. The name is probably derived from Holebourne ('the Stream in the Hollow') referring to the course of the Fleet, and later crossed by Holborn Viaduct (1869).

**Holderness** England. Low-lying peninsula and rural district in the E Riding of Yorkshire, between the North Sea and the Humber estuary, forming a fertile agricultural area, with Spurn Head at its S end. Pop. (rural district, 1961) 20,367.

**Holguín** Cuba. Town in the Oriente province, 65 m. NNW of Santiago de Cuba. Pop. (1960) 226,779. Important commercial centre. Sawmilling, tanning.

Manufactures furniture, tiles, etc. Through its port, Gibara, 19 m. NNE, it exports tobacco, coffee, maize, sugar-cane, etc. Has expanded rapidly; has notable Spanish 'colonial' buildings.

**Holland** ◊ *Netherlands*; *North Holland*; *South Holland*.

**Hollywood** (California) USA. A suburb of NW Los Angeles. Famous as the leading centre of the film industry, though most of the studios are now outside Hollywood itself. Large commercial and shopping districts, and residential areas for film actors reaching up the slopes of the near-by Santa Monica Mountains. A Greek theatre, a planetarium, the Hollywood Bowl (seating 20,000) for outdoor concerts, and many other amenities. Founded in the 1880s. Amalgamated with Los Angeles 1910.

**Hollywood** (Florida) USA. Town in SE Florida 16 m. N of Miami. Pop. (1960) 35,237. A seaside resort which developed rapidly in the 1950s. Manufactures cement, furniture, etc.

**Holyhead** Wales. Urban district in Anglesey on the N side of Holy Island. Pop. (1961) 10,408. Railway terminus, seaside resort, and packet station for Ireland, with steamer services to Dublin and Dun Laoghaire. The harbour is protected by a breakwater 1½ m. long.

**Holy Island (Lindisfarne)** England. Island 3 m. long and 1 m. wide, off the coast of Northumberland and 9½ m. SE of Berwick-on-Tweed, accessible from the mainland at low water by a causeway (1954). On the W coast is a small village. The church and monastery were founded (635) by St Aidan. St Cuthbert was one of the bishops of Lindisfarne (685–7). In 793 the settlement was destroyed by the Danes. The Lindisfarne Gospels, a 7th-cent. illuminated Latin MS. written here, is now in the British Museum. In 1083 a Benedictine priory, of which there are remains, was built on the site of the earlier cathedral.

**Holy Island (Inishcaltra)** Irish Republic. Islet in Lough Derg, Co. Clare. Remains of 4 churches dating from the 7th cent.

**Holy Island** Scotland. Small island in Buteshire, off the E coast of Arran in the Firth of Clyde.

**Holy (Holyhead) Island** Wales. Island off the W coast of Anglesey, separated from it by a narrow strait spanned by an embankment carrying the railway and road. Chief town Holyhead.

**Holy Loch** ◊ *Dunoon*.

**Holyoke** USA. Industrial town in S Massachusetts on the Connecticut R. Pop. (1960) 52,689 (about one third of Irish descent). Manufactures paper, textiles, electrical equipment, etc.

**Holywell** Wales. Urban district in Flintshire near the R. Dee estuary, 4 m. WNW of Flint. Pop. (1961) 8,459. Noted for St Winifred's Well, over which a Gothic chapel was built by Margaret, mother of Henry VII. Manufactures rayon, paper.

**Homberg** Federal German Republic. Industrial town and river port in N Rhine-Westphalia, in the Ruhr district, on the left bank of the Rhine nearly opposite Duisburg. Pop. (1963) 35,500. Coalmining centre. Iron foundries, dyeworks, textile factories.

**Homburg vor der Höhe (Bad Homburg, Homburg)** Federal German Republic. Spa in Hessen at the foot of the Taunus Mountains 8 m. N of Frankfurt. Pop. (1963) 38,200. Mineral springs rediscovered in the 19th cent. Manufactures machinery, textiles, leather goods, biscuits, etc.

**Homs (Hims)** Syria. Ancient Emesa. Capital of Homs province, on the Orontes R. Pop. (1962) 164,362. Road and rail junction in a fertile region producing cereals and fruit. Manufactures textiles, jewellery. Sugar refining, oil refining. Birthplace of Heliogabalus (Elagabalus, 204–22), the boy priest who became Roman emperor. Taken by the Arabs in the 7th cent. and later by the Turks, who retained it almost continuously till the end of the 1st World War.

**Honan** China. In Chinese, 'South of the River' (the Hwang-ho). Province in N central China. Area 64,462 sq. m. Pop. (1957) 48,670,000. Cap. Chengchow. Mountainous in the W, where outliers of the Tsinling Mountains extend halfway across it. In the E it occupies the SW part of the Great Plain of N China, which yields good crops of wheat, millet, cotton, soya beans, etc.; in the past, however, there has been constant danger from river floods and drought, and the province has suffered severely in time of famine (e.g. 1943). Chief towns Chengchow, Kaifeng, Loyang. One of the most densely populated provinces. An early centre of Chinese culture.

**Honduras** Republic in Central America. Area 43,227 sq. m. Pop. (1967) 2,440,000 (mainly mestizos). Cap. Tegucigalpa. Lang. Spanish. Rel. Roman Catholic.

Has a N coastline 350 m. long on the

Caribbean and a S coastline 40 m. long on the Pacific; bounded by Nicaragua (E and SE), Salvador (SW), and Guatemala (W). Off the Caribbean coast lie the Bay Is. (Islas de la Bahía), ceded to Honduras by Britain in 1861, forming one of the 18 departments into which the country is divided. Mainly mountainous, except for the narrow coastal strips and the undeveloped Mosquito Coast (on the Caribbean) inhabited by Indian tribes. The main cordillera of Central America traverses it, rising to over 7,000 ft. Chief rivers the Patuca, the Ulúa, and the Aguán, flowing to the Pacific. The coastal climate is hot and humid, with heavy rainfall May–Dec.; the higher land of the interior is cooler.

Chiefly agricultural. Principal exports bananas (cultivated on large American-owned plantations on the Caribbean coast), coffee. Extensive forests produce mahogany, rosewood, ebony, etc. The country ranks third (after Mexico and Peru) among silver producers in Latin America. After Tegucigalpa the most important city is San Pedro Sula.

Discovered by Columbus (1502) on his fourth voyage. Won independence from Spain 1821; a member of the Central American Federation 1823–38. The frontier with Guatemala was fixed in 1933 and that with Nicaragua in 1961.

**Honduras, British** ◊ *British Honduras.*

**Hong Kong.** British Crown Colony on the coast of Kwangtung province, in S China, consisting of Hong Kong Island, Stonecutters Island, the ceded territory of Kowloon, and the New Territories. Area 398 sq. m. Pop. (1969) 3,987,500 (98 per cent Chinese). Cap. Victoria. With its magnificent harbour between Hong Kong Island and Kowloon peninsula on the mainland, Hong Kong was long the great entrepôt for foreign trade with China, but with its expanding population in recent years other markets in the Far East have been sought and industry developed: in 1948 goods made in Hong Kong represented 15 per cent of total exports, in 1963 over 75 per cent. The main branch of industry is the manufacture of cotton goods; rubber footwear, ropes, cement, and paint are also produced, and shipbuilding and ship repairing are important. Fishing occupies a substantial part of the population. University (1912). Victoria is one of the finest cities in the East; the airport, Kai Tak, on the N shore of Kowloon Bay, has a busy international traffic. Hong Kong Island was leased to Britain in 1842, Kowloon peninsula and Stonecutters Island in 1860, and in 1898 a 99 years' lease of the New Territories was obtained. By the end of the Japanese occupation of the 2nd World War (1945) the population had been reduced to about 600,000, but the increase in the post-war years was spectacular, being largely brought about by the influx of refugees from the mainland.

**Honiara** ◊ *Guadalcanal.*

**Honiton** England. Municipal borough in Devonshire, on the R. Otter 16 m. ENE of Exeter. Pop. (1961) 4,724. Market town. Famous since Elizabethan times for the manufacture of pillow-lace, introduced by Flemish refugees.

**Honolulu** USA. State capital of Hawaii, on the S coast of Oahu. Pop. (1960) 294,194. An important seaport and centre of communications in the Pacific; airline and shipping connexions with the USA, Australia, and the Far East. Chief exports sugar, coffee, and tropical fruits (esp. pineapples). Sugar refining, fruit canning. A beautiful city; tourist trade is considerable, helped by ease of communications and a pleasant equable climate; Waikiki Beach is world-famous. To the W is the US naval base of Pearl Harbour. Seat of the University of Hawaii (1907) and of the Bernice P. Bishop Museum, founded (1889) as a memorial to Princess Bernice Panahi, the last of the Kamehameha family of Hawaiian chiefs.

**Honshu** Japan. Largest and most important of the Japanese islands, divided into 34 prefectures and containing most of the principal towns. Area 88,919 sq. m. Pop. (1960) 71,354,357.

**Hoogeveen** Netherlands. Town in Drenthe province 32 m. S of Groningen. Pop. (1968) 35,375. Food-canning and other industries.

**Hoogezand** Netherlands. Town in Groningen province 7 m. ESE of Groningen. Pop. (1968) 28,134. Manufactures machinery, tyres, etc.

**Hooghly (Hugli)** India. Most westerly and most important channel by which the Ganges R. reaches the Bay of Bengal, being thus the W boundary of the great Ganges delta, formed by the union of the Bhagirathi and Jalangi rivers; flows S for 145 m. past Chandernagore, Howrah, Calcutta, Garden Reach. Liable to silting, the Hooghly is kept open to ocean-going vessels as far as Calcutta by constant dredging.

**Hooghly Chinsura (Hooghly)** India. Town in W Bengal, on the W bank of the Hooghly 26 m. N of Calcutta. Pop. (1961) 83,104. Rice milling. Founded (1537) by the Portuguese.

**Hook of Holland (Hoek van Holland)** Netherlands. Seaport in S Holland province 17 m. WNW of Rotterdam, at the North Sea end of the New Waterway; terminus of cross-channel steamers from Harwich, England. Pop. 2,600.

**Hoover Dam** USA. Important dam on the Colorado R., in Black Canyon, on the Arizona–Nevada border, used for irrigation, hydroelectric power, and flood control, built 1931–6; 726 ft high and 1,244 ft long. First named Hoover Dam (after President Hoover), then Boulder Dam (1933–47); renamed Hoover Dam. It forms Lake Mead.

**Hopei** China. In Chinese, 'North of the River' (the Hwang-ho). Province in the NE. Area 78,242 sq. m. Pop. (1957) 43,730,000. Cap. Tientsin. Bounded on the E by the Gulf of Chihli (Po Hai). Mountainous in the N (i.e. N of the Great Wall of China) and in the W. In the S it forms part of the Great Plain of N China, where wheat, maize, groundnuts, and soya beans are cultivated. Peking is within the province but is a separate municipality.

**Horn, Cape** Chile. Rocky headland 1,390 ft high, at the extreme S end of S America, on Horn Island in Tierra del Fuego. Notorious for stormy weather and heavy seas. Discovered (1616) by the Dutch navigator Schouten; named after Hoorn (Netherlands), his birthplace.

**Horncastle** England. Urban district in Parts of Lindsey, Lincolnshire, on the R. Bain 17 m. E of Lincoln. Pop. (1961) 3,768. Market town. Long famous for its horse fair, described in George Borrow's *Romany Rye*. Brewing, malting, tanning, etc. Fruit growing in the neighbourhood. Somersby, 6 m. ENE, was the birthplace of Tennyson (1809–92).

**Hornchurch** England. Former urban district in Essex, 2 m. ESE of Romford; from 1965 part of the Greater London borough of Havering. Pop. (1961) 128,127. Mainly residential, serving as a dormitory suburb for London. Engineering. Manufactures office equipment, clothing, chemicals. The aerodrome was an important RAF fighter base in the 2nd World War.

**Hornsea** England. Urban district in the E Riding of Yorkshire, on the North Sea 13 m. NE of Hull. Pop. (1961) 5,949. Seaside resort. Just inland is Hornsea Mere, noted for herons and fish.

**Hornsey** England. Former municipal borough in Middlesex, a N suburb of London; from 1965 part of the Greater London borough of Haringey. Pop. (1961) 97,885.

**Horsens** Denmark. Port in E Jutland, on Horsens Fiord. Pop. (1965) 37,106. Manufactures textiles, machinery, tobacco products, etc. Trade in dairy produce.

**Horsham** England. Urban district in W Sussex 17 m. N of Worthing. Pop. (1961) 21,155. Railway junction. Market town. An early English church and several old houses. Christ's Hospital, the famous Blue Coat school founded by Edward VI, was moved here from London in 1902. Shelley (1792–1822) was born at near-by Field Place.

**Horta** ◊ *Azores*.

**Horwich** England. Urban district in Lancashire 5 m. NE of Wigan. Pop. (1961) 16,067. Railway workshops, cotton and paper mills.

**Hoshiarpur** India. Town in Punjab 25 m. NE of Jullundur. Pop. (1961) 50,739. Trade in grain, sugar, etc. Manufactures furniture, turpentine, rosin.

**Hot Springs** USA. Health resort in Arkansas in the Ouachita Mountains. Pop. (1960) 28,337. Named after the many thermal springs in the neighbourhood. The Hot Springs National Park was founded in 1921.

**Houghton-le-Spring** England. Urban district in NE Durham 6 m. SW of Sunderland. Pop. (1961) 31,049. Coalmining centre. A 13th-cent. church.

**Hounslow** England. Formerly a residential town in the municipal borough of Heston and Isleworth (Middlesex); from 1965 a Greater London borough including the latter and also the municipal borough of Brentford and Chiswick and the urban district of Feltham (both in Middlesex). Pop. (1963) 208,770. Once an important coaching station on the Great West Road. On Hounslow Heath, earlier the haunt of robbers and highwaymen, was marked the base-line of the first trigonometrical survey in England (1784).

**Houston** USA. Largest town and industrial centre in Texas in the SE. Pop. (1970) 1,213,064. Noted for the manufacture of chemicals based on the natural resources of the Gulf coast, i.e. sulphur, salt, petroleum, natural gas. Other products are cement, textiles, synthetic rubber, oilfield equipment, etc. An important cargo port, connected to the Gulf of Mexico by the 52-m. Houston Ship Channel. Exports petroleum, cotton, chemicals, rice, manufactured goods. Seat of the University of Houston (1934), the Texas Southern University (1947, Negro), and of the Manned Space Flight Centre (1964).

**Hove** England. Municipal borough in E Sussex, adjoining Brighton on the E. Pop. (1961) 72,843. Residential town. Seaside resort. County cricket ground and public gardens.

**Howrah** India. Important industrial town and railway junction in W Bengal, on the Hooghly R. opposite Calcutta, with which connected formerly by pontoon bridge, now by cantilever bridge. Pop. (1961) 512,598. Manufactures jute and cotton goods, hosiery, rope, chemicals, soap, etc.

**Howth** Irish Republic. Seaside town in Co. Dublin and residential suburb 8 m. ENE of Dublin with which it was incorporated in 1940, on the N side of the peninsula bounding Dublin Bay and at the foot of the Hill of Howth (560 ft). Packet station for steamers from England from 1813 until superseded by Kingstown (Dun Laoghaire) in 1833.

**Hoxton** England. District mainly in the Greater London borough of Hackney. Centre of furniture manufacture. Birthplace of Marie Lloyd (1870–1922).

**Hoylake** England. Urban district in Cheshire at the NW corner of the Wirral peninsula and 7 m. W of Birkenhead. Pop. (1961) 32,268. Seaside resort. Famous golf course.

**Hradec Králové** (Ger. **Königgrätz**) Czechoslovakia. Capital of Východočeský region at the confluence of the Orlice R. with the Elbe (Labe) R. 63 m. ENE of Prague. Pop. (1967) 64,000. Railway junction. Manufactures machinery, musical instruments, textiles, furniture, photographic equipment, etc. Gothic cathedral (14thcent.). Near by was fought the decisive Battle of Sadowa in the Seven Weeks War (1866).

**Hrvatska** ◊ *Croatia.*

**Hsinking** ◊ *Changchun.*

**Huacho** Peru. Port 70 m. NNW of Lima. Pop. 27,000. Serves the fertile cotton- and sugar-growing Huaura R. valley. Cotton-

seed-oil and soap factories. On the Pan-American Highway. Linked by rail with Lima.

**Huahine** ◊ *Society Islands.*

**Huallaga River** Peru. River 580 m. long, flowing N and NE from the high Andes of central Peru to join the Marañon R. The upper course is a mountain torrent; the lower passes through the forested Amazon lowlands.

**Huambo** ◊ *Nova Lisboa.*

**Huancayo** Peru. Capital of Junin department, 130 m. E of Lima. Pop. (1961) 46,014. In the wheat-growing Mantaro R. valley, at a height of 10,690 ft. Market town. Manufactures textiles. Flour milling. Trade chiefly in wheat, maize, and alfalfa. A well-known Sunday market, much frequented by Indians selling rugs, blankets, etc.

**Huánuco** Peru. Capital of Huánuco department 155 m. NNE of Lima. Pop. (1961) 24,606. Centre of a rich agricultural and mining area, on the upper Huallaga R. at a height of 6,271 ft in the E Peruvian Andes. Produces sugar, brandy. Founded 1539.

**Huascarán** Peru.* Extinct snow-capped volcano in the Ancash department 150 m. N of Huacho. Highest peak in the Peruvian Andes (22,205 ft). An avalanche descending its slopes buried a village and killed over 3,000 people in Jan. 1962.

**Hubli** India. Town in Mysore 12 m. SE of Dharwar, with which it was incorporated in 1961. Pop. (1961) 171,326. Trade in cotton. Railway workshops, cotton mills. Several colleges affiliated to Karnatak University (Dharwar).

**Huchow** China. Formerly Wuhing. Town in Chekiang province, 40 m. N of Hangchow. Pop. 63,000. Silk mills. To the S is the famous hill resort of Mokanshan.

**Hucknall** England. Formerly Hucknall Torkard. Urban district in Nottinghamshire 6 m. NNW of Nottingham. Pop. (1961) 23,246. Coalmining centre. Manufactures hosiery. Byron is buried in the 14th-cent. church.

**Huddersfield** England. County borough and industrial town in the W Riding of Yorkshire, on the R. Colne. Pop. (1961) 130,302. Important centre of the woollen and worsted industry with associated manufactures, e.g. dyes, carpets, clothing, textile machinery. Metal working, engineering. Development due to the introduction of the woollen trade in the 17th cent., assisted later by the proximity of coal and transportation facilities by river, canal (to the Calder Navigation), and rail. Has a church dating from the 11th cent. (rebuilt 1837). The Cloth Hall, built by Sir John Ramsden and presented to the town (1784), was demolished (1930).

**Hudson Bay** Canada. Large gulf (or inland sea) connected to the Atlantic Ocean by the Hudson Strait and to the Arctic Ocean by the Foxe Channel. Area 480,000 sq. m. At the N entrance are the Southampton, Coats, and Mansel islands. In the E are the Belcher Is., and in James Bay (SE) is Akimiski Island. There are many other islands. Churchill is the chief port on the bay, which is navigable from July to Oct. Salmon and cod fisheries are important. Named after Henry Hudson, the explorer, who discovered it in 1610. The Hudson's Bay Company (chartered 1760) held a monopoly of trading rights in the area until 1869, when its territories were transferred to the Dominion of Canada.

**Hudson River** USA. River 306 m. long, rising in the Adirondacks and flowing S, then E, then mainly S to Upper New York Bay at New York city; the final stretch (part of New York harbour) is called the North R. A commercial waterway of the first importance, linked to the Great Lakes, the St Lawrence Seaway, and L. Champlain by the New York State Barge Canal system. Chief tributary the Mohawk R. (canalized). One of the most picturesque rivers in N America. Named after Henry Hudson, the first European to explore it (1609).

**Hué** S Vietnam. Town on the Hué R., near its mouth. Pop. (1962) 103,500. Manufactures textiles, cement, etc. An ancient walled town containing royal palaces and temples. Became capital of Annam in the early 19th cent. Taken by the French in 1883, it was capital of the French protectorate till 1946, then of Central Vietnam 1946–54.

**Huelva** Spain. 1. Province in the extreme SW, in Andalusia, bordered on the W by Portugal and on the S by the Gulf of Cadiz. Area 3,893 sq. m. Pop. (1961) 399,934. The N is mountainous, forming part of the wooded Sierra Morena (here known as the Sierra de Aracena). The S consists of low plains. An important mining region, esp. for copper (Rio Tinto).
2. Capital of Huelva province, seaport on the peninsula formed by the Odiel and the Tinto river estuaries. Pop. (1967) 90,749.

Exports copper, manganese, iron and other ores, cork, wine. Also a tunny and sardine fishing centre. Fish canning, flour milling, etc. Once a Carthaginian trading centre, later a Roman colony. Near by is La Rábida monastery, where Columbus planned his first voyage, setting sail from Palos de la Frontera (1492).

**Huesca** Spain. 1. Province in the NE, in Aragon, separated from France (N) by the Pyrenees, with the highest point, Pico de Aneto, rising to 11,168 ft, descending S to the Ebro R. Area 6,054 sq. m. Pop. (1961) 233,543. Mainly agricultural; extensive irrigation. Produces cereals, wine, fruits, etc.
2. Ancient Osca. Capital of Huesca province, 42 m. NE of Zaragoza. Pop. (1961) 24,377. Trade in agricultural produce. Manufactures agricultural machinery, cement, pottery. Here Quintus Sertorius founded his school (77 B.C.) and was assassinated (72 B.C.). Has a cathedral (13th/16-cent.) and the Alcazar Real, the ancient palace used by the former university.

**Hugli** ◊ *Hooghly.*

**Huhehot** China. Formerly Kweisui. Capital of the Inner Mongolian AR and formerly capital of Suiyuan province, 270 m. WNW of Peking, with which it is linked by railway. Pop. 148,000. Industrial and commercial centre. Flour milling. Manufactures textiles, rugs, bricks and tiles, etc. Seat of the Inner Mongolia University (1957). A Mongolian religious centre and seat of the Grand Lama until the 17th cent. In 1939 the Japanese made it capital of their puppet state of Mengchiang.

**Huila** Colombia. Snow-capped volcano (18,700 ft) in the Andes 60 m. NE of Popayán. The highest peak in the Central Cordillera.

**Hull** Canada. Industrial town in SW Quebec, on the Ottawa R. at the confluence with the Gatineau R. opposite Ottawa. Pop. (1966) 60,176. Important timber, pulp, and paper centre. Manufactures matches, furniture, clothing, cement, etc. Founded (1800) by Philemon Wright. Named after Hull, England, former home of Wright's parents.

**Hull** (officially **Kingston-upon-Hull**) England. County borough in the E Riding of Yorkshire, on the N bank of the Humber at the mouth of the R. Hull. Pop. (1961) 303,268. One of the country's chief seaports. Exports manufactured goods from the N and the Midlands and imports dairy produce, timber, wool, etc. Its trawlers land a greater quantity of fish than any other British port. Manufactures vegetable oils, paints, chemicals, cement, wood products, etc. Flour milling, brewing. Trinity House, an institution for merchant seamen, was founded in 1369. The 13th-cent. Holy Trinity Church (restored) is one of the largest parish churches in England. University College (1929) became a university in 1954. Among the pupils at the grammar school (founded 1485) were Andrew Marvell and William Wilberforce (1759–1833), the abolitionist, who was born here and whose home is now a museum. Hull was presented with its charter by Edward I in 1299. The now extensive docks were begun c. 1774. Severely damaged by bombing in the 2nd World War.

**Humber River** England. Estuary of the R. Trent and the R. Ouse, flowing E for 18 m. and then SE for 19 m. to the North Sea, separating Yorkshire and Lincolnshire. Chief ports Hull, Grimsby.

**Humphrey Island** ⟡ *Cook Islands*.

**Hunan** China. In Chinese, 'South of the Lake' (i.e. Tung Ting L.). Province in S central China, with the Yangtse R. along part of its N border. Area 81,253 sq. m. Pop. (1957) 36,220,000. Cap. Changsha. Mainly hilly, it is crossed by the fertile valleys of the Siang and Yuan rivers, which drain into Tung Ting L. Rice, wheat, tea, cotton cultivated. Coal, lead, zinc, antimony mined. Chief towns Changsha, Hengyang, Changteh, Siangtan.

**Hunedoara** Rumania. Town in the Hunedoara district 82 m. E of Timisoara. Pop. (1966) 68,303. Important iron and steel centre, much expanded since the 2nd World War. Produces most of Rumania's pig iron. Also manufactures chemicals.

**Hungary** (Magyar Népköztársaság). A people's republic of SE central Europe. Area 35,912 sq. m. Pop. (1968) 10,236,000. Cap. Budapest. Lang. Magyar.

Bounded by Czechoslovakia (N), the USSR (NE), Rumania (E), Yugoslavia (S), and Austria (W). Primarily agricultural. Under the Communist régime which was established after the 2nd World War land reform has provided one of the major changes: large estates and forests were appropriated and broken up into smallholdings; in the second Five-Year Plan (1961–5), however, the emphasis was on an increase in industrial rather than agri-

cultural production. For administrative purposes the country is divided into the following 19 counties: Bács-Kiskun, Baranya, Békés, Borsod-Abaúj-Zemplén, Csongrád, Fejér, Györ-Sopron, Hajdú-Bihar, Heves, Komárom, Nógrád, Pest, Somogy, Szabolcs-Szatmár, Szolnok, Tolna, Vas, Veszprém, and Zala.

TOPOGRAPHY, CLIMATE. Hungary lies chiefly in the basin of the middle Danube, which crosses it N–S. To the E of the Danube is the Great Hungarian Plain or Alföld, which is drained also by the Tisza R.; to the W the area is crossed SW–NE by a spur of the Alps, the main part being the Bakony Forest, S of which is L. Balaton, and this line of hills continues E of the Danube and rises there to over 3,000 ft. The lowland in the NW is known as the Little Hungarian Plain or Little Alföld. Ringed by mountains, the country has a moderate continental climate, with a rainfall of 20–25 ins. annually, temperatures becoming rather more extreme to the E.

RESOURCES, PEOPLE, *etc.* In 1967 the country had 3,033 collective farms, 210 state farms, and 151 machine tractor stations, which together represented 98 per cent of its agriculture. Of the total area 56 per cent is arable land, 16 per cent pasture, and 5 per cent orchards and vineyards. Principal cereal crops maize, wheat, barley. Sugar-beet and potatoes also important. Vines are grown N of L. Balaton and on the hills of the NE, the latter producing the famous Tokay wine. Large numbers of pigs and poultry are raised, as well as sheep and cattle. During the present century irrigation and flood-control schemes have increased yields on the Alföld, but, despite the fact that agriculture forms the basis of many food processing industries, production targets in recent years have not been reached – in contrast to targets of industrial production; agriculture, in fact, is the weak section of the economy. Coal, bauxite, and petroleum are the chief minerals. Apart from Budapest, the only towns with more than 100,000 inhabitants are Miskolc, Debrecen, Pécs, and Szeged. About 60 per cent of the people live in rural areas, and nearly half of the remainder are in Budapest; such large 'towns' as Debrecen and Szeged are merely straggling collections of villages spread over a wide area. About 97 per cent of the population are Magyars (Hungarians), 2 per cent Germans, and there are small numbers of Slovaks and

Rumanians. Since 1949 all religions have had equal standing, church and state being separated; in 1956 it was estimated that 67 per cent of the people were Roman Catholic and 27 per cent Protestant (mostly Calvinist or Reformed Church). In 1948 nearly all the denominational schools were nationalized, and in 1950 a large number of Roman Catholic orders were dissolved and their property appropriated by the state.

HISTORY. The Magyars settled in the middle Danube basin in the late 9th cent. under their chieftain, Arpád. In the early 11th cent. they were converted to Christianity under St Stephen, who took the title of king. With the Arpád line extinct (1301), civil war followed, and Hungary soon came under the rule of foreign princes. Late in the 14th cent. the country achieved its greatest expansion, including the greater part of central Europe within its territory, but it was menaced from the S by the Turks, and in 1526 its army suffered utter defeat at their hands at Mohács. Hungary was now partitioned between Austria and Turkey, and by the end of the 17th cent. the Habsburgs had conquered the whole country. A revolution led by Kossuth (1848–9) was suppressed, but in 1867 the Austro-Hungarian dual monarchy was established, Hungary almost attaining equality with its neighbour. At the end of the 1st World War Hungary was proclaimed a republic, and was briefly ruled by a Communist government under Bela Kun (1919), which was followed by the regency of Admiral Horthy with the old monarchical constitution. In the 1930s it came more and more under the influence of Italy and then Germany, entered the war on their side, and was occupied by the Russian army (1944–5). In 1948 the Communists gained power, a people's republic was proclaimed (1949), and the country has since been ruled by a government of the Soviet pattern. The character of Russian domination, in fact, was exemplified in the anti-Stalinist revolution of 1956, which was ruthlessly suppressed by Russian troops and Russian tanks. Economic influence is seen in the country's foreign trade, one third of which is with the USSR and two thirds with the Communist bloc.

**Hungerford** England. Market town in SW Berkshire on the R. Kennet 8 m. WNW of Newbury. Pop. (rural district, 1961) 9,660. Noted for trout fishing. The annual Hocktide festival, on the second Tuesday after Easter, commemorates the granting of manorial rights by John of Gaunt.

**Hungnam** ⟡ *Hamhung*.

**Hunstanton** England. Urban district in Norfolk on the E shore of the Wash, consisting of New Hunstanton, the modern watering-place, and the village of Old Hunstanton, 1 m. N. Pop. (1961) 4,843. Seaside resort. Hunstanton Hall, at Old Hunstanton, mainly of the 16th cent., belonged to the Le Strange family from the Norman Conquest till 1949.

**Hunter River** Australia. River 290 m. long in New South Wales, rising in the Liverpool Range and flowing SW and then SE to the Pacific Ocean. In the lower valley there are coalfields and industrial development, mostly in the Newcastle area at its mouth.

**Huntingdon** England. Municipal borough (with Godmanchester) and county town of Huntingdonshire, on the Great Ouse and on the Roman Ermine Street 15 m. NW of Cambridge. Pop. (1961) 8,812. Market town. Connected with Godmanchester by a 14th-cent. bridge. Brewing, hosiery manufacture, etc. Birthplace of Oliver Cromwell (1599–1658), and he and Pepys were both pupils at the grammar school.

**Huntingdonshire** England. One of the smallest English counties, in the E Midlands. Area 366 sq. m. Pop. (1961) 79,879. County town Huntingdon. Low-lying and almost flat, with the NE part in The Fens, it is drained by the Nene, on the N boundary, and the Great Ouse. Mainly farming land, partly under pasture and partly used for market gardening, fruit farming, and the cultivation of cereals, sugar-beet, potatoes. Chief towns Huntingdon, Old Fletton, where bricks are made, and St Ives.

**Huntington** USA. Town in W Virginia on the Ohio R. Pop. (1960) 83,627. Commercial and industrial centre. Trade in coal. Railway engineering. Manufactures nickel products, electrical equipment, glass, cement, etc. Named after C. P. Huntington (1821–1900), an American railway builder.

**Huntington Park** USA. Industrial and residential suburb of S Los Angeles, California. Pop. (1960) 29,920. Manufactures oilfield equipment, iron and steel goods, paints, etc. Named after C. P. Huntington (1821–1900), an American railway builder.

**Huntly** Scotland. Small burgh in NW

Aberdeenshire at the confluence of the R. Deveron and the R. Bogie in Strathbogie. Pop. (1961) 3,952. Market town. Holiday and angling resort. Woollen and hosiery manufactures. The ruined Huntly Castle, formerly called Strathbogie Castle, was the seat of the Earls of Huntly. Birthplace of George Macdonald, the novelist (1824–1905).

**Huntsville** USA. Industrial town in Alabama 85 m. N of Birmingham. Pop. (1960) 72,365. Manufactures textiles, agricultural implements, etc.; rocket and guided missile centre. The cotton industry began with a mill on the Flint R. in 1818. Founded (1805) by John Hunt, a Virginian Revolutionary War veteran.

**Hupei (Hupeh)** China. Province in central China through which flow the Yangtse R. and its tributary the Han R. Area 72,375 sq. m. Pop. (1957) 30,790,000. Cap. Wuhan. Mountainous in the W, elsewhere mainly low-lying; along the Yangtse course there are many lakes. Rice, cotton, wheat cultivated. Iron ore mined. Wuhan is by far the largest town; Ichang is an important river port.

**Hurlingham** England. District in the Greater London borough of Hammersmith, containing Hurlingham Park, part of which has been converted into a housing estate and which also has the headquarters of the Hurlingham polo club, whose committee drew up the first code of rules for the game in 1874.

**Huron, Lake.** Second largest of the Great Lakes, between the USA and Canada. Area 23,860 sq. m. Bounded on the N, E, and SE by Ontario (Canada) and on the W and SW by Michigan (USA). Connected with L. Superior by the St Mary's R. and with L. Michigan by the Straits of Mackinac; it empties into L. Erie by the St Clair R., L. St Clair, and the Detroit R. Valuable fisheries. Carries heavy trade in iron ore, coal, grain, and limestone. Usually icebound from mid Dec. to mid April. Subject to violent storms.

**Hurstmonceux** ◊ *Herstmonceux.*

**Hüsten** ◊ *Neheim-Hüsten.*

**Hutchinson** USA. Industrial town in Kansas, on the Arkansas R. 44 m. NW of Wichita. Pop. (1960) 37,574. Salt mining, meat packing, flour milling, oil refining. Manufactures oil-well equipment etc. Established 1871. Named after the founder, C. C. Hutchinson.

**Hutt** ◊ *Lower Hutt.*

**Huyton-with-Roby** England. Urban district in SW Lancashire and residential suburb of Liverpool (E). Pop. (1961) 63,041. Manufactures cables, metal goods, food products, etc.

**Hvar** (Italian **Lesina**) Yugoslavia. **1.** Island of S Croatia, in the Adriatic Sea. Area 112 sq. m. Pop. (1961) 12,132. Cap. and chief port Hvar. Fishing. Grapes, olives, flowers cultivated. Popular tourist centre.
**2.** Ancient Pharos. Capital of Hvar island, on the W coast, 22 m. S of Split. Pop. 2,000. Resort and port. Fishing, boatbuilding. Founded as a Greek colony c. 390 B.C.

**Hwaining** ◊ *Anking.*

**Hwang Hai** ◊ *Yellow Sea.*

**Hwang-ho (Yellow River)** China. Second longest river in China, 2,900 m. long, rising in Tsinghai (Chinghai) province on the plateau at 14,000 ft, flowing through two lakes, Tsaring Nor and Ngoring Nor; called 'Yellow River' because of the great amounts of yellow silt (loess) which it carries down from its middle course. It flows generally E and N, but is turned S by the mountains of Shansi, here forming the boundary between this province and Shensi. After about 500 m. on this southward course through the loess plateau, it receives the Wei-ho, and turns E and then NE on to the Great Plain of N China. The silt it carries down has extended the delta and provided additional land for crops, but it also raises the river bed, necessitates the construction of embankments, and makes the river liable to cause disastrous floods. If the embankments give way, the river may change its course: in the last 4,000 years there have been 8 major changes of course. The Hwang-ho, in fact, has well merited the nickname 'China's sorrow'. Before 11 A.D. it took a northerly course, emptying into the Gulf of Chihli near Tientsin; from 11 to 1194 it flowed further S, and from 1852 it took a direct course E across the plain to the Yellow Sea; since 1947 it has flowed again to the Gulf of Chihli.

**Hyde** England. Municipal borough in NE Cheshire 7 m. ESE of Manchester. Pop. (1961) 31,710. Important cotton mills. Engineering. Manufactures rubber products, paper, etc. Coalmining in the neighbourhood.

**Hyderabad** India. Capital of Andhra Pradesh, on the Musi R. 390 m. ESE of

Bombay. Pop. (1961) 1,118,553. Industrial, commercial, and route centre. Railway engineering. Manufactures textiles, building materials, glassware, paper, etc. The old city is surrounded by stone walls, entered by 13 gates, and contains the Char Minar or Four Minarets, built in 1591, which rise from arches from which 4 of the main highways radiate. Another outstanding building is the Great Mosque, modelled on that at Mecca. Seat of the Osmania University (1918). Hyderabad was formerly capital of the state of the same name.

**Hyderabad** Pakistan. Capital of the Hyderabad Division, in W Pakistan, near the Indus R. and 95 m. NE of Karachi. Pop. (1961) 416,441. Industrial and commercial centre. Manufactures textiles, machinery, leather, cement, etc. Trade in cereals, cotton, fruit. Seat of the University of Sind (1947) since 1951. Capital of Sind province from 1768 to 1843, when it was taken by the British, and again 1947–54.

**Hydra (Gr. Ídhra)** Greece. Island in the Aegean Sea, off the coast of Argolis. Area 18 sq. m. Pop. (1961) 2,766. Chief town Hydra (pop. 2,546), on the N coast. Fishing, tanning. Flourished under Turkish rule, when the population rose to over 30,000. Its seamen played a prominent part in the Greek War of Independence (1821).

**Hymettus (Gr. Imittos)** Greece. Mountain (3,370 ft) in Attica *nome* just E of Athens. Long famous for its honey and formerly for marble.

**Hythe** England. Municipal borough in SE Kent 4 m. W of Folkestone on the English Channel. Pop. (1961) 10,026. Seaside resort. Brewing. One of the Cinque Ports, its harbour long ago silted up. Has a miniature railway to Dymchurch and New Romney. Saltwood Castle, where the plot to murder Thomas à Becket was said to have been hatched, is 1 m. N. 3 m. W is the village of Lympne, with remains of the Roman Portus Lemanis and an airfield.

# I

Iaşi (Ger. **Jassy**) Rumania. Capital of
Iaşi district in Moldavia about 10 m. W
of the Prut R. and the USSR frontier.
Pop. (1968) 170,363. Railway junction.
Manufactures textiles, metal goods, furniture, etc. Also a commercial and cultural
centre, with a university (1860), a national
theatre, and academies of music, art, and
drama. Seat of a Roman Catholic archbishopric. Among several notable churches
is the 17th-cent. Trei Erarchi, an outstanding example of Moldavian architecture. A considerable proportion of the
population was Jewish until they were
massacred by the Germans in 1941.

**Ibadan** Nigeria. Capital of the Western
State, the largest city in W Africa, on the
main railway to N Nigeria 75 m. NE of
Lagos. Pop. (1963) 750,000. Large trade
in cacao, also in palm oil and kernels,
cotton. Fruit canning, cotton weaving.
Manufactures tobacco products, etc. The
autonomous University College of Ibadan
(founded 1948) became a full University
in 1962; it has an associated teaching
hospital (opened 1957).

**Ibagué** Colombia. Capital of the Tolima
department, on the E slopes of the Central
Cordillera at a height of 4,100 ft. Pop.
(1968) 163,661. Linked by rail and road
with Bogotá and by the Quindío Pass (W)
with Armenia. Trade in coffee etc. Flour
milling, brewing. Manufactures leather
goods etc. Founded 1550.

**Ibarra** Ecuador. Capital of the Imbabura
province, 50 m. NE of Quito at a height of
7,300 ft. Pop. 25,805. On the Pan-American
Highway. Trade in coffee, sugar-cane,
cotton, etc. Manufactures textiles, furniture,
'Panama' hats.

**Iberia** Portugal/Spain. Ancient name given
by the Greeks at first to E Spain, being
derived from the Iberus (modern Ebro) R.;
later applied to the whole Iberian Peninsula, i.e. the modern Spain and Portugal.

**Iberia** USSR. Ancient name for the
country between the Greater Caucasus
and Armenia – approximately the E
Georgian SSR of today.

**Ibiza** ◊ *Balearic Islands*.

**Ica** Peru. Capital of the Ica department, on
the Ica R. and the Pan-American Highway
160 m. SE of Lima. Pop. 45,000. Commercial and industrial centre in an irrigated
cotton- and vine-growing region. Cotton
ginning. Manufactures brandy, soap, textiles. Founded 1563. Twice destroyed by
earthquakes.

**Içá River** (Brazil) ◊ *Putumayo River*.

**Ica River** Peru. River 120 m. long, flowing
from the W Andes W and S past Ica and
entering the Pacific. Irrigates a rich agricultural valley where cotton and vines are
cultivated.

**Iceland.** Island republic in the N Atlantic
Ocean. Area 39,758 sq. m. Pop. (1967)
199,920. Cap. Reykjavik. Lang. Icelandic.
Rel. Lutheran.

Lies just S of the Arctic Circle, 600 m. W
of Norway and 500 m. NW of Scotland;
the most westerly state in Europe. It is
about 300 m. long W–E and 190 m. wide
at its greatest width, and is very sparsely
inhabited. The economy depends very
largely on fishing. For administrative
purposes it is divided into 7 districts:
Reykjanes, West, Western Peninsula,
Northland West, Northland East, East,
and South.

TOPOGRAPHY, CLIMATE. The island
consists in the main of a central, virtually
uninhabited plateau of volcanic rocks of
average height about 2,000 ft. In the S and
W of this plateau there are extensive glaciers
and snowfields, the largest being Vatnajökull (S), which rises to 6,952 ft in
Oræfajökull. There are more than 100
volcanoes, one in four of which have been
active within historic times, and an area of
about 4,650 sq. m. is covered with lava
fields; Hekla (5,110 ft), the best-known
volcano, has erupted about 20 times since
the early 12th cent. Hot springs occur in
all parts of the island. There are many lakes,
rivers, and waterfalls, and hydroelectric
power is developed. The coast is rugged
and deeply indented with fiords and bays,
esp. on the W and N. The climate of
Iceland is wet, windy, and changeable, and
for its rather high latitude mild, the N
Atlantic Drift ensuring that the S coasts
remain ice-free in winter.

RESOURCES, PEOPLE, ETC. Trees are
few, and consist mainly of birches usually
no more than 10 ft in height. Grasses are
the commonest form of natural vegetation,

providing pasture for large numbers of sheep and some cattle and horses. About six sevenths of the island is unproductive, and on the small area of cultivated land the principal crops are hay, potatoes, and turnips. Fishing is by far the most important occupation, and fish (chiefly cod and herring) and fish products constitute the greater part of the country's exports. Britain has the major share of the foreign trade, followed by the USA, USSR, and the Federal German Republic. No railways, but roads and internal airways have been developed; ponies are still used for transport in country districts. Most of the people, who are almost wholly Icelandic, i.e. Scandinavian in origin, live in the towns and villages around the W, N, and E coasts, but the only town with more than 20,000 inhabitants is the capital, Reykjavik. They are justly proud of their rich early literature, which enjoyed a revival in the 19th cent. The Althing or parliament has an upper and a lower house.

HISTORY. Settled by Norwegians in the 9th cent. Iceland had its first general assembly or Althing, which founded the republic, in 930; Christianity was introduced in 1000. Under Norwegian rule from 1262, it passed to Denmark in 1380; internal self-government was granted in 1874 and equal status in 1918, and in 1944 the republic was again proclaimed. In 1958 Iceland extended the fishery limits around the coast from 4 to 12 miles; after a prolonged dispute Britain, having gained certain concessions for British fishermen, agreed to the change in 1961. Two new volcanic islands emerged in 1963 just SW of the Vestmann Is. off the S coast.

**Ichang** China. Town in Hupei province, on the Yangtse R. just below its great gorges. Pop. 73,000. An important point of transhipment between ocean-going vessels and those which can negotiate the gorges to Chungking. Trade in tung oil, grain, etc.

**Ichinomiya** Japan. Town in Aichi prefecture, Honshu, 12 m. NNW of Nagoya. Pop. (1965) 203,745. Important textile centre (esp. woollen goods).

**Ida, Mount** ◊ Crete.

**Idaho** USA. State in the NW, bordered on the N by British Columbia (Canada), on the E by Montana and Wyoming, on the S by Utah and Nevada, and on the W by Oregon and Washington. Area 83,557 sq. m. Pop. (1970) 698,275. Cap. Boise. Admitted to the Union in 1890 as the 43rd state; popularly known as the 'Gem' state. Crossed by the Rocky Mountains; mainly mountainous, with Borah Peak (12,655 ft) the highest point. Dry continental climate, with cold winters and hot summers. Agriculture important in the S. Potatoes are a speciality of the Snake valley, and wheat, oats, barley, sugarbeet, etc. are grown. Rich in minerals; produces lead, gold, silver, zinc, copper. Many state parks and national forests, with ample facilities for fishing, hunting, ski-ing, camping. The first European explorers were Lewis and Clark (1805), followed by British and American fur traders. The first permanent settlement was at Franklin (1860).

**Idaho Falls** USA. Town in SE Idaho on the Snake R. at a height of 4,700 ft, 215 m. E of Boise. Pop. (1960) 33,161. Industrial and commercial centre in an agricultural region. Manufactures beet sugar. Flour milling etc.

**Idfu** ◊ Edfu.

**Ídhra** ◊ Hydra.

**Idumaea** ◊ Edom.

**Ieper** ◊ Ypres.

**Ife** Nigeria. Town in the Western State 45 m. E of Ibadan. Pop. (1963) 111,000. Important centre in the cacao trade. Processes palm oil and kernels. Regarded as the 'holy city' of the Yoruba tribe. University (1961).

**Ifni.** Former Spanish overseas province on the NW African coast. Area 580 sq. m. Pop. (1964) 51,517. Cap. Sidi Ifni. An enclave within Morocco, on the edge of the Sahara, it was returned to Morocco in 1969. Arid climate. Irrigation permits the cultivation of grains and vegetables. Nomadic tribes raise sheep and goats.

**Igarka** USSR. Port on the Yenisei R. N of the Arctic Circle, in the Krasnoyarsk Territory, RSFSR. Pop. 14,000 in winter, increasing to about 20,000 in summer. Sawmilling. Considerable trade in timber and graphite. Founded 1929.

**Iglesias** Italy. Town in SW Sardinia, 34 m. WNW of Cagliari. Pop. (1961) 28,004. Centre of a mining district (lead, zinc, silver). Mining school. Cathedral (13th-cent.).

**Iguassú (Iguaçu) River** Brazil/Argentina. River 750 m. long, rising in the Serra do Mar in S Brazil, flowing W, and joining the Paraná R. Forms the Brazil–Argentina frontier for the last 75 m. The famous Iguassú Falls (14 m. above the confluence) consist of a line of falls over 200 ft high, separated by rocky islands; wider and higher than Niagara Falls, they have tremendous hydroelectric power potential.

**Ijmuiden** ◊ *Velsen.*

**Ijssel (Yssel) Rivers** Netherlands. **1.** *Geldersche Ijssel*: River 72 m. long, a distributary of the Lower Rhine, branching from it just S E of Arnhem and flowing generally N through Gelderland, forming the boundary with Overijssel province, to the Ijsselmeer 4 m. N W of Kampen. **2.** *Oude Ijssel*: A tributary of the Geldersche Ijssel, rising just S W of Borken (Federal German Republic) and joining it at Doesburg. **3.** *Hollandsche Ijssel*: A short tributary of the Lek (◊ *Rhine*), joining it just E of Rotterdam.

**Ijsselmeer (Ysselmeer)** Netherlands. Shallow lake formed from the old Zuider Zee, by the construction of the Ijsselmeer Dam (Afsluitdijk), completed in 1932, which carries a road and has navigation locks and drainage sluices at both ends. Fed by the Vecht, Ijssel, and Zwartewater rivers. The lake is much smaller than the old Zuider Zee, owing to reclamation by the creation of 4 polders. Work began in 1920, and in 1930 the N W Polder and in 1942 the N E Polder were brought under cultivation; work on the S E and S W Polders continued, though delayed by flooding in the 2nd World War and in 1953; the former was completed in 1956.

**Île-de-France** France. Region in the Paris Basin, Paris being its capital, so called because the original boundaries were the Seine, Marne, Aisne, Oise, and Ourcq rivers; now divided mainly into the Hauts-de-Seine, Yvelines, Val d'Oise, Oise, and Aisne departments. It comprises rich agricultural land as well as the highly industrialized region around Paris and such forests as those of Fontainebleau and Compiègne. Part of the duchy of France in the 10th cent. Split up into the present departments 1790 and 1964.

**Îles des Saintes** ◊ *Saintes, Les.*

**Ilesha** Nigeria. Town in the Western State 60 m. E NE of Ibadan. Pop. (1960) 72,000. Trade in cacao, palm oil and kernels. Cotton weaving.

**Ilford** England. Former municipal borough in S W Essex, on the R. Roding 7 m. E NE of London, for which it is a residential suburb; from 1965 part of the Greater London borough of Redbridge. Pop. (1961)

178,210. Manufactures photographic equipment and materials, electrical equipment, etc.

**Ilfracombe** England. Urban district in N Devonshire on the Bristol Channel. Pop. (1961) 8,701. Seaside resort and former fishing port. Has a church dating from the 12th cent. Some beaches reached by tunnels.

**Ilhéus** Brazil. Seaport in Bahía 155 m. S SW of Salvador, near the mouth of the Cachoeira R. Pop. 60,000. Formerly the main export centre for cacao (which is now shipped through Salvador). Now exports piassava, timber, etc.

**Ili River.** River 869 m. long in central Asia, rising on the N slopes of the Tien Shan, flowing generally W and N W past Kuldja (Sinkiang-Uighur, China) and across the Kazakh SSR to enter L. Balkhash by a delta. Much used for irrigation.

**Ilium** ◊ *Troy.*

**Ilkeston** England. Municipal borough in Derbyshire 7 m. E NE of Derby. Pop. (1961) 34,672. Market town in a coalmining area. Manufactures rayon, hosiery, clothing, earthenware, etc.

**Ilkley** England. Urban district in the W Riding of Yorkshire, on the R. Wharfe 13 m. W SW of Harrogate. Pop. (1961) 18,519. Residential town. Mineral springs. Remains of a Roman fort (Olicana). Just S is the famous Ilkley Moor (1,560 acres).

**Illampu (Sorata), Mount** Bolivia. Highest mountain in the E Cordillera of the Andes. Two peaks: Illampu (21,275 ft) and Ancohuma (21,490 ft).

**Ille-et-Vilaine** France. Department in the N W bordering N on the Gulf of St Malo, formed in 1790 from E Brittany. Area 2,699 sq. m. Pop. (1968) 652,722. Prefecture Rennes. Drained by the Vilaine and its chief tributary the Ille. Mainly agricultural, the poor soil having been improved by fertilizers. Cereals, potatoes, apples, pears widely grown. Much cider making and dairy farming. Chief towns Rennes, St Malo (seaport), Dinard (resort).

**Illinois** USA. State in the Middle West, bounded by Wisconsin (N), L. Michigan (N E), Indiana (E), Kentucky (S), and Iowa and Missouri (W), and separated from the last two by the Mississippi R. Area 56,400 sq. m. Pop. (1970) 10,973,986. Cap. Springfield. Admitted to the Union in 1818 as the 21st state; popularly known as the 'Prairie' state. Mainly level prairie. Climate humid continental. Primarily an agricultural state, with a very large production of maize (about two thirds of the acreage), oats, hay, soya beans, wheat. Also cattle, pigs, poultry. Chief mineral bituminous coal; petroleum is found in the S. Manufacturing industries are of first importance (with nearly three quarters of the factories in the Chicago area), and include meat packing, oil refining, and the manufacture of steel, railway and electrical equipment, and agricultural machinery. Chief towns Chicago, Rockford, Peoria. The first European explorers were the French (1673). Ceded to the British 1763. Became US territory 1783.

**Illyria** Albania/Yugoslavia. Ancient, vaguely defined region along the E shores of the Adriatic Sea, extending approximately from modern Rijeka to Durrës W of the Dinaric Alps, thus comprising the W coastal strip of Yugoslavia and N Albania.

**Ilmen, Lake** USSR. Lake in the RSFSR 100 m. SSE of Leningrad, discharging through the Volkhov R. into L. Ladoga. Area 350 sq. m. Fishing. Lumbering and agriculture practised around the shores.

**Iloilo** Philippines. Seaport and commercial town in Panay, 290 m. SSE of Manila. Pop. (1960) 150,976. Exports sugar, rice, copra.

**Ilorin** Nigeria. Town 35 m. NE of Ogbomosho at a height of 1,200 ft. Pop. 41,000. Manufactures pottery and handwoven cloth.

**Imandra, Lake** USSR. Lake in the RSFSR, discharging through the Neva R. into the Kandalaksha Gulf of the White Sea. Area 330 sq. m. The new town of Monchegorsk is on its NW shore, and the Murmansk–Leningrad railway runs along its E shore.

**Imathía** Greece. *Nome* in Macedonia, formed after the 2nd World War. Area 664 sq. m. Pop. (1961) 114,150. Cap. Véroia (Verria). Produces wheat, vegetables, wine.

**Imatra** Finland. Town in the Kymi province near the USSR frontier. Pop. (1968) 35,694. Important hydroelectric power station. Metallurgical industry.

**Imbros (Imroz)** Turkey. Island in the Aegean Sea W of the Gallipoli peninsula. Area 108 sq. m. Pop. 6,000. Cap. Imroz. Cereals, olives, fruits cultivated. Occupied by Greece during the 1st World War; returned to Turkey 1923.

**Imittos** ◊ *Hymettus.*

**Immingham** England. Seaport in Parts of Lindsey, Lincolnshire, on the S bank of the Humber 6 m. NW of Grimsby. Exports coal, motor cars. Imports iron ore, timber, sulphur, etc. Development began with the opening of docks in 1912, deeper water being available here than at Grimsby. Further developed by the extension of the oil jetties (1963).

**Imola** Italy. Town in Bologna province in Emilia-Romagna, 20 m. SE of Bologna on the Aemilian Way. Pop. (1961) 51,289. Manufactures machinery, pottery, wine, etc. Cathedral (12th/13th-cent., restored); 14th-cent. citadel; Renaissance palaces.

**Imperia** Italy. Capital of Imperia province, Liguria, on the Gulf of Genoa 56 m. SW of Genoa. Pop. (1961) 34,995. Port in an olive- and vine-growing region. Formed (1923) from Porto Maurizio (now Imperia Ponente), a holiday resort with olive-oil refineries, and Oneglia (now Imperia Levante), an industrial and commercial centre with iron and steel works, fruit canning, and other industries.

**Imphal** India. Capital of Manipur Territory, on the Manipur R. 140 m. ESE of Shillong. Pop. (1961) 67,717. Commercial centre in a fertile agricultural region. Trade in rice, sugar-cane, tobacco, etc. Used as an Allied base in the Burma campaign of the 2nd World War.

**Imroz** ◊ *Imbros.*

**Inaccessible Island** ◊ *Tristan da Cunha.*

**Inari, Lake** Finland. Lake in Lapland in the extreme N. Area 535 sq. m. Hundreds of islets. Drained to Varanger Fiord by the Pasvik R. Visited by tourists mainly for fishing. On the SW shore is the village of Inari, where Lapps evacuated from the Pechenga region (USSR) were resettled after the 2nd World War.

**Ince-in-Makerfield** England. Urban district in Lancashire just S of Wigan. Pop. (1961) 18,027. Coalmining centre. Cotton mills.

**Inchcape Rock** ◊ *Bell Rock.*

**Inchon** S Korea. Formerly Chemulpo. Seaport and industrial town 25 m. WSW of Seoul, on the Yellow Sea. Pop. (1966) 528,579. Exports rice, dried fish, soya beans, etc. Manufactures steel, textiles, glass, chemicals, etc.

**Independence** USA. Industrial town in Missouri 8 m. E of Kansas City. Pop. (1960) 62,328. Manufactures agricultural machinery, cement, stoves, etc. Headquarters of the Mormon sect known as the

Reorganized Church of Jesus Christ of Latter Day Saints. Starting-point for wagon trains travelling W over the Santa Fé, Old Salt Lake, and Oregon trails 1831–44.

**India (Bharat).** Republic in S Asia, member of the Commonwealth of Nations. Area 1,262,275 sq. m. Pop. (1961) 439,235,082 (inc. Sikkim but excluding the area of Jammu and Kashmir occupied by Pakistan). Cap. New Delhi. Rel. mainly Hindu, but considerable minorities of Muslims, Christians, etc. Lang. ♢ under PEOPLE, GOVERNMENT, *etc.* below.

Second most populous country in the world. Occupies the greater part of the Indian sub-continent, Pakistan occupying the other part. Besides its frontiers with Pakistan, it borders N on Tibet (China) and Nepal, and N E on Burma, the shores of its triangular-shaped peninsula being washed by the Bay of Bengal (E) and the Arabian Sea (W). Has been described as a country of villages, and small-scale and often inefficient agriculture is by far the commonest occupation, being the means of livelihood of 70 per cent of the people. Agricultural products, in some cases processed or manufactured, also form the major part of the country's exports. The output of food crops from the millions of peasant farmers, however, is far from sufficient for the country's needs, and rice and wheat, for example, have to be imported in substantial quantities. For administrative purposes the country is divided into 17 States and 10 Union territories. The States are: Andhra Pradesh, Assam, Bihar, Gujarat, Haryana, Jammu and Kashmir, Kerala, Madhya Pradesh, Madras (Tamil Nadu), Maharashtra, Mysore, Nagaland, Orissa, Punjab, Rajasthan, Uttar Pradesh, W Bengal. The Union territories are: Andaman and Nicobar Is.; Chandigarh; Delhi; Himachal Pradesh; Laccadive, Minicoy, and Amindivi Is.; Manipur; Tripura; Dadra and Nagar Aveli; Goa, Daman, and Diu; Pondicherry.

TOPOGRAPHY, CLIMATE. India is bounded in the N by the Himalayas, the most formidable mountain barrier in the world, and within its boundaries is the great Himalayan peak of Nanda Devi (25,645 ft); few passes penetrate this mountain system, and on its N side rise the three major rivers of the sub-continent, the Indus, Ganges, and Brahmaputra. S of the fertile alluvial plain of the Ganges is the Deccan plateau, fringed by the W and E Ghats. In the N W, on the border with W Pakistan, is the Great Indian or Thar Desert, while in the N E is the Chota Nagpur plateau. The two chief W-flowing rivers are the Narmada, between the Vindhya and Satpura Ranges, and the Tapti, between the Satpura and Ajanta Ranges; the three main E-flowing rivers are the Godavari, Krishna, and Cauvery, which form wide deltas on the broad coastal plain facing the Bay of Bengal.

Generally speaking, the climate of the entire country S of the Himalayas is dominated by the monsoons and may be described as tropical monsoon in character. There are three seasons, determined by the monsoon winds, and varying to some extent with geographical location. From June to September the S W monsoon brings especially heavy rainfall to the W slopes of the W Ghats, but much less to places on the lee side of the mountains as it moves N E across the peninsula; it picks up more moisture during its passage over the Bay of Bengal and again deposits heavy rainfall over Assam, Bengal, and the S slopes of the Himalayas. In Cherrapunji, Assam, the country has what is reputed to be the world's wettest spot, with 428 ins. of rain annually: almost 200 ins. fall in June and July, while there is scarcely 1 in. in December and January together. This emphasizes the great contrast between the rainy season and the conditions of the N E monsoon which follows and continues from about October to February – a season of dry, cooler weather. Finally there is the season of hot and fairly dry weather, March–May, which precedes the burst of the S W monsoon, with its oppressive heat and torrential rains, once more. RESOURCES, ECONOMY. Rice is by far the most important subsistence crop, occupying about one quarter of the total cultivated area; it is the staple food in all the wetter parts of India, the main regions of production being the Ganges valley and the coastal plains. Millet is second in importance, being the staple food in the drier parts of the Deccan, while wheat, grown as a winter crop, is significant in the irrigated lands of the Punjab. Cotton occupies a considerable area, particularly in the W Deccan, and oilseeds (inc. groundnuts, sesamum, and linseed) almost as large an area; sugar-cane comes from the Upper Ganges region and the Punjab, and jute chiefly from W Bengal. Tea is cultivated on plantations in the Assam hills, and is second only to jute products in the country's export list. Crop yields among the peasant farmers are low, the causes including primitive agricultural methods, fragmentation of holdings, soil exhaustion, and indebtedness to the moneylender. India has the enormous total of 175 million cattle (1961), which are used primarily as draught animals, but they are of poor quality, and, being regarded as sacred by the Hindus, cannot be slaughtered and are virtually valueless as a source of food. The necessity for increasing food supplies is probably the country's most difficult economic problem: throughout history India has been subject to famine, and now an increase in food production of at least 2 per cent per year is needed to keep pace with the rising population.

Few minerals are produced on a large scale. Coal is produced mainly on the edge of the Chota Nagpur plateau, in W Bengal and Bihar; output rose from 29 million to 68 million tons between 1947 and 1967, but is still far short of the country's needs. Much of the country's iron and manganese ores is exported, and India is also one of the world's leading producers and exporters of mica. Village industries and handicrafts are still important, but there has been a considerable development of factory industries in recent years. Steel was first produced in 1933, and the village of Jamshedpur (Bihar) became a thriving iron and steel centre of nearly 300,000 inhabitants in 1961, with a number of other manufacturing industries. Textile manufacture, however, is still by far the most significant industry; jute products are manufactured, largely for export, in the Calcutta area, cotton goods in Bombay, Ahmadabad, and other large towns. Six cities, Bombay, Calcutta, Delhi, Madras, Ahmadabad, and Hyderabad, have populations of more than 1 million.

PEOPLE, GOVERNMENT, *etc.* An accurate description of the races, religions, and cultures of the peoples of India within limited space is virtually impossible. One may arrive at a satisfactory division of the country on the basis of language, but it should be remembered that some of the 845 languages and dialects are spoken by people of very different races. According to the constitution (1950) the official language of the Union is Hindi in the Devanagari script, English being used for official purposes till 1965; there are 15 recognized languages: Assamese, Bengali, Gujarati, Hindi, Kannada, Kashmiri, Malayalam, Marathi, Oriya, Punjabi, Sanskrit, Sindhi, Tamil, Telugu, and Urdu. The decision to adopt Hindi as the official language aroused great controversy.

Difficulties are immensely increased by the high illiteracy rate of 76 per cent (1961) – though this was a marked improvement on the 83 per cent of the previous census (1951). Illiteracy and religious custom together have proved considerable obstacles to social progress in India; Hindus, with their narrow rules of caste, number more than 366 million of the population, Muslims 46 million, Christians 10 million, Sikhs 7 million, Buddhists 3 million, and Jains 2 million.

The Indian Parliament consists of the President and two houses: the Upper House or Council of States, elected by members of the state legislatures, with not more than 250 members, and the Lower House or House of the People, directly elected by universal suffrage, with not more than 500 members.

HISTORY. About the aboriginal inhabitants of the Indian sub-continent (India and Pakistan together) little is known. The region was invaded by the dark-skinned Dravidians, ancestors of the principal peoples of the S, and later, *c.* 2400–1500 B.C., by waves of Aryans from the NW, the latter spreading over the N and the Deccan and intermarrying with the Dravidians; it was they, the conquerors, who introduced Brahmanism or Hinduism and the caste system. In the 6th cent. B.C. Buddhism and Jainism were introduced as reforming movements, but neither substantially displaced Hinduism. In 327 B.C. the middle Indus valley was reached by Alexander the Great, and in the following century all India except the extreme S was first unified under the great Mauryan emperor Asoka, a Buddhist. N India was not again united till the Gupta dynasty (A.D. 320–480), the 'golden age of Hinduism'. Muslim invasions from the NW began in the early 11th cent. by Mahmud of Ghazni, Muslim rule was then established in the N and the Deccan, and the finest period of Muslim India came with the founding of the Mogul empire by

Babur (1526); the empire was consolidated by his grandson Akbar the Great (1556–1605) and reached its furthest extent under Aurangzeb (1658–1707), but declined rapidly after the latter's death. Islam had been imposed on a people who tenaciously clung to the Hindu religion, and this led eventually to the partition of the sub-continent into Muslim Pakistan and Hindu India in 1947.

From the early 16th cent. Portuguese, Dutch, French, and British were establishing trading posts at various places in India, but after the Battle of Plassey (1757) the British East India Company became dominant; with the mutiny (1857–8) the Company's authority was transferred to the British Crown, and Queen Victoria was proclaimed Empress of India in 1877. The British Raj maintained peace in India and conferred other benefits such as the construction of great irrigation works and railways; but it was an alien rule, and a nationalist movement arose and gained strength, notably under the leadership of Mahatma Gandhi (1869–1948). Hindus and Muslims found themselves unable to work together in an all-Indian government and in 1947 the sub-continent was divided into the Dominions of India and Pakistan; in 1950 India declared itself a republic and in 1956 Pakistan became an Islamic republic, both remaining in the British Commonwealth.

**Indiana** USA. State in the Middle West, bounded by L. Michigan (NW), Michigan (N), Ohio (E), Kentucky (S), and Illinois (W). Area 36,291 sq. m. Pop. (1970) 5,143,422. Cap. Indianapolis. Admitted to the Union in 1816 as the 19th state; popularly known as the 'Hoosier' state. Mainly rolling prairie land, with sand dunes and glacial lakes in the N. Climate humid continental. Agriculture important. Chief crop maize; also wheat, oats, rye, tomatoes (for canning), hay. Cattle, pigs, and sheep raised. Principal mineral bituminous coal. Produces most of the limestone used in the USA for building. Numerous and important industries, esp. meat packing and the manufacture of iron and steel, motor vehicles, agricultural and electrical machinery. Chief towns Indianapolis, Gary, Fort Wayne, Evansville, South Bend. Of archaeological interest are the remains of the ancient Mound-builders' culture. The first Europeans to explore the territory were the French, who found the Miami Indians the dominant tribe. Ceded to Britain in 1763 and to the USA in 1783.

**Indianapolis** USA. State capital of Indiana, on the West Fork of the White R. in the centre of the state. Pop. (1970) 742,613. Unlike most large US cities, not on a navigable waterway, but the centre of important rail, road, and air routes. Industrial centre. Meat packing, flour milling. Manufactures chemicals, motor-car parts, machinery, etc. Seat of the Butler University (1894) and schools of the University of Indiana. Scene of an annual motor-race meeting.

**Indian Ocean.** Smallest of the world's three great oceans, bounded by Asia (N), Australia (E), Africa (W), and merging S with the Southern Ocean. Area 28 million sq. m. Its greatest depth (24,460 ft) is probably in the Sunda Trench (Indonesia); its mean depth is about 13,000 ft. S of the equator its currents have a general anti-clockwise circulation, but N of the equator they are determined largely by the SW (summer) and the NE (winter) monsoons. Most of its islands are in the W half: Madagascar and Ceylon are the principal continental islands; the Maldive, Chagos, and Cocos Is. are of coral formation; Mauritius and the Crozet Is. are of volcanic origin. It is linked with the N Atlantic by the Suez Canal, and when the latter was opened (1869) its N part became the principal shipping route between Europe and the Far East.

**Indigirka River** USSR. River 1,100 m. long in the Yakut ASSR (RSFSR), in NE Siberia, rising in the Verkhoyansk Range and flowing generally N, entering the E Siberian Sea by a broad delta. Frozen for about 9 months of the year.

**Indo-China.** Name sometimes applied to the entire peninsula between India and China, including Burma, Thailand, and the former French Indo-China, but usually restricted to the last, which consisted of the colony of Cochin China and the protectorates of Cambodia, Annam, Laos, and Tongking. In 1949 Tongking, Annam, and Cochin China formed the republic of Vietnam, which in 1954 was partitioned into N Vietnam, under Communist control, and S Vietnam.

**Indonesia.** Republic of S E Asia. Area 736,512 sq. m. Pop. (1961) 97,085,348 (two thirds of whom live on Java). Cap. Jakarta. Rel. mainly Muslim. Official lang. Bahasa

INDORE

Indonesia (a variant of Malay); 25 other languages and over 200 dialects also spoken.

Comprises the territory formerly known as the Netherlands (Dutch) E Indies. It is a large island group which may be divided into 4 main areas: the Sunda Is. (Java, Sumatra, Borneo, Celebes), the Lesser Sunda Is. (Bali, Lombok, Flores, part of Timor), the Moluccas, and W Irian (W New Guinea). Primarily agricultural, but the chief island, Java, has one of the highest densities of population in the world. Main food crop rice. Principal export rubber. For administrative purposes the country is divided into the following provinces: Atjeh, N and W Sumatra, Riau, Djambi, and S Sumatra; W, Central, and E Java; W, S, E, and Central Kalimantan (Borneo); N and S Sulawesi (Celebes); Bali; W and E Nusa Tenggara (remainder of Lesser Sunda Is.); Maluku (Moluccas); and W Irian.

TOPOGRAPHY, CLIMATE, RESOURCES. Volcanic mountain ranges cross all the larger islands, with several peaks rising to more than 10,000 ft, and the slopes are well forested. Some of the islands lie on the equator; their climate may be best described as equatorial, and is influenced largely by the monsoons. At Jakarta (Java), for instance, the mean annual temperature is 79° F, and the mean monthly temperature does not vary more than 1° F above or below that figure. Rainfall everywhere is heavy, increasing seasonally with the onset of the S W and N E monsoons and reaching well over 100 ins. annually in many areas. Food crops other than rice include maize, cassava, sugar-cane, tea, coffee; rubber is produced both on plantations and on peasant smallholdings. Petroleum is the principal mineral, the oilfields being in Sumatra, Kalimantan (Borneo), and Java; it is second only to rubber in exports, while the tin mined on Bangka and Billiton is also important. ⟡ *Java, Sumatra*, etc.

PEOPLE, GOVERNMENT, *etc.* The people vary widely between the more advanced Javanese and the relatively primitive Dyaks of Borneo; the main ethnic groups are the Achinese, Bataks, and Menangkabaus of Sumatra, the Javanese and Sundanese of Java, the Madurese of Madura, the Balinese of Bali, the Sasaks of Lombok, the Menadonese and Buginese of Celebes, the Ambonese of the Moluccas, and the Dyaks of Borneo. Chinese, about 3 million

in number, are the most numerous of the non-indigenous peoples. About 80 per cent of the population are Muslims, and there are minorities of Christians, Buddhists, and Hindus. By the constitution of 1950 Indonesia was governed by a President and a House of Representatives, but in 1955 President Sukarno suspended the latter and in 1960 he appointed a Mutual Co-operation House of Representatives. After an abortive Communist *coup* (1965), the army took over the government; general elections were promised for 1971.

HISTORY. In early times Indonesia came under the influence of the Indian civilization, but by the end of the 16th cent. Islam, introduced earlier by Arab traders, had replaced Hinduism and Buddhism as the dominant religion. The disunited islands fell easily to European colonization, and the Dutch became the leading power in the early 17th cent. through the Dutch East India Company. There was virtually no movement towards independence for three centuries, but at the end of the 2nd World War, after the Japanese occupation, Indonesian nationalists proclaimed the new republic (1945); sovereignty was transferred in 1949, and the last region held by the Netherlands, W Irian (W New Guinea), was handed over to Indonesia in 1963.

**Indore** India. Town in Madhya Pradesh, on the Saraswati R. 210 m. ESE of Ahmadabad. Pop. (1961) 394,941. Manufactures cotton goods, hosiery, chemicals, furniture, etc. Trade in grain, cotton, oilseeds. It was made capital of the former princely state of Indore (area 9,934 sq. m.) in 1818, and was also capital of Madhya Bharat from 1948 until this state was merged in Madhya Pradesh in 1956.

**Indre** France. Department of central France, formed in 1790 from parts of Berry, Orléanais, Marche, and Touraine. Area 2,666 sq. m. Pop. (1968) 247,178. Prefecture Châteauroux. Slopes gently N W from the Massif Central to the Loire valley. Drained by the Indre and Creuse rivers. Chiefly agricultural. Produces cereals, vegetables, wine. Cattle and sheep raised. Chief towns Châteauroux, Issoudun.
**Indre-et-Loire** France. Department formed principally from Touraine, with small parts of Anjou, Orléanais, and Poitou. Area 2,377 sq. m. Pop. (1968) 437,870. Prefecture Tours. Crossed by the fertile valleys of the Loire and its tributaries, the Cher, Indre, and Vienne. Produces wine,

vegetables, flowers; many market gardens. Has many famous Loire châteaux, including Amboise, Chenonceaux, and Chinon. Chief towns Tours, Chinon.

**Indre River** France. River 160 m. long rising in the foothills of the Massif Central just N of Boussac, flowing generally NW through the Indre and Indre-et-Loire departments to join the Loire R. below Tours.

**Indus River** (Sanskrit **Sindhu**). One of the great rivers of the Indian sub-continent, about 1,700 m. long, rising in the Kailas Range of the Himalayas in SW Tibet. It flows N and W as the Senge Khambab, then NW through Kashmir between the Ladakh and Zaskar Ranges. Continuing through deep gorges and fine mountain scenery, it turns abruptly S and then crosses W Pakistan in a general SSW direction, to enter the Arabian Sea by a broad delta. In its upper course it receives the Shyok and Kabul and lower downstream the Panjnad – the combined waters of the Jhelum, Chenab, Ravi, Beas, and Sutlej, the 5 rivers of the Punjab. Below this confluence is the great Sukkur Barrage, whence irrigation water is supplied to the plains of Sind. The river is little used for navigation. In prehistoric times it contained one of the earliest highly organized civilizations, which lasted from *c.* 3000 to 1500 B.C., known as the Indus Valley civilization. Mohenjo-Daro and Harappa are important archaeological sites.

**Inglewood** USA. Residential and industrial suburb 9 m. SW of Los Angeles, California. Pop. (1960) 63,390. Manufactures aircraft, metal goods, pottery. Oil refining. The Hollywood Park racecourse is near by.

**Ingolstadt** Federal German Republic. Town in Bavaria on the Danube R. 45 m. N of Munich. Pop. (1963) 64,600. Manufactures textiles, textile machinery, etc. Railway engineering. Capital of a duchy from the 13th to the 15th cent.; also the seat of a university from 1472 to 1800, when this was transferred to Landshut.

**Inishcaltra** ◊ *Holy Island* (Irish Republic).

**Inland Sea** Japan. Sea between Honshu (N) and Shikoku and Kyushu (S), opening into the Sea of Japan (W) and the Pacific Ocean (E). Generally picturesque; in the central area is the Inland Sea National Park (257 sq. m.). Many important seaports and fishing ports around its shores.

**Innerleithen** Scotland. Small burgh and spa in Peeblesshire, on Leithen Water near its confluence with the R. Tweed. Pop. (1961) 2,299. Manufactures tweeds and hosiery. Said to be the site of Scott's *St Ronan's Well.*

**Inner Mongolian AR** China. Autonomous region in the NE, bounded on the N and NW by the Mongolian People's Republic and the USSR. Area 455,000 sq. m. Pop. (1957) 9,200,000. Cap. Huhehot (Kweisui). It lies mainly on the Mongolian plateau, but rises in the E to the Great Khingan Mountains and in the SW to the Ala Shan; in the S it includes the N part of the great loop of the Hwang-ho, and in the extreme E reaches the valleys of the Nun and the upper Liao. Nomadic stock rearing, chiefly of sheep, goats, horses, and camels, is the traditional occupation of the Mongolian people, but under Chinese influence agriculture is being introduced, the leading crops being millet, kaoliang, and wheat; wool, hides, and skins are exported. The region is divided into 7 *meng* or tribal leagues. It was formed in 1947, and its boundaries have been frequently changed. In 1950, for example, it comprised the N part of the former Chahar province and parts of the former W Manchuria, but in 1954 Suiyuan province and in 1955 parts of Jehol province were added.

**Innisfree** Irish Republic. Small island in Lough Gill, NE Co. Sligo. Made famous by W. B. Yeats's poem.

**Inn River.** River 320 m. long rising in Graubünden (Grisons) canton, Switzerland, and flowing generally NE through the Engadine, Tirol (Austria) past Innsbruck, and into Bavaria (Germany) to join the Danube R. at Passau; in its lower course it forms the border between Austria and the Federal German Republic. Several hydroelectric plants.

**Innsbruck** Austria. Capital of Tirol province on the Inn R. at its confluence with the Sill R. and on an important route from Germany via the Brenner Pass to Italy. Pop. (1961) 100,695. Manufactures textiles and processed foods, but famous chiefly as a tourist centre, largely due to its picturesque situation at a height of 1,880 ft surrounded by high mountains. Among the notable buildings are the 16th-cent. Franciscan Hofkirche, with the tomb of Maximilian I; 15th-cent. castle; university (founded 1677). Capital of Tirol from the 15th cent.

**Inowroclaw** (Ger. **Hohensalza**) Poland.

Town in Bydgoszcz voivodship 21 m. SW of Toruń. Pop. 53,300. Manufactures machinery, chemicals, glass, etc. Also a resort with saline springs and saltworks.

**Insterburg** ◊ *Chernyakhovsk.*

**Interlaken** Switzerland. Famous summer resort in the Bernese Alps, in Bern canton on the Aar R. at a height of 1,864 ft between lakes Thun and Brienz (hence the name). Pop. (1960) 4,800. Popular as a centre for excursions in the Bernese Oberland, with a magnificent view of the Jungfrau.

**Inuvik** Canada. Town in Mackenzie District, NW Territories, on the Mackenzie R. delta. Pop. (1966) 2,040. The first planned town in the Canadian Arctic, built on piles above the permanently frozen subsoil.

**Inveraray** Scotland. Royal burgh and county town of Argyllshire, at the mouth of the R. Aray on Loch Fyne 23 m. NNW of Greenock. Pop. (1961) 501. The 18th-cent. castle is the seat of the Duke of Argyll. Main industry herring fishing.

**Invercargill** New Zealand. Town in S Otago, S Island, on New River Harbour, Foveaux Strait. Pop. (1966) 43,530. Formerly a seaport, now silted up, its trade passing through Bluff Harbour to the S. Regional trading centre. Woollen and flour mills, breweries, sawmills.

**Invergordon** Scotland. Small burgh and former naval base in Ross and Cromarty on the N shore of Cromarty Firth 15 m. N of Inverness. Pop. (1961) 1,640. Scene of a mutiny among naval ratings 1931.

**Inverkeithing** Scotland. Small burgh and port in SW Fifeshire near the N shore of the Firth of Forth. Pop. (1961) 4,069. Shipyards, paper mills.

**Inverness** Scotland. Royal burgh and county town of Inverness-shire, at the mouth of the R. Ness and the NE end of Glen More (Great Glen). Pop. (1961) 29,773. Commercial and tourist centre and seaport, often termed the 'capital of the Highlands'. Distilling, brewing. Manufactures woollens. Well known for the purity of the English spoken here. Among its buildings is St Andrew's Episcopal Cathedral (1866). The present castle (1835) houses the county offices.

**Inverness-shire** Scotland. Largest county, bounded on the W by the Atlantic Ocean and including several of the Inner and Outer Hebrides. Area 4,211 sq. m. Pop. (1961) 83,425. County town Inverness. Mainly mountainous, occupying much of the Scottish Highlands, and has Ben Nevis (4,406 ft), the highest peak in Great Britain, and several others exceeding 3,500 ft. It is crossed NE–SW by Glen More, or the Great Glen, which extends from Moray Firth through lochs Ness, Oich, Lochy, and Linnhe to the Atlantic and is followed by the Caledonian Canal. Chief rivers the Spey, Nairn, and Findhorn. Much of its area consists of deer forests. Sheep and Highland cattle are grazed on the rough upland pastures. Hydroelectric power is developed at Lochaber, Foyers, etc. Principal towns Inverness, Fort William.

**Inverurie** Scotland. Royal burgh and market town in Aberdeenshire, 14 m. NW of Aberdeen. Pop. (1961) 5,152. The battles of Barra Hill (1307) and Harlaw (1411) were fought near by.

**Ioánnina** Greece. 1. *Nome* in Epirus bordering NW on Albania. Area 1,900 sq. m. Pop. (1961) 154,201. Mainly stock rearing (dairy produce).
2. Capital of Ioánnina *nome*, on L. Ioánnina. Pop. (1961) 34,997. Trade in cereals, wine, fruit. Seat of Ali Pasha, the 'Lion of Janina', from 1788 to 1822.

**Iona** (Celtic **Icolmkill**, 'Island of Columba's Cell') Scotland. Small island 3 m. long and 1½ m. wide in the Inner Hebrides, in Argyllshire, off the SW coast of Mull. Here in 563 St Columba landed from Ireland, founded a monastery, and began the conversion of Scotland and N England. Became the leading centre of Celtic Christianity. The monastery was plundered and burned several times by Norsemen, but was rebuilt by Queen Margaret of Scotland late in the 11th cent. On the island are the 13th-cent. cathedral church of St Mary, several Celtic crosses, and other remains. The cemetery is said to be the burial-place of many Scottish, Irish, Danish, and Norwegian monarchs. Many of the ancient buildings have been restored.

**Ionia.** Region on the W coast of Asia Minor, inhabited in ancient times by Ionian Greeks and including such cities as Ephesus, Miletus, and later Smyrna (Izmir). They came under Persian rule in the 6th cent. B.C., were taken by Alexander the Great, and retained some importance in the Roman and Byzantine Empires.

**Ionian Islands** Greece. Group of islands in the Ionian Sea up to 20 m. off the W coast, forming 4 *nome*s named after the 4 largest islands – Corfu, Levkas, Cephalonia, and Zante. Mountainous, rising to 5,315 ft in

Mt Ainos (Cephalonia), but with fertile lowlands producing wine, olive oil, and fruit. Under Venetian rule from the 15th to the end of the 18th cent. the islands temporarily passed to France, became a British protectorate 1815, and were ceded to Greece 1864. Cephalonia, Zante, and Ithaca were devastated by earthquake in 1953, 455 people being killed and some 25,000 homes completely destroyed.

**Ioshkar-Ola** ◊ *Yoshkar-Ola*.

**Iowa** USA. State in the Middle West, bounded by Minnesota (N), Wisconsin and Illinois (E), Missouri (S), and Nebraska and S Dakota (W). Area 56,280 sq. m. Pop. (1970) 2,789,893. Cap. Des Moines. Admitted to the Union in 1846 as the 29th state; popularly known as the 'Hawkeye' state. Mainly rolling plains; the hilliest region is in the NE (known locally as 'Little Switzerland'). Apart from the boundary rivers – the Mississippi (E) and the Missouri and the Big Sioux (W) – the main river is the Des Moines, crossing diagonally NW–SE. Climate humid continental; cold winters, hot summers. Agriculture is of first importance and occupies 95 per cent of the total area. Leading state for maize; oats, hay, barley, soya beans also cultivated. Livestock and poultry raised. Principal minerals bituminous coal, gypsum. Main industry the processing of farm products. Chief towns Des Moines, Cedar Rapids, Sioux City, Davenport. The first explorers were French (1673). Became part of the USA through the Louisiana Purchase (1803).

**Iowa City** USA. Town on the Iowa R. in Iowa, 24 m. SSE of Cedar Rapids. Pop. (1960) 33,443. Varied minor industries. Seat of the University of Iowa (1847). Formerly (1839–57) state capital.

**Ipin** China. Formerly Suifu, Süchow. River port in Szechwan at the confluence of the Yangtse and Min rivers. Pop. 178,000. Commercial centre for Yunnan and Tibet.

**Ipoh** Malaysia. Largest town in Perak, Malaya, 110 m. NNW of Kuala Lumpur. Pop. (1957) 125,770 (70 per cent Chinese). Important tin-mining centre. Rubber plantations in the neighbourhood.

**Ipswich** Australia. Town in SE Queensland on the Bremer R. 20 m. WSW of Brisbane. Pop. (1966) 54,531. Chief coalmining centre in the state. Woollen mills, clothing factories, railway workshops.

**Ipswich** England. Saxon Gipeswic. County town and county borough in E Suffolk at the head of the R. Orwell estuary. Pop. (1961) 117,325. Port and industrial centre. Manufactures agricultural machinery, fertilizers, electrical equipment, tobacco products, plastics. Brewing, flour milling, printing. Its long history is illustrated by many old buildings, e.g. Wolsey's Gateway, part of the college that the Cardinal (1473–1530) had planned for his birthplace, and Sparrowe's House and Christchurch Mansion (both 16th cent.). The Saxon name means 'the Village on the Gipping', the latter being the name for the upper course of the Orwell.

**Iquique** Chile. Capital of the Tarapacá province; seaport in the N, 125 m. S of Arica, on the edge of the Atacama Desert. Pop. (1966) 48,000. Modern docks. Practically rainless; water is piped from the Pica oasis 50 m. SE. Linked by rail with the nitrate fields. Exports nitrates, iodine, salt. Fish canning. Sugar and oil refining.

**Iquitos** Peru. Capital of the Loreto department in the NE, on the left bank of the Amazon R. Pop. (1965) 66,000. Head of navigation for large Amazon steamers; accessible from the Atlantic (2,300 m. distant). Exports rubber, timber, tagua nuts, etc. Sawmilling. Cotton ginning.

**Iráklion (Candia, Herakleion)** Greece. Formerly Megalokastron ('Great Fortress'). Capital of the Iráklion *nome*, on the N coast of Crete. Pop. (1961) 64,492. The largest city on the island, a seaport, with considerable coastal trade. Exports raisins, olive oil, wine, etc. Manufactures soap, leather, wine. The museum contains Minoan antiquities from Knossos, of which it was the ancient port. Taken in the Saracen conquest of Crete *c.* 823. Passed from the Venetians to the Turks 1669. Severely damaged during the German invasion in the 2nd World War (1941).

**Iran (Persia,** Persian **Keshvaré Shahanshahiyé Irân).**\* Large kingdom in SW Asia. Area 627,000 sq. m. Pop. (1966) 25,781,090. Cap. Tehran. Lang. mainly Persian. Rel. mainly Shia Muslim.

Bounded by the USSR and the Caspian Sea (N), Afghanistan and W Pakistan (E), the Gulf of Oman and the Persian Gulf (S), and Iraq and Turkey (W). Hemmed in by lofty mountain ranges, the country is somewhat isolated, and much of its area is desert; the economy is heavily dependent on its rich oilfields, which have put it in sixth place among world oil producers. It is divided for administrative purposes into

13 *ustán* or provinces which are known by number and name: (1) Gilán, (2) Mázandarán, (3) E Azerbaijan, (4) W Azerbaijan, (5) Kermanshah, (6) Khuzistan, (7) Fars, (8) Kerman, (9) Khorasan, (10) Esfahan (Isfahan), (11) Kurdistan, (12) Sistan and Baluchistan, (13) Central Province, including Tehran.

TOPOGRAPHY, CLIMATE, *etc.* Consists of an extensive central plateau at 3,000–5,000 ft almost surrounded by mountains: in the N the Elburz Mountains, rising to 18,380 ft in the extinct volcano Damavand; in the W and S the Zagros Mountains and their extensions, rising to 14,920 ft in Zard Kuh, and in the E a number of ranges close to the country's E border. The plateau sinks to about 2,000 ft in the great saline desert known as the Dasht-i-Kavir and its continuation the Dasht-i-Lut. The largest of the salt lakes is L. Urmia, in the NW. Few perennial streams. On the plateau the climate is arid and continental, with hot summers and cold winters. The humid subtropical conditions along the N slopes of the Elburz Mountains, which are well forested, are in marked contrast to the dry desertlike climate experienced S of the range, on the plateau, where the rainfall rarely exceeds 13 ins. annually and falls almost entirely in winter; the Persian Gulf coast is hot and oppressive during its long summer.

RESOURCES, ECONOMY. Rice is cultivated along the Caspian coast, wheat and barley in the drier areas. Cotton is the most important cash crop. Sugar-beet and dates are also produced. Large numbers of sheep and goats are raised, much of the wool being used in the making of carpets and rugs. In the limited fertile areas agricultural methods are usually primitive; irrigation is largely by *qanats* or underground channels leading from the mountain slopes; absentee landlordism restricts progress, and land reforms are difficult to implement. The country's economy was transformed by the discovery of oil in Khuzistan (1908), and the then Anglo-Persian Oil Company played a significant part in the commercial development of Iran. Pipelines link the oilfields with the great refinery at Abadan, and petroleum represents 80–90 per cent by value of total exports. Coal, iron, lead, and other minerals are produced on a small scale. Few good roads and only one cross-country railway, linking the Caspian with the Persian Gulf through Tehran (completed 1938). The largest cities are Tehran, Tabriz, Isfahan, and Meshed, each with more than $\frac{1}{4}$ million inhabitants.

PEOPLE, GOVERNMENT, *etc.* Most of the people are Shia Muslims, but the Kurds, about 850,000 in number, belong to the Sunni sect; there are also about 50,000 Armenians, mostly Gregorians with a much smaller number of Roman Catholics, and 40,000 Jews. Primary-school education is officially compulsory, but there are places for only about two thirds of the children of school age, and illiteracy is estimated at 60 per cent of the population. Since 1906 Iran has been a constitutional monarchy, with a National Assembly or Majlis of elected representatives and a Senate, convened for the first time in 1950, consisting of 30 members nominated by the Shah and 30 elected by the people.

HISTORY. About the middle of the 2nd millennium B.C. Aryan tribes, including the Medes and Persians, overran the country from the E. In the 6th cent. B.C. the Persians under Cyrus, who inhabited the S, overthrew the Medes and formed an empire which included Babylonia, Syria, and Asia Minor and later Egypt, NW India, Thrace, and Macedonia. In the following century, however, both Darius I and Xerxes I failed in their expeditions against the Greeks, and the empire began to decay. It was conquered by Alexander the Great (331–323 B.C.), passed to Seleucus and his successors, and was ruled by the Parthians from 138 B.C. to A.D. 226. They in turn were overthrown by the Sassanids, a native Persian dynasty founded by Ardashir, who revived a true Persian empire which was overthrown (642) by the Arabs; the latter converted the country to Islam, though some pockets of the Zoroastrian and other native religions survived. Parts of Iran were ruled by various Turkish, Persian, and Tatar dynasties, and in the 13th cent. the country was conquered by the Mongols of Genghis Khan. The Safavid dynasty ruled 1499–1736, including the great Shah Abbas I (1587–1628), and was followed by an outstanding warrior, Nadir Shah (1736–47). From 1794 the Qajar dynasty reigned until 1925, when its last member Ahmed was deposed and Riza Khan Pahlevi, a soldier, was proclaimed Shah. During the 2nd World War Riza Shah showed sympathy with the Axis cause and was forced to abdicate in favour of his son (1941). In 1951 foreign oil interests were expropriated, with disastrous effects on the country's economy, but from 1954 the industry was controlled by an international consortium of oil companies, 50 per cent of the profits accruing to Iran. In an earthquake disaster in the Hamadan–Kazvin-Saveh area (NW) in 1962 many villages were destroyed and about 10,000 people were killed.

**Irapuato** Mexico. Town in Guanajuato state, on the central plateau at a height of 5,660 ft. Pop. 35,000. Flour milling, iron founding, tanning, etc. Manufactures cigarettes. Trade in fruit, tobacco, cereals, etc.

**Iraq (Ar. Al Jumhouriya al 'Iraqia).\*** Republic of SW Asia. Area 169,240 sq. m. Pop. (1965) 8,261,527. Cap. Baghdad. Lang. mainly Arabic. Rel. predominantly Muslim.

Corresponds roughly to the ancient Mesopotamia, the land 'Between the Rivers' (i.e. the Tigris and Euphrates). Within the lower basin of the two rivers the soil is fertile and has considerable agricultural potentialities, only realizable with irrigation. Without irrigation much of the country, in addition to its desert fringe, remains unproductive; petroleum is nowadays its chief source of wealth, representing 90 per cent or more of its exports. It is divided for administrative purposes into 14 provinces or *liwas*: Arama, Arbil (Erbil), Baghdad, Basra, Diyala, Diwaniya, Hilla, Karbala, Kirkuk, Kut, Mosul, Nasiriyah, Ramadi, and Sulaimaniya.

TOPOGRAPHY, CLIMATE, RESOURCES. Consists of 3 main regions: the NE highlands, rugged and sparsely wooded, with scattered pastures, home of the Kurds; the desert region of the W and S, part of the vast Syrian Desert; and lower Iraq, the lower basin of the Tigris and Euphrates. Summers are hot and winters cool. Ranges of temperature are considerable; only in the highland areas does the rainfall exceed 10 ins. annually. Duststorms in the S half of the country are an unpleasant feature of an otherwise not unhealthy climate. The main oilfields are round Kirkuk, which has pipelines to Tripoli (Lebanon) and Banias (Syria), Khanaqin, and Ain Zalah, NW of Mosul; there is a refinery at Daura, near Baghdad (opened 1955). Dates, produced in the irrigated belt along the Shatt-al-Arab, are an important export crop, providing about four fifths of the world's trade in dates; wheat and barley are other leading crops. Large numbers of sheep and goats are raised. Efforts have been made in recent times to restore the ancient irrigation system; outstanding among the projects is the great Hindiya Barrage on the Euphrates.

PEOPLE, GOVERNMENT, *etc.* About 94 per cent of the people are Muslim, and there is a small Christian minority. Few Jews remain after the mass emigration to Israel (1950–51). The Kurds, who have aspirations for autonomy, represent about 15 per cent of the total population. Iraq, formerly a kingdom, became a republic in 1958 after an army *coup d'état* in which the King was assassinated, and in the new constitution it was described as 'an integral part of the Arab nation'; the first revolutionary régime was itself overthrown in 1963.

HISTORY. For early history ◊ *Babylonia, Assyria, Mesopotamia, Turkey.* Iraq was freed from Turkish domination in the 1st World War and became an independent Arab state under British mandate (1927), and when the mandate lapsed (1932) was admitted to the League of Nations. During the 2nd World War a pro-German *coup d'état* was put down by British forces (1941) and in 1943 Iraq declared war on the Axis powers; it joined the Arab League (1945) and took part in the unsuccessful war on Israel (1948). Its short history has been characterized by political instability.

**Irawadi River** ◊ *Irrawaddy River.*

**Irbid** Jordan. Town in the N, 44 m. N of Amman. Pop. (1967) 63,000. Commercial centre. Trade in grain etc.

**Ireland** (Irish **Éire**, whence the poetic **Erin**). Second largest island of the British Isles, lying W of Great Britain, from which it is separated by the North Channel, the Irish Sea, and St George's Channel. It is partitioned, 26 counties forming the Irish Republic, and 6 (as Northern Ireland) an integral part of the United Kingdom of Great Britain and Northern Ireland (see below).

TOPOGRAPHY, CLIMATE. Structural similarities between the two islands suggest that Ireland was once joined to Great Britain. The central part of Ireland consists of a plain which stretches W–E from coast to coast and includes the extensive Bog of Allen. Outside this central plain is a broken rim of mountains. In the N are the Derryveagh Mountains, the Sperrin Mountains, the Mountains of Antrim, and the Mourne Mountains; in the SE are the Wicklow Mountains, which rise to 3,039 ft in Lugnaquillia, and in the SW the picturesque Mountains of Kerry, which include Macgillycuddy's Reeks, with Carrantuohill (3,414 ft), the highest peak in Ireland. The longest river is the Shannon, which traverses the central plain N–S; others are the Foyle and the Bann, flowing to the N coast, the Lagan and the Liffey to the E, and the Barrow, the Suir, and the Blackwater to the S coast. Of the inland lakes or loughs the most extensive are Neagh, the largest in the British Isles, Erne (Upper and Lower), Ree, and Derg. The W coast in particular is deeply indented, with such inlets as Bantry Bay, Dingle Bay, the Shannon estuary, Galway Bay, and Donegal Bay; the many offshore islands include Valentia, the Aran Is., and Achill Island. Inlets on other coasts, however, are of greater economic importance – Lough Foyle (N), Belfast Lough and Dublin Bay (E), and Cork Harbour (S). Ireland's insular position on the NW fringe of Europe ensures a mild, equable, humid climate, with about 60 ins. of rain annually in the W, considerably more in the mountains, decreasing to 30 ins. in the E: a climate which favours vegetation, gives a fresh, green appearance to the land and justifies the nickname of the 'Emerald Isle'.

HISTORY. Long before the Christian era Ireland was invaded by Celtic tribes, and the island was divided into kingdoms which were nominally subject to an Ard-ri or High King at Tara and were frequently at war with one another. Christianity was introduced mainly through the work of St Patrick in the 5th cent., and for the succeeding two centuries Ireland was a centre of culture; settlers and missionaries, of whom the best known was St Columba, were sent to Britain. Towards the end of the 8th cent. Norse raiders began to settle at various places around the coast, and founded Dublin and other towns, but they were decisively defeated by Brian Boru, High King of Ireland, at Clontarf (1014). In 1169 the Normans under Richard Strongbow, Earl of Pembroke, invaded Ireland, thus initiating the bitter Anglo-Irish struggles which were to continue for well over 7 centuries. At Drogheda in 1495 was enacted the hated Poynings' Law, which subordinated the Irish legislature to the English. Henry VIII attempted to pacify the Irish chiefs with titles, but only created dissension within the clans. Elizabeth used force to put down rebellions;

Irish land was confiscated, and settlers were planted in Ireland – notably Scottish Protestants in Ulster, whose arrival was to lead to the long conflict between Northern and Southern Ireland. The confiscation of Ulster was largely responsible for the rebellion of 1641, which lasted for more than 10 years but was ruthlessly crushed by Cromwell. Irish support of James II's cause also ended in failure and defeat at the Battle of the Boyne (1690). Through the penal laws the Catholic majority were now harassed and oppressed at every turn; Irish agriculture was deliberately stifled, and the condition of the peasants was made wretched.

Partial independence was granted to the Irish parliament by the Act of Renunciation (1783). Pitt united the British and Irish parliaments (1801), but lost the support he had gained from many Catholics when he failed to redeem his promise of Catholic emancipation. The Catholic Relief Act (1829), however, permitted Catholics to enter parliament; in 1869 the Protestant Church of Ireland was disestablished. Meanwhile, the potato famine (1846–7) had struck the country, causing the deaths of hundreds of thousands from starvation and disease, and the emigration of about $1\frac{1}{2}$ millions, mainly to the United States; the final result was that the population was almost halved. In the political sphere such revolutionary movements as the Society of United Irishmen in the 1790s and Young Ireland in the 1840s achieved less for Ireland than the activities of such patriots as Grattan, O'Connell, and Parnell. Largely because of Parnell's determination, Gladstone was compelled to introduce the Land Act (1881), which made broad concessions to the Irish tenant, but his Home Rule Bill was rejected twice (1886, 1893). The Third Home Rule Bill was passed in 1914 but did not come into operation owing to the outbreak of the 1st World War. During that war the Easter Rising in Dublin (1916) was put down, heralding several years of bitter Anglo-Irish conflict. In the S the Sinn Fein party gained increasing power in the republican movement. The first Dail or Parliament of the Irish Republic was set up in Dublin in 1918. By the Government of Ireland Bill, passed at Westminster in 1920, two parliaments were to be established, one for the 26 counties of the south and the other for the remaining 6 counties of Ulster – but

Sinn Fein refused to co-operate. When the Northern Ireland parliament came into being, the 6 counties remained a part of the United Kingdom of Great Britain and Northern Ireland but enjoyed a substantial measure of autonomy. At length, after numerous acts of terrorism by both sides, a truce was arranged between the British and the southern Irish (1921), resulting in the Anglo-Irish Treaty. Southern Ireland was given a status resembling that of the Dominions and was called the Irish Free State; in 1937 it was renamed Eire, and in 1949 it became completely independent as the Republic of Ireland or Irish Republic.
REPUBLIC OF IRELAND. Republic comprising all Ireland except 6 counties in Ulster, which constitute Northern Ireland. Area 26,600 sq. m. Pop. (1966) 2,884,002. Cap. Dublin. Lang. Irish, English. Rel. predominantly (95 per cent) Roman Catholic.

The names of the 4 historic provinces, Ulster, Leinster, Munster, and Connacht (Connaught), are still used, though they have limited significance. For administrative purposes the country is divided into 26 counties and 4 county boroughs: *Ulster* (in part): Cavan, Donegal, Monaghan. *Leinster*: Carlow, Dublin, Kildare, Kilkenny, Laoighis, Longford, Louth, Meath, Offaly, Westmeath, Wexford, Wicklow; Dublin City (county borough). *Munster*: Clare, Cork, Kerry, Limerick, Tipperary, Waterford; Cork, Limerick, and Waterford Cities (county boroughs). *Connacht*: Galway, Leitrim, Mayo, Roscommon, Sligo.

The Parliament consists of the President, who is elected for 7 years, the House of Representatives or Dáil Éireann, elected by adult suffrage, and the Senate or Seanad Éireann, partly elected and partly nominated. Although Irish is the first official language and English the second, about four fifths of the people normally speak English and only one fifth Irish; nevertheless, the Irish language forms an essential part of the curriculum in all state schools. Probably the most eloquent testimony to the country's sad history has been the steady decline in population since the mid 19th cent. (see HISTORY above): in 1841 there were 6,528,799 inhabitants, but the numbers fell to 3,221,823 (1901) and 2,968,420 (1936).

Agriculture is by far the most important occupation, about two thirds of the land being under crops and pasture. Principal crops cereals, potatoes, turnips, hay. Cattle, sheep, pigs, poultry extensively raised; livestock (chiefly cattle) represent more than one quarter of the total exports. There is little coal in the republic, but hydro-electric resources have been developed and peat is widely used as a fuel. Industries in general are on a small scale, and are connected mainly with agriculture, e.g. brewing, distilling, biscuit manufacture. Growing tourist trade. About half of the country's foreign trade is with Great Britain. Apart from Dublin, which has almost one fifth of the total population, the only other towns with more than 50,000 inhabitants are Cork and Limerick.
NORTHERN IRELAND. Area 5,462 sq. m. Pop. (1961) 1,425,462. Cap. Belfast. Lang. English. Rel. mainly (59 per cent) Protestant. Comprises 6 of the 9 counties of Ulster (Antrim, Armagh, Down, Fermanagh, Londonderry, Tyrone), together with the county boroughs of Belfast and Londonderry. Since 1931 it has had its own parliament at Stormont, near Belfast, consisting of an elected House of Commons, and a Senate, mainly elected; it also returns 12 members to the UK House of Commons at Westminster. Executive power is vested in the Governor, who represents the Crown and holds office for 6 years.

Primarily agricultural. Principal crops barley, oats, potatoes, flax (which supplies the linen industry). Pigs, poultry, sheep, and cattle raised in large numbers; dairy produce and other goods are exported mainly to Britain. Little coal, and few other mineral resources. Industries are centred chiefly on Belfast and Londonderry. The population, like that of the 26 counties of the republic, fell from the mid 19th cent. onwards; from 1,648,945 (1841) to 1,236,952 (1901). During the present century, however, it has slowly but steadily risen. In contrast to the republic, the majority of the people are Protestants, composed of Presbyterians, Church of Ireland, and Methodists; about 35 per cent are Roman Catholics. The traditional animosity between Protestants and Roman Catholics led to civil disturbances 1969–70.
**Irian Barat** ♢ *New Guinea.*
**Irish Sea** Arm of the Atlantic Ocean, about 100 m. N–S and 120 m. W–E, separating England, Wales, and Scotland from Ireland. Connected with the Atlantic Ocean by the North Channel on the N and by St George's Channel on the S.

Irkutsk USSR. Capital of Irkutsk region, RSFSR, on the Angara R. at its confluence with the Irkut R., 40 m. below its exit from the SW end of L. Baikal. Pop. (1970) 451,000. A major Siberian industrial centre. Important airport. Motor-car assembly and other engineering, mica processing, sawmilling, flour milling, meat packing, etc. Power derived from the Cheremkhovo coalfield and the hydro-electric plant on the Angara R. (1956). University (1918). Founded 1652. Increased in importance rapidly with the construction of the Trans-Siberian Railway (1898).

Irlam England. Urban district in Lancashire, on the Manchester Ship Canal 8 m. WSW of Manchester. Pop. (1961) 15,365. Industrial centre. Manufactures soap, margarine, paper.

Iron Baron ⟡ Middleback Range.

Iron Gate (Iron Gates) Rumania/Yugoslavia. Gorge of the Danube R. about 2 m. long on the border between Rumania and Yugoslavia, between Orşova and Turnu-Severin (Rumania). Made navigable 1896.

Iron Knob ⟡ Middleback Range.

Iron Monarch ⟡ Middleback Range.

Irrawaddy (Irawadi) River Burma. Main river and country's economic artery, rising in two headstreams, the Mali and the Nmai, which unite above Myitkyina, and flowing about 1,250 m. generally SSW through the entire length of Burma. Below the confluence the river continues past Bhamo, the head of navigation, flows through spectacular defiles, and reaches Mandalay before receiving its chief tributary, the Chindwin, on the right bank; it then flows between the Arakan Yoma and the Pegu Yoma, past Yenangyaung and Prome, and about 180 m. from the coast divides across its delta, to enter the Andaman Sea across a broad front of forests and mangrove swamps.

Irtysh River USSR. River 1,840 m. long, rising in the Altai Mountains of Sinkiang-Uighur (China), flowing W, and entering L. Zaisan in the Kazakh SSR. It continues in a general NNW direction past Semipalatinsk, Omsk (RSFSR), and Tobolsk, to join the Ob, of which it is the chief tributary. Among its own main tributaries are the Ishim and the Tobol. Navigable for small craft below L. Zaisan April–Nov.

Irvine Scotland. Royal burgh in Ayrshire, on the R. Irvine near its mouth on the Firth of Clyde. Pop. (1961) 16,910. Port and industrial town. Iron founding, saw-milling. Manufactures chemicals, hosiery, etc. Exports tar, cement, etc. Birthplace of John Galt (1779–1839).

Irvington USA. Formerly Camptown. Industrial town just W of Newark, New Jersey. Pop. (1960) 59,379. Manufactures tools, machinery, paint, etc. Originally settled (1692) as Camptown; renamed (1852) after Washington Irving.

Isabela Island ⟡ Galápagos Islands.

Isar River Austria/Federal German Republic. River, 163 m. long, rising in the Austrian Tirol and flowing generally NNE into Bavaria, past Munich to join the Danube R. just below Deggendorf. Provides power for hydroelectric plants.

Isca ⟡ Caerleon.

Ischia Italy. 1. Island of volcanic origin off the coast of Campania at the NW entrance to the Bay of Naples. Area 18 sq. m. Pop. 32,000. Rises to 2,589 ft in Monte Epomeo. With its mineral springs and its scenic beauty, an increasingly popular resort. Produces olives, fruits, wine.
2. Chief town of Ischia island, on the NE coast. Pop. 7,000. Exports wine. Settled by the Greeks c. 500 B.C. but later abandoned owing to volcanic eruption.

Iseo, Lake Italy. Lake in Lombardy 16 m. long and up to 3 m. wide 18 m. E of Bergamo. The Oglio R., tributary of the Po, enters at the N end and leaves at the S end. In the centre is an island rising to 1,834 ft in Monte Isola.

Isère France. Department in the SE, formed (1790) from part of Dauphiné. Area 3,179 sq. m. Pop. (1968) 768,450. Prefecture Grenoble. Mountainous; includes part of the Massif du Pelvoux (SE) (13,461 ft). Bounded on the W by the Rhône, it comprises most of the upper course of the Isère and is drained also by the latter's tributaries the Drac and Romanche, providing much hydroelectric power. Wheat, vines, tobacco, etc. cultivated in the valley. Cattle, sheep, and horses raised. Chief towns Grenoble, Vienne.

Isère River France. River 179 m. long, rising in the Graian Alps near the Italian border and flowing generally W and SW to join the Rhône R. near Valence. Several hydroelectric plants along its upper course.

Iserlohn Federal German Republic. Industrial town in N Rhine-Westphalia 15 m. SE of Dortmund. Pop. (1963) 56,300. Manufactures wire, springs, needles, brass and bronze goods, etc. Famous in medieval times for the manufacture of armour.

**Isfahan (Esfahan, Ispahan)** Iran. Ancient Aspadana. Capital of Isfahan province and the country's second largest city, on the Zayindeh R. 200 m. S of Tehran. Pop. (1966) 575,001. Manufactures textiles, carpets and rugs, and brocade. Famous for its inlaid and ornamental work. A city of great charm and beauty. At the centre is the imposing Maidan-i-Shah, a rectangular space on the S side of which is the famous 17th-cent. Masjid-i-Shah (royal mosque) – an outstanding example of Persian architecture, covered with enamelled tiles. Almost equally beautiful is the Lutfullah mosque, with its blue-tiled dome, on the E side; on the W side the Ali Kapu gate leads to the former royal gardens and the throne room of Shah Abbas, the Chehil Sutun (forty pillars). The magnificent avenue, Chahar Bagh (four gardens), leads past the Madrassa Madur-i-Shah, built (1710) as a theological college, to the Ali Verdi Khan bridge and the suburb of Julfa, which was founded by Armenians in the early 17th cent. The city was taken by Timur and its inhabitants massacred 1387. It prospered and became a great capital under Shah Abbas I, but fell to the Afghans (1722) and never fully recovered its former glory.

**Iskenderun** Turkey. Formerly Alexandretta. Capital of Hatay province, 70 m. W S W of Gaziantep. Pop. (1965) 70,000. Seaport, naval base. Railway terminus. It was long the port of Aleppo and N Syria. With the sanjak of Alexandretta (now the province of Hatay), it was part of Syria 1920–39.

**Islamabad** Pakistan. New capital, in W Pakistan just NE of Rawalpindi. Pop. (1967) 226,000. First Cabinet meeting of the Pakistan government held here 1967.

**Islay** Scotland. Island in Argyllshire, in the Inner Hebrides, off the SW coast of Jura, from which it is separated by the Sound of Islay, 1 m. wide. Area 234 sq. m. Pop. (1961) 3,866. Main occupations fishing, stock rearing, dairy farming, whisky distilling. Chief towns Port Ellen, Bowmore.

**Isleworth** ▷ *Heston and Isleworth.*

**Islington** England. Former metropolitan borough of N London, including Holloway, Highbury, and Canonbury; from 1965 a Greater London borough including Finsbury. Pop. (1963) 261,822. Both residential and industrial. Royal Agricultural Hall (1861); Holloway and Pentonville prisons.

**Ismail** ▷ *Izmail.*

**Ismailia** United Arab Republic. Town in Lower Egypt, half-way along the Suez Canal on the NW shore of L. Timsah, 45 m. S of Port Said. Pop. (1960) 111,000. On the Ismailia (Fresh Water) Canal. Railway centre, linked with Cairo, Port Said, and Suez. Built (1863) by the former Suez Canal Company. Scene of the first campaign against malaria by the elimination of the anopheles mosquito.

**Isna** ▷ *Esna.*

**Isola Bella** ▷ *Borromean Islands.*

**Ispahan** ▷ *Isfahan.*

**Isparta** Turkey. Capital of Isparta province 185 m. ESE of Izmir. Pop. (1965) 43,000. Manufactures carpets.

**Israel.** Republic of S W Asia. Area 7,993 sq. m. Pop. (1968) 2,737,900 (2,383,900 Jews, 286,600 Muslims, 70,600 Christians, 33,100 Druses). Cap. Jerusalem. Official lang. Hebrew, Arabic.

The modern state of Israel, like Palestine and Canaan before it, occupies a strip of land in S W Asia between the Mediterranean and the Jordan valley, with a triangular wedge of desert, the Negev, extending S to the Gulf of Aqaba. Bounded by Lebanon (N), Syria (NE), Jordan (E) and by Egypt (W), which also occupied the so-called Gaza strip along the S W coast. Farming important: many small industries have been developed following the large influx of Jews in recent years; over three quarters of the Jewish population, in fact, are classified as urban.

TOPOGRAPHY, CLIMATE. The fertile coastal plain rises E to the highlands of Galilee (N) and Judaea (S), the hill country in the region of Nablus and Hebron being now occupied by Jordan; the highest point is Har Meiron (3,963 ft) in Upper Galilee, in the extreme N. Mt Carmel, rising to 1,732 ft, interrupts the coastal plain in the N. Only a part of the Jordan valley, which is mostly below sea level, lies within Israel, and other streams, including the Kishon, are intermittent. On the coastal plain the climate is Mediterranean, with hot dry summers, the rain falling mainly in winter and increasing S–N; the hill country is cooler and has a moderate winter rainfall, but the Jordan valley and the Negev are arid. L. Tiberias (Sea of Galilee) lies 696 ft below sea level entirely within Israel; Tiberias is a popular winter resort because of its mild climate at that season. Only the S W shore of the Dead Sea belongs to Israel, and here, at

1,286 ft below sea level, the climate is hot and oppressive.

AGRICULTURE, RESOURCES. On the fertile coastal plain agriculture is intensive and includes mixed farming, poultry farming, viticulture, and the growing of citrus fruits (grapefruit, oranges), the last providing one of the country's principal exports. Wheat, barley, and olives are also cultivated, and farming has been taken into the N Negev with the help of the Yarkon Negev water pipeline. There are several different types of rural settlement in Israel, among them the *kibbutz* and *kvutsa*, communal collective settlements, the *moshav ovdim*, a workers' co-operative smallholders' settlement, and the *moshav shitufi*, a communal co-operative settlement. The chief mineral resources are the salt deposits of the Dead Sea, from which potash and other chemicals are extracted. Among the industries textile manufacture has developed considerably; fruit canning and processing and diamond polishing are significant. Tel Aviv–Jaffa is the largest town, and others with more than 100,000 inhabitants are Haifa and Jerusalem (new city).

PEOPLE, GOVERNMENT, ETC. The creation of the new state of Israel (1948) led to a complete change in the composition of the people. In 1947, under the mandate, well over half the population were Muslims; they numbered more than 1 million, while there were only 615,000 Jews, the great majority of whom had entered as immigrants since 1917. When Israel was attacked by the neighbouring Arab states (1948–9), about 900,000 Arabs left the country, and in the three succeeding years (1948–51) 703,000 Jewish immigrants entered, with the result that Jews now constitute about 90 per cent of the population. The republic has a single-chamber parliament, the Knesset, consisting of 120 members elected for 4 years by universal direct suffrage.

Many religions are represented in Israel, for it is a holy land of the Jewish, Muslim, and Christian faiths, and there is complete freedom of worship and provision for the observance of days of rest and Holy Days by all faiths. Religious affairs, under the supervision of a special Ministry, are under the control of the different ecclesiastical authorities: the Jewish faith is governed by the Sephardic and Ashkenasic Chief Rabbis, for Eastern and Western Jews respectively, the Muslim by the Kadi, and the Christian by the heads of the various communities; in 1957 the Druses were recognized as an autonomous religious community. Education is free and compulsory from 5 to 14 years of age, and among schools under government supervision are 174 Arab schools.

HISTORY. On account of its strategic position Palestine was long disputed by the rulers of the E Mediterranean lands, and the Plain of Esdraelon, with Megiddo, was one of the great battlegrounds of history. A Hebrew kingdom was established, but after the reign of Solomon this was divided into Israel and Judah, the former being destroyed by Assyria in the 8th cent. B.C. and the latter by Babylonia in the 6th cent. B.C. In the 4th cent. B.C. Palestine was conquered by Alexander the Great. Under the Maccabees in the 2nd cent. B.C. the Jews achieved independence, but by 63 B.C. they had yielded to Rome, even though the Herods were nominally kings. Jewish revolts were cruelly suppressed; in the first the Temple was destroyed (A.D. 70), and with the second (A.D. 132) all hopes of an independent Jewish state were crushed. Palestine was conquered in turn by the Muslims under the Caliph Omar (636), the Seljuk Turks (1072), the Crusaders (1099), Saladin (1187), and the Ottoman Turks (1516). The centuries of mainly Turkish rule brought about a disastrous decline in the country's agricultural prosperity.

In the 1st World War (1917–18) Palestine was taken from the Turks by the British. By the Balfour Declaration (1917) Britain expressed herself in favour of the establishment of a Jewish national home in Palestine, and under the British mandate (1920) Jewish immigration was encouraged. In spite of conflict between Jews and Arabs, much economic progress was made, and tension was reduced with the onset of the 2nd World War. After the war, however, Britain refused to allow unlimited Jewish immigration, acts of terrorism were committed and severely countered, the mandate was surrendered, and the Jewish state of Israel was proclaimed (1948). Troops from the neighbouring Arab states invaded Israel but were repulsed, and in 1950 the capital was moved from Tel Aviv to Jerusalem, although the old part of the city remained in Jordanian hands. Trouble with the Arab states again came to a head in 1956, when Egypt nationalized the Suez

Canal and denied its use to Israeli ships; Israeli troops occupied the Gaza strip and the Sinai peninsula, and inflicted considerable losses on the Egyptian forces, but later withdrew. The continuing influx of immigrants put a severe strain on the country, and, although the economy became more viable, economic stability is only maintained by substantial financial help from abroad, mainly from the USA. War with neighbouring Arab states (esp. the United Arab Republic, Jordan, and Syria) again broke out in June 1967, but ended quickly with complete military victory for Israel. Sporadic fighting continued, however, esp. along the Suez Canal (after Israel had occupied the Sinai peninsula) and the Jordan frontier.

**Issyk-Kul** USSR. Large mountain lake in the Kirghiz SSR, in a deep basin, at 5,200 ft above sea level, between the Kungei Ala-Tau (N) and Terskei Ala-Tau (S) ranges. Area 2,390 sq. m. Fed by many streams from the mountain slopes. Its slightly salty waters abound with fish.

**Issy-les-Moulineaux** France. Suburb of SW Paris, in the Hauts-de-Seine department, on the left bank of the Seine R. Pop. (1968) 51,666. Manufactures cars, aircraft, electrical equipment, etc.

**Istanbul** Turkey. Formerly Constantinople. Capital of Istanbul province, on both sides of the Bosporus at the entrance to the Sea of Marmara. Pop. (1965) 1,743,000. Chief seaport. Industrial and commercial centre. Manufactures textiles, glassware, leather goods, cement, etc. Handles most of the country's imports and a considerable part of the exports. Fishing. Tourist centre. On the European side is the terminus of the former Orient Express route (from Paris); at Haydarpasa on the Asiatic side is the starting point of the railway to Baghdad. Like Rome, it is built on seven hills, standing between the Sea of Marmara and its magnificent harbour, the Golden Horn, an inlet of the Bosporus. To the N of the Golden Horn are the suburbs of Galata (commercial quarter) and Pera (European quarter), while on the opposite side of the Bosporus is Üsküdar, or Scutari (industrial centre). Istanbul has one of the world's outstanding buildings and the glory of Byzantine art in the Church of St Sophia, which after the Turkish conquest was converted to a mosque and was embellished with minarets; it was built by Justinian in the 6th cent. The most notable of the later mosques date from the 16th cent., among them those of Suleiman I and Bayezid II; these and others give the city its remarkable skyline of domes and minarets. Although the loss of the Balkan provinces after the 1st World War led to the transference of the capital to Ankara (1923), Istanbul remained an important cultural centre, with a university (founded 1453; secularized 1933) and a technical university (founded 1773; reorganized 1944). It has always been a cosmopolitan city, and Greeks, Armenians, and Jews still form a large part of its population.

Constantinople, the name by which it was known until 1930, was founded (A.D. 328) by Constantine the Great on the site of ◊ *Byzantium* as the new capital of the Roman Empire. It was strongly and skilfully fortified by a series of concentric walls, erected at various times from the reign of Constantine, each new wall reflecting the continued growth of the city. Although attacked by Avars in 627, by Saracens in the 7th and the 8th cent., and by Bulgarians in the 9th and the 10th cent., it did not fall until 1204, when it was taken by the forces of the 4th Crusade and made the seat of a Latin Empire. Recovered by the Byzantines 1261. Fell to the Turks 1453, to flourish again as capital of the Ottoman Empire for more than 4 centuries.

**Istria** Yugoslavia. Peninsula in the N Adriatic Sea, mainly in Yugoslavia; Austrian for most of the period from 1797 to the end of the 1st World War, when it was ceded to Italy. At the end of the 2nd World War (1947), it passed to Yugoslavia, except for the Free Territory of Trieste, which in 1954 was divided between Italy and Yugoslavia. Principal occupations agriculture (cereals, olive oil, wine), fishing. Chief towns Pula, Opatija.

**Itabira** ◊ *Vitória* (Brazil).

**Itajaí** Brazil. Seaport in the Santa Catarina state (SE), at the mouth of the Itajaí Açu R. Pop. 39,000. Serves a fertile agricultural region inhabited largely by Germans and Italians. Exports timber, sugar, tobacco, etc.

**Italy** (Italian **Repubblica Italiana**). Republic of S Europe. Area 116,280 sq. m. Pop. (1966) 53,639,000. Cap. Rome. Rel. predominantly Roman Catholic.

Occupies a long peninsula extending SE from the Alps (N) into the Mediterranean Sea, separating the Tyrrhenian Sea (W) from the Adriatic Sea (E), and including the large islands of Sicily, from which it is separated at the 'toe' by the narrow Strait of Messina, and Sardinia, as well as many smaller islands. In the N the formidable barrier of the Alps forms its boundary with France, Switzerland, Austria, and Yugoslavia. Primarily agricultural, but there has been considerable industrialization in the N, largely through the development of hydroelectric power. For administrative purposes the country is divided into the following 19 regions: Piedmont, Valle d'Aosta, Liguria, Lombardy, Trentino-Alto Adige, Veneto, Friuli-Venezia Giulia, Emilia-Romagna, Marches, Tuscany, Umbria, Latium, Campania, Abruzzi e Molise, Apulia, Basilicata, Calabria, Sicily, and Sardinia. Enclaves in Italy are the republic of San Marino, near Rimini, and the Vatican City, in Rome.

TOPOGRAPHY, CLIMATE. Along Italy's N frontier the Alps curve round in a vast arc from the Riviera to the Gulf of Trieste, and are penetrated by several international railways and roads: their highest peak, Mont Blanc (15,781 ft), is on the Franco-Italian frontier, while Monte Rosa (15,217 ft) is on the Swiss-Italian frontier, the loftiest mountain entirely in Italy being Gran Paradiso (13,324 ft), in the Graian Alps. On the S slopes of the Rhaetian Alps are the beautiful Italian lakes, Maggiore, Lugano, Como, and Garda, the first two shared with Switzerland. Within the curve formed by the Alps and the Apennines is a fertile plain, broadening out towards the Adriatic and consisting mainly of the basin of the Po R., which receives numerous tributaries from both mountain systems. The Apennines, continuing from the Maritime Alps, where the mountains come close to the sea, form the backbone of peninsular Italy and extend to the S extremity of Calabria – the 'toe' of Italy. They form a broad, irregular mountain system, of considerably lower elevation than the Alps, only approaching 10,000 ft in Monte Corno (9,560 ft) in the Gran Sasso d'Italia. Of several volcanic centres the best known are Vesuvius, overlooking the picturesque Bay of Naples, Etna in Sicily, and Stromboli in the Lipari Is. On both sides of the Apennines the generally narrow coastal plains widen here and there, e.g. in Campania and Apulia, but the majority of the rivers S of the Po basin are necessarily short and of little value for navigation, the most important being the Tiber and the Arno. Climate varies according to position and altitude. In the N the Riviera coast, for example, is famed for its mild winters, but the Po basin has a continental type of climate, with cold winters. Towards the S the climate becomes gradually warmer and more Mediterranean in character; S of Rome winters are mild and summers hot, while the rain falls mainly in the cooler months. At times the *sirocco*, a hot enervating wind from the Sahara, sweeps over S Italy, while the N Adriatic coast is affected in winter by the cold *bora* from the NE.

RESOURCES, PEOPLE, ETC. The fertile basin of the Po covers less than one fifth of the country but has about two fifths of its population and economically is the principal region; it produces the bulk of the wheat, maize, rice, hemp, sugar-beet, and vines. In the S olives and citrus fruits are cultivated, but the land is much less productive. Agriculture here has long suffered from backward methods, the division of land into large, neglected estates, overpopulation, and poverty; combative measures include the reclamation of such areas as the Pontine Marshes, formerly notorious for malaria, and the allocation of smallholdings to the peasants. Sulphur and mercury are exported, but Italy is generally poor in minerals; the lack of coal and oil has been offset by the development of hydroelectric power, particularly in the N, where the chief industries are concentrated. Milan and Turin are the great industrial centres and Genoa is their port. Of the other leading cities Rome is the capital and Naples the main industrial centre and seaport of the S. Italy has to import large quantities of foodstuffs and raw materials as well as certain manufactures, and normally has an adverse trade balance. This is largely made up by the mercantile marine, the fourth largest in Europe, and by the millions of tourists who visit the country annually to enjoy such world-renowned resorts as Venice and Capri and the art treasures of Florence, Pisa, and many other historic centres. Despite the country's long tradition of culture, there is still illiteracy, chiefly in the S. By a treaty between the Holy See and the State (1929), the Roman Catholic is the only State religion, and 99·6 per cent of the people are Roman Catholics. The Italian Parliament comprises a Chamber of Deputies, elected for 5 years by universal suffrage, and a Senate, elected for 6 years, while the President holds office for 7 years. HISTORY. The history of Italy from the 5th cent. B.C. to the 5th cent. A.D. is largely that of ◊ *Rome*. With the fall of the Roman Empire of the west (476), Italy came under the rule of the Ostrogoths and then the Lombards, and in 800 Charlemagne was crowned Emperor by the Pope. In 962 it became part of the Holy Roman Empire, and for the next 3 centuries its history reflected the struggle between the Empire and the papacy. At the beginning of the 14th cent. there were 5 major powers in Italy: the kingdom of Naples, the papal states, and the city-republics of Milan, Florence, and Venice, and in spite of the constant rivalry and conflict between them, it was in the 14th–16th cent. that Italy made its great contribution to European culture in the Renaissance. Spain and Austria now exercised the dominating influence; by the mid 18th cent. Naples, Sicily, and Parma were held by the Spanish Bourbons, Milan and Tuscany by Austria, Sardinia and Piedmont by Savoy, while central Italy was occupied by the papal states and Venice survived as a republic (till 1797). Under the Napoleonic régime Italy was unified, but disintegrated again on the fall of Bonaparte. Democratic and nationalist ideals introduced by the French, however, led to the *Risorgimento* movement. Unification was at last achieved by Victor Emmanuel II of Sardinia, assisted by Cavour and Garibaldi, and in 1861 he became king of united Italy; by the defeat of Austria, Venetia was secured (1866), and then Rome was added (1870). In 1882 Italy concluded the Triple Alliance with Germany and Austria, and embarked on colonial expansion with the annexation of Eritrea and part of Somaliland. The attack on Abyssinia was defeated at Adowa (1896), but the war with Turkey (1911–12) yielded Libya. In the 1st World War Italy joined the Allies (1915), and received S Tirol, Trieste, Istria, the Dodecanese and other small territories, while Fiume (Rijeka) was seized by d'Annunzio (1921). Political and industrial unrest, seething for some years, paved the way for a Fascist régime, and an aggressive foreign policy expressed itself in the conquest of Abyssinia (1935–6) and Albania (1939) and the entry into the 2nd World War (1940) on the side of Germany. Defeat in Africa and the invasion of Sicily (1943) brought about the downfall of Mussolini and the end of his grandiose schemes for a colonial empire, and until 1945 Italy was a battlefield; Victor Emmanuel III abdicated (1946), to be followed later in the same year by his son and successor, Umberto II, and a republic was proclaimed. By the peace treaty (1947) Italy lost her colonial possessions; most of Venezia Giulia went to Yugoslavia, small frontier districts to France, and Trieste became a Free Territory – to be divided between Yugoslav and Italian administration in 1954.

**Ithaca** (Gr. **Itháki**) Greece. One of the Ionian Is., off NE Cephalonia, reputed to have been the home of Homer's Odysseus (Ulysses). Area 33 sq. m. Pop. 5,800. Chief town Itháki. Produces olive oil, wine, currants. Devastated by earthquake 1953.

**Ithaca** U S A. Town in New York at the S end of Cayuga L. Pop. (1960) 28,799. Manufactures adding machines, fire-arms, etc. Situated in the beautiful scenery of the Finger Lakes region, with gorges and waterfalls. Seat of Cornell University (1865).

**Itzehoe** Federal German Republic. Ancient town in Schleswig-Holstein, on the Stör R. 32 m. NW of Hamburg. Pop. (1963) 36,900. Manufactures cement, machinery, fishing nets, etc. The oldest town in the *Land*; grew up round a 9th-cent. castle.

**Ivano-Frankovsk** USSR. Formerly Stanisławów, Stanislav. Industrial town in the Ukrainian SSR 70 m. SSE of Lvov. Pop. (1970) 105,000. Railway engineering, oil refining. Manufactures machinery, textiles, etc. An old Polish town, it reverted to Poland after the 1st World War (as Stanisławów) but was ceded to the USSR in 1945.

**Ivanovo** USSR. Formerly (1861–1932) Ivanovo-Voznesensk. Capital of the Ivanovo region in the central European RSFSR, on the Uvod R. 160 m. NE of Moscow. Pop. (1970) 419,000. The earliest and still the major centre of the cotton industry; also manufactures textile and other machinery and chemicals. Founded in the 14th cent. A commercial centre by the 17th cent. United (1861) with Voznesensk to form the town of Ivanovo-Voznesensk; renamed 1932.

**Iviza** ◊ *Balearic Islands*.

**Ivory Coast** (Fr. **Côte d'Ivoire**). Republic on the Gulf of Guinea; formerly a French overseas territory in French W Africa.

Area 124,510 sq. m. Pop. (1965) 3,840,000 (14,500 Europeans). Cap. Abidjan. Bounded by Mali and Upper Volta (N), Ghana (E), and Guinea and Liberia (W). The E of the coast is lagoon-fringed. From the coastal plain the land rises to a plateau 1,000 ft high which in the W reaches 4,000 ft. The Bandama, Comoé, and Sassandra rivers, impeded by rapids, are of little value for navigation. Hot humid climate with heavy rainfall. Largely tropical rain-forest. Exports hardwoods (e.g. mahogany); also bananas, cacao, coffee. Food crops cassava, maize, millet, rice, yams. Cotton cultivated in the savannah (N). Port Bouet (outport of Abidjan) is linked by rail with the interior, esp. Bouaké, and with Bobo-Dioulasso and Ouagadougou in the Republic of Upper Volta. Assinie and Grand Bassam, on the coast, were ceded to France in 1842, but the French did not occupy the territory until 1882. Became a colony and was incorporated into French W Africa 1904. Opted to become a member of the French Community 1958. Became an independent member of the UN 1960.

**Ivry-sur-Seine** France. Suburb of SE Paris, in the Val-de-Marne department, on the left bank of the Seine R. Pop. (1968) 60,616. Largely industrial. Manufactures chemicals, cement, earthenware, etc. Engineering.

**Iwakisan** ◊ *Hirosaki.*

**Iwo** Nigeria. Town in the Western State 25 m. NE of Ibadan. Pop. (1960) 100,000. Trade in cacao, palm oil and kernels. Cotton weaving, dyeing.

**Iwo Jima** ◊ *Volcano Islands.*

**Ixtaccihuatl** Mexico. In Aztec, 'White Woman'. Snow-capped dormant volcano (17,338 ft) 38 m. SE of Mexico City. Three separate summits, giving it the appearance of a hooded figure (hence the name).

**Izabal, Lake** Guatemala. Formerly Golfo Dulce. Country's largest lake, in the E, draining into the Caribbean Sea by the Rio Dulce, 30 m. long and up to 12 m. wide. Well known for its beauty.

**Izhevsk** USSR. Capital of the Udmurt ASSR (RSFSR), on the Izh R. 350 m. ENE of Gorki. Pop. (1970) 422,000. Railway junction. Important metallurgical centre. Manufactures agricultural machinery, fire-arms, lathes, etc. Sawmilling, brickmaking, flour milling. Founded 1760.

**Izmail (Ismail)** USSR. Capital of the Izmail region, Ukrainian SSR, in Bessarabia, on the Kiliya (Chilia) branch of the Danube R. 120 m. SW of Odessa. Pop. 47,000. Port. Commercial centre. Flour milling, tanning, etc. Trade in cereals, hides, etc. After being taken by Russia (1770), was twice transferred to Rumania (1856, 1918); returned to the USSR 1944.

**Izmir** Turkey. Formerly Smyrna. Capital of Izmir province and country's third largest city, at the head of the Gulf of Izmir on the Aegean Sea. Pop. (1965) 411,600. Seaport and naval base. Important exports of tobacco, figs, cotton, etc. Also an industrial centre. Manufactures textiles, soap, tobacco products, leather goods, etc. University (1955). Founded by Greeks and later conquered by the Romans. An early centre of Christianity. In 1424 it was taken by the Turks, who held it till 1919, when it was occupied by Greek forces. Restored to Turkey 1923.

**Izmit** Turkey. Capital of Kocaeli province, at the head of the Gulf of Izmit on the Sea of Marmara. Pop. (1965) 90,000. In a tobacco-growing region. Manufactures cement, chemicals, etc. Also a minor port.

# J

**Jabalpur (Jubbulpore)** India. Industrial town and important railway junction in Madhya Pradesh 150 m. NNE of Nagpur. Pop. (1961) 295,375. Manufactures cement, glass, textiles, etc. Seat of an agricultural university (1963).

**Jablonec (Ger. Gablonz)** Czechoslovakia. Town in N Bohemia, on the Nisa (Neisse) R. 55 m. NE of Prague. Pop. (1961) 27,533. Important centre of the glass industry. Also well known for imitation jewellery. Manufactures textiles.

**Jachymov (Ger. Joachimsthal)** Czechoslovakia. Town in W Bohemia, in the Erzgebirge, 12 m. N of Karlovy Vary. Pop. 8,000. Important centre of pitchblende mining, producing uranium, radium, and other metals. In the 16th cent. it was noted for its silver mines, and a silver coin struck here was known as the Joachimsthaler, the name being abbreviated to *thaler*, which was later modified to dollar.

**Jackson (Michigan)** USA. Industrial town and railway centre in the S, on the Grand R. Pop. (1960) 50,720. Manufactures motorcar and aircraft parts, clothing, lawn mowers, etc. Railway engineering. The Republican Party was founded here (1854).

**Jackson (Mississippi)** USA. State capital, on the Pearl R. Pop. (1960) 144,422. Chief industrial and commercial centre of the state. Manufactures glass, textiles, cottonseed oil, etc. Noteworthy buildings are the old Capitol (1839) and the Governor's mansion (1842). Named after Andrew Jackson, the 7th US President.

**Jackson (Tennessee)** USA. Town in the W, on the S Fork of the Forked Deer R. Pop. (1960) 33,849. Manufactures textiles, furniture, toys, etc. Trade in timber, cotton, maize, etc.

**Jacksonville** USA. One of the chief commercial towns on the S Atlantic coast, on the St John's R. in NE Florida. Pop. (1970) 513,439. Deep-water port. Exports timber, fruit, etc. Boatbuilding, fishing, canning. Manufactures wood products, glassware, cigars, etc. A tourist resort. Named after Andrew Jackson, the 7th US President.

**Jadida, El (Mazagan)** Morocco. Atlantic seaport 60 m. WSW of Casablanca. Pop. (1960) 40,302. Exports cereals, eggs, etc.

from the fertile Doukkala. Founded (1502) by the Portuguese. Lost some of its importance with the development of Casablanca. ⟡ *Morocco*.

**Jadotville** Congo (Kinshasa). Town 65 m. NW of Lubumbashi (Elisabethville), with which it is connected by rail. Pop. (1966) 102,000. Chiefly important as a centre of copper and cobalt production; the country's first electrolytic copper refinery was opened here 1929. Railway engineering.

**Jaén** Spain. 1. Province in Andalusia. Area 5,207 sq. m. Pop. (1961) 736,391. Mountainous, bounded by the Sierra Morena (N) and the Sierra de Segura (E). Drained by the Guadalquivir R. and its tributaries. Occupations mining (chiefly lead) and agriculture, with large production of olive oil. Principal towns Jaén, Linares. 2. Capital of Jaén province 43 m. NNW of Granada. Pop. (1967) 71,508. Trade in olive oil. Manufactures chemicals, brandy, leather, etc. Renaissance cathedral (16th/18th-cent.). Liberated from the Moors by Ferdinand III of Castile 1246.

**Jaffa** Israel. Ancient Joppa. Port on the Mediterranean coast just S of ⟡ *Tel Aviv* (with which it was incorporated 1949), now largely superseded by Haifa; formerly exported the famous Jaffa oranges from its open roadstead. Destroyed by Vespasian A.D. 68. Twice changed hands between Crusaders and Muslims in the 12th cent. Most of its predominantly Arab population left the town in 1948.

**Jaffna** Ceylon. 1. Peninsula at the N extremity of the island, separated from the rest of Ceylon by the Jaffna Lagoon and from India by Palk Strait. Intensively cultivated and densely populated, chiefly by Ceylon Tamils. 2. Town in the Northern Province, on the Jaffna peninsula and Jaffna Lagoon. Pop. (1963) 94,248. Minor port. Trade in small vessels, chiefly with S India. Has a 17th-cent. Dutch fort.

**Jagannath** ⟡ *Puri.*

**Jagersfontein** S Africa. Small diamond-mining town in the Orange Free State 65 m. SW of Bloemfontein, at a height of 4,600 ft. Pop. (1960) 3,885. Two famous diamonds, the 'Excelsior' (971 carats) and the 'Jubilee' (634 carats), were found in the mine (opened 1870).

**Jagua Bay** ◊ *Cienfuegos*.

**Jaipur** India. Capital of Rajasthan and formerly of the princely state of Jaipur, 150 m. SW of Delhi. Pop. (1961) 403,444. Well planned, commercially important. Trade in grain, wool, cotton, etc. Manufactures carpets, blankets, metal goods, etc. Has the former maharajah's palace. Seat of Rajasthan University (1947).

**Jakarta (Djakarta)** Indonesia. Formerly Batavia. Capital of the republic, on the coast of NW Java facing the Java Sea, its port at near-by Tanjungpriok. Pop. (1961) 2,973,052. Exports rubber, tea, etc. Railway engineering, tanning, sawmilling. Manufactures textiles, soap, etc. Has an old town (founded 1619), with a few Dutch colonial buildings still surviving, and a modern residential area. Seat of the University of Indonesia (1947).

**Jalalabad** Afghanistan. Capital of Nangrahar province, 75 m. E of Kabul on the Kabul R. at a height of 2,000 ft. Pop. (1965) 44,000. Trading centre for an agricultural region producing dried fruits, grain, almonds, etc. Seat of Nangrahar University (1963). Defended for 5 months by British troops in the 1st Afghan War (1841–2).

**Jalapa (Jalapa Enríquez)** Mexico. Capital of Veracruz state, in the Sierra Madre Oriental 50 m. NW of Veracruz, at a height of 4,680 ft. Pop. (1960) 66,269. Health resort in a picturesque setting, well-known for its flowers. Sugar refining, flour milling, coffee roasting, etc. Gave its name to jalap, a drug formerly produced here from the roots of a climbing plant.

**Jalisco** Mexico. Maritime state in the W. Area 30,933 sq. m. Pop. (1969) 3,344,000. Cap. Guadalajara. Mainly mountainous, crossed NW–SE by the Sierra Madre Occidental. Sugar-cane, cotton, tobacco cultivated in the hot coastal regions, cereals and beans on the uplands. Mercury, gold, silver, lead, zinc, and copper mined. The L. Chapala area is a tourist attraction.

**Jalpaiguri** India. Town in W Bengal, on the Tista R. 48 m. SE of Darjeeling. Pop. (1961) 48,738. Commercial centre. Trade in rice, tea, etc.

**Jamaica.** Third largest island in the Caribbean, in the Greater Antilles 90 m. S of the E end of Cuba; an independent member of the British Commonwealth. Area 4,411 sq. m. Pop. (1968) 1,893,000 (about 1 per cent of European stock, 78 per cent Negro, 18 per cent coloured). Cap. Kingston. Predominantly mountainous; the main range running W–E across the island ends in the Blue Mountains, with Blue Mountain Peak (7,520 ft) the highest point. Climate tropical along the coast (the temperature often exceeds 90° F in the daytime, but falls considerably at night); the mountains are cooler. Rainfall varies widely from place to place. Occasionally hurricanes cause great damage; a particularly severe one occurred in 1944. There were destructive earthquakes in 1692 and 1907. The economy depends largely on agriculture. Principal crop sugar-cane, bananas taking second place; coffee, cacao, coconuts, citrus fruits, and tobacco also important. The world's largest exporter of bauxite; some is processed into alumina. Gypsum also mined. Industrial output consists largely of products made from the crops, e.g. rum and molasses from sugar; copra, cigars, and fruit juices also exported. The tourist industry is of increasing importance, aided by the pleasant climate and the many attractive bays, together with the development of air communications, esp. with the USA. Kingston has a fine harbour; other ports are Montego Bay and Port Antonio. Spanish Town is the second largest town (after Kingston). For administrative purposes the island is divided into 3 counties, containing 14 parishes in all.

Discovered (1494) by Columbus, who named it St Jago, but the native Arawak name Xaymaca (anglicized to Jamaica) was adopted. A Spanish colony from 1509 to 1655, when it was captured by the English; formally ceded to England 1670. Slavery was abolished in 1833; the violence that followed culminated in the insurrection of 1865, after which representative government was suspended for 20 years. In 1944 self-government was introduced; in 1958 the West Indies Federation was established, but in 1962 Jamaica opted out and achieved complete independence within the British Commonwealth.

**Jambi (Djambi)** Indonesia. Town in Sumatra, on the Batang Hari R. 120 m. NW of Palembang. Pop. (1961) 113,000. Minor port. Trade in rubber, timber, rattan, etc. Also called Telanaipura.

**James Bay** Canada. S extension of ◊ *Hudson Bay*. Shallow, containing many islands, notably Akimiski. Discovered

(1610) by Henry Hudson; named after Thomas James, who explored it (1631). The railway from Cochrane (Ontario) to Moosonee, the new port on the bay, was completed in 1932.

**James River** USA. River in Virginia, 340 m. long, formed by the union of the Jackson and the Cowpasture rivers, flowing generally ESE past Richmond, the head of navigation, to Newport News on the estuary. Along its lower course is the region where the first permanent English settlement in the New World was established.

**Jamestown** (New York) USA. Industrial town on L. Chautauqua. Pop. (1960) 41,818 (predominantly of Swedish extraction). Manufactures furniture, washing and milking machines, textiles, toys, etc. Named after James Prendergast, an early settler.

**Jamestown** (Virginia) USA. Ruined village on Jamestown Island (1,560 acres) in the James R. Famous as the site of the first permanent English settlement in the New World, established 14 May 1607. Named after King James I. Incorporated in the Colonial National Historical Park 1936.

**Jammu** India. 1. Province of the state of Jammu and ◊ *Kashmir*. Area 12,378 sq. m. 2. Capital of Jammu province and winter capital of the state of Jammu and Kashmir 95 m. S of Srinagar on the Tavi R. Pop. (1961) 102,738. Terminus of a railway from Sialkot (Pakistan), now disused. Manufactures rubber products, leather, pottery, etc. Trade in grain and cotton.

**Jamnagar** India. Town in Gujarat, on the Kathiawar peninsula. Pop. (1961) 139,652. Trade in oilseeds, cotton, millet, vegetables. Manufactures textiles, leather, cement, metal goods, etc. Founded 1540, it was capital of the former princely state of Nawanagar.

**Jamshedpur** India. Industrial town in SE Bihar 140 m. WNW of Calcutta. Pop. (1961) 291,791. Has the country's chief iron and steel works, founded (1909) by the Tata family near the coal and iron fields of the Bihar–W Bengal region. This was responsible for the rapid growth of the former village, and Jamshedpur now manufactures tinplate, steel wire, agricultural implements, locomotives, etc.

**Jamuna** ◊ *Ganges*.

**Janesville** USA. Commercial town in S Wisconsin, on the Rock R. 58 m. SW of Milwaukee. Pop. (1960) 35,164. In a dairy-farming and tobacco-growing region.

Manufactures cars, textiles, fountain pens, etc.

**Janina** ◊ *Ioánnina* (2).

**Jan Mayen** Norway. Island in the Arctic Ocean between Iceland and Spitsbergen, belonging to Norway. Area 144 sq. m. Mountainous; the ice-covered extinct volcano Beerenberg rises to 7,470 ft. Named after one of its discoverers, the Dutch captain Jan May, who established a whaling station here (1614). The Norwegians have maintained a meteorological station on the island since 1921. Officially annexed to Norway 1929.

**Japan.** Country of E Asia. Area 142,727 sq. m. Pop. (1967) 100,160,000. Cap. Tokyo. Rel. mainly Shintoist and Buddhist, with Christian minority.

A crescent-shaped archipelago off the E coast of Asia consisting of 4 main islands, Hokkaido, Honshu, Shikoku, and Kyushu, and many smaller islands. In the N it is separated from Sakhalin (now wholly owned by the USSR) by La Pérouse Strait, and in the SW from Korea by Korea Strait. All arable land is intensively cultivated; the Japanese fishing catch is the second largest in the world; but the outstanding feature of the country's economy is the high degree of industrialization: in manufacture of both iron and steel and textiles the Japanese have become one of the world's leading nations, and the recovery of their basic industries after the destruction of the 2nd World War has been remarkable. For administrative purposes the country is divided into 46 prefectures: Hokkaido; Aomori, Akita, Iwate, Yamagata, Miyagi, Fukushima, Niigata, Ishikawa, Toyama, Nagano, Gumma, Tochigi, Ibaraki, Chiba, Kanagawa, Tokyo, Saitama, Yamanashi, Shizuoka, Aichi, Gifu, Fukui, Shiga, Mie, Nara, Wakayama, Osaka, Kyoto, Hyogo, Tottori, Okayama, Shimane, Hiroshima, and Yamaguchi (all on Honshu); Kagawa, Tokushima, Kochi, and Ehime (on Shikoku); Oita, Fukuoka, Saga, Nagasaki, Kumamoto, Miyazaki, and Kagoshima (on Kyushu).

TOPOGRAPHY, CLIMATE, *etc.* Mountain ranges run through the 4 main islands, sending out lateral branches and rising in the famous Fujiyama on Honshu to 12,395 ft; the latter, a sacred peak, is volcanic, like many others, including several which are still active. Japan is notoriously subject to earthquakes, an average of 4 shocks daily being experienced in some parts of the country. The earthquakes are especially prevalent along the Pacific seaboard, where the mountains shelve steeply down to the Japan Trench, which reaches a depth of 5,673 fathoms; some of the earthquakes have reached the magnitude of national disasters, the worst being that of 1923 in Sagami Bay, when 91,344 lives were lost. Rivers are generally short, the longest being the Ishikari-gawa on Hokkaido (227 m.), but they are extensively used for hydroelectric power development.

The climate is dominated by the monsoons: the SE monsoon brings heavy summer rains, while the NW monsoon makes the winters relatively cold in the centre and N. Temperatures vary considerably from N to S, particularly in winter; rainfall is plentiful everywhere, and exceeds 80 ins. annually in many areas in the S. Typhoons occur in the late summer and autumn and are a great hazard to crops.

RESOURCES, PEOPLE, GOVERNMENT. Agriculture is practised mainly in the coastal plains and valleys, though the hill slopes are terraced wherever practicable; only 16 per cent of the land area is classified as arable. Indeed so little suitable land is available that farming is based on the smallholding, the average area of which is 2 acres; after the 2nd World War land hunger was appeased to some small extent by distributing over 5 million acres from large estates to tenant farmers. Rice is the staple food crop, occupying more than half the cultivated area, and wheat, barley, sweet potatoes, sugar-beet, soya beans, apples, and mandarins are important; mulberry trees are grown for the raising of silkworms. The forests are exploited, and in a country with little stock rearing the fisheries provide food items of outstanding value. Japan has few mineral resources; petroleum, coal, and iron ore, as well as raw cotton and wool, are major imports. Besides Tokyo, the chief towns are Osaka, Nagoya, Yokohama, Kyoto, and Kobe, each with a population over 1 million.

The Japanese give the appearance today of a homogeneous people, but stem from a mixture of Malay, Manchu and Korean stocks, the original inhabitants, the Ainu, having survived only in small numbers on Hokkaido. Shinto is the oldest religion, and was supported by the state from the 1930s till 1945; many Japanese are Buddhists, and there are about 670,000 Christians. Before the 2nd World War they were governed according to the constitution of 1889, modelled on that of Prussia, but the new constitution of 1947 deprived the Emperor of his 'divine' attributes as well as all political power, abolished the peerage, and extended the franchise to women. Legislative power now rests with the House of Representatives, elected by all over the age of 20 years, and the House of Councillors (Upper House), and executive power with the Prime Minister and the Cabinet.

HISTORY. Little is known of early Japan until the 6th cent. A.D., when Buddhism was introduced and Chinese culture was generally adopted. A feudal system developed, real power being held by rulers known as shoguns, the first to take this title being Yoritomo of the Minamoto family (1192). The first Europeans to make contact with Japan were the Portuguese (1542), followed by Spaniards, Dutch, and English, but within a century only the Dutch were allowed to trade and no Japanese were permitted to leave the islands. For about two centuries Japan remained in isolation, till in 1853 the United States insisted on opening up trade, and the last shogun was compelled to abdicate (1867). Feudalism was abolished, executive power was restored to the Emperor, and a parliament was established (1889). Modern industries were developed, trade expanded, and a policy of aggression was pursued – through wars with China (1894–5) and Russia (1904–5), both of which brought territorial gains. Having supported the Allied cause in the 1st World War, Japan received the German Pacific islands as mandates. Extreme nationalist elements gained control in Japan, and the puppet state of Manchukuo was set up in Manchuria (1931); then the war with China was renewed (1937); Japan entered the 2nd World War by attacking Pearl Harbour (1941). Most of SE Asia was occupied by the Japanese but gradually lost, and surrender came after the dropping of atomic bombs on Hiroshima and Nagasaki (1945). A new and democratic constitution was put into effect in 1947 and Japan was admitted to the United Nations in 1956.

**Japan, Sea of.** Arm of the Pacific Ocean between the islands of Japan and the mainland of Asia (USSR, Korea). Area

389,000 sq. m. Important fishing region.
**Jaraguá** ♢ *Maceió*.
**Jarrow** England. Municipal borough in
NE Durham, on the R. Tyne estuary 5 m.
E of Newcastle upon Tyne. Pop. (1961)
28,752. Industrial town and port. Ship-
repairing yards, oil installation. Exports
coal. In 681 Benedict Biscop founded a
monastery in which the Venerable Bede
lived, worked, and died. The town suffered
severely from unemployment after the 1st
World War, when the shipyards closed
down, but revived somewhat when they
were reopened in the 2nd World War.
**Jarvis Island** ♢ *Line Islands*.
**Jasna Góra** ♢ *Częstochowa*.
**Jasper National Park** Canada. The second
largest of the country's scenic National
Parks, in W Alberta, bordering the Banff
National Park. Area 4,200 sq. m. Noted
for wild life, some of the highest peaks in
the Canadian Rockies, waterfalls, and
glaciers, inc. the famous Columbia ice
field. Established 1907. Well provided with
camping sites and other facilities. Jasper
is the chief tourist centre.
**Jassy** ♢ *Iaşi*.
**Játiva (Játiba)** Spain. Ancient Saetabis.
Town in Valencia province 34 m. SSW of
Valencia. Pop. 18,000. Produces brandy,
leather, cement, etc. Home of several of
the Borgia family in the 15th and 16th
cent. Birthplace of Pope Alexander VI
(1431–1503) and Ribera, the painter
(1588–1652).
**Jaunpur** India. Town in Uttar Pradesh, on
the Gumti R. 35 m. NW of Varanasi
(Benares). Pop. (1961) 61,851. Manufactures perfumes. Well-known for its ancient
buildings, inc. the 15th-cent. Jama Masjid
and other mosques, the 15th-cent. baths of
Ibrahim Shah, and the 16th-cent. bridge
over the Gumti R.
**Java** Indonesia. The country's most productive and most populous island, also the
most important politically and culturally;
lies SE of Sumatra. Area (with Madura)
51,032 sq. m. Pop. (1961) 63 million (almost two thirds of the total population).
The narrow island is traversed by a
volcanic mountain chain, with several
peaks exceeding 10,000 ft and a number
of active volcanoes, inc. the constantly
steaming Mt Bromo; the coastal plain is
wider in the N than the S, and the numerous
rivers are short. Its climate is equatorial,
the mean monthly temperatures at Jakarta,
e.g., varying only between 78° and 80° F,

but the heat is much reduced by altitude.
The N coast receives its rain mainly from
the NW monsoon (Dec.–Mar.), the S
coast from the SE monsoon (April–Oct.);
the humidity is high, thunderstorms are
frequent, and the annual rainfall is moderate
to heavy. There is a rich tropical vegetation,
though much of the forest on the plains
and lower mountain slopes has been cleared
for cultivation; teak is one of the most
valuable timbers, and forest exploitation
is carefully controlled to prevent soil
erosion and flooding.
Rice is the principal food crop, and
maize, cassava, sweet potatoes, and coconuts are also grown on smallholdings;
rubber, coffee, tea, sugar-cane, and cinchona (quinine) are chiefly plantation
crops. Despite the fact that a great part of
its surface is mountainous, Java is one of
the most densely populated agricultural
regions in the world. The difficulty of
producing sufficient food for the rapidly
increasing population, in fact, has led to
the settlement of tens of thousands of
Javanese elsewhere in Indonesia in recent
years. Oil is produced in N central Java,
near Rembang. Jakarta, the national
capital, Surabaya, and Semarang, all on
the N coast, are the chief seaports, and
Bandung and Jogjakarta are important
inland towns. The island is divided administratively into the three provinces of W
Central, and E Java.
**Java Sea**. Section of the Pacific Ocean,
between Borneo (N) and Java (S), connected with the Celebes Sea by the Strait of
Macassar, with the Indian Ocean by Sunda
Strait, and with the S China Sea by Kari-
mata Strait. Area about 120,000 sq. m.
Scene of a Japanese naval victory in the
2nd World War (1942).
**Jebel Aulia** Sudan. Village on the White
Nile 28 m. S of Khartoum, near a hill of
the same name. Pop. 3,600. Site of a storage
dam (completed 1937) which makes possible the irrigation of half a million acres
of the Nile valley.
**Jebel Yusha** ♢ *Gilead*.
**Jedburgh** Scotland. Royal burgh and county
town of Roxburghshire, on the Jed Water,
tributary of the R. Tweed, 41 m. SE of
Edinburgh. Pop. (1961) 3,647. Manufactures tweeds, woollen and rayon goods.
Remains of a 12th-cent. Augustinian
abbey. Became notorious (somewhat unjustly) for 'Jeddart [Jedburgh] justice', by
which a prisoner was hanged first and tried

later. Birthplace of Sir David Brewster (1781–1868).

**Jedda** ◊ *Jidda*.

**Jefferson City** USA. State capital of Missouri, on the Missouri R. 136 m. ESE of Kansas City. Pop. (1960) 28,228. Manufactures electrical goods, shoes, clothing. Printing. Seat of Lincoln University, founded (1866) for Negroes by two regiments of Negro infantry.

**Jelenia Góra** (Ger. **Hirschberg**) Poland. Industrial town in the Wroclaw voivodship, on the Bobrawa R. 60 m WSW of Wroclaw. Pop. (1968) 55,700. Manufactures textiles, paper, machinery, glass, etc. Returned to Poland from Germany after the 2nd World War.

**Jelgava** (**Yelgava, Mitau**) USSR. Industrial town in the Latvian SSR 30 m. SW of Riga. Pop. 36,000. Manufactures linen and woollen goods, rope, bricks and tiles, soap, etc. Sugar refining. Founded in the 13th cent. Became capital of Kurland (Courland) 1561. Later passed to Russia (1795).

**Jena** German Democratic Republic. Town in the Gera district, 23 m. WNW of Gera on the Saale R. Pop. (1965) 84,256. Home of the famous Zeiss optical and precision instrument factories, founded in 1846 and partly removed by the Russians after the 2nd World War. Also manufactures machinery, chemicals. Seat of a celebrated university (1558) at which Hegel and Schiller taught. Napoleon defeated the Prussians on the N outskirts of the city (1806).

**Jenolan Caves** Australia. Series of limestone caves in New South Wales 12 m. SE of the village of Oberon, in the Blue Mountains, and 70 m. WNW of Sydney. A famous tourist attraction, with magnificent stalactites and stalagmites and a natural tunnel 300 ft high. Made national property 1866.

**Jerba** ◊ *Djerba*.

**Jerez de la Frontera** (**Jerez**) Spain. Town in Cádiz province, Andalusia, 15 m. NE of Cadiz. Pop. (1967) 145,574. In a fertile agricultural region producing vines, cereals, olives, etc. A world-famous centre of the wine industry, having given its name to sherry. Also manufactures bottles, casks, etc. A picturesque town of white buildings, with many *bodegas* (wine-lodges) where the sherry is made and stored, and many fine churches. Taken by the Moors 711; recaptured by Alphonso X of Castile 1264.

**Jericho** Jordan. Village in the Jordan valley 15 m. ENE of Jerusalem at 825 ft below sea level and 7 m. from the N end of the Dead Sea. The first Canaanite city to be captured by the Israelites; later destroyed and rebuilt several times, as recent excavations have shown. Herod the Great made it his winter residence and died here.

**Jersey** England. Largest of the Channel Is., 15 m. W of the French coast. Area 45 sq. m. Pop. (1961) 63,345. Cap. St Helier (S coast). The island has a southward slope, with some fine cliff scenery in the N, and a mild climate, and has become very popular with holidaymakers. The original home of Jersey cattle and woollen 'jerseys'; the knitting of the latter is no longer important. Exports early potatoes and tomatoes. French is the official language, but English is commonly spoken.

**Jersey City** USA. Industrial town in New Jersey on the peninsula between the Hackensack and the Hudson rivers, opposite Manhattan, with which it is connected by ferry, tunnel, and subway. Pop. (1960) 276,101. Meat packing, oil refining. Manufactures foundry and paper products, metal goods, ink, chemicals, cigarettes, etc.

**Jerusalem** Israel/Jordan. Ancient city in central Palestine, in hill country at a height of 2,500 ft; formerly capital of the British mandated territory of Palestine, but since 1948 divided into the new city (Israel) and the old city (Jordan). Pop. (new city) 181,000; (old city) 60,000. Holy to both Jews and Christians; contains several Muslim shrines. Most of the sacred places of the three religions are in the old city, which is enclosed by walls built in the 16th cent. by Selim I, and contains the 7th-cent. Mosque of Omar (on the site of Solomon's temple) near which is the Wailing Wall, sacred to the Jews. Other places of religious interest are the Church of the Holy Sepulchre, around which are monasteries and chapels of various Christian denominations, the Garden of Gethsemane, and the Mt of Olives. In the new city (W), built mainly since the mid 19th cent., are the 14th-cent. citadel, the former buildings of the Israeli parliament, the Archaeological Museum, and many churches and synagogues. Here, too, are the city's modern industries, which include printing, metal working, and the manufacture of pharmaceutical and food products and leather goods.

The history of Jerusalem probably extends through more than 4,000 years; David made it his capital, Solomon developed it and built the Temple. In 586 B.C. it was taken by Nebuchadnezzar and many of its inhabitants were deported to Babylon, but its walls were rebuilt by Nehemiah (c. 444 B..C). It was again captured by Alexander the Great (332 B.C.), by Ptolemy I of Egypt (320 B.C.), and by Antiochus Epiphanes (168 B.C.), who destroyed the city and the Temple. Under Herod the Great the Temple was rebuilt, the fortifications restored and a new city was created, only to be destroyed yet again by Titus in A.D. 70; sixty years later Hadrian established the city of Aelia Capitolina on the site, with a temple to Jupiter in the place of the earlier Jewish Temple. In the 4th cent. under Constantine the Church of the Holy Sepulchre was built where the present church stands, but in the 7th cent. the Muslims took Jerusalem, made it one of their most sacred cities after Mecca, and erected the Mosque of Omar. Apart from the period after its capture by the Crusaders (1099–1187), the city remained almost continuously in Muslim hands, from 1517 under the Turks, until taken by the British in 1917. After the partition of Palestine the new city was made capital of Israel (1950). The new building of the Knesset (the Israeli Legislative Assembly) was inaugurated in 1966. After the Israeli-Arab war (1967), the entire city was occupied by Israeli forces.

**Jervis Bay** Australia. Inlet on the coast of New South Wales, with two small peninsulas to the N and S of the entrance. Part of the S peninsula and harbour was transferred to the Commonwealth as an outlet port (1915), 85 m. ENE of the Australian Capital Territory (♢ Canberra); area 28 sq. m.

**Jesselton** ♢ Kota Kinabalu.

**Jethou** ♢ Channel Islands; Guernsey.

**Jewish AR USSR.** Autonomous Region in the Khabarovsk Territory, RSFSR, bordered (S) across the Amur R. by Heilungkiang (China). Area 13,895 sq. m. Pop. (1968) 174,000 (128,000 Russians, 15,000 Jews, 14,000 Ukrainians). Cap. Birobidzhan. Agriculture (cereals, soya beans) is important. Also some lumbering and mining. Established as a Jewish National District 1928. Became an Autonomous Region 1934.

**Jhang-Maghiana** Pakistan. Town in W Pakistan 120 m. WSW of Lahore. Pop.

(1961) 94,971. Manufactures textiles, pottery, leather and metal goods, etc. Trade in cereals, wool.

**Jhansi** India. Market town and railway junction in Uttar Pradesh 130 m. SW of Kanpur. Pop. (1961) 140,217. Trade in grain, oilseeds, etc. Manufactures brassware. Founded in the 17th cent.

**Jhelum** Pakistan. Town in W Pakistan, on the Jhelum R. 103 m. NNW of Lahore. Pop. (1961) 52,585. Trade in timber. Manufactures textiles.

**Jhelum River.** The most westerly of the 5 rivers of the Punjab, 450 m. long, rising in Kashmir and flowing first NW past Srinagar, then W and generally SSW into W Pakistan, across the plains of the Punjab to join the Chenab R. Much used for irrigation. Near its banks Alexander the Great defeated Porus (326 B.C.). The Mangla Dam (W Pakistan), the world's largest earth-filled dam, built to store water for hydroelectric power and irrigation, was inaugurated 1967.

**Jibuti** ♢ Djibouti.

**Jidda (Jiddah, Jedda)** Saudi Arabia. Chief seaport of Hejaz, on the Red Sea 40 m. W of Mecca. Pop. 150,000. Principal port of entry for pilgrims to Mecca, said to exceed 100,000 annually, and connected by a good motor road with the city. Also imports manufactured goods for Saudi Arabia. Walled town with a large souk (bazaar).

**Jihlava** Czechoslovakia. Town in W Moravia, on the Jihlava R. 50 m. WNW of Brno. Pop. (1967) 38,000. Once important for silver mining, now an industrial and commercial centre. Manufactures textiles, leather goods, furniture, etc. Trade in cereals, timber.

**Jinja** Uganda. Lake port on the N shore of L. Victoria, at the outlet of the Victoria Nile near the Owen Falls and dam. Pop. (1961) 29,741. Linked by rail with Kampala (45 m. NE). Has expanded rapidly owing to industrial development resulting from the Owen Falls hydroelectric scheme (opened 1954). Copper smelting, sugar refining, brewing. Manufactures textiles, tobacco products, etc.

**Joachimsthal** ♢ Jachymov.

**João Pessôa** Brazil. Formerly Paraíba. Capital of Paraíba state, 11 m. above the mouth of the Paraíba R. (NE). Pop. (1960) 135,820. Exports (through its outport Cabedelo) sugar, cotton. Manufactures cement, footwear, cigars, etc. Renamed

(1930) in honour of a patriot killed in the Vargas revolution.

**Jodhpur** India. Commercial town and railway junction in Rajasthan 175 m. WSW of Jaipur. Pop. (1961) 224,760. Formerly capital of the princely state of Jodhpur. Trade in cotton, wool, hides, etc. Manufactures textiles, tools, cutlery, etc. Dominated by a red sandstone fort containing the handsome Maharajah's palace. University (1962). Gave its name to a type of riding breeches, introduced into Britain in the late 19th cent. Founded in the mid 15th cent.

**Jogjakarta (Djokjakarta)** Indonesia. Town near the S coast of Java 170 m. WSW of Surabaya. Pop. (1961) 313,000. In an intensively cultivated region producing rice, sugar-cane, rubber, tobacco, etc. Manufactures textiles, tobacco products, leather; also famous for batik work. Seat of the Gadjah Mada University (1949) and the State Institute of Islam (1960). Provisional capital of Indonesia 1945–50.

**Johannesburg** S Africa. Largest city in the republic, in the Transvaal, on the Witwatersrand 800 m. NE of Cape Town at a height of 5,750 ft. Pop. (1967) 1,294,800 (773,400 Bantu, 407,000 whites). Centre of the world's richest goldmining area. A conurbation of large mining towns stretches from Krugersdorp (W) to Springs (E). Mainly modern; many skyscrapers and notable buildings, e.g. City Hall, Municipal Art Gallery, Public Library, S African Institute of Medical Research. Anglican and Roman Catholic cathedrals. Seat of the University of Witwatersrand (1922), formerly the School of Mines and Technology (1903). Engineering, diamond cutting. Manufactures textiles, foodstuffs, furniture, etc. Important rail, road, and air transport centre. Founded (1886) after the discovery of gold; grew rapidly and became S Africa's chief commercial and industrial centre.

**Johnson City.** Town in Tennessee 85 m. ENE of Knoxville. Pop. (1960) 31,935. Manufactures hardwood flooring, textiles, plastics, etc.

**Johnstone** Scotland. Small burgh in Renfrewshire 3 m. WSW of Paisley. Pop. (1961) 18,369. Industrial centre. Manufactures machine tools, carpets, laces, etc.

**Johnstown** USA. Industrial town in Pennsylvania at the confluence of the Conemaugh R. and Stony Creek, 53 m. E of Pittsburgh. Pop. (1960) 53,949. Manufactures machinery, iron and steel goods, chemicals, etc. Coalmining in the neighbourhood. Named after Joseph Jahns, a Swiss pioneer settler (1791).

**Johore** Malaysia. The most southerly state of Malaya, separated from Singapore island by the narrow Johore Strait. Area 7,330 sq. m. Pop. (1967) 1,297,962. Cap. Johore Bahru. Generally low-lying and forest-covered. Produces rubber, copra, pineapples, iron ore, bauxite. First came under British protection in 1885.

**Joinvile (Joinville)** Brazil. Industrial town in Santa Catarina state (SE). Pop. 56,500. Brewing, maté processing. Manufactures textiles, plastics, furniture, etc. Exports (through its port, São Francisco do Sul) timber, maté tea, etc. Founded by German settlers in the mid 19th cent.

**Joliet** USA. Railway centre and industrial town in NE Illinois on the Des Plaines R. Pop. (1960) 66,780. Manufactures machinery, chemicals, paper, etc. Railway engineering, oil refining. Bituminous coalmines and limestone quarries in the neighbourhood. Named after Louis Joliet, a French-Canadian explorer.

**Jönköping** Sweden. Capital of Jönköping county, at the S end of L. Vätter. Pop. (1968) 53,815. Industrial town; the chief centre of Swedish match manufacture. Also manufactures paper, textiles, machinery.

**Jonquière** Canada. Town in Quebec 9 m. W of Chicoutimi. Pop. (1966) 29,663. Large pulp mill; railway engineering. Named after the Marquis de la Jonquière.

**Joplin** USA. Industrial town in SW Missouri 140 m. S of Kansas City. Pop. (1960) 38,958. Manufactures leather goods, mining machinery, etc. Formerly an important centre of lead and zinc mining.

**Joppa** ◊ *Jaffa.*

**Jordan.*** Independent kingdom of SW Asia. Area 36,715 sq. m. Pop. (1967) 2,100,801. Cap. Amman. Lang. Arabic. Rel. predominantly Muslim. Officially named the Hashemite Kingdom of the Jordan. Formerly Transjordan.

Borders on Syria (N), Iraq (NE), Saudi Arabia (E and S), and Israel (W). Some agriculture in the W, but most of Jordan is desert; the country has few resources, the value of imports is many times that of exports, and the economy has been sustained only by means of financial aid from abroad – largely from the US and Britain. For administrative purposes it is divided into the Desert Area and the districts of Ajlun, Amman, Balqa, Karak, Ma'an, Jerusalem, Hebron, Jenin, Zarqa.

TOPOGRAPHY, CLIMATE, *etc.* Part of Jordan lies W of the Jordan R. and includes most of the uplands of Samaria and Judaea and the old city of Jerusalem, the former rising to 3,087 ft in Mt Ebal, near Nablus. To the E of the hills is the deep Jordan valley, El Ghor, leading S to the Dead Sea, 1,286 ft below sea level, and then via the Wadi Araba to the Gulf of Aqaba, where Jordan has its single seaport, Aqaba: the entire depression forms part of the Great Rift Valley which extends into E Africa. To the E of the Jordan valley the country becomes a barren plateau which merges with the Syrian Desert. In the hill country of the W the climate is of a dry Mediterranean type, with an average of 20 ins. of rain falling mainly in winter and spring, followed by a hot rainless summer; on the plateau the rainfall amounts to only a few ins.

RESOURCES, PEOPLE, *etc.* Wheat and barley are grown in the W, vines in the extreme N, and there is usually a surplus of fruit and vegetables for export, while numbers of sheep and goats are raised; only about 5 per cent of the land, however, is under cultivation. Chief mineral resources phosphates (an important export) and potash from the Dead Sea. Amman, the only town with more than 200,000 inhabitants, is connected by motor roads with the other chief towns, which include Jerusalem (old city), Nablus, and Zarqa. The Hejaz railway is out of use S of Ma'an, but plans have been made (1963) to rebuild the line to Mecca and Medina (Saudi Arabia).

Almost half the population occupy 6 per cent of the area, in the W; there are about 55,000 nomadic Bedouin, while the 550,000 refugees from Israel, victims of the Arab-Jewish war of 1948 who were accommodated mainly in emergency camps, have placed a severe strain on the economy. The great majority of the people are Sunni Muslims, and there are some 40,000 Christian Arabs. The legislature consists of a lower house of 60 members elected by male suffrage and a senate of 30 members nominated by the King.

HISTORY. Part of the Ottoman Empire from the 16th cent. In 1923 Transjordan became a semi-independent emirate under Abdullah ibn Hussein whilst remaining a British mandated territory. In 1946, after supporting the Allies in the 2nd World War, the mandate was terminated and Abdullah took the title of King of the Hashemite Kingdom of Jordan. In 1950, after its troops had occupied much of E central Palestine, designated by the UN as Arab territory, that area was formally annexed; lying W of the Jordan, it has since been known as W Jordan, the former emirate being E Jordan. Suffered complete military defeat by Israel in the short Arab-Israeli war of June 1967; after the war all Jordanian territory W of the Jordan R. was occupied by Israeli forces.

**Jordan River.** Principal and only perennial river of Israel and Jordan, about 200 m. long, rising in several headstreams in Syria and Lebanon and flowing through the marshy L. Hula to the Sea of Galilee (L. Tiberias). It then meanders S through the depression known as El Ghor to the Dead Sea, 1,286 ft below sea level, both lying in a great rift valley. It thus descends about 3,000 ft in its short course and is unnavigable; in its lower reaches it is muddy and foul. Hydroelectric power station at Naharayim. During the British mandate of Palestine it formed much of the latter's E border, but after the partition (1948) a considerable area W of the river was annexed by Jordan; it now forms part of the Israel–Jordan and Israel–Syria borders. The main crossing point is the Allenby Bridge on the Jerusalem–Amman road (Jordan).

**Jos** Nigeria. Town on the ◊ *Bauchi (Jos) Plateau* at a height of 4,100 ft, 145 m. SSE of Kano. Pop. (1960) 39,000. A major centre of the tin-mining industry. Linked by rail with the main line from Port Harcourt to Kaduna.

**Jostedalsbre** Norway. Largest snowfield on the mainland of Europe, about 340 sq. m. in area, W of the Jotunheim Mountains, rising to 6,834 ft. Many glaciers descend from it into neighbouring valleys. At the E foot is the village of Jostedal.

**Jotunheimen (Jotunheim Mountains)** Norway. In Norwegian, 'Home of the Giants'. Highest mountain range in Scandinavia, between Jostedalsbre and Gudbrandsdal, the loftiest peaks being Galdhöpiggen (8,097 ft) and Glittertind (8,045 ft).

**Juan de Fuca Strait** Canada/USA. Channel 80 m. long and 15 m. wide, separating Vancouver Island (Canada) from the state of Washington (USA). Named after a Greek sailor, Apostolos Valerianos, reputed to have discovered it (1592) while serving Spain as Juan de Fuca. Rediscovered by Capt. Charles Barkley 1787.

**Juan Fernández Islands** S Pacific Ocean. Group of 3 volcanic islands belonging to Chile 400 m. W of Valparaiso. The largest is Más-a-Tierra (in Spanish, 'Nearer Land'; area 36 sq. m.; pop. about 500; main occupation lobster fishing). Más-a-Fuera ('Farther Out') is 100 m. W; it is well wooded. The Santa Clara islet lies SW of Más-a-Tierra. Alexander Selkirk's stay on Más-a-Tierra (1704–8) is supposed to have inspired Defoe's *Robinson Crusoe*.

**Juan-les-Pins** France. Fashionable resort in the Alpes-Maritimes department, on the French Riviera just SSW of Antibes, of which it forms part.

**Jubaland** Somalia. Former province of Kenya; ceded to Italy in 1925, incorporated into Italian Somaliland in 1926. Semi-arid except for the fertile Juba valley. Main occupation cattle and camel rearing.

**Juba River** Somalia. River over 1,000 m. long formed by the union of the Ganale and the Dawa rivers, rising in the Ethiopian Highlands, leaving Ethiopia near Dolo, flowing S across Somalia, and entering the Indian Ocean 10 m. NE of Kismayu. Navigable for dhows as far upstream as Bardera. Cotton, maize, and rice cultivated in the valley.

**Jubbulpore** ◊ *Jabalpur*.

**Júcar River** Spain. River 314 m. long in the E, rising in the Montes Universales, flowing S past Cuenca and then turning E to enter the Mediterranean at Cullera. Used for irrigation and hydroelectric power.

**Juiz de Fora** Brazil. Industrial town in Minas Gerais, on the Rio de Janeiro–Belo Horizonte road and railway, and on the Paraibuna R. Pop. 136,000. Manufactures textiles, but esp. knitted goods. Sugar refining. Brewing. Trade in coffee, tobacco, etc.

**Jujuy** Argentina. Capital of Jujuy province in the NW, at a height of 4,127 ft, on the Río Grande de Jujuy. Pop. 52,000. Flour milling, sawmilling. Trade in wheat, maize, livestock. Founded 1593.

**Jullundur** India. Town and railway junction in Punjab 50 m. ESE of Amritsar. Pop. (1961) 222,569. Manufactures textiles,

hosiery, agricultural implements, etc. Trade in wheat, sugar-cane, cotton.

**Jumet** Belgium. Town in Hainaut province 3 m. N of Charleroi. Pop. (1968) 28,637. Coalmining. Manufactures glass.

**Jumna (Jamuna, Yamuna) River** India. Chief tributary of the Ganges R., 860 m. long, rising in the Himalayas in the Tehri-Garhwal district (Uttar Pradesh) and flowing generally SW and then S along the Punjab–Uttar Pradesh border, past Delhi, turning SE past Agra and Etawah to join the Ganges just below Allahabad. It feeds the E and W Jumna Canals, which irrigate large areas, near the point where it leaves the Siwalik Hills for the plains.

**Junagadh (Junagarh)** India. Town in Gujarat 58 m. SSW of Rajkot. Pop. (1961) 74,298. Trade in cotton, millet, sugar-cane, etc. Manufactures pharmaceutical products, metal goods, etc. Was capital of the former princely state of Junagadh.

**Jundiai** Brazil. Industrial town in São Paulo state, 33 m. NW of São Paulo. Pop. 85,000. Manufactures cotton goods, steel, matches, pottery. Trade in grapes, coffee, grain.

**Juneau** USA. State capital of Alaska, in the SE, on the Gastineau Channel. Pop. (1960) 6,797. An ice-free port. Salmon canning, sawmilling. Founded (1880) after the discovery of gold in the district. Named after Joe Juneau, who helped to start the gold rush.

**Jungfrau** Switzerland. Mountain (13,642 ft) in the Bernese Oberland 11 m. SSE of Interlaken. First ascended (1811) by the Meyer brothers. A rack railway, the highest in Europe, was built (1896–1912) from Kleine Scheidegg to the Jungfraujoch, the col between the Jungfrau and the Mönch, whence there are magnificent views.

**Junín** Argentina. Market town and railway junction 145 m. W of Buenos Aires. Pop. 60,000. Trade in grain, cattle. Railway engineering. Manufactures pottery, furniture.

**Jura** France. Department in the E, in Franche-Comté, bordered on the E by Switzerland. Area 1,951 sq. m. Pop. (1968) 233,547. Prefecture Lons-le-Saunier. Largely occupied by the Jura (Mountains) and drained by the Doubs and Ain rivers, it is an agricultural department; cereals etc. grown (W); wines and cheeses (Gruyère, etc.) produced. Chief towns Lons-le-Saunier, Dôle.

**Jura** France/Switzerland. System of parallel

mountain ranges about 150 m. long and 40 m. wide along the Franco-Swiss border, on average 2,000–2,500 ft in height but rising to 5,653 ft in Crêt de la Neige and 5,643 ft in Reculet. Extends through the French departments of Jura, Doubs, and Ain and the Swiss cantons of Basel, Solothurn, Neuchâtel, and Vaud, and continues NE beyond the Rhine R. as the Swabian Jura and the Franconian Jura. Belonging geologically to the Alpine system, the limestone formations of the Jura gave the Jurassic period its name. The Doubs and Ain rivers rise here, draining longitudinal valleys on the French side, and there are many transverse gorges (*cluses*); the waterfalls, limestone caves, and forested slopes attract many tourists. An important region for the manufacture of watches and clocks, esp. at La Chaux-de-fonds and Le Locle, both in Switzerland.
**Jura** Scotland. Island in Argyllshire, in the Inner Hebrides, separated from the mainland by the Sound of Jura. Area 147 sq. m. Pop. (1961, with island of Colonsay) 420. Crossed by a range of hills rising to 2,571 ft in the Paps of Jura. Main occupations fishing and crofting. Off the N coast, between Jura and Scarba, is the whirlpool of Corrievreckan.

**Juramento River** ⟡ *Salado River*.
**Juruá River** Brazil/Peru. River 1,200 m. long, rising in E Peru near the Brazil frontier, flowing generally NE through dense forests, and joining the Amazon (Solimões) below Fonte Boa.
**Jutland** (Danish **Jylland**). Peninsula of N Europe bounded by the Skagerrak (N), the Kattegat and Little Belt (E), and the North Sea (W), comprising the continental part of Denmark and most of the German *Land* of Schleswig-Holstein; at the N end separated by Lim Fiord from Mors, Vendsyssel and Thy islands. Area (Danish Jutland) 11,400 sq. m. The peninsula is low-lying, rising to only 564 ft, with sand dunes on the W coast and fiords on the E coast. Principal occupation dairy farming, esp. in the more fertile E half. The biggest naval engagement of the 1st World War, the Battle of Jutland, was fought off NW Jutland (1916).
**Jyväskylä** Finland. Town in the Vaasa province, near the N end of L. Päijänne 80 m. NNE of Tampere. Pop. (1968) 55,328. Railway junction. Centre of a wood-pulp, paper, and plywood industry. Also manufactures matches, margarine. University (1958).

# K

**K2** ◊ *Godwin Austen.*

**Kabardino-Balkar ASSR USSR.** Autonomous republic of the RSFSR, on the N slopes of the Caucasus. Area 4,825 sq. m. Pop. (1970) 589,000. Cap. Nalchik. Contains Mt Elbruz (18,481 ft), the highest peak in the Caucasus and in Europe. Cereals cultivated. Cattle and horses raised. Important molybdenum and tungsten mining at Tyrny Auz.

**Kabinda** ◊ *Cabinda.*

**Kabul** Afghanistan. Capital of Afghanistan and of Kabul province, on the Kabul R. 140 m. WNW of Peshawar (Pakistan), with which it is linked through the Khyber Pass. Pop. (1965) 450,000. In a valley at a height of 5,900 ft just below the Kabul R. gorge. The commercial and cultural centre of Afghanistan. Manufactures textiles, leather, footwear, matches, furniture, etc. University (1932). Just W of the city is the tomb of Baber, who made it the capital of the Mogul Empire (1504). Long of strategic importance; the major invasions of India by Alexander the Great, Genghis Khan, Baber, and others passed through it.

**Kabul River** Afghanistan. River 315 m. long, rising in the Paghman Mountains W of Kabul and flowing generally E to join the Indus R. near Attock (W Pakistan). With its tributaries it waters Kabul province. Hydroelectric plant at Sarobi.

**Kabwe** Zambia. Formerly Broken Hill – named after Broken Hill (Australia). Administrative headquarters of the Central Province, 70 m. N of Lusaka on the railway. Pop. (1961) 31,000 (inc. about 5,000 Europeans). Mining town, producing lead, zinc and vanadium. Supplied with power from the Mulungushi and Lunsemfwa hydroelectric stations. A skull of prehistoric man, *Homo rhodesiensis*, was discovered here 1921.

**Kabylia** Algeria. Highland coastal region between Algiers and Annaba (Bône). Divided into two areas, Great Kabylia (W) and Little Kabylia (E). Produces olives, figs, wheat, wine, cork. The Kabyles are a Berber people, who long resisted the French; though Muslim, they are monogamous, and the women are unveiled. Poverty is widespread, and male emigration has been considerable, chiefly to Algerian and French towns.

**Kadiyevka** USSR. Town in the Ukrainian SSR, in the Donets basin 28 m. W of Lugansk. Pop. (1970) 137,000. A major coalmining centre. Metallurgical and chemical industries.

**Kaduna** Nigeria. Town in central Nigeria, 45 m. SSW of Zaria. Pop. (1963) 43,000. Railway junction. Manufactures cotton goods, furniture, etc. Trade in cotton, grain, etc.

**Kaesong** N Korea. Town 30 m. NW of Seoul, near the S Korean border. Pop. 200,000. Famous for its porcelain. Trade in ginseng. Capital of Korea in the 10th–14th cent. Many temples and other ancient buildings were destroyed in the Korean War (1950–51).

**Kaffa** Ethiopia. Forested highland province (SW) at a height of 8,000 ft, with peaks rising to over 10,000 ft, bordering on Sudan. Area 19,000 sq. m. Pop. 1,500,000. Main waterway the Omo R. (E), emptying into L. Rudolf. Home of the coffee plant, growing wild on the mountain slopes ('coffee' probably derives from 'Kaffa'). Produces coffee, cereals, beeswax. Formerly an independent kingdom. Conquered by Menelik and incorporated into Ethiopia 1897.

**Kafue River** Zambia. River 600 m. long rising on the Congo (Kinshasa) frontier W of Lubumbashi (Elisabethville), flowing generally S and E, and joining the Zambezi R. just below Chirundu (Rhodesia). In its lower course it flows through the Kafue Gorge, site of a projected hydroelectric power station.

**Kagera River.** River 300 m. long in central Africa formed by the union of the Ruvuvu and the Nyavarongo rivers, flowing N along the Rwanda–Tanzania frontier, turning E and forming part of the Tanzania–Uganda frontier, and entering L. Victoria near the frontier.

**Kagoshima** Japan. Capital of Kagoshima prefecture, in S Kyushu on the W coast of Kagoshima Bay. Pop. (1965) 328,444. Minor seaport. Near by is the volcanic peak Sakurajima. Manufactures textiles, metal goods, etc. Important in feudal times.

**Kaieteur Falls** ◊ *Essequibo River.*

**Kaifeng** China. Historic city in Honan province, near the Hwang-ho 45 m. E of Chengchow. Pop. 299,000. Commercial centre. Trade in wheat, groundnuts, fruits, etc. Manufactures chemicals, agricultural machinery. Long in danger from Hwang-ho floods, it was nevertheless an important route centre in early times and in the 10th–12th cent. was the Imperial capital. Eclipsed in recent times by Chengchow.

**Kaikoura Ranges** New Zealand. Two mountain ranges in the NE of the S Island: the Inland and the Seaward Kaikouras, running SW–NE and separated by the lower valley of the Clarence R. Highest peak Tapuaenuku (9,465 ft).

**Kailas Range** Tibet. Mountain range in the SW containing the sources of the Indus and the Brahmaputra rivers; N of L. Manasarowar is one of its highest peaks, Kailas (22,028 ft), while at the E end of the range is Lombo Kangra (23,165 ft). Kailas is sacred to both Buddhists and Hindus.

**Kaimanawa Mountains** New Zealand. Range extending 60 m. E and S of L. Taupo, in the centre of the N Island. Rises to 5,665 ft.

**Kainji Dam** ◊ *Niger River.*

**Kairouan (Kairwan, Qairwan)** Tunisia. Muslim holy city 70 m. S of Tunis. Pop. (1966) 82,299. Founded (671) by the Arab conqueror Sidi Okba. A major place of pilgrimage. Several outstanding mosques (open to non-Muslim visitors), esp. the Great Mosque or Mosque of Sidi Okba. Manufactures carpets, rugs, leather goods. Trade in cereals, olives, wool.

**Kaiserslautern** Federal German Republic. Industrial town in the Rhineland-Palatinate, on the Lauter R. 30 m. W of Ludwigshafen. Pop. (1963) 86,900. Road and rail junction. Manufactures textiles, tobacco products, furniture, etc. Name derived from the Emperor (Kaiser) Frederick I, who built a castle here in the 12th cent.

**Kakinada** India. Formerly Cocanada. Seaport in Andhra Pradesh 250 m. ESE of Hyderabad. Pop. (1961) 122,865. Exports cotton, groundnuts, etc. Cotton and flour milling.

**Kalahari (Kalahari Desert).** Semi-desert region at a height of 3,000–4,000 ft, mainly in Botswana. Mean annual rainfall 5–10 ins. The Molopo R. and other streams dry up as they cross the region. Vegetation principally short grass; scattered acacias and thorn bushes. Home of the nomadic Bushmen; some cattle and sheep are reared. The Kalahari National Park (SW) has gemsbok, springbok, ostriches, and other native fauna.

**Kalámai (Kalamáta)** Greece. Capital of the Messenia *nome* in the SW Peloponnese, port on the Gulf of Messenia. Pop. (1961) 38,007. Exports citrus fruits, olives, and other local produce. Flour milling. Manufactures cigarettes.

**Kalamazoo** USA. Industrial town in Michigan, on the Kalamazoo R. 48 m. S of Grand Rapids. Pop. (1960) 82,089. Chief industry paper making. Manufactures pharmaceutical products, fishing tackle, etc. The name is a shortened form of 'Kee-Kalamazoo' ('Where the Water Boils in the Pot'), applied to the river by local Indian tribes.

**Kalat** Pakistan. Division of W Pakistan, in the SW, bounded by Afghanistan (N), the Arabian Sea (S), and Iran (W). Area 98,975 sq. m. Pop. 589,000. Generally mountainous and infertile. Cereals and fruit produced in the valleys. The former princely state of Kalat, in Baluchistan, nominally under the Khan of Kalat, had a much smaller area than the present Division.

**Kalemie** Congo (Kinshasa). Formerly Albertville (renamed 1966). Town and port in the E, on the W shore of L. Tanganyika, linked by rail with the interior via Kabalo (on the Lualaba R.) and by lake steamer with Kigoma (Tanzania) – terminus of the railway from Dar-es-Salaam. Pop. 12,000. Manufactures cotton goods.

**Kalgan** China. Former capital of Chahar province, 100 m. NW of Peking in Hopei province. Pop. 229,000. Commercial and route centre, often termed the 'gateway to Mongolia', linked by road through Inner Mongolia with Ulan Bator (Mongolia). Trade in tea, sugar, cotton goods, etc. from China, and hides, wool, etc. from Mongolia. Manufactures cotton goods. Tanning. Divided into Chinese and Mongol sections.

**Kalgoorlie** Australia. Goldmining town in Western Australia 340 m. ENE of Perth. Pop. (Kalgoorlie-Boulder, 1966) 19,892. First proclaimed a town in 1895 following the Coolgardie gold rush of 1892, mining having begun in 1893. Water is piped here nearly 350 m. from Mundaring Weir in the Darling Range, and power is generated by a local plant with coal from Collie (Western Australia). Junction on the Trans-

Australian Railway. Airport. Flying Doctor centre. Combined with Boulder 1947.

**Kalimantan** Indonesia. The Indonesian part of the island of ♦ *Borneo*. ♦ *Indonesia*.

**Kalinin** USSR. Formerly Tver. Capital of the Kalinin region (RSFSR), at the confluence of the Volga and the Tversta rivers 105 m. NW of Moscow. Pop. (1970) 345,000. Industrial centre and river port. Manufactures railway rolling stock, textiles, clothing, plastics, leather goods, etc. Founded in the 12th cent. as Tver, it was capital of the independent principality of Tver from *c.* 1240 till nearly the end of the 15th cent. Renamed, along with the region, in 1933 in honour of M. I. Kalinin (1875–1946), former president of the USSR.

**Kaliningrad** USSR. Formerly Königsberg. Capital of the Kaliningrad region (RSFSR), on the Pregel R. near its mouth in the Frisches Haff. Pop. (1970) 297,000. Ice-free Baltic seaport, linked by deep-water channel 29 m. long with the outport of Baltiisk. Exports grain, flax, lentils, timber, etc. Also an important industrial centre. Paper and flour milling. Manufactures machinery, chemicals, food products, etc. Many of its old buildings, inc. the 14th-cent. Gothic cathedral, were damaged in the 2nd World War. Immanuel Kant (1724–1804) was born here and taught at the university, which was founded (1544) as a Lutheran institution and was housed in new buildings in 1865. The city itself grew up (as Königsberg) around the castle built (1255) by the Teutonic Knights, consisting at first of three separate towns, Altstadt, Löbenicht, and Kneiphof (united 1724). Joined the Hanseatic League 1340. Residence of the grand masters of the Teutonic Knights from 1457 and of the dukes of Prussia 1525–1618. Became capital of the province of E Prussia. Renamed when the latter passed to the USSR (1946).

**Kalisz** Poland. Ancient Calissia. Town in the Poznań voivodship, on the Prosna R. 60 m. W of Lodz. Pop. (1968) 79,300. Industrial centre. Manufactures textiles, foodstuffs, leather, etc. One of the oldest towns in Poland, having been identified with the Calissia of Ptolemy; many archaeological remains have been found here.

**Kalmar** Sweden. Capital of Kalmar county in the SE, partly on the mainland and partly on a small island in Kalmar Sound, opposite Öland. Pop. (1968) 37,965. Seaport. Shipbuilding. Manufactures matches, paper, etc. The Kalmar Union (1397), by which Sweden, Norway and Denmark were united in one kingdom, was signed in the great 12th-cent. castle (rebuilt in the 16th and 17th cent.).

**Kalmuk ASSR** USSR. Autonomous republic in the SE European RSFSR bounded by the lower Volga R., the Caspian Sea, and the Manych R. Area 29,300 sq. m. Pop. (1970) 268,000. Cap. Elista. Largely barren steppe. Main occupation sheep rearing. Some fishing. Its people, the Kalmuks, are Mongols of Buddhist faith, descendants of 17th-cent. immigrants; originally nomadic, many have been settled by the Soviet government.

**Kaluga** USSR. Capital of the Kaluga region (RSFSR), on the Oka R. 100 m. SSW of Moscow. Pop. (1970) 211,000. Industrial and commercial centre. Sawmilling, brewing, railway engineering. Manufactures iron and steel goods, bricks, matches, glass, etc. Founded in the 14th cent.

**Kalyan** India. Town in Maharashtra 28 m. NE of Bombay. Pop. 59,000. Rice milling. Manufactures rayon, bricks and tiles, etc.

**Kalymnos (Kalimnos)** Greece. Island in the Dodecanese. Area 41 sq. m. Pop. 13,600. Chief town Kalymnos, near the SE coast. Produces olive oil, citrus fruits.

**Kamakura** Japan. Town in the Kanagawa prefecture in central Honshu, 12 m. S of Yokohama. Pop. (1965) 118,329. Mainly residential. Famous for its Daibutsu (Great Buddha), a 13th-cent. bronze figure 42 ft. high. Founded in the 7th cent. Capital of the Minamoto and Hojo shoguns 1192–1333; declined later with the expansion of Tokyo.

**Kamaran Islands.** Group of islands in the Red Sea off the coast of Yemen, until 1963 a dependency of Aden; formerly a Turkish possession, occupied by the British in 1915. Opted to remain with the Southern Yemen Republic in 1967. Area 22 sq. m. Pop 1,500. The main island, Kamaran, has an airfield and a quarantine station for pilgrims to Mecca.

**Kamarlu** ♦ *Artaxata*.

**Kama River** USSR. River 1,200 m. long in the European RSFSR, rising in the N of the Udmurt ASSR, flowing first N and turning E and then S to Perm (Molotov); from here it flows generally SW to join the Volga R. below Kazan. Since the construction of the dam near Perm it has provided hydroelectric power. Navigable for about half the year. Carries a considerable volume of traffic, esp. timber (by ship and raft).

**Kamchatka** USSR. Region in the Khabarovsk Territory, in the extreme NE of RSFSR, including Kamchatka peninsula, the Komandorski Is., and the Chukot and Koryak National Areas. Area 490,425 sq. m. Pop. (1970) 287,000. Chief town Petropavlovsk-Kamchatski. Mountainous, with several volcanoes, 13 of which are active, the highest being Klyuchevskaya Sopka (15,666 ft). Agriculture possible only in the S. Main occupations hunting, fishing. Some of the people are still nomadic.

**Kamenets Podolsky** USSR. Town in the Ukrainian SSR, on the Smotrich R. 95 m. WSW of Vinnitsa. Pop. 38,000. Industrial centre; sawmilling, brewing, etc. Once capital of the province of Podolia.

**Kamensk-Uralski** USSR. Industrial town in the Sverdlovsk region (RSFSR), 80 m. ESE of Sverdlovsk. Pop. (1970) 169,000. Important centre of bauxite mining and aluminium refining. Manufactures machine tools, pipes, etc. Founded 1682. Developed chiefly in the late 1930s.

**Kamet** India. Himalayan peak (25,447 ft) in the SE of the Zaskar Range, in NW Uttar Pradesh near the Tibet border. The first mountain over 25,000 ft to be climbed (by F. S. Smythe, 1931).

**Kamloops** Canada. Town in British Columbia, at the confluence of the N and S Thompson rivers and the junction of the Canadian Pacific and Canadian National railways. Pop. (1966) 24,000. Lumbering. Marketing of livestock, fruit, vegetables. The name is a corruption of the Indian word 'cumcloups' ('meeting of the waters').

**Kampala** Uganda. Capital and chief commercial centre, on the railway from Mombasa (Kenya), 20 m. NNE of Entebbe at a height of 3,900 ft. Pop. (1965) 77,000. The former headquarters of the Kabaka (king) of Buganda are at Mengo, 6 m. SW. On the NW outskirts is the Makerere University College (1961), centre of higher education for E Africa. Coffee and tobacco processing. ◊ *Jinja.*

**Kampen** Netherlands. Town in Overijssel province, on the Ijssel R. near the Ijsselmeer. Pop. (1968) 29,041. Manufactures cigars, enamelware, etc. Gothic church (14th-cent.). Member of the Hanseatic League in the 15th cent.

**Kamyshin** USSR. Town and river port in the Volgograd region (RSFSR), on the Volga R. opposite Nikolayevski. Pop. 55,000. In an agricultural area noted for water melons. Trade in melons, grain, timber. The Volga is dammed here to irrigate a large area and supply hydroelectric power for the lumber and flour mills.

**Kanazawa** Japan. Capital of the Ishikawa prefecture, Honshu, 100 m. NNW of Nagoya. Pop. (1965) 335,825. Industrial centre. Manufactures textiles, machinery, porcelain, lacquer ware, etc. Outstanding landscape garden.

**Kanchenjunga (Kinchinjunga).** Third highest mountain in the world (28,168 ft), in the Himalayas on the Nepal–Sikkim border, visible in all its majestic beauty from Darjeeling. First climbed (1955) by an English expedition.

**Kanchipuram.** India. Formerly (till 1949) Conjeeveram. Sacred Hindu town in Madras, 40 m. WSW of Madras, known as 'the Benares of the South'. Pop. (1961) 92,714. Manufactures silk and cotton fabrics and saris. Remarkable for its many temples, among them those to Vishnu and Siva dating from the Pallava kings of the 7th and 8th cent. A.D., whose capital it was.

**Kandahar** Afghanistan. Capital of Kandahar province and the country's second largest city, 295 m. SW of Kabul at a height of 3,400 ft. Pop. (1965) 115,000. Chief commercial centre in the S, in a fertile region. Textile and fruit-canning industries. The citadel and the tomb of Ahmed Shah are the only noteworthy buildings; about 4 m. W are the ruins of old Kandahar, destroyed by Nadir Shah (1738). It had a violent history, changing hands many times. The first capital of modern Afghanistan in the 18th cent. Occupied by the British 1839–42 and 1879–81.

**Kandavu** ◊ *Fiji Islands.*

**Kandersteg** Switzerland. Village in the Bern canton, at a height of 3,900 ft; the highest station on the railway from Berne to Brig, at the N end of the Lötschberg tunnel. Pop. (1960) 933. Resort, winter-sports centre.

**Kandy** Ceylon. Town in Central Province, on the Mahaweli Ganga at a height of 1,600 ft 60 m. ENE of Colombo. Pop. (1963) 67,768. Important centre of the tea trade, in a scenically beautiful district. Famous for a Buddhist temple where a reputed tooth of Buddha is preserved.

Formerly capital of the kingdom of Kandy, it became British in 1815.

**Kangaroo Island** Australia. Island 90 m. long and 30 m. wide in S Australia, in the Indian Ocean 25 m. S of Yorke Peninsula. Chief settlement Kingscote. Has a large reserve (Flinders Chase) for native flora and fauna. Barley cultivated. Sheep raised. Salt and gypsum produced.

**Kankakee** USA. Town in Illinois on the Kankakee R. 52 m. S of Chicago. Pop. (1960) 27,666. Manufactures agricultural machinery, furniture, stoves, etc.

**Kankakee River** USA. River 230 m. long, rising near South Bend in Indiana, flowing SW and then NW, and joining the Des Plaines R. to form the Illinois R. Used by early settlers as a connecting link between the Mississippi and the Great Lakes.

**Kankan** Guinea. Market town 300 m. ENE of Conakry, with which it is linked by railway. Pop. (1964) 29,100. Trade in rice and other agricultural produce.

**Kano** Nigeria. Chief town in northern Nigeria, 550 m. NE of Lagos. Pop. (1963) 150,000. Trade in cotton, groundnuts, hides and skins, etc. Manufactures cotton goods, leather, furniture, soap, etc. For centuries an important centre of caravan routes; now also an international airport. The new town has developed outside the mud wall 13 m. long surrounding the old town. Occupied by the British (to suppress the slave trade) 1903.

**Kanpur (Cawnpore)** India. City in Uttar Pradesh, on the Ganges R. 44 m. SW of Lucknow. Pop. (1961) 895,106. Important railway and road junction. Leading industrial centre. Manufactures textiles (chiefly cotton goods), leather goods, chemicals, soap, etc. Engineering, flour milling, sugar refining. Trade in grain, oilseeds, cotton, sugar, etc. Seat of an Indian Institute of Technology (1960). Developed quickly after being ceded to the British (1801) and again after the 1st World War. Scene of one of the worst episodes of the Indian Mutiny (1857), when hundreds of women and children were massacred on the river bank after a promise of safe conduct; a memorial church and memorial gardens now stand there.

**Kansas** USA. Central state, bounded by Nebraska (N), Missouri (E), Oklahoma (S), and Colorado (W). Area 82,276 sq. m. Pop. (1970) 2,222,173. Cap. Topeka. Admitted to the Union in 1861 as the 34th state; popularly known as the 'Sunflower' state. Mostly consists of gently undulating prairie land; the highest point is 4,135 ft, near the W border. Climate continental, with extremes of summer heat and winter cold. Mainly agricultural, with over 90 per cent of the area devoted to crops and livestock. Main crop wheat; sorghums and maize also important. Chief minerals petroleum, natural gas, coal. Oil refineries. Manufactures machinery, transportation equipment, food and dairy products. Chief towns Wichita, Kansas City, Topeka. First explored by the Spaniards during Coronado's expedition (1540–41). French explorers came in the 17th cent. Ceded to Spain 1762; transferred to France 1800. Acquired by the USA through the Louisiana Purchase (1803).

**Kansas City (Kansas)** USA. Industrial city at the confluence of the Kansas and the Missouri rivers, opposite Kansas City (Missouri). Pop. (1960) 121,901. Oil refining, food processing. Manufactures chemicals, cars, etc.

**Kansas City (Missouri)** USA. Industrial city on the Missouri R., at the confluence with the Kansas R. Pop. (1960) 475,539. Important market and distribution centre for agricultural produce. Headquarters of the livestock industry. Meat packing, flour milling. Manufactures agricultural machinery, cars, refrigerators, etc. Seat of the University of Kansas City (1929), which became part of the University of Missouri in 1963.

**Kansas River** USA. River 170 m. long in NE Kansas, formed by the union of the Smoky Hill and the Republican rivers, flowing E to join the Missouri R. between Kansas City (Kansas) and Kansas City (Missouri).

**Kansk** USSR. Industrial town in the Krasnoyarsk Territory (RSFSR), on the Kan R. and the Trans-Siberian Railway 110 m. E. of Krasnoyarsk. Pop. 74,000. In a lignite-mining region. Manufactures textiles etc. Sawmilling, food processing.

**Kansu** China. Province in the NW between Tibet and Inner Mongolia. Area 151,000 sq. m. Pop. (1957) 12,800,000 (inc. many Muslims). Cap. Lanchow. Largely rugged mountain and plateau, containing part of the Nan Shan; also suffers from precarious rainfall. Where irrigation is possible, cereals, opium, melons, etc. are grown. Crossed by important caravan routes to Sinkiang-Uighur, Inner Mongolia, and Tibet.

**Kantara, El** ◊ *Qantara, El.*

**Kanye** Botswana. Town in the SE 70 m. NNW of Mafeking (S Africa). Pop. (1964) 34,045. Capital of the Bangwaketse tribe.

**Kaohsiung** Taiwan. Seaport on the SW coast 30 m. S of Tainan. Pop. (1968) 663,388. Exports sugar, rice, salt, etc. Also an industrial centre. Oil refining. Manufactures textiles, chemicals, cement, fertilizers, etc. Developed under Japanese rule (1895–1945).

**Kaolack** Senegal. River port 85 m. ESE of Dakar on the Saloum R. Pop. (1965) 69,500. Linked by rail with the line from Dakar to Bamako (Mali). Market centre. Considerable exports of groundnuts. Saltworks.

**Kapfenberg** Austria. Town in Styria, on the Mürz R. 25 m. NNW of Graz. Pop. (1961) 23,894. Important iron and steel works and paper mills.

**Kaposvár** Hungary. Capital of Somogy county, on the Kapos R. 29 m. NW of Pecs. Pop. (1968) 50,000. In a wine- and tobacco-producing region. Sugar refining, flour milling.

**Kara Bogaz Gol** USSR. Shallow gulf on the E side of the Caspian Sea, in the Turkmen SSR, about 8,000 sq. m. in area, enclosed except for a narrow strait. As a result of rapid evaporation, there are extensive deposits of chemical salts (esp. Glauber's salt), which are exploited.

**Karachayevo-Cherkess** AR USSR. Autonomous region in the S European RSFSR, part of Stavropol Territory. Area 5,442 sq. m. Pop. (1970) 345,000. Cap. Cherkessk. First formed in 1922, a Karachai AR was separated from it in 1926, but this was dissolved (1943) owing to the people's collaboration with the Germans; the present AR was re-established 1957.

**Karachi** Pakistan. Chief seaport and former capital, in W Pakistan on the Arabian Sea NW of the Indus delta. Pop. (1961) 1,912,598. Exports grain, cotton, oilseeds, hides, wool, etc. Also a naval base. Manufactures textiles, chemicals, cement, metal goods. University (1951). Important international airport. Developed rapidly as a port from the mid 19th cent. after harbour improvements and the construction of the railway, and again expanded on becoming capital of Pakistan (1947). In 1948 the city with a surrounding area and some neighbouring islands (total area 812 sq. m.) was made federal territory, but in 1962 this was again incorporated in W Pakistan.

**Karafuto** ◊ *Sakhalin.*

**Karaganda** USSR. Capital of the Karaganda region, Kazakh SSR, 490 m. NNW of Alma-Ata. Pop. (1970) 522,000. Centre of the important Karaganda coal basin, which supplies coking coal to the Ural metallurgical industry. Manufactures iron and steel, cement, etc. Founded 1928. Developed rapidly after the construction of the railway (1931).

**Kara-Kalpak** ASSR USSR. Autonomous republic in NW Uzbek SSR. Area 63,920 sq. m. Pop. (1970) 702,000. Cap. Nukus. Contains parts of the Ust Urt and Kyzyl Kum deserts and the lower basin of the Amu Darya and its delta on the Aral Sea. Cereals, fruits, and cotton cultivated by irrigation along the Amu Darya. Fisheries in the Aral Sea. Became an autonomous region in the Kazakh Autonomous Republic in 1925, and an autonomous republic in 1932, joining the Uzbek SSR 1936.

**Karakoram (Karakorum).** Mountain system in N Kashmir extending about 300 m. NW–SE. Contains some of the world's highest peaks, including Godwin Austen or K2 (28,250 ft) and several others over 24,000 ft, and many great glaciers. Separated from the W Himalayas by the Indus R. The principal pass is the Karakoram Pass (18,290 ft), on the main trade route between Kashmir and China.

**Karakorum** Mongolia. Ruins of the capital of Genghis Khan, on the Orkhon R. 200 m. WSW of Ulan Bator. Established in the early 13th cent. When the capital was moved to Peking by Kublai Khan (1267), the town declined and was later abandoned. About 25 m. NW there had been another Karakorum, capital of the Uighur kingdom in the 8th–10th cent.

**Kara-Kul** USSR. Mountain lake with no outlet, in the Tadzhik SSR, on the plateau between the Pamirs and the Alai Mountains at a height of nearly 13,000 ft, one of the highest in the world. Area 140 sq. m.

**Kara-Kum** USSR. Desert in the Turkmen SSR, S and SE of the Ust Urt plateau and between the Caspian Sea and the Amu Darya. Area 110,000 sq. m. Much of it is covered with shifting sands (the name means 'black sands'), but it contains the Tedzhen and Murgab oases. The Kara-Kum Canal from the Amu Darya, extending 500 m. through the oases to Ashkhabad, was constructed 1954–62 and is used for irrigating an extensive area.

**Kara Sea.** Part of the Arctic Ocean off the N coast of the RSFSR, between Novaya Zemlya and Severnaya Zemlya. Navigable when ice-free, usually for a few weeks in late summer. Receives the Ob and Yenisei rivers. Chief port Novy Port.

**Karbala (Kerbela)** Iraq. Capital of Karbala province, 55 m. SSW of Baghdad. Pop. 61,000. Commercial town and pilgrimage centre for Shia Muslims, with the tomb of Husain, martyr and grandson of Mohammed, who was killed here in 680. Trade in dates, wool, hides, etc.

**Karditsa** Greece. 1. *Nome* in SW Thessaly. Area 936 sq. m. Pop. (1961) 153,007. Mainly agricultural. Cereals cultivated. Livestock raised.
2. Capital of the Karditsa *nome*. Pop. (1961) 18,543. Trade in cereals, vegetables, livestock, etc.

**Karelian ASSR** USSR. Autonomous republic of RSFSR between the White Sea and Lakes Ladoga and Onega, and bounded on the W by Finland. Area 69,000 sq. m. Pop. (1970) 714,000 (Russians, Karelians, and Finns). Cap. Petrozavodsk. It is linked geologically with Finland, and on its surface there are many marshes and over 2,000 lakes; its boundary with the Leningrad region (RSFSR) in the S passes through the largest of these, Ladoga and Onega. Almost 70 per cent of the land consists of coniferous forests, and lumbering, sawmilling, and the manufacture of wood pulp, paper and other wood products (furniture, plywood, veneers, etc.) are the main industries, while hydroelectric power is developed from its rivers. Iron and lead-zinc ores are mined, and mica and various building stones are quarried. Petrozavodsk and other industrial centres are linked by the White Sea–Baltic Canal and the Murmansk Railway, and the former in particular greatly stimulated the economic development of the republic. Considerable fishing both on the White Sea coast and in the lakes and rivers.

The Karelians, who are closely related to the Finns, have been known since the 9th cent. Their territory came under Russian rule, and under the Tsars was backward and ill-developed. Before the Revolution of 1917 it was known as Olonetz province. In 1917 it became part of the RSFSR and in 1923 the Karelian ASSR. After the Soviet-Finnish war (1940) it was increased by nearly all the land ceded by Finland and was made the Karelo-Finnish SSR. In 1946, however, the S part was transferred to the RSFSR, and in 1956 its status was altered to that of an Autonomous Republic within the RSFSR once more.

**Karelian Isthmus** USSR. Strip of land between the Gulf of Finland and L. Ladoga, under Soviet control since the Russo-Finnish War (1939–40), having been incorporated into the Leningrad region (RSFSR). Of great strategic importance for the defence of its chief city, Leningrad; other important town Vyborg.

**Kariba, Lake** Rhodesia/Zambia. Lake along the Zambezi R. on the Rhodesia–Zambia frontier, 175 m. long and 12 m. wide. Created by the building of the Kariba dam across the Zambezi for hydroelectric power development (begun 1955, first power available 1959). The Kariba Dam scheme involved the evacuation of 40,000 Africans from the inundation area, and also large numbers of wild animals (marooned on temporary islands). The installation is linked with Salisbury and Bulawayo (Rhodesia) and with Lusaka and the Copper Belt (Zambia).

**Karl-Marx-Stadt** German Democratic Republic. Formerly (until 1954) Chemnitz. Capital of the Karl-Marx-Stadt district, at the foot of the Erzgebirge 37 m. WSW of Dresden. Pop. (1968) 294,942. An important centre of the textile industry (cotton, wool, rayon, etc.). Also manufactures textile machinery, chemicals, glass, etc. Coal and lignite fields near by. Most of its old buildings were destroyed in the 2nd World War.

**Karlovac** Yugoslavia. Town in Croatia 30 m. SW of Zagreb. Pop. (1961) 40,180. Manufactures textiles, footwear, etc. Trade in grain, wine, honey, timber.

**Karlovy Vary (Ger. Karlsbad, Carlsbad)** Czechoslovakia. Famous spa in W Bohemia, on the Ohře R. 68 m. WNW of Prague. Pop. (1967) 46,000. Many warm springs, the waters being taken for their medicinal properties; also exported. Manufactures porcelain, glass, footwear. Here were framed the Karlsbad Decrees (1819) limiting the freedom of German and Austrian universities after the murder of Kotzebue.

**Karlsbad** ◊ *Karlovy Vary*.

**Karlskoga** Sweden. Industrial town in Örebro county 25 m. W of Örebro. Pop. (1968) 38,203. Manufactures steel, chemicals. In its suburb Bofors, which gave its name to the Bofors gun, there is an important armament works.

**Karlskrona** Sweden. Capital of Blekinge county in the SE, on the Baltic coast 110 m. ENE of Malmö. Pop. (1968) 37,249. Seaport with a fine harbour, inc. dry docks cut out of granite. Exports granite, timber, dairy produce, etc. Air base. Since 1680 the main Swedish naval base. Metal working, brewing, sawmilling, granite quarrying. Manufactures naval equipment.

**Karlsruhe** Federal German Republic. Industrial town in Baden-Württemberg 4 m. E of the Rhine R. and 40 m. WNW of Stuttgart. Pop. (1968) 253,282. Former capital of Baden. Railway engineering. Manufactures machinery, cement, furniture, cosmetics, etc. Linked by canal with the Rhine, it has an important river trade. Severely damaged in the 2nd World War. Birthplace of Karl Benz, the engineer (1844–1929).

**Karlstad** Sweden. Capital of Värmland county, on the N shore of L. Väner and on Tingvalla island at the mouth of the Klar R. Pop. (1968) 53,208. Industrial town and port. Timber, pulp, and textile mills. Manufactures machinery, leather goods, matches, etc. Here the union of Norway and Sweden was dissolved (1905).

**Karnak** United Arab Republic. Village on the E bank of the Nile in the Qena governorate in Upper Egypt. On the N part of the site of ancient Thebes.

**Karnal** India. Town in Punjab, near the Jumna R. 74 m. N of Delhi. Pop. (1961) 72,109. Manufactures cotton goods, footwear, etc.

**Kärnten** ◊ *Carinthia*.

**Kárpathos** Greece. Island in the Dodecanese, in the Aegean Sea about 30 m. SW of Rhodes. Area 112 sq. m. Pop. 6,700. Chief town Pigádhia. Cereals, olives, grapes cultivated. Sheep and goats raised.

**Karpeńision** ◊ *Evritania*.

**Karroo** S Africa. Two semi-desert plateaux in the S of the Cape Province. The Little (Southern) Karroo, at a height of 1,000–2,000 ft, is separated from the coastal plain by the Langeberg range and from the Great (Central) Karroo (N) by the Zwarteberg range. The Great Karroo, at a height of 2,000–3,000 ft, extends as far N as the Nieuwveld range and like the Little Karroo is crossed by ranges of hills. Mainly dry grassland. Sheep and goats reared. Irrigation makes the cultivation of cereals and citrus fruits possible. The dry healthy climate has made some of the towns, e.g. Beaufort West, Graaff Reinet, popular resorts. The High Veld of S Africa, N of the Great Karroo, mainly at a height of 4,000–6,000 ft, is sometimes called the Northern Karroo.

**Kars** Turkey. Capital of Kars province, 105 m. ENE of Erzurum. Pop. (1965) 41,000. Manufactures woollen goods, carpets. Ceded to Russia 1878. Returned to Turkey 1921.

**Karst** Yugoslavia. Arid limestone plateau in the Dinaric Alps (NW), with an uneven topography of ridges and closed hollows, sinks, underground streams, and little surface drainage, and caves containing stalactites and stalagmites, these last being well exemplified at Postojna. The term, derived from the Serbo-Croat *kras*, has been applied to limestone areas of similar topography in other parts of the world.

**Karun River** Iran. River 530 m. long in the SW, rising in the Zardeh Kuh of the Zagros Mountains and flowing generally W, at first through deep gorges, then turning S and entering the plain near Shushtar; divides into two channels which reunite further S, and flows past Ahwaz to enter the Shatt-al-Arab at Khorramshahr. Navigable to Ahwaz.

**Karviná (Karvinná)** Czechoslovakia. Coal-mining town in the Severomoravský region, in the Ostrava-Karviná coal basin 8 m. E of Ostrava. Pop. (1967) 73,000. Associated gas, coke, iron, and chemical industries.

**Karyai** ◊ *Athos, Mount*.

**Kasai** Congo (Kinshasa). Former province, from 1967 divided into W and E Kasai, in the SW, bordering on Katanga. Area 124,000 sq. m. Cap. Luluabourg. An agricultural region, but with some mineral resources, esp. most of the world supplies of industrial diamonds, washed from the many rivers. Food crops cassava, yams, maize, etc. Cotton and coffee also cultivated. Cattle raised. After Congo (Kinshasa) became independent it attempted secession (like Katanga); a Baluba chief was proclaimed king of South Kasai in 1960, but the régime was dissolved in 1961. There were further revolts against the central government in 1962 and 1963.

**Kasai River** Angola/Congo (Kinshasa). River 1,300 m. long, rising in Angola, flowing N as part of the frontier with Congo (Kinshasa), and joining the Congo R., of which it is a main tributary. Navigable for 480 m. above the confluence; a main trade artery, joined by many navigable streams, rich in alluvial diamonds.

**Kashan** Iran. Town 110 m. S of Tehran at a height of 3,200 ft. Pop. (1966) 81,651. In an oasis where wheat, melons, and figs are grown. Famous for rugs and carpets. Also manufactures cotton and silk goods, copperware.

**Kashgar** China. Town in an oasis of W Sinkiang-Uighur A R, at the W end of the Tarim Basin 450 m. SW of Kuldja. Pop. 91,000. A caravan centre linked with the Kirghiz SSR (USSR) by the Torugart Pass. Manufactures textiles, rugs, etc. Trade in wool, cotton, tea, etc. Visited *c.* 1275 by Marco Polo. Taken by the Chinese in 1759, it has remained almost continuously in their hands.

**Kashmir** (officially **Jammu and Kashmir**). State in the N W of the Indian sub-continent, since partition (1947) disputed by India and Pakistan. Area 86,024 sq. m., of which about 31,250 sq. m. in the N and W are occupied by Pakistan. Pop. (Indian area, 1961) 3,560,976.. Capitals Srinagar (summer), Jammu (winter). Almost entirely mountainous, with the Karakoram system separated by the Indus R. from the Himalayas, both extending N W–S E across Kashmir; the former includes such peaks as K 2 (28,250 ft) and Rakaposhi (25,550 ft), while at the W end of the latter is Nanga Parbat (26,660 ft). It is also crossed by the valley of the Upper Jhelum, the beautiful Vale of Kashmir. About 5 per cent of the land is cultivated, and here rice, maize, and wheat are grown; cattle, sheep, and goats are raised. Kashmir is famous for a fine wool (Cashmere) obtained from the undercoat of its goats. The state includes the provinces of Jammu and Kashmir.

Kashmir became part of the Mogul Empire 1586. Ceded to the Afghans 1756. Taken by the Sikhs under Ranjit Singh 1819. Later rulers were Hindu Maharajahs, while the people were predominantly Muslim, so that both India and Pakistan claimed the territory at the partition (1947). The Maharajah acceded to India, fighting broke out, the dispute was brought before the U N and a cease-fire agreement took effect (1949); attempts to arrange a plebiscite, however, failed. In 1956 the constituent assembly of Indian Kashmir declared Jammu and Kashmir to be an integral part of India; meanwhile, the area occupied by Pakistan, known as Azad Kashmir (Free

Kashmir), was administered by a provisional government at Muzaffarabad.

**Kassala** Sudan. Capital of Kassala province, on the Gash R. 255 m. E of Khartoum and 15 m. from the Ethiopian frontier. Pop. (1964) 49,000. On the Sennar–Port Sudan railway. Centre of an important cotton-growing area. Founded (1840) by the Egyptians as a military post. Captured by the dervishes 1885; recovered by the Italians 1894; ceded to Egypt 1897. Briefly in Italian hands during the 2nd World War (1940–41).

**Kassel (Cassel)** Federal German Republic. Industrial town in Hessen, on the Fulda R. 92 m. NNE of Frankfurt. Pop. (1968) 211,586. Manufactures locomotives and railway rolling stock, machinery, scientific and optical instruments, chemicals, textiles, etc. As a centre of aircraft and tank production in the 2nd World War, it was heavily bombed and suffered severe damage, many of its historic buildings being destroyed. Capital of the former electorate of Hesse-Kassel and of the Prussian province of Hesse-Nassau (1866–1945).

**Kastoría** Greece. 1. *Nome* in Macedonia bounded on the N W by Albania. Area 667 sq. m. Pop. (1961) 47,344. Wheat and tobacco cultivated.
2. Capital of Kastoría *nome*, on a peninsula of L. Kastoría 90 m. W of Thessaloníki. Pop. (1961) 9,468. Trade in wheat, wine, etc.

**Katanga** Congo (Kinshasa). Province in the S E bordered by Zambia (E, S), Angola (S W). Area 191,827 sq. m. Pop. 1,853,000. Cap. Lubumbashi (Elisabethville). Mainly comprises the Katanga plateau, at a height of 3,000–6,000 ft. Wooded savannah drained by the Lualaba R. (W headstream of the Congo R.), the Luvua and the Lukuga rivers, and other affluents of the Upper Congo. Food crops cassava, plantains, yams. Cattle raised. Important chiefly for its great mineral wealth, esp. cobalt, copper, uranium. Also produces coal, manganese, silver, zinc. Mining was developed mainly by the Union Minière du Haut Katanga (chiefly Belgian). Main industry the smelting of copper and other metallic ores. Manufactures chemicals. Chief industrial centres Lubumbashi, Jadotville. Linked by rail with Angola and Zambia. After Congo (Kinshasa) became independent (1960) Katanga seceded; Katangan troops fought against the Congolese army and then

385                                                KAYSERI

against UN forces, which invaded Katanga in 1962. The Katangan government accepted proposals for reunification, and the region was reconstituted a province (1967).

**Katerini** Greece. Capital of Pieria *nome*, in Macedonia, 35 m. SW of Thessaloníki. Pop. (1961) 28,824. Agricultural centre. Trade in wheat, vegetables, wine, etc.

**Kathiawar.** India. Peninsula in the W between the Gulfs of Cambay and Kutch. Now part of Gujarat.

**Katmai, Mount** USA. Active volcano (7,000 ft) in S Alaska, in the Aleutian Range, with a crater 3,700 ft deep and 2½ m. across. Erupted violently in 1912; Kodiak Island was blanketed with ash, and the Valley of Ten Thousand Smokes, a region of 72 sq. m. punctured by thousands of fumaroles, was formed. The Katmai National Monument (4,215 sq. m.) was established in 1918.

**Katmandu (Kathmandu)** Nepal. Capital of the kingdom, on the Baghmati R. in the Nepal Valley at a height of 4,270 ft. Pop. 195,000. Royal palaces and many temples, inc. a 16th-cent. wooden temple from which its name (which means 'Wooden Temple') is derived. Founded in the 8th cent. Taken by Gurkhas 1768; has since remained the capital. A new 70 m. highway to the Tibet (Chinese) frontier was opened in 1967.

**Katowice** Poland. Formerly (1953–6) Stalinogrod. Capital of the Katowice voivodship, 44 m. WNW of Cracow. Pop. (1968) 292,300. Important industrial centre and railway junction in a coal- and iron-mining district. Manufactures iron and steel, machinery, chemicals, bricks, etc. Became a town 1867; passed from Germany to Poland (1921) with the partition of Upper Silesia.

**Katrine, Loch** Scotland. Picturesque freshwater lake 8 m. long and 1 m. wide, mainly in SW Perthshire, projecting SE into the Trossachs, and drained by the R. Teith. Made famous by Scott's *Lady of the Lake*. Main source of Glasgow's water supply since 1859, its level having been raised considerably for this purpose.

**Katsina** Nigeria. Town in the N, 90 m. NW of Kano. Pop. (1963) 56,000. Commercial centre and a Hausa cultural centre. Enclosed by a partly ruined mud wall. Trade in groundnuts, cotton. Crafts include metal and leather working, pottery manufacture.

**Kattegat.** Strait 150 m. long and 40–80 m. wide between Sweden and Jutland (Den-

mark), connected on the N to the Skagerrak at the Skaw and on the S to the Baltic Sea.

**Katwijk Aan Zee** Netherlands. Seaside resort in S Holland province, at the mouth of the Old Rhine (Oude Rijn) 5 m. NW of Leiden. Pop. (1968) 34,730.

**Kaufbeuren** Federal German Republic. Town in Bavaria, on the Wertach R. 48 m. WSW of Munich. Pop. (1963) 37,000. Manufactures textiles. Dyeing, printing, brewing, etc.

**Kaunas** (Russian **Kovno**) USSR. Town in the Lithuanian SSR, on the Neman R. at its confluence with the Viliya R. Pop. (1970) 309,000. Manufactures agricultural implements, metal goods, chemicals, textiles, etc. Seat of the University of Vytautas the Great (1922). Since its foundation in the 11th cent. it has often been partly or completely destroyed in war; it was an important commercial centre even in medieval times. Between the two world wars (1918–40) it served as provisional capital of Lithuania (Vilnius (Vilna) being then in the hands of Poland); restored to the USSR 1944.

**Kaválla** Greece. 1. *Nome* in Macedonia on the Aegean Sea, including the offshore island of Thásos, ceded to Greece after the Balkan War of 1912–13. Area 838 sq. m. Pop. (1961) 140,445. Noted for tobacco cultivation.

2. Ancient Neapolis. Capital of Kaválla *nome*, port on the Gulf of Kaválla. Pop. (1961) 44,406. Exports tobacco. Ruled by the Turks until 1912, then three times occupied by Bulgarians. Birthplace of Mehemet Ali (1769–1849), who founded a Turkish school here.

**Kaveri River** ◊ *Cauvery River*.

**Kavieng** ◊ *New Ireland*.

**Kavirondo** Kenya. 1. Shallow gulf in the NE of L. Victoria. Connected to the Lake by a strait 3 m. wide. The port of Kisumu stands on the shore.

2. Area round the Kavirondo gulf. The name derives from the Kavirondo, a local tribe.

**Kawar** ◊ *Bilma*.

**Kawasaki** Japan. Industrial town in Kanagawa prefecture, Honshu, between Tokyo and Yokohama. Pop. (1965) 854,776. Shipbuilding, engineering. Manufactures steel, textiles.

**Kayseri** Turkey. Ancient Caesarea Mazaca. Capital of Kayseri province, just N of Erciyas Daği (12,850 ft) at a height of 3,400 ft. Pop. (1965) 126,700. Manufactures textiles, carpets and rugs, tiles, etc. Trade in grain, fruit, vegetables. Ancient capital of Cappadocia.

**Kazakh SSR (Kazakhstan)** USSR. Second largest constituent republic, in Central Asia, bounded on the E by China. Area 1,048,070 sq. m. Pop. (1970) 12,850,000 (mainly Kazakhs, Russians, and Ukrainians). Cap. Alma-Ata. Essentially a dry steppe region, with the Caspian lowlands, the Ust Urt plateau and the Turanian basin in the W half, and rising in the E and S to the Altai Mountains, the Tarbagatai Range and other highlands of Central Asia. Extends round part of the Caspian and Aral Seas. Contains L. Balkhash. Longest river the Syr Darya, which flows into the Aral Sea. Climate continental, with extremes of summer heat and winter cold; over much of the area the rainfall is 10 ins. annually or less, rising to about 20 ins. only in the mountains. Divided administratively into 16 regions: Akmolinsk, Aktyubinsk, Alma-Ata, Chimkent, Dzhambul, E Kazakhstan, Guryev, Karaganda, Kokchetav, Kustanai, Kzyl-Orda, N Kazakhstan, Pavlodar, Semipalatinsk, Taldy-Kurgan, Uralsk.

The chief occupation was formerly nomadic cattle rearing, and Kazakhstan is still noted for the large numbers of sheep, cattle, and pigs raised on its state and collective farms, but it now also produces important crops of wheat and other cereals, sugar-beet, and cotton. Much virgin land was brought under cultivation in the 1950s and a considerable area is irrigated. Rich in mineral resources: coal is mined in the Karaganda basin, oil along the Emba R. (W), copper at Kounradski and Dzhezkazgan; lead, zinc, nickel, and manganese also produced. Many new industries have been opened up in recent years; principal manufacturing centres Alma-Ata, Karaganda, Semipalatinsk, Chimkent, Petropavlovsk. The region became part of Russian Turkestan in the 19th cent., the Kirghiz ASSR (1920), Kazakh ASSR (1925) – within the RSFSR. Became a constituent republic 1936.

**Kazan** USSR. Capital of the Tatar ASSR (RSFSR), on the Kazanka R. at the confluence with the middle Volga R. Pop. (1970) 869,000. Railway and automobile engineering, oil refining. Manufactures typewriters, musical instruments, chemicals, textiles, etc. Seat of a state university (1804) and a branch of the USSR Academy of Sciences. It is a city where western and eastern influences have mingled, and there are Muslim mosques as well as Orthodox churches; its famous Kremlin has the Suyumbeka Tower (246 ft). Became capital of the Kazan khanate in the 15th cent. Taken by Ivan the Terrible 1552; commercial importance increased thereafter. Suffered severely during the revolution of 1917 and again in the ensuing famine (1921).

**Kazan-retto** ◊ *Volcano Islands.*

**Kazerun** Iran. Town in Fars province, 55 m. W of Shiraz at a height of 2,800 ft. Pop. (1966) 39,758. In a region producing tobacco, rice, opium, cotton. Near by are the ruins of ancient Shapur.

**Kazvin (Qazvin)** Iran. Town in Gilan province, 90 m. WNW of Tehran at the S foot of the Elburz Mountains at a height of 4,150 ft. Pop. (1966) 103,791. Manufactures carpets and rugs, textiles, soap. Trade in silk, rice, etc. Founded in the 4th cent. by Shapur II; made the national capital in the 16th cent. by Tahmasp I. It has been frequently damaged by earthquakes.

**Kearny** USA. Industrial town in New Jersey, on the Passaic R. just E of Newark. Pop. (1960) 34,472. Manufactures metal goods, chemicals, etc.

**Kecskemét** Hungary. Capital of Bács-Kiskun county 50 m. SE of Budapest. Pop. (1968) 74,000. In a fertile fruit-growing region. Trade in fruit, cereals, cattle. Manufactures agricultural implements, wine, brandy, fruit and vegetable preserves, textiles, leather, etc. Birthplace of József Katona, the playwright (1791–1830).

**Kedah** Malaysia. State in NW Malaya bordering NE on Thailand. Area 3,660 sq. m. Pop. (1967) 925,105 (65 per cent Malay, 20 per cent Chinese). Cap. Alor Star. Rice and rubber cultivated. Tin and tungsten mined. Under British protection from 1909, when it was transferred from Thailand, it was one of the unfederated Malay States till 1947.

**Kediri** Indonesia. Town in E Java 50 m. SW of Surabaya. Pop. (1961) 159,000. Commercial centre in a region producing sugar, rice, rubber, coffee, etc.

**Keele** ◊ *Newcastle-under-Lyme.*

**Keelung (Kilung)** Taiwan. Chief seaport, on the N coast 15 m. ENE of Taipei, with which it is connected by railway. Pop. (1968) 294,883. Exports sugar, tea. Shipbuilding, flour milling. Manufactures cement, chemicals, fertilizers.

**Keewatin** Canada. The E mainland District of the NW Territories (except the Melville and Boothia peninsulas), including the islands of Hudson Bay. Area 228,160 sq. m. Pop. 2,400. Chief occupation fur trapping by Indians and Eskimos, who make up the greater part of the scattered population. The name is a Cree Indian word meaning 'the north wind'.

**Keighley** England. Municipal borough in the W Riding of Yorkshire, on the R. Aire 8 m. NW of Bradford. Pop. (1961) 55,852. Important centre of the woollen and worsted industry. Also manufactures machine tools, textile machinery, etc. Within the borough is ◊ *Haworth*.

**Keith** Scotland. Small burgh in Banffshire, on the R. Isla 17 m. WSW of Banff, with Fife Keith on the opposite bank. Pop. (1961) 4,208. Manufactures woollen goods. Whisky distilling. The Roman Catholic church has an altarpiece, *The Incredulity of St Thomas*, presented by Charles X of France. Birthplace of James Gordon Bennett (1795–1872).

**Kelantan** Malaysia. State in NE Malaya bordering (NW) on Thailand. Area 5,750 sq. m. Pop. (1967) 677,205 (90 per cent Malay). Cap. Kota Bharu. Produces rice, rubber, copra. Transferred from Thailand to Britain 1909; one of the unfederated states till 1947.

**Kells** ◊ *Ceanannus Mór*.

**Kelso** Scotland. Small burgh and market town in Roxburghshire, at the confluence of the R. Tweed and the R. Teviot. Pop. (1961) 3,964. Manufactures agricultural implements etc. Important ram sales. Ruins of the 12th-cent. abbey founded by David I. James Thomson, the poet (1700–1748), was born in near-by Ednam.

**Kemerovo** USSR. Formerly Shcheglovsk. Capital of the Kemerovo region, RSFSR, on the Tom R. Pop. (1970) 385,000. Important coalmining centre in the Kuznetsk Basin. Manufactures chemicals, fertilizers, plastics, agricultural machinery, etc. Founded c. 1840.

**Kemi** Finland. Town and port in the Lappi province near the mouth of the Kemi R. 60 m. NNW of Oulu. Pop. (1968) 30,259. Exports timber. Sawmilling.

**Kempten** Federal German Republic. Town in SW Bavaria, on the Iller R. 53 m. SSW of Augsburg. Pop. (1963) 44,500. Chief commercial centre of the Allgäu. Trade in dairy produce, timber. Manufactures textiles, paper, etc.

**Kenadsa** ◊ *Colomb-Béchar*.

**Kendal** England. Municipal borough in Westmorland, on the R. Kent 21 m. N of Lancaster. Pop. (1961) 18,595. Manufactures footwear, textiles, etc. Has a church dating in part from the 13th cent. and the ruins of a Norman castle where Catherine Parr, Henry VIII's last queen, was born. The woollen industry was introduced by Flemish immigrants in the 14th cent., and later the town was noted for a coarse cloth known as 'Kendal green'. Birthplace of Sir Arthur Eddington, the astronomer (1882–1944).

**Kenilworth** England. Urban district in Warwickshire 5 m. SW of Coventry. Pop. (1961) 14,427. Market town. Light engineering etc. Its ruined castle (founded in the 12th cent.) was presented by Queen Elizabeth I to Robert Dudley, Earl of Leicester, who entertained her here; it is described in Scott's *Kenilworth*.

**Kénitra** ◊ *Mina Hassan Tani*.

**Kennedy, Cape** USA. Formerly Cape Canaveral. Cape on the E coast of Florida, 150 m. SSE of Jacksonville. Site of the USAF Missile Test Centre. US earth satellites and lunar and stellar probes have been launched and men put into orbit round the earth and sent to the moon from the site. Renamed after the assassination of President J. F. Kennedy (1963).

**Kennington** England. District in the London borough of Lambeth, with the famous cricket ground, The Oval. Birthplace of Viscount Montgomery of Alamein (1887–    ).

**Kenosha** USA. Industrial town and port in SE Wisconsin, on L. Michigan. Pop. (1960) 67,899. Manufactures cars, furniture, hosiery, etc. First settled in 1832, as Pike Creek. Named Southport in 1837; incorporated in 1850, as Kenosha, an Indian word meaning 'pike' (probably the source of the 1832 name).

**Kensal Green** England. District in NW London, partly in Hammersmith and partly in Kensington, with a cemetery (laid out 1832) containing the graves of many famous men, inc. Thackeray, Trollope, Leigh Hunt, Hood, Wilkie Collins, Balfe, Cardinal Manning.

**Kensington and Chelsea** England. Royal borough of W London (from 1965), mainly residential, comprising the former metropolitan boroughs of Chelsea and Kensington. Pop. (1963) 217,976. Kensington Palace, originally Nottingham House, was purchased by William III, and later Queen Anne, George II, and Queen Victoria, who was born here, resided in it. Its grounds are now Kensington Gardens (274 acres), a public park adjoining Hyde Park, in which are the Round Pond, the Orangery, and the famous *Peter Pan* statue by Frampton; just S of them are the Albert Hall and Albert Memorial. South Kensington is a centre of museums and colleges, inc. the Victoria and Albert, Natural History, and Science Museums, the Royal College of Art, the Imperial College of Science and Technology, and the Royal Geographical Society.

**Kent** England. County in the SE lying between the Thames estuary (N) and the English Channel (S). Area 1,525 sq. m. Pop. (1961) 1,701,083. County town Maidstone. The chalk ridge of the N Downs curves round from the NW, near Westerham, where it exceeds 800 ft, to the white cliffs of Dover, and in the SW is part of the once forested Weald; otherwise, the county is mostly low-lying, and in the S is the almost flat, fertile Romney Marsh, famous for its sheep. Apart from the Thames, the principal rivers are the Medway, Stour, Darent, and Cray. Off the N coast are the Isle of Thanet, Isle of Sheppey, and Isle of Grain, all separated from the mainland by narrow channels or rivers and linked with the mainland by rail and road. Often termed 'the Garden of England', it is well-known for its orchards (apples, cherries), hop gardens, and oast-houses; but there is also considerable cereal cultivation and market gardening. Inland from Deal is the E Kent coalfield. Chalk, sand, and gravel are quarried. In the Medway area there are important cement and paper industries. Brewing is centred chiefly on Maidstone. Chatham has a naval dockyard, Rochester engineering works, Gravesend is a river port, and Dover and Folkestone are linked with the continent by cross-Channel services. Margate, Ramsgate and other coastal towns are popular resorts, while Canterbury is much visited for its famous cathedral, the mission of St Augustine here (597) making it the centre of the English Church. Kent, the first part of the country to be colonized by the Romans, became a kingdom of Anglo-Saxon Britain in the 5th cent. with approximately its present boundaries.

**Kentish Town** England. District in the London borough of Camden, with many workers' homes but also industrialized, a considerable area being occupied by railway sidings and marshalling yards.

**Kentucky** USA. State in S central USA, bounded by Ohio and Indiana (N), by W Virginia and Virginia (E), Tennessee (S), and by Missouri and Illinois (W). The N boundary is formed by the Ohio R. and the W boundary by the Ohio and Mississippi rivers. Area 40,395 sq. m. Pop. (1970) 3,160,555. Cap. Frankfort. Admitted to the Union in 1792 as the 15th state; popularly known as the 'Bluegrass' state, because of the abundance of bluegrass in its central area. Drained by the Licking, Kentucky, Green, and other rivers to the Ohio and Mississippi. The highest area is in the SE, with Big Black Mountain rising to 4,145 ft. Well-known for its limestone caves, the most famous being the Mammoth Cave. The climate is marked by hot summers and short cold winters, when heavy snowfalls may occur. Rainfall moderate and well distributed. Largely agricultural. Chief crops tobacco (by far the most important), maize, wheat, soya beans, apples, and bluegrass seed. Agriculture has suffered considerably from soil erosion. The state has long been famous for its horses. Principal mineral coal; petroleum, natural gas, and fluorspar also important. Leading manufacturing centres Louisville (where the Kentucky Derby is run), Lexington, Covington.

The territory was first explored by the English in 1750. After Daniel Boone's expeditions (beginning 1769), Boonesborough was founded (1775) and many new settlers came in from the E. From 1776 to 1792 it was part of Virginia and then became a separate state. During the American Civil War, Kentucky's loyalties were sharply divided between North and South. In the 1930s unemployment and bad living conditions in the coalfields led to violence and bloodshed, resulting in a US Senate investigation (1937).

**Kentucky River** USA. River 260 m. long, formed by the union of the North Fork and Middle Fork rivers (both rising in the Cumberland Mountains), flowing NW through Kentucky, and joining the Ohio R. at Carrollton.

**Kenya.** Republic in E Africa, member of

the British Commonwealth. Area 224,960 sq. m. Pop. (1968) 9,948,000 (9,671,000 Africans). Cap. Nairobi. Crossed by the equator. Bounded by Ethiopia and Sudan (N), Uganda and L. Victoria (W), Tanzania (S), and by the Indian Ocean and Somalia (E). A coastal strip 10 m. wide (the former Protectorate) extends from the Tanzania frontier to Kipini at the mouth of the Tana R. The N (about three fifths) is arid and sparsely peopled (largely by nomads). The S (far more important) has a low marshy coastal belt, rising to a high plateau dominated by the great volcanic cones of Mt Kenya and Mt Elgon. The W is crossed N–S by the Great Rift Valley, with a chain of lakes inc. Lakes Rudolf (the largest), Baringo, Nakuru, Naivashi, and Magadi. Along the E flanks of the Great Rift Valley are the steep Kikuyu and Laikipia escarpments; farther E are the Aberdare Mountains, rising to 13,000 ft. The SW upland climate is favourable to Europeans, and the region is the principal area of white settlement (the 'white highlands'). The nights are pleasantly cool; at Nairobi the mean annual temperature is only 63° F and the annual range about 7° F (the coastal strip, however, has a mean annual temperature of nearly 80° F). Owing to the range of altitudes, Kenya produces a wide variety of crops, esp. coffee, maize, pyrethrum, sisal, tea in the highlands (SW), and in the lowlands cotton and sugar-cane. Cattle raising is important to the Africans; there has been a noteworthy increase in dairy farming among Europeans also. The forests are mainly in the highlands, at 6,000–10,000 ft, with bamboos at the higher levels, camphor trees and cedars below.

Famous for big game, e.g. large herds of antelope and zebra, also the giraffe, elephant, rhinoceros, lion, leopard, and many other species. Hunting is strictly regulated. The Tsavo National Park and the Nairobi National Park help to preserve wildlife. Little mineral exploitation except the production of carbonate of soda from L. Magadi. Industries have expanded since the 2nd World War, though still on a small scale, e.g. cement manufacture, meat packing, flour milling, coffee and sisal preparation. Principal exports (mainly from European farms) coffee, hides and skins, meat and meat preparations, pyrethrum extract, sisal, tea. The main railway links Mombasa (chief seaport) with Nairobi and continues across Uganda; there are branch lines to L. Magadi, Kisumu, and the N of Tanzania.

Most of the people belong to various Bantu tribes (e.g. Kikuyu, Luo); others are Nilotic (e.g. Kavirondo, Nandi, Suk, Turkana) or Hamitic (e.g. Masai, Somali, Galla). The remainder are Indians, Pakistanis, Goanese (192,000 in all), Arabs (39,000, concentrated in the coastal strip) and Europeans (42,000, mostly British). The lingua franca is Swahili, a Bantu language with many Arabic words.

The coastal strip was long under the influence of Arab traders. Through the Imperial British East Africa Company, Britain leased the N from the Sultan of Zanzibar and began to open up the hinterland towards the end of the 19th cent. The frontier between British E Africa and German E Africa (later Tanganyika, now Tanzania) was fixed in 1890; Kenya became a British Crown Colony (except the leased coastal strip, which became the Kenya Protectorate) in 1920. ⟨⟩ *Jubaland* was ceded to Italy in 1925. White settlers entered in considerable numbers from the early years of the 20th cent. Their interests have frequently conflicted with those of the Africans, largely because of their occupation of extensive areas of land; Kikuyu discontent led to campaigns of violence by the secret Mau Mau organization (1952–4) but these were gradually suppressed. The first elections of African representatives to the Legislative Council took place in 1957 and the state of emergency came to an end in 1960. African leaders played an increasing part in preparations for independence; among political difficulties was a desire for secession on the part of the Arabs in the Protectorate and the Somali in the Northern Province. The former Protectorate was ceded to Kenya in 1963. An independent member of the British Commonwealth since 1963 and of the U N since 1964.

**Kenya, Mount** Kenya. Extinct volcano 80 m. N N E of Nairobi, just S of the equator; the second highest mountain in Africa, rising to 17,058 ft. The crater is much eroded, and there are 15 glaciers, most of which end at 14,000–15,000 ft. From 5,000 ft to 11,000 ft the slopes are forested. Discovered (1849) by Ludwig Krapf, a German missionary; first climbed by Sir Halford Mackinder (1899).

**Kerala** India. State in the SW, bounded

on the W by the Arabian Sea (Malabar Coast), created in 1956 and consisting of most of the former state of Travancore-Cochin together with parts of the Malabar district and S Kanara, previously in Madras. Area 15,002 sq. m. Pop. (1961) 16,903,715 (the highest population density of any state). Cap. Trivandrum. Hilly in the E, it rises to 8,841 ft in Anai Mudi and includes the Cardamom Hills, but most of its area consists of plains where the chief crops are rice, coconuts, tapioca, rubber, and pepper. Chief towns Trivandrum, Cochin (chief port), Kozhikode, Alleppey. Claims the highest literacy rate of all states, 47 per cent (1961).

**Kerbela** ◊ *Karbala*.

**Kerch** USSR. Seaport on a small bay in Kerch Strait, at the E end of the Kerch Peninsula in the Ukrainian SSR. Pop. (1970) 128,000. Main industrial centre of the Crimea. Manufactures iron and steel from iron ore mined just S; also ships iron ore to the mainland. Ship repairing, fishing and fish canning, railway engineering. Founded by Greeks from Miletus in the 6th cent. B.C.; has many features of archaeological interest.

**Kerch Peninsula** USSR. Peninsula 60 m. long and up to 30 m. wide in E Crimea, in the Ukrainian SSR, between the Sea of Azov (N) and the Black Sea (S); separated from the mainland by Kerch Strait and joined to the rest of the Crimea by an isthmus 10 m. wide. Important iron-ore deposits. Chief town Kerch.

**Kerch Strait** USSR. Ancient Bosporus Cimmerius. Shallow strait 25 m. long and up to 9 m. wide, connecting the Black Sea with the Sea of Azov and separating E Crimea from the mainland.

**Kerguelen Islands** Indian Ocean. Archipelago consisting of one large volcanic island (Kerguelen or Desolation Island) and about 300 small islands, at 40°–50° S lat., 68°–70° E long. in the Indian Ocean. Total area 2,700 sq. m. Pop. 85. Forms part of the French Southern and Antarctic Territories. The main island rises to over 6,000 ft and is partly covered with snowfields and glaciers; famous for its unique Kerguelen cabbage. Discovered by de Kerguelen 1772. Occupied by France 1949.

**Kerkira** ◊ *Corfu*.

**Kerkrade** Netherlands. Town in Limburg province, 15 m. E of Maastricht on the W German frontier. Pop. (1968) 50,206. Coalmining centre.

**Kermadec Islands** SW Pacific Ocean. Group of volcanic islands belonging to New Zealand, 600 m. NE of Auckland. Area 13 sq. m. Mountainous and fertile, but only Raoul (Sunday) Island, the largest (11 sq. m.), is inhabited, serving as a meteorological station. Annexed by New Zealand 1887.

**Kerman** Iran. Capital of Kerman province, 270 m. ENE of Shiraz at a height of 5,600 ft. Pop. (1966) 118,344. Commercial centre and road junction. Manufactures carpets, shawls, brassware. Surrounded by walls of sun-baked clay. Has an 11th-cent. mosque (restored).

**Kermanshah** Iran. Capital of Kermanshah province, 250 m. WSW of Tehran at a height of 4,850 ft. Pop. (1966) 187,930 (largely Kurds). Commercial and route centre in a fertile agricultural region. Sugar refining, flour milling. Also has an oil refinery linked by pipeline with the Naft-i-Shah oilfield.

**Kerry** Irish Republic. County in Munster province, in the SW. Area 1,815 sq. m. Pop. (1966) 112,785. Cap. Tralee. The coastline is much indented, the main inlets being Tralee Bay, Dingle Bay, and Kenmare R.; there are many offshore islands. Inland is the range Macgillicuddy's Reeks, rising to 3,414 ft in Carrantuohill, the highest point in Ireland. Fishing, farming, and catering for holidaymakers are important occupations. Noted for its beautiful scenery, particularly in the district round the lakes of Killarney; among the resorts are Tralee, Ballybunion, Killarney, and Listowel.

**Keswick** England. Urban district in S Cumberland, on the R. Greta near the N end of Derwentwater. Pop. (1961) 4,752. Tourist centre and market town, with a lead-pencil factory. The home of Southey was at Crosthwaite near by; he is buried in the parish church there.

**Kettering** England. Municipal borough in Northamptonshire 13 m. NNE of Northampton. Pop. (1961) 38,631. Important centre of leather and footwear manufacture. Also manufactures machine tools, clothing, etc. Baptist Missionary Society founded here in 1792.

**Kew** England. Residential district in the London borough of Richmond-upon-Thames, on the S bank of the R. Thames. The world-famous Kew Gardens (officially the Royal Botanic Gardens) (288 acres), containing hothouses, conservatories, museums, etc., were founded in 1759 and presented to the nation in 1840. Here is Kew Palace, home of George IV when Prince of Wales. Just S W of the Gardens is Kew Observatory.

**Keweenaw Peninsula** USA. Peninsula in Michigan, curving N E into L. Superior, and tapering off to Keweenaw Point. Formerly well known for its copper; rich deposits of the metal were worked by the Indians before the arrival of European explorers.

**Key West** USA. Southernmost city of the USA, in S Florida on the island of Key West, the most westerly of the ◊ *Florida Keys*. Pop. (1960) 33,956. A naval and air station, and a coastguard base. Cigar manufacture, fishing, and the processing of turtles for soup. Popular tourist resort. Terminus of the highway spanning the Florida Keys from the mainland. Discovered by Spanish sailors in the early 16th cent. The haunt of pirates and smugglers in the 17th and 18th cent.

**Khabarovsk** USSR. Capital of Khabarovsk Territory, RSFSR, on the Amur R. at the point where the river is crossed by the Trans-Siberian Railway. Pop. (1970) 437,000. Chief industrial centre in E Siberia. Oil refining, tanning, brewing, flour milling. Manufactures machinery, chemicals, etc. Trade in furs. Named after the Russian explorer Khabarov, who built a fort here (1652). Became the administrative centre of the Russian Far East 1880; increased in importance after being reached by the railway (1937).

**Khairpur** Pakistan. 1. Division of W Pakistan, in the Sind region. Area 20,449 sq. m. Pop. (1961) 3,133,712. Climate hot and arid, but cereals, cotton, etc. cultivated by irrigation from the Lloyd (Sukkur) Barrage.
2. Capital of the Khairpur division, 15 m. S S W of Sukkur. Pop. (1961) 34,144. Manufactures carpets, textiles, etc. Former capital of Khairpur state.

**Khakass AR** USSR. Autonomous region in the Krasnoyarsk Territory, RSFSR, on the upper Yenisei R. Area 23,855 sq. m. Pop. (1970) 446,000 (about equally Khakass and Russian). Cap. Abakan. Dairy farming and lumbering are important occupations; coal and other minerals are produced. Formed 1930.

**Khanty-Mansi NA** USSR. National Area in W Siberia, in the Tyumen Region (RSFSR). Area 215,000 sq. m. Pop.

(1970) 272,000 (Russian, Khanty (E), Mansi (W)). Cap. Khanty-Mansiisk, at the confluence of the Ob and Irtysh rivers. Fishing, lumbering, etc.

**Khanty-Mansiisk** ◊ *Khanty-Mansi N A.*

**Kharagpur** India. Town in W Bengal 70 m. W S W of Calcutta. Pop. (1961) 147,253. Industrial centre. Railway junction. Railway and other engineering, rice milling, etc.

**Kharga Oasis (Great Oasis)** United Arab Republic. Largest and southernmost of the Egyptian oases, occupying a depression in the Libyan Desert 100 m. long N–S and up to 50 m. wide E–W. Pop. 11,000 (mainly Berber). Chief town El Kharga, 110 m. W S W of Nag Hammadi on the Nile, with which it is linked by rail. Chief products dates, cereals.

**Kharkov** USSR. Capital of the Kharkov Region, Ukrainian SSR, at the confluence of two small tributaries of the N Donets R., 260 m. ESE of Kiev. Pop. (1970) 1,223,000. Important railway and road junction and major industrial centre, specializing in heavy engineering. Manufactures tractors and other agricultural machinery, coalmining, oil-drilling, and electrical equipment, locomotives, machine tools, etc., also chemicals and textiles. Seat of a university (1804), with many technological and other educational institutions. Founded in the mid 17th cent. Became capital of the Ukraine 1765. Grew rapidly in the latter half of the 19th cent. with the development of the Donets coalfield and the Krivoi Rog iron deposits, which fed its metallurgical industries. Capital of the Ukrainian SSR 1920–34, being superseded by Kiev. Severely damaged in the 2nd World War.

**Khartoum** Sudan. Capital of Sudan and of Khartoum province, on the left bank of the Blue Nile just above the confluence with the White Nile. Pop. (1964) 135,000 (with Khartoum North and Omdurman, 360,000). The largest trade centre, esp. for cotton. Connected with Khartoum North by a rail and road bridge across the Blue Nile and with Omdurman by a bridge across the White Nile. Terminus of railways from Port Sudan and El Obeid (via Sennar), and from Wadi Halfa. Steamer services up the White Nile to Kosti and thence to Juba. The Gordon Memorial College and Kitchener School of Medicine were amalgamated into the University College of Khartoum in 1951.

Founded (1822) by the Egyptians after their conquest of the Sudan. Developed quickly as a general and slave market. Destroyed by the Mahdists in 1885 (when General Gordon was killed), but recaptured by Anglo-Egyptian forces under Lord Kitchener in 1898; Kitchener drafted the new layout in the form of a Union Jack.

**Khartoum North** Sudan. Town in Khartoum province, on the right bank of the Blue Nile opposite Khartoum, with which it is linked by bridge. Pop. (1964) 58,000. River dockyards and workshops. Trade in cotton, cereals, etc.

**Khasi Hills** India. Range of hills in Assam extending over 100 m. W–E and rising to 6,300 ft. Cherrapunji, on the S slope, is said to have the world's heaviest rainfall, 428 ins. annually.

**Khaskovo (Haskovo)** Bulgaria. Capital of Khaskovo province, 45 m. ESE of Plovdiv. Pop. (1965) 57,682. Centre of the tobacco trade. Manufactures cigarettes, carpets, woollen goods, etc.

**Khatanga River** USSR. River 400 m. long in NE Krasnoyarsk Territory, RSFSR, formed by the union of the Kotui and Moiero rivers and flowing N and NE to enter the Laptev Sea by a long estuary. Well stocked with fish.

**Kherson** USSR. Capital of the Kherson region, Ukrainian SSR, port on the Dnieper R. 18 m. from the mouth. Pop. (1970) 261,000. Exports grain, timber. Flour milling, brewing, shipbuilding. Manufactures machinery, textiles, food products. So named because it was believed to be the site of the Greek colony of Chersonesus Heracleotica, but the present city was founded in 1778 by Potemkin as a naval base and seaport.

**Khingan Mountains** China. Two mountain ranges, the Great Khingan and Little Khingan Mountains. The former extend NNE for about 700 m. along the E edge of the Mongolian plateau to the Amur R., rising to 6,670 ft; from their extension, the Ilkhuri Shan, the latter extend SE parallel to and S of the Amur R., rising to 4,660 ft. The Great Khingan Mountains are well forested, and lumbering is important.

**Khiva** USSR. Town in the Uzbek SSR, in the fertile Khiva oasis 25 m. from the left bank of the Amu Darya (Oxus), by which it is irrigated. Pop. (1964) 20,500. Manufactures carpets, textiles. Remains of the former khan's palace, mosques, etc.

Khiva was a powerful kingdom in the 10th–13th cent. but was conquered by Genghis Khan (1220), Timur (1379), and the Uzbeks (1512). In the late 16th cent. the town of Khiva became capital of the khanate of Khiva, which was taken by the Russians in 1873; in 1920 the khan was deposed and the Khorezm Soviet People's Republic was established. In 1924 the territory was divided between the Uzbek and Turkmen SSR.

**Khmelnitsky** USSR. Formerly Proskurov. Capital of the Khmelnitsky region (formerly Kamenets Podolsk), in the Ukrainian SSR, on the Southern Bug R. 170 m. WSW of Kiev. Pop. (1970) 113,000. Railway junction. Engineering, furniture, and food-processing industries.

**Khoper River** USSR. River 600 m. long in RSFSR, rising 26 m. WSW of Penza and flowing generally SSW to join the Don R. Unnavigable. Ice-bound for about 3 months annually.

**Khorog** ◊ *Gorno-Badakhshan AR*.

**Khorramshahr (Khurramshahr)** Iran. Formly Mohammerah. Port in Khuzistan province, on the Shatt-al-Arab at the confluence with the Karun R. Pop. (1966) 95,100. Handles the major part of the country's overseas trade. Exports dates, cotton, hides and skins, etc. Linked by pipeline with the oilfields and by rail and road with Ahwaz and Tehran. The port was modernized during the 2nd World War, being on one of the lend-lease routes to the USSR.

**Khotan** China. Town in SW Sinkiang-Uighur AR 240 m. SE of Kashgar, on the S edge of the Tarim Basin and on the ancient Silk Road. Pop. 50,000. Manufactures cotton and silk goods, carpets. Famous for its jade. The Khotan oasis, in which it stands, produces cereals, cotton, fruits. In early times a centre of Buddhist learning. Visited by Marco Polo 1274.

**Khurramabad** Iran. Town in Khuzistan 150 m. N of Ahwaz. Pop. (1966) 59,578. Commercial centre. Trade in wool, fruit, etc.

**Khurramshahr** ◊ *Khorramshahr*.

**Khyber Pass.** Defile 33 m. long through the Safed Koh range between Afghanistan and Pakistan, joining the valley of the Kabul R. with the Peshawar plains and the Indus valley. Flanked by high, barren cliffs, narrowing to 15 ft at one point, it carries a railway and a road. Important strategically and as a trade route. The sur-

## 393

rounding country is inhabited by Afridis.

**Kiangsi** China. Province in S central China. Area 66,880 sq. m. Pop. (1957) 18,610,000. Cap. Nanchang. Mountainous in the S, it consists essentially of the basin of the Kan R., which flows NNE to the extensive Poyang L. It is a leading rice producer, and cotton, tea, and tobacco are grown. Coal and tungsten are important minerals. Principal towns Nanchang, Kiukiang.

**Kiangsu** China. Maritime province in the E. Area 39,000 sq, m. Pop. (1957) 45,230,000. Cap. Nanking. Consists mainly of a flat alluvial plain which includes the Yangtse delta, and is crossed N–S by the Grand Canal, linking the Kaoyu and Tai lakes. Rice, cotton, and mulberry trees (for silk production) are grown. Densely populated. Several large cities: Shanghai, Nanking, Wusih, Chinkiang.

**Kicking Horse Pass** Canada. Pass in the Rocky Mountains, on the border of Alberta and British Columbia, 35 m. NW of Banff at a height of 5,339 ft. On the route followed by the Canadian Pacific Railway. Discovered (1859) by Sir James Hector, geologist of the Palliser expedition; so named because he was kicked by his horse when crossing the mountains at this point.

**Kidderminster** England. Municipal borough in Worcestershire on the R. Stour 13 m. N of Worcester. Pop. (1961) 40,822. Noted since 1735 for the carpet industry, introduced from Flanders. Also manufactures textile machinery, woollen goods, etc. Birthplace of Sir Rowland Hill (1795–1879), who introduced the penny post (1840).

**Kidwelly** Wales. Municipal borough in Carmarthenshire, on Carmarthen Bay 5 m. NW of Llanelli. Pop. (1961) 2,879. A silted-up harbour. Castle (13th-cent.). Limestone quarrying etc.

**Kiel** Federal German Republic. Capital of Schleswig-Holstein, on the Kieler Förde at the E end of the Kiel Canal. Pop. (1968) 269,626. Chief German naval base until 1945, when the shipyards were dismantled. Chief industries shipbuilding, engineering; also flour milling, brewing, fishing, etc. University (1665). Entered the Hanseatic League 1284. Naval base established 1871. Severely damaged in the 2nd World War. The first W European nuclear vessel, a 15,000-ton ore carrier, was launched here in 1964.

**Kiel (North Sea–Baltic) Canal** Federal German Republic. Formerly the Kaiser Wilhelm Canal. Waterway 61 m. long connecting the Elbe estuary on the North Sea with the Kieler Förde on the Baltic Sea. Built 1887–95 to permit movement of the German fleet between the two seas and later widened. Given international status by the Treaty of Versailles (1919), but this was repudiated by Hitler in 1936.

**Kielce** Poland. Capital of the Kielce voivodship, 94 m. S of Warsaw in the low hills of Gory Swietokrzyskie. Pop. (1968) 117,800. Railway junction. Brewing, tanning, flour milling, sawmilling, etc. Manufactures textiles, cement. Founded (1173) by a bishop of Cracow.

**Kiev** USSR. Capital of the Ukrainian SSR (since 1934) and of the Kiev region, the third largest city of the USSR, on the right bank of the Dnieper R. Pop. (1970) 1,632,000. River port. Important railway and road junction. Industrial centre. Flour milling, sugar refining, tanning. Manufactures machinery, chemicals, textiles, clothing, footwear, etc. Also a leading cultural centre, with a university, transferred here in 1833, the Ukrainian Academy of Sciences, and many other educational institutions. Among its historic buildings are the Byzantine Cathedral of St Sophia and the Pechersky monastery, with its caves and catacombs, which in pre-revolution times was visited by over 200,000 pilgrims annually and has since been adapted to secular uses; both date from the 11th cent. Kiev is built mainly on bluffs overlooking the river, but the ancient Podol, where the famous 'contract fair' was held, stands on lower ground. Known as 'the mother of Russian cities', it was founded some time before the 9th cent., and in 988 its ruler, Prince Vladimir, embraced Christianity and made it the first home of the Greek Church in Russia. With its considerable transit trade along the Dnieper, on the route between Scandinavia and Byzantium, the city and its principality flourished, but after its capture by Bogolyubski (1169) and its destruction by the Tatars (1240) it declined. Held by Lithuania (1320–1569) and Poland (1569–1654) and was then annexed to Russia. Its commercial prosperity revived in the 19th cent. and sugar refining and other industries developed, but it suffered cruelly in the revolution and again in the 2nd World War. After liberation from the Germans its population had fallen to

200,000. The city's underground railway began to operate in 1960.

**Kigali** Rwanda. Capital of the republic, 110 m. NNE of Usumbura (Burundi). Pop. 7,000. Commercial centre. Trade in coffee, hides, cattle.

**Kikinda** (Hungarian **Nagykikinda**) Yugoslavia. Formerly Velika Kikinda. Town in Vojvodina 52 m. NE of Novi Sad near the Rumanian border. Pop. (1961) 34,059. Railway junction. Trade in wheat, flour.

**Kildare** Irish Republic. **1.** County in Leinster province. Area 654 sq. m. Pop. (1966) 66,404. County town Naas. Generally lowlying and fertile, it has part of the Bog of Allen in the N and the Curragh (noted for its racehorses) in the centre. Drained by the Liffey and Barrow rivers. Cattle and horses raised. Potatoes and cereals grown.
**2.** Market town in Co. Kildare, 29 m. WSW of Dublin. Pop. (1966) 2,731. Grew up round a monastery founded (490) by St Brigid. The 13th-cent. cathedral, destroyed in 1641 by Cromwell, was rebuilt 1683–6 and again in 1875.

**Kilimanjaro, Mount** Tanzania. Extinct volcano in the NE, near the Kenya frontier 290 m. NNW of Dar-es-Salaam. Two peaks: Mt Kibo (19,340 ft) the highest peak in Africa, permanently snow-capped, and Mt Mawenzi (17,300 ft). From 4,000 to 6,000 ft the slopes are planted with coffee, sisal, bananas, maize. From 6,000 to 10,000 ft there are forests; above this level there are grasslands, to about 12,000 ft. Discovered (1848) by Johannes Rebmann and Ludwig Krapt, German missionaries. Summit first reached by Hans Meyer (1889).

**Kilindini** ◊ *Mombasa.*

**Kilkenny** Irish Republic. **1.** Inland county in Leinster, in the SE. Area 796 sq. m. Pop. (1966) 60,463. Mainly hilly, rising to 1,694 ft in Mt Brandon (SE). Drained by the Nore, Barrow, and Suir rivers. Oats, barley, and potatoes cultivated and cattle reared in the fertile valleys.
**2.** County town of Co. Kilkenny, on the R. Nore 64 m. SW of Dublin. Pop. (1966) 10,052. Brewing, tanning, etc. Limestone quarrying in the neighbourhood. One of Ireland's oldest towns, once capital of the ancient kingdom of Ossory. It has the 13th-cent. Protestant cathedral (restored) of St Canice, after whom the town is named (*Cill Chainnigh* – 'Church of St Canice'), the 19th-cent. Roman Catholic Cathedral of St Mary, a 12th-cent. castle rebuilt in the

19th cent., and 13th-cent. Dominican and Franciscan abbeys.

**Killarney** Irish Republic. Market town and tourist centre in Co. Kerry, in a district renowned for its scenic beauty. Pop. (1966) 6,877. Has a 19th cent. Roman Catholic cathedral and bishop's palace. Manufactures footwear etc. Near the town are the three famous Lakes of Killarney, Upper, Middle, and Lower, the last, also known as Lough Leane, being by far the largest. Also in the neighbourhood are the Gap of Dunloe, between Carrantuohill (3,414 ft) and Purple Mountain (2,739 ft), and the ruins of the 14th-cent. Muckross Abbey.

**Killiecrankie Pass** Scotland. Wooded pass in Perthshire 3 m. NW of Pitlochry, through which the R. Garry flows, used by road and railway. At its N end was fought the Battle of Killiecrankie (1689), in which Claverhouse (Bonnie Dundee) defeated William III's forces under Mackay but was himself killed.

**Kilmarnock** Scotland. Large burgh in N Ayrshire, on Kilmarnock Water near its confluence with the R. Irvine. Pop. (1961) 47,509. Industrial town in a coalmining region. Railway and other engineering. Manufactures carpets, knitwear, whisky. Here the first edition of Robert Burns's poems was published (1786); in Kay Park is the Burns Memorial museum, which has many of his MSS. and relics. Birthplace of Alexander Smith, the poet (1830–67).

**Kilrush** Irish Republic. Small port and seaside resort in Co. Clare, on the Shannon estuary. Pop. (1966) 2,734. Scattery Island offshore has remains of ancient churches etc.

**Kilsyth** Scotland. Small burgh in Stirlingshire 13 m. NNE of Glasgow. Pop. (1961) 9,831. Industrial centre in a coalmining region. Manufactures hosiery. In 1645 Montrose defeated the Covenanters near by.

**Kilung** ◊ *Keelung.*

**Kilwinning** Scotland. Small burgh in Ayrshire, on the R. Garnock 9 m. WNW of Kilmarnock. Pop. (1961) 7,287. Engineering, worsted spinning. The reputed birthplace of Scottish freemasonry. Ruins of a 12th-cent. abbey dedicated to St Winnin – hence the name.

**Kimberley** Australia. District in the N of Western Australia consisting of rugged mountains surrounded by a grassland belt of potentially fertile country, drained by the Fitzroy, Ord, and other rivers; often referred to as the Kimberleys (W and E).

Gold (discovered 1882) mined at Hall's Creek. The first great cattle drive from New South Wales to the Kimberleys was made by the MacDonald brothers (1883); in recent years the Air Beef project, whereby livestock and carcases are flown, has made such long drives unnecessary.

**Kimberley** S Africa. Town in Cape Province 540 m. NE of Cape Town at a height of 4,012 ft. Pop. (1967) 95,100 (29,010 whites, 20,000 coloured, 45,000 Bantu). One of the world's chief diamond-mining centres. Also metal working. Manufactures cement, furniture, clothing. Founded 1870. The three main mining camps developed into the town, incorporated into Cape Colony in 1880. The two financial groups controlling the mines amalgamated, and the entire diamond production came into the hands of De Beers Consolidated Mines Ltd (1899). Became an important railway centre: linked with Cape Town 1885, Johannesburg 1906, and Bloemfontein 1908. Besieged for 5 months during the Boer War (1899–1900).

**Kincardine** Scotland. Small town in SW Fifeshire, on the Firth of Forth. Pop. 2,000. In a coalmining district, at the N end of a road bridge (1936).

**Kincardineshire (The Mearns)** Scotland. County in the E, bordering E on the North Sea. Area 382 sq. m. Pop. (1961) 48,810. County town Stonehaven. Hilly in the W and NW (Grampians), with Mt Battock rising to 2,555 ft. Low-lying and fertile along the coast and in the Howe of the Mearns, an extension of Strathmore. The Dee and the N Esk rivers form the N and S boundaries respectively. Sheep raised on the uplands. Cereals, root crops cultivated. Sea and salmon fishing.

**Kinchinjunga** ◊ *Kanchenjunga.*

**Kineshma** USSR. Industrial town in the Ivanovo region, RSFSR, on the Volga R. 50 m. ENE of Ivanovo, for which it is the river port. Pop. 85,000. Textile centre. Also paper, sawmilling, and other industries.

**King Edward VII Land** ◊ *Ross Dependency.*

**Kinghorn** Scotland. Royal burgh in S Fifeshire, on the Firth of Forth 3 m. S of Kirkcaldy. Pop. (1961) 2,112. Manufactures golf clubs. Monument near by to Alexander III, thrown from his horse and killed here in 1286.

**Kingsbridge** England. Urban district in S Devonshire, at the head of Kingsbridge Estuary 10 m. WSW of Dartmouth.

Pop. (1961) 3,283. Market town. Flour milling, brewing.

**Kings Canyon National Park** USA. Region of peaks, canyons, and corries on the W slopes of the Sierra Nevada, in California. Area 708 sq. m. Traversed by the Middle and South Forks of the Kings R., from which it takes its name. In the SW are stands of giant sequoia trees. Established 1940.

**Kingscote** ◊ *Kangaroo Island.*

**King's Lynn (Lynn Regis, Lynn)** England. Municipal borough in Norfolk, on the Great Ouse R. just S of the Wash. Pop. (1961) 27,554. Market town. Beet-sugar refining, canning, brewing, engineering. Manufactures food products. Among its buildings are the 12th-cent. Church of St Margaret, the 13th-cent. Greyfriars Tower, the 15th-cent. Red Mount Chapel, and the 17th-cent. Custom House. Important from Saxon times; in medieval times a leading port. Birthplace of George Vancouver (1758–98) and Fanny Burney (1752–1840).

**Kingsport** USA. Industrial town in Tennessee, on the Holston R. 87 m. ENE of Knoxville. Pop. (1960) 26,314. Manufactures paper, chemicals, textiles, etc.

**Kingston** Canada. Port in Ontario, at the NE end of L. Ontario. Pop. (1966) 59,004. Manufactures locomotives, mining machinery, aluminium goods, man-made fibres, chemicals, etc. Seat of the Queen's University (1841) and the Royal Military College (1875). Capital of United Canada 1841–4. Originally settled by the French in 1673, as Fort Frontenac. Destroyed by the English in 1758, it was refounded in 1782 by United Empire Loyalists and given its present name (after King George III).

**Kingston** Jamaica. Capital and largest city, on the SE coast; one of the chief ports of the W Indies, with a deep, land-locked harbour. Pop. (1967) 204,449. Headquarters of the coffee trade. Industries largely concerned with the processing of the island's agricultural produce. Manufactures cigars and cigarettes, matches, jam, clothing. Also brewing, fruit canning. Seat of the Institute of Jamaica; the University of the West Indies is at Mona, 4 m. NE. Founded 1692, after the destruction of Port Royal by earthquake. Superseded Spanish Town as the official capital 1872. Hurricanes have caused great damage at times. The earthquake of 1907 caused much destruction. There were serious fires in 1780, 1843, 1862, and 1882.

Kingston (New York) USA. Industrial town on the Hudson R. 88 m. N of New York city. Pop. (1960) 29,260. Manufactures clothing, bricks and tiles, cement, etc. Originally settled in 1652 by the Dutch. The Senate House, built in 1676, was the meeting-place of the first state legislature.

Kingston (Pennsylvania) USA. Town on the Susquehanna R. opposite Wilkes-Barre. Pop. (1960) 20,261. Anthracite mining. Railway engineering. Manufactures cigars, hosiery, etc. The Indians and British defeated a much smaller force of Americans here (1778).

Kingston-upon-Hull ◊ Hull.

Kingston-upon-Thames England. Former royal borough in Surrey, from 1965 a royal borough of London, on the S bank of the R. Thames, including Malden and Coombe and Surbiton. Pop. (1963) 145,977. Mainly residential, with varied industries. Saxon kings were crowned here, and the Coronation Stone is near the Guildhall (opened 1935).

Kingstown ◊ St Vincent.

Kingussie Scotland. Small burgh and tourist resort in Inverness-shire, on the R. Spey 29 m. SSE of Inverness. Pop. (1961) 1,079. In a sheep-farming district. Ruthven, on the opposite bank of the Spey, was the birthplace of James 'Ossian' Macpherson (1736–96).

Kinlochleven Scotland. Small town in Argyllshire at the head of Loch Leven and at the mouth of the R. Leven 9 m. SE of Fort William. Pop. 3,700. Important hydroelectric plant and aluminium works.

Kinross Scotland. Small burgh and county town of Kinross-shire, on the W shore of Loch Leven. Pop. (1961) 2,365. Textile mills.

Kinross-shire Scotland. Small county SE of Perthshire. Area 82 sq. m. Pop. (1961) 6,704. County town Kinross. Near its centre is Loch Leven, with the island on which Mary Queen of Scots was imprisoned.

Kinsale Irish Republic. Small fishing port and holiday resort in Co. Cork, on the R. Bandon estuary. Pop. (1966) 1,592. The liner Lusitania was torpedoed off the Old Head of Kinsale (S) in 1915.

Kinshasa Congo (Kinshasa). Formerly Léopoldville. Capital, on the left bank of the Congo R. just below Stanley Pool. Pop. (1967) 902,000. A centre of air, river, and rail routes. Connected by rail with Matadi, 90 m. down the river. The largest city and chief commercial centre.

Manufactures textiles, footwear, etc. One of the most modern cities in Africa, with wide avenues lined with tropical trees and plants. Seat of the Lovanium University (1954). Founded (1887) by Stanley; named after Léopold II of Belgium. Replaced Boma as capital of the Belgian Congo in 1929. Renamed Kinshasa 1966.

Kintyre Scotland. Peninsula in S Argyllshire extending 42 m. SSW from Tarbert. Mainly hilly, rising to 1,462 ft; the Mull of Kintyre, 13 m. across the North Channel from N Ireland, in the S. Chief town Campbeltown.

Kioga (Kyoga), Lake Uganda. Shallow, swampy lake 80 m. long, with several long arms, in the middle course of the Victoria Nile. Area 1,700 sq. m. Navigable by vessels of shallow draught. Steamer services.

Kirghiz SSR (Kirghizia) USSR. Constituent republic in Central Asia, bounded on the SE by China. Area 76,460 sq. m. Pop. (1970) 2,933,000 (40 per cent Kirghizians, 30 per cent Russians, 11 per cent Uzbeks). Cap. Frunze. Mountainous, lying at the W end of the great Tien Shan system and rising in the E, near the Chinese border, to 24,406 ft in Pobeda; in the NE is the extensive L. Issyk-Kul, surrounded by mountains. Climate and natural vegetation vary considerably with altitude. Stock rearing has long been the main occupation, sheep being by far the most numerous, with cattle, pigs, goats, horses, and yaks – the last in the higher districts unsuitable for other animals. Agriculture has been developed in the valleys in recent years and is largely mechanized. Chief crops wheat, maize, sugar-beet, cotton. Some coal, oil, and other minerals are produced. Principal towns Frunze, Osh. Kirghizia became an autonomous region of the RSFSR 1924, an ASSR 1926, and a constituent SSR of the USSR 1936.

Kirin China. 1. Province in E central Manchuria (NE). Area 72,000 sq. m. Pop. (1957) 12,550,000. Cap. Changchun. Mountainous in the SE, where it borders on Korea and the USSR. In the NW it forms part of the Manchurian plain. Wheat, millet, and soya beans grown on the plains. Timber and coal and other minerals are obtained from the highlands. Chief towns Changchun, Kirin.
2. Town and river port in Kirin province, on the Sungari R. 60 m. E of Changchun. Pop. 247,000. Sawmilling. Manufactures

chemicals, paper, matches, cement, etc., power being derived from the hydro-electric plant at Fengman. Trade in timber, grain, tobacco. Founded 1673. Developed industrially with the advent of the railway from Changchun (1912).

**Kirkby-in-Ashfield** England. Urban district in Nottinghamshire 11 m. NNW of Nottingham. Pop. (1961) 21,690. Coalmining, brickmaking.

**Kirkcaldy** Scotland. Royal burgh, port, and industrial town in S Fifeshire, on the Firth of Forth. Pop. (1961) 52,371. Sometimes known as the 'Lang Toun' because of its main street, which runs nearly 4 m. along the coast. Important centre of linoleum manufacture. Textile and engineering industries. Coalmining in the neighbourhood. Birthplace of Adam Smith, the economist (1723–90).

**Kirkcudbright** Scotland. Royal burgh and county town of Kirkcudbrightshire, 25 m. SW of Dumfries. Pop. (1961) 2,446. Market town. Ruins of a 16th-cent. castle and of the 12th-cent. Dundrennan Abbey (4½ m. SE).

**Kirkcudbrightshire** Scotland. County in the SW, bordering S and SE on the Irish Sea and Solway Firth and forming the E part of Galloway. Area 899 sq. m. Pop. (1961) 28,877. County town Kirkcudbright. Upland in the N and W, with Merrick rising to 2,764 ft. Drained by the Dee and its tributaries. Main occupations cattle and sheep rearing. Chief towns Castle Douglas, Dalbeattie, Kirkcudbright.

**Kirkenes** Norway. Port in Finnmark county in the extreme NE, on an arm of Varanger Fiord near the USSR border. Pop. 4,000. Exports iron ore from the near-by mines. A German submarine base in the 2nd World War, it was largely destroyed by bombing, but has been rebuilt.

**Kirkintilloch** Scotland. Small burgh in a detached portion of Dunbartonshire 6 m. NE of Glasgow. Pop. (1961) 18,257. Industrial centre. Iron founding, engineering (esp. switchgear). Its Gaelic name means 'the Fort at the End of the Ridge', referring to the fort here on the Wall of Antoninus.

**Kirkuk** Iraq. Capital of Kirkuk province, in the NE, 150 m. N of Baghdad. Pop. (1965) 167,413. Important chiefly as the centre of a rich oilfield (discovered 1927) with pipe-lines leading to Tripoli (Lebanon) and Banias (Syria), as well as a third, out of use since the Arab-Israeli War in 1948,

to Haifa (Israel). Also a market town. Trade in sheep, grain, fruit.

**Kirkwall** Scotland. Royal burgh, port, and county town of Orkney, on Mainland. Pop. (1961) 4,315. Largest town in the Orkneys. Fishing. Distilling. Exports agricultural produce, whisky, etc. Its outstanding building is the Cathedral of St Magnus (founded 1137), and there are ruins of the bishop's palace.

**Kirov** USSR. Formerly Khlynov (till 1780), Vyatka (1780–1934). Capital of Kirov region, RSFSR, on the Vyatka R. 270 m. NE of Gorki. Pop. (1970) 332,000. Important railway junction. Railway engineering. Manufactures machine tools, agricultural implements, textiles, matches, footwear, etc. Founded by Novgorod merchants in the 12th cent. Annexed by Moscow 1489.

**Kirovabad** USSR. Formerly Elisavetpol (till 1920), Gandzha (1920–35). The second largest town in the Azerbaijan SSR, on the Trans-Caspian Railway and the Baku-Batumi oil pipeline 110 m. SE of Tiflis. Pop. (1970) 190,000. Industrial and commercial centre in a fruit-growing district. Manufactures textiles, wine, etc. An ancient town which changed hands many times, it became Russian in 1804. Birthplace of the Persian poet Nizami (1140–1202).

**Kirovograd** USSR. Formerly Elisavetgrad (till 1924), Zinovievsk (1924–36), Kirovo (1936–9). Capital of the Kirovograd region in the Ukrainian SSR, 160 m. SE of Kiev. Pop. (1970) 189,000. Manufactures agricultural machinery, soap, clothing, etc. Sawmilling, brewing. Trade in grain.

**Kirriemuir** Scotland. Small burgh and market town in Angus 5 m. WNW of Forfar. Pop. (1961) 3,485. Jute mills. Birthplace of Sir J. M. Barrie (1860–1937), and the 'Thrums' of his stories.

**Kiruna** Sweden. Town in Norrbotten county in the N. Pop. (1968) 28,968. Important iron-mining centre, famous for the purity of its ore, sent by rail to Luleå, 165 m. to the ESE, and Narvik (Norway), 89 m. to the WNW, for export. Stands between the two great ore-bearing mountains of Kiirunavaara and Luossavaara.

**Kiryu** Japan. Town in central Honshu, in Gumma prefecture 60 m. NNW of Tokyo. Pop. (1965) 127,880. Manufactures textiles, esp. rayon and silk.

**Kisangani** Congo (Kinshasa). Formerly (till 1966) Stanleyville. Formerly capital of the Haut Congo province, on the upper

Congo R. below Stanley Falls. Pop. (1966) 150,000. Route centre, with an important airport; the river port at the head of steam navigation (from Kinshasa), and terminus of the railway from Ponthierville circumventing Stanley Falls. Commercial and tourist centre. University (1963). During the Congolese civil war Gizenga set up a local government in 1960, but his forces surrendered to the central government and he was dismissed in 1962. In 1963–4 the rebels under Gbenye again established a local government, but the town was recaptured by white mercenary paratroopers.

**Kiselevsk** USSR. Town in the Kemerovo region, RSFSR, 25 m. NW of Prokopyevsk. Pop. (1970) 126,000. A coalmining centre in the Kuznetsk basin.

**Kish** Iraq. Ancient Sumerian city near the Euphrates R. 10 m. E of Hilla, which flourished in the 4th millennium B.C. and was last mentioned in the 6th cent. B.C. Among finds revealed by 20th-cent. excavations was an extensive collection of pottery dating from the early Sumerian.

**Kishinev** (Rumanian Chişinău) USSR. Capital of the Moldavian SSR, on the Byk R. 100 m. WNW of Odessa. Pop. (1970) 357,000. Commercial centre in a rich agricultural region (grain, fruit, wine). Important food-processing plants. Manufactures leather, footwear, hosiery, etc. Founded 1436. Annexed to Russia in 1812 and became capital of Bessarabia. Scene of a notorious pogrom (1903). Ceded to Rumania in 1918, but returned to the USSR in 1940.

**Kiskunfélegyháza** Hungary. Market town and railway junction in Bács-Kiskun county 15 m. SSE of Kecskemet. Pop. 33,000. Trade in fruit, wine, tobacco. Important cattle market. Flour milling.

**Kislovodsk** USSR. Town and health resort in the Stavropol Territory, RSFSR, in a deep valley of the N Caucasus at a height of 2,690 ft 18 m. WSW of Pyatigorsk. Pop. 79,000. Famous for mineral waters, bottled and sold throughout the USSR. Sanatoria, convalescent homes, baths.

**Kistna River** ⇨ Krishna River.

**Kisumu (Port Florence)** Kenya. Town in Nyanza province, port at the head of the Kavirondo gulf on the NE shore of L. Victoria 165 m. WNW of Nairobi. Pop. (1962) 23,200. Fishing. Once the terminus of the railway from Mombasa; the Nakuru–Kisumu section is now a branch line off the main route through Uganda.

**Kitakyushu** Japan. City in N Kyushu formed in 1963 by the union of the five towns, ⇨ Moji, ⇨ Kokura, ⇨ Tobata, ⇨ Yawata, ⇨ Wakamatsu, and given special autonomous rights. Pop. (1965) 1,042,389. All except Kokura are modern industrial cities and have little charm. Seat of the Kyushu Institute of Technology (1909).

**Kitchener** Canada. Industrial town in S Ontario, 34 m. WNW of Hamilton. Pop. (1966) 93,255. Tanning, brewing, meat packing. Manufactures lorries, trailers, textiles, furniture, etc. Originally settled in 1800 by Mennonites from Pennsylvania; first called Sand Hills, later Ebytown. In 1824, because of the large influx of German immigrants, renamed Berlin. In 1916 the name was changed in honour of Lord Kitchener (drowned at sea in that year).

**Kitimat** Canada. Port in British Columbia, at the head of the Douglas Channel, 70 m. ESE of Prince Rupert. Pop. 15,000. A gigantic aluminium smelter, the largest in the world (begun 1951) receives power from the Kemano hydroelectric station 48 m. away. The smelter opened in 1954 and the first shipload reached Vancouver in 1955.

**Kitwe** Zambia. Town in the Western Province, 30 m. WNW of Ndola, on a branch railway. Pop. (1963) 101,600 (12,000 Europeans). Commercial centre for the near-by copper-mining centre Nkana; the two together form the largest town in the Copperbelt. Minor industries.

**Kitzbühel** Austria. Former copper-mining town in E Tirol 50 m. ENE of Innsbruck. Pop. 7,000. Now a resort and winter-sports centre.

**Kiukiang** China. River port in N Kiangsi, on the Yangtse-kiang 80 m. N of Nanchang. Pop. 121,000. Trade in rice, tea, tobacco, cotton, etc. Manufactures cotton goods etc. Flour milling. Became a treaty port 1861. To the S are the Lu Shan, rising to 4,900 ft, and the summer resort of Kuling, with famous alpine botanical gardens (1934).

**Kivu** Congo (Kinshasa). Province in the E. Area 100,030 sq. m. Pop. (1967) 2,168,533. Cap. Bukavu. Cattle are raised by the Bantu tribes in the E highlands, and coffee, pyrethrum, cinchona, and other crops are produced by European settlers. Tin mining. The major part of the Albert National Park (the principal Congolese national park, area 3,900 sq. m.), which contains most of the Ruwenzori highlands and the Semliki R., is within the province. The W (in the Congo basin) is covered by dense tropical rain-forest.

**Kivu, Lake** Congo (Kinshasa)/Rwanda. Lake in the W branch of the Great Rift Valley between L. Tanganyika and L. Edward, 55 m. long and up to 30 m. wide, at a height of 4,829 ft (the highest lake in Africa). Drains S into L. Tanganyika through the Ruzizi R. Steamer services. Main ports Bukavu and Goma in Congo (Kinshasa) and Kisenyi in Rwanda. Discovered (1894) by Count von Götzen.

**Kizil Irmak River** Turkey. River 700 m. long (the longest in Asia Minor), rising in the Kizil Dagh and flowing in a wide curve across the Anatolian plateau, first S W, then N W, and finally N E to the Black Sea.

**Kladno** Czechoslovakia. Industrial town in the Středočeský region, Bohemia, 15 m. WNW of Prague. Pop. (1967) 55,000. Coalmining and metallurgical centre. Important iron and steel industry.

**Klagenfurt** Austria. Capital of Carinthia province on the Glan R. near the E end of the Wörthersee. Pop. (1961) 69,218. Resort, in beautiful mountain scenery. Manufactures metal and leather goods, chemicals, etc. A well-planned town, it has lost many of its old buildings in various fires, but still has the 16th-cent. Landhaus and Lindwurmbrunnen (winged dragon fountain).

**Klaipéda** USSR. Formerly Memel. Baltic seaport in the Lithuanian SSR at the entrance to the Kurisches Haff (Courland Lagoon). Pop. (1970) 140,000. Shipbuilding, fish canning, flour milling. Manufactures wood pulp, paper, plywood, textiles, soap, etc. Trade in timber, grain, fish. Founded (1252) by the Teutonic Knights; passed to Prussia (as Memel), and came under Lithuanian rule in 1924 (◊ *Memel Territory*).

**Klerksdorp** S Africa. Town in the Transvaal 100 m. WSW of Johannesburg at a height of 4,350 ft, on the left bank of the Schoonspruit, 10 m. above the confluence with the Vaal R. Pop. (1968) 59,970. Goldmining and agricultural centre. Railway junction. The first Boer settlement in the Transvaal, founded 1839.

**Kleve** ◊ *Cleves.*

**Klondike River** Canada. River 100 m. long in Yukon Territory, flowing W to join the Yukon R. at Dawson; it gives its name to the gold-producing region to the S. Gold was discovered on Bonanza Creek, a tributary, in 1896, and the Klondike gold rush began. Dawson rapidly grew from a few houses to a town of over 20,000 people; but gold production reached its maximum in 1900 and has steadily declined since.

**Klosterneuburg** Austria. Town on the Danube R. on the N outskirts of Vienna. Pop. (1961) 22,787. Wine making. Has a magnificent Augustinian monastery, the oldest and one of the wealthiest in Austria, founded by Leopold the Holy in 1106, with the Leopold Chapel containing the 12th-cent. altar by Nicholas of Verdun.

**Klyuchevskaya Sopka** USSR. Highest active volcano on the mainland of Asia (15,666 ft), in the Kamchatka peninsula 220 m. NNE of Petropavlovsk.

**Knaresborough** England. Urban district in the W Riding of Yorkshire, on the R. Nidd 3 m. ENE of Harrogate. Pop. (1961) 9,311. Market town. Resort. Tanning etc. Limestone quarrying in the neighbourhood. Has a ruined castle (mainly 14th-cent.) and the Dropping Well, with petrifying properties, near which is Mother Shipton's Cave, where the 15th/16th-cent. prophetess was supposed to have been born.

**Knob Lake** ◊ *Schefferville.*

**Knockmealdown Mountains** Irish Republic. Range extending 18 m. E–W along the border between Co. Tipperary and Co. Waterford and rising to 2,609 ft.

**Knossos (Cnossus)** Crete. Ancient city near the N coast, 4 m. SE of Iráklion, its port. Centre of a Bronze Age civilization, occupied well before 3000 B.C. Excavations, especially by Sir Arthur Evans (1851–1941), revealed many archaeological treasures, including the great palace (2000–1400 B.C.), from which a great deal of information about the Minoan civilization has been obtained. Destroyed by fire *c.* 1400 B.C., but its ruins were inhabited till Roman times. ◊ *Crete.*

**Knoxville** USA. Industrial town and river port in E Tennessee, on the Tennessee R. Pop. (1960) 111,827. In a region of coal, iron, and zinc mines and marble quarries. Trade in tobacco etc. Manufactures textiles, cement, furniture, etc. Seat of the University of Tennessee (1794). Headquarters of the Tennessee Valley Authority (TVA). First settled 1786. State capital 1796–1812 and 1817–19.

**Knutsford** England. Urban district in Cheshire 14 m. SSW of Manchester, for which it is a residential suburb. Pop. (1961)

9,389. Manufactures textiles, paper. Mrs Gaskell's 'Cranford'. The name is supposed to be derived from 'Canute's Ford' (though there is no evidence that it was inhabited before the Norman Conquest).

**Kobarid** (Italian **Caporetto**) Yugoslavia. Village in NW Slovenia, on the Isonzo R. near the Italian frontier. Formerly in Italy; ceded to Yugoslavia 1947. Scene of the disastrous defeat of the Italians by the Austro-German army in the 1st World War (1917).

**Kobe** Japan. Capital of Hyogo prefecture, in SW Honshu 19 m. W of Osaka on Osaka Bay. Pop. (1965) 1,216,579. Important seaport and industrial centre, extending 9 m. along the coast. Exports textiles, ships, metal goods, etc. Shipbuilding (esp. important), engineering, sugar refining. Manufactures iron and steel, chemicals, textiles, rubber products, etc. In the rapid growth of the city the old port of Hyogo was absorbed in 1878. Severely damaged by bombing in the 2nd World War.

**Köbenhavn** ⟡ *Copenhagen.*

**Koblenz** ⟡ *Coblenz.*

**Kochi** Japan. Capital of Kochi prefecture, in S Shikoku. Pop. (1965) 217,894. Seaport. Exports dried fish (bonito), coral, paper, etc.

**Kodiak Island** USA. Island 100 m. long in Alaska, in the Gulf of Alaska. Pop. (1960) 2,628. Hilly, with a deeply indented coastline. The first European settlement in Alaska was that of the Russians under Shelekhov at Three Saints Bay (1784); this was moved to Kodiak on the NE coast (1792), which was the headquarters of the Russian-American Company until it moved to Sitka. Kodiak town is a fishing port; salmon canneries.

**Kodok** Sudan. Formerly Fashoda. Small town on the left bank of the White Nile 390 m. S of Khartoum. Pop. 3,000. Its temporary occupation by Marchand, a French officer, caused a diplomatic crisis between England and France (the 'Fashoda incident') in 1898.

**Kofu** Japan. Capital of Yamanashi prefecture, in central Honshu 68 m. W of Tokyo. Pop. (1965) 172,454. Industrial centre. Manufactures silk goods, glassware, saké, food products, etc.

**Kohat** Pakistan. Town in Dera Ismail Khan Division, W Pakistan, 30 m. S of Peshawar. Pop. (1961) 49,854. Trade in grain, salt, etc. Minor industries. Linked with Peshawar by road through the Kohat Pass.

**Kohima** ⟡ *Nagaland.*

**Kokand** USSR. Town in the Uzbek SSR, in the fertile Fergana Valley. Pop. (1970) 133,000. Sugar refining, flour milling. Manufactures textiles, superphosphates, etc. Trade in cotton. Has the former khan's palace. An ancient town, it was capital of the powerful khanate of Kokand in the 18th cent. Taken by the Russians 1876.

**Kokomo** USA. Industrial town in Indiana 50 m. N of Indianapolis. Pop. (1960) 47,197. Manufactures iron, steel, and brass products, motor-car and tractor parts, plastics, etc. Named after a Miami Indian chief, Kokomoko. One of the first practical motor-cars was built and tested here by Elwood Haynes (1894).

**Koko Nor** China. Salt lake in NE Tsinghai (Chinghai) province about 50 m. WNW of Sining at a height of over 10,000 ft. Area 1,600 sq. m. Shallow and variable in extent.

**Kokura** Japan. Industrial town and seaport in Fukuoka prefecture, N Kyushu, 40 m. NE of Fukuoka. Pop. (1960) 286,476. Manufactures steel, chemicals, textiles, porcelain. Merged (1963) with the neighbouring towns of Moji, Tobata, Yawata, and Wakamatsu to form the new city of Kitakyushu.

**Kola Peninsula** USSR. Peninsula in the Murmansk region, RSFSR, between the Barents Sea (N) and the White Sea (S), and mainly N of the Arctic Circle. Area 50,000 sq. m. A low plateau mainly of granite and gneiss, with tundra in the N and thin forests in the S and with many lakes, the largest being L. Imandra. In recent years it has become an important mining region, producing apatite, nepheline, etc. in the Kirovsk area, the minerals being exported from Kandalaksha. Chief town and seaport Murmansk, on Kola Bay (N).

**Kolar Gold Fields** India. Country's most important goldmining centre, in Mysore 45 m. E of Bangalore. Pop. (1961) 146,811. Produces about 90 per cent of India's gold. Also textile manufactures, tanning, and other industries.

**Kolarovgrad** Bulgaria. Formerly (till 1950) Shumen. Capital of Kolarovgrad province, 52 m. W of Varna. Pop. (1965) 59,362. Manufactures metal and leather goods. Trade in cereals, wine. Founded in the 10th cent. Taken by the Turks 1387. Fell to the Russians (1878) and was ceded to Bulgaria.

**Kolberg** ⟡ *Kolobrzeg.*

**Kolding** Denmark. Town and port in E

401                                          KÖNIGGRÄTZ

Jutland, on Kolding Fiord (Little Belt).
Pop. (1965) 37,093. Manufactures machinery, cement, etc. Ruins of the 13th-cent.
castle, Koldinghus, lie NW.
**Kolhapur** India. Town in Maharashtra
180 m. SSE of Bombay. Pop. (1961)
187,442. Manufactures textiles, pottery,
matches, etc. Formerly capital of Kolhapur, largest of the Deccan states, and
once an important religious centre, with
many Buddhist remains.
**Köln** ⋄ *Cologne.*
**Kolobrzeg (Ger. Kolberg)** Poland. Baltic
seaport and seaside resort in the Koszalin
voivodship. Pop. 23,800. Manufactures
machinery. An ancient town; has a 14th-
cent. red-brick church. Before 1945 it was
in German Pomerania, but the German
population was evacuated after the 2nd
World War, and its population fell from
37,000 in 1939 to 3,000 in 1946.
**Kolomna** USSR. Industrial town in the
Moscow region, RSFSR, on the Moskva
R. near the confluence with the Oka R.
65 m. SE of Moscow. Pop. (1970) 136,000.
Important railway engineering centre;
manufactures locomotives, wagons, diesel
engines, textile machinery. Founded in the
12th cent., it suffered repeatedly from the
Tatar invasions.
**Kolomyya (Polish Kolomyja)** USSR. Town
in the Ukrainian SSR, on the Prut R. Pop.
40,000. Formerly in Poland (from 1919)
but ceded to the USSR in 1945. Railway
junction. Trade in agricultural produce.
Metal working, oil refining. Manufactures
textiles, chemicals, etc.
**Kolwezi** Congo (Kinshasa). Town in the S
of Katanga, 90 m. W of Jadotville. Pop.
48,000. Commercial and transport centre
for an important mining region producing
copper and cobalt.
**Kolyma Range** USSR. Mountain range in
the N Khabarovsk Territory, RSFSR, extending 500 m. NE between the Kolyma R.
and the Sea of Okhotsk.
**Kolyma River** USSR. River 1,600 m. long
in N Khabarovsk Territory and Yakut
ASSR, RSFSR, rising in the Cherski
Range and flowing generally N and NE to
the East Siberian Sea, passing in its upper
course through the Kolyma goldfields.
Navigable for about 1,000 m. in summer.
**Komandorski (Commander) Islands** USSR.
Group of islands in the Khabarovsk Territory, RSFSR, between the Kamchatka
peninsula and the Aleutian Is., the largest

being Bering and Medny. Main settlement
Nikolskoye. Home of fur seals.
**Komati River** Moçambique/S Africa. River
500 m. long rising in SE Transvaal, flowing
generally E through N Swaziland, crossing
into Moçambique at Komatipoort (on the
railway from Johannesburg to Lourenço
Marques), taking a wide curve N, E, and
then S and entering the Indian Ocean at
Delagoa Bay. Navigable from the mouth to
Komatipoort.
**Komi ASSR** USSR. Autonomous republic of NE European RSFSR. Area
160,540 sq. m. Pop. (1970) 965,000. Cap.
Syktyvkar. Consisting mainly of the basins
of the Pechora, Vychegda, and upper
Mezen rivers, it is generally low-lying, but
rises to over 5,000 ft along the E border in
the Ural Mountains. Most of it is forested,
there is a considerable stretch of tundra in
the N, and the relatively small farming area
is devoted chiefly to stock rearing, with
reindeer raising and fishing in the tundra.
Coal is produced in the Pechora basin
(Vorkuta) and oil at Ukhta, both industries
having been stimulated by the construction
of the railway across the republic. Timber
is floated down the rivers to the coast.
**Komintern** ⋄ *Novoshakhtinsk.*
**Komi-Permyak NA** USSR. National
Area in E European RSFSR, in the Perm
Region. Area 12,000 sq. m. Pop. (1970)
212,000 (mainly Permyak). Cap. Kudym-
kar (95 m. NW of Perm). Largely forested:
provides timber for cellulose and paper
mills.
**Kommunizma (Kommunizma Peak)** USSR.
Formerly Garmo Peak, then Stalin Peak.
Highest mountain in the USSR (24,590 ft),
in the Tadzhik SSR, in the Akademiya
Nauk Range of the Pamirs.
**Komotíni** Greece. Capital of the Rodhopi
*nome* in Thrace. Pop. (1961) 29,734.
Market town. Trade in cereals, tobacco,
vegetables, etc. Formerly under Turkish
and Bulgarian rule.
**Komsomolsk       (Komsomolsk-on-Amur)**
USSR. Industrial town in the S Khabarovsk Territory, RSFSR, on the Amur R.
175 m. NE of Khabarovsk, with which it is
linked by rail. Pop. (1970) 218,000.
Founded (1932) by the Komsomol or Communist Youth League; developed rapidly
as a centre of heavy industry for the Soviet
Far East. Shipbuilding, sawmilling. Manufactures steel, wood pulp, paper, chemicals.
**Konakry** ⋄ *Conakry.*
**Königgrätz** ⋄ *Hradec Králové.*

P.E.P.—21

**Königsberg** ◊ *Kaliningrad.*

**Königshutte** ◊ *Chorzów.*

**Konstantinovka** USSR. Town in the Ukrainian SSR, in the Donbas 36 m. N of Donetsk. Pop. (1970) 106,000. Important metallurgical centre. Manufactures iron and steel, chemicals, glass, etc.

**Konstanz** ◊ *Constance.*

**Konya** Turkey. Ancient Iconium. Capital of Konya province, 145 m. S of Ankara at a height of 3,300 ft on the edge of the central plateau. Pop. (1965) 157,900. Manufactures textiles, carpets, leather goods, etc. Trade in grain, wool, mohair, etc. Ancient capital of Lycaonia; visited by St Paul. Conquered by the Seljuk Turks in the 11th cent.; under them it became capital of the sultanate of Iconium or Rum and reached the peak of its fame in the 13th cent.

**Kootenay River** Canada/USA. River 407 m. long, rising in SE British Columbia (Canada), flowing S through Montana and Idaho (USA), where it is known as the Kootenai, and then turning NW to form the Kootenay L. in British Columbia, by which it is connected with the Columbia R. Around the upper reaches is the Kootenay National Park (543 sq. m.), established in 1920 to preserve the wildlife and beautiful scenery of the area. The headquarters is the small town and resort of Radium Hot Springs.

**Kopeisk** USSR. Formerly Ugolnye Kopi, Goskopi, Kopi. Town in the Chelyabinsk region, RSFSR, just S of Chelyabinsk. Pop. (1970) 156,000. Important lignite-mining centre. Renamed in the 1930s.

**Koptus** ◊ *Coptos.*

**Korat** ◊ *Nakhon Ratchasima.*

**Körçë** Albania. Capital of the Körçë region and district in the SE. Pop. (1967) 46,000. Market town in a cereal-growing area. Flour milling, brewing, sugar refining. Orthodox and Muslim religious centre. The fifth largest town in Albania.

**Korčula** (Italian **Curzola**) Yugoslavia. Island in the Adriatic Sea 27 m. long and 5 m. wide. Area 107 sq. m. Pop. 27,000. Chief town Korčula on the E coast, a port and seaside resort. Main occupations fishing, cultivation of vines, olives, etc., marble quarrying.

**Korea** (Korean **Choson**, Japanese **Chosen**). Peninsula in E Asia between the Yellow Sea and the Sea of Japan, bounded on the N by China and the USSR, the border being marked largely by the Yalu and Tumen rivers.

TOPOGRAPHY, CLIMATE. Korea is almost hemmed in by mountains in the N and has a mountainous backbone extending N–S through the peninsula near the E coast; the highland scenery has great beauty, but no peak rises above 8,500 ft. The E coast is rocky, and the principal harbours are on the W and S coasts; there are more than 3,000 offshore islands, the majority uninhabited. In climate Korea resembles N China, with hot, rainy summers and dry, cold winters.

RESOURCES, PEOPLE. About two thirds of the population are engaged in farming. Main food crop rice; barley, wheat, soya beans, tobacco, and cotton are also cultivated. Most of the mining as well as the heavy industries is located in N Korea, which produces coal, iron ore, lead, gold, and other minerals; S Korea produces tungsten and some coal. The Korean people are distinct from both the Chinese and Japanese and their language is not related to any other. They developed a phonetic alphabet *c.* 1400. Literacy is fairly high. Confucianism was introduced as the official religion of the Yi dynasty which came to power in 1392, but was subsequently mixed with Buddhism; there are about 1½ million Christians.

HISTORY. Korea has a very ancient history, with traditions and a culture of its own although subject to Chinese and Japanese influence. It was subject to attacks by the Chinese, Manchus, and Japanese and was for long a vassal of Manchu China and kept so segregated as to be known as the Hermit Kingdom. After the Sino-Japanese War (1894–5) Japan compelled China to give up control of Korea, and after the Russo-Japanese War (1904–5) annexed the country (1910), and brought to an end the Yi dynasty which had ruled since 1392. At the end of the 2nd World War American troops occupied the S and Russian troops the N (1945), the peninsula being divided along the 38th parallel. In 1948 two separate régimes were established, the Republic of Korea in the S and the People's Republic of Korea in the N. In 1950 N Korean troops invaded the S without warning, but were driven back by UN forces to the Manchurian border; Chinese troops now supported the N, and advanced far into the S, only to be driven back to the 38th parallel again. In June 1951 a cease-fire was called and 2 years later an armistice was signed, the boundary running across

the 38th parallel; Korea and the Korean people had suffered grievously in the war. S KOREA. Area 38,452 sq. m. Pop. (1966) 29,207,856. Cap. Seoul. Other important towns Pusan, Taegu, Inchon. After a great deal of internal disorder, the economy being dependent on UN and US aid, a group of officers seized power in 1961 and new elections were held in 1963. Industrial development has been made difficult by lack of raw materials and power resources, formerly supplied from the N.
N KOREA. Area 46,814 sq. m. Pop. (1966) 12,500,000. Cap. Pyongyang. In 1946 all estates exceeding 12½ acres were divided among smallholders and landless peasants; agriculture has been largely mechanized. The N has all the large hydroelectric power stations in Korea, the majority of the metallurgical and cement works, and the only oil refinery, industries having been developed initially by the Japanese. Its economy has been supported by loans from China and the USSR.

**Koriyama** Japan. Industrial town in the Fukushima prefecture, Honshu, 27 m. S of Fukushima. Pop. (1965) 223,182. Manufactures textiles, chemicals, machinery, etc.

**Koryak NA USSR.** National Area in NE Siberia, in RSFSR, including the isthmus and the N part of the Kamchatka peninsula. Area 152,000 sq. m. Pop. (1970) 31,000. Cap. Palana. Its people are mainly Koryaks, who gain a livelihood by reindeer breeding, fishing, and hunting.

**Kos** ◊ *Cos.*

**Kosciusko, Mount** Australia. Highest peak in Australia (7,328 ft), on a high plateau of the Australian Alps, New South Wales, 90 m. SSW of Canberra. Winter-sports centre. Named after the Polish patriot and statesman Tadeusz Kosciuszko (1746–1817). ◊ *Snowy Mountains.*

**Košice** Czechoslovakia. Capital of the Východoslovenský region, in Slovakia on the Hernád R. Pop. (1967) 112,000. Manufactures textiles, machinery, fertilizers, food products, etc. The inner old town was built round the 14th/15th-cent. Gothic cathedral. Transferred from Hungary to Czechoslovakia in 1920.

**Köslin** ◊ *Koszalin.*

**Koso Gol** (Höbsögöl) Mongolia. Lake in the extreme N at a height of 5,300 ft, its N end near the USSR frontier. Area 1,200 sq. m. Well stocked with fish. Frozen for 4–5 months annually. Drains S to the Selenga R.

**Kosovo-Metohija** Yugoslavia. Autonomous region in SW Serbia, bordering SW on Albania. Area 3,997 sq. m. Pop. (1961) 963,565 (mainly Albanians). Cap. Priština. A plateau drained by the S Morava, Ibar, and White Drin rivers; in the fertile valleys it produces cereals, tobacco, fruits, etc., and sheep are raised. Under the Turks till 1913, it was then divided between Serbia and Montenegro. Became an autonomous region 1946.

**Kostroma** USSR. Capital of the Kostroma region, RSFSR, at the confluence of the Volga R. with the Kostroma 45 m. ENE of Yaroslavl. Pop. (1970) 223,000. Famous since the 16th cent. for linen. Also manufactures clothing, footwear, paper, excavators, etc. Flour milling, sawmilling. Has a 13th-cent. cathedral within the kremlin. Founded in the mid 12th cent.

**Kostroma River** USSR. River 250 m. long flowing generally SW across the Kostroma region (RSFSR) to join the Volga R. at Kostroma.

**Koszalin** (Ger. **Köslin**) Poland. Capital of the Koszalin voivodship, 90 m. NE of Szczecin. Pop. 60,600. Manufactures agricultural machinery, cement, bricks, etc. Formerly in Pomerania (Germany); passed to Poland after the 2nd World War.

**Kotabaru** ◊ *New Guinea.*

**Kotah** India. Town in Rajasthan, on the Chambal R. 160 m. SW of Gwalior. Pop. (1961) 120,345. Manufactures textiles. Trade in grain, cotton, oilseeds, etc. It was capital of the former Rajput state of Kotah.

**Kota Kinabalu** Malaysia. Formerly Jesselton. Capital and chief seaport of Sabah, on the W coast facing the S China Sea. Pop. (1960) 21,497. Exports timber, rubber. Rice milling. Fishing. Replaced Sandakan as capital of British North Borneo 1947.

**Köthen** German Democratic Republic. Industrial town and railway junction in the Halle district, 20 m. N of Halle. Pop. (1965) 38,205. Engineering, sugar refining. Manufactures textiles etc. Capital of the duchy of Anhalt-Köthen 1603–1847.

**Kotka** Finland. Seaport and capital of the Kymi province in the SE, built on an island in the Gulf of Finland. Pop. (1968) 33,553. Exports timber, wood pulp, and paper. Flour milling, sugar refining. Manufactures wood pulp and paper.

**Kotlas** USSR. Town in the Archangel region, RSFSR, on the N Dvina R. near the confluence with the Vychegda R. Pop.

39,000. Minor port. Shipbuilding, flour milling, etc.

**Kotor Gulf** Yugoslavia. Picturesque inlet of the Adriatic Sea, surrounded by mountains and forming a sheltered harbour, with Kotor and other small towns on its shores.

**Kottbus** ◊ *Cottbus*.

**Kovno** ◊ *Kaunas*.

**Kovrov** USSR. Industrial town and railway junction in RSFSR, on the Moscow–Gorki railway and the Klyazma R. 40 m. ENE of Vladimir. Pop. (1970) 123,000. Railway engineering. Manufactures metal goods, textiles, etc.

**Kowloon** China. Town on Kowloon peninsula, in SE China, opposite Victoria on Hong Kong island and forming part of the British Crown Colony of Hong Kong. Pop. 700,000. The colony's main industrial area. Manufactures cotton goods, rubber footwear, cement, ropes, etc. Important commercial centre, with accommodation for ocean-going ships and a railway link with Kwangchow (Canton). On its NE outskirts is Kai Tak airport.

**Kozáni** Greece. **1**. *Nome* in Macedonia with the Pindus Mountains on the W and drained by the Aliákmon R. Area 2,372 sq. m. Pop. (1961) 190,607. Mainly agricultural. Produces wheat, tobacco, cheese.
**2**. Capital of Kozáni *nome*, at a height of 2,350 ft on the Aliákmon R. Pop. (1961) 17,651. Market town. Hydroelectric plant on the river.

**Kozhikode** India. Formerly Calicut. Seaport in Kerala, on the Malabar coast 170 m. SW of Bangalore. Pop. (1961) 192,521. Exports copra, coconuts, coffee, tea, etc. Manufactures coir rope and mats, soap, hosiery, etc. Sawmilling. The manufacture of calico (called after its earlier name) is now almost extinct. Visited by Vasco da Gama 1498; later trading posts were established here by the Portuguese (1511), English (1664), French (1698), and Danes (1752). Taken in 1765 by Hyder Ali, who expelled the merchants and destroyed coconut palms, pepper vines, etc. in order to keep away Europeans.

**Kra Isthmus** Thailand. The narrowest part of the isthmus which joins the Malay peninsula to the mainland of Asia, 30–50 m. wide, in S Thailand. A ship canal across it has been twice planned and abandoned.

**Kragujevac** Yugoslavia. Town in Serbia 60 m. SSE of Belgrade. Pop. (1961) 52,792. Industrial centre. Manufactures munitions, and has an arsenal. Also vegetable canning,

flour milling. Capital of Serbia 1818–29.

**Krakatao (Krakatoa)** Indonesia. Small volcanic island in Sunda Strait, between Java and Sumatra. Its volcano erupted with great violence in 1883, blowing away the entire N part of the island; the noise of the explosion was heard nearly 3,000 m. away; volcanic dust spread round the world and gave brilliant sunsets; more than 36,000 people were drowned in tidal waves. There have been minor eruptions in the present century (1927–9).

**Kraków** ◊ *Cracow*.

**Kramatorsk** USSR. Industrial town in the Ukrainian SSR, in the Donbas 110 m. SSE of Kharkov. Pop. (1970) 151,000. Important centre for the manufacture of iron and steel, mining and other machinery, excavators, machine tools, cement. Railway engineering.

**Krasnodar** USSR. Formerly (till 1920) Ekaterinodar (Yekaterinodar). Capital of the Krasnodar Territory, RSFSR, on the lower Kuban R. 160 m. SSW of Rostov. Pop. (1970) 465,000. Important industrial centre, mainly engaged in food processing (butter, flour, meat, etc.). Oil refining (connected by pipeline with the Maikop oilfields), railway engineering. Manufactures chemicals, machinery, machine tools, etc. Railway junction. Founded (1794) as a fort under Catherine II.

**Krasnovodsk** USSR. Port in the Turkmen SSR on the SE coast of the Caspian Sea. Pop. 42,000. Trade in oil, cotton, grain, timber. Oil refining (connected by pipeline with the Nebit-Dag oilfield), ship repairing, fish canning. Terminus of the Trans-Caspian Railway. Founded (1717) as a fort under Peter the Great.

**Krasnoyarsk** USSR. **1**. Large territory in central Siberia (RSFSR), including the Taimyr and Evenki National Areas and the Khakass AR. Area 928,000 sq. m. Pop. (1970) 2,962,000. Extends from the Taimyr peninsula in the N through tundra, coniferous forests, and wooded steppes to the Sayan Mountains in the S, and contains the vast Yenisei basin. Wheat and sugar-beet are grown and dairy cattle are reared in the S. Produces gold. Crossed by the Trans-Siberian Railway. Principal towns Krasnoyarsk, Kansk, Igarka (chief port).
**2**. Capital of Krasnoyarsk territory, on the Yenisei R. and the Trans-Siberian Railway. Pop. (1970) 648,000. Industrial centre. Manufactures agricultural and other machinery, locomotives, cranes, cement,

textiles, paper, etc. Railway engineering, sawmilling, flour milling. Also the centre of gold production and has a gold-refining plant. Founded 1628. Expanded rapidly with the construction of the railway.

**Krefeld** Federal German Republic. Industrial town in N Rhine-Westphalia 4 m. W of the Rhine R. and 13 m. NW of Düsseldorf. Pop. (1968) 223,920. Manufactures textiles, clothing, steel, machinery, chemicals, etc. Dyeing, printing. In the Middle Ages it was already a flourishing town; developed with the establishment of the textile industry by Huguenots. First it specialized in linen weaving, then this was superseded by silk, and in more recent times rayon has taken the place of the latter. In 1929 Ürdingen on the Rhine was incorporated with it.

**Kremenchug** USSR. Industrial town, river port, and railway junction in the Ukrainian SSR, on the Dnieper R. 165 m. ESE of Kiev. Pop. (1970) 148,000. Metal working, sawmilling, food processing. Manufactures agricultural machinery, textiles, etc. A hydroelectric power station was completed in 1960, and the canal also constructed made the Dnieper navigable for large vessels from Kanev (65 m. SE of Kiev) to the Black Sea. Founded 1571.

**Krems** **(Krems-an-der-Donau)** Austria. Town in Lower Austria, on the Danube R. 35 m. WNW of Vienna. Pop. (1961) 21,046. Manufactures leather goods, jam. Trade in wine, fruit.

**Kreuznach** ♢ *Bad Kreuznach.*

**Krishna (Kistna)** River India. River 800 m. long rising in the W Ghats in SW Maharashtra and flowing generally ESE across India to the Bay of Bengal, which it enters by a broad delta. Irrigation canals of the delta are linked with those of the Godavari delta. Only a short length of the river is navigable.

**Kristiansand** Norway. Capital of Vest-Agder county, at the mouth of the Otra R. on the Skagerrak. Pop. (1968) 53,736. Seaport. Industrial town. Exports timber, metals, fish. Copper and nickel smelting, woollen milling, brewing, etc. Founded 1641. Rebuilt in stone after disastrous fire in 1892.

**Kristianstad** Sweden. Capital of Kristianstad county, on the Helge R. 55 m. E of Hälsingborg. Pop. (1968) 42,456. Manufactures textiles. Engineering, flour milling, sugar refining. Founded (1614) as a Danish fortress, it changed hands twice and

was finally acquired by Sweden (1678).

**Kristiansund** Norway. Capital of Möre og Romsdal county on four small North Sea islands connected by bridges and ferries, 85 m. WSW of Trondheim. Pop. (1969) 18,588. Fishing port. Fish canning and processing etc. Severely damaged in the 2nd World War when occupied by the Germans; rebuilt later.

**Krivoi Rog** USSR. Town in the Ukrainian SSR, on the Ingulets R. 90 m. WSW of Dnepropetrovsk. Pop. (1970) 573,000. Important iron-mining centre; still produces about half the country's iron ore. Manufactures iron and steel, machine tools, chemicals, etc.

**Krk** Yugoslavia. Island in the N Adriatic Sea SSE of Rijeka. Area 165 sq. m. Pop. 14,500. Chief town and port Krk (pop. 2,800). Vineyards, olive groves. Several bathing resorts. From the early 19th cent. it was successively ruled by Italy, France, and Austria; passed to Yugoslavia 1918.

**Kronshtadt (Kronstadt)** USSR. Naval base and port on Kotlin Island in the Gulf of Finland 14 m. W of Leningrad, RSFSR. Pop. 50,000. Fortifications, arsenal, docks, shipyards. Icebound for about 5 months annually. Kotlin was taken from Sweden by Peter the Great in 1703, and he constructed docks and a fortress on it; for a time Kronshtadt functioned as a commercial port for St Petersburg (Leningrad), but the construction of a deep-sea canal to the latter (1875–85) reduced its importance in this respect. Naval mutinies took place at Kronshtadt in 1905, 1906, 1917, and 1921, the last being against the Soviet government.

**Kroonstad** S Africa. Town in the Orange Free State, 120 m. NNE of Bloemfontein, on the Vals R. (a tributary of the Orange R.) at a height of 4,491 ft. Pop. (1968) 50,700 (16,500 Europeans). Railway junction. Agricultural and educational centre. Resort. Engineering, flour milling. Manufactures clothing.

**Kropotkin** USSR. Town in the Krasnodar Territory, RSFSR, on the Kuban R. 80 m. ENE of Krasnodar. Pop. 54,000. Railway engineering. Trade in agricultural produce (cereals, vegetable oils, meat, etc.).

**Kruger National Park** S Africa. Wildlife sanctuary along the NE Transvaal frontier with Moçambique, 200 m. long and 30–60 m. wide. Founded (1898) by President Kruger as the Sabi game reserve. Later enlarged and renamed. Contains almost every species of game native to S Africa. A great tourist attraction.

**Krugersdorp** S Africa. Town on the Witwatersrand 20 m. WNW of Johannesburg, at a height of 5,709 ft. Pop. (1967) 100,525 (62,000 Bantu, 35,000 whites). A gold, uranium, and manganese mining centre. Railway junction. Metal working. Chemical industry. Named after President Kruger.

**Kuala Lumpur** Malaysia. Federal capital and capital of Selangor state, Malaya, on the Klang R. Pop. (1968) 592,785 (mainly Chinese). Commercial centre in a tin-mining and rubber-growing area. Linked by rail and road with Port Swettenham. Well planned and modern, with fine public buildings. Became capital of the Federated Malay States (1896), of the Federation of Malaya (1948), and of the Federation of Malaysia (1963).

**Kuban River** USSR. The ancient Hypanis of Herodotus and Strabo. River 560 m. long rising in glaciers W of Mt Elbruz in the Greater Caucasus. A mountain torrent in its upper course, it flows N past Armavir, becomes a sluggish, meandering stream as it crosses the steppes in its lower course, turns W past Kropotkin and Krasnodar, and enters the Sea of Azov and the Black Sea by a broad, swampy delta. Its valley is a fertile agricultural region producing cereals, sunflowers, cotton, etc.

**Kubena, Lake** USSR. Lake in the Vologda region, RSFSR, with an outlet via the Sukhona R. to the N Dvina R. Area 140 sq. m. Linked by canal with the Sheksna R. and thus with the Mariinsk canal system.

**Kuch Bihar** ▷ *Cooch Behar*.

**Kuching** Malaysia. Capital of Sarawak, port on the Sarawak R. 15 m. above the mouth. Pop. (1967) 70,000, inc. many Chinese. Exports rubber, pepper, sago flour. Minor industries.

**Kudymkar** ▷ *Komi-Permyak NA*.

**Kuenlun** ▷ *Kunlun*.

**Kufra (Kufara) Oases** Libya. Group of 5 oases in the Libyan Desert (S Cyrenaica), an important centre of the Senussi. Produces dates, barley. Camel rearing. Junction of caravan routes from the Mediterranean coast, United Arab Republic, and Chad.

**Kuh-e-Sahand** ▷ *Tabriz*.

**Kuibyshev** USSR. Formerly Samara. Capital of the Kuibyshev region, RSFSR, on a large loop of the Volga R. at the confluence with the Samara R. Pop. (1970) 1,047,000. Important industrial and com-

mercial centre. Oil refining, flour milling, etc. Manufactures aircraft, locomotives, tractors, cables, chemicals, textiles, etc. Considerable trade in cereals. Also a river port, airport, and railway junction. Site of an important hydroelectric power station. Founded 1586; fortified chiefly to protect traffic along the Volga. During the 2nd World War it expanded greatly, in the main because of the transference here of the Soviet government owing to the German assault on Moscow. Industrial expansion continued after the war. Renamed (1935), after the Soviet leader V. V. Kuibyshev.

**Kuldja** (Chinese **Ining**) China. Town in NW Sinkiang-Uighur AR, on the Ili R. 40 m. from the USSR border. Pop. 108,000. Trade in tea, livestock, etc. Tanning. Stands on the caravan route to Alma-Ata (USSR).

**Kumamoto** Japan. Capital of Kumamoto prefecture, in W Kyushu. Pop. (1965) 407,047. Food processing. Manufactures textiles. Seat of Kumamoto Medical University (1949). Grew up round the 16th-cent. castle.

**Kumasi** Ghana. Second largest city, capital of Ashanti, 125 m. NW of Accra. Pop. (1960) 190,323. Important road and rail junction connected by main lines to Accra and Takoradi. Weaving, metal working, and other crafts. Important trade in cocoa. Seat of the Kwame Nkrumah University of Science and Technology (1961), formerly the Kumasi College of Technology. The old town was almost destroyed by the British in 1874. Modern development dates from the building of the railway from Sekondi (1903).

**Kumbakonam (Combaconum)** India. Ancient town in Madras, on the Cauvery R. delta 160 m. SSW of Madras. Pop. (1961) 96,746. Manufactures textiles, metal goods. Cultural centre with a Sanskrit library; also many temples. Capital of the Chola kingdom in the 7th cent.

**Kunene (Cunene) River** Angola. River 600 m. long, rising near Nova Lisboa, flowing generally S and then W, in its lower course forming the frontier between Angola and SW Africa, and entering the Atlantic. Descending to the coastal plain by a number of falls, it diminishes in volume as it crosses an arid region; the mouth is closed at low water.

**Kungur** USSR. Town in the Perm region, RSFSR, 48 m. SSE of Perm. Pop. 65,000.

Long famous for leather goods. Gypsum quarrying near by. Founded c. 1640.

**Kunlun (Kuenlun).** Great mountain system in central Asia lying between the plateau of Tibet (S) and the Tarim Basin (N) and extending well over 1,000 m. E from the Pamirs. Highest peak Ulugh Muztagh (25,338 ft). The most northerly range, the Altyn Tagh, passes E into the Nanshan; farther S the system is continued in the complex ranges of E Tibet and W China.

**Kunming** China. Formerly Yunnan (Yunnanfu). Capital of Yunnan province 390 m. SW of Chungking, just N of L. Tien Chih at a height of 6,300 ft. Pop. 880,000. Commercial, cultural, and route centre; terminus of the Burma Road. Manufactures textiles, chemicals, cement, machinery, etc. Seat of Yunnan University (1934). Developed rapidly with the construction of the railway to Hanoi (1910), and during the 2nd World War was an important supply base.

**Kuopio** Finland. Capital of the Kuopio province, on L. Kallavesi 210 m. NE of Helsinki. Pop. (1968) 55,067. Commercial and tourist centre. Woodworking industry. Manufactures plywood, doors, bobbins, etc.

**Kupang** ◊ *Timor.*

**Kurdistan.*** The land inhabited by the Kurds comprising the mountain and plateau region of SE Turkey and the adjoining parts of Iran, Iraq, and Syria. The Kurds are a semi-nomadic pastoral people, well known for their fiercely independent spirit; they are mainly Sunni Muslims, and speak Kurdish, an Indo-European language somewhat similar to Persian. They probably number 5 million, of whom nearly half live in Turkey. Their claims for autonomy after the 1st World War were never realized, and revolts in Turkey in 1925 and 1930, in Iran in 1946, and in Iraq in 1962 were suppressed. Iran has a province of Kurdistan, its capital Sanandaj.

**Kure** Japan. Seaport and naval base in Hiroshima prefecture, SW Honshu, 15 m. SSE of Hiroshima. Pop. (1965) 225,012. Shipbuilding (esp. oil tankers), engineering. Manufactures iron and steel, machinery.

**Kurgan** USSR. Capital of the Kurgan region, RSFSR, on the Tobol R. and the Trans-Siberian Railway 160 m. E of Chelyabinsk. Pop. (1970) 244,000. Meat packing, flour milling, tanning. Manufactures agricultural machinery. Trade in agricultural produce. Founded in the 17th cent.

**Kuria Muria Islands.** Group of 5 islands in the Arabian Sea, off the S coast of Muscat and Oman, the largest and only inhabited one being Hallaniya. Area 28 sq. m. Pop. 85. Ceded to Britain by the Sultan of Oman (1854) for a cable station; administered through Aden. Returned to the Sultan of Muscat and Oman 1967.

**Kuril (Kurile) Islands.** USSR. Chain of 32 small islands extending from the S end of the Kamchatka peninsula to Hokkaido (Japan), in the Sakhalin region, RSFSR. Area 6,020 sq. m. Pop. 18,000. Of volcanic origin, with several active volcanoes; the two southernmost are forested. Climate characterized by cool, foggy summers. Main occupations fishing, hunting, lumbering, and sulphur mining. Discovered (1634) by the Dutch navigator Martin de Vries, passed to Japan 1875; surrendered to the USSR after the 2nd World War (1945).

**Kurisches Haff (Courland Lagoon,** Russian **Kurskiy Zaliv)** USSR. Large coastal lagoon formerly in E Prussia but since the 2nd World War in the Lithuanian SSR and RSFSR; separated from the Baltic Sea, except for a narrow outlet, by the Kurische Nehrung (Courland Spit, Kurskaya Kosa), a sandy spit 72 m. long and 1–2 m. wide. On the low E shore of the lagoon is the delta of the Neman R.

**Kurland** ◊ *Courland.*

**Kurnool** India. Town in Andhra Pradesh, on the Tungabhadra R. 110 m. SSW of Hyderabad. Pop. (1961) 100,815. Commercial centre in an agricultural region. Manufactures textiles, carpets, leather, etc.

**Kuroshio (Kuro Siwo, Japan Current).** In Japanese, 'Black Stream' (because of its dark blue colour). Warm ocean current in the Pacific Ocean flowing N and NE past the S and E coasts of Japan, to which it gives heat. Similar to the Gulf Stream of the Atlantic.

**Kurow** ◊ *Waitaki River.*

**Kursk** USSR. Capital of the Kursk region, RSFSR, on the Seim R. 125 m. W of Voronezh. Pop. (1970) 284,000. Railway junction. Manufactures machinery, electrical equipment, clothing, flour, sugar, alcohol, etc. Also a market town in a rich agricultural region. Trade in cereals, sugarbeet, etc. An ancient town, founded in the 9th cent.

**Kurzeme** ◊ *Courland.*

**Kusaie Island** ◊ *Caroline Islands.*

**Kustanai** USSR. Capital of the Kustanai region, in the Kazakh SSR, on the Tobol

R. 150 m. SE of Chelyabinsk. Pop. (1970) 123,000. Industrial and commercial centre in an agricultural region. Flour milling, tanning, meat packing. Trade in grain, cattle. Founded 1871.

**Kutaisi** USSR. Industrial town in the Georgian SSR, on the Rion R. 120 m. WNW of Tbilisi (Tiflis). Pop. (1970) 161,000. In a region of citrus-fruit and vine growing and market gardening. Manufactures chemicals, textiles, etc. Vehicle assembly. Ancient capital of Imeritia (W Georgia).

**Kut-al-Amara (Kut-al-Imara)** Iraq. Capital of Kut province, on the Tigris R. 100 m. SE of Baghdad. Pop. 27,000. Trade in grain, dates. During the 1st World War it was the scene of General Townshend's victory over the Turks (1915); subsequently he was besieged there for many months and finally surrendered (1916). The Kut barrage across the Tigris, built to provide irrigation, was opened in 1939.

**Kutch (Cutch), Rann of** India. Extensive waste of mud and salt flats in NW Gujarat, consisting of the larger area or Great Rann just S of the Pakistan border and the smaller area or Little Rann to the SE. During the rainy season it becomes a salt-marsh and in the dry season a salt-encrusted desert. It was probably once a shallow arm of the Arabian Sea. Some salt is worked. It is an area of dispute between India and Pakistan, and there was fighting here between Indian and Pakistani forces April–June 1965.

**Kuwait. 1.** Independent Arab state on the NW coast of the Persian Gulf. Area 9,375 sq. m. Pop. (1965) 468,389. Bounded on the N and W by Iraq and on the S by Saudi Arabia and a neutral zone jointly owned by the two countries. Mainly desert. Its economy was transformed by the discovery of the Burgan oilfield, where production began in 1946 and rapidly expanded. Kuwait became the world's fourth largest producer in the 1950s. The oilfields are connected by pipelines to the port of Mina al Ahmadi, where some of the petroleum is refined. Under British protection from 1914, but the independence of the sheikhdom was recognized by Britain in 1961.
**2.** Capital of Kuwait, on the Persian Gulf 75 m. S of Basra (Iraq). Pop. (1965) 99,633. Port, with a good natural harbour. Its entrepôt trade has declined with the development of the oil industry. Boat-building (Arab dhows).

**Kuznetsk** USSR. Town in the Penza region, RSFSR, 65 m. E of Penza. Pop. 57,000. Tanning, brickmaking. Manufactures agricultural machinery, rope, etc. Trade in cereals, salt, etc.

**Kuznetsk Basin** USSR. Important coal-mining area in the Kemerovo region, RSFSR, E and SE of Novosibirsk, with enormous reserves. Principal mines around Anzhero-Sudzhensk and Kemerovo. Great industrial development has also taken place here, Kuzbas coal being exchanged for iron ore from Magnitogorsk, through the Ural-Kuznetsk Combine, and more recently iron ore from Temir Tau has been utilized. Non-ferrous metallurgy draws on local supplies of copper, manganese, etc. Chief industrial centre Novokuznetsk.

**Kvarner (Quarnero)** Yugoslavia. Gulf in the N Adriatic Sea separating Istria (W) from the island of Cres (E).

**Kwajalein** ◊ *Marshall Islands.*

**Kwangchow** China. Formerly Canton. Capital of Kwangtung province, on the Pearl or Canton R. at the head of the delta and 90 m. NW of Hong Kong. Pop. (1957) 1,840,000. Chief seaport, industrial and commercial centre of S China, linked by rail with Peking and also with Kowloon (Hong Kong). Has a considerable river trade; through harbour improvements, esp. since 1949, has become accessible to ocean-going vessels. Manufactures textiles (cotton, silk), chemicals, machinery, cement, matches, paper. The walls of the old city were destroyed (1921) and replaced by boulevards, while broad streets were constructed and public parks laid out, and the city was largely modernized. One of its outstanding features was the new Bund or waterfront, lined with offices, restaurants, bazaars, etc., similar to the famous Bund of Shanghai. The European business and residential quarter was on the small island of Shamien in the Pearl R. Seat of the Sun Yat-sen University, founded (1924) by Dr Sun Yat-sen, and Chinan University (1958).

A city of some importance in China from the 3rd cent. B.C., Kwangchow was visited by Hindu and Arab traders in the 8th–10th cent. and was the first Chinese seaport to be in regular contact with Europeans – the Portuguese in the 16th and the British in the 17th cent. It was involved in the Opium War between Britain and China (1841–2), as a result of which it became one of the first treaty ports (1842); but its commercial importance was affected by the development of Hong Kong in the later 19th cent. Its former name, Canton, was a European corruption of Kwangtung, and no doubt the independent outlook of the Cantonese was largely due to their early association with foreigners; they played a significant part in the revolution of 1911 under the leadership of Sun Yat-sen, whose principles of nationalism, democracy, and social reform were accepted first by the Kuomintang and later by the Communists. The city was occupied by the Japanese 1938–45 and was taken over by the Communists in 1949; its foreign treaty-port rights were abolished in 1943.

**Kwangsi-Chuang A R** China. Autonomous region in the S bordering on N Vietnam. Area 85,000 sq. m. Pop. (1957) 19,390,000. Cap. Nanning. Generally hilly, it occupies the basin of the upper Si-kiang, and in the valleys of this river and its tributaries rice is the main crop; the W is inhabited by aboriginal tribes. Chief towns Nanning, Kweilin.

**Kwangtung** China. Maritime province in the S, on the S China Sea, including the Luichow peninsula, Hainan, and many offshore islands. Area 89,000 sq. m. Pop. (1957) 37,960,000. Cap. Kwangchow (Canton). Generally hilly. Drained by the lower Si-kiang, the Pei-kiang, and the Han rivers. The climate is of the tropical monsoon type and rainfall is everywhere abundant. Rice, silk, sugar-cane, tobacco, and many varieties of fruit are produced; timber is floated down the rivers from the interior. Chief mineral tungsten. Kwangchow (Canton) is the leading industrial centre, and Swatow is also an important town. On the coast are the only remaining foreign enclaves in China, Macao (Portuguese) and Hong Kong (British). It was in Kwangtung that Sun Yat-sen began his revolutionary activities (1911).

**Kweichow** China. Province in the S W on a lofty plateau between the Yangtse-kiang and the Si-kiang. Area 65,000 sq. m. Pop. (1957) 16,890,000. Cap. Kweiyang. Rice is cultivated in the valleys and maize on the plateau, while tung oil is produced in the forests. Some mercury mined. Miao aborigines form the majority of the rural population on the plateau.

**Kweilin** China. Town in the Kwangsi-Chuang A R, on the Kwei R. 240 m. N W of Kwangchow (Canton). Pop. 145,000. Trade in rice, beans, etc. In a limestone region famous for its unusual karst scenery. Formerly capital of Kwangsi province.

**Kweisui** ◊ *Huhehot*.

**Kweiyang** China. Capital of Kweichow province, 220 m. S of Chungking at a height of 3,400 ft. Pop. 504,000. Important road junction. Manufactures iron and steel, machinery, textiles, glass, paper, matches, chemicals. Trade in grain, hides, etc. Seat of Kweichow University (1958).

**Kwinana** Australia. New town in Western Australia 17 m. S of Fremantle. Pop. (1964) 4,500. Large oil refinery, steel mill, cement works. Cockburn Sound was dredged to form a deep-water harbour.

**Kyle of Lochalsh** Scotland. Small fishing port and railway terminus in S W Ross and Cromarty, at the entrance to Loch Alsh. Pop. 1,500. Car ferry to Kyleakin, Skye.

**Kyoga, Lake** ◊ *Kioga, Lake*.

**Kyoto** Japan. Capital of Kyoto prefecture, Honshu, 230 m. W S W of Tokyo and near L. Biwa, with which it is connected by canal. Pop. (1965) 1,364,977. Important manufacturing centre famous for its craft industries – porcelain, lacquer ware, dolls, fans, silk goods, brocades, etc. Also manufactures textiles, chemicals, machinery, etc. The chief Buddhist centre, it has many temples and shrines as well as the former imperial palace. An important tourist centre, often known as 'the Florence of the East'. University (1897). Founded 793; Japanese capital until 1868.

**Kyushu** Japan. Southernmost of the 4 main islands, including about 370 small islands and divided into 7 prefectures. Area 16,247 sq. m. Pop. (1960) 12,903,515. Much of it is mountainous, and it rises to 5,544 ft in the volcanic Mt Aso; there are many hot springs. In the Chikuho Basin it has the country's chief coalfield, while near by is the important region of heavy industry centred on Kitakyushu.

**Kyzyl Kum** USSR. Means 'Red Sand'. Desert in the Kazakh and Uzbek SSRs, SE of the Aral Sea between the Amu Darya and the Syr Darya, consisting largely of sand dunes, with patches of bare rock.

# L

**Laaland (Lolland)** Denmark. Island in the Baltic Sea S of Zealand, with the German Fehmarn Is. to the SW. Area 480 sq. m. Pop. 87,000. Low-lying, rising to only 100 ft. Cereals, sugar-beet cultivated. Chief towns Maribo, Nakskov.

**La Asunción** ◊ *Margarita Island.*

**Labrador** Canada. Extensive coastal territory in the E; the most northerly district of the Newfoundland province. Area 110,000 sq. m. Pop. (1966) 21,157 (inc. about 2,600 Eskimo, chiefly scattered along the N coast). Formerly considered to be the whole peninsula between Hudson Bay and the Gulf of St Lawrence (over 500,000 sq. m.); most of this now belongs to Quebec. The present coast extends NW from Blanc Sablon (at the entrance to the Straits of Belle Isle) to Cape Chidley (at the entrance to Hudson Strait); it is deeply indented, cold and bleak, and swept by the Labrador Current. Of the rivers the Churchill (Hamilton) is the most important, with great hydroelectric potentialities. The climate is harsh, with long winters and short cool summers; heavy snowfalls occur in the interior. Main occupation cod fishing; herring and salmon fisheries also important. Some trapping of fur-bearing animals. Forests cover considerable areas, but more important are the vast iron ore deposits. The first shipment of ore from the deposit near Schefferville was sent in 1954; other deposits are being worked.

The Labrador coast was probably the first part of the American continent to be sighted by Europeans (a party of Norsemen *c.* 986). Rediscovered by John Cabot 1498. Became British 1763. Has been under the jurisdiction of Newfoundland continuously since 1809. The boundary with Quebec was finally settled in 1927.

**Labrador Current.** A cold ocean current flowing past the coasts of Labrador and E Newfoundland, from Baffin Bay and SW Greenland. Widening as it proceeds S, it meets the ◊ *Gulf Stream* off the Grand Banks (where fogs are caused by the merging of cold and warm waters). Carries icebergs into the main shipping lanes between N America and Europe.

**Labuan** Malaysia. Island off the SW coast of Sabah (N Borneo), Malaysia. Area 35 sq. m. Pop. (1960) 14,904 (mainly Malays and Chinese). Chief town Victoria (pop. 3,213). Produces copra, rubber, sago. Ceded to Britain by the Sultan of Brunei 1846. Became part of the new colony of North Borneo (renamed Sabah 1963) in 1946.

**Laccadive Islands** India. Group of 14 coral islands and several reefs in the Arabian Sea, about 200 m. W of the Malabar coast, forming a Union Territory with the Minicoy and Amindivi Is. Area (Territory) 11 sq. m. Pop. (1961) 24,108 (almost entirely Muslim). Chief lang. Malayalam. Main products copra, coir. Centre of administration Kozhikode (Kerala).

**La Ceiba** Honduras. Caribbean port. Pop. (1966) 31,951. Exports coconuts, bananas, etc. Flour milling, tanning. Manufactures footwear, soap, etc.

**Lachine** Canada. Industrial town, port, and resort in Quebec, on the S coast of Montreal Island. Pop. (1966) 43,155. At the SW end of the Lachine Canal. Manufactures iron and steel, wire, tyres, chemicals. First settled 1675. The name is said to refer ironically to La Salle's dream of finding a westward route to China (La Chine).

**Lachlan River** Australia. River 920 m. long in New South Wales, rising in the Great Dividing Range near Gunning, flowing NW and then SW to join the Murrumbidgee R. Wyangala Dam and Reservoir (1935) above Cowra is used to irrigate an extensive area.

**Lackawanna** USA. Industrial town in New York just S of Buffalo. Pop. (1960) 29,564 (about 30 per cent of Polish and Hungarian origin). Important steel industry.

**Laconia** ◊ *Lakonia.*

**La Crosse** USA. Town in Wisconsin, on the Mississippi R. at its confluence with the Black and La Crosse rivers. Pop. (1960) 47,575. Commercial centre in a dairy-farming region. Manufactures agricultural equipment, motor-car parts, footwear, etc. Named by early French fur traders after a game played by the Winnebago Indians resembling the French game 'la crosse'.

**La Cumbre** ◊ *Uspallata Pass.*

**Ladakh (Ladak)** India. District in NE

Kashmir bounded on the N by Sinkiang-Uighur and E by Tibet (China). Area 45,762 sq. m. Pop. 195,000. Cap. Leh. Geographically belongs to Tibet. The Upper Indus valley which traverses it stands at a height of 11,000 ft near Leh, and surrounding mountain ranges rise on average to 19,000 ft. The W part, known as Baltistan, contains the highest peaks of the Karakoram, including K2 (28,250 ft). The Balti, who represent about four fifths of the total population, are Muslims; the Ladakhi are Buddhists. Chief towns Leh, Skardu. Wheat and other cereals cultivated. Sheep and goats raised.

**Ladakh Range** India. Mountain range in E Kashmir extending 200 m. SE just N of and parallel to the upper Indus R., on the S side of which are the Zaskar Mountains. Includes peaks exceeding 20,000 ft.

**Ladoga, Lake** USSR. Lake in the NW of RSFSR, the largest in Europe, 125 m. long and up to 80 m. wide. Area 7,000 sq. m. Lakes Onega, Ilmen (USSR), and Saimaa (Finland) drain into it. Discharges by the Neva R. into the Gulf of Finland. Frozen from about December to March; navigation also impeded by storms and fogs. Canals along the S shore carry considerable traffic between the Volga R. and the Baltic Sea. Fishing important. A species of seal provides evidence of its former association with the Arctic Ocean. The Russo-Finnish border passed NE–SW through the lake until 1940. During the siege of Leningrad (1941–3) such provisions as reached the city were transported over the frozen lake.

**Ladrone Islands** ◇ *Mariana Islands.*

**Ladysmith** S Africa. Town in Natal, on the Klip R. 120 m. NW of Durban at a height of 3,284 ft. Pop. (1968) 32,750. A railway junction on the main line from Durban, which bifurcates here to the Transvaal and the Orange Free State. Railway engineering. Manufactures textiles, clothing, etc. During the S African War it was besieged by the Boers Nov. 1899–Feb. 1900, and was relieved by Sir Redvers Buller's force.

**Lafayette** (Indiana) USA. Town on the Wabash R. 60 m. NW of Indianapolis. Pop. (1960) 42,330. Market for grain, cattle, pigs. Meat packing. Manufactures electrical equipment, machinery, pharmaceutical products, etc. Seat of the Purdue University (1874).

**Lafayette** (Louisiana) USA. Formerly

**Vermilionville.** Town on the Vermilion R. 52 m. WSW of Baton Rouge. Pop. (1960) 40,400. Commercial centre for an agricultural and mining region. Sugar refining, cotton and cottonseed processing, etc. Also a centre of the oil industry. French is widely spoken. Founded (as Vermilionville) 1824; renamed (1884) after the Marquis de La Fayette (1757–1834).

**Lagan River** Northern Ireland. River 45 m. long rising near Ballynahinch, Co. Down, and flowing NW and then NE past Lisburn to Belfast Lough at Belfast. Linked by canal with Lough Neagh.

**Lågen River (Gudbrandsdalslågen)** Norway. River 120 m. long, rising N of the Jotunheim Mountains and flowing generally SSE through the Gudbrandsdal to L. Mjosa.

**Lågen River (Numedalslågen)** Norway. River 200 m. long, rising in the Hardangervidda and flowing generally SSE through the Numedal to the Skagerrak at Larvik.

**Lagôa dos Patos** ◇ *Pelotas*; *Pôrto Alegre*; *Rio Grande.*

**Lagoon Islands** ◇ *Ellice Islands.*

**Lagos** Nigeria. Capital and chief seaport, on an island in a lagoon on the coast of the Gulf of Guinea. Pop. (1963) 450,000. Reached from the Bight of Benin by a channel dredged through the sand bar at the entrance to the lagoon; linked by a 2,600-ft bridge with Iddo Island, in turn linked with the mainland by bridge. Exports palm oil and kernels, groundnuts, cocoa, etc. Brewing, sawmilling. Manufactures soap etc. Seat of a university (1962).

**La Guaira** Venezuela. Chief seaport, on the Caribbean Sea 7 m. N of Carácas in the Federal District. Pop. 20,000. Excellent harbour, accommodating the largest ships. Exports coffee, cacao, tobacco, etc. Linked by motorway with Carácas. Founded 1577.

**Lahore** Pakistan. Capital of W Pakistan and of Lahore division, and the country's second largest city, near the Ravi R. 650 m. NE of Karachi. Pop. (1961) 1,296,477. Important industrial, commercial, and route centre. Railway engineering. Manufactures textiles, carpets, metal goods, footwear, etc. Seat of a university (1882). Much of its architecture is undistinguished, but the Badshahi Masjid of Aurangzeb and the tomb of Ranjit Singh are notable, and to the E of the city are the famous

Shalamar gardens, created by Shah Jahan in 1637. Probably founded before the 7th cent., Lahore became capital of the Ghaznevid and Ghori lands in India in the 11th and 12th cent. and of the Sikh empire of Ranjit Singh in the 18th cent. Came under British rule 1846; was capital of the former province of Punjab before the partition of India (1947).

**Lahti** Finland. Town in the Häme province, at the S end of the L. Päijänne waterway 57 m. NE of Helsinki. Pop. (1968) 85,409. Sawmilling. Manufactures furniture, plywood, spools, matches, glass. Also a winter-sports resort.

**Laibach** ◊ *Ljubljana.*

**Laindon** ◊ *Basildon.*

**Lake Charles** USA. Town in SW Louisiana, on the Calcasieu R. (widened into L. Charles with a 35-ft channel to the Gulf of Mexico). Pop. (1960) 63,392. Exports petroleum, timber, rice, cotton. Oil refining, sawmilling, cotton ginning. Named after an 18th-cent. Spanish settler, Carlos Salia, who changed his name to Charles Sallier.

**Lake District** England. Picturesque region of lakes and mountains in the NW in N Lancashire, W Westmorland, and S Cumberland, about 30 m. N–S and 25 m. W–E. The principal lakes are: in the centre Derwentwater, Thirlmere, Grasmere, and Rydal Water; in the N Bassenthwaite; in the E Ullswater and Hawes Water; in the S Windermere, Esthwaite Water and Coniston Water; in the W Wast Water, Ennerdale Water, Crummock Water, and Buttermere. Scafell (3,210 ft), Helvellyn (3,118 ft), and Skiddaw (3,053 ft) are the highest mountains. Waterfalls and dales add beauty to the scenery, and in spite of the rather heavy rainfall the region is popular with tourists. Many literary associations, esp. with Wordsworth, Southey, and Coleridge – the so-called Lake Poets.

**Lakeland** USA. Town in Florida 35 m. ENE of Tampa. Pop. (1960) 41,350. In a region of many small lakes, hence the name. Centre of the citrus-fruit industry. Packing plants, canneries. Also a resort.

**Lake of the Woods** Canada/USA. Lake on the Canada–USA frontier, in Minnesota (USA) and Manitoba and Ontario (Canada). Area 1,485 sq. m. In a beautiful pine-forest region, with thousands of islands. Fed from L. Rainy by the Rainy R. and drained into L. Winnipeg by the

Winnipeg R. A popular tourist region.

**Lakewood** USA. Town in Ohio, on L. Erie just W of Cleveland, of which it is a residential suburb. Pop. (1960) 66,154. Manufactures tools, hardware, plastics, etc.

**Lakonia (Laconia)** Greece. *Nome* in the SE Peloponnese. Area 1,453 sq. m. Pop. (1961) 118,449. Cap. Sparta. Mainly agricultural. Produces citrus fruits, wheat, olives, etc. Sheep and goats raised.

**Laleham** ◊ *Staines.*

**Lambayeque** ◊ *Chiclayo.*

**Lambeth** England. Former metropolitan borough of S London, bordering N on the R. Thames and extending S to the county boundary, including the districts of Kennington, Vauxhall, Brixton, and part of Norwood; from 1965 a Greater London borough including the E part of Wandsworth. Pop. (1963) 340,762. Here the Thames is crossed by the Vauxhall, Lambeth, Westminster, and Waterloo road bridges and the Charing Cross railway bridge. Also has London's largest railway station, Waterloo; near by is the Old Vic Theatre, famous for its Shakespearian productions and now the home of the National Theatre. At the end of Westminster Bridge stand the London County Hall on one side and St Thomas's Hospital on the other; downstream is the Royal Festival Hall, a modern concert hall (1951), and upstream Lambeth Palace, London residence of the Archbishop of Canterbury, which has the 15th-cent. Lollard's Tower, once a prison for heretics, and since 1867 has been the scene of the periodic Lambeth Conferences, assemblies of Anglican bishops. Lambeth was formerly the site of Vauxhall Gardens, the Regency amusement centre, and includes the Oval, the famous cricket ground.

**Lamia** Greece. Capital of Phthiotis *nome* 100 m. NW of Athens. Pop. (1961) 22,353. Market town. Trade in wheat, olive oil, etc. Gave its name to the Lamian War (Antipater took refuge and was besieged here 323 B.C.).

**Lamington, Mount** Papua. Volcano in the Owen Stanley Range NE of Port Moresby which erupted violently in Jan. 1951 and killed over 4,000 people.

**Lampedusa** Italy. Largest of the Pelagian Islands, in the Mediterranean Sea between Malta and Tunisia. Area 8 sq. m. Pop. 4,000. Fishing, sardine canning. During the 2nd World War it was heavily bombed; surrendered to the Allies June 1943.

**Lampeter** Wales. Municipal borough in Cardiganshire, on the R. Teifi 24 m. E of Cardigan. Pop. (1961) 1,853. Market town. Seat of St David's College (1822), a centre for training students for holy orders.

**Lanark** Scotland. Royal burgh and county town of Lanarkshire, near the R. Clyde 22 m. SE of Glasgow. Pop. (1961) 8,436. Market town. Textile mills. New Lanark, 1 m. S, was built by the socialist reformer Robert Owen (1784). The Falls of Clyde are 2 m. S.

**Lanarkshire** Scotland. Inland county in the S, drained by the R. Clyde and its tributaries. Area 879 sq. m. Pop. (1961) 1,626,317 (of whom more than 1 million are in Glasgow). County town Lanark. In the N it is low-lying and fertile, but it rises to over 2,000 ft in the centre and S, and Leadhills, in the Lowther Hills (S), at 1,350 ft is the second highest village in Scotland, being exceeded only by near-by Wanlockhead, in Dumfriesshire (1,380 ft). Oats are cultivated, tomatoes and small fruits grown, and cattle, sheep, and the famous Clydesdale horses raised. The N became highly industrialized owing to the presence of coal and iron deposits (the former now declining and the latter exhausted); thus the county contains almost one third of the population of Scotland. Besides Glasgow, the leading manufacturing centres are Motherwell and Wishaw, Coatbridge, Hamilton, Airdrie, Rutherglen, and the 'new town' of East Kilbride.

**Lancashire** England. County in the NW bounded on the W by the Irish Sea. Area 1,878 sq. m. Pop. (1961) 5,131,646 (the greatest of any county in the UK). County town Lancaster. Hilly in the E and N, where Furness, which contains the S part of the Lake District, is separated from the rest of the county by Morecambe Bay. Chief rivers the Mersey, Ribble, and Lune. The Pennine moorlands are of little value agriculturally, but in the more fertile lowlands of the SW oats and potatoes are cultivated, and dairy farming and pig and poultry rearing are important, esp. on the Fylde peninsula. Lancashire is famous chiefly for its manufactures, however, based on the coalfield of the SE, which has a declining output. S Lancashire became the world's leading cotton spinning and weaving region, but the loss of overseas markets has led to a considerably reduced production and reorganization of the industry. Engineering, shipbuilding, and the manufacture of rayon and other textiles, paper, chemicals, glass, and hosiery are also of great significance. The largest towns, Liverpool and Manchester, are among the country's leading seaports, the latter being accessible by the Manchester Ship Canal; other industrial centres, all with a population exceeding 100,000, are Blackpool (better known as a seaside resort), Bolton, Salford, Oldham, St Helens, Preston, Blackburn. In 1351 Lancashire became a county palatine; the Duchy of Lancaster is vested in the Crown, and its Chancellor holds Cabinet rank in HM government.

**Lancaster** England. Municipal borough and county town of Lancashire, on the R. Lune 20 m. N of Preston. Pop. (1961) 48,887. Textile centre; manufactures rayon and cotton goods, linoleum, furniture, plastic products, etc. Castle (partly 13th-cent.) on the site of a Roman camp; Church of St Mary (mainly 15th-cent.); 15th-cent. grammar school. University (1964). Created a city 1937. Birthplace of William Whewell (1794–1866) and Sir Richard Owen (1804–92).

**Lancaster** (Ohio) USA. Town on the Hocking R. 26 m. SE of Columbus. Pop. (1960) 29,916. Manufactures machinery, footwear, glass, etc. Birthplace of General William T. Sherman (1820–91).

**Lancaster** (Pennsylvania) USA. Town 60 m. W of Philadelphia. Pop. (1960) 61,055. Important market town in a fertile agricultural district. Manufactures linoleum, electrical goods, watches, etc. Laid out 1730. Named after Lancaster, England. State capital 1799–1812.

**Lanchow** China. Capital of Kansu province, on the Hwang-ho 700 m. WSW of Peking at a height of 5,200 ft. Pop. 700,000. Important route, commercial, and cultural centre. The famous Silk Road to Sinkiang starts here, and it is the centre of caravan trade with Tibet, India, and the USSR; also the terminus of the Paotow railway, linking NW China with Inner Mongolia. Tobacco processing, oil refining. Manufactures oilfield equipment, chemicals, cement, textiles, soap, matches, etc. Seat of a university.

**Landau** Federal German Republic. Town in the Rhineland-Palatinate, 18 m. NW of Karlsruhe. Pop. (1963) 30,000. Trade in wine, grain, etc. Brewing. Manufactures tobacco products, furniture, etc.

**Landes** France. **1.** Department in the SW, formed (1790) from parts of Guienne, Gascony, and Béarn, occupying most of the Landes region. Area 3,615 sq. m. Pop. (1968) 277,381. Prefecture Mont-de-Marsan. Drained by the Adour R. and its tributaries. Soil generally infertile; only the hilly Chalosse region is intensively cultivated; sheep rearing is important. Industries sawmilling and the manufacture of turpentine, resin, etc. Chief towns Mont-de-Marsan, Dax.
**2.** Region in the SW extending along the Bay of Biscay, mainly the Landes department, but also occupying parts of the Gironde and Lot-et-Garonne departments. Formerly a waste of marsh and moorland, with a strip of sand dunes, many over 150 ft high, along the coast, separating a number of lagoons (the largest being the Arcachon Basin) from the sea. The dunes were fixed by the planting of pine forests, yielding timber, turpentine, resin, etc.

**Land's End** England. Ancient Bolerium. Granite headland 60 ft high on the coast of W Cornwall, the westernmost extremity of England. The Longships lighthouse is 1 m. W.

**Landshut** Federal German Republic. Town in Bavaria, on the Isar R. 38 m. NE of Munich. Pop. (1963) 50,600. Industrial centre. Manufactures metal goods, chemicals, soap, etc. Brewing, tanning. Above the town is the 13th-cent. castle of Trausnitz; among other notable buildings is the 14th/15th-cent. Gothic Church of St Martin. Seat of the University of Ingolstadt (1800–1826).

**Landskrona** Sweden. Seaport in Malmöhus county on The Sound, 21 m. NNW of Malmö. Pop. (1968) 32,125. Tanning, flour milling, sugar refining. Manufactures fertilizers. Offshore is the island of Ven, site of Tycho Brahe's observatory.

**Langdale Pikes** England. Two peaks in the Cumbrian Mountains, Lake District, on the Westmorland border 3 m. W of Grasmere: Harrison Stickle (2,403 ft) and Pike-o'-Stickle (2,323 ft).

**Langeland** Denmark. Island in the Baltic Sea between Fyn and Laaland islands, 32 m. long and up to 7 m. wide. Area 110 sq. m. Pop. 18,000. Chief town Rudköbing. Fertile. Cereals cultivated.

**Langholm** Scotland. Small burgh in Dumfriesshire, on the R. Esk 24 m. ENE of Dumfries. Pop. (1961) 2,369. Market town. Manufactures tweeds, leather.

**Languedoc** France. Region and former province in the S, bounded approximately by the Massif Central, the Rhône R., the Gulf of Lions, and the foothills of the Pyrenees, now divided into the departments of Ardèche, Gard, Hérault, Lozère, Aude, and Tarn, and parts of Haute-Garonne, Haute-Loire, Pyrénées-Orientales, and Ariège. Important wine-producing region. Chief towns Toulouse (the historic capital), Montpellier, Nîmes, Béziers, Carcassonne. The name derives from *Langue d'oc*, referring to the Provençal tongue (*langue*) in which *oc* meant 'yes' – as distinct from the *Langue d'oil* (present-day *oui*) of the centre and north.

**Lansing** USA. State capital of Michigan (since 1847), on the Grand R. 80 m. WNW of Detroit. Pop. (1960) 107,807. Noted for the manufacture of cars. Also produces buses, lorries, gas engines, fire-fighting equipment, tools, etc. First settled 1837. Industrial development came with the railways; the manufacture of railway carriages was the leading industry until 1901, when the automobile industry superseded it.

**Laoag** Philippines. Port in NW Luzon, on the Laoag R. 5 m. from the mouth. Pop. (1961) 50,096. In a region producing rice, maize, sugar, etc., which it exports. Manufactures cotton goods.

**Laoighis (Leix)** Irish Republic. Formerly Queen's County. Inland county in Leinster province. Area 664 sq. m. Pop. (1966) 44,595. County town Port Laoighise (Maryborough). Generally flat and boggy; hilly in the SE and NW, where it rises to 1,700 ft in the Slieve Bloom Mountains. Main occupations agriculture, dairy farming.

**Laon** France. Prefecture of the Aisne department, 29 m. NW of Reims on an isolated hill 330 ft above the surrounding plain. Pop. (1968) 28,613. Manufactures metal goods, sugar. Outstanding buildings are the 12th/13th-cent. former cathedral and the bishop's palace. Fortified by the Romans. From the end of the 5th cent., when it became a bishopric, it was one of the chief towns of the Franks. In the Hundred Years War it passed from Burgundian to English to French hands.

**Laos.\*** Kingdom of SE Asia. Area 88,780 sq. m. Pop. (1962) 2,200,000. Cap. Vientiane. Bounded by China (N), N and S Vietnam (E), Cambodia (S), and Thailand and Burma (W). Apart from the valley of the Mekong (which forms much of the W boundary) and its tributaries, the country is mountainous. Principal food crop rice. Produces maize, tobacco, coffee. Teak is floated down the Mekong from the forests in the N. Most of the people belong to the Lao and other Thai groups; Lao is the official language. Became a French protectorate 1893, and an independent sovereign state within the French Union 1949. In 1953 Communist Vietminh forces from Vietnam, aided by Pathet Lao rebels, invaded Laos, but in the following year both Vietminh and French Union troops withdrew from the country. Disorders continued, and in 1960 civil war broke out; a ceasefire was arranged in 1961, however, and a government of National Union was formed in 1962.

**La Paz** Bolivia. Capital of La Paz department, in the steep-sided valley of the La Paz R. at a height of 12,000 ft (1,200 ft below the bleak Altiplano). Pop. (1967) 482,367. Seat of government; *de facto* capital of Bolivia since 1898 (though Sucre is still the nominal capital). The highest large city in the world. Its airport on the Altiplano at over 13,000 ft is the world's highest commercial airfield. Commercial centre. Trade in the products of the Andean valleys and the Altiplano. Tanning, brewing, flour milling. Manufactures textiles, chemicals, etc. Seat of a university (1830). Founded (1548) by the Spaniards. Named La Paz de Ayacucho (1827) after the battle for independence.

**Lapland.** Extensive region in N Europe inhabited by the Lapps, covering the N parts of Norway, Sweden, and Finland and the extreme NW of the USSR, mainly within the Arctic Circle but of undefined limit in the political sense. In the W it is mountainous, rising to 6,965 ft in Kebnekaise and 6,857 ft in Sarektjåkko, both in Sweden. The N is mainly tundra, while the S is densely forested, and there are many lakes and rivers. Many of the Lapps, who are of Mongolian stock and number about 34,000 (20,000 in Norway), are nomadic, making seasonal migrations with their reindeer herds between the lowlands and the mountains; others, who gain a livelihood by fishing or hunting, are settled in villages. They were frequently the prey of their more powerful neighbours, and were largely absorbed, and their population declined long before the legislation of a more tolerant age gave them protection. In Swedish Lapland are some of the richest deposits of iron ore in the world, chiefly at Kiruna and Gällivare, and other minerals are exploited elsewhere.

**La Plata** Argentina. Formerly (1952–5) Eva Perón. Capital of the Buenos Aires province, near the Río de la Plata 33 m. SE of Buenos Aires. Pop. (1960) 330,310. Exports products of the pampas (meat, grain, wool) through its port Ensenada. Meat packing, oil refining, flour milling. Manufactures cement, textiles. Seat of a university (1897). Modern and well planned. Founded 1882.

**Larache (El Araish)** Morocco. Port in the NW, on the Atlantic coast 43 m. SSW of Tangier. Pop. 42,000. Exports cork, wool, etc. Fishing. Orchards and market gardens in the neighbourhood. Under Spanish protection 1912–56.

**Laramie** USA. Town in Wyoming, on the Laramie R. 43 m. WNW of Cheyenne at a height of 7,145 ft. Pop. (1960) 17,520. Commercial and route centre in a stock-rearing area. Railway engineering. Manufactures cement etc. Seat of the University of Wyoming (1887).

**Laramie Mountains** USA. A range of the Rocky Mountains in SE Wyoming, extending into N Colorado. Highest point Laramie Peak (10,272 ft).

**Laramie River** USA. River 210 m. long rising in the Front Range, Colorado, flowing N and NE past Laramie (Wyoming), and joining the N Platte R. at Fort Laramie.

**Laredo** USA. Town in SW Texas, on the Rio Grande opposite Nuevo Laredo (Mexico), with which it is connected by two international bridges. Pop. (1960) 60,678. Commercial centre for an agricultural and oil-producing region. Oil refining, meat packing, canning, etc. Also a tourist resort on the Inter-American Highway. Founded (1751) by the Spanish. Captured by Texas Rangers 1846.

**Largo** Scotland. Fishing village and resort in SE Fifeshire, on the Firth of Forth. Pop. 2,000. Birthplace of Alexander Selkirk (1676–1721).

**Largs** Scotland. Small burgh in Ayrshire, on the Firth of Clyde 11 m. SSW of Greenock. Pop. (1961) 9,100. Port. Seaside resort. Here Alexander III of Scotland defeated Haakon IV of Norway (1263).

**Larisa (Larissa)** Greece. **1.** *Nome* in E Thessaly. Area 2,080 sq. m. Pop. (1961) 237,683. Contains the fertile basin of the Peneus R.; produces wheat, citrus fruits, olives, etc.
**2.** Capital of Larisa *nome*, on the Peneus R., 35 m. NW of its port, Volós. Pop. (1961) 55,733. Trade in agricultural produce. Railway junction. Manufactures textiles. Important city in ancient Thessaly from the 6th cent. B.C. Taken by the Turks 1393; passed to Greece 1881.

**Larkana** Pakistan. Town in W Pakistan, in the Khairpur division 150 m. N of Hyderabad. Pop. (1961) 48,008. Manufactures metal goods, textiles.

**Larne** Northern Ireland. Municipal borough in Co. Antrim, at the entrance to Lough Larne 18 m. NNE of Belfast. Pop. (1961) 16,341. Seaport, tourist centre. Steamer connexion to Stranraer (Scotland) and transport ferry service to Preston (England). Bauxite refining. Manufactures linen, clothing, cement.

**La Rochelle** France. Prefecture of the Charente-Maritime department, on the Bay of Biscay. Pop. (1968) 75,497. Fishing and commercial port. Tourist centre. Manufactures fertilizers, plastics, cement. Shipbuilding, fish processing and canning, sawmilling, etc. Exports brandy, wine. Among its buildings are the 14th-cent. Tower of St Nicholas, the 15th-cent. Lantern Tower (once used as a lighthouse) and the 18th-cent. cathedral. From the 14th to the 16th cent. it was a leading French seaport; it became a Huguenot stronghold, but fell to Richelieu after a long siege (1627–8). Its trade declined when France lost Canada, and never fully recovered despite the construction of its outport, La Pallice, for accommodation of the larger ocean-going vessels.

**La Romana** Dominican Republic. Seaport in La Altagracia province, 64 m. E of Santo Domingo. Pop. (1960) 24,058. Exports sugar. Sugar refining, flour milling, coffee and tobacco processing.

**Las Alpujarras** Spain. Mountainous region in Andalusia, in the Granada and Almería provinces between the Sierra Nevada and the coast. Fertile valleys. Scene of strong resistance by the Moors after the fall of Granada (1492); they were not subdued till 1571.

**Las Cruces** USA. Market town in S New Mexico, on the Rio Grande. Pop. (1960) 29,367. In a stock-rearing and agricultural region. Founded 1848. Seat of the New Mexico State University (1959).

**La Serena** Chile. Capital of the Coquimbo province, 225 m. N of Valparaiso. Pop. (1960) 55,708. Resort. Market town. Trade in fruit, flowers, etc. Picturesque, with old-world charm; beach and casino at near-by Peñuelas. Founded 1543. Severely damaged by earthquake 1922.

**Lashio** Burma. Town in Shan State 130 m. NE of Mandalay, with which it is connected by rail. Pop. 5,000. Also terminus of the Burma Road to Chungking (China).

**Lasíthi** Greece. *Nome* in E Crete, with Mt Dhikti or Lasíthi (7,048 ft) in the extreme W. Area 738 sq. m. Pop. (1961) 73,843. Cap. Ayios Nikolaos. Olives, carobs, wheat, etc. cultivated. Sheep and goats raised.

**Las Palmas** Spain. **1.** Spanish province in the Canary Is. Area 1,569 sq. m. Pop. (1961) 453,793. Consists of the islands of Gran Canaria, Lanzarote, and Fuerteventura and the small barren islands of Alegranza, Roque del Este, Roque del Oeste, Graciosa, and Montaña Clara y Lobos.
**2.** Capital of Las Palmas province, on the island of Gran Canaria. Pop. (1967) 244,354. Largest city in the Canary Is. Its fertile valley is famous for palms (hence the name). Mild subtropical climate; a popular resort, esp. during winter (mean temp. Jan. 63° F). Its port, La Luz, is an important fuelling station. Exports fruit, vegetables, wine.

**La Spezia** Italy. Capital of La Spezia province, Liguria, 50 m. ESE of Genoa on the Gulf of Spezia. Pop. (1968) 129,312. Since 1861 Italy's chief naval base, with shipyards and arsenal, severely damaged in the 2nd World War. Also manufactures electrical equipment, textiles, porcelain, etc. Oil refining. At near-by Lerici Shelley spent his last months before being drowned off the coast.

**Las Vegas** USA. Town in SE Nevada, at a height of 2,030 ft. Pop. (1960) 64,405. Commercial centre for a mining and agricultural region. More famous as a resort, esp. for the gambling casinos. First settled (1855) by Mormons. Later abandoned, it was permanently settled in 1905, with the arrival of the railway.

**Latakia (Ar. El Ladhiqiya)** Syria. Ancient Laodicea ad Mare. Capital of Latakia province, 85 m. WSW of Aleppo. Pop. (1962) 68,498. The chief seaport. Exports the famous Latakia tobacco, also grain, cotton, etc. Flourished under the Romans and under the Crusaders. Declined in the 16th cent., but revived later with the development of the tobacco trade. Since 1950 improvements have been made in its harbour in order to divert Syrian trade to it from Beirut (Lebanon).

**Latin America.** A convenient term for all countries S of the US–Mexico frontier (except the W Indies). Includes Mexico (part of the N American subcontinent), Central America, and S America. The majority of the population are Spanish-speaking, but the language of the largest country, Brazil, is Portuguese. Dutch, English, and French are spoken in Surinam, Guyana, and French Guiana respectively. Various Indian languages survive in (e.g.) Bolivia, Chile, Peru. ◊ *Argentina*; *Bolivia*; *Brazil*; *British Honduras*; *Chile*; *Colombia*; *Costa Rica*; *Ecuador*; *Guatemala*; *Guyana*; *Honduras*; *Nicaragua*; *Panama*; *Paraguay*; *Peru*; *Salvador*; *Uruguay*; *Venezuela*.

**Latium** Italy. Region of ancient Italy S of the Tiber R. Originally the home of the Latini, but after conquest by the Romans it included also lands of neighbouring tribes, the Rutuli, Hernici, Volsci, and Aurunci.

**Latium** (Italian **Lazio**) Italy. Region of modern Italy more extensive than ancient Latium, comprising the provinces of Frosinone, Latina, Rieti, Roma, and Viterbo. Area 6,634 sq. m. Pop. (1961) 3,922,783. Cap. Rome. Includes the coastal plain between the Fiora R. (N) and the Garigliano R. (S) and the W slopes of the Apennines. Land has been reclaimed in Campagna di Roma and the Pontine Marshes. Cereals, vines, olives, etc. cultivated.

**Latvian SSR (Latvia)** USSR. Constituent republic on the Baltic Sea and the Gulf of Riga, bounded by the Estonian SSR (N), RSFSR (E), and the Lithuanian SSR (S). Area 25,590 sq. m. Pop. (1970) 2,365,000 (62 per cent Letts, 27 per cent Russians). Cap. Riga. Mostly low-lying and flat, with a small area in the extreme E rising to 1,000 ft. Chief river the Western Dvina (Daugava). About one quarter of the land is forested and yields a considerable output of timber; an almost equal area is cultivated. Main crops oats, barley, rye, potatoes, flax. Leading agricultural occupations dairy farming, cattle and pig rearing. In 1967 there were 196 state farms and 769 collective farms. Under the Soviet régime farming has been largely mechanized, but the country has also been changed from mainly agricultural to mainly industrial: the urban population, 35 per cent of the total in 1939, represented 63 per cent by the end of 1967. Dairy produce, timber, paper, textiles, footwear, electrical and telephone equipment are among the principal products. Riga is the chief seaport; Liepaja and Ventspils are also ports, and Daugavpils (Dvinsk) and Jelgava are important inland towns.

The land was inhabited by the Letts from about the 10th cent., but they were a disunited people and until the 20th cent. remained subject to foreign domination: in the 13th and 14th cent. to the Teutonic Knights and thereafter to Russia, Poland, and Sweden, to be incorporated in Russia in 1721. Although the Letts were long in a condition of serfdom, under Russian rule their economy developed, and by the end of the 19th cent. nearly one quarter of the country's exports passed through Latvian ports. Independence came at last at the end of the 1st World War (1918), but with it the decline of much of its industrial and commercial prosperity – even though agriculture still flourished. In 1940 Latvia was annexed by the USSR, and in the 2nd World War the country was devastated, as it had been in the 1st World War.

**Lauder** Scotland. Small burgh in W Berwickshire, on Leader Water, in Lauderdale. Pop. (1961) 597. Scene of the hanging (at Lauder Bridge) of James III's favourites (1482).

**Launceston** Australia. Second largest city in Tasmania, in the N at the confluence of the N Esk and S Esk rivers where they form the Tamar R., 40 m. from the open sea. Pop. (1966) 60,453. Commercial centre with a mainland trade, esp. through Melbourne. Exports agricultural produce etc. Sawmilling, brewing, flour milling. Manufactures woollen goods etc. Founded 1805.

**Launceston** England. Municipal borough in E Cornwall, on the R. Kensey. Pop. (1961) 4,518. Market town. Tanning. Formerly (till 1837) the county town. George Fox the Quaker was imprisoned here (1656) for 'disturbing the peace' in St Ives.

**Laurel** USA. Town in Mississippi, on Tallahala Creek, 28 m. NNE of Hattiesburg. Pop. (1960) 27,989. Commercial centre. Trade in timber. Manufactures fibre-board, furniture, etc. Oil refining.

**Laurentides Park** Canada. Provincial park in Quebec, N of Quebec city. Area 4,000 sq. m. Rises to 3,845 ft. Over 1,500 lakes, many streams. A game reserve for moose, deer, etc. Hunting forbidden, but fishing for speckled trout is a popular sport. Hotels and fishing camps. Established 1895.

**Laurium** Greece. Ancient town in Attica, 26 m. SE of Athens. Once famous for its silver mines, an important source of revenue to Athens. Site of the small modern seaport of Lávrion (pop. 6,600).

**Lausanne** Switzerland. Capital of Vaud canton, on the N shore of L. Geneva. Pop. (1969) 139,300. Tourist resort. Industrial and commercial centre. Printing, woodworking. Manufactures leather goods, clothing, chocolate, biscuits, etc. Trade in wine. A hilly city, divided by two short rivers into three sections, the old Cité, the Bourg (the commercial quarter), and St Laurent; the upper part is connected by funicular railway with Ouchy, its port on the lake. Educational centre. The university (founded 1891 but existing as a college since 1537) has a valuable library and art museum; there is also a School of Technology. The principal building is the cathedral (12th/13th-cent., restored), standing 500 ft above the lake. Castle (15th-cent.). Seat of the Swiss Federal Supreme Court and of the International Olympic Committee. Originally stood on the shore of the lake, SW of its present situation, but when it was destroyed in the 4th cent. the inhabitants founded a new town on the hill of the Cité. This later combined with two other settlements, the Bourg and St Laurent. The bishopric was established in the 6th cent. Protestantism introduced 1536. Became capital of the new canton of Vaud 1803. Scene of the Conference of Lausanne between the Allies and Turkey 1922–3. Birthplace of the author Benjamin Constant (1767–1830).

**Lausitz** ◊ *Lusatia*.

**Lauterbrunnen** Switzerland. Summer resort in the Bern canton, on the White Lütschine R. in the Bernese Alps 6 m. S of Interlaken. Pop. 2,610. The walls of the valley, the Lauterbrunnental, are steep-sided and deep, and the floor is often in shadow; many waterfalls, e.g. the Staubbach and Trümmelbach.

**Laval** France. Capital of Mayenne department, on the Mayenne R. 43 m. E of Rennes. Pop. (1968) 49,052. Textile centre, well known for linen since the 14th cent. Manufactures cotton goods, hosiery, leather goods, furniture. Cheese making. Its 'old'

castle dates from the 11th and 12th cent. cathedral partly of the 12th cent.

**Lavongai Island** ◊ *Bismarck Archipelago*.

**Lávrion** ◊ *Laurium*.

**Lawrence** (Kansas) USA. Town on the Kansas R. 33 m. WSW of Kansas City. Pop. (1960) 32,858. Mainly a residential and cultural centre in a rich agricultural region. Flour milling. Manufactures pipe organs etc. Seat of the University of Kansas (1865).

**Lawrence** (Massachusetts) USA. Industrial town on the Merrimack R., which provides hydroelectric power. Pop. (1960) 70,933. Important woollen and worsted manufacturing centre. Also manufactures clothing, cotton and leather goods, etc. Named after Abbott Lawrence, a Boston financier who helped to plan the city as an industrial centre.

**Lawton** USA. Town in Oklahoma 80 m. SW of Oklahoma City. Pop. (1960) 61,697. Industrial centre in an agricultural region. Manufactures cottonseed oil, leather goods, etc. Flour milling, meat packing, etc. Granite and limestone quarries near by. The Fort Sill military reservation is 4 m. N.

**Lea (Lee) River** England. River 46 m. long rising near Dunstable (Beds.) and flowing SE and S past Hertford and Ware, along the Greater London – Essex boundary, to the R. Thames at Blackwall. Source of water supply for London. The Lea valley is well known for the cultivation of tomatoes, flowers, etc. in glasshouses.

**Leamington Spa** England. Municipal borough and health resort in Warwickshire, on the R. Leam 8 m. S of Coventry, conveniently near Warwick, Kenilworth, and Stratford-on-Avon. Pop. (1961) 43,236. Engineering. Manufactures gas cookers, motor-car parts, etc. It has saline springs, the waters being taken at the Royal Pump Room. Of little importance till the end of the 18th cent., when the first baths were built, it was visited by Queen Victoria in 1838 and was thereafter officially known as Royal Leamington Spa.

**Leatherhead** England. Urban district in Surrey, on the R. Mole at the foot of the N Downs. Pop. (1961) 35,554. Largely residential. Engineering. Manufactures cigarette lighters etc. A 14th-cent. church.

**Lebanon.** Small republic in SW Asia. Area 3,400 sq. m. Pop. (1967) 2,179,000. Cap. Beirut. Lang. Arabic.

Bounded by Syria (N and E), Israel (S), and the Mediterranean Sea (W). Primarily agricultural, though only about one quarter of its area is cultivated. The considerable adverse balance of trade is offset largely by receipts from foreign tourists and Lebanese living abroad.

TOPOGRAPHY, CLIMATE, RESOURCES. Largely mountainous: the Lebanon Mountains extend throughout the country near and parallel to the coast; the fertile Bekaa valley lies between this range and the Anti-Lebanon. The climate is Mediterranean, with hot dry summers and mild rainy winters, but varies much with altitude. In the Bekaa valley cereals (esp. wheat), wines, oranges, lemons, and other fruits are cultivated. The forests, including the famous Cedars of Lebanon, have been much depleted by reckless exploitation and the depredations of goats, of which there are large numbers. Industries are on a small scale, but there are oil refineries at Tripoli and Saida (Sidon), oil being brought by pipelines, to the former from Iraq and the latter from Saudi Arabia. Beirut is the chief seaport and has an important international airport; Tripoli is the only other town with as many as 100,000 inhabitants.

PEOPLE, GOVERNMENT. Christianity has been established in Lebanon since early times, and about half the population are Christians (the majority Maronites, the remainder Eastern Orthodox, Greek and Roman Catholics, Armenians, etc.). Almost one half of the people are Muslims, about equally divided between Sunnis and Shiites, and there are many Druses. The Legislature consists of the Chamber of Deputies, elected for 4 years by universal adult suffrage; the Executive includes the President (a Maronite Christian) and the Prime Minister (a Sunni Muslim), while the Speaker is a Shia Muslim.

HISTORY. After the 1st World War Lebanon was put under French mandate (for earlier history ⟡ *Syria*). During the 2nd World War its independence was proclaimed (1941), but this did not become effective until 1944. In 1958 a Muslim revolt broke out but was suppressed after American forces had been landed at the President's request. Lebanon is a member of the UN and of the Arab League.

**Lebanon** USA. Town in Pennsylvania 70 m. WNW of Philadelphia. Pop. (1960) 30,045. Manufactures iron and steel goods, textiles, electrical equipment, etc. Developed largely because of local iron deposits.

**Lebda** ⟡ *Leptis Magna*.

**Lecce** Italy. Capital of Lecce province, in Apulia, 25 m. SSE of Brindisi. Pop. (1961) 75,297. Market town. Trade in olive oil, tobacco, and other products of the region. Manufactures papier-mâché toys, pottery, etc. Has many buildings in rococo style, built of the local yellow stone, inc. the 17th-cent. cathedral.

**Lecco** Italy. Town in Como province in Lombardy, on the SE branch of L. Como (L. Lecco). Pop. (1961) 48,230. Industrial and tourist centre. Iron and brass founding. Manufactures textiles etc. Important cheese market; exports esp. Gorgonzola cheese.

**Lech River** River 177 m. long rising in the Vorarlberg Alps (Austria), flowing generally NE to the German border, then N past Füssen and Augsburg to join the Danube below Donauwörth.

**Le Creusot** France. Industrial town in the Saône-et-Loire department, 48 m. SW of Dijon. Pop. (1968) 34,109. Situated on a coalfield, it has important iron and steel works. Manufactures locomotives, armaments, machinery, etc., the industry having been founded (1836) by the Schneider brothers. Severely damaged by bombing in the 2nd World War.

**Ledbury** England. Market town in Herefordshire, on the R. Leadon 12 m. ESE of Hereford. Pop. (1961) 3,632. Trade in cider and perry. Limestone quarried in the neighbourhood. Many timbered buildings, inc. the 17th-cent. market house. Birthplace of John Masefield (1878–1967).

**Leeds** England. County borough in the W Riding of Yorkshire, on the R. Aire. Pop. (1961) 510,597. Important industrial centre, linked by canal with both Liverpool and Goole. From the 14th cent. it had a prosperous woollen industry, which in more recent times developed into the manufacture of ready-made clothing, now the largest single industry. With the Industrial Revolution engineering assumed great importance, and today diesel engines, textile and printing machinery, agricultural implements, and electrical equipment are produced. Other industries include printing, tanning, and the manufacture of footwear, furniture, chemicals, glass. The university (1904) was formerly the Yorkshire College of Science. St John's Church exemplifies the 17th-cent. Gothic style, but the majority of the city's notable buildings are modern: the Town Hall (1858), with its large public hall; the Civic Hall (1933), housing municipal offices; and various housing estates – together with the famous Headingley cricket ground. The remains of the 12th-cent. Kirkstall Abbey, beside the R. Aire to the NW, and the park and fine mansion of Temple Newsam, which dates from the 17th cent. and is 3 m. E, both belong to Leeds.

**Leek** England. Urban district in N Staffordshire 8 m. NE of Stoke-on-Trent. Pop. (1961) 19,173. Manufactures textiles, clothing. Near by are the ruins of the 13th-cent. Cistercian abbey of Dieulacresse.

**Lee River** ◊ *Lea River*.

**Leeuwarden** Netherlands. Capital of Friesland province, 34 m. W of Groningen. Pop. (1968) 87,414. Railway and canal junction. Important cattle market. Trade in dairy and agricultural produce. Boatbuilding, iron founding. Manufactures clothing, footwear, furniture, etc. Has the 16th-cent. Kanselary and the museum of the Frisian Society.

**Leeuwin, Cape** Australia. Cape in the extreme SW of Western Australia at the W end of Flinders Bay. Lighthouse. Notorious for stormy weather and dangerous currents.

**Leeward Islands** (Pacific) ◊ *Society Islands*.

**Leeward Islands** W Indies. Chain of islands in the lesser Antilles, extending SE from Puerto Rico to the Windward Islands. 1. Former British colony: Antigua, St Kitts (St Christopher)-Nevis-Anguilla, Montserrat, British Virgin Islands; in W Indies Federation 1958–62, Antigua and St Kitts became associated states of Britain 1967. Area 422½ sq. m. Pop. (1960) 130,258. 2. The US Virgin Islands. 3. Guadeloupe and dependencies (French). 4. The Dutch islands of St Eustatius, Saba, and part of St Martin (divided with France). The islands are generally fertile, producing sea-island cotton, molasses, tropical fruits; also salt. Discovered (1493) by Columbus. Long in dispute between England and France. The present disposition was made in 1815. Dominica was transferred from the Leeward Is. colony to the Windward Is. in 1940.

**Legaspi** Philippines. Capital and chief seaport of Albay province, in SE Luzon. Pop. (1960) 60,768. Exports copra, abacá (Manila hemp).

**Leghorn** (Italian **Livorno**) Italy. Capital of Livorno province, Tuscany, on the Ligurian Sea 13 m. SSW of Pisa. Pop. (1961) 159,973. Resort. Seaport. Exports wine, olive oil, coral goods. straw hats, marble,

etc. Shipbuilding, flour milling, engineering. Manufactures soap, cement, etc. Many of its old buildings were destroyed or severely damaged by bombing in the 2nd World War. Birthplace of Pietro Mascagni, the composer (1863–1945).

**Legnano** Italy. Industrial town in Milano province, Lombardy, on the Olona R. 16 m. NW of Milan. Pop. (1961) 42,460. Manufactures textiles, shoes, soap, etc. Engineering. Near by Frederick Barbarossa was defeated by the Lombard League (1176).

**Legnica** (Ger. **Liegnitz**) Poland. Industrial town in the Wroclaw voivodship 40 m. WNW of Wroclaw. Pop. 74,600. Manufactures textiles, chemicals, paints, machinery, etc. Capital of the duchy of Liegnitz from the 12th to the 17th cent. Passed to Prussia 1742. In the 2nd World War it was severely damaged, and afterwards was ceded to Poland.

**Leh** India. Capital of the Ladakh district, Kashmir, just N of the Indus R. and 160 m. E of Srinagar, at a height of 11,500 ft in the Ladakh Range. Pop. 3,000. Commercial centre on a trade route between India and Tibet. Has a Buddhist monastery.

**Le Havre** ◊ *Havre, Le*.

**Leicester** England. Ancient Ratae Coritanorum or Ratae. County borough and county town of Leicestershire, on the R. Soar. Pop. (1961) 273,298. Industrial centre. Manufactures chiefly hosiery and footwear; also textiles, elastic fabrics, etc. Engineering, brewing. Standing on the ancient Fosse Way, it has among its Roman remains the Jewry Wall, parts of the Forum, and baths. Among the old churches are those of St Nicholas, which has Roman building materials, St Mary de Castro, and St Martin, which has been the cathedral since 1926. The Great Hall of the 12th-cent. Norman castle is preserved as part of an 18th-cent. brick building, and is used now as an assize court. The Guildhall and Trinity Hospital date from the 14th cent. Thomas Cook organized the first rail excursion, from Leicester to Loughborough and back, in 1841. University College (founded 1921) was raised to the status of a university in 1957.

**Leicestershire** England. A midland county. Area 832 sq. m. Pop. (1961) 682,196. County town Leicester. Generally low and undulating, it is bisected S–N by the R. Soar, which separates Charnwood Forest (912 ft) from the E uplands (755 ft). Much of the land is devoted to dairy farming, Stilton cheese being produced near Melton Mowbray, and to cattle and sheep rearing. Cereals cultivated in the W. Well known for fox-hunting, the famous Quorn hunt being located at the village of that name. Coal mined around Coalville. Main industrial centres Leicester, Hinckley, Loughborough.

**Leiden (Leyden)** Netherlands. Ancient Lugdunum Batavorum. City in S Holland province, on the Oude Rijn (Old Rhine) R. 10 m. N E of the Hague. Pop. (1968) 102,972. Educational and industrial centre. Printing and publishing. Manufactures blankets, cigars, etc. Famous university, founded (1575) by William of Orange as a reward for the heroic defence of the city against the Spaniards (1574). In this siege Leiden was saved by the piercing of the dikes, which flooded the surrounding area and enabled the ships of the Beggars of the Sea to bring relief. The Leyden jar was invented at the university (1745); among its celebrated scholars were Grotius and Goldsmith. St Peter's Church dates from the 14th cent. and St Pancras' Church from the 15th cent.; several 16th- and 17th-cent. buildings. Important for its weaving from the 14th cent. but the industry had declined by the 18th cent. For 11 years it was the home of the Pilgrim Fathers before they sailed for America (1620). Birthplace of Rembrandt (1606–69), Jan van Goyen (1596–1658), and Jan Steen (1626–79).

**Leigh** England. Municipal borough in Lancashire 11 m. W of Manchester. Pop. (1961) 46,153. In a coalmining district. Cotton and rayon industry. Manufactures machinery, etc.

**Leighton Buzzard** England. Urban district in SW Bedfordsire 11 m. WNW of Luton. Pop. (1961) 11,649. Market town. Sand quarrying, engineering. Manufactures bricks, cement. A 14th-cent. market cross.

**Leinster** Irish Republic. Province comprising the whole E and SE part of the republic and including the counties of Carlow, Dublin, Kildare, Kilkenny, Laoighis, Longford, Louth, Meath, Offaly, Westmeath, Wexford, and Wicklow. Area 7,580 sq. m. Pop. (1966) 1,414,415 (about 40 per cent in the city of Dublin). Mainly agricultural.

**Leipzig** German Democratic Republic. **1.** Administrative district, one of the three into which the *Land* of Saxony was divided

(1952). Area 1,915 sq. m. Pop. (1968) 1,507,873.
**2.** Capital of Leipzig district, at the confluence of the Elster, Pleisse, and Parther rivers 90 m. SSW of Berlin. Pop. (1968) 591,538. Industrial, commercial, and cultural centre. Manufactures textiles, machinery, chemicals, electrical equipment, musical instruments, leather goods, glass, etc. Famous for its industrial fairs, its trade in furs, and its book publishing. Its old or inner city, with narrow streets and 16th- and 17th-cent. houses, surrounded by inner and outer suburbs, was severely damaged by bombing in the 2nd World War. Among its ancient buildings are the 15th-cent. Thomaskirche, where J. S. Bach was organist, the 13th-cent. Paulinerkirche (restored), the 17th-cent. Johanneskirche, the 16th-cent. Gothic Rathaus, and Auerbach's Keller, immortalized in Goethe's *Faust*; the new Gewandhaus, famed for its concerts, dates from 1884. The university was founded (1409) by a secession of German students from Prague. First mentioned as a town in the 11th cent. Rapidly became important as a commercial centre. Suffered severely in the Thirty Years War. Scene of the Battle of the Nations (1813), in which Napoleon was defeated. Birthplace of Wagner (1813–83) and Leibniz (1646–1716), and home for a time of Mendelssohn and Schumann.

**Leith** Scotland. Port in Midlothian, on the S shore of the Firth of Forth, incorporated in Edinburgh in 1920. Second to Glasgow among Scottish seaports. Flour milling, brewing, whisky distilling. Manufactures paper, chemicals. Trinity House was founded in 1558 as a home for sailors, but later became the licensing authority for pilots.

**Leitha River** Austria/Hungary. River 110 m. long rising in E Austria and flowing generally E into NW Hungary to join the Danube. Formerly part of the boundary between Austria and Hungary.

**Leitrim** Irish Republic. County in Connacht extending SE from Donegal Bay. Area 589 sq. m. Pop. (1966) 33,470. County town Carrick-on-Shannon. Hilly and barren in the N (rising to 2,113 ft in Truskmore), lower in the S. Many lakes, the largest Lough Allen. Main occupations dairy farming, cattle rearing, potato cultivation.

**Leix** ◊ *Laoighis.*
**Leixões** ◊ *Oporto.*

**Le Mans** ◊ *Mans, Le.*

**Lemnos (Limnos)** Greece. Island in the N Aegean Sea. Area 175 sq. m. Pop. 22,000. Chief town Kastron. Mountainous, with fertile valleys where fruits, cereals, etc. are cultivated.

**Lena River** USSR. Country's longest river (2,650 m.), the most easterly of the three great Siberian rivers, rising just W of L. Baikal. Flows generally NE past Kirensk, Olekminsk, and Yakutsk, then turns N and enters the Laptev Sea by an extensive delta, draining an area of over 900,000 sq. m. Chief tributaries the Vitim, Olekma, Aldan, and Vilyui. Navigable for more than 2,400 m., but at the delta completely ice-bound for all but 3 months (July–Oct.). Gold has long been produced along the river and its tributaries.

**Leninabad** USSR. Formerly (till 1936) Khojent. Town in the Tadzhik SSR, on the Syr Darya 125 m. NNE of Dushanbe. Pop. (1970) 103,000 (mainly Tadzhiks). Manufactures textiles, clothing, footwear. An ancient city. Taken by the Russians 1866.

**Leninakan** USSR. Formerly Aleksandropol. Town in the NW of the Armenian SSR 55 m. NW of Yerevan. Pop. (1970) 164,000. Manufactures textiles, carpets. Sugar refining. Founded (1837) as the fortress Aleksandropol; renamed after the Revolution.

**Leningrad** USSR. Formerly St Petersburg (1703–1914), Petrograd (1914–24). Capital of the Leningrad region, RSFSR, at the mouth of the Neva R. on the Gulf of Finland. Pop. (1970) 3,950,000. The second largest city of the USSR, an important seaport, railway and industrial centre. Ship-building (inc. hydrofoils). Manufactures machinery, chemicals, textiles, clothing, cigarettes, etc. Considerable fur trade. Became important as a seaport through the construction of a ship canal (1888) linking it with the outport and naval base of Kronshtadt, and except when icebound (Dec.–March) exports timber, phosphates, etc. Connected by the Neva R. and canal with the Volga. The city is built mainly on the left bank of the Neva and on the islands formed by the various channels of the delta. Renowned for its wide boulevards and many fine buildings of the 18th and early 19th cent., esp. the Admiralty buildings, the baroque Winter Palace (now a museum), the Peter and Paul fortress, and the cathedral. It has long rivalled Moscow as a cultural centre, with a university (1819), many other educational institutions, and the famous Hermitage, with its outstanding collection of European painting and sculpture, as well as many museums. Also the traditional home of the Russian ballet.

Founded (1703) by Peter the Great on a marshy, low-lying site: so many workers died in erecting the city on piles that it was said to have been 'built on bones'. At various times it has suffered from floods. The site was chosen as a 'window looking on Europe' and an outlet to the Baltic, and under Peter the Great and his successors the city was developed as an up-to-date western capital and a centre of art and culture. It succeeded Moscow as Russian capital and remained so for over two centuries (1703–1917). In the late 19th cent. it developed as an industrial centre, and the wretched condition of the factory workers, in sharp contrast to the splendours of the court, led to the revolutions of 1905 and 1917. Renamed (1924) after Lenin, the revolutionary leader. During the 2nd World War the city was virtually isolated from the rest of the USSR and withstood continual shelling and bombing from Aug. 1941 to Jan. 1944. The atomic icebreaker *Lenin* (launched 1957) sailed on her maiden voyage from Leningrad in 1959.

**Leninsk-Kuznetski** USSR. Industrial town in the Kemerovo region, RSFSR, in the Kuznetsk basin, 20 m. S of Kemerovo. Pop. (1970) 128,000. Coal- and iron-mining centre. Railway engineering, brick-making, sawmilling, etc.

**Lens** France. Town in the Pas-de-Calais department, 17 m. SW of Lille. Pop. (1968) 42,019. Mining centre on the leading French coalfield. Manufactures chemicals, metal goods, etc. Virtually destroyed in the 1st World War; severely damaged again in the 2nd World War.

**Leoben** Austria. Town in Styria, on the Mur R. 26 m. NW of Graz. Pop. (1961) 36,257. Lignite-mining centre. Iron founding, brewing. Has a school of mining.

**Leominster** England. Municipal borough in Herefordshire, on the R. Lugg 12 m. N of Hereford. Pop. (1961) 6,403. Market town. Manufactures agricultural machinery, cider, etc. Several old timbered buildings.

**Leominster** USA. Industrial town in N Massachusetts, 6 m. SSE of Fitchburg. Pop. (1960) 27,929. Manufactures plastics, furniture, toys, etc.

**León** (Officially **León de los Aldamas**) Mexico. City in Guanajuato state, in the

Río Turbio valley at a height of 6,182 ft. Pop. (1969) 341,400. Important commercial and industrial centre in a mining and agricultural region. Manufactures footwear and leather goods, textiles, cement, etc. Flour milling, tanning. Founded 1576. Has frequently suffered from floods, but now protected by a dam.

**León** Nicaragua. Capital of the León department, 50 m. NW of Managua. Pop. (1964) 61,649. The country's cultural centre and the second largest city. Manufactures leather goods, footwear, soap, etc. Founded (1524) 20 m. away at the foot of the volcano Momotombo; destroyed by earthquake and moved to its present site 1610. Still has the appearance of an old 'colonial' city. Seat of a university (1812), which became part of the National University in 1952. Capital of the Republic until 1857.

**León** Spain. 1. Region and former kingdom in the NW, comprising the present-day provinces of León, Palencia, Salamanca, Valladolid, and Zamora. One of the earliest Christian kingdoms of Spain following the liberation from the Moors, having been established early in the 10th cent. Finally united with Castile 1230.
2. Province in the NW, mountainous in the N (Cantabrian Mountains) and W (Montañas de León); the remainder is on the central plateau. Area 5,432 sq. m. Pop. (1961) 584,594. Mainly agricultural. Coalmining in the N.
3. Capital of León province, 80 m. NW of Valladolid. Pop. (1967) 92,814. Manufactures textiles, leather, pottery, etc. Trade in agricultural produce. Cathedral (12th/14th-cent.), an outstanding example of Spanish Gothic. Capital of the kingdom of León early in the 10th cent. Declined after the union with Castile (1230).

**Léopold II, Lake** Congo (Kinshasa). Lake in the W, 80 m. long N–S and 30 m. wide at its N end, shallow and irregular in shape. Fed chiefly by the Lokoro and the Lukenye rivers. Drains into the Kasaï R. via the Fimi R. Discovered (1882) by Stanley.

**Léopoldville** ⟡ *Kinshasa.*

**Lepaya** ⟡ *Liepaja.*

**Leptis Magna** Libya. Ancient town, now known as Lebda, just E of Homs, in Tripolitania. Founded by Phoenicians from Sidon and paid tribute to Carthage. Its Roman remains are among the most important in N Africa, and have been excavated since 1911, chiefly by Italian archaeologists.

**Le Puy** ⟡ *Puy, Le.*

**Lerici** ⟡ *La Spezia.*

**Lérida** Spain. 1. Province in the NE, in Catalonia, bounded on the N by France and Andorra. Area 4,659 sq. m. Pop. (1961) 333,765. Drained by the Segre R. and its tributaries. Mainly agricultural. Produces wine, olive oil, etc.
2. Ancient Ilerda. Capital of Lérida province, on the Segre R. 83 m. WNW of Barcelona. Pop. (1967) 75,467. Manufactures textiles, paper, etc. Tanning. Old cathedral (13th-cent.), last used for public worship in 1707, and a new 18th-cent. cathedral. Captured by the Romans (49 B.C.), the Moors (714), the French (1707, 1810). By reason of its strategic position frequently attacked and besieged.

**Lérins, Îles de** France. Two islands and two islets 3 m. SE of Cannes. On Ste-Marguerite is the fort in which the 'Man in the Iron Mask' and Marshal Bazaine were imprisoned. On St-Honorat is a monastery founded at the beginning of the 5th cent.

**Lerwick** Scotland. Small burgh and county town of the Shetland Is. (Zetland County), on the E coast of Mainland. Pop. (1961) 5,906. Fishing centre and chief port for the islands. Hand-knitting.

**Lesbos (Lesvos)** Greece. 1. Island in the Aegean Sea off the coast of Asia Minor (Turkey). Area 630 sq. m. Pop. 117,000. On the fertile lowlands wheat, olives, citrus fruits, and wine are produced. Reached the peak of its prosperity in the early 6th cent. B.C., esp. under Pittacus, of whom the lyric poets Alcaeus and Sappho were contemporaries. Became a member of the Delian League. Passed from Byzantium to a Genoese family (1354) and then to the Turks (1462); regained by Greece 1913. Sometimes known by the name of its chief town, Mytilene (Mitilíni).
2. *Nome* comprising the islands of Lesbos, Lemnos, and Hagios Eustratios. Area 836 sq. m. Pop. (1961) 140,144. Cap. Mytilene.

**Lesina** ⟡ *Hvar.*

**Leskovac** Yugoslavia. Industrial town in S Serbia, 23 m. S of Niš on the S Morava R. Pop. (1961) 34,396. Manufactures textiles, soap, furniture, etc.

**Lesotho (Basutoland)** Africa. Kingdom in southern Africa, formerly the British High Commission Territory of Basutoland, enclosed by three provinces of the Republic of S Africa (Orange Free State, Natal, Cape Province). Area 11,716 sq. m. Pop. (1966)

969,634 (the great majority Basuto, a branch of the Bechuana family of Bantu, many employed in S Africa; only about 2,000 Europeans – government officials, missionaries, traders). Cap. Maseru, linked with S Africa by rail. Mainly a high dissected plateau; the Maluti Mountains in the N rise to over 9,000 ft and another great escarpment, the Drakensberg, forms the E frontier and rises to over 10,000 ft in Mont-aux-Sources (10,822 ft). In the W is a belt of lower land (5,000–6,000 ft), the most accessible part of the country. The Orange R. rises in the NE, flows to the SW, and with its tributaries drains almost the whole country. The climate is dry and bracing and the rainfall variable, averaging about 30 ins. annually, mainly in the summer months. On the grasslands sheep and goats are raised. Chief exports wool, mohair. Principal crops maize, kaffir corn, wheat. It has suffered from soil erosion, combated by reforestation, terracing, construction of irrigation dams, etc. The land is the common property of the nation, held in trust by the chiefs: no European settlement is permitted.

From the early 19th cent. the Basuto constantly quarrelled with the Boers and the British. After defeat by the Boers they came under British protection (1868) at the request of Moshesh, the paramount chief. The territory was annexed to Cape Colony in 1871 but restored to direct British control in 1884. Became one of the three British High Commission Territories in Southern Africa (the others were the Bechuanaland Protectorate and Swaziland). Constitutional reforms creating an executive council and a partly elected national council were introduced in 1960. Internal self-government was granted in 1965, and the paramount chief Moshoeshoe II took the title of king. Became the Kingdom of Lesotho and an independent member of the Commonwealth in 1966.

**Lesvos** ◊ *Lesbos*.

**Leszno (Lissa)** Poland. Market town in the Poznań voivodship, 42 m. SSW of Poznań. Pop. (1968) 32,700. Flour milling. Manufactures machinery, footwear, etc. Returned by Prussia to Poland 1919.

**Letchworth** England. Urban district in Hertfordshire 14 m. NNW of Hertford. Pop. (1961) 25,515. Engineering, printing. Manufactures corsets, rubber products, etc. The first 'garden city' in England, founded 1903.

**Lethbridge** Canada. Formerly Coalbanks. Town in Alberta, on the Oldman R. 110 m. SSE of Calgary. Pop. (1966) 37,186. Coal-mining and market centre in an irrigated agricultural and ranching region. Vegetable canning, food processing, etc. Founded in the 1870s as Coalbanks: renamed 1885.

**Leuven** ◊ *Louvain*.

**Levadia** ◊ *Boeotia*.

**Levant.** Name for the coastlands of the E Mediterranean, in Turkey, Syria, Lebanon, and Israel, or, in a wider sense, for all the countries around the coasts of this region from Greece to the United Arab Republic inclusive. The Levant States were the lands in the original French mandate over Syria (1920).

**Leven** Scotland. Small burgh in E Fifeshire, at the mouth of the R. Leven on the Firth of Forth. Pop. (1961) 8,872. Seaside resort. Manufactures golf clubs. Sawmilling, engineering.

**Leven, Loch** Scotland. 1. Sea loch on the Argyllshire–Inverness-shire border, extending about 9 m. E from Loch Linnhe, with Kinlochleven at its head.
2. Inland lake in E Kinross-shire $3\frac{1}{2}$ m. long and 2 m. wide. Noted for trout fishing. On Castle Island is the ruined castle where Mary Queen of Scots was imprisoned (1567–8).

**Leven River** Scotland. 1. River 7 m. long in Dunbartonshire, flowing S from Loch Lomond at Balloch to the R. Clyde at Dumbarton. The Vale of Leven has an important textile printing and dyeing industry.
2. River 15 m. long in Kinross and Fife, flowing E from Loch Leven to the Firth of Forth at Leven.

**Leverkusen** Federal German Republic. Industrial town and river port in N Rhine-Westphalia, on the right bank of the Rhine R. 5 m. N of Cologne. Pop. (1968) 106,707. Important centre of the chemical industry. Also manufactures machinery, textiles. etc.

**Levittown** USA. Residential town in New York, on Long Island 32 m. E of New York city. Pop. (1960) 65,276. A large planned suburb of New York, developed (1947–51) by the firm of Levitt and Sons Inc.

**Levkás** (Italian **Santa Maura**) Greece. 1. One of the Ionian Islands, off the coast of Acarnania, forming a *nome* with the islands of Ithaca and Meganesi. Area 214 sq. m. Pop. (1961) 28,969. Chief products currants, olive oil, wine.

**2.** Capital of Levkás *nome*, on the NE coast of Levkás island. Pop. (1961) 5,329.

**Lewes** England. Municipal borough and county town of East Sussex, on the R. Ouse 8 m. ENE of Brighton in the S Downs. Pop. (1961) 13,637. Market town. Manufactures agricultural machinery etc. Remains of a Norman castle, which once guarded the gap through the Downs, and of an 11th-cent. Cluniac priory; house of Anne of Cleves, now a museum. At the Battle of Lewes (1264) Simon de Montfort and the rebel barons defeated Henry III. Birthplace of George Baxter (1805–67), the engraver and printer.

**Lewisham** England. Former metropolitan borough in SE London, including the districts of Catford, Forest Hill, Hither Green, and Lee, and, among open spaces, part of Blackheath; from 1965 a Greater London borough including Deptford. Pop. (1963) 289,857. Mainly residential.

**Lewiston** USA. Town in SW Maine, on the Androscoggin R. (from which hydro-electric power is derived) opposite Auburn. Pop. (1960) 40,804. Long important in the textile industry. Also manufactures clothing, footwear, etc.

**Lewis-with-Harris** Scotland. Largest and northernmost of the Outer Hebrides, separated from the mainland by the Minch. Area 825 sq. m. Pop. (1961) Lewis 16,700, Harris 3,285. Chief town Stornoway. Divided by Loch Resort (W), an isthmus, and Loch Seaforth (E) into a larger N part, Lewis, in Ross and Cromarty, and a smaller S part, Harris, in Inverness-shire. The island is hilly, esp. in Harris, which rises to 2,622 ft; much of the land consists of peat bog and bleak moorland. Among the crofters the main occupations are fishing, sheep and cattle rearing, and the spinning and weaving of the famous Harris tweed. Stornoway, on the E coast, is a herring port.

**Lexington** (Kentucky) USA. Town in the heart of the Bluegrass region 70 m. ESE of Louisville. Pop. (1960) 62,810. Chief US centre for breeding thoroughbred horses. Important market for tobacco, livestock, bluegrass seed. Manufactures electrical and electronic equipment, furniture, etc. Seat of the University of Kentucky (1865). Two race tracks (running and trotting). Among many outstanding racehorses bred in the neighbourhood was the famous stallion Man o'War.

**Lexington** (Massachusetts) USA. Residential town 10 m. NW of Boston. Pop. (1960) 27,691. Famous as the scene of the Battle of Lexington (1775), the first armed conflict in the American War of Independence.

**Leyden** ◊ *Leiden*.

**Leyland** England. Urban district in Lancashire 5 m. S of Preston. Pop. (1961) 19,241. Industrial centre. Important manufacture of commercial motor vehicles (lorries, buses); also of tyres, textiles, paint.

**Leyte** Philippines. Island between Luzon and Mindanao. Area 2,785 sq. m. Pop. (1960) 1,177,000. Chief town Tacloban. Main products rice, copra, abacá. During the 2nd World War the Japanese suffered a severe defeat in the Battle of Leyte Gulf (1944).

**Leyton** England. Former municipal borough in Essex on the R. Lea, forming a NE suburb of London and including the residential district of Leytonstone; from 1965 part of the Greater London borough of Waltham Forest. Pop. (1961) 93,857. Manufactures cables, furniture, etc.

**Lhasa** Tibet. Capital of Tibet (now an autonomous region of China) on the Kyichu R. 250 m. NE of Darjeeling (India) at a height of 12,000 ft. Pop. 50,000. Chief centre of Lamaism. Main commercial centre of Tibet. Trade in grain, wool, furs, tea, salt, etc. Minor weaving and other industries. Dominated by the great Potala, formerly the official residence of the Dalai Lama. In the centre of the city is the Jokang temple, an important centre of Buddhist pilgrimage built originally in the 7th cent. In the neighbourhood are the three leading lamaseries of Tibet: Drepung, Sera, and Ganden. Became capital of Tibet in the 7th cent. Under Chinese rule, with the rest of Tibet, 1720–1912. Owing to its inaccessibility and its hostility to foreigners, it was long known as the 'Forbidden City'. Again came under Chinese control in 1951 (◊ *Tibet*).

**Liaoning** China. Province in the NE (Manchuria), bordering SE on N Korea. Area 58,000 sq. m. Pop. (1957) 24,090,000. Cap. Shenyang (Mukden). With highlands in the W and E, it is crossed in the centre by the broad plains formed by the Liao R., where cereals and soya beans are cultivated; in the SE is the Liaotung peninsula. Contains the principal mining and industrial region of Manchuria, with the great coalmining centre of Fushun and the steel centre of Anshan. Leading seaport Lü-ta (Port Arthur–Dairen).

**Liaoyang** China. Town in Liaoning province 40 m. SSW of Shenyang on the S Manchuria Railway. Pop. 160,000. Trade in cotton. Textile manufactures, flour milling. Scene of an important Japanese victory in the Russo-Japanese War (1904).

**Libau** ◊ *Liepaja*.

**Liberec** (Ger. **Reichenberg**) Czechoslovakia. Town in Bohemia, on the Neisse R. 55 m. NE of Prague. Pop. (1967) 71,000. Leading centre of the textile industry. Manufactures textile machinery, footwear, etc. Cloth manufacture was introduced in the 16th cent., and the town's prosperity is shown in such buildings as the 17th-cent. castle and the Renaissance town hall. Prior to the 2nd World War it was a centre of the Sudeten German movement.

**Liberia.** Negro republic on the W coast of Africa. Area 43,000 sq. m. Pop. (1967) 1,099,000. Cap. Monrovia.

Bounded by Sierra Leone (W), Guinea (N), and the Ivory Coast (E). From the coastal plain the country rises inland, reaching a height of over 6,000 ft on the Guinea frontier. The climate is equatorial, with rainfall exceeding 100 ins. annually along the coast, decreasing inland. Largely covered with tropical rain-forest. Chief crops rice, cassava, coffee, sugar-cane. In 1925 an American company was granted a concession to establish rubber plantations, which employ about 35,000 men. Rubber was long the major export, but has been superseded by iron ore. A concession to work the Bomi Hills iron deposits was given to an American company, and a 40-m. railway was built to carry the ore to Monrovia (1951). Diamonds, palm kernels, and coffee are also exported. Apart from the Bomi Hills mineral line, Liberia has no railways, and there are few roads. The free deep-water port of Monrovia was opened in 1948. Liberia has the largest merchant navy in the world (1970), consisting almost entirely of vessels registered under a 'flag of convenience'.

Liberia originated in 1822 when the American Colonization Society settled freed American slaves near Monrovia, and the descendants of these settlers, known as Americo-Liberians and numbering about 20,000, have remained the governing group. The majority of the people consist of native tribes: Kru, famed for their seamanship, Mandingos, who are Muslims, and others, principally pagan, speaking 28 different dialects. Liberian independence was declared in 1847. The rule of the Americo-Liberians often discriminated against the native tribes, and investigations into charges of forced labour and slavery led to the resignation of the President and Vice-President in 1931. More enlightened policies were followed, and tribal representatives played an increasing part in government; the franchise was granted to men and women of the tribes by 1947. Liberia has always maintained close ties with the USA. The constitution is based on that of USA, English is the official language, and considerable financial and technical help has been received from the USA.

**Libreville** Gabon. Capital, near the equator on the estuary of the Gabon R. Pop. (1965) 31,000. Seaport. Exports timber, palm oil and kernels. Sawmilling, plywood manufacture. Founded (1848) when slaves were freed and put ashore here by a French frigate (hence the name).

**Libya.** Republic of N Africa. Area 679,358 sq. m. Pop. (1964) 1,559,399. Joint capitals Tripoli, Benghazi. Lang. Arabic. Rel. Muslim.

Bounded by Egypt and Sudan (E), Niger and Chad (S), and Tunisia and Algeria (W). Almost entirely desert. Only in narrow coastal fringes round Tripoli and Benghazi does the rainfall exceed 8 ins. annually, and agriculture is limited to these areas and scattered oases. Main products wheat, barley, olives, and oranges along the coast, dates in the oases. In the semi-desert zone esparto grass is grown and goats and sheep are grazed. S of this belt of scrub is an enormous expanse of rocky, stony, and sandy desert, with oases such as Ghadames, Ghat, Murzuk, Kufra. A rich oilfield was discovered at Zelten in 1959, and the oil terminal at Marsa el Brega, at the head of the 104-m. pipeline, was opened in 1961. Oil has also been discovered in other parts of Tripolitania and Cyrenaica. Sponge and tunny fishing are important on the coast. Chief towns Tripoli, Benghazi, Misurata, Homs. Railways merely link Tripoli and Benghazi with neighbouring towns. A motor road, opened by the Italians in 1937, runs along the coast W from Tripoli to Tunis (Tunisia) and E through Homs and

Misurata to Benghazi, Tobruk, and Alexandria (Egypt).

After being under Turkish domination from the 16th cent., Libya was annexed by Italy (1912). A period of colonization followed, and about 90,000 Italian peasants had been settled by 1938. When the Italians and Germans were driven out in the 2nd World War (1942–3), Tripolitania and Cyrenaica came under British and the Fezzan under French military government. Libya became an independent kingdom in 1951, with the Amir of Cyrenaica as its first king. The monarchy was overthrown by military *coup* in 1969, and the king left the country.

**Libyan Desert.** The most easterly part of the Sahara, extending over E Libya, W Egypt, and N W Sudan to the Nile valley. Largely a sandy waste, rainless for years at a time. Principal oases Siwa, Bahariya, Farafra, Dakhla, Kharga (Egypt) and Kufra (Libya). The N part, where there was much fighting in the 2nd World War (1940–44), is sometimes known as the ◊ *Western Desert*.

**Licata** Italy. Ancient Phintias. Seaport at the mouth of the Salso R., in Agrigento province, S Sicily. Pop. (1961) 38,655. Refines and exports sulphur. Off its coast the Romans defeated the Carthaginian fleet in 256 B.C. Landing-place for US forces in the 2nd World War (1943).

**Lichfield** England. Municipal borough in Staffordshire 12 m. SW of Burton-on-Trent. Pop. (1961) 14,077. Market town. Brewing, engineering. The famous cathedral with its three spires, dating from the 13th and 14th cent., suffered severely at the hands of the Parliamentary forces in the Civil War, but was restored in the 19th cent. Also celebrated for its associations with Dr Johnson (1709–84), who was born here, and whose house is now a museum.

**Liddel Water** Scotland. River 21 m. long rising on Peel Fell (1,975 ft) in Roxburghshire and flowing SW to join the R. Esk 2 m. S of Canonbie. Its valley is known as Liddesdale or Liddisdale.

**Lidice** Czechoslovakia. Small coalmining village 4 m. E of Kladno, in Bohemia, whose name became world known when (June 1942) the occupying German forces announced that, as a reprisal for the assassination of Gauleiter Heydrich, all the men and many women had been shot, the remaining women sent to concentration camps and children to 'correction schools';

the village itself was completely destroyed. As a gesture of sympathy several places abroad were renamed in its honour, e.g. Lidice, Illinois, USA. In June 1947 delegations from many countries attended a ceremony marking the rebuilding of the village near by.

**Liechtenstein.** Independent principality in central Europe, bounded on the W by the Rhine R., separating it from Switzerland, on the E by the Austrian province of Vorarlberg. Area 64 sq. m. Pop. (1960) 16,495 (German-speaking and mainly Roman Catholic). Cap. Vaduz. Largely mountainous, with the Rhätikon Alps in the S, rising to 8,432 ft in Naafkopf. Cattle rearing and the cultivation of cereals and vines are important occupations, while there are small textile and other industries. Founded (1719) by the union of the Vaduz and Schellenberg countships. Later belonged to the German Confederation; became independent 1866. Since 1868 it has had no army, and was neutral in the 2nd World War.

**Liège** (Flemish **Luik**) Belgium. **1.** Province in the E, bounded on the E by the Federal German Republic. Area 1,526 sq. m. Pop. (1968) 1,019,105. The N is a fertile agricultural region; in the S at the foot of the Ardennes dairy farming is important; the centre, along the Meuse and Vesdre rivers, is a coalmining and industrial area. Formerly ruled by prince-bishops; became part of Belgium 1830. Chief towns Liège, Verviers.

**2.** Capital of Liège province, on the Meuse R. at the confluence with the Ourthe R. 55 m. ESE of Brussels. Pop. (1968) 152,488. Centre of coalmining and of iron, steel, and armament manufacture. Also produces machinery, machine tools, chemicals, glass, tyres, etc. University (1817). Cultural centre of French-speaking Belgium. Among its noteworthy buildings are the Cathedral of St Paul (partly 13th-cent.) and the 16th-cent. Palais de Justice. Birthplace of César Franck (1822–90).

**Liepaja (Lepaya,** Ger. **Libau) USSR.** Baltic seaport in the Latvian SSR 126 m. WSW of Riga. Pop. (1969) 88,000. Exports timber, grain, etc. Manufactures steel and steel products, agricultural machinery, linoleum, etc. Flour milling, brewing, etc. Passed to Russia 1795; developed rapidly as one of her main ice-free ports after the arrival of the railway (1871). In independent Latvia 1920–40.

**Lierre** (Flemish **Lier**) Belgium. Industrial town in Antwerp province, at the confluence of the Grande Nèthe and Petite Nèthe rivers 9 m. SE of Antwerp. Pop. (1968) 28,600. Manufactures cutlery, tools, etc.

**Liffey River** Irish Republic. River 50 m. long rising in the Wicklow Mountains and flowing generally W into Co. Kildare, then NE and E through Dublin to Dublin Bay. Important hydroelectric plant at Poulaphouca Falls.

**Lifu** ⋄ *Loyalty Islands*.

**Liguria** Italy. Region in the NW between the Ligurian Alps and the Ligurian Apennines on the N and the Gulf of Genoa on the S, comprising the provinces of Genoa, Imperia, La Spezia, and Savona, and including the Italian Riviera. Area 2,098 sq. m. Pop. (1961) 1,717,630. Produces olives, vines, fruits, flowers. Industries include shipbuilding, iron and steel and chemical manufactures. The ancient Ligures occupied a much larger area than the present region, even in Roman times. By the treaty of 1947 a small mountainous area on the W border was ceded to France.

**Ligurian Sea** Italy. Arm of the Mediterranean Sea lying between Liguria, Tuscany, and Corsica and including the Gulf of Genoa (N); separated from the Tyrrhenian Sea by the Tuscan Archipelago.

**Lihou** ⋄ *Guernsey*.

**Lille** France. Prefecture of the Nord department, on the canalized Deule R. Pop. (1968) 194,948. Major industrial and commercial centre, particularly important for the manufacture of textiles (cotton, woollen, linen and rayon goods). Also large metallurgical and engineering industries (locomotives, machinery, etc.). Brewing, sugar refining. Manufactures chemicals, biscuits, etc. Obtains coal for its industries from the coalfield just S. Among its notable buildings are the citadel, built by Vauban, and the Bourse (both of the 17th cent.), and a famous art museum. University (1887). In the 14th cent. Charles V of France handed Lille to the dukes of Burgundy, under whom it prospered, and from them it passed in turn to Austria, Spain, and to France (1668). Severely damaged in both world wars. Birthplace of General de Gaulle (1890–1970).

**Lima** Peru. Capital of Peru and of the Lima department, on the Rimac R. on a wide, gently sloping plain W of the Andean foothills, 8 m. E of Callao, its port. Pop. (1965) 1,795,100. Largest city and chief commercial centre, with four fifths of the country's industry. Manufactures textiles, furniture, soap, etc. Oil refining, tanning, brewing, flour milling. Climate dry, with mild winters. Mean annual rainfall less than 2 ins. but fogs and drizzle occur in winter and the sky is often overcast. Founded (1535) by Pizarro, who named it the 'City of the Kings' and laid the cornerstone of the cathedral. Today modern office buildings and hotels mingle with old Spanish churches and houses. In colonial times it was the chief city of Spanish S America. Seat of the San Marcos university (1551), the oldest in the continent. The Central Railway climbs spectacularly to the highland mining centres; the Pan-American Highway links it with coastal towns. Several resorts near by. Pachacámac, with Inca and pre-Inca remains, is 12 m. S.

**Lima** USA. Industrial town in Ohio, on the Ottawa R. 78 m. NW of Columbus. Pop. (1960) 51,037. Oil refining. Manufactures machine tools, diesel engines, chemicals, electrical equipment, etc.

**Limassol** Cyprus. Ancient Lemessus. Seaport on Akrotiri Bay on the S coast. Pop. (1967) 49,000. Exports wine, carobs. Manufactures brandy, perfumes, cigarettes, etc. Tourist centre; second largest town. Here Richard I of England married Berengaria of Navarre (1191).

**Limavady** Northern Ireland. Urban district in Co. Londonderry, on the R. Roe 15 m. ENE of Londonderry. Pop. (1961) 4,324. Market town. Here the *Londonderry Air* was first noted down from a travelling fiddler (1851). Birthplace of William Massey (1856–1925), the New Zealand statesman.

**Limbourg** (Flemish **Limburg**) Belgium. **1.** Province in the NE, bounded on the N and E by the Netherlands. Area 930 sq. m. Pop. (1968) 638,593. Cap. Hasselt. Agricultural, with coalmining in the Campine (Kempen) region. In 1839 the old duchy of Limburg was divided between Belgium and the Netherlands, Belgium taking the part W of the Meuse R., except for a small area around the town of Limbourg which passed to Liège province. ⋄ *Limburg*.
**2.** Old town in Liège province, on the Vesdre R. 4 m. ENE of Verviers. Pop. 5,000. Until 1648 capital of the duchy of

Limburg. The new town, with textile industry, is known as Dolhain.

**Limburg** Netherlands. Province in the SE, bounded by Belgium (W and S) and the Federal German Republic (E). Area 840 sq. m. Pop. (1968) 985,738. Cap. Maastricht. Cereals, sugar-beet, fruit cultivated. In the S are the country's chief coalmines. In 1839 the old duchy of Limburg was divided between Belgium and the Netherlands, the latter taking the part lying E of the Meuse R. ⬧ *Limbourg*.

**Limehouse** England. District in the London borough of Tower Hamlets, with docks, wharves, warehouses, and sailors' institutes and containing London's Chinese quarter. The name probably derives from the limekilns that once stood in the district. Severely damaged by bombing in the 2nd World War.

**Limeira** Brazil. Industrial town in São Paulo state, 32 m. NW of Campinas. Pop. 50,000. In an orange-growing region. Fruit packing. Manufactures coffee-processing machinery, matches, hats, etc.

**Limerick** Irish Republic. 1. County in Munster in the SW, bounded on the N by the R. Shannon estuary. Area 1,037 sq. m. Pop. (1966) 137,357. Mainly an undulating plain, containing most of the fertile Golden Vale, but mountainous in the S; in the SE rises to 3,015 ft in Galtymore (Galty Mountains). Dairy farming, stock rearing. Salmon fishing.
2. County town of Co. Limerick, on both banks of the R. Shannon at the head of the estuary. Pop. (1966) 55,912. Seaport. Tanning, bacon curing, brewing, flour milling, etc. Manufactures butter, tobacco products. Divided into English Town, Irish Town, and Newtown Pery. Outstanding buildings are the 12th-cent. Protestant cathedral, 19th-cent. Roman Catholic cathedral, and the remains of the Norman King John's castle. At Ardnacrusha, 2 m. N on the R. Shannon, is the country's major hydroelectric power station. Originally a Danish settlement; taken by Brian Boru and became capital of the kingdom of Munster. Captured by the English 1174. William III besieged the city, and resistance was ended by the Treaty of Limerick (1691), subsequently broken, granting political and religious freedom.

**Limin Vatheos** ⬧ *Samos*.

**Limnos** ⬧ *Lemnos*.

**Limoges** France. Ancient Augustoritum,

Lemovices. Prefecture of the Haute-Vienne department, on the Vienne R. Pop. (1968) 135,917. Important centre of the porcelain industry, using local kaolin. Also manufactures footwear, paper, textiles, etc. Cathedral (13th/16th-cent.), two 13th-cent. bridges over the Vienne, and a museum with a fine ceramics collection. Converted to Christianity by St Martial in the 3rd cent. In 1370 it was burned and its population massacred by the Black Prince, and it frequently suffered in religious wars. Turgot (1727–81), intendant of Limoges for 13 years (1761–74), did much to aid its recovery, including the introduction of porcelain manufacture. Birthplace of Pierre Auguste Renoir (1841–1919).

**Limón (Puerto Limón)** Costa Rica. Capital of the Limón province, on the Caribbean Sea 70 m. E of San José. Pop. (1963) 29,079. Second largest city and chief Caribbean seaport. Exports coffee, bananas, coconuts, etc. Also a popular resort.

**Limousin** France. Former province in the W of the Massif Central, now forming the department of Corrèze and part of Haute-Vienne. Largely occupied by the infertile Monts du Limousin. Annexed to the crown by Henri IV (1589) but remained economically backward until the introduction of reforms by Turgot, intendant of ⬧ *Limoges*.

**Limpopo (Crocodile) River** Moçambique/Rhodesia/S Africa. River 1,000 m. long, rising in the Transvaal, flowing N and then SE in a wide curve through southern Africa; forms the frontier between S Africa and Rhodesia, flows generally SE through Moçambique, and enters the Indian Ocean 85 m. NE of Lourenço Marques. Navigable for about 100 m. above the mouth. The region of its lower course is well watered and fertile.

**Linares** Chile. Capital of the Linares province, in the central valley 170 m. SSW of Santiago. Pop. 51,000. Market town. Trade in cereals, wine, vegetables.

**Linares** Spain. Town in Jaén province in Andalusia, in the foothills of the Sierra Morena 25 m. NNE of Jaén. Pop. (1967) 61,593. Important lead-mining centre. Lead smelting. Manufactures metal goods, chemicals, etc.

**Lincoln** England. Ancient Lindum Colonia. County borough and county town of Parts of Lindsey, Lincolnshire, on the R. Witham at the confluence with the R. Till. Pop. (1961) 77,065. Manufactures agricultural implements, excavating machinery, pumps, feed cakes, food products, etc. Famous chiefly for its cathedral, originally built 1075–90 and restored 1922–32, one of the finest in the country, with its 271-ft central tower containing the bell 'Great Tom of Lincoln' and one of the original copies of Magna Carta (1215). Also has a castle begun by William the Conqueror, the Jew's House, and other Norman remains. Was a British fortress, then the Roman settlement of Lindum Colonia.

**Lincoln** USA. State capital of Nebraska, in the SE. Pop. (1960) 128,521. Railway, commercial and industrial centre for an agricultural region. Food processing, flour milling, etc. Manufactures agricultural machinery, office equipment, etc. The state Capitol (completed 1934) is an impressive building with a 400-ft central tower. Seat of the University of Nebraska (1871) and the Nebraska Wesleyan University (1887).

**Lincolnshire** England. Second largest county in England (after Yorkshire), bounded on the N by the Humber estuary and on the E by the North Sea. Area 2,662 sq. m. Pop. (1961) 743,383. Apart from the chalk escarpment of the Lincoln Wolds in the E, it is mostly low-lying and fertile; in the SE around the Wash is a considerable area of the Fens, drained by the Witham, Welland, and Nene rivers and many canals. Sandy shores have given rise to such seaside resorts as Skegness and Cleethorpes. Sheep and cattle reared. Cereals, potatoes, sugar-beet cultivated. Iron ore mined. Scunthorpe is a centre of the iron and steel industry, Grimsby an important fishing port. Divided administratively into 3 areas: 1. Parts of Lindsey, area 1,520 sq. m., pop. 504,678, county town Lincoln. 2. Parts of Kesteven, area 724 sq. m., pop. 135,317, county town Sleaford. 3. Parts of Holland, area 418 sq. m., pop. 103,388, county town Boston.

**Linden** USA. Town in New Jersey 18 m. SW of Newark. Pop. (1960) 39,931. Oil refining. Manufactures chemicals, clothing, beverages, etc.

**Lindisfarne** ◊ *Holy Island* (England).

**Línea, La (La Línea de la Concepción)** Spain. Town and port in Cádiz province just N of Gibraltar, from which it is separated by a neutral strip and which it supplies with fruit and vegetables. Pop. (1961) 59,456.

**Line Islands** Pacific Ocean. Group of coral islands in the Central Pacific strung across the equator roughly between 150° W and 160° W long., including Palmyra and Jarvis, both belonging to the USA, and Flint, Vostok, Caroline, Starbuck, and Malden, all belonging to Britain and administered by the High Commissioner for the Western Pacific. Christmas, the largest Pacific atoll (area 223 sq. m., pop. 452), Fanning (area 12 sq. m., pop. 521) and Washington (area 3 sq. m. pop. 355) form part of the ◊ *Gilbert and Ellice Islands* colony. They produce copra from coconut plantations; the others are virtually uninhabited.

**Lingfield** England. Village in SE Surrey, on the R. Eden 9 m. SE of Reigate. Pop. (1961) 7,907. A 15th-cent. church. Race-course.

**Lingga Archipelago** Indonesia. Group of islands off the E coast of Sumatra. Area 840 sq. m. Pop. 31,000. Largest islands Lingga and Singkep. Main products sago, copra, tin.

**Linköping** Sweden. Capital of Östergötland county, 100 m. SW of Stockholm. Pop. (1968) 78,032. Railway junction. Industrial centre. Railway engineering, brewing, etc. Manufactures aircraft, cars, textiles, tobacco products. Romanesque cathedral (12th/15th-cent.).

**Linlithgow** Scotland. Royal burgh and county town of W Lothian, 16 m. W of Edinburgh. Pop. (1961) 4,327. Manufactures paper, shoes. Whisky distilling. Mary Queen of Scots (1542–87) was born in the now ruined Linlithgow Palace.

**Linlithgowshire** ◊ *West Lothian.*

**Linnhe, Loch** Scotland. Sea loch on the W coast in Argyllshire and Inverness-shire at the SW end of Glenmore, with Fort William near its head. At its mouth is ◊ *Lismore Island.* ◊ *Caledonian Canal.*

**Linz** Austria. Capital of Upper Austria (Oberösterreich), on the Danube R. 100 m. W of Vienna. Pop. (1961) 195,978. Busy river port and industrial centre. Manufactures steel, machinery, chemicals, textiles, paper, etc. Connected by bridges with the left-bank suburb of Urfahr. Gothic cathedral (completed 1924).

**Lions (Lion), Gulf of** France. Ancient Sinus Gallicus. Wide bay of the Mediterranean extending from the Franco-Spanish border (W) to Toulon (E). Chief port Marseille.

**Lipa** Philippines. Town in Batangas province, Luzon, 40 m. SSE of Manila. Pop. (1960) 69,342. Trade in sugar, abacá, maize, tobacco, etc. Manufactures textiles.

**Lipari Islands** Italy. Ancient Aeoliae Insulae (Aeolian Islands). Volcanic group off the N coast of Sicily comprising 7 islands and many islets. Area 44 sq. m. Pop. 12,000. Chief town Lipari, on the island of Lipari. Stromboli and Vulcano are active volcanoes, and the highest peak (3,150 ft) is on Salina. Exports pumice stone, wine, fruit.

**Lipetsk** USSR. Town in the Lipetsk region, RSFSR, on the Voronezh R. 70 m. NNE of Voronezh. Pop. (1970) 290,000. Important iron-mining centre. Manufactures pig-iron, tractors, chemicals, etc. Founded in the 18th cent., it has long been famous for its chalybeate springs and is a health resort.

**Lippe** Federal German Republic. Former principality between Hanover and Westphalia, with capital Detmold; since 1945 part of N Rhine-Westphalia. Area 469 sq. m. A region of small but prosperous farms; also has valuable deciduous forests.

**Lippe River** Federal German Republic. River 147 m. long in N Rhine-Westphalia rising in the Teutoburgerwald and flowing generally W past Lippstadt and Hamm to join the Rhine R. at Wesel. Declined in importance with the construction (1930) of the parallel Lippe Canal (Hamm–Wesel).

**Lippstadt** Federal German Republic. Town in N Rhine-Westphalia, on the Lippe R. 23 m. E of Hamm. Pop. (1963) 38,500. Iron founding, metal working. Manufactures wire, textiles, etc. Founded 1168.

**Lisbon** (Portuguese **Lisboa**) Portugal. Ancient Olisipo. Capital of Portugal and of the Lisboa district, on the right bank of the Tagus R. estuary at the point where the latter narrows from nearly 7 m. to 2 m. in width. Pop. (1960) 802,230. The country's chief seaport, accessible to large vessels in spite of the bar at the river mouth. Exports wine, olive oil, cork, etc. Also the leading industrial and commercial centre. Manufactures textiles, chemicals, pottery, paper, etc. Lisbon has a magnificent situation (esp. as viewed from the Tagus), built largely in white stone and rising in terraces from its shores. The pride of the city is the fine Avenida da Liberdade, 300 ft wide and nearly 1 m. long, running in a straight line from the Rossio square to the Edward VII Park – the Champs Élysées of Lisbon; the most romantic part is the Alfama or old town, in the E, with its narrow alleys and its cathedral, founded in the 12th cent. and twice rebuilt. S of the Rossio is the Cidade Baixa or lower town, reconstructed in rectangular form by the Marquis de Pombal after the disastrous earthquake of 1755. In the W is the famous Hieronymite monastery, with its lovely cloisters, and near by the Torre de Belém, a beautiful white tower and celebrated landmark from the 16th cent. – both close to the spot whence Vasco da Gama sailed on his famous voyage. Recaptured from the Moors 1147. Became capital in the 13th cent. Acquired great wealth with the establishment of Portuguese colonies in Africa and India in the 16th cent. The Salazar bridge over the Tagus, linking Lisbon with Almada, the longest suspension bridge in Europe, was inaugurated in 1966. Suffered disastrous floods, with the loss of 464 lives, in 1967.

**Lisburn** Northern Ireland. Urban district in Co. Antrim, on the R Lagan 8 m. SW of Belfast. Pop. (1961) 17,691. A centre of the linen industry, developed in the late 17th cent. by Huguenots. Also manufactures furniture. Jeremy Taylor was bishop at the 17th-cent. Protestant cathedral, and died here in 1667.

**Lisdoonvarna** Irish Republic. Resort and well-known spa, in Co. Clare 18 m. NW of Ennis. Sulphur and chalybeate springs.

**Lisieux** France. Town in the Calvados department, on the Touques R. 27 m. E of Caen. Pop. (1968) 25,223. Manufactures textiles. Brewing, tanning, etc. Large trade in dairy produce, esp. Camembert cheese. The shrine of St Thérèse (canonized 1925) is a place of pilgrimage. Severe damage was inflicted on the town, including the 12th-cent. Church of St Peter (formerly a cathedral), during the 2nd World War (1944).

**Liskeard** England. Municipal borough in Cornwall 11 m. ESE of Bodmin. Pop. (1961) 4,490. Market town. Formerly a tin-mining centre.

**Lismore** Australia. Market town and river port in New South Wales, on the Richmond R. 95 m. S of Brisbane. Pop. (1966) 19,740. Centre of a dairy-farming region. Manufactures butter. Exports dairy produce, sugar-cane, etc.

**Lismore** Irish Republic. Market town in Co. Waterford, on the R. Blackwater 35 m. WSW of Waterford. Pop. (1966) 894.

Protestant cathedral of St Carthagh (17th-cent.) and a 19th-cent. Roman Catholic cathedral. Despite repeated Danish raids in the 9th and 10th cent., the 7th-cent. monastery founded by St Carthagh became a famous cultural and religious centre. Birthplace of Robert Boyle (1627–91).

**Lismore Island** Scotland. Island in Argyllshire, at the entrance to Loch Linnhe, 9½ m. long and up to 1½ m. wide. Several ruined castles; the 13th-cent. cathedral (restored) is now used as the parish church. A valuable collection of Gaelic poetry was made by a 16th-cent. Dean of Lismore.

**Lissa** (Poland) ◊ *Leszno*.

**Lissa** (Yugoslavia) ◊ *Vis*.

**Listowel** Irish Republic. Market town in Co. Kerry, on the R. Feale 40 m. W S W of Limerick. Pop. (1966) 2,822. Remains of a castle of the Desmonds.

**Lithgow** Australia. Town in New South Wales, in the Blue Mountains 70 m. W N W of Sydney. Pop. (1966) 13,167. Coalmining centre. Manufactures small-arms, woollen goods. Sawmilling, brick-making, etc.

**Lithuanian SSR (Lithuania,** Lithuanian **Lietuva)** USSR. Constituent republic of USSR, bordering W on the Baltic Sea and S W on Poland. Area 25,170 sq. m. Pop. (1970) 3,129,000 (79 per cent Lithuanians, the remainder mostly Russians and Poles). Cap. Vilnius. Mainly low-lying and flat, rising to about 1,000 ft in the morainic hills in the S E, with many small lakes and marshes. Drained by the Neman R. and its tributaries. It has a moderate continental climate, approaching the maritime along the coast, with an annual rainfall of 20–25 ins. Only about 16 per cent of the country is still forested, nearly three quarters of its area being devoted to arable and pasture land, but considerable industrialization has taken place under the Soviet régime; the urban population has risen from 23 per cent (1937) to 47 per cent (1968). Main agricultural products rye, oats, potatoes, sugar-beet, dairy produce. Pigs and poultry raised. Vilnius, Kaunas, Klaipéda (Memel; the leading seaport), Šauliai, and Panevežys are the principal towns, their chief industries the manufacture of textiles, footwear, and paper. Lithuanian is the oldest Indo-European language still extant, and resembles ancient Sanskrit, and its literature, like that of the Letts (Latvia), is rich in ballads and folk tales.

A grand duchy in the 13th cent., Lithuania extended from the Baltic to the Black Sea in the 15th cent. and was united to Poland 1385–1795. By the partitions of Poland most of Lithuania passed to Russia, but oppression led to a strong nationalist movement, and in 1918 Lithuania was proclaimed a republic. Its area was reduced when Poland seized Vilnius (1920) and increased when Lithuania occupied Memel (now Klaipéda) (1923). In 1940 it was made a constituent republic of the USSR, but during the 2nd World War it was occupied by German forces (1941–4) and great suffering was inflicted on the country and its people.

**Little America** ◊ *Ross Dependency*.

**Little Belt** (Danish **Lille Baelt**) Denmark. Strait about 30 m. long and up to 18 m. wide between Jutland and Fyn island and connecting the Kattegat with the Baltic Sea.

**Littlehampton** England. Urban district in W Sussex, at the mouth of the R. Arun. Pop. (1961) 15,647. Seaside resort. Minor port. Boatbuilding.

**Little Rock** USA. State capital of Arkansas, on the Arkansas R. Pop. (1960) 107,813. Largest city in the state. Important commercial centre for an agricultural and mining region. Trade in cotton, bauxite, coal. Manufactures clothing, wood and cottonseed products, building materials, etc. Negroes form about one quarter of the population. There have been serious race riots, esp. 1957–9. The name derives from the smaller of two rocky formations on the banks of the Arkansas R., called La Petite Roche by the French explorer Bernard de la Harpe (1722).

**Liuchow** China. Town in the Kwangsi-Chuang A R, on the Liu-kiang 130 m. N E of Nanning. Pop. 159,000. Road and railway junction. River port. In a picturesque mountainous region. Has a famous 9th-cent. temple (restored). Developed into an important industrial centre in the 1960s: manufactures machinery, chemicals, textiles, food products, etc.

**Liverpool** England. County borough in S W Lancashire, on the right bank of the Mersey estuary 30 m. W of Manchester. Pop. (1961) 747,490. The second most important seaport in Great Britain and a major industrial centre. Flour milling, sugar refining, electrical engineering. Manufactures chemicals, soap, margarine, etc. Merseyside generally is important for the tanning of leather. With its 7 m. of docks extending along the Mersey as far as Bootle, Liverpool exports an immense variety of manufactured goods from the North and Midlands, esp. textiles and machinery. Both its own docks and those of Birkenhead, with which it is linked by ferryboat and road tunnel, are administered by the Mersey Docks and Harbour Board (established 1858). Liverpool is not a city of historic buildings, possessing scarcely anything earlier than the 18th cent.; outstanding are the Anglican cathedral (designed by Sir G. G. Scott; begun 1904), the Roman Catholic cathedral (designed by Sir E. Lutyens; begun 1933 and opened in 1967), the Town Hall (1754), St George's Hall (1854), the Royal Liver Building, the Cunard Building, and the Walker Art Gallery. Many of the city's buildings were destroyed or severely damaged by bombing in the 2nd World War. The university, founded as a university college in 1881, was chartered in 1903 and developed rapidly in the 1920s. Probably founded by Norsemen in the 8th cent. but not mentioned by name until late in the 12th cent. Liverpool was granted its first charter by King John (1207). Its development as a seaport was at first slow, but in 1709 the first wet dock in Britain was built here, and later the growth of trade with the American colonies and the W Indies gave a great impetus to its expansion; the slave trade was especially lucrative until its abolition (1807). The industrialization of S Lancashire assisted its export trade; it became the main importing centre for raw cotton, and superseded Bristol as the leading seaport on the W coast of Britain.

**Livingston** Scotland. Former village in W Lothian, 15 m. WSW of Edinburgh, designated a 'new town' with a target pop. of 70,000 by 1985. Pop. (1969) 8,500.

**Livingstone** Zambia. Chief town of the Southern Province, near the N bank of the Zambezi R. Pop. (1962) 32,000. Only 7 m. from the Victoria Falls, it has become a tourist centre. Rhodes–Livingstone Museum, which contains relics of the explorer. Important airport. Capital of Northern Rhodesia 1907–35, then replaced by Lusaka.

**Livonia** USSR. Former province of Russia, divided (1918) between Estonia and Latvia, Riga having been its historic capital. Originally inhabited by the now extinct Livs, it was ruled successively by the

Germans, Poles, and Swedes before passing to Russia (1721).

**Livorno** ◊ *Leghorn.*

**Lizard Point** England. Southernmost point of Great Britain, in S W Cornwall. Famous for its fine coastal scenery and serpentine rock. Two lighthouses. Near by is the village of Lizard Town.

**Ljubljana** (Ger. **Laibach**) Yugoslavia. Capital of Slovenia, on the Ljubljanica R. near the confluence with the Sava R. Pop. (1961) 134,169. Industrial, commercial, and route centre. Manufactures machinery, chemicals, textiles, paper, etc. The Slovenian cultural centre; seat of a university (first founded 1595, reorganized 1954). It was capital of Illyria (1816–49) and later of Carniola. Scene of the Congress of Laibach (1821). Suffered severely from an earthquake (1895).

**Llanberis** Wales. Small town in Caernarvonshire 8 m. ESE of Caernarvon at the W end of Llanberis Pass. Pop. (1961) 2,330. In a slate-quarrying district. Chief base for the ascent of Snowdon, with a mountain railway to the summit.

**Llandaff** Wales. Town in Glamorganshire 3 m. NW of Cardiff (of which a suburb since 1922) on the R. Taff. Pop. (1961) 19,850. The bishopric was created in the 6th cent., the oldest in Wales. The 12th-cent. cathedral fell into decay, to be restored in the 19th cent.; it was then severely damaged in the 2nd World War, the new restoration being completed in 1960.

**Llandovery** Wales. Municipal borough in NE Carmarthenshire, on the R. Towy. Pop. (1961) 1,898. Market town. Well-known public school (1848).

**Llandrindod Wells** Wales. Urban district in W Radnorshire. Pop. (1961) 3,248. Spa, famous since the late 17th cent. for its mineral springs.

**Llandudno** Wales. Urban district in NE Caernarvonshire, on a peninsula just E of the R. Conway mouth. Pop. (1961) 17,852. Seaside resort on a bay between Great Orme's Head (NW) and Little Orme's Head, having developed from a fishing village from the mid 19th cent.

**Llanelli** Wales. Municipal borough in SE Carmarthenshire, on Burry Inlet of Carmarthen Bay 10 m. WNW of Swansea. Pop. (1961) 29,994. Seaport. Important centre of tinplate manufacture at near-by Trostre; also steel milling, copper refining, chemical and pottery manufacture.

**Llanfairfechan** Wales. Urban district in Caernarvonshire, on Conway Bay 8 m. S W of Llandudno. Pop. (1961) 2,861. Seaside resort.

**Llanfairpwll** Wales. Village in S E Anglesey 2 m. W of Menai Bridge, made famous by an 18th-cent. poet-cobbler who lengthened its name to Llanfairpwllgwyngyllgogerchwyrndrobwlltysiliogogogoch ('St Mary's Church in the hollow of the white hazel near to the rapid whirlpool of Llandysilio of the red cave').

**Llangollen** Wales. Urban district in Denbighshire, on the R. Dee 9 m. S W of Wrexham, in the picturesque Vale of Llangollen. Pop. (1961) 3,050. Summer resort. Market town. Manufactures flannel. The ruined 13th-cent. Cistercian Valle Crucis Abbey is just N W, and there is a 14th-cent. bridge over the river.

**Llanidloes** Wales. Municipal borough in S Montgomeryshire on the R. Severn. Pop. (1961) 2,375. Formerly a centre of lead mining and flannel weaving. Tanning. Scene of Chartist riots in 1839.

**Llanquihue, Lake** Chile. Lake in the Llanquihue and Osorno provinces (S), 15 m. N of Puerto Montt. Area 329 sq. m.; the largest lake in Chile. Drains to the Pacific through the Maullín R. A picturesque resort area, with wooded hills. The volcano Osorno (8,790 ft) lies to the E.

**Llanrwst** Wales. Urban district in Denbighshire, on the R. Conway 10 m. S of Conway. Pop. (1961) 2,571. A 15th-cent. church, believed to contain the tomb of Llewellyn ap Iorwerth.

**Llantrisant** ◊ *Glamorgan*.

**Lleyn Peninsula** Wales. Hilly peninsula in S W Caernarvonshire, between Caernarvon Bay and Cardigan Bay, rising to 1,849 ft. Pwllheli is on the S coast.

**Lloyd (Sukkur) Barrage** Pakistan. Irrigation dam across the Indus R. just below Sukkur, completed in 1932; water supplied to 7 canals. Area irrigated 5,450,000 acres. It has greatly increased the production of cotton, wheat, and other crops in Sind, where agriculture used to depend on inundation canals.

**Llwchwr (Loughor)** Wales. Urban district in W Glamorganshire, on the estuary of the R. Llwchwr 6 m. W N W of Swansea. Pop. (1961) 24,903. Coalmining and tin-plate industries.

**Lobito** Angola. Chief seaport. Pop. (1960) 79,600. One of the best harbours on the African Atlantic coast, with a protective sandspit; built mainly on reclaimed land. Bulk-loading facilities. Connected by rail with Beira (Moçambique), Katanga (Congo (Kinshasa)), Malawi, Rhodesia, Zambia; the Atlantic terminus for the trans-Africa railway (from ◊ *Benguela*, 18 m. S), to the building of which (1929) it owes its rapid commercial development. Exports coffee, cotton, maize, ores, salt, sisal, sugar.

**Lob Nor** ◊ *Lop Nor*.

**Lobos (Seal) Islands** Peru. Two groups of small islands off the N coast. Rich guano deposits, accumulated in the dry climate.

**Locarno** Switzerland. Resort in Ticino canton, at the N end of L. Maggiore 12 m. W of Bellinzona. Pop. (1969) 13,400. Taken from the Milanese by the Swiss (1512) but built in Italian style. Scene of the Locarno Conference (1925).

**Lochaber** Scotland. District in S Inverness-shire around Ben Nevis, consisting of mountains, moors, and glens and well known for its wild and picturesque scenery. The lochs provide water for the Lochaber hydroelectric scheme.

**Lochgelly** Scotland. Small burgh in Fifeshire 6 m. W N W of Kirkcaldy. Pop. (1961) 9,114. In a coalmining district. Loch Gelly is just to the S E.

**Lockerbie** Scotland. Small burgh in Dumfriesshire, in Annandale 10 m. E N E of Dumfries. Pop. (1961) 2,826. Market town. Noted for its sheep sales.

**Lockport** U S A. Industrial town in New York, on the Erie Canal 21 m. N N E of Buffalo. Pop. (1960) 26,443. Manufactures paper, wallboard, etc. Named after the series of locks which take the canal through a deep limestone gorge.

**Locle, Le** Switzerland. Town in Neuchâtel canton, 9 m. W N W of Neuchâtel near the French border. Pop. (1969) 15,200. Important watch-making centre, the industry having been established in 1705. Technical school for watch-makers.

**Lod** ◊ *Lydda*.

**Lodi** Italy. Town in Milano province in Lombardy, on the Adda R. 18 m. S E of Milan. Pop. (1961) 38,158. In a rich dairy-farming district. Large trade in cheese, esp. Parmesan. Manufactures linen, silk, majolica, etc. Cathedral (12th-cent.). Founded (1162) by Frederick Barbarossa. Here Napoleon defeated the Austrians (1796).

**Lódź** Poland. Second largest city in Poland, 77 m. W S W of Warsaw. Pop. (1968) 747,700. Leading centre of the textile industry. Also manufactures clothing, electrical and metal goods, etc. With its satellite towns, Łęczyca, Pabianice, and Zgierz, it is a province in its own right. University (1945). The city is laid out in blocks about the main street, which is nearly 7 m. long. Formerly a mere village, it developed rapidly in the early 19th cent. with the introduction of German weavers and became the 'Manchester of Poland'.

Lofoten Islands Norway. Group of islands off the NW coast, forming part of Nordland county, separated from the mainland by Vest Fiord and entirely within the Arctic Circle. Chief islands Austvågöy, Vestvågöy, Moskenesöy, Flakstadöy; chief town Svolvaer (Austvågöy). A partly submerged mountain range, rising to 3,811 ft on Austvågöy, they enjoy mild winters owing to the influence of the N Atlantic Drift. To the E and N is the Vesterålen group, often included with the Lofoten Is.; chief island Hinnöy. The waters off the two groups form one of the world's richest cod and herring fisheries, and in the spring thousands of fishermen from all parts of Norway come here. Fish curing and the preparation of cod-liver oil are important occupations in the fishing villages. Total area (two groups) about 1,600 sq. m. Pop. c. 30,000.

Logan, Mount Canada. Peak in S W Yukon, in the St Elias Mountains (19,850 ft). The highest in Canada and the second highest in N America. Named after Sir William E. Logan (1798–1875), Director of the Geological Survey of Canada 1842–69.

Logroño Spain. 1. Province in Old Castile, mountainous in the S W, rising to 7,562 ft in the Sierra de la Demanda, and descending to the fertile plain of La Rioja along the Ebro R. Area 1,985 sq. m. Pop. (1961) 229,852. Mainly agricultural. Produces wine, olive oil, cereals.
2. Capital of Logroño province, on the right bank of the Ebro R. 100 m. NW of Zaragoza. Pop. (1967) 75,157. Fruit canning, flour milling, etc. Important trade in wine. An ancient walled town, it has a bridge spanning the Ebro which dates back to the 12th cent. and several old churches.

Loire France. Department on the E margin of the Massif Central, formed from the old province of Lyonnais. Area 1,853 sq. m. Pop. (1968) 722,383. Prefecture St Étienne. Drained S–N by the Loire R. Rises to the Monts du Forez in the W and the Monts du Beaujolais and the Monts du Lyonnais in the E. Cereals, vines, etc. cultivated in the lowlands. An important coalfield in the St Étienne district; many metallurgical and textile plants. Chief towns St Étienne, Roanne.

Loire-Atlantique France. Formerly Loire-Inférieure. Department in S Brittany, crossed E–W by the Loire R. estuary and by its tributaries the Erdre and the Sèvre-Nantaise. Area 2,693 sq. m. Pop. (1968) 861,452. Prefecture Nantes. Many salt marshes along the coast; France's largest lake, Grand-Lieu (21 sq. m.), lies S of the Loire estuary. Wheat, vines, sugar-beet, and potatoes widely cultivated. Industry concentrated in Nantes and St Nazaire.

Loire River France. Ancient *Liger*. Longest river in France (627 m.), rising on the volcanic Mont Gerbier de Jonc in the Massif Central. From its source it flows generally NNW to Orléans, where it turns SW to Tours and then W to enter the Bay of Biscay by an estuary. Along its course are the fertile regions of Sologne, Berry, and Beauce, and the towns of Roanne, Nevers, Orléans, Tours, Nantes, and the estuary port of St Nazaire. With its tributaries, the chief of which are the Allier, Cher, Indre, Vienne, and Maine, it drains an area of over 46,000 sq. m., more than one fifth of France. Except for the lower reaches it is only seasonally navigable; in summer it becomes shallow and thin, but since the Middle Ages several of the towns on its banks have had to be protected from the sudden and treacherous floods to which it is subject.

Loiret France. Department formed from Orléanais province, drained E–W by the Loire R. Area 2,630 sq. m. Pop. (1968) 430,629. Prefecture Orléans. Mainly agricultural, producing wheat, sugar-beet, apples, vines, etc., and containing parts of Beauce, Gâtinais and Sologne. Chief towns Orléans, Montargis.

Loir-et-Cher France. Department formed from Orléanais, drained by the Loire R. and also by the Loir (N) and the Cher (S). Area 2,479 sq. m. Pop. (1968) 267,896. Prefecture Blois. In the N is part of the fertile Beauce, where wheat is grown, and in the S is the less productive Sologne region. Many famous châteaux, inc. those of Chaumont, Cheverny, and Montrichard. Chief towns Blois, Vendôme.

Loir River France. River 190 m. long rising in the Collines du Perche (Eure-et-Loir department) and flowing generally S and W to join the Sarthe R. near Angers.

Lokeren Belgium. Town in E Flanders

province 12 m. ENE of Ghent. Pop. (1968) 26,569. Industrial centre. Manufactures textiles, lace, etc.

**Lolland** ◊ *Laaland*.

**Lombardy** (Italian **Lombardia**) Italy. Region in the N, bordering N on Switzerland, and extending N–S from the Alps to the Po R. Area 9,190 sq. m. Pop. (1961) 7,390,492. Comprises the provinces of Bergamo, Brescia, Como, Cremona, Mantua, Milan, Pavia, Sondrio, and Varese. The mountainous N half, with lakes Como and Iseo and parts of Garda, Lugano, and Maggiore, attracts large numbers of tourists and has many hydroelectric plants, while the S half is the Lombard plain. The region is drained by the Po and its tributaries the Adda, Oglio, Chiese, Lambro, Serio, and Mella. Agriculture is important and is assisted by irrigation; maize, wheat, rice, wine, and cheese are produced and mulberries are grown for sericulture. Lombardy is also Italy's chief industrial region, manufacturing textiles, iron and steel, chemicals, etc. Trade is encouraged by the convergence of such important Alpine passes as Simplon, St Gotthard, Bernina, and Splügen on to the Lombard plain, and particularly on to Milan. In the 12th cent. the cities of the Lombard plain formed the Lombard League, and defeated Frederick I at Legnano (1176). Later the region was ruled successively by Spain, Austria, France, and Austria again, to become part of Italy in 1859.

**Lombok** Indonesia. Island of the Lesser Sundas between Bali and Sumbawa. Area 1,825 sq. m. Pop. 1,252,000. Mountainous, rising to 12,224 ft in Mt Rindjani. Main products rice, coffee. Chief town Mataram, capital of the province of W Nusa Tenggara and seat of the new provincial university. The flora and fauna of Lombok are transitional between Asiatic and Australian.

**Lomé** Togo. Capital and chief seaport, on the Bight of Benin 105 m. ENE of Accra (Ghana). Pop. (1966) 80,000. Exports cocoa, coffee, palm kernels, copra, etc. Linked by air with Paris, Dakar, Abidjan, etc.

**Lomond, Loch** Scotland. Largest lake in Scotland, between Dunbartonshire and Stirlingshire, 22 m. long N–S, 5 m. wide in the S narrowing to 1 m. in the N; several inlets, the outlet being the short R. Leven emptying into the Clyde estuary at Dumbarton. Receives the outfall of the Loch Sloy hydroelectric scheme. Well-known for its scenic beauty, it has many mountains around its banks and wooded islands in its waters. One of the mountains is Ben Lomond (3,192 ft), on its E side in Stirlingshire.

**London** Canada. Town in SW Ontario, on the Thames R. Pop. (1966) 194,416. Important commercial and industrial centre, described as 'a microcosm of Canadian life'. Over 500 diversified industries. Tanning, printing, brewing. Manufactures textiles, electrical equipment, food products, leather goods, etc. Seat of the University of Western Ontario (1878). Named after London, England. Chosen (1792) as the site of the future capital of Upper Canada.

**London** England. Ancient Londinium. Capital of England and the United Kingdom and chief city of the British Commonwealth, on both banks of the R. Thames. One of the world's greatest cities, the country's chief seaport and leading financial, commercial, industrial, and cultural centre. Also the hub of the country's rail and road systems and of national and international airways.

The City of London is the ancient city and the heart of London, situated on the N bank of the Thames. It has an area of only 677 acres and its night population, i.e. the permanent residents, is only 4,767 (1961), but with the vast influx of office and other workers the daytime population is said to exceed 1 million. It is the financial and commercial headquarters of the country and the Commonwealth, in which are situated the Bank of England, joint stock and merchant banks, discount houses, the Stock Exchange, and insurance organizations, including the famous Lloyd's. In the City there are 81 Livery Companies, the oldest being the Mercers' (1393); they succeeded the ancient trade guilds, play a considerable part in the administration of the City, and are responsible for the choice of Lord Mayor. The Guildhall and the Mansion House, official residence of the Lord Mayor, are in the City, as also is St Paul's Cathedral. This great example of Renaissance architecture, designed by Wren, begun in 1675, and completed in 1710, is 500 ft long and has a dome 364 ft high.

The former Administrative County of London, on both sides of the river, with the City covered an area of 117 sq. m. and had a population (1961) of 3,195,114. While the Corporation of the City of London retained administrative powers within its own square mile, the County was governed by the London County Council, formed in 1888. It was divided into 28 metropolitan boroughs. On 1 April 1965, however, the LCC was succeeded by the Greater London Council, created under the London Government Act (1963), which became responsible for a far greater area than the old County of London (see below).

Within the old County of London, in the City of Westminster, are the Houses of Parliament, and near by is Whitehall, with many of the government offices; off Whitehall in Downing Street is the residence of the Prime Minister. Buckingham Palace, built in 1703 by the Duke of Buckingham, has been the London residence of the monarch since 1837. County Hall, seat of the Greater London Council on the South Bank of the Thames, stands at the opposite end of Westminster Bridge from the Houses of Parliament. Of the many theatres, the Royal Opera House (Covent Garden) is a centre of opera and ballet, and the Old Vic, now housing the National Theatre, is the traditional home of Shakespeare productions. Shopping centres, both fashionable and popular, include Bond St, Regent St, and Oxford St, and Piccadilly and the Strand are equally well-known thoroughfares. Mayfair and Belgravia are fashionable residential districts, while Bloomsbury has a more intellectual character. In the latter area is the British Museum, while in South Kensington is a group which includes the Victoria and Albert, Natural History, and Science Museums. Among the many famous art collections are those of the National Gallery, in Trafalgar Square, and the Tate Gallery. Outside the city the most famous church is Westminster Abbey. The University of London, incorporated in 1836, includes University and King's Colleges and the London School of Economics, and in number of students is by far the largest university in the country.

The most famous of the open spaces in London are Hyde Park and Kensington Gardens; Regent's Park has its Open-Air Theatre and the Zoo, and St James's Park its wildfowl. Below Teddington the course of the Thames is controlled by the Port of London Authority (1908), whose headquarters are in the City. The system of docks includes the Surrey Commercial Docks (scheduled for closure in 1970), the E India, W India and Millwall Docks, the large Royal Victoria, Royal Albert and King George V Docks, and Tilbury Docks. The Port of London handles about 40 per cent of the country's imports, including both foodstuffs and vast quantities of raw materials for the wide variety of industries in the London area.

The area now administered by the Greater London Council includes the former County of London, almost the whole of Middlesex, and parts of Kent, Surrey, Essex, and Hertfordshire. It covers an area of 620 sq. m. and has a population (1963) of 7,979,616. It is divided into the following 32 Greater London boroughs: City of Westminster, Camden, Islington, Hackney, Tower Hamlets, Greenwich, Lewisham, Southwark, Lambeth, Wandsworth, Hammersmith, Royal Borough of Kensington and Chelsea, Waltham Forest, Redbridge, Havering, Barking, Newham, Bexley, Bromley, Croydon, Sutton, Merton, Royal Borough of Kingston-upon-Thames, Richmond-upon-Thames, Hounslow, Hillingdon, Ealing, Brent, Harrow, Barnet, Haringey, Enfield. The Greater London borough councils were first elected in 1964.

HISTORY. London probably did not exist in the time of Julius Caesar, but it had already acquired some importance as a commercial centre when it was sacked by Boadicea (A.D. 61). The Romans then built a wall, portions of which remain, around the city, enclosing an area of about $\frac{1}{2}$ sq. m. After their withdrawal, London disappeared from history for almost two centuries but under Alfred the Great its commercial prosperity revived, and William the Conqueror granted it a charter and built the White Tower, nucleus of the Tower of London. In 1191 the City received its present form of government, and elected its first mayor in 1193; Westminster, meanwhile, became the seat of national government. In the time of Elizabeth I London acquired great wealth and power, and later played a considerable part in the struggle against the Stuarts. After the Restoration it suffered two major disasters, the Great Plague (1665) and the Great Fire (1666); the rebuilding was largely in the hands of Wren. The City began to lose its residential character in the 17th cent., railway transport led to the rapid growth of suburbs in the 19th cent., and the general movement of population towards the perimeter of Greater London and beyond has continued. During the 2nd World War many of London's historic buildings were destroyed or severely damaged by air raids, flying and rocket bombs; about 30,000 of its citizens were killed and over 50,000 injured. In the subsequent period of rebuilding, many large blocks of offices and flats were erected. One of the noteworthy new buildings was the Post Office Tower, 620 ft high, just N of Oxford St, the tallest building in London and in Great Britain, completed in 1964, opened in 1965. The first new Underground railway to be built for over 60 years, the Victoria line, was opened in 1969.

**Londonderry (Derry)** Northern Ireland. **1.** County in the NW, bounded on the N by the Atlantic Ocean and on the W by Co. Donegal (Irish Republic). Area 814 sq. m. Pop. (1961) 111,565. (Both figures exclude Derry city.) County town Londonderry (Derry city). The surface is generally hilly, rising to 2,240 ft in Mt Sawel in the Sperrin Mountains in the S. Drained by the Foyle (W), the Bann (E), and the Roe (S–N) rivers. The NW boundary passes through Lough Foyle, the SE through Lough Neagh. Oats, potatoes, and flax cultivated. Industries are concentrated on Derry city and Coleraine. The English name derives from the grant of land around the two towns to the Corporation of the City of London in 1613.
**2.** County town of Co. Derry, county borough, on the W bank of the R. Foyle 4 m. from the mouth (Lough Foyle). Pop. (1961) 53,744. Seaport. Industrial centre. Manufactures shirts, collars, other clothing, and linen. The city walls (completed 1618) and the Protestant cathedral of St Columba (1633) are memorials to the work of the Irish Society, representing the Corporation of London, which was granted lands at Derry (afterwards called Londonderry) in 1613. Other buildings are the Roman Catholic cathedral, St Eugene (1873), the Guildhall (1912), and Magee University College (since 1951 affiliated to Queen's University, Belfast). Derry originated with an abbey founded (546) by St Columba. The name derives from the Irish *doire* ('Oak Wood'). From the 9th to the 11th cent. it was frequently raided and taken by the Danes. 'Planted' with Scottish Presbyterians in the 17th cent. it underwent a long siege (1688–9) by the army of James II, but held out (under the leadership of Reverend George Walker), earning the cognomen of the 'Maiden City'.

**Londrina** Brazil. Town in the N of the Paraná State. Pop. 77,000 (many Germans and Slavs). In a region of rapid development since the introduction of coffee to Paraná. Trade also in cotton, oranges, etc. Founded 1932.

**Long Beach** USA. Tourist resort and industrial town in California 18 m. S of Los Angeles. Pop. (1960) 344,168. Excellent recreational amenities. Varied industries: oil refining, fish and fruit canning; manufactures aircraft, tyres, chemicals, soap, etc. It has a large fishing fleet, and a fine deepwater harbour protected by Catalina Island. Exports petroleum, cement. Named because of the 7 m. bathing beach.

**Long Branch** USA. Seaside resort in New Jersey 40 m. ENE of Trenton, one of the oldest in the USA. Pop. (1960) 26,228. Manufactures clothing, rubber products, etc. Fishing. First settled 1740.

**Longchamp** France. Fashionable racecourse SW of the Bois de Boulogne, Paris, where the race for the Grand Prix is run in June.

**Long Eaton** England. Urban district in SE Derbyshire, near the R. Trent 6 m. SW of Nottingham. Pop. (1961) 30,464. Formerly important in the lace industry. Now manufactures electrical equipment, hosiery, upholstery, food products, etc. Near by at Toton are the country's largest railway marshalling yards.

**Longford** Irish Republic. **1.** County in Leinster, bounded on the SW by Lough Ree. Area 403 sq. m. Pop. (1966) 28,989. Generally low-lying except in the N, where it rises to 912 ft. Contains much bog, with pastures for cattle rearing in the S. Oats and potatoes cultivated. Drained by the Shannon and its tributaries.
**2.** County town of Co. Longford, on the R. Camlin 60 m. W of Drogheda. Pop. (1966) 3,454. Market town. A 17th-cent. castle; 19th-cent. Roman Catholic cathedral.

**Long Island** USA. Island in New York state, 118 m. long and 12–23 m. wide, extending ENE from the mouth of the Hudson R.; separated from the mainland by Long Island Sound. Many resorts and residential towns, especially in the E. The W part (comprising the boroughs of Brooklyn and Queens) is essentially part of New York city. Famous resorts include Coney Island (Brooklyn), Fire Island, and Long Beach. Two airports: La Guardia (New York municipal), John F. Kennedy (New York international).

**Longleat** ◊ *Warminster*.

**Longton** England. Town in NW Staffordshire, in the Potteries district; since 1910 part of Stoke-on-Trent. Porcelain was first made here in the mid 18th cent. at Longton Hall by William Littler.

**Longview** USA. Town in Texas, 125 m. E of Dallas. Pop. (1960) 40,050. On an oilfield. Oil refining. Manufactures chemicals, oilfield equipment, etc. Grew rapidly after the discovery of oil (1930).

**Looe** England. Urban district in Cornwall, at the mouth of the R. Looe 13 m. W of Plymouth. Pop. (1961) 3,878. Consists of W and E Looe, on opposite banks of the river, both fishing ports and resorts.

**Lop Nor (Lob Nor)** China. Depression in E Sinkiang-Uighur AR, at the E end of the Tarim Basin, once filled by a large lake but now largely dried, consisting of small temporary lakes which move their location owing to the changes in the course of the Tarim R. This apparent movement of the lake was observed by the explorers Przhevalski (1876) and Sven Hedin (1928).

**Lorain** USA. Industrial town in Ohio, at the mouth of the Black R. on L. Erie. Pop. (1960) 68,932. Excellent harbour. Trades largely in coal and iron ore. Shipbuilding. Manufactures iron and steel goods, machinery, cranes, clothing, etc.

**Lorca** Spain. Ancient Eliocroca. Town in Murcia province 37 m. SW of Murcia. Pop. (1967) 61,445. Industrial centre. Manufactures fertilizers, woollen goods, footwear, etc. Tanning, flour milling, brandy distilling. Trade in agricultural produce. Built on a hill crowned by a medieval castle. Several baroque churches.

**Lord Howe Islands** ◊ *Solomon Islands*.

**Loreto** Italy. Town in Ancona province, in The Marches, 13 m. SSE of Ancona. Pop. 9,000. Famous place of pilgrimage because of the Santa Casa (Holy House), believed to be the home of the Virgin Mary miraculously transported here from Nazareth late in the 13th cent. A church, begun in 1468, was built round it.

**Lorient** France. Fishing port in the Morbihan department, on an inlet of the Bay of Biscay 70 m. SE of Brest. Pop. (1968) 68,960. Fish canning. Manufactures nets, rope, etc. Founded by the Compagnie des Indes Orientales (1664) for trade with the Orient, and named L'Orient. Taken over by the French government (1782) and

became an important naval base. During the 2nd World War it was a German submarine base, and was almost completely destroyed by Allied bombing, but was subsequently rebuilt.

**Lorraine** (Ger. Lothringen) France. Region and former province in the E, bounded on the N by Belgium and Luxembourg and on the NE by W Germany, now divided into the departments of Moselle, Meurthe-et-Moselle, Meuse, and Vosges. Consists in the main of a low plateau rising in the E to the Vosges and cut S–N by the valleys of the Meuse and Moselle. Varied agriculture; coal mined in the NE on the extension of the Saar coal basin; but the extremely rich iron ore deposits around Longwy, Thionville, Briey, and Nancy are by far the most important resource. Prior to the 9th cent. a part of the kingdom of Lotharingia. Divided (960) into the duchies of Upper and Lower Lorraine. The latter became Brabant (now in Belgium and the Netherlands) and the former, from the 11th cent. known simply as Lorraine, was united to France in 1766 as a province, with Nancy as capital. In 1871 the present Moselle department (largely German-speaking) was united with Alsace to form the German imperial territory of Elsass-Lothringen; it reverted to France in 1919, but was again annexed to Germany (1940–44) and returned to France after the 2nd World War. Lorraine suffered severely in both world wars.

**Los Alamos** USA. Town in New Mexico 24 m. NW of Santa Fé, at a height of 7,300 ft. Pop. (1960) 12,584. Famous for the US government atomic-energy laboratories, where the first atom bomb was made during the 2nd World War; later the first H-bomb was made here.

**Los Andes** Chile. Town in the Aconcagua province, 45 m. N of Santiago. Pop. 33,000. On the Trans-Andean railway. In a district producing cereals, wine, and fruit.

**Los Angeles** USA. City in S California, on the Pacific coast, largest in the state and third largest in the USA. Pop. (1970) 2,782,400. By incorporating neighbouring towns it has become the USA's largest city in area, 452 sq. m. A major seaport. Several airports. The favourable 'Mediterranean' climate attracts residents and tourists in large numbers. The long hours of sunshine, dry dependable weather, and beautiful scenery have helped to promote its major industry, the production of films.

Oil refining and aircraft manufacture rank next in importance; there are many other industries. Seat of the University of California (1919), the Methodist University of Southern California (1879), and the Loyola University of Los Angeles (1912, Roman Catholic). Some early-19th-cent. buildings survive, including the old Plaza church (1818) and the Avila Adobe (1818), the oldest house in the city. Within the city boundaries there are many districts which have retained a separate identity, e.g. Hollywood, Beverly Hills, Burbank, Pasadena, Santa Ana, Santa Monica. Several foreign communities, e.g. Chinese, Japanese, Mexican, Negro, have their own districts.

Founded (1781) by Franciscan fathers; the full name is El Pueblo Nuestra Señora la Reina de los Angeles de Porciuncula. Became capital of the Mexican state of California in 1845, but was captured by US forces in 1846, during the Mexican War. The advent of the railways and the discovery of oil in the late 19th cent. stimulated its growth. Then came the film industry in the early 1900s and the aircraft industry after 1920. Since the 2nd World War the increase in population and prosperity has been remarkable.

**Los Islands** Guinea. Group of islands near Conakry, the five most important being Tamara, Factory, Crawford, White, Coral. Chief products bauxite, palm kernels. They were British possessions from 1818 to 1904, when they were ceded to France.

**Lossiemouth and Branderburgh** Scotland. Small burgh in Morayshire, at the mouth of the R. Lossie on Moray Firth. Pop. (1961) 5,855. Fishing port. Resort. Lossiemouth has a well-known golf course. Birthplace of J. Ramsay MacDonald (1866–1937).

**Lostwithiel** England. Market town in Cornwall, on the R Fowey 5 m. SSE of Bodmin. Pop. (1961) 1,954. Fishing port. One of the four Cornish 'Stannary towns', with the monopoly of minting tin coinage.

**Lot** France. Department in the SW, formed (1790) from the Quercy district of the old Guyenne province, sloping NE–SW from the Massif Central to the Garonne valley, with the limestone Causses in the centre. Area 2,018 sq. m. Pop. (1968) 151,198. Prefecture Cahors. Drained by the Lot and Dordogne rivers. Cereals, vines, fruits cultivated; sheep and cattle raised. Chief towns Cahors, Figeac.

**Lota** Chile. Seaport in the Concepción province, 20 m. SSW of Concepción. Pop. 52,000. Important coalmining centre and bunkering port for coastal vessels. Copper smelters. Ceramics factory.

**Lot-et-Garonne** France. Department in the SW, formed (1790) from parts of Gascony and Guyenne provinces. Area 2,079 sq. m. Pop. (1968) 290,592. Prefecture Agen. Drained by the Garonne and its tributaries the Lot, Gers, and Baïse, in whose fertile valleys wheat, maize, tobacco, vines, plums, and vegetables are grown and cattle and poultry are raised. Chief towns Agen, Villeneuve-sur-Lot, Marmande.

**Lothians, The** Scotland. Area in the SE including the counties of W Lothian, Midlothian, and E Lothian. Formerly it constituted the entire area between the Firth of Forth and the R. Tweed, and formed part of the kingdom of Northumbria, but it was annexed to Scotland in 1018.

**Lot River** France. River 298 m. long, rising in the Lozère department and flowing W, crossing the limestone Causses by a deep gorge, and joining the Garonne R.

**Lötschberg Tunnel** Switzerland. Railway tunnel 9 m. long in the Alps, linking Thun (Bern canton) and Brig (Valais canton) and reaching 4,078 ft. Lies beneath the Lötschen Pass (8,829 ft). Built 1906–12.

**Loughborough** England. Municipal borough in Leicestershire, on the R. Soar 10 m. NNW of Leicester. Pop. (1961) 38,621. Engineering. Manufactures hosiery, shoes, electrical equipment, pharmaceutical products. There is also a bell-founding industry, the great bell of St Paul's, London, having been cast here (1881). Has a famous College of Technology (1909), which attained university status in 1964, and a teacher training college.

**Loughor** ◊ *Llwchwr*.

**Loughrea** Irish Republic. Market town in Co. Galway, on the N shore of Lough Rea 21 m. ESE of Galway. Pop. (1966) 3,001.

**Louisiade Archipelago** SW Pacific Ocean. Chain of volcanic islands and coral reefs in the SW Pacific SE of New Guinea. Part of the Australian Trust Territory of Papua. Gold obtained on many islands. Named (1768) by de Bougainville after Louis XV. During the 2nd World War the Americans won an important naval and air battle over the Japanese in the Coral Sea off Misima island (1942).

**Louisiana** USA. State on the Gulf of

Mexico (S) and bordered by Arkansas (N), Mississippi (E), and Texas (W). Area 48,523 sq. m. Pop. (1970) 3,564,310 (nearly one third Negroes, descendants of former slaves). Cap. Baton Rouge. Admitted to the Union in 1812 as the 18th state; popularly known as the 'Pelican' state. Part of the Gulf coastal plain; the highest point is only 535 ft above sea level, and the average elevation is about 100 ft above sea level. Floods from the Mississippi (whose delta is within Louisiana) present a serious problem; hundreds of miles of levees have been constructed. Along the Red R. (which bisects the state) there are several lakes. The Gulf coast is indented with numerous bays and lagoons. Climate humid sub-tropical; summers are hot and long, winters mild and short. Rainfall averages 50–55 ins. annually. Forests cover 56 per cent of the state, but farming is the main occupation. Leading crop cotton; sugar-cane, rice, and maize also important. The chief factor in the economy is petroleum production, mainly in the Gulf region. There are also rich sulphur and salt mines. Industries are concerned largely with farm produce (e.g. sugar refining), petroleum, and lumber. Largest town New Orleans, followed by Shreveport, Baton Rouge, Lake Charles.

Named Louisiana after Louis XIV; the French originally gave the name to the entire Mississippi basin. The first settlement in the present state was made at New Orleans (1718). The region E of the Mississippi was ceded to Britain in 1763 and became US territory in 1783. The region W of the Mississippi (a vast territory of 885,000 sq. m.) was sold by France to the USA in 1803 (the Louisiana Purchase). Out of this area the Territory of Orleans was organized in 1804; it became the state of Louisiana in 1812.

**Louis Trichardt** ◊ *Zoutpansberg*.

**Louisville** USA. Industrial and commercial town in N Kentucky, on the Ohio R., whose falls provide hydroelectric power. Pop. (1960) 390,639. Important trade in tobacco. Whisky distilling, meat packing, flour milling. Manufactures tobacco products, textiles, chemicals, etc. University (1837). Near by is the Churchill Downs racecourse, scene of the Kentucky Derby since 1875. Named after King Louis XVI of France, in recognition of the French help given to the American colonies during the American War of Independence. The city has at times suffered severely from the flooding of the Ohio R., esp. in 1937.

**Lourdes** France. Town in the Hautes-Pyrénées department, at the foot of the Pyrenees 10 m. SSW of Tarbes. Pop. (1968) 18,310. Here in 1858 an illiterate peasant girl, Bernadette Soubirous, had visions in a grotto of the Virgin Mary. A church was built near the spot (1862) and the fame of Lourdes as a place of miraculous cures rapidly grew. It is today the leading place of Catholic pilgrimage and annually attracts thousands of pilgrims, invalids, and tourists.

**Lourenço Marques** Moçambique. Capital, chief seaport, and largest city, on Delagoa Bay. Pop. 184,000. Excellent harbour. Much of its trade consists of imports for S Africa. Connected by rail with the Transvaal, Rhodesia, and Swaziland. Manufactures furniture, footwear, cement, etc. Also a popular holiday resort, with a pleasant winter climate. Named after a Portuguese trader who explored the area (1544). Superseded Moçambique as capital 1907.

**Lourenço Marques Bay** ◊ *Delagoa Bay*.

**Louth** England. Municipal borough in Parts of Lindsey, Lincolnshire, on the R. Lud 24 m. ENE of Lincoln. Pop. (1961) 11,556. Market town. Malting, brewing. Manufactures agricultural machinery. Has a 15th-cent. church with a 300-ft spire, and a 16th-cent. grammar school. About 1 m. E are the ruins of the 12th-cent. Cistercian Louth Park Abbey.

**Louth** Irish Republic. County in Leinster, the smallest in Ireland, bounded on the E by the Irish Sea and extending from Carlingford Lough (N) to the R. Boyne (S). Area 317 sq. m. Pop. (1966) 69,519. County town Dundalk. Generally low-lying and flat but rising to over 1,900 ft in the N. Drained by the Fane, Lagan, and Dee rivers. Main occupations fishing, cereal and potato cultivation, cattle rearing. Industrial centres Dundalk, Drogheda.

**Louvain** (Flemish **Leuven**) Belgium. Town in Brabant province, on the Dyle R. 15 m. E of Brussels. Pop. (1968) 32,224. Railway junction. Brewing, distilling, engineering. Its world-famous university was founded in 1426; the university library was destroyed by the Germans (1914), rebuilt with the aid of international donations, chiefly from the USA (1921–8), and again destroyed by the Germans in 1940. Prior to being a seat of learning, Louvain was a centre of the wool trade, and from the 11th to the 15th cent. was capital of the duchy of Brabant, being then replaced by Brussels.

**Lowell** USA. Industrial town in Massachusetts, on the Merrimack R. Pop. (1960) 92,107. Famous as a textile centre; the first mills were established in 1822. Also manufactures electrical equipment, chemicals, plastics, etc. Named after Francis Cabot Lowell, a pioneer in cotton manufacture. Birthplace of J. A. M. Whistler (1834–1903).

**Lower Hutt** New Zealand. Town in the SW of the N Island, 7 m. NE of Wellington. Pop. (1966) 57,337. Important industrial centre. Meat freezing, vehicle assembly, engineering. Manufactures textiles, clothing, furniture, etc. Industries mainly located in the lower valley of the R. Hutt near the N shore of Port Nicholson.

**Lower Saxony (Ger. Niedersachsen)** Federal German Republic. *Land* formed in 1946 from the former Prussian province of Hanover and the *Länder* of Oldenburg, Schaumburg-Lippe, and most of Brunswick. Area 18,262 sq. m. Pop. (1968) 6,993,200. Cap. Hanover. Borders E on the German Democratic Republic, N on the North Sea, and W on the Netherlands, and includes the E Frisian Is. The central area comprises much heath and moor, including Lüneburg Heath, and the region is drained by the Ems, Weser, Aller, and Elbe rivers. Farming is the main occupation except in the wooded Harz Mountains of the extreme SE. Chief towns Hanover, Brunswick, Osnabrück, Oldenburg, Salzgitter, Wilhelmshaven. After the 2nd World War the population increased greatly owing to the influx of refugees from the GDR.

**Lowestoft** England. Municipal borough in E Suffolk 9 m. S of Yarmouth. Pop. (1961) 45,687. Fishing port. Resort and yachting centre. Lowestoft Ness, on the North Sea, is England's most easterly point. Shipbuilding. Fishing and fish canning, tourism. Manufactures electrical equipment. In the late 18th cent. a type of china was made here and was named after it.

**Loyalty Islands** SW Pacific Ocean. Group of coral islands E of New Caledonia, of which they are a dependency. Area 800 sq. m. Pop. (1963) 13,617 (chiefly Melanesians). Three main islands, Maré, Lifu, and Uvéa, and many small islands. Export copra.

**Loyang** China. Town in Honan province, 70 m. W of Chengchow on the Lo-ho, a tributary of the Hwang-ho. Pop. 171,000. Commercial and industrial centre. Trade in cereals, cotton, etc. Manufactures tractors, machinery, ball bearings, etc. In early times the capital of various dynasties. Site of China's first tractor plant (1955). Has developed rapidly since 1949.

**Lozère** France. Department in the S of the Massif Central, formed from part of the Languedoc province. Area 2,000 sq. m. Pop. (1968) 77,258; one of the most sparsely populated regions of France. Prefecture Mende. Mountainous, rising to over 5,000 ft in the Monts de la Margeride (N). Drained by the Allier, Lot, and Tarn rivers, the last-named cutting a remarkable gorge in the limestone Causses. Sheep and dairy cattle raised. Cereals and fruit grown. Chief towns Mende, Marvejols.

**Lualaba River** Congo (Kinshasa). The W headstream of the Congo R., rising in Katanga province near the Zambia border and flowing generally N. After passing through a region of marshes and lakes, it is joined by the Luvua R., the E headstream of the Congo R. Known as the Lualaba as far as Kisangani (Stanleyville), 1,100 m. from its source, below which it becomes the Congo. Navigable downstream from Bukama.

**Luanda (São Paulo de Luanda)** Angola. Capital and seaport 210 m. SSW of Matadi. Pop. 300,000. Terminus of a railway to the interior (Malange). Exports coffee, cotton, etc. Oil refining. Manufactures cement, tobacco products, footwear, etc. Founded 1575. Centre of the slave trade to Brazil in the 17th and 18th cent. Declined in the late 19th cent. Development was restarted after the 2nd World War, but that of Lobito was more rapid and extensive. Trade and industry suffered from the Angola rebellion (1962).

**Lubbock** USA. Town in NW Texas, 225 m. WNW of Fort Worth. Pop. (1960) 128,691. Commercial centre for the S Plains area. Important market for cotton; also trade in cattle, poultry, grain, etc. Founded 1891. The first citizens were ranchers, buffalo hunters, and trail drivers. Expanded rapidly after the 2nd World War.

**Lübeck** Federal German Republic. Seaport in Schleswig-Holstein, on the Trave R. 10 m. from its mouth on the Baltic Sea and near the border of the German Democratic Republic. Pop. (1968) 242,677. Linked by canal with the Elbe R. Exports fertilizers, machinery, etc. Shipbuilding, engineering. Manufactures steel, machinery, textiles, wood products, etc. Cathedral (founded 1173); 13th-cent. Marienkirche; 13th/16th-cent. town hall; two 15th-cent. gates. Many of its buildings were damaged in the 2nd World War. Founded 1143. Became the chief city of the Hanseatic League; the last diet was held here in 1630. Remained a free Hanseatic city until 1937, when it was incorporated in Schleswig-Holstein. Birthplace of Thomas Mann (1875–1955).

**Lublin** Poland. Capital of the Lublin voivodship, on the Bystrzyca R. 100 m. SE of Warsaw. Pop. (1968) 234,300. Railway junction. Industrial and commercial centre. Manufactures agricultural machinery, electrical equipment, textiles, glass, etc. Flour milling, sugar refining. Seat of the Marie Curie-Sklodowska University (1944). Cathedral (16th-cent.). Temporary seat of the Polish government in 1918 and again in 1944.

**Lubumbashi** Congo (Kinshasa). Formerly Elisabethville. The second largest city; capital of the Katanga province, at a height of 4,000 ft. Pop. (1966) 233,000. Connected by rail with Zambia and Angola. Founded 1910. Grew rapidly with the development of copper mining by the Union Minière du Haut Katanga. Roman Catholic cathedral. Hospitals, schools, factories. Important airport. Copper smelting, food processing, brewing, printing, flour milling. Scene of fighting between Katangese troops and UN forces 1960–61.

**Lucania** ◊ *Basilicata*.

**Lucca** Italy. Capital of Lucca province, in Tuscany, in the valley of the Serchio R. 10 m. NE of Pisa. Pop. (1961) 88,428. Noted for olive-oil production. Also manufactures silk, macaroni, wine, etc. In its cathedral, which was begun in the 11th cent., is a cedar crucifix believed to have been brought miraculously to Lucca in 782. Several old churches and palaces. Scene of Julius Caesar's conference with Pompey and Crassus (56 B.C.).

**Lucena** Spain. Town in Córdoba province, in Andalusia, 36 m. SSE of Córdoba. Pop. (1961) 28,387. Manufactures earthenware jars for oil and wine storage, and produces wine, brandy, olive oil.

**Lucerne** (Ger. **Luzern**) Switzerland. Canton in central Switzerland, lying to the NW of the Lake of Lucerne. Area 577 sq. m. Pop. (1969) 284,000 (mainly Roman Catholic and German-speaking). Mountainous in the S. Agricultural and pastoral, with a large area of forests. Drained by the Reuss and the Kleine Emme rivers. One of the Four Forest Cantons; joined the Swiss Confederation in 1332.
2. Capital of Lucerne canton, on the Reuss R. at the point where it leaves the Lake of Lucerne. Pop. (1969) 74,100. One of the country's largest and most popular resorts. Manufactures aluminium goods, sewing machines, chemicals, etc. Fine views of the mountains, with the Rigi and Pilatus near by. In the town are the 17th-cent. Hofkirche and town hall, now housing the cantonal museum, and the famous Lion of Lucerne monument (sandstone) to the Swiss Guard. Grew round an 8th-cent. Benedictine monastery, and developed with the opening of the St Gotthard Pass in the 13th cent.

**Lucerne, Lake** (Ger. **Vierwaldstättersee**) Switzerland. In German, 'Lake of the Four Forest Cantons'. An irregular-shaped lake, at a height of 1,434 ft, bordering on the Four Forest Cantons – Unterwalden, Uri, Schwyz, and Lucerne. Area 43 sq. m. Fed from the S and drained from the NW by the Reuss R. With its picturesque scenery it is a popular tourist area, the resorts on its shores including Lucerne, the principal town, Weggis, Brunnen, and Flüelen. The best known of the neighbouring mountains are the Rigi (N) and Pilatus (SW).

**Luchow** China. Formerly Luhsien. River port and commercial town in Szechwan province, at the confluence of the Yangtse-kiang and the To-kiang 85 m. WSW of Chungking. Pop. 289,000. Trade in sugar, salt, tung oil.

**Luck** ◊ *Lutsk*.

**Luckenwalde** German Democratic Republic. Town in the Potsdam district, 23 m. SSE of Potsdam. Pop. (1965) 29,239. Manufactures textiles, paper, metal goods, etc. Brewing. During the Nazi régime it was the site of a concentration camp.

**Lucknow** India. Capital of Uttar Pradesh, on the Gumti R. 260 m. SE of Delhi. Pop. (1961) 595,440. Railway engineering. Manufactures paper, chemicals, carpets, copper and brass articles, etc. Trade in grain, oilseeds. Also an educational centre. University (1920). Capital of the Nawabs of Oudh 1775–1856. One of its outstanding buildings is the great Imambara or mausoleum of Asaf-ud-Daula. The defence and relief of the residency were dramatic episodes of the Indian Mutiny (1857).

**Lüdenscheid** Federal German Republic. Town in N Rhine-Westphalia 20 m. ESE of Wuppertal. Pop. (1963) 58,500. Industrial centre. Manufactures aluminium, hardware, plastics, etc.

**Ludhiana** India. Industrial and commercial town in Punjab 75 m. SE of Amritsar. Pop. (1961) 244,032. Railway junction. Manufactures hosiery, textiles, furniture, machinery, agricultural implements, etc. Trade in grain, cotton. Seat of an agricultural university (1962).

**Ludlow** England. Market town in Shropshire, on the R. Teme near the confluence with the R. Corve 23 m. S of Shrewsbury. Pop. (1961) 6,774. Important in medieval times on account of its position on the Welsh border, and among its buildings are the remains of the 11th/16th-cent. castle, and the 13th/15th-cent. parish church. A. E. Houseman (1859–1936), author of *A Shropshire Lad*, is buried here.

**Ludwigsburg** Federal German Republic. Town in Baden-Württemberg, near the Neckar R. 7 m. N of Stuttgart. Pop. (1963) 75,500. Manufactures metal goods, pianos and organs, textiles, etc. Founded in the early 18th cent. by the Duke of Württemberg; grew up round the ducal palace.

**Ludwigshafen** Federal German Republic. Town and river port in Rhineland-Palatinate, on the left bank of the Rhine R. opposite Mannheim. Pop. (1968) 172,963. A major centre of the German chemical industry. Manufactures dyes, plastics, fertilizers, pharmaceutical products, machinery, motor-car bodies, etc. Brewing, flour milling. Severely damaged by bombing in the 2nd World War.

**Lugano** Switzerland. Town in Ticino canton, on the N shore of L. Lugano near the Italian border. Pop. 22,500. Italian in appearance and character, it is a popular resort amid beautiful lake and mountain scenery, with Monte San Salvatore (3,002 ft) and Monte Brè (3,061 ft) near by. From 1848 to 1866 it was Mazzini's base in his struggle to expel the Austrians from Lombardy.

**Lugano, Lake** Italy/Switzerland. Long, narrow, irregularly shaped lake partly in Switzerland and partly in Italy, between L. Maggiore and L. Como. Area 19 sq. m. Fed by numerous mountain torrents. Drained by the Tresa R. into L. Maggiore. The chief town on the lake is Lugano.

**Lugansk** USSR. Formerly (1935–62) Voroshilovgrad. Capital of the Lugansk region, Ukrainian SSR, on the Lugan R., a tributary of the N Donets, in the Donbas mining area. Pop. (1970) 382,000. Industrial centre. Manufactures locomotives, steel pipes, coalmining machinery, ball bearings, etc. Brewing, flour milling. The first iron foundry was set up (1795) by an Englishman, Gascoyne, using local coal. After 1923 the town developed rapidly.

**Lugo** Spain. 1. Province in Galicia, in the NW, bordering N on the Bay of Biscay. Area 3,815 sq. m. Pop. (1961) 479,530. Mountainous, with broken, rocky coastline; drained by the Miño R. and its tributaries. Agriculture, fishing, lumbering. 2. Capital of Lugo province, on the Miño R. 50 m. SE of Corunna. Pop. (1967) 67,918. Market town. Tanning, flour milling. Manufactures textiles etc. Has Roman walls; 12th-cent. bridge across the Miño; 12th-cent. Gothic cathedral (much modernized).

**Luik** ◊ *Liège*.

**Luleå** Sweden. Capital of Norrbotten county, on the Gulf of Bothnia at the mouth of the Lule R. Pop. (1968) 36,296. Seaport, icebound Dec.–April. Exports iron ore from Gällivare and Kiruna, timber floated down the Lule, wood pulp, etc. Manufactures iron and steel, wood pulp.

**Lule River** Norway/Sweden. River 280 m. long rising just inside the Norwegian border and flowing SE through Stora Lule L. across Norrbotten to the Gulf of Bothnia at Luleå. Important hydroelectric plants derive power from falls at Porjus and Harspranget. Much timber floated downstream to Luleå.

**Luluabourg** Congo (Kinshasa). Town on the Lulua R., a tributary of the Kasai R., 500 m. ESE of Kinshasa. Pop. (1966) 141,000. Commercial and route centre on the Lubumbashi–Port Francqui railway. One of the chief strongholds of the Baluba tribe. Scene of fighting between Baluba and Lulu tribesmen in 1960.

**Lulworth** England. Two villages, E and W Lulworth, in the Wareham and Purbeck rural district, Dorset. The small seaside resort of W Lulworth stands near Lulworth Cove, a circular land-locked inlet surrounded by high cliffs of great beauty.

**Lund** Sweden. Town in Malmöhus county 10 m. NE of Malmö. Pop. (1968) 50,669.

Cultural centre with a university founded in 1668 and an Institute of Technology (1961). Printing and publishing, sugar refining. Manufactures paper, furniture, etc. Cathedral (11th-cent.) with an exceptionally large crypt and a medieval astronomical clock.

**Lundy** England. Rocky island 3 m. long and about $\frac{1}{2}$ m. wide off the N Devon coast 11 m. NNW of Hartland Point at the entrance to the Bristol Channel. Once the haunt of pirates and smugglers; has a ruined castle and is a sanctuary for gannets, guillemots, puffins, and razorbills. Two lighthouses.

**Lüneburg** Federal German Republic. Town in Lower Saxony, on the Ilmenau R. 25 m. SE of Hamburg. Pop. (1963) 60,900. Manufactures chemicals, ironware, clothing, cement, etc. Also a resort with saline springs. The churches of St John, St Michael and St Nicolas and the great 13th/18th-cent. town hall are outstanding. A leading member of the Hanseatic League. Capital of the duchy of Brunswick-Lüneburg 1235–1369.

**Lüneburg Heath** (Ger. **Lüneburger Heide**) Federal German Republic. Sandy region in Lower Saxony between the Elbe and the Aller rivers, largely covered with heather and scrub. Sheep raised. Potatoes and honey produced.

**Lünen** Federal German Republic. Industrial town in N Rhine-Westphalia, on the Lippe R. just NE of Dortmund. Pop. (1963) 72,200. Coalmining centre. Iron founding. Manufactures glass, aluminium.

**Lunéville** France. Town in the Meurthe-et-Moselle department, 19 m. ESE of Nancy. Pop. (1968) 25,367. Manufactures porcelain, textiles, etc. Railway engineering. The treaty of Lunéville between France and Austria was signed here (1801).

**Lunghai Railway** China. Chief E–W railway of central China, running from Lienyunkang on the Yellow Sea to Lanchow, where it links up with the Lanchow-Sinkiang Railway. At Chengchow it crosses the Peking–Kwangchow (Canton) Railway and at Paoki the new N–S trunk line (to Chungking).

**Lurgan** Northern Ireland. Municipal borough in Co. Armagh, just S of Lough Neagh 19 m. WSW of Belfast. Pop. (1961) 17,873. Centre of the linen industry since the early 17th cent. Also manufactures nylon fabrics, handkerchiefs, etc.

**Lusaka** Zambia. Capital, 30 m. N of the Kafue R. at a height of 4,200 ft. Pop. (1968) 154,000. Linked by road across the Zambezi with Salisbury (Rhodesia) and by rail with Bulawayo (Rhodesia). Commercial centre in an agricultural region. Manufactures cement, tobacco products, etc. Seat of the University of Zambia (1966). Became capital of Northern Rhodesia 1935. Raised to the status of a city 1960.

**Lusatia** (Ger. **Lausitz**) German Democratic Republic/Poland. Former district between the Elbe and the Oder rivers and N of the Lausitz Gebirge, since 1946 divided between the GDR and Poland, the latter receiving the portion E of the Neisse R. By the 15th cent. Upper Lusatia, including the towns of Bautzen, Görlitz, and Zittau, and Lower Lusatia, including Cottbus and Forst, were identified. After changing hands several times, both districts passed to Saxony (1635); but in 1815 Lower Lusatia and much of Upper Lusatia were incorporated in Prussia.

**Lü-ta** China. Formerly Port Arthur–Dairen, later Lushun-Talien. Municipality of Liaoning province at the S end of the Liaotung peninsula, formed from the ports of Port Arthur and Dairen. Pop. (1957) 1,508,000. Port Arthur (Lushun), an important naval base, was leased to Russia (1898), captured by the Japanese in the Russo-Japanese War (1905), and retained until 1945; it became a joint Soviet-Chinese naval base, but was returned to China in 1954. Dairen (Talien), 23 m. ENE of Port Arthur, is the chief seaport of Manchuria and an important industrial centre; it exports soya bean products, grain, and coal, and its industries include shipbuilding, railway engineering, oil refining, soya-bean processing, etc. Leased to Russia with adjoining territory (1898), it was taken by the Japanese (1904) and expanded rapidly under their rule. After the 2nd World War it formed a municipality with Port Arthur.

**Luton** England. Municipal borough in Bedfordshire, on the R. Lea 18 m. S of Bedford. Pop. (1961) 131,505. Industrial centre. Important motor vehicle works. Also manufactures ball bearings, refrigerators, vacuum cleaners, etc. Engineering, brewing. Long the centre of the straw-plaiting industry, introduced in the reign of James I, but the manufacture of straw hats was replaced by that of felt hats.

**Lutsk** (Polish **Luck**) USSR. Town in the Ukrainian SSR, on the Styr R. 85 m. NE of Lvov. Pop. (1968) 94,000. Manufactures agricultural machinery. Flour milling, tanning, etc. Has a cathedral and a ruined 16th-cent. castle. Passed from Poland to Russia 1791, returned to Poland after the 1st World War and again passed to Russia after the 2nd World War. In the 1st World War it was the scene of a great Russian offensive (1916).

**Lutterworth** England. Small town in S Leicestershire 6 m. NNE of Rugby. Pop. (1961) 3,730. Hosiery and engineering industries. The Church of St Mary has relics of John Wyclif, who was rector here 1374–84.

**Luxembourg. 1.** Grand duchy and independent state in W Europe, bounded by the Federal German Republic (E), France (S), and Belgium (W). Area 999 sq. m. Pop. (1968) 335,234 (about 98 per cent Roman Catholic and mostly speaking the Letzeburgesch dialect). Cap. Luxembourg. In the N it is crossed by the Ardennes and rises to over 1,800 ft. The S is gently undulating. Drained by tributaries of the Moselle, which forms part of its E boundary. About half of its area is under cultivation. Chief crops oats, potatoes, wheat, some wine being also produced. The principal resource is the iron ore which is mined in the SW on the extension of the Lorraine fields; this forms the basis of the important iron and steel industry, centred on Esch-sur-Alzette. Industries are concentrated in the capital and the much smaller towns of Differdange, Dudelange, and Pétange. It is governed by a constitutional monarchy under a Grand Duke or Duchess with a Chamber of Deputies elected for 5 years. A county in the 11th cent., when it included the present Luxembourg province of Belgium. Became a duchy 1354. From the 15th cent. it was held by the House of Habsburg, apart from brief intervals, until the Congress of Vienna (1815), when it was made a grand duchy and passed to William I of the Netherlands; in 1839 it lost the present Luxembourg province of Belgium. Personal union with the Netherlands ended in 1890 on the death of William III, and a collateral branch of the House of Nassau became the ruling line. In both world wars the country was occupied by the Germans. In 1922 it entered into a customs union with Belgium, and in 1948 the two countries with the Netherlands formed the Benelux Customs Union.

**2.** Capital of Luxembourg, on a rocky plateau above the Alzette R. Pop. (1968) 77,105. Industrial centre, the industries being mostly situated in the valley. Brewing, tanning. Manufactures chemicals, pottery, etc. Has a 16th-cent. ducal palace and a 17th-cent. cathedral. Became one of the strongest fortresses in Europe, but the fortifications were demolished under the Treaty of London (1867).

**Luxembourg** Belgium. Province in the SE in the Ardennes. Area 1,706 sq. m. Pop. (1968) 219,368. Cap. Arlon. Largely wooded with some agriculture. Iron ore mined in the extreme S.

**Luxor** ⟡ *Thebes.*

**Luzern** ⟡ *Lucerne.*

**Luzon** Philippines. Largest and most important island of the archipelago, in the N. Area 40,420 sq. m. Pop. 11 million. Largely mountainous, it rises to 9,612 ft in Mt Pulog. In the fertile Cagayan valley rich crops of rice, abacá, sugar-cane, and tobacco are produced. Chief mineral chrome ore. Has the old capital, Manila, and the new capital, Quezon City. Scene of fierce fighting in the 2nd World War.

**Lvov** (Polish **Lwów**, Ger. **Lemberg**) USSR. City in the Ukrainian SSR, capital of the Lvov region, 300 m. WSW of Kiev. Pop. (1970) 553,000. Communications and industrial centre. Oil refining, motor-vehicle assembly. Manufactures agricultural machinery, railway equipment, textiles, chemicals, glass, etc. Roman, Armenian, and Greek cathedrals. University (1661). Founded in the 13th cent. Became capital of the Austrian province of Galicia 1772. Returned to Poland 1919. Ceded to the USSR 1945.

**Lyallpur** Pakistan. Town in W Pakistan 75 m. WSW of Lahore. Pop. (1961) 426,000. Flour and oilseed milling, engineering, cotton ginning, etc. Important trade in grain.

**Lydd** England. Municipal borough in S Kent 7 m. E of Rye (Sussex) and a 'member' of the Cinque Port of New Romney, though now 3 m. from the sea. Pop. (1961) 2,685. Market town with an airport (Ferryfield) for cross-channel car and passenger traffic. Gave its name to the explosive lyddite, first tested here.

**Lydda (Lod)** Israel. Town and railway junction 11 m. SE of Tel Aviv. Pop. 18,000. The country's chief international airport. Traditional birthplace of St George. Destroyed by Vespasian (A.D. 68) and

447

LYUBERTSY

rebuilt by Hadrian. Destroyed again by Saladin (1191) and rebuilt by Richard Cœur de Lion.

**Lydia.** Ancient country on the W coast of Asia Minor which became a wealthy kingdom in the 7th cent. B.C., its capital at Sardis. Its last king was Croesus, who was conquered by Cyrus the Great of Persia (546 B.C.).

**Lyme Regis** England. Municipal borough in W Dorset, on Lyme Bay. Pop. (1961) 3,533. Seaside resort. Small port. Has a picturesque harbour and curved breakwater, known as the Cobb, the scene of Monmouth's landing (1685). Here Mary Anning (1799–1847), a native, discovered the first ichthyosaurus (1811).

**Lymington** England. Municipal borough in SW Hampshire, at the mouth of the R. Lymington on the Solent. Pop. (1961) 28,642. Market town. Holiday resort. Yacht-building. Ferry service to Yarmouth, Isle of Wight.

**Lynchburg** USA. Town in Virginia, on the James R. 44 m. ENE of Roanoke. Pop. (1960) 54,790. In a picturesque location in the foothills of the Blue Ridge. An important market for tobacco. Manufactures footwear, textiles, clothing, metal goods, etc. Named after John Lynch, Quaker of Irish origin, who established a ferry (1757) and built a tobacco warehouse on the hill.

**Lynmouth** ◊ *Lynton*.

**Lynn (Lynn Regis) (England)** ◊ *King's Lynn*.

**Lynn** USA. Industrial town and port in E Massachusetts, on an arm of Massachusetts Bay. Pop. (1960) 94,478. Noted as a centre of footwear manufacture dating from 1636. Also manufactures electrical equipment, shoemakers' tools, etc. First settled in 1629, as Saugus. Renamed in 1637, after Lynn Regis (King's Lynn), England, the home of the town's pastor.

**Lynton** England. Village and resort in N Devonshire 12 m. E of Ilfracombe near the Bristol Channel, forming an urban district with Lynmouth. Pop. (urban district, 1961) 1,918. Lynton is on a cliff 430 ft above Lynmouth, which has a harbour and is at the mouth of the E and W Lyn rivers. Near by is the Doone Valley, described in R. D. Blackmore's *Lorna Doone*. In 1952 31 people were killed and much damage was caused in Lynmouth when the R. Lyn flooded.

**Lyonnais** France. Former province bounded on the E by the Saône and Rhône rivers, and on the W by the Monts du Forez. United to the crown 1307. Became the Rhône-et-Loire department 1790 and the present departments of Rhône and Loire 1793.

**Lyons (Fr. Lyon)** France. Ancient Lugdunum. Capital of the Rhône department and the third largest city in France, at the confluence of the Rhône and Saône rivers. Pop. (1968) 535,000. A leading textile centre from the 15th cent., specializing in silk manufacture, largely replaced in recent years by rayon, nylon, and other synthetic fibres. Engineering. Also manufactures cars, cables, chemicals (esp. those used in the textile industry), hosiery, clothing, etc. Divided by the two rivers into the central area, the commercial and shopping quarter, on the tongue of land between them; the old town, on the W bank of the Saône; and the new town, E of the Rhône, with residential and industrial suburbs. Within the central district are the 17th-cent. hôtel de ville and Palais des Arts, the 11th-cent. Church of St Martin d'Ainay (restored), and the 15th-cent. Church of St Nizier, and in the old town the 12th/15th-cent. Cathedral of St Jean and the Church of Notre Dame de Fourvière, perched on the hill of that name (960 ft). Lyons is an important road and rail centre, a financial centre, with the headquarters of the Crédit Lyonnais, one of France's leading banks, and a cultural centre, with a university (1808). Founded (43 B.C.) as a Roman colony. The first place in Gaul to be converted to Christianity, in the 2nd cent. The silk industry was introduced by Italians. During the Revolution (1793) it was partly destroyed after an insurrection. Birthplace of Claudius (10 B.C.–A.D. 54), Ampère (1775–1836), Jacquard (1752–1834), inventor of the loom named after him, and Puvis de Chavannes (1824–98).

**Lytham St Anne's** England. Municipal borough in W Lancashire, consisting of Lytham, on the estuary of the R. Ribble, and St Anne's, just WNW on the Irish Sea. Pop. (1961) 36,222. Seaside resort. Manufactures pharmaceutical products, footwear. Has a famous golf-course.

**Lyubertsy** USSR. Industrial town in the Moscow region, RSFSR, 12 m. SE of Moscow. Pop. (1970) 139,000. Manufactures machinery, electrical equipment, plastics, etc.

# M

**Maarianhamina** ◊ *Ahvenanmaa*.

**Maas River** ◊ *Meuse River*.

**Maastricht** Netherlands. Capital of Limburg province, 15 m. NNE of Liège (Belgium) on the Maas R. Pop. (1968) 94,986. Railway and canal junction and industrial centre, of considerable strategic importance because of its proximity to the Belgian and German borders. Manufactures cement, textiles, glass, china, paper, etc. Brewing, tanning. The Church of St Servatius, founded in the 6th cent., is the oldest in the country. It also has an old town hall of the 15th cent. (now a museum) and a new town hall (17th-cent.).

**Mablethorpe and Sutton** England. Urban district in Parts of Lindsey, Lincolnshire, 21 m. SE of Grimsby. Pop. (1961) 5,389. Seaside resort. Severely damaged by flooding 1953.

**McAllen** USA. Town in S Texas 54 m. WNW of Brownsville, near the Rio Grande and the Mexican frontier. Pop. (1960) 32,728. Commercial centre. Winter resort. Trade in citrus fruits, vegetables, etc. Oil refining, food processing.

**Macao** China. Portuguese overseas province in SE China 40 m. W of Hong Kong, from which it is separated by the estuary of the Pearl or Canton R. Area 6 sq. m. Pop. (1960) 169,299. Consists of the town of Macao and the small islands of Taipa and Colôane. Considerable transit trade with China. Exports salted and fresh fish. Manufactures cement, metal goods, etc. Leased from China by the Portuguese 1557; recognized as Portuguese territory by China 1887. Declined in the late 19th cent. with the rapid development of Hong Kong.

**Macapá** Brazil. Capital of the Amapá territory (NE), on the N channel of the Amazon delta. Pop. 33,000. On the equator. Trade in rubber, cattle, etc. Modern town with old fortifications. Revived owing to manganese mining to the NW.

**Macassar (Makassar)** Indonesia. Capital of S Sulawesi (Celebes) province, on the SW coast of Celebes. Pop. (1961) 384,159. Chief seaport and largest town of the island. Exports coffee, gums, copra, spices, etc. First settled by the Portuguese; taken over by the Dutch 1667.

**Macclesfield** England. Municipal borough in Cheshire, on the R. Bollin 16 m. SSE of Manchester. Pop. (1961) 37,578. Important centre of the silk industry since the mid 18th cent. Also manufactures rayon, nylon, and cotton goods, textile machinery, paper, plastics, etc. To the E is the bleak moorland area of Macclesfield Forest.

**Macdonnell Ranges** Australia. System of mountain ranges in the S of the Northern Territory, rising to nearly 5,000 ft at the highest point. Alice Springs stands near a gap through the mountains.

**Macduff** Scotland. Small burgh in NE Banffshire, on the Moray Firth, at the mouth of the R. Deveron. Pop. (1961) 3,479. Fishing port. Seaside resort.

**Macedonia.** Region in SE Europe to the NW of the Aegean Sea, divided politically between Greece, Yugoslavia, and Bulgaria. Mainly mountainous, rising in several parts to over 8,000 ft. Economy primarily pastoral (sheep and goats) and agricultural (tobacco, wheat, etc.). An ancient kingdom, under Philip II it ruled the whole of Greece through his victory at Chaeronea (338 B.C.). By military conquest his son, Alexander the Great, extended the Macedonian Empire over Egypt, Asia Minor, and Persia to India. After Alexander's death, however, the Empire disintegrated, and in the 2nd cent. B.C. Macedonia itself was conquered by the Romans. In the 6th cent. A.D. it was permanently settled by Slavs. Passed to the Bulgarians and Serbs, and was held by the Turks from the 15th to the 20th cent. (1912).

**Macedonia** Greece. Division of N Greece, comprising the *nome*s of Kastoria, Kozani, Florina, Pella, Pieria, Kilkis, Thessaloniki (Salonika), Chalcidice, Mt Athos, Serrai, Drama, Kavalla, and Imathia. Area 13,380 sq. m. Pop. (1961) 1,890,654.

**Macedonia** Yugoslavia. Most southerly of the six constituent republics of Yugoslavia, bounded by Bulgaria (E), Greece (S), and Albania (W). Area 10,229 sq. m. Pop. (1961) 1,406,003. Cap. Skoplje. Mainly mountainous, practically comprising the basin of the upper Vardar. Agriculture (cereals, tobacco, cotton) and stock rearing (sheep and goats). Chromium mined near Skoplje. Other towns Bitolj, Prilep.

**Maceió** Brazil. Capital of the Alagôas

state (NE), 120 m. SSW of Recife. Pop. (1960) 170,134. Exports cotton and sugar, through Jaraguá harbour (just E). Sugar refining, distilling, sawmilling. Manufactures textiles, soap, tobacco products, etc. Has many well-preserved colonial buildings and a lighthouse on a low hill near the middle of the town.

**Macerata** Italy. Capital of Macerata province in The Marches, 22 m. S of Ancona. Pop. (1961) 38,338. Market town. Manufactures musical instruments, agricultural machinery, textiles, etc. Stands on a hill over 1,000 ft above sea level. Surrounded by medieval walls. University (1290).

**Macgillicuddy's Reeks** Irish Republic. Mountain range in Co. Kerry rising to 3,414 ft in Carrantuohill, the highest peak in Ireland. Extends 7 m. W from the Gap of Dunloe, just W of the Lakes of Killarney.

**Machu Picchu** Peru. Ruined Inca city in the Cuzco department, 55 m. NW of Cuzco on a mountain saddle at a height of 6,700 ft. Terraced slopes descend to the Urubamba R. One of Peru's great tourist attractions. Discovered (1911) by Dr Hiram Bingham of Yale University.

**Machynlleth** Wales. Urban district in Montgomeryshire 8 m. ENE of Aberdovey. Pop. (1961) 1,903. Market town. Tourist centre. Owen Glendower summoned a parliament here in 1403.

**Mackay** Australia. Port on the coast of Queensland 180 m. NW of Rockhampton. Pop. (1966) 24,566. Exports sugar and some copper and gold from near-by workings. Sugar refining, sawmilling.

**McKeesport** USA. Industrial town in Pennsylvania, on the Monongahela R. 10 m. SE of Pittsburgh. Pop. (1960) 45,489. In a coalmining region. Manufactures iron and steel products, inc. pipes and tubes, tinplate, boilers, heating equipment, etc. Named after David McKee, an Irishman who settled here 1755.

**Mackenzie** Canada. The W mainland District of the NW Territories. Area 527,490 sq. m. In the W are the Mackenzie Mountains, rising to over 9,000 ft. E of them is the valley of the Mackenzie R. Main lakes the Great Bear Lake and the Great Slave Lake. Oil produced and refined at Norman Wells. Gold mined in the Yellowknife district. Main occupation of the Indian and Eskimo inhabitants fur trapping. The fisheries of the Great Slave Lake are also commercially important. Over 6,000 reindeer are maintained in the Mackenzie delta region, and 10,000 buffalo are protected in the Wood Buffalo National Park. Important trading posts include Fort Smith, Aklavik, Coppermine. Formed 1895; named after the Mackenzie R.

**Mackenzie** Guyana. Mining centre 67 m. up the Demerara R. Pop. 15,000. In forest country near large deposits of bauxite, which is loaded on to ocean-going vessels for export.

**Mackenzie River** Canada. River 1,100 m. long, in the NW Territories, flowing from the Great Slave Lake generally NW to the Beaufort Sea of the Arctic Ocean, with a delta over 110 m. long. Chief tributaries the Liard, Peace, Athabaska, and Slave rivers. The Mackenzie–Slave–Peace–Finlay rivers form a continuous waterway of more than 2,500 m., the longest river system in Canada, of which over 1,900 m. are navigable. The navigation season is from early June to mid Oct. Named after Sir Alexander Mackenzie (1764–1820), who explored the river to its mouth (1789).

**McKinley, Mount** USA. Peak in central Alaska, in the Alaska Range and the Mt McKinley National Park, the highest in N America (20,269 ft). Named (1896, by W. A. Dickey, a prospector) first Denali and then McKinley after President McKinley (1843–1901). First climbed (1913) by Hudson Stuck and his party.

**McMurdo Sound** ◊ *Ross Dependency.*

**Mâcon** France. Prefecture of the Saône-et-Loire department, on the Saône R. 40 m. N of Lyons. Pop. (1968) 35,264. Commercial centre. Trade in Burgundy wine. Manufactures cognac, casks, hardware, etc. Birthplace of Lamartine (1790–1869).

**Macon** USA. Town in Georgia at the head of navigation on the Ocmulgee R. 75 m. SE of Atlanta. Pop. (1960) 69,764. River port. Manufactures clothing, chemicals, metal goods, etc. Seat of Mercer University (1833). Named after Nathaniel Macon (1758–1837), an American politician.

**Macquarie Island** Australia. Volcanic island 800 m. SE of Tasmania, to which it belongs, with a meteorological station but otherwise uninhabited.

**Macquarie River** Australia. River 590 m. long rising in the Blue Mountains, New South Wales, and flowing NW to the Darling R. through sheep-rearing and grain-growing country.

**MacRobertson Land** ◊ *Australian Antarctic Territory.*

**Macroom** Irish Republic. Market town in

Co. Cork, on the Sullane R. 20 m. W of Cork. Pop. (1966) 2,224. Trade in dairy produce, potatoes, etc. Salmon and trout fishing centre.

**Madagascar** ◊ *Malagasy Republic.*

**Maddalena Island** Italy. Island 8 sq. m. in area, largest of the archipelago off the NE coast of Sardinia. Pop. 12,000. Chief town and port La Maddalena, formerly an important naval base. Fishing. Maddalena is linked by causeway with the neighbouring island of Caprera, which attracts visitors to see Garibaldi's home and tomb.

**Madeira** N Atlantic Ocean. Ancient Insulas Purpurariae ('Purple Islands'). Volcanic archipelago 400 m. W of the coast of Morocco, forming the Funchal administrative district of Portugal. Total area 305 sq. m. Pop. (1964) 269,769. Cap. Funchal. Two inhabited islands: Madeira, Porto Santo. Two uninhabited groups: the Deserta Is., the Selvagen Is. Madeira (the largest island and by far the most important) is mountainous, rising in the Pico Ruivo to 6,106 ft. Luxuriant vegetation. The picturesque rugged basalt peaks, deep wooded ravines, and precipitous sea cliffs, with the exceptionally mild climate, have made it a world-renowned health and tourist resort. The lower slopes are carefully terraced and irrigated. Principal crops vines (for the famous Madeira wine), sugar-cane, early vegetables for the European market; also bananas, pineapples, and other fruits. Dairy cattle raised. Oxen are widely used as draught animals. Abundant fish, esp. tunny, mackerel. Embroidery work is done by the women and wickerwork by the men.

The islands were probably known to the Romans. Rediscovered (uninhabited) by João Gonçalvez Zarco, who sighted Porto Santo in 1418, brought settlers on the orders of Prince Henry the Navigator, and discovered Madeira in 1420. Portuguese colonization proceeded rapidly; Funchal was founded in 1421. Madeira was twice occupied by the British (1801, 1807–14).

**Madeira River** Brazil. River 2,000 m. long (with the Mamoré) in the NW, formed by the union of the Mamoré and the Beni rivers near the Bolivia–Brazil frontier, flowing NE and joining the Amazon R. 85 m. E of Manáus.

**Madeleine, La** France. Site of archaeological importance in the Dordogne department, on the Vézère R., giving its name to the Magdalenian culture. Near by are other sites, including the Cro-Magnon and Le Moustier caves.

**Madhya Pradesh** India. Largest state of the Indian Union, mainly on the N Deccan plateau, bounded on the N by Uttar Pradesh. Area 171,217 sq. m. Pop. (1961) 32,372,408 (mainly Hindi-speaking). Cap. Bhopal. In the W it is crossed by the Vindhya and Satpura ranges; most of the state is at an altitude of more than 1,000 ft. Drained to the W by the Narmada R. and to the E by the Mahanadi. Monsoon climate with 45–50 ins. of rain annually. About four fifths of the population are dependent on agriculture. Principal crops rice, wheat, oilseeds, cotton. More than one quarter of the state is covered by forests, which are the chief source of teak in India. Madhya Pradesh supplies the greater part of India's manganese ore; coal and iron ore also mined. Chief towns Bhopal, Nagpur, Gwalior, Jabalpur, Ujjain, Raipur. Formed originally from the Central Provinces and Berar, Madhya Pradesh became a constituent state under its present name in 1950 and was much enlarged, absorbing most of the former state of Madhya Bharat, in 1956.

**Madinet al-Shaab** ◊ *South Yemen.*

**Madison** USA. State capital of Wisconsin, on the isthmus between L. Mendota and L. Monona. Pop. (1960) 126,706. Commercial centre for a rich dairy-farming region. Manufactures electrical equipment, machinery, etc. Seat of the University of Wisconsin (1848), on the wooded shores of L. Mendota. Named after President Madison (1751–1836).

**Madiun** Indonesia. Town in Java, 90 m. WSW of Surabaya. Pop. (1961) 123,373. Commercial centre in a region producing sugar-cane, rice, coffee, etc. Railway engineering.

**Madras (Tamil Nadu)** India. 1. Constituent state of the Indian Union, in the SE, less than half its former area owing to the formation of Andhra Pradesh (1953) and various boundary adjustments. Area 50,331 sq. m. Pop. (1961) 33,686,953 (mainly Tamil-speaking). With a coastal plain 50–150 m. wide along the Coromandel Coast, facing the Bay of Bengal, it is mountainous in the W, rising to more than 8,000 ft in the Nilgiri Hills and the Palni Hills. Nearly two thirds of the people are engaged in agriculture. Leading crops rice, millets, groundnuts, cotton. Chief towns Madras, Madurai, Coimbatore, Tiruchirapalli,

Salem. The first trading post was established by the British in 1611; by 1801 they were in control of practically the whole area. In 1937 Madras was made an autonomous province and in 1950 a constituent state of the republic of India.

2. Capital of Madras, the fourth largest city of India, on the Coromandel Coast. Pop. (1961) 1,729,141. Chief seaport of Madras and the third leading seaport of India. Exports hides and skins, groundnuts, cotton, etc. Also an industrial centre. Engineering. Manufactures cement, chemicals, textiles, clothing, etc. University (1857). The main commercial section, George Town, lies W of the harbour, while the residential districts are largely in the S, where, too, is the Roman Catholic cathedral of S Thomé, traditional burial-place of St Thomas. Founded by the British E India Company (1640) as Fort St George.

**Madre de Dios River** Bolivia/Peru. River 600 m. long, rising in the Cordillera de Carabaya in SE Peru, flowing N and NE, and joining the Beni R. in N Bolivia.

**Madrid** Spain. 1. Province in central Spain, in New Castile. Area 3,089 sq. m. Pop. (1961) 2,606,524. Lies on the dry central plateau or Meseta, with the Sierra de Guadarrama rising to 8,100 ft on its NW boundary and the Tagus (Tajo) R. in the extreme S.

2. Capital and largest city of Spain and of Madrid province, near the centre of the peninsula at a height of about 2,100 ft, on the small Manzanares R. Pop. (1967) 2,866,728. Spain's chief centre of communications by road, rail, and air. Also an industrial centre. Flour milling, printing. Manufactures aircraft, electrical equipment, agricultural machinery, leather goods, etc. Because of its altitude and its exposed situation, the city has a rigorous continental climate, with hot summers and cold winters. Relatively few buildings of outstanding architectural interest, but in the Prado it possesses one of the world's finest art collections, with works by Velazquez, El Greco, and other Spanish masters; there are art treasures, too, in the 18th-cent. former royal palace, built on the site of the old Moorish alcázar. In contrast to the narrow streets of old Madrid (in the W and SW) is the newer part of the city (in the N and E) which has developed rapidly in the present century and has such broad thoroughfares as the Paseo del Prado. At the centre of the city is the largest and busiest plaza, the Puerta del Sol, named after one of the city gates which formerly stood here. To the NW of the latter is the university (1508). Madrid was taken from the Moors in 1083, was made capital by Philip II in 1561, and, apart from one brief interval (1601–6), has remained so ever since. During the Spanish Civil War (1936–9) it withstood the Nationalist siege for 2½ years.

**Madura** Indonesia. Island off the NE coast of Java. Area 1,762 sq. m. Pop. 2 million. It has an undulating surface, rising to over 1,500 ft. Salt, rice, maize, and cassava produced. Cattle rearing important.

**Madurai** India. Formerly Madura. Industrial town in Madras, on the Vaigai R. 265 m. SW of Madras. Pop. (1961) 424,180. Manufactures textiles, brassware, etc. Has a mainly 16th-cent. temple famous for its elaborate carving and ancient palaces. Capital of the Pandya dynasty from the 5th cent. B.C. to the 14th cent. A.D.

**Maebashi** Japan. Capital of the Gumma prefecture, 65 m. NW of Tokyo. Pop. (1965) 198,745. Centre of sericulture and the silk industry. University (1949).

**Maelström** Norway. Name originally applied to the strong tidal current, Moskenstraumen, in the Lofoten Is. between Moskenesöy and Mosken, its danger having been considerably exaggerated. Later applied to strong whirlpools elsewhere.

**Maesteg** Wales. Urban district in Glamorganshire 5 m. E of Port Talbot. Pop. (1961) 21,652. In a coalmining district.

**Mafeking** S Africa. Town in the N of the Cape Province near the frontier of Botswana. Formerly the Bechuanaland Protectorate's extra-territorial administrative headquarters. Pop. (1960) 8,279. Commercial centre. Railway engineering. During the Boer War a British force (under Baden Powell) was besieged for seven months (1899–1900); the rejoicings when the siege was raised gave the English language the verb 'to maffick'.

**Magadan** USSR. Seaport and airport in the Khabarovsk Territory, RSFSR, on the Sea of Okhotsk. Pop. (1970) 92,000. Ship repairing, fishing, etc. Founded 1932.

**Magadi, Lake** Kenya. Lake 30 m. long in the Great Rift Valley, 50 m. SW of Nairobi near the Tanzania frontier. Carbonate of soda is extracted. Magadi town is on the E shore.

**Magaliesberg Range** ◊ *Rustenburg.*

**Magallanes** ◊ *Tierra del Fuego.*

**Magdalena River** Colombia. The most important river in Colombia, 950 m. long, rising in the Central Cordillera in the Cauca department, flowing N, and entering the Caribbean. The upper river soon descends, to follow a wide level-floored rift valley between the Central and the E Cordilleras, emerges to wind sluggishly across a marshy plain, and falls only 200 ft in the last 100 m. Ships travel 570 m. to the rapids near Honda, above which the river is navigable to Neiva. Carries a large proportion of Colombia's trade. Oilfield in the lower middle valley. Coffee growing is important on the slopes of the upper middle valley.

**Magdalen Islands** Canada. Group of 16 islands in the Gulf of St Lawrence, in Quebec. Area 102 sq. m. Pop. 9,000 (largely French-Canadian stock). Main occupation fishing (lobsters, herring, cod, mackerel).

**Magdeburg** German Democratic Republic.
1. District bordering W on the Federal German Republic, formed in 1952 from part of the *Land* of Saxony-Anhalt. Area 4,510 sq. m. Pop. (1968) 1,325,927.
2. Capital of Magdeburg district, on the Elbe R. 80 m. WSW of Berlin. Pop. (1968) 268,064. Railway and industrial centre in an important sugar-beet-growing region. Sugar refining. Manufactures machinery, paper, textiles, chemicals, glass, etc. Stands at the E end of the Weser–Elbe Canal, which, opened in 1938, completed the Mittelland Canal across Germany and increased the commercial importance of Magdeburg. The cathedral (13th/16th-cent.) is a mixture of Romanesque and Gothic architecture. Magdeburg was a leading member of the Hanseatic League, and its local laws, the *Magdeburger Recht*, were long the model for other European cities. During the Thirty Years War it was almost completely destroyed (1631). Severely damaged in the 2nd World War. Birthplace of Otto von Guericke (1602–86) and Baron von Steuben (1730–94).

**Magelang** Indonesia. Town in central Java, 23 m. NNW of Jogjakarta. Pop. 82,000. Commercial centre in a region producing rice, sugar-cane, tobacco, etc.

**Magellan Strait** Chile. Winding strait 370 m. long and 2–20 m. wide, between the mainland of S America and Tierra del Fuego, connecting the S Pacific with the S Atlantic. Discovered (1520) by Magellan. Punta Arenas is the only important town.

**Maggiore, Lake** Italy. Ancient Verbanus Lacus. Lake in Lombardy, with the N end in Ticino canton, Switzerland. Area 82 sq. m. Through it flows the Ticino R. and in the SW are the Borromean Is. Surrounded by mountains, on whose terraced slopes vines and olives are grown. Around its shores are such well-known resorts as Locarno, Pallanza, and Stresa.

**Magnitnaya, Mount** USSR. Mountain 2,000 ft high in the S Urals, RSFSR. Rich deposits of magnetite iron ore, supplied to Magnitogorsk.

**Magnitogorsk** USSR. Industrial town in the Chelyabinsk region, RSFSR, 130 m. SW of Chelyabinsk on the upper Ural R., here dammed to supply water. Pop. (1970) 364,000. A major metallurgical centre, using magnetite iron ore from near-by Mt Magnitnaya, coal from the Kuznetsk and Karaganda Basins, and other raw materials from the Urals and elsewhere. First developed 1929. Now has a massive complex of blast furnaces, open-hearth furnaces, steel mills, and coke batteries. Also manufactures machinery, fertilizers, cement, clothing, etc.

**Mahalla el Kubra** United Arab Republic. Town on the Nile delta 65 m. N of Cairo. Pop. (1960) 178,000. Important cotton-manufacturing centre. Cotton, cereals, and rice cultivated in the region.

**Mahanadi River** India. River 550 m. long, rising in S Madhya Pradesh 75 m. S of Raipur, flowing generally NNE and then ESE, crossing Orissa, and entering the Bay of Bengal by a broad delta below Cuttack. Used for irrigation mainly in the delta area.

**Maharashtra** India. Constituent state of the Indian Union, formed in 1960 from the S and E parts of the former Bombay state; mainly on the Deccan plateau, with a narrow coastal plain W of the Western Ghats facing the Arabian Sea. Area 118,717 sq. m. Pop. (1961) 39,553,718 (80 per cent Marathi-speaking). Cap. Bombay. Chief rivers the Godavari and the Krishna, which flow SE to the Bay of Bengal. Most of the people are engaged in agriculture; chief crops millets, rice, cotton, groundnuts. Many textile mills. Main industrial centres Bombay, Nagpur, Poona, Sholapur, Kolhapur.

**Mahmudiya Canal** ⟁ *Alexandria*.

**Maiden Castle** England. Prehistoric hill fortress in S Dorset 2 m. SW of Dorchester, occupying about 120 acres, the finest ancient earthwork in Britain. Excavations in 1934–8 showed that it was occupied in the Neolithic period, c. 2000 B.C. Later there was a fortified Iron Age village, taken by the Romans in A.D. 43.

**Maidenhead** England. Municipal borough in Berkshire, on the R. Thames 25 m. W of London. Pop. (1961) 35,374. A boating centre, mainly residential. Brewing, boatbuilding, publishing. Manufactures radio and electronic equipment, etc.

**Maidstone** England. Municipal borough and county town of Kent, on the R. Medway 30 m. ESE of London. Pop. (1961) 59,761. A market for Kent hops. Brewing. Manufactures paper, confectionery, cement, etc. Has the 14th-cent. All Saint's Church, a 15th-cent. former archbishop's palace, and a 16th-cent. mansion (museum). Cobtree Manor, the 'Dingley Dell' of Dickens's *Pickwick Papers*, is 2 m. N. Birthplace of William Hazlitt (1778–1830).

**Maiduguri** Nigeria. Town in the NE 310 m. E of Kano. Pop. (1960) 57,000 (including the near-by town of Yerwa). Market town. Trade in groundnuts, cotton, gum arabic, etc.

**Maikop** USSR. Capital of the Adygei Autonomous Region, in the Krasnodar Territory, RSFSR, on the Belaya R. 60 m. SE of Krasnodar. Pop. (1970) 111,000. Industrial centre. Manufactures food and tobacco products, furniture, leather, etc. To the SW are the Maikop oilfields. Founded 1858.

**Maine** France. Former province, divided in 1790 to form the present departments of Mayenne and Sarthe and parts of Eure-et-Loir and Orne; the capital was Le Mans. Passed to the crown 1481.

**Maine** USA. State in the extreme NE, the largest of the New England states. Area 33,215 sq. m. Pop. (1970) 977,260. Cap. Augusta. Admitted to the Union in 1820 as the 23rd state; popularly known as the 'Pine Tree' state on account of its forests. Hilly in the W, it rises to 5,268 ft in Mt Katahdin. Features resulting from glaciation include many beautiful lakes, e.g. Moosehead Lake (117 sq. m.). Chief rivers the Penobscot, the Kennebec, the Androscoggin, and the St John. Climate humid continental, with cold winters, short warm summers. Annual rainfall 40–45 ins. Forestry important. Many sawmills and pulp mills. Leading state for potatoes, grown chiefly in the Aroostook valley. Other crops oats, hay, apples, blueberries. Herring 'sardines' and lobsters are caught. Many flourishing tourist resorts in the lake and woodland regions. Main cities Portland, Lewiston, Bangor. After abortive attempts at settlement by the French, an English settlement was established (1607) near Phippsburg. Annexed by Massachusetts in 1652, Maine was part of it until 1820. The boundary with Canada was finally settled by the Webster-Ashburton Treaty (1842).

**Maine-et-Loire** France. Department formed in 1790 from S Anjou. Area 2,787 sq. m. Pop. (1968) 584,709. Prefecture Angers. Generally low-lying and extremely fertile. Drained by the Loire and its tributaries, the Mayenne, Sarthe, and Loir. Produces vines, fruits, cereals. Chief towns Angers, Saumur, Cholet.

**Main River** Federal German Republic. River 320 m. long formed by the union of the White Main and the Red Main near Kulmbach, flowing generally W, but with wide bends, past Würzburg, Aschaffenburg, and Frankfurt to join the Rhine R. just above Mainz. Navigable for about 220 m. Linked with the Danube R. via the Ludwig Canal.

**Mainz** Federal German Republic. Capital of Rhineland-Palatinate, on the left bank of the Rhine R. opposite the confluence with the Main R. Pop. (1968) 147,143. River port. Industrial and commercial centre. Manufactures chemicals, machinery, furniture, textiles, etc. Trade in wine, timber, grain. Seat of a university, founded 1477, suppressed 1798, and revived 1946. The cathedral, founded in the 10th cent. but frequently burned and rebuilt, was finally restored in the 19th cent.; this and the 17th-cent. electoral palace were severely damaged in the 2nd World War. The town grew round a Roman camp, and by the Middle Ages was an important commercial centre. An archbishopric from the 8th cent. until the early 19th cent. Birthplace of Johann Gutenberg (1398–1468), the printer.

**Maisons-Alfort** France. Suburb of SE Paris, in the Val-de-Marne department. Pop. (1968) 53,671. Manufactures cement, soap, furniture, etc.

**Maitland** Australia. Town in New South Wales, on the Hunter R. 15 m. NW of Newcastle. Pop. (1968) 23,105. Coalmining and industrial centre. Railway junction. Manufactures textiles, clothing, etc.

**Majorca** (Sp. **Mallorca**) Spain. Ancient Balearis Major. Largest of the Balearic Is., in the W Mediterranean between Minorca and Iviza. Area 1,405 sq. m. Pop. 340,000. Cap. and chief seaport Palma. A range of mountains along the NW coast, rising to 4,741 ft in Puig Mayor, shelters the island from northerly winds, and its mild climate and luxurious vegetation have made it popular with holiday-makers. Main occupation agriculture. Olives, vines, almonds, wheat, citrus fruits cultivated. Limestone caves.

**Majuba (Amajuba) Hill** S Africa. In Zulu, 'Hill of Doves'. Mountain 6,500 ft high in the Drakensberg (NW Natal) near the Transvaal border 9 m. S of Volksrust, overlooking the Laing's Nek pass. During the Boer War of 1880–81 it was the scene of the defeat of the British by a Boer force under Piet Joubert (1881).

**Majunga** Malagasy Republic. Second largest town and second seaport, on the NW coast at the mouth of the Betsiboka R. 230 m. NNW of Tananarive. Pop. (1965) 43,393. Meat packing, rice preparation. Manufactures cement, soap, etc. Exports coffee, raffia, sugar, rice, vanilla.

**Makassar** ⟡ *Macassar*.

**Makatea** ⟡ *Society Islands*.

**Makeyeyka** USSR. Formerly Dmitriyevsk. Industrial city in the Ukrainian SSR, in the Donbas. Pop. (1970) 393,000. Once a suburb of Donetsk (formerly Stalino), now a major coalmining and metallurgical centre. Iron and steel works, coking plants. Manufactures machinery, footwear, etc.

**Makhachkala** USSR. Formerly Petrovsk. Capital of the Dagestan ASSR, RSFSR, port on the Caspian Sea. Pop. (1970) 186,000. Linked by pipeline with the Grozny oilfield. Oil refining, shipbuilding, railway engineering, food processing. Manufactures textiles, footwear, etc. Crude oil and petroleum products are shipped to the Volga. Founded 1844.

**Makó** Hungary. Town in Csongrád county, on the Maros R. 17 m. E of Szeged. Pop. 34,000. Commercial centre in an agricultural and market-gardening region. Trade in cereals and vegetables, esp. onions. Flour milling. Manufactures textiles, etc. Birthplace of Joseph Pulitzer (1847–1911).

**Makran.** Coastal region of Baluchistan on the Arabian Sea, mostly in W Pakistan, but extending into Iran. Apart from the Kej valley (dates), a barren area with the Makran Coast Range and the Central Makran Range inland. Chief port Gwadar. The former princely state of Makran acceded to Pakistan in 1948.

**Malabar (Malabar Coast)** India. Coastal region in the SW extending roughly from Goa SSE to Cape Comorin and inland to the Western Ghats, now mainly in Kerala. Chief ports Cochin, Kozhikode (Calicut). Chief products rice, coconuts, spices. The first part of India to be visited by Europeans – including Vasco da Gama.

**Malacca** Malaysia. **1**. State in SW Malaya. Area 640 sq. m. Pop. (1967) 410,326 (mainly Malays and Chinese). Consists of a low coastal plain rising to low hills inland. Chief products rubber, coconuts, rice. Came into British hands as one of the Straits Settlements 1824. Joined the Federation of Malaya after the 2nd World War. **2**. Capital of Malacca, on the Strait of Malacca 125 m. NW of Singapore. Pop. 70,000. Seaport. Exports rubber, copra. Probably founded in the 14th cent. Held by the Portuguese from 1511, the Dutch from 1641, and the British from 1824. Later overshadowed by Singapore, and trade much reduced by harbour silting.

**Malacca, Strait of.** Channel between the Malay Peninsula and Sumatra, connecting the Indian Ocean with the S China Sea, with Singapore at its S end; narrows to 25 m. just NW of Malacca.

**Málaga** Spain. **1**. Province in Andalusia bordering S on the Mediterranean Sea. Area 2,813 sq. m. Pop. (1961) 775,167. Largely mountainous, rising to about 7,000 ft. Drained chiefly by the Guadalhorce R. Olives, grapes, almonds, figs, etc. grown on fertile lowlands. **2**. Ancient Malaca. Capital of Málaga province, on the coastal plain 68 m. NE of Gibraltar. Pop. (1967) 330,413. Seaport and industrial centre. Exports wine, raisins, fruits, etc. Sugar refining, wine making, distilling, brewing, etc. Manufactures textiles, cement, etc. On account of its mild winter climate it is also a popular resort. Among its old buildings are the ruined Alcázaba and Gibralfaro citadels and the Renaissance cathedral (16th/18th-cent.). Founded by the Phoenicians and held in turn by Carthaginians, Greeks, Romans, Visigoths, and Moors, to be taken in 1487 by Ferdinand and Isabella. Birthplace of Pablo Picasso (1881–    ).

**Malagasy Republic (Madagascar).** Fourth largest island in the world; in the Indian Ocean, separated from SE Africa by the Moçambique Channel. Area 228,600 sq. m. Pop. (1963) 5,862,258. Cap. Tananarive (Antananarivo). A plateau at a height of 3,000–4,000 ft extends NNE–SSW through the island and descends fairly steeply to the

E coast and more gradually to the W. The volcanic massifs Tsaratanana and Ankaratra rise to nearly 10,000 ft. A chain of lagoons off the E coast is linked by the Canal des Pangalanes, forming an important trade route. Owing to the prevailing SE Trade Wind the E has a hot wet climate; there are large areas of dense forest with valuable hardwoods. The plateau, with seasonal rainfall, is mainly savannah. The distinctive flora (e.g. the remarkable traveller's palm) and fauna (esp. the lemurs) demonstrate the long separation from the African mainland. Zebu cattle are raised on the grasslands. Principal food crops cassava, maize, rice. Cash crops coffee, sugar-cane, tobacco, vanilla; these and surplus rice are the major exports. Chief mineral graphite. The few industries are based on agricultural products, e.g. meat packing; processing sugar, rice, tapioca. Tananarive is linked by rail with Tamatave (chief seaport). Other important ports are Majunga and Diégo-Suarez. The people are predominantly Malayo-Polynesian, with Negro admixture; the Hova (Merina) form practically one quarter of the population, and the Hova language is spoken throughout the island.

The Arabs had established settlements and profoundly influenced the native peoples centuries before Diego Diaz (Portuguese) discovered the island (1500). Both France and Britain sought to influence the Hova monarchy in the 19th cent. Opposition to France's demands led to French occupation; Madagascar and its dependencies were declared a French colony in 1896. Became an overseas territory of the French Union in 1946, a member of the French Community in 1958, and (as the Malagasy Republic) an independent member of the UN in 1960.

**Malahide** Irish Republic. Seaside resort in Co. Dublin, on the Irish Sea 8 m. NNE of Dublin. Pop. (1966) 2,967. Has a 12th-cent. castle.

**Malaita** ◊ *Solomon Islands*.

**Malakoff** France. Suburb of S Paris, in the Hauts-de-Seine department. Pop. (1968) 36,297. Manufactures electrical equipment, pharmaceutical products, musical instruments, etc. Named after a fort captured by the French in the Crimean War.

**Malang** Indonesia. Town in E Java province 50 m. S of Surabaya, on a low plateau surrounded by volcanoes. Pop. (1961) 341,452. Commercial centre. Trade in coffee, rice, sugar, etc. Manufactures textiles.

**Mälar, Lake** (Swedish **Mälaren**) Sweden. Lake extending 73 m. W from Stockholm, which stands on a narrow strait connecting it with the Baltic; very irregular in shape, with over 1,200 islands. Its shores are a favourite residential area for Stockholm businessmen. Many old castles and palaces, inc. Gripsholm and Drottningholm.

**Malatya** Turkey. Ancient Melitene. Capital of Malatya province, just W of the Euphrates R. at a height of 2,900 ft 185 m. NE of Adana. Pop. (1965) 104,400. Commercial centre. Trade in opium, grain, etc. Mainly of military importance in Roman times.

**Malawi.** Formerly Nyasaland. Republic in central Africa, member of the British Commonwealth; on the W and S shores of L. Malawi (Nyasa). Area 36,686 sq. m. Pop. (1966) 4,020,724 (the great majority Bantu; 11,299 Asians; 7,395 Europeans). Cap. Zomba. Bounded by Tanzania (N and NE), Moçambique (SE, S, and SW), and Zambia (N). Part of the Great Rift Valley is occupied by L. Malawi and the Shiré R. (its S outlet), which flows through the wedge-shaped S part of the country to the Zambezi R. The W highlands (average 4,000 ft) rise to over 8,000 ft in the Nyika Plateau. The Shiré Highlands (SE), the principal area of white settlement (average 2,500 ft), rise to 9,843 ft in Mt Mlanje. In the lower and marshy SE area bordering on Moçambique are L. Chiuta and L. Shirwa. Entirely within the tropics, but temperatures are considerably modified by the altitude. The rains (esp. abundant in the highlands) fall mainly Nov.–March. The economy is agricultural. Major export crops tea, tobacco; also cotton, tung oil. Food crops beans, cassava, maize, millet, rice. A railway runs from just N of Chipoka (on L. Malawi) through Blantyre-Limbe (chief commercial centre) to Beira in Moçambique.

Although visited by the Portuguese at a much earlier date, the country was not opened up to Europeans till Livingstone had discovered L. Malawi (1859). Missions were founded 1875–6; the first European settlements were established (in the Blantyre-Limbe area) a few years later. Britain intervened to suppress Arab slave trading and prevent a Portuguese attempt to annex the S highlands. The territory became the British Central Africa Protectorate in 1891; renamed the Nyasaland Protectorate in

1907. It joined Northern Rhodesia (now Zambia) and Southern Rhodesia in 1953 in the Federation of Rhodesia and Nyasaland. African nationalists demanded universal suffrage and majority rule; there were outbreaks of violence in 1959, followed by demands for independence in 1961. The Federation broke up in 1962. Nyasaland became a self-governing member of the British Commonwealth in 1963 and (as Malawi) an independent member of the UN in 1964. Became a republic 1966.

**Malawi, Lake.** Formerly Lake Nyasa. Southernmost and third largest of Africa's great lakes, 350 m. long N–S and 10–50 m. wide W–E, in the S of the Great Rift Valley on the frontiers of Malawi (W and S), Moçambique (E), and Tanzania (NE and N), at a height of 1,550 ft. Fed by the Songwe R. and other short streams (W) and by the Ruhuhu R. (NE). Drained by the Shiré R. into the Zambezi R. The volume of the Shiré R. varies seasonally and periodically with the level of the lake. Explored by Livingstone 1859.

**Malaya, States of** Malaysia. Part of the Federation of Malaysia. Area 50,700 sq. m. Pop. (1967) 8,540,148 (50 per cent Malays, 37 per cent Chinese, 11 per cent Indians). Cap. Kuala Lumpur. Rel. chiefly Muslim.

Comprises the S part of the Malay Peninsula and is bounded by Thailand (N), the S China Sea (E), and the Strait of Malacca (W). Divided into the following 11 states: Johore, Kedah, Kelantan, Malacca, Negri Sembilan, Pahang, Penang, Perak, Perlis, Selangor, Trengganu. A relatively prosperous country, largely dependent for its wealth on rubber and tin. TOPOGRAPHY, CLIMATE. The dominating physical feature is a central range of mountains which rises to over 7,000 ft, but the highest peak in Malaya, Gunong Tahan (7,186 ft), is in another range farther E. These mountains are flanked by hills and coastal plains which are drained by innumerable rivers and streams; more than three quarters of the land is covered with jungle. The entire country lies within a few degrees of the equator, and its climate is equatorial – hot and humid throughout the year, with abundant rainfall.

RESOURCES, PEOPLE, *etc.* The Malays are essentially peasant farmers who cultivate rice, vegetables, and coconuts, but the most important agricultural product is rubber, which occupies about two thirds of all the land under cultivation. It is produced on large estates owned or managed by Europeans and also on Malay and Chinese smallholdings. Malaya is the world's leading producer, and rubber represents nearly half of the total exports. It also has the world's highest output of tin, its second most important export. On the rubber plantations large numbers of Tamils from S India are employed, in the tin mines many Chinese; in general the native Malays prefer to retain their economic independence. Other agricultural products are palm oil and kernels, copra, and coconut oil; iron ore and bauxite are important minerals. Fishing is a thriving industry around the coasts. Kuala Lumpur, Georgetown (Penang), and Ipoh are the only towns with more than 100,000 inhabitants. Most of Malaya's foreign trade passes through Singapore, its own leading ports being Penang and Port Swettenham.

The native Malays, of Mongolian origin, are Muslims, and the official religion is Islam; the large Chinese minority are mainly Buddhist, Confucian, and Taoist, and the Indians are mainly Hindu by religion. In the heart of the jungle live small numbers of such aboriginal tribes as the Senoi. By the constitution of 1956 the hereditary rulers of the Malay states elect the Supreme Head of the Federation from among themselves for a period of 5 years. Parliament consists of a Senate of 58 members and a House of Representatives of 144 members.

HISTORY. From the 9th to the 14th cent. Malaya was the centre of the Buddhist empire of Sri Vijaya, which was overthrown by the Hindu Javanese. The Muslim religion was introduced by traders from India, who found Malacca an ideal entrepôt for the spice trade, in which, by the early 16th cent., they had almost gained a monopoly. In 1511 Malacca was taken by the Portuguese, who were followed by the Dutch (1641) and the British (1824). Meanwhile Penang (1786) and Singapore (1819) were founded by the British, and in 1826 the three territories became the Straits Settlements, which were ruled from India until 1867, when they were made a Crown Colony. British influence was extended over the native states, four of which were ceded by Siam (1909), and Malaya was divided into the Federated and Unfederated Malay States and the Straits Settlements. During the 2nd World War Malaya was occupied by the Japanese (1942–5), and afterwards the Federation of Malaya was created (1948), with Singapore a Colony and later a State. Internal disorder, fomented particularly by Communist guerillas operating in the jungle, continued for some years, but did not seriously impair the country's economic recovery. In 1963 the Federation of Malaysia came into being, despite opposition from neighbouring Indonesia.

**Malay Archipelago.** Large group of islands between SE Asia and Australia, including Indonesia and the Philippines and sometimes held to include New Guinea; Malay is the most widely distributed language and is the lingua franca of much of the region.

**Malay Peninsula.** Long narrow peninsula extending S from the mainland of SE Asia, to which it is attached by the Isthmus of Kra. The N part lies in Thailand, the S part in Malaya, and at the S extremity is the island of Singapore.

**Malaysia, Federation of.** Independent federation of SE Asia, a member of the Commonwealth of Nations, consisting of the States of Malaya (West Malaysia), Sabah (N Borneo) and Sarawak (East Malaysia), formed in 1963. Total area 128,693 sq. m. Pop. (1963) 10 million. Federal cap. Kuala Lumpur.

**Malden** USA. Residential suburb of N Boston, Massachusetts. Pop. (1960) 57,676. Manufactures paint, radio and electronic equipment, rubber footwear, etc. First settled 1640. Incorporated in 1649 as Mauldon, after Maldon (Essex, England), the home of many of the early settlers.

**Malden and Coombe** England. Former municipal borough in N Surrey, 10 m. SW of London, consisting of Old and New Malden and Coombe; from 1965 part of the Greater London Royal Borough of Kingston-upon-Thames. Pop. (1961) 46,587. Mainly residential. Manufactures knitwear etc. Merton College was founded here (1264) before being transferred to Oxford. Birthplace (Coombe) of John Galsworthy (1867–1933).

**Maldive Islands.** Group of low-lying coral islands, about 2,000 in number, of which 220 are inhabited, in the Indian Ocean 400 m. SW of Ceylon. Area 115 sq. m. Pop. (1963) 96,432. Cap. Male (pop. 10,875), on the island of Male. They consist of 12 distinct clusters of atolls, largely clothed with coconut palms; coconut products are the main exports, millet and fruits are grown, and the islanders, who are Muslims,

are famed as fishermen and sailors. Formerly a dependency of Ceylon; became a British-protected sultanate 1948, then an independent republic 1968.

**Maldon** England. Municipal borough in Essex on the R. Blackwater estuary at the mouth of the R. Chelmer 8 m. E of Chelmsford. Pop. (1961) 10,507. Market town. Port. Resort. Flour milling. Manufactures machinery, wood products. Has a church with a 13th-cent. triangular tower. Beeleigh Abbey, with its remarkable chapter house, is 1 m. W.

**Male** ◊ *Maldive Islands*.

**Malegaon** India. Commercial town in Maharashtra, on the Girna R. 155 m. NE of Bombay. Pop. (1961) 121,408. Trade in fabrics, grain, etc. Manufactures textiles.

**Mali.** Republic in W Africa, formerly French Soudan. Area 464,875 sq. m. Pop. (1967) 4,700,000. Cap. Bamako. Bounded by Algeria (N), Niger (E), Upper Volta and Ivory Coast (S), Guinea (SW), Senegal (W), and Mauritania (NW). The N comprises an extensive almost uninhabited section of the Sahara. The S, mainly savannah, with a moderate rainfall, occupies much of the Upper and Middle Niger basin and the Upper Senegal basin. Over 90 per cent of the population are in the S. At Sansanding on the Niger (in the 'inland Niger delta') a large irrigation dam (completed 1946) permits the cultivation of over 100,000 acres. Chief crops cotton, groundnuts, maize, millet, rice. Chief exports groundnuts, gum arabic, dried fish, livestock (mainly sheep). A railway from Dakar in Senegal runs through Kayes and Bamako to Koulikoro. Steamers ply from Koulikoro to Timbuktu and Gao for 7 months of the year.

Occupied by the French at the end of the 19th cent. The Senegambia and Niger French Overseas Territories were established in 1902; the Upper Senegal and Niger colony created from them in 1904 was renamed French Soudan in 1920. Became a member of the French Community in 1958, a partner with Senegal in the Federation of Mali (1959–60), and an independent member of the UN in 1960. Has an agreement (1960) with Ghana and Guinea to coordinate their defence, economic, and foreign policies.

**Malines** ◊ *Mechelen*.

**Malin Head** Irish Republic. Headland 230 ft high in NE Co. Donegal, at the N extremity of Inishowen peninsula; the northernmost point in Ireland.

**Mallaig** Scotland. Village, fishing port, and railway terminus in Inverness-shire, on the Sound of Sleat. Steamer services to Skye and the Hebrides.

**Mallorca** ◊ *Majorca*.

**Mallow** Irish Republic. Market town and resort in Co. Cork, on the R. Blackwater 18 m. NNW of Cork. Pop. (1966) 5,532. Sugar refining, tanning, salmon fishing.

**Malmédy** ◊ *Eupen and Malmédy*.

**Malmesbury** England. Municipal borough in Wiltshire, on the R. Avon 14 m. WNW of Swindon. Pop. (1961) 2,606. Market town. Once famous for its silk and wool industries; now manufactures electrical equipment. The nave, now used as the parish church, is all that remains of the magnificent 12th-cent. Benedictine abbey church, where Athelstan is buried. Birthplace of Thomas Hobbes (1588–1679).

**Malmö** Sweden. Capital of Malmöhus county, on The Sound 150 m. SSE of Göteborg. Pop. (1968) 254,338. Important seaport. Exports grain, timber, dairy produce, etc. Linked by train ferry with Copenhagen (Denmark). Industrial centre. Shipbuilding, sugar refining, engineering, brewing, textile and chemical manufactures, etc. Has a 14th-cent. church, a 16th-cent. town hall, and the 15th/16th-cent. Malmöhus Castle where Bothwell was imprisoned. Founded in the 12th cent. Part of Denmark until 1658.

**Malolos** Philippines. Capital of Bulacan province, in Luzon 20 m. NNW of Manila. Pop. 48,000. Commercial centre in a rice-growing region. Temporarily the revolutionary capital 1898–9.

**Malta.** Former British crown colony, comprising the islands of Malta (95 sq. m.), Gozo (26 sq. m.), and Comino (1 sq. m.) and some inhabited islets, in the Mediterranean Sea about 60 m. S of Sicily. Total area 122 sq. m. Pop. (1967) 314,216. Cap. Valletta. English and Maltese are the official languages and Italian is also commonly spoken. The island of Malta is oval in shape and generally hilly, rising to over 800 ft in the S. Cereals and vegetables are cultivated in the shallow soil, but Malta was long important primarily as a naval base, strategically placed about halfway between Gibraltar and Suez. Valletta stands on a peninsula which separates Grand Harbour and Marsamxett (Marsamuscetto) Harbour.

Malta has numerous megalithic remains, notably at Tarxien, and was held in turn by Phoenicians, Greeks, Carthaginians, and Romans; in 870 it was conquered by the Arabs, from whom it was taken by the Sicilian Normans in 1091. Charles V granted it in 1530 to the Knights of St John, afterwards known as the Knights of Malta, but the French gained possession in 1798. Following an appeal by the Maltese people, the island was annexed to Britain in 1814. During the 2nd World War Malta was ceaselessly bombed by enemy aircraft (1940–43), and for its gallantry was awarded the George Cross (1942). After the 2nd World War it was granted a measure of self-government, and in 1964 it achieved independence within the Commonwealth; meanwhile, the economic difficulties caused by the reduction in British naval activity on the island were countered by a Five-year Development Plan launched in 1959, followed by a second Five-year Plan. The decline of Malta as a naval base was partly offset by a considerable expansion of the tourist industry. ◊ *Valletta*.

**Maltby** England. Urban district in the W Riding of Yorkshire, 6 m. E of Rotherham. Pop. (1961) 13,691. Coalmining centre.

**Malton** England. Urban district in the N Riding of Yorkshire, on the R. Derwent 17 m. NE of York, consisting of Old and New Malton. Pop. (1961) 4,430. Market town. Tanning, brewing, flour milling. Limestone quarrying in the neighbourhood. In Old Malton are the ruins of a 12th-cent. Gilbertine priory, and there is a 16th-cent. grammar school.

**Malvern** England. Urban district in Worcestershire, on the E slope of the Malvern Hills, consisting of Great Malvern, 7 m. SSW of Worcester, and the villages of Malvern Wells, Little Malvern, Malvern Link, and W and N Malvern. Pop. (1961) 24,373. Spa and resort, with medicinal springs. Ruins of an 11th-cent. Benedictine priory church; a public school (founded 1863). The annual dramatic festival (established 1928) is associated especially with the plays of G. B. Shaw.

**Malvern Hills** England. Range about 8 m. long extending N–S along the Hereford–Worcestershire border, rising to 1,395 ft in Worcestershire Beacon.

**Malvinas, Islas** ◊ *Falkland Islands*.

**Mammoth Cave** USA. A vast natural cavern, formed by the solution of limestone, in the Mammoth Cave National Park, S Kentucky. A series of subterranean caves on five levels, with high domes,

459                                    MANCHESTER

underground lakes, stalactites and stalagmites, and many remarkable limestone
formations. The principal cave is 125 ft
high and 40–300 ft wide; 150 m. of underground passages have been explored.
There are blind fish 360 ft below the surface
in the Echo R, which empties into the
Green R.

**Mamoré River** ◊ *Madeira River*.

**Man, Isle of** U K. Island in the Irish Sea
between N Lancashire and Northern
Ireland. Area 227 sq. m. Pop. (1961)
48,150. Cap. Douglas. Generally hilly,
with Snaefell reaching 2,034 ft; off the
S W coast is a small detached island, the
Calf of Man. Its equable climate and
attractive scenery have made it popular
with tourists, on whom the economy now
largely depends. Rather more than half the
island is cultivated; oats, barley, turnips,
and potatoes are the chief crops, and a
large area is under grass, mainly for sheep
and cattle. Chief towns Douglas, Ramsey,
Peel, Castletown. The island has its own
parliament, the Court of Tynwald, consisting of the Governor, with an Executive
Council, the Legislative Council, and the
elected House of Keys; it is not bound by
Acts of the Imperial Parliament unless
specially mentioned in them. Ample
evidence of prehistoric settlement on the
island. Long a dependency of Norway until,
with the Hebrides, it was ceded to Scotland (1266). Granted to the Stanley family
(the Earls of Derby) 1406; from them
passed to the Dukes of Atholl (1736) and
then to the Crown (1828). The Manx
language, akin to Gaelic, is now used only
on ceremonial occasions.

**Manaar, Gulf of** ◊ *Mannar, Gulf of*.

**Manado** ◊ *Menado*.

**Managua** Nicaragua. Capital of the
republic and of the Managua department,
on the S E shore of L. Managua. Pop.
(1964) 274,901. The country's largest city
and administrative, trade, and industrial
centre. Manufactures textiles, cement,
cigarettes, matches, etc. Seat of a Roman
Catholic university (1961). Became capital
1855. Largely destroyed by an earthquake in 1931, and badly damaged by fire
in 1936, it has been completely rebuilt.

**Managua, Lake** Nicaragua. Second largest
lake in the republic, 38 m. long and 10–16
m. wide, draining into L. Nicaragua by the
Tipitapa R. Managua is on the S E shore.

**Manama** Bahrain. Capital, at the N end
of the largest island, Bahrain. Pop. (1965)

79,098. Commercial centre and free
transit port (since 1958). Also the centre
of the much reduced pearl-fishing industry. Boatbuilding, fishing, etc.

**Manasarowar Lake** Tibet. Lake at a height
of 15,000 ft in the W Himalayas in S W
Tibet, N N E of Gurla Mandhata (25,355 ft).
Area 200 sq. m. A Hindu place of pilgrimage.

**Manáus** Brazil. Formerly Manáos. Capital
of the Amazonas state, and chief inland
trading port of the ◊ *Amazon* basin, on the
left bank of the Negro R. 12 m. above the
confluence with the Amazon, 860 m. W S W
of Belém. Pop. (1960) 175,343. Accessible
to ocean-going steamers. Exports timber,
rubber, Brazil nuts, and other forest
products. Jute milling, oil refining.
Founded 1660. Grew with the early 20th-
cent. rubber boom; some impressive
buildings, e.g. the very ornate opera
house, remain. Famous botanical gardens.

**Mancha, La** Spain. Former province in the
S part of New Castile, now comprising
Ciudad Real and parts of Albacete, Cuenca,
and Toledo provinces. An extensive, arid
plateau of average altitude about 2,000 ft,
experiencing a harsh climate. Sparsely
peopled. Some esparto grass, cereals, and
wine are produced. Because of its aridity,
many windmills are used to supply water
from underground sources. Made famous
by Cervantes as the setting of adventures
of Don Quixote de la Mancha.

**Manche** France. Department in Normandy
bordering W, N, and N E on the English
Channel ('La Manche'). Area 2,295 sq. m.
Pop. (1968) 451,939. Prefecture St Lô.
The Cotentin peninsula forms the N part,
and the W end of the Normandy Hills
extends into the S. Dairy farming is
important. Apples and other fruits,
cereals, vegetables cultivated. The island
of Mont St Michel attracts tourists. Chief
towns Cherbourg, St Lô.

**Manchester** England. County borough in
S E Lancashire 30 m. E of Liverpool.
Pop. (1961) 661,041. A great commercial
centre, at the heart of a vast conurbation
with about 3 million inhabitants, separated
from Salford by the R. Irwell, a tributary
of the R. Mersey. Important principally
as the centre of the Lancashire cotton
industry, being itself concerned mainly
with the business and warehousing aspects
of the latter; some of its industries, e.g.
the manufacture of textile machinery and

chemicals, are directly connected with textile milling. Also manufactures electrical equipment, rubber products, paper. The construction of the Manchester Ship Canal (1887–94), giving it direct access to the sea, transformed it from an inland city into one of the country's leading seaports, importing raw cotton and exporting finished textiles.

Manchester has relatively few buildings of historic interest. The 15th/16th-cent. cathedral in Perpendicular style (restored) was built as a parish church. Its university, officially the Victoria University of Manchester, developed from the Owens College (1846) and was chartered in 1880. Manchester Grammar School (founded 1519) is one of the largest and most famous schools in the country. Chetham's Hospital is now a school (founded 1653), with a famous library; other libraries are the large Central Library (1934) and the John Rylands Library, with the Althorp collection and many valuable manuscripts. The principal art collections are in the City Art Gallery and the Whitworth Gallery. Manchester is also the home of the Hallé Orchestra (founded 1857) and here the liberal daily newspaper, the *Manchester Guardian* (now the *Guardian*) was founded in 1821.

Probably the site of the Roman fort of Mancunium (whence the name Mancunians for its inhabitants), Manchester was mentioned in the Domesday Book and received its first charter in 1301. It had a woollen industry as early as the 13th cent., and later became well-known for its linen and cotton manufactures. In the mid-18th cent., with the Industrial Revolution, came the immense growth of the cotton industry, for which Manchester had the advantages of nearness to the coalfields, a humid climate, and abundant labour supply, and it became the hub of a network of roads, railways, and canals. The first passenger railway in England was opened (1830) between Manchester and Liverpool with Stephenson's *Rocket*. Meanwhile, discontent largely caused by its non-representation in parliament led to political agitation, culminating in the 'Peterloo Massacre' at St Peter's Fields (1819). With the Reform Bill of 1832 it was given two M.P.s; it continued to be a centre of liberalism and was the headquarters of the Anti-Corn Law League. In the 2nd World War it suffered severe

damage from air raids. Birthplace of David Lloyd George (1863–1945).

**Manchester** (Connecticut) USA. Industrial town on the Hockanum R. 8 m. E of Hartford. Pop. (1960) 42,102. Manufactures textiles (since the late 18th cent.), also electrical equipment, clothing, etc. First settled (1672) as part of Hartford; separated from the parent town 1823.

**Manchester** (New Hampshire) USA. Largest town in the state, on the Merrimack R. 16 m. SSE of Concord. Pop. (1960) 88,282. Industrial centre. Manufactures textiles, leather goods, electrical equipment, etc. The first cotton mill was established 1805. Named after Manchester, England (1810). Remained the leading US cotton manufacturing centre for about 100 years.

**Manchester** (New York, USA) ◊ *Niagara Falls* (USA).

**Manchester Ship Canal** England. Artificial waterway running 35½ m. generally WSW from Manchester to the Mersey estuary at Eastham. Depth 28–30 ft. Bottom width 120 ft. Construction began in 1887 and it was opened in 1894, enabling ocean-going vessels to reach Manchester – but success was only achieved in face of strong opposition and many physical difficulties, including exceptional floods and storms. In its upper part it follows the straightened beds of the Irwell and Mersey, and in the lower part, from Runcorn to Eastham, it runs along the S side of the Mersey estuary.

**Manchukuo** ◊ *Manchuria*.

**Manchuria** China. Extensive region in the NE, now partly in the Autonomous Region of Inner Mongolia and partly forming the provinces of Heilungkiang, Kirin, and Liaoning. Consists of the great central Manchurian plain, watered by the Sungari and the Liao rivers, and flanked on the W and N by the Great Khingan, Ilkhuri, and Little Khingan Mountains and on the E by the complex E Manchurian Mountains. The central plain is extremely fertile, producing soya beans, kaoliang, millet, wheat, maize, rice. Large numbers of sheep, goats, and other livestock are raised in the W. Valuable forests on the mountain slopes. Also rich in minerals, esp. coal and iron ore, which have led to the development of an important metallurgical industry in the S. Chief towns Shenyang (Mukden), Harbin, Lü-ta, Fushun, Changchun, Anshan.

The Manchus, originally of nomadic

Mongol-Tungus stock, conquered China in the 17th cent. and established the last imperial dynasty (1644), which persisted until 1911. In the late 18th cent. Chinese colonization of Manchuria began, and by the end of the 19th cent. the Chinese formed 80 per cent of the population; today they form 90 per cent of the population, and the Manchus are virtually absorbed. In 1898 Russia obtained the lease of Kwantung, at the tip of the Liaotung peninsula, but this passed to Japan after the Russo-Japanese War (1904–5). The Japanese, tempted by the agricultural and mineral wealth, occupied the whole of Manchuria in 1931 and in the following year set up the puppet state of Manchukuo. After the defeat of Japan in the 2nd World War, Manchuria was returned to China.

**Mandalay** Burma. The second largest city, on the Irrawaddy R. 350 m. N of Rangoon, with which it is linked by rail and river. Pop. (1966) 316,796. Chief route and commercial centre of Upper Burma. Manufactures silk goods, gold and silver ware, matches, etc. Fort Dufferin, the old Burmese walled and moated city at its centre, contained the wooden royal palace, which was destroyed by fire during the Japanese occupation (1942–5). Many pagodas. University (1958). Founded 1857. Last capital of the Burmese kingdom (1860–85) before annexation to British Burma.

**Mandasor (Mandsaur)** India. Town in Madhya Pradesh 75 m. NW of Ujjain. Pop. (1961) 41,876. Commercial centre. Trade in grain, cotton, textiles, etc.

**Manfredonia** Italy. Seaport in Foggia province, Apulia, on the Gulf of Manfredonia 23 m. NE of Foggia. Pop. (1961) 37,723. Fishing. Manufactures leather goods, cement, etc. Founded by King Manfred of Sicily c. 1263.

**Mangaia** ◊ *Cook Islands*.

**Mangalore** India. Seaport in Mysore, on the Malabar coast 130 m. WNW of Mysore. Pop. (1961) 142,669. Exports coffee, cashew nuts, spices, etc. Manufactures tiles, textiles, hosiery, etc. Scene of a gallant defence by the English garrison against the army of Tippoo Sultan (1784).

**Mangareva** ◊ *Gambier Islands*.

**Mangotsfield** England. Urban district in SW Gloucestershire just NE of Bristol. Pop. (1961) 24,092. Coalmining centre. Manufactures clothing, footwear, confectionery.

**Manhattan** USA. Island in New York state, a borough of New York city. Area 22 sq. m. Pop. (1960) 1,698,281. Bounded by the Harlem R. and Spuyten Duyvil Creek separating it from the Bronx (N), by the East R. separating it from the Queens and Brooklyn boroughs (E), by New York Bay (S), and by the Hudson R. separating it from New Jersey (W). Business and cultural centre of New York. The most notable educational institution is Columbia University (1745). Famous for its skyscrapers, inc. the Empire State Building (1,250 ft), the highest in the world. Named after the Manhattan Indians, who sold it to the Dutch in 1626. Contained the whole of New York city till 1874. Became one of the boroughs of greater New York 1898.

**Manica and Sofala** ◊ *Beira*; *Moçambique*.

**Manila** Philippines. Former capital and chief seaport, on Manila Bay in SW Luzon. Pop. (1960) 1,138,611. Exports sugar, abacá (Manila hemp). Coconut-oil milling, sugar refining. Manufactures textiles, cigars, etc. Seat of the University of Santo Tomas (1611), maintained by the Dominican Order, and of the University of the Philippines (1908). The short Pasig R. divides the city into the old walled city of Intramuros (S) and the modern part (N). Founded 1571. Taken by the USA during the Spanish-American War (1898). Occupied by the Japanese during the 2nd World War (1942–5), and in its defence and recapture much of the city was destroyed.

**Manipur** India. Territory in the Indian Union, in the NE, bounded on the E by Burma. Area 8,628 sq. m. Pop. (1961) 780,037 (the majority Hindus, chiefly inhabiting the central valley, with Animist Naga and Kuki tribes in the hills). Cap. Imphal. Apart from the central valley, through which the Manipur R. flows, it is mainly mountainous, rising to over 9,000 ft in the N. Rice cultivated. Teak obtained from the hill forests.

**Manisa** Turkey. Ancient Magnesia ad Sipylum. Capital of Manisa province, 20 m. NE of Izmir. Pop. (1965) 69,700. Commercial centre. Trade in grain, raisins, tobacco, olives, etc. Scene of the defeat of Antiochus the Great by the Romans (190 B.C.).

**Manitoba** Canada. Easternmost of the Prairie Provinces. Area 246,512 sq. m. Pop. (1966) 963,066. Cap. Winnipeg (the 'Gateway to the Prairies'). Mainly low-lying, rising to the W. Highest point Duck Mountain (2,727 ft). Many lakes of glacial origin; the largest are L. Winnipeg (9,904 sq. m.), L. Winnipegosis (2,086 sq. m.) and L. Manitoba (1,817 sq. m.). In the N part, in the Laurentian Shield, 45 per cent of the land is forested, one third of commercial importance. The rich soils of the SW prairie zone produce wheat, oats, barley, etc. Mineral products include nickel, copper, gold, zinc, silver, petroleum. Main industries meat packing, flour milling. The first explorer was Sir Thomas Button, who discovered the mouth of the Nelson R. in 1612. British claims to the territory were recognized by the Treaty of Paris (1763). Constituted a province of Canada 1870. The majority of the people are of British extraction, but there is a French community centred on St Boniface, many immigrants from the Ukraine, Poland, and Germany, and about 8,500 American Indians.

**Manitoba, Lake** Canada. Elongated lake in S Manitoba, 125 m. long and up to 27 m. wide, at a height of 814 ft. Receives the outflow from L. Winnipegosis and drains into L. Winnipeg by the Dauphin R.

**Manitoulin Islands** Canada/USA. Chain of islands in L. Huron, mostly in S Ontario (Canada). The largest is Manitoulin (Great Manitoulin), 80 m. long and up to 30 m. wide, the largest freshwater-lake island in the world. Others include Cockburn (in Ontario) and Drummond (in Michigan). Farming, lumbering, and fishing important. Many summer resorts.

**Manitowoc** USA. Port in Wisconsin, on L. Michigan, at the mouth of the Manitowoc R. Pop. (1960) 32,275. Shipbuilding. Manufactures aluminium goods, furniture, etc. The name is an Indian word meaning 'Land of Spirits'.

**Manizales** Colombia. Capital of the Caldas department, on the W flank of the Central Cordillera, at a height of 7,000 ft. Pop. (1968) 221,916. Route and commercial centre, in a rich coffee-growing district. Linked by railway (W) with Buenaventura. Manufactures textiles, leather goods, etc.

**Mannar (Manaar), Gulf of.** Gulf of the Indian Ocean between the coast of Madras (India) and Ceylon, lying S of Adam's Bridge; 200 m. across at its widest. Famous for pearl fisheries.

**Mannheim** Federal German Republic. Town in Baden-Württemberg, on the right bank of the Rhine R. at the confluence with the Neckar R. opposite Ludwigshafen. Pop. (1968) 323,744. River port. Considerable trade in grain and coal. Also a road and rail and industrial centre. Railway engineering. Manufactures agricultural and other machinery, electrical equipment, chemicals, textiles, tobacco products, etc. The inner old town is laid out in rectangular pattern with numbered streets; many of its old buildings, however, were destroyed or severely damaged in the 2nd World War. A settlement in the 8th cent. Residence of the Electors Palatine 1720–78.

**Manresa** Spain. Town in Barcelona province, Catalonia, on the Cardoner R. 28 m. NNW of Barcelona. Pop. 40,000. Industrial centre. Manufactures textiles, paper, leather goods, etc. Beneath one of its churches is a cave which served as a spiritual retreat for St Ignatius of Loyola.

**Mans, Le** France. Prefecture of the Sarthe department, on the Sarthe R. at the confluence with the Huisne R. Pop. (1968) 147,651. Important railway junction. Manufactures railway rolling stock, agricultural machinery, tobacco products, textiles, paper, etc. Flour milling, tanning etc. Trade in livestock, agricultural produce. The annual 24-hour sports-car race is held at Le Mans. Traces of the Roman wall are still apparent, and in the cathedral (11th/13th-cent.) is the tomb of Queen Berengaria, wife of Richard Cœur de Lion. Here the French were finally defeated in the Franco-Prussian War (1871). Birthplace of Henry II of England (1133–89).

**Mansfield** England. Municipal borough in Nottinghamshire, on the R. Maun 13 m. N of Nottingham. Pop. (1961) 53,222. Industrial centre in a coalmining district. Manufactures hosiery, footwear, etc. Has a 16th-cent. grammar school. The urban district of Mansfield Woodhouse (pop. 20,137), mainly residential, is 1½ m. N.

**Mansfield** USA. Industrial town in Ohio, 54 m. WSW of Akron. Pop. (1960) 47,325. Manufactures electrical equipment, metal goods, tyres, etc. Named after Lt-Col. Jared Mansfield, US surveyor general.

**Mansûra** United Arab Republic. Capital of the Daqahliya governorate, on the Damietta branch of the Nile. Pop. (1960) 152,000. Important railway junction. Cotton-manufacturing centre. Founded 1221. Scene of the defeat of the Crusaders under Louis IX of France (St Louis) by the Mamelukes (1250).

**Mantua** (Italian **Mantova**) Italy. Capital of Mantova province, in Lombardy, 23 m. SSW of Verona, almost enclosed by lakes formed by the Mincio R. Pop. (1961) 62,411. Tanning, brewing, sugar refining, etc. Among its buildings are the 14th-cent. ducal palace, with paintings by Rubens, El Greco, etc.; the castle; the Church of St Andrea, which has the tomb of Mantegna; and, just outside the town, the Palazzo del Tè. Governed by the Gonzaga family 1328–1708; under them attained fame as a centre of culture. Ruled by Austria for most of the 18th cent. and again 1814–66, and then passed to Italy. Birthplace of Virgil (70–19 B.C.) near by.

**Manych Depression** USSR. A broad trough 350 m. long between the Lower Don R. and the Caspian Sea, extending ESE through the Rostov region (RSFSR) and the Kalmuk ASSR. For most of the year it is dry or contains a series of salt lakes. In spring a stream, the W Manych R., flows WNW to join the Don, and another, the E Manych R., flows ESE and disappears in the arid steppe.

**Manzala (Menzala, Menzaleh), Lake** United Arab Republic. Coastal lagoon in Lower Egypt, from the Damietta branch of the Nile to the Suez Canal. Area 660 sq. m. Separated from the Mediterranean Sea by a narrow spit, at the E end of which is Port Said. Abundant fish and waterfowl. ✧ *Tanis.*

**Manzanillo** Cuba. Seaport on the SE coast, at the head of the Gulf of Guacanayabo. Pop. 51,000. Exports sugar, molasses, coffee, hides, etc. Sugar refining, sawmilling, fish canning, etc. Founded 1784.

**Maracaibo** Venezuela. Capital of the Zulia state, on the hot humid NW shores of L. Maracaibo. Pop. (1964) 457,416. With oil exploitation (from 1917) it grew from a small coffee-exporting port to an important commercial centre. The port is accessible to ocean-going vessels, since the dredging of a channel from L. Maracaibo to the Caribbean in 1956. Main export oil. Founded 1571. Seat of the University of Zulia (founded 1891, reopened 1946).

**Maracaibo, Lake** Venezuela. Lake in the NW, 130 m. long and up to 70 m. wide. Area 5,000 sq. m. Connected with the Gulf of Venezuela by a 34-mile waterway, with a dredged channel through the bar, completed in 1956. The rich oilfields beneath the lake and its margins (discovered 1917) are Venezuela's main source of revenue; thousands of derricks stand in the waters of the lake.

**Maracay** Venezuela. Capital of the Aragua state, 50 m. WSW of Carácas, just NE of L. Valencia. Pop. (1964) 142,192. Modernized under the Gómez dictatorship 1909–35. Military training centre. Manufactures textiles etc.

**Maraetai** ✧ *Waikato River.*

**Marágheh (Marágha)** Iran. Town in E Azerbaijan province 50 m. S of Tabriz. Pop. (1966) 54,106. Commercial centre in a fruit-growing district. Capital of Hulagu (grandson of Genghis Khan) in the 13th cent. Has bridges, towers, etc. dating from the 12th–14th cent.

**Marajó Island** Brazil. Large island in the Amazon delta, 180 m. long and 120 m. wide. The W is low, swampy, and covered with rain-forest, producing timber and rubber. The E is higher grassland, used for cattle rearing. Source of handsome prehistoric pottery.

**Maranhão** Brazil. State in the NE, bounded on the N by the Atlantic. Area 126,864 sq. m. Pop. (1960) 2,492,139. Cap. São Luis. The low coastal plain, with a hot humid climate, is covered with rain-forest and tall-grass savannah. In the S there is some cattle rearing on the short-grass plateaux. Agriculture (cotton, sugar-cane, etc.) in the valleys.

**Marañón River** Peru. Headstream of the Amazon R., 900 m. long, rising in small Andean lakes in central Peru, flowing N and NE, leaving the highlands by the Pongo de Manseriche Gorge, and joining the Ucayali R. in the lowlands to form the Amazon.

**Maraş** Turkey. Capital of Maraş province, 95 m. ENE of Adana on the S slope of the Taurus Mountains. Pop. (1965) 63,300. Commercial centre. Trade in wheat, cotton. In ancient times a Hittite town.

**Marathon** Greece. Village in Attica 20 m. NE of Athens. On the plain of Marathon to the SE, the Athenians under Miltiades defeated the Persians under Darius I (490 B.C.). The feat of the soldier who carried the news of the victory from Marathon to Athens has been commemorated in the marathon race of the Olympic Games since 1896.

**Marazion** England. Fishing village and holiday resort in Cornwall, on Mount's Bay 3 m. E of Penzance. Pop. 1,300. At low tide it is connected by a natural causeway to the small island of St Michael's Mount, formerly a place of pilgrimage.

**Marburg** Federal German Republic. Town in Hessen, on the Lahn R. 50 m. N of Frankfurt. Pop. (1963) 47,800. Manufactures metal goods, precision instruments, pottery, soap, etc. University (1527). The 13th-cent. Church of St Elizabeth was built by the Teutonic Knights to hold the saint's tomb. In the 13th/14th-cent. castle the famous religious debate between Luther and Zwingli took place (1529).

**Marburg** (Yugoslavia) ◊ *Maribor*.

**March** England. Urban district in the Isle of Ely, Cambridgeshire, on the Nene R. 13 m. NW of Ely. Pop. (1961) 13,119. Market town. Railway junction. Beetsugar refining. The 14th-cent. Church of St Wendreda has an outstanding timber roof.

**Marches, The** Italy. Central region bordering E on the Adriatic Sea and comprising the provinces of Ancona, Ascoli-Piceno, Macerata, and Pesaro-Urbino. Area 3,744 sq. m. Pop. (1961) 1,347,234. Cap. Ancona. Mountainous in the W (Apennines). Many river valleys and a coastal plain on which agriculture (cereals, vines, olives) and stock rearing are the main occupations.

**March River** ◊ *Morava River* (Czechoslovakia).

**Mar del Plata** Argentina. Large resort on the Atlantic coast, in Buenos Aires province, about midway between Buenos Aires and Bahía Blanca. Pop. (1960) 203,093. More than a million visitors annually. Extensive beaches, casino, night clubs, and other tourist attractions. Fish canning, meat packing, flour milling.

**Mardin** Turkey. Capital of Mardin province, 175 m. E of Gaziantep. Pop. (1965) 31,000. Market town in an agricultural region producing cereals, wool, etc. Manufactures textiles.

**Maré** ◊ *Loyalty Islands*.

**Maree, Loch** Scotland. Lake 13 m. long and up to 2 m. wide in Ross and Cromarty E and SE of Gairloch, noted for its fine scenery. Almost surrounded by mountains, inc. Ben Slioch (3,217 ft). Contains many small islands. Its sea outlet is the short R. Ewe.

**Maremma** Italy. Marshy region in S Tuscany bordering on the Tyrrhenian Sea from the Cecina R. southwards. It was fertile and well populated in Etruscan and Roman times, being drained by underground canals, but in the Middle Ages it was largely abandoned owing to malaria. From the early 19th cent. reclamation has continued with success, and large areas of malarial swamp have been converted into fertile agricultural land.

**Mareotis (Mariut), Lake** United Arab Republic. Salt lake in the Nile delta, separated from the sea by the narrow strip of land on which ◊ *Alexandria* stands.

**Margam** Wales. Site of a large steel works (opened 1951) in the municipal borough of ◊ *Port Talbot*, Glamorganshire.

**Margarita Island** Venezuela. Island off the NE coast, forming the major part of the Nueva Esparta state. Area 444 sq. m. Pop. 87,500. Cap. La Asunción (pop. 5,500). Chief port and commercial centre Porlamar (pop. 20,000). Resort area; pleasant climate. Pearl and deep-sea fishing important occupations. Discovered (1498) by Columbus.

**Margate** England. Municipal borough on the coast of the Isle of Thanet, Kent, 15 m. ENE of Canterbury. Pop. (1961) 45,708. Seaside resort, esp. popular with Londoners; good beach and piers; noted for its sea bathing since 1750. Includes the resorts of Westgate-on-Sea (W) and Cliftonville (E).

**Mari ASSR** USSR. Autonomous SSR in RSFSR, between Gorki and Kazan on the left bank of the Volga R. Area 8,955 sq. m. Pop. (1970) 685,000. Cap. Ioshkar Ola. More than half forested. Principal industries sawmilling, woodworking, and the manufacture of paper, cellulose, furniture, etc. The Mari people, of Finnish origin, were conquered by Ivan the Terrible and annexed to Russia in 1552.

**Mariana (Marianas, Marianne, Ladrone) Islands** W Pacific Ocean. Group of volcanic islands N of New Guinea and E of the Philippines; the chain runs almost N–S. Area 370 sq. m., Guam being the largest island. Pop. (1968) 10,986. Main products copra, sugar-cane, phosphates. To the E and S is the Mariana (Marianas) Trench (5,940 fathoms). Discovered (1521) by Magellan, who called them the Islas de los Ladrones ('Thieves' Islands'); under Spanish rule 1668–1898. Guam was ceded to the USA 1899; the others were sold to Germany, but were occupied by Japan from 1914 until captured by the USA (1944) and taken under UN Trusteeship (1947).

**Marianao** Cuba. Suburb of W Havana. Pop. (1960) 229,576. Largely residential. Has a fashionable beach, racecourse, casino, etc.

**Mariánské Lázně (Ger. Marienbad)** Czechoslovakia. Famous watering place in W Bohemia 33 m. WNW of Pilsen. Pop. 9,000. Several mineral springs of varied composition, known for many centuries but first achieving popularity about the end of the 18th cent.

**Maribor (Ger. Marburg)** Yugoslavia. Town in Slovenia, on the Drava R. 56 m. NNW of Zagreb. Pop. (1961) 82,560. Manufactures textiles, leather, footwear, chemicals, etc. Trade in grain, wine, timber. Its chief buildings are the cathedral (begun in the 12th cent.) and the 15th-cent. castle.

**Mariehamn** ◊ *Ahvenanmaa.*

**Marienbad** ◊ *Mariánské Lázně.*

**Mariinsk Canals** USSR. Canal system 680 m. long in RSFSR. Dates from the early 19th cent., constructed and repeatedly improved to link Leningrad with the Volga R. via the Neva, Svir, Vytegra, Kovzha, and Sheksna rivers and the Rybinsk Reservoir.

**Marion (Indiana)** USA. Town on the Mississinewa R. 45 m. SW of Fort Wayne. Pop. (1960) 37,854. Commercial centre in an agricultural region. Manufactures oilfield machinery, electrical equipment, paper, etc. Named after General Francis Marion, a soldier in the American War of Independence.

**Marion (Ohio)** USA. Town 43 m. N of Columbus. Pop. (1960) 37,079. Commercial centre in a rich farming area. Manufactures excavating and road-construction machinery, metal goods, etc. Named after General Marion (◊ *Marion,* Indiana). Home of President W. G. Harding (1865–1923).

**Maritime Provinces** Canada. Three provinces on the Atlantic seaboard: New Brunswick, Nova Scotia, and Prince Edward Island. Known as Acadia (Acadie) during the French administration. Chief cities and ports Halifax (Nova Scotia), St John (New Brunswick).

**Maritime Territory** ◊ *Primorye Territory.*

**Maritsa (Evros) River.** River 300 m. long rising in the Rila Mountains in Bulgaria, flowing E and ESE through Bulgaria past Plovdiv, then past Edirne in Turkey, then forming parts of the Greco-Bulgarian and the Greco-Turkish frontiers, turning S and SSW, and entering the Aegean Sea. Unnavigable, but used for irrigation and hydroelectric power.

**Maritzburg** ◊ *Pietermaritzburg.*

**Mariut, Lake** ◊ *Mareotis, Lake.*

**Market Bosworth** England. Small town in Leicestershire 11 m. W of Leicester. Pop. (1961) 1,250. Two m. S is Bosworth Field, scene of the battle (1485) in which Richard III was defeated and killed, to be succeeded by his conqueror the Earl of Richmond as Henry VII.

**Market Drayton** England. Market town in Shropshire, on the R. Tern 17 m. NE of Shrewsbury. Pop. (1961) 5,853. Has a 16th-cent. grammar school. Styche, near by, was the birthplace of Lord Clive (1725–74).

**Market Harborough** England. Urban district in Leicestershire, on the R. Welland 12 m. SE of Leicester. Pop. (1961) 11,556. Market town. Manufactures electrical equipment, textiles, etc. A famous fox-hunting centre. Has a 13th-cent. church.

**Market Rasen** England. Urban district in Parts of Lindsey, Lincolnshire, on the R. Rasen 14 m. NE of Lincoln. Pop. (1961) 2,257. Market town. Racecourse.

**Markinch** Scotland. Small burgh in Fifeshire, on the R. Leven 6 m. NNE of Kirkcaldy. Pop. (1961) 2,446. Distilling, paper manufacture, etc.

**Marlborough** England. Municipal borough in Wiltshire, on the R. Kennet 9 m. SSE of Swindon near Savernake Forest. Pop. (1961) 4,843. Market town in a dairy-farming region. Engineering etc. Marlborough College, the public school, was founded 1843. It contains the 18th-cent. house where James Thomson wrote part of *The Seasons.*

**Marlborough** New Zealand. Provincial district in the NE of the S Island. Area 4,220 sq. m. Pop. (1966) 29,428. Principal town Blenheim. Chief port Picton, with regular services to Wellington. Sheep rearing. Grain and fruit growing.

**Marlow (Great Marlow)** England. Urban district in S Buckinghamshire, on the R. Thames 4 m. S of High Wycombe. Pop. (1961) 8,704. Market town. Mainly residential. Brewing. Popular boating centre. The village of Little Marlow is 2 m. ENE.

**Marmara (Marmora), Sea of** Turkey. Ancient Propontis. Sea between European and Asiatic Turkey, linked with the Black

Sea by the Bosporus and with the Aegean Sea by the Dardanelles. Area 4,400 sq. m. Takes its name from its largest island, Marmara, in the W.

**Marne** France. Department in the NE, in the former Champagne province. Area 3,168 sq. m. Pop. (1968) 485,388. Prefecture Châlons-sur-Marne. Drained chiefly by the Marne R. and its tributaries, it is crossed by the infertile dry Champagne (*Champagne pouilleuse*) and the humid Champagne (*Champagne humide*); the vineyards on its hill slopes produce some of the finest champagne. Reims, Épernay, and Châlons-sur-Marne are important centres of the Champagne wine trade.

**Marne River** France. River 326 m. long rising on the Plateau de Langres, in the Haute-Marne department, flowing N and then W in a wide curve, past Chaumont, St Dizier, Vitry-le-François, Châlons-sur-Marne, Épernay, and Meaux, joining the Seine R. at Charenton-le-Pont just above Paris. Linked by canal with the Aisne, Rhine, and Rhône rivers; an important waterway. Two vital battles of the 1st World War (1914, 1918) were fought on its banks and were named after it.

**Maroni (Marowijne) River** French Guiana. River 450 m. long rising in the Tumuc-Humac Mountains and flowing generally N through tropical rain-forests to the Atlantic. Forms most of the frontier between French Guiana and Surinam.

**Maros River** ◊ *Mureş River.*

**Marowijne River** ◊ *Maroni River.*

**Marple** England. Urban district in NE Cheshire 4 m. ESE of Stockport. Pop. (1961) 16,812. Cotton manufactures.

**Marquesas (Îles Marquises) Islands** S Pacific Ocean. Group of volcanic islands 750 m. NE of Tahiti, forming part of French Polynesia. Area 492 sq. m. Pop. (1967) 5,147. Largest island Nukuhiva, second largest Hivaoa, with cap. Atuona. The S group (Mendaña Is.) was discovered by Mendaña (1595) the N group (Washington Is.) by Ingraham (1791). Passed to France in 1842, when the population was about 20,000. European diseases were largely responsible for the subsequent decrease; the people have the finest physique of all the Polynesians.

**Marrakesh** Morocco. Traditionally the southern capital; second largest city, 140 m. SSW of Casablanca at the foot of the High Atlas Mountains. Pop. (1961) 264,000. Chief commercial centre of a fertile irrigated region. Connected with Casablanca by rail. Manufactures carpets, leather goods, etc. Hot summers, mild winters; annual rainfall (mainly Nov.–April) 9 ins. Popular tourist centre. Founded 1062. The mosque and tower of Koutoubiya (still the outstanding landmark) were built by the Sultan Yakout-el-Mansour 1184–98. Became a N terminus of trans-Saharan caravan routes. Occupied by the French in 1912, since when the modern town has developed.

**Marsala** Italy. Ancient Lilybaeum. Town and port in Trapani province in W Sicily. Pop. (1961) 81,327. Considerable trade in Marsala wine. Manufactures bottles etc. Fishing. Founded in the 4th cent. B.C. The chief Carthaginian fortress in Sicily; later a Roman base for expeditions against Carthage. Named by the Saracens Marsa Ali ('the Port of Ali'). Garibaldi landed here at the opening of his campaign in Sicily (1860).

**Marseille** (English **Marseilles**) France. Ancient Massilia. Country's second largest city and principal seaport, capital of the Bouches-du-Rhône department, on the Gulf of Lions of the Mediterranean Sea. Pop. (1968) 893,771. Exports wines, liqueurs, olive oil, soap, sugar, etc. Trades chiefly with N Africa, the E Mediterranean, and the Far East. Manufactures soap and margarine, using huge imports of vegetable oils. Also oil refining, flour milling, sugar refining, ore smelting, ship repairing, chemical and glass manufactures, etc. The harbour accommodates the largest vessels, and is linked inland by the Rhône-Marseille Canal through the Rove tunnel and the Étang-de-Berre. Stands on a bay and is flanked on three sides by limestone hills. Offshore is the islet with the famous Château d'If. In spite of its long history it has few old buildings. The pilgrim Church of Notre Dame de la Garde (1864) has a gilded statue of the Virgin and replaces a 13th-cent. building on the same site; the Church of St Victor, however, dates from the 13th cent. Founded by Greeks from Phocaea c. 600 B.C. A free city under the Romans. Several times besieged and captured, it passed to France in 1481. Its modern development as a great seaport dates from the opening of the Suez Canal (1869). Birthplace of Thiers (1797–1877), Daumier (1808–79), and Edmond Rostand (1869–1918).

**Marshall Islands** W Pacific Ocean. Group

of coral islands and atolls in the W Central Pacific in two roughly parallel NW–SE chains, Ralik and Ratak, ESE of the Mariana Is. Micronesian pop. (1968) 18,998. Main export copra. Rainfall is heavy, esp. in the S atolls, and temperatures are uniformly high. Kwajalein in Ralik Chain is the largest atoll. Discovered (1526) by the Spaniards. A German protectorate 1885–1914. Occupied by the Japanese until 1944. From 1947 included in the US Territory of the Pacific Is. under UN trusteeship. US atom-bomb tests were conducted on Bikini Atoll in 1946.

**Marske** ◊ *Saltburn and Marske.*

**Martaban, Gulf of** Burma. Inlet of the Indian Ocean receiving the Salween and Sittang rivers, with the Irrawaddy delta to the W. Chief port Moulmein. The village of Martaban, at the mouth of the Salween, opposite Moulmein, probably founded in the 6th cent., was once capital of an independent kingdom; it is the terminus of a railway to Pegu.

**Martha's Vineyard** USA. Island off the Massachusetts coast, 20 m. long and 2–10 m. wide. Pop. 6,000. Formerly a whaling and fishing centre. Now mainly a resort. First visited and named by Bartholomew Gosnold (1602). Administered by New York until 1692.

**Martina Franca** Italy. Town in Taranto province, Apulia, 17 m. NNE of Taranto. Pop. (1961) 37,460. Produces wine, olive oil, etc.

**Martinique** W Indies. Island in the Windward Is. of the Lesser Antilles, between Dominica (N) and St Lucia (S); an overseas department of France. Area 420 sq. m. Pop. (1967) 320,030. Cap. Fort-de-France. Of volcanic origin, and extremely mountainous. Highest point Mont Pelée (4,429 ft), a volcano which erupted in 1902 and destroyed the town of St Pierre, killing about 40,000 people. Also suffers from hurricanes, earthquakes, and tidal waves. Principal crops sugar-cane, bananas, cacao, coffee, fruits. Main exports bananas, sugar, rum. Probably discovered by Columbus in 1502. Colonized by the French 1635. Apart from brief intervals it has remained French; became an overseas department 1946.

**Marton** ◊ *Middlesbrough.*

**Martos** Spain. Town in Jaén province, Andalusia, 10 m. WSW of Jaén. Pop. (1961) 23,990. Manufactures cement, textiles, soap, pottery. Trade in olive oil, wine. Mineral springs near by.

**Mary** USSR. Formerly Merv. Town in the Turkmen SSR, in an oasis on the Murghab R. 220 m. ESE of Ashkhabad. Pop. (1969) 61,000. On the Trans-Caspian Railway, with a branch line to Kushka. Cotton manufacturing, using cotton grown by irrigation on the oasis; also carpet manufacture, brewing, food processing. The old city of Merv, 20 m. E, according to Hindu and Arab tradition was the source of the Aryan race; in medieval times it was a centre of Muslim culture.

**Maryborough** Australia. Town and port in SE Queensland, on the Mary R. 135 m. NNW of Brisbane. Pop. (1966) 20,381. In a sugar-growing and dairy-farming region. Iron and steel manufacture, railway engineering, sawmilling. Exports sugar, pineapples, citrus fruits, timber, coal.

**Maryland** USA. A middle Atlantic state. Area 10,577 sq. m. Pop. (1970) 3,874,642. Cap. Annapolis. One of the original 13 states; popularly known as the 'Old Line' state. Extremely irregular in shape; Chesapeake Bay almost separates the two parts of the Atlantic coastal plain, known as the Eastern Shore (on Delmarva Peninsula) and the Western Shore. The shores of the bay, too, are much indented, with many river estuaries. Inland there are rolling uplands; highest point Mt Backbone (3,340 ft) in the Alleghenies, in the extreme W. Climate humid continental; temperatures are much lower in the W than in the S and E. Annual rainfall 40–45 ins. Tomatoes, maize, soya beans, and tobacco are important crops, and oysters, crabs, and clams are fished in Chesapeake Bay. Leading industrial city Baltimore. The history of Maryland began with the granting by Charles I (1632) of a charter to George Calvert, 1st Baron Baltimore. The first settlement was established at St Mary's (1634). The boundary with Pennsylvania, long in dispute, was settled in 1763–7 by the drawing of the Mason–Dixon Line. In 1790–91 Maryland ceded the 69 sq. m. on the Potomac R. which form the District of Columbia. Named after Henrietta Maria, wife of Charles I.

**Maryport** England. Urban district in W Cumberland, at the mouth of the R. Ellen on Solway Firth 26 m. SW of Carlisle. Pop. (1961) 12,334. Port. Coalmining centre. Tanning. Manufactures chemicals etc.

**Masaya** Nicaragua. Capital of the Masaya department, in the SW. Pop. (1963) 34,127.

Commercial centre for a fertile agricultural region (coffee, tobacco, etc.). Railway junction. Crater lake near by. Indian handicrafts, esp. hammocks, rope, straw hats, etc. Manufactures footwear, cigars, etc.

**Masbate** Philippines. Island betwen Negros and the S E tip of Luzon. Area 1,262 sq. m. Pop. (1960) 337,000. Cap. Masbate (pop. 32,000). Formerly one of the country's chief gold mining areas. Rice, coconuts, abacá cultivated.

**Maseru** Lesotho. Capital, 1 m. inside the W border, 80 m. E of Bloemfontein (S Africa) near the Caledon R. at a height of 4,940 ft. Pop. 10,000. Connected with Bloemfontein by rail via Marseilles.

**Mashaba** ◊ *Rhodesia.*

**Mashhad** ◊ *Meshed.*

**Mashonaland** Rhodesia. NE region, inhabited by the Mashona, a Bantu tribe. Chief town Salisbury. Administered by the British S Africa Company 1889–1923, then part of Southern Rhodesia. Other towns Umtali, Gatooma.

**Mason City** USA. Industrial town in Iowa 110 m. N of Des Moines. Pop. (1960) 30,642. Manufactures cement, bricks and tiles, etc. Named after the first settlers, who were Freemasons.

**Mason-Dixon Line** USA. State boundary between Pennsylvania (N) and Maryland (S). Surveyed (1763–7) by two English astronomers, Charles Mason and Jeremiah Dixon, it settled the long-standing dispute between Pennsylvania and Maryland. In 1779 it was extended to mark the S boundary between Pennsylvania and Virginia (now W Virginia). Total length about 240 m. Before the American Civil War it divided the slave states from the 'free' states. Later it came to distinguish the 'South' from the 'North'.

**Massachusetts** USA. State in New England, on the Atlantic. Area 8,257 sq. m. Pop. (1970) 5,630,224. Cap. Boston. One of the original 13 states; popularly known as the 'Bay' state. On the coast is Massachusetts Bay, with its two arms Boston Bay (N) and Cape Cod Bay (S). The E part belongs to the Atlantic coastal plain, the W to the New England uplands, cut by the N–S Connecticut R. Valley. Highest point Mt Greylock (3,491 ft), in the extreme N W. Climate humid continental, the long severe winter passing quickly into a hot summer. Annual rainfall 40–45 ins. Potatoes, tobacco, cranberries, and apples widely grown. Fishing for cod, haddock, etc. still important, but manufacturing is the main activity. Principal products textiles, boots and shoes, electrical machinery, paper. Chief towns Boston, Worcester, Springfield, Cambridge, New Bedford. Distinguished for its seats of higher education; has 99 degree-granting institutions. First permanently settled by the Pilgrim Fathers, who landed from the *Mayflower* at Plymouth (1620). Prominent in resistance to the English colonial policy which led to the American Revolution. United with Maine in 1691, but the union was terminated in 1820.

**Massawa** Ethiopia. Chief N seaport, in Eritrea, on the Red Sea, partly on the mainland and partly on Massawa Island. Pop. 27,000. Exports hides, coffee, etc. Occupied by the Italians 1885. Capital of Eritrea till 1900, then superseded by Asmara. Used by the Italians as a base for the expedition against Abyssinia (Ethiopia) in 1935.

**Massillon** USA. Industrial town in Ohio 7 m. W of Canton. Pop. (1960) 31,236. Manufactures special steels, hardware, etc. Founded 1826.

**Masterton** New Zealand. Town in the N Island 50 m. ENE of Wellington. Pop. (1966) 17,596. Dairy factories, meat works, woollen mills.

**Masulipatnam** India. Formerly Masulipatam or Bandar. Seaport in Andhra Pradesh, on the N side of the Krishna delta 195 m. ESE of Hyderabad. Pop. (1961) 101,417. Exports groundnuts, castor seeds, etc. Rice milling. Manufactures cotton goods. Site of the first British settlement on the Coromandel Coast (established 1611).

**Matabeleland** Rhodesia. Region in the S W inhabited by the Matabele, a Bantu tribe of Zulu origin. Chief town Bulawayo. The Matabele were driven out of Natal and the Transvaal, and settled N of the Limpopo R., absorbing the Mashona and other tribes. Administered by the British S Africa Company 1889–1923. Cecil Rhodes obtained from the Matabele chief Lobengula the right to exploit its rich gold deposits. Became part of Southern Rhodesia 1923.

**Matadi** Congo (Kinshasa). Chief seaport, on the left bank of the Congo R. just below the Livingstone Falls, 100 m. from the coast. Pop. (1958) 59,000. Head of navigation for ocean-going vessels. Linked by rail with Kinshasa. Principal exports cacao, coffee, cotton, palm oil, minerals.

**Matagalpa** Nicaragua. Capital of the Matagalpa department, the country's second largest town, 60 m. NNE of Managua. Pop. (1963) 61,383. Coffee processing, flour milling, etc.

**Matamoros** Mexico. Town in the Tamaulipas state, on the Rio Grande near the mouth, opposite Brownsville (Texas). Pop. (1969) 174,500. Cotton ginning, vegetable-oil processing, tanning, distilling, etc. Important largely as a point of entry for US tourists. Founded 1824. Named after the Mexican patriot Mariano Matamoros (1770–1814).

**Matanzas** Cuba. Capital of the Matanzas province, on the N coast 50 m. E of Havana. Pop. (1960) 83,850. Seaport. Commercial centre in a rich agricultural region producing sugar-cane, sisal, etc. Exports sugar. Sugar refining, tanning. Manufactures rayons, footwear, etc. Excellent beaches, wide avenues, handsome plazas; second only to Havana as a tourist centre. The port has a free zone (established 1934).

**Matapan (Tainaron), Cape** Greece. Southernmost point of the Peloponnese, at the extremity of the Matapan peninsula, between the Gulfs of Messenia and Laconia. During the 2nd World War a British naval force defeated the Italians near by (1941).

**Matarani** ⇨ *Mollendo*.

**Mataró** Spain. Mediterranean seaport in Barcelona province, Catalonia, 20 m. NE of Barcelona. Pop. 32,000. Manufactures textiles, knitwear, paper, soap, etc. Trade in wine etc. The Barcelona–Mataró railway was the first in Spain (1848).

**Matera** Italy. Capital of Matera province, Basilicata, 36 m. WNW of Taranto. Pop. (1961) 38,562. Trade in cereals, olive oil, etc. Manufactures macaroni, pottery, etc. Cathedral (13th-cent.). In the neighbourhood there are many caves and rock dwellings.

**Mathura** India. Formerly Muttra. Town in W Uttar Pradesh, on the Jumna R. 30 m. NW of Agra. Pop. (1961) 116,959. Trade in grain, cotton, oilseeds, etc. Manufactures chemicals, paper, textiles. Also an important Hindu religious centre; the river bank is lined with bathing ghats and temples. An early Buddhist stronghold, it was sacked by Mahmud of Ghazni (1017), Aurangzeb (1669), and the Afghans (1756).

**Matlock** England. Urban district in Derbyshire, on the R. Derwent 15 m. N of Derby, comprising Matlock and Matlock Bath. Pop. (1961) 18,486. Resort with mineral springs. Cotton and flour mills. In the vicinity are limestone cliffs and caves and petrifying springs. Arkwright established the first cotton mill in Derbyshire here (1771).

**Mato Grosso** Brazil. In Portuguese, 'Big Forest'. Large inland state on the SW plateau. Area 475,378 sq. m. Pop. (1960) 910,262 (less than 2 per sq. m.). Cap. Cuiabá. In the N, in a vast tropical rainforest, part of the Amazon basin, live many Indian tribes (not included in the census), largely untouched by western influence, under the care of the Indian Protection Service. SW lies the *pantanal*, a region near the Paraguay R. where cattle thrive in the dry season. Main occupation cattle raising. Manganese mined near Corumbá. Many other unexploited mineral resources.

**Matopo Hills** Rhodesia. Range S of Bulawayo, 50 m. long, rising to over 5,000 ft. At the point called World's View is the tomb of Cecil Rhodes.

**Matozinhos** Portugal. Fishing port and seaside resort in the Pôrto district, at the mouth of the Leça R. 5 m. NW of Oporto. Pop. (1960) 37,694. Fish canning etc.

**Matrah** Muscat and Oman. Chief commercial town in the sultanate, just W of the capital Muscat. Pop. 14,119 (Arabs, Indians, Pakistanis, Negroes). Trade in dates, limes, and other fruits. Terminus of caravan routes from the interior.

**Matsue** Japan. Seaport in Honshu, capital of Shimane prefecture, on a lagoon of the Sea of Japan 85 m. NNE of Hiroshima. Pop. (1965) 110,534. An ancient castle town, relatively little modernized. Manufactures textiles etc.

**Matsumoto** Japan. Industrial town in Nagano prefecture, Honshu, 105 m. WNW of Tokyo. Pop. (1965) 154,131. Formerly an important centre of the silk industry; now manufactures machinery, paper, etc.

**Matsuyama** Japan. Capital of Ehime prefecture, NW Shikoku. Pop. (1965) 282,644. Industrial centre and seaport. Oil refining, fruit canning. Manufactures chemicals, rayon, textiles, agricultural machinery, etc. Seat of Ehime University (1949).

**Matterhorn (Fr. Mont Cervin, Italian Monte Cervino)** Switzerland. Peak 14,690 ft high in the Pennine Alps, on the Swiss-Italian border 6 m. SW of Zermatt. First climbed (1865) by a party of five, all but Whymper being killed on the descent.

**Maturín** Venezuela. Capital of the Monagas state (NE). Pop. 53,000. Commercial centre, near the oilfields. Trade in cacao, cotton, etc.

**Mauchline** Scotland. Small market town in Ayrshire 10 m. ENE of Ayr. Pop. 4,000. Famous for its associations with Robert Burns. Near by is the farm of Mossgiel, where the poet lived 1784–8.

**Mauer** ◊ *Heidelberg*.

**Mauretania** Africa. Ancient region in the NW consisting roughly of modern Morocco and W Algeria, inhabited by the Mauri (Moors), a Berber people. In the 1st cent. B.C. there were two kingdoms, but Juba II of Numidia became ruler of the whole area (25 B.C.). Claudius annexed it to the Roman Empire (A.D. 42) and divided it into two provinces, Mauretania Tingitana (W) and Mauretania Caesariensis (E). The area prospered until the Vandal invasion in the 5th cent. A.D.

**Mauritania.** Republic in NW Africa, formerly a French overseas territory. Area 398,000 sq. m. Pop. (1968) 1,200,000 (chiefly Muslim and of Berber origin). Cap. Nouakchott. Chief seaport Port Étienne. Bounded by Algeria (N), Mali (E and S), Senegal (SW), and Spanish Sahara and the Atlantic (W). Almost entirely in the Sahara; the inhabitants are chiefly camel-rearing nomads. In the extreme S (where there is a slight rainfall) maize and millet are cultivated and cattle, sheep, and goats raised. Other important products are gum arabic, salt (from *sebkha*, saline pools), dried and salted fish. Large deposits of iron ore, now the main export, from Fort Gouraud. A French protectorate 1903–20, colony 1920–46, overseas territory 1946–58. Became a member of the French Community 1958 and an independent member of the UN 1961.

**Mauritius** (Fr. Île Maurice) Indian Ocean. Volcanic island fringed with coral reefs, about 550 m. E of the Malagasy Republic. Area 720 sq. m. Pop. (1963) 713,381. Cap. Port Louis. With its dependencies (chiefly ◊ *Rodrigues*) it was formerly a British Crown Colony. Picturesque and mountainous, rising to 2,711 ft in Piton de la Rivière Noire (SW). Under the influence of the SE trade wind the annual rainfall varies from 150 ins. on the windward side (SE) to 30–40 ins. on the leeward side (NW). Tropical cyclones are frequent, esp. Jan.–April, causing considerable damage and sometimes loss of life. The severest re-corded cyclone took place in 1960; 42 people were killed and about 70,000 made homeless. The economy depends on the sugar-cane crop; sugar usually accounts for over 95 per cent of the exports. About two thirds of the inhabitants are the descendants of Indian immigrants introduced to work on the sugar plantations in the 19th cent. There are about 16,000 Chinese. Both groups are increasing rapidly; the population density is among the highest in the world. Discovered (1505) by the Portuguese. Held by the Dutch (who named it Mauritius) 1598–1710 and by the French (who named it Île de France) 1715–1810. Ceded to Britain 1814. The main residential centre for Europeans is Curepipe, in the interior at an altitude of 1,800 ft. Became an independent member of the British Commonwealth and admitted to the UN 1968.

**May, Isle of** Scotland. Island at the mouth of the Firth of Forth, 5 m. from the Fifeshire coast. Lighthouse. Ruins of a priory dedicated to St Adrian, martyred by the Danes in the 9th cent.

**Mayagüez** (Puerto Rico) USA. Seaport on the W coast. Pop. (1960) 83,850. In an agricultural region producing sugar-cane, coffee, tobacco. Famous for embroidery and needlework. Sugar refining. Manufactures beer, rum, cigars, etc. Founded 1760.

**Maybole** Scotland. Small burgh in Ayrshire 8 m. S of Ayr. Pop. (1961) 4,677. Market town. Manufactures agricultural machinery, footwear. Once capital of the district of Carrick. The ruins of Crossraguel Abbey are 1½ m. SW.

**Mayenne** France. Department in the NW, formed chiefly from Maine. Area 2,012 sq. m. Pop. (1968) 252,762. Prefecture Laval. Generally low-lying but hilly in the NE, where it rises to over 1,300 ft. Drained by the Mayenne R. and its tributaries. Cereals, sugar-beet, cider apples grown. Cattle reared. Chief towns Laval, Mayenne.

**Mayenne River** France. River 122 m. long, rising in the Orne department and flowing W and then S past Mayenne and Laval to join the Sarthe R. above Angers, forming the Maine R. Tributaries the Varenne and the Oudon.

**Mayfair** England. Fashionable residential district in the City of Westminster, London, bounded approximately by Oxford Street (N), Bond Street (E), Piccadilly (S), and Park Lane (W). Named after the annual fair held here in May from the 16th cent. to 1809. Among its former residents were Disraeli and Beau Brummell.

**Maynooth** Irish Republic. Small market town in Co. Kildare 14 m. W N W of Dublin. Pop. (1966) 1,254. Seat of St Patrick's College (1795), the chief Roman Catholic training centre for the clergy. Near the college are the remains of Maynooth Castle, built in the 12th cent., dismantled after being besieged in 1647.

**Mayo** Irish Republic. County in Connacht bounded on the W and N by the Atlantic. Area 2,084 sq. m. Pop. (1966) 123,330. County town Castlebar. Its coastline is rugged and deeply indented, with Killala, Blacksod, and Clew bays. Achill and Clare are the largest offshore islands. The W is largely mountainous and barren, rising in the N W to 2,644 ft in Nephin, and in the S W to 2,688 ft in Muilrea and 2,510 ft in Croagh Patrick. The E is lower and more fertile, and potatoes and oats are grown and cattle, pigs, and poultry are raised. Lough Conn is wholly and Loughs Corrib and Mask are partly within the county. Chief towns Castlebar, Ballina, Ballinrobe, Westport.

**Mazagan** ◊ *Jadida, El*.

**Mazar-i-Sharif** Afghanistan. Capital of Mazar-i-Sharif province, 190 m. N W of Kabul. Pop. (1965) 40,000. Manufactures textiles, bricks. Flour milling. Trade in karakul skins, carpets. Has a famous 15th-cent. mosque, said to be the tomb of Ali, son-in-law of Mohammed, and therefore greatly venerated by Shia Muslims.

**Mazatenango** Guatemala. Capital of the Suchitepéquez department, 18 m. S of Quezaltenango. Pop. (1964) 32,416. Commercial centre in a district producing coffee, sugar-cane, cotton.

**Mazatlán** Mexico. Chief Pacific seaport, in the Sinaloa state, at the S extremity of the Gulf of California. Pop. (1960) 75,751. Exports tobacco, bananas, minerals, etc. Sugar refining, textile manufacture, flour milling, distilling. Popular resort; picturesque, with facilities for game fishing.

**Mbabane** Swaziland. Capital, 95 m. W S W of Lourenço Marques, at a height of 3,750 ft. Pop. 14,000. Some tin mining in the neighbourhood.

**Mdina** ◊ *Città Vecchia*.

**Mearns, The** ◊ *Kincardineshire*.

**Meath** Irish Republic. County in Leinster, bordering E on the Irish Sea. Area 903 sq. m. Pop. (1966) 67,323. County town Trim. In general gently undulating and fertile. Drained by the Boyne and Blackwater rivers. Potatoes and oats cultivated. Cattle and horses raised. Chief towns Trim, An Uaimh (Navan), Ceanannus Mór (Kells). Meath was once a kingdom which included Westmeath, Longford, and parts of Cavan, Kildare, and Offaly as well as the present county, and there are many tumuli, round towers, and other antiquities. By the early 17th cent. it had become established as a county.

**Meaux** France. Town in the Seine-et-Marne department, on the Marne R. and the Ourcq Canal 24 m. E N E of Paris. Pop. (1968) 31,420. Commercial and industrial centre in the Brie region, supplying the Paris markets with agricultural produce. Sugar refining, flour milling. Manufactures starch, mustard, cheese. The cathedral (13th/14th-cent.) contains the tomb of Bossuet, bishop from 1681 to 1704.

**Mecca** Saudi Arabia. Joint capital (with Riyadh) of Saudi Arabia and capital of the Hejaz, 40 m. E of Jidda, its port on the Red Sea. Pop. 200,000. The holiest city of Islam, being the birthplace of Mohammed (*c.* 569–632). Lies in a hollow surrounded by barren hills. In early times it was the hub of desert caravan routes and long before the time of Mohammed it had a reputation as a holy place; in modern times its prosperity depends very largely on visiting pilgrims (about 100,000 annually). The only notable building is the Great Mosque, which consists of a large courtyard enclosed by cloisters. At its centre is the Kaaba, a small stone building without windows, almost cubical in shape, which was a pre-Islamic temple and has been twice rebuilt. Part of the ceremonial duty of the pilgrim is to kiss the sacred black stone embedded in the S E corner of the Kaaba as he circumambulates the building seven times; this stone, probably a meteorite, is believed to have been given to Abraham by Gabriel. In the courtyard, too, are the well Zamzam, associated with Hagar and Ishmael, the reputed tombs of Hagar and Ishmael, and the Maqam Ibrahim, a sacred stone said to bear the imprint of Abraham's foot. Mecca was under the rule of the Turks from 1517 (though at times only nominally) until 1916, when they were expelled by Husain ibn Ali; the city was taken by Ibn Saud in 1924.

**Mechelen (Mechlin, Fr. Malines)** Belgium. Town in Antwerp province, on the Dyle R.

14 m. NNE of Brussels. Pop. (1968) 65,823. Once famous for its lace; now a railway junction and industrial centre. Railway engineering, motor-car assembly. Manufactures furniture, machinery, textiles, paper, etc. It is the metropolitan see. The cathedral (12th/14th-cent.) contains Van Dyck's *Crucifixion*; two other churches have Rubens masterpieces.

**Mecklenburg** German Democratic Republic. Former *Land*, in 1952 divided into the three administrative districts of Rostock, Schwerin, and Neubrandenburg. Area 8,856 sq. m. Bounded on the N by the Baltic. Flat, forming part of the N German lowlands; many lakes. Chief occupation agriculture. Principal crops rye, potatoes, sugar-beet. The capital was Schwerin; Rostock and Warnemünde were leading ports. Occupied in the 6th cent. by Slavonic tribes. Created a duchy 1348. By 1701 its lands had been divided into two duchies, Mecklenburg-Schwerin and Mecklenburg-Strelitz, later elevated to grand duchies, which joined the German Empire 1871. At the end of the 1st World War the grand dukes were deposed, and in 1934 the two states were reunited as the state of Mecklenburg. After the 2nd World War the latter became a *Land* of the German Democratic Republic, W Pomerania being included with it.

**Medan** Indonesia. Capital of N Sumatra province, on the Deli R. in NE Sumatra; its port, Belawan, is 15 m. N. Pop. (1961) 479,098. Commercial centre. Trade in tobacco, rubber. Seat of the University of N Sumatra (1952).

**Medellín** Colombia. Capital of the Antioquia department in the NW, in an enclosed valley of the Central Cordillera, on a tributary of the Cauca R. at a height of 5,000 ft. Pop. (1968) 912,982 (143,952 in 1938). Despite its remoteness, it has Colombia's main textile industries. Also manufactures steel, cement, leather goods, etc. Centre of a coffee-growing, cattle-rearing, and goldmining area. Seat of the University of Antioquia (1871). Founded 1675.

**Medford** (Massachusetts) USA. Industrial town and residential suburb of NW Boston. Pop. (1960) 64,971. Manufactures machinery, chemicals, soap, etc. Developed in the 18th and 19th cent. as a centre of shipbuilding and rum production.

**Medford** (Oregon) USA. Town on Bear Creek 120 m. S of Eugene. Pop. (1960) 25,919. Commercial centre for an agricultural region esp. noted for pears. Fruit canneries, lumber and flour mills.

**Media.** Ancient country in SW Asia inhabited by the Medes, in the area now NW Iran between the Zagros and the Elburz Mountains. With its capital Ecbatana (modern Hamadan), it became powerful in the 8th cent. B.C. and helped to overthrow the Assyrian Empire in the following cent. Conquered by Cyrus of Persia 550 B.C.; thereafter part of the Persian Empire.

**Medicine Hat** Canada. Industrial town in SE Alberta, on the S Saskatchewan R. Pop. (1966) 25,574. In a region producing natural gas and coal. Railway engineering etc.

**Medina (Ar. Al Madinah)** Saudi Arabia. Town in the Hejaz 220 m. N of Mecca, in a basin of the plateau at a height of 2,000 ft. Pop. 80,000. Sacred city of the Muslims, second only to Mecca, situated in an oasis well known for its dates and also producing cereals and fruits. Here Mohammed lived after his flight from Mecca (622) and here he died. The most important building is the Mosque of the Prophet, which is supposed to contain the tombs of Mohammed and Omar. The Hejaz Railway, built to it from Damascus (1908), is now disused, but it still receives many pilgrims. Taken by Ibn Saud 1925.

**Medina** (United Arab Republic) ◊ *Faiyum, El.*

**Mediterranean Sea.** Ancient Mare Internum. Extensive inland sea lying between Europe, Africa, and SW Asia. Area (excluding the Black Sea) 970,000 sq. m. Length W–E 2,300 m. Greatest width 800 m. Divided by a ridge from Cap Bon (Tunisia) to Sicily into a W and an E basin. Its major subdivisions, formed by various large islands and peninsulas, include the Tyrrhenian Sea, Adriatic Sea, Ionian Sea, Aegean Sea, and the Black Sea with the Sea of Azov. Connected with the Atlantic (W) by the narrow Strait of Gibraltar; with the Black Sea (NE) by the Aegean Sea, Dardanelles, Sea of Marmara, and Bosporus; and with the Red Sea (SE) by the Suez Canal and the Gulf of Suez. Among its many islands are the Balearic Is., Corsica, Sardinia, and Sicily in the W section and Malta, Crete, Cyprus, Rhodes, the Ionian Is., the Dodecanese, and the Aegean Is. in the E.

Evaporation exceeds precipitation and inflow from rivers, so that the Mediterranean has a higher salinity than the Atlantic; a current from the Atlantic therefore enters through the Strait of Gibraltar near the surface, while a return current at greater depth flows from the Mediterranean into the Atlantic. Similar opposing currents flow between the Mediterranean and the Black Sea. A further characteristic of the Mediterranean is that it is almost tideless. It experiences such a distinctive type of climate that the term 'Mediterranean climate' has been applied to similar regions in other parts of the world. In the winter it enjoys mild weather and moderate rainfall, received from depressions driven along by the prevailing westerly winds; in summer the winds have a more northerly trend, and the weather is hot, dry, and sunny. Thus there are many popular resorts along its shores, e.g. on the Riviera, while the natural vegetation of the surrounding lands consists of drought-resistant, evergreen trees and shrubs, and olives, citrus fruits, and flowers are characteristically cultivated. Among the local winds are the hot sirocco from N Africa and the cold mistral down the Rhône valley. Important tunny and anchovy fisheries.

Encouraged by its relative calmness, the Phoenicians, Greeks, Romans, Venetians, and Genoese made the Mediterranean a commercial highway; to the Romans it was *mare nostrum*. Declined in importance in the late 15th cent. with the opening of the route to India by the Cape of Good Hope, but revived with the construction of the Suez Canal (1869). Britain sought to safeguard the route by establishing naval bases at Gibraltar and Malta. The strategic importance of the Mediterranean was demonstrated in the 2nd World War.

**Medjerda River** Algeria/Tunisia. Ancient Bagradas. Principal river of Tunisia, 260 m. long, rising near Souk Ahras in N E Algeria and flowing E N E to the Gulf of Tunis 20 m. N of Tunis. The extremely fertile valley produces olives, cereals, fruits and vegetables, and provides the main route by rail and road from Algeria to Tunis.

**Médoc** France. District in the Gironde department in the S W, consisting of a strip of land extending about 50 m. along the left bank of the Gironde. Contains such famous vineyards as those of Château Margaux and Château Latour and produces some of France's finest wines (mainly red).

**Medway River** England. River 70 m. long, rising in three headstreams in Surrey and

Sussex and flowing N and E through Kent past Tonbridge, Maidstone (head of navigation), and the Medway Towns (Rochester, Chatham, and Gillingham) to enter the Thames estuary at Sheerness.

**Meerut** India. Town in Uttar Pradesh 37 m. N E of Delhi. Pop. (1961) 200,470. Flour and oilseed milling. Manufactures cotton goods, chemicals, soap, pottery, etc. Trade in cereals, sugar-cane, oilseeds, cotton. Owed its modern importance to the establishment of the former British military cantonment (1806). Here the Indian Mutiny began (1857).

**Megara** Greece. Town in the Attica *nome* 20 m. W of Athens. Pop. 15,000. Trade in wine, olive oil, etc. The ancient Megara was an influential city from the 8th cent. B.C., declined in the 5th cent., revived somewhat in the 4th cent. Founded Chalcedon, Byzantium, and other colonies.

**Megiddo** Israel. Town in ancient Palestine, at the S edge of the Plain of Esdraelon 18 m. S E of Haifa. Scene of several battles (possibly the biblical Armageddon): Thothmes III defeated the Canaanites (*c.* 1500 B.C.); King Josiah was defeated and killed by Pharaoh Necho II (609 B.C.); the British under Allenby defeated the Turks (1918).

**Meissen** German Democratic Republic. Town in the Dresden district, on the Elbe R. 14 m. N W of Dresden. Pop. 51,000. Since 1710 the centre of manufacture of the famous Dresden china, made from local kaolin. Also manufactures matches, glass, textiles, etc. Sugar refining, brewing. Founded in the 10th cent. Cathedral (13th/15th-cent.); castle (15th-cent.).

**Meknès (Mequinez)** Morocco. Former capital, 35 m. W S W of Fez, at a height of 1,700 ft on a spur N of the Middle Atlas range. Pop. (1964) 205,000. Linked by rail and road with Fez, Rabat, Casablanca. In a fertile region producing olives, cereals, vines. Manufactures pottery, leather, carpets. Became famous when the Sultan Muley Ismail built its 17th-cent. palace, for which it was called the 'Moroccan Versailles'. Occupied by the French 1911.

**Mekong River.** Great river in SE Asia, 2,500 m. long, rising in the Tanghla Range of Tsinghai (Chinghai) province (China) and flowing SE and S through deep gorges, at about 10,000 ft, across E Tibet parallel to the Yangtse (E) and Salween (W) rivers into W Yunnan province. It then forms the boundary of Laos with Burma and part of that with Thailand, continuing past Luang Prabang and Vientiane, crosses Cambodia, and in S Vietnam enters the S China Sea by an extensive delta. At Pnom Penh (Cambodia) the river is linked with L. Tonlé Sap, which pours water into it during the dry season and acts as a flood reservoir in the rainy season. For about 300 m. of its lower course the Mekong is navigable by vessels of moderate size. The delta is a great rice-growing region.

**Melanesia** W Pacific Ocean. One of the three principal divisions of the Pacific islands, the others being Micronesia and Polynesia. Inhabited by Melanesians, a dark-skinned people with frizzy hair, thick lips, and flattened nose, in general of negroid stock but often showing traces of Polynesian admixture. Melanesia includes Fiji, New Caledonia, New Hebrides, Loyalty Is., Solomon Is., Santa Cruz Is., Admiralty Is., and the Louisiade and Bismarck archipelagoes.

**Melbourne** Australia. Capital of Victoria, on the Yarra R. near the outlet into Hobson's Bay, Port Phillip Bay. Pop. (metropolitan area, 1966) 2,110,168 (66 per cent of the state population). Second city of Australia and chief seaport of the state; includes Port Melbourne and Williamstown, together handling about one quarter of the Commonwealth shipping. Most of the industries of the state are located in the city and its suburbs. Engineering, oil refining, meat processing, fruit canning. Manufactures agricultural machinery, vehicles, aircraft, electrical equipment, woollen textiles, fertilizers, soap. Exports wool, flour, dairy produce, meat, fruit, canned produce. Among its notable buildings are the Anglican and Roman Catholic cathedrals and the State Parliament House; has a famous cricket ground, the Flemington racecourse, and spacious botanical gardens. Founded 1835; soon became a commercial centre and, like the state, developed rapidly after the gold rush of 1851. University (1854). First capital of the Commonwealth 1901–27.

**Melcombe Regis** ◊ *Weymouth and Melcombe Regis.*

**Melilla** Spanish N Africa. Seaport and garrison town, on the Mediterranean coast of N Africa 160 m. ESE of Tangier; an enclave in Morocco. Pop. (1967) 74,880. Important fishing port. Exports iron ore from the Beni bu Ifrur mines (10 m. SW). Founded by the Phoenicians; later occupied by the Carthaginians and the Ro-

mans. Taken by Spain 1470; has remained Spanish despite many sieges, including that during the revolt led by Abdel Krim (1921–6; ◊ *Rif, Er*). Spanish troops withdrew from Morocco to the enclaves of Melilla and Ceuta in 1961.

**Melitopol** USSR. Town in the Ukrainian SSR, on the Molochnaya R. 70 m. S of Zaporozhye. Pop. (1970) 137,000. Manufactures agricultural machinery, diesel engines, clothing. Flour milling, meat packing.

**Melksham** England. Urban district in Wiltshire, on the R. Avon 9 m. E of Bath. Pop. (1961) 8,279. Market town. Manufactures tyres and rubber products, condensed milk. Bacon and ham curing. Formerly important in the wool trade.

**Melos (Milos)** Greece. Island of volcanic origin in the Cyclades, 14 m. long and 8 m. wide, in the Aegean Sea. Pop. 5,000. Here the statue known as the Venus de Milo, now in the Louvre, was discovered (1820).

**Melrose** Scotland. Small burgh in Roxburghshire, on the R. Tweed 6 m. NE of Selkirk. Pop. (1961) 2,133. Market town. Resort favoured by tourists wishing to explore the 'Scott country'. The ruins of the 12th-cent. Cistercian abbey, which was destroyed and rebuilt several times and in which Robert Bruce's heart is buried, became national property in 1918; it was described in Scott's *The Lay of the Last Minstrel*, while the town appears as Kennaquhair in his *The Abbot* and *The Monastery*.

**Melrose** USA. Town in Massachusetts 7 m. N of Boston. Pop. (1960) 29,619. Mainly residential. First settled *c*. 1630.

**Melton Mowbray** England. Urban district in Leicestershire 14 m. NE of Leicester. Pop. (1961) 15,913. Market town. Produces pork pies, Stilton cheese, pet foods. Also a well-known fox-hunting centre.

**Memel** ◊ *Klaipéda.*

**Memel River** ◊ *Neman River.*

**Memel Territory** (Ger. **Memelland**) USSR. Narrow strip of land in the Lithuanian SSR extending SE from the Baltic, bounded on the S by the Neman R., and including the port of Memel (now ◊ *Klaipéda*). Area 1,026 sq. m. Formerly in E Prussia; ceded by Germany after the 1st World War (1919), and was administered by France under the League of Nations. Occupied by Lithuania in 1923, however, for practically all the rural inhabitants were Lithuanians, and it was granted to that country in 1924, having the status of an autonomous region. In

1939 it was reoccupied by Germany, but at the end of the 2nd World War (1945) it was incorporated into the USSR as part of the Lithuanian SSR.

**Memmingen** Federal German Republic. Industrial town and railway junction in Bavaria 32 m. SSE of Ulm. Pop. (1963) 31,300. Manufactures textiles, machinery, soap, etc.

**Memphis** United Arab Republic. Ancient city in Egypt, on the left bank of the Nile 14 m. S of Cairo. The first capital of united ancient Egypt; probably founded by Menes, the first Pharaoh. Pyramids of the Old and Middle Kingdoms extend for 20 m. along the Nile to Giza. Under the Ptolemies, second in importance to Alexandria; finally declined when the Arabs founded El Fustat (to the N) and used its stones to build the new city (later Cairo). ⟡ *Sakkara*.

**Memphis** USA. Commercial and industrial city in SW Tennessee, on the Chickasaw bluffs, above the Mississippi R. Pop. (1970) 620,873. River port. Railway centre. Important market for cotton and timber. Manufactures agricultural machinery, tyres and other rubber products, glass, textiles, etc. Well provided with parks, museums, and art galleries. The name was suggested by the similarity of its location on the Mississippi to that of the ancient Egyptian city of Memphis on the Nile.

**Menado (Manado)** Indonesia. Capital of N Sulawesi (Celebes) province, near the E end of the NE peninsula. Pop. (1961) 129,912. Principal seaport of N Celebes. Exports copra, coffee, nutmegs.

**Menai Strait** Wales. Channel 15 m. long separating Caernarvonshire from Anglesey, crossed by a suspension bridge (road) and a tubular bridge (railway) near the small town of Menai Bridge (Anglesey).

**Menam Chao Phraya (Menam)** Thailand. The chief river, 750 m. long, rising in the N highlands near the boundary with Laos, and flowing generally S by a winding course past Ayutthaya and Bangkok to the Gulf of Siam. In its lower course, where it is much used for the transportation of rice and teak, it has a parallel branch, the Tachin, to the W. Navigable for small vessels almost throughout its length. Much fishing. Menam means 'river'.

**Mendaña Islands** ⟡ *Marquesas Islands*.

**Menderes River** Turkey. Name of several rivers, the most important being the Büyük Menderes ('Great Menderes'), in the SW, 250 m. long, flowing generally WSW through a valley where figs and olives are cultivated to the Aegean Sea. Has a winding course: the term 'meander' derives from its ancient name (Maeander).

**Mendip Hills** England. Range of hills in Somerset extending 23 m. ESE from Axbridge and rising to 1,068 ft in Blackdown. Composed mainly of carboniferous limestone; includes the famous Cheddar Gorge and numerous caves, some of which have yielded human and animal prehistoric remains.

**Mendoza** Argentina. Capital of Mendoza province, in the valley of the Mendoza R., in the Andean foothills, at a height of 2,500 ft. Pop. (1960) 109,000. Commercial centre in an irrigated region known as 'the garden of the Andes', dealing chiefly in wine. University (1939). Largely destroyed by earthquake 1861. The new planned city is characterized by broad avenues, squares, and attractive public parks.

**Mendoza River** Argentina. River 200 m. long, rising on the slopes of Mt Aconcagua, flowing E and N across the Mendoza province, and entering L. Guanacache. Followed by the Transandine railway to Mendoza. Used for hydroelectric power and irrigation.

**Mengo** ⟡ *Kampala*.

**Menindee** ⟡ *Broken Hill* (Australia).

**Menorca** ⟡ *Minorca*.

**Menton** (Italian Mentone) France. Town in the Alpes-Maritimes department 13 m. ENE of Nice on the Mediterranean coast near the Italian border. Pop. (1968) 25,271. Fashionable resort in an attractive setting, with a backcloth of mountains and subtropical vegetation including orange, lemon, and olive trees. Belonged to Monaco 1815–48, proclaimed its independence, and in 1860 was ceded to France.

**Menzala (Menzaleh), Lake** ⟡ *Manzala, Lake*.

**Mequinez** ⟡ *Meknès*.

**Merano** Italy. Town in Bolzano province, Trentino-Alto Adige, 16 m. NW of Bolzano. Pop. (1961) 30,614. Tourist centre and winter resort. Fruit canning, pottery manufacture, etc. Gothic church (14th/15th-cent.); 15th-cent. palace.

**Mercedes** (Buenos Aires) Argentina. Industrial town and railway junction in Buenos Aires province 60 m. W of Buenos Aires. Pop. 40,000. Manufactures metal goods, footwear, etc.

**Mercedes** (Villa Mercedes) (San Luis) Argentina. Railway junction and commercial town in San Luis province 60 m. ESE of San Luis. Pop. 40,000. Trade in wheat, maize, alfalfa, etc.

**Mercedes** Uruguay. Capital of the Soriano department in the SW, on the Río Negro 160 m. NW of Montevideo. Pop. 40,000. Resort. River port. Livestock centre. Trade in cereals, wool.

**Mer de Glace** France. Glacier 4½ m. long on the N slope of Mont Blanc, formed from 3 confluent glaciers: Talèfre, Leschaux, Tacul. Much visited by tourists. The Arveyron R., tributary of the Arve R., flows from it.

**Mergui Archipelago** Burma. Group of several hundred islands off the Tenasserim coast, in the Andaman Sea. Mountainous, largely covered with forest, picturesque, and sparsely populated. Products include edible birds' nests, bêche-de-mer, pearls.

**Mérida** Mexico. Capital of the Yucatán state, in the SE. Pop. (1969) 200,900. Industrial, commercial, and tourist centre. Manufactures rope, twine, sacks, etc. from the locally produced henequen sisal. Exports indigo, sugar, henequen, hides, timber, through its port Progreso. Founded (1542) on the site of a Mayan city. Some fine 16th-cent. buildings remain, including the cathedral and a Franciscan convent. In the Park of the Americas there is an open-air theatre.

**Mérida** Spain. Ancient Emerita Augusta. Town in Badajoz province, on the Guadiana R. 35 m. E of Badajoz. Pop. (1961) 34,297. Rail and road junction. Market town. Famous chiefly for its Roman remains, inc. bridge over the Guadiana, theatre, amphitheatre, and circus, a triumphal arch of Trajan, two aqueducts, and a fort which was converted into a Moorish alcázar or citadel. Founded 25 B.C. As capital of Lusitania it was one of the finest cities in Iberia, and it still prospered under the Visigoths and Moors. Taken from the latter by Alfonso IX of León (1228), and soon declined.

**Mérida** Venezuela. Capital of the Mérida state (W), at the foot of the Sierra Nevada de Mérida at a height of 5,385 ft. Pop. (1961) 40,404. Manufactures textiles, furniture, etc. Seat of the University of Los Andes (1785). Founded 1558. Often damaged by earthquakes, esp. in 1812 and 1894.

**Meriden** USA. Industrial town in Connecticut 17 m. NNE of New Haven. Pop. (1960) 51,850. Varied industries, inc. the manufacture of silverware, ball bearings, glass, electrical equipment.

**Meridian** USA. Town in Mississippi 87 m. E of Jackson. Pop. (1960) 49,374. Manufactures textiles, clothing, cottonseed oil, etc.

**Merionethshire** Wales. County bordering W on Cardigan Bay, triangular in shape. Area 660 sq. m. Pop. (1961) 39,007. County town Dolgellau. Mountainous, rising to 2,927 ft in Cader Idris. Many lakes, the largest being L. Bala. Drained by the R. Dee. Sheep and cattle raised on a small scale. Limestone and slate quarried. Chief towns Dolgellau, Barmouth, Bala, Corwen.

**Merksem** Belgium. Town in Antwerp province 2 m. NE of Antwerp. Pop. (1968) 39,659. Manufactures glassware etc.

**Meroë** Sudan. Ancient city on the right bank of the Nile near Kabushiya (120 m. NE of Khartoum). Formerly a capital of the Ethiopian kingdom (700–300 B.C.) and later of the Meroitic kingdom (till A.D. 350). The latter included the Meroë Insula ('Isle of Meroë'), the region bounded by the Nile, the Blue Nile, and the Atbara R. Excavations (chiefly 1909–14 and 1921–3) revealed the ruins of palaces and temples, with groups of pyramids near by.

**Merrimack River** USA. River 110 m. long, formed by the union of the Pemigewasset and Winnipesaukee rivers, flowing S through New Hampshire, then ENE across NE Massachusetts, and entering the Atlantic near Newburyport.

**Merse** ◊ *Berwickshire.*

**Merseburg** German Democratic Republic. Town in the Halle district, 10 m. S of Halle on the Saale R. Pop. (1965) 54,467. Tanning, brewing. Manufactures paper, machinery, etc. Cathedral (11th/16th-cent.); 15th-cent. bishop's palace.

**Mersey River** England. River 70 m. long formed by the union of the Goyt and the Etherow rivers, flowing W along the Lancashire–Cheshire border to enter the Irish Sea by a 16-m. estuary. Tributaries the Irwell and the Weaver; also joined by the Manchester Ship Canal at Eastham. Warrington, Widnes, Runcorn, Liverpool, and Birkenhead stand on its banks and make it commercially the second most important river in the country. Liverpool and Birkenhead are connected across it by railway (1856) and road (1934) tunnels.

**Mersin** Turkey. Capital of Içel province

35 m. WSW of Adana. Pop. (1965) 87,000. Chief seaport on the S coast. Exports cotton, wool, chrome, etc. Large oil refinery (opened 1962).

**Merthyr Tydfil** Wales. County borough in Glamorganshire, on the R. Taff 20 m. NNW of Cardiff. Pop. (1961) 59,008 (80,116 in 1921; 71,108 in 1931). Engineering. Manufactures washing machines, chemicals, toys, etc. Ironworks were established in the 18th cent. and the town became one of the leading iron and steel centres in Britain. Suffered severely in the economic depression between the two world wars, however; there is still coal-mining, but the town is now largely dependent on light industries. The name is supposed to be derived from St Tydfil, a Welsh princess martyred by the Saxons in the 5th cent.

**Merton** England. From 1965 a Greater London borough, in the SW, comprising the former urban district of Merton and Morden and the municipal boroughs of Mitcham and Wimbledon, all in Surrey. Pop. (1963) 188,621. Mainly residential. Manufactures toys etc. Remains of a 12th-cent. Augustinian priory where Thomas à Becket and Walter de Merton were educated.

**Meru, Mount** ◊ *Tanzania*.

**Mesa** USA. Town in Arizona, on the Salt R. 13 m. E of Phoenix. Pop. (1960) 33,772. Commercial centre. Cotton ginning, citrus-fruit packing. Manufactures helicopters. Founded (1878) by Mormons.

**Mesa Verde** USA. High plateau in SW Colorado, of great archaeological interest. Occupied for many centuries till A.D. 1300, it has well-preserved pueblos and cliff dwellings. The Mesa Verde National Park (80 sq. m.) was established (1906) in order to preserve these settlements.

**Meshed (Mashhad)** Iran. Capital of Khurasan province, 440 m. ENE of Tehran at a height of 3,200 ft. Pop. (1966) 417,171. Important commercial and industrial centre. Trade in carpets, cotton goods, etc. Manufactures rugs. Tanning, flour milling, etc. The most sacred city in Iran, for it contains the golden-domed tomb of the Imam Riza, and is a place of pilgrimage for Muslims of the Shia sect – to which most Iranians belong. University (1955). About 15 m. NW are the ruins of Tus, birthplace and burial place of Firdausi, the great Persian poet of the 10th–11th cent.

**Mesolóngion** ◊ *Missolonghi*.

**Mesopotamia.** Name applied rather loosely to a region of SW Asia between the Armenian mountains (N) and the Persian Gulf (S) and between the Syrian Desert (W) and the plateau of Iran (E), and sometimes held to correspond to modern Iraq. It belongs more strictly, however, to the N part of this area between the Tigris and the Euphrates rivers, i.e. about as far S as Baghdad. The name, derived from Greek, means 'Between the Rivers'.

**Messenia** Greece. *Nome* in the SW Peloponnese, bordering W and S on the Ionian Sea. Area 1,315 sq. m. Pop. (1961) 210,728. Cap. Kalamáta. Mainly agricultural. Produces citrus fruits, vines, olives, wheat, etc.

**Messina** Italy. Ancient Zancle. Capital of Messina province, in Sicily, on the W shore of the Strait of Messina 54 m. NNE of Catania. Pop. (1968) 269,267. Seaport. Industrial centre. Exports olive oil, wine, citrus fruits. Manufactures macaroni, chemicals, soap, etc. Twice severely damaged by earthquakes, in 1783 and 1908, the latter being particularly disastrous; the city has few old buildings, and modern structures are generally low as a precaution against further possible shocks. The cathedral was rebuilt in the original 11th-cent. style, but again suffered damage in the 2nd World War. University (1549). Colonized by Greeks in the 8th cent. B.C. Held in turn by Carthaginians, Mamertines, Romans, Saracens, Normans, and Spaniards. The last city in Sicily to be liberated by Garibaldi (1860).

**Messina, Strait of** Italy. Strait between Italy and Sicily, 20 m. long, 8 m. wide in the S but only 2 m. in the N. Feared by sailors in ancient times for its currents and whirlpools, the latter giving rise to the legend of Scylla and Charybdis.

**Meta River** Colombia/Venezuela. River 620 m. long, rising S of Bogotá, flowing NE and E across the grassy plains (llanos), and joining the Orinoco R. Forms part of the Colombia–Venezuela frontier. Floods extensively in the rainy season (May–Oct.).

**Metohija** ◊ *Kosovo-Metohija*.

**Metz** France. Ancient Divodurum, Mediomatrica. Prefecture of the Moselle department, on the Moselle R. at the confluence with the Seille R. 27 m. N of Nancy. Pop. (1968) 113,586. Centre of the Lorraine iron-mining region. Tanning, brewing flour milling, fruit and vegetable preserving. Manufactures footwear, cement, metal goods, etc. In the old town are the 13th/16th-cent. cathedral and the castellated 15th-cent. Porte des Allemands. Chief town of the ancient Mediomatrici. Became a free imperial city in the 13th cent. Annexed to France 1552. Ceded to Germany after the Franco-Prussian War (1871), but returned to France after the 1st World War (1918). Birthplace of Paul Verlaine (1844–96).

**Meudon** France. Suburb of SW Paris, on the Seine R. in the Hauts-de-Seine department. Pop. (1968) 51,481. Manufactures munitions, electrical equipment, etc. Observatory. The Forest of Meudon to the SW is a favourite resort for Parisians.

**Meurthe-et-Moselle** France. Department in Lorraine formed (1871) from parts of the old Meurthe and Moselle departments left to France after the Franco-Prussian War; bounded on the N by Belgium and Luxembourg. Area 2,036 sq. m. Pop. (1968) 705,413. Prefecture Nancy. In the main a plateau drained by the Moselle and its tributary the Meurthe, it is less important for its agriculture than for its rich iron deposits and its metallurgical industry, centred on Nancy, Longwy, and Briey. Other towns Lunéville, Toul.

**Meuse** France. Department in the NE formed mainly from Lorraine and drained by the Meuse R. Area 2,410 sq. m. Pop. (1968) 209,513. Prefecture Bar-le-Duc. Along the banks of the Meuse SSE–NNW run two ridges, the Argonne (W) and the Côtes de Meuse (E). Cereals, potatoes, and fruits cultivated in the valleys. Scene of heavy fighting in the 1st World War. Chief towns Bar-le-Duc, Commercy, Verdun.

**Meuse** (Dutch **Maas**) **River.** River 580 m. long, rising on the Plateau de Langres in the Haute-Marne department, France, flowing generally NNW between the Argonne and the Côtes de Meuse past Sedan and Mézières-Charleville. It turns N through the Ardennes, NE past Namur and Liège (Belgium) and Maastricht (Netherlands), then W to join the Waal, a distributary of the Rhine. Picturesque in the upper course. Carries a great deal of traffic in the lower reaches.

**Mexborough** England. Urban district in the W Riding of Yorkshire, on the R. Don 11 m. NE of Sheffield. Pop. (1961) 17,095. Coalmining centre. Flour milling.

**Mexicali** Mexico. Capital of the Baja (Lower) California state, in the NW, on the US frontier adjoining Calexico (California). Pop. (1969) 427,200. Commercial centre for an irrigated agricultural area producing cotton, alfalfa, dates, grapefruit, vines. Cotton ginning. Manufactures cottonseed oil, soap, etc. Almost completely Americanized.

**Mexico.** Federal republic in N America. Area 760,373 sq. m. Pop. (1969) 48,933,000. Cap. Mexico City. Lang. Spanish (and 35 differing Indian dialects).

The narrowing southern extremity of N America, between the Pacific (W and SW) and the Gulf of Mexico and the Caribbean Sea (E); bordered on the N by the USA along the Rio Grande (Río Bravo) and on the SE by Guatemala and British Honduras. Third largest country in Latin America, with the second largest population and the greatest industrial development. The great natural resources are now being increasingly utilized for the benefit of the nation as a whole. The people range from pure Indian to pure European; there is full social equality and intermarriage, and though there are wide differences in living standards these do not (as in so many other Latin American countries) coincide with race. Political and financial stability is an encouraging background for continuing progress. Administratively divided into 29 states, a Federal District (Distrito Federal) of 573 sq. m. with Mexico City, and two territories (Baja California Sur and Quintana Roo).

TOPOGRAPHY, CLIMATE. Few islands, but two large peninsulas: in the extreme NW the 760-m. peninsula of Lower California (Baja California), separated from the mainland (except in the N) by the Gulf of California; and in the SE the Yucatán peninsula, extending N from the mainland and dividing the Gulf of Mexico from the Caribbean Sea. The broad Gulf of Campeche washes the SE coast and forms an arm of the Gulf of Mexico. Extremely mountainous; the dominating physical feature is the Sierra Madre (consisting of two separate ranges, the Sierra Madre Oriental along the Gulf of Mexico and the Sierra Madre Occidental along the Pacific), covering about three quarters of the country. The highest peaks, which are in the Anáhuac region in the interior, are the three magnificent snow-capped volcanoes, Pico de Orizaba (Citlaltépetl, 18,700 ft),

Popocatépetl, and Ixtaccihuatl (the two latter both over 17,000 ft). The new volcano Paricutín was created in 1943. Apart from the Rio Grande, the chief rivers are the Río de las Balsas and the Pánuco, Grijalva, Santiago, and Conchos rivers. The largest lake is L. Chapala (417 sq. m.).

Though the Tropic of Cancer crosses the centre of Mexico, the climate is determined more by altitude than by latitude. There is a hot zone (*tierra caliente*) along the coast, at up to 3,000 ft; a temperate zone (*tierra templada*) at 3,000–6,000 ft; and a cold zone (*tierra fria*) at above 6,000 ft. Annual rainfall (mainly June-Sept.) varies from about 2 ins. in Sonora (NW) to over 120 ins. in the jungles of Tabasco (SE).

RESOURCES, PEOPLE, *etc.* Owing to the limitations imposed by climate and topography, scarcely 5 per cent of the land is under cultivation. Maize is the basic food, but production is insufficient because of primitive methods; large quantities of this and other foodstuffs have to be imported. Export crops include cotton (grown largely in Coahuila and Durango), sugar, and coffee. Half the world supply of henequen sisal is grown in the Yucatán peninsula. The Mexican aloe (maguey) is widely grown to produce the national alcoholic drink, pulque. Irrigation is important in agriculture, but the country will not be self-sufficient in food till the area irrigated is trebled. Exceptionally rich in minerals: the world's largest supplier of silver; lead, zinc, copper, sulphur, etc. also of importance. Extensive coal resources. Iron mining has a promising future: the Cerro del Mercado (outside the city of Durango) is a hill almost entirely composed of iron ore, and the Peña Colorada field in Colima has great possibilities. In 1959 uranium deposits were discovered. Though nearly all the mines are foreign-owned, the oil-fields (mainly in the E, in the Tehuantepec Isthmus and the states of Tamaulipas and Veracruz) are state-owned: the foreign companies which had developed them were expropriated in 1938. Industries are varied and scattered; iron and steel manufacture is centred at Monterrey and textiles at Puebla and elsewhere. In recent years industrial production has greatly increased. Over half a million US tourists swell the country's foreign earnings. After Mexico City, the largest cities are Guada-lajara, Monterrey, Puebla, Ciudad Juárez, León.

Spanish influence is strong, but Mexican culture and outlook is a distinctive amalgam of Spanish and Indian; in many towns buildings are designed in the Spanish-Moorish or Spanish-colonial style, though in recent years modern architecture has been introduced in the main cities, esp. in Mexico City.

HISTORY. A number of ancient civilizations have flourished in the lands occupied by modern Mexico, which takes its name from the central valley ruled by the Aztecs at the time of the coming of the Spaniards. In Yucatán, farther S, was the last centre of the Mayan civilization, then already in decline. The Aztecs, although they had neither metal tools nor the wheel, had evolved a highly sophisticated culture, marred by their obsession with the need for human sacrifice to propitiate their gods; their capital, Tenochtitlán, aroused the admiration and the cupidity of the Spanish invaders, who by 1521 destroyed both the capital and the Aztec rulers. A 300-year period of Spanish rule began. Mexican independence was regained, in 1821, when General Iturbide established his empire; when he died (1824) a republic was set up. At that time Mexico possessed large areas in what is now the USA; in 1836 Texas rebelled and formed an independent republic, joining the USA in 1845. This led to the Mexican War (1846–8), as a result of which Mexico ceded to the US all territories N of the Rio Grande. The country thus acquired its present boundaries, and, except for the brief French occupation (1864–7) under the Emperor Maximilian, it has remained a republic. After a half-century of political disorder Porfirio Díaz assumed power in 1876 and was installed as president, remaining in office (except 1880–84) until 1910. He imposed stability, encouraged foreign investment, and developed the railways and mining industries, but also ruthlessly suppressed opposition and ignored the grinding poverty of the masses. A spontaneous rebellion against his dictatorship (1910) became a revolution inaugurating the modern period of Mexican history, marking the beginning of an era of reform which has included the new constitution of 1917 and the progressive Cárdenas administration (1934–40).

**Mexico** Mexico. State on the central

plateau, comprising part of the valley of Mexico, and the Toluca Valley. Area 8,284 sq. m. Pop. (1969) 2,803,000. Cap. Toluca. The volcanoes Popocatépetl (17,887 ft) and Ixtaccihuatl (17,342 ft) are on the SE border. The Federal District, containing Mexico City, the national capital, is administratively separate. Main occupations agriculture, dairy farming, mining (silver, gold, copper, lead, zinc). Bulls for the bull-rings bred in the Toluca Valley. The most notable of Aztec and pre-Aztec remains is the Pyramid of the Sun at Teotihuacán.

**Mexico, Gulf of.** Arm of the Atlantic Ocean, bounded by the USA (N and NE) and Mexico (W and SW). Linked with the Atlantic by the Florida Strait and with the Caribbean Sea by the Yucatán Channel. Area 700,000 sq. m. The most important rivers flowing into it are the Mississippi and the Rio Grande. Shores generally low and sandy, with many lagoons; few harbours. Has considerable influence on the climate of N America; a branch of the Equatorial Current enters it via the Yucatán Channel and originates the Gulf Stream.

**Mexico City** Mexico. Capital of Mexico and of the Federal District, near the S end of the central plateau at a height of 7,400 ft. Pop. (1969) 3,484,000; Federal District (1969) 7,425,000. Dominated by the snow-capped Sierra Nevada, with the lofty volcanoes Popocatépetl and Ixtaccihuatl to the SE. Mild, healthy climate; rainfall 20–25 ins. annually. The administrative, commercial, industrial, and cultural centre. Roads, railways, and airways radiate from it. Manufactures textiles, glass, tyres, tobacco products, etc. Motor-vehicle assembly, gold and silver refining, brewing. Architecture ranges from Spanish-Baroque to modern skyscrapers; there has been much demolition and rebuilding in recent years. The cathedral, begun in 1573, stands with other public buildings (inc. the National Palace) on the Plaza Mayor (Zócalo), the central square into which many of the main streets lead. Seat of the National University (founded 1551). Also has a mint, a large bull-ring, and many interesting churches. Built on the site of the Aztec capital Tenochtitlán, captured and destroyed by Cortés 1521. Mexico's first nuclear reactor, in the mountains just W of the city, began to operate 1968.

**Mézenc, Mont** ◊ *Cévennes.*

**Mezötur** Hungary. Town in Szolnok county 24 m. ESE of Szolnok. Pop. 29,000. Agricultural centre. Trade in cereals, livestock. Flour milling. Manufactures pottery, bricks.

**Miami** USA. Largest city in Florida and famous holiday resort, on Biscayne Bay at the mouth of the short Miami R. Pop. (1960) 291,688. Warm climate and magnificent beaches. Greater Miami includes Miami Beach, Coral Gables, and Hialeah. Important airport and harbour. Varied industries. The main development came with the Florida land boom of the 1920s. University (1925), at Coral Gables.

**Miami Beach** Florida. Holiday resort on an island in SE Florida, separated from Miami by Biscayne Bay. Pop. (1960) 63,145. Connected with Miami by causeways and bridges.

**Michigan** USA. State on the Great Lakes. Area 58,216 sq. m. Pop. (1970) 8,776,873. Cap. Lansing. Admitted to the Union in 1837 as the 26th state; popularly known as the 'Wolverine' state. The Lower Peninsula (S) and the Upper Peninsula (N) are separated by the narrow Straits of Mackinac. Generally low-lying; rises to 2,023 ft in the Porcupine Mountains of the Upper Peninsula. The generally continental climate is much modified by the Great Lakes. Annual rainfall 25–35 ins. About 40 per cent of the land is cultivated. Main crops maize, oats, hay, wheat, sugar-beet, potatoes, fruits. The best farmlands are in the S part of the Lower Peninsula. Cattle and pig rearing also important. Principal mineral iron ore (from the Upper Peninsula), followed by petroleum. Leading industry automobile manufacture; produces about half the USA's motor vehicles. Chief towns Detroit, Flint, Grand Rapids, Dearborn, Lansing. First explored by the French in the early 17th cent. The first permanent settlement was established (1668) by Marquette at Sault Ste Marie. Ceded to England in 1763 and to the USA in 1783 (as part of the NW Territory). Became a separate territory in 1805, comprising only the Lower Peninsula; the Upper Peninsula was added on the attainment of statehood (1837).

**Michigan, Lake** USA. Third largest of the Great Lakes, the only one wholly within the USA, at a height of 580 ft. Area 22,400 sq. m. Linked with L. Huron by the Straits of Mackinac (NE). Carries an immense amount of shipping. Leading ports Chicago, Milwaukee. Main cargoes coal, iron ore, grain.

**Michigan City** USA. Industrial town, port, and resort in Indiana, on L. Michigan, 23 m. ENE of Gary. Pop. (1960) 36,653. Manufactures furniture, machinery, etc.

**Michoacán** Mexico. Mountainous state on the Pacific seaboard, with a narrow coastal plain. Area 23,202 sq. m. Pop. (1969) 2,452,000 (largely Tarascan Indians). Cap. Morelia. Several volcanoes, inc. Paricutín. Many large lakes. Cereals, sugar-cane, rice, tobacco, etc. cultivated. Minerals include silver, lead, copper.

**Michurinsk** USSR. Formerly Kozlov. Town in RSFSR on the Voronezh R. 42 m. WNW of Tambov. Pop. (1961) 84,000. Railway junction. Industrial centre. Railway and other engineering. Founded 1636. Became an important horticultural centre, with an experimental institute founded by the botanist Michurin, and was named after him in the 1930s.

**Micronesia** W Pacific Ocean. One of the three main divisions of the Pacific islands, in the W Pacific N of Melanesia, the others being Melanesia and Polynesia. Inhabited by Micronesians, people of medium stature, their skin of varying shades of brown, with black curly hair, a mixture of Melanesian and Polynesian strains. Micronesia includes the Caroline, Marshall, Mariana, and Gilbert Is., and Nauru Is.

**Middelburg** Netherlands. Capital of Zeeland province, on Walcheren island 4 m. NNE of Flushing. Pop. (1968) 28,416. Market town, linked by canal with Flushing. Railway engineering. Manufactures furniture etc. An important commercial centre in medieval times. Has a 12th-cent. abbey. Suffered severely in the 2nd World War.

**Middelburg** S Africa. Town in the Transvaal 80 m. E of Pretoria at a height of 5,000 ft. Pop. (1960) 12,907. On one of S Africa's richest coalfields. The district also produces cereals, tobacco, etc.

**Middleback Range** Australia. Sandstone range in S Australia, 40 m. long N–S, in the Eyre Peninsula. Rich deposits of iron ore, exported via Whyalla, mining being mainly in open workings at Iron Knob, Iron Monarch, and Iron Baron.

**Middlesbrough** England. Industrial town in the N Riding of Yorkshire, on the S bank of the Tees estuary, spanned by transporter (1911) and lift (1934) bridges. Pop. (1961) 157,038. From 1968 part of the county borough of ◊ *Teesside*. Important iron and steel centre. Also manufactures chemicals, fertilizers, etc. Harbour protected by two large breakwaters. Exports iron and steel, machinery, chemicals, etc. Imports iron ore, timber, etc. Its rapid development in the 19th cent. was due to the discovery of iron ore in the neighbouring Cleveland Hills and the opening of the Stockton–Darlington railway. Marton, 3 m. SSW, was the birthplace of Captain Cook (1728–79).

**Middlesex** England. Former county in the SE, bounded by Hertfordshire (N), Essex (E), the County of London (SE), Surrey (S), and Buckinghamshire (W); the second smallest county. Area 232 sq. m. Pop. (1961) 2,230,093. Generally lowlying, rising from the R Thames (S) to hills on the N boundary which reach 500 ft. Mainly residential and industrial. Chief municipal boroughs were Harrow, Ealing, Willesden, Hendon, Wembley. Historic buildings Hampton Court Palace, Syon House. In 1965 almost the entire county was absorbed into Greater London (◊ *London*). The only places excluded were the former urban districts of Staines and Sunbury-on-Thames (SW), which became part of Surrey, and Potters Bar (N), which became part of Hertfordshire.

**Middleton** England. Municipal borough in Lancashire, on the R. Irk 5 m. NNE of Manchester. Pop. (1961) 56,674. Manufactures textiles, textile machinery, foam rubber, etc.

**Middletown** (Connecticut) USA. Industrial town on the Connecticut R. Pop. (1960) 32,250. Manufactures textiles, hardware, etc. Seat of the Wesleyan University (1831).

**Middletown** (Ohio) USA. Industrial town on the Great Miami R. 22 m. SW of Dayton. Pop. (1960) 42,115. Steel and paper mills.

**Middle West, The** USA. Loosely, the N part of central USA: Illinois, Indiana, Iowa, Michigan, Minnesota, Ohio, Wisconsin. Sometimes understood to include other peripheral states. One of the world's chief grain-producing areas (mainly maize and wheat). Many important industrial centres in the area of the Great Lakes.

**Middlewich** England. Urban district ·in Cheshire 7 m. N of Crewe. Pop. (1961) 6,833. The middle of the three 'wiches' or salt towns – the others being Northwich and Nantwich. Salt refining. Manufactures chemicals etc.

**Midhurst** England. Small town in W Sussex, on the R. Rother 10 m. N of Chichester. Pop. (rural district, 1961) 17,370. Has a 17th-cent. grammar school and the ruins of the 16th-cent. Cowdray House. Birthplace of Richard Cobden (1804–65) near by.

**Midland** (Michigan) USA. Industrial town 19 m. NW of Saginaw. Pop. (1960) 27,779. Important chemical industry. Oil refining. Manufactures cement products, toys, etc.

**Midland** (Texas) USA. Industrial town 280 m. WSW of Fort Worth. Pop. (1960) 62,625. In an oil-producing and cattle-ranching region. Oil refining. Manufactures oilfield equipment, chemicals, etc. Expanded rapidly in the 1950s.

**Midlands** England. The central counties, corresponding roughly to the Anglo-Saxon kingdom of Mercia, which originally comprised Staffordshire, Derbyshire, and Nottinghamshire and the N parts of Warwickshire and Leicestershire. Mercia expanded far beyond this area, however, and the term is often assumed to include also parts of Northants, Rutland, Bedfordshire, and Buckinghamshire.

**Midlothian** Scotland. Formerly Edinburghshire. County bordering N on the Firth of Forth. Area 366 sq. m. Pop. (1961) 580,332 (of whom more than four fifths live in Edinburgh). Administrative centre Edinburgh. Low-lying in the N, it rises to 2,137 ft in Blackhope Scar in the Moorfoot Hills (SE) and 1,898 ft in Scald Law in the Pentland Hills (SW); short rivers include the Esk, Almond, and Water of Leith. Cereals cultivated. Dairy farming and market gardening on the N plain. Coal and oil-shale mined. Chief towns Edinburgh, Dalkeith, Musselburgh, Portobello.

**Midnapore** India. Town in W Bengal 67 m. W of Calcutta. Pop. (1961) 59,532. Commercial centre. Trade in grain, groundnuts, etc. Manufactures textiles, copper and brass ware.

**Midway Islands** N Pacific Ocean. Atoll and two small islands 1,300 m. WNW of Honolulu. Area 2 sq. m. Pop. (1960) 2,356. The outer reef is 15 m. in circumference; the lagoon is entered on the S side, between the two islands. Discovered (1859) by Captain Brooks. Annexed by the USA 1867. A naval air base was established in 1941. The Americans decisively defeated the Japanese near by in an air-sea battle in 1942, the first serious reverse for the Japanese in the Pacific.

**Mieres** Spain. Town in Oviedo province, Asturias, 9 m. SSE of Oviedo. Pop. (1967) 68,458. Industrial centre in a coal- and iron-mining region. Steel and chemical manufactures.

**Mikínai** ◊ Mycenae.

**Milan** (Italian **Milano**) Italy. Ancient Mediolanum. Capital of Milano province and the country's second largest city, on the Olona R. and on the Plain of Lombardy. Pop. (1968) 1,683,680. Important railway, road, and canal junction. The country's chief industrial, commercial, and banking centre. Printing and publishing. Manufactures textiles, locomotives, cars, chemicals, machinery, etc. Large trade in raw silk, cereals, cheese, etc. In the heart of the city is the Piazza del Duomo, at one end of which is the great Gothic cathedral, with its many turrets and pinnacles and over 4,000 statues, the third largest church in Europe, begun in 1386 and not completed till the 19th cent. Among the oldest churches are S Ambrogio, founded by St Ambrose in 386, the present Romanesque building dating from the 12th cent., and S Lorenzo, several times restored since the 6th cent.; in the former refectory near the 15th-cent S Maria delle Grazie is Leonardo da Vinci's world-famous painting of *The Last Supper*. There are notable art galleries and museums in the Palazzo di Brera, the Palazzo dell'Ambrosiana, and the Castello Sforzesco. The celebrated La Scala theatre (1778) was severely damaged in the 2nd World War, like many other historic buildings, and was rebuilt. Both the universities were founded in the 1920s. Important in Roman times. Destroyed by the Huns and later the Goths; passed to the Lombards 569. Ruled by the Visconti family 1277–1447 and by the Sforza family 1450–1535. Napoleon made it capital of the Cisalpine Republic (1797) and of the kingdom of Italy 1805–14. United with Italy 1861, and rapidly developed into an industrial city.

**Mildenhall** England. Market town in NW Suffolk, on the Lark R. 19 m. NE of Cambridge. Pop. (rural district, 1961) 20,485. Important R A F station. A valuable hoard of Roman silverware dating from the 4th cent. A.D. was discovered near by in 1942.

**Mildura** Australia. Town in Victoria, on the Murray R. 300 m. NW of Melbourne. Pop. (1966) 12,931. Centre of an irrigated region, built on gridiron pattern, amid

483 MINDORO

vineyards and orchards of citrus fruits, apricots, peaches, etc. Fruit and vegetables canned and packed; dried fruits, wool, and wheat are handled.

**Miletus** Turkey. Ancient city and seaport in Asia Minor, near the mouth of the Maeander (◊ *Menderes*) R. Leading commercial centre of Ionia, with an extensive trade in the Black Sea area, where it had founded more than 60 cities by the mid 7th cent. B.C. Also a centre of learning. Birthplace of such famous Greeks as Thales (640–546 B.C.) and Anaximander (611–547 B.C.). Its harbour was gradually silted up by the Maeander, however, and it declined.

**Milford** USA. Town in SW Connecticut, on Long Island Sound. Pop. (1960) 41,662. Resort. Oyster fisheries. Manufactures metal goods, hardware, etc. A typical old-fashioned New England town. Founded 1639.

**Milford Haven** Wales. Urban district in Pembrokeshire, on the N side of the inlet of the same name and 6 m. WNW of Pembroke. Pop. (1961) 12,802. Fishing port. Oil refining.

**Millau** ◊ *Aveyron.*

**Millwall** England. District in the Greater London borough of Tower Hamlets, on the Isle of Dogs. Contains Millwall Docks. Known as Marshwall until the 18th cent., when several windmills were set up in the area.

**Milngavie** Scotland. Small burgh in Dunbartonshire 5 m. NNW of Glasgow. Pop. (1961) 8,894. Mainly residential. Paper milling, bleaching and dyeing, etc.

**Milos** ◊ *Melos.*

**Milton** ◊ *Sittingbourne and Milton.*

**Milton Keynes** England. Site in N Buckinghamshire, nearly 22,000 acres in area, designated a 'new city'; largely in Newport Pagnell rural district, partly in Bletchley, Newport Pagnell and Wolverton urban districts, on the M1 motorway. Mainly intended to relieve congestion in Greater London. Pop. of area (1968) 41,000; anticipated pop. (A.D. 2000) 250,000.

**Milwaukee** USA. In Indian, 'Good Lands'. The largest city in Wisconsin and an important port on L. Michigan. Pop. (1970) 709,537. Large brewing and meat-packing industries. Manufactures heavy machinery, electrical equipment, leather goods, etc. Many canals and parks. Seat of the Marquette University (1881, Roman Catholic). Much of its development was due to German immigrants.

**Mina Hassan Tani** Morocco. Formerly Kénitra, Port Lyautey. Seaport on the Sebou R. 10 m. above the mouth, 25 m. NE of Rabat on the Rabat–Meknès railway. Pop. (1960) 86,775. Exports grain, cork, etc. Originally Kénitra; renamed Port Lyautey (after the French Marshal) 1932; became Kénitra again when Morocco gained independence (1956); renamed Mina Hassan Tani 1962.

**Minaragra** ◊ *Cerro de Pasco.*

**Minas** Uruguay. Capital of the Lavalleja department (SE), 65 m. ENE of Montevideo. Pop. 27,000. Granite and marble quarrying in the neighbourhood. Brewing etc. Founded 1783.

**Minas Gerais** Brazil. In Portuguese, 'Mines in General'. State in the E. Area 224,701 sq. m. (rather larger than France). Pop. (1960) 9,798,880. Cap. Belo Horizonte. Mainly plateau. Dry and usually pleasant climate. The first part of the interior to be settled, as a result of the discovery of gold and diamonds in the 18th cent. For 100 years the richest part of Brazil, centred on the earlier capital, Ouro Prêto. The gold is now largely exhausted, but the state is rich in minerals, esp. iron ore. Agriculture now well developed: maize, beans, coffee, cotton, tobacco, fruit are grown; dairy farming, cattle rearing. Belo Horizonte is a fast-growing industrial centre.

**Minch (North Minch)** Scotland. Arm of the Atlantic separating Lewis in the Outer Hebrides from the mainland, 20–46 m. wide. Continued SW by the Little Minch, 14–25 m. wide, separating Harris and N Uist from Skye.

**Mindanao** Philippines. Second largest island, at the S end of the group and NE of Borneo. Area 39,351 sq. m. Pop. 3,300,000. Chief towns Davao, Zamboanga. Irregular in shape, with several peninsulas. Densely forested. Mountainous, rising to 9,500 ft in Mt Apo, an active volcano. Abacá (Manila hemp), coconuts, rice, and maize cultivated. Gold mined.

**Minden** Federal German Republic. Town in N Rhine-Westphalia, on the Weser R. where it is crossed by the Mittelland Canal, 26 m. NE of Bielefeld. Pop. (1963) 48,900. Manufactures soap, chemicals, glass, etc. Brewing. The 11th/13th-cent. cathedral was destroyed in the 2nd World War. In 1759 the English and Hanoverians under Ferdinand, Duke of Brunswick, defeated the French here.

**Mindoro** Philippines. Island S of Luzon.

Area 3,952 sq. m. Pop. 205,000. Chief town Calapan (pop. 27,000). Interior mountainous, rising to over 8,000 ft. Rice, maize, coconuts, etc. cultivated.

**Minehead** England. Urban district in Somerset, on the Bristol Channel 21 m. NW of Taunton. Pop. (1961) 7,674. Seaside resort. Market town. A port of some importance from the 16th to the 18th cent., but later declined.

**Minho** ◊ *Entre Minho e Douro*.

**Minho River** ◊ *Miño River*.

**Minhow** ◊ *Foochow*.

**Minneapolis** USA. The largest city in Minnesota, on the Mississippi R. at the Falls of St Anthony (an important source of water power in the early development) and adjacent to St Paul; the 'Twin Cities' form the financial, commercial, and industrial centre of a large agricultural area. Pop. (1960) 482,872. One of the world's great wheat markets. Principal industry flour milling. Also manufactures other food products, agricultural machinery, clothing, etc. The silhouette of flour mills and creameries along the Mississippi has been called the 'bread-and-butter skyline'. In one of the parks are the Minnehaha Falls celebrated in Longfellow's *Hiawatha*. The beautiful L. Minnetonka is 12 m. W. Seat of the University of Minnesota (1851).

**Minnesota** USA. State in the N, on the Canadian frontier (N) and L. Superior (NE). Area 84,068 sq. m. Pop. (1970) 3,767,975. Cap. St Paul. Admitted to the Union in 1858 as the 32nd state; popularly known as the 'Gopher' state. Includes a small detached area on the W side of the Lake of the Woods, N of the 49th parallel, the most northerly part of continental USA (excluding Alaska). Mostly prairie, at a height of 1,000–1,500 ft. In the N it forms the watershed of three great drainage systems, Hudson Bay, the St Lawrence, and the Mississippi. Thousands of lakes, formed by glacial action. Climate continental. Annual rainfall 20–30 ins. Primarily agricultural. Main crops oats, maize, barley, rye. Leading state in butter production. Also produces (chiefly in the Mesabi Range) about half of the USA's iron ore. Principal towns Minneapolis, St Paul, Duluth. Early explorers were French missionaries and fur traders. The territory passed to Britain in 1763; the land E of the Mississippi was acquired by the USA in 1783 (from the British) and

that W of the river in 1803 (from the French).

**Miño (Minho) River.** River 210 m. long rising in the Sierra de Meira in Galicia (Spain), flowing generally SSW, then turning WSW past Orense and forming part of the Spanish-Portuguese border, entering the Atlantic near Caminha (Portugal).

**Minorca** (Sp. **Menorca**) Spain. Second largest of the Balearic Is. in the W Mediterranean, 25 m. ENE of Majorca. Area 271 sq. m. Pop. 43,000. Chief town and seaport Mahón. Generally low-lying, rising to only 1,107 ft in El Toro, it is exposed to north winds in winter, and has a less equable climate and less fertile soil than Majorca. Produces cereals, wine, olives. Livestock raised. Tourist industry, though much less developed than in Majorca.

**Minot** USA. Town in N Dakota, on the Souris R. 115 m. NNW of Bismarck. Pop. (1960) 30,604. Railway and commercial centre in an agricultural and lignite-mining region.

**Minsk** USSR. Capital of the Byelorussian SSR (White Russia), on the Svisloch R. Pop. (1970) 916,000. Important railway junction and industrial and cultural centre. Manufactures motor vehicles, tractors, machinery, bicycles, radio and television sets, textiles, furniture, etc. Seat of a university (1921) and the Byelorussian Academy of Sciences (1929). Conquered by Lithuania in the 14th and Poland in the 15th cent.; annexed by Russia 1793. During the 2nd World War it was almost completely destroyed, and its Jewish population, formerly 40 per cent of the total, fell to 2 per cent.

**Minya, El** United Arab Republic. Capital of Minya governorate, on the left bank of the Nile 135 m. S of Cairo. Pop. (1960) 94,000. River port. Trade in cotton and cereals. Sugar refining, cotton ginning.

**Mirfield** England. Urban district and industrial town in the W Riding of Yorkshire, on the R. Calder 4 m. NE of Huddersfield. Pop. (1961) 12,289. Railway and other engineering. Manufactures woollen goods. Seat of a theological college (Community of the Resurrection).

**Mirzapur** India. Town in SE Uttar Pradesh, on the Ganges R. 30 m. WSW of Varanasi (Benares). Pop. (1961) 100,097. Trade in grain, oilseeds, sugar-cane. Manufactures shellac, carpets, brassware. Its river banks are lined with bathing ghats and temples; within the municipality is Bindhachal, an important place of pilgrimage.

**Mishawaka** USA. Industrial town in N Indiana, on the St Joseph R. 4 m. ESE of South Bend. Pop. (1960) 33,361. Manufactures clothing, rubber products, metal goods, etc.

**Misima Island** ◊ *Louisiade Archipelago*.

**Miskito Coast** ◊ *Mosquito Coast*.

**Miskolc** Hungary. Capital of Borsod-Abaúj-Zemplén county in the NE, on the Sajó R. 90 m. ENE of Budapest. Pop. (1968) 180,000. Industrial centre, second in importance only to Budapest. Manufactures iron and steel (using local iron ore and lignite), railway rolling stock, textiles, leather goods, furniture, etc. Flour milling, wine making. Considerable trade in cattle, wine, tobacco. Seat of a technical university (1949). A 13th-cent. church and other ancient buildings.

**Mississippi** USA. State in the S, bordering SE on the Gulf of Mexico. Area 47,716 sq. m. Pop. (1970) 2,158,872 (over 900,000 Negroes). Cap. Jackson. Admitted to the Union in 1817 as the 20th state; popularly known as the 'Magnolia' or 'Bayou' state. Mainly within the Gulf coastal plain. Highest point Woodall Mountain (806 ft) in the NE. Drained (in the W) by the Yazoo R. system and the Big Black R., flowing into the Mississippi, and (in the E and S) by the Pearl, Pascagoula, and Tombigbee river systems, flowing into the Gulf of Mexico. Extensive swamps in the Mississippi flood plain. Climate humid sub-tropical, with long hot summers, short mild winters, and an annual rainfall of 50–55 ins. Over half the state is forest; lumbering important. Main occupation agriculture. Leading crop cotton, esp. in the Yazoo basin. Principal mineral products petroleum, natural gas. Chief towns Jackson, Meridian. First settled (1699) by the French at Biloxi Bay. Part of Louisiana till 1763, when France yielded her lands E of the Mississippi to Britain. On the side of the Confederacy in the American Civil War. Coast devastated by hurricane *Camille*, with much loss of life, esp. between Gulfport and Biloxi (1969).

**Mississippi River** USA. River in central USA, second in length among N American rivers only to the Missouri, its chief tributary; 2,348 m. long, rising in streams draining into L. Itasca at a height of 1,475 ft, in N Minnesota, flowing generally S, and entering the Gulf of Mexico. The Missouri R. and the lower Mississippi (from the confluence) are sometimes considered as one river, the Mississippi–Missouri, a continuous waterway 3,760 m. long (third longest in the world, after the Nile and the Amazon), whose drainage basin (third largest in the world, after those of the Amazon and the Congo) covers 1,244,000 sq. m. The lower Mississippi meanders freely in a wide flood plain and constantly changes course.

In its upper course the Mississippi descends over 60 ft in less than 1 m. at the Falls of St Anthony near Minneapolis and St Paul (as against an average descent of little more than 1 ft in every 2 m.). It is joined by the Missouri R. 17 m. above St Louis, the largest city on the river. At Cairo (Illinois) it is joined by the Ohio R. and continues past Memphis to the Red R. confluence in Louisiana, then flows SE past Baton Rouge and New Orleans, through the delta, to the Gulf of Mexico. Along the lower Mississippi flooding is a serious problem; the river is lined by artificial levees rising 20–25 ft above the natural banks. Even so, floods occasionally (e.g. 1927, 1937) inundate large areas of 'protected' land.

In Algonquin Indian, Mississippi means 'Great River'. Discovered (1541) by the Spaniard de Soto. The upper reaches were explored by Marquette and Jolliet (1673) and the lower course by La Salle (1682). Navigated by steamboats from *c*. 1820, ushering in the most colourful period in its history, richly celebrated in American literature. The development of the railways gradually diminished its navigational importance. Today its main value lies in irrigation and urban water supply.

**Missolonghi** (Gr. **Mesolóngion**) Greece. Capital of the *nome* of Aetolia and Acarnania, on the N side of the Gulf of Patras and 20 m. WNW of Patras. Pop. (1961) 11,266. Trade in agricultural produce. Famous for its defence against the Turks in 1822, 1823, and again in 1825–6. Has a monument to Byron, who died here (1824).

**Missoula** USA. Town in W Montana 95 m. WNW of Helena. Pop. (1960) 27,090. Flour milling, sugar refining. Tourist industry. Seat of Montana State University (1895).

**Missouri** USA. State in central USA,

bordered on the E by the Mississippi R. Area 69,674 sq. m. Pop. (1970) 4,636,247. Cap. Jefferson City. Admitted to the Union in 1821 as the 24th state; popularly known as the 'Bullion' or 'Show Me' state. The N consists of rolling prairies, crossed W–E by the Missouri R., which also forms part of the W boundary. The S is largely occupied by the Ozark Mountains, with an average height of c. 1,100 ft. The SE corner comes within the Mississippi flood plain. Climate generally humid continental. Annual rainfall 30–50 ins. Tall prairie grass abounds in the N and W, and helps in the raising of livestock (chiefly cattle and pigs). Leading crops maize, winter wheat, oats, soya beans. Leading state in lead production. St Louis and Kansas City, by far the largest cities, are the main industrial centres. The first European explorers were the Frenchmen Marquette and Jolliet (1673) and La Salle (1682). Belonged to Spain 1752–1800 and was then returned to France; ceded to the USA by the Louisiana Purchase (1803). In the American Civil War Confederate sympathizers were at first dominant, but the Union forces gradually gained control.

**Missouri River** USA. Chief tributary of the Mississippi R., 2,714 m. long (the longest river in N America), rising near Three Forks in the Rocky Mountains in SW Montana at a height of 4,000 ft, formed by the union of the Jefferson, Gallatin, and Madison rivers; flowing N and E through Montana, it turns S and SE, traverses N Dakota and S Dakota, forms several state boundaries, and finally crosses Missouri, flowing E to its confluence with the Mississippi 17 m. above St Louis. Tributaries include the Yellowstone, the Cheyenne, the White, the Niobrara, the Big Sioux, the Little Sioux, the Platte, and the Kansas rivers. The most important towns on its banks are Kansas City (Missouri), Kansas City (Kansas), Omaha (Nebraska). Its discharge fluctuates widely, for example increasing in the flood season at Kansas City to more than 20 times the minimum flow. Flood-control, power, and irrigation projects are now amalgamated into one overall scheme for the river basin; several dams have been constructed, e.g. Fort Peck Dam (Montana). High water is in April (from spring rain and snow melting on the plains) and June (from snow melting in the Rockies). Long used as a waterway by the Indians, it was first explored by European fur traders in the 18th cent. Steamboats were introduced in 1819, but river traffic declined with the advent of the railways. Today it is more important for irrigation and water supply than as a trade route.

**Misurata** Libya. Capital of Misurata division in Tripolitania, 120 m. ESE of Tripoli on the coast road to Benghazi. Pop. (district) 57,000; (town) 5,000. Oasis. Trade in dates, cereals, etc. Manufactures carpets, mats. The port is Misurata Marina, 7 m. E. Capital of the short-lived Republic of Tripolitania during the 1st World War.

**Mitau** ◊ *Jelgava*.

**Mitcham** England. Former municipal borough in NE Surrey 7 m. S of London, for which it is a dormitory suburb; from 1965 part of the Greater London borough of Merton. Pop. (1961) 63,653. Mainly residential. Manufactures paints, varnishes, pharmaceutical products. Formerly noted for the cultivation of lavender and other aromatic herbs.

**Mitilíni** ◊ *Mytilene*.

**Mito** Japan. Capital of the Ibaraki prefecture, 60 m. NE of Tokyo. Pop. (1965) 154,983. Ancient castle town and commercial centre. In the early 17th cent. it became the seat of one of the main branches of the Tokugawa family.

**Mitre Islands** ◊ *Solomon Islands*.

**Mittelland Canal** Federal German Republic. Canal 273 m. long consisting of the Ems–Weser and Weser–Elbe canals, linking the Rhine R. through the Rhine–Herne and Dortmund–Ems canals with the Elbe R. E of the Elbe the W–E inland waterway across Germany is completed by the Havel R. and canals to the Oder R.

**Miyazaki** Japan. Capital of the Miyazaki prefecture, in SE Kyushu 65 m. ENE of Kagoshima. Pop. (1965) 182,860. Market town. Manufactures porcelain etc. Has an important Shinto shrine. University (1949).

**Mjösa, Lake** Norway. Long narrow lake in the SE, the largest in Norway (141 sq. m.), fed by the Lågen R. from the Gudbrandsdal and drained by the Vorma R. to the Glomma R. On its shores are the towns of Lillehammer, Gjövik, and Hamar.

**Mlanje, Mount** ◊ *Malawi*.

**Moab.** Ancient country situated in the plateau area E of the Dead Sea, now in W Jordan. The inhabitants were akin to the Hebrews, though often at war with them.

The Moabite Stone from the 9th cent. B.C., found at Dibon (Dhiban) in 1868, records the successful revolt of the Moabite king, Mesha, against Israel.

**Mobile** USA. The only seaport in Alabama, on Mobile Bay in the Gulf of Mexico. Pop. (1960) 202,779. Exports cotton, timber, steel products, coal, etc. Shipbuilding, meat packing. Manufactures paper, textiles, clothing, food products, etc. Successively in French, British, and Spanish hands from 1702 to 1813, when it was seized for the USA.

**Moçambique (Mozambique).** A Portuguese overseas territory in SE Africa, on the coast of the Moçambique Channel opposite Malagasy (Madagascar). Area 302,250 sq. m. Pop. (1960) 6,592,994 (99 per cent Bantu; 50,000 Europeans). Cap. Lourenço Marques. Bounded by Tanzania (N), Malawi and Zambia (NW), Rhodesia (W), S Africa and Swaziland (SW and S). The coastal plain (much wider in the S than in the N) is fringed with mangrove swamps and rises gradually to a plateau 1,000–2,000 ft high, with heights of over 7,000 ft near the Malawi frontier. In the centre is the extensive delta of the Zambezi R. On the lowlands the climate is tropical and the annual rainfall (mainly Dec.–April) 30–60 ins. Savannah type of vegetation. Principal exports cane sugar, cashew nuts, copra, cotton, sisal. Volume of foreign trade small for such a large country. Food crops beans, maize, millet, rice. Lourenço Marques and Beira have a considerable transit trade, thanks to rail connexions with the interior; the former serves the Transvaal, Zambia, and Rhodesia, and the latter Zambia, Rhodesia, and Malawi. The ports Moçambique and Nacala (opened 1951) handle the trade of the S. Discovered (1498) by Vasco da Gama. Settlements were established by the Portuguese from 1505 onwards. The present boundaries were settled 1886–94. The Moçambique Company was granted a charter to administer the area (which later became the Manica and Sofala province, inc. Beira) in 1891. When the charter expired (1942) the territory reverted to state control.

**Moçambique (Mozambique) Channel** Indian Ocean. Strait between the SE coast of Africa and Malagasy (Madagascar), over 1,000 m. long and 250–600 m. wide. At the N end are the Comoro Is. Chief ports Moçambique and Beira on the mainland, Majunga and Tuléar in the Malagasy Republic.

**Moçâmedes (Mossamedes)** Angola. Seaport in the SW, 200 m. SSW of Benguela. Pop. 5,000. Fishing, fish canning. Linked by rail with Ghivemba in the interior. Exports cotton, fish (canned, dried, salted), hides and skins.

**Mocha (Mokha)** Yemen. Small town and seaport on the Red Sea 100 m. S of Hodeida. Pop. 5,000. Formerly exported the Arabian coffee named after it, but declined in the 19th cent. with the rise of Hodeida and Aden. Also gave its name to Mocha stones, agates used for jewellery.

**Modder River** (Cape Province) S Africa. Small holiday resort 24 m. SSW of Kimberley, near the Orange Free State border and the confluence of the Riet and Modder rivers. Pop. 500. Site of a battle during the Boer War (1899).

**Modder River** (Orange Free State) S Africa. River 190 m. long, a tributary of the Vaal R., flowing NW and W and joining the Riet R. near the small town of Modder River.

**Modena** Italy. Ancient Mutina. Capital of Modena province, in Emilia-Romagna, on the Aemilian Way 23 m. WNW of Bologna. Pop. (1968) 161,713. Industrial centre. Manufactures agricultural implements, motor vehicles, glass, macaroni, etc. Romanesque cathedral (11th/14th-cent.); 17th-cent. ducal palace. University (1678). Taken by the Romans in the 3rd cent. B.C. Ruled by the Este family from the 13th to the 19th cent.

**Modica** Italy. Market town in Ragusa province, Sicily, 4 m. SSE of Ragusa. Pop. (1961) 44,050. Trade in olive oil, wine, cheese. 6 m. SE is the Cava d'Ispica, a limestone gorge with many early Christian and Byzantine tombs and cave dwellings.

**Moeris, Lake of** ◊ *Faiyum, El.*

**Moers (Mörs)** Federal German Republic. Town in N Rhine-Westphalia, in the Ruhr region 6 m. WNW of Duisburg. Pop. (1963) 48,000. Coalmining centre. Manufactures machinery. Formerly the capital of a principality of the same name.

**Moeskroen** ◊ *Mouscron.*

**Moffat** Scotland. Small burgh and resort in Dumfriesshire, on the R. Annan 18 m. NNE of Dumfries. Pop. (1961) 1,917. Medicinal springs. Dumcrieff House, 2 m. SW, was the home of John L. McAdam, the road builder.

**Mogadishu (Mogadiscio)** Somalia. Capital

and chief seaport, serving the irrigated Webi Shebeli valley. Pop. (1965) 127,119. Taken by the Sultan of Zanzibar 1871. Sold to Italy 1905. Captured by British forces during the 2nd World War (1941). The 77-m. railway to Villabruzzi was dismantled and transported to Kenya.

**Mogador** ⟡ *Essaouira.*

**Mogilev** USSR. Town in the Byelorussian SSR, on the Dnieper R. 110 m. E of Minsk. Pop. (1970) 202,000. Railway junction. Industrial centre. Manufactures machinery, rayon, clothing, leather, etc. Has Eastern Orthodox and Roman Catholic cathedrals. Long ruled by the Poles; annexed to Russia 1772.

**Mojave (Mohave) Desert** USA. Arid region in S California forming part of the Great Basin, S of the Sierra Nevada. Area 15,000 sq. m. Average height 2,000 ft. Roughly parallel mountain ranges, with intervening wide basins. The only stream is the Mojave R., flowing generally N and mainly underground for about 100 m.

**Moji** Japan. Seaport in the Fukuoka prefecture, N Kyushu, on Shimonoseki Strait opposite Shimonoseki (Honshu), with which it is connected by railway tunnel (1942) and road tunnel (1958). Pop. 145,000. Exports coal, cement, sugar, etc. Manufactures steel. Sugar refining, brewing. Joined (1963) with neighbouring Kokura, Tobata, Yawata, and Wakamatsu to form the new city of Kitakyushu.

**Mokha** ⟡ *Mocha.*

**Mokpo** S Korea. Seaport in the SW. Pop. 130,000. Industrial centre. Cotton ginning, rice milling, etc.

**Mold** Wales. Urban district and county town of Flintshire, on the R. Alyn 10 m. WSW of Chester. Pop. (1961) 6,857. Coalmining centre. Market town. About 1 m. W is the reputed site of the battlefield of Germanus.

**Moldau River** ⟡ *Vltava River.*

**Moldavia (Rumanian Moldova)** Rumania. Former principality of SE Europe, in NE Rumania mainly between the Prut and the Siret rivers. Founded in the 14th cent., then including Bukovina and Bessarabia. Under the Turks from 1504; lost Bukovina to Austria (1775) and Bessarabia to Russia (1812), and came more and more under the influence of Russia. After the Crimean War it united with Walachia to form Rumania (1859).

**Moldavian SSR** USSR. Constituent republic of USSR, bounded on the N, E, and S by the Ukrainian SSR and on the W by Rumania, from which it is separated by the Prut R. Area 13,000 sq. m. Pop. (1970) 3,572,000 (65 per cent Moldavians, 15 per cent Ukrainians, 10 per cent Russians). Cap. Kishinev. Mainly lowlying. Covered largely with fertile blackearth soil. Drained by the navigable Dniester R. Contains almost one third of the country's vineyards, and is well known for its wine. Also produces maize, wheat, sugar-beet, sunflower seeds. Industries include canning, flour milling, sugar refining, tobacco processing. Sturgeon fisheries in the S. Principal towns Kishinev, Tiraspol, Beltsy. After Rumania had annexed ⟡ *Bessarabia* (1919), the Moldavian ASSR was formed E of the Dniester R. as part of the Ukrainian SSR. In 1940 Bessarabia was ceded to the USSR, and the part with a predominantly Moldavian population was united with most of the former Moldavian ASSR to form the present republic.

**Molfetta** Italy. Seaport and industrial town in Bari province, Apulia, 15 m. WNW of Bari on the Adriatic. Pop. (1961) 61,684. Manufactures soap, pottery, cement, etc. Exports wine, olive oil. Romanesque cathedral (12th/13th-cent.) and 18th-cent. baroque cathedral.

**Moline** USA. Industrial town, river port, and railway centre in NW Illinois, on the Mississippi R. Pop. (1960) 42,705. Sometimes called the 'Plow City'. Manufactures agricultural machinery, an industry brought in by John Deere (inventor of a steel plough) in 1847. Also manufactures tools, furniture, etc.

**Mollendo** Peru. Port in the Arequipa department (S), with an open roadstead. Pop. 14,000. Long the outlet for S Peru and Bolivia; now eclipsed by Matarani (9 m. NW), which has a sheltered harbour. Brickmaking. Fishing and fish canning.

**Mölndal** Sweden. Industrial town in Göteborg and Bohus county, 3 m. SE of Göteborg. Pop. (1968) 31,125. Manufactures textiles, paper, etc. Has the famous 18th-cent. mansion of Gunnebo.

**Molopo River** ⟡ *Botswana; Kalahari; South Africa.*

**Molotov** ⟡ *Perm.*

**Moluccas (Spice Islands)** Indonesia. Large group of islands between Celebes (W) and New Guinea (E) forming the province of Maluku. Area 33,315 sq. m. Pop. 790,000.

Cap. Amboina (Ambon), on the island of the same name. The N Moluccas include Halmahera, the largest of the Moluccas, Morotai, and the Obi and Sula Islands; the S Moluccas include Ceram, Buru, the Aru and Tanimbar Islands, and Wetar. Most of them are mountainous and some have active volcanoes; others are low-lying coral islands. Many are uninhabited. The inhabitants are of mixed Malay and other stock, the majority being Muslims. Coconut and sago palms and pepper vines are widely grown and copra and spices are important exports. The Portuguese visited the Moluccas early in the 16th cent. They were followed by the Dutch, who conquered the islands and remained in possession almost continuously from 1667 to the 2nd World War, when the group was seized by the Japanese (1942). With the end of the Netherlands E Indies, after the 2nd World War, the islands became a province of Indonesia; for a short time in 1950 an independent republic of the S Moluccas was formed on Amboina (Ambon) and Ceram.

**Mombasa** Kenya. Chief seaport, on the E side of the coral island of the same name within an inlet of the Indian Ocean, and also on the neighbouring mainland. Pop. (1962) 193,600 (122,000 Africans, 27,000 Arabs, 32,000 Indians, 4,440 Europeans). Old Mombasa harbour is used mainly by dhows, but at Kilindini in the SW of the island there is the finest modern deep-water harbour in E Africa, an important entrepôt handling the major part of the trade of Kenya, Uganda, and NE Tanzania, with all of which it is linked by rail. Exports coffee, cotton, hides and skins, pyrethrum, sisal, soda, tea. Coffee curing, brewing. Manufactures cement, glass, soap, etc. Largely oriental in character, with mosques as well as Anglican and Roman Catholic cathedrals, Arab and Indian bazaars, and the Mombasa Institute for Muslim technical education. An Arab and Persian settlement from the 11th cent. Already a busy port when visited by Vasco da Gama (1498, on his first voyage to India). Remained in Portuguese hands in the 16th–17th cent. Recaptured by the Arabs in 1698, and after changes of rulers, ceded to the British by the Sultan of Zanzibar in 1887. Capital of the British E Africa protectorate till 1907. The first oil refinery in E Africa was opened here in 1964.

**Mona** ◊ *Anglesey*.

**Monaco.** Independent principality in Europe, on the Mediterranean Sea, an enclave within the Alpes-Maritimes department of France, 9 m. ENE of Nice. Area 368 acres. Pop. (1961) 22,297 (only 3,039 Monégasques; 12,869 French, 4,217 Italians, 598 British). It is, after the Vatican, the world's smallest sovereign state. Consists of three adjoining communes or urban areas: Monaco, the capital, on a rocky headland; La Condamine, the business quarter; Monte Carlo, famous for its gambling casino and as a resort. The casino and the tourist industry, in fact, are the main sources of revenue, some income being derived from postage stamps. Monégasques are not admitted to the gambling tables, but are exempt from taxation. Perfumes are manufactured and Mediterranean fruits are grown, and in the exceptionally mild climate the vegetation is luxuriant. In the town of Monaco are a Romanesque-Byzantine cathedral, a 13th/16th-cent. palace, and the oceanographical museum founded (1910) by Prince Albert I.

In ancient times Monaco was settled by Phoenicians and later by Greeks. From 1297 it was ruled by the Genoese Grimaldi family, but was annexed to France 1793–1814 and was a Sardinian protectorate 1815–61. In 1911, by the introduction of a constitution providing for a National Council, Monaco changed from an absolute to a constitutional monarchy. Prince Rainier III suspended this constitution in 1959 but restored it in 1962. The Principality has a customs union with France and an interchangeable currency.

**Monadnock, Mount** USA. Isolated mountain (3,165 ft) in SW New Hampshire 33 m. WNW of Nashua. Gave its name to a geological feature (a hill of hard rock which has successfully resisted erosion).

**Monaghan** Irish Republic. 1. Inland county in Ulster province lying E of Co. Fermanagh (Northern Ireland). Area 498 sq. m. Pop. (1966) 45,732. Generally undulating and rising to over 1,200 ft in Slieve Beagh (NW), with a central valley, it is drained chiefly by the Blackwater and the Finn rivers; it has a number of small lakes and bogs. Oats and potatoes cultivated. Livestock reared. Chief towns Monaghan, Clones, Carrickmacross, Castleblaney.

2. County town of Co. Monaghan, on the Ulster Canal 28 m. NW of Dundalk. Pop. (1966) 4,019. Bacon and ham curing. Manufactures footwear. Has a 19th-cent.

Roman Catholic cathedral. Birthplace of Sir Charles Gavan Duffy (1816–1903).

**Monastir** ⧫ *Bitolj*.

**Monchegorsk** USSR. Town in RSFSR, on the NW shore of L. Imandra 65 m. S of Murmansk. Pop. 46,000. Copper and nickel are smelted from ores mined in the neighbourhood. Founded in the 1930s.

**Moncton** Canada. Originally The Bend. Industrial town in SE New Brunswick, on the Petitcodiac R. Pop. (1966) 45,847. Railway engineering. Manufactures clothing, hardware, etc. Renamed (1855) after General Robert Monckton.

**Monfalcone** Italy. Industrial town in Gorizia province, Friuli-Venezia Giulia, 16 m. NW of Trieste. Pop. (1961) 26,818. Important shipbuilding industry. Oil refining. Manufactures chemicals.

**Monghyr** India. Town in Bihar, on the Ganges R. 32 m. WNW of Bhagalpur. Pop. 74,000. Commercial centre. Manufactures cigarettes. Walls and ramparts of a 16th-cent. fort.

**Mongolian People's Republic.** Independent republic in E central Asia, formerly called Outer Mongolia. Area 604,095 sq. m. Pop. (1966) 1,120,000 (76 per cent Khalkha Mongols, 5 per cent Kazakhs). Cap. Ulan Bator. Lang. Mongol. Rel. Lamaistic Buddhism (reduced in influence during recent years).

Bounded by Siberia (USSR) (N), Inner Mongolia AR (China) (S), and the Sinkiang-Uighur AR (China) (W). Its vast grazing lands have made it a country of herdsmen, and it has the highest number of livestock per head of population in the world. Now closely associated, politically and economically, with the USSR. For administrative purposes it is divided into 18 provinces and two cities (Ulan Bator, Darkhan).

TOPOGRAPHY, RESOURCES, *etc*. On the whole an extensive plateau at 3,000–4,000 ft, with the lofty Altai and Khangai Mountains in the W and the Gobi desert in the S. Chief rivers the Selenga, which drains to L. Baikal, and the Kerulen, which drains to the Amur R. Exceptionally severe climate. There are forests on the mountain slopes of the NW, but pastures occupy 84 per cent of the total area, and large numbers of sheep and goats, as well as horses, cattle, and camels, are raised on co-operative and state farms. Wheat is the chief crop on the relatively small area of cultivated land. Some coal and oil produced. Most of the foreign trade is with the USSR. Main exports cattle, horses, wool, hides, meat, butter. Linked by rail with both the USSR and China.

HISTORY. In early times the Mongols were fierce nomadic raiders, attaining their greatest power under Genghis Khan, the 800th anniversary of whose birth was celebrated in the republic in 1962; his great empire extended across Asia and far into Europe. In the 13th cent. his grandson, Kublai Khan, became the first Mongol emperor of China. But the Mongol empire was short-lived; with the overthrow of the Mongol dynasty of China by the Mings, Mongolia became separated into Outer Mongolia (N) and Inner Mongolia (S). The former was a Chinese province from 1686 to 1911, when it became autonomous under the rule of the Living Buddha of Urga (Ulan Bator); when he died (1924), the Mongolian People's Republic, on the Soviet pattern, was proclaimed. Its independence was recognized by China in 1946 and the republic was admitted to the UN in 1961.

**Moni** ⧫ *Christmas Island* (Indian Ocean).

**Monmouth** Wales. Municipal borough and county town of Monmouthshire, at the confluence of the R. Wye and the R. Monnow 19 m. NE of Newport. Pop. (1961) 5,505. Market town. Remains of the ancient walls and the 12th-cent. castle where Henry V was born. Also has a 13th-cent. gateway on the bridge over the R. Monnow.

**Monmouthshire** Wales. County in the extreme SE, on the English border. Area 542 sq. m. Pop. (1961) 443,689. County town Monmouth. Bounded on the W by Glamorganshire, on the NW by Brecknockshire, and on the E by Gloucestershire (England). Especially hilly in the W, it rises to 1,955 ft in the Sugar Loaf. Drained by the Wye, Usk, Monnow (from which its name is derived), Ebbw, and Rhymney rivers. Sheep are reared and there are orchards, but far more important are the coalmines of the upland valleys of the NW, which form part of the S Wales coalfield. In addition to the traditional coalmining and iron and steel manufacture, which suffered severely in the economic depression of the 1930s, many light industries have been introduced. Largest town and seaport Newport. Other industrial centres Pontypool, Abertillery, Ebbw Vale.

**Monongahela River** USA. River 128 m. long, formed in W Virginia by the union of the Tygart R. and the W Fork, flowing generally N into Pennsylvania, and joining the Allegheny R. at Pittsburgh to form the Ohio R. An important waterway.

**Monopoli** Italy. Adriatic seaport in Bari province, Apulia, 26 m. ESE of Bari. Pop. (1961) 37,095. Exports olive oil, wine, fruit. Flour milling, food canning. Manufactures textiles, macaroni, etc.

**Monroe** USA. Industrial town in NE Louisiana, on the Ouachita R. Pop. (1960) 52,219. Manufactures carbon black, chemicals, wood pulp and paper, furniture, etc. Extensive natural-gas fields near by.

**Monrovia** Liberia. Capital and chief seaport, near the mouth of the St Paul R. Pop. 80,000. Exports mainly rubber and iron ore; also diamonds, palm oil and kernels. Named after the US President James Monroe, during whose term it was founded (1822) as a settlement for former slaves from America.

**Mons** (Flemish **Bergen**) Belgium. Capital of Hainaut province, 33 m. SW of Brussels. Pop. (1968) 27,680. Industrial centre in the Borinage coalmining region. Sugar refining. Manufactures chemicals, textiles, soap, cement, etc. Cathedral of St Waudru (15th/16th-cent.); 15th-cent. town hall. Scene of the first engagement between British and German forces in the 1st World War.

**Montana** USA. Mountain state in the NW, bordering in the N on Canada, along the 49th parallel. Area 147,138 sq. m. Pop. (1970) 682,133. Cap. Helena. Admitted to the Union in 1889 as the 41st state; popularly known as the 'Mountain' or 'Treasure' state. In the W are the Rocky Mountains (about two fifths of the state), rising to 12,850 ft in Granite Peak in the Absaroka Range (S). In the E are the Great Plains, interspersed with hills and river valleys, at an altitude of 2,000–4,000 ft. The winters are severe, with fierce snowstorms, though modified by warm chinook winds. Annual rainfall 10–15 ins. Several important irrigation projects (e.g. Fort Peck Reservoir on the Missouri R.). Dry farming is practised. Leading crops spring wheat, barley, sugar-beet. Noted for minerals; the most valuable are petroleum, copper, silver, gold. Chief towns Great Falls, Billings, Helena. White settlement began with the Louisiana Purchase (1803), by which the territory passed from France to the USA, and increased with the discovery of gold in 1858.

**Montauban** France. Prefecture of the Tarn-

et-Garonne department in the SW, on the Tarn R. 30 m. N of Toulouse. Pop. (1968) 48,555. Market town. Trade in fruit, poultry. Food processing. Manufactures textiles, furniture, etc. Early-14th-cent. brick-built bridge; 18th-cent. cathedral; fine collection of paintings by Ingres (1780–1867), who was born here. An ancient fortress, founded 1144. A stronghold of the Huguenots in the 16th and 17th cent.

**Mont-aux-Sources** ◊ *Drakensberg*; *Lesotho*; *Orange River*; *Tugela River*.

**Mont Blanc** France. Highest mountain (15,781 ft) in the Alps, and, if the Caucasus be excluded, in Europe; in the Haute-Savoie department in the massif of the same name extending into Switzerland and Italy. The Massif is nearly 30 m. long, its greatest width 10 m. There are several sharp peaks (*aiguilles*) and glaciers; the best-known glacier is the Mer de Glace. The mountain was first ascended (1786) by Dr Michel Paccard and Jacques Balmat, of Chamonix; may now be climbed with guides from the terminus of the Aiguille du Midi overhead cable-way. A 7½-m. road tunnel under it was completed in 1962 and opened to traffic in 1965.

**Mont Cenis** France. Alpine pass (6,831 ft) in the Savoie department between the Cottian and Graian Alps, on the road between Lanslebourg (France) and Susa (Italy), built (1803–10) by Napoleon. The Mont Cenis (Fréjus) railway tunnel (8½ m. long, opened 1871) is 17 m. SW.

**Montclair** USA Residential town in New Jersey 6 m. NNW of Newark. Pop. (1960) 43,129. Manufactures chemicals, paints, metal goods. Founded 1666.

**Monte Bello Islands** (Australia) S Pacific Ocean. Group of uninhabited coral islands off the NW coast of Western Australia, NNE of Onslow, the largest being Barrow Island, 12 m. long and up to 5 m. wide. Testing site for British nuclear explosions.

**Monte Carlo** Monaco. Resort on the Riviera 10 m. ENE of Nice. Famous for its gambling casino and various artistic and sports events (chiefly in the winter season), inc. an annual motor rally. ◊ *Monaco*.

**Monte Cassino** Italy. Hill 1,703 ft high overlooking the town of Cassino, in Frosinone province, Latium, 75 m. SE of Rome. On it the famous monastery was founded (c. 529) by St Benedict, who established the Benedictine Order, and this was long an important centre of learning and religion. Its buildings were three times destroyed, by the Lombards (581), Saracens (884), and by earthquake (1349). Then, in the 2nd World War, the Germans used the abbey as a stronghold, and the buildings were destroyed a fourth time by Allied air attacks; some of the MSS. and art treasures, however, were saved. The abbey was completely restored and was rededicated by Pope Paul VI in 1964.

**Monte Gargano** Italy. Mountainous peninsula in N Apulia projecting about 35 m. E into the Adriatic, rising to 3,461 ft in Monte Calvo (or Gargano). Sheep rearing. Olives and grapes cultivated. Chief town Monte Sant' Angelo.

**Montego Bay** Jamaica. Second largest town and second seaport (after Kingston), on the NW coast. Pop. (1960) 23,471. Exports bananas, sugar, etc. Most famous as a tourist resort, largely because of the exceptionally fine bathing beach. In the bay is a cluster of coral atolls, the Bogue Islets.

**Montélimar** France. Town in the Drôme department in the SE, on the Roubion R. near the confluence with the Rhône 43 m. N of Avignon. Pop. (1968) 27,483. Famous for its nougat. Food processing, silk spinning, sawmilling, tanning, etc. Once belonged to the Adhémar family, and was called Monteil d'Adhémar.

**Montenegro** (Serbo-Croatian **Crna Gora**, 'Black mountain') Yugoslavia. The smallest of Yugoslavia's constituent republics, bounded by Albania (SE) and the Adriatic Sea (SW). Area 5,343 sq. m. Pop. (1961) 471,894 (mainly Eastern Orthodox). Cap. Titograd (formerly Podgorica). Entirely mountainous, except in the extreme S around L. Shkodër (Scutari), with a few fertile river valleys; rises to over 8,000 ft in Mt Durmitor (NW) and Mt Komovi (SE). Principal occupation rearing of sheep and goats. Cereals, potatoes, tobacco, and fruits cultivated; but agriculture is primitive. Cetinje is the capital of the former kingdom. Its history is closely linked with that of Serbia, of which it was a semi-independent province (as Zeta) in the Middle Ages. After the Turks defeated the Serbs at Kosovo (1389) it retained its independence and continually resisted Turkish aggression. Became a kingdom in 1910 and fought against Turkey in the Balkan Wars and against Austria-Hungary in the 1st World War. Became a province of Yugoslavia 1918 and a people's republic after the 2nd World War (1946).

**Monterey Park** USA. Residential town in

California 6 m. E of Los Angeles. Pop. (1960) 37,821. First developed in the late 19th cent.

**Monte Rosa** Italy/Switzerland. Mountain group in the Pennine Alps, on the Italo-Swiss border, consisting of 10 peaks. Highest peak Dufourspitze (15,217 ft), first climbed (1855) by a party led by Charles Hudson, who was killed 10 years later on the Matterhorn.

**Monterrey** Mexico. Third largest city, capital of the Nuevo León state, in the fertile valley of the Santa Catarina R. at a height of 1,765 ft. Pop. (1969) 1,011,900. Important industrial centre. Large iron and steel works and lead smelters. Manufactures textiles, glass, chemicals, cigarettes, etc. Founded 1579. Much excellent architecture, both Spanish-colonial and modern. The 18th-cent. cathedral is specially noteworthy.

**Montevideo** Uruguay. Capital of Uruguay and of the small Montevideo department (256 sq. m.), on a wide bay backed by hills, on the N shore of the Río de la Plata. Pop. (1964) 1,203,700. Major seaport, handling most of Uruguay's trade. Chief exports wool, hides and skins, meat. Uruguay's only important industrial centre. Meat packing, tanning, flour milling. Manufactures textiles, footwear, soap, matches, etc. An attractive city, with fine avenues, parks, gardens, and beaches which make it a favoured summer resort. Among outstanding buildings are the cathedral (1804) and the Cabildo (town hall, 1810). Seat of the University of the Republic (1849). Founded 1726; named after the conical hill (486 ft) the Cerro, on which stands an old Spanish fort. Became capital of the republic 1828.

**Montgomery** USA. State capital of Alabama, on the Alabama R. Pop. (1960) 134,393. Manufactures fertilizers, cotton goods, etc. Trade in livestock, cotton, dairy produce. First settled 1817. Capital of the Confederate States during the American Civil War (1861).

**Montgomery** Wales. Municipal borough and county town of Montgomeryshire, near the R. Severn 19 m. SW of Shrewsbury. Pop. (1961) 970. Market town. Ruins of a 13th-cent. castle. Just E is a well-preserved section of Offa's Dyke.

**Montgomeryshire** Wales. Inland county, bordered on the E by Shropshire. Area 797 sq. m. Pop. (1961) 44,228. County town Montgomery. Mountainous, consisting mainly of bleak, barren moorland, rising to 2,713 ft in the Berwyn Mountains of the N. Several fertile valleys in the E, where oats are cultivated. Main occupation on the uplands sheep rearing. Drained by the Severn, Vyrnwy, Dovey, and Wye rivers. L. Vyrnwy supplies Liverpool with water. Slate and stone quarried. Chief towns Montgomery, Welshpool.

**Montluçon** France. Town in the Allier department, on the Cher R. 47 m. N N W of Clermont-Ferrand. Pop. (1968) 59,983. Industrial centre. Manufactures steel, chemicals, tyres, glass, etc. Became important through the discovery of coal in the Commentry area to the S E in the early 19th cent. In the upper old town are narrow streets with many 15th/16th-cent. houses.

**Montmartre** France. District in N Paris on the hill Butte de Montmartre (330 ft), the highest point of the city. Frequented by artists; noted for its night clubs and cafés. Dominated by the basilica of Sacré-Coeur; in its cemetery are the tombs of Stendhal, Berlioz, Heine, etc.

**Montparnasse** France. District in Paris on the left bank of the Seine R. Famous cafés frequented by artists and writers. Seat of the Pasteur Institute. The cemetery contains the tombs of Maupassant, Baudelaire, Saint-Saëns, etc.

**Mont Pelée** Martinique. Volcano 4,428 ft high, 15 m. N W of Fort-de-France, which erupted violently on 8 May 1902, completely destroying the town of St Pierre (then the chief commercial centre). All but one of the 28,000 inhabitants, and many thousands of others in the district, were killed. The name means 'bald mountain' and refers to the absence of vegetation.

**Montpelier** ◊ *Vermont*.

**Montpellier** France. Prefecture of the Hérault department in the S, on the Lez R. 80 m. W N W of Marseille. Pop. (1968) 167,211. Chief town of Languedoc; commercial and cultural centre. Trade in wine, brandy. Manufactures soap, chemicals, perfumes, confectionery, etc. Seat of a famous university (founded 1289). Picturesque narrow streets with 17th/18th-cent. buildings. Among its features are the Musée Fabre, the botanical garden founded in 1593, and the 14th-cent. Gothic cathedral. Purchased by Philip VI of France from Aragon 1349. Suffered much during the religious wars; supported the Huguenot cause; besieged and captured by Louis XIII 1622.

**Montreal** (Fr. **Montréal**) Canada. In French 'Royal Mountain'. Largest city in Canada, in S Quebec on Montreal Island, at the confluence of the Ottawa and St Lawrence rivers. Pop. (1966) 1,222,255 (metropolitan area 2,436,817). The second largest French-speaking city in the world (after Paris). A major seaport; the world's largest grain-shipping port. Also exports other agricultural produce, timber, paper. The harbour has 10 m. of piers and wharves, large grain elevators, cold-storage warehouses, and a floating dry dock. Closed by ice Dec.–April. Many industries. Manufactures aircraft, railway equipment, cement, plastics, clothing, footwear, etc. Canada's banking and insurance centre. Headquarters of the two principal railway systems. Built on the slopes of the extinct volcano Mt Royal (900 ft), from which the name derives, and on which is Mt Royal Park, the largest of many. Seat of the McGill University (1821, English-speaking) and the University of Montreal (1876, French-speaking, Roman Catholic). Foremost among the buildings is the Cathedral of St James (1870), copied from St Peter's, Rome. The Victoria Bridge across the St Lawrence was opened in 1860, the Jacques Cartier Bridge in 1930. Montreal Island was discovered (1535) by Jacques Cartier. A permanent settlement was founded in 1642 by Maisonneuve. Scene of the 'Expo 67' international exhibition (1967).

**Montreuil-sous-Bois** France. Suburb of E Paris, in the Seine-St Denis department. Pop. (1968) 95,859. Famous for peaches. Manufactures metal containers, chemicals, paints, glass, etc.

**Montreux** Switzerland. Town in the Vaud canton at the E end of L. Geneva, extending nearly 4 m. along the lakeside. Pop. (1969) 19,900. Tourist centre. Woodworking, printing. Includes the smaller resorts of Clarens, Caux, Les Avants, Glion, Territet, Veytaux. A mountain railway runs almost to the summit of Rochers de Naye (6,709 ft). Near by is the castle of Chillon.

**Montrose** Scotland. Royal burgh in Angus, at the mouth of the South Esk R. 26 m. N E of Dundee, on a sandy peninsula between the North Sea and Montrose Basin, a tidal lagoon. Pop. (1961) 10,702. Fishing port. Seaside resort. Flax and jute spinning, sawmilling. Birthplace of Andrew Melville (1545–1622), James Graham, 5th

Marquess of Montrose (1612–50), and Joseph Hume (1777–1855).

**Mont St Michel** France. Conical, rocky islet in the Manche department, 3 acres in area and 260 ft high, in the Bay of St Michel 8 m. WSW of Avranches. Rises abruptly above the level sands and is accessible from the mainland by a causeway. Famous for its Benedictine monastery (founded 966), whose buildings were used as a prison from the Revolution until 1863. The medieval walls may be entered by a single gateway, from which the only street leads up to the abbey, and above all other buildings is the church.

**Montserrat** British W Indies. Island in the Leeward Is., 25 m. SW of Antigua. Area 38 sq. m. Pop. (1967) 14,468. Cap. Plymouth (pop. 4,000). Volcanic and rugged, rising to 3,002 ft in Soufrière. Often subject to earth tremors. Chief occupation agriculture. Exports sea-island cotton, tomatoes, bananas, limes, etc. Discovered (1493) by Columbus, who probably named it after the Spanish monastery. Colonized by the British 1632.

**Montserrat** Spain. Ancient Mons Serratus. Mountain 4,054 ft high in Catalonia 30 m. NW of Barcelona, above the valley of the Llobregat R. The Roman name probably derives from its jagged pinnacles, precipices, and ravines. On a ledge about 2,400 ft high is the famous Benedictine monastery, reached by funicular railway and motor road. The church contains a small black image of the Virgin, Nuestra Señora de Montserrat, said to have been carved by St Luke and brought to Spain by St Peter; for centuries it has been one of the outstanding religious shrines in Spain, attracting thousands of pilgrims annually.

**Monza** Italy. Industrial town in Milano province, Lombardy, on the Lambro R. 8 m. NNE of Milan. Pop. (1961) 84,445. Manufactures textiles, hats, carpets, machinery, etc. The 13th-cent. cathedral, built on the site of a church founded (590) by the Lombard Queen Theodelinda, contains relics of her reign and also the celebrated iron crown of Lombardy, said to have been beaten out of one of the nails used in the Crucifixion. An expiatory chapel was built (1910) after the assassination here of King Umberto I (1900). Well-known motor-racing track.

**Mooltan** ◊ *Multan.*

**Moon, Mountains of the** ◊ *Ruwenzori.*

**Moorea** ◊ *Society Islands.*

**Moose Jaw** Canada. Industrial town in Saskatchewan 40 m. W of Regina. Pop. (1966) 33,417. Flour milling, meat packing, oil refining, etc.

**Moosonee** ◊ *James Bay.*

**Moradabad** India. Industrial town in Uttar Pradesh, on the Ramganga R. 100 m. ENE of Delhi. Pop. (1961) 180,100. Manufactures ornamental brassware, cotton goods, carpets. Founded 1625. Has a Jama Masjid (Great Mosque), built (1631) by Rustam Khan.

**Morar, Loch** Scotland. Lake in W Inverness-shire, 11 m. long and up to 1½ m. wide; with a depth of 987 ft the deepest lake in Scotland. At the W end is the village of Morar.

**Morava** (Ger. **March**) **River** Czechoslovakia. River 230 m. long rising in the Sudeten Mountains and flowing generally S through Moravia, then forming part of the Austro-Czechoslovak border and joining the Danube 7 m. above Bratislava. Navigable for 80 m. of the lower course.

**Morava River** Yugoslavia. Chief river of Serbia, 130 m. long, formed by the union of the S Morava and the W Morava near Stalac and flowing generally N to join the Danube R. 30 m. ESE of Belgrade.

**Moravia** Czechoslovakia. The central region, between Bohemia and Slovakia and bordering S on Austria. An extension of the Bohemian plateau, drained by the Morava R. and its tributaries and in the NE by the Oder (Odra) R. To the N are the Sudeten Mountains, to the E the Carpathians, separated by the Moravian Gate; to the W are the Moravian Heights. The centre and S are fertile agricultural areas, there are considerable mineral resources, and industries are well developed. Principal towns Brno, Ostrava, Olomouc, Gottwaldov. By the late 8th cent. the region was peopled by Slavs, who took the name of Moravians from the Morava R. Incorporated in Bohemia 1029, but became a separate Austrian crownland in 1849. In 1918 it formed a province of the new republic of Czechoslovakia, combining with Silesia in 1927. In 1949 the three former provinces of Czechoslovakia were abolished, and Moravia and Silesia no longer formed a political unit.

**Moravská Ostrava** ◊ *Ostrava.*

**Moray Firth** Scotland. Inlet of the North Sea in the NE, sometimes considered to extend seawards to a line from Duncansbay Head (Caithness) to Kinnaird's Head

(Aberdeen), sometimes only to a line from Tarbat Ness to Lossiemouth. At its head is Inverness.

**Morayshire** Scotland. Formerly Elginshire. County in the N E, on Moray Firth. Area 476 sq. m. Pop. (1961) 49,156. County town Elgin. Hilly in the S, rising to 2,329 ft in the Cromdale Hills on the Banffshire border, sloping down to a low fertile plain, the Laigh of Moray, along the coast. Drained by the Spey, Lossie, and Findhorn rivers. Main occupations cattle and sheep rearing, agriculture (chiefly oats), fishing. Salmon fishing in the Spey and Findhorn. Many whisky distilleries. Several resorts. The ancient province of Moray was much more extensive, comprising the present counties of Moray and Nairn and parts of Inverness and Banff.

**Morbihan** France. Department in Brittany in the N W, on the Bay of Biscay. Area 2,739 sq. m. Pop. (1968) 540,474. Prefecture Vannes. Its coastline is very broken, with many picturesque bays and estuaries, inc. the Gulf of Morbihan E of the Quiberon peninsula, and many offshore islands. Much of the area is unproductive, inc. the barren Landes de Lanvaux. Chief crops cereals, potatoes, cider apples. Sardine and tunny fisheries important. Chief towns Vannes, Lorient. Carnac and Locmariaquer are famous for their megalithic monuments.

**Morden** ◊ *Merton.*

**Mordovian ASSR** U S S R. Autonomous republic in central European R S F S R, in the great bend of the Volga R. E S E of Moscow. Area 10,110 sq. m. Pop. (1970) 1,030,000. Cap. Saransk. Agriculture and dairy farming are important; many of the industries are concerned with the processing of farm produce.

**Morecambe and Heysham** England. Municipal borough in N W Lancashire, on Morecambe Bay. Pop. (1961) 40,950. Consists of Morecambe, a seaside resort, and Heysham, a seaport with a steamer service to Belfast (Northern Ireland), and an oil refinery.

**Morecambe Bay** England. Inlet of the Irish Sea into N W Lancashire, separating the Furness peninsula from the rest of the county.

**Morelia** Mexico. Formerly Valladolid. Capital of the Michoacán state, 130 m. W N W of Mexico City, near the S edge of the central plateau, at a height of 6,200 ft. Pop. (1969) 153,800. Flour milling, sugar refining, tanning. Manufactures textiles, tobacco products, etc. A noteworthy cathedral (17th/18th-cent.) and many fine colonial houses. Birthplace of the Mexican patriots Itúrbide (1783–1824) and Morelos (1765–1815); named after the latter.

**Morelos** Mexico. State just S of the Federal District, mainly on the S slopes of the central plateau. Area 1,917 sq. m. Pop. (1969) 597,000. Cap. Cuernavaca. Mainly agricultural. Produces maize, rice, sugarcane, coffee, wheat, etc. Named after the Mexican patriot Morelos (1765–1815).

**Moreton Bay** Australia. Bay in S E Queensland into which the Brisbane R. empties; the penal settlement here (1824–39) led to the development of Queensland.

**Morioka** Japan. Capital of Iwate prefecture, in N E Honshu 105 m. N of Sendai. Pop. (1965) 176,966. Commercial centre. Manufactures iron goods, toys, etc.

**Morlaix** France. Port in the Finistère department in the N W, on a tidal estuary 34 m. E N E of Brest. Pop. (1968) 21,516. Exports fruit, vegetables, dairy produce. Manufactures tobacco products. Tanning, brewing, flour milling, etc. Several 15th/17th-cent. wooden houses.

**Morley** England. Municipal borough in the W Riding of Yorkshire, 4 m. S S W of Leeds. Pop. (1961) 40,322. Coalmining. Manufactures woollen goods, textile machinery, glass, etc. Birthplace of the Earl of Oxford and Asquith (1852–1928).

**Morocco.** In Arabic, 'the Farthest West'. Independent kingdom in N W Africa. Area 171,388 sq. m. Pop. (1969) 14,100,000 (predominantly Berber, with an Arab admixture). Cap. Rabat. Bounded by the Mediterranean Sea (N), Algeria (E), Spanish Sahara (S), and the Atlantic Ocean (W). Along the Mediterranean coast is the mountainous region Er Rif (the Rif). The dominating physical feature is the Atlas Mountains, forming three distinct ranges, the High Atlas, the Middle Atlas, and the Anti-Atlas, which separate the Atlantic coastlands from the Sahara. The High Atlas rise to 13,664 ft in Djebel Toubkal (the highest peak in N Africa). The S and S E fringe lies within the Sahara. Thus the climate varies from typically Mediterranean – with annual (winter) rainfall 30–35 ins. (N) – to the hot desert type with annual rainfall less than 10 ins. (extreme S and E). Agriculture is by far the most important occupation. Principal crops cereals (chiefly wheat and barley), vines, olives, almonds, citrus fruits, dates, and early vegetables for the European market. Livestock (mainly sheep and goats) are raised. The forests yield cork. Fishing is an important coastal occupation; sardines are canned at Safi. Chief export phosphates, mined at Khouribga and Youssoufia (formerly Louis Gentil), and also iron, manganese, lead ores. Chief agricultural exports citrus fruits, barley, wheat, wine, tomatoes. Dams have been constructed on several Atlantic streams (e.g. the Oum er Rbia and its tributaries) for the storage of irrigation water and the development of hydroelectric power. Casablanca, the largest city and leading seaport, handles about three quarters of the foreign trade. The principal railway runs from Casablanca through Rabat, Meknès, Fez, and Oujda, continuing through Algeria and on to Tunis, with a branch line to Tangier; the important railway from Casablanca to Marrakesh has branch lines to Oued Zem (serving the Khouribga phosphate mines) and Safi.

HISTORY. The N and W of present-day Morocco formed part of the Roman province of Mauretania. The region fell to the Vandals in the 5th cent. A.D. and was conquered in the 7th cent. by the Arabs, who imposed the Muslim religion on the native Berber; it achieved its greatest power under the Berber dynasties of the Almoravides and the Almohades in the 11th–13th cent. The Portuguese led the European penetration of Morocco by the capture of Ceuta (1415) but were dislodged from their final stronghold, Mazagan (El ◊ Jadida), 1769. French and Spanish influence conflicted with German aspirations in the late 19th and early 20th cent. The Algeciras Conference (1906) and the Agadir incident (1911) were followed by the establishment of the French and Spanish protectorates (1912). The Tangier international zone was created in 1923. Considerable economic progress was made under the first French resident general, Marshal Lyautey (1912–25), but the Berber of the Rif mountains revolted under Abdel Krim (1921), evicted the Spanish from most of Spanish Morocco, and were subjugated only by a joint Franco-Spanish expedition (1926). The Moroccan nationalist movement continued to grow; Sultan Mohammed V was deposed and exiled in 1953 but after much internal disorder was restored in 1955 (changing his title to King in 1957). France and Spain relinquished their protectorates in 1956; the international status of the Tangier zone

was abolished. Morocco became an independent member of the UN. Spain retains the Ceuta, Melilla, Alhucemas, and Peñon de Velez enclaves; Ifni was returned to Morocco in 1969.

**Morón de la Frontera** Spain. Town in Seville province, Andalusia, 35 m. SE of Seville. Pop. (1961) 35,248. Manufactures cement, ceramics, soap, etc. Trade in cereals, olive oil, wine.

**Morpeth** England. Municipal borough in Northumberland, on the R. Wansbeck 13 m. N of Newcastle upon Tyne. Pop. (1961) 12,430. Market town. Iron founding, brewing, tanning, etc. Remains of its ancient castle and the 12th-cent. Newminster Abbey.

**Mörs** ◊ *Moers*.

**Mortlake** England. District in the London borough of Richmond-upon-Thames, on the S bank of the Thames 7 m. WSW of London. Finishing point of the annual Oxford–Cambridge boat race. Famous in the 17th cent. for tapestry.

**Moscow** (Russian **Moskva**) USSR. Capital and largest city of the USSR, of the RSFSR, and of the Moscow region of RSFSR, on the Moskva R. Pop. (1970) 7,061,000. The country's chief industrial, cultural, and political centre, and the hub of routes by road, rail, air, and waterway. Principal industries the manufacture of textiles and metal goods, inc. steel, locomotives, cars, aircraft, machinery, and machine tools; also produces chemicals, rubber and leather goods, paper, cigarettes, etc. At the centre of the city is the Kremlin or citadel, triangular in shape and surrounded by a wall with 18 towers and 5 gates, one side extending along the left bank of the Moskva R. Inside the Kremlin there are many ecclesiastical buildings: the 15th-cent. Uspenski (Assumption) Cathedral, where the Tsars were crowned; the 15th-cent. Blagoveshchenski (Annunciation) Cathedral with its 9 cupolas; and the 16th-cent. Arkhangelski (Archangel) Cathedral, where many of the Tsars were buried. Other buildings in the Kremlin are the Great Palace and the Oruzheinaya Palata (Armoury), now a museum containing a vast collection of armour, costumes, crowns, etc., both of the 19th cent.; the 15th-cent. Granovitaya Palata; the lofty bell-tower of Ivan the Great, with near by the great broken Tsar Bell (cast 1735), the largest in the world; the former arsenal; and the 18th-cent. building of the

Presidium of the Supreme Soviet of the USSR. Just outside the Kremlin (E) is the enormous Red Square, traditional site of parades and demonstrations; here are the Lenin Mausoleum and the tombs of other Revolutionary leaders, the fantastic 16th-cent. Cathedral of St Basil with its coloured towers and domes, and the historical museum. This part of the city, the Kitai Gorod, formerly the commercial and banking quarter, is now occupied chiefly by government offices. Among the many museums in Moscow perhaps the most famous is the Tretyakov Gallery, which was enriched by thousands of works from private collections, and the city also has the State Opera House, the Moscow Art Theatre, and other theatres. The USSR Academy of Sciences is in Moscow, and there are two state universities, the older founded 1755. Passenger transport is served by an underground railway system, first opened in 1935, while the main streets radiate from the central Kremlin and Kitai Gorod to the suburbs, cutting across the boulevards which mark the positions of the former walls. Moscow has a central and outer airports, and traffic by waterway is served by three ports, two on the Moskva R. and the third on the Moscow-Volga Canal (opened 1937), which transformed the city into an important inland port.

Founded in the 12th cent. Capital of a small principality by the end of the 13th cent. The Kremlin was enclosed by an earth and timber wall in 1300 and in 1367 by a stone wall. In spite of destruction by Tatar invasions and fires, it expanded until in the 16th cent. it became the national capital, and Ivan IV, Prince of Moscow, took the title of Tsar. In 1703, however, Peter the Great transferred the capital to St Petersburg (now Leningrad), and the city declined. It was again burned following the Napoleonic invasion (1812), but was rebuilt, and later in the 19th cent. grew rapidly as an industrial and railway centre, becoming capital once more after the Revolution (1918). During the 2nd World War the German army was halted about 20 m. from the city centre; further rapid expansion came after the end of hostilities.

**Moselle** France. Department in the NE, in Lorraine, bordering N on Luxembourg and NE on the Federal German Republic. Area 2,405 sq. m. Pop. (1968) 971,314. Prefecture Metz. Contains part of the Lorraine iron field. Coal mined. The important metallurgical industry is concentrated in the Metz–Thionville area. Cereals, vines, hops, fruits cultivated. Chief towns Metz, Thionville.

**Moselle** (Ger. **Mosel**) **River.** River 340 m. long, rising in the Vosges and flowing generally NW past Épinal, Toul, Metz, and Thionville (France), forming part of the Luxembourg-German frontier, then turning NE past Trier (Germany) to join the Rhine R. at Coblenz. In its lower course, between Trier and Coblenz, it meanders considerably, and here on the valley slopes are grown the grapes from which the famous Moselle wines are made. Navigable to small vessels below Frouard (near Nancy). Chief tributaries the Meurthe and the Saar (Sarre). Canalization of the 168-m. stretch between Thionville (France) and Coblenz (Germany) was completed in 1964.

**Moshi** ◊ *Tanga.*

**Moskenstraumen** ◊ *Maelström.*

**Moskva River** USSR. River 310 m. long in RSFSR, flowing generally E past Moscow and Kolomna, joining the Oka R. near the latter. Linked with the Volga R. by the Moscow Canal; canalized below the junction.

**Mosquito (Miskito) Coast** Nicaragua. Strip of land about 40 m. wide along the Caribbean coast, named after the former Mosquito (Miskito) Indian inhabitants, who now have a pronounced Negro admixture. The Mosquito Reserve forms part of the departments of Zelaya and Río San Juan; chief town Bluefields. Sparsely populated. Main occupations lumbering (mahogany etc.), banana cultivation. Discovered (1502) by Columbus. Under British protection as an autonomous 'kingdom' 1655–1860. Incorporated into Nicaragua 1893. The name is also sometimes understood to include the neighbouring coastal strip of Honduras as far as Cape Camarón, formerly claimed by Nicaragua; the present boundary was fixed (1961) by a commission of the Organization of American States.

**Mossamedes** ◊ *Moçâmedes.*

**Mossel Bay** S Africa. Formerly Aliwal South. Seaport and holiday resort in the Cape Province, midway between Cape Town and Port Elizabeth. Pop. (1960) 12,178. Serves the Little Karroo region. Important oyster and other fisheries. The bay was visited by Bartholomew Diaz (1487) and by Vasco da Gama (1497). The modern town was founded in 1848.

**Mossley** England. Municipal borough in SE Lancashire, on the R. Tame 9 m. ENE of Manchester. Pop. (1961) 9,795. Textile and metal-working industries.

**Most** (Ger. **Brüx**) Czechoslovakia. Town in NW Bohemia 47 m. NW of Prague. Pop. (1967) 56,000. In a lignite-mining region. Metallurgical and chemical industries. Manufactures ceramics, glass, etc.

**Mostaganem** Algeria. Seaport on the Gulf of Arzew, 50 m. ENE of Oran, with which it is linked by rail. Pop. (1967) 64,000. Exports wine and fruits (from the neighbouring lowlands) and wool (from the Tell Atlas). Founded in the 11th cent. Enjoyed considerable prosperity under the Turks in the 16th cent. Later declined, but revived after the French occupation in 1833. A gas pipeline runs to it from Hassi Messaoud.

**Mostar** Yugoslavia. In Serbo-Croat, 'Old Bridge'. Market town in Bosnia-Hercegovina, on the Neretva R. 48 m. SW of Sarajevo. Pop. (1961) 35,284. In a fruit-growing and wine-producing region. Manufactures textiles, tobacco products. Has a fine 16th-cent. bridge, possibly built on Roman foundations (hence the name); Turkish mosques; Orthodox cathedral.

**Mosul** Iraq. Capital of Mosul province and Iraq's second largest city, on the Tigris R. 220 m. NNW of Baghdad. Pop. (1965) 243,311. Important commercial centre, near rich oilfields. Trade in grain, fruit, livestock, wool. Tanning, flour milling. Manufactures cotton goods, cement, etc. Across the river are the ruins of Nineveh. Mosul was not handed over to Iraq by Turkey till 1925, four years after the foundation of the new country. Its importance increased with the completion of the Baghdad railway through Mosul to Syria and Turkey.

**Motala** Sweden. Town in Östergötland county, where the Motala R. leaves L. Vätter. Pop. (1968) 27,887. Manufactures locomotives and railway rolling stock, machinery, radio sets, etc. Site of a hydroelectric power plant and a radio station.

**Motala River** Sweden. River 60 m. long leaving L Vätter to flow generally E through lakes Bor, Rox, and Gla, past Norrköping, and entering Bråviken (Bra Bay) and the Baltic Sea. Between lakes Vätter and Rox the Göta Canal follows its course.

**Motherwell and Wishaw** Scotland. Large burgh in Lanarkshire, the two towns being united in 1920, 11 m. ESE of Glasgow. Pop. (1961) 72,799. Coalmining, engineering. Manufactures iron and steel, machinery, bricks, etc.

**Moulins** France. Prefecture of the Allier department, on the Allier R. 56 m. NNE of Clermont-Ferrand. Pop. (1968) 27,408. Railway junction. Brewing, tanning. Manufactures hosiery, furniture, etc. Capital of the duchy of Bourbonnais in the late 15th cent. Birthplace of Marshal Villars (1653–1734).

**Moulmein** Burma. Chief town and seaport of Tenasserim, on the estuary of the Salween R. 100 m. ESE of Rangoon. Pop. (1966) 156,968. Exports rice, teak. Sawmilling, rice milling, etc.

**Mountain Ash** Wales. Urban district in Glamorganshire, on the R. Cynon 16 m. NNW of Cardiff. Pop. (1961) 29,590. Coalmining centre with new light industries.

**Mountain View** USA. Town in California 12 m. NW of San José. Pop. (1960) 30,889. Manufactures electronic components. Fruit canning, printing and publishing, etc. Near by is the Moffett Field air base.

**Mount Gambier** Australia. Town in the extreme SE of S Australia, 225 m. SSE of Adelaide. Pop. (1966) 17,146. Railway junction. Market town. Trade in timber, agricultural produce. Named after the near-by Mt Gambier, an extinct volcano with crater lakes.

**Mount Isa** Australia. Mining town in W Queensland 65 m. W of Cloncurry. Pop. (1966) 16,713. Terminus of the railway from Townsville on the E coast. Zinc, lead, and silver ores are mined from a long lode, copper from a lower level. Smelters produce metallic lead, blister copper, and zinc concentrates.

**Mount Lyell** Australia. Copper-mining centre in Tasmania 95 m. WSW of Launceston, near Queenstown. Electrolytic refinery.

**Mount Morgan** Australia. Mining town in E Queensland 22 m. SSW of Rockhampton. Pop. (1966) 4,055. Considerable gold production in the late 19th cent.; output is now small, but copper ore is mined from beneath the gold-bearing quartz.

**Mount Rushmore National Memorial** USA. Massive sculptures carved in the granite side of Mt Rushmore in the Black Hills of W South Dakota, 17 m. SW of Rapid

City. A national memorial (1,220 acres) was established in 1929. The sculptures represent the heads of four US presidents (Washington, Jefferson, Lincoln, Theodore Roosevelt); each face is 60–70 ft high. They are the work of Gutzon Borglum, who began in 1927 and continued till his death in 1941; they were completed by his son Lincoln Borglum.

**Mount Vernon** (New York) USA. Residential and industrial suburb of New York city, New York, just N of the Bronx. Pop. (1960) 76,010. Manufactures electrical equipment, metal goods, chemicals, etc.

**Mount Vernon** (Virginia) USA. National shrine, on the Potomac R. 15 m. S of Washington (DC): the estate and mansion where George Washington lived from 1747 till his death (1799). In the grounds is the tomb of George and Martha Washington and several other members of the family.

**Mourne Mountains** Northern Ireland. Range 14 m. long in Co. Down extending NE–SW between Dundrum Bay and Carlingford Lough, rising to 2,796 ft in Slieve Donard. Reputedly the most picturesque mountains in Northern Ireland.

**Mouscron** (Flemish Moeskroen) Belgium. Town in W Flanders province 32 m. SW of Ghent near the French border. Pop. (1968) 37,746. Manufactures cotton goods, carpets, etc.

**Mousehole** England. Fishing village and seaside resort in SW Cornwall, on Mount's Bay 3 m. S of Penzance. Pop. 1,300.

**Mozambique** ◊ *Moçambique*.

**Mozambique Channel** ◊ *Moçambique Channel*.

**Muchinga Mountains** ◊ *Zambia*.

**Mufulira** ◊ *Ndola*.

**Muharraq** ◊ *Bahrain*.

**Mühlhausen** German Democratic Republic. Town in the Erfurt district, on the Unstrut R. 31 m. NW of Erfurt. Pop. (1965) 46,135. Industrial centre. Manufactures textiles, machinery, furniture, etc. An ancient town, fortified in the 10th cent., with 14th-cent. churches and a 17th-cent. town hall.

**Mukden** ◊ *Shenyang*.

**Mülhausen** ◊ *Mulhouse*.

**Mülheim-an-der-Ruhr** Federal German Republic. Industrial town in N Rhine-Westphalia, on the Ruhr R. 5 m. WSW of Essen. Pop. (1968) 189,343. Coalmining centre. Max Planck Institute for coal research. Manufactures iron and steel, machinery, textiles. Brewing, tanning, etc.

**Mulhouse** (Ger. Mülhausen) France. Industrial town in the Haut-Rhin department, on the Ill R. and the Rhône–Rhine Canal. Pop. (1968) 118,558. Important textile centre. Manufactures cotton, silk, and rayon goods, also hosiery, chemicals from the potash deposits to the N, paper, machinery, etc. Engineering. Had planned residential districts for workers from the mid-19th cent. A 16th-cent. town hall. Became a free imperial city in the 14th cent. Remained a member of the Swiss Confederation 1515–1798, and then joined France. Held by Germany, with the rest of Alsace, 1871–1918.

**Mull** Scotland. Island in the Inner Hebrides, in Argyllshire, separated from the mainland by the Sound of Mull and the Firth of Lorne. Area 351 sq. m. Pop. (1961) 1,961. Chief town Tobermory (NE). Mountainous, rising to 3,169 ft in Ben More. Picturesque broken coastline. Main occupations crofting, fishing. Tobermory attracts tourists in the summer. Duart and Aros are the principal ancient castles; near the former is a lighthouse commemorating the novelist William Black (1841–98), who described the island.

**Mullingar** Irish Republic. County town of Co. Westmeath, on the R. Brosna and the Royal Canal 45 m. WNW of Dublin. Pop. (1966) 6,471. Market town. Trade in cattle, horses, dairy produce. Modern Roman Catholic cathedral. Loughs Ennell, Owel, and Derravaragh near by are well-known for their trout fishing.

**Multan** (Mooltan) Pakistan. Capital of Multan division, W Pakistan, near the Chenab R. Pop. (1961) 358,000. Trade in wheat, cotton, sugar, etc. Manufactures textiles, hosiery, carpets, etc. Natural gas for its industries is supplied by pipeline from Sui. Has the tombs of two Muslim saints and the ruins of an ancient Hindu temple.

**Mulungushi** ◊ *Kabwe*.

**München** ◊ *Munich*.

**München Gladbach** Federal German Republic. Industrial town in N Rhine-Westphalia, on the Niers R. 15 m. W of Düsseldorf. Pop. (1968) 151,954. Centre of the cotton industry. Also manufactures textile machinery, clothing, paper, chemicals, etc. Grew up round a Benedictine monastery founded in the 10th cent.

Severely damaged by bombing in the 2nd World War.

**Muncie** USA. Industrial town in Indiana, on the White R. 50 m. NE of Indianapolis. Pop. (1960) 68,603. Manufactures glassware, electrical equipment, furniture, etc.

**Mundaring** ◊ *Kalgoorlie*; *Perth* (Australia).

**Munich** (Ger. **München**) Federal German Republic. Capital of Bavaria and the second largest city of the FGR (excluding W Berlin), on the Isar R. Pop. (1968) 1,244,237. Industrial, commercial, cultural, and route centre. Brewing, printing and publishing. Manufactures precision instruments, chemicals, machinery, clothing, food products, etc. Picturesque, with fine parks, inc. the Englischer Garten; many of its famous buildings were destroyed or severely damaged in the 2nd World War, including the Alte and Neue Pinakothek (though most of their art collections were preserved); the 15th-cent. Frauenkirche; the Renaissance church of St Michael; the Glyptothek, another art museum; and the 15th-cent. old town hall. The Hofbräuhaus, scene of the Hitler Putsch of 1923, however, survived and the Bavarian National Museum was only slightly damaged. The university was transferred here from Landshut in 1826. Became the home of the Wittelsbach family (1255) and later the capital of Bavaria (1508). Under Ludwig I (1786–1868) developed into a great art centre. Headquarters of the Nazi movement from 1919. Scene of the Munich Agreement (1938).

**Münster** Federal German Republic. Industrial town in N Rhine-Westphalia, on the Dortmund–Ems Canal 38 m. W of Bielefeld. Pop. (1968) 202,644. Manufactures agricultural and mining machinery, hardware, furniture, etc. Brewing, flour milling, printing. Formerly well-known for its medieval character; many of its buildings were severely damaged in the 2nd World War, including the 13th/14th-cent. cathedral, the 14th-cent. Gothic town hall, and the university (1773). A prominent member of the Hanseatic League in the 13th and 14th cent.

**Munster** Irish Republic. Largest of the 4 provinces, comprising counties Clare, Cork, Kerry, Limerick, Tipperary, and Waterford. Area 9,315 sq. m. Pop. (1966) 859,334. One of the ancient kingdoms of Ireland, its capital being Cashel.

**Murano** Italy. Suburb of Venice, built on several islets in the lagoon, famous since the 13th cent. for its Venetian glass industry. This industry had declined by the 18th cent., but has since been revived by the manufacture of cheaper types of glass. The 9th/12th-cent. Church of SS Maria e Donato has some outstanding mosaics.

**Murchison Falls** ◊ *Nile River*; *Shiré River*.

**Murcia** Spain. **1.** Region and former kingdom in the SE, comprising the present provinces of Albacete and Murcia. Taken from the Moors 1242. Annexed to Castile 1269.
**2.** Province in the SE on the Mediterranean Sea. Area 4,369 sq. m. Pop. (1961) 800,463. Cap. Murcia. Generally mountainous. Hot dry climate; agriculture (oranges, mulberries, cereals, etc.) is largely dependent on irrigation. Lead, zinc, and other minerals produced. Chief towns Murcia, Cartagena (seaport), Lorca.
**3.** Capital of Murcia province, on the Segura R. 43 m. SW of Alicante, in the low-lying, fertile *huerta* or garden of Murcia. Pop. (1967) 261,960. Industrial centre. Has a silk industry dating from Moorish times; manufactures other textiles. Tanning, distilling, flour milling, etc. Largely modern; 14th/15th-cent. cathedral. University (1915). Under the Moors it was twice made capital of the independent kingdom of Murcia.

**Mureş** (Hungarian **Maros**) **River** Hungary/Rumania. River 550 m. long chiefly in Rumania, rising in the Carpathians and flowing generally WSW past Targu-Mureş and Arad to join the Tisza R. at Szeged (Hungary).

**Murghab** (**Murgab**) **River**. River 450 m. long in Central Asia rising in the W of the Hindu Kush and flowing W and NW across NW Afghanistan; it enters SE Turkmen SSR, turns N across the Kara Kum desert, waters the Mary oasis, and then loses itself in the desert.

**Murmansk** USSR. Capital of the Murmansk region, RSFSR, on the E shore of Kola Bay, Barents Sea, in the NW of the Kola Peninsula. Pop. (1970) 309,000. Being an ice-free port and linked by rail with Leningrad, it developed rapidly after its foundation (1915). Exports timber, apatite. Important fishing centre. Shipyards, fish canneries, sawmills, refrigeration plants, etc. Had great strategic importance in the 2nd World War as the port to which US and British supplies for the USSR were shipped by the Arctic route.

**Murom** USSR. Industrial town and railway junction in the Vladimir region, RSFSR, on the Oka R. near the confluence with the Tesha R. 180 m. E of Moscow. Pop. (1961) 81,000. Railway engineering, flax spinning, tanning, etc. One of the oldest Russian towns, founded in the 10th cent.

**Muroran** Japan. Industrial town and seaport in S Hokkaido 45 m. NNE of Hakodate. Pop. (1965) 161,252. Important iron and steel industry. Oil refining. Manufactures cement etc. Exports iron and steel, coal, timber.

**Murray River** Australia. The chief river of Australia, 1,600 m. long, rising in the Australian Alps near Mt Kosciusko, New South Wales, flowing W through a level basin and then S through L. Alexandrina to reach the Indian Ocean at Encounter Bay, S Australia. For some 1,200 m. it forms the boundary between New South Wales and Victoria, though its shallow, winding, braided course scarcely makes it ideal for this purpose. Its major tributaries are the Lachlan-Murrumbidgee from the E, the Goulburn from the S, and the lengthy but very erratic Darling from the far NE. The upper waters, snow-fed in spring, now benefit from the Snowy R. diversion scheme. About two thirds of Australia's irrigated area lies in the Murray R. basin: water is retained in major storages such as the Hume Reservoir, raised in level by barrages, weirs, and locks at various points, and distributed by diversion or pumping into and through channels. Besides grain and pastoral products (esp. wool), there is a large output of dried and canned fruits from the river basin. Hydroelectric power comes from stations on the upper river, its tributaries, and the Snowy Mountains project.

**Mürren** Switzerland. Health resort and winter-sports centre at a height of 5,415 ft in the Bernese Oberland, above the Lauterbrunnen valley and near the Jungfrau. Pop. (1960) 336. Fine mountain views. Reached by mountain railway.

**Mur (Mura) River.** River 300 m. long rising in Austria at the W end of the Niedere Tauern, and flowing generally E, then SE past Graz, forming parts of the Austro-Yugoslav and Yugoslav-Hungarian borders, and joining the Drava R. at Legrad. Navigable below Graz.

**Murrumbidgee River** Australia. River 1,050 m. long in New South Wales, rising

in the Great Dividing Range and flowing N and then W to join the Murray R. Its chief tributary is the Lachlan R. from the N. Water impounded by the Burrinjuck Dam aids irrigation in the basin, where sheep and dairy cattle graze on sown pastures, and cereals, fruits and vines, and vegetables flourish.

**Murviedro** ◊ *Sagunto*.

**Murzuk** ◊ *Fezzan*.

**Musala, Mount** ◊ *Rhodope Mountains*.

**Muscat and Oman.** * Independent sultanate in E Arabia, on the Gulf of Oman and the Arabian Sea. Area 82,000 sq. m. Pop. 750,000 (mainly Arabs, but with a substantial admixture of Negro blood). Cap. Muscat (pop. 6,208). NW of Muscat town is a fertile coastal plain famous for its dates, which ripen early and have a fine flavour. The interior, which is generally arid, consists of a plateau and a mountain range extending NW–SE and rising in some peaks to over 9,000 ft. Muscat town is now smaller and commercially less important than Matrah. The foreign trade of the sultanate is mainly with India, Burma, and Britain. Leading exports dates, limes, and other fruits. Muscat and Oman has been closely associated with Britain for more than 150 years.

**Musgrave Ranges** Australia. Much eroded mountain ranges in the NW of S Australia, extending about 200 m. along the border with the Northern Territory, rising to 4,970 ft in Mt Woodroffe.

**Muskegon** USA. Industrial town in Michigan, on L. Michigan at the mouth of the Muskegon R. Pop. (1960) 46,485. Manufactures motor-car parts, aircraft engines, metal goods, furniture, etc.

**Muskegon River** USA. River 230 m. long in Michigan, rising in L. Houghton and flowing generally SW to L. Michigan. Widens to form L. Muskegon at the mouth.

**Muskogee** USA. Town in Oklahoma near the Arkansas R., 46 m. SE of Tulsa. Pop. (1960) 38,059. Railway and commercial centre for an agricultural and oil-producing region. Oil refining, meat packing. Manufactures glassware, clothing, etc.

**Musselburgh** Scotland. Small burgh in Midlothian, on the Firth of Forth at the mouth of the R. Esk 6 m. E of Edinburgh. Pop. (1961) 17,273. Brewing. Manufactures paper, wire rope, nets, etc. Seat of Loretto School, a leading Scottish public school. Has the Jacobean mansion Pinkie

House. The Battle of Pinkie (1547) took place just SE.

**Muzaffarpur** India. Town in Bihar, on the Burhi Gandak R. 40 m. NNE of Patna. Pop. (1961) 109,048. Trade in grain, tobacco, sugar-cane, etc. Rice and sugar milling. University (1952).

**Mwanza** ◊ *Tabora*; *Victoria, Lake*.

**Mweru, Lake** Congo (Kinshasa)/Zambia. Lake 75 m. long and 30 m. wide on the frontier between Congo (Kinshasa) and Zambia, at a height of 3,050 ft. Receives the Luapula R. (a headstream of the Congo R.) in the S. Drained by the Luvua R. in the N. Discovered by Dr Lacerda (Portuguese) 1798; rediscovered by Livingstone 1867. Sir Alfred Sharpe explored the W shore 1890.

**Mycenae** Greece. Ancient city in the NE Peloponnese 17 m. SW of Corinth near the modern village of Mikinai. Ruled over by Atreus and Agamemnon, it flourished *c.* 1400 B.C. Destroyed by the people of Argos in the 5th cent. B.C. and never recovered. The excavations of Schliemann and others (begun 1874) revealed a palace, the city walls with the famous Lion Gate, and tombs.

**Myitkyina** Burma. Capital of Kachin State, on the Irrawaddy R. 250 m. NNE of Mandalay. Pop. 7,000. Market town. Linked by rail and waterway with Mandalay and Rangoon and by road with Yunnan province (China).

**Mymensingh** Pakistan. Town in E Pakistan, on an old channel of the Brahmaputra R. 70 m. N of Dacca. Pop. 45,000. Trade in rice, jute, oilseeds, etc. Engineering.

**Mysore** India. 1. Constituent state of the Indian Union, mainly on the S Deccan plateau, with a narrow plain along the Malabar Coast. Area 74,210 sq. m. Pop. (1961) 23,586,772 (of whom 60 per cent speak Kannada (Kanarese), 15 per cent Telugu). Cap. Bangalore. The average height of the plateau region is about 2,500 ft, but in the Baba Budan Hills the land rises to over 6,000 ft. The principal rivers, e.g. the Krishna and Cauvery, flow E from the Western Ghats to the Bay of Bengal. Rainfall is heavy in the hill country, where there are dense forests, producing sandalwood etc. More than three quarters of the population, however, are engaged in agriculture. Main crops rice, groundnuts, cotton, sugar-cane, coffee. All India's gold is produced in Mysore, as well as iron and manganese ore. Principal towns Bangalore, Mysore, Hubli, Mangalore, Belgaum. Originally under Hindu rule, Mysore was seized by the Muslim usurper Hyder Ali (1761). His successor, Tippoo Sultan, was defeated by the British (1799) and the former dynasty was restored. Joined the Indian Union 1947.
2. City in Mysore state, 80 m. SW of Bangalore. Pop. (1961) 253,865. Manufactures silk and cotton goods, paints, fertilizers, etc., power being derived from the Sivasamudram hydroelectric plant. Seat of a university (1916), with Bangalore. Within the fort is the former Maharajah's palace.

**Mytilene (Mitilini)** Greece. Capital of Lesbos *nome*, seaport on the SE coast of Lesbos island, in the Aegean Sea. Pop. (1961) 25,758. Trade in olive oil, citrus fruits, cereals. Built first on an offshore island, it was later linked to Lesbos by a causeway and spread along the coast.

**Mytishchi** USSR. Industrial town in the Moscow region, RSFSR, 14 m. NNE of Moscow. Pop. (1970) 119,000. Manufactures railway rolling stock, textiles, etc.

# N

**Naas** Irish Republic. County town of Co. Kildare, 18 m. WSW of Dublin. Pop. (1966) 4,529. Once the residence of the kings of Leinster. Hunting centre. Punchestown racecourse is 2½ m. S.

**Nablus (Nabulus)** Jordan. Town in the NW, in Samaria, between Mt Ebal (3,087 ft) and Mt Gerizim (2,890 ft), 31 m. N. of Jerusalem. Pop. (1961) 45,658. Manufactures soap. Built on the site of ancient Shechem; near by are the reputed Jacob's well and Joseph's tomb.

**Nadi** ◊ *Fiji Islands.*

**Nafud (Nefud)** Saudi Arabia. Large desert area consisting of sand dunes and bare rock. The main part, S of the Syrian Desert, is known as the Great Nafud, and the SE extension, which joins the Rub al Khali, as the Little Nafud or Dahna.

**Naga Hills** India. Ranges of hills in the extreme NE, on the Burmese border, which gave their name to a former district of Assam. Average height 5,000–7,000 ft. Much forested. Little developed. ◊» *Nagaland.*

**Nagaland** India. Constituent state of the Indian Union, in the extreme NE, bordered on the E by Burma, formed in 1962 from the former Naga Hills district of Assam and the former Tuensang Frontier division of the North-East Frontier Tract. Area 6,236 sq. m. Pop. (1961) 369,200. Cap. Kohima (pop. 7,246). Inhabited by the Nagas, a Tibeto-Burmese group of tribes who speak a variety of dialects; more than 50 per cent are Christians (mainly Naga Baptists). They practise shifting agriculture, growing rice, maize, and vegetables, and were formerly notorious headhunters. For some years before the formation of the state they sought independence, and the Indian government was forced to take military action against rebels. Rebel activity continued into 1964, when the first general elections were held.

**Nagano** Japan. Capital of Nagano prefecture, in central Honshu 110 m. NW of Tokyo. Pop. (1965) 172,835. Manufactures machinery, textiles, etc. Food processing. Trade in silk. Also a religious centre, with a 7th-cent. Buddhist temple.

**Nagaoka** Japan. Industrial town in Niigata prefecture, Honshu, 31 m. SSW of Niigata.

Pop. (1965) 154,752. Oil refining, engineering. Manufactures chemicals, textiles.

**Nagapattinam (Negapatam)** India. Seaport and industrial town in Madras, on the Coromandel Coast 80 m. E of Tiruchirapalli. Pop. (1961) 59,063. Exports groundnuts, cotton goods, tobacco, etc. Railway engineering etc. Site of an early Portuguese settlement (1612); taken by the Dutch (1660) and the British (1781).

**Nagar Aveli** ◊ *Dadra and Nagar Aveli.*

**Nagasaki** Japan. Capital of Nagasaki prefecture, in W Kyushu 50 m. W of Kumamoto. Pop. (1965) 405,479. Seaport. Exports coal, cement, canned fish, etc. Important shipbuilding and engineering industry (Mitsubishi). Fishing. Picturesque, in an amphitheatre facing a narrow bay. In the 16th cent. it was the only Japanese port with foreign trade, being visited first by the Portuguese and Dutch. During the 2nd World War it was largely destroyed by the second atomic bomb, which killed 26,000 people and injured over 40,000 (9 August 1945).

**Nagercoil** India. Town in S Madras 40 m. SE of Trivandrum. Pop. (1961) 106,207. Manufactures coir rope, mats, etc. Cape Comorin, the southernmost point of India, is 10 m. SE.

**Nag Hammadi** ◊ *Kharga Oasis.*

**Nagorno-Karabakh AR USSR.** Autonomous region in the Azerbaijan SSR, on the E slopes of the Lesser Caucasus. Area 1,700 sq. m. Pop. (1970) 149,000 (Armenians and Azerbaijanis). Cap. Stepanakert (pop. 30,000). Mountainous. Main products wine, silk, dairy produce. Once a separate khanate. Became an autonomous region 1923.

**Nagoya** Japan. Capital of Aichi prefecture, central Honshu, on Ise Bay 68 m. E of Kyoto. Pop. (1965) 1,935,430. Seaport, industrial centre, and Japan's third largest city. First opened to foreign trade 1907. Engineering, metal working. Manufactures machinery, porcelain, textiles, chemicals, etc. University (1939). The 17th-cent. castle was severely damaged by bombing in the 2nd World War. Also has the Buddhist temple of Higashi Honganji.

**Nagpur** India. Commercial city and railway junction in N Maharashtra 440 m.

ENE of Bombay. Pop. (1961) 643,659.
Manufactures cotton goods, hosiery, dyes,
etc. University (1923). Became capital of
the Mahratta kingdom of Nagpur (1743),
of the Central Provinces (1861), and for
a short time of Madhya Pradesh (1956).

**Nagykanizsa** Hungary. Town in Zala
county, in the SW, 65 m. WNW of
Pécs. Pop. 34,000. Manufactures footwear.
Brewing, distilling, flour milling, etc.
Trade in grain, livestock.

**Nagykikinda** ◊ *Kikinda*.

**Nagykörös** Hungary. Market town in
Szolnok county 48 m. SE of Budapest.
Pop. 30,000. Trade in fruit, wine. Flour
milling, distilling, canning.

**Nagyszeben** ◊ *Sibiu*.

**Naha** Okinawa. Seaport and largest city,
on the SW coast. Pop. (1960) 250,832.
Headquarters of the US military and the
local government of the Ryukyu Is.
Exports sugar, dried fish, etc. Manufactures textiles, pottery, etc. Before the
2nd World War it was the capital of the
Okinawa prefecture, Japan.

**Nahuel Huapí, Lake** Argentina. Andean
lake (area 205 sq. m.) at a height of 2,516
ft near the Chilean border in Neuquén and
Río Negro provinces. Resort area with a
National Park established 1903. Picturesque, with many islands; the largest,
Victoria, has a forestry research station.

**Nairn** Scotland. Small burgh and county
town of Nairnshire, at the mouth of the
Nairn R. on Moray Firth. Pop. (1961)
4,899. Fishing port. Holiday resort. Golf
courses.

**Nairn River** Scotland. River 38 m. long
rising in Inverness-shire and flowing NE
through Nairnshire to the Moray Firth at
Nairn.

**Nairnshire** Scotland. County in the NE
bordering N on Moray Firth. Area 163
sq. m. Pop. (1961) 8,421. County town
Nairn. Mountainous in the S, rising to
2,162 ft on the Inverness border. Coastal
plain in the N, drained by the Nairn and
Findhorn rivers. Main occupations agriculture (oats, turnips), cattle and sheep
rearing, fishing.

**Nairobi** Kenya. Capital, 275 m. NW of
Mombasa at a height of 5,450 ft. Pop.
(1962) 266,794 (21,477 Europeans, 86,453
Asians). Near the equator, but has a
pleasant climate on account of the altitude.
Views of Mt Kenya and Mt Kilimanjaro.
In a fertile area producing mainly coffee,
sisal, pyrethrum. Railway and other

engineering, meat packing, flour milling,
brewing. Manufactures pottery, chemicals,
soap, etc. Outside the city is the Nairobi
National Park, a game reserve. Has the
Royal College, a constituent college of the
University of E Africa (1963). Founded
(1899) as the headquarters of the Mombasa–Uganda railway. With the influx of
white settlers it rapidly became important. Replaced Mombasa as administrative
centre 1907. Attained municipal status
1919. Became a city 1950.

**Naivasha, Lake** Kenya. Lake 10 m. long
and 9 m. wide in the Great Rift Valley, at a
height of 6,187 ft. No known outlet.
On its NE shore is the small town and
resort of Naivasha, centre of a dairy-
farming and sheep-rearing area.

**Najaf (Nejef)** Iraq. Town near the Euphrates R. 90 m. S of Baghdad. Pop. (1965)
128,096. Founded by Haroun al Rashid in
the 8th cent. A famous centre of pilgrimage for the Shia Muslims, as the burial
place of Ali, Mohammed's son-in-law.

**Nakhichevan** USSR. Ancient Naxuana.
Capital of Nakhichevan ASSR, Azerbaijan
SSR, 80 m. SE of Yerevan at a height of
2,900 ft. Pop. (1970) 33,000. Flour milling,
tanning. Long disputed by Armenians,
Turks, and Persians.

**Nakhichevan ASSR** USSR. Autonomous
republic in the Azerbaijan SSR, on the
Iranian border, an enclave within Armenia.
Area 2,130 sq. m. Pop. (1970) 202,000
(mainly Azerbaijanis). Cap. Nakhichevan.
Mainly agricultural. Chief crops cotton,
tobacco. Annexed by Russia 1828. Became
an autonomous republic within Azerbaijan
1924.

**Nakhodka** USSR. Seaport in the Primorye
Territory, RSFSR, on the Pacific coast
55 m. ESE of Vladivostok. Pop. (1970)
105,000. Acts as outport for and has largely
superseded Vladivostok, owing to greater
freedom from ice in winter. Ship repairing,
sawmilling, food processing. Manufactures
plywood, matches, etc.

**Nakhon Pathom** Thailand. Capital of Nakhon Pathom province, 31 m. W of Bangkok
on the railway to Singapore. Pop. 26,000.
Market town. Trade in rice, sugar-cane,
etc. Has the largest stupa in Thailand,
built in the 19th cent. on the site of one
dating from the 6th cent.

**Nakhon Ratchasima (Korat)** Thailand.
Capital of Nakhon Ratchasima province,
on the Mun R. 140 m. NE of Bangkok.
Pop. 41,000. Railway junction. Chief com-

mercial centre of E Thailand. Trade in rice, livestock, etc. Increased in importance with the construction of the railway from Bangkok (1892) and its later extension to the N and E.

**Nakhon Sawan** Thailand. Capital of Nakhon Sawan province, on the Menam Chao Phraya just below the confluence of the Nan and Ping rivers, 135 m. N of Bangkok. Pop. 30,000. River port. Important trade in teak, floated down river.

**Nakhon Si Thammarat** Thailand. Capital of Nakhon Si Thammarat province, near the E coast of the Malay peninsula 370 m. S of Bangkok. Pop. 26,000. Market town. Trade in rice, coconuts, fruits, etc. One of the oldest towns in Thailand; capital of a kingdom until the 13th cent.

**Nakuru** Kenya. Capital of the Rift Valley province, on the N shore of L. Nakuru, 85 m. N W of Nairobi at a height of 6,000 ft. Pop. (1962) 37,900. Commercial centre in a district important for coffee, maize, pyrethrum, sisal, wheat, dairy produce.

**Nakuru, Lake** Kenya. Salt lake 8 m. long and 4 m. wide in the Great Rift Valley, with the town of Nakuru on its N shore. Famous for its bird life, esp. the flamingo.

**Nalchik** USSR. Capital of the Kabardino-Balkar ASSR, RSFSR, on the N slopes of the Greater Caucasus 105 m. W of Grozny. Pop. (1970) 146,000. Industrial centre. Flour milling, meat packing. Manufactures oilfield equipment, furniture, textiles, clothing, footwear, etc. Founded (1818) as a Russian fortress.

**Namangan** USSR. Town in the Uzbek SSR, in the fertile Fergana valley 120 m. E of Tashkent. Pop. (1970) 175,000. Cotton manufactures, food processing, etc. Trade in livestock, fruit, etc.

**Namaqualand** S Africa/SW Africa. Arid coastal region with little vegetation. Pop. 30,000 (mainly Namaquas (Namas), consisting of Hottentot tribes). Divided into two parts by the Orange R. Great Namaqualand is in the N (in SW Africa) and Little Namaqualand in the S (in the Cape Province of S Africa). Produces copper, diamonds, tungsten.

**Namen** ◊ *Namur*.

**Namhoi** ◊ *Fatshan*.

**Namib Desert** SW Africa. Desert region 800 m. long and 60 m. wide, between the plateau and the Atlantic Ocean. The coastal strip receives less than 1 in. of rain annually and is practically barren.

**Namur** (Flemish **Namen**) Belgium. **1.** Pro-

vince in the SW, bordering S on France. Area 1,413 sq. m. Pop. (1968) 381,578. Fruit growing in the fertile N, lumbering in the wooded S. Much quarrying. Drained by the Meuse and Sambre rivers. Chief towns Namur, Dinant.

**2.** Capital of Namur province, at the confluence of the Meuse and Sambre rivers 35 m. SE of Brussels. Pop. (1968) 32,418. Manufactures cutlery, glass. Tanning, flour milling, etc. Cathedral (18th-cent.). The fortifications built in the late 19th cent. were reduced by the Germans in the 1st World War (1914), and the town was severely damaged in the 2nd World War.

**Nanchang** China. Capital of Kiangsi province, on the Kan R. 170 m. SE of Wuhan. Pop. 508,000. Commercial and industrial centre. Trade in tea, rice, cotton, hemp, tobacco, etc. Manufactures machinery, chemicals, textiles, glass, pottery, paper, etc. In the Sino-Japanese War it was occupied by the Japanese (1939–45).

**Nancy** France. Prefecture of the Meurthe-et-Moselle department in the NE, on the Meurthe R. and the Marne–Rhine Canal. Pop. (1968) 127,826. Formerly capital of Lorraine. Situated near the ironfield, it has become a centre of iron and steel manufacture. Engineering. Manufactures textiles, glass, footwear, tobacco products, etc. Extraordinarily well planned; outstanding features are the Place Stanislas, with impressive 18th-cent. buildings, a triumphal arch leading from it to the Place Carrière, and the 18th-cent. cathedral. Seat of a university (1572) and a national school of forestry. Became capital of the dukes of Lorraine in the 12th cent., and developed culturally and architecturally under the last of them, Stanislas Leszczynski of Poland, in the 18th cent. Finally became French 1766.

**Nanda Devi** India. Himalayan peak (25,645 ft) in the Garhwal district, N Uttar Pradesh. First climbed (1936) by an Anglo-American expedition (Tilman and Odell).

**Nanga Parbat** India. Himalayan peak (26,660 ft) in W Kashmir, 60 m. W of Skardu. Several climbers, particularly on the German expeditions of 1934 and 1937, lost their lives in trying to reach the summit; it was finally scaled in 1953 by Buhl, an Austrian.

**Nanking** China. Capital of Kiangsu province, on the Yangtse-kiang 165 m. WNW of Shanghai. Pop. (1957) 1,419,000. River port. Industrial centre. Manufactures textiles, paper, fertilizers, etc.; it gave its name to the cloth 'nankeen'. Once one of the leading literary centres of China. University (1928). Founded (1368) on the site of a more ancient city, it was made the 'southern capital' by the first Ming emperor but was deserted for Peking in 1421. During the Taiping rebellion the city was taken by the rebels (1853), who destroyed its ancient walls and the famous 15th-cent. porcelain tower. In 1928 it was made the capital of China by the Nationalist government, but in 1937 it fell to the Japanese – the notorious 'rape of Nanking'. In 1945 the Japanese surrender in China was signed here; in 1946 it became capital, but in 1949 under the Communist régime the capital was again moved to Peking. A road-rail bridge (double-decker construction) about 4 m. long over the Yangtse, the longest in China, was opened 1968; previously trains had to be ferried across the river.

**Nanning** China. Formerly (1913–45) Yungning. Capital of the Kwangsi-Chuang A R, on the Siang R. 105 m. S W of Liuchow. Pop. 195,000. River port. Trade in rice, hides, tobacco, etc. Flour milling, sugar refining, tanning. Manufactures textiles etc. Formerly capital of Kwangsi province, it became capital of the Kwangsi-Chuang A R 1958.

**Nanterre** France. Suburb of N W Paris, in the Hauts-de-Seine department near the left bank of the Seine R. at the foot of Mont Valérien. Pop. (1968) 90,632. Metal working. Manufactures electrical equipment, hosiery, chemicals, paints, etc.

**Nantes** France. Prefecture of the Loire-Atlantique department, on the Loire R. at its confluence with the Erdre and Sèvre Nantaise rivers. Pop. (1968) 265,009. Important seaport, with outport St Nazaire. Exports petroleum products, etc. Also an industrial centre. Oil refining, flour milling, sugar refining, tobacco processing, vegetable canning, etc. Manufactures chocolate, vegetable oils, etc. Harbour accessible to ocean-going ships owing to post-war improvements. Castle founded in the 10th cent., once residence of the dukes of Brittany; 15th-cent. cathedral, not completed till the 19th cent. Before the Roman conquest of Gaul Nantes was the chief town of the Namnetes. Here Henry IV signed the famous Edict of Nantes (1598), revoked by Louis XIV in 1685. Severely damaged in the 2nd World War.

**Nantucket** USA. Island 15 m. long, off the coast of S E Massachusetts 25 m. S of Cape Cod. Low-lying. Formerly an important whaling centre. Now chiefly a summer resort.

**Nantwich** England. Urban district in Cheshire, on the R. Weaver 4 m. S W of Crewe. Pop. (1961) 10,454. Formerly important in the salt industry; now has brine baths. Tanning. Manufactures footwear, clothing. Has a 14th-cent. church.

**Napier** New Zealand. Capital of the Hawke's Bay provincial district, N Island, on the S W shore of Hawke Bay. Pop. (1966) 28,654. Serves an intensively farmed region. Wool, frozen lamb, hides and skins are exported from its port, Port Ahuriri, 2 m. distant. In 1931 it suffered considerable earthquake damage, with loss of life, the coastal area being raised 8 ft; the town was largely rebuilt.

**Naples** (Italian **Napoli**) Italy. Ancient Neapolis. Capital of Napoli province in Campania, the second seaport and third largest city of Italy, 120 m. S E of Rome. Pop. (1968) 1,263,358. Important in industry and commerce. Shipbuilding, railway and other engineering, oil refining, tomato canning. Manufactures macaroni, textiles, chemicals, coral and tortoiseshell articles, etc. Exports wine, olive oil, fruits, etc. World-famous for its beautiful site at the base and on the slopes of a volcanic ridge on the N shore of the Bay of Naples; best viewed from the sea. Divided into two crescents by a hill surmounted by a fortress (Sant' Elmo) and the promontory of Pizzofalcone; the W part is a residential district, while the E is the much larger, more crowded, and older section of the city. On the small Isola del Salvatore, joined by a causeway to the foot of the Pizzofalcone, is the Castel dell' Ovo, while near the harbour are another medieval castle, the Castel Nuovo, the Royal Palace, and the San Carlo Opera House. Among the many churches is the 13th/14th-cent. Cathedral of San Gennaro, and the city is celebrated for the Museo Nazionale, which contains most of the objects excavated at Pompeii and Herculaneum. University (1224).

Probably founded by Greeks in the 6th cent. B.C., the city surrendered to the Romans in the 4th cent. B.C. and became a fashionable resort; Virgil often stayed here and is buried near by. Neapolis long retained its Greek culture, but in the 6th cent. it was under Byzantine rule, in the 8th cent.

an independent duchy. Later it became capital of the kingdom of Naples, the latter sometimes a separate kingdom and sometimes united with Sicily, and from the end of the 15th cent. it was held for varying periods by France, Spain, and Austria, till it was taken by Garibaldi in 1860 and incorporated in Italy in 1861. Suffered severely in the 2nd World War.

**Nara** Japan. Capital of Nara prefecture, S Honshu, 18 m. E of Osaka. Pop. 116,000. In a picturesque setting, in wooded hills. Manufactures textiles, dolls and fans, etc. Chiefly important as a religious and tourist centre. The first permanent capital of Japan 709–84. Many ancient Buddhist temples (one with a massive bronze image of Buddha) and Shinto shrines.

**Narbonne** France. Ancient Narbo Martius. Town in the Aude department 5 m. from the Gulf of Lions and 24 m. N of Perpignan. Pop. (1968) 40,035. Market town. Sulphur refining, brandy distilling, flour milling. Manufactures barrels, bricks and tiles, pottery. Trade in wine, brandy, etc. The first Roman colony in Gaul; later capital of Gallia Narbonensis. The harbour, improved by the Romans, silted up in the 14th cent. Part of the former archiepiscopal palace of the 13th/14th cent. now serves as town hall.

**Narew River** Poland/USSR. River 270 m. long rising in W Byelorussian SSR, USSR, and flowing first WNW into NE Poland, then turning SSW to join the W Bug N of Warsaw.

**Narmada River** India. River 800 m. long rising in the Maikala Range 50 m. NW of Bilaspur (Madhya Pradesh) and flowing generally W and then WSW through a depression between the Vindhya and Satpura Ranges, entering the Gulf of Cambay by a broad estuary. Sacred to Hindus. Used for navigation only in the lowest section.

**Narragansett Bay** USA. Inlet of the Atlantic in the Rhode Island coast, enclosing Rhode Island, Prudence Island, Conanicut Island, and others. Mainly fishing centres and resorts around its shores. Providence stands at its head.

**Narva** USSR. Port and industrial town in NE Estonia, on the Narva (Narova) R. 8 m. from the mouth on the Gulf of Finland. Pop. (1962) 21,300. Important textile manufacturing centre; the mills derive power from the falls on the Narva R. Founded (1223) by the Danes. Scene of the

defeat of Peter the Great of Russia by the Swedes (1700); he captured the town in 1704.

**Narvik** Norway. Ice-free port on Ofot Fiord 93 m. SSW of Tromsö. Pop. (1969) 13,422. Also a railway terminus. Exports iron ore from Gällivare and Kiruna, Sweden, having developed rapidly after completion of the railway (1903). Severely damaged in the 2nd World War; taken by the Germans in 1940, recaptured by British and French forces, and then evacuated.

**Naryan-Mar** ◊ *Nenets NA.*

**Naseby** England. Village in Northamptonshire, 11 m. W of Kettering, where the Royalists under Charles I and Prince Rupert were decisively defeated by the Parliamentarians under Cromwell and Fairfax (1645).

**Nashua** USA. Industrial town in New Hampshire 15 m. S of Manchester, at the confluence of the Merrimack and Nashua rivers. Pop. (1960) 39,096. Manufactures shoes, plastics, paper, etc.

**Nashville** USA. State capital of Tennessee, on the Cumberland R. Pop. (1960) 170,874. Important road and rail junction. Industrial and commercial centre. Railway engineering, printing and publishing. Manufactures rayon, cellophane, footwear, hosiery, glass, etc. Seat of the Vanderbilt University (1873) and the Fisk University (1865, Negro). The Hermitage, formerly the plantation home of President Andrew Jackson, is 11 m. E.

**Nasik** India. Town in Maharashtra, on the upper Godavari R. 90 m. NE of Bombay. Pop. (1961) 131,103. Manufactures copper and brass ware, soap, etc. Many temples and shrines. An important centre of Hindu pilgrimage. Near by are ancient Buddhist caves dating from the 3rd cent. B.C. and later.

**Nassau** Bahamas. Capital and chief seaport, on the NE coast of New Providence Island. Pop. (1963) 57,858. Exports pulpwood, salt, crawfish, cucumbers. Mild climate, fine beaches; chiefly famous as a holiday resort, patronized esp. by American visitors. Laid out 1729. Named after King William III (of the House of Orange-Nassau).

**Nassau** Federal German Republic. Former duchy in W Germany, with capital Wiesbaden. The family of Orange-Nassau provided the present ruling houses of the Netherlands and Luxembourg. Well wooded and fertile; famous for wines and for mineral springs, esp. at Wiesbaden and

Bad Ems. In 1866 it was incorporated in the Prussian province of Hesse-Nassau and in 1945 was incorporated into Hessen.

**Natal** Brazil. Capital of Rio Grande do Norte state in the NE, on the Potengi R. near the mouth. Pop. 157,000. Seaport. Exports sugar, cotton, salt, hides, carnauba wax. Manufactures textiles. Salt refining. A large international airport (Parnamirim) 8 m. SSW.

**Natal** S Africa. The smallest and most easterly province. Area 35,284 sq. m. including Zululand (N, 10,427 sq. m.). Pop. (1960) 2,933,447 (mainly Bantu; 300,000 whites; 300,000 Indians descended from labourers brought to the sugar plantations in 1860). Cap. Pietermaritzburg. Faces the Indian Ocean and rises westwards from the narrow coastal plain to the Drakensberg. Dissected by the Tugela R. and the Buffalo, the Pongola, and other rivers. A humid sub-tropical palm belt runs along the coast, but the major part is warm temperate grassland. Sugar-cane plantations in the coastal belt. Cotton, citrus fruits, tobacco cultivated in the uplands. Maize is an important crop in the central area. Wattle (grey acacia) is grown for timber and for tannin extract (from the bark). Cattle raised. Principal mineral coal, mined at Vryheid and Utrecht (NW). Sugar refining. Manufactures wattle extract, furniture, soap, clothing, leather. Industries are largely concentrated in Durban (largest city and chief seaport) and Pietermaritzburg; both are linked with Johannesburg by rail.

Named Terra Natalis by Vasco da Gama, who sighted the coast (near Durban) on Christmas Day 1497. Port Natal, the first British settlement, was established in 1824 and the town of Durban founded in 1835. Boers trekking from the Cape defeated the Zulus and set up the Republic of Natal in 1838. Annexed by Britain 1843; became a province of the Cape Colony 1844 and a separate colony 1856. Zululand was added in 1897 and the Vryheid and Utrecht districts in 1903. Merged in the Union of S Africa, as one of the four original provinces, in 1910.

**Natanya (Nathanya)** Israel. Town and seaside resort in the Plain of Sharon 19 m. NNE of Tel Aviv. Pop. (1968) 57,900. Diamond cutting, food processing. Manufactures textiles, chemicals, etc.

**Natick** USA. Town in Massachusetts 16 m. WSW of Boston. Pop. (1960) 28,831. Manufactures footwear, metal goods, etc.

On the site of land granted to John Eliot for his 'praying Indians' (converts) in 1650.

**Natron, Lake** Tanzania. Lake in the Great Rift Valley on the Kenya frontier, 36 m. long and 15 m. wide. Deposits of salt and soda.

**Natural Bridge** USA. Village in Virginia, 26 m. NW of Lynchburg. Near by is the 'natural bridge' from which the name derives, an arch of limestone 215 ft high, with a span of 90 ft, over Cedar Creek; a road crosses the arch.

**Naucratis (Naukratis)** United Arab Republic. Ancient city in Egypt, 45 m. SE of Alexandria. Founded by the Greeks c. 615 B.C. as a trading centre, the first Greek settlement in Egypt. The site was discovered (1884) by Flinders Petrie. Excavations have revealed much Greek pottery and the remains of temples.

**Naumburg** German Democratic Republic. Town in the Halle district, on the Saale R. 25 m. SSW of Halle. Pop. (1965) 38,121. Industrial centre. Manufactures textiles, leather goods, toys. Founded in the 10th cent. by the margraves of Meissen. The 13th-cent. cathedral has an unusually large crypt.

**Nauplia (Gr. Návplion, Nauplion)** Greece. Capital of Argolis *nome*, in the E Peloponnese, a seaport on the Gulf of Argolis. Pop. (1961) 8,918. Trade in tobacco, citrus fruits, vegetables, etc. Capital of Greece 1822–34 during the War of Independence.

**Nauru** SW Pacific Ocean. Raised atoll W of the Gilbert Is. Area 8 sq. m. Pop. (1966) 6,056 (inc. 3,101 Nauruans, 1,167 Chinese, 428 Europeans). A thick phosphate layer covering the central plateau is worked, treated, and shipped by Nauruans and Chinese, but the deposits show signs of exhaustion. Discovered (1798) by Capt. Fearn. Annexed by Germany 1888. Occupied by Australia 1914. Held under League of Nations Mandate 1920–47. Since 1947 it has been jointly held by Australia, Great Britain, and New Zealand, though administered in fact by Australia. Became independent 1968.

**Navarino** ◊ *Pylos*.

**Navarra** Spain. One of the Basque provinces, extending from the W Pyrenees along the French border in the N and to the Ebro R. in the S. Area 4,056 sq. m. Pop. (1961) 402,042. Cap. Pamplona. Largely mountainous, with fertile valleys. Drained by the Ebro and its tributaries. Sugar-beet, cereals, and vines cultivated. ◊ *Navarre*.

**Navarre** France/Spain. Former kingdom of N Spain and S W France, co-extensive with the modern Spanish province of Navarra and the French department of Basses-Pyrénées. Founded in the 9th cent. from lands inhabited by the Vascones. The Spanish section, S of the Pyrenees, was annexed to Spain (1515) by Ferdinand the Catholic. The N part was incorporated in France by Henry IV (1589).

**Návplion** ◊ *Nauplia*.

**Navsari** India. Town in Gujarat 20 m. SSE of Surat. Pop. (1961) 51,300. Trade in cotton, millet, etc. Manufactures textiles, copper and brass ware, etc.

**Naxos** Greece. Largest island in the Cyclades, in the Aegean Sea. Area 169 sq. m. Pop. 19,000. Known since ancient times for its wine. Also produces fruits, olive oil, emery. Associated with the worship of Dionysus; taken by Athens in the 5th cent. B.C.

**Nayarit** Mexico. State on the Pacific seaboard. Area 10,662 sq. m. Pop. (1969) 575,000. Cap. Tepic. Largely mountainous. The narrow coastal plain is crossed by the Santiago and other rivers. Maize, cotton, tobacco, sugar-cane, coffee, etc. cultivated. Silver, lead, etc. mined.

**Nazareth** Israel. Town in Lower Galilee 19 m. ESE of Haifa. Pop. 23,000. Famous for its associations with the early life of Jesus. Main building the church on the traditional site of the annunciation.

**Nchanga** ◊ *Zambia*.

**Ndola** Zambia. Capital of the Western Province, in the Copperbelt near the frontier with Congo (Kinshasa), 165 m. N of Lusaka. Pop. (1963) 80,000 (9,000 Europeans). Commercial, industrial, and railway centre, linked with the mining centres of Mufulira, Nchanga, Nkana, and Roan Antelope, and on the railway to Lubumbashi in Congo (Kinshasa). Copper and cobalt refining, brewing, sugar refining, etc. Settled 1902; became a municipality 1932. Scene of the air crash in which the Secretary General of the UN, Dag Hammerskjöld, was killed (1961) while on his way to negotiate a cease-fire in the Katanga civil war in Congo (Kinshasa).

**Neagh, Lough** Northern Ireland. Largest lake in the British Isles, 18 m. long, 11 m. wide, bordering on counties Antrim, Down, Armagh, Tyrone, and Londonderry. Fed by the Upper Bann, Blackwater, and other rivers. Drained by the Lower Bann. Its shores are generally low and in places marshy.

**Neanderthal** Federal German Republic. Valley in N Rhine-Westphalia 7 m. E of Düsseldorf where parts of the skeleton of Neanderthal man were discovered in a limestone cave (1856).

**Neath** Wales. Municipal borough in W Glamorganshire, on the R. Neath 7 m. ENE of Swansea. Pop. (1961) 30,884. Industrial centre. Copper smelting. Manufactures tinplate, metal boxes, chemicals, etc. Remains of a 12th-cent. castle and abbey. Its port, Briton Ferry, is within the borough.

**Nebraska** USA. State in central USA, bounded on the E and N E by the Missouri R. Area 77,237 sq. m. Pop. (1970) 1,468,101. Cap. Lincoln. Admitted to the Union in 1867 as the 37th state; popularly known as the 'Tree Planters'' or 'Cornhusker' state. Much prairie land; slopes gradually from the W, where it reaches 5,424 ft, to the SE. Drained by the Niobrara and Platte rivers (tributaries of the Missouri). Climate continental; hot summers, cold winters. Annual rainfall 20–30 ins. (decreasing to the W). Primarily agricultural. Principal crops maize, wheat, oats. Large numbers of cattle and pigs raised. Main industry the processing of agricultural produce. Chief towns Omaha, Lincoln. First explored (1541) by a Spanish party under Coronado, followed by the French in the 18th cent. Passed to the USA as part of the Louisiana Purchase (1803).

**Nechako River** Canada. River 287 m. long in British Columbia, rising in the Coast Mountains, flowing N E and E, and joining the Fraser R. at Prince George. The waters have been harnessed for hydroelectric power.

**Neckar River** Federal German Republic. River 230 m. long rising in the Black Forest and flowing generally N past Tübingen and Heilbronn, turning W past Heidelberg, and joining the Rhine R. at Mannheim. Picturesque throughout its course. Meanders in its lower reaches.

**Necochea** Argentina. Seaport at the mouth of the Quequén Grande R. 200 m. E of Bahía Blanca. Pop. 30,000. Exports grain. Also a popular resort.

**Needles, The** England. Three isolated chalk rocks off the W extremity of the Isle of Wight, Hampshire, near the entrance to the Solent. Lighthouse on the most westerly rock.

**Nefud** ◊ *Nafud*.

**Negapatam** ◊ *Nagapattinam*.

**Negev (Negeb)** Israel. Desert and semi-desert region in the S, mainly limestone plateau and hill country, triangular in outline, bordering on the United Arab Republic (W) and Jordan (E). Pop. (1962) 33,000 (excluding 18,000 semi-nomadic Bedouin). Much has been done to develop agriculture by irrigation (e.g. the Yarkon Negev water pipeline), and cereals, sunflowers, sugar-beet, etc. are grown on more than 100 settlements. Oil is produced at Heletz, and the port of Eilat (Elath) has been developed on the Gulf of Aqaba. Scene of much fighting between Israeli and Egyptian forces in 1948 and again in 1967.

**Negombo** Ceylon. Town and fishing port on the W coast 20 m. N of Colombo. Pop. (1963) 47,028. Manufactures brassware etc.

**Negri Sembilan** Malaysia. State in SW Malaya (W Malaysia), on the Strait of Malacca. Area 2,565 sq. m. Pop. (1967) 510,109 (chiefly Chinese and Malays). Cap. Seremban. Chief seaport Port Dickson. Main products rice, rubber, palm oil, tin. Formed by the union of 9 small states (1889). Joined the Federated Malay States (1896) and the Federation of Malaya (1947).

**Negro, Río** ◊ *Río Negro*.

**Negropont** ◊ *Chalcis*.

**Negros** Philippines. Fourth largest island, NW of Mindanao and between Panay and Cebu. Area 5,275 sq. m. Pop. 1,875,000. Chief town Bacolod. Largely mountainous. Produces sugar-cane and rice on the coastal plains.

**Neheim-Hüsten** Federal German Republic. Industrial town in N Rhine-Westphalia, at the confluence of the Möhne and Ruhr rivers. Pop. (1963) 34,700. Manufactures electrical equipment, cables, furniture, etc.

**Neisse (Nysa) River (Glatzer/Silesian Neisse)** Poland. River 120 m. long in SW Poland, rising near the Czechoslovak frontier and flowing generally N and E past Bystrzyca Klodzka and Klodzko (Glatz) to join the Oder R. near Brzeg.

**Neisse (Nysa) River (Görlitzer/Lusatian Neisse)** Czechoslovakia etc. River 140 m. long rising in N Bohemia, Czechoslovakia, in the Isergebirge, flowing generally N, and after leaving Czechoslovakia forming the boundary between the German Democratic Republic and Poland, past Görlitz and Forst to join the Oder R. near Gubin.

**Neiva** Colombia. Capital of Huila department, on the upper Magdalena R. 150 m. SSW of Bogotá. Pop. 81,000. Trade in coffee, tobacco, cattle, etc. Manufactures

Panama hats. Founded 1539. Destroyed by Indians; refounded 1612.

**Nejd** Saudi Arabia. Central area consisting of an extensive plateau sloping gradually E from 5,000 ft to 1,500 ft and bordered on the E by Kuwait and Hasa. Area 420,000 sq. m. Pop. about 4,000,000. Cap. Riyadh. Largely desert, with many oases in the N and E where dates form the staple product. Ibn Saud, after his conquest of Hejaz (1925), united it with Nejd to form the kingdom of Saudi Arabia (1932). ◊ *Arabia*; *Saudi Arabia*.

**Nejef** ◊ *Najaf*.

**Nellore** India. Commercial town in Andhra Pradesh, on the Penner R. 95 m. NNW of Madras. Pop. (1961) 106,776. Trade in rice, oilseeds, etc. Rice and oilseed milling.

**Nelson** England. Municipal borough in Lancashire 4 m NNE of Burnley. Pop. (1961) 31,950. Manufactures cotton and rayon goods. Engineering.

**Nelson** New Zealand. **1.** Provincial district in the NW of the S Island. Area (statistical area) 6,910 sq. m. Pop. (1966) 67,208. Mostly mountainous. The Waimea Plain is the chief agricultural area, producing apples, tobacco, hops. Coal mined near Westport in the Buller R. region.
**2.** Capital of the Nelson provincial district, on the N coast of the S Island at the head of Tasman Bay. Pop. (1966) 26,233. Seaport, dealing mainly with inter-island passenger and freight traffic. Exports fruit, vegetables, tobacco, and timber, from a hinterland with intensive horticulture and market gardening. Fruit canning, sawmilling. Birthplace of Lord Rutherford (1871–1937).

**Nelson River** Canada. River 400 m. long in Manitoba flowing generally NE through L. Cross and L. Split and entering Hudson Bay. Port Nelson is a minor port at its mouth. Discovered (1612) by Sir Thomas Button.

**Neman (Lithuanian Nemunas, Ger. Memel, Polish Niemen) River** USSR. River 550 m. long rising in the Byelorussian SSR 30 m. S of Minsk. It flows generally W through the former NE Poland past Grodno, then turns N into the Lithuanian SSR; it turns W again past Kaunas and Sovetsk and enters the Kurisches Haff (Courland Lagoon) by a delta. Navigable for about 300 m. Much used for floating timber.

**Nemi, Lake** Italy. Small but picturesque crater lake in Latium, in the Alban Hills 16 m. SE of Rome. After draining (1930–31), two pleasure barges probably built for the Roman emperor Caligula were raised, but these were burned by the retreating Germans in the 2nd World War (1944).

**Nemunas River** ◊ *Neman River.*

**Nenagh** Irish Republic. Market town in Co. Tipperary, on the R. Nenagh 22 m. N E of Limerick. Pop. (1966) 4,542. Trade in dairy produce, potatoes. The circular keep of the 12th-cent. castle survives.

**Nene (Nen) River** England. River 90 m. long rising near Daventry, Northamptonshire, flowing generally E and N E past Northampton, Wellingborough, Peterborough, and Wisbech, and entering The Wash near Sutton Bridge. Below Peterborough it flows by a straightened artificial channel while the old Nene takes a longer, more southerly course, rejoining the other at Wisbech.

**Nenets NA USSR.** National Area in the extreme N of European RSFSR, in the Arkhangelsk (Archangel) Region. Area 67,000 sq. m. Pop. (1970) 39,000 (mainly Nentsy). Cap. Naryan-Mar (420 m. N E of Archangel), a small port at the head of the Pechora R. delta. Principally tundra; chief occupations reindeer herding, fishing, hunting.

**Nen River** ◊ *Nene River.*

**Nepal.** Independent kingdom of S Asia. Area 54,606 sq. m. Pop. (1964) 9,500,000. Cap. Katmandu. Lang. mainly Nepali. Rel. mainly Hindu.

On the S slopes of the Himalayas, bounded by Tibet (China) (N), Sikkim and India (E), and India (S and W). For long it was virtually isolated and little known, but in recent years it has been penetrated by the railway (1926), and Katmandu can now be reached by air or by motor road. For administrative purposes it is divided into 14 zones.

TOPOGRAPHY, RESOURCES, PEOPLE. From N to S the country consists of part of the Great Himalaya Range, with Everest (29,028 ft), Kanchenjunga (28,168 ft), and other majestic peaks, then a series of mountain ridges and valleys, and finally a strip of low-lying terai or dense tropical jungle. National life is centred on the so-called Nepal Valley, where the three chief towns, Katmandu, Patan, and Bhatgaon, are situated. Leading crops rice, maize, millet. Timber is obtained from the forests, medicinal herbs from the mountain slopes. The people are of Mongolian stock with a strong admixture of Hindu blood, and since 1769 the Gurkhas have been the dominant race.

HISTORY. The Gurkhas, a Mongol-Rajput people originally driven out of India by the Muslims, conquered the Newars of the Nepal Valley (1769), and invaded Tibet (1790), but were defeated by the Chinese; their activities along the Indian frontier brought them into conflict with Britain and they were again defeated (1816). From then the Gurkhas formed a noteworthy section of the British Indian army and still figure in several serving battalions of the British army. Ostensibly ruled by a hereditary King, but from 1846 actual power was in the hands of a hereditary Prime Minister of the Rana family. After political disturbances in 1950–51, a more democratic form of government was promised; in 1962 the King proclaimed a new constitution based on an indirectly elected legislature and in 1963 formed a National Guidance Council of 31 members. The Chinese-built road from Katmandu to Kodari, near the Chinese frontier, was opened in 1967.

**Ness, Loch** Scotland. Long narrow lake in Inverness-shire extending 24 m. N E from Fort Augustus along the Great Glen. Outlet the R. Ness, flowing 7 m. N E past Inverness to the Moray Firth. Home of the fabled 'Loch Ness monster'.

**Netherlands (Holland).** Kingdom of NW Europe. Area 13,959 sq. m. Pop. (1968) 12,661,095. Cap. Amsterdam. Rel. 38 per cent Roman Catholic, 45 per cent Protestant (various denominations).

Bounded by the North Sea (N and W), the Federal German Republic (E), and Belgium (S). Forms the lowest part of the N European Plain, about 25 per cent of the land being below sea level. Much of the country is intensively farmed, the raising of dairy cattle being especially important, but industrial and commercial activities also play a leading part in the economy. Has the highest density of population in Europe, 907 per sq. m. Divided into 11 provinces: Groningen, Friesland, Drenthe, Overijssel, Gelderland, Utrecht, N Holland, S Holland, Zeeland, N Brabant, Limburg; part of the land reclaimed from the former Zuider Zee, the S Ijsselmeerpolders, has not yet (1969) been incorporated into any province.

TOPOGRAPHY, CLIMATE. Consists substantially of the delta formed by the Rhine and Maas (Meuse) and their various arms, including the Lek, Waal, and Ijssel. Many islands in the S W (Zeeland), including

Walcheren, and the N coast is fringed by the W Frisian Is. For centuries large areas of land have been reclaimed from the sea, these so-called polders being protected from inundation by dykes, and the work is still continuing. The greatest reclamation scheme of recent times has taken place in the former ◊ *Zuider Zee*, now the Ijsselmeer, and was made possible by the construction of a long dam, the Afsluitdijk, across its entrance. The first phase of the Delta Plan, to seal off the estuaries of Zeeland and S Holland provinces from the sea by dykes, was completed in 1961; scheduled to be completed by 1978. Three main regions may thus be distinguished in the Netherlands: the strip of sand dunes along the coast, the adjoining, intensively farmed polders, and the E, formerly sandy and infertile but made productive by the use of fertilizers etc. Almost the only relief to the monotonous flatness of the surface is in the extreme S E (Limburg), where the hills rise to 1,000 ft. The climate, which is maritime temperate, resembles that of E England but is slightly colder in winter. Rainfall amounts to 25–30 ins. annually.

AGRICULTURE, INDUSTRY, PEOPLE. About 40 per cent of the land is devoted to pasture, and from the large numbers of Friesian cattle cheese (esp. the Edam and Gouda varieties), butter, and condensed milk are produced for export. Wheat, oats, rye, potatoes, and sugar-beet are cultivated; in the Haarlem neighbourhood bulbs are produced, and these, along with flowers and fresh vegetables, are also significant exports. Holland has few mineral resources, the most important being coal, which is mined in Limburg. Manufacturing industries, on the other hand, are varied, and include the manufacture of steel at Utrecht and Velsen; shipbuilding at Rotterdam, now the world's leading seaport; diamond cutting at Amsterdam, the largest city and also a seaport, accessible to ocean-going vessels by the North Sea Canal; electrical equipment at Eindhoven; textiles at Tilburg, Arnhem, and elsewhere. Margarine, spirits (gin, liqueurs), chemicals, machinery, and china (Delft) are also manufactured, and vast quantities of petroleum are refined (Rotterdam); The Hague is the seat of government, Scheveningen near by is the leading seaside resort, and Ijmuiden is the main fishing port. Transport is facilitated by the intricate system of inland waterways, the mileage of navigable rivers and canals exceeding that of either roads or railways. Holland also has the seventh largest merchant navy in Europe (excluding the USSR). Foreign trade is chiefly with the Federal German Republic, Belgium, Britain, and the USA.

The country forms a constitutional monarchy under the House of Orange-Nassau. There is a two-chamber legislature, the First Chamber consisting of 75 members elected by members of the Provincial States and the Second Chamber of 150 deputies who are elected directly with proportional representation. The largest denomination of the Protestants is the Dutch Reformed Church, to which the royal family belongs. Standards of living and of education are among the highest in Europe. HISTORY. Until the 16th cent. the Netherlands were the Low Countries – modern Holland and Belgium. In Roman times the area was divided along the Rhine: S of the river were Belgic tribes, who were conquered by Julius Caesar, while N of the river lived the Teutonic Frisians. The whole region became part of the empire of Charlemagne, then passed to Lotharingia and so to the Holy Roman Empire. In the 15th cent. it was acquired by the dukes of Burgundy and from them by the Habsburgs. When Philip II of Spain succeeded his father, Charles V (1555), he attempted to crush the Protestant faith, but met with determined opposition which culminated in the Union of Utrecht (1579); this united the seven N provinces against Spain, and they declared their independence in 1581, unrecognized by Spain until 1648, and so laid the foundation of the modern Dutch state. The S Netherlands remained under Spanish rule, and from this time its history is that of ◊ *Belgium*.

In the first half of the 17th cent. the Dutch enjoyed great prosperity, took the major share of the world's carrying trade, founded colonies in N America, W Indies, E Indies, and India, and led the world in art; in 1689 William of Orange became William III of England. But the wars with England and then France exhausted the country, and the 18th cent. was a period of decline. In 1814 the former United Provinces (Holland) and the former Austrian Netherlands (Belgium) were united under the House of Orange, but in 1830 Belgium declared its independence. During the 2nd World War the Netherlands was occupied by the Germans, while the Dutch government took refuge in England. After the war (1945) the Dutch E Indies declared its independence as the Republic of Indonesia, but of the former empire Surinam (Dutch Guiana) and the Netherlands Antilles remain; in 1954 both these territories became constituent parts of the Kingdom of the Netherlands, with full autonomy.

**Netherlands Antilles.** Formerly Curaçao. Two groups of islands (three in each) in the Caribbean Sea. Total area 394 sq. m. Pop. (1968) 213,192. Cap. Willemstad (on Curaçao). The S group, off the coast of Venezuela: Curaçao (area 183 sq. m., pop. 139,211); Aruba (area 73 sq. m., pop. 59,020); Bonaire (area 111 sq. m., pop. 7,537). This is by far the more important group, the economy depending on the refining of oil imported from Venezuela to Curaçao and Aruba. The N group, 550 m. to the NE: Saba (area 5 sq. m., pop. 1,036); St Eustatius (area 8 sq. m., pop. 1,324); Sint Maarten (area 13 sq. m., pop. 5,064), the N half of which (⇨ *St Martin*) belongs to France. This group is of small economic importance, with subsistence agriculture the main activity. Dutch is the official language in the islands; in the S group Papiamento (a tongue of mixed origin) serves as a lingua franca. A Dutch possession since the 17th cent. Made an integral part of the Netherlands in 1922, the islands were known as Curaçao until 1949, when they were officially renamed the Netherlands Antilles. Granted full autonomy in internal affairs 1954.

**Netherlands East Indies** ⇨ *Indonesia*.

**Neubrandenburg** German Democratic Republic. **1.** Administrative district formed in 1952 from part of Mecklenburg, bounded on the E by Poland. Area 4,195 sq. m. Pop. (1968) 638,265.
**2.** Capital of Neubrandenburg district, on the Tollense R. near the N end of the Tollensesee, 75 m. N of Berlin. Pop. (1965) 37,934. Manufactures machinery, paper, chemicals, etc. Has 14th-cent. walls and gates and a 13th-cent. church. Founded 1248.

**Neuchâtel (Ger. Neuenburg)** Switzerland. **1.** Canton in the Jura, bordering NW on France. Area 308 sq. m. Pop. (1969) 167,000 (mainly French-speaking and Protestant). Consists chiefly of the typical longitudinal ridges and valleys of the Jura, rising to 4,731 ft in Mont Racine. Asphalt produced in the Val de Travers. Dairy farming. Vines cultivated. Principally

famous for its watch-making industry, centred on the towns of La Chaux-de-fonds and Le Locle. Virtually independent from the 13th cent. Joined the Swiss confederation 1815.
**2.** Capital of Neuchâtel canton, on the N shore of the Lake of Neuchâtel at a height of 1,440 ft. Pop. (1969) 36,800. Manufactures chocolate, condensed milk, watches, paper, etc. Outstanding buildings are the 15th/17th-cent. castle and the Musée des Beaux Arts. The university was originally founded (as an academy) in 1838.

**Neuchâtel, Lake of** Switzerland. The largest lake wholly in Switzerland (83 sq. m.), extending 24 m. SW–NE along the S foot of the Jura. The Thièle (Zihl) R. enters at the SW and leaves at the NE end. Extensive vineyards along the NW shore.

**Neuilly-sur-Seine** France. Residential and industrial suburb of NW Paris, on the right bank of the Seine R., in the Hauts-de-Seine department. Pop. (1968) 71,215. Manufactures cars, machine tools, perfumes, etc. The first level bridge in France was constructed here across the Seine in the 18th cent. The peace treaty between the Allies and Bulgaria was signed here (1919).

**Neumünster** Federal German Republic. Industrial town in Schleswig-Holstein 20 m. SSW of Kiel. Pop. (1963) 75,000. Railway junction. Manufactures textiles, machinery, paper, etc. Grew up round a 12th-cent. monastery.

**Neunkirchen** Federal German Republic. Town in Saarland 12 m. NE of Saarbrücken. Pop. (1963) 46,100. Coalmining centre. Manufactures iron and steel.

**Neuquén River** Argentina. River 300 m. long rising in the Andes in Neuquén province near the Chilean frontier, flowing S and SE, and joining the Limay R. to form the Río Negro. Near the confluence is Neuquén (pop. 17,500), capital of the province.

**Neuruppin** German Democratic Republic. Industrial town and tourist resort in the Potsdam district, on L. Ruppin 40 m. NW of Berlin. Pop. (1965) 22,453. Printing. Manufactures dyes, starch, etc. Birthplace of Theodor Fontane (1819–98).

**Neuss** Federal German Republic. Ancient Novaesium. Industrial town in N Rhine-Westphalia, near the left bank of the Rhine R. opposite Düsseldorf. Pop. (1968) 114,003. Food processing, paper milling. Manufactures agricultural machinery, tractors, etc. A Roman camp was founded and a bridge built across the Rhine here by Drusus, brother of the Emperor Tiberius. Has the 13th-cent. Church of St Quirinus and a 17th/18th-cent. town hall.

**Neustadt-an-der-Weinstrasse** Federal German Republic. Formerly Neustadt-an-der-Haardt (Hardt). Town in the Rhineland-Palatinate at the E foot of the Hardt Mountains 16 m. SW of Ludwigshafen. Pop. (1963) 30,800. Important centre of the wine trade. Manufactures agricultural and viticultural implements, textiles, etc.

**Neustrelitz** German Democratic Republic. Residential town and resort in the Neubrandenburg district, between two small lakes, Zierker See and Glambecker See, 62 m. NNW of Berlin. Pop. (1965) 27,486. Manufactures machinery. Former capital of the grand duchy of Mecklenburg-Strelitz.

**Nevada** USA. State in the W almost wholly within the Great Basin. Area 110,540 sq. m. Pop. (1970) 481,893 (increased 70 per cent in the 1960s). Cap. Carson City. Admitted to the Union in 1864 as the 36th state; popularly known as the 'Sagebrush' or 'Silver' state. A vast plateau, but with several mountain ranges rising well above the general level of 4,000–5,000 ft, reaching 13,145 ft in Boundary Peak in the White Mountains (W), and 13,058 ft in Wheeler Peak in the Snake Range (E). Also many buttes and mesas. Apart from the Colorado R. in the extreme SE corner, most of the rivers are small and flow only in the rainy months. Climate dry continental. Annual rainfall 5–10 ins. Sheep and cattle raised. Mining has dominated the economy since the discovery (1859) of the rich Comstock lode of silver and gold. Chief minerals copper, gypsum, iron ore, gold. Leading towns Las Vegas, Reno, Carson City. Ceded to the USA by Mexico 1848. Separated from Utah Territory 1861.

**Neva River** USSR. River 46 m. long in RSFSR issuing from the SW corner of L. Ladoga and flowing W to enter the Gulf of Finland by a delta on which Leningrad stands. At the delta it branches into 5 arms, the Great and Little Neva and the Great, Middle, and Little Nevka, and is impeded by reefs and sandbanks, but a sea channel 18 m. long to Kronshtadt allows large vessels to reach Leningrad; it is frozen usually from late Nov. to late April. Carries a large volume of water, and with its low banks is subject to floods; particularly disastrous

floods took place in 1777, 1824, 1879, 1903' and 1924. Forms part of the inland waterway system connecting the Baltic Sea with the Volga R. and the White Sea.

**Nevers** France. Ancient Noviodunum. Prefecture of the Nièvre department, on the Loire R. at its confluence with the Nièvre R. 37 m. ESE of Bourges. Pop. (1968) 45,068. Light engineering. Manufactures pottery, metal goods, pharmaceutical products, etc. Among its buildings are the 11th-cent. Romanesque Church of St Étienne, the mainly 13th-cent. cathedral and the 15th/16th-cent. former ducal palace. Has yielded many Roman remains.

**Nevis** (Leeward Islands) British W Indies. Island in St Kitts/Nevis/Anguilla, 2 m. SE of St Kitts (St Christopher). Area 50 sq. m. Pop. (1966) 15,072. Cap. and chief seaport Charlestown. Roughly circular; rises to Nevis Peak (3,596 ft) in the centre. Chief products cotton, sugar-cane. Discovered (1493) by Columbus. An English colony was established 1628. In British hands since 1783. Birthplace of Alexander Hamilton (1757–1804).

**Nevis, Ben** ◊ *Ben Nevis*.

**New Albany** USA. Industrial town in Indiana, on the Ohio R. opposite Louisville (Kentucky). Pop. (1960) 37,812. Manufactures plywood, veneers, furniture, etc.

**New Amsterdam** Guyana. Seaport at the mouth of the Berbice R. 55 m. SE of Georgetown. Pop. 15,000. Centre of a district producing rice and sugar-cane. Founded by the Dutch, as Fort St Andries, 1740.

**New Amsterdam** (USA) ◊ *Buffalo*.

**Newark** (New Jersey) USA. Largest city in the state, on the Passaic R. and Newark Bay, 8 m. W of lower Manhattan (New York city). Pop. (1960) 405,220. Road, rail, and air centre. Varied industries. Manufactures electrical equipment, metal goods, fountain pens, cutlery, chemicals, food products. Founded by Puritans from Connecticut 1666. Grew rapidly in the 19th cent. Photographic film was first made here (1887). Birthplace of the novelist Stephen Crane (1871–1900).

**Newark** (Ohio) USA. Town on the Licking R. 30 m. ENE of Columbus. Pop. (1960) 41,790. Railway engineering. Manufactures lawn mowers, fibre glass, plastics, etc.

**Newark-upon-Trent** England. Municipal borough in Nottinghamshire, on the R. Devon at its confluence with an arm of the R. Trent, 16 m. NE of Nottingham. Pop.

(1961) 24,610. Engineering, brewing. Manufactures building materials (from gypsum and limestone quarried in the neighbourhood). Has a 14th/15th-cent. parish church with a spire 252 ft high; ruined castle dating from the 12th cent., where King John died (1216), besieged three times in the Civil War; 16th-cent. grammar school. Owes its early development to its position on the Roman Fosse Way; it is on the Great North Road (A1). Birthplace of Sir William Nicholson (1872–1949).

New Bedford USA. Seaport, resort, and industrial town in Massachusetts on Buzzards Bay. Pop. (1960) 102,477. Manufactures cotton goods, clothing, electrical equipment, metal goods, etc. First settled 1652. A leading whaling port from the mid 18th to the mid 19th cent.

New Brighton England. Holiday resort in Cheshire, on the Wirral peninsula, part of the county borough of Wallasey.

New Britain SW Pacific Ocean. Volcanic island, largest in the Bismarck Archipelago, to the NE of New Guinea. Area 14,100 sq. m. Pop. (1966) 154,091. Chief town Rabaul, in the NE. Mountainous, rising to 7,500 ft. Exports copra, cacao. Rabaul was a vital Japanese base in the 2nd World War. Discovered and named by William Dampier 1700.

New Britain USA. Industrial town in Connecticut 9 m. SSW of Hartford. Pop. (1960) 82,201. Known as the 'hardware city'; manufactures almost half the US output of builders' hardware. Also produces electrical equipment, ball bearings, clothing, etc.

New Brunswick Canada. One of the Maritime Provinces, on the Gulf of St Lawrence and the Bay of Fundy, bounded on the W by Maine (USA). Area 27,985 sq. m. Pop. (1966) 616,788. Cap. Fredericton. Generally low-lying, but rises to 2,690 ft in Mt Carleton. The St John is the most important of the many rivers. The most continental climate in the Maritime Provinces; annual rainfall 40–45 ins. Heavy snowfalls (100 ins. or more in the N). Despite the severe winters, the port of St John is kept ice-free by the strong tides of the Bay of Fundy. Extensive forests; lumbering and wood-pulp and paper manufacture are leading industries. Fisheries also important. Potatoes, cereals, and fruits cultivated. Coal and other minerals produced. Chief towns St John, Moncton, Fredericton. Chaleur Bay was explored by

Jacques Cartier 1534. First settlement established by the French 1604. Later formed part of the British province of Nova Scotia. The United Empire Loyalists came in force in 1783. New Brunswick left Nova Scotia, to become a separate province, 1784.

New Brunswick USA. Industrial town in New Jersey, at the head of navigation on the Raritan R., 23 m. SW of Newark. Pop. (1960) 40,139. Manufactures machinery, medical, surgical, and pharmaceutical products, etc. Seat of Rutgers University, founded, as Queen's College, 1766. First settled 1681.

Newburgh Scotland. Royal burgh in Fifeshire, on the Firth of Tay 9 m. ESE of Perth. Pop. (1961) 2,079. Fishing port. Linoleum and oilskin manufacture. The ruins of Lindores Abbey (Benedictine), founded (1178) by David, Earl of Huntingdon, are 1 m. E.

Newburgh USA. Port and industrial town in New York, on the Hudson R. 53 m. N of New York city. Pop. (1960) 30,979. Manufactures textiles, clothing, leather goods, etc. Hasbrouck House, Washington's headquarters 1782–3, is now a museum.

Newburn England. Urban district in SE Northumberland, on the R. Tyne, 5 m. W of Newcastle upon Tyne. Pop. (1961) 27,879. Coalmining and industrial centre. Engineering. Manufactures glass, bricks, etc.

Newbury England. Municipal borough in Berkshire, on the R. Kennet 15 m. WSW of Reading. Pop. (1961) 20,386. Market town. Engineering, brewing, flour milling, etc. Formerly a centre of the woollen industry; its 16th-cent. Cloth Hall is now a museum. Well-known racecourse. Two battles were fought here in the Civil War (1643, 1644).

New Caledonia SW Pacific Ocean. Volcanic island 1,000 m. E of Queensland (Australia), forming with its island dependencies a French overseas territory. Area 7,374 sq. m. Pop. (1968) 99,902 (48,073 Melanesians, 37,433 Europeans). Cap. Nouméa. Great mineral resources, esp. nickel, chromium, iron. Chief exports metallic ores, copra. The native Melanesians raise livestock and grow vegetables, maize, fruits, coffee. Discovered (1774) by Capt. Cook. Annexed by France 1853.

Newcastle Australia. Industrial city and seaport in New South Wales 75 m. NNE of Sydney at the mouth of the Hunter R. Pop. (1966) 233,967. Centre of Australia's chief coalfield, which supplies its important iron and steel works. Among the products of its heavy industries are locomotives and railway rolling stock, girders, corrugated iron, ships; manufactures textiles, fertilizers, chemicals, cement, etc. Exports coal, wool, wheat, dairy produce, etc.

**Newcastle** Northern Ireland. Urban district in Co. Down, on Dundrum Bay 28 m. S of Belfast. Pop. (1961) 3,722. Seaside resort at the foot of Slieve Donard (2,796 ft) in the Mourne Mountains.

**Newcastle** S Africa. Town in Natal at the foot of the Drakensberg at a height of 3,900 ft, 165 m. NNW of Durban. Pop. 18,000. On the railway to Johannesburg. Coalmining. Manufactures iron and steel, bricks, tiles, stoves. Butter making.

**New Castle** USA. Industrial town in Pennsylvania 44 m. NNW of Pittsburgh. Pop. (1960) 44,790. In a coal and limestone region. Manufactures tinplate, metal goods, pottery, cement, etc. Settled 1798 and named after Newcastle upon Tyne, England, by John Stewart, who built a charcoal furnace here to make pig-iron from local ore.

**Newcastle-under-Lyme** England. Municipal borough in N Staffordshire, in the Potteries, 2 m. W of Stoke-on-Trent. Pop. (1961) 76,433. Coalmining and industrial centre. Manufactures bricks and tiles, textiles, etc. Its name is due to the fact that a castle was built here in the 12th cent. to take the place of an older fortress and that it was situated under or near the former forest of Lyme. In 1932 the borough was extended to include Wolstanton, Chesterton, and Silverdale. At Keele near by the University College of N Staffordshire was opened in 1950, and became Keele University in 1962.

**Newcastle upon Tyne** England. County borough in Northumberland, on the N bank of the R. Tyne about 9 m. from the mouth. Pop. (1961) 269,389. Important industrial centre. Shipbuilding, marine and electrical engineering, flour milling. Manufactures chemicals, soap products, etc. Also a port. Exports coal, iron and steel products, etc. Stands opposite Gateshead, with which linked by tunnel and 5 bridges, inc. the old high-level bridge (1849) and the new Tyne bridge (1928). Remains of the 12th-cent. castle from which its name was taken and of the 13th-cent. town wall; the Cathedral of St Nicholas dates mainly

from the 14th cent. Seat of a university (1963), formerly King's College. The handsome appearance of the city centre is largely due to the enterprise of a local builder, Richard Grainger (1798–1861). Best-known of the many open spaces is the Town Moor (area nearly 1,000 acres). On the site of the Roman Pons Aelii, on Hadrian's Wall. First engaged in the coal trade in the 13th cent. George Stephenson's iron works were established in 1823, and here the first locomotives for the Stockton–Darlington railway were made. Birthplace of Admiral Collingwood (1748–1810), Lord Eldon (1751–1838), Lord Armstrong (1810–1910).

**New Delhi** ◊ *Delhi*.

**New England** USA. Six states in the extreme NE: Maine, New Hampshire, Vermont, Massachusetts, Rhode Island, Connecticut. Inland from the coastal plain it is crossed by the NE extension of the Appalachian system. The chief ranges are the Taconic, Green, and White Mountains and the Berkshire Hills. The humid continental climate and the generally rocky soils do not favour agriculture. The many coastal inlets meant early development of a fishing industry. The region later became highly industrialized, and is one of the most important economically in the USA; Boston (the largest city) is the financial and commercial hub. The natural beauty of the region has given rise to a flourishing tourist industry. Traditionally the New Englanders have a reputation for shrewdness, thrift, inventiveness, and a strict moral code; they are the true Yankees.

The name was given by Capt. John Smith (1614). The first English settlement was established at Plymouth (Massachusetts) in 1620, and the New England Confederation (formed by the colonies of Plymouth, Massachusetts Bay, Connecticut, and New Haven) lasted from 1643 to 1684. Later New England played a considerable part in the American Revolution. It took the Union side in the American Civil War.

**New England Ranges** ◊ *Great Dividing Range*.

**New Forest** England. Picturesque district of woodland and heath, 145 sq. m. in area, in SW Hampshire, bounded by the Solent, Southampton Water, and the R. Avon. Managed as a national park by the Court of Verderers, a remnant of the former forest administration. One quarter of the area is cultivated. Pigs, cattle, and half-wild ponies bred. Within it are the towns of Lyndhurst and Ringwood, and the whole area is designated a rural district. A royal hunting ground under the West Saxon Kings; received its name in 1079 owing to afforestation by William I. A stone marks the spot in the forest where William Rufus was killed by an arrow (1100).

**Newfoundland** Canada. Province in the extreme E, consisting of the island of Newfoundland and ◊ *Labrador*. Total area 156,185 sq. m. (Newfoundland island 42,734 sq. m.). Pop. (1966) 493,396 (inc. 21,157 in Labrador). Cap. St John's. Newfoundland island, separated from Labrador by the Strait of Belle Isle, has a much indented coastline and many off-shore islands; in the N W and S E respectively are the large Great Northern and Avalon peninsulas. The Long Range Mountains, along the Great Northern peninsula, rise to 2,666 ft in Mt Gros Morne. The maritime climate is modified by the cold Labrador Current. Annual rainfall 30–60 ins. In the centre of the island the snowfall amounts to 120 ins. Fishing (esp. cod, haddock, lobsters) and fish processing are traditionally the leading occupations, largely owing to the nearness of the Grand Banks fishing grounds. Of greater economic importance are the extensive forests; newsprint manufacture is a leading industry. Iron ore is mined, chiefly on Bell Island; other minerals are worked. Chief towns St John's, Corner Brook.

Newfoundland was discovered (1497) by John Cabot. Annexed for England by Sir Humphrey Gilbert 1583. Formal recognition of English rule was made by the Treaty of Utrecht (1713); Newfoundland was granted jurisdiction over the coast of Labrador 1809. A larger area was awarded 1927. Responsible government was maintained 1855–1934 but the Dominion was then in serious financial difficulties, and for a time Newfoundland was governed by commission. After a referendum (1949) it joined Canada (the 10th province).

**New Guinea.** World's second largest island (after Greenland), lying N of Australia, from which it is separated by the Arafura Sea and Torres Strait. Area 321,000 sq. m. Dominated by a central chain of lofty mountains: the Nassau Mountains (W) rise to 16,400 ft in Mt

Carstensz, other peaks exceed 15,000 ft, and the chain continues to the extreme S E as the Owen Stanley Range, with Mt Victoria reaching 13,363 ft. In the N there are further mountain ranges, in the S a broad plain crossed by the Fly and many other rivers. Climate equatorial, with high temperatures throughout the year and abundant rainfall (more than 100 ins. annually over most of the island). Tropical rain-forest is the predominant type of natural vegetation. Papuans, Melanesians, Malays, and Negritos form the majority of the population. Discovered by the Portuguese early in the 16th cent. So named owing to the apparent resemblance between the natives and those of the Guinea coast of W Africa. In the 19th cent. the Dutch annexed the W part (1848), Germany the N E, and Britain the S E (1884); the island is still divided politically into two areas, W and E.

*West Irian* (*Irian Barat*): Formerly Netherlands New Guinea, transferred to Indonesia (1963) and with offshore islands made a province of that republic. Area 161,000 sq. m. Pop. (1961) 758,000 (mainly Papuans). Cap. Kotabaru, formerly Hollandia (pop. 14,000). Agriculture primitive. Some oil produced.

*Papua–New Guinea*: Territory of Papua and trust territory of New Guinea, administered as one area by Australia. Area 183,540 sq. m. Pop. (1966) 2,265,594 (1,659,258 in New Guinea) (mainly Papuans and Melanesians). Cap. Port Moresby (Papua). Leading exports copra and rubber from Papua, and copra, coconut oil, cocoa, and coffee from New Guinea. Papua came under Australian control in 1906, with adjacent islands. New Guinea became an Australian mandate in 1921, a trust territory in 1946 (inc. Bismarck Archipelago, N W Solomon Is., etc.).

**Newham** England. Greater London borough formed (1965) from the former county boroughs of East Ham and West Ham, that part of the former municipal borough of Barking W of Barking Creek, and that part of the former metropolitan borough of Woolwich N of the Thames. Pop. (1963) 264,545.

**New Hampshire** USA. State in New England, bordering on Canada, with a short Atlantic coastline in the S E. Area 9,304 sq. m. Pop. (1970) 722,753. Cap. Concord. One of the original 13 states, and the 9th to ratify the Constitution (1788); popularly known as the 'Granite' state. Generally hilly, with many lakes. The White Mountains in the N rise to 6,288 ft in Mt Washington. The winters are long and rather severe. Annual rainfall 30–50 ins. There are annual snowfalls of 100 ins. or more in the mountains. Main crops hay, potatoes, market-garden produce. Manufacturing industries are concentrated chiefly in the S; leading centres Manchester, Nashua, Concord. Land granted to John Mason (1586–1635) of King's Lynn (England) in 1629 was called by him New Hampshire. The early English settlements came under the jurisdiction of Massachusetts in 1641. New Hampshire became a separate province in 1679.

**Newhaven** England. Urban district in E Sussex, on the English Channel at the mouth of the R. Ouse. Pop. (1961) 8,325. Seaport. Steamer service to Dieppe (France).

**New Haven** USA. Seaport and industrial city in Connecticut, on Long Island Sound. Pop. (1960) 152,048. Famous chiefly as the seat of Yale University (1701), named after Elihu Yale (1648–1721), one of its principal benefactors. Manufactures hardware, clocks and watches, sewing machines, fire-arms, etc. Many of the streets are broad and lined with elms. The 16-acre Green with its three churches is an outstanding feature. Birthplace of Charles Goodyear (1800–1860), inventor of the vulcanization of rubber.

**New Hebrides** S W Pacific Ocean. Group of islands about 500 m. W of Fiji under joint Anglo-French administration. Area 5,700 sq. m. Pop. (1967) 76,582 (chiefly Melanesians; about 5,500 Europeans). Cap. Vila (on Efate). Most of the islands are volcanic, and there are three active volcanoes. Largest island Espiritu Santo. Chief product smoke-dried copra; cacao, coffee, and frozen fish are minor exports. The islands were discovered (1606) by the Portuguese de Quiros. The present Anglo-French condominium was established in 1906.

**New Iberia** USA. Town in Louisiana 49 m. S W of Baton Rouge. Pop. (1960) 29,062. In a fertile agricultural region producing sugar-cane, rice, etc. Manufactures wood products, paper, etc.

**New Ireland** S W Pacific Ocean. Volcanic island, second largest in the Bismarck Archipelago, N of New Britain, from which it is separated by St George's Channel. Area 3,340 sq. m. Pop. (1966) 50,129. Mountainous in the central area. Chief town Kavieng at the N W extremity, amid numerous coconut plantations. Principal export copra.

**New Jersey** USA. A middle Atlantic state, with the Delaware R. as its W boundary. Area 7,836 sq. m. Pop. (1970) 7,091,995. Cap. Trenton. One of the original 13 states, and the 3rd to ratify the Constitution (1787); popularly known as the 'Garden' state. More than half the state lies on the Atlantic coastal plain. The coastline is characterized by sandspits, dunes, lagoons, and marshes; no good harbours. In the extreme N W are the Kittatinny Mountains, an Appalachian ridge rising to 1,803 ft in High Point. Climate humid continental; annual rainfall 40–50 ins. Market gardening and fruit and poultry farming are important. Primarily an industrial state: copper smelting and refining, oil refining. Manufactures chemicals, paints, varnishes. Chief industrial centres Newark, Jersey City, Paterson, Camden, Trenton, Elizabeth. First settled by the Dutch; became English 1664. Named in honour of Sir George Carteret (1610–80), a former governor of Jersey (Channel Is.).

**New London** USA. Seaport and summer resort in Connecticut, on the Thames R. estuary near Long Island Sound, opposite the submarine base at Groton. Pop. (1960) 34,182. Manufactures metal goods, machinery, clothing, etc. The annual Harvard–Yale boat races are held on the Thames.

**Newlyn** England. Fishing village in Cornwall, on Mount's Bay just S W of Penzance. Much frequented by artists, and gave its name to a late 19th-cent. school of painting.

**Newmarket** England. Urban district in W Suffolk 12 m. E NE of Cambridge. Pop. (1961) 11,207. A famous racing centre since the reign of James I, many racehorses being trained here. Its racecourse on Newmarket Heath is crossed by the Devil's Ditch, an ancient earthwork; here several important racing events take place, inc. the Two Thousand Guineas, One Thousand Guineas, Cesarewitch, and Cambridgeshire. As the headquarters of British horse-racing, Newmarket is the home of the Jockey Club.

**New Mexico** USA. State in the S W,

519                                                        NEWPORT NEWS

bordering in the S on Texas and Mexico. Area 121,666 sq. m. Pop. (1970) 998,257. Cap. Santa Fé. Admitted to the Union in 1912 as the 47th state; popularly known as the 'Sunshine' state. A region of high plateaux and mountains, with an average height of 5,700 ft. Several peaks in the Sangre de Cristo Mountains (N) exceed 12,000 ft. Crossed N–S by the Rio Grande; the E is drained by its tributary the Pecos. Generally dry and sunny. Annual rainfall varies from 6 ins. in the deserts (S) to 25–30 ins in the mountains (N). Chief crops cotton, wheat, grain sorghums, largely dependent on dry farming or irrigation. Many cattle and sheep raised. Mining important, esp. potash, petroleum, copper; large reserves of uranium. Largest city Albuquerque. Ceded to the USA after the Mexican War (1846–8). The Spanish-Mexican element is less dominant than formerly but still represents about one third of the total population.

New Orleans USA. Largest city in Louisiana, on the E bank of the Mississippi R. 107 m. from the mouth, with L. Pontchartrain to the N. Pop. (1970) 585,787. A major seaport. Exports petroleum, cotton, iron and steel, timber, etc. The chief commercial and financial centre in the South. Sugar and oil refining. Textile, chemical, and other industries. Low-lying, the altitude ranging from 4 ft below sea level to 15 ft above; entirely below the river high-watermark, and protected by levees. The nucleus and most interesting quarter is the Vieux Carré (French Quarter), divided from the modern American section by Canal Street; here are the historic buildings, the Cabildo (1795), now a museum, the St Louis Cathedral (1794), the Pontalba buildings (1849), and many fine 'colonial' houses. A gay and colourful city, New Orleans annually stages the most noteworthy carnival in the USA, the Mardi Gras, which takes place just before Lent. Also the home of jazz music. Seat of 3 universities: Tulane (1884), Loyola (1911, under Jesuit administration), Dillard (1869, Negro). Founded (1718) by Jean Baptiste Le Moyne, Sieur de Bienville; named in honour of the Duc d'Orléans. Became capital of the vast French colonial region of Louisiana. Transferred to Spain 1763. Returned to France 1803, but passed to the USA in the same year with the Louisiana Purchase. A section of the present-day population, the Creoles, are descended from French and Spanish settlers.

New Plymouth New Zealand. Capital of Taranaki provincial district, in the W of the N Island just N of Mt Egmont. Pop. (1966) 31,938. Market town and seaport, handling dairy produce. Founded 1841.

Newport (Hampshire) England. Municipal borough in the Isle of Wight, on the R. Medina 5 m. above its mouth. Pop. (1961) 19,482. Market town. Has a 17th-cent. grammar school and a 19th-cent. town hall designed by John Nash. Within the borough (N) is Parkhurst prison. Carisbrooke Castle is 1 m. SW.

Newport (Shropshire) England. Urban district in Shropshire 16 m. ENE of Shrewsbury. Pop. (1961) 4,370. Market town. The ruins of the 12th-cent. Lilleshall Abbey are 3 m. SSW.

Newport (Kentucky) USA. Industrial town on the Ohio R. opposite Cincinnati (Ohio) at the confluence with the Licking R. Pop. (1960) 30,070. Manufactures metal goods, clothing, food products, etc.

Newport (Rhode Island) USA. Fashionable resort and naval base on Narragansett Bay. Pop. (1960) 47,049. Manufactures precision instruments, electrical equipment, etc. Has many historic buildings and fine 'colonial' homes. Founded 1639. Joint state capital with Providence until 1900.

Newport Wales. County borough in Monmouthshire, on the R. Usk 5 m. above its entry into the Severn estuary. Pop. (1961) 108,107. Seaport with extensive docks. Manufactures iron and steel, boilers, leather goods, etc. The old parish church of St Woollos became the cathedral 1921. Owes its rapid development in the late 19th and early 20th cent. to its favourable position on a tidal river. Also stands on the important route from London and the English Midlands into S Wales.

Newport News USA. Seaport in SE Virginia, on the N side of the James R. estuary and the Hampton Roads. Pop. (1960) 113,662. Exports coal, petroleum, tobacco, etc. Important shipyards. The liners *America* and *United States* and the aircraft-carriers *Enterprise* and *Forrestal* were built here. Manufactures wood pulp and paper, machinery, etc. Settled by Irish colonists 1621. Named after Capt. Christopher Newport, commander of the first ship to reach Jamestown (1607), and Sir William Newce, who chose the site.

**Newport Pagnell** England. Urban district in N. Buckinghamshire, on the R. Ouse at its confluence with the R. Ouzel 11 m. WSW of Bedford. Pop. (1961) 4,722. Market town. Motor-car assembly.

**New Providence** ⬙ *Nassau* (Bahamas).

**Newquay** England. Urban district in Cornwall, 10 m. N of Truro. Pop. (1961) 11,877. Sheltered from the W by Towan Head. Port. Seaside resort.

**New River** England. Artificial waterway in Hertfordshire and London 24 m. long, constructed early in the 17th cent. to supply London with water. Obtains its water from springs at Amwell and Chadwell, augmented from other sources, and originally ended at New River Head, Finsbury; now ends at the Metropolitan Water Board waterworks, Stoke Newington.

**New Rochelle** USA. Suburb of New York city on Long Island Sound. Pop. (1960) 76,812. Largely residential. Manufactures heating equipment, medical supplies, etc. Founded (1688) by Huguenot refugees, who named it after their place of origin, La Rochelle (France). Once the home of Thomas Paine; contains Paine Cottage (where he lived) and the Paine Memorial House (1925).

**New Romney** England. Municipal borough in Kent, on Romney Marsh 12 m. SW of Folkestone. Pop. (1961) 2,556. Market town. One of the Cinque Ports; declined since the sea receded and now more than a mile inland.

**New Ross** Irish Republic. Market town in Co. Wexford, on the R. Barrow just below the confluence with the R. Nore. Pop. (1966) 4,568. Brewing, tanning.

**Newry** Northern Ireland. Urban district in Co. Down on the border with Co. Armagh, on the R. Newry and the Newry Canal at the head of Carlingford Lough. Pop. (1961) 12,450. Market town. Port. Manufactures linen, rope, fishing nets, etc. Birthplace of Lord Russell of Killowen (1832–1900).

**New Siberian Islands** USSR. Archipelago in the Arctic Ocean between the Laptev Sea and the E Siberian Sea, separated from the mainland by the Dimitri Laptev Strait, and in the Yakut ASSR (RSFSR). Area 11,000 sq. m. The largest islands of the central group are Kotelny, Faddeyev, and New Siberia. The De Long Is. (NE)

and Lyakhov Is. (S) are often included in the archipelago. Discovered 1770. Uninhabited. The islands have yielded much fossil ivory.

**New South Wales** Australia. State in the SE, bounded by Queensland (N), the Pacific (E), the Murray R. and Victoria (S), and S Australia (W). Area 309,433 sq. m. (inc. Lord Howe Island in the SW Pacific). Pop. (1966) 4,233,822 (excluding Canberra). Cap. Sydney. In the E the uplifted and dissected plateaux of the Great Dividing Range (e.g. the New England Range, Liverpool Range, and Blue Mountains) are flanked by a narrow coastal plain. In the SE are the higher Snowy Mountains and part of the Australian Alps. The W slopes of the Great Dividing Range are crossed by tributaries of the Murray and Darling rivers. The forested E hills and coastlands experience occasional heavy storms and droughts, but otherwise have a well-distributed, adequate rainfall with mild winters and hot summers, suitable for dairying, market gardening and horticulture. In the N sugar-cane, bananas, and citrus fruits are grown. New South Wales is the leading pastoral and agricultural state, and the inner slopes of the Murray basin, with 20–30 ins. rainfall, are the chief wool- and wheat-producing areas. Dams on the Murray, Murrumbidgee, and Lachlan rivers provide irrigation for stock, grain-, and fruit-growing districts in the W lands of low rainfall. In the NW, with under 10 ins. annually, grasslands give way to saltbush and other shrubs, which support only low-density grazing.

Some two thirds of the population live in Sydney and in the large industrial and coalmining areas centred on Newcastle and Port Kembla-Wollongong. Over half the population live in Sydney, the capital, chief seaport, and manufacturing centre. Power comes mainly from thermal stations, but the Snowy Mountains scheme is increasing the hydroelectric output. Chief exports wool, wheat, dairy produce, fruits, meat.

Discovered and named by Capt. Cook 1770. The first penal settlement was made at Sydney 1788. Became the first colony. Since federation (1901) it has ceded to the Commonwealth the Australian Capital Territory (1911) and Jervis Bay (1915).

**Newton** USA. Town in Massachusetts, on the Charles R. just W of Boston;

divided into 14 villages. Pop. (1960) 92,384. Mainly residential. Manufactures electrical equipment, plastics, knitwear, etc. Seat of the USA's first Baptist theological seminary (1825).

Newton Abbot England. Urban district in Devonshire, at the head of the R. Teign estuary 14 m. SSW of Exeter. Pop. (1961) 18,066. Market town. Malting, tanning. Racecourse (National Hunt). William III was proclaimed king here (1688) at St Leonard's Tower.

Newton Aycliffe England. Residential and industrial district in Co. Durham, 5 m. N of Darlington; a 'new town' (1947) with a planned pop. 45,000. Pop. (1968) 21,621.

Newton-le-Willows England. Formerly Newton-in-Makerfield. Urban district in S Lancashire 5 m. E of St Helens. Pop. (1961) 21,761. Industrial town. Railway engineering. Manufactures machinery, paper, glassware, etc.

Newton Stewart Scotland. Small burgh in Wigtownshire, on the R. Cree 6 m. NNW of Wigtown. Pop. (1961) 1,980. Market town.

Newtownabbey Northern Ireland. Urban district in Co. Antrim just N of Belfast, formed (1958) from Belfast rural district. Pop. (1961) 37,440.

Newtown and Llanllwchaiarn Wales. Urban district in Montgomeryshire, on the R. Severn 12 m. SW of Welshpool. Pop. (1961) 5,512. Market town. Formerly a centre of the flannel industry. Birthplace of Robert Owen (1771–1858).

Newtownards Northern Ireland. Municipal borough in Co. Down, near the N end of Strangford Lough 10 m. E of Belfast. Pop. (1961) 13,090. Manufactures linen, hosiery, etc. Grew up round a Dominican monastery (founded 1244).

New Westminster Canada. Seaport in British Columbia, on the Fraser R. 9 m. E of Vancouver. Pop. (1966) 38,013. Exports timber, grain, etc. Oil refining. Salmon, fruit, and vegetable canning, paper and flour milling. Founded 1859. Capital of British Columbia till 1866.

New York USA.* State in the NE, on the Atlantic seaboard, extending to the Great Lakes and the Canadian border in the W and N, and including Long Island close to the SE shore. Area 49,576 sq. m. Pop. (1970) 17,979,712 (second largest in the USA). Cap. Albany. One of the original 13 states, and the 11th to ratify the Constitution (1788); popularly known as the 'Empire' state. Along the N border is the St Lawrence valley and in the E the Hudson R. valley. The Mohawk R. cuts across the state W–E, providing a route for the New York State Barge Canal. N of the Mohawk are the Adirondack Mountains, rising to 5,344 ft in Mt Marcy; S is a plateau 1,000–2,000 ft high. Climate humid continental; cold winters (often with heavy snowfalls), hot summers. Annual rainfall 40–45 ins. Dairy farming is the main agricultural activity. Cereal cultivation, fruit growing (esp. around the shores of L. Ontario and L. Erie), and market gardening are important. In manufactures New York ranks first in the USA, the industries being concentrated chiefly around New York City. Other leading centres are Buffalo, Rochester, Syracuse, Yonkers, Albany, Niagara Falls (which supplies hydroelectric power), Utica. Despite its many large urban centres, the state has several regions of scenic beauty, e.g. L. Champlain, Finger Lakes, Niagara Falls, the Adirondacks, and the Catskills.

Explored in 1609 by Champlain (who discovered L. Champlain) and Henry Hudson (who sailed up the Hudson R.). The first permanent settlers were the Dutch, who established Albany as a furtrading post (1623) and founded New Amsterdam (1625) on Manhattan Island. Prominent in the Anglo-French struggles, and again in the American War of Independence. The rapid commercial expansion in the 19th cent. was largely due to the completion of the Erie Canal (1825).

New York city (New York) USA.* Largest city in the USA (and in America) and the commercial, financial, and cultural centre of the USA, on New York Bay (Atlantic coast) at the mouth of the Hudson R. Land area 299 sq. m. Pop. (1970) 7,771,730. Five boroughs: Manhattan; the Bronx; Queens (Long Island); Brooklyn (Long Island); Richmond (Staten Island). The leading seaport of the USA with a water frontage of 750 m. Handles 40 per cent by value of US overseas trade. Imports petroleum, sugar, coffee, rubber, copper, fruit. Exports machinery, grain, meat, textiles, clothing, metal goods. The chief industry is the manufacture of clothing; also furs, hats, jewellery, and leather goods. Printing and publishing, sugar refining, food processing, brewing also important. Most of these industries are concentrated in Manhattan.

Manhattan (area 22 sq. m., pop. 1,698,281) includes a few small islands, e.g. Ellis Island (formerly an important immigration station) and Bedloe's Island, renamed Liberty Island in 1960 (site of the Statue of Liberty); it is famous for its skyline of skyscrapers, esp. the Empire State Building (1931), the tallest building in the world (1,250 ft), and the Chrysler Building (1929; 1,048 ft). There are many world-renowned streets and districts, e.g. Wall Street, the financial hub, Broadway, the world's longest street (16 m.), with many theatres and other places of entertainment; Greenwich Village, the Bohemian quarter; Chinatown; Harlem, the Negro quarter; Times Square; the fashionable shopping and residential thoroughfares of Fifth Avenue, Madison Avenue, and Park Avenue; Central Park, with attractive walks and children's playgrounds; Riverside Drive, a beautifully situated residential thorough-fare extending over 6 m. along the Hudson R. embankment.

Brooklyn (area 71 sq. m., pop. 2,627,319), primarily residential, includes the amusement centre of Coney Island and is connected with Manhattan by 3 bridges and several tunnels. Queens (area 108 sq. m., pop. 1,809,578) contains New York's two airports and Flushing Meadow (site of the New York World's Fair 1939–40 and 1964–5) and is connected with Manhattan and the Bronx by 4 bridges and many tunnels. The Bronx (area 43 sq. m., pop. 1,424,815) has Bronx Park (with botanical and zoological gardens) and the Hall of Fame, includes a high proportion of Jews among its in-habitants, and is connected with Man-hattan and Queens by 3 bridges and tunnels. Richmond (area 57 sq. m., pop. 221,991), across the Narrows from Brook-lyn, is linked by ferry with Manhattan.

New York is well served by its transport system; all the boroughs except Richmond are interconnected by railways, tunnels, subways, and bridges (e.g. the George Washington, the Brooklyn, the Henry Hudson, the Manhattan, the Triborough, and the Queensborough). The Verrazano-Narrows Bridge, between Brooklyn and Richmond (Staten Island), was opened in 1964; with a total length of 13,700 ft it is the longest in the world. Twelve railway systems serve the city. There are two air-

ports, La Guardia and the International Airport (formerly Idlewild, renamed John F. Kennedy in 1963). Seat of the Columbia University (1754), the New York Univer-sity (1831), the Fordham University (1846, Roman Catholic), the City of New York University (1847), and the St John's Uni-versity (1871, Roman Catholic). Many museums, libraries, and other cultural in-stitutions. The new Metropolitan Opera House was opened in 1966. Protestant and Roman Catholic cathedrals. The United Nations headquarters is in Manhattan (1951). New York has an extremely cos-mopolitan population, with more Irish than in Dublin, as many Jews as in Israel, and more Negroes than in any other city in the world, as well as many Scandinavians, Germans, Italians, Puerto Ricans, Chinese, and others. It cannot therefore be con-sidered a typical American city.

The Dutch bought Manhattan island from the local Indians for 24 dollars' worth of beads and ribbons in 1624. Today it is the most valuable piece of land in the world; the massive phalanx of skyscrapers is a manifestation of its value. The Dutch settlement on Manhattan, New Amsterdam, was seized by the English in 1664 and re-named New York (after the Duke of York, later James II). Capital of New York state (1788–97) and Union capital (1789–90); it lost these distinctions but was already the largest city in USA. From the early 19th cent. its financial and commercial leader-ship was undisputed.

**New Zealand.** A member country of the Commonwealth of Nations in the SW Pacific. Area 103,736 sq. m. Pop. (1966) 2,676,919 (inc. 201,159 Maoris). Cap. Wellington. Rel. mainly Protestant. Lang. English, Maori.

New Zealand proper consists of the North Island (44,281 sq. m.), the South Island (58,093 sq. m.), Stewart Island (670 sq. m.), Chatham Is. (327 sq. m.), and several minor islands (320 sq. m.). The Cook Is. and the Ross dependency in the Antarctic are also under New Zealand administration. Nearly two thirds of the population of New Zealand are urban, but the economy of the country is heavily dependent on pastoral farming. The standard of living and education is high and New Zealand has been a pioneer in social services; it was the first country to introduce non-contributory old-age pensions (1898) and a comprehen-sive health service (1941).

TOPOGRAPHY. Extends for over 1,000 m. N–S with a maximum width E–W of 280 m. Its main islands and their mountain chains lie roughly SW–NE. In the S Island the Southern Alps and the Fiordland Plateau give a high relief to the W; mountain crests rise well above the snowline (about 6,000 ft), with many peaks above 10,000 ft. Mt Cook (12,349 ft) is the highest; near by is the Tasman Glacier, the longest (18 m.) of many in the Southern Alps. Ice-cut, moraine-blocked valleys and ribbon lakes drain E through deeply cut river courses. S of the Otago plateau are alluvial plains. N of the Waitaki R. soft Tertiary rocks lie E of the Alps, with rivers which have carried alluvial material to build the Canterbury Plains. E of these, Banks Peninsula is of volcanic origin, though the S Island is almost free from volcanic activity. W of the Southern Alps there are discontinuous lowlands and in the N and NE the Nelson and Blenheim lowlands.

In the N Island the lower fold mountains continue N to East Cape. To the W is a central plateau of volcanic material, with three large active volcanoes, inc. Ruapehu (9,175 ft), S of the shallow L. Taupo. Many hot springs and geysers, esp. near Rotorua. From L. Taupo the Waikato R. flows across the plateau and the lowlands in the NW, beyond which extends the Auckland Peninsula. Flanking the fold mountains and the central volcanic plateau are hill lands of soft Tertiary rocks; coastal and valley lowlands contain most of the area utilizable for agriculture and pasture.

CLIMATE, etc. The prevailing winds are westerly and the climate is broadly similar to that of Britain but with much more sunshine. The extreme N is affected by subtropical anticyclones and occasional summer storms from the tropics. Contrasts in relief cause marked rainfall and temperature differences, but on the whole the mean annual temperature ranges are everywhere small. Forests once covered half the country but large areas have been cleared for grazing; today less than one sixth of the country is forested. Most of the N Island and the W of the S Island supported dense, mixed evergreen temperate forest, with broadleafed and coniferous species, tree ferns, and many creepers. Extensive beech forests grew in the mountains of the S Island, while the E foothills and plains were mostly tussock grassland. The isolation of New Zealand from other land masses has led to the

development of many plant species not found elsewhere; tree ferns up to 50 ft high are a striking feature of the dense evergreen forest. Indigenous species include the kauri, valued for its gum. No native mammals except bats, so that wingless birds like the kiwi and weka could survive, but the introduction of stoats, cats, rabbits, and deer has upset the original ecological relationships.

HISTORY, GOVERNMENT, etc. The natives of New Zealand are the Maoris, whose Polynesian ancestors had arrived in the 10th cent. and in greater numbers in the 14th cent. Earlier Morioris were few and had retreated to the Chatham Is., where the last died in 1933. Tasman discovered New Zealand (1642) and Cook circumnavigated the islands 1769–70. Later came sealers, whalers, and kauri seekers, who lived in a state of lawlessness. It was not till 1840 that Queen Victoria assumed sovereignty, and the first Lieutenant-Governor negotiated the Treaty of Waitangi, guaranteeing Maori tribes undisturbed possession of their lands and protection under the British Crown. Permanent settlements were made at Wellington (1840), New Plymouth (1841), and Nelson (1842). In spite of difficulties over the purchase of land from the Maoris further settlements followed in various parts of the islands. In 1853 provincial councils were set up, with a central governor, legislative council, and general assembly, but aggravated land disputes (1860–79) caused fighting between the British colonists and the Maoris, terminated without rancour. In the 1860s gold rushes to Otago, Westland, and Central Auckland further accelerated settlement. Became a dominion in 1907. Government is by a House of Representatives of 80 members who provide an Executive Council to advise the Governor General, who represents the Crown. The Maoris, who have 4 representatives, are more than four times as numerous as they were in 1900, and now take an increasing part in the life of the country.

ECONOMY. Some 18 million acres of forest have been transformed into grazing; with refrigeration (introduced 1882) it became possible to export meat and butter as well as wool and cheese. Wool, dairy produce, and meat constitute over nine tenths of the country's exports by value. Excluding sown pasture, field crops take up less than one thirtieth of the occupied land. About nine tenths of the dairy cattle are in the N Island, mostly in W and NW coastal and valley lowlands where grazing on sown pastures is controlled in small paddocks and by electric fencing. Co-operative organizations run dairy factories and other aspects of farming. More than two thirds of the country's sheep graze over large holdings in hill country, as do one third of the beef cattle. The Canterbury plains and downlands support mixed farming and produce two thirds of the country's grain.

Few minerals of value. Gold production is now very small. Coal is mined in Westland, S Auckland, and S Otago. Natural gas has been found in Taranaki. Thermal power is exploited near L. Taupo. There has been considerable hydroelectric development: in the N Island, with the greater demand, the chief source is the Waikato R., and in the S Island, which has the larger potential, the principal power station is on the Clutha R. The main industries are those processing farm products. Other industries are expanding, esp. in the Auckland and Hutt valley districts, and include engineering, vehicle assembly, and the manufacture of chemicals and textiles. Road and rail communications are difficult but coastal shipping is well developed and air transport important. Chief ports Auckland, Wellington, Lyttelton, Dunedin, Bluff. The most important inland towns are Christchurch and Hamilton.

**Ngami, Lake** Botswana. Former lake S of the Okavango swamp; now a marsh. Discovered (1849) by Livingstone (who described it as a large lake).

**Niagara Falls** Canada. Town in S Ontario on the W bank of the Niagara R. opposite Niagara Falls (USA). Pop. (1966) 56,891. Important tourist centre. Hydroelectric power installation. Manufactures wood pulp and paper, fertilizers, machinery, etc.

**Niagara Falls** USA. Formerly (till 1892) Manchester. Industrial town and tourist centre in New York, on the E bank of the Niagara R. opposite Niagara Falls (Canada), with which it is connected by bridges. Pop. (1960) 102,394. Important hydroelectric plants, supplying power to the city and the state. Manufactures chemicals, electrical equipment, machinery, paper, etc. Seat of the Niagara University (1856, Roman Catholic). Founded as the village of Manchester 1806. Amalgamated with the village of Suspension Bridge 1892.

**Niagara River and Falls** Canada/USA. River 35 m. long, flowing generally N from L. Erie to L. Ontario, forming part of the frontier between New York state (USA) and Ontario (Canada). The Niagara Falls are rather more than halfway down the river; they have gradually receded upstream, at a decreasing rate. In two sections, the American (167 ft high; 1,000 ft wide) and the Canadian or Horseshoe (158 ft high; 2,600 ft wide); they are separated by Goat Island. Thousands of tourists visit the Falls every summer. The most favourable place to view them is Rainbow Bridge, a suspension bridge opened to traffic in 1941. They are even more impressive in winter, in the grip of frost and snow. Also an important source of hydroelectric power. Shipping between L. Erie and L. Ontario circumvents the Falls by using the Welland Canal (Canada).

**Niamey** Niger. Capital, on the left bank of the Niger R. Pop. (1967) 65,000. Terminus of a Trans-Saharan motor route from N Algeria. Commercial centre. Trade in hides and skins, livestock.

**Nicaragua.** Largest of the Central American republics. Area 57,143 sq. m. Pop. (1964) 1,593,007 (70 per cent *mestizo*, 17 per cent white, 9 per cent Negro, 4 per cent Indian). Cap. (and only large city) Managua. Lang. Spanish. Rel. Roman Catholic.

Has coastlines on the Caribbean (E) and the Pacific (W). Central area occupied by mountain ranges and plateaux; in the N and W there are several intermittently active volcanoes. The principal physical feature is the extensive L. Nicaragua, linked with L. Managua by the Tipitapa R. Climate is hot and humid. Annual rainfall 150 ins. or more in the Caribbean lowlands, but much less to the W of the mountains (where about 80 per cent of the people live). In the forests mahogany, cedar, and other timbers are obtained for export. Agriculture is the chief source of the country's wealth; chief export crops coffee, cotton, sugar-cane. Many cattle raised. Principal mineral gold. Industrial production accounts for only one tenth of the national income. Apart from Managua, the leading towns are León, Granada, and Masaya. For administrative purposes the country (the most thinly peopled in Central America) is divided into 16 departments and one national district. Literacy is low (less than 40 per cent) but the annual population growth is high (3·8 per cent).

Under Spanish rule 1522–1821, then independent. Part of the Central American Federation 1824–38, then became a separate republic. There have been several border disputes with Honduras and Costa Rica.

**Nicaragua, Lake** Nicaragua. Largest lake in Central America, 100 m. long and up to 42 m. wide. Separated from the Pacific by an isthmus 12 m. wide. Fed by the Tipitapa R. from L. Managua. Discharges into the Caribbean via the San Juan R. Many islands. Fish abundant.

**Nice** France. Ancient Nicaea. Prefecture of the Alpes-Maritimes department in the S E, at the mouth of the Paillon R. on the Baie des Anges of the Mediterranean Sea; fashionable resort on the French Riviera. Pop. (1968) 325,400. In a beautiful position on a small coastal plain sheltered to the N by hills rising to the mountains of the Maritime Alps; noted for its mild, sunny climate. Among its many festivals the 'battle of flowers' is the most famous. Considerable trade in Mediterranean fruits, flowers, and essential oils. Manufactures perfumes, soap, olive oil, textiles, furniture. One of the outstanding features is the Promenade des Anglais, built by the English colony in the early 19th cent. Has a cathedral and on Mont Gros (1,220 ft) an observatory. Founded by the Phocaeans from Massilia (Marseille) in the 3rd or 4th cent. B.C. Its prosperity dates from 1388, when it came under the rule of the counts of Savoy. Ceded by Sardinia to France 1860. Birthplace of Garibaldi (1807–82) and Masséna (1756–1817).

**Nicobar Islands** Indian Ocean. Group of 19 islands S of the Andaman Is., forming with the latter a centrally administered territory of India. Area 635 sq. m. Pop. (1961) 14,563. The main islands, 12 of which are inhabited, are Great Nicobar, Camotra, Nancowrie, and Car Nicobar. There is a good landlocked harbour between Camotra and Nancowrie. Coconut palms are numerous, and the coconuts provide both the main foodstuff and the leading item of trade. The people are of Mongoloid stock, akin to the Malays, and are animists. Occupied by Denmark for a considerable period, the islands were annexed by Britain 1869. During the 2nd World War they were occupied by the Japanese 1942–5.

**Nicosia** Cyprus. Capital of the republic, in the N central part of the island, 30 m. WNW of its port, Famagusta. Pop. (1967)

109,000. Trade in cereals, wine, olive oil, etc. Manufactures cigarettes, textiles, footwear, etc. Has 16th-cent. walls built by the Venetians and the former 14th-cent. Gothic cathedral of St Sophia, now a mosque.

**Nidaros** ◊ *Trondheim.*

**Nidd River** England. River 50 m. long in Yorkshire, rising on Great Whernside and flowing generally S E and E through Nidderdale and past Knaresborough to join the R. Ouse 6 m. N W of York.

**Niedersachsen** ◊ *Lower Saxony.*

**Niederwald** Federal German Republic. Hill at the S W end of the Taunus Hills in Hessen, 1,080 ft. high. The S and W slopes are covered with vineyards. On the summit is a national monument of the war of 1870–71.

**Niemen River** ◊ *Neman River.*

**Nieuport** (Flemish **Nieuwpoort**) Belgium. Fishing port in W Flanders province, on the Yser R. 10 m. SW of Ostend. Pop. (1969) 7,187. Manufactures chemicals. Rebuilt after destruction during the 1st World War. To the N W is Nieuport-Bains (Nieuwpoort Bad), a seaside resort.

**Nieuwveld Mountains** ◊ *South Africa.*

**Nièvre** France. Department formed mainly from the old province of Nivernais. Area 2,659 sq. m. Pop. (1968) 247,702. Prefecture Nevers. Rises in the E to nearly 3,000 ft in the barren but picturesque Monts du Morvan. Drained chiefly by the Loire and Yonne rivers. Cereals, potatoes, vines cultivated. Extensive forests. Some minerals, inc. coal in the Decize area. Chief towns Nevers, Fourchambault.

**Niger.** Republic in N W Africa, formerly a French overseas territory. Area 458,596 sq. m. Pop. (1964) 3,250,000 (mainly Negroes, the majority Hausa; 300,000 Tuareg in the N). Cap. Niamey. Bounded by Algeria and Libya (N), Chad (E), Nigeria and Dahomey (S), Upper Volta and Mali (W). Wooded savannah along the Niger R. and the Nigerian frontier (extreme S W and S). Cattle, sheep, and goats raised. Cotton, groundnuts (the most important export), manioc, millet, rice cultivated. Rainfall diminishes northwards; the vast N area is part of the Sahara. A number of oases in the Aïr highlands, e.g. Agadès. Niamey and Zinder (formerly caravan posts) are termini of trans-Saharan motor routes. Became a French sphere of influence in the 1890s, a territory of French West Africa 1904, a member of the French Community 1958, and an independent member of the UN 1960.

**Niger River.** River 2,600 m. long, the third longest in Africa, rising in the S highlands of Guinea, near the Sierra Leone frontier 170 m. from the Atlantic, and flowing N, NE, SE, and S in a broad semi-circular course through Mali, Niger, and Nigeria to the Gulf of Guinea. Divides into several channels below the irrigation dam at Sansanding, passing through a region of marshes and lakes extending to Kabara (port of Timbuktu), then for 500 m. flanked along the left bank by the Sahara. In various stretches impeded by rapids. The Kainji Dam, reservoir, and hydroelectric scheme, 60 m. N of Jebba, opened in 1969, is one of the largest in Africa; it provides power and irrigation water. Joined at Lokoja by its principal tributary, the Benue, navigable in the rainy season (as are the Niger's upper and lower reaches). The great delta of the Niger, with its network of 'oil rivers' (◊ *Nigeria*) entering the sea through a belt of mangrove swamps, begins S of Onitsha. First explored (1795–6, 1805) by Mungo Park. The course, long a subject of controversy, was not completely known until almost the end of the 19th cent.

**Nigeria.** Federal republic in W Africa, a member of the Commonwealth of Nations. Area 356,669 sq. m. Pop. (1963) 55,653,821. Cap. and chief seaport Lagos. Bounded by Niger (N), Chad (NE), Cameroun (E), Dahomey (W), and the Atlantic Ocean (S). Divided administratively into 12 states (1967); 6 in the former Northern Region, which occupied about four fifths of the total area and had over half the population (mainly Hausa and Fulah); 3 in the former Eastern Region (inhabited mainly by Ibo); 2 in the W (largely Yoruba), and a new Lagos state. In the tropics; humidity much higher in the S than in the N. Very hot. Annual rainfall (mainly April–Sept.) 70–140 ins. in the S but less than 25 ins. in the N. The hot dust-laden harmattan blows from the Sahara during the dry season. Along the coast are mangrove swamps (inc. much of the Niger delta); N of this is a zone of tropical rain-forest, 50–100 m. wide. The land then rises to an undulating plateau (savannah country) dissected by the Niger and Benue rivers. The extreme N is a semi-desert thorn-and-scrub region. The highest land is on the Bauchi plateau and along the Cameroun frontier (NE), with some heights above 5,000 ft. Main occupation agricul-

ture. Food crops cassava, groundnuts, maize, millet, yams. Cattle, sheep, and goats raised in the savannah. Chief agricultural exports palm kernels and oil, cacao, rubber from the S, groundnuts from the N. Petroleum (extreme S), tin ore (Bauchi plateau), and coal (Enugu, Udi) are exploited, and petroleum has become the principal export. Cotton weaving and dyeing. Manufactures soap, groundnut oil (Kano), plywood (Sapele), cigarettes (Ibadan). The main W railway runs from Lagos through Ibadan to Kaduna, where it links with the line from Port Harcourt and Enugu and continues to Zaria, whence one line proceeds NE to Kano and Nguru and another NW to Kaura Namoda. Other seaports are Burutu, Calabar, Sapele. A branch railway from Kafanchan, serving the tin mines near Jos, has been extended to Yerwa-Maiduguri.

HISTORY. When Britain first became interested in the Niger delta and its hinterland (17th cent.) the kingdom of Benin (SW) was the most powerful state in W Africa. British influence gradually prevailed over that of other powers; Lagos was annexed (1861) to check the traffic in slaves. The slave trade was abolished, and palm oil became the main article of commerce; the streams draining the Niger delta became known as the 'oil rivers', and the Oil Rivers Protectorate was formed in 1885. Renamed the Niger Coast Protectorate 1893. The Royal Niger Company was granted a charter (1886) giving it control of the delta area and the land bordering the Niger (upstream to the confluence with the Benue). On the termination of the charter the Protectorate of Southern Nigeria was formed (1900). Amalgamated with the colony of Lagos as the Colony and Protectorate of Southern Nigeria 1906. United with the Protectorate of Northern Nigeria as the Colony and Protectorate of Nigeria 1914. Became a federation (under a Governor-General) 1954, and an independent member of the British Commonwealth (1960) and of the UN (1961). Became a republic 1963. The territory of the Cameroons (formerly a German colony) was included in Nigeria for administrative purposes (under British trusteeship) from 1923; in 1961 the S voted to unite with the Republic of Cameroun, the N to join Nigeria. The Federal Prime Minister was assassinated and military government established in 1966. Eastern Nigeria seceded as the independent republic of Biafra in 1967, and war broke out between Federal Nigeria and the breakaway state, continuing till 1970.

**Nightingale Island** ◊ *Tristan da Cunha.*

**Niigata** Japan. Capital of Niigata prefecture, N Honshu, 160 m. NNW of Tokyo. Pop. (1965) 356,302. Chief seaport on the W coast of Honshu; harbour handicapped by silting and lack of shelter. Exports oil from near-by oilfield, fertilizers, etc. Also an industrial centre. Oil refining. Manufactures chemicals, machinery, textiles, etc.

**Nijmegen (Nymegen)** Netherlands. Industrial town in Gelderland province, on the Waal R. 10 m. SSW of Arnhem. Pop. (1968) 145,455. Linked with the Maas R. by the Maas–Waal Canal. Engineering, brickmaking, sugar refining. Manufactures rayon, electrical equipment, chemicals, etc. In the beautiful Valkhof park is the site of the palace built by Charlemagne (777). Seat of a Roman Catholic University (1923). The Treaty of Nijmegen between Louis XIV (France) and the Netherlands, Spain, and the Holy Roman Empire was signed here (1678).

**Nikolayev** USSR. Black Sea port in the Ukrainian SSR, on the S Bug R. at its confluence with the Ingul R. Pop. (1970) 331,000. Exports grain, sugar, metallic ores (iron, manganese), timber, etc. A naval base and the main shipbuilding centre on the Black Sea. Flour milling also an important industry; has some of the largest grain elevators in Europe. Manufactures machinery, footwear, etc.

**Nikopol** USSR. Town in the Ukrainian SSR on the right bank of the Dnieper R. 55 m. ESE of Krivoi Rog. Pop. (1970) 125,000. Important manganese-mining centre, supplying the steel plants of the Donbas and Dnepropetrovsk. Iron founding, flour milling. Manufactures machinery etc.

**Nile River** (Ar. **El Bahr** ('the River') **En Nil**). Longest river in Africa: 3,485 m. from L. Victoria. With its farthest headstream, the longest river in the world, 4,160 m. The remotest headstream is the Luvironza R. (a tributary of the Ruvuvu R.); the Ruvuvu joins the Kagera R. (the main headstream), which enters the W of L. Victoria (a vast natural reservoir, in a region of equatorial rains). At Jinja the river leaves the N side of L. Victoria, at a height of 3,700 ft, by the Ripon Falls (submerged behind the Owen Falls dam farther downstream); now called the Victoria Nile, it passes through the marshy L. Kioga, descends by the Murchison Falls, and at a height of 2,030 ft enters L. Albert, which drains the Ruwenzori highlands through L. Edward and the Semliki R. Leaving L. Albert as the Albert Nile, and after Nimule called the Bahr el Jebel, below Juba it meanders through and spreads over the sudd region; here much water is lost by evaporation and dispersal, and navigation is seriously impeded. Joined at L. No by the Bahr el Ghazal, it is then called the White Nile. Receiving the Sobat R., it flows generally N until at Khartoum it meets its most important tributary, the Blue Nile (which after rising in the Ethiopian Highlands and flowing through L. Tana has swept round in a wide SE-to-NW curve and descended over rapids and through gorges, receiving many tributaries, into Sudan). The combined river is joined by its last tributary, the Atbara R., 200 m. below the confluence of the White Nile and the Blue Nile. Crossing the Sahara in a vast S-bend, between Khartoum in Sudan and Aswan in Egypt, it passes through a narrow valley and over a series of 6 cataracts (numbered consecutively N–S) alternating with almost level stretches. It then descends by a gentler slope, through a much wider valley, to the head of the delta just below Cairo, where it divides into two main channels each 150 m. long, the Rosetta (W) and the Damietta (E).

The prosperity of Egypt, and of the N of Sudan, depends on irrigation water from the Nile; the flood waters (swollen by heavy monsoon rains in the Ethiopian Highlands during the summer) were first used, by basin irrigation, c. 4000 B.C., and the height of the annual flood has been recorded since c. 3600 B.C. The Blue Nile contributes 68 per cent of the volume of the main river at the height of the flood (late Aug. and early Sept.) but only 17 per cent at low water; the White Nile, however, is fed chiefly from the great lakes and maintains a regular flow throughout the year, so that it contributes 83 per cent of the volume of the main river at low water but only 10 per cent at the peak of the Blue Nile flood. In modern times perennial irrigation has been made possible by the construction of huge dams at Aswan and Jebel Aulia (White Nile) and Sennar (Blue Nile). There are also several regulating barrages across the river, e.g. Asyût, Esna. The need for more land under irrigation has led to further projects, e.g. the Aswan High Dam. At high water the river provides a continuous waterway from the delta up to Juba on the White Nile, though in the sudd region it is sometimes obstructed; the Blue Nile is navigable from Khartoum to Roseires (400 m.). At low water it is unnavigable (owing to the Cataracts) from Khartoum to Aswan, except in the Kareima–Kerma section between the Third and Fourth Cataracts.

The Nile Valley was the cradle of one of the earliest civilizations. The river's course was almost certainly known to the ancient Egyptians (who held it sacred) as far upstream as the junction with the Blue Nile. Herodotus followed the river as far as the First Cataract (460 B.C.) but failed to obtain reliable information on the source, which remained a matter of speculation and legend until after the explorations of Speke and Stanley in the late 19th cent.

**Nilgiri Hills.** India. Plateau mainly in W Madras rising steeply from the plain on all but the N side. Average height 6,500 ft; rises to 8,640 ft in Doda Betta.

**Nîmes** France. Ancient Nemausus. Prefecture of the Gard department, 65 m. NW of Marseille. Pop. (1968) 129,866. Tourist, commercial, and industrial centre. Trade in wine, brandy, grain. Manufactures textiles, clothing, footwear, agricultural machinery, etc. Best known, however, for its many Roman remains, the finest in France, among them the famous arena of the 1st or 2nd cent. A.D., the Maison Carrée (a temple), the temple of Diana, and the Tour Magne (Turris Magna), on the summit of Mont Cavalier, one of the barren limestone hills near the city. To the NE is the celebrated Pont du Gard. Founded by Augustus; an important city in Roman times. Flourished as a Protestant stronghold in the 16th and 17th cent. but declined after the revocation of the Edict of Nantes (1685). Birthplace of Alphonse Daudet (1840–97).

**Nimule** ◊ *Bahr el Jebel*; *Nile River*.

**Nineveh.** Ancient capital of the Assyrian Empire, on the Tigris R. opposite modern Mosul (Iraq). Attained its greatest glory in the 8th and 7th cent. B.C. under Sennacherib and Assurbanipal. Destroyed by the Medes 612 B.C. Excavations on the mound Kouyunjik have revealed palaces and temples. ◊ *Assyria*.

**Ningpo** China. Formerly (1911–49) Ninghsien. Commercial town and port in NE Chekiang province, on the Yung R. 90 m. ESE of Hangchow. Pop. 238,000. Exports tea, cotton, fish products, bamboo shoots, etc. Fishing, fish processing; manufactures textiles. Had a Portuguese trading post in the 16th cent. Became one of the original treaty ports (1842).

**Ningsia-Hui AR** China. Autonomous region in the N, S of Inner Mongolia AR. Area 25,600 sq. m. Pop. (1957) 1,810,000. Cap. Yinchwan (formerly Ningsia). Much reduced in area from the former Ningsia province; consists entirely of lofty plateau and mountain ridges, with the Hwang-ho crossing it in the N. The river valley is irrigated and crops of wheat, kaoliang, beans, etc. are grown. Rugs are woven from the wool of local sheep.

**Niort** France. Prefecture of the Deux-Sèvres department, on the Sèvre Niortaise R. 36 m. ENE of La Rochelle. Pop. (1968) 50,079. Market town. Tanning, leather dressing, glove making, etc. Madame de Maintenon (1635–1719) was born in the prison here.

**Nipigon, Lake** Canada. Lake in S Ontario. Area 1,870 sq. m. Contains about 1,000 islands and islets. Drains S into L. Superior via the Nipigon R. (30 m. long).

**Nipissing, Lake** Canada. Lake in Ontario between the Ottawa R. and Georgian Bay (L. Huron), into which it is drained by the French R. Area 330 sq. m.

**Niš** Yugoslavia. Ancient Naissus. Town in Serbia on the Nišava R. 127 m. SSE of Belgrade. Pop. (1961) 81,250. Important railway junction, with the country's largest railway workshops. Also manufactures tobacco products, textiles, etc. Trade in wine, grain. The Emperor Claudius defeated the Goths here in A.D. 269. Birthplace of Constantine the Great (c. 280–337). Near by is the famous Tower of Skulls (Čele Kula), built by the Turks after the Serbian revolt of 1809, in which they embedded more than 900 Serbian skulls.

**Nishapur** Iran. Town in Khurasan province, 40 m. W of Meshed at a height of 4,000 ft. Pop. (1966) 33,482. In a fertile region producing cereals, cotton, etc. Manufactures pottery. Birthplace and burial-place of Omar Khayyám (1050?–1122). About 20 m. NW are the famous Iranian turquoise mines.

**Nishinomiya** Japan. Industrial town in Hyogo prefecture, central Honshu, just NW of Osaka. Pop. (1965) 336,871. Famous for its saké (rice wine). Also manufactures machinery, chemicals, soap, etc. Brewing.

**Niterói** Brazil. Capital of Rio de Janeiro state, on the E shore of Guanabara Bay opposite Rio de Janeiro, to which it is linked by frequent ferry services. Pop. (1960) 228,826. Largely residential; in effect a suburb of Rio. Shipbuilding. Manufactures textiles, metal goods, matches, etc. Also a popular resort with excellent beaches.

**Nith River** Scotland. River 70 m. long rising near Dalmellington in Ayrshire and flowing generally E and then SE through Dumfriesshire (Nithsdale) past Dumfries to Solway Firth. The Afton Water joins it at New Cumnock.

**Niue (Savage) Island** S Pacific Ocean. Coral island belonging to New Zealand, 580 m. WNW of Rarotonga. Area 100 sq. m. Pop. (1968) 5,240. Chief town and port Alofi. Exports copra, bananas. Annexed 1901. ◊ *Cook Islands*.

**Nivernais** France. Region and former province, with capital Nevers, becoming a duchy in 1559 and passing to the French crown in 1669. Practically co-extensive with the modern ◊ *Nièvre* department.

**Nizhni Novgorod** ◊ *Gorky*.

**Nizhni Tagil** USSR. Industrial town in the Sverdlovsk region, RSFSR, 80 m. NNW of Sverdlovsk near the Tagil R. Pop. (1970) 378,000. Important metallurgical centre, in an iron-mining region. Manufactures railway rolling stock, aircraft, agricultural machinery, machine tools, chemicals, etc. Founded 1725 with the building of the Visokaya ironworks.

**Nizké Tatry** ◊ *Tatra Mountains*.

**Nkana** ◊ *Kitwe*; *Ndola*; *Zambia*.

**Nocera Inferiore** Italy. Town in Salerno province, Campania, 21 m. ESE of Naples. Pop. (1961) 43,050. Tomato canning. Manufactures cotton goods. To the E is the village of Nocera Superiore, near which is a circular domed church dating from the 4th cent.

**Nogales** Mexico. Town in Sonora 160 m. N of Hermosillo at a height of 3,900 ft, on the US frontier. Pop. 38,000. Market town. Trade in livestock, agricultural produce. Also a mining centre (silver, gold, etc.). Across the border is Nogales, Arizona (USA).

**Noginsk** USSR. Formerly Bogorodsk. Industrial town in the Moscow region, RSFSR, on the Klyazma R. 32 m. E of Moscow. Pop. (1970) 104,000. Important textile-manufacturing centre. Also chemical and metal-working industries. Power station supplying electricity to Moscow.

**Nome** USA. Seaport in W Alaska, on the S coast of the Seward Peninsula. Pop. (1960) 2,316. Open June–Nov. Fishing. Tourist centre. Owes its origin to the discovery of gold near by (1898). The population rose to about 20,000 in 1900.

**Nord** France. Department in the N, bounded by the North Sea (N) and by Belgium (NE and E). Area 2,229 sq. m. Pop. (1968) 2,417,899. Prefecture Lille. Generally low-lying. Drained by the Scheldt (Escaut) and its tributaries and the Sambre; served by many canals. Cereals, flax, sugar-beet, and hops cultivated. Contains much of the Franco-Belgian coalfield. Besides coalmining there are important textile and metallurgical industries. Chief towns Lille, Cambrai, Douai, Dunkirk, Valenciennes, Armentières, Roubaix, Tourcoing. Much fighting took place here in the 2nd World War prior to the Allied evacuation from Dunkirk.

**Nordenham** Federal German Republic. Fishing port in Lower Saxony, on the Weser R. 7 m. SW of Bremerhaven. Pop. (1963) 27,100. Lead and zinc smelting etc.

**Nordhausen** German Democratic Republic. Town in the Erfurt district, at the S foot of the Harz Mountains 39 m. NNW of Erfurt. Pop. (1965) 42,018. In a potash-mining district. Distilling, printing, textile manufacture, etc. Roman Catholic cathedral. Founded in the 10th cent. Became a free imperial city 1253. Passed to Prussia 1815.

**Nore** England. Sandbank in the Thames estuary off Sheerness, marked by a lightship and buoys. The name is also applied to the anchorage around it, much used by the Royal Navy in the 17th and 18th cent. A naval mutiny took place here in 1797.

**Norfolk** England. Eastern county bounded by the North Sea (N and E) and by The Wash (NW). Area 2,054 sq. m. Pop. (1961) 561,980. County town Norwich. Generally low-lying and flat, with fens in the extreme W, and mudbanks around The Wash. The coast has suffered considerably from marine encroachment. Drained by the Yare, Bure, Waveney, and Great Ouse rivers. In the E are the famous Norfolk Broads, a region of lakes popular with yachtsmen. Soils are fertile and agriculture is highly developed. Barley, wheat, sugar-beet, and turnips are important crops. Livestock, inc. many turkeys, intensively reared. Fishing, centred mainly on Yarmouth and Lowestoft. Other main towns Norwich, King's Lynn, Cromer, East Dereham.

**Norfolk** USA. Seaport in SE Virginia, on the Hampton Roads and the Elizabeth R. Pop. (1960) 305,872. Exports coal, tobacco, cotton, timber, etc. Headquarters of the US Atlantic Fleet. Extensive shipyards, foundries. Manufactures chemicals, fertilizers, textiles, cars, etc. Also a popular seaside resort. Suffered severely in the American Revolution and the American Civil War, but several buildings from the colonial period remain, including St Paul's Church (1739), which still has a British cannon-ball embedded in its walls.

**Norfolk Island** (Australia) S Pacific Ocean. Small volcanic island 900 m. ENE of Sydney, belonging to Australia. Area 14 sq. m. Pop. (1966) 1,147. Has an equable climate, fertile soil, and luxuriant vegetation. Exports citrus and other fruits. Popular with tourists. Discovered (1774) by Capt. Cook. Was a penal settlement 1788–1813 and 1826–55. Received Bounty mutineers from Pitcairn Island 1856. Transferred from New South Wales to the Commonwealth 1913.

**Norilsk** USSR. Mining town in the Krasnoyarsk Territory, RSFSR, 50 m. ESE of the Yenisei port of Dudinka, with which it is linked by rail. Pop. (1970) 136,000. Important nickel-mining centre. Nickel, gold, platinum, and copper are refined.

**Norman** USA. Town in Oklahoma 18 m. SSE of Oklahoma City. Pop. (1960) 33,412. Market town. Seat of the University of Oklahoma (1899).

**Normandy** France. Region and former province in the NW, lying between Brittany (SW) and Picardy (NE), and comprising the departments of Seine-Maritime, Eure, Orne, Calvados, and Manche. A rich agricultural area, with much dairy farming; well known for its Camembert cheese, its cider and apple brandy (from Calvados), and wheat is widely cultivated. Rouen, the chief town, at the lowest bridging-point of the Seine R., has an important textile industry. Le Havre and Cherbourg are major seaports, and Dieppe has a cross-Channel service with Newhaven. Among the many seaside resorts are Deauville, Trouville, Étretat.

Part of the Roman province of Lugdunensis Secunda. In the 9th cent. it was frequently attacked by Northmen, or Normans, after whom the province was named and who had established themselves along the Seine by the early 10th cent. In 1066 William Duke of Normandy became

William the Conqueror of England, and Normandy was united to England 1106–1204, to be renounced in 1259, retaken by Henry V, and finally restored to France except for the Channel Is. During the 2nd World War Normandy again became a battlefield (1944), when Allied forces landed on its N coast and initiated the campaign which led to the liberation of France; many of its towns and villages were devastated in the fighting.

**Normanton** England. Urban district in the W Riding of Yorkshire, 3 m. ENE of Wakefield. Pop. (1961) 18,307. Railway junction. Coalmining centre.

**Norman Wells** ◊ *Mackenzie*; *Northwest Territories*.

**Norristown** USA. Industrial town in Pennsylvania, on the Schuylkill R. 14 m. NW of Philadelphia. Pop. (1960) 38,925. Manufactures textiles, metal goods, drugs, etc.

**Norrköping** Sweden. Industrial town and seaport in Östergötland county, on the Motala R. near its mouth on the Bråvik, an inlet of the Baltic Sea. Pop. (1968) 94,345. Important textile centre (cotton, woollen, rayon goods). Manufactures paper, carpets, etc. Exports wood pulp, paper. Power for its industries is derived from the river.

**Northallerton** England. Urban district and county town of the N Riding of Yorkshire, 14 m. NNE of Ripon. Pop. (1961) 6,720. Market town. Tanning, flour milling, etc. Has a 12th/13th-cent. church with a Perpendicular tower. The English defeated the Scots at the Battle of the Standard (1138) about 3 m. N.

**North America.** Third largest of the world's six continents. Sometimes considered to comprise Canada, the USA, and Mexico, but here taken to include also Greenland, Central America, and the W Indies. Total area 9,366,000 sq. m. Pop. 313 millions. In the NW separated from Asia by the Bering Strait (55 m. wide) and in the S joined to S America by the Isthmus of Panama. Washed on the N by the Arctic Ocean, on the E by the N Atlantic Ocean, the Gulf of Mexico, and the Caribbean Sea, and on the W by the N Pacific Ocean and the Bering Strait. The dominating physical feature is the vast Western Cordillera, extending from Alaska through Canada and the USA and continued by the Sierra Madre ranges of Mexico. The E rim of the Cordillera is formed by the Rocky Mountains (the second longest mountain chain in the world); it also includes the Alaska Range (with Mt. McKinley, 20,269 ft, the highest peak in N America), the Coast Ranges, the Cascade Range, and the Sierra Nevada. Between these W ranges and the Rockies are the Columbia and Colorado Plateaux and the Great Basin in the USA; the central plateau of Mexico lies between the two ranges of the Sierra Madre. To the E of the Rockies are the Great Plains, at a height of 2,000–5,000 ft. Farther E are the lower central plains, a huge fertile area drained to the Hudson Bay by the Saskatchewan and other rivers, to the Atlantic by the Great Lakes and the St Lawrence, and to the Gulf of Mexico by the great Missouri–Mississippi R. system. Other important rivers are the Mackenzie, the Yukon, the Columbia, the Colorado and the Rio Grande. Large lakes (besides the Great Lakes) include (in Canada) Great Bear, Great Slave, Winnipeg, and Manitoba; (in the USA) Great Salt; (in Central America) Nicaragua. N of the St Lawrence R. is the Laurentian Plateau; S are the Appalachian Mountains, the principal highlands in the E of the continent, flanked by the Atlantic coastal plain, which widens to the S and continues around the Gulf of Mexico and the Caribbean Sea.

With a N–S length of over 5,000 m., the continent has a wide range of climates, from polar in the far N to humid tropical in the S, and a similar variety in the natural vegetation. S of the tundra region (along the Arctic coasts) is a wide belt of coniferous forests, extending along the W mountain slopes as far S as California. In the SW of the USA is an arid desert and semi-desert area; E of the mountains are the vast grass-covered plains. To the E of the grasslands are coniferous (N) and deciduous (S) forests, now widely cleared. Much of the S and SE of the USA is occupied by pine forests. In the more humid parts of tropical Central America and the W Indies there are tropical rainforests; here climate and vegetation are largely dependent on altitude.

N America has great economic resources. The plains produce a high proportion of the world's wheat and maize. The S of the USA is the world's leading cotton-growing area. In Central America and the W Indies coffee, cane sugar, and bananas are major export crops. There is a gigantic output (esp. in the USA) of petroleum, coal, and hydroelectric power. The USA ranks first in world output of copper and zinc, Canada in nickel, Mexico in silver, Jamaica in bauxite (for aluminium). With raw materials made available by an efficient transport system, the NE of the USA has become a leading world industrial region and the most densely populated part of the continent.

N America was peopled in prehistoric times from NE Asia, across the Bering Strait, a migration of Mongolian origin which gave rise to the Eskimos and Indians of today. The highest stage of civilization reached in pre-Columbian times was represented by the Aztec and Maya cultures, of which spectacular remains have been found in Mexico and Central America. Farther N the tribes were of a nomadic character. The first Europeans to see N America were Norsemen led by Leif Ericsson, who in the 11th cent. visited a region he called Vinland (probably on the coast of New England), but it was not until after Columbus landed in the Bahamas (1492) that Europe acquired authentic knowledge of the continent. John Cabot discovered the coast of Canada in 1497; Amerigo Vespucci (after whom the continent was named) explored parts of the S Caribbean in 1499. The Spaniards were the first Europeans to conquer and colonize; in the first half of the 16th cent. they established colonies in Mexico and Central America which were to last for 300 years. From the 17th cent. onwards the interior of present-day Canada and the USA was opened up by explorers, fur-traders, and missionaries, mainly French and English. The vast majority of immigrants were European; a 10-per-cent Negro minority grew in the USA. English became the principal language (though there is a French-speaking minority in Canada). In Mexico and Central America the peoples are largely a mixture of Indian and Spanish; the chief language here and in Cuba is Spanish. In most W Indian islands Negroes are most numerous and the commonest language is English.

**Northampton** England. County borough and county town of Northamptonshire, on the R. Nene 44 m. ESE of Birmingham. Pop. (1961) 105,361. Important centre of footwear manufacture. Tanning, engineering, brewing, etc. The 12th-cent. Church of St Sepulchre is one of the 4 round churches in England; St Peter's church also dates from the 12th cent. Many old buildings were destroyed in the fire of 1675.

**Northampton** USA. Town in Massachusetts, on the Connecticut R. 16 m. N of Springfield. Pop. (1960) 30,058. Manufactures cutlery, brushes, hosiery, etc. Seat of Smith College for women (1871). Founded 1654.

**Northamptonshire** England. County in the E Midlands. Area (excluding the Soke of Peterborough) 914 sq. m. Pop. (1961) 398,132. County town Northampton. Generally undulating, rising to 734 ft near Daventry. Drained to the Wash by the Welland and the Nene rivers. Farming is the main occupation on its fertile soil. Large numbers of cattle and sheep are raised. Chief crop wheat. A famous foxhunting county. Iron ore mined. Principal industrial towns Northampton, Kettering, Corby, Wellingborough.

**North Berwick** Scotland. Royal burgh in E Lothian, on the S shore of the Firth of Forth 19 m. ENE of Edinburgh. Pop. (1961) 4,161. Fishing port. Holiday resort. Well-known golf course. The ruins of the 14th-cent. Tantallon Castle are 3 m. E, on the cliffs.

**North Beveland** Netherlands. Island in the Zeeland province, in the Scheldt estuary. Area 35 sq. m. Produces sugar-beet, wheat, etc.

**North Borneo** ◊ *Sabah*.

**North Cape** (Norwegian **Nordkapp**) Norway. Promontory on the island of Mageröy, Finnmark county, about 1,000 ft high. Popularly supposed to be the most northerly point of Europe, but Knivskjärodden, to the W, is actually about a mile nearer the N Pole.

**North Carolina** USA. State on the SE Atlantic seaboard. Area 52,712 sq. m. Pop. (1970) 4,961,832 (about one third Negroes). Cap. Raleigh. One of the original 13 states; popularly known as the 'Tarheel' or 'Old North' state. The coast is much indented, particularly by the Pamlico and Albemarle Sounds, and fringed with a chain of sandy islands. The E half is in the Atlantic coastal plain. To the W are the Piedmont plateau and the Appalachian Mountains, rising to 6,684 ft in Mt Mitchell (the highest point E of the Mississippi). Climate humid subtropical in the SE; cooler and more continental in the mountains. Annual rainfall 45–55 ins. Agriculture important. Chief crops tobacco (leading state), cotton, groundnuts, maize. The state also ranks

first in output of mica. Manufactures cigarettes, textiles, furniture. Chief towns Charlotte, Greensboro, Winston-Salem, Raleigh. Supported the Confederate cause in the American Civil War.

**North Channel** ◊ *Irish Sea*.

**North Dakota** USA. State in the N, bounded on the N by Saskatchewan and Manitoba (Canada). Area 70,665 sq. m. Pop. (1970) 610,648. Cap. Bismarck. Admitted to the Union in 1889 as the 39th state; popularly known as the 'Flickertail' state. Generally flat; rises E–W in three plains, from the Red R. basin in the E to the Missouri plateau in the W. Highest point Black Butte (3,468 ft) in the SW. In the extreme W are the much eroded and infertile Badlands. Drained by the Missouri R. and its tributaries, with the extensive Garrison Reservoir (flood control, irrigation, hydroelectric power) on the Missouri. Climate dry continental, with extremes of heat and cold and an annual rainfall of 15–20 ins. Mainly agricultural. Chief crops barley (leading state), wheat. Largest town Fargo. The first permanent settlement was made at Pembina (1851). Dakota was organized as a separate territory in 1861, and the two states of N Dakota and S Dakota were formed in 1889.

**North Dum-Dum** ◊ *Dum-Dum*.

**Northern Ireland** ◊ *Ireland*.

**Northern Rhodesia** ◊ *Zambia*.

**Northern Territory** Australia. Territory bounded by the Timor and Arafura Seas (N), Queensland (E), S Australia (S), and Western Australia (W). Area 520,280 sq. m. Pop. (1966) 37,433 (excluding some 19,000 aborigines). Cap. Darwin. Arnhem Land in the N contains the largest aboriginal reservation in Australia; the people are semi-nomadic, wandering from the N mangrove swamps and river forests across areas of tall grass and open woodland according to the season – the monsoon rains of 40–60 ins. being followed by a long drought. To the S the rainfall decreases on the low tableland but a broad belt of grassland across the central N parts of the territory, with a rainfall of about 20 ins. annually, provides pasture for cattle, herded largely by aborigines, which roam over the vast areas of widely scattered stations. Farther inland the rainfall decreases to under 10 ins. a year; desert and semi-desert occur, but there is enough pasture for roaming livestock. Road transport by trains of trailers facilitates the carriage of cattle to terminal points. The Stuart Highway runs N from Alice Springs to the pastoral zone and Darwin; the Barkly Highway from Tennant Creek to Mt Isa links up with the Queensland transport system. Other activities are the uranium works at Rum Jungle, gold and copper mines at Tennant Creek, tungsten at Hatches Creek and Wauchope. Chief towns Darwin and Alice Springs.

The N coast was discovered by the Dutch (1623) but was not settled by the British till 1824. The territory was under New South Wales 1825–63 and under S Australia 1863–1911, being then transferred to the Commonwealth. Between 1926 and 1931 it was divided administratively into Northern Australia and Central Australia.

**Northfleet** England. Urban district in Kent, on the Thames estuary 1 m. W of Gravesend. Pop. (1961) 22,084. Manufactures cement, paper, etc.

**North Foreland** England. Chalk headland on the E coast of Kent, just N of Broadstairs. Lighthouse. ◊ *Foreland Point*.

**North Holland** (Dutch **Noordholland**) Netherlands. Province in the N W including the W Frisian islands of Texel, Vlieland, and Terschelling. Area 1,016 sq. m. Pop. (1968) 2,215,876. Cap. Haarlem. Dairy farming and cheese production are important occupations. Leading commercial centre Amsterdam. Other towns Ijmuiden, Alkmaar, Hilversum.

**North Little Rock** USA. Industrial town in Arkansas, on the Arkansas R. opposite Little Rock. Pop. (1960) 58,032. Railway engineering, sawmilling, cottonseed-oil processing, etc.

**North Miami** USA. Town in Florida 7 m. N of Miami. Pop. (1960) 28,708. Mainly residential. Some light industries.

**North Minch** ◊ *Minch*.

**North Ossetian ASSR** USSR. Autonomous republic in European RSFSR, on the N slopes of the Caucasus. Area 3,088 sq. m. Pop. (1970) 553,000. Cap. Ordzhonikidze. Agriculture includes the cultivation of maize, wheat, cotton, and fruits. Lead, zinc, and silver mined. N Ossetia became an autonomous *oblast* (region) 1924 and an autonomous republic 1936.

**North Platte River** USA. River 680 m. long, rising in the Rocky Mountains in N Colorado, flowing generally N and then E and SE, through Wyoming and Nebraska, and joining the S Platte R. at

North Platte city, forming the Platte R. Important in hydroelectric and irrigation projects, with the Pathfinder, Seminoe, and other reservoirs along its course.

**North Rhine-Westphalia** (Ger. **Nordrhein-Westfalen**) Federal German Republic. *Land* formed after the 2nd World War from the former Prussian province of Westphalia, the state of Lippe, and the N part of the former Prussian Rhine Province, including the districts of Aachen, Cologne, and Düsseldorf. Area 13,157 sq. m. Pop. (1968) 16,842,600. Cap. Düsseldorf. A highly industrialized region. Coalmining. Manufactures iron and steel, textiles. In 1949 a small area, about 36 sq. m., was lost by frontier adjustments to the Netherlands and Belgium.

**North Sea** Europe. Sea lying between Great Britain (W) and the continent of Europe (E), about 600 m. long N–S and up to 400 m. wide. Generally shallow, resting on the continental shelf which extends around the British Isles, and reaching its maximum depth (over 300 fathoms) in the Skagerrak. In its central area there are a number of banks, the principal one being the Dogger Bank; the shallow waters here have become important fishing grounds. Many busy shipping lanes cross the North Sea, and some of the world's leading seaports, notably London, Rotterdam, Antwerp, and Hamburg, stand on its shores. A new economic development has been the offshore drilling for natural gas and oil, chiefly near the E coast of England.

**North Tonawanda** USA. Industrial town and port in New York, on the State Barge canal at its junction with the Niagara R. 10 m. N of Buffalo. Pop. (1960) 34,757. Trade in timber. Manufactures paper, plastics, metal goods, etc.

**Northumberland** England. The most northerly county, bounded on the N by Scotland, across the Cheviot Hills and the R. Tweed, on the E by the North Sea. Area 2,019 sq. m. Pop. (1961) 818,988. County town Newcastle upon Tyne. Hilly chiefly in the N, where it rises to 2,676 ft in the Cheviot Hills, and in the W, where it reaches 1,702 ft in the Pennines. Drained by the Tyne, Blyth, and Coquet rivers. Much sheep rearing. Coal mined. Shipbuilding and heavy industries are concentrated on the lower Tyne. Chief towns Newcastle upon Tyne, Wallsend, Tynemouth, Berwick-on-Tweed. The most famous of the many Roman remains is

Hadrian's Wall, which crosses the county from near Haltwhistle to Wallsend.

**Northumbria** Britain. Anglo-Saxon kingdom extending from the Forth to the Humber, formed in the early 7th cent. by Aethelfrith by uniting two older kingdoms, Bernicia (N) and Deira (S). Christianity was introduced in the 8th and early 9th cent.; the kingdom gained fame as a centre of learning, and it was extended to include Strathclyde and Dalriada. In 827, however, it accepted the supremacy of Wessex, and in the late 9th cent. was conquered by the Danes.

**North Walsham** England. Urban district in Norfolk 14 m. NNE of Norwich. Pop. (1961) 5,010. Market town. The 16th-cent. grammar school was attended by Lord Nelson. Important wool-weaving centre in medieval times: Worstead, 3 m. SSE, gave its name to the cloth known as 'worsted'.

**Northwest Passage** N America. Sea route from the Atlantic Ocean to the Pacific, round the N coast of America, sought by navigators and explorers for more than three centuries before being successfully navigated. Frobisher (1576) and Davis (1585–8) reached Baffin Island, and Henry Hudson (1610) discovered Hudson Bay; further progress to the W was made by Ross and Parry in the early 19th cent. but Sir John Franklin's ill-fated expedition (1845–7) was unsuccessful, though rescue expeditions made important discoveries. It was not until Amundsen's voyage (1903–6) that the Passage was actually traversed. Owing to the prevalence of ice it can be used only when conditions are especially favourable. It was first navigated by a commercial vessel in Aug.–Sept. 1969, when the American SS *Manhattan*, an adapted oil tanker, sailed through to Point Barrow (Alaska).

**Northwest Territories** Canada. Vast administrative region in the N, consisting of the mainland N of 60° lat. (except those parts in the Yukon Territory, Quebec, and Newfoundland) and the islands of the Arctic Archipelago and the Hudson and Ungava Bays and Hudson Strait. Area 1,304,903 sq. m. Pop. (1966) 25,995 (about two thirds Eskimos and Indians). Seat of government Ottawa. Subdivided into 3 Districts: Mackenzie (SW), Keewatin (SE), Franklin (N). Mainly low-lying. In the W are the Mackenzie Mountains, rising to 9,000 ft. The W is drained by

Canada's longest river, the Mackenzie. Innumerable lakes, the largest being the Great Bear Lake and the Great Slave Lake. The winters are very cold, the summers short but warm. On the mainland the annual precipitation is 10–15 ins. but it is less on the Arctic islands; it falls mostly as snow. Chief industry goldmining, centred on Yellowknife. Oil produced and refined at Norman Wells. Fur trapping still important; the mink is the most valuable species and the muskrat the most numerous. Aircraft and caterpillar tractors are widely used for transport. The region formerly included the Prairie Provinces and the N parts of Quebec and Ontario. Passed from the Hudson's Bay Company to the Dominion of Canada 1869.

**Northwich** England. Urban district in Cheshire, at the confluence of the R. Weaver and the R. Dane 16 m. ENE of Chester. Pop. (1961) 19,374. Centre of the salt industry. Manufactures chemicals, food products, etc. Has suffered from subsidence owing to brine pumping.

**Northwood** ◊ *Ruislip-Northwood*.

**Norton-Radstock** England. Urban district in Somerset 8 m. SW of Bath. Pop. (1961) 12,782. Coalmining centre. Manufactures footwear etc.

**Norwalk** USA. Industrial town in Connecticut, on Long Island Sound 13 m. WSW of Bridgeport. Pop. (1960) 67,775. Manufactures hats, textiles, clothing, rubber products, etc. First settled in the mid 17th cent.

**Norway.** A kingdom of NW Europe. Area 125,379 sq. m. Pop. (1968) 3,802,243. Cap. Oslo. Rel. Evangelical Lutheran.

Mountainous country occupying the W part of the Scandinavian peninsula, bounded by the Skagerrak (S), the North Sea and the Norwegian Sea (W), the Arctic Ocean (N), and Sweden, Finland, and the USSR (E). Because of the high proportion of unproductive land, Norway has been compelled to rely largely on the sea for its wealth, and fishing and the activities of its merchant navy figure prominently in the economy, while many foreign tourists are attracted by its picturesque coastal scenery. For administrative purposes the country is divided into the following 20 counties or *fylker*: Oslo (city), Akershus, Östfold, Hedmark, Oppland, Buskerud, Vestfold, Telemark, Aust-Agder, Vest-Agder, Rogaland, Hordaland, Bergen (city), Sogn og

Fjordane, Möre og Romsdal, Sör-Tröndelag, Nord-Tröndelag, Nordland, Troms, Finnmark.

TOPOGRAPHY, CLIMATE. The coast is deeply indented by many fiords, some of which penetrate far into the country, the largest and best-known being the Oslo, Hardanger, Sogne, and Trondheim fiords. It is also fringed by thousands of islands, the so-called Skärgård or 'skerry fence', of which the most important are the Lofoten Is. and the Vesterålen group. From the coast the land rises steeply to plateaux and mountain ranges; in the Jotunheim Mountains is Norway's highest peak, Galdhöpiggen (8,097 ft), and immediately W is the Jostedalsbre, the largest icefield in Europe, over 300 sq. m. in area and feeding several glaciers. Between the plateaux and mountain ranges are such deep valleys as the Gudbrandsdal, Hallingdal, and Romsdal; along many of them flow swift rivers which provide hydroelectric power, the longest being the Glomma.

The distinguishing feature of the climate is the unusual mildness of the winters, for although the country extends well beyond 70° N lat., its coast is ice-free throughout the year because of the heating effects of the SW winds from the Atlantic and the N Atlantic Drift, which washes its shores. At the same time the winds bring considerable rainfall to the W coastal regions, with frequent snow in the N. A well-known phenomenon N of the Arctic Circle is the Midnight Sun. At N Cape, for example, at least part of the sun is visible continuously from the second week in May till the end of July, but in winter the sun does not rise above the horizon for over two months.

RESOURCES, PEOPLE, etc. Little more than 3 per cent of the land is cultivated, agriculture being confined to the sheltered lowlands of the SE, the valleys and the narrow ledges beside the fiords. Main crops hay, barley, oats, potatoes. Dairy farming important; much use is made of mountain pastures in the summer. Reindeer are raised by the partly nomadic Lapps of the far N. Forests cover about 23 per cent of the land area, the remainder being unproductive. The most valuable stands of timber, consisting chiefly of conifers, are in the S, and provide raw material for the manufacture of wood pulp and paper. Iron, copper, and pyrites are mined, and there has been much expansion of the electro-metallurgical (aluminium, etc.) and electro-chemical industries. Most of the large quantity of hydroelectric power produced is used in industry, but domestic consumption is also high – over 99 per cent of the population are supplied with electricity at home. Cod and herring form the major part of the catch from the North Sea fishing grounds, and whale oil is brought in from Antarctic waters, where the Norwegians play a leading role in the whaling industry. Their mercantile marine is the fourth largest in the world and has a substantial share of the international carrying trade. Leading exports metals and metal products, wood pulp and paper, fish and fish products. Foreign trade is chiefly with the Federal German Republic, Britain, Sweden. Overseas possessions include Svalbard (Spitsbergen), Jan Mayen, the whaling station of Bouvet Island (in the S Atlantic), and Queen Maud Land (in the Antarctic). Owing to the mountainous nature of the country internal communications are difficult, but the principal centres of population, Oslo, Bergen, Trondheim, and Stavanger, are seaports, and transport is mainly by sea.

With an average of 29 per sq. m., Norway has the lowest density of population in Europe apart from Iceland. Besides the Norwegians themselves, who are typically Nordic, there are about 20,000 Lapps, living mainly in Finnmark, part of Lapland, and 8,000 Finns. The Norwegian language, which is derived from the Danish, exists in two official forms: the Bokmål or Rigsmål, the literary language, and the Landsmål or Nynorsk, the more popular variant. Norway is a constitutional and hereditary monarchy. The parliament, the Storting, is divided into an upper house or Lagting and a lower house or Odelsting, 38 of the 150 members sitting in the former and the remainder in the latter.

HISTORY. In early times Norway was divided into *fylker*, each with its own king, and unity was first achieved by Harald Haarfager (872), who imposed his rule also on the Orkneys and Shetlands. After his death, however, the country was again divided, until, after much civil strife, the power of the crown was established by Haakon IV in the 13th cent.; during this latter period Iceland came under Norwegian rule. By the Union of Kalmar (1397) Norway, Sweden, and Denmark were united under a single monarch. For Norway this union continued even after Sweden achieved independence (1523) and the country became little more than a Danish province. In 1814 Norway was ceded to Sweden, but the national movement grew in strength, and in 1905 the union was dissolved and Prince Charles of Denmark was elected king as Haakon VII of Norway. A cultural revival had also developed, and was represented by the works of Ibsen, Björnson, Grieg, etc. Early in the 2nd World War the country was invaded and occupied by German troops (1940), and the king and the government took refuge in Britain. A puppet government was set up in Norway under Quisling, but a determined resistance movement against the Germans was maintained, and the Norwegian merchant navy rendered excellent service to the Allies at sea.

**Norwich** England. County town of Norfolk, and county borough, on the R. Wensum near the confluence with the R. Yare. Pop. (1961) 119,904. Industrial centre. Manufactures footwear and other leather goods, electrical equipment, mustard, starch, vinegar, etc. The cathedral (founded 1096) is one of the finest examples of Norman work in the country. Of the castle only the Norman keep remains and now houses the museum and art gallery. Also has several old churches, the 15th-cent. Guildhall, and the Maddermarket Theatre. Seat of the University of E Anglia (1963). Many buildings were damaged or destroyed in air raids during the 2nd World War. Birthplace of Elizabeth Fry (1780–1845) and Harriet Martineau (1802–76).

**Norwich** USA. Industrial town in SE Connecticut at the confluence of the Yantic and Shetucket rivers (forming the Thames). Pop. (1960) 38,506. Manufactures textiles, clothing, leather goods, etc. Birthplace of Benedict Arnold (1741–1801).

**Norwood** USA. Industrial and residential town in Ohio, within but independent of Cincinnati. Pop. (1960) 34,580. Manufactures motor vehicles, electrical equipment, footwear, etc.

**Nossi-Bé** Malagasy Republic. Fertile volcanic island off the NW coast. Area 130 sq. m. Pop. 26,000. Chief town and seaport Hellville (pop. 8,000). Main products bananas, coffee, essential oils, sugar, vanilla. Ceded to France 1840. Became a dependency of the French colony of Madagascar 1896.

**Nottingham** England. County town of Nottinghamshire and county borough, on the R. Trent. Pop. (1961) 311,645. Industrial centre, once famous for lacemaking but now more important for the manufacture of hosiery, also bicycles, cigarettes, pharmaceutical products, etc. Brewing, engineering, printing. Roman Catholic cathedral; 16th-cent. grammar school; castle (rebuilt 1674–9, burned down 1831, restored 1875–8). The University College (opened 1881) became a full university 1948. In the 9th cent. it was one of the 5 Danish boroughs. Parliaments were held here 1334, 1337, and 1357. Charles I raised his standard here (1642) at the start of the Civil War. Birthplace of William Booth (1829–1912), founder of the Salvation Army.

**Nottinghamshire** England. Inland county, largely in the valley of the R. Trent. Area 844 sq. m. Pop. (1961) 902,966. County town Nottingham. Mainly lowlying, but hilly in the SW between Nottingham and Mansfield. Parts of Sherwood Forest remain. Wheat, oats, root crops cultivated. Cattle reared. Coal mined in the W. Chief towns Nottingham, Newark, Mansfield.

**Nouakchott** Mauritania. Capital of the republic, in the W near the Atlantic coast 250 m. NNE of Dakar (Senegal). Pop. (1968) 20,000. Commercial centre on caravan routes. Trade in grain, gums, etc.

**Nouméa** New Caledonia. Formerly Port de France. Capital and chief seaport, with fine land-locked harbour, on the SW coast. Pop. 40,880 (inc. 24,192 Europeans, mainly French). Exports nickel, chrome, iron and manganese ores, and nickel matte from local smelters.

**Nouvelle Amsterdam (Amsterdam Island)** Indian Ocean. Island situated lat. 38° S, long. 78° E, from 1955 part of the ♦ *French Southern and Antarctic Territories*. Area 25 sq. m. Of volcanic origin; rises to 2,950 ft. Meteorological and research stations. Annexed by France 1843.

**Nova Goa** ♦ *Panjim*.

**Nova Lisboa (Huambo)** Angola. Future capital; town on the Bié plateau 175 m. ESE of Lobito, at a height of 5,500 ft. Pop. 16,000. On the Benguela railway to Katanga. Commercial centre. Trade in grain, hides and skins. Important railway repair shops.

**Novara** Italy. Capital of Novara province, Piedmont, 29 m. W of Milan. Pop. (1961) 87,704. Manufactures cotton and silk goods, chemicals, etc. Rice milling, map making and printing. Cathedral (rebuilt in the 19th cent.) with a 10th-cent. baptistery; mainly 16th-cent. Church of S Gaudenzio. Here the Austrians defeated the Piedmontese under Charles Albert, King of Sardinia (1849), and the latter abdicated.

**Nova Scotia** Canada. One of the Maritime Provinces, consisting of a peninsula joined to New Brunswick by the Chignecto isthmus, and Cape Breton Island. Area 21,842 sq. m. Pop. (1966) 756,039. Cap. and chief seaport Halifax. The indented coastline provides many harbours. Mainly low-lying, rising to 1,747 ft in the Cape Breton Island uplands. Drained by many small rivers and streams. Bras d'Or Lake (on Cape Breton Island) is the largest of the numerous lakes. The influence of the sea prevents temperatures from reaching the extremes experienced farther inland in the same latitudes. Precipitation is abundant, about 40–55 ins. annually. Dairy farming and fruit growing important; the Annapolis valley is noted for apple orchards. The development of the wood-pulp and paper industry has increased the value of the extensive forests. Around the coasts are fishing and fish canning and processing industries. Coal, supplying the iron and steel industry, is mined in the Sydney and Inverness fields on Cape Breton Island.

The French were the first settlers, calling the region ◊ *Acadia*. In 1621 James I of England granted the whole peninsula to Sir William Alexander, who wished to found a 'New Scotland' (the Nova Scotia of his charter). Separated from New Brunswick 1784. Cape Breton Island was incorporated 1820. Entered the Confederation, as one of the original provinces of Canada, 1867.

**Novaya Zemlya (Nova Zembla)** USSR. In Russian, 'New Land'. Arctic land in the Archangel region, RSFSR, between the Barents Sea and the Kara Sea. Area 35,000 sq. m. Consists of two large islands separated by a narrow strait, Matochkin Shar, and several smaller islands. The two main islands are about 650 m. long and 30–70 m. wide. Typical Arctic climate, with tundra vegetation in the S. The few inhabitants live by fishing, sealing, and hunting.

**Novgorod** USSR. Capital of Novgorod region, RSFSR, on the Volkhov R. near the point where it leaves L. Ilmen and 105 m. SSE of Leningrad. Pop. (1970) 128,000. Sawmilling, flour milling, brewing. Manufactures clothing, footwear, etc. Famous chiefly as one of the country's oldest towns. Within the kremlin or citadel is the 11th-cent. Cathedral of St Sophia, modelled on the cathedral of the same name in Constantinople (Istanbul). Many other ancient churches and monasteries, inc. the 14th-cent. Znamenski cathedral. Several museums. In 862 the inhabitants invited the Varangians under Rurik to Novgorod, and Rurik became the first Prince of Novgorod; this date is thus regarded as marking the foundation of the Russian state, and a monument commemorating the 1,000th anniversary was erected in 1862. In the 12th cent. Novgorod became the chief trading centre of a vast region, and was known as Novgorod Veliki ('Novgorod the Great'). In 1478 it was taken by Ivan III of Moscow, and in 1570 it was destroyed by Ivan IV ('the Terrible') and thousands of its inhabitants were slaughtered. Many of its historical buildings were severely damaged in the 2nd World War.

**Novi Sad** Yugoslavia. Capital of Vojvodina, Serbia; a river port on the Danube 45 m. NW of Belgrade. Pop. (1961) 102,469. Before the 1st World War the Serbian cultural and religious centre; now an industrial and commercial centre. Manufactures textiles, agricultural machinery, electrical equipment, pottery, etc.

**Novocherkassk** USSR. Town in RSFSR 25 m. ENE of Rostov. Pop. (1970) 162,000. Industrial centre. Manufactures locomotives, machinery, textiles, etc. Trade in wine, grain, timber. Founded 1805 as the capital and cultural centre of the Don Cossacks, succeeding Old Cherkassk, on the Don, which had suffered from frequent floods from the river.

**Novokuznetsk** USSR. Formerly Stalinsk. Industrial city in Kemerovo region, RSFSR, on the Tom R. 115 m. SSE of Kemerovo. Pop. (1970) 499,000. A leading metallurgical centre in the Kuznetsk basin. Manufactures iron and steel, aluminium, locomotives, machinery, chemicals, cement, etc. Coalmining in the neighbourhood. Formed from the old city of Kuznetsk (founded 1618) and the new industrial town of Novo Kuznetsk (founded 1929) across the river, the two uniting as Stalinsk in 1932. In the 1930s it expanded rapidly with the development of the Kuznetsk basin. Renamed 1961.

**Novomoskovsk** USSR. Formerly Bobriki (1930–34), Stalinogorsk (1934–61). Industrial town in the Moscow region, RSFSR, 120 m. SSE of Moscow. Pop. (1970) 134,000. Lignite-mining centre. Manufactures chemicals, machinery. Large coal-fed power station. Founded 1930.

**Novorossiisk** USSR. Seaport and industrial town in the Krasnodar Territory, RSFSR, on the Black Sea 60 m. WSW of Krasnodar. Pop. (1970) 133,000. Exports grain, cement, petroleum, etc. An important centre of the cement industry. Oil refining. Manufactures machine tools, agricultural machinery, bicycles, etc. Developed rapidly after the construction of the railway from Rostov (1888).

**Novoshakhtinsk** USSR. Formerly Komintern. Town in RSFSR 32 m. NNE of Rostov. Pop. (1970) 102,000. Important anthracite-mining centre in the Donets basin.

**Novosibirsk** USSR. Capital of the Novosibirsk region, RSFSR, and the largest city in Siberia, on the Ob R. and the Trans-Siberian Railway. Pop. (1970) 1,161,000. Important industrial and route centre. Manufactures agricultural and mining machinery, machine tools, lorries, bicycles, textiles, etc. Sawmilling, flour milling, brewing. Trade in grain, meat, butter, etc. Also a cultural centre; seat of a university (1959). Founded 1896. Modern in appearance. Expanded rapidly in the 1930s and again in the 2nd World War. Linked by the Turksib Railway with Central Asia and by another direct line with the Kuznetsk basin.

**Nowa Huta** Poland. In Polish, 'New Foundry'. Industrial town in the Cracow voivodship, on the Vistula R. 6 m. E of Cracow. Pop. 50,000. Important steel centre: blast furnaces, rolling mills, coke ovens. Built since 1948.

**Nowgong** India. Town in Assam 60 m. ENE of Gauhati. Pop. (1961) 38,600. Commercial centre. Trade in rice, tea, etc.

**Nowy Sącz** Poland. Town in the Cracow voivodship 45 m. SE of Cracow, in the picturesque valley of the Dunajec R. Pop. (1968) 39,300. Railway engineering. Manufactures agricultural implements, textiles chemicals, etc.

**Nubia** Sudan/United Arab Republic. Ancient state in NE Africa; region on both sides of the Nile, from Aswan to Khartoum. Divided between the S of Egypt and the N of Sudan. Includes part of the Nubian Desert and the Libyan Desert; no clearly defined boundaries. The only fertile area is the narrow irrigable strip along the Nile. Known under the Pharaohs as Cush. Incorporated in Egypt during the 18th dynasty; later formed part of Ethiopia.

**Nubian Desert** Sudan. A rocky barren waste in the NE, between the Nile valley and the Red Sea. Mainly sandstone plateau, rising in the coastal range to over 7,000 ft. The surface is scored by many wadis.

**Nueva San Salvador** ♢ *Santa Tecla.*

**Nueva Segovia** ♢ *Barquisimeto.*

**Nueva Toledo** ♢ *Cumaná.*

**Nuevo Laredo** Mexico. Town in Tamaulipas state, on the Rio Grande opposite Laredo (Texas). Pop. 29,000. Point of entry for American tourists; starting point of the road via Monterrey to Mexico City. Manufactures textiles. Flour milling etc. Trade in agricultural produce.

**Nuevo León** Mexico. State in the NE, with a narrow corridor bordering N on the Rio Grande and the USA. Area 25,136 sq. m. Pop. (1969) 1,678,000. Cap. and chief industrial centre Monterrey. Largely mountainous; crossed by the Sierra Madre Oriental. Sugar-cane (in the N irrigated areas), also cotton, tobacco, cereals cultivated. Gold, silver, lead, and copper are among the leading minerals.

**Nuku'alofa** ♢ *Tonga.*

**Nukuhiva** ♢ *Marquesas Islands.*

**Nukus** USSR. Capital of the Kara-Kalpak ASSR (Uzbek SSR), at the head of the Amu Darya delta 500 m. WNW of Tashkent. Pop. (1970) 74,000. Manufactures cotton goods, clothing, footwear, etc.

**Nullarbor Plain** Australia. Arid plain in SW South Australia and SE Western Australia, between the Great Victoria Desert and the Great Australian Bight, without trees (hence the name) or rivers. Extensive limestone areas with karst features. Vegetation consists largely of saltbush and supports only a few sheep. Crossed by the Trans-Australian Railway.

**Numidia** N Africa. Ancient kingdom, corresponding approximately to the NE of modern Algeria. After the 2nd Punic War it was united under Masinissa (previously ruler of E Numidia), who had supported Rome. His grandson Jugurtha fought the Romans and was defeated; the E then became a Roman province (Africa Nova) and the W was added to Mauretania. Prosperous under the Romans, with chief towns Cirta (▷ *Constantine*) and Hippo Regius (modern Annaba). Invaded by the Vandals in the 5th cent. A.D. and by the Arabs in the 8th. Suffered decay and mis-government until the French conquest of Algeria in the 19th cent.

**Nuneaton** England. Municipal borough in Warwickshire, on the R Anker 8 m. NNE of Coventry. Pop. (1961) 56,598. Coal-mining centre. Manufactures textiles, cardboard boxes, etc. Has the remains of a 12th-cent. nunnery after which the town was named. Arbury, now in the borough, was the birthplace of George Eliot (1819–80).

**Nuremberg (Ger. Nürnberg)** Federal German Republic. City in Bavaria, on the Pegnitz R. in the district of Middle Franconia. Pop. (1968) 465,797. Industrial and commercial centre. Centre of the toy industry. Manufactures machinery, electrical equipment, precision instruments, office equipment, pencils, etc. Brewing, distilling. Before the 2nd World War it was famous for its medieval appearance, esp. its Gothic architecture, but many of its finest buildings were destroyed by bombing; among those badly damaged were the partly 14th-cent. town hall and the Albrecht Dürer house. The principal buildings have since been restored. Grew up round the 11th-cent. castle, and in the 15th and 16th cent. was a centre of art and culture; here the first pocket watches, known as 'Nuremberg eggs', were made. Under the Hitler régime the annual Nazi rallies were held here, the anti-Semitic 'Nuremberg laws' being decreed at the 1935 congress. In 1945–6 the Nazi leaders were tried here for their war crimes.

**Nutley** USA. Town in New Jersey 7 m. N of Newark. Pop. (1960) 29,513. Mainly residential. Manufactures textiles, chemicals, paper, etc.

**Nyasa, Lake** ▷ *Malawi, Lake.*

**Nyasaland** ▷ *Malawi.*

**Nyavarongo River** ▷ *Kagera River.*

**Nyika Plateau** ▷ *Malawi.*

**Nyíregyháza** Hungary. Capital of Szabolcs-Szatmár county 45 m. ESE of Miskolc. Pop. (1968) 63,000. Market town in a district producing tobacco, wine, and fruits. Manufactures furniture, soap, cement, etc.

**Nyköping** Sweden. Capital of Södermanland county, on the Baltic coast 32 m. ENE of Norrköping. Pop. (1968) 31,226. Seaport. Industrial centre. Manufactures textiles, furniture, etc.

**Nymegen** ▷ *Nijmegen.*

**Nysa River** ▷ *Neisse River.*

# O

**Oahu** ⧫ *Hawaii*.

**Oakengates** England. Urban district in Shropshire 13 m. ESE of Shrewsbury. Pop. (1961) 12,158. Coalmines. Ironworks.

**Oakham** England. County town and urban district of Rutland 17 m. E of Leicester. Pop. (1961) 4,571. Market town. Manufactures hosiery, footwear. Ruins of a 12th-cent. castle. Birthplace of Titus Oates (1648–1705).

**Oakland** USA. Seaport and industrial centre in California, on the E shore of San Francisco Bay. Pop. (1960) 367,548. Connected with San Francisco by the San Francisco–Oakland Bay Bridge (over 8 m. long, opened 1936). Naval air station and airport. Oil refining, shipbuilding, sawmilling, food processing, motor-car assembly. Manufactures electrical equipment, glass, chemicals, etc. The residential district extends over the slopes of the Berkeley Hills, facing the Golden Gate and giving fine views of the bay. Founded 1852.

**Oak Park** USA. Town in Illinois just W of Chicago. Pop. (1960) 61,093. Mainly residential. Some light industries. Birthplace of Ernest Hemingway (1899–1961).

**Oak Ridge** USA. Town in Tennessee 17 m. WNW of Knoxville. Pop. (1960) 27,169. Site of the US Atomic Energy Commission: has the Oak Ridge National Laboratory and two uranium-processing plants. Established 1943. Its population exceeded 70,000 before the end of the 2nd World War but afterwards declined.

**Oamaru** New Zealand. Chief town and seaport of N Otago, S Island, 60 m. NNE of Dunedin. Pop. (1966) 13,186. Exports grain, flour, limestone. Woollen and flour milling, engineering, etc.

**Oaxaca (Oaxaca de Juárez)** Mexico. **1.** State in the S, on the Pacific coast. Area 36,375 sq. m. Pop. (1969) 2,170,000. Mainly mountainous, rising to 11,145 ft in Zempoaltépetl. Fertile valleys. Rice, maize, cotton, coffee, tobacco cultivated. Stock rearing important.

**2.** Capital of Oaxaca state; in the Atoyac R. valley, at a height of 5,000 ft. Pop. (1960) 68,545 (largely Mixtec and Zapotec Indians). Flour milling, cotton ginning, textile manufacture, etc. Indian handicrafts, esp. pottery, leather goods. Founded by the Aztecs in 1486. Noteworthy Spanish-colonial architecture. Birthplace of Porfirio Díaz (1830–1915). Benito Juárez (1806–72) was born in a village near by.

**Oban** Scotland. Small burgh in Argyllshire, on the Firth of Lorne. Pop. (1961) 6,859. Port. Tourist resort. Built around Oban Bay, sheltered by Kerrera island. Roman Catholic cathedral. Ruins of Dunollie Castle; 3 m. NE are those of Dunstaffnage Castle.

**Obeid, El** Sudan. Capital of the Kordofan province, 220 m. SW of Khartoum. Pop. (1964) 60,000. Linked by railway (via Wad Medani, Sennar Junction, and Er Rahad) with Khartoum. Trading centre for gum arabic, cereals, cattle. Scene of the defeat of the Egyptian forces by the Mahdi (1883); largely destroyed but later rebuilt.

**Oberammergau** Federal German Republic. Village in Bavaria, on the Ammer R. in the foothills of the Bavarian Alps 45 m. SSW of Munich. Pop. 4,700. Resort and winter-sports centre. Sawmilling, wood carving. Chiefly famous for the Passion play performed by the inhabitants every 10 years; this was instituted in 1634 as a thanksgiving for the ending of the plague known as the Black Death.

**Oberhausen** Federal German Republic. Industrial town in N Rhine-Westphalia in the Ruhr district, just NE of Duisburg on the Rhine-Herne Canal. Pop. (1968) 252,947. Coalmining centre. Zinc smelting, oil refining. Manufactures iron and steel, chemicals, glass, soap, etc. Modern, dating only from the mid 19th cent.

**Oberösterreich** ⧫ *Upper Austria*.

**Ob River** USSR. Great river of W Siberia (RSFSR) 2,100 m. long, formed by the union of the Biya and Katun rivers, both rising in the Altai Mountains and joining near Biisk. It flows generally NW and N across the W Siberian Plain to the vast Gulf of Ob, about 500 m. long, to enter the Arctic Ocean; its drainage basin covers well over 1 million sq. m. It is navigable for most of its length, as also are its chief tributaries, the Irtysh, Chulym, and Tom. The principal towns on its banks are Barnaul and Novosibirsk. In the spring its upper reaches thaw while the lower reaches are still frozen, so that large areas of coniferous forest land are flooded.

**Oceania.** A term generally applied to the islands of the Pacific Ocean which are included in Polynesia, Melanesia, Micronesia, and Australasia. Sometimes held to include also the Philippines and Indonesia, sometimes to be simply equivalent to Australasia.

**Ocean Island** ◊ *Gilbert and Ellice Islands*.

**Ochil Hills** Scotland. Range of volcanic origin 28 m. long extending WSW–ENE from just NE of Stirling to the Firth of Tay. Highest peaks Ben Cleuch (2,363 ft), King's Seat (2,111 ft).

**Ochrida** ◊ *Okhrida*.

**Odense** Denmark. Capital of Odense county, on the Odense R. in the N of Fyn island. Pop. (1965) 107,531. Port, with a ship canal to Odense Fiord. Exports dairy produce, bacon. Shipbuilding, flour milling, brewing, etc. Manufactures machinery, textiles, glass, etc. Founded in the 10th cent. Cathedral (rebuilt in the 13th cent.); restored 13th-cent. church. Birthplace of Hans Christian Andersen (1805–75).

**Odenwald** Federal German Republic. Wooded range of hills S of the Main R., extending about 50 m. W–E, mainly in Hessen. Highest point Katzenbuckel (2,054 ft).

**Oder** (Czech and Polish **Odra**) **River.** River 560 m. long rising near the SE end of the Sudeten Mountains, in Moravia, Czechoslovakia, flowing generally NE through the Moravian Gate into Poland. It turns NW past Wroclaw, then N, to enter the Baltic Sea by the Stettiner Haff; N of its confluence with the Lusatian Neisse it has formed part of the boundary between the German Democratic Republic and Poland since the 2nd World War. Connected by canals with the Katowice industrial region and with the Havel, Spree, and Vistula rivers. Chief tributaries the two Neisse rivers and the Warthe. An important commercial waterway, esp. below Wroclaw.

**Odessa** USA. Town in W Texas 300 m. WSW of Fort Worth. Pop. (1960) 80,338. Important centre of the oil industry. Oil refining. Manufactures oilfield equipment, chemicals, synthetic rubber, carbon black, etc. Trade in livestock. Expanded rapidly after the discovery of oil in the 1920s.

**Odessa** USSR. Capital of the Odessa region and Black Sea port in the Ukrainian SSR. Pop. (1970) 892,000. Exports grain, timber, wool, sugar, etc. Also an industrial centre. Sugar and oil refining, flour milling. Manufactures agricultural machinery, machine tools, chemicals, bricks, etc. Also a cultural centre with a university (1865) and many colleges, and trade schools. Picturesquely situated on a low plateau facing the sea, and has broad, tree-lined streets. Along the coast near by there are several health resorts. Founded on the site of a Greek colony, Odessos, after which it was named. Became Russian 1795. Developed rapidly in the 19th cent. as the chief Russian grain-exporting port. Its inhabitants, along with the mutineers of the battleship *Potemkin*, were involved in the 1905 revolution. In the 2nd World War it was besieged and taken by German and Rumanian forces (1941), and suffered severely during the occupation. Birthplace of Vladimir de Pachmann (1848–1933).

**Odra River** ◊ *Oder River*.

**Oeno Island** ◊ *Pitcairn Island*.

**Offaly** Irish Republic. Formerly King's County. Inland county in Leinster province. Area 771 sq. m. Pop. (1966) 51,717. County town Tullamore. Generally lowlying, with part of the Bog of Allen in the NE and the Slieve Bloom Mountains in the SE. Drained by the Shannon (on the W boundary), Barrow, Nore, and Brosna rivers. Crossed by the Grand Canal. Cattle raised. Potatoes, barley, turnips cultivated. Chief towns Tullamore, Birr, Portarlington. In the NW is ◊ *Clonmacnoise*.

**Offa's Dyke** England. Ancient earthwork extending from the mouth of the R. Dee to the R. Severn near Chepstow, believed to have been built by Offa, king of Mercia, in the 8th cent. as a boundary between the English and Welsh. Parts still form the border between the two countries.

**Offenbach** Federal German Republic. Industrial town in Hessen, on the Main R. just ESE of Frankfurt. Pop. (1968) 116,575. Chief centre of the leather industry (footwear, luggage, handbags, etc.). Manufactures machinery, metal goods, chemicals. Has a unique leather museum. Its development was largely due to the influx of Huguenots in the late 17th cent.

**Ogasawara-gunto** ◊ *Bonin Islands*.

**Ogbomosho** Nigeria. Town in the W 130 m. NE of Lagos. Pop. (1960) 140,000. In an agricultural district producing yams, cassava, cotton, etc. Cotton weaving.

**Ogden** USA. Town and railway junction in N Utah 33 m. N of Salt Lake City. Pop. (1960) 70,197. Meat packing, food processing. Manufactures clothing, cement, etc. Settled by the Mormons 1847. Developed after the completion of the Union Pacific railway (1869).

**Ogowé (Ogooué) River.** River 680 m. long, rising on the Baleke plateau in Congo (Brazzaville), flowing generally NW and W through a densely forested region in Gabon, draining a number of lakes in the lower course, and entering the Atlantic Ocean by a delta near Cape Lopez and Port Gentil. Chief tributaries the Lolo and the Ivindo. Navigable throughout the year below Lambaréné. Important timber trade along the lower course.

**Ohio** USA. State bordering on L. Erie in the N. Area 41,222 sq. m. Pop. (1970) 10,542,030. Cap. Columbus. Admitted to the Union in 1803 as the 17th state; popularly known as the 'Buckeye' state. Along the S boundary is the Ohio R.; a range of hills running WSW from the NE corner forms a watershed between the Allegheny Mountains to the E and the prairies to the W. Climate humid continental (cold winters, warm summers) but less extreme round the shores of L. Erie. Annual rainfall 30–40 ins. Agriculture important. Chief crops maize, wheat, oats, soya beans (largely fed to livestock: cattle, pigs, and wool-bearing sheep). Coal is the outstanding mineral. A leading industrial state. Manufactures iron and steel, machinery, rubber products (tyres, inner tubes, etc.), motor vehicles and parts, paper. Industries are centred on Cleveland, Cincinnati, Columbus, Toledo, Akron, Dayton, Youngstown, Canton. Ceded to Britain in 1763 and to the USA in 1783. Became part of the NW Territory 1787.

**Ohio River** USA. River 980 m. long, principal E tributary of the Mississippi, formed by the union of the Allegheny and Monongahela rivers at Pittsburgh (Pennsylvania), flowing generally SW, and joining the Mississippi at Cairo (Illinois). Navigable from 100 m. below Pittsburgh. The tributaries from the N include the Miami, Scioto, Beaver, Muskingum, and Wabash, and from the S the Big Sandy, Licking, Kentucky, Salt, Green, Cumberland, and Tennessee. Lost much trade to the railways, but still carries considerable cargoes of coal, coke, cement, sand, etc. Dams, reservoirs, and levees have been constructed as a protection against floods, which were especially destructive in 1913, 1936, and 1937.

**Ohre River** ♢ *Cheb*.

**Ohrid** ♢ *Okhrida*.

**Oiapoque River** ♢ *Oyapock River*.

**Oil Islands** ♢ *Chagos Archipelago*.

**Oirot** A R ♢ *Gorno-Altai A R*.

**Oise** France. Department in the N, forming parts of the Île-de-France and Picardy. Area 2,273 sq. m. Pop. (1968) 540,988. Prefecture Beauvais. Mostly low-lying; large areas of woodland including the Forest of Compiègne. Forms much of the lower basin of the Oise R. Wheat, sugarbeet, fodder crops, fruits cultivated. Cattle rearing and dairy farming important. Racing stables in the Chantilly district. Chief towns Beauvais, Compiègne.

**Oise River** France. River 188 m. long rising in the Belgian Ardennes and flowing generally SW into France, past Compiègne, joining the Seine R. just below Pontoise. Navigable upstream to Noyon, thence paralleled by a lateral canal. Also linked by canals with the Somme, Scheldt (Escaut), and Sambre rivers. Chief tributary the Aisne R.

**Oita** Japan. Capital of Oita prefecture, on the NE coast of Kyushu. Pop. (1965) 226,415. Industrial town and minor seaport. Manufactures metal goods, paper. Reached its greatest importance in the 16th century.

**Okanagan Lake** Canada. Long (70 m.), narrow lake in S British Columbia, drained S by the Okanagan R., a tributary of the Columbia R. The Okanagan valley is famous for fruit growing (esp. apples), the chief town being Penticton.

**Oka River** (Irkutsk) USSR. River 500 m. long in the Irkutsk region, RSFSR, rising in the E Sayan Mountains and flowing generally N to join the Angara R.

**Oka River** (Kursk) USSR. River 900 m. long in the European RSFSR, rising in the Kursk region and flowing N past Orel, then E and NE past Kaluga, Serpukhov, Kolomna, and Ryazan to join the Volga R., of which it is the chief right-bank tributary, at Gorky. Main tributaries the Moskva and the Klyazma. Although frozen for 5 months or more annually, it is an important waterway, esp. for the transportation of wheat and timber.

**Okavango (Okovango) River.** River 1,000 m. long, rising on the Bié Plateau in Angola as the Cubango R., flowing generally SE to the SW Africa frontier and across the Caprivi strip, and entering the Okavango Swamp N of L. Ngami in Botswana.

**Okayama** Japan. Capital of Okayama prefecture, SW Honshu, on the Inland Sea 70 m. W of Kobe. Pop. (1965) 291,816. Port. Industrial town. Manufactures agricultural implements, cotton goods, porcelain, etc.

**Okazaki** Japan. Town in Aichi prefecture, Honshu, 20 m. SE of Nagoya. Pop. (1965) 194,408. Manufactures textiles, chemicals, machinery, etc. Grew up around the 15th-cent. castle.

**Okeechobee, Lake** USA. Lake 35 m. long and 32 m. wide in S Florida; the second largest freshwater lake entirely in the USA. Receives the Kissimmee R. from the N. Drains to the Atlantic through the Everglades. Good fishing (pike, bass, etc.).

**Okefenokee Swamp** USA. A famous swamp mainly in SE Georgia but partly in NE Florida. Area about 600 sq. m. Much of it is in the Okefenokee National Wildlife Refuge (established 1937). Alligators, deer, bears, raccoons, snakes, and many species of birds (inc. the ibis).

**Okhotsk, Sea of.** Arm of the NW Pacific Ocean, on the E coast of Siberia and almost enclosed by the Kamchatka peninsula, the Kuril Is., and Sakhalin. Area 600,000 sq. m. Icebound in the N Nov.–May.

**Okhrida (Ochrida, Ohrid)** Yugoslavia. Town in Macedonia, on the NE shore of L. Okhrida. Pop. 13,000. Commercial and fishing centre. Tourist resort. Picturesque, Turkish in appearance. Originally a Greek colony; settled by Slavs in the 9th cent. The most famous building is the 11th-cent. Church of St Sophia.

**Okhrida (Ochrida, Ohrid), Lake** Albania/Yugoslavia. Lake on the Yugoslav-Albanian border, at a height of 2,280 ft and exceptionally deep (maximum 962 ft); 19 m. long and 8 m. wide. Famed for the unusual clarity of its water (sometimes down to 65 ft), its scenic beauty, its fishing, and the many historic churches and monasteries on its shores. On its NE shore is the town of Okhrida.

**Okinawa.** Largest and most important of the Ryukyu Is., 330 m. SSW of Kyushu (Japan). Area 454 sq. m. Pop. (1965) 758,777. Cap. Naha City. Sugar-cane, sweet potatoes, rice cultivated. During the 2nd World War it was the scene of bitter fighting between American and Japanese forces (1945). Still an important American military base.

**Oklahoma** USA. State in the S, with the Red R. along the S boundary and the 'panhandle' in the NW. Area 69,919 sq. m. Pop. (1970) 2,498,378. Cap. Oklahoma City. Admitted to the Union in 1907 as the 46th state; popularly known as the 'Sooner' state. Mainly plains, sloping downwards from the NW (where the Black Mesa rises to 4,978 ft) to the SE. Parts of the Boston and Ouachita Mountains in the E. Drained chiefly by the Arkansas R. and its tributaries the Cimarron, the North Canadian, and the Canadian. Climate continental; cool winters, hot summers, and a generally light rainfall, increasing W–E. Originally cattle country. The main occupation is now agriculture, though cattle rearing is still important. Chief crops winter wheat, sorghum, cotton. Rich in minerals, esp. petroleum and natural gas. Principal industry oil refining. Largest cities Oklahoma City and Tulsa ('the oil capital of the world'). First explored by the Spaniards. Passed from France to the USA under the Louisiana Purchase (1803). Before the American Civil War most of Oklahoma was known as 'the Indian Territory'; a large area was opened to white settlers in 1889, some of whom, having illegally entered ahead of time, were called 'Sooners' (hence the popular name). The 68,689 Indians (1960) still represent a higher proportion of the total population than in any other state.

**Oklahoma City** USA. State capital of Oklahoma, on the N Canadian R. at a height of 1,200 ft. Pop. (1960) 324,253. Industrial and commercial centre in an agricultural and oil-producing region. Oil refining, flour milling, meat packing, printing and publishing, etc. Manufactures oilfield equipment, aircraft. Seat of the Oklahoma City University (1904). Founded 1889 as a pioneer city, acquiring a population of about 10,000 (under tents) in a single day.

**Okovango River** ⟡ *Okavango River*.

**Öland Island** Sweden. Long, narrow island in Kalmar county, in the Baltic Sea, separated from the mainland by Kalmar Sound (3–18 m. wide). Area 520 sq. m. Pop. 26,000. Chief town Borgholm (pop. 2,000). Farming and limestone quarrying are important occupations. Popular with tourists in the summer. Borgholm has the ruins of a 13th-cent. castle.

**Oldbury** England. Industrial town in Worcestershire 5 m. WNW of Birmingham. Pop. (1961) 53,935. Manufactures glass and steel products, chemicals, machinery, etc.

From 1966 part of the county borough of ♢ *Warley*.

**Oldenburg** Federal German Republic. **1.** Former *Land*, since the 2nd World War part of Lower Saxony. Area 2,084 sq. m. Before 1937 it consisted of three parts: Oldenburg proper, an enclave on the North Sea in Hanover province; Birkenfeld, an enclave in Rhine province; Lübeck district. Birkenfeld and Lübeck districts became part of Prussia 1937. A county in the 11th cent. In 1448 Count Christian became king of Denmark. Became a grand duchy 1815. Joined the German Empire 1871. Its capital was Oldenburg.

**2.** Former capital of the Oldenburg *Land*, in Lower Saxony on the Hunte R. 26 m. WNW of Bremen. Pop. (1968) 130,555. Market town. Railway junction. Manufactures textiles, dyes, ceramics, glass, etc. Food processing. Has the 17th-cent. former palace of the grand dukes, now a museum.

**Oldham** England. County borough in SE Lancashire 6 m. NE of Manchester. Pop. (1961) 115,426. Important centre of the cotton industry, esp. spinning. Also manufactures textile and other machinery, electrical equipment, plastics, clothing, etc. Linen weaving was introduced in the early 17th cent. to be followed by cotton in the 18th cent., and the town prospered with mechanization. With the decline of the cotton trade in the present century, the earlier specialization proved a liability.

**Olekma River** USSR. River 700 m. long in RSFSR, rising in the Yablonovy Range and flowing generally N through the N Chita region and the Yakut ASSR, and joining the Lena R. below Olekminsk. The basin is important for goldmining.

**Oléron** France. Island in the Bay of Biscay, in the Charente-Maritime department opposite the mouth of the Charente R., separated from the mainland by the narrow Pertuis de Maumusson. Area 68 sq. m. Pop. 14,000. Oyster beds. Produces early vegetables. Chief towns Le Château d'Oléron, St Pierre.

**Olímbos** ♢ *Olympus*.

**Olives, Mount of (Olivet)** Jordan. Ridge 2,680 ft high, just E of the Old City of Jerusalem, separated from it by the valley of Kidron. At its foot is the Garden of Gethsemane. Associated with many biblical stories.

**Olmütz** ♢ *Olomouc*.

**Olney** England. Market town in Bucking-hamshire, on the R. Ouse 10 m. WNW of Bedford. Pop. (1961) 2,337. William Cowper lived here (1767–86) and assisted John Newton, the curate, in writing the *Olney Hymns*.

**Olomouc** (Ger. **Olmütz**) Czechoslovakia. Industrial town in Moravia, on the Morava R. 41 m. NE of Brno. Pop. (1967) 78,000. Manufactures food products (e.g. malt, sugar, beer, confectionery), agricultural machinery, cement. Seat of a university, founded 1573, later reduced to the theological faculty, but refounded 1946. Among historic buildings are the 14th-cent. Gothic cathedral (restored) and the 15th-cent. town hall with its famous astronomical clock. The recognized capital of Moravia until 1640.

**Olsztyn** (Ger. **Allenstein**) Poland. Capital of the Olsztyn voivodship in the NE, 88 m. ESE of Gdańsk. Pop. (1968) 89,700. Before 1945 in E Prussia. Manufactures machinery, leather, etc. Founded by the Teutonic Knights in the 14th cent.

**Olympia** Greece. Ancient city in Elis in the W Peloponnese, at the confluence of the Cladeus R. with the Alpheus R. 42 m. S of Patras. Site of the ruined temple of Zeus, with the statue of Zeus by Pheidias (destroyed), one of the Seven Wonders of the World. Founded *c.* 1000 B.C. Scene of the Olympic Games, held every 4 years from 776 B.C. Near by is the modern village of Olympia, with a museum containing many famous sculptures, inc. the Hermes of Praxiteles.

**Olympia** USA. State capital of Washington, at the S end of Puget Sound. Pop. (1960) 18,273. Seaport. Exports timber, fish (esp. oysters). Spectacular mountain scenery. Founded 1850.

**Olympus** (Gr. **Olímbos**) Greece. Mountain ridge near the Aegean coast, on the border between Thessaly and Macedonia, rising to 9,550 ft, the country's highest summit. Snow-capped for much of the year. Traditional home of the gods, esp. of Zeus.

**Olympus, Mount** ♢ *Cyprus*.

**Omagh** Northern Ireland. County town and urban district in Co. Tyrone, on the R. Strule 27 m. S of Londonderry. Pop. (1961) 8,107. Market town. Trade in cattle, potatoes, oats. Manufactures milk products.

**Omaha** USA. Largest city in Nebraska, on the Missouri R. Pop. (1960) 301,598. Railway junction. Lead smelting, oil refining, meat packing. Manufactures agricultural machinery, paints, beverages, etc. Seat of the Creighton University (1878) and the Municipal University (1930). Named after the Omaha Indians. Founded 1854. Developed as a river port, but the trade now depends much more on the railways.

**Oman*** ◊ *Muscat and Oman.*

**Oman, Gulf of.** Arm of the Arabian Sea, in the NW, 300 m. long, between Oman and Iran, leading through the Strait of Hormuz to the Persian Gulf.

**Omdurman** Sudan. Town 5 m. NW of Khartoum, with which it is connected by a bridge across the White Nile. Pop. (1964) 167,000. Famous for native markets. Trade in hides, gum arabic, livestock. The Mahdi made Omdurman (then a village) his capital in 1884; his successor the Khalifa was utterly defeated by Anglo-Egyptian forces (under Lord Kitchener) at the Battle of Omdurman (1898). The Mahdi's tomb was destroyed, but rebuilt in 1947.

**Omsk** USSR. Capital of the Omsk region, RSFSR, at the confluence of the Irtysh R. and the Om R. and on the Trans-Siberian Railway 375 m. W of Novosibirsk. Pop. (1970) 821,000. In a flat treeless steppe. Industrial and route centre. Manufactures agricultural and other machinery, locomotives, synthetic rubber, tyres, motor vehicles, etc. Food processing, brewing. Also an important oil-refining centre, being the terminus of the country's longest pipeline, from Tuimazy (Bashkir ASSR), completed in 1955. Founded (1716) as a fortress. Expanded rapidly with the advent of the railway and again in the 2nd World War.

**Omuta** Japan. Port and industrial town in Fukuoka prefecture, W Kyushu, 35 m. S of Fukuoka. Pop. (1965) 193,875. In a coalmining region. Exports coal. Zinc refining. Manufactures chemicals, machinery, cotton goods, dyes, etc.

**Onega, Lake** USSR. Lake mainly in the Karelian ASSR (RSFSR); the second largest in Europe. Area 3,817 sq. m. The N coast is much broken. Many islands. Drains into L. Ladoga via the Svir R. Connected by canals with the Volga R. and the White Sea. Frozen from about mid Dec. to mid May. Principal town on the shores Petrozavodsk (W). Large quantities of fish caught.

**Onega Bay (Onega Gulf)** USSR. Inlet of the White Sea (SW) 110 m. long and up to 50 m. wide. At its head (SE), at the mouth of the Onega R. (not connected with L. Onega), is the small seaport of Onega (pop.

18,000): exports timber, has a sawmilling industry.

**Onitsha** Nigeria. Town in the S, on the left bank of the Niger R. 45 m. WSW of Enugu. Pop. (1963) 77,000. Commercial centre. Trade in cassava, maize, palm oil and kernels, yams.

**Ontario** Canada. The second largest province (if freshwater area included), lying between Hudson Bay and James Bay (N) and the Great Lakes (S). Area 412,582 sq. m. Pop. (1966) 6,960,870. Cap. Toronto (second largest city in Canada). The province extends 1,050 m. N–S and 1,000 m. W–E, with the great majority of the population concentrated in the SE between the Great Lakes, the St Lawrence R., and the Ottawa R. To the N it slopes down to the sparsely inhabited lowlands around Hudson Bay and James Bay. Numerous rivers and lakes. Apart from the Great Lakes (none of which lies wholly in Ontario), the largest are L. Nipigon, the Lake of the Woods (shared with Manitoba and Minnesota (USA)), L. Seul, L. Nipissing, and L. Abitibi. Owing to the great range of latitude, the climate is extremely varied, but in general it is continental, with cold winters and warm or hot summers, though in the S it is tempered by proximity to the Great Lakes. Annual rainfall 20–40 ins. (with considerable depths of snow in winter). About two thirds of the province is covered by forests; both softwood and hardwood timber are produced, and wood pulp and paper manufacture are important. Principal crops in the S are cereals, fruit, vegetables, tobacco. Dairying and stock rearing important. In mineral production Ontario is Canada's leading province: nickel, uranium, copper, and gold rank highest in value. Also has the greatest industrial output among the provinces, with abundant hydroelectric power. Highly diversified industries. Meat packing, flour milling and cheese and butter making depend on agriculture. Also manufactures cars, machinery, railway equipment, textiles, etc. Toronto, Hamilton, London, and Windsor (the main industrial centres) are all in the tapering peninsula between L. Ontario, L. Erie, and L. Huron; Hamilton and Toronto are important lake ports. On the Ottawa R is Ottawa, the federal capital.

The interior was first explored (1615) by Champlain; fur traders and missionaries followed. The territory was ceded by France to Britain in 1763. By the constitution of 1791 Canada was divided into Upper Canada (Ontario) and Lower Canada (Quebec); the two were united 1840–67, but Ontario then became one of the four original provinces of the confederation. The boundaries were extended to Hudson Bay in 1912.

**Ontario** USA. Town in S California 33 m. E of Los Angeles. Pop. (1960) 46,617. Commercial centre in a region producing vines, citrus fruits, etc. Manufactures aircraft parts, electrical equipment, etc.

**Ontario, Lake** Canada/USA. The smallest and most easterly of the Great Lakes, elliptical in shape, at a height of 246 ft above mean sea level. Area 7,313 sq. m. Connected (SW) with L. Erie through the Niagara R., by which it receives water from the other Great Lakes; the Niagara Falls are circumvented by the Welland Canal. Discharges (NE) into the St Lawrence R., and so to the Atlantic. Main ports Hamilton, Toronto, Cobourg, and Kingston in Ontario (Canada), Rochester and Oswego in New York (USA). Main cargoes coal, grain, timber. The lake freezes only near the shore, but harbours are closed from mid Dec. to mid April. Along the SW shore there is a noted fruit-growing district. Discovered (1615) by Étienne Brûlé. The French had fully explored the N shore by 1668.

**Ontong Java Islands** ◊ *Solomon Islands.*

**Oostende** ◊ *Ostend.*

**Oosterhout** Netherlands. Town in N Brabant province 6 m. NNE of Breda. Pop. (1968) 29,625. Manufactures footwear, tobacco products, etc.

**Ootacamund** India. Hill station in Madras, in the Nilgiri Hills at a height of 7,200 ft. Pop. (1961) 50,140. Has a mean annual temperature of 58° F. Also noted for hunting and fishing. Cinchona and tea plantations near by. Popularly known as Ooty.

**Opatija (Abbazia)** Yugoslavia. Town in Croatia, on the Kvarner Gulf 7 m. W of Rijeka. Pop. 12,000. Popular seaside resort, picturesquely situated at the foot of Mt Učka (4,500 ft). Belonged to Austria; ceded to Italy (1924), then to Yugoslavia (1947).

**Opava (Ger. Troppau)** Czechoslovakia. Industrial town in the Severomoravský region, on the Opava R. 18 m. WNW of Ostrava. Pop. (1967) 46,000. Manufactures textiles, knitwear. Sugar refining, brewing, etc. Founded in the 13th cent. Formerly capital of Austrian Silesia.

**Opole (Ger. Oppeln)** Poland. Capital of the Opole voivodship in the S, on the Oder R. 53 m. SE of Wroclaw. Pop. (1968) 84,900. Industrial and commercial town. Manufactures cement, lime, chemicals, soap, etc. Brewing, flour milling. Trade in grain, livestock, etc. Capital of the duchy of Oppeln 1163–1532; passed to Austria and then to Prussia (1742). Capital of the German province of Upper Silesia 1919–45.

**Oporto (Portuguese Pôrto)** Portugal. Second largest city in Portugal and port on the Douro R. 3 m. above the mouth. Pop. (1960) 303,424. Artificial harbour for large vessels at Leixões, 5 m. NW on the Atlantic. Famous for port wine, shipped largely to Britain; also exports fruits, olive oil, cork, etc. Manufactures textiles, clothing, pottery, tobacco products, etc. Sugar refining, brewing. Built above the Douro gorge, largely in granite, and is connected by the double-deck Dom Luis I bridge (1881–5) with its S suburb, Vila Nova de Gaia, where vast quantities of wine are stored. An outstanding landmark is the Torre dos Clerigos, a granite tower 246 ft high; other buildings include the 14th-cent. cathedral (much modernized) and the 12th cent. São Martinho church. University (1911).

**Oppeln** ◊ *Opole.*

**Orádea** Rumania. Capital of the Bihor district, in the NW on the Crişul Repede R. near the Hungarian frontier. Pop. (1968) 130,321. Railway junction. Manufactures machinery, textiles, glass, pottery, etc. Trade in livestock, fruit, wine. An old town with a bishopric dating from 1080. Ceded to Rumania by Hungary 1919.

**Oran** Algeria. Capital of the Oran department, seaport, and Algeria's second largest city, on the Gulf of Oran (an inlet of the Mediterranean Sea). Pop. (1967) 324,000. Chief exports wine, wheat, early vegetables (from the Tell Atlas), wool, esparto grass (from the High Plateaux). Flour milling, fruit and fish canning, iron smelting. Manufactures textiles, footwear, glass, cigarettes, etc. Receives natural gas by pipeline from the Hassi R'Mel field. Linked by railway with Algiers and (via Tlemcen and Oujda) with Morocco. Founded early in the 10th cent. A prosperous commercial centre in the 15th cent. Fell to the Spaniards 1509; except for a period in Turkish hands (1708–32), held by Spain till shortly after much of the town had been destroyed by earthquake (1790). In Turkish hands again, it was occupied by the French 1831. Expanded rapidly; the port was developed in the late 19th cent. Much of the French fleet anchored in the Gulf of Oran during the 2nd World War (1940), and was partially destroyed by British warships to prevent its capture by the Germans. Taken by Allied forces 1942.

**Orange** Australia. Town on the Central Tableland of New South Wales 125 m. WNW of Sydney. Pop. (1966) 22,200. Railway junction. Market town in sheep-farming and fruit-growing country. Manufactures woollen goods.

**Orange** France. Ancient Arausio. Town in the Vaucluse department 14 m. N of Avignon. Pop. (1968) 25,630. Minor industries. Notable Roman remains, inc. a triumphal arch, a theatre, and an amphitheatre. Once capital of the small principality of Orange, to which was added through marriage the countship of Nassau in the 16th cent.; the descendants of the union became the Dutch royal family, the House of Orange.

**Orange** (California) USA. Town in the S, 3 m. N of Santa Ana. Pop. (1960) 26,444. In an orange-growing region (hence the name). Citrus-fruit packing etc.

**Orange** (New Jersey) USA. Industrial town 4 m. NW of Newark. Pop. (1960) 35,789. Manufactures chemicals, clothing, aircraft parts, etc. With its neighbours East, West, and South Orange and Maplewood it is known as 'the Oranges'.

**Orange** (Texas) USA. Port and industrial town 23 m. E of Beaumont at the head of the Sabine R. waterway to the Gulf of Mexico. Pop. (1960) 25,605. Boatbuilding. Manufactures chemicals, paper, etc.

**Orange Free State** S Africa. Province between the Orange R. and the Vaal R. Area 49,866 sq. m. Pop. (1960) 1,386,547 (1,083,886 Bantu). Cap. Bloemfontein. Bounded by the Transvaal (N), Natal and Lesotho (E), and the Cape Province (SW and S). High, mainly grass-covered plateau, at a height of about 5,000 ft. The surface is broken by low ridges and isolated hills (*kopjes*) and drained by the Caledon and Modder rivers, and by other tributaries of the Orange and the Vaal. Livestock (esp. sheep) raised. Wheat, maize, fruits cultivated, esp. in the wetter areas (E). Gold production has increased greatly since the exploitation of the Odendaalsrus goldfield began (1946). Diamonds mined in the Jagersfontein area. Coalmining in the N (chiefly in the Coalbrook district). Industrial development still on a small scale;

Kroonstad is an important agricultural and railway centre, Welkom an important goldmining centre.

The Orange R. was first crossed by Europeans in the late 18th cent. European settlements (established in the early 19th cent.) increased considerably from 1836 onwards, after the Great Trek. The area between the Orange and Vaal rivers and E to the Drakensberg was proclaimed a British possession (1848) by Sir Harry Smith (then Governor of Cape Colony) as the Orange River Sovereignty, but British sovereignty was withdrawn and the Orange Free State declared an independent republic 1854. Joined in the 1899–1902 Boer War on the Boer side. Annexed by Britain as the Orange River Colony 1900. Granted self-government 1907. Became a province in the new Union of S Africa (resuming its former name of the Orange Free State) 1910.

**Orange River.** River 1,300 m. long, the longest in S Africa, rising in the Drakensberg at Mont-aux-Sources, flowing SW through Lesotho, continuing generally W and NW (forming the boundary between Cape Province and the Orange Free State and between Cape Province and SW Africa) and entering the Atlantic Ocean at Alexander Bay (where the mouth is obstructed by a sand bar). Principal tributaries the Vaal and the Caledon. In the winding lower course, passing through an arid region, it loses much water by evaporation. Below Upington it plunges 480 ft over the Aughrabies Falls.

**Ord River** Australia. River 300 m. long in the NE of Western Australia, flowing E and then N through rugged cattle country to Cambridge Gulf, near Wyndham.

**Ordzhonikidze** USSR. Formerly Vladikavkaz ('Key to the Caucasus'), Dzaudzhikau. Capital of the North Ossetian ASSR, RSFSR, on the Terek R., where it issues from the Caucasus, at a height of 2,345 ft. Pop. (1970) 236,000. The N terminus of the Georgian Military Highway to Tbilisi (Tiflis), which was opened in 1864 and led to its expansion. Important metallurgical plants for refining zinc, lead, and silver from the Sadon mines. Also food processing, woodworking, glass manufacture. 25 m. SSW is Kazbek peak (16,545 ft). Founded (1784) as a small fortress.

**Örebro** Sweden. Capital of Örebro county at the W end of L. Hjälmar. Pop. (1968) 87,430. Railway junction. Centre of the country's shoe industry. Also manufactures paper, soap, etc. An old town, dating from the 11th cent. Its castle on an island in the Svartå R. has been the scene of many diets. Chiefly modern in appearance, however, having been rebuilt after a fire (1854). **Oregon** USA. State in the NW, on the Pacific Ocean. Area 96,981 sq. m. Pop. (1970) 2,056,171. Cap. Salem. Admitted to the Union in 1859 as the 33rd state; popularly known as the 'Beaver' state. The Cascade Range, running N–S parallel to the coast, divides it into two contrasting climatic zones. The W has a maritime temperate climate; the E is a larger dry upland region. Annual rainfall varies from 70 ins. or more in the coastal zone to 10–20 ins. in the dry zone. Famed for its mountain and lake scenery, the Cascade Range averages 5,000–7,000 ft, and includes Mt Hood (11,245 ft) and Mt Jefferson (10,495 ft). Also running parallel to the coast is the Coast Range, which links up with the Cascades in the Klamath Mountains (S). In the NE are the Blue Mountains. The leading timber state; has over 30 million acres of forests. Agriculture important. E of the Cascades wheat growing and stock rearing predominate. To the W cereals, fruit, and vegetables are the main crops; the Willamette valley is particularly noted for its orchards and market gardens. Industries are based on the processing of farm and forest produce. Chief towns Portland, Eugene, Salem. The Oregon country was jointly held by Britain and the USA 1818–46. Became a territory 1848. The population rapidly increased in the 1840s with the influx of settlers arriving by the Oregon Trail.

**Orekhovo-Zuyevo** USSR. Town in RSFSR, on the Klyazma R. 55 m. E of Moscow. Pop. (1970) 120,000. Railway junction. Important centre of the cotton industry. Also sawmilling, flour milling, etc.

**Orel (Oryol)** USSR. Capital of the Orel region (RSFSR), on the Oka R. 205 m. SSW of Moscow. Pop. (1970) 232,000. Road, railway, and industrial centre. Iron founding, flour milling, meat packing. Manufactures textile machinery etc. On the Moscow–Kharkov railway. Founded 1564.

**Orenburg** USSR. Formerly (1938–58) Chkalov (in honour of V. P. Chkalov, the Russian airman). Capital of the Orenburg region, RSFSR, on the Ural R. 210 m. ESE of Kuibyshev. Pop. (1970) 345,000. Much increased in importance since the

opening of the railway to Tashkent (1905). A major agricultural and flour-milling centre. Trade in grain, hides, meat, wool, textiles, livestock. Railway engineering, sawmilling, brewing. Manufactures metal goods, clothing, etc. Founded (1743) as a fortress.

**Orense** Spain. **1.** Province in Galicia (NW), on the Portuguese border. Area 2,694 sq. m. Pop. (1961) 451,474. Generally mountainous. Drained by the Miño R. and its tributaries. Agriculture in the valleys: cereals, potatoes, flax, etc. cultivated; cattle reared. **2.** Capital of Orense province, on the Miño R. 44 m. ENE of Vigo. Pop. (1967) 71,768. Sawmilling, tanning, flour milling, etc. Has warm springs, known from Roman times, and a remarkable 13th-cent. bridge over the river. Destroyed by the Moors in the 8th cent. Restored by Alfonso III of Asturias in the 9th cent.

**Öresund** ◊ *Sound, The.*

**Orihuela** Spain. Town in Alicante province, on the Segura R. in a fertile irrigated region 30 m. SW of Alicante. Pop. (1961) 44,830. Trade in fruit, olive oil, wine, cereals. Manufactures textiles, leather goods, furniture, etc. Seat of a university 1568–1835. Cathedral (14th/16th-cent., restored).

**Orinoco River** Venezuela. One of the great rivers of S America, 1,300 m. long, rising in the Serra Parima in the SE, following a C-shaped course W, N, and E, and entering the Atlantic by a wide delta through many navigable channels. In its middle course are the Atures and Maipures rapids. Linked by the 200-m. Casiquiare with the Rio Negro and Amazon. Navigable for small vessels to the Maipures rapids, about 900 m. from the mouth. Ciudad Bolívar is the main commercial centre for the Orinoco basin, but the flow is sometimes so reduced through seasonal variation that goods have to be transhipped at San Felix. Industrial development is taking place in the lower course near the Caroní R. junction. The Angostura suspension bridge linking Ciudad Bolívar and Soledad, the first across the river, was opened in 1967.

**Orissa** India. State in the E, on the Bay of Bengal. Area 60,162 sq. m. Pop. (1961) 17,548,846. Cap. Bhubaneswar. Mainly hilly, with a coastal plain and the valley and delta of the Mahanadi R. Chief occupation agriculture, about four fifths of the population being engaged in rice cultivation. Extensive sal forests. Iron and manganese ores and coal mined. Principal towns Cuttack, Bhubaneswar. Fell in the Mogul conquest 1568. Later passed to the Mahrattas (1742) and the British (1803). In 1912 the province of Bihar and Orissa was created, but in 1936, owing to the intense nationalism of the Oriyas, Orissa became autonomous. Acceded to India 1947, was enlarged by the addition of several native states (1949).

**Orizaba** Mexico. Town in Veracruz state 60 m. WSW of Veracruz, at a height of 4,200 ft. Pop. 70,000. Chief centre of the textile industry. Also manufactures paper, tobacco products, etc. Railway engineering, brewing. Trade in sugar, tobacco, coffee, maize. In magnificent scenery, with the Pico de Orizaba (Citlaltépetl) 18 m. N. A resort, with a mild healthy climate.

**Orizaba, Pico de (Citlaltépetl)** Mexico. In Aztec, 'Star Mountain'. Extinct snow-capped volcano 18 m. N of Orizaba town; the highest peak in Mexico (18,700 ft). Last erupted in the 16th cent. First climbed 1848.

**Orkney Islands** Scotland. Group of about 70 islands forming a county, separated from Caithness (mainland) by Pentland Firth. Total area 376 sq. m. Pop. (1961) 18,743 (21,255 in 1951). County town Kirkwall. Principal islands Mainland (or Pomona), S Ronaldsay, Westray, Sanday, Stronsay, Hoy. Generally low-lying, though Hoy rises to 1,565 ft. Bleak and treeless, but the climate is relatively mild. Main occupation fishing, poultry farming. Stromness is the only burgh besides Kirkwall, both on Mainland. There are prehistoric remains, including the standing stones at Stenness (Mainland). The islands were conquered by Harold Haarfager (875) and remained under Norse rule until 1468, when they were pledged to James III of Scotland by Christian I of Denmark.

**Orlando** USA. Town in Florida, 77 m. ENE of Tampa. Pop. (1960) 88,135, having increased rapidly in recent years. Commercial centre for the surrounding citrus-fruit-growing and market-gardening region. Fruit packing and canning. Manufactures machinery, clothing, etc. Also a resort, in a district with many lakes.

**Orléanais** France. Region and former province on both sides of the Loire R., now forming Loiret and Loir-et-Cher and parts of Eure-et-Loir and Yonne departments. Included Beauce, Sologne, and part of Gâtinais. The capital was Orléans.

**Orléans** France. Ancient Genabum, Cenabum. Prefecture of the Loiret department, on the Loire R. 70 m. SSW of Paris. Pop. (1968) 100,134. Important railway and road junction. Food processing. Manufactures blankets, knitwear, machinery, tobacco products, etc. Trade in wine and cereals from the surrounding agricultural region. The old city lies along the right bank of the river and is surrounded by boulevards, beyond which are the modern suburbs. The Cathedral of Ste Croix, destroyed by Huguenots in 1567, rebuilt in the 17th–19th cent., was severely damaged in the 2nd World War; among the old houses are those of Diane de Poitiers and Joan of Arc. In the 7th cent. it became the chief residence, after Paris, of the French kings. In 1428–9 it was besieged by the English and Burgundians and was relieved by Joan of Arc – an event celebrated annually in the city. Became the Huguenot headquarters and was again besieged (1563), by the Catholics under Francis, Duke of Guise, who was assassinated here.

**Ormskirk** England. Urban district in SW Lancashire 12 m. NNE of Liverpool. Pop. (1961) 21,815. In a potato-growing district. Metal working, flour milling, etc. Near by are the remains of the 12th-cent. Burscough Priory.

**Orne** France. Inland department in Normandy, named after the Orne R. Area 2,372 sq. m. Pop. (1968) 288,524. Prefecture Alençon. Undulating, crossed by the Normandy and Perche Hills, rising to 1,368 ft in the Forest of Écouves. Noted for the powerful Percheron horses, bred here; products include cereals, cider apples, Camembert cheese. Chief towns Alençon, Flers, Bagnoles (spa).

**Orohena, Mount** ◊ *Tahiti*.

**Orontes River.** River in SW Asia, 230 m. long, rising near Baalbek (Lebanon) and flowing generally N past Homs and Hama (Syria), turning SW past Antioch (Antakya) in Turkey to the Mediterranean Sea. Practically unnavigable, but used for irrigation, esp. in Syria, where large wooden water-wheels (*norias*) driven by the current are used to raise and distribute the river water.

**Oropeza** ◊ *Cochabamba*.

**Oroya** Peru. Town in Junín department in the Andes, at a height of 12,200 ft at the confluence of the Mantaro and Yauli rivers, 75 m. ENE of Lima, to which it is connected by rail and road. Pop. 35,000.

Important metallurgical centre (copper, zinc, lead, silver); smelting, copper refining. Ores brought from Cerro de Pasco and other mining centres.

**Orpington** England. Former urban district in NW Kent; from 1965 part of the Greater London borough of Bromley. Pop. (1961) 80,277. Mainly residential. Gave its name to a breed of chickens. The famous Biggin Hill RAF fighter station of the 2nd World War is 5 m. SW.

**Orsha** USSR. Town in the Vitebsk region, Byelorussian SSR, on the Dnieper R. 50 m. S of Vitebsk. Pop. (1970) 101,000. Railway junction. Industrial centre. Meat packing, flour milling, brewing. Manufactures textiles etc.

**Orsk** USSR. Industrial town in the Orenburg region, RSFSR, on the Ural R. 175 m. ESE of Orenburg. Pop. (1970) 225,000. Manufactures locomotives, agricultural machinery, etc. Meat packing, flour milling. Terminus of a pipeline from the Emba oilfield, and oil refining is an important industry; nickel and other metals are also refined. Expanded greatly just before and again after the 2nd World War.

**Orta, Lake** Italy. The most westerly of the Italian Alpine lakes, draining into L. Maggiore. Area 7 sq. m. On the island of San Giulio is a church dating from the 4th cent.

**Oruro** Bolivia. Capital of the Oruro department in the Altiplano at a height of 12,160 ft 125 m. SE of La Paz. Pop. (1967) 91,911 (mainly Indian). Commercial and railway centre in a mining district (tin, silver, copper, tungsten). Tin smelting, flour milling, brewing, etc. University (1892). Founded in the early 17th cent. as Real Villa de San Felipe de Austria. First important as a silver-mining centre. Declined as the output of silver decreased in the 19th cent., but revived with the development of tin mining.

**Orvieto** Italy. Town in Terni province, Umbria, on an isolated rock at a height of 1,030 ft near the Paglia R. 60 m. NNW of Rome. Pop. (1961) 25,088. Market town. Well known for its wine and pottery. Has an outstandingly beautiful cathedral, begun in the late 13th cent., the exterior in black and white marble, with frescoes by Fra Angelico and Luca Signorelli. Near by is the 13th/14th-cent. Palazzo Papale containing a museum with Etruscan relics.

**Oryol** ▷ *Orel*.

**Osage River** USA. River 500 m. long, rising in E Kansas, flowing generally E on a meandering course into Missouri, and joining the Missouri R. below Jefferson City. The Bagnell Dam (1931) in Missouri forms the artificial Lake of the Ozarks, 130 m. long; its power station supplies electricity to St Louis.

**Osaka** Japan.* Capital of Osaka prefecture and Japan's second largest city, in S Honshu 250 m. WSW of Tokyo. Pop. (1965) 3,156,201. Important seaport on Osaka Bay. Great industrial and commercial centre. Exports textiles, machinery, metal goods. Sometimes called the 'Manchester of Japan' because of its many cotton mills. Also manufactures steel, machinery, chemicals, electrical equipment, cement, etc. University (1931). A 16th-cent. castle (rebuilt) and many Buddhist and Shinto temples. Heavily bombed in the 2nd World War.

**Osh** USSR. Capital of the Osh region, Kirghiz SSR, 185 m. SW of Frunze. Pop. (1970) 120,000. On the Uzbek border and at the E end of the fertile Fergana valley. Silk manufacturing, food processing, etc. In the neighbourhood is a peculiarly shaped rock called Takht-i-Suleiman (Solomon's Throne), well known in Muslim legend.

**Oshawa** Canada. Port and industrial town in Ontario, on L. Ontario 27 m. ENE of Toronto. Pop. (1966) 78,082. Manufactures motor vehicles, glass, plastics, textiles, metal and leather goods, etc.

**Oshkosh** USA. Town in Wisconsin on the W shore of L. Winnebago, 75 m. NNW of Milwaukee. Pop. (1960) 45,110. Manufactures machinery, leather goods, clothing, etc. Formerly important in the lumber industry.

**Oshogbo** Nigeria. Town in the SW 125 m. NE of Lagos. Pop. (1960) 123,000. On the railway to the N. Commercial centre. Trade in cacao, palm oil and kernels. Cotton weaving.

**Osijek** Yugoslavia. Ancient Mursa. Town in NE Croatia and port on the Drava R. 105 m. NW of Belgrade. Pop. (1961) 73,125. Tanning, sugar refining, flour milling. Manufactures textiles, furniture, etc. Trade in grain, fruit, timber, plum brandy, etc. Had a fortress in Roman times.

**Oslo** Norway. Formerly (1624–1925) Christiania. Capital of Norway, chief industrial centre, and ice-free seaport at the head of Oslo Fiord, an inlet of the Skagerrak. Pop. (1968) 484,275. Exports timber, wood pulp, paper, fish. Manufactures electrical equipment, machinery, chemicals, etc. On Karl Johans Gate, the main thoroughfare, are the university (1811), the Storting (parliament) building (1866), the national theatre (1899), and the royal palace (1848). The great city hall (1931–50) and the 13th-cent. Akershus fortress overlook the harbour; the famous sculptures by Gustav Vigeland are in the Frogner Park. Oslo was founded by Harald Hardrada (1048) E of the Aker R., but, after being destroyed by fire (1624), the city was rebuilt on the W side as Christiania by Christian IV.

**Osnabrück** Federal German Republic. Industrial town in Lower Saxony 58 m. NE of Dortmund. Pop. (1968) 140,227. Manufactures iron and steel, machinery, turbines, motor-vehicle bodies, textiles, paper, etc. Has a 13th-cent. Roman Catholic cathedral and a 15th/16th-cent. Gothic town hall, damaged in the 2nd World War. A member of the Hanseatic League; reached the peak of its prosperity in the 15th cent.

**Osorno** Chile. Capital of Osorno province, in the Chilean lake district 50 m. SSE of Valdivia. Pop. 90,000 (largely of German descent). Market town. Flour milling, meat packing, sawmilling. Trade in grain, livestock, etc. Founded 1558. Destroyed by Araucanian Indians; refounded 1776. Received many German immigrants in the late 19th cent.

**Osorno, Mount** Chile. Volcanic peak 8,790 ft high, on the E shore of L. Llanquihue, in the Chilean lake district.

**Oss** Netherlands. Town in N Brabant province 25 m. NE of Tilburg. Pop. (1968) 37,850. Industrial centre. Manufactures margarine, pharmaceutical products, electrical equipment, etc.

**Ossetia** ◊ *North Ossetian ASSR; South Ossetian AR.*

**Ossett** England. Municipal borough in the W Riding of Yorkshire, 3 m. W of Wakefield. Pop. (1961) 14,729. Woollen and leather industries etc. Coalmining in the neighbourhood.

**Ostend** (Fr. **Ostende,** Flemish **Oostende**) Belgium. Seaport and holiday resort in W Flanders province, on the North Sea 13 m. W of Bruges. Pop. (1968) 57,765. Exports cement, chemicals, fish, etc. Belgium's chief fishing centre. Important

railway terminus. Fish curing and canning, shipbuilding. Manufactures fertilizers. Linked by steamer service (car ferry) with Dover (England). Among its attractions as a resort are the casino and the racecourse. Early in the 1st World War it was occupied by the Germans and used as a submarine base.

**Östersund** Sweden. Capital of Jämtland county, on the E shore of L. Storsjö 100 m. NW of Sundsvall. Pop. (1968) 26,620. Industrial centre on the railway from Sundsvall to Trondheim (Norway). Manufactures machinery, furniture, etc.

**Ostia** Italy. Port of ancient Rome on the S mouth of the Tiber R. Probably the first Roman colony, dating from the 4th cent. B.C. Claudius and Trajan built new harbours, and it flourished in the 2nd and 3rd cent. A.D. but then declined. Fortified by Gregory IV 830. The castle was built (1483–6) by Julius II, whilst Cardinal, but it never regained its former importance. Since 1854 its ruins have been systematically excavated, and it provides an excellent example of a Roman town. Lido di Roma, the modern seaside resort, stands 2 m. from the ruins.

**Ostrava** Czechoslovakia. 1. *Moravská Ostrava*: Capital of the Severomoravský region, on the Moravian bank of the Ostravice R. near its confluence with the Oder R. Pop. (1961) 235,000. Important iron and steel industry; also manufactures railway rolling stock, tinplate, cranes, boilers, chemicals, etc.
2. *Slęzska Ostrava*: Coalmining town on the Silesian side of the Ostravice R. opposite Moravská Ostrava. Pop. (1961) 22,000. Combined pop. (1967) 270,000.

**Ostrów Wielkopolski** Poland. Town in the Poznań voivodship 67 m. SE of Poznań. Pop. (1968) 48,300. Railway junction. Manufactures agricultural machinery, chemicals, etc. Trade in agricultural produce.

**Oswestry** England. Market town in Shropshire 16 m. NW of Shrewsbury. Pop. (1961) 11,193. Light engineering, malting, tanning, etc. Named after St Oswald, Christian king of Northumbria, killed here (642) whilst warring with Penda, king of Mercia. Birthplace of Sir H. Walford Davies (1869–1941) and Wilfred Owen (1893–1918).

**Oświęcim** (Ger. **Auschwitz**) Poland. Town in the Krakow (Cracow) voivodship 34 m. W of Cracow. Pop. 39,000. Manufactures chemicals, metal goods, etc. During the 2nd World War, as Auschwitz, it was the site of a notorious concentration camp where the Germans practised mass extermination; 4 million people, mainly Jews, are estimated to have been murdered here.

**Otago** New Zealand. Provincial district in the S of the S Island. Area (statistical area) 14,070 sq. m. Pop. (1966) 183,477. In addition, the statistical area Southland (S) has area 11,460 sq. m.; pop. (1966) 102,686. Includes the high country of the Southern Alps in the N W, Fiordland in the S W. Long glacial lakes. The rivers drain E across dissected central plateaux and fertile lowlands. Chief towns Dunedin, with Port Chalmers, and Invercargill, served by Bluff. Produces wool, fruits, dairy produce.

**Otaru** Japan. Seaport on the W coast of Hokkaido 25 m. WNW of Sapporo. Pop. (1965) 196,762. Exports coal, timber, fertilizers. Fishing, fish processing, engineering. Manufactures rubber products etc.

**Otley** England. Urban district in the W Riding of Yorkshire, on the R. Wharfe 9 m. NW of Leeds. Pop. (1961) 11,930. Manufactures woollen goods, leather, printing machinery. Birthplace of Thomas Chippendale, the cabinet-maker (1718–79).

**Otranto** Italy. Ancient Hydruntum. Fishing port in Lecce province, Apulia, on the Otranto Strait. Pop. (1961) 4,065. Has a cathedral (11th-cent.) and the ruined castle which provided the title for Horace Walpole's novel *The Castle of Otranto*. Important port in Roman times. Destroyed by the Turks (1480) and never recovered its former importance.

**Otranto Strait** Italy. Strait 45 m. wide connecting the Ionian Sea with the Adriatic, between the 'heel' of Italy (Cape Otranto) and S Albania.

**Otsu** Japan. Capital of Shiga prefecture, Honshu, at the S end of L. Biwa just E of Kyoto. Pop. (1965) 121,000. A historic town and tourist centre in a picturesque region. Trade in rice etc. Manufactures chemicals, textiles.

**Ottawa** Canada. Capital of Canada, in SE Ontario, on the Ottawa R. opposite Hull (Quebec). Pop. (1966) 290,741 (about 30 per cent French-speaking, approximately the national average). Impressively situated on hills overlooking the river. Canada's political, social, and cultural centre. River port and important centre of the lumber industry; the output of the sawmills is enormous. Other leading industries pulp and paper milling, woodworking, flour milling, watch making. Manufactures leather goods, matches, metal products. Hydroelectric power for factories and mills comes from the Chaudière and Rideau Falls. Much has been done in recent years to improve the amenities and appearance of the city by laying out parks and scenic drives. It is dominated from Parliament Hill by the group of Gothic-style Parliament buildings; the originals (1859–65), burned down in 1916, were rebuilt in the same style. Other notable buildings include Rideau Hall (the Governor-General's residence), the Anglican and Roman Catholic cathedrals, the National Victoria Museum, and the National Art Gallery; also the government offices, Ottawa University (1866), and Carleton University (1942).

The site was discovered (1613) by Champlain, but the city's origin dates from 1826, when a town grew up round the headquarters of the British army engineers who were constructing the Rideau Canal, and was named Bytown after Colonel By, the commanding officer. Became a city in 1854, and was renamed Ottawa after the river. Chosen as capital of Canada by Queen Victoria 1858. Became capital of the Dominion 1867.

**Ottawa River** Canada. River 696 m. long, chief tributary of the St Lawrence R., rising on the Laurentian Plateau in Quebec and flowing W to L. Timiskaming, then generally S E and E past Pembroke and Ottawa, and joining the St Lawrence W of Montreal. For most of its course it forms the boundary between Ontario and Quebec. It expands into a large number of lakes, including the Grand Lake Victoria, L. Simard, L. Quinze, L Timiskaming, L. Allumette, L. Chats, L. Deschênes, and Two Mountains Lake. Many rapids, but it is navigable up to Ottawa for vessels of 9-ft draught, and is connected with L. Ontario by the Rideau Canal. Its chief importance today is for the transportation of lumber and the production of hydroelectric power; the valley has become a region of considerable industrial activity. Named after the Ottawa Indians. A major factor in Canada's early development, as the highway for fur traders, missionaries, and explorers. First explored by Étienne

Brûlé (1610) and Champlain (1613). The canoe, the first recognized means of transport, was succeeded by the steamboat, which gave way to the railways in the 1870s.

**Ottery St Mary** England. Urban district in Devonshire, on the R. Otter 11 m. E of Exeter. Pop. (1961) 4,121. Market town. Has a church begun in 1260 and built on the lines of Exeter cathedral. Birthplace of S. T. Coleridge (1772–1834).

**Ottumwa** USA. Town in Iowa, on the Des Moines R. 78 m. SW of Cedar Rapids. Pop. (1960) 33,871. Manufactures agricultural machinery, furniture, dairy products. Meat packing.

**Ötztal Alps.** Alpine range on the Austro-Italian border but mainly in the Austrian Tirol. Highest peak Wildspitze (12,382 ft).

**Ouachita River** USA. River 600 m. long rising in the Ouachita Mountains of W Arkansas, flowing generally SE and then S to join the Red R. in E Louisiana.

**Ouagadougou** Upper Volta. Capital; terminus of the railway from Abidjan in Ivory Coast (520 m. SSW). Pop. (1967) 79,500. Commercial centre in an agricultural region. Trade in groundnuts, millet, shea nuts, livestock. Vegetable-oil extraction, cotton ginning. Manufactures soap, textiles.

**Oudenarde** (Flemish **Oudenaarde**) Belgium. Town in E Flanders province, on the Scheldt R. 15 m. SSW of Ghent. Pop. (1969) 22,035. Brewing. Manufactures textiles. Has a 16th-cent town hall. Here in 1708 the English and Austrians under Marlborough and Prince Eugene defeated the French under Vendôme.

**Oudh** India. Region in central Uttar Pradesh, associated historically with the ancient kingdom of Kosala. Annexed by Britain (1856). One of the centres of the Indian Mutiny (1857–8). Joined with Agra 1877; renamed the United Provinces of Agra and Oudh 1902. The name United Provinces was changed to Uttar Pradesh in 1950.

**Oudtshoorn** S Africa. Town in Cape Province, 225 m. ENE of Cape Town on the Little Karroo. Pop. (1960) 22,186. In an ostrich-farming district. Manufactures furniture, footwear, tobacco products. The famous limestone Cango Caves, with remarkable stalactites and stalagmites, are 17 m. N at the foot of the Swartberg Range.

**Ouessant** ◊ *Ushant.*

**Oujda (Ujda)** Morocco. Capital of Oujda province, 225 m. ESE of Tangier near the Algerian frontier. Pop. (1964) 149,300. On the main Casablanca–Tunis railway, with a branch line to the S serving the coal mines of Jerada and the manganese mines of Bou Arfa. Important commercial centre. Trade in wine, citrus fruits, early vegetables, cereals (from the surrounding area); and sheep and wool (from the interior). Permanently occupied by the French 1907. Has since grown rapidly.

**Oulu (Uleåborg)** Finland. Capital of the Oulu province, at the mouth of the Oulu R. on the Gulf of Bothnia. Pop. (1968) 83,190. Seaport. Railway junction. Exports timber, tar, wood products, etc. Shipbuilding, sawmilling, tanning, etc. Manufactures fertilizers. University (1958). Has a 19th-cent. cathedral.

**Oulu River** Finland. River 65 m. long issuing from the NW end of L. Oulu (area 387 sq. m.) and flowing NW to the Gulf of Bothnia at Oulu. Used for lumber transportation. At Pyhä Falls, 20 m. SE of Oulu, is a hydroelectric plant.

**Oundle** England. Urban district in Northamptonshire on the R. Nene 9 m. E of Corby. Pop. (1961) 2,546. Market town. Has a 14th-cent. church and a well-known public school (founded 1556).

**Ouro Prêto** Brazil. In Portuguese, 'Black Gold'. Town in the Minas Gerais state (of which it was capital 1823–97) 42 m. SE of Belo Horizonte at a height of 3,500 ft. Pop. 21,000. Founded 1701, on the discovery of gold. Declined from the mid 18th cent. Some goldmining continues in the neighbourhood, also iron and manganese mining. Manufactures textiles etc. Has retained its colonial architecture virtually intact, with many splendid baroque churches, and was decreed a national monument 1933. Many examples of the work of the famous architect and sculptor Antonio Francisco Lisbôa (1738–1814), better known as O Aleijadinho ('Little Cripple'). Seat of the School of Mining and Metallurgy (1876).

**Ouse River** (Sussex) England. River 30 m. long, rising 6 m. SSW of Crawley, flowing E and then S past Lewes, cutting through the S Downs, and entering the English Channel at Newhaven.

**Ouse River** (Yorkshire) England. River 61 m. long, formed by the union of the Ure and the Swale rivers near Boroughbridge, flowing generally SE past York,

Selby, and Goole, joining the R. Trent and forming the Humber estuary. Chief right-bank tributaries the Nidd, the Wharfe, the Aire, and the Don rivers (all, like the Ure and the Swale, rising in the Pennines). Chief left-bank tributary the Derwent.

**Ouse River, Great** England. River 156 m. long, rising near Brackley in Northamptonshire, flowing generally E, NE, and then N, past Buckingham, Bedford, Huntingdon, Ely, and King's Lynn, and entering the Wash 3 m. NNW of King's Lynn. As it crosses the Fens it follows its natural course and also two straight artificial channels, the 'Bedford Rivers'.

**Ouse River, Little** England. River 24 m. long, rising in Suffolk, flowing mainly WNW along the Norfolk–Suffolk border, and joining the Great Ouse.

**Outer Mongolia** ▷ *Mongolian People's Republic.*

**Ovalle** Chile. Town in Coquimbo province, on the Limarí R. 175 m. N of Valparaiso. Pop. 47,000. In a fruit-growing, sheep-rearing, and mining district. Founded (1831) by President Ovalle.

**Ovamboland** SW Africa. District in the N, bordered N by Angola; the most densely populated part of the territory. The Etosha Pan (a marshy salt lake) is in the S. Inhabited by Ovambo and other tribes. Main occupations cattle rearing and the cultivation of maize, kaffir corn, etc.

**Overijssel** Netherlands. Province in the E, bordering E on the Federal German Republic and NW on the Ijsselmeer. Area 1,471 sq. m. Pop. (1968) 895,916. Cap. Zwolle. Drained by the Ijssel and Vecht rivers. Largely agricultural, with dairy farming predominating. Important textile industry. Chief towns Enschede, Zwolle, Hengelo, Deventer, Almelo.

**Oviedo** Spain. 1. Province in the NW on the Bay of Biscay, co-extensive with Asturias. Area 4,207 sq. m. Pop. (1961) 989,344.

2. Capital of Oviedo province, 15 m. SW of the port of Gijón. Pop. (1967) 137,339. Industrial centre. Manufactures iron and steel, armaments, metal goods, chemicals, cement, glass, etc. University (1604). Has a 14th-cent. Gothic cathedral, and the 9th-cent. Cámara Santa, which contains valuable relics. Founded in the 8th cent. Became capital of the Asturian kingdom during the time of Alfonso II (789–842). Declined in the 10th cent.

**Ovoca River** ▷ *Avoca River.*

**Owen Falls** ▷ *Nile River; Jinja.*

**Owensboro** USA. Town and river port in Kentucky, on the Ohio R. 77 m. WSW of Louisville. Pop. (1960) 42,471. In a region producing oil and natural gas. Trade in tobacco, maize, oil, sand and gravel, etc. Manufactures electric lamps, furniture, building materials, etc.

**Oxford** England. County borough and county town of Oxfordshire, on the R. Thames (or Isis) at the confluence with the R. Cherwell 50 m. WNW of London. Pop. (1961) 106,124. Famous chiefly for its university, but in recent years with considerable industrial development in the suburbs. Manufactures cars, refrigerators, electrical equipment, etc. Also a busy market town and route centre.

Almost all the colleges of the university have some architectural distinction, their hall, chapel, and lawned quadrangle. As academic institutions University (1249), Balliol (1263), and Merton (1264) are the oldest, though the last-named claims to be the oldest college, as it was the first to be organized on collegiate lines, and it is the oldest architecturally. St Edmund Hall, also dating from the 13th cent., is the only survivor of the early academic halls, and other colleges, with their dates of foundation, are as follows: Exeter (1314), Oriel (1326), Queen's (1340), New (1379), Lincoln (1427), All Souls (1437), Magdalen (1458), Brasenose (1509), Corpus Christi (1516), Christ Church (1546), Trinity (1554), St John's (1555), Jesus (1571), Wadham (1610), Pembroke (1624), Worcester (1714), Keble (1870), Hertford (1874), St Peter's Hall (1926), Nuffield (1937), St Antony's (1950), Wolfson (1966). The colleges for women, who were admitted to degrees from 1920, are Somerville and Lady Margaret Hall (1879), St Hugh's (1886), St Hilda's (1893), and St Anne's (1952). Among the non-collegiate buildings are the Bodleian Library (1602), the Ashmolean Museum (1682, the first public museum in England), the Sheldonian Theatre (1668, designed by Wren and used for university ceremonies), and the Radcliffe Camera (1737). Ecclesiastical buildings include the 11th-cent. St Michael's Church and the 13th-cent. St Mary the Virgin Church.

Mentioned in the 10th cent., Oxford became prominent in the 13th cent., when the first colleges of the university were founded and several parliaments met here

– notably that of 1258 which forced the Provisions of Oxford on Henry III. In the Civil War it was the Royalist headquarters and surrendered only in 1646. Modern industrial development began when William Morris, later Viscount Nuffield, set up his automobile factory in the suburb of Cowley (1912).

**Oxfordshire** England. County in the S Midlands. Area 749 sq. m. Pop. (1961) 309,458. County town Oxford. Bounded on the S by the R. Thames, it is drained by tributaries of the latter, the Windrush, Evenlode, Cherwell, and Thame. In the W are the Cotswolds, in the SE the Chilterns, rising to over 800 ft, and between is the broad and gently undulating Oxfordshire clay vale. On the fertile soil cereals are grown and dairy and beef cattle and sheep raised. Mainly rural. Principal towns Oxford, Banbury, Witney, Henley-on-Thames.

**Oxnard** USA. Market town in S California 53 m. WNW of Los Angeles. Pop. (1960) 40,265. In a fertile agricultural region producing sugar-beet, citrus fruits, vegetables, etc. Sugar refining, vegetable canning, etc.

**Oxus River** ◊ *Amu Darya.*

**Oyapock (Oiapoque) River** French Guiana/Brazil. River about 300 m. long, rising in the Tumuc Humac Mountains in SW French Guiana, flowing generally NNE and forming most of the boundary with Brazil, entering the Atlantic near Cape Orange.

**Oyo** Nigeria. Town in the SW, 105 m. NNE of Lagos. Pop. (1963) 72,000. Commercial centre. Trade in cacao, palm oil and kernels. Cotton weaving.

**Ozark Mountains (Plateau)** USA. A dissected plateau, mainly in Missouri but reaching its greatest altitude in Arkansas, where the Boston Mountains rise to over 2,000 ft. Important deposits of lead, barytes, and other minerals. Development has been slow, chiefly owing to poor soil and inadequate communications.

# P

**Paarl** S Africa. Town in Cape Province 34 m. ENE of Cape Town, on the Great Berg R. Pop. (1968) 49,640. An important wine-making centre; has the world's largest wine cellars. Fruit farms, vineyards, tobacco plantations in the neighbourhood. Jam making, fruit canning, flour milling. Manufactures tobacco products, textiles, etc. Founded (1690) by Huguenots, who introduced the vine from France.

**Pabianice** ◊ *Łódź*.

**Pacaraima Mountains** ◊ *Sierra Pacaraima*.

**Pachacámac** ◊ *Lima* (Peru).

**Pachuca** Mexico. Capital of Hidalgo state, on the central plateau at a height of 8,000 ft, 55 m. NNE of Mexico City. Pop. 70,000. Important silver-mining and silver-refining centre. Also manufactures woollen goods, leather, etc. The silver mines, known to the Indians in pre-Columbian times, were worked by the Spaniards for some years before the town was founded (1534).

**Pacific Ocean.** World's largest ocean, lying between Asia and Australia (W) and N and S America (E). Area, with peripheral seas, about 70,000,000 sq. m. In the N it is almost landlocked, being connected with the Arctic Ocean only by the Bering Strait, but in the S its boundary is indeterminate. At its greatest width, approximately along the parallel of latitude 5° N, it measures about 11,000 m., and it is about 10,000 m. N–S. With an average depth of just over 14,000 ft it is also the world's deepest ocean. Around its edge are a number of exceptionally deep trenches, of which the outstanding example is the Marianas Trench, where the bathyscaphe *Trieste* reached the record depth of 35,800 ft (6¾ m.) in 1960. Another remarkable feature of the Pacific is the immense number of islands of volcanic and coral origin, esp. in the S and W, the majority of them comprising Oceania – in the region frequently termed the South Seas. N of the equator the main ocean currents of the Pacific circulate in a clockwise direction and include the Kuroshio and California Currents; S of the equator the circulation is anti-clockwise, and here the currents include the Peruvian or Humboldt and the E Australian currents. In general the

salinity of the Pacific is rather less than that of the Atlantic. Whilst the density of shipping lanes is nowhere as great as in the N Atlantic, the commercial importance of the Pacific increased considerably with the opening of the Panama Canal (1914). Regular air services began to operate across the Pacific in 1935.

**Padang** Indonesia. Seaport on the W coast of Sumatra 40 m. S of Bukit Tinggi. Pop. (1961) 143,699. Exports coal, coffee, copra, rubber, etc. Trading post established here by the Dutch 1667.

**Paddington** England. Former metropolitan borough in W London, mainly residential, including Bayswater and Maida Vale; since 1965 part of the London borough City of Westminster. Pop. (1961) 115,322. Contains Paddington Station, terminus of the Western Region of British Rail. Tyburn Tree, the gallows which once stood near Marble Arch, was demolished 1759. Alexander Fleming discovered penicillin (1928) in St Mary's Hospital here.

**Paderborn** Federal German Republic. Town in N Rhine-Westphalia 23 m. SSE of Bielefeld. Pop. 42,000. Manufactures agricultural machinery, textiles, cement, etc. A historic town; Charlemagne held a diet here (777) and later made it a bishopric. Seat of a university 1614–1819. Many of its ancient buildings, inc. the 11th/13th-cent. cathedral, were severely damaged in the 2nd World War.

**Padiham** England. Urban district in Lancashire 3 m. WNW of Burnley. Pop. (1961) 9,893. Manufactures cotton and rayon goods, furniture. Engineering, coal-mining, etc.

**Padova** ◊ *Padua*.

**Padstow** England. Market town in N Cornwall, on the estuary of the R. Camel, which, having silted, has caused its decline as a port. Pop. (1961) 2,676. Seaside resort.

**Padua** (Italian **Padova**) Italy. Ancient Patavium. Capital of Padova province, Veneto, 23 m. W of Venice. Pop. (1968) 221,447. Manufactures machinery, refrigerators, chemicals, furniture, plastics, etc. A picturesque city, with fine squares, arcaded streets, and several bridges crossing the branches of the Bacchiglione R. The university, at which Galileo taught

(1592–1610), was founded in 1222. Has the oldest botanical gardens in Europe (1545). The outstanding church is the 13th/14th-cent. basilica of St Anthony, near which is the famous equestrian statue by Donatello. Other historic buildings include the Palazzo della Ragione with its great hall, and the Palazzo del Capitanio, residence of the Venetian governors. A wealthy city in Roman times. Independent from the 12th to the 14th cent. Held by the Carrara family 1318–1405, and was then ruled by Venice until 1797. Birthplace of Livy (59 B.C.–A.D. 17).

**Paducah** USA. River port in SW Kentucky, on the Ohio R. at the confluence with the Tennessee R. Pop. (1960) 34,479. Important trade in tobacco. Manufactures hosiery, textile machinery, etc. Site of an atomic energy plant.

**Paestum** Italy. Originally Poseidonia. Ancient Greek city in Campania 22 m. SE of Salerno, founded c. 600 B.C. as a Sybarite colony and called Poseidonia. Flourished as an independent city for about 200 years, then fell to the Lucanians. Came under Roman rule 273 B.C., being renamed Paestum; praised by Latin poets for its roses. Sacked by the Saracens 871. By the 16th cent. it was deserted. Among Greek remains are three Doric temples and most of the city wall; the forum and an amphitheatre date from Roman times.

**Pago Pago** Samoa. Chief port in American Samoa, in the SE of Tutuila Island, ceded to the USA (1872) as a naval base and coaling station. Pop. (1960) 1,251. Powerful radio station. Commercial airport.

**Pahang** Malaysia. Largest state in Malaya (W Malaysia), on the S China Sea. Area 13,873 sq. m. Pop. (1967) 425,552 (mainly Malays and Chinese, with some aboriginal Senoi). Cap. Kuala Lipis. Consists largely of the basin of the 270-m.-long Pahang R. Chief products rubber, tin.

**Pahlavi** ◊ *Bandar Pahlavi.*

**Paignton** England. Seaside resort in Devonshire, on Tor Bay 2 m. SSW of Torquay, from 1968 in the county borough of ◊ *Torbay.* Pop. (1961) 30,289. Has the Bible Tower, part of the ancient palace of the Bishops of Exeter: so called because it was believed (wrongly) that Miles Coverdale (1488–1569), a Bishop of Exeter, made his translation of the Bible here.

**Painter, Mount** ◊ *Flinders Range.*

**Paisley** Scotland. Large burgh in Renfrew-shire, on the White Cart R. near its confluence with the R. Clyde 6 m. WSW of Glasgow. Pop. (1961) 95,753. Industrial town, noted for the manufacture of cotton thread; also bleaching, dyeing, engineering. Manufactures textiles, starch, cornflour, preserves, etc. Once famous for Paisley shawls and for its linen and silk gauze, but these are no longer produced. Among noteworthy buildings are the Coats memorial church and the observatory. The abbey was founded in 1163, destroyed by the English in 1307, and rebuilt later by the Stuart kings. Birthplace of Robert Tannahill (1774–1810), Alexander Wilson, the American ornithologist (1766–1813), and John Wilson ('Christopher North') (1785–1854).

**Paita** Peru. Town in the Piura department in the NW, 40 m. W of Piura. Pop. 37,000. A small but important port, being the outlet for a cotton-growing region. Exports chiefly cotton, also hides, wool, Panama hats.

**Pakistan\***. Federal republic of S Asia and member of the Commonwealth of Nations. Area 365,929 sq. m. Pop. (1961) 93,720,613. Provisional cap. Rawalpindi; new cap. Islamabad. Official languages English, Urdu, Bengali. Rel. 88 per cent Muslim, nearly 12 per cent Hindu.

Consists of two provinces in the N part of the Indian sub-continent, W and E Pakistan, separated by about 850 m. of Indian territory. W Pakistan (area 310,403 sq. m.; pop. 42,880,378) is bounded by Afghanistan (NW and N), Kashmir (NE), more than one third of which is occupied by Pakistan, India (E), the Arabian Sea (S), and Iran (W); it is divided administratively into 12 Divisions – Peshawar, Dera Ismail Khan, Rawalpindi, Sargodha, Lahore, Multan, Bahawalpur, Khairpur, Hyderabad, Quetta, Kalat, Karachi. E Pakistan (area 55,126 sq. m.; pop. 50,840,235), which corresponds in the main to E Bengal, is bounded by India (W, N, and E), Burma (SE), and the Bay of Bengal (S); it is divided administratively into 4 Divisions – Dacca, Chittagong, Rajshahi, Khulna.

TOPOGRAPHY, RESOURCES, *etc.* W Pakistan is mountainous in the N, where the E Hindu Kush rise to 25,260 ft in Tirich Mir, and the W, where are the Sulaiman, Kirthar, and other ranges; the remainder consists of fertile plains watered by the Indus and its tributaries, with the Thar Desert in the E. There is also considerable desert in the SW, and the rainfall varies from below 5 ins. annually there to 20–25 ins. in the NE. Agriculture occupies the vast majority of the population, and is almost completely dependent on irrigation by the great rivers; wheat is the principal crop, followed by cotton and rice. Karachi, the chief seaport, was formerly the federal capital; other important towns are Lahore, the provincial capital, Rawalpindi, the provisional federal capital, Hyderabad, Lyallpur, Multan, and Islamabad, the new capital.

E Pakistan is generally low-lying, with hills only in the S E, and occupies the major part of the great Ganges–Brahmaputra delta. Has a tropical monsoon climate, with high temperatures and a heavy rainfall. Over 80 per cent of the people are engaged in agriculture; rice is the main food crop, and the province produces about four fifths of the world output of jute. Dacca is the provincial capital and Chittagong the chief seaport. The coastal region was devastated by cyclones and tidal waves, with the loss of thousands of lives, esp. in the Chittagong–Cox's Bazar area (1963, 1965) and the Barisal district (1965).

PEOPLE, GOVERNMENT, etc. When the former India was partitioned (1947) Pakistan was created from the areas where Muslims formed the majority of the population and, as a result, it comprises the two widely separated regions of W and E Pakistan. In the former Urdu is the principal spoken language and in the latter Bengali, while English is used for many official purposes. The literacy rate is only about 16 per cent, and is slightly the higher in E Pakistan (1961). As in India, one of the most difficult problems facing the new country was the rehabilitation of millions of refugees from across the border; externally, the outstanding problem has been the continuing dispute with India over ◊ Kashmir. At first a Dominion of the British Commonwealth, Pakistan was proclaimed an Islamic republic 1956. In 1958 martial law was declared, the central and provincial governments were dismissed, and all political parties were abolished in an attempt to create order out of the political and economic chaos into which the country had sunk. In 1962 a new constitution was proclaimed, the legislature consisting of 75 members each from E and W Pakistan and 6 women elected by the provincial assemblies, the President being head of both the state and the executive. (For history prior to 1947, ◊ India.)

Palau Islands W Pacific Ocean. Group of 4 volcanic islands, 4 coral islands, and an atoll in the W Caroline Is., 500 m. E of the Philippines. Pop. (1968) 11,904. Exports copra, tapioca, dried fish. A Japanese stronghold in the 2nd World War, taken by the USA 1944.

Palawan Philippines. The most westerly of the country's large islands, between the S China Sea (W) and the Sulu Sea (E). Area 5,747 sq. m. Pop. 67,000. Cap. Puerto Princesa (pop. 15,000). A mountain range runs through the island, rising to 6,839 ft in Mt Mantalingajan. Largely forested. Produces coconuts, rice, rubber.

Palembang Indonesia. Capital of S Sumatra province, on the Musi R. 50 m. from the mouth. Pop. (1961) 474,971. Port. Commercial centre. Important oil refineries near by. Exports petroleum products, rubber, etc.

Palencia Spain. 1. Inland province in Old Castile (though sometimes considered part of León). Area 3,096 sq. m. Pop. (1961) 231,977. Crossed by the Cantabrian Mountains in the N, the remainder being dry, barren plateau, drained by the Pisuerga and Carrión rivers, with fertile valleys where cereals, fruits, vegetables are cultivated.
2. Capital of Palencia province, on the Carrión R. 28 m. NNE of Valladolid. Pop. 41,000. Railway engineering, tanning, flour milling. Manufactures soap, textiles, etc. The Gothic cathedral (14th/16th-cent.) has paintings by El Greco and Zurbarán. The university, believed to be the oldest in Spain, was founded in 1208 and removed to Salamanca in 1239.

Palermo Italy. Ancient Panormus. Capital of Palermo province and of the region of Sicily, on the NW coast and on the edge of the Conca d'Oro plain. Pop. (1968) 651,227. Seaport. Industrial centre. Exports fruit, olive oil, wine. Shipbuilding. Manufactures steel, glass, chemicals, furniture, etc. The earliest buildings date from the time of the Norman kings, many of whose tombs are in the 12th-cent. cathedral, founded by an Englishman, Archbishop Walter of the Mill, and built in mixed Norman and Saracen styles. Other churches and also palaces of architectural interest. University (1805). Near by are Monte Pellegrino (2,000 ft) and the resort of Mondello beach. Belonged to Carthaginians, Romans,

Byzantines, Saracens, and then Normans, who made it capital of the kingdom of Sicily; attained its greatest glory under the Emperor Frederick II (1194–1250). Liberated from the Bourbons by Garibaldi 1860. Birthplace of Cagliostro (1743–95).

**Palestine** ◊ *Israel*.

**Palk Strait.** Channel between SE India and N Ceylon, 33 m. wide at its narrowest. Named after Sir Robert Palk, Governor of Madras 1763–6.

**Pallas** ◊ *Ballymahon*.

**Palma** (Canary Islands) ◊ *Santa Cruz de Tenerife*.

**Palma (Palma de Mallorca)** Spain. Capital of Majorca and of the Baleares (Balearic Is.) province, at the head of the Bay of Palma in the SW of Majorca. Pop. (1967) 199,032. Seaport. Exports almonds, fruits, wine, etc. Manufactures cement, paper, textiles, shoes, glass, etc. Mild climate and attractive situation on the bay; best known as a tourist resort. Noteworthy buildings are the Gothic cathedral (13th/17th-cent.), the adjacent Almudaina castle (a former Moorish palace), and the 15th-cent. Lonja or old exchange. Founded as a Roman colony. Liberated from the Moors (1229) by James I of Aragon. Birthplace of Raimon Lull (1235–1315), whose tomb is in the Church of St Francis.

**Palm Beach** USA. Expensive and luxurious winter resort in SE Florida, on the E shore of L. Worth, a sea lagoon, and 67 m. N of Miami. Pop. (1960) 6,055 (permanent residents). Connected by bridges to West Palm Beach, on the opposite shore of the lagoon, a winter resort and commercial town (pop. 56,208).

**Palmer Peninsula** ◊ *Graham Land*; *Bellingshausen Sea*.

**Palmerston** ◊ *Darwin*.

**Palmerston North** New Zealand. Chief town on the Manawatu R. plains in the N Island, on the Manawatu R. 80 m. NNE of Wellington. Pop. (1966) 46,816. Railway junction in dairying and sheep-farming country. Manufactures clothing, furniture.

**Palmira** Colombia. Town in the Valle del Cauca department 20 m. NE of Cali at a height of 3,500 ft. Pop. 124,000. Commercial centre. Trade in tobacco, coffee, sugarcane, cereals, rice.

**Palm Springs** USA. Exclusive winter resort in S California 76 m. E of Santa Ana. Pop. (1960) 13,468. Sulphur springs in the neighbourhood. Developed in the 1930s, when the mild climate and picturesque situation attracted Hollywood actors.

**Palmyra** Syria. Ancient city and oasis 130 m. NE of Damascus, known as early as the 12th cent. B.C.: the biblical Tadmor ('City of Palms'). Reached the height of its power and commercial importance in the 3rd cent. A.D. until the ambitions of Queen Zenobia provoked Rome: in 272 it fell to and was partly destroyed by Aurelian. Later, when under the Arabs, it was sacked by Tamerlane. Near the remains of the great Temple of the Sun, which testify to its former splendour, today lies the insignificant village of Tadmor, through which passes the Kirkuk–Tripoli oil pipeline.

**Palmyra Island** ◊ *Line Islands*.

**Palo Alto** USA. Attractive residential town in California 27 m. SE of San Francisco, near the S end of San Francisco Bay. Pop. (1960) 52,287. Seat of Stanford University (1891).

**Palomar, Mount** USA. Mountain 6,126 ft high, in S California 45 m. NNE of San Diego. Site of the Mt Palomar Observatory (at 5,600 ft), famous for its 200-in. reflecting telescope, the largest in the world, installed 1947–8.

**Palos de la Frontera** Spain. Small town in Huelva province on the Río Tinto estuary. Pop. 1,900. Former port (now silted up), from which Columbus sailed to discover America (1492) and to which he returned (1493); also where Cortés landed (1528) after his conquest of Mexico.

**Pamir (Pamirs).** Dissected plateau in Central Asia, mainly in the Gorno-Badakhshan AR of the Tadzhik SSR, USSR, but extending into Afghanistan and Sinkiang-Uighur (China). Consists of a series of high mountain valleys (the true 'Pamirs') at 12,000–14,000 ft, largely covered with grass on which the nomadic Kirghiz pasture their sheep, goats, and other livestock, flanked by lofty mountain ranges. The highest peaks are in the Akademia Nauk Range, which contains Peak Kommunizma (24,590 ft), the loftiest in the USSR.

**Pampeluna** ◊ *Pamplona* (Spain).

**Pamphylia.** Ancient region in Asia Minor, to the S of Pisidia, now in Turkey. Among its cities were Perga and Olbia. Under the Romans it was held to include Pisidia.

**Pamplona** Colombia. Town in the Norte de Santander department in the E Cordillera 36 m. S of Cúcuta at a height of 7,200 ft. Pop. 26,000. Commercial centre. Trade in coffee, cacao, cereals, etc. Textile industry, brewing, distilling. Founded 1548. Suffered severely from earthquakes 1644, 1875.

**Pamplona (Pampeluna)** Spain. Ancient Pompaelo. Capital of Navarra province, on the Arga R. 90 m. NNW of Zaragoza. Pop. (1967) 129,048. Flour milling, tanning. Manufactures textiles, soap, paper, etc. The mainly 14th/15th-cent. Gothic cathedral is remarkable for the 18th-cent. façade and the fine cloisters. On the feast of St Fermin a bull fight is held for which the bulls run through the streets to the ring. An old Basque town, rebuilt (68 B.C.) by Pompey the Great and named Pompaelo after him. Later became capital of the kingdom of Navarre, and was fortified and improved by Charles III (1361–1425). Under Philip II (1556–98) it became the best fortified city in Spain.

**Panama.** Republic in Central America. Area (excluding the ◊ *Panama Canal Zone*) 28,575 sq. m. Pop. (1960) 1,075,541 (65 per cent *mestizo* or mixed, 14 per cent Negro, 11 per cent white, 9 per cent Indian). Cap. Panama City. Lang. Spanish. Rel. Roman Catholic.

Lies between the Caribbean Sea (N) and Pacific Ocean (S), bordered by Costa Rica (W) and Colombia (E); roughly coincides with the Isthmus of Panama and connects Central and S America. The Caribbean coast is indented by the Mosquito Gulf; on the Pacific coast are the Gulf of Panama, the Azuero Peninsula, and the Gulf of Chiriqui (in which is the largest island, Coiba, used as a penal colony). There are narrow coastal lowlands, but the interior is mountainous; the highest peak is the inactive volcano Chiriqui (11,410 ft). Climate in the lowlands tropical, temperature averaging 82° F, with little seasonal variation; much cooler in the mountains. Annual rainfall varies from about 70 ins. on the Pacific coast to 160 ins. on the Caribbean coast. Timber (chiefly mahogany) produced from the extensive forests. Leading export bananas; rice, maize, and coffee grown for domestic consumption. Sea fisheries are important, with shrimps the second most valuable export. Divided administratively into 9 provinces.

First explored by the Spaniards (1501); Columbus claimed the region for Spain (1502). Buccaneers (including Drake in the 16th cent. and Morgan in the 17th) raided and looted the ports and coastal settlements. Placed under the Viceroyalty of New Granada 1739. After Spain had relin-

quished control (1821) it joined the federation of Colombia, Venezuela, and Ecuador (dissolved 1830). Became a province of Colombia until Colombia refused to allow the USA to construct the canal across the isthmus and Panama declared its independence (1903). Although the Panama Canal has benefited the country economically, it has split Panama into two parts; from time to time nationalist opinion has demanded that the Canal Zone should be placed under Panamanian control.

**Panama, Gulf of.** Inlet of the Pacific in SE Panama, 120 m. wide. At the head is the Bay of Panama, with Panama City and Balboa. Contains the ◊ *Pearl Islands*.

**Panama, Isthmus of.** Narrow neck of land between the Caribbean Sea and the Pacific Ocean (Gulf of Panama), crossed by the Panama Canal. The term is sometimes applied to the entire territory of the Republic of Panama.

**Panama Canal** Central America. Ship canal across the Isthmus of Panama connecting the Atlantic Ocean with the Pacific, 40 m. long from coast to coast; runs generally NW–SE (the Pacific entrance is farther E than the Caribbean entrance). Passage takes 7 or 8 hours; vessels move in both directions, as all the locks are double. A ship entering from the Caribbean is raised to 85 ft above sea level by the three sets of the Gatun Locks, crosses the artificial L. Gatun (about 24 m.), goes through the Gaillard Cut, and finally passes through the Pedro Miguel Locks and the two sets of the Miraflores Locks to the short sea-level canal leading to the Pacific. Constructed 1904–14. The first ship passed through in Aug. 1914. The idea of a canal dates from the Spanish explorers of the 16th cent. The USA became increasingly interested in the 19th cent. as settlers moved to the far west. After an abortive attempt by a French company (1880–89), the USA secured (1903) from the new republic of Panama the lease in perpetuity of the Panama Canal Zone. Work began in 1904. A fixed bridge 1 m. long over the Pacific entrance was opened at Balboa in 1962; it links the two parts of the Republic of Panama and the N and S American sections of the Pan-American Highway.

**Panama Canal Zone** USA. Administrative region of the USA, a strip of land about 10 m. wide along the Panama Canal, bordered on each side by the Republic of Panama. Area 647 sq. m. (land 372 sq. m.).

Pop. (1960) 42,122. Includes the canal ports of Cristóbal (Caribbean) and Balboa (Pacific); Panama City and Colón are geographically within the Zone but are Panamanian. There is no privately owned land; sites may be leased to individuals or companies.

**Panama City** Panama. Capital of Panama and of the Panama province. Pop. (1960) 273,440. Geographically within the Panama Canal Zone, but administratively and politically separate. Industrial and route centre. Its port is Balboa. Manufactures clothing, shoes, beer, etc. Seat of the University of Panama (1935). The ruins of the old city (founded in 1519 and destroyed by Henry Morgan, the buccaneer, in 1671) are 5 m. NE. The city was rebuilt on its present site in 1673. Became capital of Panama 1903.

**Panama City** USA. Port and resort in NW Florida, on St Andrew Bay, Gulf of Mexico. Pop. (1960) 33,275. Sawmilling. Manufactures paper. Fishing.

**Panay** Philippines. Island between Mindoro and Negros. Area 4,744 sq. m. Pop. 1,712,000. Chief town Iloilo. Mountainous in the W, rising there to 6,724 ft. Lower and more fertile in the E. Chief products rice, copra.

**Pančevo** Yugoslavia. Town in Vojvodina 11 m. ENE of Belgrade. Pop. (1961) 46,679. Railway junction. Flour milling etc.

**Panjim (Nova Goa)** India. Capital of the Union Territory of Goa, Daman, and Diu. Pop. 32,000. Commercial centre. Port. Trade in rice, fish, salt, etc. Velha Goa (Old Goa), the former capital, is now mainly in ruins. Has the church of Bom Jesus (1594–1603), with the tomb of St Francis Xavier, and the convent of St Francis, a converted mosque. Founded 1440. Taken by Albuquerque 1510. Declined after the removal of the capital to Panjim (formerly a suburb) in 1759.

**Pannonhalma** ◊ *Győr*.

**Pantelleria (Pantellaria)** Italy. Ancient Cossyra. Mediterranean island 63 m. SW of the SW coast of Sicily. Area 32 sq. m. Pop. 10,000. Chief town and port Pantelleria, on the NW coast. Volcanic, with fumaroles and hot springs. Fertile but lacking fresh water. Produces wine, cereals. An important Italian base in the 2nd World War; it was virtually destroyed by bombing and surrendered in 1943.

**Pánuco River** ◊ *Mexico*.

**Paotow** China. Town in the Inner Mongolia

AR just N of the Hwang-ho and 85 m. W of Huhehot. Pop. 149,000. Important route and commercial centre. Connected by rail with Peking and with Lanchow, thus linking up the great E–W and N–S trunk lines of China. Trade in wool, hides, cereals, etc. Steel industry developed in the late 1950s. Also manufactures rugs, soap, etc.

**Papal States** Italy. Territories of central Italy formerly ruled by the Pope, constituting an area of 15,700 sq. m. in the mid 19th cent. In 1860 parts and in 1870 the remainder were incorporated into Italy. By the Lateran Treaty (1929) the Pope was recognized as sovereign of the ◊ *Vatican City*.

**Papeete** ◊ *Tahiti*.

**Papua** ◊ *New Guinea*.

**Pará** Brazil. Large state in the N, lying in the Amazon basin and consisting mainly of tropical rain-forest. Area 481,744 sq. m. Pop. (1960) 1,550,935. Cap. Belém. Produces rubber, Brazil nuts, medicinal plants, tropical hardwoods, jute, and skins. Transportation chiefly by water.

**Paraguay.** Inland republic of S America. Area 157,047 sq. m. Pop. (1962) 1,816,890. Cap. Asunción. Rel. Roman Catholic. Languages Spanish, Guaraní.

Bounded by Bolivia (N and NW), Brazil (E), and Argentina (SE, S, and W). Has much good agricultural land, but in spite of its potentialities for agricultural development the general standard of living, health, and education is low, largely as a result of involvement in disastrous wars, and the difficulty of communications with other countries. The population is remarkably homogeneous, the original Spanish minority having been absorbed by the indigenous Indians. Most Paraguayans are bilingual, but a majority speak Guaraní in preference to Spanish.

TOPOGRAPHY, CLIMATE, *etc.* The Paraguay R. receives water from the interior of Brazil and flows S through Paraguay, dividing the country into two contrasting parts. To the W lies the sparsely inhabited scrub forest of the Gran Chaco, while to the E is a richer area containing most of the population, with gently rolling hills, flat moist plains, and the edge of the Paraná plateau, where the forests yield yerba maté and timber. Climate sub-tropical, with hot summers and mild winters. Rainfall generally plentiful, ranging from 30 ins. annually in the W to 80 ins. in the E.

RESOURCES, *etc.* Quebracho trees from

the E Chaco are used mainly for tanning, hides being the chief product from the rough grazing areas of these plains. The only well-organized agricultural lands are E of the Paraguay R., esp. near Asunción. Maize is the principal subsistence crop; rice, cotton, sugar-cane, tobacco, oranges, and other fruits also grown. S of the capital the grasslands support cattle for the production of leather and dried meat, and small areas produce cotton and oranges. SE of Asunción, near Villarrica, tobacco, vines, cotton, oranges, and sugar-cane are cultivated. Main exports meat products, timber, quebracho extract, cotton. Road and rail communications are poor; access to the sea is principally by rivers draining into the Río de la Plata system. Asunción, the leading port and commercial centre and only large city, on the Paraguay R., is 950 m. from the ocean. It is linked by rail with Encarnación, on the Alto Paraná R., where a ferry connects with the Argentine system.

HISTORY. The peaceable Guaraní Indians, unlike the warlike tribes farther S, did not oppose the Spaniards who founded Asunción (1537), which they used as a springboard for further colonization of ◊ *Buenos Aires* (Argentina) in 1580. Paraguay subsequently came under the viceroyalty of Peru and then of La Plata (1776); the Jesuits, who had established many well-organized settlements in which the Indians lived free from exploitation by the Spanish landowners, were expelled in 1767. Independence from Spain was achieved in 1811, but the third dictator Solano López led the country into a tragic war against Brazil, Argentina, and Uruguay (1865–70) in which more than half the population and nearly all able-bodied males were killed. In a later war with Bolivia, ended in 1935, over rival claims in the Chaco, Paraguay was victorious and gained possession of a considerable area – but at the price of exhaustion. An authoritarian régime followed, civil war broke out in 1947, and subsequent political stability has been precarious. The country is divided into two parts, the 'Oriental', E of the Paraguay R., comprising 13 departments, and the 'Occidental', W of the river, with 3 departments.

**Paraguay River.** River 1,300 m. long, rising in the central Mato Grosso (Brazil), near Diamantino, descending to wooded, swampy lowlands and flowing generally S, joining the Alto Paraná in the SW corner of Paraguay to form the Paraná R. Navigable by small craft as far upstream as Cáceres (Brazil) and by larger vessels to Concepción, though it winds greatly; an important means of communication, esp. to Paraguay. Divides the Paraguayan Chaco to the W from the richer pastoral and agricultural lands to the E, and forms part of the boundary of Paraguay with both Brazil and Argentina.

**Paraíba** Brazil. State in the NE consisting of a narrow coastal plain backed by a hilly region of uncertain rainfall, partly irrigated, with much *sertão* ('backwoods'). Area 21,760 sq. m. Pop. (1960) 2,018,023. Cap. João Pessoa. Important cotton-growing state; also produces sugar-cane, tobacco, pineapples.

**Paraíba do Norte River** Brazil. River 200 m. long, rising near the Paraíba–Pernambuco border and flowing generally ENE to the Atlantic below João Pessoa.

**Paraíba do Sul River** Brazil. River 600 m. long, rising in the Serra do Mar near São Paulo and flowing NE to the Atlantic below Campos. Its valley carries the road and railway between São Paulo and Rio de Janeiro and contains the Volta Redonda steelworks.

**Paramaribo** Surinam. Capital and chief seaport, on the Surinam R. 17 m. from the mouth. Pop. (1962) 123,000. Exports coffee, citrus fruits, timber, bauxite, etc. Dutch in appearance, with many canals.

**Paramé** ◊ *St Malo*.

**Paraná** Argentina. Formerly Bajada de Santa Fé. Capital of Entre Ríos province and port on the left bank on the Paraná R. opposite Santa Fé, to which it is linked by ferry. Pop. 174,000. Commercial centre for an extensive grain and cattle area. Has the famous Urquiza Park and a noteworthy cathedral. Capital of Argentina 1853–62.

**Paraná** Brazil. State in the S, to the E of the Paraná R., consisting of a narrow coastal lowland and an interior dissected plateau. Area 77,027 sq. m. Pop. (1960) 4,110,000, showing rapid growth (almost doubled 1950–60) due largely to European immigrants. Cap. Curitiba. Well-wooded, with extensive stands of Paraná pines. Coffee grown on the fertile *terra roxa* in the N; cotton, citrus fruits, maté, and timber are also important products.

**Paraná River.** River 1,800 m. long formed by the union of the Rio Grande and the Paranaíba R. on the plateau of SE Brazil, being known in its upper course as the Alto

Paraná. It flows generally S, receives several long tributaries that cross the tablelands of Paraná and São Paulo from the E, descends the Guaíra Falls (known in Brazil as Sete Quedas), and forms the Brazil–Paraguay boundary. It then turns W, in this section forming the Paraguay–Argentina boundary, and below the confluence with the Paraguay is called the Paraná. Two main navigable channels pass through the delta and meet the Uruguay R. in the La Plata estuary. River ports, serving as outlets for the pampas and industrial centres, lie along the lower Paraná, among the most important being Santa Fé, Paraná, and Rosario.

**Pará River** Brazil. Navigable arm of the Amazon R. delta S and E of Marajó island, about 200 m. long and 40 m. wide at the mouth. Joined by the Tocantins R. from the S.

**Pardubice** (Ger. **Pardubitz**) Czechoslovakia. Town in NE Bohemia, on the Elbe R. 60 m. E of Prague. Pop. (1967) 66,000. Railway junction. Industrial centre. Oil refining, brewing, etc. Cathedral (13th-cent., restored).

**Paricutín, Mount** Mexico. Volcano in Michoacán state, formed in a cultivated field on 20 Feb. 1943 after a week of earth tremors. Steam forced its way out of the ground, and by the evening black smoke was belching from a hole, while stones and cinders were thrown up. By the next morning a cinder cone 25 ft high had built up round the vent, and grey ash covered the countryside for miles around; the village of Paricutín was later buried under lava. At the end of a year the volcano had risen, from its base at 7,380 ft above sea level, to a height of 8,200 ft. Activity ceased in 1952.

**Paris** France. Ancient Lutetia. Capital of France and from 1964 a department, and the country's largest city, built on both sides of a meander in the Seine R. just below its confluence with the Marne R., at the centre of the Paris Basin; the only French city with more than 1 million inhabitants. Pop. (1968) 2,590,771. Greater Paris, however, may be considered to include the whole of the former Seine department, with a population of over 5½ million, giving a combined population of almost one sixth of that of France. Administration is in the hands of a prefect and a prefect of police, both appointed by the Minister of the Interior, and the city is divided into 20 *arrondissements* or districts, grouped in 9 sectors, each with its own mayor; the sectors elect their own representatives to the Municipal Council of 90 members.

Besides dominating France by virtue of its size, Paris is also the centre of its principal railways, roads, and airways, with 7 main railway termini and two airports (Orly and Le Bourget), and is the junction of many important routes between N, W, and S Europe. Less dependent commercially on its river than London is on the Thames, but the Seine carries a considerable volume of barge traffic, making it the country's leading inland port, and it is linked by canals with all the main rivers of France. Of the 33 bridges spanning the Seine (three for pedestrians only) the oldest and most famous is the 16th/17th-cent. Pont Neuf, which connects the Île de la Cité with both banks of the river. Communications include an underground railway system, the Métropolitain (Métro). In addition to being the administrative, business, and financial centre of France Paris has many industries, being esp. famed for luxury goods, e.g. jewellery, cosmetics, perfume, *haute couture* – which form a significant part of French exports. A major part of the French motorcar industry is in the region of Paris, and this together with factories for aircraft, metal goods, chemicals, etc. is located in the suburbs – e.g. Boulogne-Billancourt, Issy-les-Moulineaux, Suresnes. With its variety of attractions – historic buildings, outstanding museums and art collections, theatres, a vast array of hotels and restaurants, and a wide range of amusements – Paris is also a mainstay of another of France's chief sources of income, the tourist trade.

A characteristic of Paris is the combination of spaciousness and compactness in which the old mingles with the modern in a remarkably integrated way, partly due to the planning of Haussmann, partly a result of the expansion of the city in concentric rings from the early Gallo-Roman town on the Île de la Cité. Most of the old Paris lies within the Grands Boulevards, which roughly occupy the site of the 14th–17th-cent. ramparts. Beyond these are the first suburbs, the *faubourgs*, around which is another ring, the *boulevards extérieurs*, built over the 18th-cent. ramparts; beyond these are the more recent suburbs, incorporated into the city in 1860 as *arrondissements* XII–XX, extending to the boulevards which mark the line of fortifications erected after 1860 and demolished in 1919 to provide for housing developments, open spaces, and, in the S, for the Cité Universitaire. The Île de la Cité is the true heart of Paris; on it stands the cathedral of Notre-Dame (1163–1240), with its magnificent façade and two great towers. Most of the island is occupied by massive buildings of the Palais de Justice, among which stand the 13th-cent. Sainte-Chapelle, a gem of Gothic architecture, and the Conciergerie, where Marie Antoinette was imprisoned. The Île de la Cité is connected by bridge with the Île St-Louis, which has several fine 17th- and 18th-cent. buildings. Near by on the right bank of the Seine is the Louvre, certainly the supreme art gallery and museum in France, and possibly in the world. W of the Louvre are the beautiful Tuileries gardens; the Place de la Concorde, the greatest of the Parisian squares, with the 75-ft Luxor obelisk; then the Avenue des Champs-Elysées, leading to the Place de l'Étoile, on which 12 avenues converge, and the Arc de Triomphe, with the tomb of the Unknown Soldier. To the W and E of the city lie the Bois de Boulogne and the Bois de Vincennes. Just N of the Louvre is the Palais-Royal, in the SW wing of which is the Comédie-Française, linked by the Avenue de l'Opéra; also on the right bank is the Place de la Bastille, site of the notorious prison destroyed in the Revolution. N of the Grands Boulevards is Montmartre, the highest part of Paris (426 ft), crowned by the church of Sacré-Coeur. On the left bank the Boulevard St Michel or Boul' Mich leads S from the Île de la Cité to the Latin Quarter, with the Sorbonne or University of Paris, one of the oldest in the world (founded 1150). S of the river, too, are the Panthéon, the Chamber of Deputies, the Eiffel Tower, the principal landmark of Paris (984 ft), and the district of Montparnasse, SW of the Luxembourg Palace, which has replaced Montmartre to some extent as the artistic centre of Paris.

The city is named after its early inhabitants, the Parisii, the Gallic tribe whose original village on the Île de la Cité spread to the left bank after the Roman conquest, when it was called Lutetia. The town was captured by the Franks and in the 6th cent. became the residence of the Merovingian king Clovis. It was later repeatedly attacked and destroyed by the Norsemen, who were finally beaten off, and Capet chose Paris as the capital of his kingdom in 987 A.D. It

grew rapidly in the 12th and 13th cent. and from then on remained the focus of the life and history of France. Notre-Dame and the fortress of the Louvre were built and the university was founded. The city came under attack in the Hundred Years War and was for a time occupied by the English. A period of great development came in the Renaissance period under Francis I and Marie de Medici when the Louvre was rebuilt, and the Tuileries, Luxembourg, and Hôtel de Ville constructed. It suffered tragedy in the massacre of the Huguenots (1572) and allowed Henry IV to enter the city only after a public declaration of his conversion to Roman Catholicism ('Paris is well worth a Mass'). In the 17th and 18th cent. Paris grew in size and amenities, its cultural life flourished, and the splendour of the court increased until Louis XIV moved to Versailles. The storming of the Bastille in Paris signalled the beginning of the French Revolution followed by the execution of Louis XVI, the Reign of Terror, and the meteoric career of Napoleon Bonaparte. The revolutions of 1830 and 1848 caused no damage to the city and from 1855 Baron Haussmann, Prefect of the Seine, carried out the bold planning which characterizes modern Paris. In the Franco-Prussian war (1870–71) Paris was besieged for 4 months and after capitulation was further damaged during the suppression of the Commune. In the 1st World War the German advance was halted a few miles from Paris. Undefended in the 2nd World War, it was occupied by the Germans 1940–44, suffering only minor damage.

**Paris Basin** France. Saucer-shaped depression in the N, drained by the Seine R. and its tributaries, the Somme R., and the middle course of the Loire R. At the heart of the central area, the Île de France, is Paris. Surrounding this area are concentric chalk and limestone escarpments, most apparent to the E, where the Champagne wine country is situated. Much of the Paris Basin is very fertile and esp. productive of wheat and dairy produce.

**Paris-Plage** ⟫ *Touquet, Le.*

**Parkersburg** USA. Industrial town in W Virginia, on the Ohio R. at the confluence with the Little Kanawha R. Pop. (1960) 44,777. In a region producing oil and natural gas. Manufactures oilfield equipment, shovels, glassware, etc. First settled 1785. Chartered 1820.

**Parma** Italy. Capital of Parma province, in Emilia-Romagna, on the Parma R. and the Aemilian Way. Pop. (1968) 167,988. Manufactures machinery, glass, food products, etc. Trade in grain, livestock, Parmesan cheese and other dairy produce. The 11th-cent. Romanesque cathedral has Correggio's famous fresco of the Assumption decorating the dome. Other outstanding buildings are the octagonal 12th/13th-cent. baptistery, the 16th/17th-cent. Church of San Giovanni Evangelista with more frescoes by Correggio, and the wooden Teatro Farnese (repaired after 2nd World War damage). A Roman colony from 183 B.C. A cultural centre in medieval times; the university was founded 1502.

**Parma** USA. Town in N Ohio just S of Cleveland. Pop. (1960) 82,845. Mainly residential. Manufactures motor-vehicle parts, machine tools, etc. Grew rapidly in the 1950s.

**Parnaíba** Brazil. Town in Piauí state near the mouth of the Parnaíba R. Pop. 40,000. Commercial centre for the entire state. Exports cotton, sugar, carnauba wax, cattle.

**Parnaíba River** Brazil. River 750 m. long, rising in the Serra das Mangabeiras and flowing generally NNE, forming the boundary between the Maranhão and Piauí states.

**Parnassus, Mount** Greece. Mountain 8,061 ft high, in the NW of Boeotia *nome* 45 m. NW of Corinth. One of the holiest mountains of ancient Greece, sacred to Dionysus, Apollo, and the Muses, with Delphi and the Castalian spring on its S slopes.

**Pärnu (Pyärnu)** USSR. Seaport in the Estonian SSR, at the mouth of the Pärnu R. on Pärnu Bay, Gulf of Riga, 73 m. S of Tallinn. Pop. (1962) 36,300. Exports timber, flax, etc. Sawmilling. Manufactures textiles, leather goods, etc. Founded 1255.

**Páros** Greece. Aegean island in the Cyclades. Area 64 sq. m. Pop. (1961) 7,800. Rises to a central peak 2,451 ft high, on the N side of which are the quarries of white Parian marble, used by sculptors from the 6th cent. B.C.

**Parsonstown** ◊ *Birr.*

**Parthia.** Ancient kingdom in SW Asia, roughly co-extensive with the modern Khurasan in NE Iran, founded by Arsaces in 248 B.C. and reaching its greatest power under Mithridates I and II in the following two centuries. Its rule was extended over the whole of Persia and present-day Iraq to the Euphrates, and its mounted bowmen, formidable in battle, were frequently successful against the Romans. The Parthian kingdom fell in A.D. 226 to the Sassanids, and was annexed to Persia. Among the capitals of Parthia were Hecatompylos and Ctesiphon.

**Pasadena** USA. Mainly residential town in California just NE of Los Angeles. Pop. (1960) 116,407. Some light industries. Seat of the California Institute of Technology (1891). The Henry E. Huntington Library and Art Gallery and the pine-clad Mt Wilson and Mt Lowe, each with an observatory, are near by. Pageants, football matches, and similar events are held in the famous Rose Bowl, an amphitheatre seating 85,000 people. The Tournament of Roses, a fiesta dating to 1890, is held every New Year's Day.

**Pasargadae.** Ancient city in Persia 60 m. NE of the modern Shiraz, built by Cyrus the Great after his victory over Astyages and made his capital. Among the remains are the tomb and palace of Cyrus. Later replaced as capital by Persepolis.

**Pas-de-Calais** France. Department in the N bounded to the N by the Straits of Dover (in French, 'Pas de Calais'), formed (1790) from Artois and part of Picardy. Area 2,607 sq. m. Pop. (1968) 1,397,159. Prefecture Arras. Cereals, sugar-beet, flax, hops cultivated, but it is mainly industrial, with the emphasis on coalmining, metallurgy, and textile manufactures. Chief towns Calais and Boulogne, both seaports, Arras, Béthune, St Omer, Lens. Le Touquet is a well-known seaside resort. Suffered severely in both world wars.

**Pasley, Cape** ◊ *Great Australian Bight.*

**Passaic** USA. Industrial town in New Jersey, on the Passaic R. 9 m. N of Newark. Pop. (1960) 53,963. Manufactures textiles, rubber and leather products, radio and television equipment, etc. Settled by the Dutch 1678.

**Passau** Federal German Republic. Town in Bavaria at the confluence of the Danube with the Inn and Ilz rivers 70 m. SE of Regensburg near the Austrian frontier. Pop. (1963) 31,200. Picturesque river port and tourist centre. Manufactures agricultural machinery, tobacco products, paper. Brewing, tanning. The cathedral stands in the old town, on the tongue of land between the Danube and the Inn. Colonized by the Romans. The bishopric was founded 738.

**Pasto** Colombia. Capital of Nariño department, 165 m. SSW of Cali at a height of 8,500 ft. Pop. (1968) 112,876. Commercial centre for an agricultural and cattle-rearing region. Food processing. Manufactures hats, wooden bowls (decorated with locally made varnish), etc. University (1962). Founded 1539. Has lost its former colonial character.

**Paston** England. Village in Norfolk 17 m. NNE of Norwich. Here lived the Paston family, whose correspondence (1422–1509) became known as the Paston Letters, documents of great historical importance (now mainly in the British Musem).

**Patagonia** Argentina/Chile. Originally the most southerly part of S America – S of about 39° S lat. – including Argentine and Chilean territory, but now applied usually to the E or Argentine part. This consists mainly of a semi-arid tableland extending for 1,000 m. S of the Limay and Negro rivers to the Strait of Magellan. The plateau rises from the coast by low terraces to the base of the Andes. In the S the W part overlooks a depression, interrupted by Andean spurs and containing volcanic debris and glacial material. Large lakes extend from the Andes into this trough; several drain W, and rivers such as the Chico, Chubut, and Deseado flow in deep trenches across the plateau.

Patagonia is shielded from the prevailing westerly winds by the Andes and is affected by the cold Falkland current to the E, so that little rain falls in the cool winters or warm summers. Vegetation consists largely of tussock grass and small shrubs; extensive sheep farming is the main occupation, cattle being raised in the moister W parts. Many settlers came from Britain, including the Welsh who founded Trelew, Puerto Madryn, etc.; others came from the pampas and from S Chile. Comodoro Rivadavia is Argentina's chief source of petroleum, sending oil to La Plata and piping gas to Buenos Aires; coal in the S (Río Turbio) is sent by rail to Río Gallegos for dispatch to the pampas ports. High-grade iron ore lies to the S of the Negro.

Chilean Patagonia has good grassland and supports large numbers of sheep, with cattle in the piedmont area. Punta Arenas exports wool, skins, and frozen meat and was a point of entry for early colonists. Oil is obtained from Chilean Tierra del Fuego. The boundary between Chile and Argentina was fixed by treaty in 1881, but the demarcation was not completed till 1907.

**Paternò** Italy. Town and resort in Catania province, E Sicily, just to the S of Mt Etna. Pop. (1961) 42,935. In a region producing citrus fruits and wine. Has a 14th-cent. castle and cathedral.

**Paterson** USA. Industrial town in NE New Jersey, on the Passaic R., deriving hydroelectric power from the falls. Pop. (1960) 143,663. A leading centre for silk weaving and dyeing, which have declined somewhat in recent years. Manufactures textile machinery, plastics, clothing, rubber products, etc. One of the first American factory strikes took place in a cotton mill here (1828); workers left their looms to demand a reduction of daily hours of work from 13½ to 12.

**Patiala** India. Town in Punjab 130 m. NNW of Delhi. Pop. (1961) 125,234. Trade in cotton, grain, etc. Manufactures metal goods, textiles, footwear, etc. Seat of the Punjabi University (1962). Formerly capital of Patiala state and of the Patiala and E Punjab States Union.

**Patmos** Greece. Aegean island in the N Dodecanese. Area 13 sq. m. Pop. 2,600. Chief town Patmos, on the SE coast. Here St John the Divine wrote the Revelation whilst in exile. The monastery of St John was founded in the 11th cent. to commemorate his stay on the island.

**Patna** India. Capital of Bihar, on the Ganges R. 290 m. NW of Calcutta. Pop. (1961) 363,700. Railway junction. Manufactures brassware, carpets, furniture, etc. Trade in rice, oilseeds, etc. University (1917). Contains the mosques of Husain Shah and Sher Shah and a Sikh temple.

**Patras** (Gr. **Pátrai**) Greece. Capital of Achaea *nome* on the Gulf of Patras in the NW Peloponnese. Pop. (1961) 94,758. Seaport. Exports chiefly currants, also olive oil, wine, tobacco. Flour milling. Manufactures textiles. The Greek War of Independence began here (1821).

**Patras** (Gr. **Pátrai**), **Gulf of** Greece. Inlet of the Ionian Sea on the W coast, linked by a narrow strait to the Gulf of Corinth (E). Patras is on the SE shore.

**Pau** France. Prefecture of the Basses-Pyrénées department, on the Gave de Pau R., tributary of the Adour, 95 m. WSW of Toulouse. Pop. (1968) 76,227. Tourist resort. Engineering, tanning, brewing, flour milling. Manufactures textiles, footwear, etc. Trade in wine, foodstuffs. Was the capital of Béarn and from 1512 residence of the French kings of Navarre.

**Paulo Afonso Falls** Brazil. Falls on the lower São Francisco R. 195 m. from the mouth, consisting of rapids and three cascades together 270 ft high. The large hydroelectric power station supplies much of NE Brazil. The surrounding area has been made a National Park.

**Pavia** Italy. Ancient Ticinum. Capital of Pavia province, in Lombardy, on the Ticino R. 20 m. S of Milan. Pop. (1961) 74,962. Railway and road junction. Market for the agricultural produce of the Po valley (cereals, wine, etc.). Manufactures textiles, sewing machines, agricultural machinery, furniture, etc. Cathedral (15th-cent.); among the many famous churches that of San Michele dates from the 11th and 12th cent. An early centre of learning; its law school was probably founded in the 9th cent. and became the university in 1361. The 14th-cent. covered bridge across the Ticino was severely damaged in the 2nd World War (1944). The magnificent Carthusian monastery of Certosa di Pavia is 5 m. N. Francis I of France was defeated and captured here by the Emperor Charles V (1525). Under Spanish, French, and Austrian rule in turn in the 18th cent.; passed to Italy 1859.

**Pavlodar** USSR. Capital of the Pavlodar region, Kazakh SSR, on the Irtysh R. 250 m. ENE of Tselinograd. Pop. (1970) 187,000. Meat packing, milk canning, flour milling, etc. Has grown rapidly since the 2nd World War.

**Pawtucket** USA. Industrial town in NE Rhode Island, on the Blackstone R. at a 50-ft waterfall. Pop. (1960) 81,001. Manufactures textiles, textile machinery, machine tools, etc. The first water-power cotton mill in the USA was built here (1790).

**Paysandú** Uruguay. Capital of the Paysandú department, on the Uruguay R. 210 m. NW of Montevideo. Pop. (1964) 60,000. Important port and meat-packing centre. Manufactures soap, leather, footwear, textiles, etc.

**Peace River** Canada. River 1,195 m. long, formed by the union at Finlay Forks of two headstreams, the Finlay and the Parsnip, both rising in the Rocky Mountains; flowing generally E and N through British Columbia and Alberta by a fertile valley, it joins the Slave R.

**Peak District** England. Hilly district in the Pennines in N Derbyshire, rising to 2,088 ft in Kinder Scout 10 m. N of Buxton. The N part is known as the High Peak. Many limestone caves, the best known being Peak Cavern, near Castleton.

**Pearl Harbour** USA. Major US naval and air base in the Pacific, on the S coast of Oahu, Hawaii. On 7 Dec. 1941 the Japanese made a surprise attack, without previous declaration of war (repeating the pattern of their attack on Russia in 1905), using aircraft and submarines which sank or put out of action a great part of the US fleet. This precipitated US entry into the 2nd World War.

**Pearl Islands** (Sp. **Archipiélago de las Perlas**) Panama. Group of about 180 islands in the Gulf of Panama. Pearl fishing. Sea angling. Chief islands San Miguel (Isla del Rey), San José, Pedro González.

**Peć** Yugoslavia. Formerly Ipek. Town in Kosovo-Metohija, Serbia, 77 m. NW of Skoplje. Pop. (1961) 28,297. Much of the town is oriental in appearance, with narrow, winding streets, mosques, and Turkish houses. Seat of the Serbian patriarchs for over 300 years between the 14th and the 18th cent.; their 13th-cent. monastery stands above the town. Freed from Turkish rule 1913.

**Pechora River** USSR. River 1,100 m. long in N European RSFSR, rising in the N Urals and flowing generally N and W through coniferous forest and tundra, entering the Gulf of Pechora on the Barents Sea by a delta. When ice-free (June–Sept.) it carries cargoes of timber, coal, furs, fish.

**Peckham** England. District formerly in the metropolitan borough of Camberwell, SE London; from 1965 in the Greater London borough of Southwark. Includes Peckham Rye Common and Park (113 acres).

**Pecos River** USA. River 740 m. long, rising in N New Mexico in the Sangre de Cristo Range, flowing generally SSE through New Mexico and Texas, and joining the Rio Grande. Important dams provide irrigation water for a large agricultural region.

**Pécs** (Ger. **Fünfkirchen**, 'Five Churches') Hungary. Capital of Baranya county in the S, on the S slopes of the Meczek Hills. Pop. (1968) 140,000. Industrial town in a coal-mining area. Manufactures clothing, leather goods, porcelain, tobacco products, soap, etc. Trade in wine. Has a magnificent 11th-cent. cathedral, rebuilt in the 19th cent. The university, founded 1367, lapsed in 1526, and was revived in 1921. Under Turkish rule 1543–1686.

**Peebles** Scotland. Royal burgh and county town of Peeblesshire, on the R. Tweed 21 m. S of Edinburgh. Pop. (1961) 5,545. Market town. Resort. Manufactures woollen goods. Has the remains of the 13th-cent. Cross Kirk, which was supposed to have contained a fragment of the Cross. Became a royal burgh 1367. Birthplace of William (1800–1883) and Robert Chambers (1802–71), the publishers.

**Peeblesshire (Tweeddale)** Scotland. Inland county in the Southern Uplands. Area 347 sq. m. Pop. (1961) 14,117. Mainly hilly, rising to 2,754 ft in Broad Law (S). Drained by the R. Tweed and its tributaries. Chief occupation sheep rearing. Woollen goods manufactured in the principal towns, Peebles and Innerleithen.

**Peel** England. Port and seaside resort on the W coast of the Isle of Man 10 m. WNW of Douglas. Pop. (1961) 2,487. Fishing. Remains of a 13th/14th-cent. cathedral. Just off shore, and connected with the mainland by causeway, is St Patrick's Isle, almost entirely occupied by the ruins of Peel Castle; here St Patrick is believed to have founded the first church on Man.

**Peenemünde** German Democratic Republic. Village in Rostock district, on the NW of Usedom island at the entrance to the Peene R. estuary from the Baltic Sea. Site of a research station for rockets and guided missiles in the 2nd World War, captured by Russian forces in 1945.

**Pegu** Burma. Ancient town on the Pegu R. 45 m. NE of Rangoon. Pop. 47,000. Manufactures pottery. The outstanding building is the Shwe-mawdaw pagoda, 324 ft high, and there is a large recumbent figure of Buddha. Founded in the 6th cent. Became capital of a united Burma in the early 16th cent. Destroyed in the mid 18th cent., but was rebuilt and became the capital of Pegu province.

**Pegu Yoma** Burma. Range of hills 250 m. long extending N–S parallel to and E of the lower Irrawaddy R. Generally below 1,000 ft, but rising to 4,985 ft in Mt Popa, an extinct volcano. Teak forests.

**Peipus, Lake** USSR. Lake between the Estonian SSR and RSFSR, consisting of two basins: L. Peipus proper (L. Chudskoye), the larger (N), and L. Pskov (S), connected by a strait 15 m. long. Total area 1,356 sq. m. Empties by the Narova

(Narva) R. into the Gulf of Finland. The shores are flat and marshy or sandy. Frozen Dec.–March.

**Pekalongan** Indonesia. Seaport in Central Java province, on the Java Sea 55 m. W. of Semarang. Pop. (1961) 102,380. In a district producing rice, sugar cane. Exports sugar.

**Pekin** USA. River port and industrial town in Illinois 9 m. S of Peoria. Pop. (1960) 28,146. Trade in grain, livestock. Manufactures food products, metal goods, etc.

**Peking (Peiping)** China. Capital of the republic (means 'northern capital'), in Hopei province 70 m. NW of Tientsin. Pop. (1958) 5,420,000. China's political and cultural centre. Seat of the People's University of China (founded 1912 by Sun Yat-sen) and Peking University (founded 1898). Also an important railway junction and airport. Printing and publishing, tanning, food processing. Manufactures machinery, machine tools, textiles, etc. Consists of the Inner or Tartar City (N) and the adjacent Outer or Chinese City (S), both walled, the former enclosing the Imperial City, which in turn contains the Purple or Forbidden City (now a museum). Within the Inner City are some of the most famous buildings of China, such as the Hall of Classics and the beautiful Temple of Confucius, as well as 7 artificial lakes and several imperial palaces. In the Outer City, which includes the commercial quarter, is the Temple of Heaven, standing in a large park.

Founded near the site of a much older city known as Chi, Peking rose to greatness when Kublai Khan made it his capital (1267). Known to the Mongols as Khanbalik (Cambaluc) and to the Chinese as Tatu, it was visited and described in all its magnificence by Marco Polo. In 1368 it was replaced by Nanking, but again became capital in 1421 and was renamed Peking. Remained capital of China under the Manchu dynasty (1644–1911) and then under the new republic until 1928, when it was renamed Peiping, the government being transferred by the Nationalists to Nanking. During the Sino-Japanese War it was occupied by the Japanese (1937–45). In 1949 it fell to the Chinese Communists, who made it capital of the new People's Republic of China under its old name of Peking.

**Pella** Greece. 1. *Nome* in Macedonia, bordering N on Yugoslavia. Area 1,082 sq. m. Pop. (1961) 133,128. Cap. Edessa.

Largely mountainous. Produces cotton, wheat, tobacco, etc.

**2.** Ancient town 7 m. ESE of the modern Giannitsa (Yiannitsa) and near the modern village of Pella. Capital of Macedonia under Philip II. Birthplace of Alexander the Great (356–323 B.C.).

**Peloponnese** (Gr. **Peloponnisos,** 'the Island of Pelops') Greece. Formerly Morea, probably from its resemblance in shape to a mulberry leaf. The S peninsula of the country, joined to central Greece by the Isthmus of Corinth. Area 8,354 sq. m. Pop. (1961) 1,092,822. Largely mountainous, with deeply indented S and E coasts. Vines, citrus fruits, and olives cultivated. Sheep and goats raised.

**Pelotas** Brazil. Seaport in Rio Grande do Sul state, on the São Gonçalo Canal near the entrance to the lagoon Lagôa dos Patos. Pop. 130,000. Exports meat products, wool, hides, etc. Meat packing, flour milling, tanning, etc. Manufactures soap, footwear, furniture.

**Pemba** Tanzania. Coral island in the Indian Ocean 25 m. NNE of Zanzibar. Area 380 sq. m. Pop. (1967) 164,243 (mainly Bantu; many Arabs). Cap. Chake Chake. Produces most of the world's cloves. Also exports copra. ⬦ *Zanzibar and Pemba.*

**Pembroke** Wales. Municipal borough in Pembrokeshire, on Milford Haven 9 m. W of Tenby. Pop. (1961) 12,737. Market town. Engineering etc. Dominated by the 11th-cent. castle. Near by are the remains of the 11th cent. Monkton Priory. A government dockyard was established in 1814 and closed in 1926, the new town that grew around it being called Pembroke Dock (1 m. NW); it was used as a naval base in the 2nd World War. Birthplace of Henry VII (1457–1509).

**Pembrokeshire** Wales. County in the extreme SW on St George's Channel and the Bristol Channel. Area 614 sq. m. Pop. (1961) 93,980. County town Haverfordwest. Hilly in the NE, rising to 1,760 ft in Mynydd Prescelly. In the N drained by the R. Teifi. Inlets in its rugged coast include St Brides Bay and Milford Haven. Stock rearing, agriculture, and fishing are important occupations; some coal mined. Chief towns Haverfordwest, Pembroke, Tenby; Fishguard and Milford Haven are ports. Popular tourist area. An early centre of Celtic Christianity and was known to the Welsh as Dyfed.

**Penang** Malaysia. State in Malaya (W Malaysia) consisting of the island of Penang, off the NW coast in the Strait of Malacca, and a mainland strip formerly known as Province Wellesley. Area 398 sq. m. Pop. (1967) 752,059. Largely forested and rising to 2,700 ft, the island has rubber and coconut plantations on its lower ground. On the island is the capital, officially George Town but always known as Penang, the chief seaport of N Malaya. Formerly one of the Straits Settlements; joined the Federation of Malaya 1948.

**Penarth** Wales. Urban district in SE Glamorganshire, 3 m. S of Cardiff on the Bristol Channel at the mouth of the R. Taff. Pop. (1961) 20,897. Seaside resort. Port.

**Pendlebury** ⬦ *Swinton and Pendlebury.*

**Penge** England. Former urban district in NW Kent 3 m. W of Bromley; from 1965 part of the Greater London borough of Bromley. Pop. (1961) 25,726. Mainly residential; a dormitory suburb of SE London. Manufactures electrical equipment etc. Site of the Crystal Palace (1854) until its destruction by fire (1936). Now site of the Crystal Palace National Recreation Centre.

**Penistone** England. Urban district in the W Riding of Yorkshire, on the R. Don 12 m. NW of Sheffield. Pop. (1961) 7,071. Steel mills.

**Penmaenmawr** Wales. Urban district in Caernarvonshire, on Conway Bay 6 m. SW of Llandudno. Pop. (1961) 3,754. Seaside resort. At the foot of Penmaenmawr headland (1,500 ft) on which stood the ancient British fortress of Dinas Penmaen.

**Pennine Range (Pennines, Pennine Chain)** England. System of hills extending from the Cheviot Hills in the N to the valley of the R. Trent in the S, being separated from the former by the Tyne Gap. Forms the watershed of the main rivers of N England, and is sometimes termed 'the backbone of England'. Separated from the mountains of the Lake District by the Eden and Lune rivers, is cut by the Yorkshire dales and farther S by the Aire Gap, and ends in the S with the Peak District of Derbyshire. Highest peak is Cross Fell (2,930 ft), in the loftier N section; other heights are Mickle Fell (2,591 ft), Whernside (2,419 ft), Ingleborough (2,373 ft); in the lower S part is The Peak (2,088 ft). Moorland and rough pasture, where sheep are grazed, occupy most of the upper region, and the wild scenery here, the picturesque dales, the limestone caves, and underground streams attract many tourists. Reservoirs in the upland valleys provide a water supply for industrial areas on both sides of the Pennines. A 250-m. footpath along the Pennines, the Pennine Way, was opened in 1965; it extends from Edale (Derbyshire) to Kirk Yetholm (Roxburghshire), and passes through three National Parks, the Peak District, the Yorkshire Dales, and Northumberland.

Pennsylvania USA. State in the NE, bordered on the NW by L. Erie. Area 45,333 sq. m. Pop. (1970) 11,663,301. Cap. Harrisburg. One of the original 13 states and the second to ratify the constitution (1787); popularly known as the 'Keystone' state (from its originally central position). Almost entirely within the Appalachian Mountains system; contains the Allegheny Plateau and parts of the Allegheny Mountains, including the highest point, Mt Davis (3,213 ft). Principal rivers the Delaware (on the E boundary), the Susquehanna, and the Ohio (formed by the union of the Allegheny and the Monongahela, in the W). Climate humid continental. Annual rainfall 35–50 ins. Extensive forests yield a variety of hardwoods. Main crop hay; vegetables and fruit important. Second in mineral wealth only to Texas; esp. rich in coal, both anthracite (of which it is the main US source) and bituminous coal. Natural gas and petroleum also obtained. Second in value of manufactures only to New York; the great iron and steel industry centred on Pittsburgh produces 30 per cent of the total US steel output. Philadelphia, the largest city and 4th largest in the USA, is a great textile centre. Other important industrial towns are Erie, Scranton, Allentown. Originally settled by the Swedes (1643), who were dispossessed by the Dutch (1655). William Penn received a grant of land, which included most of the present state, in 1681; he named it Pennsylvania (Penn's woods).

Penrhyn Island ◊ Cook Islands.

Penrith England. Urban district in Cumberland 17 m. SSE of Carlisle. Pop. (1961) 10,931. Tourist centre for the lake District. Brewing, tanning, engineering. Has a ruined 14th-cent. castle. In St Andrew's churchyard are two monuments probably dating from the 10th cent., 'Giant's Grave' and 'Giant's Thumb'. Just NE is Penrith Beacon (937 ft) and 5 m. SW is Ullswater.

Penryn England. Municipal borough in Cornwall, at the head of the R. Penryn estuary 2 m. NW of Falmouth. Pop. (1961) 4,448. Market town. Port. A centre of the granite-quarrying industry.

Pensacola USA. Seaport and naval air base in NW Florida 53 m. ESE of Mobile (Alabama). Pop. (1960) 56,752. Fishing, fish canning. Manufactures furniture, paper, etc. First settled (1559) by the Spaniards. Changed hands several times between Spain, France, and Britain. Finally acquired by the USA 1821.

Penticton Canada. Town in S British Columbia, on the Okanagan R. near the S end of Okanagan Lake. Pop. (1966) 15,330. Commercial centre in a fruit-growing region. Fruit packing and canning etc.

Pentland Firth Scotland. Channel 20 m. long and up to 8 m. wide between Caithness on the mainland and the Orkney Is. Notorious for its rough seas. Contains the islands of Stroma, Swona, and the Pentland Skerries.

Pentland Hills Scotland. Range extending 16 m. SW from just S of Edinburgh. Highest point Scald Law (1,898 ft).

Pentonville England. District in the London borough of Islington where Lenin lodged whilst in London. The famous Pentonville prison is in Caledonian Road. Birthplace of John Stuart Mill (1807–73).

Penza USSR. Capital of the Penza region, RSFSR, on the Sura R. 130 m. NNW of Saratov. Pop. (1970) 374,000. Railway junction. Industrial centre. Sawmilling, engineering. Manufactures watches, paper, matches, cement, etc. Trade in grain, timber. Founded in the 17th cent.

Penzance England. Municipal borough in SW Cornwall, on Mount's Bay. Pop. (1961) 19,433. Fishing port. Resort. Sends locally-grown early vegetables and flowers (inc. those from the Scilly Is.) by rail to London and elsewhere. Birthplace of Sir Humphrey Davy (1778–1829).

Peoria USA. Town in Illinois, on the Illinois R. where it widens to form L. Peoria, 63 m. N of Springfield. Pop. (1960) 103,162. Manufactures agricultural machinery, food products, washing machines, radio equipment, etc. Trade in grain, livestock. Seat of the Bradley University (1897).

Pepel ◊ Freetown.

Perak Malaysia. The most populous state in Malaya (W Malaysia); borders N on Thailand and W on the Strait of Malacca. Area 7,980 sq. m. Pop. (1967) 1,636,605. Cap. Taiping. Consists mainly of the basin of the Perak R. Rises to over 7,000 ft in the interior. The chief tin-mining state. Also produces rice, rubber, copra. Chief towns Taiping, Ipoh.

**Pereira** Colombia. Town in Caldas department, 25 m. SW of Manizales at a height of 4,800 ft. Pop. 184,000. Commercial centre. Trade chiefly in coffee and cattle. Coffee processing, brewing. Manufactures clothing etc. Founded 1863.

**Perekop Isthmus** USSR. Isthmus, 4 m. wide at its narrowest, joining the Crimea to the mainland of the Ukrainian SSR. Scene of heavy fighting between German and Russian forces in the 2nd World War. On it is situated a strategically important village of the same name.

**Pereyaslavl-Ryazanski** ◊ *Ryazan*.

**Pergamum (Pergamus).** Ancient Greek city in W Asia Minor, now occupied by the modern town of Bergama, 50 m. N of Izmir, in Turkey. Among the ruins excavated here were the great altar of Zeus, the temple of Athena, and the famous library. Attained its highest splendour in the 3rd and 2nd cent. B.C. as capital of the kingdom of Pergamum, which was bequeathed to the Romans in 133 B.C. by Attalus III and part of which became the Roman province of Asia.

**Périgord** France. Region in the old Guienne province, now mostly in the Dordogne department, consisting of dry limestone plateaux with the fertile valleys of the Dordogne and Isle rivers. Famous for truffles. Has yielded many important prehistoric remains.

**Périgueux** France. Prefecture of the Dordogne department, on the Isle R. 50 m. SW of Limoges. Pop. (1968) 40,091. Famous for *pâté de foie gras* and truffles. Trade in grain, wine, poultry, etc. Manufactures hardware, cutlery, chemicals, etc. Besides the modern town there are two old districts – the old Roman town and the medieval town known as Le Puy-St Front. In the last-named are the 12th-cent. cathedral of St Front, restored in the 19th cent., and the remains of a 6th-cent. basilica. In the Roman town is the 11th/12th-cent. Church of St Étienne, once the cathedral. Among the Roman remains are the amphitheatre and the tower of Vésone, the latter probably part of a temple in the Roman town (Vesunna). Taken by the English 1356; returned to France in the reign of Charles V.

**Perim.** Island in the strait of Bab-el-Mandeb off the SW coast of the Arabian peninsula. Area 5 sq. m. Pop. 1,700. Rocky, barren, and crescent-shaped. Formerly important as a coaling station (1883–1936), but its operations were transferred to Aden. Occupied by the British in 1799, abandoned, then reoccupied in 1857, and became part of Aden. From 1963 it was administered by the Commissioner for Kamaran and Perim. In 1967 it became part of the republic of S Yemen.

**Perlis** Malaysia. The smallest and most north-westerly state of Malaya (W Malaysia), bounded on the NE and NW by Thailand. Area 310 sq. m. Pop. (1967) 117,606 (80 per cent Malay). Cap. Kangar. Main products rice, rubber, tin. Transferred by Siam to Britain 1909. Became one of the non-federated Malay States. Joined the Federation of Malaya 1948.

**Perm** USSR. Formerly (1940–62) Molotov. Capital of the Perm region, RSFSR, on the Kama R. Pop. (1970) 850,000. Important railway junction. River port. Railway engineering, sawmilling, tanning. Manufactures agricultural equipment, excavators, aircraft and tractor parts, fertilizers, paper, matches, etc. University (1916). The town developed industrially with the building of copper works (1723) but its greatest expansion came in the 20th cent., after the 1st World War and again after the 2nd World War. In geology the Permian System of rocks was named after the Perm region because of their great development there.

**Pernambuco** Brazil. State in the NE with a narrow humid coastal zone, a drier intermediate zone, and a dry interior (the *sertão*) which suffers periodic droughts. Area 37,458 sq. m. Pop. (1960) 4,136,900. Cap. Recife. Produces sugar, tropical fruits, cotton.

**Pernik** Bulgaria. Formerly (1949–62) Dimitrovo. Town in Sofia province on the Struma R. 17 m. WSW of Sofia. Pop. (1965) 75,884. Coalmining and industrial centre. Manufactures iron and steel, cement, glass, etc. Engineering. Expanded rapidly after the 2nd World War.

**Perpignan** France. Prefecture of the Pyrénées-Orientales department, near the Gulf of Lions and the Spanish border, on the Têt R. and on the Paris–Barcelona railway. Pop. (1968) 104,095. Tourist and commercial centre. Trade in wine, fruits, olives. Cathedral (14th/16th-cent.); large citadel enclosing the castle (13th cent.). Founded in the 10th cent. Capital of the kingdom of Majorca (1278–1344) and in the 17th cent. of the province of Roussillon.

**Persepolis** Iran. Ancient city of Persia 30 m. N E of the modern Shiraz. Capital of the Persian Empire, founded by Darius. The ruins of many of its great buildings still stand on a large terrace approached by a remarkable flight of steps. Among the remains are the hall of the 'Hundred Columns' and the palaces of Darius and his successors, built in marble from the neighbouring mountains. In the mountains themselves are the tombs of ancient Persian kings, inc. Darius. Persepolis was attacked and partly destroyed by Alexander the Great (330 B.C.) and thereafter declined. Extensively excavated in the 1930s and is today a tourist attraction.

**Pershore** England. Market town in Worcestershire, on the R. Avon 8 m. S E of Worcester. Pop. (rural district, 1961) 17,599. Centre of a soft-fruit-growing (chiefly plums) and market-gardening area.

**Persia** ◊ *Iran.*

**Persian Gulf.** Extensive but shallow arm of the Arabian Sea between Iran and Arabia, linked with the Arabian Sea by the Strait of Hormuz and the Gulf of Oman. Area 90,000 sq. m. Notorious for its extremely hot, humid summers. The only significant river that it receives is the Shatt-al-Arab, which brings it the waters of the Tigris, Euphrates, and Karun. Its once-famous pearl fisheries are now in decline, and it is far more important for the vast oilfields around its shores.

**Perth** Australia. Capital of Western Australia, on the N bank of the Swan R. 12 m. from the mouth of a shallow tidal estuary. Pop. (1966) 499,494. Administrative, commercial, and industrial centre serving a vast territory, from its immediate agricultural hinterland to the huge N W cattle stations and inland goldfields. Manufactures textiles, clothing, furniture, cars, fertilizers, flour, cement. Seat of the University of Western Australia (1911). The city and its suburbs are well spaced, with numerous parks, about a wide stretch of the river. Its port, Fremantle, at the river mouth, and Kwinana, to the S, are expanding industrial centres. The water supply comes chiefly from the Canning Dam and Mundaring Reservoir on short rivers to the W and S W.

Terminus of the Trans-Australian railway. Important airport. Founded 1829.

**Perth** Scotland. Formerly St Johnstoun. Royal burgh and county town of Perthshire, on the R. Tay. Pop. (1961) 41,199. Important dyeing industry. Whisky distilling. Manufactures textiles, carpets. One of its few architectural links with the past is the 15th-cent. Church of St John, where John Knox preached his famous sermon against idolatry (1559). Capital of Scotland from the early 12th cent. till 1437, when James I was assassinated here.

**Perth Amboy** U S A. Seaport and industrial town in New Jersey, at the mouth of the Raritan R. 17 m. S S W of Newark. Pop. (1960) 38,007. Copper smelting, oil refining. Manufactures metal products, chemicals, plastics, etc. Founded 1683. Grew as a coal-exporting centre in the late 19th cent.

**Perthshire** Scotland. County in central Scotland. Area 2,493 sq. m. Pop. (1961) 127,018. Mainly mountainous, much of its area being within the Grampians. Highest peaks include Ben Lawers (3,984 ft), Ben More (3,843 ft), and Schiehallion (3,547 ft); in the S E are the Ochil and Sidlaw Hills. Drained by the R. Tay, with its tributaries the Earn and the Tummel, and the R. Forth, along the S boundary. Endowed with many beautiful glens and lochs (Tay, Rannoch, Earn, Katrine, etc.); a favourite tourist area, the Trossachs being particularly well known. Resorts include Crieff, Dunblane, Pitlochry, Callander; other towns Perth, Blairgowrie. There are extensive deer forests, many sheep are grazed, and on the fertile lowlands of Strathmore, Strathearn, and the Carse of Gowrie oats, root crops, and fruit (esp. raspberries) are cultivated. Hydroelectric power is developed.

**Peru.** *Republic in the W of S America. Area 496,093 sq. m. Pop. (1961) 10,016,322 (excluding nomadic jungle Indians). Cap. Lima. Rel. mainly Roman Catholic. Languages Spanish; Quechua, Aymará (Indian).

Bounded on the N by Ecuador and Colombia, E by Brazil, S E by Bolivia and S by Chile; has a Pacific seaboard about 1,400 m. long on the W. A country of great contrasts in relief, climate, vegetation, and population. Much of it is unsuitable for agriculture and transport between regions is difficult. Mineral resources are considerable. The Indians who make up nearly half the population have a low standard of living either by way of subsistence farming or in the mining industry. The majority of the prosperous classes live in Lima. Peru's economy and international trade have been amongst the most stable in Latin America.

TOPOGRAPHY, CLIMATE. Third in size of the S American countries (larger than the Iberian peninsula). Consists of a dry coastal plain which quickly rises to the Sierra (average height 13,000 ft), covering about half the area of the country, beyond which is the *montaña*, the forested part of the Andes, an area of potential riches which has scarcely been tapped. The narrow coastal plain, 1,400 m. long and about one ninth of the total area of Peru, holds 30 per cent of the population: it is desert, being shielded from the rain-bearing Trade Winds by the Andes. The cold Peruvian sea current causes low cloud and mist but scarcely any rain. Few of the short streams are perennial, but there are productive irrigated regions at intervals. East of this strip rise the Andean Cordilleras, where the rivers traverse broad valleys at 10,000–15,000 ft and plunge through great canyons to the E lowlands. The W Cordillera is the highest, with Huascarán rising to 22,205 ft. In the S are volcanic peaks such as the perfect snow-capped cone of El Misti (19,166 ft). In this region the boundary with Bolivia crosses the deep freshwater L. Titicaca, at a height of 12,506 ft. There are great climatic differences between the high, bleak Andean plateaux, the milder sheltered basins, and the deep tropical valleys farther E. In the highlands the rain falls mainly Oct.–April, annual amounts varying between 20 and 50 ins., with the E generally wetter than the W. Dense forests up to 11,000 ft make journeys through the E Andean slopes, the *montaña*, difficult. A great river system drains N through the lowland forests, the Apurimac and Urubamba joining at about 11° S to form the Ucayali, which joins the Marañón near 4° S to form the Amazon in the NE.

RESOURCES, PEOPLE, *etc.* Some three fifths of the population live in the highlands; almost half are Indians who speak Quechua or Aymará, one third *mestizo*, and about one tenth whites. The political and commercial life of the country is dominated by those of European descent; for most of the highland Indians life is primitive and has changed little for centuries. Their staple foods are maize and potatoes and they chew coca leaves to alleviate some of their hardships. Many migrate to the coast, and as a result the suburbs of Lima are overcrowded. Wool of the sheep, alpaca, and llama flocks is sent to highland markets. Arequipa and Lima have textile industries. Cotton and sugar-cane are important crops, being grown mainly on irrigated land; rice and coffee are also produced. There has been a great expansion in the fishing industry in recent years, largely for the production of fish-meal; on offshore islands guano has accumulated in the dry climate from multitudes of seabirds: this is now worked by a government monopoly and the birds are protected. A variety of minerals is obtained in the highlands: Cerro de Pasco is important for copper, lead, zinc, and silver; bismuth, gold, and vanadium are also mined. Coal is sent to the Oroya smelting centre; petroleum is found in the far N, near the coast, and in the E *montaña*. Coal and iron deposits in the Santa R. valley supply the steelworks of Chimbote (opened 1958). Callao is the leading seaport, the main exports being copper, cotton, sugar, and fish products; Iquitos, a port on the upper Amazon, is the principal outlet to the E.

HISTORY. The coastal area of Peru produced some of the earliest cultures of S America, and from the end of the 11th cent. the Inca civilization was based on Cuzco. This planned society controlled extensive territories with the help of a common religion, centrally organized production and consumption, and an efficient road system. Pizarro reached Peru in 1532 and seized Cuzco, executing the Inca monarch Atahualpa at Cajamarca; in 1535 Lima was founded and with Callao became a focal point for Spanish settlement and political power. Wheat and barley were added to maize and potatoes as highland crops; horses, sheep, and cattle were introduced. Huge estates were granted to individual Spaniards, to be worked by Indian labour; other Indians worked communally, paying rent to Spanish landlords, and others provided forced labour in the mines. The hard conditions and diseases greatly reduced the population; meanwhile, the lowland irrigated areas suffered neglect. In 1820 San Martín landed in S Peru and in the following year proclaimed Peruvian independence, but much of the country remained under Spanish control until Bolívar and Sucre won decisive battles (1824). From

1864 to 1879 Peru was nominally at war with Spain. In the War of the Pacific (1879–83) Peru and Bolivia were defeated by Chile, losing the S nitrate fields, but Peru regained the S oasis of Tacna in 1929. Boundary disputes with Colombia and Ecuador were settled by the League of Nations (1934 and 1942 respectively). In 1962 torrential rains on Huascarán started an avalanche of snow and rocks which killed 3,000–4,000 people.

**Perugia** Italy. Ancient Perusia. Capital of Perugia province, in Umbria, E of L. Trasimeno on a group of hills above the Tiber valley. Pop. (1968) 123,280. Manufactures chocolate, woollen goods, furniture, etc. Trade in grain, wine, olive oil. Gothic cathedral (14th/15th-cent.); the Palazzo Comunale, with its valuable art collection, dates from the 13th cent. University (1276). Was an important Etruscan city and has Etruscan, Roman, and medieval remains. Taken by the Romans 40 B.C. Later ruled by the Popes (9th cent. A.D.). Became the centre of the Umbrian school of painting, whose outstanding figure was Perugino (1450–1524), born near by.

**Perugia, Lake** ◊ *Trasimeno, Lake.*

**Pesaro** Italy. Capital of Pesaro e Urbino province, in The Marches, 22 m. SE of Rimini on the Adriatic coast. Pop. (1961) 65,973. Port. Seaside resort. Manufactures majolica, agricultural machinery, soap, etc. Has a 15th-cent. ducal palace and fortress, and a school of music endowed by Rossini (1792–1865), who was born here.

**Pescadores.** Group of about 60 islands off the W coast of Formosa (Taiwan), the largest and most important being Penghu. Area 49 sq. m. Pop. 86,000. Main occupations fishing, fish processing. With Formosa they were ceded to Japan by China 1895. Since the 2nd World War they have been controlled by Chiang Kaishek and the Chinese Nationalist Government on Formosa.

**Pescara** Italy. Capital of Pescara province in Abruzzi e Molise, at the mouth of the Pescara R. on the Adriatic coast. Pop. (1968) 110,648. Port. Seaside resort. Manufactures furniture, soap, glass, textiles, etc. Birthplace of Gabriele d'Annunzio (1863–1938).

**Peshawar** Pakistan. Capital of the Peshawar Division, W Pakistan, 230 m. NW of Lahore. Pop. (1961) 213,000. Important commercial centre, particularly for trade between Pakistan and Afghanistan, being 11 m. E of Jamrud, at the entrance to the Khyber Pass. Rice milling. Handicraft manufacture of textiles, pottery, leather goods, copperware, etc. University (1950).

**Petah Tiqva (Petah Tikva)** Israel. Town on the Plain of Sharon 7 m. E of Tel Aviv. Pop. (1968) 73,500. Industrial centre. Manufactures textiles, chemicals, furniture, etc.

**Peterborough** Canada. Industrial town and railway junction in S Ontario, on the Otonabee R. 70 m. NE of Toronto. Pop. (1966) 56,177. Manufactures clocks and watches, knitwear, electrical machinery, dairy equipment, hardware, etc. Canada's largest cereal and flour mill.

**Peterborough** England. Originally Medehamstede. Municipal borough and county town of the Soke of Peterborough, in Northamptonshire, on the R. Nene 36 m. NE of Northampton. Pop. (1961) 62,031. Railway junction and industrial centre at the W edge of the Fens. Engineering, beet-sugar refining, brickmaking (at Fletton). Manufactures textiles. The cathedral, the third church on the same site, was begun in the 12th cent. and has been much restored; it contains the tomb of Catherine of Aragon, and Mary Queen of Scots was buried here (1587–1612). Also has a 15th-cent. church (St John's) and a market hal dating from 1671. A Saxon village before the abbey was founded here (655).

**Peterborough, Soke of** England. Administrative county consisting of the borough of Peterborough and adjacent land. Area 84 sq. m. Pop. (1961) 74,442. A flat, low-lying region between the Welland and the Nene rivers, part of the Bedford Level. The former area of jurisdiction ('soke') of the Benedictine abbey founded here in 655.

**Peterhead** Scotland. Small burgh in Aberdeenshire, on the North Sea 28 m. NNE of Aberdeen. Pop. (1961) 12,497. Formerly engaged in whaling; now a herring-fishing port. Fish canning and curing, engineering. Also granite quarrying and dressing. Founded 1587. Landing place of the Old Pretender (1715).

**Peterlee** England. Town in Co. Durham 10 m. E of Durham City, founded in 1948 in the rural district of ◊ *Easington.* Pop. (1968) 21,720. In a coalmining district. Planned pop. 30,000.

**Petersburg** USA. Industrial town in Virginia, on the Appomattox R. 23 m. S of Richmond. Pop. (1960) 36,750.

Manufactures tobacco products, luggage, textiles, optical goods, etc. Withstood a long siege by Federal troops (1864–5) in the American Civil War.

**Petersfield** England. Urban district in Hampshire 15 m. NNE of Portsmouth. Pop. (1961) 7,379. Market town. Once engaged in the woollen industry. Buriton, an early home of Edward Gibbon, is 2 m. SSE.

**Petra** Jordan. Ancient city in a basin on the E side of the Wadi el Araba, in the SW. Capital of the Nabataeans and an important centre of caravan trade. Flourished from the 1st cent. B.C. to the 3rd cent. A.D. Annexed to the Roman Empire A.D. 106. Declined as Palmyra grew in importance, and was forgotten until its ruins were discovered by Burckhardt (1812). These ruins include temples, houses, and a great theatre, carved out of the multi-coloured, largely red rock.

**Petrograd** ◊ *Leningrad.*

**Petropavlovsk** USSR. Capital of the N Kazakhstan region, Kazakh SSR, on the Ishim R. and at the junction of the Trans-Siberian Railway and the Transkazakh Trunk Line. Pop. (1970) 173,000. Commercial centre. Trade in grain, furs, textiles, etc. Meat packing, flour milling, tanning.

**Petropavlovsk (Petropavlovsk-Kamchatski)** USSR. Capital of the Kamchatka region, Khabarovsk Territory, RSFSR, on the SE coast of the Kamchatka peninsula. Pop. (1970) 154,000. Naval base and chief seaport of the peninsula. Shipbuilding, fish canning, sawmilling, etc.

**Petrópolis** Brazil. Town in Rio de Janeiro state 27 m. NNE of Rio de Janeiro at a height of 2,700 ft. Pop. 120,000. Fashionable summer resort with picturesque mountain scenery. Brewing. Manufactures textiles, chemicals. Has a cathedral in Gothic style and an Imperial Museum which has many relics of the Brazilian emperors Dom Pedro I and Dom Pedro II; it was named after the latter.

**Petrovsk** ◊ *Makhachkala.*

**Petrozavodsk** USSR. Formerly Kalininsk (1930s). Capital of the Karelian ASSR, RSFSR, on the W shore of L. Onega 185 m. NE of Leningrad. Pop. (1970) 185,000. Industrial centre. Sawmilling, mica processing. Manufactures machinery, furniture, cement, skis, etc. University (1940). Named Petrozavodsk ('Peter's Works') in 1777 after the ironworks founded here (1703) by Peter the Great.

**Pevensey** England. Village in E Sussex 4 m. NE of Eastbourne. Landing place of William the Conqueror (1066). Once a port and member of the Cinque Port of Hastings, but declined on the recession of the sea. The ruined, mainly 13th-cent. castle stands within an outer wall of Roman origin.

**Pforzheim** Federal German Republic. Town in Baden-Württemberg, on the Enz R. at its confluence with the Nagold R., at the N edge of the Black Forest. Pop. (1963) 86,100. Leading centre of the jewellery industry. Also manufactures clocks and watches, precision instruments, machinery, tools, etc. Training school for precious-metal working.

**Phenix City** USA. Residential and industrial town in E Alabama, on the Chattahoochee R. opposite Columbus (Georgia), of which it is a suburb. Pop. (1960) 27,630. Manufactures wood products etc.

**Phet Buri** Thailand. Capital of Phet Buri province, 70 m. SW of Bangkok. Pop. 53,000. Remains of ancient Brahman and Buddhist temples in the neighbourhood.

**Philadelphia** USA. Largest city in Pennsylvania, and 4th largest in the USA, on the Delaware R. at the confluence with the Schuylkill R. Pop. (1970) 1,926,529. A leading seaport, second in importance to New York, with 37 m. of waterfront along the two rivers. Exports petroleum products, coal, grain, timber, flour, manufactured goods. Imports mainly raw materials. Has a large US Navy yard, a mint, and arsenals. Many industries. Oil refining, shipbuilding, metal working, printing and publishing. Manufactures railway carriages, buses, electrical appliances, machinery, textiles, clothing, leather goods, paper. Laid out in gridiron pattern: the great N–S and E–W axes are Broad Street and Market Street. A famous thoroughfare is the wide tree-lined Benjamin Franklin Parkway; halfway along this is Logan Circle, the 'Piccadilly Circus' of Philadelphia. Many famous and historic buildings. The City Hall, topped by a statue of William Penn, rises to 548 ft; its predecessor, the old City Hall (1791), still stands. The most famous building, however, is Independence Hall (1732–41), the old State House of Pennsylvania, where the Declaration of Independence was adopted and signed (1776) and the US constitution was drawn up. Seat of the

University of Pennsylvania (1740), the Temple University (1884), and the Drexel Institute of Technology (1891).

Founded (1682) by William Penn, who named his city Philadelphia ('City of Brotherly Love') to emphasize the religious and political tolerance he intended to promote. As many European Protestant religious sects were suffering persecution, settlers were attracted to the new city; it rapidly became the leading commercial and cultural centre in the American colonies, and was the federal capital 1790–1800. The Quaker influence of the founder is still in evidence, as is also the somewhat conservative and sedate outlook of the inhabitants. A further characteristic distinguishing Philadelphia from most other large American cities is the preponderance of houses as against apartments.

**Philae** United Arab Republic. Small island in the Nile, above the First Cataract. Celebrated for the ancient temples to Isis and other deities. Since the completion of the Aswan Dam, submerged each year except July–Oct. (when the sluices are open).

**Philippeville** ⋄ *Skikda*.

**Philippi** Greece. Ancient city in Macedonia 10 m. NW of the modern Kavalla. Here Brutus and Cassius were defeated by Octavius and Antony (42 B.C.), and St Paul first preached in Europe (A.D. 53); he addressed his Epistle to the Philippians to converts here.

**Philippines, Republic of the.** A republic of SE Asia. Area 115,707 sq. m. Pop. (1960) 27,087,685. Cap. Quezon City. Lang. English, Spanish, and many native languages. Rel. 83 per cent Roman Catholic, 10 per cent Philippine Independent Church.

A group of over 7,000 islands and islets of the Malay Archipelago, in the SW Pacific, the largest and most important being Luzon (N) and Mindanao (S), followed by Samar, Negros, Palawan, Panay, Mindoro, Leyte, Cebu, Bohol, and Masbate. Formosa lies to the N and Indonesia to the S. Entirely within the tropical zone, the islands have extensive areas of forests, but the economy depends chiefly on agriculture, the principal products being rice, Manila hemp (abacá), copra, sugar-cane, maize, tobacco. Divided for administrative purposes into 65 provinces.

TOPOGRAPHY, CLIMATE. The Philippine Is. are the upper portions of partly submerged mountain chains, mostly volcanic in origin but sometimes overlaid with coral. Ranges of mountains traverse the larger islands, and volcanoes are conspicuous features of the landscape; Mt Apo (9,690 ft), an active volcano in SE Mindanao, is the highest point in the Philippines. There are several lakes, including Laguna de Bay on Luzon and L. Lanao on Mindanao. The longest river is the Cagayan, 220 m. in length, on Luzon. The climate, which is hot and humid on the plains but cooler in the mountains, is determined mainly by the NE and SW monsoons, which bring abundant rainfall to the windward sides of the islands; in general, then, the year is divided into a rainy and a 'dry' season. Typhoons are most frequent in the N islands and earthquakes are common.

RESOURCES, PEOPLE, GOVERNMENT. About 44 per cent of the land area is covered with forests, which furnish constructional and cabinet hardwoods – a significant export, as well as rattans, bamboos, tan and dye barks, and dye woods. Rice and maize are the principal food crops, though more rice has to be imported; the leading cash crops are coconuts, from which copra, coconut oil and desiccated coconut are obtained, sugarcane and abacá, and these, along with certain minerals, inc. gold and silver, are the other main exports. Water buffaloes or carabaos are widely employed in the rice fields, and large numbers of pigs are raised. Most of the country's foreign trade is with the US. Manila, until 1948 the capital, is the largest city and chief seaport; other important towns are the near-by Quezon City, the new capital, Cebu, Davao, Basilan, and Iloilo.

The majority of the population, known as Filipinos, belong to the Malay racial group, but in places reveal an admixture of Chinese and Spanish blood; in the mountains there are still small numbers of aboriginal Negritos. Over 10 million people speak English, about ½ million Spanish, and about 70 native languages are also spoken; in 1946 Tagalog, a Malayan dialect, was made the official language. The head of government is the President, who is elected for 4 years, and the legislature consists of a Senate of 24 members and a House of Representatives of 104 members, elected by male and female adult literates – who number about 8½ million (1961).

HISTORY. The Philippine Is. were discovered (1521) by Magellan, who was killed here. From 1565 the Spaniards gradually conquered the islands, converting the people to Roman Catholicism, and ruled them almost continuously until 1898. Then, following the Spanish-American War, the Philippines were ceded to the USA; in 1934 they were granted commonwealth status and in 1946 complete independence. During the 2nd World War they were invaded by the Japanese (1941) and occupied till 1944.

**Philistia.** Ancient region in SW Palestine comprising fertile lowlands along the Mediterranean coast, inhabited in Old Testament times by Philistines, now in Israel. The chief towns, Gaza, Ashkelon, Ashdod, Ekron, and Gath, formed a confederacy. In its Greek form, Palaestina, it gave its name to Palestine.

**Phnom Penh** ◊ *Pnom Penh.*

**Phocis (Phokis, Fokis)** Greece. *Nome* in central Greece bordering on the Gulf of Corinth (S). Area 806 sq. m. Pop. (1961) 47,491. Cap. Amphissa (pop. 6,076). Mountainous. Main occupation stock rearing. Ancient Phocis (larger than the present *nome*) included Delphi, but the Phocians were defeated by Philip II of Macedon, and finally lost the sanctuary in the 4th cent. B.C.

**Phoenicia.** Ancient region of the E Mediterranean roughly constituting the coastlands of modern Syria and Lebanon and lying N of Mt Carmel. Its Semitic inhabitants, the Phoenicians, were organized in city states ruled by hereditary kings, and by the 13th cent. B.C. they had become the outstanding navigators and merchants of the Mediterranean area. Their chief cities were Tyre and Sidon (Saida), and others included the present-day Beirut and Acre. They established colonies on many Mediterranean islands, e.g. Cyprus, Rhodes, Crete, Sicily, as well as in Spain and N Africa, e.g. Carthage, traded as far afield as the British Isles and the Baltic, and may even have sailed their small ships round the coasts of Africa. They became famous for their glassware and metal goods and for the Tyrian purple with which they dyed cloth, but probably their greatest legacy to mankind was their development of an alphabet. The Phoenicians were long independent, and survived the attacks of Assyrians and Babylonians, but in the 6th cent. B.C. they were incorporated into the Persian empire. From that time until they finally came under Roman rule (64 B.C.) the cities retained much of their commercial importance, but the Phoenician civilization was gradually waning and becoming superseded by that of Greece.

**Phoenix** USA. State capital and largest city in Arizona, on the Salt R. at a height of 1,090 ft. Pop. (1970) 580,275. Commercial centre for an irrigated agricultural region producing citrus fruits, cotton, alfalfa, and other crops. Flour milling, brewing, fruit canning. Manufactures steel and aluminium products, leather goods; Indian handicrafts. The warm dry climate has promoted the tourist industry. Within the city limits is La Ciudad, a collection of prehistoric Indian pit-dwellings excavated in 1927.

**Phoenix Islands** S Pacific Ocean. Group of 8 coral islands. Area 11 sq. m. Pop. (1963) 1,014. The two most important, Canton and Enderbury, were placed under joint Anglo-American control (1939); the remainder belong to the Gilbert and Ellice Is. colony. Canton, formerly an important trans-Pacific airline base, is now, owing to use of long-range jet aircraft, no longer on scheduled flights. The islands export copra.

**Phrygia.** Ancient region in central Asia Minor, now Turkey, inhabited by people speaking an Indo-European language and probably coming from Thrace or Macedonia before 1200 B.C. Flourished in the 8th cent. B.C. under kings named alternately Gordius and Midas. Later superseded by Lydia.

**Phthiotis (Fthiotis)** Greece. *Nome* in central Greece bordering E on the Gulf of Euboea. Area 1,669 sq. m. Pop. (1961) 159,373. Cap. Lamia. Mainly mountainous. Wheat and cotton cultivated in the Sperkhios R. valley.

**Phuket (Puket)** Thailand. Seaport on Phuket island, off the W coast of the Malay peninsula 440 m. SSW of Bangkok. Pop. 26,000. Exports tin ore, of which the island has rich deposits, and rubber.

**Piacenza** Italy. Ancient Placentia. Capital of Piacenza province, in Emilia-Romagna, on the Po R. 40 m. SE of Milan. Pop. (1968) 101,607. Manufactures macaroni, agricultural machinery, leather goods, etc. Has a 12th/13th-cent. cathedral (restored) with a campanile 223 ft high, the 11th-cent. San Antonio church, and the massive Palazzo Farnese, begun 1558 and never completed. One of the first Roman colonies in N Italy (218 B.C.), and the Roman influence may be seen in the rectangular pattern of streets in the centre, through which passes the Aemilian Way. United with Parma to form the duchy of Parma and Piacenza 1545.

**Piatra Neamț** Rumania. Capital of Neamț district; resort in a wooded part of Moldavia, on the Bistrița R. Pop. (1968) 48,103. Woodworking, food processing. Manufactures textiles, pharmaceutical products, etc. Trade in wine, timber.

**Piauí** Brazil. State in the NE with a very short coastline, lying E and S of the Parnaíba R., rising inland gradually to a plateau with open grasslands. Area 96,261 sq. m. Pop. (1960) 1,263,368. Cap. Teresina. Stock raising important. Cotton and tobacco cultivated. Exports babassu nuts, carnauba wax, oiticica oil, etc.

**Piave River** Italy. River 140 m. long, rising in the Carnic Alps and flowing generally SW past Belluno, then SE to the Adriatic 20 m. ENE of Venice. Scene of much fighting in the 1st World War.

**Pica** ◊ *Iquique.*

**Picardy** France. Region and former province in the N, now forming the Somme and parts of the Pas-de-Calais, Aisne, and Oise departments. Fertile agricultural region. Textile industry, centred on Amiens. Annexed to France 1477. Scene of heavy fighting in the 1st World War.

**Pichincha** Ecuador. Volcano (15,672 ft) 6 m. NW of Quito, with a large crater. In the battle of Pichincha fought near by (1822) Sucre defeated the Spanish and won independence for Ecuador.

**Pickering** England. Urban district in the N Riding of Yorkshire 23 m. NE of York. Pop. (1961) 4,193. Market town. Tourist centre for the Yorkshire moors. Has a ruined mainly 14th-cent. castle where Richard II was imprisoned.

**Pico** ◊ *Azores.*

**Picton** ◊ *Marlborough* ( New Zealand).

**Piedmont** (Italian **Piemonte**) Italy. Region in the N, bounded on the NE by Switzerland and on the W by France, consisting of the upper basin of the Po R. Area 9,817 sq. m. Pop. (1961) 3,889,962. Mainly agricultural. Industries are centred largely on Turin, the chief city. From early in the 11th cent. it was associated with the house of Savoy.

**Piedras Negras** Mexico. Town in Coahuila state, on the Rio Grande and on the US frontier opposite Eagle Pass (Texas). Pop. 28,000. Commercial centre in an agricultural and stock-rearing region, on a busy route from the USA into Mexico. Coal, silver, zinc, and copper mined in the neighbourhood.

**Piemonte** ◊ *Piedmont.*

**Pieria** Greece. *Nome* in Macedonia on the Aegean Sea. Area 593 sq. m. Pop. (1961) 97,505. Cap. Katerini. A narrow coastal plain; mountainous inland, with Mt Olympus (9,550 ft) in the S.

**Pierre** USA. State capital of S Dakota, on the E bank of the Missouri R. opposite Fort Pierre at a height of 1,440 ft. Pop. (1960) 10,088. Commercial centre for an agricultural region producing grain and livestock.

**Pietermaritzburg (Maritzburg)** S Africa. Capital of Natal province, 44 m. WNW of Durban at a height of 2,218 ft. Pop. (1967) 110,950 (45,350 whites, 33,350 Bantu, 26,350 Asians). Important railway centre amid fine mountain scenery. Manufactures wattle extract, furniture, footwear, metal goods, etc. Anglican and Roman Catholic cathedrals, the Voortrekker and Natal museums, and a section of the University of Natal. Sometimes called the 'City of Flowers' because of its many beautiful gardens. Founded (1838) by Voortrekker Boers; named after their leaders Pieter Retief and Gert Maritz.

**Pietersburg** S Africa. Town in the N of the Transvaal 155 m. NE of Pretoria, at a height of 4,270 ft. Pop. (1968) 36,274. Mining centre (gold, asbestos), in a district also important for dairy farming and the cultivation of fruit, cotton, tobacco.

**Pikes Peak** USA. Mountain (14,110 ft) in central Colorado, in the Front Range of the Rocky Mountains. Named after Zebulon Pike, who discovered it (1806). Somewhat lower than many other peaks in Colorado, but well known chiefly because of its isolated position; it commands extensive views from the summit. A popular tourist attraction. Ascended by a cog railway and a road.

**Pila** (Ger. **Schneidemühl**) Poland. Industrial town and railway junction in the Poznań voivodship 52 m. N of Poznań. Pop. (1968) 42,300. Manufactures agricultural machinery, textiles, etc. Formerly a German border town; after 1945 in Poland. Largely destroyed in the 2nd World War.

**Pilatus, Mount** Switzerland. Mountain 5 m. SSW of Lucerne, rising to 6,994 ft. Ascended by rack-and-pinion railway. Owes its name to the legend that the body of Pontius Pilate lay in a lake (now dry) on the mountain.

**Pilcomayo River.** River 1,000 m. long, rising in the Bolivian Andes near L. Poopó, flowing generally SE and forming part of the Argentina–Paraguay boundary, joining the Paraguay R. near Asunción.

**Pilgrims' Way** England. Track from Winchester, in Hampshire, to Canterbury, in Kent, by which medieval pilgrims journeyed from S and W England to see the shrine of Thomas à Becket in Canterbury Cathedral. The route had been in use in much earlier times. Much of it has been preserved, or can be traced.

**Pillars of Hercules** ◊ *Gibraltar*.

**Pilsen** (Czech **Plzeň**) Czechoslovakia. Capital of the Západočeský region in W Bohemia, at the confluence of the Radbuza and Mze rivers. Pop. (1967) 143,000. Famous for its beer and for the great metallurgical works, producing armaments, machinery, locomotives, cars, etc. Also manufactures clothing, pottery, leather goods, paper, etc. Commercial centre for a fertile agricultural region, with cereal and cattle markets. Largely modern; 13th-cent. Gothic church with a 325-ft tower, and a 16th-cent. town hall.

**Piltdown (Pilt Down)** England. Common 2 m. W of Uckfield, E Sussex, where parts of the skull of the 'Piltdown man' (Eoanthropus) were found in 1911. In 1953, however, the discovery was proved to be a hoax, the jawbone being that of a modern ape.

**Pimlico** England. District in the City of Westminster, London, on the N bank of the Thames. Mainly residential. Contains Victoria Station, a terminus of the Southern Region of British Rail.

**Pinar del Río** Cuba. Capital of the Pinar del Río province (W), 100 m. WSW of Havana. Pop. 39,000. Famous for cigars and cigarettes, made from tobacco grown in the Vuelta Abajo region. Also manufactures furniture, pharmaceutical products.

**Pindus (Gr. Píndhos) Mountains** Greece. Range of mountains about 100 m. long, running NNW–SSE along the border between Epirus and Thessaly, rising to 8,652 ft in Smólikas in the N.

**Pine Bluff** USA. Town in Arkansas, on the Arkansas R. 39 m. SSE of Little Rock. Pop. (1960) 44,037. In a cotton-growing region. Railway engineering, cotton and timber processing. Manufactures chemicals etc.

**Pinkie** ◊ *Musselburgh*.

**Pinner** England. Residential district in the Greater London borough of Harrow. Has a 14th-cent. church.

**Pinsk** USSR. Town in Byelorussian SSR, in the Pripet Marshes 135 m. SSW of Minsk. Pop. 42,000. Manufactures furniture, paper, matches, soap, leather, etc. Founded in the late 11th cent. Passed from Poland to Russia 1795. Restored to Poland 1918. Ceded to the USSR again 1945.

**Piotrków Trybunalski** Poland. Town in the Lódź voivodship 27 m. SSE of Lódź. Pop. (1968) 58,300. Flour milling, sawmilling, tanning, brewing. Manufactures textiles, agricultural machinery, etc. One of the oldest towns in Poland, founded in the 12th cent. Was the meeting place of several diets in the 15th and 16th cent.

**Piraeus** (Gr. **Piraiévs**) Greece. Seaport in Attica *nome*, 5 m. SW of Athens and within the metropolitan area. Pop. (1961) 813,957. The country's leading port and industrial centre. Exports wine, olive oil, etc. Shipbuilding, oil refining, flour milling. Manufactures fertilizers, textiles, etc. Founded in the 5th cent. B.C. as the port of Athens, it was linked with that city by the famous Long Walls, which were destroyed along with Piraeus by Sulla 86 B.C. It then declined, but was refounded as the port of modern Athens in 1834, and grew rapidly with the capital in the 19th cent.

**Pirmasens** Federal German Republic. Town in Rhineland-Palatinate 42 m. SW of Ludwigshafen. Pop. (1963) 53,100. Important for the manufacture of footwear and leather goods. Reputedly founded by St Pirmin in the 8th cent.

**Pirna** German Democratic Republic. Industrial town in the Dresden district, on the Elbe R. 13 m. SE of Dresden. Pop. (1965) 41,894. Manufactures rayon, paper, electrical equipment, glass, pottery, etc. Has a 16th-cent. church, town hall, and castle (Sonnenstein).

**Pisa** Italy. Capital of Pisa province, in Tuscany, on the Arno R. 7 m. from the mouth and 45 m. WSW of Florence (Firenze). Pop. (1968) 101,935. Manufactures textiles, bicycles, pottery, etc., but is better known for its historic monuments. Four of the most famous of these are grouped round the Piazza del Duomo:

the 11th/12th-cent. cathedral, with its three bronze doors; the 12th/13th-cent. baptistery, with its tall dome and hexagonal pulpit by Niccolò Pisano; the Campo Santo, or cemetery, created in the 12th cent. with earth from the Holy Land, and surrounded by galleries containing priceless frescoes; and the Leaning Tower, a campanile, begun in 1173, 180 ft high and 14 ft out of the perpendicular. Galileo (1564–1642), who was born here, was a student and a lecturer at the university (founded 1338). A flourishing maritime republic in the 11th and 12th cent. Defeated by Genoa at the Battle of Meloria (1284), and its final decline from greatness came when it fell to the Florentines (1509). It declined as a port when the river silted, and its trade was transferred to Leghorn (Livorno). The Campo Santo and many ancient churches and other buildings were severely damaged by bombing in the 2nd World War.

**Pisco** Peru. The chief seaport between Callao and Mollendo, in the Ica department 140 m. SSE of Lima. Pop. 28,000. Serves the irrigated agricultural lands and the mines of the interior. Exports cotton, copper and lead concentrates, etc. Manufactures cotton goods, cottonseed oil. Gave its name to Pisco brandy.

**Pishpek** ◊ *Frunze*.

**Pistoia** Italy. Capital of Pistoia province, Tuscany, at the foot of the Apennines 21 m. NW of Florence. Pop. (1961) 84,561. Manufactures macaroni, agricultural machinery, textiles, musical instruments, etc. Cathedral (13th-cent.) with a fine silver altar and a 218-ft campanile, an octagonal baptistery in black and white marble, and several noteworthy churches and palaces. The site of the Roman Pistoriae, it was here that Catiline was defeated and killed (62 B.C.).

**Pitcairn Island** S Pacific Ocean. Volcanic island about midway between Australia and S America. Area 2 sq. m. Pop. (1970) 80. Fruit and vegetables are sold to passing ships. Discovered (1767) by Carteret; occupied in 1790 by mutineers from H M S *Bounty* with women from Tahiti. By 1856 the island was overpopulated and the inhabitants were transferred to Norfolk Island, but many returned. The uninhabited neighbouring islands of Henderson, Ducie, and Oeno were annexed in 1902. Since 1952 the island has been administered by the Governor of Fiji.

**Pitești** Rumania. Capital of the Argeș district, in Walachia, on the Argeç R. 68 m. WNW of Bucharest. Pop. (1968) 65,782. Railway junction. Market town. Manufactures textiles, pottery, etc. Flour milling.

**Pitlochry** Scotland. Small burgh in Perthshire, on the R. Tummel 24 m. NNW of Perth. Pop. (1961) 2,501. A resort amid fine highland scenery, near the Pass of Killiecrankie. Trout and salmon fishing.

**Pitsea** ◊ *Basildon*.

**Pitt Island** ◊ *Chatham Islands*.

**Pittsburgh** USA. City in SW Pennsylvania at the confluence of the Allegheny and the Monongahela rivers (which form the Ohio R.). Pop. (1970) 512,676. Important industrial and transportation centre, second largest city in the state. In one of the world's richest coal regions. With adjacent industrial towns, it produces a large proportion of the US output of iron and steel. Manufactures a vast range of goods, e.g. electrical equipment, petroleum products, machinery, railway equipment, glassware, tinplate. Once the dirtiest and most disagreeable of US cities, named 'Smoky City'; a vigorous smoke-abatement campaign and a growth of civic spirit have completely transformed it. Seat of the University of Pittsburgh (1787), the Duquesne University (1878, Roman Catholic), and the Carnegie Institute of Technology (1900). The French Fort Duquesne was captured and renamed Fort Pitt by the British (1758). The settlement which grew around the fort in the modern business district (the 'Golden Triangle') was called Pittsburgh. River trade and later the railways promoted rapid expansion. Birthplace of Stephen Foster (1826–64), the composer.

**Pittsfield** USA. Industrial town in W Massachusetts, between the headstreams of the Housatonic R. 42 m. NW of Springfield. Pop. (1960) 57,879. Manufactures electrical equipment, textiles, paper, chemicals, etc. Also a tourist centre for the Berkshire Hills. Named after the elder Pitt.

**Piura** Peru. Capital of the Piura department in the NW, 130 m. NNW of Chiclayo. Pop. 43,000. Commercial centre for a large oasis irrigated by the Piura R. where long-staple cotton, rice, and sugarcane are grown. Trade in cotton etc. Cotton ginning. Manufactures cottonseed oil. Founded 1532, the oldest Spanish city in Peru; many colonial buildings.

**Plainfield** USA. Industrial and residential town in New Jersey 16 m. SW of Newark. Pop. (1960) 45,330. Manufactures printing and other machinery, tools, concrete products, clothing, etc.

**Plassey** India. Village in W Bengal, on the Bhagirathi R. 32 m. NNW of Krishnanagar. Scene of Clive's victory over Suraj-ud-Dowlah (1757), which led to the passing of Bengal to Britain.

**Plata, Río de la** ◊ *Río de la Plata.*

**Plataea** Greece. Ancient city in S Boeotia, near Mt Cithaeron, whose inhabitants fought with the Athenians at Marathon (490 B.C.). They incurred the enmity of Thebes, however, and their city was twice destroyed (427 and 373 B.C.) but was rebuilt by Philip and Alexander of Macedon and was inhabited till the 6th cent. A.D.

**Plate, River** ◊ *Río de la Plata.*

**Platte River** USA. River 310 m. long in Nebraska, formed by the union of the N Platte and S Platte rivers at North Platte, flowing generally E through an agricultural region, and joining the Missouri R. at Plattsmouth 15 m. S of Omaha. Total length, with the N Platte, 920 m. Unnavigable, owing to shallowness. Used for irrigation and hydroelectric power.

**Plauen** German Democratic Republic. Industrial town in the Karl-Marx-Stadt district, on the Elster R. 60 m. SSW o Leipzig. Pop. (1965) 81,239. Manufactures textiles (curtains, embroidery, lace, etc.), textile machinery, machine tools, paper, etc. The textile industry dates from the 15th cent. Formerly capital of the region known as Vogtland.

**Pleskau** ◊ *Pskov.*

**Pleven (Plevna)** Bulgaria. Capital of Pleven province in the N, 85 m. NE of Sofia. Pop. (1965) 79,234. Manufactures textiles, agricultural machinery, cement, leather, etc. Trade in wine, cattle. In 1877, during the Russo-Turkish war, it was the scene of two battles and a siege in which Osman Pasha, the Turkish general, was engaged.

**Plock** Poland. Town in the Warsaw voivodship, on the Vistula R. 60 m. WNW of Warsaw. Pop. (1968) 66,200. Flour milling, fruit canning. Manufactures agricultural implements. Trade in cereals. The cathedral (12th-cent., restored) has tombs of the Polish kings.

**Ploești** Rumania. Capital of the Prahova district, in Walachia, 35 m. N of Bucharest. Pop. (1968) 154,414. Leading centre of the Rumanian petroleum industry. Oil refineries; pipelines to Giurgiu, Bucharest, and Constanța. Also manufactures chemicals, textiles, hardware, cardboard, leather, etc. Frequently bombed by the Allies during the 2nd World War.

**Plovdiv** Bulgaria. Ancient Philippopolis. Capital of Plovdiv province, on the Maritsa R. 84 m. ESE of Sofia. Pop. (1965) 222,737. Bulgaria's second largest city, industrial and commercial centre. Manufactures chemicals, textiles, soap, furniture, cigarettes. Flour milling, tanning, etc. Trade in wheat, tobacco, attar of roses, etc. Taken by Philip II of Macedon in the 4th cent. B.C. (hence its ancient name). Formerly capital of Eastern Rumelia; ceded to Bulgaria 1885.

**Plymouth** (British W Indies) ◊ *Montserrat* (British W Indies).

**Plymouth** England. County borough in S Devonshire, at the head of Plymouth Sound, since 1914 comprising the Three Towns of Plymouth, Stonehouse, and Devonport. Pop. (1961) 204,279. Long important as a naval base, second only to Portsmouth, and a seaport. Manufactures chemicals, food products, etc. Engineering, brewing, boatbuilding. Stands on the broad tongue of land between the estuaries of the Plym and the Tamar, the latter known as the Hamoaze. The old town extends N from the ridge of Plymouth Hoe, where Drake played his famous game of bowls as the Armada approached. On the Hoe is Smeaton's tower, the upper part of the earlier Eddystone Lighthouse, and near by are the Marine Biological Laboratory and Sutton Pool, whence the *Mayflower* left on its voyage to America. At Devonport are large naval dockyards and barracks and at Stonehouse the Royal William Victualling Yard. A noteworthy building in Plymouth is the 19th-cent. Roman Catholic cathedral in Early English style.

Known as Sutton in the Middle Ages, Plymouth was given its present name in the 15th cent. Associated with the seafaring adventures of Drake, Hawkins, Raleigh, Grenville, and others, in Elizabethan times it became the country's leading port. The community known as the Plymouth Brethren was so called in 1830, when the Rev. J. N. Darby converted many Plymouth people to his beliefs. Became a city 1928; the title of Lord Mayor was granted 1935. During the 2nd World War the city was severely damaged in air raids (1941), and the centre was replanned and rebuilt. Devonport was the birthplace of Capt. R. F. Scott (1868–1912), the Antarctic explorer.

**Plymouth** USA. Town in Massachusetts, on Plymouth Bay 35 m. SE of Boston. Pop. (1960) 6,488. Fishing. Manufactures rope, textiles. A popular resort, famous as the place where the Pilgrim Fathers landed from the *Mayflower* (21 Dec. 1620). The first permanent colonist settlement in New England. Plymouth Rock (the granite boulder on which according to legend the Pilgrims stepped ashore) was replaced (1880) on the spot it had originally occupied. Many other historic relics.

**Plymouth Sound** England. Inlet of the English Channel between Cornwall and Devon, 3 m. wide at the entrance, into which flow the Tamar and the Plym rivers. Plymouth is at its head. In it is Drake's or St Nicholas' Island. An important roadstead, it is sheltered from SW gales by a breakwater 1 m. long with a lighthouse at its E end.

**Plynlimmon** Wales. Mountain 2,468 ft high on the borders of Cardigan and Montgomery, on which the Severn, Wye, and other rivers rise.

**Plzeň** ◊ *Pilsen.*

**Pnom Penh (Phnom Penh)** Cambodia. Capital of Cambodia, at the confluence of the Mekong and Tonlé Sap rivers and at the head of the Mekong delta. Pop. (1962) 403,000. Commercial and road centre and river port. Accessible to smaller ocean-going ships via the Mekong (through S Vietnam). Linked by road with the new Cambodian seaport of Sihanoukville. Trade in dried fish, rice, etc. Rice milling, textile manufacture, etc. Seat of a Buddhist university (1960). A picturesque city, founded in the 14th cent., it has an early 19th-cent. royal palace and a royal pagoda.

**Pobeda Peak** USSR. Highest peak of the Tien Shan mountain system (24,406 ft), in the E Kirghiz SSR. Discovered 1943.

**Pocatello** USA. Town in SE Idaho, on the Portneuf R. at a height of 4,460 ft. Pop. (1960) 28,534. Railway junction. Railway engineering, flour milling, etc. Trade in dairy produce etc. Founded (1882) as a tent colony.

**Pocklington** England. Market town in the E Riding of Yorkshire, 12 m. ESE of York. Pop. (rural district, 1961) 13,933. The 16th-cent. grammar school was attended by William Wilberforce.

**Podgorica** ◊ *Titograd.*

**Podolia** USSR. Region in the SW Ukrainian SSR between the Dniester and S Bug rivers. Chief towns Vinnitsa, Kamenets-Podolski. From the 13th cent. ruled mainly by Lithuania and Poland. Became Russian 1793.

**Podolsk** USSR. Industrial town in the Moscow region, RSFSR, 26 m. S of Moscow on the Pakhra R. Pop. (1970) 169,000. Railway engineering. Manufactures oil-refining machinery, sewing machines, cables, lime, cement, etc.

**Point Barrow** USA. The most northerly point on the Arctic coast of Alaska. US meteorological station (established 1882–3). US naval base 6 m. S (1944). Starting-point of Sir Hubert Wilkins's historic flight to Spitsbergen (1928).

**Pointe-à-Pitre** Guadeloupe. Chief seaport and largest town, in the SW of Grande Terre island. Pop. (1967) 29,538. Exports bananas, sugar-cane, rum, coffee, etc. Sugar milling, rum distilling.

**Pointe Noire** Congo (Brazzaville). Chief seaport, 240 m. WSW of Brazzaville. Pop. (1959) 56,865. Connected by rail with Brazzaville. Important airport. Exports palm oil and kernels, cotton, rubber, timber (mahogany, okoumé). Also handles much of the foreign trade of Gabon. Manufactures aluminium goods.

**Poitiers** France. Ancient Limonum. Prefecture of the Vienne department, at the confluence of the Clain and Boivre rivers 100 m. ESE of Nantes. Pop. (1968) 74,852. Market town. Trade in wine, wool, honey, etc. Manufactures chemicals, brushes, hosiery, etc. A picturesque town, with a 12th/14th-cent. cathedral; the baptistery of St John, built in the 4th cent. and enlarged in the 7th cent. – probably the oldest religious building in France; and the 11th/12th-cent. Notre-Dame-la-Grande church. University (1431). Named after its Gallic founders, the Pictavi or Pictones. In 732 Charles Martel defeated the advancing Muslims at Moussais-la-Bataille to the NE. At Poitiers in 1356 the English under the Black Prince defeated and captured John II of France. Capital of the old province of Poitou till 1790.

**Poitou** France. Region and former province in the W, now forming the departments of Vendée, Deux-Sèvres, and Vienne, with capital Poitiers; part of Aquitaine. The name was derived from the Pictavi or Pictones, the Gallic tribe living here in pre-Roman times.

**Pokrovsk** ◊ *Engels.*

**Pola** ◊ *Pula.*

**Poland.** Republic in E central Europe. Area 120,733 sq. m. Pop. (1968) 32,305,000. Cap. Warsaw. Rel. mainly Roman Catholic. Lang. Polish (Slavonic, but written in the Roman alphabet).

Bordered by the Baltic Sea and bounded by the USSR (NE and E), Czechoslovakia (S), and the German Democratic Republic (W). Consists in the main of a low, undulating plain dotted in the N with lakes of glacial origin. In the S is a low plateau, and along the Czechoslovak border the Sudeten Mountains and the Carpathians form a mountain barrier rising to over 8,000 ft in the High Tatra. Principal river the Vistula, which rises in the W Beskids (Carpathians) and flows S–N, passing through Cracow and Warsaw. The Oder and Neisse rivers form most of the boundary with the German Democratic Republic, and the W Bug, a tributary of the Vistula, part of the boundary with the USSR. Both the Vistula and the Oder, the chief waterways, are usually frozen for about 2 months each year. Climate continental, with cold winters and warm summers, extremes of temperature becoming more marked from N to S and from W to E. A moderate rainfall of 20–25 ins. annually is well distributed through the year.

RESOURCES, PEOPLE, *etc.* About 25 per cent of the country is forested, the pine and birch predominating. Arable land occupies rather more than twice this area; agriculture is still of great importance. Principal crops rye, potatoes, oats, wheat, barley, sugar-beet. Large numbers of cattle, pigs, and sheep raised. Most of the farms are still privately held. A profound change has taken place in Poland's economic structure since the 2nd World War; 61 per cent of the population gained a living by agriculture in 1939, but only 34 per cent in 1965. The country's industrial capacity was much increased by the acquisition of Silesian mining and manufacturing centres – e.g. Bytom (Beuthen), Gliwice (Gleiwitz), Zabrze (Hindenburg) – from Germany after the 2nd World War. This is the great coal-mining region of Poland; the output of coal rose from 38 million tons in 1939 to 124 million tons in 1967, and coal is the main export. Lignite, oil and natural gas, salt, iron, lead, and zinc are also mined. The leading manufactures are iron and steel, railway rolling stock, machinery, glass, and chemicals, largely centred on the Silesian coalfield, while the textile industry is concentrated here and in the Łódź region. Ninety per cent of industry is nationalized or State-controlled; all branches of industry are developed according to a planned economy. The value of the coal, coke, lignite, machinery, and railway equipment exports now far exceeds that of dairy produce and other foodstuffs. Over half of Poland's trade is with the USSR, the German Democratic Republic, and Czechoslovakia. Chief seaports Gdynia, Gdańsk (Danzig), Szczecin (Stettin).

In 1939 the population was 35 million, including more than 3 million Jews, but that of post-war Poland (1946), reduced by about 28,000 sq. m., was only 24 million. During the German occupation the Jews were systematically exterminated, the death camp at Oświecim (Auschwitz) being especially notorious; only about 100,000 survived. Most of the Poles living in the area ceded to the USSR were transferred to the districts gained from Germany, from which the Germans were expelled. As a result the population is now predominantly Polish, with small minorities of 180,000 Ukrainians, 165,000 Byelorussians, 3,000 Germans, and 31,000 Jews. The density of population is greatest in the industrial regions of Silesia, Warsaw, and Łódź. Fifty-one per cent of the people are now classified as urban, and the number of towns with more than 100,000 inhabitants has risen from 8 (1950) to 23 (1968); the largest are Warsaw, Łódź, Cracow, Wroclaw (Breslau), Poznań, Gdańsk, Szczecin, and Katowice. Education is free and compulsory up to the age of 14; there are 8 universities and 16 technical universities. For administrative purposes the country is divided into 17 voivodships or provinces and 5 cities of voivodship status. HISTORY. The story of Poland begins with the introduction of Christianity to this W Slavonic people in the latter part of the 10th cent. In 1025 one of their princes, Boleslaus I, became the first king, ruling an area extending from the Baltic Sea to the Carpathians and from the Elbe R. to the Bug R. With the death of Boleslaus III (1138) the kingdom was partitioned into independent principalities, lost power, and was raided by Tatars and threatened by the Teutonic Order. Poland was saved, however, by Wladislaus I, who reunited Great and Little Poland, and by his son, Casimir the Great (1333–70), who gave the country 37 years of peace. With the union of Poland and Lithuania by the accession of Wladislaus II (1386–1434), the threat from the Teutonic Order was removed when they were utterly defeated at Tannenberg (1410). By the Union of Lublin (1569) Poland absorbed Lithuania and at this time reached its widest limits, extending from the Baltic to the Black Sea. In 1573 the monarchy became elective, and the period of glory, with Poland's prestige high and arts and sciences flourishing, was followed by two centuries of conflict and finally humiliation. The Ukrainian Cossacks under Chmielnicki rebelled, and the country was attacked by Sweden and Russia and lost considerable territory. Taking advantage of the ensuing chaos, Frederick II of Prussia and Catherine II of Russia arranged the First Partition of Poland (1772), by which Prussia gained W Prussia, Russia much of Lithuania, and Austria most of Galicia. A new constitution making the monarchy hereditary only led to the Second Partition (1793), by which Russia took all the E provinces and Prussia further territory in the W, so that Poland was now reduced to one third of her former area. Kosciuszko heroically led an insurrection and won early successes, but was defeated by overwhelming Russian forces and taken prisoner at Maciejowice. The Third Partition followed (1795): Prussia received W Masovia with Warsaw, Austria W Galicia and S Masovia, and Russia the rest of the country. Thus Poland was effaced from the map of Europe for more than a century.

By the Peace of Tilsit (1807) Napoleon created the grand duchy of Warsaw under the King of Saxony as a buffer state, but with his defeat it disappeared. The Congress of Vienna (1815) established a nominally independent state in personal union with Russia, the W went to Prussia and Galicia to Austria, while Cracow, at first a city republic, was annexed by Austria (1848). After the insurrections of 1830 and 1863 had been crushed, Russian Poland became virtually a province of Russia, and the history of each section of the Polish people followed that of the country into which they had been incorporated.

During the 1st World War Polish troops under Pilsudski fought with Germany and Austria against Russia, and Polish independence, promised by all three countries, was established by the peace treaties.

Poland gained access to the Baltic by the Polish Corridor and regained Prussian Poland and part of Silesia. Dissatisfied with the placing of the Polish-Russian border along the Curzon Line, however, Poland made war on Russia and by the Treaty of Riga (1921) secured most of its claims, having also seized the Vilna region from Lithuania (1920). More than one third of the population now consisted of minorities – Germans, Ukrainians, Byelorussians, Jews, and Lithuanians. In 1926 Pilsudski overthrew the government by a military *coup d'état* which made him a virtual dictator. The 2nd World War was precipitated by the German invasion of Poland (1 Sept. 1939) when the Poles rejected Hitler's demands concerning Danzig, and 16 days later Russian troops invaded from the E. Polish resistance was soon crushed, and the country was partitioned between Germany and the USSR. In 1941 Germany attacked Russia and occupied the whole of Poland. Meanwhile, a Polish government in exile was set up in London; an underground movement operated in Poland; many Poles escaped and formed substantial contingents which fought in N Africa and France. By the Potsdam Conference (1945) Poland ceded 67,936 sq. m. in the E to the USSR and received 39,705 sq. m. in the W from Germany, the Polish-E German border running along the Oder and Neisse rivers. In 1947 'free' parliamentary elections were held in the familiar atmosphere of Communist coercion, a government was formed largely from members of the 1944 provisional Lublin government, and Poland became a Soviet satellite; large numbers of Poles still abroad refused to return to their native land. A new constitution was promulgated in 1952, and after the Poznań riots (1956) and the 'bloodless revolution' against Stalinism, Wladyslaw Gomulka took control of the Communist Party, and Poland succeeded in regaining a measure of freedom greater than that in any of the other 'people's democracies'. The church retains considerable influence, and agriculture remains largely under individual ownership modified by peasant co-operatives and many large state farms.

Polotsk USSR. Town in the Byelorussian SSR, on the W Dvina R. 60 m. WNW of Vitebsk. Pop. 44,000. Railway junction. Industrial centre. Sawmilling, oil refining, flour milling. An ancient town, probably founded in the 9th cent; was a large and important commercial centre under Poland in the 16th cent. Declined, chiefly because of fires and plagues; passed to Russia 1772.

**Polperro** England. Fishing village and resort in E Cornwall, on the S coast 5 m. E of Fowey. Popular with artists.

**Poltava** USSR. Town in the Ukrainian SSR, on the Vorskla R. 190 m. ESE of Kiev. Pop. (1970) 220,000. Commercial centre in a fertile region producing sugarbeet, wheat, fruits, etc. Flour milling, tanning, meat packing, brewing. Manufactures textiles. In a battle near by Peter the Great of Russia defeated Charles XII of Sweden (1709).

**Poltoratsk** ◊ *Ashkhabad*.

**Polygyros** ◊ *Chalcidice*.

**Polynesia** Pacific Ocean. One of the three main divisions of the Pacific islands, in the central and SE Pacific, the others being Melanesia and Micronesia. Inhabited by Polynesians, a tall, well-built people with a light brown skin and straight or wavy hair, who probably colonized the islands from Asia, though their origins are still not conclusively established. The island groups lie within the New Zealand–Hawaii–Easter Island triangle, and include the groups of Hawaii, Samoa, Tonga, and Tokelau, and also Tubuai, Tuamotu, Society, Marquesas, Cook, Ellice and Easter islands. Ethnologically the New Zealand Maoris are of Polynesian stock. A great number of the islands are volcanic summits, surrounded by coral reefs, while some are low coral atolls. ◊ *French Polynesia*.

**Pomerania** ◊ *Pomorze*.

**Pomfret** ◊ *Pontefract*.

**Pomona** USA. Town in California 26 m. E of Los Angeles. Pop. (1960) 67,157. Commercial centre for a fruit-growing and agricultural region, and in recent years an outer residential suburb of Los Angeles. Citrus-fruit canning. Manufactures water pumps, paper products, etc.

**Pomorze** (**Pomerania**, Ger. **Pommern**) German Democratic Republic/Poland. Region in N central Europe bordering N on the Baltic Sea and extending W from the lower Vistula R. beyond the lower Oder R. to include Rügen Island and Stralsund; now mainly in Poland, with a small area in the NE of the German Democratic Republic. A mainly flat, low-lying agricultural region. Chief crops rye, potatoes, oats. In 1919, after the 1st World War, part of it formed the Polish Corridor and was in the Pomorze voivodship (province), separating the German E Pomerania (Hinterpommern) from E Prussia. In 1945, after the 2nd World War, E Pomerania passed to Poland and W Pomerania (Vorpommern), i.e. Pomerania W of the Oder R., to the German Democratic Republic, except for the district round Szczecin (Stettin) which also became Polish. By 1950 the larger Polish Pomerania was divided into the four voivodships Gdańsk, Bydgoszcz, Szczecin, and Koszalin.

**Pompeii** (Italian **Pompei**) Italy. Ancient city in Campania, near the Bay of Naples and the foot of Vesuvius and 14 m. SE of Naples. A military colony was settled here by Sulla (80 B.C.) and the population had been Romanized by A.D. 63, when a violent earthquake caused damage. In A.D. 79 the city was buried under a mass of cinders and ash thrown out in the great eruption of Vesuvius; judging by the number of bodies found during subsequent excavations, about 2,000 people must have perished – probably about 10 per cent of the population. Pompeii was rediscovered in 1748 and the excavations began in 1763, revealing a wealth of information about Roman life in the 1st cent. A.D. The city was roughly oval, about 2 m. in circumference, with 8 gates and well-paved streets. There were fine public buildings and villas ornamented with remarkable murals and mosaics; many of the works of art were removed after excavation to museums. The much smaller Herculaneum was buried by the same eruption of Vesuvius.

**Ponape Island** ◊ *Caroline Islands*.

**Ponce** Puerto Rico. Seaport and second largest city, on the S coast 50 m. WSW of San Juan. Pop. (1960) 145,586. Exports sugar, tobacco, textiles, rum. Sugar refining, rum distilling, brewing, fruit canning. Manufactures textiles, shoes, cement, etc. A picturesque city, with attractive squares, avenues, parks, and 'colonial' mansions. Named after Juan Ponce de León (1460–1521), the Spanish explorer who conquered Puerto Rico (1509) and was appointed governor.

**Pondicherry** India. 1. Territory of the Indian Union, on the Coromandel coast of the SE, including Karikal, Mahé, and Yanaon. Area 185 sq. m. Pop. (1961) 369,072. Main food crop rice; groundnuts and sugar-cane also cultivated. Founded (1674) by the French, it was the chief French settlement in India till 1954, when it was transferred to India. Became a Union Territory 1962.

**2.** Capital of Pondicherry territory, and formerly of French India, on the Coromandel Coast 85 m. SSW of Madras. Pop. (1961) 40,421. Seaport and commercial centre. Exports groundnuts. Manufactures cotton goods.

**Pongo de Manseriche Gorge** ◊ *Marañon River*.

**Ponta Delgada** ◊ *Azores*.

**Ponta Grossa** Brazil. Town in Paraná state 65 m. WNW of Curitiba at a height of 2,900 ft. Pop. 79,000. Commercial centre in a region important for rice and tobacco cultivation, pig rearing, lumbering. Trade in timber, maté. Meat packing, sawmilling, etc.

**Pontchartrain, Lake** USA. Shallow lake 40 m. long and 25 m. wide in SE Louisiana just N of New Orleans. Linked by navigable canal with the Mississippi R. and via L. Borgne with the Gulf of Mexico by the deltaic channels Rigolets and Chef Menteur.

**Pontefract (Pomfret)** England. Municipal borough in the W Riding of Yorkshire 11 m. SE of Leeds. Pop. (1961) 27,114. Market town. In a coalmining region. Well known for its liquorice sweetmeats known as Pontefract or Pomfret cakes. Tanning, brewing, engineering, etc. Market gardening in the neighbourhood. An 11th-cent. castle, now in ruins, where Richard II was imprisoned and murdered (1400).

**Pontevedra** Spain. **1.** Province in the NW on the Atlantic Ocean, in Galicia, bordering S on Portugal along the Miño R. Area 1,427 sq. m. Pop. (1961) 680,229. Largely mountainous. Deeply indented coastline. Main occupations agriculture, fishing. Chief port Vigo.

**2.** Capital of Pontevedra province, seaport at the head of the Ría de Pontevedra. Pop. (1967) 63,315. Fishing, boatbuilding. Manufactures pottery, leather, etc. Trade in livestock, fruit, cereals, wine. A Roman bridge of 12 arches, the Pons Vetus (from which it takes its name), spans the Lerez R., on which it stands. Medieval fortifications; a 16th-cent. church.

**Pontiac** USA. Industrial town in Michigan on the Clinton R. 24 m. NW of Detroit. Pop. (1960) 82,233. An important centre of the motor-car industry. Manufactures lorries, buses, rubber products, paint, etc. Founded 1818. Carriage making in the late 19th cent. led to the modern automobile industry.

**Pontianak** Indonesia. Capital of W Kalimantan province (W Borneo), at the mouth of a distributary of the Kapuas R. Pop. (1961) 150,220. Seaport. Exports timber, copra, etc.

**Pontine Marshes**. Italy. Low-lying coastal region along the Tyrrhenian Sea, in Latium, extending NW–SE from Cisterna di Latina to Terracina. Fertile and well-peopled in early Roman times; later abandoned owing to the unhealthy marshes. Several attempts at reclamation were made, but a drainage system was not completed until the Fascist régime, when large estates were divided into smallholdings and the rural town of Littoria (now Latina) was established (1932), to be followed by Sabaudia (1934) and others. Cereals, sugar-beet, vines, fruits, and vegetables cultivated.

**Pontresina** Switzerland. Summer resort and winter-sports centre in Graubünden (Grisons) canton, at a height of 5,915 ft in the Upper Engadine 5 m. E of St Moritz. Pop. (1960) 1,067. Many peaks in the Bernina Alps are easily accessible.

**Pontus**. Ancient region in NE Asia Minor bordering the Black Sea, now in Turkey. Became a kingdom *c.* 300 B.C. and was an important power under Mithridates the Great, who was defeated by Pompey (65 B.C.). His son Pharnaces was defeated by Julius Caesar (47 B.C.) and Pontus gradually lost its identity.

**Pontypool** Wales. Urban district in Monmouthshire 8 m. NNW of Newport. Pop. (1961) 39,879. Coalmining. Manufactures steel, tinplate, nylon. Tinplate was first made here, in the late 17th cent.

**Pontypridd** Wales. Urban district in Glamorganshire, on the R. Taff at the confluence with the R. Rhondda 11 m. NW of Cardiff. Pop. (1961) 35,536. Coalmining. Iron and brass founding. Manufactures chains, cables, chemicals. Varied light industries at the Treforest trading estate, established in the 1930s to relieve unemployment. There is a single-arch bridge (built 1755) across the R. Taff.

**Poole** England. Municipal borough in Dorset on Poole Harbour, an inlet of the English Channel, 5 m. W of Bournemouth. Pop. (1961) 88,088. Seaport. Holiday resort. Boatbuilding, engineering. Manufactures pottery (from local clay), chemicals, etc. Considerable tourist trade in the neighbourhood. There are town cellars of the 15th cent. and, on one of the islands in Poole Harbour, a Tudor castle.

**Poona** India. City in Maharashtra, in the Western Ghats at a height of 1,850 ft 78 m. S E of Bombay. Pop. (1961) 597,562. Military station. Commercial centre. Trade in grain, cotton, etc. Manufactures cotton goods, paper, chemicals, soap, etc. University (1948). Has a pleasant, healthy situation, and during British rule in India was made the hot-weather capital of the Bombay Presidency; it came to be a symbol of what was most superficial and reactionary amongst the British community in India. Seat of the Mahratta rulers in the 18th cent.

**Poopó, Lake** Bolivia. Shallow lake at a height of 12,100 ft on the Altiplano about 35 m. S of Oruro. Fed by the Desaguadero R. from L. Titicaca (360 ft higher). Area 980 sq. m.

**Popayán** Colombia. Capital of the Cauca department, at the foot of the volcano Puracé (16,110 ft) 80 m. S of Cali at a height of 5,774 ft. Pop. 63,000. Cultural and commercial centre in a coffee-growing region. Flour milling, tanning, etc. A picturesque city with fine colonial buildings, distinguished old monasteries, etc. University (1640). Founded (1536) by Benalcázar. Birthplace of Francisco José de Caldas (1771–1815), the famous Colombian scientist.

**Poplar** England. Former metropolitan borough in E London on the N bank of the R. Thames, including the Isle of Dogs, Bow, Millwall, and Blackwall, also the East and West India and Millwall Docks; from 1965 part of the London borough of Tower Hamlets. Pop. (1961) 66,417. Linked with Greenwich by the Blackwall Tunnel under the R. Thames. Largely industrial. Manufactures matches, paper, clothing, etc. Heavily damaged in air raids during the 2nd World War.

**Popocatépetl, Mount** Mexico. In Aztec, 'Smoking Mountain'. Dormant volcano 42 m. S E of Mexico City, the second highest peak in Mexico (17,887 ft). A snow-capped cone, with a large crater. The lower slopes are green with conifers. There was a minor eruption in 1920, and sulphur (which has never been fully exploited) is continually deposited from the vapour which still rises from the crater. Probably first ascended by one of Cortés' soldiers (1519); frequently climbed since.

**Porbandar** India. Seaport in Gujarat, on the Kathiawar peninsula 90 m. S W of Rajkot. Pop. (1961) 74,476. Exports cotton, salt, etc. Manufactures textiles, cement, etc. Birthplace of Mahatma Gandhi (1869–1948).

**Pori** (Swedish **Björneborg**) Finland. Industrial town and seaport in Turku-Pori province in the S W, on the Kokemäki R. near the mouth on the Gulf of Bothnia. Pop. (1968) 70,957. Exports timber, wood products. Copper refining. Manufactures wood pulp, paper, textiles, matches, etc.

**Po River** Italy. Longest river in Italy (417 m.), rising on Monte Viso in the Cottian Alps, and flowing E and N E past Turin and Chivasso, then E past Piacenza and Cremona to enter the Adriatic by a large delta. Its drainage basin covers about 27,000 sq. m. and includes almost the whole broad plain between the Alps and the Apennines – economically the country's most important region. In its lower course the river has raised its bed above the level of the surrounding country, so that its banks have had to be artificially strengthened, but this has also facilitated irrigation. Its Alpine tributaries, among them the Ticino, Adda, and Mincio, are generally longer, swifter, and more important than those rising in the Apennines.

**Porjus** Sweden. Village in Norrbotten county on the Lule R. 120 m. N W of Luleå. Site of a great hydroelectric power station supplying power to the Luleå–Narvik railway and the iron mines of Kiruna and Gällivare.

**Porlamar** ◊ *Margarita Island.*

**Porsgrunn** Norway. Industrial town and seaport in Telemark county 68 m. S W of Oslo. Pop. (1968) 31,765. Manufactures fertilizers, electrical equipment, etc.

**Port Adelaide** Australia. Chief seaport of S Australia, 7 m. N W of Adelaide on Gulf St Vincent. Pop. 35,000. Has inner and outer harbours. Exports wheat, flour, wool, fruit. Iron smelting. Manufactures chemicals, cement.

**Portadown** Northern Ireland. Municipal borough in Co. Armagh, on the R. Bann 24 m. W S W of Belfast. Pop. (1961) 18,605. Railway junction. Fruit canning, bacon curing. Manufactures linen, clothing, carpets, etc. Has famous rose nurseries.

**Portage la Prairie** Canada. Town in Manitoba, on the Assiniboine R. 51 m. W of Winnipeg. Pop. (1966) 13,012. Engineering, brickmaking. Formerly the starting point of a portage route for fur traders to L. Manitoba.

**Port Ahuriri** ◊ *Napier.*

**Port Alberni** Canada. Port in British

Columbia, on Vancouver Island 88 m. NW of Victoria. Pop. (1966) 18,538. Lumbering, fishing, Exports timber.

**Portarlington** Irish Republic. Town in Co. Laoighis, on the R. Barrow and on the boundary with Co. Offaly. Pop. (1966) 2,048. Market town in a cereal- and potato-growing region. The first Irish power plant to use peat for fuel was built here (1948).

**Port Arthur** Canada. Lake port and industrial town in W Ontario, on the NW shore of L. Superior. Pop. (1966) 48,340. Ships grain, iron ore. Large grain elevators, pulp and paper mills, shipyards. Just S is the twin town of Fort William.

**Port Arthur** (China) ◊ *Lü-ta.*

**Port Arthur** USA. Port in SE Texas on the W shore of L. Sabine. Pop. (1960) 66,676. Connected with the Gulf of Mexico by the Sabine–Neches Waterway. Exports petroleum, grain, timber, etc. Oil refining. Manufactures chemicals, rubber products, etc.

**Port Augusta** Australia. Port and railway junction in S Australia at the head of Spencer Gulf 170 m. NNW of Adelaide. Pop. (1966) 10,128. Exports wool, wheat. Large thermal power station. Engineering.

**Port-au-Prince** Haiti. Capital and chief seaport, on the Gulf of Gonaïves on the W coast. Pop. (1963) 250,000 (mostly Negro and mulatto). Good natural harbour. Rum distilling, sugar milling, brewing. Manufactures textiles, etc. Seat of the University of Haiti (1944). Cathedral (18th-cent.). Has often been damaged by earthquakes and fires.

**Port Blair** ◊ *Andaman Islands.*

**Port-Bouet** ◊ *Abidjan.*

**Portchester** ◊ *Fareham.*

**Port de France** ◊ *Nouméa.*

**Port Elizabeth** S Africa. Seaport in the Cape Province, on the W shore of Algoa Bay, 425 m. E of Cape Town. Pop. (1967) 374,066 (148,712 Bantu, 116,979 whites, 103,979 Cape coloured). Exports fruits, hides and skins, mohair, wool. Motor-car assembly. Manufactures tyres, leather, furniture, clothing, etc. Fruit and jam canning, flour milling. The Addo Elephant National Park is 30 m. N. Fort Frederick was built in 1790; the town was founded by British settlers in 1820, planned by Sir R. Donkin, and named after his wife. The port developed rapidly with the construction of the modern harbour and the railway to Kimberley.

**Port Francqui** Congo (Kinshasa). Town in Kasai West province, on the right bank of the Kasai R. just above the confluence with the Sankuru R. 365 m. E of Kinshasa. Pop. 4,000. River port. Terminus of the railway from S Katanga.

**Port Fuad** ◊ *Port Said.*

**Port Glasgow** Scotland. Large burgh in Renfrewshire, on the R. Clyde estuary 3 m. ESE of Greenock. Pop. (1961) 22,551. The former outport of Glasgow, but its trade declined after the improvement of the river channel. Now important for shipbuilding, engineering, etc. Manufactures rope, twine, canvas.

**Port Harcourt** Nigeria. Seaport in the SE (Biafra), on the Bonny R. arm of the Niger R. delta 270 m. ESE of Lagos. Pop. (1963) 75,000. Exports palm oil and kernels, groundnuts, cacao, tin (from Bauchi), coal (from Enugu, Udi). Also a centre for the near-by oilfield, from which natural gas is piped to an industrial estate. Manufactures cement, tyres, cigarettes, etc. Built during the 1st World War (1914). Named after the then Colonial Secretary, Sir William Harcourt.

**Porthcawl** Wales. Urban district in Glamorganshire, on the Bristol Channel 14 m. SE of Swansea. Pop. (1961) 11,082. Seaport. Seaside resort.

**Port Huron** USA. Lake port and industrial town in SE Michigan, on the St Clair R., which connects L. Huron with L. Erie via L. St Clair and the Detroit R.; opposite Sarnia (Canada), with which it is connected by road bridge and railway tunnel. Pop. (1960) 36,084. Manufactures metal goods, paper, cement, etc. A summer lake resort.

**Portici** Italy. Town in Napoli province, Campania, on the Bay of Naples 4 m. SE of Naples. Pop. (1961) 50,373. Fishing, silk weaving, tanning, etc. Has a former royal palace (built 1738). Destroyed in the eruption of Vesuvius 1631. Terminus of the first railway in Italy (1839), from Naples to Portici.

**Portishead** England. Urban district in N Somerset, on the Severn estuary 8 m. WNW of Bristol. Pop. (1961) 6,440. Seaport. Resort. The docks form part of the Port of Bristol.

**Port Jackson** Australia. A deep, silt-free drowned valley in New South Wales, forming an excellent land-locked harbour for Sydney. The many inlets allow long wharves with deep water alongside. Spanned by Sydney Harbour Bridge (1932),

1,650 ft long, linking the city with its N suburbs.

**Port Kembla** Australia. Industrial town and port, centre of heavy industry in New South Wales, 45 m. SSW of Sydney, forming part of Greater Wollongong. Important iron and steel industry. Also copper refining, tinplate, wire and cable, fertilizer manufacture, etc. Chief residential area Wollongong, 5 m. N.

**Port Kennedy** ◊ *Thursday Island*.

**Portland** (Maine) USA. Largest city and chief seaport of the state, on a peninsula on Casco Bay. Pop. (1960) 72,566. Excellent harbour. Exports timber, grain. Manufactures paper, footwear, furniture, textiles, etc. Fishing. Founded by the English (1632) as Falmouth. Destroyed by Indians and French, and later by a British fleet. State capital 1820–31. Birthplace of Henry Wadsworth Longfellow (1807–82).

**Portland** (Oregon) USA. Largest city in the state, in the NW, on the Willamette R. near the confluence with the Columbia R. Pop. (1960) 372,676. Port; excellent freshwater harbour, served by ocean-going vessels. Exports timber, grain, flour, etc. Manufactures wood products, paper, furniture, etc. Flour milling, meat packing. Seat of the University of Oregon's medical and dental schools and of the University of Portland (1901, Roman Catholic). Founded 1845. Named after Portland, Maine. Grew rapidly during the California and Alaska gold rushes.

**Portland, Isle of** England. Rocky peninsula on the coast of Dorset connected with the mainland by the ridge of shingle known as Chesil Bank (Beach). Area 4½ sq. m. Forms an urban district with pop. (1961) 11,542. At the S end is Portland Bill, with a lighthouse. The highest point is the Verne (N). Also on the island are Portland Castle, built by Henry VIII in 1520, and the former convict prison, since 1921 a Borstal institution. Portland Harbour, on the NE side, is a naval base protected by great breakwaters. The island consists largely of a mass of limestone, which has been long quarried for building stone and was used in the construction of St Paul's Cathedral and many other London buildings.

**Portlaoighise** Irish Republic. Formerly Maryborough. County town of Co. Laoighis 48 m. WSW of Dublin. Pop. (1966) 3,434. Flour milling, malting. Manufactures woollen goods. Has re-

mains of a fort erected in the reign of Mary Tudor.

**Port Louis** Mauritius. Capital and chief seaport, on the NW coast. Pop. (1967) 136,200. Small but excellent harbour. Large exports of sugar. Railway engineering. Manufactures cigarettes, matches, soap, etc. Dominated by the Citadel (1830). Has Anglican and Roman Catholic cathedrals. Founded by Mahé de La Bourdonnais *c.* 1735. Achieved city status 1966.

**Port Lyautey** ◊ *Mina Hassan Tani*.

**Portmadoc** Wales. Urban district in Caernarvonshire, on Tremadoc Bay 16 m. SSE of Caernarvon. Pop. (1961) 3,419. Seaport. Market town. Resort. Exports slate.

**Port Mathurin** ◊ *Rodrigues*.

**Port Moresby** New Guinea. Capital of the Australian Trust Territory of Papua–New Guinea, in the SE of the island of New Guinea. Pop. (1966) 42,133. Chief seaport. Exports copra, rubber. Airport. Important Allied base in the 2nd World War.

**Port Nicholson** ◊ *Lower Hutt*.

**Port Nolloth** ◊ *South Africa*.

**Pôrto** ◊ *Oporto*.

**Pôrto Alegre** Brazil. Capital of Rio Grande do Sul state, at the N end of the Lagôa dos Patos 150 m. NNE of Rio Grande, its outport. Pop. (1960) 617,629 (many of German and Italian descent). A modern city of rapid growth. Seaport. Important commercial centre. Exports meat products, hides, wool, etc. Meat packing, tanning, brewing. Manufactures textiles, chemicals, etc. An attractive city amid picturesque scenery. Seat of two universities (1936, 1948). Founded 1742.

**Portofino** ◊ *Rapallo*.

**Port of Spain** Trinidad and Tobago. Capital, chief seaport, and largest city, on the Gulf of Paria in the NW of Trinidad. Pop. (1960) 93,954. A sheltered but shallow harbour. Exports petroleum products, sugar, rum, cacao, etc. Rum distilling, brewing, sawmilling, etc. Manufactures cement, cigarettes, etc. One of the finest and cleanest cities in the W Indies, in a beautiful setting, with many parks and squares, attractive streets, and noteworthy public buildings. Government House is in the famous Botanical Gardens, near the Queen's Park Savannah, a large recreation ground. Anglican and Roman Catholic cathedrals; an important mosque. Replaced St Joseph as capital 1783.

**Porto Novo** Dahomey. Capital and seaport on the N shore of a coastal lagoon, 50 m. W of Lagos (Nigeria). Pop. (1965) 74,500. Linked by rail with the seaport of Cotonou and with Pobé in the interior. Exports palm oil and kernels, cotton, kapok. Has lost trade to Cotonou.

**Porto Rico** ◊ *Puerto Rico*.

**Pôrto Velho** Brazil. Capital of the remote forested Amazonian territory of Rondônia, 500 m. SSW of Manáus at the head of navigation on the Madeira R. Pop. 23,000. Terminus of the railway bypassing the Madeira R. rapids. Trade in rubber, timber, medicinal plants.

**Portoviejo** Ecuador. Capital of Manabí province, on the coastal plain 80 m. NNW of Guayaquil. Pop. (1966) 96,651. Market town; trade in coffee, cacao, etc. Manufactures baskets, Panama hats.

**Port Phillip Bay (Port Phillip)** Australia. Large inlet off Bass Strait in S Victoria, 35 m. N–S and 40 m. W–E, with Melbourne at its head and Geelong on Corio Bay (W).

**Port Pirie** Australia. Seaport in S Australia, on Germein Bay leading to Spencer Gulf, 125 m. NNW of Adelaide. Pop. (1966) 15,549. Receives metal concentrates from Broken Hill; its smelters produce lead bullion and extract silver, zinc, and gold. Also exports wheat, wool. Manufactures chemicals.

**Portree** Scotland. Chief town of the Isle of Skye, Inverness-shire, on the Sound of Raasay 20 m. NW of Kyle of Lochalsh. Pop. 800. Fishing port. Resort.

**Portrush** Northern Ireland. Urban district in Co. Antrim 30 m. ENE of Londonderry. Pop. (1961) 4,263. Seaside resort and centre for the Giant's Causeway, 7 m. ENE. The ruins of the 14th-cent. Dunluce Castle are 2 m. E.

**Port Said** United Arab Republic. Seaport and important fuelling station (coal, oil), at the Mediterranean entrance to the Suez Canal, 100 m. NE of Cairo on a narrow strip of land between L. Manzala and the sea. Pop. (1960) 244,000. Linked by rail with Suez and Cairo (via Ismailia). Large entrepôt trade. Exports cotton. Manufactures chemicals, cigarettes. Salt panning. Founded 1859, when the Suez Canal was begun. Named after Said Pasha (then Khedive of Egypt). On the W breakwater is a gigantic statue of Ferdinand de Lesseps, who planned the Canal. On the opposite bank is Port Fuad (opened 1926).

**Portslade-by-Sea** England. Urban district in E Sussex, on the English Channel just W of Hove. Pop. (1961) 15,750. Minor port. Manufactures electrical equipment etc.

**Portsmouth** England. County borough in SE Hampshire, on Portsea Island at the entrance to Portsmouth Harbour opposite Gosport. Pop. (1961) 215,198. The country's chief naval base, with Nelson's flagship, H.M.S. *Victory*, in dry dock near the entrance to the Royal Dockyard. Consists of Landport, Portsea, Cosham, and Southsea, the last a residential district and popular seaside resort. Since 1927 the Church of St Thomas, dating from the 12th cent. (restored), has been the cathedral; also a modern Roman Catholic cathedral. Portsmouth, nicknamed 'Pompey', became important as a naval base in the reign of Henry VIII. Suffered serious damage from bombing during the 2nd World War. Birthplace of Charles Dickens (1812–70), George Meredith (1828–1909), Sir Walter Besant (1836–1901), and Isambard Brunel (1806–59).

**Portsmouth** (New Hampshire) USA. The only seaport in the state, in the SE, at the mouth of the Piscataqua R. Pop. (1960) 25,833. Summer resort. Manufactures footwear etc. Several 18th-cent. and early 19th-cent. houses. Naval base, with a submarine-building and repair yard, on an island in the Piscataqua R. (on the Maine side), where the Treaty of Portsmouth ending the Russo-Japanese War was signed (1905). State capital 1679–1775.

**Portsmouth** (Ohio) USA. Industrial town on the Ohio R. at the confluence with the Scioto R. Pop. (1960) 33,637. Railway engineering. Manufactures iron and steel, footwear, furniture, etc.

**Portsmouth** (Virginia) USA. Seaport and industrial town on the Elizabeth R. opposite Norfolk. Pop. (1960) 114,773 (about 40 per cent Negroes, employed in the factories, harbour, Navy Yard, and fishing industry). Exports cotton, tobacco, etc. Food processing, railway engineering. Manufactures cottonseed oil, chemicals, fertilizers, hosiery, etc. The Norfolk Navy Yard on the E waterfront is one of the most important in the USA; in the American Civil War it was evacuated by Federal troops (1861) but was retaken in 1862.

**Portstewart** Northern Ireland. Urban district in Co. Londonderry 28 m. NE of Londonderry. Pop. (1961) 3,950. Seaside resort.

**Port Sudan** Sudan. Chief seaport, a fuelling station (coal, oil), on the Red Sea. Pop. (1964) 57,000. Terminus of the railway from the Nile valley and Khartoum (via Haiya Junction). Handles almost all Sudan's foreign trade. Exports cotton, cotton and sesame seeds, gum arabic, hides and skins. Cotton ginning. Salt panning. Founded 1906, superseding Suakin.

**Port Sunlight** ◊ *Bebington*.

**Port Swettenham** ◊ *Malaya*; *Selangor*.

**Port Talbot** Wales. Municipal borough in Glamorganshire, on Swansea Bay 7 m. ESE of Swansea, formed in 1921 from the town of Aberavon and the urban district of Margam. Pop. (1961) 50,223. A port serving the coalmining and metallurgical industries; large imports of iron ore. Important steelworks, one of the largest in Europe. New harbour to accommodate large ore vessels opened 1970.

**Portugal.** Republic in SW Europe. Area (inc. Madeira and the Azores) 34,831 sq. m. Pop. (1960) 8,889,392. Cap. Lisbon. Rel. predominantly Roman Catholic.

Occupies the W part of the Iberian peninsula. Bounded by Spain (N and E) and the Atlantic (S and W). Primarily agricultural, with important forests and fisheries, and the economy is largely based on the export of three products, cork (from the cork oak), sardines, and port wine, while there is an increasing revenue from the tourist industry. Continental Portugal is divided for administrative purposes into the following 18 districts: Aveiro, Beja, Braga, Bragança, Castelo Branco, Coimbra, Évora, Faro, Guarda, Leiria, Lisboa, Portalegre, Pôrto, Santarém, Setúbal, Viana do Castelo, Vila Real, Viseu. The Atlantic islands of the Azores and Madeira are politically an integral part of the country; the former are divided into the three districts of Angra do Heroismo, Horta, and Ponta Delgada, while the latter is known as the district of Funchal.

TOPOGRAPHY, CLIMATE. Physically Portugal may be regarded as a W extension of Spain, with mountain ranges running generally NE–SW across the country, rising in the Serra da Estrêla to 6,532 ft. The four principal rivers, the Minho (◊ *Miño*), Douro, Tagus, and Guadiana, are also mainly Spanish. Because of the country's geographical position, facing the Atlantic, most of Portugal enjoys an equable, temperate climate, with a moderately heavy rainfall. In the Algarve, in the extreme S, on the other hand, both climate and vegetation are sub-tropical in character and are reminiscent of N Africa.

RESOURCES, PEOPLE, *etc.* On the plains and in the valleys of the W the leading crops are wheat, maize, vines, and olives. Port from the Douro valley is the most important wine, but many others are produced. The wooded slopes of the interior produce more cork than the rest of the world; resin from the numerous pines is another significant export. Around the coasts many men are employed in the fishing industry, and the sardines which represent the chief part of the catch are canned at Setúbal and other coastal towns. It is indicative of Portuguese maritime interests that the two largest cities by far – the only two with more than 50,000 inhabitants – are Lisbon, the capital, and Oporto, both seaports; they are also the main industrial centres, chiefly manufacturing textiles. Minerals are little exploited, owing to poor communications and lack of fuel. Development of the tourist industry is most apparent on the so-called Portuguese Riviera, W of Lisbon, where Estoril is the leading centre.

The Portuguese people are basically of Iberian descent, with an admixture of Suevi and Visigoths in the N and Moors, Jews, and even Negroes, the last imported as slaves, in the S. There is still a 30-per cent illiteracy rate, in spite of the establishment of compulsory education in 1911. Under the present constitution the National Assembly consists of 130 deputies elected by direct suffrage for 4 years; in recent years, however, a single list of candidates has been presented, and legislation has often been by government decree. Portuguese overseas possessions, Angola, Moçambique, Cape Verde Is., Portuguese Guinea, São Tomé and Principe, Macao, and Timor are all represented in the National Assembly. Portuguese India was incorporated into the Indian Union in 1961.

HISTORY. The early history of Portugal was that of the Iberian peninsula as a whole, most of the country being incorporated with part of W Spain in the Roman province of Lusitania. The Moors defeated the Visigoths, who had later overrun the peninsula, and they in turn were vanquished (1139) by Alfonso I; he proclaimed himself king, though Portugal was not finally cleared of the Moors for another century. In 1386, after English archers had assisted in the defeat of Castile, the alliance between Portugal and England was confirmed, and John I married the daughter of John of Gaunt. Now began the most illustrious period of Portuguese history, initiated by Prince Henry the Navigator, son of John I: the Azores, Madeira, and the Cape Verde Is. were colonized, the Cape of Good Hope was rounded by Bartholomew Diaz (1488), and the route to India was discovered by Vasco da Gama (1498), Brazil was acquired (1500), and the Portuguese Empire was founded. The period of glory, however, was short-lived. In 1580 Philip II of Spain seized the throne, and Portuguese independence was not again recognized by the Spaniards till 1668. The country suffered severely in the War of the Spanish Succession and the Peninsular War, later from civil war and dictatorships, and Brazil was lost. In 1908 King Carlos was assassinated, and with the revolution of 1910 the republic was set up, the Roman Catholic Church was disestablished, and religious orders were expelled. The constitution of 1933 established a corporative state; Dr Salazar, the Prime Minister, became virtually a dictator. He only relinquished office in 1968, after a serious operation, at the age of 79.

**Portuguese Guinea.** Portuguese overseas territory in W Africa, bounded by Senegal (N) and Guinea (E and SE). Area (inc. the Bijagós Is.) 13,948 sq. m. Pop. (1960) 519,229. Cap. and chief seaport Bissau. Tropical monsoon climate. Annual rainfall (mainly May–Nov.) 50–80 ins. The coast is fringed with mangrove swamps. Inland the rain-forest gradually passes into savannah. Main products palm oil and kernels, rice, copra, beeswax, groundnuts, hides. Discovered (1446) by the Portuguese sailor Nuño Tristão. Important in the slave trade in the 17th and 18th cent.

**Posadas** Argentina. Capital of Misiones province, on the Alto Paraná R. 185 m. E of Corrientes. Pop. 45,000. Linked by ferry with Encarnación (Paraguay). River port. Trade in rice, tobacco, maté, etc. Meat packing, flour milling.

**Poseidonia** ◊ *Paestum.*

**Posen** ◊ *Poznań.*

**Posillipo (Posilipo)** Italy. Ridge in Campania extending SW from Naples, pene-trated by a tunnel (the Grotto of Posillipo) through which passes the road from Naples to Pozzuoli. Famed for its beauty; the village of Posillipo, which has remains of Roman villas, is still a fashionable residential area.

**Postojna** Yugoslavia. Small town in Slovenia 25 m. SW of Ljubljana. Pop. 4,000. Famous caves, the largest in Europe, containing stalactites and stalagmites of fantastic shapes, in the limestone Karst region. Here was first discovered the remarkable amphibious creature *Proteus anguinus.*

**Potchefstroom** S. Africa. Town in the Transvaal on the Mooi R. above the confluence with the Vaal R. 70 m. WSW of Johannesburg, at a height of 4,436 ft. Pop. (1968) 52,780. In an agricultural district where wheat, maize, and alfalfa are cultivated and dairy cattle raised. Educational centre. Seat of a university (1951) and of an agricultural college and government experimental farm. Founded (1838) by Hendrik Potgieter. The oldest town and first capital of the Transvaal.

**Potenza** Italy. Capital of Potenza province, in Basilicata, on a hill above the Basento R. at a height of 2,700 ft 55 m. E of Salerno. Pop. (1961) 43,545. Market town. Largely destroyed by the earthquake of 1857 and again damaged by earthquake in 1910.

**Poti** USSR. Seaport in the Georgian SSR, on the Black Sea at the mouth of the Rion R. 40 m. N of Batumi. Pop. (1964) 42,500. Exports chiefly manganese from the Chiatura mines. Fish canning, ship repairing, etc. The neighbouring marshes (Colchis) have been largely drained.

**Potidaea** Greece. Ancient city in Macedonia, on the Kassandra isthmus of the Chalcidice Peninsula. Founded from Corinth; its opposition to the Athenian League led to the Peloponnesian War. Captured by the Athenians 429 B.C. Destroyed by Philip II of Macedon 356 B.C.; later rebuilt by Cassander.

**Potomac River** USA. River in the E, 287 m. long, formed by the union of the N and S branches (from the Allegheny Mountains), flowing NE and then generally SE, and entering Chesapeake Bay. In the upper course it forms the boundary between Maryland and W Virginia, and in the lower course that between Maryland and the District of Columbia on one side and Virginia on the other. Cuts a picturesque gorge through the Blue Ridge Mountains at Harper's Ferry, where it receives its main tributary, the Shenandoah. Washington (D.C.), 115 m. upstream from the mouth, stands at the head of navigation for shipping; the Great Falls of the Potomac R., a series of cascades and rapids in a 200-ft gorge, are 15 m. above the city. The river has many historical associations: on the right bank below Washington (D.C.) is George Washington's estate of Mount Vernon (Virginia).

**Potosí** Bolivia. Capital of the Potosí department, in the Andes at a height of 13,340 ft 55 m. SW of Sucre. Pop. (1967) 73,923. One of the highest towns in the world. Founded 1545; became famous for its rich silver mines. As the lodes deteriorated, the population declined (from 150,000 in the mid 17th cent. to 8,000 by 1825). Revived with the development of tin mining in the Cerro de Potosí. Also manufactures footwear, furniture, etc. University (1571). Has many colonial buildings, including the famous Casa Real de Moneda or Mint (1572), and a 19th-cent. cathedral.

**Potsdam** German Democratic Republic. **1.** Administrative district, one of the three into which the former *Land* of Brandenburg was divided in 1952. Area 4,849 sq. m. Pop. (1968) 1,134,388.

**2.** Capital of Potsdam district and formerly of Brandenburg, on the Havel R. 16 m. SW of the centre of Berlin. Pop. (1968) 110,617. Residential and industrial. Manufactures chemicals, precision instruments, soap, furniture, etc. Railway and other engineering. Formerly the residence of Prussian kings and German emperors, it became the centre of Prussian militarism, reflected even in the uniformity of its streets. Frederick the Great left his mark in the palace and park of Sans Souci (1745–7), and most of the noteworthy buildings date from the 18th cent. Scene of the Potsdam Conference of Truman, Stalin, and Attlee (1945). Later became the headquarters of the Soviet army in Germany.

**Potteries** England. District in N Staffordshire in the upper Trent valley, 9 m. long (NW–SE) and about 3 m. wide, including Stoke-on-Trent, Hanley, Burslem, Tunstall, Longton, Fenton, etc., amalgamated in 1910 as Stoke-on-Trent. The country's leading area for china and earthenware manufacture. Newcastle-under-Lyme,

though not a pottery-manufacturing town, lies on its W edge. The modern pottery industry dates from *c.* 1769, when Josiah Wedgwood founded his works at Etruria (now in Hanley); Wedgwood and Minton are the outstanding family names associated with it. Local coal and coarse clay were long important raw materials, but fine china clay is imported from Cornwall and Dorset.

**Potters Bar** England. Former urban district in N Middlesex, transferred to Hertfordshire in 1965 when most of Middlesex was absorbed into the Greater London Council area. Mainly residential.

**Pottstown** USA. Industrial town in Pennsylvania, on the Schuylkill R. 32 m. NW of Philadelphia. Pop. (1960) 26,144. Manufactures iron and steel goods, tyres, etc. The first ironworks in Pennsylvania were established here *c.* 1720.

**Poughkeepsie** USA. Industrial town in New York, on the Hudson R. 68 m. N of New York city. Pop. (1960) 38,330. Manufactures dairy machinery, ball bearings, business machines, precision instruments, etc. Settled by the Dutch 1687.

**Poverty Bay** New Zealand. Inlet on the E coast of the N Island where Capt. Cook first landed in New Zealand (1769); so named because he could not obtain provisions there. Gisborne is on its N coast.

**Poyang Lake** China. Shallow lake in N Kiangsi province, connected by canal with the Yangtse R. In summer it receives the latter's flood waters and reaches its maximum dimensions (80 m. by 40 m.); in winter considerably diminished. Receives one major river, the Kan-kiang, from the S. Gradually decreasing in area owing to deposition of sediment.

**Poznań** (Ger. **Posen**) Poland. Capital of the Poznań voivodship, on the Warta R. 180 m. W of Warsaw. Pop. (1968) 455,500. Important railway junction, industrial and commercial centre. Manufactures machinery, railway rolling stock, boilers, bicycles, tyres, glass, chemicals, etc. Brewing, distilling. One of the oldest cities in Poland and an archiepiscopal see since the 10th cent. The 16th-cent. town hall and the 18th-cent. cathedral were severely damaged in the 2nd World War and rebuilt. University (1919). Founded before Poland was Christianized. Its later history was largely a reflection of the Polish struggle against the Germans. Birthplace of Field Marshal von Hindenburg (1847–1934).

**Pozzuoli** Italy. Ancient Puteoli. Port in Napoli province, Campania, 7 m. WSW of Naples. Pop. (1961) 51,308. Iron and steel works. A Roman seaport, having been colonized in the 2nd cent. B.C.; its remains include an amphitheatre and the so-called Temple of Serapis (a market-place). Gave its name to *pozzuolana*, the volcanic ash found here and used, as in Roman times, for making cement. Near by is the crater Solfatara, which emits sulphurous jets and has given its name to this type of volcanic feature. Pozzuoli was twice severely damaged by earthquake (1198, 1538). ⇨ *Posillipo*.

**Prague** (Czech **Praha**) Czechoslovakia. Capital of Czechoslovakia and of the Středočeský region, in central Bohemia on the Vltava R. Pop. (1967) 1,030,000. Industrial, commercial, and route centre. Manufactures machinery, cars, aircraft, clothing, chemicals, paper, etc. Brewing, food processing, printing and publishing. Also a leading cultural centre. Seat of the Charles University (1348) and a technical university (1707). A city of outstanding architectural interest; has a 14th-cent. town hall, severely damaged in the 2nd World War; the 15th-cent. Týn church – the former Hussite religious centre containing the tomb of Tycho Brahe; the 15th-cent. Powder Tower; the Hradčany Palace, once residence of the kings of Bohemia and now of the Czechoslovak president; and the cathedral of St Vitus, begun in 1344 and completed in 1929. The most famous of the 12 bridges spanning the Vltava R. is the 14th-cent. Charles Bridge. Of more modern structures, the gigantic Masaryk or Strahov Stadium accommodates 200,000 people. German colonists were settled in Prague in the 11th and 13th cent., and the rivalry between Czechs and Germans was largely responsible for the reformist preaching of John Huss; the Defenestration of Prague (1419) led to the Hussite Wars, and a later Defenestration (1618) to the Thirty Years War. Long remained the centre of Czech nationalism, and when Czechoslovakia achieved independence (1918) it became the capital.

**Praia** ⇨ *Cape Verde Islands*.

**Prato** Italy. Town in Firenze province, Tuscany, on the Bisenzio R. 9 m. WNW of Florence. Pop. (1968) 134,207. Centre of the woollen industry. Manufactures textile machinery, furniture, etc. The 12th/15th-cent. cathedral has frescoes by Filippo Lippi and an open-air pulpit by Donatello and Michelozzo; several other noteworthy churches.

**Prayag** ⇨ *Allahabad*.

**Přerov** Czechoslovakia. Town in Moravia, on the Bečva R. 14 m. SE of Olomouc. Pop. (1967) 36,000. Manufactures machinery, textiles, etc.

**Prescot** England. Urban district in SW Lancashire 8 m. E of Liverpool. Pop. (1961) 13,077. Manufactures electric cables, watch movements, tools.

**Prešov** Czechoslovakia. Town in Slovakia, on the Torysa R. 20 m. N of Košice. Pop. (1967) 40,000. Railway junction. Market town. Distilling. Manufactures linen etc. Founded by Germans in the 12th cent. Almost completely rebuilt since a disastrous fire in 1887.

**Prespa, Lake.** Lake mainly in Macedonia, Yugoslavia, with the SW part in Albania and the SE part in Greece; at a height of 2,800 ft. Area 110 sq. m. Drained by underground channels to L. Okhrida, 6 m. W.

**Pressburg** ⇨ *Bratislava*.

**Prestatyn** Wales. Urban district in Flintshire 4 m. ENE of Rhyl. Pop. (1961) 10,771. Market town. Seaside resort.

**Presteigne** Wales. Urban district and county town of Radnorshire, on the R. Lugg 19 m. NW of Hereford. Pop. (1961) 1,190. Market town. Has a 15th-cent. parish church.

**Preston** England. County borough of Lancashire, on the R. Ribble 27 m. NW of Manchester. Pop. (1961) 113,208. Port. Engineering. Manufactures textiles (cotton, rayon), machinery, electrical equipment, motor vehicles, footwear, chemicals, etc. Trade in agricultural produce, livestock. Has the Harris Museum and Art Gallery and a grammar school founded in the 16th cent. The epithet 'proud Preston' dates from the 18th cent., when it acquired a reputation for its fashionable society. Birthplace of Richard Arkwright (1732–92), inventor of the spinning frame, Francis Thompson (1859–1907), the poet, and Robert W. Service (1874–1958), the Canadian author.

**Prestonpans** Scotland. Small burgh in E Lothian, on the Firth of Forth 8 m. E of Edinburgh. Pop. (1961) 3,104. Coalmining, brewing. Manufactures soap, bricks and tiles. At the Battle of Prestonpans (1745)

Prince Charles Edward defeated the English forces under Sir John Cope. The name derives from the pans, or ponds, in which salt was formerly obtained from seawater by evaporation.

**Prestwich** England. Municipal borough in Lancashire 4 m. NNW of Manchester, of which it is a suburb. Pop. (1961) 34,191. Mainly residential. Manufactures textiles (cotton, rayon).

**Prestwick** Scotland. Small burgh in W Ayrshire, on the Firth of Clyde 2 m. NNE of Ayr. Pop. (1961) 12,564. Seaside resort. Well-known golf course. International airport, developed during the 2nd World War as a transatlantic terminal.

**Pretoria** S Africa. Administrative capital, also capital of the Transvaal, 32 m. NNE of Johannesburg at a height of 4,600 ft. Pop. (1967) 479,739 (254,000 white, 205,739 Bantu). Important railway centre. Railway engineering. Manufactures cement, leather, chemicals. S Africa's largest steelworks is 5 m. W. Seat of the University of Pretoria (1930) and the Radcliffe Observatory (1937). President Kruger's house is a national monument. Famous for its jacaranda-lined streets; the trees bloom Oct.–Nov. Founded 1855. Named after the Boer Leader Andries Pretorius. Became the administrative capital of the new Union of S Africa 1910. Voortrekker Monument (1949), commemorating the S African *voortrekkers* (pioneers) of 1834–8, is 4 m. S.

**Préveza** Greece. 1. *Nome* in Epirus on the Ionian Sea. Area 425 sq. m. Pop. (1961) 62,387. Mainly mountainous. Produces olive oil, citrus fruits, cereals. Fishing.

2. Capital and chief port of Préveza *nome*, at the entrance to the Gulf of Arta. Pop. (1961) 11,172. Exports olives and olive oil, citrus fruits, etc.

**Pribilof (Fur Seal) Islands** USA. Group of 4 islands in the Bering Sea off SW Alaska. Area 65 sq. m. Pop. about 550 (entirely Aleuts and government officials, no others being permitted to reside on the islands). Only St Paul and St George are inhabited. Important for trade in seal furs; a major breeding ground for the Alaskan fur seal, recognized as an international seal reserve. Until the Pacific Sealing Convention (1911) the seal was threatened with extermination. Named after Gerasim Pribilof, the Russian who discovered them (1786).

**Prilep** Yugoslavia. Market town in Macedonia 45 m. S of Skoplje. Pop. (1961) 39,611. In an agricultural region. Important trade in tobacco. Birthplace of the 14th-cent. Serbian national hero, Marko Kralyević, the ruins of whose fortress lie just NE.

**Primorye (Maritime) Territory** USSR. Territory in RSFSR, in SE Siberia, on the Sea of Japan opposite S Sakhalin and Hokkaido (Japan). Area 65,000 sq. m. Pop. (1970) 1,722,000. Cap. Vladivostok. Includes part of the Sikhote Alin Range (E) and the lowlands beside the Ussuri R. and L. Khanka (W) along the border with Manchuria. Produces coal and other minerals, timber.

**Prince Albert** Canada. Town in Saskatchewan, on the N Saskatchewan R. 83 m. NNE of Saskatoon. Pop. (1966) 26,269. Commercial centre for N Saskatchewan. Woodworking, tanning, etc. Founded (1866) as a mission station.

**Prince Edward Island** Canada. The smallest province in Canada, in the Gulf of St Lawrence. Area 2,184 sq. m. Pop. (1966) 108,535. Cap. Charlottetown. Generally low-lying. The coastline is deeply indented, with sandy beaches in the N and low cliffs of red sandstone in the S. Maritime climate, milder than that of the neighbouring mainland. Annual rainfall 40 ins. Dairy farming, cattle rearing, agriculture, fishing (esp. lobsters). A train ferry connects Port Borden with Cape Tormentine (New Brunswick). Discovered by Jacques Cartier in 1534. Annexed by France 1603 (as Île St Jean). Ceded to Britain 1763. Remained part of Nova Scotia until it became a separate colony (1769). Many Scottish and Irish immigrants settled here in the early 19th cent. Joined the Confederation of Canada 1873.

**Prince George** Canada. Town in British Columbia, on the Fraser R. at its confluence with the Nechako R. 325 m. N of Vancouver. Pop. (1966) 24,471. Commercial centre for a mining and lumbering region. Founded as a fur-trading post in the early 19th cent.

**Prince of Wales Island** ⟡ *Endeavour Strait*.

**Prince Rupert** Canada. Seaport in British Columbia near the mouth of the Skeena R., on an island connected to the mainland by a bridge. Pop. (1966) 14,677. Exports grain. Serves mining, lumbering, and farming communities. Important halibut and salmon fisheries. Fish canning, pulp milling. W terminus of the Canadian National Railway's northern route.

**Princess Elizabeth Land** ⟡ *Australian Antarctic Territory*.

**Princeton** USA. Residential town in New Jersey, on the Millstone R. 11 m. NE of Trenton. Pop. (1960) 11,890. Famous as the seat of Princeton University, opened at Elizabeth (1747), moved to Newark (1748), and then to Princeton (1756), and known as the College of New Jersey until 1896. Settled by Quakers 1696. Incorporated 1813. Birthplace of Paul Robeson (1898–    ).

**Principe** ⟡ *São Tomé and Principe*.

**Pripet** (Russian **Pripyat**) **River** USSR. River 500 m. long rising in the NW Ukrainian SSR just E of the Bug R., flowing generally ENE into the Byelorussian SSR, then turning E and SE to join the Dnieper R. Navigable for much of its course and linked by canals with the Bug and the Neman rivers. Around the upper course of the river and its tributaries are the Pripet Marshes, a wooded, swampy area in which flax, potatoes, etc. are cultivated near scattered villages; before the 2nd World War it was in Poland. The chief town here is Pinsk.

**Pristina** Yugoslavia. Capital of Kosovo-Metohija, Serbia, 50 m. NNW of Skoplje. Pop. (1961) 38,593. Market town in an agricultural district. Oriental in character and appearance; under Turkish rule until 1912. The remarkable 14th-cent. monastery of Gračanica is 4 m. SW.

**Prokopyevsk** USSR. Coalmining town in the Kemerovo region, RSFSR, in the Kuznetsk Basin, 17 m. WNW of Novokuznetsk. Pop. (1970) 275,000. Linked by rail with Novokuznetsk and also with the Trans-Siberian Railway.

**Prome** Burma. River port on the Irrawaddy R. 150 m. NNW of Rangoon, with which it is connected by rail. Pop. 37,000. An ancient town with the famous Shwe Tsandaw pagoda on a near-by hill.

**Proskurov** ⟡ *Khmelnitsky*.

**Prostějov** (Ger. **Prossnitz**) Czechoslovakia. Town in Moravia 10 m. SW of Olomouc. Pop. (1967) 36,000. Brewing. Manufactures textiles, clothing, footwear, etc.

**Provence** France. Ancient Provincia. Region and former province in the SE, bounded by Italy (E), the Mediterranean Sea (S), and the Rhône R. (W); now forms the Bouches-du-Rhône, Var, and Basses-Alpes and parts of the Alpes-Maritimes and Vaucluse departments. Largely mountainous. Dry and sunny; the river valleys are noted for their vines, olives, and mulberries. The French Riviera is famous for its luxuriant vegetation as well as its mild climate. Became a kingdom in the 9th cent. United to the French crown 1486. The Provençal language was used from the early Middle Ages until the 16th cent., but the literature never completely died out and was vigorously revived in the 19th cent.

**Providence** USA. State capital, largest city, and seaport of Rhode Island, on the Providence R., at the head of Narragansett Bay. Pop. (1960) 207,498. Oil refining. Manufactures jewellery, textiles, textile machinery, machine tools, rubber products, etc. Seat of Brown University (1764). Founded (1636) by Roger Williams; named in recognition of 'God's merciful providence'. Many noteworthy 18th-cent. buildings. Joint state capital with Newport until 1900.

**Provo** USA. Town in Utah, on the Provo R. 39 m. SSE of Salt Lake City, at a height of 4,549 ft. Pop. (1960) 36,047. Commercial centre for an agricultural and mining region. Manufactures iron and steel, bricks and tiles, food products. Seat of the Brigham Young University (1875, Mormon). Settled by the Mormons 1849. Developed considerably after the arrival of the railway from Salt Lake City (1873).

**Prussia** (Ger. **Preussen**) Germany. Formerly the principal and largest state in Germany, bounded by the North Sea, Denmark, and the Baltic (N), Poland and Lithuania (E), Czechoslovakia, Saxony, Thuringia, Bavaria, and Hessen (S), and Alsace-Lorraine, Luxembourg, Belgium, and the Netherlands (W). Cap. Berlin. Comprised the provinces of Berlin, Brandenburg, E Prussia, Hanover, Hesse-Nassau, Pomerania, the Rhine, Saxony, Schleswig-Holstein, Silesia, and Westphalia, and the enclave of Hohenzollern (until the 2nd World War); a number of small states (e.g. Anhalt, Brunswick) formed enclaves within its territory. Mostly in the N German plain. Agriculture varied from the cultivation of rye and potatoes in the less fertile soils of the N and E to that of wheat and barley in the S and W. Its wealth consisted chiefly in manufactures, based on the rich coalfields of the Ruhr, the Saar, and Silesia, and centred on the great industrial cities of Berlin, Breslau (⟡ *Wroclaw*),

Cologne, Düsseldorf, Essen, Dortmund, Duisburg, Wuppertal, and many others. Industrial efficiency was aided by an excellent system of communications, with a network of roads and railways and inland waterways (inc. the Rhine, Elbe, and Oder rivers and inter-connecting canals).

Prussia was formed early in the 17th cent. by the union of the Mark of Brandenburg and the state of the Teutonic Order, through the marriage of John Sigmund, Elector of Brandenburg, to Anna, daughter and heiress of Albert Frederick, Duke of Prussia and last Grand Master of the Teutonic Order. Under Frederick William, the Great Elector (1640–88), Further Pomerania (Hinterpommern) and the prince-bishoprics of Hallerstadt, Magdeburg, and Minden were acquired, and the foundations of Prussia's military strength were laid. His son, Frederick III (1688–1713), took the title 'King in Prussia' (1701); his grandson, Frederick William I (1713–40), consolidated the wealth and military power of the kingdom, which were utilized by Frederick the Great (1740–86) to annex Silesia (Sląsk), E Frisia, and most of W Prussia. Utterly defeated by Napoleon at Jena (1806), Prussia nevertheless played a considerable part in his overthrow, and after the Congress of Vienna (1815) regained lost territories and acquired the Rhine province and Westphalia, N Saxony, and Hither Pomerania (Vorpommern). Now a powerful European state, it took the lead in the creation of the German Zollverein. The 1848 Revolution was crushed, but Frederick William IV refused the imperial crown offered him by the Frankfurt National Assembly. His successor, William I (with Bismarck as chancellor from 1862), defeated Denmark and then Austria, acquiring Schleswig-Holstein, Hanover, Hesse-Nassau, and the city of Frankfurt-am-Main. Prussia now dominated the extensive N German Confederation. After the Franco-Prussian War (1870–71) William I became Emperor of Germany; the subsequent history of Prussia is substantially that of Germany. At the end of the 1st World War Prussia joined the Weimar Republic (1918). On the re-creation of Poland (1919) E Pomerania (Pomorze) became E Prussia, Poland having only a 10-m.-wide strip (the Polish Corridor) giving her access to the sea. From 1933, under the Nazi régime, Prussia lost its semi-independence **la** the centralized Third Reich. After the 2nd World War it was dissolved; most of E Prussia and the lands E of the Oder-Neisse (Odra-Nysa) line were restored to Poland and the N part of E Prussia was ceded to the USSR; the remainder of Prussia was broken up into various *Länder* in E and W Germany.

**Prut River** Rumania/USSR. River 530 m. long, rising in the Carpathians in the SW Ukrainian SSR, flowing generally N and then E past Kolomyya and Chernovtsy, then generally SSE, forming the Rumania–USSR border, and joining the Danube R. 8 m. E of Galaţi (Rumania).

**Przemyśl** Poland. Town in the Rzeszow voivodship in the SE, on the San R. near the Ukrainian SSR frontier. Pop. (1968) 52,400. Flour milling, sawmilling, tanning, etc. Manufactures machinery. An ancient town, probably dating from the 8th cent. Occupied by Austria 1773–1915. Ceded to Poland 1919.

**Psiloríti** ◊ *Crete*.

**Pskov (Pleskau)** USSR. Capital of the Pskov region, RSFSR, on the Velikaya R. near its mouth in L. Pskov 165 m. SW of Leningrad. Pop. (1970) 127,000. Railway junction. Industrial centre in an important flax-growing region. Manufactures linen, rope, agricultural machinery, leather, etc. One of the oldest Russian cities. Has many churches and monasteries dating from the 14th and 15th cent. A prosperous and commercially important city in the Middle Ages. Annexed to Moscow 1510; thereafter declined.

**Pskov, Lake** ◊ *Peipus, Lake*.

**Pucallpa** Peru. Town in the Loreto department, on the Ucayali R. 300 m. NE of Lima. Pop. 30,000. Accessible from Iquitos by river steamer. Linked with Lima by the Andean highway since 1944. Sawmilling. Trade in agricultural produce. Reached by pipeline from the Ganzo Azul oilfield to the SSW.

**Pudsey** England. Municipal borough in the W Riding of Yorkshire, 3 m. E of Bradford. Pop. (1961) 34,825. Important woollen industry; also engineering, tanning. Famous as the home of two outstanding Yorkshire and England county cricketers, H. Sutcliffe and Sir Leonard Hutton.

**Puebla** Mexico. 1. State on the central plateau. Area 13,126 sq. m. Pop. (1969) 2,803,000. Largely mountainous; Mexico's 3 highest peaks, Pico de Orizaba, Popocatépetl, and Ixtaccihuatl, are on its borders. Mainly agricultural. Produces maize, wheat, sugar-cane, tobacco, etc. Minerals include gold, silver, copper.

**2.** Formerly Puebla de los Angeles, later Puebla de Zaragoza. Capital of Puebla state, on the central plateau at a height of 7,100 ft, 65 m. ESE of Mexico City. Pop. (1969) 383,900. Manufactures textiles, cement, glazed tiles, pottery, articles in onyx (quarried locally), etc. Picturesque; known as 'the City of Churches'. The 16th/17th-cent. cathedral is one of the finest ecclesiastical buildings in Latin America, noteworthy for its work in marble and onyx. Has the Teatro Principal, one of the oldest theatres on the continent (built 1790). University (1537).

**Pueblo** USA. Industrial town in Colorado, on the Arkansas R. at a height of 4,700 ft 105 m. SSE of Denver. Pop. (1960) 91,181. Known as 'the Pittsburgh of the West' because of the large iron and steel industry. Also oil refining, meat packing, etc.

**Puerto Barrios** Guatemala. Capital of the Izabal department, on the Caribbean coast 150 m. NE of Guatemala City. Pop. (1964) 32,071. The country's chief seaport. Exports coffee, bananas, etc. Oil refining.

**Puerto Cabello** Venezuela. The second most important seaport, in Carabobo state on the Caribbean coast 20 m. N of Valencia. Pop. 48,000. Exports coffee, cacao, hides, etc. Manufactures soap, candles, etc. Flour milling.

**Puerto de Santa María** (commonly **El Puerto**) Spain. Seaport in Cádiz province, Andalusia, at the mouth of the Guadalete R. on the Gulf of Cadiz. Pop. (1961) 35,505. Important trade in sherry. Manufactures alcohol, liqueurs, soap, etc. Tanning, fish canning. Has many sherry bodegas.

**Puerto la Cruz** Venezuela. Town and oil-exporting port in Anzoátegui state in the NE, 6 m. NNE of Barcelona. Pop. 45,000. Terminus of oil pipelines from the E llanos. Large oil refineries.

**Puerto Limón** ◊ *Limón.*

**Puerto Mexico** ◊ *Coatzacoalcos.*

**Puerto Montt** Chile. Capital of Llanquihue province and seaport on Reloncaví Sound, 115 m. SSE of Valdivia. Pop. 65,000. The S terminus of the country's railway system. Serves a sheep-farming area and Chiloé Island. Resort, with access to fine mountain scenery and the Chilean lake district. Founded (1853) by German immigrants.

**Puerto Ordaz** ◊ *Venezuela.*

**Puerto Princesa** ◊ *Palawan.*

**Puerto Rico** (W Indies) USA. Formerly (1898–1932) Porto Rico. Island and territory of the USA, with Commonwealth status since 1952; the smallest and most easterly of the Greater Antilles. Area (with offshore islands) 3,435 sq. m. Pop. (1960) 2,349,544. Cap. San Juan. Mostly mountainous, rising to over 4,000 ft in the Cordillera Central. Climate tropical but pleasant, with little seasonal variation. Annual rainfall 60–70 ins. Main agricultural product sugar-cane (at one time virtually the only crop); pineapples, citrus fruits, coffee, tobacco also grown. Industries (sugar and tobacco processing etc.) are chiefly concentrated in San Juan, Ponce, and Mayagüez. Discovered (1493) by Columbus on his second voyage; settled (1508) by one of his companions, Juan Ponce de León, the first governor. Ceded by Spain to the USA (1898) after the Spanish-American War. The density of population, 687 per sq. m. (1960), is one of the highest in the world. Serious unemployment problems; many Puerto Ricans have emigrated to the USA.

**Puerto Varas** Chile. Town in the Chilean lake district, in Llanquihue province 12 m. N of Puerto Montt on the shore of L. Llanquihue. Pop. 27,000. Tourist centre.

**Puget Sound** USA. Inlet of the Pacific Ocean in NW Washington, extending 100 m. S from the Juan de Fuca Strait (by which it is connected with the Pacific, through the Admiralty Inlet) to Olympia. Several islands. Chief ports Seattle, Tacoma.

**Puglia** ◊ *Apulia.*

**Pukapuka** ◊ *Cook Islands.*

**Puket** ◊ *Phuket.*

**Pula** (Italian **Pola**) Yugoslavia. Ancient Pietas Julia. Seaport in NW Croatia near the S end of the peninsula of Istria; also a modern tourist resort. Pop. (1961) 37,403. Taken by the Romans 178 B.C.; has many Roman remains, including a fine amphitheatre. Captured by the Venetians 1148. An Austrian naval base 1856–1918, then became capital of the Italian province of Pola and later of Istria. Passed to Yugoslavia 1947.

**Punjab.** In Sanskrit, 'Five Waters'. **1.** Former province of NW India, divided in 1947 between India and Pakistan, the E part to the former and the W part to the latter. The Sanskrit name refers to the five tributaries of the Indus R. – Jhelum, Chenab, Ravi, Beas, and Sutlej – which flow through it. On the irrigated lands (*doabs*) between the rivers, wheat is the out-

standing crop, and cotton, maize, rice, and sugar-cane are also grown. About two thirds of the people are dependent on agriculture. After the break-up of the Mogul Empire the Sikhs became the dominant power in the Punjab, but after the death of Ranjit Singh (1839) the Sikh Wars (1845–9) led to the annexation of the region to British India and the Punjab became a province. In 1901 the N W Frontier Province and in 1912 Delhi were detached from it. Constituted an autonomous province 1937. At the partition (1947) W Punjab became the Pakistani province of Punjab, and now comprises the Divisions of Rawalpindi, Lahore, Multan, and Bahawalpur in W Pakistan. Area 70,178 sq. m. Pop. (1961) 19,377,000. Chief towns Lahore, Rawalpindi, Multan, Islamabad. E Punjab became the Indian province of Punjab and later a state ($\diamond$ below).
2. Constituent state of the Indian Union bounded on the W by Pakistan. Area 47,205 sq. m. Pop. (1961) 20,306,812. Cap. Chandigarh. Mainly agricultural; crops as above. Chief industry the manufacture of textiles. Principal towns Chandigarh, Amritsar, Ludhiana, Jullundur, Patiala. With the creation of the new state of Haryana and the reorganization of Punjab as a Punjabi-speaking state (1966), Punjab lost about 18,000 sq. m. of territory and 8½ million people, mainly to Haryana.

**Punta Arenas** Chile. Capital of Magallanes province and seaport on Magellan Strait. Pop. 55,000. Port of call for ships passing between the Atlantic and the Pacific. Centre of a sheep-farming area. Exports wool, meat. Coal mined near by. Known as the most southerly city in the world.

**Puntarenas** Costa Rica. Capital of the Puntarenas province, on the Pacific coast 50 m. W of San José. Pop. (1963) 25,979. The country's chief Pacific seaport. Exports coffee, bananas, etc. Tuna fishing and processing. Manufactures soap, etc.

**Puracé, Mount** $\diamond$ *Popayán.*

**Purbeck, Isle of** England. Peninsula in S Dorset, 12 m. long and 7 m. wide, S of Poole Harbour. St Alban's Head is at the S end. Purbeck marble (limestone) is quarried. Principal towns Swanage, Corfe Castle.

**Purfleet** $\diamond$ *Thurrock.*

**Puri (Jagannath)** India. Commercial town and seaside resort in E Orissa, 45 m. S of Cuttack. Pop. (1961) 60,815. Handicraft industries. Sometimes known as Jagannath (Juggernaut); famous chiefly for its temple of Jagannath (meaning 'lord of the world'), built in the 12th cent. During the annual car festival the image of the god is dragged through the town on a large cart by pilgrims.

**Purley** $\diamond$ *Coulsdon and Purley.*

**Purús River** Brazil/Peru. River 2,000 m. long rising in the Peruvian Andes, flowing N E through the tropical rain-forest of N W Brazil, and joining the Amazon R. 110 m. W S W of Manáus.

**Pusan** S Korea. Country's chief seaport and second largest city, on the S E coast. Pop. (1966) 1,429,726. Exports rice, fish, soya beans, etc. Also a railway and industrial centre. Railway engineering, shipbuilding, rice milling, salt refining. Manufactures textiles. A centre of Japanese influence from the end of the 16th cent. During the Korean War (1950–52) it was the chief supply base for the U N troops.

**Puteaux** France. Industrial suburb in W Paris, on the left bank of the Seine R., in the Hauts-de-Seine department. Pop. (1968) 38,014. Engineering, printing. Manufactures perfumes etc.

**Puteoli** $\diamond$ *Pozzuoli.*

**Putney** England. Residential district in the London borough of Wandsworth, in S W London, on the S bank of the R. Thames. Putney Bridge, across the Thames, is the starting point of the Oxford and Cambridge annual boat race. Putney Heath, once a haunt of highwaymen, adjoins Wimbledon Common. Birthplace of Thomas Cromwell (1485–1540) and Edward Gibbon (1737–94).

**Putumayo River.** River 980 m. long rising in the Colombian Andes and flowing generally E S E, forming most of the Colombia–Peru boundary. It then enters Brazil (where it is called the Içá R.) and joins the Amazon R. Its basin consists of dense, sparsely populated tropical rain-forest: the scene of the Putumayo rubber scandal (1910–11).

**Puy, Le (Le Puy en Velay)** France. Prefecture of the Haute-Loire department, near the Loire R. 36 m. S W of St Étienne. Pop. (1968) 29,549. Famous for its lace; also produces liqueurs. Has a 12th-cent. Romanesque cathedral, and, on the summit of a tall slender rock, the Church of St Michel d'Aiguilhe.

**Puy-de-Dôme** France. Department in central France, mainly in Auvergne and partly in Bourbonnais, in the N part of the Massif Central. Area 3,095 sq. m. Pop.

(1968) 547,743. Prefecture Clermont-Ferrand. In the W are the Auvergne Mountains, with the volcanic Puy de Sancy (6,187 ft) and Puy de Dôme (4,806 ft), on the summit of which are a meteorological observatory and the ruins of a Roman temple. In the E are the Forez Mountains rising to 5,381 ft. Between these highlands is the fertile plain of the Limagne, watered by the Allier and Dore rivers, where vines, fruits, and cereals are cultivated and cattle and sheep are raised. There are spas with mineral springs in the Auvergne Mountains. Coal mined. Industries concentrated mainly in Clermont-Ferrand and Thiers.

**Puy de Sancy** ◊ *Puy-de-Dôme*.

**Pwllheli** Wales. Municipal borough in Caernarvonshire, on Cardigan Bay 19 m. SSW of Caernarvon. Pop. (1961) 3,642. Port. Seaside resort.

**Pyärnu** ◊ *Pärnu*.

**Pyatigorsk** USSR. In Russian, 'Five Mountains'. Town in the Stavropol Territory, RSFSR, in the N Caucasus 90 m. SE of Stavropol. Pop. 69,000. There are five peaks around it (hence its name). Spa, with sanatoria and sulphur springs. Metal working. Manufactures furniture, clothing, etc. The poet Lermontov (1814–41) was killed here in a duel.

**Pylos** Greece. Ancient town in the SW Peloponnese, at the N entrance to Pylos Bay, where the Athenians defeated the Spartans in 425 B.C. In the Middle Ages it was renamed Old Navarino. A new town, now known as Pílos, grew up on the S shore of the bay. At the Battle of Navarino (1827) in Pylos Bay, a British, French, and Russian fleet defeated a Turkish and Egyptian fleet.

**Pyongyang** N Korea. Capital of N Korea, on the Taedong R. 125 m. NW of Seoul. Pop. 940,000. Industrial centre in an anthracite-mining area. Sugar refining. Manufactures textiles, chemicals, paper, matches, etc. Hydroelectric power derived from plants on the Yalu R. University (1946). Reputedly founded in the 12th cent. B.C.; has remains of the ancient walls. Suffered severely during the Japanese invasion (1592), the Sino-Japanese War (1894), the Russo-Japanese War (1904), and again in the Korean War (1950–52).

**Pyrenees** (Fr. **Pyrénées**, Sp. **Pirineos**) France/Spain. Mountain range in SW Europe extending about 275 m. W–E from the Bay of Biscay to the Mediterranean Sea, separating the Iberian peninsula from France. The central Pyrenees, in the E of which is the small state of Andorra, form the widest and highest part of the range, with such peaks as the Pico de Aneto (11,168 ft) and Monte Perdido (10,997 ft). The W Pyrenees are much lower, in general 3,000–4,500 ft, descending gradually W, while the E Pyrenees fall abruptly from 9,000 ft to the Mediterranean coast. Outstanding features of the Pyrenees are the mountain torrents (*gaves*) on the French side, where most of the resorts and spas are situated; the natural amphitheatres (*cirques*), caused by glacial action, at the upper ends of many valleys; and the small number of passes, among them Perthus (915 ft), the lowest, Roncesvalles (3,468 ft), and Somport (5,354 ft). There has been considerable development of hydroelectric power on both sides of the range.

**Pyrénées-Orientales** France. Department in the S, bordered by the Gulf of Lions (E) and Spain (S), formed in 1790 mainly from Roussillon. Area 1,600 sq. m. Pop. (1968) 281,976. Prefecture Perpignan. The W part is occupied by the E Pyrenees, with Pic Carlitte rising to 9,583 ft, the E part by a coastal plain crossed by the Agly, Têt, and Tech rivers. Vineyards, orchards, olive groves, and market gardens abound in the valleys and lowlands; wine is a particularly important product. Several spas.

**Pyrgos** ◊ *Elis*.

# Q

Qairwan ◊ *Kairouan.*

**Qantara, El (El Kantara)** United Arab Republic. Village on the Suez Canal 24 m. S of Port Said. On the ancient caravan route between Egypt and Syria. Terminus of the railway to Jerusalem, built by the British during the 1st World War.

**Qatar.** Independent sheikhdom under British protection, on the E coast of Arabia, occupying a peninsula projecting into the Persian Gulf and bounded on the landward side by Saudi Arabia. Area 4,000 sq. m. Pop. (1969) 80,000. Cap. Doha. Consists largely of stony desert. Many of the Arab tribesmen are camel breeders. Main product petroleum. Dukhan (W), the chief oilfield centre, is linked by pipeline with Umm Said (SE), the oil port.

**Qattara Depression** United Arab Republic. Arid depression in the Libyan Desert 30 m. S of El Alamein, about 180 m. long (NE–SW) and 75 m. wide, 436 ft below sea level at the lowest point. Contains an extensive area of salt marsh. During the 2nd World War it was the S flank of the Allied defence line at El Alamein, the soft sand making it an impassable obstacle to military vehicles. ◊ *Western Desert.*

Qazvin ◊ *Kazvin.*

**Qena** United Arab Republic. Capital of Qena governorate, on the E bank of the Nile, on the railway 120 m. SE of Asyût. Pop. (1960) 58,000. Market town. Trade in cereals, dates. Famous for porous pottery, made into water jars and bottles. Terminal of the road from Port Safaga on the Red Sea.

**Qishm** Iran. Island in the Strait of Hormuz, Persian Gulf, 65 m. long and up to 20 m. wide. Pop. 15,000. Chief town Qishm (pop. 6,000). The largest island in the Persian Gulf. Fishing, salt mining. Cereals, dates cultivated.

Qishn ◊ *Socotra.*

**Quantock Hills** England. Range in Somerset 9 m. long, extending SE from near Watchet, rising to 1,261 ft in Will's Neck.

Quarnero ◊ *Kvarner.*

**Quebec** Canada. Largest province in the E, bounded on the S by Maine, New Hampshire, Vermont, and New York (all USA). Area 594,860 sq. m. Pop. (1966) 5,780,845. Cap. Quebec. Includes Anticosti and the Magdalen Is. in the Gulf of St Lawrence, and several islands in the St Lawrence R. The greater part lies within the Canadian Shield. S of the St Lawrence R. are the Notre Dame Mountains (an extension of the Appalachian system), continued into the Gaspé Peninsula, which has the highest point in the province, Mt Jacques Cartier (4,160 ft). Innumerable lakes, including L. Mistassini (840 sq. m.) and L. Minto (485 sq. m.). Climate very varied, but generally continental. Annual rainfall 40 ins. in the S, 15 ins. in the N (including abundant snowfalls). Immense areas of forest, the basis of the leading industry, the manufacture of wood pulp and paper, in which it holds first place among the provinces. Agriculture (cereals, hay, etc.) and stock rearing are important in the S. Mineral resources include the vast iron-ore deposits of Ungava (NE), gold, copper, and asbestos. Hydroelectric power is extensively developed. About one third of the industrial capacity is located in Montreal; other chief centres Quebec, Sherbrooke, Trois Rivières. Most of the population are of French descent and French-speaking. Known under French rule as New France (or Canada). Passed to Britain 1763. Became a province of the Dominion of Canada 1867. Acquired the territory of Ungava 1912.

**Quebec City** Canada. Capital of Quebec province, on the St Lawrence R. at the confluence with the St Charles 140 m. NE of Montreal. Pop. (1966) 166,984. Important port, but closed by ice Dec.–April. Exports timber, grain. Industrial centre. Manufactures wood pulp and paper, newsprint and paper products, clothing, food products, etc. Built around Cape Diamond, a cliff rising 333 ft above the St Lawrence R., on the summit of which is the Citadel (built 1823–32). Now divided into the upper town and the lower town. Below the Citadel are the Château Frontenac (a hotel) and the Dufferin Terrace (a well-known promenade). Many of the notable buildings date from the 17th cent., among them the Hôtel-Dieu hospital (1639) and the Chapel of Notre Dame des Victoires (1688). Like Montreal, a leading French Canadian cultural centre: seat of the Laval University

(Roman Catholic, 1852). More than 80 per cent of the population are French-speaking. There are both Anglican and Roman Catholic cathedrals. 7 m. above it is the cantilever Quebec Bridge (completed 1917) across the St Lawrence.

Jacques Cartier visited the site (1535) but the real founder was Samuel Champlain, who in 1608 built a fort where the lower town now stands. The British under General Wolfe defeated the French under Montcalm on the near-by Plains of Abraham (1759). Quebec (capital of New France since 1663) became capital of the new British colony of Quebec in 1763 and of Lower Canada in 1791. On the founding here of the Confederation of Canada (1867) it was made capital of the newly constituted province of Quebec.

**Quedlinburg** German Democratic Republic. Town in the Halle district, on the Bode R. 45 m. NW of Halle near the Harz Mountains. Pop. (1965) 30,834. A market town. Horticulture. Minor industries. Fortified in 922 by Henry I, whose tomb is in the 11th/12th-cent. Church of St Servatius. Birthplace of Friedrich Klopstock (1724–1803), the poet, and Karl Ritter (1779–1859), the geographer.

**Queenborough** England. Small port in Kent, on the W coast of the Isle of Sheppey. Pop. (1961) 3,044. From 1968 part of the municipal borough of ◊ *Queenborough in Sheppey*. Founded by Edward III; named after Queen Philippa.

**Queenborough in Sheppey** England. Municipal borough in Kent formed (1968) from the former municipal borough of Queenborough, the urban district of Sheerness, and the rural district of Sheppey. Pop. (1968) 28,630.

**Queen Charlotte Islands** Canada. Archipelago of about 150 islands off the coast of British Columbia, separated from the mainland by Hecate Strait. Area 3,780 sq. m. Pop. 3,000. Chief islands Graham, Moresby. Main occupations fishing, lumbering.

**Queen Charlotte Sound** Canada. Stretch of water in the Pacific between the Queen Charlotte Is. (NW) and Vancouver Island (SE), in British Columbia; leads SE into Queen Charlotte Strait, which separates Vancouver Island from the mainland.

**Queen Elizabeth Islands** Canada. Northernmost islands of the Canadian Arctic archipelago, lying N of 74° N lat. A separate group since 1953, part of the Franklin District of the NW Territories; 19 main islands. The largest are Ellesmere, Devon, Melville, and Axel Heiberg.

**Queensbury and Shelf** England. Urban district in the W Riding of Yorkshire, 3 m. N of Halifax. Pop. (1961) 9,268. Woollen and worsted manufactures.

**Queensferry (South Queensferry)** Scotland. Small burgh in W Lothian, on the Firth of Forth 8 m. WNW of Edinburgh. Pop. (1961) 2,929. Here are the Forth railway bridge and the new Forth road bridge. On the opposite side is N Queensferry.

**Queensland** Australia. Second largest state in the Commonwealth, comprising the whole NE, bounded by Torres Strait (N), the Pacific Ocean (E), New South Wales (S), and the Northern Territory (W). Area 667,000 sq. m. Pop. (1966) 1,663,685. Cap. Brisbane. Off the Pacific coast is the Great Barrier Reef.

The Great Dividing Range, with its diversity of plateau levels, runs roughly parallel to the E coast. Drained E by tributaries of the Burdekin and Fitzroy rivers, N to the Gulf of Carpentaria by the Mitchell, Flinders, and others, and SW to the L. Eyre basin or the Darling R. by rivers of intermittent flow. Much hill country lies close to the coast, with river valleys and coastal plains supporting the bulk of the population. Two plateau regions stand out: the fertile, basalt-capped Darling Downs in the S, and the higher Atherton Plateau in the N, with Mt Bartle Frere (5,287 ft) the highest point. Inland the plains are underlain by the Great Artesian Basin.

The coastal hills bear eucalypt forest, but dense rain forests cover the wetter slopes and deltas in the N. In the E sugar-cane is a major crop, esp. between Mackay and Cairns, and bananas, pineapples, and pawpaws flourish. In the drier valleys cotton is grown, while groundnuts and tobacco are widely cultivated. Dairying is important on the southern lowlands and on the cooler, moist Atherton Plateau, dairying and wheat growing on the Darling Downs. Inland, on grasslands with scattered eucalypts, artesian water helps to maintain cattle in the N and sheep and cattle farther S. Ports such as Rockhampton and Brisbane have large meat works. Considerable timber reserves in the state. Important mineral centres are Mt Isa–Cloncurry, with copper, lead, zinc, and silver; Mt Morgan, near Rockhampton, with copper and gold; tin is found in the N parts of the Great Divide, bauxite at Weipa, uranium at Mary Kathleen. The Ipswich–Toowoomba area, with its coal, is an expanding industrial zone; oil was discovered at Moonie (S) in 1961 and was first pumped to Brisbane in 1964. Food processing is the main industry, and the leading exports are meat, sugar, dairy produce, wool, and minerals – reflecting the dependence on agriculture and mining. Brisbane has over 40 per cent of the state population; inland the population is sparse.

Although Capt. Cook sailed along the E coast in 1770, little was known of Queensland until Flinders visited Moreton Bay (1802) and Oxley ascended the Brisbane R. (1823). A penal settlement was established at Moreton Bay 1826–42, Queensland being then part of the New South Wales colony. Became a separate colony 1859, and a state of the Commonwealth 1901.

**Queenstown** (Irish Republic) ◊ *Cóbh*.

**Queenstown** (New Zealand) ◊ *Wakatipu, Lake*.

**Queenstown** S Africa. Town in the Cape Province 100 m. N W of East London at a height of 3,550 ft. Pop. (1968) 42,977 (11,302 whites). Centre of a wheat-growing, cattle-rearing, and wool-producing region. Founded 1853.

**Quequechan** ◊ *Fall River*.

**Quercy** France. Region in the SW, now forming the Lot and part of the Tarn-et-Garonne departments, divided in the Middle Ages into Upper Quercy, with capital Cahors, and Lower Quercy, with capital Montauban; mainly in the Causses, crossed by the fertile Lot valley. Sheep reared. Produces wine, fruits. A Protestant stronghold in the 16th cent.

**Querétaro** Mexico. 1. State mainly on the central plateau. Area 4,432 sq. m. Pop. (1969) 467,000. Climate generally dry and sub-tropical. Crops include maize, wheat, fruits. Opals, mercury, etc. mined.
2. Capital of Querétaro state, 120 m. N W of Mexico city at a height of 6,100 ft. Pop. 68,000. Manufactures cotton goods, pottery. Outstanding buildings are the 16th-cent. cathedral (much restored) and the federal palace. Receives water by an 18th-cent. aqueduct. Centre of the movement for independence: here Hidalgo y Costilla's rising against the Spaniards was plotted (1810). The Emperor Maximilian was shot here (1867).

**Quetta** Pakistan. Capital of the Quetta Division in W Pakistan, 265 m. W of Multan in a mountainous region at a height of 5,500 ft. Pop. (1961) 107,000. Military station and commercial centre on the route through the Bolan Pass to Afghanistan. Trade in carpets, wool, etc. Engineering, flour milling, etc. Fruits are grown and coal mined in the neighbourhood. Came under British administration 1876. The Indian Army Staff College was established here 1907. Almost destroyed in 1935 by an earthquake, which killed thousands of the inhabitants.

**Quezaltenango** Guatemala. Capital of the Quezaltenango department, the second largest city, 70 m. WNW of Guatemala City, at a height of 7,656 ft. Pop. (1964) 56,921. Textile and flour milling, brewing, etc. Largely destroyed by an eruption of the near-by volcano Santa María in 1902.

**Quezon City** Philippines. New capital of the republic, in Luzon just N E of Manila, which it replaced (1948). Pop. (1960) 397,990. Chiefly residential. Named after Manuel Luis Quezon (1878–1944), first president of the Commonwealth of the Philippines. Seat of the University of the Philippines (1908).

**Quibdó** Colombia. Capital of Chocó department, on the Atrato R. 200 m. W N W of Bogotá. Pop. 43,000. Centre of platinum and gold mining. In the tropical rain-forest.

**Quilmes** Argentina. Seaside resort on the Río de la Plata 9 m. SE of Buenos Aires. Pop. (1960) 318,144. Also an important industrial centre. Oil refining, brewing. Manufactures textiles, glass, metal goods, etc. W. H. Hudson (1841–1922), the naturalist, was born near by.

**Quilon** India. Seaport in Kerala, on the Malabar coast 35 m. N W of Trivandrum. Pop. (1961) 91,018. Exports copra, coir, etc. Manufactures textiles, coir rope and mats, etc.

**Quimper** France. Prefecture of the Finistère department, on the Odet R. 32 m. SSE of Brest. Pop. (1968) 57,678. Industrial, commercial, and tourist centre. Famous for its Breton pottery. Also manufactures hardware, cider. Noteworthy 13th/16th-cent. Gothic cathedral. Inhabited in Roman times. Later became capital of Cornouailles.

**Quincy** (Illinois) USA. Town on the Mississippi R. 95 m. W of Springfield. Pop. (1960) 43,793. Manufactures agricultural machinery, footwear, clothing, chemicals, etc. Once an important river port; declined with the passing of the steamboat.

**Quincy** (Massachusetts) USA. Industrial town on Massachusetts Bay 8 m. SSE of Boston. Pop. (1960) 87,409. Shipbuilding, granite quarrying. Manufactures machinery, hardware, food products, etc. Birthplace of John Adams (1735–1826) and John Quincy Adams (1767–1848).

**Quintana Roo** Mexico. Federal territory in the SE, in the E of the Yucatán peninsula. Area 19,630 sq. m. Pop. (1969) 80,000. Cap. Chetumal. Low-lying, largely tropical jungle and swamp. Underdeveloped. Main products chicle, copra, henequen.

**Quito** Ecuador. Capital of the republic and of Pichincha province, at the foot of Pichincha volcano at a height of 9,350 ft. Pop. (1962) 348,151. In an Andean basin dominated by snow-capped peaks. Although only 15 m. from the equator, because of its altitude it has a pleasant, temperate climate with warm days and cool nights and a mean annual temperature of 55° F. The country's chief textile centre. Brewing, flour milling, tanning, etc. Manufactures clothing, footwear, soap. Many attractive parks and gardens and much old-world charm. Outstanding buildings are the cathedral, the archbishop's palace, the Jesuit church (La Compañía), the great church and monastery of San Francisco, and the Central University of Ecuador (founded 1787). The Pan-American Highway passes through it from Colombia to Peru. Once inhabited by Quitu Indians, after whom it is named; captured by the Incas and later by the Spaniards (1533) to become capital of the presidency of Quito under the viceroyalty of Peru.

**Qum** Iran. Holy city and route centre 75 m. SSW of Tehran. Pop. (1966) 133,941. Manufactures footwear, pottery. Sacred to Shia Muslims, it has the golden-domed shrine of Fatima, sister of the Imam Riza, and the tombs of many other saints.

**Qurna** ◊ *Thebes* (United Arab Republic).

# R

**Raasay** Scotland. Island in the Inner Hebrides, in Inverness-shire, separated from the E coast of Skye by the Sound of Raasay and from the mainland by the Inner Sound. Area 28 sq. m. Pop. 300. Rises to 1,456 ft in the SE.

**Rabat** Morocco. Capital, chief residence of the King of Morocco, on the Atlantic, at the mouth of the Bou Regreg R., on the main railway from Casablanca (through Oujda) to Algiers. Pop. (1961) 261,450. Flour milling. Manufactures textiles, bricks, hand-made Moroccan rugs. Overshadowed in trade and industry by Casablanca, but a city of considerable charm. The harbour is obstructed by a bar; a bridge (1957) now prevents seaborne trade. The walled old town is dominated by the 12th-cent. Hassan tower, a minaret 180 ft high, near a ruined mosque. University (1957). Became important with the establishment of the French protectorate (1912).

**Rabaul** New Britain. Seaport in the NE of New Britain, in the Bismarck Archipelago. Pop. (1966) 10,589. Exports copra, cacao. Formerly capital of the Territory of New Guinea. Set amid active volcanoes, it was severely damaged by eruptions in 1937. Also suffered from bombardments during the 2nd World War, when it was occupied by the Japanese (1942–5).

**Racibórz** (Ger. **Ratibor**) Poland. Town in the Opole voivodship in the S, on the Oder R. 42 m. SSE of Opole. Pop. (1968) 38,900. River port. Railway junction. Manufactures machinery, electrical equipment, soap, etc. Capital of an independent principality 1288–1532. Later in the Prussian province of Silesia.

**Racine** USA. Industrial town and port in Wisconsin, on L. Michigan 23 m. SSE of Milwaukee. Pop. (1960) 89,144. Manufactures agricultural machinery, electrical equipment, hardware, paints and varnishes, etc. Developed chiefly in the mid 19th cent. with the coming of the railway and improvement of the harbour.

**Radcliffe** England. Municipal borough in SE Lancashire 7 m. NNW of Manchester. Pop. (1961) 26,720. Engineering. Manufactures textiles (cotton, rayon), chemicals, paper, etc.

**Radium Hill** Australia. Small mining settlement in S Australia 60 m. SW of Broken Hill. Mine worked in the 1920s for radium, abandoned 1930, reopened 1952 for uranium but closed 1961. ⟡⟩ *Flinders Range.*

**Radium Hot Springs** ⟩ *Kootenay River.*

**Radnor** Wales. Small market town (New Radnor) and village (Old Radnor, 2 m. ESE) in Radnorshire 22 m. NW of Hereford. Pop. (rural district, 1961) 2,050.

**Radnorshire** Wales. County bordering E on the English counties of Shropshire and Hereford. Area 470 sq. m. Pop. (1961) 18,431. County town Presteigne. Hilly, rising to 2,166 ft in Radnor Forest. Bounded on the S by the R. Wye and on the NE by the R. Teme. Main occupations sheep and cattle rearing. Reservoirs in the Elan valley provide Birmingham with water. Llandrindod Wells is a spa.

**Radom** Poland. Industrial town and railway junction in the Kielce voivodship 60 m. S of Warsaw. Pop. (1968) 152,500. Manufactures agricultural machinery, leather, glass, wire, nails, etc. One of the oldest towns in Poland. New Radom was founded (1340) by Casimir the Great, King of Poland. Held by Austria from 1795 and by Russia from 1815; returned to Poland 1918.

**Ragusa** Italy. Capital of Ragusa province, in Sicily, on the Irminio R. 34 m. WSW of Syracuse. Pop. (1961) 57,311. Important oil-producing and asphalt-mining centre. Oil refining. Manufactures cement, textiles, etc. In the lower town was the ancient Hybla Heraea, where Hippocrates of Gela fell (491 B.C.).

**Ragusa** (Yugoslavia) ⟩ *Dubrovnik.*

**Rahway** USA. Industrial and residential town in New Jersey, 11 m. SSW of Newark. Pop. (1960) 27,699. Manufactures machinery, chemicals, rubber products, drugs, etc.

**Raiatea** ⟩ *Society Islands.*

**Raichur** India. Town in Mysore 160 m. ENE of Hubli. Pop. (1961) 63,329. Commercial centre. Trade in cereals, cotton, etc. Cotton ginning.

**Rainier, Mount** USA. Highest mountain in the Cascade Range (14,408 ft), in Washington 40 m. SE of Tacoma. Famous for 26 great glaciers and many permanent icefields. The Mt Rainier National Park (377 sq. m.) was established in 1899.

**Rainy Lake** Canada/USA. Lake on the boundary between Ontario (Canada) and Minnesota (USA). Area 345 sq. m. The Rainy R., 85 m. long, flows from it, generally W, forming part of the Canada–USA frontier, and enters the Lake of the Woods.

**Raipur** India. Commercial town and railway junction in E Madhya Pradesh 165 m. E of Nagpur. Pop. (1961) 139,792. Trade in rice, oilseeds, etc. Engineering, rice and oilseed milling. Has the ruins of a 15th-cent. fort and several ancient temples.

**Rajahmundry** India. Town in Andhra Pradesh, at the head of the Godavari R. delta 215 m. ESE of Hyderabad. Pop. (1961) 130,002. Trade in rice, salt. Manufactures cotton goods, paper, tiles, etc. Passed to the French 1753 and the British 1758.

**Rajasthan** India. Constituent state in the Indian Union, in the NW, bordering W on W Pakistan. Area 132,152 sq. m. Pop. (1961) 20,155,602. Cap. Jaipur. Its W part occupies much of the Thar Desert and is separated from the more fertile E by the Aravalli Range, which rises to 5,650 ft in the extreme S. Rainfall varies from 5–10 ins. (W) to 50 ins. or more (S). Most of the people are engaged in agriculture; wheat, maize, millets, and cotton are cultivated. Chief towns Jaipur, Ajmer, Jodhpur, Bikaner, Kotah, Udaipur. Formed in 1948 and 1949 from a number of former princely states of Rajputana. Boundary adjustments were made in 1950 and 1956. The Rajputs, although a minority, are the dominant race.

**Rajkot** India. Commercial town and railway junction in Gujarat, in the Kathiawar peninsula 125 m. WSW of Ahmadabad. Pop. (1961) 193,498. Trade in cotton, grain, etc. Oilseed and flour milling, tanning. Manufactures chemicals etc. Was capital of the former princely state of Rajkot (282 sq. m.).

**Rajputana** ◊ *Rajasthan.*

**Rajshahi** Pakistan. Capital of the Rajshahi Division, E Pakistan, on the Ganges R. 125 m. WNW of Dacca. Pop. 40,000. Commercial centre. Trade in rice etc. University (1953).

**Rakahanga** ◊ *Cook Islands.*

**Rakiura** ◊ *Stewart Island.*

**Raleigh** USA. State capital of N Carolina, 180 m. ENE of Charlotte. Pop. (1960) 93,931. Printing and publishing. Manufactures textiles, cottonseed oil, etc. Important trade in tobacco. Seat of the Shaw University (1865, Negro) and other educational institutions.

**Ralik Chain** ◊ *Marshall Islands.*

**Rama's Bridge** ◊ *Adam's Bridge.*

**Ramat Gan** Israel. Industrial town on the Plain of Sharon just E of Tel Aviv. Pop. (1968) 106,800. Manufactures textiles, food products, furniture, etc. Seat of the religious Bar-Ilan University (1955). Founded 1921.

**Rampur** India. Commercial town in Uttar Pradesh 110 m. E of Delhi. Pop. (1961) 135,407. Trade in grain, cotton, sugarcane, etc. Sugar refining, metal working. Manufactures chemicals, pottery. Was capital of the former princely state of Rampur.

**Ramsbottom** England. Urban district in SE Lancashire, on the R. Irwell 7 m. NE of Bolton. Pop. (1961) 13,813. Manufactures textiles, paper, soap, etc. Engineering.

**Ramsey** England. Urban district in Huntingdonshire 9 m. NNE of Huntingdon. Pop. (1961) 5,697. Market town. Has the remains of the 10th-cent. Benedictine abbey and the partly Norman Church of St Thomas à Becket.

**Ramsey** Isle of Man. Port and seaside resort on the NE coast 12 m. NNE of Douglas. Pop. (1961) 3,764. Mooragh Park has a marine lake and other attractions.

**Ramsgate** England. Municipal borough in E Kent, in the Isle of Thanet. Pop. (1961) 36,906. Fishing and yachting port and popular seaside resort, its harbour protected by stone piers. Its development as a resort dates from the late 18th cent. Many improvements have been made in the 20th cent. During the 2nd World War the town was severely damaged in air raids; 3 m. W is the famous wartime RAF station of Manston. Near by at Ebbsfleet, on Pegwell Bay, the Saxons under Hengist and Horsa are supposed to have landed in 449 and St Augustine in 597.

**Rancagua** Chile. Capital of O'Higgins province, in the central valley 50 m. S of Santiago. Pop. (1960) 61,832. Commercial and industrial centre in an agricultural region. Manufactures tractors. Flour milling, fruit and vegetable canning. Also a railway junction, linked with the large El Teniente copper mine.

**Rance River** France. River 62 m. long in the Côtes-du-Nord department, flowing

E and N and entering the Gulf of St Malo by an estuary 12 m. long. The world's first marine power station using the energy of the tides was opened on the estuary just above St Malo in 1966.

**Ranchi** India. Commercial town in Bihar, on the Chota Nagpur plateau at a height of 2,000 ft 70 m. NW of Jamshedpur. Pop. (1961) 122,416. Trade in rice, maize, oilseeds, cotton, etc. University (1960). Hot-weather seat of the State government.

**Rand** ◊ *Witwatersrand.*

**Randers** Denmark. Capital of Randers county in E Jutland, at the mouth of the Gudenaa R. and at the head of Randers Fiord. Pop. (1965) 42,923. Port and industrial town. Manufactures gloves, railway rolling stock, etc. Brewing, distilling. Although dating from the 11th cent., it has a modern appearance. Has a 15th-cent. church.

**Randfontein** S Africa. Goldmining town in the Transvaal, on the Witwatersrand 20 m. W of Johannesburg at a height of 5,600 ft. Pop. (1968) 46,370.

**Rangihaute** ◊ *Chatham Islands.*

**Rangoon** Burma. Capital and chief seaport of Burma, on the Rangoon R. 21 m. from its mouth. Pop. (1963) 687,708. Exports rice, cotton, teak. Rice milling, oil refining (at Syriam), sawmilling, engineering. Manufactures matches, soap, etc. Linked by rail with Prome and Mandalay, and by canal with the Irrawaddy and Sittang rivers. Important airport. University (1920). Dominated by the impressive and ornate gold-covered Shwe Dagôn pagoda, 368 ft high and standing on high ground; the pagoda contains relics of Buddha, and is one of the country's principal shrines. Many fine public buildings. Owed its development to its rebuilding by Alompra, founder of the last Burmese dynasty (1753). Taken by the British 1824 and again in 1852. Became capital of all Burma in 1886. In recent times it has been a cosmopolitan rather than a purely Burmese city. Severely damaged in the 2nd World War during the Japanese occupation (1942–5).

**Rannoch, Loch** Scotland. Lake in NW Perthshire extending W from Kinloch Rannoch, about 9 m. long and 1 m. wide, fed by the R. Ericht and other streams and drained by the R. Tummel. The surrounding district is known as Rannoch. S and W is the wild, bleak Rannoch Moor.

**Raoul Island** ◊ *Kermadec Islands.*

**Rapallo** Italy. Port and resort in Genova province, Liguria, on the Gulf of Rapallo 17 m. ESE of Genoa. Pop. (1961) 20,606. Beautifully situated on the Riviera di Levante, in a region producing vines, olives, flowers. Manufactures olive oil, wine, cement, etc. Two treaties were signed here: between Italy and Yugoslavia (1920) and between Russia and Germany (1922). Near by is the small and now fashionable resort of Portofino.

**Rapid City** USA. Town in S Dakota, in the Black Hills 145 m. WSW of Pierre. Pop. (1960) 42,399. Commercial centre in an agricultural and mining region. Manufactures cement, bricks and tiles. Flour milling, sawmilling.

**Rappahannock River** USA. River 210 m. long in Virginia, rising in the Blue Ridge and flowing generally SE to Chesapeake Bay. Chief tributary the Rapidan R. Scene of severe fighting during the American Civil War.

**Rarotonga** ◊ *Cook Islands.*

**Ras al Khaimah** ◊ *Trucial States.*

**Rasht** ◊ *Resht.*

**Ras Tanura** Saudi Arabia. Oil port on the Persian Gulf 25 m. N of Dhahran. Oil brought by pipelines from the Dhahran, Abqaiq, and Qatif oilfields is refined here, and also shipped from the marine terminal.

**Ratak Chain** ◊ *Marshall Islands.*

**Rathenow** German Democratic Republic. Town in the Potsdam district, on the Havel R. 45 m. WNW of Berlin. Pop. (1965) 28,974. Important centre for optical and precision instruments. Also manufactures agricultural machinery, chemicals, etc.

**Rathlin Island** Northern Ireland. Island off the N coast of Co. Antrim, 6 m. long and L-shaped. St Columba founded a church here in the 6th cent. Refuge of Robert Bruce in 1306: traditionally the scene of his encounter with the persevering spider.

**Ratibor** ◊ *Racibórz.*

**Ratisbon** ◊ *Regensburg.*

**Ratlam** India. Town in Madhya Pradesh 70 m. NW of Indore. Pop. (1961) 87,472. Railway junction. Commercial centre. Trade in cotton, grain, etc. Manufactures textiles. Was capital of the former princely state of Ratlam.

**Rauma River** ◊ *Romsdal.*

**Ravenna** Italy. Capital of Ravenna province, in Emilia-Romagna, 42 m. ESE of Bologna and 5 m. from the Adriatic Sea, with which it is connected by canal. Pop.

(1968) 128,878. Varied industries; trade in agricultural produce. Rich in Byzantine art, esp. famous for its mosaics. Among its outstanding buildings, several of which were damaged in the 2nd World War, are the 5th-cent. mausoleum of Galla Placidia, the 5th/6th-cent. churches of S. Giovanni Evangelista, S. Apollinare Nuovo, and S. Vitale – the last-named with fine mosaics, and the 18th-cent. cathedral. Here, too, is the tomb of Dante. Just outside the city is the mausoleum of Theodoric the Ostrogoth (454–526), with its massive dome cut from a single block of stone. In Roman times a seaport and naval base, it was made capital by Honorius early in the 5th cent. Became the seat of the exarchs from Constantinople 553–752. Ceded to the Papal States 1509. Passed to Italy 1860.

**Ravensburg** Federal German Republic. Industrial town in Baden-Württemberg 47 m. SSW of Ulm. Pop. (1963) 31,800. Engineering. Manufactures textiles, pharmaceutical products, etc. Founded in the 11th cent.

**Ravi River.** River 450 m. long in NW India and W Pakistan; one of the 5 rivers of the Punjab, rising in the Pir Panjal Range of the Himalayas, flowing generally W and SW past Lahore and joining the Chenab R. Feeds the Upper Bari Doab irrigation canal. Navigable below Lahore.

**Rawalpindi** Pakistan. Formerly the provisional federal capital; capital of the Rawalpindi Division of W Pakistan, 160 m. NNW of Lahore. Pop. (1961) 340,175. A military station and commercial and industrial centre. Trade in grain, wool, timber, etc. Oil refining, railway engineering. Manufactures chemicals, furniture, etc. Became temporary capital (in place of Karachi) in 1959, pending the building of the new capital, Islamabad, near by.

**Rawmarsh** England. Urban district in the W Riding of Yorkshire, 2 m. NNE of Rotherham. Pop. (1961) 19,603. Coalmining, iron founding.

**Rawson** Argentina. Capital of Chubut province (Patagonia), near the Atlantic coast 345 m. SSW of Bahía Blanca. Pop. 2,500. Market town. Trade in grain, sheep, etc. Named after one of its Welsh founders (1865).

**Rawtenstall** England. Municipal borough in Lancashire, on the R. Irwell 6 m. SSW of Burnley. Pop. (1961) 23,869. Manufactures cotton and woollen goods, carpets, footwear.

**Ré, Île de** France. Island in the Charente-Maritime department, in the Bay of Biscay W of La Rochelle, separated from the mainland by the Pertuis Breton. Area 30 sq. m. Pop. 9,000. Fishing, salt panning. Vines and early vegetables cultivated.

**Reading** England. County borough and county town of Berkshire, at the confluence of the R. Thames and the R. Kennet 38 m. W of London. Pop. (1961) 119,870. Industrial centre. Railway junction. Biscuit manufacture. Seed nurseries. Brewing, engineering, printing, etc. The University Extension College (founded 1892) became an independent university in 1926, and has been specially known for its work in agriculture. Has a grammar school founded in 1485 (rebuilt) and a municipal museum which contains Roman remains from near-by Silchester; there are also remains of the Benedictine abbey founded (1121) by Henry I. Here the imprisoned Oscar Wilde wrote the *Ballad of Reading Gaol*. A 13th-cent. Reading monk is said to have composed *Sumer is icumen in* here. Occupied by Danes in the 9th cent., it was burned in 1006. From the 12th to the 16th cent. it was the scene of a protracted struggle between the abbey and the merchant guild. Birthplace of Archbishop Laud (1573–1645).

**Reading** USA. Town in Pennsylvania, on the Schuylkill R. 46 m. NW of Philadelphia. Pop. (1960) 98,177. Railway engineering. Manufactures metal goods, machinery, optical goods, hosiery, etc. Its population has a large element of Pennsylvania Germans.

**Recife (Pernambuco)** Brazil. Capital of Pernambuco state in the NE, of which it is the chief seaport and largest city. Pop. (1960) 797,234. Exports sugar, grown on the neighbouring coastlands, rum and molasses, cotton, timber, fruit, coconuts, etc. Sugar refining, cotton milling, pineapple canning. Manufactures textiles, cement, etc. Built in three parts, on the mainland, on a peninsula, and on an island, with waterways bridged by modern roads running through the city; hence sometimes called the 'Venice of Brazil'. Naval station. Important airport. Many noteworthy old churches. First settled (*c.* 1535) by the Portuguese.

**Recklinghausen** Federal German Republic. Industrial town in N Rhine-Westphalia, in the Ruhr district 12 m. NW of Dortmund. Pop. (1968) 126,412. Coal mining, iron founding, brewing. Manufactures coal-tar products, mining machinery, soap, cement, etc.

**Recôncavo** ◊ *Bahia*.

**Redbridge** England. Greater London borough (1965) comprising the former municipal boroughs of Ilford and Wanstead and Woodford and parts of Chigwell (the Hainault Estate area) and Dagenham (the N part of Chadwell Heath ward), all in Essex. Pop. (1963) 248,569.

**Redcar** England. Seaside resort in the N Riding of Yorkshire, 7 m. NE of Middlesbrough, of which it is a growing residential satellite. Pop. (1961) 31,460. Manufactures steel, chemicals, etc. Racecourse. From 1968 part of the county borough of ◊ *Teesside*.

**Red Deer** Canada. Town in Alberta, on the Red Deer R. 82 m. N of Calgary. Pop. (1966) 26,171. Railway junction. market town.

**Redditch** England. Urban district in Worcestershire 12 m. S of Birmingham. Pop. (1961) 34,077. Manufactures needles, springs, clips, washers, fishing tackle, etc.

**Rede River** England. River 21 m. long in Northumberland rising on Carter Fell in the Cheviot Hills and flowing SE and S through the picturesque Redesdale, joining the R. Tyne at Redesmouth.

**Redhill** England. Residential town in Surrey forming the E part of the municipal borough of ◊ *Reigate*. Developed after the construction of the London–Brighton railway.

**Redlands** USA. Town in California 60 m. E of Los Angeles. Pop. (1960) 26,829. Largely residential. Packing and trade centre for the citrus fruit (chiefly oranges) cultivated in the region. Seat of the Baptist University of Redlands (1907).

**Redondo Beach** USA. Town in California 16 m. SW of Los Angeles on the Pacific Ocean. Pop. (1960) 46,986. Originally developed as a commercial port in the late 19th cent.; now mainly a residential and tourist centre.

**Red River** USA. Tributary of the Mississippi R., 1,000 m. long, rising on the Llano Estacado and flowing generally E across NW Texas, forming the Texas–Oklahoma boundary, then turning SE across SW Arkansas and Louisiana to join the Atchafalaya and the Mississippi rivers. On the Texas–Oklahoma border is Denison Dam (completed 1943) for flood control and hydroelectric power, which

impounds L. Texoma (223 sq. m.), one of the country's largest reservoirs. In its lower course the river is sluggish and meandering; silt and falling trees have always impeded navigation.

**Red River of the North** USA/Canada. River 350 m. long, formed by the union of the Otter Tail and the Bois de Sioux rivers (in N Dakota), flowing generally N, forming the border between N Dakota and Minnesota, entering Manitoba (Canada), and emptying into L. Winnipeg. Joined by the Assiniboine R. at Winnipeg. The valley includes some of the best farming land in N America; wheat is cultivated on a large scale.

**Redruth** England. Market town in Cornwall 15 m. ENE of Penzance, now part of the urban district of Camborne-Redruth (◊ *Camborne*). Long a centre of Cornish tin mining. Brewing, tanning, etc. Here William Murdock first used coal gas for lighting purposes (1792).

**Red Sea.** Sea 1,500 m. long and up to 210 m. wide between NE Africa and SW Asia, extending SSE from Suez to the Strait of Bab el Mandeb. Divides in the N into the Gulf of Aqaba and the Gulf of Suez, which are separated by the Sinai peninsula. Linked by the Gulf of Suez via the Suez Canal with the Mediterranean Sea, and by the Strait of Bab el Mandeb with the Gulf of Aden and the Indian Ocean. Forms part of the ◊ *Great Rift Valley*. Both coasts fringed by coral reefs; few indentations. In the S are the Dahlak Archipelago and the Farasan Is. Receives few rivers, rainfall is scanty and evaporation considerable; the salinity is high. Chief ports Suez (United Arab Republic), Port Sudan (Sudan), Massawa (Ethiopia), Jidda (Saudi Arabia). An important trade route from early times, it declined after the discovery of the route to India via the Cape of Good Hope (1497), but became one of the world's busiest shipping lanes after the opening of the Suez Canal (1869).

**Redwood City** USA. Port and residential and industrial town in California 24 m. SSE of San Francisco. Pop. (1960) 46,290. Exports oil, salt, etc. Manufactures cement, leather, electronic equipment, etc. Named for its connexion with the redwood timber trade.

**Ree, Lough** Irish Republic. Lake 17 m. long and up to 7 m. wide on the R. Shannon between Counties Roscommon, Longford, and Westmeath. Many small islands. Trout fishing.

**Reef Islands** ◊ *Solomon Islands*.

**Regensburg (Ratisbon)** Federal German Republic. Ancient Castra Regina. Town in Bavaria, on the Danube R. at the confluence with the Regen R. 65 m. NNE of Munich. Pop. (1968) 125,000. River port. Railway junction. Manufactures machinery, pencils, soap, furniture. Brewing, sugar refining, etc. Noteworthy buildings are the Gothic cathedral (founded 1275), the Romanesque churches of St James and St Emmeran, and the partly 14th-cent. town hall, where the Imperial Diet met 1663–1806, and there are Roman remains. An important stronghold of the Romans. Seat of the dukes of Bavaria in the Middle Ages, and a free imperial city from 1245, but declined in commercial importance in the 15th cent. and suffered severely in the Thirty Years War.

**Reggio di Calabria** Italy.* Ancient Rhegium. Capital of Reggio di Calabria province, in Calabria, on the Strait of Messina. Pop. (1968) 163,133. Seaport. Exports citrus fruits, olive oil, wine, figs, etc. Fruit canning. Manufactures olive oil, macaroni, furniture, etc. It suffered severely, with great loss of life, from the earthquakes of 1783 and 1908.

**Reggio nell'Emilia** Italy. Capital of Reggio nell'Emilia province, in Emilia-Romagna, on the Aemilian Way 38 m. WNW of Bologna. Pop. (1968) 125,889. Manufactures locomotives, aircraft engines, agricultural machinery, cement, wine, etc. Cathedral (13th-cent., restored in the 15th and 16th cent.); Renaissance palaces. Birthplace of Lodovico Ariosto (1474–1533), the poet.

**Regina** Canada. Capital of Saskatchewan province, in the S. Pop. (1966) 131,127. In the heart of a large wheat-growing area. The major commercial centre for Saskatchewan, and one of the world's largest distribution centres for farm implements. Also distributes cars, hardware, chemicals, etc. Oil refining. Manufactures cement, paints and varnishes, furniture, footwear. The W headquarters of the Royal Canadian Mounted Police.

**Regnitz River** Federal German Republic. River 40 m. long in Bavaria formed by the union of the Pegnitz and Rednitz rivers at Fürth, flowing N to join the Main R. near Bamberg.

**Reichenbach** German Democratic Republic. Industrial town in the Karl-Marx-Stadt district, 11 m. SW of Zwickau. Pop. (1965) 29,536. Textile centre; manufactures cotton, woollen, rayon goods, also machinery. Printing and dyeing.

**Reichenbach** (Poland) ◊ *Dzierzoniow*.

**Reichenberg** ◊ *Liberec*.

**Reigate** England. Municipal borough in Surrey 20 m. S of London at the foot of the North Downs, including the newer town of Redhill. Pop. (1961) 53,710. Mainly residential. The Priory is on the site of a 13th-cent. Augustinian foundation. In the parish church is the tomb of Lord Howard of Effingham.

**Reims (Rheims)** France. Ancient Durocortorum. Town in the Marne department on the Vesle R. 82 m. ENE of Paris. Pop. (1968) 158,634. Leading centre of the country's champagne industry. Manufactures wine-growing equipment, wine bottles, woollen goods, biscuits, etc. Flour milling, sugar refining, engineering. There are vineyards on the near-by hills; the wine is stored in great caves cut in the chalk. The famous 13th/14th-cent. Gothic cathedral was seriously damaged in the 1st World War but was completely restored by 1938. University (1547). Was capital of the Remi, after whom it was named, before the Roman conquest. In 496 Clovis I was crowned king of the Franks in the earlier cathedral, and the coronation of later French kings took place here. Almost completely destroyed by the Germans during the 1st World War. Birthplace of Jean Baptiste Colbert (1619–83).

**Reindeer Lake** Canada. Lake in NE Saskatchewan and NW Manitoba, 145 m. long and up to 40 m. wide, draining S to the Churchill R. by the Reindeer R. Many small islands.

**Reirson Island** ◊ *Cook Islands*.

**Remscheid** Federal German Republic. Industrial town in N Rhine-Westphalia, on the Wupper R. 6 m. S of Wuppertal. Pop. (1968) 132,855. Important steel centre. Manufactures machine tools, cutlery, tools, drills, agricultural implements, etc. Linked with Solingen by bridge across the Wupper R. Severely damaged by bombing in the 2nd World War. The suburb of Lennep was the birthplace of W. K. Röntgen (1845–1923), the physicist.

**Renaix** ◊ *Ronse*.

**Rendsburg** Federal German Republic. Industrial town and railway junction in Schleswig-Holstein, on the Kiel Canal 18

m. W of Kiel. Pop. (1963) 35,100. Iron founding, shipbuilding. Manufactures machinery, fertilizers, etc. Founded in the 13th cent. Passed to Prussia 1866.

**Renfrew** Scotland. Royal burgh and county town of Renfrewshire, on the R. Clyde, 5 m. WNW of and virtually a suburb of Glasgow. Pop. (1961) 17,946. Shipbuilding, engineering. Manufactures tyres, etc.

**Renfrewshire** Scotland. County in the SW bounded on the N by the Clyde estuary and on the W by the Firth of Clyde. Area 240 sq. m. Pop. (1961) 338,815. County town Renfrew. Hilly in the W and SE but mainly low-lying. Dairying and the cultivation of oats and potatoes important. Industries concentrated in Paisley, Greenock, Port Glasgow.

**Renkum** Netherlands. Town in Gelderland province 7 m. W of Arnhem. Pop. (1968) 32,815. Manufactures rubber and paper products. Has the memorial to the British airborne forces involved in the Battle of Arnhem in the 2nd World War.

**Rennes** France. Ancient Condate. Prefecture of the Ille-et-Vilaine department, at the confluence of the Ille and the Vilaine rivers. Pop. (1968) 188,515. Important route and commercial centre. Printing, engineering, tanning. Manufactures cars, footwear, hosiery, chemicals, etc. Trade in agricultural produce. Also the cultural centre of Brittany, with a university (1735). The outstanding building is the 17th-cent. parliament house, now the law courts, where the famous Dreyfus case was conducted; this is one of the few important buildings to survive the great 7-day fire of 1720. The cathedral was rebuilt 1787–1844. Severely damaged in the 2nd World War.

**Reno** USA. Commercial town and resort in W Nevada, on the Truckee R. at a height of 4,500 ft. Pop. (1960) 51,470. Meat packing, flour milling. Manufactures bricks and tiles, metal products, etc. Seat of the University of Nevada (1874). Perhaps best known as a centre for gambling, which is legalized, and for divorce, which the state law makes easily obtainable.

**Repton** England. Small town in Derbyshire 4 m. NE of Burton-upon-Trent. Pop. 2,000. Has a famous public school (founded 1557), which incorporates parts of a 12th-cent. Augustinian priory. Once the capital of Mercia and seat of a bishop.

**Republican River** USA. River 450 m. long rising in NE Colorado, flowing generally ESE through Nebraska and Kansas, joining the Smoky Hill R. at Junction City, and forming the Kansas R.

**Resht (Rasht)** Iran. Capital of Gilán province 150 m. NW of Tehran near the Caspian Sea. Pop. (1966) 141,756. Trade in agricultural produce, esp. rice, grown in the district. Manufactures textiles, hosiery, carpets, etc.

**Resina** Italy. Town in Napoli province, Campania, at the foot of Vesuvius 5 m. SE of Naples, partly on the site of ancient Herculaneum. Pop. (1961) 45,148. Tanning etc. Resort, with some noteworthy modern villas. Destroyed by the eruption of Vesuvius in 1631.

**Resistencia** Argentina. Capital of Chaco province 10 m. W of Corrientes, served by the port of Barranqueras (on the Paraná R.). Pop. 94,000. Trade in cotton, timber, livestock, hides. Meat packing, sawmilling, etc.

**Reşiţa** Rumania. Capital of Caraş-Severin district, 47 m. SE of Timişoara. Pop. (1968) 58,679. Important iron and steel industry. Also manufactures machinery, electrical equipment, etc.

**Restigouche River** Canada. River 130 m. long in N New Brunswick, flowing generally NE, forming part of the New Brunswick–Quebec border, and emptying into Chaleur Bay. Salmon fishing.

**Retalhuleu** Guatemala. Capital of Retalhuleu department, 80 m. W of Guatemala city. Pop. 29,000. Commercial centre in a region producing coffee and sugar-cane.

**Retford (East Retford)** England. Municipal borough in Nottinghamshire, 8 m. E of Worksop on the R. Idle. Pop. (1961) 17,788. Market town. Iron founding, flour milling, paper manufacture, etc. Has a grammar school founded in the 16th cent.

**Rethímni** Greece. *Nome* in W central Crete. Area 570 sq. m. Pop. (1961) 69,843. Cap. Rethimnon. Mainly agricultural. Cereals, vines, olives, etc. cultivated. Sheep and goats reared.

**Rethimnon** Greece. Capital and chief port of Rethímni *nome*, Crete, on the N coast 29 m. ESE of Canea (Khanía). Pop. (1961) 14,999. Trade in cereals, wine, olive oil.

**Réunion.** Formerly Bourbon. Island in the Indian Ocean 110 m. SW of Mauritius, an overseas department of France. Area 969 sq. m. Pop. (1969) 430,000. Cap. St Denis. Of volcanic origin, rising to 10,069 ft in the Piton des Neiges; the somewhat lower Fournaise is a still active volcano which erupted in 1925–6. Subject to the SE Trade Wind and at times to destructive cyclonic storms, it has a much heavier rainfall on the windward than on the leeward side. Sugar-cane is by far the most important crop; chief exports sugar and rum. Chief towns St Denis (pop. 85,444), St Paul (43,129), St Pierre (40,355), and St Louis (26,663). Discovered by the Portuguese in the early 16th cent. Annexed by France 1643. Renamed 1848. Became an overseas department 1947.

**Reus** Spain. Town in Tarragona province, Catalonia, 57 m. WSW of Barcelona. Pop. (1961) 41,014. Manufactures textiles, agricultural machinery, leather goods, etc. Trade in wine and fruit. Its commercial prosperity dates from the arrival of an English colony in the mid 18th cent. Birthplace of General Prim (1814–70) and Mariano Fortuny (1838–74), the artist.

**Reuss** Federal German Republic. Two former small principalities, Reuss-Greiz and Reuss-Schleiz-Gera, both incorporated in Thuringia in 1920. The house of Reuss dated from the 12th cent. By custom all the male members of the two branches of the family (which survived till the present century) were named Heinrich, and were distinguished by numbers.

**Reutlingen** Federal German Republic. Industrial town in Baden-Württemberg 18 m. S of Stuttgart on the N edge of the Swabian Jura. Pop. (1963) 70,600. Manufactures textiles, textile machinery, leather, paper, etc.

**Revel** ◊ *Tallinn*.

**Revelstoke** Canada. Town in British Columbia, on the Columbia R. and on the Trans-Canada Highway 95 m. ENE of Kamloops. Pop. (1966) 4,791. A supply centre for a lumbering and mining region. Tourist centre for the Mt Revelstoke National Park.

**Revere** USA. Town in Massachusetts 5 m. NE of Boston. Pop. (1960) 40,080. A coastal resort, sometimes termed 'the Coney Island of Boston', with the popular Revere Beach. Manufactures electrical equipment, chemicals, etc.

**Reykjavik** Iceland. Capital of the republic, on Faxa Fiord on the SW coast. Pop. (1967) 80,090. Chief seaport; a commercial and fishing centre. Exports fish and fish products. Fish processing and canning, shipbuilding. Manufactures textiles, rope, etc.

University (1911). Lutheran and Roman Catholic cathedrals. The hot springs in the vicinity provide a natural hot-water supply for the city. Founded in the 9th cent.

**Rezaiyeh** ◊ *Rizaiyeh*.

**Rhadames** ◊ *Ghadames*.

**Rhayader** Wales. Market town in Radnorshire, on the R. Wye 26 m. ESE of Aberystwyth. Pop. (rural district, 1961) 4,083. To the SW are the reservoirs of the Elan valley, which provide Birmingham with water.

**Rheims** ◊ *Reims*.

**Rheingau** Federal German Republic. District extending about 15 m. along the right bank of the Rhine R. from Biebrich (near Wiesbaden) to Assmannshausen. Famous for its wines, inc. Johannisberger and Steinberger.

**Rheinhausen** Federal German Republic. Industrial town in N Rhine-Westphalia in the Ruhr, on the Rhine R. opposite Duisburg. Pop. (1963) 70,600. Coalmining. Manufactures iron and steel, briquettes, mining machinery, armatures, concrete products, barrels, etc.

**Rheinland-Pfalz** ◊ *Rhineland-Palatinate*.

**Rhein River** ◊ *Rhine River*.

**Rheydt** Federal German Republic. Industrial town in N Rhine-Westphalia 15 m. WSW of Düsseldorf. Pop. (1963) 96,000. Manufactures textiles, machinery, cables, chemicals, soap, etc. From 1929 to 1933 it was incorporated with München-Gladbach, just N, and known as Gladbach-Rheydt. Severely damaged in the 2nd World War.

**Rhine–Herne Canal** Federal German Republic. Important Ruhr waterway 24 m. long, from Duisburg to Herne, thus forming part of the Mittelland Canal. Completed 1914.

**Rhineland** Federal German Republic. The region on both banks of the Rhine R. in W Germany, comprising parts of the *Länder* of N Rhine-Westphalia, Rhineland-Palatinate, Hessen, and Baden-Württemberg. Sometimes the name refers only to the former Prussian Rhine Province.

**Rhineland-Palatinate** (Ger. **Rheinland-Pfalz**) Federal German Republic. *Land* formed in 1945 from Rhenish Palatinate and parts of Hessen and the former Prussian provinces of the Rhine and Hesse-Nassau. Area 7,666 sq. m. Pop. (1968) 3,625,400. Cap. Mainz.

**Rhine Province** Federal German Republic. Formerly the most westerly province of Prussia, constituted in 1824 from a large number of independent principalities. Cap. Coblenz. It was divided into 5 administrative districts: Aachen, Düsseldorf, Cologne, Coblenz, and Trier, the first three of which were incorporated into N Rhine-Westphalia in 1945, and the last two into Rhineland-Palatinate.

**Rhine–Rhône Canal** France/Federal German Republic. Waterway leading from the Rhine R. via the Ill R. to Strasbourg, thence by artificial channel parallel to the Ill via Mulhouse to the Doubs, Saône, and Rhône. Constructed 1784–1833. Of limited use to modern canal transport.

**Rhine** (Ger. **Rhein**, Fr. **Rhin**, Dutch **Rijn**) River. River 820 m. long in central and W Europe, flowing from the Alps generally NNW to the North Sea, through one of the continent's most highly industrialized and densely populated regions; commercially Europe's most important waterway. Formed from two principal headstreams: the Hinter Rhein issues from glaciers of the Rheinwaldhorn at a height of 7,270 ft; the Vorder Rhein rises in L. Toma at a height of 7,690 ft. The two unite 6 m. WSW of Chur, and the Rhine proper then flows N between Switzerland (W) and Liechtenstein and Austria (E) into L. Constance; then it passes Schaffhausen, descends 70 ft at the famous Rhine Falls, and continues W along the Swiss-German border to Basle (head of navigation). It turns N through the rift valley and forms part of the Franco-German border (receiving the Ill, the Neckar, and the Main), enters Germany, at Mainz turns W to Bingen. From here to Bonn it travels 80 m. NW (receiving the Moselle at Coblenz) through the picturesque Rhine gorge, with such legendary landmarks as the Lorelei, its high banks in places covered with vineyards and crowned with ancient castles. Beyond Bonn it passes Cologne and Düsseldorf, receives the Ruhr at Duisburg, and below Emmerich enters the Netherlands; it then turns W, and crosses the extraordinarily complex delta which it shares with the Meuse (Maas). From the Lower Rhine (the more northerly of its two principal arms) the Ijssel branches N to the Ijsselmeer; the Lower Rhine itself becomes the Lek, passes Rotterdam as the New Maas, and enters the North Sea at Hook of Holland. The Waal (the southerly principal arm) takes about two thirds of the water and with the Maas enters the North Sea by the Hollandsch Diep.

In Roman times the Rhine formed the E frontier of Gaul. For centuries it has had great strategic importance, esp. to France and Germany; to the Germans 'Father Rhine' is a national symbol. Declared free to international shipping 1868. Linked by canals with many other European rivers, it carries an immense volume of traffic, esp. between the Rhine–Ruhr industrial region and Rotterdam. Principal cargoes coal, iron ore, grain.

**Rhode Island** USA. State in New England, bordering S on the Atlantic Ocean. Area 1,214 sq. m. Pop. (1970) 922,461. Cap. and chief seaport Providence. One of the original 13 states, the 13th to ratify the Constitution (1790); popularly known as 'Little Rhody', being the smallest state, though also the most densely populated. Mainly low-lying. Its outstanding feature is Narragansett Bay, which penetrates 30 m. inland to Providence, where it receives the Blackstone R. The chief island in the bay is Rhode, on which is the town of Newport. Climate humid continental. Annual rainfall about 40 ins. Famous for poultry (esp. the Rhode Island Red) but primarily industrial, chiefly in the manufacture of textiles. Leading industrial centres Providence, Pawtucket, Warwick, Cranston. The coast was explored by Verrazano in 1524, but the first permanent white settlement was made in 1636 by Roger Williams at Providence. The first colony to declare its independence.

**Rhodes** (Gr. **Ródhos**) Greece. **1.** Largest island in the Dodecanese, and the most easterly in the Aegean Sea, 10 m. from the Turkish coast. Area 542 sq. m. Pop. 59,000. Crossed N–S by mountains rising to nearly 4,000 ft at the highest point. Well-watered and fertile. Produces cereals, fruits, wine. **2.** Capital of Rhodes and of the Dodecanese *nome*, at the NE extremity of the island. Pop. (1961) 27,393. Manufactures cigarettes, brandy, etc. Trade in fruit, tobacco, grain. Surrounded by walls and towers, it rises from the main harbour in the form of an amphitheatre, and has a medieval appearance, the Street of the Knights with its old houses being especially picturesque. Founded 408 B.C. In the following century it attained great commercial prosperity, but in 227 B.C. suffered severely from an earthquake which destroyed the Colossus of Rhodes, a statue 105 ft high of the god Helios, one of the Seven Wonders of the ancient world. It declined, was taken by the Knights of St John 1309, by the Turks 1523, and by the Italians 1912. Ceded to Greece 1946.

**Rhodesia.** Former British self-governing colony in central Africa; called Southern Rhodesia until the independence of Zambia (formerly Northern Rhodesia) in 1964. Area 150,333 sq. m. Pop. (1968) 4,670,000 (237,000 Europeans). Cap. Salisbury. Bounded by Moçambique (N and E), S Africa (S, the Limpopo R.), Botswana (SW), and Zambia (NW, the Zambezi R.). Consists of a broad ridge of the High Veld running SW–NE at a height of 4,000–6,000 ft., flanked by the Middle Veld at 3,000–4,000 ft, with the Low Veld along the Limpopo and Zambezi Rivers; the highest land, in the Inyanga Mountains near the Moçambique frontier, rises to over 8,500 ft. The climate varies with the altitude and the latitude; well-marked dry (April–Oct.) and rainy (Nov.–March) seasons. Annual rainfall from 20 ins. (W) to 40 ins. (E). Mostly savannah. Chief crops maize, tobacco. Main export tobacco; also asbestos from Mashaba and Shabani, chrome ore from Selukwe, coal from Wankie, gold from many districts. Cattle rearing. The European farmers are concentrated on the High Veld. Chief towns Salisbury (linked with Beira in Moçambique) and Bulawayo, both railway centres. Famous ruins dating from the 18th cent. at Zimbabwe near Fort Victoria. The warlike Matabele invaded the region and absorbed the Mashona tribe in the 19th cent. Administered by the British S Africa Company 1889–1923. Became a self-governing colony (as Southern Rhodesia) 1923. Federated with the then Northern Rhodesia (now Zambia) and Nyasaland (now Malawi) 1953, but the Federation broke up in 1962 and the other two states became fully independent in 1964. The Rhodesian government declared independence in 1965 (UDI). ⟡ *Mashonaland*; *Matabeleland*.

**Rhodesia, Northern** ⟡ *Zambia*.

**Rhodesia, Southern** ⟡ *Rhodesia*.

**Rhodesia and Nyasaland, Federation of** ⟡ *Malawi*; *Rhodesia*; *Zambia*.

**Rhodope** Greece. *Nome* in Thrace, bounded on the N by Bulgaria and on the S by the Aegean Sea. Area 984 sq. m. Pop. (1961) 109,194. Cap. Komotíni. The N is occupied by part of the Rhodope Mountains, the S by a coastal plain on which tobacco and other crops are grown.

**Rhodope Mountains.** Mountain system in the Balkan Peninsula extending SE from SW Bulgaria along the Bulgarian-Greek border. Highest peak Mt Musala (9,596 ft) in the Rila Mountains (Bulgaria).

**Rhondda** Wales. Municipal borough in Glamorganshire extending along the valleys of the Rhondda Fawr and Rhondda Fach rivers, in the E of the S Wales coalfield, including the coalmining centres of Pentre, Treherbert, Treorchy, Tonypandy, and Maerdy. Pop. (1961) 100,314 (141,346 in 1931). The district suffered severely from the depression of the 1930s, when nearly half the male insured workers were unemployed. After the 2nd World War several light industries were established here.

**Rhône** France. Department in Lyonnais, bounded on the E by the Saône and Rhône rivers. Area 1,104 sq. m. Pop. (1968) 1,325,611. Prefecture Lyons. Largely mountainous; the Monts du Beaujolais rise to over 3,000 ft. Vines and fruits grown in the Saône–Rhône valley. Industries concentrated in Lyons and Villefranche-sur-Saône.

**Rhône River** France/Switzerland. River 504 m. long, one of the most important in Europe, rising in the Rhône glacier at the foot of the Furka Pass in the E of Valais canton (Switzerland), flowing WSW and then NW to L. Geneva, which it leaves at Geneva to enter France, cutting through several narrow gorges (*cluses*) between the Jura and the Alps. At Lyons it receives its chief tributary, the Saône, and turns S along a valley between the Massif Central (W) and the French Alps (E); receiving the Isère, Durance, and other tributaries, it flows past Vienne, Valence, and Avignon to Arles, where it divides into the Grand Rhône and the Petit Rhône, which enclose the delta of the Camargue and enter the Gulf of Lions. Navigation is limited, but the river is now much utilized for hydroelectric power. The great dam and power station at Génissiat was started by the Compagnie Nationale du Rhône in 1937 and opened in 1948; a group of 20 power stations was then planned for the lower valley, and the first – at Donzère-Mondragon, with a 17-m. canal for navigation – was opened in 1952. For centuries the Rhône–Saône valley has been the principal route between the Mediterranean and N France.

**Rhum** ⟡ *Rum*.

**Rhyl** Wales. Urban district in Flintshire, at the mouth of the R. Clwyd 26 m. WNW of

Chester. Pop. (1961) 21,825. Seaside resort. Developed in the 19th cent. from a small fishing village.

**Rhymney** Wales. Urban district in Monmouthshire, on the R. Rhymney 4 m. E N E of Merthyr Tydfil. Pop. (1961) 8,859. Coalmining centre. Light engineering etc.

**Riau Archipelago** ◊ *Riouw Archipelago*.

**Ribble River** England. River 75 m. long rising in the Pennines in the W Riding of Yorkshire, flowing generally S past Settle and then S W through Lancashire, past Preston, entering the Irish Sea by an estuary between St Anne's and Southport.

**Ribeirão Prêto** Brazil. Town in São Paulo state 190 m. N N W of São Paulo at a height of 1,900 ft. Pop. 119,000. In a rich coffee-growing region. Commercial centre serving São Paulo and the neighbouring states. Trade in coffee, cotton, sugar, grain. Cotton milling, distilling, brewing. Manufactures steel, agricultural machinery.

**Richborough** England. Ancient Rutupiae. Small port in Kent, on the R. Stour about 1 m. N of Sandwich, of which it is a suburb. Was Caesar's chief port and a military base. Several Roman remains. In the 1st World War it was again brought into use, as a supply port for the British Expeditionary Force.

**Richmond** England. Municipal borough in the N Riding of Yorkshire, on the R. Swale 11 m. S W of Darlington. Pop. (1961) 5,764. Market town. Trade in agricultural produce. Has the ruins of an 11th-cent. Norman castle, the tower of a 13th-cent. Franciscan abbey, a grammar school dating from the 14th cent. and refounded in 1567, and the Georgian Theatre (1788), one of the oldest in the country.

**Richmond** (California) U S A. Industrial town and seaport 10 m. N N W of Oakland on San Francisco Bay. Pop. (1960) 71,854. Oil refining, motor-car assembly, railway engineering. Manufactures chemicals, electronic equipment, metal goods, etc.

**Richmond** (Indiana) U S A. Industrial town 68 m. E of Indianapolis. Pop. (1960) 44,149. Manufactures machine tools, agricultural implements, motor-car parts, etc.

**Richmond** (Virginia) U S A. State capital, at the head of navigation of the James R. Pop. (1960) 219,958. Seaport. Commercial and cultural centre. Exports tobacco, grain, coal, etc. Major tobacco market. Tobacco processing. Manufactures chemicals, food products, textiles, paper, etc. Among the famous buildings are the state Capitol (1785–92), St John's Church (1741), and the White House of the Confederacy, now a Confederate museum. Important educational centre; seat of the University of Richmond (1832) and the Virginia Union University (1865, Negro). Became capital of the Confederate states 1861; in 1865 it was evacuated and set on fire by the Confederates, about one third of the city being destroyed.

**Richmond-upon-Thames** (Richmond) England. Formerly Sheen. Former municipal borough in N Surrey, on the R. Thames 8 m. W S W of London; from 1965 a Greater London borough including the former municipal boroughs of Barnes (Surrey) and Twickenham (Middlesex). Pop. (1963) 181,581. Mainly residential. Also a popular resort for Londoners; the attractions, besides the river, include Richmond Park (2,350 acres), the Royal Botanic Gardens (Kew), and Ham Common and Ham House (Ham). The present Richmond Park was added to the Old Deer Park by Charles I (1637). White Lodge, in the park, built for George II, was the birthplace of Edward VIII. The Star and Garter Home for disabled soldiers and sailors stands on the site of the hotel of the same name. Renamed (1500) by Henry VII after his earldom in Yorkshire, and the Palace of Sheen was the residence of several monarchs from Edward III onwards.

**Rickmansworth** England. Urban district in S W Hertfordshire 4 m. W S W of Watford at the confluence of the R. Chess and the R. Gade with the R. Colne. Pop. (1961) 28,442. Mainly residential. Basing House was the home of William Penn (1672–6). Near by is Moor Park, with the 18th-cent. mansion and well-known golf courses.

**Riesa** German Democratic Republic. Town in the Dresden district, on the Elbe R. 25 m. N W of Dresden. Pop. (1965) 41,014. River port, railway junction, and industrial centre. Sawmilling, brewing. Manufactures iron and steel, glass, soap, furniture, etc. Trade in petroleum, grain, etc.

**Rieti** Italy. Ancient Reate. Capital of Rieti province, in Latium, on the Velino R. 16 m. S E of Terni. Pop. (1961) 35,441. Manufactures textiles, olive oil, macaroni, etc. Roman remains; 13th-cent. cathedral and episcopal palace.

**Rif, Er** Morocco. Mountain range near the Mediterranean coast, rising to over 8,000 ft, extending 200 m. S and then E from Ceuta on the Strait of Gibraltar to the lower

Moulouya valley near the Algerian border. Inhabited by the Riffs, Berbers who (under the leadership of Abdel Krim) successfully rebelled against French and Spanish rule in 1921–6. ♢ *Melilla*.

**Riga** USSR. Capital and chief seaport of the Latvian SSR, on the W Dvina R. 8 m. above the mouth (on the Gulf of Riga). Pop. (1970) 733,000. Exports timber, flax, paper, butter, eggs. Manufactures footwear, cement, rubber products, telephone equipment, paper, textiles, etc. Shipbuilding. Outports at Daugavgriva and Bolderaja. The harbour is closed by ice for about 4 winter months. In the old Hanse town on the right bank of the river are the 15th/16th-cent. castle built by the Grand Master of the Knights of the Sword, the 15th-cent. House of the Blackheads (a corporation of foreign merchants), the 13th-cent. cathedral of St Mary (burned in the 16th cent. but rebuilt and later restored), and the 15th-cent. Church of St Peter with a steeple 412 ft high. University (1919). Bathing beaches in the vicinity. Founded in the mid 12th cent. Joined the Hanseatic League 1282 and soon became prosperous through trade. Later it passed in turn to Poland (1561), Sweden (1621), and Russia (1710). Became Russia's second most important Baltic port (after St Petersburg, now Leningrad). Capital of independent Latvia from 1919. Occupied by the Russians 1940 and by the Germans 1941–4.

**Riga, Gulf of** USSR. Inlet of the Baltic Sea into the coasts of Estonia and Latvia, about 100 m. long and 60 m. wide, with the Estonian islands of Saaremaa, Hiiumaa, and others across its entrance. Icebound Jan.–April. Chief port Riga.

**Rigi** Switzerland. Mountain ridge in the Alps, between the lakes of Lucerne, Zug, and Lauerz, reaching 5,908 ft at the highest point (Kulm). Ascended by rack-and-pinion railway. A popular excursion for tourists from Lucerne.

**Rijeka** (Italian **Fiume**) Yugoslavia. The country's chief seaport, in Croatia, on the Adriatic Sea. Pop. (Rijeka-Sušak, 1961) 100,989. Also an industrial centre. Shipbuilding, oil refining. Manufactures machinery, chemicals, tobacco products, etc. Now includes the E suburb of Sušak, whence the medieval castle and church of Trsat can be reached, the latter a place of pilgrimage. Became a free port 1723. Annexed to Hungary 1779. Claimed by Yugoslavia and Italy in 1919, it was seized

by d'Annunzio, and again by the Fascists in 1922, and was annexed to Italy in 1924. Sušak was developed as a Yugoslav port, but in 1947 Fiume (now Rijeka) was transferred to Yugoslavia, and the two towns were reunited.

**Rijn River** ♢ *Rhine River*.

**Rijswijk (Ryswick)** Netherlands. Town in S Holland province just SE of The Hague. Pop. (1968) 48,476. Largely residential. Manufactures furniture etc. The Treaty of Ryswick (1697) was signed here.

**Rikitea** ♢ *Gambier Islands*.

**Rila Mountains** ♢ *Rhodope Mountains*.

**Rimac River** Peru. River 80 m. long rising in the W Cordillera of the Andes, flowing WSW to the Pacific near Lima. Lower course used for irrigation. With its tributary the Santa Eulalia it supplies power for hydroelectric plants.

**Rimini** Italy. Ancient Ariminum. Town in Forlì province, Emilia-Romagna, on the Adriatic 65 m. SE of Bologna. Pop. (1968) 111,622. Popular seaside resort, port, and railway junction. Manufactures textiles, shoes, macaroni, etc. Popularity as a summer resort largely due to its extensive beaches. Has a triumphal arch built by Augustus, but its finest building was the Renaissance Church of S Francesco or Tempio Malatestiano (completed 1450), severely damaged, like much of the rest of the town, in the 2nd World War. An important route centre in Roman times, being a seaport and standing at the junction of the Aemilian Way to Piacenza and the Flaminian Way to Rome. Passed to the Malatesta family 1237, and was ruled by them until 1509, when it became a papal possession.

**Riobamba** Ecuador. Capital of Chimborazo province, at a height of 9,000 ft in a high Andean basin SE of Mt Chimborazo and 105 m. S of Quito. Pop. (1966) 61,393. Manufactures textiles, carpets, footwear, etc. Has a picturesque weekly fair, held in the main plazas, made colourful by Indians from the surrounding agricultural region.

**Rio Branco** (river) Brazil. River 400 m. long formed from several headstreams, including the Uraricuera and the Tacutu, rising in the Sierra Pacaraima and flowing S to join the Rio Negro.

**Rio Branco** (territory) ♢ *Roraima*.

**Río Bravo** ♢ *Rio Grande* (Mexico/USA).

**Río Colorado** Argentina. River 530 m. long formed on the Mendoza–Neuquén border by the union of the Río Grande and the Barrancas. Flows S E to the Atlantic Ocean. Often regarded as dividing the pampas (N) from Patagonia (S).

**Río Cuarto** Argentina. Town in Córdoba province, on the Río Cuarto 130 m. S of Córdoba. Pop. 70,000. Commercial and industrial centre and garrison town. Trade in cereals and other agricultural produce. Manufactures cement, textiles, etc.

**Rio da Dúvida** ◊ *Roosevelt River*.

**Rio de Janeiro** Brazil. 1. Usually known as Rio. Chief seaport and former capital of Brazil, capital of Guanabara state, on the S W shore of Guanabara Bay. Pop. (1960) 3,223,408. Exports coffee, sugar, iron ore, etc. Manufactures clothing, furniture, chemicals, cigarettes, etc. Flour milling, sugar refining, railway engineering. The city, in an outstandingly beautiful setting, first occupied only the narrow alluvial plain along the coast, but it has now spread farther inland. Stands against a background of towering mountains, extending about 6 m. around the bay; its best-known strip of coastline is the famous Copacabana beach facing the Atlantic. The highest peak, the Corcovado (2,300 ft), surmounted by a giant figure of Christ, dominates the whole; the entrance to the great landlocked harbour is overshadowed by the conical Sugar Loaf Mountain or Pão de Açúcar (1,230 ft). Some of the adjacent hills have been appropriated as shanty towns, in which about half a million of the poor of Rio live. Lies just within the tropics, but the hot humid climate is tempered by sea breezes.

Many buildings remain from the colonial period, including a number of fine churches, and there are also tall modern structures, many of considerable architectural merit. Numerous distinguished squares, parks, and gardens, including the Botanical Gardens (founded 1808), with their avenues of lofty Royal Palms. Seat of the University of Brazil (1920) and the Catholic University of Rio de Janeiro (1940). Has good communications by sea, air, and land with much of the interior and the coast, and handles a great deal of the country's domestic coastal trade. Two airports: the Santos Dumont for internal airlines, standing on Guanabara Bay, and the larger Galeão airport for international traffic, located on an island in the bay. Linked by ferries with Niterói on the opposite side of the bay.

Discovered by the Portuguese (Jan. 1502) and mistakenly thought to be at the mouth of a river; hence the name, 'River of January'. First settled (1555) by the French, but they were driven out by the Portuguese 1567, and Rio became the capital of the southern province of Brazil. Replaced Salvador (Bahia) as the colonial capital of all Brazil, and remained capital under the Empire and the Republic till Brasilia was inaugurated in 1960.

2. State on the Atlantic coast. Area 16,564 sq. m. Pop. (1960) 3,402,728. Cap. Niterói. Largely mountainous; crossed by the Serra do Mar and drained by the Paraíba R. and its tributaries. Produces coffee, citrus fruits, sugar-cane, etc. Much recent industrial development, including steel manufacture at Volta Redonda. Guanabara state, with the city of Rio de Janeiro, forms an enclave within it.

**Río de la Plata (River Plate)** Argentina/ Uruguay. Estuary of the Paraná and Uruguay rivers between Uruguay (N) and Argentina (S), extending about 160 m. S E to the Atlantic, 20 m. in width at its head broadening to 60 m. between Montevideo and the Argentine shore and 140 m. at the E end. Much silt is brought down by the rivers and deposited on the banks, esp. in the S; the water is relatively shallow, and continuous dredging of channels is necessary. Discovered by Diaz de Solis 1516. Explored by Magellan 1520. During the 2nd World War (Dec. 1939) a naval action took place off its mouth after which the German pocket battleship *Graf Spee*, unable to leave the river, was scuttled.

**Río de Las Balsas** ◊ *Mexico*.

**Río de Oro** ◊ *Spanish Sahara*.

**Rio Grande** Brazil. Seaport in Rio Grande do Sul state, at the entrance to the Lagôa dos Patos, 150 m. S S W of Pôrto Alegre, whose outport it is. Pop. 88,000. Exports meat products, hides, etc. Meat packing, fish and vegetable canning, oil refining. Manufactures textiles, footwear, etc. Founded 1737.

**Rio Grande (Río Bravo)** Mexico/U S A. Known in Mexico as the Río Bravo (Río Bravo del Norte). River 1,880 m. long, rising in the San Juan Mountains in S W Colorado, flowing S E across Colorado and then almost due S through New Mexico, and for its remaining 1,300 m. generally S E, forming the U S A–Mexico frontier, and ultimately discharging into the Gulf of Mexico. The Big Bend National

Park (1,082 sq. m.) in Texas is a wild region of desert and mountains in the wide angle formed along the lower course. Not used for navigation, but has been dammed for irrigation, flood control, and hydroelectric power. The largest dam is the Elephant Butte Dam in New Mexico, which impounds a lake 200 sq. m. in area, irrigating half a million acres. Chief tributary the Pecos R., which joins it below the Big Bend.

**Rio Grande do Norte** Brazil. State in the NE 'shoulder'. Area 20,482 sq. m. Pop. (1960) 1,157,258. Cap. Natal. Consists mainly of plateau with a semi-arid climate, and a more humid sandy coastal plain. Important salt works. Also produces sugar-cane, cotton, carnauba wax, hides.

**Rio Grande do Sul** Brazil. The southernmost state, bounded on the W by Argentina and on the S by Uruguay. Area 109,066 sq. m. Pop. (1960) 5,448,823. Cap. Pôrto Alegre. Main occupation stock rearing, but cereals, fruit, and wine production are of growing importance. In the N lumbering and maté gathering. The state has absorbed large numbers of German and Italian immigrants.

**Río Muni** ◊ *Equatorial Guinea.*

**Río Negro** Argentina. River in Patagonia 400 m. long formed by the union of the Neuquén and Limay rivers, flowing E and SE through irrigated fruit-growing lands to the Atlantic N of the Gulf of San Matías. Irrigation is made possible by the great Río Negro dam near the town of Neuquén.

**Rio Negro** Brazil. River 1,300 m. long rising in E Colombia (where it is known as the Guainía), flowing generally E and SE, a major tributary of the Amazon. Forms part of the Colombia–Venezuela border and enters Brazil in the densely forested Amazon basin. Joins the Amazon about 10 m. below Manáus, where its blue-black waters mingle with the light, silt-choked flow of the main river. Its system is linked with that of the Orinoco R. by the Casiquiare.

**Río Negro** Uruguay. River 500 m. long rising in Brazil 15 m. E of Bagé and flowing generally WSW across Uruguay to join the Uruguay R. A dam in the middle course (with hydroelectric installation) creates an artificial lake 87 m. long and 18 m. wide.

**Rion (Georgian Rioni) River** USSR. River 180 m. long in the W Georgian SSR, rising in the Caucasus and flowing gener-

ally WSW past Kutaisi (near which is a hydroelectric plant) to enter the Black Sea at Poti. In its lower course it flows through the Colchis marshes.

**Río Tinto** Spain. River 60 m. long in Huelva province, in the SW, near the source of which is the famous copper-mining town of Río Tinto.

**Riouw (Riau) Archipelago** Indonesia. Group of islands off the E coast of Sumatra at the S entrance to the Strait of Malacca. Area 2,280 sq. m. Pop. 298,000. Tin and bauxite are mined on Bintan, the largest and most important island, which has the chief town, Tandjungpinang.

**Ripley** England. Urban district in Derbyshire 9 m. NNE of Derby. Pop. (1961) 17,601. Coalmining, ironworking, engineering, knitwear manufacture.

**Ripon** England. Municipal borough in the W Riding of Yorkshire, on the R. Ure 21 m. NW of York. Pop. (1961) 10,490. Cathedral city and resort. Tanning, brewing, etc. Manufactures paints, varnishes. Its cathedral or minster, in various architectural styles and with a Saxon crypt, was built between the mid 12th and early 16th cent. In the market square is the 13th-cent. Wakeman's (Mayor's) House. The ruins of the famous 12th-cent. Fountains Abbey are 3 m. SW. In medieval times Ripon was noted for spurs.

**Ripon Falls** ◊ *Nile River.*

**Risca** Wales. Urban district in Monmouthshire, on the R. Ebbw 5 m. WNW of Newport. Pop. (1961) 14,008. Coalmining etc.

**Risdon** Australia. Oldest settlement in Tasmania (1803), on the left bank of the Derwent R. estuary opposite Hobart. Large electro-metallurgical works producing zinc, with cadmium, sulphuric acid, superphosphate, and other by-products.

**Rivera** Uruguay. Capital of Rivera department, 260 m. N of Montevideo on the Brazilian frontier. Pop. (1964) 40,000. Trade in grain, cattle, fruit, vegetables. Manufactures textiles.

**Riverina** Australia. Region in New South Wales between the Lachlan-Murrumbidgee (N) and the Murray R. (S). Consists of flat fertile grassy plains, important for sheep rearing and wheat cultivation. Much of the arable land is irrigated.

**Riverside** USA. Residential town and resort in California, on the Santa Ana R. 48 m. E of Los Angeles. Pop. (1960) 84,332. Important centre for the packing and distribution of citrus fruits. Also manufactures aircraft engines, paints, etc. Seat of the citrus experiment station of the University of California (1907). Founded 1870. The cultivation of the navel orange was introduced from Brazil (1873); the parent tree is still preserved.

**Riviera** France/Italy. Narrow strip of coast between the mountains and the sea around the Gulf of Genoa, generally considered to extend from Hyères, at the W end of the French Riviera (Côte d'Azur), to La Spezia, at the E end of the Italian Riviera. Renowned for its scenery, its mild winter climate, and its sub-tropical vegetation; has become one of the leading playgrounds of Europe, with numerous resorts. On the French Riviera are Nice, Cannes, Menton, Antibes, Juan-les-Pins, Monte Carlo (Monaco). Genoa divides the Italian Riviera into the Riviera di Ponente (W), which has San Remo, Bordighera, Imperia, and Ventimiglia, and the Riviera di Levante (E), with Rapallo, Portofino, and Sestri Levante. From Nice to Genoa runs the famous road, built by Napoleon, the Corniche or Grande Corniche; between Nice and Menton are two parallel roads, the Moyenne and Petite Corniche. Throughout the Riviera vines, olives, and citrus fruits are cultivated, and flowers are grown, partly for the preparation of perfumes.

**Riyadh** Saudi Arabia. Capital of Nejd and joint capital (with Mecca) of Saudi Arabia, in an oasis in the centre of the country 500 m. ENE of Mecca. Pop. 300,000. Formerly a walled city surrounded by groves of date palms, it has been greatly modernized and enlarged in recent years. Grew to importance early in the 19th cent. when it became the headquarters of the Wahhabi movement. Linked by railway (completed 1951) with Dammam on the Persian Gulf. Airport.

**Rizaiyeh (Rezaiyeh)** Iran. Formerly Urmia. Capital of W Azerbaijan province, just W of L. Urmia and 70 m. WSW of Tabriz. Pop. (1966) 110,419. Commercial centre in an agricultural region producing cereals, fruits, tobacco, etc. Possible birthplace of Zoroaster.

**Roan Antelope** ◊ *Ndola*.

**Roanne** France. Industrial town in the Loire department, on the Loire R. 43 m. WNW of Lyons. Pop. (1968) 54,748. Important textile industry; also manufactures paper, leather goods, tiles, etc.

Terminus of the Roanne–Digoin Canal, which runs parallel to the Loire.

**Roanoke** USA. Formerly Big Lick. Town in SW Virginia on the Roanoke R. Pop. (1960) 97,110. Industrial centre and railway junction, in the natural amphitheatre formed by the Blue Ridge and the Allegheny Mountains. Railway engineering. Manufactures textiles, chemicals, etc. Founded 1834 and named because of its salt deposits. Renamed 1882.

**Roanoke Island** USA. Island 12 m. long and 3 m. wide off the coast of N Carolina, to which Raleigh sent unsuccessful expeditions (1585, 1587), attempting to establish an English colony. The disappearance of the would-be colonists is annually commemorated by performances of *The Lost Colony*, a historical drama by Paul Green (1937).

**Roanoke River** USA. River 410 m. long rising in SW Virginia, flowing generally ESE into N Carolina, and entering Albemarle Sound.

**Robin Hood's Bay** England. Picturesque fishing village in the N Riding of Yorkshire, 5 m. SE of Whitby, on an inlet of the same name which is fringed by high cliffs.

**Robson, Mount** Canada. Highest peak in the Canadian Rocky Mountains (12,972 ft), in E British Columbia near the Alberta border. Surrounded by the Mt Robson Provincial Park, 65 m. long and up to 20 m. wide.

**Rochdale** England. County borough in SE Lancashire, on the R. Roch 10 m. NNE of Manchester. Pop. (1961) 85,785. Important centre of the cotton industry, esp. spinning; also manufactures woollen, rayon, and asbestos goods. Engineering. Here the Equitable Pioneers Society (Rochdale Pioneers) founded the co-operative movement of Great Britain (1844). Birthplace of John Bright (1811–89).

**Rochefort-sur-Mer (Rochefort)** France. Port in the Charente-Maritime department, on the Charente R. 10 m. above the mouth on the Bay of Biscay. Pop. (1968) 34,780. Fish processing, sawmilling. Developed by Colbert in the 17th cent. but later superseded as a naval base by Brest. Birthplace of Pierre Loti (1850–1923).

**Rochester** England. Ancient Durobrivae. Municipal borough in N Kent, on the S side of the Medway estuary, adjoining Chatham. Pop. (1961) 50,121. Industrial centre. Manufactures agricultural machinery, air-conditioning equipment, cement, etc. In the 11th cent. Bishop Gundulf built a cathedral on the site of one founded (604) by St Augustine; part of his work survives in the present building. Also remains of the 12th-cent. Norman castle. St Bartholomew's Hospital (now in modern buildings) was founded in 1078 and King's School in 1544. Charles Dickens lived at Gad's Hill, just NW. Borstal is SW of the town. A Roman stronghold, important as the site of the bridge carrying Watling Street over the Medway.

**Rochester** (Minnesota) USA. Town 70 m. SSE of St Paul. Pop. (1960) 40,663. Commercial centre in an agricultural region. Manufactures dairy products etc. Chiefly famous for the Mayo clinic, founded in 1889 and now internationally known.

**Rochester** (New York) USA. Industrial town and port on L. Ontario at the mouth of the Genesee R., whose falls provide hydroelectric power. Pop. (1960) 318,611. Manufactures cameras, photographic equipment, optical appliances, thermometers, office equipment, etc. In a fruit-growing and market gardening region. Known as 'the Flower City' because of its many industries. University (1850).

**Roche-sur-Yon, La** France. Prefecture of the Vendée department, on the Yon R. 38 m. S of Nantes. Pop. (1968) 38,749. Market town. Railway junction. Flour milling, tanning. After being almost destroyed (1794), it was rebuilt by Napoleon (1805) and for a time was known as Napoléon-Vendée.

**Rockall** N Atlantic Ocean. Rocky islet 240 m. W of the Outer Hebrides. Also a sea area NW of Ireland used in meteorological forecasts.

**Rockford** USA. Industrial town in Illinois, on the Rock R. 80 m. WNW of Chicago. Pop. (1960) 126,706. Manufactures machine tools, agricultural machinery, hardware, hosiery, furniture, paints, etc. Hydroelectric power is derived from a dam on the Rock R. Founded (1834) as a stage-coach ford; hence the name.

**Rockhampton** Australia. Seaport and commercial town in E Queensland 40 m. up the Fitzroy R. from Keppel Bay. Pop. (1966) 45,349. Exports meat, hides, copper, gold, coal from an extensive hinterland. Large meat works downstream. Founded 1858 after an unsuccessful gold rush.

**Rock Hill** USA. Town in S Carolina 77 m.

N of Columbia. Pop. (1960) 29,404. Manufactures textiles, paper, etc. Seat of the Winthrop College for women (1886).

**Rock Island** USA. Town in Illinois, on the Mississippi R. near the confluence with the Rock R., adjoining Moline and opposite Davenport (Iowa). Pop. (1960) 51,863. Railway engineering. Manufactures electrical and agricultural equipment, hardware, clothing, footwear, etc. On the island of the same name in the Mississippi is the main US arsenal (established 1862). With Moline, E Moline, and Davenport (Iowa) the town forms the group known as the Quad Cities.

**Rocky Mount** USA. Town in N Carolina, on the Tar R. 50 m. ENE of Raleigh. Pop. (1960) 32,147. Railway engineering, tobacco processing, cotton milling, etc. Important trade in tobacco and cotton.

**Rocky Mountains (Rockies)** N America. Vast mountain system in W Canada and USA, extending from the Yukon to New Mexico; the backbone of the Continent, divisible into four sections: the Canadian Rockies and the N, Central, and S Rockies of the USA.

The Canadian Rockies (the boundary between British Columbia and Alberta for about half of their 900 m.) contain many glaciers, lakes, and icefields, now preserved for sport and recreation in National and Provincial Parks (e.g. Jasper, Banff, etc.). Passes include the Vermilion (5,376 ft), Kicking Horse (5,339 ft), and Crow's Nest (4,450 ft).

In the US Rockies there are 20 or more principal ranges of complex structure, the N, Central, and S sections corresponding approximately with the states of Montana (N), Wyoming (central), and Colorado, Utah, New Mexico (S). The Glacier National Park in the N contains magnificent glacier and lake scenery and has 26 peaks over 9,000 ft. In the Central Rockies, the rugged Teton Range has probably the finest scenery in the entire mountain system; the Grand Teton rises to 13,747 ft. The Sawatch Range of the S Rockies contains the highest peak of all, Mt Elbert (14,431 ft), and several others over 14,000 ft. Some geographers consider the ranges of Yukon and Alaska as part of the Rockies; in this case Mt Logan (19,850 ft) is the highest peak.

**Rodez** ◊ *Aveyron.*

**Ródhos** ◊ *Rhodes.*

**Rodrigues (Rodriguez)** Mauritius. British

island in the Indian Ocean 350 m. ENE of Mauritius, of which it is a dependency. Area 40 sq. m. Pop. (1968) 21,595. Chief town Port Mathurin (pop. 600). Volcanic in origin; rises to 1,300 ft in Mt Limon. Frequently subject to tropical cyclones. Chief products maize, fruit, tobacco, salted fish. Discovered by the Portuguese 1645. Taken by the British 1810.

**Roermond** Netherlands. Industrial town in Limburg province, on the Maas R. at the confluence with the Roer R. 28 m. NNE of Maastricht. Pop. (1968) 37,011. Manufactures textiles, bicycles, paper. Flour milling, brewing, etc Trade in agricultural produce. Has a 13th-cent. Romanesque church.

**Roggeveld Mountains** ⋄ *South Africa.*

**Rohtak** India. Town in Punjab 40 m. N W of Delhi. Pop. (1961) 88,193. Commercial centre. Trade in grain, cotton, oilseeds, etc. Cotton ginning.

**Romagna** Italy. Region of N Italy, now the E part of the Emilia-Romagna region, comprising the provinces of Forlì and Ravenna and part of Bologna. Long formed part of the Papal States.

**Roman** Rumania. Town in the Neamţ district (Moldavia), on the Moldava R. near its confluence with the Siret R. 35 m. WSW of Iaşi. Pop. 32,000. Railway junction. Industrial centre. Flour milling, sugar refining, etc.

**Romania** ⋄ *Rumania.*

**Rome** (Italian **Roma**) Italy. Capital of Italy and of the Latium region and Roma province, on both banks of the Tiber R. 17 m. from the mouth, in the Campagna di Roma. Pop. (1968) 2,630,535. Port Civitavecchia. Called 'the Eternal City'; one of the world's outstanding historical, religious, cultural, and art centres. Also an important centre of roads, railways, and airways. Large tourist trade. Film production. Printing and publishing. Manufactures machinery, furniture, cement, glass, silverware, etc. Many of the inhabitants work in government offices. On the right bank of the river are the Vatican City, with St Peter's Church, and the old Trastevere quarter. On the left bank is the main part of the city, centred on the Piazza Venezia, with the large monument to Victor Emmanuel II and the Palazzo Venezia. Broad avenues radiate from the square. The Via dei Fori Imperiali (opened by Mussolini in 1932) leads past the Imperial Fora and the Roman Forum,

containing the city's principal relics of ancient Rome, to the Colosseum, near which is the 4th-cent. Arch of Constantine; to the S are the Baths of Caracalla and the Appian Way. From the Piazza Venezia the Corso Vittorio Emanuele runs W and then N W to the Tiber, through the Campo Marzio quarter, which contains the Farnese, Spada, and other Renaissance palaces and the Pantheon. One bridge across the river leads to St Peter's and another to the Castel Sant' Angelo. The main thoroughfare, the Via del Corso, runs N from the Piazza Venezia to the Piazza del Popolo, E of which is the Villa Borghese (Villa Umberto I), the largest and finest of the public parks, with the art museum of the Casino Borghese. E of the Via del Corso are the Quirinal palace (begun in 1574, the residence formerly of the king and now of the president of Italy) and the Piazza di Spagna, whence a flight of 137 steps ascends to the Church of Santa Trinitá dei Monti and the Villa Medici. Near by are the house where the poet John Keats died, and Rome's most famous fountain, the Fontana di Trevi (1762), standing before the Palazzo Poli.

Among the many churches (about 450 in all) there are 5 patriarchal basilicas: St Peter's, in the Vatican City; San Giovanni in Laterano (St John Lateran), the cathedral of Rome, with the Lateran Palace; San Lorenzo fuori le Mura (St Lawrence outside the Walls); San Paolo fuori le Mura (St Paul outside the Walls); and Santa Maria Maggiore (St Mary Major). Except for the last-named, the basilicas and ancient churches were built on the sites of martyrs' tombs. San Paolo (the largest church in Rome after St Peter's) was founded by the Emperor Constantine over the grave of the Apostle; Santa Maria Maggiore dates from 352 and has the highest campanile in Rome. Of the others, San Pietro in Vincoli (St Peter in Chains) was reputedly founded (442) to hold the chains that bound St Peter in captivity. Besides the university (founded 1303) Rome has many colleges for the training of Roman Catholic clergy, academies of fine arts and music, and numerous museums, art galleries, and libraries.

According to tradition Rome was founded by Romulus in 753 B.C. In the 8th cent. B.C. the Tarquins took the settlement on the Palatine Hill (one of the famous Seven Hills, the others being the Capitoline (NW), Quirinal, Viminal, Esquiline, Caelian, and Aventine, extending N–SW in an outer curve) and it became the chief centre of Latium. About 500 B.C. the Romans overthrew their Etruscan rulers and established the Republic, which endured for over 4 centuries. The administration was in the hands of two consuls (chief magistrates) and a Senate (council of elders). A series of campaigns led to Rome's supremacy over the known world: in Italy the Samnites and the people of Etruria, Umbria, Lucania, Apulia, and Picenum were subdued; the Greek cities of the S and later Cisalpine Gaul (Lombardy) were conquered. The three Punic Wars (264–241, 218–201, and 149–146 B.C.) resulted in the annexation of Spain, Sicily, Sardinia, Corsica, and N Africa. During the 2nd cent. B.C. Syria and Macedonia were conquered and Greece and Egypt became subject to Rome. While the legions won military glory abroad, however, suffering and discontent were rife among the common people at home; the attempts at agrarian reform by Tiberius and Gaius Gracchus led to their assassination. In 60 B.C. Pompey, Crassus, and Julius Caesar formed the First Triumvirate; by 51 B.C. Caesar had conquered Gaul as far as the Rhine. He became master of Rome but was assassinated (44 B.C.). Peace was not established until his nephew Octavian had defeated Antony and Cleopatra at Actium (31 B.C.) and (as Augustus) assumed absolute power. He inaugurated two centuries of peace (the '*Pax Romana*') under which the Empire enjoyed its greatest prosperity and reached its farthest expansion, including Armenia and Mesopotamia (E), N Africa (S), Spain and Gaul (W), and Britain, Pannonia, and Dacia (N). After the death of Marcus Aurelius (A.D. 180), however, there came a century of conflict and disorder; the strength of the Empire declined as barbarian invasions increased. In 337 Constantine I moved his capital to Byzantium (which he renamed Constantinople), leaving the Empire permanently divided into East and West. Rome was sacked by Goths and Vandals in the 5th cent. and in 476 the last Emperor of the West was deposed. In the W the bishops of Rome (later the popes) took over the imperial power; by the 10th cent. they were under the control of the leading families of Rome. The Eastern Empire survived until 1453, when Constantinople fell to the Turks. The medieval Holy Roman Empire was an attempt to revive the Western Empire. Under the popes of the Renaissance Rome became a great centre of art and culture. In 1870 the city, all that remained of the Papal States, was made capital of the new kingdom of Italy, and the pope retired to the Vatican. The Lateran Treaty (1929) recognized the Vatican City as a sovereign state. During the 2nd World War Rome suffered little damage.

**Rome** (Georgia) USA. Industrial town at the confluence of the Etowah and Oostanaula rivers 55 m. NW of Atlanta. Pop. (1960) 32,226. Manufactures cotton and rayon goods, hosiery, paper, agricultural machinery, etc. Founded 1834.

**Rome** (New York) USA. Industrial town on the Mohawk R. 14 m. WNW of Utica. Pop. (1960) 51,646. Important copper and brass-working industry. Manufactures cables, wire, machinery, vacuum cleaners, etc.

**Romford** England. Former municipal borough in SW Essex 12 m. ENE of London; from 1965 part of the Greater London borough of Havering. Pop. (1961) 114,579 (35,918 in 1931). Largely residential. Brewing, engineering. Manufactures pharmaceutical and plastic products. Birthplace of Francis Quarles (1592–1644), the poet.

**Romney** ◊ *New Romney.*

**Romney Marsh** England. Level stretch of drained marshland mainly in S Kent, between Winchelsea (Sussex) and Hythe, now used as sheep pasture. Much of it was once covered by the estuary of the R. Rother, but a great storm (1287) diverted the river from New Romney to Rye, and the subsequent recession of the sea led to the decline of New Romney, Rye, and Winchelsea as seaports. Part of Romney Marsh was reclaimed in Roman times.

**Romsdal** Norway. Valley of the Rauma R. in the SW, mainly in Möre og Romsdal county, about 60 m. long, with several waterfalls and flanked by lofty mountains including Romsdalshorn (5,102 ft). The Rauma R. enters the sea by Romsdal Fiord.

**Romsey** England. Municipal borough in Hampshire, on the R. Test 8 m. NW of Southampton. Pop. (1961) 6,229. Market town. Brewing, tanning. Has a 12th-cent.

Norman church built over the church of a 10th-cent. Benedictine nunnery. Birthplace of Sir William Petty (1623–87).

**Roncesvalles (Fr. Roncevaux)** Spain. Village in Navarra province 22 m. NE of Pamplona and 5 m. from the French frontier, at a height of 3,220 ft in the Pyrenees. Its pass is famous as the scene of the defeat of Charlemagne and the death of Roland.

**Ronda** Spain. Town in Málaga province, Andalusia, on the Guadiaro R. 40 m. W of Málaga. Pop. 31,000. Flour milling, tanning. Trade in olives, wine, leather, etc. A picturesque town, divided into two parts by the Tajo de Ronda, a deep gorge crossed by an 18th-cent bridge. The old town, S of the Tajo, is Moorish in character and has the alcazaba or fortress; the new town, to the N, dates from the 15th cent. Birthplace of Vicente Espinal (1551–1624), the poet.

**Rondônia** Brazil. Formerly Guaporé. Federal territory in the W, bounded on the W and S by Bolivia. Area 93,815 sq. m. Pop. (1960) 70,783. Cap. Pôrto Velho. Largely tropical rain-forest. Chief products rubber, Brazil nuts. Some Bolivian trade passes along the Madeira–Mamoré railway, which by-passes the Madeira R. rapids, through Pôrto Velho. Established 1943. Renamed 1956.

**Ronse (Fr. Renaix)** Belgium. Town in E Flanders province 35 m. WSW of Brussels. Pop. (1968) 25,255. Textile industry.

**Roodepoort-Maraisburg** S Africa. Town in the S of the Transvaal, on the Witwatersrand 9 m. W of Johannesburg, at a height of 5,725 ft. Pop. (1967) 115,600 (51,100 Bantu, 61,200 whites). Goldmining and residential centre. Includes the towns of Roodepoort, Florida, and Maraisburg.

**Roorkee** India. Town in Uttar Pradesh 22 m. ESE of Saharanpur. Pop. (1961) 33,651. Workshops of the Upper Ganges Canal. Seat of Roorkee University (1948), formerly the Thomason College of Civil Engineering (1847).

**Roosendaal** Netherlands. Industrial town and railway junction in N Brabant province 12 m. WSW of Breda. Pop. (1968) 45,038. Railway engineering, sugar refining. Manufactures cigars, furniture, etc.

**Roosevelt (Teodoro) River** Brazil. Formerly Rio da Dúvida. River 500 m. long rising in the Serra dos Parecis (Rondônia) and flowing N to join the Aripuana R. Explored

(1914) by Theodore Roosevelt and named after him.

**Roquefort-sur-Soulzon (Roquefort)** France. Village in the Aveyron department 9 m. SSW of Millau, long famous for its cheese, made principally from ewes' milk and ripened in limestone caves near by. Pop. (1968) 1,349.

**Roraima** Brazil. Formerly Rio Branco. Federal territory in the N, in the basin of the Rio Branco. Area 88,820 sq. m. Pop. (1960) 29,489. Cap. Boa Vista (pop. 10,000). Formed 1943 from part of Amazonas. Chiefly undeveloped tropical rain-forest. Some stock rearing on the higher savannah round Boa Vista.

**Rosario** Argentina. River port in Santa Fé province, on the Paraná R. 170 m. NW of Buenos Aires. Pop. (1960) 671,582. Second largest city in Argentina. Railway, industrial, and commercial centre. Sugar refining, meat packing, flour milling, brewing, etc. Manufactures bricks, furniture, etc. Terminus for the pampas railways. Exports wheat, meat, hides, etc.

**Roscoff** France. Fishing port and resort in the Finistère department 12 m. NW of Morlaix. Pop. (1968) 3,838. Trade in market-garden produce, esp. onions – sold in England by Breton onion-sellers.

**Roscommon** Irish Republic. 1. Inland county in Connacht, bounded on the E by the R. Shannon and on the SW by the R. Suck. Area 951 sq. m. Pop. (1966) 59,217. Partly hilly, rising to 1,082 ft in the Bralieve Mountains in the extreme N. Many lakes, including Lough Key and parts of Loughs Gara, Allen, Boderg, and Ree. Most of it lies within the limestone plain of central Ireland and is largely devoted to pasture for cattle and sheep.
2. County town of Co. Roscommon, 17 m. NW of Athlone. Pop. (1966) 1,659. Market in livestock and agricultural produce. Ruins of the large 13th-cent. castle and the Dominican priory.

**Roscrea** Irish Republic. Market town in the extreme N of Co. Tipperary on the Little Brosna R. Pop. (1966) 3,511. Malting, bacon and ham curing. Has a ruined 12th-cent. Augustinian priory. To the W is the modern Cistercian Abbey of Mt St Joseph.

**Roseau** ◊ *Dominica*.

**Rosenheim** Federal German Republic. Industrial town and railway junction in Bavaria, on the Inn R. 32 m. SE of Munich. Pop. (1963) 32,000. Manufactures chemicals, textiles, etc. Salt works.

**Roskilde** Denmark. Port in Zealand, at the S end of Roskilde Fiord 19 m. WSW of Copenhagen. Pop. (1965) 37,102. Tanning, meat canning. Manufactures agricultural machinery, paper. Capital of Denmark till 1443; in its 13th-cent. cathedral (later restored and enlarged) are the tombs of most of the Danish kings. The Peace of Roskilde (1658) between Denmark and Sweden was signed here.

**Ross and Cromarty** Scotland. Highland county extending from the Minch (W) to Moray Firth (E) and including Lewis (but not Harris) and several other islands of the Hebrides. Area 3,089 sq. m. Pop. (1961) 57,607. County town Dingwall. Rugged and mountainous, rising to 3,877 ft in Carn Eige. Many lakes, including the beautiful Loch Maree, Loch Fannich, and Loch Luichart. Deeply indented coastline. Much of the county consists of deer forests; on the E lowland (including the Black Isle), which is the most fertile area, oats and turnips are cultivated. Large flocks of sheep raised on the uplands. Chief towns (all small) Stornoway, Dingwall, Tain, Invergordon.

**Ross Dependency** Antarctica. The New Zealand sector of Antarctica, from 160° E to 150° W long. and S of 60° S lat., including the snow- and ice-covered mainland area, the Ross Sea and various islands, also the coastal regions of Victoria Land and King Edward VII Land. Area about 160,000 sq. m. The huge inlet of the Ross Sea gives a relatively short approach to the S Pole, hence the use of the coast for such bases as Little America for the Byrd 1929 expedition, and the McMurdo Sound bases for the Commonwealth Trans-Antarctic Expedition of 1957-8. Extensive surveying and mapping were carried out in 1958-9. Whaling vessels regularly visit its territorial waters. Placed under New Zealand jurisdiction 1923.

**Rossendale** England. District in E Lancashire comprising the municipal boroughs of Bacup, Haslingden, and Rawtenstall.

**Ross Island** Antarctica. Island in the Ross Sea off Victoria Land, containing the active volcano Mt Erebus (13,202 ft) and Mt Terror (10,750 ft).

**Rosslare** Irish Republic. Small resort in Co. Wexford 5 m. SE of Wexford. Rosslare Harbour, 3 m. SE, is the port for steamer services (with car ferry) to Fishguard (Wales).

**Ross-on-Wye** England. Urban district in Herefordshire, on the R. Wye 11 m. SSE

of Hereford. Pop. (1961) 5,643. Market town. Manufactures cider, leather. In the 14th-cent. church the philanthropist John Kyrle (1637-1724), Pope's 'Man of Ross', is buried.

**Ross Sea** Antarctica. Large inlet in the coast of the Ross Dependency between Cape Adare and Cape Colbeck, containing Ross Island.

**Rostock** German Democratic Republic. **1.** Administrative district, one of the three into which the *Land* of Mecklenburg was divided in 1952. Area 2,729 sq. m. Pop. (1968) 849,058.

**2.** Capital of Rostock administrative district, at the head of the estuary of the Warnow R. 8 m. from the Baltic. Pop. (1968) 188,820. Port, with outport at Warnemünde. Railway junction. Commercial centre. Shipbuilding, fishing, fish processing, brewing. Manufactures agricultural machinery, chemicals, etc. University (1418). Has a 14th-cent. Gothic town hall and several old churches. The Heinkel aircraft works here were heavily bombed in the 2nd World War. The port was much enlarged and improved in the 1960s. Birthplace of Marshal Blücher (1742-1819).

**Rostov-on-Don (Rostov)** USSR. Capital of the Rostov region, RSFSR, on the Don R. 25 m. from the mouth on the Sea of Azov. Pop. (1970) 789,000. Port. Railway junction. Major industrial and commercial centre. Overseas trade handled mainly by Taganrog. Linked via the Volga–Don Canal with Volgograd. Shipbuilding. Manufactures agricultural machinery, locomotives, chemicals, tobacco products, textiles, leather goods, etc. Includes the former Armenian suburb of Nakhichevan. Seat of a state university (1917). Founded 1761. Important for grain exports in the 19th cent. During the 2nd World War it was twice taken by the Germans and suffered considerable damage.

**Roswell** USA. Town in New Mexico, on the Rio Hondo 170 m. SE of Albuquerque. Pop. (1960) 39,593. Commercial centre in a district irrigated by artesian water. Trade in wool. Oil refining, food processing, etc.

**Rosyth** Scotland. Naval base and dockyard in Fifeshire, on the Firth of Forth 2 m. S of Dunfermline, with which it was incorporated in 1911. Much used in the 1st World War.

**Rothamsted** England. Estate 4 m. NW of St Albans, Herts, where Sir John Bennet Lawes (1816-1900) carried out his soil researches, and founded (1843) the now famous experimental station.

**Rotherham** England. County borough in the W Riding of Yorkshire, on the R. Don at the confluence with the R. Rother, 5 m. NE of Sheffield. Pop. (1961) 85,346. Industrial town. Important iron foundries and steel mills. Manufactures machinery, brassware, glass, etc. Coalmining in the neighbourhood. Has a 15th-cent. church, restored in the late 19th cent., and a grammar school founded in the 15th cent. The 15th-cent. Chantry Bridge over the Don was rebuilt in 1930.

**Rotherhithe** England. District in the London borough of Southwark, on the S bank of the R. Thames. Contains the Surrey Commercial Docks. Linked with Shadwell by the Rotherhithe Tunnel.

**Rother River** (Derbyshire-Yorkshire) England. River 21 m. long, flowing generally N through Derbyshire and Yorkshire and joining the R. Don at Rotherham.

**Rother River** (Hampshire-Sussex) England. River 24 m. long, rising 5 m. NNE of Petersfield in Hampshire, flowing S and then E past Midhurst in Sussex, and joining the R. Arun 7 m. N of Arundel.

**Rother River** (Kent-Sussex) England. River 31 m. long, rising just W of Mayfield, flowing E and then S, forming part of the Kent–Sussex boundary, and entering the English Channel near Rye. Before its diversion by the great storm of 1287, it flowed through Romney Marsh and entered the Sea at New Romney.

**Rothesay** Scotland. Royal burgh and county town of Buteshire, on the E coast of Bute island. Pop. (1961) 7,656. Fishing port. Resort. Ruins of an 11th-cent. castle.

**Rothwell** (Northamptonshire) England. Urban district in Northamptonshire 3 m. WNW of Kettering. Pop. (1961) 4,766. Manufactures footwear, clothing, etc. Has a 13th-cent. church.

**Rothwell** (Yorkshire) England. Urban district in the W Riding of Yorkshire, 4 m. SE of Leeds. Pop. (1961) 25,360. Coalmining centre. Manufactures rope etc. Engineering.

**Rotorua** New Zealand. Health resort and tourist centre S of L. Rotorua, N Island, 120 m. SE of Auckland. Pop. (1966) 25,954. In a district of hot springs and geysers, the water being used medicinally and for bathing; sanatorium on the S shore of the lake. Also renowned for its scenic beauty; near by there are Maori show-place villages.

**Rotterdam** Netherlands. Country's chief seaport, in S Holland province on the New Maas R. Pop. (1968) 710,871. Also handles considerable overseas trade for the Federal German Republic, exporting Ruhr coal as well as margarine, dairy produce, etc. from the Netherlands. Industrial centre. Important oil refineries and shipyards. Engineering, brewing, distilling. Manufactures margarine and other food products, soap, chemicals, etc. Chartered 1328. Expanded most in the 19th cent. after the construction of the New Waterway (1872) made it accessible to the largest oceangoing vessels; became the leading European seaport. Its importance as a seaport was much increased by the development of Europoort, near the North Sea entrance to the New Waterway, in the 1960s, enabling it to secure a still greater share of the overseas trade of western Europe. During the 2nd World War (1940) the centre of the city was destroyed by German bombing; it was entirely rebuilt after the war. Birthplace of Erasmus (1466–1536) and Pieter de Hooch (1629–?), the painter.

**Rotuma** ⟫ *Fiji Islands*.

**Roubaix** France. Industrial town in the Nord department, near the Belgian frontier 6 m. NE of Lille. Pop. (1968) 114,774. With its twin town Tourcoing, just NNW, it is the chief centre of the woollen industry. Also manufactures other textiles, clothing, carpets, textile machinery, rubber and plastic products, etc.

**Rouen** France. Ancient Rotomagus. Prefecture of the Seine-Maritime department, on the Seine R. 70 m. NW of Paris. Pop. (1968) 124,577. Port. Industrial centre. Exports mainly manufactured goods. Imports coal, oil. Oil refining. Manufactures textiles (esp. cotton goods), paper, chemicals, etc. A considerable trade in wines and spirits. Great historical interest; many of its finest buildings were damaged in the 2nd World War, inc. the 13th/16th-cent. cathedral, the 15th/16th-cent. Church of St Maclou, and the Gothic Palais de Justice; the 14th/16th-cent. Church of St Ouen and the 14th-cent. Tour de la Grosse Horloge (clock tower) were unharmed. Became capital of Normandy in the 10th cent.; here William the Conqueror died (1087). Held by the English 1419–49; Joan of Arc was tried and burned here 1431. An important British military base in the 1st World War. Birthplace of Corneille (1606–84) and Flaubert (1821–80).

**Rouergue** ◊ *Aveyron.*

**Roulers** (Flemish **Roeselare**) Belgium. Industrial town in W Flanders province 28 m. WSW of Ghent. Pop. (1968) 40,091. Manufactures textiles (chiefly linen), carpets. Severely damaged in the 1st World War.

**Roumania** ◊ *Rumania.*

**Roumelia** ◊ *Rumelia.*

**Rourkela** India. Industrial town in N Orissa, near the W Bengal border and 95 m. WSW of Jamshedpur. Pop. (1961) 90,287. Important iron and steel industry.

**Roussillon** France. Region and former province in the S, roughly corresponding to the modern department of Pyrénées-Orientales. Cap. Perpignan. Long in the possession of Aragon; passed to France (1659) by the Treaty of the Pyrenees.

**Rouyn** Canada. Mining town in W Quebec near the Ontario border, on L. Osisko. Pop. (1966) 18,581 (chiefly French Canadian). Produces chiefly copper, but also gold, silver, and zinc. Founded as a village 1922. Just NW is the twin town of Noranda.

**Rovaniemi** Finland. Town in the Lappi province on the Kemi R. 105 m. N of Oulu, just S of the Arctic Circle. Pop. (1968) 27,832. Commercial and winter-sports centre; often known as 'the gateway to Lapland'. Trade in timber, furs. Scene of the annual Ounasvaara International Winter Games.

**Rovereto** Italy. Industrial town in Trento province, Trentino-Alto Adige, 14 m. SSW of Trento. Pop. (1961) 25,638. Manufactures textiles, paper, leather goods, etc. Castle (15th-cent.).

**Rovigo** Italy. Capital of Rovigo province, Veneto, 37 m. SW of Venice. Pop. (1961) 45,649. Manufactures rope, furniture, etc. Sugar refining etc. Remains of a 10th-cent. castle; 16th-cent. Renaissance palace.

**Rovno** USSR. Capital of the Rovno region, Ukrainian SSR, 110 m. ENE of Lvov. Pop. (1970) 116,000. Railway junction. Industrial centre. Manufactures machinery, textiles, food products, etc. Passed from Poland to Russia 1793; returned to Poland 1921; ceded to the USSR 1945.

**Rovuma River** ◊ *Ruvuma River.*

**Rowley Regis** England. Industrial town in Staffordshire, on the R. Stour 7 m. WNW of Birmingham. Pop. (1961) 48,166. Coalmining, metal working, engineering, etc. A stone quarried locally for roadmaking is known as Rowley rag. From 1966 part of the county borough of ◊ *Warley.*

**Roxburghshire** Scotland. County in the SE, its E and S boundaries on the English border. Area 666 sq. m. Pop. (1961) 43,171. County town Jedburgh. Mainly hilly. Drained by the Tweed, Teviot, and Liddel rivers. Sheep rearing is an important occupation; manufactures tweeds and other woollen goods. Chief towns Jedburgh, Hawick, Kelso, Melrose.

**Royal Oak** USA. Town in Michigan 12 m. NNW of Detroit. Pop. (1960) 80,612 (25,087 in 1940). Mainly residential. Manufactures tools, paint, etc.

**Royston** (Hertfordshire) England. Urban district in Hertfordshire 18 m. N of Hertford. Pop. (1961) 6,160. Market town.

**Royston** (Yorkshire) England. Urban district in the W Riding of Yorkshire, 3 m. NNE of Barnsley. Pop. (1961) 8,490. In a coalmining region.

**RSFSR** (**Russia**; **Russian Soviet Federated Socialist Republic**) USSR. Largest of the constituent republics; about 76 per cent of the total area and 55 per cent of the total population. Area 6,501,500 sq. m. Pop. (1970) 130,090,000. Cap. Moscow. Administratively divided into 6 Territories, 49 Regions, 16 Autonomous Republics, 5 Autonomous Regions, 10 National Areas. Stretches 5,000 m. W–E from the Gulf of Finland to the Pacific Ocean, and up to 2,500 m. N–S from the Arctic Ocean to the Caucasus, the Caspian Sea, and the Altai and Sayan Mountains and the Amur R., which form the USSR border with China and Mongolia. The W belongs to the vast plain of E Europe, separated by the Urals from the W Siberian Plain, E of which is the Central Siberian Plateau; farther E, beyond the Lena R., is a great system of fold mountains in E Siberia, including the Verkhoyansk and Anadyr Ranges (N) and the Yablonovy and Sikhote Alin Ranges (S). In Europe the principal rivers are the Volga, the Don, and the N Dvina, and in Asia the Ob, Yenisei, Lena, and Amur. The huge L. Baikal (deepest freshwater lake in the world) lies S of the Central Siberian Plateau.

A land of such enormous extent exhibits much variety in climate and natural vegetation. In the extreme N, along the Arctic coast, is a belt of tundra; S of this is a far wider belt of coniferous forests (taiga) extending W–E across the entire republic. S of the forests (in the European part and in W Siberia) is a zone of mid-latitude grasslands (steppes) including the N portion of the fertile black-earth region. In the extreme S there are patches of arid semi-desert and desert.

The Moscow region has coniferous forests (N) and fertile steppes (S) where wheat, sugar-beet, and sunflowers are cultivated. This is the true heart of historic Russia and of the modern USSR, the political, cultural, and industrial hub of the nation, with several of the leading cities: Moscow, Gorki, Yaroslavl, Ivanovo, Tula. Lignite from the Moscow–Tula basin and peat from the N provide some of the power for the textile and metal industries of the region. In the Leningrad region (NW) there are shipbuilding and other industries at Leningrad, second only to Moscow among Soviet cities. The region along both banks of the Volga is partly forest and partly steppe, and produces crops of cereals, potatoes, hemp, etc. There are important industries at Kuibyshev, Volgograd, Kazan, and Saratov. In the Urals area minerals are the principal source of wealth: to the W and S of the mountains petroleum is obtained from the rich Volga–Ural oilfield (the 'second Baku'); also coal, iron, copper, nickel, and other metallic ores, supplying the great metallurgical industries of Sverdlovsk, Chelyabinsk, Perm, Magnitogorsk, etc. RSFSR produces about 70 per cent of the USSR's total industrial and agricultural output.

The carrying-out of the successive plans for the industrialization of the USSR has involved the creation of many new large towns and the rapid expansion of others in the republic, e.g. Magnitogorsk, Nizhni Tagil, and Berezniki (in the Urals), Novomoskovsk (Moscow region), and several in Siberia. Density of population is highest in the W, S, and central areas of European RSFSR. About four fifths of the population are Russians, but RSFSR has the greatest mixture of nationalities of all the republics: there are 38 national minorities, inc. Tatars, Jews, Poles, Bashkirs, Udmurts, Yakuts, Ossetians, most of them living in their own Autonomous Republics or Regions. ⟐ *Bashkir, Buryat, Chuvash, Dagestan, Kabardino-Balkar, Kalmuk, Karelian, Komi, Mari, Mordovian, North Ossetian, Tatar, Tuva, Checheno-Ingush, Udmurt, Yakut ASSRs, Siberia.*

**Ruanda-Urundi** ⟐ *Rwanda*; *Burundi*.

**Ruapehu** New Zealand. Highest mountain in the N Island (9,175 ft), an intermittently active volcanic peak in Tongariro National Park, SSW of L. Taupo, with a crater lake at the summit.

**Rub' al Khali.** In Arabic, 'Empty Quarter'. Vast desert in S Arabia, mainly in Saudi Arabia. Area about 300,000 sq. m. Consists partly of stony desert, partly of sandy desert, with large dunes in the E. First crossed (1931) by Bertram Thomas. In recent years has been explored for oil.

**Rubicon** (Italian **Rubicone**) **River** Italy. Short river in ancient Italy flowing NE to the Adriatic 8 m. NW of Rimini. It formed the S boundary of Cisalpine Gaul, and when Julius Caesar crossed it with his troops (49 B.C.) his action was tantamount to a declaration of war against Pompey and the Senate – hence the phrase 'crossing the Rubicon' for taking an irrevocable step.

**Rubtsovsk** USSR. Industrial town in the Altai Territory, RSFSR, near the Kazakhstan border 80 m. NNE of Semipalatinsk. Pop. (1970) 145,000. Manufactures tractors, farm implements, etc. Flour milling.

**Rudolf, Lake** Ethiopia/Kenya. Lake in the Great Rift Valley 155 m. long and up to 35 m. wide, at a height of 1,230 ft; mainly in Kenya, with the N tip in Ethiopia. Fed by the Omo and the Turkwell rivers. No visible outlet. Gradually diminishing and becoming increasingly saline owing to evaporation. Well stocked with fish, including the large Nile perch. Discovered (1888) by Count Teleki. Named after the Crown Prince of Austria.

**Rudolstadt** German Democratic Republic. Town in the Gera district, on the Saale R. 35 m. WSW of Gera. Pop. (1965) 30,087. Tourist and industrial centre. Manufactures porcelain, chemicals, etc. Seat of the counts of Schwarzburg-Rudolstadt 1599–1918.

**Rueil-Malmaison** France. Suburb 8 m. WNW of Paris, in the Hauts-de-Seine department. Pop. (1968) 62,933. Manufactures photographic equipment, pharmaceutical products, cement, etc. In a church rebuilt by Napoleon III is the tomb of the Empress Josephine; near by is the Château Malmaison, once a favourite residence of Napoleon I and later of Josephine.

**Rufiji River** Tanzania. River 375 m. long, flowing generally NE and E and entering the Indian Ocean by a delta 90 m. S of Dar-es-Salaam. Navigable by small craft for most of its course. Chief tributary the Great Ruaha R. Rice is grown in the lower valley.

**Rufisque** Senegal. Minor seaport 10 m.

ENE of Dakar. Pop. (1965) 48,300. Manufactures cement, groundnut oil, cotton goods, footwear, pharmaceutical products. Tanning, engineering.

**Rugby** England. Municipal borough in Warwickshire, near the R. Avon 11 m. E of Coventry. Pop. (1961) 51,651. Important railway junction. Engineering. Cattle market. Probably best known for its famous public school (founded 1567), which gained renown under the headmastership of Dr Thomas Arnold (1795–1842) and inspired Thomas Hughes's *Tom Brown's Schooldays*; here William Webb Ellis initiated the game of Rugby football (1823). One of the school's many famous pupils was Rupert Brooke (1887–1915), who was born at Rugby. Also birthplace of Sir Norman Lockyer (1836–1920), the astronomer. Hillmorton, 2 m. ESE, has the GPO radio station.

**Rugeley** England. Urban district in Staffordshire, on the R. Trent 8 m. ESE of Stafford. Pop. (1961) 13,012. Market town. Iron founding, tanning, etc.

**Rügen** German Democratic Republic. Island in the Rostock district, in the Baltic Sea opposite Stralsund, separated from the mainland by the narrow Strelasund (Bodden). Area 358 sq. m. Chief town Bergen. Irregular in shape, with a deeply indented coastline. Main occupations fishing, agriculture. Several seaside resorts. Connected to the mainland by a causeway (1936). Arkona, in the extreme N, has the remains of ancient fortifications and a temple, destroyed by the Danes in 1168. Passed to Pomerania 1325, to Sweden 1648, and to Prussia 1815.

**Ruhr** Federal German Republic. Leading industrial region of W Germany, in N Rhine-Westphalia, substantially in the valley of the Ruhr R. and based on its rich coalfields but in fact extending N to the Lippe R. and S to the Wupper R. It stretches W–E from Duisburg to Dortmund and includes Oberhausen, Essen, Gelsenkirchen, and Bochum, forming one great conurbation intersected by numerous railways, roads, and waterways (including the Rhine–Herne and Dortmund–Ems canals). Industrial development came in the 19th cent. with large-scale coalmining and iron and steel manufacture, and much of the postwar prosperity of the Federal German Republic has been due to the revival of these industries after the widespread destruction of the 2nd World War.

**Ruhr River** Federal German Republic. River 145 m. long, rising in the Sauerland, flowing N and then generally W past Witten and Mülheim, and joining the Rhine R. at Duisburg.

**Ruislip-Northwood** England. Former urban district in Middlesex, 14 m. WNW of London, of which it forms an outer suburb; from 1965 part of the Greater London borough of Hillingdon. Pop. (1961) 72,541. Mainly residential. Some light industries in Ruislip. At Ruislip Lido is a boating lake and reservoir.

**Rukwa, Lake** Tanzania. Shallow lake in the SW 80 m. long and up to 20 m. wide, at a height of 2,602 ft. Fed by the Songwe and the Momba rivers. No outlet.

**Rum (Rhum)** Scotland. Island in the Inner Hebrides, in Inverness-shire, S of Skye. Area 42 sq. m. Mountainous, rising to 2,659 ft in the SE.

**Rumania (Romania, Roumania).*** Republic in SE Europe. Area 91,671 sq. m. Pop. (1968) 19,540,000. Cap. Bucharest. Rel. mainly Eastern Orthodox.

Bounded by the USSR and the Black Sea (N and E), Bulgaria (S), and Yugoslavia and Hungary (W). Primarily agricultural. Agriculture (along with other industries) was nationalized (1948) after the end of the 2nd World War when the people's republic was formed. Divided administratively (from 1968) into 39 districts.

TOPOGRAPHY, CLIMATE. Crossed N–S by the Carpathians and E–W by the Transylvanian Alps; the two ranges form a great arc which encloses the Bihor Mountains and the plateau of Transylvania. The Carpathians rise to over 7,000 ft; several peaks in the Transylvanian Alps exceed 8,000 ft. To the E and S of the mountains are the plains of Moldavia and Walachia and the low plateau of the Dobrogea (Dobruja); to the W the lowlands merge with the adjoining plains of Yugoslavia and Hungary. The Danube (which forms most of the frontiers with Yugoslavia, Bulgaria, and the Ukrainian SSR) empties into the Black Sea by a broad delta and is an important artery of trade. Of the other rivers, the Prut and the Siret are tributaries of the Danube; the Mureş flows W to join the Tisza. Climate continental, with hot summers and cold winters. Annual rainfall 20–30 ins. on the plains, substantially more in the mountains.

RESOURCES, PEOPLE, *etc.* The fertile Moldavian and Walachian plains form one of Europe's leading granaries. Principal crops maize, wheat; sugar-beet, vines, and deciduous fruits also widely grown. Large numbers of sheep, cattle, pigs and poultry raised, chiefly in Transylvania. In 1967 there were 4,679 collective farms and 731 State farms; collectivization of agriculture was stated to be complete in 1962. Extensive forests in Transylvania supply an important timber industry. Chief mineral petroleum, produced mainly from wells around Ploeşti. Industries (which have expanded more rapidly than agriculture under the Communist régime) include iron and steel manufacture and flour milling; leading inland centres are Bucharest, Cluj, Timişoara. Main ports Constanţa (on the Black Sea), Brăila and Galaţi (on the Danube). Chief exports cereals, oil, timber. About 40 per cent of the foreign trade is with the USSR.

The population includes a number of minorities, with over 1,500,000 Hungarians, nearly 400,000 Germans, 150,000 Jews, and many Ukrainians, Yugoslavs, Russians, and Tatars. In 1948 the Uniate (Greek Catholic) Church, with more than 1 million members, broke with the Vatican and was reincorporated in and increased the predominance of the Eastern Orthodox Church; all denominations, however, are under the control of the State. The Grand National Assembly, elected for 4 years from the single list of the Communist-dominated Popular Democratic Front, sits twice a year and delegates its legislative rights between sessions to the State Council.

HISTORY. Modern Rumania corresponds roughly to the Roman province of Dacia (A.D. 107–275), and from the Romans are derived the country's present name and to a considerable extent the major Rumanian element in the population and their language. After the withdrawal of the Romans the area was overrun by Goths, Huns, Bulgars, Slavs, etc. The principalities of Walachia and Moldavia were founded in the late 13th and early 14th cent. Walachia became subject to the Turks in the 15th cent. and Moldavia in the 16th. The two principalities were united as Rumania (1859) with Alexander Cuza as prince, but he was deposed (1866) and Prince Charles of Hohenzollern-Sigmaringen elected as Carol I. Rumania's independence was recognized 1878. Rumania supported the Allied cause in the 1st World War, and was rewarded with Bessarabia and Transylvania. The 1930s saw the rise of fascism. Carol II established a dictatorship in 1938 but was forced to abdicate (1940) after Bessarabia, Transylvania, and southern Dobrogea had been lost to the USSR, Hungary, and Bulgaria respectively. After the 2nd World War Transylvania was restored. King Michael returned to the country and held elections but in 1947 he was compelled to abdicate and the republic was established. The former political parties were abolished, and the Communists took control. After following Soviet policy, Rumania began to take a more independent line from 1963, increasing trade with non-communist countries as well as with the USSR, maintaining a neutral position in the Sino-Soviet dispute and even attempting to mediate between the disputants. Meanwhile, the country enjoyed one of the highest rates of economic growth in the world.

**Rumelia (Roumelia)** Bulgaria/Turkey. Name formerly used for Turkish possessions in the Balkan Peninsula, inc. Thrace and Macedonia. Eastern Rumelia, an autonomous province of the Turkish Empire 1878–85, is now S Bulgaria.

**Rum Jungle** Australia. Uranium-mining centre in the Northern Territory about 50 m. S of Darwin. Discovered 1949. A treatment plant was opened and regular shipments begun in 1955; then the stockpile built up by 1958 was treated 1958–62, when mining recommenced.

**Runcorn** England. Urban district in Cheshire, on the R. Mersey and the Manchester Ship Canal 11 m. ESE of Liverpool. Pop. (1961) 26,035. River port. Industrial town. Manufactures chemicals, rope, etc. Tanning, metal working. Linked by railway bridge and high-level bridge (1961) with Widnes. Its importance dates from the construction of the Bridgwater Canal (1773), which here enters the Mersey.

**Runnymede** England. Meadow on the S bank of the R. Thames, in Egham, Surrey. Either here or on Magna Carta island, in the river, King John granted Magna Carta (1215). Presented to the nation in 1929. Near by are the war memorial to the Commonwealth Air Forces (1953) and the national memorial to President J. F. Kennedy (1965).

**Ruse (Russe, Turkish Ruschuk)** Bulgaria. Capital of Ruse province, on the right bank of the Danube R. opposite Giurgiu (Rumania). Pop. (1965) 128,384. Port.

Industrial and commercial centre. Exports cereals. Sugar refining, tanning, flour milling, brewing. Manufactures textiles, soap, tobacco products, etc. A fortified town in Roman times. Developed as a port in the 17th cent. under Turkish rule. Ceded to Bulgaria 1877.

**Rushden** England. Urban district in Northamptonshire 4 m. E of Wellingborough. Pop. (1961) 17,370. Manufactures chiefly footwear.

**Russe** ◊ *Ruse*.

**Russia** ◊ *RSFSR*; *Union of Soviet Socialist Republics*.

**Russian Soviet Federated Socialist Republic** ◊ *RSFSR*.

**Rustenburg** S Africa. Town in the SW Transvaal 60 m. W of Pretoria, near the foot of the Magaliesberg Range. Pop. (1968) 36,202. Commercial centre in a region where citrus fruits, tobacco, and cotton are grown and chrome, platinum, and nickel mined. Citrus packing, tobacco processing.

**Rutba (Rutbah, Rutba Wells)** Iraq. Frontier post (military, customs) with hotel on the trans-desert routes from Baghdad to Damascus and Jerusalem, 235 m. W of Baghdad in the Syrian desert. The most westerly permanently inhabited place in Iraq, with well water sufficient only for a small community.

**Ruthenia** Czechoslovakia/USSR. Ethnological region in central Europe, mostly now incorporated in the Zakarpatskaya (Transcarpathia) Region in the Ukrainian SSR. At the E extremity of Czechoslovakia, on the S flanks of the Carpathians. Includes the small towns of Uzhgorod and Mukachevo. The mountain slopes are forested. Cereals, potatoes, etc. cultivated on the plains. Lumbering and agriculture, the main occupations, have always been notoriously primitive. Belonged to Hungary from the late 14th cent. to 1918, and to Czechoslovakia 1918–39; during the latter period many improvements in the economy were made. Again occupied by Hungary in 1939 but was ceded to the USSR in 1945. The majority of the people are Ruthenians, closely related to the Ukrainians.

**Rutherglen** Scotland. Royal burgh and industrial town in Lanarkshire, on the R. Clyde 3 m. SE of Glasgow. Pop. (1961) 25,067. Engineering. Manufactures chemicals, paper, etc. Here was signed the treaty between the Scots and the English (1297) which led to the betrayal of Wallace.

**Ruthin** Wales. Municipal borough in Denbighshire, on the R. Clwyd 7 m. SSE of Denbigh. Pop. (1961) 3,502. Market town. Ruined 13th/14th-cent castle and a 14th-cent. church.

**Ruthven** ◊ *Kingussie*.

**Ruthwell** Scotland. Village in Dumfriesshire, near the Solway Firth 9 m. SE of Dumfries. Well-known for the Runic cross, probably of the 8th cent., now in the parish church.

**Rutland (Rutlandshire)** England. Smallest county in England, in the Midlands. Area 152 sq. m. Pop. (1961) 23,956. County town Oakham. Drained by tributaries of the R. Welland, which forms the SE boundary. Mainly agricultural; wheat and barley are the principal crops and Stilton cheese is made. Uppingham has a well-known public school.

**Ruvuma (Rovuma) River** Moçambique/Tanzania. River 500 m. long rising in S Tanzania E of L. Malawi (Nyasa), flowing generally E (forming most of the Moçambique–Tanzania frontier), and entering the Indian Ocean just N W of Cape Delgado.

**Ruwenzori** Congo (Kinshasa)/Uganda. Mountain massif 70 m. long and up to 30 m. wide on the Congo (Kinshasa)–Uganda frontier between L. Albert and L. Edward, rising in Mt Stanley to 16,794 ft. By day the higher parts are almost completely enveloped in cloud; the climate is extremely humid. Clearly-marked zones of natural vegetation, from dense equatorial forests at the foot to snowfields and glaciers in the upper regions. Discovered (1889) by Sir Henry Stanley. The main peaks were scaled by the Duke of Abruzzi's expedition (1906). Generally identified with the 'Mountains of the Moon' which were once believed to be the source of the Nile.

**Rwanda.** Republic in central Africa. Area 10,169 sq. m. Pop. (1965) 2,903,000 (mainly Hutu, with some Tutsi and 50,000 pygmies). Cap. Kigali. Bounded by Uganda (N), Tanzania (E), Burundi (S), and Congo (Kinshasa) (W). Upland plateau country, at a height of 4,000–6,000 ft. Long-horned cattle raised. Chief food crops maize, manioc, beans. Some mineral production. Exports coffee. Formerly a kingdom and part of German E Africa (1899–1917); Belgian-administered (as part of Ruanda-Urundi) under a League of Nations mandate (1923) and as a UN Trust Territory (1946–62). A referendum (1961) declared against the retention of the monarchy and a republic was proclaimed. Became an independent member of the UN 1962. The invasion of the country (from ◊ *Burundi*) by Tutsi émigrés (1963-4) caused panic which resulted in the massacre of thousands of Tutsi and the flight of thousands more to Burundi [and Congo (Kinshasa).

**Ryazan** USSR. Formerly (till 1778) Pereyaslavl-Ryazanski. Capital of the Ryazan region, RSFSR, near the Oka R. 115 m. SE of Moscow. Pop. (1970) 351,000. Flour milling, tanning. Manufactures agricultural machinery, footwear, clothing, chemicals, etc. Originally founded in the 11th cent. about 30 m. SE, capital of the Ryazan principality; moved to its present site in the 13th cent.

**Rybinsk** USSR. Formerly (temporarily) Shcherbakov. River port and industrial town in the Yaroslavl region, RSFSR, on the Volga R. near the point where it issues from the Rybinsk Reservoir. Pop. (1970) 218,000. Site of dam and hydroelectric station. Shipbuilding, flour milling, tanning, sawmilling. Manufactures matches, wire, etc. Trade in grain, petroleum, timber. Linked with Leningrad by the Mariinsk canal system. Its importance increased with the filling of the Rybinsk Reservoir (1941).

**Rybinsk Reservoir** USSR. Large artificial reservoir in RSFSR, 70 m. long and up to 30 m. wide, formed (1941) by the damming of the upper Volga R. at the confluence with the Suda and the Sheksna rivers.

**Rydal** England. Village in Westmorland just NW of Ambleside, on the small lake Rydal Water. Has Rydal Mount, Wordsworth's home from 1813 till his death (1850).

**Ryde** England. Municipal borough on the NE coast of the Isle of Wight overlooking Spithead, 5 m. SW of Portsmouth. Pop. (1961) 19,796. Seaside resort. On the site of the old village of La Rye or La Riche. Near by are the ruins of Quarr Abbey (founded 1132).

**Rye** England. Municipal borough in E Sussex on the R. Rother 10 m. NE of Hastings. Pop. (1961) 4,429. Market town and tourist centre, built on a hill. Has the 12th-cent. Ypres Tower, the remains of a 14th-cent. Augustinian friary, old timbered houses and steep cobbled streets. Was a member of the Cinque Port of Hastings, but declined in the 16th cent. as the sea began to recede. Birthplace of John Fletcher (1579-1625), the dramatist.

**Ryswick** ◊ *Rijswijk*.

**Ryukyu Islands.** Archipelago SW of Japan between Kyushu and Formosa in a chain 700 m. long. Area 848 sq. m. Pop. (1963) 908,000. Larger islands mountainous and volcanic. Principal crops sweet potatoes, sugar-cane. Main island Okinawa, with chief town Naha City. Japanese from 1879. After the 2nd World War they came under US jurisdiction, though the Amami-Oshima group (N) was returned to Japan in 1953.

**Rzeszów** Poland. Industrial town, capital of the Rzeszów voivodship, on the Wislok R. 92 m. E of Cracow. Pop. (1968) 77,300. Manufactures aircraft engines, agricultural machinery, bricks, etc.

**Rzhev** USSR. Town and river port in the Kalinin region, RSFSR, on the Volga R. 75 m. SW of Kalinin. Pop. 47,000. Railway junction. Sawmilling, distilling. Manufactures agricultural machinery, paper, linen, etc.

# S

**Saale River** German Democratic Republic/ Federal German Republic. River 265 m. long, sometimes known as the Saxonian (Thuringian) Saale to distinguish it from the much shorter Franconian Saale; rises in the Fichtelgebirge and flows generally N past Hof, Saalfeld, Rudolstadt, Jena, and Halle to join the Elbe R. 13 m. NE of Bernburg. Navigable for 120 m. to Naumburg.

**Saalfeld** German Democratic Republic. Town in the Gera district, on the Saale R. Pop. (1965) 31,048. In an iron-mining region. Manufactures machine tools, textiles, electrical equipment, etc. An ancient town, it has a 13th-cent. Gothic church and a 16th-cent. Gothic town hall.

**Saarbrücken** Federal German Republic. Capital of Saarland, on the Saar R. Pop. (1968) 133,360. Industrial centre in an important coalmining region. Iron and steel industry. Manufactures machinery, cement, clothing, paper, soap, etc. Brewing, printing. There was a bridge across the Saar here in Roman times – hence its name. Passed from France to Prussia 1815. Became capital of Saarland 1919.

**Saaremaa** (Russian **Sarema**) USSR. Island of the Estonian SSR, in the Baltic Sea at the entrance to the Gulf of Riga. Area 1,050 sq. m. Pop. 56,000. Chief town Kuressaare on the S coast, a port and resort. Low-lying. Main occupations farming, fishing. Passed to Denmark (1561), Sweden (1645), Russia (1721), Estonia (1918).

**Saarland** Federal German Republic. *Land* bordering on France (S and SW) and Luxembourg (W). Area 991 sq. m. Pop. (1968) 1,131,300. Cap. Saarbrücken. Chiefly important for its rich coalfield, on which an important iron and steel industry is dependent, iron ore being imported from Lorraine. Drained by the Saar R. Chief towns Saarbrücken, Saarlouis. In 1919 the Saar Territory was placed under League of Nations control, France being accorded the right to exploit the coalmines for 15 years. As the result of a plebiscite it was returned to Germany in 1935. After the 2nd World War it was in the French occupation zone, in 1947 gained independence (inc. economic union with France), and in 1957 was returned to Germany.

**Saarlauten** ♢ *Saarlouis*.

**Saarlouis** Federal German Republic. Formerly Sarrelouis and (1936–45) Saarlauten. Industrial town in Saarland, on the Saar R. 13 m. NW of Saarbrücken. Pop. (1963) 36,800. Manufactures steel, glass, pottery, etc. Coalmining in the neighbourhood. Founded (1681) by Louis XIV, and named after him Sarrelouis. Ceded to Prussia 1815. Birthplace of Marshal Ney (1769–1815).

**Saar** (Fr. **Sarre**) **River** France/Federal German Republic. River 149 m. long rising in the Vosges and flowing generally N through the Moselle and Bas-Rhin departments (France) past Sarreguemines (head of navigation); then crosses the German border past Saarbrücken, and turns NW through Saarland to join the Moselle R. 6 m. SW of Trier.

**Saba** Arabia. Ancient kingdom in SW Arabia, the biblical Sheba, corresponding to the modern Yemen, Asir, etc. The Sabaeans were known in the 8th cent. B.C.; their capital was Marib and another important city was Sana. In the 4th cent. A.D. they were conquered by the Ethiopians. The last native king was killed A.D. 525.

**Saba** (Netherlands Antilles) ♢ *Netherlands Antilles*.

**Sabadell** Spain. Industrial town in Barcelona province, Catalonia, 11 m. N of Barcelona. Pop. (1967) 140,601. Important textile industry. Also manufactures textile machinery, dyes, paper, fertilizers, etc. Flour milling, distilling, sawmilling.

**Sabah** Malaysia. Formerly North Borneo. A state of Malaysia, comprising the N part of Borneo with offshore islands, including Labuan. Area 29,388 sq. m. Pop. (1966) 577,812 (68 per cent. Borneans, 23 per cent Chinese). Cap. Jesselton. Largely mountainous, rising to 13,697 ft in Mt Kinabalu, the highest peak in Borneo. Climate hot and humid, with a heavy rainfall. Chief products and exports timber, rubber, copra. Principal towns Kota Kinabalu, Sandakan.

**Sabará** Brazil. Once an important goldmining centre in Minas Gerais 8 m. ENE of Belo Horizonte. Pop. 17,000. Remains a picturesque relic of an 18th-cent. mining town with interesting old churches and a museum. Rich iron deposits exist near by.

**Sabine Hills** (Italian **Monti Sabini**) Italy. Range in the Apennines NE of Rome, rising to 4,488 ft in Monte Pellecchia.

**Sabine River** USA. River 500 m. long, rising in NE Texas, flowing generally SE and S, forming the boundary between Texas and Louisiana below Logansport (Louisiana), and discharging through the Sabine Lake into the Gulf of Mexico.

**Sable Island** Canada. Crescent-shaped sandy island in the Atlantic, 20 m. long and 1 m. wide, 180 m. ESE of Halifax, in Nova Scotia. Scene of many shipwrecks; long called 'the graveyard of the Atlantic'. The exposed part of a large sandbank or shoal; gradually shrinking. Two light-houses.

**Sachsen** ◊ *Saxony*.

**Sacramento** USA. State capital of California (since 1854) and river port on the Sacramento R. 75 m. NE of San Francisco. Pop. (1960) 191,667. Food-processing plants: large packing and canning factories for fruit, vegetables, dairy products. Railway engineering. Manufactures soap, furniture, etc. Chief building the State Capitol (1874). First settled 1839. Suffered disastrous floods three times and a great fire between 1849 and 1853. Terminus of the Pony Express (1860) and the first trans-continental railway (1869).

**Sacramento River** USA. Longest and most important river in California, 390 m. long, rising in the Klamath Mountains, flowing generally S and emptying into San Francisco Bay. The Sacramento valley (N) and the San Joaquin valley (S) form California's great Central Valley, irrigated by the Shasta Dam (on the upper Sacramento) and the Keswick Dam (below the Shasta). The two dams also play a vital part in supplying the Central Valley with hydro-electric power and in flood control. Chief tributaries the McCloud and the Pit, from the Cascade Range, the Feather and the American, from the Sierra Nevada.

**Saffron Walden** England. Municipal borough in Essex 14 m. SSE of Cambridge. Pop. (1961) 7,810. Market town, noted for saffron culture from Edward III's reign till *c.* 1770. The 15th-cent. church contains the tomb of Lord Audley, chancellor to Henry VIII. Remains of a 12th-cent. castle. Audley End, a Jacobean mansion built by the 1st Earl of Suffolk

on the ruins of an ancient abbey, is 1 m. SW.

**Safi** Morocco. Atlantic seaport 80 m. WNW of Marrakesh. Pop. (1965) 100,000. Linked by rail with Youssoufia (phosphate mining) and the Ben Guérir junction on the main Marrakesh–Casablanca line. Exports large quantities of phosphates. Important fishing port. Sardine canning, boat-building, pottery manufacture. A large chemical plant for producing fertilizers, sulphuric acid, etc. was inaugurated in 1965.

**Sagar** ◊ *Saugor*.

**Saginaw** USA. Town in Michigan on the Saginaw R. 15 m. above the mouth (on L. Huron). Pop. (1960) 98,265. Commercial and industrial centre in an agricultural region. Oil wells and salt and coal deposits near by. Manufactures machinery, tools, furniture, paper, etc.

**Saginaw River** USA. River 22 m. long in Michigan, flowing generally NNE past Saginaw and Bay City, and entering Saginaw Bay (a SW arm of L. Huron).

**Saguenay River** Canada. River 475 m. long in Quebec, its farthest headstream the Peribonca R., leaving L. St John by the Grande Décharge and the Petite Décharge (which later unite), flowing ESE, and entering the St Lawrence R. near Tadoussac. Important hydroelectric power stations at Isle Maligne and Chute à Caron (above Chicoutimi), on the Grande Décharge. Widens to as much as 2 m. below Chicoutimi, flowing between banks rising to over 1,600 ft in Cape Trinity and Cape Eternity.

**Sagunto** Spain. Ancient Saguntum. Formerly Murviedro. Town in Valencia 16 m. NNE of Valencia. Pop. 27,000. Manufactures iron and steel, hardware, tiles, etc. Exports iron ore etc. Was allied to Rome, and was taken by the Carthaginians under Hannibal (219–218 B.C.) at the start of the 2nd Punic War. Near by are the remains of a large Roman theatre.

**Sahara** N Africa. The largest desert in the world. Area over 3 million sq. m. Extends across N Africa from the Atlantic to the Red Sea; the E part includes the Libyan Desert (W of the Nile) and the Arabian Desert and the Nubian Desert (E of the Nile). Bounded by the Atlas Mountains in Morocco, Algeria, and by the Mediterranean Sea in Libya, United Arab Republic (N), and merging into Sudan and the basin of the Niger R. (S). Mainly plateau, at a height of 1,000 ft, surmounted by the Ahaggar Mountains, the Aïr Highlands, and the Tibesti Highlands, descending in NE Algeria and Tunisia to a depression (partly below sea level) containing the salt lakes Chott Melrhir and Chott Djerid. Annual rainfall (irregular, in short violent thunderstorms) less than 10 ins. Daily range of temperature extreme, sometimes from well over 100° F by day to near freezing at night. Hot dust-laden winds (e.g. sirocco, khamsin) originate in the desert. Three types of surface: *erg* (shifting sand dunes), *hammada* (rock), *reg* (boulders and stones). Wind erosion is considerable. No permanent streams (apart from the Nile and the Niger, near the E and the S flanks respectively). In the oases (which derive water from wadis or from subterranean sources) date palms abound and cereals, Mediterranean fruits, and vegetables are grown; chief export dates. Elsewhere vegetation is meagre or absent. The traditional mode of transport, the camel caravan travelling from oasis to oasis, has lost importance with air routes and the Trans-Saharan motor services from N Algeria to Niamey and Zinder, but the long-planned Trans-Saharan railway from Ghazaouet in Algeria has only reached Abadla (S of Colomb-Béchar). Along the S margins the inhabitants are mainly Sudanese Negroes; elsewhere Arabs and Berber predominate. Among the nomadic peoples, the Berber Tuareg ('people of the veil') of the Ahaggar and Aïr highlands are noteworthy. The Tibesti region (inhabited by the Tibbu) is one of the few parts where Negroes form the majority.

**Saharanpur** India. Commercial town and railway junction in NW Uttar Pradesh 95 m. NNE of Delhi. Pop. (1961) 185,213. Trade in grain, sugar-cane, etc. Railway engineering, paper milling, wood carving. Manufactures cigarettes, hosiery.

**Saïda (Sidon)** Lebanon. Small seaport on the Mediterranean 25 m. SSW of Beirut. Pop. (1963) 22,000. Exports citrus fruits, apricots, etc. Has an oil refinery, handling petroleum received by pipeline from Saudi Arabia. Sidon was once the chief city of Phoenicia, older than Tyre, which it colonized. Excavations from the mid 19th cent. onwards revealed many valuable sarcophagi in a Phoenician necropolis. In ancient times the city was an important commercial centre, but it had a stormy

history, being taken by Assyrians, Babylonians, Persians, Romans, Crusaders, and Muslims. In recent times it has been superseded by Beirut.

**Saigon** S Vietnam. Capital and chief port of S Vietnam, on the Saigon R. 34 m. from the S China Sea. Pop. (with Cholon, 1962) 1,400,000. Exports rice, dried fish, copra, rubber. Distinguished by fine boulevards and public gardens. University (1917). To the SW it adjoins Cholon, with which it has been combined in one administrative unit since 1932, and the two cities form the country's main industrial region. Rice milling, brewing, distilling. Manufactures soap, rubber products, textiles. Formerly capital of Cochin-China, the French colony which became S Vietnam after the 2nd World War.

**St Agnes** ⟡ *Scilly Isles*.

**St Albans** England. Municipal borough in Hertfordshire 19 m. NNW of London. Pop. (1961) 50,276. Market town. Printing. Manufactures hosiery, electrical equipment, rubber products, etc. Just W, across the R. Ver, is the site of the important Roman city of Verulamium; the remains include part of the wall, a mosaic pavement, a hypocaust, and a theatre, and there are further relics in a museum. The famous Benedictine abbey was founded (793) by Offa, King of Mercia, in honour of St Alban (after whom the town was named), martyred here *c*. 303. The church (built partly with bricks and stone taken from Verulamium), consecrated 1116, is still largely early Norman; much restored 1871–85, it became a cathedral in 1877. The 10th-cent. Church of St Michael has the tomb of Francis Bacon, Viscount St Albans. The school (also originally founded in the 10th cent.) was refounded under Edward VI. Scene of a Yorkist victory (1455) and a Lancastrian victory (1461) in the Wars of the Roses. Birthplace of Sarah Jennings, Duchess of Marlborough (1660–1744).

**St Andrews** Scotland. Royal burgh in E Fifeshire, on the North Sea 10 m. SE of Dundee. Pop. (1961) 9,888. Market town. Resort. Has the Royal and Ancient Golf Club (founded 1754), headquarters of the game. The university (founded 1411) is the oldest in Scotland. The town church was originally founded in the 12th cent. There are ruins of a cathedral (founded 1159) and a 13th-cent. castle. Created a royal burgh 1124.

**St Asaph** Wales. Cathedral city and rural district in Flintshire 5 m. SSE of Rhyl. Pop. (rural district, 1961) 9,478. The cathedral, largely destroyed by Owen Glendower (1402), was restored in the 19th cent. It was dedicated to a 6th cent. bishop here.

**St Augustine** USA. Holiday resort in Florida 37 m. SSE of Jacksonville. Pop. (1960) 14,734. Oldest town in the USA; founded 1565, by Pedro Menéndez de Avilés.

**St Austell** England. Market town in Cornwall 12 m. ENE of Truro and NW of St Austell Bay. Pop. (1961) 25,027. Chiefly important as the centre of the china clay industry; large white refuse heaps in the neighbourhood. From 1968 part of the municipal borough of St Austell with Fowey. Combined pop. (1968) 29,430.

**St Bernard Passes. 1.** *Great St Bernard*: Alpine pass (8,100 ft) on the Swiss-Italian border, on the road between Martigny and Aosta over the SW Pennine Alps. The hospice here, founded *c.* 1050 by St Bernard of Menthon, was run by Augustinian monks who became famous for their rescue of travellers, assisted by the St Bernard dogs which were reared for this work. The pass was crossed by Napoleon I and his army (1800). The Great St Bernard road tunnel, 3½ m. long, was completed in 1962, opened to traffic 1964.

**2.** *Little St Bernard*: Alpine pass (7,178 ft) on the Franco-Italian border S of the Mont Blanc massif, on the road between Bourg St Maurice and Aosta. Less frequented than the Great St Bernard Pass. The hospice here was also founded by St Bernard of Menthon. This was probably the pass crossed by Hannibal when he invaded Italy.

**St Boniface** Canada. Industrial town in Manitoba, on the Red R. opposite Winnipeg. Pop. (1966) 43,214. Meat packing, flour milling, oil refining. Manufactures paint, soap, etc. Centre of French Canadian culture in Manitoba. Roman Catholic cathedral. Founded by missionaries 1818.

**St Brieuc** France. Prefecture of the Côtes-du-Nord department, near the English Channel 58 m. NW of Rennes. Pop. (1968) 54,763. Manufactures brushes, hosiery, furniture, etc. Fishing from its port, Le Légué. Cathedral (13th-cent., restored). Founded by and named after St Briocus, a Welsh missionary who came here in the 5th cent.

**St Catharines** Canada. Industrial town in S Ontario, on the Welland Canal 33 m. ESE of Hamilton. Pop. (1966) 97,101. Centre of a fruit-growing region; popularly called 'the Garden City'. Engineering, fruit and vegetable canning. Manufactures electrical equipment, motor-car parts, hardware, etc.

**St Christopher** ◊ *St Kitts.*

**St Clair, Lake** Canada/USA. Lake on the border between S Ontario (Canada) and SE Michigan (USA). Area 432 sq. m. Fed by the St Clair R. from L. Huron, drained by the Detroit R. to L. Erie. The St Clair R. has a deepened channel for shipping.

**St Clair Shores** USA. Town in Michigan, on the W shore of L. St Clair 12 m. NE of Detroit. Pop. (1960) 76,657, having increased rapidly (19,823 in 1950). Mainly residential. Boating centre.

**St Cloud** France. Suburb of W Paris, in the Hauts-de-Seine department on a hill overlooking the Seine R. Pop. (1968) 28,560. Has the Sèvres porcelain factory, but is largely residential. The famous 17th-cent. palace was destroyed in the siege of Paris (1870). Named after St Clodvald (Cloud), who built a monastery here in the 6th cent.

**St Cloud** USA. Commercial and industrial town in Minnesota, on the Mississippi R. 60 m. NW of Minneapolis. Pop. (1960) 33,815. Centre of an agricultural region. Produces canned vegetables, beverages, etc. Railway engineering. Granite quarried near by for buildings and monuments.

**St Croix** W Indies. Largest of the US Virgin Is. Area 82 sq. m. Pop. (1960) 14,973. Cap. Christiansted (pop. 5,088). Tourist centre. Chief occupations cattle rearing, cultivation of sugar-cane, vegetables; rum distilling.

**St Cyr-l'École (St Cyr)** France. Small town in the Yvelines department 3 m. W of Versailles. Pop. (1968) 17,037. Once famous for the military school, founded (1808) by Napoleon. The buildings were completely destroyed in the 2nd World War (1944), and the school was transferred to Coëtquidan, in the Morbihan department.

**St David's** Wales. Village and cathedral city in Pembrokeshire 13 m. WNW of Haverfordwest. Pop. 1,500. Famous for its cathedral, built from *c.* 1180 onwards, partly from local sandstone, in medieval times an important place of pilgrimage. Near by are the ruins of the 14th-cent. Bishop Gower's palace.

**St Denis** France. Industrial town and N suburb of Paris, on the Seine R. in the Seine-St Denis department. Pop. (1968) 100,060. Manufactures railway rolling stock, barges, boilers, diesel engines, chemicals, glass, pottery, liqueurs, etc. The 12th/13th-cent. Gothic abbey church contains the tombs of many French kings, including Louis XII, Francis I, and Henry II. The 7th-cent. Benedictine abbey was founded by Dagobert at the place where St Denis was buried.

**St Denis** (Réunion) ◊ *Réunion.*

**St Dizier** France. Town in the Haute-Marne department, on the Marne R. and the Marne–Saône Canal 62 m. SE of Reims. Pop. (1968) 39,034. Manufactures nails, wire, tools, hardware, etc.

**St Elias Mountains** USA. Mountains in SE Alaska and SW Yukon, continued NW by the Wrangell Mountains. Highest peaks Mt Logan (19,850 ft, the second highest mountain in N America) and Mt St Elias (18,008 ft). The flow of ice from the Mt St Elias area forms the world's largest icefield outside polar regions, and includes the great Malaspina glacier (area 1,500 sq. m.) extending 50 m. along the seaward base.

**Saintes, Les (Îles des Saintes)** W Indies. Archipelago of islets, between Dominica and Guadeloupe, a dependency of Guadeloupe (French). Area 5½ sq. m. Pop. (1967) 3,269. Of volcanic origin. Main occupations stock rearing, fishing. The two principal islands are Terre-de-Bas and Terre-de-Haut.

**St Étienne** France. Prefecture of the Loire department, on the Furens R. 31 m. SW of Lyons. Pop. (1968) 216,020. Industrial town in an important coalmining region. Manufactures iron and steel, machinery, armaments, silk and rayon goods, glass, pottery, etc. Has a famous School of Mines (1816). The manufacture of firearms dates from the 16th cent. and that of ribbons, trimmings, etc. from the early 17th cent.

**St Eustatius** ◊ *Netherlands Antilles.*

**St Ferdinand** ◊ *Florissant.*

**St Francis River** USA. River 470 m. long flowing generally S through SE Missouri and NE Arkansas, forming part of the boundary between the two states, and joining the Mississippi R. 50 m. SW of Memphis (Tennessee).

**St Gall** (Ger. **Sankt Gallen**) Switzerland. **1.** Canton in the NE, bordering N (in part) on L. Constance and E on Austria and Liechtenstein. Area 777 sq. m. Pop. (1969) 378,000. Mountainous in the S. Largely industrial in the centre and N, producing muslin, lace, embroidery. The people are almost all German-speaking and the majority are Catholics.
**2.** Capital of St Gall canton, in the N. Pop. (1969) 80,200. Industrial town. Important cotton industry. Also manufactures chemicals, chocolate, biscuits, etc. Seat of a School of Economics and Social Sciences (1899). Its abbey has a famous library with valuable incunabula and early MSS. The town grew up round the Benedictine abbey, which was founded in the 8th cent. on the site of the cell of the 7th-cent. Irish hermit, St Gall. In 1805 the abbey was secularized.

**St George's** ◊ *Grenada.*

**St George's Channel** (Bismarck Archipelago) ◊ *New Ireland.*

**St George's Channel** British Isles. Channel linking the Irish Sea and the Atlantic Ocean, separating SE Ireland from Wales, at its narrowest only 46 m. wide.

**St Germain-en-Laye (St Germain)** France. Town in the Yvelines department, an outer suburb 12 m. WNW of Paris on the Seine R. Pop. (1968) 41,190. Largely residential and a favourite resort for Parisians. Manufactures musical instruments, hosiery, chocolate. Just N is the Forest of St Germain (area 15 sq. m.) with the famous terrace overlooking the Seine. The Treaty of St Germain (1919) between the Allied powers and Austria was signed here. Birthplace of Claude Debussy (1862–1918).

**St Gotthard Pass** Switzerland. Important pass (6,916 ft) over the Lepontine Alps, on the road from Andermatt to Airolo which was constructed 1820–30. Below the pass is the St Gotthard railway tunnel (constructed 1872–80), at 9¼ m. the second longest in the Alps and reaching a maximum height of 3,786 ft, on the main Lucerne–Milan line.

**St Helena** S Atlantic Ocean. Volcanic island and British colony 1,200 m. W of the coast of Angola. Area 47 sq. m. Pop. (1967) 4,707 (chiefly of mixed European, Asian, and African origin). Cap. and port Jamestown. Mountainous, rising to 2,704 ft in Diana's Peak; deep gorges are cut into the slopes by rapidly flowing streams. Climate tempered by the SE Trade Wind. Chief crop flax. Exports fibre, rope, twine. Dependencies are Ascension Island (1922) and Tristan da Cunha, Gough Island, Nightingale Island, and Inaccessible Island (1938). Discovered (1502) by the Portuguese. Became famous as the place of exile of Napoleon from 1815 till his death (1821). Declined as a port of call with the opening of the Suez Canal (1869), but is an important cable station.

**St Helens** England. County borough in SW Lancashire 10 m. ENE of Liverpool. Pop. (1961) 108,348. The chief centre in England for the manufacture of crown, plate, and sheet glass. Also produces chemicals, pharmaceutical products, soap, etc. Iron founding; coalmining in the neighbourhood. Birthplace of Sir Thomas Beecham (1879–1961).

**St Helier** Channel Islands. Chief town of Jersey, on the S coast and on the E side of St Aubin's Bay. Pop. 26,500. Popular seaside resort. Market town. Trade in early potatoes, vegetables, cattle. On a rocky islet W of the harbour is the 16th-cent. Elizabeth Castle, in which Prince Charles, later Charles II, took refuge in 1646 and 1649. In the town is the house where Victor Hugo lived 1852–5. Near the castle is the Hermitage, with the remains of the reputed cell of St Helier.

**St Hyacinthe** Canada. Industrial town in Quebec, on the Yamaska R. 32 m. ENE of Montreal. Pop. (1966) 23,781. Manufactures woollen goods, footwear, furniture, organs, etc. Roman Catholic cathedral.

**St Ives** (Cornwall) England. Municipal borough on St Ives Bay 7 m. NNE of Penzance. Pop. (1961) 9,337. Fishing port. Holiday resort. Has long been a haunt of artists. Believed to take its name from St Ia, an Irish martyr who came to Cornwall in the 5th cent.

**St Ives** (Huntingdonshire) England. Municipal borough on the Great Ouse 5 m. E of Huntingdon. Pop. (1961) 4,076. Market town. A picturesque 15th-cent. bridge across the river carries a chapel, restored in 1689. In medieval times the Easter fair brought merchants here from a wide area.

**St Jean** (**St Johns**) Canada. Town in Quebec, on the Richelieu R. 20 m. SE of Montreal. Pop. (1966) 27,784. Manufactures textiles, paper, sewing machines, etc. Terminus of the first Canadian railway, to Montreal (1836).

**St Jean de Luz** France. Fishing port and popular seaside resort in the Basses-Pyrénées department, on the Bay of Biscay 12 m. SW of Bayonne. Pop. (1968) 11,035. Its fishing vessels were the first to sail to the Newfoundland cod-fishing grounds (1520).

**St John** Canada. Largest city in New Brunswick, at the mouth of the St John R. on the Bay of Fundy. Pop. (1966) 51,567. Important seaport, esp. in winter, when it remains ice-free. One of the world's largest dry docks, which can accommodate the largest liners. Exports vast quantities of timber, as well as grain, minerals, etc. Manufactures cotton goods, bricks and tiles, wood pulp and paper. Oil and sugar refining. Terminus of the Canadian Pacific Railway and the Canadian National Railway. Named after the river. Has suffered from several disastrous fires, esp. in 1877, when over half the city was destroyed; the wooden buildings were then replaced by stone and brick.

**St John, Lake** Canada. Lake in SE Quebec, fed by the Peribonca and other rivers. Area 375 sq. m. Only outlet the Saguenay R., by two channels (Grande Décharge, Petite Décharge). The district has many paper mills and is a popular tourist region.

**St John Island** ◊ *Virgin Islands of the USA*.

**St John River** Canada/USA. River 418 m. long, rising in several branches in Maine (USA) and Quebec, flowing NE and then E, forming part of the international frontier between Maine and New Brunswick, then turning generally SE through New Brunswick, past Fredericton, to enter the Bay of Fundy at St John. Navigable for small vessels as far as Fredericton. Near St John are the famous Reversing Falls, where the strong tides of the Bay of Fundy cause the river to reverse its flow at high tide. Discovered (1604) by Champlain and de Monts.

**St John's** (British W Indies) ◊ *Antigua*.

**St John's** (Newfoundland) Canada. Provincial capital of Newfoundland, on the E coast of the Avalon Peninsula, in the SE. Pop. (1966) 79,884. The island's largest city and chief seaport. A fine harbour approached through The Narrows, flanked by cliffs 500–600 ft high. Centre of the Newfoundland fishing fleet; principal catch cod and herring. Fish processing. Manufactures fishing equipment, marine engines, textiles, footwear, etc. Anglican and Roman Catholic cathedrals. First settled by Devonshire fishermen in the 16th cent. Sir Humphrey Gilbert landed here and claimed Newfoundland for Queen Elizabeth I in 1583. The city was devastated by fires in 1816, 1846, and 1892; stone buildings then replaced wooden.

**St Johns** (Quebec, Canada) ◊ *St Jean*.

**St John's Wood** England. Residential district in the Greater London borough of the City of Westminster, just W of Regent's Park. Contains Lord's cricket ground, headquarters of the MCC, authority for the game.

**St Joseph** (Michigan) USA. Port in the SW at the mouth of the St Joseph R. on L. Michigan. Pop. (1960) 11,755. Centre of a fruit-growing area.

**St Joseph** (Missouri) USA. River port on the Missouri R. 48 m. NNW of Kansas City. Pop. (1960) 79,673. Trade in livestock. Meat packing, flour milling, etc. The E terminus of the Pony Express (1860). Later became an important railway centre.

**St Joseph River** USA. River 210 m. long, rising in the S of Michigan, flowing generally W, with a southward curve into the N of Indiana, and discharging into L. Michigan at St Joseph.

**St Just** (St Just-in-Penwith) England. Urban district in Cornwall 7 m. W of Penzance. Pop. (1961) 3,636. Market town. Has an amphitheatre called St Just Round where medieval Cornish miracle plays were performed.

**St Kilda** Scotland. Largest of a group of small islands in the Outer Hebrides, Inverness-shire, 40 m. WNW of N Uist, 3 m. long and 2 m. wide. Now uninhabited, the population of 36 having been evacuated at their own request in 1930. Bird sanctuary (gannets, puffins, etc.).

**St Kitts** (St Christopher) British W Indies. Island formerly (with Nevis and Anguilla) in the British colony of the Leeward Is. Area 68 sq. m. Pop. (1966) 37,150. Cap. Basseterre (pop. 15,897). Of volcanic origin; crossed by mountains which rise to 3,792 ft in Mt Misery. Principal export cane sugar, shipped through Basseterre. First settled (1623) by the British. Three times seized by the French; finally ceded to Britain 1783. St Kitts–Nevis–Anguilla became an associated state within the Commonwealth 1967.

**St Laurent** Canada. Industrial and residential town in Quebec, on Montreal island 6 m. W of Montreal city. Pop. (1966) 59,479. Engineering. Manufactures chemicals, textiles, etc. Founded 1845.

**St Lawrence River and Seaway** Canada/ USA. One of the greatest rivers and waterways in N America and the world. The river issues from the NE end of L. Ontario and flows generally NE for 750 m. to the Gulf of St Lawrence; it forms the easternmost link in the St Lawrence Seaway, 2,480 m. long, which enables ocean-going vessels to reach

the W end of L. Superior. The first 114 m. of its course form the Canada–USA frontier; entering Canada, for a short distance it forms the Ontario–Quebec boundary, but most of its course is in Quebec. On leaving L. Ontario it passes through the Thousand Islands, a well-known tourist region; narrowing, it enters the turbulent International Rapids, and passes 7 other rapids, including the Coteau, the Cedars, the Cascades, and the Lachine (circumvented by canals), before reaching Montreal. It widens to form L. St Francis and then L. St Louis. Near Montreal it is joined by the main tributary, the Ottawa R.; thereafter the course is gentler and more winding. Widening again, it forms L. St Peter (Lac St Pierre), and below Quebec widens considerably into a tidal estuary 400 m. long and from 3 to 70 m. wide. Main tributaries the Ottawa, the St Maurice, the Saguenay, the Chaudière, and the Richelieu rivers. The islands include Montreal Island (on which Montreal stands) and Anticosti Island (at the mouth). Near Quebec is the famous Quebec Bridge (1917); other bridges are the Victoria Bridge (1898) and the Jacques Cartier Harbour Bridge (1930) at Montreal, the Roosevelt Bridge (1934), and the Thousand Islands Bridge (1938). Main cities Quebec, Montreal, Trois Rivières, Sorel (Quebec); Kingston, Brockville, Cornwall (Ontario); Ogdensburg (New York). The heavily wooded valley contains many lumbering centres and paper mills; the river provides abundant hydroelectric power.

Jacques Cartier first ascended the St Lawrence in 1535. Colonization began with the founding of Quebec by Champlain (1608). The French used the river as a fur-trade route; explorers and missionaries also made use of it. French possession of the valley ended when Canada was surrendered to the British (1763). Since the early 19th cent. all disputes between Canada and the USA regarding the use and navigation of the river have been settled by arbitration. Improvements on the waterway have been continuous. The work has consisted in dredging the natural channel between Quebec and Montreal and in making and improving the canals which circumvent the rapids. These improvements culminated in the St Lawrence Seaway, opened (1959) by Queen Elizabeth II and President Eisenhower. Ocean-going vessels can now bring cargoes of iron ore, grain, coal, petroleum, and petroleum products from Great Lakes ports; by facilitating such exports the Seaway has had a profound effect on the economy of Canada and the USA.

**St Louis** (Réunion) ⋄ *Réunion*.

**St Louis** Senegal. Seaport on the small island of St Louis in the Senegal R. estuary, 110 m. NE of Dakar, with which it is connected by rail. Pop. (1960) 47,900. Exports groundnuts, hides and skins, etc. Manufactures textiles. Founded 1659. First capital of French W Africa (1895–1902). Capital of Senegal until replaced by Dakar in 1958.

**St Louis** USA. Largest city in Missouri, on the right bank of the Mississippi R. 10 m. downstream from the confluence with the Missouri, opposite East St Louis (Illinois). Pop. (1970) 607,718. Major centre of communications and trade (rail, road, river, and air), with 19 m. of river frontage, including the harbour. Important international trade in fur pelts. Also handles grain, timber, wool, livestock. Oil refining, meat packing, brewing, distilling. Manufactures motor vehicles, aircraft, electrical equipment, machinery, chemicals, etc. Seat of the St Louis University (1818) and Washington University (1857). Episcopalian and Roman Catholic cathedrals. The most noteworthy of many parks is Forest Park (1,380 acres), with a large open-air theatre. Founded as a French fur-trading post 1764. Named after Louis IX of France (St Louis). Retained its French character till the 19th cent. Prosperity came with the Mississippi steamboats (1817); tobacco and other industries soon began to operate. A century of growth and progress was celebrated in 1904 with the St Louis Fair (officially, the Louisiana Purchase Exposition).

**St Louis Park** USA. Town in Minnesota just SW of Minneapolis. Pop. (1960) 43,310. Largely residential. Manufactures metal goods etc. First settled 1854.

**St Lucia** British W Indies. Island in the former British colony of the Windward Is., between Martinique (N) and St Vincent (S). Area 238 sq. m. Pop. (1965) 100,000. Cap. Castries (pop. 40,000). Of volcanic origin; mountainous, rising to 3,145 ft in Mt Gimie. More spectacular are the forest-clad cones of the Gros Piton (2,619 ft) and Petit Piton (2,461 ft), rising sheer from the sea in the SW. Famous for hot sulphur springs and solfataras. Chief exports bananas, sugar, coconut products. Became an associated state within the Commonwealth 1967.

**St Malo** France. Seaport on the English Channel at the mouth of the Rance R. in the Ille-et-Vilaine department. Pop. (1968) 43,722. Trade particularly with Southampton (England). Exports early vegetables, fruit, dairy produce, etc. Fishing is important, and there is a considerable tourist industry here and in neighbouring St Servan and Paramé. Stands on a rocky island connected with the mainland by a causeway, the Sillon. Many of the old buildings within its ramparts were destroyed or severely damaged in the 2nd World War. Flourished from the 15th to the 18th cent. largely owing to the activities of its privateers. Birthplace of Jacques Cartier (1491–1557) and Chateaubriand (1768–1848).

**St Martin (Sint Maarten)** W Indies. Island in the Leeward Is., since 1648 divided between France and the Netherlands. The N belongs to France and is a dependency of Guadeloupe: area 20 sq. m., pop. 4,502. The S is part of the Netherlands Antilles: area 13 sq. m., pop. (1968) 5,064. Little cultivable land. Chief export salt, from the coastal lagoons. Principal settlements Marigot (French), Philipsburg (Dutch).

**St Martin's** ⋄ *Scilly Isles*.

**St Marylebone** England. Former metropolitan borough in NW London, bounded on the S by Oxford Street and on the W by Edgware Road; from 1965 part of the Greater London borough of the City of Westminster. Pop. (1961) 68,834. Within it lie most of Regent's Park, with the Zoological Gardens, Lord's cricket ground (in St John's Wood), and Harley Street and Wimpole Street, famous for their doctors. The name is derived from that of the church, St Mary at Bourne, the latter referring to the Tyburn, a stream which flowed S through the borough to the Thames.

**St Mary Peak** ⋄ *Flinders Range*.

**St Mary's** ⋄ *Scilly Isles*.

**St Maur-des-Fossés (St Maur)** France. Suburb of SE Paris within a loop of the Marne R. in the Val-de-Marne department. Pop. (1968) 77,569. Manufactures hosiery, toys, furniture, electrical equipment, etc.

**St Maurice River** Canada. River in Quebec, 325 m. long, flowing generally SE and S, through the Gouin Reservoir and smaller lakes, and joining the St Lawrence R at Trois Rivières. Every year millions of logs are floated down it to the many pulp and paper mills along the banks. Important hydroelectric power stations at Shawinigan Falls, Grand'mère, etc. The power resources have attracted plastics, chemical, and aluminium industries.

**St Mawes** England. Small fishing port and resort in Cornwall, on St Mawes Harbour 2 m. E of Falmouth. Has a castle built by Henry VIII standing opposite Pendennis Castle, Falmouth.

**St Michael's Mount** England. Rocky island off the shore of Mount's Bay, Cornwall, connected at low tide with Marazion, on the mainland, by a natural causeway. Surmounted by a castle, now used as a residence, and there is also the 15th-cent. Chapel of St Michael, in the battlemented tower of which is 'St Michael's Chair' (actually the stone frame of an old lantern). In Edward the Confessor's reign the priory was granted to the Benedictine abbey of Mont St Michel, but in Henry V's time, with the dissolution of the alien houses, it was transferred to the abbey of Sion. Since 1659 the island has belonged to the St Aubyn family.

**St Michel, Mont** ◊ *Mont St Michel.*

**St Moritz** Switzerland. Resort in Graubünden (Grisons) canton, in the upper Engadine on the Inn R. Pop. 2,500. Especially famous as a winter-sports centre, originally known (16th cent.) for its mineral springs. Consists of the village St Moritz-Dorf (6,080 ft) and the spa St Moritz-Bad (5,824 ft), on the N and SW shores respectively of the small L. of St Moritz.

**St Nazaire** France. Seaport in the Loire-Atlantique department at the mouth of the Loire R. 32 'm. WNW of Nantes. Pop. (1968) 64,003. The outport of Nantes, accommodating the largest vessels. Has the country's main shipyards, constructing ships for the navy and the mercantile marine. Also manufactures steel, fertilizers, etc. Marine engineering, brewing, vegetable canning. During the 2nd World War it was used by the Germans as a submarine base, and as such was repeatedly bombed and almost completely destroyed; the shipyards were again in operation by 1948. Here the liners *Normandie* (1935) and *France* (1961) were built.

**St Neots** England. Urban district in Huntingdonshire, on the R. Ouse 8 m. SSW of Huntingdon. Pop. (1961) 5,570. Market town. Paper manufacture, brewing. Has a 15th/16th-cent. Perpendicular church and a 16th-cent. stone bridge.

**St Niklaas** (Fr. **St Nicolas**) Belgium. Town in E Flanders province 12 m. WSW of

Antwerp. Pop. (1968) 48,873. Textile industry (cotton, linen, rayon); manufactures carpets, bricks, pottery, etc. Also a market for the fertile Waasland.

**St Omer** France. Town in the Pas-de-Calais department, on the Aa R. 23 m. SE of Calais. Pop. (1968) 19,957. In a market-gardening area. Manufactures hosiery, soap, etc. Sugar refining, brewing, etc. Its outstanding building is the 13th/15th-cent. Gothic basilica of Notre Dame, a cathedral 1559–1801. During the 1st World War St Omer was the British GHQ 1914–16.

**Saintonge** France. Region and former province in the W, N of the Gironde estuary, forming most of the present Charente-Maritime department and part of the Charente department. Cap. Saintes. Low-lying and mainly agricultural, noted for its cognac.

**St Ouen** France. Suburb of N Paris in the Seine-St Denis department. Pop. (1968) 48,886. Railway engineering. Manufactures machine tools, chemicals, etc. Here Louis XVIII signed the Declaration of St Ouen (1814), promising the nation a constitution.

**St Pancras** England. Former metropolitan borough of NW London; from 1965 part of the Greater London borough of Camden. Pop. (1961) 125,278. Included Camden Town, Kentish Town, and parts of Highgate (N) and Bloomsbury (S), also the great railway termini of Euston, St Pancras, and King's Cross. Many of its working population are employed on the railways. Among open spaces are Parliament Hill and Fields, Ken Wood, and part of Regent's Park.

**St Paul** (Réunion) ◊ *Réunion.*

**St Paul** USA. State capital of Minnesota, on the Mississippi R. at the confluence with the Minnesota R. adjoining Minneapolis. Pop. (1960) 313,411. The 'Twin Cities' are the commercial and industrial centre of an extensive agricultural region. St Paul has a large trade in livestock. Motor-car assembly, oil refining, meat packing, food processing, brewing, printing and publishing, etc. Manufactures refrigerators, electronic equipment, chemicals. Seat of the Hamline University (1854). The Roman Catholic cathedral (1915) is outstanding among the buildings.

**St Paul Island** Indian Ocean. Island situated lat. 39° S, long. 78° E, from 1955 part of the ◊ *French Southern and Antarctic Territories.* Area 3 sq. m. Of volcanic origin; uninhabited. Annexed by France 1843.

**St Peter Port** Channel Islands. Chief town and seaport of Guernsey, on the E coast. Pop. 16,000. The harbour is protected by breakwaters. Exports tomatoes, vegetables. Castle Cornet, defending the harbour, dates partly from the 12th cent. and the Church of St Peter partly from the 14th cent. Elizabeth College was founded in 1563. Hauteville House, home of Victor Hugo 1856–70, is now a museum.

**St Petersburg** USA. Winter resort in W Florida, on Tampa Bay 16 m. SW of Tampa. Pop. (1960) 181,298. Known as 'the Sunshine City'; numerous recreational amenities. Some minor industries.

**St Petersburg** (USSR) ◊ *Leningrad.*

**St Pierre** Martinique. Town on the coast at the foot of the volcano Mont Pelée. Pop. 6,200. Chief industry rum distilling. Founded 1635. Formerly the chief town; its population was 28,000 in 1900, but it was suddenly destroyed by an eruption of Mont Pelée (1902); only one citizen is believed to have survived. Now of minor importance. Birthplace of the Empress Josephine (1763–1814), consort of Napoleon I.

**St Pierre** (Réunion) ◊ *Réunion.*

**St Pierre and Miquelon** N America. A French overseas territory; island group off the S coast of Newfoundland. Total area 93·5 sq. m. Total pop. (1967) 5,235. Cap. St Pierre (on St Pierre Island), with a permanently ice-free harbour. Some sparsely inhabited rocky islets (including the Île aux Marins) and two main islands: St Pierre group (area 10 sq. m., pop. 4,614); Miquelon group (area 83 sq. m., pop. 621). Miquelon's two parts, Grande Miquelon (N) and Petite Miquelon (S), are now joined by a mudbank (Isthme de Langlade). Often shrouded in fog. Thin soil, scanty vegetation. Main occupation cod fishing. A French possession almost continuously since 1660.

**St Pölten** Austria. Industrial town and railway junction in Lower Austria 33 m. W of Vienna. Pop. (1961) 40,112. Manufactures textiles, machinery. Grew up round an abbey founded in the 9th cent. and dedicated to St Hippolytus (of which the name is a corrupted version).

**St Quentin** France. Ancient Augusta Veromanduorum. Industrial town in the Aisne department, on the Somme R. 80 m. NE of Paris. Pop. (1968) 66,161. Important textile industry, specializing in the manufacture of curtains, muslin, etc. Also manufactures chemicals, machinery, etc. Grew from the 7th cent. as a place of pilgrimage round the tomb of St Quentin. Here the French were defeated by the Spaniards (1557) and the Prussians (1871); the Battle of St Quentin in the 1st World War (March 1918) saw the beginning of the great German counteroffensive.

**St Servan** ◊ *St Malo.*

**St Thomas Island** ◊ *Virgin Islands of the USA.*

**St Tropez** France. Fishing port and seaside resort in the Var department on the French Riviera 28 m. SW of Cannes. Pop. (1968) 6,151.

**St Vincent** British W Indies. Island in the Windward Is., with dependencies in the Grenadines. Total area 150 sq. m. Total pop (1966) 90,000. Cap. and chief port Kingstown (pop. 20,688). Of volcanic origin; crossed by a mountain range rising to 4,048 ft in Soufrière. Chief exports bananas, arrowroot starch. Sea-island cotton cultivated. Ceded to Britain 1763. Became an associated state within the Commonwealth 1969.

**St Vincent, Cape** Portugal. Headland at the SW extremity of Portugal. Lighthouse, on a cliff 175 ft high. Scene of the defeat of the Spanish fleet by Admiral Sir John Jervis (later Earl St Vincent) in 1797.

**St Vincent, Gulf** Australia. Inlet of the Indian Ocean just E of Yorke Peninsula, S Australia, about 95 m. long and up to 40 m. wide. Adelaide is near the E shore.

**Sais** United Arab Republic. Ancient city site 55 m. SE of Alexandria on the Rosetta branch of the Nile. Capital of lower Egypt in the 7th and 6th cent. B.C.

**Sakai** Japan. Industrial town in Osaka prefecture, on Osaka Bay just S of Osaka. Pop. (1965) 466,398. Manufactures chemicals, fertilizers, machinery, aluminium products, hosiery, etc. Formerly an important port; declined when its harbour became silted up.

**Sakhalin** USSR. Island off the E coast of Siberia, in the Sea of Okhotsk, forming a region of the Khabarovsk Territory, RSFSR, separated from Hokkaido (Japan) by La Pérouse Strait. Area 29,700 sq. m. Pop. (1970) 616,000. Has a central N–S valley flanked by parallel mountain ranges, that in the E rising to 6,604 ft in Mt Nevelski. Climate cold and inhospitable, with frequent fogs; much of the island is covered with tundra and forest. Main occupation fishing. Rye, oats, potatoes, and vegetables are grown in the S. Some coal and oil produced. Settled by the Russians in the mid 19th cent.; became a place of exile for Tsarist prisoners. After the Russo-Japanese War (1905) the S part of the island was occupied by Japan, and was known as Karafuto, but it was returned to the USSR after the 2nd World War (1945).

**Sakkara (Saqqara)** United Arab Republic. Village in the Giza governorate 15m. SW of Cairo. Pop. 8,000. Principal necropolis (with Giza) of ancient ◊ *Memphis*. Famous for its step pyramids.

**Salaberry de Valleyfield** ◊ *Valleyfield*.

**Salado River** Argentina. River 415 m. long, flowing generally SE along a shallow course through the Buenos Aires province and entering the Río de la Plata.

**Salado (Chadileufú, Desaguadero) River** Argentina. River 850 m. long, rising in the Andes, flowing SSE (as the Desaguadero R.) and forming the boundary between the Mendoza and San Luis provinces, disappearing in the marshes of La Pampa. Later (as the Chadileufú R.) reaches the Colorado R. and the Atlantic in times of high water.

**Salado (Juramento) River** Argentina. River 1,250 m. long, rising in the Andes (as the Juramento R.), flowing SE through the Salta, Santiago del Estero, and Santa Fé provinces, and joining the Paraná R. at Santa Fé.

**Salamanca** Spain. 1. Province in León, bordering W and NW on Portugal. Area 4,754 sq. m. Pop. (1961) 405,729. Consists of plateau and mountains, rising to 5,653 ft in the S; within the basin of the Duero (Douro) R. Mainly agricultural.

2. Capital of Salamanca province, on the Tormes R., a tributary of the Duero (Douro). Pop. (1967) 113,510. Important railway and road centre. Manufactures chemicals, etc. Tanning, brewing, flour milling. A city of outstanding historic and artistic interest, centred on the great arcaded Plaza Mayor. Has a Roman bridge retaining many of the original arches, an old 12th-cent. Romanesque cathedral and a new 16th/18th-cent. cathedral, the 16th-cent. Casa de las Conchas – its façade decorated with shells – and many other fine old buildings. Taken by Hannibal (222 B.C.) and later by Romans, Visigoths, and Moors. The university (founded c. 1230 by Alfonso IX of León) won European fame,

but declined with the city after the mid 16th cent. In the Battle of Salamanca (1812) Wellington decisively defeated the French under Marmont.

**Salamís** Greece. Island in the Aegean Sea off the coast of Attica just W of Piraeus. Area 36 sq. m. Off the NE coast the Greeks under Themistocles won a naval victory over the Persians under Xerxes (480 B.C.).

**Salcombe** England. Urban district in Devonshire, on the W side of Salcombe Harbour 17 m. SW of Dartmouth. Pop. (1961) 2,558. Market town, fishing port, seaside resort.

**Saldanha Bay** S Africa. Sheltered inlet of the Atlantic Ocean 60 m. NNW of Cape Town. Arid hinterland. Formerly used by whalers; now a naval training base. Fish canning.

**Sale** Australia. Chief market town of Gippsland, Victoria, 115 m. E of Melbourne. Pop. (1966) 8,640. In dairy-farming country. Linked by canal with the Gippsland lakes. Trade in grain, livestock. Flour and woollen mills; dairy and bacon factories.

**Sale** England. Municipal borough in Cheshire 5 m. SW of Manchester, of which it is a residential suburb. Pop. (1961) 51,317.

**Salé** Morocco. Seaport on the Atlantic coast, just NE of Rabat. Pop. (1960) 75,799. Fish canning. Manufactures carpets, pottery, etc. The home of pirates, the celebrated Sallee Rovers, in the 17th cent.

**Salem** India. Industrial town and railway junction in Madras, in a picturesque valley SW of the Shevaroy Hills and 170 m. SW of Madras. Pop. (1961) 249,145. Manufactures cotton goods.

**Salem (Massachusetts)** USA. Industrial town on Massachusetts Bay 15 m. NE of Boston. Pop. (1960) 39,211. Manufactures textiles, electric lamps, footwear, etc. One of the oldest towns in New England. Among the buildings are the Custom House (1819) and the 17th-cent. birthplace of Nathaniel Hawthorne (1804–64). Founded 1626. Became notorious in 1692 for the witchcraft trials, when 19 people were hanged. Its early maritime prosperity declined in the 1820s.

**Salem (Oregon)** USA. State capital, on the Willamette R. 43 m. SSW of Portland. Pop. (1960) 49,142. Flour milling, fruit and vegetable canning, meat packing. Manufactures metal goods, paper, etc. Seat of the Willamette University (1842).

**Salerno** Italy. Capital of Salerno province, in Campania, on the Gulf of Salerno 30 m.

ESE of Naples. Pop. (1968) 144,981. Port. Industrial centre. Electrical engineering, tomato canning, flour milling, tanning. Manufactures textiles, etc. The university (founded in the 9th cent., the earliest in Europe), with a famous medical school, was overshadowed by Naples University from the 13th cent.; it was closed in 1811 but refounded in 1944. The 11th-cent. cathedral was restored in the 18th cent. Scene of Allied landings in the 2nd World War (1943).

**Salford** England. County borough in SE Lancashire, on the R. Irwell opposite Manchester, with which it forms a continuous urban area. Pop. (1961) 154,963. Has the principal docks of the Manchester Ship Canal. Important industrial centre. Electrical engineering. Manufactures textiles, textile machinery, chemicals, clothing, electrical equipment, tyres, etc. Roman Catholic cathedral (1848). Birthplace of James Joule (1818–89), the physicist.

**Salgótarján** Hungary. Capital of Nógrád county, 55 m. NE of Budapest near the Czechoslovak border. Pop. (1968) 35,000. Industrial and mining centre. Manufactures iron and steel, machinery, etc. Coal and lignite mined in the neighbourhood.

**Sali** ◊ *Dugi Otok.*

**Salina** USA. Town in Kansas, on the Smoky Hill R. 85 m. NNW of Wichita. Pop. (1960) 43,202. Commercial centre in an agricultural region. Important flour-milling industry. Manufactures agricultural machinery, cement, bricks and tiles, etc.

**Salinas** USA. Town in California 46 m. SSE of San José. Pop. (1960) 28,957. Centre of a cattle-rearing and market-gardening area (lettuces, celery, etc.). Beet-sugar refining.

**Salisbury** England. Municipal borough and county town of Wiltshire, on the R. Avon at the confluence with the R. Wylye 20 m. NW of Southampton. Pop. (1961) 35,471. Market town. Brewing, carpet manufacture, etc. Famous chiefly for the magnificent mainly 13th-cent. cathedral, in Early English style, with the highest spire in England (404 ft). The library has valuable Anglo-Saxon manuscripts. Three ancient parish churches, St Martin, St Thomas, St Edmund; 15th-cent. banqueting hall of John Halle, part of a cinema since 1930; Audley House (16th-cent.). 2 m. NNW is Old Sarum, site of an important early fortress and settlement known to the Romans as Sorbiodunum. All that now

remains is a bare conical mound; the site, abandoned in the 13th cent. when New Sarum (Salisbury) was built, was in ruins by the 16th cent.

**Salisbury** Rhodesia. Capital, 230 m. NE of Bulawayo at a height of 4,825 ft. Pop. (1968) 383,500 (96,000 Europeans, 280,000 Africans). Linked by rail with Bulawayo and Beira (in Moçambique). Centre of a goldmining and agricultural area. Important trade in tobacco. Tobacco curing, grading, packing; flour milling, sugar refining, brewing. Manufactures clothing, furniture, fertilizers, etc. Founded 1890. Named after Lord Salisbury (then Prime Minister).

**Salisbury Plain** England. Region of open chalk downs about 20 m. long and 10 m. wide in Wiltshire. Largely used as a military training ground. Includes Stonehenge.

**Salonika** ◊ *Thessaloniki.*

**Salta** Argentina. Capital of Salta province in the NW, in the irrigated Lerma valley at a height of 3,895 ft. Pop. (1960) 121,491. Commercial centre in a picturesque region. Trade in tobacco, livestock, agricultural produce. Meat packing, flour milling, tanning. Founded 1582. Several old colonial buildings. Stands on the narrow gauge Transandine railway to Antofagasta (Chile), opened 1948.

**Saltaire** ◊ *Shipley.*

**Saltash** England. Municipal borough in Cornwall, on the estuary of the R. Tamar 4 m. NW of Plymouth. Pop. (1961) 7,420. Port. Market town. The estuary is crossed here by Brunel's Royal Albert railway bridge (1859) and the Tamar suspension bridge (1961); the latter replaces the ancient Saltash ferry.

**Saltburn and Marske** England. Urban district in the N Riding of Yorkshire, 10 m. E of Middlesbrough. Pop. (1961) 12,482. Consists of the small town and seaside resort of Saltburn-by-the-Sea and the village of Marske-by-the-Sea, about 2 m. WNW.

**Saltcoats** Scotland. Small burgh and seaside resort in Ayrshire, on the Firth of Clyde 13 m. NNW of Ayr. Pop. (1961) 14,187. Formerly important for saltworks.

**Saltillo** Mexico. Capital of Coahuila state, at a height of 5,244 ft 48 m. WSW of Monterrey. Pop. (1969) 135,400. Commercial, industrial, and mining centre. Manufactures textiles, clothing, ceramics, etc. Famous for woollen shawls (*sarapes*). Cathedral (18th-cent.). Founded 1586.

**Salt Lake City.** USA. State capital of Utah, on the Jordan R. 9 m. SE of the Great Salt

Lake, at a height of 4,200 ft. Pop. (1960) 189,454. Important route centre. Leading commercial and industrial centre of Utah. Oil refining, copper smelting and refining. Manufactures textiles, metal goods, food products, etc. Seat of the University of Utah (1850). A city of wide avenues in a splendid setting of mountain scenery, with the Wasatch Range to the E and SE rising to 12,000 ft. Founded (1847) by the Mormon leader Brigham Young as the Mormon capital. Notable buildings include the Mormon Temple (1893) and the Mormon Tabernacle (1867).

**Salto** Uruguay. Capital of the Salto department and river port at the head of navigation on the Uruguay R. opposite Concordia (Argentina). Pop. 60,000. Commercial and industrial centre in a stock-rearing and fruit-growing district. Trade in agricultural produce. Meat packing, flour milling.

**Salvador (El Salvador).** Smallest and most densely populated republic in Central America, facing the Pacific Ocean; no Caribbean coastline. Area 8,236 sq. m. Pop. (1961) 2,510,984 (over 90 per cent 'mestizos', mixed white and Indian). Cap. San Salvador. Official language Spanish. A country of volcanic mountains, fertile upland plains, and a hot humid coastal belt. The volcanoes include Santa Ana (7,818 ft, the highest) and Izalco (6,184 ft, active 1770–1956). Chief river the Lempa, of little navigational value but used since 1954 for hydroelectric power. Several picturesque lakes. Agriculture is the basis of the economy, coffee accounting for about 75 per cent of the exports. Cotton also cultivated and exported. The world's main source of balsam. Rice, maize, etc. produced for home consumption. Important towns are Santa Ana, San Miguel. 52 per cent of the population are illiterate (1961). Divided administratively into 14 departments: Ahuachapán; Cabañas; Chalatenango; Cuscatlán; La Libertad; La Paz; La Unión; Morazán; San Miguel; San Salvador; San Vicente; Santa Ana; Sonsonate; Usulután. Conquered by Pedro de Alvarado 1524; under Spanish rule till 1821. Joined the Central American Federation 1824; became an independent republic 1839. A great rise in population followed the development of coffee-planting in the late 19th cent. Several towns in the SE were severely damaged by earthquakes in 1951.

**Salvador** Brazil. Formerly Bahia. Capital of Bahia state, on a peninsula separating Todos Santos Bay from the Atlantic Ocean, 800 m. NNE of Rio de Janeiro. Pop. (1960) 655,735. Seaport. Exports cocoa, sugar, tobacco. Sugar refining, flour milling. Manufactures cigars and cigarettes, textiles, cement, etc. Consists of a lower town, built round the harbour, and a modern residential upper town. Has several 17th and 18th-cent. churches and other buildings. Seat of the primate of Brazil and of the University of Bahia (1946). Founded 1549. Capital of Brazil until 1763.

**Salween River.** Great river of SE Asia, 1,750 m. long, rising in the Tanglha Range in E Tibet, flowing generally SE in a deep gorge, for a time parallel to the gorges of the upper Mekong and Yangtse rivers. Then turns S through Yunnan province (China) and enters Burma, cutting another gorge through the Shan plateau and reaching the Gulf of Martaban near Moulmein. Frequently impeded by rapids; navigable for only about 70 m. above its mouth.

**Salzach River** Austria. River 130 m. long rising in the Hohe Tauern, flowing E and then N through Salzburg province past Salzburg to join the Inn R. 31 m. NNW of Salzburg.

**Salzburg** Austria. 1. Province bordering NW on the Federal German Republic. Area 2,762 sq. m. Pop. (1961) 347,292. Chiefly mountainous, containing the Hohe Tauern and part of the Niedere Tauern in the S, with glaciers and snowfields, rising to well over 10,000 ft. Drained by the Salzach R. and its tributaries. Cattle reared on the Alpine pastures. Produces timber. Salt mining. Industries centred on Salzburg. Thriving tourist trade.

2. Capital of Salzburg province, on both banks of the Salzach R. 155 m. WSW of Vienna. Pop. (1961) 108,114. Tourist centre. Brewing. Manufactures metal goods, textiles, etc. Dominated by the Hohensalzburg (11th/16th-cent. castle). Among other noteworthy buildings are the 17th-cent. cathedral, the old and new residences of the archbishops, a 13th-cent. Franciscan church, the 8th-cent. Benedictine monastery (round which the city grew up), and a Mozart house and museum. Birthplace of Mozart (1756–91). The university (founded 1623) was reduced to a theological seminary in 1810. Much visited because of the annual music festival and the associations with Mozart. The new opera house was inaugurated in 1960.

**Salzgitter** ◊ *Watenstedt-Salzgitter.*

**Salzkammergut** Austria. Mountain and lake area in the E Alps in Upper Austria, Styria, and Salzburg, crossed by the Traun R. Among its lakes are Attersee and Traunsee. Highest peak Dachstein (9,830 ft). Once important for salt production. Now a tourist region with Bad Ischl its chief centre. Other leading occupations stock rearing, forestry.

**Samar** Philippines. Third largest island, separated from S Luzon by the San Bernardino Strait. Area 5,181 sq. m. Pop. 928,000. Cap. Catbalogan (pop. 33,000). Mountainous and forested, rising to 2,800 ft. Frequently subject to typhoons. Little developed. Produces abacá, copra, rice.

**Samara** ◊ *Kuibyshev.*

**Samaria** Jordan. Ancient city in Palestine on the site of the modern village of Sabastiya (W Jordan) 6 m. N W of Nablus. Founded in the 9th cent. B.C. by Omri, who made it capital of his N kingdom of Israel. Captured and colonized by Assyria (722 B.C.). Fell to Alexander the Great (331 B.C.). Later destroyed by John Hyrcanus, rebuilt by Herod the Great; according to tradition here were the tombs of Elisha and John the Baptist. Excavations begun in 1908 revealed the palace of Omri and other valuable remains.

**Samarkand** USSR. Ancient Maracanda. Capital of the Samarkand region, Uzbek SSR, in the fertile valley of the Zeravshan R. at a height of 2,358 ft and on the Trans-Caspian Railway 170 m. S W of Tashkent. Pop. (1970) 267,000. Brewing, distilling, flour milling, tobacco processing. Manufactures textiles, clothing, chemicals, footwear, etc. Trade in grain, fruits, karakul lambskins. Seat of an Uzbek state university (1933). Divided into an old quarter, which has many historic buildings, and a new Russian town. Among the famous buildings are the mausoleum of Tamerlane, the *madrassa* or Muslim college of Bibi-Khanum, both dating from the early 15th cent. and other *madrassas*, all centred round the Rigistan or main square. Ancient capital of Sogdiana; stands in a strategic position among the W spurs of the Tien Shan. Destroyed by Alexander the Great 329 B.C. As Samarkand it was taken by the Arabs (A.D. 712) and became a centre of Arab culture, but was destroyed by Genghis Khan in 1220; it again flourished under Tamerlane, who made it his capital and constructed mosques, palaces, and gardens within its walls. Later ruled by the Chinese and the emirs of Bukhara, and fell to the Russians in 1868; its population, about 500,000 in 1220, was only 60,000 in 1900. Capital of the Uzbek SSR 1925–30 and has once more revived and expanded.

**Samarra** Iraq. Holy city of the Shia Muslims, on the Tigris R. 70 m. N N W of Baghdad. Has a golden-domed mosque of the 17th cent. and the remains of a much earlier mosque. Also extensive ruins of ancient Samarra, capital of the Abbasid dynasty 836–76.

**Sambre River** Belgium/France. River 118 m. long rising in the Aisne department (France), flowing generally E N E past Maubeuge, entering Belgium, continuing past Charleroi and joining the Meuse R. at Namur. Navigable from Landrecies and linked by canal with the Oise R.; also joins the Charleroi–Brussels Canal.

**Samoa** S Pacific Ocean.* Group of islands 450 m. E N E of Fiji. Mainly mountainous and of volcanic origin. Climate tropical, with heavy rainfall. Samoans are Polynesian, akin to the New Zealand Maoris. Chief occupations agriculture (taro, breadfruit, yams, etc.), fishing. Discovered (1722) by the Dutch. Divided politically into Western Samoa and American Samoa. 1. *Western Samoa*: Independent state consisting of two principal islands, Savai'i and Upolu, two smaller islands, Manono and Apolima, and several uninhabited islets. Total area 1,097 sq. m. Pop. (1966) 131,379. Cap. and chief seaport Apia, on Upolu. Savai'i (area 662 sq. m., pop. 36,161) rises to 6,094 ft and Upolu (area 435 sq. m., pop. 95,218) to 3,608 ft. Chief exports copra, bananas, cocoa. A German protectorate 1899–1914. Administered by New Zealand under League of Nations mandate 1920–47 and under UN Trusteeship Agreement 1947–62. Became independent 1962.

2. *American Samoa*: US territory (since 1899) consisting of the principal island Tutuila and several smaller islands. Total area 76 sq. m. Pop. (1960) 20,051. Cap. and chief seaport Pago Pago, on Tutuila. Tutuila (area 43 sq. m., pop. 17,250) rises to 2,141 ft. Chief export canned fish (mainly tuna).

**Samos** Greece. Island in the Aegean Sea separated from the W coast of Turkey by a strait about 2 m. wide, forming a *nome* with neighbouring islands. Area 300 sq. m. (Samos alone 190 sq. m.). Pop. (1961) 52,034. Cap. Limin Vatheos (pop. 5,469). Largely mountainous, but fertile. Produces wine, olive oil, tobacco, citrus fruits. Attained its greatest prosperity under the tyrant Polycrates in the 6th cent. B.C. Birthplace of Pythagoras.

**Samothrace** (Gr. **Samothráki**) Greece. Island in the NE Aegean Sea 27 m. SSW of Alexandroúpolis, in the Évros *nome*. Area 70 sq. m. Pop. 3,800. Mountainous, rising to 5,249 ft in Fengári, the highest peak in the Aegean islands. Chief occupations goat rearing, sponge fishing. It was early ' an important centre of worship of the Cabeiri. The famous statue, the Winged Victory of Samothrace (discovered 1863) is now in the Louvre, Paris.

**Samsö Island** Denmark. Island in the Kattegat, between Jutland and Zealand. Area 43 sq. m. Pop. 5,900. Mainly agricultural.

**Samsun** Turkey. Ancient Amisus. Capital of Samsun province, a Black Sea port 205 m. ENE of Ankara. Pop. (1965) 107,500. In the chief tobacco-growing region. Exports tobacco, cereals. Tobacco processing. At first overshadowed by Sinope, it superseded the latter in the 13th cent.

**Sana (San'a)** Yemen. Capital of Yemen, on a plateau at a height of 7,500 ft 90 m. ENE of its port, Hodeida, with which it is connected by a mountain road. Pop. 80,000. Handicraft industries include weaving and the manufacture of jewellery. Contains the palace of the former Imam, the citadel, the Great Mosque (with a model of the Kaaba of Mecca), and several other mosques. A capital at various times from the 4th cent. A.D.; became capital of Yemen when Turkish rule ended after the 1st World War (1918). A large, but backward, Jewish community had lived in Sana for centuries until the creation of Israel led to their expulsion or withdrawal (1948).

**San Andrés y Providencia (St Andrew's and Old Providence) Islands** Colombia. Two islands in the Caribbean, off the Mosquito Coast of Nicaragua, with several coral reefs; an intendancy of Colombia. Area 21 sq. m. Pop. (1964) 16,731. Cap. San Andrés. Export coconuts, copra, oranges.

**San Angelo** USA. Town in W Texas, on the Concho R. 185 m. NW of San Antonio. Pop. (1960) 58,815. Important wool and mohair market in a ranching and farming area. Cotton ginning, oil refining, meat packing, etc.

**San Antonio** Chile. Seaport and holiday resort in Santiago province 37 m. S of Valparaiso. Pop. 65,000. Exports agricultural products of the central valley (cereals, wine, etc.).

**San Antonio** USA. Third largest city in Texas, on the San Antonio R. 195 m. W of Houston. Pop. (1970) 650,188 (about 40 per cent Mexican). Route, commercial, and industrial centre. Trade in cattle, wool, cotton, etc., Meat packing, oil refining, food processing, brewing, etc. Seat of St Mary's University (1852) and Trinity University (1869). Military and air force bases in the neighbourhood. Founded (1718) by the Spaniards. Named after the original mission of San Antonio de Valero, whose chapel is the historic ◊ *Alamo*. Part of the city is Mexican in character, and Spanish is widely spoken.

**San Bernardino** USA. Town in California, 50 m. E of Los Angeles in the fertile San Bernardino valley. Pop. (1960) 91,922. Important packing and marketing centre for citrus fruits. Railway engineering. Manufactures cement, food products, etc.

**San Bruno** USA. Town in California 10 m. S of San Francisco. Pop. (1960) 29,063. Largely residential. Printing etc. Site of San Francisco international airport and Tanforan racecourse.

**San Buenaventura (Ventura)** USA. Coastal town in California 62 m. WNW of Los Angeles. Pop. (1960) 29,114. In an agricultural (citrus fruits, lima beans, etc.) and oil-producing district. Exports oil.

**San Cristóbal** Venezuela. Capital of Táchira state, near the Colombian border 200 m. S of Maracaibo at a height of 2,700 ft. Pop. (1964) 129,159. Commercial and route centre in a coffee-growing region, serving the W llanos. Tanning, distilling. Manufactures cement. Has a cathedral partly rebuilt in colonial style (1961). Founded 1561.

**San Cristóbal Island** ◊ *Galápagos Islands*.

**Sancti Spiritus** Cuba. Town in Las Villas province 50 m. SE of Santa Clara. Pop. (1960) 37,740. Commercial centre in an agricultural region. Trade in sugar-cane, tobacco, cattle. Tanning. Manufactures cigars, dairy products, etc. Many narrow, winding streets, with 16th/17th-cent. churches and houses. Founded 1516.

**Sancy, Puy de** ◊ *Puy-de-Dôme*.

**Sandakan** Malaysia. Seaport and largest town in Sabah, on the E coast. Pop. (1960) 29,291. Exports rubber, timber, etc. Sawmilling, fishing.

**Sandbach** England. Urban district in Cheshire 5 m. NE of Crewe. Pop. (1961)

9,856. A picturesque market town, best known for its production of salt. Manufactures lorries, chemicals, etc. Two Saxon crosses in the market place were reconstructed (1816) after being demolished.

**Sandhurst** (Australia) ◊ *Bendigo*.

**Sandhurst** England. Village in SE Berkshire 10 m. SE of Reading. Seat of the Royal Military Academy, founded (1799) as the Royal Military College and combined (1946) with the Royal Military Academy, Woolwich; has the National Army Museum.

**San Diego** USA. Seaport in California, on San Diego Bay 110 m. SSE of Los Angeles. Pop. (1970) 675,788. Excellent natural harbour. Exports canned fish, cotton, and other agricultural produce. Important tuna fishing and canning; also aircraft manufacture, fruit and vegetable processing, shipbuilding, etc. A leading US naval base. With its mild, equable climate and game-fishing and bathing facilities, it has become a popular resort. The first Californian mission, San Diego de Alcalá, was founded here in 1769, and the city was named after it.

**Sandown-Shanklin** England. Urban district on the E coast of the Isle of Wight. Pop. (1961) 14,257. Consists of the towns and seaside resorts of Sandown and Shanklin. Both have sandy beaches. Shanklin, with the Chine, a wooded cleft in the sandstone, and some thatched cottages, is the more picturesque.

**Sandringham** England. Village in Norfolk 7 m. NE of King's Lynn. Sandringham Hall is a residence of the royal family, the estate having been acquired by Edward VII when Prince of Wales (1863). George VI (1895–1952) was born and died here.

**Sandusky** USA. Town in Ohio, on Sandusky Bay (L. Erie) 50 m. W of Cleveland. Pop. (1960) 31,989. Lake port, resort, and industrial centre. Manufactures paper products, crayons, toys, etc.

**Sandviken** Sweden. Town in Gävleborg county 13 m. WSW of Gävle. Pop. (1968) 25,497. Important steel industry.

**Sandwich** England. Municipal borough in E Kent, on the R. Stour 11 m. E of Canterbury. Pop. (1961) 4,234. Resort, golfing centre. One of the Cinque Ports, in the Middle Ages it was a leading port for trade with the continent, but by the end of the 16th cent. the harbour was silted up and practically useless; it was saved from complete decline by the settlement of wool weavers from Flanders. Buildings include the 14th-cent. Fisher Gate and the 13th-cent. chapel of St Bartholomew's Hospital.

**San Felipe** Chile. Capital of Aconcagua province, at a height of 2,087 ft 45 m. N of Santiago. Pop. 27,000. Agricultural and mining centre.

**San Fernando** Argentina. Seaport and NW suburb of Buenos Aires on the Río de la Plata. Pop. 30,000. Industrial centre. Manufactures footwear, furniture, etc. Fish canning.

**San Fernando** Chile. Capital of Colchagua province, at a height of 1,100 ft in the central valley 80 m. S of Santiago. Pop. 38,000. Market town. Trade in cereals, wine, fruit, etc. Founded 1742.

**San Fernando** Spain. Seaport in Cádiz province, Andalusia, on the Isla de León 8 m. SE of Cádiz. Pop. (1967) 61,330. An arsenal founded 1790. Distilling, tanning, etc. Salt produced in the neighbourhood.

**San Fernando** Trinidad. Seaport on the Gulf of Paria (SW). Pop. (1960) 39,830. Second largest town in Trinidad. Exports petroleum products, sugar. Main industry sugar refining.

**San Francisco** USA. Seaport (with fine land-locked harbour) and second largest city in California, on the Pacific coast 350 m. NW of Los Angeles. Pop. (1970) 704,209. At the end of a peninsula, bounded by the Pacific (W), the Golden Gate (N), and San Francisco Bay (E). A great cosmopolitan city and a commercial and financial centre, the hub of a group of cities round San Francisco Bay. Exports iron and steel products, oil, canned fruit and fish, cereals, etc. Shipbuilding, oil refining, food processing and canning, sugar refining, printing and publishing. Manufactures clothing, furniture, etc. Seat of the University of San Francisco (Roman Catholic, 1930) and of schools of the University of California. Within the city are the 'Latin Quarter', with French, Spanish, Italian, and Portuguese colonies, and Chinatown, the largest Chinese settlement outside the Far East. The city's cable-cars, a unique form of public transport necessitated by its hilly location, are a source of pride to the natives and entertainment to visitors. Transportation to and from the city has been greatly facilitated by the bridges to Oakland and across the Golden Gate. Founded 1776, when the Spanish mission of San Francisco de Asís was established. A disastrous earthquake and fire (1906) destroyed much of the city, but within three years it was rebuilt in brick, steel, and concrete.

**Sangihe (Sangi) Islands** Indonesia. Group of volcanic islands NNE of Celebes. Area 314 sq. m. Pop. 86,000. Chief town and seaport Tahuna, on the largest island, Great Sangihe. Chief products sago, nutmeg, copra.

**Sangre de Cristo Mountains** USA. In Spanish, 'Blood of Christ'. Range of the Rocky Mountains, extending 210 m. N–S through S Colorado and N New Mexico, so named because of the reddish colour of the snow-capped peaks seen at sunrise. Highest mountain Blanca Peak (14,317 ft). Several others exceed 13,000 ft.

**San Joaquin River** USA. River 320 m. long in California, in the S part of the Central Valley, rising in the Sierra Nevada, flowing SW and then NNW to join the Sacramento R. just E of Suisun Bay. The fertile irrigated valley is one of the USA's richest farming regions.

**San José** Costa Rica. Capital of Costa Rica and of San José province, on the central plateau at a height of 3,800 ft. Pop. (1962) 164,241. Costa Rica's chief industrial and commercial centre. Coffee and cacao processing, flour milling, fruit and vegetable canning. etc. Seat of the University of Costa Rica (1843). Laid out on a rectangular pattern; the architecture is a mixture of Spanish-colonial and modern American, and the buildings include a cathedral and a national museum. Founded 1738.

**San José** (Panama) ⟡ *Pearl Islands*.

**San José** USA. Town in California, in the fertile fruit-growing Santa Clara Valley 40 m. SE of San Francisco. Pop. (1960) 204,196. A leading world fruit-canning and dried-fruit-packing centre. Meat packing, brewing, etc. Manufactures electrical equipment, aircraft parts, etc. Founded 1777. Prospered rapidly with the California Gold Rush (1849). State capital 1849–51.

**San José de Cúcuta** ⟡ *Cúcuta*.

**San Juan** Argentina. Capital of San Juan province, 100 m. N of Mendoza at a height of 2,100 ft. Pop. 142,000. Commercial centre in a wine-growing region where the water of the San Juan R. is used for irrigation. Trade in wine, frozen meat, dried fruit, dairy produce, etc. Founded 1562. Severely damaged by earthquake 1944. Birthplace of Domingo Sarmiento (1811–88), educationist and statesman.

**San Juan** Puerto Rico. Capital and chief seaport, on the NE coast. Pop. (1960) 451,658. Exports coffee, sugar, and tobacco to the USA. Sugar refining, rum distilling, brewing. Manufactures cigars, cigarettes. The older part of the city is situated on an island, connected by two bridges to the mainland, where the residential quarters are now located. La Fortaleza, the governor's residence, was built *c*. 1530; Casa Blanca (1523); cathedral (begun 1512). Seat of the University of Puerto Rico in Río Piedras, now incorporated in San Juan. Named after Juan Ponce de León, who founded the city (1521) and is buried in the cathedral.

**San Juan River** Nicaragua. River 120 m. long flowing generally ESE from L. Nicaragua to the Caribbean Sea, forming part of the Nicaragua–Costa Rica frontier.

**San Juan River** USA. River 400 m. long rising in the San Juan Mountains of SW Colorado, flowing generally W, and joining the Colorado R. in S central Utah. On the Colorado Plateau it passes through a series of spectacular twisting canyons (incised meanders) known as the Goosenecks. Unnavigable. Used for irrigation.

**Sankt Gallen** ⟡ *St Gall*.

**San Leandro** USA. Town in California immediately SE of Oakland. Pop. (1960) 65,962. Food processing. Manufactures tractors, electrical equipment, etc. Noted for the annual cherry and flower festival, exhibiting the produce of the surrounding district.

**Sanlúcar de Barrameda** Spain. Seaport and resort in Cádiz province, Andalusia, on the estuary of the Guadalquivir R. 17 m. N of Cádiz. Pop. (1961) 40,335. Exports wine (manzanilla). Flour milling, distilling, etc. Site of a Roman settlement. Became important in the late 15th cent. A 16th-cent. hospital founded by Henry VIII for English sailors. Here Columbus embarked on his third voyage (1498) and Magellan on his circumnavigation of the world (1519).

**San Luis** Argentina. Capital of San Luis province just S of the Sierra de San Luis at a height of 2,500 ft 160 m. ESE of Mendoza. Pop. 38,000. Trade in grain, wine, livestock. Hydroelectric station and irrigation dam near by. Onyx quarrying. Founded (1596) by Martin de Loyola, governor of the captaincy general of Chile.

**San Luis Potosí** Mexico. 1. A central state. Area 24,417 sq. m. Pop. (1969) 1,436,000. Mountainous; crossed by the Sierra Madre Oriental. The N part is arid, the SE fertile and irrigated. Chiefly a mining state (silver). Coffee and tobacco grown in the SE.

**2.** Capital of San Luis Potosí state, on the plateau at a height of 6,158 ft 225 m. NW of Mexico City. Pop. (1969) 189,700. Railway and commercial centre. Smelting and metal refining (silver, arsenic, etc.). Manufactures textiles, clothing, footwear, brushes, ropes, etc. Has a noteworthy cathedral and government palace. Famous for the multi-coloured glazed tiles in many of the old buildings.

**San Marino. 1.** Independent republic within Italy, near the Adriatic coast 9 m. SSW of Rimini. Area 24 sq. m. Pop. (1968) 18,360. Main occupations agriculture, stock rearing. Exports wine, textiles, building stone (quarried on Mt Titano). The smallest republic in Europe and claims to be the oldest in the world, having been founded (according to tradition) by St Marinus, a Christian stone-cutter, in the 4th cent. Governed by a Grand Council of 60 members.

**2.** Capital of San Marino republic, on Mt Titano, linked by road with Rimini. Pop. (1968) 4,150. In its principal church is the tomb of St Marinus.

**San Mateo** USA. Residential town in California, on San Francisco Bay 15 m. S of San Francisco. Pop. (1960) 69,870. In a horticultural and market-gardening district. First settled (1851) by John B. Cooper, a deserter from the British Navy.

**San Miguel** (Panama) ◊ *Pearl Islands*.

**San Miguel** Salvador. Capital of the San Miguel department, at the foot of the volcano San Miguel (7,120 ft) 70 m. ESE of San Salvador. Pop. (1961) 82,974. Flour milling. Manufactures cotton goods, rope, etc. Trade in cereals, cotton, sisal, etc. Cathedral (18th-cent.). Founded (1530) by Spanish settlers.

**San Nicolás** Argentina. River port and industrial town in Buenos Aires province, on the Paraná R. 38 m. SE of Rosario. Pop. 55,000. Trade in meat, hides, wool, grain. Has a large steel plant (1962) and power station. Founded 1748.

**San Pablo** Philippines. Town in Luzon 47 m. SSE of Manila. Pop. 71,000. Commercial centre. Trade in copra, rice, etc.

**San Pedro de Macorís** Dominican Republic. Capital of the San Pedro de Macorís province 40 m. E of Santo Domingo. Pop. (1960) 40,943. Caribbean seaport. Exports sugar, molasses. Sugar and flour milling, tanning. Manufactures clothing, soap, etc.

**San Pedro Sula** Honduras. Capital of the Cortés department and second largest town in Honduras, 105 m. NW of Tegucigalpa. Pop. (1966) 98,104. Industrial and commercial centre in a region producing bananas, sugar-cane, etc. Flour milling, tanning, brewing. Manufactures soap, cigarettes, furniture, etc. Founded 1536.

**Sanquhar** Scotland. Royal and small burgh in Dumfriesshire, on the R. Nith 24 m. NW of Dumfries. Pop. (1961) 2,182. Coal-mining, brick making in the neighbourhood. The 'Declarations of Sanquhar' were affixed to the market cross by covenanters (1680, 1685) renouncing allegiance to Charles II and James II respectively.

**San Rafael** Argentina. Town in Mendoza province 125 m. SSE of Mendoza. Pop. 46,000. In an area irrigated for vines, fruit, cereals. A commercial centre. Meat packing, fruit drying and canning, wine making.

**San Remo** Italy. Port and resort in Imperia province, Liguria, on the Italian Riviera (Riviera di Ponente) 70 m. SW of Genoa. Pop. (1961) 55,209. Trade in flowers, olives, fruit, etc. The old town with its narrow streets stands above the modern town of hotels, villas, and gardens, which was severely damaged in the 2nd World War. Cathedral (13th-cent.).

**San Salvador (Watling (Watlings) Island)** Bahamas. Island in the central Bahamas. Area 60 sq. m. Pop. (1963) 968. Scene of Columbus's first sight of land on the American continent (1492).

**San Salvador** Salvador. Capital, also capital of the San Salvador department, at a height of 2,237 ft at the foot of the dormant volcano San Salvador. Pop. (1961) 255,744. The country's largest city and chief commercial and industrial centre. Manufactures textiles, clothing, cigars and cigarettes, soap, etc. Meat packing, flour milling. Seat of the National University (1841). Has repeatedly suffered from earthquakes (esp. 1854); the frequent rebuilding has given it a modern appearance. Founded 1525. Capital from 1841.

**San Sebastián** Spain. Capital of Guipúzcoa province, on the Bay of Biscay at the mouth of the Urumea R. Pop. (1967) 157,928. Port. Popular seaside resort. Fishing. Manufactures soap, cement, glass, paper, etc. Situated on a narrow peninsula at the foot of Monte Urgull, which is topped by a fortress; the old town is separated from the new town by the Alameda (avenue) crossing the peninsula. The municipal museum has paintings by Goya and El Greco.

**San Severo** Italy. Town in Foggia province, Apulia, 18 m. NNW of Foggia. Pop. (1961) 48,443. Produces wine, olive oil, macaroni, etc. Brickmaking.

**Santa Ana** Salvador. Capital of the Santa Ana department, 32 m. NW of San Salvador, at a height of 2,120 ft. Pop. (1961) 121,095. Salvador's second largest city. Chief industry coffee processing; also sugar milling, brewing. Manufactures textiles, leather goods, cigars, etc. Claims to have the world's largest coffee mill (El Molino). Cathedral (Spanish Gothic).

**Santa Ana** USA. Town in California, at the foot of the Santa Ana Mountains 28 m. SE of Los Angeles. Pop. (1960) 100,350. Main industry fruit packing and canning (citrus and deciduous fruits). Beet-sugar refining.

**Santa Barbara** USA. Residential town and resort in California, on the Pacific coast 87 m. WNW of Los Angeles. Pop. (1960) 58,768. In a district noted for citrus fruits and flowers. Fine beach and a beautiful setting, with a mild climate, luxuriant subtropical vegetation, and picturesque buildings in the Spanish style. The principal historic building is the Santa Barbara Mission, completed in 1820 to replace an earlier one destroyed by earthquake in 1812. Founded 1782.

**Santa Barbara Islands** USA. Group of 8 main islands and several uninhabited islets off the Pacific coast of S California. The N group includes San Miguel, Santa Rosa, Santa Cruz, Anacapa; the S group has Santa Catalina, San Clemente, San Nicolas, Santa Barbara. Santa Catalina, the largest, is a well-known resort with fine bathing beaches and deep-sea fishing.

**Santa Catarina** Brazil. Maritime state in the S. Area 36,455 sq. m. Pop. (1960) 2,146,909. Cap. Florianópolis. Narrow coastal lowlands with lagoons and offshore islands; to the W the Serra do Mar and the plateau. Forested in the N; grassy areas in the S. Economy largely based on maize cultivation and pig rearing. Coal mined in the SE. Many German and Italian immigrants.

**Santa Clara** Cuba. Capital of the Las Villas province, on the plateau 160 m. ESE of Havana. Pop. (1960) 142,176. Important route and commercial centre in an agricultural region. Trade in coffee, sugar-cane, tobacco. Manufactures cigars, leather, etc.

Some fine old 'colonial' buildings. Founded 1689.

**Santa Clara** USA. Town in California immediately NW of San José. Pop. (1960) 58,880. Main industry fruit packing and canning. Manufactures machinery, chemicals, etc. University (1851). Expanded rapidly in the 1950s: pop. (1950) 11,702.

**Santa Clara Island** ◊ *Juan Fernández Islands*.

**Santa Cruz** Bolivia. Capital of Santa Cruz department, 190 m. ESE of Cochabamba, at a height of 1,575 ft. Pop. (1967) 96,000. Commercial centre. Trade in rice, sugarcane, etc. Sugar milling, tanning, distilling, etc. Since 1953 linked by road with Cochabamba, by rail with Corumbá (Brazil) and with Aguaray (Argentina), leading to much expansion. University (1880). Founded (1560) in the uplands; removed to its present site 1595.

**Santa Cruz** USA. Town in California, on Monterey Bay 60 m. SSE of San Francisco. Pop. (1960) 25,596. Holiday resort: bathing beaches, deep-sea fishing, yachting. Fishing, fish canning, market gardening, cement manufacture.

**Santa Cruz de Tenerife** Canary Islands. **1.** One of the two Spanish provinces; the four main W islands (Tenerife, Gomera, Palma, Hierro). Area 1,238 sq. m. Pop. (1961) 490,655.
**2.** Capital of Santa Cruz de Tenerife province, on the island of Tenerife. Pop. (1967) 169,695. Important fuelling station (oil, coal) for ships travelling from Europe to S Africa and S America. Excellent harbour. Oil refinery. Exports bananas, tomatoes, potatoes. Has developed considerably as a resort.

**Santa Cruz Islands** ◊ *Solomon Islands*.

**Santa Cruz River** Argentina. River 200 m. long in Santa Cruz province in Patagonia, rising in L. Argentino and flowing E to the Atlantic.

**Santa Fé** Argentina. Capital of Santa Fé province and river port on the Salado R. 100 m. N of Rosario. Pop. (1960) 199,179. Serves a grain-growing and stock-rearing area. Flour milling, tanning, etc. Manufactures dairy produce. Cathedral. University (1920). Founded 1573.

**Santa Fé** USA. State capital of New Mexico, at a height of 7,000 ft 55 m. NE of Albuquerque. Pop. (1960) 34,676. Tourist and commercial centre, of great historical interest. Among notable buildings are the 17th-cent. adobe Palace of the Governors and the Cathedral of St Francis (1869). Founded (1609) by the Spaniards. Headquarters of Spanish, Indian, Mexican, Confederate, and US governors in turn. W terminus of the Santa Fé Trail in the 19th cent. Developed with the coming of the railway (1880).

**Santa Isabel** ◊ *Fernando Póo.*

**Santa Maria** (Azores) ◊ *Azores.*

**Santa Maria** Brazil. Town in Rio Grande do Sul state 160 m. W of Pôrto Alegre. Pop. 50,000. Railway junction. Trade in agricultural produce. Railway engineering, brewing, tanning, etc.

**Santa Marta** Colombia. Capital of the Magdalena department, on a deep bay NW of the Sierra Nevada de Santa Marta in the N. Pop. (1962) 64,000. Important banana port. Also exports coffee, hides. Founded 1525. Sacked many times in the early colonial period. Simón Bolívar died at a hacienda near by (1830).

**Santa Monica** USA. Residential town and resort in California 15 m. W of Los Angeles. Pop. (1960) 83,249. Beautifully situated on Santa Monica Bay near the picturesque Santa Monica Mountains. Bathing beaches, yachting, fishing facilities. Manufactures aircraft, plastics, cosmetics, etc.

**Santander** Spain. 1. Province in Old Castile on the Bay of Biscay. Area 2,042 sq. m. Pop. (1961) 432,132. Crossed W–E by the Cantabrian Mountains, which rise to over 8,600 ft in the Picos de Europa (W). Main occupations mining (iron, zinc, lead), fishing, stock rearing.
2. Capital of Santander province, on an inlet of the Bay of Biscay. Pop. (1967) 136,069. Important seaport and resort. Exports minerals, wine, wheat. Shipbuilding, oil refining, tanning. Manufactures chemicals, cables, machinery, etc. A disastrous fire (1941) destroyed much of the city and the necessary rebuilding has given it a modern appearance.

**Santa Rosa** USA. Town in California, 50 m. NNW of San Francisco. Pop. (1960) 31,027. In a fruit-growing region. Fruit canning and drying, wine making, etc. Scene of the plant-breeding experiments of Luther Burbank (1849–1926).

**Santa Tecla (Nueva San Salvador)** Salvador. Capital of La Libertad department, 7 m. W of San Salvador at a height of 3,000 ft. Pop. (1961) 40,817. An attractive residential and commercial centre in a coffee-growing and stock-rearing region. Founded (1854) to replace San Salvador as capital

when the latter was destroyed by earthquake; San Salvador was rebuilt by 1859, however, and became capital again.

**Santee River** USA. River 143 m. long in S Carolina, formed by the union of the Congaree and the Wateree rivers, flowing SE to the Atlantic. Part of a large hydroelectric and waterway development (1939–42): the Santee Dam forms L. Marion, 40 m. long and up to 12 m. wide.

**Santiago** Chile. Capital of the republic and of Santiago province, on the Mapocho R. at a height of 1,950 ft. Pop. (1960) 1,169,481. Beautifully situated on a wide plain at the foot of the Andes, it has a colonial nucleus, but is essentially a modern city. Its industries (textiles, clothing, footwear, chemicals, metal goods, food products, etc.) produce more than half the national output. Linked by rail through the central valley with the N and S, with its port Valparaiso 60 m. to the WNW, and by the Transandine Railway with Argentina. Seat of a state (1842) and a Roman Catholic (1888) university. Cathedral, originally built in 1619 and several times reconstructed; many fine parks and squares. Its principal thoroughfare is the Avenida Bernardo O'Higgins (the Alameda), over 2 m. long. Founded (1541) by Pedro de Valdivia.

**Santiago de Compostela (Santiago)** Spain. Ancient Campus Stellae. City in Corunna province, Galicia, 35 m. SSW of Corunna. Pop. (1961) 57,165. The most famous place of pilgrimage in Spain since medieval times; the 11th/13th-cent. Romanesque cathedral contains the tomb of St James, patron saint of Spain. Besides the cathedral, with its finely sculptured 12th-cent. Pòrtico de la Gloria, there is a noteworthy archbishop's palace. University (1501). Trade in cereals, fruit, wool. Caters for tourists. Brewing, distilling. Manufactures linen, soap, paper, matches.

**Santiago de Cuba** Cuba. Capital of the Oriente province, on the S coast 480 m. ESE of Havana. Pop. (1960) 166,384. Major seaport and industrial centre. Exports tobacco and cigars, sugar, rum, mineral ores, etc. Sugar milling, tanning, rum distilling, brewing. Manufactures cigars, soap, perfumes, etc. Picturesquely situated in a natural amphitheatre, approached from the sea by a narrow channel 5 m. long. Among the notable buildings are the large cathedral and the university (1947). Founded (1514) by Diego Velázquez, who is buried in the cathedral.

**Santiago del Estero** Argentina. Capital of Santiago del Estero province, on the Río Dulce 90 m. SE of Tucumán. Pop. (1960) 103,115. Commercial centre. Trade in cotton, cereals, livestock. Flour milling, tanning, textile manufacture. Founded (1553) by settlers moving S from Peru.

**Santiago de los Caballeros (Santiago)** Dominican Republic. Capital of Santiago province, 90 m. NW of Santo Domingo. Pop. (1960) 84,000. Important commercial centre, in a fertile agricultural region producing coffee, rice, tobacco, etc. Coffee and rice milling. Manufactures cigars and cigarettes, furniture, pottery, etc. Founded (c. 1500) by Bartholomew Columbus. Rebuilt after the earthquake of 1564.

**Santiago River** ♦ *Mexico.*

**Santo Domingo** Dominican Republic. Formerly (1936–61) Ciudad Trujillo. Capital and chief seaport, on the S coast. Pop. (1960) 477,782. Exports sugar, cacao, coffee, etc. Distilling, brewing, tanning, etc. Manufactures soap. In the 16th-cent. Renaissance cathedral is the reputed tomb of Columbus. In many ways a typical Spanish colonial town. University (1538). Founded (1496) by Bartholomew Columbus. Suffered severely in a hurricane (1930) and was largely rebuilt. Renamed after President Rafael Trujillo Molina 1936; when he was assassinated (1961) the old name was restored.

**Santorin** ♦ *Thíra.*

**Santos** Brazil. Seaport in São Paulo state 33 m. SE of São Paulo. Pop. (1960) 262,048. Serves São Paulo city and is linked with it by rail and road over the steep Serra do Mar. The world's leading coffee port. Also exports sugar, bananas, citrus fruits, cotton, etc. Has a modern, well-equipped harbour and is served by the Cubatão hydroelectric power station, 6 m. to the NW.

**San Vicente** Salvador. Capital of the San Vicente department, at the foot of the volcano San Vicente (7,132 ft) 27 m. ESE of San Salvador. Pop. (1961) 34,723. In an agricultural region producing coffee, sugar-cane, tobacco, etc. Manufactures textiles, leather goods, hats, etc. Founded (1634) on the site of Tehuacan, an ancient Aztec city. Capital 1832–9.

**São Francisco River** Brazil. River 2,000 m. long rising in the Serra da Canastra in SW Minas Gerais, flowing generally NNE and then E, forming the Bahia–Pernambuco and Alagôas–Sergipe boundaries, to enter the Atlantic 55 m. NE of Aracajú. Navigable by small vessels in much of the middle course; in the lower course impeded by rapids and the Paulo Afonso Falls (hydroelectric plant).

**São Jorge** ♦ *Azores.*

**São Luís** Brazil. Capital and chief seaport of Maranhão state, on São Luís island 300 m. ESE of Belém. Pop. 139,000. Exports cotton, babassu oil, hides and skins, etc. Cotton milling, sugar refining, distilling. Founded (1612) by the French; named after Louis XIII.

**São Miguel** ♦ *Azores.*

**Saône-et-Loire** France. Department in E central France, in Burgundy. Area 3,331 sq. m. Pop. (1968) 550,362. Prefecture Mâcon. Bordered on the W by the Loire, and extending E beyond the Saône into Bresse, it is crossed by the Canal du Centre, which links the two rivers. Rises to 2,959 ft in the Monts du Morvan in the extreme NW. Varied and prosperous agriculture; well known for its red wines. Important industries, esp. coalmining (Montceau-les-Mines, Autun) and iron and steel manufactures (Le Creusot). The wine trade is centred on Mâcon; Chalon-sur-Saône is an important agricultural centre.

**Saône River** France. River 280 m. long rising in the Monts Faucilles, in the Vosges department. The chief tributary of the Rhône, it flows generally SSW past Chalon-sur-Saône, Mâcon, and Villefranche to join the Rhône R. at Lyons. Its own principal tributaries are the Doubs and the Ognon. Its valley forms part of the important route to Marseille, and it is connected by canals with the Moselle, Marne, Loire, Seine, Meuse, and Rhine rivers.

**São Paulo** Brazil. 1. State in the SE, with an outlet to the sea at Santos; in size about equal to the UK. Area 95,453 sq. m. Pop. (1960) 24,848,194. Apart from the small coastal strip, which has the advantage of a practicable approach to the interior plateau traversed by rail and road, it consists of a tableland drained W to the Paraná R., with an equable climate and rainfall adequate for all crops. The most populous and highly developed state in Brazil; bears comparison in standards of living and productivity with many advanced countries. Much of its soil is the fertile *terra roxa* so well suited for coffee growing, and its development as the main coffee-producing area led to massive immigration, mainly from S Europe and Germany, in the 19th

cent. Remains the leading coffee-producing state, but cotton, oranges, bananas, and other agricultural crops are of importance. Also the leading industrial state.
2. Capital of São Paulo state, on the plateau at a height of 2,700 ft in a small basin W of the escarpment (Serra do Mar) and 33 m. N W of its port Santos. S America's leading industrial centre and one of the world's most rapidly growing cities: pop. (1874) 25,000; (1920) 579,000; (1960) 3,825,351. A city of modern buildings, with a highway network and two airports, served by power from the Cubatão and Tietê valley hydroelectric plants. Manufactures textiles, clothing, paper, chemicals, metal goods, cars, machinery, etc. Seat of two universities (1934, 1946). Has two excellent collections of pictures, both modern and old masters, and the famous Butanta Institute where snake serums are produced. The new cathedral is an outstanding building; recreational centres include the Municipal Theatre, the Municipal Stadium, and the Jockey Club racecourse. Founded (1554) by Jesuits on the site of an Indian village. The original settlers came from S Portugal and were ambitious, energetic people, bands of whom ('bandeirantes') pressed on into the interior; the 'Paulistas' have remained the most enterprising of all Brazilians.

**São Paulo de Luanda** ♢ *Luanda*.

**São Tomé and Principe** Gulf of Guinea. Two islands of volcanic origin, respectively 180 and 125 m. W of the African coast, forming with the small islands of Pedras Tinhosas and Rolas an overseas province of Portugal. Area 372 sq. m. Pop. (1960) 63,485. Cap. São Tomé (pop. 7,813), on São Tomé island, which is by far the largest island and has most of the population. Chief product cacao; also exports coffee, copra, palm oil, cinchona. Discovered 1471.

**Sapele** ♢ *Nigeria*.

**Sapporo** Japan. Capital of Hokkaido prefecture, in the S W of the island 95 m. N N E of Hakodate. Pop. (1965) 794,901. Industrial and cultural centre. Flour milling, brewing, sawmilling. Manufactures agricultural machinery, etc. Seat of Hokkaido University (1918).

**Saqqara** ♢ *Sakkara*.

**Saragossa** ♢ *Zaragoza*.

**Sarajevo** Yugoslavia. Capital of Bosnia and Hercegovina, 125 m. S W of Belgrade, on the Miljacka R. Pop. (1961) 175,424. Busy commercial centre. Manufactures chemi-cals, carpets, pottery, tobacco products, etc. Flour milling, brewing, engineering. Largely Oriental in appearance, with its numerous mosques, it is the centre of the Muslim faith in Yugoslavia; also has Roman Catholic and Orthodox cathedrals. The finest mosque is the Begova Džamia (1530), built by Husref Bey and containing an early copy of the Koran. The assassination of the Archduke Francis Ferdinand in Sarajevo (1914) led to the 1st World War.

**Saransk** USSR. Capital of the Mordovian ASSR, RSFSR, 155 m. SSE of Gorky. Pop. (1970) 190,000. Industries mainly concerned with the processing of agricultural produce (grain, sugar-beet, hemp, dairy produce, etc.). Also manufactures agricultural machinery, electrical equipment, etc. Founded 1641.

**Sarapul** USSR. River port in the Udmurt ASSR, RSFSR, on the Kama R. 33 m. SE of Izhevsk. Pop. (1961) 76,000. Manufactures leather, footwear, rope, etc. Trade in grain, timber.

**Sarasota** USA. Winter resort on Sarasota Bay, SW Florida, 45 m. S of Tampa. Pop. (1960) 34,083. Exports citrus fruit, vegetables. Has the famous Ringling museums.

**Saratoga Springs** USA. Famous resort in New York state 30 m. N of Albany. Pop. (1960) 16,630. State-owned mineral springs; the water is bottled and distributed to other parts of the USA. A favourite retreat for authors and artists. Well known for its summer race meetings.

**Saratov** USSR. Capital of the Saratov Region, RSFSR, on the Volga R. 215 m. SW of Kuibyshev. Pop. (1970) 758,000. Important industrial centre. Manufactures tractors and combine harvesters, diesel engines, railway rolling stock, ball bearings, etc. Has an oil refinery and produces natural gas, and is linked by pipeline with Moscow. Flour milling, sawmilling. Seat of a university (1919), and technical and other educational institutions. Several museums. Founded (1590) on the left bank of the Volga R.; moved to its present site on the higher right bank in the 17th cent. Birthplace of Nikolai Chernyshevski (1828–89).

**Sarawak** Malaysia. Former British colony in N W Borneo, now part of the Federation of Malaysia, bounded on the E and S by Kalimantan (Indonesian Borneo). Area 48,250 sq. m. Pop. (1967) 903,000 (297,000 Chinese, 262,000 Sea Dayaks, 163,000 Malays, 75,000 Land Dayaks). Cap. Kuching. Low-lying around the coast;

mountainous and forested inland. Mainly agricultural; chief products rubber, timber, pepper, sago. Principal towns Kuching, Sibu. In 1841 the territory was granted to Sir James Brooke by the Sultan of Brunei, in return for help in quelling a revolt, and the former became rajah. It was gradually enlarged and in 1888 became a British protectorate. During the 2nd World War it was occupied by the Japanese (1941–5). In 1946 Sarawak was ceded by the last rajah to Britain and became a Crown colony. Joined the new Federation of Malaysia 1963.

**Sardes (Sardis)** Asia Minor. Ancient city in W Asia Minor, capital of Lydia; a small village in modern Turkey 35 m. E N E of Izmir. Captured by Persians, Athenians, and Romans. An early centre of Christianity, it was one of the Seven Churches of Asia. Destroyed by Tamerlane (1402).

**Sardinia** (Italian **Sardegna**) Italy. The second largest island in the Mediterranean, separated from Corsica (N) by the Strait of Bonifacio, $7\frac{1}{2}$ m. wide. Area 9,196 sq. m. Pop. (1961) 1,413,289. Cap. and chief seaport Cagliari. With some neighbouring small islands, an autonomous region; divided into 3 provinces, Sassari (N), Nuoro, Cagliari (S). Largely mountainous and wild, rising to 6,017 ft in the Monti del Gennargentu, near the centre. Hot dry summers follow mild winters. Annual rainfall 15–25 ins. in the lowlands, higher in the mountains. Agriculture is most successful in the fertile Campidano plain (S W), where cereals, grapes (for wine), and olives are grown and sheep and goats raised. One of Italy's chief mining areas, esp. for zinc and lead; chief centres Cagliari, Sassari, Iglesias. Evidence of the earliest inhabitants of the island is seen in the strange stone dwellings called *nuraghi*. Fell to the Carthaginians (*c*. 500 B.C.) and to the Romans (238 B.C.). Invaded by Saracens in the 8th–11th cent. Disputed by Pisa and Genoa in the 11th–14th cent. Passed to the House of Savoy as part of the Kingdom of Sardinia 1720. Incorporated into the newly united Italy 1861.

**Sardis** ◊ *Sardes*.

**Sarema** ◊ *Saaremaa*.

**Sark** (Fr. **Sercq**) England. Smallest of the four main Channel Is., 6 m. E of Guernsey. Area 2 sq. m. Pop. (1961) 556. Consists of Great Sark (N) and Little Sark (S), connected by an isthmus, the Coupée. The interior is reached by tunnels from the harbour at Creux (E). Main occupations farming, fishing, tourism. Much natural beauty within a small compass. Motor traffic not allowed. The island, which has a semi-feudal constitution, is governed by a hereditary seigneur or dame.

**Sarnath** India. Site, in Uttar Pradesh 4 m. N of Varanasi (Benares), of the Deer Park where Buddha preached his first sermon after the enlightenment. The ruins include an Asokan pillar. Museum.

**Sarnia** Canada. Industrial town and port in Ontario, on the St Clair R. opposite Port Huron in Michigan. Pop. (1966) 54,552. Trade in coal, grain, timber. A major oil-refining centre. Much of the petroleum from the Alberta oilfields is refined here; a pipe-line was completed in 1953. A natural-gas pipeline has been laid to Toronto and Montreal. A great concentration of petrochemical industries has developed. Manufactures synthetic rubber.

**Sarrelouis** ◊ *Saarlouis*.

**Sarre River** ◊ *Saar River*.

**Sarthe** France. Department in the W, in Maine, drained by the Sarthe R. and its tributaries the Huisne and the Loir. Area 2,411 sq. m. Pop. (1968) 461,839. Prefecture Le Mans. Mainly low-lying and agricultural. Produces cereals, hemp, cider apples, pears. The famous Percheron horses are raised. Chief towns Le Mans, La Flèche.

**Sarthe River** France. River 177 m. long, rising in the Perche Hills and flowing S W and S past Alençon and Le Mans to join the Mayenne R. above Angers and form the Maine R.

**Sarum** ◊ *Salisbury* (England).

**Sasebo** Japan. Seaport and naval station in N W Kyushu, in the Nagasaki prefecture 33 m. N N W of Nagasaki. Pop. (1965) 247,069. Exports coal. Shipbuilding, engineering, etc. Severely damaged by bombing during the 2nd World War, but quickly revived.

**Saskatchewan** Canada. Central province of the three Prairie Provinces, bounded on the S by Montana and N Dakota in the USA. Area 251,700 sq. m. Pop. (1966) 955,344. Cap. Regina. The N half (a region of coniferous forest, lake, and swamp, containing most of L. Athabasca and Reindeer L.) is drained by the Churchill R. and its tributaries. To the S the forests give way to open prairie and the land gradually rises, reaching 4,546 ft in the S W. Climate continental; long cold winters, short hot sunny summers. Annual rainfall only 10–15 ins. Wheat is the mainstay of the agriculture; the province produces about two thirds of Canada's output. Principal minerals petroleum (SW), uranium (NW), copper. Chief towns Regina, Saskatoon. First explored by white fur traders in the late 17th cent. The District of Saskatchewan was formed (1882) as part of the NW Territories. Became a separate province 1905.

**Saskatchewan River** Canada. River formed by the union of the N and the S Saskatchewan rivers. The N Saskatchewan, 760 m. long, rises near Mt Saskatchewan in the Rocky Mountains in SW Alberta and flows generally E in a winding course past Edmonton and Prince Albert. The S Saskatchewan, 865 m. long (from the farthest headstream), is formed from the Bow and the Oldman rivers in S Alberta and flows generally E and NE past Saskatoon. After their junction 30 m. E of Prince Albert, the Saskatchewan R. proper flows 370 m. E to the NW end of L. Winnipeg.

**Saskatoon** Canada. Second largest city in Saskatchewan, on the S Saskatchewan R. 145 m. NW of Regina. Pop. (1966) 115,892 (113 in 1900; 12,004 in 1911). Distribution centre for a large agricultural region. Flour milling, meat packing, brewing, oil refining, etc. Seat of the University of Saskatchewan (1907).

**Sassari** Italy. Capital of Sassari province, in Sardinia, 11 m. SE of Porto Torres, its port. Pop. (1968) 102,798. Second largest city in Sardinia. Produces cheese, macaroni, olive oil, etc. In the main a modern town, it has a cathedral and a university (1677).

**Satpura Range** India. Range of hills of average height 2,000–3,000 ft, rising to over 4,000 ft, between the Narmada and Tapti rivers. Extends about 600 m., partly along the boundary between Madhya Pradesh and Maharashtra.

**Satu Mare** Rumania. Town in the extreme NW, on the Someş R. near the Hungarian frontier. Pop. (1968) 71,196. Manufactures textiles, machinery, furniture, toys, etc. Trade in agricultural produce.

**Saudi Arabia.** Kingdom in SW Asia. Area 927,000 sq. m. Pop. (1966) 6,870,000. Joint capitals Riyadh, Mecca. Rel. Muslim.

Occupies most of the peninsula of Arabia; bounded by Jordan, Iraq, Kuwait and two neutral zones (N); the Persian Gulf (E); the Trucial States, Muscat and Oman, and S Yemen (SE and S); and by Yemen and the Red Sea (W). Most of the country consists of desert, agriculture being possible only in the upland regions of Asir (SW) and in the oases, but since the 2nd World War the exploitation of the oilfields has brought great wealth to the ruler. For topography, climate, etc., ♢ *Arabia.*

RESOURCES, PEOPLE, *etc.* Oil production is centred on Dhahran, on the Persian Gulf. Some of the crude oil is refined at Ras Tanura and on Bahrain Island, some is sent by the Trans-Arabian pipeline (1,068 m.) to Saida (Lebanon), and some is shipped from the Persian Gulf. In the oases of both the Hejaz and Nejd dates form the main crop, and in the latter wheat, barley, coffee, and limes are produced. The chief products of the nomadic Bedouin tribes are hides, wool, and clarified butter, obtained from their camels, sheep, and goats. Formerly much of the national income was derived from visitors to Mecca and Medina. Mecca is the capital of the Hejaz, Jidda the chief seaport, and Medina and Taif important towns; Riyadh is the capital of Nejd, Hofuf and Buraida are important towns, and Dammam the chief seaport. There are roads from Jidda to Mecca and Medina and a railway from Dammam to Riyadh; Dhahran is the principal airport.

Nejd has a population of about 4 million, Hejaz 2 to 3 million, most of them being Sunni Muslims. Oil revenues have provided amenities for some in the shape of water supply, medical and educational services, while the oil companies have assisted the government with irrigation schemes which have brought desert land into cultivation. Justice is administered by religious courts according to the religious law of Islam.

HISTORY. Hejaz and Nejd were united by Ibn Saud (1926), who founded the kingdom of Saudi Arabia (1932) and later played a leading part in the formation of the Arab League (1945). He was succeeded (1953) by his son, Saud ibn Abdul-Aziz, but the latter gradually relinquished power to another son, the Emir Faisal, who became Prime Minister and Minister for Foreign Affairs in 1962, governing through a Council of Ministers.

**Saugor (Sagar)** India. Town in N Madhya Pradesh 90 m. NW of Jubbulpore, picturesquely situated in the Vindhya Hills at a height of 1,700 ft, beside a small lake. Pop. (1961) 85,491. Trade in wheat, cotton, oilseeds. Minor industries. University (1946).

**Sault Sainte Marie** Canada. Port in Ontario, on the St Mary's R. connecting L. Superior (W) and L. Huron (E), opposite the twin city of Sault Sainte Marie in Michigan. Pop. (1966) 74,594. Resort. Industrial centre. Railway engineering. Manufactures steel, wood pulp and paper, etc. The rapids are circumvented by a canal; this canal and the canal on the US side are known as the Soo Canals. 'Sault' is old French for water-fall or rapids.

**Sault Sainte Marie** USA. Port in Michigan, on the St Mary's R. connecting L. Superior (W) and L. Huron (E), opposite the twin city of Sault Sainte Marie in Ontario. Pop. (1960) 18,722. Manufactures carbide, leather goods, textiles, etc. A resort, with hunting and fishing facilities. The rapids are circumvented by a canal (1919).

**Saumur** France. Town in the Maine-et-Loire department 27 m. SE of Angers, at the confluence of the Loire and the Thouet rivers and on an island in the former. Pop. (1968) 23,175. Industrial and market town, famous for the sparkling white wines made in the district. Also manufactures brandy, liqueurs, leather, rosaries, etc. Has the 11th/15th-cent. Church of Notre Dame de Nantilly, an 11th/16th-cent. castle, and the well-known cavalry school (founded 1768). As a centre of Protestantism it suffered severely from the revocation of the Edict of Nantes, losing more than half its population.

**Sauternes** France. Village in the Gironde department 24 m. SSE of Bordeaux. Has given its name to the well-known white wines of the district, which includes the vineyards of the world-famous Château d'Yquem.

**Savage Island** ◊ *Niue Island*.

**Savai'i** ◊ *Samoa*.

**Savannah** USA. River port in Georgia, on the Savannah R. 18 m. from the mouth. Pop. (1960) 149,245. Exports naval stores, raw cotton. Important industrial centre. Shipbuilding. Sugar refining. Pulp and paper milling. Manufactures cottonseed oil, ferti-lizers, chemicals, etc. Mild climate, sub-tropical vegetation. Broad avenues, parks. Many historic buildings. Popular resort. Port of departure (1819) of the *Savannah*, the first steamship to cross the Atlantic (25 days to Liverpool).

**Savannah River** USA. River 314 m. long, formed by the union of the Tugaloo and the Seneca rivers, forming the Georgia–South Carolina boundary, flowing generally SE past Augusta and Savannah (both in Georgia), and entering the Atlantic. Navi-gable for barges below Augusta. Much used for hydroelectric power.

**Sava (Save) River** Yugoslavia. River 580 m. long rising in two headstreams in the Kara-wanken Alps, flowing generally ESE through Slovenia and Croatia, forming part of the boundary of Croatia with Bosnia, and joining the Danube R. at Belgrade. Chief tributaries the Una, Vrbas, Bosna, Drina. Navigable below Sisak.

**Save River** ◊ *Sava River*.

**Savoie** (Italian **Savoia**, English **Savoy**) France. 1. Former duchy in the SE, now divided into two departments, Haute-Savoie (N) and Savoie (S); bounded by L. Geneva (N), Switzerland (NE), and Italy (E). Mainly in the Savoy Alps, with the Mont Blanc massif in the E, and the Graian Alps in the SE. Cap. Chambéry. Cattle rearing and dairy farming important; many tourist centres and hydroelectric stations. Lost much of its area to Switzerland and France after 1472. Became part of the King-dom of Sardinia 1720 and again in 1815; finally returned to France in 1860, when the present departments were created.
2. Department forming the S part of the former duchy of Savoie. Area 2,389 sq. m. Pop. (1968) 288,921. Prefecture Chambéry. Bounded by Italy on the E and SE, it is mountainous, lying almost entirely in the Savoy Alps, and rising to 12,428 ft in Mont Pourri. Drained by the Isère R. Linked with Piedmont (Italy) by the Mont Cenis and Little St Bernard passes. Dairy pro-duce and wine are important products; hydroelectric plants supply power for metallurgical and chemical industries. Chief towns Chambéry, Aix-les-Bains (a well-known spa).

**Savona** Italy. Capital of Savona province, in Liguria, on the Gulf of Genoa 24 m. WSW of Genoa. Pop. (1961) 72,115. Sea-port. Exports pottery, glassware, etc. Also the main industrial centre of the Riviera di Ponente. Manufactures iron and steel, pottery (important since the 16th cent.), glass, bricks, etc. Long a rival of Genoa, it had lost the struggle by the 16th cent.

**Savu (Sawu) Islands** Indonesia. Group of islands in the Lesser Sundas, between Sumba and Timor. Area 231 sq. m. Pop. 34,000. Chief island Savu (area 160 sq. m.; pop. 29,000). Main products copra, rice, tobacco.

**Saxe-Altenburg** German Democratic Republic. Former duchy (1603–72 and again 1825–1918); incorporated into the province of ◊ *Thuringia* 1918.

**Saxe-Coburg-Gotha** German Democratic Republic. Former duchy, formed (1826) when Ernest III of Saxe-Coburg received the duchy of Gotha and became Ernest I, Duke of Saxe-Coburg-Gotha. In 1918 his successor abdicated, and in 1920 Coburg was incorporated into ◊ *Bavaria*, Gotha into ◊ *Thuringia*.

**Saxe-Meiningen** German Democratic Republic. Former duchy founded (1681) by a son of the Duke of Saxe-Gotha, comprising the district round Meiningen. In 1826 it acquired the duchy of Saxe-Saalfeld and other territory, but in 1920 was incorporated into ◊ *Thuringia*.

**Saxe-Weimar-Eisenach** German Democratic Republic. Former grand duchy, formed (1728) by the union of the duchies of Saxe-Weimar and Saxe-Eisenach. In the late 18th cent. under Duke Charles Augustus, its capital, Weimar, became one of the leading intellectual centres of Europe, with Goethe and Schiller among its scholars. At the Congress of Vienna (1815) it was raised to the status of a grand duchy. Incorporated into ◊ *Thuringia* 1920.

**Saxony** (Ger. **Sachsen**) German Democratic Republic. Former *Land* of Germany and later (1946–52) of the GDR. Area 6,562 sq. m. Pop. (1950) 5,682,802. Cap. Dresden. Borders S on Czechoslovakia. In the S it includes much of the Erzgebirge and its foothills; descends in the N to the N European plain. Historically the name has been used of two distinct areas. It was originally applied to a region in the NW, roughly corresponding to the present *Land* of ◊ *Lower Saxony* (Federal German Republic), between the North Sea, the Rhine, and the Elbe. The Saxons who inhabited this area were conquered by Charlemagne. The first duchy of Saxony was created in the 9th cent. Duke Henry I the Fowler was elected German king in 919; he and his successors ruled until 1002. The duchy was broken up in 1180, and the title passed to Bernard, a son of Albert the Bear of Brandenburg, along with the small regions of Lauenburg and Wittenberg. From 1260 the territories were divided into the duchies of Saxe-Lauenburg and Saxe-Wittenberg; in 1356 the duke of the latter was made Elector. When the line became extinct (1423) Frederick, Margrave of Meissen, added Saxe-Wittenberg to Meissen and Thuringia

and became the Elector Frederick I of Saxony. Many changes took place in the succeeding centuries. The Electors of Saxony were kings of part of Poland 1697–1763. The Elector Frederick Augustus III assumed the title of King (1806), but lost the N part of his kingdom, which became a province of Prussia. Subsequently Saxony was a member of the Confederation of the Rhine (1815), the North German Confederation (1866), and the German Empire (1871). At the end of the 1st World War King Frederick Augustus III abdicated and a republic was proclaimed. After the 2nd World War the republic, with part of the Prussian province of Lower Silesia, became the *Land* of Saxony; the former Prussian province of Saxony, with the state of Anhalt, became the *Land* of Saxony-Anhalt, both in the GDR (1946). In 1952 Saxony was replaced by the administrative districts of Leipzig, Dresden, and Karl-Marx-Stadt, and Saxony-Anhalt by Halle and Magdeburg.

**Sayan Mountains** USSR. Mountain system in the extreme S of RSFSR, consisting of the Eastern Sayan Mountains, which extend SE from the Yenisei R. to the USSR–Mongolia border and rise to 11,457 ft in Munku Sardyk; and the Western Sayan Mountains, extending ENE from the Altai Mountains to the E Sayan Mountains and rising to over 9,000 ft. The region yields timber as well as gold, silver, lead, coal.

**Scafell** (**Scaw Fell**) England. Mountain mass in Cumberland, in the Lake District, 10 m. WNW of Ambleside. Comprises Scafell Pike (3,210 ft), the highest peak in England, and Scafell (3,162 ft), joined by the narrow ridge of Mickledore, together with Great End (2,984 ft) and Lingmell (2,649 ft). Belongs to the National Trust.

**Scandinavia.** Geographically considered, Scandinavia is the peninsula of NW Europe comprising the two countries of Norway and Sweden, bounded by the Arctic Ocean (N), the Norwegian Sea (W), and the Baltic Sea and Gulf of Bothnia (E). From the cultural and historical standpoint, however, Denmark as well as Iceland and the Faeroes should also be included. Finland too is sometimes regarded as part of the Scandinavian region.

**Scapa Flow** Scotland. Stretch of sea in the Orkneys bounded on the N by Mainland, on the E and SE by Burray and S Ronaldsay, on the W and SW by Hoy. Area 50 sq. m. In the early part of the 1st World War it was the chief base of the British Grand Fleet; here most of the ships of the interned German High Sea Fleet were scuttled by their crews (1919). Again a naval base in the 2nd World War.

**Scarborough** England. Municipal borough in the N Riding of Yorkshire, on the North Sea 40 m. N of Hull. Pop. (1961) 42,587. Seaside resort and fishing port on the peninsula between North Bay and South Bay and extending inland and along both bays. Minor industries. Crowning the peninsula are the remains of the 12th-cent. castle, built on the site of a 4th-cent. Roman signal station. The spa contains gardens, theatre, concert hall, etc. Bombarded by German warships in the 1st World War; suffered from air raids in the 2nd World War. Birthplace of Lord Leighton (1830–96) and Dame Edith Sitwell (1887–1964).

**Scarborough** (W Indies) ◊ *Tobago.*

**Scaw Fell** ◊ *Scafell.*

**Schaffhausen** Switzerland. **1.** Small canton in the N, N of the Rhine R. and almost surrounded by territory of the Federal German Republic. Area 115 sq. m. Pop. (1969) 73,000 (German-speaking, mainly Protestant). Its forests are an important source of revenue. Hydroelectric power is derived from the famous Rhine falls. Industry is concentrated in Schaffhausen. Joined the Swiss Confederation 1501.
**2.** Capital of the Schaffhausen canton, on the right bank of the Rhine R. Pop. (1969) 38,900. Industrial centre, obtaining hydroelectric power from the Rhine falls. Manufactures metal goods, textiles, etc. Medieval and modern buildings are intermingled, among the former being the 11th/12th-cent. Romanesque minster, formerly a Benedictine monastery.

**Schaumburg-Lippe** Federal German Republic. Former state between Westphalia and Hanover, now incorporated in Lower Saxony. Area 131 sq. m. Mainly agricultural; coalmining around Bückeburg, the capital.

**Schefferville** Canada. Formerly Knob Lake. Town in E Quebec near the Labrador border. Pop. (1966) 3,086. The settlement developed in the early 1950s to mine the rich local iron-ore deposits. The railway for transporting the ore to the seaport of Sept Îles was opened in 1954. Also has an airport. Incorporated 1955.

**Scheldt** (Fr. **Escaut**; Flemish, Dutch **Schelde**) **River.** River 270 m. long rising in the Aisne department (France), flowing generally NNE past Valenciennes, then crossing Belgium past Tournai, Ghent, and Antwerp. Below Antwerp its estuary, the Western Scheldt, enters Dutch territory, separating S Beveland and Walcheren islands from the mainland; the Eastern Scheldt, once a N branch of the estuary, is linked with the Western Scheldt by the S Beveland Canal. In 1648 the Dutch reserved the right to close the Scheldt, but in 1863 navigation was declared free. Chief tributary the Lys. A bridge 3 m. long (the longest in Europe) across the Eastern Scheldt, linking the islands of N Beveland and Schouwen-Duiveland, was opened in 1965.

**Schenectady** USA. Industrial town in New York state, on the Mohawk R. 15 m. NW of Albany. Pop. (1960) 81,682. Largely dependent on the manufacture of electrical equipment and locomotives. Seat of the Union University (1795). Originally settled by the Dutch (1661). Grew rapidly after the coming of the railways in the 1830s.

**Scheveningen** Netherlands. Popular seaside resort and fishing port in S Holland province 2 m. NW of The Hague, of which it is a suburb. Much of it was destroyed in the 2nd World War.

**Schiedam** Netherlands. Town and river port in S Holland province 3 m. W of Rotterdam. Pop. (1968) 82,596. Famous for its gin industry, connected with which are manufactures of glass, bottles, crates, corks, etc. Also has shipyards, chemical works, etc.

**Schiphol** ◊ *Amsterdam.*

**Schleswig** Federal German Republic. Fishing port, residential and industrial town in Schleswig-Holstein, at the W end of the Schei, an inlet of the Baltic, 27 m. NW of Kiel. Pop. (1963) 33,600. Manufactures leather goods, chemicals. Tanning, flour milling. Capital of Schleswig-Holstein 1879–1917. Birthplace of A. J. Carstens (1754–98), the German painter.

**Schleswig-Holstein** Federal German Republic. *Land* bounded on the N by Denmark and mainly occupying the S part of the Jutland peninsula, fringed by the N Frisian Is. (W) and Fehmarn Island (E). Area 6,045 sq. m. Pop. (1968) 2,499,700. Cap. Kiel. Low-lying. Drained by the Elbe R. (which forms much of the S border) and the Eider R. Crossed by the Kiel Canal linking the Elbe estuary with the Baltic Sea. Main occupation agriculture. Rye, wheat, and potatoes cultivated. Many cattle and pigs reared. The irregular Baltic coastline provides excellent natural harbours; the three chief towns (Kiel, Lübeck, Flensburg) are all seaports. For centuries the duchies of Schleswig and Holstein were associated with the Danish Crown. The Danish-German dispute (the 'Schleswig-Holstein Question') came to a head with the death of Frederick VII of Denmark (1863); the duchies were occupied by Prussian and Austrian troops (1864), and, after the Austro-Prussian War (1866), annexed to Prussia. After the 1st World War a plebiscite restored N Schleswig to Denmark (1920). The present Schleswig-Holstein became a *Land* of the Federal German Republic in 1949.

**Schönebeck** German Democratic Republic. Industrial town and river port in the Magdeburg district 9 m. SSE of Magdeburg. Pop. (1965) 44,302. Salt works. Manufactures chemicals, explosives, machinery, etc.

**Schuylkill River** USA. River 130 m. long in Pennsylvania, flowing generally SE, through an anthracite-mining region, past Reading, and joining the Delaware R. at Philadelphia. Navigable by barges for nearly 100 m. upstream.

**Schwaben** ◊ *Swabia*.

**Schwäbisch Gmünd** ◊ *Gmünd*.

**Schwarzwald** ◊ *Black Forest*.

**Schweinfurt** Federal German Republic. Industrial town in NW Bavaria, on the Main R. 23 m. NE of Würzburg. Pop. (1963) 57,800. Manufactures paints and dyes, machinery, ball bearings, etc. Founded in the late 8th cent. Became a free imperial city in the late 13th cent.

**Schwerin** German Democratic Republic. Capital of the Schwerin district, on the SW shore of L. Schwerin 45 m. SW of Rostock. Pop. (1965) 91,210. Manufactures furniture, soap, pharmaceutical products, etc. Has a mainly 15th-cent. brick-built cathedral. Founded in 1161, it was capital of the county of Schwerin, of the duchy (later republic) of Mecklenburg-Schwerin, and then of the *Land* of Mecklenburg.

**Schwyz** Switzerland. 1. Canton in central Switzerland bordering the Lakes of Zürich, Lucerne, and Zug. Area 351 sq m.. Pop. (1969) 85,500 (German-speaking, Catholic). Mountainous, esp. in the S; much of its area consists of pastures, on which cattle are raised, and forests. In 1291 it created the league with Uri and Unterwalden which formed the basis of Swiss independence;

gave its name (in the form of Schweiz) to that of the whole confederation.
2. Capital of the Schwyz canton, 15 m. E of Lucerne. Pop. (1969) 12,500. Picturesque tourist centre at the foot of the Gross Mythen (6,240 ft).

**Sciacca** Italy. Seaport in Agrigento province, Sicily, 45 m. SSW of Palermo. Pop. (1961) 31,365. An ancient town surrounded by 16th-cent. walls. Sulphur springs 3 m. E.

**Scilly Isles** England. Group of about 140 small granitic islands and islets 28 m. WSW of Land's End, 5 being inhabited: St Mary's, the largest, with Hugh Town, the only town, Tresco, St Martin's, St Agnes, and Bryher. Area 6 sq. m. Pop. (1961) 2,273. With their mild equable climate, they have become famous for the cultivation of early flowers (esp. daffodils, narcissi) and also attract holiday-makers. The gardens of Tresco Abbey are subtropical in character and unique in the British Isles. The islands were the scene of many wrecks, and on a rock to the SW is the well-known Bishop Rock lighthouse. They were also notorious for smuggling. Among prehistoric remains there is a remarkable barrow on Samson Island – the island described in Besant's *Armorel of Lyonesse*.

**Scone** Scotland. Parish in SE Perthshire consisting of the villages of Old Scone and New Scone, the latter 2 m. NE of Perth. Old Scone was the Pictish and later the Scottish capital, where the kings of Scotland were crowned 1157–1488 and Charles II in 1651. The Coronation Stone ('Stone of Destiny') on which they were crowned was taken by Edward I of England to Westminster Abbey (1297) and placed beneath the coronation chair; it was removed from there by Scottish nationalists (1950) but recovered later.

**Scoresby Sound** Greenland. Deep inlet into the E coast, about 200 m. long. Many fiords, which receive glaciers from the interior ice-cap. At the entrance (N side) is the small settlement of Scoresbysund. Named after William Scoresby (1789–1857), the Arctic explorer.

**Scotland.** The N part of Great Britain, including many islands, e.g. the Inner and Outer Hebrides, the Orkneys, the Shetland (Zetland) Is. Area 30,405 sq. m. Pop. (1961) 5,178,490. Cap. Edinburgh. Rel. mainly Presbyterian. Bounded by the Atlantic (W and N), the North Sea (E), and England (S). Almost the entire N half is occupied by the

Highlands, scenically beautiful but sparsely populated and in the main suitable only for rough pasture. The majority of the population are concentrated in the industrial area of the Central Lowlands. Divided administratively into 33 counties: Aberdeenshire; Angus; Argyllshire; Ayrshire; Banffshire; Berwickshire; Buteshire; Caithness; Clackmannanshire; Dumfriesshire; Dunbartonshire; East Lothian; Fifeshire; Inverness-shire; Kincardineshire; Kinross-shire; Kirkcudbrightshire; Lanarkshire; Midlothian; Morayshire; Nairnshire; Orkney; Peeblesshire; Perthshire; Renfrewshire; Ross and Cromarty; Roxburghshire; Selkirkshire; Stirlingshire; Sutherland; West Lothian; Wigtownshire; Zetland (Shetland). For topography, climate, etc. ◊ *Great Britain*.

RESOURCES, PEOPLE, *etc.* Nearly two-thirds of the land surface is classified as rough grazing land; less than one fifth is arable. Main crops oats, potatoes, turnips. Stock rearing is important; Scottish breeds of cattle, notably the Aberdeen Angus beef cattle and the Ayrshire dairy cattle, have won a world reputation. Large numbers of sheep, bred for meat as well as wool, in the E of the Southern Uplands (e.g. Roxburghshire). In the Highlands and the islands the poverty of resources led to crofting (a type of subsistence farming); the consequent low standard of living has caused a gradual drain of population. The fishing industry has declined since the 1st World War but Scotland still produces nearly one third of the British catch; herring predominate, and Aberdeen is the leading port.

The coalfields of Ayrshire, Lanarkshire, Fifeshire, Midlothian, and Clackmannan formed the basis of the industrial development in the Central Lowlands, exemplified esp. in the great shipbuilding industry along the Clyde estuary, engineering and textile manufacture in the Glasgow area, woollens and tweeds in the Tweed basin, jute in Dundee, beer in Edinburgh. Whisky distilling is a leading industry. Hydroelectric power has been developed in the Highlands and is utilized in part for aluminium production. The railway network is relatively sparse, esp. in the Highlands; N of the Caledonian Canal the W coast is reached at only two points, Mallaig and Kyle of Lochalsh. The roads are good; the route from Edinburgh to the NE has been much improved by the opening of a road bridge

near the famous railway bridge across the Forth (1964).

More than one fifth of the population live in the largest city, Glasgow, and more than one third in the conurbation of central Clydeside. Edinburgh, Aberdeen, and Dundee are the only towns besides Glasgow with over 100,000 inhabitants. The number of people in the Highlands who speak only Gaelic is now (1961) reduced to 1,000 and those who speak both Gaelic and English to 77,000. Scotland is represented at Westminster by 71 members in the House of Commons. The Secretary of State for Scotland has a seat in the Cabinet and is assisted at the Scottish Office by a Minister of State. The principal church is the Church of Scotland, Protestant in theology and Presbyterian in organization; the United Free Church of Scotland which seceded in 1843 was reunited with it in 1929.

HISTORY. The Romans, who invaded England under Julius Caesar in 55 B.C., were unable to penetrate Scotland until A.D. 80, when Agricola began his campaign against the northern tribes. Neither the victory at Mons Graupius nor the building of Antoninus's Wall between the Firths of Clyde and Forth (A.D. 142) was sufficient to hold the Caledonians permanently; by the end of the 2nd cent. the Romans had withdrawn to Hadrian's Wall in the N of England. In the 6th cent. Scotland was occupied by Picts (N), Scots from Ireland (W), Britons (SW), and Angles (SE). The first unifying influence came in 563, with the spread of Christianity by the Irishman St Columba (who had been preceded by St Ninian and St Kentigern); his missionaries travelled far and wide from the settlement on Iona. An army from Northumbria marched as far as the Firth of Forth but was defeated by the Picts (685). Kenneth MacAlpine, King of the Scots, united his people with the Picts in 844. Malcolm II inflicted a further defeat on the Northumbrians (1018) and occupied the SE; his grandson Duncan succeeded to Strathclyde in the SW, uniting the Picts, the Scots, the Britons, and the Angles of mainland Scotland. The islands were still held by the Norsemen: the Hebrides were not recovered till the 13th cent. and the Orkneys and the Shetlands till the 15th.

With Malcolm III's marriage to the English princess Margaret (sister of Edgar Atheling; later St Margaret) the kingdom began to lose its purely Celtic character:

English was spoken at court, the Church was Anglicized, Anglo-Norman nobles settled in the S and sometimes married Celtic ladies, and a form of feudalism was established. Under David I (1124–53, a son of Malcolm and Margaret) Scotland was united, a central government was organized, and trade developed, esp. with England. By the end of the 13th cent. the English language was spoken over most of Scotland S of the Highlands. Anglicization of the Scots, however, did not win their friendship. When Edward I of England claimed overlordship of Scotland and gave the crown to John Balliol, the latter made an alliance with France; the Scots rose under William Wallace, who was captured and executed (1305). Robert Bruce continued the struggle for independence, was crowned at Scone (1306), and utterly defeated the English at Bannockburn (1314). Scottish independence was recognized by England in 1328; the first Stewart, Robert II, came to the throne in 1371. James IV married Margaret Tudor, daughter of Henry VII of England, but the ensuing peace was short-lived; he was killed at the disastrous defeat at Flodden (1513), as was his son, James V, at Solway Moss (1542). French Catholic influence grew under the regency of Mary of Guise (mother of Mary Queen of Scots) but aroused the opposition of people and nobles. The Reformation gained ground and Protestantism was established as the national religion in 1560. After civil war in the reign of Mary (and of Elizabeth I of England) James VI of Scotland became James I of England (1603). There was a temporary union under Cromwell (1651–60) and much civil dissension throughout the Restoration period. Under Queen Anne of England the two Parliaments were united (1707). Opposition to the Act of Union was largely responsible for the Jacobite risings (1715 and 1745) against the Hanoverian Protestant succession in favour of the exiled Stewarts. The economic benefits of the union ultimately became apparent in a great expansion of commerce; with the Industrial Revolution came the development of the coal, iron, shipbuilding, and textile industries in the Central Lowlands. Scotland's justifiable grievance over her poor political representation at Westminster was rectified by successive Reform Acts in the 19th cent. Today a Scottish nationalist movement still demands a separate Parliament for Scot-

land, but since the Union the country's history has been continually woven more closely into that of England.

**Scranton** USA. Industrial town in Pennsylvania, on the Lackawanna R. 105 m. NNW of Philadelphia. Pop. (1960) 111,443. Important centre in an anthracite-mining region. Manufactures textiles, clothing, metal goods, plastics, etc. Seat of the University of Scranton (1888, Roman Catholic).

**Scunthorpe** England. Municipal borough in Parts of Lindsey, Lincolnshire, 23 m. W of Grimsby, including Frodingham. Pop. (1961) 67,257 (33,761 in 1931). An important iron and steel centre, it expanded rapidly owing to exploitation of the iron ore deposits in the neighbourhood; has blast furnaces, rolling mills, etc. Engineering. Manufactures clothing etc.

**Scutari** (Albania) ⟡ *Shkodër*.

**Scutari** (Turkey) ⟡ *Istanbul*.

**Scutari, Lake** ⟡ *Shkodër, Lake*.

**Scythia.** Ancient region in SE Europe, on the steppes N of the Black Sea between the Carpathians and the Don R. Its people, the Scythians, flourished between the 7th and 3rd cent. B.C., and were superseded by the Sarmatians.

**Seaford** England. Urban district in E Sussex 8 m. W of Eastbourne. Pop. (1961) 10,994. Seaside resort. Formerly at the mouth of the R. Ouse and was a member of the Cinque Port of Hastings, but the river changed course to Newhaven in the 16th cent. and the decline of Seaford as a port, already begun two centuries earlier, was hastened. Its revival as a watering-place began in the early 19th cent.

**Seaforth, Loch** Scotland. Inlet into the SE coast of Lewis with Harris, Outer Hebrides, forming part of the boundary between them and extending 15 m. inland.

**Seaham** England. Urban district in Durham 6 m. S of Sunderland. Pop. (1961) 26,048. Coalmining centre which includes Seaham Harbour, built in 1828 to export coal. At Seaham Hall (1 m. N) Byron was married (1815).

**Sea Islands** USA. Chain of islands off the coasts of S Carolina, Georgia, and N Florida, between the mouths of the Santee and the St John's rivers. Low-lying and sandy on the seaward side. The long-stapled 'Sea Island' cotton was formerly grown, but its cultivation was given up (for mixed farming) after destruction by the boll weevil in the 1920s.

**Seal Islands** ◊ *Lobos Islands*.

**Seathwaite** England. Village in Cumberland, in the Lake District 9 m. SSW of Keswick; said to be the wettest place in England, with a mean annual rainfall of 130 ins.

**Seaton Carew** ◊ *West Hartlepool*.

**Seaton Valley** England. Urban district in Northumberland 7 m. NNE of Newcastle upon Tyne. Pop. (1961) 26,086. Consists of a group of coalmining villages, including Seaton Delaval and Cramlington.

**Seattle** USA. Largest city in Washington, on the isthmus between Puget Sound and L. Washington. Pop. (1970) 524,263. Important seaport, trading esp. with Alaska and the Far East. Exports timber, canned and fresh fish, fruit, etc. The industrial, commercial, and financial capital of the Pacific NW. Shipbuilding. Aircraft manufacture. Food canning. Seat of the University of Washington (1861) and the Seattle University (1852, Roman Catholic). Became a boom town with the Alaska gold rush (1897). Expanded again with the opening of the Panama Canal (1914). Fine views of the Olympic Mountains (W) and the Cascade Ranges (E). Site of the first World's Fair in the USA since 1939–40, opened in 1962; the 600-ft Space Needle, the tallest US building W of the Mississippi, was left as a permanent feature.

**Sebastopol** ◊ *Sevastopol*.

**Sebha** ◊ *Fezzan*.

**Sebta** ◊ *Ceuta*.

**Secunderabad** India. Former town and cantonment in Andhra Pradesh just N of Hyderabad, in which it is now incorporated. Commercial centre. Railway junction. Founded 1806.

**Sedan** France. Town in the Ardennes department on the Meuse R. 53 m. NE of Reims near the Belgian frontier. Pop. (1968) 24,499. Manufactures woollen goods, machinery, chemicals, mirrors, etc. For some time an independent principality; passed to the French crown 1642. A Protestant stronghold in the 16th and 17th cent.; Huguenot weavers laid the foundations of its prosperity. During the Franco-Prussian War (1870) the French were decisively defeated at the Battle of Sedan. In the 2nd World War the Germans broke through the French lines here (1940).

**Sedbergh** England. Market town in the W Riding of Yorkshire, 8 m E of Kendal. Pop. (rural district, 1961) 3,293. Woollen industry. Has a well-known public school (founded 1525).

**Sedgemoor** England. Former marshy area, now drained, in Somerset 3 m. ESE of Bridgwater, where the forces of James II defeated the Duke of Monmouth (1685).

**Sedgley** England. Urban district in Staffordshire 3 m. S of Wolverhampton. Pop. (1961) 27,927. Coalmining. Manufactures fireclay.

**Segovia** Spain. 1. Province in Old Castile on the Meseta, with the Sierra de Guadarrama, rising to 8,100 ft, in the SE separating Old from New Castile. Area 2,683 sq. m. Pop. (1961) 195,602. Mainly agricultural: cereal cultivation, sheep rearing.

2. Capital of Segovia province, 42 m. NW of Madrid. Pop. (1961) 33,360. A town of great historical and architectural interest. Flour milling, tanning, etc. Manufactures pottery. Stands on a rocky ridge above the Eresma R. and a tributary, at a height of 3,276 ft, dominated by the mainly 15th-cent. Alcazar (restored) and the 16th-cent. Gothic cathedral. Another noteworthy feature is the Roman aqueduct, which still supplies the city with water.

**Seine** France. Former department in the centre of the Paris Basin, the smallest in area but the most populous. Dissolved 1964 with the creation of 7 new departments in the Paris district.

**Seine-et-Marne** France. Department in the Paris Basin formed (1790) mainly from Île-de-France and Champagne. Area 2,290 sq. m. Pop. (1968) 604,340. Prefecture Melun. Drained by the Seine and Marne and their tributaries. Between these two important rivers is the fertile Brie region, famous for its wheat and other crops and its cheeses; the department supplies many food products to the Paris markets. Principal forest that of Fontainebleau. Chief towns Melun, Fontainebleau.

**Seine-et-Oise** France. Former department in the Paris Basin formed (1790) from part of Île-de-France. Dissolved 1964 with the creation of 7 new departments in the Paris district.

**Seine-Maritime** France. Formerly Seine-Inférieure. Department in E Normandy bounded on the NW and N by the English Channel and on the S by the Seine R. and its estuary. Area 2,448 sq. m. Pop. (1968) 1,113,977. Prefecture Rouen. Flax and other crops are cultivated on the chalky Caux plateau (W), dairy cattle are raised in the Bray district (E), and the valley of the meandering Seine R. is well wooded. Industry and trade concentrated in Rouen, Le Havre, Dieppe.

**Seine River** France. One of the chief rivers, 479 m. long, rising on the Plateau de Langres, flowing generally NW across the Paris Basin, crossing Champagne, turning WSW below Troyes, then NW again, meandering through Paris and the Île-de-France to Normandy past Rouen, and entering the English Channel by an estuary between the ports of Le Havre (N) and Honfleur (S). Tributaries include the Aube, the Marne, and the Oise on the right bank and the Yonne on the left, forming an important network of waterways. Linked by canals with the Scheldt (Escaut), the Meuse, the Rhine, the Rhône, and the Loire. Navigable for ocean-going vessels as far as Rouen and for barges (partly by lateral canal) as far as Bar-sur-Seine.

**Seine-St Denis** France. Department just NE of Paris, formed in 1964 when the former Seine and Seine-et-Oise departments were reorganized. Area 91 sq. m. Pop. (1968) 1,251,792. Prefecture Bobigny.

**Sekia el Hamra** ◊ *Spanish Sahara*.

**Sekondi** Ghana. Capital of the Western Region, seaport 5 m. NE of Takoradi, with which it is linked by rail. Pop. (1960) 34,513. The Gold Coast colony's chief port after the construction of the railway to the interior, it was superseded by Takoradi in 1928. The two became a single municipality in 1946.

**Selangor** Malaysia. One of the best developed states in Malaya (W Malaysia), on the Strait of Malacca. Area 3,167 sq. m. Pop. (1967) 1,408,881 (50 per cent Chinese). Cap. Kuala Lumpur, also capital of Malaya and Malaysia. Chief products rubber, tin. Main port Port Swettenham.

**Selborne** England. Village 4 m. SSE of Alton, Hampshire, where Gilbert White (1720–93), author of *The Natural History and Antiquities of Selborne*, was born, lived for much of his life, and is buried.

**Selby** England. Urban district in the W Riding of Yorkshire, on the R. Ouse 12 m. S of York. Pop. (1961) 9,869. Market and industrial town. Flour milling, beet-sugar refining. Manufactures oilcake etc. The Church of St Mary and St German, which belonged to a Benedictine abbey founded (1069) by William the Conqueror, was much damaged by fire in 1906 and later restored. Reputed to be the birthplace of Henry I (1068–1135).

**Selenga River.** River 750 m. long rising in the N Mongolian People's Republic and flowing generally ENE to the USSR frontier, then turning N through the Buryat ASSR, past Ulan Ude to L. Baikal. Navigable in summer along the Russian section.

**Seleucia.** Name of several ancient cities founded in the 4th and 3rd cent. B.C. and called after Seleucus Nicator.

1. *Seleucia on the Tigris.* City founded 312 B.C. by Seleucus Nicator, 20 m. SE of modern Baghdad (Iraq), as his capital. An important river port with a pop. of about 600,000. Ctesiphon, on the opposite bank of the river, was made capital by the Parthians, and in A.D. 164 Seleucia was destroyed by the Romans.

2. *Seleucia Pieria.* City just N of the mouth of the Orontes R., in modern Turkey, founded 300 B.C. Port of Antioch. Was largely destroyed by earthquake (A.D. 526); the remains of walls, temples and other buildings have been excavated.

**Selkirk** Scotland. Royal burgh and county town of Selkirkshire, on Ettrick Water. Pop. (1961) 5,634. Market town. Manufactures tweeds, woollen goods. Once famous for its 'souters' (shoemakers). The Common Riding (June), when the bounds are ridden by horsemen, commemorates the Battle of Flodden, where the 'souters' fought valiantly. Andrew Lang (1844–1912) was born here, and both he and the explorer Mungo Park (1771–1806) were educated at the grammar school.

**Selkirk Mountains** Canada. Mountain range 200 m. long in SE British Columbia, extending NNW into the great bend of the Columbia R. W of the Rocky Mountains. Highest peak Mt Sir Sandford (11,590 ft). Several others exceed 10,000 ft.

**Selkirkshire** Scotland. County in the Southern Uplands, drained by the Tweed R., Ettrick Water, Yarrow Water. Area 267 sq. m. Pop. (1961) 21,055. County town Selkirk. Generally hilly, the highest point being Broad Law (2,754 ft) on the Peeblesshire border, it was once densely wooded, containing the Stewart hunting ground, Ettrick Forest. Main occupation sheep farming. James Hogg (1770–1835), the 'Ettrick Shepherd', was born and is buried at Ettrick. Chief towns Selkirk, Galashiels.

**Selma** USA. Town in Alabama, on the Alabama R. 40 m. W of Montgomery. Pop. (1960) 28,385. In a fertile agricultural region (cotton, pecan nuts, etc.).

Food processing, sawmilling, etc. Seat of the Selma University for Negroes (1878). Scene of anti-segregation demonstrations in 1965.

**Selsey** England. Seaside resort in W Sussex 7 m. S of Chichester. Pop. 4,000. Site of an abbey founded by St Wilfrid in the 7th cent. Just S, at the tip of the Selsey peninsula, is the headland of Selsey Bill.

**Semarang** Indonesia. Capital of Central Java province and seaport on the Java Sea 260 m. ESE of Jakarta. Pop. (1961) 503,153. Exports sugar, copra, kapok, tobacco, etc. Shipbuilding, railway engineering. Manufactures textiles, electrical equipment, etc. Seat of the University of Diponegoro (1960).

**Semipalatinsk** USSR. Capital of the Semipalatinsk region, Kazakh SSR, on the Irtysh R. and the Turksib Railway 520 m. NNE of Alma Ata. Pop. (1970) 236,000. Industrial and route centre. Meat packing, flour milling, tanning, etc. Founded 1718.

**Semliki River** ◊ *Albert, Lake*; *Edward, Lake*; *Nile River*.

**Semmering Pass** Austria. Alpine pass (3,215 ft) 12 m. WSW of Neunkirchen, in Lower Austria, leading into Styria. In a tourist district popular with the Viennese.

**Semnan** Iran. Town in the Central Province, 105 m. E of Tehran at a height of 3,700 ft at the foot of the Elburz Mountains. Pop. (1966) 31,058. Commercial centre in a tobacco-growing region. Manufactures rugs.

**Sendai** Japan. Capital of Miyagi prefecture and chief city in N Honshu, 190 m. NNE of Tokyo. Pop. (1965) 481,013. Food processing. Manufactures metal goods, textiles, pottery, etc. Seat of Tohoku University (1907).

**Senegal**. Republic in W Africa, formerly a French colony. Area 76,104 sq. m. Pop. (1965) 3,500,000. Cap. Dakar. Bounded by Mauritania (N, the Senegal R.), Mali (E), Guinea, Portuguese Guinea (S). Surrounds Gambia (W). Generally flat terrain; mainly savannah. Food crops maize, millet. Chief exports groundnuts, groundnut oil, oilcake. Occupied by the French in the mid 19th cent. Became part of French W Africa (cap. St Louis) 1895. Dakar became capital 1902. Joined the French Community 1958 and the Federation of Mali 1959. Became an independent member of the UN 1960.

**Senegal River**. River in W Africa 1,050 m. long, formed by the union of the Bafing and the Bakhoy rivers. Rises in the Fouta Djallon highlands, flows generally NW and is joined by the Falémé R., forms the Mauritania–Senegal frontier, turns W, and enters the Atlantic below St Louis. Navigable July–Oct. as far as Kayes (in Mali) which is linked by rail with Bamako on the Niger R.

**Senge Khambab** ◊ *Indus River*.

**Senigallia** Italy. Ancient Sena Gallica, later Sinigaglia. Town in Ancona province, Marches, 17 m. WNW of Ancona. Pop. (1961) 35,337. Port. Seaside resort. Manufactures macaroni etc. Birthplace of Pope Pius IX (1792–1878).

**Senlis** France. Town in the Oise department 27 m. NNE of Paris. Pop. (1968) 11,169. A market town and resort surrounded by forests (Hallatte, Chantilly, Ermenonville). Manufactures furniture, rubber products. Has Gallo-Roman walls and the 12th/16th-cent. early Gothic Church of Notre Dame, formerly a cathedral.

**Sennar** Sudan. Town on the left bank of the Blue Nile 160 m. SSE of Khartoum. Pop. 8,000. Linked by rail (through Sennar Junction) with Khartoum, El Obeid, and Kassala. The Sennar Dam (formerly called the Makwar Dam; completed 1925) is part of the Gezira irrigation scheme. Old Sennar (6 m. NNW) was the capital of the ancient kingdom of Sennar in the 16th–19th cent.

**Sens** France. Ancient Agedincum. Market town in the Yonne department on the Yonne R. 38 m. WSW of Troyes. Pop. (1968) 24,563. Tanning, flour milling. Manufactures footwear, brushes, etc. Trade in wine, grain, timber, etc. Its 12th/16th-cent. cathedral is one of the earliest Gothic buildings in France. An important road centre in Roman times. United to the French crown 1055.

**Senta** (Hungarian **Zenta**) Yugoslavia. Town in Vojvodina, on the Tisza R. 24 m. SE of Subotica. Pop. (1961) 25,062. Railway junction. Flour milling. Here the Austrians under Prince Eugene defeated the Turks (1697).

**Seoul** S Korea. Formerly (1910–45) Keijo. Capital, in the Han R. valley 25 m. ENE of Inchon, its seaport. Pop. (1966) 3,805,261. Industrial centre. Tanning, flour milling, railway engineering. Manufactures textiles. Also a cultural centre. Seat of 4 universities (1905, 1919, 1946, 1956). Has remnants of the ancient walls, and has been much modernized in the 20th cent. Became capital of Korea in the late 14th cent. As

Keijo, seat of Japanese government 1910–45. Became capital of S Korea 1948. Suffered severely in the Korean War (1950–51).

Sept Îles (Seven Islands) Canada. Port in E Quebec, on the N shore of the St Lawrence R. estuary. Pop. (1966) 18,950. Terminus of the railway from the Schefferville (Knob Lake) iron mines (1954). Dock capacity 10 million tons of shipping annually.

Sequoia National Park USA. Park on the W slopes of the Sierra Nevada, California, from the upper Kings R. (N) to the upper Tule R. (S). Area 602 sq. m. Established (1890) to preserve remarkable groves of sequoia trees, which are found in the W half, W of the N–S granite ridge known as the Great Western Divide, at heights of 4,000–8,000 ft. The largest trees are about 300 ft tall and are probably 1,500 to 3,000 years old.

Seraing Belgium. Industrial town in Liège province, on the Meuse R. 3 m. SW of Liège. Pop. (1968) 40,850. Coalmining. Manufactures steel, locomotives, machinery, glass. Its industrial expansion was due to John Cockerill, an Englishman, who founded the iron and steel works (1817); the first Belgian locomotive was built at these works in 1835.

Serampore India. Industrial town in W Bengal, on the Hooghly R. 12 m. NNW of Calcutta. Pop. (1961) 91,521. Important for jute and cotton milling. A Danish settlement from 1755; purchased by Britain 1845.

Serbia Yugoslavia. Constituent republic of Yugoslavia, including the autonomous province of Vojvodina and the autonomous region of Kosovo–Metohija. Area 34,107 sq. m. Pop. (1961) 7,642,227. Cap. Belgrade, also the federal capital. Bounded on the N by Hungary, on the E by Rumania and Bulgaria, and on the SW by Albania. Although generally mountainous, it is in the main agricultural, producing wheat, maize, vines, etc. Minerals include copper and antimony. Chief towns Belgrade, Niš, Kragujevac, Leskovac. The Serbs settled here in the 7th cent., were converted to Christianity in the 9th cent., and founded an independent kingdom; but after their defeat at Kosovo (1389) they were subject to the Turks. They regained their independence in 1878, forming a kingdom in 1882, but friction with Austria led to the 1st World War, after which they became the nucleus of the new Kingdom of the Serbs, Croats, and Slovenes, or Yugoslavia (1918).

Sercq ◊ Sark.

Seremban Malaysia. Capital of the state of Negri Sémbilan, in Malaya, 45 m. SE of Kuala Lumpur. Pop. 35,000. Linked by rail with Port Dickson. Centre of a region producing rubber and tin.

Seret River ◊ Siret River.

Sergipe Brazil. Second smallest state, in the NE. Area 8,490 sq. m. Pop. (1960) 760,273. Cap. Aracajú. A low coastal plain rising to a low plateau inland. Produces sugar-cane, coconuts, cotton, rice in the lowlands. Cattle raised on the plateau.

Seria Brunei. Town on the coast 55 m. SW of Brunei. Pop. 20,000. Centre of an important oilfield. Much oil exported; remainder sent by pipeline to the refinery at Lutong (Sarawak).

Seringapatam (Srirangapatnam) India. Former capital of Mysore state (1610–1799), on an island in the Cauvery R. 7 m. NNE of Mysore. Pop. 8,000. Famous for its fortress, taken by the British in 1799, and for the tombs of Tippoo Sultan and his father, Hyder Ali.

Serov USSR. Industrial town in the Sverdlovsk region, RSFSR, 190 m. N of Sverdlovsk. Pop. (1970) 100,000. Important metallurgical centre. Manufactures special steels etc.

Serowe Botswana. Town in the E 270 m. NNE of Mafeking (S Africa). Pop. (1964) 34,182. Capital of the Bamangwato tribe. Market town.

Serpukhov USSR. Industrial town in RSFSR, on the Oka R. at the confluence with the Nara R. 60 m. S of Moscow. Pop. (1970) 124,000. Important textile centre (cotton, wool, flax). Sawmilling, metal working, etc. Trade in grain, timber, etc. From the 14th to the 16th cent. its fortress protected Moscow from the S.

Sérrai (Serres, Seres) Greece. 1. Nome in Macedonia bounded on the N by Bulgaria. Area 1,566 sq. m. Pop. (1961) 248,045. Drained by the Struma R. Produces cotton, tobacco, cereals.
2. Ancient Sirrhae. Capital of Sérrai nome, 43 m. NE of Thessaloníki. Pop. (1961) 40,063. Commercial centre in a fertile region known to the Turks as the Golden Plain. Trade in tobacco, cotton, cereals. Manufactures cotton goods, cigarettes.

Sète (Cette) France. Seaport in the Hérault department 18 m. SW of Montpellier, on a narrow strip of land separating the Étang de Thau from the Gulf of Lions. Pop. (1968) 41,044. Chief Mediterranean seaport after

Marseille. Exports wine, petroleum products, etc. Fishing. Oil refining, distilling. Manufactures chemicals, cement, wine casks. Founded (1666) by Colbert and developed as the terminus of the Canal du Midi, which, with the Rhône–Sète Canal, links it with the interior. Severely damaged in the 2nd World War. Birthplace of Paul Valéry (1871–1945), the poet.

**Sete Quedas** ◊ *Paraná River*.

**Sétif** Algeria. Town in the NE at a height of 3,500 ft, 20 m. S of Djebel Bator (6,575 ft) and 70 m. WSW of Constantine. Pop. (1967) 98,000. On the railway from Algiers to Constantine and Tunis. Grain and livestock market. Flour milling.

**Settle** England. Small town in the W Riding of Yorkshire, on the R. Ribble 13 m. NW of Skipton. Pop. (rural district, 1961) 13,782. At the foot of Castleberg cliff in a picturesque limestone region. Market town. Tanning, cotton milling. An excellent centre for seeing the limestone country of the Pennines: Ingleborough, Penyghent, Ribblesdale, Malham Cove, etc.

**Setúbal** Portugal. Capital of the Setúbal district, on the N side of the Bay of Setúbal (the estuary of the Sado, Marateca, and São Martinho rivers) 18 m. SE of Lisbon. Pop. (1960) 44,605. Seaport. Exports oranges, grapes, wine, salt. Fishing. Sardine canning, boat-building. Manufactures fertilizers, cement, etc. Has a 16th-cent. castle built by Philip III of Spain, but most of its old buildings were destroyed in the earthquake of 1755.

**Sevastopol (Sebastopol)** USSR. Seaport on the SW coast of Crimea, in the Ukrainian SSR. Pop. (1970) 229,000. An excellent natural harbour; leading naval base and shipbuilding centre. Fish processing, tanning, flour milling, etc. Has a famous marine biological station. Popular seaside resort. On the peninsula just W are the ruins of an ancient Greek colony founded in the 5th cent. B.C. During the Crimean War it was captured and destroyed by British, French, and Turkish forces after an 11-month siege (1854–5), and scarcely a dozen buildings escaped unharmed. During the 2nd World War it fell to the Germans after an 8-month siege (1942).

**Seven Islands** ◊ *Sept Îles*.

**Sevenoaks** England. Residential urban district in Kent 20 m. SE of London. Pop. (1961) 17,604. Market town. Pleasantly situated in the North Downs. Has a school founded (1432) by Sir William Sevenoke,

and the 'Vine', said to be the oldest cricket ground in England. To the E is Knole, a mansion built partly in the 15th cent. by Archbishop Bourchier.

**Severn River** England/Wales. River 210 m. long rising on the NE slope of Plynlimmon, in SW Montgomeryshire, Wales, flowing generally NE at first and then following a roughly semicircular course and entering the Bristol Channel. The chief towns on its course are Welshpool (Wales) and Shrewsbury, Worcester, Tewkesbury, and Gloucester (England). Its main tributaries are the Vyrnwy, Stour, Teme, and Warwickshire Avon; it is joined by the Wye and Bristol Avon at about the point where its estuary enters the Bristol Channel. The canals which link it with the Thames, Trent, and other rivers are little used, but the Gloucester and Berkeley Canal (from Sharpness) allows small vessels to reach Gloucester. Owing to its funnel-shaped estuary, the Severn is subject to a high bore which may travel as far upstream as Tewkesbury. The new road suspension bridge over the river between Aust (Glos.) and Beachley (Mon.) was opened in 1966, replacing the old ferry service for cars and passengers.

**Seville (Sp. Sevilla)** Spain. **1.** Inland province in Andalusia. Area 5,408 sq. m. Pop. (1961) 1,234,435. Drained by the Guadalquivir R. Mainly agricultural; produces olive oil, wine, cereals, etc.
**2.** Ancient Hispalis. Capital of Seville province, the chief city of Andalusia, on the Guadalquivir R. 54 m. from the Atlantic Ocean. Pop. (1967) 598,327. A major port and industrial centre. Exports wine, olives and olive oil, citrus fruits, cork. Manufactures textiles, pottery, pharmaceutical goods, soap, etc. This colourful city is best known for its many historical and artistic associations. Its 15th/16th-cent. Gothic cathedral, one of the largest churches in the world, has a campanile of Moorish origin, the Giralda, 295 ft high, and is decorated with works by Murillo and other great Spanish painters. Near by are the 12th-cent. Alcazar, probably the outstanding monument to the Moorish occupation; the Lonja or exchange, containing the priceless Archives of the Indies; and the 17th-cent. archbishop's palace. There are paintings by the Spanish masters in many of the churches as well as in the museum. University (1502). Captured by Julius Caesar 45 B.C. Prospered under the Moors (712–1248), declined, flourished in the 16th and 17th cent.

again declined, but has again revived in the 20th cent. Birthplace of Velázquez (1599–1660) and Murillo (1617–82).

Sèvres France. Suburb WSW of Paris, in the Hauts-de-Seine department on the Seine R. Pop. (1968) 20,288. Famous for the manufacture of porcelain, established here in 1756, the factory being in the park of St Cloud. A ceramics museum and school.

Seward USA. Town and port in Alaska, at the head of Resurrection Bay 75 m. S of Anchorage. Pop. 2,000. Terminus of the Alaska Railway from Fairbanks. Supply centre for the interior and for visiting hunters and fishermen.

Seychelles Indian Ocean. Group of 85 islands and islets 600 m. NE of the Malagasy Republic, forming a British Crown Colony. Area 100 sq. m. Pop. (1967) 48,730. Cap. Victoria (pop. 12,000) on Mahé (56 sq. m.), the largest and most important island. Other islands Praslin, La Digue, Silhouette. Export copra, cinnamon, etc. Fishing; breadfruit is an important food. First occupied by the French. Taken by the British 1794. A dependency of Mauritius 1814–1903, and then became a separate Crown Colony.

Sfax Tunisia. Seaport and second largest city, on the N shore of the Gulf of Gabès 135 m. SSE of Tunis. Pop. (1966) 249,991. Linked by rail with Tunis and Gafsa (phosphate mines). Exports phosphates, olive oil, sponges, etc. Fishing (octopuses, sponges). Manufactures olive oil, soap, etc. Consists of a modern quarter built in European style and an Arab town enclosed by the ancient walls.

's Gravenhage ⇨ Hague, The.

Shadwell England. District in the Greater London borough of Tower Hamlets (E), on the N bank of the R. Thames adjoining Wapping.

Shaftesbury England. Municipal borough in Dorset, on a hill 18 m. WSW of Salisbury. Pop. (1961) 3,366. Market town. Remains of an abbey founded (880) by Alfred the Great, whose daughter was the first abbess. Known locally by its old name, Shaston.

Shahjahanpur India. Town in Uttar Pradesh 43 m. SE of Bareilly. Pop. (1961) 110,432. Sugar milling etc. Trade in grain, sugarcane, etc. Named after Shah Jahan, in whose reign it was founded (1647).

Shaker Heights USA. Residential town in NE Ohio just SE and virtually a suburb of Cleveland. Pop. (1960) 36,460. Expanded rapidly in the 1920s.

Shakhty USSR. Formerly Aleksandrovsk-Grushevsky. Industrial town in the Rostov region, RSFSR, 40 m. NE of Rostov. Pop. (1970) 205,000. Important coalmining centre in the E of the Donets Basin. Manufactures machinery, clothing, furniture, etc.

Shanghai China. The largest city in China and one of the world's principal seaports, in SE Kiangsu but an independent municipality; stands on the Hwang-pu R. 14 m. from its junction with the Yangtse R. estuary and 165 m. ESE of Nanking. Pop. (1957) 6,900,000. Its importance as a seaport is due largely to the vast, populous hinterland of the Yangtse valley and its favourable position for trans-Pacific and coastal trade. Exports raw silk, hog bristles, tea, tung oil, etc. Also a major industrial centre. Important textile manufactures (cotton, wool, silk). Also shipbuilding, engineering, tanning, rice milling; manufactures chemicals, matches, paper. As a cultural centre second only to Peking. Seat of the Futan University (1905) and several other educational institutions; important publishing industry. Most of the city is on a tidal flat on the left bank of the Hwang-pu at the mouth of Soochow Creek, and its commercial life is centred round the confluence in the former International Settlement, where banks, business houses, hotels, and large stores line the boulevards and streets; here is its best-known thoroughfare, the famous Bund or waterfront. Factories and warehouses are clustered in Hongkew, in the NE part of the former Settlement, and in the suburb of Pootung, on the opposite bank of the Hwang-pu; the residential districts are in the outer suburbs.

A mere fishing village in the 11th-cent., walled only in the 14th cent., Shanghai was still of small significance till the mid 19th cent. Then the Treaty of Nanking (1842) opened it to foreign trade, and the British (1843) and US (1862) Concessions were consolidated into the International Settlement (1863), which, with the French Concession (1849), enjoyed autonomy and extra-territorial rights. In 1941 the city was taken by the Japanese, and the International Settlement (1943) and the French Concession (1946) were relinquished. In 1949 the Communists entered Shanghai, and foreign business interests were thereafter compelled to withdraw.

**Shanklin** ♢ *Sandown-Shanklin.*

**Shannon River** Irish Republic. Chief river of Ireland, 240 m. long, rising on Cuilcagh Mountain, Co. Cavan, and flowing generally S through Loughs Allen, Boderg, Forbes, Ree, Derg to Limerick. Here it turns W into a wide estuary, nearly 60 m. long, entering the Atlantic Ocean between Co. Clare (N) and Counties Limerick and Kerry (S). Chief tributaries the Suck, Brosna, Little Brosna, Deel. Principal towns on the banks Carrick-on-Shannon, Athlone, Limerick. At Ardnacrusha, 3 m. N of Limerick, is Ireland's main hydro-electric power station. At Rineanna, 13 m. W of Limerick, is Shannon airport.

**Shansi** China. Inland province in the N, bounded on the N by Inner Mongolia. Area 60,394 sq. m. Pop. (1957) 15,960,000. Cap. Taiyuan. Generally mountainous; bordered on the W and S by the Hwang-ho and crossed by the Fen-ho. Rainfall is somewhat uncertain, but wheat, millets, and other crops are cultivated. Extensive deposits of coal, with important mines at Tatung.

**Shan State** Burma. Constituent part of the Union, in the E, bounded on the E by China and on the SE by Laos and Thailand. Area 58,000 sq. m. Pop. 1,700,000 (largely Shans, a Thai people who are migrants from SW China). Consists essentially of the Shan plateau, with an average height of 2,000–4,000 ft, cut N–S by the gorge of the Salween R. Formerly divided into 6 Northern and 36 Southern Shan States, which were semi-independent, but in 1922 these were united into the Federation of Shan States. When Burma became independent (1947) they were combined with the Wa States of the extreme NE to form the Shan State.

**Shantung** China. Maritime province in the E, including the Shantung peninsula jutting E into the Yellow Sea. Area 59,174 sq. m. Pop. (1957) 54,030,000. Cap. Tsinan. Much of the province consists of the fertile alluvial plain of the lower Hwang-ho, but there are mountains in the central area and the peninsula where deforestation has led to serious soil erosion. Wheat, millet, kaoliang, and groundnuts cultivated on the lowlands. Considerable deposits of iron ore and coal. Chief towns Tsingtao, Tsinan.

**Shap** England. Village in Westmorland 10 m. SSE of Penrith. Pop. 1,150. Granite quarrying. Remains of the 13th-cent. Shap Abbey.

**Shari (Chari) River** Central African Republic/Chad. River 1,400 m. long rising in the N of the Central African Republic, flowing generally NW, passing through Chad, forming part of the Chad–Cameroun border, and entering L. Chad (of which it is the principal feeder) by a broad delta.

**Sharja (Sharjah).** Seaport on the Persian Gulf 8 m. NE of Dubai and chief town of the sheikhdom of Sharja and Kalba, one of the Trucial States of E Arabia under British protection. Pop. 5,000.

**Sharon** Israel. Plain in the W between the Mediterranean Sea (W) and the hills of Samaria (E), extending from Haifa in the N to Tel Aviv in the S. Generally fertile. Important occupations the cultivation of citrus fruits and vines, mixed farming, poultry rearing.

**Sharon** USA. Industrial town in Pennsylvania, on the Shenango R. near the Ohio border. Pop. (1960) 25,267. Manufactures steel, textiles, chemicals, etc.

**Shasi** China. River port in Hupei province, on the Yangtse R. 120 m. WSW of Wuhan. Pop. 86,000. Textile manufactures, flour milling. Trade in cotton, grain.

**Shatt-al-Arab** Iraq. River 120 m. long in the SE formed by the union of the Euphrates and Tigris rivers, flowing SE past Basra (Iraq), Khorramshahr and Abadan (Iran) to the Persian Gulf. Flanked by marshes and date groves. The lower part forms the Iraq–Iran border.

**Shawinigan** Canada. Industrial town in Quebec, on the St Maurice R. 18 m. NW of Trois Rivières. Pop. (1966) 30,777. Manufactures wood pulp and paper, aluminium, chemicals, textiles, etc. Power is derived from the large hydroelectric plants at the falls.

**Shcherbakov** ♢ *Rybinsk.*

**Sheba** ♢ *Saba.*

**Sheboygan** USA. Port and industrial town in Wisconsin, on L. Michigan at the mouth of the Sheboygan R. 50 m. N of Milwaukee. Pop. (1960) 45,747. Centre of a dairy-farming region. Trade in cheese. Manufactures furniture, footwear, knitwear, etc. Called 'the city of cheese, chairs, children, and churches'.

**Sheen** ♢ *Richmond-upon-Thames.*

**Sheerness** England. Town in Kent, in the NW of the Isle of Sheppey. Pop. (1961) 14,123. Port formerly with a naval dockyard, in the old section known as Blue Town, founded (17th cent.) and fortified to protect the entrance to the R. Thames and the R. Medway. The modern part of the town, which functions as a holiday resort, is divided into Banks Town, Marine Town, and Mile Town. From 1968 part of the municipal borough of ◊ *Queenborough in Sheppey.*

**Sheffield** England. County borough in the W Riding of Yorkshire, on the R. Don at the confluence with the Sheaf 33 m. ESE of Manchester. Pop. (1961) 493,954. A leading iron and steel centre, esp. for the manufacture of special steels, e.g. stainless steel. Produces cutlery, tools, machinery, bicycles, rails, armour plate, etc. Manufactures silverware, glassware, optical instruments, food products. The 14th/15th-cent. cruciform parish church of St Peter and St Paul became the cathedral in 1914. Many other notable public buildings, inc. the City Hall (1932), the Ruskin Museum, and the Graves Art Gallery. The university (1905) began as Firth College, founded (1879) by a steel manufacturer. Iron was already being smelted here at the time of the Norman Conquest, the essential raw materials being available near by. Celebrated for its cutlery by the 14th cent. With the Industrial Revolution the steel industry expanded rapidly; an outstanding development was Bessemer's establishment of a steelworks (1860) to manufacture cheap steel by his own process. Many further improvements were made in subsequent years. Severely damaged by bombing in the 2nd World War.

**Sheksna River** USSR. River 100 m. long rising in L. Beloye, RSFSR, and flowing generally S to the Rybinsk Reservoir, forming part of the Mariinsk canal system. Before the filling of the Rybinsk Reservoir (1941) it joined the Volga R. at Rybinsk.

**Shellharbour** Australia. Town in a coal-mining district of New South Wales 15 m. S of Wollongong. Pop. (1968) 26,600.

**Shenandoah National Park** USA. Park in N Virginia in the Blue Ridge Mountains. Area 302 sq. m. Established 1935. Heavily forested, renowned for its scenery. Highest point Hawksbill Mountain (4,049 ft). The Skyline Drive runs its entire length (105 m.).

**Shenandoah River** USA. River 55 m. long, formed by the union of the North Fork and the South Fork, flowing generally NE through Virginia and W Virginia to join the Potomac R. near Harper's Ferry. The picturesque Shenandoah Valley is noted for orchards and pastures. Scene of much fighting in the American Civil War.

**Shensi** China. Province in the NW, with the Great Wall running near its N boundary with Inner Mongolia. Area 75,580 sq. m. Pop. (1957) 18,130,000. Cap. Sian. Largely mountainous, esp. in the S, where it is crossed W–E by the Tsinling Shan; N of the latter is the valley of the Wei-ho (also extending W–E), where Sian and Paoki (railway junction) are situated. Wheat, millet, cotton, fruits cultivated. Large coal deposits.

**Shenyang** China. Formerly Mukden. Capital of Liaoning province in the NE (Manchuria), on the Hun-ho, tributary of the Liao-ho, 390 m. ENE of Peking. Pop. (1957) 2,411,000. Chief commercial centre in the NE. Important railway junction. Trade in grain, soya beans, etc. Engineering. Manufactures textiles, chemicals, matches, paper, etc. In the 17th cent. the Manchu capital, and at times known as Fengtien, it expanded rapidly after Manchukuo was founded by the Japanese (1932).

**Shepparton** Australia. Town and railway junction in Victoria, on the Goulburn R. 100 m. NNE of Melbourne. Pop. (1966) 17,523. In a rich irrigated agricultural and stock-rearing district which yields wheat, wool, dairy produce, wine, etc. Fruit canning, meat packing.

**Sheppey, Isle of** England. Island 10 m. long and up to 4 m. wide off the N coast of Kent, in the Thames estuary, separated from the mainland by a narrow channel, the Swale. Low-lying and fertile. Produces cereals, vegetables. The large flocks of sheep justify the name, which means 'Island of Sheep'. Chief towns Sheerness, Queenborough. In 1968 the rural district of Sheppey became part of the municipal borough of ◊ *Queenborough in Sheppey.*

**Shepshed** England. Urban district in Leicestershire 4 m. W of Loughborough. Pop. (1961) 7,179. Manufactures hosiery.

**Shepton Mallet** England. Urban district in Somerset 16 m. SSW of Bath at the foot of the Mendip Hills. Pop. (1961) 5,518. Market town. Bacon and ham curing, brewing, glove making. Has a market cross dating from 1500, a church with a 13th-cent. oak roof, and a 17th-cent. grammar school.

**Sherborne** England. Urban district in Dorset, on the R. Yeo 5 m. E of Yeovil. Pop. (1961) 6,062. Market town. Glove making, engineering etc. Once capital of Wessex, it became the seat of a bishopric under St Aldhelm (705); the see was transferred to Old Sarum 1075. The Abbey church is a magnificent example of the Perpendicular style; some of the other Abbey buildings are now occupied by the well-known Sherborne School, founded in the 16th cent.

**Sherbrooke** Canada. Industrial town in Quebec, on the St Francis R. 80 m. E of Montreal. Pop. (1966) 75,690 (about 80 per cent French-speaking). Manufactures hosiery, textiles, clothing, leather goods, mining machinery, etc. Metropolis of the Eastern Townships. Commercial centre of a dairy-farming region. Seat of the Sherbrooke University (1954, Roman Catholic).

**Sheringham** England. Urban district in Norfolk, on the North Sea coast 4 m. WNW of Cromer. Pop. (1961) 4,836. Small fishing port (lobsters). Seaside resort.

**'s Hertogenbosch (Den Bosch)** Netherlands. Capital of N Brabant province, at the confluence of the Dommel and Aa rivers 30 m. SSE of Utrecht. Pop. (1968) 80,425. Railway junction. Industrial centre. Manufactures bicycles, cigars, etc. Famous 14th/16th-cent. Gothic cathedral. Birthplace of Hieronymus Bosch (1450–1516), the painter.

**Sherwood Forest** England. Ancient forest in Nottinghamshire stretching between Nottingham and Worksop, a royal hunting ground and well known as the traditional home of Robin Hood and his men. Most of the original forest has long since been cleared, but portions remain – principally in the Dukeries.

**Shetland Islands (Shetlands, Zetland)** Scotland. Archipelago of over 100 islands and islets NE of the Orkneys, the largest being Mainland, Yell, and Unst, forming the county of Zetland. Area 551 sq. m. Pop. (1961) 17,809. County town Lerwick. The islands are bleak, almost treeless, and largely infertile. Shetland ponies, sheep, and cattle raised. Important occupations fishing, fish curing, and knitting; Fair Isle is famous for its characteristically patterned knitted goods. Under Scandinavian rule 875–1468 (◊ *Orkney Islands*); the people still show evidence of their Norse origin in custom and speech.

**Shibin el Kôm** United Arab Republic. Capital of the Menûfiya governorate, on the Nile delta 35 m. NW of Cairo. Pop. (1960) 55,000. Rail centre in an agricultural area producing cereals, cotton. Manufactures cigarettes, textiles.

**Shifnal** England. Market town in Shropshire 16 m. ESE of Shrewsbury. Pop. (rural district, 1961) 14,234. Has a 12th-cent. church. In the neighbourhood is the 18th-cent. Haughton Hall.

**Shigatse** China. Commercial town in Tibet (now an autonomous region of China), in the SE, near the Tsangpo (Brahmaputra) R. 135 m. WSW of Lhasa, to which it is second only in importance. Pop. 20,000. Just SW is the famous monastery of Tashi Lumpo.

**Shihkiachwang** China. Town in Hopei province 165 m. SW of Peking. Pop. 598,000. Railway junction. Industrial and commercial centre. Railway engineering. Manufactures textiles (cotton), machinery, etc. Only a small village at the beginning of the century, it developed rapidly with the building of the railways.

**Shikarpur** Pakistan. Town in the Khairpur Division, W Pakistan (N Sind), 20 m. NW of Sukkur. Pop. 63,000. Commands the trade route through the Bolan Pass. Trade in grain, precious stones, etc. Engineering, rice and flour milling. Manufactures cotton goods, carpets, etc.

**Shikoku** Japan. Smallest of the country's 4 main islands, S of Honshu and E of Kyushu. Area (with offshore islands) 7,248 sq. m. Interior mountainous and heavily forested. Rice, tobacco, and soya beans grown on the lowlands. Divided into 4 prefectures: Kagawa, Tokushima, Kochi, Ehime. Chief towns Matsuyama, Takamatsu.

**Shildon** England. Urban district in Durham 2 m. SSE of Bishop Auckland. Pop. (1961) 14,372. Coalmining centre which includes New Shildon. Railway engineering.

**Shillelagh** Irish Republic. Village in Co. Wicklow, on the R. Shillelagh 42 m. SSW of Dublin. An ancient oak forest. Gave its name to an Irish cudgel, originally oak and later blackthorn.

**Shillong** India. Capital of Assam, at a height of 4,978 ft in the Khasi Hills 310 m. NE of Calcutta. Pop. (1961) 102,398. Resort. Commercial centre. Trade in rice, cotton, fruit, etc. Became capital of the Khasi States in 1864 and of Assam in 1874. Largely destroyed by earthquake (1897) and rebuilt.

**Shimoga** India. Town in Mysore on the Tunga R. 155 m. NW of Bangalore. Pop. (1961) 63,764. Cotton ginning, rice milling.

**Shimonoseki** Japan. Seaport and industrial town in the extreme SW of Honshu, in Yamaguchi prefecture. Pop. (1965) 254,380. Connected with Kitakyushu (Kyushu) by rail and road tunnels beneath Shimonoseki (Kammon) Strait. Shipbuilding, engineering, metal working. Fishing, fish processing. Manufactures textiles, chemicals. The treaty ending the

Sino-Japanese War was signed here (1895).

**Shipka Pass** Bulgaria. Pass (4,166 ft) through the Balkan Mountains on the road between Kazanluk and Gabrovo. Scene of fierce battles in the Russo-Turkish War (1877–8).

**Shipley** England. Urban district in the W Riding of Yorkshire, on the R. Aire 3 m. NNW of Bradford. Pop. (1961) 29,762. Manufactures woollen and worsted goods. Engineering etc. Includes the model town of Saltaire, built (1853) by Sir Titus Salt for his mill workers.

**Shiraz** Iran. Capital of Fars province, at a height of 5,000 ft on a plain surrounded by mountains 110 m. ENE of Bushire. Pop. (1966) 269,865. Commercial centre in an agricultural region producing cereals, sugar-beet, vines, etc. Manufactures textiles, rugs and carpets, cement, etc. University (1948). A picturesque city with a pleasant climate. At times the capital of Persia. Birthplace of two great Persian poets, Sadi (1184–1291) and Hafiz (1300–1388), whose tombs are features of the town.

**Shiré Highlands** Malawi. Uplands in the S, to the E of the Shiré R., at a height of about 3,000 ft, rising in parts to 5,800 ft. The main area of tea and tobacco cultivation. ⟡ *Malawi*.

**Shiré River** Malawi/Moçambique. River 370 m. long, a tributary of the Zambezi. The only outlet of L. Malawi (Nyasa), from which it flows generally S. In the middle course it forms cataracts and rapids; the most famous are the Murchison Falls. Leaving Malawi near Port Herald, it enters Moçambique and joins the Zambezi near Vila Fontes, 100 m. from the Indian Ocean.

**Shizuoka** Japan. Capital of Shizuoka prefecture, SE Honshu, 90 m. SW of Tokyo. Pop. (1965) 367,705. Commercial and industrial centre in a tea-growing region. Trade in tea, oranges. Tea processing and packing. Manufactures machinery, chemicals, etc. University (1949).

**Shkodër** (Italian **Scutari**) Albania. Capital of the Shkodër region in the NW, at the SE end of L. Shkodër where the Bojana R. leaves the lake. Pop. (1967) 50,000. Manufactures textiles, cement, etc. Trade in wool, grain, tobacco, etc. Has an ancient Venetian citadel and a Roman Catholic cathedral. Once capital of Illyria; taken by the Romans 168 B.C., later held by Serbs, Venetians, and Turks.

**Shkodër, Lake** Albania/Yugoslavia. Largest lake in the Balkan peninsula, on the Yugo-slav-Albanian border but mainly within Yugoslavia. Area 135 sq. m. Average depth normally 20–25 ft but deeper and more extensive after winter rains. Picturesque, well stocked with fish. Fed by the Morača R. Formerly an inlet of the Adriatic, but is now separated from the latter by an alluvial isthmus and is drained by the Bojana (Buenë) R.

**Shoeburyness** England. Former urban district in Essex, since 1933 incorporated in Southend-on-Sea (3 m. W), on the N side of the Thames estuary and near the promontory of Shoeburyness, well known for its school of gunnery.

**Sholapur** India. Industrial town and railway junction in Maharashtra, 225 m. SE of Bombay. Pop. (1961) 337,583. Important cotton industry. Also manufactures carpets, glass, leather goods, etc. Trade in grain, cotton, oilseeds.

**Shoreditch** England. Former metropolitan borough in E London, N of the R. Thames, including Hoxton; from 1965 part of the Greater London borough of Hackney. Pop. (1961) 40,465. Residential and industrial; furniture making and printing important. The Geffrye Museum has an interesting collection of furniture and woodwork. The first theatre in London was built here by James Burbage in 1576.

**Shoreham-by-Sea** England. Urban district in W Sussex, near the mouth of the R. Adur 6 m. W of Brighton. Pop. (1961) 17,391. Seaport. Old Shoreham was an important port in medieval times, but its harbour was silted up and it was superseded by New Shoreham and is now 1 m. inland. The urban district includes Kingston-by-Sea. Near by is Lancing College, the public school. Charles II escaped to France from Shoreham in 1651.

**Shreveport** USA. Industrial town in Louisiana, on the Red R. 210 m. NW of Baton Rouge. Pop. (1960) 164,372. Centre of an oil and natural-gas region. Important oil refineries and railway workshops. Manufactures cotton goods, wood products, etc.

**Shrewsbury** England. County town and municipal borough of Shropshire, on the R. Severn, partly within a southward loop of the river. Pop. (1961) 49,726. A picturesque and historic market town. Engineering, tanning, brewing, etc. Outstanding among its buildings is the 11th-cent. red sandstone castle, restored by Telford and belonging to the corporation, and there are many fine half-timbered houses and two ancient bridges, the English and the Welsh. Its early importance was due to its commanding position with respect to routes into Wales and along the border; in the more peaceful days of the late Middle Ages and Tudor and Elizabethan times, when commerce took the place of conflict with the Welsh, it prospered, and in the late 16th cent. were erected such buildings as the Market Hall and Ireland's and Owen's mansions. The famous public school (founded 1552) was attended by Sir Philip Sidney, Samuel Butler – author and grandson of a headmaster of the school – and Charles Darwin (1809–82), who, like Admiral John Benbow (1653–1702), was a native of Shrewsbury.

Shropshire England. County in the W Midlands, bounded on the W and NW by the Welsh counties of Radnor, Montgomery, Denbigh, and Flint. Area 1,347 sq. m. Pop. (1961) 297,313. County town Shrewsbury. To the N and E of the Severn, which crosses the county, it is generally low-lying and level apart from the isolated Wrekin (1,334 ft), but to the S and W of the river it is hilly, rising to 1,792 ft in the Clee Hills and 1,696 ft in Long Mynd. Mainly agricultural, with dairy farming in the lowlands (N) and cattle and sheep rearing on the uplands (S). The coal measures around Coalbrookdale are virtually exhausted, but there are still vestiges of the former iron industry. Castles at Ludlow, Shrewsbury, Bridgnorth, and elsewhere, in varying stages of preservation, testify to the stormy border history of the region. Chief towns Shrewsbury, Wenlock, Wellington, Oakengates, Oswestry.

Shumen ♦ Kolarovgrad.

Sialkot Pakistan. Town in the Lahore Division (Punjab), W Pakistan, 65 m. NNE of Lahore. Pop. (1961) 164,346. Manufactures sports goods, textiles, carpets, leather goods, etc. Trade in grain and sugar-cane. The shrine of Guru Nanak is a Sikh place of pilgrimage.

Siam ♦ Thailand.

Sian China. Formerly Changan, Siking. Capital of Shensi province, in the NW, 530 m. SW of Peking in the valley of the Wei-ho. Pop. (1957) 1,310,000. Important route centre, on the Lunghai railway (E–W trunk line). Industrial and commercial centre. Flour milling, tanning. Manufactures iron and steel, textiles, chemicals, cement, etc. Trade in grain, tea, tobacco, etc. Seat of the North-Western University (1937). An ancient walled city, at various times capital of China from the 3rd cent. B.C. Visited by Marco Polo in the 13th cent. In the provincial museum is a Nestorian stone tablet with a lengthy inscription dating from the 8th cent. Here in 1936 Chiang Kai-shek was kidnapped by Chang Hsueh-liang, an incident which resulted in the former combining with the Communists against the Japanese.

Siangtan China. Town in Hunan province, on the Siang R. 20 m. SSW of Changsha. Pop. 184,000. Manufactures textiles, cement, electrical equipment, etc. Trade in rice, tea, tung oil, etc. Mao Tse-tung (1893–    ) was born in a village near by.

Šibenik Yugoslavia. Adriatic seaport in Croatia 31 m. NW of Split. Pop. (1961) 26,253. Exports timber, bauxite, etc. Manufactures textiles, chemicals, etc. An ancient town, once the residence of the Croatian kings. Has a remarkable cathedral, begun in the 15th cent., built entirely in the local stone.

Siberia USSR. Region approximating to the Asiatic part of RSFSR, extending from the Ural Mountains to the Pacific Ocean and from the Arctic Ocean to the mountains and deserts of Central Asia. Area about 5,200,000 sq. m.

TOPOGRAPHY, CLIMATE, etc. May be divided into three main regions. In the W is the W Siberian Plain, a great flat area occupying the Ob R. basin and bounded by the Urals (W) and the Yenisei R. (E), to the S of which are the lofty Altai and W Sayan Mountains on the Mongolian border. Central Siberia has a much narrower plain along the Arctic Ocean, to the S of this the enormous Central Siberian Plateau, and to the S again the E Sayan Mountains, being bounded by the Lena R. E Siberia is a mainly highland region which includes the Yablonovy, Stanovoi, Verkhoyansk, Cherski, Kolyma, and Anadyr Ranges and the mountainous Kamchatka peninsula. All the main rivers of Siberia except the Amur flow into the Arctic Ocean and are frozen for most of the year. In the S is the world's deepest lake, L. Baikal. The climate is of the extreme continental type, with warm summers and exceptionally cold winters: Verkhoyansk, the so-called 'cold pole' of the earth, has a mean January temperature of −59° F. Precipitation is generally light, varying between 10 and 20 ins. annually. Along the Arctic coast the natural vegetation consists essentially of the mosses and lichens of the tundra, beneath which is a permanently frozen subsoil; to the S is the vast belt of taiga or coniferous forest, occupying most of Siberia; in the S W are the steppes, or grasslands, which have largely been cultivated.

RESOURCES, PEOPLE. Fishing is important along the Pacific coast and among the indigenous Chukchee, Koryak, and other tribes of the far N, many of whom also breed reindeer. Timber is exploited in the taiga and is transported down the Yenisei, for example, for export through the port of Igarka. Large quantities of furs are obtained from the forest animals. In the fertile soils of the S W, where agriculture is concentrated, wheat and oats are leading crops; beef and dairy cattle and sheep are raised in the S and S W. Mineral resources are considerable, the Kuznetsk coal basin having given rise to an important metallurgical industry. Iron ore is worked in the same region, and gold is widely distributed. From the First Five-year Plan (1928–32) industrial development was fostered by the Soviet government, was continued during the 2nd World War, and proved of great economic significance to the country when the German armies swept over European Russia to the gates of Moscow and Stalingrad (Volgograd).

The population is clustered mainly round the Trans-Siberian Railway and its branch lines, and here the principal cities, inc. Novosibirsk and Omsk, are to be found, with Vladivostok, terminus of the railway, the chief Pacific seaport; at the W end, in the Urals, the great centres of Sverdlovsk and Chelyabinsk form part of another important industrial region linked closely with the Kuznetsk Basin. A considerable majority of the population is of Russian origin, the native peoples largely inhabiting their National Areas – the Evenki, Koryak, Taimyr, and other National Areas, and the Autonomous Regions and Autonomous Republics.

HISTORY. The Russian conquest of Siberia began in 1581, when Cossacks led by Yermak crossed the Urals and took the khanate of Sibir. By 1639 the Russians, encountering little opposition from the natives, had reached the Sea of Okhotsk, and in 1648 Dezhnev sailed through the Bering Strait. Two centuries later Russian peasants had been settled along the left bank of the Amur R., a *fait accompli* recognized by China in 1860; the construction of the Trans-Siberian Railway

(1892–1905) led to settlement on a much larger scale. Under the Tsars, however, Siberia was treated more as a region of exile for political prisoners than as a region of development. During the Revolution and the ensuing Civil War many areas were controlled by the counter-revolutionaries, but when order was restored the planned economic development of Siberia was undertaken and has since continued, before and during the 2nd World War, with the help of forced labour and young volunteers, and accompanied by various administrative adjustments.

**Sibiu** (Ger. **Hermannstadt,** Hungarian **Nagyszeben**) Rumania. Capital of the Sibiu district, Transylvania, 135 m. NW of Bucharest. Pop. (1968) 115,156. Manufactures machinery, textiles, electrical equipment, paper, etc. Tanning, brewing, distilling. Picturesquely situated in a fertile valley. A Roman colony, resettled in the 12th cent. by colonists from Nuremberg, and has retained a medieval German appearance. Has a 14th/16th-cent. Gothic Protestant church, a 15th-cent. town hall, and a large Orthodox cathedral.

**Sibu** Malaysia. Town in Sarawak, on the Rajang R. 115 m. NE of Kuching. Pop. (1962) 29,630. Commercial centre. Accessible to large steamers. Trade in rubber, rice, sago, etc.

**Sicily** (Italian **Sicilia**) Italy. The largest and most populous island in the Mediterranean; with the small Lipari and Egadi Islands, Pantelleria, and Ustica, an autonomous region of Italy. Area (region) 9,926 sq. m. Pop. (1961) 4,711,783. Cap. Palermo. Divided into 9 provinces. Separated from mainland Italy by the narrow Strait of Messina. Ranges of mountains rising to over 6,000 ft run W–E across the N. The highest point is Mt Etna (10,741 ft), N of Catania, the only extensive plain. The coast is generally rocky and steep in the N and NE, flat in the S and SE. Summers are hot and dry and occasionally subject to the sirocco; winters are mild and rainy. Citrus and other fruits, vines, olives, cereals, and vegetables are cultivated on the coastal plains, but agriculture is backward and there is much poverty. Important tunny fisheries. Long one of the world's main sources of sulphur, but output has declined recently. A productive oilfield has been opened up in the SE. Industries are centred mainly on Palermo, Catania, and Messina.

Among the earliest inhabitants were the Siculi (after whom the island is named). The Phoenicians established trading posts along the coast, notably on the site of modern Palermo. They were followed from the 8th cent. B.C. by the Greeks, who founded settlements in the E and SE at Syracuse, Catania, Messina, etc. In the 5th cent. B.C. the Carthaginians crossed from Africa and occupied the W; after their defeat Sicily became a Roman colony (241 B.C.). After the fall of the Roman Empire it was conquered by Vandals (A.D. 440), Byzantines (535), Saracens (9th cent.), and, in the 11th cent., by the Normans, under whom it was for the first time both united and independent. Ruled by the Aragonese from the early 14th cent. and by Spain from the early 16th cent. and again 1738–1806. Formed, with Naples, the Kingdom of the Two Sicilies (1815). Garibaldi liberated it from the Bourbons (1860) and it was incorporated into Italy. During the early years of the 20th cent. there was considerable emigration. Under the Fascist régime the notorious Mafia (a secret society dating from the 15th cent.) was suppressed (1927). Occupied by the Allies (1943) in the 2nd World War.

**Sidcup** England. A mainly residential district, formerly part of the urban district of Chislehurst and Sidcup, in NW Kent; since 1965 the urban district has been divided between the Greater London boroughs of Bexley (N of the A20 road) and Bromley (S of the A20 road). Manufactures electrical, radio, and television equipment.

**Sidi-Bel-Abbès** Algeria. Town in the NW 30 m. S of Oran. Pop. (1967) 101,000. Commercial centre. Trade in cereals, wine, olives, livestock. Flour milling. Manufactures cement, furniture. Ancient walled town; became famous as the headquarters of the French Foreign Legion.

**Sidlaw Hills** Scotland. Range extending SW–NE through E Perthshire and SW Angus, rising to 1,492 ft.

**Sidmouth** England. Urban district in Devonshire, on Lyme Bay at the mouth of the R. Sid 13 m. ESE of Exeter. Pop. (1961) 11,139. Market town and seaside resort in a sheltered position between red sandstone cliffs. The Norman Lockyer observatory (1912) was attached to Exeter University in 1948.

**Sidon** ◊ *Saida*.

**Sidra, Gulf** of Libya. Ancient Syrtis Major. An inlet of the Mediterranean Sea stretch-

ing 300 m. from Benghazi (Cyrenaica) to Misurata (Tripolitania). Tunny and sponge fisheries. The coast is mainly desert. ◊ *Gabès, Gulf of*.

**Siebengebirge** Federal German Republic. In German, 'Seven Mountains'. Range of hills of volcanic origin extending along the right bank of the Rhine R. S of Bonn. Rises to 1,522 ft in Ölberg. Drachenfels (1,067 ft) is the best-known peak.

**Siedlce** Poland. Industrial town and railway junction in the Warsaw voivodship 55 m. E of Warsaw. Pop. (1968) 38,700. Manufactures cement, glass, soap, leather, etc. Under Austrian and then Russian administration during the Partitions of Poland; restored to the newly re-formed Poland 1921. Before the Nazi occupation (1939–44) about half the population were Jews.

**Siegburg** Federal German Republic. Industrial town and railway junction in N Rhine-Westphalia, on the Sieg R. 6 m. ENE of Bonn. Pop. (1963) 34,100. Manufactures machinery, chemicals, furniture, etc. Founded in the 11th cent. Flourished in the 15th and 16th cent. because of its pottery. Has a Benedictine abbey founded in the 11th cent.

**Siegen** Federal German Republic. Industrial town in N Rhine-Westphalia 45 m. ENE of Bonn on the Sieg R. Pop. (1963) 49,600. In an iron-mining region. Manufactures iron and steel etc. Birthplace of Rubens (1577–1640).

**Siena** Italy. Capital of Siena province, in Tuscany, 32 m. S of Florence. Pop. (1961) 61,453. In a beautiful setting on three hills. Much of the ancient walls and gates is preserved. Famous for its art treasures, esp. the many examples of medieval architecture: the 13th/14th-cent. cathedral, an outstanding example of Italian Gothic; the 13th/14th-cent. Gothic Palazzo Pubblico; the San Domenico, San Francesco, and other churches. In the Piccolomini Library adjoining the cathedral are Pinturicchio's celebrated 16th-cent. frescoes. Many paintings of the Sienese school. University (1300). A historic horse race is held annually in the Piazza del Campo in which horses from the 17 districts compete for the *palio* (banner). An Etruscan city, Siena was a Roman colony in the time of Augustus. The chief banking and trading centre in Italy in the early 13th cent., came into conflict with Florence, and gradually lost political power through military defeat and internal dissension. Birthplace of St Catherine of Siena (1347–80).

**Sierra de Guadalupe** Spain. Mountain range in Cáceres province in the W, about 30 m. long and rising to 4,734 ft, between the Tagus and Guadiana rivers. The small town of Guadalupe in the range has a 14th-cent. monastery, built to contain the shrine of Our Lady of Guadalupe. Guadalupe Hidalgo (Mexico) was named after it.

**Sierra de Guadarrama** Spain. Mountain range NW and N of Madrid extending about 110 m. NE along the border of Madrid and Segovia provinces, rising to 8,100 ft in the Peñalara. Well forested; yields much timber. Several winter-sports centres and sanatoria on its slopes.

**Sierra Leone.** Independent state in the Commonwealth of Nations, formerly a British colony and protectorate, in W Africa, bounded by Guinea (N and E), Liberia (SE), and the Atlantic Ocean (SW). Area 27,925 sq. m. Pop. (1963) 2,183,000. Cap. Freetown. Much of the coastline is flat and lined with mangrove swamps, but inland the country rises to a plateau with peaks exceeding 6,000 ft. Climate hot and humid; Freetown receives more than 150 ins. of rain in the year, mostly May–Oct. In the dry season the dust-laden harmattan blows from the Sahara. Before standards of hygiene and medicine had been improved, the region was considered so unhealthy for non-Africans that it was known as 'the white man's grave'.

Timber is obtained from the tropical rain-forests. Fishing important along the coast. Principal food crop rice. Exports palm kernels and some cocoa, but these are far exceeded in value by the chief minerals, diamonds and iron ore. Most of the foreign trade is with Great Britain. Among the various Negro tribes the majority are pagans, and there are many Christians and a minority of Muslims. Some are the descendants of former slaves who were settled on the Sierra Leone peninsula (Freetown) in 1787, the district being made a colony 20 years later; the much larger hinterland was made a protectorate in 1896. Became independent 1961. Divided administratively into three provinces: Northern, Eastern, and Southern.

**Sierra Madre** Mexico. Principal mountain system of Mexico, dominating the country and profoundly influencing many aspects of Mexican life; extends 1,500 m. SE from the N border. Three main ranges: the

Sierra Madre Oriental (E) parallel to the coast of the Gulf of Mexico; the Sierra Madre Occidental (W), wider and more spectacular, parallel to the Gulf of California and the Pacific coast; the Sierra Madre del Sur (S). The three enclose the great central plateau. Highest peak the Pico de Orizaba (Citlaltépetl) (18,700 ft).

**Sierra Morena** Spain. Broad mountain range in the S, forming the watershed between the Guadiana and the Guadalquivir rivers. It is a considerable barrier between Andalusia and the N, with a mean height of about 2,500 ft. Important mineral deposits, chiefly of copper, lead, silver, mercury.

**Sierra Nevada** Spain. In Spanish, 'Snowy Range'. High mountain range in the S, in Andalusia, extending about 60 m. W–E and rising to 11,421 ft in Mulhacén, the highest peak in Spain, and to 11,128 ft in the Picacho de Veleta. Many summits permanently snow-capped – hence the name.

**Sierra Nevada** USA. Mountain range extending 400 m. NW–SE through E California, between the Central Valley (W) and the Great Basin (E). A massive block of the earth's crust with a steep escarpment along the E edge. Includes Mt Whitney (14,495 ft), the highest peak in the USA outside Alaska. Several other peaks exceed 14,000 ft. Also contains three of the USA's most famous National Parks, the Yosemite, Sequoia, and King's Canyon.

**Sierra Pacaraima** Brazil/Venezuela. Mountain range forming part of the Venezuela-Brazil frontier, rising to 9,219 ft in Mt Roraima at the E end. Forms the watershed between the Orinoco and Amazon basins.

**Sihanoukville** Cambodia. Formerly Kompong Som. New seaport on the Gulf of Siam 90 m. WSW of Pnom Penh. Pop. 11,000. Built with French aid and opened in 1960. Linked by road with Pnom Penh, which it is replacing as the principal seaport. Handled 21,600 tons in 1961, 545,200 tons in 1967. Exports rice, rubber, etc.

**Sikhote Alin Range** USSR. Mountain range in the Primorye and Khabarovsk Territories, RSFSR, extending 750 m. parallel to and near the Pacific coast from Vladivostok to Nikolayevsk, near the mouth of the Amur R. Rises to over 6,000 ft. Largely forested. Mineral resources (coal, iron, lead, zinc, etc.).

**Si-kiang** China. The most southerly of the country's three great rivers, 1,200 m. long, rising in E Yunnan as the Hungshui, flowing generally E, and then turning S to enter the S China Sea. Chief tributaries the Siang, Kwei and Pei, the last-named joining it near the head of the delta. Important waterway, with Kwangchow (Canton), Hong Kong, and Macao around the delta and mouth.

**Sikkim** India. Protectorate of India, on the S slopes of the E Himalayas between Nepal and Bhutan, bounded on the N and NE by Tibet (China). Area 2,818 sq. m. Pop. (1961) 161,080 (75 per cent Nepalese). Cap. Gangtok. Entirely mountainous, rising to 28,168 ft in Kanchenjunga on the W border. Several other peaks exceed 20,000 ft. Much forested, rich in flora. Chief crops rice, maize, fruits. The State religion is Buddhism, but the majority of the people are Hindu. Passed from British to Indian protection 1950; the Maharaja is assisted in administration by an Indian civil servant.

**Silchester** England. Village in Hampshire 6 m. N of Basingstoke on the site of the Roman town of Calleva Atrebatum. Excavated 1889–1909; the remains were placed in Reading Museum.

**Silesia** (Polish **Śląsk**, Ger. **Schlesien**, Czech **Slezsko**). Region of E central Europe, in the basin of the upper Odra (Oder) R., bordering on the Sudeten and W Beskid Mountains (S). Mainly in SW Poland, with much smaller areas in N central Czechoslovakia and the German Democratic Republic. The mountain slopes are forested. The fertile lowlands produce cereals, potatoes, flax, sugar-beet. The wealth of the region is based on the rich coalfield in the SE of Polish Silesia; iron, lead, and zinc are also mined. Important metallurgical industries are centred on Wroclaw, Katowice, Zabrze, Bytom, Chorzów, Gliwice, Sosnowiec (all Polish). Chief towns in Czechoslovakian Silesia are Opava and Slezska Ostrava.

Peopled in early times by Slavonic tribes. Part of Poland by the 11th cent. Became a separate principality; divided into several smaller units in the 12th cent. The Silesian dukes invited German settlers, and transferred their allegiance to Bohemia in the 14th cent. Passed to the Habsburgs 1526. Suffered severely in the Thirty Years War (1618–48). Frederick II of Prussia claimed and annexed the greater part of Silesia in 1740. After the 1st World War the part which had been left to Austria passed mainly to Czechoslovakia and the E of Prussian Silesia was restored to re-created

Poland. At the end of the 2nd World War the whole of Prussian Silesia except a small area W of the Nysa (Neisse) R. was restored to Poland, becoming the voivodships of Wroclaw, Opole, Katowice, and part of Zielona Góra.

**Silk Road.** Ancient caravan route linking China with India and the West. From Lanchow, in Kansu province, it runs generally NW, passing N of the Nan Shan. A branch leaves N for Urumchi (Sinkiang-Uighur AR) and the USSR, and the road itself forks, one route continuing N of the Takla Makan desert through Aksu to Kashgar, the other S of the desert through Khotan and Yarkand to Kashgar.

**Silsden** England. Urban district in the W Riding of Yorkshire, 4 m. NNW of Keighley. Pop. (1961) 5,142. Manufactures textiles.

**Simbirsk** ◊ *Ulyanovsk.*

**Simferopol** USSR. Capital of the Crimea region, Ukrainian SSR, on the Salgir R. 35 m. NE of Sevastopol. Pop. (1970) 250,000. Industrial centre, in a district famous for fruits, vines, vegetables, tobacco. Fruit and vegetable canning, flour milling, tanning, etc. The Tatar settlement of Akmechet: renamed after the Russian conquest of the Crimea (1784). Before 1945 it was the capital of the Crimean ASSR.

**Simla** India. Capital of Himachal Pradesh, situated just within Punjab 170 m. N of Delhi. Pop. (1961) 42,597. A hill station in a beautiful position on a ridge of the lower Himalaya at a height of 7,000 ft. Trade in grain, timber, etc. Minor industries. Under British rule it was the summer residence of the Viceroy and government.

**Simonstown** S Africa. Town and naval base on False Bay 20 m. S of Cape Town. Pop. (1963) 10,220 (5,120 Europeans). Headquarters of the S African Navy. Fish oil refining. Seaside resort on the S outskirts. Named after Simon van der Stel, governor of the Cape 1679–99; established as a naval base 1814. Ceded to Britain by the Cape Province 1898. Transferred to S Africa 1957.

**Simplon Pass** Switzerland. Alpine pass between the Pennine and Lepontine Alps followed by the road from Brig to Domodossola (Italy), built (1800–1807) by Napoleon. The hospice is at a height of 6,565 ft. The road passes through a tunnel and the wild Gondo gorge. To the NE is the Simplon Tunnel, the longest railway tunnel in the world (12¼ m.) and the lowest Alpine tunnel (2,313 ft), through Monte Leone, opened in 1906.

**Sinai** United Arab Republic. Triangular peninsula in the extreme NE, separated from the rest by the Gulf of Suez and the Suez Canal. Area 23,000 sq. m. Pop. (Sinai province, 1960) 50,000. Chief town El Arish (pop. 11,000) on the railway and the coast. Bounded on the E by the Gulf of Aqaba and by Israel. Politically part of the United Arab Republic but geographically in Asia rather than Africa. A belt of sand dunes runs along the N coast; the central area consists of the plateau of El Tih, and the S is a mountainous region rising to 8,652 ft in Jebel Katrin, just N of which is Jebel Musa (7,497 ft), the 'Mount of Moses' (often identified with Mt Sinai, mentioned in the Old Testament as the site of the Giving of the Law to Moses, though Jebel Serbal (6,730 ft) has also been identified as Mt Sinai). The N coastal strip (formerly a trade route between Egypt and Palestine) is crossed by the railway built during the 1st World War from El Qantara to Jerusalem. The peninsula as a whole is barren: waterless apart from a number of wadis, it is inhabited mainly by nomads. Turquoise and copper were mined by the ancient Egyptians. Some manganese, iron, and oil are now produced in the W. Occupied by Israeli forces after the 1967 war.

**Sinaloa** Mexico. State in the NW extending NW–SE between the Pacific Ocean (W) and the Sierra Madre Occidental (E). Area 22,582 sq. m. Pop. (1969) 1,185,000. Cap. Culiacán. Principal seaport Mazatlán. Chief occupations mining (silver, gold, etc.), agriculture. Cereals cultivated on the uplands, sugar-cane, cotton, etc. on the lowlands.

**Sind** Pakistan. Former province of British India, mainly comprising the lower Indus R. valley and now occupying the SE part of W Pakistan. Area 50,000 sq. m. The central plain, irrigated through the Lloyd (Sukkur) Barrage and the Ghulam Muhammad (Kotri) Barrage, produces wheat, rice, cotton, etc. Rainfall is very light, and except for the irrigated lands the region is arid. The W is hilly and the E reaches the edge of the Thar Desert. Karachi stands on the coast; Hyderabad, Sukkur, and Shikarpur are the chief inland towns.

**Sindhu** ◊ *Indus River.*

**Singapore.** Republic in the British Commonwealth, island and city at the S end of the Malay Peninsula, from which it is separated by the narrow Johore Strait, crossed by a causeway carrying a road and a railway. Area 225 sq. m. Pop. (1967) 1,955,600 (1,454,500 Chinese; 283,500 Malays; 159,400 Indians and Pakistanis; 18,900 Europeans). On the N coast of the island is the naval and air base and on the S side is the city of Singapore. The latter is a seaport of outstanding importance on the route from Europe and India to the Far East, possessing a fine, almost land-locked harbour; it has a great entrepôt trade and exports rubber, tin, and copra from Malaya. Industries include tin smelting, on the offshore island of Pulau Brani, rubber processing, pineapple canning, sawmilling. Seat of the University of Singapore (1962) and the Nanyang University (1956). On the island of Singapore, which has a hot, humid climate throughout the year, there are market gardens, rubber and coconut plantations.

Destroyed by the Javanese in the 14th cent., Singapore was inhabited by only a few fishing people when Sir Stamford Raffles secured the island from the Sultan of Johore (1824). Became one of the Straits Settlements (1826) and rapidly superseded Penang and Malacca in commercial importance. In the 2nd World War it was taken by the Japanese (1942). Became a British Crown Colony (1946) and then a self-governing state (1957), joining the Federation of Malaysia in 1963. Seceded from the Federation and became an independent republic 1965.

**Sinhailien** China. Town in Kiangsu province 320 m. E of Chengchow. Pop. 208,000. Commercial centre, on the Lunghai railway from Lienyunkang, its seaport, to Chengchow and Sian. Trade in cereals, cotton, etc.

**Sining** China. Capital of Tsinghai (Chinghai) province, on the Sining R. at a height of 7,500 ft 120 m. WNW of Lanchow. Pop. 94,000. Commercial centre. Trade in cereals, wool, salt, timber. Textile manufacture, tanning.

**Sinkiang-Uighur AR** China. Autonomous region in the NW, bounded by Mongolia (NE), Tibet and Kashmir (S), and by the USSR (W and NW). Area 636,000 sq. m. Pop. (1957) 5,640,000. Cap. Urumchi (Tihwa). Corresponds roughly to the historic Chinese Turkestan and is divided by the Tien Shan into Dzungaria (N) and the

Tarim Basin (S). The latter, which is much the larger, is a region of internal drainage containing the great sandy Takla Makan desert and, in the NE, the Turfan depression. Rainfall is scanty throughout the region and temperatures are extreme. Wheat, maize, cotton, and fruits are cultivated in the oases and mountain valleys, deriving water from the melting snows on the surrounding heights. Livestock raised by the nomads of Dzungaria. The people are mainly Turkic Uighurs, with Kazakh and Chinese minorities. The principal oasis towns of the Tarim Basin are Kashgar, Yarkand, and Khotan, in the SW. In the past the Chinese hold over the region was precarious, and in the economic sphere a greater influence was often exercised by the Russians; but with the establishment of the Communist régime (1950) the Chinese undertook the planned development of the region, an initial step being the construction of the Lanchow–Sinkiang railway.

**Sint Maarten** ◊ *St Martin.*

**Sintra (Cintra)** Portugal. Picturesque town in the Lisboa district 14 m. WNW of Lisbon. Pop. 8,000. On the Serra da Sintra, which rises to 1,772 ft in Cruz Alta and is largely covered with pines, cork oaks, and other trees. Its beauty has been celebrated by many poets and authors, including Camões and Byron. The outstanding building in the town is the 14th/15th-cent. royal palace, in Moorish and Gothic styles, with two great conical chimneys. On a near-by height is the fantastically designed 19th-cent. Pena palace, and on another the remains of the Moorish castle. The Convention of Cintra (1808), signed by Britain, Portugal, and France, provided for the evacuation of Portugal by the French army.

**Sinuiju** N Korea. Capital of N Pyongan province, on the Yalu R. opposite Antung (China). Pop. 200,000. Industrial and commercial centre. Sawmilling. Manufactures paper, rayon, etc.

**Sion** Switzerland. Ancient Sedunum. Capital of the Valais canton, on the Rhône R. 42 m. SE of Lausanne, at a height of 1,700 ft. Pop. (1969) 21,600. Built around two low hills; on one are the remains of the castle of Tourbillon, on the other those of the castle of Valère (Valeria). Woodworking, printing, etc. Trade in wine, fruit, vegetables. An ancient town: seat of a bishopric in the 7th cent.

**Sioux City** USA. Town in Iowa, on the Missouri R. 150 m. WNW of Des Moines.

Pop. (1960) 89,159. Large trade in livestock, grain. Meat packing, flour milling. Manufactures dairy products, clothing, etc.

**Sioux Falls** USA. Largest town in S Dakota, on the Big Sioux R. near the Minnesota and Iowa borders. Pop. (1960) 65,466. Named after a series of cascades, which provide hydroelectric power. Meat packing. Manufactures biscuits, soap, etc.

**Sir Edward Pellew Group** ◊ *Carpentaria, Gulf of.*

**Siret (Russian Seret) River** Rumania/USSR. River 280 m. long, mainly in Rumania; rises on the E slopes of the Carpathians in the Ukrainian SSR and flows generally SSE to join the Danube R. just above Galaţi.

**Sitapur** India. Town in Uttar Pradesh 55 m. NNW of Lucknow. Pop. (1961) 53,884. Railway junction. Commercial centre. Trade in grain, oilseeds, etc. Important eye hospital.

**Sitka** USA. Port in Alaska, on the W coast of Baranof Island in the Alexander Archipelago. Pop. (1960) 3,237. Excellent harbour. Main industries fishing, fish canning, sawmilling. Manufactures wood pulp. Capital of Russian America until 1867. The original Russian settlement (New Archangel), built in 1799, was moved to the present site (1804) by Alexander Baranof. Scene of the formal transfer of Alaska from Russia to the USA (1867). Remained capital of Alaska till 1906, then replaced by Juneau. An important US naval base in the 2nd World War.

**Sittard** Netherlands. Market town in Limburg province, 14 m. NE of Maastricht. Pop. (1968) 33,804. Tanning etc. Coalmining in the neighbourhood.

**Sittingbourne and Milton** England. Urban district in Kent 10 m. ENE of Maidstone. Pop. (1961) 23,616. Market town in a fruit growing district. Manufactures paper, cement, bricks.

**Sivas** Turkey. Ancient Sebasteia. Capital of Sivas province, in the valley of the Kizil Irmak at a height of 4,400 ft 220 m. E of Ankara. Pop. (1965) 108,300. Trade in agricultural produce. Manufactures carpets, textiles, etc. Has outstanding buildings erected by the Seljuk sultans in the 13th cent. Here Mustafa Kemal held a national congress (1919), leading to the revolution which gave to Turkey its modern shape.

**Siwa (Siwah)** United Arab Republic. Oasis in the Libyan Desert 295 m. WSW of

Alexandria, near the Libya–Egypt frontier. Pop. 1,000. In a depression about 100 ft below sea level; many salt lakes and ponds. Dates and olives cultivated. Once famous for the oracle temple of Jupiter Ammon, visited by Alexander the Great (331 B.C.). ⟡ *Western Desert.*

**Siwalik Range** India/Nepal. Range of hills extending 1,000 m. WNW–ESE parallel to and S of the Himalayan system, from Kashmir through Punjab, Uttar Pradesh, and Nepal. Average height 2,000–3,500 ft.

**Skagerrak** Denmark/Norway. Strait about 80 m. wide between Norway and Denmark (Jutland), continuing to the SE as the Kattegat.

**Skagway** USA. Port in SE Alaska, at the head of the Chilkoot Inlet on the Lynn Canal. Pop. 750. Terminus of the railway from Whitehorse, Yukon (Canada). During the Klondike gold rush (1897–8) it had a floating population of 10,000–20,000.

**Skara Brae** Scotland. Prehistoric village on the W coast of Mainland, in the Orkneys, revealed after a storm in 1851, subsequent excavations discovering several stone huts and a section of street. Coarse pottery was found, but there was no evidence that the people had possessed textiles, metals, or grain.

**Skeena River** Canada. River 360 m. long in British Columbia, rising in the Stikine Mountains, flowing S and SW, and entering the Hecate Strait on the Pacific Ocean 15 m. SE of Prince Rupert.

**Skegness** England. Urban district in Lincolnshire, 37 m. ESE of Lincoln on the North Sea coast. Pop. (1961) 12,843. Popular seaside resort with extensive sands, a pier, and a holiday camp near by.

**Skellefte River** Sweden. River in the N, 250 m. long, rising near the Norwegian frontier and flowing SE through Lakes Hornavan, Uddjaur, and Storavan to the Gulf of Bothnia. Much used for transporting logs. Near its mouth is the port of Skellefteå, which exports timber, tar, and metallic ores.

**Skelton and Brotton** England. Urban district in the N Riding of Yorkshire, 9 m. E of Middlesbrough. Pop. (1961) 13,186. In a former iron-mining district. Its castle was a haunt of Laurence Sterne and the 'Demoniac' Club.

**Skibbereen** Irish Republic. Market town in Co. Cork, on the R. Ilen 41 m. SW of Cork. Pop. (1966) 2,028. Trade in agricultural produce. The district suffered severely in the famine of 1847.

**Skiddaw** England. Mountain 3,054 ft high in Cumberland, in the Lake District 3 m. N of Keswick. Bassenthwaite Lake is 2 m. W.

**Skien** Norway. Capital of Telemark county, on the Skien R. 63 m. SW of Oslo. Pop. (1968) 44,213. River port. Industrial centre. Sawmilling, tanning. Manufactures wood pulp and paper etc. The gateway to the beautiful mountain and lake scenery of Telemark. Birthplace of Henrik Ibsen (1828–1906).

**Skikda** Algeria. Formerly Philippeville. Sea port 35 m. NNE of Constantine, with which it is connected by rail. Pop. (1967) 85,000. Exports wine, citrus fruits, early vegetables, dates from the Saharan oases, iron ore, marble. Built on the site of the Roman Rusicada. Founded 1838.

**Skipton** England. Urban district in the W Riding of Yorkshire, 16 m. NW of Bradford. Pop. (1961) 12,988. The chief market town of the Craven district. Manufactures textiles. Limestone quarrying near by. Part of the castle dates from the 11th cent.

**Skíros** ⟡ *Skyros.*

**Skoplje (Skopje)** Yugoslavia. Capital of Macedonia, on the Vardar R. Pop. (1961) 171,893. Important railway and road junction; a commercial and industrial centre in a fertile valley producing grain, tobacco, etc. Flour milling, brewing, wine making. Manufactures cigarettes, carpets, cement, etc. It was divided into old and new sections by the ancient river bridge. In 1963 it was largely destroyed by an earthquake which killed more than 1,000 people, rendered the majority of the inhabitants homeless, devastated the old Turkish quarter (including the famous caravanserai of Kuršumli Khan), and wrecked most of the mosques, churches, and other leading buildings. Near by are the ruins of the ancient Scupi, destroyed by earthquake (518). Became the capital of Serbia in the 14th cent., was renamed Üsküb when captured by the Turks, and was returned to Serbia in 1913. A new iron and steel works was opened in 1967.

**Skövde** Sweden. Town in Skaraborg county 45 m. NNW of Jönköping. Pop. (1968) 28,028. Manufactures chemicals, cement, etc.

**Skye** Scotland. Largest island in the Inner Hebrides, in Inverness-shire, reached from the mainland by car ferry from Kyle of

Lochalsh. Area 643 sq. m. Pop. (1961) 7,765 (23,082 in 1841; 9,908 in 1931). Chief town Portree, on the E coast. Coast deeply indented with sea lochs. In the S are the gaunt Cuillin Hills, rising to 3,309 ft in Sgurr Alasdair; in the N The Storr reaches 2,360 ft. Sheep and cattle reared, but both crofting and fishing are declining as the tourist industry increases in importance. In the NW is Dunvegan Castle, home of the Macleods for well over 7 centuries.

**Skyros (Skíros)** Greece. Island in the N Sporades, in the Aegean Sea and in Euboea *nome*. Area 79 sq. m. Pop. 3,000. Mainly agricultural, producing wheat, olive oil, etc. Burial-place of Rupert Brooke (1887–1915).

**Śląsk ◊ Silesia.**

**Slave (Great Slave) River** Canada. River 260 m. long in the NW Territories, leaving the NW end of L. Athabaska, flowing NNW, receiving the Peace R., and entering the Great Slave Lake.

**Slavonia** Yugoslavia. Region in Croatia mainly between the Drava R. (N) and the Sava R. (S). Chief town Osijek. Mostly low-lying and fertile. Its history has closely followed that of Croatia: in 1699 it was returned to Hungary by the Turks; became an Austrian crownland 1848–9; restored to Hungary 1868; became part of Yugoslavia 1918.

**Slavyansk** USSR. Industrial town in the Ukrainian SSR, in the Donbas, 60 m. NNW of Donetsk. Pop. (1970) 124,000. Manufactures chemicals, glass, porcelain, salt, etc. Mineral springs near by. Founded 1676.

**Sleaford** England. Urban district in Lincolnshire, on the R. Slea 17 m. SSE of Lincoln. Pop. (1961) 7,834. Market town. Manufactures agricultural machinery. The Church of St Denis, with an early 15th-cent. carved oak rood screen, is noteworthy.

**Sligo** Irish Republic. 1. County in Connacht, bounded on the N by the Atlantic Ocean. Area 694 sq. m. Pop. (1966) 53,561. The chief inlets into the low, sandy coast are Sligo and Killala Bays. In the W the Slieve Gamph or Ox Mountains rise to 1,778 ft in Knockalongy, and in the NE is Benbulbin (1,722 ft). Cattle raised. Potatoes cultivated. On Inishmurray island are the remains of 6th-cent. buildings.
2. County town of Co. Sligo and port at the mouth of the R. Garavogue. Pop. (1966) 13,424. Flour milling, brewing, bacon and

ham curing, etc. Its ruined abbey was founded in the 13th cent., rebuilt in the 15th cent., and burned in 1641. The Roman Catholic cathedral was built 1869–74. Near by, on the hill Carrowmore, are megalithic remains including three dolmens and a stone circle.

**Sliven** Bulgaria. Capital of Sliven province, at the S foot of the Balkan Mountains 62 m. WNW of Burgas. Pop. (1965) 68,331. Industrial centre. Manufactures woollen goods, carpets, wine, etc. Picturesquely situated, it stands in an important strategic position and was frequently involved in Balkan conflicts.

**Slough** England. Municipal borough in SE Buckinghamshire 19 m. W of London. Pop. (1961) 80,503. A modern industrial town. Manufactures paints, plastics, food products, pharmaceutical goods, aircraft and automobile parts, radio and television sets, etc. Its rapid growth dates from the 1920s, when an industrial estate was established here. Home of the Herschel family, the astronomers; birthplace of Sir John Herschel (1792–1871).

**Slovakia** Czechoslovakia. The most easterly part of the republic, bounded on the N by Poland, on the E by the USSR (Ruthenia), and on the S by Hungary. Cap. Bratislava. Largely mountainous, rising to 8,737 ft in the High Tatra (N) and sloping S towards the Danube valley. Principal occupation farming. Part of Hungary before 1918, but then became a province of Czechoslovakia. During the 2nd World War it was nominally independent, but was reincorporated into Czechoslovakia in 1945. Abolished as an administrative unit 1949.

**Slovenia** Yugoslavia. Constituent republic in the NW bounded by Austria (N), Hungary (NE), and Italy (W). Area 7,796 sq. m. Pop. (1961) 1,591,523. Cap. Ljubljana. Mostly mountainous: the Karawanken Mountains in the N, the Julian Alps in the NW, with the highest peak Triglav (9,396 ft). Principal rivers the Sava and Drava. Potatoes, cereals, and vegetables grown. Cattle raised. Forestry important. Coal, lead, and mercury mined. Chief towns Ljubljana, Maribor. Under the Habsburgs from the 14th cent. Became a province of Yugoslavia 1918. After the 2nd World War, when it was divided between Germany, Italy, and Hungary, it was restored to Yugoslavia, being made a people's republic in 1946.

**Slubice** ◊ *Frankfurt-an-der-Oder*.

**Slupsk** (Ger. **Stolp**) Poland. Town in the Koszalin voivodship, on the Slupia R. 70 m. WNW of Gdańsk (Danzig). Pop. (1968) 65,300. Manufactures chemicals, agricultural machinery, etc.

**Smethwick** England. Industrial town in Staffordshire, 3 m. W of and virtually a suburb of Birmingham. Pop. (1961) 68,372. Manufactures glass, lighthouse equipment, metal goods, etc. At the Soho ironworks near by James Watt and Matthew Boulton worked together to produce the first steam engines. From 1966 part of the county borough of ◊ *Warley*.

**Smolensk** USSR. Capital of the Smolensk region, RSFSR, on the Dnieper R. 230 m. WSW of Moscow. Pop. (1970) 211,000. Important railway junction and industrial centre. Manufactures linen, textile and other machinery, clothing, footwear, furniture, etc. Flour milling, brewing, sawmilling. Within the city are the remains of an old kremlin, and it also has a 17th/18th-cent. cathedral. Founded in the 9th cent.; soon became an important commercial centre. Napoleon defeated the Russians here (1812), and there was heavy fighting again in the 2nd World War. In each conflict the city was all but destroyed. Birthplace of K. D. Glinka (1867–1927), the soil scientist.

**Smyrna** ◊ *Izmir*.

**Snake River** USA. Chief tributary of the Columbia R., 1,038 m. long, rising in the Yellowstone National Park in NW Wyoming, flowing S then W, crossing S Idaho in a gigantic arc, turning N to form part of the borders between Idaho and Oregon and Washington, and discharging into the Columbia R. The largest and deepest of its many gorges is the Grand Canyon (Hell's Canyon), more than 100 m. long and in places over 1 m. deep. At e.g. American Falls and Twin Falls dams have been constructed for hydroelectric power and irrigation.

**Sneeuwberg Mountains** ◊ *South Africa*.

**Snowdon** Wales. Mountain in Caernarvonshire broken up into 5 peaks, one of which at 3,560 ft is the highest in Wales and England. At its foot are the passes of Llanberis, Aberglaslyn, and Rhyd-ddu. There is a magnificent view from the summit, and it offers slopes of varying difficulty to the climber. Ascended by rack-and-pinion railway from Llanberis (the only mountain railway in Britain). The National Park of Snowdonia (established 1951) includes a wide area around Snowdon.

**Snowy Mountains** Australia.* Part of the Australian Alps in the SE, mainly in SE New South Wales near the Victoria border. In no sense 'alpine', they consist of a much dissected tableland with a general elevation of 3,000–6,000 ft, with Mt Kosciusko, summit of a block, rising to 7,328 ft. Snow-covered in winter; the melt water increases the volume of the rivers in spring. The Snowy Mountains hydroelectric scheme conserves much of this water and diverts the ◊ *Snowy River* headwaters.

**Snowy River** Australia. River 260 m. long, rising in the Snowy Mountains in the SE and flowing generally S to Bass Strait. Its waters were long unused in a region with a severe water shortage. Now, under the ◊ *Snowy Mountains* scheme, its upper waters are diverted from large new storages W to the Murray R. and N to the Murrumbidgee via its tributary, the Tumut. When the full scheme is completed, the capacity of the associated power stations will be greater than all the hydroelectric stations previously installed in the Australian Commonwealth. The first hydroelectric power from the Snowy Mountains scheme was fed into the New South Wales grid in 1957. The last mountain tunnel carrying water from the E to the W side of the Snowy Mountains was completed in 1967.

**Sobat River** Ethiopia/Sudan. Tributary of the Nile, formed by the union of the Pibor and the Baro rivers and several smaller streams, 460 m. long from the source of the Baro to the confluence with the Nile. Joins the White Nile just above Malakal. Navigable during flood time (June–Dec.) as far as Gambela in Ethiopia (on the Baro). Flow retarded by swamps; makes its main contribution to the Nile flood water late in the season (Nov.–Dec.).

**Soche** ◊ *Yarkand*.

**Sochi** USSR. Resort on the Black Sea, in the Krasnodar Territory, RSFSR, 110 m. SSE of Krasnodar. Pop. (1970) 224,000. One of the leading Russian seaside resorts, with many hotels, sanatoria, etc. Manufactures food and tobacco products.

**Society Islands** French Polynesia. Two groups of islands, some volcanic and some coral, the Windward Is. (Îles du Vent) and the Leeward Is. (Îles sous le Vent), in the S Pacific. 1. *Windward Islands*: Area 455 sq. m. Pop. (1967) 61,519. Main island ◊ *Tahiti*, its chief town Papeete (pop. 22,000);

other islands Moorea, Makatea. 2. *Leeward Islands*: Area 161 sq. m. Pop. (1967) 15,337. Main islands Huahine, Raiatea.

The group was discovered in 1767 and visited by Capt. Cook (1769) with a member of the Royal Society – hence the name. Became a French protectorate in 1843 and a colony in 1880. Now part of the overseas territory of French Polynesia. Chief products phosphates, copra, vanilla.

**Socotra (Soqotra, Sokotra)** Indian Ocean. Island 150 m. ENE of Cape Guardafui (Somalia). Area 1,400 sq. m. Pop. 12,000. Chief town Tamrida (Hadibo). Part of the Mahri Sultanate of Qishn and Socotra, from 1967 in the Republic of S Yemen. A barren plateau, with a ridge rising to nearly 4,700 ft. Along the coast and in the fertile valleys dates and gums are produced and livestock raised. Held briefly by the Portuguese (16th cent.). Placed under British protection 1886.

**Södertälje** Sweden. Town in Stockholm county 18 m. WSW of Stockholm. Pop. (1968) 52,503. On the Södertälje Canal, linking L. Mälar with the Baltic. Manufactures textiles, chemicals, matches, etc.

**Soest** Federal German Republic. Industrial town and railway junction in N Rhine-Westphalia 28 m. E of Dortmund. Pop. (1963) 34,200. Manufactures machinery, electrical equipment, soap, etc. In the Middle Ages an important Hanseatic town.

**Soest** Netherlands. Town in Utrecht province 9 m. NE of Utrecht. Pop. (1968) 33,190. Manufactures dairy products etc. Birthplace of Sir Peter Lely (Pieter van der Faes, 1618–80), the artist.

**Sofia** Bulgaria. Ancient Serdica. Capital and largest city, in the W, at a height of 1,800 ft. Pop. (1965) 800,953. Important railway junction on the route from Belgrade to Istanbul. Two airports. Industrial centre. Manufactures machinery, textiles, electrical equipment, chemicals, etc. In the main a modern city in appearance, it has a 19th-cent. cathedral and a university (1880); among its older buildings are the Chapel of St George, originally a Roman bath, the 6th-cent. Church of St Sophia, the Black Mosque, now an Orthodox church, and the Banyabashi mosque. Colonized by the Romans A.D. 29. Sacked by the Huns 447. Under Turkish rule for nearly five centuries. Passed to Bulgaria 1877 and became the national capital. Much damaged in the 2nd World War.

**Sogne Fiord** Norway. The country's longest (110 m.) and deepest fiord, its mouth 46 m. N of Bergen. Penetrates almost to the Jotunheim Mountains, with many long arms extending N and S. Its magnificent scenery attracts many summer tourists.

**Sohag** United Arab Republic. Capital of Sohag governorate, on the W bank of the Nile and on the railway, 50 m. SE of Asyût. Pop. (1960) 62,000. Cotton ginning. Pottery manufacture. Ruins of ancient Coptic churches.

**Soho** England. District in the City of Westminster, London, between Regent Street and Charing Cross Road, well known for its foreign restaurants, with theatres (Shaftesbury Avenue) and film company offices (Wardour Street). Many French Protestants settled here in the late 17th cent., and it still has a sufficiently high proportion of foreign residents to be called London's 'Latin Quarter'. The name is probably derived from an old hunting cry.

**Soissonnais** France. Region in the Paris Basin NE of Paris, traversed by the Aisne R. Chief town Soissons. Dairy produce, grain, and sugar-beet are important products.

**Soissons** France. Ancient Noviodunum, later Augusta Suessionum. Town in the Aisne department on the Aisne R. 57 m. NE of Paris. Pop. (1968) 27,641. Market town. Trade in agricultural produce from Soissonnais. Manufactures boilers, agricultural implements, rubber products, etc. Cathedral (12th/13th-cent.), and the ruined abbey of St Jean-des-Vignes, both damaged in the world wars, and the ruined abbey of St Médard, where Merovingian kings were buried. Under the Romans became the second capital of Gallia Belgica. In the Middle Ages and subsequently it suffered often in time of war.

**Sokoto** Nigeria. Town in the NW, on the Kebbi R. (a tributary of the Sokoto) 230 m. WNW of Kano. Pop. (1963) 50,000. Commercial centre. Trade in cotton, rice, etc. Formerly capital of the Sokoto province. In the 19th cent. capital of the Sokoto (Fulah) empire.

**Sokotra** ♦ *Socotra*.

**Solent, The** England. Channel about 15 m. long between the Isle of Wight and the mainland of Hampshire; the main route from the W English Channel to Southampton and Portsmouth.

**Soleure** ♦ *Solothurn*.

**Solihull** England. County borough in Warwickshire 7 m. SE of Birmingham. Pop. (1961) 96,010. Important manufactures of cars, machinery, etc. Has a 13th/15th-cent. church.

**Solikamsk** USSR. Town in the Perm region, RSFSR, 115 m. N of Perm. Pop. 82,000. A mining and industrial centre. Manufactures chemicals from locally mined potash and common salt, also magnesium, etc. Founded as a salt-mining centre in the 15th cent.

**Solingen** Federal German Republic. Industrial town in N Rhine-Westphalia 13 m. ESE of Dusseldorf. Pop. (1968) 173,417. Famous for its cutlery industry (knives, scissors, razor blades, etc.) since early medieval times, when the manufacture of sword blades is supposed to have been introduced from Damascus. Also manufactures agricultural machinery, bicycles, etc.

**Solo** ◊ *Surakarta.*

**Sologne** France. Region in the SSW of the Paris Basin, between the Loire and Cher rivers. A gently undulating plain with many marshes and a large area of forest. Cereals and vegetables cultivated. Small market towns with minor industries.

**Solomon Islands** SW Pacific Ocean. Archipelago of volcanic islands SE of the Bismarck Archipelago. Total area 15,600 sq. m. Pop. about 220,000 (mainly Melanesian, with Polynesians on the outlying islands). The N Solomons form part of the Trust Territory of New Guinea under Australian administration, and include the largest island, Bougainville, with Buka and adjacent atolls. Area 4,100 sq. m. Pop. (1966) 72,490. The remainder form a British protectorate, administered by the High Commissioner for the Western Pacific, and include Guadalcanal, Malaita, and several other islands; the Lord Howe group or Ontong Java; the Santa Cruz Is., Tikopia, the Mitre Is., the Duff Is., and the Reef group. Area 11,500 sq. m. Pop. (1968) 148,800. Cap. Honiara, on Guadalcanal.

Most of the islands are mountainous, rising to 10,170 ft in Mt Balbi, on Bougainville, and are densely forested. Climate hot and humid, with heavy rainfall. Coconuts, sweet potatoes, bananas, etc. cultivated. Chief export copra. Discovered (1568) by the Spaniard Mendaña. Divided between Germany and Britain 1886; a British protectorate was established over most of the islands in 1893, but the N Solomons

remained German until 1920, when they were mandated to Australia.

**Solothurn** (Fr. **Soleure**) Switzerland. **1.** Canton in the NW, crossed by the Jura and containing part of the fertile Aar R. valley. Area 306 sq. m. Pop. (1969) 228,000 (mainly Roman Catholic and German-speaking). Agricultural and industrial. Chief towns Solothurn, Olten, Grenchen. Joined the Swiss Confederation 1481.
**2.** Capital of Solothurn canton, on the Aar R. 18 m. NNE of Bern. Pop. (1969) 19,100. Industrial centre. Manufactures watches, precision instruments, textiles, etc. One of the oldest towns in Switzerland; has an 18th-cent. cathedral and many other noteworthy buildings.

**Solway Firth** England/Scotland. Inlet of the Irish Sea separating Cumberland (England) from Dumfriesshire and Kirkcudbrightshire (Scotland). At its head it receives the Esk and Eden rivers, and it broadens out to a width of 22 m. Being funnel-shaped, it has strong tides.

**Somalia (Somali Republic).** Republic in NE Africa occupying the 'Horn' of Africa. Area 246,200 sq. m. (former British Somaliland, 68,000 sq. m.). Pop. (1964) 2,350,000. Cap. and chief seaport Mogadishu. Created by the union of the former Italian-administered Trust Territory of Somalia with the former British Somaliland protectorate. In the N the coastal plain is narrow, rising abruptly to a plateau which reaches 7,900 ft; in the S it is much wider and the land generally lower. Climate hot and arid. Main occupation nomadic stock rearing. Along the Webi Shebeli and the Juba rivers in the S there are plantation crops, grown by irrigation (sugar-cane, bananas, durra, maize). The dominant native people are the Somali, Muslims of mixed Negro and Hamitic origin. Hargeisa was formerly the capital, and Berbera the chief seaport, of British Somaliland. The region became an Italian sphere of influence in the late 19th cent. and the colony of Italian Somaliland after the 1st World War. Jubaland was ceded (from Kenya) by Britain in 1925. Taken by Britain during the 2nd World War (1941); returned to Italian trusteeship 1950. With the British Somaliland protectorate (under British influence since the early 19th cent.) it formed the new republic, and became an independent member of the UN, in 1960. There have been continuing frontier disputes with Kenya.

**Somaliland, French** ◊ *French Territory of the Afars and the Issas.*

**Sombor** Yugoslavia. Market town in Vojvodina 35 m. SW of Subotica. Pop. (1961) 37,760. Trade in grain, cattle. Flour milling. Manufactures dairy products.

**Somersby** ◊ *Horncastle.*

**Somerset (Somersetshire)** England. County in the SW, bounded on the N by the Bristol Channel. Area 1,613 sq. m. Pop. (1961) 598,556. County town Taunton. In the W and SW are the moorland stretch of Exmoor (with Dunkery Beacon rising to 1,706 ft), the Quantock Hills, and the Blackdown Hills; between these uplands and the Mendip Hills to the NE is the formerly marshy plain crossed by the Parret, Tone, and Brue rivers now drained by numerous ditches. Largely a dairy-farming county; Cheddar cheese is esp. well known. Sheep reared. Cider apples grown. Tourists are attracted by the coastal resorts (e.g. Weston-super-Mare, Burnham-on-Sea, Minehead), by the natural beauties of Cheddar Gorge and Wookey Hole in the Mendips, and by the ancient and picturesque towns of Bath, Wells, and Glastonbury. Other important towns are Taunton, Bridgwater, Yeovil, and Norton-Radstock (near which there is a small coalfield). Keynsham is a fast-growing S suburb of Bristol (which is mainly in Gloucestershire).

**Somerville** USA. Town in Massachusetts, on the Mystic R. just NW of Boston. Pop. (1960) 94,697. Mainly residential. Meat packing. Manufactures paper products, textiles, furniture, etc.

**Somme** France. Department in the N, in Picardy, on the English Channel, crossed by the Somme R. Area 2,424 sq. m. Pop. (1968) 512,113. Prefecture Amiens. Low-lying, flat, and fertile. Produces wheat, sugar-beet, cider apples, vegetables. Chief towns Amiens, Abbeville.

**Somme River** France. River 152 m. long rising in the Aisne department and flowing generally W past St Quentin, Amiens, and Abbeville to enter the English Channel by an estuary. Linked by canals with other waterways in the N. The scene of an extended engagement of the 1st World War (1916).

**Sonora** Mexico. State in the NW, bordered by Arizona, USA (N), and the Gulf of California (W). Area 70,484 sq. m. Pop. (1969) 1,249,000. Cap. Hermosillo. Chief seaport Guaymas. Mountainous except for the narrow coastal plain; traversed by the Sierra Madre Occidental. Drained and irrigated by the Magdalena, Sonora, Yaqui, and Mayo rivers. Mainly arid; subtropical conditions near the coast, and a more temperate climate at higher altitudes. Rich in minerals, esp. copper (at Cananea, N), silver, gold, lead, zinc. Crops grown in the irrigated valleys include sugar-cane, rice, alfalfa, wheat.

**Son River** India. River 470 m. long rising in N Madhya Pradesh, flowing generally ENE and joining the Ganges above Patna. Used for irrigation in its lower course (NW Bihar).

**Sonsonate** Salvador. Capital of the Sonsonate department in the SW, 36 m. W of San Salvador. Pop. (1961) 35,351. Commercial centre. Trade in hides, livestock, agricultural produce. Manufactures cotton goods, cigars, etc. Has a cathedral with many cupolas. Founded 1524. Capital of Salvador 1833-4.

**Soo Canals** ◊ *Sault Sainte Marie* (Canada).

**Soochow** China. Formerly (1912-47) Wuhsien. Town in S Kiangsu province, on the Grand Canal 50 m. W of Shanghai. Pop. 474,000. Manufactures textiles (cotton, silk). Trade in rice etc. Situated in a picturesque region near Tai L. (Tai Hu); many canals (called 'the Venice of China'). It is one of the most ancient of Chinese cities, probably founded in the 5th cent. B.C. Many gardens, temples and pagodas, including a nine-storey pagoda. A treaty port in 1896. Largely superseded as an industrial and commercial centre by Wusih (25 m. NW).

**Sopot** Poland. Seaport on the Gulf of Gdańsk 7 m. NNW of Gdańsk. Pop. (1968) 46,500. Formerly a seaside resort; now part of the developing industrial and commercial conurbation of Gdańsk-Gdynia-Sopot.

**Sopron** Hungary. Industrial town and railway junction in Györ-Sopron county 50 m. W of Györ near the Austrian frontier. Pop. 42,000. Manufactures chemicals, textiles, etc. Sugar refining. Has several old churches. Occupied since pre-Roman times. Assigned to Austria after the 1st World War but returned to Hungary (1921) after a plebiscite.

**Soqotra** ◊ *Socotra.*

**Sorata, Mount** ◊ *Illampu, Mount.*

**Soria** Spain. 1. Province in Old Castile in the N part of the Meseta. Area 3,977 sq. m.

Pop. (1961) 147,052. Crossed by the Duero (Douro) R., it is a dry, infertile, sparsely inhabited region. Sheep rearing important. 2. Capital of Soria province, on the Duero (Douro) R. at a height of 3,450 ft. Pop. (1961) 19,301. Has 12th/13th-cent. Romanesque churches. Flour milling, tanning. Manufactures tiles etc.

**Sorocaba** Brazil. Town in São Paulo state 55 m. W of São Paulo. Pop. 119,000. In a rich cotton-, coffee-, and orange-growing region. Orange packing, railway engineering. Manufactures textiles, fertilizers, cement, etc.

**Soroka** ◊ *Belomorsk.*

**Sorrento** Italy. Town in Napoli province, Campania, on the S shore of the Bay of Naples. Pop. 29,000. Picturesquely situated on a cliff-lined peninsula separating the Bay of Naples from the Gulf of Salerno. A popular resort because of its climate and its position. Well known since Roman times for its wine. Birthplace of Torquato Tasso (1544–95), the poet.

**Sorsogon** Philippines. Seaport and capital of Sorsogon province, S E Luzon, on Sorsogon Bay. Pop. (1960) 35,548. Exports Manila hemp, copra.

**Sosnowiec** Poland. Industrial town in the Katowice voivodship 6 m. ENE of Katowice. Pop. (1968) 142,900. Iron founding. Manufactures machinery, chemicals, textiles, bricks, etc. Developed in the late 19th cent. with the exploitation of the near-by coalmines.

**Sound, The (Öresund)** Denmark/Sweden. The most easterly of the straits linking the Kattegat with the Baltic Sea, between Zealand (Denmark) and Sweden; about 70 m. long and 3 m. wide at its narrowest. Tolls were collected at Helsingör (Denmark) from ships passing through 1429–1857.

**Souris River** Canada/USA. River 450 m. long rising 14 m. N of Weyburn, Saskatchewan, flowing generally S E into N Dakota (USA), then turning N and N E and joining the Assiniboine R. 21 m. SE of Brandon, Manitoba.

**Sousse (Susa)** Tunisia. Ancient Hadrumetum. Seaport on the Gulf of Hammamet 63 m. SSE of Tunis. Pop. (1966) 82,666. Exports olive oil, phosphates. Main industry olive-oil production. Seaside resort. In the old town are the Great Mosque and the Ksar er Ribat, a square fortress, both dating from the 9th cent. Founded by the Phoenicians in the 9th cent. B.C. Later a

Carthaginian and then a Roman colony. Rebuilt by Justinian and named Justinianopolis. Restored and fortified by the Aghlabid rulers of Kairouan in the 9th cent.

**South Africa.** Republic in the southernmost part of Africa, between the Atlantic and the Indian Oceans; more than twice the size of France. Area 471,445 sq. m. Pop. (1967) 18,298,000 (12,465,000 Negroes; 3,481,000 whites; 1,805,000 coloured; 547,000 Asians, mainly Indians). Capitals Pretoria (administrative) and Cape Town (legislative); seat of judiciary Bloemfontein.

Bounded by Moçambique, Rhodesia (Limpopo R.), and Swaziland (NE), Botswana (Bechuanaland Protectorate) (Limpopo and Molopo rivers) and SW Africa (Orange R.) (N and NW). Four provinces: the Cape Province (including the Transkeian Territories); Natal (including Zululand); the Orange Free State; and the Transvaal. Dependencies: Marion Island and Prince Edward Island (1,200 m. SE of Cape Town, annexed 1947). Enclaves: Lesotho (Basutoland) and Walvis Bay (SW Africa). The most developed country in the continent, with a generally equable climate, valuable mineral resources, esp. gold and diamonds (the export of which generates most of the foreign exchange), varied agricultural products, and a growing industrial base. Early colonized by the Dutch and other European settlers. Later there was considerable British immigration. Sparsely peopled when the first white settlers arrived, but there was a large influx of Africans (from parts farther N) as mining developed a demand for abundant labour, and these labourers are now the majority of the population.

TOPOGRAPHY. Part of the vast African tableland, rising from a narrow coastal plain to a series of plateaux at a height of 2,000–6,000 ft, including the Little (S) Karroo, the Great (Central) Karroo, and the N Karroo (High Veld); this last occupies most of the N of the republic. The upland grasslands (the Veld, chiefly in the Orange Free State and the Transvaal) are classified as Low Veld at heights of 500 to 2,500 ft, as Middle Veld from 2,500 to 4,000 ft and as High Veld from 4,000 to 6,000 ft. The plateaux are fringed by escarpments, rising in the 1,400-m. Drakensberg (E) to over 11,000 ft and descending sharply to the coast. Turning W from the

S end of the Drakensberg are the Stormberg, Sneeuwberg, and Nieuwveld Mountains, continued to the N by the Roggeveld Mountains. This configuration makes most of the rivers short and swift (esp. in the E). Even the principal rivers (the Orange R. flowing W to the Atlantic, its tributary the Vaal R., and the Limpopo R.) are of little value for navigation. The coast has few good natural harbours.

CLIMATE. The extreme S of the Cape Province has a Mediterranean climate with winter rains (April–Oct.) and summer drought. Elsewhere winter is the dry season and rain falls mainly in summer. Temperatures are very uniform (owing to the compensating effects of altitude and latitude) so that Cape Town's mean annual temperature is 62·3° F and Pretoria's 63·5° F (850 m. NE but at a height of 4,471 ft). The Natal coastal lowlands are humid and sub-tropical; Durban's mean annual rainfall is 43 ins. As the inland plateau lies in the rain shadow of the Drakensberg, rainfall decreases westwards (32 ins. Johannesburg, 16 ins. Kimberley, 2 ins. Port Nolloth). In general the climate is favourable to Europeans; the long hours of sunshine and the clear dry atmosphere have led to the establishment of many health resorts in the interior.

RESOURCES, ECONOMY. The natural vegetation changes gradually (E–W with the rainfall) from the Natal palm belt to poor grassland and scrub in the Karroo plateaux. In the former, sugar-cane is the main crop. Farther W (on the slopes of the Drakensberg) Australian wattle is grown. Maize ('mealies') is the chief crop, esp. in the 'maize triangle' (Transvaal and Orange Free State) on the High Veld. 'Kaffir corn' (sorghum) is extensively grown by the Africans. The fertile region around Cape Town is famous for grapes (and wine) and citrus fruits (which from this and other areas are significant exports). Wheat, cotton, and tobacco are also cultivated; the agricultural area is being gradually increased by irrigation. Much of the land is better suited to pastoral farming; large flocks of merino and karakul sheep provide wool and 'Persian lamb' skins. Mohair is obtained from Angora goats. Important fisheries. Crawfish are canned and exported. The whaling fleet (operating from Durban) brings in large quantities of whale products.

The prosperity of S Africa is based on its enormous wealth in minerals. The Witwatersrand is the world's richest goldfield – about a third of the world output; half or three quarters of the value of S Africa's exports. The newer goldfield in the Odendaalsrus-Welkom area in the Orange Free State (opened 1946) is also rich. Uranium has become an extremely valuable by-product of the goldmining industry, and the Kimberley diamond fields are famous. Other minerals include copper, asbestos, platinum, manganese. Coal is not abundant; required in increasing amounts for the country's industrial development, it is mined chiefly in the Witbank (Transvaal) and the Vryheid (Natal) districts. The principal centre of the expanding iron and steel industry is Pretoria. The Witwatersrand (with its string of large towns, from Krugersdorp through Johannesburg to Springs) is the leading industrial region, manufacturing chemicals, cement, railway equipment, textiles, clothing, and other consumer goods. Cape Town and Durban (the chief seaports) are important industrial centres. In Port Elizabeth tyres are manufactured and cars assembled. In addition to being the most industrialized country in the continent, S Africa has the largest network of railways, almost entirely state-owned: total length 13,564 m. Johannesburg is the hub of many international and national airlines.

SOCIAL SYSTEM, EDUCATION. Eleven universities. Five university colleges for non-whites (three of them founded 1960). A university college for Indians, in Durban, opened 1961. For the white population schooling is compulsory, but the educational level of the native and coloured people is extremely low; the inequality in educational opportunity exemplifies the great contrast between the social and cultural standards of the white minority and the non-white majority.

Another complicating factor is the division between the whites who are English-speaking and those who are Afrikaans-speaking. Both Afrikaans (derived from Dutch) and English are official languages. Many of the whites are bilingual; 57 per cent use Afrikaans and 39 per cent English as their 'home' language.

The region was probably once inhabited by the Bushmen (non-Negro), few of whom now remain; the Hottentots (possibly of mixed Bushman and Hamitic origin) survive only in South-west Africa. Bantu (from the NE) have replaced these aboriginal peoples and are now the majority of the population; the Cape Coloured (a mingling of white, Negro, and Asian stock) are found chiefly in the Cape Province. The Indians (originally introduced as indentured labour) are mainly in Natal.

HISTORY. The region first came to the notice of Europeans when Bartholomew Diaz rounded the Cape of Good Hope (1488). As a supply station on the route to India the Cape steadily increased in importance. Britain seized it in 1620, but Jan van Riebeeck founded the first permanent settlement (for the Dutch E India Company) at Cape Town (1652). Britain again took possession of the Cape in 1806. The Great Trek, which began in 1836, was a mass exodus of Dutch peasant farmers (Boers) N and E into the interior, where they set up the republics of the Orange Free State and the Transvaal; these Boer states, with the Cape Colony and Natal (made a British Crown Colony in 1856), were later to become S Africa. Gold was discovered on the Witwatersrand in 1886; the ill-feeling aroused by the influx into the Transvaal of British immigrants (called '*Uitlanders*' by the Boers) culminated in the Boer War (1899–1902). The two Boer republics were annexed to Britain as Crown Colonies in 1902, became self-governing in 1907, and were joined with the Cape of Good Hope and Natal in the Union of South Africa in 1910. Boer generals (e.g. Botha and Smuts) became prominent statesmen; but the two main political parties (the United S African Party – headed by Smuts – and the Nationalist Party) reflected the continuing cleavage between the British and the Boers. The Nationalist Party opposed entry into the 2nd World War on the Allied side, but Smuts prevailed. The Nationalist Party came to power in 1948 and (under the leadership of Verwoerd and with the support of the Dutch Reformed Church) developed the policy of apartheid. The electorate voted by a narrow majority in 1960 for S Africa to become a republic (the Afrikaners were mainly in favour and the English-speaking minority opposed); it left the British Commonwealth in 1961. Prime Minister Verwoerd was assassinated in 1966.

**Southall** England. Former municipal borough in Middlesex 11 m. W of London; from 1965 part of the Greater London borough of Ealing. Pop. (1961) 51,337. Industrial and residential. Manufactures heavy commercial vehicles, food products, pharmaceutical goods, etc.

**South America.** The more southerly of the two continents of the Western Hemisphere and the fourth largest of the six continents. Area 6,872,000 sq. m. Pop. (1961) 149 millions (after Australasia the most sparsely populated continent). Divided politically into the republics of Argentina, Bolivia, Brazil, Chile, Colombia, Ecuador, Paraguay, Peru, Uruguay, Venezuela; Guyana (formerly British Guiana); the colonies of Surinam (Dutch Guiana) and French Guiana. The chief neighbouring islands, excluding the W Indies, are the Falkland Is., off the S E coast, and the Galápagos Is. (Ecuador).

TOPOGRAPHY, CLIMATE. A gigantic mountain system, the Andes, extends over 4,000 m. along the W coast from the Strait of Magellan to the Caribbean Sea, broadening out in Bolivia to a width of about 400 m. and enclosing lofty plateaux and the large lakes Titicaca and Poopó, branching out in Colombia (N) into three separate Cordilleras. It is the world's longest mountain system and after the Himalayas the highest, with many peaks exceeding 20,000 ft, including several volcanoes; Aconcagua (22,835 ft) is the highest peak in the Western Hemisphere. The extensive Brazilian plateau (E), rising towards the Atlantic coast to over 9,000 ft, and the Guiana Highlands (N) form the ancient core of the continent, being composed of granites, gneisses, and schists, overlain in parts by sandstone. Between these highlands are three great river basins: the Orinoco (N), covering the grassy plains (*llanos*) of Venezuela; the Amazon, with a vast network of rivers forming tenuous lines of communication through the *selvas*, the world's largest area of tropical rainforest; the Paraná–Paraguay, draining the Gran Chaco (N) and part of the pampas (S), its combined rivers opening out into the estuary of the R. Plate (Río de la Plata).

More than two thirds of the continent lies within the tropics, but it extends well into the temperate zone (S); as it tapers sharply southwards, however, in its higher latitudes maritime influences are clearly apparent, and no region has a high range of temperatures. In the tropical highland areas the climates may be classified according to altitude as *tierra caliente* (hot), *tierra templada* (temperate), and *tierra fria* (cool). The equator crosses the

N part of the continent, and most of the Amazon basin has an equatorial climate, with constantly high temperatures and abundant rainfall; N and S of the hot humid rain-forest, on the tropical grass-lands, the climate shows marked dry and rainy seasons, with summer rainfall maxima, passing S to the warm temperate climate of the pampas, with a moderate, well-distributed rainfall. The climatic pattern W of the Andes is very different from that to the E. In the extreme N the coastal areas are hot and rainy, but the W seaboard of Peru and N Chile, not subject to rain-bearing winds, comprises the arid Atacama Desert. S of the desert is the sub-tropical region of central Chile, with winter rainfall; S Chile, its Andean slopes clothed with forests, has copious all-year rainfall from the prevailing westerlies. Patagonia, on the E side of the Andes and in their rain shadow, consists mainly of steppe and desert.

RESOURCES, PEOPLE, etc. The importance of agriculture in the S American economy is reflected in the leading exports: coffee from Brazil and Colombia, grains, meat, hides from Argentina and Uruguay, cocoa from Brazil, cotton and sugar from Peru. With certain exceptions, mineral resources are only partially developed. Venezuela is the world's third largest producer of petroleum; Bolivia has a significant output of tin and Chile of copper and nitrates. The continent is poor in coal, and the development of hydroelectric power has scarcely begun. Industrial development, also in its infancy, is still concentrated in the national capitals and seaports. In many countries large areas are served by neither railways nor roads, a result in part of the difficult topography, which in turn has stimulated the development of airlines. Argentina, Brazil, and Venezuela are responsible for about three quarters of the exports of the continent; trade between the republics is very limited.

Vast areas of the interior are practically uninhabited, and the only densely popu-lated regions occur as small, isolated pockets, usually near the coast. Though rightly regarded as an under-populated continent, in the 1950s and 1960s S America had a higher population growth than any other major world region, and in Rio de Janeiro, São Paulo, and Buenos Aires, each with over 3 million inhabitants, it has the three largest cities in the southern continents. In many countries mestizos, of mixed European and Indian blood, form the majority of the population, and there are large numbers of Negroes and mulattoes in Argentina and Brazil. In Argentina and Brazil, esp. the former, the peoples are predominantly of European origin; in Bolivia and Peru they are mainly Indian. Of the millions of immi-grants to S America in recent times, chiefly to Brazil and Argentina, the majority have been Italian, Spanish, and Portuguese.

HISTORY. S America was probably dis-covered by Columbus in 1498, and its modern history begins with the agreed division of the continent between Portugal and Spain, the former to receive the E part (later Brazil) and the latter the remainder. The Spanish conquistadors vanquished the Incas of Peru and the Chibchas of Colom-bia, plundered their mineral wealth, con-verted them to Christianity, and main-tained colonial rule by a system of viceroyalties. One colony after another gained independence from Spain in the 1820s under the leadership of Bolívar and San Martín; Brazil became temporarily an Empire in 1822 and a republic in 1889. Only the Guianas remained the colonial possessions of Britain, the Netherlands, and France; British Guiana has since become the independent Guyana (1966). Since achieving independence, the re-publics have frequently suffered from political instability and social unrest, at times from disastrous wars. In both world wars they generally supported the Allied cause, and after the 2nd World War they showed little sympathy for Communism.

Southampton England. City and county borough in Hampshire at the head of Southampton Water on the peninsula between the estuaries of the R. Test and the R. Itchen. Pop. (1961) 204,707. Chief British passenger seaport; terminal of the most important transatlantic shipping lines. The double tides caused by its position opposite the Isle of Wight (S) are advantageous. The King George V graving dock was constructed (1933) to take the world's largest vessels. Imports fruit, vegetables, meat, wool, etc. Flour milling, yacht building. Manufactures marine engines, electrical equipment, cables. Large oil refinery at Fawley on Southampton Water. Evidence of its long history may still be seen in parts of the medieval walls, the 14th-cent. Bar Gate, the 12th-cent.

house known as King John's Palace, and other old buildings. The University College (founded 1850) became a university 1952. The Pilgrim Fathers sailed from here (1620) for Plymouth on the first stage of their voyage to America. Severely damaged by bombing in the 2nd World War. Raised to city status 1964. Birthplace of Sir John Millais (1829–96) and George Saintsbury (1845–1933).

**Southampton Island** Canada. Island in the E Keewatin District, NW Territories, at the entrance to Hudson Bay. Area 16,936 sq. m. Pop. (inc. Eskimo) about 200. Permanent white settlements only at Coral Harbour and Munn Bay, on the S coast.

**South Arabia, Federation of** ◊ *South Yemen.*

**South Australia** Australia. State in the central S part of the continent, bounded by the Northern Territory (N), Queensland, New South Wales, and Victoria (E), the Indian Ocean (S), and Western Australia (W). Area 380,070 sq. m. Pop. (1966) 1,091,875 (excluding about 5,500 aborigines). Cap. Adelaide. Has a varied topography. The W is part of the old western plateau, overlain by flat sediments of the arid Nullarbor Plain. In the S and centre considerable faulting in late Tertiary times has given a series of peninsulas, low mountain blocks, and drowned gulfs. Inland of Spencer Gulf are lakes, swamps, and salt flats, while farther inland L. Eyre, 39 ft below sea level, intermittently receives water from a vast inland drainage area. E of the Mt Lofty Range is the W part of the Murray basin, with the river flowing S to Encounter Bay. Kangaroo Island is a S extension of the Mt Lofty Range.

Winter depressions are fairly frequent S of 32° S lat., the climate being of 'Mediterranean' type. To the N and W there is a light and erratic rainfall averaging under 10 ins. annually. The arid interior carries only coarse spinifex and low acacias, the Nullarbor Plain saltbush and small shrubs. These are empty lands, crossed by the Trans-Australian Railway and the road and railway to Alice Springs; between the two is Woomera, on a missile range. Bordering the moister SE is a zone of grassland with acacias (mulga); the SE highlands bear mainly open eucalypt woodland.

The 'Mediterranean' region is the chief agricultural area, growing wheat, barley, fruit, vines. There are numerous sheep, though away from the SE their density is

low. Along the Murray R. is much irrigated land with fruit and vine growing and dairy farming; wheat is cultivated on improved soils S of the Murray R. 'bend'. The extreme S is cooler and moister and has timber plantations and sawmills, and near Mt Gambier specializes in potatoes and vegetables.

The Middleback Range is a major source of iron ore, and Whyalla consequently has become an iron-smelting centre with shipyards. Port Pirie, across Spencer Gulf, has metal and chemical works. Low-grade coal is mined 200 m. N at Leigh Creek. The most industrially developed part, however, is in and near Adelaide, E of Gulf St Vincent, with Elizabeth, a new, planned, light industrial town. Adelaide contains over 60 per cent of the state population. Port Adelaide is the principal port. The chief agricultural exports are wool, wheat, fruit, wine, the mineral exports iron, pyrites, salt, limestone.

The S coast of S Australia was explored (1802) by Flinders. In 1836 the territory was proclaimed a British crown colony, to become a state of the Commonwealth in 1901.

**South Bend** USA. Town in Indiana, on the south bend of the St Joseph R. (hence the name) 75 m. ESE of Chicago. Pop. (1960) 132,445. Manufactures cars, aircraft equipment, agricultural machinery, clothing, toys, etc. Seat of the University of Notre Dame (1842).

**South Beveland** Netherlands. Peninsula in the Zeeland province, in the Scheldt estuary. Area 135 sq. m. Vegetables, red currants, raspberries cultivated. Crossed by a ship canal and linked by railway with the mainland and Walcheren.

**South Carolina** USA. State in the SE, bordered on the E by the Atlantic. Area 31,055 sq. m. Pop. (1970) 2,522,881 (inc. 850,000 Negroes). Cap. Columbia. One of the original 13 states; popularly known as the 'Palmetto' state. About two thirds of the area is the low-lying coastal plain. Highest point Sassafras Mountain (3,560 ft), in the Blue Ridge. Chief rivers the Savannah, the Santee, the Pee Dee, the Edisto. Offshore lie the Sea Is. (shared with Georgia and Florida). Climate humid subtropical, with hot summers and mild winters. Annual rainfall 45–50 ins. Agriculture important. Main crops tobacco, cotton, maize, soya beans. Stock rearing is a major occupation. The forests produce oak, poplar, pine, etc. Industries (principally cotton milling and wood processing) centred on Columbia, Charleston (chief seaport), Greenville. Settled first by the Spaniards (1526), then by the English (1670). Played a leading part in the American Civil War, on the side of the Confederates, as a large slave-owning state; the first to secede from the Union (1860).

**South Dakota** USA. N central state. Area 77,047 sq. m. Pop. (1970) 661,406 (inc. *c.* 25,000 Indians). Cap. Pierre. Admitted to the Union in 1889 as the 40th state; popularly known as the 'Sunshine' or 'Coyote' state. Mostly in the Great Plains; largely treeless short-grass prairie. Highest point Harney Peak (7,242 ft), in the Black Hills (SW); also in the SW are the heavily-eroded Badlands. Roughly bisected by the Missouri R. Climate continental; hot summers and bitterly cold winters with heavy snowfalls. Annual rainfall 15–25 ins. Primarily agricultural. Chief crop maize, followed by oats and wheat. Large numbers of cattle, sheep, and pigs reared. Leading state in gold production (Black Hills). Largest towns Sioux Falls, Rapid City. Explored by the French (1742); first settlement a fur-trading post (1817), later known as Fort Pierre. The Dakota Territory was created in 1861; this was divided into the states of N Dakota and S Dakota in 1889.

**South Dum-Dum** ◊ *Dum-Dum*.

**Southend-on-Sea** England. County borough in SE Essex, on the N side of the Thames estuary 35 m. E of London. Pop. (1961) 164,976. Residential town and seaside resort, popular with Londoners. Includes Leigh-on-Sea, Westcliff, Thorpe Bay, Shoeburyness, etc. The tide recedes for nearly a mile, but the pier, over 1¼ m. long, accommodates steamers at all tides. Airport near by. Manufactures radio and television sets, electrical equipment, pharmaceutical goods, etc.

**Southern Alps** New Zealand. Mountainous 'backbone' in the W of the S Island, running NE–SW about 200 m. Average crest height over 8,000 ft; many peaks exceed 10,000 ft. The central snowfields near Mt Cook (12,349 ft) feed great glaciers such as the Tasman Glacier, 18 m. long and 1 m. wide; ice-cut, moraine-blocked valleys and long ribbon lakes lie along the E flanks.

**Southern Ijssellakepolders** Netherlands. Polder lands reclaimed from the former Zuider Zee (now Ijsselmeer) and drained in 1957, not incorporated in a province. Area 207 sq. m. Pop. (1968) 10,451.

**South Foreland** England. Chalk headland on the E coast of Kent, 3 m. ENE of Dover. Lighthouse.

**Southgate** England. Former municipal borough in Middlesex, 9 m. N of London; from 1965 part of the Greater London borough of Enfield. Pop. (1961) 72,051. Mainly residential.

**South Gate** USA. Industrial town in California 6 m. S of Los Angeles. Pop. (1960) 53,831. Manufactures chemicals, tyres, furniture, building materials, etc.

**South Georgia** S Atlantic Ocean. Island in the S Atlantic about 800 m. E of the Falkland Is. and a dependency of this British colony. Area 1,600 sq. m. Till 1965 an important whaling base, with summer pop. exceeding 500. Pop. (1967) 22. Mountainous, snow-covered most of the year, with glaciers. Claimed for Britain by Capt. Cook 1775. Claimed by Argentina.

**South Holland** Netherlands. Province bounded on the W by the North Sea. Area 1,085 sq. m. Pop. (1968) 2,922,450. Cap. The Hague. Mainly below sea level, being protected along the coast by dunes. Drained by distributaries of the Rhine delta. The most densely populated province in the country. Chief towns The Hague, Rotterdam, Dordrecht, Leiden, Delft. Dairy farming and market gardening are important.

**Southland** ◊ *Otago*.

**South Molton** England. Market town in Devonshire 24 m. NW of Exeter. Pop. (1961) 2,994. Centre for Exmoor. Flour milling etc.

**South Orkney Islands** S Atlantic Ocean. Island group in the S Atlantic 450 m. SW of South Georgia. Area 240 sq. m. Formerly a dependency of the British ◊ *Falkland Islands* colony; since 1962 part of British Antarctic Territory. A whaling base. Discovered 1821. Claimed by Argentina.

**South Ossetian AR** USSR. Autonomous region in the Georgian SSR, on the S slopes of the Great Caucasus. Area 1,505 sq. m. Pop. (1970) 100,000 (mainly Ossetian). Cap. Tskhinvali (Stalinir). Mountainous. Main occupations stock rearing (sheep, goats), lumbering. Established 1922.

**Southport** England. County borough in W

Lancashire, on the Irish Sea 16 m. N of Liverpool. Pop. (1961) 81,976. Seaside resort with an extensive promenade and a long pier; famous golf course (Royal Birkdale). Engineering. Manufactures hosiery and knitwear, confectionery, etc.

**South Sandwich Islands** S Atlantic Ocean. Group of small volcanic islands in the S Atlantic 450 m. ESE of South Georgia; a dependency of the British ◊ *Falkland Islands* colony. Area 130 sq. m. Discovered (1775) by Capt. Cook. Claimed by Argentina.

**South San Francisco** USA. Industrial town in California 9 m. S of San Francisco on San Francisco Bay. Pop. (1960) 39,418. Meat packing. Manufactures steel, chemicals, paint, etc.

**South Shetland Islands** S Atlantic Ocean. Group of islands in the S Atlantic off the NW coast of Graham Land; Deception is volcanic. Area 1,800 sq. m. Formerly a dependency of the British ◊ *Falkland Islands* colony; since 1962 part of British Antarctic Territory. Discovered 1819 and claimed for Britain by Capt. William Smith.

**South Shields** England. County borough in NE Durham on the S side of the Tyne estuary, opposite North Shields (in Tynemouth), with which it is connected by ferry. Pop. (1961) 109,633. Seaport. Resort. Industrial centre. Shipbuilding, marine engineering. Manufactures glass, chemicals, paint, biscuits. Coal exports, once important, have declined in recent years. The first lifeboat was launched here (1790). Birthplace of Ernest Thompson Seton (1860–1946).

**South Suburban** India. Town in W Bengal just SW of Calcutta, of which it is virtually a suburb. Pop. (1961) 185,811. Rice milling. Manufactures chemicals etc.

**Southwark** England. Greater London borough (1965) on the S bank of the R. Thames comprising the former metropolitan boroughs of Bermondsey, Camberwell, and Southwark. Pop. (1963) 312,687. Connected with the City of London by Blackfriars, Southwark, and London bridges. Has a 13th-cent. cathedral containing the tombs of John Fletcher and Philip Massinger, the dramatists; 19th-cent. Roman Catholic cathedral; Guy's Hospital (1721). Includes Bankside, site of the Globe Theatre, with which Shakespeare was associated, now dominated by a large power station: near by was the Clink Prison for heretics, which gave rise to the expression 'in the clink' (in prison). From medieval times Southwark was famous for its inns, and the 17th-cent. George, the last galleried inn in London, still survives.

**Southwell** England. Town in Nottinghamshire 12 m. NE of Nottingham. Pop. (rural district, 1961) 45,818. Flour milling. Manufactures hosiery. The minster (built 12th/14th cent.) was elevated to a cathedral in 1884. The remains of the 15th-cent. palace of the Archbishops of York were incorporated into a residence for the Bishop of Southwell. Brackenhurst, just S, was the birthplace of Viscount Allenby (1861–1936).

**South-West Africa.\*** UN mandated territory, disputedly administered by ◊ *South Africa*, bounded by Angola (N, Cunene R. and Okavango R.), Botswana (E), and S Africa (SE and S, Orange R.); the narrow Caprivi Strip (Caprivi Zipfel) extends E to the Zambezi R. (Zambia). Area 318,261 sq. m. (inc. Walvis Bay, an enclave of S Africa). Pop. (1960) 525,064 (73,154 whites). Cap. Windhoek. Part of the plateau of southern Africa, rising sharply from the arid coastal plain of the Namib Desert to an average height of 3,500 ft. No permanent streams of importance; many salt-water depressions (the largest is the Etosha Pan) in the N and E. Rainfall increases E from the coast (Swakopmund 0·7 in.) to the plateau (Windhoek 14 ins.); it reaches 20 ins. in the N but decreases again on the Kalahari plateau. Mostly poor grassland and scrub. Main occupation stock rearing: cattle in the N and centre, sheep and goats in the drier S (large numbers of karakul sheep, from which 'Persian lamb' skins are obtained for export). Principal export alluvial diamonds (recovered near Lüderitz and at the mouth of the Orange R.). Copper, lead, and zinc mined in the Grootfontein district. Chief seaport Walvis Bay. Other ports Swakopmund, Lüderitz. All three are linked by rail with Windhoek and the S African railway system. Most of the inhabitants are Bantu, chiefly Ovambo, Herero, Namaqua (Hottentots), with scattered groups of Bushmen.

The first European to visit the territory was Bartholomew Diaz, who landed at Lüderitz (Angra Pequena) in 1486. Britain annexed Walvis Bay in 1878. Germany established a settlement at Lüderitz in 1883 and created the colony of German SW Africa in 1892; after the 1st World

War the League of Nations mandated the territory to administration by the then Union of S Africa. After the 2nd World War, S Africa passed a SW Africa Affairs Amendment Act; in 1950, however, the International Court of Justice ruled that SW Africa was still under international mandate from the UN, and that S Africa was not competent to modify the international status of the territory without UN consent. S Africa left the British Commonwealth in 1961, and the status of the SW Africa territory was reviewed by the International Court of Justice, which announced (1966) that it could not give a decision.

**Southwold** England. Municipal borough in E Suffolk 11 m. SSW of Lowestoft. Pop. (1961) 2,228. Seaside resort. Has a Perpendicular 15th-cent. church.

**South Yemen.** Formerly the Federation of South Arabia. Republic in SW Asia, in S Arabia. Area 61,890 sq. m. Pop. 1,500,000. Cap. Madinet al-Shaab (formerly Al Ittihad), just NW of Aden. The Federation of S Arabia consisted of 17 states within the British Commonwealth, including ◊ *Aden*, in 1963. There were repeated political disturbances in the 1960s; eventually the country was taken over by the National Liberation Front, British troops were withdrawn, and the Republic of South Yemen was proclaimed (1967), ending 129 years of British rule. The people of the islands of Kamaran and Perim opted to remain with the Republic.

**Sovetsk** USSR. Formerly Tilsit. Industrial town in the Kaliningrad region, RSFSR, on the Neman R. 60 m. ENE of Kaliningrad. Pop. 60,000. Manufactures cheese, wood pulp, leather, soap, etc. Trade in dairy produce. Founded in the 13th cent.; later in the German province of E Prussia (as Tilsit). By the Treaty of Tilsit (1807), signed by Russia, France, and Prussia, the last-named lost almost half her territory. After the 2nd World War it passed to the USSR and was renamed.

**Soviet Central Asia** ◊ *Central Asia, Soviet.*

**Soviet Union** ◊ *Union of Soviet Socialist Republics.*

**Sowerby Bridge** England. Urban district in the W Riding of Yorkshire, on the R. Calder 3 m. SW of Halifax. Pop. (1961) 16,224. Manufactures textiles, carpets, chemicals.

**Spa** Belgium. Tourist and health resort famous for its mineral springs (discovered in the 14th cent.), in Liège province 7 m. S of Verviers in wooded hills. Pop. 9,000. Esp. fashionable in the 18th cent. Has given its name to all such resorts.

**Spain.** State in SW Europe. Area (inc. the Balearic and Canary Is.) 194,945 sq. m. Pop. (1968) 32,411,407. Cap. Madrid. Rel. Roman Catholic.

Occupies most of the Iberian peninsula, from the Bay of Biscay and the Pyrenees (N, which it shares with France) to the Strait of Gibraltar (S) and from the Atlantic (W) to the Mediterranean (E), with Portugal (W) occupying most of the Atlantic section. Almost isolated from the rest of Europe by the Pyrenees; in many respects has a closer affinity with N Africa. The interior consists of a vast plateau, the Meseta, at an average height of 2,000 ft, crossed by several lofty mountain ranges. Mainly agricultural; famous for oranges, olive oil, and wine (sherry). Also rich in mineral resources. Divided administratively into 50 provinces: Álava, Albacete, Alicante, Almería, Ávila, Badajoz, Baleares (Balearic Is.), Barcelona, Burgos, Cáceres, Cádiz, Castellón, Ciudad Real, Córdoba, La Coruña, Cuenca, Gerona, Granada, Guadalajara, Guipúzcoa, Huelva, Huesca, Jaén, León, Lérida, Logroño, Lugo, Madrid, Málaga, Murcia, Navarra, Orense, Oviedo, Palencia, Las Palmas and Santa Cruz de Tenerife, Pontevedra, Salamanca, Santander, Segovia, Sevilla, Soria, Tarragona, Teruel, Toledo, Valencia, Valladolid, Vizcaya, Zamora, Zaragoza (Saragossa).

TOPOGRAPHY, CLIMATE. To the N of the Meseta are the fold mountain ranges of the Pyrenees, rising to 11,168 ft in the Pico de Aneto, and the rather lower Cantabrian Mountains, which at few points exceed 8,000 ft. S of the Meseta, near the Mediterranean coast of Andalusia, is another fold range, the Sierra Nevada; here Mulhacén (11,421 ft) is the highest peak in mainland Spain. Between the Pyrenees and the Meseta are the plains of Aragón, drained by the Ebro R. Between the Sierra Nevada and the S edge of the Meseta (the Sierra Morena) are the fertile plains of Andalusia, drained by the Guadalquivir R. Narrow plains extend along the E and SE coasts, broadening somewhat around Valencia, Alicante, Almería, and Málaga. Across the Meseta itself the Douro, Tagus, and Guadiana rivers have cut deep valleys; between the Douro (Duero) and the Tagus (Tajo) are the ridges of the Sierra de

Gredos and the Sierra de Guadarrama, both rising to over 8,000 ft, and between the Tagus and the Guadiana the lower Sierra de Guadalupe and the Montes de Toledo. Much of the coastline is steep and rocky; the best natural harbours are the narrow inlets (rias) of the NW, where the ports of Vigo and Corunna are situated. The climate in the NW and N is W European, with a moderate well-distributed rainfall; the S and SE coastal plains are Mediterranean, hot and dry in summer and mild and rainy in winter. On the great Meseta the climate is continental with extreme temperatures, hot in summer and cold in winter, and generally light rainfall, in some areas less than 15 ins. annually.

RESOURCES, PEOPLE, etc. Productive agricultural land is about equally divided between crops and pasture. Of the cereals the most important is wheat (grown esp. in Old Castile and Andalusia), followed by barley. Rice is produced in the irrigated S and SE, where cotton and sugar-cane are also cultivated and Elche has the only groves of date palms in Europe. Spain is a leading world producer of olives, grown mainly in Andalusia. Vineyards in all regions; Jerez is famous for sherry, Almería for table grapes, and Valencia for raisins. Oranges come largely from the irrigated *huertas* of the Mediterranean coastlands. Esparto grass is a product of the plateau. Sheep are numerous; Spain is the original home of the famous wool-producing merino breed. There are more pigs than cattle, and more mules and donkeys than horses. The importance of agriculture is seen in the exports, where oranges, olive oil, and wine are the leading items. Iron ore (mined in the Cantabrian Mountains) is exported chiefly to Britain. Coal, copper, mercury, zinc, and lead are also produced, mainly in the Cantabrians and the Sierra Morena. Catalonia is the principal industrial region, specializing in cotton goods; Barcelona is the second largest city and chief seaport.

Agriculture is backward and resources generally ill developed, partly owing to poor communications: the relief is unfavourable to railways, and the rivers are virtually useless for navigation. Another contributory cause is the low cultural level of the peasant population; the illiteracy rate was still 14 per cent in 1960 although primary education is compulsory and free. The tourist trade has recently expanded

considerably, esp. along the Mediterranean coast (Costa Brava) and in the Balearic Is. (Majorca). Castilian Spanish is the language of literature and of most of the people; Catalan (NE, allied to Provençal), Galician (NW, akin to Portuguese), and Basque (unlike any other language) are spoken in their respective regions. The Roman Catholic church was disestablished in 1931 but was restored to its former position by the Franco régime after the civil war.

HISTORY. Palaeolithic Man has left his mark in the famous rock paintings of Altamira, 18 m. WSW of Santander. Much later the S and E were inhabited by Iberians (from N Africa) and the N and W by Celtic tribes from beyond the Pyrenees; Greek writers of the 3rd cent. B.C. described the mingled peoples of the Meseta as Celtiberians. Colonies were established by the Phoenicians (notably at Cádiz), the Greeks, and the Carthaginians, who conquered most of the peninsula in the 3rd cent. B.C. The end of the 2nd Punic War (201 B.C.) was followed by the Romanization of the peninsula, which was divided into the provinces of Tarraconensis (N, E, and SE), Lusitania (roughly modern Portugal), and Baetica (roughly Andalusia). After the collapse of the Roman Empire it was invaded by the Suevi, the Vandals, and the Visigoths in the 5th cent. A.D. A Muslim army under Tarik crossed from N Africa and defeated Roderick, the last Visigoth king (711); the Moors soon conquered most of the peninsula and established a separate Caliphate, with Córdoba as capital. Charlemagne also gained a temporary foothold in the Spanish March (NE) in the 8th cent. Under Moorish rule agricultural methods were improved, new industries introduced, and the arts encouraged, but the Christians advanced S and by the mid 13th cent. had assumed control of the entire country apart from the kingdom of Granada. Two powerful Christian states, Aragón and Castile, emerged from the conflict; they were united by the marriage of Ferdinand II of Aragón to Isabella of Castile (1474). Granada was conquered in 1492 and in the same year Columbus's voyage led to the acquisition of most of Central and S America. Charles V was elected Emperor (of the Holy Roman Empire) in 1519; Naples and Milan were annexed, Burgundy and the Netherlands became Spanish provinces, and Spain was the foremost country in Europe. Under Philip II the union with Portugal (independent since the 12th cent.) added the Portugese overseas possessions to the Spanish Empire (1581). But the Netherlands continued permanently in revolt, the Armada was defeated (1588), the constant wars brought on economic exhaustion (worsened by the expulsion of the Moors and the Jews), and by the 17th cent. the power of Spain was declining. Portugal became independent again in 1640. Spain lost the Netherlands, Milan, Naples, Sardinia, and Sicily in the early 18th cent. A century later it was occupied by French troops, and Napoleon ejected the Bourbon monarchy, declaring his brother Joseph King of Spain. The French were evicted by the Peninsular War, with British assistance. The remaining American colonies rebelled (1821–4); most of Latin America was independent by 1825. Spain suffered severely from civil wars, revolutions, and dictatorships during the 19th cent. Puerto Rico, Cuba, and the Philippines were lost in the Spanish-American War (1898). Primo de Rivera's dictatorship (1923–30) could not save the monarchy; Alfonso XIII abdicated and a republic was established in 1931. A liberal government was elected in 1936 but a military revolt (headed by General Franco) broke out in Spanish Morocco and was followed by a rebel invasion. In the ensuing civil war (1936–9) the rebels were aided by Germany and Italy and the republicans by the USSR and an International Brigade. The rebels were victorious and a totalitarian régime was established with the quasi-fascist Falange the only political party and General Franco as 'El Caudillo'; in 1947 he announced that Spain was to become a monarchy again, the succession after his death (by king or regent) to be determined by a Regency Council.

**Spalato** ◊ *Split*.

**Spalding** England. Urban district in Lincolnshire, on the R. Welland 14 m. SSW of Boston. Pop. (1961) 14,821. Market town in a region growing potatoes, sugar-beet, and bulbs. Sugar refining, fruit and vegetable canning, engineering, etc. Has a 13th-cent. parish church and the 15th-cent. Ayscoughfee Hall, where Maurice Johnson founded (1710) the 'Gentlemen's Society of Spalding', to which Newton, Addison, Pope, and other men of science and letters belonged.

Much visited in spring for the near-by tulip fields.

**Spandau** Federal German Republic. Residential and industrial suburb in W Berlin, at the confluence of the Havel and Spree rivers. Pop. 166,000. The favourite residence of the electors of Brandenburg. Surrendered to Prussia 1813. Incorporated into Berlin 1920.

**Spanish Guinea** ◊ *Equatorial Guinea*.

**Spanish Sahara.** Overseas province in W Africa, bounded by Morocco (N), Algeria (NE), and Mauritania (E and S). Area 102,680 sq. m. Pop. (1967) 48,607 (largely nomadic). Cap. El Aaiún (pop. 9,812). Two districts: El Aaiún (N) and Villa Cisneros (S). Formerly two zones: Sekia el Hamra (N), Rio de Oro (S). Desert; several oases. Spain ceded the strip between latitude 27°40′ N and Wad Draa to Morocco in 1958. ◊ *Ifni*.

**Sparta** (Gr. **Spárti**) Greece. Capital of Lakonia *nome*, on the Eurotas R. 90 m. SSE of Patras. Pop. (1961) 10,412. Commercial centre. Trade in citrus fruits, olive oil. Just S are the ruins of ancient Sparta (Lacedaemon), which was founded by the Dorians. Sparta was ruled by two hereditary kings; under the constitution, attributed to Lycurgus, citizens were trained for war from an early age, and were taught indifference to pain or death: they distinguished themselves in battle but contributed little to Greek literature and art. Reached the height of its power in the Persian Wars (500–449 B.C.) and the Peloponnesian War (431–404 B.C., when it defeated Athens and became the most powerful city-state in Greece). Defeated by Thebes at Leuctra (371 B.C.) and later compelled to submit to Philip II of Macedon, after which it declined. The modern town was founded 1834.

**Spartanburg** USA. Town in S Carolina 88 m. NW of Columbia. Pop. (1960) 44,352. A leading textile centre and railway junction. Many cotton mills. Manufactures clothing, food products, electrical equipment, etc.

**Spenborough** England. Municipal borough in the W Riding of Yorkshire, in the Spen valley 9 m. SW of Leeds. Pop. (1961) 36,412. Includes the towns of Cleckheaton, Gomersal, Liversedge, Birkenshaw, and Hunsworth. Manufactures woollen goods, machinery, etc.

**Spencer Gulf** Australia. Inlet of the Indian Ocean in the coast of S Australia, between

Eyre Peninsula and Yorke Peninsula, 200 m. long and up to 75 m. wide, with Port Augusta, Port Pirie, and Whyalla on its shores.

**Spennymoor** England. Urban district in Durham 5 m. S of Durham. Pop. (1961) 19,104. Coalmining etc. **Speyer** Federal German Republic. Ancient Noviomagus, Augusta Nemetum. Town in Rhineland-Palatinate, on the left bank of the Rhine R. 12 m. S of Ludwigshafen. Pop. (1963) 39,800. Manufactures tobacco products, paper, footwear, bricks, etc. Sugar refining, brewing. Famous Romanesque cathedral of sandstone, øriginally built 1030–61, and many times restored, with the tombs of 8 German emperors. Was a bishopric by the 7th cent. Became a free imperial city 1294. Many imperial diets were held here, and it was the seat of the imperial supreme court 1527–1689, but it did not recover altogether from the destruction wrought by the French in 1689.

**Spey River** Scotland. River 107 m. long rising in Inverness-shire 10 m. SSE of Fort Augustus and flowing generally NE, through Strathspey and past Kingussie, Aviemore, and Fochabers to Moray Firth. Swiftly flowing; well known for its salmon.

**Spezia, La** ◊ *La Spezia*.

**Spice Islands** ◊ *Moluccas*.

**Spion Kop** S Africa. Hill near the Tugela R. 24 m. WSW of Ladysmith. Scene of a battle (1900) in which the British were defeated by the Boers while trying to raise the siege of Ladysmith.

**Spitalfields** England. District in the Greater London borough of Tower Hamlets, E London. Named after the priory and hospital or 'spital' of St Mary (founded 1197). Manufactures footwear, furniture. Formerly noted for the silk industry, introduced by Huguenot refugees in the 17th cent.

**Spithead** England. Anchorage in the Solent, off Portsmouth. Scene of many naval pageants, and of a historic mutiny (1797). The name is sometimes wrongly applied to the E half of the Solent.

**Spitsbergen (Svalbard)** Norway. Archipelago in the Arctic Ocean belonging to Norway and about 400 m. N of that country, consisting of West Spitsbergen, Northeast Land, Edge Island, Barents Island, and several smaller islands, together with Bear Island to the S. Area 23,979 sq. m. Pop. (1968) 2,808 (908 Norwegian, 1,900 Russian). The chief island, W Spitsbergen (15,200 sq. m.), is deeply indented with fiords, and rises to 5,633 ft in Mt Newton; its W coast is kept ice-free about April–Sept. by the N Atlantic Drift. There are coalmines, 3 Norwegian and 3 Russian, on this island; 2 Norwegian and 1 Russian are not now worked. Used by whalers in the 17th cent.; awarded to Norway 1920 and formally taken over by that country 1925.

**Split** (Italian **Spalato**) Yugoslavia. Chief seaport on the Dalmatian coast, in Croatia 160 m. SE of Rijeka. Pop. (1961) 99,614. Stands on a small peninsula; has an excellent harbour. Also a tourist centre. Shipbuilding, fish canning. Manufactures cement, carpets, etc. Grew up in and around the great palace built (A.D. 295–305) by Diocletian, who was born in a near-by village. Many parts of this massive structure, which covers about 9½ acres and is an outstanding example of Roman architecture, are still well preserved. In the 7th cent. the palace was occupied by refugees from neighbouring Salona, who thus established the modern Split. The city passed to Venice (1420–1797), Austria (1815–1919), and then to Yugoslavia.

**Splügen Pass** Switzerland. Alpine pass (6,944 ft) in Graubünden (Grisons) canton, on the Swiss-Italian border, linking the village of Splügen (Switzerland) with Chiavenna (Italy).

**Spokane** USA. Industrial town in Washington, on the Spokane R. 235 m. E of Seattle. Pop. (1960) 181,608. Commercial centre for a large agricultural, lumbering, and mining region. Aluminium works and plants for processing meat, wheat, dairy produce, timber, etc. Largely destroyed by fire (1889) but rapidly rebuilt.

**Spoleto** Italy. Ancient Spoletium. Town in Perugia province, Umbria, 33 m. SSE of Perugia. Pop. 40,000. Manufactures textiles, leather, etc. Has a Roman bridge and remains of a theatre and amphitheatre, a 12th-cent. cathedral with frescoes by Filippo Lippi, and medieval churches. An important town in Roman times; repulsed Hannibal (217 B.C.). Became capital of an independent duchy in the 6th cent. A.D.

**Sporades** Greece. Scattered islands of the Aegean Sea outside the Cyclades, generally divided into two groups. 1. N Sporades, NE of Euboea, including Skíathos, Skopelos, and Skíros. 2. S Sporades, now generally known as the ◊ *Dodecanese*, off the SW coast of Asia Minor, with Samos, Icaria, etc.

**Spree River** German Democratic Republic. River 247 m. long rising in the Dresden district and flowing generally N and NW past Bautzen and Cottbus, and through Berlin to join the Havel at Spandau. Below Cottbus is the Spreewald, a popular resort area for Berlin people.

**Springfield** (Illinois) USA. State capital, on the Sangamon R. 180 m. SW of Chicago. Pop. (1960) 83,271. Manufactures agricultural machinery, electrical equipment, food products, footwear, etc. Home (1837–61) and burial-place of Abraham Lincoln.

**Springfield** (Massachusetts) USA. Industrial town on the Connecticut R. 78 m. WSW of Boston. Pop. (1960) 174,463. Manufactures electrical machinery, machine tools, fire-arms, etc. Printing and publishing. Founded 1636. Seat of an armoury dating from 1794. Home of the famous Springfield rifle.

**Springfield** (Missouri) USA. Town in the SW, in the Ozark Mountains 150 m. SSE of Kansas City. Pop. (1960) 95,865. Commercial and industrial centre in a poultry-farming, dairying, and stock-rearing agricultural region. Railway engineering. Manufactures typewriters, furniture, clothing, etc.

**Springfield** (Ohio) USA. Industrial town on the Mad R. 44 m. W of Columbus. Pop. (1960) 82,723. Manufactures motor vehicles, agricultural machinery, electrical appliances, etc.

**Springs** S Africa. Industrial town in the Transvaal, in E Witwatersrand (Rand) at a height of 5,300 ft 25 m. ESE of Johannesburg. Pop. (1967) 142,320 (93,534 Bantu). Important goldmining centre, with uranium extraction; coal also mined in the neighbourhood. Manufactures mining machinery, electrical equipment, glass, paper, etc.

**Spurn Head** England. Headland of sand and shingle at the S end of Holderness, in the E Riding of Yorkshire, across the entrance to the Humber estuary; narrow but about 4 m. long (from Kilnsea). Has 2 lighthouses and a bird-migration observatory.

**Srinagar** India. Summer capital of Jammu and Kashmir, on the Jhelum R. at a height of 5,250 ft 400 m. NNW of Delhi. Pop. (1961) 285,257. Manufactures carpets, leather goods, copperware. Picturesque, with the river, spanned by 9 wooden bridges,

winding through; centre of houseboat excursions through the beautiful Vale of Kashmir. Seat of the University of Jammu and Kashmir (1948).

**Srirangapatnam** ♢ *Seringapatam.*

**Stade** Federal German Republic. Town in Lower Saxony, on the Schwinge R. near the Elbe estuary 23 m. WNW of Hamburg. Pop. (1963) 31,400. River port. Manufactures chemicals, leather goods, etc. Formerly an important commercial centre.

**Staffa** Scotland. Uninhabited island in the Inner Hebrides, Argyllshire, 8 m. W of Mull. Well known for its basalt caves, esp. the remarkable Fingal's Cave, 227 ft long and with an entrance 66 ft high.

**Stafford** England. County town in Staffordshire, municipal borough on the R. Sow (tributary of the R. Trent). Pop. (1961) 47,814. Market town. Important footwear industry; also manufactures chemicals, electrical goods, etc. Engineering. Richard Brinsley Sheridan, the dramatist, was its MP 1780–1806; of the already important boot and shoe industry he said, 'May its trade be trod underfoot by all the world'. The unfinished 19th-cent. castle was intended to replace a Norman predecessor. Birthplace of Izaak Walton (1593–1683).

**Staffordshire** England. County in the W Midlands. Area 1,153 sq. m. Pop. (1961) 1,733,887. County town Stafford. Hilly in the N, rising to 1,756 ft in Axe Edge, with Cannock Chase in the centre, in the main it is a gently undulating plain drained by the R. Trent and its tributaries. Mainly industrial, with the N Staffordshire coalfield and the Potteries in the N, and the S Staffordshire coalfield and the Black Country in the S. Chief manufacturing centres Stoke-on-Trent, Wolverhampton, Walsall, West Bromwich, Smethwick, Stafford, Newcastle under Lyme, Burton-upon-Trent.

**Staines** England. Urban district in Surrey, at the confluence of the R. Colne with the R. Thames; includes Ashford, Stanwell, and Laleham (birthplace of Matthew Arnold, 1822–88). Pop. (1961) 49,259. Largely residential. Manufactures linoleum, paint, etc. Has reservoirs for the London water supply. An important bridging point since Roman times; the present granite bridge was designed by Rennie (1831). Transferred from Middlesex to Surrey with the administrative reorganization of Greater London (1965).

**Stalin** (Bulgaria) ♢ *Varna.*

Stalin (Rumania) ⟡ *Braşov*.

Stalin (USSR) ⟡ *Donetsk*.

Stalinabad ⟡ *Dushanbe*.

Stalingrad ⟡ *Volgograd*.

Stalinir ⟡ *Tskhinvali*.

Stalino ⟡ *Donetsk*.

Stalinogorsk ⟡ *Novomoskovsk*.

Stalinogrod ⟡ *Katowice*.

Stalinsk ⟡ *Novokuznetsk*.

Stalybridge England. Municipal borough in Cheshire, on the R. Tame 7 m. E of Manchester. Pop. (1961) 21,940. Engineering. Manufactures cotton goods, metal products, etc.

Stamford England. Municipal borough in Lincolnshire, on the R. Welland 11 m. WNW of Peterborough. Pop. (1961) 11,743. Market town. Manufactures agricultural machinery, concrete products. Has several old buildings, including Brasenose Gateway, which recalls the Oxford students who seceded in 1333 and set up their headquarters here. The 15th-cent. Browne's Hospital is one of the almshouses or 'Callises', named after the wool merchants of Calais. Near by is Burghley House, built by Lord Burghley in the 16th cent., containing a famous art collection.

Stamford USA. Town in SW Connecticut, on Long Island Sound 20 m. WSW of Bridgeport. ?op. (1960) 92,713. Industrial, commercial nd residential centre. Manufactures chemicals, ball bearings, machinery, etc. Founded 1641.

Stamford Bridge England. Village in the E Riding of Yorkshire, on the R. Derwent 7 m. ENE of York, where Harold II of England defeated his brother Tostig and Harald Hardrada, King of Norway, in 1066, prior to being himself defeated by William of Normandy at the Battle of Hastings 3 weeks later.

Standerton S Africa. Market town in the Transvaal, on the Vaal R. at a height of 5,000 ft 92 m. SE of Johannesburg. Pop. (1960) 16,868 (6,698 Europeans). In an agricultural region. Coalmining in the neighbourhood.

Stanislav ⟡ *Ivano-Frankovsk*.

Stanley (Durham) England. Urban district in Durham 8 m. NNW of Durham. Pop. (1961) 46,280. In a coalmining region.

Stanley (Yorkshire) England. Urban district in the W Riding of Yorkshire, 2 m. NE of Wakefield. Pop. (1961) 16,749. In a coalmining district.

Stanley (Falkland Is.) ⟡ *Falkland Islands*.

Stanley Falls Congo (Kinshasa). Series of 7 cataracts on the Lualaba (Congo) R.' between Kisangani (Stanleyville) and Ponthierville. The total fall is only 200 ft in 56 m., but they render this part of the river unnavigable; a railway therefore links the two towns. Below the falls the Lualaba is known as the Congo R.

Stanley Pool Congo (Brazzaville)/Congo (Kinshasa). Lake formed by the widening of the Congo R. 350 m. above the mouth, 18 m. long (E–W) and 15 m. wide (N–S). Kinshasa (Leopoldville) in Congo (Kinshasa) is on the SW shore and Brazzaville in Congo (Brazzaville) on the W. The large swampy island of Bamu (area 70 sq. m.) divides the Congo into N and S branches, of which the latter is always navigable. The lake was discovered (1877) by Stanley.

Stanleyville ⟡ *Kisangani*.

Stanmore (Great Stanmore) England. Town within the Greater London borough of Harrow. Pop. 31,000. Largely residential. Contains the 18th-cent. Bentley Priory (RAF) and the Royal National Orthopaedic Hospital.

Stanovoi Range USSR. Mountain range in the SE of the RSFSR, extending 500 m. E from the Olekma R. and continued NNE by the Dzhugdzhur Range. Rises to 8,143 ft in Skalisty Mt and forms part of the watershed between rivers flowing to the Arctic and the Pacific.

Staples, The ⟡ *Farne Islands*.

Stara Planina ⟡ *Balkan Mountains*.

Stara Zagora Bulgaria. Ancient Augusta Trajana. Formerly Eski-Zagra. Capital of Stara Zagora province 50 m. ENE of Plovdiv. Pop. (1965) 88,522. Manufactures fertilizers, textiles, etc. Flour milling, brewing, distilling, tanning. Trade in wheat, wine, attar of roses. Called by the Turks Eski-Zagra until it was ceded to Bulgaria (1877).

Stassfurt German Democratic Republic. Town in the Magdeburg district 20 m. SSW of Magdeburg. Pop. (1965) 25,803. Important centre of potash and rock-salt mining. Manufactures chemicals.

Staten Island USA. Island in SE New York, co-extensive with Richmond borough of New York city. Area 57 sq. m. Pop. (1960) 221,991. Separated from New Jersey by the Kill van Kull and the Arthur Kill channels, both spanned by bridges, and from Long Island (NY) by the Narrows. Largely residential. Resorts and bathing beaches on the E shore. Several industries, inc. shipbuilding, oil refining, printing, paper manufacture.

**Stavanger** Norway. Capital of Rogaland county, in the SW, and a seaport on Bökn Fiord. Pop. (1968) 80,781. Fishing centre with an important fish-canning industry. Also shipbuilding, woodworking, etc. One of the oldest towns in Norway; probably founded in the 8th cent., but the present town is modern. Famous 11th-cent. cathedral of St Swithin, founded by the English bishop Reinald.

**Staveley** England. Urban district in Derbyshire 4 m. NE of Chesterfield. Pop. (1961) 18,071. Coalmining centre. Manufactures iron, chemicals.

**Stavropol** USSR. 1. Formerly N Caucasus Territory (1924–37), Ordzhonikidze (1937–43). Territory in RSFSR, N of the Caucasus. Area 29,500 sq. m. Pop. 2,306,000. Drained by the Kuma, Kuban, and other rivers. Has a dry climate but is irrigated. Main occupations agriculture (wheat, maize, etc.), sheep rearing. Formed 1924. Chief towns Stavropol, Pyatigorsk.
2. Formerly (1930s–1943) Voroshilovsk. Capital of the Stavropol Territory, 190 m. SE of Rostov. Pop. (1970) 198,000. Flour milling, tanning. Manufactures agricultural machinery, textiles, etc. Trade in grain, livestock. Natural gas produced in the neighbourhood. Founded 1777.

**Steiermark** ♢ *Styria.*

**Stellenbosch** S Africa. Town in Cape Province 25 m. E of Cape Town. Pop. (1968) 29,900 (13,900 Europeans). In a picturesque region of vineyards and orchards. Mainly residential. Wine making, sawmilling. Manufactures bricks and tiles. Educational centre: seat of the University of Stellenbosch (1918). Famous for its oak-lined avenues. The oldest settlement in S Africa after Cape Town: founded 1679 by Simon van der Stel.

**Stelvio Pass** Italy. Pass between the Italian-Swiss frontier and the Ortler group (12,792 ft): third highest Alpine road pass (9,052 ft), linking Merano with Tirano (both in Italy).

**Stendal** German Democratic Republic. Industrial town and important railway junction in the Magdeburg district, 35 m. NNE of Magdeburg. Pop. (1965) 35,931. Railway engineering, metal working, sugar refining, etc. Founded in the 12th cent.; became capital of the Altmark. Birthplace of J. J. Winckelmann (1717–68).

**Stenness** Scotland. Parish in Mainland, in the Orkneys, 9 m. W of Kirkwall. Has two groups of standing stones in circles, the Ring of Brogar and the Ring of Stenness.

**Stepanakert** ♢ *Nagorno-Karabakh AR.*

**Stepney** England. Former metropolitan borough in E London extending N from the R. Thames and including Whitechapel, Shadwell, Wapping, Spitalfields, and Limehouse; from 1965 part of the Greater London borough of Tower Hamlets. Pop. (1961) 91,940. Industrial and residential. Contains the Tower of London, St Katharine and London Docks (closed); along its W boundary runs Middlesex Street (Petticoat Lane), famous for its Sunday morning market. Severely damaged by bombing in the 2nd World War. Probable birthplace of Edmund Spenser (*c.* 1552–1599), in E Smithfield.

**Sterlitamak** USSR. Industrial town and river port in the Bashkir ASSR, RSFSR, on the Belaya R. 85 m. S of Ufa. Pop. (1970) 185,000. Heavy engineering. Manufactures synthetic rubber, chemicals, cement, clothing, food products, etc.

**Stettin** ♢ *Szczecin.*

**Stettiner Haff** German Democratic Republic/Poland. Lagoon 34 m. long (W–E) separated from the Baltic Sea by Usedom and Wolin islands; divided between Poland and the German Democratic Republic. The Oder R. flows into it below Szczecin (Stettin).

**Steubenville** USA. Industrial town in E Ohio, on the Ohio R. 34 m. W of Pittsburgh. Pop. (1960) 32,495. Manufactures steel, tinplate, electrical equipment, pottery, etc.

**Stevenage** England. Urban district in Hertfordshire 28 m. N of London. Pop. (1961) 42,964 (7,168 in 1951). Formerly a small market town, but developed after 1946 as a satellite town to London. Planned pop. 105,000. Manufactures school furniture and equipment, etc. Has a 13th-cent. church and a modern parish church (1960).

**Stevenston** Scotland. Small burgh in Ayrshire 10 m. WNW of Kilmarnock. Pop. (1961) 10,174. Near by, at Ardeer, is an important explosives factory.

**Stewart Island (Rakiura)** New Zealand. Volcanic island S of the S Island, separated from the mainland by the Foveaux Strait. Area 670 sq. m. Pop. 350. Mountainous, rising to over 3,000 ft. The small settlement of Oban is in the NE. Purchased (1864) from the Maoris, who call it Rakiura.

**Stewarton** Scotland. Small burgh in Ayrshire 5 m. N of Kilmarnock. Pop. (1961) 3,387. Hosiery and dyeing industries.

**Steyning** England. Small picturesque market town in W Sussex 10 m. WNW of Brighton. Pop. 2,500. In the 11th cent. it was a flourishing port, but it declined when the sea receded. Chanctonbury Ring (783 ft) is 2 m. W.

**Steyr** Austria. Town in Upper Austria at the confluence of the Enns and the Steyr rivers 18 m. SSE of Linz. Pop. (1961) 38,306. Centre of the iron and steel industry; manufactures motor vehicles, bicycles, ball bearings, machinery, etc.

**Stilton** England. Village in Huntingdonshire 6 m. SSW of Peterborough. Gave its name to the famous Stilton cheese, which is made principally in Leicestershire.

**Stirling** Scotland. Royal burgh and county town of Stirlingshire, on the R. Forth 30 m. WNW of Edinburgh. Pop. (1961) 27,553. Manufactures agricultural machinery, carpets, etc. Once the gateway to the Highlands by its 15th-cent. Old Bridge, it is dominated by the ancient castle where Alexander I of Scotland died and where Mary Queen of Scots and James VI were crowned. Other notable buildings are the unfinished 16th-cent. Mar's Work and the 17th-cent. Argyll's Lodging, now a hospital. The 220-ft Wallace Monument (1869) is 1½ m. NE.

**Stirlingshire** Scotland. County in central Scotland bounded on the W by Loch Lomond. Area 451 sq. m. Pop. (1961) 194,858. County town Stirling. Mountainous in the NW, with Ben Lomond (3,192 ft) on the fringe of the Grampians, and hilly in the S, with the Campsie Fells, rising to 1,896 ft in Earl's Seat, and the Kilsyth Hills. Drained by the Forth, Endrick, and Carron rivers. Agriculture (oats, potatoes) and coalmining important; iron working at Carron and Falkirk, oil refining at Grangemouth. Three great battles in the struggle for Scottish independence were fought here: Stirling Bridge (1297), Falkirk (1298), Bannockburn (1314).

**Stockholm** Sweden. Capital and an important seaport, on the E coast. Pop. (1968) 767,606. The main industrial, commercial, and cultural centre. Shipbuilding, flour milling, brewing. Manufactures iron and steel, machinery, cables, telephones, textiles, chemicals, etc. Exports timber, paper, etc. Beautifully situated between L. Mälar and its outlet to the Baltic Sea, the Saltsjö, partly on a group of islands and partly on the adjacent mainland; has been called the Venice of the North. The oldest part is on the island of Staden, with the Royal Palace (1754), the 17th-cent. House of the Nobles, and the 13th-cent. Church of St Nicholas (Storkyrka). On the near-by Riddarholm island is the 13th-cent. Franciscan church where the Swedish kings are buried. Mainly a modern city; among the outstanding buildings are the City Hall (1911–23), the Houses of Parliament (1905), and the Stadium (1912). Founded 1255. Already an important commercial centre in the Middle Ages. Capital of the rural district of Stockholm (county status).

**Stockport** England. County borough in Cheshire, with the N part in Lancashire, at the point where the R. Tame and the R. Goyt join to form the R. Mersey. Pop. (1961) 142,469. Industrial town. Manufactures cotton goods, hats, textile and electrical machinery, chemicals, plastics, paper, etc. A high railway viaduct (1,780 ft long) crosses the valley which was the site of the old town.

**Stocksbridge** England. Urban district in the W Riding of Yorkshire, 8 m. NW of Sheffield. Pop. (1961) 11,137. Coalmining. Metal working.

**Stockton** USA. Inland port in California 70 m. SSE of Sacramento, at the head of navigation of the San Joaquin R. Pop. (1960) 86,321 (about 10 per cent Mexican). A deep-water channel, navigable for most ocean-going vessels, extends E from the river to the town centre. Exports the agricultural produce of the San Joaquin valley. Manufactures agricultural machinery, motor-boats. Food processing etc.

**Stockton-on-Tees** England. Industrial town in Durham, on the R. Tees 3 m. WSW of Middlesbrough. Pop. (1961) 81,198. Industrial centre. Engineering, ship repairing, etc. Expanded after the opening of the Stockton–Darlington railway (1825), the first passenger line in the country. Formerly an important port but was superseded by Middlesbrough. From 1968 part of the county borough of ◊ *Teesside*. Birthplace of Thomas Sheraton (1751–1806), the furniture designer.

**Stoke Newington** England. Former metropolitan borough of N London; from 1965 part of the Greater London borough of Hackney. Pop. (1961) 52,280. Contains Clissold Park and the 18th-cent. Clissold Mansion; also large waterworks of the Metropolitan Water Board.

**Stoke-on-Trent** England. County borough in Staffordshire on the R. Trent, formed (1910) by amalgamation with Burslem, Fenton, Hanley, Longton, and Tunstall – the 'Five Towns' immortalized by Arnold Bennett – becoming a city in 1925. Pop. (1961) 265,506. Centre of the pottery industry and practically co-extensive with the Potteries; associated with such famous manufacturers as Wedgwood, Spode, and Minton. Also engineering, tyre, and cable works. Coalmining in the neighbourhood. About 5 m. W is Keele (♢ *Newcastle under Lyme*). Josiah Wedgwood (1730–95) was born at Burslem and Arnold Bennett (1867–1931) at Hanley.

**Stoke Poges** England. Village in Buckinghamshire 2 m. N of Slough. Its churchyard was probably the scene of Thomas Gray's *Elegy*, and in it the poet is buried.

**Stolberg** Federal German Republic. Industrial town in N Rhine-Westphalia 7 m. E of Aachen. Pop. (1963) 38,200. Metal working, chemical manufacture, etc.

**Stolp** ♢ *Slupsk*.

**Stone** England. Urban district in Staffordshire on the R. Trent 7 m. S of Stoke-on-Trent. Pop. (1961) 8,791. Market town. Manufactures pottery. Has the remains of a 7th-cent. abbey. Birthplace of Peter de Wint (1784–1849), the painter.

**Stonehaven** Scotland. Small burgh and county town of Kincardineshire, 14 m. SSW of Aberdeen. Pop. (1961) 4,500. Fishing port. Holiday resort. Manufactures fishing nets, leather, etc. The ruined Dunnottar Castle is 1 m. S on a rocky cliff above the sea.

**Stonehenge** England. Chief prehistoric monument in the British Isles, on Salisbury Plain 3 m. W of Amesbury in Wiltshire. A circular earthwork over 300 ft in diameter, enclosing the remains of 4 series of stones: 2 outer circles, a horseshoe, and an inner oval. The outermost circle (100 ft in diameter) originally had 30 upright stones, of an average height of over 13 ft; the 16 which are still standing are secured by stone lintels, each dovetailed with its neighbour. The second circle (over 76 ft in diameter) originally had more than 40 stones; 9 upright and 11 fallen remain.

The horseshoe-shaped group comprises 5 large trilithons, only two of them standing, 22 ft high. Within the inner oval is the 'Altar Stone'. From the NE, Stonehenge is approached by a track called 'the Avenue', first completely revealed by aerial photography (1921), flanked by ditches 72 ft apart at the Stonehenge end. The existing monument probably dates from the Bronze Age, in the 2nd millennium B.C., and was religious in purpose. New evidence published in 1959 suggested that the trilithons were erected about 3,670 years ago. Stonehenge was presented to the nation in 1918.

**Stony Stratford** ♢ *Wolverton*.

**Stormberg Mountains** ♢ *South Africa*.

**Stornoway** Scotland. Small burgh and chief town on the E coast of Lewis with Harris, in the Outer Hebrides (Ross and Cromarty). Pop. (1961) 5,221. Fishing port. Manufactures Harris tweeds.

**Stourbridge** England. Municipal borough in Worcestershire, on the R. Stour 10 m. WSW of Birmingham. Pop. (1961) 43,917. Industrial town. Ironworks. Manufactures glass (first made in 1556), firebricks, etc.

**Stourport-on-Severn** England. Urban district in Worcestershire, at the confluence of the Worcestershire Stour with the R. Severn 10 m. N of Worcester. Pop. (1961) 11,751. A river port, but less important in this respect than formerly. Manufactures carpets, iron goods, etc.

**Stour River** (Dorset-Hampshire) England. River 55 m. long, flowing SE and joining the East Avon R. near Christchurch.

**Stour River** (Essex-Suffolk) England. River 47 m. long, formed from several headstreams, flowing E along the Essex-Suffolk border and entering the North Sea at Harwich.

**Stour River** (Oxfordshire-Warwickshire) England. River 20 m. long, flowing generally NW and joining the Upper Avon R.

**Stour River** (Worcestershire) England. River 20 m. long, flowing W and SW past Stourbridge and joining the R. Severn at Stourport-on-Severn.

**Stour River, Great** England. River in Kent 40 m. long, formed by the union of two headstreams at Ashford, then flowing NE past Canterbury, and dividing, one branch flowing into Pegwell Bay and the other reaching the sea near Reculver.

**Stowmarket** England. Urban district in E Suffolk, on the R. Gipping 11 m. NW of

Ipswich. Pop. (1961) 7,790. Market town. Manufactures chemicals, agricultural implements, etc.

**Strabane** Northern Ireland. Urban district in Co. Tyrone, at the confluence of the R. Finn and the R. Mourne, which form the R. Foyle. Pop. (1961) 7,786. Market town. Manufactures shirts and collars. Trade in oats, potatoes, etc. A salmon-fishing centre.

**Stralsund** German Democratic Republic. Seaport and railway centre in the Rostock district, on an arm of the Baltic Sea opposite Rügen Island, with which it is connected by a causeway carrying railway and road. Pop. (1965) 67,888. Shipbuilding, fish curing, metal working, sugar refining, etc. Manufactures machinery. Among its many old and picturesque buildings are the 14th-cent. town hall and several Gothic churches. Founded 1209. An important member of the Hanseatic League. Passed to Sweden (1648), France (1807), Denmark (1814), and Prussia (1815).

**Stranraer** Scotland. Royal burgh and seaport in Wigtownshire, at the head of Loch Ryan. Pop. (1961) 9,249. Has a steamer service to Larne (Northern Ireland). Also a market town. Fishing. Ruins of a 15th-cent. castle.

**Strasbourg** (Ger. **Strassburg**) France. Ancient Argentoratum. Prefecture of the Bas-Rhin department, on the Ill R. and the Rhine R. Pop. (1968) 254,038. Industrial, commercial, and cultural centre of Alsace. Also an important river port and railway junction. Brewing, tanning, fruit and vegetable canning, flour and paper milling, printing. Manufactures metal goods, electrical equipment, chemicals, soap, foodstuffs, etc. Famous for its *pâté de foie gras*. Trade in Alsatian wines, vegetables, iron ore, potash, etc. Its position on the Rhine and on the Marne–Rhine and Rhône–Rhine canals has made it France's leading inland port. Notable buildings are the 11th/15th-cent. cathedral, with a remarkable spire 466 ft high and the famous astronomical clock, and the university (founded 1567). Became a free imperial city in the 13th cent. Taken by Louis XIV 1681. Surrendered to the Germans, after siege, in 1871; returned to France 1919. Birthplace of Generals Kléber (1753–1800) and Kellermann (1735–1820), and of Gustave Doré (1832–83), the artist.

**Stratford** Canada. Town in Ontario, on

the Avon R. 56 m. WNW of Hamilton. Pop. (1966) 23,068. Railway engineering, flour milling. Manufactures textiles, furniture, agricultural machinery, etc. Has an annual Shakespearian festival.

**Stratford** USA. Resort in SW Connecticut, on Long Island Sound at the mouth of the Housatonic R. Pop. (1960) 45,012. Boatbuilding. Manufactures chemicals, hardware, etc.

**Stratford-upon-Avon** England. Municipal borough in Warwickshire, on the R. Avon. Pop. (1961) 16,847. Market town. Brewing and a few light industries. Celebrated chiefly as the birthplace of Shakespeare (1564–1616), visited by thousands of tourists each year. Among the many buildings closely associated with the poet is the half-timbered house where he was born, containing a museum. New Place, which he bought in 1597 and to which he retired (1610), was destroyed (1759), but its garden remains, and adjoining the latter is Nash's House, where his granddaughter, Elizabeth Hall, lived. The beautiful Holy Trinity Church has the graves of Shakespeare and his wife, Anne Hathaway. About 1 m. W is Anne Hathaway's Cottage. The Memorial Theatre (built 1877) was destroyed by fire (1926), but a new theatre was opened in 1932 and regularly presents seasons of Shakespeare's plays. In addition to its Shakespearian connexions, Stratford, an ancient town, has a fine 16th-cent. stone bridge of 14 arches crossing the river, and is set in picturesque countryside.

**Strathclyde** Scotland. Ancient kingdom in the SW, mainly in the Clyde basin, its capital being Dumbarton. Finally incorporated in Scotland in the 11th cent.

**Strathmore** Scotland. Broad vale extending SW–NE between the Grampians (N) and the Sidlaw Hills (S). Well known for its fertile soil and its scenery.

**Straubing** Federal German Republic. Ancient town in Bavaria, on the Danube R. 23 m. ESE of Regensburg. Pop. (1963) 36,700. Manufactures machinery, chemicals, textiles, etc. Brewing, tanning. Trade in grain, wine, cattle. Birthplace of Joseph von Fraunhofer (1787–1826), the physicist.

**Streatham** England. Residential district in SW London, formerly in the metropolitan borough of Wandsworth; from 1965 in the Greater London borough of Lambeth. Contains Streatham Common (68 acres).

**Street** England. Urban district in Somerset

11 m. E of Bridgwater. Pop. (1961) 6,660. Market town. Manufactures footwear, leather goods.

**Stresa** Italy. Port and resort in Novara province, Piedmont, on the W shore of L. Maggiore. Pop. (1961) 4,839. Famous for its beautiful scenery. The Conference of Stresa (1935) between Italy, France, and Britain was held on Isola Bella, in the Borromean Is. (in L. Maggiore).

**Stretford** England. Municipal borough in Lancashire 4 m. SW of Manchester, on the Bridgewater Canal. Pop. (1961) 60,331. Varied industries, inc. those on the Trafford Park industrial estate. Has the Lancashire County cricket ground, Old Trafford.

**Stromboli** Italy. The most northerly of the Aeolian or Lipari Is., N of Sicily in the Tyrrhenian Sea. Area 5 sq. m. Pop. 1,200. Famous for its active volcano (3,038 ft), the stream of incandescent lava being an impressive sight at night.

**Stromness** Scotland. Small burgh on the SW coast of Mainland, in the Orkneys. Pop. (1961) 1,477. Fishing port. 5 m. E are the standing stones of ♢ *Stenness*.

**Stroud** England. Urban district in Gloucestershire, on the R. Frome 8 m. S of Gloucester. Pop. (1961) 17,461. Market town. Formerly an important centre of the West of England cloth industry, famous for its scarlet dyes; still specializes in the manufacture of uniform cloth etc. Also produces plastics.

**Stuart** ♢ *Alice Springs*.

**Stuttgart** Federal German Republic. Capital of Baden-Württemberg, on the Neckar R. Pop. (1968) 613,775. Railway junction. Industrial and commercial centre. Important publishing trade. Manufactures machinery, scientific and optical instruments, clocks and watches, musical instruments, chemicals, leather goods, textiles, paper, etc. Two of its three medieval churches and the Akademie, where Schiller studied, were destroyed by bombing in the 2nd World War. Several other buildings, most of which date from the 19th cent., were severely damaged. Formerly less important than its present suburb, Cannstatt, but expanded rapidly in the 19th cent. Became a town in the mid 13th cent., having originated in a stud farm ('*Stuten Garten*') of the Counts of Württemberg, and was capital of Württemberg from 1482. Birthplace of Hegel (1770–1831).

**Styria** (Ger. **Steiermark**) Austria. Province in the SE, bordering S on Yugoslavia. Area 6,326 sq. m. Pop. (1961) 1,137,865. Cap. Graz. Mainly mountainous, esp. in the N, it includes the E part of the Niedere Tauern, and slopes generally to the SE. Drained by the Mur, Enns, Mürz, and Raab rivers. Forestry, lignite and iron mining important. Agriculture in the SE. Industry concentrated mainly in Graz. Part of the duchy of Carinthia under Charlemagne; in the 13th cent. it passed to the Habsburgs. Its S part was ceded to Yugoslavia in 1919.

**Suakin** Sudan. Port on the Red Sea 35 m. SSE of Port Sudan. Pop. 6,000. Chief port on the African Red Sea coast until the founding of Port Sudan; now decayed. The entrance to the harbour is obstructed by a coral reef.

**Subotica** Yugoslavia. Market town and railway junction in N Vojvodina, near the Hungarian frontier. Pop. (1961) 75,036. Flour milling, meat packing. Manufactures chemicals, furniture, footwear, etc.

**Suceava** Rumania. Capital of the Suceava district, on the Suceava R. 72 m. WNW of Iaşi. Pop. (1968) 40,441. Market town. Flour milling, tanning, etc. A historic town; capital of Moldavia 1388–1565.

**Süchow** China. Formerly Tungshan (1912–45). Town in NW Kiangsu province, 215 m. ESE of Chengchow. Pop. 676,000. Important railway junction, at the point where the Tientsin–Shanghai line crosses the Sinhailien-Chengchow–Lanchow line. Manufactures textiles. Flour milling etc. Scene of a major battle in the Chinese civil war (1948).

**Sucre** Bolivia. Formerly Chuquisaca. Legal capital of Bolivia and capital of the Chuquisaca department, 270 m. SE of La Paz (the actual seat of government), at a height of 9,000 ft in the E Andes. Pop. (1962) 54,270. Long isolated, now linked to Potosí by rail and road. Commercial centre for agricultural produce. Seat of the Supreme Court, a university (1624), and an archbishopric. Has a fine 17th-cent. cathedral. Founded 1538. Renamed (1839) after Bolivia's first president, Antonio José de Sucre (1795–1830).

**Sudan.** In Arabic, 'Black'. **1.** Extensive region in N Africa, between the Sahara and the tropical rain-forests, stretching from the Atlantic to the Ethiopian highlands; plateaux 1,000–1,500 ft high, drained by the Nile, the Niger, and the Senegal rivers, and in the centre by those flowing into the L. Chad depression. The name refers to the local Negro tribes: 'the Country of the Blacks'.

**2.** Republic in N E Africa. Area 967,500 sq. m. Pop. (1964) 13,011,000 (over two thirds Muslim Arabs and Nubians (N), with pagan Nilotic and Negro tribes (S)). Cap. Khartoum. Bounded by the United Arab Republic (N), Ethiopia (E), Kenya, Uganda, Congo (Kinshasa) (S), the Central African Republic, Chad (W), and Libya (N W). Mainly plateaux, descending from over 1,500 ft where the Nile enters from Uganda (S) to below 600 ft where the Nile leaves for Egypt (N). The highest parts are the Lolebai Mountains, rising to 10,456 ft in the extreme S, and the Etbai Mountains (Red Sea coast), with Jebel Erba reaching 7,273 ft. The Nile river system provides the chief physical features and trade routes. In the S the Bahr el Jebel is joined by the Bahr el Ghazal to form the White Nile (S) which joins the Blue Nile at Khartoum. The Sobat and Atbara rivers (the other two important right-bank tributaries of the Nile) also join the main river in Sudan. The climate everywhere is tropical; annual rainfall increases southwards, from negligible amounts in the N, and 5 ins. at Khartoum, to 40–50 ins. in the S (where there are well-marked dry and rainy (summer) seasons). Vegetation ranges from xerophytic desert plants and scrub (N) to wooded savannah (S). Agriculture is practised on irrigated land, esp. on the Gezira plain beside the Blue Nile (watered from the Sennar dam). Cotton is by far the most important export crop. Durra (millet) is the staple food crop. Gum arabic (from a species of acacia tree growing in the Kordofan province) is collected for export. In addition to the steamer services up the White Nile and Blue Nile, Khartoum and the adjoining towns of Khartoum North and Omdurman are linked by rail with El Obeid, Kassala, Port Sudan (the principal seaport), Sennar, and N to Wadi Halfa.

Conquered and unified by Mehemet Ali of Egypt in 1820–22. The successful Mahdist revolt (1881–98) caused the withdrawal of Egyptian forces after the defeat of the Mahdi's successor near Omdurman (1898), but the Anglo-Egyptian condominium in Sudan was established. It was reaffirmed in 1936, but abrogated by Egypt in 1951. A new constitution was agreed by Britain and Egypt in 1952.

Became an independent republic in 1956. ♢ *Nubia*.

**Sudbury** Canada. Town in Ontario 210 m. N N W of Toronto. Pop. (1966) 84,888 (44,000 in 1951). In a rich mining region, producing most of the world's nickel, also lead, zinc, copper, silver, gold, platinum. One of the world's leading nickel smelting and refining centres. Engineering, sawmilling, etc. University (1957).

**Sudbury** England. Municipal borough in W Suffolk, on the R. Stour 14 m. S of Bury St Edmunds. Pop. (1961) 6,643. Market town. Manufactures rayon, coconut matting. The 'Eatanswill' of *Pickwick Papers*. Has three 15th-cent. Perpendicular churches and many old half-timbered houses. Birthplace of Thomas Gainsborough (1727–88).

**Sudetenland** ♢ *Sudeten Mountains*.

**Sudeten Mountains** Czechoslovakia. Mountain system along the N E frontier consisting of several ranges, rising to its highest point in the Schneekoppe (5,259 ft) in the Riesengebirge. Rich in mineral resources, esp. coal. Sudetenland, named after the mountains, was the area on the fringes of Bohemia and Moravia that was formerly inhabited mainly by Germans; it was annexed by Hitler in 1938 but returned to Czechoslovakia in 1945 when the Germans were expelled.

**Suez** United Arab Republic. Port at the head of the Gulf of Suez and at the S end of the Suez Canal 70 m. E S E of Cairo. Pop. (1960) 203,000. Linked by rail with Cairo and Port Said. An important oilfuelling station; two oil refineries. Manufactures fertilizers. Until the Israel-Arab war (1967) was handling a growing proportion of Egypt's trade. The water supply formerly came from a near-by oasis (the 'Springs of Moses') whose water Moses is said to have miraculously sweetened; it now comes from the Fresh Water Canal. Suffered considerably during and after the Israeli-Arab war, inc. partial destruction of the oil refineries.

**Suez, Gulf of** United Arab Republic. The N W arm of the Red Sea, 170 m. long and up to 25 m. wide. Linked with the Mediterranean by the Suez Canal.

**Suez Canal** United Arab Republic. Ship canal 103 m. long in N E Egypt connecting the Mediterranean with the Gulf of Suez (Red Sea): Port Said is at one end (N) and Suez at the other (S). Built by the French engineer Ferdinand de Lesseps; opened

1869. Passes through L. Timsah and the Bitter Lakes; without locks. Minimum width 197 ft; average time of transit just over 11 hours. Deepened to take vessels of 37-ft draught. By the Convention of Constantinople (1888), open to the vessels of all nations and free from blockade. Formerly owned by the Suez Canal Company, in which Britain held the controlling interest (from 1875). The Canal Zone was occupied by British troops till 1954, then evacuated, under an Anglo-Egyptian agreement; the Canal was nationalized by the Egyptian government in 1956, and a Franco-British military expedition was sent against Egypt in Oct. but withdrawn in Dec. Israeli troops invaded the frontier lands but withdrew in 1957. In 1958 Egypt agreed to pay compensation (over a period of 6 years) to the shareholders of the Suez Canal Company (whose concession was to have ended in 1968). The canal was closed, several vessels having been sunk, from the Israeli-Arab war of June 1967.

**Suffolk** England. County in the E, bordering E on the North Sea. Area 1,482 sq. m. Pop. (1961) 472,665. Generally low and undulating, it rises in the S W to 420 ft in the chalk hills of the E Anglian Heights. Coastline flat and marshy. Separated from Norfolk (N) by the Little Ouse and Waveney rivers and from Essex (S) by the Stour; other rivers are the Deben, Orwell, and Alde. Primarily agricultural. Chief crops wheat, barley, sugar-beet. Suffolk punch horses are still raised, and Newmarket is an important centre for the breeding and training of racehorses. Industries are mainly related to agriculture, and include beet-sugar refining and the manufacture of agricultural implements and fertilizers. For administrative purposes the county is divided into: 1. *E Suffolk*: Area 871 sq. m. Pop. 342,696. Chief towns Ipswich (county town), Lowestoft (fishing port), Felixstowe (resort). 2. *W Suffolk*: Area 611 sq. m. Pop. 129,969. County town Bury St Edmunds.

**Suhl** German Democratic Republic. Capital of the Suhl district, in the Thuringian Forest 30 m. S W of Erfurt. Pop. (1965) 28,177. Manufactures motor cycles and cycles, pottery, etc. Once famous for the manufacture of fire-arms.

**Suir River** Irish Republic. River 85 m. long rising in N Tipperary and flowing S and then E past Clonmel to Waterford

Harbour, where it joins the R. Barrow, **Sukhumi** USSR. Ancient Dioscurias. Formerly Sukhum-Kaleh. Capital of the Abkhazian ASSR, in the Georgian SSR on the Black Sea 100 m. N N W of Batumi. Pop. (1970) 102,000. Seaport and health resort. Metal working. Processing of fruit, tobacco and fish. Has a famous botanical garden. An ancient Greek colony; later the Turkish fortress of Sukhum-Kaleh. Passed to Russia 1810.

**Sukkur** Pakistan. Town in the Khairpur Division (N Sind), W Pakistan, on the Indus R. 230 m. N E of Karachi. Pop. 77,000. Trade in grain, oilseeds, etc. Manufactures textiles, leather goods, cement, etc. Just below it is the famous ◊ *Lloyd* (Sukkur) *Barrage* across the Indus.

**Sulaimaniya** Iraq. Capital of Sulaimaniya province 135 m. E S E of Mosul near the Iranian frontier. Pop. 48,000. Market town. On trade routes with Iran.

**Sulaiman Range** Pakistan. Barren mountain range in W Pakistan extending 180 m. N–S along the E border of the Quetta Division, rising to 11,085 ft in Takht-i-Sulaiman (N).

**Sulu Archipelago** Philippines. Group of islands lying S W of Mindanao and extending to within 20 m. of the coast of N E Borneo. Area 1,087 sq. m. Pop. 295,000. Chief town Jolo, on Jolo Island. Most of the 400 islands are of volcanic origin, others are coral. Pearl fishing and the cultivation of rice and coconuts are important. The islands were ceded to the Philippines by the former Sultan in 1940.

**Sumatra** Indonesia. Large island in the Greater Sunda Is. lying across the equator, separated from Malaya (NE) by the Strait of Malacca and from Java (SE) by Sunda Strait. Area 164,000 sq. m. Pop. (1961) 15,700,000. A belt of mountains, the Barisan Mountains, extends parallel to the W coast from N to S, the highest of its many volcanic peaks being Kerintji (12,484 ft); off the S end of Sumatra is the volcanic island of Krakatao. The mountains descend steeply to the W coast, but slope more gradually through a belt of hill country to the coastal lowlands in the E. Climate equatorial, with high temperatures throughout the year and a heavy all-year rainfall derived from both S W and N E monsoons. Dense forests clothe much of the interior, and the flora is extraordinarily varied. Main subsistence crop rice; rubber, tobacco, tea, coffee, copra, palm oil produced for export. Principal minerals petroleum, coal. Economically the island is less developed than Java.

Divided administratively into the following provinces: Atjeh (cap. Banda Atjeh), N Sumatra (cap. Medan), W Sumatra (cap. Bukit Tinggi), Djambi (cap. Telanaipura), S Sumatra (cap. Palembang). The provincial capitals are the chief towns. The majority of the population, predominantly Muslim, consist of different tribes of Malays, among the most important being the Achinese (N), the Batak, around L. Toba, and the Menangkabau (W); Arabs, Chinese, and Indians have settled around the coasts. In the 8th cent. Palembang was the capital of a powerful Hindu kingdom, but in the 13th cent. the Muslim religion was introduced by the Arabs and spread over the island. The Dutch arrived at the end of the 16th cent., and gradually extended their control over all the native states. In 1945 most of Sumatra joined the new Republic of Indonesia, and the entire island was united in 1950.

**Sumba** Indonesia. Formerly Sandalwood Island. Island in the Lesser Sunda Is., separated from Flores and Sumbawa (N) by Sumba Strait. Area 4,306 sq. m. Pop. 182,000. Chief town Waingapu (pop. 2,200). Formerly an important source of sandalwood. Rice cultivated; copra exported. Livestock raised.

**Sumbawa** Indonesia. Island in the Lesser Sunda Is., between Lombok and Flores. Area 5,695 sq. m. Pop. 315,000. Cap. Raba. Generally mountainous, rising to 9,353 ft in Mt Tambora (N). Rice cultivated; cattle raised. Chief towns Raba, Bima, Sumbawa.

**Sumer.** Region of Mesopotamia (modern Iraq) occupying the S part of Babylonia, where a civilization developed in the 5th millennium B.C. Its people, the Sumerians, who were non-Semitic, invented the cuneiform system of writing.

**Sumgait** USSR. Industrial town in the Azerbaijan SSR 15 m. NW of Baku. Pop. (1970) 124,000. Manufactures chemicals, synthetic rubber, etc., using the products of the Baku oilfields.

**Sumy** USSR. Capital of the Sumy region, in the Ukrainian SSR 195 m. ENE of Kiev. Pop. (1970) 159,000. Sugar refining, sawmilling, tanning. Manufactures agricultural machinery, fertilizers, textiles, food products, etc. In a fertile farming region where wheat and sugar-beet are the chief crops. Founded 1658.

**Sunbury-on-Thames** England. Urban district 15 m. WSW of London, formerly in Middlesex; transferred to Surrey with the formation of the Greater London Council (1965) and the disappearance of Middlesex. Pop. (1961) 33,403. Largely residential. Includes Shepperton (film studios), the large Queen Mary Reservoir (Metropolitan Water Board), and Kempton Park racecourse.

**Sunda Islands** Indonesia. Island group comprising the W part of the Malay Archipelago, between the S China Sea and the Indian Ocean. 1. *Greater Sunda Is.*: Borneo, Java, Sumatra, and Celebes, with adjacent islands. 2. *Lesser Sunda Is.*: Islands E of Java, the most important being Bali, Lombok, Sumbawa, Sumba, Flores, and Timor.

**Sundarbans.** Region in the S of the Ganges delta, in E Pakistan and adjoining W Bengal (India), extending 150 m. along the coast and up to 50 m. inland. Swampy, with a network of tidal rivers and creeks, much of it covered with mangroves and other trees. It is gradually being reclaimed and brought under cultivation.

**Sunday Island** ◊ *Kermadec Islands*.

**Sundbyberg** Sweden. Town in Stockholm county 5 m. NW of Stockholm. Pop. (1968) 28,661. Manufactures chemicals, paper, etc.

**Sunderland** England. County borough in NE Durham, at the mouth of the R. Wear. Pop. (1961) 189,629. Seaport; has exported coal since the 14th cent. Important shipbuilding and ship-repairing industry. Manufactures machinery, pottery, glass, chemicals, paper, etc. Its dependence on coalmining and coal exports aggravated the effects of the economic depression of the 1930s. In the suburb of Monkwearmouth (N of the Wear) are remains of the Benedictine monastery founded (674) by St Benedict Biscop, incorporated in St Peter's Church. Sunderland also includes Bishopwearmouth, Southwick, and Pallion. Birthplace of Sir Henry Havelock (1795–1857) and Sir Joseph Swan (1828–1914). The Venerable Bede (672–735) was born near by.

**Sundsvall** Sweden. Seaport in Västernorrland county, on the Gulf of Bothnia 210 m. NNW of Stockholm. Pop. (1968) 62,278. Important exports of timber and wood pulp. Icebound in winter. Sawmilling.

Manufactures wood pulp and paper. Founded (1621) by Gustavus II.

**Sungari River** China. River 1,150 m. long in the NE (Manchuria), rising in the Changpai Shan in SE Kirin province and flowing first NW past the Fengman Dam and hydroelectric power station, with the large Sungari Reservoir, just above Kirin. At the confluence with the Nun R. it turns sharply ENE past Harbin and Kiamusze to join the Amur R. near Tungkiang. Ice-free May–Oct.

**Sunnyvale** USA. Town in California 13 m. WNW of San José. Pop. (1960) 52,898 (9,829 in 1950). Fruit canning. Manufactures electronic equipment, guided missiles, etc. Industries expanded rapidly in the 1950s.

**Suomi** ◊ *Finland*.

**Superior** USA. Port in NW Wisconsin at the W end of L. Superior. Pop. (1960) 33,563. With the near-by port of Duluth, the W terminus of the St Lawrence Seaway. Ships vast quantities of iron ore from Minnesota and grain from the Middle West. Shipbuilding, oil refining, railway engineering, flour milling, brewing.

**Superior, Lake** Canada/USA. The most westerly and the largest of the Great Lakes and the largest freshwater lake in the world; in central N America, 600 ft above sea level (at the surface). Area 32,483 sq. m. (about two thirds in the USA). Bounded by Ontario (N and E), Michigan and Wisconsin (S), and Minnesota (W). The water is deep and clear; greatest depth 1,333 ft. Never freezes completely, but its temperature does not rise much above freezing point even in summer, though it tempers the winter cold and summer heat of the districts around the shores. Gales frequent in autumn. The navigation season is about 8 months, mid April to mid Dec.

Fed by about 200 rivers, including the Nipigon and the St Louis. Drains into L. Huron and L. Michigan at the SE end via the St Mary's R.; canals constructed around the rapids at Sault Ste Marie enable ships to enter and leave it. Isle Royale (USA) is the largest of the many islands. The N shore has deep bays and high cliffs rising to 1,500 ft; the low and sandy S shore has the famous red-sandstone Pictured Rocks, 300 ft high, so called from the effects of wave action. The main Canadian ports are Fort William and Port Arthur; main US ports Duluth,

Superior, Ashland, Marquette. Grain, timber, and iron ore and copper ore are the principal eastbound cargoes, and coal the chief westbound cargo. Discovered (1623) by the French explorer Étienne Brûlé.

**Sur** ◊ *Tyre*.

**Surabaya** Indonesia. Capital of E Java province, on the Madura Strait near the mouth of the Kali Mas R. Pop. (1961) 1,007,945. Important seaport and naval base. Handles nearly half of Java's exports. Exports sugar, tobacco, coffee, etc. Also an industrial and commercial centre. Shipbuilding and ship repairing, railway engineering, oil refining. Manufactures textiles, glass, chemicals, tobacco products, etc. Seat of a branch of the Airlangga University. During the 2nd World War it was captured by the Japanese (1942) and was severely damaged by bombing.

**Surakarta (Solo)** Indonesia. Town in central Java, on the Solo R. 30 m. ENE of Jogjakarta. Pop. (1961) 367,626. Trade in rice, sugar, tobacco, etc. Textile manufacture, tanning. Has the former Sultan's palace.

**Surami Mountains** ◊ *Caucasus* (3).

**Surat** India. Industrial city in Gujarat, on the Tapti R. 14 m. from the mouth. Pop. (1961) 288,026. Engineering. Manufactures cotton and silk goods, paper, soap, etc. Trade in cotton, grain. During the reigns of Akbar, Jahangir, and Shah Jahan it was an important seaport and the chief commercial centre in India. Here the English established their first trading post in India (1612), but the city declined when the headquarters of the E India Company was transferred to Bombay (1687). Has revived somewhat in the 20th cent.

**Surbiton** England. Former municipal borough in N Surrey, on the R. Thames; from 1965 part of the Royal Borough of Kingston-upon-Thames (Greater London). Pop. (1961) 62,940. Light engineering. Mainly a dormitory suburb of London. Includes Chessington, headquarters of the Ordnance Survey Dept.

**Suresnes** France. Industrial suburb of W Paris, in the Hauts-de-Seine department on the Seine R. Pop. (1968) 41,263. Manufactures cars, bicycles, chemicals, perfumes, etc.

**Surinam (Dutch Guiana).** Self-governing territory of the Netherlands on the NE coast of S America, bounded by French Guiana (E), Brazil (S), and Guyana

(W). Area 70,087 sq. m. Pop. (1967) 345,000 (about 45 per cent Negroes and mulattoes, 30 per cent Indians, 18 per cent Indonesians, about 5,000 Amerindians, and Chinese and European minorities). Cap. and chief seaport Paramaribo. Consists of 3 main regions: coastal lowlands (N), where sugar-cane, rice, and citrus fruits are produced; an intermediate savannah region; densely forested highlands (S). Climate tropical and humid, with abundant rainfall. Bauxite, chiefly from Moengo and Paranam, represents over 75 per cent of total exports. Divided administratively into 8 districts. Ceded by Britain to the Netherlands by the Peace of Breda (1667). Twice subsequently in British hands; returned to the Netherlands 1815. Became a self-governing part of the kingdom of the Netherlands 1950.

**Surrey** England. County in the SE bounded on the N by the R. Thames. Area 722 sq. m. Pop. (1961) 1,733,036. County town Guildford. The NE is almost entirely urban, forming part of Greater London, but the county is crossed E–W by the chalk ridge of the North Downs, which has such well-known heights as the Hog's Back and Box Hill. Highest point Leith Hill (965 ft), farther S. The two chief rivers cut through the North Downs, the Wey near Guildford and the Mole between Dorking and Leatherhead, to join the Thames. Although the county is mainly residential, market gardening and dairy farming are important, sheep are grazed on the Downs, and fuller's earth is obtained at Nutfield. Industries are concentrated mainly in the NE, where Croydon, Kingston-upon-Thames, and other districts became part of Greater ◊ *London* in 1965.

**Susa** Iran. Capital of ancient Elam, 16 m. SSW of the modern Dizful near the Karcheh R. Destroyed by the Assyrians 645 B.C.; was restored and became capital of Persia. Excavations begun in the mid 19th cent. yielded remains of the palace of Darius I and considerable pottery, coins, etc. The modern village of Shush is near by.

**Susa** (Tunisia) ◊ *Sousse*.

**Susiana** ◊ *Elam*.

**Susquehanna River** USA. River 444 m. long, rising in Otsego Lake (NY), flowing generally S through New York and Pennsylvania, and entering the head of Chesapeake Bay. Not navigable. Several hydroelectric power stations.

**Sussex** England. County in the SE, bounded on the S by the English Channel. Area 1,457 sq. m. Pop. (1961) 1,075,893. Its outstanding feature is the chalk ridge of the South Downs, running WNW–ESE and ending in the cliffs of Beachy Head; they descend steeply on the N side to the Vale of Sussex, N of which is the Weald, where the Forest Ridges rise to nearly 800 ft. Highest point in the county Blackdown (918 ft) in the NW. Chief rivers the Arun, Adur, Ouse, and Rother. Cereals and root crops are grown, and fruit and hops in the E. Cattle and sheep raised. Extensive woodlands. The many coastal resorts include Brighton, Hove, Hastings, Eastbourne, Worthing; Newhaven is the principal channel port. Famous for its iron industry from Roman times till the early 19th cent. Divided for administrative purposes into: E Sussex (area 829 sq. m.; pop. 664,669; county town Lewes) and W Sussex (area 628 sq. m.; pop. 411,224; county town Chichester).

**Sutherland** Scotland. County in the N, bounded on the N and W by the Atlantic and on the SE by the North Sea. Area 2,028 sq. m. Pop. (1961) 13,442. County town Dornoch. Mountainous, rising to 3,273 ft in Ben More Assynt. Many lochs (Shin, Assynt) and extensive deer forests but little cultivated land. The N and W coasts are rocky and deeply indented with sea lochs, and in the extreme NW is the formidable Cape Wrath with its lighthouse. Chief rivers the Oykell, Brora, and Helmsdale. Sheep rearing and fishing are practised but most of the people gain a meagre living as crofters. The population has been steadily falling over the past century.

**Sutlej River.** Longest of the 5 rivers of the Punjab (900 m.), rising in Manasarowar Lake in SW Tibet and flowing WNW and then generally SW, crossing Himachal Pradesh and the plains of Punjab (India), entering W Pakistan, and finally joining the Chenab R. Chief tributary the Beas. Much used for irrigation: many dams, inc. the Bhakra Dam on the upper Sutlej, for irrigation and hydroelectric power (1954).

**Sutton** England. Greater London borough (from 1965), about 12 m. SSW of central London, comprising the former municipal boroughs of Beddington and Wallington, Sutton and Cheam, and the urban district of Carshalton, all in Surrey. Pop. (1963) 169,019. Mainly residential.

**Sutton Coldfield** England. Municipal borough in Warwickshire 7 m. NE of Birmingham. Pop. (1961) 72,143. Largely residential. Manufactures machinery, pharmaceutical products, etc. Has a television transmitter and the 2,090-acre Sutton Park. New Hall, 1½ m. SE, is an inhabited medieval mansion.

**Sutton-in-Ashfield** England. Urban district in Nottinghamshire 13 m. NNW of Nottingham. Pop. (1961) 40,438. Manufactures hosiery, metal containers, etc. Coalmining in the neighbourhood. Has a 13th-cent. church (restored in the 19th cent.).

**Suva** Fiji. Capital and chief seaport, on the SE coast of Viti Levu. Pop. (1966) 54,157. Extensive harbour. Manufactures coconut oil, soap. Exports sugar, coconut oil, gold. Proclaimed a city 1953.

**Suwannee River** USA. River 250 m. long, rising in the Okefenokee swamp (SE Georgia), following a winding course generally S, across N Florida, and entering the Gulf of Mexico. Famous as the 'Swannee River' of Stephen Foster's song *The Old Folks at Home*.

**Suzdal** USSR. Small town in the Vladimir region, RSFSR, 20 m. N of Vladimir. Founded in the 11th cent.; became an important religious centre with an ancient cathedral and monasteries. Extensive restoration during the 1960s.

**Svalbard** ◊ *Spitsbergen*.

**Svendborg** Denmark. Capital of Svendborg county in SE Fyn 25 m. SSE of Odense. Pop. (1965) 23,729. Seaport, yachting centre, and industrial town. Shipbuilding, brewing. Manufactures textiles, machinery, etc. Picturesque; many half-timbered houses.

**Sverdlovsk** USSR. Formerly Ekaterinburg. Capital of the Sverdlovsk region, RSFSR, in the E foothills of the central Ural Mountains. Pop. (1970) 1,026,000. Important railway junction and industrial centre. Large metallurgical plants. Manufactures steel, mining and heavy engineering equipment, ball bearings, lathes, railway rolling stock, aircraft, chemicals, clothing, furniture, etc. Copper smelting, gem cutting and polishing. W terminus of the Trans-Siberian Railway; also links the other Ural industrial towns with W Siberia. Principal cultural centre of the Urals. University (1920). Founded (1721)

as Ekaterinburg (after the Empress Catherine I); renamed 1924. Tsar Nicholas II and his family were executed here (1918). Its industrial importance began with the building of the first ironworks (1725). Expanded rapidly after the construction of the Trans-Siberian Railway (1895) and again with the development of the metallurgical industry during the 1930s and the 2nd World War.

**Svir River** USSR. River 140 m. long in RSFSR, flowing WSW from L. Onega past the Svirstroi hydroelectric plant to L. Ladoga. Forms part of the Mariinsk canal system.

**Svolvaer** Norway. Chief town of the Lofoten Is., on the SE coast of Austvågöy. Pop. 3,000. Fishing port and centre of the Lofoten cod fisheries. Manufactures cod-liver oil, fertilizer, etc.

**Swabia (Ger. Schwaben)** Federal German Republic. Region in the SW, approximating to the area now occupied by S Baden-Württemberg and SW Bavaria. The name derives from Suevi, the tribe once living here. A medieval duchy originating early in the 10th cent. Belonged to the house of Hohenstaufen from 1079 to 1268, when it was divided up.

**Swadlincote** England. Urban district in Derbyshire 4 m. SE of Burton-upon-Trent. Pop. (1961) 19,222. Coalmining. Manufactures sanitary ware etc.

**Swakopmund** SW Africa. Town on the Atlantic coast 175 m. W of Windhoek. Pop. (1960) 4,763. Chief port during the German administration; now closed, owing to the silting of the harbour. Railway terminus. Holiday resort. Salt pans to the N.

**Swale River** England. River 75 m. long in the N Riding of Yorkshire, rising in the Pennines near the Westmorland border and flowing E past Richmond, then SSE through the Vale of York, joining the R. Ure to form the R. Ouse.

**Swanage** England. Urban district in Dorset, on Swanage Bay (Isle of Purbeck) 7 m. S of Poole. Pop. (1961) 8,112. Seaside resort; a picturesque, cliff-lined coast and a sandy beach.

**Swanland** Australia. The SW and the most populous part of Western Australia; also its most fertile region, with a 'Mediterranean' climate, including a number of perennial rivers and considerable stretches of forest, mostly the hardwood eucalypts, jarrah and karri. Perth stands on the Swan

R. and Fremantle at its mouth. Products include wheat, wool, timber, fruit, vines, tobacco, dairy produce.

**Swansea** Wales. County borough in Glamorganshire, at the mouth of the R. Tawe on Swansea Bay. Pop. (1961) 166,740. Seaport. Exports anthracite from the S Wales coalfield, tinplate, etc. Imports ¢ in ore, timber, etc. An important centre of tinplate manufacture. Foundries smelting zinc, copper, tin, nickel. Manufactures chemicals etc. Within the borough are the oil refinery of Llandarcy and the seaside resort of The Mumbles. Seat of the University College of Swansea (1920), a constituent college of the University of Wales. Ruins of a 14th-cent. castle. Severely damaged by air raids during the 2nd World War. Birthplace of Beau Nash (1674–1761).

**Swatow** China. Seaport, industrial and commercial town in Kwangtung province, at the mouth of the Han R. 220 m. E of Kwangchow (Canton). Pop. 200,000. Exports sugar, tobacco, fruit, etc. Manufactures pharmaceutical products, matches, cigarettes, pottery, etc. Opened to foreign trade 1858; became an important emigration port. Thousands of lives were lost when a tidal wave swept over the town after a particularly fierce typhoon (1922).

**Swaziland.** Former British protectorate, now a kingdom, in SE Africa bounded on the N, W, and S by the Transvaal and on the E by Zululand (Natal) and Moçambique. Area 6,705 sq. m. Pop. (1966) 389,492 (the great majority Swazi, members of a Bantu tribe akin to the Zulu). Administrative capital Mbabane. Divided into 3 regions extending N–S: the high veld over 4,000 ft in the W, then the middle veld, and finally the low veld at about 1,000 ft in the E. The Komati and the Usutu, flowing W–E, are the main rivers. Rainfall abundant on the high veld (W) but generally light on the low veld (E). Principal food crop maize. Sugar, rice, and cotton grown for export. Large numbers of cattle raised. Chief mineral asbestos.

The Swazi gained independence from the Zulus early in the 19th cent., and this independence was recognized by the British (1881) and the Boers (1884). In the Boer War the Swazi sided with the British, and in 1906 their land was made a British protectorate under the High Commissioner for S Africa. From 1967 governed by a House of Assembly of 24 elected and 6 nominated members and a Senate of 12 members. Gained full independence and admitted to the United Nations 1968.

**Sweden.** A kingdom occupying the E part of the Scandinavian peninsula of N Europe. Area 173,620 sq. m. Pop. (1968) 7,892,774. Cap. Stockholm. Rel. predominantly Lutheran.

Bounded by Finland, the Gulf of Bothnia, and the Baltic Sea (E), The Sound, the Kattegat, and the Skagerrak (SW), and Norway (W). A large area of forests and rich deposits of iron ore; these resources have strongly influenced the external trade. Outstanding in the provision of social security and exceptionally high standards of education and material welfare. Administratively divided into 24 counties ('*läner*'): Stockholm (city and county), Uppsala, Södermanland, Östergötland, Jönköping, Kronoberg, Kalmar, Gotland, Blekinge, Kristianstad, Malmöhus, Halland, Göteborg och Bohus, Älvsborg, Skaraborg, Värmland, Örebro, Västmanland, Kopparberg, Gävleborg, Västernorrland, Jämtland, Västerbotten, Norrbotten. Stockholm city and county united 1968.

TOPOGRAPHY, CLIMATE. Mountains extend along most of the W frontier (with Norway), rising to their highest points (N) in Kebnekaise (6,965 ft) and Sarektjåkko (6,857 ft), and slope E down to a narrow coastal plain along the Gulf of Bothnia; mostly low-lying and level S of lat. 60° N. Four main regions. Norrland (the most northerly) occupies over half of the total area and is drained by many roughly parallel and swiftly flowing rivers which in their upper courses widen into long narrow lakes, e.g. the Torne, the Lule, and the Ångerman; in summer, logs cut from the vast coniferous forests are floated down the rivers, which are also utilized for the development of hydroelectric power. Immediately S of Norrland are the central lowlands (Svealand), another region of numerous lakes; the largest are Väner, Vätter, Mälar, and Hjälmar, linked with one another by rivers and canals. The Göta R. connects the Kattegat with L. Väner, which is linked with the Baltic Sea by the Göta Canal through L. Vätter. Götaland (S) is made up of two regions: the low plateau of Småland, rising to 1,237 ft, and the fertile low-lying peninsula of Skåne (extreme S). Apart from Skåne, the coast of Sweden (like that of Norway) is fringed with innumerable small islands; the largest are Gotland and Öland (in the Baltic).

Sweden is almost 1,000 m. long N–S; climatic conditions therefore vary considerably. In the far N winters are much colder and longer and summers much shorter and cooler than in the S; in general the climate is transitional between the relatively mild maritime type of Norway (W) and the continental type of Finland (E). The mean temperature for Feb. (the coldest month) is everywhere below freezing point; E coast ports are closed by ice for varying periods of the winter, but Göteborg (Gothenburg) (SW) is ice-free all the year. Annual rainfall is 15–25 ins. and increases generally N–S, with a much greater proportion of snow in the N.

RESOURCES, PEOPLE, etc. About 56 per cent forested; the great majority of the trees are pine and spruce. Lumbering, woodworking, pulp making, and paper milling are important occupations, esp. in Norrland. Timber, wood pulp, and paper represent nearly one third of the exports. Much of the timber is also manufactured into matches (at Jönköping) and furniture. About 9 per cent of the land is cultivated; agriculture is most successful in Skåne. Chief crops oats, barley, wheat, potatoes, sugar-beet, hay. Dairy farming important. Iron ore of high grade is mined at Gällivare and Kiruna (in Lapland) and exported via Luleå on the Gulf of Bothnia in summer and via Narvik (in Norway) in winter. Also deposits of iron ore in Svealand, as well as copper, lead, zinc. The iron ore and imported coal are raw materials for the highly important steel and metallurgical industries, in the manufacture of certain products of which (e.g. electrical machinery, telephone equipment, ball bearings, lighthouse apparatus, cream separators) Sweden specializes; these rank high in the export list. Swedish glassware and porcelain are also world-famous. Almost all the power required for industry and other purposes is derived from water; there are particularly important hydroelectric installations at Trollhättan on the Göta R. and Porjus on the Lule R., the former supplying power to most of S Sweden and the latter to the iron mines of Gällivare etc. and to the Luleå–Narvik railway. More than half the railway system is electrified. More telephones in proportion to population than any other country except the USA. Foreign trade is principally with the Federal German Republic and Britain.

The three leading cities, Stockholm, Göteborg (which has the greatest trade), and Malmö, are also the chief seaports. The urban population of Sweden rose from 11 to 52 per cent of the total 1862–1962, and about two thirds of the population became dependent on industry and commerce for a livelihood. Apart from about 30,000 Finns and 4,000 Lapps (in the N) the people are almost entirely of Teutonic stock. The standard of education is high and there is practically no illiteracy. Sweden is a constitutional monarchy; executive power is vested in the King, acting through a Council of State responsible to the parliament ('Riksdag'), which consists of two chambers (elected by proportional representation): the First Chamber, indirectly elected (151 members for 8 years), and the Second Chamber, elected by universal suffrage (233 members for 4 years).

HISTORY. In early times Svealand was occupied by the Suiones (or Svear) and Götaland by the Götar; by the 7th cent. A.D. the two peoples had merged, with the Lapps inhabiting the N. The S part of Sweden was united under one king in the 12th cent. Christianity was firmly established and Finland conquered. By the Union of Kalmar (1397) Sweden, Norway, and Denmark were united under a Danish dynasty, but with little support from the Swedes. Gustavus Vasa was elected king of Sweden in 1523 and as Gustavus I developed trade and military strength, and adopted the Lutheran religion; he is regarded as the founder of modern Sweden. Under Gustavus Adolphus (Gustavus II) Sweden attained its greatest power: Ingermanland, Karelia, most of Livonia, Pomerania, and Bremen were acquired in the 17th cent. and the Danes driven from Skåne; Livonia was ceded to Sweden in 1660. After the death of Charles X Swedish power began to wane; there were military defeats, and under the Peace of Nystad (1721) most continental possessions were lost. Gustavus III assumed absolute power, but a new constitution (the basis of the present monarchy) was adopted (1809) when Napoleon declared Marshal Bernadotte King of Sweden. Sweden was joined in 'personal union' with Norway in 1814 (unpopular with the Norwegians, this was ultimately dissolved in 1905). Bernadotte joined the last coalition against Napoleon, was confirmed as King in the post-Napoleonic settlement, and founded the present dynasty, as Charles XIV (1818), in succession to the childless Charles XIII. The later 19th and early 20th cent. saw increasing industrialization, the rise of the Social Democratic party, and the evolution of today's comprehensive system of social welfare. Throughout both world wars Sweden remained neutral.

**Świdnica** (Ger. **Schweidnitz**) Poland. Market town in the Wroclaw voivodship 30 m. SW of Wroclaw. Pop. 46,000. Manufactures textiles, agricultural machinery, chemicals, furniture, etc. Brewing, tanning. Founded in the 13th cent. Temporarily capital of an independent principality. Passed to Prussia 1742. Transferred to Poland after the 2nd World War.

**Swilly, Lough** Irish Republic. Long narrow sea inlet into the N coast of Co. Donegal extending nearly 30 m. inland from the entrance between Fanad Head and Dunaff Head.

**Swindon** England. Municipal borough in NE Wiltshire. Pop. (1961) 91,736. Railway junction and market town (Old Swindon). Important railway workshops of the Western Region, British Rail. Manufactures clothing, electronic equipment, etc. Many new industries established in recent years. Grew rapidly from a village with the establishment of the GWR locomotive and wagon works. Has an outstanding Railway Museum (opened 1962). Richard Jefferies (1848–87) was born at Coate Farm (1½ m. SE).

**Swinemünde** ◊ *Świnoujście.*

**Świnoujście** (Ger. **Swinemünde**) Poland. Fishing port and seaside resort on the Baltic coast of Usedom Island, in the Szczecin voivodship 37 m. NNW of Szczecin. Pop. (1968) 25,300. Formerly in Prussia, it was a German naval base in the 2nd World War, when it was largely destroyed. Ceded to Poland 1945.

**Swinton** England. Urban district in the W Riding of Yorkshire, 9 m. NE of Sheffield. Pop. (1961) 13,420. Coalmining. Manufactures glass, pottery (once famous for Rockingham ware).

**Swinton and Pendlebury** England. Municipal borough in SE Lancashire 4 m. NW of Manchester. Pop. (1961) 40,450. Coalmining. Engineering. Manufactures cotton goods, electrical equipment (inc. batteries), chemicals, etc.

**Switzerland** (Ger. **Schweiz**, Fr. **Suisse**, Italian **Svizzera**). A small inland republic in W Europe. Area 15,941 sq. m. Pop. (1969) 6,224,000. Cap. Bern. Languages German 69 per cent; French 19 per cent; Italian 10 per cent; Romansch 1 per cent. Religions Protestant 53 per cent; Roman Catholic 45 per cent.

Bounded by the Federal German Republic (N), Austria and Liechtenstein (E), Italy (S), and France (W). Very mountainous, with varied scenic beauties; the outstanding playground of Europe, attracting large numbers of tourists in both summer and winter. Tourism is an extremely important part of the economy. A confederation of 22 cantons, three of them divided into 'half-cantons', making 25 in all: Zürich, Bern, Luzern (Lucerne), Uri, Schwyz, Unterwalden (Obwalden and Nidwalden), Glarus, Zug, Fribourg, Solothurn, Basel (Basel-Stadt and Basel-Land), Schaffhausen, Appenzell (Ausser-Rhoden and Inner-Rhoden), St Gallen, Graubünden (Grisons), Aargau, Thurgau, Ticino (Tessin), Vaud, Valais, Neuchâtel, Geneva.

TOPOGRAPHY, CLIMATE. Three distinct regions, all running SW–NE: the Jura; the Central Plateau; the Alps. The Jura extend along the frontier with France, with several peaks exceeding 5,000 ft. Agriculture and forestry are important, as is watch making, the main export industry. On the Central Plateau (between the Jura and the Alps), the main industrial region, are the principal lakes: Constance, Zürich, Lucerne, Neuchâtel, Geneva. Well over half the country is occupied by the ranges of the Alps. N of the Rhône R. are the Bernese Alps, which contain the Finsteraarhorn (14,022 ft) and the Jungfrau (13,763 ft). S of the Rhône are the Pennine Alps, in which are the Matterhorn (14,780 ft) and the Dufourspitze of Monte Rosa (15,203 ft, the highest peak wholly in Switzerland). The mountains to the E are rather less lofty, though the Piz Bernina in the Bernina Alps (SE) rises to 13,304 ft. There are hundreds of glaciers among the Alpine peaks; among the many world-famous resorts are St Moritz, Davos, Zermatt, Interlaken, Arosa. On the S frontier (where parts of L. Maggiore and L. Lugano lie in Switzerland) the beautiful Alpine zone with its snow-covered peaks changes to a region of almost sub-tropical vegetation. The Alps are cut W–E by the deep valleys of the upper Rhône and the

Rhine; the Inn flows NE through the Engadine to the Danube and the Ticino flows S to the Po.

The distinguishing feature of the climate is the great variation with altitude, e.g. at Basle (909 ft) the mean temperatures are 32° F in Jan. and 66° F in July while at Säntis (8,202 ft) they are respectively 17° F and 41° F. The mean annual rainfall is 33 ins. at Basle, 100 ins. at Säntis; at the latter the majority of the precipitation falls as snow, with depths sometimes exceeding 40 ft. In the Alpine region the danger from avalanches is increased by the warm dry wind called the föhn.

RESOURCES, PEOPLE, etc. About 24 per cent of the land is unproductive and a roughly equal area is forested; about half the remainder is pasture land. In summer the mountain pastures ('alps') high above the valley farms are used for grazing dairy cattle. Much of the cheese, butter, and condensed milk is exported. Chief crops wheat, barley, potatoes. Wine is produced in most cantons. The country, however, is far from self-sufficient in foodstuffs, esp. cereals. Principally an industrial country, even though minerals and other raw materials have to be imported; the Swiss have concentrated on the manufacture of goods of high value relative to their bulk. Leading exports machinery, scientific instruments, clocks and watches, chemicals and dyes, textiles, clothing, footwear. Hydroelectric power is extensively developed; 3,153 m. of the 3,185 m. of railway track are electrified. An outstanding source of income is the 5,000,000 or so foreign tourists who visit Swiss resorts each year.

French is the principal language in the W cantons, Italian in Ticino, Romansch (made the fourth official language 1937) in parts of Graubünden (Grisons), and German elsewhere. The most densely populated cantons are Geneva and Zürich, and the least populated the Alpine cantons (Graubünden, Uri, Valais). Largest towns Zürich, Basle, Geneva, Bern, Lausanne. No state religion: each canton maintains its own clergy and its extremely efficient educational system. The banking and insurance organizations are famous. Legislative authority is vested in a parliament of two chambers: the 'Ständerat' (Council of States) with 44 members (two for each whole canton), and the 'Nationalrat' National Council), with 200 members directly elected for 4 years (in proportion to the population of the cantons).

HISTORY. Inhabited in early times by the Helvetii. Conquered by the Romans 58 B.C. After the fall of the Roman Empire, it was overrun by the Burgundii and Alemanni in the 5th cent., and in the 6th cent. passed to the Franks. Part of the Holy Roman Empire from 1033. The first movement towards political unity came in 1291, when the three forest cantons (Uri, Schwyz, Unterwalden) formed a defensive league against the Habsburg overlords. After a great victory at Morgarten (1315) they were joined by five others; further defeats of the Austrians followed (1386, 1388). Charles of Burgundy was vanquished in 1477; there were 13 cantons in the league by 1513. Largely through the activities of Calvin in Geneva and Zwingli in Zürich Switzerland played a great part in the Reformation during the 16th cent. and suffered considerable religious discord. Neutrality was maintained in the Thirty Years War; Swiss independence of the Holy Roman Empire was recognized by the Peace of Westphalia (1648) which ended the war.

The French Revolution brought an invasion by French troops (1798); the Swiss Confederation was dissolved and replaced by the French-dominated Helvetic Republic. The Confederation was restored in 1815 with 22 cantons and its present boundaries; the powers guaranteed its perpetual neutrality. Seven Catholic cantons concluded a separate alliance (the 'Sonderbund') and threatened to secede (1845) but were defeated. A new constitution was adopted in 1848; this was superseded (1874) by the present constitution, which increased the powers of the central government and introduced the principle of the referendum. Swiss neutrality was preserved in both world wars though the country suffered grave economic losses. It was the seat of the League of Nations (from 1920), and is the headquarters of several international organizations, esp. at Geneva, e.g. the International Red Cross, the International Labour Organization (1919), the World Health Organization (1946).

Sybaris Italy. Ancient Greek city of great wealth, in the S, on the Gulf of Tarentum (Taranto), founded c. 720 B.C. Its inhabitants, the Sybarites, were well known for their luxury and voluptuousness.

Destroyed in a war with Crotona 510 B.C.
Sydney Australia. Capital of New South
Wales, largest city and chief seaport in
Australia, mainly on the S shore of Port
Jackson. Pop. (1966) 2,444,735. Developed
from an early settlement at Sydney Cove
(1788). Its fine silt-free harbour has a
depth of 40 ft to wharves which extend
along inlets of the drowned valley. Serves
an extensive hinterland, handling a large
volume of exports, esp. wheat and wool
from the Murray basin, but also from the
E coastlands. Lies on a great coal basin,
with deep mines within the city limits. Iron
and steel, tinplate, and the products of
heavy industries are obtainable from Newcastle or Port Kembla, and Sydney is able
to provide consumer goods for its own
growing population and also for its hinterland. Metal working, oil refining, food
processing, brewing. Manufactures machinery, scientific apparatus, clothing,
textiles, leather goods, furniture, paper,
chemicals, bricks. Australia's chief wool-
selling centre.

Most of the industrial development is S
of the harbour, the N side having remained
largely residential; the two areas are
connected by the celebrated harbour
bridge (completed 1932), 3,770 ft in total
length. There are excellent beaches and
resorts close to the city, mainly E, including the famous Bondi beach, and it is
well provided with open spaces, such as
Centennial Park, Moore Park, and the
botanical gardens. Many of its public
buildings are impressive, among them the
University (founded 1850), the Anglican
and Roman Catholic cathedrals, and the
National Art Gallery. Water comes from
a complex system of reservoirs, large
supplies being dammed back along the
Nepean and other rivers. The metropolitan area now extends S to Botany Bay,
with its 48 municipalities covering 685
sq. m.
Sydney Canada. Seaport and industrial
town in Nova Scotia, on the NE coast of
Cape Breton Island. Pop. (1966) 32,767.
Exports coal. Imports iron ore and lime-
stone from Newfoundland. Coalmining.
Manufactures steel, chemicals, bricks, etc.
Founded (1784) by United Empire Loyalists.
Syene ◊ Aswan.
Syktyvkar USSR. Capital of the Komi
ASSR, RSFSR, on the Vychegda R.
220 m. NNE of Kirov. Pop. (1970) 125,000.

Mainly a centre of the timber trade. Sawmilling, boatbuilding, fur processing.
Manufactures wood pulp and paper.
Sylhet Pakistan. Chief town of the tea-
producing district of Sylhet, in E Pakistan,
on the Surma R. 120 m. NE of Dacca.
Pop. (1961) 37,740. Formerly in Assam;
transferred to Pakistan at the partition of
India (1947).
Symond's Yat England. A famous view-
point on the R. Wye where the river,
flowing through a narrow gorge, describes
a loop nearly 5 m. long around Huntsham
Hill, curving back to within 600 yards of its
former course. The Yat, or Gate, is 6 m.
SSW of Ross, in Herefordshire.
Syracuse (Italian Siracusa) Italy. Capital of
Siracusa province, on the SE coast of
Sicily. Pop. (1968) 100,654. Seaport. Exports olive oil, wine. Fisheries, saltworks.
Manufactures chemicals, cement. On the
small island of Ortygia, connected by
bridge with the mainland, are the cathedral,
the ruins of the Temple of Apollo, the
fountain of Arethusa, and the Maniace
castle erected by the Emperor Frederick II.
On the mainland are the famous Greek
theatre, a Roman amphitheatre, the fortress
of Euryalus, built by Dionysius, and a cave
with remarkable acoustic properties known
as 'Dionysius' Ear'. Syracuse was founded
on Ortygia by Greek colonists from
Corinth in 734 B.C. Became an important
cultural centre under Hiero I (478–467
B.C.), with Aeschylus and Pindar at his
court. Withstood a siege from the Athenians (415–413 B.C.) and attained its greatest
power under Dionysius I (406–367 B.C.).
Besieged and taken by the Romans (214–
212 B.C.); Archimedes was killed during the
plunder of the city. Now it became a mere
provincial city, and lost still more of its
former glory when assaulted by the Saracens (A.D. 878).
Syracuse USA. Industrial town in New
York, at the S end of L. Onondaga 135 m.
E of Buffalo. Pop. (1960) 216,038. Manufactures machinery, metal goods, typewriters, chemicals, etc. University (1849).
Salt production was the main industry in
the early 19th cent. but declined after
1870.
Syr Darya USSR. Ancient Jaxartes. River
1,400 m. long in Soviet Central Asia,
rising as the Naryn R. in the E Kirghiz
SSR S of L. Issyk Kul. Flowing generally
W and SW and cutting through wild
gorges, it enters and irrigates the fertile

Fergana valley, in the Uzbek SSR. It then turns NW across SW Kazakh SSR, where the Kyzyl Kum desert extends to its left bank, and enters the Aral Sea (NE) by a delta.

**Syria.** Republic of SW Asia. Area 71,210 sq. m. Pop. (1966) 5,634,000. Cap. Damascus. Lang. Arabic. Rel. mainly Muslim.

Bounded by Turkey (N), Iraq (E), Jordan (S), and Israel, Lebanon, and the Mediterranean Sea (W). Essentially an agricultural and pastoral country, though much of its area consists of desert. Divided for administrative purposes into the following districts: Damascus, Hama, Homs, Der'a, Aleppo, Latakia, Deir ez Zor, Soueida (Jebel ed Druz), Hassakeh, Raqqa, Idlib, Kiniatira, Tartus.

TOPOGRAPHY, CLIMATE, *etc.* In the W mountain ranges run more or less parallel to the coast, the highest being the Anti-Lebanon, on the Lebanon border, which rises to 9,232 ft in Mt Hermon; in the SW, near the Jordan border, the Jebel ed Druz exceeds 5,500 ft. The plateau of the Syrian Desert, occupying most of the central area, descends E to the basin of the Euphrates, which flows NW–SE across the E region. Along the coast the climate is Mediterranean, but inland the temperatures become more extreme and the rainfall decreases from 30 ins. or more near the sea to less than 10 ins. annually in the desert.

RESOURCES, PEOPLE, *etc.* In the fertile and well-watered regions (i.e. along the coast, in the Euphrates valley, and around Damascus) wheat and barley are the principal food crops, and vines, olives, tomatoes, and apricots are widely cultivated. Cotton has become the leading cash crop and is by far the most important export; others are wool, cereals, and tobacco (grown around Latakia). Mineral resources are probably limited but have not been fully explored. There is very little manufacturing, and this only in Damascus, Aleppo, and Homs; apart from these Hama is the only town with more than 100,000 inhabitants. Four pipelines cross Syria from the oilfields of Iraq to the coast and provide revenue.

Practically all the people are Muslims, the majority belonging to the Sunni sect, with substantial minorities of Alawites and Druses (heretical Muslim sects), the latter dwelling in the Jebel ed Druz. There are nearly half a million Christians, the principal denominations being the Greek Orthodox and Greek Catholic, the Armenian Orthodox and Armenian Catholic, and the Syrian Orthodox. Most of the people are peasants; there are some Bedouin. The standard of living is generally low, especially among the Bedouin tribes. The illiteracy rate is high.

HISTORY. The region known historically as Syria included modern Syria, Lebanon, Israel, and Jordan, i.e. all the lands along the Mediterranean coast; it was inhabited from very early times, and occupied by many peoples. Here the Phoenicians established their trading posts along the coasts, mainly in present-day Lebanon. Its geographical position and the fertility of its coastlands made it an object of conquest, and it was ruled by Assyria, Babylonia, Egypt, Persia, Macedonia, and the Seleucidae; Antioch, on the Orontes, was founded and made capital by Seleucus Nicator (301 B.C.) and became an important province of the Roman Empire, passing, on the division of the latter, to Byzantine rule. In the 7th cent. A.D. it was conquered by the Arabs (636) and was largely converted to the Muslim religion. Continued to prosper even through the Crusades, but never fully recovered from the fierce Mongol invasions of the 13th cent. A province of the Ottoman Empire 1516–1918. After the 1st World War France was given a mandate over Syria and Lebanon (1920) but found it difficult to govern. Following a serious Druse rebellion (1925) the Lebanon was made a separate state (1926); the sanjak of Alexandretta was ceded to Turkey 1939. During the 2nd World War British and Free French troops ejected the Vichy French and Syria was proclaimed independent (1941). The republic joined the UN and the Arab League, and took part in the unsuccessful Arab war on Israel (1948). Joined Egypt in the United Arab Republic in 1958, but the new régime rapidly became unpopular; after an army revolt it withdrew from the UAR (1961) and proclaimed its separation, being readmitted to the UN and the Arab League. Political stability has not been a feature of independence, and orderly government has been interrupted by several *coups d'état*. In the Israeli–Arab war of June 1967 the Syrian forces were quickly defeated.

**Syros** (Gk **Síros**) Greece. Island in the Cyclades, in the Aegean Sea. Area 33 sq. m.

Pop. 30,000. Chief town and port Syros (Hermoupolis) (pop. 16,971). Mainly mountainous; produces grain, fruits, wine.

**Syzran** USSR. Town in the Kuibyshev region, RSFSR, on the right bank of the Volga R. Pop. (1970) 174,000. Important river port, railway junction, and industrial centre. Oil refining. Manufactures machinery, building materials, clothing, etc. Founded (1684) as a fortress. Developed in the 19th cent. as a grain market and expanded rapidly with the oil industry in the 1930s.

**Szczecin** (Ger. **Stettin**) Poland. Capital of the Szczecin voivodship, on the Oder R. 17 m. above the mouth in Stettiner Haff. Pop. (1968) 331,700. Important Baltic seaport and industrial centre. Exports coal, timber, etc. Shipbuilding. Manufactures synthetic fibres, paper, fertilizers, cement, etc. A Wendish settlement as early as the 9th cent. Joined the Hanseatic League 1360. Passed to Prussia (1720), becoming capital of the province of Pomerania, and to Poland (1945). Severely damaged in the 2nd World War. Birthplace of Catherine the Great of Russia (1729–96).

**Szechwan** China. Province in the SW; the most populous of all provinces and regions. Area 222,000 sq. m. Pop. (1957) 72,160,000. Cap. Chengtu. Mainly mountainous, rising in the W to the lofty Tibetan plateau. Crossed SW–NE by the Yangtse R.; the heart of the province is the Red Basin, where the density of population reaches and in parts even exceeds 1,000 per sq. m. In this fertile region rice, maize, sugar-cane, beans, and tobacco are cultivated, and tung oil is an important export product. Chengtu is now linked by railway with the chief port, Chungking, on the Yangtse R.

**Szeged** Hungary. Town in (but independent of) Csongrád county, near the confluence of the Tisza and Maros rivers 100 m. SSE of Budapest. Pop. (1967) 120,000. Commercial and industrial centre in an agricultural region. Flour and paprika milling, brewing, sawmilling. Manufactures textiles, footwear, tobacco products, etc. University (1921). The country's second largest city until 1950, when its area was reduced by excluding some of its many constituent villages.

**Székesfehérvár** Hungary. Ancient Alba Regia. Capital of Fejér county 37 m. SW of Budapest. Pop. (1968) 68,000. Market town. Trade in wine, tobacco. Manufactures footwear etc. Aluminium works. Coronation and burial place of Hungarian kings from the 11th to the 16th cent.

**Szolnok** Hungary. Capital of Szolnok county, at the confluence of the Tisza and Zagyva rivers 50 m. ESE of Budapest. Pop. (1968) 59,000. Railway junction. River port. Flour milling, sawmilling, brickmaking, etc.

**Szombathely** Hungary. Capital of Vas county, in the W near the Austrian frontier. Pop. (1968) 60,000. Industrial town in a fertile fruit-growing region. Manufactures textiles, agricultural machinery, etc. Flour milling, sawmilling. Built on the site of a Roman settlement. Became the seat of a Roman Catholic bishopric 1777.

# T

**Tabasco** Mexico. State in the SE on the Gulf of Campeche, bordered on the SE by Guatemala. Area 9,783 sq. m. Pop. (1969) 691,000. Cap. Villahermosa. Mainly low-lying and covered by jungle; many swamps, lagoons, and watercourses. Climate hot and humid. The forests provide dyewoods and other valuable timber. Crops include rice, sugar-cane, bananas.

**Table Mountain** S Africa. Mountain 3,567 ft high in Cape Province overlooking Table Bay and Cape Town; the N end of the range which terminates (S) in the Cape of Good Hope. Flat-topped; the summit is often covered, esp. in summer, by a white cloud (called the 'Tablecloth') overhanging the precipitous N face. A cable railway (completed 1929) runs from Cape Town to the summit, where the view S includes the whole of the Cape Peninsula; from one point the Atlantic Ocean and the Indian Ocean may both be seen.

**Tabora** Tanzania. Town 450 m. WNW of Dar-es-Salaam at a height of 3,900 ft. Pop. 15,000. On the railway to Kigoma on L. Tanganyika, with a branch line to Mwanza on L. Victoria. Agricultural market. Trade in cotton, millet, groundnuts, etc. Founded in the early 19th cent.; became a centre of the slave trade.

**Tabriz** Iran. Capital of E Azerbaijan province and Iran's third largest city, 325 m. NW of Tehran at a height of 4,400 ft just N of the volcanic Kuh-e-Sahand (12,172 ft). Pop. (1966) 468,459. Important market town in a fertile agricultural region. Manufactures carpets, textiles, leather goods, soap. Trade in dried fruit, almonds, etc. University (1947). Has the ruins of the famous 15th cent. Blue Mosque and an old citadel of massive proportions. An ancient city, Tabriz was several times almost destroyed by earthquakes.

**Tacna** Peru. Capital of the Tacna department, at 1,800 ft in the Andean foothills 30 m. N of Arica (Chile), to which it is linked by railway. Pop. 34,000. Serves an irrigated area where tobacco, cotton, and sugar-cane are cultivated. Held by Chile 1883–1929.

**Tacoma** USA. Seaport and industrial town in Washington, on Commencement Bay in Puget Sound, 25 m. S of Seattle. Pop. (1960) 147,979. Exports timber, grain, flour, phosphates, refined copper, etc. Manufactures chemicals, clothing, food products, etc. Copper smelting, woodworking, flour milling, boatbuilding, etc.

**Tadmor** ◊ *Palmyra*.

**Tadoussac** Canada. Village in SE Quebec on the Saguenay R. near the confluence with the St Lawrence R. Pop. (1966) 1,059. Reputedly the site of the earliest European settlement in Canada: a house was built here in 1600 by Pierre Chauvin.

**Tadzhik SSR** USSR. Constituent republic in Soviet Central Asia, bounded on the E by Sinkiang-Uighur AR (China) and on the S by Afghanistan. Area 55,240 sq. m. Pop. (1970) 2,900,000. Cap. Dushanbe. A lofty mountain and plateau region of the Pamir and Alai systems, with two of the country's highest peaks, Peak Kommunizma (24,590 ft) and Lenin Peak (23,386 ft), the lowest valleys of the Pamirs being 11,000 ft or more above sea level. The only true lowlands are its section of the Fergana Valley (N) and the valley of the Amu Darya (SW), which forms the S boundary with Afghanistan. Includes the Gorno-Badakhshan AR. Main occupations agriculture, stock rearing. Cotton is the most important crop; wheat, maize, fruits (inc. grapes), and vegetables are grown. Large numbers of sheep and cattle are raised, the Gissar sheep in the S being noted for its meat and fat; karakul sheep are bred for their wool. Since the Revolution agricultural methods have been greatly improved with the introduction of tractors and combine harvesters, the extension of irrigation and electric power; mineral resources have been tapped and industries established. Illiteracy, almost complete under the Tsars, has been practically eradicated. About 53 per cent of the people are Tadzhiks, who are Sunni Muslims speaking a language similar to Persian; most of the remainder are Uzbeks, Russians, and Ukrainians. Chief towns Dushanbe, Leninabad. The republic was founded (1924) as an ASSR within the Uzbek SSR. Became a separate constituent republic 1929.

**Taegu** S Korea. Commercial town in the SE, 55 m. NNW of Pusan on the railway to Seoul. Pop. (1966) 847,494. In an agricultural region producing grain, tobacco, fruits. Textile industry.

Taganrog USSR. Seaport in the Rostov region, RSFSR, on the Gulf of Taganrog, an arm of the Sea of Azov. Pop. (1970) 254,000. Exports grain and coal from its 3 harbours. More important now as an industrial centre. Manufactures iron and steel goods, inc. agricultural machinery, hydraulic presses, tools, boilers, etc. Founded as a fortress by Peter the Great 1698. Twice lost to the Turks; finally annexed to Russia 1769. Birthplace of Chekhov (1860–1904).

Tagus (Portuguese Tejo, Sp. Tajo) River Portugal/Spain. River 565 m. long rising in the Montes Universales of E Spain (Teruel), flowing first NW, then generally SW and W across the Meseta and past Toledo. In Estremadura it again passes through a mountainous region and is impeded by rapids, forms the boundary between Spain and Portugal for about 30 m., and finally enters an extensive estuary on the N shore of which is Lisbon. Navigable to small vessels only as far upstream as Abrantes (Portugal). The Salazar bridge over the estuary, linking Lisbon with Almada, the Setúbal peninsula, and the S, the largest suspension bridge in Europe, was inaugurated in 1966.

Tahiti (French Polynesia) S Pacific Ocean. Largest and most important island of French Polynesia, in the Windward Is. (◊ Society Islands). Area 402 sq. m. Pop. (1967) 61,519. Cap. Papeete (pop. 22,278), also capital of French Polynesia. Mountainous, the higher of its two ancient volcanoes, Mt Orohena, reaching 7,339 ft. Exports phosphates, copra, vanilla. Discovered 1767. After an unsuccessful attempt at colonization by the Spaniards, was a French protectorate (1843–80) and was then ceded to France.

Taichung Taiwan. Market town 85 m. SW of Taipei. Pop. (1968) 389,306. In an agricultural region producing rice, sugar-cane, jute, etc. Sugar refining, distilling.

Taif Saudi Arabia. Town in the Hejaz, in an oasis at a height of 5,200 ft 40 m. ESE of Mecca. Pop. 30,000. Summer resort.

Taimyr USSR. 1. Peninsula on the Arctic coast of Siberia (RSFSR) between the Kara Sea and the Laptev Sea; the Byrranga Mountains extend across it and Cape Chelyuskin is at its N extremity. The Taimyr R. (330 m.) flows NE and N through L. Taimyr to the N coast.

2. National Area in the N Krasnoyarsk Territory, RSFSR, almost co-extensive with the Taimyr peninsula. Area 336,000 sq. m. Pop. (1970) 38,000. Cap. Dudinka. Consists mainly of tundra. The inhabitants are chiefly nomadic Samoyeds. Main occupations hunting, fishing, reindeer breeding. Also called Dolgano-Nenets NA.

Tain Scotland. Small burgh in Ross and Cromarty, near the S shore of Dornoch Firth. Pop. (1961) 1,699. An ancient town, with the ruins of St Duthus' Chapel. The remains of Fearn Abbey are 4 m. SE.

Tainan Taiwan. Market town in the SW, 25 m. N of Kaohsiung. Pop. (1968) 429,374. Iron working, rice and sugar milling, etc. A cultural centre. Formerly capital of the island, replaced by Taipei.

Tainaron, Cape ◊ Matapan, Cape.

Taipei Taiwan. Capital of the island, in the N on the Tanshui R. 15 m. WSW of its port, Keelung. Pop. (1968) 1,221,112. Commercial centre. Trade in rice and tea, processed here. Coalmining in the neighbourhood. Replaced Tainan as capital 1885. Developed under Japanese rule 1895–1945. Became useless as a seaport owing to silting of the harbour.

Taiwan (Formosa). Island off the coast of SE China, from which it is separated by the Formosa Strait. Area 13,890 sq. m. Pop. (1968) 13,297,000. Cap. Taipei. Has great scenic beauty – hence the name Formosa, given by the Portuguese who discovered it (1590). A mountain range crosses it N–S, the slopes descending steeply to the nearer E coast and more gently to the W, with Yu Shan rising to 12,959 ft and several peaks exceeding 10,000 ft; the mountains are densely forested. The Tropic of Cancer passes through the island, and the climate is tropical, with abundant rainfall received from the SW and NE monsoons; occasional typhoons. More than half the population are dependent on agriculture. Main food crops rice, sweet potatoes. Chief export sugar; camphor is still a product of some importance. Chief towns Taipei, Kaohsiung, Tainan, Taichung. Chinese settlement of Taiwan began in the 17th cent. and now only a small minority of aborigines remains in the mountainous interior. Ceded to Japan 1895; returned to China after the 2nd World War (1945). Became the last territory of the Chinese Nationalist government when Chiang Kai-shek withdrew there in

1950, the Chinese Communists dominating the mainland. The USA furnishes considerable financial aid and military support.

**Taiyuan** China. Formerly Yangkü. Capital of Shansi province, on the Fen-ho at a height of 2,600 ft, 255 m. SW of Peking. Pop. (1957) 1,020,000. Industrial centre in a coalmining district. Manufactures iron and steel, agricultural and textile machinery, textiles, cement, paper, etc. An ancient city, walled in the 14th cent. to protect it against Mongol attacks; many historical relics in the Shansi provincial museum. Occupied by the Japanese 1937–45.

**Tajo River** ◊ *Tagus River*.

**Takamatsu** Japan. Capital of Kagawa prefecture, on the N coast of Shikoku 85 m. WSW of Osaka. Pop. (1965) 243,423. Seaport and industrial centre. Exports tobacco, rice, etc. Manufactures wood pulp and paper, cotton goods, fans and parasols, lacquer ware, etc. Famous for the landscape gardens in Ritsurin Park, a tourist attraction.

**Takaoka** Japan. Industrial town in Toyama prefecture, W Honshu, 25 m. ENE of Kanazawa. Pop. (1965) 139,500. Manufactures cotton goods, lacquer ware, etc.

**Takasaki** Japan. Town in Gumma prefecture, central Honshu, 60 m. NW of Tokyo. Pop. (1965) 173,887. Manufactures textiles, machinery, etc. Flour milling.

**Takla Makan** China. Extensive sandy desert in the Sinkiang–Uighur AR, lying S of the Tien Shan and occupying the major part of the Tarim Basin, with the Tarim R. flowing along its N edge. Uninhabited because of its shifting sand dunes. Principal oases around its margins are Yarkand (W) and Khotan (SW).

**Takoradi** Ghana. Chief seaport (a single municipality with Sekondi), on the Gulf of Guinea 115 m. WSW of Accra. Pop. (1960) 41,000. Linked with the interior by the important railway to Kumasi. The modern harbour (opened 1928) is protected by two breakwaters; has ample storage facilities for oil, timber, cacao, etc. Exports cacao, diamonds, gold, manganese, timber. Handles most of the overseas trade. Cocoa processing, sawmilling. Manufactures cigarettes.

**Talara** Peru. Seaport in the Piura department 55 m. NW of Piura, in the NW desert region. Pop. 60,500. Centre of the Peruvian petroleum industry, linked by pipelines with the oilfields. Peru's second port by virtue of the oil exports. Oil

refining. Water is piped 25 m. from the Chira R.

**Talca** Chile. Capital of Talca province, 155 m. SSW of Santiago in the central valley. Pop. (1966) 72,000. Important industrial centre in a wine-producing area. Manufacturers matches, footwear, paper, tobacco products, etc. Flourmilling, distilling, tanning. Founded 1692. Destroyed by earthquake (1928) and since rebuilt. Chile's independence was proclaimed here (1818).

**Talcahuano** Chile. Seaport and naval station in Concepción province, on Concepción Bay 8 m. NNW of Concepción. Pop. (1966) 75,000. Excellent harbour and dry docks. Exports timber, wool, hides, etc. Imports iron ore for a modern steel plant. Fishing and fish canning, flour milling, oil refining.

**Tallahassee** USA. State capital of Florida, in the NW 160 m. W of Jacksonville. Pop. (1960) 48,174. Commercial centre. Woodworking, meat packing. Seat of the Florida State University (1857) and the Florida Agricultural and Mechanical University (1887, for Negroes). Settled by Spaniards in the 16th–17th cent.

**Tallinn (Tallin)** USSR. Formerly Revel. Capital and chief seaport of the Estonian SSR, on the S coast of the Gulf of Finland. Pop. (1970) 363,000. Exports timber, paper, textiles. Manufactures cotton goods, paper, cement, etc. The port is kept open for most of the winter by ice-breakers. In the upper old town is the 13th-cent. Danish castle. Founded by the Danes 1219. Joined the Hanseatic League 1285. Taken by Russia 1710. Capital of Estonia 1919–40. Severely damaged in the 2nd World War.

**Tamale** Ghana. Capital of the Northern Region 270 m. NNW of Accra. Pop. (1960) 40,327. Market town. Trade in groundnuts, rice, cotton, etc. Cotton milling, shea-nut processing.

**Tamar River** Australia. River in N Tasmania formed by the union of the N Esk and the S Esk rivers at Launceston, flowing generally NNW to Bass Strait and forming a navigable 40-m. waterway; has a winding course, tidal throughout.

**Tamar River** England. River 60 m. long flowing generally SSE and forming part of the boundary between Cornwall and Devon, entering Plymouth Sound by its estuary, the Hamoaze. A road suspension bridge across the river between Devonport

(Devon) and Saltash (Cornwall), replacing the ferry, was opened in 1961.

**Tamatave** Malagasy Republic. Seaport on the E coast (Indian Ocean) 140 m. ENE of Tananarive and connected with it by rail. Pop. (1965) 49,387. The deep-water harbour was completed in 1935. Exports coffee, rice, sugar, etc. Meat packing etc. Destroyed by hurricane 1925; later replanned and rebuilt.

**Tamaulipas** Mexico. State in the NE, bordering N on the USA (across the Rio Grande) and E on the Gulf of Mexico. Area 30,734 sq. m. Pop. (1969) 1,487,000. Cap. Ciudad Victoria. On the coast, where there are many lagoons, the climate is hot and humid; the W, in the Sierra Madre Oriental, is more temperate. Petroleum from the Tampico region is the chief resource. Crops include cotton, sugar-cane, tobacco. Main industries are located in Tampico, Nuevo Laredo (in the NW 'panhandle'), Ciudad Victoria, Matamoros.

**Tambo River** ◊ *Apurímac River.*

**Tambov** USSR. Capital of the Tambov Region, RSFSR, on the Tsna R. 160 m. WSW of Penza. Pop. (1970) 229,000. Railway junction. Industrial centre in a fertile black-earth agricultural region. Flour milling, sugar refining, distilling. Manufactures machinery, chemicals, synthetic rubber, textiles, etc. Founded (1636) as a fortified Muscovite outpost.

**Tamil Nadu** ◊ *Madras.*

**Tammerfors** ◊ *Tampere.*

**Tampa** USA. Seaport and second largest city in Florida, on an inlet in Tampa Bay on the W coast. Pop. (1960) 274,970. Exports chiefly phosphates and canned grapefruit. Principal cigar-making centre in the USA. Also fruit canning, shipbuilding, meat packing. A tourist resort. Seat of the University of South Florida (1960) and the University of Tampa (1931).

**Tampere (Tammerfors)** Finland. Second largest city, in the Häme province 100 m. NNW of Helsinki. Pop. (1968) 150,022. Industrial centre, deriving hydroelectric power from the Tammerkoski rapids, between Lakes Näsi and Pyhä. Also a railway junction. Manufactures textiles, railway rolling stock, wood pulp and paper, footwear, etc. The textile industry was founded by a Scotsman in the early 19th cent. Chiefly modern; has a 20th-cent. cathedral and an open-air theatre with revolving auditorium.

**Tampico** Mexico. Important seaport in Tamaulipas state, in the NE, on the Pánuco R. Pop. (1969) 155,300. Exports petroleum and petroleum products etc. Oil refining, boatbuilding, sawmilling. Manufactures chemicals etc. Popular winter resort; famous for tarpon fishing.

**Tamworth** Australia. Market town and railway junction in New South Wales, on the Peel R. 190 m. N of Sydney. Pop. (1966) 21,682. Flour milling, sawmilling. Manufactures furniture etc.

**Tamworth** England. Municipal borough in Staffordshire, on the R. Tame 13 m. NE of Birmingham. Pop. (1961) 13,555. Market town. Manufactures cars, clothing, bricks and tiles, etc. Has a castle overlooking the confluence of the Tame and the Anker, a 14th-cent. church, and 17th-cent. almshouses built by Thomas Guy, founder of Guy's Hospital, London.

**Tana (Tsana), Lake** Ethiopia. Ethiopia's largest lake, 50 m. long and up to 40 m. wide, S of Gondar at a height of 6,004 ft. Fed mainly by the Little Abbai R. (SW). Drained by the Blue Nile (SE). Site of a projected dam to control irrigation in the UAR (Egypt) and Sudan.

**Tananarive (Antananarivo)** Malagasy Republic. Capital and chief commercial and industrial centre, on the interior plateau at a height of 4,800 ft 140 m. WSW of Tamatave, to which it is linked by rail. Pop. (1965) 321,654. Manufactures footwear, clothing, soap. Flour milling, meat packing. The Republic's main educational centre; seat of a university (1961) and an agricultural college. Founded in the 17th cent. by a Hova chief. Occupied by the French 1895.

**Tana River** Kenya. River 440 m. long rising in the Aberdare Mountains, flowing generally E and S and entering the Indian Ocean at Kipini. Navigable for small vessels in the lower course.

**Tandil** Argentina. Resort and market town in Buenos Aires province, just N of the Sierra del Tandil 190 m. SSW of Buenos Aires. Pop. 70,000. In a dairy-farming region. Granite quarries in the neighbourhood.

**Tanga** Tanzania. Second seaport, on the Indian Ocean 120 m. N of Dar-es-Salaam. Pop. (1960) 38,000. Exports sisal, copra, coffee. Terminus of the railway to Moshi (Kilimanjaro), Arusha.

**Tanganyika** ◊ *Tanzania.*

**Tanganyika, Lake.** Second largest lake in

Africa and second deepest (4,700 ft) in the world (after L. Baikal), 420 m. long and 30–45 m. wide, in the Great Rift Valley at a height of 2,515 ft. Borders on Burundi (NE), Tanzania (E), Zambia (S), and Congo (Kinshasa) (W). Around the lake the land rises abruptly in places to over 8,000 ft. The Ruzizi R. (N, outlet of L. Kivu) is the main feeder. The Lukuga R. (W, flowing to the Congo R. basin), the only outlet, often silts up and raises the surface level. Principal lake ports Kalemie (Congo (Kinshasa)), Bujumbura (Burundi), and Kigoma (Tanzania). Discovered by Burton and Speke 1858. Later explored by Livingstone and Stanley, whose famous meeting (1871) took place at Ujiji, on the E shore.

**Tangier** Morocco. Seaport on the N coast, at the W entrance to the Strait of Gibraltar. Pop. (1961) 166,290. Commercial centre with minor industries, e.g. soap manufacture. Important tourist trade. Significance as a seaport has declined. Linked by rail with the main Casablanca–Tunis line through Morocco. Held in turn by Romans, Vandals, Byzantines, and Arabs. Taken by the Portuguese 1471. Then successively in Spanish, Portuguese, and English hands; abandoned by the English 1684. The International Zone of Tangier, providing for its neutrality and its government by an international commission, was established 1923. Occupied by Spain during the 2nd World War 1940–45. The international status was restored in 1945 but abolished when Morocco became independent (1956). Became the summer capital 1961. Declared a free port 1962.

**Tanimbar Islands (Timorlaut)** Indonesia. Group of islands in the S Moluccas about 250 m. ENE of Timor. Area 2,172 sq. m. Pop. 32,000. Largest island Jamdena. Chief products copra, sago.

**Tanis** United Arab Republic. Ancient Egyptian city in the Nile delta (where the modern village of San el Hagar stands). Flourished in the 21st Dynasty. Abandoned when threatened with flooding from L. Manzala. Excavations by Flinders Petrie (and later P. Montel) have revealed tombs, statues, and inscriptions.

**Tanjore** ◊ *Thanjavur.*

**Tannenberg** (modern **Stębark**) Poland. Village in the Olsztyn voivodship 25 m. SW of Olsztyn (Allenstein). Scene of two famous battles: the Teutonic Knights were routed by the combined forces of Poland

and Lithuania under King Jagiello (1410); the Russians were defeated by the Germans in the 1st World War (1914).

**Tanta** United Arab Republic. Capital of the Gharbiya governorate, 50 m. NNW of Cairo in the Nile delta. Pop. (1960) 184,000. Important railway junction and commercial centre. Cotton ginning, cotton-seed-oil extraction. Manufactures soap. Noted for its fairs and Muslim festivals.

**Tanzania.** Republic in E Africa, a member of the British Commonwealth. Area 361,800 sq. m. (20,650 sq. m. water). Pop. (1967) 12,231,342 (10,351,900 Africans and Arabs, 104,300 Indians and Pakistanis, 17,500 Europeans). Cap. Dar-es-Salaam. Bounded by Kenya, Uganda (N), the Indian Ocean (E), Moçambique, Zambia, Malawi (S), Congo (Kinshasa) (W, L. Tanganyika), Rwanda, Burundi (NW). Includes much of Lakes Victoria, Tanganyika, and Malawi, and several smaller lakes, e.g. Rukwa, Natron, etc. From the narrow coastal plain the land rises gradually to a plateau of average height 3,500 ft, dominated by the volcanic peaks of Kilimanjaro (19,565 ft) and Meru (14,979 ft) in the NE and rising to 9,715 ft in the Kipingere Mountains, N of L. Malawi. Climate tropical, with distinct rainy (summer) and dry seasons. Annual rainfall exceeds 60 ins. in the highlands and is 30–40 ins. on much of the plateau. Natural vegetation principally of the savannah type. Subsistence crops grown by the Africans include maize, millet, and groundnuts, with rice along the coast. Large numbers of cattle, sheep, and goats reared. Leading export crop sisal; cotton and coffee also important. Chief minerals diamonds, gold.

In the 16th and 17th cent. the Portuguese exercised influence over the coastal towns, which later became the centres of Arab trade in ivory and slaves. In the 19th cent. Germany took an increasing interest in the territory; in 1885 it was declared a protectorate as German E Africa, and the coastal strip was acquired from the Sultan of Zanzibar in 1890. After the 1st World War (renamed Tanganyika Territory) it became a mandated territory administered by Britain, except for the NW region, which was made the Belgian mandated territory of Ruanda-Urundi. After the 2nd World War, it became a UN Trust Territory (as Tanganyika) administered by Britain (1946) and an independent member of the UN 1961. In 1964 Zanzibar united with it and the new state was named Tanzania.

**Taormina** Italy. Picturesque winter resort in Messina province, on the E coast of Sicily 27 m. SSW of Messina. Pop. (1961) 8,072. Famous for the large Greek theatre, rebuilt by the Romans; also has the Church of S Pancrazio, built into a temple of the 3rd cent. B.C., and the 14th-cent. Palazzo Corvaia. Founded early in the 4th cent. B.C.

**Tapajós River** Brazil. Tributary of the Amazon R., 500 m. long, formed by the union of the São Manuel and Juruena rivers, flowing generally NNE past the Fordlandia and Belterra rubber plantations to join the Amazon at Santarém.

**Tapti River** India. River 440 m. long rising in the Satpura Range in S Madhya Pradesh and flowing generally W past Burhanpur and Surat to the Gulf of Cambay. Lower course navigable only to small vessels.

**Tara** Irish Republic. Village in Co. Meath 6 m. SSE of Navan (An Uaimh). The Hill of Tara (507 ft) was the residence of the Irish High kings until c. 560. On the hill are 6 raths or earthworks, within the largest of which, the King's Rath, stands a pillar-stone, called the Lia Fáil (Stone of Destiny), on which the monarchs were crowned. According to another story the true Stone of Destiny was taken to Scone, Scotland, and later to Westminster Abbey.

**Tarabulus** ◊ *Tripoli*.

**Taranaki** New Zealand. Provincial district in the W of the N Island. Area (statistical area) 3,750 sq. m. Pop. (1966) 101,104. Cap. and chief port New Plymouth. The pastoral region encircling Mt Egmont has many dairy factories producing butter and cheese. Inland as far as the upper Wanganui R. is hill country where sheep are reared.

**Taranto** Italy. Ancient *Tarentum*. Capital of Ionio province, Apulia, 48 m. SSE of Bari on the Gulf of Taranto. Pop. (1968) 214,705. Important naval base with shipyards and arsenal; also a seaport. Exports wine, olive oil. Oysters and mussels cultivated. Manufactures furniture, glass, footwear, etc. Excellent museum of antiquities. Was a powerful city in Magna Graecia but declined in Roman times. Destroyed by the Saracens and rebuilt in the 10th cent. Gave its name to the dance, the tarantella. The largest integrated steelworks in Italy was inaugurated here in 1965.

**Tarascon** France. Town in the Bouches-du-Rhône department, on the left bank of the Rhône R. opposite Beaucaire and 13 m. SW of Avignon. Pop. (1968) 10,857. Manufactures textiles, furniture. Trade in fruit, vegetables. Has a 14th/15th-cent. castle and the Church of St Martha. Immortalized in Alphonse Daudet's satirical *Tartarin de Tarascon*.

**Tarawa** (Gilbert and Ellice Islands) W Pacific Ocean. Atoll consisting of a group of islets surrounding a lagoon in the W Central Pacific; capital of the colony. Pop. 5,000. Exports copra, mother-of-pearl. Occupied by the Japanese 1941; captured by US marines 1943.

**Tarbes** France. Prefecture of the Hautes-Pyrénées department, on the Adour R. 75 m. WSW of Toulouse. Pop. (1968) 59,432. Tourist centre. Trade in horses, farm produce. Tanning, sawmilling. Manufactures footwear, harness, furniture, machinery, etc. Seat of a bishopric dating from the 5th cent.; has a partly 13th-cent. cathedral. Was capital of the old countship of Bigorre. Birthplace of Théophile Gautier (1811–72) and Marshal Foch (1851–1929).

**Taree** Australia. Town in E New South Wales, on the Manning R. 85 m. NE of Newcastle. Pop. (1966) 10,559. Dairy factories.

**Târgu-Mureş** Rumania. Capital of the Mureş district, on the Mureş R. 80 m. NW of Braşov. Pop. (1968) 92,104. Market town. Sugar refining, brewing. Manufactures fertilizers, furniture, soap, etc. Trade in timber, grain, wine. Has a 15th-cent. Gothic church.

**Tarifa** Spain. Minor seaport in Cadiz province, on the Strait of Gibraltar. Pop. (1961) 17,469. The most southerly town in Spain. Fishing centre. Trade in oranges, cereals. Tanning, fish canning. Moorish in appearance, with white houses and narrow, winding streets. Taken by the Moors 711. Recaptured by Sancho IV of Castile 1292.

**Tarija** Bolivia. Capital of the Tarija department, in the basin of the Guadalquivir R. 180 m. SSE of Sucre at a height of 6,250 ft. Pop. (1967) 26,787. Market town. Trade in local agricultural produce (cereals, potatoes, etc.). Noteworthy cathedral. University (1886). Founded by the Spanish 1574: one of the oldest settlements in Bolivia.

**Tarim Basin** China. Vast depression in the Sinkiang-Uighur AR, extending about

900 m. E–W and up to 300 m. N–S, enclosed by the Tien Shan (N), the Altyn Tagh and Kunlun Shan (S), and the Pamirs (W), and largely occupied by the Takla Makan desert. The Tarim R. flows generally E about 1,000 m. along the N margin of the desert and finally disappears in the Lop Nor basin. Khotan, Yarkand, Kashgar, and Aksu are important oases along the edge of the Tarim Basin.

**Tarn** France. Department in Languedoc on the edge of the Massif Central (E) and the basin of Aquitaine (W), reaching a height of 4,134 ft in the Monts de Lacaune in the extreme SE. Area 2,232 sq. m. Pop. (1968) 332,011. Prefecture Albi. Drained by the Tarn R. and its tributary the Agout. Cereals and vegetables cultivated. Cattle and sheep raised. Coalmines. Varied industries. Chief towns Albi, Castres.

**Tarn-et-Garonne** France. Department in the SW, formed from parts of Guienne, Gascony, and Languedoc. Area 1,441 sq. m. Pop. (1968) 183,572. Prefecture Montauban. Drained by the Garonne, Tarn, and Aveyron rivers. Generally fertile; produces cereals, vines, plums, etc. Chief towns Montauban, Moissac.

**Tarnopól** ◊ *Ternopol*.

**Tarnów** Poland. Industrial town and railway junction in the Kraków voivodship, on the Biala R. 48 m. E of Cracow. Pop. (1968) 83,700. Manufactures agricultural machinery, glass, etc. Gothic cathedral (15th-cent.); 14th-cent. town hall.

**Tarn River** France. River 234 m. long, rising on Mont Lozère in the Cévennes and flowing generally W through the limestone Causses, forming the picturesque Tarn gorge, past Millau, Albi, and Montauban to join the Garonne R. below Moissac.

**Tarquinia** Italy. Formerly Corneto. Town in Viterbo province, Latium, 45 m. NW of Rome. Pop. (1961) 11,856. Impressively situated on a rocky height overlooking the Tyrrhenian Sea. Manufactures cement, paper. Has 12th/13th-cent. Romanesque-Gothic churches and the 15th–cent. Vitelleschi palace containing a museum with Etruscan antiquities. To the SE is the necropolis from the ancient Etruscan city of Tarquinii, which flourished in the 8th–6th cent. B.C. and was the leading city of Etruria.

**Tarragona** Spain. 1. Province in the NE, in Catalonia, bordering on the Medi-

terranean Sea. Area 2,426 sq. m. Pop. (1961) 362,679. Mountainous inland. Coastal plain containing the delta of the Ebro R. Produces wine, olive oil, almonds, fruit, etc. Chief towns Tarragona, Reus. 2. Ancient Tarraco. Capital of Tarragona province, a Mediterranean seaport 50 m. WSW of Barcelona. Pop. (1967) 64,192. Exports large quantities of wine. Manufactures pharmaceutical products, electrical equipment, liqueurs, etc. The old town stands on a steep hill overlooking the sea, and is enclosed by ruined walls with a cyclopean lowest course of massive unhewn blocks surmounted by Roman masonry. Also has a Roman aqueduct and a 12th/13th-cent. cathedral. Taken by the Romans in the 3rd cent. B.C.; made capital of the province of Hispania Tarraconensis by Augustus (26 B.C.).

**Tarrasa** Spain. Industrial town in Barcelona province, Catalonia, 13 m. NNW of Barcelona. Pop. (1967) 123,112. Manufactures textiles, textile machinery, dyes, fertilizers, etc.

**Tarsus** Turkey. Market town in Içel province (S), 22 m. W of Adana. Pop. (1965) 57,000. Trade in wheat, barley, fruits, etc. There are ruins of the ancient city, which flourished in Roman times and was famous as the birthplace of St Paul – who described himself as a 'citizen of no mean city'.

**Tartu** (Ger. **Dorpat**) USSR. Formerly Yuryev. Industrial city, the second largest in the Estonian SSR, on the Ema R. 100 m. SE of Tallinn. Pop. (1964) 77,000. Manufactures agricultural machinery, textiles, cigars and cigarettes, etc. Seat of a famous university, founded in 1632 by Gustavus Adolphus of Sweden, moved in 1699, and restored in 1802, with an observatory and botanical gardens. Cathedral (13th-cent., restored) on one of the city's two hills; Estonian National Museum. Founded in the 11th cent. as Yuryev. Held by Russians, Poles, and Swedes. Took its present name on passing to Estonia (1918).

**Tashkent** USSR. Capital of the Uzbek SSR and the largest city in Soviet Central Asia, in an oasis irrigated by the Chirchik R., a tributary of the Syr Darya. Pop. (1970) 1,385,000. Important route and industrial centre. Manufactures textiles (cotton), textile and agricultural machinery, leather goods, paper etc. Also a leading educational centre, with a university (1920) and the Uzbek Academy of Sciences

(1943) in the new Russian town; the old Oriental town to the SW has the ruins of ancient *madrassas* (Muslim seminaries). Coal is produced (Angren); hydroelectric plants in the district. Probably founded in the 7th cent. Taken by the Russians 1865. Expanded rapidly after being reached by the Trans-Caspian Railway (1898). Capital of the former Turkestan SSR 1918–24 and of the Uzbek SSR from 1930.

**Tasman Glacier** ♢ *Southern Alps.*

**Tasmania** Australia. Island and state of the Commonwealth, separated from the mainland by Bass Strait, 150 m. wide. Area (inc. adjacent islands) 26,215 sq. m. Pop. (1966) 371,435. Cap. Hobart. A compact island with a central plateau of hard old rocks, an extension of the E highlands of the mainland. The plateau (about 3,000 ft, with peaks rising above 5,000 ft) has shallow lakes. Rivers descend steeply from the plateau, the chief being the Derwent, flowing to a broad estuary in the SE, and the Tamar, in the N; the coastal plains are narrow.

Lying in a zone of prevailing westerlies and depressions, the W has a high rainfall, mostly over 80 ins. a year; the sheltered E is drier, averaging below 30 ins. except for the NE highlands. Mean monthly temperatures are about 45°–60° F. Eucalypts cover much of the island, furnishing timber, wood pulp, and paper. The wetter, cooler parts have beech, pine, and yew, and the SW supports a tangle of 'horizontal scrub' where the rare Tasmanian wolf still lives.

The chief agricultural regions are: the N coastal area, with mixed farming, dairying, and cultivation of potatoes and vegetables; the central lowlands, with sheep rearing; the SE, with sheep and cattle rearing; the Derwent and Huon valleys, with cultivation of apples, pears, berry fruits, and hops. Large mineral deposits in the NE and NW, where coal occurs, enable Tasmania to produce more tin and tungsten than any other state and also export zinc, copper, lead, and silver. Large quantities of ores and concentrates are received for electrolytic refining, esp. zinc at Risdon and aluminium at Bell Bay. Many hydroelectric stations on and around the central plateau. Chief exports metals, wool, temperate fruits and vegetables, timber.

Discovered by Tasman 1642; named Van Diemen's Land. Visited by Capt. Cook 1777. Used as a penal colony 1803–53,

and was then renamed Tasmania. Became a state of the Commonwealth 1901. The last of the Tasmanian aborigines died in 1876.

**Tasman Sea** Australia. Part of the Pacific Ocean between SE Australia and Tasmania (W) and New Zealand (E); to the N is the Coral Sea and to the SW the Indian Ocean.

**Tatabánya** Hungary. Capital of Komárom county 30 m. W of Budapest. Pop. (1968) 63,000. Lignite-mining centre. Brickmaking etc.

**Tatar ASSR** USSR. Autonomous republic in RSFSR, occupying a region round the middle Volga and lower Kama rivers. Area 26,250 sq. m. Pop. (1970) 3,131,000 (46 per cent Tatar, 43 per cent Russian). Cap. Kazan. Wheat, rye, and oats cultivated. Petroleum and other minerals produced. Industry is concentrated in Kazan. The Tatars, Muslim by religion, are mainly descendants of Mongols and Bulgars.

**Tatra (Czech Tatry) Mountains** Czechoslovakia/Poland. The highest mountain group in the Carpathians, known as the High Tatra (Vysoké Tatry), on the border of Slovakia and Poland, rising to 8,737 ft in Gerlachovka. Scenically beautiful, with many summer resorts and winter-sports centres. To the S is the Low Tatra (Nizké Tatry), a parallel range reaching 6,709 ft.

**Tatung** China. Town in N Shansi province 175 m. W of Peking. Pop. 229,000. Coalmining and industrial centre. Railway and other engineering. Manufactures cement, chemicals, mining machinery.

**Taunton** England. Municipal borough and county town of Somerset, on the R. Tone 38 m. SW of Bristol. Pop. (1961) 35,178. Market town in the picturesque vale of Taunton Dean. Manufactures shirts, collars, gloves, leather, etc. Remains of the 12th-cent. castle; the Great Hall where Judge Jeffreys held his 'Bloody Assize' after Monmouth's ♢ *Sedgemoor* rebellion (1685). Taunton School was founded in 1522.

**Taunton** USA. Industrial town in Massachusetts, on the Taunton R. 31 m. S of Boston. Pop. (1960) 41,132. Manufactures textile machinery, plastics, jewellery, silverware, etc. Formerly an important port.

**Taunus** Federal German Republic. Range of hills in Hessen extending 45 m. ENE from the Rhine R., rising to 2,887 ft in the Grosser Feldberg. Wine produced on the

S slopes (Rheingau). Mineral springs; well-known spas of Wiesbaden, Bad Homburg, Bad Nauheim.

**Taupo, Lake** New Zealand. Largest lake in the country, 25 m. long and up to 18 m. wide, in the centre of the N Island. In a volcanic area with hot springs. Source of the Waikato R. On the NE shore is the small town of Taupo.

**Tauranga** New Zealand. Port in Tauranga Harbour, Bay of Plenty, N Island, 100 m. SE of Auckland. Pop. (1966) 23,380. The harbour lies behind the bar of Matakana Island and is approached through a tidal channel. Centre of a region noted for citrus fruits, esp. lemons. Exports dairy produce, meat, timber.

**Taurus Mountains** Turkey. Mountain system in the S extending SE from L. Eğridir, then curving E and NE parallel to the Mediterranean coast, forming the S rim of the Anatolian plateau. Many peaks exceed 10,000 ft; Ala Dağ rises to 12,251 ft and the detached Erciyas Daği to 12,850 ft. To the NE it is continued as the so-called Anti-Taurus.

**Tavastehus** ◊ *Hämeenlinna.*

**Taveuni** ◊ *Fiji Islands.*

**Tavistock** England. Market town in Devonshire, on the R. Tavy 12 m. N of Plymouth. Pop. (1961) 6,086. Manufactures agricultural implements, chemicals. Built round a 10th-cent. abbey. Formerly a tinmining centre; one of the four stannary towns of Devon. Sir Francis Drake (1542–96) was born near by.

**Tavoy** Burma. 1. Port in Tenasserim, at the head of the Tavoy R. estuary 175 m. S of Moulmein. Pop. 40,000. Coastal trade. Rice milling, sawmilling.

2. Island in the N Mergui Archipelago 65 m. S of the town of Tavoy in the Andaman Sea.

**Taw River** England. River in Devonshire 50 m. long, rising on Dartmoor and flowing generally N past Barnstaple to the estuary in Bideford Bay, Bristol Channel.

**Tayport** Scotland. Small burgh in Fifeshire, on the Firth of Tay 3 m. ESE of Dundee. Pop. (1961) 3,151. Seaside resort.

**Tay River** Scotland. River in Perthshire, the longest in Scotland (118 m.), rising on Ben Lui on the Argyllshire border. Known as the Fillan from its source to Loch Dochart, and from here to Loch Tay (14½ m. long) as the Dochart. Below Loch Tay it flows generally E and SE past Aberfeldy, Dunkeld, and Perth, to enter its tidal estuary, the Firth of Tay (25 m. long). At Dundee it is crossed by the Tay Bridge (railway), which replaces the one blown down with a train in 1879, and a new road bridge opened in 1966. Chief tributaries the Tummel and the Earn. Famous for its salmon.

**Tbilisi** (Russian **Tiflis**) USSR. Capital of the Georgian SSR, on the Kura R. Pop. (1970) 889,000. Commercial, cultural, and route centre, on the Baku–Batumi trunk railway and at the S end of the famous Georgian Military Highway. Engineering, woodworking. Manufactures textiles, textile machinery, electrical equipment, etc. Derives power from the great Zemo-Avchala hydroelectric station. Trade in carpets, textiles, dried fruits, etc. Sheltered by the Caucasus foothills and rising in terraces above the river valley; has an old Oriental section with narrow streets and a bazaar and a new Russian area of wide roads and modern buildings. University (1918). The Sion cathedral dates from the 5th cent. and the Armenian cathedral of Van from the 15th cent. Founded in the 4th cent. Capital of Georgia in the 5th cent. Destroyed and rebuilt several times before passing to Russia (1800). Became capital of the Georgian SSR in 1936, when the name was officially changed from Tiflis to the Georgian Tbilisi.

**Tczew** Poland. Industrial town and railway junction in the Gdańsk voivodship, on the Vistula R. 20 m. SSE of Gdańsk. Pop. (1968) 38,900. Manufactures building materials, agricultural machinery, etc. Railway engineering, sugar refining. Founded in the 13th cent. Passed to Prussia 1772. Returned to Poland 1919.

**Tebessa** Algeria. Ancient *Theveste.* Town at the E end of the Saharan Atlas Mountains 100 m. SE of Constantine. Pop. 20,000. Important mining centre (phosphates). Manufactures carpets. Trade in wool, esparto grass, etc. Notable Roman remains in the neighbourhood, including the 3rd-cent. arch of Caracalla.

**Teddington** England. Residential district in Twickenham, in the London borough of Richmond-upon-Thames, on the R. Thames 12 m. WSW of London. Contains Bushy Park and the National Physical Laboratory. Teddington Lock, the largest on the Thames, marks the tidal limit of the river; above it the river is controlled by the Thames Conservancy Board, below it by the Port of London Authority.

**Tees River** England. River 70 m. long rising on Cross Fell and flowing generally E, forming the Durham–Westmorland and then the Durham–Yorkshire boundary, passing Barnard Castle, Stockton-on-Tees, Thornaby-on-Tees, and Middlesbrough to enter the estuary on the North Sea.

**Teesside** England. County borough in the N Riding of Yorkshire and Co. Durham, formed in 1968 from the former county borough of Middlesbrough, the municipal boroughs of Redcar, Thornaby-on-Tees and Stockton-on-Tees, and the urban districts of Billingham and Eston. Pop. (1968) 392,990.

**Tegucigalpa** Honduras. Capital of the republic and of the Francisco Morazán department, on the Choluteca R. at a height of 3,200 ft. Pop. (1966) 190,844. Food processing, brewing, distilling, textile manufacture, etc. Has no railway. Seat of the National University (1847). The chief building is the 18th-cent. domed and double-towered cathedral. Founded (1578) as a gold- and silver-mining centre. Became capital 1880.

**Tehran (Teheran)** Iran. Capital, at the S foot of the Elburz Mountains at a height of 3,800 ft. Pop. (1966) 2,803,130. Iran's largest city and leading industrial and route centre, at the intersection of railways N–S from the Caspian Sea to the Persian Gulf and E–W from Meshed to Tabriz. Manufactures textiles, carpets, chemicals, glass, etc. University (1935). The city extends N up the lower slopes of the Elburz Mountains into the district of Shemran, a favourite residential area in the summer. Although the lower, S part is still typically Oriental, the central area was transformed after 1925 by Riza Shah: broad avenues, open squares, and modern buildings were constructed. In the heart of the city is the large square known as the Maidan Sepah, and S of this is the old royal palace with the famous Peacock Throne, brought by Nadir Shah from India. Became capital of Persia 1788. During the 2nd World War it was occupied by Russian and British forces. Scene of the Tehran Conference between Stalin, Churchill, and Roosevelt (1943).

**Tehuacán** Mexico. Town in Puebla state 70 m. SE of Puebla at a height of 5,500 ft. Pop. 32,000. Health resort. Mineral springs, the water from which is bottled and widely distributed.

**Tehuantepec, Isthmus of** Mexico. Isthmus 130 m. wide in E Veracruz and Oaxaca, between the Gulf of Campeche on the Gulf of Mexico (N) and the Gulf of Tehuantepec on the Pacific Ocean (S). The N is swampy and jungle-covered; in the S are the foothills of the Sierra Madre. An inter-oceanic railway (completed 1907) links the ports of Salina Cruz (S) and Coatzacoalcos (N).

**Teignmouth** England. Urban district in Devonshire, at the mouth of the R. Teign. Pop. (1961) 11,576. Seaside resort. An important seaport in the Middle Ages.

**Teign River** England. River 30 m. long, rising on Dartmoor and flowing SE past Newton Abbot to the English Channel at Teignmouth.

**Tejo River** ⋄ *Tagus River*.

**Telanaipura** ⋄ *Jambi*.

**Tel Aviv** Israel. Largest city and the chief industrial and commercial centre of Israel, on the Mediterranean coast 35 m. NW of Jerusalem. Pop. (1968) 388,000. Manufactures textiles, metal goods, food products, chemicals, etc. The main centre of modern Israeli culture and seat of a university (1953); its appearance is entirely modern. Founded 1906. Absorbed the former Arab town of Jaffa 1949.

**Tel el Amarna** United Arab Republic. The collection of ruins and rock tombs on the E bank of the Nile 40 m. NNW of Asyût. Site of the city of Akhetaton, built by Ikhnaton *c.* 1370 B.C. to replace Thebes as his capital. Excavations in the late 19th cent. revealed much information about the ancient city.

**Tema** Ghana. Seaport 17 m. ENE of Accra. Pop. (1960) 26,860. The harbour was opened in 1962, and has since taken the traffic formerly handled by the 'surf' ports of Accra, Keta, Winneba, and Cape Coast. Fishing. Oil refining.

**Témbi (Tempe) Gorge (Vale of Tempe)** Greece. The picturesque gorge in Thessaly, 5 m. long, through which the Peneus (Piniós) R. flows, between Mt Ossa and Mt Olympus. Sacred to Apollo, and an important route into Thessaly.

**Tempe** USA. Town in Arizona on the Salt R. 8 m. E of Phoenix. Pop. (1960) 24,897. Commercial centre. Flour milling etc. University (1885).

**Temple** USA. Town in Texas 113 m. S of Fort Worth. Pop. (1960) 30,419. Commercial and industrial centre in an agricultural region. Manufactures furniture, footwear, cottonseed oil, etc.

**Temuco** Chile. Capital of Cautín province, on the Cautín R. 380 m. SSW of Santiago. Pop. 109,000. Market town in an agricultural and forest region producing cereals, apples, timber. Tanning, flour milling, sawmilling. A market for the Araucanian Indians. A treaty with the Araucanians ending the Indian wars was signed here (1881).

**Tenasserim** Burma. Region in the S consisting of a coastal strip extending from Moulmein (N) to Victoria Point (S) on the Isthmus of Kra. Main products rice, teak, tin, tungsten. Chief towns Moulmein, Tavoy, Mergui.

**Tenasserim River** Burma. River in Tenasserim 250 m. long, flowing first S and then NW and entering the Andaman Sea near Mergui.

**Tenby** Wales. Municipal borough in Pembrokeshire 9 m. E of Pembroke, on a headland overlooking Carmarthen Bay, Bristol Channel. Pop. (1961) 4,752. Seaside resort. Has two sandy beaches and a harbour. Just NE are the ruins of the 12th/13th-cent. castle.

**Tenerife** Canary Islands. Largest of the islands, between Gomera (W) and Gran Canaria (E); part of the Spanish province of Santa Cruz de Tenerife. Area 795 sq. m. Pop. 350,000. Cap. Santa Cruz. Rises to 12,172 ft in the volcanic Pico de Teide. The mild climate makes it a popular resort. In the fertile valleys bananas, tomatoes, early fruits and vegetables are grown.

**Tennessee** USA. State in S central USA, bordered (W) along the Mississippi R. by Arkansas and Missouri. Area 42,246 sq. m. Pop. (1970) 3,838,777. Cap. Nashville. Admitted to the Union in 1796 as the 16th state; popularly known as the 'Volunteer' state. In the E are the Unaka and Great Smoky Mountains of the Appalachian ranges; Clingmans Dome rises to 6,642 ft. Farther W is the Cumberland Plateau, at about 1,800 ft. The land then slopes W to the Mississippi R. Largely drained by the Tennessee R. and its tributaries; the N is drained by the Cumberland R. (also a tributary of the Ohio). Short mild winters, hot summers. Rainfall plentiful, about 50 ins. annually. Agriculture important. Chief crops cotton, maize, tobacco, hay. Cattle, pigs, and poultry extensively reared. Coal, zinc, pyrites, and phosphates mined. E Tennessee is an important industrial area (textiles, chemicals, etc.); principal centres Memphis, Nashville, Chattanooga, Knoxville. The state has derived great economic benefit from the Tennessee Valley Authority (TVA) set up in 1933, a multi-purpose project for developing the Tennessee R. valley in the interests of transport, flood control, and hydroelectric power, which operates mainly in Tennessee but extends into neighbouring states. Associated with TVA was the large fertilizer plant at Muscle Shoals, and 27 dams were built on the Tennessee R. and its tributaries. TVA has also been concerned with afforestation and soil conservation in the area, and is an excellent example of the benefits of regional planning. The first permanent settlement in Tennessee was made by Virginians (1769). The region became part of the USA in 1783. In the American Civil War it was on the Confederate side.

**Tennessee River** USA. River 652 m. long, formed by the union of the Holston and the French Broad rivers near Knoxville in Tennessee, flowing generally SW past Knoxville and Chattanooga, turning WNW in N Alabama and re-entering Tennessee, and finally entering Kentucky to join the Ohio R. at Paducah. The drainage basin occupies about 38,500 sq. m.; the area has been developed by the Tennessee Valley Authority (♦ *Tennessee*).

**Tenterden** England. Municipal borough in Kent 9 m. SW of Ashford. Pop. (1961) 4,935. Market town. In the 15th cent. it was made a member of the Cinque Port of Rye, for the sea was then only 2 m. S. Reputed birthplace of William Caxton (1422–91).

**Tepic** Mexico. Capital of Nayarit state, at the foot of the extinct volcano Sanganguey 120 m. NW of Guadalajara. Pop. 54,000. Market town. Sugar refining, rice milling, cotton ginning, etc. Founded 1531.

**Teplice** (Ger. **Teplitz**) Czechoslovakia. Industrial town in NW Bohemia 10 m. W of Ústi-nad-Labem. Pop. (1967) 52,000. Manufactures glass, pottery, textiles, cement, etc. Also a watering-place with thermal mineral springs.

**Teramo** Italy. Capital of Teramo province in Abruzzi e Molise, on the Tordino R. 30 m. NW of Pescara. Pop. (1961) 41,899. Market town. Manufactures textiles, macaroni, etc. Romanesque-Gothic cathedral (14th-cent.). A famous astronomical observatory is near by.

**Terceira** ♦ *Azores*.

**Terek River** USSR. River 370 m. long in the Georgian SSR, rising in the Caucasus in glaciers on Mt Kazbek, flowing NNW through the Daryal Gorge past Ordzhonikidze, then E and NE, forming a swampy delta about 70 m. wide on the Caspian Sea. Used for irrigation along the lower course and for hydroelectric power on its headstreams.

**Teresina** Brazil. Capital of Piauí state, on the Parnaíba R. 200 m. SE of São Luís, to which it is linked by railway. Pop. 110,000. Trade in cattle, hides and skins, rice, cotton. Sugar refining. Manufactures textiles, soap, etc.

**Terni** Italy. Ancient Interamna Nahars. Capital of Terni province, in Umbria, on the Nera R. 46 m. NNE of Rome. Pop. (1968) 103,936. Railway junction. Industrial centre. Manufactures iron and steel, armaments, locomotives, turbines, chemicals, etc. Roman remains. Cathedral (13th-cent., restored in the 17th cent.). Near by are the famous waterfalls, Cascata delle Marmore, which supply hydroelectric power for the factories. Founded in the 7th cent. B.C. Birthplace of Marcus Claudius Tacitus, Roman emperor A.D. 275–6.

**Ternopol (Tarnopól)** USSR. Capital of the Ternopol Region, Ukrainian SSR, on the Seret R. 75 m. ESE of Lvov. Pop. (1963) 61,000. Railway junction. Market town. Flour milling. Manufactures agricultural machinery, cement, etc. Founded (1540) by Jan Tarnowski (Polish). Taken by the Russians in the 1st World War; returned to Poland 1919; ceded to the USSR 1945.

**Terracina** Italy. Town in Latina province, Latium, on the Gulf of Gaeta 60 m. SE of Rome. Pop. (1961) 29,751. Port. Seaside resort. Fishing etc. Roman remains include an amphitheatre and baths; the modern *piazza* was the Roman forum.

**Terranova di Sicilia** ♢ *Gela.*

**Terre Haute** USA. Town in Indiana, on the Wabash R. 70 m. WSW of Indianapolis. Pop. (1960) 72,500. Manufactures bricks and tiles, chemicals, plastics, glass, etc. Birthplace of Theodore Dreiser (1871–1945).

**Terror, Mount** ♢ *Ross Island.*

**Teruel** Spain. 1. Province in Aragón. Area 5,713 sq. m. Pop. (1961) 215,183. Mountainous and largely barren, rising to over 6,000 ft in the S and SW. Has few good roads or railways; one of the most sparsely populated provinces in Spain. 2. Capital of Teruel province, on the Turia

R. 135 m. E of Madrid. Pop. (1961) 19,726. Market town. Manufactures soap, tiles, etc. The old walled town has narrow streets and a 16th-cent. cathedral.

**Tessin** ♢ *Ticino.*

**Teton Range** USA. Range of the Rocky Mountains, mainly in NW Wyoming, just S of Yellowstone National Park and now mainly in the Grand Teton National Park. Highest peak Grand Teton (13,766 ft). Noted for scenic beauty; much frequented by climbers, hikers, and campers.

**Tettenhall** England. Town in Staffordshire 2 m. WNW of Wolverhampton, from 1966 part of the county borough of Wolverhampton. Pop. (1961) 14,800. Mainly residential.

**Tetuán** Morocco. Capital of Tetuán province, formerly capital of Spanish Morocco, 20 m. S of Ceuta and 6 m. WSW of Río Martín (its port on the Mediterranean), to both of which it is linked by rail. Pop. (1964) 117,000. Manufactures textiles, soap, leather goods. The modern town was founded at the end of the 15th cent. by Jewish refugees from Portugal.

**Teuco River** ♢ *Bermejo River.*

**Tevere River** ♢ *Tiber River.*

**Teverone River** ♢ *Aniene River.*

**Tewkesbury** England. Municipal borough in Gloucestershire, on the R. Severn at the confluence with the Warwickshire Avon. Pop. (1961) 5,814. Market town. Flour milling. Has many timbered houses, but the principal feature is the fine Norman abbey church, consecrated 1123, with 14th-cent. additions. The Yorkist victory at the Battle of Tewkesbury (1471) brought the Wars of the Roses to an end.

**Texarkana** USA. Town partly in NE Texas and partly in SW Arkansas (hence the name). Pop. (1960) 50,006 (30,218 in Texas, 19,788 in Arkansas). Manufactures wood products, cottonseed oil, textiles, etc.

**Texas** USA. State in the S and SW, the second largest in the USA (after Alaska), bordered on the S along the Rio Grande by Mexico, and on the SE by the Gulf of Mexico. Area 267,339 sq. m. Pop. (1970) 10,989,123. Cap. Austin. Admitted to the Union in 1845 as the 28th state; popularly known as the 'Lone Star' state. Largely plains and flat tablelands. In the W is the Llano Estacado (Staked Plain), a rather dry, short-grass region at a height of 3,000–4,000 ft; in the SW, between the Rio Grande and its tributary the Pecos, are the Sacramento Mountains, rising to 8,751 ft in Guadalupe Mountain, the highest point in the state. The coast is fringed with many long narrow islands, lagoons, and bays. Along the N border is the Red R. (a tributary of the Mississippi); rivers draining to the Gulf of Mexico are the Rio Grande, the Colorado, the Brazos, the Trinity, the Sabine. The climate varies from humid sub-tropical on the coastal plain to dry continental (the N W 'panhandle'). Has the highest value of agricultural produce in the USA, despite serious soil erosion in some areas. Chief crop cotton, in which it leads the USA, as it does also in sorghum; also has the greatest number of cattle and sheep in the USA. Petroleum and natural gas (of which it is by far the leading producer) are the most important mineral products. Industries are mainly the processing of the agricultural and mineral products; leading centres Houston (chief seaport), Dallas, San Antonio, Fort Worth, El Paso, Austin, Corpus Christi. Large numbers of Mexicans work in Texas; there are over 1 million Negroes. The mixed population and stormy history make it one of the most colourful of the states. Once part of Mexico; won its independence in 1836 and later joined the Union (1845).

**Texas City** USA. Industrial town and seaport in Texas, on Galveston Bay 6 m. N W of Galveston. Pop. (1960) 32,065. Tin smelting, oil refining. Manufactures chemicals. Exports petroleum products, chemicals, sulphur, etc. Virtually destroyed by explosions and fires in 1947; later rebuilt.

**Texoma, Lake** ◊ *Red River.*

**Thailand.** Formerly Siam. Kingdom in SE Asia. Area 198,250 sq. m. Pop. (1960) 26,257,916. Cap. Bangkok. Lang. Thai. Rel. mainly Buddhist.

Occupies part of the Indo-Chinese and Malay peninsulas. Bounded by Laos (NE and E), Cambodia (SE), the Gulf of Siam and Malaya (S), and the Andaman Sea and Burma (W). As in other monsoon countries of SE Asia, the main crop is rice, of which it normally produces a considerable surplus; it is one of the chief rice-exporting lands. Divided for administrative purposes into 71 provinces.

TOPOGRAPHY, CLIMATE. Geographically the country falls into 4 main regions. The N consists of a series of parallel hill ranges and valleys with a general N–S trend, the hills rising to 8,452 ft in Doi Inthanon

(NW). Four of the principal valley streams join to form the Chao Phraya R. Teak is a valuable product of the highland forests. Central Thailand is a broad alluvial plain watered mainly by the Chao Phraya – the great rice-growing area. The E consists of a shallow basin surrounded by hills and drained to the Mekong on the E border, a thinly populated region of poor soils and inhospitable climate. S Thailand comprises a narrow strip of land along the W shores of the Gulf of Siam, continuing S across the Isthmus of Kra into the N part of the Malay peninsula, a picturesque region of palm-fringed beaches and inland forests.

The climate is of the monsoon type and much resembles that of India: a dry cool season Nov.–Feb. (NE monsoon), followed by a hot dry season March–May, and then by a hot rainy season June–Oct. (SW monsoon); in the S temperatures show little variation throughout the seasons. Rainfall amounts to 40–80 ins. annually.

RESOURCES, PEOPLE, *etc.* About 85 per cent of the people are engaged in agriculture and fishing, and rice and fish are the staple foods; rice also represents one third of the country's exports. Irrigation projects, notably the construction of a dam on the Chao Phraya (1957), have considerably increased the area of cultivated land on the Central Plain. There has also been some diversification in products, with rubber, sugar-cane, maize, and copra increasing in importance; rubber is now second to rice among the exports. Teak is floated from the forests of the NW down the Chao Phraya to Bangkok or down the Salween to Moulmein (Burma) for export. Tin and wolfram (tungsten), mined in the S, are the leading mineral exports. Bangkok, which handles most of the country's foreign trade, is linked by rail with Chiang Mai (N), with the Malayan railway system (S), and with Laos and Cambodia at the respective frontiers. Away from the railways and rivers, buffalo and bullock carts are widely used for transport.

Commerce is largely in the hands of the Chinese, who form about 6 per cent of the population; the smaller minority of Muslim Malays, like the Thai or Siamese themselves, are mainly peasant farmers and fishermen. Most of the Thai, who constitute nearly 90 per cent of the total population, profess Buddhism, and elementary education in the villages has been almost exclusively conducted by the Buddhist monasteries. The monarchy, formerly absolute, has been constitutional since 1932.

HISTORY. The Thai people first occupied the country in the 13th cent., when they were driven out of SW China by Kublai Khan. About a century later (1350) Ayutthaya was made capital and the first king of Siam was crowned. Then followed a long series of wars with neighbouring peoples, particularly the Burmese, who finally destroyed Ayutthaya (1767). In 1782 the present dynasty was founded by an army general and Bangkok became the new capital. During the 19th cent. Siam was brought increasingly into contact with French and British interests, and was compelled to cede Laos and parts of Cambodia to the former (1893–1907) and 4 Malay states to the latter (1909). After a *coup d'état*, constitutional government was introduced in 1932. During the 2nd World War Siam supported Japan, and annexed parts of Laos, Cambodia, Malaya, and Burma, all of which were returned in 1946. The country was virtually ruled by dictatorship from 1947, but the 1932 constitution was restored in 1951. Elections did not lead to political stability, the National Assembly was dissolved (1958), and an interim constitution was 'decreed (1959). In 1939 it was declared that the name of the country, previously Siam, would henceforth be Thailand, and this was reaffirmed in 1949.

**Thame** England. Urban district in SE Oxfordshire, on the R. Thame 12 m. E of Oxford. Pop. (1961) 4,197. Market town. Has a 16th-cent. grammar school which was attended by John Hampden.

**Thame, River** England. River 30 m. long, flowing generally SW through Buckinghamshire and Oxfordshire past Thame to join the R. Thames near Dorchester.

**Thames, Firth of** ◊ Hauraki Gulf.

**Thames, River** England. The chief (though not the longest) river, 210 m. from Thames Head to the Nore, rising on the SE slope of the Cotswold Hills in 2 headstreams: the Thames (Isis), with its source at Thames Head 3 m. SW of Cirencester; the Churn, with its source at Seven Springs 4 m. SSE of Cheltenham. The Churn joins the Thames near Cricklade; the Coln and the Leach join it near Lechlade. Flowing generally ENE, the Thames receives the Windrush and turns SE past Ox-

ford, receiving first the Cherwell and then the Thame (above and near Oxford the main stream is often called the Isis). Receiving the Kennet at Reading, it follows a winding course, generally E, past Windsor, Kingston-on-Thames, London, Tilbury, and Southend-on-Sea, and enters the North Sea by a wide estuary at the Nore. Below Reading the chief tributaries are the Colne, the Lea, and the Roding on the left bank and the Wey, the Mole, the Darent, and the Medway on the right. Joined by several canals; navigable for barges as far as Lechlade. Ships of 800 tons can reach London Bridge; the largest ocean-going vessels can dock at Tilbury. Tidal as far as Teddington; above this point it is controlled by the Thames Conservancy Board (1857) and below it by the Port of London Authority (1908). The stretch of water between London Bridge and Tower Bridge is called the Pool of London. The economic importance of the Thames is due to the vast amount of trade passing through the Port of London, Britain's leading seaport. Above London the Thames has much attractive scenery and is noted for angling; it is also the chief boating river in England. Scene of the annual Henley Regatta and of the Oxford and Cambridge boat race (Putney–Mortlake).

**Thana** India. Town in Maharashtra, 20 m. NNE of Bombay. Pop. (1961) 101,107. Trade in rice, sugar-cane. Manufactures textiles (cottons, woollens), matches, etc.

**Thanet, Isle of** England. Island forming the NE corner of Kent, from which it is separated by the two branches of the R. Stour. Contains the seaside resorts of Ramsgate, Broadstairs, Margate, and Westgate. The N Foreland is at the NE extremity.

**Thanjavur** India. Formerly Tanjore. Industrial town in Madras 180 m. SSW of Madras. Pop. (1961) 111,099. Rice milling. Manufactures cotton and silk goods, jewellery, inlaid copperware, etc. The last capital of the Hindu Chola dynasty, it has a large 11th-cent. temple and a 16th-cent. rajah's palace.

**Thar (Great Indian) Desert** India/Pakistan. Sandy desert mainly in NW Rajasthan (India) but extending into the adjoining areas of W Pakistan. Rainfall irregular and generally less than 10 ins. annually. Sparsely populated. Chief town Bikaner.

**Thásos** Greece. Island in Kaválla *nome*, in the N Aegean, 15 m. SE of Kaválla. Area

154 sq. m. Pop. 16,000. Rises to nearly 4,000 ft. Produces olive oil, wine. Colonized from Paros in the 8th cent. B.C. Once famous for its goldmines. Fell to the Turks 1455; returned to Greece 1913.

Thebes Greece. Important city in ancient Greece, in Boeotia 35 m. NW of Athens. Founded by Cadmus, after whom the citadel Cadmeia was named. In the 6th cent. B.C. it led the Boeotian League. Animosity towards Athens led the Thebans to support Sparta in the Peloponnesian War, but they turned against their allies and destroyed Spartan power at Leuctra (371 B.C.) under the leadership of Epaminondas and Pelopidas. With the Athenians, they were defeated by Philip II of Macedon at Chaeronea (338 B.C.), and the city was destroyed by Alexander the Great. The modern town of Thívai was built on the site. Birthplace of Pindar (c. 518–438 B.C.).

Thebes United Arab Republic. Ancient capital of Upper Egypt, on the banks of the Nile 310 m. SSE of modern Cairo. The site is now occupied by Luxor, Karnak, and Qurna. Referred to in Homer's *Iliad* as a city of '100 gates', probably because of its numerous temples (with gates). In the Eleventh dynasty it began to develop into an important city; from about 1600 B.C. it became the capital of the Eighteenth, Nineteenth, and Twentieth dynasties and the centre of the worship of Ammon. When the new Empire began to decay, Thebes lost much of its importance; it was destroyed by the Assyrians (668 B.C.) and by the Romans (29 B.C.), and a few years later had become merely a collection of villages. Many outstanding archaeological discoveries have been made in the ruins of Thebes, among them the tomb of Tutankhamen (1922); much of the material is now housed in the Cairo Museum. The modern Luxor, a winter resort, has a population of about 30,000.

Thera ◊ *Thíra.*

Thermopylae Greece. Pass in E central Greece 10 m. SE of Lamía, famous for the heroic defence by Leonidas and his 300 Spartans against the Persians under Xerxes (480 B.C.). Here, too, in 279 B.C. the Greeks checked the Gauls for several months, to be ultimately defeated.

Thessaloniki (English Salonika) Greece. 1. *Nome* in Macedonia to the N of the Chalcidice peninsula. Area 1,897 sq. m. Pop. (1961) 542,880. Cereals, vines cultivated.

2. Ancient Therma. Capital of Macedonia and of the Thessaloniki *nome.* Pop. (1961) 377,026. Seaport at the head of the Gulf of Salonika, with a free zone; second city of Greece and an industrial centre. Exports tobacco, hides, metallic ores, etc. Manufactures textiles, metal goods, chemicals, cigarettes, etc. Flour milling, tanning, etc. Also an important railway and airline centre. University (1925). Has several Byzantine churches, though much of the old city was destroyed in the disastrous fires of 1890 and 1917. The ancient town was so named because of neighbouring hot springs; it was refounded in the 4th cent. B.C., as Thessalonica. It became important because of its position on the Roman Via Egnatia, the highway linking the Adriatic with Constantinople. St Paul, visiting the Christians here, addressed two epistles to the Thessalonians. Taken by the Turks 1430; passed to Greece 1912. In the 1st World War it was the base for the Allied Salonika campaigns against the Bulgarians. Birthplace of Kemal Atatürk (1881–1938).

Thessaly (Gk Thessalía) Greece. Regional division of E central Greece. Area 5,308 sq. m. Pop. (1961) 694,461. Consists of fertile lowlands in the centre drained by the Peneus (Pinios) R., surrounded by mountains. Wheat, tobacco, olives cultivated. Chief towns Vólos, Lárissa, Tríkkala, Kardítsa. Divided administratively into the Karditsa, Lárissa, Magnesia, and Tríkkala *nomes.*

Thetford England. Municipal borough in Norfolk, at the confluence of the Thet and Little Ouse rivers 28 m. SW of Norwich. Pop. (1961) 5,398. Market town. Light engineering etc. Its chief historical feature is the large mound known as Castle Hill, probably dating from the 6th cent. Ruins of a Cluniac priory (founded 1104). In the 14th cent. it had 20 churches and 8 monasteries. Birthplace of Thomas Paine (1737–1809).

Thetford Mines Canada. Town in Quebec 50 m. S of Quebec. Pop. (1966) 21,614. An important centre of the asbestos industry; the world's largest asbestos deposits (discovered 1876) are in the neighbourhood.

Thiès Senegal. Town 32 m. ENE of Dakar. Pop. (1965) 69,000. Railway junction. Market town. Trade in groundnuts, rice, fruit, etc. Manufactures fertilizer from phosphates quarried in the neighbourhood.

Thionville France. Town in the Moselle

department in Lorraine, on the Moselle R. 18 m. N of Metz. Pop. (1968) 38,469. Industrial centre. Manufactures iron and steel, metal goods, cement, etc.

**Thíra (Thera)** Greece. Formerly Santorin. Volcanic island in the Cyclades in the S Aegean Sea 70 m. N of Crete. Area 29 sq. m. Pop. 10,000. Rises to 1,860 ft. Produces wine.

**Thirlmere** England. Lake 3 m. long in the Lake District, Cumberland, 4 m. SSE of Keswick. Provides Manchester with part of its water supply.

**Thirsk** England. Market town in the N Riding of Yorkshire, 21 m. NNW of York. Pop. (rural district, 1961) 13,060. Flour milling etc. Has a well-known racecourse.

**Thonburi** Thailand. Second largest city, on the Chao Phraya R. opposite Bangkok, with which it is connected by 3 bridges. Pop. (1968) 540,300. Rice milling, sawmilling. Capital 1767–82, being succeeded by Bangkok.

**Thorn** ⟡ *Toruń*.

**Thornaby-on-Tees** England. Industrial town in the N Riding of Yorkshire, on the R. Tees 3 m. WSW of Middlesbrough. Pop. (1961) 22,786. From 1968 part of the county borough of ⟡ *Teesside*. Heavy engineering, iron founding, flour milling. Linked by bridge with Stockton-on-Tees.

**Thornton Clevelys** England. Urban district in W Lancashire, comprising the market town of Thornton, 3 m. S of Fleetwood, and the seaside resort of Clevelys, on the Irish Sea. Pop. (1961) 20,642.

**Thousand Islands** Canada/USA. Group of about 1,700 small islands and islets in the St Lawrence R. near the E end of L. Ontario, mainly in Ontario (Canada) and the remainder in New York (USA). Popular resort area.

**Thrace (Gk. Thráki)** Greece. Region in the extreme NE, bordering N on Bulgaria and E on Turkey, comprising the *nome*s of Évros, Rhodope, and Xánthi. Area 3,315 sq. m. Pop. (1961) 356,708. Chief town Komotíni. Produces tobacco, wheat, cotton, etc. In ancient times it occupied a much larger area, extending N to the Danube R. and E to the Black Sea.

**Three Rivers** ⟡ *Trois Rivières*.

**Thun** Switzerland. Town in the Bern canton, on the Aar R. where the latter leaves L. Thun (NW). Pop. (1969) 36,000. Manufactures metal goods, watches, clothing, etc. Has a 12th-cent. castle.

**Thun, Lake (Ger. Thunersee)** Switzerland.

Lake in the Bern canton 11 m. long and 2 m. wide at a height of 1,837 ft. Picturesque; popular with tourists. It is entered in the SE by the Aar R., connecting it with L. Brienz, and the river leaves it in the NW near Thun.

**Thurgau** Switzerland. Canton in the NE bordering N on L. Constance. Area 388 sq. m. Pop. (1969) 187,000 (German-speaking). Cap. Frauenfeld. Hilly but fertile, especially in the Thur R. valley. Produces cereals, vines. Textile industry. Became a canton of the Swiss Confederation 1803.

**Thuringia** German Democratic Republic. Former *Land* in GDR, bounded by Saxony (E), Bavaria (S), and Hessen (W). Hilly, crossed NW–SE by the Thuringian Forest and drained by the Saale, Werra, and White Elster rivers. Fertile, producing cereals, sugar-beet, and fruit. Important textile, glass, and other industries. When the lands belonging to the Saxon house of Wettin were divided (1485) most of Thuringia went to the Ernestine branch, and later it was divided into a number of duchies, including Saxe-Coburg, Saxe-Gotha, and Saxe-Meiningen. Thuringia became a state under the Weimar Republic in 1920, a *Land* of the German Democratic Republic in 1945, and was reorganized into the 3 administrative districts of Erfurt, Gera, and Suhl 1952.

**Thuringian Forest (Ger. Thüringerwald)** German Democratic Republic. Wooded mountain range extending about 70 m. NW–SE between the Werra R. and the Thuringian Saale, rising to 3,222 ft in Beerberg. Picturesque; several resorts.

**Thurles** Irish Republic. Town in Co. Tipperary, on the Suir R. 23 m. NNW of Clonmel. Pop. (1966) 6,747. Hunting and fishing centre, with a beet-sugar refinery and a racecourse. Has a 19th-cent. cathedral in Romanesque style and a ruined 12th-cent. castle; 4 m. S is the famous ruined Holy Cross Abbey, dating from the 12th cent.

**Thurrock** England. Urban district in Essex on the N bank of the R. Thames, formed (1936) from the urban districts of Grays Thurrock, Purfleet, and Tilbury, and other districts. Pop. (1961) 114,302. Manufactures cement etc. Docks and passenger landing stage at Tilbury (Port of London). Oil refineries at Shell Haven, Coryton. A road tunnel (opened 1963) links Essex and Kent, from Purfleet to Dartford.

**Thursday Island** Australia. Small island in

Queensland, in Torres Strait, 15 m. NW of Cape York. Pop. (1966) 2,551. Chief town, Port Kennedy, a centre of pearl and trepang ('bêche-de-mer') fishing.

**Thurso** Scotland. Small burgh in N Caithness, on Thurso Bay at the mouth of the R. Thurso. Pop. (1961) 8,038. Market town. Port. The most northerly town on the Scottish mainland. Steamers sail to Orkney. Dounreay, 8 m. W, is the site of an experimental atomic power station.

**Tiber** (Italian **Tevere**) **River** Italy. Italy's most famous river, 252 m. long, rising in the Tuscan Apennines and flowing generally S past Rome and Ostia to the Tyrrhenian Sea. Chief tributary the Nera. It has two mouths, the N mouth at Fiumicino being navigable for 21 m. to Rome owing to canalization.

**Tiberias** Israel. Town in the NE, on the W shore of the Sea of Galilee (L. Tiberias) 33 m. E of Haifa, at 680 ft below sea level. Pop. 20,000. Health resort, with medicinal springs. Founded by Herod Antipas *c.* A.D. 21, and named after the Emperor Tiberius, the town became a centre of Jewish learning; it became the seat of the Sanhedrin late in the 2nd cent., and the Talmud was completed here (*c.* 400). Taken by the Arabs 637.

**Tiberias, Lake** ♢ *Galilee, Sea of.*

**Tibesti Highlands** Chad/Libya. Saharan mountain region of volcanic origin; mainly in N Chad but extending NE into Libya. Highest peak Emi Koussi (11,200 ft). Dates and cereals grown in scattered fertile oases. Camels, donkeys, sheep, and goats raised. The people are mainly nomadic Tibbu and Arabs. ♢ *Sahara.*

**Tibet** China. Autonomous Region in the SW, bounded on the S by India, Bhutan, Sikkim, and Nepal, and on the W by Kashmir. Area 470,000 sq. m. Pop. 1,270,000. Cap. Lhasa. The most extensive high plateau region in the world, with an average height of over 12,000 ft, lying between the Kunlun Mountains (N) and the Himalayas (S). A number of still loftier mountain ranges with a general E–W trend cross the tableland. In the S, on the border with Nepal, is Everest (29,028 ft), and there are several other peaks exceeding 20,000 ft. Many salt lakes are scattered about the plateau, the largest being Nam Tso in the SE. Some of the great rivers of S and SE Asia have their source here: the Indus and Sutlej rise in the SW, the Salween in the E, while the

Tsangpo (Brahmaputra) flows generally E across S Tibet. The Mekong, Yangtse, and Hwang-ho rise in the extension of the Tibetan plateau in neighbouring Tsinghai (NE). Climate unusually rigorous, with long cold winters and short hot summers and an annual rainfall which reaches 10–15 ins. in places but is elsewhere considerably less. Temperatures vary greatly with altitude, and there are marked differences between day and night and between sun and shade temperatures.

Much of the land, especially in the N, is treeless and barren. A scanty grass is the most widespread type of natural vegetation, and there are considerable woodlands in the E. Agriculture is possible in the more favoured parts of the S and E, where the rains of the summer monsoon can penetrate the river valleys, and barley, wheat, peas, and beans are grown. The Tibetans, many of whom are nomadic, raise large numbers of yaks (which are invaluable beasts of burden on the steep highland tracks), ponies, donkeys, and sheep; these animals provide wool, hides, and yak hair for export. Principal minerals borax, soda, and salt; alluvial gold is widely distributed. Leading towns Lhasa, Shigatse, and Gyangtse, all in the S. Trade is mainly conducted by animal and sometimes by human transport over rough tracks and mountain passes, but a motor road has been constructed between Lhasa and Lanchow, on the Chinese railway system, and an air service between Lhasa and Peking was inaugurated in 1957.

The Tibetan people are of Mongoloid stock. Their religion is Lamaism, derived from the Mahayana form of Buddhism. Religion occupies a dominant place in their lives, and about one fifth of the male population are lamas, dwelling in hundreds of monasteries scattered throughout the country. From the mid 17th cent. until recent years Tibet was a theocracy, ruled by the Dalai Lama as head of the Lamaist religion, assisted by the Panchen Lama and a council of 4 ministers. Since the country was invaded (1950) effective government has been in the hands of the Chinese.

The known history of Tibet commences in the 7th cent. A.D., when it was a powerful independent kingdom; in the following century it exacted tribute from China. Buddhism was introduced from India, and an alphabet based on Sanskrit made possible the translation of the Buddhist scriptures into Tibetan. Various reforms were effected, and in the 17th cent. the grand lama of Lhasa took the title of Dalai Lama, with the chief abbot of the Tashi Lumpo lamasery, the Panchen Lama, as second in command. From 1720, when a Chinese army invaded Tibet and took Lhasa, the country was ruled, at least nominally, by the Manchu dynasty. Various Jesuits, Capuchins, and others entered Tibet, and in the late 18th cent. Britain made contact with the country from India. In the 19th cent. Europeans were systematically excluded and Lhasa became the 'forbidden city'. In 1904 the Younghusband expedition to Lhasa enforced the establishment of trading posts at Yatung, Gyangtse, and Gartok, and Britain recognized Chinese sovereignty over Tibet; when the Manchu dynasty came to an end, however, all Chinese officials and troops were expelled (1912). In 1918 the Chinese unsuccessfully attacked Tibet over the division of the country into Inner Tibet, under Chinese authority, and Outer Tibet; in 1920 Sir Charles Bell was invited by the Dalai Lama to Lhasa to assist in effecting a settlement. In 1922 Lhasa was linked by telegraph with India. Chinese Communist forces invaded Tibet in 1950; resistance to the Chinese developed into open rebellion, which was quickly suppressed (1959), and the Dalai Lama fled to India. Became an Autonomous Region of China 1965.

**Ticino** (Ger. *Tessin*) Switzerland. Canton in the S. Area 1,086 sq. m. Pop. (1969) 242,000 (Italian-speaking, Roman Catholic). Cap. Bellinzona. Mainly mountainous, with the Lepontine Alps in the N. Drained by the Ticino and Maggia rivers. Vines and tobacco grown in the valleys; the sheltered shores of L. Maggiore and L. Lugano enjoy a delightful Mediterranean type of climate and have many resorts. Chief towns Bellinzona, Lugano, Locarno. The canton was formed and became a member of the Swiss Confederation in 1803.

**Ticino River** Switzerland. River 161 m. long, rising in the Lepontine Alps and flowing generally S through Ticino canton and L. Maggiore into Italy to join the Po R. just below Pavia. Much used for irrigation in its lower course.

**Tien Shan.** Great mountain system in Central Asia extending about 1,500 m. generally WSW-ENE from the Kirghiz SSR (USSR) through the Sinkiang-Uighur AR (China) to the Mongolian border. Highest peaks Pobeda (24,406 ft) and Khan Tengri (23,616 ft). In the W it divides into a number of different mountain ranges, of which the most south-westerly are by some considered part of the Pamir-Alai system.

**Tientsin** China. Capital of Hopei province and the third largest city in China, on the Grand Canal and on the Hai-ho at the confluence with several tributaries, 70 m. SE of Peking. Pop. (1957) 3,220,000. Important railway junction and industrial centre. Manufactures iron and steel, chemicals, textiles (cottons, woollens), leather goods, matches, glass, etc. Food processing, engineering. It is the port of Peking, with outports 30 m. downstream at the mouth of the Pei-ho. Exports hog bristles, wool, skins, etc. Usually kept open for 2 months in winter by icebreakers. Seat of Nankai University (1919). Tientsin had relatively little importance till it was occupied by British and French forces and opened to foreign trade (1858–61). After the Boxer Rebellion (1900), during which it suffered severely, its ancient walls were pulled down and the city was reconstructed. Occupied by the Japanese 1937–45.

**Tierra del Fuego** Argentina/Chile. Archipelago at the S extremity of S America, separated from the mainland by the Strait of Magellan. Total area 27,476 sq. m., the major W part in Chile (in Magallanes province) and the E part in Argentina (Tierra del Fuego province). The N of the main island (18,000 sq. m.) is mainly flat, treeless tableland; in the S, Andean mountains run E, presenting sheer rock walls broken by fiords to the sea. Main occupations sheep farming, lumbering, oil production. Chief towns Punta Arenas (Chile), Ushuaia (Argentina).

**Tiflis** ◊ *Tbilisi.*

**Tigris River.** River in SW Asia 1,150 m. long, rising in E Turkey and flowing generally SE past Diarbakir, where for a short distance it forms the border with Syria; it then continues SE through Iraq, more or less parallel to the Euphrates R., past Mosul and Baghdad. It is joined by the Euphrates near Al Qurna, and the river, from this point known as the Shatt-al-Arab, enters the Persian Gulf. Liable to floods in the late spring when the snows in the Turkish mountains melt: reaches its highest level in April, its lowest in Sept.–Oct. Navigable by shallow-draught vessels to Baghdad. Together with the Euphrates, the Tigris embraces the land of Mesopotamia ('the Land between the Rivers') which they have irrigated from time immemorial. Today various barrage schemes permit the irrigation of increasing areas in Iraq.

**Tikopia** ◊ *Solomon Islands*.

**Tijuana** Mexico. Town in the NW of Baja California on the Tijuana R. and on the US–Mexico frontier 12 m. SE of San Diego (California). Pop. (1969) 354,800. Tourist resort, catering largely for Americans; gambling casinos, racecourses, and other amenities.

**Tilburg** Netherlands. Industrial town and railway junction in N Brabant 20 m. WNW of Eindhoven. Pop. (1968) 150,282. Important centre of textile manufacture. Dyeing, tanning, etc.

**Tilbury** ◊ *Thurrock*.

**Tillicoultry** Scotland. Small burgh in Clackmannanshire 3 m. NE of Alloa at the S foot of the Ochil Hills. Pop. (1961) 3,963. Woollen and paper milling.

**Tilsit** ◊ *Sovetsk*.

**Timaru** New Zealand. Seaport, railway junction, and market town in the S Island 95 m. SW of Christchurch. Pop. (1966) 27,306. In a sheep-rearing and grain-producing area. Exports wool, grain, chilled and frozen meat. Also a holiday resort.

**Timbuktu (Tombouctou)** Mali. Town 450 m. NE of Bamako, 6 m. N of the Niger R. Pop. (1967) 9,000. For centuries a centre of caravan routes and a slave market, also trading in salt, cereals, livestock. Changed hands many times; then its prosperity declined with the abolition of the slave trade and again with the diminishing importance of the desert caravans. Seized by the French 1893.

**Timgad** Algeria. Ancient Thamugas. Ruined city 18 m. ESE of Batna, on the lower N slopes of the Aurès Massif. Founded by Trajan A.D. 100. Destroyed by the Berber in the 7th cent. Excavations begun in 1881 revealed important Roman remains, including Trajan's triumphal arch, restored 1900.

**Timişoara (Hungarian Temesvár)** Rumania. Capital of the Timiş district, 260 m. WNW of Bucharest. Pop. (1968) 182,096. Railway junction. Manufactures textiles, footwear, chemicals, etc. Trade in grain. Seat of a university (1945) and of Roman Catholic and Orthodox bishops. It was a Roman settlement, became Hungarian in the 11th

cent., was taken by the Turks (1552), and was annexed to Rumania from Hungary after the 1st World War.

**Timmins** Canada. Town in Ontario, on the Mattagami R. 130 m. N of Sudbury. Pop. (1966) 29,303. A commercial centre for the Porcupine goldmining region. Founded in 1911 for workers in the Hollinger goldmine.

**Timor.** Largest and most easterly of the Lesser Sunda Is., in the Malay Archipelago, divided politically between Indonesia and Portugal. Area 13,071 sq. m. Pop. 1,300,000. Mountainous, rising to 9,678 ft in Ramelau (Portuguese Timor). Chief products copra, sandalwood, coffee. 1. *Portuguese Timor*: Area 7,332 sq. m. Pop. 517,000. Cap. and seaport Dili. Occupies the E part of the island and an enclave on the NW coast of Indonesian Timor.
2. *Indonesian Timor*: Area 5,765 sq. m. Pop. 823,000. With adjacent islands, including Roti and Savu, forms the province of E Nusa Tenggara, of which the island's chief town, Kupang (pop. 15,000), is capital. The island of Timor was divided between Portugal and the Netherlands by treaty (1859). The Dutch part passed to Indonesia 1950.

**Timorlaut** ◊ *Tanimbar Islands*.

**Tinnevelly** ◊ *Tirunelveli*.

**Tintagel** England. Village in Cornwall 17 m. WNW of Launceston. The rugged promontory of Tintagel Head is near by. Here are the remains of Tintagel Castle, the legendary birthplace of King Arthur. The ruins of an early Celtic monastery were also unearthed on the site.

**Tintern Abbey** Wales. Famous ruined abbey in Monmouthshire, on the R. Wye 4 m. N of Chepstow. Founded (1131) by Walter de Clare for Cistercian monks; it inspired Wordsworth's poem, *Lines Composed a Few Miles above Tintern Abbey*.

**Tipperary** Irish Republic. 1. Inland county in Munster. Area 1,643 sq. m. Pop. (1966) 122,812. County town Clonmel. Mountainous in parts, with the Knockmealdown Mountains rising to 2,609 ft (S) and the Galty Mountains to 3,015 ft in Galtymore (SW). Along its W border are Lough Derg and the R. Shannon, and it is drained by the latter and the R. Suir and their tributaries. In the SW is part of the fertile Golden Vale, where dairy farming is the main occupation; potatoes and sugar-beet are cultivated. There are minor industries in the main towns, which include Clonmel, Cashel, Tipperary, Carrick-on-Suir, Nenagh, Roscrea.

2. Market town in Co. Tipperary 21 m. WNW of Clonmel. Pop. (1966) 4,507. In a dairy-farming region. Manufactures condensed milk.

**Tipton** England. Industrial town in Staffordshire, in the Black Country 4 m. SSE of Wolverhampton, from 1966 part of the county borough of ◊ *Dudley*. Pop. (1961) 38,091. Iron founding, engineering. Manufactures electrical equipment, metal goods, etc.

**Tiranë (Tirana)** Albania. Capital, 19 m. E of Durrës (its port) and linked with it by railway. Pop. (1967) 169,000. On the edge of a fertile plain. Manufactures textiles, soap, cigarettes, etc. Largely modern; has several mosques. University (1957). Founded by the Turks in the 17th cent.

**Tiree** Scotland. Low windswept island in the Inner Hebrides, in Argyllshire, 14 m. W of N Mull. Area 30 sq. m. Pop. (with Coll, 1961) 1,143. Visited by many migratory birds.

**Tirol (Tyrol)** Austria. Province in the W, bordering N on the Federal German Republic and S on Italy. Area 4,884 sq. m. Pop. (1961) 462,899. Cap. Innsbruck. Almost entirely mountainous, with the Zillertal Alps, the Ötztal Alps (rising to 12,461 ft in the Gross Glockner), and part of the Rhaetian Alps in the S, the Lechtal Alps in the NW. Drained SW–NE by the Inn R. The famous Brenner Pass (S), between the Zillertal and Ötztal Alps, links Innsbruck with Bolzano (Italy). Cereals cultivated; dairy cattle raised. The picturesque scenery attracts many tourists. After the unsuccessful rebellion of the peasants, led by Andreas Hofer, against Bavarian rule established by Napoleon (1805), the whole Tirol was restored to Austria in 1814. After the 1st World War, however, S Tirol, including a mainly German-speaking area, was awarded to Italy by the Treaty of St Germain (1919), reducing its area by half, and this left E Tirol, with capital Lienz, separated from the present province.

**Tiruchirapalli (Trichinopoly)** India. Industrial town and railway junction in Madras, on the Cauvery R. 190 m. SW of Madras. Pop. (1961) 249,862. Railway engineering. Manufactures textiles, cigars, gold and silver ware. In the town is the Rock of Trichinopoly, 273 ft high, ascended by an ornamental stone staircase and surmounted by a temple.

**Tirunelveli (Tinnevelly)** India. Town in Madras 90 m. SSW of Madurai. Pop. (1961) 87,988. Sugar refining. Here St Francis Xavier first preached in India, and there are important mission stations.

**Tisza (Ger. Theiss) River** USSR/Hungary/ Yugoslavia. River 610 m. long rising in the NE Carpathians in the W Ukrainian SSR and flowing generally W and then S, crossing the Hungarian plain. Passing through Szeged, it joins the Danube below Novi Sad (Yugoslavia). Important fisheries. In Yugoslavia it is linked by canals with the Danube and with Timişoara (Rumania). Navigable by steamers to Szolnok (Hungary).

**Titicaca, Lake** Bolivia/Peru. Largest lake in S America (area 3,500 sq. m.), and at 12,500 ft the highest in the world, crossed by the boundary between Peru and Bolivia. Consists of the large NW lake Chucuito and the smaller SE lake Uinamarca joined by a narrow strait; drained S by the Desaguadero R. to L. Poopó. Terraces and old shore-lines show that it was more extensive in the past. The great depth of the lake (1,200 ft) keeps it at an even all-year temperature of 11° C, which modifies the climate and makes agriculture (barley, potatoes, etc.) possible on the surrounding land. Small steamships ply between Peru and Bolivia, forming a 50-m. water link in a rail system from La Paz (Bolivia) to terminals in Peru (Mollendo, Matarani). The ships were built in Britain and assembled from sections carried from the Peruvian coast.

**Titograd** Yugoslavia. Formerly Podgorica. Capital of Crna Gora (Montenegro), on the Morača R. 180 m. SSW of Belgrade. Pop. (1961) 30,657. Manufactures tobacco products. Although largely destroyed in the 2nd World War and later rebuilt, it retains the old Ljubić mosque and other Turkish buildings. Renamed (1948) in honour of Marshal Tito.

**Tiverton** England. Municipal borough in Devonshire, on the R. Exe 12 m. N of Exeter. Pop. (1961) 12,296. Market town. Formerly important in the woollen trade; in the 19th cent. it became famous for lace manufacture. Remains of the 12th-cent. castle. Near by is the well-known Blundell's school (founded 1604), described in *Lorna Doone*.

**Tivoli** Italy. Ancient Tibur. Town in Roma province, Latium, on the Aniene R. 17 m.

ENE of Rome. Pop. (1961) 34,067. In a picturesque situation overlooking the river. Manufactures paper, footwear, etc. It is esp. famous for the remains of Hadrian's Villa, the beautiful 16th-cent. Villa d'Este with terraced gardens, and the waterfalls which now provide hydroelectric power. It was a favourite resort of wealthy patricians in the days of the Roman Empire.

**Tjirebon (Cheribon)** Indonesia. Seaport in W Java province, on the Java Sea 130 m. ESE of Jakarta. Pop. (1961) 158,299. Exports copra, rubber, etc. Manufactures textiles, cigarettes. At the near-by village of Linggadjati the Tjirebon Agreement between Indonesia and the Netherlands, recognizing the Republic of Indonesia, was signed in 1946.

**Tlaxcala** Mexico. 1. The smallest state, in central Mexico. Area 1,555 sq. m. Pop. (1969) 454,000. Mountainous. Mainly agricultural. Chief crops cereals and maguey (from which the liquor pulque is made).
2. Officially Tlaxcala de Xicohténcatl. Capital of Tlaxcala state, 60 m. E of Mexico City, on the central plateau at a height of 7,350 ft. Pop. 5,071. The Church of San Francisco, founded (1521) by Cortés, is the oldest in the Americas. On a near-by hill is the famous Sanctuary of Ocotlán.

**Tlemcen** Algeria. Ancient Pomaria. Town in the Tell (NW) 70 m. SW of Oran, near the Morocco frontier. Pop. (1967) 80,000. Linked by rail with Oran and Oujda (Morocco). In a fertile region where olives, fruits, and cereals are cultivated. Large trade in agricultural produce, wool, sheep. Manufactures hosiery, footwear, furniture. Handicraft industries, e.g. carpets, rugs, brassware. Architecturally one of the most famous of Arab towns, the mosques, minarets, etc. dating from the Middle Ages. Flourished from the 13th to the 16th cent. Declined after capture by the Turks (1553). Occupied by the French 1842, but has remained a predominantly Muslim town.

**Tobago** W Indies. Island NE of Trinidad, part of the state of Trinidad and Tobago, a member of the British Commonwealth. Area 116 sq. m. Pop. (1960) 33,333 (mainly West Indians of African descent). Chief town Scarborough (pop. 2,500). Main products cacao, coconuts, limes. Discovered (1498) by Columbus. Ceded to Britain 1814. Amalgamated with ◊ *Trinidad* (1888) as a British Crown Colony.

**Tobata** ◊ *Kitakyushu.*

**Tobermory** Scotland. Small burgh on the N coast of the island of Mull, Argyllshire. Pop. (1961) 668. Fishing port. Resort. A Spanish galleon was sunk in the bay in 1588, and several attempts have been made to recover the supposed treasure.

**Tobol River** USSR. River 800 m. long rising in the S Ural Mountains in the N Kazakh SSR and flowing generally NNE past Kustanai and Kurgan to join the Irtysh R. at Tobolsk.

**Tobolsk** USSR. Town in the Tyumen region, RSFSR, at the confluence of the Irtysh and Tobol rivers 120 m. NE of Tyumen. Pop. (1962) 45,000. Sawmilling. Trade in fish, furs. Founded in 1587, it has an old fortress of the reign of Peter the Great built in the style of the Moscow Kremlin. It was long the chief administrative and commercial centre of W Siberia, but it declined when the Trans-Siberian Railway was built.

**Tobruk** Libya. Small port in E Cyrenaica, 225 m. E of Benghazi, on the coast road. Pop. 5,000. A supply port in the 2nd World War, changing hands 5 times; finally taken by the British 1942.

**Tocantins River** Brazil. River 1,680 m. long rising in Goiás state on the central plateau, flowing generally N to join the Pará R. 50 m. WSW of Belém. Chief tributary the Araguaia R. Navigable by ocean-going ships for about 130 m. to Tucuruí; from here a railway circumvents a series of rapids to Jatobá.

**Tocopilla** Chile. Port in Antofagasta province, on the arid N coast 110 m. N of Antofagasta. Pop. 22,000. Exports nitrates and iodine from the caliche fields inland. Supplies electric power to the Chuquicamata coppermine, from which it takes copper ores for smelting and export. Fishing industry.

**Todmorden** England. Municipal borough in the W Riding of Yorkshire, on the R. Calder 7 m. SE of Burnley. Pop. (1961) 17,416. Manufactures cotton goods, textile machinery.

**Togliatti** USSR. Formerly Stavropol; renamed 1964 in honour of Palmiro Togliatti (1893–1964), the Italian Communist leader. River port near the S end of the Kuibyshev Reservoir (Volga R.), RSFSR, 40 m. WNW of Kuibyshev. Pop. (1970) 251,000. Industrial centre. Ship repairing, engineering, food processing. Manufactures chemicals, synthetic rubber,

737

furniture, etc. Expanded rapidly in the 1960s: pop. (1959) 72,000.

**Togo.** Republic in W Africa, on the Gulf of Guinea (Slave Coast), bounded by Upper Volta (N), Dahomey (E), and Ghana (W). Area 22,000 sq. m. Pop. (1966) 1,680,000 (almost entirely Africans). Cap. and chief seaport Lomé. Both the N and the S are lowlands; the central area is crossed SSW–NNE by mountains rising to nearly 3,000 ft. The N is savannah; the S is tropical rain-forest, fringed by coastal lagoons. Cacao, palm kernels, and copra are the main products in the S, and coffee is grown on the interior uplands; these are the main agricultural exports. Increasing quantities of phosphates have been mined in recent years, and are now the leading export. Subsistence crops include manioc, maize, rice. Lomé is linked by rail with Blitta and Palimé in the interior and with Anécho along the coast.

Togoland was annexed by Germany in 1884, but the N frontiers of the protectorate were not fixed till 1899. After the 1st World War it was divided and placed under British (W) and French (E) League of Nations mandate. British Togoland was administered as part of the Gold Coast (now Ghana) and joined Ghana when it became independent (1956). The remainder became a UN Trust Territory administered by France (1946) and an independent republic in 1960.

**Tokaj (Tokay)** Hungary. Town in Borsod-Abauj-Zemplen county at the confluence of the Tisza and Bodrog rivers. Pop. 5,000. From the vineyards in the neighbourhood, on the slopes of the Hegyalja, comes the famous Tokay wine.

**Tokat** Turkey. Capital of Tokat province, 50 m. NNW of Sivas. Pop. (1965) 35,000. Manufactures copper ware, leather goods, etc.

**Tokay** ◊ *Tokaj*.

**Tokelau (Union) Islands** S Pacific. Group of 3 atolls (Atafu, Nukunono, Fakaofo) 300 m. N of W Samoa. Area 4 sq. m. Pop. (1967) 1,883. Exports copra. Formerly part of the Gilbert and Ellice Is. Colony. Transferred to New Zealand 1926; became part of New Zealand 1949.

**Tokushima** Japan. Capital of Tokushima prefecture, in NE Shikoku 70 m. SW of Osaka. Pop. (1965) 193,206. Seaport. Large market town. Manufactures cotton goods, saké, etc.

**Tokyo** Japan. Formerly Yedo. Capital of Japan, virtually co-extensive with Tokyo prefecture, and from the standpoint of population the world's largest city, in central Honshu at the mouth of the Sumida R. on Tokyo Bay. Pop. (1965) 10,348,975. Important seaport since the deepening of the harbour, handling mainly coastal shipping; its port amalgamated with Yokohama as Keihin in 1941. Also the leading Japanese business centre; has a great variety of industries. Shipbuilding, engineering, printing and publishing. Manufactures textiles, chemicals, cars, etc. All road distances in Japan are measured from the famous Nihonbashi, or Bridge of Japan, over the Sumida R.; the Shiba and Ueno are the most celebrated of the many parks. Seat of Tokyo University (1877, a former Imperial University) as well as three other universities (1875, 1946, 1949) and an Institute of Technology (1881). Probably founded towards the end of the 12th cent. and known as Yedo, it was not important until about four centuries later, when its castle was occupied by the first of the Tokugawa shoguns. In 1868, with the abolition of the shogunate, it replaced Kyoto as imperial capital and was renamed Tokyo ('Eastern Capital'). In 1923 an earthquake and the ensuing fire destroyed much of the city and killed tens of thousands of its inhabitants. Reconstruction followed rapidly, being largely designed to prevent a recurrence of the disaster, and massive modern buildings arose, dwarfing the ancient temples; the city again suffered severely, however, in the 2nd World War from American air raids.

**Tolbukhin** Bulgaria. Formerly Bazargic, Dóbrich. Market town in the NE, in S Dobruja 26 m. NNW of Varna. Pop. (1965) 55,111. Manufactures textiles, furniture, etc. Flour milling. Since being under Turkish rule (till 1878), it has passed between Rumania and Bulgaria, belonging to the latter since 1940. Formerly called Bazargic and then Dóbrich, it was renamed (1949) after the Soviet Marshal Tolbukhin, who captured it from the Germans during the 2nd World War.

**Toledo** Spain. 1. Province in New Castile, in central Spain. Area 5,925 sq. m. Pop. (1961) 521,637. Generally mountainous, with the Montes de Toledo (S) rising to over 4,500 ft. Watered by the Tagus (Tajo) R. and its tributaries. Sheep and goats raised. Wheat, barley, etc. cultivated.

**2.** Ancient Toletum. Capital of Toledo province, on the Tagus R. 40 m. SSW of Madrid. Pop. (1961) 40,651. Still famous for its swords, as it was 2,000 years ago; also manufactures fire-arms, textiles, etc. Stands on a granite hill flanked on 3 sides by the Tagus, with narrow, winding streets. With its historic buildings and its many art treasures, one of Spain's outstanding cities. Its archbishop is the primate of Spain, and the magnificent 13th-cent. cathedral is notable for stained-glass windows, tapestries, paintings (El Greco, Goya, Rubens), etc. The house where El Greco (1542–1614) lived is now a museum; many fine churches and two Moorish bridges. Captured by the Romans in the 2nd cent. B.C. Became capital of the Visigothic kingdom. After being recaptured from the Moors (1085), capital of Spain. Declined when Philip II moved the capital to Madrid (1561).

**Toledo** USA. Important Great Lakes port in Ohio, at the W end of L. Erie. Pop. (1960) 318,003. Trade in coal, oil, agricultural produce, etc. Also a railway, industrial and commercial centre. Shipbuilding. Manufactures cars, glass, machine tools, machinery, etc. University (1872).

**Tolpuddle** England. Village in Dorset 7 m. ENE of Dorchester. Made famous by the 'Tolpuddle Martyrs', agricultural labourers who were condemned to transportation in 1834 for forming a trade union.

**Toluca (Toluca de Lerdo)** Mexico. Capital of Mexico state, 40 m. WSW of Mexico City at a height of 8,660 ft. Pop. (1960) 71,026. Manufactures textiles, food products, pottery, etc. Brewing, distilling. The Toluca valley breeds bulls for Mexican bullfights.

**Tomaszów Mazowiecki** Poland. Industrial town in the Lódź voivodship, on the Pilica R. 30 m. SE of Lódź. Pop. (1968) 54,500. Manufactures textiles, bricks, etc. Tanning, flour milling.

**Tombouctou** ⟡ *Timbuktu.*

**Tomsk** USSR. Capital of the Tomsk region, RSFSR, on the Tom R., a tributary of the Ob R., and on a branch of the Trans-Siberian Railway 120 m. NE of Novosibirsk. Pop. (1970) 339,000. Industrial centre. Manufactures machinery, electrical equipment, ball-bearings, matches, etc. Also an educational centre, with a university (1888) and other academic institutions. Founded 1604. Developed in the early 19th cent. when gold was dis-

covered in the neighbourhood; became a leading commercial centre. Declined when bypassed by the Trans-Siberian Railway and revived again on being associated with the development of the Kuznetsk Basin.

**Tonbridge** England. Urban district in Kent, on the R. Medway 12 m. SW of Maidstone. Pop. (1961) 22,141. Market town. Manufactures cricket balls. Printing, sawmilling, etc. Has the remains of a Norman castle, and a well-known public school (founded 1553).

**Tonga (Friendly Islands)** S Pacific Ocean.* Group of about 150 coral and volcanic islands, SE of Fiji, in 3 main groups, Tongatabu (S), Ha'apai (centre), and Vava'u (N), forming an independent Polynesian kingdom and British protectorate. Area 270 sq. m. Pop. (1966) 77,429 (mostly Tongans and almost half on Tongatabu, the largest island). Cap. Nuku'alofa, on Tongatabu. Climate is healthy, and they are free of malaria; temperatures range from 52° to 84°F. Principal exports copra, bananas. Discovered by the Dutch (1616); visited (1773) by Capt. Cook, who named them the Friendly Is. English Methodist missionaries arrived in 1822; the ruler King George I was converted to Christianity in 1831, to be followed by his people. In 1862 a constitutional monarchy was established, preparing the way for the present form of democratic government. The group came under British protection in 1900.

**Tongareva** ⟡ *Cook Islands.*

**Tongariro** ⟡ *Ruapehu.*

**Tongatabu** ⟡ *Tonga.*

**Tonlé Sap, Lake** Cambodia. Lake in the central plains, linked with the Mekong R. by the Tonlé Sap R. Area (dry season) about 1,000 sq. m. In the rainy season (July–Oct.) the Mekong R. discharges into the lake, which expands to 4,000 sq. m. or more and acts as a vast flood reservoir. In the dry season (Nov.–June) the lake discharges into the Mekong R. Fishing important; considerable trade in live, dried, and smoked fish.

**Toowoomba** Australia. Town in Queensland 70 m. W of Brisbane. Pop. (1966) 52,120. Market town for the Darling Downs. Butter, cheese, and clothing factories, iron foundries and machine shops. Coalmines in the neighbourhood. Trade in wool, wheat, dairy produce.

**Topeka** USA. State capital of Kansas, on the Kansas R. 60 m. W of Kansas City.

Pop. (1960) 119,484. Industrial and commercial centre in an agricultural region. Manufactures tyres etc. Railway engineering, flour milling, meat packing, printing and publishing, etc. Seat of the Washburn University (1944).

**Tor Bay** England. Inlet in the S coast of Devonshire between the headlands of Hope's Nose and Berry Head. Torquay, Paignton and Brixham (together forming the county borough of Torbay) are on its shore.

**Torbay** England. County borough in Devonshire formed in 1968 from the former municipal borough of Torquay and the urban districts of Paignton and Brixham. Pop. (1968) 100,680.

**Torino** ◊ *Turin.*

**Torne** (Finnish **Tornio**) **River** Finland/Sweden. River 300 m. long rising in N Sweden, passing through L. Torne, flowing generally S E to form part of the Swedish-Finnish border, and entering the Gulf of Bothnia. The towns of Haparanda (Sweden) and Tornio (Finland) are at the mouth.

**Toronto** Canada. Capital and largest city of Ontario, second largest city in Canada (after Montreal), at the mouth of the Humber R. on the N shore of L. Ontario. Pop. (1966) 664,584; (metropolitan area) 2,158,496. Important industrial, commercial, and financial centre. Varied industries. Shipbuilding, railway engineering, printing and publishing, meat packing, food processing, etc. Manufactures agricultural machinery etc. Cheap electric power supplied from Niagara Falls. The finest natural harbour on the Great Lakes; handles an immense volume of freight, esp. wheat and other agricultural produce. Educational and cultural centre; the university was founded in 1827 (as King's College). Anglican and Roman Catholic cathedrals and many churches. Outstanding buildings are Osgoode Hall and the fantastic Casa Loma (originally built as a residence, at a cost of 3 million dollars). Lakeside bathing beaches. Numerous parks: High Park is the largest; Queen's Park contains the provincial parliament building; the annual Canadian National Exhibition is held in Exhibition Park.

The name Toronto is derived from a Huron Indian expression probably meaning 'Meeting Place'. Fort Toronto, a French fur-trading post, was established in 1749; it was soon occupied by the British. Became capital of Upper Canada (1793) as York, but when incorporated as a city (1834) the name Toronto was restored. Became capital of Ontario in 1867 and then began to acquire a metropolitan character. The first underground railway was opened in 1954.

**Torquay** England. Town in Devonshire, on Tor Bay 18 m. S of Exeter, from 1968 part of the county borough of ◊ *Torbay.* Pop. (1961) 53,915. Popular seaside resort and yachting centre well known for its mild climate. It has Torre Abbey, founded in the 12th cent., and within the borough are Babbacombe, a smaller resort, Cockington, with a forge, and Kent's Cavern (stalactites), where prehistoric remains were discovered in the 19th cent.

**Torrance** USA. Industrial and residential town in California, 15 m. SSW of Los Angeles. Pop. (1960) 100,991. Oil refining, railway engineering, etc.

**Torre Annunziata** Italy. Seaport and industrial town in Napoli province, Campania, on the Bay of Naples 11 m. SE of Naples. Pop. (1961) 58,400. Manufactures macaroni, fire-arms, etc.

**Torre del Greco** Italy. Seaport, resort, and industrial town in Napoli province, Campania, on the Bay of Naples 7 m. SE of Naples. Pop. (1961) 77,576. Coral fishing and working, macaroni manufacture, etc. Built on the 1631 lava stream from Vesuvius, it has often been damaged by earthquakes and eruptions.

**Torreón** Mexico. Town in Coahuila state, 200 m. W of Monterrey. Pop. (1969) 243,200. In the cotton- and wheat-growing Laguna district. Silver, zinc, and copper mines in the neighbourhood. Textile and flour milling, brewing. Manufactures chemicals.

**Torres Strait** Australasia. Channel between the S coast of New Guinea and the N coast of Cape York Peninsula, about 90 m. wide, connecting the Arafura Sea (W) and the Coral Sea (E). Discovered (1606) by the Spanish navigator Torres.

**Torridge River** England. River 40 m. long in Devonshire rising near the Cornish border and flowing ESE and then NNW past Great Torrington and Bideford to the R. Taw estuary.

**Torrington** (England) ◊ *Great Torrington.*

**Torrington** USA. Industrial town in Connecticut, on the Naugatuck R. 22 m. W of Hartford. Pop. (1960) 30,045. Manufactures hardware, machinery, electrical appliances, etc. Birthplace of John

Brown (1800–1859), the famous abolitionist.

**Tortosa** Spain. Ancient Dertosa. Port in Tarragona province, on the Ebro R. 22 m. above its mouth. Pop. (1961) 43,267. Flour milling. Manufactures soap, pottery, etc. Built largely of granite, the town has a 14th-cent. cathedral occupying the site of a 10th-cent. mosque. An important town under the Moors.

**Tortuga** Haiti. In Spanish, 'Turtle'. Island off the NW of Haiti. Area 70 sq. m. Pop. 12,000. Haunt of English and French buccaneers in the 17th cent.

**Toruń (Ger. Thorn)** Poland. Industrial town and railway junction on the Vistula R. in the Bydgoszcz voivodship 27 m. ESE of Bydgoszcz. Pop. (1968) 124,100. Manufactures machinery, chemicals, textiles, etc. Sawmilling. Trade in grain, timber. University (1945). Founded by the Teutonic Order in the 13th cent. Became an important Hanseatic town, but declined after the Partitions of Poland. Was included (as Thorn) in Prussia 1815–1918. Birthplace of Copernicus (1473–1543).

**Totnes** England. Municipal borough in Devonshire, on the R. Dart 7 m. WSW of Torquay. Pop. (1961) 6,064. Market town. Flour milling, brewing, etc. Has the ruins of a Norman castle, a 15th-cent. church, and a 16th/17th-cent. guildhall, as well as two of the four original town gates. Trout and salmon fishing in the river.

**Tottenham** England. Former municipal borough in Middlesex; from 1965 part of the Greater London borough of Haringey. Pop. (1961) 113,126. Largely residential, with some industry (furniture etc.). The 16th/18th-cent. mansion Bruce Castle (in Bruce Castle Park) now houses a museum.

**Tottori** Japan. Capital of Tottori prefecture, in W Honshu on the Sea of Japan 92 m. WNW of Kyoto. Pop. (1965) 108,864. Seaport. Industrial centre. Manufactures textiles, paper, etc.

**Touggourt** Algeria. Town and oasis 120 m. S of Biskra, with which it is linked by railway. Pop. (1961) 26,000. Commercial centre. Trade in dates etc. Vast numbers of date palms in the oasis. On the oil pipeline from Hassi Messaoud to Bougie.

**Toulon** France. Important naval base on the Mediterranean Sea, in the Var department 29 m. ESE of Marseille. Pop. (1968) 178,489. Has an excellent roadstead, sheltered by hills and a breakwater. Industries, shared by La Seyne-sur-Mer (3 m. SW), include shipbuilding and ship repairing; manufactures armaments. The arsenal and fortifications were constructed by Vauban in the 17th cent. after Henry IV had encouraged its development as a naval base. In 1942 the French fleet was scuttled here to prevent it from falling into German hands.

**Toulouse** France. Ancient Tolosa. Prefecture of the Haute-Garonne department in Languedoc, on the Garonne R. and the Canal du Midi. Pop. (1968) 380,340. Important commercial and industrial centre on the route to the Mediterranean through the Gate of Carcassonne. Trade in the agricultural produce of Aquitaine. Flour milling, tanning, printing. Manufactures aircraft, chemicals, agricultural machinery, electrical equipment, footwear, hosiery, etc. Seat of France's second oldest university (founded 1230). Has a magnificent 11th/ 13th-cent. Romanesque basilica, St Sernin; a 13th/16th-cent. Gothic cathedral, St Étienne; the 13th-cent. church of the Jacobins; the 18th-cent. Capitole (town hall); several outstanding Renaissance mansions. Was capital of the Visigoths (419–507), of the Kingdom of Aquitaine (781–848), and of the comté of Toulouse until it passed to the French crown (1271). Scene of many battles and massacres during the papal crusade against the Albigenses, whose headquarters it was. Continued to play an important political role in S France until the French Revolution (1790). Expanded rapidly with the development of roads and railways in the 19th cent.

**Toungoo** Burma. Town on the Sittang R. 150 m. N of Rangoon. Pop. 32,000. Rice milling, sawmilling. Once capital of an independent kingdom.

**Touquet, Le** France. Seaside resort in the Pas-de-Calais department 15 m. S of Boulogne. Pop. (1968) 4,403. With adjoining Paris-Plage, it is often known as Le Touquet-Paris-Plage. Severely damaged in the 2nd World War.

**Touraine** France. Former province corresponding approximately to the present department of Indre-et-Loire, with capital Tours. Drained by the Loire R. and its tributaries, the Cher, Indre, and Vienne. Took its name from the Turones, the tribe inhabiting it when Caesar conquered Gaul. The famous châteaux were built when French monarchs and aristocrats came to live in the region.

**Tourcoing** France. Industrial town in the Nord department 8 m. NNE of Lille. Pop. (1968) 99,369. With its twin town of Roubaix (just SSE), produces most of France's woollen goods. Also manufactures carpets, clothing, cotton goods, leather, etc.

**Tournai (Flemish Doornik)** Belgium. Industrial town in the Hainaut province, on the Scheldt R. 12 m. ESE of Roubaix (France). Pop. (1968) 33,518. Manufactures carpets, hosiery, cement, leather, etc. The famous cathedral, dating from the 11th cent., is part Romanesque, part Gothic.

**Tours** France. Ancient Caesarodunum. Prefecture of the Indre-et-Loire department, on the strip of land between the Loire and the Cher rivers near the confluence 128 m. SW of Paris. Pop. (1968) 132,861. Manufactures agricultural machinery, fertilizers, cement, textiles, pottery, etc. Trade in wine, brandy, etc. Popular tourist centre for the famous castles of the Loire valley. Has a 12th/16th-cent. Gothic cathedral, a 17th/18th-cent. former archbishop's palace (now an art museum), and several 15th-cent. houses. Fell to the Visigoths in the 5th cent. and to the Franks in the 6th. Charles Martel defeated the Moors about 30 m. S of the town at the so-called Battle of Tours (732). A silk industry was established by Louis XI, but this declined after the revocation of the Edict of Nantes (1685) and the flight of the Huguenot weavers. Birthplace of Honoré de Balzac (1799–1850).

**Towcester** England. Small market town in Northamptonshire 8 m. SSW of Northampton. Pop. (rural district, 1961) 15,198. Site of a Roman station (on Watling Street). Claims to be the 'Eatanswill' of *Pickwick Papers*.

**Townsville** Australia. Seaport in NE Queensland, on Cleveland Bay 690 m. NW of Brisbane. Pop. (1966) 56,687. The second port in the state, serving a vast hinterland in the N. Receives minerals from the Mt Isa–Cloncurry region and cattle from the E highlands and the Great Artesian Basin. Exports wool, frozen meat, sugar, metals, minerals. Meat works, copper refinery. Founded (1864) by Robert Towns, an Englishman.

**Toyama** Japan. Capital of Toyama prefecture, Honshu, on Toyama Bay 110 m. N of Nagoya. Pop. (1965) 239,809. Leading centre for the manufacture of patent

medicines and drugs; also manufactures textiles, chemicals, machinery, etc.

**Toyohashi** Japan. Industrial town in Aichi prefecture, Honshu, 40 m. SE of Nagoya. Pop. (1965) 238,672. Food processing, metal working. Manufactures cotton goods.

**Trabzon (Trebizond)** Turkey. Capital of Trabzon province, on the Black Sea coast 105 m. NW of Erzurum. Pop. (1965) 65,500. Port, modernized since the 2nd World War. Exports tobacco, hazel nuts, flour, etc. Food processing etc. A Greek colony of the 8th cent. B.C. Rose to greatness when it became the capital of an empire, founded by Alexius Comnenus, which lasted from 1204 to 1461, when it was taken by the Turks.

**Trafalgar, Cape** Spain. Headland on the Atlantic coast of Cadiz province near the Strait of Gibraltar. Scene of the decisive naval victory of the British fleet which ended Napoleon's sea power and in which Nelson was mortally wounded (1805).

**Trail** Canada. Industrial town in SE British Columbia, on the Columbia R. near the US frontier. Pop. (1966) 11,600. Smelting of lead, zinc, copper, silver, etc. Manufactures chemicals.

**Tralee** Irish Republic. County town of Kerry, on the R. Lee near Tralee Bay, with which it is connected by ship canal. Pop. (1966) 11,213. Market town. Manufactures hosiery, etc. Exports dairy produce. The port of Fenit, birthplace of St Brendan (483–578), is 7 m. W.

**Tranent** Scotland. Small burgh in E Lothian, 8 m. E of Edinburgh. Pop. (1961) 6,317. Coalmining centre.

**Trani** Italy. Adriatic seaport in Bari province, Apulia, 27 m. WNW of Bari. Pop. (1961) 38,129. Produces wine. Has a 12th/13th-cent. Romanesque cathedral and a 13th/16th-cent. castle. It framed the first of the medieval codes of maritime law (1063).

**Transcaucasia** USSR. Territory lying S of the Caucasus, formed into the Federal Republic of Transcaucasia in 1917, splitting in the following year into the republics of Georgia, Azerbaijan, and Armenia. In 1922 the Transcaucasian SFSR was formed on Soviet lines, but in 1936 divided into the Georgian, Azerbaijan and Armenian SSRs.

**Transkeian Territories** S Africa. A division in the E of the Cape Province, between Natal and the Great Kei R. Area 16,554 sq. m. (13,916 sq. m. African reserves governed by native councils). Pop. (1960) 1,439,169 (1,407,815 African, 17,514 white, 13,840 coloured). Cap. Umtata. Four districts: Transkei, Tembuland, Pondoland, Griqualand East. Source of labour recruitment for the Witwatersrand mines. Main occupations stock raising, wool production.

**Transvaal** S Africa. Province in the NE, between the Limpopo (N) and the Vaal (S) rivers. Area 110,450 sq. m. Pop. (1960) 6,225,052. Cap. Pretoria. Largest town Johannesburg. Bounded by Rhodesia (N), Moçambique (E), Swaziland (SE), Natal and the Orange Free State (S), the Cape Province (SW), and Botswana (Bechuanaland Protectorate) (W). Mainly plateau 3,000–4,000 ft high, rising in the Witwatersrand (E and S) to over 5,000 ft. Consists very largely of the High Veld. The Kruger National Park is in the NE. Cattle raised on the grasslands. Principal crop maize ('mealies'). Citrus fruits and tobacco grown on irrigated land. Great mineral wealth, esp. gold (the Witwatersrand produces one third to one half of the known world output), with uranium a valuable by-product from the goldmines; also asbestos, chromium, coal, copper, diamonds, iron, manganese, nickel, platinum. Manufactures iron and steel, cement, machinery, chemicals, explosives. Johannesburg is the largest town in S Africa; other important towns are Benoni, Brakpan, Germiston, Krugersdorp, Roodepoort-Maraisburg, Springs. Well served by road, rail, and air services. Much of the internal trade passes through Lourenço Marques (Moçambique). First colonized by the Boer Voortrekkers, who evicted the native Matabele after making the Great Trek from Cape Colony (1836). Britain recognized its independence in 1852. Formed the South African Republic (1856) but was annexed by Britain (1877). Won self-government again 1881. The Witwatersrand goldfield was discovered in 1886; the denial of political rights to the many prospectors who flocked there from the Cape, Britain, and elsewhere ('*Uitlanders*' to the Boers) led to the Boer War (1899–1902). Then it was a self-governing British Crown Colony until it became one of the four provinces of the new Union of S Africa (1910).

**Transylvania** Rumania. Former province, separated from Moldavia (E) by the Carpathians and from Walachia (S) by the Transylvanian Alps. Mainly plateau 1,000–1,500 ft high, rising in the Bihar Mountains (W) to 6,000 ft; crossed NE–SW by the Mureş R. Largely forested. The mineral resources are as yet little exploited. Cereals, potatoes, and vines cultivated in the fertile valleys. Chief towns Cluj, Braşov. Most of the people are Rumanians, but there are considerable numbers of Hungarians and Germans. Part of the Roman province of Dacia from A.D. 103. Incorporated into Hungary early in the 11th cent. Virtually independent 1526–1699, then part of the Austro-Hungarian Empire. The Magyar element in the population worked continually for union with Hungary, ultimately gained in 1867. Ceded to Rumania (1920) after the 1st World War. Hitler awarded most of the area to Hungary (1940); it was returned to Rumania 1947. Divided into Regions (including the predominantly Hungarian Magyar Autonomous Region) 1952; changed to Districts 1968.

**Trapani** Italy. Ancient Drepanum. Capital of Trapani province in W Sicily. Pop. (1961) 77,139. Seaport. Tunny fishing. Produces salt, wine, macaroni, etc. An important Carthaginian naval base in the 1st Punic War.

**Trasimeno (Perugia), Lake** Italy. The largest lake in central Italy, in Umbria 11 m. W of Perugia. Area 50 sq. m. Drained by an artificial tunnel to a tributary of the Tiber R. On its N shore Hannibal defeated the Romans under Flaminius (217 B.C.).

**Trebizond** ◊ *Trabzon*.

**Tredegar** Wales. Urban district in Monmouthshire 16 m. NW of Newport. Pop. (1961) 19,792. Coalmining centre.

**Trelew** Argentina. Town in Chubut province (Patagonia) 10 m. WNW of Rawson. Pop. 11,500. Market town serving agricultural settlements. Sawmilling, brewing. Founded (1881) by Welshmen.

**Trengganu** Malaysia. State in Malaya (W Malaysia), on the E coast. Area 5,027 sq. m. Pop. (1967) 378,738. Cap. Kuala Trengganu. Consists of a narrow coastal plain rising inland to densely forested mountains reaching nearly 5,000 ft. Chief products rice, rubber, copra.

**Trent** (Italy) ◊ *Trento*.

**Trentino-Alto Adige** Italy. Region bordering on Switzerland and Austria and comprising the provinces of Trento and Bolzano, formerly part of Austria. Area 5,252 sq. m. Pop. (1961) 785,491 (many German-speaking).

**Trento (Trent)** Italy. Capital of Trento province, in Trentino-Alto Adige, on the Adige R. and on the Brenner Pass route through the Alps. Pop. (1961) 75,154. Electrical engineering. Manufactures chemicals, cement, etc. A picturesque town, with a 13th/16th-cent. cathedral and the 16th-cent. Church of Santa Maria Maggiore where the Council of Trent met (1545–63). Passed to Austria 1803; restored to Italy 1919.

**Trenton** USA. State capital of New Jersey, at the head of navigation on the Delaware R. Pop. (1960) 114,167. Industrial centre. Manufactures wire rope, cables, pottery, aircraft equipment, steam turbines, etc. First settled 1679. At the Battle of Trenton (1776) Washington defeated the British in the American War of Independence.

**Trent River** England. Chief river in the Midlands, 170 m. long, rising on Biddulph Moor, N Staffordshire, and flowing first SE past Stoke-on-Trent, then turning NE past Burton-on-Trent, Nottingham, Newark, and Gainsborough to join the R. Ouse 15 m. W of Hull and form the Humber. Chief tributaries the Dove, Derwent, Soar, and Devon. Linked with the Mersey by the Trent and Mersey Canal.

**Tres Arroyos** Argentina. Town in Buenos Aires province 115 m. ENE of Bahía Blanca. Pop. 40,000. Market town in a wheat-growing and stock-rearing area. Flour milling. Manufactures furniture, etc.

**Tresco** ♢ *Scilly Isles*.

**Trèves** ♢ *Trier*.

**Treviso** Italy. Capital of Treviso province, in Veneto, 17 m. NNW of Venice. Pop. (1961) 75,017. Manufactures agricultural machinery, paper, brushes, etc. The cathedral (12th-cent., later restored) contains work by Titian and by Bordone (1500–1571), who was born here. The building, along with many others, was severely damaged in the 2nd World War.

**Trichinopoly** ♢ *Tiruchirapalli*.

**Trichur** India. Town in Kerala 38 m. N of Ernakulam. Pop. (1961) 73,038. Commercial and cultural centre, with colleges affiliated to Kerala University. Manufactures cotton goods.

**Trier** (Fr. Trèves) Federal German Republic. Town in Rhineland-Palatinate, on the Moselle R. 60 m. SW of Coblenz. Pop. (1963) 87,400. Centre of the Moselle wine trade. Manufactures textiles, leather goods, etc. Named after the Treveri, a tribe of the Belgae, it was important from Roman times, and among its remains are the Porta Nigra (a fortified gate), a large amphitheatre, and baths. The cathedral, built from a Roman basilica and extended in the 11th–13th cent., has a relic, the 'Holy Coat of Trier', said to be the seamless coat of Christ. This building and many others were badly damaged or destroyed in the 2nd World War. Seat of a university from 1473 until 1797, when it was occupied by the French, and the political power of the Archbishops was finally removed. Birthplace of Karl Marx (1818–83).

**Trieste** (Slovenian Trst) Italy. Seaport on the Gulf of Trieste, on the NE coast of the Adriatic Sea, 73 m. ENE of Venice. Pop. (1968) 280,658. Important transit port for Central Europe; also an industrial centre. Shipbuilding, oil refining. Manufactures marine engines, jute products, paper, etc. The narrow, winding streets of the old town extend up Monte Giusto, on which are the cathedral and castle; near the sea is the Piazza dell' Unità. University (1924). The famous white castle of Miramare, once the home of the Archduke Maximilian who became Emperor of Mexico, is 4 m. NW. A port in Roman times. Passed to Austria in 1382 and (with brief interruptions) remained in Austrian hands till 1918. An imperial free port 1719–1891. Ceded to Italy after the 1st World War. After the 2nd World War (1947) it was made capital of the Free Territory of Trieste, which was divided into Zone A (Italian, occupied by US and UK forces), including the city of Trieste, and Zone B (Yugoslav) to the S, larger but less populous. Most of Zone A passed to Italy, and the remainder to Yugoslavia, in 1954.

**Triglav, Mount** Yugoslavia. Country's highest peak (9,396 ft), in the Julian Alps 40 m. NW of Ljubljana, near the Austrian and Italian frontiers.

**Trikkala** Greece. 1. *Nome* in Thessaly, bounded on the W by the Pindus Mountains. Area 1,328 sq. m. Pop. (1961) 142,450. Cereals and olives cultivated.
2. Capital of Trikkala *nome*, 37 m. WSW of Larissa. Pop. (1961) 27,876. Market town. Trade in cereals, tobacco, etc. Seriously damaged by earthquake in 1954.

**Trim** Irish Republic. County town of Meath, on the R. Boyne 26 m. NW of Dublin. Pop. (1966) 1,467. Market town. Trade in cereals etc. In the castle (founded in the 12th cent.) Henry of Lancaster, afterwards Henry IV, was imprisoned by

Richard II. There are also two gates of the old town wall.

**Trincomalee** Ceylon. Seaport on the NE coast. Pop. 28,000. Has one of the world's outstanding natural harbours; formerly a British naval base. Was settled by Tamils from S India: their famous Temple of a Thousand Columns, standing on a height in the E of the town, was destroyed by the Portuguese (1622), and the Dutch built a fortress on its site (1676).

**Tring** England. Urban district in W Hertfordshire 14 m. WNW of St Albans. Pop. (1961) 6,087. Near by is Tring Park with a zoological museum bequeathed (1938) by Lord Rothschild to the British Museum.

**Trinidad** W Indies. Island off the NE coast of Venezuela, part of the state of Trinidad and Tobago, an independent member of the British Commonwealth. Area 1,864 sq. m. Pop. (1965) 973,920 (mainly Negroes and Asian Indians). Cap. and chief seaport Port of Spain. Three ranges of hills cross the island E–W, the highest peaks just exceeding 3,000 ft. Climate tropical and humid; annual rainfall 50–100 ins. Chief products asphalt (from the Pitch Lake in the SW), petroleum. Two oil refineries. Leading crops sugar-cane, cacao, coconuts, citrus fruits. Discovered (1498) by Columbus. Ceded to Britain 1802. Amalgamated with Tobago as a British Crown Colony 1888. The state opted out of the short-lived Federation of the W Indies (1958–62), and became independent in 1962.

**Tripoli** (Ar. **Tarabulus**) Lebanon. Seaport on the Mediterranean coast 45 m. NNE of Beirut. Pop. (1963) 100,000. Has an oil refinery, being a terminus of the pipeline from Iraq. Manufactures textiles, soap, cement, etc. Exports citrus fruits, tobacco, etc. An ancient city, it became capital of the Phoenician federation of Tyre, Sidon, and Aradus, each with its own district in the town, and was extended and improved under the Seleucids and Romans. Taken by the Arabs 638. Destroyed by the Mamelukes 1289; rebuilt on its present site.

**Tripoli** Libya. Seaport on the Mediterranean coast 400 m. W of Benghazi. Pop. (1964) 212,577. Capital of Tripolitania; since 1952 joint capital of Libya with Benghazi, with which and other towns it is linked by a coastal road. Near a large oasis. Exports esparto grass, hides, dates, salt, sponges. Manufactures tobacco products, soap, leather, rugs and carpets, pottery. Sponge and tunny fishing. Founded about the 7th cent. B.C. by Phoenicians from Tyre and subsequently occupied by Rome; some Roman walls survive. To the E is the ancient city of Leptis Magna (also founded by the Phoenicians) with the most extensive Roman ruins in N Africa. Ruled by Turkey, and a pirate stronghold, from the mid 16th cent. Occupied by the Italians 1911; became the capital of the Italian colony of Libya. Taken by the British during the 2nd World War (1943).

**Tripolitania** Libya. Province in the NW, bounded by Cyrenaica (E), Fezzan (S), and Tunisia (W). Area 100,000 sq. m. Pop. 800,000 (mainly Muslim Arabs and Berber, with Negro admixture). Cap. and chief seaport Tripoli. Apart from the line of coastal oases (from the Tunisian border as far E as Misurata), where the annual rainfall is about 15 ins., it forms a section of the Sahara, with part of the vast rock desert Hammada el Homra (SW); the only drainage consists of wadis. Camels, sheep, and goats raised by nomads. Barley, wheat, olives, dates, and vegetables grown in the oases. Tripoli is the only deep-water port and has the few small industries.

**Tripura** India. Union Territory in the NE, bounded by E Pakistan (N, W, and S) and Assam (E). Area 4,036 sq. m. Pop. (1961) 1,142,995. Cap. and chief commercial centre Agartala (pop. 54,878). Mainly hilly, with much jungle. Chief products timber, rice, jute, cotton. Formerly a princely state, it became a centrally administered area of the Indian Union in 1949 and a Union Territory in 1956.

**Tristan da Cunha** S Atlantic Ocean. Group of volcanic islands about halfway between S Africa and S America; since 1938 a dependency of St Helena. The largest island, Tristan, in the N (area 16 sq. m.), has a central volcanic cone 7,640 ft high, often snow-capped, with a crater lake. Potatoes are grown and cattle, sheep, and pigs are raised on the NW plateau, and there is fishing. It was discovered (1506) by the Portuguese Tristão da Cunha. The first permanent settler was Thomas Currie (1810), others arriving from 1817 onwards; the population increased from 109 in 1880 to 281 in 1960. In 1961 a volcanic eruption made it necessary to evacuate the inhabitants to Britain; two years later, after the cessation of danger, the majority elected to return to Tristan (1963). Other islands in the group are Gough, Inaccessible, and Nightingale Islands, all un-inhabited.

**Trivandrum** India. Capital of Kerala, near the Malabar coast 130 m. SW of Madurai. Pop. (1961) 239,815. Manufactures textiles, coir ropes and mats, copra, soap, etc. Centre of Malayalam culture; seat of Kerala University (1937). Has an old Hindu temple.

**Trnava** Czechoslovakia. Market town in Slovakia 27 m. NE of Bratislava. Pop. (1967) 36,000. In a fertile agricultural region. Sugar refining, brewing. Manufactures fertilizers, textiles, etc. Detached from Hungary 1920.

**Trois Rivières (Three Rivers)** Canada. Industrial town in Quebec, on the St Lawrence R. at its confluence with the St Maurice R. 80 m. NE of Montreal. Pop. (1966) 57,540. A leading world centre of newsprint production. Iron founding. Manufactures textiles, clothing, electrical equipment, etc. Hydroelectric power is derived from the St Maurice R.

**Trollhättan** Sweden. Industrial town in Älvsborg county, on the Göta R. 42 m. NNE of Göteborg. Pop. (1968) 40,803. Manufactures machinery, chemicals, cellulose, etc. The river here descends 108 ft in 6 falls, supplying power for an important hydroelectric plant, which in turn provides electricity for much of S Sweden as well as for the town's industries.

**Tromsö** Norway. Capital of Troms county, in the N, on an island just off the coast. Pop. (1968) 36,340. Fishing and sealing port. Fish processing, tanning. Largest town N of the Arctic Circle. Has an Arctic museum.

**Trondheim** Norway. Formerly Nidaros, Trondhjem. Capital of Sör Tröndelag county, on Trondheim Fiord and at the mouth of the Nid R. Pop. (1968) 120,818. Important seaport and fishing centre. Shipbuilding, fish canning, metal working. Manufactures margarine, soap, etc. Exports wood pulp, paper, fish, metals. The cathedral, dating from the 11th cent., is reputedly the finest church in Norway. Seat of the Norwegian Institute of Technology (1900). Founded (996) as Nidaros by Olaf Tryggvason; capital until 1380. Renamed Trondhjem in the 16th cent., Nidaros (1930–31), and then Trondheim.

**Troödos Mountains** ◊ *Cyprus.*

**Troon** Scotland. Small burgh in Ayrshire 6 m. N of Ayr. Pop. (1961) 9,932. Seaside resort. Exports coal. Engineering.

**Troppau** ◊ *Opava.*

**Trossachs** Scotland. In Gaelic, 'the Bristly Country'. Picturesque wooded glen in SW Perthshire, between Loch Achray and Loch Katrine, with Ben Venue (2,393 ft) to the SW. Described in Scott's *The Lady of the Lake* and *Rob Roy.*

**Trouville** France. Popular seaside resort and fishing port in the Calvados department at the mouth of the Touques R. opposite Deauville. Pop. (1968) 6,577.

**Trowbridge** England. Urban district in Wiltshire 8 m. ESE of Bath. Pop. (1961) 15,833. Market town. Manufactures woollen goods. Bacon and ham curing, brewing, etc. George Crabbe (1754–1832) is buried in the parish church. Birthplace of Sir Isaac Pitman (1813–97).

**Troy.** Ancient Troja, Ilium. Ancient city in Asia Minor, just SE of the entrance to the Dardanelles from the Aegean Sea, in the region known as Troas. Excavations begun by Schliemann in 1872 revealed 9 successive cities on the site, of which the Homeric Troy (c. 1200 B.C.) was probably the 7th.

**Troy** USA. Industrial town in New York, at the head of steamboat navigation on the Hudson R. 7 m. NNE of Albany. Pop. (1960) 67,492. Manufactures clothing (esp. shirts and collars), fire hydrants, brushes, etc. Home of Samuel Wilson (1816–1906), reputedly the original of 'Uncle Sam'.

**Troyes** France. Prefecture of the Aube department, on the Seine R. 90 m. ESE of Paris. Pop. (1968) 77,009. Road and railway junction. Industrial town. Manufactures knitwear, hosiery, paper, textile machinery. Dyeing, flour milling. Has a 13th/16th-cent. cathedral and many churches famous for their stained-glass windows, some of which were damaged in the 2nd World War. The bishopric was created in the 4th cent. Became capital of Champagne, and its medieval fairs were renowned – it gave its name to the standard troy weight; its trade suffered severely, however, from the revocation of the Edict of Nantes (1685). Probable birthplace of the medieval poet, Chrétien de Troyes.

**Trucial States.** Group of 7 British-protected Arab sheikhdoms in E Arabia, on the Persian Gulf between Qatar (W) and Muscat and Oman (E). Area 32,300 sq. m. Pop. 180,200 (about 10 per cent nomads). The Sheikhdoms are Abu Dhabi, Dubai, Sharja and Kalba, Ajman, Umm al Qaiwain, Ras al Khaimah, Fujairah. Chief town and port Dubai (pop. 60,000). Main occupations fishing, trading. The sheikhdoms are bound by treaty with Britain, who assumes responsibility for external affairs and defence. The first agreement was signed in 1820. The coast was once known with some justification as the Pirate Coast. After the announcement of the coming British withdrawal from the Persian Gulf, the 7 Trucial States formed a federation with Bahrain and Qatar (1968).

**Trujillo** Peru. Capital of La Libertad department, in the NW on the coastal plain 8 m. NNW of its port Salaverry on the Pan-American Highway. Pop. (1965) 123,500. Important commercial and industrial centre in an irrigated region producing sugar-cane and rice. Manufactures soap, candles, cocaine, etc. Food processing, tanning, brewing. A picturesque city, it has a cathedral, a university (1824), and many colonial buildings. Founded 1535.

**Truk Islands** W Pacific Ocean. Group of volcanic and coral islands, about 100 in all, in the E Caroline Is. Pop. (1968) 26,368. Export copra, dried fish. Important Japanese naval base during the 2nd World War.

**Truro** England. Municipal borough and administrative centre of Cornwall, on the Truro R. 8 m. N of Falmouth. Pop. (1961) 13,328. Market town. Manufactures pottery, biscuits, etc. The bishopric was established in 1876 and the cathedral was built in Early English style. Birthplace of Henry Martyn (1781–1812), the missionary.

**Tsamkong (Chankiang)** China. Seaport in Kwangtung province, on the NE coast of the Luichow peninsula. Pop. 166,000. Developed as a seaport 1954–7. A railway links it with Litang (Kwangsi-Chuang AR) in the interior.

**Tsana, Lake** ◊ *Tana, Lake.*

**Tsangpo River** ◊ *Brahmaputra River.*

**Tsaritsyn** ◊ *Volgograd.*

**Tselinograd** USSR. Formerly Akmolinsk. Capital of the Tselinny (Virgin Land) Territory and the Tselinograd region, Kazakh SSR, on the Ishim R. 120 m. NW of Karaganda. Pop. (1970) 180,000. Important railway junction, industrial and commercial centre. Meat packing, flour milling, tanning. Manufactures agricultural machinery. Founded 1830. Renamed Tselinograd 1961.

**Tsinan** China. Capital of Shantung province, just S of the Hwang-ho and 225 m. S of Peking. Pop. (1957) 862,000. Rail-

way junction. Industrial centre. Railway engineering, flour milling. Manufactures machinery, textiles, paper, cement, etc. Ancient city, probably inhabited for over 3,000 years. Opened to foreign trade 1904. Occupied by the Japanese 1937–45.

**Tsinghai (Chinghai)** China. Province on the NE border of Tibet, including much of the former NE Tibet. Area 278,000 sq. m. Pop. (1957) 2,050,000. Cap. Sining. Consists largely of a lofty, barren plateau crossed by the Nan Shan, which rises to over 20,000 ft, and the Bayan Khara Shan. In the N is the Tsaidam, a desolate swampy depression, and in the NE another basin occupied by the lake Koko Nor or Tsinghai, after which the province is named. Main occupation herding, esp. sheep.

**Tsingtao** China. Seaport and industrial town in Shantung province, on the peninsula at the entrance to Kiaochow Bay 275 m. SE of Peking. Pop. (1957) 1,121,000. Has an excellent, deep-water harbour. Exports soya beans, groundnuts, etc. Manufactures textiles, machinery, cement, soap, etc. Railway engineering, flour milling. Seat of Shantung University (1926). Passed to Germany (1898) as part of the Kiaochow lease and was quickly developed. Returned to China 1922.

**Tsitsihar** China. Formerly (1913–47) Lungkiang. Town in Heilungkiang province (Manchuria), on the Nun-kiang 175 m. NW of Harbin. Pop. (1957) 668,000. Flour milling, soya-bean processing. Manufactures chemicals, matches. Trade in grain etc. Famous autumn fairs. Capital of Lungkiang province in Manchukuo 1934–46.

**Tskhinvali** USSR. Formerly (1936–61) Stalinir (Staliniri). Capital of the S Ossetian Autonomous Region (Georgian SSR), 55 m. NW of Tbilisi. Pop. (1970) 30,000. Fruit canning etc.

**Tsu** Japan. Capital of Mie prefecture 52 m. E of Osaka. Pop. (1965) 117,210. Industrial centre. Manufactures textiles etc. Ancient temples.

**Tsushima** Japan. Group of 5 islands in Nagasaki prefecture, between Kyushu (Japan) and S Korea 80 m. WNW of Kitakyushu. Area 271 sq. m. Pop. (1960) 69,556. Chief town Izuhara. Main occupation fishing. During the Russo-Japanese War the Russian fleet was utterly defeated by the Japanese near by (1905).

**Tuam** Irish Republic. Market town in Co. Galway 19 m. NNE of Galway. Pop.

(1966) 3,624. Sugar refining. Has a Protestant cathedral (founded 1130) and a Roman Catholic cathedral.

**Tuamotu Islands** ◊ *French Polynesia.*

**Tuapse** USSR. Seaport in the Krasnodar Territory, RSFSR, on the Black Sea 65 m. S of Krasnodar. Pop. (1962) 42,000. Exports petroleum products. Oil refining; terminus of pipelines from the Grozny and Maikop oilfields.

**Tübingen** Federal German Republic. Town in Baden-Württemberg, on the Neckar R. 19 m. SSW of Stuttgart. Pop. (1963) 53,300. Printing and publishing. Manufactures textiles, precision instruments, etc. Seat of a university (founded 1477), whose school of theology led by F. C. Baur achieved fame in the 19th cent. Has a 15th-cent. town hall and church and a 16th-cent castle. Birthplace of Ludwig Uhland (1787–1862), the poet.

**Tubuai Islands** ◊ *Austral Islands.*

**Tucson** USA. Industrial and commercial town and popular health and holiday resort in Arizona, 110 m. SE of Phoenix at a height of 2,400 ft. Pop. (1960) 212,892 (45,454 in 1950). Railway engineering, flour milling. Manufactures electronic equipment, bricks and tiles, etc. Seat of the University of Arizona (1891). Expanded rapidly in the 1950s.

**Tucumán** Argentina. Capital of Tucumán province, at the foot of the E Andes in the most populous region of the NW. Pop. (1960) 287,004. Commercial and industrial centre in a region producing sugar-cane, maize, rice, etc. Sugar refining, flour milling, distilling. An attractive city (the 'garden of Argentina') with many colonial buildings. Cathedral. University (1914). Founded 1565. Moved to its present site 1580.

**Tugela River** S Africa. River 300 m. long in Natal, rising on Mont-aux-Sources in the Drakensberg. It soon plunges over the escarpment in a series of falls, passing through a beautiful wooded gorge, then flowing generally E and emptying into the Indian Ocean 50 m. NE of Durban. Various battles were fought in its upper basin during the Zulu War (1879; ◊ *Zululand*).

**Tula** USSR. Capital of the Tula region, RSFSR, 105 m. S of Moscow. Pop. (1970) 462,000. Railway junction. Industrial centre. Manufactures pig iron, firearms, agricultural machinery, samovars, etc., fuel being derived from the local Moscow–Tula lignite basin. Sugar refining, flour milling. The 16th-cent. kremlin, in the centre of the city, was restored after the 2nd World War. Founded in the 12th cent. Became an important iron-working centre in the 17th cent., after Boris Godunov had established the first gun factory (1595). Industrial expansion was considerable in the 19th cent.

**Tullamore** Irish Republic. County town of Offaly, on the Grand Canal 50 m. W of Dublin. Pop. (1966) 6,654. Market town. Brewing, distilling, bacon curing. At Durrow Abbey (4 m. N), founded by St Columba in the 6th cent., the 7th-cent. *Book of Durrow* (now in the Trinity College Library, Dublin) was written.

**Tulle** France. Prefecture of Corrèze department 47 m. SSE of Limoges. Pop. (1968) 21,324. Market town. Manufactures firearms, textiles, etc.; gave its name to the fabric 'tulle', first produced here. Has a 12th/14th-cent. cathedral.

**Tulsa** USA. Industrial town in Oklahoma, on the Arkansas R. 105 m. NE of Oklahoma City. Pop. (1960) 261,685. A leading centre of the oil industry in a rich oil-producing region; sometimes called the 'oil capital of the world'. Manufactures oilfield equipment, aircraft, machinery, metal goods, glass, etc. Grew rapidly after the discovery of oil (1901).

**Tumaco** Colombia. Pacific port in the Nariño department on a small offshore island 190 m. SW of Buenaventura. Pop. 49,000. Exports coffee, tobacco, tagua nuts, etc. Climate hot and humid.

**Tummel River** Scotland. River 55 m. long in Perthshire, flowing generally E from Loch Rannoch through Loch Tummel, turning SE past Pitlochry to join the Tay R. near Ballinluig. Near Pitlochry it has been dammed as part of a hydroelectric scheme, creating the new Loch Faskally.

**Tunbridge Wells** England. Municipal borough in SW Kent 15 m. SW of Maidstone. Pop. (1961) 39,855. A spa owing its popularity to a chalybeate spring, whose medicinal value was discovered by Lord North in 1606. Among subsequent notable visitors were Henrietta Maria, Charles II and Catherine of Braganza, Dr Johnson, David Garrick, and Beau Nash, and it reached the height of its fame in the latter half of the 18th cent. Its outstanding feature, now as then, is the colonnaded, tree-lined promenade known as the Pantiles. Manufactures biscuits, bricks. 'Tunbridge ware', articles made in wood-mosaic, was well known for three centuries.

**Tung Ting Lake** China. Extensive shallow lake in N Hunan province, 115 m. SW of Wuhan. Fed by the Siang and Yüan rivers, with an outlet (N) to the Yangtse R. Area (in winter) 1,500 sq. m. During the summer it receives the flood waters of the Yangtse R. and more than doubles in size. It is slowly filling up owing to deposition of silt.

**Tunis** Tunisia. Capital and chief seaport, on a shallow lagoon, the Lake of Tunis (El Bahira) at the head of the Gulf of Tunis on the Mediterranean Sea. Pop. (1966) 642,384. Linked with its outport La Goulette by a channel 6 m. long through the lagoon. The E terminus of the main railway through Morocco and Algeria; also connected by rail (S) with Sousse, Sfax, Gabès, Gafsa. Favourably situated for Mediterranean trade: serves the Tell, the Medjerda valley, the plateau, and the coastal lowlands. Exports phosphates, iron ore, Mediterranean fruits, dates, olive oil, esparto grass. The chief commercial and industrial centre. Food processing, brewing. Manufactures soap, footwear, cement, etc. The ruins of ancient Carthage, with which it is connected by electric railway, are 9 m. NE.

**Tunisia.** Republic in NW Africa. Area 63,362 sq. m. Pop. (1966) 4,457,862 (numerous French and Italian settlers). Cap. and chief seaport Tunis. Bounded by the Mediterranean Sea (N and E), Libya (SE), and Algeria (W). The main regions are the N highlands (an extension of the Tell Atlas); the irrigated Medjerda valley (wheat, barley); the Cape Bon peninsula (citrus fruits); the Sahel (E lowlands) (olives); the central plateau (with the E–W depression containing the shallow salt lakes of Chott Djerid, Gharsa, Fedjedj); and the S Sahara, with oases (dates). Chief mineral exports phosphates (mined around Gafsa) and iron ore and lead (NW). Chief agricultural exports olive oil, wine, wheat, barley. Tunis, the E terminus of the trunk line through Morocco and Algeria, is linked by rail along the E coast with Sousse, Sfax, and Gabès, with branch lines to the mining districts, the Tozeur oasis, and the Muslim holy city of Kairouan. Bizerta (a naval and air base) was retained by France until 1963.

After having been long dominated by Carthage, became the Roman province of 'Africa' in the 2nd cent. B.C. and served as a granary for Rome. Taken in turn by Vandals in the 5th cent., Byzantines in the 6th, and Arabs in the 7th; became most powerful under the Berber Hafsid dynasty in the 13th–16th cent. Under Turkish suzerainty became a haunt of pirates; European powers intervened, and France established a protectorate in 1881. Scene of much bitter fighting during the 2nd World War; the Axis troops finally surrendered in 1943. The nationalists forced France to grant internal autonomy in 1955 and independence in 1956. The Bey was deposed and a republic set up in 1957. Conditions of housing, nutrition, and education are being energetically improved.

**Tunja** Colombia. Capital of the Boyaca department, at a height of 9,250 ft in the E Cordillera 80 m. NE of Bogotá. Pop. 53,500. Market town. Founded by the Spanish (1539) on the site of one of the Chibcha capitals. Much fine architecture of the early colonial period.

**Tunstall** ◊ *Stoke-on-Trent.*

**Tura** ◊ *Evenki NA.*

**Turfan** China. **1.** Formerly Lukchun. Depression in the Sinkiang-Uighur AR between the Tien Shan (N) and the Kuruk Tagh (Dry Mountains). Its lowest point is 980 ft below sea level. Rain almost unknown. Fruits (esp. grapes), cotton, cereals cultivated by irrigation.
**2.** Chief town of the Turfan Depression, 90 m. SE of Urumchi, on the Lanchow–Urumchi railway. Pop. 20,000. Manufactures cotton goods.

**Turin** (Italian **Torino**) Italy. Ancient Augusta Taurinorum. Capital of Piedmont and of the Turin province, the fourth largest city in Italy, at the confluence of the Po R. with the Dora Riparia. Pop. (1968) 1,131,621. Important industrial and route centre. Has Italy's chief motor-car plants; also manufactures aircraft, textiles, clothing, leather goods, plastics, confectionery, paper, etc., utilizing considerable hydroelectric power from the rivers. Its wide, straight streets cutting one another at right-angles are a relic of Roman times. Among its noteworthy buildings are the 15th-cent. cathedral, with its façade of white marble and a chapel containing the shroud in which Christ's body was reputedly wrapped after the Crucifixion; the Palazzo Madama and Palazzo Carignano, both now housing museums; the 19th-cent. Mole Antonelliana, also used as a museum and said to be the highest brick-built edifice in Europe (544 ft); and the university (founded 1404). Became a Roman colony under Augustus. Capital of the kingdom of Sardinia 1720. Capital of Italy 1861–4. Severely damaged in the 2nd World War.

**Turkestan.** Extensive region in Central Asia, between Siberia (N) and Iran, Afghanistan and Tibet (S), and between the Caspian Sea (W) and Mongolia and the Gobi desert (E). Politically divided into W or Russian Turkestan or Soviet Central Asia and E or Chinese Turkestan, which is now usually regarded as co-extensive with the Sinkiang-Uighur AR. The name means 'Land of the Turks', but there are many non-Turkish peoples in the region. Russian Turkestan includes the broad plain often known as the Turanian Basin, lying W of the Tien Shan and the Pamir–Alai mountain systems, with the Kara Kum and Kyzyl Kum deserts, and watered by the Syr Darya and Amu Darya. There are settlements along these rivers, but the population is concentrated mainly in the high valleys of the SE, esp. the fertile Fergana Valley, where water from the mountain streams is available for irrigation. Under the Tsarist régime Russian Turkestan was divided into the Khanate of Khiva, the Emirate of Bukhara, and the Governor-Generalship of Turkestan, but after the Revolution the area was redistributed on a nationality basis among the Kazakh, Kirghiz, Tadzhik, Turkmen, and Uzbek SSRs. Agricultural and industrial development followed and was greatly stimulated by the construction of the famous Turkestan–Siberian or Turksib Railway. Chinese Turkestan is centred on the Tarim Basin, S of the Tien Shan, but is generally held to include also Dzungaria, in the N of the Sinkiang–Uighur AR. The majority of the peoples of Turkestan are Muslims, and a form of Turkish provides a *lingua franca*; in the Chinese region they have frequently come into conflict with their rulers, the last serious Muslim rebellion in Sinkiang taking place in the 1930s.

**Turkey.** A republic mainly in SW Asia, with a small area in SE Europe. Area 301,302 sq. m. Pop. (1965) 31,391,207. Cap. Ankara. Lang. mainly Turkish. Rel. 99 per cent Muslim.

The major part, about 97 per cent of the total area, consists of Asia Minor, which is bounded by the Black Sea (N), the USSR and Iran (E), Iraq, Syria, and the Mediterranean Sea (S), and the Aegean Sea (W). This region is separated from Turkey in Europe by the Bosporus, the Sea of Marmara, and the Dardanelles. The European part occupies E Thrace, bounded by Bulgaria (N) and Greece (W). Turkey is primarily an agricultural and pastoral country; where irrigation is practised the soil is fertile, but only about 20 per cent of the land is cultivated and a much greater area is used as pasture. Modernization is slowly taking place, largely through foreign aid. For administrative purposes the country is divided into 67 *ils* or provinces.

TOPOGRAPHY, CLIMATE. The Anatolian Plateau, which forms the greater part of Turkey in Asia, has an average height of about 3,000 ft and is bounded in the N by a series of ranges known as the Pontic Mountains and in the S by the Taurus Mountains, the former roughly parallel to the Black Sea coast and the latter to the Mediterranean coast. Towards the E the Taurus, the parallel Anti-Taurus, and the Pontic Mountains converge and rise to the knot of the Armenian highlands, which contain the country's highest peak, Mt Ararat (16,916 ft), and its largest lake, L. Van. The most important rivers, the Euphrates and the Tigris, flow generally S from E Anatolia to Syria and Iraq; the longest river entirely in Turkey is the Kizil Irmak, which enters the Black Sea – but none of the many Turkish rivers is navigable. On the plateau the climate is dry, with hot summers and cold winters, and only the limited plains along the W and S coasts enjoy a Mediterranean type of climate; rainfall is heaviest along the E Black Sea coast.

RESOURCES, PEOPLE, GOVERNMENT. Of the grain crops wheat and barley occupy by far the greatest acreage. These and other cereals are grown mainly for domestic consumption, and the country is better known for its export crops, the chief of which is tobacco, cultivated particularly in the Samsun district. Cotton, grown largely in the Adana district, and hazelnuts, from the NE coastal region, are also important exports, and grapes (partly for sultanas), olives, citrus fruits, and figs are produced on the W and S coastal plains. In recent years considerable tracts of land have been distributed among peasants who were either landless or owned areas that were inadequate for subsistence. Large flocks of sheep and goats, including the Angora goats which yield mohair, are raised on the plateau. There are probably substantial mineral resources, hitherto little worked owing to poverty of communications. Turkey is one of the world's leading producers of chrome ore; coal, lignite, iron ore, and petroleum are exploited. Industries are still at an early stage of development, and many of them, like the mines and forests, are owned by the state. They are situated mainly in Istanbul (the leading seaport), Ankara, Izmir (Smyrna; also an important seaport), and Adana. Main steel plants at Karabük and Ereğli (1965); chief hydroelectric power station at Hirfanli (1960), on the Kizil Irmak.

The largest minority in the population of Turkey are the Kurds, who dwell mostly in the E provinces, and, like the Turks themselves, are Sunni Muslims; they number about 2,180,000 (1965). Of the smaller minorities the most numerous are the Arabs, Circassians, Greeks, Armenians, and Georgians. Although the people are so predominantly Muslim, Islam has not been recognized as the state religion since 1928. Many of the more progressive elements were lost to the country through the enforced emigration of Greeks in the 1920s and the earlier massacres and emigration of Armenians. Nevertheless, the literacy rate rose from 11 per cent in 1927, when long overdue reforms were just beginning to take effect, to 49 per cent in 1968; elementary education is compulsory and in state schools free. Since 1928 the Latin script has been in use, and since 1929 the publication of books in Arabic characters has been forbidden. By the 1961 constitution legislative power is vested in the Grand National Assembly (450 members), and executive power in the President of the Republic and the Council of Ministers. Women have had the franchise since 1934 and the ballot has been secret since 1948. HISTORY. Among the many early civilizations in Anatolia was the Hittite, which flourished in the 2nd millennium B.C., and the ruins of such cities as Troy and Ephesus bear witness to the importance of the region. In the 11th cent. A.D. the conquerors were the Seljuk Turks, who spread W from the deserts of Turkestan and established a powerful empire, to be followed by the Ottoman or Osmanli Turks, themselves driven W by the Mongols. Osman I

(Othman), leader of the Ottomans, took the title of Sultan, and thus founded the Ottoman Empire, which was to survive for more than 6 centuries till the end of the 1st World War. The Ottomans invaded Europe, taking Constantinople (Istanbul) in 1453; by the mid 16th cent. they had conquered the Balkan Peninsula and most of Hungary, as well as Syria, Egypt, Arabia, Mesopotamia, and Tripolitania. In 1683, however, they were defeated outside Vienna, and the long period of decline began. Britain and France, seeking to curb the expansion of Russia, fought with Turkey in the Crimean War (1854–6) – but the Turks were gradually being forced back towards the Bosporus. The Greeks won their independence (1829) and by the Treaty of Berlin (1878), following revolts in the Balkans and another war with Russia, so also did Serbia, Rumania, and Bulgaria. Despite the efforts of the nationalistic Young Turks, the country suffered further humiliation when Tripolitania was seized by Italy (1911–12) and the army was driven out of Albania and Macedonia and utterly defeated in the Balkan War (1912–13). In the 1st World War Turkey took sides with Germany; at the end Syria, Palestine, Mesopotamia (Iraq), and Arabia were lost. The Turks now found an outstanding leader in Mustafa Kemal, later known as Kemal Atatürk; he became the first President of the Republic (1923) when the Sultanate was abolished, and with dictatorial powers he inaugurated a drastic policy of westernization. During the 2nd World War Turkey remained neutral.

**Turkmen SSR** USSR. Constituent republic of the USSR, in Central Asia, bounded on the W by the Caspian Sea and on the S by Iran and Afghanistan. Area 188,400 sq. m. Pop. (1970) 2,158,000. Cap. Ashkhabad. Consists mainly of an arid lowland, almost 80 per cent of its area being occupied by the Kara-Kum desert, and the population is concentrated in oases along the Amu Darya, Murghab, and Tedzhen rivers and in the foothills of the Kopet Dagh Mountains (S). Irrigation has been much improved, esp. with the construction of the Kara-Kum Canal from the Tedzhen oases to the Amu Darya (1954–60), later extended to Ashkhabad (1961–2). Cotton is the most important crop, maize the chief grain; sericulture and fruit and vegetable growing are important. Karakul and other

751TUVA ASSR

sheep, goats, and cattle and a special breed of Turkoman horses are raised. Fishing and fish canning along the Caspian Sea coast. Considerable mineral resources; oil is produced in the Nebit Dag district and sodium sulphate around the Kara Bogaz Gol. Leading industrial centres (all on the Trans-Caspian Railway) Ashkhabad, Chardzhou, Mary. About 70 per cent of the population are Turkmens (who are Sunni Muslims), 17 per cent Russians, and 8 per cent Uzbeks. Until conquered by the Russians (1881), the Turkmen tribes were largely nomadic; their republic was founded 1924.

Turks and Caicos Islands W Indies. Two groups of islands, geographically part of the Bahamas; a British Crown Colony. Area 166 sq. m. Pop. (1960) 5,716. Chief town Grand Turk, on Grand Turk Island. The Turks Islands Passage, 22 m. wide, separates the Turks Is. (E) from the Caicos Is. (W). There are about 30 islands, of which 6 are inhabited. The centre of government is at Grand Turk. Largest island Grand Caicos, 25 m. long and 12 m. wide. Severe damage is caused from time to time by hurricanes, recently esp. in 1945 and 1960. Principal industry salt panning. Main exports salt, crawfish. Discovered (1512) by Juan Ponce de León. First settled (1678) by Bermudians (who established the salt-panning industry). Placed under the Bahamas (1799), then under Jamaica (1873). Became a British Crown Colony when Jamaica became independent (1962).

Turku (Swedish Åbo) Finland. Capital of Turku-Pori province, Finland's third largest city, on the Gulf of Bothnia 95 m. WNW of Helsinki. Pop. (1968) 149,078. Seaport with a harbour kept open throughout the winter. Industrial and cultural centre. Exports timber, butter, etc. Shipbuilding, sawmilling, sugar refining, etc. Seat of Swedish (1919) and Finnish (1922) universities; an earlier university (founded 1640) was moved to Helsinki after Turku was almost destroyed by fire in 1827. Founded 1229. Capital of Finland until 1812.

Turnhout Belgium. Industrial and market town in Antwerp province 25 m. ENE of Antwerp. Pop. (1968) 37,803. Manufactures paper, playing cards, textiles, agricultural implements, cement, bricks, etc. The town hall was once a palace of the dukes of Brabant.

Turnu Severin Rumania. Ancient Drobeta, Turris Severi. Capital of Mehedinţi district, in Walachia, on the Danube R. below the Iron Gate (Yugoslav frontier). Pop. (1968) 46,010. River port. Shipbuilding, railway engineering, etc. Trade in cereals, petroleum, etc. Near by are the remains of Trajan's bridge (A.D. 103) over the Danube, parts of which are sometimes visible.

Turriff Scotland. Small burgh in Aberdeenshire 31 m. NNW of Aberdeen. Pop. (1961) 2,686. Market town. Engineering. Scene of the first engagement of the Civil War in Scotland, called the 'Trot of Turriff' (1639).

Tuscaloosa USA. Industrial town in Alabama, on the Black Warrior R. 50 m. SW of Birmingham. Pop. (1960) 63,370. Oil refining. Manufactures cotton goods, paper, tyres, etc. Seat of the University of Alabama (1831). State capital 1826–46.

Tuscany (Italian Toscana) Italy. Region in central Italy bordering W on the Ligurian and Tyrrhenian Seas, corresponding roughly to the ancient Etruria and comprising the provinces of Apuania, Arezzo, Florence (Firenze), Grosseto, Leghorn (Livorno), Lucca, Pisa, Pistoia, and Siena. Area 8,876 sq. m. Pop. (1961) 3,267,374. Cap. Florence. Mainly mountainous. Drained chiefly by the Arno R. and its tributaries. Wheat, vines, and olives cultivated. Most of Italy's iron ore (island of Elba) and mercury (Siena) are mined here. Chief towns Florence, Leghorn, Pisa, Lucca, Siena. A grand duchy from 1567 almost continuously until 1860; it then joined the kingdom of Sardinia, and that of Italy in 1861.

Tuticorin India. Seaport in Madras, on the Gulf of Mannar 80 m. S of Madurai. Pop. (1961) 124,230. Exports cotton goods, coffee, etc. Also a railway terminus. Manufactures cotton goods. Salt works. Founded in the 16th cent. by the Portuguese; long held by the Dutch.

Tuttlingen Federal German Republic. Town in Baden-Württemberg, on the Danube R. 58 m. SSW of Stuttgart. Pop. (1963) 25,400. Manufactures surgical instruments, footwear, etc.

Tutuila Island ◊ Samoa.

Tuva ASSR USSR. Autonomous republic in RSFSR, situated between the Sayan mountains (N) and the Tannu Ola Mountains (S) and bounded on the S by the Mongolian People's Republic. Area 65,810 sq. m. Pop. (1970) 231,000. Cap. Kyzyl.

Extensive pastures. Main occupation cattle rearing. The Tuvans, who form about three quarters of the population, are a Turkic people who were formerly ruled by tribal chiefs. Their region was a Chinese dependency, became a Russian protectorate (1914), gained independence as the Tannu Tuva People's Republic (1921), and was incorporated into the USSR (1944) as an Autonomous Region. Raised to the status of Autonomous Republic 1961.

**Tuxtla Gutiérrez** Mexico. Capital of Chiapas state, in the S, 440 m. ESE of Mexico City at a height of 1,750 ft. Pop. 41,000. Market town in an agricultural region producing coffee, sugar cane, tobacco, etc.

**Tuz, Lake** Turkey. Salt lake in central Turkey, 65 m. SSE of Ankara at a height of 2,900 ft. Area 625 sq. m. in winter, much reduced in summer. Large quantities of salt produced.

**Tuzla** Yugoslavia. Town in Bosnia-Hercegovina W of the Majevica (mountain range) 50 m. NNE of Sarajevo. Pop. (1961) 53,008. In a district producing salt, lignite, coal.

**Tver** ◊ *Kalinin.*

**Tweeddale** ◊ *Peeblesshire.*

**Tweed River** England/Scotland. River 97 m. long rising in SW Peeblesshire in Tweed's Well, flowing first NE across the county. It turns E through the counties of Selkirk and Roxburgh, then NE, forming part of the boundary between Scotland and England, and finally E again, to cross Northumberland for about 3 m. and enter the North Sea at Berwick-on-Tweed. Chief tributaries are the Ettrick Water, Teviot, and Till. Cereals and root crops are grown in its lower valley, the Merse. Sheep are raised on the surrounding hills; several small towns on its banks have become woollen-manufacturing centres, esp. Peebles and Galashiels. The name 'tweed' for woollen cloth is believed to derive from a misreading of 'tweel' (Scottish for twill) by association with the river.

**Twickenham** England. Former municipal borough in Middlesex, on the N bank of the R. Thames 11 m. WSW of London; from 1965 part of the Greater London borough of Richmond-upon-Thames. Pop. (1961) 100,822. Mainly residential. Hampton, Hampton Wick, and Teddington were added to the borough in 1937. Contains the English Rugby Football Union ground, Hampton Court Palace, and Bushy Park.

**Tyburn Brook** England. Short stream in W London, flowing S from Hampstead towards the R. Thames, now an underground sewer. Gave its name to Tyburn gallows (near the modern Marble Arch), used for public executions until 1783.

**Tyler** USA. Town in Texas 95 m. ESE of Dallas. Pop. (1960) 51,230. Famous chiefly for its rose-growing industry. Also oil refining, iron founding, food processing. Manufactures cottonseed oil, clothing, etc. Has an annual rose festival (Oct.).

**Tynemouth** England. County borough in Northumberland, at the mouth of the R. Tyne 7 m. ENE of Newcastle upon Tyne. Pop. (1961) 70,112. Seaside resort. Residential and industrial town. Includes North Shields, which is largely industrial: ship repairing, engineering, etc. Ruins of an ancient priory and castle.

**Tyne River** England. River formed by the union of the N Tyne, which rises in the SW Cheviot Hills and flows 32 m. SE, and the S Tyne, which rises near Cross Fell and flows 33 m. N and E. The two rivers join 2 m. above Hexham, and the Tyne then flows 30 m. E past Blaydon, Newcastle upon Tyne, Gateshead, Wallsend, Hebburn, Jarrow, and South Shields to the North Sea at Tynemouth. The valleys of the two headstreams are picturesque, but the Tyne for the last 18 m. of its course, where it forms the boundary between Northumberland and Durham, passes through a region of collieries, shipyards, and factories.

**Tyre (Ar. Sur)** Lebanon. Ancient Phoenician city and seaport 45 m. SSW of Beirut, now a small commercial town. Pop. 12,000. Trade in cotton, tobacco. Originally built on an island, but accumulation of sand has turned this into a peninsula. Probably founded in the 15th cent. B.C. One of its kings, the biblical Hiram, traded with Solomon, and built a causeway linking the island with the mainland. Its island fortress gave it a strong defence, and in the 6th cent. B.C. it withstood siege by Nebuchadnezzar for 13 years. It was taken and destroyed by Alexander the Great, however, after 7 months' siege. Tyre quickly recovered, and flourished again under the Seleucids and the Romans, acquiring fame for its silks and its Tyrian purple dye. It was taken by the Arabs in the 7th cent. A.D., and by the Crusaders (1124); in 1291 it was destroyed by the Muslims and never completely recovered.

**Tyrol** ◊ *Tirol.*

**Tyrone** Northern Ireland. County W of Lough Neagh, bordered by Co. Donegal in the Irish Republic (W). Area 1,218 sq. m. Pop. (1961) 133,930. County town Omagh. Hilly; the Sperrin Mountains along the N boundary rise to 2,240 ft in Sawel. Oats and potatoes cultivated. Dairy cattle raised.

**Tyumen** USSR. Capital of the Tyumen region, RSFSR, on the Tura R. 180 m. E of Sverdlovsk. Pop. (1970) 269,000. Industrial centre. Linked by rail with Sverdlovsk and Omsk. Tanning, sawmilling, boatbuilding. Manufactures carpets, chemicals, etc. One of the oldest towns in Siberia (1585). For 3 centuries the gateway to Siberia, till superseded by Chelyabinsk with the building of the Trans-Siberian Railway. From 1964 the centre of a region producing oil and natural gas.

# U

**UAR** ◊ *United Arab Republic*.

**Ubangi River**. River 700 m. long in Central Africa, formed by the union of the Mbomu and the Uèle rivers, flowing generally W along the frontier between Congo (Kinshasa) and the Central African Republic, turning S near Bangui, forming the frontier between Congo (Kinshasa) and Congo (Brazzaville), and joining the Congo R. W of L. Tumba. Navigable in parts of the upper and lower courses.

**Ube** Japan. Town in Yamaguchi prefecture, Honshu, on the Inland Sea 75 m. WSW of Hiroshima. Pop. (1965) 158,985. Coalmining and industrial centre. Manufactures chemicals, cement, etc. Railway entineering.

**Úbeda** Spain. Town in Jaén province, Andalusia, 28 m. NE of Jaén. Pop. (1961) 28,956. Manufactures olive oil, soap. Tanning, flour milling, distilling. Has ancient Moorish walls and Renaissance architecture.

**Uberaba** Brazil. Town in Minas Gerais state 260 m. W of Belo Horizonte at a height of 2,300 ft. Pop. 72,000. Important rail and road junction; centre of a cattle-rearing and agricultural region. Sugar milling. Manufactures lime.

**Ucayali River** Peru. River 1,000 m. long, formed in the E Peruvian *montaña* by the union of the Apurímac and the Urubamba rivers, flowing generally N to join the Marañón R. and form the main course of the Amazon R. Navigable for 600 m.

**Udaipur** India. Town in S Rajasthan, at the S end of the Aravalli Hills 215 m. SW of Jaipur. Pop. (1961) 111,139. Trade in grain and cotton. Minor industries. Standing at a height of 2,469 ft, it is beautifully situated in the wooded hills, and on its W side is the picturesque L. Pichola, on whose two small islands there are palaces of the 17th and 18th cent. Capital of the former princely state of Udaipur (Mewar) 1568–1948; has a 16th-cent. maharana's palace.

**Uddevalla** Sweden. Industrial town and railway junction in Göteborg och Bohus county, on Byfiord, 44 m. N of Göteborg. Pop. (1968) 36,480. Manufactures textiles, paper, matches, etc.

**Udine** Italy. Capital of Friuli-Venezia Giulia and Udine province, 62 m. NE of Venice. Pop. (1961) 86,188. Industrial centre. Manufactures textiles, paper, furniture, pharmaceutical products, etc. Sugar refining, tanning. Has a 13th-cent. Romanesque cathedral standing in an arcaded square, a 15th-cent. Gothic town hall, and a 16th/18th-cent. archbishop's palace with frescoes by Tiepolo.

**Udmurt ASSR USSR**. Formerly Votyak AR. Autonomous republic in RSFSR, W of the Urals between the Vyatka and Kama rivers. Area 16,250 sq. m. Pop. (1970) 1,417,000 (52 per cent Udmurts, 43 per cent Russians) Cap. Izhevsk. Consists largely of forests, which provide timber. Chief crop flax; rye, oats, potatoes also cultivated. Industries largely centred in Izhevsk. The Udmurts, formerly known as Votyaks, were colonized by the Russians in the 16th cent., and the Votyak Autonomous Region was constituted in 1920. In 1932 the name was changed to Udmurt, and in 1934 it was raised to the status of an Autonomous Republic.

**Uèle River** Congo (Kinshasa). River 750 m. long in Central Africa, rising NW of L. Albert near the frontier between Congo (Kinshasa) and Uganda as the Kibali R., flowing NW, then taking a meandering course W through an important cotton-growing region and joining the Mbomu R. at Yakoma to form the Ubangi R.

**Ufa USSR**. Capital of the Bashkir ASSR, RSFSR, at the confluence of the Ufa and Belaya rivers. Pop. (1970) 773,000 (246,000 in 1939). Oil-refining centre, connected by pipeline with the Volga–Ural oilfield. Also a railway junction and industrial town. Engineering, sawmilling, food processing. Manufactures chemicals, machinery, electrical equipment, paper, matches, etc. University (1957). Founded in the 16th cent.; became a commercial centre on the route to Siberia. Became capital of the Bashkir ASSR 1922. Birthplace of S. T. Aksakov (1791–1859).

**Ufa River USSR**. River 450 m. long, rising in the S Urals, flowing NW and then SSW to join the Belaya R. at Ufa. Extensively used for floating timber.

**Uganda**. Republic in E Africa, a member of the British Commonwealth. Area

93,981 sq. m. (13,680 sq. m. water and swamp, with part of lakes Victoria, Albert, and Edward and the whole of L. Kioga). Pop. (1963) 7,189,600 (7,093,000 Africans, 82,000 Indians, 10,000 Europeans, many of them Polish refugees; nearly half the Africans are Bantu, the others of Nilotic, Hamitic, and Sudanese tribes). Cap. Kampala. Bounded by Sudan (N), Kenya (E), Tanzania and Rwanda (S), and Congo (Kinshasa) (W). Four provinces: Northern, Eastern, Western, and ◊ *Buganda*; the last was formerly a native kingdom (cap. Entebbe) under a Kabaka (king).

Part of the E African plateau, at a height of 3,000–4,500 ft, with the Ruwenzori highlands (16,794 ft) near the Congo (Kinshasa) frontier, Mt Elgon (14,178 ft) on the Kenya frontier, and other peaks, far above this level. Climate tropical. Annual rainfall 40–55 ins. with two rainy seasons, March–May and Sept.–Nov. In the wooded savannah (covering much of the country) elephant, buffalo, antelope, and other game abound. Main exports cotton and coffee, the former wholly and the latter very largely grown by Africans. Tea and tobacco also produced. Food crops bananas, maize, millet. Chief minerals copper and cobalt, obtained at Kilembe. The railway from Mombasa (Kenya) is now extended to near-by Kasese. Industrial expansion is planned, utilizing hydroelectric power from the Owen Falls scheme.

The Englishman John Speke was the first European to explore the region (1862). Buganda came under the control of the Imperial British E Africa Company in 1890 and a British protectorate was proclaimed in 1894; adjoining territories were added in 1896. From 1948 the technical services (railways, mail, customs, etc.) were co-ordinated with those of Tanganyika (now Tanzania) and Kenya, under the E Africa High Commission, reorganized as the E African Common Services Organization in 1961. Became an independent member of the UN 1962. The Kabaka of Buganda, who had been President of all Uganda, was deposed in 1966 and fled the country; his office was taken over by the then Prime Minister, Dr Milton Obote.

**Uist, North and South** Scotland. Islands in the Outer Hebrides, in Inverness-shire, N Uist being 8 m. SW of Harris across the Sound of Harris. N Uist, 17 m. long and 13 m. wide, is swampy and hilly, rising

to 1,138 ft in Ben Eaval, in the E, and here are the sea lochs Maddy and Eport. Pop. (1961) 1,921. Chief village Lochmaddy. Just S is the smaller island of Benbecula. S again is S Uist, 22 m. long and 8 m. wide, which rises to 2,034 ft in Ben More and has the sea lochs Eynort and Boisdale. Pop. (1961) 3,983. Chief village Lochboisdale. Main occupations on both islands crofting and fishing. S Uist was the birthplace of Flora Macdonald (1722–90).

**Uitenhage** S Africa. Town in Cape Province 18 m. NW of Port Elizabeth. Pop. (1968) 65,460 (22,000 white). Railway engineering. Manufactures textiles, tyres, etc. Founded 1804.

**Ujda** ◊ *Oujda*.

**Ujiji** Tanzania. Small port on the E shore of L. Tanganyika. Pop. 12,000. Once a centre of the Arab slave and ivory trade. Famous as the place where Livingstone was found by Stanley (1871).

**Ujjain** India. Town in Madhya Pradesh, on the Sipra R. 35 m. NNW of Indore. Pop. (1961) 144,161. Trade in grain, cotton, etc. Manufactures textiles, hosiery, tiles, etc. A sacred city of the Hindus and a well-known place of pilgrimage. Seat of Vikram University (1957). An ancient city, it was capital of the former Gwalior state in the second half of the 18th cent.

**UK** ◊ *United Kingdom*.

**Ukrainian SSR (Ukraine)** USSR. Constituent republic. Area 231,990 sq. m. Pop. (1970) 47,136,000 (77 per cent Ukrainians, 17 per cent Russians). Cap. Kiev. Bounded by the Sea of Azov and the Black Sea (S) and by Rumania, Moldavia, Hungary, Czechoslovakia, Poland (SW and W). Divided into 25 Regions: Cherkassy, Chernigov, Chernovtsy, Crimea, Dnepropetrovsk, Donetsk, Ivan Franko, Khmelnitsky, Kharkov, Kherson, Kiev, Kirovograd, Lugansk, Lvov, Nikolayev, Odessa, Poltava, Rovno, Sumy, Ternopol, Vinnitsa, Volhynia, Zakarpatskaya, Zaporozhye, Zhitomir.

The richest agricultural region in the USSR; the Donets basin is one of the leading coalfields. Highly important deposits of iron ore at Krivoi Rog and of manganese at Nikopol. Great iron and steel industry. Principally lowland, with a section of the Carpathians in the extreme W in Zakarpatskaya (the Transcarpathian Region, ◊ *Ruthenia*). Chief rivers the Dniester, the S Bug, the Dnieper and its tributaries, and the N Donets. Three main natural regions: the level and often marshy forests of the NW; the wooded steppes of the central area (including some of the rich black-earth soils); the true black-earth steppes of the S. One of the USSR's main granaries, producing nearly a quarter of its grain (wheat, maize) and half its sugar-beet, as well as potatoes, sunflower seeds, dairy produce, etc. About three quarters of the area is under cultivation; in 1968 there were 9,639 collective farms and 1,418 State farms. The Donets basin produces over one third of the USSR's coal. Manufactures iron and steel, machinery, chemicals, food products. Principal towns Kiev, Kharkov, Donetsk, Odessa (chief seaport), Dnepropetrovsk, Lvov (ceded from Poland in 1945), Zaporozhye, Krivoi Rog. On the Dnieper is the famous Dneproges dam.

The N and W formed part of Kievan Russia (which had Kiev as its capital) from the 9th cent. The area was devastated by the Tatar invasion of the 13th cent. Under Polish rule after the union of Lithuania and Poland (1569); many of the peasants fled to the Dnieper and beyond and set up rebel 'Cossack' communities. Russia annexed Kiev and the Ukraine E of the Dnieper in 1667, and the remainder by the Partitions of Poland (1793–5). The 19th-cent. Ukrainian nationalist movement favoured unity with Germany rather than Russia. The Ukrainian SSR, proclaimed in 1917, became part of the USSR on its creation in 1923. By the settlement after the 2nd World War it now includes N Bukovina, part of Bessarabia, the Transcarpathian Region, and the SE of prewar Poland. The Moldavian ASSR was separated and became the Moldavian SSR in 1940. The Crimea was incorporated (from RSFSR) in 1954. Suffered severely in the 2nd World War; occupied by the Germans 1941–4. Theoretically has the right of secession from the USSR.

Ulan Bator Mongolia. Formerly (until 1921) Urga. Capital of the Mongolian People's Republic, 280 m. S of Ulan-Ude (USSR) at a height of 4,300 ft. Pop. (1966) 250,000. The chief industrial and commercial centre. Manufactures woollen goods, saddles, footwear, etc. Linked by rail with Ulan-Ude and the Trans-Siberian Railway, and with Peking (China). Also a cultural centre; seat of the National Choibalsan University (1942). Founded in the mid 17th cent.

Ulan-Ude USSR. Formerly Verkhne-Udinsk. Capital of the Buryat ASSR (RSFSR), on the Selenga R. at the confluence with the Uda R. 135 m. E of Irkutsk. Pop. (1970) 254,000. Industrial centre. Railway engineering, sawmilling, meat packing. Manufactures woollen goods, glass, etc. Also an important route centre on the Trans-Siberian Railway; the railway and road to Ulan Bator (Mongolia) carry considerable trade.

Uleåborg ◊ Oulu.

Ullapool Scotland. Fishing village and resort in Ross and Cromarty, on Loch Broom 45 m. NW of Inverness. Fine mountain and coast scenery.

Ullswater England. Scenically beautiful lake 7½ m. long and ½ m. wide on the Cumberland–Westmorland border 5 m. SW of Penrith, in the Lake District.

Ulm Federal German Republic. Industrial town and railway junction in Baden-Württemberg, on the Danube R. 46 m. SE of Stuttgart. Pop. (1963) 94,400. Manufactures metal goods, textiles, cement, etc. Brewing, tanning. An ancient town; many of its historic buildings were damaged in the 2nd World War, but the dominating 14th-cent. cathedral was unscathed. Its tower, not completed till 1890, is the highest in Germany (528 ft). An important trade centre in the Middle Ages; became a free imperial city in 1155. Linked with Neu-Ulm (pop. 25,100) on the opposite bank of the Danube in Bavaria by 4 bridges. Birthplace of Albert Einstein (1879–1955).

Ulster Ireland. The NE province of ancient Ireland. Nine counties: Antrim, Armagh, Down, Fermanagh, Londonderry (Derry), Tyrone (Northern Ireland); Cavan, Donegal, Monaghan (Irish Republic). Area 8,556 sq. m. Pop. (1961) 1,642,986 (Northern Ireland 1,425,462; Irish Republic 217,524). Largely agricultural. Important shipbuilding, linen, and other industries, centred chiefly on Belfast. Throughout the 17th cent. most of the land was confiscated and distributed among English and Scottish settlers (the 'Plantation'). The Unionist Protestant party violently opposed the Home Rule movement 1885–1920; Ireland and Ulster were partitioned by the 1921 Government of Ireland Act, establishing 6 counties as Northern Ireland and the remaining 26 as the Irish Free State (since 1948 the Irish Republic).

Ulverston England. Urban district in

Lancashire 8 m. NE of Barrow-in-Furness. Pop. (1961) 10,515. Market town. Engineering, tanning, etc. Birthplace of Sir John Barrow (1764–1848), the explorer.

**Ulyanovsk** USSR. Formerly (until 1924) Simbirsk. Capital of the Ulyanovsk region, RSFSR, on a hill above the right bank of the Volga R., between this river and the Sviyaga R. 110 m. NW of Kuibyshev. Pop. (1970) 351,000. River port. Railway junction. Industrial centre. Manufactures machinery, motor vehicles, etc. Sawmilling, tanning, brewing, flour milling. Founded 1648. Renamed after Lenin (V. I. Ulyanov, 1870–1924), who was born here; also birthplace of Ivan Goncharov (1812–91).

**Umbria** Italy. Region in central Italy in the Apennines, comprising the provinces of Perugia and Terni. Area 3,281 sq. m. Pop. (1961) 788,546. Largely mountainous. Drained by the upper Tiber. Contains L. Trasimeno. Produces cereals, wine, olive oil. Some industry at Terni. The Umbrians allied themselves with Rome early in the 3rd cent. B.C. The Umbrian school of painting of the 15th–16th cent. included Perugino and Raphael.

**Umeå** Sweden. Capital of Västerbotten county, at the mouth of the Ume R. 140 m. NE of Sundsvall. Pop. (1968) 51,952. Port. Industrial centre. Exports timber, tar. Manufactures machinery, wood pulp, furniture.

**Umm Said** ◊ *Qatar.*

**Umtali** Rhodesia. Town 130 m. SE of Salisbury near the Moçambique frontier at a height of 3,550 ft. Pop. (1968) 53,500 (43,000 Africans). Market town on the Beira–Salisbury railway. Engineering. Manufactures textiles, clothing, etc. Gold mining in the neighbourhood.

**Umtata** S Africa. Capital of the Transkeian Territories and of the Tembuland district, Cape Province, on the Umtata R. 115 m. NNE of East London. Pop. (1960) 12,287. Terminus of the railway from East London. Has an Anglican cathedral.

**Ungava** Canada. District in N Quebec around Ungava Bay, including the Ungava Peninsula (W). Area 351,780 sq. m. Pop. 3,000. Immense iron-ore resources. Annexed to Quebec 1912.

**Union City** USA. Industrial town in New Jersey just N of Jersey City. Pop. (1960) 52,180. Manufactures textiles, electrical equipment, pharmaceutical products, etc.

**Union Islands** ◊ *Tokelau Islands.*

**Union of Soviet Socialist Republics (USSR, Soviet Union).** By far the largest single country in the world, occupying more than one seventh of the world's land surface. Area 8,649,512 sq. m. Pop. (1970) 241,748,000 (55 per cent Russians, 18 per cent Ukrainians, 4 per cent Byelorussians, etc.). Cap. Moscow. Languages Russian and the local national languages.

Bounded by the Arctic Ocean (N) and the Pacific (E). Most of the S frontier is with China and Mongolia and the remainder with Afghanistan, Iran, and Turkey. The W frontiers are with Rumania, Hungary, Czechoslovakia, Poland, Finland, and Norway. Politically one of the two principal world powers (the other being the USA). The leading communist state, but this is being challenged by China, the world's most populous country. Before the Revolution primarily agricultural; one of the Soviet régime's outstanding achievements has been its transformation into a predominantly industrial state. Industrial production, 42 per cent of the total in 1913, was 77 per cent in 1962. With its great natural resources, virtually self-sufficient. Comprises 15 constituent republics (SSRs): RSFSR (Russian Soviet Federated Socialist Republic), the largest and most populous; the Ukraine; Byelorussia; Turkmenia; Uzbekistan; Tadzhikistan; Kazakhstan; Armenia; Georgia; Azerbaijan; Kirghizia; Lithuania; Latvia; Estonia; Moldavia.

TOPOGRAPHY, CLIMATE. At its greatest width, the USSR extends from about longitude 20° E to 170° W, almost halfway round the world; and from Cape Chelyuskin, latitude 77° N, as far S as 35° N on the Afghanistan frontier. The W half mainly consists of a vast lowland area; the Ural Mountains (usually taken as the boundary between European and Asian Russia) separate the E European Plain from the W Siberian. E of the latter are the Central Siberian Plateau and then the lofty mountain ranges of the Far East with peaks exceeding 10,000 ft. The highest mountains lie along the S frontiers, e.g. the Caucasus (separating Europe from Asia) with Mt Elbruz (18,481 ft), the Pamirs and the Alai Mountains, with Peak Kommunizma (formerly Stalin Peak, 24,590 ft), the highest point in the USSR; also the Tien Shan, the Altai, the W and E Sayan Mountains, the Yablonovy and Stanovoi Ranges. Near the Caspian Sea, however, the land sinks to more than 400 ft below sea level. The USSR has some of the world's longest rivers, many of value for navigation and for electric power: in Europe the Volga, the Ural, the Dnieper, the Don, and the N Dvina; in Asia the Ob, the Yenisei, the Lena, and the Amur. Among the lakes are the Caspian Sea (the world's largest), L. Ladoga, and L Onega (Europe), and the Aral Sea, L. Baikal, and L. Balkhash (Asia).

The climate of such an enormous land mass is bound to show wide variations, but in general it is continental, with hot summers and cold winters (becoming more severe W–E). The earth's 'Cold Pole' is at Verkhoyansk (NE Siberia). Annual rainfall is heaviest along the SE shore of the Black Sea (93 ins. at Batumi); elsewhere it is 15–25 ins. (decreasing to less than 10 ins. in the dry SW). The main regions of natural vegetation are closely influenced by climate: tundra along the Arctic coast; coniferous forest (taiga) and smaller deciduous and mixed forests, about half of the total area; steppe (grasslands), including the fertile black-earth region; desert and semi-desert, in Central Asia N and E of the Caspian Sea; a relatively small Mediterranean region in S Crimea.

RESOURCES, INDUSTRY, TRANSPORT. The northern forests shelter large numbers of fur-bearing animals, e.g. fox, marten, sable, which provide pelts for the fur trade: many animals (e.g. mink) are now raised in captivity on fur farms. The forests provide enormous quantities of timber; afforestation over a wide area added further resources under the Seven-year Plan 1959–65. Though stressing the importance of industrialization, the Soviet régime has completely reorganized agriculture (which under the Tsars had been notoriously backward), putting the peasants to work on collective and State farms and introducing large-scale mechanization; there are 36,800 collective farms and 12,783 State farms. Some plans have failed (e.g. the reclamation of the 'Virgin Lands') but great increases in production have been achieved: between 1913 and 1962 the output of grain and sugar-beet was more than trebled, that of raw cotton was increased sixfold, the area of irrigated land was almost trebled, and the amount of chemical fertilizers used annually increased more than 70-fold. Other important crops are potatoes, flax, sunflowers, tobacco. Tea and citrus fruits are grown in the Black Sea area. Large numbers of cattle, sheep, and pigs are reared; the 1913 output of meat had been more than doubled and that of milk more than quadrupled by 1962.

The USSR has immense power resources. In world production of coal and petroleum it ranks first and second respectively. The main coalfields are the Donets and Kuznetsk basins and the main oilfield the Volga-Ural (the 'second Baku'). In iron-ore and manganese output the USSR leads the world. Other important minerals include bauxite, chromite, gold, phosphates. Steel output increased 18-fold 1913–62 and is now second only to that of the USA. Industry is well distributed, with particular concentration in the regions around Moscow and Leningrad (the two largest cities), the Donets basin, and the Urals. Kiev, Baku, Gorky, Tashkent, and Kharkov are all major industrial centres with more than 1 million inhabitants.

European Russia is better served with railways than Asian Russia, but the network (centred principally on Moscow and Leningrad) is tenuous compared with that of most European countries, though the mileage has been more than doubled since 1913. Important trunk lines include the Trans-Siberian route to Vladivostok (the Pacific seaport); the Trans-Caspian (linking the Caspian Sea with Central Asia); the Turkestan-Siberian ('Turksib', linking the Trans-Caspian with the Trans-Siberian); the route to Vorkuta and the N Urals; and the direct route from Moscow to the Donets basin. Of the Arctic ports, only Murmansk is ice-free throughout the winter. Odessa is the chief seaport on the Black Sea. Increasing use is made of navigable rivers and canals, though they are frozen for varying periods in the winter; the Volga–Don Canal (1952) joins the White Sea, the Baltic, the Caspian, the Black Sea, and the Sea of Azov into a single waterway system. Airways too have great significance in a country of such enormous distances.

PEOPLE, GOVERNMENT, etc. The density of population is highest in the central zone of European Russia (around Moscow) and is lowest in the tundra and forest regions of N Siberia and the deserts of Central Asia; over the USSR as a whole it is lower than for any European country except Iceland. Industrialization has brought some redistribution of population, with a general movement from the rural districts into the towns: the 1926 urban population was 18 per cent of the total, that of 1970 over 55 per cent. Many new towns have arisen in fast-developing industrial areas, e.g. Zaporozhye, Nizhni Tagil, Magnitogorsk, Kramatorsk, Novomoskovsk (European Russia); Karaganda, Novokuznetsk, Kemerovo, Frunze, Prokopyevsk, Dushanbe, Komsomolsk, Anzhero-Sudzhensk (Asian Russia), all with 1970 populations of over 100,000.

Education is free and compulsory from 7 to 15; in large towns and industrial areas the school-leaving age is 17. Besides the many universities, there are 166 Institutions of the USSR Academy of Sciences; 14 of the constituent republics have their own Academies of Sciences. Before the Revolution the great majority of the Russian people belonged to the Eastern Orthodox faith; in 1918 the Church was disestablished and all religions were given an equal status, and more than two thirds of the churches have since closed. Nominally the Russians, Ukrainians and Byelorussians are Eastern Orthodox; the Muslims (about 24 million) form the next most numerous religious group; the Lutherans are mainly in Latvia and Estonia, the Roman Catholics in Lithuania and the formerly Polish W Ukraine, the Buddhists in the Buryat, Kalmuk, and Tuva autonomous republics; there are several Jewish communities.

The basis of the economy is State ownership of the means of production, i.e. the land, mineral deposits, waters, forests, mills, factories, etc. Private enterprise on a small scale is permitted; e.g. the peasant members of collective farms may possess and use small plots of land attached to their homes. The highest legislative organ is the USSR Supreme Soviet (Council) with two chambers, the Union Council and the Council of Nationalities, both elected for four years, the former on the basis of one deputy per 300,000 population (767 members in 1966) and the latter on that of 32 deputies from each Union Republic, 11 from each Autonomous Republic, 5 from each Autonomous Region, and 1 from each National Area (750 members in 1966). The Supreme Soviet elects a Presidium to act as the supreme State authority between sessions and a Council of Ministers which has executive authority and can legislate by decree. Each Union Republic and Autonomous Republic has its own Supreme Soviet (one chamber) and its own Council of Ministers. The influence of the sole political organization, the Communist Party, is felt in most branches of national and Union life.

HISTORY. The early Slavonic peoples of the northern forests were first united by the legendary Viking chief Rurik, who ruled from Novgorod in the 9th cent. A.D. From the 10th to the 12th cent. the Russian tribes were held together under rule from Kiev. One of the Kievan rulers, Vladimir, accepted the Greek form of Christianity (988) and imposed it on his subjects. When the power of Kiev declined the political centre moved to Moscow. In the 13th cent. Russia was overrun by Mongols from the E (the 'Golden Horde'), and it was largely with Mongol help that the principality of Moscow established authority over its neighbours. Ivan III extended its boundaries, and threw off Mongol domination (1480). Ivan IV (named 'the Terrible' for his callous cruelty) took the title of Tsar and conquered Kazan and Astrakhan. A period of confusion followed his death. In 1613 the boyars (nobles) elected Michael Romanov to the throne, the first of a dynasty which was to last till 1917. At about this time serfdom was established; the peasant labourers were forbidden to move from one estate or landowner to another.

The reign of Peter the Great (1682–1725) is noteworthy for his reforms and his efforts to westernize the Russian people. With foreign assistance, he reorganized the administration. He reduced the power of the nobility and the Church, encouraged education, agriculture, industry, and external trade, introduced social changes, founded a navy, and built an entirely new capital at St Petersburg (his 'window on Europe'), all against considerable opposition from his subjects. He also defeated Sweden and acquired much of the Baltic seaboard. His foreign policy was continued by his successors. Under Catherine II (1762–96) Russia benefited territorially from the Partitions of Poland (1793–5) and also annexed the Crimea from Turkey. The reign of Alexander I (1801–25) saw Napoleon's invasion and then his retreat from Moscow; having played a major role in his downfall, Russia then enjoyed great prestige in Europe. The Tsar's early declarations of liberal policy did not result in the long-awaited reforms within Russia, however, and revolutionary ideas began to spread; some reforms were at last introduced in the reign of Alexander II (1855–81): the serfs were liberated (1861); local government (hitherto in the hands of the landowners) was reorganized through the formation of provincial councils ('zemstvos'); judicial procedure was reformed (1864); and Russia took the first hesitant steps towards industrialization. In one of a series of outrages Alexander II was assassinated. Meanwhile, Russian foreign policy led to wars with Turkey, the traditional enemy (including the Crimean War (1854–61) in which she was defeated, though indecisively), but later made extensive gains in Central Asia. The occupation of Manchuria led to the disastrous Russo-Japanese War (1904–5); Russia's rivalry with Germany and Austria (esp. in the Balkans) was largely responsible for the outbreak of the 1st World War.

Nicholas II (1894–1917) was the last of the Tsars. The 1905 revolution was ruthlessly suppressed, but the utter defeat of Russia in the 1st World War assisted the 1917 Bolshevik Revolution, led by Lenin. Despite foreign intervention by 22 nations (1918–22) and civil war (1918–24) the Soviet Union was created (1923) by the union of the Russian SFSR and the Transcaucasian, Ukrainian, and Byelorussian SSRs as the world's first communist state. On the death of Lenin (1924), Stalin assumed power and gradually stifled all opposition. Industrialization was speeded by a series of 5-year plans; agriculture was forcibly collectivized. A non-aggression pact was concluded with Germany (1939), but the German invasion (1941) brought the USSR into the 2nd World War on the side of the Allies. Having suffered terribly in the fighting, esp. in loss of manpower, it emerged from the war with considerable territorial gains: Estonia, Latvia, and Lithuania had been absorbed (1940); large areas were ceded by Poland, Rumania, and Finland, and taken from Germany; in the E, the S of Sakhalin and the Kuril Is. were taken from Japan. Communist régimes were set up in Poland, the German Democratic Republic, Czechoslovakia, Hungary, Rumania, Bulgaria, Albania, and Yugoslavia (but Yugo-

slavia was expelled from the Cominform in 1948, diplomatic relations with Albania were broken off in 1961, and Rumania began opposition to Comecon in 1963). Post-war foreign policy was characterized by hostility towards the West, esp. the USA, exemplified in a number of international incidents; after Stalin's death (1953) this policy was modified, esp. as the threat from the 'imperialist' powers seemed overshadowed by the rise of the ambitious and rapidly developing communist China on the S frontier.

United Arab Republic (Egypt).* Republic in NE Africa. Area 386,198 sq. m. Pop. (1967) 30,907,000. Cap. Cairo. Lang. mainly Arabic. Rel. 91 per cent Muslims, 8 per cent Copts.

Occupies the NE corner of Africa, the adjoining Sinai peninsula, and the narrow coastal belt of SW Palestine known as the Gaza Strip. Sinai and the Gaza Strip, however, were occupied by Israel after the 1967 war. Bounded by the Mediterranean Sea (N), Israel and the Red Sea (E), Sudan (S), and Libya (W). Home of one of the great civilizations of the past; its economy and the way of life of most of its people have changed but little throughout the centuries: agriculture is its mainstay, and it is still as much 'the gift of the Nile' as it was when Herodotus thus described it 2,400 years ago. Only about 13,500 sq. m. or 3·5 per cent of its area, comprising the Nile valley and delta and the oases, has been settled and cultivated; the remainder is desert. The delta area has long been known as Lower Egypt, and the region to the S as Upper Egypt. Divided administratively into 25 governorates: 13 in Lower Egypt, 8 in Upper Egypt, and 4 in the outer desert areas; 5 of the urban governorates, all in Lower Egypt, are based on large towns – Cairo, Alexandria, Port Said, Suez, Ismailia. Cairo is the smallest governorate and the most populous.

TOPOGRAPHY, CLIMATE. The Nile delta is a broad alluvial plain sloping gently down to the Mediterranean, where the coast is lined with sandhills behind which are a number of extensive lagoons. To reach its delta the Nile flows generally N across a low plateau, irrigating a narrow ribbon of land, in places no more than 1 m. in width, so creating with the delta an elongated, fertile oasis in what is substantially the E section of the great Sahara. To the E of the Nile valley is the Arabian

Desert, which rises to a range of mountains bordering the Red Sea, the highest peak being Shayib el Banat (7,175 ft). To the W is the Libyan Desert, the part around the Farafra Oasis being often known as the Western Desert. In the NW the Qattara Depression sinks to about 440 ft below sea level. In the NE the Sinai peninsula rises to 7,497 ft in Jebel Musa (Mt Sinai). The principal oases of the Libyan Desert are Siwa, Bahariya, Farafra, Dakhla, and Kharga; El Faiyum, with its lake Birket Qarun, lies just W of the Nile, with which it is connected by the canalized Bahr Yusef, an old branch of the river.

Everywhere in Egypt winters are mild and summers hot. Along the N coast the climate verges on the Mediterranean type, with Alexandria, for instance, receiving 8 ins. of rain entirely Oct.–April, but even as far N as Cairo the mean annual rainfall is only about 1 in., while farther S the country is virtually rainless. A hot, dry southerly wind known as the *khamsin* is sometimes experienced, chiefly in spring.

RESOURCES, TRADE. Agriculture is dependent on the flood waters of the Nile, and, while much irrigation is still carried out by primitive methods, these are being displaced by a system of dams and barrages, e.g. ◊ *Aswan*. In 1959 the UAR and Sudan concluded an agreement on the sharing of the Nile waters when the new Aswan High Dam is in operation. Cotton is by far the most important crop and represents more than two thirds of the country's exports; wheat, maize, and rice are also widely cultivated, and sugar-cane in Upper Egypt. The great majority of the *fellahin*, or peasants, own smallholdings of 1 acre or less, and even when harvests are good they are unable to rise above a bare subsistence level; attempts have been made in recent years to improve their lot by redistributing land from holdings exceeding 200 acres. Petroleum is drilled around the Gulf of Suez and phosphates are mined on the Red Sea coast. Industries, esp. textile manufactures, have developed considerably since the 2nd World War, and are concentrated in Cairo, Alexandria, Port Said, Tanta, and Mahalla el Kubra.

Alexandria handles most of the country's foreign trade, and Port Said and Suez are the chief ports on the Suez Canal. The latter was nationalized in 1956, and after the ensuing conflict, involving Israel, France, and Britain against Egypt, the

direction of Egyptian foreign trade changed. Trade with Britain and France diminished considerably, while exports to the Soviet bloc countries rose from 14 to 52 per cent and imports from 6 to 30 per cent of the total 1954–9; since 1959, however, there has been a partial recovery of trade with Britain and France.

PEOPLE, GOVERNMENT. The present population with its unchecked birth rate has a density in the settled region of nearly 2,000 per sq. m. – a density which makes urgent the extension of the area of cultivated land through such schemes as the construction of the High Dam. Most of the people are Sunni Muslims; the Copts (mainly Orthodox) are the descendants of Egyptians who were converted to Christianity in the 1st century A.D. Besides the settled population there are probably about 60,000 nomadic Bedouin. About 97 per cent of the total population are Arabic-speaking; there are small minorities of Greeks, Armenians, etc. Education is officially free and compulsory for the ages 6–12, but the illiteracy rate is still high. Since 1962 the republic has been governed by an Executive Council of 25 Ministers and a Defence Council of 20 members, the latter under the chairmanship of the President.

HISTORY. Ancient Egyptian history, from the foundation of the state until its conquest by Alexander the Great, is usually divided into 30 Dynasties. Upper and Lower Egypt were first united *c.* 3400 B.C. by the legendary Menes, whose capital was at Memphis, near Cairo. About 5 centuries later his successors were overthrown by a new king from the S who inaugurated the 4th Dynasty, during which Egyptian culture was exemplified by the building of the pyramids at Giza: monuments, magnificently preserved in the dry Egyptian climate, which have fired the imagination of men throughout the ages. But in the later years of the Old Kingdom the authority of the monarchy was challenged by a powerful nobility, and Egypt sank into a state of anarchy.

Unity was restored and the strength of the nobility reduced in the 11th and 12th Dynasties (Middle Kingdom); Thebes replaced Heracleopolis as capital, and a high standard of art was again achieved, esp. in the reign of Amenemhet III. This period of culture and material prosperity, beginning in the 22nd cent. B.C., was terminated in the 17th cent. by the conquest of Egypt by the Hyksos, or 'Shepherd Kings', a probably Semitic people from SW Asia. Within about a century the Hyksos had been expelled, and under the 18th Dynasty (New Kingdom), c. 1580–1350, a number of vigorous kings, notably Thutmosis III, founded an empire extending into Syria and Mesopotamia; this was the period of the great temples at Luxor and Karnak and the famous tomb of Tutenkhamen (excavated 1922). The reign of Amenhotep IV or Ikhnaton (1375–1358) was marked by his vain attempt to introduce religious reforms in the shape of a new monotheistic sun cult. In the 19th Dynasty Egyptian art had begun to decline, though in the military sphere Seti I and Rameses II dealt successfully with Nubians, Libyans, Syrians, and Hittites; Rameses III (1198–1167) of the 20th Dynasty was also able to repel would-be invaders. A spirit of decadence permeated the country, however, the nobles became virtually independent, and the empire gradually melted away; although the general decline was temporarily halted by various rulers, Egypt was conquered by the Assyrians in the 7th cent. and by the Persians in the 6th and 4th cent. At the second Persian conquest the last native pharaoh fled the country (341).

In 332 B.C. Alexander the Great liberated Egypt from Persian rule, and at his death (323) the country passed to his general Ptolemy, whose descendants ruled until the death of Cleopatra (30 B.C.). It was now Augustus who conquered Egypt, and under the Romans the irrigation system was improved, trade was stimulated, and for about a century the country enjoyed considerable prosperity. Christianity was now introduced, Monophysitism giving rise to the Coptic Church, but from the early years of the 3rd cent. A.D. the Christians were frequently persecuted. It was largely because of religious dissension, in fact, that Egypt, in the Eastern Empire from A.D. 395, fell easily first to the Persians (616) and then to the Arabs (639–42); the Greek and Coptic languages fell into disuse, to be replaced by Arabic, and the country was absorbed into the Islamic world. For more than three centuries (629–968) it was a province of the Eastern caliphate, and was then conquered by the Fatimites, who founded Cairo (969) and the Mosque of El Azhar and remained in power till 1171. They were replaced by Saladin, who founded the semi-independent Ayyubid dynasty, followed in its turn (1250) by the Mamelukes – former slaves who had acquired influence and now usurped the supreme power. The Mamelukes ruled until 1517, when Egypt was conquered by the Ottoman Turks.

Government by Turkish pashas was marked by corruption and assassination, while the common people at times suffered from famine and plague. In 1798 Napoleon invaded Egypt under the pretext of suppressing the still active Mamelukes and restoring Turkish authority but in fact in furtherance of his plans for world domination. By 1801 the French had been expelled by the British in company with the Turks, and after a period of anarchy a former Albanian officer, Mehemet (Mohammed) Ali, was appointed pasha (1805). He established his authority chiefly by exterminating the Mamelukes, and he imposed heavy taxes on the long-suffering *fellahin*, but at least he imposed order throughout Egypt, and he introduced cotton cultivation, improved irrigation, and expanded foreign trade. The reign of Ismail, a grandson of Mehemet Ali, who took the title of khedive in 1867, was noteworthy for the opening of the Suez Canal (1869). By reason of his extravagance he was forced to sell his Suez Canal shares to Britain, and he was deposed (1879) in favour of his son Tewfik. A military revolt (1881–2) led to British occupation of the country, while the Mahdi's rebellion in the Sudan, a part of the khedive's dominions, was put down by Lord Kitchener (1898); the Sudan now became the condominium of the Anglo-Egyptian Sudan. Meanwhile, under the wise guidance of Lord Cromer as consul general (1884–1907), Egypt enjoyed several years of peace and a continually rising prosperity. With the 1st World War the attenuated link with Turkey was broken and Egypt was declared a British protectorate. Owing to nationalist demands for independence, however, Egypt was made a constitutional kingdom under Fuad I, a son of Ismail (1922). By the Anglo-Egyptian Treaty (1936) it became a sovereign state, and the eventual withdrawal of British troops was promised; in the same year Farouk succeeded his father Fuad I as king.

During the 2nd World War Egypt was invaded by Axis forces, which were defeated by the British at El Alamein (1942) and driven out of the country. After the war relations with Britain were strained, partly owing to Egypt's claim to the Sudan, but British troops were withdrawn from Cairo and the delta in 1947, from the Canal Zone in 1954. In 1948 Egypt joined other Arab states in the attack on Israel but won only slight initial success; by the truce of 1949 the small Gaza Strip on the Mediterranean coast was occupied. At home discontent over governmental corruption and inefficiency led to a *coup d'état*: Farouk was compelled to abdicate (1952), and the monarchy was then abolished and the country declared a republic, with General Neguib as president (1953). In 1954 Neguib was forced to resign in favour of Colonel Nasser, and in 1956 a new constitution was approved, providing for a single political party, the National Union Party, its object the establishment of a socialist democratic society. Confronted with the refusal of the USA and Britain to grant financial aid for the projected Aswan High Dam, Nasser nationalized the Suez Canal (1956); Israeli forces invaded Gaza and the Sinai peninsula and were joined by British and French troops, but international pressure soon brought the conflict to an end and Egypt agreed to compensate shareholders of the old Suez Canal Company. In 1958 Egypt united with Syria to form the UAR, which then federated with Yemen as the United Arab States; in 1961, however, the Syrians, objecting to Egyptian domination and to Nasser's socialization programme, withdrew from the UAR; later in the same year Egypt ended the union with Yemen but retained the title of UAR. In the Israeli–Arab war of June 1967 the Egyptian army was quickly defeated, and retreated across the Sinai peninsula to the Suez Canal.

**United Kingdom.** The United Kingdom of Great Britain and Northern Ireland: i.e. England, Wales, Scotland, the Isle of Man, the Channel Is., and 6 of the 9 counties of Ulster. Area 94,500 sq. m. Pop. (1961) 52,828,085. Was the United Kingdom of Great Britain and Ireland 1801–1920; 'Northern Ireland' replaced 'Ireland' after the creation of the Irish Free State by the Government of Ireland Act (1921). Legislative powers for the UK as a whole are vested in the Westminster Parliament; Northern Ireland, the Isle of Man, and the Channel Is. also have their own local legislatures; that of Northern Ireland has full legislative powers except over defence and taxation.

**United States of America.** Federal republic in N America. Area (inc. Great Lakes and other inland waters) 3,775,602 sq. m. Pop. (1970) 204,500,000 (inc. 11 per cent Negroes). Cap. Washington, D.C. Lang. English. Rel. mainly Protestant and Roman Catholic.

The main part of the USA, i.e. excluding the states of Alaska and Hawaii, occupies most of the S half of N America. Bounded by Canada (N), largely along the 49th parallel and the Great Lakes, and Mexico (S), partly along the Rio Grande, lying between the Atlantic (E), the Gulf of Mexico (SE), and the Pacific (W). Alaska lies NW of Canada on the N American mainland and Hawaii in the Pacific. The fourth largest country in the world both in area and in population, but ranks first in industrial production with vast resources – its agricultural land, forests, and almost all the basic industrial raw materials. Its people enjoy an exceptionally high standard of living. Consists of the following 50 states and the District of Columbia (with dates of admission to the Union): *New England* (NE): Maine (1820), New Hampshire (1788), Vermont (1791), Massachusetts (1788), Rhode Island (1790), Connecticut (1788). *Middle Atlantic*: New York (1788), New Jersey (1787), Pennsylvania (1787). *E North Central*: Ohio (1803), Indiana (1816), Illinois (1818), Michigan (1837), Wisconsin (1848). *W North Central*: Minnesota (1858), Iowa (1846), Missouri (1821), N Dakota (1889), S Dakota (1889), Nebraska (1867), Kansas (1861). *S Atlantic*: Delaware (1787), Maryland (1788), District of Columbia (1791), Virginia (1788), W Virginia (1863), N Carolina (1789), S Carolina (1788), Georgia (1788), Florida (1845). *E South Central*: Kentucky (1792), Tennessee (1796), Alabama (1819), Mississippi (1817). *W South Central*: Arkansas (1836), Louisiana (1812), Oklahoma (1907), Texas (1845). *Mountain* (*W*): Montana (1889), Idaho (1890), Wyoming (1890), Colorado (1876), New Mexico (1912), Arizona (1912), Utah (1896), Nevada (1864). *Pacific*: Washington (1889), Oregon (1859), California (1850), Alaska (1959), Hawaii (1960). The District of Columbia is co-extensive with the capital, Washington, D.C. Outlying dependencies of the USA consist of Puerto Rico, the Virgin Is. of the US, the Panama Canal Zone, Guam,

American Samoa, and certain other Pacific islands.

TOPOGRAPHY. The Atlantic coastline is heavily indented, the largest inlet being Chesapeake Bay; at the SE corner is the long peninsula of Florida, and then follows the Gulf coast, extending W to the mouth of the Rio Grande and containing Tampa Bay, the Mississippi delta, and numerous coastal lagoons. Among the many offshore islands on the Atlantic are (N–S) Nantucket and Martha's Vineyard (Mass.), the island of Rhode Island (R.I.), Long Island and Staten Island (N.Y.), the Sea Is. and the Florida Keys. The Pacific coast is much less indented, though it contains Puget Sound (Wash.) and San Francisco Bay (Cal.); the only off-shore islands of note are the Santa Barbara Is. (Cal.) and those in Puget Sound.

The USA is a country of great mountain ranges, vast plains, and long rivers; its highest point is Mt McKinley, Alaska (20,269 ft), and its lowest point is in Death Valley, California, 280 ft below sea level. It may be divided into 7 physical regions: the Atlantic coastal plain, continuing along the Gulf of Mexico as the Gulf coastal plain; the Appalachian Mountains; the central plains; the Rocky Mountains; the basins and plateaux W of the Rockies; the Coast Ranges and other mountains and valleys of the Pacific coastal region; finally, the Great Lakes region, an extension of the Laurentian Plateau of Canada. The Atlantic and Gulf coastal plain, with its many indentations and islands, slopes gradually down to the sea and continues as a broad continental shelf. To the W is the Piedmont, a transitional zone bordering W on the Appalachian Mountains, which extend NE–SW from the St Lawrence R. to the Gulf plain; the highest peak in the Appalachians is Mt Mitchell (6,684 ft). W of the Appalachian Plateau is the great lowland region of the central plains, at 500–1,000 ft, drained by the Missouri–Mississippi system, rising W to the Great Plains, which themselves rise to about 5,500 ft in the foothills of the Western Cordillera. Here the Rocky Mountains stretch N–S across the USA from Canada, continuing in Mexico as the Sierra Madre and reaching 14,430 ft in Mt Elbert. W of the Rockies is the region of basins and plateaux, with the Columbia Plateau (N) and the Colorado Plateau (S) and in the centre the vast area of interior drainage

known as the Great Basin, containing the Great Salt Lake as well as Death Valley and other desert tracts. In the Pacific zone there are two N–S mountain belts: firstly, the Cascade Range, continued S by the Sierra Nevada, which has Mt Whitney (14,495 ft), the highest point in the USA outside Alaska; and secondly, farther W, the Coast Ranges, which in many parts slope steeply down to the ocean. Between the Sierra Nevada and the Coast Range is the elongated Central Valley of California.

Of the numerous rivers the greatest is the Mississippi, with its chief tributary the Missouri. It flows N–S from Minnesota to Louisiana and the Gulf of Mexico, thus nearly dividing the country into E and W sections; the Missouri–Mississippi, i.e. the Missouri R. together with the Mississippi from the confluence to the mouth, is about 3,760 m., a length exceeded only by the Nile and the Amazon. Other great rivers include the Colorado in the SW, the Columbia in the NW, and the Rio Grande in the S. The Great Lakes, which are partly in Canada, drain to the Atlantic via the St Lawrence R. Other notable lakes are the Great Salt Lake (Utah), L. Okeechobee (Florida), and L. Champlain (N.Y. and Vermont).

CLIMATE. Because of its great extent and varied topography the USA exhibits several different types of climate. In the E half, i.e. E of about the 100th meridian, three climatic zones may be distinguished according to latitude. The N section has a humid continental climate, with annual rainfall of 20–40 ins., generally increasing W–E, and cold winters; the zone to the S in general has a heavier rainfall and higher temperatures throughout the year; the most southerly zone has a humid sub-tropical climate, with a still more abundant rainfall (80 ins. annually along parts of the Gulf coast), warm summers, and mild winters. To the W of the 100th meridian the climate of the Great Plains is characterized by hot summers and relatively cold winters, with annual rainfall of only 10–20 ins. In the Rockies and other mountain ranges in the W the climate varies with altitude and exposure; the lowlands of the SW, shielded by the mountains from rain-bearing westerly winds, have a low rainfall, amounting to less than 10 ins. annually, and a high range of temperatures, and in this area are to be found the

765                           UNITED STATES OF AMERICA

deserts. The moisture-laden winds from the Pacific, on the other hand, deposit considerable rainfall on the windward slopes of the mountains, and in the N W coastal region annual amounts vary from 40 ins. to more than 100 ins.; the climate is mild and may be best described as maritime temperate. Much of S California enjoys a Mediterranean type of climate, with warm dry summers and mild rainy winters.
FORESTS. Forests cover about one quarter of the entire land area of the country, but of some 500 million acres so covered about one half is classified as commercial timber. Rather more than half the softwoods produced come from the Pacific states, where the giant redwoods of California and the Douglas firs are outstanding. There are also extensive forests in the N – in Michigan, Wisconsin, and Minnesota, whence come most of the hardwoods; in the S and SE various species of pine provide most of the remaining softwoods. In spite of the large areas of forests under national and state ownership, and increasing efforts at conservation, more timber is still being cut and destroyed annually than is being replanted.
AGRICULTURE. Agricultural output has increased tremendously in recent years, among the contributory causes being a successful conservation and irrigation policy, increased mechanization, the effective control of pests, the use of more suitable fertilizers, and better feeding of livestock. Since 1910 farm production has doubled, and in 1962 was 69 per cent above the 1935–9 level.

The main crops are grain, cotton, and tobacco. Maize is grown chiefly in the Corn Belt with Iowa the leading state; Kansas is the principal wheat-growing state (winter wheat), followed by N Dakota (spring wheat). Cotton is grown increasingly W of the Mississippi: Texas has the highest production, followed by California, and these two states now produce 45 per cent of the national output (1962). Tobacco is grown mainly in N Carolina and Kentucky, and Winston-Salem (N.C.) is the world's greatest tobacco market; in cotton and tobacco production the USA leads the world. Many other crops are grown on a large scale, e.g. soya beans, flax, sugar-beet, rice, potatoes. The Great Lakes region and the Atlantic coastal plain are noted for fruit and market-garden produce, the latter also producing ground-

nuts. California is famous for its grapes, citrus and other fruits. Hawaii grows sugarcane and pineapples, and the Gulf coast region sugar-cane and rice. On the Great Plains and in Texas there are huge cattle ranches: in 38 years (1930–68) the number of cattle has increased from 61 million to 109 million, but the number of sheep has fallen from 52 million to 22 million, and the number of pigs has remained about the same at 50–60 million. Dairy farming extends from the Middle Western states to New England and is especially important in Wisconsin. Agricultural output has been greatly increased through irrigation schemes, which often also include the provision of hydroelectric power, the Tennessee Valley Authority scheme being particularly noteworthy. At the same time the serious problem of soil erosion and soil depletion in certain areas, brought about largely by over-cropping, over-stocking, and deforestation, is being dealt with by Federal and state governments.
MINERALS. The USA has vast and varied mineral resources. It has long been the largest single producer of petroleum. Bituminous coal and anthracite are mined chiefly in the Appalachians and the central plains, Pennsylvania being especially noted for its anthracite. Petroleum and natural gas are produced mainly in Texas but also in California, Oklahoma, Louisiana, etc. Of the metallic minerals, iron, copper, lead, zinc, gold, and silver are the most important; iron ore comes chiefly from the L. Superior region (Minnesota, Michigan), and the non-ferrous metallic ores from the thinly populated mountain states of Arizona, Utah, Nevada, Montana, and Idaho. Non-metallic minerals include phosphates (Florida) and sulphur (Louisiana). Nevertheless the USA has to import most of its supplies of industrial diamonds, tin, and nickel, and, to satisfy the demands of industry, part of its bauxite (aluminium) and other non-ferrous ores and even iron ore.
INDUSTRIES. In industrial output the USA leads the world. The chief industrial belt is in the N E, comprising New England, the Middle Atlantic states, and most of the Middle Western States. In this area are such leading industrial centres as Detroit (automobiles), Pittsburgh and Youngstown (steel), Chicago, New York, Boston, Philadelphia, Buffalo, and many others, with an enormous range of manufactures. There are other industrial concentrations at

St Louis, Kansas City, Omaha, New Orleans, Minneapolis, Los Angeles, and San Francisco, to name only some of the major centres.

COMMUNICATIONS, TIME ZONES. The main seaports are New York, Philadelphia, Baltimore, Boston (Atlantic coast); New Orleans and Houston (Gulf coast); Los Angeles, San Francisco, Portland, Seattle (Pacific). Of the inland waterways the most important are the Great Lakes and the St Lawrence Seaway (shared with Canada) and the Mississippi. The mileage of main track railways, densest in the E, is 211,514, of roads 3,697,960; there are 8,891 airports and 452 heliports (1967). Owing to the great E–W extent, there are four different time zones, Eastern, Central, Mountain, and Pacific between the two oceans, and three further time zones in Alaska. POPULATION. In 1960, five cities – New York, Chicago, Los Angeles, Philadelphia, Detroit (in order of population) – had more than 1 million inhabitants, and 51 cities more than 250,000. The Middle Atlantic and S New England states are the most densely populated areas. Negroes number about one tenth of the total population, and are most numerous in the SE states (the 'deep south'). American Indians, descendants of the aboriginal inhabitants, numbered 523,591 in 1960; they are settled largely in Indian 'reservations' in the W states. The Chinese, some 240,000, are mainly in San Francisco and other Pacific coast cities. Japanese, almost exclusively settled on the Pacific coast, number some 260,000, while a further 200,000 of them are in Hawaii; Filipinos number over 100,000, with a further 70,000 in Hawaii. There are Mexican communities in the SW, and Spanish-speaking Puerto Ricans in New York City; in Alaska there are some thousands of Eskimos and Aleuts. Apart from such minorities, the people generally speak English.

GOVERNMENT, etc. The Federal government is based in Washington, D.C., where the President, elected every fourth year, resides and carries out his official functions, and where Congress (Senate and House of Representatives) have their sittings. The Senate consists of 2 members from each state, chosen by popular vote for 6 years, one third retiring or seeking re-election every 2 years; the House of Representatives has 435 members, elected every second year, the number from each state being dependent on its population (e.g. New York 41, California 38, Idaho 2, Wyoming 1). The form of government is based on the constitution of 17 Sept. 1787, which gives the Federal government authority in taxation, foreign affairs, the armed forces, postal services, coins, weights and measures, patents, copyright, and crimes against the US. It has sole legislative authority over the District of Columbia and overseas possessions and controls the National Parks and Indian Reservations. State legislatures, however, have power to deal with all matters not reserved for the Federal government, such as civil and criminal law, trade, transport, education, licensing, and fisheries within state waters. Each state has an elected governor and capital city, with the Capitol as the centre of administration.

HISTORY. The early history of the USA is the history of the discovery and colonization of the country by the leading maritime powers of Europe, of which three, Britain, Spain, and France, played the chief parts. It proved to be the British who exercised the most enduring influence on the new nation in the vital period of its development, so that the US inherited the English language, English habits of thought and free speech, and to some extent English culture. Probably the first Europeans to land on the mainland were the Spaniards under Ponce de León, who landed on the coast of Florida in 1513; the first permanent white settlement was established in 1565 at St Augustine, Florida. By 1540 Florida was a subject province of the Spanish domain in Mexico, the Californian coast was surveyed, and an expedition penetrated into the interior beyond the Grand Canyon of the Colorado R. – with plunder rather than settlement its main purpose. The French in their turn proved to be better explorers than colonizers: Samuel de Champlain reached lakes Huron and Ontario (1615) and paved the way for later 17th-cent. French explorers, missionaries, and fur traders who gradually traversed the vast area S of the Great Lakes to the Gulf of Mexico. In the 1680s Robert de la Salle explored the Great Lakes and the Mississippi R. and delta, taking possession of the region for France under the name of Louisiana. But French colonization was not very successful, and by 1700 there were only about 1,000 French settlers throughout this great region. The English finally proved the most successful colonists; their first permanent settlement was at Jamestown, Virginia (1607); the group of Puritans from England and Holland who landed at Plymouth, Mass., in 1620 (the famous 'Pilgrim Fathers') are widely regarded as the true founders of the US. In the 18th cent. large numbers of immigrants arrived from Germany and Ireland, but up to the end of the colonial period about four fifths of the colonists were of English or Scottish origin. There were 13 colonies, which became the 13 original states of the Union after the American War of Independence (1775–83).

The new republic acquired all the territory E of the Mississippi which had passed from France to Britain in 1763. In 1803 came the next major acquisition of territory through the Louisiana Purchase, whereby the US gained the vast region known as Louisiana (area 827,000 sq. m.) stretching from the Mississippi to the Rockies and N from the Gulf of Mexico; its boundaries were somewhat ill-defined at the time, but it was to prove a source of immense strength to the country. In 1819 Florida was purchased from Spain. In 1821 Mexico achieved independence and acquired much of the S W part of the present US from Spain; then in 1848, after the US–Mexican War (1846–8), the territory (529,000 sq. m.) was ceded by Mexico to the US. Texas (390,000 sq. m.), which had broken away from Mexico and established an independent republic (1836), was annexed in 1845. In the NW the region known as the Oregon Territory (285,000 sq. m.) was occupied jointly by the US and Britain 1818–46, but was then ceded to the US. The E part of the boundary with Canada was settled in 1842, and the W part was fixed along the 49th parallel in 1846; the US–Mexico boundary was settled in 1853–4.

From c. 1850 events began to move towards the Civil War of 1861–5: the issue being national unity, which was threatened by a dispute between the N and S states over the question of slavery. The slaves were the Negro plantation workers, descendants of African slaves shipped to N America during the colonial period. Matters came to a head when Lincoln took office as president (1861), for the S states feared that he would try to abolish slavery.

From the material standpoint the N was overwhelmingly stronger than the S, and finally the S surrendered (9 April 1865). As a result of the Civil War the slaves were liberated, but not integrated into the general society, even in the N states.

The last 40 years of the 19th cent. saw an immense expansion of the railway system. In 1860 there were 30,000 m. of railway, chiefly E of the Mississippi, but in 1900 there were nearly 200,000 m. The first transcontinental railway was completed in 1869, and settlement of the W developed rapidly as communications improved. Between 1880 and 1900 the population increased from 50 million to 75 million, and agricultural and industrial production was doubled. In 1867 Alaska was purchased from Russia and in 1898 Hawaii was annexed. As a result of the Spanish-American War Puerto Rico and the Philippines were acquired (1898); the latter became independent in 1946.

Along with the tremendous burst of economic activity that followed the Civil War, the US began to play an increasing part in world affairs – though reluctantly at first, owing to the traditional isolationism of many Americans. However, it early (1823) asserted the principle of the Monroe Doctrine, that S America should not be a European sphere of influence. It fought a war with Spain (1898) over Cuba, which became independent. The US intervened from time to time in such Latin American states as were in political turmoil. After initially proclaiming its neutrality the US entered the 1st World War in 1916 and its help proved decisive; but it failed to support President Wilson's creation, the League of Nations.

In the succeeding years, the US was overtaken (1929) by an economic depression of great magnitude; conditions improved under the New Deal policies of Franklin D. Roosevelt, but unemployment was not entirely overcome until the US entered the 2nd World War, since when the country has experienced economic growth of immense proportions.

After the 2nd World War the US found itself inextricably committed to playing a leading role in world politics – as a source of economic rehabilitation for Europe, as a major partner in the 'Free World', and as the most powerful and dynamic of the world economies. In the defence of the 'Free World', the US took costly military action in Korea in the 1950s and in Vietnam in the 1960s.

**Unna** Federal German Republic. Industrial town in N Rhine-Westphalia, in the Ruhr region 10 m. E of Dortmund. Pop. (1963) 31,000. Coalmining centre. Manufactures metal goods.

**Unterwalden** Switzerland. Canton in central Switzerland S of L. Lucerne comprising the two half-cantons of Obwalden and Nidwalden. Area 296 sq. m. Pop. (1969) 50,600 (German-speaking and Roman Catholic; about equally divided between the half-cantons). In 1291 Nidwalden formed the Everlasting League with Uri and Schwyz, to be joined later by Obwalden; with Lucerne they became the Forest Cantons.

**Upington** S Africa. Market town and railway junction in Cape Province, on the Orange R. 220 m. W of Kimberley. Pop. (1968) 26,835. Flour milling, cotton ginning. Also a tourist centre for the Aughrabies Falls (Orange R.).

**Upolu** ◊ *Samoa*.

**Upper Austria** (Ger. **Oberösterreich**) Austria. Province in the N, bordering W on Bavaria (FGR) and N on Czechoslovakıa. Area 4,625 sq. m. Pop. (1961) 1,131,623. Cap. Linz. Generally hilly, becoming mountainous in the S. Drained by the Danube, Inn, and Enns rivers. Main occupations agriculture, forestry. Industries chiefly in Linz, Wels, and Steyr. With Lower Austria it formed the nucleus of the Austrian empire of the Habsburgs.

**Upper Tunguska River** ◊ *Angara River*.

**Upper Volta.** Republic in W Africa bounded by Mali (N and W), Niger (E), and Dahomey, Togo, Ghana, and Ivory Coast (S). Area 105,839 sq. m. Pop. (1969) 5,330,000 (inc. 3,500 Europeans). Cap. Ouagadougou. Consists mainly of wooded savannah. Millets and maize important subsistence crops; groundnuts cultivated for export. Cattle, sheep, and goats raised. Chief towns Ouagadougou, Bobo-Dioulasso. Upper Volta was formed (1919) as a French colony from Upper Senegal and Niger; divided up between Ivory Coast, Sudan, and Niger (1932); formed again 1947. Became a member state of the French Community 1958; gained independence and membership of the UN 1960.

**Uppingham** England. Market town in Rutlandshire, 20 m. W of Peterborough, chiefly known for its public school (founded 1584). Pop. (rural district, 1961) 5,340.

**Uppsala** Sweden. Capital of Uppsala county, 40 m. NNW of Stockholm. Pop. (1968) 97,172. Cultural centre, with Sweden's oldest university (founded 1477), which has a famous library containing the 6th-cent. '*Codex Argenteus*' and other manuscripts; also an institute of agriculture, a botanic garden, and an observatory. The cathedral (13th/15th-cent.), where Swedish kings were formerly crowned, has the tombs of Gustavus Vasa, Linnaeus, and Swedenborg. Publishing, flour milling, etc. Old Uppsala, about 2 m. N, was a centre of pagan worship in the 9th cent.; after a destructive fire the new city grew up on its present site (13th cent.).

**Ur** Iraq. Ancient city in Sumer, the biblical Ur of the Chaldees, on a site 105 m. WNW of modern Basra, near the Euphrates R. Dates from very early times, excavations having shown that it was a prosperous city *c*. 3500 B.C., and it was the reputed home of Abraham. The outstanding ruin is the ziggurat or temple tower. After Ur had been destroyed, it was restored by Nebuchadnezzar in the 6th cent. B.C., but soon afterwards it began to decline, possibly because the Euphrates, beside which it had grown up and flourished, had changed its course; before the end of the 4th cent. B.C. it was abandoned.

**Ural Mountains** USSR. Mountain system extending over 1,400 m. N–S from the Arctic Ocean and forming part of the physical boundary between Europe and Asia. Of generally low elevation, the Urals reach their greatest height in Narodnaya (6,214 ft), in the N section; there are few other peaks exceeding 5,000 ft. Well forested. The central section contains some of the country's richest mineral deposits (inc. iron, manganese, nickel, copper), which have contributed much to the development of such great industrial centres as Sverdlovsk and Chelyabinsk; the minerals were known to exist more than 1,000 years ago but have been exploited on a large scale only since the 1930s.

**Ural River** USSR. River 1,400 m. long rising in the S Ural Mountains and flowing S past Magnitogorsk and Orsk, W past Orenburg and Uralsk, then S again to enter the Caspian Sea near Guryev. Navigable to Orenburg.

**Uralsk** USSR. Capital of the Uralsk region, Kazakh SSR, on the Ural R. 150 m. SSE of Kuibyshev. Pop. (1970) 134,000. Commercial centre in an agricultural region. Trade in cereals, livestock. Meat packing, tanning, flour milling, etc. Founded 1775.

**Uranium City** Canada. Small mining town in N W Saskatchewan, N of L. Athabaska. Pop. (1960) 4,000. Developed in the 1950s for the production of uranium concentrates.

**Urawa** Japan. Capital of Saitama prefecture, 15 m. N N W of Tokyo, of which it is a residential suburb. Pop. (1965) 221,333.

**Urbana** USA. Market town in Illinois 125 m. S S W of Chicago. Pop. (1960) 27,294. Manufactures scientific instruments, paints, etc. Seat of the University of Illinois (1867).

**Urbino** Italy. Town in Pesaro e Urbino province, in the Marches, 19 m. S W of Pesaro. Pop. 23,000. Manufactures textiles, majolica, etc. Standing on a hill, it is dominated by the 15th-cent. ducal palace; also has a cathedral. University (1506). Noted in the 15th–16th cent. for its majolica. Birthplace of Raphael (1483–1520).

**Ure River** England. River in Yorkshire 50 m. long, rising in the Pennines and flowing E and S E past Ripon to join the R. Swale and form the R. Ouse. The upper part of the valley is known as Wensleydale.

**Urfa** Turkey. Ancient Edessa. Capital of Urfa province, in the S 75 m. E of Gaziantep. Pop. (1965) 73,500. Market town. Trade in wheat, cotton, etc. Changed hands many times. Fell to the Muslims (638), the Crusaders (1097), and finally to the Turks (1637).

**Uri** Switzerland. Canton in central Switzerland. Area 415 sq. m. Pop. (1969) 34,000 (German-speaking and Roman Catholic). Cap. Altdorf. Includes the upper Reuss valley, from which rise lofty peaks and glaciers, and in the N includes part of L. Lucerne; on the S border is the St Gotthard Pass. With Schwyz and Unterwalden it formed the Everlasting League (1291), which was the foundation of the Swiss confederation, and was one of the Forest Cantons.

**Urmia, Lake** Iran. The largest lake, in the N W, at a height of 4,250 ft. Area 1,500 sq. m. (increasing at times to over 2,300 sq. m.). Saline and shallow. Has no outlet.

**Urmston** England. Urban district in S E Lancashire 5 m. W S W of Manchester. Pop. (1961) 42,983. A mainly residential suburb. Metal working, flour milling, food processing, etc.

**Uruapán** Mexico. Town in Michoacán state 190 m. W of Mexico City at a height of 5,300 ft. Pop. (1960) 45,727. Famous for articles made by local craftsmen: lacquer and glass ware, wooden and embroidered goods. Tourist centre for the volcano Paricutín.

**Urubamba River** Peru. River 450 m. long, rising in the high Andes of the S E and flowing generally N N W through gorges to join the Apurímac R. and form the Ucayali R.

**Uruguaiana** Brazil. Town in Rio Grande do Sul state, on the Uruguay R. and on the Argentine frontier 365 m. W of Pôrto Alegre. Pop. (1960) 48,358. Cattle centre. Meat packing. Manufactures leather goods, soap, etc.

**Uruguay (República Oriental del Uruguay).** The smallest republic in S America. Area 72,172 sq. m. Pop. (1963) 2,590,158. Cap. Montevideo. Lang. Spanish. Rel. mainly Roman Catholic.

Bounded by Argentina (W), Brazil (N), the Atlantic (E), and the Río de la Plata (S). Resources derived almost entirely from farming (mainly pastoral). Nearly all the people are of European stock, chiefly Italian or Spanish, and a high degree of prosperity and literacy has been achieved. The one effective 'welfare state' in America. Divided into 19 departments.

TOPOGRAPHY, CLIMATE. The S is a gently undulating plain similar to the Argentine pampas; the N is more varied, with low hills extending S from the Brazilian border. Central Uruguay is crossed from the N E by the Río Negro, which joins the Uruguay R. In its middle course a dam creates a lake 87 m. long and 18 m. wide, with a hydroelectric power plant. Climate warm, temperate, and healthy, well suited to all-year sheep and cattle grazing. Rainfall moderate and well distributed, though occasionally serious droughts occur.

ECONOMY. Except for forests along the valleys and palms in the S and E, the country remains largely natural grassland, and the economy is based on stock raising and agriculture. In the early days exports were dried and salted meat, hides, and tallow, but refrigeration led to the large-scale shipment of chilled and frozen meat. Herefords and other European breeds of cattle were introduced, the production of meat and meat extracts began at Fray Bentos in the 19th cent., and continues there and at Montevideo. Sheep rearing is extremely important, the flocks being mostly of British breeds (Corriedale, Lincoln, Romney Marsh) as well as merinos. The high wool prices of the 1950s led to a great increase in numbers, and wool is the other leading export (with meat and meat products). Livestock are reared on enclosed grasslands, sheep being rather more numerous in the N, while the best cattle pastures, including those for dairy cattle, are mainly in the S. Many roads have parallel grassy tracks for flocks and herds, and the small towns are situated at cross-roads to serve the widely spaced *estancias* or ranches. Most of the arable land lies within 50 m. of the S coast; the principal crops are wheat, maize, flax (linseed), sunflowers, and rice, and enough wine is produced for domestic consumption. Mineral exploitation is negligible. Montevideo handles most of the country's trade and has a considerable proportion of its industries: meat packing, flour milling, brewing, textile manufacture, etc. Other towns Paysandú, Salto, Rivera.

HISTORY. Uruguay was first visited in the early 16th cent. by the Spanish, to whom the region was known as the *Banda Oriental* ('East Bank', i.e. of the Uruguay R.), but a permanent settlement was not established till 1624. They were followed by the Portuguese, and a long and bitter rivalry ensued for possession of the area; in 1776 it became part of the Spanish viceroyalty of La Plata and in 1820 a province of Brazil. Led by the national hero Artigas, the Uruguayans fought for and won independence (1825), but for the remainder of the 19th cent. the country suffered from internal strife and corruption. An outstanding programme of social reform was introduced during the second administration of President Batlle y Ordóñez (1911), however, and in 1951 the individual presidency was abolished in favour of a two-party National council of 9 members. The presidential system was reintroduced in 1966.

**Uruguay River** S America. River 1,000 m. long rising in S Brazil only 40 m. from the Atlantic coast (as the Pelotas), flowing W and then SW and S, marking the Brazil–Argentina and the Uruguay–Argentina frontiers, and joining the Paraná R. to form the Río de la Plata. Navigation is im-

peded by falls and rapids above Salto (Uruguay), but the river is navigable by ocean-going ships upstream to Paysandú (Uruguay), about 130 m. from the mouth.
**Urumchi** China. Formerly Tihwa. Capital of Sinkiang-Uighur A R, in a valley through the Tien Shan at a height of 9,000 ft. Pop. 141,000. Commercial centre on the route between China (Lanchow) and the USSR. Flour milling, tanning. Manufactures chemicals, textiles, cement, etc. Small iron and steel industry. University (1960).
**USA** ◊ *United States of America.*
**Usedom (Uznam)** German Democratic Republic/Poland. Island between the Stettiner Haff and the Baltic Sea; since 1945 divided between the GDR (W) and Poland (E). Area 172 sq. m. Pop. 45,000. Chief town Swinoujście (E). Part of the ancient Polish province of Pomorze (Pomerania). In E Prussia 1919–39.
**Ushant (Fr. Ouessant)** France. Island 5 m. long and 2 m. wide, in the Finistère department off the W coast of Brittany 26 m. WNW of Brest. Pop. 2,000. Rocky coastline. Main occupation fishing. Two naval battles (1778, 1794) were fought near by between the French and the English.
**Ushuaia** Argentina. Capital of Tierra del Fuego province on Beagle Channel. Pop. 3,000. The most southerly town in the world. Centre of a sheep-rearing, lumbering, and fishing region.
**Usk** Wales. Urban district in Monmouthshire, on the R. Usk 9 m. NNE of Newport. Pop. (1961) 1,875. Market town. Has the remains of a 13th-cent. castle.
**Usk River** Wales. River 57 m. long, rising 5 m. SE of Llandovery and flowing E, SE, and S past Brecon, Abergavenny, Usk, and Caerleon to the Bristol Channel at Newport. Noted for fishing.
**Uspallata Pass (La Cumbre)** Argentina/ Chile. Pass through the Andes at a height of 12,600 ft at the foot of Mt Aconcagua. The statue 'Christ of the Andes' in the pass, dedicated in 1904, commemorates the boundary settlement between Argentina and Chile. The railway tunnel beneath the pass links Mendoza (Argentina) and Valparaiso (Chile).
**USSR** ◊ *Union of Soviet Socialist Republics.*
**Ussuri River** USSR. River 540 m. long rising in the S Sikhote Alin Range and flowing generally NNE, forming the border between the Primorye Territory, RSFSR (USSR), and Heilungkiang

province (China), to join the Amur R.; linked with L. Khanka. Used for floating timber, but frozen Nov.–April. Fighting between Russian and Chinese border guards along the river caused loss of life (1969): both sides claimed the small un-inhabited island of Damansky (Chenpao), 1½ m. long and ½ m. wide.

**Ussuriisk** USSR. Formerly Nikolsk-Ussuriiski, then (1935–62) Voroshilov. Industrial town and railway centre at the junction of the Trans-Siberian and Chinese Eastern Railways, in S Primorye Territory, RSFSR, 30 m. N of Vladivostok. Pop. (1970) 128,000. Railway engineering, saw-milling, soya bean processing, etc. Developed rapidly after the completion of the Trans-Siberian Railway (1905).

**Ústi-nad-Labem** Czechoslovakia. Capital of the Severočeský region, Bohemia, on the Elbe (Labe) R. 45 m. NNW of Prague. Pop. (1967) 73,000. Railway junction. River port. Industrial centre. Important chemical works. Manufactures textiles, machinery, rubber products, etc.

**Ust-Kamenogorsk** USSR. Industrial town in E Kazakh SSR, on the Irtysh R. 110 m. ESE of Semipalatinsk. Pop. (1970) 230,000. In a mining district (zinc, lead, copper). Metal refining and processing. Manufactures food products, clothing, furniture, etc. Large hydroelectric power station near by.

**Ust-Ordyn Buryat NA** USSR. National Area in S Siberia, in the Irkutsk Region (RSFSR). Area 8,000 sq. m. Pop. (1970) 146,000. Cap Ust-Ordynsky (45 m. NNE of Irkutsk). Largely wooded steppe. Cattle rearing, dairy farming.

**Ust-Ordynsky** ◊ *Ust-Ordyn Buryat NA.*

**Ust Urt** USSR. Desert plateau in SW Kazakh SSR and Kara-Kalpak ASSR, between the Caspian Sea and the Aral Sea. Area 90,000 sq. m. Standing at a height of about 800 ft, it is almost barren except after the scanty spring rains.

**Usulután** Salvador. Capital of Usulatán department in the SE, at the foot of the volcano Usulután. Pop. (1961) 30,465. Market town. Trade in maize, tobacco, bananas, etc.

**Usumbura** ◊ *Bujumbura.*

**Utah** USA. State in the W. Area 84,916 sq. m. Pop. (1970) 1,060,631. Cap. Salt Lake City. Admitted to the union in 1896 as the 45th state; popularly known as the 'Mormon' or 'Beehive' state. Its average altitude is about 6,000 ft. The E consists

of high plateau and the W forms part of the Great Basin; the central highlands, including the Wasatch Range, run roughly N–S through the state. In the NE the Uinta Mountains rise to 13,227 ft in Kings Peak. In the NW are the Great Salt Lake, the largest salt lake in the Americas, and the Great Salt Lake Desert. Climate dry continental, with a rainfall of less than 5 ins. annually in the W, and an average for the state of 10–15 ins. Only 24 per cent of the land area is classified as farm land, and there is considerable soil erosion; chief crops wheat, hay, sugar-beet, potatoes. Minerals important, esp. copper and gold, in which Utah ranks second in production in the USA. Bryce Canyon and Zion National Parks and other scenic areas attract tourists. Leading towns Salt Lake City, Ogden. About 70 per cent of all church members in the state are Latter-day Saints (Mormons). Utah was first settled (1847) by Mormons led by Brigham Young. Ceded to the USA by Mexico 1848; Territory of Utah formed 1850.

**Utica** USA. Town in New York, on the Mohawk R. 48 m. E of Syracuse. Pop. (1960) 100,410. Manufactures cotton goods, knitwear, clothing, machinery, etc. Industry, centred on textiles since the mid 19th cent., has become more diversified in recent years.

**Utrecht** Netherlands. **1.** The smallest province, bordering N on Ijsselmeer. Area 526 sq. m. Pop. (1968) 768,715. Heath and woodland in the E; vegetable and fruit growing and dairy farming in the SW. Industries centred on Utrecht and Amersfoort.
**2.** Capital of Utrecht province, on the Kromme Rijn (Crooked Rhine) where it divides into the Old Rhine and the Vecht, 21 m. SSE of Amsterdam. Pop. (1968) 274,388. Important railway junction. Railway engineering. Manufactures machinery, radio sets, food and tobacco products, chemicals, clothing, etc. Famous for its industrial fairs. A picturesque old city, it has a university (founded 1636), several outstanding museums, and a cathedral dating from the 13th cent. Seat of the Roman Catholic archbishop of the Netherlands. The Union of Utrecht (1579) laid the foundation of the Netherlands. The Treaty of Utrecht (1713) ended the War of the Spanish Succession. Birthplace of Adrian VI (1459–1523), the last non-Italian pope.

**Utrera** Spain. Town in Seville province, Andalusia, 18 m. SE of Seville. Pop. (1961) 41,126. Market town. Railway junction. Manufactures olive oil. Flour milling, tanning, etc. Remains of a Moorish alcazar.

**Utsunomiya** Japan. Capital of Tochigi prefecture 62 m. N of Tokyo. Pop. (1965) 265,764. Railway junction and tourist centre, terminus of a branch line to the Nikko National Park.

**Uttar Pradesh** India. State in the N, bounded on the N by Tibet (China) and Nepal. Area 113,654 sq. m. Pop. (1961) 73,746,401. Cap. Lucknow. In the NW are the Himalayas, rising to over 25,000 ft in Kamet and Nanda Devi, but the majority of the state lies in the Upper Ganges plain. Crossed by the three great tributaries, the Jumna, Gogra, and Gumti, as well as the Ganges itself. About three quarters of the population depend on agriculture. Principal crops wheat, rice, pulses, sugar·cane, oilseeds. Large numbers of cattle, used mainly as draught animals. Chief industrial centres Kanpur, Lucknow, Varanasi (Benares), Agra, Bareilly. In 1877 the provinces of Agra and Oudh were united and in 1902 their name was changed to the United Provinces of Agra and Oudh. When India became independent the states of Rampur, Benares, and Tehri-Garhwal were incorporated into the U.P. (1949); present name adopted 1950.

**Uttoxeter** England. Urban district in Staffordshire 12 m. NW of Burton-on-Trent. Pop. (1961) 8,168. Market town. Manufactures agricultural machinery, biscuits. Racecourse. Denstone College (founded 1873) is 5 m. N.

**Uvéa** ◊ *Loyalty Islands.*

**Uxbridge** England. Former municipal borough in Middlesex, on the R. Colne 15 m. WNW of London; from 1965 part of the Greater London borough of Hillingdon. Pop. (1961) 63,762. Market town. Largely residential. Brickmaking, sawmilling, engineering, etc. The Old Treaty House was the scene of the abortive negotiations between Charles I and the Parliamentarians (1645).

**Uzbek SSR** USSR. Constituent republic, in Central Asia, bounded on the S by Afghanistan. Area 173,546 sq. m. Pop. (1970) 11,963,000 (62 per cent Uzbeks, 14 per cent Russians). Cap. Tashkent. Includes the Kara-Kalpak ASSR, and is divided into the regions of Andizhan, Bukhara, Fergana, Khorezm, Samarkand, Surkhan-Darya, Syr-Darya, Tashkent. Much of it lies in the Kyzyl Kum desert, but it is watered by the Amu Darya and Syr Darya, and irrigation is highly developed. Climate dry continental, with hot summers; rainfall varies from less than 5 ins. annually in the desert (N) to 20–25 ins. in the foothills of the Pamirs and Tien Shan (SE). With the help of irrigation agriculture flourishes, esp. in the fertile Fergana Valley and the Tashkent, Khorezm, and Zeravshan oases; Uzbekistan produces about two thirds of the country's cotton and half or more of its rice and alfalfa. Also large numbers of sheep and cattle. Agriculture now highly mechanized; the land is divided into 1,029 collective farms and 321 state farms (1967). Principal minerals coal, oil. Leading industry textile manufacture (esp. cotton goods). Chief towns Tashkent (largest city in Soviet Asia), Samarkand, Andizhan, Namangan. Most of the Uzbeks, or Uzbegs, are Sunni Muslims, deriving their name from the 14th-cent. Uzbeg Khan, a chief of the Golden Horde, who introduced Islam. They divided into separate khanates and were compelled to submit to the Russians (1864–73), though Khiva and Bukhara were nominally independent till 1917. The Uzbek SSR was formed in 1924. ◊ *Turkestan.*

**Uznam** ◊ *Usedom.*

# V

**Vaal River** S Africa. River 750 m. long rising in the Drakensberg in the SE Transvaal, flowing generally WSW, forming the boundary between the Transvaal and the Orange Free State, and crossing into Cape Province to join the Orange R. The reservoir behind the Vaal Dam, where the Vaal is joined by the Wilge 20 m. SE of Vereeniging, supplies water to the Witwatersrand and irrigates 67,000 acres of land.

**Vaasa** (Swedish **Vasa**) Finland. Formerly (1852–1918) Nikolainkaupunki (or Nikolaistad). Capital of the Vaasa province, on the Gulf of Bothnia 230 m. NNW of Helsinki. Pop. (1968) 48,679. Seaport. Exports timber, tar, wood products. Ship repairing, sawmilling, flour milling, sugar refining. Manufactures textiles etc. Founded 1606. Destroyed by fire 1852; rebuilt nearer the sea and renamed.

**Vaduz** Liechtenstein. Capital of the principality, near the Rhine R. and the Swiss frontier, 23 m. SSE of St Gallen (Switzerland). Pop. (1967) 3,966. Market town. Cotton industry.

**Valais** (Ger. **Wallis**) Switzerland. Canton in the S bordering S on Italy and W on France. Area 2,021 sq. m. Pop. (1969) 193,000 (mostly French-speaking and Roman Catholic). Cap. Sion. Includes the upper Rhône valley from the source to L. Geneva, and many of the peaks of the Bernese (N) and Pennine (S) Alps – Finsteraarhorn, Matterhorn, Monte Rosa, and also the Great St Bernard and Simplon passes. Fine Alpine scenery. Lower mountain slopes forested. In the Rhône valley cereals and vines are cultivated. Principal resort Zermatt. Valais was a French department (Simplon) 1810–13, and then joined the Swiss Confederation.

**Valdai Hills** USSR. Low ridges in W RSFSR, NW of Moscow, rising at the highest point to 1,050 ft and forming the watershed to the Volga, W Dvina, and other rivers.

**Val-de-Marne** France. Department just SE of Paris, formed in 1964 when the former Seine and Seine-et-Oise departments were reorganized. Area 94 sq. m. Pop. (1968) 1,121,340. Prefecture Créteil.

**Valdepeñas** Spain. Town in Ciudad Real province, New Castile, 98 m. NE of Córdoba. Pop. (1961) 25,706. Vine-growing centre, noted for its wines and *bodegas*. Also produces olive oil, vinegar, leather, etc.

**Valdivia** Chile. Capital of Valdivia province, 460 m. SSW of Santiago on the Valdivia R., 11 m. from its port, Corral. Pop. 73,000. Industrial and commercial centre, in a rich agricultural region noteworthy for the beauty of its scenery. Tanning, flour milling, brewing. Manufactures food products, metal goods, paper, etc. University (1954). Founded (1552) by Pedro de Valdivia. Much developed by German settlers in the 1850s. Severely damaged by earthquake and tidal wave in 1960.

**Val-d'Oise** France. Department just N and NW of Paris, formed in 1964 when the former Seine and Seine-et-Oise departments were reorganized. Area 482 sq. m. Pop. (1968) 693,269. Prefecture Pontoise.

**Valdosta** USA. Town in S Georgia 155 m. SW of Savannah. Pop. (1960) 30,652. Railway junction. In a region producing cotton, tobacco, timber. Manufactures textiles, wood products, etc. First settled 1859; named after the Italian Valle d'Aosta.

**Valence** France. Prefecture of the Drôme department, on the Rhône R. 58 m. S of Lyons. Pop. (1968) 64,134. Market town. Trade in fruits, olives, wines, cereals. Manufactures rayon and silk goods, furniture, etc. Flour milling. It was important in Roman times and was the medieval capital of the duchy of Valentinois. Romanesque cathedral (11th cent., restored).

**Valencia** (Irish Republic) ◊ *Valentia*.

**Valencia** Spain. **1.** Region and former kingdom in the E, on the Mediterranean Sea, comprising the modern provinces of Castellón de la Plana, Valencia, and Alicante, formed from it in 1833. Regained from the Moors by the Cid (1094), it was taken by James I of Aragón (1238) but maintained its political identity until the 18th cent.

**2.** Province of the Valencia region. Area 4,239 sq. m. Pop. (1961) 1,429,708. Cap. Valencia. Mountainous in the interior and rising to over 4,000 ft in the NW, with a

narrow but extremely fertile coastal plain. The irrigation system derives much of its water from the Turia and Júcar rivers. Famous for its *huertas*, irrigated lands yielding more than one crop annually. Produces oranges, raisins, etc.
3. Capital of Valencia province, and the third largest city in Spain, on the Turia R. on the irrigated coastal plain. Pop. (1967) 601,414. Industrial centre and seaport (harbour 2 m. E). Exports oranges, raisins, vegetables, olive oil, wine. Bathing beaches. Shipbuilding, railway engineering. Manufactures textiles (silk, rayon, linen), chemicals, machinery, tiles, etc. In one of the porches of the 13th/15th-cent. cathedral the 'water tribunal' has met every week since 1350 to discuss irrigation problems. The Lonja de Mercadero (medieval silk mart) is perhaps finer architecturally than the cathedral. The university dates from c. 1500. The art gallery is second only to the Prado (Madrid).

**Valencia** Venezuela. Capital of Carabobo state just W of L. Valencia. Pop. (1964) 204,273. Commercial and industrial centre in the leading agricultural region (sugarcane, cotton, etc.). Tanning, sugar refining, meat packing. Manufactures textiles, leather goods, etc. Linked by road and rail with its port Puerto Cabello, 20 m. N. Founded 1555.

**Valenciennes** France. Town in the Nord department, on the Escaut (Scheldt) R. 29 m. SE of Lille. Pop. (1968) 47,464. Coalmining and industrial centre. Manufactures textiles, chemicals, etc. Engineering, sugar refining. Once famous for its lace. Passed to France 1677. The citadel was built by Vauban. Birthplace of Emperor Baldwin I (1172–1205), Froissart (1338–1410), and Watteau (1684–1721).

**Valentia (Valencia)** Irish Republic. Island 7 m. long and 2 m. wide just off the coast of Co. Kerry. Pop. (1966) 847. Terminal station of the original transatlantic cable, laid (1865) by the *Great Eastern*. Farming, fishing. Slate, once important, is no longer quarried.

**Valetta** ⟡ *Valletta.*

**Valladolid** (Mexico) ⟡ *Morelia.*

**Valladolid** Spain. 1. Province in Old Castile. Area 3,158 sq. m. Pop. (1961) 363,106. Situated on the Meseta. Drained by the Duero (Douro) R. and its tributaries. Fertile areas produce cereals, wine, etc.
2. Capital of Valladolid province, at the confluence of the Pisuerga and the Esgueva rivers 100 m. NW of Madrid at a height of 2,200 ft. Pop. (1967) 193,214. Railway junction. Industrial centre. Railway engineering, tanning, flour milling, brewing. Manufactures textiles, chemicals, metal goods, etc. Cathedral (16th-cent.), several older churches, university (founded in the 13th cent.), the house where Columbus died (1506), and the home of Cervantes noteworthy. Flourished chiefly in the 16th cent.

**Valle d'Aosta** Italy. Autonomous region (since 1948) in the NW, bordering N on Switzerland (Pennine Alps) and W on France (Graian Alps). Area 1,259 sq. m. Pop. (1961) 99,754 (mainly French-speaking). Cap. Aosta. Comprises the upper basin of the Dora Baltea R. Largely agricultural. Many hydroelectric plants.

**Vallejo** USA. Port and industrial town in California, on San Pablo Bay 20 m. N of Oakland. Pop. (1960) 60,877. Flour milling, meat packing, etc. Naval station on Mare Island. State capital for a brief period 1852–3.

**Vallenar** Chile. Town in Atacama province, in the irrigated Huasco valley 90 m. SSW of Copiapó. Pop. 31,000. On the main N–S railway; also linked by rail with its port Huasco. Market town in a wine-producing district.

**Valletta (Valetta)** Malta. Capital, chief seaport, commercial and cultural centre, built at the end of a rocky peninsula, Mt Sceberras, on the E coast, lying between Grand and Marsamxett (Marsamuscetto) Harbours. Pop. (1967) 15,279. Formerly important as a naval base, headquarters of the British Mediterranean Fleet. Repeatedly bombed during the 2nd World War (1940–43), and some of its finest buildings were destroyed or irreparably damaged. Among the famous *auberges* (lodges) built for the various nationalities of the Knights of Malta, the outstanding Auberge de Castille survived. Cathedral (1577). University (1769). Founded by and named after Jean de la Valette, Grand Master of the Knights of Malta, following the victory over the Turks (1565). After the 2nd World War, the British government decided to close the naval dockyard; it was converted to civilian use (1959) and nationalized (1968). To compensate for loss of employment, new industries were introduced, e.g. light engineering, food processing.

Valleyfield (officially Salaberry de Valley-field) Canada. Industrial town in Quebec, on the St Lawrence R. at the E end of L. St Francis 33 m. SW of Montreal. Pop. (1966) 29,111. Manufactures textiles, paper, felt, etc.

Valley Stream USA. Town in New York, on the SW coast of Long Island. Pop. (1960) 38,629. Mainly residential; an outer suburb of New York city.

Valois France. Ancient district NE of Paris, now in the Oise and Aisne departments. A county, later a duchy, it was united to the crown in 1214 and again in 1498. Its capital was Crépy-en-Valois.

Valona ◊ Vlonë.

Valparaiso Chile. Capital of Valparaiso province, on a wide bay sheltered naturally from the S and artificially from the N, 60 m. WNW of Santiago. Pop. (1966) 261,684. The leading seaport of Chile and of the W coast of S America. Important industrial centre. Sugar refining. Manufactures textiles, clothing, chemicals, leather goods, etc. Seat of a university of technology (1926) and a Catholic university (1928). Founded 1536. Has suffered many earthquakes, and was largely destroyed by that of 1906.

Valtellina Italy. Valley of the upper Adda R. in Lombardy, extending from the Ortler mountain group to L. Como. Has many hydroelectric plants and tourist resorts. Chief town Sondrio (pop. 18,944). Belonged to the Cisalpine Republic from 1797; passed to Austria (1815) and to Italy (1859).

Van, Lake Turkey. Salt lake in the E at a height of 5,600 ft, the largest in Turkey, with no outlet. Area 1,453 sq. m. The small town of Van (pop. 22,000), capital of Van province, stands near its E shore. Salt and soda are obtained from the lake water by evaporation.

Vancouver Canada. Largest city in British Columbia, the third largest in Canada, and the country's chief Pacific seaport, on Burrard Inlet of Georgia Strait. Pop. (1966) 410,375 (metropolitan area 892,286). Has an excellent natural harbour. Handles cargoes of grain, fish, minerals, timber. Commercial, financial, and industrial metropolis of W Canada. Shipbuilding, fish canning, oil refining, sawmilling. Manufactures wood pulp and paper, steel goods, furniture, chemicals, etc. Also the terminus of the transcontinental railways. International airport. Linked with the Alberta oilfields by a pipeline (completed 1953). Many fine parks and open spaces, inc. Stanley Park (900 acres). Seat of the University of British Columbia (1908). Before the 2nd World War most of its inhabitants were of British extraction, but since 1945 it has become more cosmopolitan. The first sawmills were established here in the 1860s; the city was named and incorporated in 1886.

Vancouver USA. Port and commercial town in SW Washington, on the Columbia R. opposite Portland (Oregon), with which it is connected by bridge. Pop. (1960) 32,464. Exports grain, timber. Manufactures aluminium, chemicals, paper, etc. Also a military station. Founded 1825.

Vancouver Island Canada. Largest island off the W coast of America, in SW British Columbia. Area 12,408 sq. m. Pop. (1961) 290,835. Largely mountainous and densely forested; highest peak Golden Hinde (7,219 ft) in Strathcona Provincial Park. No navigable rivers, but the indented coastline provides a number of good harbours. Esquimault, on the S coast, is the chief Canadian naval base in the Pacific. Climate mild and temperate. Main occupations lumbering, fishing and fish canning, dairy and fruit farming. Coal, gold, and copper mined. Chief towns Victoria (capital of British Columbia), Nanaimo. The island became a Crown Colony 1849; united with British Columbia 1866.

Väner, Lake Sweden. The largest lake in Sweden, in the SW. Area 2,141 sq. m. Drained SW by the Göta R. to the Kattegat. Linked with L. Vätter and the Baltic Sea by the Göta Canal. Karlstad is on the N shore.

Vannes France. Prefecture of the Morbihan department in Brittany, on the Gulf of Morbihan 60 m. SW of Rennes. Pop. (1968) 40,724. Port. Boatbuilding, tanning. Manufactures textiles etc. Cathedral (13th/15th-cent.). Capital of the Veneti before the Roman conquest.

Vanua Levu ◊ Fiji Islands.

Var France. Department in Provence on the Mediterranean Sea. Area 2,325 sq. m. Pop. (1968) 555,926. Prefecture Draguignan. Contains part of the Alpes de Provence in the N and the Monts des Maures in the S; between them is the Argens R. valley. Vines, olives, and mulberries cultivated. Extensive bauxite deposits (Brignoles). Chief towns Toulon,

Draguignan; Hyères, St Tropez, Fréjus, and St Raphael are resorts. On the transfer of the Grasse district to the Alpes-Maritimes department (1860) the river which gave it its name no longer remained within the department.

**Varanasi** India. Formerly Benares, then Benaras. Sacred Hindu city, in SE Uttar Pradesh, on the Ganges R. 70 m. E of Allahabad. Pop. (1961) 471,258. Oilseed milling, engineering. Manufactures handmade textiles, brassware, jewellery. For about 3 m. along the Ganges the left bank is lined with ghats (flights of steps), where tens of thousands of pilgrims bathe annually in the sacred river: it is the ambition of every devout Hindu to have his sins thus washed away, and at death to be cremated here and have his ashes scattered on the water. In the city there are about 1,500 Hindu temples and several mosques, including the Golden Temple (1777) and the 17th-cent. mosque of Aurangzeb. Seat of two universities, the Hindu University (1916) and the Varanasaya Sanskrit Vishwavidyalaya (1958). Dates from very early times (probably as early as the 13th cent. B.C.). For some centuries an important centre of Buddhism. Ceded to Britain 1775.

**Vardar River** Greece/Yugoslavia. Chief river in Macedonia, 210 m. long, rising in the Šar Mountains in SW Yugoslavia and flowing NNE and then SSE, past Skoplje; it enters Greece, where it is known as the Axios, and reaches the Aegean Sea near Thessaloníki (Salonika).

**Varese** Italy. Capital of Varese province, in Lombardy, 30 m. NW of Milan. Pop. (1961) 66,963. Industrial centre. Manufactures cars, machinery, textiles, footwear, etc. Has a 16th/17th-cent. basilica. L. Varese is 3 m. W.

**Varna** Bulgaria. Formerly (1949–55) Stalin. Seaport, railway terminus, and resort on the Black Sea 230 m. ENE of Sofia. Pop. (1965) 180,062. Also a commercial and industrial centre. Trade in canned fish, grain, livestock. Tanning, food processing, etc. Founded by Greeks in the 6th cent. B.C. Taken from the Turks by the Russians and ceded to Bulgaria 1877.

**Var River** France. River 84 m. long in the Alpes-Maritimes department, rising in the Maritime Alps and flowing generally SSE to the Mediterranean 4 m. SW of Nice.

**Vasa** ◊ *Vaasa.*

**Västerås** Sweden. Capital of Västmanland county, on L. Mälar 55 m. WNW of Stockholm. Pop. (1968) 108,694. Important centre of the electrical industry; manufactures motors, generators, turbines, transformers, etc., also steel and glass. Has a 13th-cent. Gothic cathedral (twice restored in the 19th cent.) and a (rebuilt) 12th-cent. castle. Several national Diets were held here, notably that of 1527 when the Reformation was introduced into Sweden by Gustavus Vasa.

**Vatican City** Italy. Sovereign papal state forming an enclave in the city of Rome. Area 109 acres. Pop. 1,000. Mainly on the W bank of the Tiber, W of the Castel Sant'Angelo. Includes the papal residence and church, and administrative buildings. In the SE is the great Piazza leading to St Peter's Church, immediately N and NW of which are the Vatican Palace and its gardens. Famous art collections; one of the world's greatest libraries. Also has extra-territorial rights over three great basilicas outside the City (St John Lateran, St Mary Major, and St Paul Outside the Walls), the palace of San Callisto, and the papal summer residence of Castel Gandolfo. Has its own railway and radio and television station; issues its own stamps and coinage. Created by the Lateran Treaty (1929) between the Pope and the Italian government.

**Vatnajökull** Iceland. Large icefield in the SE. Area 3,140 sq. m. Includes active volcanoes; rises to 6,950 ft in Öræfajökull in the extreme S.

**Vätter, Lake** Sweden. Picturesque lake, the second largest in Sweden, SE of L. Väner. Area 733 sq. m. Linked to L. Väner by the Göta Canal (W) and to the Baltic Sea via the Motala R. (E). Jönköping is at the S end.

**Vaucluse** France. Department in Provence, bounded on the W by the Rhône R. and on the S by the Durance R. Area 1,381 sq. m. Pop. (1968) 353,966. Prefecture Avignon. The W half is in the fertile, lowlying Rhône valley; the E half is crossed by ranges of the Alpes de Provence, rising to 6,273 ft in Mont Ventoux. Noted for its wines (e.g. Chateauneuf-du-Pape) and fruits; olives, mulberries, cereals also cultivated. Chief towns Avignon, Orange, Cavaillon, Carpentras. Has an enclave, the canton of Valréas, in the Drôme department.

**Vaud** (Ger. **Waadt**) Switzerland. Canton in the W, extremely irregular in shape, bordering W on France and lying mainly between L. Neuchâtel and L. Geneva. Area 1,239 sq. m. Pop. (1969) 509,000 (mainly French-speaking and Protestant). Cap. Lausanne. Mountainous in the SE but generally fertile; noted for its wines. Chief towns and resorts Lausanne, Montreux, and Vevey on L. Geneva; Yverdon on L. Neuchâtel. Joined the Swiss Confederation 1803.

**Vauxhall** England. District in the London borough of Lambeth, on the S bank of the R. Thames. Named after Vauxhall Gardens (opened *c.* 1660), much frequented as a public garden from 1732 till its closure in 1859.

**Växjö** Sweden. Capital of Kronoberg county, 120 m. SE of Göteborg. Pop. (1968) 32,886. Manufactures paper, matches etc.

**Veii** Italy. Ancient city in Etruria, in modern Latium 9 m. NNW of Rome. An Etruscan stronghold, continually at war with Rome until captured by Camillus in 396 B.C. after a long siege. Etruscan and Roman remains have been discovered.

**Vejle** Denmark. Port and industrial town in E Jutland, on Vejle Fiord. Pop. (1965) 32,021. Manufactures hardware, machinery, textiles. Trade in dairy produce.

**Velbert** Federal German Republic. Industrial town in N Rhine-Westphalia, in the Ruhr 8 m. S of Essen. Pop. (1963) 53,000. Manufactures locks, vehicle fittings, windows, etc.

**Velebit Mountains** Yugoslavia. Mountain range in the Dinaric Alps, Croatia, extending about 100 m. along the Adriatic Sea, rising to 5,768 ft in Vaganjski Vrh.

**Velebit Strait** Yugoslavia. Narrow channel about 80 m. long parallel to the Velebit Mountains and separating the mainland from the neighbouring islands of Pag, Rab, etc.

**Vélez Málaga** Spain. Town in Málaga province, Andalusia, on the Vélez R. 18 m. ENE of Málaga. Pop. (1961) 35,061. Market town in a fertile region producing vines, citrus fruits, sugar-cane, etc. Sugar refining, tanning. Manufactures soap. Served by the near-by port of Torre del Mar.

**Velika Kikinda** ◊ *Kikinda*.

**Velletri** Italy. Ancient Velitrae. Town in Roma province, Latium, in the Alban Hills 22 m. SE of Rome. Pop. (1961) 40,053. Wine-making. Railway junction. Cathedral (13th-cent., rebuilt in the 17th

cent. and seriously damaged in the 2nd World War).

**Vellore** India. Town in Madras, on the Palar R. 80 m. WSW of Madras. Pop. (1961) 113,742. Trade in agricultural produce, sandalwood, etc. Famous for its fortress and a temple of Siva.

**Velsen** Netherlands. Industrial town in N Holland province 13 m. WNW of Amsterdam, forming a municipality with the fishing port of Ijmuiden (Ymuiden) 2 m. W, on the North Sea Canal. Pop. (1968) 67,864. Important centre of the steel industry; also manufactures chemicals, cement, paper. Severely damaged in the 2nd World War.

**Ven** ◊ *Landskrona*.

**Vendée** France. Department on the Bay of Biscay, formed (1790) from part of Poitou. Area 2,709 sq. m. Pop. (1968) 421,250. Prefecture La Roche-sur-Yon. Hilly in the NE but generally low-lying. Drained by the Sèvre Nantaise, the Sèvre Niortaise, and its tributary the Vendée. Mainly agricultural. Cattle rearing. Produces wheat, fodder crops, fruit, wine. Chief towns La Roche-sur-Yon, Les Sables d'Olonne. Scene of the Vendée royalist resistance to the French Revolution (1793–5).

**Veneto** Italy. Formerly Venezia Euganea. Region in the NE comprising the provinces of Belluno, Padova (Padua), Rovigo, Treviso, Venezia, Verona, Vicenza. Area 7,094 sq. m. Pop. (1961) 3,833,837. Cap. Venice. Mountainous in the N, including the Dolomites, the Asiago Plateau, and part of the Carnic Alps. Extends to L. Garda in the SW and Austria in the NE. The fertile plain (S) is drained by the Po, Adige, Brenta, Piave, and other rivers. Produces wheat, vines, sugar-beet, hemp, etc. Chief towns Venice, Padua, Treviso, Vicenza, Verona. Lost the province of Udine after the 2nd World War (1946), when this became part of Friuli-Venezia Giulia.

**Venezia Giulia** Italy. Former region in the NE comprising the provinces of Carnaro, Gorizia, Istria, Trieste, Zara. After the 2nd World War most of the region was ceded to Yugoslavia, the remainder becoming part of Friuli-Venezia Giulia.

**Venezuela**. Republic on the Caribbean coast of S America. Area 352,143 sq. m. Pop. (1961) 7,523,999. Cap. Carácas. Lang. Spanish. Rel. Roman Catholic.

Bounded by Guyana (E), Brazil (S), and

Colombia (W). The largest exporter of petroleum in the world, statistically it has the highest per capita income of all S American countries. Agriculture and cattle raising, however, are hampered by its mountainous nature and poor communications. The discrepancies between rich and poor are great, and a third of the population are close to destitution. The cost of living is high and much of the food is imported. The country is divided into 20 states, two territories, the federal district, and the federal dependencies (islands in the Antilles).

TOPOGRAPHY, CLIMATE. In the W the E Cordillera of the Andes trends N E as the high Cordillera de Mérida, then E, where lower highlands run parallel with the coast. W of L. Maracaibo is another spur of the E Cordillera, the Sierra de Perijá, and to the N E are the Segovia Highlands. Inland the vast lowland plains or *llanos* of central Venezuela are traversed by meandering tributaries of the Orinoco R. In the S E the Guiana Highlands occupy almost half the country; rivers rising here cut deep valleys as they too flow to the Orinoco, whose C-shaped course follows the massif edge.

There are four main climatic zones (according to altitude): the *tierra caliente* up to 3,000 ft, with mean annual temperatures over 75° F, rain-forest in wet locations, cacao, bananas, and sugar-cane being cultivated; the *tierra templada*, 3,000–6,000 ft, 65°–75° F, coffee being the chief crop on forest-cleared slopes; the *tierra fria*, 6,000–10,000 ft, 55°–65° F, with cultivation of cereals; the *páramos*, alpine meadows from 10,000 ft to the snowline at about 15,500 ft. Differences in rainfall are considerable and affect vegetation and land use at all levels. In N Venezuela E to N E winds prevail, so that sometimes the E slopes bear rain-forest while the W slopes have scrub savannah. Seasonal variations are most marked in the *llanos*, which are covered with tall-grass savannah, swamp grasses, and low deciduous woodland; they are often flooded April–Oct., but are dry Nov.–March, when the green, swamp-like conditions of the hot wet season change to a landscape of dry, brown grasses, leafless trees, and cracked mud-flats. The lower Orinoco and N E Guiana Highlands carry dense rain-forest; the W Guiana Highlands have much deciduous forest and wooded savannah.

ECONOMY. Petroleum production is of first importance. Venezuela is the third largest producer and the leading exporter in the world, and petroleum represents 90 per cent of total exports. It is produced chiefly around L. Maracaibo, with other wells in the E *llanos*; foreign companies own the concessions, and the government takes well over half the profits. Pipelines run from the oilfields to refineries on the shores of L. Maracaibo, on the Paraguaná peninsula, and at Puerto la Cruz in the N E. A dredged channel (completed 1956) enables ocean-going vessels to enter L. Maracaibo, and tankers transport oil to the Dutch Caribbean islands of Curaçao and Aruba. Resources of iron ore, manganese, and bauxite are tapped on the N edge of the Guiana Highlands, formerly yielding only gold and diamonds, and iron ore is a significant export; there is a steel works at Puerto Ordaz and a hydro-electric plant on the Caroní R.

The revenue from oil aids the growth of secondary industries, though development has been very limited. Principal manufactures textiles, clothing, footwear, cement, tyres, petrochemicals. Despite the country's mineral wealth, many of the people have a low living standard, particularly those engaged in agriculture, and about half the adult population are illiterate. Coffee grown in the highlands is the principal commercial crop, cacao, sugar-cane, tobacco, and cotton are grown, and cattle are raised; large areas of the *llanos* are either undeveloped or used for rough grazing. Carácas is linked to the chief seaport, La Guaira, by a six-lane highway. Other leading towns Maracaibo, Barquisimeto, Maracay, Valencia, Puerto Cabello (port). The urban population is increasing rapidly. Nearly three quarters of the population are mestizos of Spanish-Indian stock, about one tenth are Europeans, and the remainder Amer-Indians, Negroes, and mulattoes. There has been a considerable inflow of European immigrants (some $\frac{3}{4}$ million since 1946).

HISTORY. The first settlements in Venezuela were established by the Spaniards at Cumaná (1521) and Coro (1527), on the N coast; Valencia was founded in 1555 and Carácas in 1567. They penetrated the highlands, seeking gold, but made no settlement in the Orinoco basin until the 18th cent. Resisting Spanish oppression and avarice, in 1811 Francisco de Miranda and

Simon Bolívar declared a short-lived independence which was finally won after the Spanish defeat at Carabobo (1821). In 1830, however, Venezuela seceded from the newly-formed union of Gran Colombia. There followed more than a century of civil war, dictatorships, and international disputes, though economic relief was gained with oilfield development, begun in 1918. In 1947 a new constitution provided for presidential election by popular vote, which was followed by a military *coup d'état* (1948). The head of the junta government was assassinated, however, and the promulgation of a new constitution in 1961 did not save the country from further internal strife.

**Venice** (Italian **Venezia**) Italy. Capital of the Veneto region and of the Venezia province, at the head of the Adriatic Sea, in the NW of the Gulf of Venice. Pop. (1968) 366,814. Seaport. Naval base. Industrial centre. Manufactures glassware, jewellery, textiles, furniture, etc. Oil refining, engineering, shipbuilding, printing and publishing. Most industries are located in the mainland suburbs of Porto Marghera and Mestre. The city is built on a cluster of more than 100 small islands; linked with the mainland by a railway and road bridge. The islands are divided into two groups by the Grand Canal, the main artery of traffic, winding NW–SE. About 170 smaller canals (crossed by 400 bridges) serve the Grand Canal; means of transport consist of steamers, launches and gondolas. Beside the canals are many Byzantine, Gothic, and Renaissance palaces, erected on piles driven into the soft mud. At the centre is the famous St Mark's Square (Piazza San Marco) where are the great 11th/15th-cent. Church of St Mark, the 15th-cent. Clock Tower (Torre dell' Orologio), the Campanile, the Doge's Palace, and the Bridge of Sighs (connecting the Palace with the state prison). Among the many other churches are those of SS. Giovanni e Paolo, San Salvatore, and Santa Maria della Salute. The Academy of Fine Arts has the world's finest collection of Venetian paintings, with works by Bellini, Mantegna, Titian, Veronese, Tintoretto, Giorgione, etc. 2 m. SE, on a low island between the lagoon and the Gulf of Venice, is the fashionable seaside resort, the Lido.

Founded by mainland refugees escaping from the barbarian invasions which began in the 5th cent. The first Doge was elected in 697. In its favourable position for trade between Europe and the East the city became a strong maritime and commercial power; Venetian rule extended over the E Mediterranean and the Aegean to the Black Sea. It was governed by a strict oligarchy. Defeated Genoa, her great rival, in 1380; attained the peak of prosperity in the 14th and early 15th cent. Began to decline after the discovery of the Cape route to India. Ceded to Austria by Napoleon 1797. Passed to the new kingdom of Italy 1866.

**Venlo** Netherlands. Industrial town and railway junction in Limburg province, on the Maas R. near the German frontier. Pop. (1968) 61,675. Brewing, distilling, tanning. Manufactures chemicals etc. Also a river port and market town, with a large trade in market-garden produce. Has a 16th-cent. town hall.

**Ventimiglia** Italy. Seaport in Imperia province, Liguria, on the Gulf of Genoa 8 m. W of San Remo. Pop. (1961) 21,775. Also a seaside resort (Italian Riviera) with an important flower market. Cathedral (12th-cent., restored). The ruins of the ancient Album Intimilium lie 3 m. E of the modern town.

**Ventnor** England. Urban district on the S coast of the Isle of Wight. Pop. (1961) 6,410. Seaside resort. Built on terraces above the sea, it has a mild climate and contains several hospitals and convalescent homes. To the E is Bonchurch, where Swinburne (1837–1909) is buried. To the N is St Boniface Down (787 ft), the highest point in the Isle of Wight.

**Ventura** ◊ *San Buenaventura.*

**Veracruz** Mexico. 1. State on the Gulf of Mexico and its arm, the Gulf of Campeche, including part of the Isthmus of Tehuantepec. Area 27,759 sq. m. Pop. (1969) 3,629,000. Cap. Jalapa. Extends from the coastal plain into the Sierra Madre Oriental. Mainly agricultural. Crops include cotton, sugar-cane, tobacco. Rubber, chicle, and hardwoods obtained from the forests. Oil wells along the Gulf coast. Chief towns Jalapa, Veracruz (largest city).
2. Leading seaport of Mexico, on the Gulf of Mexico in Veracruz state. Pop. (1969) 199,500. Exports coffee, chicle, vanilla, tobacco, etc. Flour milling. Manufactures textiles, chemicals, soap, etc. Also a seaside resort. Founded near by 1519. Moved to the present site 1599.

**Vercelli** Italy. Ancient Vercellae. Capital of Vercelli province, in Piedmont, on the Sesia R. 40 m. ENE of Turin. Pop. (1961) 50,907. Important trade in rice. Rice and flour milling, sugar refining, textile manufacture, etc. In the cathedral library is the Vercelli Book (*Codex Vercellensis*), an Anglo-Saxon MS. dating from the early 11th cent. Chief town of the ancient Ligurian tribe of Libici.

**Verde, Cape** Senegal. The westernmost point of Africa, a promontory 20 m. long E–W. The W tip is Cape Almadies. Dakar is on the S coast.

**Verdun** Canada. Residential suburb of Montreal, Quebec, with roughly equal numbers of French- and English-speaking inhabitants. Pop. (1966) 76,832. Incorporated as a city 1921.

**Verdun** France. Ancient Verodunum. Small industrial town in the Meuse department on the canalized Meuse R. 36 m. W of Metz. Pop. (1968) 24,716. Manufactures alcohol, clothing, furniture. The ancient town was already important by the Roman conquest. By the famous Treaty of Verdun (843) the empire of Charlemagne was divided into three parts. It was one of the Three Bishoprics (with Toul and Metz) taken by France from the Holy Roman Empire (1552). In its strategic position at the E approach to the Paris Basin, Verdun became an important French fortress. During the 1st World War it was the scene of a long and costly battle (1916), characterized by a powerful German offensive repulsed by an equally determined and courageous French resistance. The town, virtually destroyed, was rebuilt after the war, to be damaged again in the 2nd World War.

**Vereeniging** S Africa. Town in the Transvaal, on the Vaal R. 33 m. S of Johannesburg at a height of 4,750 ft. Pop. (1967) 94,546 (58,750 Bantu, 33,360 whites). Coalmining and industrial centre. Manufactures iron and steel, nuts and bolts, cables and wire, bricks and tiles, etc. The Boer War was ended by the Treaty of Vereeniging (1902).

**Verkhoyansk** USSR. Small town in the Yakut ASSR (RSFSR) on the Yana R. 420 m. NNE of Yakutsk, with which it is linked by air. Fur-trading and mining centre. Situated near the so-called 'cold pole' of the earth, with a mean Jan. temperature of −59° F but a mean July temperature of 59° F; here the lowest temperature then recorded on the earth's surface, −90° F, was registered (1892), and the temperature has since reached almost −100° F. Formerly used as a place of exile.

**Verkhoyansk Range** USSR. Range of mountains in the Yakut ASSR (RSFSR), extending about 1,000 m. W and N in an arc parallel to and E of the Lena R. Rises in the extreme SE to 8,200 ft.

**Vermont** USA. New England state, in the NE, bordering N on Quebec (Canada). Area 9,609 sq. m. Pop. (1970) 437,744. Cap. Montpelier (pop. 8,782). Popularly known as the 'Green Mountain State', it was admitted to the Union (1791) as the 14th state. Traversed N–S by the Green Mountains, which rise to 4,393 ft in Mt Mansfield. Principal river the Connecticut, which forms the E boundary. Climate humid continental; average rainfall 35–45 ins. annually. Mainly agricultural. Leading crops hay, maize, apples, potatoes; produces maple syrup and sugar. Granite and marble quarried. Flourishing tourist industry. Vermont has always been a mainly rural state; only Burlington has a population exceeding 20,000.

**Verny** ♢ *Alma-Ata*.

**Véroia (Verria)** Greece. Capital of Imathía *nome*, Macedonia, 40 m. WSW of Thessaloníki (Salonika). Pop. (1961) 25,765. Trade in cereals etc. Manufactures textiles.

**Verona** Italy. Capital of Verona province, in Veneto, on the Adige R. 66 m. W of Venice. Pop. (1968) 251,603. Hub of routes from N Italy (Milan, Venice, etc.) through the Brenner Pass. Trade in cereals. Manufactures paper, plastics, rope, etc. Printing. Renowned for its buildings, among which are the 12th/17th-cent. Romanesque cathedral, the churches of S Zeno, S Anastasia, and S Fermo Maggiore, the tombs of the della Scala family (Scaligeri), and the medieval Castel Vecchio, which houses the fine Museum of Art; many were damaged in the 2nd World War. Of the Roman remains the outstanding is the restored amphitheatre, seating about 25,000 people, where open-air performances are held during the summer. Powerful and prosperous under the Romans, it was still more important in medieval times, and at various periods was a leading centre of art. Under Austrian rule (1797–1866) it was one of the famous 'Quadrilateral' of fortresses (with Peschiera, Mantua, and Legnago). Birthplace of Paolo Veronese (1528–88).

**Verria** ◊ *Véroia*.

**Versailles** France. Prefecture of theYvelines department, a residential suburb 11 m. WSW of Paris. Pop. (1968) 94,915. Also a tourist centre, chiefly famous for the magnificent palace. Varied industries. Louis XIII had a hunting lodge built near the village in 1624; the palace was designed in the late 17th cent. for Louis XIV by Le Vau and Mansart on a grand scale and at enormous cost. Among the outstanding features are the Hall of Mirrors, the Orangery, and the gardens planned by Le Nôtre. Near by are two smaller palaces, the Grand Trianon and the Petit Trianon, the latter a favourite residence of Marie Antoinette. In the Hall of Mirrors William I of Prussia was crowned Emperor of Germany (1871) and the Treaty of Versailles between the Allied powers and Germany was signed (1919) at the end of the 1st World War.

**Verulamium** ◊ *St Albans*.

**Verviers** Belgium. Industrial town in Liège province, on the Vesdre R. 15 m. ESE of Liège. Pop. (1968) 35,335. Important woollen industry. Also manufactures textile machinery, leather goods, chemicals, chocolate, etc.

**Vesuvius** (Italian **Vesuvio**) Italy. Active volcano in Campania, near the E shore of the Bay of Naples 8 m. ESE of Naples. The cone is half enclosed by a ridge, Monte Somma (3,714 ft), which is the wall of a great prehistoric crater, and the slopes are marked by lava flows. On the W slope is a seismological observatory (established 1844). Vineyards on the fertile lower slopes produce grapes for the well-known Lacrima Christi wine. The first recorded eruption occurred in A.D. 79 and destroyed Pompeii, Herculaneum, and Stabiae. For centuries Vesuvius was then much less active, but a severe eruption occurred in 1631 and further great convulsions in 1779, 1794, 1822, 1872, 1906, 1929, and 1944. These eruptions have continually altered its height, which is now 3,891 ft; that of 1944 destroyed the funicular railway, and a chair lift now takes visitors almost to the edge of the crater.

**Veszprém** Hungary. Capital of Veszprém county, on the S slopes of the Bakony Hills 60 m. SW of Budapest. Pop. (1968) 32,000. Railway junction. Market town. Manufactures textiles, wine, etc. Seat of a technical university (chemical engineering) (1949).

**Vevey** Switzerland. Resort in Vaud canton, on the NE shore of L. Geneva 11 m. ESE of Lausanne. Pop. (1960) 16,269. Has excellent views of the mountains. Manufactures chocolate, cigars, etc.

**Viareggio** Italy. Seaside resort in Lucca province, Tuscany, on the Ligurian Sea 13 m. WNW of Lucca. Pop. (1961) 47,323. Sandy beaches sheltered by pine woods. Manufactures hosiery etc. The body of Shelley was cremated here after his death by drowning (1822).

**Viborg** Denmark. Capital of Viborg county, in Jutland 26 m. W of Randers. Pop. (1965) 24,762. Iron founding, distilling. Manufactures textiles. Has a 12th-cent. cathedral (restored in the 19th cent.).

**Viborg** (USSR) ◊ *Vyborg*.

**Vicenza** Italy. Ancient Vicetia (Vicentia). Capital of Vicenza province, in Veneto, 40 m. WNW of Venice. Pop. (1968) 109,511. Railway junction. Industrial centre. Manufactures iron and steel, machinery, furniture, glass, etc. Has a mainly 13th-cent. Gothic cathedral. Birthplace of Andrea Palladio (1518–80); has many of his most famous buildings (e.g. the Teatro Olimpico, the basilica, and the Palazzo Chiericati), several of which, with the cathedral, were severely damaged in the 2nd World War. Ruled by Austria 1797–1866.

**Vichy** France. Health resort and spa in the Allier department, on the Allier R. 30 m. NNE of Clermont-Ferrand. Pop. (1968) 33,898. Has many hotels, thermal establishments, recreational centres, etc. Vichy water, consumed for stomach and liver complaints, is bottled and exported. Manufactures pharmaceutical products. Seat of the Pétain ('Vichy') government of France during the 2nd World War (1940–44).

**Vicksburg** USA. River port in Mississippi, on the Mississippi R. near its confluence with the Yazoo R. Pop. (1960) 29,130. Trade in cattle, cotton. Manufactures cottonseed oil, clothing, chemicals, etc. In the Civil War it was a Confederate stronghold and was besieged for nearly 7 weeks before capitulating (1863). Just N is Vicksburg National Cemetery (established 1865) with over 16,000 soldiers' graves.

**Victoria** Australia. Second smallest and most densely populated state, in the SE, bounded by New South Wales (N), the

Tasman Sea, Bass Strait, and Indian Ocean (S), and S Australia (W). Area 87,884 sq. m. Pop. (1966) 3,219,526. Cap. Melbourne. The plains in the N and NW form part of the Murray Basin. S of these lies the extension of the Great Dividing Range, then there are fairly level lowlands, sometimes called the Great Valley, and still farther S the coastal uplands. Port Phillip Bay is a drowned part of the Great Valley; into it flows the Yarra R., on which Melbourne stands. The driest area is the Murray basin, but irrigation makes possible fruit orchards, vineyards, and pastures. Extensive wheatlands and sheep country lie S W of the basin and on the inner mountain slopes. E of Melbourne there is dairy farming, and fruit and vegetables are also grown in the S. Gold stimulated the early settlement of Victoria, with the rushes to Ballarat and Bendigo in the 1850s, but today the state produces little gold. Coal is mined in S Gippsland, and huge lignite deposits W of Melbourne supply power stations; hydroelectricity comes from dams on the Murray R. and its tributaries, and from the Snowy Mountains scheme. Many industries, esp. in Melbourne and at Geelong, Ballarat, and smaller towns; they include engineering, oil refining, and the manufacture of textiles, cars, aircraft, agricultural equipment, chemicals. At inland towns and ports fruit is canned, preserved, and dried. Population predominantly urban: 66 per cent of the state population live in the Melbourne metropolitan area. Exports include wool, wheat, textiles, dairy produce, canned fruit.

The first settlement was made at Portland in the SW in 1834, and in the following year Melbourne was founded. Victoria formed part of the New South Wales colony 1836–51, and was a separate colony 1851–1901. Became a state of the Commonwealth 1901, with Melbourne the Commonwealth capital until 1927.

**Victoria** Canada. Capital of British Columbia, at the SE tip of Vancouver Island facing the Juan de Fuca Strait. Pop. (1966) 57,453. Seaport and base for the fishing fleet. Exports fish, timber, cement, etc. Fish canning. Manufactures paper, matches. The provincial parliament buildings are esp. noteworthy, and there are several fine parks; the mild climate attracts many tourists. Founded (1843) by the Hudson's Bay Company as a fur-

trading post. Became capital of British Columbia 1868.

**Victoria** (Hong Kong) ◊ *Hong Kong.*
**Victoria** (Malaysia) ◊ *Labuan.*
**Victoria** (Malta) ◊ *Gozo.*
**Victoria** (Seychelles) ◊ *Seychelles.*
**Victoria** USA. Industrial town in S Texas, on the Guadalupe R. 120 m. SW of Houston. Pop. (1960) 33,047. Oil refining. Manufactures cottonseed oil, chemicals, etc. Founded (1824) by Spanish settlers.

**Victoria (Victoria Nyanza), Lake** E Africa. The largest lake in Africa and the second largest freshwater lake in the world. Area 26,828 sq. m. In the plateau basin between the E and W branches of the Great Rift Valley, at a height of 3,700 ft. Fed by the Kagera R. (often regarded as the farthest headstream of the Nile), the Katonga R., and the Mara R. Drained N from Jinja (Uganda) by the Victoria Nile. Just below Jinja is the Owen Falls dam (completed 1954), which stores the headwaters of the Nile and has raised the lake level by 3 ft. Many inlets in the shores, e.g. the Kavirondo Gulf (NE) and the Speke Gulf (SE). Many islands. Steamer services; main ports Jinja and Entebbe in Uganda, Bukoba and Mwanza in Tanzania, Kisumu in Kenya. Discovered (1858) by Speke; explored (1875) by Stanley. Originally Lake Ukerewe; renamed in honour of Queen Victoria. ◊ *Tabora.*

**Victoria Falls** Rhodesia/Zambia. Falls on the middle Zambezi R. on the frontier between Zambia and Rhodesia. Greater in height and width than Niagara Falls; divided by islets into 3 main sections, the Eastern Cataract, the Rainbow Falls, and the Main Falls. The Zambezi plunges into a great chasm over 1 m. long at right-angles to its course, about 420 ft deep at the centre. Less than 400 ft from the edge of the falls, and at the same level, are the opposite cliffs. The river leaves the chasm through a narrow opening in the cliffs (the 'Boiling Pot') and enters a winding gorge crossed by a railway and road bridge. The Victoria Falls are an important tourist attraction, esp. June–Oct., immediately after the flood period. A hydroelectric plant serves Livingstone (Zambia).

**Victoria Island** Canada. Second largest island in the Canadian Arctic Archipelago, in the SW Franklin District of the NW Territories, separated from the mainland by the Dolphin and Union Strait, Coronation Gulf, and Queen Maud Gulf. Area 80,340 sq. m. Discovered 1838.

**Victoria Land** ◊ *Ross Dependency.*

**Vienna** (Ger. **Wien**) Austria. Capital, administratively a province, mainly on the right bank of the Danube R. and on the Danube Canal, at the foot of wooded hills (the Wiener Wald). Pop. (1961) 1,627,566 (23 per cent of the national total). Commercial, industrial, and cultural centre, and one of the most beautiful cities in Europe. Route centre. Inland port. Manufactures machinery, electrical equipment, textiles, chemicals, paper, furniture, leather goods, etc. Divided into 26 Districts (*Bezirke*) grouped round the Inner City. The old ramparts enclosing the Inner City were removed (1858–60) to make way for the famous Ringstrasse boulevard within which stand most of the chief buildings. These include the Hofburg (the former imperial palace), the mainly 14th–15th-cent. Cathedral of St Stephen (with a Gothic spire 450 ft high), the Gothic *Rathaus*, the Houses of Parliament in Greek style, and the Opera House in Renaissance style. Also many fine museums and art collections. The university (1365) has a medical faculty of world reputation. Several beautiful parks and gardens, including the famous Prater. Home of Haydn, Mozart, Beethoven, Schubert; birthplace of the younger Johann Strauss (1825–99) and inevitably associated with his waltzes and other light music.

In early times a Celtic settlement. Later a Roman military town. Capital of the duchy of Austria in the 12th cent.; its importance grew during the Crusades. Passed (with the duchy) to the Habsburgs 1278. Besieged by the Turks in 1529 and 1683. Expanded rapidly in the 18th cent. The Congress of Vienna (1814–15) arranged the 'Concert of Europe' after Napoleon's defeat. After the 1st World War and the resulting dissolution of the Austro-Hungarian Empire, it became a disproportionately large capital in a small republic, losing both trade and population. There was also much destruction and suffering during and after the 2nd World War. Jointly occupied by the four Allied powers 1946–55.

**Vienne** France. Department in W central France, formed (1790) mainly from Poitou. Area 2,720 sq. m. Pop. (1968) 340,256. Prefecture Poitiers. Drained chiefly by the Vienne R. Mainly agricultural (cereals, potatoes, wines, stock rearing). Chief towns Poitiers, Châtellerault.

**Vienne** (Isère) France. Town in the Isère department on the left bank of the Rhône R. 17 m. S of Lyons. Pop. (1968) 30,276. Manufactures woollen and leather goods. Iron founding, distilling, etc. Has noteworthy Roman remains (including the temple of Augustus and Livia) and the 11th/16th-cent. church (former cathedral) of St Maurice. Originally capital of the Allobroges; became an important city in Roman Gaul.

**Vienne River** France. River 220 m. long, rising on the Plateau de Millevaches (N Corrèze) and flowing generally NNW past Limoges and Châtellerault to join the Loire R.

**Vientiane** Laos. Administrative capital of Laos, on the left bank of the Mekong R. where the latter forms the boundary with Thailand. Pop. (1963) 138,000. River port. Commercial centre. Trade in timber, resins and gums, textiles, etc. Has the former royal palace and several pagodas. It was capital of the kingdom of Vientiane from 1707, but declined after being taken by the Thais (1827), to revive in the present century as capital of all Laos.

**Viersen** Federal German Republic. Industrial town in N Rhine-Westphalia, on the Niers R. 4 m. NNW of München-Gladbach. Pop. (1963) 42,200. Manufactures textiles (velvet, cotton, linen), paper, etc.

**Vierwaldstättersee** ◊ *Lucerne, Lake.*

**Vierzon** France. Town in the Cher department at the confluence of the Cher and Yèvre rivers 17 m. NW of Bourges. Pop. (1968) 34,421. Manufactures bricks and tiles, porcelain, agricultural machinery, etc.

**Vietnam.** In Annamese, 'Land of the South'. Region in S E Asia, in the E part of the peninsula of Indo-China, comprising the former Tonkin, Annam, and Cochin-China, now divided politically into N and S Vietnam.

N VIETNAM (Democratic Republic of Vietnam). Comprises 29 provinces of N Vietnam (former Tonkin) and 4 northern provinces of Central Vietnam (N part of former Annam). Area 63,344 sq. m. Pop. (1960) 15,916,955. Cap. Hanoi. Consists in the main of the valley and delta of the Red R. and its tributaries. Separated by lofty mountains in the W from Yunnan (China) and Laos. Principal crop rice; sugar-cane and maize also cultivated. Under the Communist régime practically all the peasants have been organized in agricultural co-operatives. Principal mineral coal; phosphates are important, and tin and zinc are also produced. Hanoi and Haiphong, the chief seaport, are the leading industrial centres. Political power in N Vietnam is in the hands of the Workers' (Communist) Party, and in many respects the constitution of 1960 is similar to that of the People's Republic of China.

S VIETNAM (Republic of Vietnam). Comprises the S part of Central Vietnam (former Annam) and 23 provinces of S Vietnam (former Cochin-China). Area 66,263 sq. m. Pop. (1962) 14,200,000. Cap. Saigon. Bounded on the W by Laos and Cambodia, being separated from the former by high mountain ranges. Most of the people are concentrated in the great delta of the Mekong in the S and in the narrow coastal plains. On these lowlands rice is grown on nearly 90 per cent of the cultivated area; rubber is by far the most important export. Sugar-cane and maize are also grown, and tea and coffee at higher levels. Industries are located mainly in the Saigon-Cholon area. The only other large towns are Hué and Binh Dinh. According to the constitution of 1956 executive power is vested in the President and legislative power in a single-chamber National Assembly.

HISTORY. More than 80 per cent of the people of Vietnam are Vietnamese (Annamese), who are of Mongolian origin; there are minorities of Cambodians and Chinese, and various aboriginal tribes such as the Moi and Muong are thinly scattered over the mountainous regions. From earliest times the region was dominated by China. European influence was not established till the mid-19th cent., when a French punitive expedition was sent to avenge the death of some missionaries, and by 1884 Cochin-China was a French colony and Annam and Tonkin were French protectorates. There was considerable opposition to French rule, however, and this became active during the Japanese occupation of the 2nd World War, when the Vietminh League was founded by the Communists (1941). In 1945 a Vietnamese republic was set up by the Vietminh, but the French objected to the inclusion of Cochin-China; hostilities broke out, the French were forced to withdraw, and the country was partitioned approximately along the 17th parallel (1954). At the same time S Vietnam left the French Union and attained full sovereignty. There was much disaffection over the dictatorial methods of the President of the Republic, particularly in his persecution of the Buddhists (he was a Roman Catholic), and he was overthrown and shot in a military *coup* (1963); meanwhile, the Communist guerrillas or Vietcong, aided from N Vietnam, intensified their campaign and made steady progress. US economic and military aid was increased rapidly 1964–6 to offset the growing strength of the Vietcong. Peace talks began in Paris 1968.

**Vigevano** Italy. Industrial town in Pavia province, Lombardy, near the Ticino R. 20 m. SW of Milan. Pop. (1961) 57,069. Manufactures footwear, textiles, plastics, etc. Has a 14th-cent. castle of the Sforza family.

**Vigo** Spain. Seaport, fishing port, and resort in Pontevedra province, Galicia, on the S shore of Vigo Bay (Ría de Vigo). Pop. (1967) 179,567. A port of call for transatlantic liners, with a fine natural harbour. Fish processing, boatbuilding, oil refining, distilling. Manufactures chemicals, soap, cement, paper, etc. Attacked by Drake 1585 and 1589. A British and Dutch fleet destroyed a Spanish fleet in the bay (1702); some of the treasure of the latter is believed to be still lying there.

**Viipuri** ◊ *Vyborg*.

**Vijayavada** India. Formerly Bezwada. Commercial town and railway junction in Andhra Pradesh, on the Krishna R. 150 m. ESE of Hyderabad. Pop. (1961) 230,397. Engineering, rice and oilseed milling, etc. Also headquarters of the Krishna canal system for irrigation and navigation.

**Vila** ◊ *New Hebrides*.

**Villach** Austria. Industrial town in Carinthia, on the Drau (Drava) R. 22 m. W of Klagenfurt. Pop. (1961) 32,971. Manufactures lead products etc. Has a considerable tourist traffic; 2 m. S is Warmbad Villach, with hot mineral springs. Has a 15th-cent. Gothic church with a 315-ft tower.

**Villahermosa** Mexico. Capital of Tabasco state, on the Grijalva R. 240 m. ESE of Veracruz. Pop. 52,000. Market town. Sugar refining, distilling, etc.

**Villa María** Argentina. Market town and

railway junction in Córdoba province, on the Tercero R. 90 m. SE of Córdoba. Pop. 50,000. Manufactures textiles. Flour milling etc. Trade in grain, timber, dairy produce.

**Villarrica** Paraguay. Capital of Guairá department, 90 m. ESE of Asunción in an agricultural region. Pop. (1962) 30,761. Market town. Trade in yerba maté, tobacco, cotton, sugar-cane, etc. Flour milling, sugar refining, etc.

**Villavicencio** Colombia. Capital of Meta department, at the foot of the E Cordillera 45 m. SE of Bogotá. Pop. 44,000. Commercial centre for the llanos. Trade in cattle, hides, etc. Rice milling.

**Villeurbanne** France. Industrial suburb of Lyons (E), in the Rhône department. Pop. (1968) 122,898. Manufactures textiles, chemicals, metal goods, etc. Food processing, tanning.

**Vilnyus** (**Vilnius**, Russian **Vilna**, Polish **Wilno**) USSR. Capital of the Lithuanian SSR, on the Viliya R. Pop. (1970) 372,000. Important railway junction and industrial centre. Sawmilling, food processing. Manufactures agricultural implements, fertilizers, paper, etc. Also a cultural centre, with a university founded in 1579, closed in 1832 for political reasons, and reopened in 1920. The Roman Catholic cathedral was originally built in the 14th cent., the present structure being completed in 1801; there are also many other Roman Catholic churches, some Orthodox and Protestant churches, synagogues, and a mosque. Founded in the 10th cent. Became capital of the grand duchy of Lithuania 1323. Suffered severely in the wars following the union of Poland and Lithuania (1569), and passed to Russia in the Partition of Poland (1795). Seized by Poland 1920; restored to Lithuania 1939, succeeding Kaunas as the capital. During the German occupation of the 2nd World War the city's Jews were practically exterminated.

**Vilvoorde** Belgium. Industrial town in Brabant province 6 m. NNE of Brussels. Pop. (1968) 34,204. Oil refining. Manufactures chemicals, electrical equipment, textiles, etc.

**Viña del Mar** Chile. Residential suburb and seaside resort, one of the most popular in S America, just NE of Valparaiso. Pop. (1966) 107,563. Has many bathing beaches, parks, and hotels, a casino and a racecourse. Also an industrial and commercial centre. Sugar refining. Manufactures textiles, paint, etc. Trade in fruit, wine, vegetables.

**Vincennes** France. Suburb of E Paris, in the Val-de-Marne department. Pop. (1968) 49,297. Manufactures electrical equipment, chemicals, perfumes, rubber products, etc. Its famous castle, on the N border of the Bois de Vincennes, was begun in the 12th cent., later became a state prison, and had many distinguished inmates.

**Vindhya Range** India. Range of mountains in central India, about 600 m. long, extending ENE roughly parallel to and N of the Namada R. valley. Average height 1,500–2,500 ft. Separates the Ganges basin (N) from the Deccan (S).

**Vinnitsa** USSR. Capital of the Vinnitsa Region, Ukrainian SSR, on the S Bug R. 125 m. SW of Kiev. Pop. (1970) 211,000. Flour milling, meat packing. Manufactures machinery, fertilizers, etc. Ruled by Poland from 1569 and by Russia from 1793.

**Virginia** USA. Middle Atlantic state, roughly triangular in shape and including the S end of the Delmarva peninsula across Chesapeake Bay. Area 40,815 sq. m. Pop. (1970) 4,543,249 (900,000 Negroes). Cap. Richmond. One of the original 13 states and the 10th to ratify the Constitution (1788); popularly known as the 'Old Dominion' and 'Mother of Presidents'. Consists of three distinct regions: the low coastal plain, deeply indented with estuaries and including the marshy Dismal Swamp in the SE; to the W the gently undulating Piedmont plateau, rising from 300 ft (E) to 1,200 ft (W); and still farther W the Blue Ridge, extending about 300 m. NE–SW across the state and rising to 5,720 ft in Mt Rogers, and the ridges and valleys of the Appalachians (inc. the famous Shenandoah Valley). Chief rivers the Potomac, James, Roanoke, Rappahannock. Most of the state has a humid sub-tropical climate, with an annual rainfall of 40–50 ins. Leading commercial crop tobacco; maize, wheat, oats, groundnuts also grown. Extensive fishing in Chesapeake Bay. Most important mineral coal. Chief industrial centres Norfolk, Richmond, Portsmouth, and Newport News – the last two being ports on Hampton Roads. In historical importance Virginia is unrivalled among US states: the first permanent English settlement in America was made at Jamestown (1607), and the state produced such famous men as Washington, Jefferson, Monroe, and Robert E. Lee. In the Civil War it espoused the Confederate cause and was re-admitted to the Union in 1870.

**Virgin Islands** W Indies. Archipelago lying E of Puerto Rico and geologically similar to the Greater Antilles, belonging partly to Britain (◊ *British Virgin Islands*) and partly to the USA (◊ *Virgin Islands of the USA*).

**Virgin Islands of the USA** W Indies. Group of over 60 islands and islets between Puerto Rico and the British Virgin Is. Area 133 sq. m. Pop. (1960) 32,099. Cap. Charlotte Amalie (pop. 12,740) on St Thomas (area 27 sq. m., pop. 16,201); the other two main islands are ◊ *St Croix* and St John (area 19 sq. m., pop. 925). The remaining islets are uninhabited. Cattle rearing, rum distilling, and the cultivation of sugar-cane and vegetables are important; tourism is developing. The islands were purchased by the USA from Denmark (1917) because of their strategic position on the route from the Atlantic to the Caribbean Sea and the Panama Canal.

**Vis** (Italian **Lissa**) Yugoslavia. Island off the Dalmatian coast 33 m. SSW of Split. Area 39 sq. m. Pop. 3,000. Chief town Vis. Main occupations vine growing, fishing. The British defeated the French (1811) and the Austrians defeated the Italians (1866) in naval engagements off the island. During the 2nd World War it served as a Yugoslav partisan headquarters and supply base for a time.

**Visby** Sweden. Capital of Gotland county, on the W coast of Gotland island. Pop. 16,000. Seaport. Resort. Sugar refining, metal working. Manufactures cement. Has a medieval appearance; its walls and massive towers, the cathedral (12th/13th-cent., restored), and several other partly ruined churches all provide evidence of its former wealth. An early member of the Hanseatic League, it achieved its greatest prosperity from the 11th to the 14th cent. It changed hands between Sweden and Denmark, lost much of its trade, became Swedish again in 1645, and revived in the late 19th cent.

**Vishakhapatnam (Vizagapatam)** India. Seaport in Andhra Pradesh, on the Bay of Bengal 310 m ENE of Hyderabad. Pop. (1961) 182,002. Exports manganese, oilseeds, etc. Has a modern protected harbour (1933), an oil refinery, and the country's only major shipyards, where the first completely Indian-built steamer was launched (1948). The suburb of Waltair, a seaside resort, is the seat of Andhra University (1926).

**Vistula** (Polish **Wisła**, Ger. **Weichsel**, Russian **Visla**) River Poland. River 680 m. long rising in the W Beskids (Carpathians) and flowing generally N and NW past Cracow, Warsaw, and Toruń. Below Tczew it forms a delta, the Martwa Wisla ('Dead Vistula') and the Nogat being the main channels, and reaches the Gulf of Gdańsk. Linked with the Neman, Oder, and Bug rivers by canals; thus of considerable value to Polish trade.

**Vitebsk** USSR. Capital of the Vitebsk Region, Byelorussian SSR, on the W Dvina R. 145 m. NE of Minsk. Pop. (1970) 231,000 (inc. many Jews). Industrial centre. Manufactures agricultural machinery, linen goods, footwear, glass, furniture, etc. The chief town of the Polotsk principality, it passed to Lithuania in the 14th cent., to Poland in the 16th cent., and was finally annexed to Russia in 1772.

**Viterbo** Italy. Capital of Viterbo province, in Latium, 40 m. NNW of Rome. Pop. (1961) 50,047. Manufactures furniture, pottery, olive oil, macaroni, etc. Has a 12th-cent. cathedral; beautiful fountains. Here Pope Adrian IV (Nicholas Breakspear) enforced the homage of the emperor Frederick I; it was a favourite papal residence in the 13th cent.

**Viti Levu** ◊ *Fiji Islands*.

**Vitim River** USSR. River in S Siberia 1,100 m. long, rising on the Vitim plateau E of L. Baikal and flowing S, NE, N, and NW to join the Lena R. at Vitim. Bodaibo, on the river, is the centre of a goldmining industry.

**Vitória** Brazil. Capital of Espírito Santo state, on an island linked by bridge with the mainland, 270 m. NE of Rio de Janeiro. Pop. 85,000. A seaport. Exports iron ore from the Itabira mines, also coffee and timber. Sugar refining. Manufactures textiles, cement, etc.

**Vitoria** Spain. Capital of Álava province 32 m. SSE of Bilbao at a height of 1,750 ft. Pop. (1967) 110,869. Manufactures furniture. Tanning, flour milling, etc. Trade in cereals, potatoes, wool, wine. Has a 12th-cent. cathedral (much modified) and a 12th-cent. church. In the Peninsular War Wellington decisively defeated the French here (1813).

**Vittoria** Italy. Town in Ragusa province,

SE Sicily, 12 m. WNW of Ragusa. Pop. (1961) 45,035. Important wine trade. Manufactures alcohol, macaroni, etc.

**Vittorio Veneto** Italy. Town in Treviso province, Veneto, 23 m. N of Treviso. Pop. (1961) 27,399. Manufactures textiles, etc. Chiefly known for one of the last battles of the 1st World War, in which the Italians decisively defeated the Austrians (1918).

**Vizagapatam** ◊ *Vishakhapatnam.*

**Vizcaya** Spain. One of the ◊ *Basque Provinces*, on the Bay of Biscay. Area 858 sq. m. Pop. (1961) 754,383 (the second most densely populated province in Spain). Cap. Bilbao. Rich iron mines and an important iron and steel industry centred on Bilbao. Other towns Guernica, Durango.

**Vlaardingen** Netherlands. Port and fishing centre in S Holland province, on the New Maas R. 6 m. W of Rotterdam. Pop. (1968) 78,654. Fish processing. Manufactures fertilizers, rope, sails, soap, etc. Has a 17th cent. town hall.

**Vladikavkaz** ◊ *Ordzhonikidze.*

**Vladimir** USSR. Capital of the Vladimir Region, RSFSR, on the Klyazma R. 115 m. ENE of Moscow. Pop. (1970) 234,000. Industrial centre. Manufactures textiles, tractors, machine tools, precision instruments, etc. The kremlin (citadel), situated on a hill, contains two 12th-cent. cathedrals (restored in the 19th cent.) and there are several 12th-cent. churches. Founded in the early 12th cent., became capital of the Vladimir principality, and passed to Moscow in the 14th cent.

**Vladivostok** USSR. Capital of the Primorye Territory, RSFSR, on the Pacific coast between Amur Bay and the Golden Horn 380 m. SSW of Khabarovsk. Pop. (1970) 442,000. Chief seaport and naval base on this coast. Fishing, whaling. Exports soya-bean oil, oilcake, coal, timber, fish. Also an industrial centre and terminus of the Trans-Siberian Railway. Shipbuilding, sawmilling, fish canning, food processing, etc. Has a good natural harbour, kept open by ice-breakers in winter. Seat of a university (1923, closed 1939–56). Founded 1860. Developed rapidly after the completion of the Chinese Eastern Railway (1904).

**Vlissingen** ◊ *Flushing.*

**Vlonë (Valona)** Albania. Capital of the Vlonë district, in the SW 62 m. SSW of Tiranë. Pop. (1967) 50,000. Seaport. Market town. Exports petroleum. Linked by pipeline with the Kuçovë oilfield. Fishing, fish canning, oil-refining. Manufactures olive oil, cement. The independence of Albania was proclaimed here (1912).

**Vltava (Ger. Moldau) River** Czechoslovakia. River 270 m. long rising in the Bohemian Forest (Böhmerwald) and flowing SSE and then generally N past České Budějovice and Prague to join the Elbe (Labe) R. near Melnik. Important hydroelectric installations.

**Vojvodina** Yugoslavia. Autonomous province in N Serbia, bordering on Hungary (N) and Rumania (E). Area 8,683 sq. m. Pop. (1961) 1,854,965 (inc. Serbs, Croats, Hungarians, Rumanians, and Slovaks). Cap. Novi Sad. Generally low-lying and fertile; drained chiefly by the Danube, Sava, and Tisa (Tisza) rivers. Produces large quantities of cereals, fruit, vegetables. Chief towns Novi Sad, Subotica, Zrenjanin, Pančevo. Ceded by Hungary to Yugoslavia after the 1st World War. Became an autonomous province after the 2nd World War.

**Volcano Islands** (Japanese **Kazan-retto**) W Pacific Ocean. Group of 3 volcanic islands 750 m. S of Tokyo, the largest being Iwo Jima. Total area 11 sq. m. Pop. about 1,000. Sugar plantations. Sulphur mines. Annexed by Japan 1887. Taken by US forces in the 2nd World War, and afterwards administered by the US Navy. Returned to Japan 1968.

**Volga Heights (Volga Hills)** USSR. Hills in RSFSR extending along the right bank of the Volga R. between Gorky and Volgograd, rising to about 1,000 ft.

**Volga River** USSR. River 2,425 m. long, the longest in Europe and the most important in the USSR, navigable for almost the entire course. Rising in the Valdai Hills, it flows generally E past Kalinin, Yaroslavl, Kostroma, and Gorky to Kazan, turns S and flows past Kuibyshev (on a wide bend), Saratov, Volgograd, and Astrakhan, entering the Caspian Sea by a broad delta. Chief tributaries the Oka (right bank) and the Kama (left bank). A vast scheme for the greater exploitation of the Volga, to provide hydroelectric power, irrigate the dry wheat-growing steppes E of the middle course, and improve navigation, was undertaken in the 1930s. Between Kalinin and Gorky are the Volga Reservoir, the great Rybinsk Reservoir, the Kostroma Reservoir, and the Gorky

Reservoir. Below Gorky are the Cheboksary Reservoir and the Kuibyshev Reservoir (which extends up the Kama R.) the Saratov Reservoir, and the Volgograd Reservoir. The Moscow–Volga Canal was opened in 1937 and the Volga–Don Canal in 1952; with the Mariinsk Canal System, these made the river and the capital accessible to vessels from the White Sea, the Baltic, the Caspian, the Sea of Azov, and the Black Sea. Closed by ice 3–5 months annually, and impeded by shoals in late summer, but of paramount importance to transportation in European Russia. Below the Volgograd Reservoir it receives no tributaries, and forms a braided flood plain below sea level. The many distributaries on the delta are rich in sturgeon and other fish.

**Volgograd** USSR. Formerly Tsaritsyn, Stalingrad. Capital of the Volgograd Region, RSFSR, on the Volga R. near the junction with the Volga–Don Canal (opened 1952). Pop. (1970) 818,000. Important river port and industrial centre. Manufactures iron and steel, tractors, machine tools, oilfield machinery, railway equipment, cement, footwear, clothing. Sawmilling, oil refining. Founded (as Tsaritsyn) 1589. Became important in the 19th cent. chiefly because of its position on the Volga–Don route. Besieged by the White Army after the 1917 revolution; renamed (1925) after Stalin because of his part in the defence. Besieged by the Germans during the 2nd World War (1942–3), and seriously damaged. After a Soviet counter-attack the German army capitulated; the Battle of Stalingrad was the turning-point of the war on the Soviet front. Renamed 1961.

**Volhynia** ◊ *Volyn*.

**Volkhov River** USSR. River 140 m. long in RSFSR, rising in L. Ilmen and flowing NNE past Novgorod and Volkhov to L. Ladoga; an important waterway. Volkhov is the site of a hydroelectric power station, at the rapids, and a large aluminium plant.

**Völklingen** Federal German Republic. Industrial town in Saarland, on the Saar R. 7 m. WNW of Saarbrücken. Pop. (1963) 42,900. Coalmining. Manufactures steel, machinery, electrical equipment, cement, etc.

**Vologda** USSR. Capital of the Vologda region, RSFSR, on the Vologda R. 110 m. N of Yaroslavl. Pop. (1970) 178,000. Industrial centre. Railway junction. Railway engineering. Manufactures agricultural machinery, textiles, glass, cement, etc. Important trade in dairy produce from the surrounding area. Cathedral (16th-cent.). Founded (1147) as a colony of Novgorod, it flourished as a commercial centre in the 16th cent., declined later, and recovered with the construction of the railway to Archangel.

**Vólos** Greece. Capital of Magnesia *nome*, Thessaly, at the head of the Gulf of Vólos 100 m. NNW of Athens. Pop. (1961) 49,221. Chief seaport of Thessaly. Manufactures textiles, chemicals, cement, etc. Exports tobacco, olive oil. A relatively modern city; severely damaged in earthquakes (1954, 1955) and rebuilt.

**Volta Redonda** Brazil. Town in Rio de Janeiro state, on the Paraíba R. 60 m. WNW of Rio de Janeiro on the main Rio–São Paulo railway. Pop. 84,000. Has the country's main steel plant (largest in S America), inaugurated in 1947. Well known as a model industrial town, with the steel plant near the river and workers' homes built on the near-by wooded slopes.

**Volta River** Upper Volta/Ghana. River 700 m. long formed by the union of the Black Volta and the White Volta 40 m. NW of Yeji in Ghana, and flowing generally SE and S to the Gulf of Guinea; the most important river in Ghana. The Volta River Scheme includes a dam, which impounds a lake (area 1,900 sq. m.), and hydroelectric power station at Akosombo and an aluminium smelter at Tema to develop Ghana's bauxite resources and improve navigation. The dam and power station were completed in 1966; the first aluminium was marketed in 1967.

**Volyn (Volhynia, Wolyń)** USSR. Region in the NW Ukrainian SSR, between the Bug and the Dnieper rivers. Drained chiefly by right-bank tributaries of the Pripet R. Consists largely of marshy woodlands. The medieval Volhynia, more extensive than present-day Volyn, passed to Lithuania in the 14th cent., to Poland in the 16th cent., and to Russia in the Partitions of Poland (1795). The W part was returned to Poland in 1921, but was ceded to the USSR in 1945, as the Volyn region.

**Voorburg** Netherlands. Industrial town in S Holland province 3 m. E of The Hague. Pop. (1968) 46,703. Manufactures ball bearings, machinery, etc.

**Vorarlberg** Austria. In German, 'Before

the Arlberg' (the pass linking the province with the Tirol). Province bordering on W Germany (N), Switzerland (S and W), and Liechtenstein (SW). Area 1,005 sq. m. Pop. (1961) 226,323. Cap. Bregenz. The Rhätikon Alps and part of the Silvretta massif (rising to over 11,000 ft) lie along the S boundary, and part of the Lechtal Alps is in the NE; renowned for mountain scenery. Main occupations forestry, dairy farming, tourism.

**Voronezh** USSR. Capital of the Voronezh Region, RSFSR, on the Voronezh R. near its confluence with the Don R. Pop. (1970) 660,000. A major industrial centre and chief town of the central black-earth (chernozem) area. Manufactures synthetic rubber, tyres, machine tools, excavators, radio and television sets, etc. Seat of a university, moved here in 1918. A Russian fort was built here (1586) on the site of an 11th-cent. Khazar town, and in 1695 Peter the Great made Voronezh a shipbuilding centre; later it traded in grain and wool. The town had to be rebuilt after disastrous fires (1703, 1748, 1773).

**Voroshilovgrad** ♦ *Lugansk*.

**Vosges** France. Department lying W of the Vosges Mountains, formed (1790) chiefly from Lorraine. Area 2,279 sq. m. Pop. (1968) 388,201. Prefecture Épinal. Mainly uplands, with the Vosges Mountains forming a natural boundary in the E and the Monts Faucilles crossing the S. Drained by the Moselle, Meuse, and Meurthe rivers. Agriculture (cereals, potatoes, hops) and forestry practised. Several spas.

**Vosges (Mountains)** France. Range of mountains in the E extending about 150 m. SSW–NNE, structurally similar and roughly parallel to the Black Forest (W Germany), from which it is separated by the rift valley of the Rhine R. The mountains slope steeply down to Alsace (E) and more gently to Lorraine (W), are well forested, and rise to 4,669 ft in the Ballon de Guebwiller. The Moselle, Meurthe, and Sarre (Saar) rivers rise on their W slopes and the Ill on their E slopes.

**Votkinsk** USSR. Town in the Udmurt ASSR, RSFSR, 30 m. ENE of Izhevsk. Pop. 59,000. Railway engineering. Manufactures agricultural machinery, boilers, dredgers, etc. Founded 1759. A 500 kV. electricity transmission line between Votkinsk (hydroelectric power station) and Sverdlovsk was opened in 1962. Birthplace of P. I. Tchaikovsky (1840–93), the composer.

**Vršac** Yugoslavia. Town in Vojvodina, near the Rumanian frontier 47 m. ENE of Belgrade. Pop. (1961) 31,620. Flour milling, distilling, meat packing. Trade in wine, brandy.

**Vyatka** ♦ *Kirov*.

**Vyborg** (Finnish **Viipuri**, Swedish **Viborg**) USSR. Seaport in the Leningrad Region, RSFSR, on Vyborg Bay, Gulf of Finland, 70 m. NW of Leningrad. Pop. 51,000. Exports timber, wood products, etc. Manufactures agricultural machinery, electrical equipment, etc. Linked by canal with L. Saimaa. Grew up round a 13th-cent. Swedish castle, became a Hanseatic port, and was ceded to Russia in 1721. Passed to Finland 1812; regained by the USSR 1945.

**Vyrnwy, Lake** Wales. Artificial lake (reservoir) 4½ m. long and up to ½ m. wide in NW Montgomeryshire. Formed by damming the R. Vyrnwy (1880–90) to provide a water supply for Liverpool.

**Vyrnwy River** Wales. River 35 m. long rising 6 m. S of Bala, flowing generally ESE through Montgomeryshire, and joining the R Severn 11 m. WNW of Shrewsbury.

**Vyshni Volochek** USSR. Town in the Kalinin Region, RSFSR, 70 m. NW of Kalinin. Pop. 64,000. On the Vyshnevolotsk canal system, originally constructed by Peter the Great in the early 18th cent. to link the Volga R. with the Baltic, and now of minor importance. Sawmilling. Manufactures textiles, glass.

# W

**Waadt** ♢ *Vaud.*

**Wabash River** USA. River 475 m. long rising in Grand Lake, W Ohio, and flowing generally W and then S, forming the Indiana–Illinois boundary below Terre Haute and joining the Ohio R.

**Waco** USA. Town in Texas, on the Brazos R. 88 m. SSW of Dallas. Pop. (1960) 97,808. Important trade in cotton. Railway engineering. Manufactures glass, tyres, textiles, cottonseed oil, etc. Seat of Baylor University, the oldest in Texas (1845).

**Wadi Halfa** Sudan. Town in the N, near the Egyptian frontier on the right bank of the Nile 240 m. NNW of Atbara, about 6 m. below the Second Cataract. Pop. 11,000. Terminus of the railway from Khartoum and of steamer services from Shellal in Egypt. Important transfer point for Sudanese-Egyptian trade.

**Wad Medani** Sudan. Capital of the Blue Nile province, on the left bank of the Blue Nile on the railway from Khartoum (110 m. NW). Pop. (1964) 57,000. Centre of the Gezira irrigation scheme. Important cotton centre. Cotton ginning. Also trade in cereals etc.

**Wagga Wagga** Australia. Town in New South Wales, on the Murrumbidgee R. 100 m. W of Canberra. Pop. (1966) 25,939. Railway junction and commercial centre for a wheat-growing and dairy-farming area. Roman Catholic cathedral.

**Waikato River** New Zealand. Longest river in the country, rising in L. Taupo, N Island, and flowing 220 m. NW over a series of rapids and through gorges, across a volcanic plateau. It enters the Tasman Sea 25 m. SSE of the entrance to Manukau Harbour. Many hydroelectric power stations, inc. Arapuni and Maraetai, on the upper course. The lower plains are noted for the raising of dairy cattle and fat lambs.

**Wainganga River** India. River 400 m. long in Madhya Pradesh, rising in the Satpura Range and flowing generally S to join the Wardha R., forming the Pranhita R., a tributary of the Godavari R.

**Waingapu** ♢ *Sumba.*

**Waitaki River** New Zealand. River 95 m. long in the S Island formed by the union of the Ahuriri and Tekapo rivers, the latter being fed from Lakes Ohau, Pukaki, and Tekapo, flowing generally SE to the Pacific about 13 m. NE of Oamaru. Hydroelectric power stations at Kurow and elsewhere.

**Wakamatsu** Japan. Seaport in N Kyushu, in Fukuoka prefecture 32 m. NE of Fukuoka. Pop. 79,000. Exports chiefly coal from the Chikuho coalfield, also steel, fertilizers, etc. Merged with Moji, Kokura, Tobata, and Yawata (1963) to form the new city of Kitakyushu.

**Wakatipu, Lake** New Zealand. Picturesque, winding lake in W Otago, S Island, 50 m. long and up to 3 m. wide, at a height of 1,016 ft in a glacial valley. Has an outlet via the Kawarau R. to the Clutha R. Queenstown, a tourist centre, is on the N shore.

**Wakayama** Japan. Capital of Wakayama prefecture, S Honshu, on the Kii peninsula 35 m. SSW of Osaka. Pop. (1965) 328,649. Industrial centre. Manufactures iron and steel, textiles, chemicals, saké, etc.

**Wakefield** England. County borough and county town of the W Riding of Yorkshire, on the R. Calder 8 m. S of Leeds. Pop. (1961) 61,591. A centre of the woollen industry in a coalmining district. Also manufactures chemicals, machine tools, mining machinery, etc. Trade in agricultural produce. Has a 14th-cent. cathedral with a spire 247 ft high, a 14th-cent. chantry chapel on one of its bridges, and a 16th-cent. grammar school. Scene of a battle in the Wars of the Roses (1460), in which Richard Duke of York was defeated and killed by the Lancastrians. Birthplace of John Radcliffe (1652–1714) and George Gissing (1857–1903).

**Wake Island** N Pacific Ocean. Atoll 2,300 m. W of Hawaii. Pop. (1960) 1,097. Discovered by Capt. Wake (British) 1796; claimed by the USA 1899; made an airline base on the route to the Philippines in 1935 and a naval and air base in 1939. After a stubborn defence by US marines it fell to the Japanese (1941); recaptured 1945.

**Walachia (Wallachia)** Rumania. Region in S Rumania bounded on the N by the Transylvanian Alps and on the W, S, and E by the Danube R., which separates it from Yugoslavia, Bulgaria, and the Rumanian Dobruja respectively. Area 29,575 sq. m. Chief city Bucharest, capital of Rumania. Divided by the Olt R. into Muntenia or Greater Walachia (E) and Oltenia or Lesser Walachia. Main occupation agriculture (cereals, vines, fruit). Oil produced around Ploeşti. The principality of Walachia was founded (1290) by Radu Negru, a Transylvanian ruler, became independent in the 14th cent., then remained under Turkish rule almost continuously till the mid 19th cent. Its union with the principality of Moldavia (1859) laid the foundation of modern Rumania.

**Walbrzych (Ger. Waldenburg)** Poland. Industrial town in the Wroclaw voivodship, in the Sudeten Mountains 42 m. SW of Wroclaw. Pop. (1968) 126,200. Coalmining centre. Manufactures china, glass, linen goods, etc. Formerly in Germany (as Waldenburg); passed to Poland in 1945 after the 2nd World War.

**Walchensee** Federal German Republic. Lake in Bavaria, in the Bavarian Alps 37 m. SSW of Munich at a height of 2,630 ft. Area 6 sq. m. Has one of the country's most important hydroelectric plants.

**Walcheren** Netherlands. Island in Zeeland province, in the estuary of the Scheldt R., linked with S Beveland island and the mainland by railway and road causeways. Area 82 sq. m. Fertile; produces potatoes, sugar-beet, vegetables, etc. Chief towns Flushing, Middelburg. During the 2nd World War it was liberated from the Germans after the dykes had been breached; the island again suffered severely from the disastrous floods of 1953.

**Waldeck** Federal German Republic. Former principality, under Prussian administration from 1867. Area 420 sq. m. Pop. 92,000. Cap. Arolsen. Chiefly agricultural; produces cereals, potatoes, fruit. From 1918 to 1929 it was a *Land* of the German Republic; it then became part of Hesse-Nassau, later (1945) of Hessen.

**Waldenburg** ◊ *Walbrzych*

**Wales.** A principality; peninsula in the SW of Great Britain. Area 8,016 sq. m. Pop. (1961) 2,640,632. Cap. Cardiff. Bounded by England (E), the Bristol Channel (S), St George's Channel (W), and the Irish Sea (N). Includes the island of Anglesey off the NW coast, separated from the mainland by the Menai Strait (crossed by railway and road bridges). The county of Monmouthshire was long disputed between Wales and England but is now officially counted as part of the principality. The central mountainous counties are sparsely populated; the population is concentrated mainly in the industrial region of the S, with the density highest in Glamorganshire, where coalmining and iron and steel manufacture form the basis of the economy. Few economic ties between the N and the S: each is less closely associated with the other than with the neighbouring parts of England. Divided administratively into 12 (13) counties: Anglesey, Brecknockshire, Caernarvonshire, Cardiganshire, Carmarthenshire, Denbighshire, Flintshire, Glamorganshire, Merionethshire, (Monmouthshire), Montgomeryshire, Pembrokeshire, Radnorshire. For topography, climate, etc., ◊ *Great Britain.*

ECONOMY. The farming is mainly pastoral: less than one fifth of the land surface is arable, and most of the remainder is rough grazing land and permanent pasture, in approximately equal areas. In the mountains sheep rearing is the chief occupation; beef and dairy cattle are raised on the coastal plains of Anglesey and in the Lleyn peninsula, Pembrokeshire, and Glamorganshire. Oats, barley, and root crops are cultivated, mainly for feeding to livestock. With the Industrial Revolution the almost uniformly agricultural economy changed radically, and people crowded into the coalmining valleys of the SE. Welsh steam coal and anthracite achieved a high reputation and the S Wales coalfield became the world's chief coal-exporting region. Largely through foreign competition this overseas trade diminished to negligible proportions after the 1st World War. Local supplies of iron ore assisted the development of a great steel industry; most of the ore is now imported, but S Wales remains Britain's principal steel-producing region, with plants of outstanding importance in the Port Talbot district. Tinplate manufacture (an offshoot of the steel industry) and the smelting of zinc, copper, tin, and nickel are concentrated in the Swansea–Llanelli area; there are important oil refineries at Llandarcy and Milford Haven. S Wales suffered severely from the economic depression of the 1930s; to relieve unemployment, new trading estates were established (e.g. Treforest), new industries were introduced (e.g. nylon manufacture at Pontypool), and the steel industry was modernized. The much less important industrial region centred on Wrexham is based on the smaller N Wales coalfield. The slate quarries in the N face dwindling markets but resorts along the N coast and the district around Snowdon attract holidaymakers and climbers. The three major industrial centres – Cardiff, Swansea, and Newport (Monmouthshire) – are all in the S and are all seaports.

POPULATION. About 26 per cent of the people (1961) are Welsh-speaking (26,233 speaking Welsh only). Interest in the Welsh language (which is Celtic in origin) was stimulated by the founding (1893) of the University of Wales (which has constituent colleges at Aberystwyth, Cardiff, Bangor, and Swansea), and is maintained by the National Eisteddfod (revived in the mid 19th cent. and held annually). In general the educational system is similar to that of England, but the Welsh language is widely taught in the schools. Wales has been politically linked to England since 1536, returning members to the House of Commons at Westminster; some legislation applies to Wales alone. The strength of the Nonconformist sects in Wales is due to the Methodist movement of the 18th cent. (see below); leading denominations are the Calvinistic Methodist (Presbyterian) Church of Wales, the Methodist (Wesleyan) Church, the Baptist Church, and the Congregationalist Church. The Anglican Church of Wales was disestablished in 1914.

HISTORY. The Romans conquered and occupied Wales but made little impression. The Anglo-Saxon invasion of England was at first of no serious consequence to Wales; later the defeats at Deorham (577) and Chester (613) separated the Welsh from their compatriots in the S W (Cornwall) and the N W (Cumberland), and confined them to the mountainous W peninsula. King Offa of Mercia constructed Offa's Dyke as a defence against the Welsh in the 8th cent. During this century the Welsh Church (established 200 years earlier) established regular contact with Rome. During the 9th–11th cent. the Welsh, divided among small tribal kingdoms, were raided along the coasts by Northmen, and engaged on their landward border with the Mercians. Gruffyd ap Llewelyn (1039–63) defeated the Mercians and

temporarily united the Welsh. They continued to resist after the Norman conquest, but Llewelyn ap Gruffyd was defeated (1282) by Edward I, who had his son (born 1284 in Caernarvon Castle) proclaimed Prince of Wales in 1301; the title has been held by the eldest son of the English monarch ever since. Owen Glendower rebelled unsuccessfully in the early 15th cent. With the accession of Henry VII (part Welsh by birth) peace was established; Henry VIII incorporated Wales politically into England, and gave it parliamentary representation by the Act of Union (1536); Welsh history thereafter was approximately that of England. The Reformation hardly reached Wales. In the early 17th cent. it was mainly Royalist, but Protestant ideas began to take root during the Cromwellian era. The 18th-cent. Methodist 'revival' movement had as great an impact on Welsh life as did the Industrial Revolution; partly religious, partly educational, it produced an outstanding leader in Griffith Jones, a Carmarthenshire rector, and culminated in the Methodist Secession (1811). More recently Wales has been a stronghold of trade unionism and socialism. There has also been a revival of Welsh nationalism. To placate Welsh sentiment, a Cabinet Minister has been in charge of Welsh affairs since 1951.

**Wallachia** ◊ *Walachia*.

**Wallaroo** ◊ *Yorke Peninsula*.

**Wallasey** England. County borough in Cheshire, on the Wirral peninsula, near the mouth of the R. Mersey opposite Liverpool. Pop. (1961) 103,213. Seaside resort and residential suburb of Liverpool, including New Brighton and Egremont. Linked with Liverpool by ferry service.

**Wallingford** England. Municipal borough in N Berkshire, on the R. Thames 12 m. SSE of Oxford. Pop. (1961) 4,829. Market town. Picturesque; important in medieval times. Has a much older history than its many Georgian buildings would suggest.

**Wallis** ◊ *Valais*.

**Wallis and Futuna Islands** SW Pacific Ocean. Island group N E of Fiji, consisting of Uvéa and several uninhabited coral islets, with Futuna and Alofi to the S. Area 106 sq. m. Pop. (1962) 8,326. Cap. Matautu (Uvéa). Formed the French protectorate of the Wallis and Futuna Is. from 1842, but in 1959 their inhabitants, almost entirely Polynesians, voted overwhelmingly to become an overseas territory of the French Community.

**Wallsend** England. Municipal borough in Northumberland, on the N bank of the R. Tyne 3 m. ENE of Newcastle upon Tyne. Pop. (1961) 49,785. Shipbuilding, marine engineering, coalmining. Manufactures chemicals, ropes, etc. Stands at the E end of Hadrian's Wall – hence its name.

**Walsall** England. County borough in S Staffordshire, in the Black Country 8 m NNW of Birmingham. Pop. (1961) 117,836. Industrial town, specializing in leather goods. Also manufactures hardware, machine tools, aircraft parts, chemicals, etc. Coalmining and limestone quarrying in the neighbourhood.

**Walsingham** England. Two villages in N Norfolk. Little Walsingham, 25 m. NW of Norwich, had the 11th-cent. shrine of Our Lady of Walsingham, an important centre of medieval pilgrimages; the ruins of the priory stand in the grounds of the modern abbey. Great Walsingham is 1 m. NE. At Houghton St Giles, 1 m. SSW, is the Slipper Chapel where pilgrims (kings and commoners alike) had to leave their shoes before proceeding barefoot to the shrine.

**Waltham** USA. Industrial town in Massachusetts, on the Charles R. 10 m. W of Boston. Pop. (1960) 55,413. Famous for the manufacture of clocks and watches since the mid 19th cent. Also produces electronic equipment, precision instruments, etc. Seat of Brandeis University (1948).

**Waltham Abbey (Waltham Holy Cross)** England. Urban district in SW Essex, on the R. Lea 8 m. SW of Harlow. Pop. (1961) 11,751. Manufactures plastics, tiles, etc. Has a government explosive research establishment. It had a great 11th-cent. Augustinian abbey, founded by King Harold, the nave of which is now used as the parish church; Harold was said to have been buried here after the Battle of Hastings.

**Waltham Cross** England. Town in Hertfordshire, on the R. Lea opposite Waltham Abbey, part of the urban district of Cheshunt. Manufactures insecticides etc. So called because of its Eleanor Cross.

**Waltham Forest** England. Greater London borough (1965) comprising the former municipal boroughs of Chingford, Leyton, and Walthamstow, all in Essex. Pop. (1963) 248,422.

**Waltham Holy Cross** ◊ *Waltham Abbey.*

**Walthamstow** England. Former municipal borough in SW Essex, also a NE suburb of London; from 1965 part of the Greater London borough of Waltham Forest. Pop. (1961) 108,788. Mainly residential. Engineering, brewing, etc. Has a 16th-cent. church. Large reservoirs. Birthplace of William Morris (1834–96).

**Walton and Weybridge** England. Urban district in N Surrey on the R. Thames, including Walton-on-Thames, Weybridge (at the mouth of the R. Wey), and Hersham. Pop. (1961) 45,497. Mainly residential. Manufactures electrical equipment, bricks and tiles, aircraft. The former motor-car race track of Brooklands (opened 1907) is in Weybridge.

**Walton-le-Dale** England. Urban district in Lancashire, on the R. Ribble just SE of Preston. Pop. (1961) 19,061. Engineering. Manufactures cotton goods.

**Walton-le-Soken** ◊ *Walton-on-the-Naze.*

**Walton-on-Thames** ◊ *Walton and Weybridge.*

**Walton-on-the-Naze (Walton-le-Soken)** England. Seaside resort in NE Essex, on the North Sea 6 m. S of Harwich, forming part of the urban district of Frinton and Walton; just NE is the low headland of The Naze. Pop. (urban district, 1961) 9,571.

**Walvis Bay** SW Africa. Chief seaport, 165 m. WSW of Windhoek. Pop. (1961) 16,490 (inc. 5,067 Europeans). Terminus of the railway system, by which it is linked with Swakopmund and Windhoek. With 374 sq. m. of its hinterland it forms an exclave of Cape Province, S Africa, but is administered by SW Africa (since 1922). Exports chilled meat etc. Fishing, fish canning. Manufactures fish oil, fish meal. Annexed by Britain 1878.

**Wandsworth** England. Formerly the largest metropolitan borough of London, on the S bank of the R. Thames, including Putney, Streatham, Balham, Tooting, and part of Clapham; from 1965 a Greater London borough comprising the former metropolitan borough (except the Clapham and Streatham areas – now included in the borough of Lambeth) and the former metropolitan borough of Battersea. Pop. (1963) 335,367. Residential and industrial. Textile printing, dyeing, brewing, etc. Open spaces include Putney Heath, Tooting Common, Wandsworth Park, and parts of Richmond Park and Wandsworth

Common. Contains Wandsworth prison. Linked by Wandsworth Bridge with Fulham.

**Wanganui** New Zealand. Town and port on the SW coast of the N Island 95 m. NNE of Wellington near the mouth of the Wanganui R. Pop. (1966) 35,604. Regional centre for dairy-farming and sheep-rearing districts. Meat works, woollen mills, clothing and soap factories. Founded 1842.

**Wanganui River** New Zealand. River 140 m. long in the N Island, rising in the Rangitoto Range and flowing generally S to Cook Strait through broken hill country and forests and, on the lower plains, dairy-farming land.

**Wangaratta** Australia. Town in Victoria, on the Ovens R. 125 m. NE of Melbourne. Pop. (1966) 15,167. Manufactures textiles (woollen, rayon). Trade in livestock etc.

**Wanhsien** China. River port in Szechwan province, on the left bank of the Yangtse R. 140 m. NE of Chungking. Pop. 100,000. Trade in tung oil, hog bristles, tobacco, etc.

**Wankie** Rhodesia. Coalmining town on the railway to and 180 m. NW of Bulawayo at a height of 2,500 ft. Pop. 23,300. Developed considerably with the demand for coal by the Zambia copperbelt mines. Coke ovens, brickworks.

**Wanks River** ◊ *Coco River*.

**Wanne-Eickel** Federal German Republic. Industrial town in N Rhine-Westphalia, in the Ruhr 3 m. NNW of Bochum. Pop. (1968) 101,849. Port on the Rhine-Herne Canal. Coalmining centre. Manufactures chemicals.

**Wanstead and Woodford** England. Former municipal borough in SW Essex, on the R. Roding; from 1965 part of the Greater London borough of Redbridge. Pop. (1961) 61,259. Mainly residential. Contains Wanstead Park and most of Wanstead Flats.

**Wantage** England. Urban district in NW Berkshire 13 m. SW of Oxford on the N edge of the Berkshire Downs. Pop. (1961) 5,940. Market town. Has a 13th-cent. church and a large statue of Alfred the Great (849–900), who was born here. Also birthplace of Bishop Joseph Butler (1692–1752).

**Wapping** England. District in the London borough of Tower Hamlets (E), between the London Docks and the R. Thames.

Connected with Rotherhithe by the Thames Tunnel (1843). Has the famous 'Prospect of Whitby' inn. Near the Tunnel Pier is the site of Execution Dock, where pirates were hanged.

**Warangal** India. Town in Andhra Pradesh, 85 m. NE of Hyderabad. Pop. (1961) 156,106. Cotton milling, printing. Manufactures carpets. Trade in grain, hides, etc. Was capital of a 12th-cent. Hindu kingdom; there are a fort and remains of a temple of that period.

**Wardsesson** ◊ *Bloomfield*.

**Ware** England. Urban district in Hertfordshire, on the R. Lea 2 m. ENE of Hertford. Pop. (1961) 9,980. Brewing. Manufactures plastics etc. The 'Great Bed of Ware', in Shakespeare's *Twelfth Night*, formerly at the Saracen's Head here, is now in the Victoria and Albert Museum, London.

**Wareham** England. Municipal borough in Dorset, on the R. Frome 6 m. WSW of Poole. Pop. (1961) 3,094. Market town. Inhabited since pre-Roman times and almost surrounded by Saxon earthworks. Has the restored Saxon Church of St Martin; in the ancient Church of St Mary is the marble coffin of Edward the Martyr.

**Warley** England. County borough in S Staffordshire, formed in 1966 from the former county borough of Smethwick and the municipal boroughs of Oldbury and Rowley Regis. Pop. (1968) 168,970.

**Warminster** England. Urban district in Wiltshire, on the W edge of Salisbury Plain 19 m. WNW of Salisbury. Pop. (1961) 9,855. Market town. Bacon and ham curing. Manufactures gloves, food products, etc. Longleat, the beautiful Elizabethan mansion of the Marquis of Bath, is 4 m. WSW.

**Warren** USA. Industrial town in Ohio, on the Mahoning R. 14 m. NW of Youngstown. Pop. (1960) 59,648. Manufactures steel, machinery, electrical appliances, etc.

**Warrenpoint** Northern Ireland. Urban district in Co. Down, near the head of Carlingford Lough 6 m. SE of Newry. Pop. (1961) 3,238. Seaside resort and centre for the Mourne Mountains.

**Warrington** England. County borough in Lancashire, on the R. Mersey 16 m. E of Liverpool. Pop. (1961) 75,533. Industrial town. Iron founding, engineering, brewing, tanning. Manufactures soap, detergents, chemicals, wire, etc. An important town in Roman times; has a grammar school founded in the 16th cent.

**Warrnambool** Australia. Seaport with an artificial harbour in SW Victoria 145 m. WSW of Melbourne. Pop. (1966) 17,497. Also a commercial town and resort. Serves a rich dairy-farming and sheep-rearing region. Exports wool, butter. Manufactures butter, woollen goods.

**Warsaw (Polish Warszawa)** Poland. Capital of Poland and of the Warszawa voivodship (but independent of it), on both banks of the Vistula R. in N central Poland. Pop. (1968) 1,273,600. Route, commercial, and industrial centre. Metal working, flour milling, sugar refining, brewing, distilling. Manufactures tractors, machine tools, electrical equipment, chemicals, textiles, clothing, etc. Seat of a university (1818), of academies of arts and sciences, and of a Roman Catholic archbishopric. At first the residence of the dukes of Mazovia; became capital of Poland 1550. Taken by the Swedes (1702) and the Russians (1794). Passed to Prussia 1795. Became capital of Napoleon's 'duchy of Warsaw' in 1807 and of the post-Napoleonic 'Congress Kingdom' in 1815, but in fact remained in Russian hands until the 1917 Bolshevik Revolution. Became capital of the re-created Polish republic after the 1st World War (1919). Suffered very severely in the 2nd World War; occupied by the Germans from Aug. 1939. The Jews were enclosed in the ghetto and it was wiped out (1943); the Warsaw Rising was suppressed and the city was virtually obliterated (1944). The reconstruction began (1945) round an important E-W highway; in 6 years a new city had been built. The population increased 50 per cent 1950-62.

**Warta (Ger. Warthe) River** Poland. River 480 m. long rising 8 m. SSE of Częstochowa and flowing generally N and W past Częstochowa and Poznań to join the Oder R. at Kostrzyn. Linked by its tributary the Noteć and the Bydgoszcz Canal with the Vistula R.

**Warwick** England. Municipal borough and county town of Warwickshire, on the R. Avon 19 m. SE of Birmingham. Pop. (1961) 16,032. Engineering. Manufactures gelatine, furniture, etc. The magnificent 14th-cent castle, standing on a rock above the river, is associated with several famous Earls of Warwick and has a fine collection of armour, furniture, and pictures. It survived the disastrous fire of 1694, along with the 15th-cent. Beauchamp Chapel of St Mary's Church, the 16th-cent. Leycester Hospital, and the E and W gates of the medieval town walls, with chapels. Birthplace of Walter Savage Landor (1775-1864).

**Warwick** USA. Industrial and residential town in Rhode Island, on Narragansett Bay 10 m. S of Providence, including several villages within its limits. Pop. (1960) 68,504. Primarily a textile centre, producing cotton, silk, and rayon fabrics. Also manufactures metal goods, machinery.

**Warwickshire** England. County in the W Midlands. Area 983 sq. m. Pop. (1961) 2,023,289. County town Warwick. Generally undulating, rising to 743 ft in Edgehill in the extreme SE, it is crossed NE-SW by the R. Avon. The larger NW portion of the county so divided, drained by the Tame and other tributaries of the R. Trent, is one of the most highly industrialized regions in the world; long specializing in the manufacture of metal goods, it contains Birmingham, Coventry, Solihull, Sutton Coldfield, and Nuneaton, while Rugby and Leamington (spa) stand near the Avon. Coal is mined chiefly in the NE. To the S of the R. Avon agriculture and fruit farming are the main occupations. Warwick, Kenilworth, and Stratford-on-Avon are smaller but more picturesque and historically more interesting towns than the great industrial centres to the N. Stratford-on-Avon and the Forest of Arden are inevitably associated with the county's most distinguished son, William Shakespeare.

**Wasatch Range** USA. Range of the Rocky Mountains extending 200 m. N-S through SE Idaho to central Utah and rising to 12,008 ft in Mt Timpanogos.

**Wash, The** England. Shallow bay of the North Sea into the coasts of Norfolk and Lincolnshire, 18 m. long and up to 15 m wide. There are two navigable deep-water channels: Boston Deeps, maintained by the Witham and Welland rivers, and Lynn Deeps, by the Nene and Great Ouse rivers, giving access to the small ports of Boston and King's Lynn respectively. The Wash has long been subject to silting and covers a much smaller area than formerly; at times parts of it have been reclaimed.

**Washington** England.* Urban district in NE Durham 6 m. W of Sunderland. Pop. (1961) 18,772. Coalmining centre. The home of George Washington's ancestors before their removal to Sulgrave Manor, Northamptonshire.

**Washington** USA. State in the extreme NW, bounded on the N by British Columbia (Canada). Area 68,192 sq. m. Pop. (1970) 3,352,892. Cap. Olympia. Admitted to the Union in 1889 as the 42nd state; popularly known as the 'Evergreen' state. Its coast is heavily indented in the NW, with Puget Sound, connecting with Juan de Fuca Strait, extending 100 m. N–S. Largely mountainous, it is divided into E and W parts by the Cascade Range, which rises to 14,408 ft in Mt Rainier, its highest point. The main river is the Columbia, and such tributaries as the Snake and Spokane are also important. The climate to the E of the Cascades is dry continental and to the W maritime temperate. Forests cover more than 50 per cent of its area, and it was long the leading timber-producing state, but now ranks third to Oregon and California. Fruit, vegetables, and hops are widely grown, apples being the chief commercial crop. The fisheries are of great importance. Chief cities Seattle, which is also the leading seaport, Spokane, and Tacoma. Hydroelectric development has assisted industrial progress, esp. through the Grand Coulee and Bonneville Dams on the Columbia R. The mountain and coastal scenery is noteworthy, many resorts have sprung up, and the Olympic and Mt Rainier National Parks are justly famous. Jointly occupied by the USA and Britain from 1818, then in 1846 the 49th parallel was fixed as the US–Canadian boundary, and large-scale settlement began in the 1850s.

**Washington** (District of Columbia) USA. Capital, on the left bank of the Potomac R. at the head of navigation and 100 m. from its mouth. Pop. (1970) 764,000. The first modern city to be planned from the start as a seat of national government; regulations restrict the height of buildings, and it has no skyscrapers.

The site was designated by Act of Congress (1790) and was laid out by Andrew Ellicott from the plans of the French engineer Pierre l'Enfant commissioned by George Washington. Work began on the White House, the President's official residence, in 1792, and on the Capitol building in 1793. The Federal government moved to Washington in 1800 from Philadelphia, but the city developed very slowly. The plan was centred upon the Capitol with broad tree-lined avenues radiating from it like the spokes of a wheel; these,

however, in practice have been interrupted, e.g. by parks, which are a noteworthy feature of the city (the Potomac Park: 740 acres, including the Tidal Basin ringed with Japanese flowering cherry trees; Rock Creek Park: 1,800 acres; Anacostia Park: 1,100 acres; the National Zoological Park: 175 acres).

The Capitol, the central and dominating building, stands on a ridge 88 ft above the level of the Potomac R. With the growth of legislative business it became necessary to add extensions to it (a Senate Chamber on the N and a House of Representatives Chamber on the S side, built 1851–9); at the top of the dome is a statue of Freedom. Down Pennsylvania Avenue from the Capitol is the White House. Both buildings were burned by the British in 1814, and the White House was afterwards painted white to disguise damage – the origin of its name. In the vicinity are the buildings of the Treasury, the State Department, the Supreme Court, the Pan-American Union, and Ford's Theater, where Lincoln was assassinated (1865), now a museum. Among the many cultural and scientific institutions are the Smithsonian Institution, the Library of Congress, and the Mellon Gallery of Art, and there are 5 universities: Georgetown (1789), George Washington (1821), Howard (1867), Catholic University of America (1887), American University (1893). Of the monuments, the most striking is the Washington Monument, a white marble obelisk 555 ft high, the city's most famous landmark; others are the Lincoln Memorial and the Thomas Jefferson National Memorial.

The population of the District of Columbia has fallen slightly in recent years, and within the city itself about one half of the population is Negro. There is little industry except printing and publishing. In the main the residents are civil servants and employees of the US Government. Outside the District of Columbia proper there is a 'metropolitan area' in adjacent parts of Virginia and Maryland bringing the total population to over two million. This area serves largely as residential suburbs, but also contains important scientific and medical research institutions, and the Pentagon, the largest single building in the world, headquarters of the US military forces.

**Washington** (Pennsylvania) USA. Indus-

trial town in the SW, 23 m. SW of Pittsburgh. Pop. (1960) 23,545. Manufactures
metal goods, glass, etc.

**Washington, Mount** USA Highest peak in
the White Mountains, New Hampshire,
and in NE USA (6,288 ft). Well known for
its scenery. Rack-and-pinion railway to the
summit (opened 1869).

**Wassenaar** Netherlands. Residential town
in S Holland province 6 m. NE of The
Hague. Pop. (1968) 26,502. Bulb growing.

**Wast Water** England. Lake in SW Cumber-
land, in the Lake District 13 m. W of
Ambleside, 3 m. long and ½ m. wide and
the deepest in England (260 ft). About 2 m.
E of the N end of its valley, Wasdale, is
Scafell.

**Watchet** England. Urban district in
Somerset, on Bridgwater Bay 15 m. NW
of Taunton. Pop. (1961) 2,596. Small port.
Seaside resort.

**Watenstedt-Salzgitter** Federal German Republic. Industrial town in Lower Saxony
15 m. SSW of Brunswick. Pop (1968)
117,564. Iron and potash mining. Manufactures iron and steel, coke, chemicals,
textiles, machinery, etc. Incorporated in
1942 chiefly to exploit the rich iron
deposits of the district.

**Waterbury** USA. Industrial town in
Connecticut, on the Naugatuck R. 18 m.
NNW of New Haven. Pop. (1960) 107,130.
A leading centre of the brass industry.
Also manufactures clocks and watches,
hardware, machinery, plastics, clothing,
etc. Incorporated 1686. The brass industry
dates from c. 1800.

**Waterford** Irish Republic. **1.** County in
Munster, in the SE, bounded on the S by
the Atlantic Ocean. Area 710 sq. m. Pop.
(1966) 73,080. Largely mountainous, with
the Knockmealdown Mountains rising to
2,609 ft (NW); also the Comeragh
Mountains (2,504 ft.) and the Mona-
vullagh Mountains (2,387 ft). Drained
chiefly by the Blackwater and the Suir
rivers. The coast has many indentations,
esp. Waterford Harbour. Main occupations
dairy farming, cattle and pig rearing. Chief
towns Waterford, Dungarvan, Lismore.
**2.** County town of Co. Waterford, on the
R. Suir near the mouth on Waterford
harbour, an inlet formed by the estuaries
of the Suir, Nore, and Barrow. Pop. (1966)
29,842. Seaport. Exports cattle and dairy
produce. Bacon curing, brewing, flour
milling, etc. Among its old buildings is
Reginald's Tower (1003), and there are

Roman Catholic and Protestant cathedrals, both dating from the 18th cent. An
important Danish settlement until taken
(1171) by Strongbow, who here married
Eva, daughter of the King of Leinster.
Withstood siege by Cromwell (1649) but
fell to Ireton (1650). In the 18th cent.
famous for glass manufacture; the trade
had died out by the mid 19th cent. but is
now reviving. Birthplace of Charles Kean
(1811–68), the actor.

**Waterloo** Belgium. Small town in Brabant
12 m. S of Brussels, near which was
fought the famous battle (1815) in which
British and Prussian forces (with some
Dutch and Belgians) under the Duke
of Wellington and Blücher defeated the
French under Napoleon.

**Waterloo** USA. Formerly Prairie Rapids.
Town in Iowa, on the Cedar R. 50 m. NW
of Cedar Rapids. Pop. (1960) 71,755. Has
the famous annual National Dairy Cattle
Congress. Manufactures agricultural machinery, cement mixers, leather goods, etc.
Railway engineering, meat packing. First
settled 1845; renamed 1851.

**Waterton-Glacier International Peace Park**
Canada/USA. International park created
(1932) by the amalgamation of two
adjoining National Parks – Waterton
Lakes National Park, Alberta (204 sq.
m.) and Glacier National Park, Montana
(1,560 sq. m.). Many glaciers and lakes.
Highest peak Mt Cleveland (10,448 ft).

**Watertown** (Massachusetts) USA. Residential and industrial town on the Charles
R. just W of Boston. Pop. (1960) 39,092.
Manufactures textiles, clothing, rubber
products, etc. Founded and incorporated
1630.

**Watertown** (New York) USA. Town on the
Black R. 65 m. NNE of Syracuse. Pop.
(1960) 33,306. In a dairy-farming region.
Manufactures paper, plumbing appliances,
thermometers, etc. Founded 1800. F. W.
Woolworth, originator of the famous
stores, started business here (1878).

**Watford** England. Municipal borough in
SW Hertfordshire, on the R. Colne 16 m.
NW of London. Pop. (1961) 75,630.
Industrial and residential centre. Printing,
engineering, brewing. Manufactures paper,
office equipment, etc. Also serves as a
dormitory suburb of London, esp. since the
establishment of the LCC housing estate
at Oxhey.

**Watling (Watlings) Island** ◊ *San Salvador*
(Bahamas).

**Watling Street** England. Early English name for the Roman road linking London (Londinium), through St Albans (Verulamium), with Wroxeter (Viroconium), 4 m. ESE of Shrewsbury. Much of it is still in use today. The name is also applied to parts of the main road from London to Dover (via Canterbury).

**Wattenscheid** Federal German Republic. Industrial town in N Rhine-Westphalia, in the Ruhr 6 m. E. of Essen. Pop. (1963) 79,700. Coalmining centre. Metal working. Manufactures footwear, electrical equipment, etc.

**Waukegan** USA. Industrial and residential town and lake port in Illinois, on L. Michigan 37 m. NNW of Chicago. Pop. (1960) 55,719. Manufactures steel and asbestos products, hardware, boilers and radiators, wire, etc.

**Waukesha** USA. Town in Wisconsin, on the Fox R. 16 m. W of Milwaukee. Pop. (1960) 30,004. Trade in dairy cattle. Manufactures metal and wood products etc. Food processing. Formerly a resort; mineral spring water is bottled.

**Wausau** USA. Town in Wisconsin, on the Wisconsin R. 160 m. NNW of Milwaukee. Pop. (1960) 31,943. Brewing, granite quarrying. Manufactures electrical appliances, wood products, paper, etc.

**Wauwatosa** USA. Industrial town in SE Wisconsin just W of Milwaukee. Pop. (1960) 56,923. Manufactures metal and concrete products, chemicals, etc.

**Waveney River** England. River 50 m. long rising 8 m. SW of Diss and flowing generally NE past Diss, Bungay, and Beccles, forming much of the boundary between Norfolk and Suffolk, and entering the SW end of Breydon Water.

**Wazirabad** ◊ *Balkh.*

**Waziristan** Pakistan. Mountainous tribal region in W Pakistan, in the Dera Ismail Khan Division at the N end of the Sulaiman Range, bounded on the W by Afghanistan. Peopled mainly by Waziris, a Pathan tribe with an evil reputation for banditry. Many British military expeditions were needed to quell lawlessness in the latter half of the 19th cent.

**Weald, The** England. Region in SE England between the N and S Downs in Kent, Surrey, and Sussex. Formerly forested, supplying charcoal for the iron industry, which flourished in the 16th and the 17th cent. but had practically died out by the early 19th cent.; now the region is more important for grazing and the cultivation of hops, fruit, and vegetables. Remnants of the original woodlands exist in Ashdown, Tilgate, and St Leonards forests.

**Wear River** England. River 65 m. long rising in W Durham near the Cumberland border and flowing E and then NE, past Bishop Auckland, Durham, and Chester-le-Street to the North Sea at Sunderland. Above Bishop Auckland its valley (Weardale) is picturesque. Navigable in the lower reaches.

**Weaver River** England. River 50 m. long in Cheshire, rising 12 m. SSW of Crewe and flowing N and then NW past Nantwich, Winsford, and Northwich, to join the R. Mersey near Runcorn. Navigable below Winsford.

**Wednesbury** England. Industrial town in Staffordshire, 5 m. SE of Wolverhampton in the Black Country. Pop. (1961) 34,511. Manufactures steel tubes and other metal goods. The Church of St Bartholomew is supposed to stand on the site of a temple of Woden (hence the name Wednesbury).

**Wednesfield** England. Industrial town in S Staffordshire (the Black Country) 2 m. ENE of Wolverhampton. Pop. (1961) 32,986 (17,422 in 1951). Manufactures hardware, nuts and bolts, etc. Scene of the defeat of the Danes by the Saxons (who named it 'Woden's Field') in 910.

**Weert** Netherlands. Industrial town in Limburg province 16 m. SE of Eindhoven near the Belgian frontier. Pop. (1968) 34,919. Manufactures metal goods, textiles, etc.

**Weiden** Federal German Republic. Industrial town in Bavaria 33 m. SE of Bayreuth. Pop. (1963) 42,200. Manufactures china, glassware, textiles, etc.

**Weimar** German Democratic Republic. Industrial town in the Erfurt district, on the Ilm R. 52 m. WSW of Leipzig. Pop. (1965) 63,985. Manufactures textiles, machinery, electrical equipment, etc. Outstanding among its many famous buildings is the former grand-ducal palace (1789–1803); others include the houses of Goethe, Schiller, and Liszt and the Stadtkirche (City Church). Became important from the mid 16th cent. as capital of the duchy and then the grand duchy of Saxe-Weimar-Eisenach, later of the *Land* of Thuringia. J. S. Bach was court organist (1708–17), and in the late 18th and early 19th cent. Weimar was a leading cultural centre, esp. during the residence here of Goethe and Schiller; Franz Liszt was musical director (1848–59). At the end of the 1st World War the constitution of the new German Republic (the 'Weimar Republic') was adopted here (1919).

**Weinheim** Federal German Republic. Town in Baden-Württemberg 8 m. NE of Mannheim at the foot of the Odenwald. Pop. (1963) 28,800. Industrial centre. Resort. Tanning. Manufactures soap etc. Has a 16th-cent. Gothic town hall.

**Weirton** USA. Industrial town in W Virginia, on the Ohio R. 32 m. W of Pittsburgh. Pop. (1960) 28,201. Important steel works producing sheet steel, tinplate, etc. Also manufactures steel furniture, cement, chemicals.

**Weissenfels** German Democratic Republic. Industrial town in the Halle district, on the Saale R. 20 m. WSW of Leipzig. Pop. (1965) 46,874. In a lignite-mining region. Manufactures footwear, paper, machinery, etc. The former 17th-cent. Augustusburg palace stands above the town.

**Weisshorn** Switzerland. One of the highest peaks (14,792 ft) in the Pennine Alps, in the S, 6 m NNW of Zermatt.

**Welkom** S Africa. Town in the Orange Free State 85 m. NNE of Bloemfontein at a height of 4,500 ft. Pop. (1967) 137,358 (37,000 white, 100,000 Bantu). Residential and commercial centre serving the new goldfield, with 6 important mines in the neighbourhood.

**Welland** Canada. Town in S Ontario, on the Welland R. and the Welland Ship Canal 37 m. ESE of Hamilton. Pop. (1966) 39,960. Industrial centre. Canal port. Manufactures steel, agricultural machinery, footwear, etc.

**Welland River** England. River 70 m. long rising near Market Harborough, Northamptonshire, and flowing generally NE across Lincolnshire and past Spalding to the Wash.

**Welland Ship Canal** Canada. Canal in S Ontario joining lakes Erie and Ontario, bypassing the Niagara Falls; just over 27½ m. long, part of its course being formed by the Welland R. Constructed 1913–32 to supersede the old Welland Canal (built 1824–33). One of the world's busiest inland waterways.

**Wellingborough** England. Urban district in Northamptonshire, on the R. Ise 10 m. ENE of the confluence with the R. Nene at Northampton. Pop. (1961) 30,579. Industrial centre. Tanning, iron founding, footwear manufacture; also produces tanning chemicals, clothing, etc. Has a public school (founded 1595).

**Wellington** (Shropshire) England. Urban district 10 m. E. of Shrewsbury. Pop. (1961) 13,630. Market town. Manufactures automobile components, cranes, etc. The Wrekin (1,335 ft) is 2 m. SW; 6 m. WSW is Wroxeter.

**Wellington** (Somerset) England. Urban district 6 m. WSW of Taunton. Pop. (1961) 7,523. Market town. Manufactures woollen goods, made here since the reign of Elizabeth I. On the Blackdown Hills to the S is a monument to the Duke of Wellington, who took his title from the town.

**Wellington** New Zealand. **1.** Provincial district in the SW of the N Island. Area (statistical area) 10,870 sq. m. Pop. (1966) 523,755. Largely mountainous, esp. in the N; a fertile coastal region in the S and W, with dairy and sheep farms. Wellington (city) is in the SW.
**2.** Capital of New Zealand, on the SW shore of Port Nicholson, now Wellington Harbour, off Cook Strait. Pop. (1966) 131,843. Important seaport, with a large deep, sheltered harbour, and the city has spread among the high encircling hills. Among its outstanding buildings are the Houses of Parliament, Victoria University (1897), and the National Museum and Art Gallery. In 1872 earth movements raised the shore-line so that Lambton Quay, with large commercial and administrative buildings, now lies inland of the waterfront. Exports dairy produce, wool, meat, hides. The main industrial growth has been in the Hutt valley, just to the NE, where woollen mills, meat factories, engineering industries, vehicle assembly, rubber manufactures, and oil refineries are located. Railways to the N follow the W coast and the Hutt valley, and there are regular inter-island links by sea to Picton and by air to Nelson. Founded 1840. Succeeded Auckland as capital 1865.

**Wells** England. Municipal borough in Somerset 17 m. S of Bristol, at the S foot of the Mendip Hills. Pop. (1961) 6,691. Manufactures cheese, paper, etc. Within the borough is the ecclesiastical city, surrounded by medieval walls and containing the small but very beautiful 12th/13th-cent. cathedral, the moated bishop's palace, etc. The W front of the cathedral, which is mainly Early English in style, has 300 finely carved figures, and is attributed to Bishop Jocelyn (1206–42). Just NW is the famous limestone cave of Wookey Hole.

**Wells-next-the-Sea** England. Small port and holiday resort in Norfolk 29 m. NW of Norwich, well known for its shellfish. Pop. (1961) 2,490.

**Wels** Austria. Industrial town in Upper Austria, 15 m. SW of Linz on the Traun R. Pop. (1961) 41,060. Manufactures machinery and food products, deriving fuel from natural gas wells in the vicinity. Has a 14th-cent. Gothic church and an imperial castle.

**Welshpool** Wales. Municipal borough in Montgomeryshire, near the R. Severn 17 m. WSW of Shrewsbury. Pop. (1961) 6,332. Market town. Manufactures biscuits. To the SW are Powys (Powis) Castle, seat of the Earls of Powys, and the picturesque Powys Park.

**Welwyn Garden City** England. Urban district in Hertfordshire 6 m. NE of St Albans. Pop. (1961) 34,944. Manufactures food products, chemicals, plastics, etc. Planned (1919) by Sir Ebenezer Howard as a residential and industrial centre with an ultimate population of 50,000.

**Wembley** England. Former municipal borough in Middlesex and NW suburb of London; from 1965 part of the Greater London borough of Brent. Largely residential. Electrical engineering. Manufactures food products, industrial gases, etc. Site of the British Empire Exhibition (1924–5), many of the buildings of which were converted into factories. Wembley Stadium is the venue of the Cup Finals of the Football Association and Rugby League and international football matches; the Olympic Games were held there in 1948.

**Wenchow** China. River port in SE Chekiang province, on the Wu-kiang 15 m. from the sea and 160 m. SSE of Hangchow. Pop. 200,000. Trade in tea, timber, bamboo, oranges. Manufactures leather goods, mats, umbrellas, etc. Opened to European trade 1877.

**Wendover** England. Market town in Buckinghamshire, in the Chiltern Hills 5 m. SE of Aylesbury, on the Upper Icknield Way. Pop. (1961) 3,500. Coombe Hill (852 ft), 1½ m. WSW, presents magnificent views over the Vale of Ayles-

bury. Chequers, country residence of the British prime minister, is 2½ m. SW. Birthplace of Roger de Wendover (d. 1237), an early English historian.

**Wenlock** England. Rural borough (1966) Shropshire 11 m. SE of Shrewsbury. Pop. (1961) 14,929. Comprises Much Wenlock, a market town with the ruins of a convent founded in the 7th cent., Little Wenlock, Ironbridge, with the first iron bridge built in England (1779), Broseley, Coalbrookdale, and Madeley. Coalmining. Manufactures pottery, tiles. Wenlock Edge, a ridge rising to 867 ft, extends about 15 m. to the SW.

**Wensleydale** England. The picturesque upper valley of the R. Ure, in the N Riding of Yorkshire, widening at its lower end into the Vale of York. Famous for its cheese.

**Wernigerode** German Democratic Republic. Tourist resort in the Magdeburg district 45 m. SW of Magdeburg, at the N foot of the Harz Mountains. Pop. (1965) 32,676. Manufactures paper, chemicals, etc. Engineering. Has an ancient castle and a 15th-cent. town hall.

**Wesel** Federal German Republic. Town in N Rhine-Westphalia, near the confluence of the Rhine and Lippe rivers 17 m. NNW of Duisburg. Pop. (1963) 32,100. Railway junction. Manufactures machinery etc. Almost completely destroyed by bombing in the 2nd World War (1945) and rebuilt.

**Weser River** Federal German Republic. River 310 m. long formed by the union of the Fulda and Werra rivers at Münden, flowing generally N past Minden and Bremen, entering the North Sea at Bremerhaven. Navigable throughout; connected by the Mittelland Canal system with the Rhine, Ems, and Elbe rivers.

**Wessex** Britain. Kingdom of the West Saxons, probably founded by Cerdic around the R. Avon in Wiltshire towards the end of the 5th cent. and comprising in the first place the modern counties of Wiltshire, Hampshire, and Berkshire; Dorset, Somerset, and parts of Devonshire were added by the end of the 7th cent. Egbert (802–39) defeated Mercia and annexed Essex, Sussex, and Kent; under Alfred (871–900) Wessex controlled all England not ruled by the Danes, and its history then becomes that of England. The Wessex novels of Thomas Hardy refer mainly to Dorset.

**West Allis** USA. Industrial town in SE

Wisconsin just W of Milwaukee. Pop. (1960) 68,157. Manufactures lorries, heavy machinery, industrial gases, etc.

**West Bay** ◊ *Bridport*.

**West Bengal** ◊ *Bengal*.

**West Bridgford** England. Residential urban district of Nottinghamshire and a S suburb of Nottingham, with Trent Bridge cricket ground. Pop. (1961) 26,957.

**West Bromwich** England. County borough in S Staffordshire, in the Black Country 5 m. NW of Birmingham. Pop. (1961) 95,909. Coalmining and industrial centre. Manufactures metal goods (springs, nails, safes, stoves, weighing machines, etc.); also chemicals, paint. The picturesque 16th-cent. Oak House is now a museum.

**Westbury** England. Urban district in Wiltshire 11 m. SE of Bath. Pop. (1961) 5,409. Market town. Railway junction. Tanning. Manufactures woollen goods. To the E is the White Horse of Westbury, cut (1873) in the chalk downs over an earlier figure.

**West Covina** USA. Town in California 19 m. E of Los Angeles. Pop. (1960) 50,645. Almost entirely residential. Its working population commutes largely to Los Angeles.

**West Drayton** ◊ *Yiewsley and West Drayton*.

**Westerham** England. Market town in W Kent, on the R. Darent 5 m. W of Sevenoaks. Pop. 4,000. Birthplace of General Wolfe (1727–59), who is commemorated in Quebec House. Just S is Chartwell, home (1922–65) of Sir Winston Churchill.

**Western Australia** Australia. Largest state in Australia, W of the meridian 129° E, which separates it from the Northern Territory and S Australia. Area 975,920 sq. m. Pop. (1966) 836,673. Cap. Perth, in the only fertile and populous area, Swanland (SW). There is a great diversity of landscape and land-use. In the NE the Kimberleys consist of broken blocks of high country, much eroded and cut by river gorges; here monsoon rains support grass and permit low-density cattle rearing, with agricultural possibilities if rivers such as the Ord are utilized. To the SW are eroded plateaux such as the Hamersley Range. Summers are hot; the temperature in some parts has exceeded 100° F on more than 100 consecutive days. The SW interior has granites and gneisses at the surface, and here the spinifex and dwarf acacia give way to closer mulga and dry grassland.

The extreme SW is forested (largely with the hardwood eucalypts jarrah and karri), the climate being of 'Mediterranean' type. Main occupations dairying, lumbering, and the cultivation of citrus and other fruits and vines. Much of the inland area with a mean annual rainfall between 25 ins. and 10 ins. has been cleared for wheat and sheep farming.

Chief mineral gold, occurring mostly in a wide belt in the SW interior including such centres as Kalgoorlie, Meekatharra, Wiluna; the gold rush of 1892 saw the beginnings of large-scale goldmining at and near Kalgoorlie. Iron is mined on islands in Yampi Sound in the NW, coal comes from Collie in the SW and asbestos from the Hamersley Range. Chief commercial and administrative city Perth; at Fremantle, its port, and Kwinana, just S, industries are growing and include the manufacture of iron and steel, chemicals and textiles, and oil refining. Exports include gold, iron ore, wheat, wool, dairy produce, timber.

The first settlement was formed (1826) at Albany by convicts. In 1829 Capt. Fremantle took possession of the territory for Britain and Capt. Sterling founded the Swan River Settlement in the Perth-Fremantle area. The colony became a state of the Commonwealth of Australia in 1901.

**Western Desert** United Arab Republic. Ill-defined section of the ◊ *Libyan Desert*, on the border of Cyrenaica, containing the Siwa, Bahariya, and Farafra oases and the Qattara Depression (N). A railway runs along the coast from Alexandria through El Alamein to Matruh, and then a coastal road to Sidi Barrani and Salum (all well known in the 2nd World War).

**Western Isles** ◊ *Hebrides*.

**Western Samoa** ◊ *Samoa*.

**Westfalen** ◊ *Westphalia*.

**Westfield** (Massachusetts) USA. Town on the Westfield R. 7 m. WNW of Springfield. Pop. (1960) 26,302. Manufactures machinery, bicycles, paper, etc. Founded 1660 as a trading post.

**Westfield** (New Jersey) USA. Town 11 m. SW of Newark. Pop. (1960) 31,447. Mainly residential. Some light industries.

**West Flanders** ◊ *Flanders*.

**West Ham** England. Former county borough in SW Essex, on the N bank of the R. Thames; from 1965 part of the Greater London borough of Newham. Pop. (1961)

157,186. Includes Stratford, Forest Gate, Plaistow, Canning Town, and Silvertown, with the Royal Victoria dock and parts of the Royal Albert and King George V docks of the Port of London. Industrial and residential. Railway engineering. Manufactures rubber and jute products, chemicals, soap, etc.

**West Hartford** USA. Town in Connecticut 3 m. W of Hartford. Pop. (1960) 62,382. Mainly residential. Birthplace of Noah Webster (1758–1843), the lexicographer.

**West Hartlepool** England. Industrial town in Durham, on the S side of Hartlepool Bay 7 m. N of Middlesbrough. Since 1967 part of the county borough of ◊ *Hartlepool*. Pop. (1961) 77,073. Seaport. Shipbuilding. Manufactures machinery, paper, hosiery, cement, etc. Includes the seaside resort of Seaton Carew. In the 1st World War the town was shelled by German cruisers (1914).

**West Haven** USA. Industrial town in Connecticut, just SW of New Haven. Pop. (1960) 43,002. Manufactures textiles, aircraft parts, fertilizers, etc.

**Westhoughton** England. Urban district in Lancashire 4 m. WSW of Bolton. Pop. (1961) 16,254. Coalmining. Manufactures cotton goods, chemicals, paint.

**West Indies**. Archipelago off Central America, separating the Atlantic Ocean from the Caribbean Sea and extending in a wide arc about 2,500 m. long from near the Florida coast to near the coast of Venezuela. Consists of 3 main groups, the Greater Antilles, the Lesser Antilles, and the Bahamas. The Greater Antilles include Cuba (the westernmost and by far the largest island in the W Indies), Hispaniola, Puerto Rico, and Jamaica; the Bahamas are the northernmost group, lying E of Florida; the Lesser Antilles include the Leeward Is., the Windward Is., Barbados, Trinidad and Tobago, Margarita, and islands of the Netherlands Antilles (Curaçao, Aruba, Bonaire). All the islands have a wide measure of autonomy or are independent republics. Hispaniola is divided between Haiti (W) and the Dominican Republic (E), which, like Cuba, are independent. The USA possesses Puerto Rico and the Virgin Is. of the US; France has Guadeloupe and Martinique; the Netherlands has the Netherlands Antilles; Venezuela has Margarita and some small adjacent islands. The remaining islands, including the Bahamas, are British, either as independent members of the Commonwealth or as Crown Colonies.

Most of the W Indies are of volcanic origin, being the peaks of a submerged range of mountains; some, notably the Bahamas, are of coral formation. No important rivers, but plentiful supplies of underground water. Some of the islands are mountainous: Hispaniola has peaks exceeding 10,000 ft; the Blue Mountains of Jamaica rise above 7,000 ft. Climate tropical but tempered by the NE Trade Winds; many islands experience hurricanes Aug.–Oct. Volcanic eruptions in modern times have been confined to Martinique and St Vincent. Many fine natural harbours, inc. Havana (Cuba), Kingston (Jamaica), San Juan (Puerto Rico).

The fertile soil yields many varieties of tropical products. Main crop sugar-cane; others exported in quantity are tobacco, cacao, citrus fruits, bananas, coffee; sugar refining is a major industry; rum and lime juice are prepared for export. Jamaica has large bauxite deposits and Trinidad produces asphalt from its Pitch Lake; Curaçao and Aruba have petroleum industries of great importance. Negroes form the bulk of the population, being descendants of African slaves brought to work on the plantations; they predominate in most of the islands, though in Cuba and Puerto Rico whites of Spanish stock are in the majority. The aboriginal peoples, Arawaks and Caribs, have almost disappeared, but a few Caribs survive in Dominica.

The W Indies were discovered by Columbus, who made his first landfall in the Americas (1492) on San Salvador (Watling) Island in the Bahamas. As he believed that he had reached India by a westerly route, the islands were named 'West Indies'. Spaniards were the first Europeans to settle; in 1496 Santo Domingo, on Hispaniola, was founded as the first European town in the New World. The W Indies and the adjacent waters became the haunt of pirates and buccaneers, and continual struggles took place (esp. between the English, French, and Dutch) for possession of the islands. Slave trading began in the 1560s and grew apace in the 17th and 18th cent. Slavery was abolished in the British W Indies in 1834 and in the other islands later.

During the 19th cent. the islands of the British W Indies were made Crown Colonies, and some, e.g. Trinidad and Tobago, were combined for administrative purposes. In 1958 the Federation of the BWI was formed, with the capital at Port of Spain (Trinidad). In 1962, however, the Federation was dissolved because Jamaica and Trinidad opted out; Jamaica (1962), Trinidad and Tobago (1962), and Barbados (1966) became independent, while Antigua, Grenada, St Lucia, and other small islands were given self-government in association with Britain, i.e. became 'associated states' (1967). The US has a number of naval and air bases outside its own territory – Guantánamo Bay in Cuba and the bases in the BWI obtained in 1940–41 on a 99-year lease.

**West Irian** ◊ *New Guinea*.

**West Lothian** Scotland. Formerly Linlithgowshire. County in the Central Lowlands bordering N on the Firth of Forth. Area 120 sq. m. Pop. (1961) 92,764. County town Linlithgow. Hilly in the S. Drained by the R. Almond and the R. Avon. Largely cultivated. Produces coal, shale oil. Chief towns Linlithgow, Bathgate, Bo'ness.

**Westmeath** Irish Republic. Inland county in Leinster. Area 681 sq. m. Pop. (1966) 52,900. County town Mullingar. Generally low-lying, with a considerable area of bog; has many loughs, including Loughs Ree (on the R. Shannon), Sheelin, Derravaragh, and Ennell, all noted for their trout. Main occupations cattle rearing, dairy farming. Chief towns Mullingar, Athlone.

**Westminster** England. City and former metropolitan borough of London on the N bank of the R. Thames; from 1965 a Greater London borough comprising the former Westminster and the metropolitan boroughs of Paddington and St Marylebone. Pop. (1963) 269,379. Contains many of the chief theatres, restaurants, and shops (West End) and a large number of London's historic buildings and monuments, e.g. Buckingham Palace, St James's Palace. In front of the former, at the head of the Mall, is the Queen Victoria Memorial; near by are the royal parks, Hyde Park and the much smaller St James's Park and Green Park. Westminster Abbey (officially the Collegiate Church of St Peter), the most famous church in the British Commonwealth, stands on the site of a 7th-cent. abbey built by Sebert, king of the E Saxons, which was destroyed but rebuilt by Edward the Confessor in the 11th cent. Further rebuilding was begun in the 13th cent. Later additions include Henry VII's Chapel (16th-cent.) and the two W towers, designed by Wren (17th cent.) and completed 1740. Scene of the coronation of all English monarchs since William the Conqueror (except Edward V and Edward VIII); the burial-place of many of them, and of many other famous Englishmen, including some of the greatest poets (in 'Poets' Corner') and the Unknown Soldier. Westminster School (St Peter's College, originally attached to the Abbey and refounded by Elizabeth I in 1560) is one of the oldest and most famous English public schools, with Ben Jonson, Dryden, Wren, and Gibbon among its former scholars, but is perhaps best known to the outside world for its annual 'tossing the pancake' ceremony on Shrove Tuesday. Opposite the Abbey, in New Palace Yard, is Westminster Hall, completed in 1099, rebuilt 1394–1402, as part of the royal Palace of Westminster, which included courts of law; it has witnessed many historic events, e.g. the deposition of Richard II and the trials of Charles I and Warren Hastings (whose trial lasted 7 years). The adjoining Houses of Parliament, in imitated Perpendicular style (1840–67), are dominated by the Victoria Tower and the Clock Tower (which contains the celebrated bell Big Ben). The thoroughfare Whitehall, leading N from Parliament Square to Trafalgar Square, contains the Cenotaph war memorial and the principal government offices; close by is Downing Street, with the residences of the Prime Minister and the Chancellor of the Exchequer. In Trafalgar Square is Nelson's Column (1843) and on the N side the National Gallery (1838). From Westminster Bridge (crossing the Thames near the Houses of Parliament) the Victoria Embankment curves past the Cleopatra's Needle obelisk (brought from Egypt 1878) to Waterloo Bridge. From Trafalgar Square the Strand runs parallel to the river, with Somerset House, King's College (University of London), and the two 'island' churches, St Mary-le-Strand and St Clement Danes; just N, towards the E end of the Strand, is Covent Garden, with the extensive fruit and vegetable market and the Royal Opera House. The S side of Westminster is Pimlico, with Victoria Station and a Byzantine-style

Roman Catholic cathedral (1895–1903); in the W are many embassies and institutions, the residential districts of Belgravia and Mayfair, and the Royal Albert Hall and the Albert Memorial; in the N is the less fashionable Soho (London's 'Latin Quarter'). Piccadilly (running alongside Green Park in the N) is well known for shops and also for Burlington House, seat of the Royal Society and of the Royal Academy. Many famous buildings (including the House of Commons, Westminster School, and St Clement Danes Church) were severely damaged by bombing in the 2nd World War.

The 13th-cent. Statutes of Westminster (1275, 1285) expressed basic principles in English law. Those of 1931 defined the relationship between Britain and the Dominions, within the Commonwealth. There have been many Synods of Westminster, esp. the Westminster Assembly (1643–9), which drew up a Confession of faith accepted by the Presbyterian churches.

**Westmorland** England. County in the NW, reaching the sea in the R. Kent estuary in the extreme SW, drained also by the R. Eden. Area 789 sq. m. Pop. (1961) 67,222. County town Appleby. Largely mountain and moorland, with Helvellyn (3,118 ft) the highest point, it contains much of the Lake District, inc. Hawes Water, Grasmere, Rydal Water, and parts of Windermere and Ullswater, and so has a considerable tourist traffic. Cattle and sheep reared. Granite and limestone quarried. Kendal is the only town with more than 10,000 inhabitants.

**West New York** USA. Industrial town in NE New Jersey, on the Hudson R. opposite Manhattan. Pop. (1960) 35,547. Manufactures textiles, clothing, leather goods, toys, etc.

**Weston-super-Mare** England. Municipal borough in Somerset, on the Bristol Channel 18 m. WSW of Bristol. Pop. (1961) 43,923. Seaside resort, popular with holidaymakers from Bristol and the W Midlands.

**West Orange** USA. Town in New Jersey 5 m. NW of Newark. Pop. (1960) 39,895. Residential and industrial. Manufactures electrical equipment, machinery, etc. Home of Thomas A. Edison (1887–1931), the inventor.

**West Palm Beach** USA. Winter resort in SE Florida, on the W shore of L. Worth opposite Palm Beach, 65 m. NNE of

Miami. Pop. (1960) 56,208. Manufactures air-conditioning equipment, prefabricated buildings, etc. Has an important tourist trade.

**Westphalia** (Ger. **Westfalen**) Germany. Former province of Prussia; since 1946 part of the *Land* of N Rhine-Westphalia. In the W is the Ruhr district, one of the most important industrial regions in Europe, based on the coalfield; among its many large manufacturing towns are Cologne, Essen, Düsseldorf, Dortmund. Westphalia was originally the W part of the old duchy of Saxony. Some of the area passed to the archbishops of Cologne (1180) as the duchy of Westphalia. In 1803 the Church lands were secularized, and part of Westphalia went to Prussia. Napoleon created the kingdom of Westphalia (including territory never before associated with it) for his brother Jerome (1807). The Prussian province (cap. Münster) formed in 1816 more or less coincided with the original region. The Treaty of Westphalia (1648), concluded at Münster and Osnabrück, brought the Thirty Years War to an end.

**West Point** USA. US military reservation, home of the US Military Academy, on a plateau above the Hudson R. 8 m. SSE of Newburgh in SE New York, including Constitution Island in the Hudson R. Opened in 1802 with 10 cadets; now has about 2,500 cadets.

**Westport** Irish Republic. Market town and fishing port in Co. Mayo, on Westport Bay, an inlet of Clew Bay. Pop. (1966) 2,927. Manufactures hosiery. Has the 18th-cent. Westport House, seat of the Marquess of Sligo.

**West Virginia** USA. State in E central USA. Area 24,181 sq. m. Pop. (1970) 1,701,913. Cap. Charleston. Admitted to the Union in 1863 as the 35th state; popularly known as the 'Panhandle' state. Has two narrow extensions, the N Panhandle between Ohio and Pennsylvania and the E Panhandle between Maryland and Virginia. The Allegheny Plateau covers two thirds of its area. Highest point Spruce Knob (4,860 ft). Chief rivers the Ohio and the Potomac, on the W and N borders respectively. Climate humid continental, with a mean annual rainfall of 40–50 ins. Most important occupation mining; W Virginia ranks first among US states in coal production. Chief crops hay, maize. Large quantities of apples and peaches grown. Leading industrial centres Charleston, Huntington, Wheeling. Originally part of Virginia, the region resented domination by the E Virginians, and at the outbreak of the Civil War joined the Union (1861) and became a separate state (1863).

**Westward Ho** England. Village and small seaside resort in Devonshire, in the urban district of Northam, on Bideford Bay 2 m. NW of Bideford. Named after Charles Kingsley's novel. Rudyard Kipling was educated at the United Services College, which was formerly here.

**Wetzlar** Federal German Republic. Industrial town in Hessen, on the Lahn R. 67 m. ESE of Bonn. Pop. (1963) 37,800. Iron founding. Manufactures cameras, optical instruments, machine tools, etc. Associated with Goethe's *Werther*.

**Wexford** Irish Republic. **1.** County in Leinster, in the extreme SE, bounded on the E and S by St George's Channel. Area 908 sq. m. Pop. (1966) 83,437. In the main gently undulating; mountainous along the NW border, rising to 2,610 ft in Mt Leinster. Drained by the Slaney and Barrow (SW border) rivers. Cereals and potatoes cultivated. Dairy farming. Cattle rearing. The first Irish county to be colonized from England, the Anglo-Normans landing in 1169 at the invitation of Diarmid MacMurrough, overlord of Leinster.
**2.** County town of Co. Wexford, on Wexford Harbour, formed by the estuary of the R. Slaney. Pop. (1966) 11,542. Fishing port. Manufactures agricultural implements. Iron founding, bacon and ham curing, tanning, etc. Owing to the bar at the mouth of the estuary, Wexford declined as a seaport and was superseded by Rosslare. A Danish settlement in the 9th cent. Lost its independence (1169) when Diarmid MacMurrough and his Anglo-Norman allies captured it. Birthplace of Sir Robert M'Clure (1807–73), who won fame in the discovery of the North-west Passage.

**Weybridge** ◊ *Walton and Weybridge.*

**Weymouth** USA. Industrial town in Massachusetts, on Massachusetts Bay 11 m. SSE of Boston. Pop. (1960) 48,177. Manufactures footwear, machinery, fertilizers, etc. First colonized 1622. A tannery was established 1697.

**Weymouth and Melcombe Regis** England. Municipal borough on the coast of Dorset at the mouth of the short R. Wey (6 m.).

Pop. (1961) 40,962. Seaside resort. Packet station for the Channel Is. Boatbuilding, brewing, etc. Popularized as a resort by George III, a frequent visitor. Just S is the Isle of Portland. Birthplace of T. L. Peacock (1785–1866).

**Wey River** England. River 35 m. long formed from two streams, one rising near Alton (Hampshire) and the other near Haslemere (Surrey), flowing generally NE past Godalming and Guildford to join the R. Thames at Weybridge.

**Whangarei** New Zealand. Industrial town and port on the E coast of Auckland Peninsula, N Island, 85 m. NNW of Auckland. Pop. (1966) 27,390. Harbour improved by dredging. Exports coal, dairy produce, fruit. Manufactures glass, cement.

**Wharfe River** England. River 60 m. long in the W Riding of Yorkshire, rising 3 m. N of Pen-y-ghent and flowing generally ESE past Ilkley, Otley, and Tadcaster to join the R. Ouse just above Cawood. Its upper valley, Wharfedale, is one of the most beautiful in England.

**Wheeling** USA. Town in W Virginia, on the Ohio R. 45 m. SW of Pittsburgh, in the N Panhandle of the state. Pop. (1960) 53,400. Large iron and steel industry. Manufactures tinplate, nails, glass, tiles, etc. Founded 1769. Site of the Wheeling Conventions (1861–2) which led to the separation of W Virginia from Virginia. State capital 1863–70 and 1875–85.

**Whickham** England. Urban district in Durham 4 m. W of Gateshead. Pop. (1961) 24,791. Coalmining, metal working. Manufactures paper, printers' ink, etc.

**Whipsnade** England. Village in Bedfordshire 3 m. S of Dunstable. Has a Zoological Park of 500 acres (opened 1931 by the London Zoological Society) where animals and birds are bred and exhibited in their natural state.

**Whitby** England. Urban district in the N Riding of Yorkshire, at the mouth of the R. Esk, which divides the town into the old and new parts. Pop. (1961) 11,662. Seaside resort. Fishing port. Boatbuilding, fish curing. The manufacture of jet ornaments is still carried on. The ruins of the famous abbey, founded in the 7th cent., stand on the E cliff. Capt. Cook lived here, and the ships for his voyages were built here. Birthplace of William Scoresby (1789–1857), the Arctic explorer.

**Whitchurch** England. Market town in Shropshire 18 m. N of Shrewsbury. Pop.

(1961) 7,159. Has a 17th-cent. almshouse and several Georgian houses. Birthplace of Sir Edward German (1862–1936).

**Whitechapel** England. District in the London borough of Tower Hamlets (E), with a predominantly Jewish population. The famous Sunday morning market of 'Petticoat Lane' (Middlesex Street) is on its W boundary. Contains the Whitechapel Art Gallery.

**Whitehaven** England. Municipal borough in Cumberland, on the Irish Sea 36 m. SW of Carlisle. Pop. (1961) 27,541. Seaport. Coalmining, flour milling. Manufactures textiles, food products, chemicals. Exports coal. It expanded rapidly in the 17th cent. with the exploitation of the local coal deposits, but, being largely dependent on coal, suffered severely in the depression of the 1930s.

**Whitehorse** Canada. Capital and largest town of the Yukon Territory, on the Lewes (Upper Yukon) R. just below Whitehorse Rapids and 95 m. N of Skagway (Alaska), with which it is connected by rail. Pop. (1966) 4,771. Trading centre for a mining and fur-trapping region. Expanded during the 2nd World War (on the Alaska Highway), declined, and revived again after 1952 when it superseded Dawson as capital.

**White Horse, Vale of** England. Valley of the R. Ock, which flows ENE across NW Berkshire to join the R. Thames at Abingdon. Flat and well wooded in contrast with the Berkshire Downs to the S. Called after White Horse Hill (856 ft), in the Downs just S of the village of Uffington, which has the figure of a horse 374 ft long, cut on its N slope by removing the turf and exposing the underlying chalk; on the summit is the earthwork known as Uffington Castle. The figure is supposed to commemorate the victory of Alfred the Great over the Danes at Ashdown (871). There are similar white horses elsewhere in England, notably near Westbury (Wilts).

**White Mountains** USA. 1. Range in N New Hampshire, part of the Appalachian Mountains. A favourite resort area owing to the fine scenery. Highest peak Mt Washington (6,288 ft).
2. Range in E California and SW Nevada. Highest peak White Mountain (14,242 ft).

**White Plains** USA. Town in SE New York, on the Bronx R. 25 m. NNE of New York city. Pop. (1960) 50,485. Residential and industrial. Manufactures

clothing, plastics, food products, etc. During the American Revolution the provincial congress met here and approved the Declaration of Independence (1776), and a battle was fought between Washington and the British (1776).

**White Russia** ◊ *Byelorussia*.

**White Sea** USSR. Inlet of the Barents Sea in N European RSFSR, entered by a channel 30–90 m. wide between the Kola and Kanin peninsulas. Area 36,000 sq. m. Receives the Mezen, N Dvina, and Onega rivers. Contains the Kandalaksha, Onega, and Dvina gulfs. Principal port Archangel (Arkhangelsk). Usually frozen Oct.–May. Its commercial importance increased with the completion of the Baltic–White Sea Canal (1933).

**Whithorn** Scotland. Royal burgh in SE Wigtownshire 9 m. S of Wigtown. Pop. (1961) 986. Market town. Ruins of the 12th-cent. St Ninian's Priory, built for Premonstratensian monks. According to some authorities this was the site of the stone church called Candida Casa ('White House'), built in 397 by St Ninian, the first Christian missionary to Scotland; others place the site at the coastal village known as Isle of Whithorn, 3 m. SE.

**Whitley Bay** England. Municipal borough in Northumberland, 8 m. NE of Newcastle upon Tyne. Pop. (1961) 36,519. Seaside resort. In the borough is the coalmining town of Monkseaton.

**Whitney, Mount** USA. Highest peak in USA outside Alaska, rising to 14,495 ft. Near the S end of the Sierra Nevada, California. Discovered (1864) by Josiah D. Whitney, the geologist, and named after him.

**Whitstable** England. Urban district in Kent, near the E entrance to the Swale 6 m. NNW of Canterbury. Pop. (1961) 19,534. Seaside resort and small port, famous for at least 2,000 years for its oyster beds. The Canterbury–Whitstable railway line (1830), one of the earliest in the country, was closed to passengers in 1930.

**Whittier** USA. Town in California 11 m. SE of Los Angeles. Pop. (1960) 33,663. Residential and industrial. Manufactures tools, gas and oil heaters, etc. Founded (1887) by Quakers.

**Whittlesey** England. Urban district in the Isle of Ely 5 m. ESE of Peterborough. Pop. (1961) 9,324. Market town. Manufactures bricks and tiles. Whittlesey Mere,

6 m. SW, formerly a lake, was drained in the mid 19th cent.

**Whyalla** Australia. Port on the NW shore of Spencer Gulf, S Australia, 140 m. NNW of Adelaide. Pop. (1966) 22,126. Created as an outlet for the iron-ore mines of the Middleback Range. Manufactures iron and steel. Shipbuilding. Water is piped 220 m. from the Murray R. A new steel plant was inaugurated in 1965.

**Wichita** USA. Largest town in Kansas, on the Arkansas R. at the confluence with the Little Arkansas R. 180 m. SW of Kansas City. Pop. (1960) 254,698. Commercial and industrial centre in a wheat-growing and oil-producing region. Large trade in grain and livestock. Flour milling, meat packing, oil refining. Manufactures aircraft, chemicals, etc. Seat of the University of Wichita (1926) and Friends University (1898).

**Wichita Falls** USA. Town in Texas, on the Wichita R. 100 m. NW of Fort Worth, in a region producing oil and grain. Pop. (1960) 101,724. Oil refining, flour milling. Manufactures oilfield machinery, glass, cottonseed oil, etc.

**Wick** Scotland. Royal burgh and county town of Caithness 80 m. NE of Inverness. Pop. (1961) 7,397. Port. Fishing centre. Distilling. Manufactures hosiery, glass, etc. The harbour was built (1800) by Telford. On the cliff edge 3 m. NNE stand the ruins of the 15th-cent. Castle Girnigoe.

**Wicklow** Irish Republic. **1.** County in Leinster, in the SE, bordering E on the Irish Sea. Area 782 sq. m. Pop. (1966) 60,428. Generally mountainous apart from a narrow coastal strip, rising to 3,039 ft in Lugnaquillia (Wicklow Mountains). Main rivers the Liffey and the Slaney. Among the beautiful glens are Glendalough, Glen of the Downs, Glenmalure, and the Vale of Avoca – the river formed by the union of the Avonmore and the Avonbeg. In the NW, on the Liffey, are the Poulaphuca dam, hydroelectric power station, and reservoir (1938), which serves as a water supply for Dublin. Chief towns Wicklow, Arklow, and Bray, the last a seaside resort; the village of Shillelagh gave its name to the traditional Irish cudgel. **2.** County town of Co. Wicklow, at the mouth of the R. Vartry 27 m. SSE of Dublin. Pop. (1966) 3,340. Small seaport. Market town. Remains of the 12th-cent. Black Castle on cliffs to the S; 13th-cent. Franciscan friary.

**Widecombe-in-the-Moor** England. Village

in Devonshire on the E edge of Dartmoor 17 m. SW of Exeter. Has a 14th/16th-cent. church and a 15th-cent. church house. Immortalized in the well-known song about its annual fair.

**Widnes** England. Municipal borough in SW Lancashire, on the N bank of the R. Mersey opposite Runcorn, with which it is connected by railway and transporter bridges. Pop. (1961) 52,168. Important centre of the chemical industry. Also manufactures soap, paint, metal products, etc.

**Wien** ◊ *Vienna*.

**Wiener Neustadt** Austria. Town in Lower Austria 28 m. S of Vienna. Pop. (1961) 33,845. Industrial centre. Manufactures locomotives, railway rolling stock, machinery, leather goods, textiles, etc. Has the 12th-cent. Castle of Babenberg, converted in 1752 into a military academy and in 1919 into a school, but is chiefly modern in appearance, having been largely rebuilt in 1834 after a disastrous fire.

**Wiesbaden** Federal German Republic. Capital of Hessen, at the S foot of the Taunus Hills 20 m. W of Frankfurt. Pop. (1968) 258,178. One of the oldest and most famous watering-places in Germany, with warm springs and a mild climate. Manufactures textiles, chemicals, plastics, cement, pottery, etc. Printing. Trade in wine, fruit, vegetables. Was a well-known Roman spa, and the wall known as the 'Heidenmauer' was probably part of the fortifications erected under Diocletian (3rd cent.). By the 9th cent. it was known as Wisibada ('Meadow Bath'). Capital of the duchy of Nassau 1815–66.

**Wigan** England. County borough in Lancashire, on the R. Douglas and the Leeds–Liverpool Canal 17 m. NE of Liverpool. Pop. (1961) 78,702. Coalmining, engineering, food processing. Manufactures cotton goods, metal goods, tools, etc. The Church of All Saints has a partly 13th-cent tower. The grammar school was founded in the 16th cent.

**Wight, Isle of** England. Island and administrative county in Hampshire, separated from the mainland by the Solent (NW) and Spithead (NE), 22 m. long E–W and 13 m. wide N–S. Area 147 sq. m. Pop. (1961) 95,479. Chief town Newport. A line of chalk hills runs E–W across the island, ending in the Needles, and there are further hills in the S. The R. Medina, on whose estuary Newport stands, flows S–N, and practically bisects the island. Scenery and a mild climate have combined to make it popular with holiday-makers; among the resorts are Ryde, Sandown, Shanklin, Ventnor, and Cowes (headquarters of English yachting). Of the Roman remains the best known is the villa at Brading (discovered 1879). In Carisbrooke Castle Charles I was imprisoned before his execution.

**Wigston** England. Urban district in Leicestershire 3 m. SSE of Leicester. Pop. (1961) 21,405. Manufactures hosiery, footwear, biscuits, etc.

**Wigtown** Scotland. Royal burgh and county town of Wigtownshire, on the W shore of Wigtown Bay. Pop. (1961) 1,201. Market town. Small port. In the church-yard are buried the Wigtown Martyrs, two women Covenanters who were drowned here (1685). The ancient circle known as the Standing Stones of Torhouse is 3 m. WNW.

**Wigtownshire** Scotland. County in the extreme SW, separated from Northern Ireland by the North Channel. Area 488 sq. m. Pop. (1961) 29,107. County town Wigtown. The coast is deeply indented by Loch Ryan, Luce Bay, and Wigtown Bay. In the W is the hammer-headed peninsula known as the Rhinns of Galloway, which, with the Machers in the SE, is low-lying and fertile. Oats cultivated. Dairy farming and cattle and sheep rearing important. The N part, called the Moors, is hilly and bleak. Chief towns Wigtown, Stranraer, Newton Stewart, and Whithorn.

**Wilhelmshaven** Federal German Republic. Port in Lower Saxony, on the NW shore of the Jadebusen and at the E end of the Ems–Jade Canal 40 m. NW of Bremen. Pop. (1968) 101,932. Industrial centre. Oil refining. Manufactures chemicals, agricultural machinery, refrigerators, etc. After the harbour was opened (1869) it became the chief German naval base on the North Sea. Heavily bombed in the 2nd World War; surviving naval installations were dismantled afterwards, and new industries were introduced. Has again become a naval base.

**Wilkes-Barre** USA. Industrial town in Pennsylvania, on the Susquehanna R. 16 m. SW of Scranton. Pop. (1960) 63,551. An important anthracite-mining centre in the Wyoming Valley. Manufactures loco-motives, mining machinery, wire, electrical appliances, etc.

**Wilkes Land** ◊ *Australian Antarctic Territory.*

**Willamette River** USA. River 290 m. long in W Oregon formed by the union of the Coast Fork and Middle Fork and flowing generally N to join the Columbia R. below Portland. Provides power for various hydroelectric installations.

**Willemstad** Netherlands Antilles. Capital, on the SW coast of Curaçao. Pop. (1964) 59,586. Has an excellent natural harbour. Important refining centre for Venezuelan oil, also an entrepôt for the SE Caribbean and a popular tourist resort. Has several 17th- and 18th-cent. Dutch buildings.

**Willenhall** England. Industrial town in S Staffordshire 3 m. E of Wolverhampton. Pop. (1961) 32,317. Coalmining. Manu-factures locks, tools, hardware, car radiators, etc.

**Willesden** England. Former municipal borough in Middlesex, including the districts of Cricklewood, Neasden, Kil-burn, Brondesbury, Harlesden, and Kensal Rise; from 1965 part of the Greater London borough of Brent. Pop. (1961) 170,835. Largely residential. Food pro-cessing. Manufactures motor-car acces-sories etc.

**Williamsburg** USA. Historic town in Virginia 46 m. ESE of Richmond, forming part of the Colonial National Historical Park. Pop. (1960) 6,832. Since 1926 500 buildings have been reconstructed in colonial form, among them the Governor's Palace (1720), Raleigh Tavern, Capitol, largely through the generosity of John D. Rockefeller, Jr. First settled in 1632 and called Middle Plantation; renamed on becoming state capital (1699–1779).

**Williamsport** USA. Industrial town in Pennsylvania, on the W branch of the Susquehanna R. 70 m. WSW of Scranton. Pop. (1960) 41,967. Manufactures textiles, clothing, fire hydrants, aircraft parts, furniture, etc. A lumbering centre in the 19th cent. until the forests were depleted.

**Wilmington** England. Village in E Sussex 5 m. NW of Eastbourne. Just S is Wind-over Hill, on the slope of which is the Long Man of Wilmington, a figure about 240 ft tall, of unknown age and origin, formed by removing the turf from the underlying chalk.

**Wilmington** (Delaware) USA. Largest town and chief industrial and commercial centre of Delaware, on the Delaware R. 25 m. SW of Philadelphia. Pop. (1960) 95,827.

Important chemical industry. Also shipbuilding, tanning, meat packing. Manufactures textiles etc. First settled (1638) by Swedish colonists, it has several historic buildings including Old Swedes Church (1698).

**Wilmington (N Carolina) USA.** Chief seaport in the state, on the Cape Fear R. 115 m. SSE of Raleigh. Pop. (1960) 44,013. Exports tobacco, cotton, wood pulp, etc. Manufactures textiles, clothing, wood products, etc.

**Wilmslow** England. Urban district in Cheshire 11 m. S of Manchester. Pop. (1961) 21,393. Manufactures cotton goods, clothing, etc. Engineering.

**Wilno** ⋄ *Vilnyus*.

**Wilson USA.** Town in N Carolina 40 m. E of Raleigh. Pop. (1960) 28,753. Important trade in leaf tobacco. Tobacco processing, meat packing, flour milling, etc.

**Wilson, Mount USA.** Peak (5,700 ft) in the San Gabriel Mountains, S California, just NE of Pasadena. Famous for the Mt Wilson Observatory (1904–5), administered jointly by the Carnegie and California Institutes of Technology.

**Wilton (Wiltshire) England.** Municipal borough at the confluence of the Wylye and Nadder rivers 3 m. WNW of Salisbury. Pop. (1961) 3,404. Market town famous since the 16th cent. for carpet manufacture (esp. Wiltons and Axminsters) and long an important sheep market. Wilton House near by is associated especially with Sir Philip Sidney, whose sister, the Countess of Pembroke, entertained many of the great Elizabethan poets here, and it has several portraits by Van Dyck. Wilton was the ancient capital of Wessex, and gave its name to the county.

**Wilton (Yorkshire) England.** New industrial town in the N Riding 4 m. SSW of Redcar. Important chemical industry, producing synthetic fibres etc.

**Wiltshire** England. Inland county in the S. Area 1,345 sq. m. Pop. (1961) 422,753. County town Salisbury. Largely chalk uplands, e.g. the Marlborough Downs (N) and Salisbury Plain (S; important as a military training-ground). Also has the fertile Vales of Pewsey and Wardour. Chief rivers the Kennet, Bristol Avon, Hampshire Avon, and Wylye. Dairy farming, bacon curing. Principal crop wheat. Chief towns Swindon (the largest), Salisbury, Chippenham, Trowbridge. Stonehenge and Avebury are famous prehistoric monuments.

**Wimbledon** England. Former municipal borough in N Surrey; from 1965 part of the Greater London borough of Merton. Pop. (1961) 56,994. Mainly residential. Headquarters of the All England Lawn Tennis Club since 1877. Wimbledon Common, a large open space adjoining Putney Heath, has ancient earthworks known as 'Caesar's Camp'.

**Wimborne Minster (Wimborne)** England. Urban district in Dorset on the R. Stour 6 m. N of Poole. Pop. (1961) 4,156. Market town. Dominated by its minster, which contains the tomb of Ethelred I; also a chained library and a 14th-cent. astronomical clock.

**Winchelsea** England. Small town in E Sussex 7 m. NE of Hastings. Pop. 1,100. Once an important seaport and a member of the Cinque Port of Hastings. The old town was engulfed by the sea (1287), and the present town was laid out in the 14th cent. – an excellent example of early town planning. The remarkable Church of St Thomas à Becket was never completed.

**Winchester** England. Ancient Venta Belgarum. County town of Hampshire, a municipal borough on the R. Itchen 12 m. NNE of Southampton. Pop. (1961) 28,643. Cathedral city, route centre, and market town. Minor industries. The great cathedral, built by Bishop Walkelin (1070–98) to replace an earlier Saxon cathedral, is the longest in England and contains the mortuary chests of Saxon kings and the tombs of Isaak Walton and Jane Austen. All that remains of the Norman castle is the Great Hall, which has the so-called King Arthur's Round Table, dating possibly from the 13th cent. Also the ruins of Wolvesey Castle, a residence of the bishops. Two gates of the ancient city walls remain. The 12th-cent. Hospital of St Cross still provides a dole of bread and beer for wayfarers. An educational centre from very early times; Winchester College (founded by William of Wykeham in 1382) is the oldest English public school. Winchester was a Roman-British town, and is identified by some with Camelot. Became extremely important in Saxon times as the capital of Wessex; it rivalled London, e.g. for the crowning and burial of kings. Under the Normans it was a leading commercial centre.

**Windermere** England. Urban district in

Westmorland above the E shore of L. Windermere. Pop. (1961) 6,556. Resort. Market town. Includes Bowness on the lakeside.

**Windermere, Lake** England. Picturesque lake in Westmorland, on the border with Lancashire in the S E of the Lake District, with wooded banks and several small islands; the largest lake in England, 10½ m. long and rather less than 1 m. wide. Fed by the Rothay, Brathay, and Trout Beck. Drained by the R. Leven into Morecambe Bay. There is a steamer service in summer.

**Windhoek** S W Africa. Formerly Windhuk. Capital and chief commercial centre, in the central area 800 m. N of Cape Town at a height of 5,400 ft. Pop. (1962) 43,000 (25,000 whites). Linked by rail with Walvis Bay and with the S African system. Trade in karakul (Persian lamb) skins. Refrigerating plants. Meat canning, brewing. Manufactures bone meal. Called Windhuk when capital of German S W Africa (1892–1915).

**Windsor** Canada. Major industrial city in S Ontario, on the Detroit R. opposite Detroit (Michigan), with which it is linked by road and railway tunnels, a suspension bridge, and ferry services. Pop. (1966) 192,544. Chief industry motor-car manufacture. Also salt refining; manufactures machinery, steel products, chemicals, etc. Seat of Assumption University (1857).

**Windsor** England. Municipal borough in Berkshire, on the R. Thames 23 m. W of London and linked by bridge with Eton. Pop. (1961) 27,126. Official name New Windsor, to distinguish it from Old Windsor, 2 m. SE. The town is dominated by the royal castle, which was founded by William the Conqueror on the site of an earlier stronghold, and has since remained the principal residence of English monarchs. Here, from the top of the 230-ft Round Tower, parts of 12 counties may be seen. To the W of the Round Tower the Lower Ward contains St George's Chapel, an outstanding example of Perpendicular architecture, and the Albert Memorial Chapel; to the E the Upper Ward has the state apartments, with noteworthy paintings, furniture, etc., and the private and visitors' apartments. The Home Park, adjoining the castle, and the Great Park extend S to Virginia Water, an artificial lake. Also in Windsor is the 17th-cent. town hall built by Sir Christopher Wren, who was MP for the borough. There is a

racecourse, and steamers ply the Thames in both directions. Old Windsor, though of small importance today, has an older history than New Windsor, for in the time of Edward the Confessor it was a royal residence.

**Windward Islands** (Pacific) ◊ *Society Islands*.

**Windward Islands** W Indies. Island group of the Lesser Antilles, in the W Indies, extending 300 m. S from the Leeward Is. Consist of the following islands (N–S): Dominica, Martinique, St Lucia, St Vincent, the Grenadines, and Grenada. Of these, Martinique is a French possession (since 1816) and the remainder are British associated states. Area of the latter 821 sq. m. Pop. (1960) 316,743. The islands are volcanic in origin and have an equable tropical climate with occasional hurricanes and earth tremors; they have a rich variety of tropical flora. So named because of their location in the path of the NE Trade Winds. Most of the people are Negroes. The British colony of the Windward Is. was established 1855; cap. was St George's (◊ *Grenada*).

**Winnipeg** Canada. Capital and largest city of Manitoba, on the Red R. at the confluence with the Assiniboine R. Pop. (1966) 257,005. The country's chief wheat market and the financial and distribution centre of the Prairie Provinces, well named 'The Gateway to the West'. Has vast grain elevators, railway yards, stockyards, flour mills, and meat-packing plants. Manufactures agricultural machinery, cereal foods, clothing, etc. Seat of the University of Manitoba (1877). The first white settlement was made here by La Vérendrye (1738) and was called Fort Rouge. Winnipeg was incorporated under its present name in 1873 and developed rapidly as a railway centre, the Canadian Pacific Railway being completed in 1885. The population was 241 in 1871 and 42,340 by 1901.

**Winnipeg, Lake** Canada. Lake in S central Manitoba. Area 9,094 sq. m. Receives the surplus waters of L. Manitoba, L. Winnipegosis, and the Lake of the Woods, draining through the Nelson R. to Hudson Bay. Tributary rivers include the Red, Winnipeg, and Saskatchewan.

**Winnipegosis, Lake** Canada. Lake in S W Manitoba. Area 2,086 sq. m. Drains by the Waterhen R. to L. Manitoba and thence into L. Winnipeg.

**Winnipeg River** Canada. River 475 m. long

issuing from the N end of Lake of the Woods and flowing generally N W to the S E corner of L. Winnipeg. Several rapids on its lower course, used for hydro-electric power for industries of Winnipeg.

**Winsford** England. Urban district in Cheshire, on the R. Weaver 23 m. S W of Manchester. Pop. (1961) 12,738. Centre of the salt industry; chemical manufacture, silica and quartz processing.

**Winston-Salem** USA. Industrial town in N Carolina 67 m. NNE of Charlotte. Pop. (1960) 111,135. Formed (1913) by the union of the adjacent towns Winston and Salem. Important tobacco centre; manufactures cigarettes and pipe tobacco, also nylon yarn, hosiery, furniture, etc. Founded (1766) as the centre of a Moravian colony.

**Winterswijk** Netherlands. Town in Gelderland province 35 m. E of Arnhem near the German frontier. Pop. (1968) 26,073. Manufactures cotton goods, furniture, etc.

**Wintherthur** Switzerland. Industrial town and railway junction in Zürich canton 11 m. NE of Zürich. Pop. (1969) 94,200. Manufactures electric locomotives, diesel engines, textiles, soap, etc.

**Wirksworth** England. Urban district in Derbyshire 11 m. NNW of Derby. Pop. (1961) 4,930. Market town. Limestone quarrying; lead mines, worked from Roman times, have been abandoned. Has a 13th/14th-cent. church.

**Wirral, The** England. Peninsula in NW Cheshire between the estuaries of the R. Mersey and the R. Dee. Low-lying, once a royal forest. In the NE are Birkenhead and Wallasey, across the Mersey from Liverpool. Has given its name to an urban district centred on Heswall (W). Pop. (urban district, 1961) 21,847.

**Wisbech** England. Municipal borough in the Isle of Ely, on the R. Nene 19 m. ENE of Peterborough. Pop. (1961) 17,512. Market town and river port; also centre of a region growing bulbs, fruit, vegetables, flowers. Fruit and vegetable canning, brewing, printing. Manufactures paper, cement, etc. Birthplace of Thomas Clarkson (1760–1846), the anti-slavery agitator.

**Wisconsin** USA. A Great Lakes state, bounded on the N by L. Superior and on the E by L. Michigan. Area 56,154 sq. m. Pop. (1970) 4,366,766. Cap. Madison. Admitted to the Union in 1848 as the 30th state; popularly known as the 'Badger' state. Much of it is low-lying, but the Superior Highlands (N) rise to 1,951 ft in Sugarbush Hill, the highest point in the state. Continental climate, with hot summers and cold winters and an annual rainfall of 30–35 ins. Wisconsin leads all US states in dairy produce; cheese, butter, and milk are widely sold outside the state. Chief crops maize, oats, hay, largely for the dairying industry. Iron ore mined in the Gogebic Range (N). Chief towns Milwaukee, Madison. Exploration of the region was begun by the French (1634). Ceded to Britain 1763 and to the USA 1783. In the Civil War it supported the Union.

**Wishaw** ⟡ *Motherwell and Wishaw.*

**Wisła River** ⟡ *Vistula River.*

**Wisley** England. Village in NW Surrey 3 m. E of Woking with the gardens of the Royal Horticultural Society.

**Wismar** German Democratic Republic. Seaport and industrial town in the Rostock district 32 m. E of Lübeck. Pop. (1965) 55,062. Shipbuilding, sugar refining. Manufactures railway rolling stock, machinery, etc. A prosperous Hanse town in the 13th and 14th cent.

**Witbank** S Africa. Town in the Transvaal 65 m. E of Pretoria at a height of 5,300 ft. Pop. (1968) 39,880 (15,500 whites). The chief coalmining centre. Manufactures chemicals. Thermal electric power station, fuelled by the local coalfield.

**Witham** England. Urban district in Essex 8 m. NE of Chelmsford. Pop. (1961) 9,457. Market town. Dates from the 10th cent. Has a 13th/15th-cent. church.

**Witham River** England. River 90 m. long rising in N Rutland, flowing N into Lincolnshire, past Grantham, then E and SE past Lincoln and Boston to the Wash.

**Witney** England. Urban district in Oxfordshire 10 m. WNW of Oxford on the R. Windrush. Pop. (1961) 9,217. Market town. Long famous for the manufacture of blankets and other woollen goods. Has an old butter cross (1683) and a grammar school also dating from the 17th cent.

**Witten** Federal German Republic. Industrial town in N Rhine-Westphalia, on the Ruhr R. 8 m. SW of Dortmund. Pop. (1963) 97,400. Manufactures steel, machinery, coal-tar products, glass, etc.

**Wittenberg** German Democratic Republic. Industrial town and river port in the Halle district, on the Elbe R. 57 m. SW of Berlin. Pop. (1965) 46,846. Manufactures paper, machinery, soap, etc. Famous for its association with Martin Luther during the early years of the Reformation. In 1517 Luther nailed his Ninety-five Theses on the door of the Schlosskirche and in 1520 in the market place publicly burned the papal bull that condemned him. The university (founded 1502) was absorbed into the University of Halle in 1815.

**Wittenberge** German Democratic Republic. Industrial town in the Schwerin district, on the Elbe R. 80 m. NW of Berlin. Pop. (1965) 32,439. Railway engineering, metal working. Manufactures woollen goods etc.

**Witwatersrand** S Africa. In Afrikaans, 'White Waters Ridge'; familiarly known as the Rand. Ridge 5,000–6,000 ft high in the S of the Transvaal, extending 150 m. E–W, and centred on Johannesburg. The central part has a gold-bearing reef about 50 m. long which produces one third to one half of the world's gold; here are the large towns (E–W) of Springs, Brakpan, Benoni, Boksburg, Germiston, Johannesburg, Roodeport-Maraisburg, Krugersdorp, all linked by railway. Coal and manganese are also mined. Many industries. Gold was discovered in 1886 (when Johannesburg was founded). Mining has since extended to depths of about 9,000 ft and is considered economic to 12,000 ft.

**Wloclawek** Poland. Industrial town in Bydgoszcz voivodship, on the Vistula R. 90 m. WNW of Warsaw. Pop. (1968) 72,400. Manufactures machinery, paper, fertilizers, dyes, etc. Lignite deposits near by. Cathedral (14th-cent.).

**Woburn** England. Market town in SW Bedfordshire 12 m. NW of Luton. Pop. 950. Near-by Woburn Abbey, seat of the Duke of Bedford and occupying the site of a 12th cent. Cistercian abbey, has a famous art collection.

**Woburn** USA. Town in Massachusetts 10 m. NNW of Boston. Pop. (1960) 31,214. Residential and industrial. Manufactures leather goods, food products, etc. Birthplace of Sir Benjamin Thompson (Count von Rumford) (1753–1814), the scientist.

**Woking** England. Residential urban district in Surrey, on the R. Wey 23 m. SW of London. Pop. (1961) 67,485. Printing. Has a Muslim mosque and a museum of Eastern antiquities. Brookwood Cemetery, with the first crematorium in England and an American military cemetery, is 4 m. WSW.

**Wokingham** England. Municipal borough in Berkshire 7 m. ESE of Reading. Pop.

(1961) 11,400. Market town. Engineering. Manufactures electrical appliances etc. Picturesque 17th-cent. almshouses. Wellington College, the public school (1853), is 4 m. SSE.

**Wolds, The** England. Range of chalk hills in the E Riding of Yorkshire and Lincolnshire, running roughly parallel to the coast and rising to 808 ft in the N. The N part, usually known as the Yorkshire Wolds, is separated from the S part (the Lincolnshire Wolds) by the Humber estuary.

**Wolfenbüttel** Federal German Republic. Town in Lower Saxony, 7 m. S of Brunswick on the Oker R. Pop. (1963) 39,700. Manufactures agricultural machinery, soap, etc. Has a famous library containing many early Bibles and MSS. Grew around an 11th-cent. castle. Capital of the dukes of Brunswick-Wolfenbüttel 1671–1753.

**Wolfsburg** Federal German Republic. Industrial town in Lower Saxony 17 m. NE of Brunswick on the Weser–Elbe Canal. Pop. (1963) 74,100. Important centre of the motor-car industry (Volkswagen). Has grown rapidly with the expansion of this industry. Founded 1938.

**Wolin** (Ger. **Wollin**) Poland. Island on the Baltic coast (NW) 28 m. N of Szczecin, with Usedom (W) enclosing the Stettiner Haff. Area 95 sq. m. Chief town Wolin, a fishing port on the SE coast (pop. 2,400). Fishing and tourism are important occupations.

**Wollongong** Australia. Residential and industrial town in New South Wales 40 m. SSW of Sydney. Pop. (Greater Wollongong, 1966) 162,835. A coalmining centre. Manufactures sheet steel, wires and cables, machinery, chemicals, etc. 5 m. S is the heavy industrial centre and port, Port Kembla.

**Wolverhampton** England. County borough in Staffordshire, in the Black Country 13 m. NW of Birmingham. Pop. (1961) 150,385. Industrial centre with a considerable variety of manufactures, including bicycles, trolley-buses, tools, locks and keys, hardware, tyres, rayon, chemicals. St Peter's Church was founded in the 10th cent. and restored in the 19th, and there is a grammar school founded in the 16th cent. From the 14th to the 16th cent. it was important in the wool trade, but by the mid 18th cent. it had transferred to metal working; its principal manufacture was locks.

**Wolverton** England. Urban district in

Buckinghamshire, 17 m. N of Aylesbury on the R. Ouse. Pop. (1961) 13,116. Railway workshops. Engineering. Includes Stony Stratford (W).

**Wombwell** England. Urban district in the W Riding of Yorkshire 3 m. ESE of Barnsley. Pop. (1961) 18,701. Coal-mining, engineering. Manufactures glass.

**Wonsan** N Korea. Capital of S Pyongan province, on the E coast 95 m. E of Pyongyang. Pop. 200,000. Seaport, with a good natural harbour. Fishing. Railway engineering, oil refining, etc. Severely damaged in the Korean War (1950–51).

**Woodbridge** England. Urban district in Suffolk, on the R. Deben estuary 7 m. ENE of Ipswich. Pop. (1961) 5,927. Market town. Fruit and vegetable canning, boatbuilding. A picturesque town, it has many fine Georgian houses. Bredfield House (2 m. N) was the birthplace of Edward Fitzgerald (1809–83), translator of Omar Khayyám.

**Wood Buffalo National Park** Canada. Vast National Park in NE Alberta and S Mackenzie District, NW Territories. Area 17,300 sq. m. Contains large herds of buffalo, also bear, caribou, moose, and other animals. Established 1922.

**Woodford** ⟡ *Wanstead and Woodford.*

**Wood Green** England. Former municipal borough in Middlesex 7 m. N of London; from 1965 part of the Greater London borough of Haringey. Pop. (1961) 47,897. Mainly residential. Contains the former Alexandra Park racecourse, and Alexandra Palace, which was opened in 1873, burned, and reopened in 1878, and where the first BBC television transmitter was established (1936).

**Woodhall Spa** England. Urban district in Lincolnshire 14 m. ESE of Lincoln. Pop. (1961) 1,990. Spa: bromo-iodine springs, discovered accidentally during a search for coal. Near by is Kirkstead, with the ruins of a 13th-cent. Cistercian abbey.

**Woodstock** England. Municipal borough in Oxfordshire 8 m. NNW of Oxford on the R. Glyme. Pop. (1961) 1,808. Long known for the manufacture of gloves. Site of an old palace which was the scene of Henry II's courtship of the 'Fair Rosamond', of the birth of the Black Prince, and of the imprisonment of Elizabeth I (1554), and a royal residence until the Civil War, when it was used as a royalist garrison; it was largely destroyed by Parliament forces later. The manor was bestowed on John Churchill, Duke of Marlborough, after his victory at Blenheim (1704), and ⟡ *Blenheim Palace*, designed by Vanbrugh, was built for him. Woodstock is the scene of Scott's novel *Woodstock.*

**Wookey Hole** England. Village in Somerset 2 m. NW of Wells, named after a large natural cave formed where the R. Axe emerges from the Mendip Hills. Objects shown in the museum demonstrate that the cave was occupied in prehistoric times. Also here are handmade paper mills dating from the 17th cent.

**Wool** England. Market town in Dorset, 10 m. WSW of Poole on the R. Frome. Pop. 4,000. Has a 15th-cent. bridge; beside this is the manor house of Woolbridge, the 'Wellbridge House' of Hardy's *Tess of the D'Urbervilles.*

**Woolwich** England. Former metropolitan borough in SE London, mainly on the S bank of the R. Thames but with two detached portions on the N bank; from 1965 part of the Greater London borough of Greenwich (but excluding the portions on the N bank). Pop. (1961) 146,397. Contains the Royal Arsenal (1805), with barracks, warehouses, etc. Became important as a dockyard and naval base in Henry VIII's reign, but the Royal Dockyard was closed and converted into a military stores department in 1869. The Royal Military Academy on Woolwich Common (founded 1741) was transferred to Sandhurst (1946) on amalgamation with the Royal Military College. Within the borough are Plumstead, with Plumstead Marshes (E), and Eltham, with the former royal palace; Shooter's Hill (425 ft) was crossed by the Roman Watling Street.

**Woomera** Australia. Town in S Australia, in semi-arid country 110 m. NW of Port Augusta, from which water is piped. Pop. (1966) 4,745. Since 1946 base of the Long Range Weapons Establishment, whose range extends about 1,250 m. NW over desert land.

**Woonsocket** USA. Industrial town in Rhode Island, on the Blackstone R. 13 m. NNW of Providence. Pop. (1960) 47,080. Textile centre, producing woollen, cotton, and rayon goods; also clothing, rubber products, etc.

**Wootton Bassett** England. Market town and railway junction in Wiltshire 5 m. WSW of Swindon in a dairy-farming region. Pop. 2,400.

**Worcester** England. County borough,

WORCESTER 814

cathedral city, and county town of Worcestershire, on the R. Severn. Pop. (1961) 65,865. Industrial centre, long famous for the manufacture of gloves, china, and 'Worcester sauce'. Also produces footwear, hardware, etc. Its beautiful cathedral is mainly 14th-cent., with a Norman crypt dating from the 11th cent., the outstanding feature being the Early English choir; the Three Choirs Festival is held here once every 3 years. There are several churches of the 12th–15th cent.; among other old buildings are the Commandery, founded (1085) as a hospital by St Wulstan and rebuilt in Tudor times, and the 18th-cent. Guildhall. The King's School and the Royal Grammar School were both founded in the 16th cent. At the Battle of Worcester (1651) Cromwell finally defeated Charles II and the Scots. Birthplace of Sir Edward Elgar (1857–1934) at Broadheath (2 m. NW).

**Worcester** S Africa. Town in Cape Province 63 m. ENE of Cape Town, with which it is linked by rail, and near the Hex River Mountains. Pop. (1968) 37,250 (12,750 whites). In a fruit-growing region. Produces wine, brandy, jam, dried and canned fruit. Manufactures textiles etc. Water supply from the Hex R. and the Stettynskloof Dam (1954).

**Worcester** USA. Industrial town in Massachusetts, on the Blackstone R. 38 m. WSW of Boston. Pop. (1960) 186,587. Manufactures textiles, electrical appliances, machine tools, paper, etc. Also an important cultural and educational centre, with Clark University (1887) and several colleges; noted for its annual musical festival. Its industries developed rapidly after the construction (1828) of the Blackstone Canal, linking it with Providence (Rhode Island).

**Worcestershire** England. County in the W Midlands, including a small enclave in Staffordshire around Dudley. Area 700 sq. m. Pop. (1961) 568,642. County town Worcester. Lies largely in the valleys of the Severn and the Warwickshire Avon, but there are hills around its boundary: in the SW the Malvern Hills (1,395 ft), in the N the Clent Hills (1,035 ft) and Lickey Hills, and in the extreme SE the edge of the Cotswolds (1,048 ft). The land is fertile, and dairy farming and the cultivation of fruit, vegetables, and hops are important; the Vale of Evesham, along the R. Avon, is especially noted for plums. Salt

produced in the Droitwich area. Important industrial centres, all in the N, are Dudley, Oldbury, Halesowen, Stourbridge, Kidderminster.

**Workington** England. Municipal borough in Cumberland, at the mouth of the R. Derwent 30 m. SW of Carlisle. Pop. (1961) 29,507. Seaport. Coalmining centre. Engineering. Manufactures iron and steel etc.

**Worksop** England. Municipal borough in Nottinghamshire, on the R. Ryton 11 m. NNE of Mansfield. Pop. (1961) 34,237. Coalmining centre. Manufactures hosiery, glass, etc. Flour milling. Remains of an early 12-cent. Augustinian priory. The 19th-cent. Worksop Manor was built on the site of an earlier mansion burned down in 1761.

**Worms** Federal German Republic. Ancient Borbetomagus. Town in Rhineland-Palatinate, on the Rhine R. 12 m. NNW of Mannheim. Pop. (1963) 63,100. River port in a vine-growing and wine-producing region. Tanning. Also manufactures machinery, chemicals, cork products, etc. The 12th/14th-cent. Romanesque cathedral was seriously damaged, along with many other buildings, in the 2nd World War. Often the seat of Imperial Diets, including the famous Diet of Worms (1521) before which Luther appeared in order to defend his doctrine before the emperor Charles V.

**Worsborough** England. Urban district in the W Riding of Yorkshire 2 m. S of Barnsley. Pop. (1961) 14,577. Coalmining centre.

**Worsley** England. Urban district in SE Lancashire 6 m. WNW of Manchester. Pop. (1961) 40,948. Coalmining, engineering. Manufactures cotton goods, clothing, etc.

**Worthing** England. Municipal borough in W Sussex 10 m. W of Brighton. Pop. (1961) 80,143. Seaside resort. Residential town. Has many glasshouses, producing tomatoes etc. Also manufactures pharmaceutical products etc. The prehistoric earthworks of Cissbury Ring are 3 m. N on the South Downs; Roman remains have been found in the borough.

**Wrangel Island** USSR. Island in the Khabarovsk Territory, RSFSR, in the Arctic Ocean about 80 m. off the coast of NE Siberia. Area 1,800 sq. m. Largely consists of tundra; rises to 2,493 ft. First explored (1881) by Capt. Hooper of the US Navy. Claimed by the Russians 1924.

**Wrath, Cape** Scotland. Promontory in NW

Sutherland at the NW extremity of the mainland. Lighthouse.

**Wrekin, The** England. Isolated hill 1,335 ft high in central Shropshire 3 m. SW of Wellington.

**Wrexham** Wales. Municipal borough in Denbighshire 11 m. SSW of Chester. Pop. (1961) 35,427. Market town. Coalmining centre. Manufactures cables, chemicals, metal goods, etc. The 14th/16th-cent. parish church has a 135-ft tower and the tomb of Elihu Yale (d. 1721), founder of Yale University, USA. Wrexham is the seat of the Roman Catholic bishopric of Menevia, which includes all Wales except Glamorganshire.

**Wrocław** Poland. Formerly (Ger.) Breslau. Capital of the Wrocław voivodship, on the Oder (Odra) R. 190 m. WSW of Warsaw. Pop. (1968) 509,400. River port and important road, railway, and industrial centre. Railway engineering, food processing. Manufactures machinery, machine tools, chemicals, textiles, etc. Before 1945 it was capital of the German province of Lower Silesia. Has a 13th/15th-cent. cathedral and a 13th/15th-cent. town hall; about two thirds of the buildings were destroyed in the 2nd World War. The university, founded in 1702 and Polish since 1945, was transferred from the universities of Lwów (Lvov) and Wilno (Vilna), now Russian. Capital of the duchy of Silesia in the 12th cent. Passed to the Habsburgs in the 16th cent. and to Prussia 1742.

**Wroxeter** England. Village in Shropshire, on the R. Severn 4 m. ESE of Shrewsbury. Near by are remains of the Roman camp of Viroconium.

**Wuchang** ◊ *Wuhan.*

**Wuchow** China. Formerly (1913–46) Tsangwu. Town and river port in the Kwangsi-Chuang AR on the Si-kiang at the confluence with the Kwei R. 120 m. WNW of Kwangchow (Canton). Pop. 111,000. Manufactures textiles, chemicals. Food processing, sugar refining. Trade in grain, tung oil, bamboo, etc.

**Wuhan** China. Capital of Hupei province and the largest city in central China, on the Yangtse R. at the confluence with the Han R. Pop. (1957) 2,146,000. Formed by the union of three cities, Hankow, Hanyang, and Wuchang. Important route centre, at the point where the Peking–Kwangchow (Canton) Railway crosses the Yangtse R. Hankow is a river port,

accessible to ocean-going vessels, and the leading industrial and commercial centre of central China. Manufactures textiles, machinery, chemicals, cement. Flour milling. Trade in tea, cotton, and other agricultural produce. Its great development dates from 1858, when it was opened to foreign trade. Hanyang became the centre of an important iron and steel industry, using ore from the Tayeh iron deposits 60 m. SE, having expanded considerably after the establishment of the first modern steel works in China (1891). The steel plant was dismantled and removed to Chungking (1938); a new steel plant was established E of Wuchang in the 1950s. Wuchang, which faces the other two cities from the S bank of the Yangtse, and is linked with them by a rail-road bridge (1958), is an administrative and cultural centre, and is the seat of Wuhan University (1913). Manufactures textiles, paper. Wuhan was occupied by the Japanese 1938–45.

**Wuhing** ◊ *Huchow.*

**Wuhsien** ◊ *Soochow.*

**Wuhu** China. River port in S Anhwei, on the Yangtse R. 55 m. SSW of Nanking. Pop. 242,000. Tanning, flour milling. Manufactures textiles (cotton, silk). Important rice market; also trade in cotton etc. Opened to foreign trade 1877.

**Wuppertal** Federal German Republic. Industrial town in N Rhine-Westphalia, on the Wupper R. 17 m. E of Düsseldorf. Pop. (1968) 412,732. Important centre of the textile industry (woollen, cotton, rayon), extending about 10 m. along the Wupper valley; an overhead railway runs along the river. Also manufactures pharmaceutical products, paper, machinery, tools, rubber products, etc. Brewing, printing and publishing. Formed (1929) by the amalgamation of the two large towns of Elberfeld and Barmen and the smaller Cronenberg, Vohwinkel, Beyenburg, etc. The purity of the Wupper water led to the establishment of bleaching here in the 16th cent. During the 2nd World War the town was repeatedly bombed and suffered severe damage.

**Württemberg** Federal German Republic. Former kingdom in the SW, after 1918 a republic, bounded on the E by Bavaria and on the S and W by Baden, with the partial enclave of Hohenzollern (Prussia) in the S. Area 7,532 sq. m. Cap. Stuttgart. Mountainous and undulating, crossed SW–NE by the Swabian Jura, with the Black Forest in the W. Drained by the Neckar R. Largely agricultural. Incorporated with the duchy of Swabia in the 9th cent. By the 13th cent. it was ruled by the counts of Württemberg. Became a duchy in 1495 and a kingdom in 1806. After the 2nd World War (1945) it was divided: the N part combined with N Baden to form Württemberg-Baden; the S part with Hohenzollern became Württemberg-Hohenzollern. In 1952 these two *Länder* were combined with Baden to form Baden-Württemberg.

**Würzburg** Federal German Republic. Historic town and railway junction in NW Bavaria, on the Main R. 55 m. WNW of Nuremberg. Pop. (1968) 119,422. Centre of the wine trade. Brewing. Manufactures machine tools, chemicals, furniture, tobacco products, etc. Romanesque cathedral (11th/12th-cent. with later additions); among other ancient buildings are the Marienberg fortress, residence of the bishops 1261–1720, the later Baroque episcopal palace, the 16th-cent. Julius hospital, and the university (founded 1582). The town probably existed as early as the 7th cent.; the bishopric was founded *c.* 740.

**Wusih** China. Industrial town in S Kiangsu province, on the Grand Canal and on the Shanghai–Nanking Railway 65 m. WNW of Shanghai. Pop. 581,000. Manufactures textiles, machinery. Rice and flour milling etc. Trade in rice, wheat, etc. Has superseded Soochow as economic centre of the Tai Hu (Tai Lake) basin.

**Wyandotte** USA. Industrial town in Michigan, on the Detroit R. 10 m. SSW of Detroit. Pop. (1960) 43,519. Important chemical industry based on local salt deposits. Also manufactures toys, cement, etc.

**Wyandotte Cave** USA. Large limestone cave in S Indiana 24 m. W of Louisville. Has many imposing chambers, passages, and rock formations; one chamber is nearly 150 ft long and 55 ft wide and is surmounted by a great dome.

**Wye River** England. River 20 m. long in Derbyshire, rising on the outskirts of Buxton and flowing generally SE through the beautiful Miller's Dale and Monsal Dale, past Bakewell, and joining the R. Derwent.

**Wye River** Wales. River 130 m. long, rising on the E slope of Plynlimmon near the source of the Severn (central Wales), flowing generally SE and then S, past Rhayader, Builth Wells, Hereford, Ross-on-Wye, and Monmouth, and joining the Severn 2 m. below Chepstow. Noted for beautiful scenery, esp. between Ross and Chepstow (inc. Symonds Yat).

**Wymondham** England. Urban district in Norfolk 9 m. SW of Norwich. Pop. (1961) 5,896. Market town. Has a 17th-cent. half-timbered market cross, and a partly Norman church which was attached to a 12th-cent. Benedictine priory.

**Wyoming** USA. State in the W. Area 97,914 sq. m. Pop. (1960) 330,066. Cap. Cheyenne. Admitted to the Union in 1890 as the 44th state; popularly known as the 'Equality' state. Largely mountainous, it lies within the region of the Rocky Mountains and the Great Plains. Gannett Peak (13,785 ft) in the Wind River Mountains (W) is the highest point; Grand Teton in the Teton Mountains rises to 13,766 ft. In the E are the Great Plains, which have extensive stretches of grassland; in the NW is the Yellowstone National Park (3,485 sq. m.); in the centre and SW is the semi-desert Wyoming basin. Dry continental climate, with substantial snowfalls in winter and a rainfall of 10–20 ins. annually. Sheep and cattle reared on a large scale, the ranches being located mainly in the Great Plains, and it ranks second to Texas in wool production. Chief mineral petroleum. Cheyenne and Casper are the only towns with more than 20,000 inhabitants. First explored in the early 19th cent. Formed part of the vast territory acquired from France by the Louisiana Purchase agreement (1803). Became a territory 1869.

# X

**Xanthi** Greece. **1.** *Nome* in W Thrace, bounded on the N by Bulgaria (Rhodope Mountains) and on the S by the Aegean Sea. Area 667 sq. m. Pop. (1961) 89,613. Mainly agricultural. Produces tobacco, cereals, etc.

**2.** Capital of Xanthi *nome*, on the railway 110 m. ENE of Thessaloniki (Salonika). Pop. (1961) 26,377. Important trade in tobacco.

**Xingu River** Brazil. River 1,200 m. long rising on the Mato Grosso plateau and flowing generally N to the Amazon delta. Has a series of rapids in the middle course.

# Y

**Yablonovy (Yablonoi) Range** USSR. Range of mountains in SE Siberia (RSFSR), E of L. Baikal, extending SW–NE for about 700 m. and forming part of the watershed between rivers flowing to the Arctic and Pacific Oceans. Average height 4,000–6,000 ft.

**Yahata** ◊ *Yawata.*

**Yakima** USA. Town in Washington, on the Yakima R. 110 m. SE of Seattle. Pop. (1960) 43,284. In an irrigated agricultural region. Fruit packing, drying, and canning; flour milling etc.

**Yakut ASSR** USSR. Autonomous republic in RSFSR, in NE Siberia, bounded on the N by the Arctic Ocean and on the S by the Stanovoi Range. Area 1,197,760 sq. m. Pop. (1970) 664,000. Cap. Yakutsk. A vast, thinly populated republic entirely in the tundra and coniferous forest regions. Consists largely of the basins of the Lena, Yana, Indigirka, and Kolyma rivers, but in the E half there are the Verkhoyansk and Cherski Ranges, the latter rising to over 10,000 ft. Extreme continental climate, with exceptionally cold winters and relatively warm summers; near Verkhoyansk is the so-called 'cold pole' of the earth. The people, who are 80 per cent Yakuts and 10 per cent Russians, are mainly settled in the river valleys. Principal occupations are trapping and breeding of fur-bearing animals, fishing, the raising of reindeer and cattle, and mining (gold, tin, mica, coal). Chief products furs, gold, mammoth ivory. Some agriculture on collective and state farms. The severity of the climate and the lack of railways impede economic development, though roads and airways are established; Yakutsk, for example, is linked by air with Irkutsk. Other important towns Verkhoyansk, Vilyuisk, Olekminsk, Sredne Kolymsk. The region was taken by the Russians in the 17th cent. The Yakut autonomous republic was formed in 1922.

**Yakutsk** USSR. Capital of the Yakut ASSR, RSFSR, near the left bank of the Lena R. 1,140 m. NE of Irkutsk. Pop. (1970) 108,000. Commercial centre. Trade in furs, mammoth ivory, hides, etc. Tanning, sawmilling, brickmaking. Some of its trade is by river, which is open to navigation June–Nov., and it is linked by road with the Trans-Siberian Railway and by air with Irkutsk. A fort was founded here in 1632.

**Yallourn** Australia. Town in Victoria 78 m. ESE of Melbourne. Pop. (1966) 23,205. In a lignite-mining district. Manufactures briquettes. Lignite mines supply an important electric power station near by.

**Yalta** USSR. Town on the S coast of Crimea, Ukrainian SSR, 32 m. ESE of Sevastopol. Pop. 34,000. A leading resort enjoying a Mediterranean climate and set amid vineyards and orchards; many hotels, sanatoria, convalescent homes, etc. Wine making, fish canning. During the 2nd World War it was the scene of a historic conference between Churchill, Roosevelt, and Stalin (1945).

**Yalu River** China/N Korea. River 490 m. long rising on the S slopes of the Changpai Shan and flowing first S then W and SW past Antung (China), forming much of the border between China and N Korea, and entering Korea Bay at Tatungkow. Navigable only near its mouth. Frozen Nov.–March. Several important hydroelectric power stations; also used for floating timber.

**Yamagata** Japan. Capital of Yamagata prefecture, in N Honshu 75 m. ENE of Niigata. Pop. (1965) 193,736. Commercial centre in a region producing rice and silk. Manufactures metal goods.

**Yamaguchi** Japan. Capital of Yamaguchi prefecture, in SW Honshu 35 m. ENE of Shimonoseki. Pop. (1965) 98,977. An ancient commercial centre dating from the 14th cent.

**Yamalo-Nenets NA** USSR. National Area in the N Tyumen region, RSFSR, including the Yamal Peninsula, between the Kara Sea and the Gulf of Ob. Area 259,000 sq. m. Pop. (1970) 80,000. Cap. Salekhard. Main occupations fur trapping, reindeer breeding, fishing. Chief towns Salekhard and Novy Port, a port on the Gulf of Ob.

**Yambol** Bulgaria. Capital of Yambol province, on the Tundzha R. 50 m. W of Burgas. Pop. (1965) 58,405. Manufactures textiles, metal goods. Tanning etc. Trade in grain. First mentioned in the 11th cent. Has the ruins of an ancient stone mosque.

**Yampi Sound** Australia. Inlet in the coast

of Western Australia N of Derby. Haematite deposits on Cockatoo and other islands. There are opencast workings, crushing plant, and loading gear on Cockatoo, and the ore is carried by sea to iron and steel centres in New South Wales.

**Yamuna** ♢ *Jumna.*

**Yana River** USSR. River 700 m. long in the N Yakut ASSR (RSFSR), rising in the Verkhoyansk Range and flowing generally N to the Laptev Sea, which it enters by a broad delta. Navigable in the lower course June–Sept.

**Yangtse-kiang** China. Longest river in Asia and China's chief commercial river, about 3,400 m. long, rising on the N side of the Tanglha Range in SW Tsinghai province. It flows E and then SE across S Tsinghai into Szechwan province. As it continues S through a deep gorge, it comes within 40 m. of the almost parallel Mekong R. to the W. After taking a series of sharp curves in N Yunnan, and receiving the Yalung R., it now flows generally NE through the Red Basin of Szechwan, past Luchow, Chungking, and Wanhsien. Below the last-named town it is hemmed in again by mountains, traversing its famous gorges where navigation is impeded by dangerous rapids. In this section it is joined by a number of tributaries, including the Min and Kialing on the left and the Wu on the right bank. From Ichang, the head of navigation for ocean-going vessels, it flows alternately SE and NE until it reaches the sea, crossing fertile basins dotted with numerous lakes. Through two of these lakes, the Tungting and Poyang, which serve as overflow reservoirs for the Yangtse during the summer floods, the river receives two of its great tributaries, the Siang and the Kan respectively; at Wuhan it is joined by the Han from the NW. In the lower part of its course it flows past the city of Nanking, and enters the E China Sea by two main channels separated by Tsungming Island, the port of Shanghai being linked with it by the Hwang-pu R. In contrast to the upper part of its course, where it falls about 15,000 ft, below Wuhan its descent is little more than 1 in. per m. The Yangtse is a commercial highway of immense importance, with four of the country's greatest cities, Chungking, Wuhan, Nanking, and Shanghai, on or near its banks. It acquired still greater significance with the completion of the rail and road bridge over the river at Wuhan, on

the Peking–Kwangchow (Canton) route, in 1958. In China it is often known as the Chang-kiang ('Long River'), while along its upper course each section has its own local name.

**Yaoundé** Cameroun. Capital and terminus of the railway from Douala (125 m. W), at a height of 2,500 ft. Pop. (1965) 90,000. Commercial centre. Handles much of the trade of the Central African Republic. Manufactures soap, cigarettes, etc.

**Yap Islands** W Pacific Ocean. Group of 14 islands in the W Caroline Is., with cable and radio stations. Pop. (1968) 6,761. The Micronesian natives produce copra and dried fish. Important Japanese naval and air base in the 2nd World War. From 1946 administered by the USA.

**Yare River** England. River 50 m. long in Norfolk rising near East Dereham and flowing generally E past Norwich to Breydon Water, entering the North Sea at Great Yarmouth. Chief tributaries the Wensum, Waveney, and Bure. It is thus connected with the Norfolk Broads.

**Yarkand** (Chinese **Soche**) China. Chief town of the Yarkand oasis, in SW Sinkiang-Uighur AR 90 m. SE of Kashgar at a height of 3,900 ft. Pop. 80,000. Commercial centre. Manufactures textiles, carpets. Cereals and fruit grown in the oasis. The town stands on the W side of the Takla Makan desert and on the Yarkand R., which irrigates the oasis, and is a centre of the caravan trade between China, USSR, and Kashmir.

**Yarmouth** (Isle of Wight) England. Small port and resort on the Solent, 10 m. WSW of Cowes. Pop. 900. Linked by ferry with Lymington in Hampshire.

**Yarmouth** (Norfolk) ♢ *Great Yarmouth.*

**Yaroslavl** USSR. Capital of the Yaroslavl region, RSFSR, on the Volga R. at the confluence with the Kotorosl R. 160 m. NE of Moscow. Pop. (1970) 517,000. River port. Industrial centre. Manufactures textiles, motor vehicles, tyres, synthetic rubber, leather goods, agricultural machinery, paints, etc. Founded in the 11th cent.; became capital of a principality but was annexed by Moscow in the 15th cent. Although much of the old city was destroyed during the revolution, several churches and monasteries remain.

**Yarrow Water** Scotland. River 24 m. long in Selkirkshire, flowing generally ENE through St Mary's Loch and past the village of Yarrow to join Ettrick Water just above Selkirk. Its valley, noted for its beauty, was extolled by Wordsworth and Scott.

**Yasnaya Polyana** USSR. Village in the Tula region, RSFSR, 7 m. S of Tula. Birthplace and home of Tolstoy (1828–1910), whose house is now a museum.

**Yawata (Yahata)** Japan. Chief industrial town in Kyushu, in Fukuoka prefecture 25 m. NE of Fukuoka. Pop. (1960) 332,167. Coalmining. Important centre of the steel industry; also manufactures chemicals, cement, etc. Formerly a fishing port; grew rapidly with the steel and associated industries during the 20th cent. Severely damaged by bombing during the 2nd World War (1945). Merged (1963) with Moji, Kokura, Tobata, and Wakamatsu to form the new city of Kitakyushu.

**Yazd** ◊ *Yezd*.

**Yedo** ◊ *Tokyo*.

**Yelgava** ◊ *Jelgava*.

**Yellowhead Pass** Canada. Pass at a height of 3,700 ft between Alberta and British Columbia, in the Rocky Mountains, on the Canadian National Railway main line. The first recorded crossing was made in 1827.

**Yellowknife** Canada. Goldmining town in S Mackenzie District, Northwest Territories, on the N shore of the Great Slave Lake; also an R.C.M.P. station, with airport, school, hospital, and radio and meteorological stations. Pop. (1966) 3,741. Founded in 1935 after the discovery of gold. Largely abandoned in the early 1940s; developed again in 1944 on the discovery of a new goldmine.

**Yellow River** ◊ *Hwang-ho*.

**Yellow Sea** (Chinese **Hwang Hai**). Large inlet of the Pacific Ocean between Korea and the mainland of China, the main area being linked by the Strait of Chihli with the Gulfs of Chihli and Liaotung. The name is due to the yellow colour of the silt carried into it by various rivers. Among the rivers it receives are the Hwang-ho ('Yellow River'), Liao, and Yalu.

**Yellowstone National Park** USA. The country's oldest and largest National Park, established in 1872, mainly in NW Wyoming. Area 3,458 sq. m. Consists of volcanic plateaux of the Rocky Mountains, averaging 8,000 ft in altitude, surrounded by ranges rising to over 11,000 ft. The chief river is the Yellowstone, with its Grand Canyon, 20 m. long, and spectacular waterfalls; it feeds Yellowstone Lake

(area 139 sq. m.), which has great scenic beauty. Thousands of hot springs and about 200 geysers, the most notable being the geyser called 'Old Faithful', which erupts every hour or so. The protected wild life includes bison, moose, deer, elk, antelopes, goats, bear, and many species of birds.

**Yemen.** Republic in the S W of the Arabian peninsula. Area 75,000 sq. m. Pop. (1964) 5,000,000. Cap. Sana. Lang. Arabic. Rel. Muslim.

Bounded by Saudi Arabia (N and E), the Republic of S Yemen (S), and the Red Sea (W). It is the most fertile part of the peninsula, being substantially the Arabia Felix of the ancients, but nevertheless remains an isolated and under-developed country.

TOPOGRAPHY, RESOURCES, *etc*. A narrow coastal plain known as the Tihama, which is hot and dry, rises sharply inland to mountain and plateau exceeding 10,000 ft in places, representing the uptilted edge of the Arabian tableland. In the highlands there is a summer rainfall amounting to about 20 ins. Main food crop millet; wheat and barley are also grown, along with Mocha coffee (named after the port from which it was formerly shipped), grapes and other fruits, and *qat*, a narcotic shrub. To the E the land slopes gradually down to the vast sandy wastes of the Rub' al Khali. Besides Sana important towns are Ta'iz and the port of Hodeida. In recent years economic aid, e.g. in the building of roads, has been provided by China, the USSR, and USA, but internal trade is still largely by camel caravan. The highland population belongs to the Zaidi sect of Shias, the remainder being mainly a mixture of Sunni and Shia Muslims; most of the Jews (of whom there was an ancient and numerous community) emigrated to Israel after the Arab-Israeli war (1948).

HISTORY. The earliest known civilization of the region was that of the Minaean kingdom, which survived for more than 500 years till the mid 7th cent. B.C., to be followed by the Sabaean, till the 2nd cent. B.C., and the Himyarite, till the 6th cent. A.D. In the 7th cent. Yemen was converted to Islam, becoming a mere province of the Arab caliphate, and about three centuries later came under the control of the Zaidi dynasty, which ruled until modern times; for two periods (1538–1630, 1849–1918) the country was occupied by the Turks. Yemen became a member of the Arab

League in 1945 and of the UN in 1947. In 1958 it formed a loose confederation, the United Arab States, with the United Arab Republic (Egypt), but this was dissolved by the UAR in 1961. In 1962, shortly after the death of the reigning king, Imam Ahmed, his son was deposed by a group of army officers and a republic was proclaimed; fighting broke out between republican and royalist forces, the former being aided by Egypt and the latter by Saudi Arabia. Egyptian troops were withdrawn and peace was restored by the end of 1967.

**Yenakiyevo (Enakievo)** USSR. Formerly Rykovo (1928–35), Ordzhonikidze (1935–43). Industrial town in the Ukrainian SSR, in the Donbas 25 m. NE of Donetsk. Pop. 88,000. Important centre of the coalmining and iron and steel industries; also manufactures chemicals.

**Yenisei River** USSR. One of the longest rivers in Asiatic USSR (2,400 m.), formed in the Tuva ASSR (RSFSR) by the union of two headstreams at Kyzyl, themselves rising in the extreme S near the Mongolian border. It flows W and then for most of its course generally N, past Krasnoyarsk and Igarka, to enter the Arctic Ocean by a long estuary. Its chief tributaries are the Angara (Upper Tunguska), the Stony Tunguska, and the Lower Tunguska, all joining it by the right bank. Navigable throughout its length to Kyzyl, but the lower reaches are ice-free only July–Oct. Used chiefly for the transportation of timber and grain.

**Yentai** ◊ *Chefoo.*

**Yeovil** England. Municipal borough in Somerset, on the R. Yeo 20 m. ESE of Taunton. Pop. (1961) 24,552. Market town with a glove-making industry almost 400 years old; also manufactures cheese, aircraft, hovercraft, etc. East Coker near by was the birthplace of William Dampier (1652–1715).

**Yerevan (Erevan, Erivan)** USSR. Capital of the Armenian SSR, on the Zanga R. 110 m. S of Tbilisi (Tiflis) at a height of 3,400 ft. Pop. (1970) 767,000. Picturesquely situated in a mountainous area, with Mt Ararat (16,916 ft) 40 m. SSW (in Turkey) usually visible. Developed into a leading industrial centre. Important producer of chemicals, including synthetic rubber and plastics; also manufactures machinery, machine tools, tyres, textiles, etc. Aluminium refining. Power derived from hydro-electric plants on the Zanga R. (the Sevan-Zanga Cascade) and natural gas received by pipeline from Karadag (Azerbaijan). Cultural centre: seat of the Armenian state university (1920) and other institutions of higher education. Its outstanding building is the mosque of Hasan Ali Khan (the Blue Mosque), and there are many old Turkish and Persian buildings. Founded in the 7th cent., it often changed hands between Turks and Persians; taken by the Russians 1827. Became capital of the Armenian SSR 1920. The name was officially changed to Yerevan in 1936.

**Yerwa-Maiduguri** ◊ *Maiduguri.*

**Yezd (Yazd)** Iran. Town in Isfahan province, at a height of 3,900 ft 170 m. ESE of Isfahan, with which it is connected by road. Pop. (1966) 150,531. Manufactures textiles (inc. silks), carpets. Has part of the old walls, dating from the 12th cent., and several noteworthy mosques. Its inhabitants include many Zoroastrians, whose ancestors fled here from the Arabs.

**Yiewsley and West Drayton** England. Former urban district in Middlesex, on the R. Colne and the Grand Union Canal 15 m. W of London; from 1965 part of the Greater London borough of Hillingdon. Pop. (1961) 23,698. Largely residential. Engineering, film processing, power-tool manufacture, publishing, etc.

**Yinchwan** ◊ *Ningsia-Hui AR.*

**Yingkow** China. Formerly Newchwang. Seaport in Liaoning province, at the mouth of the Liao R. 110 m. SW of Shenyang. Pop. 200,000. Exports soya beans, grain, coal. Ice-bound for 3 or 4 months in winter. Until 1907 a major commercial outlet for S Manchuria, but then largely superseded by Dairen; now has only local trade. Manufactures soyabean oil, textiles, matches, etc.

**Ymuiden** ◊ *Velsen.*

**Yoho National Park** Canada. National Park in SE British Columbia, in the Rocky Mountains. Established 1886. Area 507 sq. m. Has some of the most spectacular scenery in the Canadian Rockies. A favourite region for mountaineers.

**Yokkaichi** Japan. Seaport, industrial and commercial town in Mie prefecture, Honshu, 22 m. SW of Nagoya. Pop. (1965) 218,985. Exports cotton goods etc. Oil refining. Manufactures textiles, chemicals, porcelain, etc.

**Yokohama** Japan. Capital of Kanagawa prefecture, central Honshu, on the W shore of Tokyo Bay 17 m. S of Tokyo. Pop. (1965) 1,788,796. The fourth largest city and one of the leading seaports, handling about 30 per cent of the total foreign trade. Main exports silk and rayon goods, canned fish. Manufactures steel, motor vehicles, chemicals. Shipbuilding, oil refining. It was only a small fishing village until 1859, when it became the first Japanese port to be opened to foreign trade. Almost destroyed by earthquake in 1923, thousands of its inhabitants being killed, but was quickly rebuilt. Severely damaged by bombing during the 2nd World War (1945).

Yokosuka Japan. Seaport and naval base in Kanagawa prefecture, on the SW shore of Tokyo Bay. Pop. (1965) 317,410. Important shipbuilding industry.

Yonkers USA. Industrial and residential town in New York, on the Hudson R. just NNE of New York City. Pop. (1960) 190,634. Manufactures carpets and rugs, clothing, cables, elevators, etc. Sugar refining. First settled (1646) by Adriaen van der Donck, a Dutch 'jonker' or young nobleman – from which the name Yonkers was evolved.

Yonne France. Department in central France formed from parts of Champagne, Burgundy, and Orléanais. Area 2,881 sq. m. Pop. (1968) 283,376. Prefecture Auxerre. Highest in the SE (Monts du Morvan), it slopes gently down to the Paris Basin and is drained S–N by the Yonne R. and its tributaries. Mainly agricultural. Produces wine, cereals, sugar-beet, etc. Chief towns Auxerre, Chablis, Sens.

Yonne River France. River 180 m. long rising in the Monts du Morvan and flowing generally NNW past Auxerre and Sens to join the Seine R. at Montereau.

York England. Ancient Eboracum. County borough and cathedral city, county town of Yorkshire but also of county status itself, on the R. Ouse at the confluence with the Foss. Pop. (1961) 104,468. Important railway junction. Railway and other engineering, sugar refining, brewing. Manufactures chocolate and confectionery, glass, furniture, etc. The old city is enclosed by walls dating mainly from the 14th cent. which are penetrated by four main gates (Bars). The great Cathedral of St Peter (generally known as York Minster) was begun in 1154, on the site of the wooden church where King Edwin was baptized by Paulinus (627), and was continued for over

3 centuries. The world-famous stained glass was carefully preserved in the Civil War and in both world wars; the celebrated Five Sisters window was restored (1925) as a memorial to the women who died in the 1st World War. Clifford's Tower (built in the 13th cent.) is the principal survival on the site of the castle erected by William the Conqueror. Among other notable buildings are the 14th/15th-cent. guest house of St Mary's Abbey (now a museum of Roman antiquities), St William's College (1453), the 14th-cent. Merchant Adventurers' Hall (restored), and the Railway Museum. The fine 15th-cent. Guildhall was destroyed (rebuilt later), and several other buildings were damaged, in the 2nd World War. University (1963).

As Roman Eboracum, it was the military capital of Britain, where Constantine the Great was proclaimed Emperor (A.D. 306). There was a Bishop of York in the 4th cent. When Britain was divided into two archiepiscopal Provinces (7th cent.) it became capital of the N Province, and has remained so (though Scotland is now excluded); the Archbishop ranks second only to the Archbishop of Canterbury in the Church of England. One of the most famous educational centres in Europe in the 8th cent. Has had a Lord Mayor since 1389 and ranked as a county since 1396. Birthplace of John Flaxman (1755–1826), the sculptor.

York USA. Town in S Pennsylvania 22 m. SSE of Harrisburg. Pop. (1960) 54,504. Manufactures refrigerators, agricultural machinery, turbines, building materials, etc.

Yorke Peninsula Australia. Peninsula between Spencer Gulf and Gulf St Vincent, S Australia. Wheat growing, sheep rearing. Chief ports Port Pirie, Wallaroo.

Yorkshire England. The largest county, in the NE, bounded on the E by the North Sea. Area 6,090 sq. m. Pop. (1961) 4,722,661. County town York. Divided administratively into the E, N, and W Ridings and the City of York, each with county status. E Riding: area 1,172 sq. m., pop. 527,051, county town Beverley. N Riding: area 2,127 sq. m., pop. 554,383, county town Northallerton. W Riding: area 2,780 sq. m., pop. 3,641,228, county town Wakefield. In the W is part of the Pennine Range, consisting of rather bleak wind-swept moors penetrated by picturesque dales (valleys), e.g. Teesdale,

Swaledale, Wensleydale, Nidderdale, Wharfedale, Airedale, all formed by tributaries of the R. Ouse. Highest peaks Mickle Fell (2,591 ft), Whernside (2,419 ft), Ingleborough (2,373 ft). E of the central Vale of York are the N Yorkshire Moors; the Cleveland Hills are separated from the Yorkshire Wolds by the Vale of Pickering. In the fertile Vale of York and Holderness excellent crops of cereals, sugar-beet, and potatoes are produced. Several popular coastal resorts, e.g. Scarborough, Whitby, Bridlington; Harrogate is a fashionable inland spa. Yorkshire is better known, however, for the important industries of the W Riding, based on the coalfield. The chief centres of woollen manufacture are Leeds, Bradford, Halifax, Huddersfield. Sheffield is the leading steel town; Middlesbrough and Rotherham are also engaged in the iron and steel industry. Hull is one of Britain's principal commercial and fishing ports.

The Vale of York carried the main road to the N in Roman times as it does today (the A1); the Romans probably used Yorkshire coal. Sheffield cutlery and Bradford woollen goods were known by the 14th cent. but the great expansion of the two major Yorkshire industries came with the Industrial Revolution.

**Yorktown** USA. Small historic town in SE Virginia, on the York R. 11 m. ESE of Williamsburg. Pop. 400. Headquarters of the Colonial National Historical Park. Famous as the scene of the British surrender at the end of the Revolutionary War (1781).

**Yosemite National Park** USA. National Park in California, on the W slopes of the Sierra Nevada. Area 1,189 sq. m. Established 1890. An outstanding feature is the Yosemite Valley, a great canyon 7 m. long, overlooked by many peaks exceeding 7,000 ft in height. The highest peaks of all are Mt Lyell (13,095 ft) and Mt Dana (13,055 ft), near the E boundary. Yosemite is probably most famous for its waterfalls, inc. Ribbon Fall (1,612 ft), the second highest single cataract in the world, and Upper Yosemite (1,430 ft); these falls are seen at their best in May and June, when swollen by melting snow. There are three groves of sequoia trees, Merced and Tuolumne (W) and Mariposa (S), the last-named including the famous Wawona or Tunnel tree, through which a road 11 ft wide was driven.

**Yoshkar-Ola (Ioshkar-Ola)** USSR. Capital of the Mari ASSR, RSFSR, 155 m. ENE of Gorky. Pop. (1970) 166,000. Industrial and commercial centre. Sawmilling, food processing. Manufactures furniture etc.

**Youghal** Irish Republic. Fishing port and seaside resort in Co. Cork, on the estuary of the R. Blackwater 27 m. E of Cork. Pop. (1966) 5,108. Well known for its lace. Manufactures carpets. Has the 15th-cent. (restored) St Mary's Church, near which is Myrtle Grove, an Elizabethan house where Sir Walter Raleigh lived intermittently (1584–97) and introduced the potato and tobacco to Ireland. Also has remains of the 13th-cent. North Abbey and the 14th-cent. St John's Abbey.

**Youngstown** USA. Industrial town in Ohio, on the Mahoning R. 57 m. NNW of Pittsburgh. Pop. (1960) 166,989. Important iron and steel centre, manufacturing a wide variety of metal products, also electrical equipment, chemicals, plastics, clothing, etc. University (1908). First settled 1796. First blast furnace built 1826.

**Ypres (Flemish Ieper)** Belgium. Town in W Flanders province, on the small canalized Yperlée R., a tributary of the Yser R., 40 m. WSW of Ghent. Pop. (1969) 18,447. Important centre of the textile industry since the Middle Ages. Three great battles were fought here in the 1st World War (1914, 1915, 1917), and the town, including its famous 13th/14th-cent. Cloth Hall and the cathedral, was almost completely destroyed. It was later rebuilt, and the Menin Gate was erected as a memorial to British soldiers killed here; to these troops the town was generally known as 'Wipers'.

**Ysselmeer** ⋄ *Ijsselmeer*.

**Yssel Rivers** ⋄ *Ijssel Rivers*.

**Yucatán** Mexico. State in the SE, forming the N part of the Yucatán peninsula. Area 14,868 sq. m. Pop. (1969) 817,000. Cap. and largest city Mérida. Flat and low-lying. Climate tropical. Chief product henequen (sisal), exported through Progreso. Sugar-cane, tobacco, maize also grown.

**Yucatán Channel** ⋄ *Mexico, Gulf of*.

**Yucatán Peninsula**. Peninsula separating the Gulf of Mexico (W) from the Caribbean Sea (E), mainly in SE Mexico but also including British Honduras and N Guatemala. Area about 70,000 sq. m. A low plateau of limestone, remarkable for the absence of surface rivers, which have underground courses in the limestone.

The peasants raise the water by innumerable windmills. In the S there are dense tropical forests yielding mahogany, dyewoods, etc. Savannah in the N W. A great centre of Mayan civilization in pre-Columbian times, as is evidenced by the ruins at Chichén Itzá and Uxmal (Yucatán, Mexico).

**Yugoslavia.** Federal republic in S E Europe, the largest country in the Balkan peninsula. Area 98,725 sq. m. Pop. (1961) 18,549,291 (mainly Serbs and Croats). Cap. Belgrade. Lang. mainly Serbo-Croat.

Bounded by Austria and Hungary (N), Rumania and Bulgaria (E), Greece and Albania (S), the Adriatic Sea (W), and Italy (N W). Consists of 6 socialist republics: Bosnia and Hercegovina; Montenegro (Crna Gora); Croatia; Macedonia; Slovenia; Serbia (with Vojvodina and Kosovo-Metohija). Extremely complex ethnically as well as physically; has had a stormy history. Primarily agricultural; almost two thirds of the population are employed on the land.

TOPOGRAPHY, CLIMATE. In the N are the Julian and Karawanken Alps; the former rise to 9,396 ft in Triglav, the highest point in Yugoslavia. From the N W, parallel to the Adriatic coastline, runs a series of limestone ridges called the Dinaric Alps, with deep gorges and little surface drainage. Behind Rijeka (N W) the mountainous region is relatively narrow; broadening rapidly to the S and E, it covers the whole of the S of the country, with many peaks over 6,000 ft. These mountains create a very difficult problem for communications between the interior and the Adriatic. For much of the coast the mountains adjoin the sea; with numerous beautiful islands of varied size and shape, e.g. Krk, Cres, Pag, Brač, Hvar, Korčula, this is one of the most picturesque littorals in Europe. The lowlands lie in the N E, a continuation of the Hungarian plain, drained by the Danube and its tributaries the Drava, the Sava, and the Tisa (Tisza). In the S the Morava flows N to the Danube the Vardar S to the Aegean Sea. Lakes Shkodër, Ohrid, Prespa, and Doiran lie across the S frontier. Climate varies from Mediterranean on the Dalmatian coast to continental on the N E plains.

RESOURCES, PEOPLE, etc. About 40 per cent of the area is classified as cultivated land. Agriculture is largely organized in peasant co-operatives. Principal crops maize, wheat. Grapes (for wine) and plums also grown. Sheep, cattle, and pigs extensively reared. Considerable forests (beech, oak, fir). Mineral resources include coal, lignite, bauxite, iron, copper, lead, zinc, chrome, antimony, petroleum. Great efforts have been made to develop industries, which are concentrated mainly in the N W; the leading centres are Belgrade, Zagreb, Ljubljana, Sarajevo. Exports, however, still consist chiefly of timber, metals, fruit, livestock, meat products. Foreign trade is principally with Italy, the Federal German Republic, and the USA.

The great majority of the population are of Slavonic stock, in 4 major groups: Serbian (42 per cent), Croatian (24 per cent), Slovene (9 per cent), Macedonian (5 per cent). Minorities include Rumanians, Albanians, Bulgarians, Czechs, Italians. Three allied languages are recognized: Serbo-Croat (the lingua franca), Macedonian, Slovene. Serb and Macedonian use the Cyrillic alphabet, Croat and Slovene the Roman. People of the Eastern Orthodox faith are mainly in Serbia, the Roman Catholics in Croatia and Slovenia, and the Muslims in Bosnia and Hercegovina. The constitution of 1945 (when the Federal People's Republic was proclaimed) was on Soviet lines, but was modified by the new constitutions of 1953 and 1963; that of 1963 changed the name of the country to the Socialist Federal Republic of Yugoslavia. All citizens over the age of 18 have the vote.

HISTORY. For early history, ◊ *Serbia*, *Croatia*, *Slovenia*, etc. After the 1st World War (which began ostensibly because of the assassination in 1914 of the Austrian Archduke Francis Ferdinand at Sarajevo) the Kingdom of the Serbs, Croats, and Slovenes was formed (1918) from Serbia, Montenegro, and regions which had formerly belonged to the Austro-Hungarian Empire (Croatia, Slovenia, and Bosnia and Hercegovina). Internal dissension among the various Slav groups caused Alexander I to establish a dictatorship in 1929 (when the name of the state was changed to Yugoslavia); he was assassinated at Marseilles in 1934, and was succeeded by his infant son, Peter II, with a regency government headed by Prince Paul. Their sympathies were with Nazi Germany; when they were ousted Yugoslavia was invaded by German troops (1941) and soon overrun. Guerrilla forces maintained a heroic resistance in the mountains, their most successful leader being the communist Josip Broz (Tito). After the end of the 2nd World War the republic was proclaimed (1945) under Marshal Tito, who welded the heterogeneous nation together by encouraging rather than suppressing regional aspirations, granting a large measure of autonomy to the 6 constituent republics. From Italy Yugoslavia received part of Venezia Giulia, the Dalmatian town of Zadar, and certain Adriatic islands (1947). Drifting away from Soviet domination, it was expelled from the Cominform (1948), and has since pursued a policy of independence, preserving friendly relations with the West but since the death of Stalin (1953) effecting a *rapprochement* with the USSR.

**Yukon** Canada. Territory in the NW, bordered on the W by Alaska. Area 207,076 sq. m. Pop. (1966) 14,382 (85 per cent whites, 14 per cent Indians). Cap. and largest town Whitehorse. Largely mountainous: in the SW are the St Elias Mountains, with Mt Logan (19,850 ft), the highest peak in Canada; along much of the E border are the Mackenzie Mountains. Chief river the Yukon. Climate Arctic, with long cold winters and short summers. Mining is the basis of the economy; chief minerals silver, gold, lead, zinc. Fur trade important. During the Klondike gold rush the population rose to 27,000 (1901).

**Yukon River** Canada/USA. River 1,979 m. long in Yukon (Canada) and Alaska (USA), its furthest headwaters being the source of the Nisutlin R. on the Yukon–British Columbia border. Flows N and NW through Yukon, past Whitehorse and Dawson, and follows a great westward curve through Alaska to empty into the Bering Sea. Navigable (June–Sept.) for 1,777 m. to Whitehorse. Tributaries include the White, Stewart, Klondike, Porcupine, and Tanana rivers.

**Yunnan** China. Province in the SW bordering W on Burma and S on Laos and N Vietnam. Area 168,000 sq. m. Pop. (1957) 19,100,000. Cap. Kunming. In the NW and W there are high forested mountain ranges and the deep gorges of the Yangtse, Mekong, and Salween. The remainder consists mainly of a plateau, cut in the SE by the valleys of the Red and Black rivers. In the valleys and on terraced hill slopes rice, wheat, barley, tea, and tobacco are grown. Tin, tungsten, and other minerals obtained. Chief towns Kunming, Mengtsz, Szemao. Among the population are many non-Chinese, including the Lolos and Shans. Scene of a Muslim rebellion (1855–72); still has a relatively high proportion of Muslims.

**Yvelines** France. Department W of Paris, formed in 1964 when the former Seine and Seine-et-Oise departments were reorganized. Area 877 sq. m. Pop. (1968) 853,386. Prefecture Versailles.

**Yverdon** Switzerland. Town in Vaud canton at the SW end of L. Neuchâtel. Pop. (1969) 20,700. Manufactures typewriters, cigars, etc. In the early 19th cent. its castle was the home of the famous Pestalozzi school.

# Z

**Zaandam** Netherlands. Industrial town and railway junction in N Holland province, near the North Sea Canal 8 m. NW of Amsterdam. Pop. (1968) 58,312. Sawmilling, oil refining. Manufactures cement, dyes, etc.

**Zabrze** Poland. Formerly (1915–45) Hindenburg. Industrial town in Katowice voivodship 11 m. WNW of Katowice. Pop. (1968) 199,300. Coalmining. Manufactures iron and steel, machinery, chemicals, glass, etc. Founded in the 14th cent. Passed to Prussia 1742. Restored to Poland after the 2nd World War (1945).

**Zacapa** Guatemala. Capital of the Zacapa department, 65 m. ENE of Guatemala City. Pop. (1964) 30,187. Railway junction. Market town. Sulphur springs.

**Zacatecas** Mexico. 1. State on the central plateau, crossed NW–SE by the Sierra Madre Occidental. Area 28,125 sq. m. Pop. (1969) 1,082,000. Cap. Zacatecas. Main resources minerals, esp. silver; also gold, zinc, lead, etc. Chief towns Zacatecas, Fresnillo.
2. Capital of Zacatecas state, 375 m. NW of Mexico City at a height of 8,000 ft in a deep gulch in the central plateau. Pop. (1960) 31,700. A silver-mining centre. Minor industries, inc. the making of *serapes* (Mexican shawls). Cathedral (17th/18th-cent.). Founded (1546) after the discovery of rich silver deposits.

**Zacatecoluca** El Salvador. Capital of the La Paz department, 27 m. SE of San Salvador. Pop. (1961) 40,424. Market town. Manufactures cotton goods, cigars, etc.

**Zadar** (Italian **Zara**) Yugoslavia. Seaport and seaside resort in Croatia, on the Adriatic Sea 95 m. SSE of Rijeka. Pop. (1961) 25,132. Noted for the manufacture of maraschino liqueur. The 9th-cent. Church of St Donat, built over a Roman forum, is one of the oldest buildings in Dalmatia; there are other medieval churches and also Roman remains. Acquired by Venice 1409. Passed to Austria 1797. Became an Italian enclave in Yugoslavia 1920. Ceded to Yugoslavia 1947, after suffering severely in the 2nd World War.

**Zagazig** United Arab Republic. Capital of the Sharqiya governorate, on the Nile delta 38 m. NNE of Cairo. Pop. (1960) 124,000. Railway and canal junction in a fertile region. Trade in cotton, grain. Cotton mills. The ruins of Bubastis are just S.

**Zagorsk** USSR. Formerly Sergiyev. Town in the Moscow region, RSFSR, 45 m. NNE of Moscow. Pop. 74,000. Famous for the monastery (*lavra*) of Troitsko-Sergiyevskaya – the Trinity Monastery of St Sergius, founded in 1340 and still visited by large numbers of pilgrims, being converted into a museum at the revolution (1917). Within the monastery were 15th- and 16th-cent. cathedrals, several churches, a bell tower 320-ft high, and the tomb of Boris Godunov, as well as ecclesiastical treasures.

**Zagreb** Yugoslavia. Capital of Croatia, on the Sava R. 105 m. ENE of Trieste. Pop. (1961) 457,499. The second largest city in Yugoslavia, and a road and railway junction on the route between Belgrade and Ljubljana. Manufactures machinery, textiles (woollen, cotton, silk, rayon), leather goods, paper, glass, furniture, chemicals, etc. Divided into the old ecclesiastical town (Kaptol), containing the Gothic cathedral, the 13th-cent. upper town, and the more modern lower town. The first two parts, originally separate walled towns and bitter rivals, united against the Turks, and as the city of Zagreb became capital of Croatia-Slavonia in 1867. Zagreb is also a Croat cultural centre. Seat of a university (1669) and of the Yugoslav Academy of Science and Arts.

**Zagros Mountains** Iran. Mountain system forming the SW edge of the plateau of Iran, extending NW–SE along the frontiers with Turkey and Iraq, and across S Iran N of the Persian Gulf. Includes several parallel ranges. Rises to 14,920 ft in Zard Kuh. Iran's main oilfields are located in the foothills of the central Zagros, in Khuzistan.

**Zákinthos** ◊ *Zante*.

**Zalaegerszeg** Hungary. Capital of Zala county, on the Zala R. 115 m. WSW of Budapest. Pop. (1968) 32,000. Market town in a stock-rearing and cereal-growing region.

**Zama (Zama Regia)** Tunisia. Ancient

village 13 m. N of the modern town of Maktar (85 m. S W of Tunis). Site of one of the decisive battles of world history, in which the Roman Scipio Africanus defeated the Carthaginian army under Hannibal (202 B.C.), thus ending the 2nd Punic War and the power of Carthage.

**Zambezi River.** Fourth longest river in Africa, 2,200 m. long, rising in the extreme N W of Zambia near the frontiers of Congo (Kinshasa) and Angola, flowing generally S E in an immense S-curve and entering the Moçambique Channel 130 m. N E of Beira. From the source, it flows S across E Angola and Barotseland, turns E S E to form the frontier between Zambia and the Caprivi Strip (S W Africa), and continues E, between Kasungula and Zumbo forming the frontier between Zambia and Rhodesia: in this section are the Victoria Falls and the Kariba hydroelectric scheme. It enters Moçambique at Zumbo; below the Kebrabasa Rapids it turns S E past Tete (head of steamer navigation) and enters the sea by a marshy delta, only one channel of which (the Chinde) is navigable. River traffic declined with the opening of the railway bridge at Sena (1935) linking Malawi (then Nyasaland) with Beira. Elsewhere along the course it is seriously impeded by rapids and falls; only limited stretches are navigable. Chief tributaries the Lungwebungu, the Luanginga, the Chobe, the Shangani, and the Sanyati on the right, and the Kafue, the Luangwa, and the Shiré (outlet of L. Malawi) on the left.

**Zambia.** Republic in central Africa, a member of the British Commonwealth. Area 288,130 sq. m. Pop. (1966) 3,894,686 (inc. 67,000 Europeans). Cap. Lusaka. Bounded by Tanzania (N), Malawi (E), Moçambique (S E), Rhodesia and S W Africa (S, Zambezi R. and Caprivi Strip), Angola (W), and Congo (Kinshasa) (N W). A rolling plateau at a height of 4,000 ft rising to over 5,000 ft in the Muchinga Mountains (E and N E). Drained principally by the Zambezi and its tributaries the Kafue and the Luangwa; the N W is drained by the Luapula (a headstream of the Congo R.) rising in L. Bangweulu. Wholly within the tropics, but climate considerably modified by altitude. Distinct rainy (Nov.–April) and dry seasons. Annual rainfall ranges from 25–30 ins. (S) to 50 ins. (N). Natural vegetation savannah; sufficient woodland in some areas for timber

exploitation. Agriculture consists mainly of the cultivation by Africans of subsistence crops, e.g. maize, millet, groundnuts. Cattle rearing is restricted to uplands not infested by the tsetse fly. Minerals are the chief source of wealth, esp. from the Copperbelt (near the Congo (Kinshasa) frontier), which provides over 80 per cent of exports; Zambia is the world's second largest producer of copper. The chief mines are at Kabwe (Broken Hill) (lead, vanadium, zinc), Roan Antelope, Nkana, Mufulira, Nchanga. Chief towns Ndola, Luanshya, Kitwe, Chingola. Livingstone (near the Victoria Falls, capital until 1935) is a well-known tourist attraction.

Explored and described by Livingstone 1851–5. Suffered from the activities of Arab slave traders in the 19th cent.; the slave trade was suppressed by the British 1891–4 and the two provinces of N E and N W Rhodesia were amalgamated (1911) as N Rhodesia. Administration transferred from the British S Africa Company (in control since 1889) to the British government 1924. Proposals for a new constitution led to disturbances in 1961, but full independence and membership of the U N were achieved without difficulty in 1964. The mineral wealth was nationalized, with moderate compensation to the British S Africa Company.

**Zamboanga** Philippines. Capital of Zamboanga province, at the S W extremity of Mindanao, on Basilan Strait. Pop. (1960) 131,411. Seaport. Exports copra, timber, abacá, etc. Founded (1635) by the Spanish.

**Zamora** Spain. 1. Province in León, in the N W, bordering W on Portugal. Area 4,082 sq. m. Pop. (1961) 301,129. Cap. Zamora. Mountainous in the N W, but chiefly plateau. Drained by the Duero (Douro) R. and its tributaries. Main occupation agriculture (cereals, vines). Sheep rearing.
2. Capital of Zamora province, on a steep hill above the Douro R. 55 m. WSW of Valladolid. Pop. (1961) 42,060. Trade in cereals, wine. Flour milling. Manufactures textiles, cement, soap, etc. Has a small but beautiful 12th-cent. Romanesque cathedral, other 12th-cent. churches, and a 14th-cent. bridge across the river.

**Zanesville** USA. Industrial town in central Ohio, on the Muskingum R. at the confluence with the Licking R. 50 m. E of Columbus. Pop. (1960) 39,077. Manufac-

tures tiles, pottery, glass, cement, etc. Birthplace of Zane Grey (1875–1939).
**Zanjan** ◊ *Zenjan.*
**Zante** (Gr. **Zákinthos**) Greece. Ancient Zacynthus. 1. The most southerly of the main Ionian Islands, 12 m. from the NW coast of the Peloponnese, forming with some small islets the *nome* of Zante. Area 158 sq. m. Pop. (1961) 35,451. Produces currants, wine, olive oil. Annexed by Rome 191 B.C. Long a Venetian possession (1482–1797). Has often suffered from earthquakes, notably in 1811, 1820, 1840, 1893, 1953.
2. Capital of Zante *nome*, on the E coast. Pop. (1961) 9,506. Seaport. Exports currants, olive oil. Flour milling. Manufactures soap. Virtually destroyed in the earthquake of 1953.
**Zanzibar** Tanzania. 1. Coralline island in the Indian Ocean, separated from the E coast of Africa by the 22-m.-wide Zanzibar Channel. Area 640 sq. m. Pop. (1967) 190,117. ◊〉 *Zanzibar and Pemba.*
2. Capital of Zanzibar island and of Zanzibar and Pemba, on the W coast of Zanzibar 45 m. N of Dar-es-Salaam. Pop. (1967) 68,400. Commercial centre, entrepôt for E African trade; the world's leading exporter of cloves. Grew in importance after becoming the Omani capital (instead of Muscat), but declined with the rise of Mombasa and Dar-es-Salaam.
**Zanzibar and Pemba** Tanzania. The islands of ◊ *Zanzibar* and ◊ *Pemba.* Area 1,020 sq. m. Pop. (1967) 354,360 (78 per cent Africans, 16 per cent Arabs). Cap. Zanzibar. Tropical climate. Fertile soil. Main crop cloves (providing the bulk of the world's supply). Coconuts and fruits also grown. Chief export cloves, clove oil; also coconuts and coconut oil, copra. The Portuguese occupied Zanzibar and Pemba early in the 16th cent. but were superseded by the Arabs (from Oman) in the 17th cent. The Sultan of Muscat made Zanzibar his capital in 1832, and the link with Oman was broken; one of his sons later became Sultan of Zanzibar. The Sultan's island possessions were proclaimed a British protectorate (as Zanzibar) in 1890, but the N of his mainland possession was purchased by Italy and the S by Germany; the central 10-m.-wide strip along the Kenya coast was leased by Britain (its administration passing to Kenya) and known after 1920 as the Kenya Protectorate. After a very brief period of indepen-

dence within the British Commonwealth (1963–4), Zanzibar united with Tanganyika as Tanzania (1964).
**Zaporozhye** USSR. Formerly (till 1921) Aleksandrovsk. Capital of the Zaporozhye Region, Ukrainian SSR, on the Dnieper R. 40 m. S of Dnepropetrovsk. Pop. (1970) 658,000. Industrial centre which has expanded rapidly in recent years, largely owing to the Dneprostroi Dam and hydroelectric power station on the Dnieper R. It has developed a great metallurgical and engineering industry, manufacturing special steels and alloys, aluminium, machinery, machine tools, wire, ballbearings, etc. The present name, meaning 'Beyond the Rapids', refers to its position below the Dnieper falls which led to the Dneprostroi power station.
**Zara** ◊ *Zadar.*
**Zaragoza** (Eng. **Saragossa**) Spain. Province in Aragón, in the NE. Area 6,615 sq. m. Pop. (1961) 656,772. Mountainous along the N, W, and S borders; consists mainly of a barren plain crossed by the Ebro R. and its tributaries. Agriculture (sugar-beet, cereals, etc.) impeded by extremes of temperature and low rainfall.
2. Ancient Caesarea Augusta or Caesaraugusta (of which the modern name is a corruption). Capital of Zaragoza province, on the Ebro R. at the confluence with the Huerva and Gállego rivers 160 m. W of Barcelona. Pop. (1967) 414,331. Important railway junction and commercial and industrial centre. Engineering, sugar refining, flour milling, wine making. Manufactures chemicals, soap, cement, etc. Has two cathedrals, the 12th/16th-cent. mainly Gothic La Seo and the 17th-cent. baroque El Pilar, named after the sacred pillar of jasper on which the Virgin is supposed to have alighted when she appeared to St James here; also the 11th-cent. castle of Aljaferia, the Lonja (Exchange), and the university (founded 1587). Capital of the kingdom of Aragón in the 12th–15th cent. but declined after the union with Castile. Goya (1746–1828) was born at the village of Fuendetodos near by.
**Zárate** Argentina. Formerly (1930–45) General José F. Uriburu. Industrial town on the Paraná R. 50 m. NW of Buenos Aires. Pop. 52,000. In an agricultural region, linked by ferry with Ibicuy. Meat packing. Manufactures paper.
**Zaria** Nigeria. Town in the N 85 m. SW of Kano. Pop. (1960) 54,000. On the main

railway from Lagos to Kano and Nguru (with a branch line to the NW with terminus at Kaura Namoda). Market town in a cotton-growing region. Railway engineering, cotton ginning, printing, tanning, etc. Seat of the University of Northern Nigeria (1962), formerly the Nigerian College of Technology.

**Zasieki** ◊ *Forst.*

**Zealand** Denmark. Largest island, between the Kattegat and the Baltic Sea, and separated from Sweden by The Sound, and from Fünen (Fyn) by the Great Belt, and connected by road and railway bridge with Falster. Area 2,709 sq. m. Pop. (1965) 2,055,040. Low and slightly undulating. Main occupations cereal cultivation, dairy farming, cattle rearing. Chief towns Copenhagen, Roskilde.

**Zeebrugge** Belgium. Seaport in W Flanders province, 9 m. N of Bruges at the N end of the Bruges–Zeebrugge canal. Exports coke, chemicals (produced here). A German naval base in the 1st World War, its entrance was closed by a British naval force in 1918.

**Zeeland** Netherlands. Province in the SW comprising a small area on the mainland bordering S on Belgium and islands in the Scheldt estuary including Walcheren, N and S Beveland. Area 684 sq. m. Pop. (1968) 298,457. Cap. Middelburg. Mainly agricultural. Cereal cultivation, dairy farming, cattle rearing. Chief towns Middelburg, Flushing (chief port).

**Zeist** Netherlands. Residential and industrial town in Utrecht province 5 m. E of Utrecht. Pop. (1968) 55,950. Manufactures pharmaceutical goods, soap, etc. Market gardening in the neighbourhood. A Moravian settlement was established here in the 18th cent.

**Zeitz** German Democratic Republic. Industrial town in the Halle district, on the White Elster R. 25 m. SSW of Leipzig. Pop. (1965) 46,524. Sugar refining. Manufactures textiles, chemicals, pianos, etc. Capital of the duchy of Saxe-Zeitz in the 17th and 18th cent. Passed to Prussia 1815.

**Zelten** ◊ *Libya.*

**Zenjan (Zanjan, Zinjan)** Iran. Town in Gilan province, 175 m. WNW of Tehran. Pop. (1966) 82,530. Manufactures cotton goods, rugs, matches, etc.

**Zenta** ◊ *Senta.*

**Zeravshan River** USSR. River 450 m. long flowing generally W through the Tadzhik and Uzbek SSRs and watering the oases of Samarkand and Bukhara, petering out in the desert before reaching the Amu Darya.

**Zermatt** Switzerland. Village and climbing centre in Valais canton, at a height of 5,315 ft at the foot of the Matterhorn (5 m. SW), with Monte Rosa also near by. Pop. (1960) 2,731. There is a rack-and-pinion railway to the summit of the Gornergrat (10,289 ft).

**Zetland** ◊ *Shetland Islands.*

**Zhdanov** USSR. Formerly Mariupol. Seaport and industrial town in the Donetsk region, Ukrainian SSR, 60 m. SSW of Donetsk on the Sea of Azov. Pop. (1970) 417,000. Exports grain, coal, salt, etc. from the near-by harbour. Fishing, fish processing. Manufactures iron and steel, machinery, chemicals, clothing, etc. Renamed (1948) after A. A. Zhdanov (1896–1948), the Soviet statesman, who was born here.

**Zhitomir** USSR. Capital of the Zhitomir region, Ukrainian SSR, on the Teterev R. 80 m. WSW of Kiev. Pop. (1970) 161,000. Road and railway junction. Industrial centre. Metal working, brewing. Manufactures furniture, clothing. Passed to Lithuania in the 14th cent., to Poland in the 16th cent., and was occupied by Russia in 1778.

**Zielona Góra (Ger. Grünberg)** Poland. Capital of the Zielona Góra voivodship 73 m. WSW of Poznań. Pop. (1968) 69,300. Industrial centre. Railway engineering. Manufactures textiles. Lignite mining in the neighbourhood. Trade in wine.

**Ziguinchor** Senegal. Port on the estuary of the Casamance R. 170 m. SSE of Dakar. Pop. (1962) 29,000. Exports groundnuts etc.

**Žilina** Czechoslovakia. Town in Slovakia, on the Vah R. 105 m. NE of Bratislava. Pop. (1967) 39,000. Railway junction. Industrial centre. Railway engineering. Manufactures paper, matches, fertilizers, etc.

**Zimbabwe National Park** Rhodesia. Site of a ruined town built by a Bantu people in the SE 15 m. SE of Fort Victoria, probably dating from the Middle Ages, consisting of dry granite walls which were apparently never roofed. The main ruins are the 'elliptical temple' (a stone kraal, not strictly elliptical); the 'acropolis' (a fortified citadel), on the summit of a granite hill; and the 'valley ruins' (smaller buildings which were probably dwellings).

Relics from Zimbabwe (pottery, metal ornaments, etc.) are now in museums at Salisbury, Cape Town, etc. The name Zimbabwe means literally 'Stone Houses'. Discovered 1868. Several excavations during the 20th cent.

**Zinder** Niger. Town in the S 460 m. E of Niamey. Pop. 15,000. Terminus of a Trans-Saharan motor route from N Algeria. Till 1926 capital of the French colony of Niger. Commercial centre. Trade in groundnuts, hides and skins, etc. Local crafts: leather goods, blankets.

**Zinjan** ◊ *Zenjan*.

**Zion National Park** USA. Reserve in SW Utah. Area 230 sq. m. Established 1919. Chief feature Zion Canyon, a gorge containing beautifully coloured rocks and unusual rock formations.

**Zipaquirá** Colombia. Town in the Cundinamarca department at a height of 8,700 ft in the E Cordillera 30 m. N of Bogotá. Pop. 29,880. In a cattle-rearing district. Has a remarkable mine containing immense quantities of rock salt, which provides raw material for the local chemical industry.

**Zittau** German Democratic Republic. Industrial town and railway junction in the Dresden district, near the Czechoslovak and Polish frontiers 50 m. ESE of Dresden. Pop. (1965) 42,876. Manufactures textiles, commercial vehicles, machinery, etc. First settled by Sorbs (Lusatian Serbs); a member of the Lusatian League (from 1346).

**Zlatoust** USSR. Industrial town in the Chelyabinsk region, RSFSR, on the Ai R. 70 m. W of Chelyabinsk. Pop. (1970) 181,000. Important centre of the iron and steel industry, esp. producing special steels; manufactures agricultural machinery, cutlery, etc. One of the older metallurgical centres.

**Zlín** ◊ *Gottwaldov*.

**Zomba** Malawi. Capital, 30 m. NE of Blantyre at a height of 3,000 ft. Pop. (1966) 19,666. On the lower slopes of Zomba Mountain, in the Shiré Highlands, in a tobacco-growing and dairy farming region. Many of its inhabitants work in government offices and on the plantations and farms.

**Zonguldak** Turkey. Capital of Zonguldak province, on the Black Sea 110 m. NNW of Ankara. Pop. (1965) 61,000. Seaport. Exports coal mined in the district. Chief industry coal processing.

**Zoutpansberg** S Africa. In Afrikaans, 'Salt Pan Mountain'. Mountain range S of the Limpopo R., in the Transvaal, extending 100 m. E–W and rising to 5,700 ft. Chief town in the district Louis Trichardt (pop. 14,800).

**Zrenjanin** Yugoslavia. Formerly Veliki Bečkerek (till the 1930s), then Petrovgrad (till 1947). Town in Vojvodina, on the canalized Begej R. 28 m. ENE of Novi Sad. Pop. (1961) 55,578. River port. Manufactures agricultural machinery, food products, etc.

**Zug** Switzerland. **1.** The smallest undivided canton, in N central Switzerland. Area 93 sq. m. Pop. (1969) 66,700 (mainly German-speaking and Roman Catholic). Joined the Swiss Confederation 1352.
**2.** Capital of Zug canton, on the NE shore of L. Zug and 15 m. S of Zürich. Pop. (1969) 23,400. Printing, woodworking. Manufactures electrical equipment, metal goods. Stands at the foot of the Zugerberg (3,261 ft). Has a 16th-cent. town hall.

**Zug, Lake** (Ger. **Zugersee**) Switzerland. Lake 9 m. long and 2½ m. wide N of L. Lucerne and mainly in Zug canton. On the NE shore is the town of Zug; to the S is the Rigi (5,908 ft).

**Zugspitze** Federal German Republic. Country's highest peak (9,721 ft), in the Bavarian Alps and on the Austrian frontier. Ascended from Garmisch-Partenkirchen (Germany) by rack-and-pinion and then cable railway, and from Ehrwald (Austria) by cable railway.

**Zuider Zee** Netherlands. Former gulf of the North Sea, probably once a lake, the coast being represented then by the line of the W Frisian Is. By the 14th cent. the sea had breached the coast and formed the shallow gulf. In 1920 work on a large-scale reclamation project was begun: the Noordholland-Wieringen Barrage (1½ m.) was completed in 1924 and the Wieringen-Friesland Barrage or Afsluitdijk (18½ m.) in 1932, sealing off the former gulf from the sea. Four polders were to be reclaimed, leaving a freshwater lake, the ◊ *Ijsselmeer*, remaining from the old Zuider Zee. The NW Polder was brought under cultivation in 1930 and the NE Polder in 1942, while in 1956 the E Flevoland part of the SE Polder was enclosed by a further dyke. The remaining part of this polder and the Markerwaard or SW Polder are also to be enclosed, the entire scheme being scheduled for completion by 1980.

**Zululand** S Africa. The NE part of Natal, bounded by Moçambique (N), Swaziland

(NW), and the Tugela R. (S). Area
10,362 sq. m. Pop. (1960) 544,429. Cap.
Eshowe. From the coastal plain, where
sugar-cane and cotton are cultivated, the
land rises to the plateau, on which cattle
are raised. Includes several game reserves.
Early in the 19th cent. the Zulu were
transformed from a small and insignificant
tribe into a powerful nation by the military
prowess of their chief, Chaka. For a time
they repulsed both Boers and British, but
in 1879 the latter defeated them at Ulundi,
and Chief Cetewayo was captured. Became a British protectorate 1887. Annexed
to Natal 1897.

**Zürich** Switzerland. 1. Canton in the N.
Area 667 sq. m. Pop. (1969) 1,100,000
(mainly German-speaking and Protestant).
Contains a considerable area of forests.
Cereals, fruit, vines cultivated. Industries
concentrated chiefly in Zürich and Winter-
thur.
2. Capital of Zürich canton, the country's
largest city, on the Limmat R. where it
leaves L. Zürich. Pop. (1969) 433,500.
The leading industrial, banking, and insurance centre. Manufactures textiles, electrical machinery, etc. Publishing, printing.
The cultural centre of German-speaking
Switzerland, with a university (1833), the
Federal Institute of Technology (1855), the
National Museum, the Central Library and
Art Gallery. Among famous buildings are
the 11th/14th-cent. Grossmünster and the
13th/15th-cent. Fraumünster, both Pro-
testant churches, and the 17th-cent. town
hall. First inhabited by prehistoric lake-
dwellers, who were followed by the
Helvetii and the Romans. Became a free
Imperial city 1218. Joined the Swiss
Confederation 1351. Played a leading
part in the Reformation, and the reformer
Zwingli (1484–1531) became pastor at the
Grossmünster in 1518; he was later killed
whilst fighting with the Protestant forces.
Birthplace of Pestalozzi (1746–1827),
Gottfried Keller (1819–90), Conrad Meyer
(1825–98).

**Zürich, Lake** Switzerland. Lake mainly in
Zürich canton, 25 m. long and up to 2½ m.
wide, at 1,332 ft above sea level, fed by the
Linth R. and drained by the Limmat R.
At its N end is Zürich. Crossed by a
causeway carrying a road and a railway
between Rapperswil (N) and Pfäffikon
(S). Although lacking the spectacular
Alpine scenery of some Swiss lakes, it is
pleasantly situated amid vineyards and
orchards.

**Zutphen** Netherlands. Industrial town in
Gelderland province, on the Ijssel R.
16 m. NE of Arnhem. Pop. (1968) 27,290.
Manufactures bricks, clothing, paper, etc.
Trade in grain, timber. Has the remains of
the ancient town walls and a 12th-cent.
church. Sir Philip Sidney was mortally
wounded here (1586).

**Zweibrücken** Federal German Republic.
Town in Rhineland-Palatinate, near the
Saarland border 23 m. SW of Kaiserslautern. Pop. (1963) 33,300. Manufactures leather goods, textiles, etc. Dates
from the 12th cent. Capital of a countship,
later a duchy. Belonged to France 1801–14,
when it was called Deux-Ponts.

**Zwickau** German Democratic Republic.
Industrial town in the Karl-Marx-Stadt
district, on the Zwickauer Mulde R. 40 m.
S of Leipzig. Pop. (1968) 127,795. In a coalmining region. Manufactures textiles
(cotton, woollen, rayon, etc.), paper,
machinery, tractors, chemicals, etc. Has the
15th/16th-cent. Gothic Church of St
Mary and a 16th-cent. town hall. The
Anabaptist movement was founded here
c. 1521. Birthplace of Robert Schumann
(1810–56).

**Zwolle** Netherlands. Capital of Overijssel
province, 21 m. NNE of Apeldoorn on the
Zwartewater. Pop. (1968) 73,253. A canal
and railway junction. Important cattle
market. Manufactures chemicals, metal
goods, dairy products, etc. Has a 14th/
15th-cent. church. Thomas à Kempis
(1380-1471) spent most of his life at the
monastery on the near-by Agnietenberg.
Birthplace of Gerard Terborch (1617–81),
the painter.

# ADDENDA

**Alpes-de-Haute-Provence** France. Department in the SE formerly known as ◊ *Basses-Alpes*.

**Andorra.** Female citizens were given the right to vote in 1970.

**Ashdod** Israel. Seaport 19 m. SSW of Tel Aviv; of Mediterranean ports second in importance to Haifa. Pop. (1969) 31,900.

**Aswan (Assuan)** United Arab Republic. With the inauguration of the twelfth and last power-generating turbine in July 1970, the Aswan High Dam was essentially completed.

**Baracaldo** Spain. Industrial town in Vizcaya province just NW of Bilbao, on the railway from Bilbao to Portugalete (its outport). Pop. (1967) 107,299. Manufactures iron and steel, machinery, etc. A well-planned town, developed during the 20th cent. round its heavy industries. Expanded considerably in the 1960s: pop. (1959) 78,626.

**Basses-Alpes** France. The department was renamed Alpes-de-Haute-Provence in 1970, on the grounds that the earlier name implied inferiority.

**Bottrop** Federal German Republic. Industrial town in N Rhine–Westphalia, in the Ruhr district just NW of Essen. Pop. (1968) 110,023. Coalmining. Manufactures steel, machinery, chemicals (coal by-products). Developed from the late 19th cent. with the coalmining industry.

**Brazil.** In 1970 Brazil extended her territorial waters from 12 m. to 200 m., thus joining ◊ *Peru* (Addenda), Chile, and Ecuador in claiming jurisdiction over the belt of sea reaching 200 m. from the coast.

**Bristol** England. The *SS Great Britain*, which had been beached in the Falkland Is. for many years, was towed 8,000 m. back to Bristol in 1970. Designed by Brunel and launched at Bristol in 1843, she had been the first screw-driven ocean-going vessel and the first one to be constructed of iron.

**California** USA. One of the fastest growing states in pop., overtook New York in the 1960s and became the most populous state in the Union. Pop. (1970) 19,696,840 (15,717,204 in 1960).

**Cambodia.** Became more deeply involved in the Vietnam war in 1970, when US and S Vietnamese troops invaded the country to attack N Vietnamese and Vietcong (Communist) bases: Cambodia had long involuntarily harboured these guerrillas. The US and S Vietnamese forces later withdrew. The monarchy was abolished and a republic proclaimed in 1970.

**Carletonville** S Africa. Town in S Transvaal 42 m. WSW of Johannesburg, on the main Johannesburg–Cape Town railway. Pop. (1967) 102,500 (80,000 Bantu, 22,000 whites). Goldmining centre on the W Witwatersrand. Light industries. District first settled 1842. Goldmining began in the 1930s; township founded 1948. Expanded rapidly in the 1960s: pop. (1960) 56,246.

**Czechoslovakia.** Serious riots took place in Prague and Brno, with some loss of life, in 1969, on the anniversary of the Soviet invasion. Soviet pressure led to political purges (1969, 1970), and the economic reforms that had been formulated before the Soviet invasion were dropped.

**Da Nang** S Vietnam. Formerly Tourane. Seaport and second largest town, 50 m. SE of Hué. Pop. (1966) 144,000. Important US air base in the Vietnam war.

**Danube River** ◊ *Rumania* (Addenda).

**Dawley** England. Urban district in Shropshire 12 m. ESE of Shrewsbury, formed (1966) from the previous urban district of Dawley (pop. (1961) 9,553) and parts of Wenlock borough and Shifnal and Wellington rural districts. It covers the original designated area (1963) of Telford New Town, to take industries and population from Birmingham and the Black Country; the area was extended (1968). Pop. (1968) 22,080. Birthplace of Matthew Webb ('Captain Webb') (1848–83), the first man to swim the English Channel (1875).

**Eilat** Israel. An oil pipeline from Eilat to Ashkelon, entirely within Israel and by-passing the Suez Canal, was opened in 1970.

**Fiji Islands** SW Pacific Ocean. Fiji gained independence, became a member of the Commonwealth, and was admitted to the UN in 1970.

**Gaberones** Botswana. Officially renamed Gaborone 1969.

**Gaborone** Botswana. Capital, formerly ◊ *Gaberones.*

**Gambia.** Proclaimed a republic 1970.

**Haverhill** England. Urban district in W Suffolk 11 m. S of Newmarket. Pop. (1961) 5,446. Market town. Industrial estate and considerable housing development: agreed with the Greater London Council to accommodate 10,000 Londoners; pop. planned to reach 18,500 by 1971 and 30,000 by 1981. Pop. (1968) 10,700.

**Hospitalet** Spain. Industrial suburb of SW Barcelona. Pop. (1967) 192,087. Manufactures textiles, chemicals, etc. Expanded rapidly in the 1960s: pop. (1959) 111,013.

**Huascarán** Peru. An avalanche, set in motion by a violent earthquake, again descended the mountain slopes, buried two towns, and killed about 20,000 people, in May 1970.

**Iran.** A large area of the NE province of Khurasan was devastated by violent earthquakes in 1968; more than 12,000 people were killed and 100,000 made homeless. There was a less severe earthquake in the same province in 1970; 175 people were killed and 2,500 made homeless.

**Iraq** ◊ *Kurdistan* (Addenda).

**Jordan.** In Aug. 1970 Jordan, with the United Arab Republic, accepted a ceasefire plan in the hostilities against Israel. In Sept. 1970 three foreign civil airliners were hijacked by Arab guerrillas (with whom the Jordanian government had maintained an uneasy truce for some time) and taken to a desert airstrip N of Amman, where they were destroyed; a brief civil war broke out, and the Jordanian army attacked and defeated the guerrillas.

**Kurdistan.** In Iraq, fighting between Kurdish nationalists and government forces ended in a truce in 1966; the Iraqi government granted recognition of the Kurdish language and Kurdish representation in the National Assembly. Complete settlement of the Kurdish problem was announced in 1970.

**Kyzyl** USSR. Formerly (till 1917) Byelotsarsk. Capital of the Tuva ASSR, RSFSR, 310 m. SSE of Krasnoyarsk, at the confluence of the two main headstreams of the Yenisei R. Pop. (1970) 52,000. Linked by road and by steamer service along the Yenisei R. with Minusinsk, by air with Krasnoyarsk. Sawmilling etc.

**Laos.** There was again civil war from 1967, with government forces engaging the Pathet Lao, and both sides receiving foreign support: the former being helped by Thai troops and US aircraft, the latter by troops from N Vietnam.

**Lappeenranta** Finland. Industrial town and lake port in Kymi province, picturesquely situated at the S end of L. Saimaa 60 m. NE of Kotka. Pop. (1969) 50,580. Sawmill-

ing. Manufactures sulphuric acid, cement, etc. In Russian hands 1743–1812. Expanded rapidly in the 1960s: pop. (1960) 21,100.

**Luang Prabang** Laos. Royal capital and river port, on the Mekong R. 135 m. NNW of Vientiane, with which also linked by road. Pop. 22,000. Trade in rice, timber, etc. Formerly capital of a kingdom of the same name.

**Miass** USSR. Town in the Chelyabinsk region, RSFSR, 50 m. WSW of Chelyabinsk. Pop. (1970) 132,000. Manufactures motor cars etc. Expanded considerably in the 1960s: pop. (1959) 98,000.

**Muscat and Oman.** Renamed the sultanate of Oman in 1970.

**Namibia** ◊ *South-West Africa.*

**New York** USA. The pop. increased by more than 1 million 1960–70, but that of California increased at a much faster rate during the decade: California thus overtook New York as the most populous state, with New York in second place.

**New York city (New York)** USA. In the 1960s the pop. of the city decreased slightly, though the pop. of the metropolitan area increased by 6.7 per cent to 11,410,000: the same outward movement of pop. as exhibited in other great cities (e.g. London) was thus continued during the decade.

**Oman.** Sultanate in E Arabia formerly known as ◊ *Muscat and Oman.*

**Osaka** Japan. Site of the 'Expo 70' international exhibition (1970).

**Pakistan.** E Pakistan was again devastated by a cyclone and tidal wave, which flooded coastal areas and islands of the Ganges–Brahmaputra delta, in 1970. Early estimates suggested that the loss of life may have been as high as $\frac{1}{4}$ million. Several nations participated in the ensuing rescue operation, dispatching food, medical supplies, etc. to the survivors. The first free elections to a National Assembly were held throughout Pakistan in Dec. 1970.

**Peru.** In 1969 US oil interests, inc. the oilfields in the N and the refinery at ◊ *Talara,* were expropriated by the Peruvian government. Several US fishing vessels were seized and fined (1969) for fishing inside the 200-m. limit of territorial waters which is claimed by Peru but not recognized by USA; this claim enables Peru to protect her important fishing industry – she is now the world's leading fishing nation. ◊ *Brazil* (Addenda). In 1970 a violent earthquake caused the worst natural disaster in the country's history, chiefly in an area 200–

250 m. N N W of Lima: about 50,000 people were killed and 800,000 made homeless, and many towns and villages were virtually destroyed, inc. Trujillo and Chimbote. As a result of the earthquake an immense avalanche of ice, snow and rocks swept down the slopes of Huascarán, buried two small Andean towns, and killed about 20,000 people.

**Reggio di Calabria (Reggio Calabria)** Italy. Serious riots took place here in 1970 over the proposal to make the smaller town of Catanzaro the capital of the region of Calabria.

**Reynosa** Mexico. Town in Tamaulipas state, on the Rio Grande (Río Bravo) 130 m. E N E of Monterrey, opposite McAllen (Texas). Pop. (1969) 150,000. Market town, on one of the main routes from the U S A into N E Mexico. Expanded rapidly in the 1960s: pop. (1960) 108,500.

**Ruda Śląska** Poland. Town in the Katowice voivodship just E of Zabrze. Pop. (1969) 140,300. Coalmining. Manufactures chemicals etc. Includes the industrial town Nowy Bytom.

**Rumania.** Heavy spring rains (1970) caused the Danube R. to rise to its highest level since records were started in 1840, and caused the country's worst floods for more than a century. Many places in the Dobruja, inc. Galaţi and Brăila, were temporarily isolated, hundreds of other towns and villages were inundated, 160 lives were lost, and tens of thousands were made homeless.

**Samoa** S Pacific Ocean. Western Samoa joined the Commonwealth of Nations in 1970.

**Severodvinsk** U S S R. Formerly Molotovsk. Seaport in the Archangel region, R S F S R, on Dvina Bay (White Sea) 25 m. W of Archangel. Pop. (1970) 145,000. Exports timber etc. Expanded rapidly in the 1960s: pop. (1959) 79,000.

**Skellefteå** Sweden. Town and port in Västerbotten county, on the Skellefte R. near the mouth. Pop. (1968) 61,949. Exports metallic ores, timber, tar. Copper and lead smelting, using ores from the near-by Boliden mines; also produces gold, silver, etc. Expanded rapidly in the 1960s: pop. (1960) 22,193.

**Skelmersdale and Holland** England. Urban district in Lancashire 6 m. W of Wigan, formed in 1968 from the urban districts of Skelmersdale and Up Holland and parts of Ormskirk urban district and Wigan rural district. Pop. (1968) 21,870. Designated for development (1961) primarily to relieve overcrowding on Merseyside. Target pop. (1980) 80,000. Engineering etc.

**Snowy Mountains** Australia. The Talbingo Dam, on the Tumut R. (a tributary of the Murrumbidgee R.), the last and largest dam in the Snowy Mountains hydroelectric and irrigation scheme, was completed in 1970.

**South-West Africa.** Also known outside S Africa as Namibia.

**Tarrasa** Spain. Ancient Egara. Industrial town in Barcelona province, 13 m. N W of Barcelona. Pop. (1967) 123,112. Manufactures textiles etc. Expanded considerably in the 1960s: pop. (1959) 86,469.

**Tonga (Friendly Islands)** S Pacific Ocean. Formerly a British protectorate (since 1900), became independent and a sovereign member of the Commonwealth in 1970.

**Tourane** ◊ *Da Nang* (Addenda).

**United Arab Republic.** Sporadic fighting with Israeli forces, chiefly across the Suez Canal, continued until a cease-fire plan was accepted by the U A R, Jordan, and Israel in Aug. 1970. President Nasser died in Sept. 1970.

**Volzhsky** U S S R. New industrial town in the Volgograd region, R S F S R, on the left bank of the Volga R. 15 m. N E of Volgograd. Pop. (1970) 142,000. Aluminium smelting; manufactures chemicals. Expanded rapidly in the 1960s: pop. (1959) 67,000.

**Washington** England. Designated a 'new town' (1964), formed from most of Washington urban district and parts of Houghton-le-Spring urban district and Chester-le-Street rural district: target pop. 80,000. Pop. (1968) 21,170.

Some other books published by Penguins are
described on the following pages

# ASIA HANDBOOK

## EDITED BY GUY WINT

*Revised and Abridged*

Factual surveys, basic information, up-to-date essays, maps, and extracts from post-war treaties and agreements concerning the whole of Asia apart from the Middle East. These explain the political, social, economic, cultural, and religious realities of a continent containing half the world's population in 'an encyclopedia which can be read'.

The contributors include C. P. Fitzgerald, Richard Harris, Geoffrey Hudson, Owen Lattimore, K. M. Panikkar, George N. Patterson, Percival Spear, Richard Storry, Hugh Tinker and many other specialists in Asiatic affairs.

NOT FOR SALE IN THE U.S.A.

# AFRICA HANDBOOK

## EDITED BY COLIN LEGUM

A modern and all-inclusive survey of the whole continent of Africa, in which experts have assembled a mass of reliable background information for the intelligent but non-expert reader. The bulk of the handbook is devoted to individual articles (with bibliographies) on each of the sixty or more independent (and often newly named) territories, colonies, and islands which make up the 'crisis continent': for each country the political development and the economic situation are outlined and the basic geographical and racial facts given. In addition there are special essays on cultural and religious subjects.

The contributors include Basil Davidson, James Duffy, Ernest Gellner, Tom Hopkinson, A. J. Hughes, Harry Land, E. G. Parrinder, Hella Pick, Tom Stacey, Clyde Sanger, and other specialists on African affairs.

NOT FOR SALE IN THE U.S.A.

# A DICTIONARY OF GEOGRAPHY

## W. G. MOORE

### Fourth Edition

This dictionary – now revised and enlarged – describes and explains such commonly met terms as the Trough of Low Pressure (from the weather forecast), a Mackerel Sky, a Tornado, the Spring Tides and hundreds of others. But there are also sections on such stranger phenomena as the Willy-willy of Australia, the Doctor of West Africa, the Plum Rains of Japan, the Volcanic Bomb, the Anti-Trades, the Bad Lands, and the Celestial Equator.

Because geography is largely a synthetic subject, the items of the dictionary are derived from many sciences, including geology, meteorology, climatology, astronomy, anthropology, biology. Even the most abstruse terms, however, are of the kind that the student is likely to meet in the course of his reading – terms that the author of geographical works employs but often has no space to define. The dictionary may thus help to clarify and systematize the reader's knowledge.

### Also available

## GEOGRAPHY OF WORLD AFFAIRS

### J. P. COLE

Now very fully revised, this is a superlative background book to 'fill in' the daily news

### and

## GEOGRAPHY OF THE U.S.S.R.